Oxford Dictionary of
National Biography

Volume 28

Oxford Dictionary of National Biography

IN ASSOCIATION WITH

The British Academy

From the earliest times to the year 2000

Edited by

H. C. G. Matthew

and

Brian Harrison

Volume 28

Hooppell–Hutcheson

OXFORD

UNIVERSITY PRESS

OXFORD
UNIVERSITY PRESS

Great Clarendon Street, Oxford OX2 6DP

Oxford University Press is a department of the University of Oxford.
It furthers the University's objective of excellence in research, scholarship,
and education by publishing worldwide in

Oxford New York

Auckland Bangkok Buenos Aires Cape Town
Chennai Dar es Salaam Delhi Hong Kong Istanbul Karachi
Kolkata Kuala Lumpur Madrid Melbourne Mexico City Mumbai Nairobi
São Paulo Shanghai Taipei Tokyo Toronto

Published in the United States
by Oxford University Press Inc., New York

British Library Cataloguing in Publication Data
Data available

Library of Congress Cataloging in Publication Data
Data available: for details see volume 1, p. iv

ISBN 0-19-861378-4 (this volume)
ISBN 0-19-861411-X (set of sixty volumes)

Text captured by Alliance Phototypesetters, Pondicherry
Illustrations reproduced and archived by
Alliance Graphics Ltd, UK
Typeset in OUP Swift by Interactive Sciences Limited, Gloucester
Printed in Great Britain on acid-free paper by
Butler and Tanner Ltd,
Frome, Somerset

LIST OF ABBREVIATIONS

1 General abbreviations

AB	bachelor of arts
ABC	Australian Broadcasting Corporation
ABC TV	ABC Television
act.	active
A$	Australian dollar
AD	*anno domini*
AFC	Air Force Cross
AIDS	acquired immune deficiency syndrome
AK	Alaska
AL	Alabama
A level	advanced level [examination]
ALS	associate of the Linnean Society
AM	master of arts
AMICE	associate member of the Institution of Civil Engineers
ANZAC	Australian and New Zealand Army Corps
appx *pl.* appxs	appendix(es)
AR	Arkansas
ARA	associate of the Royal Academy
ARCA	associate of the Royal College of Art
ARCM	associate of the Royal College of Music
ARCO	associate of the Royal College of Organists
ARIBA	associate of the Royal Institute of British Architects
ARP	air-raid precautions
ARRC	associate of the Royal Red Cross
ARSA	associate of the Royal Scottish Academy
art.	article / item
ASC	Army Service Corps
Asch	Austrian Schilling
ASDIC	Antisubmarine Detection Investigation Committee
ATS	Auxiliary Territorial Service
ATV	Associated Television
Aug	August
AZ	Arizona
b.	born
BA	bachelor of arts
BA (Admin.)	bachelor of arts (administration)
BAFTA	British Academy of Film and Television Arts
BAO	bachelor of arts in obstetrics
bap.	baptized
BBC	British Broadcasting Corporation / Company
BC	before Christ
BCE	before the common (*or* Christian) era
BCE	bachelor of civil engineering
BCG	bacillus of Calmette and Guérin [inoculation against tuberculosis]
BCh	bachelor of surgery
BChir	bachelor of surgery
BCL	bachelor of civil law

BCnL	bachelor of canon law
BCom	bachelor of commerce
BD	bachelor of divinity
BEd	bachelor of education
BEng	bachelor of engineering
bk *pl.* bks	book(s)
BL	bachelor of law / letters / literature
BLitt	bachelor of letters
BM	bachelor of medicine
BMus	bachelor of music
BP	before present
BP	British Petroleum
Bros.	Brothers
BS	(1) bachelor of science; (2) bachelor of surgery; (3) British standard
BSc	bachelor of science
BSc (Econ.)	bachelor of science (economics)
BSc (Eng.)	bachelor of science (engineering)
bt	baronet
BTh	bachelor of theology
bur.	buried
C.	command [identifier for published parliamentary papers]
c.	*circa*
c.	*capitulum pl. capitula*: chapter(s)
CA	California
Cantab.	Cantabrigiensis
cap.	*capitulum pl. capitula*: chapter(s)
CB	companion of the Bath
CBE	commander of the Order of the British Empire
CBS	Columbia Broadcasting System
cc	cubic centimetres
C$	Canadian dollar
CD	compact disc
Cd	command [identifier for published parliamentary papers]
CE	Common (*or* Christian) Era
cent.	century
cf.	compare
CH	Companion of Honour
chap.	chapter
ChB	bachelor of surgery
CI	Imperial Order of the Crown of India
CIA	Central Intelligence Agency
CID	Criminal Investigation Department
CIE	companion of the Order of the Indian Empire
Cie	Compagnie
CLit	companion of literature
CM	master of surgery
cm	centimetre(s)

Cmd	command [identifier for published parliamentary papers]		edn	edition
CMG	companion of the Order of St Michael and St George		EEC	European Economic Community
			EFTA	European Free Trade Association
Cmnd	command [identifier for published parliamentary papers]		EICS	East India Company Service
			EMI	Electrical and Musical Industries (Ltd)
CO	Colorado		Eng.	English
Co.	company		enl.	enlarged
co.	county		ENSA	Entertainments National Service Association
col. *pl.* cols.	column(s)		ep. *pl.* epp.	*epistola(e)*
Corp.	corporation		ESP	extra-sensory perception
CSE	certificate of secondary education		esp.	especially
CSI	companion of the Order of the Star of India		esq.	esquire
CT	Connecticut		est.	estimate / estimated
CVO	commander of the Royal Victorian Order		EU	European Union
cwt	hundredweight		ex	sold by (*lit.* out of)
$	(American) dollar		excl.	excludes / excluding
d.	(1) penny (pence); (2) died		exh.	exhibited
DBE	dame commander of the Order of the British Empire		exh. cat.	exhibition catalogue
			f. *pl.* ff.	following [pages]
DCH	diploma in child health		FA	Football Association
DCh	doctor of surgery		FACP	fellow of the American College of Physicians
DCL	doctor of civil law		facs.	facsimile
DCnL	doctor of canon law		FANY	First Aid Nursing Yeomanry
DCVO	dame commander of the Royal Victorian Order		FBA	fellow of the British Academy
DD	doctor of divinity		FBI	Federation of British Industries
DE	Delaware		FCS	fellow of the Chemical Society
Dec	December		Feb	February
dem.	demolished		FEng	fellow of the Fellowship of Engineering
DEng	doctor of engineering		FFCM	fellow of the Faculty of Community Medicine
des.	destroyed		FGS	fellow of the Geological Society
DFC	Distinguished Flying Cross		fig.	figure
DipEd	diploma in education		FIMechE	fellow of the Institution of Mechanical Engineers
DipPsych	diploma in psychiatry			
diss.	dissertation		FL	Florida
DL	deputy lieutenant		*fl.*	*floruit*
DLitt	doctor of letters		FLS	fellow of the Linnean Society
DLittCelt	doctor of Celtic letters		FM	frequency modulation
DM	(1) Deutschmark; (2) doctor of medicine; (3) doctor of musical arts		fol. *pl.* fols.	folio(s)
			Fr	French francs
DMus	doctor of music		Fr.	French
DNA	dioxyribonucleic acid		FRAeS	fellow of the Royal Aeronautical Society
doc.	document		FRAI	fellow of the Royal Anthropological Institute
DOL	doctor of oriental learning		FRAM	fellow of the Royal Academy of Music
DPH	diploma in public health		FRAS	(1) fellow of the Royal Asiatic Society; (2) fellow of the Royal Astronomical Society
DPhil	doctor of philosophy			
DPM	diploma in psychological medicine		FRCM	fellow of the Royal College of Music
DSC	Distinguished Service Cross		FRCO	fellow of the Royal College of Organists
DSc	doctor of science		FRCOG	fellow of the Royal College of Obstetricians and Gynaecologists
DSc (Econ.)	doctor of science (economics)			
DSc (Eng.)	doctor of science (engineering)		FRCP(C)	fellow of the Royal College of Physicians of Canada
DSM	Distinguished Service Medal			
DSO	companion of the Distinguished Service Order		FRCP (Edin.)	fellow of the Royal College of Physicians of Edinburgh
DSocSc	doctor of social science			
DTech	doctor of technology		FRCP (Lond.)	fellow of the Royal College of Physicians of London
DTh	doctor of theology			
DTM	diploma in tropical medicine		FRCPath	fellow of the Royal College of Pathologists
DTMH	diploma in tropical medicine and hygiene		FRCPsych	fellow of the Royal College of Psychiatrists
DU	doctor of the university		FRCS	fellow of the Royal College of Surgeons
DUniv	doctor of the university		FRGS	fellow of the Royal Geographical Society
dwt	pennyweight		FRIBA	fellow of the Royal Institute of British Architects
EC	European Community		FRICS	fellow of the Royal Institute of Chartered Surveyors
ed. *pl.* eds.	edited / edited by / editor(s)			
			FRS	fellow of the Royal Society
Edin.	Edinburgh		FRSA	fellow of the Royal Society of Arts

FRSCM	fellow of the Royal School of Church Music		ISO	companion of the Imperial Service Order
FRSE	fellow of the Royal Society of Edinburgh		It.	Italian
FRSL	fellow of the Royal Society of Literature		ITA	Independent Television Authority
FSA	fellow of the Society of Antiquaries		ITV	Independent Television
ft	foot *pl.* feet		Jan	January
FTCL	fellow of Trinity College of Music, London		JP	justice of the peace
ft-lb per min.	foot-pounds per minute [unit of horsepower]		jun.	junior
FZS	fellow of the Zoological Society		KB	knight of the Order of the Bath
GA	Georgia		KBE	knight commander of the Order of the British Empire
GBE	knight or dame grand cross of the Order of the British Empire		KC	king's counsel
GCB	knight grand cross of the Order of the Bath		kcal	kilocalorie
GCE	general certificate of education		KCB	knight commander of the Order of the Bath
GCH	knight grand cross of the Royal Guelphic Order		KCH	knight commander of the Royal Guelphic Order
GCHQ	government communications headquarters		KCIE	knight commander of the Order of the Indian Empire
GCIE	knight grand commander of the Order of the Indian Empire		KCMG	knight commander of the Order of St Michael and St George
GCMG	knight or dame grand cross of the Order of St Michael and St George		KCSI	knight commander of the Order of the Star of India
GCSE	general certificate of secondary education		KCVO	knight commander of the Royal Victorian Order
GCSI	knight grand commander of the Order of the Star of India		keV	kilo-electron-volt
GCStJ	bailiff or dame grand cross of the order of St John of Jerusalem		KG	knight of the Order of the Garter
			KGB	[Soviet committee of state security]
GCVO	knight or dame grand cross of the Royal Victorian Order		KH	knight of the Royal Guelphic Order
			KLM	Koninklijke Luchtvaart Maatschappij (Royal Dutch Air Lines)
GEC	General Electric Company		km	kilometre(s)
Ger.	German		KP	knight of the Order of St Patrick
GI	government (*or* general) issue		KS	Kansas
GMT	Greenwich mean time		KT	knight of the Order of the Thistle
GP	general practitioner		kt	knight
GPU	[Soviet special police unit]		KY	Kentucky
GSO	general staff officer		£	pound(s) sterling
Heb.	Hebrew		£E	Egyptian pound
HEICS	Honourable East India Company Service		L	lira *pl.* lire
HI	Hawaii		l. *pl.* ll.	line(s)
HIV	human immunodeficiency virus		LA	Lousiana
HK$	Hong Kong dollar		LAA	light anti-aircraft
HM	his / her majesty('s)		LAH	licentiate of the Apothecaries' Hall, Dublin
HMAS	his / her majesty's Australian ship		Lat.	Latin
HMNZS	his / her majesty's New Zealand ship		lb	pound(s), unit of weight
HMS	his / her majesty's ship		LDS	licence in dental surgery
HMSO	His / Her Majesty's Stationery Office		*lit.*	literally
HMV	His Master's Voice		LittB	bachelor of letters
Hon.	Honourable		LittD	doctor of letters
hp	horsepower		LKQCPI	licentiate of the King and Queen's College of Physicians, Ireland
hr	hour(s)		LLA	lady literate in arts
HRH	his / her royal highness		LLB	bachelor of laws
HTV	Harlech Television		LLD	doctor of laws
IA	Iowa		LLM	master of laws
ibid.	*ibidem*: in the same place		LM	licentiate in midwifery
ICI	Imperial Chemical Industries (Ltd)		LP	long-playing record
ID	Idaho		LRAM	licentiate of the Royal Academy of Music
IL	Illinois		LRCP	licentiate of the Royal College of Physicians
illus.	illustration		LRCPS (Glasgow)	licentiate of the Royal College of Physicians and Surgeons of Glasgow
illustr.	illustrated			
IN	Indiana		LRCS	licentiate of the Royal College of Surgeons
in.	inch(es)		LSA	licentiate of the Society of Apothecaries
Inc.	Incorporated		LSD	lysergic acid diethylamide
incl.	includes / including		LVO	lieutenant of the Royal Victorian Order
IOU	I owe you		M. *pl.* MM.	Monsieur *pl.* Messieurs
IQ	intelligence quotient		m	metre(s)
Ir£	Irish pound			
IRA	Irish Republican Army			

m. *pl.* mm.	membrane(s)
MA	(1) Massachusetts; (2) master of arts
MAI	master of engineering
MB	bachelor of medicine
MBA	master of business administration
MBE	member of the Order of the British Empire
MC	Military Cross
MCC	Marylebone Cricket Club
MCh	master of surgery
MChir	master of surgery
MCom	master of commerce
MD	(1) doctor of medicine; (2) Maryland
MDMA	methylenedioxymethamphetamine
ME	Maine
MEd	master of education
MEng	master of engineering
MEP	member of the European parliament
MG	Morris Garages
MGM	Metro-Goldwyn-Mayer
Mgr	Monsignor
MI	(1) Michigan; (2) military intelligence
MI1c	[secret intelligence department]
MI5	[military intelligence department]
MI6	[secret intelligence department]
MI9	[secret escape service]
MICE	member of the Institution of Civil Engineers
MIEE	member of the Institution of Electrical Engineers
min.	minute(s)
Mk	mark
ML	(1) licentiate of medicine; (2) master of laws
MLitt	master of letters
Mlle	Mademoiselle
mm	millimetre(s)
Mme	Madame
MN	Minnesota
MO	Missouri
MOH	medical officer of health
MP	member of parliament
m.p.h.	miles per hour
MPhil	master of philosophy
MRCP	member of the Royal College of Physicians
MRCS	member of the Royal College of Surgeons
MRCVS	member of the Royal College of Veterinary Surgeons
MRIA	member of the Royal Irish Academy
MS	(1) master of science; (2) Mississippi
MS *pl.* MSS	manuscript(s)
MSc	master of science
MSc (Econ.)	master of science (economics)
MT	Montana
MusB	bachelor of music
MusBac	bachelor of music
MusD	doctor of music
MV	motor vessel
MVO	member of the Royal Victorian Order
n. *pl.* nn.	note(s)
NAAFI	Navy, Army, and Air Force Institutes
NASA	National Aeronautics and Space Administration
NATO	North Atlantic Treaty Organization
NBC	National Broadcasting Corporation
NC	North Carolina
NCO	non-commissioned officer
ND	North Dakota
n.d.	no date
NE	Nebraska
nem. con.	*nemine contradicente*: unanimously
new ser.	new series
NH	New Hampshire
NHS	National Health Service
NJ	New Jersey
NKVD	[Soviet people's commissariat for internal affairs]
NM	New Mexico
nm	nanometre(s)
no. *pl.* nos.	number(s)
Nov	November
n.p.	no place [of publication]
NS	new style
NV	Nevada
NY	New York
NZBS	New Zealand Broadcasting Service
OBE	officer of the Order of the British Empire
obit.	obituary
Oct	October
OCTU	officer cadets training unit
OECD	Organization for Economic Co-operation and Development
OEEC	Organization for European Economic Co-operation
OFM	order of Friars Minor [Franciscans]
OFMCap	Ordine Frati Minori Cappucini: member of the Capuchin order
OH	Ohio
OK	Oklahoma
O level	ordinary level [examination]
OM	Order of Merit
OP	order of Preachers [Dominicans]
op. *pl.* opp.	opus *pl.* opera
OPEC	Organization of Petroleum Exporting Countries
OR	Oregon
orig.	original
OS	old style
OSB	Order of St Benedict
OTC	Officers' Training Corps
OWS	Old Watercolour Society
Oxon.	Oxoniensis
p. *pl.* pp.	page(s)
PA	Pennsylvania
p.a.	per annum
para.	paragraph
PAYE	pay as you earn
pbk *pl.* pbks	paperback(s)
per.	[during the] period
PhD	doctor of philosophy
pl.	(1) plate(s); (2) plural
priv. coll.	private collection
pt *pl.* pts	part(s)
pubd	published
PVC	polyvinyl chloride
q. *pl.* qq.	(1) question(s); (2) quire(s)
QC	queen's counsel
R	rand
R.	Rex / Regina
r	recto
r.	reigned / ruled
RA	Royal Academy / Royal Academician

RAC	Royal Automobile Club
RAF	Royal Air Force
RAFVR	Royal Air Force Volunteer Reserve
RAM	[member of the] Royal Academy of Music
RAMC	Royal Army Medical Corps
RCA	Royal College of Art
RCNC	Royal Corps of Naval Constructors
RCOG	Royal College of Obstetricians and Gynaecologists
RDI	royal designer for industry
RE	Royal Engineers
repr. *pl.* reprs.	reprint(s) / reprinted
repro.	reproduced
rev.	revised / revised by / reviser / revision
Revd	Reverend
RHA	Royal Hibernian Academy
RI	(1) Rhode Island; (2) Royal Institute of Painters in Water-Colours
RIBA	Royal Institute of British Architects
RIN	Royal Indian Navy
RM	Reichsmark
RMS	Royal Mail steamer
RN	Royal Navy
RNA	ribonucleic acid
RNAS	Royal Naval Air Service
RNR	Royal Naval Reserve
RNVR	Royal Naval Volunteer Reserve
RO	Record Office
r.p.m.	revolutions per minute
RRS	royal research ship
Rs	rupees
RSA	(1) Royal Scottish Academician; (2) Royal Society of Arts
RSPCA	Royal Society for the Prevention of Cruelty to Animals
Rt Hon.	Right Honourable
Rt Revd	Right Reverend
RUC	Royal Ulster Constabulary
Russ.	Russian
RWS	Royal Watercolour Society
S4C	Sianel Pedwar Cymru
s.	shilling(s)
s.a.	*sub anno*: under the year
SABC	South African Broadcasting Corporation
SAS	Special Air Service
SC	South Carolina
ScD	doctor of science
S$	Singapore dollar
SD	South Dakota
sec.	second(s)
sel.	selected
sen.	senior
Sept	September
ser.	series
SHAPE	supreme headquarters allied powers, Europe
SIDRO	Société Internationale d'Énergie Hydro-Électrique
sig. *pl.* sigs.	signature(s)
sing.	singular
SIS	Secret Intelligence Service
SJ	Society of Jesus
Skr	Swedish krona
Span.	Spanish
SPCK	Society for Promoting Christian Knowledge
SS	(1) Santissimi; (2) Schutzstaffel; (3) steam ship
STB	bachelor of theology
STD	doctor of theology
STM	master of theology
STP	doctor of theology
supp.	supposedly
suppl. *pl.* suppls.	supplement(s)
s.v.	*sub verbo* / *sub voce*: under the word / heading
SY	steam yacht
TA	Territorial Army
TASS	[Soviet news agency]
TB	tuberculosis (*lit.* tubercle bacillus)
TD	(1) *teachtaí dála* (member of the Dáil); (2) territorial decoration
TN	Tennessee
TNT	trinitrotoluene
trans.	translated / translated by / translation / translator
TT	tourist trophy
TUC	Trades Union Congress
TX	Texas
U-boat	*Unterseeboot*: submarine
Ufa	Universum-Film AG
UMIST	University of Manchester Institute of Science and Technology
UN	United Nations
UNESCO	United Nations Educational, Scientific, and Cultural Organization
UNICEF	United Nations International Children's Emergency Fund
unpubd	unpublished
USS	United States ship
UT	Utah
v	verso
v.	versus
VA	Virginia
VAD	Voluntary Aid Detachment
VC	Victoria Cross
VE-day	victory in Europe day
Ven.	Venerable
VJ-day	victory over Japan day
vol. *pl.* vols.	volume(s)
VT	Vermont
WA	Washington [state]
WAAC	Women's Auxiliary Army Corps
WAAF	Women's Auxiliary Air Force
WEA	Workers' Educational Association
WHO	World Health Organization
WI	Wisconsin
WRAF	Women's Royal Air Force
WRNS	Women's Royal Naval Service
WV	West Virginia
WVS	Women's Voluntary Service
WY	Wyoming
¥	yen
YMCA	Young Men's Christian Association
YWCA	Young Women's Christian Association

2 Institution abbreviations

All Souls Oxf.	All Souls College, Oxford
AM Oxf.	Ashmolean Museum, Oxford
Balliol Oxf.	Balliol College, Oxford
BBC WAC	BBC Written Archives Centre, Reading
Beds. & Luton ARS	Bedfordshire and Luton Archives and Record Service, Bedford
Berks. RO	Berkshire Record Office, Reading
BFI	British Film Institute, London
BFI NFTVA	British Film Institute, London, National Film and Television Archive
BGS	British Geological Survey, Keyworth, Nottingham
Birm. CA	Birmingham Central Library, Birmingham City Archives
Birm. CL	Birmingham Central Library
BL	British Library, London
BL NSA	British Library, London, National Sound Archive
BL OIOC	British Library, London, Oriental and India Office Collections
BLPES	London School of Economics and Political Science, British Library of Political and Economic Science
BM	British Museum, London
Bodl. Oxf.	Bodleian Library, Oxford
Bodl. RH	Bodleian Library of Commonwealth and African Studies at Rhodes House, Oxford
Borth. Inst.	Borthwick Institute of Historical Research, University of York
Boston PL	Boston Public Library, Massachusetts
Bristol RO	Bristol Record Office
Bucks. RLSS	Buckinghamshire Records and Local Studies Service, Aylesbury
CAC Cam.	Churchill College, Cambridge, Churchill Archives Centre
Cambs. AS	Cambridgeshire Archive Service
CCC Cam.	Corpus Christi College, Cambridge
CCC Oxf.	Corpus Christi College, Oxford
Ches. & Chester ALSS	Cheshire and Chester Archives and Local Studies Service
Christ Church Oxf.	Christ Church, Oxford
Christies	Christies, London
City Westm. AC	City of Westminster Archives Centre, London
CKS	Centre for Kentish Studies, Maidstone
CLRO	Corporation of London Records Office
Coll. Arms	College of Arms, London
Col. U.	Columbia University, New York
Cornwall RO	Cornwall Record Office, Truro
Courtauld Inst.	Courtauld Institute of Art, London
CUL	Cambridge University Library
Cumbria AS	Cumbria Archive Service
Derbys. RO	Derbyshire Record Office, Matlock
Devon RO	Devon Record Office, Exeter
Dorset RO	Dorset Record Office, Dorchester
Duke U.	Duke University, Durham, North Carolina
Duke U., Perkins L.	Duke University, Durham, North Carolina, William R. Perkins Library
Durham Cath. CL	Durham Cathedral, chapter library
Durham RO	Durham Record Office
DWL	Dr Williams's Library, London
Essex RO	Essex Record Office
E. Sussex RO	East Sussex Record Office, Lewes
Eton	Eton College, Berkshire
FM Cam.	Fitzwilliam Museum, Cambridge
Folger	Folger Shakespeare Library, Washington, DC
Garr. Club	Garrick Club, London
Girton Cam.	Girton College, Cambridge
GL	Guildhall Library, London
Glos. RO	Gloucestershire Record Office, Gloucester
Gon. & Caius Cam.	Gonville and Caius College, Cambridge
Gov. Art Coll.	Government Art Collection
GS Lond.	Geological Society of London
Hants. RO	Hampshire Record Office, Winchester
Harris Man. Oxf.	Harris Manchester College, Oxford
Harvard TC	Harvard Theatre Collection, Harvard University, Cambridge, Massachusetts, Nathan Marsh Pusey Library
Harvard U.	Harvard University, Cambridge, Massachusetts
Harvard U., Houghton L.	Harvard University, Cambridge, Massachusetts, Houghton Library
Herefs. RO	Herefordshire Record Office, Hereford
Herts. ALS	Hertfordshire Archives and Local Studies, Hertford
Hist. Soc. Penn.	Historical Society of Pennsylvania, Philadelphia
HLRO	House of Lords Record Office, London
Hult. Arch.	Hulton Archive, London and New York
Hunt. L.	Huntington Library, San Marino, California
ICL	Imperial College, London
Inst. CE	Institution of Civil Engineers, London
Inst. EE	Institution of Electrical Engineers, London
IWM	Imperial War Museum, London
IWM FVA	Imperial War Museum, London, Film and Video Archive
IWM SA	Imperial War Museum, London, Sound Archive
JRL	John Rylands University Library of Manchester
King's AC Cam.	King's College Archives Centre, Cambridge
King's Cam.	King's College, Cambridge
King's Lond.	King's College, London
King's Lond., Liddell Hart C.	King's College, London, Liddell Hart Centre for Military Archives
Lancs. RO	Lancashire Record Office, Preston
L. Cong.	Library of Congress, Washington, DC
Leics. RO	Leicestershire, Leicester, and Rutland Record Office, Leicester
Lincs. Arch.	Lincolnshire Archives, Lincoln
Linn. Soc.	Linnean Society of London
LMA	London Metropolitan Archives
LPL	Lambeth Palace, London
Lpool RO	Liverpool Record Office and Local Studies Service
LUL	London University Library
Magd. Cam.	Magdalene College, Cambridge
Magd. Oxf.	Magdalen College, Oxford
Man. City Gall.	Manchester City Galleries
Man. CL	Manchester Central Library
Mass. Hist. Soc.	Massachusetts Historical Society, Boston
Merton Oxf.	Merton College, Oxford
MHS Oxf.	Museum of the History of Science, Oxford
Mitchell L., Glas.	Mitchell Library, Glasgow
Mitchell L., NSW	State Library of New South Wales, Sydney, Mitchell Library
Morgan L.	Pierpont Morgan Library, New York
NA Canada	National Archives of Canada, Ottawa
NA Ire.	National Archives of Ireland, Dublin
NAM	National Army Museum, London
NA Scot.	National Archives of Scotland, Edinburgh
News Int. RO	News International Record Office, London
NG Ire.	National Gallery of Ireland, Dublin

NG Scot.	National Gallery of Scotland, Edinburgh
NHM	Natural History Museum, London
NL Aus.	National Library of Australia, Canberra
NL Ire.	National Library of Ireland, Dublin
NL NZ	National Library of New Zealand, Wellington
NL NZ, Turnbull L.	National Library of New Zealand, Wellington, Alexander Turnbull Library
NL Scot.	National Library of Scotland, Edinburgh
NL Wales	National Library of Wales, Aberystwyth
NMG Wales	National Museum and Gallery of Wales, Cardiff
NMM	National Maritime Museum, London
Norfolk RO	Norfolk Record Office, Norwich
Northants. RO	Northamptonshire Record Office, Northampton
Northumbd RO	Northumberland Record Office
Notts. Arch.	Nottinghamshire Archives, Nottingham
NPG	National Portrait Gallery, London
NRA	National Archives, London, Historical Manuscripts Commission, National Register of Archives
Nuffield Oxf.	Nuffield College, Oxford
N. Yorks. CRO	North Yorkshire County Record Office, Northallerton
NYPL	New York Public Library
Oxf. UA	Oxford University Archives
Oxf. U. Mus. NH	Oxford University Museum of Natural History
Oxon. RO	Oxfordshire Record Office, Oxford
Pembroke Cam.	Pembroke College, Cambridge
PRO	National Archives, London, Public Record Office
PRO NIre.	Public Record Office for Northern Ireland, Belfast
Pusey Oxf.	Pusey House, Oxford
RA	Royal Academy of Arts, London
Ransom HRC	Harry Ransom Humanities Research Center, University of Texas, Austin
RAS	Royal Astronomical Society, London
RBG Kew	Royal Botanic Gardens, Kew, London
RCP Lond.	Royal College of Physicians of London
RCS Eng.	Royal College of Surgeons of England, London
RGS	Royal Geographical Society, London
RIBA	Royal Institute of British Architects, London
RIBA BAL	Royal Institute of British Architects, London, British Architectural Library
Royal Arch.	Royal Archives, Windsor Castle, Berkshire [by gracious permission of her majesty the queen]
Royal Irish Acad.	Royal Irish Academy, Dublin
Royal Scot. Acad.	Royal Scottish Academy, Edinburgh
RS	Royal Society, London
RSA	Royal Society of Arts, London
RS Friends, Lond.	Religious Society of Friends, London
St Ant. Oxf.	St Antony's College, Oxford
St John Cam.	St John's College, Cambridge
S. Antiquaries, Lond.	Society of Antiquaries of London
Sci. Mus.	Science Museum, London
Scot. NPG	Scottish National Portrait Gallery, Edinburgh
Scott Polar RI	University of Cambridge, Scott Polar Research Institute
Sheff. Arch.	Sheffield Archives
Shrops. RRC	Shropshire Records and Research Centre, Shrewsbury
SOAS	School of Oriental and African Studies, London
Som. ARS	Somerset Archive and Record Service, Taunton
Staffs. RO	Staffordshire Record Office, Stafford

Suffolk RO	Suffolk Record Office
Surrey HC	Surrey History Centre, Woking
TCD	Trinity College, Dublin
Trinity Cam.	Trinity College, Cambridge
U. Aberdeen	University of Aberdeen
U. Birm.	University of Birmingham
U. Birm. L.	University of Birmingham Library
U. Cal.	University of California
U. Cam.	University of Cambridge
UCL	University College, London
U. Durham	University of Durham
U. Durham L.	University of Durham Library
U. Edin.	University of Edinburgh
U. Edin., New Coll.	University of Edinburgh, New College
U. Edin., New Coll. L.	University of Edinburgh, New College Library
U. Edin. L.	University of Edinburgh Library
U. Glas.	University of Glasgow
U. Glas. L.	University of Glasgow Library
U. Hull	University of Hull
U. Hull, Brynmor Jones L.	University of Hull, Brynmor Jones Library
U. Leeds	University of Leeds
U. Leeds, Brotherton L.	University of Leeds, Brotherton Library
U. Lond.	University of London
U. Lpool	University of Liverpool
U. Lpool L.	University of Liverpool Library
U. Mich.	University of Michigan, Ann Arbor
U. Mich., Clements L.	University of Michigan, Ann Arbor, William L. Clements Library
U. Newcastle	University of Newcastle upon Tyne
U. Newcastle, Robinson L.	University of Newcastle upon Tyne, Robinson Library
U. Nott.	University of Nottingham
U. Nott. L.	University of Nottingham Library
U. Oxf.	University of Oxford
U. Reading	University of Reading
U. Reading L.	University of Reading Library
U. St Andr.	University of St Andrews
U. St Andr. L.	University of St Andrews Library
U. Southampton	University of Southampton
U. Southampton L.	University of Southampton Library
U. Sussex	University of Sussex, Brighton
U. Texas	University of Texas, Austin
U. Wales	University of Wales
U. Warwick Mod. RC	University of Warwick, Coventry, Modern Records Centre
V&A	Victoria and Albert Museum, London
V&A NAL	Victoria and Albert Museum, London, National Art Library
Warks. CRO	Warwickshire County Record Office, Warwick
Wellcome L.	Wellcome Library for the History and Understanding of Medicine, London
Westm. DA	Westminster Diocesan Archives, London
Wilts. & Swindon RO	Wiltshire and Swindon Record Office, Trowbridge
Worcs. RO	Worcestershire Record Office, Worcester
W. Sussex RO	West Sussex Record Office, Chichester
W. Yorks. AS	West Yorkshire Archive Service
Yale U.	Yale University, New Haven, Connecticut
Yale U., Beinecke L.	Yale University, New Haven, Connecticut, Beinecke Rare Book and Manuscript Library
Yale U. CBA	Yale University, New Haven, Connecticut, Yale Center for British Art

3 Bibliographic abbreviations

Adams, *Drama* — W. D. Adams, *A dictionary of the drama*, 1: *A–G* (1904); 2: *H–Z* (1956) [vol. 2 microfilm only]

AFM — J O'Donovan, ed. and trans., *Annala rioghachta Eireann / Annals of the kingdom of Ireland by the four masters*, 7 vols. (1848–51); 2nd edn (1856); 3rd edn (1990)

Allibone, *Dict.* — S. A. Allibone, *A critical dictionary of English literature and British and American authors*, 3 vols. (1859–71); suppl. by J. F. Kirk, 2 vols. (1891)

ANB — J. A. Garraty and M. C. Carnes, eds., *American national biography*, 24 vols. (1999)

Anderson, *Scot. nat.* — W. Anderson, *The Scottish nation, or, The surnames, families, literature, honours, and biographical history of the people of Scotland*, 3 vols. (1859–63)

Ann. mon. — H. R. Luard, ed., *Annales monastici*, 5 vols., Rolls Series, 36 (1864–9)

Ann. Ulster — S. Mac Airt and G. Mac Niocaill, eds., *Annals of Ulster (to AD 1131)* (1983)

APC — *Acts of the privy council of England*, new ser., 46 vols. (1890–1964)

APS — *The acts of the parliaments of Scotland*, 12 vols. in 13 (1814–75)

Arber, *Regs. Stationers* — F. Arber, ed., *A transcript of the registers of the Company of Stationers of London, 1554–1640 AD*, 5 vols. (1875–94)

ArchR — *Architectural Review*

ASC — D. Whitelock, D. C. Douglas, and S. I. Tucker, ed. and trans., *The Anglo-Saxon Chronicle: a revised translation* (1961)

AS chart. — P. H. Sawyer, *Anglo-Saxon charters: an annotated list and bibliography*, Royal Historical Society Guides and Handbooks (1968)

AusDB — D. Pike and others, eds., *Australian dictionary of biography*, 16 vols. (1966–2002)

Baker, *Serjeants* — J. H. Baker, *The order of serjeants at law*, SeldS, suppl. ser., 5 (1984)

Bale, *Cat.* — J. Bale, *Scriptorum illustrium Maioris Brytannie, quam nunc Angliam et Scotiam vocant: catalogus*, 2 vols. in 1 (Basel, 1557–9); facs. edn (1971)

Bale, *Index* — J. Bale, *Index Britanniae scriptorum*, ed. R. L. Poole and M. Bateson (1902); facs. edn (1990)

BBCS — *Bulletin of the Board of Celtic Studies*

BDMBR — J. O. Baylen and N. J. Gossman, eds., *Biographical dictionary of modern British radicals*, 3 vols. in 4 (1979–88)

Bede, *Hist. eccl.* — *Bede's Ecclesiastical history of the English people*, ed. and trans. B. Colgrave and R. A. B. Mynors, OMT (1969); repr. (1991)

Bénézit, *Dict.* — E. Bénézit, *Dictionnaire critique et documentaire des peintres, sculpteurs, dessinateurs et graveurs*, 3 vols. (Paris, 1911–23); new edn, 8 vols. (1948–66), repr. (1966); 3rd edn, rev. and enl., 10 vols. (1976); 4th edn, 14 vols. (1999)

BIHR — *Bulletin of the Institute of Historical Research*

Birch, *Seals* — W. de Birch, *Catalogue of seals in the department of manuscripts in the British Museum*, 6 vols. (1887–1900)

Bishop Burnet's History — *Bishop Burnet's History of his own time*, ed. M. J. Routh, 2nd edn, 6 vols. (1833)

Blackwood — *Blackwood's [Edinburgh] Magazine*, 328 vols. (1817–1980)

Blain, Clements & Grundy, *Feminist comp.* — V. Blain, P. Clements, and I. Grundy, eds., *The feminist companion to literature in English* (1990)

BL cat. — *The British Library general catalogue of printed books* [in 360 vols. with suppls., also CD-ROM and online]

BMJ — *British Medical Journal*

Boase & Courtney, *Bibl. Corn.* — G. C. Boase and W. P. Courtney, *Bibliotheca Cornubiensis: a catalogue of the writings … of Cornishmen*, 3 vols. (1874–82)

Boase, *Mod. Eng. biog.* — F. Boase, *Modern English biography: containing many thousand concise memoirs of persons who have died since the year 1850*, 6 vols. (privately printed, Truro, 1892–1921); repr. (1965)

Boswell, *Life* — *Boswell's Life of Johnson: together with Journal of a tour to the Hebrides and Johnson's Diary of a journey into north Wales*, ed. G. B. Hill, enl. edn, rev. L. F. Powell, 6 vols. (1934–50); 2nd edn (1964); repr. (1971)

Brown & Stratton, *Brit. mus.* — J. D. Brown and S. S. Stratton, *British musical biography* (1897)

Bryan, *Painters* — M. Bryan, *A biographical and critical dictionary of painters and engravers*, 2 vols. (1816); new edn, ed. G. Stanley (1849); new edn, ed. R. E. Graves and W. Armstrong, 2 vols. (1886–9); [4th edn], ed. G. C. Williamson, 5 vols. (1903–5) [various reprs.]

Burke, *Gen. GB* — J. Burke, *A genealogical and heraldic history of the commoners of Great Britain and Ireland*, 4 vols. (1833–8); new edn as *A genealogical and heraldic dictionary of the landed gentry of Great Britain and Ireland*, 3 vols. [1843–9] [many later edns]

Burke, *Gen. Ire.* — J. B. Burke, *A genealogical and heraldic history of the landed gentry of Ireland* (1899); 2nd edn (1904); 3rd edn (1912); 4th edn (1958); 5th edn as *Burke's Irish family records* (1976)

Burke, *Peerage* — J. Burke, *A general [later edns A genealogical] and heraldic dictionary of the peerage and baronetage of the United Kingdom* [later edns *the British empire*] (1829–)

Burney, *Hist. mus.* — C. Burney, *A general history of music, from the earliest ages to the present period*, 4 vols. (1776–89)

Burtchaell & Sadleir, *Alum. Dubl.* — G. D. Burtchaell and T. U. Sadleir, *Alumni Dublinenses: a register of the students, graduates, and provosts of Trinity College* (1924); [2nd edn], with suppl., in 2 pts (1935)

Calamy rev. — A. G. Matthews, *Calamy revised* (1934); repr. (1988)

CCI — *Calendar of confirmations and inventories granted and given up in the several commissariots of Scotland* (1876–)

CClR — *Calendar of the close rolls preserved in the Public Record Office*, 47 vols. (1892–1963)

CDS — J. Bain, ed., *Calendar of documents relating to Scotland*, 4 vols., PRO (1881–8); suppl. vol. 5, ed. G. G. Simpson and J. D. Galbraith [1986]

CEPR letters — W. H. Bliss, C. Johnson, and J. Twemlow, eds., *Calendar of entries in the papal registers relating to Great Britain and Ireland: papal letters* (1893–)

CGPLA — *Calendars of the grants of probate and letters of administration* [in 4 ser.: *England & Wales, Northern Ireland, Ireland*, and *Éire*]

Chambers, *Scots.* — R. Chambers, ed., *A biographical dictionary of eminent Scotsmen*, 4 vols. (1832–5)

Chancery records — chancery records pubd by the PRO

Chancery records (RC) — chancery records pubd by the Record Commissions

CIPM	*Calendar of inquisitions post mortem*, [20 vols.], PRO (1904–); also *Henry VII*, 3 vols. (1898–1955)
Clarendon, *Hist. rebellion*	E. Hyde, earl of Clarendon, *The history of the rebellion and civil wars in England*, 6 vols. (1888); repr. (1958) and (1992)
Cobbett, *Parl. hist.*	W. Cobbett and J. Wright, eds., *Cobbett's Parliamentary history of England*, 36 vols. (1806–1820)
Colvin, *Archs.*	H. Colvin, *A biographical dictionary of British architects, 1600–1840*, 3rd edn (1995)
Cooper, *Ath. Cantab.*	C. H. Cooper and T. Cooper, *Athenae Cantabrigienses*, 3 vols. (1858–1913); repr. (1967)
CPR	*Calendar of the patent rolls preserved in the Public Record Office* (1891–)
Crockford	*Crockford's Clerical Directory*
CS	Camden Society
CSP	*Calendar of state papers* [in 11 ser.: *domestic, Scotland, Scottish series, Ireland, colonial, Commonwealth, foreign, Spain* [at Simancas], *Rome, Milan,* and *Venice*]
CYS	Canterbury and York Society
DAB	*Dictionary of American biography*, 21 vols. (1928–36), repr. in 11 vols. (1964); 10 suppls. (1944–96)
DBB	D. J. Jeremy, ed., *Dictionary of business biography*, 5 vols. (1984–6)
DCB	G. W. Brown and others, *Dictionary of Canadian biography*, [14 vols.] (1966–)
Debrett's Peerage	*Debrett's Peerage* (1803–) [sometimes *Debrett's Illustrated peerage*]
Desmond, *Botanists*	R. Desmond, *Dictionary of British and Irish botanists and horticulturists* (1977); rev. edn (1994)
Dir. Brit. archs.	A. Felstead, J. Franklin, and L. Pinfield, eds., *Directory of British architects, 1834–1900* (1993); 2nd edn, ed. A. Brodie and others, 2 vols. (2001)
DLB	J. M. Bellamy and J. Saville, eds., *Dictionary of labour biography*, [10 vols.] (1972–)
DLitB	Dictionary of Literary Biography
DNB	*Dictionary of national biography*, 63 vols. (1885–1900), suppl., 3 vols. (1901); repr. in 22 vols. (1908–9); 10 further suppls. (1912–96); *Missing persons* (1993)
DNZB	W. H. Oliver and C. Orange, eds., *The dictionary of New Zealand biography*, 5 vols. (1990–2000)
DSAB	W. J. de Kock and others, eds., *Dictionary of South African biography*, 5 vols. (1968–87)
DSB	C. C. Gillispie and F. L. Holmes, eds., *Dictionary of scientific biography*, 16 vols. (1970–80); repr. in 8 vols. (1981); 2 vol. suppl. (1990)
DSBB	A. Slaven and S. Checkland, eds., *Dictionary of Scottish business biography, 1860–1960*, 2 vols. (1986–90)
DSCHT	N. M. de S. Cameron and others, eds., *Dictionary of Scottish church history and theology* (1993)
Dugdale, *Monasticon*	W. Dugdale, *Monasticon Anglicanum*, 3 vols. (1655–72); 2nd edn, 3 vols. (1661–82); new edn, ed. J. Caley, J. Ellis, and B. Bandinel, 6 vols. in 8 pts (1817–30); repr. (1846) and (1970)
DWB	J. E. Lloyd and others, eds., *Dictionary of Welsh biography down to 1940* (1959) [Eng. trans. of *Y bywgraffiadur Cymreig hyd 1940*, 2nd edn (1954)]
EdinR	*Edinburgh Review, or, Critical Journal*
EETS	Early English Text Society
Emden, *Cam.*	A. B. Emden, *A biographical register of the University of Cambridge to 1500* (1963)
Emden, *Oxf.*	A. B. Emden, *A biographical register of the University of Oxford to AD 1500*, 3 vols. (1957–9); also *A biographical register of the University of Oxford, AD 1501 to 1540* (1974)
EngHR	*English Historical Review*
Engraved Brit. ports.	F. M. O'Donoghue and H. M. Hake, *Catalogue of engraved British portraits preserved in the department of prints and drawings in the British Museum*, 6 vols. (1908–25)
ER	The English Reports, 178 vols. (1900–32)
ESTC	*English short title catalogue, 1475–1800* [CD-ROM and online]
Evelyn, *Diary*	*The diary of John Evelyn*, ed. E. S. De Beer, 6 vols. (1955); repr. (2000)
Farington, *Diary*	*The diary of Joseph Farington*, ed. K. Garlick and others, 17 vols. (1978–98)
Fasti Angl. (Hardy)	J. Le Neve, *Fasti ecclesiae Anglicanae*, ed. T. D. Hardy, 3 vols. (1854)
Fasti Angl., 1066–1300	[J. Le Neve], *Fasti ecclesiae Anglicanae, 1066–1300*, ed. D. E. Greenway and J. S. Barrow, [8 vols.] (1968–)
Fasti Angl., 1300–1541	[J. Le Neve], *Fasti ecclesiae Anglicanae, 1300–1541*, 12 vols. (1962–7)
Fasti Angl., 1541–1857	[J. Le Neve], *Fasti ecclesiae Anglicanae, 1541–1857*, ed. J. M. Horn, D. M. Smith, and D. S. Bailey, [9 vols.] (1969–)
Fasti Scot.	H. Scott, *Fasti ecclesiae Scoticanae*, 3 vols. in 6 (1871); new edn, [11 vols.] (1915–)
FO List	*Foreign Office List*
Fortescue, *Brit. army*	J. W. Fortescue, *A history of the British army*, 13 vols. (1899–1930)
Foss, *Judges*	E. Foss, *The judges of England*, 9 vols. (1848–64); repr. (1966)
Foster, *Alum. Oxon.*	J. Foster, ed., *Alumni Oxonienses: the members of the University of Oxford, 1715–1886*, 4 vols. (1887–8); later edn (1891); also *Alumni Oxonienses ... 1500–1714*, 4 vols. (1891–2); 8 vol. repr. (1968) and (2000)
Fuller, *Worthies*	T. Fuller, *The history of the worthies of England*, 4 pts (1662); new edn, 2 vols., ed. J. Nichols (1811); new edn, 3 vols., ed. P. A. Nuttall (1840); repr. (1965)
GEC, *Baronetage*	G. E. Cokayne, *Complete baronetage*, 6 vols. (1900–09); repr. (1983) [microprint]
GEC, *Peerage*	G. E. C. [G. E. Cokayne], *The complete peerage of England, Scotland, Ireland, Great Britain, and the United Kingdom*, 8 vols. (1887–98); new edn, ed. V. Gibbs and others, 14 vols. in 15 (1910–98); microprint repr. (1982) and (1987)
Genest, *Eng. stage*	J. Genest, *Some account of the English stage from the Restoration in 1660 to 1830*, 10 vols. (1832); repr. [New York, 1965]
Gillow, *Lit. biog. hist.*	J. Gillow, *A literary and biographical history or bibliographical dictionary of the English Catholics, from the breach with Rome, in 1534, to the present time*, 5 vols. [1885–1902]; repr. (1961); repr. with preface by C. Gillow (1999)
Gir. Camb. opera	*Giraldi Cambrensis opera*, ed. J. S. Brewer, J. F. Dimock, and G. F. Warner, 8 vols., Rolls Series, 21 (1861–91)
GJ	*Geographical Journal*

Gladstone, *Diaries*	*The Gladstone diaries: with cabinet minutes and prime-ministerial correspondence*, ed. M. R. D. Foot and H. C. G. Matthew, 14 vols. (1968–94)
GM	*Gentleman's Magazine*
Graves, *Artists*	A. Graves, ed., *A dictionary of artists who have exhibited works in the principal London exhibitions of oil paintings from 1760 to 1880* (1884); new edn (1895); 3rd edn (1901); facs. edn (1969); repr. [1970], (1973), and (1984)
Graves, *Brit. Inst.*	A. Graves, *The British Institution, 1806–1867: a complete dictionary of contributors and their work from the foundation of the institution* (1875); facs. edn (1908); repr. (1969)
Graves, *RA exhibitors*	A. Graves, *The Royal Academy of Arts: a complete dictionary of contributors and their work from its foundation in 1769 to 1904*, 8 vols. (1905–6); repr. in 4 vols. (1970) and (1972)
Graves, *Soc. Artists*	A. Graves, *The Society of Artists of Great Britain, 1760–1791, the Free Society of Artists, 1761–1783: a complete dictionary* (1907); facs. edn (1969)
Greaves & Zaller, *BDBR*	R. L. Greaves and R. Zaller, eds., *Biographical dictionary of British radicals in the seventeenth century*, 3 vols. (1982–4)
Grove, *Dict. mus.*	G. Grove, ed., *A dictionary of music and musicians*, 5 vols. (1878–90); 2nd edn, ed. J. A. Fuller Maitland (1904–10); 3rd edn, ed. H. C. Colles (1927); 4th edn with suppl. (1940); 5th edn, ed. E. Blom, 9 vols. (1954); suppl. (1961) [see also *New Grove*]
Hall, *Dramatic ports.*	L. A. Hall, *Catalogue of dramatic portraits in the theatre collection of the Harvard College library*, 4 vols. (1930–34)
Hansard	*Hansard's parliamentary debates*, ser. 1–5 (1803–)
Highfill, Burnim & Langhans, *BDA*	P. H. Highfill, K. A. Burnim, and E. A. Langhans, *A biographical dictionary of actors, actresses, musicians, dancers, managers, and other stage personnel in London, 1660–1800*, 16 vols. (1973–93)
Hist. U. Oxf.	T. H. Aston, ed., *The history of the University of Oxford*, 8 vols. (1984–2000) [1: *The early Oxford schools*, ed. J. I. Catto (1984); 2: *Late medieval Oxford*, ed. J. I. Catto and R. Evans (1992); 3: *The collegiate university*, ed. J. McConica (1986); 4: *Seventeenth-century Oxford*, ed. N. Tyacke (1997); 5: *The eighteenth century*, ed. L. S. Sutherland and L. G. Mitchell (1986); 6–7: *Nineteenth-century Oxford*, ed. M. G. Brock and M. C. Curthoys (1997–2000); 8: *The twentieth century*, ed. B. Harrison (2000)]
HJ	*Historical Journal*
HMC	Historical Manuscripts Commission
Holdsworth, *Eng. law*	W. S. Holdsworth, *A history of English law*, ed. A. L. Goodhart and H. L. Hanbury, 17 vols. (1903–72)
HoP, *Commons*	*The history of parliament: the House of Commons* [1386–1421, ed. J. S. Roskell, L. Clark, and C. Rawcliffe, 4 vols. (1992); 1509–1558, ed. S. T. Bindoff, 3 vols. (1982); 1558–1603, ed. P. W. Hasler, 3 vols. (1981); 1660–1690, ed. B. D. Henning, 3 vols. (1983); 1690–1715, ed. D. W. Hayton, E. Cruickshanks, and S. Handley, 5 vols. (2002); 1715–1754, ed. R. Sedgwick, 2 vols. (1970); 1754–1790, ed. L. Namier and J. Brooke, 3 vols. (1964), repr. (1985); 1790–1820, ed. R. G. Thorne, 5 vols. (1986); in draft (used with permission): 1422–1504, 1604–1629, 1640–1660, and 1820–1832]
IGI	*International Genealogical Index*, Church of Jesus Christ of the Latterday Saints
ILN	*Illustrated London News*
IMC	Irish Manuscripts Commission
Irving, *Scots.*	J. Irving, ed., *The book of Scotsmen eminent for achievements in arms and arts, church and state, law, legislation and literature, commerce, science, travel and philanthropy* (1881)
JCS	*Journal of the Chemical Society*
JHC	*Journals of the House of Commons*
JHL	*Journals of the House of Lords*
John of Worcester, *Chron.*	*The chronicle of John of Worcester*, ed. R. R. Darlington and P. McGurk, trans. J. Bray and P. McGurk, 3 vols., OMT (1995–) [vol. 1 forthcoming]
Keeler, *Long Parliament*	M. F. Keeler, *The Long Parliament, 1640–1641: a biographical study of its members* (1954)
Kelly, *Handbk*	*The upper ten thousand: an alphabetical list of all members of noble families*, 3 vols. (1875–7); continued as *Kelly's handbook of the upper ten thousand for 1878* [1879], 2 vols. (1878–9); continued as *Kelly's handbook to the titled, landed and official classes*, 94 vols. (1880–1973)
LondG	*London Gazette*
LP Henry VIII	J. S. Brewer, J. Gairdner, and R. H. Brodie, eds., *Letters and papers, foreign and domestic, of the reign of Henry VIII*, 23 vols. in 38 (1862–1932); repr. (1965)
Mallalieu, *Watercolour artists*	H. L. Mallalieu, *The dictionary of British watercolour artists up to 1820*, 3 vols. (1976–90); vol. 1, 2nd edn (1986)
Memoirs FRS	*Biographical Memoirs of Fellows of the Royal Society*
MGH	Monumenta Germaniae Historica
MT	*Musical Times*
Munk, *Roll*	W. Munk, *The roll of the Royal College of Physicians of London*, 2 vols. (1861); 2nd edn, 3 vols. (1878)
N&Q	*Notes and Queries*
New Grove	S. Sadie, ed., *The new Grove dictionary of music and musicians*, 20 vols. (1980); 2nd edn, 29 vols. (2001) [also online edn; see also Grove, *Dict. mus.*]
Nichols, *Illustrations*	J. Nichols and J. B. Nichols, *Illustrations of the literary history of the eighteenth century*, 8 vols. (1817–58)
Nichols, *Lit. anecdotes*	J. Nichols, *Literary anecdotes of the eighteenth century*, 9 vols. (1812–16); facs. edn (1966)
Obits. FRS	*Obituary Notices of Fellows of the Royal Society*
O'Byrne, *Naval biog. dict.*	W. R. O'Byrne, *A naval biographical dictionary* (1849); repr. (1990); [2nd edn], 2 vols. (1861)
OHS	Oxford Historical Society
Old Westminsters	*The record of Old Westminsters*, 1–2, ed. G. F. R. Barker and A. H. Stenning (1928); suppl. 1, ed. J. B. Whitmore and G. R. Y. Radcliffe [1938]; 3, ed. J. B. Whitmore, G. R. Y. Radcliffe, and D. C. Simpson (1963); suppl. 2, ed. F. E. Pagan (1978); 4, ed. F. E. Pagan and H. E. Pagan (1992)
OMT	Oxford Medieval Texts
Ordericus Vitalis, *Eccl. hist.*	*The ecclesiastical history of Orderic Vitalis*, ed. and trans. M. Chibnall, 6 vols., OMT (1969–80); repr. (1990)
Paris, *Chron.*	*Matthaei Parisiensis, monachi sancti Albani, chronica majora*, ed. H. R. Luard, Rolls Series, 7 vols. (1872–83)
Parl. papers	*Parliamentary papers* (1801–)
PBA	*Proceedings of the British Academy*

Pepys, *Diary* — *The diary of Samuel Pepys*, ed. R. Latham and W. Matthews, 11 vols. (1970–83); repr. (1995) and (2000)

Pevsner — N. Pevsner and others, Buildings of England series

PICE — *Proceedings of the Institution of Civil Engineers*

Pipe rolls — *The great roll of the pipe for . . .*, PRSoc. (1884–)

PRO — Public Record Office

PRS — *Proceedings of the Royal Society of London*

PRSoc. — Pipe Roll Society

PTRS — *Philosophical Transactions of the Royal Society*

QR — *Quarterly Review*

RC — Record Commissions

Redgrave, *Artists* — S. Redgrave, *A dictionary of artists of the English school* (1874); rev. edn (1878); repr. (1970)

Reg. Oxf. — C. W. Boase and A. Clark, eds., *Register of the University of Oxford*, 5 vols., OHS, 1, 10–12, 14 (1885–9)

Reg. PCS — J. H. Burton and others, eds., *The register of the privy council of Scotland*, 1st ser., 14 vols. (1877–98); 2nd ser., 8 vols. (1899–1908); 3rd ser., [16 vols.] (1908–70)

Reg. RAN — H. W. C. Davis and others, eds., *Regesta regum Anglo-Normannorum, 1066–1154*, 4 vols. (1913–69)

RIBA Journal — *Journal of the Royal Institute of British Architects* [later *RIBA Journal*]

RotP — J. Strachey, ed., *Rotuli parliamentorum ut et petitiones, et placita in parliamento*, 6 vols. (1767–77)

RotS — D. Macpherson, J. Caley, and W. Illingworth, eds., *Rotuli Scotiae in Turri Londinensi et in domo capitulari Westmonasteriensi asservati*, 2 vols., RC, 14 (1814–19)

RS — Record(s) Society

Rymer, *Foedera* — T. Rymer and R. Sanderson, eds., *Foedera, conventiones, literae et cuiuscunque generis acta publica inter reges Angliae et alios quosvis imperatores, reges, pontifices, principes, vel communitates*, 20 vols. (1704–35); 2nd edn, 20 vols. (1726–35); 3rd edn, 10 vols. (1739–45), facs. edn (1967); new edn, ed. A. Clarke, J. Caley, and F. Holbrooke, 4 vols., RC, 50 (1816–30)

Sainty, *Judges* — J. Sainty, ed., *The judges of England, 1272–1990*, SeldS, suppl. ser., 10 (1993)

Sainty, *King's counsel* — J. Sainty, ed., *A list of English law officers and king's counsel*, SeldS, suppl. ser., 7 (1987)

SCH — Studies in Church History

Scots peerage — J. B. Paul, ed. *The Scots peerage, founded on Wood's edition of Sir Robert Douglas's Peerage of Scotland, containing an historical and genealogical account of the nobility of that kingdom*, 9 vols. (1904–14)

SeldS — Selden Society

SHR — *Scottish Historical Review*

State trials — T. B. Howell and T. J. Howell, eds., *Cobbett's Complete collection of state trials*, 34 vols. (1809–28)

STC, 1475–1640 — A. W. Pollard, G. R. Redgrave, and others, eds., *A short-title catalogue of . . . English books . . . 1475–1640* (1926); 2nd edn, ed. W. A. Jackson, F. S. Ferguson, and K. F. Pantzer, 3 vols. (1976–91) [see also Wing, *STC*]

STS — Scottish Text Society

SurtS — Surtees Society

Symeon of Durham, *Opera* — *Symeonis monachi opera omnia*, ed. T. Arnold, 2 vols., Rolls Series, 75 (1882–5); repr. (1965)

Tanner, *Bibl. Brit.-Hib.* — T. Tanner, *Bibliotheca Britannico-Hibernica*, ed. D. Wilkins (1748); repr. (1963)

Thieme & Becker, *Allgemeines Lexikon* — U. Thieme, F. Becker, and H. Vollmer, eds., *Allgemeines Lexikon der bildenden Künstler von der Antike bis zur Gegenwart*, 37 vols. (Leipzig, 1907–50); repr. (1961–5), (1983), and (1992)

Thurloe, *State papers* — *A collection of the state papers of John Thurloe*, ed. T. Birch, 7 vols. (1742)

TLS — *Times Literary Supplement*

Tout, *Admin. hist.* — T. F. Tout, *Chapters in the administrative history of mediaeval England: the wardrobe, the chamber, and the small seals*, 6 vols. (1920–33); repr. (1967)

TRHS — *Transactions of the Royal Historical Society*

VCH — H. A. Doubleday and others, eds., *The Victoria history of the counties of England*, [88 vols.] (1900–)

Venn, *Alum. Cant.* — J. Venn and J. A. Venn, *Alumni Cantabrigienses: a biographical list of all known students, graduates, and holders of office at the University of Cambridge, from the earliest times to 1900*, 10 vols. (1922–54); repr. in 2 vols. (1974–8)

Vertue, *Note books* — [G. Vertue], *Note books*, ed. K. Esdaile, earl of Ilchester, and H. M. Hake, 6 vols., Walpole Society, 18, 20, 22, 24, 26, 30 (1930–55)

VF — *Vanity Fair*

Walford, *County families* — E. Walford, *The county families of the United Kingdom, or, Royal manual of the titled and untitled aristocracy of Great Britain and Ireland* (1860)

Walker rev. — A. G. Matthews, *Walker revised: being a revision of John Walker's Sufferings of the clergy during the grand rebellion, 1642–60* (1948); repr. (1988)

Walpole, *Corr.* — *The Yale edition of Horace Walpole's correspondence*, ed. W. S. Lewis, 48 vols. (1937–83)

Ward, *Men of the reign* — T. H. Ward, ed., *Men of the reign: a biographical dictionary of eminent persons of British and colonial birth who have died during the reign of Queen Victoria* (1885); repr. (Graz, 1968)

Waterhouse, *18c painters* — E. Waterhouse, *The dictionary of 18th century painters in oils and crayons* (1981); repr. as *British 18th century painters in oils and crayons* (1991), vol. 2 of *Dictionary of British art*

Watt, *Bibl. Brit.* — R. Watt, *Bibliotheca Britannica, or, A general index to British and foreign literature*, 4 vols. (1824) [many reprs.]

Wellesley index — W. E. Houghton, ed., *The Wellesley index to Victorian periodicals, 1824–1900*, 5 vols. (1966–89); new edn (1999) [CD-ROM]

Wing, *STC* — D. Wing, ed., *Short-title catalogue of . . . English books . . . 1641–1700*, 3 vols. (1945–51); 2nd edn (1972–88); rev. and enl. edn, ed. J. J. Morrison, C. W. Nelson, and M. Seccombe, 4 vols. (1994–8) [see also *STC, 1475–1640*]

Wisden — *John Wisden's Cricketer's Almanack*

Wood, *Ath. Oxon.* — A. Wood, *Athenae Oxonienses . . . to which are added the Fasti*, 2 vols. (1691–2); 2nd edn (1721); new edn, 4 vols., ed. P. Bliss (1813–20); repr. (1967) and (1969)

Wood, *Vic. painters* — C. Wood, *Dictionary of Victorian painters* (1971); 2nd edn (1978); 3rd edn as *Victorian painters*, 2 vols. (1995), vol. 4 of *Dictionary of British art*

WW — *Who's who* (1849–)

WWBMP — M. Stenton and S. Lees, eds., *Who's who of British members of parliament*, 4 vols. (1976–81)

WWW — *Who was who* (1929–)

Hooppell, Robert Eli (1833–1895), antiquary and Church of England clergyman, born in the parish of St Mary, Rotherhithe, London, on 30 January 1833, was the son of John Eli Hooppell, carpenter, and his wife, Mary Ann. He was educated at Queen Elizabeth's Free Grammar School, Horsleydown, and was admitted sizar at St John's College, Cambridge, on 30 June 1851. He was also a scholar of the college. In 1855 he graduated BA, being fortieth wrangler in the mathematical tripos, and in 1856 he obtained a first class in moral science. He proceeded MA in 1858, LLD in 1865, and was admitted *ad eundem* at Durham in 1876. He married at Broxbourne, Hertfordshire, on 20 June 1855, Margaret, daughter of Samuel and Elizabeth Hooppell of Fishleigh, Devon.

From 1855 to 1861 Hooppell was second and mathematical master at Beaumaris grammar school. He later used his mathematics for a statistical paper on the Contagious Diseases Acts read to the British Association in 1871. He was ordained deacon in 1857 and priest in 1859, and from 1859 to 1861 he served as English chaplain at Menai Bridge. In 1861 he was appointed first principal of Winterbottom Nautical College, South Shields, and he remained in that position until 1875, when he was instituted to the rectory of Byers Green, co. Durham. For the last year or two of his life he was in delicate health, and wintered at Bournemouth.

Hooppell served on the committee which superintended the excavation of the Roman camp at South Shields. His paper on the discoveries there (*Natural History Transactions of Northumberland*, 7, 1882, 126–42) was the prelude to a lecture, published in 1879, on *Vinovium, the Buried Roman City at Binchester*, between Bishop Auckland and Byers Green, and in 1891 *Vinovia, a Buried Roman City*, with thirty-eight illustrations. The substance of this treatise appeared in the journal of the British Archaeological Association, and he contributed to the same journal for 1895 a paper on 'Roman Manchester and the roads to and from it'. From 1877 he read papers on the names of Roman stations to the Newcastle Society of Antiquaries, and he contributed to the *Archaeologia Aeliana* and the *Illustrated Archaeologist*. His work on Vinovia has been largely superseded by later scholarship. His address, as president of the Tyneside Naturalists' Field Club, is in the *Natural History Transactions of Northumberland* (7.187–206), and after his death there was published in 1898 a volume entitled *Rambles of an Antiquary*, comprising papers published in the *Newcastle Courant* in 1880 and 1881, chiefly on the antiquities of Northumberland and Durham.

Hooppell also published, in addition to several individual sermons, *Reason and Religion, or, The Leading Doctrines of Christianity* (1867; 2nd edn, 1895) and *Materialism: Has it any Real Foundation in Science?* (2nd edn, 1874). He died at The Burlington, Oxford Road, Bournemouth, on 23 August 1895, and was buried in Bournemouth cemetery. His wife, two sons, and a daughter survived him.

W. P. COURTNEY, rev. H. C. G. MATTHEW

Sources *Journal of the British Archaeological Association*, new ser., 1 (1895), 280 · *Proceedings of the Society of Antiquaries of Newcastle upon Tyne*, 7 (1895–6), 156 · *Newcastle Weekly Courant* (31 Aug 1895) · Venn, *Alum. Cant.* · CGPLA Eng. & Wales (1896)

Wealth at death £3303 15s. 10d.: administration with will, 23 March 1896, CGPLA Eng. & Wales

Hooten [Hooton; *née* Carrier], **Elizabeth** (d. 1672), Quaker preacher, first appears as Elizabeth Carrier on 11 May 1628 at Ollerton, Nottinghamshire, when she married Oliver Hooten (d. 1657), a prosperous farmer. Their son Samuel was baptized at Ollerton on 4 May 1633, but they subsequently moved to Skegby near Mansfield. There were at least five other children: Thomas (*bap.* 1636), John (*bap.* 1639), Josiah (*bap.* 1641), Oliver, and Elizabeth.

After leaving the Church of England at an unknown date, Hooten appears to have been active in her local Baptist community and perhaps as a preacher, but according to her son Oliver, writing years later in 1686 or 1687, 'after some time finding them that they were not upright hearted to the Lord but did his work negligently' (Mack, 146), she parted company with them. She may have been the first person to be 'convinced' by George Fox about 1647. Initially, Oliver Hooten seems to have opposed his wife's new beliefs 'in so much that they had like to have parted' (ibid., 197), but some time in the next decade he turned Quaker himself, for his death is recorded in the Quaker digest registers for the Nottinghamshire and Derbyshire quarterly meeting. Fox wrote in his journal that about 1649 Elizabeth's 'mouth was opned to preach y[e] gospell' (Fox, *Journal*, 2.325). Gerard Croese noted in 1696 that she 'was the first of her sex among the Quakers who attempted to imitate men, and preach' and suggested that she was a role model for women: 'after her example, many of her sex had the confidence to undertake the same office' (Croese, 37). Hooten was obviously very close to Fox in the late 1640s and an important figure in the incipient movement. About 1649 or 1650 he appointed a meeting at her home in Skegby, where he miraculously healed a woman.

Hooten soon troubled the authorities with her preaching and her protestations against the corruption of the clergy and magistrates. Her first recorded imprisonment appears to have been in Derby about 1651 for reproving a minister. In 1652 she was imprisoned in York Castle for admonishing a minister and his congregation in Rotherham at the close of their worship. With other Quakers, including Mary Fisher and Thomas Aldam, she was a signatory to *False Prophets and False Teachers* (1652), a tract attacking paid ministry, written in the castle. Her experiences at York led her to write to Oliver Cromwell criticizing the legal system. She noted that many murderers 'escaped throughe frends & money, & pore people for Lesser facts are put to death', while lamenting that in prison many 'Lighe worse than doggs for want of strawe' (Manners, 10). In 1653 Fox was imprisoned in Carlisle for preaching with other leading Quakers including Hooten, James Nayler, and William Dewsbury. After delivering the Quaker message at a church in Beckingham, Lincolnshire, in 1654, Hooten was imprisoned for five months, becoming the first to suffer for Friends in that county. She served a further three weeks in Lincoln in 1655 for 'exhorting the people to repentance' (Besse, 1.346). Harsh treatment by a female gaoler prompted her to write once again 'to him in Authority' (presumably meaning Cromwell), condemning prison conditions (Manners, 15). In 1660 Hooten was back in Nottinghamshire where a man named Jackson, the minister for Selston, violently assaulted her, allegedly without provocation, while she was walking along the road.

Hooten's husband died on 30 June 1657. Four years later, in 1661, she travelled to America with Joane Brooksup or Brooksop. Her son Samuel opposed the undertaking, but later supported her decision and eventually preached in America himself. Arriving at Boston, via Virginia, they were imprisoned by Governor Endicott and then driven for two days out into the wilderness and left to starve. They managed to make their way to Rhode Island, from where they obtained a passage to Barbados, before returning once again to Boston 'to testify against the spirit of persecution there predominant' (Besse, 2.229). Apprehended by a constable, they were then put on board a ship for Virginia and eventually returned to England.

Once there, Hooten repeatedly petitioned Charles II in the hope that she would be able to live more comfortably on a proposed return trip to America. In 1662 she handed letters to the king in St James's Park, causing a stir among bystanders because she did not kneel. Receiving no reply, she continued to harangue Charles and was, she recalled, 'moved to goe amongst them againe at Whitehall in sacke-cloathe and ashes' (Manners, 37). Hooten eventually obtained a royal licence to settle in any of the American colonies, and sailed to Massachusetts with her daughter, Elizabeth. She asked the Boston authorities on numerous occasions for a house, a place for Friends to meet, and land for a burial-ground, but was refused in spite of the king's recommendations. Hooten afterwards travelled eastwards and was imprisoned first at Hampton and then at Dover for her activities against ministers. Next, at Cambridge, she called people to repentance as she walked through the streets and was imprisoned yet again for two days and nights in 'a noisome, stinking dungeon', without food or water (Bishop, 99). A magistrates' order that she be whipped through the three towns of Cambridge, Water Town, and Dedham 'was rigorously executed' (Besse, 2.229). Once again she was sent out into the wilderness on horseback yet managed to make her way back to Rhode Island, later returning to a place near Cambridge with her daughter and an old woman named Sarah Coleman. After further whippings, Hooten returned to Boston, where she was sent to the house of correction, then again whipped through three towns (Roxbury, Dedham, and Medfield) and cast out into the wilderness. After further imprisonment in Boston and Rhode Island she was warned that she faced execution or branding should she ever return. In 'Some more of the sufferings of Elizabeth Hooten' in George Bishop's *New England Judged* (1667) she described how she was able to withstand this constant string of punishments, writing through God-given strength.

Hooten then returned to England and resumed her work as an itinerant preacher. The Quaker historian William Sewel noted at the time that he had 'several times seen her in England in a good condition' (Sewel, 570). In 1663 she suffered the distraint of three mares and other losses which made it very difficult for her to continue farming. In 1667 she wrote a letter to Friends condemning John Perrot, the Quaker schismatic, and his followers and linked them with Ranterism. In 1670 she published an address of her own in Thomas Taylor's *To the King and both Houses of Parliament*, in which she criticized the authorities for the severity of persecution against Quakers ensuing from the second Conventicle Act. Hooten was a fairly prolific letter writer, who often petitioned the authorities, as she did the king for the release of Margaret Fox from Lancaster Castle. Her letters, which include many to other Friends, are of considerable importance for the insights they provide into the 'radicalism' of early Quakerism. Perhaps surprisingly, she published very little; apart from the aforementioned works, she was signatory to a testimony for William Simpson contained in *A Short Relation Concerning the Life and Death of William Simpson* (1671).

On 11 August 1671 Hooten crossed the Atlantic for the last time, on this occasion with George Fox and other Friends, including Solomon Eccles and William Edmunson. They passed from Barbados to Jamaica, where at Port Royal Hooten died in February 1672. Her cause of death is unclear, though a testimony from the Quaker James Lancaster recorded that her body was weak and swollen and she was unable to speak. She was buried in Jamaica.   CAROLINE L. LEACHMAN

Sources E. Manners, 'Elizabeth Hooten: first Quaker woman preacher (1600–1672)', *Journal of the Friends' Historical Society*, suppl. 12 (1914) · G. Bishop, *New England judged*, pt 2 (1667) · J. Besse, *A collection of the sufferings of the people called Quakers*, 2 vols. (1753) · *The journal of George Fox*, ed. N. Penney, 2 vols. (1911) · P. Mack, *Visionary women: ecstatic prophecy in seventeenth-century England* (1992) · C. Trevett, *Women and Quakerism in the 17th century* (1995) · G. Croese, *The general history of the Quakers* (1696) · J. Gough, *The history of the people called Quakers*, vols. 1 and 2 · W. Sewel, *The history of the rise, increase, and progress of the Christian people called Quakers* (1799), vol. 1 · G. Fox, *The short and itinerary journals of George Fox*, ed. N. Penney (1925) · J. Smith, ed., *A descriptive catalogue of Friends' books*, 1 (1867) · Quaker digest registers, RS Friends, Lond. · 'Dictionary of Quaker biography', RS Friends, Lond. [card index]
Archives RS Friends, Lond., corresp. and papers | RS Friends, Lond., A. R. Barclay MSS, letters · RS Friends, Lond., portfolio MSS, 3/2–6, 28–30, 32–42, 44, 46–79

Hooton, Charles (c.1813–1847), novelist and journalist, was born about 1813 but his origins and early life are otherwise obscure. In 1836, while editing a newspaper in Leeds, Hooton published *The Adventures of Bilberry Thurland*. In 1837 he moved to London and published in *Bentley's Miscellany* a novel called *Colin Clink* (republished 1841). As the sub-editor of the *True Sun*, Hooton wrote a series of articles on the subject of political economy. In 1840 he edited another short-lived paper, *The Woolsack*, in which he attacked the abuses of the court of chancery. Following the collapse of *The Woolsack*, Hooton left for Texas, where for nine months he attempted to live off the land, farming, hunting, and fishing. He afterwards undertook newspaper work in New Orleans, New York, and Montreal, but his failing health prompted him to return to England. He wrote a series of ballads for the *New Monthly Magazine* illustrative of American life and literature, and a novel called *Launcelot Wedge*, which was running in *Ainsworth's Magazine* at the time of his death (republished 1849). Hooton's account of his experiences in the United States and Canada was published posthumously as *St Louis' Isle, or, Texiana* (1847). He died, apparently unmarried, from an accidental overdose of morphine at his residence in Nottingham on 16 February 1847. According to a late twentieth-century assessment of his writing, 'his sub-Dickensian fiction, though quirky, has its powerfully atmospheric and comic moments' (Sutherland, 305).

FRANCIS WATT, *rev.* CHARLES BRAYNE

Sources *New Monthly Magazine*, new ser., 80 (1847), 397–8 · *GM*, 2nd ser., 27 (1847), 442–3 · *Annual Register* (1847), 211 · J. Sutherland, *The Longman companion to Victorian fiction* (1988)

Hopcyn ap Tomas ab Einion (*fl.* 1337–1408), literary patron, lived at Ynys Forgan (rather than Ynys Dawy as previously believed), a house at the lower end of the Swansea valley, in the medieval lordship of Gower. His *floruit* date is defined by a document witnessed by his father in 1337 and a deed transferring land by Hopcyn to his son Tomas in 1408. There is, as yet, no other record documentation for Hopcyn ap Tomas or his estate but other evidence, mostly circumstantial, indicates that he was probably a leading figure in local (especially legal) administration, a person of substance, and certainly a literary patron with whom can be associated a number of fourteenth-century Welsh manuscripts, the most significant of which is the Red Book of Hergest (Bodl. Oxf., MS Jesus College 111).

Written about 1400, this is one of the most important of all Welsh manuscripts, containing, as it does, a well-planned representative collection of medieval Welsh literature. With the exception of legal texts the whole range of secular Middle Welsh writing is to be found here: early and court poetry, contemporary praise poetry, prose narratives, both traditional *mabinogion* and recently translated Old French texts, a compilation of Welsh history from the siege of Troy containing versions of Geoffrey of Monmouth's *Historia regum Britanniae* and of the *Brut y tywysogyon* (down to 1282), triadic and other legendary, prophetic, and moral compilations, medical, geographical and utilitarian texts, and a copy of a bardic grammar. The book has been planned as a library of classical and contemporary Welsh literature and learning and in concept reflects the knowledgeable interests of a single patron able to draw on substantial material and literary resources. Five praise poems in the book, by different poets, are addressed to Hopcyn together with a light-hearted piece listing the pet hates of his craftsman. Though much of this poetry is stereotyped eulogy some references suggest a more personal and active involvement in contemporary literary culture and in bardic discussions. (It may be significant that the craftsman's hates included poets and rhymesters.) Two of the poems specify the nature of some of the books in Hopcyn's library— *Elucidarium*, Greal, Annales, Law. In 1403 'Hopkyn ap Thomas of Gower' was summoned to Carmarthen by Owain Glyn Dŵr to be consulted by him on the outcome of his current campaign since Hopcyn was held to be 'maister of Brut', that is, an acknowledged interpreter of prophetic verse and other utterances. Another Welsh manuscript (Philadelphia Public Library Company, MS 86800), containing fragments of the historical compilation found in the red book, has a colophon stating that the scribe— Hywel Fychan ap Hywel Goch—copied the text for 'his master' Hopcyn ap Tomas.

Hywel is the main scribe of the red book and his work is also found in a number of other manuscripts, some of which contain versions of the texts mentioned as being in Hopcyn's library. Hywel also wrote the Red Book of Talgarth (Aberystwyth, NL Wales, Llanstephan MS 27), an anthology of religious texts (including *Elucidarium*), apparently for one Rhys ap Tomas ab Einion, who may have been Hopcyn's brother. The Ynys Forgan family appear to have been genuine bookmen and Hopcyn's support of poets and scribes was being undertaken more from personal interest than simply as a social duty. Such clear evidence for the literary activity of the gentry class is uncommon but perhaps it should not be inferred that Hopcyn's interests were unusual. He may have been typical of gentry patronage of literature in the late fourteenth and fifteenth centuries.

The eighteenth-century forger Edward *Williams, 'Iolo Morganwg' (1747–1826), knew of the poems referred to above and used them to compose an imaginary account of Hopcyn's role in Welsh literature. He also asserted, without genuine evidence, that Hopcyn's grandfather was *Einion Offeiriad.

BRYNLEY F. ROBERTS

Sources C. James, '"Llwybrau wybodau, llên a llyfrau": Hopcyn ap Thomas a'r traddodiad llenyddol Cymraeg', *Cwm Tawe*, ed. H. T. Edwards (1993), 4–44 · B. F. Roberts, 'Un o lawysgifau Hopcyn ap Tomas o Ynys Dawy', *BBCS*, 22 (1966–8), 223–8 · G. J. Williams, *Traddodiad llenyddol Morgannwg* (1948), 9–14 and *passim* · G. Charles-Edwards, 'The scribes of the Red Book of Hergest', *National Library of Wales Journal*, 21 (1979–80), 246–56 · G. Charles-Edwards, 'Hywel Vychan: Red Book and White Book', *National Library of Wales Journal*, 21 (1979–80), 427–8 · P. Morgan, 'Glamorgan and the Red Book', *Morgannwg*, 22 (1978) · J. Rhys and J. G. Evans, eds., *The text of the Mabinogion and other tales from the Red Book of Hergest* (1887) · J. Rhys and J. G. Evans, eds., *The text of the Bruts from the Red Book of Hergest* [1890] · J. G. Evans, ed., *The poetry in the Red Book of Hergest* (1911) · T. Jones, ed. and trans., *Brut y tywysogyon, or, The chronicle of the princes: Red Book of Hergest* (1955)

Hope family (*per. c.*1700–1813), merchants and merchant bankers, of Amsterdam and London, came to prominence with **Archibald** [i] **Hope** (1664–1743). The son of Henry [i] Hope (1630–1688), a merchant of Rotterdam and London, Archibald was baptized in 1664 at the Scottish church in Rotterdam in the Netherlands. Although based in Amsterdam he and his family were of Scottish origin and claimed ancestral links to Sir Thomas [i] Hope [see Hope, Sir Thomas, of Craighall (1573–1646)], lord advocate, and the earls of Hopetoun, and were connected through business to the City of London. In the second half of the eighteenth century their merchant bank of Hope & Co. emerged as Europe's most powerful, in particular raising huge sums for kings and governments throughout Europe and beyond to the United States.

Archibald [i] continued his father's business, but experienced greater success. In 1694 he married Anna Claus (d. 1752), daughter of an Amsterdam button maker, and they had at least eight sons and two daughters. In due course Archibald was succeeded in business by his sons Isaac (d. 1766) and Zachary (1711–1770). However, it was his second son, **Archibald** [ii] **Hope** (1698–1733), who laid the merchant bank's foundations. In 1720 he became apprenticed to his uncle, an Amsterdam stockjobber, and swiftly got involved in banking business. In 1726 he married a merchant's daughter, Geertruyd Reessen (1702–1726); they had no children.

His brother, **Thomas** [ii] **Hope** (1704–1779), joined him about 1724, followed soon after by another brother, **Adrian** [i] **Hope** (1709–1781), but Archibald's contribution was cut short by his untimely death in Rotterdam on 28 March 1733. In consequence, the merchant banking house was restyled Thomas and Adrian Hope. These two brothers developed the business so that during the Seven Years' War (1756–62) it became one of Amsterdam's most successful. Thomas married in 1727 Margareta Marcelis, daughter of an Amsterdam merchant and soap boiler, and they had one son, John. Adrian did not marry.

Thomas achieved great commercial influence and overshadowed Adrian. The newly restored stadholder, William IV, appointed him his representative director of the major trading company the West Indische Compagnie, and also to his committee to plan for Dutch economic resurgence. Thomas proposed limited free trade as a stimulus to regeneration, but his plans were cut short by William's death in 1751. He then withdrew from the company but in 1756 joined the more important Oost Indische Compagnie and from 1766 to 1770 represented on its board the new stadholder, William V.

In mid-1762 Thomas and Adrian restyled their firm Hope & Co. and admitted as partners the former's only son, **John Hope** (1737–1784), and an American nephew, **Henry** [iii] **Hope** (1735–1811). Buttressed by his father's wealth and commercial influence, John was destined to play a prominent role in Dutch society and politics and gradually withdrew from the firm's day-to-day management. His marriage in 1763 to Philippina Barbara van der Hoeven (c.1738–1789), daughter of Rotterdam's burgomaster, was his first step to membership of the Netherlands' political élite. They had at least three sons: Thomas *Hope (1769–1831), Adrian [ii] (1772–1834), who became insane, and Henry Philip *Hope (1774–1839) [see under Hope, Thomas (1769–1831)], a partner of Hopes.

William V arranged for John's membership of Amsterdam's Vroedschap (council) as an alderman from 1768 to 1784, and from the late 1760s through to his death in 1784 he acquired estates and great houses, not least Nederhorst den Berg Castle, near Hilversum. In 1770 he succeeded his father as a director of the Oost Indische Compagnie.

John's American cousin Henry was the son of Henry [ii] Hope, elder brother of Thomas [ii] and Adrian [i] Hope. His father had settled at Boston, Massachusetts, about 1730, and Henry was probably born there. He moved to England about 1748 in order to complete his education. In 1754 young Henry joined Gurnell, Hoare & Co., London merchants, and about 1760 entered the London house of Hope & Co. as a clerk.

From 1762 until the early 1780s these four partners developed Hopes into Europe's leading merchant bank. Adrian and especially Thomas consistently provided over 80 per cent of the capital, largely through the plough-back of profits, and this rose from just over 4 million guilders in 1762 to 10.3 million in 1780. In the process, the Hope partners accumulated great wealth, distributing over 500,000 guilders annually in ten years and under 400,000 in only four.

The Hopes' merchanting business was broadly based, embracing all types of goods traded in markets across Europe and North and Central America. Occasionally they entered into trading speculations of immense size, as in 1787 when they endeavoured, albeit with limited success, to control the international cochineal market. From 1768 the business of financing sovereign clients through the issue of their bearer bonds supplemented the traditional merchanting business and became a major source of prestige. The Hope family's early clients included the kingdom of Sweden, for which 14.5 million guilders was raised in twelve loans between 1768 and 1787; the elector of Bavaria, for whom 400,000 guilders was provided in 1771 on security of his crown jewels; and the republic of Poland, for which 2.6 million guilders was raised in 1772. These were huge sums and were often provided at crucial moments in the histories of these countries. Initially Hopes sought out its clients; by the 1780s, such was their power, the statesmen of Europe beat a path to Hopes.

Henry, 'singularly even, mild, engaging and amiable' (Buist, 16), was the leader in developing this business, benefiting from a neutrality afforded by his American origins. Following Thomas's death in 1779 and Adrian's in 1781, his role became vital and more so when John died unexpectedly in 1784 aged forty-seven. The huge breach their deaths made in Hopes' leadership was never made good. John's sons were then minors but when of age they showed little inclination towards business. For his part, Henry remained a bachelor.

In July 1782 Henry's part-solution was to admit **John Williams Hope** (1757–1813). This young Cornishman, born at St Ewe and employed in Hopes' counting house as a clerk, was the son of William Williams, rector of St Ewe, and of Elizabeth, daughter of Francis Gregor of Trewarthenick. He deeply impressed Henry, who encouraged his marriage in 1782 to his heiress, Anne (1763–1820), daughter of his sister Henrietta Maria and her husband, John Goddard of Rotterdam and Woodford Hall, Essex. Williams thereupon changed his surname to Williams Hope and was admitted a partner. John Williams Hope failed to meet expectations, however, excelling as a 'desk man' who 'ran the office precisely and with pleasure' (Buist, 17) yet who lacked the dynamism and enterprise which were to be found in his wife. This imbalance of temperament made for a turbulent marriage, culminating in Anne's elopement in 1808 with Baron von Dopff, whom she married in 1813. There were at least two children from the marriage of John Williams Hope and Anne: Henrietta, who married the seventh earl of Athlone, and **William Williams Hope** (1802–1855). Inheriting a large fortune, W. W. Hope purchased Rushton Hall in Northamptonshire, but spent most of his life in fashionable Paris. A noted eccentric, he was said to possess a magnificent set of diamonds, which he often wore on his own person. Detesting male society, W. W. Hope was also reputed to maintain a coterie of eighteen ladies, distinguished by their musical or artistic attainments. He died at his mansion, 131 rue Dominique, Faubourg St Germain, Paris, on 21 January 1855.

From the 1780s, Henry [iii] Hope reigned supreme over his house, his only rival, from the 1790s, being **Pierre César Labouchère** (1772–1839). This son of a Huguenot cloth merchant was born at The Hague in 1772 and, after service in his uncle's merchant house at Nantes, joined Hopes as a clerk in 1790; he received procuration three years later although he was not made a partner until 1802.

Throughout the stormy 1780s, when the Netherlands suffered the destructive forces of opposing political factions, more than ever Henry fell back upon his Anglo-American origins. 'For not being obliged either by status or duty to take sides', he reckoned, 'I have observed a strict neutrality' (Buist, 42); he thereby retained his freedom of action. His bond-issuing business prospered. Russia was now the major client; between 1787 and 1793 eighteen bond issues, raising the immense sum of over 50 million guilders, were arranged. A thankful Empress Catherine offered Henry a barony, which he refused. Of his great wealth he made little secret. Much of it was ploughed into his great neo-classical palace of Welgeleegen, Haarlem, built between 1785 and 1790 and based upon the work of Palladio. Henry filled it with great pictures and sculpture; in 1802 he made it over to John Williams Hope.

No protective neutrality was possible following the invasion of the Netherlands by the armies of revolutionary France in 1794. To preserve life and limb from a new terror, the Hopes fled abroad with Henry, Williams Hope, and P. C. Labouchère settling in London in 1794. Henry, anticipating a long stay, took a residence in Harley Street, adding a wing to accommodate his 372 pictures, acquired a country seat at East Sheen, and entered into an alliance with the merchant bank of Sir Francis *Baring.

The two houses had done business since the 1760s but now grew closer, with Barings benefiting from use of Hopes' evacuated capital. Their remarkable similarity of outlook was further strengthened when P. C. Labouchère married Francis Baring's daughter, Dorothy (b. 1771), in 1796. The couple had two sons, the eldest of whom, Henry *Labouchere (1798–1869), became a Liberal politician and was ennobled as the first Baron Taunton. Together the houses ploughed £100,000 into land purchases in New

England in 1796, arranged a loan for the court of Lisbon in 1802—the proceeds of which were paid as a war levy to Napoleon—and, more importantly, arranged $11.25 million finance for the United States' purchase of Louisiana from France in 1803–4.

Henry Hope, Williams Hope, and Labouchère returned to Amsterdam in 1802 to resuscitate Hope & Co., although much of their capital remained in London in the house of Henry Hope & Co. Quickly it recovered its former pre-eminence by continuing the work, begun in London, of funding war levies imposed by France on its enemies and allies alike, in particular Spain and Prussia. Notwithstanding their strong London links, Henry Hope and Labouchère did this with the tacit support of Napoleon and his lieutenants such as G. J. Ouvrard; they must be regarded as major financiers of the French wars.

But it was their Indian summer; by 1808 Hopes was a spent force. In that year, spurred on by his unhappy marriage and increasingly at odds with his partners, Williams Hope left to live in England; Henry was now over seventy; Labouchère sought early retirement, and died in January 1839; and no Hope children showed interest in succeeding their fathers despite John Hope's heirs' owning much of the capital. Crisis point was reached when Henry died in 1811 and Williams Hope, known simply as John Hope since Henry's death, died two years later, on 12 February 1813 at his home in Harley Street, London. He was buried at St Ewe, Cornwall. The insistence of John Hope's widow on the immediate withdrawal of her husband's capital resulted in Hopes' acquisition by Sir Francis Baring's son, Alexander *Baring, in 1813. It was the end of a dynasty.

The Hope family had been lured from their business by prospects of prestige and enjoyment to be found elsewhere. The eldest son of John Hope (1737–1784), Thomas *Hope (1769–1831), an influential figure in English connoisseurship, provides the most telling yet distinguished example. Born at Amsterdam on 30 August 1769, he was the eldest of three brothers who together inherited their father's substantial interest in Hopes but was never active in its management. Instead he turned to the study of classical architecture and civilization and from 1787 spent eight years travelling and studying in Mediterranean countries. In 1795 he settled in London, living in Duchess Street from 1799, and won recognition as an informed scholar, writer, collector, enlightened patron, proponent of neo-classicism, and influencer of taste. He was 'entirely devoted to the arts' (Watkin, 13).

The Hopes, of Scottish descent and with enduring business and cultural links with Britain, were one of Europe's greatest banking dynasties. Their rise during the Seven Years' War and the immense financial power they exercised from then until almost the end of the Napoleonic era were based upon their command of the Amsterdam capital market and their expertise as merchant traders. Their clients included numerous European kings and governments for whom they made bond issues; the finance they provided at vital moments, not least during the Napoleonic wars, influenced international relations. Their accumulation of great wealth enabled their acquisition of estates and works of art as well as their distinguished connoisseurship and patronage; but ultimately this distracted them from their business and undermined its strength. JOHN ORBELL

Sources M. G. Buist, *At spes non fracta: Hope & Co., 1770–1815* (1974) · D. Watkin, *Thomas Hope, 1769–1831, and the neo-classical idea* (1968) · C. H. Wilson, *Anglo-Dutch commerce and finance in the eighteenth century* (1941) · P. Ziegler, *The sixth great power: Barings, 1762–1929* (1988) · S. Baumgarten, *Le crépuscule néo-classique: Thomas Hope* (1958) · T. L. Ingram, 'A note on Thomas Hope of Deepdene', *Burlington Magazine* (Aug 1980) · ING Barings, London, Barings archives, DEP 74, DEP 193.40 · *DNB* · private information (2004)
Archives Gemeentearchief, Amsterdam · ING Barings, London, Barings archive
Likenesses C. Alexander, portrait, 1763 (Adrian Hope), NG Scot. · C. Alexander, portrait, 1763 (John Hope) · C. H. Hodges, print, 1776 (Henry Hope; after lost painting by J. Reynolds), ING Barings, London · B. West, group portrait, 1802, Museum of Fine Arts, Boston · A. Kauffmann, portrait (John Williams Hope), ABN-AMRO? · G. Sanders, portrait (Archibald Hope), Dulwich Picture Gallery, London · portrait (P. C. Labouchère), ING Barings, London

Hope, Adrian (1709–1781). *See under* Hope family (*per. c.*1700–1813).

Hope, Sir Alexander (1769–1837), army officer, was born on 9 December 1769, the second son of John Hope, second earl of Hopetoun (1704–1781), who had been lord of police for Scotland, and his third wife, Lady Elizabeth (1737–1788), the second daughter of Alexander Leslie, fifth earl of Leven and Melville. Hope was educated at home, and, together with his elder half-brother John *Hope, afterwards the fourth earl, he travelled on the continent with their tutor, Dr John Gillies (1747–1836).

In 1786 Hope became an ensign in the 63rd foot, was made lieutenant in the 64th foot two years later, and in 1791 raised an independent company, which was called up. On 20 July 1791 Hope was appointed lieutenant and captain 1st foot guards. He was one of the officers selected to serve in the light infantry companies which were first added to the regiment in 1793. He served in Flanders in 1794 as brigade-major of the guards, under Major-General Gerard Lake, and afterwards as aide-de-camp to Major-General Sir Ralph Abercromby. In the same year he became a major in the 81st foot, and a lieutenant-colonel in the 2nd battalion of the 90th foot from where he transferred in December to the 14th foot while still with the retreating army in the Netherlands. He commanded the 14th during the attack from Buren on Gueldermasen on 8 January 1795. During this action, Hope was severely wounded by a ball which lodged deep in his shoulder, destroying his arm and causing permanent lameness. He received a pension as a consequence.

Hope, who was a strong supporter of the younger Pitt, sat as MP for Dumfries in 1796. He went on to represent Linlithgowshire between 1802 and 1834. He married Georgina Alicia, the daughter of George Brown of Ellistown, on 23 October 1805; they had five sons and a daughter.

He was appointed lieutenant-governor of Tynemouth

Sir Alexander Hope (1769–1837), by Sir Thomas Lawrence, 1810

and Cliff Fort in 1797, and then of Edinburgh Castle in 1798. He was brigade-major and assistant adjutant-general of the eastern district in 1798–9. Aged thirty, he was exceptionally young to hold this post. He became a brigadier-general in 1807, and a major-general in 1808. In June 1811 Hope, who was then deputy quartermaster-general at the Horse Guards, under Sir Robert Brownrigg, was appointed governor of the Royal Military College, Sandhurst. In January 1813 he was sent on a special mission to Sweden to determine the strength of the forces that could co-operate in the forthcoming allied campaign in Germany. Back at Sandhurst, Hope proposed changes in the entrance exam and raising standards for commissioning, given his belief that many applicants 'from want of education in childhood either failed to enter, or are rejected after the probationary year' (Shepperd, 43). In 1819 Hope left Sandhurst to return to his previous post as lieutenant-governor of Edinburgh Castle. He became lieutenant-governor of Chelsea Hospital in 1826, and after serving as colonel of the 5th West India regiment, then of the 74th (Highland) regiment, became colonel of the 14th foot in 1835.

On 30 June 1824 Oxford conferred on Hope the honorary degree of DCL. On the same day, his eldest son, John Thomas Hope, of Christ Church (who died while lieutenant-colonel of the Fife militia in 1835), recited his Newdigate prize poem, 'The Arch of Titus'. James Robert Hope-*Scott of Abbotsford was his third son.

It has been reported that Hope held rank in the Austrian army (Ornsby, 59–60). The Austrian war office did not maintain an army list before 1820; but the archives of the financial department confirm that no officer of the name served between 1773 and 1840. Hope died, a full general and GCB at the lieutenant-governor's house, Chelsea Hospital, London, on 19 May 1837; he was buried in the family vault at Abercorn, Linlithgowshire. His wife survived him.   H. M. CHICHESTER, rev. S. KINROSS

Sources GM, 2nd ser., 7 (1837) • A. Shepperd, Sandhurst (1980) • GEC, Peerage • R. Ornsby, Life of J. R. Hope-Scott, 1 (1884) • F. W. Hamilton, The origin and history of the first or grenadier guards, 2 (1874) • T. C. W. Blanning, The French revolutionary wars, 1787–1802 (1996) • GM, 2nd ser., 8 (1837), 423

Archives NA Scot., corresp. and papers • NRA Scotland, priv. coll., political and legal corresp. and papers | BL, letters to Hudson Lowe • Hants. RO, corresp. with William Wickham • NA Scot., corresp. with Lord Melville • NL Scot., letters to Lord Lynedoch

Likenesses F. H. Fuger, portrait, 1801, Hopetoun House, West Lothian • T. Lawrence, oils, 1810, Hopetoun House, West Lothian [see illus.] • T. Lawrence, portrait, Royal Military Academy, Sandhurst, Berkshire

Hope, Alexander James Beresford Beresford (1820–1887), politician and author, was born on 25 January 1820, the youngest son of Thomas *Hope (1769–1831), art collector, of Deepdene, Surrey, and his wife, Louisa (d. 21 July 1851), youngest child of William Beresford, first Baron Decies, archbishop of Tuam. Louisa Hope later married, on 29 November 1832, William Carr *Beresford, Viscount Beresford (1768–1854). Henry Thomas *Hope was his elder brother. On inheriting the English estates of his stepfather, Alexander Hope took the additional name of Beresford before that of Hope (30 May 1854). After a prizewinning career at Harrow School and Trinity College, Cambridge (matriculated 1837, BA 1841, MA 1844), he became MP for Maidstone (1841–52; 1857–65), for Stoke-on-Trent (1865–8), and eventually for Cambridge University (1868–87). He married, on 7 July 1842, Lady Mildred Arabella Charlotte Henrietta Cecil (1822–1881), eldest daughter of James, second marquess of Salisbury, and sister of Robert, third marquess of Salisbury, later prime minister. She was for many years a leader of London society; they had three sons and seven daughters.

Describing himself as a 'Conservative, yet liberal and unshackled by party', Beresford Hope consistently supported the established church, 'both as a divine institution, and as an estate of the realm' (WWBMP, 31). He voted for agricultural protection in 1846, 'on the ground *solely* of a previous appeal not having been made to the constituencies'; and he opposed a graduated income tax in the 1840s, secret ballots in the 1850s, and electoral reform in the 1860s (Dod's Parliamentary Companion, 1858, 1870, 1881). Throughout his career he strongly supported church rates and denominational education, and was conspicuously hostile to the disestablishment of the Irish church. He spoke out for the rights of the south as well as the north in the American Civil War, and he vehemently attacked successive bills to legitimize marriage with a deceased wife's sister. In all this he seldom adopted an orthodox party line, and he often opposed Disraeli, as in April 1867 when he famously described the tory leader as an 'Asian mystery'. Such attitudes hardly made for a successful parliamentary career, and towards the end of his life he readily acknowledged his failure. 'I could have imagined myself', he admitted, 'measuring swords with Gladstone, or Disraeli, or Carlyle, or Tennyson, or Montalembert. Now I

shall die a second rate notoriety … "the rich Mr. Beresford Hope"' (Law and Law, 126, 232).

Beresford Hope was a prolific journalist and an architectural pundit of considerable influence. Having inherited a fortune in 1841, a great London mansion (Arklow House, Connaught Place) in 1843, and sizeable estates in Kent and Staffordshire (Bedgebury Park and Beresford Hall), he placed his resources at the service of the Gothic revival. He was an outspoken president of the Royal Institute of British Architects in 1865–7, co-proprietor of—and regular contributor to—the Saturday Review from 1855, and for many years a committed chairman (1846 onwards) and president (1859 onwards) of the Ecclesiological (previously Camden) Society. In all these roles he aimed to expand the language of architectural form, linking English and European styles, and hoped even to integrate the practice of architecture and engineering. He was William Butterfield's patron at St Augustine's, Canterbury—in 1844 he had purchased the ancient buildings as a college for missionary clergy—and (not without quarrels) at All Saints, Margaret Street, London; he was Gilbert Scott's advocate in the battle for the Foreign Office design in 1858; and he was William Burges's champion in the law courts competition of 1867. And even when the Gothic revival began to wane, he remained in church-building matters an adherent of 'creative restoration'; in fact he denounced William Morris's 'anti-scrape' doctrine as a 'Gospel of Death' (The Athenaeum, 571). Beresford Hope's support for Burges's plan to complete St Paul's Cathedral with a full-blown scheme of mural decoration was too 'creative' for most classicists. And his support for Butterfield's abstracted polychromy proved too 'progressive' for many Goths. Yet although he was a Gothicist to his heart's core, he eventually discovered Gothic principles—of skyline, composition, and planning—in Venice and Amsterdam alike, and in seventeenth-century Paris and fifteenth-century Bruges. Almost everywhere, in fact, except in Palladianism and neo-classicism. The result was a new, assimilative approach to style which he formulated in a series of articles and pamphlets, and which he christened 'progressive eclecticism' (A. B. Hope, The Common Sense of Art, 1858). Ironically, it was this approach—fusing medieval and Renaissance traditions in pursuit of a new synthesis—which first recreated the Gothic revival in the 1860s, then destroyed it in the 1870s. Modern Gothic gave way to Queen Anne.

In the politics of ecclesiology Beresford Hope played an ambivalent role. Although he will be forever linked with Benjamin Webb and John Mason Neale—the high-church trinity of Trinity College, Cambridge—his churchmanship was rather different to theirs. He was less of a sacramentalist than Neale, less of a ritualist than Webb. He was, after all, a layman. His Anglicanism was establishmentarian, moderate, paternal, tory. He was a high-churchman of the Hook and Hooker type—rather different from being a ritualist.

In private Beresford Hope could be humorous, even quixotic; but as a public figure he was not helped by an awkward manner and an over-elaborate style of speech.

Disraeli sarcastically alluded to his 'Batavian graces', a reference to Hope's Dutch ancestry and stilted delivery (Kebbel, 1.600). Even so, as a churchman, as a critic, most of all as a patron, he has his place in architectural history.

Besides numerous essays, reviews, and pamphlets—notably *Public Offices and Metropolitan Improvements* (1857), *The Common Sense of Art* (1858), *The Condition and Prospects of Architectural Art* (1863), *The World's Debt to Art* (1863), and *The Art Workman's Position* (1864)—Beresford Hope was the author of *The English Cathedral of the Nineteenth Century* (1861), *Worship in the Church of England* (1874), and two novels, *Strictly Tied Up* (1880) and *The Brandreths* (1882). He was a privy councillor (1880), a trustee of the British Museum and the National Portrait Gallery, and a fellow of various learned societies; he was awarded honorary doctorates by Oxford (1848), Cambridge (1864), Washington (1879), Tennessee (1879), and Dublin (1881). Beresford Hope died at Bedgebury Park, Cranbrook, Kent, on 20 October 1887, and was buried six days later at Kilndown, Kent. His fortune had been great, but after a lifetime of patronage he left only £78,270.   J. MORDAUNT CROOK

Sources H. W. Law and I. Law, *The book of the Beresford Hopes* (1925) · *DNB* · J. M. Crook, 'Progressive eclecticism: the case of Beresford Hope', *Architectural Design*, 53 (1983), 56–62 · Venn, *Alum. Cant.* · Boase, *Mod. Eng. biog.* · *Parliamentary Pocket Companion* (1858) · *Dod's Parliamentary Companion* (1870) · *Dod's Parliamentary Companion* (1881) · *The Athenaeum* (29 Oct 1887), 571 · T. E. Kebbel, *Selected speeches of the earl of Beaconsfield*, 1 (1882) · *WWBMP*, 1.31 · Burke, *Gen. GB* (1937) · GEC, *Peerage*

Archives priv. coll., corresp. relating to St Columba's College | BL, corresp. with W. E. Gladstone, Add. MS 44213, fols. 227–357 · JRL, letters to E. A. Freeman · Lancing College, letters to Nathaniel Woodard · LPL, corresp. with E. W. Benson · LPL, corresp. with A. C. Tait · LPL, letters to Christopher Wordsworth · Trinity Cam., letters to William Whewell

Likenesses Ape [C. Pellegrini], caricature, chromolithograph, NPG; repro. in *VF* (10 Sept 1870) · E. Edwards, carte-de-visite, NPG · C. Martin, oils, RIBA

Wealth at death £78,270 4s. 11d.: resworn probate, May 1888, *CGPLA Eng. & Wales* (1887)

Hope [*née* Fulton], **Anne** (1809–1887), historian, was born on 7 September 1809 at Calcutta, where her father, John Williamson Fulton (1769–1830), was a merchant; he was a founder of the firm of Mackintosh, Fultons and McClintock. Her mother was Anne (1780?–1845), daughter of Robert Robertson and widow of Captain John Hunt of the Bengal army. The younger Anne was the third of five daughters; she had two brothers. At an early age she was sent from India to Lisburn, co. Antrim, where her father's family resided, and on her parents' return home in 1820 settled with them in 4 Upper Harley Street, London, where she met friends of her father, who included Daniel O'Connell, John Lawless, and other Irish parliamentary leaders.

On 10 March 1831 Anne Fulton married James *Hope MD (1801–1841), a physician at St George's Hospital specializing in heart disease; she assisted him with some of his publications. After his death in 1841 she prepared a memoir of him, which was edited by Dr Klein Grant and published in 1842. Anne Hope devoted herself to the education of her only son, Sir Theodore Cracraft Hope (*b.* 1831),

who joined the Bombay civil service in 1853. Letters which she addressed to him were published in 1843 under the title *On Self-Education with Formation of Character*.

Ill health compelled Hope to spend much time in Madeira between 1842 and 1850, and she remained an invalid for the rest of her life. She became interested in ecclesiastical history, and completed in 1850, but did not publish, a work on the early Christian church. This research interest led her to convert to Roman Catholicism about 1846. She met W. G. Ward and John Dalgairns, fellow converts. She developed close links with the Oratorians, of which congregation Dalgairns was a member, and, for a while, she lived in Edgbaston, near the Birmingham Oratory, where John Henry Newman and Dalgairns were then based. Dalgairns became her chief literary adviser and counsellor. In a spirit of devotion to her adopted church, she published *The Acts of the Early Martyrs* (1855), which was based on Paul de Ribadeneira's *Flores sanctorum*, and intended for the use of oratory schools. It was republished several times within three years. This frankly hagiographical volume was followed in 1859 by a life of St Philip Neri, the founder of the Oratorians. Hope's next two publications were her most substantial: the *Life of St Thomas à Becket* (1868) and *The Conversion of the Teutonic Races* (2 vols., 1872). Both were scrupulously based on medieval chronicles and saints' lives, and showed wide reading, but exhibited little critical sense, being as credulous as they were learned. Dalgairns contributed a preface to each work. In 1878 she published *Franciscan Martyrs in England* and between 1874 and 1878 she also wrote seven contributions to the *Dublin Review*, including a reply to J. A. Froude's attack on Thomas a Becket. She spent her later years in Torquay, at the Hermitage, St Mary Church, and continued to work in old age, employing an amanuensis. She was examining material relating to the recently beatified English martyrs within a week of her death at home on 12 February 1887. The Catholic historian, Abbot Francis Gasquet, edited and published this manuscript as *The First Divorce of Henry VIII* (1894).

[ANON.], *rev.* ROSEMARY MITCHELL

Sources Gillow, *Lit. biog. hist.* · *The Tablet* (19 Feb 1887), 303 · Burke, *Gen. Ire.* · W. G. Gorman, *Converts to Rome* (1910), 141 · *WI*, 2, 953 · private information (1891)

Wealth at death £5001 6s. 8d.: probate, 5 April 1887, *CGPLA Eng. & Wales*

Hope, Anthony. See Hawkins, Sir Anthony Hope (1863–1933).

Hope, Archibald, Lord Rankeillor (1639–1706). *See under* Hope, Sir John, Lord Craighall (1603x5–1654).

Hope, Archibald (1664–1743). *See under* Hope family (*per.* c.1700–1813).

Hope, Archibald (1698–1733). *See under* Hope family (*per.* c.1700–1813).

Hope, Charles, first earl of Hopetoun (1681–1742), politician, was born on 14 August 1681 into a distinguished legal family, the only son of John Hope of Hopetoun (1650–1682), landowner, and Lady Margaret Hamilton (1649–

Charles Hope, first earl of Hopetoun (1681–1742), by William Aikman

1711), eldest daughter of John, fourth earl of Haddington. Helen *Hope, countess of Haddington, was his elder sister. He was educated in Edinburgh and attended the university from 1692, though he did not graduate. On 31 August 1699 he married Lady Henrietta Johnstone (1682–1750), only daughter of William, first marquess of Annandale; they had four sons and nine daughters.

Hope was elected a parliamentary commissioner for Linlithgowshire in 1702. From 6 July 1704 he sat as a peer, having been created on 15 April 1703 earl of Hopetoun, Viscount Aithrie, and Lord Hope and sworn of the privy council. He was a strong supporter of the Union. From 1715 to 1742 he was lord lieutenant of the county of Linlithgow, and in 1723 was appointed lord high commissioner to the general assembly of the Church of Scotland. He was a Scottish representative peer from 1722 to 1742; a lord of police from 1734; invested in the Order of the Thistle in 1738; and governor of the Bank of Scotland from 1740. A ministerial dependant, in 1721 Hopetoun received £3000 from the secret service fund.

Hopetoun died at his home, Hopetoun House, Linlithgowshire, on 2 February 1742, and was buried at Abercorn church, Linlithgowshire, on 26 February. He was survived by his wife, who died on 25 November 1750, and by his second son, John (1704–1781), who succeeded him to the earldom.

T. F. HENDERSON, rev. MAIRIANNA BIRKELAND

Sources GEC, *Peerage* · W. Ferguson, *Scotland: 1689 to the present* (1968); pbk edn (1978) · G. Donaldson and R. S. Morpeth, *A dictionary of Scottish history* (1977) · *Scots peerage* · private information (2004)

Archives NRA Scotland, priv. coll., papers | NA Scot., letters to duke of Montrose
Likenesses D. Allan, oils, after 1742 (after W. Aikman?), Hopetoun House, West Lothian · W. Aikman, oils, Hopetoun House, West Lothian [see illus.]

Hope, Charles, Lord Granton (1763–1851), judge, was born on 29 June 1763, the eldest son of John *Hope (1739–1785), MP for Linlithgowshire (and great-grandson of Charles Hope, first earl of Hopetoun), and his wife, Mary (1741/2–1767), only daughter of Eliab Breton of Forty Hill, Enfield, and granddaughter of Sir William Wolstenholme, bt. Sir John *Hope, army officer, and Vice-Admiral Sir William Johnstone *Hope were his brothers. He was educated at Enfield grammar school, and afterwards at Edinburgh high school, where in 1777 he became the Latin dux. After studying law at Edinburgh University he was admitted an advocate on 11 December 1784, and on 25 March 1786 was appointed a depute advocate. Although not an outstanding lawyer he was an accomplished public speaker at tory political meetings. On 5 June 1792 he became sheriff of Orkney, and in the following year, on 8 August 1793, he married his cousin, Lady Charlotte Hope (1771–1834), the second daughter of John, second earl of Hopetoun, and his third wife, Lady Elizabeth Leslie, second daughter of Alexander, fifth earl of Leven and Melville. They had four sons and eight daughters; the eldest boy was John *Hope (1794–1858), and the youngest girl was Louisa Octavia Augusta *Hope (1814–1893).

In June 1801 Hope was appointed lord advocate in the Addington administration in place of Robert Dundas of Arniston and shortly afterwards was presented with the freedom of the city of Edinburgh for his assistance to the magistrates in obtaining a bill for the poor of the city. At the general election in July 1802 he was returned to the House of Commons for Dumfries district, but resigned when Henry Dundas was made a lord, and was returned unopposed for the city of Edinburgh in January 1803. As lord advocate Hope saw through the House of Commons the Scotch Parochial Schoolmasters' Act which compelled heritors to build houses with two rooms for the schoolmasters. His only speech to be reported in the *Parliamentary Debates* was delivered in his own defence in the debate on Whitbread's motion for the production of papers relating to Hope's censure of a Banffshire farmer named Morison, who had dismissed his servant for attending drills of a volunteer regiment. Hope made an ingenious defence, and gave a lively description of the duties of his office. Though the case against him was strong, the motion was defeated by 159 to 82.

On 20 November 1804 Hope was appointed an ordinary lord of session and lord justice clerk in the place of Sir David Rae, Lord Eskgrove, and assumed the title of Lord Granton. He took his seat on the bench on 6 December 1804. On 12 November 1811 he succeeded Robert Blair of Avontoun as lord president of the court of session, being succeeded as lord justice clerk by David Boyle. In 1820 he presided at the special commission for the trial of high treason at Glasgow and his *Charge Delivered to the Grand Jury of the County of Stirling on 23 June 1820* was published (1820). On 17 August 1822 he was admitted to the privy council at Holyroodhouse. On 29 July 1823 he was appointed, together with his eldest son John, on the commission of inquiry into the forms of process and the course of appeals in Scotland. His *Notes by the Lord President on the Subject of Hearing Counsel in the Inner House* were published as a pamphlet (1826). When James Graham, third duke of Montrose, died in December 1836, Hope became lord justice general, when the post was combined by statute with the office of lord president of the court of session.

Hope was a man of imposing presence, with a magnificent voice, which, according to Lord Cockburn, 'was surpassed by that of the great Mrs Siddons alone' (*Memorials*, 160). Though politically partisan, and without tact or judgement, 'his integrity, candour, kindness, and gentlemanlike manners and feelings gained him almost unanimous esteem', according to Cockburn (*Journal*, 1, 308–9). His charges to juries were persuasive and impressive. Lockhart left a graphic account of Hope's imposing bearing on the bench in *Peter's Letters to his Kinsfolk* (2, 1819, 102–8).

When the volunteer movement began during the Napoleonic wars, Hope enlisted as a private in the first regiment of Royal Edinburgh volunteers. He was afterwards appointed lieutenant-colonel of the corps, and performed his duties for several years, until the regiment was disbanded for the second time in 1814. He daily inspected the volunteers on duty at Edinburgh Castle while the regular troops were on duty in the western counties. Hope's famous regimental orders of 18 October 1803 are given at length in Cockburn's *Memorials* (pp. 187–94).

Hope retired from the bench in the autumn of 1841 and was succeeded as lord president by David Boyle. He died at his home, Granton House, 12 Moray Place, Edinburgh, on 30 October 1851 and was buried on 4 November in the mausoleum at Hopetoun House. His wife predeceased him on 22 January 1834.

G. F. R. BARKER, *rev.* HUGH MOONEY

Sources GM, 2nd ser., 36 (1851), 649 · *Annual Register* (1851), 44–5 · J. Haydn, *The book of dignities: containing rolls of the official personages of the British empire* (1851) · Burke, *Peerage* · *Lord Cockburn's memories of his time* (1856) · *Journal of Henry Cockburn: being a continuation of the 'Memorials of his time', 1831–1854*, 2 vols. (1874) · R. Douglas, *The peerage of Scotland*, 2nd edn, ed. J. P. Wood, 1 (1813), 745–6, 750 · 'Report from commissioners: forms of process, and course of appeals, Scotland', *Parl. papers* (1824), vol. 10, no. 241 · J. G. Lockhart, *The life of Sir Walter Scott*, [new edn], 10 vols. (1902)

Archives BL, corresp. with Sir Robert Peel, Add. MSS 40268–40608, *passim* · NA Scot., corresp. with Lords Melville · NL Scot., letters to Lord Melville · NL Scot., letters incl. Lord Rutherfurd · NRA Scotland, priv. coll., letters to William Adam · Sandon Hall, Staffordshire, Harrowby Manuscript Trust, letters to and from Richard Ryder, letters to second Viscount Melville

Likenesses C. M. Hope, lithograph, BM · J. Kay, three etchings, NPG; repro. in J. Kay, *A series of original portraits and caricature etchings*, 2nd edn (1842) · H. Raeburn, portrait, Boston Museum of Fine Arts · H. Raeburn, portrait, Scot. NPG · J. Watson-Gordon, portrait, Parliament Hall, Edinburgh

Wealth at death £27,848 19s. 0½d.: confirmation, 2 Jan 1852, NA Scot., SC 70/1/74, pp. 389–95

Hope, Frederick William (1797–1862), entomologist and collector of insects and engravings, was born on 3 January 1797 at 37 Upper Seymour Street, Portman Square, London, the second son of John Thomas Hope (1761–1854) of Netley Hall, Shropshire, and Ellen Hester Mary, only child of Sir Thomas Edwardes, seventh baronet, rector of Frodesley, Shropshire, and Tilston, Cheshire. He was privately educated under the Revd Delafosse of Richmond, Surrey, and after entering Christ Church, Oxford, in 1817, graduated BA in 1820, and MA in 1823. He then took holy orders, becoming for a time curate of the family's living at Frodesley.

At Oxford, Hope became interested in natural science, especially entomology, and with his considerable means was able to accumulate a great collection of insects. He also collected prints, amassing 140,000 portraits, 70,000 topographical engravings, and more than 20,000 natural history engravings. On 6 June 1835, at Marylebone church, Middlesex, Hope married Ellen, younger daughter of George Meredith of Nottingham Place, Marylebone; they had no children.

Hope travelled to France, Switzerland, Germany, and Holland but owing to his poor state of health was compelled at times to reside on the Mediterranean. From 1840 to 1862 he spent most of his time at Naples and Nice, bases which provided him with the opportunity to study fish and Crustacea. These studies formed the basis for his work *Catalogo dei crostacei Italiani e di molti altri del Mediterraneo* (1851).

In 1849 Hope executed a deed of gift giving his collections of fish, Crustacea, birds, shells, books, and 230,000 pictures to the University of Oxford. However, the original deed of gift was not accepted by convocation until April 1850, owing to almost continual, and at times frustrating, discussion between Hope and the university over the details. For many years afterwards both Hope and his wife (who shared his interest in natural history) continued to add entomological and other zoological specimens to the Oxford collections. In 1855, when construction of the new museum at Oxford was started (later the Oxford University Museum of Natural History), Hope was awarded the honorary degree of DCL by the university, no doubt in recognition of his generous donation.

Hope was also keen to establish a new chair of zoology at Oxford. Negotiations had begun by 1856, and in 1860 endowment for the Hope professorship of zoology was agreed. In January 1861 John Obadiah Westwood was nominated by Hope and appointed as first Hope professor of zoology; in turn the Hope department of zoology was founded. Furthermore in 1857, in line with Hope's recommendations, Westwood took up the curatorship of the Hope entomological specimens.

Hope's correspondence with naturalists was extensive, and his London residence was often used as their meeting-place. He often associated with Charles Darwin, with whom he would go 'entomologizing', and he contributed valuable information to the works of others, including Gravenhorst, Shuckard, and Schönberr. He was author of about sixty papers on entomology, chiefly in the Entomological Society's *Transactions*. Hope's major work was probably *The Coleopterist's Manual* (1837–40); his entomological collection also formed the basis of Westwood's catalogues of Hemiptera (1837–1842?), and lucanoid Coleoptera (1845).

Hope was early elected a fellow of the Linnean Society (1822) and the Royal Society (1834), and took an active part in founding the Zoological and Entomological societies (1826 and 1833, respectively). He served as treasurer, then vice-president (1833–4, 1837–8, and 1841–3), of the Entomological Society, and was its president in 1835–6, 1839–40, and 1845–6. He also received many awards and honours from a number of institutions both at home and abroad.

Hope died at his residence, 37 Upper Seymour Street, Portman Square in London, on 15 April 1862. In accordance with his wishes, his widow, Ellen, gave an additional endowment to the professorship which he had founded at Oxford, a stipend for the keeper of his collection of engravings, and further funding for maintaining and expanding the portrait and entomological collections. Hope's print collection later went to the university's Ashmolean Museum; in the late 1990s a vast number of his entomological specimens and archives could still be found in the Hope department at Oxford University's Museum of Natural History.　　　　　　　　YOLANDA FOOTE

Sources *GM*, 3rd ser., 12 (1862), 785–8 · T. J. Pettigrew, 'Obituary notice of the Rev. Fred. Wm. Hope', in J. O. Westwood, *Thesaurus Entomologicus Oxoniensis* (1874), [xvii]–xxi · A. Z. Smith, *A history of the Hope entomological collections in the University Museum, Oxford* (1986) · Ward, *Men of the reign* · Boase, *Mod. Eng. biog.* · Foster, *Alum. Oxon.* · *CGPLA Eng. & Wales* (1862)
Archives DWL, notebook · Oxf. U. Mus. NH, Hope Library, corresp., notebooks, and papers; registers and drawings | Oxf. U. Mus. NH, letters to J. C. Dale
Likenesses L. C. Dickinson, oils, 1864, Oxf. U. Mus. NH · L. C. Dickinson, oils, AM Oxf. · J. Dickson, lithograph, NPG · M. & N. Hanhart, lithograph (after drawing by J. Dickson), RS · W. Raddon, engraving, RS · W. Raddon, line print, BM · chalk drawing, Bodl. Oxf.
Wealth at death under £20,000: probate, 21 May 1862, *CGPLA Eng. & Wales*

Hope, George (1811–1876), agriculturist, was born on 2 January 1811 at West Fenton, East Lothian, the second of the seven sons and a daughter of Robert Hope (*d.* 1852), tenant farmer, and his second wife, Christian, *née* Bogue, daughter of a farmer of Stevenson Mains. The Hopes were descended from a Dutch officer who had come over with William of Orange and afterwards settled near Edinburgh. Robert Hope was a great reader and his children had access to more books, newspapers, and periodicals than was normally the case in a household impoverished by the low prices resulting from poor weather and the corn laws. From his earliest days George found himself opposed to the shorter catechism, which he failed to master at Dirleton and Haddington schools, preferring mathematics, and toryism, whose sentiments he encountered in *Blackwood's Magazine*.

Hope left school at fourteen to work for Alexander Donaldson, a lawyer, and attended classes in the evenings.

After four years he was obliged to take over Fenton Barns (near Gullane, East Lothian), 653 acres previously farmed by his late half-brother, but he always considered his time with Donaldson to have been of great value. After two or three years he had the offer of a good situation in Australia, but he declined this as his mother was unwell and did not want him to leave the district. Fenton Barns was on heavy clay soil, which yielded a poor crop in good years and nothing worth harvesting in wet years. The remedy lay in under-drainage, but so costly a cure had to wait until money was available; meanwhile George Hope set about improving his land by means of crop rotation, assisted by generous applications of the new manure, Peruvian guano. Soon his yields increased and his livestock flourished.

Hope found many influential men in Scotland and England who shared his strong unitarian and political opinions, and he counted Richard Cobden and John Bright among his friends. He supplemented his income by reviewing for *The Scotsman*, and his prize-winning essay opposing the corn laws was published in 1842; this brought him £30, and was inserted in whole or in part in many other newspapers. On 8 July 1844 Hope married Isabella Peterkin, daughter of an Edinburgh solicitor; they had several children, some of whom died in childhood from diphtheria and scarlet fever.

Continuous manuring, the installation of land drains, and careful husbandry eventually brought Fenton Barns to prosperity and Hope even leased additional nearby land to cultivate. His fame spread, bringing visitors from the United States of America, Sweden, Denmark, and Russia. In 1870 he received a diploma constituting him a member of the Royal Swedish Academy of Agriculture. He was one of the deputies of the Highland Society, taking livestock to the International Show in Paris, in June 1856. At home Hope opposed the game laws, which denied tenants the right to take game on their land. He was also against the Scottish law of hypothec, which allowed a landlord to distrain the produce of any tenant who failed to pay his rent, even when that produce had passed into other hands.

Hope stood twice for parliament. In 1865 he contested East Lothian, where he lost to Lord Elcho, a candidate with local influence; in 1875 he contested East Aberdeenshire, where he was not well known, and where his outspoken and unorthodox religious opinions, along with his support for disestablishment, roused the clergy to a furious canvass against him. The seat was easily won by Sir Alexander Gordon, second son of the fourth earl of Aberdeen. Hope's stand for parliament cost him dear. Like all tenant farmers, he lacked security of tenure: in 1875 his lease at Fenton Barns was due to expire and his application to renew was refused. The news of the treatment meted out after the Hope family had transformed the sour land of Fenton Barns into one of Britain's model farms, admired across northern Europe, caused a sensation throughout the land, reaching even to the houses of parliament. George Hope took a new farm at Bordlands, near Noblehouse, Peeblesshire, and ran an outlying sheep farm at Glencotho, Lanarkshire. But although in the last summer of his life he managed to visit both Glencotho and his son's border farms, he grew weaker; and by the autumn he had lost all interest in his former concerns. He died at Bordlands on 1 December 1876 and was buried at Dirleton, East Lothian. His wife survived him.

ANITA MCCONNELL

Sources C. Hope, *George Hope of Fenton Barns* (1881) • J. A. S. Watson and M. E. Hobbs, *Great farmers*, 2nd edn (1951) • C. S. Orwin and E. H. Whetham, *History of British agriculture, 1846–1914* (1964) • J. A. Symon, *Scottish farming* (1959) • *WWBMP* • parish register (birth), Dirleton • parish register (baptism), Dirleton • d. cert. • *CCI* (1877)
Likenesses G. Reid, portrait, Scot. NPG
Wealth at death £14,654 13s. 5d.: confirmation, 25 Jan 1877, *CCI* • £2330 19s.: additional estate, 17 July 1877, *CCI*

Hope, Helen, countess of Haddington (*bap.* **1677**, *d.* **1768**), forester, was baptized on 28 September 1677 at Kirkliston, Linlithgowshire, the elder child and only daughter of John Hope of Hopetoun (1650–1682) and his wife, Lady Margaret Hamilton (*d.* 1711), eldest daughter of John Hamilton, fourth earl of Haddington. Her father was drowned on his way back to Scotland with the duke of York (later James VII and II) when she was five and her brother Charles *Hope, later first earl of Hopetoun, was less than a year old. It was therefore her mother who arranged her marriage in 1696 to Helen's sixteen-year-old first cousin, Thomas *Hamilton, sixth earl of Haddington (1680–1735). Her portrait, painted by Sir John de Medina two years earlier, shows a slim, brown-haired young woman with a wide forehead, long nose, full lower lip and an air of sprightly determination.

The young couple began their married life at Leslie House in Fife and the eldest of their four surviving children, Charles *Hamilton, Lord Binning, was born the following year. In 1700 they moved to the earl's family home of Tyninghame House in Haddingtonshire. The estate there had been leased out for several years to careless tenants, who had neglected it, and Helen was immediately struck by the lack of trees. When questioned about this the local people asserted that there was no point in planting young saplings, for the salt sea air and the cold east winds would inevitably destroy them.

By his own account the earl would have left the situation as it was. Writing a description of his activities for the benefit of his grandchildren, he later confessed: 'I took pleasure in sports, dogs and horses but had no manner of inclination to plant, inclose or improve my grounds'. His wife, however, was of a different disposition. He went on:

> But as your grandmother was a great lover of planting, she did what she could to engage me to it, but in vain. At last she asked leave to go about it, which she did, and I was much pleased with some little things that were both well laid out and executed, though none of them are now to be seen, for when the designs grew more expensive we were forced to take away what first was done.   (Fraser, 1.243)

The earl gradually forgot his horses and dogs and decided to lay out a fashionable 'wilderness'. As soon as that was done, Helen announced that she would like to enclose the Muir of Tyninghame, a piece of rough ground extending to more than 300 acres Scots. Her husband was doubtful. 'It seemed too great an attempt and almost

everybody advised her not to undertake it as being impracticable, of which number I confess I was one' (Fraser, 1.244). Once more, however, she managed to persuade him, he soon joined her in planning walks through the plantation on the Muir, and eventually 'an incredible number of trees was planted' (ibid.) on what had been a stretch of barren waste. Helen then renamed the area Binning Wood in honour of her ten-year-old elder son, who shared her enthusiasm for planting.

The earl was now reading everything he could find about the cultivation of trees, and he gained great fame throughout the country for his planting activities, writing the learned treatise on the subject in which he paid his handsome tribute to his countess. As Mr MacWilliam, fellow improver, whimsically noted in his engagingly entitled *Essay on the Dry Rot*:

> Thus can good wives, when wise, in every station
> On man work miracles of reformation
> And were such wives more common, their husbands would
>   endure it
> However great the malady, a loving wife can cure it
> And much their aid is wanted, we hope they'll use it fairish
> While [until] barren ground, where wood should be, appears
>   in every parish
> (Fraser, 1.260)

Helen's husband died in 1735. She survived him for more than thirty years, dying in her house at Edinburgh on 19 April 1768 at the age of ninety. She was buried with her husband at Tyninghame.

ROSALIND K. MARSHALL

Sources *Scots peerage*, 4.321–2, 493 • W. Fraser, *Memorials of the earls of Haddington*, 2 vols. (1889), vol. 1, pp. 239–61 • Thomas, sixth earl of Haddington [T. Hamilton], *Treatise on the manner of raising forest trees* (1761) • NA Scot., Edinburgh register of testaments, 18/4/1769
Likenesses J. de Medina, oils, 1694, priv. coll. • J. de Medina, oils, 1696–9, priv. coll. • negative (of portrait, 1694), Scot. NPG; repro. in R. K. Marshall, *Women in Scotland, 1660–1760* (1979), 46 [exhibition catalogue, Edinburgh, 1976]
Wealth at death household furnishings valued at £355 19 s. 7d.; books valued at £2 sterling: inventory, NA Scot., Edinburgh register of testaments, 18 April 1769, CC8/8/121; Fraser, *Memorials*, 260

Hope, Lady Henrietta (*c.***1750–1786**), benefactor, was born in Scotland, the second daughter of John, second earl of Hopetoun (1704–1781), and his first wife, Lady Anne Ogilvy (*d.* 1759), the second daughter of James, earl of Findlater and Seafield. Her family consisted of eighteen brothers and sisters: nine full siblings and nine half-siblings. Recently converted, possibly through Darcy, Lady Maxwell, it was probably in October 1772 that she first met Willielma Campbell, Viscountess Glenorchy, and they became inseparable friends. Lady Glenorchy valued her advice greatly. In 1780 her father allowed Henrietta to join Lady Glenorchy, and on 17 May they left Edinburgh for London, where they visited Selina, countess of Huntingdon. Here Lady Glenorchy was taken ill, but by the end of June was well enough to travel on to Exmouth, Exeter, and Bath. From here they went to Hawkestone, Shropshire, to stay with Jane Hill, sister of the evangelical preacher Rowland Hill, before returning via Buxton to Scotland until November, when Lady Glenorchy returned to Bath. Lord Hopetoun having died in early 1781, his large family was dispersed, with Lady Henrietta going to London, where she made her home with Lady Glenorchy.

Both were keen to promote the cause of religion and, as they travelled around 'taking the waters' for their health, they either visited churches Lady Glenorchy had already founded or started others. In 1784 Lady Glenorchy purchased a house in Matlock for use as a church and the following summer the friends took up residence there before going on to Bristol Hotwells in late September or early October. Here Henrietta's already poor health deteriorated; she became dropsical and suffered terribly during November and December before her death on 1 January 1786. The two ladies had planned to build a chapel at Hotwells, and Lady Henrietta left £2500 towards the venture. Lady Glenorchy described the plan for 'a neat place of worship, plain but elegant and which will be a suitable monument for my dear friend, Lady Henrietta, and which I mean to call Hope Chapel' (Lady Glenorchy to Lady Maxwell, 26 Feb 1786, Jones, 508–9). The building of the chapel was started, but Lady Glenorchy died on 17 July 1786 and her executrix, Lady Maxwell, carried out the friends' wishes. The structure, known as Hope Chapel, was opened on Granby Hill, Bristol, in August 1788. Lady Henrietta was described as having 'a happy temper and high accomplishments, she was distinguished for sagacity and prudence, talents which she inherited from her father' (*The Life and Times of Selina, Countess of Huntingdon*, 2 vols., 1840).

E. DOROTHY GRAHAM

Sources *Scots peerage* · T. S. Jones, *The life of Willielma, Viscountess Glenorchy* (1822) · E. D. Graham, 'The contribution of Lady Glenorchy and her circle to the evangelical revival', BD diss., U. Leeds, 1965 · D. P. Thomson, *Lady Glenorchy and her churches: the story of 200 years* (1967) · 'The correspondence of the Revd. Brian Bury Collins, M.A.', ed. A. M. Broadley, *Proceedings of the Wesley Historical Society*, 9 (1914), 25–35, 49–58, 73–85 · J. F. Nicholls and J. Taylor, *Bristol past and present*, 3 vols. (1881–2) · W. Atherton, 'A sketch of the life and character of Lady Maxwell', *Arminian Magazine*, 39 (1816), 721–31, 801–14, 881–92 · J. Lancaster, *The life of Darcy, Lady Maxwell, of Pollock: late of Edinburgh compiled from her diary and correspondence, and from other authentic documents*, 2nd edn (1826)
Wealth at death over £2500: Jones, *Life of Willielma*; Thomson, *Lady Glenorchy*, 56

Hope, Henry (1735–1811). *See under* Hope family (*per. c.*1700–1813).

Hope, Sir Henry (1787–1863), naval officer, was the eldest son of Captain Charles Hope RN, who died commissioner at Chatham on 10 September 1808, and his wife, Susan Anne (*d.* 1802), daughter of Admiral Herbert *Sawyer. He was cousin of Sir William Johnstone Hope, and great-grandson of Charles Hope, first earl of Hopetoun. Hope entered the navy in 1800 on the *Kent*, commanded by his cousin, W. J. Hope. After serving off the Egyptian coast, he was moved into the *Swiftsure* with Captain Hallowell, and was made prisoner when she was captured on 24 June 1801. He afterwards served in the *Leda* on the Mediterranean and home stations, and in 1804 in the *Atlas*, again with his cousin, W. J. Hope.

On 3 May 1804 Hope was promoted lieutenant of the *Adamant*. In 1805, in the *Narcissus*, he was present at the capture of the Cape of Good Hope, and on 22 January 1806 was made commander and appointed to the sloop *Espoir* in the Mediterranean. On 24 May 1808 he was posted to the *Glatton*, and afterwards commanded the frigates *Leonidas*, *Topaze*, and *Salsette*, all in the Mediterranean, cruising successfully against French privateers. During the latter half of 1811, in the *Salsette*, he was senior officer in the Greek archipelago, and at the request of Stratford Canning, the ambassador at Constantinople, on 29 November, drove on shore at Nauplia a French privateer which had taken refuge under the guns of the Turkish batteries.

In May 1813 Hope was appointed to the *Endymion* (48 guns); this was one of the few British frigates carrying 24-pounders, and it was thought it might contend on somewhat equal terms with the large American frigates. After eighteen months on the North American station, on the morning of 15 January 1815, she was in company with a small squadron under Captain John Hayes off Sandy Hook, New Jersey, when they sighted the American frigate *President* (56 guns). The accident of position and her superior sailing enabled the *Endymion* to bring her to action, while the other British ships were some distance astern. It was already dusk, and it seemed possible that the *President* might escape in the dark. The *Endymion*, however, stuck closely to the fleeing enemy even though her own rigging was so cut that about nine o'clock she was obliged to drop astern to repair damages. By then the *President* had received such damage that, on the *Pomone* and *Tenedos* coming up an hour later, she at once surrendered. To claim that the *Endymion* took the *President* single-handedly is an absurd exaggeration. Although her consorts had a very small share in the action, their close proximity, especially that of the *Majestic*, a cut-down 74-gun ship, terribly hampered the *President*'s manoeuvres and, by compelling her to defend herself in a running fight, enabled the *Endymion* to take up a deadly position on her quarter. Otherwise the result might have been different: the *Endymion* was smaller, less heavily armed, with a weaker crew; and, gallant officer and fine seaman as Hope was, Commodore Stephen Decatur, who commanded the *President*, also had a high reputation in the United States Navy. Despite this the victory, the first by a British force over one of the American super-frigates, was very welcome in Britain. Hope was the popular hero of the episode. The Admiralty gave him the gold medal, and the war medal to the *Endymion* alone. The merchants of Bermuda presented Hope with a complimentary letter and a silver cup, and the officers with a second cup, 'to be considered as attached to that or any future ship which might bear the gallant name of *Endymion*'. In June 1815 Hope was nominated a CB, but he had no further service.

Hope married, on 21 July 1828, his first cousin, Jane Sophia, youngest daughter of his mother's brother, Admiral Sir Herbert Sawyer KCB. There were no children, and she died in August 1829. Hope served as naval aide-de-camp to the sovereign from 1831 to 1841; he became rear-admiral in 1846, vice-admiral on 2 April 1853, KCB on 5 July 1855, and admiral on 20 January 1858. He died at Holly Hill, Southampton, on 23 September 1863. Hope left personal property valued at under £70,000, of which he bequeathed nearly half to religious and charitable societies, including £4000 each to the Church Missionary Society, the Bible Society, and the London City Mission.

The capture of the *President* was deemed an event worthy of celebration; the *Endymion* was rebuilt and remained in service until 1860, while a replica of the *President* was added to the navy list. Both ships were frequently sent to the North American station as talismans. Hope was also a talisman, although he had a large fortune, and chose not to go to sea again; his contemporaries believed he had won 'perpetual fame' (O'Byrne, 438).

J. K. LAUGHTON, *rev.* ANDREW LAMBERT

Sources A. T. Mahan, *Seapower in its relations to the war of 1812* (1905) · J. Marshall, *Royal naval biography*, suppl. 1 (1827), 314–17 · *GM*, 3rd ser., 15 (1863), 777 · logs of HMS *Endymion*, *Pomone*, *Tenedos*, PRO · O'Byrne, *Naval biog. dict.* · Boase, *Mod. Eng. biog.* · *Dod's Peerage* (1858) · *CGPLA Eng. & Wales* (1863)

Wealth at death under £70,000: probate, 7 Oct 1863, *CGPLA Eng. & Wales*

Hope, Henry Philip (1774–1839). *See under* Hope, Thomas (1769–1831).

Hope, Henry Thomas (1808–1862), patron of the arts and politician, was born in London, probably in Duchess Street, on 30 April 1808, eldest of the three sons of Thomas *Hope (1769–1831), of the Amsterdam banking family, and his wife, Louisa (*d.* 1851), daughter of William de la Poer Beresford, first Baron Decies, and his wife, Elizabeth. Hope's inheritance of money, property, and art collections from his father and his uncle, Henry Phillip Hope (*d.* 1839), led to bitter estrangement from his brothers, who included Alexander James Beresford *Hope, but allowed him as 'one of the richest commoners of the kingdom' (Watkin, 26) to follow his political and cultural interests in a style of enlightened opulence.

Hope was educated at Eton College (*c.*1823) and at Trinity College, Cambridge (1825–9). His first parliamentary seat was the rotten borough of East Looe (1829–32), purchased by his parents, who hoped to exchange his political services for a peerage for his father. The tactic failed, though Henry became briefly a groom of the bedchamber (1830). He opposed parliamentary reform, asserting that his constituents were under 'no other influence than that of kindliness and respect' (*Hansard 3*, 22 July 1831). East Looe lost its separate representation in 1832, and Hope sought an alternative seat, standing unsuccessfully for Gloucester in December 1832 and Marylebone in March 1833, before being elected as a Conservative at Gloucester in April 1833, largely because of his spending and his whig opponents' squabbling. He represented it for fifteen years in all—1833–7, 1838–41, and 1847–52. He was, however, a shy man who seldom spoke in the Commons, and he is memorable, not as parliamentarian, but as patron and host.

In spending and in commitment, Hope prided himself on always 'doing more rather than less of what I promised' (Hope to Disraeli, 23 Feb 1854). He had diverse interests, being a founder of the Art Union of London (1836) and the Royal Botanical Society, vice-president of the Society of Arts, and president of the Surrey Archaeological Society. He kept his own accounts and was an early promoter (1833) of the London and Westminster Joint Stock Bank. In his London house on Duchess Street, he entertained sumptuously among his art treasures; guests, Disraeli reported in 1834, 'supped off gold and danced in the Sculpture Gallery' (*Disraeli Letters*, 1.322 and n.13). At Deepdene (demolished in 1969), in Surrey, visiting aristocrats, diplomats, and politicians occupied luxurious suites, and strolled among more statues and pictures; even so, their host's conversation, sophisticated and learned, was 'the finest thing in it' (L'Estrange, 2.305). From 1836 he continued his father's remodelling of Deepdene into 'the most perfect Italian palace' (*Disraeli Letters*, 3.1104), adding (probably to his own design) impressive reception rooms and a spectacular two-storey galleried entrance hall. By 1840 his modifications made it a pioneering example of Victorian Italianate architecture and landscaping.

In this appropriately picturesque setting, Hope played Maecenas to political idealists, such as Young England in 1842–4, or the Spanish Carlists in 1846. Disraeli began *Coningsby* there in September 1843, but in dedicating it to Hope he was acknowledging more than hospitality and encouragement: in 1842, his seat in parliament had been saved by Hope's willingness to accede to an informal agreement between the party election agents that the Liberal candidates would drop their petition against Disraeli's election at Shrewsbury in return for Hope's withdrawing his petition against the successful Liberal candidates at Gloucester. Ten years later, he was still supporting Disraeli's political views with financial contributions to Disraeli's newspaper, *The Press*. Nevertheless, it was as a Conservative free-trader that he was re-elected for Gloucester in 1847, and as a Peelite that he was defeated in July 1852.

Meanwhile, Hope bought an 18,000 acre Irish estate, Castle Blayney, co. Monaghan, partly to show how to improve a neglected property. He was an organizer of the Great Exhibition of 1851, while constructing (1849–51) a palatial French-designed mansion at 116 Piccadilly (later the Junior Athenaeum). Lavishly decorated, it reputedly cost £30,000 (about one third of his annual income) and again anticipated architectural style rather than merely following contemporary taste. It housed his collection of Dutch and Italian masters, which he opened to the public. Also in 1851, he married Anne Adele Bichat (*d.* 1887), daughter of Joseph Bichat; she was already mother of his daughter, Henrietta Adele (1843–1913). Shortly afterwards Isambard Kingdom Brunel persuaded him to chair the Eastern Steam Navigation Company, rightly judging that Hope's perseverance and ability to raise funds would surmount the problems which surrounded the building of Brunel's largest ship, the *Great Eastern*. Henrietta Hope named it in November 1857. Hope thankfully resigned his position in 1858.

In 1861 the family at last obtained the title which Hope's father had wanted, when Henrietta Hope married Lord Lincoln (later sixth duke of Newcastle). In effect, Hope saved the dukedom, paying Lincoln's debts with £35,000 and an allowance of between £10,000 and £12,000. Hope died, after a long illness, on 4 December 1862 at 116 Piccadilly, London. Probably to preserve them from his brothers, his money (sworn at under £300,000) and a life interest in his landed properties were secured to his wife.

MARY S. MILLAR

Sources D. Watkin, *Thomas Hope, 1769–1831, and the neo-classical idea* (1968), 3–28, 182–91 · *Benjamin Disraeli letters*, ed. J. A. W. Gunn and others (1982–), vols. 1–6 · H. T. Hope, correspondence with Disraeli and Mrs Disraeli, Bodl. Oxf., Dep. Hughenden HB/VI/16, 33, 46–7, B XXI/H/649–661, D/III/C/1048–58, E/VI/O/11 · *ILN* (4 July 1857), 22 · *ILN* (3 April 1858), 352 · *The Times* (5 Dec 1862) · A. G. L'Estrange, ed., *The friendships of Mary Russell Mitford: as recorded in letters from her literary correspondents*, 2 (1882), 303–05 · *Disraeli, Derby and the conservative party: journals and memoirs of Edward Henry, Lord Stanley, 1849–1869*, ed. J. R. Vincent (1978) · L. T. C. Rolt, *Isambard Kingdom Brunel* (1957), 238–86 · *Disraeli's reminiscences*, ed. H. M. Swartz and M. Swartz (1975) · *DNB* · *VCH Gloucestershire*, vol. 4 · G. Smythe, 'In the house of Maecenas', *Temple Bar*, 34 (1872), 186–91 · Venn, *Alum. Cant.* · Boase, *Mod. Eng. biog.*

Archives Bodl. Oxf., Hughenden MSS

Likenesses engraving (after portrait), repro. in Monypenny and Buckle, *The life of Benjamin Disraeli*, 2 (1912), facing p. 198 · engraving (after photograph by Mayall), repro. in *ILN* (3 April 1858), 352

Wealth at death under £300,000: probate, 25 Feb 1863, *CGPLA Eng. & Wales*

Hope, James. *See* Johnstone, James Hope-, third earl of Hopetoun and *de jure* fifth earl of Annandale and Hartfell (1741–1816).

Hope, Sir James, of Hopetoun, appointed Lord Hopetoun under the protectorate (1614–1661), industrialist and political radical, was born on 4 July 1614, the sixth son of Sir Thomas *Hope of Craighall, lord advocate (1573–1646), and Elizabeth (*d.* 1660), daughter of John Bennet of Wallyford, Haddingtonshire. Sir John *Hope and Sir Thomas *Hope of Kerse were his brothers. Entering Edinburgh University in 1632, he graduated on 25 July 1635 and continued his studies in law at Orléans from February 1636 to October 1637. On 14 January 1638 he married Anna (*d.* 1656), daughter of the wealthy Edinburgh merchant and goldsmith Robert Foulis, an heiress through whom he acquired several mining properties in Lanarkshire commonly known as the Leadhills. Hope's mercantile concerns were extensive. He had an abiding interest in mining, trade, shipping, and technology, in many ways anticipating the improvers of the eighteenth century: extensive material survives at Hopetoun House detailing his business interests, including contracts (usually to supply lead ore to Holland), bonds, directives to his factors about building and draining mines, mending the highway leading from the mines to port, and a strikingly wide range of titles, assignations, discharges, translations, declarations, and investments. Given his expertise in metals and technology, it is hardly surprising that the covenanting government appointed him master of the mint in 1641. That year he was also knighted.

Like his father and most of his brothers, Hope was deeply religious and an active participant in the covenanting revolution, but by the late 1640s an apocalyptic spirituality led him and his elder brother John to expectations

Sir James Hope of Hopetoun, appointed Lord Hopetoun under the protectorate (1614–1661), by unknown artist

of far-reaching reform. Both eventually became republicans and ardent supporters of the British Commonwealth that emerged in 1652. James Hope has the unique distinction of being part of what can only be called the 'left opposition' in the most radical parliament in Scottish history (the Whiggamores Parliament of 1649) where he became *persona non grata*, and shortly thereafter a member of the 'left opposition' within the most radical parliament in English history (Barebone's Parliament of 1653), from which he was ejected at gunpoint. In both parliaments he served on the centrally important law reform committees. He was directly involved in the administration of the state in both countries, serving on the committee of estates in Scotland, on the council of state in England.

Between 1649 and 1651 both Hopes opposed Scotland's treaty with Charles II, foreseeing rightly that it would lead to a disastrous war with the new English republic. They repeatedly urged the marquess of Argyll and Charles to come to terms with the London government, proposals that very nearly landed the brothers in gaol. Argyll denounced Hope as 'a maine enemie to king and kingdom' and a 'plotter and contriver, assister and abettor of all the mischiefs that hes befallen the kingdom', while Charles subsequently threatened to hang the brothers from the other end of the same rope by which he would hang Oliver Cromwell (*Historical Works of Balfour*, 4.173).

It is against this background of self-deception and the political catastrophe deriving from it, that in late December 1651 Hope and John Swinton of Swinton agreed to join John Hope at Craighall, his home in Fife, to consider a new beginning for Scotland. On 1 January 1652 they were joined by major-generals John Lambert and Richard Deane and other leading English officers for 'consultations about politique affairs'. It is unfortunate and yet not altogether surprising that the extensive entry in Hope's diary about the Craighall meeting has been mutilated, but it is likely that the matters discussed ranged from the practical (the surrender of Dumbarton Castle which was commanded by Hope's brother-in-law Sir Charles Erskine of Alvath), to the establishment of a new structure of government within Scotland, the tender for union, and the larger aspirations and apocalyptic hopes which all of these people shared (Firth, *Scotland and the Commonwealth*, 30, 43).

In May 1653 Hope joined his brother on the commission of justice for Scotland—the republic's equivalent to the court of session, the members of which were addressed in the manner of the lords of session. Cromwell, who had met Hope during the Scottish campaign, also wanted him in the new 'British' assembly which would now replace the Long Parliament. Hope arrived in London just in time for its opening on 4 July. Shortly thereafter he made what has been described as a 'speech for the Jews'—undoubtedly a plea for Jewish readmission into the newly emerging Britain. His remarks clearly spoke to the universal reconciliation expected at the 'end of days' and provide an indication of his apocalyptic hopes. Such a speech fitted the mood in Barebone's Parliament and must have shared much with Cromwell's well-known and highly prophetic address to it. It is not surprising then that Hope joined the council of state ten days later. The only Scot on the council and with unique legal expertise, he served, effectively, as the secretary of state for Scotland.

In addition to serving on the controversial committee to codify the law, Hope was extremely active in a broad spectrum of the Commonwealth's administrative matters, ranging from military supply to censorship, mental health, legal procedures, and specialist Scottish business. He and his three Scottish colleagues were inevitably concerned to introduce emergency measures to repair the shattered Scottish economy and 'the destitute conditione' of the Scottish people (*CSP dom.*). In all of this there was the central preoccupation of a new Scotland within a new world, and an act of union would naturally be all important. Inescapably, the debates about the Anglo-Scottish union would be protracted and complex, and, as he noted to Erskine on 24 September, he did not expect a bill to emerge before December, if then (Erskine-Murray MSS, 5155, fol. 151). Such devotion to duty went well beyond the standards of seventeenth-century parliaments; like more radical members (and in contrast to traditional attitudes), Hope appears to have viewed his office as a public trust rather than as property.

Similarly Hope appears to have associated himself consistently with far-reaching reform: he was personally and presumably politically attracted to the Kent radical Thomas St Nicholas. On 1 November 1653 both failed to secure re-election to the council as a result of their radicalism. In the parliament's famous final division, the Scottish votes made the difference (three radicals, one conservative), a circumstance which inevitably provoked considerable comment. In contrast with that of his three colleagues, the forcible dissolution of parliament forever ended Hope's public career. He apparently had a confrontation with Cromwell on the matter, so spectacular that he was immediately disgraced and discharged from all public office. As he commented in a private petition to the protector two years later, he had hoped to find 'in my private statione a hydeing place untill the indignation should be overpast' (Hopetoun House, Linlithgow MSS, bundle 648). More important, as with so many people in Britain, the failure of this parliament had cooled his prophetic vision and qualified his hopes: incremental improvement, not revolution; 'present dispensations', not a new heaven, a new earth. Probably as much as anyone Hope embodies the disappointments and transvaluations of the 'British revolution'. He now focused his formidable energies into commercial and industrial activity, and his concern with government was limited to personal matters: securing his family's traditional immunities from lead ore export duties and acquiring government support for new mining ventures. Mineral discoveries at home might compensate for the failure of the republic's 'Western Design' at Hispaniola.

Hope was a respected and apparently a genuinely likeable man—even Cromwell continued to like him. His old colleague John Swinton let him know in 1657 that no less a figure than Major-General Lambert had regretted his removal from public office. Not surprisingly, Hope's name came up from time to time as a possible appointment to the Scottish commission—only to be specifically rejected in 1655 by the president of the new Scottish council, the conservative Lord Broghill. By this time Hope avowed he had 'no scruple to serve under this or any other power whatsoever in such publict imployments', an outlook a long way from his earlier stance. Regarded by English republicans as 'a knowne Commonwealthes man', in March 1660 Hope was at last appointed once again to the commission, but neither he nor his fellow appointees ever actually served the rapidly disintegrating regime (Firth, *Scotland and the Protectorate*, 385).

His first wife having died in 1656, Hope had married on 29 October 1657 Lady Mary, eldest daughter of William *Keith, sixth Earl Marischal. On 23 November 1661 he died at the Granton home of his elder brother Alexander from a fever contracted during a trip to Holland, and was buried at Cramond church. His second wife survived him, and his son John (1650–1682) succeeded to the Hopetoun estate.

ARTHUR H. WILLIAMSON

Sources A. H. Williamson, 'Union with England traditional, union with England radical: Sir James Hope and the mid-seventeenth-century British state', *EngHR*, 110 (1995), 303–22 · Hopetoun House, West Lothian, Linlithgow MSS · 'The diary of Sir James Hope, 1646–1654', ed. J. B. Paul, *Miscellany … III*, Scottish History Society, 2nd ser., 19 (1919), 99–168 · NL Scot., Erskine-Murray MSS 5071, 5155 · 'The diary of Sir James Hope', ed. P. Marshall, *Miscellany … IX*, Scottish History Society, 3rd ser., 50 (1958), 129–97 · APS, 1648–60, 2 · *The historical works of Sir James Balfour*, ed. J. Haig, 4 (1825) · *CSP dom.*, 1652–4 · *Diary of Sir Archibald Johnston of Wariston*, 2, ed. D. H. Fleming, Scottish History Society, 2nd ser., 18 (1919) · C. S.

Terry, ed., *The Cromwellian union: papers relating to the negotiations for an incorporating union between England and Scotland, 1651–1652*, Scottish History Society (1902) · C. H. Firth, ed., *Scotland and the Commonwealth: letters and papers relating to the military government of Scotland, from August 1651 to December 1653*, Scottish History Society, 18 (1895) · C. H. Firth, ed., *Scotland and the protectorate: letters and papers relating to the military government of Scotland from January 1654 to June 1659*, Scottish History Society, 31 (1899) · D. Laing, ed., *A catalogue of the graduates ... of the University of Edinburgh*, Bannatyne Club, 106 (1858) · J. Nicoll, *A diary of public transactions and other occurrences, chiefly in Scotland, from January 1650 to June 1667*, ed. D. Laing, Bannatyne Club, 52 (1836)

Archives Hopetoun House, West Lothian, Linlithgow MSS · NA Scot., Register House, register of the committee of estates · priv. coll., papers relating to office as master of the mint in Scotland · U. Edin. L., student notebook, MS Dc.8.168 · U. St Andr. L., business letter-books | NL Scot., Erskine-Murray MSS

Likenesses oils, Hopetoun House, West Lothian [*see illus.*]

Wealth at death over £10,000—est. moveable wealth, 2 May 1662; revised upwards, 20 Jan 1664: NA Scot., CC 8/8/70, fols. 289–90

Hope, James (1764–1847), United Irishman, son of a fugitive highland covenanter who had settled in the north of Ireland as a linen weaver, was born in the parish of Templepatrick, co. Antrim, on 25 August 1764. With only fifteen weeks of formal schooling, he was apprenticed to linen weaving at the age of ten. In due time he became a journeyman weaver. The commercial distress prevalent in the north of Ireland, as a result of the American War of Independence, convinced Hope that the fundamental question of the time was social rather than political, and only to be solved by restoring to the people 'their natural right of deriving a subsistence from the soil on which their labour was expended'. But it was the religious feuds between the Peep-o'-Day Boys and the Defenders, nowhere more bitter than in his own neighbourhood, that first seriously attracted his attention to politics. He threw himself with enthusiasm into the movement for a union between the Roman Catholics and Presbyterians, aimed at an extension of civil and religious freedom among all classes of the community, and he became a member of the Roughford volunteer corps, and at a later period a member of the Mallusk Society of United Irishmen. On the reconstruction of the United Irish Society in 1795, he consented, though reluctantly, to take the oath of secrecy and fidelity, and was appointed a delegate to the upper baronial committee of Belfast.

Firmly in the confidence of United Irish leaders such as Henry Joy McCracken and Thomas Russell, Hope's chief role in the society was as a messenger and organizer, extending the movement outside Ulster. In the spring of 1796 he was sent to Dublin to spread the principles of the society among the workers of the capital. For a time he lived at Balbriggan, working as a silk weaver; but his motives were suspected by the Orangemen in the factory, and he moved to Dublin, to work in the liberties as a cotton weaver. Here he managed to found a branch society, but when he was suspected of being a castle spy, he narrowly escaped assassination, and returned to Belfast. On the outbreak of the rebellion in Ulster in 1798 he remained true to his principles, and took part in the battle

of Antrim (7 June). After lurking about in the neighbourhood of Ballymena and Belfast for four months, he made his way undetected to Dublin in November 1798. Here he was joined in the following summer by his family; but for four years he lived in continual expectation of being arrested. While in Dublin he became acquainted with Robert Emmet in 1803, and assisted him in his plot, but he took no part in the insurrection, being at the time engaged with Russell in organizing a rising in co. Down. After the failure of Emmet's rebellion he avoided arrest, and on the political amnesty that followed the death of Pitt and the accession to office of Fox and Grenville in 1806, he returned to Belfast, and resumed his work as a linen weaver. For a time he was employed by Mary Ann McCracken, the sister of Henry Joy McCracken, and later as a clerk for Joseph Smyth, publisher of the *Belfast Almanac*. In 1843 he wrote his memoirs at the request of R. R. Madden.

Hope was of medium height, slightly but firmly built, and of a modest and retiring disposition, known among his comrades as the Spartan. He married the daughter of his first employer, Rose Mullen, who died in 1831, after bearing four children. He died in Belfast in 1847 and was buried at Mallusk, co. Down.

Hope's 'Memoirs', printed in Madden's *United Irishmen*, provide a rare testament to the social radicalism and expectations of lower-class supporters of the United Irish movement. A persistent theme is the betrayal of the rank-and-file members by timid but opportunistic middle-class leaders. His firsthand account of the battle of Antrim appears in Madden's chapter on Henry Joy McCracken.

ROBERT DUNLOP, *rev.* NANCY J. CURTIN

Sources R. R. Madden, *The United Irishmen: their lives and times*, 3rd ser., 7 vols. (1842–6) · E. Black, 'James Hope, 1764–1847: United Irishman', *Irish Sword*, 14 (1980–81), 65–8 · J. Smyth, *The men of no property* (1992) · M. Elliott, *Partners in revolution: the United Irishmen and France* (1982) · N. J. Curtin, *The United Irishmen: popular politics in Ulster and Dublin, 1791–1798* (1994)

Archives TCD

Likenesses W. C. Nixon, portrait, 1840, Ulster Museum, Belfast · T. W. Huffam, mezzotint, pubd 1843, NG Ire. · death mask, Ulster Museum, Belfast · group portrait, lithograph (*The United Irish patriots of 1798*), NPG

Hope, James (1801–1841), physician and cardiologist, was born at Stockport, Cheshire, on 23 February 1801, son of Thomas and Ann Hope. His father was a wealthy merchant and manufacturer. After attending Macclesfield grammar school from 1815 to 1818 Hope entered Edinburgh University in 1820, received his medical degree in 1825, and immediately spent some months at St Bartholomew's Hospital in London, whence he obtained a year later the diploma of the Royal College of Surgeons. This was followed by a year at La Charité in Paris as a clinical clerk of M. Chomel. He subsequently spent another year on a medical tour of the continent, visiting Switzerland, Germany, Italy, and the Netherlands. Having returned to England in 1828 he rapidly established himself in practice in the fashionable part of London, at 13 Lower Seymour Street, Portman Square. At the same time he continued his studies as a pupil at St George's Hospital and passed with ease the Royal College of Physicians examinations as a licentiate. Having learned of the value of Laënnec's discovery of auscultation while in Paris, Hope championed its use from his very first days in practice. His acute hearing and aptitude for discerning the nuances of musical tones and rhythms worked to his advantage in the new art of auscultation.

Hope's interests encompassed the exciting and rapidly developing elements of physical diagnosis, clinicopathological correlations, and a pathophysiological approach to clinical diagnosis. What Laënnec did for the clinical diagnosis of pulmonary disease, Hope did for diseases of the heart and aorta.

Hope's doctoral thesis, 'Aneurism of the aorta', contained illustrations and descriptions rivalling those of Scarpa in scope and accuracy of anatomical details. While engaged as house physician and house surgeon to the Royal Infirmary, Edinburgh, he completed in 1829 four papers on aneurisms of the aorta for publication in the *London Medical Gazette*, based on his personal observations. The same journal published a year later four more papers dealing chiefly with the sounds of the heart and their physiological basis. On 10 March 1831 he married Anne (1809–1887) [*see* Hope, Anne], the well-educated daughter of John Williamson Fulton, a prosperous merchant then of Harley Street, London, and his wife, Anne, *née* Robertson.

Meanwhile Hope was busy with his own private dispensary. He also discharged his duties as physician to the Marylebone Infirmary where, from 1831, he was in charge of ninety beds, and gave lectures in his home, at St George's Hospital, where he was assistant physician from 1834, and at the Aldersgate Street school of medicine. Despite this heavy load, which eventually took a toll on his health, he managed to publish during 1833 and the following year his *Principles and Illustrations of Morbid Anatomy*. It is ironic that this great physician, who described so well so many anatomical abnormalities, had a marked aversion to dissection, but through unremitting discipline made dissection part of his daily routine.

Hope was the first accurately to time the first and second heart sounds. His report that the second sound was related to the closure of the aortic and pulmonic valves antedated phonocardiographic and electrocardiographic evidence. Hope's continuing investigations into the cause of heart sounds involved vivisection, which led to a controversy in 1835 with C. J. B. Williams. Four years later this controversy erupted into opposition, albeit briefly, on the part of Williams towards the appointment of Hope as full physician at St George's Hospital. From this time on Hope's health declined dramatically owing to consumption, until he was unable finally to fulfil his duties.

Hope was well aware of the different physiological pathways for the development of myocardial dilatation or hypertrophy. He agreed with his contemporaries that a stenosed valve caused thickening of the muscle because of the increased force needed to drive the blood through the constricted orifice, while a valve that leaked during diastole brought about a softening of the muscle wall due to volume overload and the wall's stretching, with a resultant dilatation of the chamber. However, he was unaware that a common cause of hypertrophy was systemic hypertension. He introduced semantic confusion with the term 'myosclerosis'. Acknowledging it as another cause of myocardial enlargement, he failed to delineate precisely what the term meant or what its aetiology was.

Hope's most important contribution was probably his tome on cardiovascular physiology and clinicopathological correlations. Published initially in 1832 it was entitled *A treatise on the diseases of the heart and great vessels, comprising a new view of the heart's action*. It was widely acclaimed and went through three editions during his lifetime. A fourth edition was published eight years after his death in a much reduced form and without the highly valued plates of the previous editions. The treatise was based on a thousand cases, and is a good example of how systematic clinical observation can be used to further the understanding of pathophysiology. Of note was the detailed information on acute pericarditis and inflammatory pericardial effusion and the association of both with rheumatic fever. He also emphasized that mitral stenosis was often associated with an irregular pulse. The text described in detail the volume and contour of the arterial pulse in the presence of other valvular lesions, and outlined the quantitative relationship between the aortic and mitral lesions and pulse volume. Corrigan's classic account of the rapid pulse of aortic insufficiency was anticipated by Hope. He was also the first to note the early diastolic pulmonary murmur heard in association with pulmonary hypertension, later called the Graham–Steell murmur. At one time this murmur carried the eponym of Hope. He antedated apex cardiography with his excellent descriptions of precordial movements in the presence of aortic aneurism as well as in a number of cardiac abnormalities. Hope also described the employment of the fingers as a pleximeter in percussion of the chest, considering it superior to all other methods; his method is still in use today. Finally, the treatise contained a clear presentation of the materia medica favoured in the treatment of heart disease at the time. However, he followed the blood-letting practice of the age.

Hope was elected FRS in 1832; he was also a fellow of the Royal College of Physicians and a corresponding member of several foreign societies. His non-cardiological publications included *Inflammation of the Brain*, which appeared in Tweedie's Library of Medicine, and *Notes on the Treatment of Chronic Pleurisy*, which he finished just four days before his death, on 13 May 1841 at Clare House, Hampstead, from pulmonary tuberculosis. He was buried at Highgate cemetery. His widow wrote a memoir that went through four editions. Sir Theodore Cracraft Hope (1831–1915) was their only surviving child.

W. A. GREENHILL, rev. LOUIS J. ACIERNO

Sources L. J. Acierno, *The history of cardiology* (1994) · J. Hope, *A treatise on the diseases of the heart and great vessels, comprising a new view of the heart's action*, 3rd edn (1849) · R. J. Mann, 'Historical vignette. Scarpa, Hodgson, and Hope: artists of the heart and great vessels',

Mayo Clinic Proceedings, 49 (1974), 890–92 • A. E. Hope, *Memoir of the late James Hope, M.D., physician to St George's Hospital*, 4th edn (1848) • H. M. Korns, 'A brief history of physical diagnosis', *Annals of Medical History*, 3rd ser., 1 (1939), 54 • A. Leatham, 'Auscultation and phonocardiography: a personal view of the past 40 years', *British Heart Journal*, 57 (1987), 397–403 • *GM*, 2nd ser., 15 (1841), 666 • Munk, *Roll*, 4.22–3 • d. cert.
Likenesses T. Phillips, oils, 1841, RCP Lond. • H. S. Ball, stipple, 1842 (after T. Phillips), Wellcome L. • T. Bridgford, lithograph, Wellcome L.

Hope, James (1803–1882), lawyer and political agent, was born on 28 May 1803, the third son of the Right Honourable Charles *Hope of Granton (1763–1851), judge and lord president and lord justice general of the court of session from 1811 to 1841, and his wife, Lady Charlotte Hope (1772–1834), daughter of John, second earl of Hopetoun. His family formed part of the extended Dundas connection that dominated Scottish political and legal life in the late eighteenth and early nineteenth centuries. His mother was the half-sister of Jane, the second wife of the politician Henry Dundas, first Viscount Melville (1742–1811), and his elder brother was John *Hope (1794–1858), dean of the faculty of advocates and later a judge. On 2 December 1828 James Hope married Elizabeth (d. 1880), daughter of David *Boyle, later Lord Shewalton (1772–1853), a former protégé of Henry Dundas, who had been lord justice clerk since 1811 and was to succeed Hope's father as lord president in 1841. Few men beginning a legal career in Edinburgh in the 1820s could have been as well connected, even though by the end of the decade the influence of the Dundas faction had greatly diminished. In January 1828 Hope was in the final year of an apprenticeship to prepare him for admission to the Society of Writers to the Signet. The head of the society, the keeper of the signet, was William Dundas, the tory MP for Edinburgh. When Dundas appointed James Hope as one of two joint deputy keepers on 12 January 1828 the members of the society protested at his imposing on them a twenty-four-year-old who had not yet completed his apprenticeship. Henry Cockburn recalled that there was a 'little bit of rebellion' in the society and the writers 'got into a blaze and expectorated in resolutions and protests' (*Memorials … by Henry Cockburn*, 449). Hope, duly admitted to the society on 4 July 1828, was joint deputy keeper until 1850 and then sole deputy keeper until his death in 1882, by which time he was possibly the last office holder in Scotland to owe his position to Dundas patronage.

During the agitation for parliamentary reform in 1831–2 Hope was active in the tory opposition to the measure. He helped to organize the 'great constitutional meeting' held in Edinburgh on 28 November 1831, and when the Scottish Reform Act passed in the summer of 1832 he was appointed election agent for Sir George Clerk of Penicuik, MP for Midlothian in the Dundas interest since 1811. After Clerk's defeat at the general election in December 1832, Hope continued as agent for Clerk and the Conservative supporting gentlemen of the county. His primary objective was to increase the number of Conservative supporters enrolled at the annual registration court and to restrict the number the whigs could enrol (Brash, xxxviii–xlvii).

Hope had some success in 1833 and 1834, which may have helped Clerk to regain his seat for the county by a small margin at the election in January 1835, but the whigs had the better of that year's registration contest when Hope said he spent an average of ten hours a day in court for eleven days. In April 1835 Hope wrote a 'Memorandum for the private consideration of those principally interested in maintaining the conservative interest in the county of Mid Lothian' (Brash, 22–5) in which he proposed that a credit of several thousand pounds should be obtained at one of the banks to fund the buying-up of properties to keep them out of the hands of opponents and to enable supporters to gain qualifications. The duke of Buccleuch approved the plan and a credit of £5000 was established at the Royal Bank of Scotland. Hope arranged the purchase of several properties and began the preparation of voting qualifications for registration in 1836, some of which were considered by the select committee on fictitious votes (Scotland) in 1837–8. By then Hope had ceased to be the Conservative agent. The county gentlemen decided they required an agent of a more bustling and active disposition, more ready to mix with 'men of inferior rank' (Brash, 86). A prolonged dispute over Hope's accounts and who was responsible for paying them, in which Hope involved his brother, the dean of the faculty, contributed to his being replaced in June 1836, but although he took no further part in Midlothian county politics, issues connected with the settlement of his accounts or the properties acquired with the cash credit obtained in 1835 at his suggestion troubled the county gentlemen and the duke of Buccleuch until at least the early 1850s.

Hope appears to have devoted the rest of his career to professional activities including his duties for over half a century as deputy keeper of the signet. At his death the society formally acknowledged the respect and esteem in which he was held. His marriage to Elizabeth Boyle, which lasted until her death in 1880, produced four sons and three daughters. James Hope died on 14 February 1882 at his residence, Avenel, in Edinburgh.   J. I. BRASH

Sources J. I. Brash, ed., *Papers on Scottish electoral politics, 1832–1854*, Scottish History Society, fourth ser., 11 (1974) • [F. J. Grant], *A history of the Society of Writers to Her Majesty's Signet* (1890) • *Memorials of his time, by Henry Cockburn* (1856) • *Law Times* (25 Feb 1882) • NA Scot., Buccleuch MSS, GD 224 • NA Scot., Clerk of Penicuik MSS, GD 18 • 'Select committee on the registering of fictitious votes in Scotland', *Parl. papers* (1837–8), vol. 14, no. 590 • Burke, *Peerage* (1900)
Archives BL, corresp. with H. Bonham-Carter • NA Scot., Buccleuch MSS, GD 224 • NA Scot., Clerk of Penicuik MSS, GD 18
Wealth at death £21,990 13s. 3d.: confirmation, 19 June 1882, *CCI* • £0: supplementary inventory, 14 Sept 1882, *CCI* • £3073 6s. 9d.: additional inventory, 30 July 1884, *CCI* • £1460: second additional inventory, 5 Sept 1885, *CCI*

Hope, Sir James (1808–1881), naval officer, born on 3 March 1808, was the son of Rear-Admiral Sir George Johnstone Hope (1767–1818), who as a captain commanded the *Defence* at Trafalgar, and his first wife, Lady Jemima Hope Johnstone, fifth daughter of James Hope Johnstone, third earl of Hopetoun. Admiral Sir Henry Hope (1787–1863) was James Hope's first cousin. In August 1820 Hope entered the Royal Naval College, Portsmouth, and in June 1822 was appointed to the frigate *Forte* going out to the West Indies; afterwards he served in the *Cambrian* in the Mediterranean and was promoted lieutenant on 9 March 1827. On 16 September he was appointed to the *Maidstone*, but a fortnight later was transferred to the *Undaunted*, which carried Lord William Bentinck out to India as governorgeneral. In August 1829 Hope was appointed flag lieutenant to the earl of Northesk, then commander-in-chief at Plymouth, and on 26 February 1830 he was promoted commander. From 1833 to 1838 he commanded the *Racer* on the North America and West Indies station and was posted on 28 June 1838. On 16 August 1838 he married the Hon. Frederica Kinnaird, daughter of Charles Kinnaird, eighth Lord Kinnaird; the couple had no children. In December 1844 he commissioned the steam frigate *Firebrand* for service on the South American station, and on 20 November 1845 played a prominent part in the engagement with the batteries at Obligado on the River Parana in Argentina. Hope was nominated a CB on 3 April 1846. During the Crimean War from 1854 to 1856 he commanded the *Majestic* in the Baltic, but without opportunity of personal distinction. On 19 November 1857 he attained the rank of rearadmiral. In March 1859 he was appointed commander-inchief in China and on 16 April reached Singapore, where he relieved Sir Michael Seymour.

The Second Opium War had formally ended in a treaty signed at Tientsin (Tianjin) on 26 June 1858, the ratifications of which were to be exchanged at Peking (Beijing) within a year. It was, however, rumoured at Shanghai that the British and French ministers would not be permitted to go to Peking. On 17 June 1859 the *Chesapeake*, flying Hope's flag, anchored in the Po Hai (Bohai), and Hope went at once in the gunboat *Plover* to the mouth of the Peiho (Beihe) to inform the governor of the forts of the ambassadors' approach and to see for himself what the passage was like. He found that it was blocked and the forts guarding it strengthened. On 19 June the allied ministers arrived off the bar of the Peiho, but as the obstructions prevented their passing up the river, and they were told to go to the Pehtang (Beitang), 9 miles further north, contrary as they thought to the terms of the treaty, they formally requested Hope to clear the way for them. This accordingly he undertook to do, and on 25 June he attempted, and failed, to force the passage. The Chinese defended resolutely. Three British ships were sunk and more disabled; 89 men were killed and 345 wounded, including Hope, who was seriously injured. It was a significant rebuff to British arms.

This repulse of British forces gave rise to the allegation that they were treacherously attacked, and that the guns were manned by Europeans—Russians more especially— or Americans. Such allegations were unfounded: for even admitting that the attack was a violation of the treaty, it was understood by Hope that the treaty was to be violated; and he approached the boom knowing that he would have to fight his way. The passage which Hope tried to force had been forced by Seymour only the year before; and it had

often been pointed out that to attack the Chinese forces twice in the same way on the same ground was likely to lead to serious fighting. Despite the tactical error, which led the prime minister, Lord Palmerston, to doubt his suitability for such a high command, Hope's exploits aroused great popular enthusiasm in Britain. It was decided that the treaty must be ratified at Peking, and a strong military expedition was sent out by the allied powers. Hope had meantime gone to the vicinity of Ningpo (Ningbo), where he remained to revive his health. In 1860 he oversaw local transport arrangements, and by the end of June the troops were landed at the mouth of the Pehtang. By 1 August all was ready for the advance. On 20 September they attacked and stormed the fort on the north side of the Peiho. When that was captured the southern forts were at once evacuated, the obstacles were removed from the mouth of the river, and on the 23rd Hope went up to Tientsin, where he for the most part remained until the treaty was signed at Peking on 24 October. On 9 November 1860 he was nominated a KCB and in the following year received the grand cross of the Légion d'honneur. In the spring of 1862 he co-operated with the Chinese imperial troops under Ward, the American general, in driving back the Taipings from the areas near Shanghai and Ningpo. Several of their positions were taken by storm, and on different occasions there was severe though irregular fighting during which Hope was wounded by a musket shot. The situation was still very unsettled when, in the autumn, he was relieved by Rear-Admiral Kuper.

Despite reservations about his diplomatic skills, towards the end of 1863 Hope was appointed commander-in-chief in North America and the West Indies, where the American Civil War was still raging. His command there was uneventful. He became vice-admiral on 16 September 1864, GCB on 28 March 1865, and returned to England in spring 1867. From 1869 to 1872 he was commander-in-chief at Portsmouth and was thus, in October 1870, called on to preside at the court martial which inquired into the loss of the *Captain*. He became admiral on 21 January 1870; was appointed principal aide-de-camp in February 1873; was retired, on reaching seventy, in March 1878; and on 15 June 1879 was advanced to the honorary rank of admiral of the fleet. In 1877 he married his second wife, Elizabeth Reid Cotton, daughter of General Sir A. Cotton; she survived him. During his later years his health was poor, and he lived in comparative retirement. He died, childless, at his home, Carriden House, Bo'ness, Linlithgowshire, on 9 June 1881. Hope was an officer of great personal courage but lacked the intellectual and diplomatic skills required for high command.

J. K. LAUGHTON, *rev.* ANDREW LAMBERT

Sources G. S. Graham, *The China station: war and diplomacy, 1830–1860* (1978) · U. Southampton L., Broadlands MSS · Bucks. RLSS, Somerset papers · O'Byrne, *Naval biog. dict.* · Boase, *Mod. Eng. biog.* · Burke, *Peerage* (1879) · Kelly, *Handbk* (1879) · *The Times* (10 June 1881)
Archives Bucks. RLSS, letters to duke of Somerset · Devon RO, letters to duke of Somerset · NA Scot., corresp. with Robert Saunders-Dundas

Likenesses J. S. Hodges, portrait, *c*.1857, NMM · G. F. Clarke, portrait, Admiralty, Portsmouth

Hope, Sir James Archibald (1785–1871), army officer, was the son of Lieutenant-Colonel Erskine Hope, 26th (Cameronians) regiment, and great-grandson of Sir Thomas Hope of Craighall, Fife, eighth baronet. In January 1800 he was appointed ensign in the 26th (Cameronians), then at Halifax, Nova Scotia, of which his father was junior major. He became lieutenant in the regiment in 1801 and captain in 1805. He served with his regiment in Hanover in 1805–6, was a deputy assistant adjutant-general under Lord Cathcart at Copenhagen in 1807, and was on the staff of Sir John Hope, later fourth earl of Hopetoun, in Sweden in 1808, in Spain in 1808–9 (including the battle of Corunna), and with the Walcheren expedition. He was aide-de-camp to General Thomas Graham at Barossa, and brought home the dispatches and the 'eagle' captured by the 87th regiment. He was afterwards with Graham at Ciudad Rodrigo and Badajoz.

When Graham went home on sick leave during Wellington's advance against the forts of Salamanca, Hope was appointed an assistant adjutant-general, and he was present at Salamanca, Burgos, Vitoria, San Sebastian, and the passage of the Bidassoa. He was afterwards selected to act as assistant adjutant-general and military secretary to Marshal Beresford, who was in command of an army corps. With this corps Hope saw the later campaigns, including the battle of the Nivelle, Nive, Orthez, and Toulouse. He was made a brevet major in March 1811 and lieutenant-colonel in January 1813, and was promoted on 25 July 1814 from the Cameronians to captain and lieutenant-colonel 3rd foot guards. In that regiment he served twenty-five years, retiring on half pay unattached on 1 November 1839. He became brevet colonel in 1830 and major-general in 1841, and was employed as major-general on the staff in Lower Canada, 1841–7; he was appointed colonel in the 9th regiment in 1848, becoming lieutenant-general in 1851 and general in 1859.

Hope was a GCB, and had the Peninsular gold cross and clasp for Vitoria, Nivelle, Nive, Orthez, and Toulouse. He was married, and had three children. He died at his residence, Balgowan House, Pittville, Cheltenham, on 30 December 1871, aged eighty-six.

H. M. CHICHESTER, *rev.* JAMES FALKNER

Sources *Army List* · *The Times* (Jan 1872) · *Hart's Army List* · *The dispatches of … the duke of Wellington … from 1799 to 1818*, ed. J. Gurwood, 4: *Peninsula, 1790–1813* (1835), 698 · *Colburn's United Service Magazine*, 3 (1849), 142
Archives NAM, military papers | NA Scot., letters to Sir Alexander Hope · NL Scot., corresp. with Lord Lynedoch
Likenesses attrib. A. H. Lawrence, oils, *c*.1850; Christies, 1 March 1963
Wealth at death under £20,000: resworn probate, June 1873, *CGPLA Eng. & Wales* (1872)

Hope [*formerly* Hope-Scott], **James Fitzalan**, **first Baron Rankeillour** (1870–1949), politician, was born in London on 11 December 1870, the second of the two sons (his elder brother died in infancy) in the family of six children of James Robert Hope-*Scott, QC (1812–1873). His mother, who died nine days after his birth, was Lady Victoria Alexandrina Fitzalan-Howard (1840–1870), eldest daughter of the fourteenth duke of Norfolk [*see* Howard, Henry Granville Fitzalan-] and was his father's second wife. His father died when James was two and the children went to live at Arundel with his grandmother, the dowager duchess of Norfolk (Duchess Minna). Her son, the fifteenth duke of Norfolk, after his marriage bought for her the estate of Heron's Ghyll at Uckfield which had been created by Coventry Patmore. There the children, who later reverted to their father's original name of Hope, grew up. Hope became so attached to Heron's Ghyll that after the death of his grandmother he persuaded his uncle to keep the property so that he might purchase it when he came of age.

Hope was educated at the Oratory School, Birmingham, and went to Christ Church, Oxford, in 1889, but ill health prevented him from completing his degree. He then served as private secretary to his uncle when postmaster-general, and was also for some years assistant honorary secretary at the Conservative central office. On 15 November 1892 he married Mabel Ellen (*d.* 1938), daughter of Francis Henry Riddell, of Cheeseburn Grange, Northumberland. They had three sons and one daughter.

After unsuccessfully contesting the Elland division of Yorkshire in 1892 and Pontefract in 1895, Hope entered parliament in 1900 as Conservative member for the Brightside division of Sheffield, and held various parliamentary private secretaryships to Conservative ministers until the political landslide of 1906 when he lost his seat. He was returned unopposed, however, for the Central division of Sheffield at a by-election in 1908. On the formation of the coalition government in 1915 he was one of the Conservative whips; from 1916 until 1919 he was a junior lord of the Treasury, and in 1919 he was appointed parliamentary and financial secretary to the Ministry of Munitions.

It was noted of Hope that during 'his career in Parliament he rarely took part in debates' (*The Times*, 15 Feb 1949, 7), and any further political aspirations he may have had were put on one side in 1921, when, at the request of the prime minister, Lloyd George, he accepted the post of chairman of ways and means and deputy speaker, and in that office he remained, except during the first Labour government in 1924, until 1929. He was sworn of the privy council in 1922. His tenure of office as deputy speaker was marked particularly by clashes with the Labour Party, especially those led by James Maxton. In March 1925 he suspended from the house the Labour member David Kirkwood in a manner considered even by his Conservative colleagues to have been 'unnecessarily sharp' (*Real Old Tory Politics*, 219). There continued to be an atmosphere of antagonism between Hope and the Labour Party, and in 1926 several Labour members proposed a motion of censure against him for not having maintained 'the high traditions of the Chair for impartiality' (*The Times*, 15 Feb 1949, 7). This move the Conservatives needed to counter with their own motion of confidence. Some Labour members also began to run a minor public campaign against Hope. The partisan climate that existed with Hope in the chair led to moves within his own party for his removal from the post. Robert Sanders wrote that he himself was approached in 1924 and 1925 with the possibility of his taking over if Hope was moved.

In 1928 J. H. Whitley resigned the speakership, and Hope would normally have been expected to move with little opposition into the position. But he stood aside. He was quick to counter the suggestion that he did this because he was 'out of favour with the opposition and, therefore, was unlikely to be elected unanimously' (*The Times*, 4 March 1943, 7), and stated instead that his decision was 'based upon the purely personal ground that from close observation and understudy I had conceived the strongest repugnance for the life involved' (*The Times*, 12 March 1943, 5). He continued to act as chairman until the general election of 1929 when, having given up his Sheffield constituency, he stood for a Walthamstow division and was defeated.

Hope was raised to the peerage as Baron Rankeillour of Buxted, Sussex, on 28 June 1932. He served on the joint select committee on India, and with Lord Salisbury and others was one of the die-hard opponents of moves towards Indian self-government. He took an active share in putting forward amendments during the passage of the Government of India Bill in 1935. He was generally a regular contributor to the House of Lords debates.

Outside his political life Hope was a prominent layman in the Roman Catholic world with a membership of various Catholic associations. He also took up the Catholic cause in his contributions to debates in the Lords, particularly in regard to the Education Bill of 1944. He was a keen classicist, often quoting from Horace and Juvenal, and to the end of his life he read the epistles and gospels in Greek. He was said to have an astonishing memory and to be able to quote whole sentences from books which he had not read for years. He was also a man given to little show of emotion and was, in many ways, a solitary figure. Following the death of his first wife he married, on 15 September 1941, Lady Beatrice Minny Ponsonby Kerr-Clark (*d.* 1966), daughter of Ponsonby William Moore, the ninth earl of Drogheda and widow of Captain Struan Robertson Kerr-Clark, of the Seaforth Highlanders. They had no children. He died at St Mary's Hospital, Paddington, London, on 14 February 1949 and was buried at Heron's Ghyll on 17 February. He was succeeded by his eldest son, Sir Arthur Oswald James Hope (1897–1958).

GEOFFREY THROCKMORTON, *rev.* MARC BRODIE

Sources *The Times* (15 Feb 1949) · *The Times* (4 March 1943) · *The Times* (12 March 1943) · J. Foster, *Oxford men, 1880–1892: with a record of their schools, honours, and degrees* (1893) · *Real old tory politics: the political diaries of Robert Sanders, Lord Bayford, 1910–35*, ed. J. Ramsden (1984) · R. Blake, *The unknown prime minister: the life and times of Andrew Bonar Law* (1955) · Burke, *Peerage*
Archives HLRO, corresp. with Andrew Bonar Law
Likenesses W. Stoneman, photograph, 1932, NPG
Wealth at death £48,597 8s. 5d.: probate, 22 April 1949, *CGPLA Eng. & Wales*

Hope, Sir John, **Lord Craighall** (1603x5–1654), advocate, was the eldest son of Thomas, later Sir Thomas *Hope of Craighall, Fife (1573–1646), lord advocate, and Elizabeth (*d.* 1660), daughter of John Bennet of Wallyford, near Haddington; Sir Thomas *Hope (1606–1643) and Sir James *Hope (1614–1661) were his younger brothers. He was educated for the law, and rapidly acquired a thriving practice. In 1632 Hope was knighted and appointed an ordinary lord of session, assuming the title of Lord Craighall, and taking his seat on 27 July. He married Margaret, daughter of Sir Archibald Murray of Blackbarony, in the same year. The couple had two sons and six daughters.

In common with his father, Craighall was sympathetic to the aims of the national covenant. He was a close associate of Archibald Johnston of Wariston (a leader of the covenanting movement, and lord advocate in 1646), who attended the baptism of his daughter Helen in June 1638. In September, Craighall refused to subscribe Charles I's alternative king's covenant, unless the general assembly approved the document. In 1640 he was a member of the committee of estates charged with the defence of the kingdom against Charles, and in 1641 was reappointed ordinary lord of session. Craighall was one of the commissioners for the visitation of St Andrews in 1644 (at which date he succeeded his brother Sir Thomas Hope of Kerse as a commissioner for the plantation of kirks), and was appointed to the privy council in 1645.

Latterly, Craighall joined the Cromwellian administration of Scotland, and was reputedly of the opinion that Charles II ought 'to treat with Cromwell for the one halff of his cloake before he lost the whole' (Anderson, *Scot.*

Sir John Hope, Lord Craighall (1603x5–1654), by George Jamesone

nat., 2.490). In May 1652 he was one of eight commissioners appointed by the new regime to manage Scottish affairs. The appointment caused a rift with his former colleague Johnston of Wariston, who wrote that Craighall gained little 'comfort' from his employment, 'which he took to provyde his children, [but] in al apearance hes lost mor be the superiorities [than] gotten be his fees'. Indeed, he noted, the family 'looked very ruynous' by 1654. Nevertheless, on hearing of Craighall's 'fayling and wearying away' of a violent 'seaknesse' Wariston joined a 'great multitude about [his old friend's] bed' in Edinburgh (*Diary of Sir Archibald Johnston*, ed. Fleming, 167, 240–43). Craighall died, at 'about midnight', on 28 April 1654, and was survived by his wife.

Their second son, **Archibald Hope**, Lord Rankeillor (1639–1706), was lord of session in 1689 and lord of justiciary in 1690. Adopting the title of Lord Rankeillor, he was appointed to the privy council in 1696, and was a commissioner to parliament in 1706. With his wife, Margaret, *née* Aytoun, he had a son, Sir Thomas *Hope, eighth baronet. He died on 10 October 1706.   VAUGHAN T. WELLS

Sources *Diary of Sir Archibald Johnston of Wariston*, 1, ed. G. M. Paul, Scottish History Society, 61 (1911) · *Diary of Sir Archibald Johnston of Wariston*, 2, ed. D. H. Fleming, Scottish History Society, 2nd ser., 18 (1919) · M. D. Young, ed., *The parliaments of Scotland: burgh and shire commissioners*, 1 (1992) · *Scots peerage* · Anderson, *Scot. nat.* · J. R. Young, *The Scottish parliament, 1639–1661: a political and constitutional analysis* (1996) · *DNB*

Likenesses G. Jamesone, oils, priv. coll.; on loan to Scot. NPG [*see illus.*]

Hope, John. *See* Bruce, Sir John Hope, of Kinross, seventh baronet (1684?–1766).

Hope, John (1725–1786), physician and botanist, was born in Edinburgh on 10 May 1725, the son of Robert Hope (d. 1742), surgeon, and Marion Glass of Sauchie, Stirlingshire, and grandson of Archibald Hope, Lord Rankeillor (1639–1706), judge of session. He was educated locally and from the age of about fifteen read medicine, partly under Charles Alston at Edinburgh University, and about 1748–9 in Paris, where he studied botany under Bernard de Jussieu at the Jardin du Roi. In 1750 he was awarded MD at Glasgow University and, in 1762, elected a fellow of the Royal College of Physicians of Edinburgh. He married Juliana, daughter of John Stevenson, later professor of physic at Glasgow, on 28 February 1760. They lived close to the junction of High School Yards and High School Wynd. Hope practised medicine in Edinburgh, being appointed a physician to the Royal Infirmary and, in 1784, became president of the college. He was active in inducing the town council to improve the sanitation of the city and became a governor of the Orphan College, a member of the university senate and a foundation fellow of the Royal Society of Edinburgh. He was a member of the Hollandsche Maatschappij der Wetenschappen, Haarlem, and was elected FRS 1767.

With David Hume, Adam Smith, and others, Hope was a founder, in 1754, of the Select Society, inaugurated by Allan Ramsay: his intellectual passion was botany. In 1761 he was appointed Alston's successor as professor of botany and materia medica and also king's botanist for Scotland and superintendent of the royal garden in Edinburgh. In the winter sessions he lectured on materia medica, in the summer on botany, being, with Thomas Martyn at Cambridge, the first in Britain to teach the Linnaean system. After seven years he persuaded the council to divide his duties between two professors, so that he gave up the former and was appointed regius professor of medicine and botany in 1768. Besides medical income, he was earning some £300 (sterling) a year—from course fees, the chair (£77), and the garden post (£50), now assured for life.

Hope established a botanical garden to replace the polluted Royal Abbey Garden and the Town Garden at Trinity Hospital, which was on swampy ground (now Waverley Station). He moved the rarer plants to a 5 acre site with poor but varied soil north of Leith Walk, receiving grants from the Treasury in 1763, 1774, and, with the lobbying of Joseph Banks, 1781. This garden (now the Royal Botanic Garden) was not merely for the demonstration of materia medica but had greenhouses, ponds, and groves and, as in Paris, was arranged on botanical rather than medical principles. He introduced uniform Linnaean nomenclature ahead of Paris and, in 1779, at his own expense, set up to Robert Adam's design a monument to Linnaeus. In 1763–4 he organized the first British syndicate for importing plant material, especially from North America, where its first collector was John Bartram of Philadelphia, who had been recommended by Benjamin Franklin; in 1766 Hope toured English gardens to gather more. He was particularly concerned to introduce the medicinal Chinese rhubarb (*Rheum palmatum*) and asafoetida (*Ferula persica*), publishing on these topics, if little else, though he intended to prepare a Scottish flora with the help of his students. Hope advised Banks on botanists, notably his pupil Archibald Menzies, for voyages of exploration and for the growing network of botanical gardens centred on Kew: William Wright on Jamaica, George Young (d. 1803) on St Vincent, and a certain Munro on Grenada were all his pupils, as were Richard Pulteney, Richard Salisbury, James Edward Smith, Francis Buchanan-Hamilton, and William Roxburgh.

Hope's contribution to science was the building up, in little more than twenty years, of an influential school of botanists, some of whom were to be the driving force for forest conservation in India, and one of the leading botanical gardens in Europe. His attempt to develop a natural classification of plants matured through another pupil, his successor, Daniel Rutherford, who in turn lectured to Robert Brown who re-established the natural system in 1810. Hope's lectures, which stressed the importance of anatomical and physiological work, though not oratorical, were scholarly and well attended; in 1780 some fifty-nine students took his botany course.

Hope was known for his common sense and generosity and for his simple and unostentatious lifestyle. He died in Edinburgh on 10 November 1786 and was buried in the family plot in Greyfriars churchyard there. He was survived by four sons, the third of whom, Thomas Charles *Hope, became professor of chemistry at Glasgow and later Edinburgh. Hope's estate, some £12,000 Scots, went to his wife, who already owned land near the botanical garden. Hope was commemorated in *Hopea*, first used for the tropical tree genus now called *Symplocos*, but later applied by Roxburgh, as today, to a south-east Asian genus of timber-trees (*Dipterocarpaceae*).   D. J. MABBERLEY

Sources A. G. Morton, *John Hope* (1986) · *The Banks letters*, ed. W. R. Dawson (1958) · D. J. Mabberley, *Jupiter botanicus: Robert Brown of the British Museum* (1985) · R. H. Grove, *Green imperialism: colonial expansion, tropical island Edens, and the origins of environmentalism, 1600–1860* (1995) · will, PRO, PROB 11/1154, sig. 275
Archives NA Scot., corresp. and papers · NL Scot., housekeeping book · Royal Botanic Garden, Edinburgh, notes and drawings · RS, papers · U. Aberdeen L., lecture notes · U. Edin., clinical casebook · Wellcome L., lecture notes | Linn. Soc., corresp. with Richard Pulteney · NL Scot., corresp. with Robert Liston · RBG Kew, corresp. with Sir Joseph Banks · Royal Botanic Garden, Edinburgh · Royal College of Physicians of Edinburgh, corresp. relating to Royal College of Physicians of Edinburgh
Likenesses J. Kay, caricature, etching, 1785, NPG; repro. in Morton, *John Hope*
Wealth at death £12,000 Scots: Morton, *John Hope*

Hope, John (1737–1784). *See under* Hope family (*per. c.*1700–1813).

Hope, John (1739–1785), writer and politician, was born on 7 April 1739, the second son of Charles Hope (afterwards Hope-Vere) and Catherine Weir, and grandson of Charles *Hope, first earl of Hopetoun. He was educated at the Revd Andrew Kinross's academy at Enfield, Middlesex, and was sent to Holland in 1752 to learn business with distant kinsmen, the Hopes of Amsterdam. He returned in 1759 and engaged in mercantile pursuits in London, apparently with no great success. On 2 June 1762 Hope married Mary (1741/2–1767), only daughter of Eliab Breton of Forty Hill, Middlesex. Mary committed suicide at Brockhall, Northamptonshire, on 25 June 1767, at the age of twenty-five, and was buried nearby at Norton. Her husband erected a monument with a rhyming epitaph to her memory in the south transept of Westminster Abbey (Neale, 2.257). Their three sons, Charles *Hope (1763–1851), John *Hope (1765–1836), afterwards knighted; and William Johnstone *Hope (1766–1831), also afterwards knighted, are separately noticed.

In 1768 Hope was chosen by the influence of his uncle, John Hope, second earl of Hopetoun, to succeed his father as MP for Linlithgowshire. The earl allowed him an annuity of £400 to defray his expenses. In 1770 he was unseated on the petition of his opponent, James Dundas. He had lost favour, both with his patron and with the majority of the House of Commons, for his equivocal support for the government in the Wilkes affair. This was demonstrated by his voting for Wilkes on the question of the Middlesex election on 8 May 1769, and to this he attributed the loss of his seat. 'It was chiefly in your cause I suffered', he wrote to Wilkes (letter to John Wilkes, BL, Add. MS 30871, fol. 132).

The majority of Hope's writing appeared in print after the end of his political career—although his first book of poetry and his first contributions to periodicals are dated as early as 1769. He wrote on a variety of contemporary issues in a wide range of genres, but was primarily an essayist and a poet. Almost all of Hope's work originally appeared unsigned, under his initials, or pseudonymously, in popular periodicals of the day—in the *Public Advertiser* (1769–72), *Town and Country Magazine* (1769–84), *Westminster Magazine* (1773–81, under the name The Leveller), and the *Lady's Magazine* (1776–8). Some of these contributions he later reprinted under his own name in his *Thoughts in Prose and Verse Started in his Walks* (1780). Pitcher notes, however, that Hope 'contributed more to the magazines than he cared to preserve' and attributes to him the anonymously published satire *Sketches from Nature in High Preservation* (1779) (*N&Q*, new ser., 45/1, 1998, 77–81). In this work, which went through fourteen editions in its first year in print, a sketch of 'John H—e, esq.' appears in two scenes, representing 'Patience' and 'Paul Writing to the Ephesians and Philippians, while Prisoner at Rome'. The *Gentleman's Magazine* also credits Hope with the authorship of the *New Margate Guide* (1780). Hope died on 21 May 1785 at Newcastle upon Tyne of a 'mortification in his bowels' (*GM*, 1st ser., 55/2, 1785, 665).

FRANCIS WATT, *rev.* JEFFREY HERRLE

Sources *GM*, 1st ser., 55 (1785), 665 · *N&Q*, 6 (1852), 18, 39–40 · E. W. Pitcher, 'On the miscellaneous works of John Hope (1739–1785)', *N&Q*, 243 (1998), 77–81 · J. Hope, letter to John Wilkes, 1770, BL, Add. MS 30871, fol. 132 · *N&Q*, 12 (1855), 42 · *N&Q*, 5 (1852), 582 · J. P. Neale, *The history and antiquities of Westminster Abbey and Henry the Seventh's chapel, their tombs, ancient monuments, and inscriptions* (1856), 2.257 · S. Halkett and J. Laing, *A dictionary of the anonymous and pseudonymous literature of Great Britain*, 3 (1885) · HoP, *Commons*, 1754–90
Archives BL, letter to John Wilkes, Add. MS 30871, fol. 132

Hope, John, fourth earl of Hopetoun (1765–1823), army officer, the son of John Hope, second earl (1704–1781), and his second wife, Jean (*d.* 1767), daughter of Robert Oliphant of Rossie, Perthshire, was born at Hopetoun House, Abercorn parish, Linlithgowshire, on 17 August 1765. He was the elder half-brother of generals Sir Alexander *Hope and Charles Hope (*d.* 1825). Educated at home, he travelled on the continent with his brother Alexander and their tutor, Dr John Gillies, who later became the historiographer royal for Scotland.

Hope is reported to have served for a short time as a volunteer. He was appointed cornet in the 10th light dragoons on 28 May 1784. He then became a lieutenant in the 100th foot, and later in the 27th Inniskillings, a captain in the 17th light dragoons (later lancers) in 1789, major in the 1st Royals foot in 1792, and lieutenant-colonel of the 25th foot on 26 April 1793. A tory, he was elected MP for Linlithgowshire in 1790, and again in 1796.

When the Mediterranean and channel fleets under lords Hood and Howe put to sea in April–July 1793 the 25th foot was one of the regiments that embarked so as to compensate for the shortfall in marines. Hope remained in headquarters at Plymouth until December 1794, by which time independent companies had been drafted into the regiment, increasing it to two battalions. On 9 February 1795 he sailed as commander of ten companies of the regiment for the West Indies. On reaching Grenada on 30 March he was invalided home. He returned to the West Indies in 1796 as adjutant-general under Sir Ralph Abercromby. He took part in the capture of the French and Spanish West Indies in 1796–7, and was repeatedly praised by Abercromby and other senior officers. He returned home in 1797.

In August 1799 Hope was deputy adjutant-general of the advanced force sent to the Netherlands under Abercromby. However he received a severe wound in the ankle during the landing on The Helder, and was sent home. On 27 August 1799 he was promoted from the 25th foot to colonel of the North Lowland fencible infantry (raised in 1794 and disbanded in 1802). At the end of September he returned to the Netherlands as adjutant-general of the main body of the expeditionary force under the duke of York. He was present at the second battle of Bergen (2 October) and the battle of Castricum (6 October). He was also one of the officers assigned to arrange the convention of Alkmaar.

Hope was adjutant-general to Abercromby in the Mediterranean in 1800, and in the Egyptian expedition of 1801. At the battle of Abu Qir (20 and 21 March) Hope was severely wounded; Abercromby was killed. On his recovery he asked for the command of a brigade, and was appointed to one composed of two of the army's most distinguished regiments, the 28th foot and 42nd highlanders. His brigade joined the army outside Cairo, and he was sent by General Hutchinson to arrange the terms of surrender of the French garrison. He later did the same in Alexandria. Hope had married first, on 17 August 1798, his cousin, Elizabeth, fifth and youngest daughter of the Hon. Charles Hope-Vere of Craigiehall, and sister of John Hope (1739–1785). She died childless on 20 March 1801. He married second on 9 February 1803, Louisa Dorothea (d. 1836), daughter of Sir John Wedderburn, bt. They had eleven children.

Hope became a major-general in 1803, commanded a brigade in the eastern district of England under Sir J. H. Craig during the invasion alarms of 1803–5, and in 1805 was appointed lieutenant-governor of Portsmouth, resigning in the same year to join the expedition to Hanover under Lord Cathcart. He became a lieutenant-general in 1808, was deputy commander of the troops sent to Sweden under Sir John Moore, and in August 1808 he landed in Portugal. He was in command at Lisbon when the French evacuated the city, and had the difficult task of restraining the local population from exacting revenge upon their erstwhile occupier. He was present during the negotiations of the controversial convention of Cintra (24 August 1808).

When Moore advanced into Spain, Hope commanded one of the army's two divisions. Having crossed the River Tagus he was forced to make a circuitous 380-mile journey through Elvas, Badajoz, Talavera, and Escorial with all twenty-four of Moore's guns, his trains and his few cavalry. During this period Hope negotiated with representatives of the Spanish junta, but refused to take his troops into Madrid. He linked up with Moore near Salamanca on 4 December and confirmed that Napoleon was concentrating on Madrid and had no immediate intention of moving west. Hope then took part in the retreat to Corunna. He commanded the British left at the battle of Corunna (January 1809), and succeeded to overall command when Moore fell and Baird was wounded. He 'wisely decided to pursue the object for which the battle had been fought, a safe re-embarkation' (Fortescue, *Brit. army*, 6.390). It is said that he personally visited every street in the port, to ensure that no-one was left behind. He received the thanks of parliament, and was made a KB.

Hope commanded the reserve in the Walcheren expedition of 1809. Landing at Ter Goes he took up a position from which the western Scheldt was covered for the duration of the operations. He realized after only a few days that the expedition's objectives were unattainable. In 1812 he became commander of the forces in Ireland. In 1813 he was appointed to succeed Sir Thomas Graham in the Peninsular army. Instructions were received that he was to be given the command of at least a division and placed next in seniority to Wellington, though not his second in command. Hope commanded the first division at the battle of Nivelle (10 November) and at the battles of the Nive (10–13 December) in which he was wounded. Wellington wrote of him: 'I have long entertained the highest opinion of Sir John Hope, like everybody else, I suppose, but every day more convinces me of his worth. We shall lose him if he continues to expose himself as he did during the last three days. Indeed, his escape was wonderful. His coat and hat were shot through in many places, besides the wound in his leg. He places himself among the sharpshooters, without sheltering himself as they do' (*Dispatches of the Duke of Wellington*, 203).

In February 1814 Hope, with the left wing of the army, crossed the Adour. The operation to cross the river was beset with difficulties, and the French forces opposing the crossing were intimidated by the use of the Congreve rocket. Hope next blockaded the important fortress of Bayonne, an operation that lasted until the end of the war. In the final sortie of the French garrison on 14 April 1814, a futile gesture which caused needless bloodshed given that a truce had been agreed elsewhere, Hope had his horse shot under him, was wounded, and briefly taken prisoner. The surrender did not take place until 27 April 'thanks to an obdurate Bonapartist commander who demanded to see Soult's written orders' first (James, 236).

Hope's wounds prevented him from accepting command of the forces sent to America in 1814. After the war Hope was made a peer as Baron Niddry of Niddry Castle, Linlithgowshire. In 1816 he succeeded his elder half-brother, James Hope-*Johnstone, third earl of Hopetoun, in the family title. He became a full general in 1819. He had been appointed colonel-commandant of a battalion of 60th Royal Americans in 1806; from this regiment he had transferred to the colonelcy of the 92nd Gordon Highlanders, and from the 92nd, in 1820, he was appointed colonel of the 42nd highlanders. Among his many offices were those of lord lieutenant of Linlithgowshire, governor of the Royal Bank of Scotland, and captain of the royal archers. In 1822 he was offered the post of lieutenant-general of the ordnance by Wellington, then master-general, but he declined it. Hopetoun's last public duty was to attend George IV, during the king's visit to Scotland in 1822, as captain of the royal archers and gold-stick for Scotland. He entertained the king at Hopetoun House during the visit.

The pupil and friend of Abercromby, the friend of Moore, and, in Wellington's words, 'the ablest man in the Peninsular army' (*Dispatches of the Duke of Wellington*, 7.22), Hopetoun also distinguished himself in civil life, in which his soldierly mien, polished bearing, high ideal of duty, and strong common sense rendered him generally popular. He died in Paris on 27 August 1823, and was buried in the family vault at Abercorn on 1 October.

The eldest of Hopetoun's nine sons succeeded him as fifth earl of Hopetoun. Others served in the navy and army. The youngest, Brigadier-General the Hon. Adrian Hope (1821–1858), of the 60th rifles and 93rd highlanders, served until distinction in the Crimea, and commanded a brigade at the siege of Lucknow, where he was killed on 14 April 1858. H. M. CHICHESTER, *rev.* S. KINROSS

Sources GEC, *Peerage*, new edn, vol. 6 · *GM*, 1st ser., 93/2 (1823) · Fortescue, *Brit. army*, vols. 6–7, 9–10 · *The dispatches of … the duke of Wellington … from 1799 to 1818*, ed. J. Gurwood, 7: *Peninsula, 1790–1813* (1837) · *Supplementary despatches (correspondence) and memoranda of Field Marshal Arthur, duke of Wellington*, ed. A. R. Wellesley, second duke of Wellington, 15 vols. (1858–72), vols. 8–9 · C. W. C. Oman, *A history of the Peninsular War*, 1 (1902) · *The diary of Sir John Moore*, ed. J. F. Maurice, 2 (1904) · R. Glover, *Peninsular preparation: the reform of the British army, 1795–1809* (1963) · L. James, *The Iron Duke* (1992) · R. F. Weigley, *The age of battles* (Bloomington, IN, 1991) · D. Chandler, *The campaigns of Napoleon* (1966)
Archives NRA, priv. coll., diaries, corresp., military and estate papers | BL, letter to Sir John Moore, Add. MS 57541 · BL, corresp. with Robert Peel, Add. MSS 40222–40349 · NA Scot., letter to Lord Leven; corresp. with Lord Melville · Northumbd RO, Newcastle upon Tyne, letters to his sister Jane
Likenesses J. Vendramini, stipple, 1811 (after W. M. Craig), BM, NPG; repro. in *Contemporary portraits* (1811) · H. Raeburn, oils, c.1820, County Hall, Cupar, Fife · attrib. J. Watson-Gordon, oils, 1822, Hopetoun House, Lothian region · D. Wilkie, group portrait, oils, 1822–9 (*The entrance of George IV at Holyrood House*), Royal Collection · T. Campbell, statue, Royal Bank of Scotland, Edinburgh · by or after J. Hoppner, oils, Gordon Barracks, Aberdeen · J. Watson-Gordon, oils (in Archers' Company uniform), Hopetoun House, Lothian region

Hope, Sir John (1765–1836), army officer, was born on 15 July 1765, the son of the author John *Hope (1739–1785), and his wife, Mary (1741/2–1767), the only daughter of Eliab Breton of Norton, Nottinghamshire, and Forty Hill, Enfield. Charles *Hope, lord president of the court of session, and Vice-Admiral Sir William Johnstone *Hope were his brothers.

In November 1778 Hope was appointed a cadet in Houston's regiment of the Scottish brigade serving the Dutch. Having first served as a corporal and sergeant he was made an ensign in the regiment, stationed at Bergen op Zoom, in December 1779, and marched with it to Maastricht.

After a period at home he rejoined the regiment at Maastricht on the day of his promotion to captain, 26 April 1782, and withdrew from the Dutch service, receiving British half pay.

In 1787 Hope was placed on full pay as captain of the 60th Royal Americans, but his company was soon reduced. In 1788 he was appointed to a troop in the 13th light dragoons, and from November 1792 he served as aide-de-camp to Sir William Erskine (d. 1795) in the Flanders campaigns and in Germany. On 25 March 1795 Hope became a major, and on 20 February 1796 lieutenant-colonel of the 28th Duke of York's light dragoons. He commanded this regiment at the Cape of Good Hope before returning home.

In April 1799 Hope was appointed to the 37th foot in the West Indies, and in November 1804 he transferred to a battalion of the 60th foot at home, and was temporarily the assistant adjutant-general in Scotland. He was deputy adjutant-general under Lord Cathcart in Hanover in 1805, and at Copenhagen in 1807. On 20 September 1806 he married Mary, the only daughter and heir of Robert Scott of Logie. She died on 19 March 1813; they had three daughters. Hope's second marriage, on 21 April 1814, was to Jane Hester, the daughter of John Macdougall; they had five sons and five daughters and she survived her husband.

After serving as a general officer on the staff in Scotland and in the Severn district, Hope proceeded to the Peninsula, and in July 1812 commanded a brigade of the 5th division at Salamanca. He was invalided home soon afterwards, causing Wellington to write: 'Major-General Hope I am sorry to lose, as he is very attentive to his duties' (*Dispatches*, 56, 73).

Hope went on to hold brigade commands in Ireland and Scotland until being promoted to lieutenant-general in 1819. He was made colonel of the 92nd highlanders in 1820, and transferred to the 72nd highlanders in 1823. A GCH in 1820, Hope was made a knight bachelor on 30 March 1821. He died at his seat in Scotland in August 1836, aged seventy-one. H. M. CHICHESTER, *rev.* S. KINROSS

Sources GM, 2nd ser., 6 (1836) · *The dispatches of … the duke of Wellington … from 1799 to 1818*, ed. J. Gurwood, 6: *Peninsula, 1790–1813* (1836) · Fortescue, *Brit. army*, vol. 8 · R. Cannon, ed., *Historical record of the seventy-second regiment, or the duke of Albany's own highlanders* (1848) · A. J. Guy, ed., *The road to Waterloo: the British army and the struggle against revolutionary and Napoleonic France, 1793–1815* (1990) · T. C. W. Blanning, *The French revolutionary wars, 1787–1802* (1996)
Archives NMM, meteorological observations; order book | NA Scot., letters to Sir Alexander Hope · NA Scot., corresp. with first and second lords Melville

Hope, John (1794–1858), judge, was born in Edinburgh on 26 May 1794, the eldest son of Charles *Hope (1763–1851), lord president and lord justice-general of the court of session, and his wife, Charlotte (1771–1834), daughter of John Hope, second earl of Hopetoun. The lawyer James *Hope was his younger brother, and Louisa *Hope was his sister. His grandfather was John *Hope (1739–1785), MP for Linlithgowshire. He was educated partly at Edinburgh high school and he was admitted as an advocate in November 1816. Hope married Jessie Scott (d. 1872), daughter of

Thomas and Isabella Irving of Shetland, in 1824 or 1825, and they had a son who survived to maturity.

Appointed an advocate-depute under Sir William Rae, Hope came early to prominence as a defender of the then tory administration of justice in Scotland. On 25 June 1822 James Abercromby moved (unsuccessfully) in the House of Commons for the appointment of a committee of inquiry into the conduct of the lord advocate and the other law officers of the crown in Scotland in relation to their connections with the press. Specifically it was felt that an article in the *Glasgow Sentinel* attacking James Stuart of Dunearn, a whig, had shown too strong a link between the law officers and the tory press. This article had resulted in the death of the author in a duel and the trial of Stuart at the insistence of the lord advocate. Together with a colleague Hope sent Abercromby a letter of protest couched in such terms that only a warrant for their, and Abercromby's, arrest prevented further bloodshed. Hope was subsequently heard at the bar of the House of Commons in his own defence, on 17 July 1822, but, though found guilty of a breach of the privileges of the house, no further proceedings were taken in the matter.

This early incident contains good indications of Hope's character. Sir Walter Scott described Hope as 'the most hopeful young man of his time' (Lockhart, 587), talented, ambitious, and popular. On the other hand Scott commented on Hope's hot and rather hasty manner, which would get him into difficulties if not amended. In November 1822 Hope, after only a few years at the bar, was appointed solicitor-general for Scotland in Lord Liverpool's administration. He held this post until the formation of Lord Grey's ministry in 1830, when he was succeeded by Henry Cockburn.

In December 1830 Hope was elected dean of the Faculty of Advocates in succession to Francis Jeffrey, in whose favour Hope had waived his claims to this position in the previous year. As an advocate, therefore, Hope appears to have been popular among his contemporaries at the bar. He enjoyed a high reputation and a successful practice. His powerful memory, however, appears to have been used to accumulate a mass of detail. As a pleader he was not nimble, but rather a traditionalist who favoured overwhelming an opponent's argument with a battery of precedents. On paper he was accused of a lack of clarity and of being verbose. Cockburn, on a visit to an English court, made the following comparative comment on Hope's style as an advocate:

> I heard no voice strained, and did not see a drop of sweat at the bar in these eight days. Our high-pressure Dean screams and gesticulates and perspires more in any forenoon than the whole Bar of England (I say nothing of Ireland) in a reign. (*Journal of Henry Cockburn*, 1.114)

Hope's importance in Scottish history lies in the role he played in the conflict in the Church of Scotland in the period leading up to the Disruption of 1843, a role which earned him much negative comment. He was described by the Free Churchman Robert Buchanan as 'the author of the Disruption' (Buchanan, 1.315). A stout defender of the established church, whose rights and privileges he regarded as having been conferred by the state, Hope was the solitary elder who tabled fourteen reasons for dissenting against the Veto Act at the general assembly of 1834. This act gave parishioners in Scotland the power to block a patron's presentee to a vacant parish. At this point Hope apparently questioned neither the church's right to pass the act, nor its jurisdiction over spiritual appointments, but rather its right to determine who might receive a civil benefice. In 1835 Hope became legal adviser to Robert Young, the rejected presentee at Auchterarder, in a test case on the act. He then took matters on to the much more dangerous and contentious plane of church–state relations by asking the court of session to declare that the assembly's Veto Act was illegal, and that if a presentee was found to be qualified then the presbytery was bound to admit him in spite of any objections raised at parish level. The case was heard in late 1837, and the court—presided over by his father, Lord Justice-General Charles Hope—decided in early 1838 by a majority of eight to five in favour of Hope's arguments.

Hope intervened at other points in this continuing controversy, always to argue that the established church was subject to the civil authority. He achieved most public attention with the publication in 1839 of his pamphlet *A letter to the lord chancellor, on the claims of the Church of Scotland in regard to its jurisdiction, and, on the proposed changes in its polity*. Described by W. E. Gladstone as fearfully long (it ran to 290 pages), it nevertheless reached a wide and influential audience both within and outside Scotland, including key figures in the Conservative Party to whom Thomas Chalmers, Hope's leading non-intrusionist opponent in the church, was increasingly looking. Gladstone told Sir James Graham that it convinced him of the threatening nature of the Scottish church question. Graham, who was home secretary at the time of the Disruption, for his part appears to have been influenced by Hope's pamphlet into thinking that the church was affected by an undesirable democratic excitement.

Less publicly, but more effectively, Hope increasingly had the ear of Lord Aberdeen, who in 1839 and 1840 was involved in discussions with Thomas Chalmers to try to find a legislative solution to the church's problems that would save it from the interference of the civil courts. In a voluminous correspondence and in personal meetings with Aberdeen, Hope was responsible behind the scenes for souring relations between Aberdeen and Chalmers. Aberdeen, in fact, was making Hope privy to the correspondence which he was conducting with the non-intrusionist leader. Hope apparently also tried to isolate Aberdeen from other church contacts and played a part in blocking changes to his proposed legislative measure of 1840, which Robert Buchanan claimed would have averted the Disruption. Furthermore, in the months immediately preceding the Disruption in 1843, Hope continued mistakenly to advise Aberdeen, and through him the prime minister, Sir Robert Peel, that any secession from the Church of Scotland would be insignificant in size. This may have played a part in ensuring government inactivity in the matter. Small wonder that epithets such as 'mole' and 'wily and devious Kirk agent' (Maciver, 93, 110) have been applied to Hope.

These more negative views of Hope continued after he became a judge in 1841, succeeding David Boyle as lord justice-clerk and president of the second division of the court of session. This very rapid elevation excited some comment. One explanation was that Hope at the outset of his career had been offered the post of lord advocate by Canning, but had stepped aside at that point in favour of Sir William Rae. As a judge Hope was regarded as having a contempt for public opinion and a love of precedent. He was known for an arrogant manner and for making his personal dislikes obvious. His decisions were questioned on equitable if not on legal grounds. Even so, his opinions on civil questions and in medical jurisprudence enjoyed a firm reputation. *The Scotsman* thought that as a judge Hope was neither hard-hearted nor unable to pity misfortune. He also presided at nearly all the criminal trials of importance which took place in the high court of justiciary during his seventeen years in office. These included the celebrated trial of Madeline Smith for murder in 1857.

Hope died at his home, 20 Moray Place, Edinburgh, on 14 June 1858, from a sudden attack of paralysis, and was buried five days later at Ormiston Hall, near Tranent, in East Lothian. His widow died on 26 January 1872.

GORDON F. MILLAR

Sources The Times (16–17 June 1858) • *The Scotsman* (16–17 June 1858) • *The Scotsman* (21 June 1858) • *Glasgow Herald* (16 June 1858) • I. A. Muirhead, 'Chalmers and the politicians', *The practical and the pious: essays on Thomas Chalmers (1780–1847)*, ed. A. C. Cheyne (1985), 98–114 • I. F. Maciver, 'Chalmers as a "manager" of the church', *The practical and the pious: essays on Thomas Chalmers (1780–1847)*, ed. A. C. Cheyne (1985), 84–97 • F. Lyall, *Of presbyters and kings* (1980) • R. Buchanan, *The ten years' conflict*, new edn, 2 vols. (1854), vol. 1, p. 315 • G. W. T. Omond, *The lord advocates of Scotland from the close of the fifteenth century to the passing of the Reform Bill*, 2 (1883) • G. W. T. Omond, *The lord advocates of Scotland, second series, 1834–1880* (1914) • B. W. Crombie and W. S. Douglas, *Modern Athenians: a series of original portraits of memorable citizens of Edinburgh* (1882), 73–4 • F. J. Grant, ed., *The Faculty of Advocates in Scotland, 1532–1943*, Scottish RS, 145 (1944), 104 • J. G. Lockhart, *Memoirs of the life of Sir Walter Scott*, [new edn] (1845), 587 • *GM*, 2nd ser., 21 (1844), 258 • *GM*, 3rd ser., 5 (1858), 192 • *Scots peerage*, 4.499 • S. J. Brown, *Thomas Chalmers and the godly commonwealth in Scotland* (1982) • *Journal of Henry Cockburn: being a continuation of the 'Memorials of his time', 1831–1854*, 2 (1874), 114 • W. Anderson, *The Scottish nation*, 6 (1882), 495–6 • *Letters chiefly connected with the affairs of Scotland from H. Cockburn to T. F. Kennedy (1818–1852)* (1874) • *Hansard 2*, 7.1654, 1665, 1671, 1691 • S. J. Brown and M. Fry, eds., *Scotland in the age of the disruption* (1993) • G. I. T. Machin, *Politics and the churches in Great Britain 1832–1868* (1977)

Archives BL, corresp. with Lord Aberdeen, Add. MSS 43202–43206, 43327 • BL, corresp. with Sir Robert Peel, Add. MSS 40346–40596 • NL Scot., corresp. with J. G. Lockhart • NL Scot., corresp. with Lord Melville • priv. coll., letters to Sir George Sinclair • U. Edin., New Coll. L., letters to Thomas Chalmers

Likenesses B. W. Crombie, lithograph, NPG • attrib. B. W. Crombie, watercolour drawing, NG Scot. • C. Smith, oils, Parliament Hall, Edinburgh, Faculty of Advocates • C. Smith, oils, NG Scot.

Wealth at death under £25,000: probate, 18 Sept 1858, *CGPLA Eng. & Wales* • £21,318 13s. 4d.: inventory, 5 Oct 1858, NA Scot., SC 70/1/98/828

Hope, John (1807–1893), lawyer and philanthropist, was born at Dalry House, near Edinburgh, on 12 May 1807, the elder son of James Hope (d. 1842), writer to the signet, and his wife, Jane (d. 1822), daughter of James Walker of Dalry. His paternal grandfather was John *Hope (1725–1786), professor of botany at Edinburgh, and his uncle was Thomas Charles Hope (1766–1844), professor of chemistry in the same university. Hope was educated at Edinburgh high school and the University of Edinburgh, but he did not take a degree. Thereafter he studied law, and qualified as a solicitor by admission to the Society of Writers to the Signet in 1828. He completed his education by taking a grand tour in 1829–30.

Hope, who was tall and bearded, established himself as a successful solicitor during the 1830s. A combination of professional earnings and inherited resources rapidly made him a wealthy man. About 1838 he experienced an evangelical conversion, which gave him the inspiration to engage in methodical and energetic religious and philanthropic activity. He was fastidious and abstemious, and, remaining unmarried, he had ample resources to donate to the causes to which he committed himself. He took an intense interest in the welfare of numerous protégés, and energetically lobbied clergy and others to secure support for his pet schemes. In the face of the Disruption of 1843 he remained loyal to the Church of Scotland, but was critical of its lethargic response to the moral and spiritual needs he perceived.

Hope's philanthropic interests were extensive, but by the mid-1840s his overriding preoccupations became the promotion of total abstinence from alcohol, and strenuous resistance to the advance of the Roman Catholic church in Scotland. In 1847 he founded the British League of Juvenile Abstainers which aimed to promote a teetotal culture among children, as a mainspring of moral and social improvement. A great gathering of the movement in Edinburgh in July 1851 attracted 20,000 young people from numerous parts of southern and central Scotland. In 1851 he also launched a No Popery movement, sustaining protestant classes in a number of Edinburgh districts, and missions to Roman Catholics in various Scottish towns.

Hope was an autocrat and an individualist who generally preferred creating his own organizations to working through existing mechanisms. Nevertheless he saw some virtue in the political process, and served as an Edinburgh town councillor from 1857 to 1889, in which capacity he actively supported schemes for improving living and working conditions in the city. He also led military volunteer companies in the 1860s and 1870s, believing that they had an important role in instilling social discipline as well as in providing national security.

Hope's anti-Catholic and total abstinence movements declined somewhat from the 1860s, but in his later years he found fresh inspiration in a campaign for the use of unfermented wine at communion. In 1890 he set up the Hope Trust, which was intended to maintain this movement and his protestant campaigns after his death. He remained active until the end of his life and died at his home, 31 Moray Place, Edinburgh, after a short illness, on

25 June 1893, and was buried in Greyfriars churchyard, Edinburgh. He bequeathed his entire £400,000 estate to the Hope Trust in his will. This was subsequently the focus of a celebrated legal action in which his disappointed relatives alleged that he had suffered delusions regarding total abstinence and the Roman Catholic church. The matter was eventually settled out of court. Hope's sanity was not seriously in question, though he had been an undeniably eccentric figure whose preoccupations had become unfashionable by the time of his death. Nevertheless his wealth, energy, and sincere, if narrowminded, concern for the welfare of others enabled him to make a significant impact on the fabric of life in Edinburgh and beyond. The Hope Trust has continued to support the causes to which he committed himself, although legal measures were taken in the 1970s to allow a more flexible and positive interpretation of his intentions.   JOHN WOLFFE

Sources D. Jamie, *John Hope: philanthropist and reformer* (1900) · Hope MSS, NA Scot. · J. Wolffe, *The protestant crusade in Great Britain, 1829–1860* (1991) · S. Bruce, *No pope of Rome: anti-Catholicism in modern Scotland* (1985)

Archives NA Scot., corresp. and papers, incl. letter-books and writing books

Likenesses F. Trablé, photographs, 1860, NA Scot. · photograph, *c.*1865, NA Scot. · engraving (after photograph by F. Trablé), repro. in Jamie, *John Hope*, frontispiece

Wealth at death £400,000: Jamie, *John Hope*, 4

Hope, John Adrian Louis, seventh earl of Hopetoun and first marquess of Linlithgow (1860–1908), governor-general of Australia, was born on 25 September 1860 at Hopetoun House, South Queensferry, Linlithgow, Scotland, the eldest son of John Alexander Hope, sixth earl of Hopetoun (1831–1873) and sometime army officer (1st Life Guards), and his wife, Ethelred Anne Birch Reynardson (*d.* 1884). Educated at school in Brighton and then at Eton College (1874–8), he succeeded to the earldom on 2 April 1873, at the age of twelve. As a member of a family with a strong military tradition (his great-grandfather John Hope, the fourth earl, had been a distinguished general officer in the Peninsular War), he attended the Royal Military College, Sandhurst, from which he passed out in 1879. He did not, however, enter the regular army, but was gazetted in 1880 as a lieutenant in the Lanarkshire yeomanry, in which he rose to major. Later he became honorary colonel of the Forth division, Royal Engineers (volunteers) submarine miners and brigadier-general of the Royal Company of Archers (the monarch's bodyguard in Scotland). Hopetoun travelled in Turkey and Egypt in 1881 and in America in 1882. He became deputy lieutenant of the counties of Linlithgow, Lanark, Haddington, and Dumfries. Wealthy, with a large landholding of more than 42,500 acres, including rich coal deposits, he was attracted to politics, and was seen as a possible rival to his neighbour and friend the fifth earl of Rosebery. Hopetoun became junior Conservative whip in the House of Lords in 1883 and was a lord-in-waiting to the queen in 1885–6 and from 1886 to 1889. On 18 October 1886, at All Saints' Church, Knightsbridge, London, he married Hersey Alice Eveleigh-de-

John Adrian Louis Hope, seventh earl of Hopetoun and first marquess of Linlithgow (1860–1908), by Robert Brough, 1904

Moleyns (1867–1937), the daughter of the fourth Baron Ventry. In 1887–9 he was lord high commissioner to the general assembly of the Church of Scotland.

Hopetoun was selected as governor of the colony of Victoria in 1889 to succeed the experienced Sir Henry Loch and, having been appointed GCMG, arrived in Melbourne and assumed office on 28 November. Although he was not robust—the effort of shaking hands at his first levee caused him to faint—the active and youthful aristocrat proved a notable success, carrying out his duties with cheerful hospitality and easy amiability during a time of bank failures, industrial unrest, and political instability. Paul Blouët described the 'young diplomatist' in 1894 as having 'a face that is bright and smiling, an intelligent forehead, and a delicate nose and mouth. He is witty and amiable, full of life, *Grand Seigneur* to the tips of his fingers, immensely rich, and generous in proportion' (O'Rell, 193). He travelled Victoria enthusiastically, visiting all parts of the colony, and on occasion riding on horseback unheralded into outback towns. After a successful extended term he left Melbourne on 26 March 1895.

From 1895 to 1898 Hopetoun was paymaster-general in

Lord Salisbury's government. Standing as Unionist candidate for the lord rectorship of Glasgow University in 1895 he lost to H. H. Asquith. That same year he was sworn of the privy council and elected president of the Institution of Naval Architects, in which capacity he visited Germany in 1896; he presided over the International Congress of Naval Architects in London the following year. He declined the governor-generalship of Canada in 1898 and was lord chamberlain to Queen Victoria from 1898 to 1900. There was general satisfaction in the Antipodes when he was selected as first governor-general of the newly federated commonwealth of Australia. The position was an opportunity for public service in the cause of the empire for a patriot unable to take part in the Second South African War because of poor health. He was appointed knight of the Thistle and GCVO in 1900.

On the journey to Australia via India, Hopetoun contracted severe typhoid fever and Lady Hopetoun malaria. His early days in Sydney, where he arrived on 15 December looking, the local press reported, 'care-worn' and 'cadaverous', were overshadowed by anxiety about his and his wife's health and by his commissioning of William John Lyne, the premier of New South Wales, instead of Edmund Barton, to be first prime minister of Australia—an action which has become known as the Hopetoun blunder. When Lyne was unable to form a ministry, Barton took over in time for the inauguration ceremony on 1 January 1901, at which the still convalescing earl was also sworn in as governor-general. From May to July Hopetoun capably managed the tour of the duke of Cornwall and York (later George V) and the duchess to open the first parliament of the commonwealth of Australia, in Melbourne. He encountered difficulties, however, in attempting to assert a supervisory role over correspondence between state governors and the British government. A minor embarrassment arose over a speech in which he defended his ministers from accusations of dilatoriness in dispatching troops to the Second South African War, earning him a reproof from the opposition leader, George Reid.

Occupying two government houses—at Sydney and Melbourne—Hopetoun entertained lavishly and spent heavily from his private income. When the Australian parliament refused to vote him an annual allowance of £8000 in addition to his salary of £10,000, he asked the secretary of state for the colonies, Joseph Chamberlain, to recall him, and relinquished his post on 17 July 1902. Before departing he had paid for food to be distributed to the unemployed in Sydney and Melbourne and champagne to Sydney hospitals to celebrate the coronation. Despite his difficulties, Hopetoun's term had been important in establishing the parameters of the office of governor-general of Australia. The attempt to make it that of an ostentatious viceroy had been rejected. His successors profited by his experience: decoration, display, and expense were not to be required of the representative of the crown in Australia. As Alfred Deakin, later Australia's second prime minister, commented (anonymously) in the *Morning Post*, Australians had revised their estimate of the

office, 'stripping it too hastily, but not unkindly, of its festal trappings. The stately ceremonial was fitting, but it has been completed' (*Morning Post*, 2 Sept 1902).

Hopetoun was created marquess of Linlithgow on 27 October 1902 and withdrew from public life, though he was persuaded to act briefly as secretary for Scotland from February to December 1905. Questions had been raised about the appropriateness of the price he had received for the sale to the government in 1903 of property for what was to become the Rosyth naval base. From 1904 to 1908 he was deputy governor of the Bank of Scotland. He was a knight of justice and sub-prior of the order of St John of Jerusalem.

Fond of fishing and boating, Linlithgow was a regular follower of hounds all his life and a master of packs of harriers and beagles; he was known as a very bold, straight rider, although was the most hapless of huntsmen, having several serious falls. He lived a good deal in France and was said to be a proficient French scholar. He was not a fluent orator and spoke, according to the Melbourne *Argus*, with 'a suggestion of hesitancy' (*The Argus*, 2 March 1908), although this augmented his self-deprecating charm. Lady Tennyson (the wife of his successor, the second baron), writing to her mother in 1902, described him as 'a curious mixture—of simplicity & conceit—full of fun, a wonderful mimick & extremely kind and thoughtful and open', but reported that his wife suffered agony from shyness and had 'rather a melancholy expression & sad voice' (11 May 1902, Tennyson papers, MS 479/41/167).

Linlithgow died at Villa Cecil, Pau, France, of pernicious anaemia on 29 February 1908. He was survived by his wife, two sons, and a daughter (another daughter had died in infancy). After a Church of Scotland service at Hopetoun House he was interred in the family mausoleum there. He was succeeded by his eldest son, Victor Alexander John *Hope (1887–1952), second marquess of Linlithgow and viceroy of India.   CHRISTOPHER CUNNEEN

Sources NL Aus., Hopetoun House papers [microfilm reel AJCP M936, National Library of Australia] · C. Cunneen, *Kings' men* (1983) · *The Times* (2 March 1908), 5 · *The Times* (6 March 1908), 8 · *The Times* (7 March 1908), 15 · J. A. La Nauze, *The Hopetoun blunder: the appointment of the first prime minister of the commonwealth of Australia* (Melbourne, 1957) · M. O'Rell, *John Bull and Co.: the great colonial branches of the firm* (1894) · *The Argus* [Melbourne] (2 March 1908), 7 · C. Cunneen, 'Hopetoun, John Adrian Jouis Hope', *AusDB*, vol. 9 · NL Aus., Tennyson papers, MS 479 · GEC, *Peerage* · *Morning Post* (2 Sept 1902) · *Sydney Morning Herald* (16 July 1900), 7 · *Daily Telegraph* [Sydney] (17 July 1900), 5 · *Daily Telegraph* [Sydney] (13 June 1902), 5 · *Daily Telegraph* [Sydney] (20 June 1902), 5 · *Army List* (1880–1908) · *The Argus* [Melbourne] (24 July 1889), 5 · *The Argus* [Melbourne] (7 Sept 1889), 5 · *The Argus* [Melbourne] (28 Nov 1889), 8 · b. cert. · m. cert. · d. cert.

Archives Hopetoun House, near Queensferry, papers · NRA, priv. coll., corresp. and papers | BL, corresp. with Lord Ripon, Add. MS 43560 · Bodl. Oxf., corresp. with Lord Selborne · NL Aus., letters to Alfred Deakin · NL Scot., letters to Sir Charles Dalrymple · NL Scot., letters to Lord Rosebery | FILM BFI NFTVA, news footage · ScreenSound Australia, Canberra

Likenesses D. W. Stevenson, plaster bust, *c*.1891, Scot. NPG · R. Brough, oils, 1904, Hopetoun House, West Lothian [*see illus.*] · B. Rhind, statue, 1911, Melbourne, Australia · Elliott & Fry, photograph, NPG; repro. in *Our conservative and unionist statesmen*, 2

[1897] · G. Frampton, statue, Linlithgow · J. Quinn, oils, Parliament House, Canberra, Australia · Spy [L. Ward], lithograph caricature, NPG; repro. in *VF* (17 May 1900)

Wealth at death £225,985 16*s*. 3*d*.: confirmation, 11 May 1908, *CCI* · £11,004 3*s*. 7*d*.: eik additional estate, 22 June 1909, *CCI* · £921,000—gross: GEC, *Peerage*, 6.576

Hope, John Williams (1757–1813). *See under* Hope family (*per*. *c*.1700–1813).

Hope, Laurence. *See* Nicolson, Adela Florence (1865–1904).

Hope, Louisa Octavia Augusta (1814–1893), promoter of household science teaching, was the youngest of the twelve children of Charles *Hope, Lord Granton (1763–1851), the tory politician and lord president of the court of session, and of his wife (and cousin), Lady Charlotte Hope (1771–1834), second daughter of John, second earl of Hopetoun. John *Hope (1794–1858) and James *Hope were her elder brothers. Most of Louisa's childhood seems to have been spent at the family home at Granton, north of Edinburgh, where she was educated mainly by her oldest sister. Like six of her seven sisters, Louisa remained unmarried.

Louisa Hope was an evangelical who, during the Disruption crisis, shared her family's prominent commitment to the Church of Scotland. The church subsequently became the vehicle through which she advanced many of her educational ideas. In the 1840s she ran evening classes for 'maid servants and female apprentices' and she became convinced of the need for working-class girls to be provided with a more useful education. At the time less than 20 per cent of Scottish girls received school training in sewing and almost none were given guidance in cooking.

In 1849 the Church of Scotland called for the creation of female 'schools of industry', and in 1852 Louisa Hope played a leading part in the establishment of the Scottish Ladies Association for Promoting Female Industrial Education. This was an influential society composed largely of wealthy women associated with the church. Its object was to encourage the instruction of working-class girls in appropriate domestic and industrial skills and Christian beliefs, and it sought to persuade upper-class women to promote such a programme in their localities. In 1853 the association established a boarding-house in Edinburgh for young women training to become teachers. Louisa Hope published her opinions on this movement in her book *The Female Teacher: Ideas Suggestive of her Qualifications and Duties* (1853).

From childhood Louisa Hope was a close friend of Lord Aberdeen's family and it may have been her connection with the prime minister (1852–5) which resulted in her being given the 'urgent and very worrying mission [of] training nurses' in the latter part of the Crimean War. During her stay in London at this time she assisted the Revd William Gill at the National, Industrial and Sunday School in Fitzroy Square. In 1858 she organized a petition of 130 of 'the principal ladies of Scotland' protesting at the lack of needlework instruction for Scottish schoolgirls, and she wrote many letters to the press on this and related subjects (see, especially, *The Scotsman*, 18 Feb 1865).

In 1860 she submitted a paper to the Social Science Association calling for improved domestic education for girls and female teachers (see *Transactions of the National Association for the Promotion of Social Science, Glasgow Meeting* 1860, 397–404).

The activities of Louisa Hope and her friends were more influential than has sometimes been appreciated. An act of 1861 enabled grants to be made to parish schools which employed a woman to teach girls household skills, and by 1872, when Scottish elementary education came under secular control, almost 70 per cent of girls in inspected schools were being taught sewing. Moreover a tradition had been established whereby upper-class ladies lent support to female domestic training in local schools. These developments formed the foundation for the eventual full introduction of domestic science.

For many years Louisa Hope was a notable Edinburgh character. Her nephew described her as 'a strange mixture—so odd, so ugly and sometimes so disagreeable—but the cleverest of the sisters' (Hope Family MSS). Yet her delightful private memoir of her childhood shows that she was also a woman of real wit and charm. She died at her home, 11 Gloucester Place, Edinburgh, on 23 October 1893.   TOM BEGG

Sources Hope family MSS [including D. Robertson, 'Hope Annals', 2 (1911) and L. O. Hope, childhood memoir] · L. Moore, 'Educating for the "woman's sphere": domestic training versus intellectual discipline', *Out of bounds: women in Scottish society, 1800–1945*, ed. E. Breitenbach and E. Gordon (1992) · *Home and Foreign Mission Record of the Church of Scotland*, 9 (1854), 146 · *Home and Foreign Mission Record of the Church of Scotland*, 10 (1855), 95–6 · d. cert.

Archives priv. coll.

Likenesses cartoon, repro. in *The Times*

Hope, Sir Thomas, of Craighall, first baronet (1573–1646), advocate and politician, was the son of Henry Hope, an Edinburgh merchant of French descent, and his wife, Jacqueline de Tott (or de Jott). The couple witnessed the St Bartholomew's day massacre of Huguenots in Paris before fleeing to Scotland. His father was dead by the time of his graduation, as master of arts at Edinburgh University on 12 August 1592, and his mother subsequently returned to France for nearly thirty years.

Advocate and writer Hope committed himself to a career in law, but lack of means to finance further study meant that his progress was at first slow. By 21 March 1600 he had made sufficient progress to be appointed by the general assembly of the Church of Scotland to be the church's solicitor and advocate, and about the same time he entered the service of his cousin John Nicolson of Lasswade, a well-established Edinburgh writer (solicitor). Shortly before his own death he was to remember Nicolson as 'my maister, under quhom I learnit not only my calling as a citizen, but my calling as a Christian' (Fraser, 1.xxxv).

Hope married Elizabeth (*d*. 1660), daughter of John Bennet, in or before 1602 (their first child being born in June 1603), and he was admitted to the Faculty of Advocates in

Sir Thomas Hope of Craighall, first baronet (1573–1646), by George Jamesone, 1627

Edinburgh on 7 February 1605. He quickly made a name for himself through being one of the four advocates for the defence at the trial at Linlithgow on 10 January 1606 of six parish ministers accused of treason for declining to acknowledge the authority of the privy council of Scotland over the general assembly of the church. The lawyers urged their clients to submit as they had no defence, and on their refusal to do so the two most senior advocates withdrew from the case. Hope, however, led such an eloquent defence that, though his clients were found guilty, his boldness and skill made his reputation. He won for himself 'the estimatioune both of a guid man and of a guid advocate' (J. Melvill, *Autobiography*, ed. R. Pitcairn, 1842, 621). 'His pleading that day procured him great estimatioun and manie clients; and his credite has ever grown sensyne [since]' (D. Calderwood, *History of the Kirk of Scotland*, ed. T. Thomson, 8 vols., 1842–9, 6.379).

This trial 'laid the foundation of a phenomenally successful professional career' (Hope, *Major Practicks*, 1.vii), and already by 1608 Sir Thomas Hamilton, the lord advocate, who had led the prosecution at the 1606 trial, could refer to Hope as one of 'the most learned and best experienced' advocates in Scotland (J. Maidment, ed., *State Papers … of Thomas Earl of Melros*, 2 vols., 1837, 1.50). Much of the profit from his lucrative legal practice was invested in land, including the estate of Craighall in Fife, and he also remembered his old college, paying for the building of two chambers for the use of Edinburgh University in 1625–6. Hope also found time for writing, drafting his

Minor Practicks—by, according to family tradition, dictating the text to his sons while he was dressing (T. Hope, *Minor Practicks*, new edn, 1726, vii)—and compiling the *Major Practicks*, a comprehensive digest of statutes and decisions interspersed with 'practical observations' (H. Mackechnie, ed., *Introductory Survey of the Sources and Literature of Scots Law*, 1936, 36). He also published a Latin poem on the accession of Charles I, and translations into Latin of the Psalms and the Song of Solomon and a genealogy of the earls of Mar are also attributed to him.

Servant of Charles I With the accession of Charles I in 1625 Hope added public business to his private practice, being given a central role in the king's plans to revoke grants of church property to subjects. The main achievement of the complicated investigations and negotiations that followed was a settlement of the chaotic matter of teinds (tithes) in Scotland. Eventually most other property which had passed to the nobility and gentry was confirmed in their hands in a settlement ratified by the Scottish parliament in 1633. In these years Hope emerged as one of the most active and talented of the king's Scottish servants, ready to use all his skills to uphold the king's powers. His services were acknowledged by his appointment on 29 May 1626 as joint lord advocate with the elderly Sir William Oliphant (*d*. April 1628). His appointment was evidently not popular with the court of session, which was rebuked by Charles I for its treatment of him in December 1626. Further royal favour brought him admission to the Scottish privy council on 10 January 1628, and appointment as a baronet of Nova Scotia on 19 February the same year.

Hope's rise was closely connected to that of William Grahame, earl of Menteith, who was appointed president of the Scottish council in February 1628. When Menteith claimed the ancient earldom of Strathearn he was advised and encouraged by Hope, and the king recognized his title in July 1631. Hope received his reward in favours to his family. His second son, Thomas, was knighted in 1631, and his eldest, James, was appointed a judge of the court of session in 1632—though only after a delay during which Hope bombarded Menteith with grovelling pleas on his son's behalf, terrified by rumours that the post would go to a rival and begging the earl not to treat him with 'contempt and ignomie' by allowing him to be so disgraced (Fraser, 2.128–9). A major threat to Hope's reputation emerged when allegations were made that possession of the earldom of Strathearn, which he had gained for his patron, implied a claim to the throne. This led to the earl's disgrace in 1633, when he was stripped of his offices and his new title. Hope was left open to allegations that in his advice to Menteith he had put the earl's interests before those of the crown, but he survived this crisis and had the courage to help his former patron to reach a settlement with the king. A political enemy, Lord Napier, charged him with being 'a base follower of greatness, and maliciously eloquent' (M. Napier, *Memoirs of Montrose*, 2 vols., 1856, 1.110), but he showed loyalty to one fallen from greatness in a way that could have damaged his own career.

In 1634 Hope acted for the crown in the prosecution of Lord Balmerino, who was charged with leasing-making for being connected with an unpublished text critical of royal policy in religion. Hope secured Balmerino's conviction and condemnation to death on 14 November, though he was later pardoned. Thus Hope played leading roles in enforcing all the main policies—the revocation, religious reform, and the suppression of aristocratic dissent—which were central to the alienation of Scotland's landowners from the crown. But though he was zealous in upholding the civil powers of the crown, at heart he was sympathetic to those who opposed the changes in church government and worship which Charles I wished to impose. He probably expressed his reservations in council, for it seems likely that it was more than coincidence that a week after the privy council approved preliminary orders for the introduction of a new prayer book (20 December 1636) Hope heard rumours that he was to be removed from office, or have a joint lord advocate appointed to work with him. He indignantly protested, stressing 'my sufferings' and great losses—estimated at over £100,000 Scots (presumably lost private practice revenue)—in the king's service. He attributed the move to replace him to the earl of Traquair, the treasurer and Charles I's most influential Scottish adviser, who was becoming notorious for his bullying of anyone who opposed him. A report in January 1637, however, suggests that it was Hope's disagreement with Traquair over a private case that led the earl to threaten him with dismissal from office.

The troubles of 1637–1640 Such early indications of Hope's crisis of conscience lend credibility to the allegation that in April 1637 he was present at a meeting at which demonstrations to be held when the prayer book was first used were planned. Certainly in that month he went to Pencaitland to take communion according to traditional forms, and this was regarded as a public enough declaration of his dissent to earn him a rebuke from William Laud, the archbishop of Canterbury. In the months that followed the first riots against the prayer book on 23 July 1637, Hope became a major embarrassment to the regime. In September he stated that although he had consented to the imposing of the prayer book 'he meant not an active but a passive obedience to the King's desyre, and that he never intended to accept it as warrantable' (J. Gordon, *History of Scots Affairs*, 3 vols., 1841, 1.14). When in November those supplicating the king on grievances began to elect commissioners to meet in Edinburgh, he infuriated the king's supporters by declaring that their proceedings were legal, and as a privy councillor he refused to sign a proclamation of 20 February 1638 denouncing the king's opponents on the grounds that in it Traquair had exceeded the king's orders. At the end of the month he refrained from signing the national covenant, but joined other lawyers in declaring it legal and justifiable. In the opinion of royalists, he now became the covenanters' 'oracle', advising them on their policies (*Memoirs of Henry Guthry*, 26, 130).

When the marquess of Hamilton arrived in Scotland as the king's representative in May 1638 to try to reach a settlement, 'one of the greatest troubles' was that many lawyers, and especially Hope, supported the covenanters. Hamilton was ignorant of Scottish law while Hope 'was as skilled as much as any ever was', and in the privy council frequently ruled that actions proposed by Hamilton were illegal (Burnet, 53). On the issuing of the 'king's covenant' as a rival to the national covenant Hope indeed signed it, and urged others to do so. But he then declared that, contrary to the king's intentions, the new covenant bound its signatories to reject the innovations in religion that he was seeking to enforce. When the covenanters none the less decided to oppose the king's covenant, Hope declared himself 'almost stupefeit' (*Letters and Journals of Robert Baillie*, 1.474) with disappointment, because he had thought that his stratagem of imposing his interpretation of the new covenant would have forced the king to back down.

Hamilton ordered Hope to attend the Glasgow assembly in November 1638 and defend episcopacy, but he refused. When threatened with dismissal from office, he replied that Hamilton could not remove him, as his appointment had been ratified by parliament. Hamilton furiously denounced him as 'A bad and most wicked instrument', warning the king that while Hope remained in office, with his great influence in the privy council 'no thing will goe a right in your service conserning the Churche; nay, so pernicious is he, that I doe confes … that I take him to be a woorse instrument then anie Covenanter' (S. R. Gardiner, ed., *Hamilton Papers*, CS, new ser., 27, 1890, 50–51). Hope 'should be removed, for he is ill dissposed' (P. Yorke, earl of Hardwicke, *Miscellaneous State Papers*, 2 vols., 1778, 2.117). However, one of the peculiarities of Charles I was that he sometimes retained men in office even though he knew they were opposed to his plans, confident that he could make them obey. With Hope this proved a disastrous miscalculation. Not until January 1640 did he act against Hope—and even then he only banished him to his own house of Craighall. Hope responded dramatically 'I am to goo to morrow to the place of my confyning And to remayne and die thair, if so be youre majesty's plesure' (NA Scot., GD 406/1/1285, 1286). He seemed to royalists a traitor, betraying the king's regime from within, but in his own mind he was a loyal servant in civil matters, and indeed an upholder of royal power, but considered that in religion obedience to his interpretation of God's will had to overrule allegiance to the crown. In accordance with this stance he urged the earl of Rothes in January 1640 not to press the king on 'civill pointis' (constitutional reform) because this would allow the king to win support by claiming that the covenanters were attacking monarchy. 'For civill points, luik nevir to haif me to go with yow' (Hope, *Diary*, 115–16).

Parliament and the covenanters, 1640–1643 Charles I, climbing a new peak of political folly, accepted Hope's distinction between civil and religious affairs sufficiently for him to believe it safe to release Hope from his confinement so that he could represent the crown by implementing an order to postpone the session of the Scottish parliament which was due to meet on 2 June 1640. But Hope, citing technical problems about the validity of the commission under which he was supposed to act, failed to prevent parliament meeting. To royalists this was further betrayal, and the legislation subsequently passed by the parliament aimed at achieving a massive reduction in the powers of the crown. This, however, was in fact as little to Hope's taste as it was to the king's. One act abolished the civil right of officers of state, including the lord advocate, to sit in parliament, and when Hope tried to take his seat in August 1641 he was removed. He complained furiously at the loss of a traditional right of the crown's legal agent, and it was eventually conceded that he could be present in parliament when called for, to give advice or plead, but not to vote. However, when he was duly summoned his arguments in parliament were a source of irritation to the covenanters. His 'idle curiositie'—which may be interpreted as regard for legal technicalities—blocked legislation on schools and stipends. Far more significantly, at the end of the 1641 session when the king was ready to assent to legislation which amounted to a constitutional revolution at the expense of royal power, Hope urged him to include a statement reserving the crown's rights, thus indicating that royal prerogative remained undamaged. Robert Baillie interpreted this as 'idlenesse' or irresponsibility (*Letters and Journals of Robert Baillie*, 1.394, 397), but it was far more than that. It was a clear statement of Hope's constitutional beliefs in civil matters. Charles, however, ignored his advice, for making any such reservation would have led to the collapse of settlement between him and the Scots, which was vital to the king to free him to turn his attention to crises in England and Ireland.

Hope's support for royal authority led him to oppose the covenanters again in 1643. They summoned a convention of estates after the king refused permission for the Scottish parliament to meet to discuss the crisis caused by the English civil war, but Hope joined Hamilton in protesting that this could not be done without the king's sanction. It was perhaps partly this stand that led to the appointment of Hope to act as king's commissioner to the general assembly of the church which was due to meet on 2 August, though the main reason was evidently that no royalist nobles were willing to act. It was clear that, in the prevailing mood in Scotland, the assembly would favour intervening in the English war on the side of parliament, and whoever acted as commissioner would then be blamed by the king for not preventing it from doing so. The assembly proceeded to draft the solemn league and covenant. By one account Hope failed to execute the king's instructions, being so influenced by his two covenanter sons 'that he resolved to say nothing to the Church or countrey's prejudice' (*Letters and Journals of Robert Baillie*, 2.83–4), but in fact he tried to continue balancing his conflicting religious and civil allegiances, declaring 'his personal heartie consent' to the new covenant, but then as king's commissioner assenting to it only so far as it concerned religion and the liberties of the church, and refusing to accept civil alliance with the English parliament. However the covenanter leaders 'did so always

overawe his Grace, that he made us not great trouble' (*Letters and Journals of Robert Baillie*, 2.95–6).

Reputation and final years Hope's actions as king's advocate in 1637–43 were hugely damaging to Charles I, frequently preventing effective action and giving the covenanters the propaganda advantage of being able to claim that the king's senior legal adviser supported their interpretations of the law. On the occasions when he tried to support the crown's civil power he was ignored. In public he expressed his support for much of what the covenanters did concerning religion in terms of interpreting the law, but in private his religious zeal revealed itself in emotional outbursts on paper. Thus when episcopacy was declared unlawful by the 1639 general assembly Hope recorded this as being 'to the unspeakabill joy of all of them that feiris the Lord, and waittis for his salvatioun' (Hope, *Diary*, 104). However, his diary also bears evidence of the strain of trying to reconcile duty to God and king when the two were in conflict. From April 1639 he was strengthened by a voice that spoke to him, which he came to accept as divine. After praying that the king would spare the Scots from the rage of their enemies, the voice said 'I will preserve and saiff [save] my peopill'. When he prayed that God would take pity on the kirk, the voice said 'I will pitie it' and 'I will arisse' (Hope, *Diary*, 89, 96, 98). In 1641 his fear of the consequences of his actions led to bad dreams in which he was lost in mist or darkness, or was accused of treason. An unsympathetic nineteenth-century editor reacted to Hope's voices and dreams by denouncing him for being 'degraded ... by strange and humiliating indications of weakness and credulity' (Hope, *Diary*, v), but they may now be recognized as symptoms of the intense conflicts of loyalties he was experiencing.

In his last years Hope played little part in public affairs: the covenanting regime which ruled the country employed their own procurators of state in legal matters. In February 1646, in anticipation of his death, he recommended that he be succeeded as lord advocate by Thomas Nicolson, his cousin, because of ties of blood and Hope's respect for Nicolson's dead father and uncle. If he declined, Sir Archibald Johnston of Wariston was to have the office (Fraser, 1.xxxv). In the event Wariston was appointed—but Nicolson succeeded him in 1649. On 1 October 1646, in Edinburgh, after a few days' illness, Hope died 'about 10 a clocke at night' (J. Hope, 'Diary', *Miscellany of the Scottish History Society*, 9, 1958, 194) after giving his blessing to his family. Contemporaries agreed in accepting that he had been a remarkably talented and successful lawyer, but disagreed as to whether he had treacherously betrayed his king, or admirably put conscience before any worldly considerations. His diary makes clear his love and concern for the advancement of his family. Six of his children reached adulthood. The two daughters married a knight and a lord; three sons—Sir James *Hope of Hopetoun (1614–1661), Sir John *Hope, Lord Craighall (d. 1654), and Sir Thomas *Hope of Kerse (1606–1643)—became judges in the court of session, the fourth the king's cup-bearer. This was to be the foundation for a remarkable dynasty of eminent Scottish lawyers in the following centuries.   DAVID STEVENSON

Sources G. W. T. Omond, *The lord advocates of Scotland from the close of the fifteenth century to the passing of the Reform Bill*, 2 vols. (1883) · DNB · W. Fraser, ed., *The Red Book of Menteith*, 2 vols. (1880) · *Diary of the public correspondence of Sir Thomas Hope*, ed. [T. Thomson], Bannatyne Club, 76 (1843) · D. Stevenson, *The Scottish revolution, 1637–44: the triumph of the covenanters* (1973) · D. Stevenson, 'A lawyer and his loyalties: Sir Thomas Hope of Craighall', *King or covenant?* (1996), 105–14 · G. Burnet, *The memoires of the lives and actions of James and William, dukes of Hamilton and Castleherald* (1677) · *The memoirs of Henry Guthry, late bishop*, 2nd edn (1747) · *The letters and journals of Robert Baillie*, ed. D. Laing, 3 vols. (1841–2) · T. Hope, *Hope's 'Major practicks', 1608–33*, ed. J. A. Clyde, 2 vols., Stair Society, 3–4 (1937–8) · 'Twenty-four letters of Sir Thomas Hope, 1627–1646', ed. R. Paul, *Miscellany … I*, Scottish History Society, 15 (1893), 73–139 · *Reg. PCS*, 1st ser. · *Reg. PCS*, 2nd ser. · J. Dennistoun, ed., *The Coltness collections, MDCVIII–MDCCCXL*, Maitland Club, [58] (1842) · C. Rogers, ed., *The earl of Stirling's register of royal letters relative to the affairs of Scotland and Nova Scotia from 1615 to 1635*, 2 vols. (1885) · private information (2004) [Anne Hope] · D. Laing, ed., *A catalogue of the graduates … of the University of Edinburgh*, Bannatyne Club, 106 (1858), 10 · J. Row, *The history of the Kirk of Scotland, from the year 1558 to August 1637*, ed. D. Laing, Wodrow Society, 4 (1842) · T. Craufurd, *History of the University of Edinburgh from 1580 to 1646* (1808) · G. Crawford, *The peerage of Scotland: containing an historical and genealogical account of the nobility of that kingdom* (privately printed, Edinburgh, 1716) · NA Scot., GD 406/1/343, 406/1/1285, 406/1/1286
Archives NL Scot., deeds and corresp. · NRA Scotland, priv. coll., legal papers | NA Scot., corresp. with seventh earl of Glencairn, GD 39 · NA Scot., letters to the earl of Strathearn and others, GD 22
Likenesses G. Jamesone, oils, 1627, Scot. NPG [*see illus.*] · G. Jamesone, oils, priv. coll.; repro. in D. Thomson, *The life and art of George Jameson* (1974)

Hope, Sir Thomas, of Kerse (1606–1643), politician and judge, was born on 6 August 1606, the second son of Sir Thomas *Hope of Craighall (1573–1646), future lord advocate, and his wife, Elizabeth (d. 1660), daughter of John Bennett of Wallyford, Haddingtonshire. Sir James *Hope of Hopetoun and Sir John *Hope, Lord Craighall, were his brothers. He graduated from the University of Edinburgh in 1625 and was admitted advocate on 17 July 1631. He had received a grant of the lands and barony of Kerse in 1625 and was knighted, as Sir Thomas Hope 'of Wester Granton', by Charles I at Innerwick on 16 July 1633. He married Helen, third daughter and coheir of Adam Rae of Pitspindie.

Hope played an active part in public affairs, sitting in the Scottish parliament of 1639–41 as commissioner for Clackmannanshire. In 1639, during the first bishops' war, he held joint command of General Leslie's lifeguard, raised by the college of justice, and in 1640–41 commanded the general's lifeguard of horse, again raised from the college, and won praise for his conduct at Newburn. He was named to the 1640 committee of estates, and as collector-general of the tenth and twentieth pennies, raised in 1640–41 to support the Scottish war effort. In September 1641 he proposed in parliament, as speaker for the barons or freeholders, that the estates should appoint officers of state and privy councillors by ballot, though the

proposal was lost. He was prominent in opposing Charles's demand for a public inquiry into the 'incident', and was the author of the compromise effected between the king and the estates with reference to the appointment of Loudoun as chancellor. On 13 November 1641 the estates agreed his appointment as an ordinary lord of session, one of four chosen to replace royalist incumbents, and he was named lord justice-general by the king. At the same time he was chosen as one of the conservators of the peace, the body established under the treaty of London to liaise with the English parliament, and acted as a commissioner to treat with Westminster for the suppression of the Irish rising. He was a member for Stirlingshire in the convention of estates of 1643 and was chosen to negotiate with English parliamentary representatives, negotiations which would culminate in the solemn league and covenant. He was, however, replaced owing to ill health and died at Edinburgh on 23 August 1643. He was succeeded by his eldest son, Thomas, who was himself succeeded by his younger brother, Alexander, first baronet. Hope left two legal works in manuscript, the 'Law repertorie' and a two-volume commentary on books 12–24 of Justinian's *Digest*, held by the National Library of Scotland.

J. A. HAMILTON, *rev.* SHARON ADAMS

Sources M. D. Young, ed., *The parliaments of Scotland: burgh and shire commissioners*, 1 (1992) · G. Brunton and D. Haig, *An historical account of the senators of the college of justice, from its institution in MDXXXII* (1832) · J. M. Thomson and others, eds., *Registrum magni sigilli regum Scotorum / The register of the great seal of Scotland*, 11 vols. (1882–1914), vols. 8, 11 · F. J. Grant, ed., *The Faculty of Advocates in Scotland, 1532–1943*, Scottish RS, 145 (1944) · D. Laing, ed., *A catalogue of the graduates … of the University of Edinburgh*, Bannatyne Club, 106 (1858) · *The historical works of Sir James Balfour*, ed. J. Haig, 2–3 (1824) · *Scots peerage* · J. R. Young, *The Scottish parliament, 1639–1661: a political and constitutional analysis* (1996) · E. M. Furgol, *A regimental history of the covenanting armies, 1639–1651* (1990) · D. Stevenson, ed., *The government of Scotland under the covenanters*, Scottish History Society, 4th ser., 18 (1982)
Likenesses G. Jamesone, portrait, Hopetoun House, Edinburgh

Hope, Sir Thomas, eighth baronet (c.1681–1771), agricultural improver and politician, was born at the family home of Rankeillor in Fife, the second son of a distinguished lawyer, Archibald *Hope of Rankeillor, Lord Rankeillor (1639–1706) [*see under* Hope, Sir John, Lord Craighall], and Margaret, daughter of Sir John Aytoun, their first son having died in infancy. It was intended that he too was to enter the legal profession; his education is largely unknown but he was admitted advocate on 10 July 1701. He married Margaret (d. 1743), eldest daughter of James Lowis of Merchiston, on 16 March 1702.

Hope was appointed commissioner of supply for Fife in 1695 and justice of the peace for the county in 1706. He succeeded to the title and estates on the death of his father, on 10 October 1706. Commissioner to the Scottish parliament for Fife from 1706 to 1707, he was opposed to the Union with England and ceased to be a commissioner following the union of parliaments. However, he remained involved in local administrative matters.

Throughout most of his adult life, Hope took an interest in agriculture; as early as 1699 he was appointed to the

Scottish privy council's 'committee anent the export of wool'. His estate in Fife was described as a 'very handsome house with a good deall of inclosures and regular planting about them' (Mitchell, 379). He was one of the founders of the Society of Improvers in the Knowledge of Agriculture, established in Edinburgh in June 1723 and one of Europe's earliest agricultural societies. The society elected Hope its first president and had initially some 300 members, drawn largely from the Scottish landowning class. It counted among its number forty peers, including the marquess of Lothian, the dukes of Hamilton and Atholl, and the earls of Hopetoun, Ilay, Kinnoul, and Stair. The poet Allan Ramsay was an admirer of the society and dedicated to it his poem, 'The Pleasures of Improvements in Agriculture' (*The Works of Allan Ramsay*, ed. A. M. Kinghorn and A. Law, 6, 1974, 129). In 1724 the society published a *Treatise concerning the manner of fallowing of ground, raising of grass seeds and training of lint and hemp, for the increase and improvement of the linnen manufactures in Scotland*; this was largely the work of Hope, aided by Robert Maxwell of Arkland, the secretary of the society.

Many of the ideas of the society were later put into action by the board of trustees for manufacturers, which was set up in 1727, largely because many of the trustees were also members of the society. Hope himself was one of the original members of the board of trustees for manufacturers. Maxwell erroneously claimed that the foundation of the board of trustees was largely the result of the society's efforts. Hope was appointed to the subcommittee for linen and was heavily involved in the promotion of the linen industry in Scotland. A lengthy treatise on the flax industry, entitled 'Observations and directions for cultivating and raising flax', written in 1735, exists among the Hope of Craighall papers. The transactions of the society were intermittent, though a number of detailed queries on agricultural matters with a foreword by Hope was published in 1743 under the title of *Select transactions of the honourable the Society of Improvers in the Knowledge of Agriculture in Scotland*. This 450-page volume contained detailed correspondence with Jethro Tull, as well as agricultural advice on cultivation, the growing of grass and sainfoin, drainage, and fencing, and other responses to members' queries. Maxwell commented that though, in terms of agricultural proficiency, Scotland had been centuries behind England, the work of the society had reduced it to less than one. The society existed for about thirty years but petered out following the death of Hope and other more enthusiastic members.

Hope travelled extensively throughout England and continental Europe during the 1730s, noting agricultural methods. A diary of his visit to the Low Countries and northern France, undertaken in 1737, has survived among the Hope of Craighall papers. In 1722 Hope took a lease of the Burrowloch or south loch of Edinburgh, which he drained and laid out as an ornamental park; it was known then as Hope Park and subsequently as the Meadows. He built a residence there in 1740, and his wife died at Hope Park in 1743.

Hope succeeded to the baronetcy of Craighall in 1766 following the death of Sir John Hope *Bruce, his cousin. He became 'father of the bar' in Scotland as the oldest practising advocate, and by the late 1760s Hope was also the last surviving former member of the pre-Union Scottish parliament. He died at Hope Park, his house in Edinburgh, on 18 April 1771.   PETER G. VASEY

Sources Hope of Craighall muniments, NA Scot., GD 377 · M. D. Young, ed., *The parliaments of Scotland: burgh and shire commissioners*, 2 vols. (1992–3) · W. M. Bryce, 'The burgh muir of Edinburgh', *Book of the Old Edinburgh Club*, 10 (1918), 252–63 · J. E. Handley, *Scottish farming in the eighteenth century* (1953) · *Geographical collections relating to Scotland made by Walter MacFarlane*, ed. A. Mitchell, 1, Scottish History Society, 51 (1906), 379 · R. Maxwell, *The practical husbandman* (1757) · 'Observations and directions for cultivating and raising flax', 1735, NA Scot., GD 377/257 · T. Hope, 'Diary of a visit to the Low Countries and northern France', NA Scot., GD 377/271 · H. Paton, ed., *The register of marriages for the parish of Edinburgh, 1701–1750*, Scottish RS, old ser., 35 (1908)
Archives NA Scot., Hope of Craighall muniments, GD 377
Likenesses J. B. de Medina, miniatures in oils, c.1702, priv. coll.

Hope, Thomas (1704–1779). *See under* Hope family (*per. c.*1700–1813).

Hope, Thomas (1769–1831), art collector and connoisseur, was born in Amsterdam on 30 August 1769, the eldest of the three sons of John *Hope (1737–1784) [*see under* Hope family (*per. c.*1700–1813)] and his wife, Philippina Barbara van der Hoeven (c.1738–1789), daughter of Rotterdam's burgomaster. John Hope was a member of an immensely wealthy and prestigious family of Amsterdam merchants of Scottish descent, a partner in their highly successful firm, Hope & Co., and a leading figure in Dutch politics and society.

In 1784, aged fifteen, Thomas Hope shared his father's fortune with his brothers Adrian Elias (*b.* 1772) and Henry Philip (1774–1839), and seemed destined for leadership of Hope & Co. In 1790, following his mother's death, he briefly worked as a partner in its counting-house, but he was never active in its management. Indeed it appears that at some stage his mother and others had turned him against the Hope partners. Instead he took up the study of classical architecture and civilization and from 1787, apart from short periods in Amsterdam, spent eight years travelling and studying architecture in countries bordering the Mediterranean. The austere simplicity of classicism impressed him greatly but he was also infused with the romanticism of Mediterranean culture; in Turkey, for example, he adopted local dress and abandoned his Christianity. His romantic novel, *Anastasius* (1819), first published in French but subsequently in thirteen editions and in four languages, was based on the experience of these travels. He published it anonymously and for a while it was thought to be the work of Lord Byron.

In 1795, at the time of the French occupation of Amsterdam, like most of his family, Hope settled in London, living in Duchess Street from 1799 and winning recognition as a scholar, collector, writer, proponent of neo-classicism, and enlightened patron of young and promising artists and craftsmen. He said of himself that he was entirely 'devoted to the arts' (Watkin, 13); above all else he sought to influence taste. To this end he employed, systematically, his immense fortune, intellect, and energy. All was done on a grand scale and with magnificence.

On 16 April 1806 Hope married a woman of modest means, Louisa (d. 1851), the beautiful daughter of William de la Poer Beresford, archbishop of Tuam and later first Baron Decies, and niece of the first marquess of Waterford. They had at least one daughter and four sons, the former and one of the latter predeceasing Thomas. Their youngest son, Alexander James Beresford Beresford *Hope, became a notable politician and author. Louisa emerged as a glittering society hostess and their set came to include the prince and princess of Wales (later George IV and Queen Caroline), and the duke and duchess of Clarence (the future William IV and Queen Adelaide); Queen Adelaide appointed Mrs Hope a woman of the bedchamber. Thomas's preference was for the intellectual circles of exalted connoisseurship.

Hope was admitted to the Society of Dilettanti in 1800 and a year later received his first invitation to the annual dinner of the Royal Academy. Membership of the Royal Institution, the Royal Society, the Society of Arts, and the British Institution, and not least of their influential committees, followed as his reputation as an informed scholar grew. They provided him with a platform from which to influence taste and he was only held back by his widely acknowledged conceit, lack of tact, and unprepossessing appearance; he was described as ill-looking and effeminate in manner. He damaged his cause by openly lobbying the duke of Wellington, when prime minister, for a peerage.

Hope's concerns, according to his biographer Watkin, were with 'antique and modern art and with the attempt to influence the character of the latter by promoting knowledge of the former' (Watkin, 35). At the heart of his ambition was the wish to influence modern design through knowledge of the art of the ancients. Hope mastered the vast knowledge of classical art and architecture accumulated in the eighteenth century in order to interpret and publicize it. He did as much as anyone in England to promote neo-classicism but his interests were wider and more complex; he was equally a proponent of the English picturesque and linked both as valid components of a wider Romantic movement.

Hope had started to collect by 1795 when in Rome. Then, and on his many subsequent tours through southern Europe, he purchased sculpture, vases, and other antiquities. Most notably, he acquired in 1801 for £4500 a magnificent collection of classical vases from Sir William Hamilton, and by 1806 he possessed over 1500 of the highest quality. There were also examples of the very best Greek and Egyptian sculpture and, on a much smaller scale, Renaissance and baroque paintings purchased at London sales. The sculpture included magnificent Greek statues of Hygeia and Athene, regarded as the work of Pheidias or his school, discovered at Ostia in 1797.

Hope encouraged and acted as patron of little-known artists of promise. As a young man in Rome, he early recognized the great neo-classical sculptors Bertel Thorvaldsen and John Flaxman, and provided them with important commissions. By his death Hope had no fewer than eleven works by Thorvaldsen including bas reliefs of himself, his wife, and his children. From Flaxman came a marble of the *Apollo Belvedere*, a group of *Aurora and Cephalus*, and, most notably, a series of 109 drawings as illustrations to Dante's *Divine Comedy*, which confirmed Flaxman as the pre-eminent English neo-classical artist. He also commissioned works from Antonio Canova, most notably a *Venus* delivered in 1822, and from painters. Here his interests included great neo-classical history canvases commissioned from artists such as Benjamin Robert Haydon, Louis Gauffier, and Richard Westall. But in contrast, his picture purchases also encouraged the picturesque and sentimental; he acquired works from young artists such as Thomas Daniell, John Martin, and Robert Smirke.

Hope sought out and sponsored craftsmen of merit to make furniture and objects according to his own neo-classical designs for installation in his Duchess Street showcase; those who made furniture included Francis Chantrey. He also extended his patronage to innovatory engravers such as Edmund Aikin and Henry Moses and to silversmiths such as Paul Storr. Of greater note was his encouragement of the architect William Wilkins. In 1804 Hope had vigorously and successfully promoted the purity of Wilkins's Greek designs for Downing College, Cambridge. In his outspoken pamphlet *Observations on the Plans … for Downing College* (1804), Hope laid down his opposition to the Roman Doric design put forward by James Wyatt, then president of the Royal Academy; Wyatt's defeat marked Hope out as a force to be reckoned with in architectural judgement.

Hope's collection was exhibited at his town and country houses for the instruction of visitors. His Duchess Street mansion, originally designed by Robert Adam, was greatly altered and extended with the ground and first floors being equipped with large galleries of neo-classical design; one visitor referred to the house as a 'temple of art'. It was, in fact, neither home nor museum, more a place where the rich and informed were to be influenced. The rooms and galleries were lined with sculpture and paintings, vases, and other antiquities, all of exquisite quality. In 1807 he acquired a country home at Deepdene, near Dorking in Surrey, which he greatly extended in the style and setting of the picturesque. A mausoleum along with additional wings and a tower were completed in 1818 and a sculpture gallery and conservatory followed in the 1820s. All appear to have been the work of William Atkinson, with significant contributions from Hope himself.

So systematic was Hope's approach to the use of his collection as a didactic tool that entrance, at least to Duchess Street, was by admission ticket. He issued his first tickets in 1804. The recipients were sixty Royal Academicians who would be permitted, along with three friends each, to enter Duchess Street between February and March. This highlighted the seriousness with which Hope aimed to pursue his desire to influence taste, although on this occasion the absence of personal invitations along with the seeming impertinence of their young issuer was to leave the Academicians outraged. He also endeavoured to effect influence through his writings. *Household Furniture and Interior Decoration* (1807) was perhaps his most didactic and influential work and it was followed by *Costumes of the Ancients* (1809). On his deathbed he completed *Essay on the Origin and Prospects of Man* (1831).

In 1831 Hope fell seriously ill and died on 2 February at Duchess Street. On 12 February he was laid to rest in the mausoleum at Deepdene. Throughout his life Hope maintained his fortune; it is estimated to have been about £200,000 on his death. Although Duchess Street was demolished in 1851, most of its contents were retained at Deepdene and in a new London family house in Piccadilly. The major dispersal of Hope's collection occurred in 1917, when his descendants sold Deepdene and disposed of its contents by auction at Christies; Deepdene itself was demolished in 1969.

Henry Philip Hope (1774–1839), art collector, was the youngest son of John Hope and his wife, Philippina Barbara van der Hoeven. He was born in Amsterdam and educated privately at home; he probably spent some time in Brunswick with his governor before studying at Leiden University. At fifteen he was described as 'the angel of the family—an excellent heart and amiable disposition' (Ingram, 428). He was in Rome between 1795 and 1796 with his two brothers. He visited Pacetti's studio where he purchased some antiquities, a group of *Bacchus and Hope*, and a *Hermaphrodite*. Henry returned to Italy between 1796 and 1798, when he visited a number of northern cities, Naples and Rome. He was in London for the sales of the Orléans collection of paintings where he purchased approximately seven paintings to the value of £2500. He became a member of the Society of Dilettanti in 1807.

Henry Hope appears to have been close to his brother, Thomas. The latter commissioned a portrait bust of him from Flaxman, for the dining-room at Deepdene, and Henry purchased the neighbouring estate of Chart Park for Thomas. In 1819 Henry lent Thomas the Hope collection of nearly 100 paintings he had inherited. Henry also patronized contemporary artists, purchasing John Martin's *The Fall of Babylon* (exh. British Institution, 1819) for 400 guineas. He died, unmarried, in 1839. In his will, proved with two codicils on 5 May 1840, Henry Hope bequeathed most of his art collection to his nephew, Henry Thomas Hope.   JOHN ORBELL

Sources D. Watkin, *Thomas Hope and the neo-classical idea* (1968) · M. G. Buist, *At spes non fracta: Hope & Co., 1770–1815* (1974) · T. L. Ingram, 'A note on Thomas Hope of Deepdene', *Burlington Magazine*, 927 (June 1980), 427–8 · *DNB* · S. Baumgarten, *Le crépuscule néoclassique: Thomas Hope* (1958) · Colvin, *Archs.* · *GM*, 1st ser., 101/1 (1831), 368–70 · will, PRO, PROB 11.1927, fols. 290v – 293r
Archives CKS, letters to Lord Stanhope · ING Barings, London, Barings archives, bank account
Likenesses J. H. Sablet, oils, 1792, Marylebone Cricket Club, London · W. Beechey, oils, 1798, NPG; repro. in Watkin, *Thomas Hope* · A. Bnok, watercolour drawing, 1805, Brooks's Club, London, Society of Dilettanti · B. Thorvaldsen, marble bust, c.1817, Thorvaldsen Museum, Copenhagen · C. R. Bone, miniature, repro. in Watkin, *Thomas Hope*
Wealth at death approx. £200,000: Watkin, *Thomas Hope*, 27

Hope, Thomas Charles (1766–1844), chemist and educationist, was born on 21 July 1766 in Edinburgh, the third of four sons and a daughter of John *Hope (1725–1786), professor of botany at the University of Edinburgh, and his wife, Juliana, daughter of a Dr Stevenson, an Edinburgh physician. Educated mainly at the high school, Edinburgh, in 1779 he entered the university where he gave much attention to botany and chemistry. On his father's death he applied unsuccessfully for his chair. The following year, 1787, he graduated MD at Edinburgh, and through the influence of his uncle, Alexander Stevenson, professor of medicine in the University of Glasgow, was elected lecturer in chemistry and materia medica at Glasgow. In 1788 he ceased to teach materia medica and lectured on chemistry alone until 1791. Although previously a believer in the phlogiston theory, in 1788 he became the first in Britain to teach the alternative views of Lavoisier, to whose opinions he was converted by Sir James Hall (1761–1832).

In 1789 his uncle secured for Hope appointments as his assistant and successor. On Stevenson's death in 1791 Hope assumed the chair of medicine which he held until October 1795. He was physician and clinical lecturer to the Royal Infirmary, Glasgow, opened in 1794, but continued to conduct private research in chemistry. In 1793 he communicated to the Royal Society of Edinburgh, of which he had become a fellow in 1788, his paper on the first known compound of strontium. Joseph Black, professor of chemistry and medicine at Edinburgh, was so impressed by this discovery of a new chemical element that he secured for Hope, his former pupil, the post of assistant professor from November 1795. In 1797–8 Hope took over all Black's lectures and succeeded him in 1799.

As professor at Edinburgh, Hope did not neglect medicine. For several years he lectured on clinical medicine and, having been elected a fellow of the Royal College of Physicians, Edinburgh, in 1796, was its secretary (1798–1803), treasurer (1803–9), and president (1815–19). He wrote the chemical part of the tenth edition of its *Pharmacopoeia* (1817). In 1810 he was elected a fellow of the Royal Society of London. As a chemist, he was initially innovative in teaching and research. He continued to promote the new chemistry of Lavoisier, and for several years he was the only Scottish professor who advocated the geological views of James Hutton. In 1805 he published his discovery that the maximum density of water occurs not at the freezing point, 32 °F, but around 39 °F. He was also active as a consultant. In 1806 Thomas Thomson, Andrew Coventry, and he reported to the Scottish excise commissioners the results of two years' work on the differences between English and Scottish barley. In 1813 he investigated the water supply of Edinburgh so thoroughly that in 1817 he was given the freedom of the city.

However, after 1806, Hope devoted his talents mainly to improving his teaching. He had the advantage of succeeding the illustrious Black whose impeccably neat lecture demonstrations had attracted an audience of about 200. Receiving no salary, dependent on the fees paid by members of his class, and having to meet its costs, Hope sustained a testing programme: for six months for five days a week he gave spectacular and punctiliously organized lecture-demonstrations using large apparatus specially designed for the purpose. Spurning the rewards of writing textbooks, Hope reached his peak in the 1820s: his clear if pompous lectures, given from 1820 in his big room in the new Adam–Playfair building, attracted an audience of over 500 and fees of about £2000 per annum from his exceptionally heterogeneous class, which was open to any man who could pay. Numerous foreigners, from princes to ancient historians, were impressed by his chemical drama. In spring 1826 he reached the zenith of his popularity when he gave a course to which women and their beaux were admitted; the fees from the audience of over 600 enabled him in 1828 to give £800 to found a university chemistry prize. In 1826 Hope was a conspicuous protagonist in the professorial quarrelling which was endemic at Edinburgh. Publicly reviled by one colleague as a mere showman, he himself had to pay £500 to another for defamation. In 1823 he became a vice-president of the RSE.

Until 1823 Hope provided no opportunities for students to do practical work. He then grudgingly arranged for his own lecture assistant, John Wilson Anderson, to run a practical class at his own responsibility and risk. By the early 1830s Hope was under threat. In 1833 David Boswell Reid (1805–1863), then in charge of the practical class, lobbied Edinburgh town council, which supervised the university, to create a separate chair of practical chemistry. This proposal was successfully opposed by the university senate and by Hope who vigorously defended his professorial monopoly. By this point, indifferent to research, to practical chemistry, and to contact with industry, he resisted any addition to the lecturing which had brought him esteem and wealth for three decades. Next year the town council seriously considered but rejected the establishment of a separate lectureship in practical chemistry.

Hope maintained his control of practical chemistry at the cost of publicly displayed ill will, the discrediting of the university's course of practical chemistry, and a severe drop in the size of his class and income from 1833. He continued to teach until summer 1843 when he resigned his chair; his last class numbered only 118. A wealthy bachelor, he remained a leading figure in Edinburgh's polite society, and was reputed to be capable of eating eight plates of turtle. He lived in Moray Place, a select part of Edinburgh's New Town, enjoyed his vice-presidency of the Edinburgh Royal Society, and in 1837 presided by invitation over the centenary dinner of the Royal Medical Society of Edinburgh. After a long illness Hope died of paralysis on 13 June 1844 at his home. He was buried at Greyfriars churchyard, Edinburgh, on 18 June.

JACK MORRELL

Sources T. S. Traill, 'Memoir of Dr Thomas Charles Hope', *Transactions of the Royal Society of Edinburgh*, 16 (1849), 419–34 · J. B. Morrell, 'Practical chemistry in the University of Edinburgh, 1799–1843', *Ambix*, 16 (1969), 66–80 · minutes of Edinburgh Town Council, Edinburgh City Archives · minutes of the University of Edinburgh senate, U. Edin. L. · lecture notes by Hope and notes of his lectures, U. Edin. L. · V. A. Eyles, 'The evolution of a chemist: Sir James Hall … and his relations with Joseph Black, Antoine Lavoisier, and other scientists', *Annals of Science*, 19 (1963), 153–82 · W. S. Craig, *History of the Royal College of Physicians of Edinburgh* (1976) · J. Gray, *History of the Royal Medical Society, 1737–1937*, ed. D. Guthrie (1952) · J. Coutts, *A history of the University of Glasgow* (1909) · L. Horner to A. Marcet, 22 Nov 1821, NL Scot., MS 9818, fol. 91 · 'Record of interment in Greyfriars burying ground, Edinburgh, 1839–1860', Edinburgh Central Library

Archives Bodl. Oxf., lecture notes · Chemical Society of London, lecture notes · JRL, lecture notes · McGill University, Montreal, Osler Library, lecture notes · NL Scot., lecture notes · RCP Lond., lecture and case notes · Royal College of Physicians of Edinburgh, lecture and case notes · Sci. Mus., lecture notes · U. Edin. L., corresp. and papers · Wellcome L., lecture notes | Linn. Soc., corresp. with Sir James Edward Smith · NL Scot., corresp. with Robert Liston · U. Edin., Joseph Black corresp. · U. Edin. L., letters to A. I. C. Monet

Likenesses J. Kay, etching, 1817, NPG · T. Hodgett, mezzotint (after H. Raeburn), BM, RS · H. Raeburn, oils, repro. in A. Kent, ed., *An eighteenth century lectureship in chemistry* (1950)

Hope, Victor Alexander John, second marquess of Linlithgow (1887–1952), viceroy of India, was born at Hopetoun House, South Queensferry, Linlithgowshire (West Lothian), on 24 September 1887, the elder son of John Adrian Louis *Hope, seventh earl of Hopetoun, afterwards first marquess of Linlithgow (1860–1908) and first governor-general of Australia, and his wife, Hersey Alice Everleigh-de-Moleyns (1867–1937), daughter of the fourth Baron Ventry. He was educated at Eton College and in 1908 succeeded his father as second marquess. On 19 April 1911 he married Doreen Maud (1886–1965), younger daughter of Sir Frederick George Milner, seventh baronet. They had twin sons and three daughters. An active territorial, he served throughout the First World War, ending with the rank of colonel, with the Lothians and Border horse, and in command of a battalion of the Royal Scots. He was mentioned in dispatches and made an OBE (military). After the war he was civil lord of the Admiralty in the Conservative government (1922–4); deputy chairman of the Unionist Party Organization (1924–6); and president of the Navy League (1924–31). He was chairman of the Medical Research Council and of the governing body of the Imperial College of Science and Technology (1934–6). Closely interested in agriculture, he was chairman of the committee on the distribution and prices of agricultural produce (1923) and president of the Edinburgh and East of Scotland College of Agriculture (1924–33). He declined the governorship of Madras in 1924, partly to avoid separation from his school-age sons, but largely because he needed to enhance his earning capacity by commercial employment. He joined several company boards: his father had left an insufficient endowment to maintain Hopetoun House, which was closed down from time to time as an economy measure. He developed a close knowledge of India as chairman (1926–8) of the royal commission on agriculture in India and, importantly, as chairman (1933–4) of the joint select committee on Indian constitutional reform.

Victor Alexander John Hope, second marquess of Linlithgow (1887–1952), by Sir Oswald Birley, 1950

When Lord Willingdon's term as viceroy expired in April 1936 and it was expected that his successor's major task would be to give effect to the Government of India Act (1935) that emerged from the select committee's labours, Linlithgow was appointed to the viceroyalty. He would hold it for a record seven and a half year term, one of enormous stress and difficulty, both in peace and war. The act of 1935 provided for the autonomy of the eleven provinces of India, subject to 'special responsibilities' vested in the governors, and for an all-India federation of the provinces and the princely states, if enough princes agreed to accede to it. India's advance to provincial and central responsible government depended upon the willingness of her parties and princes to co-operate with the act's provisions. In the fractured polity of inter-war India, outstanding diplomatic talents were required of the incoming viceroy.

At the provincial elections of the winter of 1936–7 the Indian National Congress enjoyed an unexpected but convincing success, capturing six of the eleven provinces. Initially Congress declined to accept office unless the governors undertook not to use their special powers. Linlithgow stood by the constitution but persuaded Congress to accept office by a conciliatory clarification of the spirit in which the governors would discharge their obligations. He also pursued the path of explanation in relation to the princes' accession, dispatching emissaries to the princes in 1936 to clarify their intended position under federation.

Precious time was lost as they individually bargained for financial concessions that Linlithgow found the British government was reluctant to allow. Nor was he permitted to exert pressure upon them, from fear of provoking the 'die-hards' in British political life, who had opposed the 1935 act. By the time an instrument of accession was available for negotiation with the princes, Congress, installed in provincial government, challenged as offensive to democracy the act's provision for the states' federal representatives to be the princes' nominees. The political settlement that the act was designed to establish was further disturbed by the determination of the Muslim League, which had valued the princes' authority as a counterpoise to the predominantly Hindu and populist Congress, to renegotiate the federal scheme. Some months before the Second World War broke out the failure of the federal scheme was apparent. The communal situation was deteriorating, with the League complaining of oppression by the Congress provincial governments. Further moves were halted for the duration of the war.

Linlithgow has been criticized severely for committing India to war in 1939 without consulting the party leaders or the provincial governments, eight of which were then controlled by Congress. His action provoked Congress to seek a definition of Britain's war aims in relation to India, while the Muslim League sought to prevent any constitutional statement of which it did not approve. Linlithgow held discussions with the party leaders, according Jinnah, as president of the League, undue status as a representative and spokesman for Indian Muslims, for the League was not the governing party in any province. He has been accused of exploiting Hindu–Muslim differences and following a policy of divide and rule. In his hands the constitutional problem came to seem intractable. In the first months of the war he was unwilling to recognize India's right of post-war self-determination or to admit party leaders to his central executive, which was still functioning under the 1919 constitution. The cabinet reinforced his opposition to conciliation. During November 1939 the Congress governments withdrew from office, never to return for the duration of the war. As the war situation deteriorated in 1940, he became increasingly amenable to an accommodation with Congress, based upon a promise of Indian participation in a post-war constitution-making body and the present reconstruction of the central executive to include party leaders. He was led so far reluctantly, by the promptings of successive secretaries of state for India, Lord Zetland and Leopold Amery. He was not disappointed when Churchill himself recast the 1940 'August offer' in terms so unyielding that Congress was bound to refuse them. He now favoured meeting a challenge from Congress with a determination 'to crush the organization as a whole' (Moore, 37). When Gandhi inaugurated individual civil disobedience there were some 23,000 convictions under the Defence of India Act. In summer 1941 Linlithgow did reconstruct his executive council to include eight Indians, a majority of members, but he retained his constitutional dominance over it. He also set up a National

Defence Council with representatives of British India and the princes.

In March and April 1942 the membership and operation of the executive council became the focus of controversy between the leaders of the political parties in Britain and India. While Sir Stafford Cripps took to India a draft declaration that adumbrated a procedure for Indians to make a dominion constitution after the war—and which Gandhi dismissed as 'a post-dated cheque' (Moore, 91)—his mission was concerned essentially with attracting the leaders of the Congress and the League to the wartime executive. Linlithgow resented Cripps's discussions with the Congress leaders over the composition and operation of his council. He particularly disliked his involvement of President Roosevelt's representative, Colonel Louis Johnson, in discussions on the defence portfolio. The lengthy negotiations finally broke down through Linlithgow's unwillingness to offer such liberal assurances on decision-making procedures for his executive as he had given for the provincial executives in 1937. His wartime experience of the Congress working committee had made him mistrustful of their loyalty and sceptical of their representativeness and administrative capacity. He was also apprehensive of importing communal antagonism, which the League's growing influence in consequence of the Congress withdrawal from the constitutional field had exacerbated, into the machinery of central government. Again reinforced by Churchill, for whom the Cripps mission was an unpalatable political necessity designed to placate Indian 'moderates' and the American allies, he stood out against conciliation. Subsequently, in August, he brought the full force of the raj to bear against Gandhi's Quit India movement. The Congress leaders were detained for the duration of the war. He was impervious to the moral pressure that Gandhi's long fast in February 1943 imposed.

Linlithgow presided over both the disappointment of hopes for an all-India polity and the successful mobilization of India's men and materials for the defence of the empire on the Middle Eastern and south-east Asian fronts. The volunteer Indian army was expanded tenfold to more than 2 million men. His essential purpose was not Indian freedom but 'to hold India to the Empire' and deploy its resources to Britain's benefit. That was also the purpose of the British cabinet throughout his viceroyalty, and he was given little scope for political manoeuvring. As the viceroy of a beleaguered subcontinent he had an elevated conception of his duty and a commensurate sense of self-sufficiency. In the face of external threats and internal challenges he governed with great courage. Among historians, controversy persists over whether and how he might have done more to bridge the divisions that increasingly separated Congress and the Muslim League, and which resulted in the partition of India in 1947. While he did see the chances of all-India federation receding he was slow to recognize the widening of the communal chasm, as illustrated by the League's demand for Pakistan in March 1940, and its implications for the future of the subcontinent. He underestimated the importance of the Congress and the quality of its leaders, especially Jawaharlal Nehru. He had little regard for nationalist aspirations or integrity. He saw Nehru as 'a doctrinaire', 'an amateur' (Moore, 18), and his colleagues as 'a collection of declining valetudinarians' who 'could never run straight' (Mansergh and Lumby, 1, docs. 30, 517). They found him aloof and inflexible. Nehru described him as 'Heavy of body and slow of mind, solid as a rock and with almost a rock's lack of awareness' (J. Nehru, *The Discovery of India*, 1960 edn, 446). When he left India in October 1943 the country was on a sound war footing, though there was a calamitous famine in Bengal. It was not long before his successor, Lord Wavell, was warning the British government of the dangers of a post-war administrative breakdown and of the urgent need to reopen the political dialogue with the Indian parties.

Linlithgow was an imposing figure, 6 feet 5 inches tall, with a formidably erect upper body; poliomyelitis at the age of sixteen had left him with permanently impaired neck muscles, so that he could not turn his head without turning his shoulders. He was innately shy and appeared brusque to strangers. He conveyed an impression of dignity, with a deep voice and powerful jaw. He was, however, a wordy public speaker. To Lord Zetland, the seasoned secretary of state to whom he referred for his first four years as viceroy, he was 'wise, cautious Hopie' (R. J. Moore, *Endgames of Empire*, 1988, 69). His instincts were essentially conservative and he lacked political imagination. He had a boyish sense of fun, which breaks out in his private papers at moments of high seriousness. There he would see off the failed Cripps mission with a jocular quip, 'Goodbye Mr Cripps!' (Mansergh and Lumby, 1, doc. 517). On ceremonial occasions he and his wife, who was almost 6 feet tall, made a commanding pair. She received the CI (1936) and the kaisar-i-Hind gold medal. While he was said to dislike ostentation, the marriage celebrations of his eldest daughter in Delhi in November 1939 made, in the interests of morale, no concessions to wartime austerity. His viceregal record has been loyally defended in a study by his younger son, Lord John Hope, created Lord Glendevon (1964), a Conservative member of parliament (1945) who was minister for works in 1959–62.

On his retirement in October 1943 Linlithgow, already a KT (1928), a GCIE (1929), a PC (1935), and a GCSI (1936), was appointed KG. In 1945 he accepted the chairmanship of the Midland Bank and other important business appointments, including a directorship of Imperial Chemical Industries. He was prominent in Scottish public life. A sincere Presbyterian, he was lord high commissioner of the Church of Scotland in 1944 and 1945, chancellor of Edinburgh University from 1944 until his death, and chairman (1944–52) of the board of trustees of the National Gallery of Scotland. A keen sportsman, a bird shot of unusual skill, and a good golfer, he had been vice-lieutenant of West Lothian from 1927 and lord lieutenant from 1929, and took an active interest in the development of his extensive estates in the Scottish lowlands. He died suddenly on 5 January 1952, while out shooting at Hopetoun, and was succeeded by the elder of his twin sons.

ROBIN J. MOORE

Sources J. Glendevon, *The viceroy at bay: Lord Linlithgow in India, 1936–1943* (1971) · G. Rizvi, *Linlithgow and India: a study of British policy and the political impasse in India, 1936–43* (1978) · C. Bridge, *Holding India to the empire: the British conservative party and the 1935 constitution* (1986) · S. R. Ashton, *British policy towards the Indian states, 1905–1939* (1982) · R. J. Moore, *Churchill, Cripps, and India, 1939–1945* (1979) · N. Mansergh and E. W. R. Lumby, eds., *The transfer of power, 1942–7,* 1–4 (1970–73) · *DNB*
Archives BL OIOC, corresp. and papers relating to India, MS Eur. F 125 · priv. coll., corresp. and papers, incl. papers relating to royal commission on agriculture in India | BL OIOC, corresp. with Sir John Anderson, MS Eur. F 207 · BL OIOC, corresp. with Lord Brabourne, MS Eur. F 97 · BL OIOC, corresp. with R. H. Dorman-Smith, MS Eur. E 215 · BL OIOC, corresp. with Lord Erskine, MS Eur. D 596 · BL OIOC, corresp. with Sir G. H. Haig, MS Eur. F 115 · BL OIOC, corresp. with Sir Robert Reid, MS Eur. E 278 · BL OIOC, corresp. with Cornelia Sorabji, MS Eur. F 165 · BL OIOC, corresp. with Sir Findlater Stewart, MS Eur. D 714 · Bodl. Oxf., corresp. with Geoffrey Dawson · JRL, corresp. with Auchinleck · NA Scot., corresp. with Lord Lothian | FILM BFI NFTVA, current affairs footage · BFI NFTVA, documentary footage · BFI NFTVA, news footage
Likenesses O. Birley, oils, 1945, Marble Hall of Rashtrapathi Bhavan, New Delhi; copy, Hopetoun House, West Lothian · O. Birley, oils, 1950, HSBC Group Archives, London, Midland Bank archives [*see illus.*]

Hope, Sir William, first baronet (1664–1729), swordsman and writer, was the son of Sir John Hope (*d.* 1661) of Hopetoun, Lanarkshire, and his second wife, Lady Mary Keith, the eldest daughter of William, seventh Earl Marischal. A passionate amateur swordsman, he was one of the most prolific authors on swordplay, writing between 1687 and 1724 five books that became the unrivalled authorities on their subject for more than fifty years. He was knighted by William III before 1692 for his services to the whig party in Scotland, became a baronet in 1698, and was appointed lieutenant-governor of Edinburgh Castle. In 1705 he bought a substantial estate at Balcomie in Fife. Hope's first treatise, in which he is identified simply as 'W. H., Gent', was *The Scots Fencing Master*, published in Edinburgh in 1687. This conversation piece between scholar and master is the only work that deals with the transition rapier, a weapon described as having a blade about three quarters of an ell (34 inches) long. As illustrated in the first of twelve crudely drawn illustrations, the guard features two large rings curving out from the shell to meet a short crossbar.

Where Hope learned to fence remains a mystery, but it is evident that he was taught in the new French style rather than the traditional Italian or Spanish schools, for he advises his pupil never to put one or two fingers through the rings, as was usual in Italy and Spain, but to hold the handle firmly with the thumb on the flat part and the fingers completely around it. As well as teaching the basics of swordplay, he provided directions for duelling on horseback using pistol and sword.

In 1691 Hope published the first of three editions of a popular pocket book, *The Sword-Man's Vademecum*, in which he extolled the virtues of calmness, vigour, and judgement in all aspects of swordplay. He also gave some of the rules to be observed in his fencing school, which was open five days a week. Strict silence was imposed so that the master's 'advices and reproofs' could be heard.

Hope provided further details of the school of arms in *The Fencing Master's Advice to his Scholar* (1692), in which the rules governing the use of the foil were described for the first time, some four years before Labat in *L'art en fait d'armes*. Although hits with the foil were counted only if they arrived within the target area from neck to waistband, hits to the arms and legs were allowed, in order to accustom a man to the use of 'sharps'. The regulation dress consisted of a black velvet cap, white waistcoat, breeches of any colour and material, stockings, and walking shoes. The tips of the foils, or *fleurets* as he called them to indicate their French origin, were covered with sponge and dipped in vermilion and water, so that judges could see the effect of every thrust. Bouts were for three hits and competitors were allowed only one bout a day on account of the physical exertion demanded during contests.

The year 1692 also saw the republication of Hope's *The Scots Fencing Master* in London under the title *The Compleat Fencing Master*, to avoid any suggestion of a Scottish origin. In the same year Hope was one of a group of teachers of swordsmanship who founded the Society of Swordsmen in Scotland to encourage the art of swordplay. A subsequent bill to allow the society to examine and license suitably qualified masters twice failed in a Scottish parliament preoccupied with the issue of union with England.

In the year of the Act of Union Hope produced his most comprehensive treatise: *A New, Short, and Easy Method of Fencing* (1707), on the title-page of which he identified himself for the first time as 'Sir William Hope of Balcomie, Baronet, Late Deputy-Governour of the Castle of Edinburgh'; a second edition appeared seven years later. In 1724 Hope brought out *A Vindication of the True Art of Self-Defence* in an attempt to persuade parliament to pass a bill establishing a court of honour as a means of settling disputes, in the vain hope that this would end the practice of duelling. This appears to have been his final study, although some bibliographies list another title, *Observations on the Gladiators Stage Fighting*, as having been published in 1725; however, no copy has ever been found. A second edition of the *Vindication* (1729) was dedicated to the prime minister, Sir Robert Walpole. That year Hope died of a chill caught after overexertion while dancing.

MALCOLM FARE

Sources J. D. Aylward, *The English master of arms* (1956) · GEC, *Baronetage*

Hope, Sir William Henry St John (1854–1919), antiquary, the eldest son of the Revd William Hope (*d.* 1889), rector of St Peter's, Derby, and his first wife, Hester, daughter of the Revd John Browne Williams, vicar of Llantrisant, Glamorgan, was born at Derby on 23 June 1854. His taste for ecclesiology, inherited from his father, was developed in his school-days at St John's College, Hurstpierpoint, Sussex, where his lifelong friend Joseph Thomas Fowler was then chaplain. His earliest printed work, on the misericords in Lincoln Cathedral, was published in 1872. He entered Peterhouse, Cambridge, in 1877, and achieved some success in his excavations at Dale Abbey, near Derby, in 1878 and 1879. As an undergraduate, his knowledge of

English medieval church antiquities was recognized and respected by older scholars, and he formed close friendships with Henry Bradshaw and John Willis Clark. After graduating BA in 1881, he was for a short time an assistant master at the King's School, Rochester. His work on monastic remains continued with excavations at Lewes priory, and subsequently at Repton priory and Alnwick abbey. His increasing reputation led to his election as a fellow of the Society of Antiquaries of London in 1883, and two years later he was appointed assistant secretary of the society, the last to be resident in Burlington House.

During the twenty-five years in which Hope held this position (1885–1910) his authority in antiquarian circles was unique. His keen observation and retentive memory found exercise in many directions. While his chief interest always lay in ecclesiastical architecture, and the best work of his life was done in his researches into monastic history and buildings, he was very knowledgeable in Roman antiquities and medieval fortification. Heraldry, medieval plate, and alabaster carvings were among his studies, and upon these and several areas of ecclesiology his authority was generally recognized. His holidays from his duties at Burlington House were spent in practical work upon the remains of abbeys and castles and at meetings of archaeological societies. Among his numerous activities during this period, punctually recorded in papers contributed to *Archaeologia* and other learned publications, his part in the excavation of the Roman town of Silchester deserves special mention. In all, his writings include more than two hundred papers, many of them of considerable length.

Hope's relations with the society's secretary, Sir Hercules Read, were notoriously bad. In 1910, less than two years after Read was elected president, Hope resigned in order to have more time for his own work. He now completed his most conspicuous single achievement, a monumental work on Windsor Castle, undertaken some years previously by royal command, and, after its publication in 1913, he was rewarded in 1914 by the grant of a knighthood. He was awarded the honorary degrees of DCL from the University of Durham in 1911 and of LittD from Cambridge in 1912.

Hope was twice married: first, on 17 October 1885 to Myrrha Fullerton (d. 1903), daughter of Major-General Edward Norman Perkins; secondly, on 28 December 1910 to Mary, daughter of John Robert Jefferies, of Ipswich. There was one son from his first marriage. He died at Galewood, Stapleford, near Cambridge, where he spent the last few years of his life, on 18 August 1919, and was buried in the churchyard at Normanton, near Derby.

A. H. THOMPSON, rev. BERNARD NURSE

Sources A. H. Thompson, *A bibliography of the published writings of Sir William St John Hope* (1929) · J. Evans, *A history of the Society of Antiquaries* (1956) · *The Times* (20 Aug 1919) · *WWW* · Venn, *Alum. Cant.* · m. certs. · *CGPLA Eng. & Wales* (1919) · *Proceedings of the Society of Antiquaries of London*, 2nd ser., 32 (1919–20), 168–9 · A. H. T., *Archaeological Journal*, 76 (1919), 302–6
Archives Borth. Inst. · priv. coll. · S. Antiquaries, Lond. · St George's Chapel, Windsor Castle, Aerary · W. Yorks. AS

Likenesses G. E. K. Gray, drawing, 1912, S. Antiquaries, Lond.; repro. in Evans, *History*
Wealth at death £1751 5s. 1d.: probate, 11 Dec 1919, *CGPLA Eng. & Wales*

Hope, Sir William Johnstone (1766–1831), naval officer and politician, third son of John *Hope (1739–1785) of Craigiehall, Linlithgow, Scotland, a London merchant, and his wife, Mary *née* Breton (1741/2–1767), was born at Finchley, Middlesex, on 16 August 1766. Charles *Hope, judge, and Sir John *Hope, army officer, were his brothers. He was first cousin of Admiral Sir Henry Hope. He attended Edinburgh high school from 1774 to 1776. In January 1777 he entered the navy under his uncle, Captain Charles Hope (d. 1808), on the *Weasel*, and served with him in different ships on the home, Lisbon, and Newfoundland stations until, in October 1782, he was promoted lieutenant of the *Daedalus*, serving on the Newfoundland and home stations. In 1785 he rejoined his uncle as lieutenant of the *Sampson*, guardship at Plymouth, and in March 1786 was appointed to the frigate *Pegasus*, commanded by Prince William Henry, with whom he quarrelled, in the West Indies. In May 1787 he was moved to the *Boreas*, with Nelson as captain, and in her returned to England. In 1789 he went to Newfoundland in the *Adamant* with Sir Richard Hughes, who, in 1790, promoted him commander, and appointed him acting captain of the *Adamant*.

Hope married, on 8 July 1792, Lady Anne Hope Johnstone (d. 28 Aug 1818), eldest daughter of James Hope *Johnstone, third earl of Hopetoun; they had two daughters and four sons, of whom Sir William James Hope-Johnstone, rear-admiral, died in 1878.

In 1793 Hope commanded the fireship *Incendiary* in the channel, and on 21 March 1794 was posted to the *Bellerophon*, flagship of Rear-Admiral Pasley, with whom he served in the battle of 1 June 1794 in the north Atlantic. In January 1795 he was appointed to the *Tremendous*, but in March was moved into the *Venerable* as flag captain to Admiral Duncan. An accidental blow on the head compelled him to resign this command in September 1796; he did not serve again until February 1798, when he was appointed to the *Kent*, again as flag captain to Lord Duncan.

On the surrender of the Dutch Texel fleet on 28 August 1799, Hope was sent to England with the dispatches, when he was presented by the king with £500 for the purchase of a sword. He was shortly afterwards made a commander of the knights of St John by the tsar, whose fleet had been co-operating with the British. The *Kent* then went to the Mediterranean to join the fleet under Lord Keith, and in November 1800 received Sir Ralph Abercromby on board at Gibraltar, to sail to Egypt. In the early operations of the 1801 campaign Hope was present, but he resigned his command when the *Kent* was selected by Sir Richard Bickerton as his flagship, and returned to England.

In 1800 Hope had been elected member of parliament for the Dumfries burghs, and in October 1804 was returned for the county of Dumfries, which he continued to represent until 1830. Both constituencies were under the patronage of Henry Dundas, Lord Melville. Hope was rarely active in the house.

In the summer of 1804 Hope commanded the *Atlas* in the North Sea, but was obliged by failing health to resign. From 1807 to 1809 he was one of the lords of the Admiralty under Lord Mulgrave; in August 1812 he attained his flag, and from 1813 to 1818 was commander-in-chief at Leith. In 1815 he was appointed a KCB; in August 1819 he became a vice-admiral; and from 1820 to 1828 he was at the Admiralty, later becoming a member of council of the lord high admiral.

A well-connected Scottish conservative politician and sea officer, part of the 'Dundas despotism', Hope served as senior naval lord in the last decade of the unreformed Admiralty. In this period naval policy was largely developed by the controller of the navy, Admiral Sir Thomas Byam Martin, under the authority of the first lord, Lord Melville. The first naval lord's duties were light, and in peacetime predominantly political. Hope's unremarkable talents and advanced years proved unequal to the political tensions of the period following the collapse of Lord Liverpool's administration in 1827, and he was replaced by the more astute and effective Sir George Cockburn in March 1828. He was appointed treasurer of the Royal Naval Hospital, Greenwich, and, when that office was abolished, became one of five commissioners for managing the hospital.

On 30 October 1821 Hope married Maria *née* Eden, dowager countess of Athlone (1769/70–5 March 1851), widow of Frederik Willem van Reede, sixth earl of Athlone. They had no children. He was nominated GCB in 1825. He resigned his parliamentary seat in 1830 and died the following year, on 2 May, in Bath; he was buried at Johnstone church, Johnstone, Dumfriesshire.

J. K. LAUGHTON, rev. ANDREW LAMBERT

Sources A. D. Lambert, *The last sailing battlefleet: maintaining naval mastery, 1815–1850* (1991) · C. J. Bartlett, *Great Britain and sea power, 1815–1853* (1963) · M. Fry, *The Dundas despotism* (1992) · HoP, *Commons* · J. Marshall, *Royal naval biography*, 1/2 (1823), 507–13 · *GM*, 1st ser., 101/2 (1831), 639–40 · 'Biographical memoir of Captain William Johnstone Hope', *Naval Chronicle*, 18 (1807), 269–75
Archives NMM, letters to Sir Thomas Foley
Likenesses Bartolozzi, Landseer, Ryder & Stow, line engraving, pubd 1803 (*Commemoration of the victory of June 1st, 1794*; after *Naval victories* by R. Smirke), BM, NPG · H. R. Cook, stipple, pubd 1807 (after miniature), BM, NPG · C. Turner, mezzotint, pubd 1812 (after G. Watson), BM · portrait, repro. in *Naval Chronicle* (1807)

Hope, William Williams (1802–1855). *See under* Hope family (*per. c.*1700–1813).

Hopetoun. For this title name *see* Hope, Sir James, of Hopetoun, appointed Lord Hopetoun under the protectorate (1614–1661); Hope, Charles, first earl of Hopetoun (1681–1742); Johnstone, James Hope-, third earl of Hopetoun and *de jure* fifth earl of Annandale and Hartfell (1741–1816); Hope, John, fourth earl of Hopetoun (1765–1823); Hope, John Adrian Louis, seventh earl of Hopetoun and first marquess of Linlithgow (1860–1908).

Hopkin, Hopkin (1737–1754). *See under* Hopkin, Lewis (1707/8–1771).

Hopkin, Lewis (1707/8–1771), poet and artisan, was the youngest son of Lewis Hopkin (*c.*1675–1756) of Peterston-super-montem, Glamorgan, and Joan (1674/5–1753), daughter of William Thomas of neighbouring Penrhiwfer. One of his ancestors was the gentleman–poet Hopcyn Tomas Phylip (*d.* 1597) of Gelli'r-fid, Llandyfodwg, Glamorgan, an author of free-metre religious carols called *cwndidau*. When he was still a young man Hopkin moved to the parish of Llandyfodwg, the birthplace of many of his ancestors, and it was there, at Hendre Ifan Goch, that he lived until his death. Trained as a carpenter, he became skilled in other crafts as well, including those of glazier, stonemason, and wire-worker. In the latter part of his life he took to farming, and he also owned a fairly large country shop. According to his son, many sought his services in surveying, planning, measuring, calculating, and writing law documents. He built a house and furnished it himself.

Lewis Hopkin became a nonconformist and was a member (and possibly a deacon) of the Independent Congregational assembly at Cymer, Porth. He married Margaret (*d. c.*1775), daughter of Thomas Bevan, a member of a family of staunch Quakers. His eldest son, Lewis (1734–1789), who became minister of the Independent church at Bromyard, Herefordshire, maintained that he was so zealously religious in his latter years that he held meetings on sabbath day evenings from house to house to expound the scriptures, and that he had a pulpit from which he preached whenever he held services in his barn at Hendre Ifan Goch. He was a figure of considerable importance in the nonconformist circles of Upper Glamorgan.

Hopkin was also a prominent and influential figure in the literary revival that occurred in Glamorgan in the early eighteenth century. As a boy he had received instruction in English, writing, and mathematics, and later, by dint of his own efforts, he acquired a reasonably good knowledge of Latin, to which he also added a wide acquaintance with English literature. He also mastered the Welsh bardic craft and played a prominent role in organizing local eisteddfodau. Some of his poems appeared in various eighteenth-century almanacs and in the journal called *Trysorfa Gwybodaeth* (1770), and an elegiac *cywydd* by him was published in Carmarthen in 1769. In 1813 his son-in-law, John Miles, published a collection of his poetry under the title *Y fel gafod*. His verse reflects the resolute efforts he had made to master the intricate rules relating to *cynghanedd* and the twenty-four strict metres. He also composed some verses in English and made splendid Welsh translations of 'The Ballad of Chevy Chase' and of James Thomson's 'The History of Lavinia'. The letters he addressed to his son Lewis reflect a devout and cultured mind and clearly testify to his firm command of English. Among the works he had in his possession were English and Welsh books of a literary and devotional nature, volumes on law and medicine, *The Spectator*, and some Latin and French books. Both Edward Evan (1716–1798) and Edward Williams (Iolo Morganwg; 1747–1826) were instructed by him in the bardic craft.

Hopkin died on 17 November 1771, aged sixty-three, and

was buried with his children and ancestors in Llandy-fodwg churchyard. Among the elegies addressed to him are those composed by Edward Evan in *Afalau'r awen*, and by Iolo Morganwg under the title *Dagrau yr awen* (1772).

Only four of Lewis Hopkin's eleven children lived to maturity. Two of those who died very young were dwarfs, who grew no taller than 32 inches. The girl, named Joan, died of smallpox when she was thirteen. The boy, **Hopkin Hopkin** (1737–1754), known as Hopcyn Bach (Little Hopkin), was exhibited to various groups in London, including some members of the royal family. His weight never exceeded 17 lb, and he died in Glamorgan, 'seemingly of old age' on 19 March 1754, when he was in his eighteenth year (*GM*). His suit, 'court coat', and gauntlet are now kept in the National Museum and Gallery of Wales, Cardiff.

C. W. LEWIS

Sources L. J. Hopkin-James, ed., *Hopkiniaid Morgannwg* (1909), 70–148, 217–81 · G. J. Williams, *Traddodiad llenyddol Morgannwg* (1948), esp. 231–6, 282–91 · C. W. Lewis, 'The literary history of Glamorgan from 1550 to 1770', *Glamorgan county history*, ed. G. Williams, 4: *Early modern Glamorgan* (1974), 535–639, esp. 612–14 · *GM*, 1st ser., 24 (1754), 191 · I. C. Peate, *Guide to the collection of Welsh bygones* (1929), 79 · L. Hopkins, *Y fel gafod* (1813) · Cardiff, MS 4.877,165 [in the autograph of David Jones, Wallington] · *Trysorfa Gwybodaeth* (1770), passim · E. Evan, *Afalau'r awen*, 4th edn (1874) · I. Morganwg [E. Williams], *Dagrau yr awen* (1772)

Hopkins, Charles (1671?–1700), poet and playwright, probably born in Dublin, was the elder son of the Rt Revd Ezekiel *Hopkins (1634–1690), bishop of Derry, and his first wife, Alice (*bap.* 1645, *d.* 1681), the daughter of Samuel Moore and niece of Sir Thomas Vyner, a goldsmith. His younger brother was John *Hopkins (*b.* 1675), the writer. A number of eighteenth-century authorities state that Hopkins was born in Exeter, perhaps in 1664, but the well-documented career of his father, who left London and became the minister of St Mary Arches, Exeter, in 1666, and who accompanied John, Lord Robartes of Truro, to Ireland as the lord lieutenant's chaplain in 1669, makes this account difficult to sustain. On 7 July 1685, moreover, when his age was recorded as fourteen, Hopkins was admitted to Trinity College, Dublin. He continued his education at Queens' College, Cambridge, where he was admitted pensioner on 14 May 1687. He graduated BA in 1688/9.

Following the events of 1688, Hopkins returned to Ireland. Over his loyalties records again differ, but it is probable that he fought for the protestant cause. He subsequently settled in London, where he led a fashionably dissolute life. Although he was admitted to the Middle Temple on 17 August 1695, he moved in predominantly literary circles, counting among his acquaintance William Wycherley, William Congreve, and Thomas Southerne. Hopkins published *Epistolary Poems on Several Occasions* (1694), a collection of verses addressed to friends and patrons, including Charles Sackville, earl of Dorset, and Walter Moyle, and translations of Ovid's *Metamorphoses*, and the *Elegies* of Tibullus, which he dedicated to Anthony Hammond, the poet and pamphleteer. He further published *The History of Love. A Poem in a Letter to a Lady* (1695),

dedicated to Isabella FitzRoy, duchess of Grafton, a selection of renderings from the *Metamorphoses*, and *Heroides*, which attracted Dryden's favour and which was subsequently appended to *Ovid's Art of Love* (1709), a popular compendium of translations and paraphrases by Dryden, Congreve, Nahum Tate, and Arthur Maynwaring; *White-Hall, or, The Court of England* (Dublin, 1698), dedicated to Mary Butler, duchess of Ormond, an effusive but able Williamite panegyric which was reprinted in London the following year as *The Court-Prospect*, and which may have suggested itself to Alexander Pope during the composition of *Windsor-Forest* (1704–13; published 1713); and *The Art of Love: in Two Books: Dedicated to the Ladies* (1700), a paraphrase of parts of *Ars amatoria*, not to be confused with *The History of Love*.

The anonymous prose tract *A Letter to A. H. Esq; Concerning the Stage* (1698), a sensible contribution to the dispute which had arisen from Jeremy Collier's views on the 'immorality' of the English stage, has also been attributed to Hopkins (the initials have been thought to denote Anthony Hammond). He certainly enjoyed a parallel career as a playwright. *Pyrrhus King of Epirus* (published 1695), a tragedy—this was his only dramatic genre—appears to have been written by November 1693, but it is likely that it was first performed at Lincoln's Inn Fields in August 1695, a month when the capital was thinly peopled, as the prologue, by Congreve, elaborates. *Neglected Virtue, or, The Unhappy Conquerour* was performed at Drury Lane to no greater success, probably in February 1696, and published anonymously that same year, under the supervision of Hildebrand Horden, who took the part of Artaban, a Parthian general. *Boadicea Queen of Britain* (published 1697) played to applause at Lincoln's Inn Fields, however, probably in November 1697. Hopkins ascribed its success to the versification; he was, Dryden wrote, 'a poet who writes good verses without knowing how, or why; I mean he writes naturally well, without art or learning, or good sence' (*The Letters of John Dryden*, 1942, 124), a just, if faintly ironic, appreciation of Hopkins's undoubted abilities.

Dryden's comments, in a letter of 7 November 1699, were prompted by the opening night of what was to be Hopkins's final play, *Friendship Improv'd, or, The Female Warriour* (published 1700). It is unlikely that the author saw the production: the dedication to Edward Coke of Norfolk, written in Londonderry and dated 1 November 1699, attests to his poor health. In *A Select Collection of Poems*, John Nichols reprints a none the less characteristically poised hymn written 'about an hour before his death, when in great pain'. Hopkins died in the parish of Templemore, Londonderry, from the effects, it was stated, of a dissipated life, and was buried, presumably in Templemore, on 7 March 1700.

JONATHAN PRITCHARD

Sources A. E. Jones, 'A note on Charles Hopkins (c.1671–1700)', *Modern Language Notes*, 55 (1940), 191–4 · Venn, *Alum. Cant.* · [G. Jacob], *The poetical register, or, The lives and characters of all the English poets*, 2 vols. (1723), vol. 1, pp. 140–41; vol. 2, p. 75 · C. Hopkins, *Epistolary poems: on several occasions* (1694) · C. Hopkins, 'To Edward Coke, of Norfolk, Esq.', *Friendship improv'd, or, The female warriour: a tragedy* (1700), sigs. A2r–A3r · W. Van Lennep and others, eds., *The London stage, 1660–1800*, pt 1: *1660–1700* (1965), 429, 447, 459, 487,

516–17 • J. Nichols, ed., *A select collection of poems*, 2 (1780), 321 • J. Hutchinson, ed., *A catalogue of notable Middle Templars: with brief biographical notices* (1902), 125 • B. Maxwell, 'Notes on Charles Hopkins' *Boadicea*', *Review of English Studies*, 4 (1928), 79–83

Hopkins, Charles Plomer (1861–1922), founder of missions to seamen and trade unionist, was born on 7 March 1861 in Brewster, Massachusetts, USA, the son of an American master mariner employed for many years as a river pilot in Burma, and an English mother, Elizabeth. As a young child he and two sisters were brought to England to stay with maternal Cornish relatives, before being taken to Burma in 1867. In 1869 Hopkins travelled back to England to continue his education. He later recalled the effect on his future ministry of seeing officers' cruelty to the sailors who had befriended him on this voyage.

The dates of his attendance at Falmouth grammar school, then at Trinity College, London, after a spell in Heidelberg, are uncertain. He returned in 1882 to Rangoon as assistant organist at the Anglican pro-cathedral. Hopkins gave as the reason for his refusal of promotion as organist at Madras and of his interest in seamen an encounter with drunken midshipmen on his way to evening prayer. His discovery of their great neglect and his natural rapport with them prompted the bishop of Rangoon to appoint him to the vacant Rangoon seamen's chaplaincy, initially as a layman reading for holy orders. He was ordained deacon in 1884, and priest in 1885. Hopkins soon filled the seamen's church but his championing of seafarers' rights, especially after an incident where an overloaded ship sank, set him at odds with the shipping worthies on the chaplaincy committee. Things came to a head during the short Third Anglo-Burmese War in 1886; the bishop sent Hopkins to the seasonal chaplaincy at Akyab for six months to allow tempers to cool.

In what proved to be two years at Akyab Hopkins ran the parish, and opened a seamen's club. During this period he came to the conclusion that work among seamen could best be achieved by a band of men under religious vows. In 1888 malaria forced him to England for convalescence. He stayed briefly with the Revd Osborne Jay's parochial brotherhood, the ephemeral Society of St Paul (SSP) in Shoreditch. Within months he had taken vows and sailed to Calcutta as port chaplain and prior-provincial of the SSP, soon transmuted into his own Order of St Paul (OSP), recruited from the maritime community it sought to serve. Hopkins opened several seamen's clubs, and also established the Seamen's Friendly Society of St Paul, which grew rapidly, offering seamen-members legal protection as well as a religious rule. His bishop was in no doubt that it was a trade union. Hopkins's litigiousness (some thirty cases in five years) on behalf of seamen incensed local shipowners, some of whom, when other pressure failed, tried to get a young boy to make public accusations against him. This backfired against the instigators, and was dismissed in court, but dogged Hopkins as rumour for the rest of his life.

Hopkins returned to Britain in 1894 to strengthen his community: he opened priories at Barry in south Wales, and Greenwich, and built Alton Abbey in Hampshire as a mother house. By 1900 the Indian priories had been closed. The Colonial Clergy Act (1874) prevented his functioning publicly as a priest in England, rumour probably encouraging the archbishop of Canterbury to withhold his licence. Instead, Hopkins became increasingly involved with the National Seamen's and Firemen's Union (NSFU), meeting its president, Havelock Wilson, in 1900. In 1910 he became secretary to the international committee of seamen's unions, and in this role he announced the start of the first international strike of seamen in June 1911. He kept Hermann Jochade of the International Transport Federation informed. Hopkins toured the country as a major NSFU speaker, and was key NSFU negotiator at its resolution. After the strike was over he was appointed a trustee of the NSFU, serving until 1922 as its troubleshooter and research specialist. His close involvement with merchant navy crewing issues during the First World War was rewarded with a CBE. Two publications by Hopkins, *Altering Plimsoll's Mark* (1913) and *The National Service of British Seamen, 1914–18* (1920), offered detailed statistics and horrific examples to support the campaign to improve safety and conditions at sea. These were concerns he attempted to bring to the attention of seamen themselves with *The Seafarer's Annual* (1921).

Hopkins died at St Mawes, Cornwall, on 24 March 1922, after years of increasingly bad health, and was buried at Alton Abbey. At his death the OSP had dwindled to two brothers and one sister from a peak of around twenty members. It survived as a Benedictine community (and was depicted in fiction as the Order of St George in Compton MacKenzie's *The Altar Steps*). Although largely forgotten by the Church of England, his work influenced the formation of the Roman Catholic Œuvre de Mer (1893), a French organization for work among fishermen, and also of the Apostleship of the Sea (1895). R. W. H. MILLER

Sources R. Miller, 'Charles Plomer Hopkins and the Seamen's Union', MA diss., University of Warwick, 1993 • U. Warwick Mod. RC, NSFU papers • LMA, Family welfare association records, A/FWA/C/D251/1-2 • LPL, Davidson papers, 57, 65, 129 • records, Alton Abbey • *The Messenger* (Dec 1899) • P. F. Anson, *Irish Monthly*, 50 (1922), 404ff. • d. cert.

Likenesses photograph, repro. in *The Seaman* (31 March 1922) • photograph, Alton Abbey

Wealth at death £8754 14s. 2d.: probate, 9 June 1922, CGPLA Eng. & Wales

Hopkins, Edward (c.1602–1657), colonial governor, was probably born in Elton parish, Herefordshire, one of the seven children of Edward Hopkins and his wife, Katherine, who was the sister of Sir Henry Lello, a prosperous overseas trader. A benevolent uncle without children of his own, Sir Henry patronized his sister's family. He probably paid to educate the elder son, Henry, at Cambridge, he dowered his nieces, and he financed Edward's start as a merchant with a gift of £400. At Lello's death in 1629, Edward's brother Henry inherited the manor of Thickoe in Essex and became warden of the Fleet prison and keeper of the palace of Westminster, an ancient and profitable government sinecure that Lello had purchased for about £15,000. Edward himself inherited shares in the East India Company.

At some time in his youth Hopkins rejected 'the mixt fellowships, and other pollutions' of the Church of England and attached himself to the puritan movement (E. Hopkins and W. Goodwin, 'The epistle to the reader', [T.] Hooker, *A Survey of the Summe of Church-Discipline*, 1922). He solidified that connection in 1631 when he married Ann Yale (1615–1698), a young woman noted in puritan circles for her intense piety. She was the daughter of Thomas Yale and Ann Yale (*née* Lloyd), and by 1631 the stepdaughter of Theophilus Eaton, one of the founders of the Massachusetts Bay Company. Unfortunately, Ann Hopkins suffered from debilitating fits of depression that led eventually to insanity. Hopkins and his wife tried various cures, including medicinal waters, but nothing worked and Hopkins was never entirely able to resign himself to 'this sad and great tryall which almost overwhelmes my spiritt' (Edward Hopkins to John Winthrop, 21 June 1648, *Winthrop Papers*, 5.231). Hopkins and his wife had no children.

Hopkins joined the puritan exodus to New England in 1637 and soon settled in Hartford in the Connecticut River valley. He was involved in the emerging government of the river settlements and from 1640 he was elected almost every year as governor or deputy governor of Connecticut, often serving alongside, or in alternation with, John Haynes. He was especially important in developing the colony's economy, in helping to establish the confederation of New England, in negotiating secure boundaries with the Dutch in New Netherland, and in adding the Saybrook settlement to Connecticut. Never entirely happy in New England, Hopkins returned to England in 1652 and was quickly employed by the Commonwealth government as a naval commissioner, in which capacity he impressed sailors, collected medical supplies, paid wages, and inspected timber, among other numerous duties. He performed so well that he was named an admiralty commissioner in 1655, with a rise in salary. That same year, on the death of his brother Henry, he inherited the manor of Thickoe and the wardenship of the Fleet prison. Elected to the House of Commons for Dartmouth in 1656, he served usefully on various committees concerned with trade and the war with Spain but did not sign the protest against the way the parliament had been packed and took no part in the debate about offering a crown to Cromwell.

Hopkins probably contracted tuberculosis in his youth and his health was in rapid decline by late 1656. On 7 March 1657 he wrote his will and within a week, on 13 March, he died. He had amply provided for his 'deere distressed' wife so that she lived out a widowhood of forty years in material comfort until her death on 14 December 1698 (*New England Historical and Genealogical Register*, 38.315–17). Hopkins also left a large trust fund for the education of young men in New England, part of which was used to found the Hopkins Grammar School in New Haven, Connecticut.

Hopkins was fortunate to start life under the patronage of a rich uncle but he greatly improved that advantage. Energetic and competent, he could have wanted no better epitaph than the words of an associate: 'Mr. Hopkins … whom we all know to be a man that makes conscience of his words as well as his actions' (Edward Winslow to John Winthrop, 2 Aug 1644, *Winthrop Papers*, 4.453).

JAMES P. WALSH

Sources T. B. Davis, *Chronicles of Hopkins Grammar School* (1938) · C. Mather, 'Publicola Christianus: the life of Edward Hopkins, esq.; governour of Connecticut-colony', in C. Mather and E. W. Miller, *Magnalia Christi Americana*, ed. K. B. Murdock, new edn (1977), 246–52 · *New England Historical and Genealogical Register*, 38 (1884), 313–17 [wills of Henry Lello, Henry Hopkins, and Edward Hopkins] · *The journal of John Winthrop, 1630–1649*, ed. R. S. Dunn, J. Savage, and L. Yeandle (1996) · *Johnson's wonder-working providence of Sions saviours in New England*, ed. J. F. Jameson (1967) · *The Winthrop papers*, ed. W. C. Ford and others, 6 vols. (1929–92) · D. Pulsifer, ed., *Acts of the commissioners of the united colonies of New England* (1859), vols. 9–10 of *Records of the colony of New Plymouth in New England*, ed. N. B. Shurtleff and D. Pulsifer (1855–61) · *CSP dom.*, 1649–60 · J. H. Trumbull, ed., *The public records of the colony of Connecticut*, 1 (1850) · J. T. Adams, 'Hopkins, Edward', *DAB* · *DNB* · E. Feinstein, 'Hopkins, Edward', *ANB*

Archives Connecticut State Library, Hartford, Connecticut archives | Mass. Hist. Soc., Winthrop MSS

Wealth at death £1476 15s. 4d. in New England; plus English estate: Davis, *Chronicles*, appendix 2

Hopkins, Edward John (1818–1901), organist, born at Westminster on 30 June 1818, was the son of George Hopkins (1789–1869), a clarinet player. He was also a cousin of Edward Hopkins (1818–1842), organist of Armagh Cathedral, and of John Larkin Hopkins (1819–1873), organist of Rochester Cathedral. John Hopkins (1822–1900), organist of Rochester Cathedral, and Thomas Hopkins (*d. c.*1893), organ builder, were his brothers. After serving as a chorister at the Chapel Royal, St James's, London, from 1826 to 1834, Hopkins was organist in turn of Mitcham church, Surrey (from 1834), of St Peter's, Islington (from 1838), and of St Luke's, Berwick Street, Soho (from 1841). He twice won the Gresham prize medal, for his anthems 'Out of the deep' (1838) and 'God is gone up' (1840).

In October 1843 Hopkins was elected organist at the Temple Church, London, where he remained for fifty-five years. In 1845 he married Sarah Lovett, and in the course of time they had four sons and five daughters. He became a member of the Royal Society of Musicians in 1851, and the following year he was made an associate of the Philharmonic Society; he became a member of the society in 1864. He was also one of the founders of the College of Organists, a fellow of the Royal College of Organists, and one of the original members of the Musical Association. He later became a professor of organ at the Royal Normal College for the Blind in Norwood.

Hopkins's compositions included some 160 chants and hymn tunes, and he was one of the first to issue a series of elaborate arrangements for the organ. For the services at the Temple Church he arranged and edited a *Book of Responses*, and a collection of chants, all of which were incorporated in the *Temple Church Choral Service Book* (1867) and the *Temple Psalter* (1883). His historical prefaces to the Temple service books contained much scholarly research. He also edited Purcell's organ music and several volumes for the Musical Antiquarian Society, and contributed many articles on music to the press. Hopkins was a recognized authority on organ construction, and was perhaps best known for his book *The Organ, its History and Construction* (1855).

Hopkins received the honorary degree of MusD from the archbishop of Canterbury in 1882 and from the University of Toronto in 1886. On completing his jubilee at the Temple Church in 1893 he received a valuable testimonial from the benchers, and on his retirement in 1898 he was made honorary organist. Hopkins died at his home, 23 St Augustine Road, Camden Square, London, on 4 February 1901, and was buried five days later in Hampstead cemetery. His musical career encompassed performing at both the coronation of William IV in 1831 and Queen Victoria's diamond jubilee celebrations in 1897.

J. C. BRIDGE, rev. NILANJANA BANERJI

Sources C. W. Pearce, *Life and works of E. J. Hopkins* (1910) · *New Grove* · Grove, *Dict. mus.* · J. E. West, *Cathedral organists past and present* (1899) · Brown & Stratton, *Brit. mus.* · D. Baptie, *A handbook of musical biography* (1883)
Archives BL, letters to F. G. Edwards, Egerton MS 3092
Wealth at death £4032 19s. 2d.: resworn probate, May 1901, *CGPLA Eng. & Wales*

Hopkins, (Jane) Ellice (1836–1904), social purity campaigner, was born on 30 October 1836 at Cambridge, the youngest daughter of the four children of William *Hopkins (1793–1866), geologist and mathematician, and his second wife, Caroline Frances Boys (1799–1881). Brought up in the academic milieu of university life, she was educated at home by her parents. Her mother was an accomplished musician, although Hopkins attributed most of her own intellectual powers and oratorical ability to the scientific prowess of her father. She spent much time as a young woman in the company of Arthur Tennyson on family holidays at Farringford and Freshwater, where she also became a friend of the photographer Julia Margaret Cameron.

Sharp-witted and deeply sensitive, Hopkins remained a devout high-church spinster throughout her life. A heavily incarnational theology informed her interpretation of moral purity in significant ways, but commitment to practical reform superseded any form of religious denominationalism. Her social activism can be grouped into three broad phases. She initially entered public life as an ardent evangelist during the late 1850s, organizing numerous Bible classes and mothers' meetings, and founding a men's mission hall at Barnwell, near Cambridge. After the death of her father in 1866, she moved with her mother to Percy House, Brighton, and immersed herself in a second aspect of urban philanthropy—rescue work. She became involved with the Albion Hill Home for prostitutes, writing several fund-raising booklets for the venture. In 1872 she met the medical specialist and sexual radical James Hinton (1822–1875), an unlikely influence upon her own moral austerity, but whose entreaty to expand her endeavours against the sexual degradation of young women into a national campaign swayed the future direction of her reform efforts. The undue emphasis placed on Hinton in subsequent accounts has tended to minimalize the contribution of other, more long-standing figures in Hopkins's personal and professional life. Sarah Robinson (b. 1834), joint collaborator with her in establishing the Soldier's Institute at Portsmouth in 1874, was an innovative rescue worker whose approach affected Hopkins's own methods considerably. Bishop George Wilkinson, her spiritual mentor for over twenty years, and Annie Ridley, her closest lifelong friend, to whom she was devoted, were also frequently acknowledged as inspirational to her work.

Hopkins's success as a religious and political activist and organizer was unquestionable. In 1876 she undertook a gruelling tour of British towns, recruiting thousands of middle-class Christian women into the Ladies' Association for the Care of Friendless Girls. The associations stimulated several related female initiatives, such as the National Union of Women Workers. Hopkins's presentation of prostitution as a national moral outrage indicated a willingness to contemplate increased state legislation in the regulation of vice. She was instrumental in the passing of the Industrial Schools Amendment Act of 1880, which advocated reallocating brothel children into approved reform schools, a coercive strategy which earned her much criticism from feminist contemporaries. More popularly, she canvassed support for the Criminal Law Amendment Act of 1885, which raised the age of sexual consent from thirteen to sixteen years.

Hopkins's non-palliative, preventive approach to rescue work incorporated a radical attack upon the prevailing sexual double standard. Her essay, *A plea for the wider action of the Church of England in the prevention of the degradation of women*, submitted to convocation in July 1879, condemned ecclesiastical indifference to the plight of fallen women, challenging men to take equal responsibility for their own moral conduct. In a climate charged with scandalous revelations of child prostitution and trafficking in women, she gained unprecedented clerical support for a national agency committed to the promotion of male chastity. The resulting 1883 inauguration of the White Cross Society, co-founded by Hopkins with Bishop Joseph Lightfoot of Durham, represented the culmination of her moral reform. This concluding phase of activism established her as a major exponent and orchestrator of social purity education. Between 1883 and 1888 she addressed controversial mass meetings of men from Newcastle to Cardiff. Combining Christian morality with popular medical science, she articulated a discourse of moral Darwinism which interpreted the individual struggle against the sins of the flesh through an evolutionary schema. Personal virtue was construed as vital to imperial advance, with economic and political supremacy contingent upon the superior morality of the British people. Her polemic on male impurity yielded results which earned her the open admiration of many eminent churchmen. Bishop Lightfoot described her as having done 'the work of ten men in ten years' (Barrett, 103) and Henry Scott Holland wrote effusively of her spellbinding eloquence. Through the organizational edifice of the White Cross she gained an international reputation, writing more than forty separate titles relating to personal chastity, the sanctity of marriage, and the centrality of Christian family life. Suffering from chronic sciatica and nervous exhaustion, she was forced to retire from public life in 1888. This did not diminish the publication rate of her writings: more than 2 million of her purity pamphlets were still in circulation in 1910. In addition to prescriptive and educational literature, of which *True Manliness* (1883) was the most popular, she compiled a book of meditations for the sick and composed two volumes of poetry, *English Idylls and other Poems* being her first publication in 1865. During her final years of ill health she wrote two companion titles, *The Power of Womanhood* (1899) and *The Story of Life* (1902), the latter a remarkable attempt at early sex education. In August 1903 Hopkins suffered an attack of aphasia from which she never fully recovered. She died on 21 August 1904 from cerebral apoplexy at her home, 5 Belle Vue Gardens, Brighton.

Dominant interpretations of Hopkins's moral puritanism belie the radical implications of her sexual agenda. Her sexual politics emerged as a contending force in the regulation of late Victorian morality, forging an effective coalition between religious expectations of chastity and feminist demands for the elimination of the sexual double standard.   SUE MORGAN

Sources R. M. Barrett, *Ellice Hopkins: a memoir*, ed. H. S. Holland (1907) · J. E. Hopkins, *Work in Brighton* (1877) · J. E. Hopkins, *Man and woman: the Christian ideal* (1883) · J. E. Hopkins, *True manliness* (1883) · J. E. Hopkins, *The power of womanhood, or, Mothers and sons* (1899) · E. J. Bristow, *Vice and vigilance: purity movements in Britain since 1700* (1977) · J. R. Walkowitz, *Prostitution and Victorian society: women, class and the state* (1980) · F. Mort, *Dangerous sexualities: medico-moral politics in England since 1830* (1987) · L. Bland, *Banishing the beast: English feminism and sexual morality, 1885–1914* (1995) · S. Jeffreys, *The spinster and her enemies: feminism and sexuality, 1880–1930* (1985) · d. cert.
Archives LPL, letters to A. C. Tait and related papers
Likenesses photograph, repro. in Barrett, *Ellice Hopkins*, frontispiece
Wealth at death £793 6s. 5d.: probate, 24 Sept 1904, *CGPLA Eng. & Wales*

Hopkins, Esek (1718–1802), revolutionary naval officer, was born on 26 April 1718 in Providence, Rhode Island, the sixth of nine children of William Hopkins (*d.* 1738), farmer, and his wife, Ruth, daughter of Samuel Wilkinson and his wife, Plain. He spent his youth working on his father's farm and received little formal education. Upon his father's death, he suddenly had to make his own way in life. As two of his brothers, John and Samuel Hopkins, were masters of their own trading vessels, he also became a seafarer. Soon he was commander of a merchant ship, sailing mostly to the West Indies, and was widely recognized to be a master mariner and astute businessman. On 28 November 1741 he married Desire Burroughs; they made their home in Newport until 1748, then moved to Providence. They had ten children. During the Seven Years' War, Hopkins was a privateer, and seized a number of rich French prizes. With his wealth he purchased a

Esek Hopkins (1718–1802), by unknown engraver, pubd 1776 (after Wilkinson)

farm in North Providence, but continued to make voyages to the West Indies and Africa until 1772. At that time he gave up the sea and retired to his farm.

In the 1770s Hopkins emerged a defender of Rhode Island's rights against Britain. His experience in military and maritime affairs, plus the fact that he was the brother of a former governor, Stephen Hopkins, caused the general assembly on 4 October 1775 to give him the rank of brigadier-general and put him in charge of Rhode Island's defences. Meantime, the continental congress in Philadelphia was creating a national army and navy, with Stephen Hopkins serving on the naval committee. Not surprisingly, the committee recommended to congress that Esek Hopkins be appointed commander-in-chief of the new navy, with the title commodore. On 22 December 1775 the recommendation was accepted. In early January 1776 Hopkins reached Philadelphia and took charge of eight small vessels, including his flagship *Alfred* (24 guns), that constituted the continental navy. On 5 January he was ordered by congress to attack the enemy vessels of Lord Dunmore in Chesapeake Bay, to cruise along the southern coast, and finally to eliminate British naval power in Rhode Island waters. He was delayed by ice in the Delaware River, and did not sail until 17 February. Believing enemy forces in the Chesapeake too strong to overcome, he took advantage of a discretionary clause in his orders to set a course for Nassau, New Providence Island, Bahamas. There, in a successful amphibious operation, he captured a large store of ammunition and guns that were sorely needed by the American army.

On 17 March, Hopkins sailed for Rhode Island, experiencing an uneventful voyage until 4 April. That day, near the east end of Long Island Sound, he captured the enemy schooner *Hawk* and bomb brig *Bolton* without the loss of a single man. On 6 April, however, he fell in with the *Glasgow*, a twenty-gun frigate commanded by Captain Tyringham Howe. Although Hopkins's ships outgunned him, Howe fought courageously, damaging a number of American vessels before escaping into Newport, Rhode Island. Two days later Hopkins brought his fleet into New London, Connecticut, where he was met by a storm of criticism for his putative disobedience of orders and for allowing the *Glasgow* to escape. In June congress summoned him to Philadelphia to explain himself. Although he was warmly defended by John Adams and other New England delegates, he was so truculent in his own defence that congress on 16 August 1776 voted to censure him. He returned to Rhode Island and attempted to organize another fleet, but his inability to compete with privateers for manpower and supplies, and his anger and ineptitude, finally doomed his efforts. Although a good seaman, he was not an effective naval commander and did not know how to deal with congressmen. In December 1776 the British fleet blockaded his ships in Narraganset Bay, and in early 1777 his officers turned against him, and presented their complaints to congress. He was suspended from command on 14 May, and in January 1778 was dismissed from the service, never again to serve at sea.

Esteemed by New Englanders who believed he had been unfairly treated by congress, Hopkins served in the general assembly of Rhode Island from 1777 to 1786. He was collector of imposts in 1783 and a trustee of Rhode Island College from 1782 until his death. On 26 February 1802 he died, from the effects of a stroke, at his farm on Admiral Street, North Providence, and was buried on 2 March at God's Acre, the family cemetery in North Providence.   PAUL DAVID NELSON

Sources *The correspondence of Esek Hopkins, commander-in-chief of the United States navy, transcribed from the original manuscripts in the library of the Rhode Island Historical Society*, ed. A. S. Beck (1933) • *The letter book of Esek Hopkins, commander-in-chief of the United States navy, 1775–1777, transcribed from the original letter book in the library of the Rhode Island Historical Society*, ed. A. S. Beck (1932) • E. Field, *Esek Hopkins, commander-in-chief of the continental navy during the American Revolution, 1775 to 1778: master mariner, politician, brigadier, general, naval officer and philanthropist* (1898) • W. M. Fowler, 'Hopkins, Esek', ANB • G. W. Allen, *A naval history of the American revolution*, 2 vols. (1913) • W. J. Morgan, *Captains to the northward: the New England captains in the continental navy* (1959) • W. M. Fowler, *Rebels under sail: the American navy during the revolution* (1976) • C. H. Miller, *Admiral number one: some incidents in the life of Esek Hopkins, 1718–1802, first admiral of the continental navy* (1962) • G. H. Preble, 'Esek Hopkins, the first "commander-in-chief" of the American navy, 1775', *United Service*, 12 (1885), 137–46, 300–17
Archives Rhode Island Historical Society, Providence, papers
Likenesses T. Hart, mezzotint, 1776, repro. in Field, *Esek Hopkins* • engraving, pubd 1776 (after Wilkinson), AM Oxf., Hope collection [*see illus.*] • T. J. Heade, oils, *c.*1800–1840, Brown University, Providence, Rhode Island
Wealth at death 200 acres of land and mansion house: will in Field, *Esek Hopkins*, 248

Hopkins, Ezekiel (1634–1690), bishop of Derry, son of John Hopkins, curate of Sanford, and later rector of Pinhoe, Devon, was born at Crediton on 3 December 1634. He was educated first at Merchant Taylors' School from 1646 to 1648, then Magdalen College, Oxford, where he became a chorister in 1649, before matriculating on 19 November 1650 and graduating BA on 17 October 1653. Two years later he became an usher in the college school, and was appointed chaplain of the college in 1656, the year he proceeded MA.

At the restoration of Charles II, Hopkins travelled to London, where he became an assistant to Dr William Spurstow, one of the authors of the Smectymnuus tracts, and at that time minister of St John's, Hackney. Hopkins, who conformed after the Act of Uniformity of 1662, was elected preacher of St Edmund's, Lombard Street, or, according to one authority, St Mary Woolnoth. In 1663 he published a sermon on the death of Grevill. In 1666 Hopkins left charred and smoking London for his home county of Devon, where he was shortly afterwards chosen minister of St Mary Arches, Exeter. In 1668 he published a *Treatise on the vanity of the world*, dedicated to his wife, Alice (*bap.* 1645, *d.* 1681), only daughter of Samuel Moore of London, a niece of London goldsmith Sir Thomas Vyner.

At Exeter the eloquence and wit of Hopkins's preaching attracted the favourable attention of John, Lord Roberts, baron of Truro, who, on being appointed lord lieutenant of Ireland in 1669, made Hopkins his domestic chaplain. On 22 November 1669 Hopkins became archdeacon and treasurer of Waterford, and on 8 December he was instituted as prebendary of Rathmichael, though he was never installed there. His entry into the established church of Ireland was sufficient to protect his career prospects from the rapid decline of Lord Roberts in the king's estimation, and his replacement as chief governor.

On 2 April 1670 Hopkins was appointed dean of Raphoe, and on 29 October in the following year was consecrated bishop there. The same year, 1671, he published a sermon on submission to rulers and religious conformity which he had preached the year before at Christ Church, Dublin. In it, he inveighed against a generation of men who 'thought the debate of a rite, or the mode of discipline, cause enough to warrant arms, and blood, and the ruin of kingdoms' (Greaves, 102). Such sentiments were rather more in keeping with those of the new lord lieutenant, Lord Berkeley, than they were with those of his predecessor. Hopkins resided constantly in his diocese. He was translated to the bishopric of Derry on 11 November 1681. He contributed largely to the adornment of the cathedral of his new diocese, furnishing an organ and handsome communion plate. He also kept a sharp eye out for the discovery of presbyterian plotting.

In 1685 Hopkins married his second wife, Lady Araminta (or Aramintha) Roberts (*bap.* 1655), daughter of his former patron. On the outbreak of the rebellion in support of James II in 1688 Hopkins fled to England, having offended the apprentice boys of Londonderry by suggesting, in company with many of the leading citizens there, and in accordance with his lifelong commitment to the principle of non-resistance, that they reopen the city gates to admit Tyrconnel's garrison. In May 1689 Hopkins was attainted of treason in his absence by the patriot parliament. That September he was elected preacher of the parish church of St Mary Aldermanbury in London. Hopkins died on 19 June 1690, and was buried on the 24th in the church where he then served. He was survived by two sons by his first marriage, Charles *Hopkins and John *Hopkins. His funeral sermon was preached by Dr Richard Tenison, bishop of Clogher. Despite at least one contemporary complaint that Hopkins's preaching style was uninspiring, his works long survived him. A volume of his sermons was published by the bishop of Cork and Ross in 1692, and aside from a number of other volumes an edition of his works appeared in 1701. To these were added in 1712 his *Doctrine of the two covenants*, *Doctrine of the two sacraments*, and *Death disarmed of sting*. An edition of his works was published in four volumes by Josiah Pratt in 1809.

SEAN KELSEY

Sources DNB · J. P. Malcolm, *Anecdotes of the customs of London from the Roman invasion to the year 1700*, 3 vols. (1811), vol. 2, p. 125 · H. J. Lawlor, *The fasti of St Patrick's, Dublin* (1930) · W. A. Phillips, *History of the church of Ireland from the earliest times to the present day*, 3 vols. (1933), vol. 3, pp. 149–50 · J. B. Leslie, *Derry clergy and parishes* (1937) · A. Ford, J. McGuire, and K. Milne, eds., *As by law established: the church of Ireland since the Reformation* (1995) · R. Greaves, *God's other children: protestant nonconformists and the emergence of denominational churches in Ireland, 1660–1700* (1997) · I. McBride, *The siege of Derry in Ulster protestant mythology* (1997)
Likenesses J. Sturt, line engraving, BM, NPG; repro. in E. Hopkins, *Sermons* (1691) · M. Vandergucht, line engraving, BM, NPG; repro. in E. Hopkins, *Death disarmed* (1712)

Hopkins, Sir Frank Henry Edward (1910–1990), naval officer, was born on 23 June 1910 at The Poplars, Maldon Road, Wallington, Surrey, the fourth child and only son of Edward Frank Lumley Hopkins, solicitor, and his wife, Sybil Mary Walrond. He was educated at the Nautical College at Pangbourne, Berkshire, and joined the Royal Navy as a cadet on 16 September 1927. He served as a midshipman in the cruiser *London*, and then in destroyers before qualifying as an observer in 1934, flying from the aircraft-carriers *Furious* and *Courageous*. When war broke out in 1939, he was on the staff of HMS *Peregrine*, the naval observer school at Ford in Sussex. In 1940 he joined 826 naval air squadron, flying Fairey Albacores, covering the Dunkirk evacuation, bombing rail and road communications in Holland, and attacking enemy shipping off Zeebrugge, before operating for five months with Royal Air Force Coastal Command, making night attacks against targets in France, Belgium, and Holland. Hopkins was awarded the DSC in 1941.

In November 1940 his squadron embarked in the aircraft-carrier *Formidable* and sailed for the Mediterranean. On 28 March 1941 no. 826's aircraft made two torpedo attacks on ships of the Italian fleet off Cape Matapan. In a dusk attack, no. 826's aircraft torpedoed and crippled the heavy cruiser *Pola*. This led to a night action in which *Pola* and two more heavy cruisers, *Fiume* and *Zara*, were sunk with considerable loss of life. Hopkins was mentioned in dispatches (1941). On 6 December 1941 Hopkins took command of 830 naval air squadron, which flew Fairey Swordfish from Malta. Night after night he led his squadron on torpedo and bombing strikes which sank thousands of tons of axis shipping, seriously affecting supplies to Rommel's army in north Africa.

Late in January 1942 Hopkins led a striking force through a gale to search for a large enemy convoy on its way to Tripoli. By the time the planes found the convoy they were too short of fuel to attack so they returned to Malta, refuelled, took off again, found the convoy a second time, and sank a 13,000-ton troopship. When Hopkins landed at Hal Far, the naval air station in Malta, just after dawn, he had been in the air for more than twelve hours in flying conditions normally considered impossible. He received an immediate DSO (1942), an award which his squadron thought by no means over-generous.

Hopkins then joined the staff of the British air commission in Washington, DC, and he qualified as a pilot in 1944. As British naval air observer with the US Pacific Fleet, serving in the American carriers USS *Hancock* and *Intrepid*, he was present at the decisive defeat of the Japanese navy in the battle of Leyte Gulf in October 1944. In 1945 he went to the Royal Navy Staff College, Greenwich, London, for two years on the directing staff. He went to Washington again in 1947, for two years as assistant naval air attaché. He was awarded the American Legion of Merit in 1948.

In 1949 Hopkins joined the light fleet aircraft-carrier *Theseus* as commander (air) and served in her in the Korean War from October 1950 until April 1951. Under Hopkins, *Theseus*'s air group was particularly energetic and successful in operations over Korea and in 1950 it won the Boyd trophy, awarded annually for the most outstanding feat of airmanship. Hopkins was again mentioned in dispatches (1950).

From 1951 to 1958 Hopkins was at the Admiralty as deputy director, naval air organization and training; was captain (D) of the 2 training squadron, commanding the destroyer *Myngs*; and was at the Admiralty again as director, naval air warfare. He also recommissioned the carrier *Ark Royal*, after a long and extensive refit, successfully commanding her through a difficult period with new aircraft, radar, and flight deck equipment. He then went to the Britannia Royal Naval College, Dartmouth, as the first naval aviator and the first public-school entry officer to command the college (1958–60). In 1960 (the year he was promoted rear-admiral) he became flag officer, flying training, and in 1962 flag officer, aircraft-carriers.

Having become vice-admiral in 1962, in 1963 Hopkins was appointed deputy chief of naval staff and fifth sea lord. He now had to fight for the navy's future air power. The Royal Air Force set out to destroy plans for the projected new carrier, known as CVA 01, claiming that shore-based aircraft could do all that carrier aircraft could do, and more. When CVA 01 was cancelled in February 1966, the first sea lord and the first lord both resigned. Hopkins wanted to follow suit but was prevailed upon to stay and became commander-in-chief, Portsmouth, which he said was the most miserable appointment of his life. He was promoted admiral in 1966 and retired from the navy in

1967. He was made commander of the Swedish order of the Sword in 1954, appointed CB in 1961, and made KCB in 1964.

Hopkins worked his squadron hard, but with his reputation for gallantry and endurance he could ask anything of his aircrew. He was always introspective, and his experience with no. 830, when he risked his life almost every night, left its mark on him, but he had great personal charm and was an excellent dinner-table companion. He was a keen and expert helmsman and a member of the Royal yacht squadron.

Hopkins was a handsome man, even into old age, with sharp features, high cheekbones, and a keen gaze, quick to sum up a newcomer to ship or squadron. Although the marriage was not registered, about 1933 he married Joan Mary, *née* Ashwin (*d.* 1982), widow of Lieutenant-Commander John Standring RN. They had one daughter. They were divorced in 1937 and in 1939 he married Lois Barbara, daughter of James Robert Cook, of Cheam, Surrey, director of Cook, Hammond, and Kell, cartographers and printers. They had no children. Lois died in 1987 and he married in 1988 Georgianna Priest, the widow of an American naval officer he had met during the war. Latterly he lived half the year in Devon near Dartmouth, where his home was Kingswear Court Lodge, and half in Hawaii, USA. Hopkins died on 14 April 1990 in Hawaii, after a road accident there.   JOHN WINTON, *rev.*

Sources *Daily Telegraph* (18 April 1990) · squadron records, Fleet Air Arm Museum, Yeovilton, Somerset · memorial service address by Captain Desmond Vincent-Jones, 26 June 1990 [privately available] · *The Times* (20 April 1990) · *CGPLA Eng. & Wales* (1991) · personal knowledge (1996) · private information (1996)
Wealth at death £272,460: probate, 22 Nov 1991, *CGPLA Eng. & Wales*

Hopkins, Sir Frederick Gowland (1861–1947), biochemist, was born on 20 June 1861 at 16 Marine Parade, Eastbourne, the son of Frederick Hopkins, bookseller, and his wife, Elizabeth Stafford, *née* Gowland. From the age of six he went to Grove House School at Eastbourne. Hopkins's father died while he was still an infant, so that he had no memory of him; he was later given his father's telescope and microscope, and his papers relating to his membership of an amateur natural science group.

In 1871 Hopkins and his mother went to live with her mother and brother, James Gowland, a city merchant. He built a house in Enfield where they lived for twenty years. Hopkins attended the City of London School from 1871, but at fourteen he left, to play truant for several weeks, after which he was sent to a private school. On leaving, he spent six months in an insurance office before being articled for three years to a consulting analyst in the City, where he was conscious of learning only something of an analyst's technique and dexterity, although these he may have undervalued. With a small legacy from his paternal grandfather he entered himself at twenty for a course in chemistry at the Royal School of Mines, South Kensington, under Edward Frankland, and then, after a spell of

Sir Frederick Gowland Hopkins (1861–1947), by Meredith Frampton, 1938

analytical practice with his son, Percy Faraday Frankland, he studied at University College, London, for the associateship of the Institute of Chemistry. His performance in this examination brought him to the notice of Thomas Stevenson, Home Office analyst and lecturer at Guy's Hospital on forensic medicine. Stevenson offered Hopkins a post as his assistant, which he eagerly accepted. During his engagement in this more interesting and responsible analytical work Hopkins began to read for his BSc (London), cramming himself for matriculation and the subsequent examinations by private study, largely on daily journeys between Enfield and Guy's. He graduated in 1890, having in 1888 entered Guy's Hospital as a medical student, being immediately awarded the Gull research studentship. In 1891 he published in *Guy's Hospital Reports* a method for determining uric acid in urine, which remained standard practice for many years. Meanwhile, the work on uric acid probably drew his attention to the scale pigments in the wings of the Pieridae, a large family of common white and yellow butterflies. Years before, when he was seventeen, he had published in *The Entomologist* some observations on the purple vapour ejected by the bombardier beetle, which, as he later claimed, had made him already 'a biochemist at heart'. A preliminary note on the pigments of the Pieridae and their suggested relation to uric acid was published in 1889, and the full paper was communicated by E. R. Lankester to the Royal Society and published in their *Philosophical Transactions* of 1895. Later work, by Dr Heinrich Wieland and others, did not substantiate Hopkins's early suggestions concerning the relation of these pigments to uric acid, but towards the end of his life he returned to the subject.

After medical qualification in 1894 Hopkins became an assistant in the department of physiology at Guy's, making contacts and friendships for life with E. H. Starling, W. M. Bayliss, and others. To make ends meet he undertook a number of other part-time duties, including one which contributed to the formation of the Clinical Research Association. He found time, however, for important researches on halogen derivatives of proteins and on the crystallization of the albumins of blood serum and egg white—the latter published later, after his removal to Cambridge.

This decisive step in his career was taken in 1898 when Michael Foster invited Hopkins to become lecturer at Cambridge on chemical physiology—an aspect of the subject which had then fallen into neglect. In that year, on 14 April, he married Jessie Ann (1869–1956), daughter of the late Edward William Stevens, ship's fitter, of Ramsgate. There were three children: a son who entered the medical profession and two daughters, one of whom was the archaeologist Jacquetta *Hawkes (1910–1996).

The Cambridge lectureship, however, carried but a meagre stipend for a married man and a prospective father, and Hopkins found it necessary to supplement his income by tutorial work at Emmanuel College, which later expanded into a full tutorship. This was in addition to his primary obligation of setting up a vigorous and inspiring course of advanced study on chemical physiology, and left little time for research. He used this, however, to follow up, in logical succession from an initial chance observation in his practical class, discoveries of the nature of the reagent in the Adamkiewicz colour test for proteins, of the amino acid tryptophane responsible for the reaction, and then of the nature of the amino acids necessary in a mammalian diet for maintenance and growth. Thus he was led to a clear apprehension that a diet containing only purified proteins, fats, carbohydrates, and salts, in whatever proportions and abundance, will not suffice for complete animal nutrition, but that traces, too small to contribute to energy value, of then unknown substances present in natural, fresh foods—now known as vitamins—were also essential. Similar observations made earlier by others had been overlooked and forgotten, and Hopkins's own work on the matter suffered interruption for a year, at a critical period, through a temporary failure of health. It was generally recognized, however, that the paper which he published in 1912 in the *Journal of Physiology* was of primary importance in giving precision and focus to ideas in this field and to methods of exploring them. The award of a Nobel prize in 1929 jointly to Hopkins and Eijkman of Holland, was widely applauded.

Hopkins's lectureship had been raised to a readership in 1902, but the growing needs of his family had made the tutorial post at Emmanuel College a necessary addition. During his year of illness in 1910, due to overwork, relief from this position came with the offer from Trinity College of a praelectorship, with no formal obligation but his own researches. Hopkins was thus enabled to embark on the studies in which during the rest of his life he endeavoured to unravel successive strands in the skein of intermediary metabolism—the complex of linked chemical reactions, catalysed by intracellular enzymes, which provides the physical and energetic basis for the process of life in general and of cellular respiration in particular.

In 1914 the removal of Cambridge physiology to a fine new building enabled Hopkins, who now became professor of biochemistry, to expand into its former quarters, from the almost incredibly restricted and unsuitable ones to which his work had until then been confined. In later years he gathered a school of younger investigators, who in turn had a far-reaching effect on the development of biochemistry in this country. A much wider opportunity came in 1921 when the trustees of the late Sir William Dunn furnished money for a new institute of biochemistry at Cambridge and the endowment of a chair in that subject, which Hopkins was to hold until 1943.

Except in the one year already mentioned, Hopkins, although small and very light in physique, enjoyed unusually good health for most of his long life. During his last few years, however, he suffered from increasing disabilities, including the loss of eyesight. He continued, however, until it was no longer physically possible, to go to his laboratory and there to pursue his researches with the help of others. If he had been asked to define the central aim of his life's work, he would have named the exploration of the chemistry of intermediary metabolism, and the establishment of biochemistry as a separate discipline concerned with this active chemistry of the life process, and not merely with its fuels and end products. He lived to see the acceptance of this aim by a great army of investigators in all countries, and the identification of the parts played even by many of the vitamins in different cycles of this dynamic biochemistry.

Hopkins was a member of the first Medical Research Committee, appointed in 1913; he was knighted in 1925 and appointed to the Order of Merit in 1935. He was elected FRS in 1905, was awarded a royal medal in 1918, the Copley medal in 1926, and was president (1930–35). He was president of the British Association in 1933, and received many honorary degrees, including the DSc of Oxford (1922) and ScD of Cambridge (1933). He died at his home, Saxmeadham, 71 Grange Road, Cambridge, on 16 May 1947.   H. H. DALE, *rev.*

Sources H. H. Dale, *Obits. FRS*, 6 (1948–9), 115–45 · 'Autobiography', in J. Needham and E. Baldwin, *Hopkins and biochemistry* (1949), 1–26 · W. J. O'Connor, *British physiologists, 1885–1914* (1991), 19–21, 35–41 · J. Needham, 'Sir Frederick Gowland Hopkins', *Notes and Records of the Royal Society*, 17 (1962), 117–62 · *The Times* (17 May 1947), 7e · *The Times* (27 May 1947), 7e · *The Times* (2 June 1947), 7b · M. Dixon and C. Rimington, *Nature*, 160 (1947), 44–8 · *Journal of the Royal Society of Arts*, 95 (1946–7), 471 · E. Mellanby, 'Hopkins memorial lecture', *JCS* (1948), 713–22 · b. cert. · m. cert. · d. cert. · *CGPLA Eng. & Wales* (1948)

Archives Bodl. Oxf., corresp; relating to Society for the Protection of Science and Learning · CUL, corresp. and working papers · Medical Research Council, London, corresp. and papers · Wellcome L., MSS | CAC Cam., corresp. with A. V. Hill | FILM BFI NFTVA, documentary footage

Likenesses G. Henry, oils, 1926, U. Cam., department of biochemistry · E. Kennington, pencil drawing, 1926, Trinity Cam. · W. Stoneman, photograph, 1932, NPG · M. Frampton, portrait, 1938, RS [*see illus.*] · photogravure photograph, 1938 (after M. Frampton), Wellcome L. · E. Kapp, charcoal drawing, 1943, FM Cam. · E. Kapp, drawing, 1943, Barber Institute of Fine Arts, Birmingham · J. Palmer Clarke, photograph, Wellcome L. · F. A. Swaine Ltd, photograph, Wellcome L. · photogravure photograph, Wellcome L.

Wealth at death £14,021 7s. 7d.: probate, 12 April 1948, *CGPLA Eng. & Wales*

Hopkins, George (1620–1666). *See under* Hopkins, William (1647–1700).

Hopkins, Gerard Manley (1844–1889), poet, was born on 28 July 1844 at 87 The Grove, Stratford, London, eldest of the nine children of Manley Hopkins (1818–1897), average adjuster in marine insurance and consul-general in London for Hawaii, and his wife, Catherine (Kate; 1821–1920), daughter of Dr John Simm Smith, a fashionable family doctor, and his wife, Maria.

Youth, 1844–1863 Having left school at fourteen, and having made his way in the City of London by hard work after his father's career had failed, Gerard's father Manley started his own firm of average adjusters, about the time of his eldest son's birth. Business prospered, and Gerard was brought up in a comfortable social position and home, usually with three or four servants, though he did not mention in letters his father's job and hard path to success, and it was never assumed that he would carry on the business (his nearest brother, Cyril, fulfilled that role). His lifelong silence on his father's Hawaiian connection is also remarkable. (Manley often exaggerated the importance of this largely honorary position, which had comic and embarrassing aspects.)

Always small and delicate (at Oxford he was known as Poppy), Gerard was his mother's favourite, and was tutored by his aunts: Annie, Manley's sister, whose mawkish portrait of him, aged ten, is in the National Portrait Gallery; and Maria, Kate's sister, who encouraged his sketching, particularly of countryside and trees. Another early interest was Gothic architecture, stimulating him to focus on detail. It was a refined and lively bourgeois household, with parlour music, dramatics, humour, and poetry; Manley wrote poetry and was an avid reader who published several books and articles on insurance and a wide variety of other subjects, and passed on his mental voracity to Gerard. The family religion was conventional and domestic, moderately high-church, mainstream Anglican in its repudiation of Roman practices; there were family prayers and Bible readings daily.

In 1852 the increasingly prosperous Hopkins family moved to Oak Hill Park, Hampstead, comfortably near the countryside, the heath, with its ponds for swimming, and central London, whose cultural resources, particularly art exhibitions and churches, Gerard appreciated. Their parish church was the nearby St John's, a classical building of 1745, which Hopkins, with his Gothic prejudices, found 'dreary', and whose clergy he made fun of. After two years

Gerard Manley Hopkins (1844–1889), by Forshaw & Coles, 1880

at a private school, Hopkins in 1854 started boarding at Highgate School, whose headmaster, Dr Dyne, emphasized classics, ancient history, and divinity in preference to modern studies; though narrow, the syllabus provided Hopkins with a good grounding in the elements of language and poetry. Another major influence at school was an unconventional younger boy, Marcus Clarke, a high-spirited and gifted writer, who passed on to Hopkins his enthusiasm for contemporary English artists, especially Frederick Walker and J. E. Millais. Hopkins started writing poetic descriptions of nature and weather effects, and poems of many types and lengths. 'The Escorial' won the school poetry prize in 1860, and shortly before he left school his 'Winter with the Gulf Stream', filled with lively but discrete images, was published in the national journal *Once a Week*.

Hopkins's experimentalism, stands on principle, and rebelliousness were remembered by schoolfriends, particularly his battles with the headmaster, once because for a bet he had stopped taking liquids for three weeks. Several times threatened with expulsion, in the sixth form he became a day boy to avoid further trouble, but nevertheless won prizes and the school exhibition for a university. When nineteen, at his second attempt, he gained another exhibition, to Balliol College, Oxford.

Oxford, 1863–1867 Hopkins's moral and intellectual being was formed at Oxford University. He made deep and lasting friendships there, particularly with Robert Bridges and Mowbray Baillie, his two major correspondents in adulthood. The letters and diaries he wrote soon after his arrival in Oxford reflect his energy and breadth of interests, including frenetic socializing between studies; the voice is youthfully patronizing and self-congratulatory, in the manner of a *Punch* social cartoonist, a livelier version of what his professional artist brothers, Arthur and Everard, became.

Hopkins had gone up to Oxford in April 1863 intending to be a painter, although his surviving drawings suggest only an ordinary middle-class talent. He followed Ruskin's precepts of accurate and close observation of nature's details, and in his journal's highly distinctive verbal descriptions showed his intense desire to explore and record not merely the look but the behaviour of natural phenomena. Closely associated with this in his early diaries and journals was his creative apprenticeship in linguistics, building a useful vocabulary hoard while forming groups of words and etymological notes that go well beyond contemporary theories of onomatopoeia and word origins; in particular he listed similar sounding words of related meanings, and (several years before coining the term 'inscape') he was obsessed with the inscapes of individual words and the things they stood for.

After passing responsions, the elementary undergraduate test, Hopkins spent five terms working for classical honours moderations, which focused on the detail of major texts and accuracy of language; he was placed in the first class, and in Lent term 1865 entered Oxford's chief honours school, that of *literae humaniores*, or Greats—a pre-eminently philosophical school, with a preponderance of Plato's *Republic* and Aristotle's *Ethics*. Under Benjamin Jowett, his rigorous tutor for Greats, Hopkins became fluent in Latin and Greek, practised and spirited in thinking and writing about language, art, and poetry, and more careful about his own poetic style and exactness of expression. As a disciple of Ruskin and Pugin in their medievalist battle for Gothic architecture against Greek servility and lack of aesthetic and moral imagination, he was critical of several aspects of classical civilization, and never assimilated the methods of modern critical scholarship advocated by Jowett. Hopkins rejected also the radical social ideas of T. H. Green, Balliol's chief teacher of philosophy, who advocated personal involvement in political questions; to Hopkins, inward virtue was of pre-emptive importance. For one term Hopkins was coached by W. H. Pater of Brasenose, but direct influence is not obvious.

Although Hopkins's studies deeply affected the formal and aesthetic theories and practices of his mature poems, most of his undergraduate poetry is, though competent, not distinctly personal, and is largely derived from the Romantic poets. The first poems and dramatic fragments Hopkins wrote at Oxford are bewildering in range and number, in speed of composition, and in their intermingling with his social life. This wealth of activity and interest came to be seen by Hopkins as promiscuity; he became

afraid that he was a natural 'blackguard' (Hopkins, *Letters*, 139; *Further Letters*, 242), his self-indulgent life needing external control. Reacting strongly against contemporary liberalism and Darwinism, in his first fortnight at Oxford Hopkins had turned against the dangerously modern ethos of Balliol to the eminent high-churchmen Canon H. P. Liddon and Dr E. B. Pusey, to both of whom he confessed. He became familiar with ritualist doctrines and practices close to Roman Catholicism, making detailed daily notes of all his sins.

Most of Hopkins's 'sins' show over-scrupulousness, and that he was mainly, but not exclusively, attracted by his own sex—hardly unusual in public schools and universities of the 1860s—though no sexual acts with other people are recorded. Throughout his life he was particularly susceptible to people's looks. His close relationships were all with men, usually students with high-church leanings. He became infatuated with a sixteen-year-old schoolboy relative of Bridges, Digby Dolben, who flamboyantly leant towards Rome; Hopkins copied out Dolben's poems and took on some of his enthusiasms, particularly those for Savonarola and the Virgin Mary, before whose picture Hopkins kissed the floor each morning. He started writing poems about and practising painful physical austerities as helpful for the soul. His confessor Liddon had forbidden contact with Dolben, but Hopkins could not help continually mentioning him to friends and writing sonnets of longing and separation. He became despondent and inert, and copied into his diary John Clare's poem 'I am! yet what I am who cares or knows', which anticipates his own sonnet of 1855, 'To Seem the Stranger'. Two years later, on Dolben's death by drowning, Hopkins wrote: 'there can very seldom have happened the loss of so much beauty (in body and mind and life) … seldom … in the whole world' (Hopkins, *Letters*, 16–17).

Hopkins decided to give up the prospect of becoming a professional artist, as the passions would be too strongly involved. But his poetry writing continued, and several poems show stages of his conversion to Roman Catholicism: a Pre-Raphaelite picture of professional religious life ('The Habit of Perfection'), or religious doubt, asking similar questions to Tennyson's in *In Memoriam* ('Nondum'), or self-disgust ('Trees by their Yield'), or John Henry Newman's image of the Church of England as *The Half-Way House* between atheism and Roman Catholicism.

Hopkins's conversion anguished his parents—'O Gerard, my darling boy, are you indeed gone from me?' wrote his father (Hopkins, *Further Letters*, 97)—but, to Hopkins's surprise, they soon came to accept it, as they did later on when Gerard's sister Milicent became a high-church Anglican nun (none of his brothers retained a religious faith beyond adolescence). In 1867 Hopkins obtained first-class honours in Greats, and was offered a teaching post at the Oratory School, Birmingham, by Newman, who had received Hopkins into the Roman Catholic church, and whose spiritual autobiography, *Apologia pro vita sua*, written to gain converts of Hopkins's type, had influenced him. Hopkins was unhappy as a teacher—the only secular job he ever had—finding the self-discipline unpalatable, with few opportunities to continue self-education or to see Oxford friends. He decided to remedy feelings of aimlessness and the sordidness of ordinary life by becoming a professional religious. He burned his poems—'slaughter of the innocents', he called this act (Hopkins, *Journals and Papers*, 165)—though he had previously sent copies of them all to Bridges, and three months later remarked with pride on a peculiar beat he had introduced into his new verse. He chose the most severely disciplined of the Counter-Reformation orders, the Society of Jesus.

First, however, following the Romantic lead of Wordsworth and Ruskin, Hopkins took a walking holiday in Switzerland. There his uncensored journal writing achieved heights of liveliness and inventive imagery, using the new terms 'inscape' and 'instress'. His account includes human scenes with women as well as alpine descriptions, and makes one regret the controlled, comparatively limited subject range in his journal writing once he had become a Jesuit.

Early Jesuit years, 1868–1874 The appeal of the Society of Jesus to Hopkins was its highly structured system, as manifested in St Ignatius's spiritual exercises, of conquering oneself and regulating one's life, a counter to the undergraduate guilt and insecurity he still experienced after his conversion. But a Jesuit seminary was an encompassing institution with tensions of a community life which constricted individual personality and self; normal privacy and emotional sustenance were feared. The exercises were unsuited to his temperament, which was predisposed to melancholia. Hopkins was considered by his fellow Jesuits odd, whimsical, eccentric, too delicate; few appreciated him. He was naïvely surprised at being forbidden to take Swinburne's *Poems and Ballads* with him into the noviciate at Manresa House, Roehampton.

Hopkins resolved to keep only weather notes, but fortunately, in his second year, the journal expanded considerably into natural observations, stories, and accounts of words, dreams, and visits. In September 1870 he took his vows, and moved north to the philosophate, at Stonyhurst College, in rural Lancashire. In spite of his pessimism about the wintry climate, recording and dwelling on deaths obsessively, and finding the course hard and wearisome, while everyday life was 'as dank as ditchwater' (Hopkins, *Further Letters*, 113), his journal's extended descriptions of Stonyhurst's natural surroundings record joyful experiences, particularly around its three beautiful rivers, though most show him as lonely and intense. His dull professional life contrasted with the vivid seascapes bejewelling the journals he wrote during community holidays on the Isle of Man, excitedly conveying intense discoveries and images of the textures, shapes, and colours of sea water. 'Inscape' and 'instress' frequently occur as the looked-for and perceived qualities in nature, and he was now 'flush with a new stroke of enthusiasm' (Hopkins, *Journals and Papers*, 221) about Duns Scotus, the medieval theologian who, although disapproved of by Hopkins's superiors, helped to sanction his way of perceiving and recording nature. Hopkins had 'resolved to write no more, as not belonging to my profession' (Hopkins, *Correspondence*, 14), but nevertheless wrote some Latin and two English poems, a May exercise, officially encouraged, to honour the Virgin Mary; one of them, 'Ad Mariam', closely imitates Swinburne.

In August 1873 Hopkins was posted back to Roehampton for a year's teaching. In spite of a comparatively easy year, with exhibition visits renewing his interest in modern English painting, his teaching left him very tired and deeply cast down; however, on a summer holiday to Devon he recorded feelings of intense love for the coomb scenery around Teignmouth.

St Beuno's, 1874–1877 At the end of August 1874 Hopkins travelled to a remote part of north Wales, to study theology for four years at St Beuno's College. Again he immediately fell in love with the landscape: the glens, woods, and trees of the deep Elwy valley, and the densely wooded hills and long-drawn valley of the River Clwyd, with the Snowdonian mountain range and the sea in the distance. Hopkins felt 'an instress and charm of Wales' (Hopkins, *Journals and Papers*, 258), delighted in word-painting the countryside, and began to learn Welsh, which he associated with poetry and mythology. In spite of discouragement from his rector unless he intended to convert local Welsh speakers, Hopkins enthusiastically persisted with lessons, and tried his hand at the intricacies of classical Welsh verse.

Hopkins became fascinated by the appearance, legend, and traditions of St Winefride's Well, composed a Latin and an English poem on the saint, and planned a drama, 'St Winefred's Well' (with which he sporadically toyed for more than ten years, but never finished). However, the bleak weather, his health, and particularly his studies were sources of tension and unhappiness during his first year: he barely passed the examination.

During Hopkins's Roehampton teaching his lectures on poetry had emphasized sound, repetition, and rhyme in its widest sense of sound-similarity. Although not understanding its detailed rules, he was now attracted by the Welsh *cynghanedd* metrical form for its variety of binding and enriching systems, and its focus on sound. Poetry was spoken sound, not the printed word, which was only its representation; his own poetry, he always said, had to be read aloud. Something greater was imminent, and in December 1875, strongly affected by and seeing religious and symbolic implications in a newspaper account of a shipwreck in which five nuns lost their lives, Hopkins set to work at a poem on a modern Catholic martyrdom, using the Pindaric ode form. 'The Wreck of the *Deutschland*' is an idiosyncratic shipwreck poem, using vigorous sea, storm, and narrative description, a story of the tall nun's victory against the odds, and the poet's account of the shaping of his own dramatic conversion and discovery of God's purpose behind apparently incoherent tragedy. The powerfully awkward 'sprung rhythm', vigorous language, and personal excitement counter echoes of fatalism and disenchantment in this vast experimental poem.

Hopkins never again composed a poem of this length and ambition. The culmination and justification of his lengthy and deep poetic thinking and practice, its acceptance by his superiors would have transformed his life and future poetry, as well as giving him a new and invigorating sense of purpose in the society. But after initial encouragement the editor of *The Month* persistently delayed publication until Hopkins resigned himself to its rejection; he told a friend that the Jesuit periodical 'dared' not print it (Hopkins, *Correspondence*, 15). Representing officially sanctioned orthodoxy, the journal's decision gave Hopkins a lasting feeling of rejection by his community, and set up a barrier between himself and authority. He returned to his old guilty feeling about his art: as his poetry making was not approved, he could not allocate more than an occasional short piece of leisure time to it. The majority of his subsequent poems were sonnets, a form that Hopkins could carry in his head while officially 'recreating'. This rejection also meant that Bridges now had the crucial role of guardian of Hopkins's poetry.

Ironically, while composing his great ode, Hopkins was writing three minor and stilted occasional poems on his bishop's silver jubilee, one each in Latin, Welsh, and English; the last, published as part of a celebratory pamphlet, was one of the handful of his poems he ever saw in print. In spring 1877, although he found 'going over moral theology over and over again and in a hurry is the most wearisome work' and was so tired that he was 'good for nothing' (Hopkins, *Further Letters*, 143), he rejoiced in the first primroses, and wrote 'The Starlight Night' and 'God's Grandeur' for his mother's birthday. These started the great series of lyrical sonnets, which include 'The Lantern out of Doors', 'As Kingfishers Catch Fire', 'The Sea and the Skylark', 'Spring', 'The Caged Skylark', 'In the Valley of the Elwy', 'The Windhover' (his favourite poem of that year), 'Pied Beauty', and 'Hurrahing in Harvest'.

Many of these poems from 1877 celebrate Hopkins's joyful observations of nature. Sometimes he is at his poetic best, as in the octave of 'The Windhover', where the medley of sound-devices, the personal excitement of the narrator, and the imitation of the bird's intense hovering are simultaneously perfect, or in the successful achievement of complex, passionate argument in 'The Caged Skylark', or in the fondness, enthusiasm, and sexuality of Hopkins's most ecstatic poem, 'Hurrahing in Harvest'. But sometimes there is deep rejection of and disgust with everyday life and everything man-made, or the hidden biographical comparison between the sweet peace of the Elwy household and Hopkins's customary harsh institutional surroundings. The joyful accounts of nature throw into relief his loneliness and misanthropy; his idealism was constantly undermined by disillusion.

In July 1877 Hopkins failed his theology examination, being too Scotist for his examiners. 'Much against my inclination I shall have to leave Wales', he wrote to Bridges (Hopkins, *Letters*, 43). Not only was he unable to continue into his fourth year of theology, but he also would never reach the highest ranks and posts in the society. However he was ordained to the priesthood in September of that year, and after an operation for circumcision took his last look at Wales, the 'true Arcadia of wild beauty' (Hopkins,

Further Letters, 370) and 'always to me a mother of Muses' (Hopkins, *Letters*, 227).

'Fortune's football', 1877–1884 Each September almost every Jesuit shifted to another location, in changes known as 'general post'; a basic condition of Jesuit life, the process still hurt. The saddest of his St Beuno's poems, showing Hopkins at his most vulnerable, is 'The Lantern out of Doors', which laments being deprived of people to whom he had grown attached. In his loneliness, the only counter to his daily surroundings, which appear as 'much thick and marsh air', is the presence of some man:

> whom either beauty bright
> In mould or mind … makes rare

He wrote to his mother: 'Ours can never be an abiding city nor any one of us know what a day may bring forth' (Hopkins, *Further Letters*, 142).

In July 1883, after six years of his own constant removals, Hopkins wrote: 'I have long been Fortune's football and am blowing up the bladder of resolution big and buxom for another kick of her foot' (Hopkins, *Letters*, 183). Since leaving Wales he had been posted to Mount St Mary's College, near Sheffield, for seven months of secondary-school teaching, but having become 'very fond of the boys' (Hopkins, *Further Letters*, 158) had been given only a week's notice before being sent to Stonyhurst College to coach a few boys for external university degrees. After three months he was sent south to London to act as curate at Farm Street Church in Mayfair, where he remained for five months, before, in December 1878, becoming curate at St Aloysius's Church, Oxford. Ten months later he took up a similar position at St Joseph's Church, Bedford Leigh, in Lancashire. Then after only three months there he was posted as curate to St Francis Xavier's Church, Liverpool, where he stayed for one year and seven months, before going as relief temporary curate to St Joseph's, Glasgow, for two months. At the end of that period he started his year's tertianship at Roehampton, and having completed it was appointed teacher at Stonyhurst College again, where he remained for one year and four months. He travelled to Dublin to take up his professorship at the University College in February 1884, having been in eleven postings, in four countries, in eight years.

Hopkins was pessimistic about the Mount St Mary's post before he arrived there—'the work is nondescript', the countryside 'not very interesting' (Hopkins, *Further Letters*, 148)—and he found life at the college was 'as dank as ditchwater and has some of the other qualities of ditchwater'; he had been 'reduced to great weakness by diarrhoea' (Hopkins, *Letters*, 47). His muse had 'turned utterly sullen in the Sheffield smoke-ridden air' (ibid., 148), but he composed another shipwreck poem, 'The Loss of the *Eurydice*', much simpler than 'The Wreck of the *Deutschland*', but far less distinguished: *The Month* again rejected it for publication. Then at Stonyhurst another Marian poem, 'The May Magnificat', was refused permission to be placed before the Virgin Mary statue. Hopkins started a friendship and correspondence with one of his former Highgate teachers, Canon R. W. Dixon, by regretting the lack of due recognition suffered by writers. At Oxford Hopkins complained of overwork, illness, and disaffection from his parishioners, but wrote several poems, including 'Henry Purcell', and two, 'Binsey Poplars' and 'Duns Scotus's Oxford', expressing modern man's insensitivity to landscape and his own deep rejection of modern religion and civilization. Many poems show Hopkins's lack of inward comfort and ease. His parish work in working-class Lancashire and Glasgow was 'very wearying to mind and body', and as a sheltered middle-class southerner he was shocked to see the ghastly cost of industrial prosperity. Liverpool was 'a most unhappy and miserable spot' (Hopkins, *Correspondence*, 42), where 'one is so fagged, so harried and gallied up and down' (Hopkins, *Letters*, 110), while Glasgow was a 'wretched place' (ibid., 135) and 'repulsive to live in' (Hopkins, *Further Letters*, 248). Even less suited to these than to his other Jesuit posts, he suffered the indignity of having his Liverpool sermons censored by his rector because of incorrect theology (Scotus was, again, partly to blame). Nevertheless in the Lancashire countryside he produced the sad but charming 'Spring and Fall: to a Young Child', and by Loch Lomond his Scottish poem 'Inversnaid'.

Hopkins's tertianship at Roehampton was intended to enable him by withdrawal from the world to recover his primal Jesuit fervour; he completed his formal training as a Jesuit when he took the simple vows of a spiritual coadjutor in August 1882, fourteen years after he had entered the society as a novice. At Stonyhurst, where he taught university-standard classics, Hopkins was allowed time to write on academic subjects, and he planned a work on Greek lyric art, but was hampered by ignorance of contemporary classical scholarship, self-doubt, and 'a wretched state of weakness and weariness, I can't tell why, always drowsy and incapable of reading or thinking to any effect' (Hopkins, *Letters*, 168). He wrote the brooding 'Ribblesdale', 'The Leaden Echo and the Golden Echo', and three letters published in the scientific journal *Nature*, consisting mainly of skyscape descriptions. He started a friendship with Coventry Patmore, a Roman Catholic poet he already admired.

Dublin, 1884–1889 In spite of strong opposition from the archbishop of Dublin and his successor, Hopkins early in February 1884 was elected to a fellowship of the Royal University of Ireland, and to a junior classics chair at University College, Dublin—successor to the Catholic University of Ireland founded by Newman, and now taken over by the Irish Jesuits. It was an inauspicious appointment, Hopkins having been attacked because of his nationality, and supported by reason of his Oxford background and his salary, which was needed by the ailing college. The head of the English Jesuit province had written of his 'oddities', and an old Balliol acquaintance had supported him for his originality and 'curiously delicate perception' (White, *Hopkins: a Literary Biography*, 361), not qualities suitable for teaching and controlling students less educated and sophisticated than those he had known at Oxford.

For his first year Hopkins taught nothing but was given continuous examining, at one time having '557 papers on hand: let those who have been thro' the like say what that means' (Hopkins, *Correspondence*, 123). By April his depression was worsening: he was 'in a great weakness' (Hopkins, *Letters*, 192) and had suffered 'a deep fit of nervous prostration … I did not know but I was dying' (ibid., 193). He started writing perhaps his most intense and terrifying poem, 'Spelt from Sibyl's Leaves', in which the doomsday portent of an oracular sunset overpowers the vulnerable aesthetic qualities of nature.

In summer 1885 Hopkins wrote to Bridges of his 'continually jaded and harassed mind' (Hopkins, *Letters*, 221). More isolated than ever, he was seen unsympathetically and distantly by colleagues and pupils alike (see his sonnet 'To Seem the Stranger'). The label by which they diminished what they could not understand was that of a typical aesthetic Newmanite convert; his sense of humour was not recognized in Ireland, though it is apparent in almost every letter he wrote, even when at his most miserable: a Liverpool organist

> got drunk at the organ (I have now twice had this experience: it is distressing, alarming, agitating, but above all delicately comic; it brings together the bestial and the angelic elements in such a quaint entanglement … for musicians never play such clever descants as under those circumstances …) … He was a clever young fellow and thoroughly understood the properties of narrow-necked tubes. (Hopkins, *Letters*, 264)

Shy and effeminate, slight and not more than 5 feet 2 inches tall, he was sometimes mistaken for a teenager, although now in his forties (his glossy light-brown to tawny hair partly greying). His Oxford and Balliol mannerisms did not go down well in the comparatively primitive college, hostile towards Britain; unable to cope with classroom discipline, he was ragged by students. He was disgusted that two Irish archbishops backed rebellion against British government, and could not condone what he saw as disloyalty to the crown, but painfully admitted that home rule was inevitable because the Irish were ungovernable. After his death the few Dublin stories of him concerned his eccentricity: he had got a student to drag him on his back round a table to demonstrate Hector's death, and had once told a class that he regretted never having seen a naked woman.

But to define and explore his mental disturbances Hopkins had poetry, now his sole resource. Whereas the originality of many of his pre-Dublin poems had been compromised by the required religious conclusion, the uncontrollable strength of his psychological turmoil in Ireland took him well beyond the limits of conventional religious diagnosis and terminology; and poetry itself was driven beyond commonly recognized subject and means of expression. His 'desolate' or 'terrible' sonnets of 1885, such as 'I Wake and Feel the Fell of Dark' and 'No Worst, There is None', have become classic explorations of modern psychic despair and torment, with widely known images and phrases such as 'cliffs of fall' and 'O the mind, mind has mountains'.

Hopkins had a few friends outside Dublin, such as the

Cassidys of Monasterevin, where he composed the unfinished 'On the Portrait of Two Beautiful Young People', an elegy on human beauty, which he had previously tried to justify according to his religion's precepts in the sonnet 'To what serves mortal beauty?' Besides being obsessed by Irish politics he became more jingoistic, writing three poems on military virtues, and denigrating the lack of realism in Irish myths and the woolliness of modern Irish writing and painting, although he made an interesting and humorous collection of Hiberno-English words and phrases. On holiday in 1887, Hopkins wrote two of his most idiosyncratic poems, sonnets lengthened beyond recognition. 'Harry Plowman' is to be heard, not silently read; the man is created in natural images, sound-devices connecting different senses. In the companion piece, 'Tom's Garland', expressing Hopkins's conservative social thinking, symbols clash with realistic description, obscuring the argument.

So often in Dublin Hopkins had felt unable to 'breed one work that wakes' ('Justus tu es', l. 13), but his final group of three sonnets, composed in March and April 1889, which bewail his lack of poetic inspiration, is ironically some of his most distinguished work. Soon afterwards Hopkins caught typhoid, which developed into peritonitis, probably from the defective plumbing of the University College drains, and he died on 8 June 1889 at 85 St Stephen's Green. He was interred on 11 June in the Jesuit burial plot in the Prospect cemetery, Glasnevin, on the north side of Dublin.

Literary reputation Hopkins was soon forgotten in Dublin; twelve years after his death a student of the same college who was keen on literature reported that Hopkins was 'practically unknown'. Robert Bridges, however, on whom the poet had relied to keep, treasure, and conceivably publish the poems after Hopkins's death, believed that they must be printed, and was soon planning an edition with a short memoir. Delay was caused by his respect for the private nature of the letters, by his feeling that Hopkins's melancholia should not be publicly exposed, and by fear that the public would not understand the peculiarities of the verse. He gradually introduced small groups of the poems into anthologies, but it was not until 1916 that he received the public encouragement for which he was waiting. The sensitive, handsome, and almost complete small edition, edited and largely designed by Bridges, was published at the end of 1918. Hopkins did not use his middle name, but Bridges introduced 'Manley' on the first edition title-page to distinguish him from his nephew, also Gerard Hopkins.

The edition of 750 copies had still not sold out when, in 1930, a second edition was called for by the poetry public who were demanding new, difficult poetic voices. Advocated especially by I. A. Richards, F. R. Leavis, William Empson, and Michael Roberts, so that his poems appeared in general and modernistic anthologies, followed by university and school syllabuses, Hopkins had suddenly become a popular modern poet. It was not until the 1960s that his Victorian qualities were appreciated. In the second half of the twentieth century with both protestant and Roman Catholic faiths searching for new voices, the use of Hopkins's writings considerably increased, but there are signs that the distinctive literary qualities of his poetry, journals, and letters (he was one of the best letter writers of the nineteenth century) are being valued less, and his unorthodox characteristics hidden. As one of his biographers said, no one else writes with such strength and vivacity about the extreme human emotions of joy and pain.   NORMAN WHITE

Sources *The journals and papers of Gerard Manley Hopkins*, ed. H. House and G. Storey (1959) · *The letters of Gerard Manley Hopkins to Robert Bridges*, ed. C. C. Abbott, 2nd rev. edn (1955) · *The correspondence of Gerard Manley Hopkins and Richard Watson Dixon*, ed. C. C. Abbott, 2nd rev. edn (1955) · *Further letters of Gerard Manley Hopkins, including his correspondence with Coventry Patmore*, ed. C. C. Abbott, 2nd rev. enlarged edn (1956) · N. White, *Hopkins: a literary biography* (1992) · N. White, *Gerard Manley Hopkins in Wales* (1998) · private information (2004)
Archives Bodl. Oxf., literary MSS, papers, and corresp. · Campion Hall, Oxford, papers, incl. diaries and journals · College of Notre Dame of Maryland, corresp., literary MSS, and papers · College of the Holy Cross Library, Worcester, Massachusetts, papers · Princeton University Library, New Jersey, papers · priv. coll. · Ransom HRC, papers | Bodl. Oxf., corresp. with Robert Bridges and literary papers · U. Durham L., letters to Coventry Patmore · University College, Dublin, letters and postcards to Alexander Baillie
Likenesses photograph, 1850–59, Oxford University Press · G. Giberne, photographs, 1856–74, Ransom HRC; repro. in White, *Hopkins: a literary biography* · A. E. Hopkins, watercolour drawing, 1859, NPG · A. E. Hopkins, watercolour drawing, 1859, Bodl. Oxf. · group portrait, photograph, 1860–69, Balliol Oxf. · Hills & Saunders, albumen print, 1863, NPG · E. M. Hopkins, self-portrait, drawing, 1864, Campion Hall, Oxford · T. C. Bayfield, albumen print, 1866, NPG · group portrait, photograph, 1866, Oxford University Press · group portrait, photograph, 1879, Gonzaga University, Spokane, Crosby Library · photograph, 1879, repro. in White, *Hopkins: a literary biography* · Forshaw & Coles, two albumen prints, 1880, NPG [*see illus.*] · group portrait, photograph, 1883, Clongowes Wood College, co. Kildare · photograph, 1888, priv. coll.; repro. in White, *Hopkins: a literary biography* · A. Hopkins, portrait (aged ten), NPG · H. E. Wooldridge, oils (after photograph, 1879), priv. coll.

Hopkins, Harold Horace (1918–1994), physicist and endoscopist, was born on 6 December 1918 at 76 Argyle Street, Leicester, the youngest of six children of William Ernest Hopkins, a baker's journeyman, and his wife, Teresa Ellen, *née* Hewitt. The family were hard up, his father often being unemployed in the 1920s and 1930s, but encouraged by his mother Hopkins obtained a good education, starting at a local state elementary school. At various Sunday schools he sang in a church choir, and also went to concerts of the Leicester Symphony Orchestra. At the age of nine he won an adult verse competition. In 1929 he won a scholarship to the local technical grammar school, Gateway. His aptitude for English and foreign languages induced him to drop science, but a new headmaster persuaded him to return to it. In 1936 he went to University College, Leicester, with a scholarship; he lived at home, and graduated in physics and mathematics in 1939. As there were less than a hundred students he mixed with friends from many different disciplines, but remained faithful to his ambition to do research in physics.

In September 1939 Hopkins was directed to work for an optics company, Taylor, Taylor, and Hobson; there he had his introduction to optical design, on which he obtained his PhD in 1945. In 1941 he was briefly called up for army service, during which he 'rose rapidly to the rank of lance-corporal, temporary acting unpaid' (McCombie and Smith, 240). On 22 February 1941 he married Joan Avery Frost (b. 1920/21), a typist, daughter of Arthur Horace Frost, a motor driver. In 1947 a research fellowship took Hopkins to Imperial College, London, where he became a lecturer in optics and then a reader, achieving the degree of DSc, London, in 1950. On 22 December 1950, having obtained a divorce, he married Christine Dove Ridsdale (b. 1918/19), computer, daughter of the Revd Harold Ridsdale, a Church of England clergyman; she was a talented painter. His second wife provided the stability that was so important to him; they had three sons and a daughter. Hopkins remained at Imperial College until 1967, when he was appointed to a new chair in applied optics at Reading University. There he introduced a lens design unit and an MSc course in applied optics. He retired in 1984, having served as head of the department of physics from 1977 to 1980.

Hopkins always aimed for new results in optical theory of direct use to the design of optical instruments. His doctoral thesis was devoted to work on a small circular spot of light at the centre of the diffraction pattern of a point light source, named the Airy disc, after Sir George Biddell Airy. Hopkins's treatment of the passage of light through a system of lenses produced important advances, culminating in a book, *The Wave Theory of Aberrations* (1950). Optical science was by this time already well developed; its theoretical basis had been enriched by many people, including some of the great names in physics and mathematics. However, Hopkins realized there was still scope for further work; he returned to the fundamentals of the subject and extended its theoretical basis. After a few years his achievements in the analysis of optical systems were comparable with the wartime efforts on communication systems and radar. An important practical advance was the zoom lens. In 1948 he produced a system for the BBC that allowed a television camera to go immediately from a view of, for example, the whole cricket field to a close-up of a single player. Another practical device was the video disc, which resulted from an industrial consultancy with Phillips at Eindhoven.

In medicine Hopkins's outstanding achievements lay in the development of endoscopes, optical tubes that enable doctors and surgeons to view the inside of the body. After a period of ninety years in which there had been only minor changes, a chance meeting between Hopkins and a physician, Hugh Gainsborough, produced an important advance. Hopkins and his postdoctoral co-worker, N. S. Kapany, designed a 'fibroscope', a flexible bundle of glass fibres, 0.06 mm in diameter. Their letter to *Nature* (January 1954) brought a telephone call from an engineer in Scotland, who asked Hopkins to make a flexible fibroscope 6 feet long so that inaccessible bolts on the Forth Bridge could be inspected for corrosion. At the same time a South African gastroenterologist, Basil Hirschowitz, started making fibre bundles for a flexible gastroscope, which he

first tested on himself. Hopkins then designed a rigid endoscope, in co-operation with a Liverpool urologist, James Gow. It inspired a German manufacturer, Karl Stortz, to collaborate with Hopkins in constructing a cystoscope, first shown at an international meeting at Munich in 1967. Stortz introduced an external light source, transmitted inside the body through a bundle of glass fibres. The clear, bright images produced excellent photographs, and also enabled surgeons to view previously inaccessible parts of the body. These developments were of enormous clinical importance, and the medical profession conferred on Hopkins many of their highest awards. He became an honorary fellow of the Royal College of Surgeons and of the Royal College of Physicians, and of the national optical societies of America, India, and China. He received honorary doctorates from the universities of Besançon, Bristol, Liverpool, and Reading. In 1973 he was elected a fellow of the Royal Society, and received its Rumford medal (1984), together with the gold medal of the Royal Society of Medicine (1994).

Hopkins was a gregarious individual and a generous host, noted for his large fund of anecdotes and criticisms. Among his recreations he listed keyboard music, sailing, woodwork, and reading; he was fluent in several languages. Throughout his life he remained faithful to the socialist beliefs inculcated by his mother and his own childhood experience; while in London he was an active member of the local Labour Party. He died in Reading on 22 October 1994, and was survived by his wife and four children.

BREBIS BLEANEY

Sources C. W. McCombie and J. C. Smith, *Memoirs FRS*, 44 (1998), 239–52 · *WWW*, 1991–5 · *The Times* (3 Nov 1994) · *The Independent* (5 Nov 1994) · personal knowledge (2004) · private information (2004) · b. cert. · m. certs.

Likenesses photograph, 1984, repro. in McCombie and Smith, *Memoirs FRS*, 238 · C. Hopkins, portrait, U. Reading · photograph, repro. in *The Times* · photograph, repro. in *The Independent*

Wealth at death £221,417: probate, 24 Jan 1995, *CGPLA Eng. & Wales*

Hopkins, John (1520/21–1570), psalmist and Church of England clergyman, was born at Wednesbury, Staffordshire. Nothing is known of his family or early life. He is probably identifiable with the John Hopkins who supplicated for the degree of BA at Oxford in March 1544 (he 'determined' in 1545). After Oxford Hopkins seems to have migrated to London and become acquainted with Edward Whitchurch, printer of the 1549 Book of Common Prayer and Thomas Sternhold's *Certayne Psalmes* in English metre (STC 2419). On 22 August 1549 Whitchurch was one of the witnesses to Sternhold's will. On 24 December 1549 he published *Al such Psalmes of David as Thomas Sternehold late grome of the kinges majesties robes, didde in his life time draw into English metre*, in which Sternhold's texts were followed by a preface to the reader, signed I. H., and a separate sequence of Psalms 30, 33, 42, 52, 79, 82, and 146 (in later editions attributed to John Hopkins). These, Hopkins explained, were added 'especially to fyll up a place ... that the booke maye ryse to his juste volume', implying a commission by the printer (T. Sternhold, *Al such Psalmes*, sig.

G2*v*). There is no evidence that Hopkins knew Sternhold personally and no likelihood that they collaborated; Whitchurch provided the link between them.

Whitchurch worked in Fleet Street, which provides circumstantial evidence for identifying the psalmist with the John Hopkyns ordained deacon on 2 November 1551, and priest, on 15 May 1552, by Nicholas Ridley, bishop of London. The ordination record of 1551 gives his age (thirty) and place of birth, and describes him as resident in the parish of St Bride's (Fleet Street), London, for the past four years. Nothing is known of Hopkins's whereabouts between his ordination and his institution to the parish of Great Waldingfield, Suffolk, on 12 August 1561 by John Parkhurst, bishop of Norwich; on 11 May 1563 Hopkins was also instituted into the living of the neighbouring parish, Chilton.

During the 1550s, if not before, Hopkins may have been a schoolmaster. Edward Hake's dedication of *A Compendious Fourme of Education* (1574) reminds John Harlowe how they were 'trained up' together 'with the instructions of that learned and exquisite teacher, Maister John Hopkins, that worthy Schoolemaister, nay rather, that most worthy parent unto all children committed to his charge of education'. Hake (*b. c.*1544) came from Bishop's Stortford, Hertfordshire, and may have been at school there. He appears to be name-dropping in mentioning Hopkins, who was widely known from 1562, when John Day printed *The whole booke of Psalmes, collected into Englysh metre by T. Starnhold, J. Hopkins & others*: an amalgamation of his two earlier collections of eighty-two psalms (1561; *STC* 2429) and *The residue of all Davids psalmes in metre, made by John Hopkins and others* (1562; *STC* 2429.5).

By 1562 Hopkins had composed fifty-four new psalm versions replacing twelve of William Kethe's versions printed in 1561 (Psalms 27, 36, 47, 54, 58, 62, 70, 85, 88, 90–91, 94) and three of William Whittingham's (Psalms 50, 67, 71), whereby it seems that contributions by Marian exiles were being demoted. Hopkins also composed versions of Psalms 24, 26, 28, 31, 35, 38–40, 45–6, 48, 55–7, 59–61, 64–5, 69, 72, 74, 76–7, 80–81, 83–4, 86–7, 89, 92–3, 95–9, and 102.

Hopkins's reputation has been distorted by association with former Anglo-Genevan exiles who became the focus for non-conformity in the Elizabethan church. In part this is because, as with Sternhold, his literary reputation as a metrical psalmist was based on texts which were substantially revised by Whittingham and others for the use of the Anglo-Genevan community in 1556 (*STC* 16561; and *STC 1475–1640*, 2.87–90, table of liturgies; for the unrevised London editions printed up to 1553, see chart of editions in *STC, 1475–1640*, 1.99–103).

Hopkins's will, dated 10 October 1570, made his wife, Anne, his principal heir and sole executor, and shows a concern for the supervision of his son's education, making it more likely that the rector of Great Waldingfield was Hake's former schoolmaster. For five years after his death Hopkins willed that his son John should be brought up in learning, at the grammar school, at his wife's costs. Thereafter he left £20 'to be bestowed uppon hym in

Learninge' under the supervision of Thomas Spencer, rector of Hadleigh, Suffolk (who had supplicated for his BA degree the same date as Hopkins) or Edward Colman of Waldingfield. He also bequeathed to his son all his Latin books. He left £10 to each of his daughters, Martha and Sara, and also ten lambs to Martha 'to be delivered to her when her mother shall se good', indicating that this Suffolk pastor also tended real sheep. There were small bequests to servants and friends, and, significantly, provision of 6*s.* 8*d.* for some learned man to preach a funeral sermon in Waldingfield on the day of his burial. To Colman, who was to supervise the will, he gave his copy of 'master bolinger his sermondes upon the Revelacon in english' (H. Bullinger, *A Hundred Sermons upon the Apocalyps*, 1561), which Parkhurst had directed ministers in his diocese to procure. Hopkins was buried at Great Waldingfield on 23 October 1570.

Hopkins's literary reputation in print began with John Bale who referred to him in 1559 as 'not the least significant of British poets of our time' and one who would make the Psalms known to his posterity 'by the elegant, harmonious arrangement of words in English measures' (Bale, *Cat.*, 113). Thomas Fuller (1662) celebrated the English metrical psalms and Alexander Pope allowed that 'Hopkins and Sternhold glad the heart with Psalms' but saw their 'pathetic strains' as the means by which the 'Boys and Girls whom charity maintains / Implore your help' (A. Pope, *Imitations of Horace's Epistles*, bk 2, no. 1, lines 230–32). Sternhold and Hopkins were never partners in life, but in death their names have been inseparable. Thomas Warton's *History of English Poetry* (1774–81) suggested that Hopkins was a better English poet than Sternhold, but generally, the ballad measures and popular diction of these lyrics alienated those who aspired to more refined poetic fashions. From 1562 until the 1690s the Elizabethan metrical psalms were the best-known English verses because every English man, woman, and child sang them in church. Hopkins was the author of the largest number, 61 out of 150 psalms. RIVKAH ZIM

Sources *STC, 1475–1640* · GL, MS 9545/1, fols. 9*v*, 11*r* · Norfolk RO, DN/REG 13, book 19, fols. 55, 81 · *Reg. Oxf.*, 1.208 · will, PRO, PROB 11/52, sig. 36 · Suffolk RO, Bury St Edmunds, FL 514/4/1 · E. H. [E. Hake], 'A compendious fourme of education', *A touchstone for this time present* (1574) · R. Zim, *English metrical psalms: poetry as praise and prayer, 1535–1601* (1987) · Bale, *Cat.*, 113 · Bodl. Oxf., MS Ashmole 1126, fol. 46*v* · *DNB* · H. Robinson, ed. and trans., *The Zurich letters, comprising the correspondence of several English bishops and others with some of the Helvetian reformers, during the early part of the reign of Queen Elizabeth*, 1, Parker Society, 7 (1842), 99 · A. Pope, 'The first epistle of the second book of Horace imitated', *The poems of Alexander Pope: a one-volume edition of the Twickenham text*, ed. J. Butt (1960), 643; repr. (1970)

Hopkins, John (*b.* 1675), poet, was born on 1 January 1675, the second son of Ezekiel *Hopkins (1634–1690), bishop of Derry, and younger brother of Charles *Hopkins. A John Hopkins was admitted sizar at Jesus College, Cambridge, where he graduated BA in 1693–4, and proceeded MA in 1698. This John Hopkins was ordained deacon at Norwich in March 1698, and priest at York in September that year.

In 1698 Hopkins published two Pindaric poems: *The triumphs of peace, or, The glories of Nassaw … written at the time of his grace the duke of Ormond's entrance into Dublin*, and *The Victory of Death, or, The Fall of Beauty*, on the death of Lady Cutts. In the following year he issued *Milton's 'Paradise Lost' imitated in rhyme, in the fourth sixth and ninth Books: containing the primitive loves, the battel of the angels, the fall of man*, apologizing in the preface for his audacity on the ground that 'when I did it, I did not so well Percieve the Majesty and Noble air of Mr. Milton's *style as now I do*' (J. Hopkins, *Milton's 'Paradise Lost'*, 1699, 1).

Hopkins's last work was a collection of indifferent love-verses and translations from Ovid, *Amasia, or, The Works of the Muses* (1700), with an 'Epistle Dedicatory' to the duchess of Grafton, and dedications of particular sections to various persons of distinction. Referring in the preface to his brother's renderings of Ovid ('very well perform'd') he observes, 'mine were written in an other Kingdom before I knew of his' (sig. A4). The author's portrait, engraved by F. H. Van Hove and subscribed with his assumed name, Sylvius, is prefixed to this work.

A. H. BULLEN, rev. FREYA JOHNSTON

Sources A. Chalmers, ed., *The general biographical dictionary*, new edn, 32 vols. (1812–17) · G. Borlase, ed., *Cantabrigienses graduati … usque ad annum 1800* (1800) · Venn, *Alum. Cant.*
Likenesses M. Hove, line engraving, NPG · Sylvius [F. H. Van Hove], engraving, repro. in J. Hopkins, *Amasia, or, The works of the muses*, 3 vols. (1700)

Hopkins, John Larkin (1819–1873), organist and composer, the son of a musician, Edward Hopkins, was born in Westminster on 25 November 1819. The organist Edward John Hopkins (1818–1901) was his cousin. Two further cousins, as well as his uncle and at least one brother, were also musicians. He sang for several years as a chorister in Westminster Abbey under the supervision of James Turle, organist and master of the choristers. After leaving the abbey choir Hopkins devoted himself to the study of music, and particularly of the organ, with such success that in 1841, at the age of twenty-two, he was chosen to succeed Ralph Banks as organist of Rochester Cathedral. In 1842 he took the degree of MusB at Cambridge. He published *Five Glees and a Madrigal*, followed by a collection of the words of anthems used in Rochester Cathedral, which was published in collaboration with Revd S. Shepherd in 1847. Hopkins was also the author of *A New Vocal Tutor* (1855), cathedral services in C♭ and E♭ (1857), *A Collection of Anthems*, and several other services, songs, anthems, glees, and carols. In 1856 he was elected organist of Trinity College, Cambridge, and he resigned his appointment at Rochester. He took the degree of MusD in 1867.

Hopkins died at Ventnor, Isle of Wight, on 25 April 1873. He was survived by his wife, Mary Matilda Hopkins, who was said to have been Russian by birth and a friend of Wagner. Their son Edward Larkin Hopkins (d. 9 July 1910) became a priest.

R. F. SHARP, rev. NILANJANA BANERJI

Sources Venn, *Alum. Cant.* · Brown & Stratton, *Brit. mus.* · J. D. Brown, *Biographical dictionary of musicians: with a bibliography of English writings on music* (1886) · D. Baptie, *Sketches of the English glee composers: historical, biographical and critical (from about 1735–1866)* [1896] · D. Baptie, *A handbook of musical biography* (1883) · Grove, *Dict. mus.* · CGPLA Eng. & Wales (1873)
Wealth at death under £800: probate, 29 Nov 1873, CGPLA Eng. & Wales

Hopkins, Matthew (d. 1647), witch-finder, was the son of James Hopkins (d. 1634?), vicar of Wenham in Suffolk. His collaborator John Stearne described Matthew as 'the son of a godly minister' (Stearne, 61). James's will, proved in 1634, mentions six children, only two of whom (Thomas and James) were named. The will entrusted the upbringing of the remaining children to the clergyman's widow, which implies that Matthew was then a minor, and hence in his twenties when he flourished as a witch-finder between 1645 and 1647. Practically nothing more is known of his earlier life, and the persistent tradition that he had received legal training is apparently unfounded. But in the last two and a half years of his life Hopkins enjoyed a brief prominence in eastern England, and he is remembered as the most notorious individual in English witchcraft history.

By the winter of 1644–5 Hopkins was resident at Manningtree in Essex and, on his own account, became troubled by the activities of seven or eight supposed witches living in the town. From March 1645 these and other suspected witches were apprehended and taken to be examined by local justices of the peace, with Hopkins giving detailed evidence against several of them. Thirty-six suspected witches, all women, were eventually tried at the Essex assizes in July 1645, of whom nineteen were executed. A further nine died of disease in gaol, and six were still in prison in 1648. Only one of the accused was acquitted and released, another, Rebecca West, escaping punishment after she became the leading witness for the prosecution.

This was a serious enough local witch-hunt by English standards, but it marked the first stage of a major persecution. Witchcraft accusations spread from Manningtree to Suffolk, where over a hundred alleged witches were identified and at least forty executed, and to Norfolk, where another forty witches were tried, of whom perhaps half were executed. There were trials in Huntingdonshire, in Cambridgeshire, in a number of counties in the eastern midlands, and in several boroughs, notably Great Yarmouth, King's Lynn, Stowmarket, and Aldeburgh, with the last accusations coming in the Isle of Ely in 1647. It is likely that at least 250 people were tried as witches or subjected to preliminary investigation during this witch panic. Of these at least a hundred were executed.

The fact that the phrase 'the Hopkins witch panic' is used to describe the trials of 1645–7 demonstrates that a central role is normally attributed to Hopkins, aided by John Stearne. But even if Hopkins was a catalyst, it is clear that the necessary preconditions for a major episode of witch-hunting were present. The influences which had hitherto prevented large-scale witch persecution in England, where both trials and demonological writings had apparently passed out of fashion by the 1630s, were absent in East Anglia in the early 1640s. During the first civil war local justices of the peace were concerned

Matthew Hopkins (*d.* 1647), by unknown engraver, pubd 1647

mainly with keeping the war effort going and thus a major witch craze could gather momentum in the absence of their normal restraining hand. Moreover, the war was increasingly being seen in ideological terms, with a consequent encouragement of popular godliness. Moderate ministers had been purged in both Essex and Suffolk, and it is probably no coincidence that one of the zones of Suffolk which was to experience heavy witchcraft accusations in 1645 was the area where the iconoclast William Dowsing had been active a year earlier.

Thus Hopkins's and Stearne's claims that they operated mainly in towns which had requested their services, although perhaps overstated, are evidently not without foundation. Even during the early accusations at Manningtree, Hopkins was only one of ninety-two witnesses giving evidence against the alleged witches. It remains clear, however, that their investigative techniques were reprehensible. Suspects were 'watched', primarily to prevent them from having contact with their familiar spirits, a practice which amounted to their being subjected to severe sleep-deprivation. This, allied to interrogations which depended heavily on leading questions, led to numerous confessions of doing harm by malefic witchcraft, meeting and making a pact with the devil, having sexual intercourse with him, and varied dealings with familiar spirits. Critics, correctly, identified the advent of witch-finders as something new to England: 'such a profession or occupation', wrote the clergyman John Gaule in a pamphlet published in June 1646, 'has not been heard of heretofore' (Gaule, 88).

Hopkins's motives in witch-hunting remain obscure.

There is a strong tradition, dating from the period of the trials, that his main motive was to make money. Certainly Hopkins did receive payments from some communities for his witch-finding, but often much of the money took the form of expenses for himself, Stearne, and Mary Phillips, a Manningtree woman who acquired a considerable reputation for being able to find the witch's mark. Hopkins, as many would have thought appropriate for the son of a godly country minister, had a genuine concern about witchcraft and may well have been, initially at least, surprised to find himself the central figure in a major witch-hunt. By the time John Gaule wrote, however, Hopkins was probably growing in self-confidence and self-importance. In May 1647 he issued *The discovery of witches in answer to severall queries, lately delivered to the judges of the assize for the county of Norfolk. And now published by Matthew Hopkins, witch-finder, for the benefit of the whole kingdome.*

The East Anglian trials of 1645–7 were the only major English witch-hunts and witch-hunting in the Hopkins mode, with its unleashing of enthusiastic popular godliness and the coming to prominence of an obscure man, became one of the symbols of what polite post-Restoration society regarded as the dreadfulness of the 1640s and 1650s. To later generations Hopkins's name has become associated with bigotry and harshness, especially after the making of the 1968 film *Witchfinder General* (directed by Michael Reeves), in which Vincent Price gave a memorably robust performance as Matthew Hopkins.

There is a pleasing tradition, still repeated in modern works of reference, that Hopkins was himself swum and subsequently executed as a witch. In fact he died, according to Stearne, 'after a long sicknesse of consumption' (Stearne, 61) at Manningtree, and the parish register of Mistley with Manningtree records his burial there on 12 August 1647.   JAMES SHARPE

Sources R. Deacon, *Witch finder general* (1976) · J. Sharpe, 'England's mass witch-hunt: East Anglia, 1645–7', *Instruments of darkness: witchcraft in England, 1450–1750* (1996), 128–47 · A. Macfarlane, 'The witch-finding movement of 1645 in Essex', *Witchcraft in Tudor and Stuart England: a regional and comparative study* (1970) · M. Hopkins, *The discovery of witches* (1647) · J. Stearne, *A confirmation and discovery of witchcraft* (1648) · *A true and exact relation of the severall informations, examinations and confessions of the late witches arraigned and executed … the 29 of July 1645* (1645) · J. Davenport, *The witches of Huntingdon, the examinations and confessions, exactly taken by his majesties justices of the peace for that county* (1645) · J. Gaule, *Select cases of conscience touching witches and witchcrafts* (1646) · F. Hutchinson, *A historical essay concerning witchcraft* (1718)

Likenesses pen and watercolour drawing, NPG · woodcut, NPG; repro. in Hopkins, *Discovery* [see illus.]

Hopkins, Richard (*b.* c.1546, *d.* in or before 1596), Roman Catholic exile and translator, son and heir of Richard Hopkins, was admitted to the Middle Temple on 9 October 1560. He was a commoner of Magdalen College, Oxford (not St Alban Hall, as sometimes stated) by 1564. About 1566 Hopkins became 'wearied with the heresy' of Middle Temple, according to Anthony Wood (Wood, *Ath. Oxon.*, 1.567), and he went into exile at Louvain, where he was befriended by Thomas Harding. After a period of study in Spain he returned to Louvain by 1579, when he lodged with Anne, Lady Hungerford, the sister of Jane Dormer, duchess of Feria.

Following the advice of Thomas Harding, who had earlier urged Hopkins to undertake the translation of Spanish devotional works as being spiritually more profitable than controversy, he published at Paris in 1582 a translation of part one of the *Libro de la oración y meditación* by the Spanish Dominican Luis de Granada. This was dedicated to the benchers of the inns of court, as was his translation of part one of the same author's *Memorial de la vida Christiana*, published at Rouen in 1586. The two works, based on a scholarly recension of the Spanish text, illustrated and designed for the use of the laity, enjoyed wide popularity. The first work, *Of Prayer and Meditation*, went into eleven protestant editions between 1592 and 1634, and at least three protestant editions of the *Memoriall of a Christian Life* had been published by the end of Elizabeth's reign. The florid devotional style is thought to have influenced the language of Crashaw and Vaughan. Hopkins's translation of part two of the *Memorial* was published after his death in John Heigham's *Six Spirituall Bookes* (1611).

From 1579 Hopkins was a close associate of William Allen, and he was a leading member of the English Catholic émigré community in Flanders. As Allen's agent Hopkins was possibly involved in clandestine negotiations for peace between England and Spain about 1594. In a report drawn up for the Archduke Ernest, governor of the Low Countries, in 1594, Hopkins was described as 'a man of great loyalty and zeal in the service of God and the King' (Loomie, 'Creswell's *Información*', 472, 476). In 1596, having died in Louvain, he was listed as a deceased pensionary of the Spanish crown.   G. MARTIN MURPHY

Sources A. C. Southern, *Elizabethan recusant prose, 1559–1582* (1950), 429–31 · A. F. Allison and D. M. Rogers, eds., *The contemporary printed literature of the English Counter-Reformation between 1558 and 1640*, 2 (1994), nos. 270, 439–45 · A. F. Allison, *English translations from the Spanish and Portuguese to the year 1700: an annotated catalogue* (1974) · H. A. C. Sturgess, ed., *Register of admissions to the Honourable Society of the Middle Temple, from the fifteenth century to the year 1944*, 1 (1949), 25 · A. J. Loomie, *The Spanish Elizabethans* (1963), 251 · Gillow, *Lit. biog. hist.* · A. J. Loomie, 'Father Joseph Creswell's *Información* for Philip II and the Archduke Ernest, c. August 1594', *Recusant History*, 22 (1994–5), 465–81 · Wood, *Ath. Oxon.*, new edn, 1.567 · Foster, *Alum. Oxon.* · R. B. Wernham, *The return of the Armada: the last years of the Elizabethan war against Spain, 1595–1603* (1994), 9–10

Archives BL, intercepted letter to William Allen at Rome, dated Antwerp, 8 Jan 1594, Cotton MS Titus B. ii, fol. 224

Hopkins, Sir Richard Valentine Nind (1880–1955), civil servant, was born in Edgbaston on 13 February 1880, the son of Alfred Nind Hopkins, a businessman, and his wife, Eliza Mary Castle. He was educated at King Edward's School, Birmingham, and at Emmanuel College, Cambridge, where he was a scholar, played rugby and cricket, and obtained a first class in part one of the classical tripos (1901) and in part two of the history tripos (1902). He entered the Inland Revenue as a first division clerk in 1902 and spent his spare time at the Bermondsey Mission, where he lived for a time. While he was working on Lloyd George's land values duties his ability was noticed by Sir Robert Chalmers, chairman of the Board of Inland Revenue. With the outbreak of the First World War Hopkins

Sir Richard Valentine Nind Hopkins (1880–1955), by Walter Stoneman, 1941

and Josiah Stamp designed and administered the excess profits duty, which proved a triumphant blend of the former's theoretical talents in taxation with the latter's growing administrative capacity in allying expertise to traditional civil service values.

With the reconstitution of the Board of Inland Revenue in 1916 Hopkins became a board member and in 1922 chairman, having been appointed CB in 1919 and KCB in 1920. He gave valuable evidence before the royal commission on the income tax (1919–20); was chairman of a departmental committee asked to devise a scheme for a levy on war wealth which, in the event, was not imposed; and advised on methods of dealing with the avoidance of supertax. In 1923 he married Lucy Davis MB ChB (*d.* 1960), daughter of Francis Cripps; they had one son.

As chairman Hopkins was renowned for his skills as a negotiator and for the goodwill he generated among junior and senior colleagues alike. His work at the board taught him the practicalities of taxation, and especially the two great secrets of this department: what could be managed, and how far taxpayers could be pushed. This was vital knowledge and critical for the next stage of his career. In 1927 'Hoppy' transferred to the Treasury where the two branches of finance and supply were combined under his control. This was therefore a key appointment in the reorganization of Treasury functions and personnel initiated by its permanent secretary, Sir Warren Fisher, who had known Hopkins from his Inland Revenue days. Hopkins became second secretary in 1932 and permanent secretary in 1942, retiring three years later. He was thus for eighteen years the chief Treasury adviser on all matters concerning financial policy and the control of government expenditure. At a time when the scale of national finances and the economic role of government were transformed, he served six chancellors of the exchequer and confronted policy problems which ranged in time and scope from negotiations on reparations and war debts to the financial crisis of the early 1930s, rearmament, and finally a second war.

It was said of Hopkins that his personality was particularly well suited to the Treasury at this time:

> Never attempting to dictate or to overrule, he proceeded to build his own conception of his duties as a ready and sympathetic listener, a student of men and their doings whose impartiality and objectivity was shaded only by an innate desire to assume the best and not the worst in his fellows, and finally as a wise counsellor whose advice was never forced on his colleagues but was always available when required.   (*Public Administration*, 119)

Of the many warm tributes to Hopkins, and of the fund of stories about him, the sense of the man and the civil servant is perhaps best conveyed in his answer to a 1943 parliamentary inquiry as to where the ultimate authority lay in a disagreement over the expenditure estimates. He replied that he would 'write to the Permanent Secretary of the Ministry. If he doesn't do what we want, I'll ask him round here for tea and a chat. If it's an obdurate case, I'll send out and get a small piece of cake with the tea' (Chapman and Greenaway, 113). He was likened to one of the great Elizabethan servants of the state, who 'inclined to his master's views, but held him clearly to the basic national traditions' (*DNB*). It was in that combination of attentiveness to politics but unwavering commitment to the realities of economics and finance that his counsel was sought and privileged, notwithstanding the diverse politics and personalities of his six chancellors. In addition to politicians Hopkins also worked closely with Montagu Norman, the governor of the Bank of England: together they hammered out policies on foreign exchange and monetary policy; 'and it became a feature of London life to see the governor's car outside the Treasury shortly before six o'clock each evening' (*DNB*).

Hopkins came into the public eye as an official witness in January 1931 while giving evidence before the royal commission on unemployment insurance. The meetings of the Macmillan committee on finance and industry in 1930 attracted rather less publicity. On that occasion Hopkins became locked in battle with J. M. Keynes, who was challenging the precepts of Treasury finance. The issue of this conflict was characterized by the committee's chairman, Lord Macmillan, as 'a drawn battle' (*DNB*). Similarly Keynes's first biographer, Sir Roy Harrod, went so far as to describe Hopkins's testimony as a 'great masterpiece' and to draw attention to his being unique in his generation in meeting Keynes on the latter's chosen ground of economics, without Keynes having the better of the argument (Harrod, 373, 420, 422). Although their views were at this time widely divergent, Keynes generally excluded Hopkins from his condemnation of the dead hand of the

Treasury and of its orthodoxies. He acknowledged that Hopkins did really understand public finance. The respect was mutual, and after the outbreak of war Hopkins provided Keynes with a room at the Treasury, where Keynes could ensure that his point was properly put.

Official documents in the Public Record Office relating to Hopkins's eighteen years at the centre of British government reveal the key role he played in the transition from an essentially *laissez-faire* to a modern managed economy in Britain. These documents show that, while most of the innovations in Treasury thinking in the 1930s originated with Hopkins's deputy, Sir Frederick Phillips, it was Hopkins who was ultimately the decisive influence on policy. This was primarily due to his capacity to take up, develop, and above all express in simple but compelling terms new ideas in a manner which persuaded chancellors that Treasury policy need not be ultra-orthodox but could be more experimental, providing the niceties of fiscal prudence *appeared* to be maintained.

Hopkins's role proved particularly decisive during the Second World War. This began with his efforts to bring Keynes into the Treasury as a wartime adviser, from which ensued many critical domestic and external economic policy decisions. There were three particular strands to his influence on wartime, and above all on post-war, economic policies. First, Hopkins was instrumental in persuading the chancellor, Sir John Anderson, that beginning in 1941 budgets should be framed in a much more explicitly quantitative manner. This was made possible by the compilation of national income statistics by J. R. N. Stone and James Meade, who were themselves inspired by Keynes's *How to Pay for the War* (1940) and his analysis of an inflationary gap that had to be met by higher taxation and/ or savings. The resulting white paper, *An analysis of the sources of war finance and an estimate of the national income and expenditure in 1938 and 1940* (1941), was described by Keynes as a 'revolution in public finance' (*Collected Writings*, 22.354). Second, Hopkins chaired the official steering committee on post-war employment which, proceeding from a document first prepared by Meade, drafted what eventually became the 1944 employment policy white paper which committed government to the maintenance of a 'high and stable level of employment' after the war. Hopkins's report was described by Keynes 'as an outstanding State Paper which, if one casts one's mind back ten years or so, represents a revolution in official thinking' (*Collected Writings*, 27.364). Historians have generally concurred with this judgement, although the diffusion of Keynesian ideas into the practice of British economic policy is now judged to have been a more drawn out process, and Hopkins's draft was, in many respects, a classic civil service 'fudge', drawing upon incompatible Treasury and Keynesian views in different chapters. Third, in 1945 Hopkins chaired another official committee, the national debt inquiry, which laid the foundations for the post-war cheap money policy and marked a further stage in the absorption of Keynesian ideas into official thinking. During its deliberations Hopkins is on record as having twice read Keynes's *The General Theory of Employment, Interest and*

Money (1936) and of having used arguments and quotations from it in writing the inquiry's report. For some historians this marked the completion of the conversion of the Treasury to Keynesian ideas, a conversion all the more poignant because of Hopkins's earlier defence of the Treasury view before the Macmillan committee in 1930.

Hopkins worked in harmony with politicians, bankers, and economists, and as the Treasury's permanent secretary (1942–5) avoided the atmosphere of controversy which had marked the periods of office of his predecessors Fisher and Sir Horace Wilson in their management of the civil service. Most unusually, he was appointed to replace Wilson, who was two years his junior. He retired in 1945 and, again unusually, was sworn of the privy council; he had been promoted GCB in 1941.

After his retirement Hopkins served the Church of England as a member of the central board of finance of which, in June 1947, he became chairman. He was seen going with delight to its conferences, and said: 'I have guided or tried to guide eighteen budgets in my time, but this afternoon I shall introduce my own budget' (*DNB*). He was also a crown member of the court of the University of London, a member of the Port of London Authority, of the Imperial War Graves Commission, and of a number of government committees, and a director of several companies. He was elected an honorary fellow of Emmanuel College, Cambridge, in 1946 and was Alfred Marshall lecturer in 1946–7. Hopkins died in London on 30 March 1955.

ROGER MIDDLETON

Sources *DNB* · *The Times* (21 April 1955) · 'Sir Richard Hopkins', *Public Administration*, 34 (1956), 115–23 · R. F. Harrod, *The life of John Maynard Keynes* (1951) · G. C. Peden, 'Sir Richard Hopkins and the "Keynesian revolution" in employment policy, 1929–45', *Economic History Review*, 2nd ser., 36 (1983), 281–96 · S. Howson and D. Winch, *The economic advisory council, 1930–1939: a study in economic advice during depression and recovery* (1977) · R. A. Chapman and J. R. Greenaway, *The dynamics of administrative reform* (1980) · *The collected writings of John Maynard Keynes*, ed. D. Moggridge and E. Johnson, 22 (1978) · *The collected writings of John Maynard Keynes*, ed. D. Moggridge and E. Johnson, 27 (1980) · P. Clarke, *The Keynesian revolution in the making, 1924–1936* (1988) · A. Booth, *British economic policy, 1931–1949* (1989) · *CGPLA Eng. & Wales* (1955)
Archives PRO, official papers, T175 · PRO, papers relating to his appointment as commissioner of Imperial War Graves Commission | BL, letters to Albert Mansbridge, Add. MS 65253
Likenesses W. Stoneman, photograph, 1941, NPG [*see illus.*] · photograph, repro. in *The Times* · photograph, repro. in 'Sir Richard Hopkins'
Wealth at death £15,712 5s. 11d.: probate, 20 June 1955, *CGPLA Eng. & Wales*

Hopkins, Samuel (1721–1803), Congregationalist minister in America, was born on 17 September 1721 in Waterbury, Connecticut, the first of the nine children of Timothy Hopkins (1691–1749), farmer and justice of the peace, and his wife, Mary (*c*.1701–1744), daughter of Thomas Judd of Waterbury. He graduated with a BA from Yale College in 1741 and then studied intermittently with Jonathan Edwards for the next year and a half. He was ordained to the ministry on 28 December 1743 at the Second Congregational Church of Sheffield in Housatonic (incorporated as Great Barrington in 1761), in western Massachusetts. On

13 January 1748 he married Joanna (*d.* 1793), the daughter of Moses Ingersoll of Housatonic. They had five sons and three daughters.

Hopkins was the greatest disciple of Edwards and the most important theologian of late eighteenth-century New England. He was a chief exponent of the New Divinity, a doctrinally rigorous movement that carried out the implications of Edwards's thought. Hopkins developed an inventive synthesis of reformed theology and Enlightenment thinking to defend the rationality and ethical accountability of reformed orthodoxy. Yet the provocative nature of some of his teachings earned for his theology the derisive label of 'New Divinity' or 'Hopkinsianism'. For example, in *Sin, through Divine Interposition, an Advantage to the Universe* (1759) he reconciled the existence of evil with divine goodness and omnipotence by contending that God wilfully permitted and guided sin to produce the best possible world. And in *An Inquiry Concerning the Promises of the Gospel* (1765) he undercut the preparationist scheme of grace by arguing that unrepentant 'awakened' sinners who used the means of grace and continued to resist the gospel were more repugnant to God than the most terrible 'unawakened' sinners who shunned those means. Opposition from Dutch settlers and controversies over his theology and strict ecclesiastical policies led to his dismissal in the winter of 1769. On 11 April 1770 Hopkins became minister of the First Congregational Church in Newport, Rhode Island.

In Newport, Hopkins advanced a morally stringent concept of Christian holiness as disinterested benevolence to counter what he perceived to be a growing acceptance of selfishness in New England religion, society, and ethical discourse. In *An Inquiry into the Nature of True Holiness* (1773) he asserted that the Christian faith demanded the surrender of one's own self-interests whenever it conflicted with the good of 'being in general'. He even speculated that this might entail a willingness to be damned if God's glory would be promoted by one's eternal condemnation. Hopkins's call for radical disinterested love provided a spur to evangelical social activism and evangelism. He himself, ministering in slave-trading Newport, became one of New England's most vocal abolitionists.

Although a supporter of the American War of Independence, in his influential *A Dialogue Concerning the Slavery of the Africans* (1776) he denounced the hypocrisy of American rhetoric of liberty amid his country's continued involvement in slavery and the slave trade. Determined to generate greater good out of the evil of slavery, he tried to found a mission colony of freed slaves in Africa in order to advance the cause of Christianity.

In 1793 Hopkins published a monumental summary of New Divinity doctrines, his 1100-page *System of Doctrines*. He defended biblical authority and the value of systematic divinity in the face of an increased deist presence in the United States. His *System* was the most consequential American systematic theology of the eighteenth century.

Hopkins's first wife, Joanna, died on 31 August 1793. On 14 September 1794 he married Elizabeth West (*c*.1739–

1814). In January 1799 he was struck by paralysis, but he continued to minister until his death on 20 December 1803 in Newport, where he was buried three days later.

PETER JAUHIAINEN

Sources *The works of Samuel Hopkins, D.D.*, 3 vols. (1852) [incl. memoir by E. A. Park] · J. Conforti, *Samuel Hopkins and the New Divinity movement: Calvinism, the Congregational ministry, and reform in New England between the Great Awakenings* (1981) · P. Jauhiainen, 'An Enlightenment Calvinist: Samuel Hopkins and the pursuit of benevolence', PhD diss., University of Iowa, 1997 · S. West, *Sketches of the life of the late, Rev. Samuel Hopkins, D.D.* (1805)

Archives Newton Center, Massachusetts, Andover Newton Theological College, papers · Williams College, Williamstown, Massachusetts, journal, Williams MSS | Congregational Historical Society, Boston, MSS · Hartford Seminary Library, Hartford, Connecticut, Joseph Bellamy papers · Hist. Soc. Penn., Gratz MSS · Mass. Hist. Soc., bound MSS · Newport Historical Society, Newport, Rhode Island, First Congregational Church, Newport, R. I., papers · Rhode Island Historical Society, Providence, Rhode Island, Moses Brown papers · Yale U., Yale MSS

Likenesses J. Badger, oils, Mass. Hist. Soc.

Wealth at death near poverty: Park's memoir in *Works of Samuel Hopkins*

Hopkins, Stephen (1707–1785), revolutionary politician in America, was born on 7 March 1707 in Providence, Rhode Island, east of a former American Indian village called Mashapaug in what is today the Elmwood section of Providence. He was the second of nine children born to farmers William Hopkins jun. (*c*.1681–1738) and Ruth Wilkinson (*b.* 1686), a devout Quaker. Hopkins moved at an early age with his parents and older brother to a farm at Chopmist in a part of 'the outlands' of Providence that was incorporated as the town of Scituate in 1731. On this agricultural frontier Hopkins grew to manhood, working on his parents' farm, receiving an education from his mother, and acquiring skills as a surveyor. In 1726 he married Sarah Scott (1707–1753) of Providence with whom he had seven children in a marriage that endured until her death by suicide in 1753 after a debilitating illness. On 2 January 1755 he married Ann, *née* Smith (1717–1782), the widow of Benjamin Smith.

Though he lacked formal education, the man John Adams would later describe as a person of 'wit, humour, anecdotes, science, and learning' became the first town moderator of Scituate in 1731 at the age of twenty-four. This post was the initial step in a political career that included election to the office of speaker of the Rhode Island house of representatives (seven times), service as governor (nine one-year terms), the position of chief justice of Rhode Island's highest court (eleven years), and selection as a Rhode Island delegate to the first and second continental congresses (1774–9). The rise of Hopkins in the world of government was accompanied by a rapid ascent in the business of trade and commerce. In 1742 he moved from rural Scituate, which he represented in the state legislature, to the port town of Providence where he immediately secured election to the general assembly and resumed the post of house speaker that he first held in 1738. Hopkins formed business partnerships with prominent Newport (Rhode Island) merchant Godfrey Malbone and then with the powerful Brown family, Providence's

leading eighteenth-century entrepreneurs. Thereafter, his wealth and financial connections fuelled his rise to political prominence.

Hopkins's first significant foray into intercolonial politics came in 1754 when he represented Rhode Island at the Albany congress. Farsighted enough to see the advantages of colonial co-operation in the face of a potential war with France and practical enough to realize the potential usefulness in protecting commerce of a strong colonial navy (one of the plan's prospects), Hopkins favoured the British-promoted plan of an American colonial union and wrote a pamphlet defending his participation in the locally unpopular conclave. The plan, however, failed under the heavy weight of colonial infighting.

In 1755 Hopkins was elected to his first term as governor, a post with little constitutional power under Rhode Island's system of legislative ascendancy. None the less he began to exert considerable political strength and influence as the leader of the dominant faction in the colony's emergent two-party system—one of America's first. In this political milieu, opposing groups, one headed by Samuel Ward of Westerly and the other by Hopkins, were organized with sectional overtones. Generally speaking (though with notable exceptions) the merchants and farmers of southern Rhode Island (Ward) battled with their counterparts from Providence and its environs (Hopkins). The principal goal of these groups was to secure control of the powerful legislature. Rampant factionalism, with Hopkins usually prevailing, endured until 1768 when Ward and Hopkins agreed to retire from future gubernatorial races. In 1770 Hopkins began a six-year tenure as chief justice—an office he continued to hold even after he and his former adversary, Ward, went to Philadelphia in 1774 to represent Rhode Island's interests in the first continental congress.

When Britain began to reorganize its North American empire at the conclusion of the Seven Years' War in 1763, Hopkins began to develop and articulate economic and political proposals that ran counter to parliamentary enactments. In the radical *Providence Gazette*, which he helped to establish in 1762, Hopkins opposed the renewal of the Molasses Act of 1733 upon its expiration in 1764. He denounced the measure's 6*d*. per gallon duty on foreign molasses as destructive of Rhode Island's lucrative triangular trade with the West Indies and as a levy that diminished Rhode Island's ability to buy British manufactures or pay British creditors. The Sugar Act of 1764 reduced the duty to 3*d*., but that toll was far greater than the one half of 1 per cent duty recommended by Hopkins in his essay, and the new levy was marked by much more vigorous enforcement than the old.

Late in 1764 Hopkins penned a more elaborate analysis of imperial relations—one which shifted from a purely economic defence of colonial rights to a political and constitutional conception of the empire. In this pamphlet, *The Rights of Colonies Examined*, Hopkins repeatedly referred not merely to the economic interests of Rhode Islanders, or of the northern colonists (as in the first essay), but rather to the broad rights of 'Americans'. This treatise is notable in that it suggests a federal theory of empire, with parliament legislating on matters of imperial concern—war, trade, international relations—but with colonial assemblies possessing sovereignty in local affairs, including taxation. In 1766 this bold and defining tract was published in London under the title *The Grievances of the American Colonists Candidly Examined.*

In 1768 another Providence lawyer, Silas Downer, colleague, friend, and protégé of Hopkins, delivered a path-breaking public discourse at the local 'Liberty Tree' repudiating the recently passed Declaratory Act of 1766 (in which parliament declared its sovereignty over the American colonies in all matters, most notably taxation) and denying the authority of parliament to make any laws of any kind to regulate the colonies. In 1774 Hopkins took attorney Downer to the first continental congress to serve as secretary to the Rhode Island delegation. During the second continental congress, which convened in September 1775, Hopkins became chairman of the naval committee and secured for his brother Esek (1718–1802) the position of first commodore and commander-in-chief of the newly created continental navy; then, as chairman of the naval and marine committee, Stephen supervised the civilian administration of the American navy. In July 1776 he became one of two Rhode Island signers of the Declaration of Independence (William Ellery was the other), and he was the Rhode Island member of the thirteen-man committee that drafted the articles of confederation—America's first written constitution.

Declining health, including what was then described as 'shaking palsy', limited Hopkins's role in the events of the revolution. Despite his continuing election as a delegate, he was unable to attend sessions of the congress after 1776, but he did serve from December 1776 to May 1778 on the Rhode Island council of war, an *ad hoc* body established by the legislature to supervise and direct Rhode Island's war effort. In addition he was a delegate to the wartime convention of New England states in 1776, 1777, and 1779, serving as convention president in 1777.

In his declining years Hopkins continued his productive relationship with the powerful and versatile Brown family of Providence with whom he was bound by ties of family, religion, literary and civic projects, and commercial enterprise. In 1781 he had an unexpected visit from George Washington, who had gone to Rhode Island to consult with General Jean Baptiste de Vimeur, comte de Rochambeau, the commander of the American-allied French expeditionary force, then quartered in Newport. House guest Moses Brown, who, like Hopkins, was a leading Quaker businessman, remarked on the 'unaffected friendliness' of the two revolutionaries as they talked about the war and the forthcoming Virginia campaign. On 20 January 1782 Ann, his wife of twenty-seven years, died. By that date five of his seven children (all by his first marriage) had also predeceased him. On 13 July 1785 Hopkins—governor, jurist, legislator, patriot, pamphleteer, farmer, merchant, educator (he was the first chancellor of Brown University), amateur scientist, and civic leader—died peacefully in his Providence home, a structure now preserved as a national historic site, and was buried in Providence's north burial-ground.

PATRICK T. CONLEY

Sources P. R. Campbell, ed., *Stephen Hopkins: the rights of colonies examined* (Providence, 1974) · W. E. Foster, *Stephen Hopkins: a Rhode Island statesman*, 2 vols. (Providence, 1884) · M. Appleton, 'Stephen Hopkins', *A portrait album: four great Rhode Island leaders* (Providence, 1978), 29–59 · D. S. Lovejoy, *Rhode Island politics and the American revolution, 1760–1776* (1958) · S. V. James, *Colonial Rhode Island: a history* (1975) · 'Notes on the Hopkins family: genealogical and biographical', *Narragansett Historical Register*, 7 (1889), 137–54
Archives Brown University, Providence, Rhode Island, letters
Likenesses J. Trumbull, pen-and-ink sketch, Frick Art Reference Library

Hopkins, William (*fl.* 1674), stenographer and writing master, wrote *The flying pen-man, or, The art of short-writing by a more easie, exact, compendious, and speedy way* (1674), using a system related to those of Thomas Shelton, Jeremiah Rich, and especially Theophilus Metcalfe. Beautifully engraved with ornamental borders and a frontispiece portrait of Hopkins by Jan Drapentier, the volume contains laudatory poems by Albertus Warren, E. Coles (possibly Elisha Coles, the stenographer), and E[dward?] Beecher. The poem by Warren below the portrait notes the 'mild but serious visage' of the handsome, austere, and scholarly Hopkins, whose 'tongue for Speed' is stated to be 'matched by the pen'. Hopkins is depicted writing Psalm 117 in shorthand as he sits before a bookcase containing the titles of ten works by stenographic predecessors, among them John Willis, William Folkingham, William Mason, Rich, and Shelton. Hopkins's own subtitle pays tribute to Theophilus Metcalfe.

While *The Flying Pen-Man* contained 'nothing new in the art' (Pitman, 19), the work does present a clear exposition of his system. Hopkins provides a useful dictionary of common words, showing how they would be spelt if sounded in his shorthand system and what letters were to be omitted, and also a list of phrases commonly used in sermons, demonstrating the close link between religion and seventeenth-century stenography. In his preface, Hopkins makes an oblique reference to the advantageous secret uses of shorthand by protestant travellers and merchants abroad, stating that:

> twas a maine part of my designe in this … to accomodate our Merchants and others English in the parts beyond the Seas, with this Succinct Secret and Litle Pocket Consort, that there, in dispite of Misguided Zeal the Doctrine which is only necessary (but forbidden to be read in our Native Language on the other side of the water) may be read secretly and at pleasure with safetie because Secret.

The preface suggests that Hopkins was a fervent admirer of Sir Walter Raleigh ('S^r W R'). PAGE LIFE

Sources Wood, *Ath. Oxon.*, 2nd edn, 2.1074 · Wood, *Ath. Oxon.*, new edn, 4.681 · J. H. Lewis, *An historical account of the rise and progress of short hand* (privately printed, London, c.1825) · I. Pitman, *A history of shorthand*, 3rd edn (1891) · M. Levy, *The history of short-hand writing* (1862) · E. Arber, ed., *The term catalogues, 1668–1709*, 3 vols. (privately printed, London, 1903–6); repr. (1965), vol. 1, pp. 198, 386 · A. Paterson, 'A seventeenth-century stenographer: Theophilus Metcalfe', *Phonetic Journal*, 56 (1897), 221–2 · A. Heal, *The English writing-masters*

and their copy-books, 1570–1800 (1931); repr. (Hildesheim, 1962) · J. Westby-Gibson, *The bibliography of shorthand* (1887)
Likenesses J. Drapentier, line engraving, 1674, BM, NPG; repro. in W. Hopkins, *The flying penman, or, The art of short-writing* (1674)

Hopkins, William (1647–1700), Church of England clergyman and antiquary, was born at Evesham, Worcestershire, on 2 August 1647, and baptized on 28 August, the son of **George Hopkins** (1620–1666), clergyman and ejected minister, then vicar of All Saints, Evesham. It is not certainly known whether the wife who survived George Hopkins, Margaret, was also William's mother. George Hopkins was born at Bewdley, Worcestershire, on 15 April 1620, the son of William Hopkins (*d.* in or after 1641), who was described by Richard Baxter as 'the most eminent, wise, and truly religious magistrat of Bewdley' (Keeble and Nuttall, 1.92). George matriculated from New Inn Hall, Oxford, in 1638, graduating BA in 1641 and proceeding MA in 1648. Vicar of Evesham from 1642 he also served in the parliamentarian armies, presumably as a chaplain. Hopkins was, like his father, a friend of Baxter, who wrote a preface for his *Salvation from Sin* (1655) and later cited him as the authority for 'the certainest and fullest instance of witchcraft that ever I knew' (*Calamy rev.*, 275). In the 1650s George Hopkins was an assistant to the Worcestershire commission of ejectors and an active member of the Worcestershire association of ministers. He was ejected from his living in 1662 under the Act of Uniformity, and moved to Dumbleton, Gloucestershire. There he took the so-called Oxford oath to avoid further proscription under the Five Mile Act of 1665. He died between 2 March (when he made his will) and 30 June 1666 (when it was proved).

William Hopkins was educated at Evesham grammar school and matriculated as a commoner of Trinity College, Oxford, in October 1661. He moved to St Mary Hall in 1666, and proceeded MA in 1668. In 1671–2 he accompanied Henry Coventry (1619–1686) as his chaplain on an embassy to Sweden. Coventry returned to become secretary of state, Hopkins returned with an enthusiastic interest in the languages and history of the Germanic north. With Coventry's support he was appointed a prebendary of Worcester Cathedral, where he was installed in March 1675. He married Averill (*d.* 1691), daughter of Thomas Martin, on 3 February 1678.

From that time Hopkins worked closely with the dean of Worcester, the learned George Hickes, the nonjuror, both in the cathedral chapter and in pioneering studies of Old English. He did not, however, immediately take up residence in Worcester. The dean and chapter appointed him to the curacy of Mortlake, Surrey, in June 1678, and in 1680 he was afternoon preacher at St Lawrence Jewry, London, then newly rebuilt by Wren. He exchanged Mortlake for the vicarage of Lindridge, Worcestershire, in 1686, and then went to live in the city. He was appointed master of St Oswald's Hospital, Worcester, in 1697 but surrendered his salary there to establish an endowment for the hospital. His wife, Averill, died in 1691; he married for a second time in 1699 Elizabeth, *née* Bromley, widow of Dr Thomas Whitehorne of Tewkesbury.

Hopkins proceeded DD on 5 July 1692. He had combined his theological and his historical interests in 1686 in publishing Bertramnus of Corbie's eucharistic tract *De sanguine et corpore domini* as *The Book of Bertram or Ratramnus Concerning the Body and Blood of the Lord*, with Latin text and an English translation. In 1691 he ventured into religion and politics in *Animadversions on Mr Johnson's Answer to Jovian*. By that time George Hickes had been deprived of his deanery for not taking the oaths to William and Mary, and *Animadversions* was a contribution to a convoluted exchange on divine right and unconditional obedience between Hickes, writing as Jovian, and Samuel Johnson (1649–1703), the author of *Julian the Apostate*. Hopkins's intervention was largely a mark of his friendship with Hickes, which was evidently not impaired by his own conformity to the new regime. He was generally more concerned with scholarship than politics. He assisted Edmund Gibson, later bishop of London, in preparing *Chronicon Saxonicum* (1692) and Gibson's first translation of Camden's *Britannia*. He also provided Anthony Wood with lists of Worcester clergy and other notes for Wood's *Athenae Oxonienses*, and collected material for a history of Worcester Cathedral.

Hopkins died at Worcester of a fever on 18 May 1700, and was buried in the cathedral. There was a memorial there to him, which seems to have named only his first wife. It was later removed and lost, but was replaced in 1910 by a small brass inscription in the north transept, which probably marks the site of his grave. George Hickes published *Seventeen Sermons*, from Hopkins's papers, in 1708, prefaced by a memoir of his friend's life and work.

G. H. MARTIN

Sources DNB · Foster, *Alum. Oxon.* · Wood, *Ath. Oxon.*, new edn, vol. 4 · *The life and times of Anthony Wood*, ed. A. Clark, 5 vols., OHS, 19, 21, 26, 30, 40 (1891–1900) · W. Hopkins, *Seventeen sermons*, ed. G. Hickes (1708) · W. M. Ede, *The cathedral church of Christ and the Blessed Virgin Mary of Worcester: its monuments and their stories* [1925] · *Calamy rev.* · *Calendar of the correspondence of Richard Baxter*, ed. N. H. Keeble and G. F. Nuttall, 1 (1991)
Archives Bodl. Oxf., letters to Anthony Wood

Hopkins, William (1706–1786), religious controversialist, was born on 27 December 1706, the son of John and Gwelthean Hopkins of Monmouth. After attending Monmouth grammar school, he matriculated at All Souls College, Oxford, on 19 November 1724, and graduated BA in 1728. He was ordained deacon in St Giles-in-the-Fields, Middlesex, in March 1728; appointed curate of Waldron, Sussex, on 25 March 1729; and ordained priest on 17 March 1731. In the same year he became curate of Buxted and Cuckfield, Sussex, and an assistant master of Cuckfield grammar school; he also became vicar of the neighbouring village of Bolney. In 1753 he published anonymously *An Appeal to the Common Sense of All Christian People*, a controversial, Arian work. He also printed several pieces in the *London Magazine* in 1754 under the *nom de plume* Philalethes. He married Anna, widow of a Mr Stanbridge, and daughter of John Cook, of Bolney. Their son, William, was baptized on 10 July 1754 in Bolney; he married Philadelphia Funnell on 21 May 1781 in Cuckfield, where Hopkins had been elected schoolmaster in January 1756. Anna died in November 1782.

Hopkins published two anonymous pieces criticizing the liturgy of the Church of England in 1763 and 1765. The following year he became curate of Slaugham, Sussex, and both there and in Bolney he made alterations to the service with the help of the churchwardens. He supported the petition to parliament against compulsory subscription to the liturgy and to the Thirty-Nine Articles, and he published several letters in 1771 and 1772 in the *Lewes Journal*, signed A Sussex Clergyman. Hopkins also published 'Queries recommended to … the public with regard to the Thirty-Nine Articles', and a pamphlet against Josiah Tucker's *Apology for the Present Church of England*. His last work, issued in 1784, was a scholarly translation of Exodus. Opinion varied on the value of the work, especially the notes, because of Hopkins's Arian beliefs. After a period of mental debility Hopkins died in Cuckfield in April 1786 of 'a suppression of urine' (*Short Memoir*, 16). He was buried in Cuckfield church on 28 April.

GORDON GOODWIN, *rev.* ADAM JACOB LEVIN

Sources *A short memoir of the late William Hopkins, BA, vicar of Bolney, Sussex* (1815) • Foster, *Alum. Oxon.* • R. Williams, *Enwogion Cymru: a biographical dictionary of eminent Welshmen* (1852), 220 • *DWB*, 366 • IGI • Allibone, *Dict.* • F. J. G. Robinson and others, *Eighteenth-century British books: an author union catalogue*, 3 (1981), 168 • A. Chalmers, ed., *The general biographical dictionary*, new edn, 18 (1814), 161–2
Archives NL. Wales

Hopkins, William (1793–1866), mathematician and geologist, was born on 2 February 1793 at Kingston in Derbyshire, the only son of William Hopkins, gentleman farmer. The young Hopkins acquired agricultural skills in Norfolk prior to an unsuccessful attempt to farm a small property, purchased for him by his father, near Bury St Edmunds in Suffolk. Following the death of his first wife, a Miss Braithwaite, about 1821 Hopkins sold the farm, cleared his debts, and entered himself as an undergraduate at Peterhouse, Cambridge, in 1822. While an undergraduate he married Caroline Frances Boys (1799–1881). In 1827 he graduated seventh wrangler in the mathematical tripos, and three years later he received his MA. Since college fellowships were open only to unmarried men, Hopkins instead settled in Cambridge as a private tutor or mathematical coach whose task it was to 'drill' the most promising undergraduates for a high place in the mathematical tripos.

Hopkins quickly became one of Cambridge's most respected private tutors with the nickname 'senior wrangler maker'. He admitted that a successful private tutor could earn a comfortable £700–£800 per annum, each pupil paying upwards of £100. By 1849 he could claim nearly 200 wranglers among his pupils, of whom seventeen were senior wranglers and forty-four in one of the top three places. Among them were G. G. Stokes and William Thomson, and later pupils included James Clerk Maxwell and Isaac Todhunter. In an otherwise cold, unworldly, and monastic institution, Hopkins's humanity served to inspire his pupils. As Francis Galton later explained:

Hopkins to use a Cantab expression is a regular brick; tells funny stories connected with different problems and is no way Donnish; he rattles us on at a splendid pace and makes mathematics anything but a dry subject by entering thoroughly into its metaphysics. I never enjoyed anything so much before. (Pearson, 1.163)

Throughout a period of tripos reform during the 1840s and 1850s Hopkins sought to maintain 'the standard of acquirement in our higher class of students'. He thus opposed exclusion from the tripos of some of the more advanced branches of the mathematical sciences (including hydrodynamics). Such subjects contributed 'most to elevate and enoble the character of our mathematical studies' and were vital to that small but elite group of students who 'remain among us, and afterwards form the tutorial body of the University, occupy its important offices, and give to it its prevailing tone and character' (Hopkins, 10–12). Hopkins's primary commitment to the education of a mathematical and scientific elite differentiated him from Cambridge contemporaries such as William Whewell who sought to shape the university's ideals of a liberal education for the general body of undergraduates.

Adam Sedgwick, Cambridge professor of geology from 1819, fired Hopkins's enthusiasm for geological science from about 1833. An early paper (1834) focused on the stratification of Derbyshire and in the late 1830s Hopkins seemed a likely candidate to undertake an unpaid official survey of his native county at a time when the geological survey was in its infancy. In the event, Hopkins had more pressing commitments.

By 1835 he had read to the Cambridge Philosophical Society his first major scientific memoir which introduced a new subject, 'Researches in physical geology'. Physical geology would bring the power and prestige of mathematical analysis to bear on geological phenomena. Geological science would thereby be raised to the same high status as physical astronomy. As with the mythologized history of physical astronomy, the new geology would have three stages: first, a geometrical description of the relevant motions (analogous to Kepler's laws of planetary motion); second, postulation of a very general force that would cause the motions (analogous to gravity); and third, derivation of the actual motions from the general force according to dynamical principles. The formulation of geometrical laws of faults, fissures, mineral veins, and so on constituted the aim of his first memoir. Cautiously, Hopkins sought a very general cause, an 'elevatory force', responsible for all these phenomena wherever and whenever they occurred. He found that cause in the widely held doctrine of central heat whereby the earth, assumed to have been formed as a hot fluid mass that subsequently solidified, had undergone, and continued to experience, a progressive cooling. Like the doctrine of universal gravitation in its generality and simplicity, central heat became for Hopkins the fundamental agency of geological dynamics.

Hopkins's preferred model was of a largely solid earth containing cavities. Hot vapours or fluids forced into those cavities from below would produce elevatory pressures in local regions. This model clashed directly with the steady-state (non-progressionist) geological theory of Charles Lyell which denied the doctrine of primitive heat while upholding the notion of a largely liquid interior supporting a thin terrestrial crust less than 100 miles thick. Most of Hopkins's subsequent extensive investigations in physical geology were directed to justifying the adequacy of his model. Between 1838 and 1842 a series of papers for the Royal Society argued on mathematical grounds that the observed behaviour of the terrestrial planet around its axis (its precession and nutation) were consistent with a solid, but inconsistent with a liquid, interior. A long report to the British Association (1847) treated the phenomena of earthquakes and volcanoes within the same framework.

Guided by his one-time pupil William Thomson, Hopkins instituted a series of experiments with the assistance of James Prescott Joule and William Fairbairn in Manchester to determine the effects of enormous pressures on the melting point of substances, the results of which he interpreted as supporting the solidity of the earth. These experiments were supported by Royal Society grants. During the same period Hopkins argued that past climatic conditions, including those of an ice age, would be unaffected by the internal cooling of the earth, being due instead to changes on the surface of the earth.

Within the mid-nineteenth century British scientific establishment, Hopkins had few rivals in the field of physical geology. Only when he attempted to apply the same methods to explain the mechanism of glaciers did he find himself engaged in intense controversy with the doyen of glacial phenomena, J. D. Forbes, who regarded the subject as almost a personal possession and who resisted what he saw as an attempt at territorial annexation by a Cambridge analyst with no personal experience of his beloved alpine glaciers. Towards the end of Hopkins's life, however, William Thomson tactfully began to question his mathematical and astronomical arguments, though not his conclusions, regarding the solidity of the earth.

Hopkins received the Wollaston medal of the Royal Society in 1850 for his geological investigations, was elected president of the Geological Society in 1851 and became president of the British Association in 1853. His most enduring legacy, however, was his role in training the group of outstanding mathematical physicists (most notably Stokes, Thomson, and Maxwell) who dominated Victorian physics in the period 1850–80. Hopkins had one son and three daughters, including the social purity campaigner (Jane) Ellice *Hopkins (1836–1904), from his second marriage. His other interests included music, poetry, and landscape painting. He died in Stoke Newington on 13 October 1866, survived by his wife.   CROSBIE SMITH

Sources C. Smith and M. N. Wise, *Energy and empire: a biographical study of Lord Kelvin* (1989) · C. Smith, 'William Hopkins and the shaping of dynamical geology, 1830–1860', *British Journal for the History of Science*, 22 (1989), 27–52 · W. Hopkins, *Remarks on certain proposed regulations respecting the studies of the university* (1841) · K. Pearson, *The life, letters and labours of Francis Galton*, 3 vols. in 4 (1914–30) · S. Rothblatt, *The revolution of the dons: Cambridge and society in Victorian England* (1968) · *DNB* · J. A. Secord, 'The geological survey of Great Britain as a research school', *History of Science*, 24 (1986), 223–75 · G. K. C. Clarke, 'A short history of scientific investigations on glaciers', *Journal of Glaciology, Special Issue* (1987), 4–24 · B. Hevly, 'The heroic science of glacier motion', *Osiris*, 2nd ser., 11 (1996), 66–86

Archives CUL, letters to Sir George Stokes · CUL, letters to James Thomson and William Thomson · U. Edin. L., corresp. with Sir Charles Lyell · U. St Andr. L., corresp. with James Forbes

Likenesses oils, Peterhouse, Cambridge · woodcut, NPG

Wealth at death under £12,000: probate, 3 Jan 1867, *CGPLA Eng. & Wales*

Hopkinson, Sir Alfred (1851–1939), lawyer, was born at Manchester on 28 June 1851, the second son of John Hopkinson, mechanical engineer and sometime mayor of Manchester, and his wife, Alice, daughter of John Dewhurst, of Skipton, Yorkshire. His elder brother was John *Hopkinson (1849–1898), electrical engineer.

Hopkinson was educated at a private school in Manchester before going on in 1866 to the Owens College. In 1869 he went from there with a scholarship to Lincoln College, Oxford, where he was placed in the second class in *literae humaniores* in 1872 and in the first class in the BCL examination in 1874. He was elected to the Stowell fellowship in civil law at University College, Oxford, in 1873, and to the Vinerian scholarship in 1875. In 1873 he married Esther (d. 1931), youngest daughter of Henry Wells of Nottingham; they had four sons and three daughters. Of their sons the second, John Henry, became archdeacon of Westmorland, and the third was MP for Mossley, Lancashire.

Hopkinson was called to the bar by Lincoln's Inn in 1873 and settling in Manchester as a barrister soon acquired a considerable local practice on the northern circuit, mainly in the palatine chancery court. In addition he held a lecturership and (later at the age of twenty-four) the professorship of law at the Owens College. He resigned this chair in 1889.

In 1885 and 1892 Hopkinson stood unsuccessfully as a Liberal candidate in Manchester. After moving to London in 1889 and taking silk in 1892, however, he was elected member for the Cricklade division of Wiltshire in 1895, only to resign the seat in 1898 on his appointment as principal of the Owens College, the first constituent college of the newly formed Victoria University of which he became first vice-chancellor in 1900. In these offices he did his finest work. During the 1890s he also contributed to periodicals such as *Cornhill Magazine* and *Fraser's Magazine*.

Retiring from the vice-chancellorship in 1913, Hopkinson devoted himself to public service. His activities included visiting India to report on the University of Bombay, and at a by-election in 1926 he was once more returned to parliament as Unionist member for the Combined English Universities, finally retiring in 1929.

A man of striking physical appearance and great personal charm, Hopkinson was a principled man with a deep-rooted belief that 'the hope of mankind is in the Christian religion'. In *Rebuilding Britain: a Survey of Problems of Reconstruction* (1918) he expounded his political ideas and views of English affairs, while in *Penultima* (1930) he gave frank and refreshing expression to the views which had guided him throughout his long life.

Hopkinson was knighted in 1910 and elected an honorary fellow of Lincoln College, Oxford, in 1903. He received honorary degrees from several universities and was elected bencher of Lincoln's Inn in 1896 and treasurer in 1921. He died at Long Meadow, Bovingdon, Hertfordshire, on 11 November 1939.

ALFRED T. DAVIES, *rev.* CATHERINE PEASE-WATKIN

Sources *The Times* (13 Nov 1939) · A. Hopkinson, *Penultima* (1930) · A. Hopkinson, 'In memoriam: Alfred Hopkinson', *Alpine Journal*, 52 (1940), 114–15 · private information (1949) · personal knowledge (1949) · *Wellesley index* · *CGPLA Eng. & Wales* (1939)
Archives JRL, letters to *Manchester Guardian*
Likenesses W. Rothenstein, lithograph, *c*.1899, NPG · L. Moholy, photograph, 1937, NPG
Wealth at death £42,068 10s. 4d.: probate, 14 Dec 1939, CGPLA Eng. & Wales

Hopkinson, Bertram (1874–1918), mechanical and aeronautical engineer, was born on 11 January 1874 at Woodlea, Birmingham, the eldest son of John *Hopkinson FRS (1849–1898), electrical engineer, and his wife, Evelyn Oldenbourg. His father was himself the son of an engineer. He attended St Paul's School, London, living at home in an engineering household. Like his father, he read mathematics at Trinity College, Cambridge (1893–6), but then entered the legal profession and was called to the bar in 1897. His father's death (together with those of a brother and two sisters) in the following year led him back to engineering, and by 1903 he had achieved such success that in the same year he was elected to the Cambridge chair in mechanism and applied mechanics (that his father had once refused) at the age of twenty-nine. On 31 December 1903 he married Mariana Dulce Siemens, a distant cousin to the founders of the German firm of electrical engineers; they had seven daughters.

The mechanical sciences tripos at Cambridge, on whose curriculum Hopkinson's father had had a deep influence, consisted of papers in mathematics, mechanics, strength of materials and theory of structures, heat and heat engines, and electricity and magnetism. From the time of his predecessor, J. A. Ewing, and through the first half of the twentieth century, the teaching staff were expected to be conversant with all of these subjects (and it is perhaps not surprising that vacant posts were usually filled by those who had themselves been undergraduates at Cambridge). This polymathy is reflected in the twenty-nine items in the volume of Hopkinson's papers published posthumously in 1921. His chief investigations relate to the strength of metals under non-steady stresses (including explosive loading and studies of fatigue and hysteresis), to the magnetic properties of iron and its alloys, to a wide range of problems encountered in internal combustion engines, and to fluid motion involving singularities (sources and vortices). All of these papers combine appropriate mathematics with a clear appreciation of practical application. The Hopkinson bar, of use in the testing of materials, became a standard piece of equipment.

Hopkinson was equally clear about the ways in which

Ewing's pattern of teaching should be supported, and the Cambridge school flourished both in numbers and in reputation. He himself was elected FRS in 1910, and he became a professorial fellow of King's College, Cambridge, in 1914. On the outbreak of the First World War he was commissioned in the Royal Engineers. He immediately applied his knowledge of explosions to problems of both attack and defence; he worked on the best form of bomb to be dropped from aircraft; and other experiments led to the successful invention of a 'blister' to be added to the hull of a ship, designed to absorb the energy of an exploding torpedo or mine. He was secretary of a committee set up by the Royal Society to advise the government on the scientific problems of the war, and he also took part in an organization for dealing with enemy cipher. In 1915 he was appointed to the department of military aeronautics, where he was in charge of the supply to aircraft of all items of their armament. He established an experimental station for the Royal Flying Corps at Orford Ness, and later at Martlesham Heath, where the testing of aircraft was under his control.

This work led to Hopkinson's promotion to the rank of colonel, and to his appointment as CMG; it included the development of bombs, guns, gunsights, and ammunition, and also the systematic study of night flying, and of navigation in clouds and bad weather. He learned to fly at Orford Ness, and during the latter part of the war he made many solo flights between the stations in England and to France. He died on one of these flights, from Martlesham Heath to London, on 26 August 1918, when his Bristol Fighter crashed at High Ongar, Essex, in bad weather. He was buried at Cambridge. It is likely that, had he lived, he would not have returned to Cambridge; there were plans for a national school of aeronautical engineering, of which he was to have been head. He was survived by his wife.

JACQUES HEYMAN

Sources DNB · J. A. E., *PRS*, 95A (1918–19), xxvi–xxxvi · A. V. Hill, 'Colonel Bertram Hopkinson, an appreciation', *Alpine Journal*, 32 (1918–19), 353–6 · J. Ewing and J. Larmor, eds., *The scientific papers of Bertram Hopkinson* (1921) · T. J. N. Hilken, *Engineering at Cambridge University, 1783–1965* (1967) · T. M. Charlton, 'Professor Bertram Hopkinson', *Notes and Records of the Royal Society*, 29 (1974–5) · *CGPLA Eng. & Wales* (1918)
Likenesses A. J. Nowell, oils, 1911, U. Cam., department of engineering; repro. in *PRS*, 95A (1918–19)
Wealth at death £16,457 0s. 5d.: probate, 14 Dec 1918, CGPLA Eng. & Wales

Hopkinson [*née* Botting], **Eirene Adeline** [*known as* Antonia White] (1899–1980), novelist, was born on 31 March 1899 at 22 Perham Road, West Kensington, London, the only child of Cecil George Botting (1870–1929), classics master at St Paul's School, London, and his wife, Christine Julia Barbour White (1871–1939), governess, daughter of Henry and Clementina White. She disliked her name and was known for most of her professional life as Antonia White. Her father, a gifted but rigid man, dominated her childhood, and she would blame him for her terrifying emotional problems. In 1906 the family was converted to Roman Catholicism, and Antonia boarded at the Sacred Heart Convent, Roehampton, London (1908–14), the

Eirene Adeline Hopkinson [Antonia White] (**1899–1980**), by Sir Cedric Morris, 1936

experience on which she based her famous novel *Frost in May*. She wrote: 'I sometimes wish I'd never been brought into and up in the Catholic religion … but I can no more escape from it all than I can restore the lenses to my eyes or straighten my broken finger' (*Diaries, 1958–1979*, 11 June 1971). She was removed from school after the nuns found a 'scandalous' novel she had been writing, and this event came to symbolize the struggle between her wish to please her father and the church, and her yearning for a life of art and freedom.

Distancing herself from Cecil Botting's values, Antonia worked from the age of sixteen as a governess, clerk, and actress, and earned a good income from writing advertisements and newspaper fiction. But though this writing came easily, she found serious creative work a lifelong problem. On 28 April 1921 she married Reginald Henry (Reggie) Green-Wilkinson (*b.* 1899/1900), a part-time actor and a secretary for Anglo Continental film studios, but the marriage was annulled owing to non-consummation. This led to a breakdown, and in November 1922 she was committed for nine months to Bethlem Hospital, London, where she suffered hallucinations and was forcibly fed. Although she was not certified again, the possibility of mental illness haunted her for the rest of her life.

On 15 April 1925 Antonia married Eric Earnshaw Smith (1893/4–1972), a civil servant, with whom she had a deep platonic friendship. The marriage was permitted by the church, but within a year she had lapsed as a Catholic. As she later wrote, 'The general climate of the 1920s, the scepticism, the almost idolatrous devotion to art got under my skin' (*The Hound and the Falcon*, 155). She worked in Crawford's advertising agency, mixed with painters

and writers, and soon began to look for a more normal relationship. She was now an attractive and sophisticated woman, nothing like the girlish heroine of her novels, and had several lovers. Eventually she sought a second annulment to marry Rudolph (Silas) Glossop, a mining engineer who was the father of her daughter, the writer Susan Chitty (*b.* 1929). But instead she married, on 28 November 1930, (Henry) Thomas (Tom) *Hopkinson (1905–1990), the future editor of *Picture Post*. They had a daughter, Lyndall, born in 1931.

Antonia continued to work in women's journalism and on the fringes of the London literary world. She was quite undomestic; her children were looked after by a nurse. Her husband encouraged her to write and in 1933 she produced her best-known novel, *Frost in May*. This has been acclaimed ever since as the classic account of a Catholic education: a female, more accessible equivalent to James Joyce's *Portrait of the Artist*. But, as she complained long afterwards, 'it hangs round my neck like a withered wreath' (*Diaries, 1926–1957*, 16 Aug 1954). She could not follow up her success because her marriage was crumbling, owing to Tom's infidelity and her fears that she was again becoming mad. In 1935 she left home, became involved with various younger men, and submitted to a long course of Freudian analysis which, she felt, enabled her to stay out of asylums. She and Tom Hopkinson were divorced in 1938. She had a difficult relationship with her daughters, who lived with her only part-time. Both later wrote memoirs of her.

Antonia remained in London throughout the war, working for the BBC and later the Special Operations Executive. Her letters (1940–41) to the Catholic intellectual Peter Thorp were eventually published as *The Hound and the Falcon* (1965). Although troubled by 'the Church's rigorously repressive attitude towards so much in contemporary thought and opinion' ('Foreword' to *The Hound and the Falcon*), she started to practise her religion again. Although she had no more affairs, it remained a love–hate relationship.

In 1950 Antonia published *The Lost Traveller*, which continues the story of the Antonia-figure, now called Clara, into adulthood. But it was nothing like as good as *Frost in May*, and the reviewers said so. It was followed by two better novels, *The Sugar House* (1952) and *Beyond the Glass* (1954), dealing with her first marriage and breakdown. She tried for many years to complete Clara's story, but was never able to get much beyond her release from Bethlem in 1923. A collection of short stories, *Strangers* (1954), also contains some striking work.

The last twenty-five years of Antonia's life were the calmest, though she was still distressed by religious doubts, money problems, and her writer's block. She lived in Kensington, alone except for her cats, who inspired two charming children's books, and supported herself by translating over thirty novels from French. The beginnings of another 'Clara' novel and an autobiography were published in *As Once in May* (1983), edited by Susan Chitty. In 1978, after years of neglect, *Frost in May* was reprinted as the first Virago Modern Classic. The three sequels followed and she was applauded as one of the very few writers who could transmute personal experience into literature. She died of cancer on 10 April 1980 at St Raphael's Nursing Home, Danehill, Sussex, and therefore did not live to see her novels dramatized on BBC television in 1981. She was buried in the Catholic cemetery at West Grinstead, Sussex, close to where her father's family had lived for generations. MERRYN WILLIAMS

Sources *Antonia White: diaries*, ed. S. Chitty, 1: *1926–1957* (1991) • *Antonia White: diaries*, ed. S. Chitty, 2: *1958–1979* (1992) • A. White, *The hound and the falcon* (1965) • L. P. Hopkinson, *Nothing to forgive* (1988) • S. Chitty, *Now to my mother* (1986) • A. White [E. A. Hopkinson], *As once in May*, ed. S. Chitty (1983) • T. Hopkinson, *Of this our time* (1982) • b. cert. • m. cert. [Eirene Adeline Botting and Reginald Henry Green-Wilkinson] • m. cert. [Eirene Adeline Botting and Eric Earnshaw Smith] • d. cert. • private information (2004)
Archives priv. coll., diaries
Likenesses C. Morris, oils, 1936, NPG [*see illus.*]
Wealth at death £6884: resworn probate, 8 Oct 1980, *CGPLA Eng. & Wales*

Hopkinson, Francis (1737–1791), musician, jurist, and revolutionary politician in America, was born on 2 October 1737 in Philadelphia and baptized at Christ Church, son of Thomas Hopkinson (1709–1751), lawyer, and his wife, Mary Johnson (1718–1804), both recent émigrés from England. He was among the first generation of native-born Americans trained to cultivate the arts and sciences on their own soil. Most were gentlemen amateurs who dabbled in many arts and mastered none. Hopkinson's skill in music, graphic design, and political satire was, however, exceptional. His career was shaped by a strong-willed, widowed mother who raised two sons and four daughters. Enrolled in 1751 in the first class of the College of Philadelphia, after a year at the Academy at Philadelphia, he received a BA in 1757 and an MA in 1760; he then read law under the province's attorney-general, Benjamin Chew, passing the bar a year later and practising as a conveyancer until named collector of customs at New Salem, New Jersey, in 1763. He was able to appoint an agent as deputy to bear the brunt of the violent reaction to the hated Stamp Act, which imposed British taxation on internal colonial trade.

Between May 1766 and August 1767 Hopkinson visited Britain, haplessly seeking preferment through his mother's cousin, James Johnson, bishop of Worcester. He turned to studying drawing under Benjamin West before returning to Philadelphia and opening a dry goods (fabric) shop. On 1 September 1768 he married Ann (Nancy; 1747–1827), an heiress, daughter of Joseph Borden of nearby Bordentown, New Jersey, with whom he had five children. One, Joseph, became a congressman and wrote the lyrics for 'Hail Columbia'.

An accomplished organist, Hopkinson served as minister of music at Christ Church, Philadelphia, composing hymns and songs, among them 'My days have been so wondrous free', America's first secular song. A masque, 'The Temple of Minerva', a pastiche of others' music and his lyrics, was performed in Philadelphia during the American War of Independence.

By 1771 pacts of non-importation of British goods by American patriots had cut off supplies to Hopkinson's shop, forcing him to move to his wife's ancestral home. Two years later he was appointed to another sinecure: collector of customs at New Castle, Delaware, where pilots refused to serve ships carrying American Indian tea and so spared him the tempest then brewing at Boston over British taxes on tea. In New Jersey his father-in-law was a prominent figure in Burlington county, and his friend William Franklin was governor. He was named to a number of offices, including the governor's council in April 1774. This made him fair game for satirists, who mocked him as a witling soaring to power on a bridal veil. But by 1774 he was eyeing a broader target with an allegorical satire, *A Pretty Story*. This twenty-nine-page pamphlet, modelled on John Arbuthnot's *History of John Bull* (1712), tells how wicked stepmother (the British parliament) and evil steward (the prime minister) conspire to ruin the harmony of the ancestral farm. The pamphlet went through three editions between mid-August and December 1774. In 1776 he led New Jersey delegates to cast a crucial vote for the Declaration of Independence.

During wartime Hopkinson headed the navy board and the office accounting for loans to the new United States. In these years he maintained his residence in Bordentown, putting his home at risk from British troops and roving bands of loyalists. He also served as judge of admiralty for Pennsylvania. During 1780 he suffered the distinction of being the first American judge to be impeached. The charge that he accepted an inconsequential bribe was quickly dismissed as a political vendetta. Under the revised constitution of 1787 he was appointed to the United States court for Pennsylvania's eastern district, a position he held until his death.

Even during wartime Hopkinson pursued a virtuoso's career, composing music, inventing devices such as lamps that float on water, and serving as treasurer of the American Philosophical Society, at which he presented scientific papers. He wrote some of the most popular ballads of the war, which mostly poked fun at the British and American loyalists. The 'Camp Ballad', 'The Toast', and 'The Battle of the Kegs' were set to music and sung throughout the new nation. Under contract to congress he claimed design of the stars and stripes flag along with the seal of the United States. He also illustrated some of his newspaper satires, most notably depicting the strident tone of polemics by using size of type to fit the tone.

During the war Hopkinson used satire to compensate for his physical incapacity to fight. Afterwards he satirized such civic issues as pollution and sanitation. For these he used gentle satire that contrasted with the slashing mockery of the wartime pieces such as his 'Battle of the Kegs' (1778), a ballad triumphing over the incident in which a few kegs of powder floating down the Delaware River frightened the enemy into shooting at anything afloat. When he employed the same tone later for satires of local politicians and anti-federalists, they replied in kind, insulting his apple-sized head, tiny body, effeminate manners, presumed homosexuality, and obvious sycophancy.

Hopkinson's triumph came as the producer of a mammoth procession on the streets of Philadelphia celebrating the adoption on 4 July 1788 of the new federal constitution as a 'New roof' sustained by thirteen columns, a design he had created. He died of apoplexy on 9 May 1791 in Philadelphia and was buried there two days later at Christ Church.   P. M. ZALL

Sources G. Hastings, *Life and works of Francis Hopkinson* (1926) • P. Zall, *Comical spirit of '76: humor of Francis Hopkinson* (1976) • G. Anderson, '"The temple of Minerva" and Francis Hopkinson: a reappraisal of America's first poet-composer', *Proceedings of the American Philosophical Society*, 120 (1976), 166–77 • E. Williams, 'The fancy work of Francis Hopkinson: did he design the stars and stripes?', *Prologue*, 20 (1988), 42–52
Archives American Philosophical Society, Philadelphia, MSS • Hist. Soc. Penn., family papers • Hunt. L., MSS • L. Cong., MSS
Likenesses R. E. Pine, oils, 1785, American Philosophical Society, Philadelphia

Hopkinson, Henry Lennox D'Aubigné, first Baron Colyton (1902–1996), diplomatist and politician, was born on 3 January 1902 at 78 Holland Park, Kensington, London, the eldest of three sons of Sir Henry Lennox Hopkinson (1855–1936), solicitor and later almoner of St Bartholomew's Hospital, and his wife, Marie Ruan (d. 1949), daughter of Francis Blake Du Bois, of St Croix, Virgin Islands, and New York. He was brought up at Duntisbourne House, near Cirencester, and educated at Eton College, where he was awarded the Royal Humane Society's award for saving an airman from drowning in the Thames, and at Trinity College, Cambridge, where he read modern languages, being already bilingual in English and French. He entered the diplomatic service in October 1924 and was posted as third secretary and private secretary to the ambassador in Washington, Sir Esme Howard. There he met and on 10 November 1927 married his first wife, Alice Labouisse Eno (d. 1953), the daughter of Henry Lane Eno, a professor at Princeton University. She was an elegant hostess both in Washington and subsequently at their house in Belgravia after their return to London in 1929. They had one son, Nicholas Henry Eno (1932–1991), and a daughter, Olivia, Nicholas's twin, who died when four days old. Hopkinson's next posting was to Stockholm and when he returned again to London in 1932 it was as assistant private secretary to the foreign secretary, Sir John Simon. Postings to Cairo (where he acquired a knowledge of Arabic) and to Athens (where he acted as chargé d'affaires in 1938 and 1939) were followed by yet another private secretarial appointment in London—this time to the permanent under-secretary, Sir Alexander Cadogan.

At the age of thirty-seven in 1939 Hopkinson was thought to be too old for military service, but when he was selected to be assistant to Oliver Lyttelton, minister of state in the Middle East, Cadogan reluctantly conceded 'as a patriot, I must agree to the best man going' (*The Independent*, 8 Jan 1996). His further wartime service was in Lisbon, where he was instrumental in securing the Azores air base for the allies and where he was made CMG, and as deputy British high commissioner in Italy after the collapse of Mussolini. The war years had established his reputation as a smooth and competent supporting diplomat.

When the war ended, however, Hopkinson accepted Anthony Eden's invitation to enter politics, first as a member of the Conservative parliamentary secretariat and research department (where he had an uneasy relationship with the liberal-minded Rab Butler) and then in February 1950 as MP for Taunton. Churchill recognized him as an unusually experienced new MP and promptly made him a member of his government in November 1951, initially as a junior minister at the Board of Trade and then from May 1952 (under his wartime chief Oliver Lyttelton again) at the Colonial Office. He was made a privy councillor in 1952. As minister of state in the Colonial Office, Hopkinson toured Africa in an attempt to garner support for the short-lived Central African Federation, which was aimed partly at prolonging white domination of Southern and Northern Rhodesia as well as Nyasaland after independence. But it was the Cyprus problem that was to be Hopkinson's undoing in the House of Commons. In a debate in 1954 he effectively stated that Cyprus would never be granted independence (six years before it in fact was), and this unfortunate mis-prediction was to dog him thereafter: 'Never say never', Churchill is said to have commented. In the government reshuffle of December 1955 Hopkinson was predictably dropped and, although Eden offered him various overseas diplomatic appointments, he preferred to go to the back benches until the following year when he was created Baron Colyton and began to play an active part in the House of Lords.

Freed from office, Colyton came out in his true colours as a traditional—not to say reactionary—tory. He criticized Ian Macleod's decolonizing policies and the imposition of sanctions against Ian Smith's unilateral declaration of independence regime in Rhodesia, and he supported the regime of Dr Salazar (by whom he was awarded the grand cross of the order of Prince Henry the Navigator) in Portugal and Portuguese Africa. These views fitted well with his chairmanship of Tanganyika Concessions, with its European mining interests in Africa, and his other capitalist ventures. He became increasingly a figure of the extreme right in politics and in international business.

Colyton's first wife died in 1953 and on 11 December 1956 he married Barbara Estella Addams, the former wife of Charles Samuel Addams, the *New Yorker* cartoonist, and daughter of Stephen Barb, of New York. There were no children from this second marriage. They continued to live in the Jacobean manor house in Devon—Netherton Hall—which Colyton had purchased with his first wife and to which he was greatly attached. In the last years of his life, however, he and his second wife moved to Monte Carlo where he died aged ninety-four on 6 January 1996. His son had predeceased him, and the barony passed to his elder grandson, Alisdair John Munro Hopkinson (b. 1958).

With his conventional good looks, impeccable manners, ultra right-wing views and privileged career, Colyton appeared to many as almost a caricature of a defunct breed of tory grandee. But beneath the glossy—some said cardboard—exterior there was a sensitive man who was more vulnerable than at first appeared, and more courageous than many apparently more robust public figures.

JOHN URE

Sources H. Colyton, *Occasion, chance and change: a memoir, 1902–1946* (1993) · *WWW* · Burke, *Peerage* · *The Times* (10 Jan 1996) · *The Independent* (8 Jan 1996) · *FO List* · *The Eton register*, 8 vols. (privately printed, Eton, 1903–32) · personal knowledge (2004) · b. cert. **Archives** Bodl. RH, corresp. with Sir R. R. Welensky **Likenesses** photograph, repro. in *The Times* · photograph, repro. in *The Independent*

Hopkinson, John (1610–1680), antiquary, was born in 1610 at Lofthouse, near Leeds, Yorkshire, the second of the five sons of George Hopkinson and his second wife, Judith, daughter of John Langley of Horbury. He was a law student at Lincoln's Inn, where he also developed his antiquarian and heraldic interests. His fellow members of the inn included Charles Fairfax, Matthew Hale, and Samuel Roper, and it was in Roper's chambers there that his countryman Roger Dodsworth met William Dugdale in 1638. Hopkinson's father died about 1650, and since the son of his father's first marriage and his own elder brother had died young he inherited the family estate and settled in Lofthouse.

In 1654 William Ryley, Norroy king of arms during the Commonwealth, appointed his 'wel beloved friend' Hopkinson as his deputy in Lancashire and Yorkshire (Lancaster, 201). After the Restoration he was appointed deputy clerk of the peace for Yorkshire, a position he held until his death. When William Dugdale made his visitation of Yorkshire in 1665–6, Hopkinson attended him in the capacity of a secretary. At this time he was part of an active antiquarian network in Yorkshire and Lancashire, which included Christopher Towneley, who proposed to write a history of Lancashire. It seems inevitable, in view of his role in the evolution of county histories in other counties, that Dugdale encouraged Hopkinson to undertake a history of Yorkshire or to assist his colleague Nathaniel Johnston. A decade later Hopkinson was employed with Johnston in arranging the Talbot papers at Sheffield Castle, which were an essential source for the undertaking. Hopkinson accumulated an extensive miscellany of manuscripts, subsequently described as 'the great storehouse for the Yorkshire topographer' (J. H. Lupton, *Wakefield Worthies*, 1864, 208). Although the emphasis is on Yorkshire and genealogy, his collections also reflected his legal training, his professional role as deputy clerk of the peace, and a wider interest in recent English history.

Hopkinson never married. He died on 28 February 1680 and was buried at Rothwell, near Leeds. His collections, of which some eighty volumes survived in 1815, passed to the Richardson family, to whom he was related through the marriages of his half-sister Elizabeth and sister Jane. Through the botanist and antiquary Dr Richard Richardson of North Bierley the collections of 'Uncle Hopkinson' were made available to Ralph Thoresby for use in his own county history.

JAN BROADWAY

Sources W. T. Lancaster, ed., *Letters addressed to Ralph Thoresby* (1912) · W. Dugdale, *The visitation of the county of Yorke*, ed. R. Davies and G. J. Armytage, SurtS, 36 (1859) · *Third report*, HMC, 2 (1872), 293–300 · E. Stephens, ed., *The clerks of the counties, 1360–1960* (1961) · *DNB* **Archives** BL, collections relating to Yorkshire, Lancashire, and law of England, Add. MSS 26738–26739, 26741, 26749 · W. Yorks. AS, Bradford, antiquarian papers and collections, ref. 32D86 | Bodl. Oxf., corresp. with Nathaniel Johnston and pedigrees, MSS Top. Gen. c. 50, 53; MSS Top. Yorks. MSS c. 17–18, 29, 36; MS Eng. Hist. c. 286 · Bodl. Oxf., copy by Thomas Wilson of MS, 1745, MS Top. Yorks. b. 8

Hopkinson, John (1849–1898), electrical engineer, was born on 27 July 1849 in Manchester, the eldest of the five children of John Hopkinson, mechanical engineer, and his wife, Alice, daughter of John Dewhurst of Skipton. Sir Alfred *Hopkinson, lawyer, was his younger brother. He was educated under C. Willmore at Queenwood School, Hampshire. In 1865 he became a student at Owens College, Manchester. There he studied mathematics under Thomas Barker and, acting on his advice, entered for and won a minor scholarship at Trinity College, Cambridge, in 1867. At Cambridge he devoted himself to mathematics as his chief study, under E. J. Routh, and in 1871 he graduated from Cambridge as senior wrangler and first Smith's prizeman. While in residence at Cambridge he gained a Whitworth scholarship and proceeded to a degree in science in the University of London (1871). Shortly after his tripos he was elected a fellow of Trinity. In 1873 he married Evelyn Oldenbourg; they had six children.

In 1871 Hopkinson entered his father's works, and in 1872 he became manager and engineer in the lighthouse and optical department of Chance Brothers of Birmingham. In 1872 he first proposed the group flash system to enable mariners to distinguish one light from another. The flashes in his system were of varying length and were separated by varying intervals of darkness which characterized the lights more distinctly. His great mathematical abilities proved to be of the utmost value to him in his optical work, and later on in his electrical work. In one of his papers he proved mathematically that alternating current dynamos could be connected to work in parallel. His views on the relation of mathematics to engineering were fully explained in his James Forrest lecture delivered at the Institution of Civil Engineers in 1894 (*PICE*, 118, 1894, 530).

Stimulated by the publication of James Clerk Maxwell's *Electricity and Magnetism* in 1873, and on the advice of Sir William Thomson (Lord Kelvin), Hopkinson later performed a valuable series of experiments on the residual charge of the Leyden jar, and on the electrostatic capacity of glass in 1876–7. The results of these experiments were published in four papers in the *Philosophical Transactions of the Royal Society* (1876–81), in which he supplemented and improved Maxwell's theory of residual charge. He worked continuously on this subject almost up to the time of his death, and the last paper he published on this question was 'On the capacity and residual charge of dielectrics as affected by temperature and time' (*PTRS*, 189, 1897, 109–35).

In 1878 Hopkinson resigned his post with Chance Brothers and set up as a consulting engineer in London. In

John Hopkinson (1849–1898), by unknown photographer

the same year he was elected a fellow of the Royal Society, on whose council he served in 1886–7 and 1891–3. He continued to act as scientific adviser to Chances and was also frequently engaged as an expert witness in patent litigation.

The Paris Exhibition of 1881 brought into prominence electric lighting and electric transmission of power, and Hopkinson served as one of the judges to evaluate different electric lighting systems. Two important papers of his were read before the Institution of Mechanical Engineers in 1879 and 1880. In these he tried to clarify the theory of the dynamo machine and introduced for the first time the notion of the characteristic curve ('On electric lighting', *Proceedings of the Institution of Mechanical Engineers*, 1879, 1880). In 1882 he obtained his well-known patent for the three-wire system of distributing electricity. In 1883, in an address delivered before the Institution of Civil Engineers entitled 'Some points in electric lighting', he described his first important improvements in the dynamo. The general solution of the problem involved was fully given in a joint paper by Hopkinson and his brother, Edward Hopkinson, in 1886 ('Dynamo electric machinery', *PTRS*, 1886). The first portion of this paper was devoted to the construction of the characteristic curve for a machine of given dimensions. The second half described the actual experiments conducted on a dynamo to verify the theories set forth in the first, and investigated the causes of discrepancies.

This paper was undoubtedly the most important publication by Hopkinson on the practical applications of electricity, and laid the foundation of the accurate design of dynamos through the combination of mathematics and laboratory experiments with engineering skills.

In 1890 Hopkinson was appointed professor of electrical engineering and head of the Siemens Laboratory at King's College, London. Although he did not give lectures while in this position, it gave him the necessary facilities to conduct research on the dynamo. His direction of the laboratory was extremely valuable in stimulating the students and providing advanced students with suggestions for research. In this work he was assisted by E. Wilson, and a number of papers were published in the *Philosophical Transactions of the Royal Society* between 1894 and 1896 on their joint experiments on the effect of armature reaction, on the efficiency of transformers, and on alternating currents.

In 1885 Hopkinson published the results of a series of experiments on the magnetic properties of iron, for which he was awarded in 1890 a Royal Society medal. Between 1881 and 1883 he worked as scientific adviser to the British Edison Company. During this time he made a significant improvement on the design of Edison's early dynamo. In 1891 he was appointed by the Manchester corporation to advise on the electric lighting of the city, and he acted as consulting engineer while the work was carried out. From 1896 he also worked as consulting engineer to the corporations of Leeds, Liverpool, and St Helens to supervise their works for electric traction. In connection with the Manchester scheme he introduced an important innovation into the system of charging customers for the current used—a system which he had advocated as early as 1883. Under this system the customer had to pay 'a charge, which is calculated partly by the quantity of energy contained in the supply and partly by a yearly or other rental, depending upon the maximum strength of the current to be supplied' (Hopkinson, *Original Papers*, 1901, 1.254–68).

In the field of electric traction Hopkinson did much professional work. He was consulting engineer to the contractors for the electrical work on the City and South London Railway and in 1896 he was electrical engineer for the Kirkstall and Roundhay tramway at Leeds. He joined the Institution of Civil Engineers in 1877, and in 1895 became a member of its council. He was also a member of the Institution of Electrical Engineers, and was president in 1890 and 1896. It was owing to his initiative that the volunteer corps of electrical engineers (which sent a strong detachment for active service in South Africa in 1900) was formed, and he was appointed the first major in command of this corps.

Hopkinson was an ardent mountaineer and his holidays were usually spent climbing in Switzerland, especially in the neighbourhood of Arolla. His death, at the early age of forty-nine, was due to a terrible alpine accident. On 27 August 1898, he, his son John, and two of his daughters, died while ascending the Petite Dent de Veisivi in the Val d'Herens, an offshoot from the Rhone valley. A few days later all the bodies were recovered; they were buried in the cemetery at Territet. Hopkinson was commemorated at Cambridge by a wing of the engineering laboratory built by his widow and surviving children, including the mechanical and aeronautical engineer Bertram *Hopkinson, and at Owens College by an electrotechnical laboratory built by his father and other relatives.

Hopkinson was a man of most unusual achievements. His great powers as an experimenter in the most difficult fields of scientific research were combined with a wide practical knowledge, and in many of his papers he was able in a unique way to employ his high mathematical ability in the solution of practical problems of commercial importance. T. H. BEARE, *rev.* S. HONG

Sources B. Hopkinson, 'Memoir', in *Original papers of John Hopkinson*, 1 (1901), x–lxi · J. Greig, *John Hopkinson: electrical engineer* (1970) · B. Bowers, 'Edison and early electrical engineering in Britain', *History of Technology*, 13 (1991), 168–80 · *The Electrician* (10 Jan 1890), 236–7 · J. A. E., *PRS*, 64 (1898–9), xvii–xxiv · *CGPLA Eng. & Wales* (1898)

Archives Inst. EE, corresp. · RS | CUL, letters to Sir George Stokes

Likenesses T. B. Kennington, oils, 1900 (after photographs and portrait, c.1894), U. Cam., department of engineering · W. H. Thornycroft, marble bust, 1902, U. Cam., department of engineering · R. H. Campbell, oils, 1929, Inst. EE · R. H. Campbell, oils, Athenaeum, London · photograph, repro. in Hopkinson, 'Memoir' [*see illus.*]

Wealth at death £74,672 5s. 4d.: probate, 1 Oct 1898, *CGPLA Eng. & Wales*

Hopkinson, Sir (Henry) Thomas (1905–1990), journalist and magazine editor, was born on 19 April 1905 in Victoria Park, Manchester, the second child and second son in the family of four sons and one daughter of John Henry Hopkinson (son of Sir Alfred *Hopkinson), lecturer in classical archaeology at the University of Manchester, who soon took holy orders and eventually became archdeacon of Westmorland, and his wife, Evelyn Mary, schoolteacher, daughter of the Revd Henry Thomas Fountaine, vicar of Sutton Bridge, Lincolnshire. Hopkinson went to St Edward's School, Oxford, with the financial assistance of a wealthy uncle, Austin Hopkinson MP, and then won a classical scholarship to Pembroke College, Oxford, where he obtained a second class in classical honour moderations (1925) and a third in *literae humaniores* (1927).

For seven years Hopkinson lived in London by freelance journalism and copywriting in Crawford's advertising agency. After the publication of his first book, *A Strong Hand at the Helm* (1933), an acerbic commentary on the failings of Ramsay MacDonald's government, Hopkinson transferred in 1934 to Odhams Press, where he became assistant editor of *The Clarion*, a weekly that combined cycling news with Labour youth propaganda. In the same year this was incorporated into *Weekly Illustrated*, which Stefan Lorant, a gifted Hungarian refugee, had persuaded Odhams to launch. When in the summer of 1938 Lorant achieved the backing of Edward Hulton in launching *Picture Post*, Hopkinson joined as assistant editor, taking over as editor when Lorant, fearing a German invasion, emigrated to the USA in July 1940. The magazine had been expected to sell 250,000 copies at most; soon it was selling more than 1,500,000 a week.

Lorant was an outstanding photo-journalist and trained Hopkinson to use pictures with equal flair. Hopkinson added a campaigning streak of his own, often contrasting the lives of the rich with the reality of poverty and deprivation, picturing, he hoped, the lives of ordinary people with the eye of a Rembrandt. Hopkinson was an excellent caption writer and always stressed the need for words to reinforce the message of his pictures. He gained the affection and devotion of his staff, displaying an almost donnish approach to their work and a total lack of pretension. His cool professional judgement contrasted with some turbulence in his emotional life, just as a remarkably tidy office contrasted with the turmoil and tension needed to bring out a weekly magazine. His slightly enigmatic personality and ability to adapt to people masked his true political convictions. He certainly attempted to encapsulate the socialist dream of a more just society. As the Second World War progressed, he paid particular attention to the problems that would arise when peace finally arrived. With a talented team of photographers and reporters, hand-picked by Hopkinson, *Picture Post* became immensely influential in setting the mood of the country and may well have made a contribution to the Labour victory in the 1945 election.

Growing tension between Hulton, who was a Conservative, and Hopkinson finally came to a head in October 1950 over a powerful picture story, from photographer Bert Hardy and journalist James Cameron, highlighting the appalling plight of so-called political prisoners in Korea, some of them children, under the western-backed regime of Syngman Rhee. Hulton refused to allow the magazine to print it and, with the support of a pliant board including his second wife, Nika, sacked Hopkinson. Without his inspired editorship *Picture Post* soon lost its way and was closed in 1957. After freelancing for a few years Hopkinson joined the *News Chronicle* in 1954. He resigned two years later because he believed the paper was destroying itself. In 1957 he was asked to edit *Drum*, the African picture magazine based in Johannesburg, and he took up the post early in 1958. However, the magazine did not offer quite the same opportunities and eventually he fell out with the proprietor, resigning in 1961, after three and a half years. In March 1963 he launched the International Press Institute's training centre for black journalists in Nairobi, Kenya, staying there as director until 1966. He then moved on to the academic training of journalists, becoming senior fellow in press studies at the University of Sussex (1967–9). Finally, in 1970 he became the first director of the centre for journalism studies at University College, Cardiff, a post he held until 1975. Eventually he became the virtual godfather of photojournalism and did much to increase the standing of photographers in their profession. Hopkinson was also fairly successful as a writer of short stories and novels. As a writer he was a perfectionist, sometimes staying up all night to find the right word. He was appointed CBE in 1967 and knighted in 1978. He was an honorary fellow of the

Royal Photographic Society (1976) and won its silver progress medal (1984), and had an honorary degree of LittD from Wales (1990).

Hopkinson was always beautifully dressed, a neat composed figure with a rather florid face, which gave him the air of a countryman. In 1930 he married the novelist Antonia White (d. 1980) [see Hopkinson, Eirene Adeline], daughter of Cecil George Botting, senior classics master at St Paul's School. She became increasingly unbalanced and they were divorced in 1938. In October 1938 he married Gerti Deutsch, an Austrian photographer, whose father Victor Deutsch was a rope manufacturer. The marriage was dissolved in 1953 and in the same year he married Dorothy, daughter of Thomas Vernon, musician, and widow of Hugh Kingsmill. Hopkinson had one daughter from his first marriage and two from his second. Towards the end of his life he came to believe in reincarnation. He died of cancer on 20 June 1990, in Oxford, where his home was 26 Boulter Street, St Clements.

CHARLES WINTOUR, *rev.*

Sources T. Hopkinson, *In the fiery continent* (1962) · T. Hopkinson, ed., *Picture Post* (1970) · T. Hopkinson, *Of this our time* (1982) · *The Times* (22 June 1990) · *The Independent* (22 June 1990) · *The Independent* (23 June 1990) · *The Independent* (26 June 1990) · *CGPLA Eng. & Wales* (1991) · personal knowledge (1996) · private information (1996)
Likenesses C. Hewitt, photograph, 1950, Hult. Arch.
Wealth at death under £115,000: administration with will, 25 Jan 1991, *CGPLA Eng. & Wales*

Hopkinson, William (d. 1604), Church of England clergyman and author, perhaps came from Lincolnshire; his parentage is obscure. He matriculated as a sizar from St John's College, Cambridge, where he became a pupil of Thomas Drant, in February 1565. He was ordained deacon in May 1566 and priest in March 1567, by the bishops of Ely and Lincoln respectively, before graduating BA in 1568. In 1569, probably by now a licensed preacher, he was instituted rector of Birdham, Sussex, at the presentation of Thomas Sackville, Lord Buckhurst, and rector of Holton-cum-Beckering, Lincolnshire, at the presentation of Francis Russell, second earl of Bedford. Resigning Birdham by July 1570, he was collated by Richard Curteys, bishop of Chichester, to the prebend of Bursal in Chichester Cathedral in November 1570 and to the vicarage of Slinfold, Sussex, in March 1571 but seems never to have been inducted to either living. Curteys, however, appointed Hopkinson a commissary in the archdeaconry of Lewes, in which capacity he seems to have made use of his connections with Curteys for personal gain.

Hopkinson proceeded MA in 1571, resigning Holton-cum-Beckering in May that year, during which he also sat in convocation as a proctor for the Chichester diocesan clergy. In October he was collated by Curteys to the rectory of Warbleton, Sussex, and in March 1572 was instituted vicar of Salehurst, Sussex, at the presentation of Sir Henry Sidney. As chaplain to Curteys he was dispensed the same month to hold a third living, provided it was within 26 miles of the other two. At an unknown date he married his

wife Joan or Joanna (surname unknown); their daughter Anne was baptized at Warbleton in April 1573.

In 1576 Hopkinson joined with some of his Salehurst parishioners in signing a petition to Edmund Grindal, archbishop of Canterbury, on behalf of John Strowd, the controversial preacher of Cranbrook, Kent, who had clashed with the vicar, Richard Fletcher, and his son (also Richard), the future bishop of London. In December 1576 he was one of more than forty Sussex ministers who subscribed a testimonial to Bishop Curteys which was prefaced to Curteys's *An Exposition of Certayne Words of S. Paule, to the Romaynes* (1577). Notwithstanding his manifestly radical sympathies it was to the conformist John Aylmer, bishop of London, that Hopkinson dedicated his work *An Evident Display of Popish Practises, or, Patched Pelagianisme* (1578), a translation from the Latin of Theodore Beza, praising Aylmer's careful oversight of the clergy (including himself) who had fallen under his jurisdiction as archdeacon of Lincoln. Hopkinson was now apparently living permanently at Salehurst, keeping a curate at Warbleton, and his children were given distinctive evangelical Christian names. Between 1579 and 1592 his sons were christened Jabez, Indure, and Safe on Highe, and his daughters Persis and Renued.

After the publication in England in 1580 of the Tremellius–Junius Latin edition of the Bible a certain Mr Hopkinson wrote a short series of manuscript 'animadversions' which were highly critical of Tremellius's linguistic competence (BL, Royal MS 17 A. xliii). This man is probably identifiable with the Hopkinson who lived in Grub Street in London, 'a reader of the Hebrew tongue' and 'reputed the most famous in that language about the town', even though he was otherwise 'an obscure and simple man for worldly affairs' (Jones, 231). There is a long-standing tradition that the author of the 'animadversions' on Tremellius was William Hopkinson but it is difficult to reconcile the known facts of the latter's career with the apparent obscurity of the Grub Street linguist—except for the interesting circumstance that St John's was noted for Hebrew studies and that the Hebrew lecturer there from 1564 to 1566, when William Hopkinson was a student, was none other than Richard Curteys, the future bishop.

It may have been the steady insistence by the ecclesiastical authorities from about 1580 on the importance of the sacraments that led Hopkinson to publish *A Preparation into the Waye of Lyfe, with a Direction into the Right Use of the Lord's Supper* (1581); it concludes with the text of a letter written by Edward Dering. A new edition, published in 1583, was dedicated to Sir Henry Sidney. That year Hopkinson played a prominent role in the subscription crisis which followed hard on the heels of John Whitgift's elevation as archbishop of Canterbury. In December 1583 he was a member of the Sussex delegation which confronted Whitgift at Lambeth Palace to protest at the suspension of godly ministers. He took a leading part in the subsequent negotiations and it is indicative of his standing that when the delegation eventually consented to a modified form of subscription to Whitgift's articles his name headed the list of signatories.

Hopkinson's precise role in the radical campaigns of the 1580s remains obscure. He vacated his vicarage of Sale-hurst about February 1597, residing thereafter at Warble-ton. He was buried there on 22 November 1604, having died intestate. Letters of administration, identifying Joan as his widow and disclosing that his moveable goods had been valued at £34 10s. 6d., were granted in the arch-deaconry court of Lewes in February 1606. One Joanna Hopkinson married Richard Sharpe at Warbleton in June 1611.

DAVID J. CRANKSHAW

Sources Venn, *Alum. Cant.*, 1/2.406 · Cooper, *Ath. Cantab.*, 2.5; 3.94 · D. J. Crankshaw, 'Elizabethan and early Jacobean surveys of the ministry of the Church of England', PhD diss., U. Cam., 2000 · E. Sussex RO, MSS Par 477/1/1/1, 501/1/1; W/B3 · *Fasti Angl., 1541–1857*, [Chichester] · PRO, court of requests, proceedings, REQ 2/177/58 · J. Goring, 'The reformation of the ministry in Elizabethan Sussex', *Journal of Ecclesiastical History*, 34 (1983), 345–66 · G. Hennessy, *Chich-ester diocese clergy lists* (1900) · C. W. Foster, ed., *Lincoln episcopal records*, Lincoln RS, 2 (1912) · *Registrum Matthei Parker, diocesis Cant-uariensis, AD 1559–1575*, ed. W. H. Frere and E. M. Thompson, 1, CYS, 35 (1928); 2, CYS, 36 (1928) · R. B. Manning, *Religion and society in Elizabethan Sussex* (1969) · A. Peel, ed., *The seconde parte of a register*, 1 (1915) · G. L. Jones, *The discovery of Hebrew in Tudor England: a third language* (1983)
Archives BL, Add. MS 38492, fols. 91r–92v · BL, Royal MS 17A.xliii
Wealth at death moveable goods valued at £34 10s. 6d.: E. Sussex RO, MS W/B3, fol. 66r

Hopkirk, Thomas (1785–1841), botanist, was born at Dal-beth House, Dalbeth, near Glasgow, on 4 July 1785. His father, James Hopkirk, and his mother, Christian Glass-ford, were members of eminent Glasgow merchant fam-ilies. Hopkirk matriculated at Glasgow University in 1800. He was the pioneer botanist of west central Scotland. His *Flora Glottiana: a catalogue of the indigenous plants on the banks of the River Clyde, and in the neighbourhood of the city of Glas-gow*, published in 1813, was one of Britain's earliest regional floras and became the benchmark against which later work on the botany of Strathclyde was measured. In 1817 Hopkirk published *Flora Anomoia: a general view of the anomalies in the vegetable kingdom*, a path-finding and wide-ranging study of the abnormalities and variations of plant structure. A skilled draftsman and lithographer, he pre-pared many fine botanical illustrations, notably the plates for *Flora Anomoia*. Hopkirk was also one of the principal movers behind the foundation of the Glasgow Botanical Gardens, to which he gifted several thousand plants from his own garden at Dalbeth. In 1837 he published anonym-ously a popular botanical text *The Juvenile Calendar, or, Nat-ural History of the Year*. Elected a fellow of the Linnean Soci-ety in 1812, he received an honorary degree of LLD from Glasgow University in 1835. He was a JP for Lanarkshire.

Hopkirk moved to Ireland after 1830 and was involved for some years with the geological department of the Irish Ordnance Survey. He married, possibly while in Ireland; nothing is known of his wife except that she predeceased him, leaving at least one daughter. Hopkirk himself died in Malone, Belfast, on 23 August 1841. He has been com-memorated by the naming of Glasgow University's Hop-kirk Laboratory for taxonomic botany.

MALCOLM NICOLSON

Sources R. Turner, 'Thomas Hopkirk of Dalbeth: a sketch of his life and botanical work', *Proceedings and Transactions of the Natural History Society of Glasgow*, new ser.,1 (1884–5), 196–259 · Desmond, *Botanists*, rev. edn · *Glasgow Courier* (28 Aug 1841) · J. Britten, 'Bio-graphical index of British and Irish botanists', *Journal of Botany, British and Foreign*, 27 (1889), 113–16 · IGI
Likenesses W. Goodwin, photograph (after oil painting), repro. in Turner, 'Thomas Hopkirk of Dalbeth'

Hopley, Edward William John (1816–1869), subject painter, was born at Whitstable, Kent, but lived the early part of his life at Lewes in Sussex. He was originally des-tined for the medical profession, but soon turned to art, settled in London, and after some years won popularity as a painter of domestic subjects, and also of portraits. In 1845 he exhibited at the British Institution a picture entitled *Love Not*, and in 1854 and 1855 two pictures illus-trating the *Vicissitudes of Science: Sir Isaac Newton Explaining to Lord Treasurer Halifax his Theory of Colour* and *Michael Angelo in the Gardens of the Medici*. In 1859 he exhibited a pic-ture entitled *The Birth of a Pyramid*, the result of consider-able archaeological research and industry, which att-racted attention. He first exhibited at the Royal Academy in 1851, when he sent *Psyche*, and he was a frequent exhib-itor thereafter. His last work was a portrait of Professor Owen FRS, exhibited at the British Institution in 1869.

In 1859, prompted by 'the growing interest taken in painting by all orders of our countrymen' (Hopley, iv), Hopley published an essay in art criticism for the begin-ner, *Art, and How to Enjoy it*. In this he argued that if art were to attain its true standing in national life it must 'inculcate virtue and morality', and he looked forward to a day when 'elegant haymakers, unimpeachable market-girls, interesting ankles crossing babbling brooks … when such trash as this shall yield place on our walls to elevated moral and historical triumphs' (ibid., 19–20). A short read-ing list omitted the works of Ruskin, which Hopley con-sidered 'dangerous to the student of art', though of undoubted value to the connoisseur. He also invented a trigonometrical system of facial measurement for the use of artists, which was displayed in the fine arts department of the Great Exhibition of 1851. Towards the end of his life he lived at 14 South Bank, Regent's Park, London, where he died on 30 April 1869, apparently unmarried.

L. H. CUST, *rev.* MARK POTTLE

Sources *Art Journal*, 31 (1869), 216 · Wood, *Vic. painters*, 2nd edn · Redgrave, *Artists* · B. Stewart and M. Cutten, *The dictionary of portrait painters in Britain up to 1920* (1997) · E. Hopley, *Art, and how to enjoy it: a reply to the question 'How shall I know a good picture?'* (1859) · *The exhibition of the Royal Academy* (1854–69) [exhibition catalogues] · *Catalogue of the works of British artists in the gallery of the British Insti-tution* (1854–69) [exhibition catalogues] · CGPLA Eng. & Wales (1869)
Likenesses E. Edwards, carte-de-visite, NPG
Wealth at death under £300: probate, 4 June 1869, CGPLA Eng. & Wales

Hoppé, Emil Otto (1878–1972), photographer, was born on 14 April 1878 in Munich, Germany, the only son and elder child of Philip Hoppé, bank director, and his wife, Marie von der Porter, pianist. Soon after his birth the fam-ily moved to Vienna, where Hoppé began his formal edu-cation which he later completed in Paris and Munich. In

1900 he moved to London to work for the Deutsche Bank. In 1903, having received a camera as a birthday gift, he embarked on his career in photography. Hoppé became a member of the Royal Photographic Society in 1907, and later in that year won £100 in a photographic competition. Encouraged, he resigned his post at the bank and, using the prize-money as capital, opened a portrait studio at 10 Margravine Gardens, Baron's Court. In 1905 Hoppé married Marion Bliersbach. They had a son, Frank (*b.* 1913), and a daughter, Marion (*b.* 1916).

Hoppé co-founded the London Salon of Photography in 1910; in the following year he held his first one-man show. Over the next fifteen years he became one of London's most celebrated portraitists while also establishing himself as a skilled theatre and fashion photographer. In 1913 he moved into 7 Cromwell Place, South Kensington, the former home of the painter Sir John Millais, and to make an impression on his wealthy clientele, had it lavishly redecorated. Conversely, the studio which he used for twenty years was simple and plain, matching a style of portrait photography in which, to use his own words, 'character rather than flattery [was] the dominant note' (Hoppé, 15). He was soon in great demand and the frequent republication of his work earned him much in reproduction fees. Among the publications to take his work were *Vogue*, *Vanity Fair*, the *Illustrated London News*, and the *Tatler*.

In 1921 Hoppé photographed George V and Queen Mary at Buckingham Palace, in a style that was informal by the standards of the time. In the following year his one-man exhibition of mainly portrait photographs at the Goupil Gallery won plaudits from the critics. John Galsworthy wrote the catalogue introduction, and record audiences viewed the touring exhibition. All 221 prints from the show were purchased by a consortium of collectors under the aegis of the *Asahi Shimbun*, one of Japan's leading newspapers, and were subsequently exhibited in Tokyo and Osaka in 1923.

Hoppé photographed numerous world leaders, including Benito Mussolini and American president Calvin Coolidge; assorted royalty, both European and Asian; and many of the century's leading artists and thinkers—Vaslav Nijinsky, Albert Einstein, Ezra Pound, George Bernard Shaw, Rudyard Kipling, Somerset Maugham, and Thomas Hardy were among those who made up Hoppé's vibrant social and intellectual milieu. Hoppé once said of his aesthetic mission: 'To confirm the spirit behind the eyes is the test' (Hoppé, 15).

Hoppé has been justly praised for his portraits, but his little-known topographic works by themselves would have qualified him as an innovative modernist before the term was even coined. Hoppé's dynamic views of urban environments and industrial buildings link the late pictorialist experiments of his fellow member of the art photography group Linked Ring, Alvin Langdon Coburn, with the depression-era work of Walker Evans.

In his later years Hoppé turned his attention to landscape, travel, and news photography, capturing portraits and topographic views throughout Britain, Germany, Japan, the United States, South America, Australia, India, and Jamaica. Hoppé wrote and published extensively, producing some twenty-eight photographic books including two outstanding titles which exemplify his topographic work, *Romantic America: Picturesque United States* (1927) and *Deutsche Arbeit* (1930). He also ran a picture agency, which aided the dissemination of his work.

Hoppé died in Wildhern, Hampshire, on 9 December 1972. Cecil Beaton referred to him simply as 'the Master': elsewhere, he has been cited as the most important photographer in the world during the 1920s. He was certainly a photographer of daring vision and—from his publications, and his role in the founding of the London Salon—a significant figure in twentieth-century photography.

GRAHAM HOWE

Sources C. Beaton, introduction, in E. O. Hoppé, *Hundred thousand exposures: the success of a photographer* (1945) · *Studies in Visual Communication*, 11/2 (spring 1985), essays by B. Jay and M. Gidley, chronology and bibliography by T. Pepper · personal knowledge (2004) [Frank Hoppé, son; Michael Hoppé, grandson] · Curatorial Assistance, Inc., Los Angeles, California, E. O. Hoppé archive · *DNB* · J. Turner, ed., *The dictionary of art*, 34 vols. (1996) · *CGPLA Eng. & Wales* (1973)

Archives Curatorial Assistance, Inc., Los Angeles, archives

Likenesses C. Beaton, photograph, NPG · E. O. Hoppé, self-portrait, Curatorial Assistance Inc., Los Angeles, E. O. Hoppé archive

Wealth at death £30,036: probate, 4 April 1973, *CGPLA Eng. & Wales*

Hopper, Christopher (1722–1802), Methodist preacher, was born on 25 December 1722 at Low-Coalburn, Ryton, co. Durham, and baptized at Ryton parish church on 9 January 1723, the ninth and youngest child of Moses Hopper, a farmer, and his wife, Ann Barkiss. At about five years old he was sent to a school run by a Mr Alderson, a pious and forbidding teacher. His formal education appears to have ended with Alderson's suicide, whereupon, aged fifteen, Hopper was employed as a driver on the wagon-ways between the coal pits and the River Tyne.

In May 1742 reports began to circulate of John Wesley's preaching to great effect at Sandgate, Newcastle upon Tyne. Hopper was himself converted by the preaching of Jonathan Reeve in the spring of the following year. On 14 July 1743 John Wesley spoke at Low Spen, near Newcastle, and soon after a Methodist society was formed with Hopper as one of its leaders. He received requests to preach at such places as Blanchland, Prudhoe, Durham, and Sunderland, where on occasions he encountered violent opposition. In 1744 Hopper began work as a teacher at a school at Barlow, near Ryton. His involvement in Methodist work did not endear him to the rector and curate, and led to his being charged before the spiritual court at Durham with teaching and preaching without a licence. On 28 May 1745 he married Jane Richardson (*d.* 1755) at Ryton, and shortly afterwards the couple moved to the preacher's house at Sheephill and then, in 1748, to Allendale, Northumberland.

By this date Hopper was formally recognized as an itinerant preacher in the Newcastle circuit. From then he travelled in the northern circuits. He was a travelling preacher at Birstall, Bolton, Bradford, Liverpool, and Manchester, as well as Newcastle, and established some of the first Methodist societies in the north of England. He travelled to Ireland several times, accompanying John Wesley on a tour between April and July 1750, and was again in attendance during Wesley's pioneering visit to Scotland in April of the following year. He was appointed president of the Methodist conference at Bristol in 1780, the only person to hold this position other than Wesley in his lifetime. Following the death of Jane on 15 August 1755, Hopper had married Ann Twizell in April 1759, although no further details are known. On superannuating in 1792 Hopper moved to Bolton, where he built a house next to the chapel. Although his activities were curtailed he managed to continue preaching in the circuit and generally made annual visits into Yorkshire and adjacent circuits.

After a short illness Hopper died on 5 March 1802 at Bolton and was interred there in a vault in the new churchyard of St George's. The funeral sermon was preached by the Revd Thomas Cooper, circuit superintendent, from 2 Samuel 3: 38—'Know ye not that there is a prince, and a great man has fallen this day in Israel?'— who described Hopper as

> a good man, full of faith, and mighty in scriptures. God greatly blessed his word both to saints and sinners; graciously banished all his fears, and made him as bold as a lion in the face of all his dangers.   (Cooper, 396)

D. COLIN DEWS

Sources C. Hopper, 'The life of Christopher Hopper', *The lives of early Methodist preachers, chiefly written by themselves*, ed. T. Jackson, 2nd edn, 1 (1846) · T. Cooper, 'A funeral sermon in memory of Mr Christopher Hopper, minister of the gospel, who departed this life March 5, 1802', *Methodist Magazine*, 26 (1803), 389–97 · *The journal of the Rev. John Wesley*, ed. N. Curnock and others, 8 vols. (1909–16) · *The letters of the Rev. John Wesley*, ed. J. Telford, 8 vols. (1931) · J. Musgrave, *Origins of Methodism in Bolton* (1863) · K. B. Garlick, *Mr Wesley's preachers: an alphabetical arrangement of Wesleyan Methodist preachers and missionaries and the stations to which they were appointed, 1739–1813* (1977) · IGI
Archives JRL, Methodist Archives and Research Centre, MS material
Likenesses engraving, c.1781, repro. in *Wesleyan Methodist conference handbook* (1914), 61

Hopper [*married name* Chesson], **Eleanor Jane** [Nora] (1871–1906), writer, was born on 2 January 1871, at 8 Radnor Place, St Leonard, Devon, the daughter of Captain Harman Baillie Hopper (d. 1871), an Irish officer retired from the 31st Bengal native infantry, and his second wife, Caroline Augusta, née Francis, who was Welsh. Eight months later, Hopper died. Caroline Hopper went to live with her unmarried sister Sarah in Sussex Villas, Kensington. Nora was educated at Cumberland House, South Kensington, and lived with her mother at 36 Royal Crescent, Notting Hill, until her marriage.

Nora Hopper began to write poems at fifteen and studied folklore at the British Museum with the encouragement of Dr Richard Garnett and A. P. Graves, spending three years reading Icelandic sagas. She began to publish poems and stories in such periodicals as *The Sketch*, *Black and White*, *Household Words*, *Longman's*, *Macmillan's*, and *Chambers'* magazines, *Sylvia's Journal*, the *Yellow Book*, the *National Observer*, and *The Lyceum*.

Ballads in Prose (1894), Hopper's first book, alternated verse and prose in a *conte-fable* structure ostensibly based on Irish fairy-lore, but in fact 'spun out of the moonshine of my own brain … Irish tradition has given me nothing' she confessed (letter to Richard Garnett, 28 Jan 1895, Harry Ransom Humanities Research Center, University of Texas at Austin). That the Irishness of her work had been achieved by one who had never been there was 'a remarkable instance of temperament and interest independent and almost defiant of environment'. Home rule politics were 'meaningless in her ears, and she only becomes a partisan at the sound of "'98," or at the names of Emmett or Sarsfield' (*The Bookman*, Sept 1895).

Ballads in Prose contained naïve plagiaries of both Yeats and Katharine Tynan. Annoying as Yeats found the plagiary of his announced title *The Wind among the Reeds*, incorporated into Joseph Walter West's cover design, he reassured Hopper. He was 'haunted' by four 'strange wayward' stories which, in turn, influenced his *The Secret Rose* (1897), including 'The gifts of Aodh and Una', which inspired his plans for a Celtic mystical order. (Hopper played a minor role in its visionary experiments.)

Unequal and immature as Hopper's work was, Yeats praised *Ballads in Prose* in two lists of 'Best Irish Books' in 1895 as 'an absolute creation, an enchanting tender little book full of style and wild melancholy', leading the Irish newspapers to suspect rightly that he was booming her prematurely (*Collected Letters*, 440–43, 453n., 470n.). He included her work in *A Book of Irish Poetry* (1900) and wrote the headnote for her poems in Brooke and Rolleston's *A Treasury of Irish Poetry in the English Tongue* (1900).

Hopper's drawback was her lack of precise knowledge of Ireland. After her death Yeats thought that Irish Fairyland had spoiled her work (always excepting 'The King of Ireland's Son', which she had herself spoiled by revision, as he told her in 1898). Yet Thomas MacDonagh considered Hopper (with Lionel Johnson) as one of only few writers who were born and who lived their whole lives out of Ireland, and yet were truly Irish. Nora Hopper's work appeared in a range of publications: *Folk-Lore*, *The Celt*, *The Evergreen*, the *Cornish Magazine*, *Daily Express* (Dublin), and *New Ireland Review*.

Collections of Hopper's poems such as *Under Quicken Boughs* (1896), *Songs of the Morning* (1900), and *Aquamarines* (1902) followed, as did *The Bell and the Arrow: an English Love Story* (1905). She read at 'original nights' of the Irish Literary Society, London (1898–1901), with 'an exquisitely modulated voice, but her appearance was disappointing … rather common-looking, short and squat' (MacManus, 5). Ford Madox Hueffer (later Ford) recalled her 'quality of having existed for ever, not of having aged. Above all, it was the quality of seeming aloof … not absent-mindedness, but rather abstraction'. During a train journey, she 'was not in the carriage at all. She was, precisely, in another world, and just before we entered London, with a sudden air of "pulling herself together," she announced that she had a poem in her head' (Chesson, biographical note, xi–xii).

On 5 March 1901 at Brentford register office Hopper married (Wilfrid) Hugh Chesson (1870–1953), literary journalist and publisher's reader for T. Fisher Unwin, whom she had known since 1894. Their first child, Ann Caroline Spry, was born on 6 August 1902, followed by a son, Dermot, on 11 July 1904. They lived at Childwall, 337 Sandycombe Road, North Sheen, Surrey, Hugh Chesson's home for the next fifty years. The house belonged to Nora Chesson: she had investments of £60 a year and literary earnings of £40 a year from prolific hack work as reviewer, novelist, anthologist, versifier for children's books illustrated by Louis Wain, and paraphraser and reteller of nursery tales for Raphael Tuck & Sons. She also wrote for the *Girls' Own Paper*. 'No poet of her time contributed more to the Press', Chesson recalled, but she had become so well known as Nora Hopper that 'the press refused her the privilege of being equally well known' as Nora Chesson (Chesson, biographical note, viii). Nora Chesson wrote the libretto for O'Brien Butler's three-act opera *Muirgheis* ('The sea-swan'), produced in Dublin in 1903 and later translated into Irish by Tórna (Tadhg Ó Donnchadha), and a Celtic play 'The dark prince' (rejected for the Abbey in 1910).

On 27 June 1905 Nora Chesson applied to the Royal Literary Fund after her husband's 'complete nervous breakdown'. As her case was appraised, H. C. Beeching invoked comparisons with Christina Rossetti. In July 1905, when the first instalment (£150) of the £250 grant came, she took the family to Crockham Hill, Edenbridge, and thence to the Waverley Hotel, Lyme Regis. On 13 September 1905 she met Irish writers in Dublin for the first time, and by 9 November 1905 the Chessons were at 6 Mark Street, Portrush, co. Antrim, where her husband made 'steady progress'. Back in London, a second daughter, Dagmar, was born on 21 March 1906. On 14 April 1906 Nora Chesson died at her home in North Sheen. The death certificate lists 'old valvular disease of the heart' and 'parturition 24 days', but E. V. Lucas told the Royal Literary Fund that she died of puerperal fever. A friend, Margaret Harwood, arranged for Dermot Chesson to be adopted by her sister and brother-in-law, Alice and Graham Spence. Thereafter, Dermot had virtually no contact with his father or sisters.

Hugh Chesson's interest on the £2284 15s. 8d. left by Nora Chesson came to £74 per annum, and there were debts. Ford Madox Hueffer proposed to pay Chesson a small sum for preparing an edition of his wife's poems and to return the proceeds to a fund for the daughters, who lacked a breadwinner and a responsible parent. Five fascicles of her poems under the overall title *Selected Poems* (1906) followed. The first, *Dirge for Aoine and other Poems*, contained a biographical note by Chesson and an 'Introductory' by Hueffer. By 4 July 1906 the appeal had raised £206 9s. 6d. G. K. Chesterton, Justin McCarthy, and Richard Garnett supported a further bid to the Royal Literary Fund. £250 was added, and the fund became the Chesson Trust (£505 3s. 7d.).

Hugh Chesson 'slowly recovered from a most terrible struggle with inner forces whispering of self destruction … [feeling] not far removed from the precipice into which any mental strain might again precipitate him', as Garnett testified. His spiritualism enabled him to 'look upon his wife's death not so much as loss but as separation and that alleviated by the possibilities of continued intercourse' (Royal Literary Fund archive, London). In his introduction to her novel *Father Felix's Chronicles* (1907) Chesson claimed that his occult beliefs arose in part from his wife's visionary experiences, which involved time travel and the gift of tongues. More darkly, he hinted that she 'coveted the pain of them whom she loved' (p. 8). On 20 June 1923 Hugh Chesson married a Miss Daisy Green. By then his daughter Ann had committed suicide shortly after her marriage to Gilson MacCormack, and the discovery of his infidelity. Chesson had at least two more children, and died on 16 February 1953, aged eighty-two. Dagmar Chesson was given administration of the residue of Nora Hopper's estate at his death. She never married, but lived a bohemian life in Chepstow Villas, Bayswater, and died in 1991.

WARWICK GOULD

Sources W. H. Chesson, biographical note, in N. Chesson, *Dirge for Aoine and other poems* (1906) • W. H. Chesson, introduction, in N. Chesson, *Father Felix's chronicles*, ed. W. H. Chesson (1905) • *The collected letters of W. B. Yeats*, 1, ed. J. Kelly and E. Domville (1986) • *The Bookman* (Sept 1895) • L. MacManus, *White light and flame: memories of the Irish literary revival and the Anglo-Irish War* (1929) • Royal Literary Fund archive, London • b. cert. • m. cert. • d. cert. • d. cert. [Wilfrid Hugh Chesson]
Likenesses K. Pragnall, double portrait, photograph, 1903 (with her daughter Ann), repro. in Chesson, *Father Felix's chronicles*
Wealth at death £2284 15s. 8d.: probate, 31 May 1906, CGPLA Eng. & Wales

Hopper, Humphrey (1764/5–1844), sculptor, was baptized on 22 March 1765 at Wolsingham, co. Durham, the son of Humphrey Hopper and his wife, Margaret. He exhibited three works at the Royal Academy in 1799 and 1800, and entered the Royal Academy Schools, London, in February 1801, when his age was given as thirty-four. He won the silver medal in 1802, and the gold medal in 1803 for *The Death of Meleager*, a bas-relief. In 1802 Joseph Farington noted that Hopper 'had, it was said, been a Mason, but had industriously exerted himself to acquire a knowledge of Art' (Farington, *Diary*, 5.1944). He exhibited, not prolifically but regularly, at the Royal Academy between 1799 and 1835, giving different addresses in the parish of Marylebone, Middlesex; from 1815 he lived at 13 Wigmore Street. From 1807 to 1813 the works he exhibited included a number of mythological figures in plaster, designed to hold lamps. Usually of Bacchic figures or muses, the size of 'small life', they are normally signed and precisely dated (which indicates that he took out a patent): four survive at Lancaster House, London. The niches which held them were designed by architects such as Lewis Wyatt. For their manufacture he seems to have associated with the Gemelli family of casters in plaster.

Between 1815 and 1825 Hopper exhibited seven portrait busts of well-known men, including (in 1815 and 1817) the duke of Wellington. In 1807 he had exhibited 'monument[s] to the memory of' William Pitt and Lord Nelson, 'intended for [the] Guildhall' (*RA exhibitors*). He did not obtain those commissions but was awarded one of the national monuments in St Paul's Cathedral, that to General Andrew Hay (*d.* 1814), producing an ambitious and generally abused work in which the general is shown falling lifeless into the arms of a naked Hercules. However, his talents in works of smaller scale were appreciated, and by the 1820s and especially the 1830s he was well employed for funeral monuments, usually of moderate size and often distinguished by graceful mourning figures in traditional classical style. Such works have charm and are of fine workmanship. Humphrey Hopper died on 27 May 1844 at his home, 13 Wigmore Street, Marylebone, Middlesex, aged seventy-nine, in the presence of William Hopper of the same address.

JOHN KENWORTHY-BROWNE

Sources R. Gunnis, *Dictionary of British sculptors, 1660–1851* (1953), 209 · Graves, *RA exhibitors*, 4 (1906), 152 · J. Rutherford, *Country house lighting, 1660–1890* (1992), 135 · Farington, *Diary*, 5.1944; 6.2191, 2202 · S. C. Hutchison, 'The Royal Academy Schools, 1768–1830', *Walpole Society*, 38 (1960–62), 123–91, esp. 160 · Redgrave, *Artists*, 2nd edn, 224 · Courtauld Inst., Conway Library · *IGI* · d. cert.

Hopper, Thomas (1776–1856), architect, born in St Marylebone, Middlesex, on 5 July 1776, and baptized there on 28 July, was the eldest child of Thomas Hopper, measuring surveyor, and his wife, Ann Alexander. From an early age he assisted his clever but intemperate father, who had migrated from Rochester to London immediately after a hasty marriage. About 1806 he came to the notice of Walsh Porter, decorative consultant to the prince of Wales; Porter employed him to decorate rooms in Craven Cottage, Fulham (burned 1888), in a variety of styles: the hall Egyptian, copied from a plate in V. Denon's *Travels in Egypt* (translated 1803), with palm trees in the corners; a top-lighted Tartar chieftain's tent; and a Gothic dining-room modelled on Henry VII's Chapel. This caught the fancy of the prince, who in 1807 had Hopper design a magnificent Gothic conservatory for Carlton House, likewise in the style of Henry VII's Chapel, fan-vaulted and constructed in cast iron with coloured glass in the interstices of the vaulting ribs (dem. 1826). This made Hopper's reputation as well as bringing him further work at short-lived Carlton House.

In 1816 Hopper was elected surveyor of the county of Essex on a salary of £250 p.a., retaining the post until death. His father had speculated in building at Southend, and Hopper himself had acted as surveyor for the repair of Chelmsford parish church in 1804, under the then county surveyor. His position brought him local private commissions as well as his public ones. With his gaol at Salisbury, Wiltshire, already under construction, Hopper in a report on Essex prisons, February 1819, insisted on the need for isolating the various categories of prisoner; and on the basis of the 'separate' system he designed the forbidding Springfield gaol, Chelmsford (1822–6), at a building cost of £57,290, and houses of correction at Little Ilford (1828–31) and Chelmsford (*c.*1832–5, dem.). When the 'solitary' system was adopted, he converted Springfield to a cellular prison (1845–8), at a cost of £36,000. As surveyor to the Atlas Insurance Company, Hopper designed their Inigo Jonesian-style office in Cheapside (1834–6, cost: £12,000; altered). He also designed the Legal and General Life Insurance office in Fleet Street (dem. 1885), and altered Coutts Bank in the Strand (1838–9, dem. 1923). In the competitions for public buildings that formed such a significant feature of late Georgian architectural activity, however, Hopper was almost uniformly unsuccessful. Disappointment at failure in that for a new General Post Office, 1819–20, turned to resentment when the building erected to Robert Smirke's design 1824–8 emerged from its hoardings bearing, to Hopper's eyes, a close resemblance to his own entry. Defeated by Barry in the Houses of Parliament competition, 1835–6, Hopper was one of the most persistent and percipient critics of the competition judges, setting out detailed grounds for objection in his *Letter to the … First Commissioner of his Majesty's Works* (1837); pursued the controversy in *Hopper versus Cust, on the … Rebuilding of the Houses of Parliament* (1837); and eventually went to the considerable expense of publishing his own, amended, designs of the 'Gothic of the pure English of Edward III's time' in elephant folio (1840)—a showy, coarsely detailed work that drew on a wide selection of ecclesiastical architecture: 'Nearly every ancient edifice has been pressed into his service' (*GM*, 5, 1836, 525). Meanwhile, the announcement of a competition for rebuilding the burned Royal Exchange encouraged Hopper to publish his views on the proper way to conduct competitions in *A Letter to Lord Viscount Melbourne* (1839); and failure in the Nelson memorial competition of 1839 again drove him into print to attack 'the failures and abortions which mark the present age' (T. Hopper, *Designs for the Nelson Testimonial*, 1839). Although he had in 1826 designed Arthur's clubhouse, St James's Street (where a handsome neo-Palladian exterior, simplified by the crown surveyors, masked a Grecian interior), Hopper was unsuccessful in limited competitions for the Travellers' (1828), the Conservative (1842), and the Carlton (1844) clubhouses. For St Mary's Hospital, Paddington (1845–51), he contributed his services gratis.

Country house commissions, however, in which he established a major practice, constitute Hopper's primary role. Here he exhibited his competence in planning, and displayed to the highest degree the versatility expected of a Regency architect. An eclectic of the eclectics, he declared that the architect's business was 'to understand all styles, and to be prejudiced in favour of none' (T. Hopper, *Hopper versus Cust*, 1837, 14), as he indicated in the designs he exhibited frequently at the Royal Academy from 1833 to 1848. His internal alterations at Melford Hall, Suffolk (1813), alterations and extensions at Terling Place, Essex (1818–21), and a new house, Leigh Court, Somerset (1814), were in Greek revival style; new wings to Woolverstone Hall, Suffolk (1823), in Roman Doric (with cast-iron columns). In Tudor Gothic were Margam Abbey, Glamorgan (1830–35, gutted 1977), Easton Lodge, Essex (1847, rebuilt), and Danbury Place, Essex (1832)—where the north front was composed of elements arranged 'without any noticeable principle other than picturesqueness' (Pevsner, *Essex*,

1954, 141). Llanover House, Monmouthshire (1828–39), and Hardwick House, Hawstead, Suffolk (c.1831), were Elizabethan. Hopper remodelled Wivenhoe Park, Essex, in Jacobean (1846–9); rebuilt Amesbury House, Wiltshire (1834–40), and Kinmel Park, Denbighshire (1842–3), in neo-Palladian; and Birch Hall, Essex (1843–7, dem. 1954) in Italianate. But to a conscious exponent of the Picturesque, the Norman style offered notable advantages, and Hopper made it very much his own, for churches as well as mansions. It was unfamiliar and therefore striking; it was also in its geometrical massiveness peculiarly adapted to exploit the aesthetic of the sublime. Hopper's first important essay in this mode was Gosford Castle, co. Armagh, Ireland (1819–21), but his finest work and the outstanding exemplar of the style was Penrhyn Castle, Caernarvonshire, 1822–37, for G. H. Dawkins Pennant, owner of the great Welsh slate quarries. With a keep modelled on that of Rochester, Kent, with detailing from Castle Hedingham, Essex, rising 115 ft from the batter; and an interior drawing inspiration from ecclesiastical sources such as Durham Cathedral, but blended with detail of later periods and devices such as lighting the hall through tubes from the roof, Hopper's forms and spaces successfully exemplify Burke's aesthetic of the sublime. His characteristic richness of overall ornamentation, employing carefully studied Norman motifs, here achieves an effect that modern commentators have found Sicilian, Byzantine, or Arabic in character. Externally, the Picturesque effect is enhanced by a contrived aggregative effect from early Norman in the hall block, through the later Norman of the keep to the Gothic towers of the stable block.

In contrast to his father, Hopper 'never drank anything stronger than water' (The Builder, 14, 1856, 481), though that did not inhibit a constant flow of spirits: he displayed 'remarkable' powers of conversation and a 'most tenacious' memory; and could 'bear a marvellous amount of fatigue' (ibid.). His forceful character is illustrated by the effectiveness with which he supported his own views in consultations with clients, notably C. G. Round of Birch Hall (1842–5). The oft-repeated story that he refused a knighthood from George IV is improbable, but he may have been invited to St Petersburg by Tsar Alexander I. John Ternouth, who exhibited a bust of Hopper at the Royal Academy in 1838, is said to have given Hopper's 'form and features' to the sailor supporting a wounded mariner in his bas-relief on the east side of the base of Nelson's Column. With his wife, Anne (1783/4–1855), whom he married about 1808, Hopper had a son (an alcoholic who predeceased him) and two daughters. At the time of the 1851 census the family was living at 1 Bayswater Hill, Paddington, supported by two female servants, a housekeeper, and a coachman. Hopper died there on 11 August 1856.   M. H. PORT

Sources The Builder, 14 (1856), 481 · Dictionary of architecture, Architectural Publication Society, 4 [1882], 76 · register, St Marylebone, City Westm. AC [baptism] · IGI · census returns, 1851, PRO, HO 107/1467/240 · Colvin, Archs. · A. Searle, 'Thomas Hopper', Essex Journal, 5 (1970), 132–9 · R. Fedden, 'Thomas Hopper and the Norman revival', Studies in architectural history, ed. W. A. Singleton, 2 (1956), 581–69 · C. F. Smith, 'Thomas Hopper, 1776–1856', Essex Review, 23 (1914), 145–8 · PRO, PROB 11/2240 · T. Faulkner, An historical and topographical account of Fulham (1813) · The parish of St James, Westminster, 1/2, Survey of London, 30 (1960), 356–7, 401, 475–7, 479 · R. Evans, The fabrication of virtue (1982) · London Directory (1795–1855) · N. Burton, 'Thomas Hopper', The architectural outsiders, ed. R. Brown (1985), 114–31

Likenesses J. H. Lynch, lithograph, 1838 (after J. Ternouth), NPG · J. Ternouth, bust, 1838, RA · Miss Turner, lithograph, 1838 (after J. Ternouth), BM, NPG · J. Ternouth, bas-relief (Thomas Hopper?), Nelson's Column, Trafalgar Square, London

Wealth at death unknown but probably substantial; left £300 to a friend, and whole estate to daughter; had a coachman as well as other servants: will, PRO, PROB 11/2240; census returns, 1851, PRO, HO 107/1467/240

Hoppner, (Richard) Belgrave (1786–1872). See under Hoppner, John (1758–1810).

Hoppner, John (1758–1810), portrait painter, was born on 25 April 1758 in London, perhaps at St James's Palace, the first of the two children of John Hoppner, a surgeon, and Mary Anne (1728/9–1812). Hoppner's parents were both Germans—Bavarians according to the artist's son Belgrave—who came to England to serve in the court of George II. While Hoppner's place of birth is uncertain, he was baptized at Whitechapel, at that time a German Catholic ghetto in London, suggesting he may have been Roman Catholic.

Early years and education Having spent his childhood at court, Hoppner associated easily with royalty throughout his career. Indeed rumours began during his own life that he was an illegitimate child of George III. While Hoppner never denied them (according to some he encouraged them, certainly for reasons of publicity), there is no credible evidence for a liaison between the twenty-year-old prince of Wales and Hoppner's thirty-year-old mother. Hoppner apparently had only one sibling, Elizabeth, who married the engraver J. H. Meyer; they were the parents of the engraver Henry *Meyer.

Hoppner was a member of the Chapel Royal choir and was recommended as a 'Lad of Genius' (Farington, Diary, 2.286) to George III who provided him with an allowance. In 1775 he entered the Royal Academy Schools, winning a silver medal for drawing from life in 1778 and the gold medal for historical painting in 1781, when he completed his studies. He married Phoebe Wright (1761–1827), daughter of the wax sculptor Patience *Wright (1725–1786), on 8 July 1781 and moved into Mrs Wright's waxworks in Cockspur Street, Westminster. Upon his marriage his royal allowance ended and by all accounts he struggled for some years. By Christmas 1783 Hoppner and his wife had moved into 18–20 Charles Street, between St James's Square and the Haymarket (now demolished), a fashionable address, which added to Hoppner's financial concerns.

1780–1790 At the Royal Academy Schools Hoppner was a contemporary of Patience Wright's son Joseph; Mrs Wright's studio functioned in many ways as a salon, in particular for artistic and whig personalities. While there is no account of Hoppner at the waxworks, it was clearly through his wife's family that he acquired a number of connections, both artistic and social. Hoppner began

John Hoppner (1758–1810), self-portrait, c.1800

exhibiting at the Royal Academy in 1780, and continued annually (except in 1801 and 1808 for reasons of health) until 1809. While most of his early portraits depict gentry, by 1783 he was exhibiting portraits of nobility and in 1785 exhibited three portraits of the youngest daughters of George III, perhaps using his court connections to advantage. In 1786 he exhibited a full-length portrait of the duke of Clarence's actress mistress, *Mrs Jordan as the Comic Muse* (Royal Collection), in emulation of, or perhaps in competition with, Reynolds's celebrated portrait exhibited two years earlier, *Mrs Siddons as the Tragic Muse*.

In 1785 Hoppner published his first art criticism: unsigned reviews of works by Maria Cosway, Richard Cosway, and Benjamin West in the *Morning Post*. These were critical and condescending, though not contrary to prevailing opinion. Later revealed as the author, Hoppner was led to write his 'Address to the public' (*Morning Post*, 2 July 1785); there he described the difficulties under which he laboured when his royal allowance was withdrawn after his marriage, blaming West, who he thought was trying to rid himself of a rival.

In reality Hoppner was no one's rival in 1781, but his reputation steadily advanced throughout the 1780s. In 1787, when Gilbert Stuart abandoned London for Ireland to escape creditors, Hoppner was the artist widely considered the successor to Sir Joshua Reynolds and Thomas Gainsborough as the country's most respected portraitist. He was well connected socially; the duke of Clarence, Henry Lascelles, second earl of Harewood, Earl Grosvenor, and Viscountess Hampden all served as godparents for his children. During the late 1780s he crafted likenesses, primarily head-and-shoulders images, which were finely coloured and often noted for their dependence on Reynolds

(although perhaps he owed more to George Romney earlier in the decade). In 1790 Hoppner had been recommended to Catherine the Great as the young British artist with the most talent: 'Hoppner est celui parmi les jeunes Peintres qui parait avoir le plus de Talens' (*Soobshsheniya Gos. Ermitazha*, 44). In the Royal Academy exhibition of 1790, however, Hoppner's two subtle heads of the Horneck sisters (Taft Museum, Cincinnati, and ex Sothebys, New York, 25 April 1985) were overshadowed by the two bold full-length portraits exhibited by the 21-year-old Thomas Lawrence of Queen Charlotte (National Gallery, London) and of the actress Elizabeth Farren (Metropolitan Museum of Art, New York). Hoppner, caught unaware—as were his contemporaries—by the quality of Lawrence's work, spent the 1790s demonstrating his own powers both of painting and of attracting sitters.

1791–1800 With the fourteen paintings entered in the exhibitions of 1791 and 1792, Hoppner did indeed demonstrate the full range of his work, with ten of the sitters being royal, a royal mistress, or noble (two others were subject pictures). By 1793 he had succeeded Reynolds as portrait painter to the prince of Wales, a more popularly prestigious appointment than portraitist to the king (which went to Lawrence), and was elected an associate of the Royal Academy. In 1795 he was elected an academician and his prestige was such that the king commissioned him, rather than Lawrence, to paint a portrait of the new princess of Wales, an opportunity Hoppner lost by responding aggressively to some of the king's art criticism.

Even without the patronage of the king, Hoppner was extremely successful in the 1790s, making over £2000 a year in 1798 and £3000 in 1801. He was patronized by all sectors of society: tories and whigs, politicians, the military and clergy, the elderly, and the parents of children and young beauties. By all accounts he was handsome and a brilliant conversationalist, not only amusing and animating his sitters but active in several clubs and in the political and social life of the Royal Academy. Hoppner took an active role in running the academy, taking his turn at serving on the council and as a visitor to the schools, and with other *ad hoc* groups such as that which investigated the validity of the notorious 'Provis's process' or the 'Venetian secret', a recipe for mixing paints in the manner of Titian.

Hoppner's technique and style derived from the teachings of Reynolds, but neither in technique nor in style did he follow the elder painter slavishly. As a student and in his early maturity (when his style owed more to Romney and Johan Zoffany) Hoppner would have heard Reynolds deliver his *Discourses*; but while Reynolds held up the work of Michelangelo and the Florentine Renaissance as a model for artists, Hoppner preferred the Venetian and Flemish painters, such as Titian and Van Dyck, or the more painterly aspects of Rembrandt, all of whose works Hoppner knew at first hand from the Royal Collection; these Reynolds advocated only with caution for their 'seductive' qualities. While Reynolds taught that artists should work in an academic method of preparation with drawings and sketches, Hoppner (as did Reynolds himself) began his portraits directly from life onto the final canvas and worked them up to completion, only occasionally making a study of the sitter first. Hoppner's studio was described by the French artist Henri-Pierre Danloux in 1792:

> his gallery is small and sombre, as are all those of the English … The light came in from above and one could hardly distinguish a thing. I was surprised at this lack of light; he said to me that he could see perfectly and it was the true way of getting the effect.   (Portalis, 94)

Hoppner took an interest in younger artists, freely offering advice as he did to Turner (who gave him a watercolour in thanks for his help), or taking them into his studio, as he did with Henry Salt. Constable recorded Hoppner's help on the verso of a portrait of Richard Ramsay Reinagle (ex Sothebys, London, 10 November 1993); J. J. Halls recorded that he had an open invitation to Hoppner's studio; and David Wilkie's journals imply that he, Constable, and Benjamin Robert Haydon were all welcomed by Hoppner. Two of Hoppner's children exhibited as artists: Lascelles Hoppner (who likewise won the Royal Academy's gold medal and later took over his father's studio), and Richard Belgrave Hoppner [see below].

1801–1810 Hoppner fell from his coach and broke his arm in 1801, causing him to exhibit nothing that year, and the first decade of the nineteenth century was a period of considerable success but also of declining health. Hoppner's health had caused concern from an early age; a contemporary wrote that he became an artist because he did not have 'sufficiently good health to follow the profession of music' (Papendiek, 1.232). The diarist Joseph Farington first noted Hoppner's tenuous health in 1795, and throughout the first decade of the 1800s he records a variety of ailments, most notably with Hoppner's liver, but also including 'Hectic Fever', 'debility and want of Appetite', and 'dropsy', for which Hoppner consulted several eminent physicians, among others Matthew Baillie, Sir Everard Home, Erasmus Darwin, and William Jenner. In 1807 he complained that his health was preventing him from finishing a portrait of the prince of Wales, and he did not exhibit at the Royal Academy in 1808. In 1809 he exhibited portraits executed earlier.

Hoppner painted some of his most celebrated works between 1802 and 1807 after his only trip abroad: to Paris during the peace of Amiens. In Paris he visited the Louvre, and despite his knowledge of the old masters in the British Royal Collection he was unprepared for the quality of the works of art assembled by Napoleon. On his return Hoppner worked with new attention to primary colours and simple compositions, in particular in life-scale, head-and-shoulders portraits of men. His portraits were frequently remarked upon for their likeness, even when the composition as a whole was unsatisfactory. Referring specifically to Hoppner's portrait of William Pitt, the portraitist William Owen described Hoppner's qualities of likeness in relation to those of other artists. Owen

wondered Hoppner had dared so strongly to express a character in Mr. Pitt's countenance in which Hauteur and something of disdainful severity were so predominant.—It was the *truth* but others had as usual, when any disagreeable tendency was manifested in the countenance, endeavoured to *soften it*.   (Farington, *Diary*, 7.2693)

Hoppner's portrait of Nelson (1800–01; Royal Collection) was not only considered a good likeness, but took on an enhanced popularity when it was engraved by Charles Turner after Nelson's death and published in 1806.

Hoppner's last years were occupied by the political turmoil at the Royal Academy surrounding Benjamin West's presidency in 1805; Hoppner voted inconsistently during this period. This, combined with his increased irritability caused by health problems, caused him to paint less and write more, spending less time with his established circle of academician friends. His intellectual social life centred on younger artists, literary friends, and clubs; he was a member of the Athenian Club, the Council of Trent (limited to thirty members), and the King of Clubs. Moreover, he was proposed for the Royal Society in 1797 and the Literary Club in 1799, but was not elected to either, according to Farington, because he was an artist. He counted among his friends several eminent poets and literary critics. Hoppner painted a handful of exceptional full-length portraits, most notably of admirals Sir Samuel Hood (1807; NMM) and John Jervis, earl of St Vincent (Royal Collection), both of whom were portrayed in a sympathetic and thoughtful manner. His smaller works, particularly those portraying acquaintances, were frequently rendered in a penetrating style with clear colours—as in portraits of Sir George Beaumont (1803; National Gallery, London) or his friends from the King of Clubs such as Samuel Rogers (1809; priv. coll.). Occasionally, however, they displayed a remarkable energy of brushwork, as in portraits of the third duke of Grafton (1805) or Lady Caroline Lamb (c.1806; both priv. coll.).

Hoppner had resumed his writing career by the late 1790s, when Farington recorded his work in the *British Critic*. By that time he had also begun writing Arabic-themed poetry; at least one of these poems was published in *The Pic-Nic*. He published these verses as a group in 1805 as *Oriental Tales*, but they are better known for the notorious preface to the first edition. In the preface Hoppner justified his own style and method of painting—which had often been criticized as unfinished—in contrast to the contemporary French school, in particular the work of J. L. David and Elisabeth Vigée Le Brun (the latter then working in England), and which he savaged. In 1807 Hoppner wrote for Prince Hoare's *The Artist*, and late in his life reviewed books on art for the *Quarterly Review*.

Hoppner's art collection included a few distinguished works, among them Gainsborough's portrait of Jonathan Buttall ('The Blue Boy'; Huntington Library, San Marino, California), Van Dyck's portrait of François Langlois playing bagpipes (National Gallery, London), and a portrait of Sir Theodore Mayerne, then thought to be Rubens's original (North Carolina Museum of Art).

Hoppner's health declined substantially in the summer of 1809 on a holiday to the Isle of Wight; in June he suffered what William Gifford described as an apoplectic fit.

In mid-January 1810 he was extremely lethargic and tried to work so as to keep from sleeping constantly (Farington, *Diary*, 10.3594). He fell into a coma about three days before his death at his home, 18–20 Charles Street, London, on 23 January 1810. He was buried at St James's churchyard, Hampstead Road, London, on 29 January after a private funeral. Little public notice was taken of his death.

Reputation Owing in part to Sir Thomas Lawrence's spectacular portraits of the 1810s and 1820s, and Hoppner's own less flamboyant style, Hoppner's reputation flagged throughout most of the nineteenth century. It was revived somewhat at the turn of the twentieth century with interest in grand-manner British portraiture collected by the Rothschilds, the Huntingtons, the Mellons, and the Fricks, among others. Portraits by Hoppner that most resembled those by Reynolds were the most sought after. His full-length portrait of Lady Louisa Manners (Musée de l'Art et d'Histoire, Geneva) was sold in 1901 for 14,050 guineas, at that time the record price for a picture sold at auction. With the decline of interest in society portraiture after the First World War Hoppner's reputation all but disappeared. His one appearance in late twentieth-century popular culture was his inclusion in Alan Bennett's play *The Madness of George III* (1991); the character was written out of the subsequent film.

(Richard) **Belgrave Hoppner** (1786–1872), diplomatist, was born on 9 January 1786 in London, the second among the five children of John Hoppner and Phoebe Wright. Belgrave Hoppner, as he was known, was named after his godfather, Richard *Grosvenor, first Earl Grosvenor, whose courtesy title was Viscount Belgrave. He was educated at Eton College and received some artistic training from his father, exhibiting marine paintings at the Royal Academy, as an honorary exhibitor, in 1807, 1810, and 1811. He also exhibited twenty-one paintings at the British Institution.

Belgrave Hoppner's diplomatic career began in 1801 when he received a clerkship in the Foreign Office. He served as secretary to a variety of foreign missions in Spain, the Netherlands, and at the Council of Vienna. On 3 September 1814 he married Marie Isabelle (d. 1869/70), fourth daughter of Beat Lois May, seigneur d'Oron et de Brandis, of the canton of Bern, Switzerland, at the residence of the British ambassador in Brussels. They had a daughter, Emily. That year he was appointed consul general at Venice where his friendship with Byron, for which he is now chiefly remembered, was formed. Hoppner was on familiar terms with the poet by September 1817 when Byron leased the Hoppner villa in the Euganean Hills near Este. Byron was godfather to Hoppner's son, prompting the lines 'On the birth of John William Rizzo Hoppner' in February 1818. For six weeks from mid-May 1818 the Hoppners took temporary care of Allegra, Byron's illegitimate infant daughter with Claire Clairmont, repeating this kindness occasionally until Byron placed her in a convent. Hoppner was one of Byron's confidants during the poet's years in Italy, expressing candid disapproval of his relationship with Teresa Guiccioli, riding and swimming with him (most

notably in Venice during Byron's contest with Cavalier Angelo Mengaldo, a 4½-mile swim from the Lido to the end of the Grand Canal near Santa Chiara), administering Byron's financial affairs while the poet was living in Ravenna, and sharing Byron's then low opinion of Venice.

Belgrave Hoppner suffered from frail health (Byron noted how thin he was), a trait he shared with his father, and he blamed much of it on the Venetian climate. He frequently asked for other assignments, but retired to London in July 1825. He was appointed consul general in Lisbon in 1830 during the Portuguese civil war; at a time when there were no formal diplomatic relations with Portugal he functioned as an ambassador. He returned to London in 1833 and took on no further appointments. Hoppner's hundreds of dispatches from his appointments survive in the Public Record Office; *Voyage around the World*, his translation of Ivan Fedorovich Kruzenshtern's account, was published by John Murray in 1813 and an 'Elegy' was praised by Byron in 1817 as 'remarkably good'. His recollections and letters were the basis for much of the early biographical material for his father; his descendants own several of his letters.

Upon his retirement Hoppner lived for some years in Grenoble. By 1860 he was living in Versailles and in 1871, after his wife's death at some time between October 1869 and January 1870, he moved to Turin. He died there the following year.　　　　JOHN WILSON

Sources Farington, *Diary* · Mrs Cromarty, 'Notes taken from Mamma's anecdotes and from Uncle Belgrave's letters', BL, Add. MS 28510, fols. 237–99 · J. H. Wilson, 'The life and work of John Hoppner (1758–1810)', PhD diss., Courtauld Inst., 1992 · W. McKay and W. Roberts, *John Hoppner, R.A.* (1909); supplement (1914) · O. Millar, *The later Georgian pictures in the collection of her majesty the queen*, 2 vols. (1969) · C. Papendiek, *Court and private life in the time of Queen Charlotte*, 2 vols. (1887) · R. Portalis, *Henri-Pierre Danloux peintre de portraits: son journal durant l'émigration (1753–1809)* (Paris, 1910) · Graves, *RA exhibitors*, 4 (1906), 153–5 · J. J. Halls, *The life and correspondence of Henry Salt*, 2nd edn, 2 vols. (1834) · A. Cunningham, *The life of Sir David Wilkie*, 3 vols. (1843) · Soobshsheniya Gos. Ermitazha/Bulletin du Musée de l'Ermitage, 18 (1960), 44 · will, PRO, PROB 11/1508, fols. 209–10 · rate lists · catalogues, 1780–1810, RA · H. P. K. Skipton, *John Hoppner* (1905) · records, RA · C. S. B. Buckland, 'Richard Belgrave Hoppner', *EngHR*, 39 (1924), 373–85 · *Byron's letters and journals*, ed. L. A. Marchand, 12 vols. (1973–82)
Archives BL, Mrs Cromarty, 'Notes taken from Mamma's anecdotes and from Uncle Belgrave's letters', Add. MS 28510, fols. 237–99 · Ches. & Chester ALSS, corresp. with Sir John Leicester and receipts for payment of his pictures
Likenesses J. Hoppner, self-portrait, oils, c.1792, RA; version, NPG · H. Singleton, group portrait, oils, c.1795 (*Royal academicians, 1793*), RA · attrib. Singleton, oil study of head for his group portrait, c.1795; London Art Market, 2000 · G. Dance, chalk drawing, c.1800, RA · J. Hoppner, self-portrait, c.1800, RA [*see illus.*] · J. Hoppner, self-portrait, Parham, West Sussex · J. Hoppner, self-portrait, NG Ire.

Hopps, John Page (1834–1911), Unitarian minister, was born in London on 6 November 1834; nothing is known about his origins and upbringing other than that his father was Cordt Hopps, a stall merchant. After studying at Leicester Baptist college, in 1856 he became minister of a Baptist meeting at Hugglescote, Leicestershire. Doubts

John Page Hopps
(1834–1911), by
Museum Studio

when, during his Leicester troubles, he was reflecting gloomily on the future of Unitarianism.

An inveterate publisher of sermons, hymns, and manuals for family worship, Hopps also edited two periodicals, *The Truthseeker* from 1863 to 1887 and the *Coming Day* from 1891 until his death. But he also advocated less conventional means for spreading the Christian message. Floral Hall, opened in Leicester in 1880 to appeal to unchurched working people through flowers, music, and popular preaching, drew an estimated attendance of 40,000 in the last year of its existence; its sale in 1886, without his consent, began the series of disappointments that led to his leaving Leicester. His later campaign for 'Our Father's Church' sought to transform and transcend his own congregation to unite people from all denominations in spiritual development and social sympathy.

While honouring the Unitarian contribution to free inquiry and religious liberty, Hopps thought that Unitarian doctrine had outlived its usefulness and welcomed the Free Christian movement promoted by Martineau and his friends in the 1860s. But he moved on to new enthusiasms characteristic of a generation to whom traditional theological questions seemed increasingly irrelevant. Of these, the most remarkable was spiritualism, for which he was prepared by an early exposure to Swedenborgianism and by his mother's spiritualist experiences and to which he turned during a mental crisis in the mid-1860s. His spiritualism was consistent with his all-embracing humanitarianism and an expansive view of God as a spirit, not a person. Rejecting belief in the resurrection of the body, he was an early advocate of cremation.

Politically, Hopps was an advanced Liberal. In 1886, determined to defend W. E. Gladstone against what he saw as tory abuse, he undertook a hopeless candidacy against Lord Randolph Churchill in Paddington, losing by 2576 votes to 769. He was a strong supporter of Irish home rule—a position that weakened his standing in his Leicester congregation—land reform, anti-vivisection, and the peace movement. He frequently wrote for newspapers, among them *The Times* and the *Daily News*, and his stern criticism of British South African policy early in the new century appeared in the *New Age*, edited from 1902 to 1907 by a Unitarian minister, Harold Rylett (1851–1936).

Hopps died of heart failure on 6 April 1911 at The Roserie, his house in Broadlands Avenue, Shepperton-on-Thames. The funeral service was held on 11 April at the Woking crematorium.   R. K. WEBB

having set in, the next year he became an assistant to the Revd George Dawson (1821–1876), the great Birmingham preacher whose migration from the Baptist faith to liberal non-denominationalism was reflected in a succession of assistants making similar pilgrimages. On 13 June 1859 Hopps married Mary Jackson (1838–1902), daughter of Edward Jackson, a farmer; four children were born to the couple. Following his first wife's death, he married Alice Elizabeth Hallawell (b. 1876), the daughter of a London merchant, on 13 July 1903.

In 1860 Hopps became minister at Upperthorpe Chapel, a new Unitarian congregation in Sheffield, moving from there to Old Chapel, Dukinfield, in 1863 and in 1869 to the splendidly idiosyncratic classical chapel in St Vincent's Street, Glasgow, erected in 1856 and demolished in 1982. Known as a compelling preacher and social activist—in 1874 he was elected to the Glasgow school board, where he was an advocate of secular education—he was called in 1876 to one of the most prominent Unitarian congregations, Great Meeting, Leicester, at the large stipend of £400. There for a time he was even more successful than in Glasgow, but by 1892 tensions had set in, and he left for the Free Christian church, Croydon, where he remained until 1905, successfully building up a relatively new foundation, though he found metropolitan piety inferior to that in the midlands and the north. He then became minister at Little Portland Street, the chapel identified with the London career of James Martineau (1805–1900). On its closure in 1909 the congregation moved to University Hall in Gordon Square, where Hopps preached his last sermon on the Sunday before his death.

A slight man with a massive head and rugged face, gifted with a fine voice and a quick sense of humour, Hopps saw the preacher's art as the key to filling churches, repeatedly citing the spell-binding Baptist Charles Haddon Spurgeon (1834–1892) as proof. His buoyant personality is caught in his habit of signing letters 'Heartily yours', even

Sources *The Inquirer* (15 April 1911) · *The Inquirer* (22 April 1911) · *The Inquirer* (4 Nov 1911) · congregational records, Great Meeting, Leicester, Leics. RO · *Unitarian Herald* (6 May 1864) · *Unitarian Herald* (6 Oct 1865) · J. P. Hopps, *Spirit-life in God the Spirit: a meditation on God and immortality* (1874) · d. cert. · m. certs. · d. cert. [Mary Hopps]
Archives Leics. RO, Congregational records of the Great Meeting, Leicester
Likenesses photograph, *c*.1863, Old Chapel, Dukinfield · Museum Studio, photograph, DWL [*see illus.*] · cartoon, repro. in *The Bailie* (2 April 1873) · photograph, DWL
Wealth at death £2319 1*s.* 1*d.*: probate, 10 Oct 1911, CGPLA Eng. & Wales

Hoppus, John (*bap.* **1791**, *d.* **1875**), philosopher and Independent minister, son of John Hoppus, also an Independent minister, and his wife, Mary, was baptized in Hoxton, London, on 16 August 1791. He was educated for four years under James Bennett at the Rotherham Independent college, Yorkshire, where the views of Edward Williams, author of *Divine Equity and Sovereignty* (1813), had great influence among the students. From 1819 to 1820 Hoppus attended classes in Greek and philosophy at Edinburgh University, but he transferred his terms to Glasgow in order to attend the sermons of Thomas Chalmers, and there graduated MA in 1822. He moved to London to take charge of the Carter Lane Chapel, but resigned in 1825 owing to difficulties with his congregation, which was somewhat Arian in its views. Early in 1826 he began work as a temporary classics tutor at Highbury College. He also taught classical languages at the Baptist Academical Institution, Stepney, and took on some private tuition.

In 1827 he published an account of Francis Bacon's *Novum organon scientiarum* for the Society for the Diffusion of Useful Knowledge and in this connection he came to know Henry Brougham. Also in 1827 he was considered for the chair of logic and philosophy of mind at the fledgeling University of London, afterwards University College. His application was rejected when Brougham and James Mill supported George Grote's opposition to any minister of religion occupying a chair of philosophy. But when the post remained unfilled two years later Hoppus was reconsidered, Mill having abandoned his objection following Hoppus's assurance that he was a follower of the associationist philosopher David Hartley. He was recommended by the education committee in Grote's absence and appointed by the council, despite Grote's renewed protest, in December 1829. Grote's anger at this move contributed to his decision to resign from the council early in 1830. Hoppus's long tenure of the post was infuriating to him, and when Hoppus eventually resigned the chair in 1866 (to Grote's 'undissembled satisfaction') Grote controversially thwarted the appointment of another cleric, James Martineau, as his successor.

Hoppus 'almost killed the study of philosophy in the college' (Bellot, 111), not because he was a minister of religion but because he was an awful teacher. He did not make any original contribution to philosophy: aside from his work on Bacon his only philosophical publications appear to have been a statement of the course of study in his classes and an introductory lecture. And his lectures (planned along lines which show the influence of Dugald Stewart) were 'dull and inaudible' (Clarke, 154) and extremely poorly attended. But he was very assiduous and lectured not only on philosophy of mind and logic but also exhaustively on the history of philosophy (demonstrating a thorough knowledge of Kant and the post-Kantians) and on moral philosophy. In 1832 Hoppus married Martha Devenish (1803–1853). There were several children, including Mary Anne Martha Hoppus, who as Mary Anne Marks was the author of several volumes of fiction as well as a popular history of the corn laws and other economic

works. In 1837/8 and 1852/3 Hoppus was dean of the faculty of arts and laws. He was made LLD of Glasgow in 1839 and FRS in 1841.

In 1847 Hoppus published *The Crisis of Popular Education*, in which he expressed the view, unpopular in some dissenting circles, that government had a role to play in the provision of education. Other publications were largely religious in character. His contribution to a series of *Lectures Against Socialism* (1840), for example, was concerned only to rebut the atheistic element of Robert Owen's socialism and expressed a weakly benevolent but rather vague attitude towards Owen's philanthropy and social theory. And his pamphlet *Ireland's Misery and Remedy* (1835) explained Irish history wholly in terms of the twin vices of popery and established protestantism: for Hoppus the solution to Ireland's problems lay in its moral regeneration (conversion from Catholicism) by the missionary efforts of an army of young clerics. He died on 29 January 1875 at his home at 26 Camden Street, Camden Town, London.   W. A. J. ARCHBOLD, *rev.* C. A. CREFFIELD

Sources H. H. Bellot, *University College, London, 1826–1926* (1929) · H. Grote, *The personal life of George Grote* (1873) · M. L. Clarke, *George Grote: a biography* (1962) · *Testimonials presented to the council of the University of London in favour of J. Hoppus* (1827) · M. Hoppus, *Memorials of a wife* (1856) · *Congregational Year Book* (1876) · *CGPLA Eng. & Wales* (1875) · *IGI*
Archives UCL, SDUK MSS, letters to Society for the Diffusion of Useful Knowledge
Likenesses Fenner, Sears & Co., stipple (after J. R. Wildman), NPG
Wealth at death under £6000: probate, 24 Feb 1875, *CGPLA Eng. & Wales*

Hopson, Charles Rivington (*bap.* **1744**, *d.* **1796**), physician, was baptized at St Stephen's, Coleman Street, London, on 2 February 1744, the son of Michael and Mary Hopson. He may have been related to the publishing family of Rivington. He was educated at St Paul's School, and entered Leiden University on 1 October 1765. At Leiden he gained his MD, his dissertation (published at Leiden, 1767) being entitled *De tribus in uno*. Hopson practised in London, and for many years was physician to the Finsbury Dispensary. He wrote *An Essay on Fire* (1782) and translated works from German and Swedish, including 'A treatise on dysentery', by J. G. Zimmerman (1771), published by John and Francis Rivington. He is also credited with translations of J. G. A. Forster's *Voyages and Discoveries in the North* (1786). Hopson died on 23 December 1796.

W. A. J. ARCHBOLD, *rev.* KAYE BAGSHAW

Sources *GM*, 1st ser., 67 (1797), 80 · E. Peacock, *Index to English speaking students who have graduated at Leyden University* (1883) · *IGI*

Hopson, Edward (**1671–1728**). *See under* Hopson, Sir Thomas (*bap.* 1643, *d.* 1717).

Hopson [Hopsonn], **Sir Thomas** (*bap.* **1643**, *d.* **1717**), naval officer, was the second son of Captain Anthony Hopson (*d.* 1667) and Anne, *née* Kinge, of Shalfleet, Isle of Wight, where he was baptized on 6 April 1643. The family had settled on former monastic land at Ningwood in Henry VIII's reign, but was in reduced circumstances by the time of Hopson's birth. According to local tradition, he ran away to sea at an early age, and was certainly serving in the navy by 1666, when he became a 'particular friend' of Pepys's brother-in-law Balthazar St Michel (Heath, 210–11). He served as second lieutenant of the *Dreadnought* from May 1672 to July 1674, fighting in all the battles of the Third Anglo-Dutch War. He then served as first lieutenant of the *Dragon*, *Centurion*, and *Mary* in the Mediterranean between November 1676 and 21 March 1678. On that date Admiral Arthur Herbert, commanding the Mediterranean Fleet, gave him a commission as captain of the *Tiger Prize*. Herbert had written a little earlier that Hopson had 'as much merit as modesty, and so much of both that … any man when he becomes well known will be proud to have been the instrument of his preferment' (Herbert to Pepys, 5 March 1678, Herbert letterbook, p. 4). Hopson commanded the prize until she was paid off in August but then held no other naval command for over two years, becoming an ensign in the Portsmouth garrison in 1681. He became captain of the *Swan* on 10 January 1682, serving initially on the coast of Ireland and then as part of the fleet sent to evacuate Tangier under the command of George Legge, Lord Dartmouth. After returning to England and paying off his ship in September 1684, Hopson returned once more to his military career, becoming a lieutenant in the 1st foot guards on 30 April 1685. On 18 May 1688 James II appointed him captain of the *Bonadventure*. Despite this, he was one of the conspirators in the fleet who supported William of Orange and his old patron, Herbert, during the naval events of the revolution of 1688; he retained command of the *Bonadventure* until October 1689, forming part of the squadron that relieved Londonderry in June.

Hopson moved to the *York* on 28 October 1689 and commanded her during the battle of Beachy Head in the following summer. He moved to the *Royal Katherine* in August 1690, commanding her for two months, and then had two lengthy commissions as captain of the *Saint Michael* (1690–93), which he commanded at the battle of Barfleur (19–21 May 1692). He commanded the *Breda* from February to September 1693, serving as a rear-admiral under Sir George Rooke during the disastrous scattering of the Smyrna convoy in June, although his own conduct was not criticized. With the *Russell* as his flagship he served as vice-admiral of the squadron convoying the Mediterranean trade over the winter of 1693–4. Promoted to vice-admiral of the blue in 1694, Hopson spent much of that summer trying to trap the great French seaman Jean Bart's squadron in the channel and off Dunkirk. He was engaged on a similar service in the following year. In 1696 Hopson gave up the captaincy in the foot guards that he had held since 1692, and in 1698 he was elected MP for Newtown, Isle of Wight; he served as such until 1705, although he had an inactive parliamentary career. In 1699 he commanded a squadron successively on the Irish and French coasts, flying his flag in the *Kent*, and in 1700 went with Rooke to the Baltic to pressurize Denmark into withdrawing from the Great Northern War. In the summer of 1701 he commanded a squadron transporting troops from Ireland to the Netherlands. During the 1702 campaign Hopson served again as Rooke's vice-admiral, taking effective command of the

fleet in August when Rooke was struck with gout. At the battle of Vigo (12 October 1702) Hopson flew his flag in the *Torbay* (80 guns) and led the Anglo-Dutch line of battle into the harbour, with the *Torbay* making all sail to break the boom. She then engaged the *Bourbon* and *Espérance* before being attacked by a fireship which successfully fired her foresail. However, the fireship was a hastily converted merchantman laden with snuff, and, when she blew up, her cargo 'extinguished the flames, but almost blinded and suffocated those that were near' (Markham, 57). With 115 men killed and the *Torbay* badly shattered, Hopson moved his flag to the *Monmouth* in the latter stages of the battle. Twenty-one French and Spanish warships, and twenty lesser craft, were taken or destroyed, and Hopson justifiably received most of the credit for a famous victory. His monument in Weybridge church records that he forced the boom 'with his usual resolution and conduct, whereby he made way for the whole confederate fleet … to enter, take and destroy all the enemy's ships of war and galleons; which was the last of 42 engagements he had been in'. On his return to England, Hopson was knighted (29 November 1702) and appointed a commissioner of the navy with a salary of £500 per annum. He retained this position until 1714, also serving as governor of Greenwich Hospital from 1704 to 1708 and as colonel of the eastern regiment of the Cinque Ports militia in 1703.

Sir Thomas married Elizabeth Timbrell (d. 1740) of Portsmouth on 31 May 1680. They settled in Weybridge, Surrey, in later years, and by his will (dated 4 January 1717) Hopson bequeathed his house there to her. He also made bequests to a son, James, and to four daughters, one of whom married the naval captain John Goodall. Another son, Peregrine Thomas Hopson, became an army officer and died in 1759 as governor of Nova Scotia. Additionally, Sir Thomas made bequests to his executors, his fellow former flag officer Sir John Jennings, Captain Edward Hopson (both of Weybridge), and Brigadier William Watkins of Walton-on-Thames. Hopson died at Weybridge on 12 October 1717 and was buried in the parish church there on 17 October. Highly regarded by most of the leading admirals of the day, notably Herbert, Russell, and Rooke, Hopson seems to have been a compassionate commander who never lost sight of his roots. In 1702 he begged for the life of a captain condemned to be shot for cowardice, on the grounds that

> when I was a youth in the Isle of Wight, [I remember] that his father had the character of a very loyal gentleman … he is ancient, and has an ancient wife, and [I beg] that they may see each other before they die. (*CSP dom.*, 1702–3, 350–51)

The **Edward Hopson** (1671–1728), naval officer, mentioned in Sir Thomas's will was long conjectured to be a much younger brother or else a more distant relative. In fact he was the son of Sir Thomas's elder brother, Anthony (1640–1679), a gunner at Sandham Fort, Isle of Wight, and was at sea with his uncle in the *Swan* in 1682. Appointed lieutenant to Sir Thomas in the *Breda* in 1693, a post captain on 24 July 1696, rear-admiral in 1719, and vice-admiral in 1727, he died in command in the West Indies on 8 May 1728.   J. D. DAVIES

Sources PRO, ADM MSS, ADM 6/424 · will of Sir Thomas Hopson, PRO, PROB 11/560, fol. 263 · will of Edward Hopson, PRO, PROB 11/623, fol. 110 · will of Dame Elizabeth Hopson, PRO, PROB 11/701, fols. 433–4 · parish registers, Shalfleet and Brading, Isle of Wight RO · 'Hopson, Sir Thomas', HoP, *Commons* [draft] · *CSP dom.*, 1689–1704 · E. Lloyd, 'Weybridge parish registers', *Surrey Archaeological Collections*, 17 (1902), 41–69, esp. 54–7 · original commissions, NMM, MS ADL/Q/24 · Glos. RO, Rooke MSS · J. Ehrman, *The navy in the war of William III, 1689–1697* (1953) · H. T. Heath, ed., *The letters of Samuel Pepys and his family circle* (1955) · A. Herbert, letterbook, 1678–83, Yale U., Beinecke L., Osborn Collection, fb 96 · *Life of Captain Stephen Martin, 1666–1740*, ed. C. R. Markham, Navy RS, 5 (1895) · C. Dalton, ed., *English army lists and commission registers, 1661–1714*, 6 vols. (1892–1904)
Archives BL, King's MSS 55–59 · PRO, ADM MSS
Likenesses M. Dahl, oils, c.1705–1708, NMM
Wealth at death £1800 in bequests; plus house in Weybridge: will, PRO, PROB 11/560, fol. 263

Hopton, Arthur (*c*.1580–1614), mathematician and almanac maker, can probably be identified as the fourth son of Richard Hopton of Hopton, Shropshire, gentleman, and his wife, Anne, daughter of Thomas Walker (also known as Leigh) of Stretton in the same county. He was educated at Clement's Inn, off the Strand, Westminster, and lodged there for the rest of his life. Hopton's first publications were almanacs, calculated for Shrewsbury and the Welsh borders, and produced annually from 1606 to advertise his instruments and books. He stressed that he was writing mainly for lawyers, scholars, and clerics, with no wish 'to be praised of the multitude of meane mecanicks' (Hopton, *Almanack*, 1607, sig. Bv). The almanacs show that Hopton was familiar with the modern astronomical writings of the time. He generally accepted Copernican data on the size and distance of heavenly bodies, though unlike most of his friends he rejected Copernican heliocentrism, wavering between the geocentric systems of Ptolemy and Tycho Brahe. Hopton defended astrology and gave meteorological and medical advice, but he dismissed the judicial astrology of his age as mercenary, ignorant, and worthless. The few predictions he offered, mainly to satisfy public expectation, were generally flippant.

Hopton's main achievement lay in two substantial and important works on surveying. *Baculum geodaeticum* (1610), dedicated to Robert Cecil, earl of Salisbury, explained the use of his 'Geodeticall Staffe', and provided a lucid introduction to geometry, trigonometry, and dialling. *Speculum topographicum, or, The Topographicall Glasse* (1611), dedicated to Lord Ellesmere, the lord chancellor, described another of his instruments, a theodolite with dials and circles, enabling it to serve the functions of a quadrant and astrolabe. Hopton also included a notable defence of scientific progress, and insisted on the value of practical as much as theoretical knowledge. His instruments, made in both brass and wood, were fashioned by some of the leading craftsmen of the time—Elias Allen, John Read, and John Tompson. *A Concordancy of Yeares* (1612, and several later editions), dedicated to Sir Edward Coke, was a very different publication, a utilitarian handbook providing miscellaneous astronomical and medical data, tables of interest rates, weights and measures, the law terms, lists of peers

and bishops, and the parliamentary constituencies. Hopton designed another instrument, 'Clavis mathematica', and promised a further book to explain it, but he died before completing it. His friend Thomas Bretnor offered to teach the geometrical and astronomical applications of the instrument, which in the event was soon superseded by Gunter's sector.

Hopton was a friend of many of the leading mathematicians of his time, including Edward Wright and Mark Ridley. There is no evidence that he secured patronage from the eminent figures to whom he dedicated his works, but he was widely respected in intellectual circles. His London and Shropshire friends, mainly lawyers (among them John Selden), gentlemen, and clerics, provided admiring verses for his works. In 1613 Hopton himself wrote a commendatory verse for a volume of religious verse by his friend and kinsman Sir William Leighton. His almanacs reflect his own vigorous but moderate religious views, attacking both non-preaching pluralists and the 'sect of Puritans' (Hopton, *Almanac*, 1613, sig. C7). Hopton appears to have remained unmarried, and his almanacs contain many jocular misogynist verses. He died in the parish of St Clement Danes, London in November 1614, while still young, and was probably buried in the parish church.

BERNARD CAPP

Sources A. Hopton, *Baculum geodaeticum* (1610) · A. Hopton, *Speculum topographicum, or, The topographicall glasse* (1611) · A. Hopton, *A concordancy of yeares* (1612) · A. Hopton, *Almanack* (1606–14) · E. G. R. Taylor, *The mathematical practitioners of Tudor and Stuart England* (1954) · B. S. Capp, *Astrology and the popular press: English almanacs, 1500–1800* (1979) · Wood, *Ath. Oxon.* · F. R. Johnson, *Astronomical thought in Renaissance England* (1937) · D. W. Waters, *The art of navigation in England in Elizabethan and early Stuart times* (1958) · R. Tresswell and A. Vincent, *The visitation of Shropshire, taken in the year 1623*, ed. G. Grazebrook and J. P. Rylands, 2 vols., Harleian Society, 28–9 (1889) · W. Leighton, *The teares or lamentations of a sorrowfull soule* (1613)

Hopton, Sir Arthur (1588–1650), diplomat, was the fifth son of Sir Arthur Hopton of Witham, Somerset, and his wife, Rachel, daughter of Edmund Hall of Gretford, Lincolnshire. His father, a sheriff of Somerset under Elizabeth I, was created a knight of the Bath in 1603. Privately educated, Arthur matriculated at Lincoln College, Oxford, on 14 March 1605 but after this little is known of his activities prior to his long career representing Charles I at the court of Philip IV.

Hopton first arrived in Madrid in July 1629 as secretary to Sir Francis Cottington, who spent over a year in the negotiations for a peace treaty, which proved to be a renewal of the terms signed in London in 1604 but failed to satisfy Charles's ambition to restore the Palatinate to his brother-in-law. After Cottington left in 1630 Hopton remained as the resident agent. From the outset Hopton proved to be a diligent correspondent who provided detailed comments about events in Castile and the major decisions of Philip's powerful adviser, the count-duke of Olivares. He benefited greatly by his skill in speaking and writing Castilian, which afforded him many private talks with Olivares, as he noted in his dispatches. He was certain that Philip wanted to remain at peace with Charles, since he needed English mediation with the Dutch and naval support against France. Typically, he assured Olivares that Charles was 'more agrieved against the Hollanders than any others' (PRO, SP 94/37, fol. 20, 28 March 1634). However, he was sceptical that Castile's finances were capable of supporting a new military offensive in Catalonia: 'at the end of the year they will have neither money in their purses nor an army paid' (BL, Egerton MS 1820, fol. 340, 6 April 1634). Olivares valued Hopton's role as an informant to Charles's council, but relied on his agent in London, Necolalde, to initiate new proposals there—such as new levies of Irish troops, naval protection of shipments of silver to Flanders, or an anti-Dutch policy in herring fishing—while Hopton's opinion would not be sought until later. Accordingly, Hopton complained to Cottington that Philip's court presumed that: 'we are so much in love with their trade as it is a recompense for anything we can doe for them' (Bodl. Oxf., MSS Clarendon, vol. 17, fol. 64, 11 Aug 1635). Early in 1636 Hopton was recalled to England for a year and a half; after receiving a knighthood on 2 February 1638, he returned to Madrid as resident ambassador.

At the close of 1641, possibly to secure his pay that was usually in arrears, Hopton wrote a summary of his many duties since his arrival, preserved among the state papers. Typical for 1638 were his attempts to negotiate on the Palatinate, and on a joint policy for herring disputes, and to replace the current Spanish agent in London. In 1639 he argued for the release of English ships held in Spanish ports and defended English policy on Virginia tobacco. In 1640 he sought arbitration for English claims against Spain's overseas commerce and, in the following year, the release of ships seized, 'upon the revolting of the Portugese from … Spayne', for Charles had recognized Portugal's independence at once, to the dismay of Olivares. The crisis in Catalonia led to some of Hopton's more pessimistic observations. For example, he warned London that Olivares was stubborn rather than prudent: 'so wilful as he will break rather than bend' (PRO, SP 94/42, fol. 144, 3 April 1641). Five months later he found him 'so overlaid with care that his judgement begins to break' (PRO, SP 94/42, fol. 211, 9 Sept 1641). He reported each stage in the total eclipse of the famous count-duke and the emergence of the new clique led by Luis de Haro in 1644.

Finally, in summer 1645, Charles's official letter of recall, dated 30 December 1644, reached him. Later the council of state, led by the sixth count of Monterrey, advised King Philip that his departure gift to Hopton should be 5000 escudos (about £1250) in coin, as the ambassador was in deep financial straits from his long, rarely paid tour of duty. Hopton was the last royal ambassador until Sir Henry Bennet in 1660. He returned to England by 1648 and made his will on 10 March 1649 while living at Wisset, Suffolk. He asked to be buried in the parish church nearest to where he died. As he never married his principal heirs were a nephew, Sir Nicholas Throckmorton, who received his properties in Gloucestershire, and a sister, Margaret, Lady Bannister, who inherited properties in Herefordshire. After his death near Bampton, Oxfordshire on 6 March 1650 Hopton was buried in the nearby parish church of Black Bourton.

A. J. LOOMIE

Sources PRO, SP 94, vols. 34, 36–7, 40–42 · letter-book of Arthur Hopton as agent, 1631–6, BL, Egerton MS 1820 · Bodl. Oxf., MSS Clarendon 14–18 · Archivo General de Simancas, Estado MS, Sección de Estado, Legajo 2523 [unbound vol.] · J. H. Elliott, *The count-duke of Olivares* (1986) · A. J. Loomie, 'The Spanish faction at the court of Charles I, 1630–38', *BIHR*, 59 (1986), 37–49 · G. M. Bell, *A handlist of British diplomatic representatives, 1509–1688*, Royal Historical Society Guides and Handbooks, 16 (1990) · *DNB* · *Reg. Oxf.*, 2.281 · will, PRO, PROB 11/211, sig. 40

Archives BL, register of corresp., Egerton MS 1820 | Bodl. Oxf., Clarendon MSS, copies of many of the dispatches from Spain, vols. 14–18 · PRO, original dispatches from Spain, SP 94, vols. 34, 36–7, 40–42

Wealth at death modest income: will, PRO, PROB 11/211, sig. 40

Hopton, John (*d.* in or before **1526**), naval administrator, is of obscure origins. His father's name was William, his mother's Margaret, and his brother's Edward, but nothing else is known about them. He was in the king's service by April 1501, when he was described as 'one of the yeomen of the Chamber' in a grant of the office of porter of Warwick Castle. By 1511 he was being described as 'gentleman usher of the Chamber', a change of status which reflected the king's favour, but probably also indicated an origin in a merchant or minor gentry family. By 1514 he owned several ships of his own, and was receiving licences to trade in wool. How he achieved his seafaring experience is unclear, but by October 1511 he was deemed sufficiently expert to be named as 'chief captain of the ships which the king intends to send against pirates'. He may well have been involved with the king's ships before 1509, because in September 1512, along with John Dawtrey, Robert Brygandyne, and Sir Thomas Lovell, he presented accounts for naval expenditure going back to 1506. At about the same time he was appointed as clerk controller of the ships, with a fee of £33 6s. 8d. a year.

Over the next three years Hopton is described in different documents as captain of the *Mary John*, the *Mary Rose*, the *Lyon*, the *Dragon*, the *Alys*, and the *Great Galley*. This may indicate that he took over these ships when they were about to be laid up or decommissioned rather than that he commanded them in action. However, he was no mere administrator. In May 1513 he was appointed to command all the ships which were assembled to escort the army to Calais, although he was not described as admiral, probably because of his inadequate status. He was also paid for the wages and victuals of a crew in November 1512, which suggests an active command. In 1514 he was responsible for 'wafting', or convoying, the wool fleet to Calais, a fleet which contained at least one of his own ships. In January of that year a John Hopton was described as leading twenty-four of his own men in the 'earl of Arundel's company', but it is not certain that this reference is to the same man. In the same month the clerk controller was granted the further office of keeper of the new storehouses which had just been built at Erith and Deptford. It was in that capacity that he received and stored the rigging taken out of the king's great ships when they were laid up in July. In 1520 he was responsible for rigging the ships which accompanied Henry to the Field of Cloth of Gold, and in 1521 and 1523 he was at sea with the king's ships.

Hopton continued to keep a foot in the commercial world of London. In 1515 he was licensed to gather alms to redeem thirty persons 'imprisoned in Barbary', and there continue to be references to his ownership of ships. He was clearly a man of considerable wealth, seemingly acquired through trade. In his will of 22 June 1522 he referred to lands, tenements, and copyholds in Deptford, Stepney, Hackney, and Stratford. In 1524 he retired, possibly because of age or ill health; his clerkship was granted to Thomas Spert, and the keepership to William Gonson. By July 1526 he was dead, because his widow, Anne, was then given a pardon and release from all debts. His will, which was proved on 24 November 1526, shows him to have been a man of active but conventional piety. Apart from 100 marks as a marriage portion for his daughter, all his specific bequests were for religious purposes, in the form of masses for his own soul, those of his parents, and two other women who may have been deceased sisters. Hopton's importance is that of an active, and very early, admiralty official, who, because he seems to have belonged both to the city and the court, demonstrated through his career the links which the king used and fostered for his own service.   DAVID LOADES

Sources M. Oppenheim, *A history of the administration of the Royal Navy* (1896) · D. M. Loades, *The Tudor navy* (1992) · *LP Henry VIII*, vols. 1–4 · PRO, PROB 11/12, fols. 91v–92r · A. Spont, ed., *Letters and papers relating to the war with France, 1512–1513*, Navy RS, 10 (1897)
Wealth at death see will, PRO, PROB 11/12, fols. 91v–92r

Hopton, John (d. 1558), Dominican friar and bishop of Norwich, was probably born at Mirfield, Yorkshire, the son of William Hopton. He was a member of the Oxford Dominican convent in 1516 and of the London convent in 1520. He was ordained subdeacon in the diocese of Salisbury on 17 May 1516, and priest in that of London on 22 September 1520. He became a bachelor of theology at the University of Bologna on 5 July 1525, and a doctor in theology at the same university. Incorporated at Oxford on 27 November 1529, he obtained a doctorate in theology from that university on 8 July 1533. That same year he was university preacher on Ascension day, when he was allowed to preach an English sermon at St Frideswide's instead of a Latin one at St Mary's. He was prior of the Oxford convent in 1528, an office he still held in 1536. A dispensation to hold a benefice, granted to him on 26 June 1538, refers to him as 'Prior Provincial in England' (Chambers, 139). The abbot and convent of Westminster presented him on 24 January 1539 to the rectory of St Anne and St Agnes, Aldersgate, in London which he had vacated by September 1548. On 22 November 1540 he received a dispensation to hold an additional benefice on the ground that his rectory was worth less than £8. He held the rectory of Great Yeldham, Essex, *in commendam* from 10 February 1541 until his death, and on 27 May 1548 Princess Mary presented

him to the rectory of Great Fobbing in the same county, which he had vacated by May 1549. He also became rector of Aston Clinton, Buckinghamshire, of which Mary was granted the advowson in 1548, and vacated it on his promotion as bishop.

In Edward VI's reign, Hopton was private chaplain to Mary Tudor. In June 1549, the privy council, hearing that Mary was still having mass celebrated in her house, asked her to send Hopton to them, which she did despite her concern that the journey would threaten the life of her 'poor sick priest' (*Acts and Monuments*, 6.10). He was given detailed instructions to satisfy Mary concerning the authority of the recent Act of Uniformity, and to declare his conscience 'for the allowing of the manner of the Communion' (ibid.) as he had professed it before the council. Mary still refused to comply, and Hopton was presumably one of those chaplains who continued to celebrate mass in her household during the rest of Edward's reign in defiance of the king and the privy council.

Just over fifteen months after Mary's accession, on 28 October 1554, Hopton was consecrated bishop of Norwich, vacated by the translation of Thomas Thirlby to the richer see of Ely. Hopton took a close personal interest in proceedings against heretics. John Foxe claimed that he was a pitiless tormentor, 'in such sort, that many of them he perverted, and brought quite from the truth, and some from their wits also' (*Acts and Monuments*, 7.372), an unintended tribute to Hopton's success in recovering protestants for the Catholic faith. Foxe's own accounts of interrogations show that this was their main aim. Although Hopton tended to bluster and lose his temper when faced with obdurate nonconformists, he could also be patient, courteous, and even kind. He tried to demonstrate to some heretics the scriptural basis of transubstantiation. His most notable coup was perhaps the subscription in June 1555 by the noted evangelical preacher Thomas Rose of a statement concerning Christ's presence in the sacrament of the altar. He was not, however, always successful. Thirty-five individuals were burnt at the stake as a result of prosecutions for which he was legally responsible, though many of these victims had been arrested by enthusiastic lay supporters of persecution, especially in Suffolk. An exceptionally large number of clergy were punished for simony during Hopton's episcopate. The continued resort of formerly married clergy to their wives also presented him with a serious disciplinary problem. On 11 February 1557 the queen granted him for life the advowsons of the six prebends of Norwich Cathedral, to one of which he collated John Barret, a learned former evangelical.

Hopton's will, dated 24 August 1558, was proved on 24 January 1559. He directed that certain books of the queen's, including a Greek New Testament and Bible, should be returned to her. He willed the rest of his books to be equally divided between the black friars of Norwich when they were restored and Norwich Cathedral for a library there. He left £5 apiece to buy ornaments to Norwich Cathedral and to Mirfield church, where his father and grandfather had been buried; a richly decorated cope to

Leeds church; and to Christopher Hopton, esquire, a chalice and a cup as heirlooms, the chalice to be used in the chapel of Armley Hall. Hopton died between 1 and 8 December 1558, so deeply in debt, according to Archbishop Parker, that 'he was not able, for all his spare hospitality, to pay half what he owed' (Bruce and Perowne, 58). He was buried in Norwich Cathedral.

RALPH HOULBROOKE

Sources Emden, *Oxf.*, 4.298 · *The acts and monuments of John Foxe*, ed. J. Pratt, [new edn], 8 vols. (1877) [with introduction by J. Stoughton] · D. S. Chambers, ed., *Faculty office registers, 1534–1549* (1966) · will, PRO, PROB 11/42b, sig. 62 · act book, Norfolk RO, MS DN/ACT 7/8 · R. Houlbrooke, *Church courts and the people during the English Reformation, 1520–1570* (1979) · *Reg. Oxf.*, vol. 1 · *CPR, 1548–9; 1557–8* · Wood, *Ath. Oxon.*, new edn, 2.784–5 · *Correspondence of Matthew Parker*, ed. J. Bruce and T. T. Perowne, Parker Society, 42 (1853) · register, Norfolk RO, DN/REG/12/18, fol. 210v · F. Blomefield and C. Parkin, *An essay towards a topographical history of the county of Norfolk*, [2nd edn], 11 vols. (1805–10) · *Fasti Angl., 1541–1857*, [Ely], 37
Archives Norfolk RO, act book · Norfolk RO, register
Wealth at death see will, PRO, PROB 11/42b, sig. 62; *Correspondence*, ed. Bruce and Perowne

Hopton, Sir Owen (*c*.1519–1595), administrator, was one of five or six sons of Sir Arthur Hopton (1488–1555), courtier and administrator, of Cockfield Hall, Yoxford, Suffolk, and his second wife, Anne (*d*. in or after 1556), daughter of Sir Davy Owen of Cowdray, Sussex. The Hopton family owed its wealth to descent from an illegitimate son of Sir Robert Swillington of Yorkshire and Suffolk. Sir Arthur Hopton benefited from royal service and received grants of former monastic land. Owen Hopton's early years are obscure and nothing is known of his education, his admission to Gray's Inn in 1580 being clearly honorary. He married Anne (*d*. 1599), daughter and coheir of Sir Edward Echingham, in August 1542. They had three sons, including Arthur (*d*. 1607), and two daughters. He succeeded to his father's estates in 1555 and was knighted at Smallbridge on 13 August 1561 when Elizabeth I was on progress through Suffolk. He was part of the group of gentry from east Suffolk led by the Wentworth and Wingfield families who attempted to reinforce one another's interests, especially in garnering royal favour and patronage. Hopton was an active MP who was returned as knight of the shire for Suffolk in 1559 and 1571, and for Middlesex in 1572 and 1584. The journals of the House of Commons record him as sitting on thirteen committees discussing bills on such varied subjects as the repression of seminarists, shipping, the merchant adventurers, clerks of the market, and the court of common pleas. He was one of the commissioners who met to discuss the fate of Mary, queen of Scots, in 1572. He served as JP for Suffolk from 1554 and was of the quorum from 1562. He was appointed sheriff of Norfolk and Suffolk in 1564–5 and was a commissioner for musters for Suffolk by 1569. Hopton was named JP for Middlesex and attended the county quarter sessions from 1569. During this time of crisis men like Hopton—loyal, capable, and dependable—were more necessary than ever. In 1570, having recommended himself by the custody and care he took of Lady Katherine Grey at Cockfield, Suffolk, during the last fourteen weeks of her life in 1567–8, Hopton was

appointed by Elizabeth lieutenant of the Tower of London. His election as MP for Middlesex owed more to his new office than to anything else, and that appointment reflected the necessity of having a reliable and loyal man to watch over Thomas Howard, fourth duke of Norfolk, when the latter was a prisoner in the Tower.

The office of lieutenant of the Tower was an important one and involved Hopton in regular consultation with the privy council and others in authority. Perhaps the most grim duty he acquired was the supervision of examinations under torture, but he was also responsible for the armour and weapons housed in the Tower (though answerable to the master of the ordnance), the maintenance of order within the adjoining liberties, and conducting guided tours for foreigners. He appears to have acquitted his office with care yet found it a financial burden as it often proved extremely difficult to recover from prisoners the cost of their diets. He borrowed money and repeatedly petitioned the privy council for the release of some of his captives and for their help in recovering the money they owed him for their keep. Financial embarrassment forced Hopton to resign his office in the summer of 1590 and in March 1591 the privy council took measures to restrain his creditors from seeking 'extremities' against him (Mousley, 337).

Hopton's religious views are difficult to assess. As a loyal servant of the queen, officially he was a stout protestant and one whom John Aylmer, bishop of London, commended for his zeal. In 1589 he was a member of the high commission that forbade the entertaining of unlicensed preachers and the holding of conventicles, although previously he had permitted Andrew Melville to preach and form a congregation in the Tower church, which was an exempt jurisdiction. By the late 1580s rumours were circulating that Hopton's subordinates were 'tainted with popery' (Mousley, 336). At the same time he appears to have befriended Philip Howard, thirteenth earl of Arundel, who was a prisoner in the Tower. The earl arranged for Hopton to represent the borough of Arundel in the parliament of 1589 and it was through the assistance of Hopton's daughter Cicely that Arundel was able to attend secret celebrations of mass within the Tower. Hopton spent his final years managing his estates more efficiently and attending to local administration in Middlesex. His death was sudden as he died intestate in September 1595 and was buried in the parish church of St Dunstan, Stepney, on 26 September. His widow, Anne, was living at Wroxton, Oxfordshire, when she died in 1599.

JOHN CRAIG

Sources J. E. Mousley, 'Hopton, Owen', HoP, *Commons, 1558–1603*, 2.336–7 · D. MacCulloch, 'Catholic and puritan in Elizabethan Suffolk: a county community polarises', *Archiv für Reformationsgeschichte*, 72 (1981), 232–89 · D. MacCulloch, *Suffolk and the Tudors: politics and religion in an English county, 1500–1600* (1986) · J. J. Muskett, *Suffolk manorial families, being the county visitations and other pedigrees*, 3 vols. (1900–10) · J. Gage, *The history and antiquities of Suffolk: Thingoe hundred* (1838) · W. A. Copinger, *The manors of Suffolk*, 7 vols. (1905–11) · W. L. Rutton, 'Notes to pedigree of Hopton of Suffolk and Somerset', *Miscellanea Genealogica et Heraldica*, 3rd ser., 3 (1900), 81–3 ·

Venn, *Alum. Cant.* • W. L. Rutton, 'Lady Katherine Grey', *N&Q*, 8th ser., 8 (1895), 2–3, 82–3 • LMA, P93/DUN/274

Hopton, Ralph, Baron Hopton (*bap.* 1596, *d.* 1652), royalist army officer, was the eldest son of a wealthy landowner, Robert Hopton of Witham, Somerset, and his wife, Jane, daughter of Rowland Kemeys of Monmouthshire, and widow of Sir Henry Jones. He was baptized at Evercreech parish church on 13 March 1596. David Lloyd records that he was a child prodigy, able to read by the age of three, and educated at a Somerset grammar school and at Lincoln College, Oxford. His residence at Lincoln is attested by other sources, though there is no formal record of his studies there to compare with his unequivocal admission to the Middle Temple on 14 February 1614.

Protestant soldier and MP In 1620 Hopton volunteered for the service of the protestant queen of Bohemia, whom Lloyd attests to have escaped from Prague in November riding postilion behind Hopton, then an ensign. In 1621 he entered parliament as a client of the earl of Pembroke, sitting for Shaftesbury, and on 18 March 1623 he married Elizabeth (1591–1646), daughter of Sir Arthur Capel of Hadham, Hertfordshire, and widow of Sir Justinian Lewin; the union was childless. Established with his own estate, at Evercreech Park, Somerset, he served in 1624 as lieutenant-colonel of Sir Charles Rich's foot regiment in Count Mansfield's expeditionary force. He was returned to the parliaments of 1625 and 1628, sitting first for Bath (probably still as a Pembroke client) and then for his local town of Wells. Though active on committees, he made no impression as a speaker. Having been created a knight of the Bath on 2 February 1626 in the coronation honours list

of Charles I, he served through the 1630s as a JP and deputy lieutenant for Somerset, although his attendance at quarter sessions, at least, was sporadic.

In 1640 Hopton was returned to the Short Parliament for Somerset and to the Long Parliament for Wells, and in the latter he finally became a prominent MP. He struck at royal ministers, denouncing the Finches on 23 November 1640 and the earl of Strafford on 15 April 1641, and proposed further measures against Roman Catholics on 1 December 1640. On the other hand he defended the king's right to levy ship money and during February and March 1641 he proposed that 'abuses' be reformed in the church but that bishops retain both their religious offices and their seats in the House of Lords. This behaviour was typical of those who subsequently became royalists, as was his opposition to the grand remonstrance in November 1641. In December he opposed the royal move to place the Tower of London under the command of the extreme royalist Sir Thomas Lunsford, but on 5 January 1642 he defended the king's attempted arrest of the five members. On 4 March he opposed a declaration of both houses against the king's actions with such vehemence that the Commons committed him to the Tower for two weeks.

The outbreak of war and the western campaigns to Roundway down With that episode Hopton vanishes from the house's affairs, to reappear at York in July, as one of the king's active supporters at the outbreak of the first civil war. On 12 July he was one of a party, led by the marquess of Hertford, who left the king in order to raise a royalist army in the west country. They settled at Wells, where Hopton used his own money to recruit a horse troop. On 6

Ralph Hopton, Baron Hopton (*bap.* 1596, *d.* 1652), by unknown artist, 1637 [with his wife, Elizabeth]

August they were dislodged by superior local parliamentarian forces, and retired to Sherborne Castle. There they came under renewed attack, their enemies having been reinforced from London, and retired again to Minehead in September. From Minehead, on the 24th, Hertford shipped the infantry to safety in royalist Wales, while Hopton led the 160 horse and dragoons to the still uncommitted territory of west Cornwall.

Once at Truro, Hopton rallied the local royalists and won over public opinion by a scrupulous show of attention to legal niceties. The Cornish parliamentarians fled, and by 6 October the whole county had been secured for the king. A regular royalist army was now recruited, which by November numbered about 5000 foot and 500 horse. In that month the king commissioned Hopton to lead the horse troops, as lieutenant-general, and to command the whole force jointly with three others. This division of authority caused no trouble, because of the remarkable amity between the men involved, who reached decisions by consensus in a council of war which included all senior officers. Between November 1642 and May 1643 a military stalemate ensued, in which the royalists defeated every invasion of Cornwall but were repelled every time they marched into Devon; they were defeated at Exeter on 23 November, Modbury on 6 December, Chagford on 9 February, Plympton on 21 February, and Sourton down on 25 April, but won notable victories at Braddock Down on 18 January and Beacon Hill on 23 April. These campaigns perfected the habit of co-operation between the royalist commanders, and a related tactic of converging upon the enemy in separate columns. They proved their worth at Stratton, Cornwall, upon 16 May, when the converging-column trick overwhelmed the southwestern parliamentarian field army under the earl of Stamford.

This now laid open Devon and Somerset to a royalist advance, and the king ordered one. On 4 June, at Chard, the Cornish army united with a detachment of the royal one, the combined force coming under the renewed command of Hertford but operating through an enlarged council of war. Its immediate opponent was Sir William Waller, an old friend of Hopton who had served with him under Mansfield and now led parliament's western army; the letter which he wrote to Hopton on 16 June, upon the manner in which the conflict had separated friendships, lamenting 'this war without an enemy', remains one of the most frequently quoted documents of the war (S. R. Gardiner, *History of the Great Civil War*, 4 vols., 1901, 1.167–8). The royalists forced Waller back upon Bath, which he protected by occupying Lansdown, the steep hill above. On 5 July the Cornish foot, apparently acting without orders, stormed the hill. The royalist losses were so severe that, although victorious, they retreated eastward to Devizes, where a reinforced Waller besieged them. Hopton himself had been wounded in an arm at Lansdown, and then severely burned by the explosion of a powder cart on the following day. He was carried to Devizes, where he and his comrades were only saved by the arrival of a relief force

from the king, which combined with them to destroy Waller's army at Roundway down on 13 July 1643.

Field marshal-general This victory gave the royalists control of most of the west country, and Hopton was rewarded with the charge of its largest city, by being made lieutenant-governor of Bristol under the nominal governorship of Prince Rupert. His commission was signed on 29 July, and he devoted two months to his duties and to recovery from his injuries. On 4 September he was raised to the peerage as Baron Hopton of Stratton, and on 29 September he was commissioned as general for the counties of Dorset, Wiltshire, and Hampshire and ordered to clear these counties of the enemy before advancing on London. Although (at least by his own account) he had been the leading spirit in the Cornish army, this was the first time he had been wholly in command of a field force. Two further commissions to him on 10 and 27 October made him 'field-marshal-general' in those three counties plus Devon, Somerset, Sussex, Surrey, and Kent. Hopton's initial plan was to reduce the hostile garrisons left in Wiltshire and Dorset, but the king ordered him to push forward into Hampshire, and by mid-November he had gathered about 3000 foot and dragoons and 2000 horse at Winchester.

Hopton's opponent was Waller again, with a new army of his own based on Farnham. Having failed to tempt Sir William to battle, Hopton and his council decided in early December to garrison Arundel Castle in Sussex as a springboard for a future campaign, and scatter their army into winter quarters between there and Winchester. The mistake was serious, for Waller surprised and destroyed the central billet of royalist regiments at Alton on 13 December, and then turned on Arundel, which surrendered on 6 January 1644. These losses, and the winter weather, left Hopton paralysed at Winchester until March, when he was again reinforced by a detachment of the royal army. He commanded the combined force under the earl of Brentford, and on 29 March they engaged Waller at Cheriton, Hampshire. As at Lansdown, Sir William took the advantage of ground, and an unauthorized attack by royalist soldiers led to heavy losses among the latter. This time, however, Waller held his position and so was able to claim victory as Hopton and Brentford withdrew.

After these failures the king called off operations in the south-east, and Hopton's independent command was extinguished. His army was absorbed into the royal one, where he appears on 10 April 1644 as colonel of a horse and a foot regiment, and on 26 May he was sent back to his post at Bristol. This he fulfilled energetically until rejoining the royal field force as it moved into the west, on 15 July. In early August he led a division of it in the successful moves to encircle the earl of Essex's army at Lostwithiel, and on 14 August he was promoted its general of ordnance. In this position he served until the end of the year's campaign.

Last campaigns and exile In early 1645 Hopton was given fresh honours and a different role, as one of a council appointed to attend the prince of Wales at Bristol and to administer the royalist war effort in the west country; he was intended to be the chief military officer upon it. On 26 January he was commissioned lieutenant-general in the four western counties, on 1 March sworn of the royal privy council, and on 17 March made a member of the admiralty commission. He had begun to escort the prince into the west on 5 March, and he remained there until the end of the war. There is no doubt that he served upon the council with his usual industry and dedication, and that he made an amicable and effective working partner for its other members. His employment, however, mostly remained that of a civilian administrator, as the military operations in the region were left to local commanders. The only point at which he seems directly to have taken charge of the western field army was in early May, for the reduction of Taunton; and this failed when a parliamentarian detachment relieved the town on 11 May.

The king now sent Lord Goring to command in the region, with an ill-defined commission which caused constant friction with the prince's council, worsened in the second half of 1645 as parliament's New Model Army pushed them back first into Devon and then into Cornwall. There, in January 1646, the prince at last appointed Hopton to take overall control of the remaining royalist soldiers, and on 6 February he advanced into Devon once more with about 2000 foot and 2000 horse. At Great Torrington, on 16 January, they were overwhelmed by the New Model Army, which had more than twice their numbers, and Hopton led the remnants in full retreat to Truro. There they were trapped by the New Model, and Hopton supervised the negotiations for their surrender before following the prince into exile on 11 April.

The route of that exile lay first to Scilly and then to Jersey, where on 24 June he quitted the prince's service because the boy had decided to join his Catholic mother in France; Hopton's dislike of the Church of Rome had not greatly diminished since 1640. In March 1647 he moved to join his uncle, Sir Arthur *Hopton, at Rouen; he vanishes from sight until July 1648, when he rejoined the prince of Wales for what was intended to be an intervention in the second civil war. He remained with him during the summer's naval campaign in the North Sea, and then at The Hague, where he was appointed to the new privy council when the prince received news of his father's execution on 4 February 1649. Hopton attended Charles II as a privy councillor in France, Jersey, and back to the Netherlands in late 1649 and early 1650, to part from him finally at Breda in June 1650, as the king signed a treaty with the Scottish covenanters which Hopton believed to compromise the episcopalian Church of England. For two more years he moved about the Dutch and Spanish Netherlands; he died at Bruges, of an 'ague', on 28 September 1652. His body was kept embalmed at Helvoetsluys until 1661, when it was transferred to the parish church near his ancestral home, at Witham.

Assessment Two aspects of Hopton's character emerge most strongly from his career. One was his devotion to conscience and duty, illustrated both in his steady support for king and church and his personal piety; he punished

vice severely in his armies and delayed the battle of Beacon Hill until his soldiers had finished hearing divine service. His image in the National Portrait Gallery is dignified and sober. The other trait is his talent for teamwork; he was consistently an affable and popular member of joint commands and councils, and contributed greatly to making such arrangements successful each time he was part of one. He was also clearly a talented soldier, and his own claim to have guided the moves of the Cornish army in 1642–3 is supported by the manner in which the king especially honoured him afterwards. On the other hand, the number of occasions upon which he was surprised or outmanoeuvred—especially in Devon in 1642–3 and in Hampshire in 1643–4—suggests that he lacked the strategic insight and military imagination of a great general. His treatment by historians has been kind, largely because of their heavy reliance on his own military memoirs and the history written by his dear friend Clarendon. Clarendon's judgement was that Hopton was 'a man of great honour, integrity, and piety, of great courage and industry, and an excellent officer in any army for any command but the supreme, to which he was not equal' (Clarendon, *Hist. rebellion*, 3.312). The verdict seems wholly just.

RONALD HUTTON

Sources Bellum civile: Hopton's narrative of his campaign in the West, 1642–1644, ed. C. E. H. Chadwyck Healey, Somerset RS, 18 (1902) • Bodl. Oxf., MSS Clarendon 23–42 • Clarendon, *Hist. rebellion* • William Salt Library, Stafford, Salt MS 45 • *The Nicholas papers*, ed. G. F. Warner, 1, CS, new ser., 40 (1886) • D. Lloyd, *Memoires of the lives … of those … personages that suffered … for the protestant religion* (1668) • *Mercurius Aulicus* (1643–5) • PRO, SP16/510–511 • *A true relation of the proceedings of the Cornish forces* (1643) • *A true relation of the late victory obtained by Sir Ralph Hopton* (1643) • *The roundhead's remembrancer* (1643) • P. Young, ed., 'The vindication of Richard Atkyns, Esquire', *The civil war*, ed. P. Young and N. Tucker (1967) [The Military Memoirs] • E. Lodge, *Portraits of illustrious personages of Great Britain*, [new edn], 12 vols. in 6 (1835), vol. 7 • GEC, *Peerage* • Bodl. Oxf., MS Ashmole 832, fols. 193–4
Archives BL, letters, Add. MSS 18980–18982
Likenesses double portrait, 1637 (with his wife Elizabeth); Sothebys, 9 July 1997, lot 12 [see illus.] • oils, 1640–49, NPG

Hopton [née Harvey], **Susanna** (1627–1709), devotional writer and religious controversialist, was baptized on 27 October 1627 at St Martin-in-the-Fields, Middlesex, the daughter of Sir Simon Harvey (d. 1628), royal grocer and clerk of Greencloth, and his second wife, Ursula (1586–1671), daughter of Richard Wiseman, goldsmith, of Torrell's Hall, Willingale Doe, Essex, and his wife, Mary. Susanna Harvey was probably the youngest in a family of at least six children. Her father died when she was one year old, and by 1641 her mother had married Harcourt Leighton of Plaish, Cardington, Shropshire, a presbyterian and an officer in the parliamentary army during the civil war. Susanna, with characteristic independence, actively espoused opposing principles. Before the battle of Worcester in 1651 she and Lord Lauderdale collaborated with her future husband, Richard Hopton, in his work as a royalist agent, and at about the same period she was converted to Roman Catholicism by Father Henry Turberville, who dedicated *A Manuel of Controversies* to her in 1654.

On 14 February 1654 Richard Hopton signed an indenture to be made void if Susanna Harvey should 'Question molest or troble' him concerning 'any Engagement promise or Contract of Marriage' (Smith, 169). But whatever story lies behind this document, Susanna had her way and she and Richard Hopton were married on 13 June 1655 at St Peter Paul's Wharf, London. Richard Hopton (*c*.1610–1696) was the fifth son of Sir Richard Hopton of Canon Frome, Herefordshire. He had been called to the bar in 1648 and was to become in 1683 chief justice of the north Wales circuit. The marriage between him and Susanna, who wrote that she loved him 'truly, and passionately' (Hickes, 148), was a long and happy one. The couple had no children.

After their marriage Richard Hopton devoted 'laborious Studies, and indefatigable Pains' to reconverting Susanna to the Church of England. Like Turberville, he recognized that she 'could not forbear to examine, and judge', and encouraged her to undertake a detailed comparison of the doctrine, discipline, and worship of the two churches, and to discuss them 'with the best Divines of the Church of *England*, which our Parts afford' (Hickes, 124, 149). She returned to the Church of England about 1660. About 1661 she wrote a long controversial letter to Turberville expounding her reasons for renouncing Roman Catholicism. This was published by George Hickes in 1710 as 'A letter written by a gentlewoman of quality to a Romish priest', in *A Second Collection of Controversial Letters*. Although Susanna herself felt that her education had been neglected, a lack which she frequently lamented, and she had little knowledge of languages, Hickes thought that through studying English writers she attained a skill in divinity 'not much inferiour to that of the best Divines' (*Devotions in the Ancient Way*, sigs. a4v–5r).

Although 'her *Genius* led her to Controversie, and Dispute', Susanna Hopton was also 'a great reader, and maker of Books of Devotion' (Hickes, ix, xi–xii). In 1673 her first devotional work, *Daily Devotions*, was published anonymously; it consisted of thanksgivings, confessions, and prayers, which were largely extracted from other authors, for use throughout the day. In 1700 Hickes published her *Devotions in the Ancient Way of Offices*, a reformed version of the Roman Catholic John Austin's popular book of daily offices of 1668. Both of these works ran into many editions and during the eighteenth and nineteenth centuries her reputation flourished. After her death Nathaniel Spinckes published in 1717 her *Collection of Meditations and Devotions, in Three Parts*, containing, in addition to *Daily Devotions*, *Meditations on the Creation* and *Meditations and Devotions on the Life of Christ*. *Meditations on the Creation* was a hexameron, the meditations and prayers on each of the six days of creation concluding with a poem; both it and *Meditations and Devotions on the Life of Christ* emphasized the devotional and personal application of scriptural events. She also left a manuscript of her religious poetry. None of her published works was entirely original: they were all to varying degrees compilations from other writers, including material from the unpublished manuscripts of

Thomas Traherne, and often adapted Roman Catholic devotional sources for Anglican use.

In the 1660s and 1670s Susanna Hopton and her husband lived at Gattertop, Hope under Dinmore, Herefordshire. By the early 1680s they had moved to Kington, and there Richard died on 28 November 1696. By this date Susanna was a nonjurist sympathizer and a close friend of the nonjuring bishop George Hickes, who spent some time in hiding at her home. A long polemical letter of this period made a spirited attempt to convert her friend Thomas Geers, serjeant-at-law, to her nonjuring principles (Bodl. Oxf., MS Eng. hist. b.2, fols. 176–80). During her widowhood Susanna led a life of religious discipline, rising at four for matins 'even in her old Age, and the cold Winter Season' (Hopton, *A Collection of Meditations*, sig. A2v), worshipping five times a day, fasting, and giving alms liberally. According to William Brome, who knew her in her later years, 'Her Discourse & Stile upon serious matters was strong eloquent & nervous: upon pleasant subjects witty & facecious: & when it required an edge was as sharp as a Rasor' (Bodl. Oxf., MS Ballard 41, fol. 67), although Hickes also thought her 'very apt to be abused by crafty flattering Folks abt. her' (Smith, 171).

By 16 July 1708, when she made her will, Susanna Hopton had moved to the parish of St Peter's, Hereford. She died there 'of a very sharp Feavour' (Hickes, viii) at about 2 o'clock in the afternoon on 12 July 1709 and was buried on 14 July in the chancel of Bishop's Frome church, Herefordshire, close to her husband. Her bequests included money left in trust for suffering nonjuring clergymen, and a good collection of religious books, filled with her manuscript notes, to be distributed to those whose names she had written on their title-pages.

JULIA J. SMITH

Sources G. Hickes, *A second collection of controversial letters* (1710) · [S. Hopton], *A collection of meditations and devotions, in three parts* (1717) · W. Brome, letter to G. Ballard, 12 Feb 1742, Bodl. Oxf., MS Ballard 41, fol. 67 · G. Ballard, *Memoirs of several ladies of Great Britain* (1752) · J. J. Smith, 'Susanna Hopton: a biographical account', *N&Q*, 236 (1991), 165–72 · W. Birchley [J. Austin] and [S. Hopton], *Devotions in the ancient way of offices: with psalms, hymns and prayers for every day of the week, and every holiday in the year; reformed by a person of quality* (1700) · will and probate inventory, 1709, Herefs. RO, deanery probate records · W. R. Williams, *The history of the great sessions in Wales, 1542–1830* (privately printed, Brecon, 1899) · G. M. Yould, 'The career and writings of Dr George Hickes, nonjuror (1642–1715)', BD diss., U. Oxf., 1968 · parish register, Middlesex, St Martin-in-the-Fields, 1627

Archives Herefs. RO, MSS | Bodl. Oxf., corresp. with T. Geers [copy]

Likenesses portrait (in old age), repro. in M. H. [M. Hopton], *Froma Cannonica, or, The history of Canon Frome and the Hopton family*, facing p. 54 [1902]; stolen from Canon Frome Court, Herefordshire in 1994

Wealth at death £2544 13s. 11d.: probate inventory, filed with will of S. Hopton, Herefs. RO

Hopton, Sir Walter of (*c*.1235–1295/6), justice, was probably born in or before 1235 in Shropshire, perhaps at Hopton Castle, which his family had held since at least the mid-twelfth century as major knightly tenants of the honour of Clun. He was the son of another Walter of Hopton and his wife, Joan. The first office he is known to have held (in 1256) was the purely local one of coroner, and in 1258 he was one of the four Shropshire knights appointed to investigate grievances in the same county under the provisions of Oxford. In 1267–8 he held the rather more responsible local post of sheriff of the twin counties of Shropshire and Staffordshire. By July 1270 he had been knighted.

Hopton's first appointment as a royal justice came at the end of Henry III's reign. In 1272 he was a justice of the general eyre in Herefordshire, Staffordshire, and Shropshire. In 1274 he is to be found serving as a baron of the exchequer. Later the same year he was appointed a justice of king's bench. Hopton left king's bench in 1278 to become one of the justices of a court newly established after the treaty of Aberconwy to deal with litigation from Wales and the Welsh marches. He soon become senior justice of this court. After the completion of the Edwardian conquest of Wales the legal system was recast and Hopton ceased to be involved in Welsh legal affairs.

In 1284 Edward I appointed Hopton to a commission sent to Ireland to audit accounts there. Hopton had previously participated in late 1278 and early 1279 in two eyres of the 'southern' circuit of the general eyre. He rejoined the same circuit in 1285, part-way through the visitation of Essex, and remained on the circuit until eyres were suspended in 1289. Like most of his judicial colleagues he was also appointed in 1285 to a vacation assize circuit, and acted as a gaol delivery justice. In February 1290 he received appointment as one of two commissioners to hear complaints against the king's officials in London, but later the same month was himself convicted, with his colleagues in the 1286 Norfolk eyre, of judicial misconduct for failing to take appropriate action on two presentments made at the eyre. Initially Edward was unsympathetic to the petition in which Hopton claimed that at the material time he had not been serving as a justice, because of a bureaucratic muddle over his appointment, but by December 1290 the king had agreed that the money Hopton had already paid towards his fine should count instead towards a fine he had made to secure the wardship of the lands of his late wife. Hopton received no further judicial or administrative appointments from Edward.

With an unknown first wife Hopton had a son and heir, also named Walter. His second wife was Maud, the daughter of William Pantulf (d. 1233), who by the time of her own second marriage, to Walter (in 1282 or 1283), was sole heir to the Shropshire barony of Wem. There were no children of this second marriage. Hopton was still alive and engaged in litigation in Michaelmas term 1295, but dead by 28 September 1296.   PAUL BRAND, rev.

Sources J. C. Davies, ed., *The Welsh assize roll, 1277–1284* (1940), 86–110 · BL, Additional Roll 14987 · PRO, Assize rolls, JUST/1/743 m. 2 · P. Brand, *The making of the common law* (1992) · D. Crook, *Records of the general eyre*, Public Record Office Handbooks, 20 (1982)

Hopwood, Charles Henry (1829–1904), judge and politician, was born at 47 Chancery Lane, London, on 20 July 1829, the fifth son, in a family of eight sons and four daughters, of John Stephen Spindler Hopwood (1795–

1868), solicitor, of Chancery Lane, and his wife, Mary Ann (1799–1843), daughter of John Toole of Dublin. After education successively at Mr Mullen's private school, Acton, at King's College School, and at King's College, London, he became a student at the Middle Temple on 2 November 1850, and was called to the bar on 6 June 1853. He joined the northern circuit and obtained a good practice. He took silk in 1874, and was elected a bencher of his inn in 1876, becoming reader in 1885, and treasurer in 1895. He gained valuable early experience as a law reporter, editing two series of reports of *Registration Cases*; the first series (1863–7), in which he collaborated with F. A. Philbrick, appeared in 1868, and the second series (1868–72), in which he collaborated with F. J. Coltman, was published in two volumes between 1872 and 1879.

Hopwood came to public prominence in the early 1870s as a supporter of Josephine Butler's campaign to repeal the Contagious Diseases Acts. He also acted as counsel for trade unionists indicted for conspiracy and helped the Trades Union Congress in its efforts to achieve changes in the criminal law which were carried through in 1875. In February 1874 he was elected member of parliament for Stockport as an 'advanced Liberal'. He was defeated in the same constituency at the general election in November 1885. In July 1892 he was elected as a Gladstonian Liberal for the Middleton division of Lancashire and sat until his defeat in July 1895. During Gladstone's short ministry of 1886 Hugh Childers, the home secretary, appointed Hopwood recorder of Liverpool.

Throughout his public life Hopwood supported energetically and with singular tenacity and consistency the principle of personal liberty. He supported radical measures, but at the time of his death he was justly described as 'the last of those liberals who were all for freedom—freedom from being made good or better as well as freedom from worse oppression; freedom from state control; freedom from the tyranny of the multitude, as well as from fussy, meddlesome legislation' (*The Times*, 17 Oct 1904, 4). In parliament, as well as opposing the Contagious Diseases Acts, he attacked the Vaccination Acts, denying that it was justifiable to curtail the personal liberty of people who chose to expose themselves and others to risks of infection. He supported an amnesty for Irish prisoners, and sponsored a bill to end flogging in the army. He favoured a wide extension of the suffrage, and was an early supporter of the enfranchisement of women. After initially opposing in 1880 the atheist Bradlaugh's claim to affirm and take his seat in parliament, Hopwood (who came from an Anglican family) subsequently became one of Bradlaugh's most committed supporters. Towards the end of his life he spoke with indignation of an act forbidding—on the ground of public safety—the carrying of pistols without a licence.

As recorder of Liverpool, Hopwood was identified as the protagonist of a reaction against imposing unduly severe sentences upon criminals, and particularly opposed the imposition of long periods of imprisonment on petty offenders. He stated that during his recordership the average sentence passed decreased from one year one month and six days to two months and twenty-two days (Radzino-wicz and Hood, 746). His stand earned him much notoriety, and his opponents disputed his claim that by substituting sentences of about three months' imprisonment for sentences of about seven years' penal servitude he had greatly diminished crime within his jurisdiction. They maintained that his statistics made no allowance for the fact that the magistrates, disapproving of his reforming zeal, committed to the assizes many defendants who would in normal circumstances have been sent for trial to his sessions, and themselves dealt summarily with very many more. Hopwood, who defended his policy in a lecture to the Democratic Club entitled *Justice, not Leniency* and in an article entitled 'Crime and punishment' in the *National Review* (1893), proposed legislation in favour of short sentences, and in 1897 he founded the Romilly Society to reform the criminal law and prison administration. He sought to establish a court of appeal in criminal cases. He viewed crime as a product of material deprivation and he opposed the use of the law to enforce morality, discouraging prosecutions for such offences as keeping brothels.

Hopwood was a handsome man with a full black beard, and preserved an almost juvenile complexion to the end of his life. He had the power of attracting the warm personal regard of many of his friends, even though they did not always share his opinions. Hopwood died unmarried at his home, Northwick Lodge, 2 St John's Wood Road, London, on 14 October 1904, and his remains, after cremation at Golders Green, were buried in a family grave at Kensal Green. Francis John Stephens Hopwood, first Baron Southborough (1860–1947), civil servant, was his nephew.   M. C. CURTHOYS

Sources A. T. C. Pratt, ed., *People of the period: being a collection of the biographies of upwards of six thousand living celebrities*, 2 vols. (1897) · *Men and women of the time* (1899) · *The Times* (17 Oct 1904) · *The Times* (19 Oct 1904) · *Law Times* (22 Oct 1904), 581 · *DNB* · L. Radzinowicz and R. Hood, *A history of English criminal law and its administration from 1750*, 5: *The emergence of penal policy in Victorian and Edwardian England* (1986) · J. L. Hammond and B. Hammond, *James Stansfeld: a Victorian champion of sexual equality* (1932) · W. L. Arnstein, *The Bradlaugh case: a study in late Victorian opinion and politics* (1965) · *CGPLA Eng. & Wales* (1904)
Likenesses J. Brooks, oils, 1912; in possession of Canon Hopwood, Louth, Lincolnshire, 1912 · attrib. J. B. Kenning, Middle Temple, London
Wealth at death £38,629 1s. 5d.: probate, 15 Nov 1904, *CGPLA Eng. & Wales*

Hopwood [*née* Skene], **D. Caroline** (*d.* in or before 1801), autobiographer and schoolmistress, was the youngest of three children of a Scottish army lieutenant named Skene and his wife, the daughter of Dr Law of Carlisle, 'a woman of good natural abilities … a liberal education and a religious turn of mind' (Hopwood, 5). The sole source of information about Caroline Skene's life is her autobiography, which she began writing in 1781 as a record of her religious experiences, for the benefit of her children. In it she records that her brother died on an army expedition in Egypt and that her father died when she was eight. Her mother was 'extremely fond' of her elder sister, causing Caroline to consider herself 'not so much noticed' (ibid.).

The remarkable feature of this autobiography is its detailed recollection of periods of spiritual trial and doubt and its disabling conviction of sin and culpability; locations and names, however, are sketchy. Caroline Skene was brought up as an Anglican but, convicted 'for sin' at age seven, 'afraid to die' at eight, and unimpressed at twelve by clergymen who 'were not like the Apostle Paul' (ibid., 6), she 'became careless and indifferent about religion, dressed gay, and was fond of plays' (ibid., 7). Her family's financial problems led her to serve as housekeeper in a wealthy family for several years. Her early religious scruples re-emerged in her chalking up sins on a bedroom cupboard door, a list she rubbed off with the conviction that she was growing ever more sinful.

It is not known when Caroline Skene married Mr Hopwood, with whom she had two daughters. She continued her search for a spiritual home after her marriage. 'Not satisfied' with the Presbyterians and 'despis[ing] the Methodists as a low mean people' (Hopwood, 9), she nevertheless joined the latter in 1768. She debated with her religious teachers the issues of perfection and justification, and concluded that Methodism concentrated on 'outward atonement only' (ibid., 12); she felt 'uneasy with the Methodist principles' and their 'studied sermons' (ibid., 15). When her husband's unspecified business failed to prosper she set up a school, where she taught 'needle work of all sorts, drawing, pastry' (ibid., 17). Forsaken by the Methodists, she read John Woolman's Quaker treatise, and was persuaded by her eight-year-old daughter to hear the Quaker preacher Edmund Gurney of Norwich, whose preaching 'tendered [her] heart and opened [her] understanding' (ibid., 20). By 1781 she had endeavoured to join the Society of Friends, despite the attempts of the Methodists to dissuade her and the censure of her pupils' parents that she had changed from 'a polite, well-bred woman to a stupid Quaker' (ibid., 24). She stripped her children and herself 'of every decoration in dress' and took in only plain sewing; 'deeply affected' by the war against France and by slavery, she boycotted 'those articles produced by [slaves'] labour' (ibid., 28). Her reception among the Quakers, however, was never wholehearted and she continued to criticize 'the great insensibility and dead formality' (ibid., 34) of their meetings.

Hopwood died in Leeds in or before 1801, when her autobiography, which she had finished in 1788, was published by her relatives, together with some of her manuscript writings, principally prose meditations on such topics as the immortality of the soul, silence, and the perceptibility of good and evil, and religious poetry.

PATRICIA DEMERS

Sources *An account of the life and religious experiences of D. Caroline Hopwood of Leeds, deceased* (1801) · Blain, Clements & Grundy, *Feminist comp.*

Hopwood, Francis John Stephens, first Baron Southborough (1860–1947), civil servant, was born in Bayswater, London, on 2 December 1860, the eldest son of James Thomas Hopwood (1827–1906), a barrister who practised as an equity draftsman and conveyancer, and his wife, Anne Ellen (*d.* 1873), daughter of John Stone DL of the Prebendal House, Thame, Oxfordshire, and Long Crendon, Buckinghamshire. Charles Henry Hopwood, recorder of Liverpool, was his uncle. He was educated at King Edward VI School, Louth, of which another uncle, Canon Walter William Hopwood, was headmaster, and was admitted a solicitor in 1882. On 6 July 1885 he married Alice (d. 1889), daughter of Captain William James Smith-Neill RA and granddaughter of James George Smith Neill. They had one son and one daughter. In the year of his marriage Hopwood became an assistant law clerk to the Board of Trade; he was appointed assistant solicitor in 1888, and private secretary to the president of the board in 1892.

That year, on 28 September, following the death of his first wife, he married Florence Emily (d. 1940), daughter of Lieutenant-General Samuel Black. They had one son and two daughters. Hopwood's work during these years took him several times to Canada, Newfoundland, and the United States, and it was on his return from Newfoundland in 1891 that he alerted the Royal National Mission to Deep-Sea Fishermen, on the board of which he sat, to the need for medical services in those parts. As a result Wilfred Thomason Grenfell went out to Labrador to found his medical mission. In 1893 Hopwood was appointed secretary to the railway department of the Board of Trade, and as British delegate attended the international railway congresses in London (1895) and Paris (1900). In 1901 he became permanent secretary to the board, which he represented at several colonial conferences, and on a number of transport commissions, including the London traffic commission (1903), the canals and waterways commission (1906), and the commission on ocean freights and shipping 'rings' (1906).

In 1897 Hopwood, having attracted the attention of Joseph Chamberlain, was appointed secretary to the chairman of the Commons select committee on the Jameson raid. His special talents for working in committee and for undertaking individual tasks requiring tact and skill in negotiation were now widely recognized. He was accordingly sent in 1906 to South Africa, as a member of the committee under Sir Joseph West Ridgeway, to consider the constitutions to be given to the Transvaal and the Orange River Colony. On his return he declined the offer of a railway commissionership and became, in 1907, permanent under-secretary of state for the colonies. In this capacity he accompanied the prince of Wales to Canada in 1908. In 1910 he returned to South Africa with the duke of Connaught for the opening of the Union parliament. Between these two excursions he found time, in 1909, to serve on the royal commission on electoral reform and to undertake railway arbitration.

At the end of 1910 Hopwood resigned from the Colonial Office on being pressed, against his inclination, to become vice-chairman of the Development Commission. He therefore welcomed a temporary return to the Colonial Office in 1911 for the period of the Imperial Conference; he preferred to be in the mainstream of events and found the commission something of a backwater. When he left it the following year he might have pursued a lucrative career in the City. Instead, he continued in the public service, was sworn of the privy council, and was made an additional civil lord of the Admiralty, the first lord being his close acquaintance Winston Churchill. In 1911 Hopwood had been one of nine '"distinguished" outsiders' elected to the 'Other Club', which Churchill had founded that year with F. E. Smith (M. Gilbert, 1.11 n.2). At the Admiralty he concerned himself especially with departmental contracts. The outbreak of war in 1914 brought additional duties with the chairmanship of the Board of Trade arbitration court, the grand committee on war trade dealing with contraband and blockade, and, from 1916, the war trade advisory committee.

In February 1917 Hopwood was entrusted with an unusual and secret mission when he visited Scandinavia to investigate rumours of Austrian peace proposals. It proved impossible, however, for him to make direct contact with responsible Austrian diplomats. A few months later he was elected secretary to the Irish convention, set up by the government to explore solutions to the vexed question of Irish home rule. It was a post in which Hopwood's somewhat similar experience in South Africa and his aura of 'detached impartiality' were of value. He did not, however, share the optimistic outlook of his chairman, Sir Horace Plunkett, who wrote sanguine reports to the king while the convention was in progress. The effect of these was counterbalanced by the king's private secretary, Lord Stamfordham, who was kept informed of proceedings by Hopwood, a close friend and trusted adviser. Foreseeing trouble ahead, Hopwood wrote to Stamfordham in October 1917: 'There must be another episode of blood & tears & sorrow & shame before we can settle this difficult business' (Nicolson, 313). That autumn he was created Baron Southborough of Southborough, Kent. In 1919, as the situation in Ireland deteriorated, Southborough drew a parallel with the situation in South Africa twenty years earlier. He hoped that moderation and pragmatism might again prevail, and in a letter to The Times (30 Oct 1919) he offered his services as an intermediary between the Sinn Féin leaders and the British government. As The Times remarked, there 'was no one who could more ably and would more impartially play such a part'; but the proposal, 'frankly and honestly made', was rejected by the Irish (The Times, 30 Oct 1919). The Irish viewpoint was represented in a letter to The Times from Erskine Childers, minister for publicity in Dáil Éireann from 1919 to 1921. While acknowledging the purity of Southborough's motives, Childers doubted that he could possibly act 'merely as a private individual on the British side' (The Times, 1 Nov 1919). Moreover, a settlement would not be found in the 'small unofficial conference' that Southborough proposed, but must instead be sought at a full meeting between the British government and the elected representatives of the Irish people, namely, Sinn Féin.

In 1918, after the completion of his work in Ireland, Southborough undertook the chairmanship of the committee which went to India to report on questions of franchise in the light of the proposed Montagu–Chelmsford reforms. In the years which followed, turning his attention to business, he accepted a number of directorships, notably in 1926, at a difficult time for armament firms, the chairmanship of Sir W. G. Armstrong, Whitworth & Co. He continued for some time to give his services on public matters, acting as chairman of numerous committees of inquiry, such as those into the position of ex-servicemen in the civil service (1923), economic and social development in east Africa (1924), disinterested public-house management (1925), and British trade in China (1926). He was also at different times chairman of the British Empire League, the China Association, and the National Council for Mental Hygiene, a governor and treasurer of Wellington College, a member of the committee of the National Physical Laboratory, and an honorary member of the Institution of Electrical Engineers.

In the House of Lords Southborough took no part in politics but spoke occasionally on matters which aroused his concern. In April 1920 he moved for a committee of inquiry into the complex phenomenon of shell-shock, hoping that a remedy might be found and lessons learned for future conflicts. A consensus had emerged, he explained, that shell-shock cases were 'varying and differing types of hysteria and traumatic neurosis, common and well known in civil life, well understood by medical practitioners, and frequently met with in railway and other violent accidents' (*Hansard 5L*, cols. 1094–1100). Early in the war, though, when the condition was not well understood, it had been mistaken for loss of nerve or cowardice. For Southborough there were clear implications regarding those suffering from shell-shock who were subsequently court-martialled and punished, perhaps with death, for dereliction of duty:'I fear that, through inadvertence and want of knowledge, dreadful things may have happened to unfortunate men who had in fact become irresponsible for their actions' (ibid.). Viscount Peel, the War Office spokesman in the Lords, at once rebutted this notion, while accepting the proposal for a committee of inquiry. Southborough was given the presidency of this and wrote a lengthy two-part article on its findings, published in *The Times* on 2 and 5 September 1922. The inquiry found that the vast majority of cases, 80 per cent of the total, were due to 'emotional disturbance', the effect of fear. It concluded therefore that the term 'shell-shock' was a misnomer, and blamed the high incidence of such cases on the nature of the conscript army raised to fight the war. A *Times* leader, headlined 'Courage and character', observed that the lessons to be learned were primarily about recruitment and training: 'men can be trained, and can train themselves, to despise danger and to seek the ways of courage' (*The Times*, 2 Sept 1922). As Southborough himself observed, the committee showed a unanimity in its conclusions that had been 'wholly unexpected' two years earlier, but he defended it vigorously against the charge that it had been 'cold and unsympathetic' (*The Times*, 5 Sept 1922). For the government, though, the inquiry served a useful purpose, negating in particular any need for a review of court martial cases, and thus defusing a potential controversy that Southborough had himself primed.

In spite of his high profile on this occasion, it was seldom that Hopwood brought himself before the public eye: 'He was a civil servant all the time, and a very correct one, whose personal views and contributions to discussions or action were never trumpeted in public' (*The Times*, 18 Jan 1947). Extremely capable himself, he was quick to appreciate the diversity of talent in others, and this made him an excellent chairman of committees. He had a fine presence and a quiet, dignified, yet friendly manner, behind which lay deep resources of knowledge, wisdom, and strength of character. He was not easy to know well, for his temperament was cool and he never 'gave himself away'. He was appointed CMG (1893), CB (1895), KCB (1901), KCMG (1906), GCMG (1908), GCB (1916), GCVO (1917), and KCSI (1920). He died at 14 Campden Hill Square, London on 17 January 1947 and was succeeded in his title by his elder son, James Spencer Neill (1889–1960).

H. M. PALMER, rev. MARK POTTLE

Sources *The Times* (30 Oct 1919) • *The Times* (1 Nov 1919) • *The Times* (29 April 1920) • *The Times* (2 Sept 1922) • *The Times* (5 Sept 1922) • *The Times* (18 Jan 1947) • *The Times* (25 Jan 1947) • *Hansard 5L*, 39.1094–1100 • H. Nicolson, *King George V: his life and reign* (1952) • *The Churchill war papers*, ed. M. Gilbert, 1: *At the admiralty, September 1939 – May 1940* (1993) • private information (1959) • Burke, *Peerage* (1959) • GEC, *Peerage*

Archives Bodl. Oxf., corresp. and papers | BL, corresp. with Lord Gladstone, Add. MS 46004 • Bodl. Oxf., corresp. with Lewis Harcourt • Bodl. Oxf., corresp. with Lord Selborne • CUL, corresp. with Lord Hardinge • HLRO, corresp. with W. G. S. Adams • HLRO, corresp. with Andrew Bonar Law • NA Scot., letters to Gerald Balfour • Plunkett Foundation, Long Hanborough, Oxfordshire, corresp. with Sir Horace Plunkett • Sci. Mus., corresp. with Oswald John Silberrad • Tyne and Wear Archives Service, Newcastle upon Tyne, letters to Lord Rendel

Likenesses W. Stoneman, photograph, 1918, NPG • F. O. Salisbury, oils, 1959, Tilbury Dredging Co., London • W. Llewellyn, portrait, priv. coll. • O. Salisbury, portrait, priv. coll. • photograph, repro. in *The Times* (14 Feb 1940), 14 • photograph, repro. in *The Times* (15 Feb 1939), 20 • photograph, repro. in *The Times* (8 July 1924), 18

Wealth at death £212,791 0s. 11d.: probate, 15 April 1947, CGPLA Eng. & Wales

Hopwood, James, the elder (1745x54–1819), printmaker, was born in the late 1740s or early 1750s in Beverley, Yorkshire. According to an article in the *Literary Gazette*, he taught himself engraving around the age of forty-five and published a speculative plate by subscription in the hope of raising money to support his struggling family of six children. Although his 'little knowledge of art [was] inadequate to his purpose' (Pye, 335), Hopwood quickly followed this venture with a few further copper engravings and thus raised enough capital to move down to London in 1797. Once there he met with great competition, but he persevered and was soon employed by the well-known engraver James Heath. It is not clear whether Hopwood studied under Heath in any formal way, but his work of the following decades certainly shows the influence of Heath's highly popular sentimental vignettes and book illustrations. Hopwood was employed mainly by publishers, producing book illustrations at the more commercial end of the market, and his first London works appeared in Edward Harding's illustrated edition of Shakespeare (1798–1800). Working from the designs of artists such as Henry Corbould and Charles Heath, he then went on to contribute attractive stipple-engravings as vignettes for various fashionable magazines, such as the *Poetical Magazine* (1804). He was also successful in attracting commissions for decorative frontispieces and portraits for a number of topographical volumes, including David Hughson's *London* (1805–9) and Bernard Lambert's *The History and Survey of London* (1806).

Described as 'an inspired savage' (Pye, 336), Hopwood was a principled and outspoken man who, in 1812, defended the family of Henry Pether, another engraver, against imputations of profligacy in the face of charitable support. He produced an eloquent pamphlet entitled *A Letter to the Donors and Subscribers to the Artists' Benevolent Fund* (1812). Evidently he had never forgotten his own poverty at the start of his career, and in the following year he was elected secretary of the Artists' Benevolent Fund—a subscription society which hoped to combat 'pauperism' among artists and to alleviate their old age by providing pensions. He held this position until 1818, when, on account of ill health, he was forced to retire and become himself a recipient of the fund's charity.

Hopwood died in London on 29 August 1819 and was survived by his sons **James Hopwood the younger** (*b. c.*1795) and **William Hopwood** (1784–1853), both of whom were born in Beverley and followed in their father's footsteps as printmakers. Of these two brothers, by far the most successful was James, perhaps because he had the advantage of studying at the Royal Academy Schools. After 1801 both brothers regularly exhibited works at the Royal Academy exhibitions. While James submitted painted as well as engraved portraits, William sent in only prints that were destined to be book illustrations. Indeed, William Hopwood's career can only be traced in the few plates he produced for volumes such as R. J. Thornton's *Temple of Flora* (1799); while he did occasionally execute etchings in the more linear neo-classical style popularized by artists such as John Flaxman, he was principally a stipple-engraver.

In contrast, James Hopwood the younger was far more prolific. Although he may have been one of the last generation of stipple-engravers, he was also part of the first generation to work with steel plates, which were more durable and thus more commercially viable. He also had a delicate touch, and this was particularly suited to magazines and annuals, such as *Beauty's Costume* (1838), which were aimed at women purchasers. His career took a new turn when, in 1828, he began a series of French portraits which were published in Paris. Shortly afterwards he moved to Paris, where he found much work engraving portraits and vignettes in his characteristic blend of line-etching and stipple-engraving. He was particularly skilled in depicting facial expression as well as volume, and this is evident in the plates he contributed to *Portraits-vignettes pour l'histoire des Girondins* (1847). While James Hopwood the younger was basically a commercially orientated

engraver, he is remembered as the first master of Ferdinand Gaillard, a well-known French engraver of the later nineteenth century.   LUCY PELTZ

Sources B. Adams, *London illustrated, 1604–1851* (1983) · H. Hammelmann, *Book illustrators in eighteenth-century England*, ed. T. S. R. Boase (1975) · S. T. Prideaux, *A history of aquatint engraving* (1909) · J. Pye, *Patronage of British art: an historical sketch* (1845) · Redgrave, *Artists* · Thieme & Becker, *Allgemeines Lexikon* · H. Turnbull, *Artists of Yorkshire: a short dictionary* (1976) · *Bibliothèque Nationale, département des Estampes: inventaire du fonds français après 1800* (1958) · B. Hunnisett, *An illustrated dictionary of British steel engravers*, new edn (1989) · Graves, *Artists* · IGI

Likenesses J. H. Robinson, etching, *c.*1845 (after A. Cooper), repro. in Pye, *Patronage of British art*, 335

Hopwood, James, the younger (*b. c.*1795). *See under* Hopwood, James, the elder (1745×54–1819).

Hopwood, William (1784–1853). *See under* Hopwood, James, the elder (1745×54–1819).

Horbery, Matthew (*bap.* 1706, *d.* 1773), theologian, was born at Haxey, Lincolnshire, the son of Martin Horbery, vicar of Haxey and rector of Althorpe, and Jane Bishop. He was baptized on 9 January 1706 at Althorpe. After attending schools at Epworth and Gainsborough, Lincolnshire, he matriculated at Lincoln College, Oxford, on 26 May 1726. He graduated BA on 26 January 1730, and proceeded MA on 26 June 1733. In July 1733 he was elected to a Lincolnshire fellowship at Magdalen College. He proceeded BD on 22 April 1743 and DD on 4 July 1745.

Horbery took holy orders and gained a great reputation at the university for his preaching. Garrick, who often heard him preach at Lichfield, noted that 'he was one of the best deliverers of a sermon he had ever heard' (Nichols, 9.559). In 1735 he published *Animadversions upon a late pamphlet entitled Christian liberty asserted, and the scripture doctrine of the Trinity*. This was a defence of Daniel Waterland, who had been attacked by the Arian John Jackson. The work secured Horbery some fame as a theologian. Richard Smalbroke, bishop of Lichfield, made him his chaplain and collated him to the prebend of Bubbenhall at Lichfield on 26 July 1736, and in addition, presented him to the vicarage of Eccleshall, Staffordshire, and the perpetual curacy of Gnosall. He resigned the prebend of Bubbenhall for the prebend of Wellington on 25 June 1739, resigned Wellington for Stotfold on 31 August 1745, and Stotfold for Freford on 29 June 1749. He held Freford with the prebend of Hansacre until his death. Upon his resignation at Gnosall in 1740 he was appointed vicar of Hanbury, a position he held until his resignation in 1772. At Magdalen College he served as dean of arts (1743), bursar (1744, 1752), dean of divinity (1749), and vice-president (1750). On 14 September 1756 he married Sarah Taylor, daughter of the vicar of Chebsey, Staffordshire at Eccleshall, Staffordshire. In the same year he was presented by his college to the rectory of Standlake, Oxfordshire.

In 1744 Horbery published *An enquiry into the scripture-doctrine concerning the duration of future punishment … occasion'd by some late writings, and particularly Mr Whiston's discourse of hell-torments*. Written at the solicitation of Richard Smalbroke, the work defended the doctrine of the eternal torment of the damned; and, concerned about the possible number to be damned, Horbery reinterpreted the New Testament texts and concluded that half of humanity would be saved and half damned.

On the death in 1768 of Thomas Jenner, president of Magdalen College, Horbery declined an invitation to stand for the post. He died in Standlake on 22 June 1773 and was buried on 25 June 1773 in the chancel of the church there. A tablet in the chancel spoke of his 'eloquent and pathetic discourses from the pulpit, his learned and ingenious writings in defence of the Catholic faith, and his unaffected piety and benevolence of heart' (Macray, 5.75). For the benefit of his widow, eighteen of his sermons were edited and published by their nephew, Jeffrey Snelson, in 1774, and they were pronounced 'excellent' by Dr Johnson (Nichols, 9.560). Horbery's library was sold for £120 and 200 of his manuscript sermons were sold for 600 guineas. His collected works were published by Clarendon Press, Oxford, in two volumes in 1828.

ROBERT D. CORNWALL

Sources W. D. Macray, *A register of the members of St Mary Magdalen College, Oxford*, 8 vols. (1894–1915), vol. 5 · Foster, *Alum. Oxon.* · S. Shaw, *The history and antiquities of Staffordshire*, 1 (1798) · Nichols, *Lit. anecdotes* · *Fasti Angl.* (Hardy) · Allibone, *Dict.* · P. C. Almond, *Heaven and hell in Enlightenment England* (1994) · IGI · *The works of the Rev. Daniel Waterland*, ed. W. van Mildert, 10 vols. (1823) · DNB

Horden, Hildebrand (1675–1696), actor, was born on 16 January 1675 in London, the son of John Horden (*d.* 1690) and his wife, Elizabeth. His father was rector of Holy Trinity-the-Less and St Michael Queenhithe, and from 1681 was also vicar of All Saints, Isleworth, Middlesex. Horden had become an actor in London's United Theatre Company by 1694, when the leading players, led by Thomas Betterton, left to set up a rival company at Lincoln's Inn Fields. Horden remained with the less experienced troupe at Drury Lane and Dorset Garden and was soon entrusted with secondary roles, generally of likeable young men. Colley Cibber, also a member of the company, remembered that 'this young Man had almost every natural Gift, that could promise an excellent Actor; he had besides, a good deal of Table-wit, and Humour, with a handsom Person, and was every Day rising into publick Favour' (Cibber, 174). In September 1695 Horden created the roles of Fairly in Thomas Scott's *The Mock-Marriage* and Venutius in George Powell's adaptation of *Bonduca* by Beaumont and Fletcher. The following month he acted Vilander and spoke the prologue in Robert Gould's *The Rival Sisters*. In Thomas D'Urfey's *Don Quixote, Part 3* (November 1695) he acted Basilius ('an accomplisht Gentleman, but poor') and was joined by the young Letitia Cross in the prologue, a lively dialogue in which she encourages him to court the ladies as she courts the men, but he claims to prefer the bottle. Horden's success with audiences is shown by the number of prologues and epilogues he was given—seven during the season, more than any other member of the company. His other roles included Stanmore in Thomas Southerne's *Oroonoko* (November 1695), Thraselin in Elkanah Settle's version of *Philaster* by Beaumont and Fletcher (December 1695),

Young Worthy in Colley Cibber's *Love's Last Shift* (January 1696), Welborn in Aphra Behn's *The Younger Brother* (February 1696), Wildman in Mary Manley's *The Lost Lover* (March 1696), and Lysander in Richard Norton's *Pausanius the Betrayer of his Country* (April 1696). The anonymous author of the tragedy *Neglected Virtue, or, The Unhappy Conqueror* gave Horden his play, with the rights to any profits. Horden wrote and spoke the prologue ('The Poet shares the Praises, I the Gold') and played Artaban, whose suicide ends the play. The epilogue, spoken by the comedian Joe Haines, refers to 'Kid Horden' and his appeal to the 'Misses' in the audience. Unfortunately Horden gained little gold, for the play was a failure when it was staged in February 1696. His dedicatory letter to the printed text refers to the sport the 'poor maim'd Thing' gave to 'those wide-mouth'd Curs, the Criticks'.

On the evening of 18 May 1696 a group of actors drinking at the bar of the Rose tavern, Covent Garden, annoyed some gentlemen in an adjacent room by their noise. This led to a 'frivolous, rash, accidental Quarrel' (Cibber, 174) in which Horden was killed by Captain Burgess. Burgess was arrested, but escaped after making his keeper drunk and fled to the continent. Another gentleman, John Pitts, was acquitted, as having been 'no waies accessary thereto, more then being in company when 'twas done' (Luttrell, 126). Burgess was pardoned on his return to England in November 1697. Cibber relates how, after Horden's death, 'it was observable, that two or three Days together, several of the Fair Sex, well dress'd, came in Masks (then frequently worn) and some in their own Coaches, to visit this Theatrical Heroe, in his Shrowd' (Cibber, 174). He was buried at St Clement Danes on 22 May.

OLIVE BALDWIN and THELMA WILSON

Sources W. Van Lennep and others, eds., *The London stage, 1660–1800*, pt 1: 1660–1700 (1965) · C. Cibber, *An apology for the life of Mr. Colley Cibber* (1740) · P. Danchin, ed., *The prologues and epilogues of the Restoration, 1660–1700*, 7 vols. (1981–8), vol. 3 · *London Newsletter* (18–20 May 1696) · *Post Man* (23–6 May 1696) · *Protestant Mercury* (18–20 May 1696) · N. Luttrell, *A brief historical relation of state affairs from September 1678 to April 1714*, 4 (1857) · [C. Gildon], *The lives and characters of the English dramatick poets … first begun by Mr Langbain* [1699] · [G. Jacob], *The poetical register, or, The lives and characters of the English dramatick poets*, [1] (1719) · [J. Mottley], *A compleat list of all the English dramatic poets*, pubd with T. Whincop, *Scanderbeg* (1747) · T. Davies, *Dramatic miscellanies*, 3 (1784) · J. Milhous and R. D. Hume, eds., *A register of English theatrical documents, 1660–1737*, 1 (1991), changed to vol. 1 by CR–vxv · parish register, Holy Trinity-the-Less, 19 Jan 1675 [baptism] · parish registers, St Clement Danes, City Westm. AC, 22 May 1696 [burial] · G. Hennessy, *Novum repertorium ecclesiasticum parochiale Londinense, or, London diocesan clergy succession from the earliest time to the year 1898* (1898)

Horder, Percy Richard Morley (1870–1944), architect, was born at Torquay on 18 November 1870, the eldest son of William Garrett Horder, Congregational minister and hymnologist, and his wife, Mary Annie Morley. He was educated at the City of London School, and was then articled in the office of George Devey. About 1902, Horder's first designs for houses began to appear in the professional press. His work for the following ten years was mainly confined to houses; thereafter educational and commercial buildings appear among his commissions.

From 1919 to 1925 he worked in partnership with Briant Poulter. He was elected FRIBA in 1904, resigned in 1926, and resumed his membership from 1936 until his death. He became a member of the Art Workers' Guild in 1916, but resigned in 1930.

Horder's numerous country houses were mainly built in the home counties, the Cotswolds, and Dorset. They were carefully planned, with due regard to practical needs, and often with considerable originality. The relation of house and garden was always important and Horder's handling of building materials was extremely sensitive. For most of his houses he favoured the 'traditional' treatment then popular, with gables, dormers, prominent chimneys, mullioned windows, leaded lights, inglenooks, brick fireplaces, and panelling; but he seldom used half-timber. Among his best brick houses were a group built at Walton Heath (including one for Lloyd George), and others at Bexhill and at Hartfield in Sussex. At Greystoke, Warwick, and in several other cases, he adopted roughcast for exteriors; for houses at Charminster and Dorchester he used stone dressings with roughcasted walls; and at the Thatched House, near Guildford, he introduced elm weatherboarding and a thatch roof in conjunction with roughcast. His domestic buildings in traditional stonework included: houses at Stinchcombe, Stroud, Dursley, and Pitchford, and the Gyde Orphanage, Painswick, all in the Cotswolds, and houses at Hawes in Yorkshire, at Arnside in Westmorland, and at Minehead in Somerset. Among his successful restorations were Nettlestead Place in Kent and Brimshot Farm on Chobham Common, Surrey. For himself, he restored the Court House, East Meon, Hampshire, where he lived from about 1937 until his death. He also designed attractive groups of housing for officers' families at Morden, Surrey, and near Cambridge.

Horder's first educational building was Cheshunt College at Cambridge (1913), a college for training Congregational ministers, formerly located at Cheshunt in Hertfordshire. It was a charming traditional design carried out in local sand-coloured bricks with stone dressings. Later work at Cambridge included Westcott House, extensions to Jesus College, and the large National Institute of Agricultural Botany (1919), where Horder adopted the classical vernacular of Wren, with steep roofs and bold chimneys. This is one of his best works. At Oxford his new buildings for Somerville College (1934) complied very skilfully with the local tradition in stone; and in his little Institute for Research in Agricultural Economics he ingeniously incorporated Regency houses in a simple design.

About 1917 Horder began building shops for Boots, the chemists, the chief examples being at Bristol, Lincoln, Windsor, Brighton, and Regent Street in London. His friendship with Sir Jesse Boot (later Lord Trent) led to the important commission for Nottingham University College, where in 1925–8 he produced a great group of stone buildings in Italian Renaissance style. Much of the credit for the design of the London School of Hygiene and Tropical Medicine in Bloomsbury (1926–9), however, must be ascribed to his collaborator, Verner Owen Rees. Horder

also built St Christopher's School at Letchworth, showrooms for the Tottenham District Power Company, and a village hall at Turnham Green. Among Congregational churches designed by him are those at Brondesbury Park (1913), of brick in Italian Romanesque style; at Penge (1911), of stone in an original variant of late Gothic; and at Mill Hill (1913; dem.), a very cheap but most attractive little building. In 1925 he added a beautiful 'little church' to his late father's Victorian Gothic chapel on Ealing Green in a quasi-Byzantine style.

Horder possessed the artistic temperament in excess: he cultivated a bohemian appearance, and exasperated his clients and contractors by his erratic, wayward, and unbusinesslike habits; in his office his pupils nicknamed him 'Holy Murder'. However, he managed to retain the goodwill of his patrons, and most of those who employed him professionally continued to entrust him with commissions and to recommend him to their friends. Horder married on 6 April 1897 Rosa Catherine (b. 1872/3), daughter of Ebenezer Apperley, dental surgeon, of Stroud, Gloucestershire; they had two daughters. From about 1909 onwards he intermittently hyphened his name as Morley-Horder. He died at the Stone House, Stone, Dartford, Kent, on 7 October 1944. His wife survived him.   M. S. BRIGGS, rev. CATHERINE GORDON

Sources A. S. Gray, *Edwardian architecture: a biographical dictionary* (1985), 214–16 · *Architect and Building News* (20 Oct 1944), 51 · *The Builder*, 167 (1944), 317 · *The Times* (12 Oct 1944) · private information (1959) · *CGPLA Eng. & Wales* (1945) · m. cert.
Archives RIBA, nomination papers | FILM BFI NFTVA, documentary footage · BFI NFTVA, news footage
Likenesses C. Gardiner, oils, National Institute of Agricultural Botany, Cambridge
Wealth at death £17,237 7s. 5d.: probate, 29 Jan 1945, *CGPLA Eng. & Wales*

Horder, Thomas Jeeves, first Baron Horder (1871–1955), physician, was born on 7 January 1871 in Shaftesbury, Dorset, the fourth and youngest child of Albert Horder, a successful draper and businessman, who had married one of his assistants, Ellen Jeeves. Two years after his birth the family moved to Swindon, where Horder was later educated at the high school and quickly showed himself an exceptional pupil. At the age of fifteen he was thought to have a chest complaint and spent two years working on his uncles' farms on the Wiltshire downs. After his return home, he passed the matriculation examination of London University. He had still no idea what he wanted to do in life, except that he did not wish to enter the drapery business; it was the family doctor who suggested he take up medicine.

Horder took a correspondence course in biology with a tutorial college in Red Lion Square, London, where his papers were corrected by H. G. Wells, who is said to have noted on them that Horder was not cut out for research. Wells was later to be one of his patients. In 1891 Horder obtained an entrance scholarship to St Bartholomew's Hospital, and he was awarded the junior and senior scholarships in anatomy and physiology in 1892 and 1893. He

Thomas Jeeves Horder, first Baron Horder (1871–1955), by Sir William Nicholson, 1937

graduated BSc from London University in 1893 with second-class honours in physiology, and qualified in medicine in 1896; he went on to obtain the degree of MB, BS with first-class honours and gold medals in medicine, midwifery, and forensic medicine in 1898, and MD in 1899. He became a member of the Royal College of Physicians in 1899 and a fellow in 1906.

Horder's resident hospital experience began with his appointment as a house physician to Samuel Gee at St Bartholomew's. Gee was a gifted physician whose teaching was founded on observation and deduction at the bedside and regular attendance at the post-mortem room. He made a great impression on Horder, who published 'Clinical aphorisms from Dr. Gee's wards (1895–6)' in *St. Bartholomew's Hospital Reports* in 1896. Up to this time Horder had been uncertain whether his future lay in biology, physiology, or medicine, and it was from Gee that he learned the fascination of the art of medical diagnosis which was to be the mainspring of his career. Horder subsequently held a number of junior appointments at St Bartholomew's and at the Hospital for Sick Children, Great Ormond Street; he was demonstrator of practical pathology at St Bartholomew's in 1903 and medical registrar and demonstrator of morbid anatomy in 1904–11; he also became a member of the staff of the Royal Northern Hospital, Islington.

In later life Horder said that the three great advances of medicine in his lifetime were the integration of morbid anatomy with clinical medicine, the development of laboratory methods and the birth of clinical pathology, and the arrival of X-rays. The combination of observation at the bedside with special investigations in the laboratory was the foundation of Horder's success. When accused of forsaking the bench for the bedside, he replied: 'No, I took the bench *to* the bedside.' This was true, and people soon began to talk about Horder's box, with its syringes and needles for venous and lumbar puncture, its tubes of broth and agar for preparing cultures at the bedside, its stains, cover-glasses, and folding microscope. In much of his work he was closely associated with the brilliant pathologist and scientist Mervyn Gordon; and while Horder himself never became a research worker, together they greatly advanced the existing knowledge of cerebrospinal fever, acute rheumatism, and infective endocarditis.

Horder began making a name for himself in the early years of the twentieth century, and while still a registrar at St Bartholomew's he was able to afford a Rolls-Royce which he discreetly parked a few streets away from the hospital. His success was not altogether palatable to some of his senior colleagues, who did not like his background or his new outlook on medicine, and at times writhed under his criticism. His chance came when he was called in consultation to see Edward VII and by astute observation was able to make the correct diagnosis. 'They can hardly fail to take me now,' he said to a friend. In 1912 he was appointed assistant physician at St Bartholomew's; he became a senior physician in 1921 and retired under the age limit in 1936. He was made honorary consultant physician to the Ministry of Pensions (1939) and medical adviser to London Transport (1940–55). He was the outstanding clinician of his time and one of the personalities in medicine best known to the British public. His patients included George V, George VI, Elizabeth II, Bonar Law, and Ramsay MacDonald.

Horder was short and compact in build and his chief qualities have been described as sagacity, audacity, and humanity. The impression he gave in consultation or in committee was of organized common sense. He had the faculty of seeing the relevant facts in a clinical situation, arranging them in perspective, and comparing them with the previous data in his well-stored memory so as to arrive at the correct diagnosis. His help was widely sought in committee work and he was chairman of the Ministry of Health advisory committee (1935–9), chairman of the committee on the use of public air-raid shelters (1940), and medical adviser to Lord Woolton at the Ministry of Food (1941). He was chairman of the scientific advisory committee of the British Empire Cancer Campaign for approximately thirty years, and chairman of its grand council from 1950 to 1955. He was chairman of the Empire Rheumatism Council from its beginning in 1936 until 1953. Others of his numerous interests were the Noise Abatement League, the Family Planning Association, the Cremation Society, and the National Book League.

In his teaching Horder emphasized observation, precision, and logic. He used to say that the best book to read in medicine was the *Primer of Logic* by W. S. Jevons. Most of what he wrote was the current coin of medical literature, but his book, *Fifty Years of Medicine* (1953), which was an expanded version of his Harben lectures delivered in 1952, may still be read with pleasure, as may his occasional addresses, *Health and a Day* (1937). Horder was a rationalist who believed in the possibility of solving human problems by science, education, and reform, and he was not afraid to do battle for his beliefs. Characteristically, the title he chose for his Conway memorial lecture in 1938 was 'Obscurantism'. He was an individualist who disliked many of the features of the National Health Service and he organized the Fellowship for Freedom in Medicine, becoming its first chairman in 1948. His main interests outside medicine and public life were literature and gardening.

Horder was knighted in 1918, created a baronet in 1923, and a baron in 1933. He was appointed KCVO in 1925 and GCVO in 1938; among the honorary degrees he received were a DCL from Durham and the MD from Melbourne and Adelaide. In 1902 he married Geraldine Rose (*d.* 1954), only daughter of Arthur Doggett, of Newnham Manor, Baldock, Hertfordshire. They had two daughters and one son, Thomas Mervyn (1910–1997), chairman of the publisher Duckworth from 1948 to 1970. He died suddenly at his house, Ashford Chace, Steep, near Petersfield, on 13 August 1955, having been blessed with abundant health and vitality to the end; he was succeeded in his title by his son.   L. J. WITTS, *rev.*

Sources *The Times* (15 Aug 1955) · *BMJ* (20 Aug 1955), 493–7 · *The Lancet* (20 Aug 1955) · M. Horder, *The little genius* (1966) · private information (1971) · personal knowledge (1971)
Archives Wellcome L., papers | BL, letters relating to Havelock Ellis, Add. MS 70556 · Rice University, Houston, Texas, Woodson Research Center, corresp. with Sir Julian Huxley | FILM BFI NFTVA, documentary footage
Likenesses W. Stoneman, photograph, 1933, NPG · W. Nicholson, oils, 1937, St Bartholomew's Hospital, London [*see illus.*] · D. Gilbert, bust, exh. RA 1941, RA · O. de Wet, bronze head, *c.*1954–1955, Royal College of Physicians of Edinburgh · B. Adams, painting; exh. Royal Society of Portrait Painters, 1942
Wealth at death £83,008 10s. 4d.: administration, 24 Nov 1955, *CGPLA Eng. & Wales*

Hordern, Sir Michael Murray (1911–1995), actor, was born on 4 October 1911 at The Poplars, High Street, Berkhamsted, Hertfordshire, the youngest of the three sons (he had a younger stepsister) of Captain Edward Joseph Calverley Hordern, officer in the Royal Indian Marines, and his wife, Margaret Emily, *née* Murray, whose family had invented Milk of Magnesia. He was educated at Windlesham House preparatory school and Brighton College, where he made his first stage appearances in Gilbert and Sullivan operettas. For much of his childhood he felt very much in the shadow of his immediately elder brother, Peter, who won a rugby blue at Oxford and went on to play for England. By the time Hordern himself was of college age family funds had run low, and he went into prep-school teaching before becoming a commercial traveller for the Educational Supply Association, selling chalk

Sir Michael Murray Hordern (1911–1995), by Alistair Morrison, 1988

and blackboards by day and working at night in amateur theatricals at the St Pancras People's Theatre.

Hordern was twenty-five before he felt secure enough to abandon life as a chalk salesman and start out as an assistant stage manager at the Savoy Theatre; in the late 1930s he also found work with an East End theatre company and at the Little Theatre in Bristol. In 1940 he played PC James Hawkins, and then the Stranger, in *Without the Prince* at the Whitehall Theatre. He made his first, brief, screen appearance in 1940 with Emlyn Williams and Margaret Lockwood in the Carol Reed thriller *The Girl in the News*.

In 1940 Hordern joined the Royal Naval Volunteer Reserve, initially as a gunner. His first ship was a merchant ship carrying 10,000 tons of munitions. He later recalled:

> the second night out the convoy in which we were sailing was attacked by U-boats. We were going with the guns all night and when the sun came up the sea was completely empty. Four of the other ships around us had gone down and the others had scattered. My second night out and almost my last. I was frightened that night. That was when I grew up. (*The Times*, 25 Nov 1989)

He subsequently served on the aircraft-carrier *Illustrious* where, with another actor, Robert Eddison, he was responsible among much else for shipboard entertainments. On 27 April 1943 he married Grace Eveline Mortimer (1914/15–1986), daughter of Dudley Mortimer, schoolmaster. They had met before the war, at the Little Theatre, Bristol. They had one daughter. Hordern ended the war as a lieutenant-commander.

In 1946 Hordern returned to the stage as Torvald Helmer in *A Doll's House* at the Intimate Theatre, Palmer's Green. He continued to carve out an impressive classical stage career as a riotously comic Bottom in Purcell's *Fairy Queen* at Covent Garden (1946). He then played Richard Fenton in the long-running *Dear Murderer* at the Aldwych (1946), and Captain Hoyle in *Noose* at the Saville (1947). He spent two Christmases (1948 and 1949) at Stratford upon Avon as Mr

Toad in *Toad of Toad Hall*, and made a celebrated appearance in the film *Passport to Pimlico* (1949), as the police inspector trying unsuccessfully to restore British authority in the inner-London republic. In 1950 he joined the Alec Clunes Company at the Arts for Chekhov's *Ivanov* (1950) and John Whiting's *Saint's Day* (1951), in which he first made his name. That in turn led him back to Stratford for a 1952 *As You Like It*, in which his Jacques was reviewed by Kenneth Tynan: 'a great performance, rooted in self-disgust, but with a tattered plume of merriment capering always over his head' (*The Times*, 4 May 1995). As so often, Tynan there caught not just a performance, but the essence of an entire career.

Hordern now became established on screen as a fine if sinister character actor, with parts in *Alexander the Great* (1956), *Cleopatra* (1963), and *The Spy who Came in from the Cold* (1965), but on stage his work was always more varied, even quirky; he played in the John Mortimer comedy *The Dock Brief* (1958) as well as the première of Harold Pinter's *The Collection* (1962) and in equally early work by Tom Stoppard (*Enter a Free Man*, 1968), David Mercer (*Flint*, 1970), and Alan Ayckbourn (*Relatively Speaking*, 1967). His first *King Lear* was for Jonathan Miller at the Nottingham Playhouse in 1969, and then in 1972 he achieved true greatness in Tom Stoppard's complex *Jumpers* as George Moore, the philosophy don forever debating with himself and occasionally with a tortoise. He was still playing the role seven years later, but in starry 1980s revivals of *You Never can Tell* (1987) and *The Rivals* (1983) he was to prove equally impressive in period comedy. His last stage appearance was in a revival of *Trelawny of the Wells* in 1992, and on television he was seen a few months before his own death as the dying Featherstone in the BBC's acclaimed *Middlemarch* (1994).

Hordern's marriage was not improved by a long love affair with the actress Coral Edith *Browne (1913–1991), and he shared his later life with the actress Patricia England. His other true passion was fly-fishing, which he once expounded in a lengthy television series; he lived near the river in Bagnor, near Newbury, Berkshire, and was not best pleased to find the Watermill Theatre built on his doorstep. He was appointed CBE in 1972 and knighted in 1983. He died at the Churchill Hospital, Oxford, on 2 May 1995, and was survived by his only child, Joanna, and by the memories of millions of stage and screen audiences around the world who cherished his anarchic brilliance in both comedy and tragedy, specializing as he did in morose clergymen, bizarre diplomats, dotty generals, and tetchy fathers. A memorial service was held at St Paul's, Covent Garden, on 3 October 1995.

Hordern was offstage the least theatrical of leading men, yet established on stage and screen a career of considerable versatility and integrity in a golden age for British classical players. Once described, not entirely flatteringly, as 'the Austin Princess among British actors' (*The Times*, 4 May 1995), implying reliability but a faint lack of charisma, he in fact grew in later years into one of the great eccentrics of his profession, perched perilously somewhere half way between Alistair Sim and Alec Guinness. He played many of the great classical roles (Lear, Macbeth, Chekhov's Ivanov), but was equally loved by younger audiences for his Paddington Bear and Toad of Toad Hall.

SHERIDAN MORLEY

Sources M. Hordern, *A world elsewhere* (1993) · *The Times* (25 Nov 1989) · *The Times* (4 May 1995) · *The Times* (4 Oct 1995) · *The Independent* (4 May 1995) · *The Independent* (9 May 1995) · WWW, 1991–5 · b. cert. · m. cert. · d. cert.
Likenesses photographs, 1952–84, Hult. Arch. · A. Morrison, photograph, 1988, NPG [*see illus.*] · photograph, repro. in *The Times* (4 May 1995) · photograph, repro. in *The Independent* (4 May 1995)
Wealth at death £391,059: probate, 20 Oct 1995, *CGPLA Eng. & Wales*

Hore, Richard (*fl.* 1535–1538), mariner, was a citizen and leather-seller of London. Late in 1535 he attempted to generate interest in a voyage to the 'northwest parts of America'. Several gentlemen of the inns of court and chancery responded to his approach; their motive—being 'desirous to see the strange things of the world' (Hakluyt, 8.3)—has since inclined commentators to regard them as proto-tourists. Hore hired two vessels, the *Trinity* and the *William*. With a complement of 160, including 30 gentlemen, he departed from England at the end of April 1536. Almost two months elapsed before the ships sighted land, near Cape Breton. Moving north-eastwards without making formal observations of the coastline, they anchored for several days off Newfoundland. There they sighted, and disembarked to chase, a party of Indians, but were unable to make contact. From this point their stores failed them, and extreme solutions—as were later reported—became necessary. Several acts of murder and cannibalism apparently took place among the crew. As their number decreased, 'the officers knew not what was become of them', until one man, challenging another for a piece of meat, asked its provenance. 'If thou wouldst needs know', he was told, 'the broyled meate that I had was a piece of such a mans buttocke' (ibid., 8.5, 6). Despite Hore's exhortations to curb such unpleasantness, his mariners had reached the stage of holding a lottery to decide whom among their number should provide the next meal, when a French ship entered their harbour and was seized by the famished Englishmen. With this prize they returned to England, reaching St Ives in October 1536.

The only account of the voyage is that provided by Hakluyt, and its accuracy is highly suspect. Much of what he reported was third-hand, via his cousin, the lawyer Richard Hakluyt, from conversations with one of the gentlemen voyagers. The only original source was a surviving member of the *Trinity*'s crew, whom Hakluyt interviewed almost half a century after the voyage took place. Such evidence as exists contradicts both men's statements. Following his return Hore failed to honour his contract with the *William*'s owner, William Dolphyn, and the ship's cargo was seized. Examined in the court of admiralty, Hore claimed that he had intended a fishing voyage; and he was certainly carrying fish when he returned to England, so acts of cannibalism hardly seem to have been necessary. It may rather be the case that the voyage's unaccustomed hardships may have inclined the 'tourists' to overstate their ordeal somewhat.

In the following year Hore was before the admiralty court once more, having hired another vessel, the *Valentine*, voyaged to Portugal, and undertaken to transport several Portuguese travellers to England. In fact he kidnapped them, brought them to a haven near Cardiff, and demanded money for their release. He seems successfully to have argued himself free from custody. In September 1538 the *Valentine* was arrested upon the action of her owner, to whom Hore owed £280. Predictably her cargo of salt and wine was suspected to have been obtained dishonestly. The over-enterprising Hore thereafter disappears from extant records.   JAMES McDERMOTT

Sources R. Hakluyt, *The principal navigations, voyages, traffiques and discoveries of the English nation*, 8, Hakluyt Society, extra ser., 8 (1904) • PRO, HCA 24/2; 30/542 • E. G. R. Taylor, 'Master Hore's voyage of 1536', *GJ*, 77 (1931), 469–70 • D. B. Quinn, ed., *The Hakluyt handbook*, 2 vols., Hakluyt Society (1974) • S. E. Morrison, *The European discovery of America* (1971)

Hore-Belisha. For this title name *see* Belisha, (Isaac) Leslie Hore-, Baron Hore-Belisha (1893–1957).

Horenbout [Hornebolt], **Gerard** (*d.* 1540/41), painter, is first recorded in 1487 at Ghent in the Low Countries. His father's name, Willem, is recorded in the document of 27 August 1487 by which he became a master painter at Ghent. His family origins are otherwise obscure, but he used an elaborate coat of arms, indicating that he came from a gentle family. He had by 1517 married Margaret Svanders or de Vandere (*d.* 1529), daughter of Derick Svanders and widow of Jan van Heerweghe. He spent the latter part of his career in England at the court of Henry VIII. The children of Gerard and Margaret, Lucas *Horenbout and Susanna [*see below*], also settled in London; the 'sister Margaret' mentioned in 1537 in the will of Susanna's husband may be her sister-in-law rather than a third child.

Gerard Horenbout's documented works at Ghent include the ten cartoons for a tapestry series commissioned for the church of St Pharahildis in 1508–9 and the 'description' of part of Ghent and some surrounding villages paid for by the town authorities in 1510–11. He is known to have employed an apprentice and a journeyman with skills in manuscript illumination, and may have run a large workshop, which to some extent specialized in illumination. However, Gerard himself is normally referred to as a painter, rarely as an illuminator, and it is not certain that he himself actually contributed miniatures to the manuscripts for which he and his workshop were paid. According to Karel van Mander's *Schilder-Boeck* of 1603–4 he painted religious works for Lieven Huguenois, abbot of St Bavo in Ghent. In 1515 he was appointed 'varlet de chambre et painctre' to Margaret of Austria, ruler of the Low Countries, and is regularly mentioned in her accounts between 1516 and 1522. The works he received payment for included a design for a church window and a work of embroidery showing the holy family in a garden, as well as that most often associated with him, completion of the illuminated manuscript known as the 'Sforza Hours' (BL, Add. MS 34294), begun for Bona Sforza in Milan about 1490. In 1522 Margaret of Austria purchased from him a portrait of Christian II of Denmark, who had recently visited the Low Countries. There is no further reference to Gerard Horenbout at Ghent, but Albrecht Dürer recorded meeting him at Antwerp in 1521.

Gerard Horenbout is recorded as a 'paynter' in the service of Henry VIII, in the accounts of the treasurer of the chamber between October 1528 and April 1531, in receipt of monthly payments of 33s. 4d. This record leaves open the possibility that he entered the king's service as early as 1525, since although there are no extant references to Gerard Horenbout in the accounts of the treasurer of the chamber between January 1522 and October 1528, these accounts do not survive as a complete sequence (there is a gap in the extant accounts between September 1525, when his son Lucas is first mentioned, and October 1528). The reasons for Gerard Horenbout's defection from the service of Margaret of Austria to that of Henry VIII remain as obscure as the work for which he was responsible in England. However, his children, Lucas and Susanna, may well have preceded him, and found royal patronage for the variety of work which Gerard Horenbout had been able to offer his former patron Margaret of Austria. Although Gerard Horenbout's name has been associated with patents and manuscripts prepared for Cardinal Wolsey, the connection remains unproven, and accounts of 1528–9 which mention a 'Gerard' or 'Garard' in fact refer to a scribe, William Gerard or Garrard. Gerard Horenbout's name is absent from the sequence of surviving royal accounts that begins in February 1538, and he died in 1540 or 1541, when his heirs paid duty on his estate in Ghent. His country of residence for the decade between 1531 and his death is uncertain, but he may have remained in England with his children. Margaret Horenbout died in 1529, and was commemorated in a brass in All Saints, Fulham.

Susanna Horenbout (*b. c.*1503, *d.* in or before 1554), painter, daughter of Gerard Horenbout and his wife, Margaret Svanders, married John Parker of Fulham, Middlesex, yeoman of the king's robes and keeper of the Palace of Westminster between 1521 and 1529. He died in 1537, and Susanna married on 22 September 1539, as his second wife, John Gilman, a gentleman of Anglesey, a vintner in the city of London and serjeant of the king's woodyard; he later became gentleman harbinger, and died in 1558. They had two children, Henry and Anne. The former later lived at Twickenham, the latter married a gentleman from Coventry.

Susanna Horenbout is first mentioned in the diary of Albrecht Dürer in May 1521, when, he states, she was about eighteen. He met her at Antwerp and bought from her an illumination of the Saviour; he expressed surprise that a woman should be capable of such work. According to Lodovico Guicciardini, in his *Descrittone di tutti i Paesi Bassi* (1567), Henry VIII attracted her to work for him in England, and she may well have been the first member of her family to arrive at the court in London. Unlike her father, Gerard, and brother, Lucas, she is not documented in the accounts of the treasurer of the chamber, but as a 'gentlewoman' received, along with her husband, John

Parker, a gift of a gilt cup from the king in the new year's ceremony of 1532. She is referred to as Parker's wife in the inscription to the brass commemorating her mother's death of 1529 in All Saints, Fulham; she may have designed the brass herself.

In October 1539 Susanna Horenbout, now the wife of John Gilman, was chosen to serve Anne of Cleves, and to accompany her on her journey to England to become Henry VIII's queen, presumably in part for her knowledge of the Dutch language. She became, briefly, one of the queen's gentlewomen of the privy chamber. By November 1543 she was in attendance on Queen Katherine Parr, and in August 1544 the privy purse accounts of Princess Mary record that Susanna received 12 yards of black satin from Mary. She may have been the 'Mrs Silynyn', one of the gentlewomen of the queen's privy chamber who attended the funeral of Henry VIII in 1547. She was dead by 7 July 1554, when her husband remarried.

The paintings mentioned in the will of Gilman's relative Gerard Legh of 1563, a 'lymned pycture of Jesus and hys mother Marye' and a 'pycture of the wyndmylle', might have been inherited from the Horenbouts, and could conceivably have been works by Susanna herself.

SUSAN FOISTER

Sources L. Campbell and S. Foister, 'Gerard, Lucas and Susanna Horenbout', *Burlington Magazine*, 128 (1986), 719–27 · C. van Mander, *Het Schilder-boek* (Haarlem, 1604)

Horenbout [Hornebolt], **Lucas** (*d.* 1544), artist, was the son of the artist Gerard *Horenbout (*d.* 1540/41), painter, who ran a large workshop in the Low Countries, notable for illumination of manuscripts, and his wife, Margaret Svanders or de Vandere (*d.* 1529), widow of Jan van Heerweghe. His sister was the artist Susanna Horenbout (*b. c.*1503, *d.* in or before 1554). He married Margaret Holsewyther (*d.* in or after 1559); they had a daughter, Jacquemine; Margaret married Hugh Haywarde (Hawarde) in 1544.

Lucas Horenbout is first documented as a 'pictor maker' in the service of Henry VIII in 1525 in the accounts of the privy chamber, according to which he received a payment of 55*s*. 6*d*. a month. These accounts do not survive as a complete sequence, but Lucas Horenbout's name recurs in the accounts for 1528, where he is given the same description and monthly payment. In 1531 and 1532 his continuing presence in England is confirmed by the fact that he was granted a licence to export 400 quarters of barley in each of these years, as well as supplying brushes to painters working at Whitehall Palace in 1531. On 22 June 1534 he was granted English denizenship, and on the same day appointed to the office of king's painter, with a grant of a tenement in Charing Cross and a licence to employ four foreign journeymen. At the traditional presentation of new year gifts to the monarch in 1539 Lucas Horenbout gave Henry VIII a fire screen of 'blew worsted' and received in return the gift of a gilt cup with a cover. Regular payments recur in the surviving series of accounts of Henry VIII from 1538 to 1544, when Horenbout died. His will dated 8 December 1543 was proved on 27 May 1544. He expressed the wish to be buried in London at St Martin-in-the-Fields.

There are no surviving documented works by Lucas Horenbout. He has usually been identified with the 'Meister Lucas' who, as van Mander stated in his life of Holbein published in 1604, taught Holbein to illuminate. This statement has usually been interpreted to mean that Lucas Horenbout taught Holbein to paint portrait miniatures, which use a technique very similar to that employed in the illumination of manuscripts. Since a surviving group of portrait miniatures of Henry VIII and his family are very different in style from those of Holbein, it has been assumed that these must be the work of Lucas Horenbout. However, although his father Gerard employed illuminators, he was not indubitably an illuminator himself, and it cannot be regarded as certain that Lucas was trained as an illuminator. The accounts of Henry VIII clearly distinguish Lucas as a 'pictor maker' from a 'lymner of bookes', which makes it clear that Lucas was not employed by Henry as an illuminator. Lucas Horenbout was not the only painter to be named as king's painter (Hans Holbein was known as king's painter during Lucas Horenbout's lifetime, and John Brown was called king's painter until 1527) but he clearly played a valued role as a court painter over a long period. His role might be tentatively distinguished from that of the English painters such as Andrew Wright who succeeded John Brown as serjeant painter in 1532; they were responsible for the range of decorative painting at court and in the royal palaces. It also appears to have differed from the role of Holbein, who produced portrait paintings of the king and of prospective wives of the king, but who received a slightly lower salary than Lucas Horenbout, and one paid quarterly rather than monthly.

Apart from the fire screen given as a new year's gift, there are few references to works which may have been produced by Lucas Horenbout. One such arises in a manuscript text of poems by the humanist and antiquary John Leland. In it Leland writes of devices such as the feathers of the prince of Wales or the phoenix—signifying the dead queen Jane Seymour—and states that these refer to works by 'lucas regius pictor'. A woodcut of the feathers of the prince of Wales reproduced in Leland's *Genethliacon* of 1543 might record a design by Lucas Horenbout of this type. A second reference to his work occurs in a payment to 'Lucas Hornebolt' in the office of revels accounts of 1542–3 for painting with black on paper to produce some 'bulls' and 'small rolls', presumably properties for an unidentified entertainment. A third is found in a payment in the accounts of Katherine Parr in May 1547 'to Lucas wyfe for makynge of the Quenes pykture and the kyngs', probably a settlement of an outstanding account from Lucas Horenbout's lifetime.

The group of portrait miniatures which have been associated with Lucas Horenbout and which may well be his work include images of Henry VIII. One of these (FM Cam.) includes a decorative border which has some of the characteristics of illuminated manuscripts from the Low Countries. Another (V&A) shows an illuminated portrait of Henry VIII within the letters patent of 1524 granting properties to Thomas Foster, comptroller of the king's works. If Lucas's work, this would presumably be a single surviving example of a number of such illuminated documents. Despite the lack of clarity concerning the precise nature of his work, it is clear that Henry VIII valued it highly, as stated in the renewed grant of office of 1544, in which the king paid tribute to his 'science and experience in the pictorial art'. SUSAN FOISTER

Sources L. Campbell and S. Foister, 'Gerard, Lucas and Susanna Horenbout', *Burlington Magazine*, 128 (1986), 719–27 · will, LMA, DL/C/355/Lucas Hornebolt/1544/May

Horenbout, Susanna (*b. c.*1503, *d.* in or before 1554). *See under* Horenbout, Gerard (*d.* 1540/41).

Horlick, Sir James, first baronet (1844–1921), health drink manufacturer, was born at Ruardean, near Cinderford, Gloucestershire, on 30 April 1844, the third of four sons born to James Horlick, saddler, and his wife, Priscilla Griffiths. He was educated in Andover, Hampshire, and, having to look outside the small family concern for a career, in 1862 became an assistant to a homoeopathic chemist in London, qualifying as a pharmacist seven years later. In 1873 he married Margaret Adelaide (*d.* 1925), eldest daughter of William Burford, a builder of Leicester; they had three sons, the youngest of whom died in the First World War.

Horlick and his wife soon emigrated to the United States, where his younger brother William had been an accountant since 1869. While working for the Mellin Company in Chicago, makers of a powdered malt and bran baby food, Horlick devised an improved version; in 1874 he and William patented this as a 'new food' for infants and invalids (especially dyspeptics). Two years later they built a factory in Racine, Wisconsin. William oversaw production and the accounting side, while James took charge of marketing.

Their preparation rapidly became popular throughout North America and was exported to Britain. By 1882, when the brothers enlarged the factory, William was developing a new variety of the product, a malt extract with a milk base. Although it secured a number of strong medical recommendations, James was dubious and William patented the process on his own. In fact, it was such a triumph that in 1885 the Horlicks Food Company was incorporated, with James as president and William as the company secretary.

James returned to England in 1890, to open up the market in Europe and also in the British empire. He soon saw the advantages of producing in England, but William—a naturalized American citizen since the late 1880s—proved hesitant. It was not until 1905 that a Horlicks factory opened, in Slough, Buckinghamshire, technical help being provided from Wisconsin. James had to agree to meet any losses. In the event, success followed, thanks partly to publicity about the use of Horlicks on polar expeditions such as that headed by Roald Amundsen. During the First World War it was supplied in quantity to the armed forces.

Meanwhile Horlick was achieving recognition in British society, most notably in agricultural circles. In 1898 he

Sir James Horlick, first baronet (1844–1921), by Spy (Sir Leslie Ward), pubd 1909

bought an extensive property at Cowley, Gloucestershire, becoming lord of the manor there. He was appointed a justice of the peace for the county in 1900 and high sheriff and a deputy lieutenant in 1902. At Cowley Manor and on his Sussex estate, at Forest Row, he bred shorthorn cattle and Oxford Down sheep. These he exhibited both at the Gloucestershire Agricultural Society, of which he was president, and at the Royal Agricultural Society of England's shows, where he was awarded prizes or commendations every year between 1903 and 1914. He was an active patron of many of the county's rural associations.

These agricultural pursuits were intended partly to provide the company with the milk it required; the product's main ingredient came from maltings Horlick owned in Norfolk. They also gained him a baronetcy for public services in 1914. By then he was an establishment figure, an Anglican, a true Conservative, albeit on the tariff reform wing, who in 1920 had the organ of Gloucester Cathedral restored in memory of his dead son. However, his outside activities clearly hampered the company's development. It now relied wholly on the malted milk product, vulnerable because it was twice as expensive as its main rival Ovaltine, recently brought over from Switzerland where it had been invented. Neither James nor William took steps to diversify into other food products as a form of insurance. After a decade or more of expansion, therefore, the English branch began to lose its momentum after 1918. The septuagenarian Horlick's health was by then rapidly deteriorating, and he died at his London home, 2 Carlton House Terrace, on 7 May 1921. He was succeeded as second baronet by his son, Sir Ernest Burford Horlick.

T. A. B. CORLEY

Sources C. Murphy, 'Horlick, Sir James', *DBB* · V. Ward, 'Marketing convenience foods between the wars', *Adding value: brands and marketing in food and drink*, ed. G. Jones and N. J. Morgan (1994) · Burke, *Peerage* · *WWW* · *Who was who in America*, 1 (1943) · *The Times* (10 May 1921) · 'Horlick', *A supplement to the Oxford English dictionary*, ed. R. W. Burchfield, 4 vols. (1972–86)
Likenesses Spy [L. Ward], engraving, NPG; repro. in *VF* (10 March 1909) [*see illus.*]
Wealth at death £450,481 5*s.* 5*d.*: probate, 17 Sept 1921, *CGPLA Eng. & Wales*

Horman, William (1457–1535), schoolmaster and grammarian, came from the parish of St Thomas, Salisbury, Wiltshire, and was admitted as a scholar of Winchester College in 1468. He was promoted to be a scholar of New College, Oxford, in 1475 and a fellow two years later, graduating BA in 1480 and MA about three years later. In 1484 he was ordained subdeacon at Oxford, and priest probably soon afterwards. Horman resigned his fellowship in February 1486 to become headmaster of Eton College, the college subsequently presenting him to its rectory of East Wretham, Norfolk, in 1494. In March 1495 he moved to the headmastership of Winchester, which he held until 1501, returning to Eton as a fellow of the college in the following year and resigning East Wretham at about the same time. He spent the rest of his life in the college, becoming vice-provost in later years, and died there on 12 April 1535. He was buried in the college chapel beneath a tombstone containing a memorial brass, depicting him as a priest in mass vestments with an inscription in Latin verse. During his life he collected manuscripts and printed texts, twenty-seven of which have been recorded, and also owned equipment for binding books. He gave eighteen items from his library to Eton, probably in 1533–4, chiefly works of theology but also of medicine. By his will, which was made on 9 November 1534, he further bequeathed the college a liturgical manual, a chalice and paten, a silver cup, and the apparel for an altar.

Horman had wide scholarly interests, and the Tudor bibliographer John Bale credits him with twenty-nine works on subjects including Latin literature, history, medicine, and theology, as well as a Latin elegy on the death of his friend William Lily (d. 1522), the grammarian and high-master of St Paul's School, London. He published only four titles, however, the earliest, a *Dialogus lingue et ventris*, appearing about 1494. The other three lay in the field of grammar where, like his contemporaries John Anwykyll, John Holt, and John Stanbridge, he sought to bring humanist standards to the teaching of Latin in England through the composition of school textbooks. The first of these, an *Introductorium lingue Latine*, was published

in 1494 and reissued in 1499, and the second, a large collection of *Vulgaria* (English sentences with model Latin translations), appeared in 1519. The contract for the *Vulgaria* is still extant, and shows that Horman paid the London printer Richard Pynson 8*s.* a ream to publish 800 copies of the work using three typefaces. The book is an encyclopaedic collection of sentences arranged in thirty-five chapters, covering religion, manners, learning, domestic life, and recreations, and provides an admirable survey of the culture of early Tudor England. The work contained commendatory poems by Lily, and was sold for about 5*s.* When it appeared, however, Robert Whittington, the leading writer of school grammars, posted scornful verses on the door of St Paul's School, ridiculing the work and its price. This led Horman to publish his final work, *Antibossicon*, jointly with Lily, in 1521, attacking Whittington's own abilities as a grammarian and pouring scorn on his claim to be the 'chief poet of England'. Horman reissued his *Vulgaria* in 1530 and his will provided for a third edition which did not, however, appear. His interest in school education was thus a unifying element of his life, although he did not hold a major teaching post after his mid-thirties.

NICHOLAS ORME

Sources Emden, *Oxf.*, 2.963–4 · Winchester College archives, 21850, fol. 129*r* · Bale, *Index*, 129–30 · *STC*, 1475–1640, nos. 13807-11 · W. Horman, *Vulgaria* (1519); repr. (1975) · *The Vulgaria of John Stanbridge and the Vulgaria of Robert Whittinton*, ed. B. White, EETS, old ser., 187 (1932) · *LP Henry VIII*, 3/1, no. 337

Horn, Alexander [*name in religion* Maurus] (1762–1820), Benedictine monk and political agent, was born in northeast Scotland on 28 June 1762, the son of Alexander Horn and Jeanette, his wife (d. 1807). His father was descended from the Horns, lairds of Westhall (Oyne, Aberdeenshire). He entered Regensburg seminary in December 1772, took the Benedictine habit and religious name Maurus in 1778, and was professed on 29 September 1779. He was ordained priest, probably about 1785.

Clearly possessing academic ability, about 1789 Horn was apparently considering work on Marianus Brockie's *Monasticon Scoticum*. At this time the Scots' monastic library was being praised in print by visiting bibliophiles. Horn was librarian in 1790 and had bought incunables, and later was to receive great praise for his work as librarian. His interests, however, widened. From about 1790 he acted as agent in Regensburg, seat of the imperial diet, for the British ambassador in Munich, and in 1791 published anonymously a tract condemning France's activities against the empire: *Kurze and unparteiische Darstellung aller Tractaten und Verträge, auf welche Frankreich seine dermaligen Angriffe auf das deutsche Reich gründen sucht*. Another such paper was delivered by his fellow Scottish monk Ildephonse Kennedy to the Bavarian Academy of Sciences in Munich. Horn now cultivated influential people, had close ties with the princely family of Thurn and Taxis—his brother, also a monk, was later *Hofrat* (court official) and confessor to them—and led a social life, being described by an English visitor in late 1794 as 'such a wild young fellow, that it is a real shame that he should have the monkish habit' (Fremantle, 2.9). John Robison's sensational work published in 1797 on the alleged international conspiracy of freemasons, illuminati, and Jacobins contained important material supplied by Horn.

In 1799 Horn travelled with the British ambassador in Munich to England, where he had dealings with members of William Pitt's cabinet, particularly Earl Spencer, then returned to Regensburg as official British agent. This was the time of secularization of religious houses in south Germany. Horn used his bibliographical expertise to deal in rare books and manuscripts, including some from these houses, and helped to build up Spencer's magnificent collection. When in 1802 secularization in Regensburg itself became imminent, he appealed to the British government on behalf of the Scots monastery and (with more success) to the cardinal protector of Scotland in Rome, as the Scots abbey enjoyed exemption from all church authority except the Holy See. He and his abbot, Benedict Arbuthnot, also sought the aid of Napoleon's Scottish Catholic generals, Macdonald and Lauriston. In the event the monastery continued in being, though with restrictions.

In 1804 Napoleon succeeded in having the British ambassador expelled from Munich. Horn was then British chargé d'affaires in Regensburg (1804–6), dealing most successfully with the diet and heading a network of informants. When Rome in 1805 intervened at Napoleon's request, he chose to give up his monastic commitments and continue his political work. Having for a time acted clandestinely in Regensburg, he went to Austria as a British diplomat and agent. His reports from Linz, Vienna, and Prague show him to have been an acute observer in close touch with important political and military persons. In 1808–10 he was the sole British diplomat in central Europe. When Austria fell in 1810, he went to London and received a generous government pension.

Horn's later years are obscure. After returning to Regensburg in December 1813 he was expelled by order of Montgelas. He then lived with a pension at Frankfurt am Main. At some point he married a Baroness von Gumppenberg. In April 1820, with permission from Munich, he planned to return to Regensburg with the princess of Thurn and Taxis, but died, either shortly before or after, on 16 April. He is included in the monastic necrology, indicating that he was reconciled with the church authorities or perhaps, in such traumatic times for monasticism, was not considered an apostate from religion.

MARK DILWORTH

Sources L. Hammermayer, 'Die europäische Mächte und die Bewahrung von Abtei und Seminar der Schotten in Regensburg (1802/03)', *Verhandlungen des Historischen Vereins für Oberpfalz und Regensburg*, 106 (1966), 291–306 · L. Hammermayer, 'Benedikt Arbuthnot (1737–1820)', *Beiträge zur Geschichte des Bistums Regensburg*, 23–4 (1989–90), 469–87 · P. J. Anderson, ed., *Records of the Scots colleges at Douai, Rome, Madrid, Valladolid and Ratisbon*, New Spalding Club, 30 (1906) · M. Dilworth, 'Two necrologies of Scottish Benedictine abbeys in Germany', *Innes Review*, 9 (1958), 173–203 · *The Wynne diaries*, ed. A. Fremantle, 2 (1937) · A. Ross, 'Three antiquaries', *Innes Review*, 15 (1964), 122–39, esp. 127–30 · P. A. Lindner, *Die Schriftsteller … des Benediktiner-Ordens … Bayern*, 2 vols. (Regensburg, 1880), vol. 2, pp. 232–9; appx 2, 122 · F. K. G. Hirsching, *Versuch einer Beschreibung sehenswürdiger Bibliotheken Teutschlands*, 4 vols. (1786–91), 3.650–69 · K. A. Baader, *Reisen durch verschiedene Gegenden Deutschlandes in Briefen*, 2 vols. (1795–7), 2.413–16
Archives Scottish Catholic Archives, Edinburgh, letters

Horn, Andrew (c.1275–1328), administrator and chronicler, probably belonged to a long-established London family, but his relationship to any of the earlier and numerous Horns of London and Southwark is unknown; his father may have been Edmund Horn (d. after 1296), whose tenement, probably in Bridge Street, was owned by Andrew's brother Simon in 1314. Two brothers—a fishmonger Simon, and William, rector of Rotherhithe—are mentioned in his will, together with a nephew and niece, William Doget and Christina. A son was born to him in 1305 according to the *Annales Londonienses*, but died a few weeks later; his wife's name is not known, though she evidently predeceased him. He is otherwise first mentioned as warden of the fishmongers' guild in 1307, and as a 'fishmonger of Bridge Street', liable for a modest contribution of 5s. to the subsidy of 1319, and as witness to a number of Bridge House deeds from 1321 to 1327. At his death he owned two tenements, one in the parish of St Magnus in Bridge Street, probably his principal residence, and the other in Lucas Lane, in the parish of St Leonard at Eastcheap. That he practised as a fishmonger is evident from the suits brought against him in 1307 and 1315 for giving short weight in his fish baskets; but his compilations show that, from 1311 at latest, his interests, and probably his career, were increasingly formed by the practice of law and the defence of city privileges in the London courts. His access to city muniments implies that he had some position in the legal world of the Guildhall before he was elected chamberlain on 16 January 1320, a position he held until his death, which occurred between 9 and 23 October 1328.

As city chamberlain Horn belonged to the administrative and judicial rather than the aldermanic world of London, though he co-operated with the popular regime of his fellow fishmonger, the mayor Hamo Chigwell, in its careful response to the attempts by Edward II's regime to undermine the liberties of the city embodied in the highly provocative eyre of 1321. Horn was now London's permanent financial and judicial officer; some of his accounts appear in the London letter-books, though the sums at his disposal were small, and his discretion was limited by the city auditors. His court probably took more of his time and attention: his compilations have a direct bearing on its business, much of which is referred to in the letter-books. It applied city customary law, modified by royal statute and city ordinances; records of all three of these categories appear in his collections.

Horn's literary activity largely consisted of making collections of documents, but he was evidently responsible for the *Annales Londonienses* and a narrative of the eyre of 1321. His compilations, which he left to the Guildhall together with a copy of Henry of Huntingdon's *Historia Anglorum*, are, first, the *Liber Horn*, a volume of statutes originally prefaced by a statement of London legal practice drawn up in 1311, and then massively enlarged by new statutes, records of London cases, and other documents. It is the most comprehensive of all statute collections, and the only source of some lesser Edwardian statutes. Second, a volume of legal texts now divided into two manuscripts at Corpus Christi College, Cambridge, which was originally made about 1313, and contained the *Mirror of Justices*, *Britton*, and the early thirteenth-century text *Leges Anglorum*, with his own attempt to continue it. His copies rescued both the *Mirror* and *Leges Anglorum* from oblivion, and show Horn discovering the body of Old English law on which, he believed, London's liberties reposed. Third, *Liber legum regum antiquorum*, a more formal collection of history, political advice, law, custom, and precedent drawn up about 1322, and now distributed among several volumes in the Cotton collection, an Oriel College manuscript, and the *Liber custumarum*; in its original state it probably included the *Annales Londonienses*, and his narrative of the London eyre of 1321. This collection exemplified Horn's conception of civic custom as an integral part of the fundamental law laid out in the Old English law books. His hand is also likely to be that of the annotator of an older text of the *Leges Anglorum* in the Cotton collection, the *Liber ordinationum* in the London Records Office, and BL, Additional Charter 3153, a copy of the London eyre roll of 1276.

Horn's original compositions are less extensive. He wrote an account of the London eyre of 1321, composed of selections from the official roll that touched on city privilege, strung together with a skeletal narrative: a technical document, it is at once learned in city customary law and practical for future proceedings. He also made a version of part of the *Trésor* of Brunetto Latini, which described the Italian city office of *podestà*, adapted to apply to the election and conduct of a mayor of London. This tract, too, was drawn up for detailed implementation. He was almost certainly the author of *Annales Londonienses*, a version and continuation of the Westminster *Flores historiarum* in which much London material has been incorporated, and which from 1307 to 1317, when it ends, is an original composition. In this text the author, though writing from a London perspective, showed his sympathy with the lords ordainer and expressed his hope, at least in 1312, that Edward II would prove a second Alexander after all. In all his works Horn's developing sense of a bedrock of English customary law, its deepest stratum being the Mosaic law, and the Anglo-Saxon law books its authentic statement, enabled him to see English history as a continuous whole, further defined by the events of his time; its underlying principles provided for him an entirely practical guide in the defence of London privileges. He had perhaps the most coherent and comprehensive notion of specifically English liberties of any writer before the seventeenth century.   JEREMY CATTO

Sources *Liber Horn, Liber ordinationum, Liber custumarum*, CLRO · *Liber legum regum antiquorum*, BL, Cotton MS Claudius D.ii · *Liber legum regum antiquorum*, Oriel College, Oxford, MS 46 · *Leges Anglorum*, BL, Cotton MS Titus A.xxvii · London eyre roll, 1276, BL, Add. charter 3153 · *Mirror of justices*, CCC Cam., MS 70 · *Leges Anglorum*, CCC Cam., MS 258 · W. Stubbs, ed., *Chronicles of the reigns of Edward I and Edward II*, 1, Rolls Series, 76 (1882) · H. T. Riley, ed., *Munimenta Gildhallae Londoniensis*, 3 vols. in 4, Rolls Series, 12 (1859–62) · R. R. Sharpe, ed., *Calendar of wills proved and enrolled in the court of husting, London, AD 1258 – AD 1688*, 1 (1889), 344–5 · R. R. Sharpe, ed., *Calendar of letter-books preserved in the archives of the corporation of the City of London*, [12 vols.] (1899–1912) · N. R. Ker, 'Liber custumarum and other manuscripts formerly at the Guildhall', *Guildhall Miscellany*, 1/3 (1954), 37–45 · J. Catto, 'Andrew Horn: law and history in fourteenth-century England', *The writing of history in the middle ages*, ed. R. H. C. Davis and J. M. Wallace-Hadrill (1981), 367–91

Archives BL, Cotton MS Claudius D.ii · CCC Cam., MS 70 · CCC Cam., MS 258 · CLRO, 'Liber Horn', 'Liber ordinationum', 'Liber custumarum' · Oriel College, Oxford, MS 46 | BL, Cotton MS Titus A.xxvii · BL, Add. charter 3153

Wealth at death wealthy

Horn, Charles Edward (1786–1849), composer and singer, born in the parish of St Martin-in-the-Fields, London, on 21 June 1786, was the eldest son of Charles Frederick *Horn (1762–1830) and his wife Diana Dupont. After moving to England in 1782, his father was appointed music master to Queen Charlotte in 1789. Charles Edward Horn was taught music by his father, and also studied briefly, in Bath in 1808, with Venanzio Rauzzini. He began his career as a cello and double bass player in London theatres, and made his singing début at the Lyceum on 26 June 1809, in M. P. King's *Up All Night*. In 1810 he left the stage to take singing lessons from Thomas Welch, but in the same year his comic opera *Tricks upon Travellers* and his 'dramatic romance' *The Magic Bride* were produced at the Lyceum. During the next four years he wrote or collaborated in some nine stage works, of which *The Devil's Bridge* (1812) was particularly successful; it was frequently revived in England, Ireland, and the USA. He also began composing glees and songs.

In 1814 Horn made his mark as a singer, in the part of Seraskier in Storace's *The Siege of Belgrade*. Good acting and a wide vocal range rather than quality of voice brought him moderate success for the next ten years, but his popularity increased greatly after a highly acclaimed performance as Caspar in an English version of Weber's *Der Freischütz* at Drury Lane in 1824. He composed some eighteen stage works during those years. Although most are a heterogeneous mixture of original and borrowed music, many contain the simple but effective solo and concerted songs that were an essential feature of successful English operas at that period. 'On the banks of Allen Water', from *Rich and Poor*, and the duet 'I know a bank', from *The Merry Wives of Windsor*, quickly became popular, while the ballad 'Cherry Ripe', apparently written for Madame Vestris to sing in *Paul Pry* (1826), with which Horn was otherwise unconnected, almost attained the status of a folk-song. Charles Mackay recalled in 1841 that, for a time,

> 'Cherry Ripe!' 'Cherry Ripe!' was the universal cry of all the town. Every unmelodious voice gave utterance to it; every crazy fiddle, every cracked flute, every wheezy pipe, every street-organ was heard in the same strain, until studious and quiet men stopped their ears in desperation, or fled miles away into the fields and woodlands to be at peace. This plague lasted for a twelvemonth, until the very name of cherries became an abomination in the land. (Mackay, 627)

'Cherry Ripe' involved Horn in an action for plagiarism with Thomas Attwood, from one of whose songs he was supposed to have derived the melody, but he was acquitted of the charge.

In 1827 Horn travelled to New York, where he sang, produced *The Devil's Bridge* (known there since 1820), staged arrangements of operas by Mozart, Rossini, Storace, Mayr, and Weber, and performed his cantata *The Christmas Bells*. Soon after his return to London in 1830 his opera *Honest Frauds*, in which Maria Malibran enjoyed great success with the song 'Deep, Deep Sea', was staged. During 1831–2 he was music director at the Olympic Theatre. In 1832 he was again in New York, where he became music director of the Park Theatre. He produced there his opera *Nadir and Zulika* and also arranged works by Mozart and Rossini. Two of his glees from this period, 'Wisdom and Cupid' (1834) and 'Forest Music' (1835), earned him prizes in America. After losing his voice through illness in 1835 he went into partnership in a music business with W. J. Davis; from 1836 he managed it alone as Horn's Music Store, at 411 Broadway. His compositions of these years include the oratorio *The Remission of Sin* (1835), considered by a New York paper to be the first oratorio composed in America, and his last operas, *Ahmed al Ramel* (1840) and *The Maid of Saxony* (1842). In 1842 he also helped to found the New York Philharmonic Society.

After returning to London in 1843 Horn became director of music at the Princess's Theatre. His American oratorio, revised and retitled *Satan*, was given by the London Melophonic Society in 1845, and a second oratorio, *Daniel's Prediction*, was performed at the Hanover Square Rooms in 1847 without much success. He then returned to America, where he was offered the directorship of the Boston Haydn and Handel Society on 23 July 1847; commenting on this, *The Athenaeum* (20, 15 May 1847, 1226) described him as 'the best of our ballad composers … who, if trained under a better dispensation might have done much for English music'. He was married twice, first to a Miss Rae, then to Maria Horton (*d.* 1887); a son, also Charles Edward, became a tenor. Charles Horn senior died in Boston on 21 October 1849.   CLIVE BROWN

Sources R. A. Montague, 'Charles Edward Horn: his life and works', PhD diss., Florida State University, 1959 · [J. S. Sainsbury], ed., *A dictionary of musicians*, 2 vols. (1825) · D. Baptie, *Sketches of the English glee composers: historical, biographical and critical (from about 1735–1866)* [1896], 114–15 · H. C. Lahee, *Annals of music in America* (1922) · E. W. White, *The rise of English opera* (1951) · J. Mattfeld, *A handbook of American operatic premières, 1731–1962* (1963) · C. Mackay, *Memoirs of extraordinary popular delusions* (1841)

Archives Yomiuri Nippon Symphony Orchestra, Tokyo, Japan, Nanki Collection, account of C. F. Horn · Yomiuri Nippon Symphony Orchestra, Tokyo, Japan, Nanki Collection, letter (draft), 1830

Likenesses S. De Wilde, watercolour drawing, 1811, Garr. Club · J. McDougall, lithograph, BM · Pocock, oils (as Seraskier in *The siege of Belgrade*), Royal Society of Musicians, London

Horn, Charles Frederick (1762–1830), musician, was born on 24 February 1762 in Nordhausen, Germany, the third of four children of 'John' (presumably Johann) Wolfgang Horn (1737–1798) and his wife, Sophia Dorothea, *née* Shenaman (1735–1793x9). His father intended him to become a surveyor and destroyed his clavichord so that he

would concentrate upon that career, but was unable to stop him from studying music with the Nordhausen organist Christoph Gottlieb Schröter (1699–1782). Schröter had had contact with Johann Sebastian Bach years earlier and presumably brought Bach's music to Horn's attention.

On Schröter's death Horn decided to travel to Paris to further his studies and to earn his livelihood as a musician. *En route* he was persuaded to travel to London instead by a stranger, who after accompanying him there stole most of his money. Knowing no English and unsure whether to stay, Horn was wandering about London when he bumped into a man who swore in German. Horn confessed his plight, and the man kindly took him to Longman and Broderip's music shop, where Horn sat down at a piano. Impressed by his pianistic skills, the proprietor had him play for the Saxon ambassador and amateur musician Count John Maurice de Brühl (1736–1809), on whose recommendation Granville Leveson-Gower, first marquess of Stafford (1721–1803), engaged Horn as music master of his daughters at his Staffordshire estate, Trentham Hall.

There Horn met Diana Dupont (1764–1831), the daughters' governess and French teacher. They were married on 28 September 1785. As a consequence of her pregnancy the couple removed to London, where, in May 1786, Horn published his six sonatas op. 1, and on 21 June their first child, the composer and singer Charles Edward *Horn, was born. The Horns had six further children: Frederick Thomas, born in 1787; William, born in 1792, who published and sold music in London from about 1817 to 1836; Henrietta Elizabeth, born in 1789; George John (1790–1820); and two other daughters.

The subscribers to Horn's op. 1 included, besides musicians such as Muzio Clementi and Johann Peter Salomon, many members of the nobility and gentry. One of them, Lady Caroline Waldegrave, recommended Horn to Queen Charlotte, who had not employed a music master since the death of Johann Christian Bach in 1782. The queen appointed Horn to instruct her twice a week from 20 October 1789 to 9 October 1793, during which time he and his family had a home in Windsor as well as one in London. From June 1789 to October 1812 he taught music also to the royal princesses.

Horn published numerous musical compositions, a treatise on harmony, and arrangements of works by Haydn, Mozart, and Ignace Joseph Pleyel, but is remembered today chiefly as a pioneer in the introduction of J. S. Bach's music to England. In 1807 he published an arrangement for four instruments of twelve of Bach's organ fugues. After meeting Samuel Wesley in 1808, Horn provided the manuscript from which the two of them in 1809–11 issued the first complete edition anywhere of six organ trios by Bach. They proceeded to publish by subscription a 'new and correct' edition of Bach's '48' in four volumes, which was reprinted several times after its initial release in 1810–13. Horn desired to publish all of Bach's works, including a translation by his friend Edward Stephenson, a banker, of the life of Bach written in German by Johann Nicholas Forkel. Although Wesley described Horn as 'indefatigable' these grand plans did not succeed.

The Horns returned to Windsor in June 1824 when George IV, who had subscribed to Horn's op. 1 as prince of Wales, appointed him organist of St George's Chapel in Windsor Castle. According to his son's memoir, when Horn heard the news of George IV's death on 26 June 1830 he declared that his task was done. He died at Windsor on 3 August 1830 and was buried on 7 August in St George's Chapel. His estate was valued at £450. His widow died in 1831 and was buried at St George's Chapel on 20 August 1831.   MICHAEL KASSLER

Sources *Charles Edward Horn's memoirs of his father and himself*, ed. M. Kassler (2003) · [C. E. Horn], 'Biographical notice of the lately deceased Charles Frederick Horn', *The Harmonicon*, 8 (1830), 400–01 · C. E. Horn, narrative journal, Yomiuri Nippon Symphony Orchestra, Tokyo, Japan, Nanki Collection · M. Kassler and P. Olleson, *Samuel Wesley (1766–1837): a source book* (2001) · E. H. Fellowes, *Organists and masters of the choristers of St George's Chapel in Windsor Castle* (1939) · M. Kassler, 'Horn, Charles Frederick', *New Grove*, 2nd edn [incl. list of Horn's musical works] · *Court and private life in the time of Queen Charlotte, being the journals of Mrs Papendiek*, ed. V. D. Broughton, 2 vols. (1887) · E. H. Fellowes and E. R. Poyser, eds., *The baptism, marriage, and burial registers of St George's Chapel, Windsor* (1957) · S. M. Bond, ed., *The monuments of St George's Chapel, Windsor Castle* (1958)
Archives U. Glas., Euing Collection, letter to Mr Sainsbury, 1823
Wealth at death £450: administration, PRO, PROB 6/206, fol. 178v

Hornblower, Jabez Carter (1744–1814), steam engineer, was born on 21 May 1744 at Broseley, Shropshire, the eldest son of Jonathan *Hornblower (1717–1780), mechanical engineer, and his wife, Ann Carter (1723–1802). In the year following his birth, his father moved to Cornwall. Jabez was brought up to be a lawyer by his maternal grandfather, Thomas Carter, but at nineteen decided to become an engineer. His first wife was Mary St John and, after her death, he married Ann Hanbury at St Leonard's, Bridgnorth, on 24 September 1787. In 1775 Hornblower was employed to erect a Newcomen engine in the Netherlands for regulating the level of the canals in Rotterdam. He faced considerable difficulties because he spoke no Dutch and had few skilled workmen. The engine first worked a few days before 15 March 1776 but the complicated system of three beams and multiple pumps never functioned properly although the steam engine performed well. He returned to Cornwall where he invented a form of flash steam boiler. He was employed on erecting the Boulton and Watt engine at Ting Tang but was dismissed because, although a good and conscientious engineer, he had the unfortunate propensity of upsetting people. Possibly to prevent him taking the secrets of the Watt engine to Holland, he was offered employment at Soho in Birmingham. In the early part of 1779 he was erecting engines at Donnington Wood and Ketley, but here again he had to be replaced. In 1780 he upset the proprietors of the lead mine at Penrhyn on the Llŷn peninsula, and was replaced once more, although here he may not have been to blame because some parts were delayed in transit.

Hornblower was not offered further employment with Boulton and Watt and in November 1780 was at Broseley.

He helped his brother Jonathan *Hornblower (1753–1815) with his compound engine and appeared in Birmingham recruiting engine men and smiths in August 1784. He turned to civil engineering at Truro, Tewkesbury, and Northleach. In 1788 he was declared bankrupt while in business at Gloucester. By 1790 he had moved to London as a manufacturer of engines and machinery. He went into partnership with J. A. Maberley, a London currier, and his son, who had purchased Isaac Mainwaring's patent for a double cylinder steam engine. Mainwaring's engine had two ordinary atmospheric cylinders, but those built by Hornblower had a condenser and enclosed cylinders with steam pushing down the pistons. By 1796 five of these engines had been erected, two in London, one in Canterbury, and two in co. Durham.

Boulton and Watt considered that Hornblower's improvements infringed Watt's 1769 patent and injunctions were issued in January 1796. Hornblower and Maberley sought to become licensees of Boulton and Watt but negotiations came to nothing and Boulton and Watt started legal proceedings. The case began in the court of common pleas in December 1796. Judgment was given in favour of Boulton and Watt but an appeal was lodged. Hornblower and Maberley had the support of the Cornish mining interests but the king's bench upheld Watt's patent in 1799. After this Hornblower spent some time in a debtor's prison. In 1800 he patented a machine for glazing calico which, although a technical success, brought little financial gain. He contributed various essays to *Nicholson's Journal*: 'Description of an hydraulic bellows' (1802), 'Of a measuring screw' (1803), 'Account of a machine for sweeping chimneys by a blast of air' (1804), 'On the measure of force by horse power' (1805), and 'On the measure of mechanical power'. Other articles appeared in Olinthus Gregory's *Treatise of Mechanics* and in 1808 in *The First Report on Highways*. In 1809 he was recommending cast-iron rails for waggonways because this was a useful way of storing the iron until needed. He went to Sweden to erect a large malting and brewing establishment which he had designed, and returned in 1813. He died at London on 11 July 1814.   RICHARD L. HILLS

Sources T. R. Harris, 'The Hornblower family', *Journal of the Trevithick Society*, 4 (1976), 7–44; 5 (1977), 67–9 · H. Torrens, 'Jonathan Hornblower (1753–1815) and the steam engine: a historiographic analysis', *Perceptions of great engineers: fact and fantasy*, ed. D. Smith (1994), 23–34 · A. P. Woolrich, 'Hornblower and Maberley engines in London, 1805', *Transactions* [Newcomen Society], 56 (1984–5), 159–68 · J. Tann, 'Mr. Hornblower and his crew: steam engine pirates at the end of the 18th century', *Transactions* [Newcomen Society], 51 (1979–80), 95–109 · A. Rees, 'Steam engine', in A. Rees and others, *The cyclopaedia, or, Universal dictionary of arts, sciences, and literature*, 45 vols. (1819–20) · T. R. Harris, *Arthur Woolf: the Cornish engineer, 1766–1837* (1966) · H. W. Dickinson and R. Jenkins, *James Watt and the steam engine* (1927); facs. edn (1981) · J. Farey, *A treatise on the steam engine* (1827); facs. edn in 2 vols. (1971) · C. E. Lee, 'Some railway facts and fallacies', *Transactions* [Newcomen Society], 33 (1960–61), 1–16 · L. F. Lorre, 'The first steam engine of America', *Transactions* [Newcomen Society], 10 (1929–30), 15–27
Archives Birm. CL, Boulton and Watt collection · Birm. CL, James Watt MSS

Likenesses portrait, repro. in R. Stuart, *Historical and descriptive anecdotes of steam-engines and of their inventors and improvers* (1829), 2.364 • portrait, repro. in *Journal of the Trevithick Society*, 5 (1977), 69

Hornblower, Jonathan (1717–1780), engineer, was born on 30 October 1717 at Broseley, Shropshire, the eldest son of Joseph Hornblower (1696?–1762), engine builder, and his first wife, Rebecca. His father went to Cornwall in 1725 to erect a Newcomen engine at Wheal Rose, near Truro, followed by others. In 1748 his father settled at Salem, Chacewater, Cornwall, and died at Bristol in 1762. Jonathan also became an erector of Newcomen engines and presumably was trained under his father but there are no details of his early schooling or career. He erected Newcomen engines in Derbyshire, Shropshire, and Wales before moving in 1745 to Cornwall with his brother, Josiah Hornblower (1729–1809) [*see below*], where he was to remain for the rest of his life. Here he installed steam engines on William Lemon's copper mines in Gwennap and elsewhere, probably using five cylinders supplied by the Coalbrookdale Company in 1742. By 1758 he may have erected twenty engines and by 1775 he and his associates may have been responsible for most of the forty then in Cornwall of which only eighteen were still working, owing to the high price of fuel. By this time he was recognized as one of the leading engineers there.

Hornblower became engineer to many Cornish mines, such as Wheals Virgin, Maid, Sparnon, and Carharrack. In October 1776 he enquired about the terms on which Boulton and Watt would supply one of their improved engines for Ting Tang. James Watt came to Cornwall to supervise the erection of this engine and one at Chacewater which were both first tested on 30 July 1778. Hornblower co-operated with Watt in the erection of all the first seven or eight Boulton and Watt pumping engines in Cornwall, later acting as that company's resident engineer. He gave Watt a great deal of advice and was on intimate terms with him until his death. Watt reported to Boulton that Hornblower 'seems a very pleasant sort of old Presbyterian' (Boulton MSS, Watt to Boulton, 9 Aug 1777).

Hornblower took a prominent part in establishing the Baptist Society in Cornwall by starting weekly conversation meetings for hymn singing and prayer at Chacewater in 1761, where he was largely instrumental in building the meeting-house. He married Ann (1723–1802), the daughter of Thomas Carter, a lawyer at Broseley. They had six sons, including the steam engineers Jabez Carter *Hornblower and Jonathan *Hornblower, and seven daughters. The fifth, Joanna, died at the age of three, but all the rest, who were given Christian names beginning with 'J', outlived him. Hornblower became ill during the winter of 1779 and, although he made a partial recovery, died of 'stone' on 7 December 1780 at Whitehall, near Scorrier, Cornwall.

Josiah Hornblower (1729–1809) was born on 23 February 1729 in Shropshire, the fourth son of Joseph Hornblower. He accompanied his brother to Cornwall in 1745 and assisted in his engine building business. Joseph Hornblower and his sons were given the task of superintending the order for an engine to drain the Schuyler copper mine at New Barbadoes Neck (later North Arlington), New Jersey. Josiah accompanied the parts from London, sailing in the ship *Irene* on 6 June 1753. The weather encountered was so severe that the voyage took thirteen weeks instead of the usual six, and Hornblower arrived at New York on 9 September. He developed such a dread of crossing the ocean that he remained in America for the rest of his life. The parts were successfully transhipped to the mine but, through lack of skilled mechanics, the engine did not start working until 12 March 1755. Josiah Hornblower accepted Colonel John Schuyler's offer to superintend both engine and mine. Then, in 1761, he took a fourteen-year lease with a partner, John Stearndall. However, the engine and house were badly damaged by fire in July 1768 so that underground working ceased although that on the surface continued. Hornblower extended the lease for a further ten years but the American War of Independence caused disruption. In 1792 new lessors employed him to restore the engine and become superintendent but he retired in September 1794. However, he helped to establish a workshop at Belleville, New Jersey, where some of the earliest American steam engines were built.

Hornblower lived at Belleville where he also operated a ferry and a general store. He obtained a reputation as a good engineer and mathematician. He supported the colonists in their revolutionary struggle, becoming a representative for several sessions in the Congress of the United States, a member of the state legislature, speaker of the house of assembly, New Jersey, and one of the judges of the court and justice of the peace for this state. By 1755 he had married Elizabeth, daughter of Colonel W. Kingsland; they had eight sons and four daughters. He died at Belleville on 21 January 1809.

RICHARD L. HILLS

Sources R. Jenkins, 'Jonathan Hornblower and the compound engine', *Transactions* [Newcomen Society], 11 (1930–31), 138–55 • T. R. Harris, 'The Hornblower family', *Journal of the Trevithick Society*, 4 (1976), 7–44 • L. F. Lorre, 'The first steam engine of America', *Transactions* [Newcomen Society], 10 (1929–30), 15–27 • W. J. Rowe, *Cornwall in the age of the industrial revolution* (1953); 2nd edn (1993) • D. B. Barton, *The Cornish beam engine: a survey of its history and development in the mines of Cornwall and Devon from before 1800 to the present day*, 2nd edn (1969) • Birm. CL, James Watt MSS, 4/36 • Birm. CL, Matthew Boulton MSS • H. S. Torrens, 'Some newly discovered letters from Jonathan Hornblower (1753–1815)', *Transactions* [Newcomen Society], 54 (1982–3), 189–200
Archives Birm. CL, James Watt MSS • Royal Institution of Cornwall, Truro, Hornblower–Clarke letters
Likenesses portrait, repro. in *Journal of the Trevithick Society*, 5 (1977), 66, pl. 1

Hornblower, Jonathan (1753–1815), steam engineer, was born on 5 July 1753 at Chacewater, Cornwall, the sixth child and fourth son of Jonathan *Hornblower (1717–1780), steam engine builder, and his wife, Ann Carter. Jabez Carter *Hornblower (1744–1814) was his brother. He was probably educated at Truro grammar school before being apprenticed to a plumber or brazier at Penryn, Cornwall, and lived at Trelever where he was baptized on 25 July 1773. He was following his trade in 1779 at Penryn when he supplied some copper pipes for the engine at Poldory mine which his father was erecting for Boulton and Watt. He married Rosamund (either Phillips or Mudge) who died in 1779, and then in 1786 Elizabeth Jordan, who died four years later, leaving two daughters.

Hornblower always claimed that he formed his concept of the compound steam engine, in which the steam first went into a high-pressure cylinder and then was expanded in a second, low-pressure, cylinder, in 1776, before he had seen a Watt engine. His father thought that the friction would be too great if the tops of the cylinders were enclosed and the piston rods passed through stuffing boxes so that steam could be used to push the pistons down. After seeing this on Watt's engines he, however, revived his ideas and built a larger model, probably followed by a full-size engine at Wheal Maid in 1779. The steam was condensed in a surface condenser in the bottom of the second, low-pressure, cylinder but an accident smashed this. Then he employed a jet which was prevented from cooling the whole cylinder, first by a perforated plate which restricted it to the bottom and then by making the jet pass horizontally across the base. He obtained a patent in 1781 (no. 1298) in which John Winwood of Bristol acquired a two-fifths share. Their first engine, erected for a coal mine at Radstock in 1782, did not perform well. Another may have been erected in that area and he continued to experiment on a third at Penryn. He wrote a description of his engine for Howard's *Royal Cyclopaedia* for which the date of publication is usually given as 1788, but 1792 is more likely. The article shows that he had a good understanding of the properties of steam.

Hornblower was able to persuade the adventurers of Tincroft mine to erect one of his engines in 1791. Accounts of the performance of this engine vary, some saying it was better than one of Boulton and Watt's and others worse. By 1794 he had erected a further nine engines in Cornwall but their designs of condensing apparatus drew closer to Watt's. Watt had realized the threat that Hornblower's engine posed as early as 1782 but it would have been very difficult to prove that the method of condensing infringed Watt's 1769 patent. However, when Hornblower applied to parliament in 1792 for an extension of his 1781 patent, Boulton and Watt raised such effective opposition that the bill was withdrawn. They were considering possible prosecution in 1799 but never did take it to court. Either the threat of prosecution, or Watt's patent of the parallel motion for rotative engines, may have caused Hornblower to abandon reciprocating engines and turn to rotary types. He patented two designs, one in 1798 and the other in 1805. In spite of many experiments neither was a success but he would not take the advice of Davies Gilbert to concentrate on high-pressure engines (which was where the future lay). Possibly too self-opinionated and concentrating too much on his own ideas, in the last years of his life Hornblower became rather disillusioned, especially after the death of his second wife. In his later life he became interested in astronomy. His foundry and works at Penryn flourished for he left a considerable estate, not far below £10,000, when he died at Penryn on 23 February 1815.   RICHARD L. HILLS

Sources R. Jenkins, 'Jonathan Hornblower and the compound engine', *Transactions* [Newcomen Society], 11 (1930–31), 138–55 · T. R. Harris, 'The Hornblower family', *Journal of the Trevithick Society*, 4 (1976), 7–44 · H. Torrens, 'Jonathan Hornblower (1753–1815) and the steam engine: a historiographic analysis', *Perceptions of great engineers: fact and fantasy*, ed. D. Smith (1994), 23–34 · D. B. Barton, *The Cornish beam engine: a survey of its history and development in the mines of Cornwall and Devon from before 1800 to the present day*, 2nd edn (1969) · A. C. Todd, *Beyond the blaze: a biography of Davies Gilbert* (1967) · W. J. Rowe, *Cornwall in the age of the industrial revolution* (1953); 2nd edn (1993) · G. S. Howard, 'Hydraulics', *The new royal cyclopædia, and encyclopædia, or, Complete, modern, and universal dictionary of arts and sciences*, 3 vols. (1788) · E. Galloway, *History and progress of the steam engine: with a practical investigation of its structure and application* (1830) · J. Tann, 'Mr. Hornblower and his crew: steam engine pirates at the end of the 18th century', *Transactions* [Newcomen Society], 51 (1979–80), 95–109 · A. Rees, 'Steam engine', in A. Rees and others, *The cyclopaedia, or, Universal dictionary of arts, sciences, and literature*, 45 vols. (1819–20) · J. Farey, *A treatise on the steam engine* (1827); facs. edn in 2 vols. (1971) · R. L. Hills, *Power from steam: a history of the stationary steam engine* (1989)
Archives Royal Institution of Cornwall, Truro, corresp. | Birm. CA, corresp. with J. Watt and Gleig, and papers relating to his patent bill · Birm. CL, Boulton and Watt collection · NL Scot., Rennie MSS
Wealth at death under £10,000: J. S. P. Buckland, 'The Hornblower family – additional notes', *Newcomen Society Bulletin*, 129 (1984), 4–5

Hornblower, Josiah (1729–1809). *See under* Hornblower, Jonathan (1717–1780).

Hornby, Albert Neilson (1847–1925), cricketer, was born on 19 February 1847 at Blackburn, Lancashire, the sixth son of the seven sons and four daughters of William Henry *Hornby (1805–1884), a cotton spinner and MP for Blackburn (1857–69), and his wife, Margaret Susannah (*d.* 1898), daughter of Edward Birley of Kirkham, Lancashire. He was educated at Harrow School, at which time the Little Wonder, as he was called, weighed less than 6 stone, 'bat and all'. His wiry and agile physique, and perhaps rather simian features, led to his also being nicknamed Monkey. After a brief encounter with Oxford University in 1865, he joined the prosperous family cotton business. A rich man, he was able to devote his life to cricket, and he completed the family transition from milling folk to country gentry. The Hornbys moved in 1861 to rural Nantwich in Cheshire, where Hornby lived for the rest of his life. In 1876 he married Ada Sarah, the wealthy daughter and eldest surviving child of Herbert *Ingram of Rickmansworth, Hertfordshire, founder of the *Illustrated London News*. They had four sons, of whom the eldest, Albert Henry, (1877–1952) played cricket for Lancashire and captained the team from 1908 to 1914.

Hornby was a dashing, impetuous front-foot batsman, and earned a reputation as the maestro of the short single. He played in 437 first-class matches, including three test matches, making 16,109 first-class runs at an average of 24. In 1881, his finest year, he became the first Lancashire batsman to make 1000 runs (1534, average 40) in a season. He formed a typical amateur–professional, one might even say cavalier–roundhead, opening partnership with the prudent stonewaller Richard Barlow, an association affectionately commemorated in verse by Francis Thompson in his poem 'At Lord's' ('My Hornby and my Barlow long ago').

Having captained the MCC at Lord's in 1878, when the Australians famously won, Hornby led England in the famed 'Ashes' test at the Oval in 1882. He captained Lancashire from 1880 to 1893 and in 1897–8, and introduced a more modern concept of team-building, with an Australian-style emphasis on fielding: Hornby himself was an adept cover point and took 313 catches in the course of his career. Under his strict discipline, Lancashire flourished, winning the county championship in 1881, 1882 (jointly), 1889, and 1897.

Hornby was president of Lancashire from 1894 to 1916 and was unyielding in his autocratic influence, becoming easily the club's most powerful figure. His appearance was austere, with his dark hair closely cropped and severely parted, and with a neatly kept moustache. In character loyal, irascible, and valiant, he once made a perilous citizen's arrest during a Sydney crowd disturbance in 1879. W. G. Grace claimed that Hornby's energetic chases among spectators led to the formal acknowledgement of boundaries, and he certainly grasped the requirements of a modern spectator sport, and attempted to create entertaining and successful teams.

Hornby also played football for Blackburn Rovers; he was nine times an England rugby union international; he boxed, he shot, and he was an enthusiastic huntsman. As well as having a cricket field beside his stately home, he kept a sprightly stud of hunters. The 'Squire of Lancashire' was injured hunting, and it is thought that the internal injuries he sustained on that occasion eventually contributed to his death. He died after a period of illness, on 17 December 1925, at his home, Parkfield, Wellington Road, Nantwich; he was buried nearby in Acton churchyard. ERIC MIDWINTER

Sources P. Bailey, P. Thorn, and P. Wynne-Thomas, *Who's who of cricketers* (1984) · *Wisden* (1926) · private information (2004)
Likenesses photographs, Marylebone Cricket Club (Lord's) Library, London · photographs, Lancashire County Cricket Library, Old Trafford, Manchester
Wealth at death £6420 16s. 5d.: probate, 4 March 1926, *CGPLA Eng. & Wales*

Hornby, Albert Sydney [nicknamed Ash] (1898–1978), grammarian and lexicographer, was born on 10 August 1898 at Melville Cottage, Garden Lane, Chester, the eldest of the four children of Joseph Sidney Hornby (1871–1940), publisher's agent, and his wife, Margaret Ann Kitchen (1872–1966). Joseph was a Methodist lay preacher and his son in due course married in the Primitive Methodist Chapel in Chester, though perhaps out of filial loyalty rather than from firm conviction. Hornby was never a regular churchgoer, and in later years he was a declared agnostic. Hornby attended Chester grammar school, and in 1919, after war service in the Royal Navy, entered University College, London, where he read English. He graduated in 1922, and the following year was recruited to teach English at the Oita Higher Commercial School on the

Albert Sydney Hornby (1898–1978), by unknown photographer

island of Kyushu. Shortly after marrying Ida Louise Arnold (1896–1940) on 17 January 1924, Hornby set out with her on the long sea-journey to Japan.

Hornby had been recruited to teach English literature, but he was quickly drawn to teaching language, recognizing that this was the more urgent need in Japanese schools and colleges. As he later recalled, 'I found that [my students] read with some understanding ... but that their knowledge of the English language was very limited indeed. ... they'd say to me, "Where went you yesterday?" and that kind of thing' (Hornby and Ruse, 2). He therefore decided to concentrate on language and leave the teaching of literature to the Japanese professors. It was the same sure sense of prior need which led him to support the movement for the reform of English language teaching in Japan led by Harold E. Palmer, who had been appointed linguistic adviser to the Japanese government in 1922, and who a year later was made director of the newly established Tokyo Institute for Research in English Teaching (IRET).

Though geographically remote from the centre of these developments, Hornby quickly began to acquire an understanding of linguistics, initially through reading. But he also started to correspond with Palmer, and 'through my correspondence with him I became more and more interested in linguistics, especially linguistic methodology'

(Hornby and Ruse, 2). By 1931 Hornby was already publishing textbooks and was soon to contribute articles on linguistic themes to the IRET *Bulletin*. Palmer was sufficiently impressed to invite him, in the spring of that year, to help compile a list of 'collocations', or set phrases of various kinds. This project, which had been initiated at IRET in 1927, but to which Hornby made a major contribution, culminated in 1933 in the publication of the *Second Interim Report on English Collocations*, the first linguistically based analysis of English phraseology ever to appear. In 1934, and at Palmer's instigation, Hornby moved to Tokyo, followed by his wife and two daughters, Phyllis and Margaret. Later he held two posts simultaneously, one at the government school of foreign languages in Tokyo, the other at the Tokyo higher normal school, a leading teacher training institution.

As well as teaching, or supervising the teaching of others, at two centres, Hornby was now simultaneously engaged in research projects set up at the institute. Moreover, as Palmer's designated successor he eventually assumed other burdens as well. In March 1936 Palmer retired, and from one day to the next Hornby became *de facto* head of research at the institute, editor of its *Bulletin*, and the inheritor of plans—already tentatively discussed with the Tokyo publisher Kaitakusha—for a monolingual dictionary for advanced learners, eventually published in 1942 as the *Idiomatic and Syntactic English Dictionary* (*ISED*) and later, by Oxford University Press, as *A Learner's Dictionary of Current English* (1948).

The design of this dictionary and the leading role in its compilation and two subsequent revisions (Hornby's co-authors on *ISED* were Edward Gatenby and Harold Wakefield) are without doubt Hornby's greatest achievements, and those for which he is chiefly remembered. Yet here we are faced by a curious paradox. Although it would be no exaggeration to say that lexical research begun in the late 1920s (including the work on collocations already referred to) gave birth to English as a foreign language (EFL) lexicography, Hornby and Palmer do not seem to have become aware until about 1936 that nothing other than an innovative *dictionary* could draw together, satisfactorily for the student, the manifold details of structure and usage which the research had brought to light.

The actual direction taken by IRET research into the vocabulary of English also gave particular shape and emphasis to the design of the new work. Although the needs of its users as readers were not neglected, Hornby came to lay particular stress on their needs as writers. This emphasis partly came about through the attention given at IRET to research on 'vocabulary control', a systematic attempt to identify those relatively few words which carry the main burden of everyday communication. Though the vocabularies delimited in this way varied from 1000 to 3000 items, they were alike in containing a nucleus of 'structural' words (prepositions, auxiliary verbs, articles, and so on) and of items which, while not structural, formed part of very many stock phrases. They included the 'heavy-duty' verbs 'come', 'go', 'put', 'set', and 'take'. Both these categories pose severe problems for learners

attempting to write in English, and it is not surprising that information designed to help students overcome them should feature strongly in the new dictionary.

Shortly after the bombing of Pearl Harbor in December 1941, British nationals were repatriated by the Japanese, in the first instance to the United States. As their mother, Ida, had died in 1940, Phyllis and Margaret Hornby were part of this early exodus, and were taken care of in America by a missionary family. In the meantime Hornby himself had been interned—being confined in a German Jesuit monastery. Here he was well treated, and his friend and publisher Naoe Naganuma also did what he could to make conditions tolerable. Eventually Hornby was repatriated aboard the same Red Cross ship as the diplomatic staff.

On his return to England in 1942, Hornby was recruited by the British Council and spent the rest of the war in Persia, teaching at the University of Tehran and at the Anglo-Persian Institute. It was in the council's offices in Tehran that Hornby met the vivacious and delightfully forthright Marian de la Motte (1899–1987), daughter of Vital de la Motte. They married on 14 July 1944. It was Marian who decided that A. S. Hornby would henceforth become Ash, the nickname by which he was later universally known.

In 1945 Hornby was appointed to the headquarters of the British Council in London and to the not entirely congenial post of linguistic adviser. Remote from the classroom, and sensing that 'whatever knowledge I might possess was not being used in the right way', Hornby sought permission from the council to start up a periodical which, like the IRET *Bulletin*, would be devoted to problems of English language teaching (Hornby, 3). *English Language Teaching*—issued at low cost to make it accessible to the teachers of the third world with whom Hornby's sympathies chiefly lay, and with articles designed to appeal to teachers everywhere—was duly launched under his editorship in October 1946. *English Language Teaching* (or *English Language Teaching Journal*, as it later became) eventually acquired a reputation for combining expert practical advice with contributions from linguists written in a style accessible to the lay reader. According to his daughter Phyllis, Hornby was also at this time making a major contribution to the BBC series *English by Radio* (for this reason often called *Hornby by Radio*), though in her view he never received official credit for his leading role.

In 1950 Hornby resigned as editor of *English Language Teaching* to concentrate on full-time writing. His publisher, Eric Parnwell, had suggested that he might like to work in the country, producing smaller, lower-level dictionaries based on the major work but also preparing a number of language courses, including the *Oxford Progressive English for Adult Learners*, a three-volume course published from 1954 onwards. For variety, Hornby occasionally undertook a long lecture tour overseas for the British Council. During the earlier part of this period Hornby and his wife were living at Shermanbury, in Surrey, but they later moved to Appledore, in Kent, and later still to Willersey, in Worcestershire. At Willersey, especially, Hornby was able to indulge to the full a lifelong passion for gardening.

In 1954 Hornby published *A Guide to Patterns and Usage in English*, a practical grammar whose approach to analysis and tabular style of presentation reflected the methods employed in the *Advanced Learner's Dictionary* (as it was now named). The patterns were also a central feature of *Oxford Progressive English* and of his practical coursebook for teachers, *The Teaching of Structural Words and Sentence Patterns* (1959–62).

The intense activity characteristic of Hornby in his fifties and sixties is somehow at odds with the genial but mild and self-effacing teacher and scholar who appears in photographs taken in an *English by Radio* studio or during an overseas lecture tour. But a kind of quiet tenacity was needed to carry through the ambitious projects of the post-war years, a period in which he completed one radical revision of the *Advanced Learner's Dictionary* (in 1963) almost single-handed, and, beyond the normal age of retirement, undertook a further revision of the major work (published in 1974) and an intermediate adaptation (the *Oxford Student's Dictionary*, 1978).

Hornby seems to have been unaware of, or even to have played down, the part played by sheer professionalism in his remarkable career. Modesty goes some way to explain this, but also discernible is a quintessentially English suspicion of the expert, and of theory divorced from practice. Hornby saw himself as 'a simple teacher', yet this limiting description is belied by his linguistic scholarship (the *Report on Collocations* is masterly in its overall plan and detailed structuring); his firm and enthusiastic commitment to applied research; and his pioneering editorship of *English Language Teaching*, one result of which was to bring to a readership of practising teachers the developing alliance between linguists and language-teaching professionals. As it happens, these various achievements all bear witness to his particular strength, an extraordinary ability to link theory and practice, and to bring each of his skills as lexicographer, grammarian, and teacher 'to bear succinctly and illuminatingly on the others' (Quirk, 1974).

Hornby's influence on English language teaching has been further extended through the work of the A. S. Hornby Educational Trust, which he himself set up in 1961. This was a far-sighted and generous initiative whereby a substantial part of his income from royalties was set aside to improve the teaching and learning of English as a foreign language, chiefly by providing grants to enable teachers of English from overseas to come to Britain for advanced professional training. Thanks to the trust, hundreds of teachers have been able to develop their teaching expertise through British Council summer schools and postgraduate courses in linguistics and English as a foreign language at British universities.

Hornby's pre-eminence in the field of learner lexicography and language teaching methodology was recognized towards the end of his life by the award of several honours. He was appointed OBE (1964) and made a fellow of University College, London (1975), and a master of arts of the University of Oxford. Shortly before his death from cancer on 13 September 1978, at the University College Hospital, the volume *In Honour of A. S. Hornby*, edited by Peter Strevens and with contributions by many of his friends and former colleagues, was presented to him to mark his eightieth birthday.

A. P. COWIE

Sources A. P. Cowie, *English dictionaries for foreign learners: a history* (1999) • A. P. Cowie, 'A. S. Hornby, 1898–1998: a centenary tribute', *International Journal of Lexicography*, 11 (1998), 251–68 • A. S. Hornby and [C. Ruse], *Hornby on Hornby and the advanced learner's dictionary* (1974) • P. Strevens, ed., *In honour of A. S. Hornby* (1978) • A. S. Hornby, 'Looking back', *English Language Teaching*, 21 (1966), 3–6 • Y. Ogawa, 'Hornby osei: a tribute from Japan', *In honour of A. S. Hornby*, ed. P. Strevens (1978), 8–10 • P. Collier, D. Neale, and R. Quirk, 'The Hornby educational trust: the first ten years', *In honour of A. S. Hornby*, ed. P. Strevens (1978), 3–7 • J. Brown, preface, *In honour of A. S. Hornby*, ed. P. Strevens (1978), vii–xi • R. Quirk, signed tribute on the dust jacket, *Oxford advanced learner's dictionary*, ed. A. S. Hornby, rev. 3rd edn (1974) • private information (2004) [Marian Hornby, widow; Phyllis Willis, daughter; R. Smith] • b. cert. • m. certs. • d. cert. • index of consular births and deaths, Family Records Centre, London

Archives priv. coll., corresp.

Likenesses photograph, repro. in Stevens, *In honour of A. S. Hornby* [see illus.]

Wealth at death £132,371: probate, 8 Dec 1978, *CGPLA Eng. & Wales*

Hornby, Frank (1863–1936), toy manufacturer, was born at 77 Copperas Hill, Liverpool, on 15 May 1863, the only son of the three children of John Hornby, provisions dealer, and his wife, Martha Thomlinson. He was educated at local council schools until he obtained employment as a shipping clerk, working with several companies until he was thirty-eight. In 1887 he married Clara Walker, daughter of William Godefroy, mariner and customs worker. They had a daughter who died at fourteen, and two sons (who both became directors of Meccano Ltd).

Always interested in mechanical devices, experimenting in his home workshop Hornby developed the Meccano construction idea by using metal strips perforated with holes at half inch intervals and assembled with screws and nuts. Wheels, rods, cranks, and other components were added so that, with instruction manuals, boys (girls were never specified in the advertising) could build the illustrated models. Hornby obtained his first patent in 1901; the following year sets, produced in rented premises and marketed as 'Mechanics Made Easy', appeared in Liverpool toyshops. In 1908 Meccano Ltd was registered and, within five years, manufacturing plants were established in Paris, Berlin, Barcelona, and Elizabeth in New Jersey. The success of Hornby's invention was due largely to the principle of gradation from simple sets to larger ones with more complicated mechanisms. Over many years Meccano became widely used by designers to demonstrate ideas useful in mechanical research.

In 1914 Meccano Ltd moved to a purpose-built factory at Binns Road in Liverpool which by 1928 employed over 1200 people supplying Meccano sets to agents and distributors all over the world, including the Soviet Union and China. To publicize Hornby's business, *Meccano Magazine* was founded in 1916 and continued publication (usually monthly in up to seventeen languages) for over fifty years.

Prior to 1914 clockwork toys had been manufactured

Frank Hornby (1863–1936), by unknown photographer

Likenesses photograph, repro. in K. D. Brown, *The British toy business: a history since 1700* (1996) [*see illus.*]
Wealth at death £231,536 17*s.* 1*d.*: probate, 5 Nov 1936, *CGPLA Eng. & Wales*

Hornby, Sir Geoffrey Thomas Phipps (1825–1895), naval officer, second son of Admiral Sir Phipps *Hornby (1785–1867) and his wife, Sophia Maria Burgoyne (*d.* 1860), sister of Field Marshal Sir John Fox Burgoyne, was born at Winwick, Lancashire, on 20 February 1825. James John *Hornby was his younger brother. He attended Winwick grammar school and Southwood's School, Plymouth (1832–7). Hornby entered the navy in March 1837 on the *Princess Charlotte*, flagship of Sir Robert Stopford in the Mediterranean; he served in the Syria campaign of 1840, and remained with his ship until she was paid off in August 1841. After spending six months at Woolwich Dockyard, where his father was superintendent, he was appointed in early 1842 to the *Winchester*, flagship of Rear-Admiral Josceline Percy, at the Cape of Good Hope. Hornby was promoted lieutenant of the *Cleopatra* (Captain Christopher Wyvill (1792–1863)) on 15 June 1844, and served on the anti-slavery patrol on the east coast of Africa. He was sent to the Cape in command of a prize in the summer of 1846, and returned to England in the following spring. In August his father accepted the post of commander-in-chief in the Pacific, primarily to advance his son's career. He took him as his flag lieutenant, and on 12 January 1850 Geoffrey was promoted commander of the flagship *Asia* (84 guns). In the summer of 1851 the *Asia* returned to England. Hornby went with his cousin Lord Stanley for a tour in India but his health broke down, and he was obliged to return home. In 1852 his father was a lord of the Admiralty in Lord Derby's administration; on the government's downfall he secured Hornby's promotion to captain on 18 December 1852. In 1853 Hornby married Emily Frances, daughter of the Revd John Coles of Ditcham Park, Hampshire, and sister of Captain Cowper-Coles; they had three sons and two daughters. One of their sons, Robert Stewart Phipps Hornby CMG, became captain in the navy; and in 1900 an elder son, Edmund John Phipps Hornby, won the Victoria Cross while serving in South Africa as a major in the artillery.

Having become the youngest full captain in the navy, Hornby, a Conservative related to Lord Derby, spent many years on half pay; the last year of this period was spent at the Royal Naval College, Portsmouth. Then, in August 1858, during Lord Derby's second ministry, he was appointed to the *Tribune*. He joined her at Hong Kong in October, and was sent with a detachment of marines to Vancouver Island, because of the dispute with the United States over San Juan, an island between Vancouver and the mainland. The island was awarded to the United States in 1872; but in 1859 the difficulty was tided over mainly owing to Hornby's tact. The *Tribune* was ordered home to repair serious defects, and arrived at the end of July 1860. In March 1861 Hornby went out to the Mediterranean to command the *Neptune*, an old three-decker converted into a screw two-

mainly in Germany and Hornby shrewdly foresaw that, with the war over, there would be a demand for such toys made in England. In 1920 Meccano Ltd produced the first Hornby model trains, replicas of British trains with authentic colours and lettering used by the railway companies of the time. All kinds of rolling-stock, signal-boxes, stations, level-crossing gates, complementary buildings, and scenery were added to increase the realism of railway modelling. Clockwork was eventually replaced by low-voltage electric power to drive the engines and automate switching-points on the railway track. In 1933 the 'Dinky' range was introduced, with miniatures of cars, lorries, trucks, motor cycles, farm machinery, rural animals, and other models. When Hornby died at the height of his company's success, the annual output of his factories totalled millions of Meccano sets, Hornby trains, and Dinky toys, which had become household names throughout the world. By then 2000 employees were engaged at Binns Road, made up of management, designers, production workers, and marketing and advertising specialists.

In 1931 Hornby won the House of Commons seat of Everton for the Conservative Party. It was a short and not very effective venture; he resigned before the 1935 general election because of business pressures, declining health, and failing eyesight. Hornby died on 21 September 1936 at the David Lewis Northern Hospital, Liverpool. He was survived by his wife.

Meccano continued to be made in Liverpool until 1979, when falling sales caused the factory to be shut down. The firm was bought by Nikko, a Japanese toy manufacturer, in 2000, and Meccano sets were still being manufactured in France and Argentina.   A. A. WARDEN, *rev.*

Sources M. P. Gould, *Frank Hornby* (1915) · F. Hornby, 'The life story of Meccano', *Meccano Magazine* (March 1917–April 1922) · *Liverpool Daily Post* (18 Aug 1928) · *Liverpool Daily Post* (12 Sept 1935) · *Liverpool Daily Post* (21 Sept 1936) · *Liverpool Daily Post* (11 Nov 1936) · *The Times* (22 Sept 1936) · B. N. Love, *Model building in Meccano* (1971) · B. Huntington, *Along Hornby lines* (1976) · P. Randall, *The products of Binns Road* (1981)

Sir Geoffrey Thomas Phipps Hornby (1825–1895), by Elliott & Fry

decker, and manned by 'bounty' men, whom he characterized as 'shameful riffraff'. Here he came under the command of Sir William Fanshawe Martin, and witnessed Martin's attempts to develop steam manoeuvres. At the time Hornby thought them needlessly complicated and probably dangerous; but in later life he seems to have better recognized the difficulties with which Martin had to contend, and to have acknowledged their merit. This practice led to his own profound studies of the subject and to his future excellence in the management of fleets.

In November 1862 the *Neptune* returned to England, and in the following March Hornby was appointed to the *Edgar* as flag captain of Rear-Admiral Sidney Colpoys Dacres, commanding the channel squadron. In September 1865 Hornby was appointed to the *Bristol* as a first-class commodore for the west coast of Africa, where he continued until the end of 1867; his health, and his private affairs after his father's death, forced him to return to England early in 1868. On 1 January 1869 he was promoted rear-admiral, and appointed to command the flying squadron, which he did for two years. From 1871 to 1874 he commanded the channel squadron, being entrusted with the first heavy weather trials of the epochal battleship *Devastation*. From 1875 to 1877 he was one of the lords of the Admiralty, a position which, to a man of active habits, proved very irksome, the more so because he disagreed with the Admiralty's methods of conducting naval business. His time, he complained, was so taken up with many little details that he was unable to give proper consideration to important affairs. For this he blamed the reforms introduced by Hugh Childers in 1869, and in consequence he and admirals Key and Beauchamp Seymour agreed to refuse the post of senior naval lord without the promise of a major enquiry and additional naval assistance. Key broke this agreement in 1879. On 13 January 1877 Hornby wrote that he had left the Admiralty with less regret and more pleasure than he had left any other work with which he had previously been so long connected. It was thus that, when offered the choice of being first sea lord or commander-in-chief in the Mediterranean, he unhesitatingly chose the latter, and he was accordingly appointed early in January 1877, having been promoted vice-admiral on 1 January 1875.

With his flag in the *Alexandra* Hornby arrived at Malta on 18 March, and took up the command, which he held during the Russo-Turkish War (1877–8); and in February 1878, the Russian army having advanced to within what seemed striking distance of Constantinople, Hornby was ordered by Disraeli's cabinet to take the fleet through the Dardanelles. The Turkish governor and government protested, but they made no attempt to oppose the passage, though Hornby went through prepared to use force if necessary. His services and tact were rewarded by the KCB in August 1878. In June 1879 he was promoted admiral, and in February 1880 he returned to England. In 1881 he was appointed president of the Royal Naval College, Portsmouth; thereafter he was regularly consulted by the Admiralty on all issues of policy. In November 1882 he became commander-in-chief at Portsmouth, a position he held for the customary three years. In the summer of 1885 he left Portsmouth for a few weeks to command the Baltic fleet assembled during the Panjdeh crisis. After the crisis abated Hornby and his flag captain, John Fisher, carried out a series of experiments on the attack and defence of harbours using mines and torpedoes. On 19 December 1885 he was appointed GCB, with especial reference to his summer 'work in command of the evolutionary squadron'; and on 18 January 1886 he was appointed first and principal naval aide-de-camp to the queen.

Hornby now proposed to settle down on his estate at Lordington, near Emsworth, Hampshire. Although he continued to farm his own land, and to take much interest in county affairs, the welfare of the service always had prior claims. From 1884 Hornby took the lead in providing naval support for the 'big navy' agitation. He directed his followers, notably Captain John Fisher, to provide W. T. Stead with the material for his 1884 *Pall Mall Gazette* articles, and he continued to speak publicly on the subject after the Conservatives returned to power. Since his time at the Admiralty in the mid-1870s Hornby had believed the navy was too small. For him this was not a party political issue, and he refused to be silenced by the Conservatives. Here the defection of his cousin the fifteenth earl of Derby to the Liberals helped him. Supported by the London chamber of commerce Hornby continued to urge increased provision for the defence of trade. His efforts were in part responsible for the Naval Defence Act of 1889 and the Spencer programme of 1894. He even accepted the presidency of the Navy League. On 1 May 1888 he was promoted admiral of the fleet, and in 1889, and again in 1890, he was appointed aide-de-camp to Kaiser Wilhelm II during his visits to Britain. In 1891 he was officially sent, at the Kaiser's invitation, to the German manoeuvres in Schleswig-Holstein. Although he recovered from a serious illness in 1888, and from a severe accident in the early spring of 1891, he was then considerably aged. The death of his wife in January 1892 was a further shock. In February 1895, on his seventieth birthday, he was retired. On 3 March he died of influenza at Little Green, Lordington, Sussex. After his cremation at Woking his ashes were buried at Compton, Sussex, on 9 March.

While president of the Royal Naval College, Portsmouth, Hornby delivered there, in the spring of 1882, a short course of lectures on 'exercising squadrons', the notes of which were printed for the use of officers. During his later years he wrote occasionally in *The Times* and the monthly reviews on professional subjects. For many years he was recognized in the navy as the highest authority on tactics and strategy, though, except as a boy at Acre in 1840, he had never seen a shot fired in war. Almost all his service had been in flagships, and thus he had exceptional familiarity with fleets, and received the traditions and reflections of past generations.

Hornby dominated the navy between 1875 and 1885, and even in his last years remained a major influence on it, through his followers and his successful exploitation of the 'big navy' propaganda. His career had been made by two men: his father, who twice took posts that his age and health would otherwise have led him to refuse, in order to secure his son's early promotion; and his relative Lord Derby. As a result in 1852 Hornby, at the age of twenty-seven, had become the youngest captain in the navy. This provided him with experience of command, and the relative youth for a long and active flag career. Although considered the finest fleet commander of the era, Hornby was equally influential in issues of ship design and strategy. Throughout his career he stressed the importance of efficiency, order, and discipline, and he helped to raise standards in all areas. He led the movement that would transform the Victorian navy into the modern service that went to war in 1914.

J. K. LAUGHTON, *rev.* ANDREW LAMBERT

Sources Mrs F. Egerton, *Admiral of the fleet: Sir Geoffrey Phipps Hornby, a biography* (1896) · A. J. Marder, *The anatomy of British sea power*, American edn (1940) · R. F. MacKay, *Fisher of Kilverstone* (1973) · P. H. Colomb, *Memoirs of Admiral the Right Honble. Sir Astley Cooper Key* (1898) · J. B. Hattendorf and others, eds., *British naval documents, 1204–1960*, Navy RS, 131 (1993) · S. R. B. Smith, 'Public opinion, the navy and the City of London: the drive for British naval expansion in the late nineteenth century', *War & Society*, 9/1 (1991) · *CGPLA Eng. & Wales* (1896) · personal knowledge (1901) · *The Times* (4 March 1895) · *Army and Navy Gazette* (9 March 1895)
Archives NMM, corresp. and papers | BL, letters to Sir A. H. Layard, Add. MSS 39012–39034, *passim*
Likenesses Elliott & Fry, photograph, NPG [*see illus.*] · photographs, repro. in Egerton, *Admiral of the fleet*
Wealth at death £27,339 16s. 1d.: resworn probate, July 1896, CGPLA Eng. & Wales

Hornby [Horneby], **Henry** (*c.*1457–1518), college head, was the son of George and Emma Hornby, probably of West Deeping, Lincolnshire, where a George Hornby was keeper of horses to Lady Margaret Beaufort and Thomas, Lord Stanley in 1483. Henry graduated BA at Cambridge in 1479, MA in 1481, and DTh in 1495 or 1496. His first recorded living was the vicarage of St James, East Deeping, Lincolnshire, which he vacated in 1481; he was dean of St Chad's, Shrewsbury, from 1494, and rector of Burton Bradstock, Dorset, from 1495 until his death, and held many other livings for varying lengths of time.

In 1494 Hornby was also presented to the rectory of Trefdreyr in Cardigan by Lady Margaret Beaufort, who was that year made by the pope official patron of the feast of the Name of Jesus. Hornby is thought to have composed an office for the feast about 1488, while he was a student of theology. After gaining his doctorate Hornby rapidly gained an important position in Lady Margaret's household, as dean of chapel, secretary, and, after 1504, chancellor. His household career was paralleled by distinguished collegiate appointments. He was admitted master of Peterhouse, Cambridge, in 1501, in succession to Thomas Denman, Lady Margaret's physician. In 1502, after she had drawn up new statutes for Tattershall College, Lincolnshire, Hornby was appointed warden. In 1509 he was preferred as dean of Wimborne Minster, Dorset, where Margaret had left provision in her will for the foundation of a chantry with a grammar school attached. Hornby held these offices for his life, except in the period 1508–12, when his friend Edmund Hanson held the wardenship of Tattershall.

After Lady Margaret's death in 1509 Hornby began the task of aiding Richard Fox (d. 1528) and John Fisher (d. 1535), her other principal executors, to complete the transformation of St John's Hospital, Cambridge, into a new college in accordance with her will. He maintained a watching brief on the progress of St John's, and on the difficult negotiations for removing the remaining brethren of the hospital to Ely and compensating them with pensions. On 29 July 1516 he and John Fisher, representing the other executors of Lady Margaret, installed Alan Percy as master of the college, along with thirty-one fellows. At some date before his death Hornby gave £10 to St John's towards glazing the chapel windows.

In 1514 Hornby founded a chantry to commemorate himself, his family, friends, and benefactors, including Lady Margaret. It was to be served by a priest–fellow of Peterhouse, whose stipend was drawn from the profits of the manor of Chewell in Haddenham and its neighbourhood, Cambridgeshire, which Hornby bought for the college. The land also provided the salary of a schoolmaster to teach grammar at Baston, near the Deepings, Lincolnshire. This school was administered until at least 1542 by the Guild of the Blessed Virgin Mary at Baston, of which

Hornby was alderman. By a fuller agreement in 1516 Peterhouse was also to celebrate the anniversary of Hornby's death. Land at Caldecote, Cambridgeshire, was also granted by him in 1517 to Clare College to support a chantry with similar aims.

Under the terms of Hornby's final will, proved 16 March 1518, books were left to both colleges, and support provided for poor scholars both of Peterhouse and in the university at large. Hornby was probably buried in Little St Mary's, Cambridge, though no memorial now remains. Bale ascribes to him authorship of a *Historia nominis Iesu*, which is most likely the same as the office that he allegedly composed *c*.1488, and a *Historia visitationis beatae Mariae virginis*. His date of death has been recorded by many authorities as 12 February 1518, but no contemporary evidence for this has been found.

MALCOLM G. UNDERWOOD

Sources Emden, *Cam.* · will, PRO, PROB 11/19, sig. 6 · Peterhouse, Cambridge, Misc. Boston [*recte* Baston] School 1 · Peterhouse, Cambridge, collegium E2 · Peterhouse, Cambridge, Haddenham C10 · register, St John Cam., C7.2 · register of leases, Clare College, Cambridge, safe C, 5/1 · T. A. Walker, *A biographical register of Peterhouse men*, 1 (1927) · J. Bale, *Illustrium Maioris Britannie scriptorum ... summarium* (1548) · Bale, *Cat.*, vol. 2 · *An inventory of the historical monuments in the city of Cambridge*, Royal Commission on Historical Monuments (England), 2 (1959) · R. W. Pfaff, *New liturgical feasts in later medieval England* (1970) · account of the farmer at West Deeping, Lincolnshire, 1483, PRO, SC 6/909/16

Archives Peterhouse, Cambridge, collegium E2; Haddenham C10; Misc. Boston [*recte* Baston] School 1

Likenesses panel portrait, *c*.1560, Peterhouse, Cambridge

Hornby, James John (1826–1909), college head, born at Winwick, Lancashire, on 18 December 1826, was the third and youngest son of Admiral Sir Phipps *Hornby (1785–1867) and his wife, Sophia Maria (*d.* 1860), daughter of Lieutenant-General John Burgoyne (1722–1792). Sir Geoffrey Thomas Phipps *Hornby was his brother. He was entered as an oppidan at Eton College in 1838, and after a successful career as a scholar and as a cricketer went to Balliol College, Oxford, in 1845, where he gained a first class in the final classical school in 1849, and rowed in the Oxford eight in 1849 and 1851. After graduating BA in 1849, in which year he was elected a founder's fellow of Brasenose College, and proceeding MA in 1851, he was ordained in 1855. He was principal of Bishop Cosin's Hall at Durham University from 1853 to 1864, when he returned to Oxford, becoming classical lecturer and junior bursar at Brasenose. He was a university proctor in 1866.

In 1867 Hornby was appointed second master at Winchester College, but shortly after was appointed headmaster of Eton on the resignation of Edward Balston (1817–1891). For several generations the headmaster, who was the subordinate officer of the provost, had been an Eton colleger and scholar of King's College, Cambridge. Under the 1868 Public Schools Act the whole administration of Eton was changed; in particular the headmaster's position became one of increased independent authority. In these altered circumstances Hornby entered upon his duties early in 1868. The appointment of an oppidan, an

James John Hornby (1826–1909), by John Caswall Smith, 1899

Oxonian, and a man of aristocratic birth and high social connections, who had not served his apprenticeship as an Eton master, marked the new era in the history of the school.

Hornby immediately made changes in the school curriculum, introducing compulsory French and science, and enabling the senior boys to take modern subjects, such as political economy. He paid out of his personal funds for the chemistry laboratory, which opened in 1869. An army class was instituted for boys preparing for entry to Sandhurst or Woolwich. A daily morning service in chapel was introduced, and the Eton Mission at Hackney Wick was founded in 1880. An accomplished sportsman, Hornby encouraged organized games. He was a progressive rather than a radical reformer, with a tendency to become more conservative as the years went on; in a conflict over tutorial authority between the classical and non-classical masters he firmly supported the continued subordination of the latter to the classicists. Hornby was swift to assert his authority over his staff. Two popular masters were removed in rapid succession, William Johnson (later Cory) in 1872 and Oscar Browning in 1875. Browning's dismissal occasioned a public controversy. Both masters had cultivated close relations with the boys, and both seem to have fallen foul of Hornby's muscular conception of manliness and his rigid determination in matters of purity. Another unconventional master, the socialist James Leigh Joynes (1853–1893), was forced to resign in 1882.

Despite his experience as an Oxford proctor, Hornby

was not an effective disciplinarian, and academic standards were low. Many of those initiatives which he did carry through were attributed to the energy of Edmond Warre, a housemaster and Hornby's successor as headmaster. His courtesy and sympathetic manner, together with a strong sense of humour, helped him to maintain a personal popularity, but colleagues noted a dilatoriness and indolence, complaints of which grew after his appointment, on Gladstone's recommendation, as provost of Eton in succession to C. O. Goodford in 1884. He held the provostship until his death. His tenure of this dignified post, less arduous than the headmastership, was characterized by what Edward Lyttelton described as 'a courteous immobility' (Card, 80).

Complaints of Hornby's administrative indolence contrasted with his lifelong bodily vigour. From 1854 to 1867 he distinguished himself as one of the pioneers of alpine climbing, and was a member of the Alpine Club from December 1864 until his death. He made many new ascents, which called for the highest physical and mental qualities in a mountaineer. After his appointment to Eton, his athletic feats were chiefly confined to skating, in which he was proficient up to the date of his death. Although he did not pretend to any literary gifts, he was an accomplished scholar and an admirable public speaker. Hornby, who proceeded DD at Oxford in 1869 and was created honorary DCL of Durham in 1882, was appointed honorary chaplain to Queen Victoria in 1882, and in 1901 to Edward VII, who made him CVO in 1904. Shortly after his appointment to the headmastership Hornby married, in 1869, Augusta Eliza (d. 1891), daughter of the Revd J. C. Evans of Stoke Poges. They had three sons and two daughters. He died at The Lodge, Eton College, on 2 November 1909, and was buried at Eton cemetery.

L. H. CUST, rev. M. C. CURTHOYS

Sources *The Times* (3 Nov 1909) · [C. B. Heberden], ed., *Brasenose College register, 1509–1909*, 2 vols., OHS, 55 (1909) · O. E. [H. S. S. Salt], *Eton under Hornby* (1910) · D. W. Freshfield, 'In memoriam: J. J. Hornby', *Alpine Journal*, 25 (1910–11), 46–9 · T. Card, *Eton renewed: a history from 1860 to the present day* (1994)
Likenesses J. Collier, oils, exh. RA 1898, Eton · J. C. Smith, photograph, 1899, NPG [*see illus.*] · Spy [L. Ward], caricature, watercolour study, NPG; repro. in *VF* (31 Jan 1901) · wood-engraving (after photograph by Hills & Saunders), NPG; repro. in *ILN* (25 Jan 1868)
Wealth at death £23,511 5s.: probate, 24 Dec 1909, CGPLA Eng. & Wales

Hornby, John (*fl.* 1350–1375), Carmelite friar, and religious controversialist, entered the Carmelite order at Boston, Lincolnshire, and then studied at York, where he was ordained acolyte on 18 September 1350, subdeacon on 18 December 1350, deacon on 11 June 1351, and priest on 24 September 1351. He incepted as a doctor of theology at Cambridge, where he was regent master of theology in 1374. At that period, the increasing influence of the Carmelite order, and its claim to have been founded by the prophet Elijah, were leading to criticism from the other mendicant orders. In Cambridge a fierce attack on the order was led by a Dominican, John Stokes, who, apart from denying its Old Testament origins, asserted that the Carmelites had never been fully confirmed by the church,

and that their title, Brothers of the Virgin Mary, referred not to the Blessed Virgin but to Mary of Egypt, a converted prostitute. Hornby defended his order in a public debate before the chancellor, John Donewych, and the assembled doctors of the university. Armed with copies of papal privileges and other documents, Hornby answered Stokes's attacks with such effect that the chancellor issued a solemn decree in favour of the Carmelites in the church of Little St Mary's on 23 February 1375.

Hornby's *Determinaciones ac conclusiones* survive in a single copy, dated 1439 (Bodl. Oxf., MS e Museo 86, fols. 176–211). There are some repetitions and lacunae in this text, which suggest that it may have been based upon Hornby's own preparatory notes for the debate. The text has never been printed although its contents are discussed in detail by J. P. H. Clark. Hornby's arguments bear witness to the fierce determination of the Carmelites to assert their Old Testament origins, and the difficulties they experienced in justifying their historical pretensions. The only other surviving work by Hornby is part of a sermon on the Carmelite order, preached 'to the people' following the debate. It has been edited by Clark. Bale records some lectures on theology with incipit by Hornby, but other attributions by him and later authors are spurious.

Of Hornby's later career nothing is known except that it is claimed that he died in his home convent of Boston, where he was buried. His fame rests almost exclusively on his defence at Cambridge, and news of his success spread rapidly. The text of the university decree (printed in the *Speculum Carmelitanum*, ed. J. B. de Cathaneis, Venice, 1507, fols. 80v–81v) was frequently quoted in other works defending the order.

RICHARD COPSEY

Sources J. P. H. Clark, 'A defence of the Carmelite order by John Hornby, O.Carm., AD 1374', *Carmelus*, 32 (1985), 73–106 · Emden, *Cam.*, 314 · J. Bale, BL, Harley MS 3838, fols. 76v–77, 184 · Bale, *Cat.*, 1.480 · Bodl. Oxf., MS e Museo 86, fols. 176–213 · Borth. Inst., Reg. 10 Zouche, fols. 49, 50, 52, 53 · J. Bale, Bodl. Oxf., MS Bodley 73 (SC 27635), fols. 2, 108v, 112v, 138, 196v · A. Staring, 'Hornby, John', *Dictionnaire d'histoire et de géographie ecclésiastiques*, ed. A. Baudrillart and others, 24 (Paris, 1992), 1134 · C. de S. E. de Villiers, *Bibliotheca Carmelitana*, 2 vols. (Orléans, 1752); facs. edn, ed. P. G. Wessels (Rome, 1927), vol. 2, pp. 8–9

Hornby, Sir Phipps (1785–1867), naval officer, born at Winwick, Lancashire, on 27 April 1785, was the fifth son of Geoffrey Hornby (1750–1812), rector of Winwick, and his wife, Lucy Stanley (d. 1833), daughter of James Stanley (styled Lord Strange) and sister of Edward, twelfth earl of Derby. His sister Charlotte Margaret married her cousin Edward, thirteenth earl of Derby. This family connection dominated Hornby's political life and led to his changing from whig to tory with Lord Stanley in 1834.

Hornby was educated at Sunbury, and entered the navy in May 1797, on the frigate *Latona* with Captain John Bligh, just before the outbreak of the mutiny at the Nore, in the Thames estuary in May–June 1797, which he witnessed. With Bligh he served in the *Romney*, *Agincourt*, and *Theseus*, chiefly on the coast of North America and in the West Indies. In 1804 he was sent out to the Mediterranean, where he joined the *Victory* off Toulon, and on 1 August was promoted from her by Nelson to be lieutenant of the *Excellent*, with Captain Frank Sotheron. The promotion was confirmed on 16 November, and Hornby, continuing in the *Excellent*, was employed throughout 1805 and 1806 in the operations on the coast of Italy, including the defence of Gaeta and the capture of Capri.

On 15 August 1806 Hornby was promoted to the command of the armed vessel *Duchess of Bedford*, and in her fought a sharp action in the Strait of Gibraltar with two heavy spanish privateers, which he succeeded in beating off. In February 1807 he was moved to the sloop *Minorca*, in which he several times fought Spanish gunboats off Cadiz, and in 1809 was employed in the Adriatic. On 16 February 1810 he was advanced to post rank, and, after a short period in command of the *Fame* (74 guns) off Toulon, was appointed to the *Volage*, a small frigate of 22 guns. It was in the *Volage*, on 13 March 1811, that Hornby took part in the brilliant frigate action off Lissa in the Adriatic, for which, with the other captains, he received the gold medal. The *Volage* had thirty-three wounded, including Hornby, and thirteen killed. He afterwards commanded the frigates *Stag* (36 guns), at the Cape of Good Hope, and the *Spartan* (38 guns) in the Mediterranean, where he co-operated with Tuscan troops in taking Elba from the French, for which he received the Austrian order of St Joseph of Würzburg. On 4 June 1815 he was nominated a CB.

Hornby married, on 22 December 1814, Sophia Maria (*d.* 1860), eldest daughter of Lieutenant-General John *Burgoyne (1723–1792). They had five daughters and three sons: Captain John Phipps (1820–1848) of the Royal Engineers, Admiral Sir Geoffrey Thomas Phipps *Hornby (1825–1895), and James John *Hornby (1826–1909), provost of Eton.

After paying off the *Spartan* in the summer of 1816, Hornby had no further service until 1832, when he was appointed superintendent of the Royal Naval Hospital and victualling yard at Plymouth, from which post he was transferred in January 1838 to Woolwich, as superintendent of the dockyard. He was comptroller-general of the coastguard from December 1841 until he became rear-admiral on 9 November 1846. From August 1847 to August 1850 he was commander-in-chief in the Pacific, with his flag in the *Asia* (80 guns), a post he accepted in order to promote his son to commander, and between March 1852 and January 1853 he was one of the lords of the Admiralty on the duke of Northumberland's board. On the fall of Lord Derby's government his son was promoted captain. On 7 April 1852 Hornby was nominated a KCB; he became vice-admiral on 21 January 1854, admiral on 25 June 1858, and was made a GCB on 28 June 1861. He died at his home at Little Green, near Petersfield, Hampshire, on 19 March 1867. J. K. LAUGHTON, rev. ANDREW LAMBERT

Sources Mrs F. Egerton, *Admiral of the fleet: Sir Geoffrey Phipps Hornby, a biography* (1896) · T. Pocock, *Remember Nelson: the life of Captain Sir William Hoste* (1977) · Herefs. RO, Pakington MSS · O'Byrne, *Naval biog. dict.* · Boase, *Mod. Eng. biog.* · *WWW, 1897–1915* · *GM*, 4th ser., 3 (1867), 671
Archives NMM, letter-books, corresp., and papers
Likenesses J. Lavery, oils, RA

Wealth at death under £70,000: probate, 27 May 1867, *CGPLA Eng. & Wales*

Hornby, (Charles Harold) St John (1867–1946), businessman and private printer, was born on 25 June 1867 at Much Dewchurch, Herefordshire, the eldest son of the Revd Charles Edward Hornby, then a curate, and his wife, Harriet, daughter of the Revd Henry Turton, vicar of Betley, Staffordshire. He was educated at Harrow School and, from 1887, at New College, Oxford, where he read classics, taking a first class in moderations in 1888 and a third class in finals in 1890. He rowed for New College, and in 1890 was stroke in the university boat. In 1890–91 he travelled round the world with a friend, another former member of the New College rowing eight, W. F. D. (Freddy) Smith (later Viscount Hambleden). He married Cicely, daughter of Charles Barclay, a director of the National Provincial Bank, in 1898. They had three sons and two daughters.

Hornby was called to the bar in 1892, but soon afterwards was invited by Freddy Smith to become a partner in his family firm, W. H. Smith & Son, wholesalers and retailers of newspapers and books. In recruiting his college rowing friend into the family firm Smith, as a fourth-generation heir to the business, exemplified the arbitrary approach to the selection of top management which has often been cited as a reason for Britain's relative economic decline during the twentieth century; but he had chosen wisely, and Hornby ascended rapidly to a dominant position in the firm. After starting training in January 1893, Hornby rose to become a salaried partner in 1894 and a profit-sharing partner in 1896. He was quickly given increasing responsibility for handling the firm's external relations. This included dealing with the new breed of newspaper and magazine proprietors, such as Alfred Harmsworth, whose brashness was antipathetic to the older partners; Hornby succeeded in establishing friendly relations with them. It also included negotiating the renewal of contracts with the railway companies for the operation of bookstalls and the sale of advertising spaces which at that time constituted the bulk of the firm's business.

The railway companies, finding profits hard to earn at the turn of the century, wanted ever higher rents from W. H. Smith. Hornby had the task of trying to keep their demands within bounds that would allow W. H. Smith a reasonable return. When the managers of the Great Western Railway and the London and North Western Railway, representing between them about one-third of W. H. Smith's railway business, insisted on what he considered to be uneconomic levels of rent, Hornby was unable to conclude acceptable new contracts with them in 1905. The other partners backed his judgement and prepared to switch their business in those areas from bookstalls to bookshops off railway property. The firm already operated a few shops, and Hornby, anticipating the possible loss of the contracts, had set men scouting for possible shop sites, but it was still a considerable challenge to transfer so many of the firm's outlets while keeping the daily business of newspaper distribution running smoothly. Hornby relished a challenge: in ten weeks, 144 new shops were opened on the territory of the two railway companies.

This most dramatic episode in the firm's history pointed the way to the future structure of its business, centred on shops rather than stalls, and established Hornby's position as the strategist of the firm. During the First World War he bore even more responsibility, as four of the six partners left on military service. He continued to be the dominant figure in W. H. Smith, which became a private company in 1929 following the death of Freddy Smith, Viscount Hambleden. Freddy's heir, William (Billy) Hambleden, though no mere figurehead, felt no need to challenge Hornby's position. Forceful as he was, Hornby considered himself to be part of a team, and he took an interest in bringing on talented managers.

For many years Hornby's major relaxation outside business was his private press, the Ashendene Press. He first set up a hand press at his father's house in Ashendene, Hertfordshire, in 1895. In 1899, the year after his marriage, he moved his press to his new home, Shelley House on Chelsea Embankment, and continued to produce highly regarded limited editions from there until 1935. He had two typefaces specially designed for his press, Subiaco and Ptolemy. His passion for fine printing and bookbinding was reflected in his attitude to the printing department of W. H. Smith—where concern for high standards of design and workmanship was allowed for some time to prevail over profitability.

Hornby died at his home, Chantmarle, Cattistock, Dorchester, on 26 April 1946. His clear and perceptive mind, his energetic, decisive, and determined character, and shrewd business sense, made him the most influential figure in W. H. Smith in the twentieth century. After his death, the directors formally recorded in their minutes: 'To him more than anyone else is due the expansion of the Firm of W. H. Smith & Son since he first entered it fifty-three years ago' (W. H. Smith archives, Y. 123, fol. 285). One of his sons, Michael, became a director of W. H. Smith; Michael's son Simon also later joined the firm, becoming chief executive and then chairman.

Christine Shaw

Sources C. Wilson, *First with the news: the history of W. H. Smith, 1792–1972* (1985) · C. H. St J. Hornby: an anthology of appreciation (privately printed, London, 1946) · C. H. St J. Hornby: jubilee celebrations, 1 January 1943 (privately printed, London, 1943) · DNB · d. cert.
Archives W. H. Smith Group plc, Milton Hill House, Abingdon, Oxfordshire, letter-books | BL, corresp. with Sir Sidney Cockerell, Add. MSS 52724–52725 · BL, corresp. with Lord Northcliffe, Add. MS 67172
Likenesses W. Rothenstein, chalk drawing, 1923, NPG · W. Coldstream, portrait, W. H. Smith plc · photograph, NPG
Wealth at death £1,005,724 11s. 3d.: probate, 21 Aug 1946, CGPLA Eng. & Wales

Hornby, William (*fl.* 1618–1622), poet, was, according to his own account, educated at Peterborough Free School, of which he gives an amusing account of its overbearing regime and the pupils' riotous reaction to such discipline in his *Horn-Book*. He is the author of the rare verse *The Scourge of Drunkennes* (1618), on the title-page of which is a woodcut of a wild man holding a scourge in his right hand and a pipe in his left. Another edition was issued in 1619; the text was dedicated to Hornby's kinsman Henry Cholmely and was prefaced by a metrical address, 'To all the Impious and relentlesse-harted Ruffians and Roysters under Bacchus Regiment: *Cornu-apes* [i.e. Horn-bee] wisheth remorse of Conscience and more increase of Grace', and by some verses to Drunkenness. The poem entitled 'The scourge of drunkennes' follows 'Cornu-Apes his Farewell to Folly, or his Metamorphosis'. The verses reveal a distinctly personal bias. Amid humorous descriptions of the appearance of drunkards are autobiographical passages relating long struggles towards self-reform. Two short poems, entitled 'A Meditation of the Flesh and Spirit' and 'A Prayer Against Temptation', are appended.

Hornby published one other work, a whimsical poem called *Hornbyes Horn-Book* (1622), of which the British Library possesses the sole extant copy. Conceived to instruct young scholars in a plain and simple style the book was dedicated to Sir Robert Carr, later second baronet, of Sleaford, Lincolnshire; Sir Rochester Carr, the future fifth baronet; and Thomas Grantham, heir to Sir Thomas Grantham of Goltho, Lincolnshire. Both were major gentry families who were politically highly active during the period. Robert had only just entered his teens in 1622, and Thomas's education was to be concluded by a continental tour commencing in February 1626.

A. H. Bullen, *rev.* Elizabeth Haresnape

Sources W. Hornby, *Hornbyes horn-book* (1622) [sole extant copy in BL] · T. Corser, Collectanea Anglo-poetica, or, A ... catalogue of a ... collection of early English poetry, 8, Chetham Society, 102 (1878), 289–92 · C. Holmes, Seventeenth-century Lincolnshire, History of Lincolnshire, 7 (1980) · APC, 1625–6, 348

Hornby, William Henry (1805–1884), cotton spinner and manufacturer, was born on 2 July 1805 in King Street, Blackburn, one of seven children (two of whom died in infancy) of John Hornby (1763–1841), cotton spinner and manufacturer, and his wife, Alice Kendall (d. 1827), daughter of Daniel Backhouse. During the early nineteenth century John Hornby and his business partner, John Birley, operated as cotton manufacturers, putting out to handloom weavers from their warehouse in Clayton Street, Blackburn. In 1828, they extended their activities by building a small cotton spinning mill alongside the River Blakewater at Brookhouse, half a mile or so from the town centre. Even at this late date, the mill was water-powered. By 1830, however, the partnership had been dissolved, control passing to William Henry Hornby and his partners, John Newsham and William Kenworthy.

Of the young Hornby, little is known. By repute he was a man of forceful character, who was a keen athlete and games player. Probably he entered his father's business during the 1820s, and may have helped to establish the Brookhouse venture. But the only certain detail of his early life is his marriage to Margaret Susannah Birley on 19 May 1831. She was the daughter and sole heir of Edward Birley of Kirkham, nephew of John Birley, erstwhile partner of William Henry's father. The union produced seven sons, including the cricketer Albert Neilson *Hornby, and four daughters.

The Brookhouse business prospered, power-looms being installed in 1830, and a steam engine in 1841. By the early 1850s, the works comprised the original mill and four others. It had also become associated with improvements to the power-loom, which greatly improved its efficiency; some of these were patented by William Kenworthy, along with James Bullough, one of the firm's employees. In 1847 the firm employed 1400 people, placing it among the largest concerns in the Lancashire cotton industry.

Brookhouse mills being in a somewhat remote location, the partners provided housing on site for their employees and, by 1847, had built several blocks of two-up two-down terraces, accommodating over 180 families. They also financed the provision of community facilities, most notably a British Society school in 1839, and, two years later, a walled stadium for outdoor games. Such acts have been viewed as examples of the employer paternalism that may have emerged strongly in Lancashire's cotton districts at this time. They allowed industrialists like Hornby to imitate and rival the actions of landed society and, perhaps, lessened class conflict. But in any case Hornby's relationship with his workforce was much the stronger because of his support for the Ten Hours Bill.

True to the traditions of his family, Hornby espoused the causes of toryism and Anglicanism, though he played a fuller role in politics than in religion. Following the passage of the 1832 Reform Act, Blackburn's tories founded the Operative Conservative Association, appointing Hornby, then aged twenty-seven, its vice-chairman. In this capacity, he helped his younger brother, John, to become one of the town's two tory MPs at the 1841 election. Feelings between rival factions in the town ran high at election times and Hornby suffered his share of intimidation. Thus, during both the 1841 and 1853 campaigns, his opponents threw stones at his house, breaking the windows and, on the second occasion, forcing his wife and children to escape by the back door.

At the time of Blackburn's incorporation in 1851, William Henry Hornby had acquired considerable wealth and social standing. He was perhaps the town's biggest employer and certainly one of its major property owners. He was also a director of the Lancashire and Yorkshire Railway Company and a county magistrate. He plainly lived in some style: his King Street household included nine resident servants, including a butler, a coachman, a groom, and a cook. With such advantages, Hornby was well placed to accept office as Blackburn's first mayor in 1852, when he was also appointed a borough alderman. Meanwhile, he continued to play a leading role in local parliamentary campaigns, offering himself unsuccessfully as a candidate in the 1853 election, but being returned unopposed four years later. He was re-elected in 1859 and 1865, and though topping the poll in the 1868 election—the first under the extended franchise brought in by the 1867 Reform Act—he and his fellow victor were subjected to a petition against their return on the grounds of voter intimidation. Following an inquiry held in Blackburn town hall, the charge was upheld and the two were unseated. However, the family interest at Westminster was maintained: Hornby's son Edward was successful when the election was rerun in 1869.

Following his defeat, Hornby, then in his early sixties, partially withdrew from public and business activities, spending his remaining years at Poole Hall, his Cheshire country seat at Nantwich. However, he retained his interest in the magistracy, sitting for Cheshire as well as Lancashire, and by the late 1870s, he had accepted the position of Lancashire's deputy lieutenant. He died at Poole Hall on 5 September 1884, in his eightieth year. His body was returned to Blackburn by train and, amid scenes of great public mourning, was interred on 11 September in the family vault at St John's Church.

J. GEOFFREY TIMMINS

Sources *Blackburn Standard* (6–20 Sept 1884) · Hornby family (newspaper cuttings file), Blackburn Public Library · W. A. Abram, *A history of Blackburn, town and parish* (1877) · P. Joyce, *Work, society and politics* (1980) · G. C. Miller, *Blackburn: the evolution of a cotton town* (1951) · J. D. Marshall, 'Colonisation as a factor in the planting of towns in north-west England', *The study of urban history* [Leicester 1966], ed. H. J. Dyos (1968), 215–30 · *Ordnance survey of England and Wales: Blackburn*, Ordnance Survey (1847), sheet 2 [5 feet: mile] · Blackburn rate book, 1851/2, Blackburn Reference Library · M. Rothwell, *A guide to the industrial archaeology of Blackburn*, 1: *The textile industry* (1985) · D. Beattie, *Blackburn* (1992) · *Pigot's Directory* (1830–31) · census returns for Blackburn, 1851 · CGPLA Eng. & Wales (1885)
Likenesses bronze statue, 1912, King William Street, Blackburn, Lancashire · portrait, repro. in *Blackburn Times* (12 Jan 1889)
Wealth at death £250,638 17s. 8d.: probate, 9 Jan 1885, CGPLA Eng. & Wales

Horne, Benjamin (1698–1766), coal factor, was born on 8 September 1698 at Arundel, Sussex, the ninth of ten children of Thomas Horne (*d.* 1718), a glover of that town, and his wife, Susannah (*d.* 1734), both Quakers. In 1719 he set up in business in London as a coal factor—buying coal by the chaldron or by the entire cargo from the northern colliers, and selling it into the City and suburbs. At first he operated from wharves east of the Tower; later he transferred to Billingsgate. At this time the Quakers were no longer being persecuted and Horne was among those who were able to prosper in business. About 1724 he married Mary (*c.*1707–1782), daughter of Simeon Warner of Bermondsey, where they soon settled and raised seven children.

When the lightermen who brought the coal from ship to shore combined to demand premiums from the shipmasters, which greatly increased the price of coal to consumers, Horne and several other factors set up an office in the Dog tavern, Billingsgate, in 1728, to act as agents for the masters and evade these extra charges. Objections to the high price of coal by the principal industrial consumers—brewers, soapboilers, and dyers—led to the passing of an act in 1729 allowing any coal trader to maintain his own wharves, lighters, and other craft. This licence was of considerable benefit to such as Horne. When he gave evidence to a House of Commons inquiry in 1730 he claimed that with others he had a concern in over forty collieries to the value in 1727 of £48,262. He also held a joint interest in collieries at West Denton, Northumberland, which he leased to a local operating miner.

In 1742 the customs department uncovered a huge fraud which had continued since 1724. It transpired that shipmasters left bonds with the factors to pay the customs duty when their deliveries had been assessed, so that they were not delayed from returning north. In fact many of these duties had never been paid, the factors having retained the bonds. Horne was one of those found to be owing considerable sums, though he was able to pay when charged. Horne later retired to High Cross, Tottenham, where he died on 25 May 1766. He was interred at the Quaker burial-ground, Long Lane, Bermondsey, leaving, it was said, an estate said to be worth over £70,000 (*GM*, 439).

Horne's eldest son, Thomas (1725–1802), was apprenticed to his father's friend Caleb Smith, coal merchant of Bankside and his partner in the colliery venture. Smith was in the Clothworkers' Company and Thomas took his freedom by serviture in 1753, the first of a long line of Hornes to serve on the livery of that company; succeeding generations entered into various partnerships with other coal companies, and eventually became part of the Charrington group.   ANITA McCONNELL

Sources R. Smith, *Sea-coal for London* (1961) · E. Fraser-Stephen, *Two centuries in the London coal trade* (1952) · *The Pedigree Register*, 2 (March 1913), 363–73 · *JHC*, 21 (1727–32), 517 · *GM*, 1st ser., 36 (1766), 439

Wealth at death over £70,000

Horne, Benjamin Worthy (1804–1870), coach proprietor, was the eldest son of William Horne, and his wife, Mary. William Horne (1783–1828) was originally a painter, and entered the innkeeping and coaching trade following an advantageous marriage to Mary Worthy, daughter of a wealthy wheelwright. Subsequently, in 1812, he purchased the Golden Cross inn, Charing Cross. Other inn yards were later acquired too, as well as stables for 200 horses at Barnet. In 1819 he had about 400 horses at work, and in 1827 between 700 and 800 horses.

Benjamin Horne took over the business when his father died in 1828. In 1836 he was the second largest coach proprietor (after William Chaplin), and had ninety-five coaches, including five mail coaches, leaving London every day. Horne was an exceptionally aggressive competitor, and he generally had sufficient resources to win any contest. Harper described him as:

> a tall, lathy, irritable man, of eager face, quick, nervous speech, and rapid walk, with something of a military air in his alert, upright figure … Horne must always expend his energies on the minor details of his extensive business, and himself do work that would have been better delegated to subordinates. … Up early, no day was long enough for him, and he economised time by taking no regular meal until evening. He was generally to be seen eating his lunch out of a paper bag as he swung furiously along the streets. … Although there was no keener or more ruthless man of business … he was privately a considerate and kindly man, helpful and charitable to those less successful than himself. (Harper, 2.221–2, 225)

On 4 November 1830 he married Catherine Larkin at St Nicholas's Church, Rochester; they had at least nine children.

It was apparently his friend William Chaplin who persuaded him to adapt to the railways instead of opposing them. Certainly Horne was aware by 1835 of the probability of coach businesses being 'annihilated by steam some few years hence'. He joined with his brother Henry and William Chaplin in the firm of Chaplin and Horne, which in 1840 became carrying agent to the Grand Junction Railway (later the London and North Western Railway or LNWR), and was also active on other railways. In 1858 he described himself as the managing partner, and was constantly in and out of the LNWR yards at Euston and Camden. When the railway took in hand the goods department at Camden, citing inefficiency, he challenged the railway at law and, although he lost, was regarded as having vindicated the firm. He also continued his coaches where they could still pay their way, and, in 1843, considered himself the largest coach proprietor. He had an estate at Highlands near Mereworth, Kent, and a London residence at 33 Russell Square, and he died at the latter on 14 April 1870, aged sixty-six. He was survived by his wife.   DORIAN GERHOLD

Sources C. G. Harper, *Stage-coach and mail in days of yore*, 2 (1903), 210–25 · 'Select committee … on the turnpike roads and highways', *Parl. papers* (1819), 5.352–3, no. 509 · 'Commissioners of inquiry into … mail coach contracts', *Parl. papers* (1835), 48.435–9, 457–61, no. 313 · will, 1870 · *IGI* · Lords evidence on Northampton and Peterborough Railway Bill, HLRO, 1843, vol. 2, 17 June, 217 · Commons evidence, HLRO, 1858, vol. 45, 4 May, 1 · G. L. Turnbull, *Traffic and transport: an economic history of Pickfords* (1979), 110, 120, 130–32 · *Robson's London Directory* (1836) · will of William Horne, PRO, PROB 11/1745, 303 · d. cert.

Likenesses photograph, repro. in Harper, *Stage-coach and mail*, 221

Wealth at death under £120,000: probate, 7 May 1870, *CGPLA Eng. & Wales*

Horne, Donald (1787–1870), lawyer and political agent, was born on 20 May 1787 at Stanstill in Caithness, the second son of John Horne (*c*.1753–1823), of Stirkoke. If, as is likely, he was the Donald Horne baptized at Halkirk, Caithness, on 26 May, his mother was named Elizabeth Williamson. He was educated in Musselburgh and at Edinburgh University, and was admitted writer to the signet on 6 July 1813, after serving an apprenticeship to his uncle, James Horne of Langwell, also writer to the signet. He became his uncle's partner and a prominent figure in the legal fraternity. In April 1821 Scott's biographer, John Gibson Lockhart, wrote to his wife while on circuit from Edinburgh that he was on his way to Inverness to 'rejoin the great Donald Horne' (Lochead, 86). On 28 May 1821 Horne married Jane (1797/8–1834), daughter of Thomas Elliot Ogilvie of Chesters in Roxburghshire, whose family had close associations with the dukes of Buccleuch. They had several children. She died aged thirty-six on 30 May 1834 shortly after giving birth to a stillborn son. General Henry Sinclair *Horne, Baron Horne (1861–1929), was their grandson.

Horne was for several years in the 1820s solicitor for the excise but was disappointed in his hopes of becoming crown agent in 1828. He also engaged in a variety of other activities: in 1822 he was one of the original partners of the Australia Company of Edinburgh and Leith; in 1831 he was listed as a director of the Edinburgh and Leith Glass Company; he served in the Edinburgh squadron of the yeomanry cavalry from 1822 to 1845; and in 1825 was master of the Caledonian masonic lodge (Macmillan, 374, 393; Tancred, 262). When his uncle died in 1831 Horne inherited the Langwell estate near Berriedale in Caithness, which James Horne had purchased from Sir John Sinclair in 1813 for £40,000. Langwell was famous for its sheep and Horne became a director of the Highland and Agricultural Society. He sold the estate to the fifth duke of Portland in 1857 for £90,000 (Groome, 4.466; Tancred, 262–3).

After the passing of the Scottish Reform Act in 1832 Horne applied his considerable energies to Conservative politics in several counties from the borders to his native Caithness. He was among the first to recognize that weaknesses in the drafting of the act could be turned to advantage. In March 1833, only weeks after the general election at which the tory party was defeated in most Scottish counties, Horne wrote a 'Memorandum for the private consideration of those principally concerned in maintaining the conservative interest in the county of Midlothian' (Brash, 6–8). He argued that by purchasing properties and making votes the tories could regain the county 'notwithstanding of the Reform Bill'. Subsequently Horne was responsible for complex transactions by which, in counties such as Roxburgh and Selkirk, votes of questionable validity were prepared for the annual registration of electors, often in the form of multiple joint-qualifications on a single property. Horne's expert knowledge of these practices led to his appearance as a principal witness before the select committee on fictitious votes (Scotland) in 1837–8.

Horne acted as a political agent for the fifth duke of Buccleuch, who on account of his extensive landholdings and great wealth was regarded by many Conservatives in south-eastern Scotland as their natural leader and a fruitful source of electoral funding. Between 1834 and 1840 Horne compiled for the duke increasingly comprehensive surveys of Conservative election prospects in the Scottish counties and burghs (Brash, 220–78). It seems probable that some of Horne's information was passed to Francis Bonham, the Conservative Party's political secretary at the Carlton Club. Horne himself was considered sufficiently important to be elected a member of the Carlton in 1838. He handled a great part of the money the duke of Buccleuch and others invested in electoral politics in the 1830s, but by the early 1840s, even though the Conservatives had regained the majority of Scottish counties, the duke was increasingly impatient with what he saw as Horne's extravagance and delay in accounting for his expenditure. Horne ceased to be his agent in 1842 and took no further part in electoral politics, though he continued to pursue his professional career. From 1845 he was the legal agent in Edinburgh for the British Fisheries Society, a position in which he took an increasingly influential

role (Dunlop, 169–70). He was also solicitor in Scotland for the commissioners of woods and forests from 1843 to 1865, after which he retired owing to failing health.

Horne died on 23 June 1870 at his home, 10 Atholl Crescent, Edinburgh, and was buried in St John's Episcopal churchyard. George Tancred wrote of him:

[he] was a man of no ordinary stamp. He had unbounded energy and extraordinary mental vigour. He possessed a peculiar faculty of extracting information from those with whom he conversed, even when there might be an unwillingness to communicate it. (Tancred, 26)

J. I. BRASH

Sources J. I. Brash, ed., *Papers on Scottish electoral politics, 1832–1854*, Scottish History Society, 4th ser., 11 (1974) · G. Tancred, *The annals of a Border club* (1899) · [F. J. Grant], *A history of the Society of Writers to Her Majesty's Signet* (1890) · NA Scot., Buccleuch MSS, GD 224 · 'Select committee on the registering of fictitious votes in Scotland', *Parl. papers* (1837), vol. 12, no. 215; (1837–8), vol. 14, no. 590 · M. Lochead, *John Gibson Lockhart* (1954) · D. S. Macmillan, *Scotland and Australia, 1788–1850* (1967) · J. Dunlop, *The British Fisheries Society, 1786–1893* (1978) · F. H. Groome, ed., *Ordnance gazetteer of Scotland*, new edn, 6 vols. (1894–5) · *IGI* · gravestone, St John's Episcopal churchyard, Edinburgh · d. cert.
Archives NA Scot., Buccleuch MSS, GD 224
Wealth at death £47,825 16s. 1d.: confirmation, 7 Sept 1870, NA Scot., SC 70/1/149/756–765

Horne, George (1730–1792), bishop of Norwich, was born at Otham, near Maidstone, on 1 November 1730, the eldest surviving son of the Revd Samuel Horne (*c*.1693–1768), rector of the parish, and Anne, the youngest daughter of Bowyer Handley (*d*. 1787). He received his early education from his father, and was then sent for two years to Maidstone School. He won a 'Maidstone scholarship' at University College, Oxford, whence he matriculated on 17 March 1746. Among his undergraduate contemporaries were Charles Jenkinson, later first earl of Liverpool, and William Jones, his future chaplain and biographer. Horne graduated BA in October 1749, and was elected to a Kentish fellowship at Magdalen College in 1750. He graduated MA in 1752, and was ordained by the bishop of Oxford in 1753.

Horne pursued an academic career in the university for the next three decades; he was junior proctor in 1758, was awarded the DD in 1764, and was elected president of Magdalen College by a convincing majority in 1768. He married, on 12 June that same year, Felicia (*bap*. 1741), the daughter of Philip and Felicia Burton of Eltham, Kent. They had three daughters. With his girls Horne could be a playful and amusing father, and his satisfying family life was a constant source of relief from his public career.

Apart from his work in the university, Horne made no less a mark as a controversialist against a number of varied antagonists including William Law, David Hume, and Adam Smith. He started by helping his lifelong friend William Jones produce an *Answer to Dr. Clayton's Essay on Spirit* in 1752. The tract had a Trinitarian emphasis that was a recurrent theme in most of Horne's writings; the three-person Godhead was, he opined, 'the root of the Xtn Religion' (Magdalen College, MS 449, fol. 10, commonplace book, *c*.1755). Guided by his tutors, George Watson and Benjamin Holloway, and encouraged by Jones, Horne

George Horne (1730–1792), by unknown artist, 1790–92

became an apologist in the 1750s for the physico-theological writings of John Hutchinson in which he found a scriptural emphasis that had no equivalent for him in Newtonian science. He published anonymously *A Fair, Candid, and Impartial Statement of the Case between Sir Isaac Newton and Mr Hutchinson* (1753), attempting to show that the work of both men could be reconciled. When the 'Hutchinsonians' in the university were attacked for their ungenerous attitudes towards their opponents in an anonymous pamphlet called *A Word to the Hutchinsonians*, Horne replied with *An Apology for Certain Gentlemen in the University of Oxford, Aspersed in a Late Anonymous Pamphlet* (1756). While Horne disagreed with Hutchinson's more fanciful interpretations of Hebrew etymology, he was concerned at the plan of Benjamin Kennicott and some of his friends to collate the Hebrew Bible on the basis of an extended range of manuscript sources so as to reform the text and prepare it for a new translation into the English language. Horne produced *A View of Mr Kennicott's Method of Correcting the Hebrew Text* in 1760 to voice these concerns, but it did not prevent the two men from living in Oxford on amicable terms. Horne preserved an essentially typo-logical view of the Bible throughout his life, insisting that 'the Scripture allegories are … equally true in the letter and in the spirit of them' (*A Commentary on the Book of Psalms*, 2 vols., 1776, 1.xxxvii).

Horne combined his Hutchinsonianism with a high-churchmanship that drew inspiration from late Stuart times and the nonjurors in particular. Along with other contemporaries such as Samuel Horsley, he reinvigorated the Caroline theologico-political tradition. He constantly insisted that whereas governors should not abuse power,

subjects should obey, for rebellion was a greater offence than bad government (see sermon xvi, 'Submission to government', *Discourses on Several Subjects and Occasions*, 1793–4, vol. 4). Horne particularly appreciated the polemical writings of Charles Leslie on which, to begin with at least, he modelled his own. Leslie's *Freeholder* inspired Horne's own journalistic efforts early in his career under the pseudonym Nathaniel Freebody in the *General Evening Post*, *St James's Chronicle*, and elsewhere. He also responded to the piety and orthodoxy found in William Law's earlier writings, and was upset to find him in old age attracted by Behmenism, 'falling from the heaven of Christianity into the sink and complication of Paganism, Quakerism, and Socinianism, mixed up with chemistry and astrology by a possessed cobbler' (Jones, 1.cxxxv). Horne accordingly issued *Cautions to the readers of Mr. Law, and, with very few varieties, to the readers of Baron Swedenborg* (1758), to which was added *A Letter to a Lady on the Subject of Jacob Behmen's Writings*. Horne's early Hutchinsonianism had something in common with Methodism in its insistence on spiritual religion and its high regard for scripture, and he disapproved of the expulsion of the six Methodist students from St Edmund Hall, Oxford. He had his differences with John Wesley but, when bishop of Norwich, raised no objection when the Methodist leader requested permission to preach in his diocese.

Horne's Oxford career reached its height in the 1770s and he was vice-chancellor of the university from 1776 until 1780. Despite his official duties Horne continued to defend the church establishment and orthodox tenets from being undermined, taking a leading role in obstructing reformers during the attempts of 1772–3 to place subscription on a more modern basis, including the proposed abolition of the matriculation oath of adherence to the Thirty-Nine Articles. His supposedly anonymous *Letter to the Rt. Hon. Lord North* as chancellor of the university, urging him to defend the established church—'the public subject of daily, blasphemous invective' (6)—was both popular and effective. Influenced by James Beattie's *Essay on the Nature and Immutability of Truth* (1770), in 1777 he issued the anonymous *Letter to Dr. Adam Smith LL.D … by one of the People called Christians*, a witty and acerbic attempt at turning on its head Smith's account (in a letter to the printer William Strahan) of David Hume's virtuous life and death, with Horne presenting Hume as a man 'possessed with an incurable antipathy to all that is called RELIGION' (p. 10). Horne's reputation as a preacher, convinced monarchist, and defender of religious orthodoxy did not go unnoticed at court and he was chaplain in ordinary to George III from 1771 to 1781. North's dual position as premier and chancellor of Oxford enhanced Horne's patronage prospects further, especially after his sermon before the House of Commons at St Margaret's, Westminster, for the fast day of 3 February 1780. After some delay, in September 1781 he was awarded the deanery of Canterbury in his home county.

Horne retained the presidency of Magdalen after appointment to the deanery and spent much time riding between Oxford and Canterbury. As dean he took a keen interest in the management of the cathedral and its music (a new organ was built), preached on behalf of several charitable societies, and became a public advocate of Sunday schools. His polemical output also continued, with *Letters on Infidelity* (1784), addressed to 'W. S. Esqr.', his cousin and friend, William Stevens, the treasurer of Queen Anne's Bounty. The letters had a range of targets including Hume, Voltaire, and d'Alembert, and were written in a sprightly style intended for a general audience. His greatest concern in this decade was the threat posed to orthodoxy by the dissemination of Socinianism by Joseph Priestley and his allies. Horne was vehemently opposed to Priestley's attacks on Christian orthodoxy and the Anglican establishment (especially his direct efforts to reach a student audience with *Letters to the young men who are in a course of education for the Christian ministry at the universities of Oxford and Cambridge*) and rushed out *A Letter to the Reverend Doctor Priestley, by an Undergraduate* (1787) as a response castigating Priestley's errors—'You have now outstripped Socinus and all his followers' (4)—and wittily restating the case for Nicene Christianity with more than a touch of the *faux-naif*. It followed on from his two important sermons in Canterbury Cathedral in 1786, the first preached on Trinity Sunday, the second the following Sunday at the archbishop's primary visitation, similarly reasserting Trinitarian doctrines and characterizing the church's adversaries as 'shrewd, active, busy, bustling, and indefatigable' ('The duty of contending for the faith', *Sixteen Sermons on Various Subjects and Occasions*, 1793, 393). Horne contemplated a more extended defence of Christ's divinity against the Unitarians which was barely started on his death. Another project left uncompleted was a reply to Edward Gibbon. Horne was an avid reader of the *Decline and Fall*. Though he admired Gibbon's diligence and the breadth of his scholarship, Horne found wearisome Gibbon's 'covert way of sneering at Jewish & Xtian institutions under cover of heathen' (CUL, Add. MS 8134, B(1), 317).

Horne's health collapsed in the late 1780s just as his name was being associated with a number of vacant bishoprics. In February 1790, after much hesitation on his part, he was offered and accepted Norwich (consecrated 6 June), and resigned the presidency of Magdalen the following April. He was able to accomplish little during what proved to be an eighteen-month episcopate: 'Taking my seat in the House of Lords when I should be taking my rest in the grave' (CUL, Add. MS 8134, A/6), was his melancholy note to himself. Yet he placed his influence in the upper house behind the cause of the Scottish nonjuring bishops to whom he had first been introduced when they came south in 1789 to petition parliament (unsuccessfully) for relief from the legal penalties still incurred by their church. Horne's health did not improve at Norwich, and he barely had time to write a *Charge* (1791), addressed to his diocesan clergy. It contains the best summary of his mature beliefs against the background of the French Revolution, and he remained adamant that 'true religion and true learning were never yet at variance' (p. 7). He suffered a paralytic stroke on a journey to Bath from which he

never fully recovered. He died there on 17 January 1792, and was buried in the Burton family vault in Eltham churchyard. His wife survived him. There is a marble tablet to his memory on a pillar on the north side of the choir of Norwich Cathedral.

Horne was renowned as a preacher, and his earnest but entertaining sermons were in print throughout his lifetime. Among the public at large he was perhaps best known for his *Commentary on the Book of Psalms* (1776), a book which was nearly twenty years in preparation, and showed up what his friend and admirer, Hannah More (Horne's youngest daughter, Sally, attended the Mores' school near Bristol), called his 'sweet and devout spirit' (More, 2.407). It is partly devotional and partly exegetical, working on the principle that the psalms cannot be understood except in relation to Messianic prophecies and their fulfilment. His stress on revelation rather than natural religion was a constant feature of his theology here as elsewhere. His high-churchmanship, with no doubts about the validity of confession, prayers for the dead, and the honouring of saints, provides an important link between the nonjurors and the Oxford Movement. Though constantly aware of what there remained to do— 'The enemies of Religion are awake, let not her friends sleep', he implored (*A Letter to Adam Smith*, 1777, ii)—he sought out a wide audience and was one of the most resourceful and respected polemicists for Christian orthodoxy of his day: 'Best way to be civil and courteous,' he wrote, 'but nothing further' (CUL, Add. MS 8134, B(7), commonplace book, p. 18, 4 Jan 1788). He never produced the systematic work of theology long expected of him and he was not in the first flight as a philosopher, as his critique of Hume's *Dialogues Concerning Natural Religion* in the *Letters on Infidelity* reveals. Nevertheless his taste for paradox, irony, and the *reductio ad absurdum* made him a feared opponent, just as his combination of 'a playful fancy with a serious heart' (CUL, Add. MS 8134, N8, 'Character of the late bishop of Norwich by Samuel Parr') made him a delightful friend. He was slightly above average height. 'His countenance was remarkably expressive, and bespoke the sweetness of his temper' (Todd, 254).   NIGEL ASTON

Sources *Memoirs of the life, studies and writings of … George Horne*, ed. W. Jones, 2nd edn, 6 vols. (1799) · Foster, *Alum. Oxon.* · *Fasti Angl.* (Hardy), 1.34; 3.499, 563 · E. Hasted, *The history and topographical survey of the county of Kent*, 2nd edn, 5 (1798), 517, 519 · H. J. Todd, *Some account of the deans of Canterbury* (1793) · J. M. Cooper, *The lives of the deans of Canterbury, 1541–1900* (1900) · H. More, *Memoirs*, ed. W. Roberts, 4 vols. (1834) · N. Aston, 'Horne and heterodoxy: the defence of Anglican beliefs in the late Enlightenment', *EngHR*, 108 (1993), 895–919 · N. Aston, 'Infidelities ancient and modern: George Horne reads Edward Gibbon', *Albion*, 27 (1995), 561–82 · N. Aston, 'The dean of Canterbury and the sage of Ferney: George Horne looks at Voltaire', *Crown and Mitre*, ed. N. Yates and W. Jacob (1993) · A. Robinson, 'George Horne, bishop of Norwich and president of Magdalen', *Magdalen College Record* (1987), 40–46 · J. Gregory, 'Canterbury and the ancien régime: the dean and chapter, 1660–1828', *A history of Canterbury Cathedral, 598–1982*, ed. P. Collinson and others (1995), 204–55 · N. Aston, 'George Horne, bishop of Norwich, 1790–92', *Norfolk Archaeology*, 42 (1994–7), 283–95 · J. V. P. [J. V. Price], 'Horne, George', *The dictionary of eighteenth-century British philosophers*, ed. J. W. Yolton, J. V. Price, and J. Stephens (1999) · C. B. Wilde, 'Hutchinsonianism, natural philosophy and religious controversy in eighteenth-century Britain', *History of Science*, 18 (1980), 1–24 · C. D. A. Leighton, 'Hutchinsonianism: a counter-Enlightenment reform movement', *Journal of Religious History*, 23 (1999), 168–84 · J. C. D. Clark, *English society, 1688–1832: ideology, social structure and political practice during the ancien régime* (1985) · W. R. Ward, *Georgian Oxford: university politics in the eighteenth century* (1958) · B. W. Young, *Religion and Enlightenment in eighteenth-century England: theological debate from Locke to Burke* (1998) · P. B. Nockles, *The Oxford Movement in context: Anglican high churchmanship, 1760–1857* (1994) · G. Horne, commonplace book, Magd. Oxf., MS 449 · CUL, Add. MS 8134

Archives CUL, corresp. and papers · Magd. Oxf., corresp. and papers | BL, letters to George Berkeley, Add. MSS 39311–39312 · BL, letters to Charles Poyntz · LPL, Moore MSS

Likenesses oils, 1790–92, Canterbury Cathedral, deanery [*see illus.*] · T. Olive, oils, 1792, Magd. Oxf. · T. Olive?, portrait, University College, Oxford

Horne, Henry Sinclair, Baron Horne (1861–1929), army officer, the third son of Major James Horne (1822–1872) of Stirkoke, and his wife, Constance Mary (*d*. 1908), daughter of Edward Warner of Cheltenham, was born at Stirkoke on 19 February 1861. He was educated at Harrow School (1874–6) and at the Royal Military Academy, Woolwich (1878–80), from which, in May 1880, he received a commission in the Royal Artillery. He was at first posted to the garrison artillery, from which in 1883 he was transferred to the mounted branch, and after serving as adjutant of artillery brigades in both branches, he was promoted captain in 1888. In September 1890 he was appointed staff captain, Royal Artillery, at Meerut, and two years later he became adjutant of the Royal Horse Artillery (RHA) at Kirkee. He returned to England in 1896 and was soon afterwards posted to J battery, RHA, with which he remained until he was promoted major in 1898. On 1 July 1897 he married Kate, daughter of George McCorquodale of Newton-le-Willows, Lancashire, and widow of William John Sinclair Blacklock. They had a daughter, also Kate.

On the outbreak of the Second South African War in 1899 Horne was given command of an ammunition column and landed in Natal on 15 November of that year; soon afterwards he moved to Cape Colony in order to join the cavalry division under Major-General (later Sir) John French. With the cavalry division Horne took part in the operations which resulted in the relief of Kimberley (15 February 1900), the occupation of Bloemfontein (13 March), and in the advance from Bloemfontein into the Transvaal. In May 1900 he was given command of R battery, RHA, which was attached to French's 3rd cavalry brigade, and with that battery he took part in the occupation of Johannesburg (31 May), the battle of Diamond Hill (11–12 June), and the operations in the Wittebergen, which resulted in the surrender of General M. Prinsloo (25–9 July). From that time until the end of 1901 Horne was employed with mounted columns in the Orange River Colony and Cape Colony, and from January 1902 he was in command of remount depots. For his services he was mentioned in dispatches and received the brevet of lieutenant-colonel and the queen's medal with five clasps, and the king's medal with two clasps.

After three years in charge of the artillery depot at Weedon, Horne was promoted regimental lieutenant-

Henry Sinclair Horne, Baron Horne (1861–1929), by John Singer Sargent, *c*.1922

colonel in November 1905, and was given successively the command of field artillery and horse artillery brigades in Ireland. He was gazetted brevet colonel in May 1906, and in the following September was appointed staff officer for horse and field artillery at Aldershot. In May 1912 he was appointed inspector of horse and field artillery with the rank of brigadier-general, and on the outbreak of the First World War in August 1914 he went to France as brigadier-general commanding the Royal Artillery (BGRA), 1st corps, under Sir Douglas Haig.

At the beginning of the retreat from Mons (24 August 1914) Horne was appointed by Haig to command his rearguard. He rendered conspicuous service throughout the retreat, in the battle of the Marne (5–9 September), the battle of the Aisne (12–15 September), and in the first battle of Ypres (19 October – 22 November). In October he was promoted major-general as a reward for distinguished service in the field, and at the end of the year he was made CB. In January 1915 Horne was placed in command of the 2nd division of the 1st corps, and he led it in the operations about Givenchy in March 1915, in the battle of Festubert (15–25 May), and in the battle of Loos (25 September – 8 October). It was on his suggestion that as a result of experience gained at Festubert the system of command of the artillery was changed.

In November 1915 Horne was chosen by Lord Kitchener to accompany him to the Dardanelles, when the question of the evacuation of the Gallipoli peninsula was at issue. After the evacuation had been successfully carried out he was again employed by Lord Kitchener to devise a scheme for the defence of the Suez Canal, and when that task was completed he was given command in January 1916, with the temporary rank of lieutenant-general, of the new 15th corps in the northern sector of the canal defences. In March 1916 the 15th corps was moved to France, where it joined the Fourth Army, commanded by Sir Henry Rawlinson, which was preparing for the battle of the Somme (1 July – 30 September). The chief achievements of Horne's corps in that battle were the capture of Fricourt (2 July) and of Flers (15 September) which saw the first use of tanks. In September he was created KCB, and after the capture of Flers he was promoted commander of the First Army with the temporary rank of general.

As part of the campaign designed by General Nivelle, the commander-in-chief of the French armies, for the spring of 1917, the British army undertook the battle of Arras, in which the most important share, the assault on the Vimy Ridge, fell to the First Army. General Nivelle's staff was sceptical of a British success and openly critical of Horne's plans. Horne was also hampered at this critical time by the pain from a broken bone in his leg caused by a fall from his horse, but he overcame these difficulties and stuck to his plans, and the capture of the Vimy Ridge (9–10 April), in which the Canadian corps took the chief part, was the outstanding success won by the British army up to that time in the war. Owing to the failure of Nivelle's attack the operations on the Arras front had to be continued well into May, several weeks beyond the period which had been proposed. Thereafter Haig began to transfer troops to his northern flank in preparation for the battles of Messines and Passchendaele, and the role of the First Army became one of attracting the attention of the Germans to itself with reduced troop levels, a part which Horne skilfully played until October 1917, when the Canadian corps was taken from him for the battle of Passchendaele.

The winter of 1917–18 was devoted to preparations for meeting the great German attack expected in the spring. The brunt of the German effort fell on the armies further south, but on 28 March a heavy German attack was made on the Vimy Ridge and successfully beaten off. On 9 April another German attack on the Lys front fell on the Portuguese divisions attached to Horne's army, just at the time when arrangements for the relief of those divisions had been completed. The Germans broke through, and the situation again became highly critical, but the resolute stand of the 55th division of the First Army at Givenchy saved the Vimy Ridge, and Horne was the only British army commander who was not forced by the German offensive to move his headquarters to the rear.

After May 1918 the German efforts were directed against the French, and the First Army was given a breathing space in which to recover and prepare for attack in its turn. After Rawlinson's victory at Amiens on 8 August, the Germans began to withdraw from the great salient which they had created in the north in the spring, and towards the end of August the First Army began an advance which was to be continuous until the signing of the Armistice on 11 November. On 2 September Horne's army, in co-operation with the Third Army on its right, broke through the Drocourt–Quéant section of the Hindenburg line. This success was followed on 27 September by the forcing of the Canal du Nord. Then in swift succession Lens (3 October), Douai (17 October), and Valenciennes (2 November) were captured, and the advance of the First Army ended with the occupation of Mons two and a half hours before the Armistice became effective.

Horne was promoted substantive lieutenant-general in 1917, and substantive general in 1919. He was created KCMG in 1918 and GCB in 1919. For his services in the war he received the thanks of both houses of parliament, was raised to the peerage as Baron Horne of Stirkoke, and given a grant of £30,000. He also received many foreign decorations, including the Légion d'honneur. The University of Oxford conferred on him the honorary degree of DCL, the universities of Cambridge and Edinburgh that of LLD, and the borough of Northampton made him a freeman. In 1918 he was made colonel commandant of the Royal Artillery.

Soon after his return to England Horne was appointed general officer commanding-in-chief, eastern command, in which capacity he was actively concerned with the problems of demobilization and of the reorganization of the army. In 1920 he was appointed aide-de-camp general to George V. After refusing offers of governorships abroad, he retired from the army in May 1926, and in the same month he was appointed master gunner, St James's Park. He interested himself actively in service charities, particularly those of the Royal Artillery, the British Legion, and the National Association for the Employment of Soldiers, Sailors, and Airmen. He became governor and commandant of the Church Lads' Brigade, and took a prominent part in the affairs of his county, Caithness, of which he was deputy lieutenant. In 1929 he was made colonel of the Highland light infantry, in which his father had served. He died suddenly while shooting on his estate at Stirkoke on 14 August 1929, and was buried at Wick, Caithness. His peerage became extinct. After his death his tenants, on their own initiative, railed off the place on Stirkoke Moor where he died and planted the area with flowers.

Horne's career closely followed that of Douglas Haig, with whose views he usually concurred. Haig's influence runs like a motif through Horne's wartime career. Horne began the war as BGRA to Haig's 1st corps. He was given command of 2nd division, in January 1915, shortly after Haig's promotion from general officer commanding 1st corps (in which 2nd division served) to general officer commanding First Army. Promotion to the command of 15th corps, in January 1916, followed shortly after Haig succeeded French as commander-in-chief. Horne's final promotion, in September 1916, was to Haig's former command at the First Army. Horne was a conscientious and practical professional of limited vision. He understood the importance of administration and was meticulous in his preparations. He was fortunate in often having under his command the excellent Canadian corps, though his handling of it was exemplary. He was also fortunate in his subordinates, especially his innovative artillery commander, Major-General E. W. Alexander VC, who served with him at 15th corps and First Army, and his chief of staff at First Army, Major-General Sir Hastings Anderson. Horne was a handsome man of soldierly bearing, with a strong face which increasingly displayed evidence of the strains of command. His intellect was commonplace—Liddell Hart thought him stupid—but he possessed unusual determination, a high sense of duty, and uncompromising integrity. Iron self-control allowed him to overcome a tense, highly-strung temperament which made sleep difficult, and a physical constitution which was never robust. F. B. MAURICE, *rev.* J. M. BOURNE

Sources J. E. Edmonds, ed., *Military operations, France and Belgium*, 14 vols., History of the Great War (1922–48) · H. Uniacke and H. Anderson, *General the Lord Horne of Stirkoke* [n.d.] · *The private papers of Douglas Haig, 1914–1919*, ed. R. Blake (1952) · [H. Uniacke], 'General the Lord Horne', *Army Quarterly*, 19/1 (Oct 1929) · Lord Horne [H. S. Horne], *Reminiscences of the South African War* (1900) · H. Anderson, 'Lord Horne as an army commander', *Journal of the Royal Artillery*, 56 (1930), 407–18 · GEC, *Peerage* · *CGPLA Eng. & Wales* (1929)

Archives IWM, corresp., orders, etc. | FILM IWM FVA, actuality footage · IWM FVA, documentary footage · IWM FVA, news footage | SOUND IWM SA, oral history interview

Likenesses J. H. Lander, oils, *c.*1908, Stirkoke House, Wick, Caithness · F. Dodd, charcoal and watercolour drawing, 1917, IWM · W. Stoneman, photograph, 1917, NPG · J. S. Sargent, group portrait, oils, 1922 (*General officers of World War I*), NPG · J. S. Sargent, oils, *c.*1922, Scot. NPG [*see illus.*] · photograph, 1929, repro. in *The Times* (15 Aug 1929), 12 · O. Birley, oils, Stirkoke House, Wick, Caithness · O. Birley, oils, Royal Artillery Institution, Woolwich, London · O. Birley, oils, Harrow School War Museum, Middlesex · J. S. Sargent, group portrait, oil study (*General officers of World War I*), NPG · photograph, repro. in E. Wyrall, *The history of the second division*, 2 vols. (1921–2), vol. 1, p. 174

Wealth at death £13,820 7*s.* 9*d.* effects in England: probate, 3 Dec 1929, *CGPLA Eng. & Wales*

Horne, Herbert Percy (1864–1916), architect, art collector, and art historian, was born at 10 Russell Square, London, on 18 February 1864, the son of Horace Horne (*d.* 1894), architect, and his wife, Hannah Louisa Gibson (*d.* 1903). After attending Miss Moore's day school in Hereford Square and Kensington grammar school, he was articled to the London architect George Vigers.

In the early 1880s Horne began working for A. H. Mackmurdo, a very intellectual architect with strong social concerns, and in the mid-1880s they went into partnership. Thus he was probably involved from the start with the Century Guild, a loose association of architects, designers, and craftsmen set up by Mackmurdo about 1882; the artist Selwyn Image was also involved. The guild proposed to make architecture and the decorative arts 'the sphere, no longer of the tradesman, but, of the artist' (Century Guild prospectus, William Morris Gallery, K339). This was the language of William Morris and the arts and crafts movement, and Horne owed some allegiance to Morris at this stage. But he had probably already read Walter Pater's *Studies in the History of the Renaissance*, and discovered a less social, more exclusively aesthetic philosophy.

Horne made important designs for textiles and wall-coverings for the Century Guild, but the work with which his name was most closely associated was the editing of the *Century Guild Hobby Horse* which he shared with Mackmurdo. This finely printed quarterly magazine of art and literature ran, with gaps and a change of title, from 1884 to 1894. Its layout, from the issue of January 1888 onwards, was something of a milestone in British graphic design, presenting type, paper, and illustrations as a coherent whole. Horne, along with the engraver Emery Walker, may have been responsible for this. In the *Hobby Horse* he published lyric poems in which the imagery is both religious and sensuous, and thoughtful, discriminating essays which manage to embrace both the rational disciplines of English classical architecture and the visionary work of William Blake. The seventeenth century was his ideal moment in English culture, Robert Herrick and Inigo Jones his heroes. Meeting him in 1888, Bernard Berenson admired the range of Horne's talents and thought he might become William Morris's successor, 'the great man of the next generation' (E. Samuels, *Bernard Berenson*, 1979, 62).

This was Horne by day. By night he could be found in the saloon bar of The Crown in Charing Cross Road, with Lionel Johnson, Ernest Dowson, and Arthur Symons, Bohemian poets and littérateurs, or lecturing on art to the people of the East End, or escorting young dancers from the music-hall with Stewart Headlam and Selwyn Image. Headlam and Image were engaged in a peculiar Christian crusade against puritanism; Horne was perhaps naturally at home in the *demi-monde*. He seems to have lived with his parents, from about 1880 in Bedford Park in west London, and later at 14 Cheyne Walk, Chelsea; but in the 1890s he also had chambers in King's Bench Walk, Temple, with Chippendale furniture and chiaroscuro woodcuts after Raphael and Mantegna, an aesthete's retreat. He had many mistresses during his life, but no lasting relationship, and he was, perhaps, bisexual. Dark, reticent, worldly-looking, with pale skin and disturbingly red lips, he appears in memoirs of the nineties as a figure of more weight than warmth. To Arthur Symons and Edgar Jepson he seemed cold and self-restrained; William Rothenstein noted his secretiveness. But W. B. Yeats praised his knowledge and taste; and both Arnold Dolmetsch, the pioneer of the revival of early music, and the artist Lucien Pissarro—Frenchmen struggling to establish themselves in London—had reason to be grateful to Horne for his early support.

The partnership with Mackmurdo was dissolved about 1892, and most of Horne's work as an architect and designer did not extend beyond the middle of the 1890s. In the early 1890s he designed several books which combine elegance with self-conscious archaism. His most substantial building was the Chapel of the Ascension in Hyde Park Place, Bayswater Road, London, designed in 1889–90 along loosely quattrocento lines to provide wall space for the fervently evangelical paintings of Frederic Shields. (The chapel was bombed in 1940 and demolished in 1969.) These were years of transition; Horne was moving away from architecture and design towards critical writing, art-historical scholarship, and collecting and dealing in art. His imagination now dwelt more readily in fifteenth-century Italy than in seventeenth-century England. And he was seen less often in The Crown. If he made new friends, they were critics and dealers in art such as Roger Fry and Bernard Berenson. About 1894 he was asked by the publishers George Bell & Sons to write a short book on Botticelli in a popular series. He decided instead to write a long and definitive book, and as a result began to spend part of the year in Florence.

The pull of Florence was strong. Art history took more of Horne's time in the early 1900s, and about 1904 he sold his English watercolours, including an important collection of the work of Alexander Cozens, to Edward Marsh, and moved permanently to Florence. In 1908 George Bell & Sons published his *Alessandro Filipepi Commonly called Sandro Botticelli, Painter of Florence* in a small edition of 240 copies. It was a big, expensive book, designed by Horne with all the old, mannered elegance of the *Hobby Horse*, a narrative of Botticelli's life and work studded with lyrical descriptions of the major paintings. Like Fry, Horne was concerned with formal qualities, but also with attribution, studying characteristic details in the manner of Berenson and Giovanni Morelli. What distinguished Horne's work was the thoroughness of his archival research and the severely factual nature of his narrative. '"What is it that we really know?" is the question always in Mr. Horne's mind' wrote Roger Fry in a review (*Burlington Magazine*, 13, 1908, 84). Though it was written about a hundred years ago, when English art-historical scholarship was not even in its infancy, the book survives today as one of the standard works on Botticelli, challenged only in details by subsequent research, though not always studied at first hand. For John Pope-Hennessy it was 'the best monograph in English on an Italian painter' (Pope-Hennessy, ix), while Fritz Saxl, lecturing in London in 1944—before the rise of Anthony Blunt—described Horne as 'the most accomplished historian of art whom this country has ever produced' (Saxl, 332).

Saxl spoke movingly of the passage in Horne's life from London to Florence, from a connoisseur in the mould of Walter Pater to an art historian devoted to archival research, but he suggested perhaps too movingly the single-mindedness of Horne's new life: 'Day after day he would go to the archives' (Saxl, 335). In fact, Horne lived much the same life in Florence as he had in London: he had his mistresses; he did some designing, including several distinguished typefaces; and he was busier than ever collecting and dealing in works of art, working in an edgy, unstable triangle with Roger Fry and Bernard Berenson, easing the passage of works of art from Italy to Britain and the United States. He lived by himself in lodgings on the Lung'arno degli Archibusieri, waiting to find a fine house which he could afford to buy. Eventually, in 1911, he purchased the fifteenth-century Palazzo Corsi on the corner of the via de' Benci and set about restoring it and filling it, not only with his own important collection of works of art, but also with furniture and household objects appropriate to its date. He would create a house of the quattrocento, an interior which might embody the civilizing values of the Florentine Renaissance. It would also be the last stage in the series of transformations that were his life.

Horne did not move into the palazzo until 1915, by which time he was seriously ill and often confined to two small, plain rooms at the very top, where he was part host, part caretaker of the riches on the floors below. Aby Warburg visited him in 1915 and found him 'very ill, exceedingly noble, and divorced from everything material' (Saxl, 342). A year later, when he was clearly dying, Mary Berenson persuaded him to write a will, and he bequeathed the palazzo and its contents to the Italian state. It is now open to the public as the Museo Horne.

Horne died, unmarried, at his palazzo in Florence, on 14 April 1916. The funeral was, according to Mary Berenson, 'rather awful, the assistance being chiefly Sods (excuse the word) and dealers, … myself and one or two Museum officials of grubby aspect' (*Mary Berenson*, 208). He was buried in the Gli Allori protestant cemetery in Florence.

ALAN CRAWFORD

Sources I. Fletcher, *Rediscovering Herbert Horne: poet, architect, typographer, art historian* (1990) • L. Morrozzi, *Le carte archivistiche della Fondazione Herbert P. Horne* (1988) • L. Morrozzi, 'Horne, Herbert', *The dictionary of art*, ed. J. Turner (1996) • J. F. Codell, 'Herbert Percy Horne: the critic as artist', PhD diss., University of Indiana, 1978 • 'Letters from Herbert Horne to Roger Fry', ed. D. Sutton, *Apollo*, 122 (1985), 136–56 • F. Saxl, 'Three "Florentines": Herbert Horne, Aby Warburg, Jacques Mesnil', *Lectures*, 2 vols. (1957), 1.331–44 • S. Evans, 'Century Guild inventions: the Century Guild of Artists at the International Inventions Exhibition, London, 1885', *Journal of the Decorative Arts Society*, 21 (1997), 46–53 • P. Stansky, *Redesigning the world: William Morris, the 1880s, and the arts and crafts* (1985) • J. Pope-Hennessy, introduction, in H. P. Horne, *Botticelli: painter of Florence* (1980) • M. Campbell, *Dolmetsch: the man and his work* (1975) • *Mary Berenson: a self-portrait from her letters and diaries*, ed. B. Strachey and J. Samuels (1983); repr. (1985) • A. Symons, *The memoirs of Arthur Symons: life and art in the 1890s*, ed. K. Beckson (1977) • *The letters of Lucien to Camille Pissarro, 1883–1903*, ed. A. Thorold (1993) • b. cert. • papers relating to A. H. Mackmurdo and the Century Guild, William Morris Gallery, Walthamstow • CGPLA Eng. & Wales (1917) • DNB

Archives Museo Horne, Florence, corresp., diaries, draft writings, drawings, and research notes | Bodl. Oxf., diaries and letters of Selwyn Image, and corresp. with Robert Bridges and Bertram Dobell • Harvard University, near Florence, Italy, Center for Italian Renaissance Studies, letters to Bernard Berenson and Mary Berenson • William Morris Gallery, Walthamstow, papers relating to A. H. Mackmurdo and the Century Guild

Likenesses photograph, c.1882, William Morris Gallery, London • M. Beerbohm, caricature, c.1906, Museo Horne, Florence, Italy, Fondazione Horne • M. Harris Brown, oils, Museo Horne, Florence, Italy, Fondazione Horne • photograph, repro. in Fletcher, *Rediscovering Herbert Horne*, 1

Wealth at death £7001 0s. 4d.: administration with will, 15 March 1917, CGPLA Eng. & Wales

Horne, John (bap. 1616, d. 1676), clergyman and ejected minister, was baptized on 10 August 1616 at Long Sutton, Lincolnshire, the son of Christopher Horne. He matriculated at Trinity College, Cambridge, in 1633, graduated BA in 1637, and was ordained deacon and priest in 1639 at Peterborough. After his marriage (probably but not certainly to his wife at the time of his death, Esther (d. 1687)) and serving as preacher at Sutton St James, Lincolnshire, he moved in 1643 to All Saints, King's Lynn, where he was beneficed as rector in 1646 and ejected in 1662.

Horne went to Lynn under the aegis of its governor, Valentine Walton, Cromwell's brother-in-law, who in 1643 had bested the town's royalists. Horne's dedication in *The Open Door* (1650) acknowledged Walton's favour and that of Lynn's puritan MPs Miles Corbet and Thomas Toll. Like Horne's other works, written over a quarter of a century, *The Open Door* joyously proclaimed the possibility of universal redemption. His belief that doctrines of election and reprobation lacked biblical basis, strongly stated in *A Caveat to All True Christians* (1651), seems Arminian but did not necessarily eschew Calvin. In 1656 Horne's *Brief Instructions for Children* argued that Christ's death ransomed 'all men, none excepted' although most would be doomed for wilfully sinning 'against Christ's light and grace' (Horne, *Brief Instructions*, 21). Richard Baxter and 'Dr. Amirald', Horne contended, agreed with 'the Universality of the Grace and love of God' (ibid., title-page). Horne unsuccessfully urged the influential Baxter to publish on the subject. Baxter believed in general redemption but felt God would probably save an elect group regardless. Amirald, or Amyraldus (Moïse Amyraut; 1596–1664), professor at Saumur in France, argued that a misunderstood Calvin had seen the possibility of universal redemption although many, known to an omniscient God, would die unrepentant.

Neither Baxter nor Amyraldus was as liberal on redemption as Horne. Baxter, like John Davenant, distinguished between sufficient and efficient grace. To take advantage of the grace sufficiently given, sinful men needed the redeeming efficient grace, which God dispensed at will. Thus, Baxter's universalism was hypothetical. Horne's was not. *The Brazen Serpent* (1673) assures readers that God wants all men to have eternal life, as John 3: 14–15 asserts. To that end God sent his Son to be the medium for salvation of any and all who believe. As believers they would try to follow gospel directives like loving one's neighbour, but faith was the key. Amyraldus, too, believed that God wished men to be saved. However, he found that God created the conditions for faith in some, the elect, but not in others.

With *The Open Door* Horne had joined the national debate on redemption. This, his best-known book, responded to John Owen's attack on the universalism of Horne's associate Thomas Moore senior (1593–1672). At some point early in his ministry Horne had become linked to Moore, the universalist vicar of St Mary's, Whittlesey, Cambridgeshire. In 1654 Horne entered the debate again, digressing in *A Consideration of Infant Baptism* to deplore the Calvinist George Kendall's attack on the Arminian John Goodwin. Kendall replied vituperatively (G. Kendall, *Sancti sanciti*, 1654, 145, 155), and Goodwin in turn defended the 'godly and grave' Horne (J. Goodwin, *Triumviri*, 1658, 240).

Much about the readership of Horne, Moore, and Moore's son, Thomas junior (*d.* 1668), is unknown. However, the eastern fens held concentrations of their followers called universalists, Mooreians, revelators, or

manifestarians, presumably awaiting 'the manifestation of the children of God' (Romans 8: 19). Their universalism attracted Quaker and Baptist recruiters, engaging Horne and Moore junior from 1655 to 1660. Horne debated with the Quaker George Whitehead, posted anti-Quaker warnings, and published three anti-Quaker tracts insisting on biblical authority and on perfectibility only after death. Whitehead responded, championing the inner light and temporal perfectibility. These issues, infant baptism, and non-separation also fuelled Horne's arguments with Baptists, including Thomas Grantham.

Cited in 1661 for disregarding the prayer book, Horne refused the oath of uniformity in 1662. Ejected but tolerated, he continued to publish and to attend services at All Saints while leading about 100 universalists in his 'society', twice on Sundays and three times during the week (Turner, 1.96–7). In 1672 he and Charles Phelps were licensed as Independent teachers.

Horne

> was a man of great charity, commonly emptying his pocket of what money he had in it amongst the poor when he went into the town; giving to any such miserable object as presented, the first piece of silver that came to hand, be it what it would.   (E. Calamy, *The Nonconformist's Memorial*, 2 vols., 1775, 2.195)

His generosity was legendary in Lynn, where his son John (1643–1732) became usher (1668), then headmaster (1678–1728) of the grammar school. Horne died at King's Lynn on 14 December 1676, two years after his second son, Thomas. He was buried there in St Nicholas, as was his widow, Esther, in 1687. He also left behind two daughters, Sarah and Ann, land at Sutton and Gosberton, Lincolnshire, and a thriving universalist society under Phelps. Eventually some of these universalists left the Church of England entirely, while the church absorbed many others; Phelps's son was ordained in 1709.

SHEILA McISAAC COOPER

Sources Calamy rev. · J. Horne, *Brief instructions for children: wherein, the chief grounds of the Christian religion are plainly, though briefly, laid down, as may best sute the capacity of children though not unusefull for the view and consideration of those that are grown men*, 2nd edn (1656) · J. Horne, *Thyra aneōgmenē: the open door for Man's app[r]oach to God* (1650); reissued as *Universal redemption* (1656) · J. Horne, *A caveat to all true Christians … together with some brief directions for their orderly walkings* (1651) · D. D. Wallace, *Puritans and predestination: grace in English protestant theology, 1525–1695* (1982) · Venn, *Alum. Cant.* · G. F. Nuttall, 'John Horne of Lynn', *Christian spirituality: essays in honour of Gordon Rupp*, ed. P. Brooks (1975), 233–47 · *The Christian progress of that ancient servant and minister of Jesus Christ, George Whitehead*, ed. [J. Besse?] (1725) · G. F. Nuttall, 'Appendix: the manifestarian controversy', *Early Quaker letters from the Swarthmore manuscripts to 1660* (1952), 293–7 · B. G. Armstrong, *Calvinism and the Amyraut heresy: protestant scholasticism and humanism in seventeenth-century France* (1969) · W. M. Lamont, *Richard Baxter and the millennium: protestant imperialism and the English revolution* (1979) · I. Morgan, *The nonconformity of Richard Baxter* (1946), 77–80 · G. L. Turner, ed., *Original records of early nonconformity under persecution and indulgence*, 3 vols. (1911–14) · J. Horne, *Diatribē peri paido-baptismou, or, A consideration of infant baptism* (1654) · J. Horne, *The divine wooer, or, A poem setting forth the love and loveliness of the Lord Jesus, and his great desire of our welfare and happiness, and propounding many arguments full of weight and power to persuade souls to the faith and obedience of him; and answering divers objections that are made there-against, and that hinder many there-*

from (1673) · parish register, King's Lynn, St Nicholas, 1676 [burial] · will

Horne, John (1848–1928), geologist, was born at Campsie, Stirlingshire, on 1 January 1848, the son of a farmer, James Horne, and his wife, Janet, *née* Braid. He attended Glasgow high school and Glasgow University, where he studied under Lord Kelvin, but did not graduate. He left the university at the age of nineteen to take an appointment with the geological survey, where he spent his whole working life.

Horne's early surveying was carried out in the Silurians of the southern uplands and among the metamorphic rocks and the Old Red Sandstone country round the Moray Firth. During vacations he and other surveyors sometimes conducted independent research. For example, with his friend Benjamin Neeve *Peach, Horne worked on glacial problems in northern Scotland, and he visited the Carpathians with Robert Logan Jack. Such work could be and was published outside the official channels of the survey.

Horne's scientific partnership with Peach was one of the most successful in the annals of Scottish geology. In 1883 they were sent by the survey's director-general, Archibald Geikie, to examine the rocks of the north-west highlands, for which Geikie and Roderick Murchison had proposed a structure in the 1860s. This structure had been challenged by James Nicol, but the Murchison–Geikie view prevailed until the early 1880s when Charles Callaway and Charles Lapworth independently arrived at alternative models that were much the same. After two seasons in the field, and influenced by his findings, Peach and Horne arrived at an interpretation similar to Lapworth's, and Geikie had to make an embarrassing climb-down. The name and reputation of the survey were subsequently restored, however, by the brilliant field mapping of Peach and Horne, who worked out the complex structures in great detail. It was Horne who first changed his mind about the 'official' structure.

Peach and Horne then had to examine the rocks of the southern uplands, where the structural interpretations offered by Geikie, partly based on the fieldwork of Jack, had also been challenged by Lapworth. In the southern uplands, as in the north-west highlands, the structures were found to be much more complex than originally realized, because of repeated reverse faulting. Two large memoirs, *The Silurian Rocks of Britain*; volume 1, *Scotland* (1899) and *The Geological Structure of the North-West Highlands* (1907), gave permanent expression to the notable fieldwork of Horne and his co-workers.

In 1901 Horne was promoted to assistant director of the geological survey with responsibility for Scotland, in which position he served with distinction until his retirement in 1911. During this period much work was done on the Scottish coalfields. After retirement Horne was active in Edinburgh intellectual life, and he collaborated with Peach on a synthetic treatise on Scottish geology. Unfortunately, this was much delayed, as a result of disagreements (at the scientific level only) between the authors as to the origin of the 'Moine Schists' of northern Scotland. The work eventually appeared posthumously in 1930.

Besides tectonics, much of Horne's work was concerned with glaciation and relatively recent geological phenomena. He also published a significant paper with Edward Greenly on the metamorphic rocks of eastern Sutherland (1896).

Horne was elected FRS (1900), and received honorary degrees from Aberdeen, St Andrews, and Edinburgh. With Peach, he was awarded the Geological Society's Murchison medal (1899), and (again with Peach) the Wollaston medal (1921). Horne presided over the geological section of the British Association (1901), and was president of the Royal Society of Edinburgh (1915–19). He was married to Anna Leyland, daughter of Henry Taylor of Pernambuco, Brazil. They had two sons and a daughter. His wife died in 1926 and Horne himself died at his home, 20 Merchiston Gardens, Edinburgh, on 30 May 1928. He was buried in Edinburgh. DAVID OLDROYD

Sources J. S. F. [J. S. Flett], *PRS*, 104B (1929), i–viii · J. W. Gregory, *Quarterly Journal of the Geological Society*, 85 (1929), lx–lxii · T. J. Jehu, *Proceedings of the Royal Society of Edinburgh*, 48 (1927–8), 201–8 · E. B. Bailey, *Scottish Geographical Magazine*, 44 (1928), 226–8 · J. W. Gregory, *Nature*, 121 (1928), 991–2 · R. Campbell, 'John Horne and his contribution to geological science', *Transactions of the Edinburgh Geological Society*, 12 (1929), 267–79 [contains list of publications] · M. Macgregor, *Geological Magazine*, 65 (1928), 381–4 · 'Notable geologist: the late Dr John Horne, work for Scottish research', BGS, 1/205, fol. 38 [newspaper cutting] · 'Noted geologist. The late Dr John Horne. Loss to Scottish science', *Glasgow Herald* (31 May 1928) · D. R. Oldroyd, *The highlands controversy: constructing geological knowledge through fieldwork in nineteenth-century Britain* (1990) · E. Greenly, *A hand through time*, 2 (1938), 506–14 · *DNB*

Archives BGS · BGS, Edinburgh | BGS, letters to John Flett · BGS, letters to Finlay Kitchin · BGS, letters to Benjamin Peach · BGS, letters to Jethro Teall · Elgin Museum, letters to George Gordon

Likenesses group portrait, photograph, c.1885 (*The bandits of Inchnadamph, or, The secret of the north-west highlands*), BGS, Edinburgh, LSA 364.14 · S. H. Reynolds, double portrait, photograph (with B. N. Peach), repro. in Oldroyd, *Highlands controversy*, 272 · A. S. Watson, photograph, repro. in Jehu, 'John Horne' · group photograph (with staff), repro. in Oldroyd, *Highlands controversy*, 166 · photograph, repro. in J. S. F., *PRS*

Wealth at death £2292 3s. 11d.: confirmation, 24 July 1928, *CGPLA Eng. & Wales*

Horne, (Charles) Kenneth (1907–1969), comedian, was born on 27 February 1907 at Ampthill Square, London, the youngest in the family of three sons and four daughters of (Charles) Sylvester *Horne (1865–1914), Congregational minister, and his wife, Katharine Maria (1870–1958), daughter of Herbert Hardy Cozens-*Hardy, later first Baron Cozens-Hardy, master of the rolls. Horne was educated at St George's School, Harpenden, Hertfordshire, at the London School of Economics, and at Magdalene College, Cambridge. Though popular with contemporaries and a fine sportsman (he gained a tennis half-blue at Cambridge), he did not have a spectacular academic career, and was sent down from the university in December 1927.

Through the influence of his uncle, Austin Pilkington, a director of the Pilkington Glass Company, Horne secured a job as a progress clerk with the Triplex Safety Glass Company in 1928. On 20 September 1930 he married Lady Mary

(Charles) Kenneth Horne (1907–1969), by Lewis Morley, 1960s

Pelham-Clinton-Hope (*b.* 1910), second daughter of the eighth duke of Newcastle, but the marriage was annulled in 1933. On 5 September 1936 he married (Margaret) Joan (*b.* 1915/16), daughter of Ernest Burgess, chairman and managing director of a Birmingham firm of brass founders. In 1938 Horne enlisted in the Royal Air Force Volunteer Reserve. He was commissioned as acting pilot officer and posted to 911 squadron (barrage balloons). He served in the RAF throughout the war, reaching the rank of wing commander, and on demobilization in 1945 he rejoined Triplex Glass as sales director. He was divorced in the same year, and married, on 2 November 1945, Marjorie Mallinson (*b.* 1909/10), widow of Lieutenant George Ambler Thomas and daughter of Harry George Sadler, civil servant. Horne himself had no surviving children, but his third wife had a daughter from her previous marriage. His business career continued to flourish after the war and he became managing director of the British Industries Fair (1954–6) and chairman and managing director of the Chad Valley Toy Company (1956–8), among other directorships. He gave up his business interests in 1958, when he was partially incapacitated by coronary thrombosis.

From 1940, when he made his first appearance over the airwaves as quizmaster in the BBC radio series *Ack, Ack, Beer, Beer*, Kenneth Horne was a constant broadcaster, and in 1943, by then stationed at the Air Ministry in London, he created and wrote with Squadron Leader Richard *Murdoch (1907–1990) the radio series *Much Binding in the Marsh*, a take-off based on a fictitious RAF station, which ran until 1950. He was subsequently the eponymous Ken of the comedy radio series *Beyond our Ken* (1958–64), which claimed up to 10 million listeners. *Round the Horne* succeeded *Beyond our Ken* in 1965, and achieved international audiences. Frequently repeated on the radio, the scripts (by Marty Feldman and Barry Took) were published in the 1970s and again in the following decade, and the BBC released recordings of the shows on cassette. Horne's

rich, fruity voice and warm patrician manner made him the ideal link man and that, coupled with a mischievous sense of humour, ensured that any programme in which he was involved was the better for his presence. He was, his obituarist wrote, 'a master of the scandalous double-meaning delivered with shining innocence … [and of] the excruciating schoolboy pun' (*The Times*). He also chaired a television quiz show, *Celebrity Challenge*, and the radio programme *Twenty Questions*, and his skill in handling staff and co-directors in industry transferred successfully to his broadcasting career. His notably temperamental co-star, Kenneth Williams, paid tribute to 'his unselfish nature, his kindness, tolerance and gentleness [which] were an example to everyone' (*Kenneth Williams Diaries*, 345). Kenneth Horne died on 14 February 1969 at St George's Hospital, Westminster, having suffered a second heart attack during the awards presentations of the Guild of British Film and Television Producers at the Dorchester Hotel, London.   BARRY TOOK

Sources *The Times* (15 Feb 1969) · N. Hackforth, *Solo for Horne* (1976) · Burke, *Peerage* (1967) · m. cert. · d. cert. · *The Kenneth Williams diaries*, ed. R. Davies (1993) · *WWW* · personal knowledge (2004) · *CGPLA Eng. & Wales* (1969)
Archives FILM BFI NFTVA, documentary footage · BFI NFTVA, record footage |SOUND BL NSA, 'Bow dialogues', 16 Jan 1968, C812/19 C11 · BL NSA, documentary recordings · BL NSA, performance recordings
Likenesses group portrait, photograph, 1949, Hult. Arch. · double portrait, photograph, 1953 (with R. Murdoch), Hult. Arch. · L. Morley, photograph, 1960–69, NPG [*see illus.*]
Wealth at death £78,945: probate, 30 April 1969, *CGPLA Eng. & Wales*

Horne, Richard Hengist [*formerly* Richard Henry] (1802–1884), writer, was born at Edmonton, Middlesex, on 31 December 1802, the eldest of the three sons of James Horne (*d.* 1810), quartermaster in the 61st regiment of foot, and his wife, Maria, *née* Partridge (*c.*1782–1847). After his father's death he was brought up in the Edmonton home of his paternal grandmother, Sarah Tice, and was educated at the Revd John Clarke's school in Enfield and then (probably) at the Edmonton grammar school before entering the Royal Military College, Sandhurst, in April 1819. At Sandhurst he failed to shine (except in military drawing) and was withdrawn at the end of his probationary year.

Early in 1825 Horne obtained, through family connections, an appointment as midshipman in the navy and saw action at the siege of Vera Cruz. He returned to England—after working his way through the United States and Canada—in late 1826 or early 1827 and began his writing career by publishing a lengthy Shelleyan poem, 'Hecatompylos', in *The Athenaeum* in June 1828. Thereafter, for some years, he worked on a variety of projects, made acquaintances in the literary world, and produced occasional pieces for magazines and newspapers (notably the *True Sun*). The discovery, in 1832, that much of his patrimony had been muddled away by the trustee provided a stimulus to more energetic exertion, and his first book, *The Exposition of the False Medium and Barriers Excluding Men of Genius from the*

Public (a timely argument for the establishment of an institution to relieve impoverished geniuses), appeared in the summer of 1833. The book was gleefully savaged by John Wilson in *Blackwood's Edinburgh Magazine*, but it earned a favourable review from William Johnson Fox, and Horne was soon an intimate member of Fox's circle at Craven Hill and a regular contributor to the *Monthly Repository*, the editorship and joint ownership of which he assumed in 1836 (selling it on to Leigh Hunt in the following year).

After publishing in 1834 an inadequately disciplined satire on the forces of English conservatism entitled *The Spirit of Peers and People*, Horne turned his attention, as did so many of his contemporaries, to the composition of ambitious blank verse historical dramas with morally ambivalent protagonists. *Cosmo de' Medici* appeared in 1837 and was closely followed by *The Death of Marlowe*, in which the dramatist improbably expires in a duel over the honour of his beloved courtesan Cecilia. Although Horne besieged the actor–manager William Macready, neither play was staged, and the same fate befell *Gregory VII* (1840). Work on these high-reaching projects was interspersed with more mundane labours: in 1841 Horne not only edited a selection of modernized tales from Chaucer but also published a mediocre biography of Napoleon, for which much of the research had been completed by his close friend Mary Gillies. Also in 1841 he was appointed a sub-commissioner on the royal commission for the investigation of the employment of children in mines and factories; his subsequent report on the appalling conditions he found in the industrial north inspired 'The Cry of the Children' (1843) by Elizabeth Barrett, with whom he had begun a prolific epistolary friendship in 1839.

In 1843 Horne published the work for which he is best-known, the three-book epic *Orion*. This poem, broadly of the Spasmodic school, more credibly imagines the torments and distractions which befall genius than the precise nature of its enduring achievements. It was glowingly reviewed (by, among others, Edgar Allan Poe), and its public reputation was cannily enhanced by Horne's decision to price copies at a farthing, gaining him the nickname the Farthing Poet. His next undertaking, however—an edited collection of critical essays on his contemporaries entitled, in imitation of his idol Hazlitt, *A New Spirit of the Age* (2 vols., 1844)—predictably elicited a deluge of abuse from its victims, and Horne, naïvely surprised, decamped hastily on a tour of Germany (where he began *The Good Natured Bear*, the first of three engaging children's stories). Although *A New Spirit* had alienated many former friends, he retained some influential contacts, and in December 1845 Dickens, with whom he had been acquainted since the late 1830s, appointed him to the staff of the *Daily News* as branch editor for Ireland, in which capacity he covered the opening stages of the great famine.

In the autumn of 1846 Horne returned to London and shortly afterwards began work on *The Dreamer and the Worker* (serialized in the *Shilling Magazine* in 1847; 2 vols., 1851), a novel which in its preface claims affinities with Mrs Gaskell's *Mary Barton* and Charles Kingsley's *Alton Locke* and which asserts a crucial role for the visionary poet

in improving the condition of England. On 17 June 1847, after a brief courtship, Horne married Catherine Clare St George Foggo (*b. c.*1825), daughter of David Foggo. The couple went to live in Finchley, Middlesex, and Horne (the last of whose private income had evaporated earlier in the year when the Mines Royal cancelled their dividend) redoubled his efforts to secure a comfortable maintenance from his writing. Another play, *Judas Iscariot* (1848), enjoyed the usual lack of success, but in 1850 a Christmas book, *The Poor Artist, or, Seven Eyesights and one Object* (an interesting fable on relativity of vision), so impressed Dickens that he appointed Horne to a sub-editorship of *Household Words*. Horne worked hard in his new post, producing a wide range of topical articles (and appearing as a member of Dickens's private theatrical troupe), but by 1852 he was enmeshed in disagreements with W. H. Wills and, spurred by the discovery of gold in Australia, he decided to accompany William Howitt to the diggings in Victoria, though he continued to contribute to *Household Words*.

Shortly after his arrival in Australia in September 1852, Horne was appointed to command a private gold escort between Bendigo and Melbourne, but in June 1853 he acquired (through a distant relative in the Colonial Office) an official post as assistant commissioner for crown lands at Heathcote, whence he was soon afterwards transferred to Waranga. Here, in March 1854, he received a letter from his wife, whom he had left in some financial distress in England, requesting a formal separation. Shattered by the news, he neglected his duties and in September was dismissed from the commission and the magistracy. He now decided to exploit his literary reputation (an Australian edition of *Orion* appeared in 1854) and to consolidate his acquaintance among Melbourne's cultural élite. One of his new friends, the lawyer Archibald Michie, gave him work as his counsel clerk and encouraged him to stand as a candidate for Rodney in the 1856 election (he came last); another, Charles Gavan Duffy, got him appointed to the commission for water and sewerage, a position in which he was able to support a brief relationship with a woman called Jessie Taylor, who gave birth, in February 1857, to a son christened Percy Hazlitt; the child died in September. The commission was abolished in 1859 and thereafter, for four years, Horne lived from hand to mouth, delivering series of lectures, composing his partly autobiographical *Australian Facts and Prospects* (1859), standing again (even more disastrously) for parliament, arranging for a belated staging of *The Death of Marlowe* at Melbourne's Theatre Royal in 1860, and, finally, petitioning the Royal Literary Fund for assistance, a petition strongly supported by Dickens in 1862. A part of such money as he managed to procure had to be remitted to his estranged wife and more was used to support a milliner named Mary Jane Hill (or Hull) with whom he lived for a time in a cottage in Robe Street, St Kilda, Melbourne.

In 1863 Horne was appointed (after much importunity) registrar of mines at the Blue Mountain goldfield, where he completed his poetic drama *Prometheus the Fire-Bringer*

(1864) which inventively features a sub-chorus of troglodytes, and did little official work, preferring to spend his time in Melbourne (where he may have had another short-lived child called Bella Isolda, whose death he recorded in February 1867 and whose mother's name is unknown). He was dismissed from his registrarship in 1868 and sailed for England in June of the following year.

On his return to London Horne (who had unaccountably changed his middle name to Hengist in 1867) found himself a largely forgotten figure. He took rooms in Northumberland Street and began to re-establish contact with the literary scene, forming acquaintances with younger writers such as Swinburne, arranging for reprints of his earlier work, editing his correspondence with Elizabeth Barrett, and publishing reminiscences in any magazine which would take them. Dickens, however, now refused to associate with him, as he was angry with Horne's lack of substantial support for his wife while he was in Australia. In 1874 financial pressures were relieved when Horne was granted a civil-list pension of £50. (The sum was doubled six years later.) He was still indefatigably producing poetic dramas: *Laura Dibalzo* appeared in 1880, *Sithron the Star-Stricken* in 1883. In February 1884 he became seriously ill at his lodgings at 16 Trinity Hill, Margate, Kent (where he had for some time been spending several months of each year), and his condition, diagnosed as general inflammation of the mucous membrane, worsened in March. Horne died in his sleep at 16 Trinity Hill on 13 March 1884 and was buried in Margate cemetery.

Horne was a talented and versatile writer who aspired to the condition of genius. A belated Romantic who had seen Hazlitt on his deathbed, worshipped Shelley, and once, according to his own account, thrown a snowball at Keats, he adjusted reluctantly and awkwardly to the demands of professional authorship, reserving his most intense energies for ambitious projects for which he lacked the critical self-awareness to bring to success. He believed passionately in the social efficacy of poetry, but his attempts to clarify the objectives it might serve dissolve into visionary generality. Nevertheless, his delusions of vatic grandeur, while they excited the ridicule of more earthbound contemporaries, helped to sustain him through a long and often unhappy life: like his own Orion, he could, he believed, look forward to the consolations of immortal fame.   ROBERT DINGLEY

Sources A. Blainey, *The Farthing Poet: a biography of Richard Hengist Horne, 1802–1884* (1968) · C. Pearl, *Always morning: the life of Richard Henry 'Orion' Horne* (1960) · R. H. Horne, *Australian facts and prospects* (1859) · R. G. Laird, 'Richard Henry (Hengist) Horne', *Victorian poets before 1850*, ed. W. E. Fredeman and I. B. Nadel, DLitB, 32 (1984), 154–60 · E. J. Shumaker, *A concise bibliography of the complete works of Richard Henry (Hengist) Horne (1802–1884)* (1943) · M. Fisher, 'Introduction', in R. H. Horne, *Memoirs of a London doll* (1967) · K. J. Fielding, 'Charles Dickens and R. H. Horne', *English*, 9 (1952), 17–19 · J. Lucas, 'Politics and the poet's role', *Literature and politics in the nineteenth century*, ed. J. Lucas (1971), 7–43 · I. Armstrong, *Victorian poetry: poetry, poetics, and politics* (1993) · A. Lohrli, ed., *Household Words: a weekly journal conducted by Charles Dickens* (1973) · CGPLA Eng. & Wales (1884)
Archives BL, papers, Add. MSS 47444–47445 · BL, letters to Royal Literary Fund, loan 96 · Hunt. L., letters and papers · Hunt. L., papers · Mitchell L., NSW, papers · State Library of Victoria, Melbourne, corresp. · UCL, SDUK MSS, letters to Society for the Diffusion of Useful Knowledge · UCL, letters · University of Melbourne Library, corresp. | BL, corresp. with Leigh Hunt, Add. MSS 38109–38110, 38523 · BL, letters to Marianne Hunt, Add. MSS 38109–38110 · BL, letters to Macmillans, Add. MSS 55253–55255 · Herts. ALS, letters to Lord Lytton · NL NZ, Turnbull L., letters to Henry Edwards, William Fox, and Robert Browning · Trinity Cam., letters to Lord Houghton · U. Birm. L., letters to Harriet Martineau · U. Leeds, Brotherton L., letters to Sir Edmund Gosse · University of Melbourne Library, letters to W. H. Archer and H. T. Dwight
Likenesses M. Gillies, oils, *c.*1840, NPG · Elliott & Fry, photograph, 1882–3, repro. in Pearl, *Always morning*, facing p. 151 · M. Gillies, wash drawing, BM · W. J. Linton, woodcut, BM · C. Summers, marble plaque, Mitchell L., NSW · C. Summers, plaster medallion, NPG · C. Summers, plaster medallion, Keats House, Hampstead · daguerreotype, University of Melbourne · stipple and line engraving (after daguerreotype by Paine of Islington), NPG
Wealth at death £106 1s. 11d.: probate, 17 May 1884, CGPLA Eng. & Wales

Horne, Robert (1513×15–1579), bishop of Winchester, was the son of John Horne of Cleator, Cumberland.

Education and early career Horne studied at St John's College, Cambridge, and graduated BA in 1537, proceeding MA in 1540, BTh in 1546, and DTh in 1559. He was elected a fellow of the college on 25 March in either 1536 or 1537, was senior bursar in 1544, and Hebrew lecturer in 1545–6. On 3 October 1548, presented by Sir Richard Rich, he was instituted to the vicarage of Matching, Essex, which he resigned before 27 February 1553. Soon after July 1547 he received a licence to preach under the great seal. Archbishop Cranmer collated him on 8 May 1550 to the rectory of All Hallows, Bread Street, London, where he became a well-known evangelical preacher. He had resigned this living by 10 March 1552. In November 1551 Horne was one of three evangelical divines chosen to confute the views of three imprisoned religious conservatives in disputations on the eucharist staged on Sir William Cecil's initiative in preparation for the parliamentary debate on the introduction of a new prayer book. He was one of six divines instructed by the privy council on 21 October 1552 to consider forty-five articles of religion, which he also signed.

Meanwhile, in view of his erudition and the rarity of good ministers of the gospel in the north, Horne had been appointed dean of Durham by the crown on 18 November 1551. He was also collated to the prebend of Bugthorpe in York Minster on 28 April 1552, but had already resigned it by 15 October following. On 18 February 1552 the privy council wrote to the prebendaries of Durham warning them to conform themselves to Horne's orders in religion and divine service, and requiring them to receive and use him well. At Durham, Horne allegedly had the tomb of St Cuthbert in the cloister garth pulled down, had some stained glass windows illustrating Cuthbert's miracles smashed, and broke up the Corpus Christi shrine in St Nicholas's Church with his own feet. According to Edward VI's journal, on 11 October 1552 Horne revealed a plot by the earl of Westmorland in 1551 to gain popular support with a proclamation to raise the face value of coins called

Robert Horne
(1513×15–1579), by
Marcus Gheeraerts
the elder, 1576
[detail from
*Procession of the
Knights of the Garter*]

the king who were so besotted with wives and children that they forgot their poor neighbours and the duties of their calling.

Exile and return After Queen Mary's accession, according to his own account, Horne set out for London as soon as he learned that he had been excepted from the queen's pardon. Summoned to appear before the privy council, he learned that Cuthbert Tunstall had caused two noblemen to charge him with preaching heresy. Tunstall accused Horne of infecting the whole diocese of Durham with new learning, claimed that he was not an Englishman born, that he had exercised Tunstall's office, and that he had brought his wife into Durham Cathedral, where no woman had been before. Stephen Gardiner then falsely charged him with failing to answer three letters commanding him to appear before the council. Hearing on 30 October that the queen had confiscated all his goods at Durham and that he was to be committed to the Tower the following day for ignoring her letters (and also as a supposed Scot), he decided to flee abroad. He justified his actions in a pugnacious apology, printed late in that year, together with his translation *Certaine Homilies of M. Joan Calvine* exhorting Christians to fly outward idolatry and suffer persecution. He defended himself and his fellow preachers against the charge that they were carnal flatterers and heretics who dared not defend their doctrines, and justified his decision to marry: God had not given him the gift of chastity. The former rulers, far from taking the evangelical preachers to be flatterers, blamed them for too boldly and plainly rebuking their sins. The exiles had fled the realm because they knew protestants would be denied an impartial hearing.

After visiting Pietro Martire Vermigli (known as Peter Martyr) in Strasbourg, Horne went to Zürich, arriving on 5 April 1554. There, he and his wife Margery (surname unknown) headed a list of twelve petitioners to the magistrates to be allowed to stay in the city. On 13 October fourteen Zürich exiles, including Horne, declined to join the English church in Frankfurt unless its use of the 1552 Book of Common Prayer was guaranteed. This was ensured by the triumph of Richard Cox and his supporters in March 1555. Then on 5 April Horne joined Cox and his leading supporters notifying Calvin of their resolve to maintain the second Edwardian prayer book after purging it of its most controversial observances. Horne was chosen to be the reader of the Hebrew lecture in the English congregation at Frankfurt, and on 1 March 1556 he succeeded David Whitehead as its pastor, but only after he had been cleared, at his own insistence, of rumours tending to the discredit of his ministry.

On 13 January 1557 a quarrel between Horne and Thomas Ashley, followed on 17 January by an accusation that Ashley had slandered the pastor and elders, led to a serious dispute over discipline and authority in the congregation. At first the issue was the validity of the proceedings against Ashley undertaken by Horne and the ministers, elders, and deacons. Ashley and his supporters held that the latter could not proceed in a matter in which they themselves were a party, while Horne held that they

down by the crown. On 28 October the duke of Northumberland envisaged in a letter to Cecil that Horne might become the bishop of a much reduced diocese of Durham, but by 3 December he had decided that this 'peevish dean' was unsuitable. Northumberland had been informed that Horne 'on his ale bench' had let it be understood that he would refuse the promotion if he might not have it according to his own will (*CSP dom.*, Edward VI, 278). Four days later he complained to Cecil about a letter of Horne's claiming that he could not tell whether the duke was a dissembler in religion. Horne, Northumberland told Cecil on 2 January 1553, was greedy, malicious, and an open evil speaker. Implicitly he classed him as one of the new obstinate doctors, and as one of those lately promoted by could, having received their authority from the whole church. Horne and the elders unwillingly agreed that the whole church might meet to resolve the controversy, but faced with a majority decision that they were not competent judges in Ashley's case, they resigned their ministry on 2 February. They then allegedly obstructed attempts to make peace and draw up a new discipline.

The most important objections made by Horne and his associates to the new discipline focused on the articles concerning the authority of the ministers and the congregation, and the management of the church's funds, especially for poor relief. They thought one minister should be pre-eminent (the new discipline established parity between two) and strongly criticized the weight given to majority decisions of the congregation. The majority, headed by David Whitehead, claimed that Horne aimed to rule the roost, with his close ally Richard Chambers exercising control over the church's funds. This would give them lordship over the poor, and through them over the congregation as a whole. Horne and Chambers suddenly left Frankfurt shortly after 10 June. Chambers wrote to his former associates from Strasbourg on the 20th claiming that he had collected alms for deserving English exiles in general, never for the Frankfurt church in particular. The two men later travelled together to distribute funds to the exile churches in Aarau and Geneva. In 1558 Horne was registered as a student at the University of Basel. According to John Jewel he left Strasbourg for England on 21 December, a month after Elizabeth's accession, together with Edwin Sandys and others.

The Elizabethan settlement On 29 March 1559 Horne gave the third of the Eastertide sermons at St Mary Spital in London; it was the first of several sermons which he delivered at the Spital, Paul's Cross, and the court in the early years of Elizabeth's reign. He was one of the nine men chosen to debate three key questions with Roman Catholic churchmen in the Westminster Abbey disputation attended by the privy council and the two houses of parliament which began at the end of March. In response to Henry Cole's rather heated opening discourse Horne read a prepared statement defending the use of a vernacular liturgy. He was appointed in late June to the commissions for the royal visitations of Cambridge University and Eton College and of the dioceses of London, Norwich, and Ely.

On 31 October 1559 Horne received a pardon (formally attributed to the queen's affection for him) for leaving the realm without licence, and his forfeited goods were restored to him together with the arrears of revenue from his deanery, to which he was restored. He soon returned north. The duke of Norfolk, Elizabeth's lieutenant-general there, urgently recommended to Cecil on both 10 January and 16 February 1560 that a commission should be granted to Horne enabling him to tackle the religious disorder in the north-east. On 18 February Horne himself complained to Cecil of the deplorable state of religion in those parts. He pointed out that three Durham prebendaries had refused the oath of supremacy, and named replacement candidates, men who (he implied) would be workmen suitable for the task of planting knowledge and

virtue. He also sought Cecil's help in recovering goods and books unjustly taken from him by the three prebendaries and Thomas Watson, his successor as dean in 1553. Horne and Thomas Sampson, a canon of Durham, later visited Berwick and preached there to very good effect, according to letters sent to William Cecil by Sir Francis Leek on 17 September and 2 October 1560.

Horne as diocesan: combating Catholicism Horne was offered the bishopric of Durham as early as autumn 1559, but seems not to have accepted it, and by 6 November 1560 he was reported to have accepted Winchester instead. He was formally nominated on 24 November and consecrated on 16 February 1561, aged either forty-six or forty-seven. He also became prelate of the Order of the Garter, an office customarily held together with that see. In the case of Winchester, as in that of Durham, the government envisaged the retention of extensive episcopal properties by the crown. Not long after paying the first instalment of his first fruits at Michaelmas 1561, however, Horne petitioned for release from two further instalments on the grounds that his revenues had been overvalued by £180. He was also burdened with £600 of annuities and urgently needed to spend £300 on repairs. The government appears to have responded by allowing Horne, in return for a yearly pension of £400, to administer and profit from the lands which (technically speaking) it had withheld from the see. The bishopric's valuable Somerset properties were restored in law by letters patent in 1575, but the pension, or 'Taunton rent', remained payable.

Writing to Cecil during his primary visitation on 8 June 1561 Horne recorded mixed impressions of his new diocese. The ministers who had appeared before him had proved conformable. Several clergy, however, had failed to appear, and many churches either lacked incumbents or were too poor to support a minister at all. By 29 August Horne had come to see the importance of co-operation with the JPs. He reported that he and the gentlemen of his division of Hampshire had charged the constables, tithingmen, and most substantial inhabitants to return certificates of breaches of statutes. He and other justices who had followed his example had found more disorders in religion by this method than he could do in his visitation by means of the churchwardens, because fines were so much more feared than excommunication. Many justices, however, were opposed to this course of action. More seriously, a great man who had ruled Hampshire the previous year, probably John Paulet, Lord St John, the eldest son of the marquess of Winchester, had expressed his dislike of Horne, and had done him grievous injury. Even after some changes during the next three years the Hampshire commission of the peace still contained a minority of men disaffected to the established religion, according to Horne's detailed report to the privy council of November 1564. The conservative group proved strong enough to secure the return of Winchester's grandson Sir John Berkeley as one of the knights of the shire in a sharply contested by-election in November 1566. Horne, however, managed to prevent the addition of more associates of the

Paulets to the commission of the peace in 1569, and Winchester's death in March 1572 hastened the eclipse of the conservative group in the government of Hampshire. In Surrey, where Horne knew of no 'mislikers' in 1564, he had a valuable ally and friendly correspondent in William More of Loseley.

Support for the old religion was strong in Hampshire; of 243 principal inhabitants of the county listed in 1572, 143 were believed to have Catholic leanings. Soon after his arrival in Winchester, Horne appears to have ordered incumbents and churchwardens to send in regular lists of non-communicants. The number of citations for not receiving communion or not coming to church increased sharply in 1570, and though it soon declined, remained somewhat higher thereafter than during the 1560s. Horne recognized Winchester itself as a major centre of religious conservatism. In November 1564 he told the privy council that nearly all who bore authority there were addicted to the old superstition. He and his officials worked hard to suppress such traditional popular observances as midsummer bonfires and bell-ringing on the night of All Saints.

Horne enjoined that several conservative clergy of the diocese who had either performed proscribed rituals or upheld Catholic doctrines should preach against specified Catholic beliefs or practices, and especially the 'usurped jurisdiction' of the papacy. He soon identified some priests in Winchester Cathedral as sources of superstition and popery in the city, and in his May 1562 injunctions for the cathedral required that a twice weekly divinity lecture be established, that a sermon be preached there every Sunday, and that each prebendary should preach in person at least annually. Minor canons and choristers were to be examined regularly on a set programme of biblical reading. During his visitation of the cathedral in 1563 Horne personally carried out such an examination. When four of the resident prebendaries admitted that they had not preached in person he laid down who was to preach each Sunday during the next quarter, and ordered that each preacher certify his compliance within three days of the due date. During his 1571 cathedral visitation Horne found continuing neglect of preaching and study, while the dean, Francis Newton, was charged with favouring superstitious religion more than the true.

Reforming the ministry Horne vigorously pursued the goal of a learned and preaching ministry. Numerous visitation presentments of men who had failed to catechize or provide sermons reflect the steady pressure exerted by Horne and his chancellors. Horne's 1570 visitation articles show that he expected all clergy under the degree of MA to read a chapter of the Bible in Latin and English every day. Their progress was to be assessed in quarterly deanery synods by the archdeacons. More detailed orders for an exercise of the clergy in Winchester archdeaconry were issued in 1573, including a programme of reading for both beneficed clergy and curates. Meetings of the clergy of each deanery were in future to take place every six weeks, and every quarter the beneficed clergy were to exhibit notes of all the sermons preached in their parishes.

Despite Horne's readiness to preside over his own consistory court when necessary, the success of his programme of reform depended in large measure on those who held office under him. George Acworth, his chancellor from 1562 to about 1570, had initially conformed under Mary before going abroad to study in Padua and elsewhere, and eventually left Winchester in some dissatisfaction. His successor was John Kingsmill, member of a family which included some of the staunchest supporters of protestantism in Hampshire. Horne inherited as his principal registrar John Cooke, who allegedly so abhorred the 'pure religion' which Horne sought to promote that he tried to discredit the bishop by spreading a rumour that he had been seen in adultery. For this Cooke was eventually compelled by the privy council to do penance at Paul's Cross. In August 1564 Horne instituted proceedings against Stephen Cheston, archdeacon of Winchester, the validity of whose collation to the archdeaconry in 1554, following the deprivation of the future martyr John Philpott, he may have impugned. Cheston, however, survived in place until his death in 1572. Horne complained in 1573 that he had hitherto had little help from his archdeacon of Surrey. He also felt strongly the inadequacy of the church courts and their chief sanction, excommunication, as he made clear to Cecil in January 1570. He therefore requested an ecclesiastical commission, and ecclesiastical commissioners were certainly active in Hampshire during the 1570s, though no commission has been found.

The bishop of Winchester's ecclesiastical jurisdiction over the Channel Islands was confirmed in 1568. Huguenot ministers had already established reformed churches there early in Elizabeth's reign. In August 1565 the privy council attempted to impose a compromise by which the churches in St Helier and St Peter Port were allowed to follow the order of service used in the French church in London while the other parishes of the islands used the Book of Common Prayer. Various cases of local religious conflict came to Horne's notice. Peter Pelley, of whom the dean of Guernsey had already complained to Cecil in 1565, admitted to Horne in 1569 that he had not received communion in St Peter Port for seven years. He was not a member of the reformed church there, he said, and he disliked the way they celebrated communion. In April 1568 Horne received a complaint that the Norman-born minister of St Helier, Thomas Jone, had railed against the queen's injunctions and against those who refused to attend his services. He had excommunicated one of these men, the complainant Hugh Peryn, of St Martin's parish. In 1569 the synod of the islands drew up a scheme of ecclesiastical discipline which it resolved to present to Horne. A synod, with the governors of both islands present, formally adopted it in 1576. In January 1576 (or possibly 1577) Horne responded in the most friendly fashion to an appeal for help from the colloquy of Guernsey, faced with resistance to its authority from one Elie Bonamy, and wrote on its behalf to Thomas Leighton, governor of the island.

Horne and Oxford University Horne, who was incorporated DTh of Oxford University on 9 July 1567, had visitorial jurisdiction over a number of Oxford colleges. He began his first college visitation in September 1561. Finding the general level of theological knowledge in the university rather low he restricted himself to securing acceptance of the queen's supremacy, the prayer book, and the royal injunctions, and refrained from pushing even these requirements too far. The very unsatisfactory president of Corpus Christi was persuaded to resign soon after the visitation. Thomas Greenaway, elected on Horne's initiative in 1562, quarrelled with the fellows and resigned in 1568. The queen's nominee as his successor, William Cole (one of Horne's fellow Zürich exiles), was at first shut out of the college. Royal commissioners, including Horne, then visited Corpus, installed Cole, and expelled three Catholic fellows. Cole was later accused of defrauding the college, and allegedly had some difficulty in dissuading Horne from removing him.

At New College only the warden and nine fellows took the required oaths in 1561; two fellows protested that only the mass was allowed by their statutes. When Acworth visited the college in 1566 twenty-three fellows refused to subscribe the articles of religion. The expulsion of nearly half the fellowship during the first decade of Elizabeth's reign gradually made the college more conformable. All the fellows of Trinity subscribed the articles of religion in 1566, but in 1570 Horne rebuked them for keeping popish ornaments and monuments, and in 1571 six fellows resigned or were removed.

Only at Magdalen did Horne find a preponderance of members forward in religion in 1561. He ordered the deprivation of the president, Thomas Coveney, and Lawrence Humphrey, another Zürich exile, was elected shortly afterwards, and soon became one of the leaders of Oxford resistance to the cap and surplice. This did not prevent Horne's presenting him to a living in the diocese of Salisbury, to the dismay of Bishop John Jewel, who told Matthew Parker on 22 December 1565 that he would not institute him without the archbishop's explicit consent. In September 1566 Acworth formally ordered all the fellows of Magdalen to wear the surplice on Sundays and festivals. In 1575 Horne supported Humphrey against a rebellion by several Magdalen fellows who accused their president of covetousness, mismanagement, and breach of college statutes.

Horne and national affairs The Spanish ambassador, Alvaro de la Quadra, reported to Philip II on 5 May 1561 that Horne was one of those bishops who were meeting daily with William Cecil and Nicholas Bacon to discuss the question of admitting the papal nuncio Martinengo, sent to announce the forthcoming third session of the Council of Trent. The following day he knew that they had decided not to do so. (According to de la Quadra, writing on 25 March, Cecil had then used 'insulting words' to Horne because of his preaching against conciliar authority.) Horne also had important dealings with some of the most eminent surviving Catholic churchmen. John Feckenham, deprived abbot of Westminster, was in October 1563 entrusted to his custody. They discussed matters of religion daily until the end of the following January, when Horne reported his hopes of Feckenham's conformity,

much to the latter's discomfiture. Relations between the two thereafter deteriorated until Horne complained about Feckenham to the privy council and he was returned to the Tower in October 1564. Early in 1565 Feckenham published a book purporting to contain scruples about the royal supremacy which Horne had failed to resolve, to which in 1566 Horne published a vigorous response claiming that Feckenham had never presented his arguments against the supremacy in the form of such scruples. He proceeded to refute them point by point, concluding with a rebuttal of Feckenham's complaint of ill treatment at his hands.

In April 1564 Horne had Edmund Bonner, formerly bishop of London and now a prisoner in the Marshalsea in Southwark, and as such resident in Winchester diocese, summoned to take the oath of supremacy. Bonner refused and was indicted in queen's bench, but the prosecution was thwarted by an ingenious objection to Horne's episcopal authority. The oath was not tendered to him again. In 1572 Horne was given temporary custody of John Lesley, bishop of Ross, Mary Stuart's ambassador in England, but he wrote to Burghley on 14 November 1573 begging for deliverance from this troublesome responsibility. The privy council committed Thomas Watson, the former bishop of Lincoln, to Horne's charge in 1577–9.

If Horne's attitude to Catholicism was clear, his response to protestant nonconformity was more equivocal. Writing to Rudolf Gwalther of Zürich on 17 July 1565 he referred to the papists' efforts to exploit the controversy about square caps and surplices which had recently arisen in England, and told Gwalther that he and his colleagues had complied with the requirement to wear them lest their enemies should take possession of their places on their refusal. They hoped to have the relevant clause of the Act of Uniformity repealed in the next session of parliament, but if this could not be achieved he thought that they should nevertheless continue in the ministry. Along with Matthew Parker and four other bishops Horne subscribed the *Advertisements* concerning uniformity in the clergy's ministry and apparel drawn up in response to the queen's demand. Their publication in 1566 was followed by a purge of non-subscribers in the diocese of London.

On 6 February 1567 Horne joined Edmund Grindal in writing to the leaders of the Zürich church asserting that the ministers of the Church of England might wear the vestments prescribed only for the sake of order by public authority, and expressing their impatience with those who for the sake of a trivial scruple divided and endangered a church in which pure doctrine was preached. In the spring of 1571 Horne preached on the subject at Paul's Cross along with his colleagues Jewel and Cox. Yet despite his increasingly harsh words about vestiarian nonconformists, whom he regarded as vainglorious and contentious, Horne never approved of the vestments. In August 1571 he admitted as much to Heinrich Bullinger, and indeed, there is little evidence of proceedings against vestiarian nonconformists in Winchester diocese during Horne's episcopate.

In 1574, allegedly at Horne's suggestion, Parker ordered

a metropolitical visitation of Winchester diocese, with George Acworth acting as his commissary-general. Obedience, Parker told Burghley on 11 April 1575, had greatly improved as a result, even though Horne had been told that 'his clergy was sifted, and the thorn was put in his foot'; but, Parker had been informed, Horne would 'so pluck it out that it should be so in other men's feet that they should stamp again' (*Correspondence*, 478). The Isle of Wight and other places in the diocese had already abandoned their obedience. He was almost certainly referring to nonconformists. Parker condemned such a policy of working secretly against the queen's religion. It is hard to avoid the conclusion that he associated Horne with this policy.

International involvements Whatever his misgivings about the vestiarian policy Horne certainly regarded the Church of England as reformed in essentials. He assured Bullinger in December 1563 that all England had the same ecclesiastical doctrine as Zürich. The gospel was flourishing in England, he told Rudolf Gwalther in August 1576. The queen was intent upon its advancement both at home and abroad. She had always abominated popery from her infancy, and would never admit Lutheranism, a great disturber of Christianity. Horne, as this letter suggests, was a strong supporter of the international reformed cause. During a Spital sermon on 12 April 1563 his call for assistance to French refugees helped raise £45. When in 1567 a group of French-speaking protestant refugees hoped to establish a community in Southampton, they looked to Horne to support their economic and fiscal as well as religious requests to the town corporation and privy council, and on 30 June the bishop duly appealed to Cecil to allow them to gather in one church and live under godly discipline. He assigned them the chapel of St Julien in God's House Hospital, and attended their first service on 28 October. On 23 November 1572 Antonio Fogaça reported to the duke of Alva, the Spanish viceroy of the Netherlands, that one Henry Horne, a nephew of the bishop's (and his servant, according to a later letter), was being employed in a most secret mission from the queen to the three protestant electors of the empire. Juan de Salvatierra told Philip II the following 9 April that Horne had joined other bishops in petitioning Elizabeth to help William of Orange and the Huguenot leader, the comte de Montgommery. Faced with the queen's reluctance to become directly involved Horne had allegedly raised £35,000, and Sandys of London £20,000, for the cause.

As a subscriber to the *Advertisements* of 1566 Horne was described as a commissioner in causes ecclesiastical, and he was certainly appointed to the commissions for the southern province in 1572 and 1576. The revision of the books of Isaiah, Jeremiah, and Lamentations in the Bishops' Bible, published in 1568, was entrusted to him. He allegedly took the main part in compiling the canons of 1571, along with Richard Cox and Matthew Parker. On 1 July 1572 he and Parker made an award between Thomas Cooper, bishop of Lincoln, and the archdeacon of Lincoln, John Aylmer, concerning their exercise of ecclesiastical jurisdiction.

Death and assessment Horne's wife died not long before 23 January 1576. On 28 February 1579 Horne himself was reported to be very infirm. In his will, dated 29 March 1579, he named four daughters as residuary legatees. Anne was married to John Dayrell or Darrell of Caleshill, Mary to John Hales of Tenterden, Margery (born in Frankfurt) to Thomas Dayrell of Lillingstone Dayrell, and Rebecca (then pregnant) to Henry Heyman of Sellinge. Elizabeth, possibly his eldest daughter, who married George Acworth on 24 December 1564, and then Anthony Dering of Charing about 1586, was not named. Horne also left bequests to three grandsons (all called 'nephews'), Paul and George Dayrell and Richard Acworth, to several servants, to Winchester Cathedral (all his historical books), to Magdalen and St Cross hospitals near Winchester, and to the poor of Durham. (He had already, in 1574, given seventy-two books to the library of Cambridge University.) He appointed as his executors John Watson and John Ebden, respectively dean and archdeacon of Winchester, together with his sons-in-law John Dayrell and John Hales. Horne wished to be buried before the pulpit in Winchester Cathedral without pomp or ceremony. At his death he owed the crown £1100; he had fallen into arrears in his payment of tenths, and had allegedly invested large sums in his daughters' dowries.

Horne died at Winchester Place in Southwark on 1 June following and was buried at Winchester; his will was proved on the 27th. A brief memorial inscription in his cathedral describes him as an outstanding doctor of theology and a former exile in Christ's cause. The most incisive contemporary appraisal of Horne was written by John Joscelin, Matthew Parker's biographer. Joscelin wrote that he was 'of great mind and profound genius, sagacious in detecting, skilful in preventing the arts of the adversaries; diligent in preaching, prompt and keen in disputing' (Dixon, 5.302); in his diocese he curbed the more powerful and inflexible papists, but treated the rest very gently. Widely respected for his learning and administrative ability Horne was also disliked by those who suffered from his pugnacity and his strong authoritarian streak. His vigorous commitment to the reformed cause, his tireless support for it both within his diocese and elsewhere, and a good relationship with William Cecil made him one of the more effective of early Elizabethan bishops. He was out of sympathy with the policy of enforcing vestiarian uniformity, yet his letters evince an underlying confidence in Elizabeth I.   RALPH HOULBROOKE

Sources Cooper, *Ath. Cantab.* · R. Horne, *Certaine homilies of M. Joan Calvine, conteining profitable and necessarie admonition for this time, with an apologie of Robert Horn* (1553) · W. Whittingham, *A brief discours off the troubles begonne at Franckford in Germany, Anno Domini 1554: Abowte the booke off off [sic] common prayer and ceremonies* (1574) · H. Robinson, ed. and trans., *The Zurich letters, comprising the correspondence of several English bishops and others with some of the Helvetian reformers, during the early part of the reign of Queen Elizabeth*, 2 vols., Parker Society, 7–8 (1842–5) · *Correspondence of Matthew Parker*, ed. J. Bruce and T. T. Perowne, Parker Society, 42 (1853) · *CSP dom.*, rev. edn, 1547–53 · will, PRO, PROB 11/61, fol. 26 · H. Robinson, ed. and trans., *Original letters relative to the English Reformation*, 1 vol. in 2, Parker Society, [26] (1846–7) · R. Horne, bishop's register, Hants. RO, Winchester diocesan records, 21M65.A1/26 · visitation books, Hants. RO,

Winchester diocesan records, MS 21M65/B1/9–14 · act books, consistory court office, Winchester, Hants. RO, Winchester diocesan records, MS 21M65/C1/7–20 · R. A. Houlbrooke, *Church courts and the people during the English Reformation, 1520–1570* (1979) · *Hist. U. Oxf.* 3: *Colleg. univ.* · R. H. Fritze, 'The role of family and religion in the local politics of early Elizabethan England: the case of Hampshire in the 1560s', *HJ*, 25 (1982), 267–87 · R. Horne, *An answeare made by Rob. Bishoppe of Wynchester, to a booke entituled, The declaration of suche scruples, and staies of conscience, touching the othe of the supremacy, as M. John Fekenham, by wrytinge did deliver unto the L. Bishop of Winchester: with his resolutions made thereunto* (1566) · J. E. Paul, 'Hampshire recusants in the time of Elizabeth I, with special reference to Winchester', *Proceedings of the Hampshire Field Club*, 21 (1958–60), 61–81 · R. W. Dixon, *History of the Church of England*, 6 vols. (1878–1902) · *Athenae Oxonienses ... containing the life of Wood*, ed. P. Bliss, another edn, [1] (1848) · J. Strype, *Annals of the Reformation and establishment of religion ... during Queen Elizabeth's happy reign*, new edn, 4 vols. (1824) · B. Usher, 'Durham and Winchester episcopal estates and the Elizabethan settlement', *Journal of Ecclesiastical History*, 49 (1998), 393–406 · *CSP Spain, 1558–79* · *CSP for., 1558–61* · A. Spicer, *The French-speaking reformed community and their church in Southampton, 1567–c.1620*, Southampton Records Series, 39 (1997) · H. Gee, *The Elizabethan clergy and the settlement of religion, 1558–1564* (1898) · *APC, 1542–80* · J. Strype, *The life and acts of Matthew Parker*, new edn, 3 vols. (1821) · F. Heal, *Of prelates and princes: a study of the economic and social position of the Tudor episcopate* (1980) · A. J. Eagleston, *The Channel Islands under Tudor government, 1485–1642: a study in administrative history* (1949) · C. M. Dent, *Protestant reformers in Elizabethan Oxford* (1983) · *Fasti Angl., 1541–1857, [Canterbury]* · *Holinshed's chronicles* (1804) · R. Newcourt, *Repertorium ecclesiasticum parochiale Londinense*, 2 vols. (1708–10)

Archives Hants. RO, Winchester diocesan archive, records of his episcopate, including his register (A1/26), visitation books (B1/9–14), and consistory court office act books (C1/7–20), 21M65

Likenesses M. Gheeraerts the elder, group portrait, etching, 1576, BM [*see illus.*] · R. White, line engraving (after 'Holbein'), BM, NPG; repro. in Burnet, *History of the Reformation* (1681) · oils, Trinity Hall, Cambridge

Horne, Robert (1564/5–1640), Church of England clergyman, was the student of Newcastle who matriculated 'pleb. fil.' at Magdalen Hall, Oxford, aged sixteen, on 25 February 1581, graduating BA in 1584 and MA in 1587. After serving as chaplain of Magdalen College (1585–95) Horne was presented to the rectory of Ludlow by the earl of Essex and instituted on 17 November 1596, and it was almost certainly he who had married Mary Amyas of Ludlow on 13 January 1594. Horne scorned the surplice and opposed signing the cross in baptism, views which soon led to trouble with the church courts. In 1601, after the Essex rebellion, the crown acquired the advowson of Horne's rectory; on 5 December 1604 Thomas Crowther succeeded him there.

Horne still had influential friends, including Richard Atkyns of Tuppe Leigh, Gloucestershire, member of the council in the marches of Wales, and recorder for Ludlow in 1601. To him Horne dedicated *The Christian Governour* (1614). Atkyns also knew Sir John Dannet, lord of the nearby manor of Westhope, who in his will (1607) provided that during the lifetime of his widow Horne should have continuing maintenance, and bequeathed him a ring on which were inscribed the words 'Praise God'. It was 'from Mrs Danet's house near Ludlow', that Horne signed his *Of the Rich Man and Lazarus* in 1619. Between 1618 and 1626 he was also busy transcribing manuscripts, including letters of Ralegh and Bacon, and of the puritan John Burgess. In 1626 Agnes Dannet died, without providing for the minister.

However, Horne found other patrons. In private letters in 1626–7 he referred to Lady Brilliana Harley as 'that elect lady' (Eales, 48–9). He dedicated his *History of the Woman of Great Faith* (1632) to her, and acknowledged Sir Richard Harley as his patron. There, as elsewhere in his writings, Horne was elaborately deferent to those whom God had placed in high authority; pious, puritan, and conservative, he urged all men to 'submit to that estate that God hath laide upon them'. But in practice this was chiefly directed at 'our unthankful poor', men who responded to charitable gifts 'not humbly with prayer, nor dutifully with thanks, but with proud and insolent replyings' (*Rich Man and Lazarus*, 41). Horne also edited the sermons of Richard Eedes.

Horne's association with Ludlow church continued: in 1629, a kneeling place was granted to 'Robert Horn minister of God's word for term of his natural life' (Jones, 139). Horne may have spent his last years at or near Ludlow; he was buried there on 28 October 1640.

E. T. BRADLEY, *rev.* STEPHEN WRIGHT

Sources E. H. Martin, 'History of the manor of Westhope', *Transactions of the Shropshire Archaeological and Natural History Society*, 3rd ser., 9 (1909), 147–248 · W. G. D. Fletcher, 'Institutions of Shropshire incumbents', *Transactions of the Shropshire Archaeological and Natural History Society*, 3rd ser., 8 (1908), 39–54 · M. A. Faraday, *Ludlow, 1085–1660* (1991), 11, 71 · H. T. Weyman, 'Recorders of Ludlow', *Transactions of the Shropshire Archaeological and Natural History Society*, 2nd ser., 11 (1899), 301–30 · J. Eales, *Puritans and roundheads: the Harleys of Brampton Bryan and the outbreak of the English civil war* (1990), 48–9 · Bodl. Oxf., MS Rawl. B. 151 · L. Jones, 'Churchwardens' accounts of the town of Ludlow', *Transactions of the Shropshire Archaeological and Natural History Society*, 2nd ser., 2 (1890), 105–40 · W. P. W. Phillimore, ed., *Diocese of Hereford*, 13: *Ludlow registers*, Shropshire Parish Registers, (privately printed, London, 1912), 368 · *Reg. Oxf.*, 2/2, 95, 2/3, 119 · J. R. Bloxam, *A register of the presidents, fellows ... of Saint Mary Magdalen College*, 8 vols. (1853–85), vol. 2, p. 129 · *DNB*

Archives Bodl. Oxf., MS Rawl. B. 151

Horne, Robert Stevenson, Viscount Horne of Slamannan (1871–1940), politician and businessman, was born on 28 February 1871 at Slamannan, Stirlingshire, the youngest son of Robert Stevenson Horne (1830–1887), Church of Scotland minister of the parish of Slamannan, and his wife, Mary, daughter of Thomas Lochhead of Toward, Argyll. In each of his successive careers—academic, legal, administrative, political, and business—he displayed the ambition, intellectual application, practical common sense, and social assurance common among Scottish 'sons of the manse'. He was educated at George Watson's College, Edinburgh, and at the University of Glasgow, where he excelled in student politics as well as in his studies, becoming president of the university Conservative club. After obtaining first-class honours in mental philosophy in 1893 and a university fellowship in 1894, he spent a year as philosophy lecturer at the University College of North Wales, Bangor. From 1896 to 1900 he was an examiner at the University of Aberdeen (of which he was

Robert Stevenson Horne, Viscount Horne of Slamannan (1871–1940), by Lafayette, pubd 1922

lord rector in 1921–4), but had already switched to a legal career.

Horne joined the Scottish bar in 1896 and became one of its leading advocates, specializing in commercial and shipping cases, and was made king's counsel in 1910. With his personal circumstances secure, he stood as Conservative candidate for Stirlingshire in the two general elections of 1910, but without success. His opportunities to break into new areas of activity came with the First World War, and he seized them with remarkable personal success. After briefly serving as secretary to the agricultural section of the national service department, he worked under Eric Geddes as a director of railways behind the western front, with the honorary rank of lieutenant-colonel in the Royal Engineers. In 1917 he followed Geddes to the Admiralty, first as assistant inspector-general of transportation, then in 1918 as director of the department of materials and priority, and ended the war as director of the labour department and third civil lord. His considerable organizational abilities, confident handling of men, and personal congeniality had impressed the Conservative Party leaders and especially Lloyd George, who rewarded him with a KBE in 1918 and with rapid ministerial advancement.

Returned as Conservative MP for Hillhead, Glasgow, at the 1918 election, Horne had the unusual distinctions of his first political office being in the cabinet and of entering the House of Commons with immediate front-bench status. In the post-war coalition government he occupied successively three posts with strategic importance during the troubles of reconstruction. As minister of labour from 1919 to 1920 he dealt with a wave of industrial unrest, deploying his skills from wartime manpower management to ease negotiations with trade union leaders and assist quick settlements in major coal, railways, and road transport disputes. In February 1919 he opened the National Industrial Conference, but shared the cabinet disinclination to enforce an industrial concordat; and as the unrest persisted his sympathies gave way to lurid fears that trade union militancy indicated revolutionary intentions. Faced with imminent expiry of temporary unemployment payments intended to facilitate demobilization, he was responsible for the Unemployment Insurance Act of 1920, which extended the limited pre-war scheme to cover the majority of workers. This was both the basis of the inter-war system of unemployment insurance and the source of its chronic difficulties: conceived during the short-lived economic boom, it proved to be actuarially flawed once persistent depression and high unemployment began later in the year, plunging the insurance fund into persistent deficit.

On becoming president of the Board of Trade in March 1920 Horne addressed the delicate issue of trade policy, negotiating, against die-hard Conservative criticism, a trade agreement with Soviet Russia and preparing, against Coalition Liberal opposition, protective and anti-dumping measures in the Dyestuffs Act and the Safeguarding of Industries Bill, eventually carried by his successor, Stanley Baldwin. Horne also had ministerial responsibility for the coal industry, resisting the miners' associations' pressure for nationalization and handling renewed disputes over wages.

On his appointment as chancellor of the exchequer in April 1921 Horne was still engaged with a threatened national coal strike, and the budget statement of that year had to be introduced by his predecessor, Austen Chamberlain. By now the economic downturn had become severe, and intense pressure had developed from business, taxpayers groups, the Conservative Party, and Conservative newspapers for reductions in government expenditure and taxation. Horne became the chancellor most associated with Treasury deflation and the financial constriction of reconstruction policies. His attempts to make cuts in his own unemployment insurance scheme were politically unacceptable to the cabinet. But he cut expenditure on housing, ending the Addison scheme; and he acquiesced in the appointment of a non-ministerial economy committee (the 'Geddes axe') and supervised cabinet economy committees to impose education and civil service cuts. Consequently in his 1922 budget he could reduce the standard rate of income tax from 6s. to 5s., though he retained some flexibility for social service expenditure by suspending the sinking fund.

During the post-war years Horne also took London 'society' by storm. Urbane, affable, and ever cheerful, a good mimic and excellent raconteur, he became an habitué of nightclubs and parties, a favourite with political hostesses, and a renowned and often risqué after-dinner speaker. Though never marrying, he was a social success with women, not least as an accomplished dancer. In a 1923 doggerel he was:

> beaming Bert
> That incorrigible flirt
> Who loved to dance at all the Balls
> In London's noble marble Halls.
> (Bridgeman MSS)

His political strength came from great competence, versatility, and coolness in resolving difficulties as they arose, which made little impression on the wider public mind but won ministerial and parliamentary admiration. By 1922 he was a member of the inner government leadership. He shared in the abortive attempt to perpetuate the coalition at the next general election, and after the Conservative Party rebellion at the Carlton Club meeting of 19 October 1922 joined other 'Chamberlainite' Conservative former ministers in refusing to join Bonar Law's Conservative government.

Out of office, Horne's experience in commercial law, finance, and government, and his political and social contacts, were highly attractive in the City and in commerce. He soon had seven directorships and the chairmanship of the National Smelting Company, at this time reliant upon government co-operation for its survival, and these and their large accumulated income became a counter-attraction to politics. Along with loyalty to other 'Chamberlainites', they were a factor in his refusing the chancellorship of the exchequer when Baldwin became prime minister in May 1923. He rejoined the front bench when the Conservative leadership reunited in early 1924, but after the party's election victory in October declined an offer of the lesser, and lesser paid, office of minister of labour. Baldwin deplored this preference for private income before public service, reinforcing a moral disapproval of Horne's lifestyle and frequent switches of directorships in search of higher fees, including a brief vice-chairmanship of Baldwins Ltd. He concluded that Horne was 'that rare thing—a Scotch cad' (Middlemas and Barnes, 282), and never considered him for office again. Horne thereafter established a place among the business élite, usually sitting on between ten and fifteen boards, notably Lloyds Bank and Commercial Union Assurance Company, the Suez Canal Company, and the P. & O. Navigation Company, and at the time of his death occupying six chairmanships, including those of the Burma Corporation (from 1926), Zinc Corporation (1927), Imperial Smelting Corporation (1929), and the Great Western Railway (1934).

Even so Horne never withdrew wholly from politics, retaining his parliamentary seat and enjoying his status as a senior back-bencher, representing the sophisticated face of business politics, offering his patronage to younger MPs, and prepared, if circumstances—particularly Baldwin's removal—became propitious, to return to high government office. When Conservative Party troubles resumed after the 1929 election, he took a prominent part in various protectionist movements and emerged as a potential rival to Baldwin, but ultimately felt bound in June 1930 to defend him against Beaverbrook's

attempt to dictate party policy. In the later 1930s he was loosely associated with Churchill's criticism of the pace of rearmament and appeasement, and as political excitements intensified came to regret leaving the House of Commons as Viscount Horne of Slamannan in May 1937. After the outbreak of war in 1939 he was a member of Lord Salisbury's 'watching committee', critically scrutinizing Chamberlain's war policies. He died on 3 September 1940 at Farnham, Surrey, after an operation for appendicitis.

PHILIP WILLIAMSON

Sources *The Times* (4 Sept 1940) · *The Times* (11 Sept 1940) · *The Times* (13 Sept 1940) · *Directory of Directors* · M. Cowling, *The impact of labour, 1920–1924: the beginning of modern British politics* (1971) · K. O. Morgan, *Consensus and disunity: the Lloyd George coalition government, 1918–1922* (1979) · B. B. Gilbert, *British social policy, 1914–1939* (1970) · R. Lowe, *Adjusting to democracy: the role of the ministry of labour in British politics, 1916–1939* (1986) · P. Williamson, *National crisis and national government: British politics, the economy and empire, 1926–1932* (1992) · T. Jones, *Whitehall diary*, ed. K. Middlemas, 3 vols. (1969–71) · K. Middlemas and J. Barnes, *Baldwin: a biography* (1969) · Shrops. RRC, W. C. Bridgeman MSS · GEC, *Peerage* · Burke, *Peerage* (1939) · G. Channon, 'Horne, Robert Stevenson', *DBB* · *DNB* · *WWW*
Archives U. Glas., corresp. and lecture notes | HLRO, corresp. with Lord Beaverbrook · HLRO, corresp. with Andrew Bonar Law · HLRO, corresp. with David Lloyd George, etc. · Lpool RO, corresp. with seventeenth earl of Derby · NA Scot., corresp. with Lord Elibank · NL Scot., letters to Lord Beaverbrook · U. Birm., A. Chamberlain MSS | FILM BFI NFTVA, news footage
Likenesses W. Stoneman, photographs, 1918–39, NPG · I. Opffer, chalk drawing, 1931, NPG · T. Cottrell, print on cigarette card, NPG · H. J. Gunn, oils, Scot. NPG · Lafayette, photograph, NPG; repro. in *ILN* (29 April 1922) [*see illus.*] · B. Partridge, caricature, pen-and-ink drawing, NPG; repro. in *Punch* (10 May 1922)
Wealth at death £64,923 8s. 6d.: confirmation, 7 Jan 1941, *CCI*

Horne, (Charles) Silvester (1865–1914), Congregational minister and politician, was born in Cuckfield, Sussex, on 15 April 1865, the youngest of three sons and four children of Charles Horne (1829–1903), Congregational minister and later editor of the *Newport Advertiser*, and his wife, Harriet Simpson, daughter of the superintendent of government tobacco warehouses in Liverpool. Educated at Newport grammar school, Horne joined Newport's Congregational church, and, with the ministry in mind, went to Glasgow University (MA, 1886) and then Mansfield College, Oxford, where he took the three-year college course in theology. In 1887 he was invited to Kensington chapel, where he was ordained on 17 October 1889: determined that Horne should be its minister, Kensington waited eighteen months for him to complete his course. In August 1892 he married Katharine Maria (1870–1958), elder daughter of Sir Herbert Hardy (later first Baron) Cozens-*Hardy MP, later master of the rolls. They had three sons and four daughters.

Horne arrived at Kensington the freshest star in the nonconformist firmament; he left heir presumptive to Hugh Price Hughes and John Clifford. He galvanized his congregation, as admired for his campaigns to students or country towns as for his commemorative services. He wrote a novel, *A Modern Heretic* (1893), as well as *A Manual of Church Fellowship* (1893) and popular histories of the London Missionary Society (1895) and the free churches (1903). Thus he became known, and he declined repeated calls to important churches before accepting the challenge of the debt-burdened Whitefield's Tabernacle in Tottenham Court Road, London.

Horne moved there in September 1903 to promote a mission modelled on Wesleyan central halls. The Whitefield's combination of Congregationalism and club-cum-business house for Christ, captured in its banner (a knight ascending to shining towers burdened by a broken comrade) and its motto 'No quest, no conquest', appeared to be effortless.

In 1910, at the height of the New Theology controversy, Horne became chairman of the Congregational Union of England and Wales, his friendship with the chief protagonists preventing undue bloodletting. He was now a national figure, a passive resister, pro-Boer, and a rumbustious electioneer, fighting as a Progressive in London and being urged to fight in Birmingham. In December 1909 invitations to become their MP came from both Merthyr and Ipswich. Encouraged by friends who saw him as a nonconformist Lord Hugh Cecil (later Baron Quickswood), Horne stood for Ipswich.

Horne sat from January 1910, the first nonconformist MP in pastoral charge since Praisegod Barebones. He gained no instant parliamentary fame, although he was a useful back-bencher; and there is some evidence that his arguments were instrumental in moving the mind of Asquith (a distant connection of Katharine Horne) towards the granting of universal suffrage. His maiden speech was on the Congo and his last was on home rule for Ireland. In between he delivered speeches on peace, colonial exploitation, and Welsh disestablishment.

Horne, whose passion was golf, seemed forever off in a taxi to address a meeting somewhere. He attracted children and men, but women were less at ease with him. He was a poor but amusing correspondent. Oddly for so fluent a man he wrote his sermons in advance of delivery, and he also prayed with his eyes open, which added to the impact of his public prayer. In London he lived at Campden Hill Gardens and later at Ampthill Square. He built The Bluff at Sheringham and the White House at Church Stretton, whose architect, P. R. Morley Horder, collaborated with him in plans and designs for *The Institutional Church* (1906). His youngest son was (Charles) Kenneth *Horne (1907–1969), a notable radio comedian.

By 1914 Horne was faltering, for his effortlessness was illusory. The voice which had charmed his early hearers grew hoarse. The techniques of the pulpit were too dominant for Westminster, and those of the platform worried Whitefield's. Their doubts shook him. He resigned from Whitefield's and intended to resign from parliament, and went to lecture at Yale University on 'The romance of preaching'. After Yale he travelled to Canada. He died on 2 May 1914 while standing on deck as his steamer entered Toronto harbour. His body was returned to Church Stretton for burial, where he was also commemorated by a village institute designed by Morley Horder.

CLYDE BINFIELD, rev.

Sources W. B. Selbie, *The life of Charles Silvester Horne* (1920) • C. Binfield, *So down to prayers: studies in English nonconformity, 1780–1920*

(1977) • J. C. Binfield, 'Horne, Charles Silvester', *BDMBR*, vol. 3, pt 1 • private information (1993) [Ronald Cozens-Hardy Horne and others] • *WWW* • *CGPLA Eng. & Wales* (1914)
Archives BLPES, corresp. with E. D. Morel
Likenesses H. G. Rivière, oils, 1904, Castlegate Congregational Centre, Nottingham • R. Haines, photograph, repro. in Selbie, *Life*, frontispiece
Wealth at death £8450 19s. 5d.: probate, 1 July 1914, *CGPLA Eng. & Wales*

Horne, Thomas (1610–1654), headmaster, son of William Horne of Cassall, Nottinghamshire, was born at West Hallam, Derbyshire. He matriculated at Magdalen Hall, Oxford, on 28 January 1625, graduating BA on 14 February 1629 and proceeding MA on 4 July 1633. After keeping a private school in London, he was then master of the free school, Leicester, for about two years, and of Tonbridge School from 1640 to 1648. In 1648 he succeeded George Goad as master of Eton College, where Robert Boyle was his pupil.

Horne was the author and translator of several popular school books. His translations of Jan Comenius's *Janua linguarum* in the Latin, English, French, and Spanish version of 1634 and the bilingual version of 1636 went through several editions, as did his *Cheiragōgia, sive, Manuductio*, first published in 1641.

Horne died at Eton College on 22 August 1654 and was buried on 24 August in the college chapel. Two of Horne's sons became distinguished scholars. One, William, a scholar of Eton, graduated BA in 1660 and proceeded MA in 1664 from King's College, Cambridge, was elected fellow, and became assistant master at Eton and afterwards master of Harrow. The other, Thomas, also a scholar of Eton, graduated BA in 1662 and proceeded MA in 1666 from King's College, Cambridge, where he was elected a fellow. He became chaplain to the earl of St Albans and was senior proctor at Cambridge in 1682, when he also was appointed fellow of Eton. He published several sermons.

E. T. BRADLEY, rev. S. E. MEALOR

Sources *Athenae Oxonienses ... containing the life of Wood*, ed. P. Bliss, another edn, [1] (1848) • Wood, *Ath. Oxon.: Fasti*, new edn • J. Nichols, *Queries proposed to the nobility, gentry and clergy of Leicestershire* [1787] • W. Combe, *The history of the colleges of Winchester, Eton and Westminster* (1816) • T. Harwood, *Alumni Etonenses, or, A catalogue of the provosts and fellows of Eton College and King's College, Cambridge, from the foundation in 1443 to the year 1797* (1797) • H. C. Maxwell Lyte, *A history of Eton College, 1440–1875* (1875) • W. O. Hughs-Hughes, ed., *The register of Tonbridge School from 1820 to 1886* (1886) • S. Rivington, *The history of Tonbridge School*, 4th edn (1925) • *STC, 1475–1640* • Wing, *STC*

Horne, Thomas Hartwell (1780–1862), biblical scholar and bibliographer, was born in Chancery Lane, London, on 20 October 1780, the son of William Horne, a barrister's clerk and the eldest of six. He was educated successively at a dame-school at Eversley, Hampshire, then at a boys' school in London, and at Christ's Hospital, where he remained from 1789 to 21 October 1795, and was awarded a senior scholarship (deputy Grecian). He overlapped as a student at Christ's Hospital with Samuel Taylor Coleridge, who was head Grecian. In the summer of 1790 Coleridge taught him, among other skills, the Greek alphabet.

The early death of his parents meant that he was unable

to go to university. Since he was also sickly, he needed to choose a career which would not tax his physical energies. In 1796 he became a barrister's clerk and began to write in order to supplement his low wages. His first publication, when he was aged only eighteen, was *A Brief View of the Necessity and Truth of the Christian Revelation* (1800 and 1802). It was at this point that the idea of writing a complete introduction to the study of the scriptures was conceived, a project that would take seventeen years. Soon afterwards he became a Wesleyan Methodist, remaining in communion with the Wesleyans until ordination in the Church of England became a possibility. He continued to work as a clerical and literary assistant in various fields and to various people: to Dr Willich (doctor of medicine); to William Cruise, a Catholic barrister; to Charles Butler, a Catholic historian, and from 1806 to 1809 as private clerk to Joseph Butterworth. Various publications, medical, legal, and historical, were produced under his editing and supervision, and some were translated by him. In 1814 he published his impressive *Introduction to the Study of Bibliography* (2 vols.). Meanwhile he devoted himself late at night and early in the morning to editing or compiling works on varied subjects such as grazing (*The Complete Grazier* was published anonymously in 1805), theology, law, Sunday schools (*Hints on the Formation and Management of Sunday Schools* was published anonymously in 1807), topography, and bibliography.

In 1808 Horne was recommended by Butterworth to compile the indexes of the catalogue of the Harleian manuscripts in the British Museum. After its completion he continued to be employed in the record office at the Chapter House, Westminster. In 1812 he married Sarah, eldest daughter of John Millard, solicitor. They had two daughters, one of whom, Sarah Anne, later became the mother of the Old Testament scholar T. K. Cheyne. In 1816 he began work on the index to the *Rotuli Scotiae in turri Londonensi et in domo capitulari Westmonasteriensi asservati*, and from 1817 to 1819 was junior clerk at the record office.

In 1818 Horne published the first edition of *An Introduction to the Critical Study and Knowledge of the Holy Scriptures* (3 vols., 1818; 4 vols., 1821). The research for this substantial work, which provided a mine of bibliographical information, had taken him from 1801 to 1812, and the writing took a further five years. It rapidly became the standard textbook for the study of the scriptures in all English-speaking Anglican colleges and universities and underwent several editions in the 1820s, and further editions later. It was a popular work also in the United States of America. While it was clearly the work of an orthodox scholar, he recognized the difficulties presented by a plain reading of the text. Although Horne sought to deal with these by correcting the traditional text in order to restore unity, for example by rearranging the order, his study acknowledged issues of a critical nature and the focuses of source criticism. For this reason, Joseph M'Caul would describe him as 'the nursing-father of modern English biblical criticism' (Cheyne, viii). However, the content of the volume rewritten by the critical scholar Samuel

Davidson (the tenth edition, 1856), and the controversy which ensued, dismayed him, and he dissociated himself from Davidson and his work.

The popularity of the *Introduction* afforded Horne an honorary MA in 1818 from King's College, Aberdeen, and also influenced W. Howley, bishop of London, in his decision to ordain him to the curacy of Christ Church Greyfriars in 1819. In November 1833 he became rector of the parish of St Edmund the King with St Nicholas Acons in the City of London. In 1831 he became a prebendary in St Paul's Cathedral.

Until 1823 Horne had been sub-librarian to the Surrey Institution. From 1824 until his retirement in 1861, at eighty-one, he was senior assistant librarian in the department of printed books in the British Museum. There he worked five days a week, combining this with his duties as rector and with his literary activities. While working on the second edition of his *Introduction* he was appointed in 1821 to the task of compiling a classified catalogue of Queens' College Library, Cambridge, and three years later undertook to compile a similar catalogue of the printed books in the British Museum. This work was eventually abandoned in favour of a rival alphabetical catalogue. In 1822 he was admitted to the Eclectic Society, and in March 1828 was elected a fellow of the Society of Antiquaries. In 1829 he took the degree of BD at St John's College, Cambridge, as a 'ten year man'. At his suggestion, the commemoration of the publication of the English Bible by Myles Coverdale was celebrated in 1835. Alongside his biblical scholarship, he published several polemical works, including *Deism Refuted, or, Plain Reasons for being a Christian* (1819), and *Romanism Contrary to the Bible* (1827). He continued to provide bibliographical sources: *A Compendious Introduction to the Study of the Bible* appeared in 1827 and *A Manual of Biblical Bibliography* in 1839.

Horne's wife, Sarah, died on 7 July 1858 and he suffered himself from a respiratory disease. He died at his home, 47 Bloomsbury Square, London, on 27 January 1862, and was buried in the cemetery at Nunhead on 3 February.

JOANNA HAWKE

Sources *Reminiscences, personal and bibliographical, of Thomas Hartwell Horne*, ed. S. A. Cheyne (1862) • *GM*, 3rd ser., 12 (1862), 504–8 • J. Rogerson, *Old Testament criticism in the nineteenth century: England and Germany* (1984), 182–4 • J. Davson, 'Critical and conservative treatments of prophecy in nineteenth-century Britain', DPhil diss., U. Oxf., 1991, chap. 1 • [T. T. Shore], ed., *Cassell's biographical dictionary* (1867–9) • Allibone, *Dict.* • C. Knight, ed., *The English cyclopaedia: biography*, 6 vols. (1856–8)

Archives BL, corresp. and papers, Add. MS 46844

Likenesses H. Adlard, line engraving (after photograph), BM; repro. in Cheyne, ed., *Reminiscences*, frontispiece • J. Cochrane, stipple and line engraving (after photograph), NPG

Wealth at death under £4000: probate, 22 Feb 1862, *CGPLA Eng. & Wales*

Horne, Sir William (1774–1860), barrister and politician, was the second son of the Revd Thomas Horne (d. 1826), who kept a private school, Manor House, Chiswick, where Lord Lyndhurst was educated. He was admitted a student at Lincoln's Inn on 3 June 1793 and called to the bar on 23 June 1798. On 12 August 1799 he married Ann (d. 12 Nov

1849), daughter of James Hesse of Bedfordshire; they had at least four sons and several daughters. In 1818, on losing his seat in the Commons, he became a king's counsel, and on 6 November 1818 was made a bencher of his inn. He was a distinguished leader in the court of chancery for many years before being appointed attorney-general to Queen Adelaide in 1830. When Brougham became lord chancellor a law officer was necessary to assist him in the court of chancery, and Horne was appointed. He became solicitor-general on 26 November 1830, and was knighted at that time; but his abilities made him no match for Sugden in the courts, and in the House of Commons he was deficient in adroitness. He sat for Helston in Cornwall from 1812 to 1818, and when he became an officer of the crown a seat was found for him first at Bletchingley, Surrey, which he held from 18 February to the dissolution on 23 April 1831, and then for Newtown in the Isle of Wight for the parliament of 1831–2. After the Reform Act he represented the new constituency of Marylebone (1832–4). When Denman succeeded as lord chief justice, Brougham made a vain attempt to induce Sir John Bayley to retire from the court of exchequer to make way for Horne there. Horne was appointed attorney-general (November 1832) with John Campbell as solicitor-general. Campbell was not long in pressing his claims to promotion, and Bayley was at last forced into resignation in Horne's favour (February 1834). Horne's opposition to capital punishment prevented him going on circuit or sitting in a criminal court. After a conversation with the lord chancellor, he imagined that the court was to be remodelled, and that he would not be called upon to undertake these duties; but this plan, if ever entertained by Brougham, proved impracticable, and Horne was told that he must either resign or be superseded. He replied 'with great spirit' that he would vacate his office, and thereupon withdrew to private practice. After several years he accepted from Lord Cottenham, on 23 July 1839, the post of master in chancery which he held until 1853. Horne, whose country house was Ponfield, Herefordshire, died at his London home, 49 Upper Harley Street, on 13 July 1860. Campbell acknowledged Horne's 'many valuable qualities', and Brougham referred to the 'abominable treatment of Horne' and his 'admirable and truly unexampled behaviour'. Horne's third son, Francis Woodley Horne, a major in the 7th hussars, was killed in the Indian mutiny on the River Rapti in 1858, and is commemorated on a tablet in Little Berkhamsted church (Cussans, vol. 2, pt 2, 168).

W. P. COURTNEY, rev. H. C. G. MATTHEW

Sources The Times (14 July 1860) · T. Martin, Lord Lyndhurst (1883) · D. Le Marchant, Life of … third Earl Spencer (1876) · H. P. Brougham, The life and times of Henry, Lord Brougham, ed. W. Brougham, 3 vols. (1871) · GM, 2nd ser., 12 (1839), 194 · GM, 2nd ser., 32 (1849), 665 · Life of John, Lord Campbell, lord high chancellor of Great Britain, ed. Mrs Hardcastle, 2 vols. (1881) · HoP, Commons · J. E. Cussans, History of Hertfordshire, 3 vols. (1870–81) · The Greville memoirs, 1814–1860, ed. L. Strachey and R. Fulford, 8 vols. (1938) · CGPLA Eng. & Wales (1860)
Likenesses G. Hayter, group portrait, oils (The House of Commons, 1833), NPG

Wealth at death under £30,000: probate, 20 Aug 1860, CGPLA Eng. & Wales

Horne, Sir William Cornelius Van (1843–1915), railway builder and financier in Canada, was born on 3 February 1843 at Chelsea, Will county, Illinois, USA, the eldest son of Cornelius Covenhoven Van Horne, lawyer, and his second wife, Mary Minier Richards. His father's ancestors had emigrated from the Netherlands to New Amsterdam in 1635, and on his mother's side he came partly of German, partly of French stock. From 1849 to 1857 he attended the public schools of Chelsea and Joliet, Illinois. He then became a telegraph operator on the Chicago and Alton Railway, one of the lines which was opening up the west, and by energy and ability rose steadily. Van Horne married in March 1867 Lucy Adaline, only daughter of Erastus Hurd, civil engineer, of Galesburg, Illinois. They had one son and one daughter.

From 1874 to 1879 Van Horne was general manager of the Southern Minnesota Railway, and from 1879 to 1881 general superintendent of the Chicago, Milwaukee, and St Paul line. In 1881 he accepted the general managership of the newly formed Canadian Pacific Railway, the construction of which was one of the terms upon which British Columbia had entered the Canadian federation. Van Horne pushed construction at such a frenetic pace that the last spike of the main line was driven on 7 November 1885, some six years ahead of schedule. In 1884 he became vice-president of the company, and in August 1888 he was succeeded as general manager by Thomas George Shaughnessy. From 1888 to 1899 he was president of the company, and from 1899 to 1910 chairman of the board of directors. From the first he saw that settlement must go hand in hand with construction, and showed foresight and ingenuity in encouraging immigration to the vast Canadian west.

Van Horne became a naturalized Canadian in 1888, and in 1894 was created an honorary KCMG. From 1884 onwards he lived in Montreal, but he travelled so regularly that he claimed to have covered more miles than any other living man. Despite his American origins, Van Horne came to recognize himself as a Canadian, and even intervened in Canadian politics from time to time if his own interests were materially affected. He was, for example, influential in the defeat of trade reciprocity with the United States in 1891 and 1911. From 1900 until his death he was increasingly interested in the development of Cuba. He was both founder and president of the Cuba Company, building the country's first trans-island railway. He died at the Royal Victoria Hospital in Montreal on 11 September 1915, after an operation for an internal abscess. He was survived by his wife, and was buried at Joliet, Illinois, USA, on 15 September.

Van Horne was tall and strong, and despite his enormous girth had great physical vitality and power of work. In his later years he became even more corpulent, but his energy never slackened. After a hard day's work he would spend the night at chess or poker, and turn to the next day's work with unexhausted ardour. Less concerned with systematic organization and management, his great ability lay in his demonic energy and his charismatic hold over those who worked for him, and he is now recognized as one of the great railway builders of North America. His interests were very wide; he had great natural talent as a watercolourist, and made large collections of old masters, pottery, and palaeontological specimens. He was a member of the Unitarian church.

W. L. GRANT, *rev.* GREGORY P. MARCHILDON

Sources W. Vaughan, *The life and work of Sir William Van Horne* (1920) · W. K. Lamb, *History of the Canadian Pacific Railway* (1977) · D. Cruise and A. Griffiths, *Lords of the line: the men who built the CPR* (1988) · P. Berton, *The last spike: the great railway, 1881–1885* (1971) · J. A. Eagle, *The Canadian Pacific Railway and the development of western Canada, 1896–1914* (1989) · G. D. Taylor and P. A. Baskerville, *A concise history of business in Canada* (1994) · M. Bliss, *Northern enterprise: five centuries of Canadian business* (1987) · C. L. Sibley, 'Van Horne and his Cuban railway', *Canadian Magazine*, 41 (1913), 444–51
Archives Canadian Railroad Historical Association | Canadian Pacific Railway Archives, Montreal, CPR MSS · James Jerome Hill Reference Library, St Paul, Minnesota, J. J. Hill MSS · NA Canada, Canadian Pacific Railway (CPR) MSS
Likenesses photograph, NA Canada; repro. in Eagle, *The Canadian Pacific railway* · photograph, repro. in Vaughan, *Life and work*, introduction, 84, 132 · photographs, repro. in Cruise and Griffiths, *Lords of the line*, 120, 134, 220

Hornebolt, Gerard. *See* Horenbout, Gerard (*d.* 1540/41).

Horneby, Henry. *See* Hornby, Henry (*c.*1457–1518).

Horneck, Anthony (1641–1697), Church of England clergyman, was born at Bacharach in the Lower Palatinate in 1641, the son of Phillip Elias Horneck, the recorder of the town, and his wife, Anna Sophia, *née* Grammartz. Anthony's father educated him for the Reformed ministry under Friedrich Spanheim at Heidelberg. Like many Lutheran and Reformed theologians at that time Horneck came to England to continue his studies in 1660. On 21 December 1663 he was incorporated at Oxford MA from Heidelberg, and three days later was entered at Queen's College, Oxford, where he caught the eye of the provost, Thomas Barlow, who had the reputation of being a stiff Calvinist and also a patron of needy scholars.

Horneck's reputation was based partly on his expertise in oriental languages, and partly on a personal piety which he sustained lifelong. Ecclesiastical preferment, none of it very lucrative, followed: Barlow appointed him college chaplain; Lincoln College presented him to the Oxford living of All Saints'; in 1670 the duke of Albemarle (to whose son he had been a tutor) presented him to the living of Dolton, Devon, and got the bishop of Exeter to grant him a prebend in the cathedral worth £20 p.a. In 1669 he returned to the Palatinate, where his preaching at the court of the elector, Charles Lewis, was well received. In 1671 he was appointed preacher in the Savoy and in February the following year married Jane Boulton (*b.* 1649/50), who was to outlive him. Horneck was an outspoken critic of pluralities and non-residence, and although his new appointment carried almost no income and involved his renting a house, he resigned the parish of Dolton. He soon had a family of four children (among them the satirist and poet Philip *Horneck), but his fidelity to the protestant

Anthony Horneck (1641–1697), by Robert White, pubd 1706 (after Mary Beale)

interest cost him the support of prospective patrons. In 1693 the Russell family, dukes of Bedford, prevailed on Queen Mary to grant him a prebend in Westminster Abbey, and in 1694 arranged for him to exchange his Exeter prebend for another exiguous one at Bath and Wells.

Bishop Kidder, Horneck's biographer, regarded him as 'a true son of the Church of England equidistant from the innovations of Rome and from Enthusiasm' (Kidder, xxvi); in fact he brought the equipment of an adherent of the Reformed orthodox party to bear on a church situation in England dominated by the prospect of a Catholic succession to the crown, a prospect actually realized in his lifetime in his native Palatinate. In the seventeenth century both the Lutheran and the Reformed orthodox parties displayed an unparalleled enthusiasm for Rabbinic and Hebrew studies; and this was the strongest feature of Horneck's intellectual equipment, and led to the award of a Cambridge DD in 1681. Like the protestant orthodox generally, he depended excessively for his leverage upon conscience upon the assertion that the ultimate day of judgment was at hand, and like them was prepared to soften the asceticism for which he called by classifying as things indifferent a more liberal list of worldly pleasures than would have been countenanced by the pietists of the next generation.

Horneck shared the protestant orthodox belief in witches, contributing an appendix of Swedish cases to Joseph Glanville's *Saducismus triumphatus* (2nd edn, 1682). In the orthodox manner again he increased the appeal of his preaching by calling upon the mysticism which formed an important component of popular religion. The great object of his ministry was so to internalize protestant principles in his flock as to stay them in the event of a failure of the protestant succession. A 'florid, fervent and pathetique' (Kemble, 193) style of preaching gathered a large congregation in the Savoy, and his monthly communions were noted not merely for their devotion but for the unheard of proportion they bore to the congregations at the normal preaching services. In the same way he began religious societies for young men, with strict rules, and after 1689 supported the movement for the reformation of manners. Burnet noted:

> things of that kind had been formerly practised only among the puritans and dissenters; but these were of the church, and came to their ministers to be assisted with forms of prayer and other directions; they were chiefly conducted by Dr Beveridge and Dr Horneck. (*Burnet's History*, 709)

Much of Horneck's literary output was devoted to working out rules of life for ordinary Christians, and his *Fire of the Altar*, a work designed to assist the devout communicant, ran to at least fourteen editions. In the end Horneck received his reward: in 1693 he became chaplain to William III and the first of a series of court chaplains and German preachers in the Savoy who played a distinguished role in British religious life for most of the eighteenth century. Always ascetic, usually eating in the evening only 'an Apple or two, with a little Bread, and small Ale or Milk-Water' (Kidder, 1.xxvi) and finally giving up wine, he laboured tirelessly, despite the fact that the stone latterly made both walking and riding in a coach agony to him. Over Christmas 1696 he worked desperately hard, and his health declined rapidly. He died near the Savoy on 31 January 1697 and was buried in Westminster Abbey before an enormous funeral congregation. **W. R. WARD**

Sources R. B. Hone, *Lives of eminent Christians* (1834–43), 2.305–68 · W. J. Loftie, *Memorials of the Savoy* (1871) · F. W. B. Bullock, *Voluntary religious societies, 1520–1799* (1963) · G. V. Portus, *Caritas Anglicana* (1912) · J. Glanville, *Saducismus triumphatus, or, Full and plain evidence concerning witches and apparitions*, trans. A. Horneck, 2nd edn, 2 pts (1682) · A. Horneck, *Delight and judgment* (1684) · A. Horneck, *The happy ascetick* (1681) · J. Spurr, *The Restoration Church of England, 1646–1689* (1991) · *Bishop Burnet's History of his own time*, new edn (1875) · J. M. Kemble, ed., *State papers and correspondence illustrative of the social and political state of Europe from the revolution to the accession of the house of Hanover* (1857) · R. Kidder, 'Life of the author', in A. Horneck, *Several sermons upon the fifth of St Matthew*, 2nd edn (1706) · private information (2004) [Scott Kisker] · *DNB* · will, PRO, PROB 11/438, sig. 94 · J. L. Chester and J. Foster, eds., *London marriage licences, 1521–1869* (1887)
Likenesses R. White, line engraving, pubd 1706 (after M. Beale), BM, NPG [*see illus.*]

Horneck, Philip (1673/4–1728), journalist, was born in London, the son of Anthony *Horneck (1641–1697), clergyman and author of devotional works, and his wife, Jane,

née Boulton (b. 1649/50). His early education was at the Charterhouse; he was admitted to St John's College, Cambridge, on 1 November 1690, aged sixteen, migrated to Sidney Sussex College on 26 May 1697, and was awarded a Cambridge LLB in 1698. He was ordained deacon in the London diocese on 7 May 1698 and became chaplain to Francis, second Baron Guilford. His first publication was a sermon (1699) on the death of his patron's young wife. He may be the Philip Horneck who was listed as a naval chaplain in 1709.

Horneck displayed his whiggism in a feeble *Ode* published by Curll in March 1709, addressed to Thomas, earl of Wharton (1648–1715), and, far more outspokenly, in a vituperative twice-weekly satirical journal, the *High German Doctor*, which ran from 30 April 1714 to 12 May 1715 and was reprinted with additions, alterations, and a large explanatory index in 1715 and 1719–20. This journal's anti-Jacobite frenzy reflects in extreme form the political uncertainties and fears of the months surrounding Queen Anne's death and the Hanoverian succession. Using the fiction that tory ministers are quack doctors Horneck attacks Oxford ('Doctor Hermodactyl') and Bolingbroke ('Harry Gambol') as well as Jacobite high-churchmen such as Atterbury ('Frank Scammony'). His few glancing blows at their friend Pope are slight and incidental, but were enough to provoke sharp replies in at least three prose pieces by Pope in 1715 and at last to earn Horneck immortality in *The Dunciad* (1728, 3.146).

Horneck's earthly reward was to be appointed solicitor to the Treasury on 18 January 1716 at a salary of £500 per annum. He promptly expressed his gratitude in a flatulent *Votive Ode* (February 1716) wishing prosperity to the royal family. He had a law degree but the appointment was probably a sinecure. It did not free him completely from financial troubles, for in September 1721 he was committed to the king's bench prison for various debts (Rogers, 304). He died, unmarried, on 13 October 1728 and was succeeded in his Treasury office by his friend and fellow *Dunciad* victim Edward Roome (d. 1729). **JAMES SAMBROOK**

Sources Venn, *Alum. Cant.* · J. C. Sainty, ed., *Treasury officials, 1660–1870* (1972), 133 · P. Rogers, *Grub Street: studies in a subculture* (1972), 304 · J. L. Chester and J. Foster, eds., *London marriage licences, 1521–1869* (1887) · *The High German Doctor and the English fool*, satirical engraving, Bodl. Oxf., Douce prints a.49, fol. 162 · *The memoirs of Martinus Scriblerus*, ed. C. Kerby-Miller (1950), 116, 241 · *The prose works of Alexander Pope*, 1, ed. N. Ault (1936), 179, 206–7 · J. V. Guerinot, *Pamphlet attacks on Alexander Pope, 1711–1744* (1969), 18–19, 27, 32 · *N&Q*, 2nd ser., 9 (1860), 419 · *N&Q*, 3rd ser., 6 (1864), 92 · G. Taylor, *The sea chaplains* (1978)

Hornel, Edward Atkinson (1864–1933). *See under* Glasgow Boys (*act.* 1875–1895).

Horner, Arthur Lewis (1894–1968), trade unionist and communist, was born at Merthyr Tudful, Glamorgan, on 5 April 1894, the eldest son in a family of seventeen children, eleven of whom died at birth or in early childhood. His father, James Horner, was a railwayman from Northumberland and his mother, Emily, came from Llandrindod Wells in mid-Wales. Horner was brought up

Arthur Lewis Horner (1894–1968), by Bassano

against a background of religious nonconformity and the emerging Independent Labour Party (ILP) and was greatly influenced by the Christian socialism of Keir Hardie, Merthyr's MP. His father's involvement with the Co-operative Society, the Rechabites, and the Temperance Society, and his parents' adherence to the Baptist cause (the Church of Christ) were also formative influences. Horner was educated at elementary schools in Merthyr until he was twelve, but had already worked part-time from the age of eight for a grocer and a barber. Between 1908 and 1915 he was, at different times, a railway platform boy, a shop assistant (several times), a travelling salesman, and a grocer's haulier.

By the time Horner was fifteen he was known as the 'Welsh boy preacher' although he was also actively involved in boxing, football, and foot-racing—all of which provided him with a physical hardness that was to prove useful in the coming decades. In 1911 he was awarded a two-year scholarship at the Training Centre of the Church of Christ in Birmingham but stayed only six months. As late as 1913, however, he was associated with the Christadelphian sect. The turning point in his career came when chapel deacons tried to censor his sermons for being too political and pacifist.

In May 1916 Horner entered the coal industry as a surface worker at Ynys-hir's Standard colliery in the Rhondda Fach and began his lifelong commitment to the miners' cause as an activist in the South Wales Miners' Federation (SWMF). He had joined the ILP as early as 1909, and was subsequently influenced by the Unofficial Reform Committee's pamphlet, *The Miners' Next Step* (1912), which emphasized the primacy of trade unionism in the process of political change: the syndicalist perspective it embodied continued, despite his later avowed communism, to be a major influence on him throughout his life. This outlook was reinforced by the influence of Noah Ablett, one of the authors of *The Miners' Next Step*, whose Marxist Plebs' League classes he attended.

When war broke out in 1914 Horner opposed it on political and religious grounds but, as the anti-war movement developed alongside the rising tide of industrial militancy, Horner adopted an increasingly revolutionary position through his membership of the Rhondda Socialist Society. He was forced to move first to Lewis Merthyr colliery and then to Mardy colliery because of his anti-war and industrial activities. In the midst of all this turmoil, on 8 June 1916 he married Ethel Mary (*née* Merrick), who remained his most important personal and political supporter; they had three daughters.

Hunted by police for evading military service, Horner exchanged one assumed name (Arthur T. Johns) for another (Jack O'Brien) and fled to Ireland to join the Irish Citizen Army in 1918. On his return in August he was sentenced to six months' hard labour. On release he was again arrested, handed over to the military, court-martialled for incorrigible misconduct in refusing to serve in the armed forces, and sentenced to two years' hard labour. He derived the title of his autobiography *Incorrigible Rebel* (1960) from this charge. While in Carmarthen gaol he was elected checkweighman at Mardy colliery assisted by Ablett and his friend Charlie Jones: he was released under the 'Cat and Mouse' (introduced before the war to deal with hunger-striking suffragettes) following his hunger strike. So began his association with Mardy, soon to be described as 'Little Moscow': the pit, the lodge, the town, the party, and Horner were for the coming decades to be inextricably linked.

Arthur and Ethel Horner became foundation members of the Communist Party (CP) when the Rhondda Socialist Society joined the new organization in 1920. By 1923 he was a part-time member of the political bureau and following the arrest of the CP leadership in 1925 became head of the industrial department. Moreover through his leading role in the miners' minority movement and membership of the executive of the SWMF (1925–7) and the Miners' Federation of Great Britain (MFGB; 1926–7) he was by the mid-1920s the most prominent communist trade unionist in the country.

Horner's uncompromising position over the 1926 miners' lock-out meant that he increasingly parted company with such erstwhile allies as Aneurin Bevan in south Wales and nationally with A. J. Cook, secretary of the MFGB. Excluded from key forums locally and nationally in the late 1920s, Horner focused his attention on the CP and the National Unemployed Workers' Movement, unsuccessfully contesting parliamentary elections in Rhondda East in 1929, 1931, and 1933. He was also a leader of the 1927 hunger march. During this difficult period of rising unemployment, trade union retreat, and the growth of European fascism, he came into conflict with his own party over the demand of the Communist International (CI) for independent revolutionary trade unions. He was called to Moscow in 1931 to explain the so-called deviation of 'Hornerism' following his removal from the leadership of the minority movement. The CI acknowledged that there was no deviation but Horner was guilty of indiscipline.

Horner's troubles were compounded in this period with the expulsion of the Mardy lodge in 1930 for continued support of the minority movement and the Communist Party and in 1932 by his imprisonment for leading a demonstration against the action of bailiffs in Mardy. All this was happening against the continuing social and industrial decline of the locality. Paradoxically the prison sentence provided a lifeline. As prison librarian, he read widely, including the Bible, and deepened his knowledge of Clausewitz and Marx. Moreover he achieved renewed public prominence through a nationwide campaign for his release. Having gained a remission of his sentence, he narrowly lost a parliamentary by-election in 1933. With his election very shortly after this as a miners' agent in the more prosperous western anthracite district he once again focused his attentions on his main political interest, the miners' union. This provided the springboard for his election as the first communist president of the SWMF in 1936. His presidency was distinguished by a wide range of achievements: the first major restructuring of coalfield wages in Britain in 1937; the elimination of the 'company' union in 1938 and growing left–right political unity with support for the united front; and the leading of international solidarity campaigns, notably support for the Spanish republican cause in Spain, which he visited on two occasions.

With the outbreak of war in 1939 Horner was again in conflict with the CP in refusing to accept the change of line in characterizing it as an imperialist war. His unequivocal opposition to fascism led him, on the fall of France, to be involved in secret government preparations for resistance and was also responsible for his condemnation of unofficial strikes. In the closing year of the war he played a crucial role with Sam Watson of Durham in the creation of the National Union of Mineworkers (NUM) whose constitution was a balance between national unity and regional autonomy.

With the coming of peace, Horner's standing was such that he was appointed national coal production officer in 1945 and elected general secretary of the NUM by a large majority in 1946; he was able to play a crucial role in the shaping of the new National Coal Board (NCB) in 1947. Through his close association with Emanuel Shinwell (minister of fuel and power) Horner was not only the outstanding figure in shaping the early years of the NUM and the NCB but also played a not insignificant part, given the importance of coal, in the rebuilding of the post-war British economy.

However, the broad political unity within the labour movement and more specifically in the NUM was shattered with the onset of the cold war. In particular, Horner's public support for a communist-led miners' strike in France in 1948 was condemned by his own right-wing dominated national executive which thereafter prevented him from being the public political spokesman of the union. Further conflicts over German rearmament and the Hungarian uprising put him under more pressure, even though he criticized the execution of Imre Nagy in 1956. He nevertheless remained a member of the Communist Party until his death. Although his outstanding abilities were widely acknowledged, he was prevented from taking the seat on the general council of the Trades Union Congress which was, by custom and practice, reserved for the miners' general secretary.

Despite these difficulties, Horner's period as general secretary was one of considerable achievement, with the NUM centrally involved in every aspect of the nationalized industry: indeed much of the miners' charter which he had been asked to draft in 1945 had been won by the time of his retirement. He continued to play the leading role in negotiations with the NCB; his grasp of the issues and his negotiating abilities evidently made him indispensable. The 'third day wage structure' was a particular milestone in preparing the way for the elimination of the divisive piece-work system. It was a particular personal pleasure for him to be succeeded in 1959 by his close friend and fellow communist from south Wales, Will Paynter.

On his retirement from the NUM Horner was awarded the freedom of his native Merthyr Tudful. Despite a life of conflict, his personal charm and honesty meant that he made few enemies. He died on 4 September 1968 at his Middlesex home, 21 Eversley Avenue, Wembley. His wife predeceased him on 9 February 1965. A tablet was erected in their memory at Golders Green crematorium with the following inscription: 'In memory of Arthur Horner, Miners' Leader, 1894–1968 and Ethel his wife. Their God was a man covered in coaldust.' HYWEL FRANCIS

Sources U. Wales, South Wales Miners' Library, South Wales Coalfield collection, Arthur Horner MSS · R. Frankenburg, interviews, 1957, U. Wales, South Wales Miners' Library · private information (2004) · DLB · A. Horner, Incorrigible rebel (1960) · H. Francis and D. Smith, The Fed: a history of the south Wales miners in the twentieth century (1980) · m. cert. · CGPLA Eng. & Wales (1968) · DNB

Archives U. Hull, Brynmor Jones L., corresp. with R. Page Arnot · U. Wales, South Wales Miners' Library, South Wales Coalfield collection, corresp. and papers

Likenesses Bassano, photograph, NPG [see illus.] · Kazatkin, portrait, U. Wales, South Wales Miners' Library · photographs, Trades Union Congress, London

Wealth at death £1169 0s. 6d.: probate, 4 Oct 1968, CGPLA Eng. & Wales

Horner [née Graham], **Frances Jane**, Lady Horner (1854/5–1940), hostess and patron of the arts, the fourth daughter and sixth of the eight children of William Graham (1818–1885), MP, India merchant, and art patron, and Jane Catherine, daughter of John Lowndes of Renfrewshire, was educated by governesses in her evangelical, Presbyterian family home at Langley Hall, near Manchester, and then at

Frances Jane Horner, Lady Horner (1854/5–1940), by Sir Edward
Coley Burne-Jones, 1879

54 Lowndes Square, London. Excluded from fashionable
life by her father's connections with trade, Frances Graham initially owed her position in society to friendship
with the Tennant sisters (whose father was also in business and also a Liberal MP for Glasgow), to friendship with
the Gladstone–Lyttelton circle, and, most importantly, to
her connections with the artist Edward Burne-Jones.

William Graham, a patron of modern British painting,
introduced his daughter at an early age to the studios of
his protégés, including Rossetti and Burne-Jones through
whom she also became acquainted with John Ruskin.
Burne-Jones developed a passion for Frances Graham,
designed 'Sirens for her girdle, Heavens and Paradises for
her prayer-books' (Burne-Jones, 2.130–31), wrote to her
constantly, and included her likeness in a number of his
pictures, including *The Golden Staircase* (1880) and *The Spirit
of the Downs* (1883). Occasioning despair in the married
Burne-Jones (who commented, 'she has gone and married
a market gardener'; ibid.), she married into an unexcep-
tionable English county family in the person of John Francis Fortescue Horner (1842–1927), barrister, of Mells Park,
Frome, Somerset, on 18 January 1883; her husband was
knighted in 1907. Of their four children, the eldest son,
Edward, was killed in 1917, and the younger, Mark, died at
sixteen in 1908. Their younger daughter, Katharine, married Raymond Asquith, son of Herbert Henry Asquith; he
also was killed in the war.

At Mells, Frances Horner continued to play host to the
artistic and intellectual friends who had surrounded her
in London, where she had been one of the first young
unmarried women to entertain her own guests. Both she
and her husband were part of the informal aristocratic
group, the Souls, who shared her artistic interests and dislike of the 'sporting set'. Edwin Lutyens described her as 'a
political intriguer', but commented that 'her bias [was]
born of friends and not conviction' (*Letters of Edwin Lutyens*,
218–19). For H. H. Asquith she acted as confidante, and
throughout the 1890s he corresponded with her regularly.
R. B. Haldane, whom she had introduced to upper-class
society, attributed his acceptance of the War Office in 1905
to her decisive influence.

A needlewoman of considerable skill—one of her
embroideries, executed to a design by Burne-Jones, hangs
in St Andrew's Church, Mells—Frances Horner contributed mainly to the arts as a patron. She was principally
responsible for several significant memorial commissions
in the village and church at Mells, by Burne-Jones, Alfred
Munnings, Eric Gill, William Nicholson, and, most
importantly, Edwin Lutyens. The latter's design for the
memorial to Edward Horner, an equestrian statue by Munnings atop a Lutyens plinth, has been described as 'one of
Lutyens's best and most moving tributes to the waste of
life in the Great War' (*Letters of Edwin Lutyens*, 371–2).

Widowed in 1927, Lady Horner lived on at the Manor
House, Mells, with her daughter, Katharine Asquith, until
1940, when she died on 1 March at the age of eighty-five.
She had been appointed OBE in 1919, and for a time was a
JP. In 1933 she published a volume of memoirs under the
title *Time Remembered*.   K. D. REYNOLDS

Sources F. Horner, *Time remembered* (1933) · G. Burne-Jones,
Memorials of Edward Burne-Jones, 2 vols. (1904) · *The letters of Edwin
Lutyens to his wife Lady Emily*, ed. C. Percy and J. Ridley (1985) · J. Abdy
and C. Gere, *The Souls* (1984) · P. Fitzgerald, *Edward Burne-Jones*
(1975) · *Mary Gladstone (Mrs Drew): her diaries and letters*, ed. L. Masterman (1930) · H. C. G. Matthew, 'H. H. Asquith's political journalism', *BIHR*, 49 (1976), 146–51 · R. Jenkins, *Asquith* (1964) · *Raymond
Asquith: life and letters*, ed. J. Jolliffe, new edn (1987) · m. cert. · d.
cert. · will · Burke, *Gen. GB* (1914)
Archives Bodl. Oxf., corresp. with Margot Asquith
Likenesses E. C. Burne-Jones, portrait, 1879; Christies, 10 March
1995 [*see illus.*] · photograph, repro. in M. Asquith, *Autobiography*, 1
(1920), facing p. 200
Wealth at death £40,843 2s. 7d.: probate, 6 June 1940, *CGPLA Eng.
& Wales*

Horner, Francis (1778–1817), politician, was born at his
parents' home in St David Street, Edinburgh, on 12 August
1778, the eldest son and first surviving of seven children of
John Horner and his wife, Joanna, daughter of John Baillie, writer to the signet, of Gladsmuir, Haddington. His
father, who outlived him until 1829, sold Scottish linens to
London wholesale drapers. The survivor of his two
brothers was the educationist Leonard *Horner.

Education and early career A delicate child, Horner went to
school locally in 1784 and proceeded to Edinburgh high
school in 1786. After being dux of rector Adam's class in
1792 he matriculated in November at Edinburgh University. His mother had intended him for the kirk, but with
paternal encouragement he preferred the law, aspiring

Francis Horner (1778–1817), by Sir Henry Raeburn, 1812

beyond that to public life, funded by his profession. He gained approbation from Professor Dugald Stewart as an intellectual all-rounder, and left in 1795 to sojourn with the Revd John Hewlett, under whose tutelage at Shackle-well, Middlesex, he nearly lost his Scots accent. Unimpressed by Westminster oratory, he nevertheless included political economy in an ambitious plan of studies on returning to Edinburgh in 1797. He joined the Speculative Society with his former playmate and future rival Henry Brougham, and was also active in the Academy of Physics, the Chemical and Literary societies, and others. In May 1799 he emerged from political quietism to record in his journal that he espoused 'the ancient Whig politics of England, which are at present so much out of fashion, being hated by both parties' (Horner, *Memoirs*, 1.79). An essay on the role of political opposition was later burnt by him, but he admitted that 'the history of Britain during the eighteenth century haunts me like a dream, and I am alternately intoxicated with visions of historic laurels and of forensic eminence' (ibid., 1.116). His mentors were David Hume and the French physiocrats. In June 1800 he passed advocate but found little business, and relished only his philosophical and scientific pursuits. His friends were Lord Webb Seymour, Lord Henry Petty, and Sydney Smith. After attending Dugald Stewart's lectures on political economy, he became critical of his ability to sustain 'one regular persevering train of thought' (ibid.), and decided to switch to the English bar.

The *Edinburgh Review* and whig politics Horner entered Lincoln's Inn on 26 April 1802, and while in London became acquainted with the whig lawyers and literati Romilly,

Abercromby, Mackintosh, and Sharp, who welcomed him as a 'Northern Light'. His entitlement to this was manifest when later that year he helped to found the *Edinburgh Review*, for whose editor, Francis Jeffrey, he was to supply fourteen articles in the next few years. Those on the currency and the grain trade indicated the budding political economist. In March 1803 Horner left Edinburgh for London, 'fixed for life' (Horner, *Memoirs*, 1.215). Taking up residence at Garden Court in the Temple, he was soon to be joined by his parents in London. At his first business appearance in the House of Commons on 1 April 1803, he spoke to a committee on 'manure, and a turnpike road' (ibid.), and when appearing at the bar of the Lords on 16 May 1804, he was tongue-tied, but he was consoled by an East India Company commission to draw up a policy report (unidentified). Even before he was established professionally he was inveigled into Foxite politics by the crisis of 1804, during which he attended debates: 'all my feelings carry me towards that party and all my principles confirm the predilection' (ibid., 1.254). He needed to find a whig patron to get into parliament. This ambition now took precedence and he failed to review Malthus's *Essay on Population* for the *Edinburgh Review*, writing only sparingly for it henceforward, while seeking to maintain his influence over editorial policy. His friend Sydney Smith was sure he would succeed in public life: 'Horner pleases the best judges and does not offend the worst' (N. C. Smith, ed., *The Letters of Sydney Smith*, 1953, 1.102). When his friends entered government on Pitt's death in 1806 he accepted a modest place at the board of inquiry into the nawab of Arcot's debts; resigning in 1809 he decried it as a 'blunder in my plans' (Horner, *Memoirs*, 1.467). Dismayed by Fox's death and conscious of his preference for an opposition role, he was found a seat in parliament in the 1806 election by Lord Henry Petty. It was for St Ives, a pocket borough placed at government disposal by Sir Christopher Hawkins. The berth was paid for by Lord Kinnaird, but a feeble contest sent Horner to Cornwall, where he shook hands with an electorate 'stinking with brine and pilchard juice' (ibid., 1.381).

Horner's maiden speech was on the Scottish Clergy Bill on 27 January 1807, but at this stage he preferred the experience of committee work on poor-law reform and finance. He helped Henry Bankes bring in a bill curtailing offices reserved in advance for holders, and defended it on 24 April. Meanwhile the 'ministry of all the talents' had been dismissed, and Horner, already a member of the Whig Club, revised for publication a threepenny pamphlet drafted by Henry Bennet and entitled *A Short Account of a Late Short Administration*. He was found a seat at the 1807 election for another pocket borough, Wendover. The patron, Lord Carrington, was an ally of the outgoing premier Lord Grenville. Within weeks Horner was called to the bar, and went the western circuit, which ruled out constant attendance at Westminster. There he opposed the control of trade by export licence to counter Bonaparte's continental system in 1808 and, critical of the naval battering of Copenhagen, voted for Whitbread's peace motion. He supported Catholic relief and his role model Romilly's bid to reform criminal law. Joining the whig aristocratic haunt of Brooks's Club in May 1808, he was further taken up by Lord Holland, Fox's nephew, who infected Horner with his enthusiasm for the Spanish revolt against Bonaparte. This was not expressed in the house, though he revised a memoir of Holland's on Spain for publication, as it ran contrary to the Grenvillite stance. News of the retreat from Corunna added heartache to a bout of illness: Horner, who had recently moved to Lincoln's Inn, saw that he was 'made, or educated, for the sunshine of an improving community' (Horner, *Memoirs*, 1.445), which eluded him. Personable, and enjoying Lady Holland's admiration, he remained a solemn bachelor, relying on Holland House as his social forum. Apart from his own 'indolence, fastidiousness, dread of failure, etc', he deplored the lack of a 'popular' (ibid.) party leader, and voted rather than spoke for opposition questions. When he spoke he made no headway in the 1809 session with his advocacy of Anglicizing the Scottish judicial system, his renewed attack on export licences, or his defence of the Sale of Offices Prevention Bill.

While Horner was disdainful of Spencer Perceval's ministry and ruled out any whig flirtation with it unless Catholic relief were conceded, he engineered a cross-party issue on which to display his talent when he moved for a committee of inquiry into the high price of bullion on 1 February 1810. With Horner in the chair, the committee reported on 8 June, and Horner admitted that it had more the air of a dissertation than was desirable, so he delayed its publication until August while testing the reactions of likely critics. Its argument was that there had been an excessive issue of paper money since the stoppage of cash payments by the Bank of England in 1797, and that bullion importation was the solution. Horner proposed the repeal of restrictions on cash payments on 20 February 1811, and on 6 May produced sixteen resolutions in favour, only to see them thwarted by ministerial counter-resolutions on 26 June. Even the whig managers, Ponsonby and Tierney, disliked his insistence on resumption of cash payments in two years, but his reputation was established, not helped, he thought, by a two-party system which prevented topics from being debated on their merits, of which the inquiry into the bungled Walcheren expedition struck him as a prime example. He had no time, however, for radical courses, and regretted that the house had not itself handled the 'too popular' (Horner, *Papers*, 642) Sir Francis Burdett's breach of privilege. His visit to Ireland in the summer of 1810 confirmed his view that Catholic relief was essential, but he was observed to have become 'impatient of contradiction' (S. H. Romilly, ed., *Letters to 'Ivy' from the First Earl of Dudley*, 1905, 118). He spoke for opposition on the regency question on 20 December 1810, and it is interesting that he made no set speech, as he had to recollect it afterwards for Cobbett's *Debates*. The whigs saw him as financial secretary to the Treasury if they returned to power, though the Irish secretaryship was also suggested. He disliked whig dalliance with the ministry or with George Canning, then in opposition, and if they merged with Canning threatened to follow Whitbread, despite their now contrary views on peace prospects. His own major effort in 1812 was against the issue of fresh paper currency, on 20 April, though he was also a critic of legislation against Luddite machine breakers on 5 May. Canning's support on the bullion and Catholic questions removed his objection to alliance with him, but it fell through, as did a temporary reconciliation with Brougham, who had made Horner's former topic of the export licence trade his claim to fame, and eschewed the middle course Horner found more tactful as a Grenvillite nominee. Thus he felt obliged to speak on 7 May against a radical whig attack on a sinecure held by Lord Grenville, and was spared any embarrassment arising out of a motion entrusted to him on 15 June to charge the regent's secretary's salary to the privy purse, because the regent swallowed the proposal in advance.

Later political career and political economy Horner did not contest the election of 1812 when Lord Carrington transferred his seat to a nephew, and he had no prospect of being returned 'in the more regular and desirable way' (Horner, *Memoirs*, 2.128). Holland, seeking a seat for him, feared that 'the bullion question is unpopular in exact proportion to its merit' (BL, Holland MSS, Add. MSS 51917, Lord Holland's memo, 1813), and Horner judged that Grenvillite hostility to parliamentary reform would encumber him if he were seated by them. Yet it was Grenville's brother Buckingham who returned him for St Mawes on 17 April 1813, at the cost of an election dinner only. He was to resign if they differed politically. His late entry into the house left Horner little chance to trumpet their agreement on Catholic relief, but he was in time to criticize the East India Company's trade monopoly, and to advocate a presbyterian chaplaincy in India on 14 June. He supported Whitbread's peace bid on 30 June, but once more changed his mind to align himself with the hawkish Grenvilles. He was a consistent opponent of the protectionist corn laws in 1813–14, and, echoing Grenville in the Lords, he quizzed Castlereagh on his failure to obtain universal abolition of the slave trade during peace negotiations on 28 June. A continental tour in the summer of 1814 revived his interest in foreign affairs, and in November he three times assailed the peace settlement, referring privately to 'the plunder of Europe' by the 'robbers of Vienna'. Encouraged by Ponsonby, he attacked ministers on the conduct of the naval war with the United States on 1 December, but this initiative petered out when peace was made early in 1815. Speeches of his against the loss of Genoan independence and against the corn laws raised whig hopes that he would become a powerful debater: the City of London voted thanks to him for his critique of protectionism on 20 March 1815. His condemnation of extradition of Spanish liberals from Gibraltar had enough bite to irritate the Spanish king. On 7 March he urged government to force the bank to resume cash payments, and two days later carried an amendment enjoining this when market and Royal Mint prices of gold were equal.

Horner defended London petitions against renewal of

hostilities with France, on Bonaparte's return, and the likely tax burden, on 1 and 5 May 1815, and went on to oppose the Bourbon restoration in Naples. His hostility to restoration of the Bourbons in France had already caused friction with the Grenvilles: on 8 April he offered to resign his seat, but was induced by Lord Grenville to bide his time, as the opposition was in disarray. On 28 April he voted for Whitbread's motion against resumption of war, and told his patron he would resign when two motions he had in hand were presented. Bonaparte's defeat obviated this, but on 1 February 1816, with due notice to Grenville, he attacked the regent's speech, and several times that month voiced his hostility to a reactionary peace settlement, with the overblown military establishment and concomitant tax load at home it entailed. The impact of these speeches was by no means limited to his whig coterie. That session, too, he satisfied his ambition to do something for Ireland, when his bill regulating Irish grand juries on indictments, using proposals pamphleted by Thomas Spring Rice, became law (56 Geo. III c.87). He was thwarted, by 146 votes to 73, when he tried to forestall the renewal of the Bank Restriction Act on 1 May, nor could he induce the house to authorize cash payments in two years, or oblige the bank to prepare for this, on 3 and 8 May. But he returned to the fray against the Aliens Bill and on behalf of the Spanish liberals on 27 May, and concluded his session by championing Catholic emancipation on 25 June.

Death and publications Horner's exertions intensified a pulmonary complaint, and, advised to winter in a warmer climate, he went to Pisa with his brother in October. There he rallied, and returned to his studious aspirations, but never recovered. On 21 December 1816 he penned a political testament to Lord Holland, urging the whigs to occupy the high ground of constitutional liberty everywhere. He died at Pisa on 8 February 1817. The tribute due to a talent tragically cut short was paid to him in the Commons on 3 March. He was buried in the protestant cemetery in Leghorn. It was on Horner's departure for Italy that David Ricardo was urged to enter parliament. He did so, stepping into the shoes of 'the first man in England to make the doctrine of political economy intelligible to the House of Commons' (*Westminster and Foreign Quarterly Review*, 58, July 1852, 105), as Lord Campbell later characterized Horner. By 1819 Robert Peel, a near contemporary on the opposite side in politics, gave decisive support to resumption of cash payments, underlining the force of Horner's arguments. His political acumen was however obscured by the sanitized version of his life at length published in 1843, for want of a more eligible biographer, by his brother. His first publication, a translation with a memoir of the author of Leonard Euler's *Algebra*, in 1797, had been anonymous, but was acknowledged in the 1822 edition. His articles for the *Edinburgh Review* are listed in the *Wellesley index*, with further information on them available in the work of F. W. Fetter in the source list below and in the anthology of his writings first listed. His brother

included the 1807 pamphlet and the most important parliamentary speeches, and most of Horner's youthful journal, in his biography, and the omissions which prevented this giving a balanced view of his political motions are largely supplied in *The Horner Papers* (1994).

ROLAND THORNE

Sources *The Horner papers: selections from the letters and miscellaneous writings of Francis Horner, MP, 1795–1817*, ed. K. Bourne and W. B. Taylor (1994) · *Memoirs and correspondence of Francis Horner, MP*, ed. L. Horner, 2 vols. (1843); another edn (1849); 2nd edn (1853) · *Annual Biography and Obituary*, 2 (1818), 252–74 · F. W. Fetter, *The economist in parliament, 1780–1868* (1980) · *The economic writings of Francis Horner in the Edinburgh Review, 1802–6*, ed. F. W. Fetter (1957) · F. W. Fetter, 'The bullion report re-examined', *Quarterly Journal of Economics* (1941–2), 655–66 · *GM*, 1st ser., 87/1 (1817), 275 · Lord Brougham, *Statesmen of the time of George III*, 2nd ser. (1839), 170–82 · *EdinR*, 78 (1843), 261–99 · J. Clive, *Scotch reviewers: the Edinburgh Review, 1802–1815* (1957) · 'Horner, Francis', HoP, *Commons* · S. Hollander, *The economics of David Ricardo* (1979) · S. Collini, D. Winch, and J. Burrow, *That noble science of politics* (1983)

Archives BLPES, corresp. and papers · Trinity Cam., corresp. and papers | BL, corresp. with John Allen, Add. MS 52180 · BL, letters to Lord Grenville, Add. MS 58977 · NL Scot., corresp. relating to Academy of Physics · NL Scot., letters to Archibald Constable · NL Scot., letters to Lady Anna Maria Elliot · NL Scot., letters to James Reddie · priv. coll. · U. Durham L., letters to Earl Grey

Likenesses J. Henning, wax medallion, 1806, Scot. NPG · H. Raeburn, oils, 1812, NPG; copy, NG Scot. [*see illus.*] · F. Chantrey, marble bust, 1818, Scot. NPG · F. Chantrey, statue on monument, 1820, Westminster Abbey, London · portrait, 1820 (after Raeburn), Speculative Society Hall, Edinburgh · F. Chantrey and H. C. Englefield, portrait, 1823, protestant cemetery, Leghorn (Livorno), Italy, Horner monument · S. W. Reynolds, mezzotint, pubd 1843 (after Raeburn), BM, NPG · J. Henning, chalk drawing, Scot. NPG · H. Raeburn, oils, Scot. NPG · group portrait (Raeburn family in 1876; after Raeburn), priv. coll.

Wealth at death professional earnings modest; received financial support from father when necessary

Horner, (Norman) Gerald (1882–1954), physician and medical editor, was born on 1 January 1882 at High Street, Tonbridge, Kent, the son of Arthur Claypon Horner, medical practitioner, and his wife, Frances, formerly Cundell (*née* Cooper). He was normally known by his middle name, Gerald, or as 'NG'. His father, who died while he was a child, had served with the Red Cross during the Franco-Prussian War and as medical officer and naturalist on two Arctic expeditions. From 1891 to 1899 Horner was educated at Tonbridge School, where his father held the post of medical officer; he then went to Gonville and Caius College, Cambridge, where he read natural sciences (1899–1902). After graduating with a second-class degree he undertook his medical training, at St Bartholomew's Hospital, London. He also gained his first experience of medical journalism, as assistant editor of the *St Bartholomew's Hospital Journal*. He qualified MRCS and LRCP in 1906. In 1910 he graduated MB BCh, from Cambridge. He was awarded the degree of MD in 1922 with a thesis on the history of the general practitioner in England. In his youth Horner was a capable cricketer and an enthusiastic performer of amateur dramatics, in which he excelled as a female impersonator.

In London, after a short spell as house surgeon at Westminster Hospital, Horner returned to St Bartholomew's where, briefly, he was both house physician and editor of its journal. He then combined general practice with clinical assistantships at both St Bartholomew's and Shadwell Children's Hospital in east London. Meanwhile he retained his links with medical journalism, first as a contributor and then as an assistant editor of Sir Henry Burdett's weekly journal for GPs, *The Hospital*. On 4 August 1911 Horner married Grace Malleson Fearon (1890/91–1950), daughter of Walter Malleson Fearon, a woman of powerful personality. In the same year he gave up clinical practice to become assistant editor of *The Lancet*. One of his first duties was to cover the national health-insurance struggle. In 1915 he left *The Lancet* to take up a commission in the Royal Army Medical Corps (RAMC). He attained the rank of captain and for two years served in France, including on the Somme. In 1917 his wife, aware that her husband did not wish to return to *The Lancet* on leaving the army, took it upon herself to ask the editor of the *British Medical Journal* (BMJ), Sir Dawson Williams, to arrange her husband's release from the RAMC and appoint him to an assistant editorship. These arrangements having been made, Horner stayed with the *BMJ* until his retirement in 1946. He was editor from 1928, though for several years before his departure the journal was effectively run by his successor, Hugh Clegg.

Horner faced several difficulties during his years at the *BMJ*. As assistant editor he had to shoulder much of the editorial responsibility for producing it as Williams's health declined. As his own health failed, particularly following the detachment of his right retina in 1940, he carried the substantial burden of having to run the journal under wartime conditions. Moreover he had major difficulty as editor in his inability to escape the conviction that he was unworthy to succeed his mentor, Williams. Nevertheless, under his editorship the *BMJ* had its successes. Most significantly it carried many important scientific papers. Horner also oversaw the major design changes of 1936–7, in which a new front cover was introduced featuring a design by Eric Gill and a typeface designed by Stanley Morison. Additionally, the *BMJ*'s circulation rose substantially during Horner's editorship, though this had more to do with rising membership of the British Medical Association (the journal was a benefit of membership) than with the journalistic quality.

Overall, however, Horner cannot be counted a successful editor of the *BMJ*. His successor observed that he 'did nothing except sit there and shift columns'; the journal 'wasn't being edited and people were beginning to complain' (Clegg MSS). Under Horner's direction the *BMJ* became staid and unimaginative, and as such it reflected the personality of its editor. Kind and courteous, Horner possessed an understated sense of humour, but he was also extremely diffident, painfully sensitive to criticism, pedantic, indecisive, and wholly undynamic. Shortly after his appointment as editor *The Times* suggested that the responsibility of editing the *BMJ* was 'well-nigh crushing' (28 Feb 1928). Sadly, Horner was well and truly crushed.

Horner became honorary FRCP in 1939 and FRCS in 1942. Towards the end of the Second World War he began

to live at the Savile Club, possibly because he and his wife had separated. He had a keen interest in the history of medicine and was, successively, honorary secretary and vice-president of the Royal Society of Medicine's history of medicine section. Although he wrote very little outside the pages of the journals with which he was editorially connected, in retirement he briefly assisted in the compilation of Sir Arthur MacNulty's official medical history of the Second World War. Following several years of illness, Horner died of broncho-pneumonia, pulmonary oedema, and coronary thrombosis at St Pancras Hospital, London, on 7 March 1954. He was cremated at Golders Green crematorium on 12 March. His only child, a son, survived him.

P. W. J. BARTRIP

Sources *BMJ* (13 March 1954), 648–50 · P. Bartrip, *Mirror of medicine: a history of the British Medical Journal* (1990) · *Nature*, 173 (1954), 614–15 · Munk, *Roll* · *St Bartholomew's Hospital Journal*, 58 (1954), 121–2 · *St Bartholomew's Hospital Journal*, 58 (1954), 182–3 · *WWW* · *The Lancet* (13 March 1954), 577 · *BMJ* archives, Clegg MSS · *BMJ* (3 April 1954), 823 · *BMJ* (20 March 1954), 708 · R. S. Stevenson, *Goodbye Harley Street* (1954) · b. cert. · m. cert. · d. cert. · Tonbridge School archives · Gon. & Caius Cam. · *The Times* (13 March 1954)
Archives British Medical Association, London, archives
Likenesses photograph, repro. in *BMJ*
Wealth at death £7787 4s. 11d.: probate, 6 May 1954, *CGPLA Eng. & Wales*

Horner, Leonard (1785–1864), factory inspector, geologist, and educationist, was born on 17 January 1785 at St George's Square, Edinburgh, the third and youngest son of John Horner (d. 1829), a wealthy whig linen merchant, and his wife, Joanna, née Baillie. In his youth his circle of acquaintances included James Mill, Henry Brougham, Henry Cockburn, and Francis Jeffrey. Subsequently, several of these aided Horner's professional advancement. In 1799, on leaving Edinburgh high school, Horner entered Edinburgh University, where he studied moral philosophy, political economy, science, and mathematics. He was taught chemistry by Thomas Hope, who awakened in him a lifelong passion for geology.

In 1803 Horner left university to become a partner in his family's business. In 1804 he accompanied his father to London to help manage its metropolitan branch. In 1806 he married the daughter of a Yorkshire landowner, Anne Susan Lloyd (d. 1862); they had six daughters and a son who died in childhood. The decline of the linen trade prompted Horner to become an underwriter at Lloyd's insurance office. The venture was unsuccessful and in 1814, following heavy losses which his father made good, he returned to Edinburgh where he lived until 1827. In 1816–17 he accompanied his ailing brother, Francis *Horner, on a tour of Italy, in the course of which Francis died. Many years later Horner, who published a memoir of his brother in 1843, described this event as 'the greatest calamity of my life'. During his period in Edinburgh, Horner played an active part in the city's political and educational reform movements. In 1821 he founded the Edinburgh School of Arts, one of the earliest mechanics' institutes. It later became Heriot-Watt College (1885) and

Leonard Horner (1785–1864), by unknown artist

Heriot-Watt University (1966). He was one of the promoters of the Edinburgh Academy, founded in 1823 as a rival to the Edinburgh high school.

Throughout adulthood Horner retained a keen interest in scholarship, particularly geology. In 1808, in its second year of existence, he became a fellow of the Geological Society. He remained an active member for the rest of his life, becoming one of its secretaries (1810–14) and later president (1845–6 and 1860–61). In 1813 he was elected fellow of the Royal Society. During his second presidency of the Geological Society he allowed women to attend meetings, a concession which was reversed soon after his term of office ended. Horner encouraged several promising young geologists, among whom was his future son-in-law, Charles Lyell. In 1835 he helped establish the Geological Survey of Great Britain.

In 1827 some of Horner's Scottish whig friends invited him to be the first warden and secretary of the newly created University of London at a salary of £1200 p.a. Horner's four years at the university brought him into conflict with the academic staff. Although this clash owed much to the financial and constitutional problems which beset the university, Horner's dictatorial approach to his duties also played a part. His resignation in 1831 was partly a consequence of chronic ill health, but his father's death, in 1829, had provided him with an inheritance sufficient to

enable him to eschew uncongenial paid employment. Free from university entanglements, Horner took his family on a tour of continental Europe. In August 1831 he settled in Bonn where, for some eighteen months, he studied the geology of the Rhineland. In April 1833 he returned to public life when his whig connections secured his appointment to the royal commission on the employment of children in factories.

The commissioners accepted that the existing factory acts had been largely ineffective owing to the lack of viable enforcement provisions. In an attempt to supply this deficiency they recommended the appointment of full-time salaried inspectors. Before serving on the royal commission Horner had shown no real interest in the factory question. Although not one of the initial appointees, he became inspector for Scotland, northern Ireland, and the four northernmost counties of England in November 1833. His remuneration was £1000 p.a., from which travelling and certain other expenses had to be met. From 1837 Horner's district comprised Lancashire, much of Yorkshire, Cumberland, Durham, Northumberland, and Westmorland. Horner remained an inspector until his retirement in 1859. Throughout his tenure of office he was an energetic and uncompromising official who, to some extent, was the unofficial leading inspector. While he was neither hostile to manufacturers' desires to maximize their profits, nor quick to prosecute, Horner was determined to ensure that factory workers benefited from the legal protections conferred by parliament. As a result he came into conflict with some manufacturers, notably over their use of the 'relay system' for circumventing restrictions on hours of work. In the 1850s he clashed with the National Association of Factory Occupiers on the question of industrial safety. On occasion he criticized the magistracy's lax attitude towards factory offences. A supporter of factory schools, he published a translation (1838) of Victor Cousin's *De l'instruction publique en Hollande* as a contribution to the contemporary debate on popular education. After a visit to the continent in 1838 he published *On the Employment of Children in Factories in the United Kingdom and in some Foreign Countries* (1840). Between 1840 and 1843 Horner was a member of the children's employment commission, the reports of which contributed to the extension of state regulation of the workplace.

After his retirement Horner devoted his time to geology. The results of the investigations which he had directed into the rate of alluvial deposition in the Nile valley were published in the *Philosophical Transactions of the Royal Society* (1855 and 1859). His presidential address to the Geological Society in 1861 described the evidence for the existence of the human race at a much earlier date than traditional biblical chronology allowed. He wintered in Florence during 1861–2, when he translated P. Villari's life of Girolamo Savonarola; the work was published in 1863.

Horner died on 5 March 1864 at 60 Montagu Square, London, and was buried at Brookwood cemetery, Woking. His wife had predeceased him on 22 May 1862. In *Capital* Karl Marx praised his 'invaluable service to the English working-class' (4th edn, 1891, bk I, pt iii, n. 10). A stained-glass window in York Minster memorializes Horner's efforts on behalf of working people.   P. W. J. BARTRIP

Sources K. M. Lyell, ed., *Memoir of Leonard Horner* (1890) • B. Martin, 'Leonard Horner: a portrait of an inspector of factories', *International Review of Social History*, 14 (1969), 412–43 • C. M. Brown, 'Leonard Horner, 1785–1864: his contribution to education', *Journal of Educational Administration and History*, 17 (1985), 1–10 • W. J. Hamilton, *Quarterly Journal of the Geological Society*, 21 (1865), xxx–xl • *PRS*, 14 (1865), v–x • H. H. Bellot, *University College, London, 1826–1926* (1929) • PRO, HO 87, HO 45; LAB 15
Archives BGS, accounts • GS Lond., corresp. and papers • NL Scot., corresp. and papers • Som. ARS, geological descriptions of the western part of Somerset | BL, corresp. with Sir Robert Peel, Add. MSS 40369–40567, *passim* • GS Lond., letters to Roderick Impey Murchison • LUL, corresp. with Augustus De Morgan • NL Scot., letteers to A. J. G. Marcet; letters to Lord Minto • Sci. Mus., corresp. with Thomas Andrews • U. Edin., New Coll. L., letters to Thomas Chalmers; letters to Sir Archibald Geikie • U. St Andr. L., corresp. with James David Forbes • UCL, letters to Lord Brougham; letters to James Loch; letters to Society for the Diffusion of Useful Knowledge • Wellcome L., letters to Dionysius Lardner
Likenesses S. Williams, woodcut, BM • drawing?, Heriot-Watt University Archive [*see illus.*] • wood-engraving, NPG; repro. in *ILN* (1846–7)
Wealth at death under £18,000: probate, 13 April 1864, *CGPLA Eng. & Wales*

Horner, William George (1786–1837),

mathematician and schoolteacher, was the son of William Horner (1746/7–1826), a native of Ireland who became an itinerant preacher in 1770. Brought to England by Wesley, the elder Horner officiated as a regular minister until 1819. Horner was educated from 1794 until 1800 at Kingswood School, near Bristol, which Wesley had established; he was assistant master there in 1800–04, then, at the age of nineteen, its headmaster, on an annual salary of £50.

In 1809 Horner left Kingswood to found his own school, The Seminary, at 27 Grosvenor Place, Bath; he was headmaster there until his death. A man of high intellectual powers, he suffered from irritability and impatience, and he applied the cane freely to those pupils he considered diligent yet dull. However, many benefited from his teaching and he encouraged bright boys to stay an extra year at school.

An interest in mathematics led Horner to develop a method of finding a rapid means of approximating to a root of a polynomial equation. 'Horner's method', as it became known, was conveyed to Davies Gilbert, read before the Royal Society on 1 July 1819, and published in the *Philosophical Transactions* later that year. Horner was unaware that a similar method had been practised in thirteenth-century China and rediscovered in Italy by Paolo Ruffini in 1807, as were Augustus De Morgan and J. R. Young, who popularized Horner's method among their students. Horner's work represented an early example of thinking in terms of the complexity and efficiency of algorithms, and in it for the first time in modern mathematics a suitable arrangement of data in the plane was explicitly used for economical calculation. The attribution of his name, even if historically debatable, attests to the interest taken in his finding; it joined other such methods, including that known as 'Newton–Raphson'.

In the late 1810s and later, Horner wrote a sextet of other papers on the transformation and solution of equations. He also solved some functional equations, which were popularized in Britain in the mid-1810s by Charles Babbage and John Herschel, as part of their efforts to revive English mathematics. In 1832 he published *Natural magic, a familiar exposition of a forgotten fact in optics, including strictures on A. Gellius and his interpreters.*

Horner and his wife, whose name is unknown, raised several children, one of whom, William Horner, also taught at The Seminary. Horner endured 'a lingering and painful disorder', described as 'a complication of asthma and ossification of the heart' (*Wesleyan Methodist Magazine*), and died at 27 Grosvenor Place 'after a sudden and violent stroke of illness' (*Bath Journal*), on 22 September 1837.   ANITA MCCONNELL

Sources J. L. Coolidge, *The mathematics of great amateurs* (1949), chap. 15 • *The history of Kingswood School … by three old boys* (1898) • *Bath Journal* (2 Oct 1837), 2 • *Register of Kingswood School* (1910) • R. Cooke, *The history of mathematics: a brief course* (1997), 235, 385 • F. Cajori, 'Horner's method of approximation anticipated by Ruffini', *Bulletin of the American Mathematical Society*, 17 (1910–11), 409–14 • *Wesleyan Methodist Magazine*, 60 (1837), 957 • *VCH Somerset*, 2.463 • M. E. Baron, 'Horner, William George', *DSB*

Horniblow [married name Dalton], (Emilie) Hilda (1886–1950),

chief controller of Queen Mary's Army Auxiliary Corps and educationist, was born at Sheep Street, Charlbury, Oxfordshire, on 24 June 1886, the daughter of Frederick Thomas Horniblow, stationer, and his wife, Sarah Ellen, *née* McCulloch. She was educated at Oxford high school from May 1901 until July 1902 and at University College, Reading, from 15 October 1907 to 1 July 1908. By 1914 she was assistant mistress at the municipal school, Westwood, Scarborough.

Horniblow temporarily left teaching during the First World War, joined the Women's Legion, and in August 1915 became superintendent of three kitchens, each catering for 1000 men, at Sommerdown convalescent camp, Eastbourne. After demonstrating her 'able leadership' there (Cowper, 11) she took over the running of the officers' mess at Lydd, Kent, in September 1916. By February 1917 she had been made deputy to Florence Leach, controller-in-chief of the Women's Army Auxiliary Corps (WAAC), which subsumed the women's legion, and became assistant controller of cooks. The WAAC was renamed Queen Mary's Army Auxiliary Corps (QMAAC) on 9 April 1917, when the queen accepted the title of commander-in-chief. Later in that year Horniblow was promoted chief controller of the QMAAC, on secondment to the American expeditionary force in France. She arrived at Le Havre on 9 July and on 11 July went from a new base depot at Harfleur to Tours. There, on 29 July, she and her detachment were inspected by General Pershing. On 23 September she took charge of her camp at the American record office, Bourges, where she commanded what was ultimately a 1000-strong detachment assigned to the United States army. In July 1918 she was recalled to London to replace Mrs Long, chief controller in England of the QMAAC, who had been killed when the Red Cross ship on which she was travelling was torpedoed. Horniblow was appointed OBE (1918) and CBE (military, 1919).

After the war Horniblow became headmistress of Fair Street (London county council) women's evening institute and then, in 1935, was made staff inspector for women's subjects in technical institutions. On 20 December 1941 she married a widower, John Edwin Dalton (*b.* 1875/6) OBE, a retired inspector of schools, of Menston-in-Wharfedale, Yorkshire. Hilda Dalton retired in 1942, and died at her home—5 The Crescent, Menston, Ilkley—on 2 January 1950. She was survived by her husband.

JANE POTTER

Sources b. cert. · m. cert. · d. cert. · *WWW* · S. Bidwell, *The Women's Royal Army Corps* (1977) · *Directory of women teachers* (1914) · J. M. Cowper, *A short history of Queen Mary's Army Auxiliary Corps* (1966) · M. Izzard, *A heroine in her time* (1969)
Likenesses photograph, IWM, Women's War Work archive
Wealth at death £7482 6s. 2d.: probate, 9 March 1950, *CGPLA Eng. & Wales*

Horniman, Annie Elizabeth Fredericka (1860–1937), theatre patron and manager, was born at Surrey Mount, Forest Hill, London, on 3 October 1860, the only daughter of Frederick John *Horniman (1835–1906), tea merchant and founder of the Horniman Museum, and his first wife, Rebekah Elmslie (1825–1895). Her grandfather was the Quaker tea merchant John Horniman; her father became a Congregationalist on his marriage. Both Annie and her younger brother, Elmslie, were educated privately at Surrey Mount, the family's large Victorian home in the London suburbs, which was gradually filling with the father's famous zoological and cultural collection. A German governess brought stimulating companionship and, when Annie was fourteen, a secret introduction to the theatre with a visit to *The Merchant of Venice*, against the views of her nonconformist parents that such entertainments were sinful.

Annie Horniman's father did allow her to enter the Slade School of Fine Art in 1882. She worked hard, although she eventually realized that she would never be a good painter. She devoured the opportunities now open to her—to make her own friends, to visit museums, to enjoy the theatre. She cropped her long golden hair and was given her lifelong nickname Tabbie. In her first student summer she was overwhelmed by Richter's performances of Wagner's *Ring*, which provoked annual pilgrimages to Bayreuth for thirty years, enriched by Annie's fluency in German. Her studies ended in 1888. The lonely rich girl became an independent-minded woman. She bicycled around London and twice over the Alps, outrageously in bloomers. She smoked in public and explored alternative religions. In 1889 she saw Ibsen's *An Enemy of the People* in Munich. She was there again in 1891 for the première of his *Hedda Gabler*. She gave unpaid help to the poet W. B. Yeats, typing his poems and correspondence and generally tidying his untidy life and his disorderly rooms. This close relationship was sustained for many years, despite her awareness of his selfishness, by her deep respect for his creative talents.

Horniman's absorbing preoccupation from 1890 to 1903

Annie Elizabeth Fredericka Horniman (1860–1937), by Flora Lion, *c.*1912

was as a member of the mystic religious Hermetic Order of the Golden Dawn. With friends who studied at the British Museum, including her romantic companion Nina Bergson, Yeats, and the actress Florence Farr, Annie was initiated into the mysteries of the order by its founder, the charismatic writer on magic Samuel Liddell Mathers. She devoted thirteen years of study, service, and also financial subsidy, rising through its secret hierarchies in her search for life's hidden truths. Eventually faction fighting and scandal disillusioned her and she resigned in 1903.

One by-product of these attachments was Annie Horniman's first involvement with the theatre. In 1894 Florence Farr obtained her financial backing for a season at the Avenue Theatre, made possible by a legacy from Annie's Quaker grandfather. The season opened with a new play by Yeats, *The Land of Heart's Desire*, and included the striking première of Shaw's *Arms and the Man*—his début on the public stage. Her involvement, kept secret to avoid parental dismay, was not discovered by Shaw for ten years.

In 1903 Yeats lured Annie to Dublin where he hoped her backing for productions by the Irish Literary Theatre would bring more of his poetic dramas to the stage. To her delight Yeats invited her to design his play *The King's Threshold*. Annie soon realized she was administrator rather than artist, and the atmosphere of an amateur company directed by three playwrights—Yeats, Lady Gregory, and J. M. Synge—was never congenial. She bought them an old theatre, organized and financed its renovation, guaranteed six years of subsidy, but took the boat home before the Abbey Theatre's historic opening night on 27 December 1904. The following year she paid for the actors to become professionals, but always underestimated the force of nationalist feeling and would not support political propaganda. A complete breach was inevitable and came at the end of her agreement.

Annie Horniman's greatest achievement was embodied in management of the Gaiety Theatre, Manchester, which she bought, renovated, and opened in 1908 with money left by her father, while still attending to the rumbustious affairs at the Abbey. With the young actor-director Ben Iden Payne she created an acting ensemble on forty-week contracts, with no star system, and the actors alternating between large and small parts. Dedication to the author was paramount. Shakespeare, Euripides, the 'new drama' of Ibsen and Shaw, local dramatists such as W. S. Houghton and Harold Brighouse, culled from over forty new plays she read every week, played in a repertory system, not straight runs. Wages were fair. Annie's organization was disciplined, just, happy. She managed it thoroughly, personally, without crowding her artists. 'An actor's best friend', they called her. She even paid for their coffee breaks. In 1910 Manchester University made her an honorary MA, and she proudly wore the cap and gown whenever she could. Her 'repertory' theatre became hugely influential. The refreshing ensemble delighted Manchester, British, and North American audiences, and astonished the critics. It ultimately inspired the network of subsidized regional theatres for which she endlessly campaigned in public speeches, alongside her championing of the suffragist cause.

The First World War polished off her regime and resources. She retired from the management of the Gaiety in 1921, but continued to travel and give advice—but not talks—until rheumatism immobilized her. In 1933 she was made a Companion of Honour for services to drama. She died at her last home, Acorn Bank, Shere, Surrey, on 6 August 1937, and was cremated on 10 August at Woking crematorium, where her ashes were scattered. Mourned by her audiences everywhere and by her now-famous protégés, who included Lewis Casson and Sybil Thorndike, she was remembered affectionately for her modesty, her dry sense of humour, her stunning dresses, and her fundamentally Quaker generosity to so many people, and to the art of the theatre.   PETER CHEESEMAN

Sources S. Gooddie, *Annie Horniman: a pioneer in the theatre* (1990) • R. Pogson, *Miss Horniman and the Gaiety Theatre, Manchester* (1952) • *Manchester Guardian* (9 Aug 1937) • *The Times* (9 Aug 1937) • *Evening Chronicle* (9 Aug 1937) • *Daily Herald* (9 Aug 1937) • *Gaiety Theatre* annuals, 1909–11, Man. CL, Arts Library, Manchester theatre collection, Th 792.094273 Ma21 • the Horniman festival, a scrapbook, Man. CL, Arts Library, Manchester theatre collection, Th 792.094273 H1 • A. E. F. Horniman, letters to Tom Bass, 1919–37, Man. CL, Arts Library, Manchester theatre collection, MS F927.92.Hol • miscellaneous collection of newspaper cuttings, 1907–78, Man. CL, Arts Library, Manchester theatre collection, Th 792.094273 H016 • 'A talk about the drama', Manchester Statistical Society, 14 Dec 1910, Man. CL, Arts Library, Manchester theatre collection, Th 792.094273 H09 • T. Wyke and N. Rudyard, *Manchester theatres* (1994)

Archives JRL, corresp. and papers • Man. CL, Manchester Theatre collection, MSS • NL Ire., corresp. • TCD, corresp. • Theatre Museum, London, letters | BL, letters to George Bernard Shaw, Add. MS 50538 • Man. CL, Manchester Archives and Local Studies, letters to Tom Bass • TCD, corresp. with J. M. Synge

Likenesses J. B. Yeats, oils, 1904, Abbey Theatre, Dublin • J. B. Yeats, pencil drawing, 1904, Abbey Theatre, Dublin • L. A. Bell, pastel drawing, c.1910, Tate collection • F. Lion, chalk drawing, c.1912, NPG [*see illus.*] • photographs, c.1912–1913, NPG • E. Magnus, oils, Man. CL • Matt, cartoon, repro. in *Manchester Evening Chronicle* (13 April 1908) • Studios of Guttenberg, photograph, Man. CL • photograph, Man. CL; repro. in *Gaiety Theatre Annual* (1909), 21 • photographs, Horniman Museum collection, London • photographs, JRL

Wealth at death £51,066 0s. 3d.: resworn probate, 27 Sept 1937, CGPLA Eng. & Wales

Horniman, Frederick John (1835–1906), tea merchant and founder of the Horniman Museum, London, was born on 8 October 1835 at Bridgwater, Somerset, the fourth of six children of John Horniman (1803–1893) and his wife, Ann, daughter of Thomas Smith of Witney. The first two children and the last died in infancy; young Horniman therefore had an elder brother, William Henry, and a sister, who died at the age of fourteen. John and Ann Horniman were Quakers and Horniman was educated at Friends' School, Croydon. On Frederick's birth certificate his father described himself as a cheese factor but about five years later he invented a tea-packaging machine, and when the selling of tea in sealed packets proved profitable he established the tea business of Horniman & Co. Horniman left school at the age of fourteen to join his father and by 1852 the firm had offices in the City of London at Wormwood Street and a warehouse in Shepherdess Walk.

In later years Horniman recorded that from an early age he was interested in natural history, particularly entomology, and had collected butterflies, birds' eggs, moths, and insects of all kinds. His enthusiasm for these interests seems never to have flagged but he found time in 1859, on 3 June, to marry Rebekah, daughter of John Emslie of Dalston, and he became a Congregationalist to please his wife and her parents. In 1868 his father retired and Frederick and his brother took over the increasingly successful business, with Frederick, the younger but apparently dominant partner, as chairman. Later at the opening of new premises he explained their success thus:

> We supply direct, we employ no middlemen at all, we buy for cash, and we sell for cash … we never vary our quality any more than we vary our labels and we reduced our price when the tea duty was lowered … We cut everything as fine as we can, for we think that if we always give customers the best tea at a low price we shall never lose our trade. We … made our trade by sticking to that principle and we shall never change. As a proof that our policy is the best the business grows every day.   (*St Stephen's Review*, 3 Jan 1891)

W. H. and F. J. Horniman & Co., as the business had become, was described in 1891 as the biggest tea firm in the world. The export trade alone in Horniman Pure Tea was estimated to exceed 5000 chests per week, each chest containing 100 lb of tea.

Physically, Frederick Horniman appears to have been a small man, quite bald from an early age and in middle life with a moustache and beard, which he later shaved off. Concurrently with his business activities he was collecting on an ever-increasing scale, his interests having expanded since boyhood to comprise a great variety of rare and curious objects as well as those illustrative of natural history, arts, and handicrafts from all over the world. With the wealth derived from his business he employed missionaries and travellers of all sorts as agents, and he later travelled and collected extensively himself, in 1884 making a three-month trip to India and Ceylon. Since 1868 he had been living at Surrey House, Forest Hill, but the scale of his collecting over twenty years was such that room by room the collections had taken over and eventually he moved to Surrey Mount at the top of the hill. At the end of 1890 he opened Surrey House as a free museum to the public on three days a week.

In 1895 Rebekah Horniman died; later that year Frederick was elected Liberal MP for Penryn, Falmouth, and Flushing. No sooner had he been elected than he embarked on a world tour, crossing the USA and Canada, visiting Japan, China, Burma, and India and returning home via Egypt, where he was escorted around the temples of Luxor and Karnak by Howard Carter. Back home, characteristically, he seems to have been an active MP, gaining particular popularity in the constituency by securing the passage through both houses of parliament of a bill abolishing the rector's rate, which had been, as he described it at a meeting in 1897, 'a noxious impost' on the borough since the time of Charles II.

In middle life Horniman joined the Church of England; on 30 January 1897 he married Minnie Louisa, daughter of G. W. Bennett of Charlton, Kent. With his new wife, who was some forty years his junior, he subsequently had two daughters. In the same year, to celebrate Queen Victoria's diamond jubilee, he opened a large part of the gardens of Surrey Mount to the public. By now electric light had been installed in Surrey House and the collections were said to include: birds, butterflies, Egyptian and classical antiquities, coins, manuscripts, armour, glass, porcelain, and oriental ethnography and musical instruments. Although the house had been extended so that twenty-four 'saloons' were open to the public, the collection and the numbers of people visiting it had outgrown the space available, and Frederick decided to close and demolish the existing museum and build a new one on the site. As architect he chose Charles Harrison Townsend, and the new building, consisting basically of two large galleries and a distinctive tower, which has been described as one of the few large-scale masterpieces of English free-style architecture, was completed at a cost of £40,000 in 1901. Soon afterwards it was presented, with the collections and 15 acres of gardens, to the London county council, as representing the people of London. It was recorded on a plaque at the entrance than this should be 'for ever as a free museum for their recreation, instruction and enjoyment'.

Frederick Horniman died at his home, Falmouth House, 20 Hyde Park Terrace, London, on 5 March 1906 and was buried with his first wife in Camberwell old cemetery. His son with Rebekah, Emslie John Horniman, Liberal MP for Chelsea (1906–10), added a lecture hall and library to the museum. His daughter with Rebekah, Annie Elizabeth Fredericka *Horniman (1860–1937), founder of the Abbey Theatre, Dublin, and the Repertory Theatre, Manchester, was made a Companion of Honour in 1933. Following the demise of the London county council and its successors the greater London council and the inner London education authority, the Horniman Museum and Gardens were administered by a trust and funded by the Department of National Heritage. For all the range of his interests, it can be seen that Frederick Horniman was informed by a serious purpose in his determination to build comprehensive collections in selected areas, and that determination has been built upon in the intervening years so that now each of the three collecting departments of the museum, ethnography, natural history, and musical instruments, houses material of international importance.

MICHAEL HORNIMAN

Sources *The Times* (6 March 1906) · K. Teague, *Mr Horniman and the tea trade* (1993) · Richard Quick's scrapbook, Horniman Museum, London · S. Goodie, *Annie Horniman: a pioneer in the theatre* (1990) · **Archives** Horniman Museum and Library, London, corresp. **Likenesses** M. Stewart, oils, 1891, Horniman Museum, London · B. Stone, photograph, 1897, NPG · E. Roberts, pastel drawing, 1903, Horniman Museum, London · possibly by J. W. Rollins, bronze bust, Horniman Museum, London · photographs, Horniman Museum, London **Wealth at death** £421,628 13s.: probate, 9 April 1906, *CGPLA Eng. & Wales*

Hornor, Thomas (1785–1844), surveyor and panoramist, was born on 12 June 1785 at Lowgate, Hull, where his family were Quaker grocers. He was taught surveying and engineering by his brother-in-law William Johnson. In the early 1800s he was in Manchester, surveying the property of the free grammar school, but by 1807 he was in London, living first in Kentish Town and later that year in Chancery Lane. That same year he was appointed by the vestry of St James's, Clerkenwell, to draw a large-scale plan of the parish. On 19 October 1808, well ahead of his deadline, he presented them with a huge plan measuring 81 in. by 72 in., which shows him to have been a skilled and assiduous surveyor and cartographer. The vestry was well satisfied, and Hornor particularly impressed William Cook, a local improving landowner. Under Cook's patronage Hornor set up in business at 3 Church Court, Inner Temple, from where he undertook the survey and valuation of landed properties, the division of commons, and the levelling for canals and drains. In 1813 he published a version of his Clerkenwell map, which, though decorative, remained informative and accurate. He advertised himself as a promoter of picturesque landscape gardening, having devised a new method of drawing estate plans which he called 'panoramic chorometry'. He elaborated on this technique, which he claimed reunited the arts of surveying and landscape painting, in his *Description of an Improved Method of Delineating Estates* (1813).

By 1814 Hornor was in Wales, advertising for business as a 'Pictural Delineator of Estates'. He produced some 300 to

400 watercolours, hinged cut-out books after the manner of Humphry Repton's red books, panoramas of estates, and at least four huge maps, all of which attest to his skills as surveyor, artist, and entrepreneur. He mixed with his clients as equals and grew very wealthy.

Having returned to London in 1820, Hornor lived in 2 Robert Street, Adelphi, and after 1825 at 10 Royal (or Adelphi) Terrace. Having been an irregular worshipper in Manchester, he stopped attending meeting altogether in London, and in 1822 the Society of Friends disowned him. His artistic ambitions grew with his social status and he began his most spectacular project, that of a 360 degree panorama of London with the summit of St Paul's as the viewpoint. In a cabin precariously balanced on scaffolding erected in connection with repairs to the cathedral, he sketched and measured. Although he attracted considerable publicity for his enterprise and admiration for his courage, few subscribed to his initial scheme of publishing the work as a series of prints. However, the MP and banker Rowland Stephenson sponsored the construction in Regent's Park of a dome by Decimus Burton, second in size in England only to that of St Paul's, in which Hornor's work was to be displayed. In it in 1825 the artist E. T. Parris began the daunting task of transferring views from flat sheets to 42,000 square feet of curved canvas. It was due for completion in 1827 but was far from finished by the end of 1828 when Stephenson absconded to the USA, deeply in debt. In January 1829 Hornor threw open the unfinished Colosseum to the public, who could enjoy the panorama at various levels, riding upwards in the 'ascending room', the first passenger lift in England and Hornor's own design. Income was large, but costs were larger yet, and later that year Hornor also absconded to the USA. There he did some second-rate work before dying in penury (and possibly insane) in New York city on 14 March 1844. He was interred at the Friends' burial-ground there.

The Colosseum was finished in 1831 and visitors could take delight in Hornor's pleasure gardens as well as his panorama: but, after a series of proprietors had failed to make it pay, the building and its contents were auctioned in 1868. There were no bidders for Hornor's panorama and it remained in place until 1874, when it was brought up to date and shipped to America for display on Broadway.

Hornor fell into obscurity, not least as many of his finest works remained in private hands in Wales. He was recognized as a considerable artist in the later twentieth century, when his Welsh watercolours and prints came to light, but, despite his claims to have reunited the plan and the prospect, he had no followers. He remains more a curiosity than a pioneer, and his works 'a supreme example of misdirected genius' (Hyde, 'Hornor', 32).

ELIZABETH BAIGENT

Sources R. N. Hyde, 'Thomas Hornor: pictural land surveyor', *Imago Mundi*, 29 (1977), 23–34 · R. N. Hyde, *The Regent's Park colosseum* (1982) · E. Jenkins, 'Thomas Hornor', *Glamorgan Historian*, 7 (1971), 37–50

Hornsby, Thomas (1733–1810), astronomer, the son of Thomas Hornsby (*bap.* 1704, *d.* 1771), an apothecary and later alderman, and his wife, Thomasine Forster, *née* Coulson (*bap.* 1705, *d.* 1775), was baptized in the parish of St Nicholas, Durham, on 27 August 1733. Having matriculated at Corpus Christi College, Oxford, on 1 December 1749, he graduated BA in 1753 and MA in 1757, and was elected fellow in 1760. He established his own observatory in the college and spent the rest of his life in Oxford, where he acquired a DD by diploma in 1785.

Hornsby succeeded James Bradley as Savilian professor of astronomy at the start of 1763, when the requirement of yearly courses was introduced. In the same year he became professor of experimental philosophy. His lectures, illustrated by apparatus worth £375, kept abreast of current discoveries and acquired such a reputation that Matthew Boulton, the Birmingham engineer, arranged for his son, not an undergraduate, to attend them. Hornsby's promotion enabled him to marry Ann Cherrill (*c.*1740–1812) on 18 August 1763.

The Savilian professor of geometry until 1764, Nathaniel Bliss, was a friend and scientific collaborator of George Parker, earl of Macclesfield, and it was presumably he who introduced Hornsby to Shirburn. In 1761 Bliss reported to the Royal Society the observations of the transit of Venus at Shirburn by Hornsby, together with Parker's employees Thomas Phelps and John Bartlett. In April 1763 Hornsby was elected a fellow of the Royal Society, where in December he read a paper on the parallax of the sun, a product of the transit; in 1771, following the 1769 transit, he submitted another paper on the same topic, deducing a parallax of 8.78 seconds, which has hardly been bettered.

In 1764 Hornsby's observations of the solar eclipse of 1 April were read and the following year a paper on the then forthcoming transit of Venus, in which he recommended sites for observing it. In 1769 his report of the event included observations made at Shirburn by the Macclesfields and their retainers, besides his own and those of eight others at Oxford; the latter included George Shuckburgh, Basil Nikitin (from Russia), and Samuel Horsley. Hornsby's last paper in the *Philosophical Transactions*, in 1773, gave his calculation of the proper motion of Arcturus. In his 1798 edition of Bradley's *Observations* he gave further results on proper motions, and did assert that Castor 'is a double star, properly so called' (p. xxiii), contrary to later aspersions on him.

After succeeding Bradley, Hornsby had bought an expensive 32 inch mural quadrant by the premier maker John Bird. In 1768 he petitioned the Radcliffe trustees for an observatory and instruments, which he recommended should be made by Bird, by then old and ailing; he proposed that the professor should observe continuously, and yearly give two lecture courses in practical astronomy. After approval in 1771, the foundation stone was laid in 1772, and construction proceeded.

Hornsby and his family moved into the adjoining professor's residence at the end of 1773 and observation began in January 1774, although the observatory was not fully completed until 1797. Hornsby and the trustees were fortunate in their timing, for Bird had completed the instruments by the time of his death in 1776. Constructed in London, they were transported to Oxford by barge. Of the 8 foot south mural quadrant Hornsby said, 'I scruple not to call it by far the best instrument of the kind in the world' (Guest, 241). Hornsby's (reduced) observations of 1774–98 were published in 1932.

Meanwhile, an argument had been proceeding between the board of longitude and the Royal Society on the one hand, and Bradley's family on the other, over the ownership of Bradley's Greenwich papers. In 1776 the papers were handed to the chancellor of Oxford University, the prime minister, Lord North, on condition that they should be published by the Clarendon Press. The task of editing fell to Hornsby. An inordinate delay ensued—hardly surprising considering Hornsby's commitments to lecturing and to setting up the observatory and carrying out his own observations. In addition, in 1782 he was appointed Sedleian professor of natural philosophy and in 1783 Radcliffe librarian (treated by him as a sinecure), both of which ran concurrently with his former two chairs; all were retained until his death. Another delaying factor gradually became apparent: Hornsby was suffering epileptic fits, which interrupted his work, although he fulfilled his duties when possible. By 1784 hard words were being said by the commissioners of longitude, the Greenwich personnel, and the Royal Society; suggestions were made that the papers be handed to the society for publication, or that someone else be employed at Oxford. Hornsby advanced his ill health as explanation for the delay, and as an *ex officio* commissioner managed to sit through discussions apparently without speaking, secure in the knowledge that he had the full backing of the university and of the delegates of the Clarendon Press, who were satisfied with progress. In 1793 Hornsby promised to complete within a year, but on the appointed date had to say that illness had again intervened. Finally the first volume appeared in 1798; the task of editing the second volume was passed to Abram Robertson.

The Hornsbys had twelve children between 1764 and 1783, of whom seven died in infancy. The surviving sons, educated at Christ Church, Oxford, were Thomas (1766–1832), who became vicar of Ravensthorpe, Northamptonshire, and George (1780–1837), vicar of Turkdean, Gloucestershire. Three daughters, Ann, Isabella Savil, and Charlotte, were still living in 1801. Their mother died in February 1812, aged seventy-one.

Hornsby died in Oxford on 11 April 1810, and was buried at St Giles' there on 19 April. He appears to have been an amiable man, full of enthusiasm and determination, who successfully overcame his disability. He had practical skills in the physical sciences and was a lucid lecturer. In his main field of astronomy he was a remarkably accurate observer.

On the removal of the observatory from Oxford in 1935, most of Bird's instruments went to the Museum of the History of Science, Oxford, and Hornsby's observation books were transferred to the Royal Astronomical Society. In 1973 a lunar crater was named in Hornsby's honour.

RUTH WALLIS

Sources R. Wallis, 'Cross-currents in astronomy and navigation: Thomas Hornsby, FRS (1733–1810)', *Annals of Science*, 57 (2000), 219–40 • I. Guest, *Dr John Radcliffe and his trust* (1991) • D. Howse, *Nevil Maskelyne: the seaman's astronomer* (1989) • E. G. Forbes, *Greenwich observatory*, 1: *Origins and early history (1675–1835)* (1975) • parish register, Dalton-le-Dale, co. Durham • parish registers, St Nicholas, St Oswald, and St Giles, Durham • parish register, Durham Cathedral • parish registers, St Cross, St Peter-in-the-East, and St Giles, Oxford • Foster, *Alum. Oxon.* • *GM*, 1st ser., 80 (1810), 494 • J. Bradley, *Astronomical observations made at the Royal Observatory … MDCCL to … MDCCLXII*, ed. [T. Hornsby and A. Robertson] (1798–1805) • A. E. Musson and E. Robinson, *Science and technology in the industrial revolution* (1969), 176 • will, PRO, PROB 11/1511, sig. 245
Archives Bodl. Oxf., lecture notes and papers • CCC Oxf., notes and papers • MHS Oxf., corresp. and papers • MHS Oxf., most of Bird's instruments • RAS, observation records | LPL, letters to F. Wingrave • RAS, letters to Sir William Herschel
Wealth at death see will, PRO, PROB 11/1511, sig. 245

Hornsby-Smith. For this title name *see* Smith, (Margaret) Patricia Hornsby-, Baroness Hornsby-Smith (1914–1985).

Hornung, Ernest William (1866–1921), writer, was born on 7 June 1866 at Cleveland Villas, Marton, Middlesbrough, the eighth and last child of John Peter (formerly Johan Petrus) Hornung (1821–1886) and his wife, Harriet, *née* Armstrong (1824–1896). His father, of Hungarian extraction, had transferred his trading skills to England in the mid-1840s and become a wealthy iron, coal, and timber merchant. Willie, as Hornung was known in the family circle, was small, thin, and short-sighted, and suffered from severe asthma. He was immensely fond of cricket, although his skills at the game were limited. He was educated at Uppingham School for four years, but poor health obliged him to leave in 1883. Sent to New South Wales, Australia, to recuperate, he was employed as a tutor but also worked on sheep farms and gained much useful knowledge and experience. He returned to England in 1886 to find his father bankrupt and dying.

Hornung lived for a time with his mother and sister in Twickenham, Middlesex. Abandoning hopes of being a poet, he nevertheless resolved to become a professional writer. With Australia as his favourite subject, he contributed articles and short stories to magazines and his first novel, *A Bride from the Bush*, was published in 1890. An assured, graceful comedy of manners, it was followed by seven novels with Australian settings and two collections of short stories. His books were well received and abounded in authentic Australian phraseology but freshness, adroitness of plot, and clarity of description came to be recognized as characteristic hallmarks of a Hornung novel.

Hornung lodged in west London, became acquainted with numerous authors and artists, and lived in close proximity to Oscar Wilde for a time. Although the extent of their acquaintance is difficult to gauge, he evidently felt a close affinity with the playwright and refers to him obliquely but unmistakably in several novels. Hornung married Constance Aimée Monica Doyle (1868–1924) on 27 September 1893 and thus became the brother-in-law of Arthur Conan *Doyle (1859–1930). Their relations were sometimes strained, but Conan Doyle acted as godparent to Willie and Constance's only child—Arthur Oscar Hornung (b. 24 March 1895)—and accompanied them to Rome in 1898.

Hornung now started writing stories about A. J. Raffles—former public schoolboy and varsity man, a cricketer by day and burglar by night. Published in 1899 as *The Amateur Cracksman* (impishly dedicated 'To A.C.D.'), they attracted tremendous attention. Raffles is handsome, elegant, cynical, witty, and brave. He lives at The Albany, his debonair lifestyle, fondness for Sullivan cigarettes, and prowess at the wicket concealing nerves of steel. At times of crisis he copes daringly and ingeniously. His adventures are narrated by Bunny Manders, his admiring former fag and accomplice, and a homosexual relationship is hinted at. Ostensibly a collection of cautionary tales, it ends with Bunny in chains, facing eighteen months' imprisonment, and Raffles apparently drowned. But the miscreants enjoy a second innings in *The Black Mask* (1901), although Raffles has to masquerade as an elderly invalid for much of the time and can only venture out to a very limited extent. He is killed fighting for queen and country in the Second South African War, thereby atoning for his sins, but the tales were so immensely popular that a third collection, *A Thief in the Night*, relating some earlier adventures (and bringing the total number of short stories to twenty-six), was published in 1905. The first two collections were meanwhile merged into one volume (*Raffles: the Amateur Cracksman*) in 1906. Providing romance and excitement, and cocking a snook at authority, the books were massive best-sellers. Raffles would be portrayed on the stage by Gerald Du Maurier and on the screen by John Barrymore, Ronald Colman, and David Niven, and the stories would be a popular television series in the 1970s, but many people (including Conan Doyle) expressed grave doubt about Hornung's wisdom in writing them. In a sense, Raffles and Bunny were inverted counterparts of Holmes and Watson. But they were also fictionalized versions of Wilde and Bosie (Lord Alfred Douglas). To appreciate the clearest parallel drawn by Hornung between the man-about-town playwright who led a secret life and the man-about town cricketer who led a secret life, it must be explained that in 1820 Charles Maturin (Wilde's great-uncle) published a book called *Melmoth the Wanderer*. When Wilde went into hiding as a semi-invalid after coming out of prison in 1897—fated, thereafter, to endure a shadowy existence—he called himself Sebastian Melmoth. When Raffles went into hiding as a semi-invalid after coming back to England in 1897—fated, thereafter, to endure a shadowy existence—he called himself Mr Maturin. Both Wilde and Raffles would die in 1900.

Between 1899 and 1914 Hornung wrote *Peccavi* (1900), an absorbing account of a disgraced clergyman's atonement, and several thrillers of varying quality—among them *Mr Justice Raffles* (1909), which proved a disappointment for the fans of the cracksman. He also created an Oxford-educated bushranger called Stingaree. Most of his later works showed a sad decline in quality, although *Fathers of Men* (1912), narrating the career of a former stable boy at a fictionalized Uppingham, was regarded by many critics as

a fine achievement. *Witching Hill* (1913), about strange happenings on a new housing estate, endeavoured to break fresh ground but went almost unnoticed. Its two successors were feeble productions, bringing his novel-writing career to a lacklustre conclusion.

Short, dark-haired, and dapper, Hornung grew a moustache in the 1890s and invariably wore large pebble glasses. He was a quiet man averse to public life, although active in the Society of Authors and a frequent speaker at his old preparatory school. A firm believer in the merits of discipline, his two greatest enthusiasms were cricket and the public school system. He warmly endorsed Sir Henry Newbolt's sentiments of 'Play up, play up, and play the game!' Cricket loomed large in his stories, and he was proud of his election to the MCC (1907); he also enjoyed lawn tennis and cycling and (later) motoring and skating. An amusing conversationalist, he joined the Reform Club in the mid-1890s and remained a member until elected to the Savile Club in 1913.

Hornung and his wife lived in Kensington, London, for most of their married life. They took a great interest in the education of their son, Oscar, about to enter Cambridge when war broke out in August 1914, and were stunned by his death in action in July 1915. Hornung produced a little biography of him for private circulation, joined an anti-aircraft unit, and started doing voluntary YMCA work for troops home on leave. He visited the western front and his poem about a military cemetery, 'Wooden Crosses', was published in *The Times* and subsequently as a tiny booklet in its own right. Anxious to play a more active role, he went to France for the YMCA and by Christmas 1917 was serving behind the counter in a front-line canteen in Arras. He established a lending library for the troops but in March 1918, following substantial German advances, all civilians were sent home. He wrote an account of his experiences and re-established his library in Cologne after the armistice. Returning to England in 1919, he settled down with Constance at Midway Cottage, Partridge Green, a quiet Sussex hamlet in close proximity to his brother Pitt and his family at West Grinstead. He published a slim volume of collected verse and began work on a new novel, convinced it would be the best that he had yet written.

Held in much affection by friends and relatives, Hornung was a kind, sensitive, and conscientious man, endowed with a keen sense of humour. A fictionalized version of himself in *Fathers of Men*, 'a wild impulse burning in his eyes' (Hornung, *Fathers of Men*, 344), declares that he has not always been so 'straight' as generally supposed, but stops short of saying more. Clearly, Hornung was *not* a sphinx without a secret. But, equally clearly, sentiments expressed by a character in *The Camera Fiend* (1911) are his own—'I like a man's secrets to die with him' (Hornung, *Camera Fiend*, 268). Accompanying Constance to the south of France, he caught a chill which turned into aggravated influenza and pneumonia. He died on 22 March 1921 at St Jean de Luz and was buried in its cemetery a few feet away from his friend George Gissing.

PETER ROWLAND

Sources P. Rowland, *Raffles and his creator: the life and works of E. W. Hornung* (1999) · S. R. Chichester, ed., *E. W. Hornung and his young guard, 1914* (1941) · B. M. Collin, ed., *J. P. Hornung: a family portrait* (1970) · S. R. Chichester, *'Fathers of men' by E. W. Hornung* (1942) · private information (2004) [family, friends] · b. cert. · *Yorkshire Ridings Magazine*, 14/2 (spring 1977), 17

Likenesses group portrait, photograph, 1898, repro. in J. Dickson Carr, *The life of Sir Arthur Conan Doyle* (1949), facing p. 144 · photograph, *c*.1905, repro. in Chichester, ed., *E. W. Hornung* · photograph, repro. in *ILN* (2 April 1921), 431

Wealth at death £11,907 3*s*. 5*d*.: probate, 1 June 1921, *CGPLA Eng. & Wales*

Hornyold, John Joseph (1706–1778), vicar apostolic of the midland district, was born on 19 February 1706, the eldest of the six children of John Hornyold (1679–1771), gentleman, of Blackmore Park and Hanley Castle, Worcestershire, and his wife, Mary (*d*. 1731), eldest daughter of Sir Piers Mostyn of Talacre, Flintshire. Originally destined for a worldly career, he entered the English College, Douai, on 7 August 1728 and took the student's oath on 24 December 1730. Having survived an accident that deprived him of sight in his left eye, he was ordained at Arras on 22 December 1736, and left for the English mission the following September with the hope of the college authorities that he would be 'a good missionary in the future' (*Douay College Diaries*, 214). For nearly two years he was based in Grantham, Lincolnshire, where he was noted for his pastoral zeal.

In 1739 Hornyold became chaplain to Mary, the widow of Thomas Giffard of Chillington, Brewood, Staffordshire, who lived in the dower house, called Longbirch, from 1718 until her death in 1754. After this date, and until 1804, Longbirch was rented as a residence for the vicars apostolic of the midland district. During his time as chaplain Hornyold published three works: *The Decalogue Explained* (1744), *The Sacraments Explained* (1747), and *The Real Principles of Catholics* (1749), based on the writings of his predecessor at Longbirch, John Johnson.

By 1750 Bishop John Talbot Stonor, vicar apostolic of the midland district, decided that he needed a coadjutor and that 'no body, within my acquaintance, was as fit as good Mr Hornyold' (Stonor to Mrs Giffard, 27 Sept 1750, Birmingham Archdiocesan Archives, A183). The bulls confirming Hornyold's appointment as bishop of Philomalia *in partibus infidelium* and coadjutor with right of succession were dated 20 December 1751 (ibid., A939), and he was consecrated by Bishop Stonor at Stonor Park, Oxfordshire, on 10 February 1752, succeeding to the vicariate on Stonor's death on 29 March 1756.

Hornyold continued to live at Longbirch, but was assiduous in making pastoral visits throughout his vicariate, which comprised fifteen counties and the Isle of Ely, and numbered 8760 Catholics, served by 42 secular and 48 religious priests (draft letter to Propaganda, 1773, Birmingham Archdiocesan Archives, A793). He often supplied for priests who had to be absent from their missions and, whenever possible, received newly ordained priests into his house to prepare them for their pastoral duties. His reputation was that of a quiet, hard-working prelate who continued to live as far as possible the life of a holy and dedicated pastor.

By 1765 Hornyold complained that his constitution was 'much broken', that his eyesight was failing, and, being unable to ride, he could not visit his district (J. Hornyold to T. Talbot, 15 Sept 1765, Birmingham Archdiocesan Archives, A142a). He tried to obtain Thomas Joseph Talbot as his coadjutor, offering 'with utmost Pleasure to resign the whole Government of the Distr[ict] to your Sole Care and to retire' (J. Hornyold to T. Talbot, 6 May 1766, ibid., A153), but Talbot steadfastly refused until prevailed upon by others, and he was consecrated in June 1766.

Although Talbot undertook the active care of the vicariate, Hornyold continued to interest himself in its affairs. He took over responsibility for Sedgley Park School on the death of William Errington in 1768, he bought land and caused the house and chapel at Oscott, Birmingham, to be rebuilt as a possible future residence for his successors, and he maintained a wide correspondence. 'Though he was most abstemious and mortified in his way of living,' wrote Bishop Milner, 'he was cheerful and good humoured, as his friends in general testify, and particularly those clergymen, who, in succession were his chaplains.' His health continued to decline, and he died at Longbirch on 26 December 1778, leaving the bulk of his estate, after some personal, pious, and charitable legacies, to his successor. He was buried on 30 December in Brewood parish church. JOHN SHARP

Sources Birmingham Roman Catholic Archdiocesan Archives, A and C series · J. M. [John Milner], 'The Rt Rev. John Hornyold', *Laity's Directory* (1818) · Gillow, *Lit. biog. hist.*, vol. 3 · W. M. Brady, *The episcopal succession in England, Scotland, and Ireland, AD 1400 to 1875*, 3 (1877) · G. Anstruther, *The seminary priests*, 4 (1977) · *Genealogical collections illustrating the history of the Roman Catholic families of England: based on the Lawson manuscript*, ed. J. J. Howard, H. F. Burke, and H. S. Hughes, 4 (privately printed, London, 1887) · 'Catholic chapels in Staffordshire', *Catholic Magazine*, 5 (1834), 301–24 · E. H. Burton and E. Nolan, *The Douay College diaries: the seventh diary, 1715–1778*, Catholic RS, 28 (1928)

Archives Birmingham Roman Catholic Archdiocesan Archives, papers

Likenesses Keating & Co., copper-plate engraving, 1817 (after drawing formerly in the possession of the Revd John Roe), Birmingham Roman Catholic archdiocese, archdiocesan archives; formerly in the possession of the Revd John Roe · oils, Blackmore Park, Worcestershire · woodcut, repro. in *Orthodox Journal*, 3 (1834), 161; copy, Birmingham Roman Catholic Archdiocesan Archives

Horovitz [*née* Hooker], **Frances Margaret** (1938–1983), poet and broadcaster, was born on 13 February 1938 in Princess Beatrice Hospital, Kensington, London, the elder daughter of Frank Edward Hooker (1904–1975), a management accountant for ASEA Electric, and his wife, Margaret Alice Dorothy Scroggs (*b*. 1907), daughter of Arthur William Scroggs, a valet to Sir Frederick Williams Taylor. In 1941 the family moved from London to Nottingham, where during the war Frank Hooker was manager of a munitions factory. They returned in 1947 to live in Walthamstow, east London, where from 1949 to 1956 Frances attended the Walthamstow High School for Girls. School trips to the Old Vic and a sixth-form visit to Italy introduced her to Shakespeare's plays and Renaissance

Frances Margaret Horovitz (1938–1983), by Mike Golding

painting. By the time she entered Bristol University in 1956 to read English and drama, she was determined to become an artist. Graduating from Bristol in 1959, she went on to the Royal Academy of Dramatic Art in London where, between 1959 and 1961, she starred in a number of student productions. In 1960 she met the poet Michael William Horovitz (*b.* 1935), and became one of a group of Blake enthusiasts connected with Horovitz's radical journal *New Departures*; on 12 June 1964 she married him in London. They went on to live at 29 Colville Terrace, Notting Hill, London.

As a young actress Frances Horovitz took small parts in West End productions and spent time in repertory, but her beautiful speaking voice soon caught the ear of the poet George MacBeth, who cast her in his anti-nuclear satire *The Doomsday Show* (1963), later employing her as a principal reader in the poetry programmes he was producing for the BBC. Her unsurpassed performances as a poetry reader for radio, directed first by George MacBeth and after 1976 by Fraser Steel, ceased only with the illness that preceded her death. She came to feel that poetry reading was a different discipline from acting—purer, more austere, and without egotistical self-projection. In 1975 she acted in the first performance of Ted Hughes's *Cave Birds* at the Ilkley Festival, soon afterwards beginning the long professional partnership with the literary biographer

Robert Gittings that established her as one of finest interpreters of Keats and Hardy.

Frances Horovitz's performances, live and on the radio, won her thousands of admirers, but as a poet she eschewed self-dramatization and instead drew on an instinctive, entirely uncompromised spirituality. In December 1964 she paid the first of many visits to the Carmelite priory in Aylesford, Kent. The attraction was a circle of young artists brought together by Father Brocard Sewell under the auspices of the *Aylesford Review*. Henry Williamson, who considerably influenced her, was the guiding spirit of this group which shared a reverence for the natural world and a belief that the disciplines of art had to be commensurate with the disciplines of the spirit. When, after her marriage, she began to write poetry, the *Aylesford Review* became her first publisher. *Poems* by Frances Horovitz was printed, in an edition of 526 copies, by St Albert's Press in 1967. *Poems* was followed by *The High Tower*, published by New Departures in 1970. Ten years then lapsed before Enitharmon Press brought out her third collection, *Water over Stone*, in 1980. It was during this hiatus that her poetry deepened considerably. By the time *Snow Light, Water Light* (Bloodaxe Books) was put into her hand on her deathbed in 1983, her lyrics 'Rain—Birdoswald' and 'Flowers' had established her as a lasting poet in the English mystical tradition of Traherne and George Herbert.

During the 1960s Frances Horovitz augmented her slender income by teaching English and drama part-time in a number of London schools, her favourite being the Carlyle Grammar School for Girls in Fulham. In the summer of 1970 she and her husband managed to buy Mullions, a tiny semi-detached cottage in the Slad valley, near Stroud, Gloucestershire, while still retaining their flat in London. On 27 April 1971 their son Adam was born in St Mary's Hospital, Paddington, London. With the establishment of the Arvon writing centres in the 1970s, she became a regular tutor at Lumb Bank in Yorkshire and Totleigh Barton in Devon. Shortly before Christmas 1980, with nine-year-old Adam, she went to live with the poet Roger Garfitt (*b.* 1944) in north-east England, spending much of that winter and the next in a farmhouse near the Roman fort of Birdoswald. Through the Li-Yuan-Chia (LYC) Gallery in Cumberland, she contributed poems to *Wall* (LYC Press, 1981) on the theme of Hadrian's Wall. Another LYC collaboration with Winifred Nicholson and others resulted in the landscape anthology *Presences of Nature* (Carlisle Museum and Art Gallery, 1982).

In July 1982, after a spring trip to Orkney, Frances Horovitz and Roger Garfitt moved to 2 Mount Pleasant, St Weonards, overlooking Orcop in Herefordshire. On the morning of their move, Frances learned that the pain she had been suffering in her ear was due to skin cancer. She went north again for a series of operations, but when these proved unsuccessful she was admitted in May 1983 to the Royal Marsden Hospital in Fulham, London. On 28 July her divorce from Michael Horovitz came through, enabling her to marry Roger Garfitt in her bedroom in St Weonards on 6 September 1983. Shortly afterwards she returned, much weakened, to the Royal Marsden Hospital, where she died on Sunday morning, 2 October 1983.

Frances Horovitz's death was mourned by thousands. After her funeral and burial in Orcop on Saturday, 8 October, memorial readings were held before huge audiences in Bristol and London. Two commemorative pamphlets were published: *Tenfold* (Martin Booth, 1983) and *A Celebration of and for Frances Horovitz* (New Departures, 1984). In 1985 Bloodaxe Books, in association with the Enitharmon Press, brought out her *Collected Poems*. Remembering Frances in 1996, Roger Garfitt wrote:

> When I look back at Frances, I see that her beauty was all of a piece: her poetry, her voice, her manner, the clothes she wore, the very pots she used in her kitchen. Few of us achieve such unity. Yet it's important to see the fierceness in her poetry, the cutting through to the elemental. I see the last poems not as prophetic of her early death but as the culmination of her art—the beautiful, quiet acceptance she had been working towards all her life.   (private information)

ANNE STEVENSON

Sources B. Sewell, ed., *Frances Horovitz, poet: a symposium* (1987) • M. Horovitz, ed., *A celebration of and for Frances Horovitz*, rev. edn (1984) • private information (2004) • I. Hamilton, ed., *The Oxford guide to twentieth-century poetry* (1996) • b. cert. • m. cert. • personal knowledge (2004)
Archives priv. coll.
Likenesses M. Golding, photograph, Bloodaxe Books, Tarset, Northumberland [*see illus.*] • O. Jones and others, photographs, repro. in Horovitz, ed., *Celebration of … Frances Horovitz* • J. Percival, portrait, repro. in F. Horovitz, *Water over stone* (1980), cover • photograph (aged fourteen), repro. in Sewell, ed., *Frances Horovitz, poet*
Wealth at death under £40,000: probate, 7 June 1984, CGPLA Eng. & Wales

Horrabin, James Francis [Frank] (1884–1962), socialist educator and cartoonist, was born at 12 Cromwell Road, Peterborough, on 1 November 1884, the eldest son of James Woodhouse Horrabin (*d.* 1937), a commercial traveller and later cutler, from Sheffield, and his wife, Mary Pinney (*d.* 1937), of Stamford, Lincolnshire. The family was Methodist. Horrabin attended Stamford grammar school and the Sheffield School of Art, where he studied metalwork design and met his first wife, Winifred, *née* Batho [*see* Horrabin, Winifred (1887–1971)], who was also to become a leading socialist writer. In 1906 he secured a post as staff artist on the *Sheffield Telegraph*, and in 1909 he became art editor for the *Yorkshire Telegraph and Star*. On 11 August 1911 he married Batho, and in the same year he moved to London to work on the *Daily News* (later the *News Chronicle*) and the London *Star*. For the *News Chronicle* he created the genial cartoon characters of Japhet (son of Mr and Mrs Noah and brother of Ham and Shem) and Happy (a bear). Collections of gently humorous illustrated stories, cartoon strips, and songs followed: *Japhet and Fido* (1922), *Mr Noah* (1922), *More about the Noahs—and Tim Tosset* (1922), and *The Japhet Book* (1925). *The Japhet and Happy Annual* first appeared in 1926. *The Star* featured the adventures of the two office-girls Dot and Carrie, from which collections were also published. Horrabin's connection with the two newspapers lasted nearly half a century, with a brief interlude only between 1917 and 1918, when he was a rifleman in the Queen's Westminster rifles. His Dot and Carrie strip still appeared at the time of his death in the *Evening News*, to which it had transferred after *The Star* ceased publication in 1960.

Horrabin was an illustrator of considerable talent. He was capable of detailed, accurate portraiture, though the enduring appeal of the Noah family and Dot and Carrie can be explained by populism achieved partly by naïve and simple drawings. Despite the political agenda of the newspapers in which the Noahs and Dot and Carrie appeared, these were cartoons with only a gentle social message, and they form a stark contrast to his cartoons for other working-class journals. There may have been an autobiographical element—the little wooden-top figure of Mrs Noah resembled his wife, Winifred. Horrabin became a guild socialist in 1915 and dedicated his artistic talent to working-class politics. He became a member of the Plebs League, the workers' education movement that broke away from Ruskin College in 1909, and contributed hundreds of satirical and propagandist drawings to its journal, *The Plebs*, of which he became editor in 1914. For these visual works of polemic, Horrabin relied upon a greater realism of style. His political caricatures were clear portraits, and the gentle humour of the Noahs was replaced by bitter and dark jest. Horrabin and his wife became very influential in the labour college movement. Frank Horrabin lectured in the Central Labour College, and Winifred Horrabin was honorary secretary of the Plebs League and founded the Central Labour College's Women's League in 1913 to promote the education of women workers. Fund-raising events, such as dramatic evenings, were organized jointly by the Horrabins and were crucial in keeping the Central Labour College in operation. They both regularly wrote for *The Plebs*, though Frank Horrabin contributed mostly political commentary while his wife concentrated on publicity and funding.

The Horrabins became part of a group of London-based left-wing socialists that included H. G. Wells, and in 1919 Horrabin was asked to illustrate Wells's *Outline of History*, which first appeared in 1920 and went through several revised editions. His 200-plus contributions included maps and charts and speculative reconstructions of prehistoric animal and plant life. Wells said of Horrabin that he was 'not only an illustrator but a collaborator'.

Horrabin was drawn into the circle of socialist intellectuals that lived on the Essex estates of Frances Evelyn, Lady Warwick. The circle included Wells, Robert Blatchford, Conrad Noel, and Harold and Freda Laski. In 1921 Horrabin joined the Communist Party and added Harry Pollitt to his list of friends. He continued to edit *The Plebs*, and he co-wrote *Working Class Education* (1924) with Winifred Horrabin. His theatre and book reviews viciously attacked enemies of the socialist cause, and he joined with Wells in political support of the general strike in 1926. He worked closely also with the Labour MP for Middlesbrough, Ellen Cicely Wilkinson (1891–1947), with whom he had a long-standing extramarital affair.

Through Wilkinson he briefly became interested in parliamentary politics, and he served as Labour MP for Peterborough from 1929 to 1931.

In 1932 Horrabin changed tack in several ways. He was enlisted, with other former guild socialists, by G. D. H. Cole and Margaret Cole on to the executive of the Society for Socialist Inquiry and Propaganda (he became chairman in 1936). He joined the national council of the Socialist League and took on the editorship of *The Socialist* and *Socialist Leaguer*. He relinquished his editorship of *The Plebs* to J. P. M. Millar, though his move to the Socialist League allowed him to move away from parliamentary politics and return to the promotion of the working-class movement through propagandist journalism and appearances on radio programmes such as *Your Questions Answered*. Through programmes of research, lectures, and conferences the Socialist League exerted pressure on the Labour Party and Trades Union Congress to pursue the movement's goals. Horrabin continued to propagate socialism through educational texts, illustrating Lancelot Hogben's *Mathematics for the Million* (1936) and *Science for the Citizen* (1938), and the 1939 edition of *Glimpses of World History* by Jawaharlal Nehru. Independently he produced a number of atlases. These were low-priced books, intended for adult students with small resources.

In the 1940s Horrabin turned to international socialism, and when the New Fabian Research Bureau had reformed and revitalized the Fabian Society, he collaborated with Rita Hinden and Arthur Creech Jones to create the Fabian Colonial (later Commonwealth) Bureau, providing it with *Empire*, a monthly anti-imperialist journal. In 1945 he succeeded Creech Jones as chairman of the bureau, which post he held until 1950. Horrabin also wrote a regular column for the monthly *Socialist Commentary*, edited by Hinden, but by the 1950s his health was failing, and he gradually became less politically active.

Horrabin was a tall, good-looking man with curling fair hair. His first marriage, to Winifred Batho, was dissolved in 1947. On 30 March 1948 he married Margaret Victoria McWilliams, *née* Speers (*b.* 1897/8), secretary, a widow, with whom he had been conducting an extramarital affair since his relationship with Ellen Wilkinson had ended in 1932. He had no children. Horrabin died of bronchopneumonia at his home, 16 Endersleigh Gardens, Hendon, on 2 March 1962.

MARGARET COLE, rev. AMANDA L. CAPERN

Sources B. Pimlott, *Labour and the left in the 1930s* (1977) · *The Plebs*, 1–24 (1909–32) · J. P. M. Millar, *The Plebs*, 54/4 (1962), 84–5 · J. P. M. Millar, *The labour college movement* (1979) · W. W. Craik, *The Central Labour College, 1909–29* (1964) · M. Cole, *The Times* (3 March 1962) · M. Cole, *The Times* (6 March 1962) · *The Labour who's who* (1927) · B. D. Vernon, *Margaret Cole, 1893–1980* (1986) · A. Clark, *Dictionary of British comic artists, writers and editors* (1998) · b. cert. · m. cert. [Margaret McWilliams] · d. cert. · *CGPLA Eng. & Wales* (1963)
Archives U. Hull, Brynmor Jones L., corresp. and MSS of Winifred Horrabin | SOUND BL NSA, Kingsley Martin and James Francis Horrabin, 'A new judgement on H. G. Wells', 18 Dec 1949
Likenesses photographs, 1890–99 (in infancy), U. Hull; corresp. and MSS of Winifred Horrabin · photograph, 1910–11, U. Hull · double portraits, photographs, 1911–25 (with Winifred Horrabin),

U. Hull · group portraits, photographs, *c.*1915–1939, U. Hull · photograph, 1940, U. Hull
Wealth at death £5334 11*s.*: probate, 13 June 1963, *CGPLA Eng. & Wales*

Horrabin [*née* Batho], **Winifred** [*pseud.* Freda Wynne] (**1887–1971**), socialist and journalist, was born on 9 August 1887 in Sheffield, the fourth of the six children (three died in infancy) of Arthur John Batho (1855/6–1891), postal telegraph clerk, and his wife, Lilian Outram (1858/9–1938). Her parents came from artisan families and were members of the Wicker Congregational Church. Her father sailed to South Africa on the SS *Durban* in 1890 hoping to cure his tuberculosis, but, shortly after being joined by his family, he died and was buried in Graaff-Reinet in May 1891.

Batho returned to Sheffield and attended the Central School, then the Sheffield School of Art from 1907 where she met her future husband, James Francis *Horrabin (1884–1962), the cartoonist and cartographer. Her political awakening reflected the legacy of her father's death; she became anti-Boer and felt a close affinity with the South African feminist and socialist Olive Schreiner, whose biography she began to write. Batho joined the Women's Social and Political Union and disrupted a speech by Winston Churchill in 1909 with the suffragettes' cry 'votes for women'. She 'converted' to guild socialism 'via William Morris art' (Horrabin MS DWH/1/64) and wrote a play, 'Victorian Love Story: Beloved Good', about Thomas Carlyle and his wife, Jane.

Winifred Batho and James Horrabin were married on 11 August 1911 and moved to London. Together they worked in the labour college movement: they favoured independent workers' education and published these views in *Working Class Education* in 1924. Horrabin was honorary secretary of the Plebs League and edited *The Plebs*. She joined the Communist Party and delivered a paper in 1912 to the Fabian Society in which she argued that only the destruction of private property would release women from economic slavery (*Is Woman's Place the Home?*, published in 1933). During the First World War she began writing an autobiographical novel about a wartime love affair.

In the 1920s Horrabin became internationalist and pacifist in her outlook. She visited Russia in 1926, meeting N. K. Krupskaya and making a pilgrimage to Lenin's tomb. In Poland she observed a mass trial of political dissidents. When her younger brother, Harold Batho, died from First World War injuries in 1932, she told the National Conference of Labour Women that the international working classes should resist war, choosing starvation over employment in munitions factories.

In 1937 Horrabin began reviewing films and books for *The Tribune* (she continued until 1948), beginning a long career in journalism which included travel writing, social commentary, and short stories for journals such as *Time and Tide*. She had a weekly column in the *Manchester Evening News* from 1944 under the *nom de plume* of Freda Wynne. In 1938 Horrabin's mother died, Horrabin's novel was rejected by publishers, and she was diagnosed as having an ovarian cyst. She underwent a hysterectomy in February 1939. She moved to Oxford at the outbreak of war and in March 1942 her husband, who was immersed in his second extramarital affair, asked for a separation. Despite knowledge of his adultery, she was devastated and sought psychoanalytical treatment. On 13 October 1947 the marriage was dissolved. Horrabin lived and worked for six months in Jamaica before moving to Blackheath in 1950.

Horrabin's final years were marred by loneliness and a deep sense of failure. In 1951 her elder brother, Arthur (Artie) Denton Batho, died, leaving her without family, and she never fully recovered from the dissolution of her marriage. She compiled, but did not publish, 'The Summer of a Dormouse', a series of autobiographical essays. Their significance lies in her recollection of suffragist work with Adela Pankhurst in 1909 and socialist contacts in the 1920s and 1930s such as Harold Laski and H. G. Wells. She polished her novel and gave it the title 'After which War?', but, like her play and the Schreiner biography, it remained unpublished. She died at her home, Sandycross, Ridgeway Road, Dorking, Surrey, on 24 June 1971 and was cremated at Randall's Park crematorium, Leatherhead, on 30 June. Her estate of £185 was bequeathed to Robert Alfred Blatchford.

AMANDA L. CAPERN

Sources U. Hull, Brynmor Jones L., Horrabin papers · *The Tribune* (2 July 1971) · *CGPLA Eng. & Wales* (1971) · P. M. Graves, *Labour women: women in British working-class politics, 1918–1939* (1994) · W. W. Craik, *The Central Labour College, 1909–1929: a chapter in the history of working-class education* (1964) · J. P. M. Millar, *The labour college movement* (1979) · *The Labour who's who* (1927) · m. cert. · *DNB*

Archives U. Hull, corresp., diaries, and papers

Likenesses O. Nemon, bust · bust, U. Hull, Brynmor Jones L., Horrabin MSS · photographs, U. Hull, Brynmor Jones L., Horrabin MSS

Wealth at death £185: administration with will, 16 Aug 1971, *CGPLA Eng. & Wales*

Horridge, Sir Thomas Gardner (1857–1938), judge, was born at Raikes Cottage, Tonge with Haulgh, Bolton, Lancashire, on 12 October 1857, the only son of John Horridge, chemist, and his wife, Margaret, youngest daughter of Robert Sharpe Barlow, of Bolton. Educated at Nassau School, Barnes, he was admitted a solicitor in 1879 and practised at Southport. In 1884 he was called to the bar by the Middle Temple and joined the northern circuit, practising at the local bar at Liverpool, where his Lancashire associations secured him a start.

Horridge had a good presence, self-confidence, and ability, and soon acquired a substantial practice. On 17 September 1901 he married Evelyne Emma (1876/7–1920), the youngest daughter of Melvill Sandys, of Lanarth, Cornwall, who had served in the Bengal civil service. In the same year he became queen's counsel, continuing to practise mainly on the circuit, despite being successful, especially in commercial cases. In 1907 he appeared for W. H. Lever (later Viscount Leverhulme) in his successful action for libel against the Northcliffe newspapers, one of his juniors being F. E. Smith (later earl of Birkenhead).

At the general election of 1906 Horridge entered parliament as Liberal member for East Manchester, defeating A. J. Balfour by a substantial majority. F. E. Smith entered parliament at the same time and Horridge's election oratory became one of the targets for Smith's invective in a famous maiden speech. The two men crossed swords again on the government's Trades Disputes Bill (1906) which Horridge supported, along with the old age pensions scheme.

Horridge did not stand at the general election of January 1910, and that October was appointed a judge of the King's Bench Division. He proved excellent in both jury and non-jury cases, sound, competent, dignified, and expeditious, although he was thought to be somewhat brusque in his addresses to both counsel and witnesses. He frequently dealt with bankruptcy and divorce as well as the ordinary King's Bench cases. In 1916 he took part with Sir Rufus Isaacs (later marquess of Reading) and Sir Horace Avory in the trial at bar of Roger Casement. The court's construction of the Treason Act of 1351 was upheld in the court of criminal appeal.

After his first wife's death Horridge married, on 6 August 1921, May Ethel (*b.* 1867/8), daughter of Captain Francis Pavy of London and Wroughton, Wiltshire; she was the widow of Alfred Isenberg, and had assumed the surname Markham by deed poll. There were no children of either marriage.

Horridge, who told a royal commission in 1935 that he was opposed to the introduction of a retiring age for judges, retained his position until his eightieth year, resigning in May 1937. He was sworn of the privy council on his retirement. In 1929 he became treasurer of the Middle Temple. He died at 62 Wilbury Road, Hove, Sussex, on 25 July 1938; he was survived by his second wife.

DAVID DAVIES, *rev.* HUGH MOONEY

Sources *The Times* (26 July 1938) · *Law Journal* (30 July 1938), 78, 89 · b. cert. · m. certs. · d. cert.

Likenesses P. A. de Laszlo, oils, 1917, Man. City Gall. · W. Stoneman, photograph, 1930, NPG · photograph, repro. in *Law Journal*, 89

Wealth at death £97,468 5s. 1d.: probate, 20 Sept 1938, *CGPLA Eng. & Wales*

Horrocks, Sir Brian Gwynne (1895–1985), army officer, was born at Ranniken in India on 7 September 1895, the elder child and only son of a doctor of medicine, Colonel Sir William Heaton Horrocks, and his wife, Minna, daughter of the Revd J. C. Moore, of Connor, co. Antrim, Ireland. Having been educated at Uppingham School and the Royal Military College, Sandhurst, Horrocks was commissioned into the Middlesex regiment on the outbreak of war in 1914. Captured during the battle of Ypres in October 1914, he passed the war as a prisoner of war in Germany, and was a Soviet prisoner for another eighteen months after going to Vladivostok in 1919 as a staff officer in a mission under Major-General Sir Alfred Knox to the White Russian Admiral Aleksandr Kolchak. He was awarded the MC (1919).

Horrocks spent fifteen years as an infantry captain, but such was his love of the army that he was not dismayed by the poor career prospects. In 1924 he won the British modern pentathlon championship, and took part in the Olympic Games. He married in 1928 Nancy, daughter of Brook

Sir Brian Gwynne Horrocks (1895–1985), by Walter Stoneman, 1946

army commander and Horrocks as corps commander made 'an unbeatable team'.

Horrocks was seriously wounded at Bizerte in an air raid in August 1943 as he was preparing 10th corps for the Italian campaign. Five operations and eighteen months of illness and convalescence at Aldershot followed. However, in July 1944, when Montgomery sacked the 30th corps commander after a lacklustre tank battle in Normandy, he sent for Horrocks to replace him. Everyone connected with 30th corps at the time testified to the spectacular way in which he revived the morale of his war-weary troops. Still suffering from recurrent fever, Horrocks led 30th corps in the dramatic dash from the Seine to Antwerp. Then he made a mistake by ordering his corps to rest for three days at a moment when it was imperative to rush a crossing of the wide Albert Canal while the Germans were still in confusion. Hitler used the delay to send up fresh formations, and the British drive into the Netherlands was halted.

Both the British and Polish airborne commanders in their autobiographies criticized Horrocks for failing to link up with them after the Arnhem drop in September 1944. According to some of his colleagues Horrocks was unwell, but he crossed the Nijmegen Bridge within a few hours of its capture by the grenadiers to congratulate them. The truth is Montgomery had set 30th corps an impossible task.

When the German offensive in Christmas 1944 threatened Brussels and Antwerp, Horrocks told Montgomery that the German armour should be allowed to cross the Meuse and then his corps would annihilate them on the battlefield of Waterloo. This did not appeal to Montgomery, who sent him home on compulsory sick leave. He was quickly back to lead his corps over the Rhine and in the final triumphal drive to the Elbe. Friends of General Miles Dempsey, commander of the Second Army, have criticized Horrocks during this period for bypassing Dempsey and taking his instructions direct from Montgomery. The fault lay with Montgomery who was nostalgic for his previous relationship with Horrocks in Africa. Horrocks was appointed CB in 1943, to the DSO in 1943, KBE (1945), and KCB (1949).

After the war Horrocks became general officer commanding western command in February 1946 and then general officer commander-in-chief British army of the Rhine early in 1948. The problems of defeated Germany unduly strained his health and he was invalided out of the army in 1949 with the rank of lieutenant-general.

Immediately Horrocks was offered the post of gentleman usher of the black rod in the House of Lords, which he discharged with distinction from 1949 to 1963. He also became a television star, making around forty programmes with Huw Weldon. Horrocks loved the bustle and immediacy of television and also the floods of fan mail which in no way affected his character. His media role provided a much-needed boost for the image of the peacetime army. After fourteen years as black rod, Horrocks resigned to become a director of Bovis, and to leave

Taylor Kitchin, architect, of the Local Government Board. They had one daughter who was drowned when swimming in the Thames in 1979. Having passed out of the Staff College, Camberley, in 1933 he was well poised to achieve high rank when the Second World War started in 1939.

Horrocks was something of an actor, tall and good looking with charisma and charm and a capacity to make friends, although he could sometimes quarrel. He became friendly with A. P. (later Earl) Wavell and B. L. Montgomery during peacetime exercises and shared their enthusiasm for mechanized mobile warfare at a time when some senior officers still hankered after horse cavalry. Frank Simpson had become a close friend of his at the Staff College, and during the war as director of military operations (War Office) helped Horrocks to achieve promotion.

Horrocks went to France in 1939 commanding the 2nd battalion, Middlesex regiment, and was promoted brigadier during the evacuation of Dunkirk. Soon he was a divisional commander, and in 1942 Montgomery summoned him to the western desert to command 13th corps and later 9th and 10th corps. At El Alamein and the Mareth line his troops performed magnificently, and Sir C. Denis Hamilton claimed that a combination of Montgomery as himself more time for television, sailing, and charities. He had an honorary LLD degree from Belfast. Horrocks died on 4 January 1985 in Chichester.   RICHARD LAMB, *rev.*

Sources B. Horrocks, *A full life*, 2nd edn (1974) · P. Warner, *Horrocks* (1984) · R. Lamb, *Montgomery in Europe* (1983) · IWM, Sir Frank Simpson papers · *CGPLA Eng. & Wales* (1985) · *WWW* · *The Times* (9 Jan 1985)
Archives King's Lond., Liddell Hart C., corresp. with Sir B. H. Liddell Hart · NAM, papers relating to Middlesex regiment | FILM BFI NFTVA, *Challenge*, 1966 · BFI NFTVA, *The Peacemaker*, 1968 · BFI NFTVA, news footage · IWM FVA, 'HM the king attends a church service', Army Film Unit, 15 Oct 1944, A700/177/5 · IWM FVA, 'Showing the visit of General De Vennejoul to HQ. BAOR', Army Film Unit, 20 Nov 1945, A700/445 · IWM FVA, actuality footage · IWM FVA, documentary footage · IWM FVA, news footage | SOUND BL NSA, documentary recordings · IWM SA, current affairs recording · IWM SA, documentary recording · IWM SA, oral history interview
Likenesses W. Stoneman, photograph, 1946, NPG [*see illus.*]
Wealth at death £230,865: probate, 23 April 1985, *CGPLA Eng. & Wales*

Horrocks [Horrox], **Jeremiah** (1618–1641), astronomer, was born in the first half of 1618 in Lancashire and grew up in Toxteth Park, then an isolated village about 3 miles from the port of Liverpool. It had been settled in the late sixteenth and early seventeenth centuries by several families of puritan sympathies. Horrocks's religious opinions reflected their outlook. His parents, who were of moderate means, were in all probability James Horrocks (*d.* 1641), a watchmaker, and his wife, Mary, *née* Aspinwall (*b.* 1580). Jeremiah had a younger brother, Jonas, and relatives in New England.

A passion for astronomy Horrocks was admitted sizar in Emmanuel College, Cambridge, in May 1632 and left in 1635 without taking a degree. As a sizar his tuition was remitted and he was expected to help in the college buttery or kitchen, wait on fellows at table, and act as a servant to one of the senior fellows. In a brief autobiographical sketch written when he was twenty, Horrocks tells how as a boy at Cambridge he became enamoured of astronomy and in a relatively short time, without formal instruction or the companionship of others with similar interests, mastered its principles. The intensity of his commitment to the science, he relates, was fired by ambition, pleasure in observation, contemplation of the wisdom of the Creator, and a desire to know the causes of celestial phenomena. His remarkable achievements during his short life were highly praised by the leading scientists of the seventeenth century, including Newton. By the nineteenth century the praise of astronomers and historians of astronomy had not diminished. J.-B. J. Delambre referred to him as 'a genius of the same stamp as Kepler' (Delambre, 2.499), while John Herschel called him 'the pride and boast of British astronomy' (Herschel, 86n). The Victorian era saw the rise of a special genre of Horrocks hagiography, emphasizing his pluck, perseverance, and moral rectitude, and the happy convergence in him of religious and scientific ideals, partially owing to the mistaken impression that he had been ordained.

Horrocks came to the study of his science at a time when traditional conceptions of the heavenly bodies and the nature of the universe were breaking down and a significant increase in observational precision had become an important desideratum. At Cambridge he read as widely as he could in the works of Ptolemy, Copernicus, and Tycho Brahe as well as more recent authors. His initial textbook, however, was very likely *The Strange and Dangerous Voyage of Captain James* (1633), a popular account of an expedition to find the north-west passage. It contained an appendix by Henry Gellibrand (1597–1637), Gresham professor of astronomy, which seems to have provided Horrocks with an introduction to the essential literature and instrumentation of his science.

Computing planetary tables Following Gellibrand's recommendation, Horrocks obtained Philip van Lansberge's *Perpetual Tables*, which, their author claimed, would predict accurately planetary positions for all time. When his observations made clear that Lansberge's assertions had been highly overstated, Horrocks became disenchanted, and in January 1637 concluded that Lansberge's tables should be discarded and more accurate ones created. It was presumably then that he began to compute his own, and shortly thereafter he drafted and redrafted a treatise attacking Lansberge. His annotated copy of Lansberge's book, preserved in the library of Trinity College, Cambridge, is a valuable source of information on the development of Horrocks's thought in his early period. His other early notes and manuscripts are no longer extant; those remaining were begun in the second half of 1637. They appear to be of two types: those constituting notes for his astronomical education, written in English, and several drafts in Latin of treatises begun but never completed.

Among Horrocks's earliest observations, and of a kind he was to continue to make, were lunar, solar, planetary, and stellar diameters. Contrary to contemporaneous belief, Horrocks concluded that the apparent diameters of the stars were so immeasurably small as to be equivalent to points of light. He also made corrections to stellar positions in both Ptolemy's and Tycho Brahe's star tables. Determined to put astronomical theory to observational test whenever possible, he continually compared his observations of planetary positions with their places as predicted in several different astronomical tables.

Horrocks's astronomical instruments included three cross-staffs, or astronomical radii—graduated rods with sliding cross-pieces for the measurement of celestial angles—which he built himself. He also constructed a 13 inch quadrant and purchased a telescope in 1637 and another the following year. Always concerned about the accuracy of his observations, he carefully noted his means of observation and frequently the weather. In the course of his career he made adjustments to his observations for atmospheric refraction, ocular parallax, or eccentricity of the eye (allowing for the slight distance of the centre of the eye from the observing end of the astronomical radius from which angular measures were taken), and redetermined terrestrial longitudes using lunar eclipses and also the latitudes of several places.

Conversion to Keplerian astronomy After he left Cambridge, Horrocks presumably returned to Toxteth Park. In June 1636 he began a correspondence with William Crabtree, a clothier or draper of Broughton, near Manchester, that was to give further impetus to his studies. The two men exchanged letters frequently and they occasionally visited one another. Crabtree's observations strengthened Horrocks's conviction concerning the inadequacy of Lansberge, and Crabtree persuaded his friend to investigate the astronomy of Johannes Kepler. Horrocks then began to purchase Kepler's books, acquiring all his major works in 1636 and 1637, and immersed himself in the study of Kepler's astronomy.

By the end of 1637 Horrocks had become a convinced Keplerian, accepting what would come to be called Kepler's laws—elliptical orbits, non-uniform planetary motion, and the proportionality between the squares of the planets' periods and the cubes of their distances from the sun. In Horrocks's surviving manuscripts there is no mention of Kepler's 'second law' of planetary motion, which asserts that a radius vector from the planet to the sun sweeps out equal areas in equal times. Horrocks was nevertheless familiar with it, as he would develop a geometrical solution for a means of approximating to it and used it in his theory of the moon.

Horrocks fully accepted Kepler's vision of an astronomy based on physical causes, rare at the time, as well as harmonic ones, and rejected the Peripatetic division between the celestial and terrestrial regions. The causes of the motions of the planets he held with Kepler to reside in the sun. Like Kepler, he saw a great advantage in the elimination of the traditional circles, eccentrics, and epicycles from astronomy; they were fictional devices useful only for purposes of calculation.

Size of the universe On dynamical and cosmological issues, however, Horrocks became partially dissatisfied with Kepler's quasi-magnetic causes of planetary motion, rejecting his concept of a periodic solar repulsion of the planets, and opting instead for a mechanical analogy with falling bodies and a conical pendulum. He also objected to Kepler's intimation that certain anomalies in the celestial motions might be due to accidental physical causes, and called attention to the doubt of some astronomers that astronomy would ever be established on certain principles, noting the number of frustrated attempts to make astronomical tables coincide with the heavens. Horrocks was persuaded, however, that, if rightly cultivated, astronomy would shortly attain the perfection sought.

With his telescopes Horrocks observed the planets, the sun by projection—taking note of sunspots and recording a solar eclipse—the moon, and appulses to the moon. He took great pains to improve the accuracy of his measurements of the sun's diameter and made a considerable number, as it was important for the determination of the solar parallax, the angle subtended at the sun by the earth's radius.

The effective employment of geometrical means to determine the relative distances of sun, earth, and moon

had been sought from antiquity. Horrocks found the figures given for solar parallax by earlier astronomers inadequate. Since the planetary parameters depended on it, a more precise figure for it would yield more accurate predictions of planetary positions. Realizing that the parallax was negligible and outside the range of observational precision, he nevertheless thought it possible to gain a reasonable idea of it by utilizing very precise observations and making certain harmonic assumptions. Concerned with the harmonious ordering of the universe as God's creation, Horrocks, as had Kepler before him, thought that the sizes of the planets would fit a pattern. All the planets, he concluded, seem to have apparent diameters of 30 seconds of arc when seen from the sun. Horrocks derived a figure at first of 15 seconds and then 14 seconds of arc for the solar parallax, yielding a very great increase in the size of the solar system compared to those given by earlier astronomers. Horrocks's numbers gave the distance of the earth from the sun at about two-thirds its accepted value at present.

Revising Kepler's tables Horrocks's revision of Kepler's figure of 1 minute of arc for the solar parallax led the young astronomer to effect improvements on Kepler's tables for the sun and planets. His comparison of his observations with the places predicted from Kepler's tables had shown Kepler to err by up to 1°3'. Noting also that Kepler's *Rudolphine Tables* had the vernal equinox arriving earlier than it should have, Horrocks altered Kepler's figures for the eccentricity of the earth—the distance from the sun of the centre of the earth's elliptical orbit as a fraction of the radius along its major axis. Convinced, however, of the superiority of the *Rudolphine Tables* over all others, and that they alone rested on a correct theoretical foundation, Horrocks continued to work at correcting the parameters for each of the planets based on his and Crabtree's observations. His observations led Horrocks to the conclusion that Jupiter was becoming more rapid in its mean motion and Saturn slower. He seems to have recognized that these secular retardations and accelerations were periodic and may have been caused by their influence upon one another.

Having noticed in 1637 significant departures in the moon's position from predicted places derived from Kepler's tables, Horrocks turned his attention to the theory of the moon. The moon was the celestial body offering the greatest difficulty in predicting its position on a consistent basis. By the end of 1638 Horrocks presented Crabtree with a rough draft of his 'new theory of the moon'. It was in his lunar theory that Horrocks created his most influential advance over Kepler. With Kepler, Horrocks accepted an elliptic orbit for the moon, but he advanced considerably beyond Kepler in accounting more accurately for certain lunar inequalities than anyone had up to that time, or indeed would for some time after him. Horrocks's lunar theory involved the adoption of a varying eccentricity for his elliptical lunar orbit and an oscillation of the lunar apsides—the line passing through its minimum and maximum distances from the earth—about its mean position, which underwent a slow rotation. He indicated that there must be some physical explanation for these variations, but offered none other than a hint that the periodically changing relationships between sun, earth, and moon must play some part. From the beginning Horrocks linked both empirical factors and physical hypotheses in his efforts to explain or account for the motions of the moon and its inequalities. His elliptical theory has in it the kernel of perturbation theory based on physical causes of the lunar inequalities. By 1640 he had changed a number of lunar parameters. The last stage of his theory is found in a letter of Crabtree to William Gascoigne in June or July 1642. In his last letter to Crabtree Horrocks had expressed the opinion that his lunar theory was the most important of his discoveries. Isaac Newton would later adopt Horrocks's variable eccentricity and oscillating apse-line, making only a small improvement in the efficacy of the theory.

From the summer of 1639 to the summer of 1640 Horrocks spent a year in the village of Hoole, 20 miles north of Liverpool. His employment is unknown, but he was possibly a tutor or 'reader' to the most prominent family in the village. He may have taught in the local school or had some part in the services of the local church.

Transit of Venus Horrocks continued to work at his planetary tables and, while working on the planet Venus, discovered in the autumn of 1639 that the planet would pass across the face of the sun. He computed the time of conjunction from Copernican, Tychonian, and Keplerian tables and those of Lansberge. Kepler had claimed that there would be no transit of Venus until 1761, and it was probably on his authority that no other astronomer was prepared to look for it. Having discovered an error in Venus's latitude in Kepler's tables, Horrocks realized that the planet would transit the sun on 24 November and communicated the information to Crabtree, urging that he pay particular attention to the apparent diameter of Venus.

The resulting observation led Horrocks to feel it confirmed his opinion concerning the solar parallax, but required him to revise it slightly. It also permitted him to adjust the elements of the sun, and the orbits of the earth and Venus. The transit was also observed by Crabtree, who confirmed in a general way what Horrocks had observed. While the several tables Horrocks had consulted were considerably off in predicting the time of the transit—the best of them, Kepler's *Rudolphine Tables*, erred by almost ten hours—Horrocks's corrected tables were accurate to within two minutes. The observation also confirmed, despite the opinion of Tycho Brahe, that the planets were dark bodies and not self-luminous.

Horrocks undertook to study the tides in the autumn of 1640, possibly convinced after reading Galileo's *Dialogue on the Two Great World Systems* that the motion of the earth could be proved by the tides. Liverpool is well situated for such observations, as there is a great difference between high and low water. Horrocks, however, held with Kepler that the tides are affected by the moon's attraction, but wondered if they could affect in turn the motion of the earth.

Horrocks's achievements lay hidden from the wider scientific world for several years after his death, at Toxteth Park, on 3 January 1641. Many of his papers have been lost, but during the 1660s those that survived came to the notice of some astronomers and early fellows of the Royal Society, among whom they exerted some influence on the development of predictive astronomy and celestial mechanics. It was then that Newton learned for the first time of Kepler's third law and of Horrocks's successful test of it. Horrocks's *Venus in sole visa*, a draft of a treatise on the transit of Venus, and a defence of Keplerian astronomy, was published by Hevelius in 1662. Most of the remainder of his work was published under the editorship of John Wallis by the Royal Society in 1672 and 1673 as *Opera posthuma*. It was reissued in 1678, with an appendix by John Flamsteed describing Horrocks's mature lunar theory. In the nineteenth century a memorial tablet in Horrocks's honour was placed in Westminster Abbey near the site of Newton's burial place, and the popular astronomer Moses Holden paid for another to be set up in St Michael's Church, Toxteth. WILBUR APPLEBAUM

Sources C. Wilson, 'Predictive astronomy in the century after Kepler', *Planetary astronomy from the Renaissance to the rise of astrophysics*, ed. R. Taton and C. Wilson, *The general history of astronomy*, ed. M. A. Hoskin (1989), 166–71, 197–201 · C. Wilson, 'On the origin of Horrocks's lunar theory', *Journal for the History of Astronomy*, 18 (1987), 77–94 · C. Wilson, 'Horrocks, harmonies, and the exactitude of Kepler's third law', *Studia Copernicana XVI: science and history: studies in honor of Edward Rosen*, ed. E. Hilfstein and others (1978), 235–59 · W. Applebaum, 'Horrocks, Jeremiah', *DSB* · A. Chapman, 'Jeremiah Horrocks, the transit of Venus, and the "new astronomy" in early seventeenth-century England', *Quarterly Journal of the Royal Astronomical Society*, 31 (1990), 333–57 · W. Applebaum, 'Between Kepler and Newton: the celestial dynamics of Jeremiah Horrocks', *Proceedings of the XIIIth International Congress of the History of Science* [Moscow 1971], 4 (1974), 292–9 · S. B. Gaythorpe, 'Jeremiah Horrocks: date of birth, parentage and family associations', *Transactions of the Historic Society of Lancashire and Cheshire*, 106 (1954), 23–33 · *Memoir of the life and labours of the Rev. Jeremiah Horrox: to which is appended a translation of his discourse upon the transit of Venus across the sun*, trans. A. B. Whatton (1859) · S. B. Gaythorpe, 'Jeremiah Horrocks and his "new theory of the moon"', *Journal of the British Astronomical Association*, 67 (1956–7), 134–44 · S. B. Gaythorpe, 'Horrocks's observations of the transit of Venus 1639 November 24 (O.S.)', *Journal of the British Astronomical Association*, 47 (1936–7), 60–68; 64 (1953–4), 309–15 · J. B. J. Delambre, *Histoire de l'astronomie moderne*, 2 (Paris, 1821), 499 · J. F. W. Herschel, *Treatise on astronomy* (1839), 86n. · *Jeremiae Horroccii…opera posthuma*, ed. J. Wallis (1673)

Archives CUL, Royal Greenwich Observatory archives, papers · Trinity Cam., Horrocks's annotated copy of Philip van Lansberge's *Tabulae perpetuae*

Horrocks, John (1768–1804), cotton spinner and manufacturer, was born on 27 March 1768 at Bradshaw Hall Farm, Bradshaw, near Bolton, one of five surviving children of John Horrocks (*d.* 1816), stone-quarry proprietor, and his wife, Jane, daughter of John Booth. At an early age Horrocks began work for Thomas Thomasson, a cotton carder and spinner, from the neighbouring village of Edgworth, who apparently paid for him to attend a boarding-school at Schude Hill, Manchester. However, Thomasson died in 1782 leaving debts exceeding £600, and Horrocks had to rejoin his family, now established at Edgworth. In 1787 he married an Edgworth woman, Mary Lomax; their children included two sons, Peter and John, who succeeded him in business.

Although Horrocks found work in the family quarrying business, he was keen to take advantage of the rapidly expanding cotton trade. Accordingly he began to produce and sell cotton yarn, installing spinning machinery at his father's premises. His main customer became John Watson, owner of Preston's earliest cotton-spinning mill, but the two quarrelled over yarn prices and severed their business connection. Despite this setback Horrocks persevered in the trade and in 1791 started production in Preston. He operated from premises at Turk's Head Yard, which may have been used for both carding and putting out yarn to local hand weavers.

The timing of Horrocks's new venture was propitious, since the cotton industry showed a marked upturn during the early 1790s. Eager to take full advantage of this situation he decided to expand further by building two carding and spinning mills, the horse-driven Yellow Factory in Dale Street (1791), and the adjoining Yard Factory (1792). He also entered into partnership with Richard Newsham and Thomas Greaves, who advanced some £400 to buy spinning mules, an indication of Horrocks's interest in producing finer grades of cottons.

Rising cotton exports during the mid-1790s helped Horrocks to prosper and encouraged him to embark on a further, quite remarkable, programme of spinning-mill construction in Preston. It comprised Moss Mill in 1796; Frenchwood Mill a year later; Canal Mill in 1799; and Top o'th' Yard Mill at Dale Street in 1802. Additionally, in 1796, he rebuilt the Yard Mill, which had been destroyed by fire. New partners were brought into the concern; John's brother Samuel joined in 1797, followed by John Whitehead and Thomas Miller in 1801. In 1799 the company's turnover reached an impressive £105,000, and by 1801 Horrocks was wealthy enough to build a substantial family house, Penwortham Lodge, to the south of Preston.

Although by the early nineteenth century Horrocks was moving towards factory spinning using powered machines, he remained firmly committed to hand technology in weaving. The technical inadequacies of the power-loom and the abundant supply of hand-loom weavers would have strongly influenced his decision. Many of the weavers he employed probably occupied the numerous rows of cottages with cellar loomshops that adjoined his spinning mills. Yet he also put work out to hand weavers in the surrounding country districts, establishing several warehouses from which yarn was collected and to which woven cloth was returned. Additionally he built a group of hand weaving sheds at New Preston, off New Hall Lane, perhaps anticipating that they would eventually be fitted with power-looms.

Having succeeded in business Horrocks turned to politics, and became embroiled in the bitter political feuding that had arisen in Preston between the tory-inclined corporation and the whig interests, represented by the town's most prestigious inhabitant, the earl of Derby. Preston's two parliamentary seats had long been held by the whigs, and Horrocks was persuaded to challenge them on behalf of the tories at the 1796 election. He lost narrowly, but the emergence of the new manufacturing interests in a town where all adult males could vote posed a severe threat to the whigs. As a result they came to an accommodation with the tories so that, in future, each party would nominate one candidate in an uncontested election. By this means, Horrocks was returned to parliament at the next election in 1802. Little is known of his political views, though he did support William Radcliffe's quest to curtail exports of cotton yarn in order to protect the British weaving trade.

In fact, Horrocks had little time to make any political mark. While at his London home in New Bridge Street, Blackfriars, during the early months of 1804, he became ill; his condition deteriorated and he died on 1 March from inflammation of the lungs. He was buried at St Mary's Church in Penwortham, not far from his family home.

John Ainsworth Horrocks (1818–1846), explorer and farmer, was born on 22 March 1818 at Preston, the grandson of John Horrocks, and one of eleven children of Peter Horrocks (b. 1791) and his wife, Clara, née Jupp. In 1839 he emigrated to Adelaide, South Australia, where he founded Penwortham village, 75 miles north of Adelaide. An Anglican, he remained unmarried; he died on 23 September 1846 following a gun accident during an expedition to the head of Spencer's Gulf.   J. GEOFFREY TIMMINS

Sources C. Hardwick, *History of the borough of Preston and its environs* (1857) • C. Brown, *Origins and progress of Horrocks and Company* (1925) • *A chapter in the history of the cotton industry in Lancashire,* Horrockses, Miller & Co. (1901) • D. Hunt, *A history of Preston* (1992) • A. Hewitson, *History (from AD 705 to 1883) of Preston in the county of Lancashire* (1883) • M. Burscough, *The history of Lark Hill, Preston* (1989) • A. Crosby, *A history of Preston Guild* (1991) • W. Dobson, *Parliamentary representation of Preston* (1868) • W. A. Abram, *Lancashire and Cheshire antiquarian notes: in which are included selections from 'Sketches in local history' in the Preston Guardian,* ed. W. Duncombe Pink, 2 (1886) • P. Whittle, *History of the borough of Preston* (1837) • W. Radcliffe, *Origin of the new system of manufacture, commonly called 'power-loom weaving'* (1828) • G. Timmins, *The last shift: the decline of handloom weaving in nineteenth-century Lancashire* (1993) • L. Taylor, 'Horrocks, John', *HoP, Commons, 1790–1820,* 247 • J. Statton, ed., *Biographical index of South Australians, 1836–1885,* 4 vols. (Marden, South Australia, 1986) [John Ainsworth Horrocks] • *AusDB,* vol. 1 [John Ainsworth Horrocks]
Archives Lancs. RO, Horrocks Company papers (DDHs)
Likenesses portrait, repro. in Burscough, *History of Lark Hill*
Wealth at death £150,000: Hunt, *History of Preston*

Horrocks, John Ainsworth (1818–1846). *See under* Horrocks, John (1768–1804).

Horsa (d. 455?). *See under* Kent, kings of (act. c.450–c.590).

Horsbrugh, Florence Gertrude, Baroness Horsbrugh (1889–1969), politician, was born at 2 Grosvenor Street, Edinburgh, on 13 October 1889, the daughter of Henry Moncrieff Horsbrugh, a chartered accountant, and his wife, Mary Harriet Stark Christie. She was educated at Lansdowne House, Edinburgh, and at St Hilda's in Folkestone. Her route into public life lay partly in voluntary work for the Conservative and Unionist Party in Scotland and in wartime work in the 'national kitchens' under the

Florence Gertrude Horsbrugh, Baroness Horsbrugh (1889–1969), by Walter Stoneman, 1945

Ministry of Food, for which she was appointed MBE in 1920. Although well known as a Unionist speaker, Horsbrugh struggled to enter parliament. In 1931 she won the nomination in what appeared to be the hopeless two-member seat at Dundee, where her partner was the National Liberal candidate Dingle Foot. Her sense of humour and ready wit helped her through her double ordeal as a single woman and a Conservative. Asked at a public meeting whether she would be prepared to marry a man with only 15s. a week, she replied: 'I am sorry to say no one has asked me (laughter)'. When a whispered message was received from a man in the audience, Horsbrugh announced that she had received a proposal of marriage; but 'I am going to … ask for his proposal in writing in case there is any chance of breach of promise (laughter)' (Horsbrugh MSS, 2/3). However, in the unusual circumstances of the 1931 election, which swept the National Government back into power, she succeeded in overturning a Labour majority of 14,000; Dundee returned her a second time in 1935.

As an MP, Florence Horsbrugh immediately impressed the house with a maiden speech, apparently delivered impromptu, on the Abnormal Importations Bill; in this she placed great emphasis on solving unemployment by using tariffs to exclude imported goods. She also proved to be unusually successful as a back-bencher in steering two

pieces of legislation onto the statute book. The first was the 1937 bill designed to control the sale and consumption of methylated spirits, and the second the 1939 Adoption of Children (Regulation) Bill, which arose out of her role as chair of the departmental committee on adoption societies and agencies in 1936. She was appointed CBE in 1939. She maintained her interest in international affairs by acting as a delegate to the League of Nations assembly in 1933, 1934, and 1935. This continued beyond the Second World War; in 1945 she attended the San Francisco conference at which the United Nations charter was drawn up, and she led the British delegation to the seventh session of the general conference of UNESCO in Paris. However, although appreciated by fellow parliamentarians, she attracted some criticism from feminists for failing to promote women's causes. For example, when questioned about the provision of information on birth control through local authority clinics, she said she opposed the use of taxpayers' money for purposes which were 'against the conscience of a great many people' (Horsbrugh MSS, 2/3). She insisted on being simply a member of parliament rather than a women's representative, and argued that it would not help the women's cause for members to be relegated to women's questions. In practice she concentrated on such topics as jute, canning, and fishing, which were of concern to her constituents.

Yet despite her loyalty and experience, Horsbrugh's party leaders showed themselves slow to promote her. It was only on the eve of war in 1939 that she gained a junior post as parliamentary secretary at the Ministry of Health, which she held until 1945. She became involved in schemes to evacuate children and to reform the health services. From May to July 1945 she was parliamentary secretary at the Ministry of Food. In 1946 the Royal College of Surgeons of Edinburgh made her their first female honorary fellow and in the following year Edinburgh University made her an honorary LLD. After losing her seat at Dundee in 1945 she failed to win re-election at Midlothian and Peebles in 1950. However, the death of the Conservative candidate for Manchester Moss Side shortly before polling led to her surprise nomination and return at the postponed election.

Following Churchill's narrow victory in 1951 Horsbrugh was appointed minister for education. Unhappily, while education marked the climax of her political career, it also proved to be the graveyard of her political reputation. Her dilemma lay in the fact that housing, not education, was the new government's spending priority. Denied, at least until September 1953, the status of a cabinet minister, she found herself implementing economies which reduced school-building and thus left her open to attacks about overcrowding and substandard classrooms. As a result she acquired a reputation as a weak minister: her 'vagueness seemed to spring more from a want of courage than anything else' (*Times Educational Supplement*, 3 Dec 1954). After she left office in October 1954 the economy programme was withdrawn. On her resignation from the cabinet she became a dame grand cross in the Order of the British Empire and was sworn of the privy council, and in

1959 she was made a life peer. She continued to be active in public life, and attended the Council of Europe and the Western Economic Union as a British delegate from 1955 to 1961.

As a public figure, Florence Horsbrugh enjoyed the advantage of a resonant, well-modulated voice and a tall, dignified bearing. At a time when women were often reluctant to smoke in public she became noticeable 'puffing briskly at a cigarette held levelly between the lips' (Horsbrugh MSS, 1/4). Despite a reputation for being severe in the manner of a Scottish schoolmistress, she was a good-humoured woman who enjoyed political controversy; she once described herself as 'representative of all the maiden aunts in Britain' (Horsbrugh MSS, 2/12). Although it was claimed in her obituary (*The Times*, 8 Dec 1969) that she had 'achieved many victories for feminism', these successes were of a minor or largely nominal character; for example, in 1936 she was the first woman to move the address in reply to the speech from the throne. In fact she was a beneficiary of gains made by women before and during the First World War rather than an active worker for women's causes. She died at her home in Edinburgh, 4 Merchiston Crescent, on 6 December 1969.

MARTIN PUGH

Sources CAC Cam., Florence Horsbrugh MSS · *DNB* · *The Times* (8 Dec 1969) · M. Pugh, *Women and the women's movement in Britain, 1914–1959* (1992) · b. cert. · d. cert. · *CGPLA Eng. & Wales* (1970)
Archives CAC Cam., scrapbooks, papers, and corresp.
Likenesses W. Stoneman, photograph, 1945, NPG [*see illus.*] · Maeers, photograph, 1953, Hult. Arch.
Wealth at death £42,705 11s.: confirmation, 26 Jan 1970, NA Scot., SC 70/1/1878/305 · Scottish action sealed in London, 9 Feb 1970, *CGPLA Eng. & Wales*

Horsburgh [Horsbrough], **James** (1762–1836), hydrographer and chart maker, was born at Elie, Fife, on 23 September 1762, the son of William Horsbrough, shoemaker, and his wife, Jean Given or Givan. In materials for an autobiographical account Horsburgh described them as 'pious, and respectable, but not opulent'; his mother, from accounts of her son's provision for her, continued to live in Elie with her sisters until at least 1805. After receiving instruction in mathematical science, bookkeeping, and the theory of navigation at school in Elie, Horsburgh was apprenticed at the age of sixteen to Messrs James and William Wood, of Elie, a firm which operated ships in the North Sea coal trade. His first voyages were from Newcastle and the Firth of Forth to Hamburg, Middelburg, and Ostend; he was captured with others off Walcheren by a French privateer in May 1780 and imprisoned for a short time in Dunkirk. As a seaman returning from a voyage to the West Indies in 1782 under Austrian colours, Horsburgh avoided the press-gang by masquerading as Danish in London, before taking passage to Madras and Calcutta in 1783. Deciding to remain in India, he swam from the ship as it left the Hooghly River and narrowly avoided being swept out to sea. Onshore in Calcutta he obtained employment as a rigger in the shipyard of David Briggs, a fellow townsman from Elie, and through him, in 1784, the position of third mate of the *Nancy* coasting to Tellicherry.

Horsburgh was first mate of the *Atlas* when, returning from Batavia and Bencoolen to Ceylon, the ship was wrecked on Diego Garcia. Fortunately the crew of the *Atlas* found there the ships of the Bombay expedition of 1786 (with Archibald Blair as surveyor) sent to investigate the viability of establishing a settlement, and Horsburgh returned to Bombay in the *Admiral Hughes* after spending only three days on the island.

In Bombay in 1786 Horsburgh was employed as second mate in the *Gunjavur*, a Surat ship in the country trade between India and China. Promoted to first mate when the ship reached Canton (Guangzhou), Horsburgh gained experience of shoals, winds, and currents in the China Sea during a succession of voyages for Bombay shipowners, particularly in the 1790s as first mate in the *Anna* and the *Carron* for Pestonjie Bomanjee. He made a voyage to Europe in 1796 when the *Carron* was taken up as an extra ship in Canton, and continued to the West Indies in 1797 when the ship was turned to government service as a transport before returning to India. In Bombay in April 1798 Horsburgh was appointed to the command of the *Anna*, which he held during successive voyages to Canton. Twice the *Anna* was taken up for Europe, bringing Horsburgh to London for a few months in 1799 and 1801. The *Anna* passed into the ownership of Messrs Bruce, Fawcett & Co. in Bombay in 1801, and Horsburgh became their employee. After his retirement in Canton in September 1804, he returned to Britain a passenger with Peter Heywood in the *Cirencester* in 1805.

After his shipwreck on Diego Garcia, and particularly during his time as commander of the *Anna*, Horsburgh developed his interest in scientific observation and charting. As an interested commander of a country ship regularly crossing between India and China, Horsburgh was best placed to collect information and observations bearing on the navigation of the eastern seas, and to compile charts of and sailing directions for those waters. Alexander Dalrymple, hydrographer to the East India Company, published three of his first charts, of the Straits of Macassar, of the western Philippines, and of the tract from Dampier's Strait to Batavia, after they had been officially transmitted from Canton to the East India Company. When introduced in London in 1796 to Dalrymple by a letter from James Drummond in Canton, Horsburgh provided Dalrymple with a 'Book of remarks' which Dalrymple later published for the East India Company as *Observations on the Eastern Seas* (1799). On his 1799 and 1801 visits Horsburgh was introduced to the circle which included Sir Joseph Banks, Nevil Maskelyne, and Henry Cavendish. For Cavendish he maintained, from April 1802 to February 1804, a continuous register of the barometer, taken every four hours, by day or night, at sea or in harbour, which established the diurnal variation of the barometer in open sea between 26° N and 26° S. Horsburgh's departure on retirement was delayed by his unsuccessful attempts to obtain official consent to initiate a boat survey of shoals in the China Sea, for the refinement of the charts he was constructing in Canton. On his return to London he was elected a fellow of the Royal Society in March 1806.

Without extensive wealth to remit to Europe on retirement, Horsburgh planned to capitalize on his experience by publishing privately in London a series of charts of the China Sea, Malacca Strait, and Bombay Harbour. This he did, with Heywood's help and Dalrymple's encouragement, in 1805, with the explanatory text *Memoirs Comprising the Navigation to and from China*. Much of his correspondence at this time was concerned with arrangements for publication and for sales agents in North America and Asia. Horsburgh's efforts between 1806 and 1811 were devoted to compiling comprehensive sailing directions (and accompanying charts) for the East Indies navigation, the first edition of which appeared as *Directions for sailing to and from the East Indies, China, New Holland, Cape of Good Hope, and the interjacent ports, compiled chiefly from original journals and observations made during 21 years' experience in navigating those seas*, in two parts in 1809 and 1811. Horsburgh had wished to be appointed assistant to Dalrymple, retained by the East India Company as hydrographer to 'examine the ships' journals' and to publish charts and sailing directions. After Dalrymple's sudden death following his dismissal from the parallel post of hydrographer to the admiralty, Horsburgh successfully proposed himself for the salaried post of hydrographer to the East India Company, which he took up in 1810. As hydrographer Horsburgh was primarily responsible for supervising the engraving of charts sent back to London by marine surveyors in India and ordered by the company to be published, and for examining the deposited journals of returning ships for observations which would refine the oceanic navigation charts currently in use, besides other duties of provision of information laid on him by the court. He continued privately to revise and republish his sailing directions, subsequently known as the *East India Directory*, in editions of 1816–17, 1826–7, and 1836, and revised Murdoch Mackenzie's *Treatise on Surveying* for publication in 1819. When the East India Company gave instructions in 1824 for the compilation, from the work of military surveyors, of the sheets of the *Atlas of India*, the task of supervising the engraving and publication was added to Horsburgh's responsibilities.

As with many from East India Company service overseas, Horsburgh became an old man with young children. At forty-three he married Elizabeth Longworth (*d.* 1829) on 14 October 1805, and they settled first at 6 Savile Row, Walworth. Their first daughter, Jane Frances, was born on 29 August 1808; a second daughter, Elizabeth, followed in 1815 and a son, James, in 1821 when Horsburgh himself was fifty-nine. In his reflective writings, particularly a devotional epistle to his wife and children in 1815, he clearly expected to predecease his family, but it was his wife who died first, suddenly in 1829. His edition of Nathaniel Marshall's *Treatise by St Cyprian … of the Unity of the Church*, to which he added his own appendix, represents the cautious side of his religious devotion: the incautious side showed when he felt compelled to write from East India House to alert Lord Sidmouth to the pernicious claims of Joanna Southcott.

Horsburgh died of 'hydrothorax' on 14 May 1836 at Herne Hill, Kent. When the news reached Canton in November that year, a subscription was opened for a memorial to Horsburgh, which resulted in the construction of the Horsburgh lighthouse on the rock of Pedro Branca in the eastern entrance to the Strait of Singapore, for the safety of shipping arriving from China. An equally lasting memorial was the perpetuation of his *East India Directory*, with the consent of his children (who subscribed the introduction to the second 1836 volume), by the admiralty hydrographic office, latterly an off-duty responsibility shouldered by Edward Dunsterville, chief naval assistant, which produced the fifth, sixth, seventh, and eighth editions in 1841, 1852, 1855, and 1864. With the demise of the East India Company and of the Indian navy in 1858 and 1863, many of the charts Horsburgh had published were taken over by the hydrographic office and issued as admiralty charts.   ANDREW S. COOK

Sources 'Biographical memoir of James Horsburgh, esq., hydrographer to the East India Company', *Naval Chronicle*, 28 (1812), 441–51 · *GM*, 2nd ser., 6 (1836), 98–9 · *Journal of the Royal Geographical Society*, 7 (1837), vi · A. Day, *The admiralty hydrographic service, 1795–1919* (1967) · H. R. Mill, *The record of the Royal Geographical Society, 1830–1930* (1930) · *British Library map collections in the India Office records* (1988) [CD-ROM] · *DNB* · bap. reg. Scot. · will, PRO, PROB 11/1865, sig. 487

Wealth at death see will, PRO, PROB 11/1865, sig. 487, fols. 307v–308v

Horsburgh, John (1791–1869), engraver, was born at Prestonpans, near Edinburgh, on 16 November 1791, the son of William Horsburgh, a coachman, and his wife, Margaret Weddal. His father died when he was a child. He studied drawing at the Trustees' Academy in Edinburgh and at the age of fourteen was apprenticed to the landscape engraver Robert Scott. He continued to work for Scott for several years after his apprenticeship, before establishing his own practice in Edinburgh. Horsburgh's engraving of *Whitstable* after J. M. W. Turner appeared in *Picturesque Views on the Southern Coast of England* (1826). That year he was elected a founder member (associate engraver) of the Royal Scottish Academy, but he withdrew after the first meeting along with eight others who considered the enterprise too ambitious, and was never re-elected. From 1829 he worked with steel plates: his earliest engraving on steel is *Ponte Sesto, Rome* after S. Prout (dated 28 October 1829) for T. Roscoe's *Tourist in Switzerland* (1830). He contributed fourteen illustrations to Sir Walter Scott's Waverley novels including *Convent of St. Saba* after D. Roberts; *On the Coast of Galloway* and *Cathedral of Glasgow* after C. Stanfield; and the portrait of Scott after J. W. Gordon (dated 1830) used as a frontispiece. On 10 November 1833 Horsburgh married Mary Jardine, who survived him.

Horsburgh made a series of engravings after J. M. W. Turner illustrating Scott's *Poetical Works* (1833–4) and *Prose Works* (1834–6). Further engravings after Turner appeared in *Picturesque Views in England and Wales* (1838). Other book illustrations include *Belshazzar's Feast* after J. Martin for *The Imperial Family Bible* (1844), *The Blessing* after W. Bonnar for the title-page of the *Casquet of Literature*, and *Turnberry Castle* after D. O. Hill for *Land of Burns* (1840). His portraits include *Robert Burns* after J. Taylor engraved for the Royal

Scottish Association; *James Dalrymple, Viscount Stair* after Sir J. Medina; *Robert Foulis* after J. Tassie; *Sir John Leslie* after D. Wilkie; *Charles Mackay the Actor as Baillie Nichol Jarvie in Scott's 'Rob Roy'* after Sir W. Allan; *Mark Phillips* after J. P. Gilbert; a second portrait of Scott for S. C. Hall's *Royal Gallery of Art* after T. Lawrence; *Robert Stevenson* after S. Joseph; and *John M. Vandenhoff as Hamlet* after W. S. Watson. Horsburgh's genre pictures include *Prince Charlie Reading a Dispatch* after W. Simson for the Glasgow Art Union and *Italian Shepherds* after McInnes.

For almost forty years from about 1832 Horsburgh worked, unpaid, as a respected minister in the Scotch Baptist church. In the early 1850s he retired from engraving. His sermons, together with a short memoir, were published posthumously in 1869. He died at 18 Buccleuch Place, Edinburgh, on 26 September 1869, aged seventy-seven. The Victoria and Albert Museum and the British Museum hold collections of his engravings.

Lois Oliver

Sources B. Hunnisett, *An illustrated dictionary of British steel engravers*, new edn (1989) · Thieme & Becker, *Allgemeines Lexikon* · *Engraved Brit. ports.*, vol. 2 · DNB · A. Lyles and D. Perkins, *Colour into line: Turner and the art of engraving* (1989) · d. cert. · bap. reg. Scot.
Wealth at death £1689 16s. 11d.: confirmation, 30 Nov 1869, NA Scot., SC70/1/145/830–835

Horsefield, John (1792–1854), botanist and weaver, was born on 18 July 1792, probably at Besses o' th' Barn, near Prestwich, Lancashire, the eldest son of Charles Horsefield (*b.* 1764). Born 'dead', according to his mother, he was restored to life by a medical attendant but remained a sickly child unable to tolerate the staple Lancashire diet of potatoes. When he was six he attended school for a year and learned to read despite his susceptibility to fainting fits. On one occasion he fell, unconscious, into the treadle-hole of his master, who continued to work at the loom while instructing several pupils. Though he started work as a weaver his education continued in writing and arithmetic two nights a week until about 1807 when he outstripped his teacher. Horsefield read all the books he could acquire, and found his imagination sparked by an old, unillustrated edition of Culpeper's *Herbal*. His desire to know the plants mentioned in the book was the start of the passion for botany that was to motivate him throughout his life.

Encouraged by his barely literate father, Horsefield began to participate in the network of botanical meetings and societies established in pubs by working men such as George Caley, John Dewhurst, and Edward Hobson. He was thus enabled to borrow James Lee's *Introduction to Botany* (1760), from which he learned the Linnaean system of plant classification by copying the names and characters of the twenty-four classes on to a piece of paper which he pinned to his loom and memorized while weaving. From about 1810 he regularly attended botanical meetings and rapidly showed his skills at both collecting and identifying plants, including mosses. He was the first to discover the moss *Entosthodon templetoni* in England, as recorded in William Wilson's *Bryologia Britannica* (1855), and he was held in high regard by other gentlemen botanists.

Horsefield's main achievements, however, lay less in particular discoveries than in his efforts to sustain the communal activities whereby working-men botanists exchanged knowledge and pooled funds to buy books.

Horsefield's early political impulse, expressed in his attendance at reform meetings in 1816 and his presence as an observer at the Peterloo massacre of 1819, was later channelled into working-class efforts of self-education and the right to participate in botanical culture. He nurtured artisan botany within the convivial context of the pub, founding and presiding over the Prestwich Botanical Society from 1820 and, in 1830, succeeding Hobson as president of the Sunday pub meetings at which working-men botanists from a wider region congregated. His role was to name aloud the plants gathered by those attending meetings, thus combining oral and text-based traditions of learning and ensuring that illiterates such as his own father could acquire botanical knowledge. While botanizing on Kersal Moor in 1826 he was delighted to encounter Richard Buxton whom he immediately drew into this social network. In 1847, however, he declined to collaborate with Buxton in writing a flora of Manchester. Instead his only publications are spirited defences of the self-acquired botanical skill of working men and the respect they deserved as independent participants in the science of botany. His article 'Notice of the Prestwich Botanical Society, and the Bury Botanical and Entomological Society', preceded by some critical remarks on a passage in the account of the conductor's tour in France' in the *Gardener's Magazine* (6, 1830, 392–5), was a robust reply to remarks made by John Claudius Loudon on the 'ignorance' and 'degradation' of Lancashire operatives. Similarly, the conviction in November 1850 of a publican for serving liquor on Sunday morning to working men who had arrived for a botanical meeting turned Horsefield's autobiography, published in the *Manchester Guardian* (2 March 1850; 24 April 1850; 21 December 1850; 31 December 1851), into a lively explanation of the practices of artisan botanists.

Horsefield's family shared his interest in botany: he and his future wife, Esther Eccorsley (1793/4–1872), met on the way to a botanical meeting in 1812 and were married on 20 December the same year; their two sons, James and William, became active botanists, the latter eventually serving as secretary of the Prestwich Botanical Society. While Horsefield acknowledged his 'celebrity' in botany, he was also quick to point out that 'fame is not bread' (*Manchester Guardian*, 2 March 1850). His only financial gain from his knowledge came from his skill in floriculture. Having acquired a garden in 1819, he later raised a lily *Tigridia conchiflora* which he sold to a Manchester nurseryman for £10.

A gingham weaver all his life, Horsefield suffered severe poverty, especially in his later years. In 1853 a subscription was started for his support from which he received £13 10s. before his death on 6 March 1854, when a further £37 was given to his widow. Horsefield's only property at his death consisted of thirty-seven bulbs of a new daffodil *Narcissus horsefieldii*, which were sold for £2 11s. He was buried on 10 March 1854 at the church of St Mary the Virgin, Prestwich, where his gravestone bears Charles Swain's tribute in verse, while Samuel Bamford's poem 'Lines, on the Death of the Late John Horsefield, Botanist, of Prestwich' laments the departure of one of the 'humble great'.

ANNE SECORD

Sources J. Horsefield, 'John Horsefield, the botanist [pt 1]', *Manchester Guardian* (2 March 1850) · J. Horsefield, 'John Horsefield, the botanist [pt 2]', *Manchester Guardian* (24 April 1850) · J. Horsefield, 'John Horsefield, the botanist [pt 3]', *Manchester Guardian* (21 Dec 1850) · J. Horsefield, 'Societies of Lancashire botanists in humble life', *Manchester Guardian* (31 Dec 1851) · J. Horsefield, 'Notice of the Prestwich Botanical Society, and the Bury Botanical and Entomological Society, preceded by some critical remarks on a passage in the account of the conductor's tour in France', *Gardener's Magazine*, 6 (1830), 392–5 · A. Secord, 'Science in the pub: artisan botanists in early nineteenth-century Lancashire', *History of Science*, 32 (1994), 269–315 · R. Buxton, *A botanical guide to the flowering plants, ferns, mosses, and algae, found indigenous within sixteen miles of Manchester* (1849), vi–viii · E. W. Binney, *A few remarks respecting Mr. R. Buxton, the author of 'The Manchester Botanical Guide'* (1863), 6 · 'Tigridia conchiflora "Watkinsoni"', *Paxton's Magazine of Botany*, 14 (1848), 51–2 · W. Brockbank, 'John Horsefield', *Gardeners' Chronicle*, 3rd ser., 16 (1894), 465–7 · C. W. N., 'Some old florists', *Gardeners' Chronicle*, 3rd ser., 89 (1931), 169–70 · 'Testimonial to the late John Horsefield', *Manchester Guardian* (11 March 1854) · 'The late John Horsefield', *Manchester Guardian* (11 March 1854) · S. Bamford, *Homely rhymes, poems, and reminiscences* (1864), 130–32 · L. H. Grindon, *Manchester walks and wild-flowers: an introduction to the botany and rural beauty of the district* [1859], 57–8 · gravestone, St Mary the Virgin, Prestwich, Lancashire [grave 874]
Wealth at death 'suffered severe poverty' for much of life; property at death was thirty-seven bulbs of a new daffodil sold for £2 11s.: Brockbank, 'John Horsefield'; C. W. N., 'Some old florists'

Horsell, William (1807–1863), promoter of vegetarianism, was born in Brinkworth, Wiltshire, on 31 March 1807, the son of a publican. He was probably the William Horsel baptized at Brinkworth on 12 April 1807, whose parents were named William and Elizabeth. Though raised to be an 'agriculturalist', before he was twenty he was preaching the gospel. Aware of his own taste for alcohol and having once been drunk (during his confirmation ceremony), he was drawn into the temperance movement. He pledged abstinence from spirits in 1833, and after attending a lecture by Joseph Barker he became teetotal. In April 1842 he founded a Nature's Beverage Society. He established what was probably the first British anti-tobacco society at Congleton, Cheshire, and supported the United Kingdom Alliance when it was formed.

Horsell was an early enthusiast for hydropathy. His book *The Board of Health and Longevity, or, Hydropathy for the People* (1845) was well received and was later published in America. In 1846 he settled in Ramsgate, Kent, intending to establish a hydropathic boarding-house which working men could afford. He became the manager of a 'Hydro-Vegetarian establishment' there, at Northwood Villa.

In 1847 Horsell began a thirteen-year publishing career. Initially his work was published by the radical William Shirrefs in the Isle of Man. When Manx postal privileges were abolished, he joined Shirrefs in partnership in London. There he established his own business at 13 Paternoster Row (1849–53) and also at 190½ High Holborn (1850–52). He next had offices—for a time in partnership with

William Horsell (1807–1863), by unknown engraver

Shirrefs again—at 492 New Oxford Street (1853–7). Some work was briefly published at 2 Margaret's Place, Shooter's Hill Road, Blackheath, where he lived. As editor of the *Truth-Tester, Temperance Advocate and Healthian Journal* (1847–8), he endeavoured to fulfil his intention, announced in the first number, 'to grapple with most questions affecting the social, physical, intellectual and moral Health of Man. These topics will be viewed in their relation to Christian truth and equity' (*Truth-Tester*, 1847, 3). The journal failed through lack of support. His next venture was the *Vegetarian Advocate*, the first avowedly vegetarian paper in Britain and the first organ of the Vegetarian Society (although vegetarian propaganda had appeared earlier in journals published by followers of James Pierrepont Greaves). Efforts were made to create a 'class journal more valuable to the community and increasingly useful to the principle it advocates' (preface to *Vegetarian Advocate*, 1, 1848) but circulation was small, and the arrival of an official Vegetarian Society magazine meant its demise, at some financial loss. Undeterred by these failures, Horsell continued to produce (as publisher or printer) various health, social, and moral reform papers and periodicals. These included the *Pioneer and Weekly Record of Movements*, the *Journal of Health*, and the *Temperance Star*. In total he published, or printed, some thirty journals and magazines, although few lasted long.

Horsell gave several reasons for becoming vegetarian: ill health, reading Shelley, and preparation for his hydropathic book. He became the first secretary of the Vegetarian Society in 1847; he lectured on the cause and wrote *The Science of Cooking Vegetarian Food* (1856). His Vegetarian Depôt was a forerunner of several progressive information repositories for moral and health reformers such as the Progressive Library of James Burns and the Hygienic Institute of T. L. Nichols. Horsell sold a range of Anglo-American physiological, hydropathic, phrenological, mesmeric, phonographic, religious, and 'miscellaneous' literature, equipment, and foods. The premises were shared with a homoeopathic pharmacy and phrenological museum. Later Horsell assisted with hydropathic and homoeopathic treatment.

In July 1859 Horsell formed a publishing partnership with a fellow teetotal vegetarian, Job Caudwell. They took the lease of 'large and elegant premises', at 335 Strand. The partnership was dissolved in September 1860, after which Horsell fades from the published records of the reform movements with which he had been associated. In 1863 he undertook a mission to Lagos for two Quaker women. *En route*, after lecturing at Cape Coast on the prospects for the African cotton trade, he died of a fever on board the *Just* on 23 December 1863. On Christmas day he was buried at Lagos cemetery by a fellow missionary. Horsell left a widow but no children. In his *Science of Cooking Vegetarian Food* he condemned the domestic slavery of women; he held that woman was the divinely appointed teacher of man, and advocated a greater public role for women. His wife, Elizabeth (1798–1874), actively supported her husband's reform activity. She worked with him in organizing vegetarian meetings and he published her own vegetarian manual.

Horsell's exact religious affiliations are unclear. Although he was raised an Anglican, one temperance authority lists him as the Revd William Horsell, and as a minister of an unspecified church in London about 1833 (Winskill, *Temperance Standard Bearers*). Certainly he was a minister at a chapel at Hayes, Middlesex, in 1845. It is not certain to which denomination the ministry was attached; at all events he had resigned this position by 1846, and did not allude to it subsequently. In the 1850s he endorsed spiritualism as an aid to faith.

Horsell was bearded at a time when this was widely associated with eccentricity, and a phrenological examination revealed 'large organs of Hope and Veneration' and an enthusiasm which needed to be moderated by more 'stolid minds' (*Journal of Health*, Feb 1857). He was undoubtedly an enthusiast, but he himself explained that an enthusiast was 'A Man in earnest—"zealously affected in a good thing"; a living man who can go against the stream,—who dares to be singular, and to suffer' (*The Science of Cooking Vegetarian Food*, 89).   JAMES GREGORY

Sources *Dietetic Reformer*, 2/14 (1864), 64 · *Temperance Star* (26 Feb 1864) · W. Caine, ed., *Biographical key to the picture containing one hundred and twenty portraits of temperance reformers collected by Mr Thomas Lythgoe* (1860), 76–7 · B. Lindsay, 'William Horsell', *Vegetarian Messenger*, pt 1 (March 1886), 62–4 [with portrait] · B. Lindsay, 'William Horsell', *Vegetarian Messenger*, pt 2 (May 1886), 131–5 · *Journal of Health* (Feb 1857), 121–3 · J. Belchem, '"Temperance in all things": vegetarianism, the Manx press and the alternative agenda of reform in the 1840s', *Living and learning: essays in honour of J. F. C. Harrison*, ed. M. Chase and I. Dyck (1996), 149ff. · S. Graham, *The science of human life*, ed. W. Horsell (1854) · W. Horsell, *The science of cooking vegetarian food, also, The rise and progress of the Vegetarian Society, twelve reasons for not eating flesh, and answers to twenty objections to the vegetarian practice* (1856) · journals published by Horsell, and catalogues and advertisements in books published by Horsell, 1847–60 · P. T. Winskill, *Temperance standard bearers of the nineteenth century: a biographical and statistical temperance dictionary*, 1 (1897), 61 · P. T. Winskill, *The temperance movement and its workers*, 4 vols. (1891–9), vol. 2, p. 150 · Boase, *Mod. Eng. biog.*, 5.705–6 · W. Horsell, *The board of health and longevity, or, Hydropathy for the poeple* (1845) · C. Henly, parish register transcriptions for Brinkworth, Wiltshire, www.genuki.org.uk/big/eng/WIL/Brinkworth, 20 March 2002

Likenesses W. Carter, engraving, repro. in *Journal of Health*, 121 · W. Carter, engraving, repro. in C. W. Forward, *Fifty years of food reform* (1898), 19 · engraving, Vegetarian Society, Altrincham, Cheshire [*see illus.*]

Wealth at death library detailed in *Dietetic Reformer*

Horsey family (*per. c.*1500–*c.*1640), gentry, derived its name from the manor of Horsey near Bridgwater, Somerset, which it held from the twelfth century. During the fifteenth century a succession of profitable marriages brought the family numerous additional properties in Somerset and Dorset, including Charlton Mackerell, Somerset, and Clifton Maybank, Dorset, which became the family's principal residence. **John** [i] **Horsey** (1479–1531) married Elizabeth, daughter and heir of Richard Turgis of Melcombe in central Dorset, and this brought a further large increase to the Horsey estates. He was actively involved in the royal service in both Somerset and Dorset. He served on the commission of the peace and in other public offices, and as sheriff of both counties in 1512, 1523, and 1524. Horsey was a knight of the body to Henry VIII and was present at the Field of Cloth of Gold in 1520. In 1529 he was elected to parliament as one of the county members for Dorset. When he died in 1531 he was buried in the parish church of Yetminster, near Clifton Maybank, to which he had been a generous benefactor.

It was Horsey's elder son, **Sir John** [ii] **Horsey** (*d.* 1546), who brought the family to the peak of its wealth and power, through a combination of royal service, prominence in local affairs, and astute investment in former monastic properties. He served as a JP in Somerset and Dorset, and followed his father as MP for Dorset. He was knighted on the occasion of Anne Boleyn's coronation in June 1533 and served as sheriff of Somerset and Dorset six times between 1536 and his death in 1546. He was appointed to various commissions concerned with taxation, raising forces, the security of the region, and the protection of the coasts from invasion. In 1539 he was named as a member of the short-lived council of the west.

Sir John eagerly seized the opportunities for enrichment offered by the suppression of the numerous wealthy monastic houses in Somerset and Dorset. Like many local gentlemen, he was closely involved with several monasteries for some years before the dissolution. From about 1530 he acted as steward for the estates of Sherborne, Muchelney, Athelney, and Montacute, and received an annual pension from each of these houses. In 1521 he was named as a trustee of the grammar school established at Milton Abbey by the abbot, William Middleton. He supervised the election of a new prior of Montacute on behalf of the crown in January 1531. During 1535 he was one of the commissioners appointed to compile the *valor ecclesiasticus* for Dorset.

Horsey was particularly interested in the ancient Benedictine abbey of Sherborne, which was close to Clifton Maybank and many of whose estates adjoined his own. When Abbot Meere of Sherborne resigned in 1535, Horsey made a secret offer of 500 marks to Thomas Cromwell if John Barnstaple (or Barstaple) should be elected in his place. Barnstaple was duly elected and Horsey wrote to Cromwell promising to bring him the 500 marks shortly. Following the suppression of the abbey in 1539 Horsey ensured that Barnstaple obtained the lucrative rectory of Stalbridge, Dorset, while he himself acquired the site, buildings, and many of the former estates of the abbey. In

Horsey family (*per. c.*1500–*c.*1640), by unknown sculptor [left to right: Sir John Horsey (*d.* 1546) and Sir John Horsey (*d.* 1564)]

addition, he was able to purchase some of the lands of the nunnery at Cannington, Somerset, and of the Cistercian house at Bindon, Dorset. The property at Longleat, Wiltshire, which he acquired from the estates of Hinton Charterhouse, Somerset, he rapidly sold to John Thynne, and lands at Creech on the Isle of Purbeck he sold to the Lawrence family. Always anxious to keep the goodwill of Thomas Cromwell, Horsey sold him the manor of Horton Maybank, Sussex, on remarkably advantageous terms. It is noteworthy that although he was ruthless in his pursuit of monastic spoils, Horsey's sister, Anne, had been a nun at Barking, Essex, and his daughter, Elizabeth, had been a nun at Shaftesbury, receiving an annual pension of £4 13s. 4d. at the dissolution.

The site, buildings, and some of the lands of Sherborne cost Horsey nearly £1500, and he spent a similar amount on further purchases during 1540. Some of these lands he sold immediately, including the abbey church at Sherborne, which the vicar and parishioners of Sherborne bought for about £320 to be their parish church. His success in obtaining monastic property meant that by the time of his death in 1546 the number of Horsey manors had increased fourfold and his estate included a conveniently compact block of land around Clifton Maybank. It is a sign of his increased wealth and importance that while previous members of the family had been buried in the parish church at Yetminster, Sir John was buried in the former abbey church at Sherborne. He had married Joan, daughter of a landowner named Maudlin from nearby

Corscombe. In his long will, dated three days before his death on 23 December 1546, he made generous provision for his wife and other members of the family, friends, and servants. The bulk of his estates was left to his eldest son, **Sir John** [iii] **Horsey** (*d.* 1564). The cautious wording of the will suggests that relations between father and son were not close, and that the son was not regarded as trustworthy.

The younger Sir John had spent some time in Cromwell's service and had been involved in business for the crown in Nottinghamshire, where he was a JP and commissioner for gaol delivery at Nottingham Castle during the early 1540s, although he was also listed as a Dorset justice in 1540. He had not been involved in his father's wide-ranging administrative duties in Somerset and Dorset, nor in his father's successful acquisition of former monastic land. He was knighted in 1547. Soon after his father's death in 1546 Sir John made Clifton Maybank his principal residence and began to reconstruct the house on a grand scale. Built of the golden stone from Ham Hill, it became one of the most spectacular of the group of contemporary houses in the district, which included Barrington, Melbury, and Montacute. Most of the house was demolished and various parts of it were sold in 1786. The main front was re-erected at Montacute.

Horsey displayed that strain of reckless extravagance which was soon to bring ruin to the family. He was addicted to gambling, or, as he himself expressed it, 'was oftentymes enticed and overmuche used and disposed to dyce play' (PRO, C78/19/12). His building work at Clifton Maybank and Melcombe Horsey was expensive, and the numerous law suits in which he engaged were a heavy drain on his resources. He died at Clifton Maybank on 30 January 1564 and, like his father before him, was buried at Sherborne in the former abbey church. A large monument consisting of an altar tomb, with the recumbent effigies of father and son, both in elaborate, old-fashioned armour, was erected in what became known as the Horsey aisle.

The history of the main branch of the Horsey family following the death of the second Sir John is a sorry tale of slow decline, loss of property, and eventually total ruin. In 1538 he had followed the family tradition of advantageous alliances in his marriage to Edith, daughter of Richard Phelips of Montacute; she was the widow of John Stocker, a merchant of Poole. Their son **Sir John** [iv] **Horsey** (*d.* 1589) continued the unions with local landowning families by marrying Grace, daughter of Thomas Howard, Lord Bindon, of Lulworth Castle, Dorset, on 20 October 1564. After her death on 19 August 1568 he married Dorothy, widow of Sir George Speke of Whitelackington, Somerset. There were no children from either marriage. On the death of Sir John [iv] on 12 July 1589 the Horsey property in Somerset and Dorset passed to **Sir Ralph Horsey** (*d.* 1612), son of George Horsey of Standon, Hertfordshire, and grandson of Jasper Horsey, who was the brother of the first Sir John.

By the late sixteenth century a combination of profligacy and poor estate management meant that in spite of its widespread lands the Horsey family was already encumbered with debt. Sir Ralph continued the family involvement in local government, but did nothing to clear his debts. He was knighted in 1591 and was active in raising forces for the defence of Dorset during the 1590s. He was on good terms with his neighbour Sir Walter Ralegh and was present at the supper party in 1593 the conversation at which later led to Ralegh's examination on charges of atheism. By 1601 he was forced by debt to sell the rectory and other property at Cranborne to Robert Cecil for £2000. In 1603 he sold the parsonage and lands at Sherborne. Other sales soon followed, including the family's original seat at Horsey, Somerset.

Sir Ralph married his cousin Edith, daughter of a Cornish landowner, William Mohun; she died in 1628. Their son **Sir George Horsey** (*d.* 1640) succeeded to the estates on his father's death in 1612. He married Elizabeth, daughter of Sir Thomas Freke of Shroton, Dorset. Sir George brought about the final ruin of the estate. He lost large sums of money through investment in a project inspired by Dud Dudley in the midlands to smelt iron using coal. These losses were compounded by his involvement in an ill-judged scheme to reclaim the Fleet in Dorset, an expanse of tidal water and marshland lying between Chesil Beach and the mainland, which belonged to Sir John Strangways of Melbury as part of his estate at Abbotsbury. In July 1630 Horsey and other 'adventurers', including his brother-in-law, Sir John Freke, obtained a lease to drain the Fleet, intending to emulate the contemporary drainage work in the fens. Huge sums of money were spent on major works, such as building dams, channels, and sluices. Although some initial success was achieved, during winter storms the sea inevitably poured through and over Chesil Beach, flooding the whole area. To add to the problems facing the 'adventurers', the crown claimed rights over part of the Fleet, and amid a welter of legal and technical difficulties the whole ill-conceived project collapsed. During the next few years Horsey was forced to sell the remaining estates one by one. For a time in 1638 he was imprisoned in Newgate. On his release he sought shelter in the house of his brother-in-law at Shroton. Finally he was imprisoned for debt in the county gaol at Dorchester, where he died in penury in 1640.

As a last ironic footnote to the collapse of the family's fortunes, Sir George's third son, Captain John Horsey, died on 6 August 1645 while fighting in the parliamentary army at the siege of Sherborne Castle, within sight of the former Horsey estates and little more than 3 miles from their mansion at Clifton Maybank. He was given a military funeral in Sherborne Abbey church.   J. H. BETTEY

Sources P. Webb, 'John and Jasper Horsey', *Proceedings of the Dorset Natural History and Archaeological Society*, 99 (1977), 28–32 • P. Webb, 'John and Jasper Horsey', *Proceedings of the Dorset Natural History and Archaeological Society*, 100 (1978), 22–30 • J. Fowler, *Medieval Sherborne* (1951) • R. Lloyd, *Dorset Elizabethans* (1967) • J. H. Bettey, *Suppression of the monasteries in the west country* (1989) • J. Hutchins, *The history and antiquities of the county of Dorset*, 3rd edn, ed. W. Shipp and J. W. Hodson, 4 (1874), 425–31 • *Dorset*, Royal Commission for the Historic Monuments of England, 1 (1952), 98–9, 208, 271 • A. R. Bayley, *The great civil war in Dorset, 1642–1660* (1910), 19, 22, 282 • W. H. Price, *The English patents of monopoly* (1906), 110, 197 • PRO, C 78/24/4; C 78/30/17; C 3/83/14; REQ 2/39/13; REQ 2/44/85; REQ 2/131/56; C 78/19/12; C 78/38/1; C 78/38/11; E 178/5626; E 178/6206; E 78/14/18; E 315/212; E 315/236; E 318/622; E 318/623 • J. H. Bettey, *Rural life in Wessex, 1500–1900* (1987), 25
Likenesses stone effigy, Sherborne Abbey, Dorset [*see illus.*]
Wealth at death bankrupt: Sir George Horsey

Horsey, Adeline Louisa Maria De. *See* Lancastre Saldanha, Adeline Louisa Maria de, Countess de Lancastre (1824–1915).

Horsey, Sir Edward (*d.* 1583), conspirator and soldier, was the eldest son of Jasper Horsey (*d.* 1546) of Exton, Devon, and his wife, Joan, daughter and heir of William Welford. Jasper Horsey was admitted to the Middle Temple in 1522, served in the household of the marquess of Exeter, and was a justice of the peace in Surrey during his later years. Although no daughters are known, Jasper and Joan Horsey had, in addition to Edward, three other sons named Francis, George, and John.

Little is known of Edward Horsey's early life or education. There are hints that, as a young man, he may have fought on the continent as a soldier of fortune; he may also have been part of an English embassy to France in 1551. When Queen Mary acceded to the throne in 1553 and then married Prince Philip of Spain the following year, Edward Horsey harassed the new regime by spreading rumours of a general revolt in Dorset in July 1555. After meeting in London with other malcontents a few months later, he went into exile in March 1556 with his brother Francis and there became part of a formal plot, led by Henry Dudley, cousin of the executed duke of Northumberland, to overthrow Mary and Philip. The Horsey brothers, along with fellow conspirators Dudley and Christopher Ashton, met secretly that same month with the French king Henri II to secure his promise of assistance, but by then several of the exiles' confederates in England had been seized and so the plot collapsed. Some time later in 1556 Edward Horsey married an unnamed Huguenot woman in Normandy. It was also during these years on the continent that he made the acquaintance of Henry Dudley's kinsman Robert Dudley, the future earl of Leicester and the man who later became Horsey's lifelong patron.

Horsey 'earnestly desired to be restored to his country' following Elizabeth's accession in 1558, but he was still considered an outlaw and so remained with his wife in Normandy for the next three years. While there he ingratiated himself with Elizabeth's privy council, and especially with William Cecil, by regularly reporting French 'sea matters' to the royal secretary (*CSP for., 1558–9*, 380). By summer 1562 he was Cecil's agent in the Huguenot port of Dieppe, returning only briefly to England in July to report in person to the council on the continuing religious and civil strife in France. Horsey was rewarded for his loyal services at this time with a lucrative licence to import French wines into England. He was soon ordered back to Dieppe and Rouen to help organize the Huguenot defence of those towns and, serving under the command of Robert Dudley's brother Ambrose, earl of Warwick,

Horsey led a band of soldiers into battle against French royal forces near Harfleur. He was by this time considered so 'trusty and valiant' that both Cecil and Robert Dudley came to rely upon his frequent reports from the continent. He was also a brave military commander whose troops on one occasion 'pushed with the pike against [enemy] horsemen' (*CSP for.*, *1563*, 371), and who was himself erroneously reported slain in summer 1563. When the Huguenots surrendered Dieppe to the French crown in late July of that year, Horsey agreed to serve as a treaty hostage and so found one more way to demonstrate his loyalty to his queen and her council.

That loyalty was amply rewarded when, having finally been released from French custody, Horsey was formally pardoned for his treasons against Queen Mary and was then named captain of the Isle of Wight in summer 1565. There his most pressing responsibility seems to have been the monitoring of hostile naval activity and piracy in the narrow seas around the island. In December 1568 Horsey reported to Cecil that he had seized several Spanish vessels with treasure valued at '31,000 pounds or thereabouts' (*CSP for.*, *1566–8*, 585–6), and in May 1570 he reported that 'certain men-of-war' were suspiciously sailing off Wight flying the colours of Navarre. In August 1571 Horsey was busy outfitting a 'hulk' for the use of the privateer Martin Frobisher off the Irish coast, and in autumn 1576 he was authorized by the privy council to capture French pirates operating in the channel.

As captain of the Isle of Wight, Horsey served his queen not only as a valued supply officer and troop commander, but also as an experienced ambassador to foreign courts. As a military officer, he supervised the refurbishing of defensive structures on the isle such as Carisbrooke Castle and the dilapidated fort at West Cowes. When the great northern uprising broke out in 1569, Horsey equipped and led 500 mounted troopers against the 'beastly and cowardly' insurgents (*CSP dom.*, *1547–80*, 355). A grateful monarch rewarded him with the lucrative wardship of young William Oglander, and duly repaid his expenses the following year. In 1577 and in subsequent years, Horsey procured a 'greate quantitie of saltpetre' for her majesty's gunners from a Flemish merchant named Cornelius Stephenson, who agreed to the transactions in return for the lease of some land in the New Forest area of Hampshire. A few years later the captain housed and victualled some 300 soldiers mustered to help repel an expected Spanish invasion of Ireland. On the diplomatic front, after leading embassies to Flanders in 1568 and France in 1573, Edward Horsey was sent in December 1576 to help defuse tensions between Don John of Austria and rebellious Dutch protestants in the Spanish Netherlands. His mission proved unnecessary when Don John and the states general agreed to terms on their own, but Horsey was none the less rewarded for his diplomatic services with a knighthood in December 1577.

Throughout his career Edward Horsey was a friend and client of the queen's confidant and councillor Robert Dudley, earl of Leicester, a man he had met on the continent during the time of his Marian exile. Possibly because of Leicester's influence, Horsey was appointed justice of the peace for Hampshire and Wight in 1569, a post he held until his death. During 1571–2 he was also returned to parliament, first as a burgess of the city of Southampton and then as a knight of the shire of Hampshire. In May 1573 he performed an important service for his patron when he participated in the wedding of Leicester to an attractive young widow, Lady Douglas Sheffield, with whom the earl had been carrying on an illicit affair for some years. It was Horsey's task to witness the secret ceremony at Esher, and to 'give away' Lady Sheffield, who later bore Leicester a son and who eventually sued him to protect her own honour and the rights of their son. Horsey's discreet performance of this and other missions for Leicester won him the earl's confidence and thus a respected place at court as a reliable agent of the crown.

By 1580, when probably in his fifties, Sir Edward Horsey had settled into a comfortable life at his manor of Great Haseley, near Arreton on the Isle of Wight. There he lived with a mistress named Cowsebel Mille, the widow of George Mille of Hampshire, a woman he might well have married but for the surviving French wife he had abandoned many years before in Normandy. Horsey was, however, still quite active in public affairs in these his last years. Although he was no longer personally involved in diplomatic missions to the continent, Sir Edward eagerly received letters from friends such as William Herle who wrote to catch him up on news from abroad. In November 1580 he played host to the visiting Portuguese ambassador at Great Haseley, despite the fact that many members of his household were 'down with the disease'. He seems to have contracted the plague himself that month, for Herle wrote to him soon after expressing pleasure that Horsey's 'recovery' had been so swift and complete (*CSP dom.*, *1547–80*, 687, 690). In 1581 the captain of the Isle of Wight was still responsible for suppressing piracy around his island, but he had by then entrusted this duty to his client John Story, whose negligence had encouraged an increase in such activity. In April 1582 Horsey was ordered by the privy council to prosecute a group of pirates his agents had apprehended, and to release (with vessel and goods) the French merchant who had been their recent victim.

Sir Edward fell ill again early the following year, but this time he did not recover. He died at Great Haseley in late February 1583, leaving most of his fortune and estates to his brother George, and was buried in the medieval church of St Thomas of Canterbury (rebuilt 1854) in Carisbrooke. Horsey's tomb, which can still be seen today, was fashioned of alabaster with inlaid marble, and featured an armoured effigy lying beneath a columned canopy that bore his family crest. Such a tomb was a fitting memorial to a man who had served his sovereign and his patron so well for so many years. Following his death Sir George Carew became the next captain of the Isle of Wight, and served in that position until his own death in 1603.

CLAYTON J. DREES

Sources HoP, *Commons, 1558–1603*, 2.339 · D. M. Loades, *Two Tudor conspiracies* (1965) · APC · *CSP dom., 1547–90* · *CSP for., 1553–78* · CPR, *1563–81*, esp. vols. 3, 5–6, 9 · D. C. Peck, ed., *Leicester's commonwealth:*

the copy of a letter written by a master of art of Cambridge (1584) *and related documents* (1985) • D. Wilson, *Sweet Robin* (1981) • R. H. Fritze, 'Faith and faction: religious changes, national politics, and the development of local factionalism in Hampshire, 1485–1570', PhD diss., U. Cam., 1981 • A. Kendall, *Robert Dudley, earl of Leicester* (1980) • PRO, probate 6/3, fol. 63r • W. B. Robison, 'Justices of the peace of Surrey', PhD diss., Louisiana State University, 1983 • *DNB* • *VCH Hampshire and the Isle of Wight*

Likenesses alabaster sculpture, 1582, St Thomas's Church, Newport, Isle of Wight

Wealth at death see PRO, probate 6/3, fol. 63r

Horsey, Sir George (*d.* 1640). *See under* Horsey family (*per.* *c.*1500–*c.*1640).

Horsey, Sir Jerome (*d.* 1626), traveller to Russia and diplomat, was the son of William Horsey and Elinor, daughter of William Peryam. He entered the service of the Muscovy Company as an apprentice clerk in Russia in 1572 and lived there until 1585, being employed by the Russians as emissary to England in 1580 and 1585. He acted as emissary between the two countries again in 1587 and was sent as English ambassador to Moscow in 1590–91.

As a result of these experiences, Horsey wrote a 'Relacion or memoriall abstracted owt of Sir Jerome Horsey his travells, imploiments, services and negociacions, observed and written with his owne hand; wherein he spent the most part of eighteen years tyme', a major, and still valuable, account of contemporary Russia. It was probably compiled between mid-November 1589 and late March 1590, perhaps with an eye to establishing his credentials for the embassy to Russia immediately thereafter. A later version, with some emendations and additions of later material, was compiled in the years 1603 to 1605 and then just prior to his death, and published as an addendum to the fourth edition of Samuel Purchas's *Purchas his pilgrimage, or, Relations of the world and the religious observed in all ages and places discovered from the creation unto this present* (1626). He also served as the major informant for Giles Fletcher's famous *Of the Russe Commonwealth*. Horsey claimed to know Russian (which the other Englishmen did not), but modern scholars have considerable doubt about the precision of that knowledge. In addition to Russian and English, Horsey alleged knowledge of Polish and Dutch. He was knowledgeable about English ships.

Horsey's account of Russia includes events that happened before he arrived there, such as the Livonian War (1558–83) and the Crimean Tartar invasion and burning of Moscow in 1571. Some of that information he credits to a Russian informant, Prince Ivan Fyodorovich Mstislavsky. Other insiders informed him about events in the Russian Orthodox church, such as the 1580 council convoked to limit the growth of church landholding. Horsey's account is valuable in many areas ranging from the Russian economy (products and trade) to military affairs (especially the Crimean Tartar front and the ceaseless slave raids), from the paranoid-sadistic personality of Ivan IV (Ivan the Terrible) to the machinations of Boris Godunov 'aimed at the crown'. Most interestingly, he reports opposition to Ivan

IV, but is never sufficiently precise so that confirmation is possible.

In 1580 Ivan IV sent Horsey on a secret mission to England to buy arms. Sir Edward Horsey, governor of the Isle of Wight and probably a kinsman, introduced him to Queen Elizabeth and he returned to Russia in 1581 with thirteen tall ships. On his 1585 trip to England he stopped in Riga and arranged for the return to Russia of Maria, niece of Ivan IV, who upon arrival was imprisoned in the Trinity Sergius Monastery with her daughter. Horsey expressed his regret for his role in that episode.

Horsey negotiated a new trade agreement between the Muscovy Company and Russia in 1585–7. He also acted on behalf of his alleged friend Boris Godunov, the regent for the incompetent Tsar Feodor Ivanovich. In spite of these efforts Horsey was accused by the Muscovy Company during those years of theft and trading on his own account. He had also borrowed significant funds from Russians to finance his trading enterprises. England was dependent on Russian naval stores at this time, as evident in 1588 when the Spanish armada was defeated by English ships using Russian masts, linen sails, and hemp cordage.

Horsey was sent to Russia in 1590 as England's ambassador at the urging of his patron, Sir Francis Walsingham, over the objections of the Muscovy Company. This embassy failed, and the Russians (motivated to a considerable extent by the personal animosity of their prime minister, Andrey Yakovlevich Shchelkalov) expelled him with orders that he not return. Horsey alleged that numerous attempts were made to murder him while he was still in Moscow.

Of particular interest to historians has been Horsey's account of the events of mid-May 1591, when young Dmitry Ivanovich, Ivan the Terrible's sole surviving competent son, died mysteriously in Uglich at the age of ten. Although the offspring of Ivan's seventh wife and therefore illegitimate according to Orthodox canon law, Dmitry was presumed to be the heir upon the death of Tsar Feodor (the Bellringer) Ivanovich, Ivan's mentally handicapped son (who finally died in 1598). For over four centuries debate has raged as to whether Dmitry died from falling on a knife during an epileptic fit or whether he was murdered by Boris Godunov to pave his way to the throne once Tsar Feodor, the sole survivor of the seven-centuries-old Ryurikid dynasty, expired. During the events in Uglich, Horsey was about 65 miles away in Yaroslavl and alleged he heard about the story from Dmitry's relative Afanasy Fyodorovich Nagoy soon after the event had happened. He claimed that Dmitry's throat had been cut by the son of a state secretary (*d'iak*, the official sent from Moscow to administer Uglich). The son confessed to having murdered Dmitry at the behest of Boris Godunov.

Horsey must have been one of the most abrasive individuals of his time, for he was seemingly always fighting with someone. He had especially bad relations with the English ambassador to Russia, Sir Jerome Bowes. In 1587 he was accused of fraud against the Muscovy Company and fled to the continent. He was also accused of committing unspeakable atrocities against Englishmen while he was in Russia. He seems to have got on well with Ivan the Terrible, but ultimately Boris Godunov expelled him in disgrace from Russia.

The second half of Horsey's life was less eventful than the decades of his travels and life in Muscovy. In January 1592 he married Elizabeth (*d.* 1607), daughter of Griffith Hampden of Great Hampden, a Buckinghamshire gentry family. Horsey settled down in Buckinghamshire and called it his home. Nearly a decade later he became justice of the peace, he was knighted on 23 July 1603, and he was sheriff in 1611–12. He was active among the godly in promoting a learned preaching ministry.

By unknown means Horsey secured Cornish borough seats in parliament, where he sat during the five parliaments convened in the three decades between 1592 and 1622. He represented Saltash in 1593, perhaps through the patronage of Sir Walter Ralegh, Camelford in 1597, and Bossiney in 1601, 1604, and 1614, at which times he may have been the creature of Sir William Peryam, possibly a kinsman of his mother. Early in the reign of James I Horsey was more conciliatory to the demands of the king than were other MPs. During the Addled Parliament of 1614 Horsey was an 'extreme member of the opposition' (Moir) but his sole contribution seems to have been to call the question, an illustration of his nullity at the time. In general he was hardly one of the most distinguished MPs of his time. He served on parliamentary committees for poor relief and disloyal subjects in 1593, for privileges and returns, monopolies, and Langport Eastover in 1597, and for privileges and returns again in 1601. His final parliament was that of 1621, where he sat for East Looe.

Horsey's first wife, with whom he had two sons and three daughters, died in 1607, and he married Isabella, daughter of Edward Brockett of Wheathampsted, about October 1609. He may have married a third wife, Elizabeth North, in 1619, but she is not mentioned in his will. This document, drawn up when he was 'not in perfect health', names his sons William 'whose disobedience and offences god forgive' and John, and daughters Elizabeth Duckett, Frances Knappe (who married her husband Henry 'by her owne untimely will'), and Anne Horsey (PRO, PROB 11/148, fol. 60r–v). Horsey died in January 1626 and was buried at Great Kimbell. His son John proved the will on 28 January. RICHARD HELLIE

Sources R. Virgoe, 'Horsey, Jerome', HoP, *Commons, 1558–1603* · E. A. Bond, ed., *Russia at the close of the sixteenth century*, Hakluyt Society, 20 (1856) · L. E. Berry and R. O. Crummey, *Rude and barbarous kingdom: Russia in the accounts of sixteenth-century English voyagers* (1968) · R. Croskey, 'The composition of Sir Jerome Horsey's "Travels"', *Jahrbücher für Geschichte Osteuropas*, 26 (1978), 362–75 · M. Perrie, 'Jerome Horsey's account of the events of May 1591', *Oxford Slavonic Papers*, new ser., 13 (1980), 28–49 · A. A. Sevast'ianova, 'Zapiski Dzheroma Gorseia o Rossii v kontse XVI-nachale XVII vekov. Raznovremennye sloi istochnika i ikh khronologiia', *Voprosy istoriografii i istochnikovedeniia otechestvennoi istorii: sbornik trudov*, ed. V. B. Kobrin (1974), 63–124 · T. L. Moir, *The Addled Parliament of 1614* (1958) · PRO, PROB 11/148, fol. 60r–v [Horsey's will]
Archives Norfolk RO, observations on Russian travel

Horsey, John (1479–1531). *See under* Horsey family (*per. c.*1500–*c.*1640).

Horsey, Sir John (*d.* 1546). *See under* Horsey family (*per. c.*1500–*c.*1640).

Horsey, Sir John (*d.* 1564). *See under* Horsey family (*per. c.*1500–*c.*1640).

Horsey, Sir John (*d.* 1589). *See under* Horsey family (*per. c.*1500–*c.*1640).

Horsey, John (1753/4–1827), Independent minister and tutor, was born at Ringwood, Hampshire, the son of John Horsey, Independent minister (*d. c.*1777), and his wife, Ann (1714/15–1783). Nothing is known of his early education, until he entered Homerton Academy in 1771 to prepare for the ministry. After leaving in 1775 he supplied Castle Hill Independent Chapel, Northampton, then at a low ebb. Offered its ministry the following year, he at first declined but accepted in 1777; he remained its minister for nearly fifty-one years.

Horsey was an attractive, non-sectarian preacher, with a relaxed and genial disposition. His marriage in 1779 to Hannah King (*bap.* 1753, *d.* 1825), daughter of the Revd Samuel King of Welford, further endeared him to the congregation, which grew under his gentle and cultured ministrations, 'not however distinguished by much energy' (Coleman, 31).

Philip Doddridge's theological academy moved to Daventry after his death in 1751, but when its principal, Thomas Belsham, resigned in 1789 on adopting unitarian opinions, it returned to Northampton with Horsey as principal. He inherited a theological whirlwind as the students were about equally divided between Arians, some of whom had unitarian leanings, and trinitarians. The position was compounded because Horsey refused to require his students to adopt a predetermined theological position. 'Freedom of inquiry on all subjects is the birthright and glory of a rational being. In this seminary it has been enjoyed. In this seminary it shall be enjoyed' (quoted in McLachlan, 166). It is no wonder that his critics said that it was difficult to ascertain his own views on disputed doctrines.

From 1789 lay students were no longer admitted to the academy, which henceforth consisted only of students for the ministry. The period of study was the same as at Daventry, and the subjects were almost unchanged. Horsey continued to use Doddridge's *Lectures on Pneumatology, Ethics and Divinity* as the theological textbook. It is difficult to see the ways in which Horsey created a heterodox atmosphere, although he was accused of fostering unitarian thought through his belief in the right of private judgement.

Controversy came to a peak in the session of 1797–8, when a tutor at the academy wrote to *Protestant Dissenter's Magazine* and the Coward Trustees, who maintained the academy, claiming that Socinianism was taught at the college. All the twelve students supported Horsey, but as the dispute intensified the trustees became increasingly restive. The Coward Trustees dissolved the academy at Northampton in June 1798, setting it up anew at Wymondley, Hertfordshire, the following year.

Horsey trained thirty-seven students, who included William Stevenson and William Johns, subsequently tutors at Manchester Academy, David Daniel Davis, one of the earliest professors at London University, and Lant Carpenter, one of the leading Unitarian ministers of his generation. His achievement was to lead a theological academy in revolutionary times and, by his eirenical approach, prevent it from splitting asunder.

Horsey resigned his ministry in January 1827 because of ill health and died on 12 May that year, aged seventy-three, at Northampton, where he was buried. The congregation then split apart, the seceders forming the first Unitarian congregation in Northampton, with Horsey's son and three daughters among its leading members. Like the Baptist Robert Robinson of Cambridge, Horsey was not unitarian in belief, but his open approach seemingly encouraged it in others.   ALAN RUSTON

Sources M. Deacon, *The church on Castle Hill (Northampton)* (1995), 29–34 • T. Arnold and J. Cooper, *The history of the church of Doddridge, Northampton* (1895), 164–75 • A. Ruston, 'Unitarianism in Northampton: Rev. John Horsey to Sir Philip Manfield', *Transactions of Unitarian Historical Society*, 19/4 (1987–90), 238–41 • *A history of Castle Hill Church, Northampton, 1674–1895* (1896), 42–4 • *IGI* • *Monthly Repository*, new ser., 1 (1827), 448, 609–10 • 'An address received by the late Rev. John Horsey, of Northampton, from his congregation, 1799', *Christian Reformer, or, Unitarian Magazine and Review*, 11 (1844), 1157–8 • B. Godfrey, *Castle Hill meeting: a brief history, Northampton* (1947), 44–9 • A. Sell, *John Locke and the 18th century divines* (1997), 146–7, 389 • *Congregational Magazine*, 11 (1828), 712 [suppl.] • T. Coleman, *Memorials of the Independent churches of Northamptonshire* (1853), 30–33 • J. H. Thompson, *A history of the Coward Trust: the first two hundred and fifty years, 1738–1988* (1998), 37–41 • H. McLachlan, *English education under the Test Acts: being the history of the nonconformist academies, 1662–1820* (1931), 165–9
Archives Castle Hill United Reformed Church, Northampton • DWL, Northampton MSS
Likenesses engraving, repro. in Arnold and Cooper, *History*, facing p. 164 • engraving, repro. in Deacon, *Church on Castle Hill*, 29
Wealth at death see will, Northants. RO

Horsey, Sir Ralph (*d.* 1612). *See under* Horsey family (*per. c.*1500–*c.*1640).

Horsfield, Thomas (1773–1859), physician and naturalist, was born at 42 West Market Street, Bethlehem, Pennsylvania, colonial America, on 12 May 1773, the son of Timothy Horsfield jun. and Juliana Sarah Parsons (*b.* 1738). His family had gone to America from Liverpool two generations earlier and had adopted Moravian Christianity. He was educated at schools in Bethlehem and Nazareth, Pennsylvania, before entering the University of Pennsylvania where he studied medicine. His interest in botany was shown by his MD thesis, a study of the effects of the physiologically active poison ivy, *Rhus toxicodendron* L., and other members of the Anacardiaceae.

In 1800 Horsfield voyaged to Java for the first time, where he was captivated by the complexity and abundance of tropical flora and fauna. He subsequently travelled widely throughout the island, working for the Dutch East India Company on, among other things, the toxin from the latex-producing tree *Antiaris toxicaria*. Although best known as a botanist Horsfield involved himself in all aspects of Javanese natural history; he visited many of the volcanoes, collected volcanic rocks, and, in 1803, attempted chemically to analyse the lava from the eruption of Gunung Gunter. Following the seizure of Java by the British in 1811 Horsfield came into contact with Thomas Stamford Raffles of the East India Company. In November 1812 Horsfield visited Bangka Island, known for its tin ores, and prepared a map of the island for Raffles. He also prepared a 'Mineralogical sketch [map] of the island of Java' which was published as an inset in Raffles's *History of Java* (1817). Horsfield and Raffles became friends and, together with Lady Raffles, visited Sumatra in 1818.

It was probably on Raffles's recommendation that Horsfield was appointed to a position in the company's India Museum, in Leadenhall Street, London, during 1820. From there he continued his researches and writings on the natural history of south-east Asia. He was elected a fellow of the Royal Society in 1828. He worked with the botanists J. J. Bennett (1801–1876) and Robert *Brown (1773–1858) to publish the splendidly illustrated *Plantae Javanicae rariores* (1838–52). Horsfield remained at the India Museum for thirty-nine years, until his death. During that time, in addition to his work on plants, he produced several significant zoological works including *Zoological Researches in Java* (1821–4); an account of 1827, written with N. A. Vigors, of Australian birds, published in volume 15 of the *Transactions of the Linnean Society of London*; and, with Sir William Jardine, *Illustrations in Ornithology*, published about 1830. He died on 24 July 1859 at his home, 29 Chalcot Villas, Camden Town, London, and was buried at the Moravian cemetery in Chelsea.   D. T. MOORE

Sources J. B. Stanley [J. S. Bastin], 'Horsfield in the Indies', *Straits Times Annual* (1972), 84–8 • J. S. Bastin and D. T. Moore, 'The geological researches of Dr Thomas Horsfield in Indonesia, 1801–19', *Bulletin of the British Museum (Natural History)* [Historical Series], 10 (1982), 75–115 • BL OIOC, Horsfield MSS • NHM, Horsfield MSS • *The history of the collections contained in the natural history departments of the British Museum*, British Museum, 1 (1904) • *CGPLA Eng. & Wales* (1859) • Bethlehem, Pennsylvania, USA, Moravian archives
Archives BL OIOC, corresp. and papers, MSS Eur. F 51–54; NHD 1, 9 • NHM, corresp. and papers • RBG Kew, drawings | Linn. Soc., letters to William Swainson • NHM, corresp. with Robert Brown • Oxf. U. Mus. NH, letters to J. O. Westwood
Likenesses J. Erxleben, lithograph, *c.*1843, BM, NPG; repro. in Bastin and Moore, 'The geological researches'
Wealth at death under £2000: probate, 12 Aug 1859, *CGPLA Eng. & Wales*

Horsfield, Thomas Walker (1792–1837), antiquary, was born on 6 November 1792 in Sheffield, the eldest of six children of James Horsfield, bookkeeper, and his wife, Ann Hewett. In 1814 he entered the Unitarian academy at Hackney and in 1817 he moved to Lewes, Sussex, as minister of the Westgate Chapel. He married Hannah, fourth daughter of Robert Waterhouse of Sheffield, in 1818; seven of their children were living at his death. Probably starting early in 1822 with materials collected by his publisher, the Lewes printer John Baxter (1781–1858), and augmenting these from Sir William Burrell's collections in the British Museum Library, he wrote *The History and Antiquities of Lewes and its Vicinity* (2 vols., 1824–7). The Society of Antiquaries elected him a fellow in January 1825.

Horsfield's support for radical causes, including Catholic emancipation, depleted numbers at his boarding-school and contributed to his leaving Lewes in December 1827 to become minister at the Mary Street Chapel in Taunton, Somerset. In 1832 Baxter was planning a third volume, but having in 1833 bought the copyrights to the history of western Sussex by James Dallaway (1763–1834) and Edmund Cartwright (1773–1833), he had Horsfield edit a new work, *The History, Antiquities, and Topography of the County of Sussex* (2 vols., 1835). The *History* was the first to cover every parish in Sussex. Just before it appeared Horsfield moved to Chowbent Chapel at Atherton, Lancashire. He died in Atherton on 26 August 1837. His wife survived him and later remarried.   JOHN H. FARRANT

Sources F. W. Steer, introduction, in T. W. Horsfield, *The history, antiquities, and topography of the county of Sussex*, 1 (1974) · J. H. Farrant, *Sussex depicted: views and descriptions, 1600–1800*, Sussex RS, 85 (2001), 68–71 · J. Goring, 'Why did Horsfield leave Lewes?', *Sussex Archaeological Collections*, 138 (2000), 234–5 · *IGI*
Archives E. Sussex RO, corresp.

Horsford, Sir Alfred Hastings (1818–1885), army officer, was born at Bath, the son of General George Horsford (*d.* 1840), a distinguished Antiguan officer and lieutenant-governor of Bermuda 1812–16, and his wife, Marianne. Horsford was educated at the Royal Military College, Sandhurst, and was commissioned second lieutenant in the rifle brigade on 12 July 1833. He was promoted lieutenant on 23 April 1839 and captain on 5 August 1842.

Horsford served with the 1st battalion rifle brigade in South Africa in the Cape Frontier War of 1847–8. He returned to the Cape in 1851 and commanded the battalion in the war against the Xhosa of 1852–3. He was promoted major on 26 December 1851 and lieutenant-colonel on 28 May 1853.

Horsford accompanied his battalion to the East in 1853, and served with it in Bulgaria and the Crimea, including the battles of the Alma, Inkerman, and Balaklava, and the early part of the siege of Sevastopol. He was promoted brevet lieutenant-colonel (28 November 1854), and made CB and knight of the Légion d'honneur.

Horsford was appointed one of the lieutenant-colonels of the 3rd battalion rifle brigade which formed at Portsmouth in 1855, and took a wing of the battalion out to Calcutta, landing in October 1857. He commanded the battalion in Walpole's brigade at the battle of Cawnpore and in the advance on Lucknow. From February 1858 he commanded a brigade at the siege of Lucknow and in the operations in Oudh and north of the Gogra. After the defeat of the rebels at the Rapti on 30 December 1858, Horsford's brigade was left to watch the Nepal frontier.

Horsford returned home in 1860 to become deputy adjutant-general at the Horse Guards (until 1866), brigadier-general at Aldershot 1866–9, major-general on the staff at Malta 1869–71, major-general commanding the south-eastern district at Dover 1872–4, and military

secretary at the Horse Guards 1874–80. In 1874 he represented Great Britain at the international conference on the usages of war at Brussels.

Horsford was made a KCB in 1860, and GCB in 1875. He was promoted major-general on 1 January 1868, lieutenant-general on 2 August 1875, and full general on 1 October 1877. He was a special commissioner of Chelsea Hospital, and successively colonel of the 79th Cameron Highlanders, the 14th foot, and the 2nd battalion rifle brigade. He died while on holiday at Belmaduthy House, Munlochy, near Inverness, on 13 September 1885.

H. M. CHICHESTER, *rev.* ALEX MAY

Sources *Army List* · *Hart's Army List* · J. Foster, *The peerage, baronetage, and knightage of the British empire for 1880*, [2 pts] [1880] · *ILN* (31 Oct 1885) · W. Cope, *The history of the rifle brigade* (1877) · M. Barthorp, 'The rifle brigade in South Africa, 1852–53', *JSAHR*, 53 (1975), 127–35 · W. Verner, *History and campaigns of the rifle brigade* (1912) · A. J. Smithers, *The Kaffir wars, 1779–1877* (1973) · *CGPLA Eng. & Wales* (1885)
Likenesses Vincent Brooks, Day & Son, lithographic caricature, *c.*1877 (*The beau ideal*), repro. in *VF* (3 Feb 1877) · Spy [L. Ward], chromolithograph caricature, NPG; repro. in *VF* (3 Feb 1877)
Wealth at death £10,818 7*s.* 8*d.*: probate, 12 Oct 1885, *CGPLA Eng. & Wales*

Horsford, Sir John (1751–1817), army officer in the East India Company, was born in London on 2 May 1751, son of John and Ann Horsford, of St George-in-the-East, Stepney, where he was baptized on 19 May 1751. He had a brother, James. He was sent to Merchant Taylors' School in 1759, matriculated at St John's College, Oxford, on 30 June 1768, and was a fellow there from 1768 to 1771, but never took a degree. Horsford enlisted under the assumed name of John Rover in the East India Company's Bengal artillery and sailed for India on the *Duke of Grafton* on 1 April 1772. Enquiries about him attracted the attention of Colonel Pearce, commanding the Bengal artillery. The story goes that Horsford pointed out an error in a Greek quotation in some papers he was copying for the colonel, who suddenly called him by his right name as he was leaving the room. His true identity discovered, Horsford was appointed a cadet of artillery under his real name on 9 March 1778. He was commissioned a lieutenant-fireworker (31 March 1778), first lieutenant (5 October 1778), and captain (26 November 1786).

Horsford commanded a company of Bengal artillery detached to Madras in the Third Anglo-Mysore War, under Lord Cornwallis, in 1790–92. He was promoted to major on 6 August 1801 and lieutenant-colonel on 1 May 1804. He commanded the artillery during Lord Lake's campaigns in 1803–5. In 1806 the governor-general in council recognized Horsford's ability by recommending him to the court of directors for a special allowance while he commanded the artillery in the field. He commanded a brigade and also directed the artillery at the siege of Komanur (August–November 1807), and in 1808 he succeeded to the command of the Bengal artillery, which he held until his death. He was promoted colonel on 25 July 1810 and major-general on 4 June 1811. He was not engaged in the

Nepal War, but the artillery arrangements for those operations and for the grand army under the marquess of Hastings, which subsequently took the field against the Pindaris, were directed by him. He was made a KCB on 7 April 1815, and on 28 June 1816 was appointed an extra major-general on the staff of the grand army. His last military operation was the direction of the artillery at the siege of Hathras in March 1817.

Horsford did not marry, but with his Indian partner, Sahib Jaun, he had three sons: James (d. 1845), Stephen (d. 1819), and Charles (d. 1823); and three daughters: Anne, who married Thomas Brooke Bingley, an officer in the Bengal artillery, in 1818; Eliza, who married Henry Harris, gentleman, in 1819; and Sarah. Horsford died of heart failure at Cawnpore ten days after his return from the field, on 20 April 1817; he was buried in Kacheri cemetery.

H. M. CHICHESTER, rev. ENID M. FUHR

Sources F. W. Stubbs, ed., *History of the organization, equipment, and war services of the regiment of Bengal artillery*, 1–2 (1877) · V. C. P. Hodson, *List of officers of the Bengal army, 1758–1834*, 4 vols. (1927–47) · biographical index, British Army Museum · biographical index, BL OIOC · *The Bengal obituary, or, A record to perpetuate the memory of departed worth*, Holmes & Co. (1848) · Foster, *Alum. Oxon.* · C. J. Robinson, ed., *A register of the scholars admitted into Merchant Taylors' School, from AD 1562 to 1874*, 2 (1883), 120 · *GM*, 1st ser., 87/2 (1817), 561 · IGI

Archives NAM, MS account of life and related papers · Royal Artillery Institution, Woolwich, London, papers

Horsley, Charles Edward (1822–1876), composer, the son of William *Horsley (1774–1858) and his wife, Elizabeth Hutchins Callcott (1793–1875), was born in London on 16 December 1822. Both his maternal grandfather, John Wall *Callcott, and his father were composers; his elder brother, John Callcott *Horsley, was a respected painter. Charles received his earliest musical training from his father, and, when sufficiently advanced, studied the piano under the guidance of Ignaz Moscheles. By the advice of Mendelssohn, who during his visit to England in 1832 became very intimate with the Horsley family, he was sent in 1839 to Kassel, where he was under the tuition of Moritz Hauptmann and had close contact with Spohr. From Kassel he went in 1841 to Leipzig. There he remained until 1843, enjoying the great advantage of personal instruction from Mendelssohn. Mendelssohn wrote to his friend Karl Klingemann in London on 24 January 1841:

> Horsley has now been in our circle for several weeks and delights and pleases us very much by his open, natural, fine character. I did not recognize him, and he has changed for the better so much that I would never have known him; tall, good-looking and apparently grown strong, remarkably like his father and then again like Fanny [Horsley's sister], and quite the young gentleman [*ein ganzer junger* gentleman]! He has already played several times at my apartments … His playing is musical and secure, but not yet at all polished and rounded, and whether that can be achieved in a few months seems doubtful to me, however I am working hard at it and he is such a model of diligence and eagerness, practises so much and so indefatigably that whatever is not achieved will not, I think, be the fault of either of us. His attempts at composition are also good [*brav*] and he has again written something new here. He is the most sought-after companion, the most welcome comrade and gladly seen

everywhere.   (*Felix Mendelssohns Briefwechsel*, 256, trans. C. Brown)

While in Germany Horsley wrote several instrumental works, including a trio for piano, violin, and cello, a symphony in D minor, and an overture which was produced at Kassel in 1845.

On his return to England Horsley devoted himself to teaching music, and won considerable distinction as a pianist and organist. Shortly after he settled in London, at the age of twenty-four, he achieved a success with an oratorio, *David*, and again, three years later, with a second oratorio, *Joseph*. Both works were written for the Philharmonic Society in Liverpool, where he lived from about 1850 to 1853. From 19 September 1853 until June 1857 he was organist of St John's, Notting Hill, London. In 1854 he composed an anthem for the consecration of Fairfield church, and in 1860 he produced at the Glasgow music festival a third oratorio, *Gideon*. His overture *Genoveva* was performed by the New Philharmonic Society in 1853 and another, entitled *The Merry Wives of Windsor*, was given at the Crystal Palace in 1857.

About 1866 Horsley went to Australia, and lived for some time in Melbourne, where he became organist of Christ Church, South Yarra. For the opening of Melbourne Town Hall in 1870 he wrote an ode, *Euterpe*, for soloists, chorus, and orchestra. A selection from this was performed at the Crystal Palace in March 1876. From Melbourne he proceeded in 1872 to the United States. He died in New York on 28 February 1876.

Besides those already mentioned, Horsley's compositions included music to *Comus*, which was published in New York in 1874 and much praised on its production; a song, 'The Patriot Flag', and an anthem written while he was in America; a piano concerto in C minor (1848); and a number of songs, anthems, piano pieces, and sonatas for piano, piano and flute, and piano and cello. He edited a *Collection of Glees*, by his father (1873), and his own *Text-Book of Harmony* (a rewriting of his father's *Explanation of the Musical Intervals* of 1825) was published posthumously in London in 1876.   R. F. SHARP, rev. CLIVE BROWN

Sources *New Grove* · *Dwight's Journal of Music*, 35 (1876), 195 · *Mendelssohn and his friends in Kensington: letters from Fanny and Sophy Horsley, written 1833–36*, ed. R. B. Gotch (1934) · *Felix Mendelssohns Briefwechsel mit Legationsrat Karl Klingemann in London* (1909) · *Harper's Weekly*, 20 (18 March 1876) · private information (1891)

Horsley, John (1685/6–1732), natural philosopher and antiquary, was born of unknown parentage, probably in Northumberland but possibly in Scotland. His posthumous fame as an antiquary has meant that many commentators have sought to identify his family background, but despite a number of confident suggestions none of these is verifiable. His biography has been further confused by misidentification with at least two other contemporaries of the same name: one a land agent in Widdrington who was appointed a trustee of the nonconformist chapel at Morpeth (where this Horsley ministered) on 21 July 1721, the other—possibly a graduate of the University of Edinburgh—rector of Newington, Surrey, and lecturer at St Martin-in-the-Fields, London, who married Ann

Hamilton, daughter of Professor William Hamilton; she is sometimes incorrectly named as the wife of this John Horsley.

It is known that Horsley was educated at Newcastle grammar school, and he then matriculated at the University of Edinburgh on 2 March 1699, graduating MA on 29 April 1701. He was licensed as a dissenting minister, being given pastoral charge of Morpeth, Northumberland, at least by 1709, when he was visited by Dr Edmund Calamy. He also had occasional duty at Alnwick and Widdrington. He kept an academy school in Morpeth, where his pupils included the Revd Newton Ogle, who later became dean of Winchester. Some time before 1711 he married Mary (d. 1746), with whom he had two sons (the first of whom died before his first birthday in November 1711) and six daughters.

Horsley published a number of miscellaneous pieces on religious and natural philosophical subjects, and corresponded with the Royal Society of London: a short paper appeared in the *Philosophical Transactions*, 377 (1723), 'An account of the depth of rain fallen from April 1, 1722, to April 1, 1723. Observed at *Widdrington* in *Northumberland*'. In February 1729 he visited Edinburgh where he met the antiquary Sir John Clerk. In a letter to Roger Gale, Clerk described Horsley as having 'acquired a great reputation for the mathematics, and his knowledge in all parts of philosophy' while at the university. Clerk found him

> to be much acquainted with the Greek and Roman learning, and very ready in his notions about inscriptions and the Roman stations ... He affects now and then a singularity in his readings and opinions, but this I did not wonder at, for the poor man writes for bread, and must have something new to entertain his readers. (*Family Memoirs*, 80.390–91)

Horsley subsequently began a friendly correspondence with Gale, often discoursing on Roman inscriptions. Gale put him in touch with William Stukeley, who recorded having a 'world of discourse' with him on the subject of Roman Britain when they met in February 1729 (*Family Memoirs*, 76.71). He travelled to Bath and to London in 1727 and 1728, and was elected a fellow of the Royal Society on 8 May 1729. In 1731 he began a series of public lectures on astronomical and natural philosophical subjects in Morpeth and Newcastle, which included the use of orreries and other scientific instruments, but these were ended by his sudden death in January 1732.

Horsley had been collecting material on the history of Roman Britain when, about 1727, he began working on them with a view to publication. He was assisted in various aspects of his antiquarian research by his friend and correspondent Robert Cay, and by George Mark, who was probably Horsley's assistant at his school in Morpeth. Mark helped to prepare the plans and drawings for Horsley's history, undertook archaeological tours and explorations, and made surveys, including one of Watling Street. He was also assisted by John Ward, professor of rhetoric at Gresham College, who helped revise the manuscript 'and communicated to him many important remarks for its improvement' (Nichols, *Lit. anecdotes*, 5.521). Horsley's work on Hadrian's Wall utilized material from Alexander

Gordon's *Itinerarium septentrionale* (1726), though his reliance on this book largely went unacknowledged. The *Britannia Romana, or, The Roman Antiquities of Britain* was divided into three 'books'. The first contained the history of the Romans in Britain, with accounts of the legions stationed there, the Roman stations, and a substantial description of the Roman walls; the second 'book' contained a complete collection of the Roman inscriptions and sculptures found in Britain, together with historical and critical notes; the third 'book' contained a 'Roman geography of Britain', including all the extant ancient Roman accounts of Britain. Horsley wrote that the first 'book' had cost him

> much labour and time in my study, to draw out an history of transactions, through so many ages, and at such a distance from our own times ... But I need not inform the world, that the second book was the most expensive and tedious. Several thousand miles were travelled on this account, to visit antient monuments ... I omitted no care nor pains, that was necessary to copy these with the greatest exactness, which was the principal design of the work. (Horsley, *Britannia Romana*, 1732, i)

The book's prefatory dedication to Sir Richard Ellys was written on 2 January 1732, but Horsley did not live to see the publication in early April of this, his greatest achievement. On 12 January he was, according to his friend Ward, 'suddenly and unexpectedly taken off by an apoplexy' (Hinde, 178). His exertions on his Roman history were thought to have contributed to his early death at the age of only forty-six. He died apparently better off than Clerk had found him in 1729, and 'possessed of a good fortune' (ibid., 177).

In his lifetime Horsley had made a greater name for himself as a natural philosopher than as an antiquary, and his obituary in the *Newcastle Courant* on 15 January 1732 described him as 'a great and eminent mathematician, and much esteemed by all that had the happiness of his acquaintance' (Hinde, 178). He was buried in the graveyard at Morpeth parish church on 15 January 1732. His wife survived him by nearly fifteen years and was buried on 16 November 1746. Ward wrote that Horsley's sudden death was 'not only a deplorable calamity to his numerous family, but allso ... to the publick. He had some other designs in view, which, if he had lived to effect, would, I believe, have been of service to the world' (Ward to Roger Gale, 18 Jan 1732, *Family Memoirs*, 80.407). These included the notes he had begun in the autumn of 1729 for a history of Northumberland. They were not published until 1869, as 'Materials for the history of Northumberland' (along with George Mark's 'Survey of a portion of Northumberland') in the first (and only) part of *Indebted Contributions to the History of Northumberland* (1869), edited by John Hodgson Hinde. Despite occasional inevitable errors and inaccuracies, Horsley's *Britannia Romana* was one of the major antiquarian achievements of his day. F. Haverfield in *The Roman Occupation of Britain* (1924) described it as 'till quite lately the best and most scholarly account of any Roman province that had been written anywhere in Europe' (Haverfield, 75).

DAVID BOYD HAYCOCK

Sources J. C. Hodgson, 'Remains of John Horsley the historian', *Archaeologia Aeliana*, 3rd ser., 15 (1918), 57–75 · J. H. Hinde, 'Notes on Rev. John Horsley', *Archaeologia Aeliana*, new ser., 6 (1865), 174–82 · E. Birley, *John Horsley and John Hodgson* (1958) · G. Macdonald, 'John Horsley, scholar and gentleman', *Archaeologia Aeliana*, 4th ser., 10 (1933), 1–57 · *The family memoirs of the Rev. William Stukeley*, ed. W. C. Lukis, 3 vols., SurtS, 73, 76, 80 (1882–7) · Nichols, *Lit. anecdotes*, vols. 2, 5 · F. Haverfield, *The Roman occupation of Britain* (1924) · J. M. Levine, *The battle of the books: history and literature in the Augustan age* (1991), 389–402 · *DNB*

Archives Northumbd RO, Newcastle upon Tyne, corresp. and papers · U. Edin. L., essay on barrows and other tumuli, La ii 49 | NA Scot., letters to Sir John Clerk · RS, letters to James Jurin

Wealth at death relatively wealthy: Hinde, 'Notes on Rev. John Horsley', 177

Horsley, John Callcott (1817–1903), painter, was born on 29 January 1817 at Brompton Row, London, the eldest son of William *Horsley (1774–1858), composer, and his wife, Elizabeth Hutchins Callcott (1793–1875), daughter of John Wall *Callcott (1766–1821), composer, and niece of the painter Sir Augustus Wall Callcott (1779–1844). One of Horsley's sisters married Isambard Kingdom Brunel (1806–1859), while his younger brother, Charles Edward *Horsley, was also a noted composer When he was six Horsley's family moved to 1 High Row, Kensington, London, where he was to live for the rest of his life. He attended a local school, later the site of the Carmelite priory, Kensington.

Encouraged by Augustus Wall Callcott and William Mulready, a close family friend, Horsley enrolled at Henry Sass's academy in Bloomsbury. On 14 December 1831 he entered the Royal Academy Schools and in 1832 won a silver medal for a drawing from the antique. While still a student he met his lifelong friend the painter Thomas Webster. He travelled around England in the 1830s, sketching portraits as well as Elizabethan and Jacobean houses such as Haddon Hall which featured in his first exhibited picture *Rent-Day in the Sixteenth Century at Haddon Hall, Derbyshire* (exh. British Institution, 1837; sketch for later version, York City Art Gallery). This was the first of many costume pictures illustrating domestic incidents set in sixteenth- or seventeenth-century England, the compositions of which were strongly influenced by Dutch seventeenth-century masters. Examples such as *The Morning Mail* (1865; Walker Art Gallery, Liverpool), *The Banker's Private Room: Negotiating a Loan* (1870; Royal Holloway College), and *Coming Down to Dinner* (1876; Manchester City Galleries) reveal an extensive knowledge of the work of artists such as Pieter de Hooch, in the combination of architectural elements and strong light effects used to divide and dramatize the composition, and with the use of open doors and windows revealing secondary characters or vistas to other rooms. In the early part of his career, Horsley also worked on book illustrations, including contributions to volumes such as Moxon's *Tennyson* (1857) and the Home Treasury series published in 1843 by Felix Summerly, a pseudonym used by Henry Cole, for whom he also designed, in the same year, the first commercially produced Christmas card.

Horsley was successfully involved with the competitions to decorate the new houses of parliament, winning

John Callcott Horsley (1817–1903), by Ralph W. Robinson, 1889

prizes in 1843 for his cartoon *St Augustine Preaching to Ethelbert and Bertha, his Christian Queen* (1843; V&A), in 1844 for two small frescoes, *Prayer* and *Peace*, and in 1847 for an oil, *Henry V Believing the King Dead Assumes the Crown*. Between 1844 and 1845 he executed two frescoes in the houses of parliament, *The Spirit of Religion* and *Satan Touched by Ithuriel's Spear*, a scene from Milton's *Paradise Lost*. He continued working on a grand scale at Somerleyton Hall, Suffolk, in 1851 with two wall paintings depicting scenes from the life of Alfred the Great, and worked on a scheme to paint Yealmpton church, Devon, with frescoes. The failure of the latter project was a great professional disappointment.

From 1845 Horsley worked for two years as a headmaster of the school of design at Somerset House, and on 25 August 1846 married Elvira Catherine Jenny (1821–1852), daughter of William Walter. Her death was followed in 1854 by the deaths of two of their sons from scarlet fever; their third son died in 1857. Horsley married on 13 June 1854 Rosamund (Rose) Haden (1820–1912), daughter of Charles Thomas Haden, a surgeon, and sister of the etcher Sir Francis Seymour Haden (1818–1910); they had seven children, including Walter Charles Horsley, a painter; Victor Alexander Haden *Horsley (1857–1916), a surgeon; Gerald Horsley, an architect; and Rosamund, an artist and writer.

By the late 1850s Horsley and his family were frequently visiting Cranbrook in Kent and in 1861 he bought a house there, Willesley, which was remodelled by Richard Norman Shaw between 1864 and 1870. Other artists including F. D. Hardy, Thomas Webster, and G. B. O'Neill also lived in Cranbrook, and by the early 1860s it was recognized as an artists' colony. There was no shared philosophical creed or common style but many of the artists painted local rural life and scenery. It was a sociable community with parties and amateur dramatics and, despite Horsley's somewhat stern good looks in photographs, such company obviously suited his genial temperament. Influenced by the Cranbrook artists, Horsley painted some contemporary subjects, including *Showing a Preference* (1860; one of two versions, David Scott collection) in which a young naval officer gives great attention to a girl on his right arm, while ignoring another on his left. This picture shows his fine use of bright, clear colours and, as a contemporary critic noted, his elegant ability to portray 'the incidents and mishaps of love' with a 'sly wit and quiet drollery [which] sparkles upon such scenes pleasantly and prettily' ('Royal Academy', *Art Journal*, 30, 1868, 104).

Horsley was elected an associate of the Royal Academy on 5 November 1855 and a Royal Academician on 16 December 1864. His paintings declined in popularity from the 1880s and he returned to painting portraits. He became involved in organizing and finding pictures for the old master exhibitions at the Royal Academy from 1870 until his retirement from the academy in 1897; he was also treasurer at the Royal Academy from 1882 to 1897.

A deeply religious man, Horsley expressed his views about the demeaning consequences of female artists' models posing naked, both in a letter to *The Times* in May 1885 (entitled 'A woman's plea' and signed a 'British matron', although written in fact by Horsley himself) and in a speech given to the church congress in October of that year. His opinions were ridiculed in the press, with *Punch* nicknaming him 'clothes-Horsley', and attacked by other artists, including J. A. M. Whistler, who exhibited a pastel of a nude at the Society of Artists in December 1885 with a note attached reading 'Horsley soit qui mal y pense'. Horsley died at the age of eighty-six on 19 October 1903 at 1 High Row, Kensington, London, and was buried on 22 October in Kensal Green cemetery, London. His obituary described him as 'one of the most sweet-tempered of men, and one of the most innocent' (*The Times*).

HELEN VALENTINE

Sources J. C. Horsley, *Recollections of a Royal Academician*, ed. E. Helps (1903) · A. Greg, *The Cranbrook colony: F. D. Hardy, G. Hardy, J. C. Horsley, A. E. Mulready, G. B. O'Neil, T. Webster* (1977) [exhibition catalogue, Central Art Gallery, Wolverhampton, 22 Jan – 12 March 1977; Laing Art Gallery, Newcastle upon Tyne, 26 March – 17 April 1977] · 'British artists, their style and character: no. XXV, John Callcott Horsley', *Art Journal*, 19 (1857), 181–4 · J. C. Horsley papers, 1830–1903, Bodl. Oxf. · L. Errington, *Sunshine and shadow: the David Scott collection of Victorian paintings* (1991) [exhibition catalogue, NG Scot., 11 April – 2 June 1991] · J. Chapel, *Victorian taste: the complete catalogue of paintings at the Royal Holloway College* (1982) · artist's file, archive material, Courtauld Inst., Witt Library · J. C. Horsley, *ILN* (31 Dec 1864), suppl., p. 677 · *The Times* (20 Oct 1903) · M. Girouard, 'A young architect in Kent: early Norman Shaw commissions I', *Country Life*, 154 (1973), 554–7 · J. C. Horsley members' file, RA · A. Smith, *The Victorian nude: sexuality, morality and art* (1996) · m. certs · d. cert.

Archives Bodl. Oxf., corresp. and papers

Likenesses H. J. Brooks, group portrait, oils, 1833 (*Private view of the Old Masters Exhibition, Royal Academy, 1888*), NPG · C. W. Cope, pencil drawing, *c.*1862, NPG · J. C. Watkins, carte-de-visite, 1868, RA · J. C. Horsley, self-portrait, oils, 1882, Aberdeen Art Gallery, MacDonald collection · R. W. Robinson, photograph, 1889, RA, NPG; repro. in *Members and associates of the Royal Academy of Arts* (1891) [*see illus.*] · W. C. Horsley, oils, 1891, RA · R. Cleaver, group portrait, pen-and-ink drawing, 1892 (*Hanging committee, Royal Academy, 1892*), NPG · W. C. Horsley, oils, exh. RA 1902, RA · C. W. Cope, pencil sketch, NPG · Elliott & Fry, carte-de-visite, NPG · Lock & Whitfield, woodburytype photograph, NPG; repro. in T. Cooper, *Men of mark: a gallery of contemporary portraits* (1882)

Wealth at death £22,012 9s. 2d.: probate, 21 Dec 1903, *CGPLA Eng. & Wales*

Horsley, John William (1845–1921), social reformer, was born on 14 June 1845 in Dunkirk, near Canterbury, Kent. He was the eldest son of the Revd John William Horsley (*d.* 1849), the first incumbent of Dunkirk, and his wife, Susannah, daughter of William Sankey, a Dover physician. He was educated at King's School, Canterbury, and at Pembroke College, Oxford. He matriculated in October 1863 but did not graduate, owing to loss of income. After teaching for a few years until he was old enough to be ordained in 1870, he was made assistant curate in Witney. He became curate of St Michael's, Shoreditch, in 1875, and from that time his life was devoted to the amelioration of the condition of the poor, and especially to the reclamation of prisoners. From 1876 to 1886 he was chaplain at Clerkenwell prison. Many of his suggestions for the improvement of the lot of prisoners, made while he was at this institution, although at first rejected as being impracticable, were later adopted by prison authorities.

In 1877 Horsley married Mary Sophia Codd, the eldest daughter of Captain Codd, governor of Clerkenwell prison. They had two sons and five daughters. Mary died in May 1890.

On the abolition of the Clerkenwell prison, in 1886, Horsley became the first clerical secretary of the Waifs and Strays Society, to which he devoted much time and care. His next appointment (1889) was as vicar of Holy Trinity, Woolwich. He began a vigorous campaign for improved housing and sanitation in Woolwich and afterwards became a member of the Woolwich local board and board of guardians. In 1894 he became rector of St Peter's, Walworth, where he filled the positions of chairman of the public health committee of the borough of Southwark, chairman of its largest workhouse, and, in 1909, mayor of Southwark. In 1903 he was appointed an honorary canon of Rochester, and when the new diocese of Southwark was created in 1905 he became an honorary canon of the cathedral. All these activities, over and above the heavy work connected with a large and very poor parish, proved a severe strain on his health, and in 1911 he retired to the vicarage of Detling, near Maidstone. Here he remained until June 1921, when the state of his health compelled him to resign.

Horsley was the author of a number of works on social questions, the best-known being *Practical Hints on Parochial Missions* (1877), *Jottings from Jail* (1887), *How Criminals are Made and Prevented* (1912), and *I Remember* (1911). In 1905 he was installed master of the Quatuor Coronati Lodge of freemasons, of which he had been a member since 1891.

He was also chaplain for many years to the Saye and Sele Lodge, and in 1906 was appointed grand chaplain of the freemasons of England.

Horsley was an enthusiastic alpinist and also a great authority on botany and certain genera of *Mollusca*. Every year it was his custom to take a party of his parishioners to Meiringen in Switzerland, where he would act as guide on long walks and climbs, enlivening the expedition by his extensive knowledge of the topography, fauna, and flora of the Alps. He also organized holidays in the British countryside for the poor children in his parishes.

Concerned with all matters connected with the 'moral reform' of the poor, and the improvement of their social conditions, Horsley became a total abstainer for the sake of example, and was an active member of the council of the Church of England Temperance Society. While in Woolwich he was president of the Woolwich and Plumstead Temperance Council. He wrote the annual review of Britain's criminal statistics for the National Temperance League. He was also vice-president of the Anti-Gambling League. This lover of children, who wrote that the best way to diminish crime was to work for the welfare of children, defending their rights and recognizing their importance, had the great crypt of his church in Walworth cleared of coffins and transformed into a playground for the poor children of the neighbourhood. He died at his home, Rowena, Kingsdown, near Deal, on 25 November 1921. H. B. CHAPMAN, *rev.* C. A. CREFFIELD

Sources J. W. Horsley, *I remember* (1911) · *The Times* (26 Nov 1921) · private information (1927)

Wealth at death £4486 5*s*. 5*d*.: probate, 28 Dec 1921, *CGPLA Eng. & Wales*

Horsley, Samuel (1733–1806), bishop of St Asaph, was born in St Martin's Place, London, on 15 September 1733, son of the Revd John Horsley (1699–1777), a lecturer at St Martin-in-the-Fields, and his first wife, Anne Hamilton (*d.* 1736), daughter of William *Hamilton, professor of divinity at Edinburgh University. His father came from a dissenting family but conformed to the established church in 1727. After his mother's death in 1736, before Horsley's third birthday, his father remarried; his second wife was Mary Leslie (*d.* 1787) with whom he had seven more children. Before going up to Cambridge in 1751 Samuel Horsley was educated at home by his father in the parsonage at Thorley, Hertfordshire. At first he planned a legal career and was admitted to Trinity Hall, Cambridge, on 24 October 1751 to read for a degree in civil law; neither his college nor his degree was highly regarded. On 25 January 1755 he entered the Middle Temple and returned to Trinity Hall in 1757, taking his LLB in 1758. By that time he had already decided to abandon the bar for the church; on 16 July 1758 he was ordained deacon and on 24 September 1758 ordained priest by his godfather, Zachary Pearce, bishop of Rochester. On 18 January 1759 he became rector of Newington Butts, a rural parish close to London, which his father vacated for him.

The Royal Society Despite his somewhat undistinguished career at Cambridge, Horsley was an intelligent man drawn more to intellectual pursuits than to the pastoral

Samuel Horsley (1733–1806), by Walter Stephens Lethbridge, *c.*1803

care of his parishioners. A non-resident rector, he lived in London and was elected a fellow of the Royal Society on 9 April 1767. In November of the same year he was incorporated at Christ Church, Oxford—a more likely setting than Trinity Hall, Cambridge, for one who was to become a leading high-church tory in the Caroline tradition. At Oxford he tutored Heneage Finch, eldest son of the third earl of Aylesford, who took his MA in June 1770. Horsley retained his connection with Christ Church and was made a DCL on 18 January 1774, but for the next decade it was the Royal Society which became the focus of his intellectual life. On 30 November 1771 he was elected to the council of the Royal Society, attended meetings regularly, and engaged in the scientific research of the society. On 30 November 1773 he was rewarded for his activity by being elected one of the two secretaries to the Royal Society, and he worked hard to revive and develop the society's library. In December 1775 he proposed to 'publish, by subscription, a compleat edition of all the works of Sir Isaac Newton' (Mather, 43), a task which did not in fact encompass all of Newton's work and was not completed until 1785. In the course of it he catalogued, in 1777, the Newton mathematical papers owned by the earls of Portsmouth. The five-volume *Opera omnia* of Newton, published from a heterogeneous mass of papers between 1779 and 1785, was a considerable achievement. The Royal Society's support for this work and the access it allowed him to Newton's papers in its ownership was, however, less than wholehearted, and before the edition was completed Horsley had parted company with the society on acrimonious terms. He relinquished the secretaryship and left the council as early as 30 November 1779, when the 35-year-old Joseph Banks became president of the Royal Society. When in November 1783 Banks persuaded the council to force the resignation of the mathematician Charles Hutton, Horsley led the agitation against this, believing that Banks wanted to replace mathematics with natural history as the principal focus of the society's activities. Banks easily won a vote of confidence and Horsley's appeal to public opinion in the anonymous *Authentic Narrative of the Dissentions and Debates in the Royal Society* in March 1784 alienated society members. By the spring of 1784 his career in the Royal Society was over.

Ecclesiastical career and family Although a minor pluralist Horsley was anxious to avoid any gross abuses. He retained the rectory of Newington Butts from 1759 until 1793, but took care never to occupy more than one other incumbency with it: Albury in Surrey, in the gift of the earl of Aylesford, his pupil's father, from 1774 to 1779; Thorley in Hertfordshire from 1779 to 1782; and South Weald in Essex from 1782 to 1793. He was presented to these last two parishes by his patron Robert Lowth, bishop of London. Lowth also appointed Horsley his domestic chaplain and a prebendary of St Paul's in 1777, and made him archdeacon of St Albans in 1781.

On 13 December 1774, when he became rector of Albury at the age of forty-one, Horsley married Mary Botham (*d.* 1777), the orphaned daughter of the previous incumbent at Albury, John Botham. They had two children: a daughter, Harriott, who died in infancy, and a son born on 23 February 1776 and named Heneage after Horsley's pupil and patron. Their happy marriage was soon over: Mary Horsley died in August 1777 and Horsley was left with two infant children to bring up. He married, probably in 1778, Sarah Wright (*d.* 1805), a protégée of his first wife, whose health, never good, progressively deteriorated until her death on 2 April 1805. Horsley gave close attention to his son's education: when Heneage was a student at Oxford his father wrote to him regularly and re-read Thucydides so that they could discuss the Greek text. Later, at the age of twenty-nine, Heneage was to disgrace his father by acquiring considerable debts, but the family saved him and he went on to enjoy a minor clerical career and to devote thirty-four years of his life to editing and publishing his father's writings (1810–45).

On protestant dissenters and Roman Catholics As a leading figure in the Royal Society Horsley might be regarded as part of an 'English enlightenment', but his defence of religious orthodoxy soon led him to oppose Enlightenment critiques of the mysteries of faith. For a while he found congenial company in the circle of that high-church tory, Samuel Johnson, whom he visited from March 1782 and whose conversational club he joined in December 1783. By the time of Johnson's death in 1784 Horsley was already embroiled in the six-year controversy which established him as a national figure. In 1782 his fellow scientist the Unitarian minister Joseph Priestley published *A History of the Corruptions of Christianity* which denied the doctrine of the Trinity. Horsley denounced this book in his visitation

charge as archdeacon of St Albans, on 22 May 1783, but it was Priestley who made the running in the ensuing dispute—Horsley was a reluctant participant. He was being drawn into the field of patristic scholarship in which he was no expert, although he worked hard to master it. He established an argument which appeared reputable and scholarly, and his fellow Anglicans hailed him as victor in the debate. But few modern scholars would agree with Horsley that there was no significant development in the doctrines of the church between apostolic times and the meeting of the Council of Nicea in AD 325. As well as defending the doctrine of the Trinity, Horsley also affirmed the apostolic succession of the Anglican clergy and publicly identified himself as a leading high-churchman. Intellectually he may have failed to defeat Priestley, but he emerged from the controversy in 1790 with his reputation considerably enhanced. Lord Chancellor Thurlow was impressed and ensured that he was rewarded, first with a prebend in Gloucester Cathedral on 19 April 1787, and second on 6 May 1788 by being elected bishop of St David's.

Between 1789 and 1793 Horsley opposed, consistently and vigorously, the attempts to repeal the Test and Corporation Acts: speaking in the House of Lords, writing a powerful tract, *A Review of the Case of the Protestant Dissenters* (February 1790), and in the same year instructing his clergy to vote against the pro-repeal candidate in the Carmarthen election. His arguments for the preservation of the constitution in church and state reflected the views of Edmund Burke but were probably reached independently. He believed that an established church was essential to good government, suggesting in an unpublished paper of February 1790 that every civil government needed 'to find a common measure of moral conduct universally applicable to the purpose of providing and securing the happiness and welfare of a whole community' and arguing that 'the Christian must regard the intimate and inseparable union of religion and civil government as the grand desideratum with respect to human happiness' (LPL, MS 1767, fols. 198*v*, 201*v*).

While recognizing that other denominations which taught social subordination could be useful in controlling the lower orders, Horsley opposed any moves which would weaken the position of the established church in the constitution or dilute its traditional trinitarian doctrines. In a letter of 6 July 1805 he reflected, 'if the Church of England is to be overturned or undermined it will not be by the Catholics, but by sects of a far different description' (LPL, MS 1767, fol. 15). Accordingly, while Horsley staunchly defended the established church against the claims of Unitarians and protestant dissenters, he worked for toleration for English Catholics and Scottish Episcopalians. He welcomed and defended the French émigré clergy and played a leading role in the passage of the Catholic Relief Act of 1791, ensuring that the words of the proposed oath were altered so that ultramontanes could swear with a clear conscience. He assured the House of Lords that Roman Catholics were no longer a political threat, but were 'led by the genuine principles of their religion to inoffensive conduct, to dutiful submission and cordial loyalty' (Horsley, 42). He supported the repeal of the penal laws against the Scottish Episcopalians when they formally abandoned the Jacobite succession in 1788, and agreed to pray for the Hanoverian monarchy. He used his influence to persuade a reluctant Lord Chancellor Thurlow to agree to the passage of a Relief Bill in 1792, and introduced a clause in committee which required Scottish Episcopalian clergy to subscribe to the Thirty-Nine Articles.

Opposition to political radicalism Within a year of Horsley's elevation to the bench of bishops revolution had broken out in France and Horsley's reaction to it completed the transition from enlightened Cambridge scientist to high-church tory bishop. His turn to preach the martyrdom day sermon, commemorating the execution of Charles I, in Westminster Abbey before the House of Lords, came on 30 January 1793 at the end of an intense three-month pamphlet war in England and nine days after the execution of Louis XVI in Paris, at a time when the establishment feared that revolution in Britain was close. In an atmosphere of tension and anxiety Horsley preached a powerful and emotional sermon which combined traditional Anglican political theory with anti-revolutionary oratory. A paradigm statement of the hostility of the established church to revolution, it was enthusiastically received, the congregation rising to its feet at the start of the peroration and remaining standing until the end. It was rumoured that it was to this performance that Horsley owed his appointment as dean of Westminster and his translation to the bishopric of Rochester, in November 1793. But the sermon was no piece of cynical opportunism; the views it expressed were sincerely held and entirely consistent with the bishop's actions between 1789 and 1793.

In the House of Lords Horsley supported the government with his vote until 1798. His assertion in the 1795 debate on the Treasonable and Seditious Practices Bill that the people 'had nothing to do with laws, except to obey them' led to his being satirized as the Turkish autocrat, the grand mufti (J. Debrett, *The Parliamentary Register*, second ser., 14, 1795, 88–98). In politics his closest friend was William Windham, who shared his interest in mathematics and other scholarly matters. When Pitt the younger left office, Horsley associated himself with Pitt's cousin, Lord Grenville, and joined him in attacking Addington's administration. He actively opposed the preliminaries of the peace on 3 November 1801, then was unusually absent from the house for eight months and did not vote on the ratification of the treaty of Amiens in May 1802. He desisted, however, from joining in the fatal assault on Addington, though his translation to the see of St Asaph (the wealth of which was greater than its status) on 26 June 1802 was probably more a reward for a decision already taken than a bribe. Although personal relations between the high-church bishop and the evangelical Wilberforce were uniformly bad, Horsley was an active opponent of the slave trade and spoke unequivocally against it in debates in parliament. On 5 July 1799 he

assured the Lords that he held 'no visionary notions of equality and imprescriptible rights of man' but argued that 'there is an extreme condition of subjection, to which man cannot without injustice be degraded' and that that 'is the condition of the African carried away into slavery' (Horsley, 197). The former stalwart of the Royal Society then proceeded to present a mass of scientific and geographical evidence about the Africans of Nigeria, drawn from the recent account of Mungo Park, to show that the Mandingo people were far from the savages the defenders of the slave trade argued. As dean of Westminster, Horsley's support of Warren Hastings in the impeachment proceedings was, perhaps, less principled, although he seemed genuinely to believe in the justice of Hastings's case. Hastings was a distinguished alumnus of Westminster School, where Horsley's adored son Heneage was a king's scholar; members of the bishop's family also had strong connections with the East India Company. He opposed utilitarian reform of the poor law and advocated generous Christian charity to those in need. He joined with Bishop Porteus of London and Bishop Barrington of Durham in supporting Lord Auckland's Adultery Bill of May 1800, which sought to discourage collusion in divorce cases by prohibiting the subsequent marriage of the guilty parties. He played his part in the high-church movement to provide 'free churches' for the urban poor and, as an assiduous patron of the Society for Promoting Christian Knowledge, was a strong supporter of popular education.

Christian instruction, whether in the charity school or from the pulpit, provided the social control Horsley regarded as essential to free government. His episcopal charges to his clergy showed clearly his understanding of the duty of an established church in teaching and enforcing a moral code; the revolution in France, and later the rise of Napoleon, made this more vital than ever. In his *Charge* to the clergy of Rochester in 1796 he suggested that there was a significant group in society that tolerated the Church of England and supported its establishment only so long as it fulfilled this function. If the clergy failed in their duties the church would lose both its privileges and its wealth. But his main message was a spiritual one: the French Revolution was as much an assault on the Christian religion as on government. In his 1800 *Charge* he discussed the conspiracy theory of the Abbé Barruel, who blamed the *philosophes* and the freemasons for the destruction of religion, which had opened the door to revolution. Horsley was himself a freemason belonging to a branch in Scotland; he declared his interest in the House of Lords in 1799 and tried to argue that the masons in Britain were innocent and loyal, although he conceded that some continental freemasons had been deluded by the *illuminés*. In 1800 he likened the masons to the Methodists, whose schools he claimed were under Jacobin influence although Methodism itself was ignorant of this wicked enterprise. Equating the French republic to the beast of the apocalypse, Horsley related the revolution to his millenarian thinking. While much popular millenarian thought took a radical turn in the 1790s Horsley linked it firmly to the conservative cause, arguing that the imperfections of human government must be suffered until the second coming of Christ, when the millennium of good government would be inaugurated.

The last years A large number of Horsley's writings were published during his lifetime, and more by his son after his death. Apart from a few scientific and mathematical pieces, most of them are in the form of sermons and charges, and reflect his devotion to his calling. By the standards of his day Horsley was far from being a bad bishop. Although more attracted to intellectual and political pursuits he did not neglect the pastoral needs of his clergy, and at St David's he reformed diocesan administration. His radical critics found it easy to satirize Horsley, with his bull-like features, blotchy skin, rotundity, and overindulgence in food and wine, as an arch-reactionary, but his position was more complex, subtle, and principled than they allowed.

The last two years of Horsley's life were blighted by the death of his second wife and the debts of his son. In the summer of 1805 he moved into the bishop's palace at St Asaph, with his daughter-in-law and her two daughters. Fanny Bourke had married Heneage Horsley in June 1801 and rapidly became the bishop's frequent correspondent. His warm affection for her and for his granddaughters was reciprocated, and he indulged in minor nepotism to the advantage of her family. In April 1806 he returned to London for his final parliamentary session, and died at Brighton on 4 October 1806 after a brief illness: a 'slight complaint in his bowels' which 'brought on a mortification' (*GM*, 1058). He was insolvent at the time of his death, having just failed to renew a life insurance policy for £5000, and his effects were sold to pay his creditors. His fine library of 1932 books was auctioned at Leigh and Sothebys in the Strand in May 1807 and, according to manuscript annotations in the Bodleian Library copy of the sale catalogue, made more than £1600. After a funeral service in Westminster Abbey he was buried in St Mary's, Newington Butts; when that church was demolished in 1876 to make way for a railway, his remains were removed to Thorley.   ROBERT HOLE

Sources F. C. Mather, *High church prophet: Bishop Samuel Horsley (1733–1806) and the Caroline tradition in the later Georgian church* (1992) · *GM*, 1st ser., 76 (1806), 987–90, 1057–9, 1073, 1238 · *Annual Register* (1806), 199–205 · R. Hole, *Pulpits, politics and public order in England, 1760–1832* (1989), 160–73 · LPL, Samuel Horsley MSS, MS 1767 · S. Horsley, *The speeches in parliament of Samuel Horsley*, ed. H. Horsley (1813) · *A catalogue of the entire and very valuable library of the late Right Rev. Samuel Horsley* (1807) [sale catalogue, Leigh and Sotheby, 1807] · H. H. Jebb, *A great bishop of one hundred years ago: being a sketch of the life of Samuel Horsley* (1909) · A. P. Stanley, *Historical memorials of Westminster Abbey*, 3rd edn (1869) · *DNB*

Archives BL, corresp. · LPL, corresp. and papers · RS, papers | LPL, Roundall Palmer, first earl of Selborne, MSS, MSS 1890–1893, 2809–2810 · NL Scot., corresp. with Lord Monboddo · NL Wales, letters to Isaac Williams

Likenesses Leney?, engraving, pubd 28 Feb 1799 (after R. Dighton), NPG · S. W. Reynolds, mezzotint, *c*.1799 (after Baron), BM · W. S. Lethbridge, miniature on ivory, *c*.1803, NPG [*see illus.*] · R. Dighton, cartoon, coloured etching, pubd 1809, BM, NPG; repro. in Mather, *High church prophet*, jacket · H. Meyer, mezzotint, pubd 1813 (after J. Green), BM, NPG; repro. in Mather, *High church prophet*, frontispiece · J. Stow, line engraving, pubd 1822 (after line drawing by S. Roch), BM, NPG · T. Blood, stipple (after O. Humphrey), BM, NPG; repro. in *European Magazine* (1813) · T. Dean, engraving (after J. Green), NPG · oils (after T. Green), Westminster Abbey, deanery

Wealth at death insolvent; effects sold to pay creditors: *GM*

Horsley, Sir Victor Alexander Haden (1857–1916), physiologist and surgeon, was born in 2 Tor Villas, Campden Hill, Kensington, London, on 14 April 1857, the son of John Callcott *Horsley (1817–1903), and his second wife, Rosamund Haden (1820–1912), daughter of Charles Haden MD (1786–1824) and a sister of Sir Francis Seymour Haden (1818–1910). He was the second son in a family of seven children. His childhood was spent in his father's country house at Cranbrook, Kent, and he became a day boy at Cranbrook grammar school. Between 1874 and 1880 he studied at University College Hospital medical school, where he began studies of his own in physiology and bacteriology. After qualification he became house surgeon to John Marshall and surgical registrar at University College Hospital. It was at this time that he made a long series of observations on the action of anaesthetics on his own brain. In 1882 he was appointed assistant professor of pathology, and was full professor between 1886 and 1896.

From 1884 to 1890 Horsley was professor-superintendent to the Brown Institution (University of London), a veterinary hospital and the chief centre in London of advanced research in pathology and physiology. Horsley followed three main lines of study: the action of the thyroid gland, protective treatment against rabies, and the localization of function in the brain.

In 1883 Horsley was a member of a committee appointed by the Clinical Society to investigate the action of the thyroid gland in connection with myxoedema and cretinism. His first experiments (removal of the thyroid) were made on monkeys and he proved beyond all dispute the action of the thyroid. The committee's report, published in 1898, gave a summary of myxoedema, but there is no mention of hope for a cure. Finally, in 1890, Horsley advised treatment by transplantation of a sheep's thyroid under the patient's skin, as Schiff had suggested; later came the work of George Murray and others on the administration of thyroid extract. Horsley's work does not stand absolutely alone; but it was he who founded in Britain the modern study of the thyroid gland, leading to the rational treatment of myxoedema and sporadic cretinism.

Following Pasteur's first use in July 1885 of the preventive treatment of rabies, the following year the Local Government Board appointed a commission, of which Horsley was secretary, to study and report on the treatment. After travelling to Paris with John Burdon Sanderson, Thomas Lauder Brunton, and Sir Henry Enfield Roscoe, Horsley learned the whole method. He became the only thorough student of rabies at the Brown Institution, and the only representative and interpreter of Pasteur's method in Britain. He studied the outbreak of rabies among the deer in Richmond Park in 1886–7, and in 1888 he examined and exposed the claims of a quack cure for rabies, the Bouisson bath treatment. He was chairman of

Sir Victor Alexander Haden Horsley (1857–1916), by unknown photographer

the society for the prevention of hydrophobia, and together with other members of the commission assisted the government over the enforcement of the order for the muzzling of dogs (1897).

In 1884 Horsley began his chief work in physiology, his investigations of the localization of function in the brain and spinal cord. He was associated in this work with E. A. Sharpey-Schafer, Charles Edward Beevor, Felix Semon, and his future brother-in-law, Francis Gotch. He came to the work at the time of the high tide of interest in the physiology and pathology of the brain, and his contributions to the literature of the subject were numerous and important.

In 1885 Horsley became assistant surgeon at University College Hospital (he was professor of clinical surgery between 1899 and 1906), and in 1886 he was appointed surgeon to the National Hospital for the Paralysed and Epileptic, Queen Square, London, a post which brought him the leadership in the field of cerebral surgery. There had been very few recorded cases of modern cerebral surgery, on the principles of localization of function, when Horsley was appointed to the Queen Square hospital. His experimental work on monkeys, with nothing to guide him except the localization of function, had familiarized him with cerebral surgery, and before the end of 1886 he had done ten operations at Queen Square, nine of them successful. On 9 June 1887 he removed a tumour from the spinal cord: it was the first operation of its kind. The work of these two years set Horsley in the very front of his profession, and he established an international reputation. In 1893 his experiments on the effect of bullet wounds in the brain proved that the immediate cause of death in such cases is failure, not of the heart, but of the respiration. In 1906, when the British Medical Association met in Toronto, Horsley gave the address in surgery, reviewing in it the whole field of cerebral surgery; this address is one of the most significant of his writings.

Horsley was a prolific writer; 278 items have been recorded in an unpublished bibliography of his works (Holder). He received many honours for his research; he became a fellow of the Royal College of Surgeons in 1883 and a fellow of the Royal Society in 1886, and he was knighted for his contributions to medicine in 1902. In 1887 he married Eldred Bramwell, second daughter of Sir Frederick *Bramwell (1818–1903), engineer; they had two sons and a daughter.

Horsley was active in the politics of his profession. He was president of the Medical Defence Union, served on the General Medical Council, and was one of the leaders of the British Medical Association; he was always on the side of reform inside the profession. The general election of 1910 brought Horsley into party politics, though he never entered parliament. He had no liking for compromises, and offended people by his vehemence and by his ardent and persistent support of the claims of women to citizenship. He took a leading part in the agitation against alcohol in Britain, and, with Dr Mary Sturge, published in 1907 *Alcohol and the Human Body*.

In the First World War Horsley was at first surgeon to the British hospital at Wimereux, but in May 1915 he was sent to Egypt, and in July was appointed consultant to the Mediterranean expeditionary force. In March 1916 he went to India and Mesopotamia. Both in Egypt and in Mesopotamia he fought hard to improve conditions for the wounded. He died of heatstroke, complicated by intestinal infection, at the British General Hospital at Amara, near Baghdad, on 16 July 1916. He was buried at Amara. Horsley was survived by his wife, and in 1923 the Victor Horsley memorial lectures were inaugurated at University College Hospital.

STEPHEN PAGET, rev. CAROLINE OVERY

Sources S. Paget, *Sir Victor Horsley: a study of his life and work* (1919) · J. Lyons, *The citizen surgeon: a life of Sir Victor Horsley* (1966) · E. Clarke, 'Horsley, Victor Alexander Haden', *DSB* · personal knowledge (1927) · C. J. Bond, *Recollections of student life and later days: a tribute to the memory of the late Sir Victor Horsley, FRS* (1939) · V. G. Plarr, *Plarr's Lives of the fellows of the Royal College of Surgeons of England*, rev. D'A. Power, 2 vols. (1930) · C. E. Holder, bibliography of Horsley's publications, 1949, U. Lond. · W. R. Merrington, *University College Hospital and its medical school: a history* (1976), 102–15
Archives Bodl. Oxf., corresp. and papers · UCL, corresp. and papers · Wellcome L., laboratory notebook written with Sir Felix Simon | Wellcome L., corresp. with Sir Edward Sharpey-Schafer
Likenesses group portrait, photograph, 1897, UCL · G. C. Beresford, photograph, Wellcome L. · photographs, repro. in Paget, *Sir Victor Horsley* · photographs, repro. in Lyons, *The citizen surgeon* · two photographs, Wellcome L. [*see illus.*]
Wealth at death £35,595 6s. 3d.: probate, 7 Oct 1916, *CGPLA Eng. & Wales*

Horsley, William (1774–1858), composer, the descendant of an old Northumbrian family, was born in London on 15 November 1774. He showed an aptitude for music at an early age, and when he was sixteen definitely chose it as his profession. After some training from Gardiner, a pupil of Pepusch, he was articled for five years to the pianist Theodore Smith. Smith gave him scanty instruction and treated him harshly. More profitable was his association with the three brothers Pring and John Wall *Callcott. He was encouraged by them to attempt glee writing, in which he later established his reputation. During this period he wrote a number of glees, canons, and rounds, besides several anthems and cathedral services.

In 1794 Horsley was elected to the post of organist of Ely Chapel, Holborn, and three years later, on 15 June 1797, was admitted a member of the Royal Society of Musicians. In the following year, with the co-operation of Callcott, he founded the Concentores Sodales, a club for the encouragement of glee and canon writing, which flourished, with varying fortunes, until 1847. About the same time he was appointed assistant organist to Callcott at the Asylum for Female Orphans, and in consequence resigned his post at Ely Chapel. On 8 June 1800 he took the degree of BMus at Oxford, his exercise being an anthem, 'When Israel came out of Egypt'. The next year the Vocal Concerts were revived, and Horsley wrote for them several glees and songs, as well as some instrumental pieces, including three symphonies. In 1802 he succeeded Callcott as organist to the asylum, and held the appointed until 1854. On 12 January 1813 he married Elizabeth Hutchins Callcott (1793–1875), the daughter of his friend. In the same year he joined Clementi, Bishop, Smart, Attwood, Cramer, and others in founding the Philharmonic Society. From 1812 to 1837 Horsley was also organist at the new Belgrave Chapel in Halkin Street. In 1838 he exchanged this post for that of organist to the Charterhouse.

Horsley was a member of the Society of British Musicians from 1834 to 1839, was elected member of the Royal Academy of Music at Stockholm in 1847, was a member of the Catch Club, and became a frequent visitor at the meetings of the Madrigal Society. He died on 12 June 1858, at his home, 1 High Row, Gravel Pits, Kensington, and was buried in Kensal Green cemetery. His wife survived him. His eldest son, John Callcott *Horsley RA, was well known as an artist; another son, Charles Edward *Horsley, was a composer.

Although his compositions were various, Horsley's reputation as a composer rests chiefly on his glees, in which he had few equals. Between 1801 and 1827 he published five collections, and another was issued by his son C. E. Horsley in 1873; some were also contributed to Clementi's *Vocal Harmony*, of which Horsley edited the second edition in 1830. These compositions showed great refinement of taste, and the music was well suited to the words. A very high opinion of them was held by Mendelssohn, whose friendship with Horsley dated from his first visit to England in 1829. Mendelssohn remained in close contact with Horsley and his family after he assumed the directorship of the Leipzig Gewandhaus concerts in 1835. According to J. C. Horsley in his *Recollections of a Royal Academician*:

> He carried off copies of many of the glees, for the Sing-Verein at Leipsic; and wrote afterwards to his English friend of the fact that in his absence from Leipsic the choir there had sung 'By Celia's Arbour' and other of the glees with forty voices to a part!—a misunderstanding which Mendelssohn soon corrected.

Perhaps the most popular of Horsley's glees were 'By

Celia's Arbour' (1807, words by Thomas Moore), 'See the chariot at hand', 'Mine be a cot', 'Cold is Cadwallo's tongue', and 'Oh, nightingale!' Baptie considered Horsley 'one of the most elegant learned and artistic of all the excellent glee composers our country has produced'. Horsley's church music, of which he wrote a substantial amount, did not enjoy any lasting popularity, but two of his hymn tunes, 'Belgrave' (1819) and 'Horsley' (1844), remained in use in the late twentieth century. Horsley wrote several theoretical works, the most important of which was his *Introduction to the Study of Practical Harmony and Modulation* (1847). He was also active as an editor, and revised the third edition of his father-in-law's *Musical Grammar* (1817). He also issued a collection of the latter's glees, together with a memoir and analysis of Callcott's work (1824).   R. F. SHARP, *rev.* CLIVE BROWN

Sources 'Sketch of the state of music in London', *Quarterly Musical Magazine and Review*, 5 (1823), 241–75 · *GM*, 1st ser., 83/2 (1813), 82 · *GM*, 3rd ser., 5 (1858), 94 · [J. S. Sainsbury], ed., *A dictionary of musicians*, 2 vols. (1825) · [J. W. Davison], 'William Horsley', *Musical World* (26 June 1858), 408–9 · W. A. Barrett, *English glee and madrigal writers* (1877), 38 · D. Baptie, *Sketches of the English glee composers: historical, biographical and critical (from about 1735–1866)* [1896], 82ff. · J. C. Horsley, *Recollections of a Royal Academician* (1903) · *Mendelssohn and his friends in Kensington: letters from Fanny and Sophy Horsley, written 1833–36*, ed. R. B. Gotch (1934) · private information (1891)

Archives Bodl. Oxf., diaries and papers

Likenesses G. H. Harlow, pencil, NPG · R. J. Lane, lithograph (after J. C. Horsley), BM, NPG · W. Owen, oils, NPG

Wealth at death under £6000: probate, 8 Sept 1858, *CGPLA Eng. & Wales*

Horsman, Edward (1807–1876), politician, born on 8 February 1807, was the son of William Horsman of Stirling, who died on 22 March 1845, aged eighty-six. His mother was Jane, third daughter of Sir John Dalrymple, bt, and sister of the seventh and eighth earls of Stair; she died in 1833. Horsman was entered at Rugby School at midsummer 1819, and afterwards proceeded to Trinity College, Cambridge, but did not take a degree. He was admitted an advocate of the Scottish bar in 1832, but did not continue to practise his profession for long. He was briefly a commissioner of inquiry into the Church of Scotland. As a moderate Liberal he unsuccessfully contested Cockermouth in 1835, but was returned there unopposed at a by-election on 15 February 1836, and continued to represent the constituency until 1 July 1852, when he was defeated at the general election. He was returned unopposed on 28 June 1853 for Stroud, which he represented until 11 November 1868. From 11 May 1869 to his death he was the member for Liskeard, but he had then so far separated himself from the Liberal Party that he was opposed on both occasions by more advanced members of his own party—in 1869 by Sir F. Lycett, and in 1874 by L. H. Courtney.

Early in his political career (January 1840) Horsman, when addressing his constituents at Cockermouth, denounced James Bradshaw, MP for Canterbury, for speaking ill of the queen, and for secretly sympathizing with the Chartists. A bitter correspondence was followed

Edward Horsman (1807–1876), by Southwell Brothers, c.1862–4

Horsman and Lowe were thus the original 'Adullamites', playing a central part in the fall of the Liberal government in June 1866, though Horsman continued to support Gladstone's leadership of the party in the Commons. Horsman maintained his independent attitude to the last. He best served the public by exposing jobs and other weak points in the ecclesiastical system, various of his speeches on which were published. Contemporaries felt that Disraeli's reference to him as 'that superior person' was a fair shaft (Monypenny and Buckle, 6.347).

Horsman married, on 18 November 1841, Charlotte Louisa, the only daughter of J. C. Ramsden, MP. They had no recorded children. Horsman died at Biarritz on 30 November 1876 and was buried there on 2 December. His wife died on 26 August 1895.

G. C. BOASE, rev. H. C. G. MATTHEW

Sources *The Times* (2 Dec 1876) · Boase, *Mod. Eng. biog.* · W. F. Monypenny and G. E. Buckle, *The life of Benjamin Disraeli*, 6 vols. (1910–20)
Archives Muncaster Castle, Ravenglass, political corresp. · W. Yorks. AS, Leeds, diary | BL, corresp. with W. E. Gladstone, Add. MSS 44393, 44396, 44412, 44783 · BL, letters to A. H. Layard, Add. MSS 38982, 38983, 38990 · Bucks. RLSS, letters and papers
Likenesses Southwell Brothers, photograph, c.1862–1864, NPG [see illus.] · G. Böhm, lithograph (after daguerreotype), NPG · Faustin, chromolithograph caricature (a *Figaro* cartoon), NPG · chromolithograph caricature, NPG; repro. in *VF* (10 Aug 1872) · portrait, repro. in *Graphics* (16 Dec 1876), 592, 595 · wood-engraving (after photograph), NPG; repro. in *ILN* (16 May 1857), 478, 482 · wood-engraving (after photograph by London Stereoscopic Co.), NPG; repro. in *ILN* (16 Dec 1876), 581
Wealth at death under £5000: probate, 1 Jan 1877, *CGPLA Eng. & Wales*

by a duel at Wormwood Scrubs, which was without serious results. Finally Bradshaw apologized. From September to August 1841 Horsman was a junior lord of the Treasury in Melbourne's administration. He criticized severely, and at times with personal bitterness, the ecclesiastical policy of Lord John Russell's ministry of 1847, as being far too favourable to the bishops. A vote of censure on the ecclesiastical commissioners was moved by him and rejected on 14 December 1847. On 26 April 1850, in the discussion on the Ecclesiastical Commission Bill, Horsman smartly attacked the bishops, thereby rousing Goulburn to denounce him as 'a disappointed man' foiled of his hopes of office. In March 1855, when Lord Palmerston became prime minister and the Peelites withdrew from the cabinet, Horsman was made chief secretary for Ireland, and was sworn of the privy council. He resigned the chief secretaryship after the general election in April 1857, and thenceforth assumed a more independent position in the House of Commons.

With Robert Lowe, Horsman opposed the Gladstone–Russell Reform Bill of 1866. John Bright, speaking on the second reading (13 March 1866), ascribed Lowe's hostility to Horsman's influence, and depicted Horsman as retiring 'into what may be called his political cave of Adullam, to which he invited every one who was in distress, and every one who was discontented' (*Hansard 3*, 13 March 1866).

Horsman, Nicholas (*fl.* 1654–1689), Church of England clergyman, was born in Devon, the son of a clergyman. He matriculated at Magdalen College, Oxford, on 15 March 1654, but migrated to Corpus Christi College, Oxford, in the same year. He graduated BA in January 1656 and proceeded MA in March 1659. After taking orders he became a fellow, and proceeded BD in 1667. In 1668 he added to his fellowship the prebend of Higher Line in the collegiate church of Chumleigh, Devon.

Horsman wrote *The spiritual bee, or, A miscellaney of scriptural, historical, natural observations, and occasional occurrencyes applied to divine meditations by an university pen* (1662). He made additions to the edition of Degory Wheare's *Reflectiones hyemales de ratione et methodo legendi utrasque historias civiles et ecclesiasticas* published in the same year in the form of an appendix 'Mantissa de historicis gentium particularium' ('Mantissa, or, An addition concerning the historians of particular nations, as well ancient as modern', as it was translated into English in later editions), which strengthened the book's treatment of medieval historians.

In 1669, according to Anthony Wood, 'going the college-progress [Horsman] became crazed by an unseasonable journey (late at night) through certain marshes in Kent, and so continued to his dying-day' (Wood, *Ath. Oxon.*, 4.616). This presumably malarial infection also struck down the college steward (who recovered) and a physician from the college (who died). Despite his affliction Horsman contributed to a university collection of memorial verses for Henrietta Maria published in 1670. However, his illness had left him in such a state that the college gave him an annual allowance of £55, and, again according to Wood, Horsman was 'kept distracted' near Bath before moving to Plymouth, where he was living—and is last certainly heard of—in 1689 (ibid., 4.617).

CAROLINE L. LEACHMAN

Sources Wood, *Ath. Oxon.*, new edn, 4.616–17 • J. R. Bloxam, *A register of the presidents, fellows … of Saint Mary Magdalen College*, 8 vols. (1853–85), vol. 1, pp. 72 • Foster, *Alum. Oxon.* • D. Wheare, *The method and order of reading both civil and ecclesiastical histories*, trans. E. Bohun (1694), 179

Hort, Fenton John Anthony (1828–1892), biblical scholar and theologian, was born on 23 April 1828 in Dublin, the eldest of the five children of Fenton Hort (1795–1873), a member of an Irish aristocratic protestant family, and Anne Collett (1802–1866), the daughter of a Suffolk clergyman. His father, educated at Cambridge and with private means, was active in public affairs and charitable work. His mother was gifted and intelligent, and a strong supporter of the evangelical movement; her views were dominant in the raising of Fenton, his brother, and his three sisters. In 1837 the family moved to Cheltenham, at that time a centre of the evangelical movement. After attending a preparatory school in Laleham, Middlesex, for two years, Fenton was sent to Rugby School in 1841. Here he spent his formative years, and on his own admission the school exercised a lasting impression on him. Thomas Arnold had been headmaster since 1827, and though he died in 1842 the brief personal contact along with the whole ethos of Rugby provided a liberal influence quite different from that of Hort's upbringing. Also important were the teaching of Bonamy Price, who kindled in him a love of language, and Arnold's successor, A. C. Tait, the future archbishop of Canterbury. Fenton was a promising pupil, already displaying the thoroughness and breadth of knowledge which were to characterize the mature man. Contemporaries remembered him as a rather awkward figure, not good at games, with a resolute, earnest face, blue eyes, bushy eyebrows, and black, straight hair.

University years Hort went to Trinity College, Cambridge, in 1846, where he read for the classics and mathematics tripos. From the outset his interests were wide, embracing philosophy, natural science, theology, and politics. So too was his circle of friends, among whom were John Ellerton, the Christian socialist and hymn writer, Daniel Macmillan, the publisher, Henry Bradshaw, later to be university librarian, and James Clerk Maxwell, later first professor of experimental physics at Cambridge. The intellectual promise Hort showed at Rugby was fulfilled when in 1850 he gained a first-class award in the classical tripos (illness marred his performance in the mathematics tripos), and in 1851 first classes in both the newly created moral science tripos and the natural science tripos; he also won the Whewell prize for proficiency in moral philosophy. He was elected to a fellowship at Trinity in 1852.

It was in his early years at Cambridge that Hort first met

Fenton John Anthony Hort (1828–1892), by George Percy Jacomb-Hood, 1891

Brooke Foss Westcott and Joseph Barber Lightfoot, whose friendship and collaboration were profoundly to affect his whole life and work. Westcott became his classical 'coach' in January 1850. They soon became firm friends and, when Westcott went to Harrow School as a master, regular correspondents. For almost half a century Westcott was the closest of all Hort's friends. Lightfoot was elected to a fellowship at Trinity in 1852, as Hort was. The three men, often described as the 'Cambridge triumvirate', were to work together on various projects over the next forty years.

During his undergraduate years, Hort came to question the evangelical tradition in which he had been raised. The liberal air breathed at Rugby was reinforced by other influences, among which were the writings of Samuel Taylor Coleridge; the Oxford Movement (from which he derived a 'high' view of the church and ministry); and, above all, the writings and friendship of F. D. Maurice. He first met Maurice in 1850 and through him came into contact with the early group of Christian socialists, among whom were Charles Kingsley, Thomas Hughes, and J. M. Ludlow. Hort took a lively interest in the movement of 1848–54, and though he himself could not accept the Christian socialist position he remained a candid friend of the movement. He and Maurice soon became close friends, and he was permanently influenced by Maurice's distinctive theological outlook, his quest for 'unity', and his independence from theological schools and parties.

Early career Hort held his fellowship at Trinity from 1852 to 1857, using the opportunity to read widely and thoroughly and becoming involved in the broader life of the university. In June 1851 he had joined the famous Apostles club, through which he came into contact with distinguished men from a variety of disciplines. In October 1852 he became president of the union, a recognition of his frequent contributions to union debates. Some of his contemporaries felt at this stage in his life that he was destined for a scientific career. He was already reviewing books in the *Annals of Botany*, and he examined for the natural science tripos in 1855. For all his versatility, however, two areas of study were becoming of special concern to him. One was the text of the New Testament: it was in this period that he and Westcott resolved to undertake joint editorship of a critical edition of the New Testament in Greek, a project which was to engage them for the next twenty-eight years. The other was early church history: he read widely in early Christian apologetics and edited the Hulsean prize essay written by his friend, Henry Mackenzie, entitled 'The beneficial influence of the Christian clergy on European progress in the first ten centuries'. Another interest was editing, with Lightfoot and J. E. B. Mayor, the *Journal of Classical and Sacred Philology*. This was the period of his life when Hort began the habit of sitting up far into the night to study, which was to have permanent effects on his health.

In 1853 F. D. Maurice was expelled from his chair at King's College, London, for his unorthodox views on eternal punishment. Hort had written to Maurice on this very issue four years earlier, expressing his own doubts and misgivings about the doctrine. In the controversy which ensued, he aligned himself totally with Maurice, defending him publicly, and supporting him vigorously in private correspondence. Two years later, he was actively involved in the foundation of the Working Men's College in Cambridge. This was modelled on the famous London college, of which Maurice, still active in London as chaplain of Lincoln's Inn, was now principal.

Marriage and priesthood Hort had decided to enter the church during his last year at Rugby, and he was ordained deacon at Cuddesdon, near Oxford, in 1854, and priest at Ely Cathedral in 1856. In the same year he contributed to a collection entitled *Cambridge Essays* his 'Essay on S. T. Coleridge', the fruit of some ten years' reading of Coleridge's work. This was one of the earliest attempts to interpret the thought of the poet-philosopher, who was to be seen as a seminal thinker in the twentieth century.

In June 1857 Hort married Fanny Holland, the daughter of Thomas Holland of Heighington, near Lincoln. They had five sons, one of whom died in infancy, and two daughters. Marriage meant the forfeiture of his fellowship, so Trinity presented him with the living of St Ippolyts-cum-Great Wymondley, near Hitchin, where he spent the next fifteen years. He threw himself wholeheartedly into the life of a double rural parish and was conscientious in his pastoral duties. His habitual shyness and reserve, however, made such work peculiarly difficult. Preparation of sermons was also a problem; all his life he found it hard to express himself in work prepared for public utterance or publication. The conviction grew that the life of a parish priest was not his true vocation.

The outcome of all this was that he suffered a nervous breakdown after just two years at St Ippolyts, and he was compelled on medical advice to give up parish work altogether between 1863 and 1865, spending the winters in Cheltenham and the summers in the Alps. When he eventually came back to the parish his mind turned increasingly towards Cambridge and a return to academic life.

New Testament criticism During these parish years Hort found academic work therapeutic, and he became involved in a number of projects. In 1860 he joined with Westcott and Lightfoot in another ambitious venture, a commentary scheme covering the whole of the New Testament. The aim was to provide a new type of commentary, accepting the demands of historical criticism yet recognizing that the New Testament documents were written 'from faith to faith'. Hort took the synoptic gospels, the non-Pauline literature, and Revelation, but produced very little: three fragments were published posthumously. Another scheme involved contributing a number of articles, chiefly on the early Gnostics, to Smith's *Dictionary of Christian Antiquities*. In 1870 Hort joined the New Testament Revision Company, an enterprise which was to consume a great deal of his time and energy over the next decade. The year 1871 was an 'annus mirabilis', during which Hort was both the examiner in the natural science tripos and the Hulsean lecturer at Cambridge. The lectures were published posthumously, as *The Way, the Truth, and the Life* (1893), constituting Hort's only purely theological work, in which he reflected upon the theological controversies of the 1860s—the 'Essays and reviews' and 'Origin of species' debates—in the light of the words of Jesus in John 14: 5–6. Some would regard this as his most important book, the only one which exhibited his lifelong concern for Christian apologetics and theology. Two volumes of his sermons preached at St Ippolyts were published posthumously: *Village Sermons* (1897) and *Village Sermons in Outline* (1900). These showed the influence of Maurice, which was also evident in Hort's awareness of being theologically unorthodox, apparent in his letters at this time.

University teaching The inevitable return to Cambridge and academic life came in 1872, when Hort was elected to a fellowship and lectureship in theology at Emmanuel College. A cause of particular satisfaction to him was that he was now joining his friends Lightfoot and Westcott who were, respectively, Hulsean and regius professors of divinity in the university. He moved into 6 St Peter's Terrace, Cambridge, which was to be his home for the rest of his life, and only a few doors away from Westcott. Another near neighbour was Maurice, now Knightbridge professor of moral philosophy at Cambridge. Sadly, Maurice died a few days after Hort had moved in. Hort attended his funeral in London and preached a memorial sermon in St Edward's Church, where Maurice had been incumbent, the following Sunday. Hort's wide interests and reputation for accurate scholarship meant that he was now in demand for numerous university committees and syndicates, and in 1878 he became a member of the council of the university senate. His conscientiousness in attendance meant that a great deal of his time was absorbed in such work.

During his six years at Emmanuel Hort lectured to students on New Testament subjects and on patristics. Among the former were James and Revelation 1–3, work on which was to be incorporated into his fragmentary commentaries on those books which were part of his contribution to the New Testament commentary scheme. There was also a fragment on 1 Peter. In 1876 Hort published his *Two Dissertations*, for which he obtained the degrees of BD and DD in 1875. The first was a minutely detailed examination of the reading *monogenēs Theos* ('only begotten God', John 1:18) in its scriptural context and in tradition, an exercise in the textual critical method he had been evolving in his work with Westcott. The second was an examination of the Constantinopolitan and other Eastern creeds of the fourth century—an essay on early church history and doctrine. The book was well received by scholars and contributed to Hort's growing reputation within the university.

In 1878 Hort was elected to the Hulsean professorship of divinity, a post he held for the next nine years. Now, for just one year, the triumvirate of Westcott, Lightfoot, and Hort were divinity professors together; Westcott was regius professor and Lightfoot was Lady Margaret professor, and the three names were inextricably linked. The combination was short-lived, however, for in 1879 Lightfoot was offered the see of Durham.

Principal scholarship In 1881 two of the major tasks in which Hort had been involved over the previous two decades were completed: the *Text of the Greek New Testament* appeared on 12 May, and the English Revised Version New Testament was published on 17 May. The 'Introduction' and 'Appendix' to the *Text* followed on 4 September. Both publications provoked public debate and controversy. The publication of the *Text* began a new era in textual study: building on the work of earlier textual scholars, Westcott and Hort had placed the study of the Greek New Testament on clear scientific principles. In the concise and lucid introduction Hort set out the basic principles of textual criticism and identified four principal types of text: Syrian, Western, Alexandrian, and neutral. The latter (seen most clearly in Codex Vaticanus and Codex Sinaiticus) preserved the purest, most reliable text, whereas the Syrian (the *textus receptus*) was rejected as a late, corrupt text. This was a radical solution to the textual problem of the New Testament, and it was immediately attacked by conservative scholars who defended the *textus receptus*. The Westcott and Hort text had been used in the meetings of the panel producing the Revised Version New Testament. Publication of this also provoked controversy, partly because of the 'modern' English, but also because the new text was adopted in sixty-four places in preference to other texts. Hort attended 319 out of the 363 meetings which took place over the ten years, and such conscientiousness took its toll on his health; he later claimed that he had never recovered from the strain of the revision, which involved defending his textual position. Like

the *Text*, the Revised Version was a major achievement, an anticipation of the many modern translations made in the twentieth century. When the work on the New Testament was completed, Hort was asked to join a panel producing a revised Apocrypha, and he joined Westcott and W. F. Moulton in preparing the revised version of the Wisdom of Solomon and 2 Maccabees.

In 1887 Hort was elected to the Lady Margaret professorship of divinity, a post he held until his death. His reputation as a scholar now stood at its height. His achievements in textual and translation work were widely recognized, and he received honorary degrees from the universities of Dublin (1888) and Durham (1890); bad health obliged him to decline a similar offer from the University of Oxford. His stature was acknowledged by American and German scholars and in 1889 William Sanday, biblical scholar at Oxford, claimed that Hort was the greatest scholar in England or Germany. Contemporaries recall his striking appearance at this time: the keen, spare face, the piercing eyes, the prematurely white beard, moustache, and whiskers, and the broad forehead. His lectures were not popular with undergraduates, for his method was too austere. He would take almost a whole term to introduce a subject, for instance. He was always careful not to over-influence his students. One recalled that 'he seemed to regard the formation of opinion as a very sacred thing' (Robinson and Ramsay, 69). To another, who asked him to recommend books to help him study the synoptic problem, his answer was: 'I should advise you to take your Greek New Testament, and get your own view of the facts first of all' (ibid., 69).

During his final years, Hort's lecture courses included coverage of two important subjects which became the focus of two books after his death: *Judaistic Christianity* (1894) gave his response to the theories of the Tübingen school and F. C. Baur, who argued for a second-century date for a number of New Testament books. Hort, like Westcott and Lightfoot, argued that the New Testament documents belonged to the first rather than the second century. *The Christian Ecclesia* (1897), one of Hort's most significant works, offered a survey of the history and development of the church in the New Testament. Its clarity and objectivity make it perhaps the supreme example of Hort's capacity for working in a 'dry light', but some of its conclusions upset high-churchmen.

Last years and death The final years brought increasing ill health and the break-up of the triumvirate: Lightfoot died on 20 December 1889, and Westcott was appointed to succeed him as bishop of Durham, leaving Hort the survivor of the three at Cambridge. Hort preached Westcott's consecration sermon in Westminster Abbey on 1 May 1890, but the strain of preparing for this contributed to a breakdown in health, which rendered him a semi-invalid for the last two years of his life. He gave his last lecture in April 1892, and went to Switzerland for the summer. For a time there was an improvement, but a further deterioration forced him to return home in September. His condition slowly weakened. His last piece of work was the article on Lightfoot for the *Dictionary of National Biography*, which exhausted him as had the consecration sermon for Westcott two years earlier. He died on 30 November 1892 at his home at St Peter's Terrace, Cambridge. The funeral took place on 6 December in the chapel of Emmanuel College, and he was buried in Mill Road cemetery, Cambridge.

Final assessment Hort's name will always be linked with those of Lightfoot and Westcott, with whom he shared much of his life's work, yet his churchmanship, theology, and exegesis were distinctive. In his isolation from the ecclesiastical parties of his time, and in his awareness of being unorthodox theologically and in textual matters, the influence of F. D. Maurice may be detected. He is an important link with the twentieth-century rediscovery of Maurice. A hundred years after his death, Hort's weaknesses were more apparent than they were to his contemporaries: the failure to concentrate his interests; the perfectionism which inhibited publication or public utterance; and the neglect, shared by Westcott and Lightfoot, of the Old Testament and the gospels. Yet it is clear that he was a major figure in the Victorian church; he was not merely a textual critic and New Testament scholar, but a church historian, a scientist, a philosopher, and, above all, a theologian who was deeply involved in some of the central theological issues of the nineteenth century. He was one of the last of the 'Renaissance men', before knowledge became fragmented into specialisms.

GRAHAM A. PATRICK

Sources A. F. Hort, *Life and letters of Fenton John Anthony Hort*, 2 vols. (1896) · *DNB* · G. A. Patrick, *F. J. A. Hort: eminent Victorian* (1988) · E. G. Rupp, *Hort and the Cambridge tradition* (1968) · I. M. Bubb, 'The theology of F. J. A. Hort in relation to nineteenth-century thought', PhD diss., University of Manchester, 1956 · G. A. Patrick, 'A study of the writings of F. J. A. Hort, and an assessment of him as a biblical scholar', PhD diss., U. Lond., 1978 · J. A. Robinson and W. M. Ramsay, 'The late Professor Hort', *Expositor*, 7 (1893) · W. M. Sanday, 'The future of English theology', *Contemporary Review*, 56 (1889) · W. M. Sanday, 'The life and letters of F. J. A. Hort', *American Journal of Theology*, 1 (1897) · T. B. Strong, 'Dr Hort's life and works', *Journal of Theological Studies*, 1 (1899–1900) · J. M. Creed, 'The study of the New Testament', *Journal of Theological Studies*, 42 (1941)

Archives CUL, selections from his theological corresp., Add. MS 6597 · CUL, New Testament letters, 1, Add. MS 6946 | BL, corresp. with Macmillans, Add. MS 55094 · Bodl. Oxf., corresp. of Mark Pattison, MSS 52, 54 · JRL, corresp. with Mrs S. P. Tregelles · U. Durham L., letters to J. B. Lightfoot

Likenesses G. P. Jacomb-Hood, oils, 1891, divinity school, Cambridge · G. P. Jacomb-Hood, oils, second version, 1891, Emmanuel College, Cambridge [*see illus.*] · G. P. Jacomb-Hood, oils, Trinity Cam.

Wealth at death £21,247 13s. 6d.: resworn probate, Jan 1894, *CGPLA Eng. & Wales* (1893)

Hort, Josiah (*c.*1674–1751), Church of Ireland archbishop of Tuam, was the son of John Hort of Marshfield, Gloucestershire. From 1690 to 1695 he was educated at the academy for nonconformist ministers kept by Thomas Rowe, apparently in Little Britain, London. It would appear that Hort was assisted in his studies by an exhibition from the Presbyterian Fund. Isaac Watts, one of Hort's fellow students and a lifelong friend and correspondent, described him as 'the first genius in the academy', and dedicated to

him his paraphrase from Martial in 1694. On the completion of his studies, Hort is said to have spent some time as pastor of a dissenting congregation at Newbury, but the records of the two nonconformist congregations there fail to support this. The antiquary William Cole mentions a report that Hort was a Presbyterian teacher at Soham, Cambridgeshire, while, according to Jerom Murch, Hort was assistant minister at Marshfield. However, he soon afterwards conformed to the Church of England and entered Clare College, Cambridge, in April 1704; he left Cambridge without a degree in 1705. In the same year he was ordained deacon by Bishop Moore of Norwich, and priest by Bishop Simon Patrick of Ely. He was for some time chaplain to John Hampden, MP for Buckinghamshire, and held in succession three benefices in Buckinghamshire.

In 1709 Hort went to Ireland as chaplain to the lord lieutenant, the earl of Wharton. In 1710 he was nominated by the crown to the parish of Kilskyre, diocese of Meath; as the patronage of the benefice was disputed he received no profits from it for seven years. When in 1717 the case was decided in Hort's favour, on appeal to the British House of Lords, he resigned his English benefice. In 1718 he became dean of Cloyne and rector of Louth; in 1720 he became dean of Ardagh, and on 26 February 1721 he was consecrated as bishop of Ferns and Leighlin. Archbishop William King of Dublin refused to take part in Hort's consecration as bishop because Hort, in his letters patent, was erroneously styled DD. King, however, issued a commission for the purpose; this action gave rise to the rumour that Hort had never received holy orders in the Church of England. According to Bishop Henry Downes it was rumoured at the time that the archbishops of Armagh, Dublin, and Tuam petitioned George I to recall Hort's nomination, probably on account of his early connection with nonconformists. Hort was translated to the united sees of Kilmore and Ardagh on 27 July 1727 and, retaining Ardagh *in commendam*, to the archbishopric of Tuam on 27 January 1742. About 1738 his voice failed from overexertion, and he was disabled from preaching.

On 19 February 1725 Hort married Elizabeth (*d.* 1745), daughter of the Hon. William Fitzmaurice, brother of the twentieth Lord Kerry and uncle of the twenty-first lord and first earl of Kerry. Hort had four sons and five daughters. His second son, John Hort (1731–1807), was appointed English consul-general at Lisbon in 1767, was created a baronet in the same year, and died on 23 October 1807. In 1729 Hort published his *Charge to the Clergy of Kilmore*; another charge, delivered at his primary visitation of the diocese of Tuam, was published in 1742 and was republished in the *Clergyman's Instructor* (1807). His *Volume of Sixteen Sermons* appeared in 1788 and was later issued in a second edition; many of his sermons were also printed separately. Hort died on 14 December 1751 and was buried in St George's Chapel, Dublin.

WILLIAM REYNELL, *rev.* J. FALVEY

Sources B. Bradshaw and others, 'Bishops of the Church of Ireland from 1534', *A new history of Ireland*, ed. T. W. Moody and others, 9: *Maps, genealogies, lists* (1984), 392–438 · H. Cotton, *Fasti ecclesiae*

Hibernicae, 6 vols. (1845–78) • R. Mant, *History of the Church of Ireland*, 2 vols. (1840) • Burtchaell & Sadleir, *Alum. Dubl.*, 2nd edn • J. J. Falvey, 'The Church of Ireland episcopate in the eighteenth century', MA diss., University College, Cork, 1995 • R. J. Hayes, ed., *Manuscript sources for the history of Irish civilisation*, 11 vols. (1965)

Archives NA Ire., M.2815 | BL, Sloane MS 4075 • JRL, papers of his daughter Lady Elizabeth Caldwell, incl. Hort family papers • NA Ire., M.2815

Likenesses A. Miller, mezzotint, pubd 1752 (after J. Wills), NG Ire.

Horton, (James) Africanus Beale (1835–1883), army medical officer and political economist, was born in Gloucester village, Sierra Leone, on 1 June 1835, the son of James Horton (*c.*1791–1867), a carpenter, and his wife, Nancy. Both were of Igbo descent, members of the receptive community, liberated there from slavery. Horton grew up at a time when skin colour was no barrier to advancement in Sierra Leone. He was educated in Freetown, at the Church Missionary Society Grammar School and Fourah Bay College, and, with two others, was chosen in 1855 by the War Office to train in Britain as an army medical officer. He studied at King's College, London (1855–8), then at Edinburgh University, where he took an MD in 1859.

Horton served for twenty years as a medical officer in west Africa, chiefly in the Gold Coast, during which time he participated in two of the wars against the kingdom of Asante, acted from time to time as an administrative officer, and undertook medical and geological research. In 1859 he published his doctoral thesis, a medical topography of west Africa, and later issued three more medical works—a plea for much-needed sanitary reform in west Africa, a monograph on the Guinea worm, and a textbook of tropical medicine (which went into two editions). His *Political Economy of British West Africa* appeared in 1865 and was followed by his best-known work, *West African Countries and Peoples* (1867, reprinted 1969). Subtitled *A Vindication of the African Race*, the latter begins with a refutation of contemporary racial theories, and goes on with Horton's own blueprint for the future evolution of west Africa, including substantial expenditure on education and economic development, on lines that foreshadow those followed at decolonization in the 1950s and 1960s. In 1870 he published *Letters on the Political Condition of the Gold Coast* (reprinted 1970).

Horton retired in 1880 with the rank of surgeon-major, the then equivalent of lieutenant-colonel. Having prospected for gold, he had obtained mining concessions in the Gold Coast from local rulers, and surveyed a railway route to connect them with the coast. Then, after returning to Freetown, he formed a mining company with London backers and opened a bank. But the exertions of his years of active service, coupled with constant attacks of malaria, had weakened his health, and on 15 October 1883, aged only forty-eight, he died at his home, Horton Hall, Gloucester Street, Freetown. He was buried the following day in the city's Circular Road cemetery.

Horton was twice married: on 27 March 1862 to Fannie Marietta Pratt (1843–1865), also of Igbo origin, and on 29 May 1875 to Selina Beatrice Elliot (1851–1910), from one of the Freetown settler families, with whom he had two daughters. His estate, from which he had hoped to endow a technical college, was largely dissipated after his death in lawsuits between members of his wives' families. A memorial tablet was erected to him in St George's Cathedral, Freetown. In the eighty years after his death, which saw the triumph of the racial policies he had condemned, his memory was forgotten. However, it was revived in the 1960s, since when Horton has been hailed as one of the precursors of mid-century African nationalism.

CHRISTOPHER FYFE

Sources C. Fyfe, *Africanus Horton: west African scientist and patriot* (1972) • D. Nicol, *Africanus Horton: the dawn of nationalism in modern Africa* (1969) • W. Johnston, *Roll of army medical service* (1917), no. 5903 • *African Times* (22 June 1867) • *Sierra Leone Weekly News* (16 July 1910) • *West African Reporter* (26 March 1881) • *The Watchman and West African Record* (20 Oct 1883) • admissions registers, Church Missionary Society Grammar School, Freetown, Sierra Leone; Fourah Bay College, Freetown, Sierra Leone; King's Lond.; U. Edin.

Archives PRO, CO MSS • U. Birm. L., Church Missionary Society archives

Likenesses photograph, repro. in T. J. Thompson, *The jubilee and centenary volume of Fourah Bay College, Freetown, Sierra Leone* (1930), 148

Wealth at death £3515 5*s*. 6*d*.—estate in England • £25,000—house property in Freetown and investments purchased at the London Stock Exchange: PRO

Horton, Christiana (1698/9–1756), actress, was identified by the author of *The History of the English Stage* as 'descended from a very good Family in Wiltshire' (Betterton, 163), and according to the same source started performing 'when but a Child' with Booker's strolling troupe. The *Dramatic Miscellanies* records that she married young, to a musician, who treated her 'very brutally' (Davies, 103). In 1713 she appeared as Marcia in Addison's *Cato* with 'a company of miserable strollers' at Windsor during Queen Anne's stay. It is said that her superior performance and beauty, coupled with the recommendation of powerful supporters, resulted in her engagement at Drury Lane. Alternatively, the *History* suggests that Barton Booth saw 'her act the Part of Cupid, in a Droll called *Cupid and Psyche*, in Southwark-Fair, 1714, and being pleased with her Performance, he brought her on the Drury-Lane Theatre' (Betterton, 163).

However Mrs Horton arrived at Drury Lane, her first recorded appearance was as Melinda in George Farquhar's *The Recruiting Officer* on 21 September 1714. Records for the season list her parts as Amy in Richard Brome's *The Jovial Crew* and Dorinda in William Mountfort's *Greenwich Park*. Mrs Horton remained at Drury Lane for the next twenty years, receiving a 'moderate salary' and annual solo benefits from 1715–16 onwards (Davies, 104). Noted for her beauty, she specialized in comedy and was particularly successful as the coquette, taking such roles as Millamant or Belinda in William Congreve's *The Old Bachelor*, although Henry Fielding thought her voice unsurpassed for tragic parts. Her confidence as a performer is illustrated by an incident in 1725 when she played Phillis in Richard Steele's *The Conscious Lovers*, in place of Mrs

Younger. The production was almost halted by hissing, until 'she advanced to the front of the stage, and boldly addressed the pit: "Gentlemen, what do you mean? What displeases you; my acting or my person?" This shew of spirit recovered the spectators into good humour' (Davies, 104). She was hailed by Booth and Wilks as the only fitting successor to Ann Oldfield.

In 1733 Horton was a complainant with Theophilus Cibber about the management of Drury Lane, and the following year she moved to Covent Garden. Here she took on several new parts for the season, as well as reprising such familiar roles as the Countess of Rutland in John Banks's *The Unhappy Favourite*, Lady Townly in John Vanbrugh's *The Provoked Husband*, and Mrs Sullen in Farquhar's *The Beaux' Stratagem*. Additional inducement for the move might have been the salary John Rich was offering: £250 for 1735–6, supplemented in following years with the proceeds from a spring benefit. By the 1740–41 season she was costing Rich £1 10s. per day, with a charge-free benefit of £159 17s. Rich engaged Hannah Pritchard, at the cheaper rate of £200 per annum, to play 'in the room of the said Mrs Horton in all her parts'. However, Mrs Horton had not 'engaged herself to act in the other theatre' (Vaughan, 28–30), and the two actresses shared out the leading parts between themselves. Fleetwood did engage Mrs Horton at the other theatre for the 1743–4 season, but her popularity was waning. Davies compared her acting unfavourably with Mrs Pritchard's natural and easy dialogue. Back at Covent Garden by 1746, Horton received only £3 per week, which by 1749 was reduced to £1.

'Between Mrs Woffington and Mrs Pritchard she suffered shipwreck', Rosenfeld notes. After retiring from London in 1750, Christiana Horton played Cleopatra and Estifania in John Fletcher's *Rule a Wife and Have a Wife*, among other roles, at Simpson's Theatre, Bath. Her last recorded performance in London was for her shared benefit on 20 April 1752. She received benefits from the Drury Lane company during the spring of the following two years and in 1756, although she did not perform again. She died on 4 December 1756 at the age of fifty-seven. It is only in her will that we have a record of her daughter, Penelope Wolseley, to whom she left her whole estate. Mrs Horton was buried on 8 December at St Giles-in-the-Fields, London. J. MILLING

Sources Highfill, Burnim & Langhans, *BDA* · T. Betterton, [W. Oldys and others], *The history of the English stage* (1741), 163–4 · T. Davies, *Dramatic miscellanies*, 1 (1784), 103–5 · E. L. Avery, ed., *The London stage, 1660–1800*, pt 2: *1700–1729* (1960) · S. Rosenfeld, *Strolling players and drama in the provinces, 1660–1765* (1939), 185–98 · A. Vaughan, *Born to please: Hannah Pritchard, actress, 1711–1768* (1979), 27–31 · A. H. Scouten, ed., *The London stage, 1660–1800*, pt 3: *1729–1747* (1961)

Horton, Sir Max Kennedy (1883–1951), naval officer, was born at the Maelog Lake Hotel, Anglesey, on 29 November 1883, the second son of the family of four of Robert Joseph Angel Horton, a member of the London stock exchange, and his wife, Esther Maud, daughter of William Goldsmid, also a stockbroker. In 1898 Max Horton joined the training

Sir Max Kennedy Horton (1883–1951), by Walter Stoneman, 1933

ship *Britannia* where he played for the first eleven at football and won the middle-weight boxing prize. The technical side of the navy appealed to him strongly and while a senior midshipman his thoughts turned to the new submarine branch, where in addition to the attraction of intricate machinery there would be plenty of adventure and scope for initiative. At the age of twenty-two he was given command of A.1, a submarine of 200 tons used for experimental work. He later commanded C.8, and in 1910 returned to general service for two years in the cruiser *Duke of Edinburgh* where he was awarded the Board of Trade silver medal for heroism in saving life when the P. & O. liner *Delhi* was wrecked in a gale off Cape Spartel.

In the manoeuvres of 1912 Horton, while in command of D.6, penetrated the Firth of Forth at periscope depth and torpedoed two 'hostile' warships which were above the bridge, an operation which placed him in the front rank of submarine commanders. On the outbreak of war in 1914 he was in command of E.9, a new ocean-going submarine; he took her into the fortified harbour of Heligoland; next, while on patrol outside the entrance, he sank the cruiser *Hela*, the first enemy warship to be destroyed by a British submarine, and then the destroyer S.116 a few miles from her own coast. For these achievements in the first two months of war he was appointed to the DSO and recommended for early promotion.

In October 1914 Horton, who was promoted commander at the end of the year, took E.9 into the dangerous waters of the Baltic where he sank two destroyers, torpedoed a large German cruiser, and with other British submarines disrupted the Swedish iron ore supplies to Germany. In December 1915, although the British ambassador to Russia asked specifically that he might remain in the Baltic, he was recalled to England to command J.6, a new submarine of 1200 tons. For his services to Russia he was awarded the order of St Vladimir with swords, the order of St Ann with swords and diamonds, and the order of St George. The French government made him a chevalier of the Légion d'honneur and in 1917 he was given a bar to his DSO. Always prominent in matters of design and experiment, Horton was in 1917 given command of M.1, a large submarine carrying a 12 inch gun. Her trials were successful and she was used operationally, but never fully tested in war.

In the spring of 1920, after another year in the Baltic, this time in command of a submarine flotilla with the delicate task of assisting the Baltic states against Bolshevik aggression, Horton received a second bar to his DSO and in June was promoted to captain at the age of thirty-six. As a young submarine commander Horton had the reputation of being 'a bit of a pirate' and also a gambler who played high hands at bridge and poker, but he now seemed to withdraw from his companions. He loved power and used it mercilessly, although he was tolerant when people were prepared to admit their mistakes as he admitted his own. Influenced possibly by what he had seen in Russia he feared that industrial unrest might spread to the navy and, since the incentive of war had gone, he demanded the highest standard of discipline from officers and men. In 1922 he was appointed to command a flotilla of large, fast, steam-driven submarines of the K class. They were clumsy and dangerous, and great skill was required when diving under a screen of destroyers to attack battleships moving at high speed. Horton, having no sympathy with the idea that wartime risks were not justified in peace, constantly practised his flotilla in this form of attack, impressing upon his commanders that sheer efficiency was the true safeguard against accidents, and that tolerance of inefficiency was dangerous. 'In submarines', he said, 'there is no margin for mistakes, you are either alive or dead' (Chalmers, 27).

After four years of shore service, at the Admiralty as assistant director of mobilization and at Portsmouth as chief of staff to Sir Roger Keyes, Horton went to the Mediterranean for two years in command of the battleship *Resolution*. In October 1932 he was promoted rear-admiral and he flew his flag in the battleship *Barham* in 1934 to 1935 as second in command of the Home Fleet where his duties were mainly administrative. He was appointed CB in 1934 and in 1935 returned to the Mediterranean in command of the 1st cruiser squadron, a powerful force of eight fast, heavily armed cruisers. In a period which included the Abyssinian crisis and the outbreak of the Spanish Civil War he brought his squadron to a high standard of efficiency, but his ruthlessness and blunt manner alienated him from some senior officers who maintained that equally good results could have been obtained by less rigorous methods.

Horton was promoted vice-admiral in 1936 but when in the following year he was appointed to command the Reserve Fleet many people thought that it would be his last appointment. Horton was in no way disappointed: the responsibility for bringing this heterogeneous collection of 140 ships to a state of readiness for war strongly appealed to him and by midsummer 1939 the whole fleet was ready to sail. He had been promoted KCB in the new year honours and on the outbreak of war took command of the northern patrol, responsible for intercepting merchant ships of all descriptions between Iceland and Scotland, thus enforcing a distant blockade of Germany. This dull routine was quite unsuited to a man of Horton's energy and temperament and in January 1940 he took up with alacrity the post of flag officer submarines, establishing his headquarters at Swiss Cottage where he could be in close touch with the Admiralty and also the headquarters of Coastal Command. At the end of March Horton was convinced, contrary to official opinion, that the Germans were about to invade Norway. He concentrated all his submarines in the southern approaches to the Norwegian coast with orders to sink at sight. A week later, when the invading forces appeared, his dispositions proved so effective that twenty-one enemy transports and supply ships were sent to the bottom. His submarines also sank two cruisers and severely damaged a pocket battleship. The battle cruiser *Gneisenau* was put out of action in June when it was badly needed for the invasion of England and at the end of the year the Admiralty wrote to Horton that 'The high percentage of successful submarine attacks, and the low number of material failures, contributed a remarkable achievement' (Chalmers, 103). In October 1940 Horton refused the command of the Home Fleet mainly because he would not have control of the various types of aircraft which he considered necessary. He knew that he was throwing away his chances of becoming an admiral of the fleet, but felt that he should use to the full his experience of submarine warfare. Later in the Mediterranean the submarines which he had trained and administered helped to bring Rommel's army to a standstill by wrecking transports and disrupting seaborne supplies. He also encouraged the development of midget submarines and human torpedoes.

As a submariner, Horton believed that German U-boats would be used ruthlessly in large numbers to prevent supplies coming across the Atlantic, and so reduce the army and air force to a state of impotence. He urged strongly that the Royal Air Force should share with the navy the responsibility for anti-submarine defence and both services be trained to co-operate in the use of the latest weapons. In November 1942 when the Atlantic lifeline was stretched to its limit and the U-boats were increasing their stranglehold, Horton was appointed commander-in-chief of the western approaches with responsibility for ensuring not only that the people of Britain should be fed, but also that a constant flow of troops and military supplies should be maintained in safety. Although 700,000 tons of shipping had been sunk by U-boats in November,

Horton was not dismayed. The German submarine commander-in-chief, Admiral Dönitz, had found the soft spots in the allied defence; Horton knew where to look for them in the U-boat attack. More than a hundred U-boats were working in packs in mid-Atlantic where they hoped to be out of range of allied aircraft. He told the Admiralty that the best way to defend the convoys was to reinforce their escorts with highly trained and speedy support groups working in co-operation with very long-range aircraft, and free to take the offensive against the U-boats. As a result of his representations sixteen warships were released from close escort duty; and, after being augmented by a destroyer flotilla from the Home Fleet in March 1943, all were formed into five support groups. Meanwhile, seven squadrons of very long-range and long-range aircraft had been allocated to Coastal Command for use against the U-boats, and in addition aircraft-carriers (converted merchant ships) joined Horton's command. He refused to rush his forces into action until they had been fully trained to work together, and in addition to other measures established a school of sea–air co-operation in Northern Ireland. In April 1943 the combined plan took shape: a main offensive by naval and air striking forces to destroy the U-boats in mid-Atlantic, and a subsidiary offensive by shore-based air forces to destroy U-boats near their bases in the Bay of Biscay. Surprise was achieved and success was complete. The brunt of the battle was borne by British and Canadian sea and air forces under Horton's command, the destruction of U-boats being shared equally by warships and aircraft. The spirit of the enemy was broken, and at the end of May Dönitz withdrew his U-boats from mid-Atlantic. From then onwards, Horton successfully countered all attempts by the enemy to resume the offensive. Acknowledging his request to retire at the end of the war in order to facilitate promotion, the Admiralty wrote to Horton: 'Never has this country endured so dangerous a threat to its existence, and with the overcoming of that danger your name and that of the Western Approaches Command will ever be associated' (Chalmers, 251).

A great admiral in the tradition of St Vincent rather than of Nelson, Horton had a technical knowledge and genius for detail which never obscured his eye for the main issues: he could see the wood and the trees, and his driving force saw to it that the policies he initiated were always carried through. He said himself that he could be as obstinate as two mules when he knew that he was right. Many were thankful that some of his energies were used up on the golf course to which he repaired every afternoon, returning to fight the battle of the Atlantic at night. Ruthless and intolerant of inefficiency he yet possessed an understanding and kindness of heart not always realized. He was famous for the accuracy of his hunches, not altogether attributable to knowledge and experience even at the service of a brilliant mind. He admitted that he prayed every night for guidance and foresight, and for the safe-keeping of his ships. Part Jewish, he was a deeply religious man who had leanings towards, but did not join, the Roman Catholic church. He was a perfectionist, completely repudiating half-measures, and this perhaps explains a great devotion to St Theresa of Lisieux which would have surprised his shipmates had they known of it. It was typical of Horton that they did not. He was an individualist who liked to keep sentiment away from his work and his social life apart from the navy. He passionately loved all that was beautiful, travelled as often as he could in Europe, was a devotee of opera, and had many friends in the theatrical world. His character was unusually complex and earned for him more admiration and criticism than falls to the lot of lesser men.

In June 1945 Horton was promoted GCB and in 1946 appointed Bath king of arms. The United States, France, the Netherlands, and Norway conferred upon him their highest honours and he received the honorary degree of LLD from the Queen's University, Belfast (1947). But apart from the freedom of Liverpool (1946) where he had had the headquarters of his command, no other British honour came to him. He died in London on 30 July 1951, having suffered from ill health brought on by the strain of the war and undergone five major operations. He was accorded a state funeral in Liverpool Cathedral, where a memorial to him was unveiled in 1957.

W. S. CHALMERS, *rev.*

Sources W. S. Chalmers, *Max Horton and the western approaches* (1954) · *His Majesty's submarines* (1945) [HMSO 222835 e.157] · *The battle of the Atlantic: the official account of the fight against the U-boats, 1939–1945*, Central Office of Information (1946) · S. W. Roskill, *The war at sea, 1939–1945*, 3 vols. in 4 (1954–61) · *The Times* (31 July 1951) · *WWW* · private information (1971) · personal knowledge (1971)
Archives FILM BFI NFTVA, news footage · IWM FVA, actuality footage
Likenesses W. Stoneman, photograph, 1933, NPG [*see illus.*] · O. Birley, oils, *c.*1945–1948, Royal Naval College, Greenwich · D. Wales-Smith, oils, NMM · J. Worsley, oils, Fort Blockhouse, Gosport

Horton, Percy Frederick (1897–1970), painter and art teacher, was born on 8 March 1897 at 38 Jersey Street, Brighton, Sussex, the eldest of the three sons of Percy Horton (1870–1937), bus conductor, and his wife, Ellen Marman (1866–1954). All three sons won scholarships to the Brighton municipal secondary school. Harry Horton (*b.* 1899), the middle son, became a schoolteacher and Ronald Horton (*b.* 1902), the youngest, became an artist and schoolteacher.

Percy Horton continued his studies at the Brighton School of Art from 1912 to 1916, again with a scholarship, passing the department of education drawing examination with distinction in 1914. As a student his political thinking developed into active support of socialism. He joined the Labour Party at the age of sixteen. His opposition to the First World War led him to join the No-Conscription Fellowship when conscription was introduced in 1916. There he met Lydia Sargent Smith (1886–1970x79), the daughter of George Smith, a Quaker and a prosperous corn merchant of Derbyshire. She was eleven years older than Horton, a suffragette, and one of the earliest policewomen. In 1916 she was engaged to Royle

Richmond, a conscientious objector who subsequently died in prison in December of that year. Horton and Lydia were married in 1921; they had one daughter, Kay Chaloner.

As a conscientious objector himself Horton applied for absolute exemption from any form of service which might have helped the war effort. His stand was unusual and was refused; and he was duly taken to his unit where his refusal to obey orders led to a court martial and prison. A cycle of three trials by courts martial and imprisonment ensued. He was sentenced to two years' hard labour in Calton prison, Edinburgh, the first three months being spent in solitary confinement. He remained in prison until November 1917, stitching mailbags, when he was taken to Edinburgh Hospital for an operation on his wrist. There he began to draw again, having access to materials. By then attitudes towards conscientious objectors were changing and Horton was among those who were released as being too unfit to withstand the regime of prison life. His drawings of nurses and patients drew the attention of the Scottish artist Edward Arthur Walton, and on being discharged from prison in April 1918 Walton offered Horton his home for a period of several months in which to convalesce.

After the war Horton continued his education at the Central School of Arts and Crafts in London, where he studied under Archibald Standish Hartrick and Francis Ernest Jackson from 1919 to 1920. He was the assistant art teacher at Rugby School until 1922, when he returned to the full-time study of painting. At the Central School he entered the department of education examination in painting, which he passed with distinction, and was consequently awarded a royal exhibition (only one per year was awarded) tenable at the Royal College of Art, London. There he studied with Henry Moore, Eric Ravilious, Edward Bawden, and Cyril Mahoney, becoming an associate on gaining a diploma with distinction in painting in 1924. Although prejudice against conscientious objectors meant that many schools would not employ him, the nonconformist traditions of Bishop's Stortford College enabled Horton to secure a part-time post as drawing-master.

In 1930 Horton was invited by William Rothenstein to join the teaching staff at the Royal College of Art, where he taught painting for the next nineteen years. He also taught at a working men's college, where he introduced life classes. The major influence on his work was that of Cézanne, whose paintings he had first seen in September 1919 at the exhibition 'Modern French Painting' at the Mansard Gallery in London. Horton's work, which uses the formal structure of Cézanne's perception-based realism, shows a humane concern for ordinary people whom the artist depicted with dignity in a range of social roles. Such works as *The Ironing Board* and *The Postman* (both priv. coll.) and *The Unemployed Man* (Sheffield City Art Galleries) are typical of his artistic, political, and social concerns. He joined the Artists' International Association (founded 1934), with whom he exhibited regularly, and became a member of their advisory council in 1941. During the Second World War Horton was commissioned by the War Artists' Advisory Committee to draw several portraits and paint *Blind Men Working on War Production, Lucas Factory, Birmingham* (1943, Imperial War Museum, London). When the Royal College of Art was evacuated to Ambleside, Westmorland, he divided his time between the Lake District (of which he made several paintings, and others of local people) and London. His strong opposition to fascism overcame conscientious objections to war and he joined the Home Guard.

In 1949 Horton was appointed master of drawing at the Ruskin School of Drawing at Oxford, where he remained until 1964. He executed many portraits of heads of houses at Oxford and Cambridge and in 1954 was commissioned by Exeter College, Oxford, to do a portrait of Roger Bannister after he had run his historic 4 minute mile. In 1948 he began renting a gamekeepers' tower on Lord Gage's estate, Firle Park, Sussex, which he used as a studio at weekends and during vacations, and more often after his retirement in 1964. Even after retirement he continued to teach two days a week at the Sir John Cass School, London, and at Hastings School of Art in Sussex, where he worked with Vincent Hines. Percy Horton died at St George's Hospital, Tooting, London, on 4 November 1970. Examples of his work are in the Tate collection, the Imperial War Museum, the National Portrait Gallery, the Ashmolean Museum, Oxford, and the Fitzwilliam Museum, Cambridge; and municipal galleries in Sheffield, Leeds, and Brighton.   PHILIP MORSBERGER, *rev.* JANET BARNES

Sources J. Barnes, *Percy Horton, 1897–1970: artist and absolutist* (1982) [exhibition catalogue, Sheffield City Art Galleries] · private information (2004) · *CGPLA Eng. & Wales* (1971)
Archives E. Sussex RO, personal, professional, and family records incl. sketchbooks and photos | Tate collection, corresp. with Lord Clark
Likenesses P. F. Horton, self-portrait, oils, c.1926, priv. coll. · P. F. Horton, self-portrait, oil on board, 1936, Arts Council of England collection · P. F. Horton, self-portrait, oil on paper, AM Oxf.
Wealth at death £7370: administration, 22 Feb 1971, *CGPLA Eng. & Wales*

Horton, Robert Forman (1855–1934), Congregational minister, was born in Egremont Place, St Pancras, London, on 18 September 1855, the second child and only son of Thomas Galland Horton (1828–1900), Congregational minister, and Sarah Ellen (1827–1873), second daughter of Robert Forman, hop merchant and maltster, of Derby. At the time of his birth his father was minister of Tonbridge Chapel, Euston Road, London. The family moved to Reading in 1857, and then to Wolverhampton, where T. G. Horton was minister of Queen Street Congregational Church from 1862 until 1876. In 1867 the young Horton entered Tettenhall proprietary school, which his father had helped to found as a school for the sons of nonconformists. Five years later, in the face of much criticism from fellow nonconformists, T. G. Horton sent his son to the (Anglican) public school at Shrewsbury, which he believed could provide a better preparation for the Oxford scholarship he hoped his son would win.

Robert Horton was duly awarded an open scholarship to

Robert Forman Horton (1855–1934), by Olive Edis, 1922

New College, Oxford, in 1874, and there joined the first generation of nonconformist students to whom Oxford degrees were now open without restriction. He had a brilliant undergraduate career: he gained firsts in both classical moderations (1875) and Greats (1878), was elected president of the union in 1877, and rowed for his college. In 1879 his college elected him as fellow and tutor in ancient and modern history.

During the next four years Horton divided his energies between teaching for his college, providing a forum for the nonconformist students now coming up to Oxford in increasing numbers, and preaching regularly at weekends to a new congregation gathered in Hampstead in north London, to which he had been introduced by his Oxford friend Cecil Curwen. As well as entering into the general college and university social and intellectual life, he was instrumental in the founding and leading of the Oxford University Nonconformists' Union, which flourished in the early 1880s and prepared the way for the founding of Mansfield College as a postgraduate nonconformist theological college in Oxford in 1886. When pressed to become the permanent minister of the Hampstead congregation, he faced a dilemma.

Horton's decision finally to leave the academic life of Oxford for full-time pastoral and preaching ministry in London was precipitated by the university congregation's vote to overturn convocation's decision to approve his nomination as examiner for the pass examinations paper 'The rudiments of faith and religion'. The thought of a nonconformist layman examining Anglicans in such an examination was too much for most of the Anglican clergy who formed the largest element in congregation. On 13 December 1883 Horton left Oxford for good. He was ordained on 17 January 1884 and began his full-time ministry to the congregation whose new church building, designed by Alfred Waterhouse, was opened in Lyndhurst Road, Hampstead, on 3 July 1884. His expressed desire to 'wear no clothes to distinguish me from my fellow Christians' was a gift to the caricaturist.

For the next forty-six years Horton exercised a notable ministry in London. At a time when nonconformists were at the height of their influence on political and religious life, he was regarded as an outstanding representative not only of Congregationalism but of nonconformity as a whole. With his dignified appearance and musical voice, he was a fine preacher; his sermons were evangelical in tone, intellectual in content, inspired by the missionary spirit, and challenging to social reform. He tried to bridge what he saw as the chasm developing between biblical scholars and the ordinary Bible reader (see *Inspiration and the Bible*, 1888). In 1893 he delivered the Lyman Beecher lectures at Yale University on the subject of preaching. They were published that year as *Verbum Dei*, and reissued in 1898 as *The Word of God*. There was a regular congregation of about 900 throughout most of his ministry. He built up a strong team of elders and deacons to share the work of ministry, and was unusually (for the time) supportive of the contribution of women (for some years he was a member of the council of Somerville College, Oxford). The church members included the staff of two Congregational theological colleges (Hackney and New colleges) and several other ministers out of pastoral charge, as well as many leading Congregational lay men and women. He refused many invitations to other spheres of work. He was elected chairman of the Congregational Union of England and Wales in 1903, and president of the National Free Church Council in 1905.

In the *Congregational Quarterly* (1926) Horton called for a meeting of 'Modern Free Churchmen' to present Christianity in a form equally removed 'from Romanism and from Fundamentalism', complementing the movement of Anglican Modern Churchmen; from this challenge there developed a series of annual theological conferences, in which he participated, and which did much to revitalize Congregational theology and churchmanship. His fifty books and pamphlets had wide circulation during his lifetime. Yale University awarded him an honorary DD.

Horton's closest friend during most of his life was Rosa Oakes (*née* Mellor), sister of one of his schoolfriends. He relied on her for emotional support, and from 1902 until 1910 Rosa Oakes and her husband shared his home. Eight years after Rosa Oakes's death, on 4 April 1918, at the age of sixty-two, he surprised his congregation and friends by marrying (Isabel) Violet Basden, thirty-six years his junior. They had one daughter, Genevieve. He retired in 1930, and died suddenly on 30 March 1934 at his home, Chesils, Christchurch Road, Hampstead. He was buried on 4 April. His wife died in November 1984.　　ELAINE KAYE

Sources A. Peel and J. A. R. Marriott, *Robert Forman Horton* (1937) · R. F. Horton, *An autobiography* (1917) · E. Neale, 'A type of Congregational ministry: R. F. Horton' (1855–1934) and Lyndhurst Road', *Journal of the United Reformed Church History Society*, 5 (1992–7), 215–31 · M. D. Johnson, *The dissolution of dissent, 1850–1918* (1987) · minute book of Oxford University Nonconformists' Union, Mansfield College, Oxford · J. Munson, *The nonconformists* (1991) · *Nonconformist and Independent* (10 March 1881) · *Nonconformist and Independent* (7 April 1881) · m. cert. · d. cert.

Archives DWL, Lyndhurst Road Congregational Church archive

Likenesses O. Edis, photograph, 1922, NPG [*see illus.*] · R. Haines, photograph, repro. in Horton, *An autobiography* · Langfier, photograph, repro. in Peel and Marriott, *Robert Forman Horton* · caricature, repro. in Peel and Marriott, *Robert Forman Horton*
Wealth at death £14,641 4s. 3d.: resworn probate, 14 May 1934, CGPLA Eng. & Wales

Horton, Sir Robert John Wilmot-, third baronet (1784–1841), politician and colonial governor, was born on 21 December 1784, the only son of Sir Robert Wilmot, second baronet, of Osmaston, Derbyshire, and his first wife, Juliana Elizabeth, the second daughter of John *Byron, a naval officer, and the widow of William Byron. The poet George Gordon Byron was his cousin. His mother died when he was three years old. He was educated at Eton College and at Christ Church, Oxford (BA 1806, MA 1815), where his closest friend was Reginald Heber (the future bishop of Calcutta) at Brasenose College. Wilmot was a serious student but fond of sport, an interest he maintained in his country gentleman persona throughout his life. On 1 September 1806 he married Anne Beatrix Horton (*d.* 1871), the daughter of Eusebius Horton of Catton Hall in Derbyshire, and the heir to a modest fortune. Between 1808 and 1825 they had eight children; one daughter died in 1811. In accordance with his father-in-law's will, Wilmot took the additional name of Horton by royal licence on 8 May 1823 to begin a new line of Wilmot-Hortons at Catton Hall. The house and its 1200-acre estate came into his possession with an annual income close to £2400 and a reputation for agricultural improvement and general estate welfare. It was an important support to his finances, which were never robust enough for his political and social aspirations. His wife was a renowned beauty and much admired, notably by George Canning. She inspired Byron's lines in the *Hebrew Melodies* which began

> She walks in Beauty, like the night
> Of cloudless climes and starry skies.

Her degree of intimacy with Byron was a matter of speculation and Byron was sometimes contemptuous of her husband. At the poet's death, Wilmot-Horton, under the instructions of Mrs Leigh, was made responsible for the burning of his memoirs. The manuscript had been given to Thomas Leigh, who ordered its destruction in John Murray's parlour in 1824. The episode led to acrimonious public discussion, though Wilmot-Horton acted honourably in the episode.

Early political career Wilmot-Horton nurtured intellectual and political ambitions and was not content with the role of country gentleman. He moved to London in November 1812 and immersed himself in political economy. He believed that education was the greatest civilizing influence available, and he wrote an article on the subject in the *Quarterly Review* in 1813. He also published a pamphlet in 1813 partly in support of Thomas Malthus, though he was critical of his predictions of demographic doom. He always aspired to dialogue with the political economists, the 'men of science', and he engaged the leaders in earnest theoretical debate for much of his life. His political views were moderately reformist but he was always anxious about the danger of generating social turmoil in the

Sir Robert John Wilmot-Horton, third baronet (1784–1841), by Richard James Lane, 1827 (after Joseph Slater)

process of reform. In 1814 he visited Paris. He took steps to enter parliament in 1815 through the Trentham interest in Staffordshire but was defeated, partly from a lack of funds. With the encouragement of Canning he eventually, in 1818, succeeded at Newcastle under Lyme, where the election expenses amounted to 6000 guineas. It was an insecure and expensive constituency and Wilmot-Horton, lacking a sufficient personal fortune, was always nervous of election contests. He was never a popular member but was returned unopposed in 1820; thereafter his position was rarely better than precarious. In 1819 he toured the continent, where he may have contracted venereal disease. In parliament he was close to Canning (they agreed about Catholic emancipation and reform) but proclaimed himself independent and generally in support of the government. He made his maiden speech in 1819 and developed a reputation as a reliable advocate—which gave him good standing for office, for which he was hungry. However, his electoral and financial vulnerability set limits on a career in office, since he could not afford positions which entailed new elections. Hobhouse said of him that he was 'one of those who were in the habit of eulogising things as they are' (Johnston, 58). Yet, though he was a conservative, Wilmot-Horton's genuine independence of principle unquestionably disadvantaged his political career.

Wilmot-Horton came to the notice of Henry Bathurst, who recruited him in December 1821 to replace Henry Goulbourn as under-secretary of state for war and the colonies, a post which he retained until January 1828. This, and his wife's inheritance, helped Wilmot-Horton's finances, and he acquired Sudbrooke Park at Petersham in 1825. His finances also benefited from his enthusiastic involvement in the 'bubble schemes' of 1824–5. In one of these ventures he reaped a quick profit of £12,000. These activities were curtailed by a government prohibition on further involvement. He had been so successful that in November 1825 he admitted, surprisingly, that he was richer than he needed to be. At the Colonial Office, Wilmot-Horton was responsible for radical reorganization during the 1820s, and he was full of energetic innovation at a time of greatly increased activity in the office. He was responsible for several key appointments, including those of R. W. Hay and T. F. Elliot, as junior clerk, in 1825, and for the promotion of James Stephen. He was urgent in his desire to influence policy. The pressure of work affected his health (in 1824) and temper, but he remained a lively and visible figure about society. With Bathurst in the Lords, he was the government's main spokesman on colonial policy in the Commons. Though he differed severely with Bathurst on the question of Catholic emancipation, their relations were almost always amicable.

Proponent of emigration With energy to spare, Wilmot-Horton concerned himself with some of the central questions of the day—notably reform, pauperism, and political stability—and he searched for a grand national solution. He voiced an interest in emigration as early as 1819, but it did not loom large in his thinking until 1822. His predecessors at the Colonial Office had been lukewarm in support of state experiments with the emigration of the poor, and Goulbourn had opposed such ideas. Wilmot-Horton took up the cause, and wrote a pamphlet in January 1823, *An Outline of a Plan of Emigration to Upper Canada*. State-aided emigration became his personal panacea for the nation's woes, particularly those of Ireland. He was a tenacious and somewhat eccentric advocate, urging that parishes mortgage their poor rates in order to raise loans from government to finance elaborate emigration systems to Canada. He saw mass emigration as a solution to the problems of surplus population at home and labour shortages in the colonies. It was a device for turning a curse into a blessing, a safety valve which would relieve the alarming pressure of social turmoil. He believed in colonies and thought that emigrants served larger imperial functions, and he rejected the pessimistic Malthusian proposition that emigration would always be replenished by still faster population growth. To Wilmot-Horton, excess population was a temporary problem for which emigration offered a vital solution, but only if undertaken with energy and if properly organized by government direction. He threw himself into the cause and was able to gain cabinet support for two experiments in state-aided emigration (which were only partially successful). He set up, organized, chaired, and was the leading spirit in the emigration committees of the House of Commons in 1826 and 1827. These became a vehicle for his own views and, equally, for contemporary opinion, most notably that of Malthus himself. Their recommendations supported state

intervention, and it was the first time that full-scale government action to deal with a great social problem had been considered. Wilmot-Horton was especially concerned to help the rural poor of Ireland and the unemployed weavers of the north of England. The economist J. R. McCulloch, his most enthusiastic supporter, told him that his plans would 'confer a greater benefit on the country than has ever been conferred on it by any other individual' (D. P. O'Brien, *J. R. McCulloch: a Study in Classical Economics*, 1970, 331–2), and constituted the best method of deploying government funds.

Wilmot-Horton pressed his case repeatedly and became obsessive. In 1827 he admitted that his work on emigration was damaging his health, keeping him from riding and walking. He inflated the matter to such a degree that his cabinet colleagues came to question his judgement; he became the butt of reproving and condescending comments from his contemporaries and his views were easily caricatured as 'shovelling out paupers'. In truth he was actuated by a sincere concern to alleviate poverty and promote social improvement both at home and in the colonies. He was unambiguously opposed to sending the penniless to the colonies and advocated elaborate arrangements for their reception and welfare. The likely cost of his larger proposals ran into millions of pounds, however, and taxpayers and politicians were alarmed, although he did intend his schemes to be self-financing. He practically monopolized the emigration debate in the 1820s. He was much derided in the newspapers: one of them decried his incessant advocacy of emigration as an 'amiable weakness'. He was not taken seriously, and he quite misjudged his support in the Commons. His political disappointment partly reflected the negative contemporary attitude to the colonies, but he had also failed to engage his ministerial colleagues at his own intellectual level. In 1827 Peel, who offered him consolation at other times, expressed amiable exasperation at the receipt of yet another pamphlet, exclaiming, 'I really think that some effectual stop ought to be taken forthwith to prevent every unemployed man in the country looking for relief from emigration' (L. Melville, ed., *The Huskisson Papers*, 1931, 125). Wilmot-Horton expressed himself in convoluted terms which left him open to misunderstanding and caricature. Most colleagues recoiled from his enthusiasm, and this certainly damaged his political prospects. He attempted to get a bill into parliament in 1828, but faced apathy and even derision. Although he recruited varying degrees of support in principle from David Ricardo, Thomas Tooke, James Mill, Malthus, and McCulloch, he was regarded as a zealot.

Wilmot-Horton became exceedingly disappointed by his evident failure to influence policy and withdrew from the government in 1828. He was offered the vice-presidency of the Board of Trade, but was not prepared to incur the expense of the electoral contest that it would entail. Wellington tried to induce him to return in 1828, and so did Bathurst in 1830. Wilmot-Horton despaired of achieving a post in keeping with his abilities. Political associates spoke best of him when he was out of office. In February 1831 Howick, taking up Wilmot-Horton's ideas, briefly revived the policy of parish emigration, and Sydney Smith wrote to Wilmot-Horton that, though he had been ridiculed, his advice was now being followed. In reality Edward Gibbon Wakefield soon became the alternative font of all advice on the question.

Wakefield and Gouger later acknowledged Wilmot-Horton's influence on their more successful propaganda for systematic emigration. But their doctrines had diverged sharply. After an initial flirtation they fell into conflict, which was publicly exposed in April 1830. In effect, Wilmot-Horton's jealous authority on all emigration questions was challenged and then overthrown by Wakefield, who soon chose to denigrate the work of the man who had championed the cause in the previous decade. Wakefield's doctrines were derived from different principles and required the creation of colonies on a new basis radically at odds with Wilmot-Horton's principles, which had always favoured a system of quasi-peasant proprietorship. In the refound enthusiasm for migration in the early 1830s they poured scorn on Wilmot-Horton, castigating him as 'an ignorant and meddling pretender in political economy' (*The Spectator*, 4, 1831, 207). It produced a complete rift, and the Wakefieldians took over the field. Wilmot-Horton was soon forgotten as a theorist of emigration. Nevertheless, many of his views and predictions regarding the emigration question, especially on Ireland, were painfully vindicated by events.

Pamphleteer and governor of Ceylon Wilmot-Horton was a determined and persistent pamphleteer and, apart from many papers devoted to pauperism and emigration, he wrote on Napoleon, the West Indies and slavery, Ireland and Canada, taxation, the corn laws, political economy, and the Reform Bill. Although he had some anxieties about social turmoil, he did not fear revolution and believed that education was the greatest requirement of the times. He considered that opposition to the Catholics was a consequence of ignorance among the people of England. It was his unwavering commitment to Catholic emancipation that prevented the resurrection of his career out of the emigration cul-de-sac into which he had placed himself. As Canning said, Wilmot-Horton had 'the misfortune to differ with a large and respectable body of his constituents' (Jones, 125). In May 1827 he was made privy councillor, possibly as a consolation for his failure to achieve promotion in the cabinet. He had set his heart on the Irish secretaryship, and Canning said that he would be perfect: 'but he has spoilt himself for Ireland by his Publications' (ibid.). His pamphleteering made him sound rabid. Mrs Arbuthnot described him as 'a very violent partisan of the Catholics, and has not one grain of judgment or common sense' (*The Journal of Mrs Arbuthnot, 1820–1832*, ed. F. Bamford and G. Wellesley, 2, 1950, 190). His pro-Catholic views were unpopular in his Newcastle constituency, where he could not risk expensive contests. Political advancement required re-election and a safer seat, and by October 1827, despite some urging to stay in government, he seems to have set his mind on colonial administration. Some thought he had blundered politically in 1828 and alienated Peel and Wellington, but his withdrawal from government surprised his colleagues, and many expected him to return. Wellington, Bathurst, and Peel all thought so. He believed, wrongly, that he was front runner for Canada: 'I should have no scruples about Climate, as affecting my family', he said (Jones, 83). He was deeply disappointed and exclaimed that there was 'a spell and curse' on his career. He was offered, but declined, Jamaica. In Wellington's government his views on emigration, abolition, and Catholic emancipation again excluded him from office, though he supported the government.

When Palmerston saw Wilmot-Horton in Paris in late 1829 he was 'indefatigably hammering on emigration, and writing his shorthand scribe to a skeleton' (Jones, 91). By 1830 he was opposed to extensive political reform: 'The nation was blest with a system of civic polity the most perfect of any age or any country and he believed the great mass of people duly estimated it' (ibid.). He had already decided not to contest the election of 1830. Attending one of Wilmot-Horton's lectures in 1831, Grenville reported that he was 'full of zeal and animation, but so totally without method and arrangement that he is barely intelligible' (S. L. Levy, *Nassau W. Senior, 1790–1864*, 1970, 70). Goderich was now in office and offered Wilmot-Horton the governorship of Ceylon in early 1831: he had hoped for Madras, citing his 'pecuniary embarrassments', but gladly accepted Ceylon, and served from 1831 to 1837. He became knight of the grand cross of the Royal Guelphic Order in June 1831.

In Ceylon Wilmot-Horton set about a thorough reform of the administration, reorganizing the island into five provinces. He was able to resist some of the recommendations of William Colebrooke's commission of inquiry (1831–2) into the administration and revenues of the island, which he regarded as 'crude and impractical', but not the severe budgetary cuts. He encountered further difficulties. Falling cinnamon prices damaged revenue income and caused a rapid decline in the industry; administrative expenditure was reduced, including the governor's own salary; and he was faced with an alleged plot to overthrow British rule and re-establish the kingdom of Kandy. Despite Treasury opposition and forced economies, he managed to advance important road improvements between Kandy and Trincomalee, Jaffna, and Port Pedro. He eventually saw better prospects for coffee and coconut oil production. He supervised the final abolition of slavery in Ceylon and the development of a free press (to which he contributed anonymously). He strove to improve the calibre of colonial officials.

In July 1834 Wilmot-Horton succeeded to his father's baronetcy and to the estates at Osmaston and Weston, but not to a large fortune: much of the inheritance went to the younger children of his father's second marriage. He returned to England in the autumn of 1837, and was regarded as one of the most accomplished governors of the time. On his return he was said to be 'looking rather puffy and too fat, but well'. He lived at Sudbrooke and probably continued to seek government employment, perhaps in Canada. He was opposed to Palmerston, who regarded him as 'a particularly silly fellow'. He resumed his writings, now more conservative in tone, on parliamentary reform; he still urged emigration schemes for Ireland, but with negligible impact on public opinion. In 1839 he travelled to Germany. Despite his colonial service income, he was still strapped for money in 1840.

Wilmot-Horton died at Sudbrooke on 8 June 1841 without much notice in the newspapers. He was regarded as highly articulate, a playful wit, and a good conversationalist, a pleasant clubbable type but restless by disposition. He was a charter member of Grillion's Club in 1813, with which he remained throughout his life. He was always a great believer in empire and regarded the colonies as overseas extensions of the United Kingdom. He was convinced of the essential excellence of British institutions. James Stephen described him as 'the pleasantest of companions and the most restless of politicians' (P. Knapland, *James Stephen and the British Colonial System*, 1953, 293). He did not live up to his own expectations or those of his contemporaries, and his political behaviour was too often quixotic or inept. He was possessed of a passion for 're-making the world', and he pursued too many impractical visions.

ERIC RICHARDS

Sources E. G. Jones, 'Sir R. J. Wilmot Horton, bart., politician and pamphleteer', MA diss., Bristol University, 1936 · H. J. M. Johnston, *British emigration policy, 1815–30* (1972) · D. Winch, *Classical political economy and colonies* (1965) · L. A. Mills, *Ceylon under British rule, 1795–1932* (1933) · C. R. De Silva, *Ceylon under the British occupation, 1795–1833*, 2nd edn, 2 vols. (1942) · D. M. Young, *The colonial office in the early nineteenth century* (1961) · E. F. C. Ludowyk, *The modern history of Ceylon* (1966) · R. N. Ghosh, 'Malthus on emigration and colonisation: letters to Wilmot Horton', *Economica*, new ser., 30 (1963), 45–61 · N. McLachlan, 'She walks in beauty', *London Magazine, a Monthly Review of Literature*, new ser., 30/5–6 (1990), 20–33 · J. R. Poynter, *Society and pauperism: English ideas on poor relief, 1795–1834* (1969) · C. R. Fay, *Huskisson and his age* (1951) · D. Pike, 'Wilmot Horton and the National Colonization Society', *Historical Studies: Australia and New Zealand*, 7 (1955–7), 205–10

Archives Bodl. Oxf., corresp. · Department of National Archives of Sri Lanka, corresp. and papers relating to Ceylon · Derbys. RO, corresp. and papers · PRO, corresp. and papers relating to Ceylon, CO 537/146 | BL, corresp. with William Huskisson, Add. MSS 38745–38754 · BL, corresp. with Sir Hudson Lowe, Add. MSS 20133–20233 · BL, corresp. with Robert Peel, Add. MSS 40346–40401 · Keele University Library, letters to Ralph Sneyd · LPL, corresp. with Bishop Howley · Lpool RO, letters to Lord Stanley · Mitchell L., NSW, letters from Lord Bathurst · PRO, letters to Lord Granville, PRO 30/29 · St Deiniol's Library, Hawarden, corresp. with Sir John Gladstone · Staffs. RO, Sutherland MSS; letters to Lord Hatherton

Likenesses R. J. Lane, engraving, 1827 (after J. Slater), BM [*see illus.*] · J. Doyle, pencil caricature, 1829, BM

Horton, Thomas (*bap.* 1603, *d.* 1649), parliamentarian army officer and regicide, was baptized in February 1603 at Gumley, Leicestershire, the second son of William Horton (*d.* 1638?) and his wife, Isabell Freeman. Horton was a client of Sir Arthur Hesilrige: he was once believed to have been his servant and falconer, but documents relating to property transactions confirm his position as a minor landowner in Leicestershire. Horton also witnessed numerous mortgages relating to Hesilrige's estates at Noseley in that county and in the north-east of England, underlining his literacy and numerate ability.

When civil war broke out in 1642 Horton followed Hesilrige into the parliamentarian army as his cornet. In this appointment he fought at Edgehill on 23 October, before becoming captain-lieutenant to Hesilrige's own troop in 1643. He fought in all the major engagements of Sir William Waller's army in the campaigns of 1643 and 1644, including Lansdown, Alton, Cheriton, Cropredy Bridge, and the second battle of Newbury. Upon the formation of the New Model Army in 1645 Horton's name appeared in both lists from the House of Lords; he eventually became major to Colonel John Butler, who had received command of Hesilrige's regiment upon the latter's resignation under the terms of the self-denying ordinance. At Naseby on 14 June 1645 Horton was on the extreme left wing and suffered the full impact of Prince Rupert's charge, being wounded in the rout which followed. The wound was sufficiently severe to keep Horton from the army for the rest of that summer, and during his enforced absence he married Mistress St Lo, the niece of a London businessman and friend of Hesilrige.

The end of hostilities in 1646 should have ended Horton's military career but he was now a trusted member of the army's Independent group, which was becoming more vehement with victory. When in the late spring and early summer of 1647 the quarrel between the army and the presbyterian faction in parliament broke out into open defiance, Horton signed his regiment's petition of grievances in May and by the end of the following month had replaced Butler as its colonel. In July the army council, now led by Henry Ireton, sent Horton to south Wales to secure the ports and principal garrisons against royalist insurrection, but also to prevent the Welsh soldiery from supporting the presbyterians. It was, however, already evident that Colonel Rowland Laugharne could not be trusted, but despite warnings he was left in his command, leaving Horton in a policing action against risings which were sure to come. At the close of April 1648 Horton's military strength was increased by the arrival of a small number of regular foot under Major Read and the experienced dragoons of John Okey, allowing him to move against royalist forces assembling near Carmarthen under Colonel Rice Powell. After a brief skirmish Powell disengaged and slipped into the hills; a similar indecisive move against Colonel John Poyer left Horton marching in circles until on 8 May his force met a larger, yet untrained, royalist force between St Fagans and Peterstown. After a 'sharp dispute' which lasted almost two hours, his superior regulars totally routed them, pursuing them for 7 miles and taking 3000 prisoners, including Major-General John Stradling. Tenby Castle, long held by Powell, surrendered to Horton on 31 May. Parliament ordered a thanksgiving to be observed, and settled the sequestered estates of the defeated royalists on the victors. Sir Henry Lingen, on his way to north Wales, was intercepted and after another skirmish was taken by Horton.

Horton, acting as a commissioner at the high court of justice, attended the king's trial every day and signed the death warrant [*see also* Regicides]. He also acted briefly as a commissioner for south Wales. In April 1649 his regiment was chosen for Cromwell's campaign in Ireland, but some of its officers resigned their commissions rather than go. Horton and his regiment sailed from Milford Haven at the end of August, but soon after arriving in Ireland he contracted a form of dysentery and died of 'the bloody flux'. Cromwell, writing on 25 October, reported that Horton 'is lately dead of the country-disease' (Abbott, 2.153). Horton left an only son, Thomas. His will, dated at Cardiff on 3 July 1649, was proved on 16 January 1651. By it he left 'the major-Gen. [Henry Ireton] my horse called Hesilrige', and to the major of his regiment, Thomas Pennyfeather, his carbine with a rifled barrel (will). In 1654, on the petition of his executors, £1405 was voted in satisfaction of Horton's arrears of pay. At the Restoration his name was excepted out of the Bill of Pardon and Oblivion, and his estate was forfeit.   BARRY DENTON

Sources C. H. Firth and G. Davies, *The regimental history of Cromwell's army*, 2 vols. (1940) • parish register, Gumley, Leics. RO • Leics. RO, Hazlerigg papers • E. Peacock, *The army lists of the roundheads and cavaliers* (1874), 54 • B. Denton, *Only in heaven: the life and campaigns of Sir Arthur Hesilrige, 1601–1661* (1997) • *JHL*, 5–6 (1642–4) • *JHC*, 5–8 (1646–67) • *JHL*, 10 (1647–8) • *CSP dom.*, 1648–50; 1654 • *S. W.'s exceediing good newes from South Wales* (1648) • *A great fight in Wales betwen Colonell Horton and Colonell Powell* • *A fuller relation of a great victory obtained against the Welsh forces by Col. Tho. Horton* (1648) • will, PRO, PROB 11/215, sig. 5, fols. 37v–38r • *The writings and speeches of Oliver Cromwell*, ed. W. C. Abbott and C. D. Crane, 4 vols. (1937–47), vols. 1–2 • J. Rushworth, *Historical collections*, new edn, 7 (1721), 1110 • Greaves & Zaller, *BDBR*, 2.113 • R. K. G. Temple, ed., 'The original officer list of the New Model Army', *BIHR*, 59 (1986), 50–77, esp. 63n. • personal information (2004) [Arthur J. Flint]
Wealth at death over £200: will, PRO, PROB 11/215, sig. 5, fols. 37v–38r; *CSP dom.*, 1654, 145, 202, 276

Horton, Thomas (*d.* 1673), college head, a native of London, was the son of Laurence Horton, merchant and a member of the Mercers' Company. (He must not be confused with another man of those names who was nominated to the living of Alderton, Northamptonshire, on 3 June 1646, and ejected for scandal in 1656.) He was admitted to Emmanuel College, Cambridge, on 8 July 1623 as a pensioner, graduating BA in 1626 and MA in 1630. He was a fellow of Emmanuel in 1631 and took the degree of BD in 1637. Following his subscription to the thirty-sixth canon in November 1638 Horton became one of the twelve university preachers. On 12 July 1638 he was appointed to the perpetual curacy of St Mary Colechurch, London, a donative of the Mercers' Company, and he held the living until the institution of his successor, Samuel Cheyney, on 28 November 1640. On 26 October 1641 he stood against Benjamin Witchcote (1609–1683) for the vacant professorship of divinity at Gresham College, London, and was elected.

Horton was one of the divines appointed by the parliament under the ordinance of 4 October 1644 to ordain ministers in and near London, and the following year he subscribed the City ministers' petition urging parliament to implement presbyterian government without delay. Horton preached fast sermons before parliament on 30 December 1646 and 29 September 1647. He was appointed preacher of Gray's Inn on 18 May 1647. On 19 September

1647 he was elected president of Queens' College, Cambridge, in succession to the recently deceased Herbert Palmer; he was admitted to that position on 2 October. His presbyterian but consensual outlook resembled that of his predecessor, and it appears that under Horton's leadership the college remained peaceful. He was awarded the doctorate of divinity in 1649 and was incorporated in that degree at Oxford on 9 August 1652. It was reported that following the execution of the king Horton had serious scruples about taking the engagement, but if so he was able to overcome them. His acceptance in 1650 of the vice-chancellorship involved him in leading the implementation of government regulation of publishing at the university.

Horton had already returned (perhaps during the civil war) to the parish of St Mary Colechurch, where he received for the nine months to 25 December 1649 an augmentation of £37 13s. 4d. out of the sale of the bishops' lands, and he was reported to be there still in October 1651. Also in 1651 Horton married his wife, Dorothy, and it was perhaps in connection with his marriage that in Easter term 1651 he resigned his preachership at Gray's Inn, which on 28 May 1655 honoured the 'late preacher of this society' by admitting him as a member (Foster, 272). A contemporary at Queens' reported Horton as a most jealous husband. His marriage certainly gave rise to trouble at Gresham College, where the founder's will stipulated that the professor must remain single, and the authorities accordingly declared the place vacant. However, in May 1651 Horton had managed to procure a dispensation from the committee of parliament for reforming the universities; the Gresham governors hesitated to replace him. Eventually on 19 May 1656 they elected George Gifford, but Horton was able to obtain a new dispensation, dated 26 August, from the council of state, and he remained in possession until after the Restoration.

As all of this may suggest, Horton was in good standing with the protectorate authorities. He was named as a 'trier' of candidates for the ministry under the ordinance of 20 March 1654 and also in that year was appointed a visitor of Cambridge University. He preached before the mayor and aldermen of London at the Spital on 11 April 1653, and at St Paul's on 5 November 1654. His sermon preached on Thursday 8 May 1656 to 'the native citizens of London, in their solemn assembly at Paule's' was signed 'from my study at Gresham college, 3 June 1656'. One reason for his determination to cling on at Gresham may have been the unreliability of his stipend as president of Queens'. In April 1654 he petitioned Cromwell that his stipend was a year in arrears. But the situation seems to have improved, for by an order dated 29 May 1655 Horton was paid £50 as master of Queens' College, for the year to 29 September 1656.

Horton was named by parliament as a commissioner for the approbation of ministers in the act of March 1660, but after the Restoration his fortunes declined. On 1 August he was able to obtain a dispensation from Charles II to retain his professorship, but by an order of the earl of Manchester he was removed the following day from the presidency of Queens' and Edward Martin was restored. Horton was still professor of divinity at Gresham during the Savoy conference of April 1661, to which he was nominated but which he did not attend. On 26 May 1661, however, following Gifford's petition to Charles II, the dispensation earlier granted to Horton was revoked, and Gifford was re-elected on 7 June. Horton was one of the divines ejected under the Act of Uniformity in August 1662, but conformed soon afterwards.

On 13 June 1666 Horton was admitted to the vicarage of St Helen, Bishopsgate, London, under the patronage of Sir John Langham. Here his presbyterian outlook, including a willingness to administer communion standing to those who wished it, attracted to his ministry many of a similar persuasion. He was in sufficiently good standing with the authorities, however, to be asked to preach the assize sermon at St Saviour's, Southwark, on 28 February 1671 before Sir Thomas Twisden and Sir William Morton. Horton held the living of St Helen's until his death. He was survived by his wife and his daughter Judith, and was buried in the chancel of St Helen's on 29 March 1673. Benjamin Witchcote was a witness of his will. The mathematician John Wallis, who had been under his tuition at Cambridge and was a fellow of Queens' from 1644, reported that Horton was 'very well skilled in the oriental languages, very well accomplished for the work of the ministry, and very conscientious in the discharge of it' (Horton, *One Hundred Select Sermons*, preface).

STEPHEN WRIGHT

Sources J. Ward, *The lives of the professors of Gresham College* (1740) · W. G. Searle, *The history of the Queens' College of St Margaret and St Bernard in the University of Cambridge*, 2, Cambridge Antiquarian RS, 13 (1871) · Venn, *Alum. Cant.* · J. Twigg, *A history of Queens' College, Cambridge, 1448–1986* (1987) · J. T. Cliffe, *The puritan gentry besieged, 1650–1700* (1993) · W. A. Shaw, *A history of the English church during the civil wars and under the Commonwealth, 1640–1660*, 2 vols. (1900) · will, PRO, PROB 11/342, fols. 389–90 · G. Hennessy, *Novum repertorium ecclesiasticum parochiale Londinense, or, London diocesan clergy succession from the earliest time to the year 1898* (1898) · J. F. Wilson, *Pulpit in parliament: puritanism during the English civil wars, 1640–1648* (1969) · T. Horton, *One hundred select sermons upon several texts: fifty upon the Old Testament, and fifty on the New* (1679) · T. Horton, *A sermon preached in the parish church of St Mary Saviour's in Southwark* (1671) · *Calendar of the correspondence of Richard Baxter*, ed. N. H. Keeble and G. F. Nuttall, 2 vols. (1991) · J. Foster, *Register of admissions to Gray's Inn, 1521–1881* (privately printed, London, 1887) · Wood, *Ath. Oxon.: Fasti* (1820)
Wealth at death see will, PRO, PROB 11/342, fols. 389–90

Hortop, Job (*fl.* 1550–1591), powder maker and seaman, was born in Bourne, Lincolnshire. From the age of twelve he served the queen's powder maker in Rotherhithe, London, until pressed as a gunner in the *Jesus of Lubeck* on John Hawkins's third slaving voyage (October 1567). After the disaster at San Juan d'Uloa (1568) Hortop was among those landed from the *Minion* north of the River Panuco, in Mexico. For two years he worked freely as a tinsmith and powder maker in Mexico city; by then a tall, thin, rosy-cheeked, slightly bearded figure of about twenty he was long remembered by local friars for the fireworks and set

pieces he made for their holy day celebrations. In March 1571 Hortop was sent to Spain aboard the plate fleet; he was almost hanged after a failed escape attempt in the Azores, and, after incarceration in the Casa de Contratación, Seville, was sentenced (1573) to ten years (later extended to twelve) in the galleys, followed by life imprisonment. Four years in the Inquisition's prison in Seville and a period of service with the treasurer of the royal mint ended in October 1590, when he managed to escape from San Lucar in a Flemish fly-boat, transferred to the *Dudley*, an English warship, and landed at Portsmouth on 2 December.

Hortop returned to Rotherhithe, and in 1591 he published (in two editions) an account of his 'travailes'—apart from three references in the Mexican archives, the only evidence for his life. The first edition seems to have been written from memory; the enlarged second edition (reprinted by Hakluyt in 1598) showed some revisions, possibly the result of contact with the narratives of Hawkins and Miles Phillips, published by Hakluyt in 1589, and with Anthony Goddard, who had acted as interpreter in Mexico and Spain. Hortop, clearly prone to innocent surprise and natural curiosity, delighted in anecdotes about the more outrageous beasts and reptiles he had encountered: the hippopotamus which sank a boat on the Guinea coast, the tigers lurking in the Venezuelan woods, the alligator caught with a dog as live bait at Rio de la Hacha, the adder with a coney in his mouth at Santa Marta, the river-browsing 'manatees' at Tampico, whose flesh resembled bacon, and the merman off the Bahamas. A phlegmatic traveller, he recollected the strange foods he sampled: delicate, sugary bananas; the Mexican white crab; and the multipurpose spiny Indian agave plant. Throughout his account Hortop's hero is Hawkins, though he puts a more favourable light on Drake's desertion at San Juan d'Uloa than did Hawkins's own account. Overall his version is vivid, if, written at a distance of twenty-three years, not always strictly accurate.

BASIL MORGAN

Sources R. Hakluyt, *The principal navigations, voyages, traffiques and discoveries of the English nation*, 2nd edn, 3 vols. (1598–1600); repr. 12 vols., Hakluyt Society, extra ser., 1–12 (1903–5), 445–65 · R. Unwin, *The defeat of John Hawkins* (1962) · J. A. Williamson, *Hawkins of Plymouth*, 2nd edn (1969) · G. R. G. Conway, *The rare travailes of Job Hortop* (1928) · *DNB* · J. Suarez de Peralta, *Noticias historicas de la Nueva España* (1878), 265–6 · Archivo General de Indias, Seville, MS Doc. 51-3-81-5

Horwitz, Bernard (*c.*1807–1885), chess player, was a native of the grand duchy of Mecklenburg, of Jewish descent, who learned the game under Mendheim at Berlin and became one of the seven great players known as the Pleiades. He moved about 1840 to Hamburg and to Britain about 1845. Originally an artist, he vindicated this character in later life by wearing 'hats of the most impossible shapes' (Hoffer, 755).

Horwitz repeatedly beat Henry Bird early in the latter's chess career, but was unsuccessful against Howard Staunton. Employed by J. Kling from 1852 as resident professional at his Oxford Street chess and coffee rooms, he also wrote with Kling *Studies of Endgames* and in 1851–3 issued the *Chess Player*, a periodical. In 1857 Horwitz became professional for the Manchester chess club, where he encouraged the young J. H. Blackburne. He also painted children's portraits. He married Priscilla Dey Res (*née* Goss) on 25 April 1874 and died at 27 Parkhurst Road, Bowes Park, London, on 29 August 1885. His wife survived him.

R. E. ANDERSON, *rev.* JULIAN LOCK

Sources *British Chess Magazine*, 5 (1885), 341–3, 375–7, 384–8, 397–400 · D. Hooper and K. Whyld, *The Oxford companion to chess*, 2nd edn (1992), 176–7 · L. Hoffer, 'The chess masters of today', *Fortnightly Review*, 46 (1886), 753–65 · Boase, *Mod. Eng. biog.* · H. Staunton, *The chess-player's handbook* (1847); facs. edn (1985) · P. W. Sergeant, *A century of British chess* (1934) · *ILN* (12 Sept 1885), 277 · *ILN* (19 Sept 1885), 307 · *Annual Register* (1885) · m. cert.
Likenesses A. Rosenbaum, group portrait, oils, 1880 (with Johann Zukertort), repro. in K. Matthews, *British chess* (1948), 31 · portrait, repro. in *ILN*, 8 (1846), 100

Horwood, Richard (1757/8–1803), surveyor and cartographer, the son of William and Mary Horwood, was baptized at the church of St Mary, Aylesbury, Buckinghamshire, on 26 March 1758. An elder brother Thomas was baptized at the same church on 2 April 1749. Horwood appears again at the age of twenty-one when he surveyed the estate of Trentham Hall, Staffordshire. His elder brother Thomas was the agent for the marquess of Stafford, Granville Leveson-Gower, and commissioned Richard to survey the estate in order that he might manage it more efficiently (see Staffs. RO, D 593/H/3/33 and 344, redrawn maps dated 1782). Thomas is later believed to have lived at Weston Turville Manor, 4 miles from Aylesbury.

Where Richard Horwood went immediately after this is unknown. There is no firm evidence to support speculation that he worked as a surveyor for the Phoenix Fire Office in London. In October 1790 he published a map of the area around Leicester Square and Haymarket 'as a specimen of a Plan of LONDON' in the hope of attracting subscribers from both gentry and tradesmen to enable him to produce a map of the city, which had changed very substantially since it was last mapped by John Rocque in 1738 (published 1742). In March 1791 Horwood sent the 'specimen' to the Society of Arts, knowing that since 1759 it had encouraged cartography by offering premiums, bounties, and medals for newly surveyed and accurate maps. He was thanked by the society but received no reward as only finished products were considered by them. Horwood must have raised money by subscription since the following year he published the first sheet of his map, dated 22 June 1792. Another followed in 1793 and by 1795 eight sheets were complete. Horwood sent these eight sheets to the Society of Arts and appeared before them to plead his case for some reward, but none was forthcoming and it was subscriptions, finally totalling 838 and including the king and queen and the Bank of England, and a loan of £500 from the Phoenix Fire Company, to whom the map was finally dedicated, which enabled him to complete it. The work was done by late 1799 and comprised a 'Plan of the

Cities of London and Westminster, the Borough of Southwark and parts adjoining' in thirty-two sheets. It was the largest map then printed in Britain and shows the city in extraordinary detail. Horwood attempted, in many areas successfully, to show each individual building, the first such attempt since Ogilby and Morgan's map of 1676, and he also attempted to number the buildings, an enterprise unmatched until the 1930s. He had been defeated by the sheer quantity of buildings in some areas and his publicly announced intention of showing parish boundaries had been defeated by their complexity in the City of London, although they are shown outside the City. But the results are none the less strikingly impressive. Horwood wrote of it:

> The execution of it has cost me nine years severe labour and indefatigable perseverance; and these years formed the most valuable part of my life. [I] took every angle; measured almost every line; and after that plotted and compared the work. The engraving, considering the immense mass of work, is, I flatter myself, well done.   (edited version of letter of 20 May 1800 to Society of Arts, in *Transactions of the Society of Arts*, 21, 1803, 311–13)

After importuning the Society of Arts further he was finally awarded a bounty of 50 guineas in 1803. The map is aesthetically very pleasing, but it was as a working document that it must have been appreciated by the London businesses, institutions such as parish vestries, and individuals who subscribed to it. By this time Horwood was in Liverpool where he had quickly secured official patronage for his scheme to map that city. With the promise of help from the corporation's surveyors and a subscription for ten copies from the treasurer his map of Liverpool made rapid progress. Similar in conception to his London map it was published in July 1803 in six sheets with 760 subscribers.

On 3 October 1803 Horwood died in Liverpool and was buried in Toxteth Chapel, Liverpool. The thirty-two plates of his London map passed to William Faden, the country's most important seller and publisher of large-scale maps, who realized their value as part of an original and meticulously surveyed work in an age dominated by cartographic hacks and plagiarists. Faden updated them, completed some detailed work, and added eight new plates to show new developments (particularly in the dock areas of the expanding city), this itself being a considerable geographical achievement. He published three editions (1807, 1813, 1819), of which the 1813 edition was republished in 1985 as *The A to Z of Regency London*. This last has enabled the widespread use of the map in the later twentieth century as a historical geographical source.

ELIZABETH BAIGENT

Sources E. Baigent, 'Richard Horwood's map of London: eighteenth-century cartography and the Society of Arts', *RSA Journal*, 142 (Dec 1994), 49–51 · P. Laxton, 'Richard Horwood's map and the face of London, 1799–1819', *The A to Z of Regency London* (1985), iv–xiv · P. Laxton, 'Richard Horwood's plan of London: a guide to editions and variants, 1792–1819', *London Topographical Record*, 26 (1990), 214–63 · Committee of Polite Arts, minutes, RSA, 16 March 1791, 20 Feb 1795, 12 Dec 1800, 13 May 1801, 30 April 1803 · *IGI* · F. W. Steer and others, *Dictionary of land surveyors and local map-makers of*

Great Britain and Ireland, 1530–1850, ed. P. Eden, 2nd edn, ed. S. Bendall, 2 vols. (1997) • private information (2004)

Archives RSA

Horwood, William (c.1430–1484), church musician and composer, is of unknown parentage and upbringing. During 1458–9 he was admitted to the Confraternity of St Nicholas, a guild of the clerks and professional musicians working in the parish and collegiate churches of the London region. In February 1461 he was appointed thence to Lincoln Cathedral, probably to introduce there the newly developing practices of choral polyphonic singing. However, he left Lincoln at Michaelmas 1461 and in 1462–3 was readmitted to the Confraternity of St Nicholas; he served as its master during 1474–5, in which year his wife, Agnes, also was admitted.

Later in 1475 Horwood returned to Lincoln Cathedral to occupy a newly created post of master of the music, which conferred responsibility for the direction of all performances of polyphony. His duties were to attend daily at Lady mass and the evening Marian antiphon; both were sung in the lady chapel by the choristers and the ablest vicars choral, and at the former he was both to sing and play the organ. For the choristers he was to provide a comprehensive musical training, extending to playing the organ and clavichord, and to all the styles of singing then current: plainsong, counterpoint improvised to plainsong, and 'pricksong' (singing from the written notation of polyphony). In April 1483 he also became player of the principal cathedral organ, used on Sundays and major feasts at the major services sung by the full choir. His total emoluments placed him among the highest-paid professional church musicians of his day.

In music history Horwood is very important. He was a conspicuously able composer of that generation which, by adding bass and boy treble voices to the historic core of altos and tenors, created one of the most enduring of all resources for musical performance, namely the four-part chorus of soprano, alto, tenor, and bass voices. Three Marian votive antiphons (one incomplete) and an *alternatim* Magnificat, all for five unaccompanied voices, survive in the Eton choirbook of c.1502–5. The experimental scoring and harmonic and cadential idioms of the *Salve regina* show it to be an early piece, dating perhaps from his London days. The remainder demonstrate Horwood's role in the establishment of the principal features of late fifteenth-century English style, especially its vocal scoring and its characteristic grandeur in terms of scale of composition, sonority of choral writing, and virtuosity of solo writing. A setting of a Lady mass Kyrie survives in a fragmentary state elsewhere.

At Lincoln Horwood dwelt within the cathedral close, and may have been of a somewhat irascible disposition, being fined in 1478–9 for an assault on one of the chantry priests. In the same year he was also fined, as was his daughter Joan two years earlier, for brewing and selling ale that was in contravention of the law. He died early in 1484, probably in Lincoln. He was survived by his wife, and was buried in the cathedral nave south aisle.

ROGER BOWERS

Sources Lincs. Arch., Lincoln Cathedral archives • parish register, London, Confraternity of St Nicholas, GL, MS 4889 • R. Bowers, 'Music and liturgy to 1640', *A history of Lincoln Minster*, ed. D. Owen (1994), 47–76 • F. L. Harrison, ed., *The Eton choirbook*, 2nd edn, 3 vols., Musica Britannica, 10–12 (1967–73), nos. 10, 29, 44, 52 • H. Baillie and P. Oboussier, 'The York masses', *Music and Letters*, 35 (1954), 19–30 • R. Bowers, 'To chorus from quartet: the performing resource for English church polyphony', *English choral practice, 1400–1650*, ed. J. Morehen (1995), 1–47 • H. Baillie, 'A London gild of musicians, 1460–1530', *Proceedings of the Royal Musical Association*, 83 (1956–7), 15–28

Horwood, Sir William Thomas Francis (1868–1943), army officer and police administrator, was born in November 1868, the youngest son of Charles Horwood of the Manor House, Broadwater, Sussex. At twenty he was commissioned into the 5th lancers, serving as recruiting officer and adjutant for the 49th regimental district from 1900 to 1902. After two years as brigade-major in the 24th field artillery, he moved in 1904 to the War Office, where he spent six years on administrative duties. His first experience of the police was as chief of police of the London and North Eastern Railway, a post he held from 1911 until the beginning of the First World War. From 1914 to 1915 he was deputy assistant adjutant-general at the War Office, and in 1915 was appointed provost marshal at the general headquarters of the British expeditionary force in France. He was awarded the DSO in 1917. On 27 April 1897 Horwood married Violet (1864/5–1941), eldest daughter of Lieutenant-General James George Fife, of Goring-on-Thames, Berkshire, an officer in the Royal Engineers. The couple had one daughter.

When Sir Nevil Macready was appointed commissioner of police to the metropolis in September 1918, after the first police strike and the resignation of Sir Edward Henry, the former commissioner, he chose Horwood, his former staff officer, as one of his assistant commissioners, continuing the tradition of appointing men from a military background to the highest posts in the police force. He later promoted him to the new rank of deputy assistant commissioner. Working closely with Macready, Horwood helped to restore the morale of the force after the strike, and when the police union called a second strike, in August 1919, only 5 per cent of the force went on strike, and were dismissed. He oversaw the introduction of an experimental force of women police in 1919, and the experiment with mobile patrols, which developed into the flying squad in the 1920s. When Macready was sent to command the troops in Ireland in 1920 he advised the prime minister, Lloyd George, to appoint Horwood as his successor.

Horwood was a good administrator, preferring, like his predecessors, to surround himself with military men, including Major-General Sir Wyndham Childs, appointed assistant commissioner to replace Sir Basil Thomson in 1921. One of the first problems to face Horwood in the early 1920s was that of arson attacks by Irish terrorists in London, and attacks on the families of men serving in Ireland in the Royal Irish Constabulary and the British army. Although he began a big recruiting campaign in 1920 he had to end this after the imposition of the 'Geddes axe' in

Sir William Thomas Francis Horwood (1868–1943), by Lafayette, 1928

1922 and the reduction in national expenditure, and had to cut the force by 1000, a 5 per cent reduction in strength. But following the decision of the government in 1925 to hand over the policing of naval and military establishments to the Admiralty and the War Office, 1300 policemen were able to return to regular duties, and the force was back up to strength by the time of the general strike in 1926, when the conduct of the police impressed the public. By 1927 criticism of the Metropolitan Police was growing, however, and despite the report of the Macmillan committee on the conduct and management of the police, which cleared the police of all but one of the charges in the newspapers that innocent citizens were being harassed, morale was low.

Horwood's last few months in office were overshadowed by two scandals, which gained a lot of press publicity and contributed to the worsening reputation of the force. In May 1928 allegations accusing the police of using tyrannical methods in the interrogation of a Miss Savidge led to questions in parliament, and although a commission of inquiry vindicated the police officers concerned, the government decided in August 1928 to set up the royal commission on police powers and procedure because of the criticism of police methods. The Savidge case was followed by the Goddard scandal, when Sergeant Goddard, who had had the duty of suppressing brothels and gambling dens in London, and keeping an eye on night clubs, was accused by his fellow policeman, Sergeant Joslin, of accepting bribes from bookmakers and the owners of brothels and night clubs to save themselves from police investigation. Although Horwood referred the case to the Home Office, and an inquiry found Joslin guilty of making false accusations, Goddard was later charged, and imprisoned, in 1929. In February 1928, before these scandals broke, Horwood had already announced his intention to retire in November, and the home secretary, Sir William Joynson-Hicks, decided that the Metropolitan Police needed to be headed by a strong and well-known public figure who could restore confidence in the force. He appointed General Lord Byng of Vimy to succeed Horwood as commissioner on Horwood's retirement on his sixtieth birthday.

Horwood was appointed KCB in 1921 and GBE in 1928. He had nearly died in 1922 after eating a box of poisoned chocolates sent through the post, but survived another twenty years, and died on 16 November 1943 at his home, The Hut, Coast Road, West Mersea, Essex, after a short illness. He was cremated at Golders Green on 22 November.

ANNE PIMLOTT BAKER

Sources D. G. Browne, *The rise of Scotland Yard: a history of the metropolitan police* (1956) · W. Best, 'C' or St James's: a history of policing in the West End of London, 1829–1984 (1985) · M. Fido and K. Skinner, *The official encyclopedia of Scotland Yard* (1999) · N. Macready, *Annals of an active life* (1924) · H. A. Taylor, *Jix, Viscount Brentford* (1933), chap. 23, 210–21 · *The Times* (19 Nov 1943) · WW · m. cert. · d. cert. · CGPLA Eng. & Wales (1944)

Archives HLRO, letters to David Lloyd George | FILM BFI NFTVA, news footage

Likenesses photograph, c.1923, repro. in Fido and Skinner, *Official encyclopedia*, 126 · Lafayette, photograph, 1928, NPG [*see illus.*]

Wealth at death £20,559 3s. 8d.: probate, 3 June 1944, CGPLA Eng. & Wales

Hosack, John (d. **1887**), police magistrate and author, was the third son of John R. Hosack of Glenaher, Dumfriesshire. He became a student of the Middle Temple on 26 January 1838, was called to the bar on 29 January 1841, and practised on the northern circuit and at the Liverpool sessions. Though not a QC, on 22 May 1875 he was made a bencher of his inn, and in 1877 he became police magistrate at Clerkenwell, London. He was also an examiner in international and constitutional law at the Middle Temple. Hosack was married but his wife predeceased him and there were no surviving children at his death. He died at his house, 172 Finborough Road, West Brompton, on 3 November 1887, and was buried at Lytham in Lancashire.

Hosack wrote *A Treatise on the Conflict of Laws of England and Scotland*, only one part of which was published, in 1847; *The rights of British and neutral commerce, as affected by recent royal declarations and orders in council*, 1854; *Mary Queen of Scots and her Accusers*, a defence of the queen, 1869; *On the rise and growth of the law of nations, … from the earliest times to the treaty of Utrecht*, 1882; and *Mary Stewart: a brief statement of the principal charges which have been brought against her, together with answers to the same*, published posthumously in 1888.

W. A. J. ARCHBOLD, rev. ERIC METCALFE

Sources J. Foster, *Men-at-the-bar: a biographical hand-list of the members of the various inns of court*, 2nd edn (1885) · *Law Journal* (12 Nov 1887) · catalogue [BM] · CGPLA Eng. & Wales (1888)

Wealth at death £8250 15s. 10d.: administration, 3 Jan 1888, CGPLA Eng. & Wales

Hosain, Attia Shahid (1913–1998), writer and broadcaster, was born on 20 October 1913 in Lucknow in the province of Uttar Pradesh in northern India, one of five children of Shahid Hosain Kidwai. She belonged to one of the feudal landowning families, the *talukdars*, which in the twentieth century produced many prominent and distinguished men. Her father had studied at Christ's College, Cambridge, and the inns of court, and was a friend of Motilal Nehru, the father of Jawaharlal Nehru, and well known in political circles. Her mother came from a family of scholars and poets and was the founder of an institution for women's education and welfare that was still in existence at the end of the century. Attia Hosain was only eleven years old when her father died, and her mother took over all responsibility for the estate and for her children, bringing them all up strictly according to Muslim tradition. She had English governesses and attended La Martinière School for Girls in Lucknow, but when she returned home had private tuition in Urdu and Persian and read the Koran. Hosain went on to the Isabella Thoburn College at the University of Lucknow, then the foremost college for women in India, and in 1933 became the first woman from a *talukdari* family to graduate. Nevertheless, she envied her brother who had been sent to Cambridge to study, met his friends when they returned, and was influenced by their left-wing politics and socialist and communist leanings. She attended the first Progressive Writers' Conference and could be called a fellow traveller. Although Hosain did not join the Communist Party, she remained an ardent socialist all her life.

Hosain married her cousin, Ali Bahadur Habibullah, the son of the vice-chancellor of the University of Lucknow, who was prominent in the nationalist politics of the time, and was herself swept up in the agitation for independence from British rule. Her early writing appeared in *The Pioneer*, then edited by Desmond Young, and also in *The Statesman*, the leading English newspaper in Calcutta. She was in England when India became independent in 1947, along with her husband, who was doing war repatriation work; he returned to India (and predeceased her), but she chose to remain in England with her two small children and began to earn her own living by broadcasting and presenting a women's programme on the Eastern Service of the BBC.

In 1953 Chatto and Windus published a collection of Hosain's short stories, *Phoenix Fled*, which John Connell described as 'little vignettes, precise, loving and exquisitely true in spirit and in fact'. The *Times Literary Supplement* noted her unusual distinction and charm. In 1961 she published her only novel, *Sunlight on a Broken Column*, a portrait of her native city of Lucknow and of its feudal society's struggle to change, or else to retain, its beliefs and structure during the independence movement of the twentieth century. Of this society she wrote that 'They loved the city to which they belonged, and they lived and behaved as if the city belonged to them' (Hosain, 35).

Both books are marked by a rich and graceful English prose that reflects the ornate and formal traditions of Urdu and Persian literature, by their interpretation of feudalism that was Attia Hosain's background and that she considered noble and protective at best and cruel and unjust at worst, and by her ability to create characters who were aristocrats and born of privilege as well as those who served them and lived in grinding poverty. They are prose representations of busy Mughal miniatures with all their vivid detail of a way of life that lasted many centuries in India. The books enjoyed a resurgence of interest when Virago brought out new editions in 1988.

Attia Hosain's *œuvre* is small because she was her own harshest critic and destroyed much of what she wrote. She also had a vivid, exuberant personality that enjoyed society—she counted among her many friends Cecil Day Lewis and Compton MacKenzie—and in London her Chelsea flat was open to friends and admirers from around the world. In 1961 she acted on the West End stage with Gladys Cooper in Peter Mayne's play *The Bird of Time*. Even towards the end of her life she found it difficult to refuse to receive a guest or decline an invitation. Her last public appearance, shortly before her death, was at Nehru House in London for the launch of a volume of short stories by Indian women writers living abroad; it was published as a tribute to her.

Attia Hosain died on 23 January 1998 in the Chelsea and Westminster Hospital, Chelsea, London; she was survived by her son Waris Hussein, a theatre and film director, and a daughter, Shama Habibullah, a film-maker. Attia Hosain was remembered by all who knew her for her wit, her elegance, her cosmopolitanism (she had declared 'I am a universalist-humanist'), her fierce championing of causes dear to her, and her legendary beauty that even when she was in her eighties could take one's breath away.

ANITA DESAI

Sources *The Guardian* (31 Jan 1998) · private information (2004) [A. Amer Hussein] · N. E. Bharucha, *Biblio* (July–Aug 1998) · A. Hosain, *Sunlight on a broken column* (1988) · *CGPLA Eng. & Wales* (1998) · [E. L. Sturch], review, *TLS* (4 Dec 1953), 773 · d. cert.
Wealth at death under £180,000: probate, 1998, *CGPLA Eng. & Wales*

Hose, Charles (1863–1929), colonial official and ethnologist, was born on 12 October 1863 at Willian, Hertfordshire, the second son and second child in the family of four sons and two daughters of Thomas Charles Hose, a Church of England priest, later rector of Roydon, Norfolk, and his wife, Fanny (*c.*1840–*c.*1927), daughter of Thomas Goodfellow of Hall O'Wood, Staffordshire, owner of the pottery works at Tunstall, famous for having introduced willow-pattern china into England. He spent his childhood in Norfolk, and was educated at Felsted School, Essex, before going up to Jesus College, Cambridge, in 1882.

Hose left Cambridge during his second year, without taking a degree, to take up a cadetship in the Sarawak civil service under the second raja, Sir Charles Brooke, arranged by his uncle George Frederick *Hose (1838–1922), bishop of Singapore, Labuan, and Sarawak. Before sailing for Kuching in 1884 he spent six months with the

Cleveland Mineral Railway in Yorkshire, studying surveying. In Sarawak, he was sent to the mangrove swamps of the remote Baram River district, annexed from the sultanate of Brunei in 1882, and in 1888 he was appointed officer in charge of the district. In 1891 he was made resident of the fourth division (Sarawak was divided into five administrative divisions), and from 1894 he served on the Council Negri (the state council). In the Baram, Hose forbade headhunting (although infringements were punished by allowing retaliatory headhunting raids), and he was very proud of the 1899 peacemaking at Marudi, where after four years of preparation he gathered 6000 people of the local groups still hostile to each other, and made them swear to keep the peace. This was followed by the Baram regatta, inspired by his days at Cambridge, with boat races which he hoped would divert people from headhunting. According to tradition, Raja Charles Brooke liked to have big men in his service. Hose was a big man, weighing at least 25 stone, and the story was told of how he averted a threatened rising by sending a messenger ahead with a pair of his enormous trousers, warning that the man who wore them was on his way. In 1904 Hose was promoted to the position of resident (first class) of the third division, at Sibu, on the north coast, and was made a member of the supreme council. He continued his peacemaking activities with a successful expedition against Iban rebels around Bukit Batu in 1904, and in 1907 he negotiated peace between the upper Batang Lupar Ibans and the downriver Rejang Ibans.

Far from being lonely and bored during his sixteen years in the Sarawak interior, Hose spent much of his time exploring the rain forest, collecting plants and other natural history specimens, encouraged by Raja Charles Brooke, who had founded the Sarawak Museum and wanted specimens for it. He discovered many new species of animals, insects, birds, and fish, including a species of squirrel, *Sciuropterus hosei*, and several new plants, including the flowering plant *Oberonia hosei*. He made the first map of Sarawak, which was published in 1924. Hose also became interested in ethnography, and studied the people of the Baram River area, collecting cultural specimens such as war shields, making notes, and taking photographs. He believed that social anthropology should be applied to government, and tried to put his own insights to work. He later donated some of his collections to museums in England and abroad, including the British Museum, which has the Hose collection of the life and culture of Sarawak, and the Museum of Ethnology in Cambridge, while he sold others to dealers. He wanted his observations and theories to be taken seriously by scholars, and gave hospitality to many visitors, including members of the Cambridge University Torres Strait expedition, led by Dr A. C. Haddon and including William McDougall, whom he persuaded to spend six months in the Baram on their way back to England in 1898-9. They were present at the 1899 peacemaking. After he had suffered from beriberi he did extensive research into the causes of the disease, and it was he who discovered that it was caused by eating polished rice. He read a paper on the causes of beriberi to the British Medical Association in 1905.

Raja Charles Brooke insisted that his officials remain single for at least ten years, and preferably throughout their Sarawak careers, expecting them to retire on their official pensions in their mid-forties. In 1905 Hose married Emilie (Poppy) Ellen, daughter of John Peter Ravn. They had one son and one daughter. He retired to England, settling in Norfolk, and spent the rest of his life writing and lecturing about Sarawak, while continuing to make frequent visits there. His three most important books were *The Pagan Tribes of Borneo* (2 vols., 1912), to which William McDougall added his name, copies of which Hose presented to all the leading anthropologists, and which by 1924 was required reading for cadets in the Sarawak civil service; *Natural Man* (1926), an abridged and more popular version of *The Pagan Tribes of Borneo*; and his autobiography, *Fifty Years of Romance and Research, or, A Jungle-Wallah at Large* (1927). Hose was writing at a time when fieldwork was replacing 'armchair' anthropology, and although his fieldwork was less rigorous than that of academic anthropologists, he did succeed in winning academic recognition, and some of his terminology became widely accepted, such as his use of the term 'Iban' to describe the Sea Dyaks to avoid the confusion surrounding the word 'Dyak', previously used by the English and Dutch for any of the pagan tribes, and his term 'Klemantan' for any unclassified groups. Hose also wrote the article on Sarawak in the eleventh edition of the *Encyclopaedia Britannica*.

Perhaps the most significant contribution made by Hose to the future prosperity of Sarawak was the part he played in the development of the oilfield at Miri, in the mouth of the Baram River. His predecessor as resident, Claude de Crespigny, had discovered oil in 1882, but it was Hose who followed up Crespigny's work with the help of his brother Ernest Hose, who ran the Borneo Company's rubber plantations in Sarawak. He compiled a detailed map of the oil seepages, and in 1909, with the raja's permission, took his map and samples to the Anglo-Saxon Petroleum Company (part of Royal Dutch-Shell) in London. With Dr Erb, a Swiss geologist, he travelled to Sarawak by way of the Trans-Siberian Railway, and after a successful survey the raja gave Shell the exclusive right to explore for oil. Hose was able to secure a small percentage of the profits for himself. The first well was drilled in 1910, and by 1929 Sarawak was the second largest oil-producing area in the British empire, although production declined after this.

Hose spent most of the First World War in King's Lynn, running a munitions factory. He was appointed to the Sarawak state advisory council in Westminster in 1919 (Sarawak, although not a British protectorate, had been under British protection since 1888), and he helped prepare the Sarawak pavilion for the 1924 British Empire Exhibition at Wembley. Among the many honours he received were a ScD from Cambridge University in 1900, and an honorary fellowship of Jesus College, Cambridge, in 1926. Hose died on 14 November 1929 at the Hutton Nursing Home in Purley Oaks, Surrey, following an operation. He was buried four days later at Bandon Hill cemetery in Beddington, Surrey. At his funeral the coffin was draped with the Sarawak flag.   ANNE PIMLOTT BAKER

Sources C. Hose, *Fifty years of romance and research, or, A jungle-wallah at large* (1927) [repr. 1994 with introduction by B. Durrans] • C. Hose and W. McDougall, *The pagan tribes of Borneo*, 2 vols. (1912) [repr. 1994 with intro by B. Durrans] • C. Hose, *Natural man* (1926) [repr. in 1988 with intro by B. Durrans] • R. Pringle, *Rajahs and rebels: the Ibans of Sarawak under Brooke rule, 1841–1941* (1970) • T. Harrisson and B. Brunig, 'Hose's Irrawaddy pioneers', *Sarawak Museum Journal*, new ser., 6/6 (1955), 518–21 • A. H. Moy-Thomas, 'Economic development under the second rajah, 1870–1917', *Sarawak Museum Journal*, new ser., 10/17–18 (1961), 50–58 • E. Hose, 'Notes from the old days', *Sarawak Museum Journal*, new ser., 10/17–18 (1961), 108–11 • G. C. Harper, 'The Miri field, 1910–1972', *Sarawak Museum Journal*, 20/40–41 (1973), 21–30 • S. Runciman, *The white rajahs: a history of Sarawak from 1841 to 1946* (1960) • C. Hose, 'The constitutional development of Sarawak', *Asiatic Review*, 25 (1929), 481–91 • *The Times* (15 Nov 1929) • *CGPLA Eng. & Wales* (1930)
Archives BM, department of ethnography, Photographic Library, photographs and negatives • NHM, black and white prints of photographs of the peoples, animals, and plants of Sarawak • Royal Anthropological Institute, London, photographs and negatives • U. Cam., Museum of Archaeology and Anthropology | BL, corresp. with Macmillans, Add. MS 55157
Likenesses photographs, 1907–21, repro. in Hose, *Pagan tribes of Borneo*, vol. 1, facing pp. vii, xv • wood figure, University of Pennsylvania, Philadelphia, Museum of Archaeology and Anthropology; repro. in Hose, *Pagan tribes of Borneo*, vol. 1, p xxx
Wealth at death £8382: probate, 19 Feb 1930, *CGPLA Eng. & Wales*

Hose, George Frederick (1838–1922), bishop of Singapore, Labuan, and Sarawak, was born in Brunswick Place, Cambridge, on 3 September 1838, the son of Frederick Hose, a clerk, and his wife, Mary Ann Knight. Educated at St John's College, Cambridge, where he graduated MA, he was ordained at Ely as deacon in 1861 and priest the following year. Appointed colonial chaplain at Melaka in 1868, he moved to Singapore in 1872, and two years later became Singapore's first archdeacon, responsible to Bishop Walter Chambers, who was based in Sarawak.

Hose and his gentle wife, Emily, were an intelligent, conscientious, kindly couple, and they fitted happily into Singapore society. Hose was proficient in Malay and a keen botanist, and he helped to found the public library and museum in 1874, and was the prime mover and first president of the Straits Asiatic Society, which in May 1878 was affiliated as the Straits (later Malaysian) branch of the Royal Asiatic Society.

Chambers recommended Hose as his successor, but the Society for the Propagation of the Gospel in Foreign Parts (SPG), hesitated, favouring new blood to rejuvenate the diocese. Nevertheless, Hose was eventually appointed, in December 1880, and consecrated by the archbishop of Canterbury at Lambeth Palace in London on 26 May 1881; he was enthroned as bishop of Singapore and Labuan in Singapore on 27 November 1881 and given letters patent as bishop of Sarawak from Raja Charles Brooke in Kuching on 17 January 1882.

The unwieldy diocese embraced some 120,000 square miles, with Kuching and Singapore 450 miles apart by sea, and it involved expanding responsibilities for the protected (later federated) Malay states, British North Borneo, and British communities in Siam and the East Indies. In his early years Hose achieved much, attracting many converts and improving schools in Singapore and Kuching. An enthusiastic traveller, he spent half the year in Singapore and the other half in Kuching, with annual tours to outlying Dyak missions and occasional visits to North Borneo, Labuan, and the Malay states. While the Anglican church's prime concern in British Malaya was with westerners, Hose as chaplain in Melaka had set up a mission among the Chinese, and as bishop he encouraged work among Asians in Singapore, Penang, and Kuala Lumpur. He translated the New Testament and Book of Common Prayer into Malay, ordained a few Tamil and Chinese priests, and opened new churches which conducted vernacular services. However, he favoured neither a full Asian ministry, nor the merging of European and Asian congregations.

Always overstretched, the diocese lost ground to the Roman Catholic and Methodist missionaries, who reached out to the Asian communities both in the Peninsula and in Borneo. While in England in 1901, Hose appealed in vain to the SPG for experienced recruits and more resources. Already distressed by Sarawak press criticism of Anglican schools, Hose was then grief-stricken when Emily died of cancer in Kuching in July 1904. Never a man of fire, he lost heart and let administration drift. In Borneo he left matters to the energetic Arthur Sharp, vicar-general at Kuching from 1898. However, despite Sharp's success among Asians, promoting local staff and converting many Chinese, the raja lost patience with the Anglican mission, and, with wide public support, in 1905 the archdeacon of Singapore appealed to the SPG both to send a new young bishop and to divide the see of Singapore from Borneo. This split was unanimously endorsed at a public meeting in Singapore in December 1905.

Initially Hose resisted retiring, and continued to enjoy the relaxing climate, and he planted Borneo's first rubber trees in the beautiful garden he had created with his wife. However, he supported dividing the diocese, which was agreed in principle in 1907, and finally left Kuching in December 1907. He received an affectionate farewell at Singapore's Memorial Hall, on 4 February 1908, and a memorial chalice and paten were afterwards used in his honour on special occasions at St Andrew's Cathedral. After the Lambeth conference in London, Hose submitted his formal resignation, in November 1908, and retired in England. He died at his home, the Manor House, Normandy, near Farnham, Surrey, on 26 March 1922.

C. M. TURNBULL

Sources A. F. Sharp, *The wings of the morning* (1954) • G. Saunders, *Brookes and bishops, 1848–1941: the Anglican mission and the Brooke raj in Sarawak* (1992) • B. Taylor, *The Anglican church in Borneo, 1848–1962* (1983) • *Mission Field* [monthly journal of the SPG] (May 1922) • F. G. Swindell, *A short history of St Andrew's Cathedral* (1929) • E. Green,

Borneo, the land of river and palm (1910) · W. Makepeace, G. E. Brooke, and R. St J. Braddell, *One hundred years of Singapore*, 2 vols. (1921); repr. (1991) · B. Taylor and P. M. Heyward, *The Kuching Anglican schools, 1848–1973* (1973) · M. S. Northcott, 'Two hundred years of Anglican mission', *Christianity in Malaysia: a denominational history*, ed. R. Hunt, K. H. Lee, and J. Roxborough (1991) · K. A. Loh, 'Fifty years of the Anglican church in Singapore island, 1909–1959', BA diss., University of Malaya, 1960 · B. E. K. Sng, *In his good time* (1980) · H. P. Thompson, *Into all lands* (1951) · R. Pringle, *Rajahs and rebels: the Ibans of Sarawak under Brooke rule, 1841–1941* (1970) · S. Baring-Gould and C. A. Bampfylde, *A history of Sarawak under its two white rajahs, 1839–1908* (1909) · b. cert. · d. cert.

Archives LPL, corresp. with A. C. Tait

Likenesses photograph, repro. in *Mission Field* (1895), frontispiece · photograph, repro. in Green, *Borneo*

Wealth at death £2954 3s. 6d.: probate, 27 May 1922, CGPLA Eng. & Wales

Hose, Robert John (1863–1935), banker, was born on 13 October 1863 at 201 Bethnal Green Road, London, the youngest of the three children (two boys, one girl) of Joseph Hose, a well-to-do master butcher, and his wife, Christian Anna, *née* Pringle. Hose was educated privately. He entered the City at fifteen and gained experience of South American trade and banking. His father died in 1883, leaving an estate of nearly £11,000; his mother died in 1890. In 1884 he married Victoria Rosina, known as 'Queenie' (d. 1936), daughter of Henry Boyle, gentleman; they had five sons and one daughter.

In May 1896 Hose was appointed secretary to the Bank of Tarapacá and London, a company set up in 1888 by Colonel John T. North to finance the export of nitrate from northern Chile. North died in the month that Hose was recruited. The history of the dynamic expansion of the bank mirrors Hose's relentless rise through its senior management. Within a year, he was promoted to the double role of sub-manager and secretary, and became manager and secretary in 1900. In the following year, his acquisition of the roughly coeval Anglo-Argentine Bank marked the first of the takeovers and affiliations which were to be the hallmark of his leadership. His company was then renamed the Bank of Tarapacá and Argentina, of which he became general manager and secretary in 1902.

The merger brought fresh blood, notably the Belgian, Edward Bunge, compensating for the resignation in 1903 of W. H. Young, an autobiographer as well as a banker, who had brilliantly run and extended the bank's Chilean operations since 1894. To re-establish stability and strengthen morale, Hose left England in November 1905 on a six-week tour of inspection. In 1907 his company was renamed the Anglo-South American Bank (usually shortened to the 'Anglo Bank'), reflecting the true scope of Hose's ambition. In the same year he went to New York to open an agency.

Hose next set his sights on Mexico and the northern countries of South America. In Colombia, he bought a stake in the Cortés Commercial and Banking Company, renamed the Commercial Bank of Spanish America in 1911, whose business, rooted in the financing of the coffee trade, was in need of new capital. At the same time, Hose courted the London Bank of Mexico and South America, partly to acquire its Chilean interests, which were a threat to the profitability of the Anglo Bank, of which he had become managing director in 1911. The high price which he had to pay for the Mexican bank in October 1912 was the first jolt to his expansionist aims.

The First World War aggravated, briefly, an existing weakness in some Latin American economies. However, rising commodity prices in Europe soon brightened export markets and Hose swept on in bullish style, building up the Anglo Bank's balance sheet quite dramatically from some £17 million in 1914 to £98 million in 1919–20. Early in 1918, he felt able to move from a minority holding in the Commercial Bank of Spanish America to outright control. In the same year, he became chairman and managing director of the Anglo Bank.

The immediate post-war years in Latin America consolidated a boom which had set in even before hostilities ceased in Europe. Hose cast about aggressively, seeking some entry to Brazil, the major omission in his South American domain. In 1920, when the bank's profitability and dividend payments outstripped all its Latin American competition, he abandoned agency arrangements with the London and Brazilian Bank and bought up its rival, the British Bank of South America. This bank continued under his own chairmanship. In the same year, he bought a significant private bank in Chile (Banco A. Edwards y Cía). But even then the boom was subsiding as Europe and the United States cut back on imports, and Hose fought throughout the 1920s to maintain the Anglo Bank's position. The Chilean economy suffered as the production of synthetic nitrate undercut the raw material in which the Anglo Bank had invested heavily. Hose ran into liquidity problems and faced a loan portfolio increasingly ill-secured. Recovery was also hampered by a decision he made in 1910 to set up the Anglo-South American Property Company, to which he sold his bank's branches. As this was an independent company, its assets could not be realized when the Anglo Bank was in trouble, nor was the book value of the branches marked down, to conform with the normal practice of prudential banking. Hose resigned as managing director early in 1928, but battled on as chairman until 1931. A rescue package negotiated with the Bank of England proved ineffectual. In 1936 the Anglo Bank was liquidated, certain assets passing to the Bank of London and South America.

The importance of Hose, apart from the vast achievements of his restless energy, lay in his knack of assimilating able men of different banks and races and orchestrating their varied abilities. He made mistakes, for instance locking up the value of his bank's premises by the creation of an *ad hoc* management company, but he was not responsible for the ultimate collapse of his empire. In physique, Hose had a frame to match the robustness of his policies, but his health was for some years undermined by the problems of the bank. He also overstretched himself in the number and diversity of his outside directorships. He was chairman of Combined Tin Smelters Ltd, and on the board of the London and Lancashire Insurance Company Ltd, the Antofagasta (Chili) and Bolivia Railway Company Ltd, and the Trust and Agency Company of Australasia Ltd. Hose, who had never forfeited the respect of City colleagues, died at Copenhagen on 27 August 1935. His widow died in Chislehurst, Kent, on 26 April 1936.

JOHN BOOKER

Sources Kelly, *Handbk* · *Commercial encyclopedia*, British and Latin American Chamber of Commerce (1922) · *WWW* · *Bankers' Magazine*, 140 (1935), 492 · D. Joslin, *A century of banking in Latin America* (1963) · G. Jones, *British multinational banking, 1830–1990: a history* (1993) · b. cert.
Archives Lloyds TSB, London, TSB archives, records of Anglo-South American Bank · UCL, BOLSA archive, letter-books, etc., of Anglo-South American Bank
Likenesses photograph, repro. in *Commercial encyclopedia*, British and Latin American Chamber of Commerce, 1193
Wealth at death £11,953 1s. 5d.: administration with will, 13 Nov 1935, *CGPLA Eng. & Wales*

Hosie, Sir Alexander (1853–1925), diplomatist and explorer, was born at Inverurie, Aberdeenshire, on 16 January 1853, the elder son and second child of Alexander Hosie, a farmer, and his wife, Jean, daughter of James Anderson. His father's farm did not prosper, and the family moved to Aberdeen, where the elder Alexander Hosie was accidentally killed in 1869. Hosie was educated at Old Aberdeen grammar school and at King's College, Aberdeen; he worked his way through the university by taking pupils, graduated in 1872, and was appointed sub-librarian of the university. However, in 1876 he joined the Chinese consular service, and sailed for China with his lifelong friend and future chief, Sir John Newell Jordan.

Hosie's first post, after he had finished his student interpretership at Peking (Beijing), was in Shanghai. At that time Edward Colborne Baber was the chief consular traveller of inland China, and at his suggestion Hosie was sent in 1882 on special service to Chungking (Chongqing). Isolated and lonely in this far western province of Szechwan (Sichuan), he soon realized the need, and the opportunity, of devoting himself to some absorbing preoccupation. At much risk, he set out on a series of travels in the interior, making full notes as he journeyed of the geography and products of the country. This resulted in his first book, *Three Years in Western China* (1889), which passed through two editions. In it he described for the first time the trade and showed the potentialities of those little-known regions.

On 1 December 1887 Hosie married Florence (d. 1905), daughter of John Lindsay, corn factor, of Aberdeen; they had one son. Considerations of the welfare of his family in a notoriously hostile and frequently unhealthy environment were to affect Hosie's acceptance of various postings throughout his career. He saw service in Canton (Guangzhou), Wenchow (Wenzhou), Chefoo (Yantai), Amoy (Xiamen), Tamsui (Danshui), and Wuhu, and in 1894 went north to take charge of the consulate at Newchwang (Yingkou) during the difficult days of the Sino-Japanese War. In 1897 he was sent south to Pagoda Anchorage and

then, as consul, to Wuchow (Wuzhou), a port much harassed by river pirates. After the Boxer uprising (1900), during which he was on home leave, he went north to take charge again at Newchwang. He travelled extensively in Manchuria, and in 1901 produced his book *Manchuria: its People, Resources, and Recent History*, which passed through two editions. His official duties were concerned with the defence of British trade in Manchuria against the diplomatic and military inroads on Chinese sovereignty of Russia and Japan; but he was always proud that he on one occasion received the thanks of the Chinese government for his effective defence of the Chinese maritime customs on behalf of China, at a time when Chinese officials had fled before Japanese troops.

In 1903 Hosie was appointed first consul-general at Chengtu (Chengdu) in Szechwan. The boat which took him up the Yangtze (Yangzi) River was wrecked, he narrowly escaped with his life, many of his goods were lost, and his books had ten days' soaking at the bottom of the river. He used his term at Chengtu to compile a white paper on the products of the province, which in 1922 he republished in book form as *Szechwan: its Industries and Resources*. He journeyed to the verge of the forbidden land of Tibet, and brought to official notice the boundary-stone which was to figure largely in the tripartite boundary discussions at Darjeeling in 1914. From 1908 to 1912 Hosie was given the rank of consul-general at Tientsin (Tianjin), but did not proceed to that post; and from 1905 to 1909 was retained as acting commercial attaché to the legation at Peking, in which post he did much pioneer work on behalf of trade. In 1907 he was knighted.

In 1908 the government of India offered to stop the export of opium to China if China abandoned the cultivation of the opium poppy. Hosie was appointed commissioner to arrange proceedings, and in 1909 was British delegate at the Shanghai International Opium Commission, which led to his being sent in the following year, at the request of the Indian government, to visit the chief opium-growing provinces of China in order to monitor progress. He published an account of his investigations as *On the Trail of the Opium Poppy* (2 vols., 1914), which included much information on agricultural and other economic products.

Hosie retired in 1912, having travelled in each of the twenty-two provinces of China, except Sinkiang (Xinjiang). He settled at Sandown, Isle of Wight, where he was active in public affairs. On 2 January 1913 he married Dorothea [see below], daughter of William Edward Soothill (1861–1935), a Methodist missionary in China and professor of Chinese at Oxford University, and his wife, Lucy Farrar. In 1919 he revisited China on a trade commission, and was retained as special attaché in Peking until early in 1920. In 1922, as a result of his many hardships, his right foot was amputated. Aided by his second wife, he edited Philips's *Commercial Map of China* (1922), the authoritative economic map of China, a work of great accuracy and research.

Interested in botany, Hosie sent thousands of specimens to Kew, Hong Kong, and Singapore, especially from

Szechwan. About 1905 or 1906 the Kew authorities requested Sir Ernest Satow, then minister in Peking, that his services might be specially requisitioned for this work, and they named an order of tropical tree, *Ormosia hosiei*, after him. In 1885 he had been proposed as the recipient of the Royal Geographical Society medal, which was, however, awarded to H. M. Stanley, who found David Livingstone in that year. In 1913 Aberdeen University conferred on him the honorary degree of LLD. Hosie died at Coleford, Broadway, Sandown, on 10 March 1925.

He was survived by his second wife, **Dorothea Hosie**, Lady Hosie (1885–1959). She had been born in Ningbo, China, and educated at Newnham College, Cambridge, before marrying Hosie, who was considerably her senior. She had assisted her father by editing several of his works of Chinese scholarship for publication, and likewise assisted her husband. After Hosie's death, however, she published several works on China in her own right, including *Brave New China* (1938); she contributed the memoir of Sir John Jordan to the *Dictionary of National Biography*. President of the National Free Church Women's Council in 1932–3, she published *Jesus and Woman* (1946; rev. edn, 1956), which also had an American edition. A lecturer on Chinese affairs and a member of the Isle of Wight educational committee 1916–24, in 1938 she took up the post of vice-principal at Brampton Down Girls' School in Folkestone, which she retained until 1946. She died at the General Infirmary, Salisbury, on 15 February 1959.

W. E. SOOTHILL, rev. K. D. REYNOLDS

Sources private information (1937) • personal knowledge (1937) • P. D. Coates, *The China consuls: British consular officers, 1843–1943* (1988) • Burke, *Peerage* (1924)
Archives RGS, Manchuria travel diary | Mitchell L., NSW, letters to G. E. Morrison
Wealth at death £1671 13s. 9d.: probate, 31 March 1925, *CGPLA Eng. & Wales* • £4795 3s. 0d.—Dorothea Hosie: probate, 1 April 1959, *CGPLA Eng. & Wales*

Hosie, Dorothea, Lady Hosie (1885–1959). *See under* Hosie, Sir Alexander (1853–1925).

Hosier, Arthur Julius (1877–1963), farmer and engineer, was born on 16 October 1877 at Shawford, Somerset, the twelfth and youngest child of Joshua Hosier, tenant dairy farmer, and his second wife, Sarah Fricker, a farmer's daughter from Frome. His was the fourth generation of farmers in the family but his father did not prosper in the profession. Having failed as an arable farmer in the difficult years of the 1880s, Joshua Hosier took to dairy farming in the 1890s when at Atworth, near Melksham in Wiltshire. This proved to be no more successful and he was forced to take a small, poor-quality and under-capitalized farm on which Arthur Hosier began to learn his trade. Yet from humble beginnings Hosier built up in his lifetime a farming complex which by 1954 extended to 22,000 acres, much of which he and his family owned.

Hosier's farm apprenticeship was hard. From the age of nine he helped with the milking, morning and evening. Despite a successful record at Bradford-on-Avon grammar school, much of his time was diverted to farm work. As well as helping with harvesting, he learned to operate a steam-powered threshing engine which, on leaving school at thirteen, he and his brother took away for long periods on contract work. In 1896 he and a brother were successful tenant farmers, selling milk at 5d. per gallon. Five years later, aged twenty-four, Hosier had his own tenancy, and by 1910 he was farming some 600 acres. In 1901 Hosier married Ruth (d. 1950), the daughter of George William Smith, a tenant farmer, of Broad Blunsdon. They had two sons and three daughters. In 1953 Hosier married Florence Joyce Orchard, of Collingbourne, with whom he had one daughter.

Hosier's early interest in machinery continued with a number of inventions, such as the first side-rake and a mechanical milk filter, for which he was awarded a medal at the 1904 London Dairy Show. In the same year he took over an engineering business following the death of his brother-in-law, Uriah Whatley. The engineering knowledge he gained, particularly regarding well-boring, was to prove very useful later in his farming career.

In 1910 Hosier returned to farming with his brother Joshua to grow corn on a large scale. Succeeding as arable farmers, they had sufficient capital in 1920 to purchase the 1700 acre Wexcombe estate, in a poor downland area near Marlborough in Wiltshire, worth about £5 per acre.

Wexcombe was to become Hosier's home for the rest of his life and where he was to develop the open-air dairying system for which he is best known. He foresaw that, with the end of the war, the importation of cheap cereals would soon resume. Convinced that the future lay with low-cost milk production he set out on a new venture, despite the topographical problems posed by an estate on derelict downland with few buildings, a poor water supply, and no roads. The Hosier system, as it is better known, derived from necessity and a knowledge of practices in Australia (possibly from his brother Sidney, who had emigrated there in 1919). The essence of the system was a portable milking installation (or 'bail') that could be drawn by a tractor and used in the fields. The original design provided six stalls abreast and formed part of a four-wheeled structure with a roof. A converted shepherd's hut was used to house machinery, including the engine and vacuum pump, and also a boiler to produce hot water for cleaning and sterilizing, a dynamo for lighting, and later a refrigeration unit for cooling the milk. The bail was moved daily by a tractor or winch about its own length. This low-cost production system was ideally suited to the prevailing economic circumstances and was profitable even though milk prices had collapsed after the war from 2s. 6d. per gallon to as little as 6d. Milk was sold to London, initially by Hosier himself, using a lorry, and later by United Dairies, who bought him out.

Following the first experiment in 1922, Hosier's system was operated throughout the year, even in the hardest winters. At its peak, there was a milking herd of 300 cows (mainly humble Irish heifers—that is, non-pedigree all-purpose animals) for which Hosier required five milking bails and only sixteen regular farm staff. The combination of open-air conditions and meticulous attention to hygiene resulted in high-quality milk, including grade A

(T. T.) milk for which he gained a better price. His profitability—varying from 3s. 3d. to 8s. 6d. per gallon—owed much to the greatly reduced labour costs and minimal expenses on buildings and equipment compared with the conventional cowshed system. The bail system was taken up by other innovative farmers, such as the Strattons in Wiltshire. By 1930 there were some eighty-six farms using the Hosier system and producing enough milk to supply a town the size of Leicester. Ten years later there were almost 200 farmers using the system in Wiltshire and the surrounding counties. Indeed the Second World War provided a further spur to its wider adoption. Although limited in application to light soil districts and to larger farms with good water supplies, its impact was considerable and the development of liquid milk production in these areas is comparable in its significance to the transformation of Essex farming before the First World War.

Hosier did not neglect his farming in the broader sense. At Brunton, a mixed farm of 1500 acres bought in 1929, he developed a system of 'alternate husbandry', which allowed for ploughing up pasture and grassing down arable land as opportunity offered. This gave him scope for more new ideas, such as ploughing, pressing, seeding, and harrowing in one operation, and the invention of many devices for bush clearance, hay and silage making, and cereal harvesting. As part of the so-called 'apex fold' system, he designed a portable poultry unit enabling some 5000 laying hens to accompany each dairy herd, using the same land. His concern with land reclamation was clearly demonstrated following his acquisition of more than 800 acres of derelict land at Hipponscombe in the mid-1930s.

Hosier was an outstanding pioneer. His love of hard work and his flair for original thought lasted until his death. He was a reserved man, with a deep-rooted aversion to officialdom and committees. His relationship with the National Union of Farmers was an uneasy one because of his highly individualistic and innovative nature. Nevertheless he gave freely of his knowledge to young farmers and was generous in support of charities. He was a Methodist lay preacher throughout his life. In 1949 he was appointed OBE and in 1951 Cambridge University conferred on him the honorary degree of LLD. Hosier died at Wexcombe House, Wexcombe, on 3 April 1963. He was survived by his second wife.   DAVID TAYLOR

Sources The Times (6 April 1963) · A. J. Hosier and F. H. Hosier, Hosier's farming system (1951) · C. S. Orwin, A pioneer of progress in farm management (1931) · R. N. Dixey and M. Messer, Open air dairying: a survey of farms using milk bails in 1932 (1933) · R. N. Dixey, Open air dairy farming: a survey of farms using milking bails in 1940–1941 (1942) · DNB · private information (1995) · d. cert. · CGPLA Eng. & Wales (1963)
Archives Sci. Mus., papers relating to his inventions
Wealth at death £86,853 18s. 6d.: probate, 4 Nov 1963, CGPLA Eng. & Wales

Hosier, Francis (bap. 1673, d. 1727), naval officer, born at Deptford, and baptized at St Nicholas's Church, Deptford Green, on 15 April 1673, was a son of Francis Hosier, clerk of the cheque at Gravesend and agent victualler at Dover, and his wife, Elizabeth, née Hawes. He entered the navy about 1685 and in 1692 was appointed lieutenant of the Neptune, which carried Sir George Rooke's flag at Barfleur.

Hosier's first command was the smack Abraham's Offer in July and August 1694. In 1695 he commanded the Portsmouth Prize, and he took post from 27 June 1696, when he was appointed to the Winchelsea (32 guns). In December 1698 he commanded the Trident Prize; on 12 January 1704 he was appointed to the Burlington (50 guns), and in 1706 he was moved into the Salisbury (50 guns), in which, in October 1707, he brought home from the Isles of Scilly the body of Sir Cloudesley Shovell. Early in 1710, in company with the St Albans off Cape Clear, he captured the large French ship Heureux, which was taken into the navy as the Salisbury Prize. On 4 July 1710 he married Diana Pritchard (d. 1742) with whom he had a daughter. In the following year he went to the West Indies to reinforce Commodore James Littleton, and took a distinguished part in the action with the Spanish galleons off Cartagena on 27 July.

In June 1713 Hosier was appointed to the Monmouth; but at the accession of George I, under suspicion of being an opponent of the Hanoverian succession, he, with several others, was suspended from the service during the king's pleasure. He was reinstated in his rank on 5 March 1717. On 6 March 1719 he was appointed to the Dorsetshire with the temporary rank of rear-admiral, on the special staff of James, third earl of Berkeley. This was only until 15 April, and on 8 May he was promoted rear-admiral of the white. By August he was commanding a division in the Baltic, and he remained there in 1720 and 1721, flying his flag in the Prince Frederick.

On 16 February 1723 Hosier was advanced to vice-admiral of the blue; and on 9 March 1726 he was appointed to command a squadron sent to the West Indies, to prevent the Spaniards sending home treasure. The treasure ships were at Portobello, and when Hosier signified the object of his coming, they were dismantled and the treasure sent back to Panama. Hosier, however, decided to keep up a close blockade of Portobello, in the course of which, while lying at the Bastimentos, a virulent fever broke out among the crews of the squadron. By December the state of all the ships was alarming. With great difficulty they were taken to Jamaica, where they were cleared out, and new men entered to replace the dead. However, the contagion remained, and during the spring and summer, while the squadron was blockading Havana or Vera Cruz, the same mortality continued. Hosier himself at last fell a victim, and after ten days' sickness died at Jamaica on 25 August 1727. In all the fever carried off 4000 men, some fifty lieutenants, and eight or ten captains and flag-officers, including Hosier's immediate successors, Commodore Edward St Lo and Vice-Admiral Edward Hopson. Hosier's body was embalmed, and sent to England by the sloop Happy, and he was buried 'with great funeral pomp' in the church of St Nicholas at Deptford Green on 8 February 1728. The sum of £500 was expended on the ceremony. Although Hosier died intestate, administration of his estates was eventually granted in 1739 to his cousin John Hawes, who claimed to be his only next of kin: this seems to have led to a litigation with Hosier's wife, which was still ongoing at her death in 1742.

Hosier was given a posthumous fame out of all proportion to his actual achievements by the publication in 1740 of Richard Glover's poem 'Admiral Hosier's Ghost'. This was a blatantly political piece which sought to misrepresent Hosier's fate to support then current attacks on the Walpole government, ascribing his death to his resentment at the inactivity forced on him by government orders and his inability to prevent the devastation of his fleet by disease. In the poem Hosier's ghost appeared to his successor in the West Indies, Edward Vernon, who had just captured Portobello:

Heed, Oh heed, our fatal story—
I am Hosier's injur'd ghost—
You, who have now purchased glory
At this place where I was lost,
Though in Portobello's ruin
You now triumph, free from fears,
When you think on our undoing,
You will mix your joy with tears! …
See these mournful spectres sweeping,
Ghastly o'er this hated wave,
Whose wan cheeks are stained with weeping:
These were English captains brave.
Mark those numbers pale and horrid—,
Who were once my sailors bold,
Lo, each hangs his drooping forehead,
While his dismal tale is told. …
Unrepining at thy glory,
Thy successful arms we hail;
But remember our sad story,
And let Hosier's wrongs prevail.
After this proud foe subduing,
When your patriot friends you see,
Think on vengeance for my ruin,
And for England shamed in me.
(Lonsdale, 332–3)

J. K. LAUGHTON, rev. J. D. DAVIES

Sources Hosier's letters to the admiralty, 1726–7, PRO, admiralty MSS, esp. ADM 1/230, ADM 6/424, ADM 8 · R. Glover, 'Admiral Hosier's ghost', *The new Oxford book of eighteenth-century verse*, ed. R. Lonsdale (1984) · papers relating to Hosier's command, BL, Add. MS 33028, fols. 48–174 · list of captains, 1688–1715, NMM, Sergison MS SER/136 · *Report on the manuscripts of Lord Polwarth*, 2, HMC, 67 (1916) · *Report on the manuscripts of Lady Du Cane*, HMC, 61 (1905) · W. L. Clowes, *The Royal Navy: a history from the earliest times to the present*, 7 vols. (1897–1903), vol. 3 · will, PRO, PROB 6/115, fol. 53; 6/119, fol. 7v · will, PRO, PROB 11/720 [Diana Hosier], fol. 298 · parish register, Deptford, St Nicholas, LMA [baptism, death, death of wife] · parish register, Fleet Street, St Bride, LMA, 4 July 1710 [marriage] · Pepys, *Diary*, 10.192–3

Archives BL, Add. MS 33028 · East Riding of Yorkshire Archives Service, Beverley, orders to Captain Henry Medley · PRO, Admiralty MSS

Hosken, James (1798–1885), naval officer and developer of ocean steam navigation, was born at Plymouth on 6 December 1798. His father, a warrant officer, served with distinction through the American War of Independence and the French Revolution, and was present at seventeen general actions, from St Lucia in 1778 to that off Cape Finisterre in 1805. He died at Penryn, Cornwall, on 20 June 1848, aged ninety-one.

James Hosken entered the navy in 1810 as midshipman on the *Formidable*, and served in the Baltic, the Mediterranean, and North Sea until the peace of 1815. Afterwards he served in the *Pique* in the West Indies from 1816 to 1819, for three years in the channel in the brig *Wolf*, and from 1824 to 1828 in the revenue cutter *Scout*, against smugglers. On 9 August 1828 he was promoted lieutenant of the bomb-vessel *Aetna* in the Mediterranean.

In 1831 Hosken transferred to mercantile service. In 1832 he had command of the packet *Tyrian*, carrying the mails to Brazil, and from 1833 to 1836 of a merchant ship trading from Liverpool to South America. In 1837 he devoted himself to the study of the marine steam engine, and towards the end of the year was appointed to the command of Isambard Kingdom Brunel's *Great Western*, a large paddle-steamer built in Bristol to solve the question of the practicability of ocean steam navigation. After going from the Thames to Bristol she left for New York on 8 April 1838 and arrived on the 23rd—a great experiment brought to success. The *Sirius*, which had left Cork some four days before the *Great Western* left Bristol, arrived two hours earlier, making the passage with difficulty in nineteen days, four days more than the *Great Western*. Soon the *Great Western's* fifteen days were reduced to thirteen, and in 1839, after such a run out, 18–31 May, Hosken was presented by the passengers with a telescope, inscribed with a record of the then unparalleled achievement. In November 1843 he was presented with a gold watch by the underwriters of Lloyd's, in testimony of their high opinion of his skill and care 'in having successfully navigated the Great Western steamship sixty-four passages between England and America'.

Hosken's reputation was then high; he had been repeatedly thanked by the Admiralty for information on steam navigation and the screw-propeller. In 1844 he was appointed to command Brunel's Bristol-built, six-masted 'leviathan' the *Great Britain*, the biggest vessel in the world, the first large iron vessel, and the first large screw vessel, regarded as one of the wonders of the world. When she went to London in April 1845 the queen and the prince consort visited her, and Hosken, by her majesty's command, was presented. At Plymouth, Dublin, and Liverpool she was visited by crowds. The *Great Britain* sailed from Liverpool for New York in August 1845, and after making three or four trips was stranded on a sandy beach in Dundrum Bay, co. Down, Ireland, on the night of 22 September 1846. She had left Liverpool the previous morning; the weather became very thick, and Hosken assumed that the light on St John's Point, at the entrance of the bay, was on the Calf of Man, which they had passed four hours before. Hosken blamed his chart, but the stranding was clearly his fault, and raised doubts about his navigational skill. Months afterwards the ship was refloated and repaired, but, understandably, Hosken had no further employment in the merchant service.

From 1848 to 1849 Hosken was, through the patronage of Sir James Brooke, harbour master, postmaster, and chief magistrate at Labuan, off Borneo, then lately ceded to Britain. He also had some correspondence about 1850 with Henry Labouchere, afterwards Lord Taunton, on the

Mercantile Marine Bill, then before the House of Commons. In 1851 he was appointed to command the dispatch vessel *Banshee* in the Mediterranean, and afterwards in the channel. In September 1853 he was promoted commander, and in the Baltic campaigns of 1854–5 commanded the hospital ship *Belle-Isle*. At the end of the Crimean War he was employed in the *Belle-Isle* bringing home troops. In June 1857 he was promoted captain, and he retired in January 1868. He became rear-admiral in 1875, and vice-admiral in August 1879, and, having preserved his faculties to great age, died at his home, 9 Apsley Terrace, Ilfracombe, Devon, on 2 January 1885. He was twice married, and had at least one child. His second wife, Elizabeth Ann, survived him, and in 1889 privately published *Autobiographical Sketch of the Public Career of Admiral James Hosken*.

J. K. LAUGHTON, *rev.* ANDREW LAMBERT

Sources E. Corlett, *The iron ship: the history and significance of Brunel's 'Great Britain'* (1975) · D. Griffith, *Brunel's Great Western* (1981) · A. Tyrell and M. Tyrell, 'The Hosken family papers', *Mariner's Mirror*, 74 (1988), 273–82 · G. Farr, *The steamship Great Britain* (1970) · *Autobiographical sketch of the public career of Admiral James Hosken*, ed. [E. A. Hosken] (privately printed, 1889) · *Annual Register* (1846) · *Nautical Magazine*, 15 (1846), 616 · O'Byrne, *Naval biog. dict.* · Boase, *Mod. Eng. biog.* · *CGPLA Eng. & Wales* (1885)

Archives priv. coll.

Wealth at death £813 17s. 5d.: probate, 13 March 1885, *CGPLA Eng. & Wales*

Hoskier, Herman (1832–1904), merchant banker, was one of at least two sons and daughters of Herman Christian Hoskier, merchant, then based in Christiania, Norway. In 1840 Hoskier's family moved to Copenhagen and by 1846 he and his brother, Emile, were at school in Berlin. About 1848 he went to study in Florence. From an early age his outlook was cosmopolitan and he enjoyed fluency in at least French and English. On 8 February 1860, when working at Mobile in the USA, he married Elizabeth Catherine Byrne of New Orleans.

Hoskier's career began in 1850 with a short stint as a clerk in the Algiers branch of his father's house, H. C. Hoskier & Son of Paris. Later that year he travelled to New York to join the merchants Dutilh & Co. and in 1851 and 1853 spent time in London, latterly with C. Hambro & Co., which at this time rescued his father's firm from ruin. Everard Hambro, later head of Hambros, became a close friend, and later Hoskier's executor. In 1854 Hoskier established Dutilh's Liverpool office, remaining as manager until 1857 and becoming friendly with Stewart Henry Brown.

Brown was a junior partner in Brown Shipley & Co., the British end of the Brown family's leading north Atlantic merchant banking business, and in 1859 Hoskier was appointed Browns' agent at Mobile, dealing largely in cotton. Despite the outbreak of the civil war and the imposition of a blockade, Hoskier managed to secure the passage to Browns in Liverpool of some 30,000 bales of cotton, 'nearly the whole … balance of the year's cotton crop' (Crosby Brown, 275) thereby ensuring large profits on their sale in Britain. In June 1861 Hoskier, with his wife and child, undertook a hazardous journey to New York,

from where he sailed to join Browns in Liverpool. Early in 1864 Hoskier and his colleague Mark Collet established Brown Shipley's London house, and Hoskier was a partner from 1866. The business flourished in those years, but Hoskier 'carries a heavy workload' and was 'disposed to stand for what he considers his rights & to go if he does not get them' (Kouwenhoven, 143). It was not surprising, therefore, that Hoskier in 1880 retired early from Brown Shipley, owing to a combination of ill health 'and other circumstances' (ibid.) and having 'sufficient for his wants' (Guildhall MS 20111–20112).

By then Hoskier's transformation from merchant to merchant banker was complete and in the last two decades of the nineteenth century he established a well-founded reputation as a financier. The Union Bank of London, one of London's largest banks, appointed him a director in 1881, and he served until his death, but he declined its governorship in 1893. In 1886 he was appointed London director, largely concerned with finance, of Arthur Guinness Son & Co. Ltd, one of the largest brewing businesses, on the eve of its flotation and on the recommendation of his friend Lord Revelstoke of Barings. Revelstoke reckoned him a 'first class man, clever, a gentleman and good at accounts' (History of Guinness). He served for a time as London agent for the Banque de Paris et des Pays Bas and he was closely connected with his brother's Parisian bank, Emile Hoskier & Cie.

Hoskier was at his most influential in the 1880s and 1890s, when he brought together underwriting syndicates for bond issues and other transactions in securities. His intimate connections with Brown Shipley, Hambros, Barings, and the Banque de Paris meant that he was able to act as an informal intermediary, in return for a one to two per cent commission. During the Baring crisis of 1890, the Bank of England, perhaps unaware of his friendship with Revelstoke, wanted him to investigate Barings' books, but his co-investigator, Bertram Currie, rejected him on account of an obvious conflict of interest.

After 1864 Hoskier lived at Queenswood, Blackheath, Roehampton, and finally at Coney Hill, Hayes Common, Kent. He had two sons, and at least one daughter. He died on 7 May 1904 at the Royal Pavilion Hotel, Folkestone, having been taken there the previous December after falling ill while travelling to Biarritz. Hoskier was survived by his wife.

JOHN ORBELL

Sources J. C. Brown, *A hundred years of merchant banking: a history of Brown Brothers and Company, Brown Shipley and Company and the allied firms* (privately printed, New York, 1909) · A. Ellis, *Heir of adventure: the story of Brown, Shipley & Co., merchant bankers* (privately printed, London, 1960) · J. A. Kouwenhoven, *Partners in banking: an historical portrait of a great private bank, Brown Brothers, Harriman & Co., 1818–1968* (1968) · 'History of Guinness', London, Guinness archives · d. cert. · will

Archives GL, Brown Shipley archives, corresp. · GL, Hambros archives, corresp. · ING Barings, London, Barings archives, corresp.

Likenesses photograph, repro. in Brown, *A hundred years of merchant banking*

Wealth at death £211,027 7s. 6d.: probate, 4 June 1904, *CGPLA Eng. & Wales*

Hosking, William (1800–1861), architect and civil engineer, was born on 26 November 1800 at Buckfastleigh, Devon, the eldest son of John Hosking, at one time a woollen manufacturer in Devon, and his wife, Anne Elizabeth, *née* Mann. Owing to business losses the father accepted a government office in New South Wales, and with his wife and his three sons, William, Peter Mann, and John, went to Australia in 1809. In Sydney William was apprenticed to a general builder and surveyor, and for nearly four years he worked with his own hands 'in actual constructions, which involved most of the handicrafts employed by the engineer and architect' (*Introductory Lecture at King's College*, 1841, 9).

In 1819 Hosking returned with his parents to Britain, and in 1820 he was articled for three years to W. Jenkins, architect, of Red Lion Square. He subsequently travelled with Jenkins's son John for a year in Italy and Sicily, studying architecture and making drawings. Following this trip they jointly published *A Selection of Architectural and other Ornaments, Greek, Roman and Italian* (1827), and Hosking exhibited drawings of ancient monuments in Italy and Sicily at the Royal Academy and the Suffolk Street gallery. In Suffolk Street he also exhibited designs, chiefly of domestic buildings. On 14 February 1830 he was elected FSA. In 1834 he was appointed engineer to the Birmingham, Bristol, and Thames junction, afterwards called the West London Railway, and designed for it, in 1838–9, the arrangement at Wormwood Scrubs by which the Paddington Canal was carried over the railway, and a public road over the canal. The structure was altered in 1860, but when first executed attracted considerable attention. On 3 September 1836 Hosking married Elizabeth (1809–1877), second daughter of the printer William *Clowes; they had ten children, eight of whom survived him. During 1843 he was engaged in planning and taking levels for a projected branch railway (afterwards abandoned) between Colchester and Harwich. He was elected a fellow of the Institute of British Architects on 16 January 1835, and was a member of council for the session 1842–3.

In January 1829 Hosking delivered a course of six lectures on architecture at the Western Literary Institution in Leicester Square, in which he discussed the modern buildings of the metropolis in a judicious tone. In 1840 he became professor of the 'art of construction, in connection with civil engineering and architecture' at King's College, London, a professorship which was altered the following year into that of the 'principles and practice of architecture and of engineering constructions'. This he held until his death. When the Metropolitan Building Act of 1844 was passed he was appointed senior official referee, and he retained the post until the office was superseded by the act of 1855. In 1842, in conjunction with John Britton, he made drawings and drew up detailed reports for the restoration of St Mary Redcliffe Church at Bristol. An abstract, with engraved plan and views of the church, was printed for the vestry in 1842, and on 5 December 1842 he read a paper on the subject at the RIBA. An elevation of the west front of the church, with the tower and spire as proposed, drawn by J. Benson, was exhibited in the Royal

Academy in 1843. Among many other works Hosking designed a residence for W. Redfern, Campbellfield, New South Wales, in 1830; Trinity Congregational Chapel, Poplar (1840–41; bombed 1944), to which he afterwards added a minister's residence; and the buildings in Abney Park cemetery, Stoke Newington (1841).

Hosking's most important publications were his works on bridges. His first publication on the subject, *Preliminary Essay on Bridges* was privately printed in 1841 and reprinted a year later (again privately), with additional essays on the practice and architecture of bridges. In 1843 he published *The Theory, Practice, and Architecture of Bridges*, the theory being supplied by J. Hann. Hosking claimed to have first suggested groining a bridge arch, or carrying a groining through the length of a series of arches. He recommended the placing of parapets upon a corbelled cornice, and showed that the thickness and extension of bays might be reduced without imperilling the structure's strength. He also published *A Guide to the Proper Regulation of Buildings in Towns* (1848), dealing with the prevention of fire and with methods to avert the danger of cholera. A second edition, entitled *Healthy Homes*, appeared in 1849. In a pamphlet, *Some Observations upon the Recent Addition of a Reading-Room to the British Museum* (1858), accompanied by plans and elevations, Hosking set out his claim to be considered the originator of the scheme to increase the accommodation of the British Museum by the erection of a circular building, a modified copy of the Pantheon in Rome, in the unoccupied quadrangle. He submitted his drawings to the trustees of the museum on 30 November 1849, and an account of the scheme, with some discussion, appeared in *The Builder* (22 June 1850, 295–6). When Sydney Shirke's plan for the reading-room was adopted in 1854, Hosking regarded it as 'an obvious plagiarism' of his own suggestion and design, and the matter caused him bitter disappointment.

Hosking wrote the articles on 'Architecture' and on 'Building' for the seventh edition of the *Encyclopaedia Britannica*. These were illustrated from drawings by Hosking and Jenkins, and reappeared in the eighth edition; the article on 'Architecture' included a supplement written in 1853, and articles on 'Construction' and 'The drainage of towns' were also added. Many of the plates were retained in the ninth edition to illustrate the rewritten articles. Hosking's articles were republished in a separate volume in 1832, 1846, 1860, and (revised by Arthur Ashpitel) in 1867. He was preparing an enlarged and improved edition of them at the time of his death. He read papers to the Society of Antiquaries (*Archaeologia*, 23, 1831, 85, 411); and to the RIBA (1842–3). In 1844 he read a paper at the Institution of Civil Engineers, 'On the introduction of constructions to retain the sides of deep cuttings in clays or other uncertain soils', printed in the *Minutes of Proceedings* of the institution (3, 1844, 355–67).

True to his position at King's College, Hosking sought to maintain a unity between architecture and engineering, against the general tendency of his time towards specialization. He sometimes spoilt his case by his tendency to be querulous, or even litigious. He died at his home, 23

Woburn Square, London, on 2 August 1861, in his sixty-first year. His widow lived until 17 August 1877. Both were buried at Highgate old (west) cemetery.

BERTHA PORTER, rev. ROBERT THORNE

Sources *The Builder*, 2 (1844), 274 · *The Builder*, 8 (1850), 295–6 · *The Builder*, 19 (1861), 560 · *The Athenaeum* (11 March 1829), 157–8 · *ILN* (28 April 1855), 403 · F. W. Sims, *Public works of Great Britain* (1838), 66–8 and pl. lxxiii–lxxiv · J. Rondelet, *Traité théorique et pratique de l'art de bâtir* (1847), 1.213 and pl. xcvi · A. Ashpitel, *Treatise on architecture* (1867) · J. M. Crook, 'Architecture and history', *Architectural History*, 27 (1984), 555–78 · S. Porter, ed., *Poplar, Blackwall and the Isle of Dogs: the parish of All Saints*, [1], Survey of London, 43 (1994), 135–7 · P. Joyce, *A guide to Abney Park cemetery* (1984) · IGI
Archives RIBA
Wealth at death £10,000: probate, 29 Aug 1861, *CGPLA Eng. & Wales*

Hoskins, Anthony (1568/9?–1615), Jesuit, was born in Hereford, 'descended from a high family' (Foley, 7.373). He entered the English College, Douai, on 17 April 1590 and went on to the English College, Valladolid, on 26 March 1591. He entered the Society of Jesus at Valladolid on 4 March 1593. His name is given in the Jesuit records at the English College, Seville, in 1599, at Madrid in the same year, and at St Omer in 1602. He was sent on the English mission in 1603 and was professed of the four vows in London on 1 May 1609. All this time nothing remarkable is recorded of him save that he was a man 'of remarkable piety and prudence' (Foley, 6.521). It was no doubt for these virtues that he was called to Brussels in 1610 to be vice-prefect of the English mission in the Spanish Netherlands.

Hoskins's two contributions to the controversies of the time were both published from the St Omer press in 1611. To rebut the accusations made against the Jesuits of complicity in the assassination of the French king, Henri IV, in 1610, Hoskins compiled in English translation *The apologies of the most Christian kings of France and Navarre, Henry IV and Lewis XIII … for the fathers of the Society of Jesus*. He also joined in the controversy being waged, notably between King James and Cardinal Bellarmine, concerning the oath of allegiance, by abridging his fellow Jesuit Leonard Lessius's *Defensio potestatis summi pontificis* (1611) in English translation as *A briefe and cleare declaration of sundry pointes absolutely dislyked in the lately enacted oath of allegiance* under the initials H. I.

Hoskins's translations of Catholic devotional literature included a modernized version of Richard Whitford's old translation of Thomas à Kempis's *Imitatio Christi* (1531?), which he brought out with great success in 1611 under other initials, B. F. or F. B. By 1636 it had gone into eight editions and has been considered the model followed by all subsequent translators of the work. Hoskins was moved to Madrid on 26 January 1613 as vice-prefect of the English mission in Spain. On 9 April 1615 he was appointed rector of the English College of St Alban at Valladolid, and died there on 20 September 1615 'deeply regretted' (Foley, 7.373).

W. A. J. ARCHBOLD, rev. PETER MILWARD

Sources Gillow, *Lit. biog. hist.*, 3.406–7 · H. Foley, ed., *Records of the English province of the Society of Jesus*, 6 (1880), 521–2; 7 (1882–3), 373 · C. Dodd [H. Tootell], *The church history of England, from the year 1500, to the year 1688*, 2 (1739), 416–17 · P. Milward, *Religious controversies of the Jacobean age* (1978), 101–2 · T. M. McCoog, *English and Welsh Jesuits, 1555–1650*, 2 vols., Catholic RS, 74–5 (1994–5) · T. H. Clancy, *A literary history of the English Jesuits: a century of books, 1615–1714* (1996) · E. Henson, ed., *The registers of the English College at Valladolid, 1589–1862*, Catholic RS, 30 (1930)

Hoskins, Sir Anthony Hiley (1828–1901), naval officer, born at North Perrott, near Crewkerne, Somerset, on 1 September 1828, was fourth son of Henry Hoskins (1790–1876), rector of North Perrott, and his wife, Mary, daughter of William Phelips of Montacute. After briefly attending Winchester College (1841–2) Hoskins entered the navy in April 1842, with a proficiency in classical learning unusual for his age. He remained on his first ship, the *Conway*, for some years, participating in fights with Arab slavers off the east coast of Africa and in the attack on Tamatave, Madagascar. Afterwards, in the *President*, he continued on the same station on similar service. On 26 May 1849 he was made lieutenant, and, while in the *Castor* on the Cape station, was lent to Sir Henry Smith as aide-de-camp during the Cape Frontier War of 1851–2. In 1857 he took the gunboat *Slaney* to China, taking part in the capture of Canton (Guangzhou) on 28 December. For this he was promoted to commander, on 26 February 1858, but remained in the *Slaney*. In May he was in the Gulf of Po Hai (Bohai), and was present at the capture of the Taku (Dagu) forts and in the operations in the Peiho (Beihe) leading to the occupation of Tientsin (Tianjin). On 12 December 1863 he was promoted captain.

From 1869 to 1872 Hoskins commanded the *Eclipse* on the North American station, and in 1873–4 the *Sultan*, in the Channel Fleet; from 1875 to 1878 he was commodore in Australian waters. In 1877 he was appointed a CB; he became a rear-admiral on 15 June 1879, and from 1880 was a lord commissioner of the Admiralty. From this post, in 1882, he was sent to the Mediterranean, after the bombardment of Alexandria, to secure the Suez Canal and act as second in command. On his return, in the winter, he was nominated KCB, and until June 1885, when he became vice-admiral, he was superintendent of naval reserves. He was then for nearly four years a junior naval lord of the Admiralty. From March 1889 he was commander-in-chief in the Mediterranean until June 1891, when he was promoted admiral, and was appointed senior naval lord of the Admiralty.

At the Admiralty, Hoskins had proved to be a capable and successful second naval lord under Lord George Hamilton and Admiral Hood. When Hamilton compared the two admirals he found Hoskins 'more adaptable and versatile' than Hood, but 'with less motive power' (Hamilton, 87). This limitation was exposed by his later term as senior naval lord under Lord Spencer. Hoskins's views were moderate on most issues, though he was a disciple of the pure 'blue water' strategy of the day that opposed all forts. However, his term in the Mediterranean left him anxious for the squadron there, to the extent of urging the need for a 25 per cent superiority over the French fleet as the only alternative to the complete abandonment of that sea on the outbreak of war in favour of a defensive concentration in the channel. His moderate views on the shipbuilding effort required in 1892–3 did not find favour with his more dynamic colleagues, Admiral Sir Frederick Richards and Captain John Fisher. Even before Hoskins retired, Richards and Fisher had taken control of policy, and they secured the 'Spencer programme' of 1894. A talented and able officer, Hoskins proved ill suited to high command afloat or ashore: he made little impression in the Mediterranean, and none at the Admiralty.

Hoskins retired on reaching the age limit, on 1 September 1893; he was nominated GCB in November. He then lived mostly in London, taking much interest in naval and geographical societies.

Hoskins married, on 27 October 1865, Dorothea Ann Eliza (d. 7 Oct 1901), second daughter of the Revd Sir George Stamp Robinson, seventh baronet. They had no children. He died at Pleystons Capel, near Dorking, Surrey, on 21 June 1901, and was buried at North Perrott. Stern, strict, and even severe in service relations, he was, in private, most genial.

J. K. LAUGHTON, rev. ANDREW LAMBERT

Sources A. J. Marder, *British naval policy, 1880–1905: the anatomy of British sea power* [1940] · G. Hamilton, *Parliamentary reminiscences and reflections*, 2: 1886–1906 (1922) · R. F. MacKay, *Fisher of Kilverstone* (1973) · *The Red Earl: the papers of the fifth Earl Spencer, 1835–1910*, ed. P. Gordon, 2 vols., Northamptonshire RS, 31, 34 (1981–6) · P. H. Colomb, *Memoirs of Admiral the Right Honble. Sir Astley Cooper Key* (1898) · CGPLA Eng. & Wales (1901) · *Navy List* · *The Times* (22 June 1901) · *The Times* (27 June 1901) · W. L. Clowes, *The Royal Navy: a history from the earliest times to the present*, 7 vols. (1897–1903), vols. 6–7 · J. B. Wainewright, ed., *Winchester College, 1836–1906: a register* (1907)
Archives U. Mich., Clements L., letter-books
Likenesses H. T. Wells, oils, 1901 (Grillion's Club series) · Spy [L. Ward], chromolithograph caricature, NPG; repro. in *VF* (28 April 1883) · Walery, photograph, NPG
Wealth at death £20,399 6s. 7d.: probate, 25 Oct 1901, CGPLA Eng. & Wales

Hoskins, John (1566–1638), poet and judge, was the second son of John Hoskins (d. 1607), a yeoman farmer of Monkton, or Mouncton, near Llanwarne, Herefordshire, and his wife, Margery (née Jones) (fl. 1534–1617). Aubrey claims that Hoskins did not learn to read until he was ten, but then 'at the yeare's end, entred into his Greeke grammar' (*Brief Lives*, 1.416). After a brief stay at Westminster School, Hoskins entered Winchester College in 1579; there 'the flower of his time' (ibid., 1.417) is still remembered by a wall-painting with accompanying Latin verses, both of his composition, which depict the leading characteristics of the 'trusty servant'.

Hoskins went up to New College, Oxford, in 1585, graduating BA in 1588 and MA in 1592. While a burgeoning literary reputation secured his appointment to the licensed jester role of *terrae filius* at that year's graduation ceremony, his 'bitterly satyrical' (*Brief Lives*, 1.417) personal attacks, possibly on the recently deceased university chancellor Christopher Hatton, saw him expelled from both his college fellowship and the university. Exiled to Somerset as a schoolteacher, Hoskins began to compile a Greek lexicon, complete to the letter M, which Aubrey sighted but is now lost; like most of his writings, apart from some commendatory verses, this did not appear in print during his lifetime.

Legal career In March 1593 Hoskins took his first step towards a new career by admission to the Middle Temple. There he was bound with John Davies, a former New College contemporary, and associated with other wits and 'ingeniose persons' (*Brief Lives*, 1.417) including Richard Martin, Benjamin Rudyerd, and James Whitelocke, while also cultivating some court connections. Along with much occasional verse both Latin and English, and a 'Tufftaffity speech' written for the Middle Temple Christmas revels of 1597–8 (Osborn, chap. 8), his most substantial surviving work from these years is the *Directions for Speech and Stile*, an elaborate treatise on rhetoric, which exists in several manuscript versions as well as modern editions, and was extensively plagiarized by Ben Jonson, who later acknowledged Hoskins's influence as his literary 'father'.

Called to the bar in 1600, Hoskins was married on 1 August the following year to Benedicta (d. 1625), the well-to-do daughter of Robert Moyle and widow of a fellow Middle Templar, Francis Bourne. Through the favour of William Herbert, earl of Pembroke, this propitious match was shortly followed by Hoskins's appointment as deputy steward (or recorder) of Hereford, where he leased and subsequently purchased a substantial house, and was returned to parliament in 1604. From the start Hoskins showed himself a busy committee man and a vigorous debater, prominent in attacking the economic exploitation of royal prerogative powers by imposition, the Merchant Adventurers Company, pre-emption, and purveyors, while supporting restrictions on the jurisdiction of the council in the marches of Wales. His poetic and satirical powers also continued to flourish, notably in the composition of a much copied verse sequence 'on the fart in the Parliament house' (1607) and a Latin 'Convivium philosophicum' celebrating Tom Coryate and other frequenters of the Mitre tavern, including his fellow lawyer-MP Christopher Brooke, the poet John Donne, and the artist Inigo Jones. 'In short', as Aubrey put it, 'his acquaintance were all the witts then about the towne' (*Brief Lives*, 1.418).

From 1604 onwards a thread of anti-Scottish prejudice ran through Hoskins's parliamentary speeches; his suggestion at the close of the 1610 session that remittances to Edinburgh were the prime cause of the king's indebtedness impressed the French ambassador as nothing short of an incitement to mob violence. In 1614 Hoskins's voicing of similar sentiments figured largely in the precipitate dissolution of the Addled Parliament. Responding to a royal message that the session would end forthwith unless supply were granted, Hoskins delivered a vehement denunciation of royal financial policy, adding that the king should 'send all strangers home to their countries' (Jansson, 422–3), lest a bloodbath ensue. Much of this speech seems to have been based on a text supplied by Sir Charles Cornwallis, an ally of Henry Howard, earl of Northampton, although its provocative references to 'a

Sicilian Vespers or a Parisian Matins' (Birch, 1.346) were almost certainly Hoskins's own work.

Royal disfavour Whether Hoskins was acting largely on his own initiative, or as Northampton's instrument, the immediate consequences of this outburst were markedly more severe than those which had followed his public indiscretions at Oxford two decades before. Having provided James with a convenient pretext for the summary dissolution of parliament, in the face of the Commons' refusal to censure Hoskins, the latter found himself imprisoned in the Tower, displaced from his recordership, and put off the commission of the peace. Despite serving a year-long 'close' captivity behind boarded-up windows, Hoskins was evidently permitted some interaction on literary matters at least with his fellow prisoner Walter Ralegh, as well as family visits. Yet even after his conditional release following repeated submissive apologies, backed by the intercession of his wife and others, Hoskins remained in deep disfavour. His election as mayor of Hereford in 1616 was specifically countermanded by royal letter, and early the next year he was again brought before the privy council in connection with a 'rime or libel' (*Letters of John Chamberlain*, 2.52), avoiding further proceedings only through the good offices of his friend Lionel Cranfield and the 'truly noble Earle of Buckingham' (Whitlock, 516).

These unfortunate experiences, coupled with growing domestic responsibilities, evidently discouraged Hoskins from seeking re-election in 1621, when his avowed concern was rather to prevent the manner of his imprisonment being raised as a parliamentary grievance. By now he had joined the Middle Temple's governing bench, delivering his reading in Lent 1620 (on 31 Eliz. I, c. 11, forcible entries) at which the entertainment, notable for 'abundance, yea superfluity', attracted Buckingham and 'a reasonable portion of Lords' (Osborn, 50). Further professional preferment soon followed, together with the purchase of a substantial estate at Morehampton, Herefordshire; in June 1621 Hoskins, now restored to royal favour, became second judge on the Carmarthen circuit, 'by the meanes of the Marquesse Buckingham, my lord President [Henry Montague, or possibly William Compton, first earl of Northampton] & the Mr of the wardes [Cranfield]' (Osborn, 51). The hopes of further promotion raised by this appointment were at least partially fulfilled in June 1623, when Hoskins was joined to a general call of serjeants-at-law.

Final years Following his wife's death in 1625 and his remarriage to the well-to-do widow Isabel Barrett, *née* Risely (*d.* 1634), on 10 December 1627, Hoskins represented Hereford for a final term in the 1628 parliament. Less active and generally more moderate than before, Hoskins nevertheless played a not unimportant part in facilitating passage of the petition of right, as chairman of the committee of the whole. In the second session he followed a largely Erastian and anti-Arminian line, besides attacking official lenience towards popish priests, although his own religious sympathies were sufficiently broad to permit

him to compose an English anthem for Hereford Cathedral, thereby offending (according to Aubrey) the puritanical Sir Robert Harley.

Despite gradually failing health, Hoskins continued to ride the circuits and travel to London, usually accompanied by his son, until at the Hereford assizes 'a massive countrey fellowe trod on his toe, which caused a gangrene' (*Brief Lives*, 1.422). Hoskins died on 27 August 1638 at Morehampton and was buried at nearby Dore Abbey. An attractive portrait miniature by his namesake, the painter John Hoskins, bears on its back a pen-and-ink sketch of a family group, with the annotation 'J Hoskins by himself'; this has been plausibly identified as representing our subject, his first wife, and his two step-children about 1618. Both depict a man with dark hair, a lively expression, and a prominent nose, the sketch being less idealized than the professional portrait. Aubrey, who derived much of his relatively extensive memoir from Hoskins's son Benedict (1609–1680), mentions various works now lost, including a book of poems 'bigger than Dr Donne's poemes' lent by the son 'to he knows not who', and 'a method of the lawe (imperfect)' (ibid., 1.418, 421).

John Hoskins the younger (1581–1631), Church of England clergyman and author, was a younger brother of Serjeant John Hoskins. Following in his elder sibling's footsteps, John entered Winchester College in 1593 and proceeded to New College, Oxford, matriculating on 2 November 1599 (despite John's attempts to procure his admission the previous year). As a fellow of New College Hoskins graduated BCL in 1606 and DCL in April 1613. Six months earlier he had become vicar of Ledbury, a wealthy benefice near Hereford, where he held a series of prebendary stalls in the cathedral. In 1615 Hoskins published a volume entitled *Sermons Preached at Paul's Crosse and Else-where*, dedicated to Lord Keeper Ellesmere. He also served as chaplain to the family friend Bishop Robert Bennett, as royal chaplain, and as master of St Oswald's Hospital, near Worcester. In 1616 Dr Hoskins married Frances Bourne (*fl.* 1601–1632), who thus became wife of the brother of her own step-father (John Hoskins senior); they had four sons and a daughter before John died on 8 August 1631 at Ledbury where he was also buried.   WILFRID PREST

Sources *Brief lives, chiefly of contemporaries, set down by John Aubrey, between the years 1669 and 1696*, ed. A. Clark, 2 vols. (1898) • B. W. Whitlock, *John Hoskyns, serjeant-at-law* (1982) • L. B. Osborn, *The life, letters and writings of John Hoskyns* (1937) • W. R. Prest, *The rise of the barristers: a social history of the English bar, 1590–1640* (1986) • Baker, *Serjeants* • [J. P. Ferris], 'Hoskins, John', HoP, *Commons, 1604–29* [draft] • *The letters of John Chamberlain*, ed. N. E. McClure, 2 vols. (1939) • M. Jansson, ed., *Proceedings in parliament, 1614 (House of Commons)* (1988) • T. Birch, ed., *The court and times of James the First*, 2 vols. (1849) • J. H. Baker, *Readers and readings in the inns of court and chancery*, SeldS, suppl. ser., 13 (2000) • C. S. Russell, *The Addled Parliament of 1614: the limits of revision* (1992) • Foster, *Alum. Oxon.* • DNB • admon, PRO, PROB 6/14A, fol. 77r [John Hoskins the younger]

Archives BL, papers • Herefs. RO, family and estate papers • NRA, priv. coll., personal and family papers

Likenesses J. Hoskins, miniature • J. Hoskins, self-portrait, group portrait, repro. in Whitlock, *John Hoskyns*, xi; formerly? in possession of duke of Buccleuch

Wealth at death PRO, C 142/60/99, cited in Baker, *Serjeants*, 519; will, PRO, PROB 11/178, sig. 127, repr. in Osborn, *Life*, 241–2 • John

Hoskins: administration, PRO, PROB 6/14A, fol. 77*r* · probably moderately well-to-do, owning lands in Monmouthshire and Herefordshire besides Morehampton estate (which he purchased for some £3000 in 1621): Whitlock, *John Hoskyns*, 561–2

Hoskins, John, the younger (1581–1631). *See under* Hoskins, John (1566–1638).

Hoskins, John [*known as* John Hoskins the elder, Old Hoskins] (*c.*1590–1665), miniature painter, was born perhaps in Wells, Somerset, the son of a John Hoskins of whom almost nothing is known except that he died, presumably a debtor, in the Fleet prison in London, from where he was buried on 3 May 1610. The circumstances and main events of the personal life of the miniaturist are still largely obscure but he is thought to have had relatives both in Wells and among a network of Hoskinses and Coopers in Surrey. From among the latter his sister Barbara, who must have been close in age to her brother, found her husband, Richard Cooper, whom she married on 1 September 1607 at the church of St Nicholas Cole Abbey, near Blackfriars, the same year that her father was first recorded as being in the Fleet. Barbara was the mother of Samuel *Cooper and Alexander *Cooper, the miniaturists, but she and her husband either died early or otherwise relinquished responsibility for the boys, who were brought up by their uncle John Hoskins.

The lack of records suggests that the males, at least, of the Hoskins family married outside London. John Hoskins himself seems to have married twice, for his son, also John [*see below*] and also a miniaturist, was born about 1617 to a wife of whom nothing is known. His putative second wife, Sarah, certainly gave birth to a daughter, Christiana, on 24 January 1654. Indirect evidence suggests that the family continued to live in Blackfriars, a district outside the jurisdiction of the Painter–Stainers' Company and therefore much favoured by immigrant artists such as Van Dyck. From at least 1634, however, Hoskins lived and worked as a miniaturist in Bedford Street, Covent Garden, and was granted by the king on 30 April 1640 an annuity of £200 for life, 'provided that he work not for any other without his Majesty's licence'. After the first instalment, in the changed political and economic circumstances of the 1640s, the annuity was not paid. Hoskins made his will on 30 December 1662. He died on 22 February 1665, said to be sick and impoverished, and was buried the same day at St Pauls, Covent Garden. His widow, Sarah, 'an almswoman', was buried there on 19 February 1669. According to Buckeridge's additions to de Piles, Hoskins was 'bred a Face-Painter in Oil, but afterwards taking to Miniature he far exceeded what he did before' (de Piles, 437). Documented paintings by Hoskins on loan to Norwich Castle Museum (Moore and Crawley 84–7, nos. 18–19, reproduced pl. 55–6), of Sir Hamon Le Strange (*c.*1583–1654) and his wife, Alice (*d.* 1656), are still in the possession of the family. The household accounts of Sir Hamon, now in the Norfolk Record Office, record payments:

June 1st 1617 to Mr Hoskins in part of £4, for drawing of 2 pictures £2-4-0. Sepr 8. To Hoskins in full payment of £4 for drawing of 2 pictures £1-16-0. For a case and a cord for 2

pictures 1s/7d. Oct 10th. For bringing the 2 pictures from London to Limm 1/9. (Singh, 1.316–7)

On the evidence of these certain works Hoskins would have been influenced by William Larkin, whose formulae for the arrangement and representation of his sitters, as well as handling of the paint, Hoskins at this time evidently followed.

Early works Hoskins's earliest miniatures, of which there are examples in the Victoria and Albert Museum, London, date from *c.*1615 and reinforce the sense of an early relationship with Larkin. He was clearly by that date already a fully competent exponent of the technical mystery of the miniaturist, which he probably learned directly from Nicholas Hilliard. Certainly the *Unknown Woman* of *c.*1615 (V&A) is very close to Hilliard in technique, and the use of Hilliard's trade secrets—for example, a way of simulating jewels by building up molten resins on a bed of burnished silver—was still evident in another *Unknown Woman* of the early 1620s (also V&A). There is internal evidence that he may after 1620 have been the part-author of one of the manuscript handbooks on the techniques of painting in both oil and miniature, the so-called Gyles manuscript (BL, MS Harley 6376), a recension of the well-known technical treatise by Nicholas Hilliard, adapted by Edward Norgate (Murrell, 59–62; Norgate, ed. Muller and Murrell, 239). The author of this part of the manuscript gives firsthand testimony of the studio practice of Nicholas Hilliard and of a painter in oils described as 'my Master Mr Martins the elder', probably Daniel Mytens (*c.*1590–1647), who arrived in England about 1618. Possibly Hoskins studied also under this brilliant exponent of the new baroque court portraiture. Later he certainly copied a Mytens portrait of Charles I in several miniature versions (for example, those at Madresfield Court, Worcestershire; the Pierpont Morgan Library, New York; and the V&A). By this time Hoskins's activity must have been predominantly in miniature.

The best way of learning to draw well is to be taught by a good Artist that is able to direct you and shew you where you ere … for you are not able to see your owne faults at the first. Yea many a time a stander by may spy a fault in the worke of a good workeman. Be not out of hope although your draught comes far short of your patterne at the first, For daily practise with a Continued resolution and intention of the minde … And once in fower or five years time you may be a good draughtsman. (Norgate, ed. Muller and Murrell)

In his treatise Norgate called Hoskins one of the 'doctors' of miniature (Norgate, ed. Muller and Murrell, 70), and there is evidence also among the Hoskins miniatures of the early 1620s that he studied the work of Isaac Oliver very closely, using a version of his firm, dark stipple to produce a more highly modelled effect for certain sitters, such as James I (versions in the Royal Collection and the V&A). Throughout the 1620s and 1630s, working as Peter Oliver did for Charles I and visibly responding to the different influences of the immigrant painters in large, such as Paul van Somer and Daniel Mytens, Hoskins developed from these sources his own version of a stipple technique, minutely polychromatic in brown, sanguine, blue, yellow, and opaque white. This technique, once perfected, remained stable until at least the end of the 1630s.

Major works Far more than Peter Oliver, who was his close contemporary and potential rival for court patronage in the 1620s, Hoskins remained a face painter. Although a *Venus, Mercury and Cupid*, after Correggio, survives at Burghley House neither Hoskins nor any of his family seems to have been seriously involved in the copying of the old masters in the Royal Collection. Oliver's absorption in that highly rewarded enterprise left the field of miniature portraiture open to Hoskins. In the 1630s, however, Hoskins too showed great ambition, enlarging both the size of his miniatures and their scope, by pioneering in particular the use of landscape or sky backgrounds. The work of this period is marked by vivid consciousness of Wenceslas Hollar as well as of the newly arrived genius Anthony Van Dyck, whose portraits of courtiers Hoskins frequently copied. A fine example showing both these developments is the *Katherine Bruce, Mrs Murray* of 1638, in the collection of the Victoria and Albert Museum at Ham House in Surrey. Norgate commented: 'As for *Lanscape* behind pictures they are very excellent, when well done, and the ground large enough to afford roome' (Norgate, ed. Muller and Murrell, 77). These large miniatures represent the high point of Hoskins's œuvre and one of the high points of British seventeenth-century art. They represent a continuation of Hilliard's practice of painting the most important sitters in an enlarged format and in a naturalistic setting. Finished across much of the surface to a very high degree, these miniatures must have been extremely expensive to produce, especially so of time.

From the 1630s also date the works that have long been recognized as problematic: not clearly by the same hand, variable in conception, style, and quality, and marked with at least three different forms of monogram or signature. There is evidence that Hoskins had too much work to do himself. Lord Wentworth, later earl of Strafford, wrote to his agent on 17 August 1636: 'I pray to get Hauskins to take my picture in little from my original that is at length [by Van Dyck], and to make it something like those that he last drew, and desire Sir Anthony from me to help him' (Smith, 181). And to his wife, from London on 29 June 1636:

> My picture in great you have, and one in little if I can possibly procure it; but Mr Hoskins hath so much work as I fear he will not have time to spare. I have promised one to another … uniform, and have courted the gentleman and yet cannot get his promise for that. (Lady Burghclere, *Strafford*, 1931, 2.13)

In these circumstances Hoskins seems to have employed his nephews Samuel and Alexander Cooper, and David *Des Granges, who married a certain Judith Hoskins in January 1636, to help meet demand. Demand naturally encouraged an increase in supply, and from the 1640s miniatures bearing Hoskins's monograms were rarely painted in the immensely demanding technique, and never on the scale, of the great works of the 1630s. A pensioned servant of the crown, after *c*.1642 Hoskins may

willingly have passed the leading role to his nephew Samuel Cooper, who was by this time established in his own house and signing his own work. A rare example of work plausibly attributable to the elder Hoskins after this watershed is the *Mrs Henderson* of 1649, at Ham House. The extent to which his own son, John Hoskins the younger, was responsible for the miniatures signed with IH monograms after *c*.1645 is still a major crux of scholarly debate about seventeenth-century miniatures. A school of thought holds that Old Hoskins, aged about fifty-five, re-invented himself, discovering a new and bolder brushwork and different iconographic idiom, and continuing work as before. According to this view the younger Hoskins was not a serious miniaturist.

John Hoskins the younger (b. *c*.1617) was born evidently to his father's putative first wife; he was left a legacy of £20 in his father's will and married, on 7 February 1670, Grace, elder daughter of Thomas Beaumont, a lay vicar-choral of Wells Cathedral and probably also a surgeon or apothecary. With her he had seven children and was, under his mother-in-law's will, the executor and residuary legatee of her estate, which he wound up after her death in 1692. He was mentioned in Samuel Cooper's will, which he witnessed, and was subsequently named as legatee of the residue of Samuel Cooper's studio, under the will of Christiana, Cooper's widow, dated 16 May 1693. The date and place of his death are not known. A record of legal proceedings in York, dated 1658, shows that his normal residence was in Durham Yard, near to his father in Bedford Street. This document states that he was aged forty-one, implying that he was born in 1616 or 1617, but since the document also gives the age of the Coopers slightly inaccurately it may not be reliable. A portrait believed to be of him, possibly by Samuel Cooper, is the recto of the *Dead Baby* (priv. coll.; exh. NPG, 1974, no. 138).

That the younger Hoskins painted miniatures and was, like his father, highly regarded for this accomplishment is indicated by William Sanderson: 'For Miniature or Limming, in watercolours, Hoskins and his son (if my judgement faile not) incomparable'. A portrait (priv. coll.) signed with the monogram traditionally associated with the younger Hoskins and inscribed '*Ipse*' may be a self-portrait, and there are impressive miniatures similarly signed at Madresfield Court (*Princess Elizabeth*, 1645) and in the Victoria and Albert Museum (*Sir John Wildman*, 1647); others, all following a formula in which the figure is viewed somewhat from below and dated variously in the later 1640s and through the 1650s, appear frequently on the market. The *Unknown Man*, signed and dated '*IH Aetatis 81 1661*', at Chatsworth in Derbyshire, so far appears to be the latest miniature of this group. It is surely likely to be by the younger Hoskins, aged about forty-four, rather than by his father, aged about seventy-one.

A reference to the younger Hoskins, as 'Mr Cooper's cousin Jacke', present at Pepys's midsummer dinner party in 1668, the year before his marriage, characterizes him as one of a group 'all eminent men in their way'. If another reference is to him rather than his father he evidently practised also in the newly fashionable tonal medium of 'crayons'. Aubrey records Robert Hooke observing: 'John Hoskins the painter, being at Freshwater to drawe pictures … grinding chalke, ruddle and coale' into a sort of pastel to be applied with the brush (*Brief Lives*, ed. Clark, 409; *Brief Lives*, ed. Lawson Dick, 49). Referred to by his relatives as 'Jack's son', he is probably the author of a pastel portrait of Cooper in the Victoria and Albert Museum. But Hoskins the younger, who was clearly a man of substance, should probably be thought of as a brilliant amateur exponent of these gentle arts, not a professional limner like his father.   JOHN MURDOCH

Sources *Brief lives, chiefly of contemporaries, set down by John Aubrey, between the years 1669 and 1696*, ed. A. Clark, 2 vols. (1898) · *Aubrey's Brief lives*, ed. O. L. Dick (1949) · [B. Buckeridge], 'An essay towards an English school of painting', in R. de Piles, *The art of painting, with the lives and characters of above 300 of the most eminent painters*, 3rd edn (1754), 354–439 · A. Moore and C. Crawley, *Family and friends: a regional survey of British portraiture* (1992) · F. D. Singh, *Portraits in Norfolk houses*, ed. E. Farrer, 2 vols. (1928) · E. Norgate, *Miniatura, or, The art of limning*, ed. M. Hardie (1919) · E. Norgate, *Miniatura, or, The art of limning*, ed. J. M. Muller and J. Murrell (1997) · B. S. Long, *British miniaturists* (1929) · M. Edmond, 'Limners and picturemakers', *Walpole Society*, 47 (1978–80), 60–242, esp. 113–23 · M. Edmond, 'Samuel Cooper, Yorkshireman—and recusant?', *Burlington Magazine*, 127 (1985), 83–5 · W. Sanderson, *Graphice: the use of the pen and pensil, or, The most excellent art of painting* (1658) · G. Reynolds, *English portrait miniatures* (1952); rev. edn (1988) · J. Murdoch, 'Hoskinses and Crosses: work in progress', *Burlington Magazine*, 120 (1978), 284–90 · J. Murdoch, *Seventeenth-century English miniatures in the collection of the Victoria and Albert Museum* (1997) · J. Murrell, *The way howe to lymne, Tudor miniatures observed* (1983) · F. W. F. Smith, earl of Birkenhead, *Strafford* (1938) · E. Reynolds, *The sixteenth and seventeenth century miniatures in the collection of her majesty the queen* (1999), nos. 72–92
Likenesses S. Cooper? or J. Hoskins the younger?, portrait, exh. NPG 1974, priv. coll.; on recto of *Dead baby* · J. Hoskins, self-portrait, watercolour miniature, Buccleuch estates, Selkirk · J. Hoskins the younger, self-portrait (John Hoskins the younger), priv. coll.

Hoskins, John, the younger (b. c.1617). *See under* Hoskins, John (c.1590–1665).

Hoskins [Hoskyns], **Sir John**, **second baronet** (1634–1705), lawyer and natural philosopher, was born in Herefordshire on 23 July 1634, the eldest son of Sir Bennet Hoskins, first baronet (d. 1680), of Harewood and Morehampton Park, Herefordshire, barrister and MP for Wendover (1640) and Hereford (1640–48), and the grandson of Sergeant John *Hoskins. He was first educated by his mother, Anne (d. in or before 1655), the daughter of Sir John Bingley of Temple Combe, Somerset, and then at Westminster School. Following in his father's footsteps he was called to the bar at the Middle Temple although there is little evidence that he practised. He was knighted in 1676 and held the office of master in chancery from 1676 to 1703. He had an excellent reputation as a lawyer and performed his duties in chancery with integrity according to Roger North, the brother and biographer of Lord Keeper Francis North Guildford, an intimate friend of Hoskins. Like many generations of Hoskinses before him he also served as the MP for Hereford (1685–7) and became the second baronet of Harewood and Morehampton Park after his father's death in 1680. On 29 August 1671 he married Jane

(d. 1724), the daughter of Sir Gabriel Lowe of Gloucestershire. They had five children, four sons and a daughter.

It was not, however, his skill at the practice of law or politics but his interest in natural philosophy that distinguished Hoskins among his contemporaries. From an early age he showed an interest in the new experimental philosophy and became one of the original fellows of the Royal Society of London when it was incorporated in 1663. While he was not known to have participated in many meetings, he attended regularly, recruited many new members, and occasionally used his knowledge of the law to the society's benefit. With the endorsement of John Evelyn he succeeded Christopher Wren as president of the Royal Society in 1682 and resigned one year later. His short tenure was marked by the revival of the society's *Philosophical Transactions* in January 1683. He then served as secretary to the society from 1685 to 1687. His researches were mainly horticultural: he was particularly interested in the art of grafting and searched for ways to preserve plants against the cold.

Outside the Royal Society Hoskins was a noted conversationalist and a favourite dinner companion. He frequently dined with the likes of Robert Hooke, John Aubrey, and Lord Keeper Guildford. Roger North notes that 'these two often gott to supper together, and the conversation was intirely upon experimentall philosofye, astronomy, etc.' (North, 242). He was also a regular attender at John Harrington's nightly philosophical discussions. In his description of Hoskins Granger reported that 'there was nothing at all promising in his appearance: he was hard-favoured, affected plainness in his garb, walked the street with a cudgel in his hand, and an old hat over his eyes. He was often observed to be in a reverie: but when his spirits were elevated over a bottle, he was remarkable for his presence of mind, and quickness of apprehension, and became the agreeable and instructive companion' (Granger, 4.315). Hoskins died on 12 September 1705 and was succeeded in his titles by his eldest surviving son, Bennet. There is a contemporary portrait of Hoskins by the English engraver Robert White.   G. S. MCINTYRE

Sources C. R. Weld, *A history of the Royal Society*, 2 vols. (1848) · R. North, *The life of the Lord Keeper North*, ed. M. Chan (1995) · J. Granger, *A biographical history of England, from Egbert the Great to the revolution*, 4th edn, 4 (1804) · *Brief lives, chiefly of contemporaries, set down by John Aubrey, between the years 1669 and 1696*, ed. A. Clark, 2 vols. (1898) · T. Birch, *The history of the Royal Society of London*, 4 vols. (1756–7); repr. with introduction by A. R. Hall (1968) · Burke, *Peerage* (1956) · *The diary of Robert Hooke … 1672–1680*, ed. H. W. Robinson and W. Adams (1935) · *The correspondence of Henry Oldenburg*, ed. and trans. A. R. Hall and M. B. Hall, 13 vols. (1965–86) · *Engraved Brit. ports.*, vol. 2 · *Diary of John Evelyn*, ed. W. Bray, 1–2 (1889) · M. Hunter, *The Royal Society and its fellows, 1660–1700: the morphology of an early scientific institution*, 2nd edn (1994)
Archives Bodl. Oxf., letters to John Aubrey
Likenesses R. White, line engraving, BM; copy, pubd 1800, BM · pen-and-ink drawing (after engraving), NPG

Hoskins, Percy Kellick (1904–1989), journalist, was born on 28 December 1904 at Bothenhampton, Burton Bradstock, Bridport, Dorset, the son of John Hoskins, chief officer of coastguards, and his wife, Sarah Rose Trevett. After a career of sixty years reporting crime, Hoskins rejoiced in his boast that a life so devoted to crime and punishment should have begun on Holy Innocents' day in Bridport, where once they made the hangman's rope. He was educated locally at Bridport. Hoskins was nineteen when he went to London to join the *Evening Standard* as a reporter. Nine years later he was crime reporter on the *Standard*'s sister paper, the *Daily Express*. His catalogue of successes was formidable. He wrote the first account of the disappearance of Guy Burgess and Donald Maclean, the Foreign Office diplomats who defected to Moscow. But his most memorable case was his campaign in support of Dr John Bodkin *Adams, a fashionable Eastbourne doctor. In the years up to 1956 a number of wealthy widows living in the district had died. There was much local gossip; then an inquest on one widow brought about a police inquiry and Scotland Yard was called in. The national newspapers printed sensational accounts of the affair. There was talk of the exhumation of ten women, of the wills of 400 people being examined, even of the possibility of a local 'Bluebeard'.

Hoskins was suspicious of the briefings that the police were giving to newspapers and decided that the rumour and vilification of Dr Adams had reached a point where a fair trial might be impossible. With the backing of his editor, Edward Pickering, he launched a one-man campaign attacking trial by newspaper. The *Daily Express* stood alone. Even the proprietor, Lord Beaverbrook, had doubts. On his morning walks with the editor, he would repeatedly say, 'I hope and pray you are right' (private information).

On 19 December 1956 Dr Adams was charged with the murder of an eighty-year-old woman patient. In March 1957 his trial opened at the Old Bailey. It proved to be a chapter in legal history. Lord Devlin was the judge; the attorney-general, Sir Reginald Manningham-Buller, prosecuted, with Melford Stevenson QC as his junior. Geoffrey Lawrence QC defended. The weight of evidence seemed to be going against the doctor when Lawrence dramatically produced the diaries kept by the nurses going back several years which contradicted claims of improper administration of drugs. On 9 April 1957 Dr Adams was found not guilty. On that day Hoskins received a telephone call from Lord Beaverbrook: 'Two men have been acquitted today: Adams and Hoskins'—a phrase that Hoskins adapted for his own sparkling book on the trial.

The importance of the Bodkin Adams case, and Hoskins's part in it, was demonstrated by the fact that it brought about a fundamental change in criminal law. The Tucker committee was set up and its findings resulted in the Criminal Justice Act of 1967 laying down a change to the restrictions on the reporting of proceedings in magistrates' courts, leaving the choice of publicity or no publicity to the defence. It also highlighted the medical and ethical problems a doctor faces in treating aged and sick patients—a dilemma brilliantly expounded by Lord Devlin in his book *Easing the Passing* (1986).

For some years Hoskins was chairman of the Crime Reporters' Association and was largely responsible for improving relations between police and the press. He was a regular lecturer at police colleges and training schools.

He married while still a young man, but the relationship was not long-lasting. The couple nevertheless had a daughter. One of Hoskins's great strengths as a newspaperman was the wide circle of contacts and friends that he maintained in many fields, and in this he was greatly helped by his subsequent partner, Jeannie Fettes Smith (1909–1986). Although the couple never married, this was not publicly known; and she took his name by deed poll. Jeannie Hoskins was the founder of Celebrity Services, which looked after the London schedules for visiting politicians, film stars, and actors. Consequently, on any night in their flat at 55 Park Lane, one was liable to encounter high-ranking police officers, ministers of the crown, publishers, Hollywood beauties, and editors.

Hoskins was president of the Saints and Sinners Club, which he had founded with Jack Hylton, the band leader, in 1947, an organization which raised many hundreds of thousands of pounds for charity, and endowed the Percy Hoskins scholarship at Sheffield University's School of Journalism. The club also raised more than £40,000 to endow the Jeannie Hoskins memorial suite in King's College Hospital, London, and later, in 1991, sponsored two suites with full intensive care facilities in memory of Hoskins. For his work in journalism and for charity he was made CBE in 1976.

All this daily activity and Hoskins's frequent visits to health farms had little effect on his Alfred Hitchcock-like figure. His rich Dorset burr stayed with him, as did a magnificent bass voice that came from years of church-choir training. He was capable on occasions of bursting into song—a Stanford or a Mendelssohn anthem or an operatic aria. He wrote several books dealing with crime, including *No Hiding Place* (1951), a title made famous in a television series.

Hoskins died at his home, 65 Kingsway Court, Queens Gardens, Hove, on 5 February 1989 from cerebral thrombosis. He was cremated in Hove. Jeannie Hoskins had died three years earlier in 1986.   EDWARD PICKERING

Sources personal knowledge (2004) · private information (2004) · P. Hoskins, *Two men were acquitted* (1984) · *The Times* (7 Feb 1998) · b. cert. · d. cert. · *CGPLA Eng. & Wales* (1989)
Likenesses photographs, Times Picture Library, London · thirty photographs, Express Picture Library, London
Wealth at death £180,611: probate, 25 April 1989, *CGPLA Eng. & Wales*

Hoskins, Samuel Elliott (1799–1888), physician, was born at Guernsey in February 1799, the son of Samuel Hoskins, businessman, of Honiton, London, and Guernsey, and his wife, Elizabeth Oliver. Hoskins was educated at Topsham and Exeter, and being destined for the Guernsey bar was placed under Advocate Charles de Jersey; however, after a year's probation Hoskins abandoned the law for medicine. From 1818 to 1820 he studied at the united hospitals of Guy's and St Thomas's, London. He became a licentiate of the Society of Apothecaries in 1821, a member of the Royal College of Surgeons in 1822, and an extra-licentiate of the Royal College of Physicians in 1834, of which he was elected fellow in 1859. While a student he came to know Astley Cooper, Coleridge, Charles Lamb, De Quincey,

Thomas Talfourd, and Douglas Jerrold. After passing his surgical examination he returned to Guernsey and entered into partnership with his former instructor, Dr Brock, having declined the offer of an assistant surgeoncy in the foot guards. Hoskins studied for a short time in Paris in 1827, and settled finally in the Channel Islands. In 1830 he married Harriet Rowley (d. 12 March 1889), daughter of Thomas and Harriet Le Merchant MacCulloch. They had one son.

Soon after his return to the Channel Islands Hoskins developed a chart of stethoscopic signs. This research was published in 1830 under the title, *A stethoscopic chart in which may be seen at one view the application of auscultation and percussion to the diagnosis of thoracic disease*. Hoskins also carried out an investigation into the solubility of calculi within the body. This involved a translation of Scharling's work on vesical calculi. Hoskins's results, presented to the Royal Society and published in 1843 in its *Philosophical Transactions*, gained his election to a fellowship on 25 May 1843. His other work involved observations on the climatology of Guernsey, and was regarded by contemporaries as unique. At the request of the Epidemiological Society he wrote a paper on the origin and progress of cholera and smallpox in 1849. He also carried out research into the causes of the failure of the percussion caps of the 46th regiment; this was confirmed by Faraday, and approved by the duke of Wellington.

In 1859 Hoskins retired from his profession, leaving his practice in the hands of his partner, Dr de Lisle, and devoted himself to historical research. He published a number of historical works including *The Carved Oak Chests of the Channel Islands* and *The Outposts of England*. His work entitled *Charles the Second in the Channel Islands* (2 vols., 1854) was well known to contemporaries. Hoskins died on 12 October 1888 at York Place, Candie Road, Guernsey, and was buried in Candie cemetery. His wife died five months later.   G. C. BOASE, *rev.* CLAIRE E. J. HERRICK

Sources BMJ (27 Oct 1888), 969–70 · The Lancet (27 Oct 1888), 845 · Munk, Roll · The Times (19 Oct 1888), 5 · PRS, 45 (1888–9), 47 · CGPLA Eng. & Wales (1888)

Wealth at death £4308 3s. 10d. effects in England: probate, 8 Nov 1888, CGPLA Eng. & Wales

Hoskins, William George (1908–1992), historian of the English landscape, was born on 22 May 1908 in Exeter, the eldest of four sons of William George Hoskins (1873–1955), baker, and his wife, Alice Beatrice (1879–1966), daughter of John Dymond of Silverton, Devon. He was born at his grandparents' house, 54 St David's Hill. His parents lived in Little Silver. His grandfather, William George Hoskins (1835–1904) was also an Exeter baker. At three years of age he first attended Hoopern Street infants' school, next the Episcopal infants' school, and from 1915 the Episcopal Boys' School. In the summer of 1918 he won a scholarship to Hele's School, Exeter. He entered the University College of Exeter in 1925, and completed the BSc (Econ) degree in 1927, aged nineteen years. He immediately began research for the MSc (Econ), completing in 1929 a thesis, 'The rise and decline of the serge industry in the south-west of England'.

Hoskins taught for one year at Exeter, and moved in 1930 for another year to Bradford Technical College, teaching economics and commercial subjects for the BComm degree. Stronger but latent interests were already evident in his attendance at lectures by Arthur Raistrick on local archaeology. In 1931 he was appointed assistant lecturer in economics in the department of geography and commerce at Leicester University College, but later gave his opinion of economics as distasteful, arid, and wrongheaded. More congenial from the beginning was his voluntary teaching of evening students at Vaughan Working Men's College, which had become an extramural department of the University College; here he gave courses on the antiquities and archaeology of Leicestershire, and took students to museums and into the country on fieldwork. These interests were much stimulated by a flourishing archaeological society in Leicestershire, and a rich collection of books on local history, bestowed on the college library by Thomas Hatton.

Hoskins's post was impermanent and insecure, and to improve his prospects elsewhere he completed in 1937 a PhD thesis (as a London University external student) entitled 'The ownership and occupation of land in Devonshire, 1650–1800'. By 1938 he was responsible for most of the teaching for the BSc (Econ) and BComm degrees, and by 1941 was single-handed in the department. But the college could not secure his deferment from military service and the department closed. In July 1941 he was called to work as a statistician with the Central Price Regulation Committee of the Board of Trade in London, and so remained until 1945. He detested London, but spent his leisure in libraries, the Public Record Office, and bookshops, gathering local material on Devon and Leicestershire, and publishing articles which exploited in a fresh way local documents such as wills, probate inventories, and poll tax and subsidy lists. One essay on the deserted villages of Leicestershire coincided with a similar investigation in Warwickshire by Maurice Beresford and the two scholars thereby opened up the possibilities of landscape history in a direction which excited immediate attention, and had wide repercussions thereafter for history and archaeology. Hoskins's work on probate inventories also revealed their value in elucidating local farming specialities and the layout of domestic buildings; so he launched agricultural history and the study of vernacular architecture on new and broader paths with far-reaching consequences.

After the war Hoskins debated a different career, in the civil service, in local government, or in educational administration, but the planned expansion of university education, and the urgings of R. H. Tawney, persuaded him to accept an invitation to return to Leicester in January 1946. Jack Simmons was appointed to head the department of history in 1947, and since he was also a Devon man with a strong interest in landscape and buildings, as well as being a specialist in colonial history and railways, the two formed a strong alliance in promoting local history. Further powerful support came from the principal of the college, F. L. Attenborough, originally an Anglo-Saxon historian, who was a fine photographer, and who accompanied Hoskins on many of his exploratory journeys through the midland countryside. Attenborough proposed the setting up of a department of English local history to allow Hoskins freedom for his research; it was established in 1948. This move was a milestone in claiming for local history a respectable place in academic studies, though that place was not generally conceded until decades later, when the published results of many local studies were seen to revise, even overturn, many old historical platitudes.

Publications for the Festival of Britain in 1951 brought an invitation to Hoskins to write two books in a series, About Britain, for which he wrote *Chilterns to Black Country* (1951) and *East Midlands and the Peak* (1951), thereby venturing into less familiar territory. He had already in 1946 published *Heritage of Leicestershire* and through a correspondence initiated by a reader who happened to be lecturing at the Leicester School of Architecture, struck up a warm, admiring friendship with Hope Bagenal, architect, and expert on building acoustics, who had a philosophy that saw 'the essence of civilisation' in common things. He exhorted Hoskins to be more meditative and leisurely in his judgements, curbing his inclination to be 'impatient and swift'. Something of that influence is defined in Hoskins's dedication of his comprehensive survey of Devon to 'Hope Bagenal, Poet and Topographer'.

Bagenal's architectural expertise and questionings sharpened Hoskins's attention and skills when inspecting buildings, and expanded his thinking generally on the connections between economic development and phases of building activity. He published in 1953 a seminal article, 'The rebuilding of rural England, 1570–1640', which galvanized research on its bold proposition, and, although the claim for a fundamental 'rebuilding' of rural England in that period has been refined and modified since then, the essay stands as another challenging and path-breaking guide into new historical territory.

Hoskins's letters between 1947 and 1951 glitter with zest for new projects in local history, some of which foundered, some of which flourished. Out of all this emerged his history of *Devon* (1954), for which he visited all 450 parishes in the county, travelling by bus, train or on foot, positively relishing the 'feast of solitude'. He never learned to drive a car, though he used one later, driven by his wife. The Victoria County History of Leicestershire was restarted through his efforts and he became for a while the editor, though his attempt to restart the *Victoria County History* of Devon failed, as did the plan to found a record society for Leicestershire.

Hoskins remained the single member of his college department until an enquiry by the Clapham committee into the future of economic and social history resulted in money being allocated to promote research, and through G. D. H. Cole's prodding he was encouraged to apply for a grant to his department. Knowing the relatively unexploited richness of Lincolnshire archives, he applied this money to set up a research fellowship for the study of Lincolnshire agrarian history, to which Joan Thirsk was appointed in 1951. But before she took up the post, Hoskins's growing reputation in the academic world had resulted in an invitation to take up the readership in economic history at Oxford University. He accepted, and although in the event the Oxford history syllabus had no room to accommodate local history, he gained wider renown for his radio broadcasts and his membership (with Dudley Stamp) of the royal commission on common land (1955–8), and graduate students who were inspired by his teaching and chose research subjects under his influence congregated around him. The access to libraries and time for research were Oxford privileges which enabled Hoskins to write many articles and books between 1951 and 1965. One of these was *The Midland Peasant* (1957), a work of high scholarship and an influential model of an academic village history. It traced economic and social changes in the Leicestershire village of Wigston Magna, from the Anglo-Saxon period until 1900, when Wigston supported far more people, but 'a whole culture, a qualitative civilisation, had perished to bring about this quantitative triumph' (W. G. Hoskins, *The Midland Peasant*, 1957, 282). More conspicuously successful with the general reader was *The Making of the English Landscape* (1955), offering a historical account and explanation for the man-made features of the English countryside. Readers learned how to ask questions and search for answers about familiar local scenes; to many it opened new worlds.

Work in the civil service had emboldened a quiet, reserved person into one who wrote more rapidly, and revealed some strong prejudices against trends in the modern world. Hoskins's writing became lively, colourful, sometimes poetic, and always friendly towards the common reader. His lecturing style similarly inspired the imagination of his hearers, and still warmer responses came from those who heard his radio talks for the BBC after he had moved to Oxfordshire, and in the 1970s when he gave two series of television programmes, showing sites of historic significance while standing out in all weathers, rubicund, benign, usually smiling, though he was once ankle deep in river water.

Hoskins's unease at Oxford mounted in the 1960s; he saw it as a privileged place; he was not offered a college fellowship but was a guest only at All Souls College. In 1965 he returned to Leicester University as Hatton professor of English history, devised a one-year MA course in local history, but resigned in 1968 'in despair' (*WW*), unwilling to submit to administrative burdens that impeded research. He lived until his death in Devon, first in Exeter, then Stoke Canon, and finally in Cullompton.

Hoskins married on 4 February 1933 Frances Ethel Jackson of Leicester, always known as Jane; they had a son, William Dommett (1935–1987) and daughter Susan Mary (*b.* 1944). Jane was patient and self-effacing, and catered for Hoskins's growing indulgence in good food and wine; she enabled him, on his own admission 'to live and work in Victorian comfort' (dedication to *The Shell Guide to Leicestershire*, 1970). Hoskins had moved from Oxfordshire to Exeter in 1955 and in 1963, in alliance with the new Civic

Society, of which he was a founder member, he battled against a redevelopment of its Guildhall area. Incautious criticisms of the city's planning committee resulted in a libel suit which he settled out of court, to his cost. He was an acknowledged authority on historic buildings, gave much advice to Devon county council, and saved many threatened buildings from destruction.

Hoskins was elected fellow of the British Academy in 1969, was appointed CBE in 1971 'for his services to local history', and received in his honour a Festschrift in 1974, which gives a full bibliography of his writings; in this year too he was awarded an honorary DLitt by Exeter University. He enjoyed an active, contented retirement for some years, but from 1979 minor strokes changed his personality, leaving him irascible and often melancholy. His interest in local history ceased and he turned to reading the classics of English literature and books on modern politics that provoked his familiar humorous grin, and witty and wickedly acerbic comments. He died of pneumonia at the Old Vicarage Nursing Home at Cullompton, Devon, on 11 January 1992. For reasons unknown to his family, he asked for his ashes to be scattered at Brampford Speke, and his wish was carried out, on 5 February 1992; George Gissing had described it as 'the most perfect village I ever saw'. His wife died three months later on 14 April 1992.

Hoskins was no international traveller, preferring to explore England, loving Devon, and best of all Exeter; he often cited Horace's lines in relation to Exeter—'it is that corner of the world above all which has a smile for me'. But his studies ranged widely within England, and by capturing a wide audience through his attractive writing, and by deepening public understanding of its historic landscapes, he contributed immeasurably to current knowledge and concern to conserve the environment.

JOAN THIRSK

Sources private information (2004) [Mrs Susan Hewitt, Okehampton, Devon] · J. Thirsk, 'William George Hoskins, 1908–1992', *PBA*, 87 (1995), 339–54 · priv. coll., Hoskins MSS · *The Times* (15 Jan 1992) · *Daily Telegraph* (14 Jan 1992) · J. Thirsk, *The Independent* (14 Jan 1992) [additional note by M. W. Beresford, 15 Feb 1992] · *The Guardian* (14 Jan 1992) · personal knowledge (2004) · C. Phythian-Adams, 'W. G. Hoskins and the local springs of English history', *The Historian* [London], 45 (1995), 9–12 · WW

Archives Devon RO · Exeter Central Library, Westcountry Studies Library, typescript thesis, notes on St Giles in the Wood · priv. coll., letters · University of Leicester, Centre for English Local History, corresp., notebooks, diaries, and papers

Likenesses photograph, University of Leicester, Centre for English local history

Wealth at death approx. £50,000: private information

Hoskyns, Chandos Wren (1812–1876), agriculturist, was born on 15 February 1812 in Herefordshire, the second son of Sir Hungerford Hoskyns, seventh baronet (1776–1862), of Harewood and Morehampton Park, Herefordshire, and his wife, Sarah *née* Philips (d. 1860). He was educated at Shrewsbury School and at Balliol College, Oxford, and obtained a second class in classics in 1834. He then entered the Inner Temple and was called to the bar in 1838. Although he did not long practise law, he later took a close interest in the legal aspects of agricultural affairs. On 20

April 1837 he married Theodosia Anna Martha, the daughter and heir of Christopher R. Wren, the last direct descendant of the celebrated architect. They had a daughter, Catherine. Hoskyns assumed the additional surname of Wren by royal licence on 15 April 1837, and after his marriage took charge of his wife's extensive family estate of Wroxall Abbey, Warwickshire. His wife's illness interrupted Hoskyns's legal career, and for several years he resided with her in Madeira and other health resorts. Following her death on 25 March 1842, Hoskyns married, on 9 July 1846, Anna Fane (d. 1881), daughter of Charles Milner Ricketts; they had a son and two daughters.

Hoskyns made extensive contributions to the *Agricultural Gazette* from its inception in 1844, and was concerned to improve the popularity and accessibility of agricultural writing. In the preface to his *A Short Enquiry into the History of Agriculture in Ancient Medieval and Modern Times* (1849)—originally a course of lectures given at the Manchester Athenaeum—he made the observation that, 'English publishers say, despondingly, that agriculturists are not a reading class. What have they ever had to make them so?' His work had a wry character and exhibits a humour reminiscent of his ancestor, Sergeant John Hoskins. The best exemplar of his agricultural writing is *Talpa, or, The Chronicles of a Clay Farm*; it was published as a book in 1852, having first appeared in series form in the *Agricultural Gazette* of 1847. His other early contributions to the paper include 'Anomalies of agriculture' and 'Tales of a landlord'. Hoskyns also made a number of contributions to the *Journal of the Royal Agricultural Society of England*, which he helped to edit (with H. S. Thompson and Thomas Dyke Acland) between 1855 and 1858 following the death of the society's first editor, Philip Pusey.

Hoskyns was interested in all forms of agricultural progress and in the 1850s campaigned for the official collection of agricultural statistics. His lifelong associate and friend John Chalmers Morton (editor of the *Agricultural Gazette*, 1844–88) recognized him as helping to bring about an early acceptance of free-trade opinion among agriculturists. Later he turned his attention to the land laws and land system in England. In a number of publications—*Land in England, Land in Ireland, and Land in other Lands* (1869), *The Land Laws of England: Systems of Land Tenure in Various Countries* (1870), and *A Catechism on the English Land System* (1873)—he advocated an extensive reform of the real property laws of the country, a restriction of entail, and a reduction in the cost of land transfer. Hoskyns also wrote the introductory essay, and the contributions on education and the landlord, for Morton's *Cyclopaedia of Agriculture*, published in 1855. Hoskyns took a close interest in history, and his published lecture *The Battle Line of History* (1864) is a good example of his numerous attempts to popularize the subject. Hoskyns represented the City of Hereford in parliament from 1869 to 1874, but made little impression in the House of Commons apart from some contributions on agricultural topics. He died at 41 Eccleston Square, London, on 28 November 1876, having suffered a growth in his larynx for eighteen months.

NICHOLAS GODDARD

Sources *Agricultural Gazette* (7 Jan 1871) · *Agricultural Gazette* (9 April 1877) · J. S. Arkwright, 'Introductory note', in C. W. Hoskyns, *Talpa, or, The chronicles of a clay farm: an agricultural fragment* (1903) · Burke, *Peerage* · d. cert.
Archives Hereford RO, family estate papers
Likenesses engraving (after photograph), repro. in *Agricultural Gazette* (7 Jan 1871)
Wealth at death under £20,000: probate, 29 Dec 1876, *CGPLA Eng. & Wales*

Hoskyns, Sir Edwyn Clement, thirteenth baronet (1884–1937), theologian, was born on 9 August 1884 at St Clement's vicarage, Notting Hill, London, the eldest child and only son of Edwyn Hoskyns (1851–1925), Church of England clergyman, and his wife, Mary Constance Maude, only daughter of Robert Benson, of London. His father was the second bishop of Southwell (1904) and twelfth baronet (1923–5). Hoskyns was educated at Haileybury College, and at Jesus College, Cambridge, where he took a second in history. Decisively for his future development, Foakes-Jackson, dean of Jesus, sent him to the University of Berlin for the year 1906–7. After a year at Wells Theological College, he was ordained deacon in 1908 and undertook a curacy at St Ignatius, Sunderland. He became warden of Stephenson Hall, Sheffield, in 1912 and a chaplain to the forces in 1915. There he was much loved and won the MC. On his return he took up a fellowship at Corpus Christi College, Cambridge, and became, over the years, dean of chapel, librarian, and president. In 1922 he married Mary Trym Budden (*d.* 1995), a young research fellow in mathematics at Newnham. They had four sons and a daughter. She was a suffragist and more to the left politically than he. Hoskyns was canon theologian of Liverpool Cathedral, 1932–5.

B. H. Streeter said that Corpus, Cambridge, was the only college in either ancient university which took the teaching of theology seriously. It was tory in politics in contrast to King's, but its theology was liberal Catholic as represented by the work of its fellow and future master the scientist Will Spens, in his book *Belief and Practice* (1915), which placed the warrant for Catholic faith neither in scripture nor in the oracular pronouncements of a supposedly infallible *magisterium*, but in continuing religious experience. Hoskyns at first taught in this vein, but gradually there was a change due to his German encounters, his friendship with Gerhard Kittel, his emphasis on the study of words, and his reading of the second edition of Karl Barth's *Der Römerbrief* (1919) which he brilliantly translated into English as *Commentary on Romans* in 1933. He moved from a religion of experience to one of revelation through history received by faith. Liberalism, he argued, both Catholic and protestant, could not withstand what the gospels actually said. As he wrote in his essay 'The Christ of the synoptic gospels', 'The contrast is not between the Jesus of history and the Christ of faith, but between the Christ humiliated and the Christ returning in glory' (Selwyn, 176).

Hoskyns regarded the Bible as a unity held together by the scarlet thread which ran throughout humanity, which was sin; and yet when sin seemed triumphant and Christ crucified, it proclaimed the forgiveness and the victory of God. The Bible was 'difficult, strange and foreign' to us, not because it came from a different culture, but because its message was delivered from outside all human culture. It was history, 'rough, crude history', yet it needed the non-historical to make sense of it and theology to control its fragmentary and incomplete details.

> The visible, historical Jesus is the place in history where it is demanded that men should believe … and, where, if they believe, the fragmentary story of his life is woven into one whole, manifesting the glory of God and the glory of men who have been created by him. (Hoskyns, *Fourth Gospel*, 85)

The theme of the church and the meaning of life was 'crucifixion–resurrection'. This was 'the song which is sung, whether it be recognised or not, by the whole world of men and of things in their tribulation and their merriment' (Hoskyns, *Cambridge Sermons*, 93).

Hoskyns's teaching was very different from that of the Cambridge theology faculty as a whole, which was of sound, sometimes rather arid scholarship, free of rhetoric but also anxious to take natural theology seriously and bring Christianity into line with scientific discovery and contemporary thought. His lectures and tutorials intoxicated many, some of whom discovered their vocation as New Testament scholars. Others counted the clichés. He discovered a literary partner in Francis Noel Davey, who, as far more than an amanuensis, wrote *The Riddle of the New Testament* to his instructions in 1931 and edited and completed *The Fourth Gospel* (1940) after Hoskyns's death. He also partly finished what should have been Hoskyns's masterpiece *Crucifixion–Resurrection*, which was not published until 1981, something of a torso with some dazzling insights.

A lovable man, with wide interests in music and literature, Hoskyns read the *Farmer and Stockbreeder* as well as the Bible. He revolted against Anglo-Catholic pietism in his dedication to biblical theology. His friendship with Kittel, notoriously a Nazi supporter, tinged him with anti-semitism. Much has happened in New Testament scholarship since his time; and in spite of his biblical and patristic knowledge he seems an amateur compared with the vast erudition of scholars today. Yet Hoskyns cannot be written off. Some of the issues which concerned him remain subjects for debate, and no one would question his assertion that 'The figure of Jesus as the embodiment of the Word of God controls the whole matter of the Christian religion' (Hoskyns, *Fourth Gospel*, 163), even though they might differ as to whether the New Testament view of Jesus was wholly authentic. He may have got to the heart of Christian theology and ethics.

Hoskyns died on 28 June 1937 from pneumonia, while recovering from a nervous breakdown, at the Flower House, Beckenham Hill Road, London. This was only six weeks before his fifty-third birthday, and he left much unfinished, not least the chapters on the resurrection in *Crucifixion–Resurrection*. He was succeeded as fourteenth baronet by his eldest son, Chandos Wren Hoskyns, who was killed in the Second World War. Hoskyns was buried at Grantchester churchyard, Cambridge and the words 'Crucifixion–resurrection' were inscribed on the gravestone.   GORDON STEVENS WAKEFIELD

Sources G. S. Wakefield, 'Edwyn Clement Hoskyns', in E. C. Hoskyns and F. N. Davey, *Crucifixion–resurrection* (1981), 27–81 · C. Smyth, 'Edwyn Clement Hoskyns, 1884–1937', in E. C. Hoskyns, *Cambridge sermons* (1938), vii–xxviii · R. H. Fuller, 'Sir Edwyn Hoskyns and the contemporary relevance of biblical theology', *New Testament Studies*, 30 (1984), 331–4 · C. Evans, 'Crucifixion–resurrection: some reflections on Sir Edwyn Hoskyns as theologian', *Epworth Review* (May 1983), 73 · M. Cowling, *Religion and public doctrine in modern England*, 1 (1980) · D. M. Mackinnon, 'Crucifixion–resurrection', *Themes in theology, the three-fold cord: essays in philosophy, politics and theology* (1987), 196–207 · R. E. Parsons, *Sir Edwyn Hoskyns as biblical theologian* (1985) · T. E. B. Howarth, *Cambridge between two wars* (1978) · *WWW* · *The Times* (30 June 1937) · private information (2004) [the late Mary, Lady Hoskyns; Dr Noel Davey; Prof. C. F. Evans] · E. G. Selwyn, ed., *Essays Catholic and critical* (1926) · E. C. Hoskyns, *The fourth gospel*, ed. F. Noel (1947) · *CGPLA Eng. & Wales* (1937)
Archives Queen's College, Birmingham
Wealth at death £26,472 16s. 7d.: resworn probate, 25 Aug 1937, *CGPLA Eng. & Wales*

Hoste, Dirick (c.1588–1663), merchant and financier, was born in Middelburg, Netherlands, the son of Jacques Hoste (b. 1545), a merchant, and his wife, Barbara Henricksen. His father and grandfather had fled Oudenarde in Flanders for religious reasons in the wake of the 'Wonderyear' of 1566—the failed protestant insurrection in the Netherlands. The family settled in London in 1567, then around 1580 moved to Middelburg in Zeeland, where Dirick and his twin brother, Jacques, were born. By 1607 Dirick had arrived in London and on 12 October 1613, at Austin Friars, he married Jane van Meteren or Desmaistres (1596–1661), the daughter of the wealthy immigrant London brewer James van Meteren. They lived in Abchurch Lane, near London Bridge. Despite his family's roots in the cloth trade Hoste focused on general overseas trade. In 1615 he became a member of the East India Company, and by 1625 he belonged to a group of Dutch and Flemish merchants who supplied the king of Spain with gunpowder, cordage, and iron for his ports in Africa. His many international trading contacts made it easy for him to operate as a successful banker and financier, and among his customers were the royal physician Sir Théodore de Mayerne and the Spanish ambassadors to London. According to John Aubrey, the Spanish customs farmers who financed the Catholic imperial armies in the Netherlands and Germany during the Thirty Years' War kept their cash on deposit with him. Considering Hoste's strong commitment to the Calvinist cause, this is somewhat surprising. From the outset he was an active member of the Dutch Reformed church in London, where he was elected deacon in 1627. A year later he was promoted to the eldership, thus following in the footsteps of his father, who had regularly served the reformed church in Middelburg in this capacity between 1597 and 1605. He was prominently involved in two of the major collections for persecuted Calvinist brethren abroad—in 1630 he was one of four elders responsible for the second English collection for refugee Calvinists from the German palatinate, while in

1643 he was among the four parliamentary commissioners appointed to raise funds for suffering Irish protestants in the Netherlands. In this latter enterprise he was joined by the City radical and colonizer Maurice Thomson, with whom he had already co-operated closely in the mercantile field.

Hoste played a major role within the Dutch Reformed church in London for at least two decades. In 1646 he was chosen, together with the minister Cesar Calandrini, to negotiate with the Independent and Baptist leaders Sidrach Simpson and William Kiffin on behalf of the church. In 1649, on account of his excellent relations with the speaker of the House of Commons, William Lenthal, and the radical London mercer Colonel Edmond Harvey, he was able to help the many weavers within the Dutch community who had come under attack from the Weavers' Company. In addition he found time to publish, in an English translation, *Of Death, a True Description* (1629), written by his friend and consistorial colleague Jacob Cool. During the civil war and interregnum, in 1643–5 and again in 1651–2, he lived in Middelburg, where he owned several houses. By 1654, however, he had retired permanently to his country house in Mortlake in Surrey. Of his thirteen children only four survived childhood: Joanna, who married Peter vander Put; James, who married Elizabeth Sleigh; Theodorus, who married Anne Chilcott; and Mary, who married Sir Stephen Langham. Hoste died a wealthy man in Mortlake in March 1663, and was buried there on 24 March.   OLE PETER GRELL

Sources R. E. G. Kirk and E. F. Kirk, eds., *Returns of aliens dwelling in the city and suburbs of London, from the reign of Henry VIII to that of James I*, Huguenot Society of London, 10/3 (1907), 153, 165, 271 · J. H. Hessels, ed., *Ecclesiae Londino-Batavae archivum*, 3 vols. (1887–97) · *Brief lives, chiefly of contemporaries, set down by John Aubrey, between the years 1669 and 1696*, ed. A. Clark, 2 vols. (1898) · O. P. Grell, *Dutch Calvinists in early Stuart London: the Dutch church in Austin Friars, 1603–1642* (1989) · O. P. Grell, *Calvinist exiles in Tudor and Stuart England* (1996) · R. Brenner, *Merchants and revolution: commercial change, political conflict, and London's overseas traders, 1550–1653* (1993) · will, PRO, PROB 11/310, fol. 36 · registers (birth, baptism, marriage), 1884, Dutch Reformed Church, Lymington
Likenesses C. Jonson, two double portraits (with his wife); priv. coll. [stolen, 1992] · photographs, Courtauld Inst.
Wealth at death approx. £10,000: will, PRO, PROB 11/310, fol. 36

Hoste, Sir George Charles (1786–1845), army officer, third son of the Revd Dixon Hoste, rector of Tittleshall, Norfolk, and of Margaret, daughter of Henry Stanforth of Salthouse, Norfolk, and brother of Captain Sir William *Hoste, RN, first baronet, was born on 10 March 1786. After attending the Royal Military Academy, Woolwich, he was commissioned second lieutenant in the Royal Engineers on 20 December 1802. His further commissions were: lieutenant, 21 December 1802; second captain, 18 November 1807; captain, 21 May 1812; brevet major, 17 March 1814; lieutenant-colonel, 29 July 1825; brevet colonel, 28 June 1838; colonel, 23 November 1841.

After service at Portsmouth and Dover, Hoste went to the Mediterranean in April 1805, and accompanied the expedition under Lieutenant-General Sir James Craig in

November to co-operate with the Russians in the protection of the kingdom of Naples. He landed at Castellamare and took part in the subsequent withdrawal to Messina in January 1806. At the end of June he served in Calabria under Sir John Stuart, and was present at the battle of Maida on 4 July and at the siege of Scylla Castle from 12 to 23 July, when it capitulated. He returned with Stuart to Messina.

In March 1807 Hoste accompanied the expedition under Major-General McKenzie Fraser to Egypt, landed at Abu Qir on the 16th, and took part on the 18th in storming the defence of Alexandria, which capitulated, and was occupied on 22 March. In April he took part in the siege of Rosetta until the costly retirement to Alexandria, and, on the evacuation of Egypt, returned to Sicily with the troops in September. He was engaged during 1808 and 1809 in improving the defences and communications of the east of Sicily to resist attack. The surrender of Capri to Marshal Murat in October 1808 led to an expedition under Sir John Stuart in the following June to the Bay of Naples, when Hoste was engaged in the capture of Ischia and Procida on 25 October. He was present at the siege of the castle of Ischia, which capitulated on 30 October, after which he returned with the expedition to Messina.

In May 1810 Hoste was on board the frigate HMS *Spartan*, commanded by Captain Jahleel Brenton, on scouting duty, when off the Bay of Naples on 3 May she was attacked by a French squadron. At Brenton's request Hoste took command of the quarter-deck guns. After a successful action, in which the *Spartan* lost ten killed and twenty-two wounded, she sailed in triumphantly with her prize, *La Sparvière*, to the mole of Naples, where Murat had watched the fight. In his dispatch Brenton spoke highly of Hoste's services and King Ferdinand conferred upon him the knighthood of the third class of the royal Sicilian order of St Ferdinand and of Merit 'for great courage and intrepidity'. He was permitted by the prince regent to accept and wear the insignia.

In December 1810 Hoste left Sicily for Gibraltar, and in May 1811, having returned to England, was stationed at Landguard Fort. On 4 January 1812 he accidentally killed his younger brother, Charles Fox, when out shooting. He married, on 9 July 1812, Mary, only daughter of James Burkin Burroughes of Burlingham Hall, Norfolk; they had four sons and two daughters. In November 1813 Hoste accompanied the expedition to the Netherlands, landing on 24 November and marching to Delft. He was engaged under Sir Thomas Graham, later Lord Lynedoch, in the bombardment of Antwerp in February 1814 until it was abandoned, and in the night assault on Bergen-op-Zoom on 8 March, when he led the third column, consisting of about one thousand men of the guards under Colonel Lord Proby, into the town. At daybreak, owing to contradictory orders, the assaulting columns were withdrawn when the fortress was within their grasp. Hoste was favourably mentioned by Graham in dispatches, and received a brevet majority.

After the peace Hoste returned to England in May and resumed his duties in the eastern military district, from which he was called a year later to join the Waterloo campaign in June 1815. Hoste was appointed commanding royal engineer of the 1st army corps commanded by the prince of Orange, in which capacity he was present at the battle of Waterloo on 18 June, at the assault of Péronne on the 26th, and at the occupation of Paris on 7 July. He was mentioned in dispatches and made a CB, military division (22 June 1815), on the recommendation of Wellington. In November 1815 he was one of the British commissioners appointed to take over French fortresses for occupation by the allies.

In February 1816 Hoste returned to England, and for the next nine years was employed in the Medway and Thames military districts, after which he went on service to Canada in 1825 and to Ireland in 1828. On the accession of William IV in 1830 he was appointed gentleman usher of the privy chamber to Queen Adelaide. He served as commanding royal engineer of the eastern, western, and Woolwich military districts successively. He died at his residence, Mill Hill, Woolwich, on 21 April 1845, and was buried in Charlton churchyard, Kent, where a tomb marked the grave.   R. H. VETCH, *rev.* JAMES FALKNER

Sources *Army List* · W. Porter, *History of the corps of royal engineers*, 2 vols. (1889) · *LondG* (27 Nov 1811) · J. Philippart, ed., *The royal military calendar*, 3rd edn, 5 vols. (1820) · *Hart's Army List* · *Annual Register* (1845) · *GM*, 1st ser., 80 (1810), 574–5 [copy of Hoste's account of naval encounter at Grao] · *GM*, 1st ser., 85/2 (1815), 629 · Burke, *Peerage* · *European Magazine and London Review*, 62 (1812), 71

Likenesses W. Salter, group portrait, oils (*Waterloo banquet at Apsley House*), Wellington Museum, Apsley House, London · W. Salter, oils (study for *Waterloo banquet*), NPG

Hoste, Sir William, first baronet (1780–1828), naval officer, descended from a sixteenth-century Flemish refugee family, was the second son of Dixon Hoste, rector of Godwick and Tittleshall in Norfolk, and his wife, Margaret Stanforth, of Salthouse. He was born at Ingoldisthorpe, the property of his father, on 26 August 1780. Hoste was intended for a naval career from the age of five, when his name was entered in the books of the *Europa* as a captain's servant. In 1787, when seven years old, he went to boarding-school in King's Lynn; later he attended Paston School, North Walsham. War with France in 1793 provided the opportunity to launch his naval career, and his father's patron, Thomas Coke of Holkham, secured the 'interest' of Captain Nelson, son of the parson of nearby Burnham Thorpe, who took him as a captain's servant in the *Agamemnon* in April 1793. Hoste continued with Nelson, almost without interruption, for the next five years, following him from the *Agamemnon* to the *Captain*, to the *Irresistible*, and to the *Theseus*, and being present in the two actions off Toulon on 14 March and 13 July 1795, in the battle off Cape St Vincent, and, though not landed, at Santa Cruz. Hoste rapidly endeared himself to Nelson: 'without exception one of the finest boys I ever met with' (*Nelson's Letters*, 223); 'his gallantry never can be exceeded, and … each day rivets him stronger to my heart' (Hoste, 1.67). Under his mentor's guiding hand promotion came quickly. He was raised to midshipman by captain's authority on 1 February 1794, appointed acting lieutenant after

Sir William Hoste, first baronet (1780–1828), by William
Greatbach, pubd 1833

the slaughter at Santa Cruz in July 1797, and, with the aid
of his *Europa* time, confirmed as lieutenant on 8 February
1798. Continuing in the *Theseus* with Captain R. W. Miller,
he took part in the battle of Abu Qir Bay after which
Nelson took the opportunity to promote him to the command of the brig *Mutine* in succession to Capel, who left
her at Naples, where Hoste was received with enthusiasm,
the queen presenting him with a diamond ring. He
rejoined the fleet off Cadiz, where his promotion was confirmed on 3 December 1798. He continued to command
the *Mutine* for the next three years under Nelson and afterwards under Lord Keith, to whom he was comparatively
unknown. To the chagrin of Hoste and his distant mentor
his promotion stalled until, probably at Nelson's prompting, on 7 January 1802 he was posted by Lord St Vincent,
first lord of the Admiralty, though the promotion did not
reach him until May. Meanwhile, having been sent to
Alexandria, he contracted malaria, followed by inflammation of the lungs, which left lasting ill effects. Convalescence at Athens with Lord and Lady Elgin provided an education in 'the beautiful remains of antiquity' (Hoste,
1.173–4). After receiving his commission to the frigate
Greyhound at Malta he completed his classical education
with the envoy at Florence, Sir Francis Drake, while
employed on the coast of Italy; he did not return with the
Greyhound to England until April 1803.

In November 1804 Hoste was appointed to the *Eurydice*,
in which he cruised on the coast of Africa as far as Goree,
and, returning to Portsmouth, took out a convoy to Malta.
In September 1805 Nelson summoned him to the fleet off
Cadiz, where, after a typically aggressive action in which

he captured four merchant vessels and a privateer from a
coastal convoy, his patron moved him (13 October) into
the *Amphion* (36 guns), 'one of the finest and most desirable ships on the station' (Hoste, 1.249). Having been dispatched on a diplomatic mission to Algiers, he only
learned of Trafalgar and the death of his patron on his
return to Gibraltar on 9 November. 'Not to have been in it',
he wrote to his father, 'is enough to make one mad; but to
have lost such a friend besides is really sufficient to almost
overwhelm me' (Hoste, 1.251).

In 1806 the *Amphion* was on the coast of Naples and Sicily
under the orders of Sir W. Sidney Smith, and on 30 June
she was used to help transport the little army which, on 4
July, won the battle of Maida, and afterwards co-operated
with General Brodrick in the capture of Reggio, Cotrone,
and other places on the Calabrian coast. In June 1807 the
Amphion returned to England, and after she had undergone a six-month dockyard refit Hoste sailed again for the
Mediterranean at the express request of the station commander because 'he is active, vigilant and knows the
coast, and more depends upon the man than the ship'
(Hoste, 1.299). A bold attempt to seize the armed storeship
Baleine, lying in the Bay of Rosas, under three heavy batteries (12 May 1808) earned the warm approbation of Colling-
wood, who in June sent him to the Adriatic, 'the best
cruise in his command' (Hoste, 1.316), where, sometimes
under the orders of a senior officer, but also often independently, he carried on a successful partisan war, destroying signal stations, cutting out gunboats, taking many
prizes, and virtually stopping the coasting trade. From 23
June 1808 to Christmas day 1809 the *Amphion* took or destroyed 218 of the enemy's vessels. 'It looks well on paper',
Hoste wrote, 'but has not put much cash in our pockets,
owing to the difficulty attending their being sent to port'
(Hoste, 2.12). At Christmas 1809 the *Amphion* and a sloop
dominated the Adriatic despite far superior enemy numbers. Having been joined by the *Active* (36 guns) and the
Cerberus (32 guns), he harassed the French positions with
renewed vigour. On 23 April 1810 he wrote: 'We have been
very fortunate since we left Malta in March, and have
taken and destroyed forty-six sail of vessels, some of
which are very good ones, and will bring us in a little pew-
ter' (Hoste, 2.21).

In 1810 Napoleon determined to clear the British from
the Adriatic and built up a frigate squadron at Venice and
Ancona under one of his most aggressive frigate commanders, Bernard Dubourdieu, who in September raided
Hoste's base at Lissa during his absence. In November 1810
the British squadron was joined by the *Volage* (22 guns);
after being driven to Malta to refit, it arrived again off
Lissa on 11 March 1811, just as Dubourdieu sailed from
Ancona with the intention of occupying the island. He
had with him three French 44-gun frigates and three Venetian frigates, one of which was also of 44 guns, with five
smaller vessels, carrying some 500 troops. On the morning of 13 March 1811 the two squadrons came in sight of
each other. Hoste was outnumbered by six frigates to four
and by 276 guns and 2000 men to 124 guns and 900 men,

but he sought action with the assuredness of his mentor and model, whose spirit he invoked to inspire his crews with the signal 'Remember Nelson'. Dubourdieu, in the *Favourite*, leading down to the English line, attempted, after a short cannonade, to board the *Amphion*. But a howitzer, loaded to the muzzle with musket-bullets, slaughtered the boarding party crowded on *Favourite*'s forecastle; Dubourdieu himself was killed; and partly from the loss of men, partly from the damage to her rigging, partly too from Hoste's alert reversal of his squadron's course, the French ship went ashore, where she was abandoned and set on fire. Meanwhile Hoste found himself attacked on each side by Dubourdieu's supports, the French frigate *Flore* and the Venetian *Bellona*. Again skilful manoeuvring enable him to pass round *Flore* and use her as a shield from *Bellona*'s fire until, after an extremely sharp action, the *Flore* surrendered to the *Amphion* (although she afterwards escaped); a few minutes later Hoste was able to rake the *Bellona*, which also surrendered. The *Corona*, another Venetian, after having been warmly engaged with the *Cerberus*, surrendered to the *Active*, while the two remaining enemy frigates fled. Hoste himself was severely wounded by the explosion of a chest of musket cartridges and by a musket shot in his right arm, and the total British losses were 190 killed and wounded; those of the enemy amounted to upwards of 700. Owing to the vast numerical superiority of the enemy and the decisive result, the action off Lissa was considered one of the most brilliant naval achievements of the war. Hoste and his colleagues received the gold medal, and the first lieutenants were promoted. The four frigates with their prizes arrived at Malta on 31 March, when the garrison spontaneously turned out to cheer them.

The *Amphion* was in such bad condition that she was ordered to England; she arrived in June, and at the Admiralty Hoste was told to choose his ship and station. He was appointed to the frigate *Bacchante* (38 guns) but a year passed before she was ready. In June 1812 she sailed for the Mediterranean, from where Hoste was again sent into the Adriatic under the orders of Rear-Admiral Fremantle, who had with him three battleships and six or seven frigates. The *Bacchante* was frequently detached on independent cruises; among many actions, on 18 September 1812 she captured eight gunboats, with their convoy of eighteen trading vessels, on the coast of Apulia; and on 11 June 1813, at Giulia Nova, near Ancona, she captured a flotilla of seven gunboats with seventeen vessels in convoy. Greater fame came out of his element when, in December 1813, Hoste was sent to assist the Austrians in clearing the French from their strongholds on the Dalmatian coast. Operating at one of the most delicate international nerve-ends of Europe, Hoste by-passed diplomatic problems by allowing Ragusan rebels to fly the flag of their old republic while himself flying the flags of Russia, patron of the Montenegrins, and of Austria, the anticipated recipient of the area. In conjunction with the Montenegrins he attacked Cattaro, which surrendered on 5 January 1814, as soon as Hoste had, in what was denounced as 'a most

unmilitary way of proceeding' (Hoste, 2.248), established a battery of heavy guns, mortars, and rockets on the top of a rugged hill which dominated the enemy's position but was accessible to naval working parties drilled at hauling heavy weights by block and tackle. From Cattaro Hoste immediately crossed over to Ragusa, which also surrendered on the completion of a battery on the top of a supposedly inaccessible hill. For his exploits the Austrian emperor made him a knight of the order of Maria Theresa on 23 May 1814.

The labour of these sieges, the hardships, and the exposure to wet and cold undermined Hoste's health, already feeble, and he was invalided to England. On 23 July 1814 he was made a baronet, and at the same time was granted the augmentation to his arms, which included the words 'Lissa' and 'Cattaro'. In 1815 he was made a KCB. After his return to England his health remained delicate, and for many years he had no service. On 17 April 1817 he married Lady Harriet Walpole, fourth daughter of the second earl of Orford; they had three sons and three daughters. His eldest son, William Legge George, second baronet (1818–1868) became a rear-admiral. In 1822 Hoste accepted the command of the guardship *Albion* at Portsmouth, and in 1825 he was appointed to the yacht *Royal Sovereign*. A cold, caught in January 1828, settled on his lungs, and he died of tuberculosis in London on 6 December 1828; he was buried in St John's Chapel, near Regent's Park.

Hoste's successes in the Adriatic, his victory at Lissa, and his capture of Cattaro gave him a naval reputation far beyond that of any other officer of his age and rank. Aristocratic and naval families had crowded to entrust their sons' naval education to him. A devoted professional yet with a social assurance embellished by classical knowledge, he kept out of politics, following Nelson's advice that sailors had no business with party; the one cause he championed after 1815 was the ending of impressment. In his private life his letters show him as affectionate, tenderly attached to his family, and sacrificing opportunities of self-enrichment to help his spendthrift father, to whom, it was said, he applied £50,000 out of the £60,000 he gained in the Adriatic.

J. K. LAUGHTON, rev. MICHAEL DUFFY

Sources T. Pocock, *Remember Nelson: the life of Captain Sir William Hoste* (1977) · *Memoirs and letters of Captain Sir William Hoste, Bart*, ed. H. Hoste, 2 vols. (1833) · G. H. Hoste, *Service afloat, or, The naval career of Sir William Hoste* (1887) · *Nelson's letters to his wife and other documents, 1785–1831*, ed. G. P. B. Naish, Navy RS, 100 (1958) · W. James, *The naval history of Great Britain, from the declaration of war by France in 1793, to the accession of George IV*, [3rd edn], 6 vols. (1837) · D. Syrett and R. L. DiNardo, *The commissioned sea officers of the Royal Navy, 1660–1815*, rev. edn, Occasional Publications of the Navy RS, 1 (1994) · J. Marshall, *Royal naval biography*, 2/1 (1824), 470–81
Archives Nelson Museum and Local History Centre, Monmouth, papers · NMM, papers
Likenesses attrib. S. Lane, oils, *c*.1815, NMM · T. Campbell, statue, St Paul's Cathedral, London · W. Greatbach, line engraving, BM, NPG; repro. in Hoste, ed., *Memoirs and letters* [see illus.]
Wealth at death at marriage eleven years before death had £12,000 capital, and wife brought dowry of £13,000: Pocock, *Remember Nelson*

Hotchkis, Thomas (*c*.1611–1693), Church of England clergyman, was probably born in Whitchurch, Shropshire, about 1611, the son of John Hotchkis (1574/5–1666). His mother, whose name is unknown, was still alive in 1655. He was admitted a sizar at Corpus Christi College, Cambridge, in 1627 and graduated BA in 1631 and MA in 1634. He may have been married by this time, to Grace (*d*. 1688), and had a son, Joshua, the first of eight children. In 1637 he was appointed rector of Stanton Fitzwarren, Wiltshire, although he had no known association with the county. This living he was to hold for the rest of his life, as a presbyterian who conformed at the Restoration. He considered himself 'an obscure countrey-Minister', which he largely remained, but notice was taken of him by some of the principal Wiltshire presbyterians, including Peter Ince who wrote of him that 'he has generally the reputation of a godly man but has been counted one that did in all things keep the orthodox company' (*Calendar*, 2.156, 1.128). Hotchkis signed the *Concurrent Testimony* of the ministers of Wiltshire in 1648, and in the same year was nominated as a minister for the triers of the Marlborough classis, one of the four classes established for presbyterian church organization in Wiltshire.

Hotchkis's correspondence with Richard Baxter, some of which survives, reveals his readiness to gain Baxter's approval for his few writings. In 1654 Hotchkis penned a tract, 'An exercitation concerning the nature of forgiveness of sin', which he intended generally as an attack on antinomianism, and specifically as a forthright reply to a treatise by William Eyre, curate of St Thomas's, Salisbury, which had defended solefidianism. Hotchkis had circulated the manuscript of 'Exercitation' among his neighbouring clergy, including Adoniram Byfield and Humphrey Chambers, but it received little commendation. Baxter proved more sympathetic when he received it in January 1654, and its publication in the following year probably owed much to his contribution of a prefatory epistle. The tract elicited an attack from William Robertson, and although Hotchkis was quick in writing an answer to Robertson he was probably dissuaded by Baxter from publishing it. Baxter was less supportive of Hotchkis's second part to the 'Exercitation' as well as, in 1673, an untitled discourse on the sabbath, neither of which was published, although in 1675 Hotchkis found a publisher for *Reformation or Ruin*, a series of his sermons on Leviticus.

Indeed, the manuscript on the sabbath succeeded only in eliciting Baxter's rebuke for its acerbic criticism of Obadiah Grew: 'And what use is it to tell men that by Law he is not one of the church of England?' (*Calendar*, 2.154). Hotchkis defensively replied that he had never knowingly criticized Baxter or any other nonconformist minister (and indeed that he had been lent Grew's book, with which his argument was theological, over what he saw as its antinomian tendencies, by a nonconformist chaplain). He emphasized his admiration for and engagement with the works of Baxter, John Howe, and Thomas Manton. He did, however, demur from a passage of Baxter's which seemed to assert 'the ejected ministers to be in the right, or true

Ministers of those parishes, out of which by the present law of our kingdom they are ejected' (ibid., 156).

In his only other work, *A Discourse Concerning the Imputation of Christ's Righteousness to Us*, which appeared in two parts in 1675 and 1678, Hotchkis re-entered a familiar theological controversy, first attacking the solefidian doctrines elucidated in John Troughton's *Lutherus redivivus: of the Protestant Doctrine of Justification by Faith Alone* (1677) and John Owen's *On Communion with God* (1657) and Owen's later *Doctrine of Justification by Faith* (1677). A synoptic assessment of the merits of Hotchkis's literary works is provided by Baxter's polite judgement of him as:

> a grave, pious, sober divine, not so quick and sharp as deliberately judicious and solid, not made so much for words as matter, nor to please men's ears with smoothness and eloquence as to inform their judgements by a plain discovery of practical truths. (*Calendar*, 1.140)

Hotchkis drew up his will on 23 November 1691. His only bequests related to his theological books, the authorship of which reflected his literary and doctrinal tastes. Most of these tomes, including bibles, notes on the Westminster assembly, Thomas Watson's *The Art of Divine Contentment*, and works by Baxter, Dr Gough, and 'the most pious and judicious' William Allen were left to his son-in-law Thomas Hippesley. Hotchkis was buried at Stanton Fitzwarren on 22 September 1693, having been predeceased by his wife and three of his children.

HENRY LANCASTER

Sources *Calendar of the correspondence of Richard Baxter*, ed. N. H. Keeble and G. F. Nuttall, 2 vols. (1991) · Wood, *Ath. Oxon.*, new edn · Venn, *Alum. Cant.*, 1/2.412 · C. Whiting, *Studies in English puritanism* (1931) · *Diaries and letters of Philip Henry*, ed. M. H. Lee (1882) · W. Masters, *Notes on the ancient church of St. Leonard, Stanton Fitzwarren* (1913) · T. Hotchkis, *An exercitation concerning the nature of forgiveness of sin* (1655) · PRO, PROB 11/417, fol. 90v · *The county of Wilts divided into four classes* (*c*.1650) · parish register, Stanton Fitzwarren, Wiltshire, 1693 [burial]
Archives DWL, letters to R. Baxter
Wealth at death bequests of books: will, PRO, PROB 11/417, fol. 90v

Hotham, Beaumont, second Baron Hotham (1737–1814), judge, was born on 5 August 1737 at Innaresk, Edinburgh, the fourth of five sons of Beaumont Hotham (1698–1771), a customs commissioner at Edinburgh who became Sir Beaumont Hotham, seventh baronet, in 1767, and his wife, Frances (*d*. 1771), daughter of the Revd William Thompson, of Welton, Yorkshire. He entered Westminster School in 1745 and there formed a lifelong friendship with William Henry Cavendish Cavendish-Bentinck, the future third duke of Portland and prime minister. He matriculated at Trinity Hall, Cambridge, in 1754 but left after two years without taking a degree, having proceeded to the Middle Temple, which he had entered on 20 January 1753. He was called to the bar in 1758 and then attempted, without much success, to establish a law practice. On 6 June 1767, at St Clement Danes, London, he married Susanna (1737–1799), younger daughter of Sir Thomas Hankey and widow of James Norman; they had four sons, one of whom was Sir Henry *Hotham (1777–1833), naval

Beaumont Hotham, second Baron Hotham (1737–1814), by Valentine Green, pubd 1796 (after Nathaniel Dance)

officer, and three daughters. By all accounts Hotham was a loving husband and a devoted father.

Hotham's schoolfriend Portland appointed him auditor of his estates and acted as his political mentor, installing him from 1768 to 1775 as MP for Wigan, Lancashire, a borough with independent-minded burgesses whose support could not be taken for granted. Through Portland Hotham was tied to the rudimentary party formed around Charles Watson-Wentworth, second marquess of Rockingham; like many in that opposition group he cared even less for William Pitt, earl of Chatham, than he did for administration leaders. He was active in the Commons (twenty-four speeches are recorded) but he preferred tempered remark to heated exchange, took no hardline stands, had little taste for political intrigue, and put friendship over faction. Twice offered a potentially lucrative commissioner's post with the East India Company by Lord North he demurred, but then accepted a place on the exchequer court, rose to the bench on 17 May 1775, and was knighted on the same day.

North's offers had probably been inspired as much by Hotham's good sense and even-handedness as by desire to woo a member of the opposition. Hotham showed that the attributes that had inhibited his law practice and kept him on the fringe in the Commons helped him to succeed as a judge. Although he did not consider himself a legal scholar—it was said that if faced with an objection on a point of law in a civil case he would send the cause to arbitration—he did hold some progressive views. For instance he supported the right of juries in libel cases to decide questions of law as well as matters of fact, which put him in line with Sir William Blackstone but at odds with William Murray, first earl of Mansfield, and he took a common-sense approach in his rulings. As an assize judge on the western circuit, in March 1777 he presided at the trial of James Aitken, infamous as the arsonist 'John the Painter'. The records for this trial—one of the few pled before Hotham for which details survive—show how, like many judges of his generation, he used the bench as pulpit to preach the need for retributive justice. However, Isaac Espinasse recalled:

> The capital conviction of a prisoner seemed to go to his heart, and in passing sentence on them his language was impressively affecting. His humanity often turned the course of rigid justice, and made the administration of it yield to his feelings. (Espinasse, 188)

In the trial for murder of a young Irish officer called Purefoy who had killed his superior, Colonel Roper, in a duel Hotham told the jury that if they acquitted Purefoy they would 'do an act lovely in the eyes of God and man' (ibid., 190); the jury duly acquitted the defendant.

That Hotham was occasionally overturned on appeal made him no different from his peers. He was proud of his stamina in riding the circuit as well as sitting for the exchequer, and retired on 23 January 1805 only because he felt that he no longer had the strength to continue. As a judge he had been determined to remain detached from politics. His only public involvement off the bench had come in April 1783, when at Portland's request he agreed to act as one of three commissioners for the great seal. The fall of Portland's coalition ministry in December brought an end to that duty. According to family tradition, in 1783 he had declined Portland's offer of a British peerage and the lord chancellorship of Ireland, the former because of the financial burden that it would place on his heirs, the latter because he felt unqualified and had no desire to leave home anyway.

As the fourth of five sons Hotham had once lamented to Portland the disadvantage of his birth order. His third brother, Admiral William *Hotham, had been made an Irish baron in 1797 with remainder to the heirs male of his father, but as his second brother, Sir John Hotham, ninth baronet, bishop of Clogher, had left a son, Sir Charles Hotham, tenth baronet, it was assumed that Sir Charles would inherit the peerage. However, Sir Charles died childless in 1811, and following William's death in 1813 Hotham succeeded to the title and estates. Hotham now added to his residence in Bloomsbury Square, London, his country house in Hampton, Middlesex, and various properties across the Thames from Hampton in East Molesey, Surrey, the family's extensive holdings in Yorkshire, including their seat at South Dalton. For the ten months that he had left in life he remained in Middlesex, troubled by rheumatism and gout but otherwise enjoying his retirement. He died on 4 March 1814 at his home in Hampton, having provided generously for family and servants in his will. Six days later he was buried alongside his wife and two of his children in the family vault at St Mary the Virgin, East Molesey, after—as he had requested—a very simple service. The church was rebuilt from 1865 and it is no longer clear where the bodies were reinterred. Beaumont *Hotham (1794–1870), his grandson, succeeded to the titles and estates. **NEIL L. YORK**

Sources A. M. W. Stirling, *The Hothams*, 2 vols. (1918) · B. Hotham, letters to Charles Hotham, U. Hull, Brynmor Jones L., Hotham family archive, DDHO/4 · A. Collins, 'Genealogical and historical account of the family of Hotham, of Scarborough, in the county of York', emendations by F. Hotham, U. Hull, Brynmor Jones L., DDHO/17/9 · *Strictures on the lives and characters of the most eminent lawyers of the present day* (1790), 169–74 · N. L. York, *Burning the dockyard: John the Painter and the American revolution*, Portsmouth Papers, 71 (2001) · B. Hotham, letters to the duke of Portland, U. Nott. L., Hallward Library, Portland MSS, PWF · *Pages and portraits from the past: being the private papers of Sir William Hotham*, ed. A. M. W. Stirling, 2 vols. (1919) · GEC, *Peerage*, 6.578 · L. B. Namier, 'Hotham, Beaumont', HoP, *Commons, 1754–90* · [I. Espinasse], 'My contemporaries: from the note-book of a retired barrister', *Fraser's Magazine*, 7 (1833), 188–90 · Burke, *Peerage* (1990) · IGI · Sainty, *Judges* · parish register, St Clement Danes, 6 June 1767 [marriage] · parish register, East Molesey, St Mary the Virgin, 10 March 1814 [burial]
Archives BL, letters to Lord Auckland, Add. MSS 34412–34460, *passim* · U. Hull, Brynmor Jones L., letters to his brother, Sir Charles Hotham · U. Nott., Hallward Library, letters to the third duke of Portland, PWF
Likenesses V. Green, mezzotint, pubd 1796 (after N. Dance), BM, NPG, AM Oxf. [*see illus.*] · N. Dance, portrait, Dalton Hall, Yorkshire · G. Stuart, portrait, Dalton Hall, Yorkshire
Wealth at death over £20,000: will, PRO

Hotham, Beaumont, third Baron Hotham (1794–1870), army officer and politician, was born on 9 August 1794 at Lullingstone Castle, Kent, the elder son of Beaumont Hotham (1768–1799)—eldest son of Beaumont *Hotham, second Baron Hotham (1737–1814) and a lieutenant-colonel in the Coldstream Guards—and his wife, Philadelphia (*d.* 1808), daughter of Sir John Dixon Dyke, third baronet (1732–1810). He was educated at Westminster School (1806–8) and the Royal Military College, Great Marlow, and on 27 June 1810 was commissioned ensign in the Coldstream Guards. He served in the Peninsular War from 1812 to 1814, was wounded at Salamanca, and was present at the battle of Waterloo. He succeeded as third Baron Hotham on his grandfather's death (4 March 1814).

Hotham was placed on half pay on 14 October 1819 (gaining the rank of colonel in June 1838, major-general in November 1851, and lieutenant-general in August 1858). He was a tory MP for the scot and lot borough of Leominster, Herefordshire, from March 1820 to April 1831, and though defeated at the general election, was returned at a by-election in December 1831, and continued to represent that borough until the dissolution in July 1841. He sat for the East Riding of Yorkshire from July 1841 to the dissolution in November 1868, when he retired. He voted against Lord Derby's Reform Bill in March 1859. He was gazetted general on 12 January 1865. He resided at South Dalton Hall, Beverley, Yorkshire, and was patron of four livings. He died on 12 December 1870, at Sand Hutton, near York, while on a visit to Sir James Walker, and was buried in the family vault in South Dalton church, East Riding of Yorkshire, on 20 December. Hotham was not married, and was succeeded in the peerage by his nephew Charles (1836–1872), the fourth son of Rear-Admiral George Frederick Hotham (1799–1856).

ROGER T. STEARN

Sources ILN (31 Dec 1870) · *The Times* (14 Dec 1870) · *The Times* (21 Dec 1870) · GEC, *Peerage* · Burke, *Peerage* · *Old Westminsters*, vol. 1 · *Dod's Peerage* (1858) · HoP, *Commons, 1790–1820*, vol. 2 · WWBMP, vol. 1 · Boase, *Mod. Eng. biog.* · CGPLA Eng. & Wales (1871)
Archives U. Hull, Brynmor Jones L., corresp. and papers, DDHO 8 | BL, corresp. with Sir Robert Peel, Add. MSS 40367–40605
Likenesses Grant, portrait, priv. coll. · G. Hayter, group portrait, oils (*The House of Commons, 1833*), NPG · W. Salter, oils (*Waterloo Banquet at Apsley House*), Wellington Museum, Apsley House, London; oil study, NPG
Wealth at death under £500,000: probate, 10 Jan 1871, CGPLA Eng. & Wales

Hotham, Charles (1615–1672), ejected minister and author, was born on 12 May 1615 at Scorborough, near Beverley, Yorkshire, the third son of Sir John *Hotham, first baronet (1589–1645), politician and parliamentarian army officer, and his second wife, Anne (1593–*c.*1624), daughter of Ralph Rokeby of York, secretary to the council of the north. After attending Westminster School he matriculated as a pensioner from Peterhouse, Cambridge, on 22 November 1631, migrated to Christ's College on 7 May 1632, and graduated BA in 1636 and proceeded MA in 1639. During his student days he contributed to a compilation of verse entitled *Carmen natalitium ad cunas illustrissimae principis Elisabethae* (1635). He was appointed vicar of Hollym, Yorkshire, on 5 November 1640, and his father deeded him the advowson on 29 October 1641. He subsequently received his father's interest in the advowsons of Wigan, Lancashire (14 December 1644), and Beswick, Yorkshire (24 December 1644). During the siege of Hull during the civil war he was with his father, and he testified on the latter's behalf at his trial in 1644.

Hotham resigned his living at Hollym in 1644 to accept an appointment from the earl of Manchester as fellow of Peterhouse. Two years later he served as university preacher and proctor, and on 3 March 1646 he engaged in a debate at Cambridge over whether the soul was directly created by God and infused into the body, or was transmitted from parent to child. He concluded that 'the Soule's Traduction from the Parents, and its Creation by God, are not onely either of them probable, but both true'. His account of the debate, published in 1648 as *Ad philosophiam Teutonicam manuductio*, revealed his indebtedness to Jakob Boehme's *Three Principles of the Divine Essence* as well as his facility in Greek and Latin; he may have known Hebrew, though he used only a single word of it in this book. Henry More contributed commendatory verse to the volume, and an English translation, *An Introduction to the Teutonick Philosophie* (1654), was prepared by Hotham's brother Durant *Hotham (1616/17–1691). Hotham's interests also encompassed astrology, chemistry (for the study of which he constructed a laboratory in his rooms at Peterhouse), and mathematics, including plans for an edition of the works of Jeremiah Horrocks.

After Hotham preached against the engagement in 1649 or 1650, the commissioners visiting Cambridge ordered him not to do so again on pain of permanent exclusion from the pulpit. On 27 March 1651 he petitioned the parliamentary committee for the reform of the universities, complaining that Lazarus Seaman, master of Peterhouse, had assumed the sole power of convoking and dissolving college meetings, proposing questions for discussion, refusing at times to heed the will of the majority, and wielding veto power. He sought a remedy akin to that granted to London's common council in 1648, including the termination of veto authority and an agreement to convene a meeting when requested by two or more of the seven fellows. The attack on Seaman may have been rooted in the dissatisfaction of Hotham and other intruded fellows with their stature and remuneration as well as his anger about the expulsion of one of his students from a fellowship on grounds of malignancy and scandalous behaviour. After he appeared before the committee on 10 April, it agreed to review the statutes of every college. Concerned that Seaman would delay the investigation, Hotham published *The Petition and Argument*, including records of what had transpired before the committee and the 1648 act concerning the common council. Incensed at this breach of parliamentary privilege, the committee required his appearance on 22 May, at which time he admitted authorship. Resolving that *The Petition* was scandalous and a violation of privilege, the committee deprived him of his fellowship on the 29th. In *A True State of the Case of Mr. Hotham* (1651) he protested, citing lack of due process, blaming Seaman's evil influence, and attaching a statement dated 12 June from thirty-three colleagues, including Henry More, Ralph Cudworth, and Samuel Cradock, attesting to his good character, 'strictness in Religion', and affection to parliament (pp. 14–15). The same year he published *Corporations Vindicated in their Fundamental Liberties*, reiterating his objections to veto power and his support for the rule of the majority, but also warning against the danger of parliamentary committees that acted arbitrarily and failed to manifest concern for people's rights. Proclaiming himself a defender of liberty and property, he called for the relief of those who were oppressed by poverty, and he denounced both illegal monopolies and the delay of justice. With an eye to his own circumstances, he demanded Seaman's removal because of his 'prodigious non-residencies' (p. 46) and sought permission to present his case to parliament.

On 22 July 1652 Hotham was presented under the great seal to the rectory of Nunburnholme, Yorkshire, succeeding Philip Ford. Following the death of John Bridgeman, bishop of Chester, Hotham was appointed rector of Wigan on 5 January 1653 by his father's trustees. The following year he published a translation of Boehme's *A Consolatory Treatise of the Four Complexions*, noting that this required skill in 'the language of Angells' as well as Dutch, assistance in which he obtained from a scholar at Peterhouse. 'For the Angelique, my way was a little smoothed by my former Perusall of this Authors other original writings that speak the same language' (A5r). In fact, he was one of the early disciples of Boehme in England. He followed this work in 1656 with a commendatory verse to An *Ingenious Poem, called the Drunkards Prospective* by one of his parishioners, Major Joseph Rigbie (Rigby), whom he lavishly praised:

> Let *Hercules* labors silent be,
> Yours live to immortality.
> (p. 31)

On 15 September that year Hotham married Elizabeth (*d.* 1685), daughter of Stephen Thompson of Humbleton, Yorkshire, at Wigan; they had a son, Charles, and two daughters, Charlotte and Mary.

At the Restoration the crown presented the rectory of Wigan to John Burton, but Hotham was reinstalled on 3 August 1660, thanks to the efforts of his father's trustees, and a royal warrant ensued on 29 September, revoking an earlier grant to Burton. However, Hotham was ejected in 1662 for nonconformity, at which time George Hall succeeded him. On 9 January 1668 Hotham was elected a fellow of the Royal Society, presumably because of his interest in astronomy and chemistry. On 28 February 1670 he and William Edwards were appointed ministers to Bermuda. Responsible for preaching at Warwick and Paget, Hotham could not be assigned elsewhere without his consent. On 28 June 1670 the governor and council reported that the two ministers were 'well approved of amongst us' (Lefroy, 1.704–5). Hotham died in Bermuda on 3 March 1672 and was buried there two days later. In his will, dated 15 February 1672 and proved in London on 2 March 1674, he instructed that his astrological books be burned 'as monuments of lying vanity and Remnants of the heathen Idolatry', but he bequeathed his astronomy books to the 'publick Library' of Bermuda and left his 'Chimicall Iron Tooles' to Dr John Troutbeck of London (PRO, PROB 11/344, fol. 282v). He owned property in the Holderness district of Yorkshire, which he bequeathed to his son along with the advowson of Hollym, though he had sold the manor of Weeton in the East Riding in 1669. His widow was buried at Little Driffield, Yorkshire, on 29 April 1685. Their son, Charles (*d.* 1723), succeeded his cousin as fourth baronet in 1691, became a brigadier-general in 1710, and sat as MP for Scarborough (1695–1702) and Beverley (1702–23).

RICHARD L. GREAVES

Sources Calamy rev. · Venn, *Alum. Cant.*, 1/2.412 · will, PRO, PROB 11/344, fols. 281v–283r · A. M. W. Stirling, *The Hothams*, 1 (1918), 116–23 · *CSP dom.*, 1660–61, 278, 324 · J. H. Lefroy, *Memorials of the discovery and early settlement of the Bermudas or Somers Islands*, 2 vols. (1878–9), vol. 1, pp. 704–5; vol. 2, p. 307 · VCH *Lancashire*, 4.59–60, 63 · DNB · Walker rev., 393 · T. Birch, *The history of the Royal Society*, 4 vols. (1968), vol. 2, p. 236 · VCH *Yorkshire East Riding*, 5.144 · J. B. Mullinger, *The University of Cambridge*, 3 (1911), 393–419
Archives U. Hull, family MSS | BL, Add. MSS 36792, fol. 48 · PRO, state papers, domestic, 29/16/89, 29/19/60
Wealth at death approx. £300; plus land in Holderness; also tithes and perpetual advowson of vicarage of Hollym, Yorkshire; also cattle and tobacco in Bermuda; also books and chemical instruments: will, PRO, PROB 11/344, fols. 281v–283r

Hotham, Sir Charles (1806–1855), naval officer and colonial governor, was born at Thornham, Norfolk, on 14 January 1806. He was the eldest son of the Revd Frederick Hotham (1774–1854) and his wife, Anne Elizabeth, the eldest daughter of Thomas Hallett Hodges of Hemsted Place,

Kent. The Yorkshire family of Hotham had a tradition of distinguished naval service. One of Charles's uncles was Vice-Admiral Sir Henry *Hotham, who foiled Napoleon's attempt to escape to America after the French defeat at Waterloo. Charles's maternal grandmother was the sister of John Cartwright and Edmund Cartwright.

In 1808 Frederick Hotham and his family moved to Dennington, Suffolk. He was educated at Westminster School (1814–18) and the naval college at Portsmouth (1818–20). At the age of fourteen Charles went to sea as a naval volunteer. After five years' service in the North Sea and the Mediterranean he was made a lieutenant. In 1833 he reached the rank of captain, but because of the peacetime reduction in naval forces it was not until December 1842 that he received his next posting. He was appointed to the *Gorgon*, a steamship in the fleet stationed in South America. The fleet, commanded by Commodore Purvis, protected British residents of Buenos Aires and Montevideo whenever there were outbreaks of violence between these rival Spanish and Portuguese communities. In 1845 Hotham led a force of six British warships that joined with the French navy to destroy a Spanish blockade across the Parana River. He was appointed KCB on 9 March 1846.

Later in the same year Hotham was promoted to the command of a squadron engaged in combating the slave trade on the west coast of Africa. During his two years in command the squadron captured 173 slave ships and released more than 15,000 slaves, a result surpassing that achieved by most of his predecessors. Illness forced his return to England in April 1849.

Three years later Hotham went back to South America on a brief, but highly successful, diplomatic mission. He hoped this would lead to another naval appointment, but instead he was offered the lieutenant-governorship of the Australian colony of Victoria. This he reluctantly accepted.

On 10 December 1853 Hotham married Jane Sarah Holbech (1817–1907), the widow of Hugh Holbech and daughter of Samuel Hood, the second Viscount Bridport. The Hothams arrived in Melbourne on 22 June 1854. They were warmly received, but the new governor soon faced serious problems. The discovery of gold three years previously had disrupted the orderly growth of the colony. Charles La Trobe, Hotham's predecessor, had imposed a monthly licence fee on gold-diggers, in order to raise urgently needed revenue. The diggers thought the fee unjust and expected Hotham to abolish it without delay, but his inexperience as a civil administrator made him slow in implementing reforms. He distrusted the colonial secretary and was at first unwilling to delegate responsibility to members of the legislature whom he barely knew.

A crisis occurred late in November 1854, when the diggers at Ballarat publicly burned their licence certificates in defiance of the goldfields officials, whom they believed to be corrupt. They barricaded themselves into a section of the goldfields known as the Eureka lead and prepared for battle. On 3 December the Eureka stockade was stormed by soldiers and police. Thirty diggers and five soldiers were killed.

This episode caused Hotham to be unfairly reviled as a tyrant; his promotion to the full status of governor on 23 May 1855 was ignored by the public. He continued to work diligently, preparing Victoria for the transition to responsible government late in 1855. In November he wrote to the secretary of state for the colonies requesting permission to relinquish the post of governor a year later, when the new government would be well established; he hoped to return to naval service. But before the letter reached England, Hotham was dead. He contracted pneumonia and died in Melbourne on 31 December 1855. Following a funeral service at St James's Cathedral, Melbourne, he was buried in the city's general cemetery on 4 January 1856.

SHIRLEY ROBERTS

Sources S. Roberts, *Charles Hotham, a biography* (1985) · G. Serle, *The golden age: a history of the colony of Victoria, 1851–1861*, new edn (Carlton, VIC, 1977) · C. Lloyd, *The navy and the slave trade* (1949) · H. G. Turner, *A history of the colony of Victoria*, 2 vols. (1904) · G. W. Rusden, *History of Australia*, 3 vols. (1883) · W. Hadfield, *Brazil, the River Plate and the Falkland Islands* (1854) · A. C. Key, *Narrative of the recovery of HMS Gorgon* (1847) · W. L. Clowes, *The Royal Navy: a history from the earliest times to the present*, 7 vols. (1897–1903) · W. Kelly, *Life in Victoria, or, Victoria in 1853 and Victoria in 1859, showing the march of improvement*, 2 vols. (1859)
Archives U. Hull, Brynmor Jones L. | Hants. RO, Harris MSS · PRO, Admiralty records, letters and dispatches to the secretary of state for foreign affairs, and Colonial Office MSS CO 309/26–38 · University of Melbourne, Trinity College, Rusden MSS
Likenesses portrait, *c.*1841–1842, repro. in Roberts, *Charles Hotham*, 36 · J. H. Lynch, lithograph, 1859, NPG
Wealth at death under £20,000: PRO, death duty registers

Hotham, Durant (1616/17–1691), biographer, was the fifth son of Sir John *Hotham (1589–1645) of Scorborough, Yorkshire, and his second wife, Anne Rokeby (*d. c.*1624). He was educated privately by a Mr Sugden at Scorborough, and subsequently at Westminster. Admitted to Christ's College, Cambridge, on 7 May 1632, aged fifteen, he received his BA in 1637 and MA in 1640. On 6 January 1641 he entered the Middle Temple. He became involved in his father's disgrace, his letters and papers were seized (June 1643), and he was summoned to attend parliament. After being examined, he was soon discharged, though he received strict injunctions not to join his father. However, he conducted his father's defence at his court martial in the Guildhall in December 1644.

On 23 August 1645 Hotham married Frances (1625–1693), daughter of Richard Remington of Lund, Yorkshire; the couple had seven sons and four daughters, all of whom died young. For many years he lived at Lockington in Yorkshire, engaged in scientific pursuits. His short hagiographical account of the German mystic Jakob Boehme, based on Abraham von Frankenberg's biography, was first published as *The Life of one Jacob Boehmen* in 1644 and reissued ten years later as an appendix to the English translation of Boehme's commentary on the book of Genesis. Although Hotham is also said to have translated in 1654 his brother Charles Hotham's introduction to Boehme's theosophy, *Ad philosophiam Teutonicam manductio* (1648), there is no evidence for this in modern catalogues.

Hotham was a justice of the peace, probably the Justice

Hotham whom George Fox met in 1651, describing him as a 'well-wisher' to the Quakers. In his judicial capacity in 1654 Hotham pursued a band of robbers as far as London, returning them to Yorkshire for trial, and on 15 September 1656, under the provisions of the 1653 Civil Marriage Act, officiated at the marriage of his brother Charles at Wigan, thereby indicating his sympathy with the puritan hostility to ecclesiastical marriage. Hotham died in the parish of St James, Westminster, in 1691, and was buried in the church. Administration of his estate was granted to his widow in 1692.

GORDON GOODWIN, rev. B. J. GIBBONS

Sources A. M. W. Stirling, *The Hothams*, 2 vols. (1918) • J. Peile, *Biographical register of Christ's College, 1505–1905, and of the earlier foundation, God's House, 1448–1505*, ed. [J. A. Venn], 2 vols. (1910–13) • *The diary and correspondence of Dr John Worthington*, ed. J. Crossley and R. C. Christie, 2 vols. in 3, Chetham Society, 13, 36, 114 (1847–86) • *CSP dom.*, 1652–3 • D. Hotham, *The life of Jacob Behmen* (1654)
Archives U. Hull, Brynmor Jones L., corresp. and papers

Hotham, Sir Henry (1777–1833), naval officer, youngest son of Beaumont *Hotham, second Baron Hotham (1737–1814), and his wife, Susanna (1737–1799), second daughter of Sir Thomas Hankey, and widow of James Norman, was born on 19 February 1777, and, after passing through the Royal Naval Academy at Portsmouth, entered the navy in 1790 on the *Princess Royal*, then carrying his uncle's flag. He afterwards served in the *Lizard* in the channel, and the *Lapwing* in the Mediterranean; in 1793 he was moved into the *Victory*, Lord Hood's flagship, and in her was present at the occupation of Toulon and the operations in Corsica. After the capture of Bastia in May 1794, he was promoted lieutenant of the *Aigle* on 6 June, with Captain Samuel Hood. After the capture of Calvi he was moved again into the *Victory*, and, when Lord Hood went home, into the *Britannia*, the flagship of his uncle, who became commander-in-chief, and speedily promoted his nephew to command of the sloop *La Flèche*, taken at Bastia. On 13 January 1795 Hotham was posted to the frigate *Mignonne* (32 guns), taken at Calvi; but the *Mignonne* not being fit for service, he was permitted to join the *Egmont* as a volunteer, and in her was present in the action of 13 July off the Hyères. In September he was appointed to the *Dido* (28 guns), in which—as afterwards in the *Blanche*—he continued attached to the Mediterranean Fleet until towards the end of 1798, when he was sent home in charge of convoy. From 1799 to 1801 he commanded the frigate *Immortalité* (36 guns), and cruised successfully in the Bay of Biscay, gaining familiarity with the enemy coast.

On the renewal of the war in 1803 Hotham was appointed to the *Impérieuse* (40 guns), and in the following March was turned over to the *Révolutionnaire* (44 guns). In her he was employed during the year on the coast of North America, but in 1805 was again on the home station, and on 4 November was with Sir Richard Strachan when he captured the small French squadron which had escaped from Trafalgar. In March 1806 Hotham was appointed to the *Defiance* (74 guns), and for many months commanded the squadron blockading Lorient; in 1808 he had command of the squadron employed on the north coast of Spain, and

on 24 February 1809 was with Rear-Admiral Stopford in the Bay of Biscay, when he drove ashore three French frigates from the roadstead of Les Sables d'Olonne. During the rest of the year, and the early part of 1810 Hotham continued in the *Defiance*, employed in the Bay of Biscay, and on the coast of Spain. In August 1810 he was moved into the *Northumberland* (74 guns), and again employed off Brest, Lorient, and Rochefort.

During this long service Hotham and Mr Stewart, the master of the *Northumberland*, acquired an intimate knowledge of the French coast, which proved all-important when in May 1812 he was specially detached from the fleet to look out for two frigates and a brig, which had been for several months the scourge of British commerce in the Atlantic, especially off the Azores. On 22 May they were sighted by the *Northumberland* some 10 miles to the south of Île de Groix, sailing for the port of Lorient. Hotham, by a piece of brilliant seamanship, aided by his knowledge of the pilotage, not only prevented their gaining the port, but drove them on shore, and, anchoring near them, succeeded in destroying the two frigates; the brig was afterwards floated off and taken into the harbour. It was a service praised by Lord Keith for the courage, skill, and extraordinary management of all concerned. Hotham's application helped to promote improved gunnery.

In 1813 Hotham was appointed captain of the fleet on the North America and West Indies station, with Sir John Warren, and afterwards with Sir Alexander Cochrane; towards the end of the year he hoisted a broad pennant on the *Superb* as second in command on the station. On 4 June 1814 he was advanced to flag rank, and on 2 January 1815 was nominated a KCB. On his return to England, just as war again broke out, he was appointed to command a squadron in the Bay of Biscay, and it was mainly through his knowledge of the station that Bonaparte's idea of escaping to America was rendered impossible. The *Bellerophon*, which received Bonaparte's surrender, was acting under his orders. On 31 August 1815 he struck his flag. Hotham married, on 6 July 1816, Lady Frances Anne Juliana Rous (d. 31 Jan 1859), eldest daughter of the first earl of Stradbroke; they had three sons.

From March 1818 to March 1822, and again from 1828 to 1830, Hotham was a lord of the Admiralty. Although a tory he was offered a seat on the whig board of 1830, but refused to serve under Sir Thomas Hardy, a junior officer. He became a vice-admiral in May 1825, and in January 1831 was appointed commander-in-chief in the Mediterranean. After a two days' illness, he died at Malta on 19 April 1833. A monument to his memory was erected on the baracca by a subscription among the officers on the station. An officer with a genius for coastal operations and onshore navigation, Hotham was one of the captains who transformed the Royal Navy from a sea-control fleet into a power-projection force.

J. K. LAUGHTON, rev. ANDREW LAMBERT

Sources C. J. Bartlett, *Great Britain and sea power, 1815–1853* (1963) • A. D. Lambert, *The last sailing battlefleet: maintaining naval mastery, 1815–1850* (1991) • J. Ralfe, *The naval biography of Great Britain*, 1 (1828) • J. Marshall, *Royal naval biography*, 1/2 (1823), 615–21 • *United*

Service Journal, 3 (1834), 369 • W. James, *The naval history of Great Britain, from the declaration of war by France in 1793, to the accession of George IV*, [5th edn], 6 vols. (1859–60), vols. 4–5 • *GM*, 1st ser., 103/2 (1833) • Burke, *Peerage* (1959)

Archives U. Hull, Brynmor Jones L., official and private corresp., letter- and order books, journals, diaries, etc. | BL, Martin MSS • Cumbria AS, Carlisle, corresp. with Sir James Graham • NA Scot., corresp. with Lord Melville • NL Scot., letters to Sir Alexander Cochrane • NMM, letters to Lord Keith

Hotham, John (*d.* 1337), administrator and bishop of Ely, was the son of Alan and Matilda Hotham, and was born at Trehouses in Hotham, Yorkshire. He would appear to have had important connections, however, for a mortuary roll describes him as 'brought up in the houses of kings and nobles' (Sheppard, 2.116). He was certainly the nephew of William Hotham, archbishop of Dublin (*d.* 1298), and made his early career in Ireland. First recorded as an attorney at the Irish exchequer in 1291, he represented William de Valence, earl of Pembroke (*d.* 1296), and his sister Agnes there from 1293 to 1296. By 1305 he was a baron of the Irish exchequer. At the end of his reign Edward I promised him a benefice worth at least 60 marks. Hotham came to England in July 1308, but the following January returned to Ireland, where he probably met and secured the patronage of Piers Gaveston (*d.* 1312), then in exile. In May 1309 he obtained a dispensation to retain a series of mainly Irish benefices to the value of £39, and in the same month was appointed chancellor of the Irish exchequer on the recommendation of William Melton (*d.* 1340), who later, as archbishop of York, addressed him as 'our friend'. He held this post until January 1310.

In November 1309 Hotham came to England, where he received his first English appointment, that of escheator north of Trent, which he held from December 1309 to February 1311. His later promotion should probably be attributed primarily to his links with Gaveston. In December 1310 Edward II ordered that Hotham be assigned benefices to the very high value of £300, and shortly afterwards, on 30 January 1311, he was presented to the York prebend of Stillington, valued in 1291 at £46 13s. 4d. yearly. Before Gaveston went into exile, in October 1311, he appointed Hotham one of his attorneys. It was doubtless his association with Gaveston, for whom he had deputized as keeper of the forest north of Trent, that led the ordainers to demand his removal from office and the court. Accordingly on 2 December 1311 he surrendered his keepership of the forest to the ordainer Henry Percy (*d.* 1315). But royal grants early in 1312 of the church of Cottingham in Yorkshire, and of the custody of Leixlip near Dublin, signified that his career was far from over, and on 13 December 1312 he was appointed chancellor of the exchequer, a post he held until June 1316. He accompanied the king on his visit to France in June 1313.

In August 1314 Hotham was sent to Ireland to see how much money could be raised for the king. He remained there until the end of November, and was sent back again in the wake of the invasion of Edward Bruce in 1315, in September receiving virtually viceregal powers to co-ordinate resistance to the Scots and to remove inefficient officials. He fortified Dublin, shored up the loyalty of the Irish magnates after Edward Bruce's triumph at Ardscull in January 1316, and complained of the dire state of Irish finances. Royal patronage secured him the bishopric of Ely on his return to England. He was elected in June 1316 and consecrated at Canterbury on 3 October. At the end of the year he was nominated to the mission to Avignon led by the earl of Pembroke, one object of which was to secure the promotion as archbishop of Dublin of Alexander Bicknor (*d.* 1349), for whom Hotham had deputized as treasurer of the Irish exchequer in the latter part of 1309. After his return from Avignon, on 27 May 1317 Hotham was appointed treasurer of England. This was in contravention of the ordinances, and as such a sign that the king was reasserting himself. In June 1318 he gave up this post to become chancellor. He was prominent in the negotiations with the earl of Lancaster that led to the treaty of Leake in August 1318, and was one of the standing council appointed as a result of that treaty. The York parliament of October 1318 confirmed his appointment as chancellor; and he was one of the committee appointed there to reform the royal household, a measure achieved by the household ordinance of December 1318.

The hostile author of the *Flores historiarum* attributes the removal of government to York in September 1319 to Hotham, who on 12 September was present at the disastrous battle of Myton, where untrained forces gathered by the archbishop of York were routed by Scottish invaders. In December he was one of those commissioned to sue for a truce with the Scots, but in January 1320 he was replaced as chancellor, and his prominence in government grew less. The Bridlington chronicle reports that, after the fall of Leeds Castle in Kent in late October 1321, he was attached, summoned to London, and fined. No reason is given. On 1 December he made a show of his loyalty to the king by being one of only five bishops to attend the ecclesiastical assembly that declared illegal the exiling of the Despensers. Consequently, on 6 December his debts to the crown were respited.

In January 1323 Hotham was sent to Gascony, to settle disputes between the barons there, and to seek their aid against the Scots. It would appear that, despite being pressed for debts of more than £1000 in April 1324, Hotham was still close to the king in 1325. However, on Queen Isabella's invasion in September 1326, he quickly joined her. It may be that his temporalities had been distrained as a result of failure to account for earlier periods of royal service. His role in Edward II's deposition is unclear, but in its aftermath he was appointed chancellor for the second time on 28 January 1327, and held the post until 1 March 1328. He attended Edward III's coronation on 1 February 1327, and entertained Edward's future queen, Philippa of Hainault, at his residence in Holborn on her arrival in England in December, but after 1328 he took little further part in government.

In 1329 Hotham granted the manor of Cuckney to Welbeck Abbey; among those for whom he stipulated prayers were his uncle William Hotham, the countess of Pembroke, Gaveston, and John Wogan, justiciar of Ireland during much of his official career there. He retained his interests in Ireland, obtaining a third of the Irish lordship of Kilkenny for £100 p.a. from Eleanor Despenser in 1329. During his episcopate the central tower of Ely Cathedral collapsed and the building of the octagon was commenced. Although the octagon was the sacrist's rather than the bishop's achievement, Hotham was responsible for the restoration of three bays of the chancel. For the last two years of his life he suffered from paralysis. He appointed coadjutors on 26 August 1336; one of them was his nephew, Alan. He died at his house at Somersham in Huntingdonshire on 14 January 1337 and was buried in Ely Cathedral on the east side of the altar in the choir.

M. C. BUCK

Sources *Chancery records* · J. R. S. Phillips, 'The mission of John de Hotham to Ireland, 1315–1316', *England and Ireland in the later middle ages*, ed. J. Lydon (1981), 62–85 · [H. Wharton], ed., *Anglia sacra*, 2 vols. (1691) · F. R. Chapman, ed., *Sacrist rolls of Ely*, 2 vols. (1907) · J. B. Sheppard, ed., *Literae Cantuarienses: the letter books of the monastery of Christ Church, Canterbury*, 3 vols., Rolls Series, 85 (1887–9) · H. R. Luard, ed., *Flores historiarum*, 3 vols., Rolls Series, 95 (1890) · W. Stubbs, ed., *Chronicles of the reigns of Edward I and Edward II*, 2 vols., Rolls Series, 76 (1882–3) · R. M. Haines, *Archbishop John Stratford: political revolutionary and champion of the liberties of the English church*, Pontifical Institute of Medieval Studies: Texts and Studies, 76 (1986) · exchequer, king's remembrancer's memoranda rolls, PRO, E.159 · J. Bentham, *The history and antiquities of the conventual and cathedral church of Ely*, ed. J. Bentham, 2nd edn (1812) · J. L. Grassi, 'Royal clerks from the archdiocese of York in the fourteenth century', *Northern History*, 5 (1970), 12–33, esp. 19–22, 30 · Rymer, *Foedera* · *CEPR letters* · *CDS*, vol. 3 · G. A. Holmes, 'Judgment on the younger Despenser, 1326', *EngHR*, 70 (1955), 261–7 · J. R. Maddicott, *Thomas of Lancaster, 1307–1322: a study in the reign of Edward II* (1970) · R. Frame, *English lordship in Ireland, 1318–1361* (1982) · T. Astle, S. Ayscough, and J. Caley, eds., *Taxatio ecclesiastica Angliae et Walliae auctoritate P. Nicholai IV*, RC (1802), 297

Hotham, Sir John, first baronet (1589–1645), parliamentarian army officer, was born about July 1589, the eldest son of John Hotham (d. 1609) of Scorborough, Yorkshire, and his third wife, Jane, daughter of Richard Legard of Rysome, Yorkshire. Hotham was lineally descended from a Norman family that had settled in Scorborough, near Beverley, in the twelfth century. His father was sheriff of Yorkshire in 1584, and sat as MP for Scarborough in 1584, and Hedon in 1586. On 16 February 1607 Hotham married Katherine, daughter of Sir John Rodes (or Rhodes) of Barlborough, Derbyshire. She had died by 16 July 1614, when he married his second wife, Anne Rokeby (b. 1593), daughter of Ralph Rokeby of York, the secretary to the council of the north. Hotham was knighted on 11 April 1617.

Supporter of Wentworth Drawn to soldiering since his youth, Hotham enlisted in Mansfeld's Rhineland army in 1619, but he had returned to England by November 1621 when he was added to the East Riding bench. On 4 January 1622 he was created a baronet. At some point during the latter half of the 1620s, his second wife having died, he married Frances Legard (bap. 1604), daughter of John Legard of Ganton, Yorkshire; his fourth marriage, on 27 October 1631, was to Catherine (d. 1634), daughter of Sir

William Bamborough of Howsham, Yorkshire, widow of Sir Thomas Norcliffe of Langton, Yorkshire; and his fifth, on 7 May 1635, was to Sarah Anlaby, daughter of Thomas Anlaby of Etton, Yorkshire. The lands and money acquired by these marriages enabled Hotham to enlarge his already substantial estate. He was the East Riding's leading supporter of Sir Thomas Wentworth in his power struggle with Sir John Savile, and as MP for Beverley in 1625, 1626, and 1628 he associated with the 'country' interest at Westminster and was 'in all things … opposite to the duke [of Buckingham]' (*CSP dom.*, 1625–6, 447). Although appointed a loan commissioner in 1627, he refused to pay and was removed from the bench and briefly imprisoned. When Wentworth became president of the council of the north in 1628 he restored Hotham—his 'true servant' (BL, Add. MS 15858, fol. 31)—to the bench and appointed him governor of Hull. In 1635 Wentworth secured the withdrawal of a case in Star Chamber against Hotham for his 'rigorous and undue proceedings' (*The Fairfax Correspondence: Memoirs of the Reign of Charles I*, ed. G. W. Johnson, 2 vols., 1848, 1. 226–7) in the collection of ship money during his term as sheriff of Yorkshire in 1634–5.

The onset of the bishops' wars put strain on Hotham's support for 'thorough', and in 1638 he began to question the orders and authority of Sir Edward Osborne, the vice-president of the council of the north. Wentworth conceded that Hotham showed 'more Will and Party' than he could wish, but maintained that he was 'very honest, faithful and hearty … and to be won and framed as you please with good Usage' (Radcliffe, 2.288). Early in 1639, when the crown proposed replacing Hotham as governor of Hull, Wentworth leapt to his defence:

> I do know his Faithfulness to be such, as I durst answer for him with my Life; nor am I ignorant that in Party he is very eager … yet it were very easy to have him as forward in the King's Party … he is as considerable a Person in that Way as any other Gentleman in the north of England; and therefore it were … not well utterly to cast him off and discourage him, as by taking the Government of that Town you shall infallibly do.   (Radcliffe, 2.310–11)

Wentworth was ignored, however, and the result was as he predicted. By early 1640 Hotham, with his cousin and friend Sir Hugh Cholmley, headed the opposition to ship money in the East Riding and was removed from all commissions.

The Short and Long parliaments In the elections to the Short Parliament Hotham was returned once again for Beverley. He supported Pym and those members who called for redress of grievances before supply, and repeatedly insisted that only the removal of military charges, as well as ship money, would satisfy his own region. The retention of military charges was vital for the king's forthcoming campaign against the Scots, and shortly after parliament was dissolved Hotham and Henry Belasyse were summoned before Charles and the privy council to answer for their speeches in the Commons. Their responses were deemed so undutiful that they were committed to the Fleet for ten days.

During the second bishops' war Hotham and Cholmley

played a leading role in representing Yorkshire's grievances to the king. They drafted the county's petition of 28 July 1640 (described by Wentworth as 'mutinous'), and probably that of 24 August, asserting, in the face of an empty exchequer and the threat of Scottish invasion, the impossibility of mustering Yorkshire's militia without pay. In September they helped organize another petition from the Yorkshire gentry, requesting that Charles summon parliament. The king accused Hotham and Cholmley of being 'the cheife cause and promoters of all the petetions from the County', and warned them that if they had a hand in any more he would hang them (Binns, 102).

Hotham retained his seat in the elections to the Long Parliament, and soon emerged as one of the most active and vocal men in the house. Between November 1640 and March 1642 he made numerous contributions to debate; was named to over 100 committees; reported and/or managed thirty conferences; and was frequently employed as a messenger to the Lords. Hotham, his son-in-law Sir Philip Stapilton [see Stapleton, Sir Philip], and Cholmley were among the most influential of the 'northern men' at Westminster, and possessed 'a numerous train which attended their motions' (Clarendon, *Hist. rebellion*, 1.309, 421). On several issues, particularly when it came to improving the kingdom's revenues, Hotham was aligned with Pym and his 'junto'. But his commitment to the rule of law and lack of sympathy for godly reformation prevented him from moving too closely into Pym's orbit. Hyde believed it was merely hatred of Strafford and fear of punishment for his rigorous proceedings over ship money that pushed Hotham into the parliamentarian camp. Cholmley took a more generous view:

> he was a man that loved liberty, which was an occasion to make him join at first with the Puritan party, to whom after he became nearer linked merely for his own interest and security; for in more than concerned the civil liberty he did not approve of their ways.   (Scrope and Monkhouse, 2.185)

Hotham's main concern at Westminster was the supply and disbandment of the English and Scottish forces in the northern counties; and as chairman of the committee for the king's army he made numerous reports concerning the state of the kingdom's finances. Despite supporting efforts to raise money for the armies he objected to Pym's motion of 20 February 1641 that the City be compelled to lend money, as contrary to the liberties of the subject. He subsequently opposed the impressment of soldiers for Ireland on the same grounds. On 7 April he testified against Strafford at the latter's trial, apparently with rather less enthusiasm than was credited to him by Clarendon, and supported the bill of attainder. Hotham criticized the 'Brownists', yet was convinced that Laudian prelates were involved in a Jesuit-inspired conspiracy to subvert protestantism and the people's liberties. He played a leading role in the Commons' efforts to suppress popery at court and in the kingdom generally, and on 19 July seconded a motion for gelding priests and Jesuits. He backed Pym over the grand remonstrance, but repeatedly urged leniency for the army plotters, and opposed Scottish involvement in suppressing the Irish rising (a course favoured by Pym) as 'a dishonour to our nation' (*Journal*, ed. Coates, 91).

Governor of Hull On 11 January 1642, following an attempt by the king to seize Hull and its magazine, the Commons ordered Hotham to secure the town using the trained bands, though it was actually his son, Captain John *Hotham, who carried out this order. Hotham senior did not assume his command as the town's parliamentary governor until mid-March. When the king appeared before Hull on 23 April, Hotham, his resolve stiffened by the Hull MP Peregrine Pelham, shut the gates in his face. Kneeling on the walls, Hotham protested his loyalty but asserted that he could not admit the king without breach of the trust reposed in him by parliament. He was also swayed by rumours (almost certainly false) of a plot to murder him should the king gain admission. Charles demanded Hotham's exemplary punishment, and declared him a traitor. But the two houses responded that Hotham had merely obeyed their commands, and that declaring him a traitor constituted a high breach of parliamentary privilege.

In May Hotham foiled a plot to betray Hull, but conspired to the same end with George Digby, who had been taken prisoner and brought to Hull in June. Digby apparently persuaded him that by surrendering Hull he would both prevent a civil war and gain honour and riches for himself. Hotham allegedly expressed dissatisfaction with parliament's bellicose stance, and promised that if the king made a show of investing Hull 'he should think he had discharged his trust to the Parliament, as far as he ought to do' and would surrender the town immediately (Clarendon, *Hist. rebellion*, 2.259–67). Hotham released Digby, who persuaded the king to make an armed approach on Hull. But Hotham evidently had second thoughts about betraying the town, for the king's army was fiercely resisted and forced to raise its siege in July.

Hotham's dismay at the slide towards civil war re-surfaced early in October, when he wrote to the speaker and the earls of Northumberland and Holland asking them to use their influence for a negotiated settlement. He remained convinced that if the king's evil counsellors were removed then Charles would clearly see the 'glorious mixture and temperament of a just prerogative and a people's liberties' (Brynmor Jones Library, DDHO/1/57). A further letter to the speaker, dated 4 January 1643, urging 'peace and unity' (BL, Add. MS 18777, fol. 121v), was allegedly suppressed by the Commons (*Mercurius Aulicus*, 8–14 Jan 1643, 21). By late 1642 Hotham was engaged, through his son, in secret negotiations with the earl of Newcastle. This 'treaty' with Newcastle, besides helping to keep Hull and the Hotham estates free from royalist attack, was an expression of Hotham's growing disenchantment with the parliamentarian cause and leadership, which was exacerbated by his son's quarrel with Ferdinando, Lord Fairfax, over 'superiority of commands' in Yorkshire (*JHC*, 2, 1640–42, 923).

Parliament's inability to meet Hotham's constant demands for money during the winter and spring of 1643 put further strain on his relations with the parliamentary leadership. In mid-February Pym received 'another angry letter' from Hotham to the effect that unless the houses sent down money quickly 'they must not blame him if he took that course which God had put into his mind for the cause' (*Mercurius Aulicus*, 19–25 Feb 1643, 102, BL, E246/41). The defection of Cholmley to the royalists in March aroused further 'jealousies' against Hotham at Westminster (*Certaine Letters Sent from Sir John Hotham, Young Hotham, the Major of Hull, and Others*, 1643, 1, 4, 5), even though he was instrumental in recovering Scarborough for parliament. Nevertheless he and his son were willing to treat with the queen after she landed at Bridlington, and in April he declared to Newcastle that if Charles had offered reasonable terms in the Oxford negotiations, 'I should, with my life and fortunes, more willingly have served him than ever I did any action in my life' (J. L. Sanford, *Studies and Illustrations of the Great Rebellion*, 1858, 554). Cholmley, however, believed that the Hothams were 'cautious of being engaged too far, having an eye at the inclination of the Scots' (Scrope and Monkhouse, 2.182).

Defection The imprisonment of Captain Hotham by Cromwell and Colonel John Hutchinson at Nottingham in June seems to have snapped the last links in Hotham's loyalty to parliament. After Captain Hotham managed to escape, his father congratulated him on foiling the 'great Anabaptists' at Nottingham, and implied that he was preparing to defect to the royalists (Brynmor Jones Library, DDHO/1/42). Alerted to Hotham's intrigues, the Commons sent instructions to Sir Matthew Boynton to seize Hull, which was accomplished by the townspeople on 29 June. Hotham fled to Beverley but was apprehended and conveyed with his son to London.

Hotham was expelled from his seat on 7 September 1643 and sent to the Tower. The seizure after Marston Moor of some of the Hothams's letters to Newcastle provided solid evidence of their treachery, and in November and December 1644 they were tried by a court martial presided over by Sir William Waller. In his defence Hotham emphasized the extreme latitude of his instructions as Hull's governor, and claimed that he was the victim of a conspiracy by Lord Fairfax's supporters, chiefly John Alured and Thomas Stockdale (Brynmor Jones Library, DDHO/1/35, 38). The court martial was not convinced, and on 7 December sentenced him to death—as it did Captain Hotham shortly afterwards. Sir John petitioned the Lords that either his own or his son's life might be spared, 'that this whole family … may not be cut off root and branch' (*JHL*, 1644–5, 7.116–17). The Lords reprieved him twice, but when his friends among the parliamentary Presbyterians forced a Commons vote on 30 December on whether to spare him, they were defeated by 94 votes to 46—the majority tellers being Cromwell and his fellow Independent Sir John Evelyn. Hotham went to the block at Tower Hill on 2 January 1645, the day after his son, protesting his innocence to the last. He was buried the same day at All Hallows Barking.

Assessment Hotham appeared to contemporaries as a man mastered by pride and ambition, and yet at the same time shrewd and with at least the capacity for sound judgement. Sir Henry Slingsby thought him 'covetous & ambitious', but acknowledged that he was 'not easily led to beleive as another doth, or hold an opinion for the authors sake' (*The Diary of Sir Henry Slingsby*, ed. D. Parsons, 1836, 91, 92). Hyde described him as 'a rough and rude man; of great covetousness, of great pride and great ambition; without any bowels of good nature, or the least sense or touch of generosity', yet conceded that 'his parts were … composed and judged well; he was a man of craft' (Clarendon, *Hist. rebellion*, 2.261–3). Cholmley's assessment of Hotham was probably nearest the mark:

> Sir John was a man of good understanding and ingenuity, yet of a rash and hasty nature, and so much wedded to his own honour, as his passion often over ballanced his judgement, and yet he was able to give good counsel and advice, where his own interest was not concerned.   (Scrope and Monkhouse, 2.185)

Hotham's lands were worth £3000 a year, and his personal estate about £10,000. At his death he left stock in money, goods, and merchandise in the East India Company and elsewhere 'employed in the way of trade or interest' (Cliffe, 92). In May 1645 the sequestration on his property was lifted and the bulk of his estate passed to his grandson, Sir John Hotham, second baronet.

Hotham's five marriages produced sixteen children, of whom seven died young. The six sons and three daughters who survived childhood included his eldest son (with his first wife) John Hotham and the Behmenists Durant *Hotham, lawyer, landowner, and East Riding magistrate, and Charles *Hotham, ejected minister, sons of Sir John and his second wife.   DAVID SCOTT

Sources HoP, *Commons, 1690–1715* [draft] · *JHC*, 2–4 (1640–46) · *JHL*, 4–7 (1628–45) · U. Hull, Brynmor Jones L., Hotham MSS, DDHO · R. Scrope and T. Monkhouse, eds., *State papers collected by Edward, earl of Clarendon*, 3 vols. (1767–86), vol. 2, pp. 181–6 · G. Radcliffe, *The earl of Strafforde's letters and dispatches, with an essay towards his life*, ed. W. Knowler, 2 vols. (1739) · *The memoirs of Hugh Cholmley* (1787) · Clarendon, *Hist. rebellion* · *The journal of Sir Simon D'Ewes from the beginning of the Long Parliament to the trial of the earl of Strafford*, ed. W. Notestein (1924) · *The journal of Sir Simon D'Ewes from the first recess of the Long Parliament to the withdrawal of King Charles from London*, ed. W. H. Coates (1942) · W. H. Coates, A. Steele Young, and V. F. Snow, eds., *The private journals of the Long Parliament*, 3 vols. (1982–92) · J. T. Cliffe, *The Yorkshire gentry from the Reformation to the civil war* (1969) · J. Rushworth, *Historical collections*, new edn, 3–5, 8 (1721), vols. 3–5, 8 · PRO, C 142/319/179 · *Dugdale's visitation of Yorkshire, with additions*, ed. J. W. Clay, 3 (1917), 260–64 · P. Roebuck, *Yorkshire baronets, 1640–1760* (1980)
Archives U. Hull, Brynmor Jones L., corresp. and papers incl. some relating to his trial | BL, Harley MSS 162, 163, 164, 476–479, 1601; Add. MSS 14828, 15858, 18777, 64807 · PRO, C 142/319/179, C 181/2–5, C 231/4–5
Likenesses attrib. T. Simon, silver medal, 1645, NPG · T. Simon, sculpture, silver medal, BM · R. Walton, etching, NPG
Wealth at death landed estate £3000 p.a.; personal estate approx. £10,000 in 1643: Cliffe, *Yorkshire gentry*, 92, 110, 352; Brynmor Jones Library, DDHO/1/35, 77

Hotham, John (1610–1645), parliamentarian army officer, was the eldest son of Sir John *Hotham (1589–1645) and his first wife, Katherine Rodes. Although he was admitted to Gray's Inn on 12 April 1628 his vocation was soldiering, and in the spring of 1629 he and Thomas Fairfax travelled into the Low Countries, where they obtained captaincies under Lord Vere in the army of the prince of Orange. Hotham had returned to England by 13 January 1631, when he married Frances Wray (1611–1635), daughter of Sir John *Wray of Glentworth, Lincolnshire. His second marriage, which occurred in 1636, was to Margaret Watkinson, daughter of Thomas, Viscount Fairfax of Emley, Yorkshire; and by June 1643, Margaret having died, he had taken as his third wife Isabel Anderson, daughter of Sir Henry Anderson of Long Cowton, Yorkshire.

In the elections to the Short and the Long Parliament in 1640 Hotham was returned for Scarborough on his father's interest. In between he signed the three Yorkshire petitions to the king of July, August, and September, complaining about illegal billeting, and pleading poverty in the face of royal commands to mobilize the county's trained bands against the Scots. Impatient of parliamentary procedure, Hotham played a relatively minor role in the Long Parliament. He shared his father's zeal for the suppression of Catholicism and the removal of the king's evil counsellors, but not his concern for the rule of law, expressing the hope in 1642 that the Commons would 'not stand upon the nicety of the law nor lawyers' (*Private Journals of the Long Parliament*, 1.318, 322). He participated in the Commons' attack upon the earl of Strafford, Francis, Lord Cottington, and Edward, Lord Littleton, and backed John Pym over the grand remonstrance. But unlike most of those associated with Pym's 'junto', Hotham was unenthusiastic about root and branch religious reform.

On 12 January 1642 Hotham was assigned the vital task of securing Hull and its magazine—his father, who had been appointed the town's governor the day before, being unable to leave Westminster until mid-March. On receiving his orders Hotham reportedly declared 'Mr Speaker! Fall back, fall edge, I will go down and perform your commands' (Rushworth, 4.496). With the 'well management of threats and [en]treaties' (Brynmor Jones Library, Hotham papers, DDHO/1/35) he garrisoned the town with some of the East Riding trained bands, and by late July, when he was commissioned a captain of horse in the earl of Essex's army, he was effectively second-in-command at Hull. Indeed, according to Clarendon, Pym's junto realized that Sir John Hotham 'was not possessed with their principles in any degree', and used 'Captain Hotham' (as he was generally styled), 'in whom they most confided', to spy on his father (Clarendon, *Hist. rebellion*, 1.523–4).

Late in September Hotham led about 500 horse and foot into the West Riding, and on 4 October he stormed Cawood Castle in defiance of the treaty of neutrality that the commander of parliament's forces in Yorkshire, Ferdinando, Lord Fairfax, had agreed with the West Riding royalists. Both Hotham and his father publicly condemned the treaty, and were supported by the Westminster militants. From mid-October Hotham joined with Fairfax to drive the royalists out of Leeds and to impede the earl of

Newcastle's advance into Yorkshire. But he resented Fairfax's authority over him, regarding himself as far better commander-in-chief material, and Fairfax was soon complaining of his refusal to obey orders.

With his father's support Hotham began corresponding secretly with the earl of Newcastle late in 1642, using possession of Hull to barter for pardon and reward. Pique and self-interest aside, Hotham was motivated by a desire for a 'happy peace'; fearing either tyranny if king or parliament became 'absolute conquerors', or that the 'necessitous people of the whole kingdom will presently rise in mighty numbers and … set up for themselves to the utter ruin of all nobility and gentry' (*Portland MSS*, 1.87). In February 1643 he had a 'private conference' with the queen, through Newcastle (*The Weekly Account*, 18–24 Dec 1644), and allegedly demanded titles for himself and his father, senior military command, and £20,000 (Scrope and Monkhouse, 2.182–3). Newcastle and the queen clearly expected him to have defected by late March, and accused him of 'disaffection' (Brynmor Jones Library, Hotham papers, DDHO/1/25). But the Hothams were keen to 'linger out the treaty … for the better accomplishing their own ends', and to make certain that they were not deserting the stronger party (Scrope and Monkhouse, 2.183).

Early in April Hotham led his forces into Lincolnshire, where his kinsmen, the Wrays, had secured him the generalship of the county's forces. Once in Lincolnshire he endeavoured to subvert the local parliamentarian leaders, and by the end of May had begun a 'private treaty' with the queen at Newark (Hutchinson, 128–9). He also allowed his men to plunder indiscriminately, informing Colonel John Hutchinson that 'he fought for liberty and expected it in all things' (ibid., 129). Suspecting that he was disloyal, Cromwell and Hutchinson obtained a parliamentary order for his arrest, and on 22 June he was seized and imprisoned in Nottingham Castle on charges of plundering parliament's supporters, desertion in battle, and maintaining correspondence with the enemy. Hotham immediately wrote to the queen for help, promising to deliver up Hull, Lincoln, and Beverley to the king. Soon afterwards he managed to escape and fled to Lincoln, where he wrote to parliament, claiming that Cromwell had employed an 'Anabaptist' and a captain 'who was lately but a yeoman' to slander him (BL, Harley MS 164, D'Ewes diary, fol. 234). This view of Cromwell and his men as 'a company of Brownists, Anabaptists, [and] factious, inferior persons' (*A Continuation of Certaine Speciall and Remarkable Passages*, 29 June–6 July 1643, 2–3) was shared by his father. Hotham then returned to Hull, resolving to have nothing more to do with 'the popularity' (Rushworth, 5.746 [2nd pagination]), and resumed his correspondence with Newcastle. But on 29 June the townsmen seized him in his chambers, and he and his father were conveyed to London.

Whether Hotham had ever possessed a coherent plan to defect to the king, or had simply been hedging his bets and letting events dictate his ultimate allegiance, is difficult to judge. What is certain is that he underestimated the intelligence and resolve of 'the popularity', and over-estimated his ability to continue deceiving them with impunity.

Hotham was expelled from the Commons on 8 September 1643, and his personal estate (valued at £7000 by his wife) was confiscated. He was not brought to trial until 9 December 1644, when the court martial that had sentenced his father to death two days earlier commenced proceedings against him. He constructed a clever defence, producing many witnesses, deporting himself with 'submissiveness and respect' (Scrope and Monkhouse, 2.184) and implying that the fault lay mostly with his father. But the court was not convinced, and on 24 December he too was sentenced to death. He petitioned both houses asking that his sentence be commuted to a fine or banishment, but according to Sir Hugh Cholmley fewer than six MPs spoke up for him (ibid., 185). On 1 January 1645, after a short speech protesting his innocence and reproaching parliament for continuing the war, he was beheaded at Tower Hill. He was buried at All Hallows Barking by the Tower, along with his father, who was executed on 2 January.

Hotham made a bad impression on contemporaries. Clarendon thought him full of 'pride and stubborness' (Clarendon, *Hist. rebellion*, 3.527); and Cholmley described him as 'a very politic and cunning man, [who] looked chiefly at that which stood most with his own particular interest' (Scrope and Monkhouse, 2.186). Both men believed that Hotham senior would have declared for Charles in the summer of 1642 if his loyalty had not been blunted by his son's self-interest. Hotham was certainly more active in treating with Newcastle, and unlike his father made no effort to urge MPs to an accommodation with the king. Indeed in April 1643 he denounced the Oxford negotiations. Nevertheless he seems to have had a genuine desire for a speedy settlement, if only to forestall further social upheaval. His eldest son, Sir John Hotham, second baronet, represented Beverley in the Cavalier Parliament.   DAVID SCOTT

Sources HoP, *Commons, 1640–60* [draft] · *The manuscripts of his grace the duke of Portland*, 10 vols., HMC, 29 (1891–1931), vol. 1, p. 89 · U. Hull, Brynmor Jones L., Hotham MSS, DDHO · Clarendon, *Hist. rebellion* · R. Scrope and T. Monkhouse, eds., *State papers collected by Edward, earl of Clarendon*, 3 vols. (1767–86), vol. 2, pp. 181–6 · *JHC*, 2–4 (1640–46) · J. Rushworth, *Historical collections*, new edn, 3–5 (1721) · G. W. Johnson and R. Bell, eds., *The Fairfax correspondence*, 4 vols. (1848–9), vol. 3 · L. Hutchinson, *Memoirs of the life of Colonel Hutchinson*, ed. J. Hutchinson, new edn, ed. C. H. Firth (1906) · *Certaine letters sent from Sir John Hotham, Young Hotham, the major of Hull, and others* (1643) · *A most true relation of the great and bloody battell fought by Capt. Hotham with 1000 foote* (1642) [Thomason tract E 129(9)] · *Speciall Passages and Certain Informations* (4–11 Oct 1642) [Thomason tract 121(32)]; (15–22 Nov 1642) [E 127(35)]; (11–18 April 1643) [E 97(8)]; (28 Feb 1643/4–7 March 1643/4) [E 92(82)] · *A true and perfect relation of a victorious battell obtained against the earl of Cumberland* (1642) [Thomason tract E 126(5)] · *A true and perfect relation of the taking of a great ship* (1642) [Thomason tract E 121(21)] · *A true and exact relation of the several passages at the siege of Manchester ... also a protestation of Master Hotham* (1642) [Thomason tract E 121(45)] · *A Continuation of Certaine Speciall and Remarkable Passages* (10–14 Oct 1642) [Thomason tract E 122(14)] · *A Continuation of Certaine Speciall and Remarkable Passages* (29 June–6 July 1643) [Thomason tract E 59(13)] · *The Weekly Account, Containing Certain Speciall and Remarkable Passages* (18–24 Dec 1644) [Thomason tract E 22(8)] · *Certaine Informations from Severall Parts of the Kingdome* (19–26 June 1643) [Thomason tract E 56(2)] · *More plots found out and plotters apprehended: a true relation of the discovery of a most desperate and dangerous plot* (1643) [Thomason tract E 59(2)] · *Mercurius Britanicus* (5–12 Sept 1643) [Thomason tract E 67(8)] · *Kingdomes Weekly Intelligencer* (11–18 April 1643) [Thomason tract E 97(9)] · parliamentary diary of Sir Simonds D'Ewes, BL, Harley MSS 162–164 · BL, Harley MSS 476, 479, 5047 · parliamentary diary of Walter Yonge, BL, Add. MS 18777 · BL, Add. MS 28082, fol. 80v · PRO, SP28/143, p. 8 · W. H. Coates, A. Steele Young, and V. F. Snow, eds., *The private journals of the Long Parliament*, 3 vols. (1982–92)
Archives Bodl. Oxf., letters · U. Hull, Brynmor Jones L., papers
Likenesses attrib. T. Simon, silver medal, 1645, NPG · T. Simon, silver medal, NPG · R. Walton, etching, NPG
Wealth at death approx. £7000—personal estate: J. W. Clay, *Abstracts of Yorkshire wills*, Yorkshire Archaeological Society Record Series, 9 (1890), 43

Hotham, Sir Richard (1722–1799), merchant and founder of the resort of Bognor, was born in York on 5 October 1722, the youngest of five children (of whom only he and his sister survived infancy) of Joseph Hotham, gentleman, and his wife, Sarah Bradley. In 1791 Sir Richard erected a memorial to his parents at Skelton church, near York.

Nothing is known of Hotham's early years, but at some time he established himself as a hatter and hosier in Serle Street, Lincoln's Inn, London, and later, about 1750, in the Strand, advertising his wares by circulating copper tokens in London and the provinces. About 1760 his interests extended to chartered shipping with the East India Company and he was the author of two pamphlets, *Reflections upon East India Shipping* (1773) and *A Candid State of Affairs Relative to the East India Shipping* (1774), which sharply criticized the company's bad management.

In 1764 Hotham purchased Moat House Farm, Merton, which he rebuilt as Merton Place, later the home of Lord Nelson. He sold this in 1792 but retained one field of the enlarged estate, on which he built his own house, Merton Grove, at Wimbledon. He was knighted on 12 April 1769, allegedly for expressing the loyalty of Surrey to King George III during the agitation by John Wilkes, and appointed sheriff of Surrey, 1770–71. He conducted a prolonged dispute with Wimbledon vestry committee over developing a public highway to Wandsworth.

In 1780 Hotham was elected MP for Southwark, defeating Henry Thrale and thereby provoking the contempt of Dr Samuel Johnson. He was a member of the Whig opposition and of the St Alban's tavern group, which attempted a union of parties. After narrowly losing the 1784 by-election, Hotham visited Sussex, where he embarked upon the ambitious scheme of transforming the fishing hamlet of Bognor into the select watering place of 'Hothamton'. Some 1600 acres of land were purchased and the building of several mansions and terraces commenced in January 1787. The licensing of his own private chapel was the subject of an acrimonious dispute with the vicar of South Bersted. Having created his sea-bathing resort, this enterprising and sometimes contentious individual achieved the recognition he sought: the patronage of the upper classes. Substantial debts led to the dispersal of his

Sir Richard Hotham (1722–1799), by William Dudman, 1796

estates after his death, but Bognor's reputation for health and respectability continued to attract royalty and nobility.

Hotham married on 3 December 1743, by licence at Chelsea Hospital Chapel, Frances Atkinson, of Stockton-on-Tees, with whom he had a son John, who died in 1751. She was buried on 14 August 1760 in St Martin-in-the-Fields, Westminster, where on 7 April 1761 he married Barbara (*b.* 1733), daughter of Joseph Huddart, tradesman, and his wife Patience, *née* Rash. She died without issue at Brompton on 1 February 1777 and was buried a week later. Hotham had adopted, unofficially, arms similar to those of the Hotham baronetcy, to which he was not connected. George Romney painted his portrait in 1793. Romney at first declined the commission, but 'he was pleased with the cheerful adventurous disposition of that commercial Knight, whom he afterwards painted at full length in London' (Hayley, 175). Hotham died in Bognor on 13 March 1799 and was buried in the local parish churchyard of South Bersted.   R. IDEN, *rev.*

Sources G. Young, *A history of Bognor Regis* (1983) · J. B. Davis, *The origin and description of Bognor, or Hothamton* (1807) · HoP, *Commons, 1754–90* · *GM*, 1st ser., 40 (1770) · *GM*, 1st ser., 47 (1777), 95 · *GM*, 1st ser., 69 (1799) · parish register, York, Holy Trinity, King's Court, Borth. Inst. · parish register, Skelton, near York, Borth. Inst. · Chelsea Hospital marriage register, PRO, RG4/4330 · parish register, South Bersted, Sussex, W. Sussex RO · W. Hayley, *Life of George Romney* (1809), 175 · private information (2004) [Susanna Fisher] · R. Iden, 'The two wives (and one son) of Sir Richard Hotham', *Newsletter* [Bognor Regis Local History Society], 45 (Aug 2001) · *A history of Lord Nelson's Merton Place* (1998) · R. Iden, 'Sir Richard Hotham's chapel at Bognor', *Sussex Archaeological Collections*, 134 (1996), 179–83 · parish register of St Martin-in-the-Fields, City Westm. AC

Likenesses G. Romney, portrait, 1793 · W. Dudman, portrait, 1796, Bognor Regis town hall [*see illus.*]

Hotham [Hothum], **William of** (*c.*1255–1298), Dominican friar and archbishop of Dublin, took his name from Hotham in the East Riding of Yorkshire. A William Hotham is included among the fellows of Merton College, Oxford in 1291, but this was a nephew, who became chief baron of the Irish exchequer. Another nephew was John *Hotham, bishop of Ely, who also had connections with Ireland. Exactly when William of Hotham entered the Dominican convent at Oxford is not known, but he was lecturer on the *Sentences* (*cursor de sentenciis*) and assistant (*socius*) to Adam de Lakeor, the regent master, in 1269; in the same year he acted as one of his house's representatives in settling a dispute with the Franciscans concerning the latter's observance of evangelical poverty. He was possibly at the York convent in 1270–71, when he received money from Archbishop Walter Giffard. BTh by 1269, Hotham was lecturing on the *Sentences* at Paris *c.*1275 and incepted as DTh there.

Between 1282 and 1287 Hotham was provincial of the order in England, during which time he took part in disputations at Oxford. As a Dominican theologian he was thrust into the vortex of the controversy that was sweeping through the universities of Oxford and Paris on account of the influx of Aristotelian ideas, their mediation through such Arabic commentators as Averroes and Avicenna, and the synthesis of pagan and Christian philosophy undertaken by Thomas Aquinas. There was increasing concern that the conclusions of philosophers in the arts faculty of Paris, arrived at by reason, were in conflict with the theologians, for whom philosophy was of necessity subordinate to faith. Aquinas, himself a Dominican, sought at Paris to reconcile accepted Augustinian teaching with the newly accessible corpus of Aristotle's works. Although he argued against certain of Averroes's philosophical opinions, some of his own propositions were to come under attack from Franciscans and Dominicans alike, and after his death were condemned at both Paris and Oxford in 1277.

Hotham could well have taught theology to his fellow Dominican Richard Knapwell and, if he is correctly identified as 'Willelmus predicator', presided over that scholar's *vesperies*—the disputation held the day before his inception. He must therefore have been well acquainted with the views expressed by his confrère, indeed was probably in sympathy with them. Knapwell, in the course of attempting to reconcile traditional teaching with Thomist tenets, published his *Notabilia* about 1280, and was almost certainly the author of the *Correctorium corruptorii quare*, composed about 1283 as a riposte to the critique of Thomist propositions of the Franciscan William de la Mare. In any case, Hotham rushed to assert the orthodoxy of his order, which by that time had approved Thomism, but had not made it obligatory. On 22 October 1284 he appeared at Sonning, Berkshire, for the consecration of Walter Scammel, bishop of Salisbury, and took the opportunity to acquaint Archbishop John Pecham with the misgivings of the Oxford Dominicans, who feared that on coming to the university the archbishop would repudiate their teaching. Hotham made a vain attempt to dissuade Pecham from following his predecessor at Canterbury, Robert Kilwardby, a Dominican, who in 1277 had forbidden—allegedly with the concurrence of the Oxford masters—the teaching at the university of certain of Aquinas's philosophical propositions. However, Kilwardby stopped short of declaring them heretical. Pecham, a Franciscan who had engaged in disputations with Aquinas at Paris, upheld against the latter the concept of the plurality of forms, and singled out the doctrine of the unity, or unicity, of form in man—a single form for each being, based on Aristotle's teaching—for special condemnation. On 24 November 1285 Hotham vigorously defended his order's position before the university, claiming that hostility against it was being fostered by the Franciscans and by Pecham's councillors, an allegation already circulating in the university in an anonymous pamphlet.

Aroused by Hotham's denunciation, the archbishop in a letter to the Oxford chancellor accused the provincial of misrepresentation, and his order of hubris, in claiming to have special access to doctrinal truth. In reiterating Kilwardby's prohibition, Pecham claimed to have acted solely in accordance with his own conscience. While in London for the parliament of April 1286 the archbishop summoned a special convocation. On the 30th, sitting judicially in the church of St Mary of the Arches in the presence of three suffragans, of the Oxford chancellor, and of others including Hotham, he condemned various theses advanced by Knapwell, among them that of unity of form, declaring them to be heretical. Hotham, arguing that the archbishop had exceeded his authority in thus condemning a Dominican, launched an appeal to the curia. The hearing was delayed by the death of Honorius IV on 3 April 1287, and with the accession of Nicholas IV—a Franciscan sympathetic to Pecham—Knapwell was put under a ban of silence.

Hotham was released from his position as provincial of England by the general chapter of the order which assembled at Bordeaux in May 1287, and was appointed professor of theology in Paris, presumably in the expectation that he would sustain Thomist views. The studium had been disrupted by internal disturbances (perhaps against the friars), but Hotham, possibly detained by royal business at home, did not assume his chair. In consequence he was censured in the succeeding general chapter at Lucca (1288). Re-elected to the provincialate in 1290, Hotham retained the office until he became archbishop.

Following Edward I's conquest of Scotland Hotham encouraged the settlement of Dominicans in that country. In 1291 he acted as arbiter in a dispute between the archbishop of York, John Romanus, and his suffragan, Antony (I) Bek, bishop of Durham. Two years later he was himself in dispute with the archbishop about the licensing of friars to hear confessions within the latter's jurisdiction.

Apart from his work for the Dominican order and his involvement in theological controversy, Hotham acted as a trusted royal clerk. In 1282 he accompanied the king to north Wales, and in March 1289 was with him in Gascony. He had earlier come to England with papal letters about the sexennial tenth in aid of the Holy Land, and between 8 May and 31 December 1289 he returned to Rome to seek a dispensation for the proposed marriage of the king's son, Edward, to Margaret of Scotland, to reach a settlement about arrears of the annual tribute due to the curia, and to seek permission for the diversion of the crusading tenth to the king's use. The English Dominicans were prominent in the promotion of the crusade, so it is not surprising that their provincial was at the royal manor of Clipstone, Nottinghamshire, when on 14 October 1290 Edward I swore to take the cross. Three years later, when the Spaniard Pedro Martinez da Luna offered to place 100 knights under the king's banner, he suggested that Hotham be sent with the king's response.

During 1291 and 1292 Hotham acted as an arbitrator in the business of the Scottish succession, the Great Cause, and on 4 August 1295 preached before the king and the cardinals sent by Boniface VIII to plead for peace between Edward and Philippe IV of France. In 1295, with his fellow Dominican Thomas Jorz, he was deputed to explain the king's affairs at a general chapter of the Dominicans scheduled to meet in Strasbourg, although in the event the death of the master-general meant that no meeting was held. In August 1297 he accompanied Edward I to Flanders and played a prominent part in presenting the English case at Courtrai and Tournai which led to an agreement to accept the arbitration of Boniface between the English king and Philippe IV. He was the principal member of the delegation to Rome that accepted Pope Boniface's award of 30 June 1298.

Boniface, who wrote appreciatively of Hotham's virtues, provided him to the see of Llandaff on 16 September 1290, but Hotham excused himself by reason of his ignorance of Welsh and his recent reappointment as provincial prior. On the annulment of the election of Thomas Chadworth to the archbishopric of Dublin he was provided to the see by a bull of 24 April 1296. His temporalities were restored on 23 November 1296, and he had livery on 2 February in the following year. He was consecrated at Ghent in December 1296 at the hands of Antony Bek, with whom he was friendly. The last of ten Dominicans to be raised to the episcopate in western Christendom during the thirteenth century, he did not reach his see but died at Dijon on 27 August 1298. His nephew John, the future bishop of Ely, was with him at the time and acted as one of his executors. His body was buried in the church of the Blackfriars in London.

Early in the fourteenth century Bernard Gui remarked that Hotham was 'a great master of theology, noted throughout the order' (Hinnebusch, 387 n. 148). The chronicler Nicholas Trevet regarded him as a man of acute mind, genial, placid, sincerely religious, and acceptable to all. In modern times he has been acclaimed as 'one of the greatest Dominicans of the thirteenth century' (Hinnebusch, 386). Despite his scholarly reputation little of his literary output has survived. In fact only a *Quodlibet* delivered during his regency in Paris, and preserved in a single manuscript in the Bibliothèque Nationale, is ascribed to him without reservation. The Stams catalogue (*Catalogus Stamsensis scriptorum ordinis Praedicatorum*) states that he wrote a commentary on the first book of the *Sentences*, as well as other pieces including one *De unitate formarum*. There is a difference of opinion as to whether he can be identified as Guillelmus Hedonensis or Willelmus Predicator. If so, some surviving *quaestiones* may be his, as well as a tract *De anima*. Some of his sermons have been preserved in manuscripts at the Bibliothèque Nationale, Worcester Cathedral Library, and elsewhere. His activities as a royal clerk have been criticized by M. H. MacInerny, the historian of the Irish Dominicans, on the grounds that he was too blind a follower of royal policies. At the time there was also concern within the order itself about the preoccupation of its members with secular concerns and episcopal functions. ROY MARTIN HAINES

Sources *Chancery records* · W. A. Hinnebusch, *The early English Friars Preachers* (1951) · M. H. MacInerny, *History of the Irish Dominicans*, 1 (1916) · D. E. Sharp, *Franciscan philosophy at Oxford in the thirteenth century*, British Society of Franciscan Studies, 16 (1930) · F. C. Copleston, *A history of philosophy* (1966), 2: *Mediaeval philosophy: Augustine to Scotus* (1966) · G. Leff, *Paris and Oxford universities in the thirteenth and fourteenth centuries* (1968) · H. Rashdall, *The universities of Europe in the middle ages*, ed. F. M. Powicke and A. B. Emden, new edn, 3 (1936) · A. G. Little and F. Pelster, *Oxford theology and theologians*, OHS, 96 (1934) · J. C. Russell, 'Dictionary of writers of thirteenth century England', *BIHR*, special suppl., 3 (1936) [whole issue] · P. Glorieux, *Répertoire des maîtres en théologie de Paris au XIIIe siècle*, 1 (Paris, 1933) · P. Glorieux, 'Comment les thèses Thomistes furent proscrites à Oxford, 1284–6', *Revue Thomiste*, 10 (1927), 259–91 · M. D. Chenu, 'La première diffusion du Thomisme à Oxford: Knapwell et ses *Notes* sur les "Sentences"', *Archives d'Histoire Doctrinale et Littéraire du Moyen Âge*, 3 (1928), 185–200 · J. Quétif and J. Echard, *Scriptores ordinis praedicatorum recensiti*, 1 (Paris, 1719) · N. Trevet, *Annales sex regum Angliae, 1135–1307*, ed. T. Hog, EHS, 6 (1845) · B. M. Reichert, ed., *Acta capitulorum generalium ordinis praedicatorum*, 3 (Rome, 1898) · D. L. Douie, *Archbishop Pecham* (1952) · Emden, *Oxf.*, 2.970–71 · *The chronicle of Walter of Guisborough*, ed. H. Rothwell, CS, 3rd ser., 89 (1957) **Archives** Bibliothèque Nationale, Paris, MS nat. lat. 15805 · Bibliothèque Nationale, Paris, nat. lat. 14947; 15005, 15971 · CCC Oxf., MS 107 · Gon. & Caius Cam., MS 342 · Worcester Cathedral, MS Q46, etc.

Hotham, William, first Baron Hotham (1736–1813), naval officer, was born on 8 April 1736, the third son of Sir Beaumont Hotham, seventh baronet (1698–1771), a descendant of Sir John Hotham, first baronet (d. 1645), and his wife, Frances, daughter of the Revd William Thompson of Welton. He received his early education at Westminster School, entered the Royal Naval Academy at Portsmouth in 1748, and in 1751 was appointed to the *Gosport* on the North American station. He afterwards served in the *Advice* in the West Indies, and the sloop *Swan* in North America, and passed his examination on 7 August 1754. On 28 January 1755 he was promoted lieutenant of the *St George*, flagship of his patron, Sir Edward Hawke, with whom he moved into the *Namur*, the *Antelope*, and the *Ramillies*, and by whom he was promoted to the command of a 10-gun polacca. From her he was appointed to the sloop *Fortune*, and pending her return to port he was placed in temporary command of the *Syren* (20 guns), in which he fought a sharp but indecisive action with the frigate

Télémaque (26 guns). After joining the *Fortune* he fell in with a large French privateer which he carried by boarding. For this service he was made captain in the frigate *Gibraltar* on 17 August 1757; in November he was appointed to the *Squirrel*, and on 17 April 1758 to the *Melampe* (36 guns), employed during the next twelve months in the North Sea. On 28 March 1759, while in company with the *Southampton*, the *Melampe* fell in with two French frigates of superior force, one of which, the *Danaë*, was captured after an action lasting through the night. The *Melampe* was afterwards attached to the Grand Fleet under Hawke, but was principally employed in independent cruising, though forming part, in April 1761, of the squadron engaged under Augustus Keppel in the capture of Belle Île. On 20 May 1761 Hotham was moved into the frigate *Aeolus*, and, continuing until the end of the Seven Years' War on the same service, was very successful in the capture or destruction of the enemy's privateers and merchant ships.

From 1766 to 1769 Hotham commanded the guardship *Hero* at Plymouth, and in her, in the spring of 1769, went out to the Mediterranean, with the relief for the garrison of Minorca. From 1770 to 1773 he commanded the *Resolution* at Portsmouth. In 1776 he was appointed to the *Preston* (50 guns) and, with a commodore's broad pennant, escorted a large troop convoy to North America where he played a major role in Lord Howe's capture of New York. In 1777, when Howe was absent on the expedition against Philadelphia, Hotham was left senior officer at New York, and, in co-operation with Sir Henry Clinton the elder, was endeavouring to secure a passage up the Hudson River when news arrived that Lieutenant-General John Burgoyne had surrendered at Saratoga. Continuing at New York, in the following July Hotham took part under Howe in the preparations for the defence of Sandy Hook against the expected attack of d'Estaing and in the subsequent operations off Rhode Island. After the scattering of the fleets by the storm of 12 August, the *Preston* fell in with the *Tonnant* (80 guns) alone and disabled, and boldly engaged her until the arrival of some of the *Tonnant*'s consorts compelled Hotham to retire. He was then sent to the West Indies in command of a reinforcement for Samuel Barrington, and took part in the brilliant action in the Cul-de-Sac of St Lucia on 15 December 1778.

During the summer of 1779 Hotham was stationed at Barbados, and early in 1780 he moved his broad pennant to the *Vengeance* (74 guns), in which he assisted in the several engagements with the French fleet on 17 April, and 15 and 19 May. When Rodney afterwards proceeded to the coast of North America Hotham was left senior officer at the Leeward Islands, and was in Port Castries of St Lucia during the hurricane of 10–12 October. The *Vengeance* was blown from her anchors and tailed on to the rocks, but by cutting away her masts and throwing her after guns overboard, she got off, and, the wind veering, escaped without further damage. It was, however, found necessary for her to go to England, and in the following spring Hotham was sent home in charge of the convoy from St Eustatius. Of the departure and the wealth of this convoy the French had fairly accurate intelligence, and dispatched a squadron of eight ships of the line besides frigates, under the command of M. de la Motte Picquet, to waylay it on its approach to the channel. In this they fully succeeded. Every available English ship had gone with Vice-Admiral George Darby to the relief of Gibraltar, and on 2 May Motte Picquet intercepted the convoy some 60 miles to the west of the Isles of Scilly. Hotham, whose force consisted of two ships of the line and three frigates, was powerless. He signalled the merchant ships to disperse and make the best of their way independently, and for the men-of-war to close with the *Vengeance*. The French, however, avoided the battleships and gave chase to the richly laden merchant ships, many of which they captured. The remainder got into the Irish port of Berehaven, where they were joined by the commodore.

In 1782 Hotham, again as commodore, commanded the *Edgar* in the Grand Fleet under Howe at the relief of Gibraltar and the skirmish with the allies off Cape Spartel. On 24 September 1787 he was promoted rear-admiral of the red, and during the Spanish armament of 1790 he hoisted his flag on board the *Princess Royal*. On 21 September 1790 he became vice-admiral of the blue, and in February 1793, with his flag in the *Britannia*, he went out to the Mediterranean as second in command under Lord Hood, with whom he co-operated during the campaigns of 1793 and 1794, more especially in taking charge of the blockade of the French fleet in Golfe Jouan in the autumn of 1794. When Hood went to England for his health, Hotham was left in temporary command. His exhausted fleet lacked a base, stones, men, and even firewood. He had no reliable allies, and no more than perfunctory instructions from home. Despite being personally ill-equipped for the complex political and diplomatic tasks of this large station, Hotham carried the burden of the war for twelve months under the most adverse circumstances. In March 1795 the fleet was at Leghorn, when Hotham learnt that the French were again at sea. In terms of numbers the French fleet was equal to that of the British, but of the crews more than three-quarters of the French were at sea for the first time, and were ignorant of their duties. On 12 March the two fleets were in sight of each other, and the French commander, who understood the inferiority of his ships, resolved to avoid an action. But the wind and various accidents during the night retarded his retreat. A partial and very straggling encounter followed, in which Captain Horatio Nelson of the *Agamemnon* secured the honours of the day. It was renewed again on 14 March, when two of the French ships, the *Ça-Ira* and *Censeur*, were cut off and captured. The rest escaped, for the British fleet was scattered and of inferior speed, and Hotham refused to risk the command of the Mediterranean by undertaking a pursuit in the light, variable breezes that came and went without warning. So slowly was the fleet moving that Nelson came on board the flagship, to press for a pursuit—but as Hotham could see, the clean-hulled French ships were out of reach. It appeared, however, from the admiral's dispatch that the French fleet was numerically equal or superior, and its real inferiority was not known at

home; two ships had been captured, and the victory won for Hotham and his comrades the thanks of both houses of parliament. On 16 April Hotham was advanced to the rank of admiral. However, the sacking of Hood on the eve of his return caused the already exhausted Hotham to suffer a nervous breakdown. On 13 July 1795 he again fell in with the French fleet, under somewhat similar circumstances, in nearly the same locality, and with nearly the same result. After a long, and very slow chase the *Alcide* (74 guns) struck her flag, but before she was taken possession of she caught fire and was totally destroyed, the greater part of her crew perishing with her; some 200 were taken up by the British boats. With a numerical superiority of twenty-three ships against seventeen, Hotham would have brought on a decisive action, had the wind lasted.

Hotham had been left to exercise the responsibility of the chief command by Hood's dismissal. He had done a solid professional job, leaving the station in better shape than he found it, having twice beaten a flighty enemy. A good officer and a man of undaunted courage, he had on several occasions done admirably in a subordinate rank and though some found him wanting in the energy, force of character, and decisiveness requisite in a commander-in-chief he was only ever the stand-in. In November 1795 he was relieved by Sir John Jervis, and returned to England. He saw no further service. On 7 March 1797 the king raised him to the peerage of Ireland as Baron Hotham of South Dalton, near Hull; and on the death of his nephew, the son of his second brother, he also succeeded as the eleventh baronet (18 July 1811). He died, unmarried, at his home, South Dalton Hall, on 2 May 1813, and was buried at South Dalton church; the titles passed to his younger brother, Beaumont *Hotham (1737–1814).

Hotham had been commended by lords Hawke, Howe, Rodney, and Hood. There was no finer captain or junior admiral in the navy of his day, but he was not equipped for the wide-ranging, complex demands of the Mediterranean command. Very few men were.

J. K. LAUGHTON, *rev.* ANDREW LAMBERT

Sources U. Hull, Brynmor Jones L., Hotham MSS, DDHO · NMM, Hamilton MSS · PRO, Admiralty records · A. M. W. Stirling, *The Hothams*, 2 vols. (1918) · *The dispatches and letters of Vice-Admiral Lord Viscount Nelson*, ed. N. H. Nicolas, 7 vols. (1844–6) · A. T. Mahan, *Life of Nelson* (1897) · W. James, *The naval history of Great Britain, from the declaration of war by France, in February 1793, to the accession of George IV, in January 1820*, [2nd edn], 6 vols. (1826) · BL, Spencer MSS · memorial, South Dalton church, Yorkshire

Archives U. Hull, Brynmor Jones L., corresp. and papers | BL, Spencer MSS · Glos. RO, letters to Francis Reynolds · NMM, corresp. with Sir William Hamilton · PRO, corresp. with F. J. Jackson, FO 353 · PRO, corresp. with Rodney and letters to admiralty, PRO 30/20

Likenesses portrait, priv. coll.

Hotham, Sir William (1772–1848), naval officer and courtier, was born on 12 February 1772, the second son of General George Hotham and his wife, Diana, youngest daughter of Sir Warton Pennyman, bt. He was a nephew of William *Hotham, first Baron Hotham, and was educated at Westminster School. He entered the navy in 1786, on the *Grampus*, with Captain Edward Thompson, in which he made a voyage to the Guinea coast. He afterwards served at Portsmouth, in the West Indies, and in the channel. He was promoted lieutenant on 27 October 1790 when in the *Princess Royal* under his uncle's flag. In the following years he was employed on the coast of North America and in the West Indies, and in January 1794 he joined the *Victory*, carrying Lord Hood's flag in the Mediterranean. In the following May he served on shore at the siege of Bastia, under the immediate orders of Nelson, and on 12 August was promoted to the command of the sloop *Eclair*. On 7 October he was advanced to post rank, and appointed to the frigate *Cyclops* (28 guns), which continued attached to the Mediterranean Fleet until the beginning of 1796, when she was sent home with dispatches and paid off.

In January 1797 Hotham was appointed to the *Adamant* (50 guns), in the North Sea. When the mutiny broke out the *Adamant* was the only ship, besides the *Venerable*, which did not join it, and for several weeks these two ships alone maintained the blockade of the Texel [*see* Duncan, Adam, Viscount Duncan]. After sharing in the glories of Camperdown on 11 October 1797, the *Adamant* was attached to the squadron off Le Havre, under Sir Richard Strachan, and towards the end of 1798 was sent out to the Cape of Good Hope, where she was principally employed in the blockade of Mauritius. On 12 December 1799, in company with the *Tremendous*, she drove ashore and destroyed the French frigate *Preneuse*. The *Adamant* continued on this service until September 1801, when she was sent home with convoy and was paid off.

In March 1803 Hotham was appointed to the *Raisonnable* (64 guns), employed to watch the enemy's flotilla at Boulogne. His health gave way, and in 1804 he resigned his command, and retired for a while from active service. On 1 June 1804 he married Anne (*d.* 21 Aug 1827), daughter of Sir Edward Jeynes. They had one daughter and four sons. After his marriage, Hotham was for a short time in command of the sea fencibles of the Liverpool district, and of the yacht *Royal Sovereign*, until his promotion to rear-admiral on 4 December 1813. For several years he was attached to the court as gentleman-in-waiting, and in his leisure wrote a gossipy book, 'Characters, Principally Professional', which was left in manuscript. In January 1815 he was nominated a KCB, and on 19 July 1821 became vice-admiral. In 1835 he married Jane Pettiward *née* Seymour, widow of Roger Pettiward. He became an admiral on 10 January 1837, and on 4 July 1840 he was nominated a GCB. He died at Windsor on 31 May 1848, and was buried in the family vault at Binfield, Berkshire, on 7 June.

J. K. LAUGHTON, *rev.* ANDREW LAMBERT

Sources O'Byrne, *Naval biog. dict.* · J. Ralfe, *The naval biography of Great Britain*, 3 (1828), 336 · J. Marshall, *Royal naval biography*, 1 (1823), 580 · *Journal of the Royal Geographical Society*, 20 (1850), xxxiv · *GM*, 2nd ser., 30 (1848), 203–4

Likenesses G. Noble and J. Parker, group portrait, line engraving, pubd 1803 (*Commemoration of 11th Oct 1797*; after *Naval victories* by J. Smart), BM, NPG · oils, *c*.1840 (after G. Hayter), NMM

Hothby, John (*c*.1430–1487), composer and music theorist, was the son of William Hothby (*d.* in or before 1473), and on the evidence of his later career was born about 1430.

John joined the Carmelite order at an unknown date, and may be identifiable with the John Otteby, Carmelite friar of the Oxford convent, who was ordained subdeacon on 18 December 1451 in Northampton. Before settling in Lucca he had, by his own account (preserved in his so-called *Epistola*), travelled in Italy, the German empire, France, Great Britain (*Britania magiore*), and Spain. He studied at the University of Pavia, probably in the early 1460s; in 1469 he is called a *lector* in sacred theology. In February 1467, already a *magister*, he was installed as chaplain and *magiscolus* at Lucca Cathedral, with the obligation to teach plainchant and polyphony; he also taught grammar and mathematics. An earlier connection with Florence seems to be indicated by the letter he wrote to Lorenzo de' Medici in 1469 on behalf of a friend. From 1469 he was paid by the Lucca city government to teach publicly as *doctor musicae*.

None of Hothby's nine treatises exists in definitive form; they survive in multiple versions, with different titles, in both Latin and Italian and sometimes a mixture of the two; most seem to have been taken down as lecture notes, sometimes in faulty, even incomprehensible, form. Five different versions of his teachings on notation are extant, and six of his counterpoint treatises. *Quid est proportio* (BL, Add. MS 10336, fols. 58–73*v*), a work on proportions related to the ratios of intervals, appears to be his only treatise copied in England. The rather sketchy nature of these works suggests that they supplemented lectures based primarily on Guido d'Arezzo, who wrote in the early eleventh century, and Johannes de Muris, who died about 1350.

Two treatises of a more speculative cast, and also the most substantial of Hothby's works, are the Italian *Calliopea legale* and the related Latin *Tractatus quarundam regularum artis musicae*. These too exist in several versions with differing titles and order of material. Here, side by side with explanations of the fundamentals of music, Hothby develops advanced ideas, clothed in enigmatic terminology, on the tonal system: his division of the gamut into quarter-tones (demonstrated on his own instrument) anticipates developments of nearly a century later. He has commonly been considered a conservative, since his teachings are based firmly on Boethius, Guido, and Johannes de Muris and he entered into polemics with the radical contemporary theorist Bartolomé Ramos de Pareja; if his idiosyncratic terminology was meant to mask his avant-garde notions, it largely succeeded.

Like many theorists, Hothby also composed. Only nine, mostly undistinguished, works remain (all edited by Albert Seay); six are sacred, the others secular, on Italian texts. Copied in Ferrara by another Carmelite theorist, they were probably written before Hothby came to Lucca; the English idiom is noticeable. One of these compositions, *Ora pro nobis*, which involves complex proportions, evidently had a didactic motivation. A rota demonstrating the note values of the mensural system, referred to by later writers, is now lost.

Hothby's fame as a teacher may have been the reason for his journey to England in March 1486, which was made at the request of Henry VII, as a credential letter by the

government of Lucca attests. He died in England or Brittany (*in Brittania*) in October or November 1487; if Brittany, then it was on the return trip to Lucca, where his post was held open for him for two years. His successor was appointed on 16 November 1487.
BONNIE J. BLACKBURN

Sources *The musical works of John Hothby*, ed. A. Seay, Corpus Mensurabilis Musicae, 33 (1964) · J. Hothby, *De arte contrapuncti*, ed. G. Reaney, Corpus Scriptorum de Musica, 26 (1977) · J. Hothby, *Opera omnia de musica mensurabili*, ed. G. Reaney, Corpus Scriptorum de Musica, 31 (1983) · J. Hothby, *Tres tractatuli contra Bartholomaeum Ramum*, ed. A. Seay, Corpus Scriptorum de Musica, 10 (1964) [incl. *Epistola*] · J. Hothby, *La calliopea legale*, ed. T. L. McDonald, Corpus Scriptorum de Musica, 42 (1997) · J. Hothby, *Quid est proportio*, BL, Add. MS 10336, fols. 58–73v · J. Hothby, *Tractatus quarundam regularum artis musicae*, BL, Add. MS 36986, fols. 2–24v · L. Nerici, *Storia della musica in Lucca* (1879) · Emden, *Oxf.*, 2.969, 1409 · G. Reaney, 'The musical theory of John Hothby', *Revue Belge de Musicologie*, 42 (1988), 119–33 · G. Reaney, 'The manuscript transmission of Hothby's theoretical works', *A Festschrift for Albert Seay*, ed. M. D. Grace (1982), 21–31 · A. Seay, 'Florence: the city of Hothby and Ramos', *Journal of the American Musicological Society*, 9 (1956), 193–5 [incl. letter to Lorenzo de'Medici] · A. Seay, 'The *Dialogus Johannis Ottobi Anglici in arte musica*', *Journal of the American Musicological Society*, 8 (1955), 86–100 · U. Kornmüller, 'Johann Hothby: eine Studie zur Geschichte der Musik im 15. Jahrhundert', *Kirchenmusikalisches Jahrbuch*, 8 (1893), 1–23 · A. W. Schmidt, *Die 'Calliopea legale' des Johannes Hothby* (1897) · T. L. McDonald, 'The *Musica plana* of John Hothby', PhD diss., Rutgers University, 1990

Hothum, William of. *See* Hotham, William of (*c.*1255–1298).

Hotine, Martin (1898–1968), geodesist and photogrammetrist, was born at 9 Wymond Street, Putney, on 17 June 1898, the tenth child and fourth son of Frederick Martin Hotine, a retired army officer and journalist, and his wife, Mary Louisa Golder. After an education at Southend high school and the Royal Military Academy, Woolwich, he was commissioned into the Royal Engineers on 6 June 1917, the head of his entry. He saw active service in Persia, Iraq, and India, and then went up to Magdalene College, Cambridge, although he abandoned his studies without obtaining a degree. In 1924 Hotine married Kate Amelia, daughter of George Pearson, of Rochford, Essex; they had three daughters.

In 1925 Hotine was appointed research officer to the air survey committee. Although the subject was new to him he devoted his mathematical ability, experimental aptitude, and energy to photogrammetry, that is, the technique of using photographs to ascertain measurements relating to what is photographed, used especially in surveying and mapping. In 1927–31 he was attached to the geographical section of the general staff (GSGS) at the War Office, but retained his interest in photogrammetry and his *Surveying from Air Photographs* (1931) was the standard textbook in English for many years, describing the methods favoured in Britain which did not rely on the expensive equipment used in continental Europe. From 1931 to 1933 Hotine was in Tanganyika on observation for the measurement of the 30th arc of meridian and this practical work aroused his interest in geodesy and developed

his appreciation of the basic survey needs of less economically developed countries. From 1934 until 1939 he served in the Ordnance Survey where he initiated the retriangulation of Great Britain, completed in 1962. In spite of severe financial restrictions he insisted on the highest technical standards; he regarded it as essential that the triangulation stations be recoverable and the pillars on hill tops throughout the United Kingdom are monuments to his vision.

When war broke out in 1939 Hotine was appointed deputy director of survey in the British expeditionary force and, later, deputy director (surveys) east Africa command, whence he returned to England in 1941 to become director of military survey, the officer commanding Geographical Section General Staff responsible for the army's maps and the RAF's aeronautical charts. He retained this post, with the rank of brigadier, until 1946. He developed close co-operation with the United States army map service, ensuring that the results of the surveying and cartographic work of each country was available to the armed forces of the other.

In 1946 Hotine became the first director of the directorate of colonial (geodetic and topographical) surveys (after 1957 directorate of overseas (geodetic and topographical) surveys). The concept of the organization—a large, centrally organized body whose surveyors would be highly mobile and whose remit was imperial and, in particular, which was not under the auspices of the Ordnance Survey—was his own, and 'Hotine's private army', as the directorate became known, achieved much, not least because of his enthusiasm and vision. The survey's main effort was devoted to the production of general topographical maps of increasing detail as time went on, but in addition to general mapping, he fostered special activities such as resource and land use surveys. His method was to combine aerial photography with field surveying as the only way to cover large areas at a high standard of accuracy. While at the directorate, Hotine was president of the very successful Commonwealth survey officers' conference in 1955, 1959, and 1963.

Hotine was keenly interested in geodesy and geodetic survey was an important part of the directorate's work. Hotine himself was especially interested in three-dimensional geodesy, which was assuming increasing importance as satellite imagery advanced, and in the mathematics of projection systems. He retired from the directorate in October 1963 and within a month became a member of the research staff of the United States coast and geodetic survey, working in Washington, DC, and then of the United States environmental science services administration, working at Boulder, Colorado. During his five years in America, which his daughter considered among the happiest of his life and the climax of his career (*The Times*, 7 Dec 1968), he wrote his major scientific work, *Mathematical Geodesy* (1969).

Hotine was appointed CBE in 1945 and CMG in 1949, the year in which he retired from the army. In 1947 he was awarded the founder's medal of the Royal Geographical Society and in the same year became an officer of the

American Legion of Merit. In 1955 he was the first recipient of the president's medal of the Photogrammetric Society of London. The gold medal of the Institution of Royal Engineers was awarded to him in 1964, and in 1968, the day before he died, he was awarded the gold medal of the American department of commerce. He died in Woking on 12 November 1968.

Hotine could be acerbic and outspoken in his official correspondence but in his ideas, scientific and otherwise, he was often ahead of his time. As early as 1949 he wrote: 'Racial co-operation is particularly important in the Colonies … Treat members of other races just exactly as you would treat Englishmen' (in Macdonald, 67). He was less enlightened in his insistence that surveyors' wives should not accompany their husbands on tour and his policy led to many resignations before it was abandoned in 1956.

The directorate which Hotine established and ran became associated with a style of development which fell from favour—the dam on the River Volta (Gold Coast) with its associated reduction of bauxite, and the east African groundnut scheme were just two schemes which rested on the directorate's surveys—but this does not undermine the general use of maps for development nor the dedication of the people who produced them. Hotine was a passionate defender of both and as a 'consummate politician' (McGrath, 20) was able to realize his vision at a time of considerable uncertainty and flux in Britain's relationship with her colonies and former colonies. That the directorate was closed in 1985 was no poor reflection on him or his staff but a simple recognition that times had changed. ELIZABETH BAIGENT

Sources A. Macdonald, *Mapping the world: a history of the directorate of overseas surveys, 1946–1985* (1996) · G. McGrath, 'Mapping for development: the contributions of the directorate of overseas surveys', *Cartographica*, 20, nos. 1–2 (1983) [*Cartographica* monograph 29–30] · *The Times* (13 Nov 1968) · *The Times* (20 Nov 1968) · *The Times* (7 Dec 1968) · b. cert. · *CGPLA Eng. & Wales* (1969) · 'Directorate of overseas surveys', *Nature*, 199 (1963), 1230–31 · *Royal Engineers Journal*, new ser., 83 (1969), 74–7 · *WWW* · *DNB* · private information (2004) [R. T. Porter] · M. Hotine, 'Letters home', *Royal Engineers Journal*, new ser., 103 (1989), 136–8; new ser., 104 (1990), 154–8; new ser., 106 (1992), 233–9
Archives Ordnance Survey, Southampton, papers | IWM, letters to his wife [microfilm]
Likenesses L. M. Carmichael, oils, 1963, repro. in Macdonald, *Mapping the world*, frontispiece · photographs, repro. in Macdonald, *Mapping the world*, pl. 1, 10
Wealth at death £10,976: probate, 6 May 1969, *CGPLA Eng. & Wales*

Hoton, Richard (*d.* 1308), prior of Durham, derived his surname from Hutton in the parish of Guisborough. He was possibly uncle of the John who in 1335 gave the family's land in Hutton to Guisborough Priory. When Antony (I) *Bek was chosen bishop of Durham on 9 July 1283, Hoton was the seventh and last elector (*compromissarius*) selected by the monks. Before 1286 he had succeeded Roger of Methley as sub-prior, and when at his enthronement at Durham Bishop Bek forced the resignation of Richard of Claxton as prior, Hoton maintained that he, as sub-prior,

should continue to have jurisdiction over the monks in accordance with precedent, whatever arrangements the bishop might make over estate management during the vacancy. Bishop Bek, however, succeeded in cowing the monks into accepting Henry of Horncastle, prior of Coldingham, as keeper of both jurisdictions until the re-election on 11 January 1286 of Hugh of Darlington (previously prior between 1258 and 1272). The new prior transferred Hoton first from the sub-priorship to the tiny dependent cell of Lytham in Lancashire, and then to Coldingham as a simple monk. Four years later Darlington resigned a second time, and on 24 March 1290 Hoton was elected prior of Durham. He was an effective administrator, maximizing the priory's extensive revenues, which in 1293/4 amounted to £3985 according to the bursar's calculations. He started reclamation of Spennymoor, with its coal reserves, and bought at Oxford a house for Durham monks studying at the university—its site is now occupied by Trinity College. In November 1291 he and the Durham monks were licensed by Bishop Bek to have free warren at Westoe and Wardley, and free chase at Muggleswick; while their acquisition of Houghall was confirmed.

These courteous relations were brought to an abrupt end in May 1300, when the bishop announced his intention to make a formal visitation of his cathedral priory on the grounds of complaints about Hoton's administration. Hoton asserted that there was precedent only for a personal visit, by the bishop alone, and appealed to the courts of York, Canterbury, and Rome. Bek forthwith excommunicated Hoton and his adherents, the priory was blockaded, and its lands seized. In June 1300 Edward I tried to intervene, but bishop and prior remained intransigent. On 10 August the prior of Lindisfarne, Henry of Lusby, was nominated by Bek to succeed Hoton. On 21 August the monastery was stormed, and on 24 August Hoton was dragged from his choir stall and imprisoned. The following December Hoton escaped from his confinement and his wrongs were presented before Edward I and Boniface VIII (*r.* 1294–1303). In February 1302 Hoton was restored. The case, however, was reopened in the curia, and in July 1302 Boniface issued an ordinance, 'Debent', allowing Bek to visit accompanied by four clerks, including a notary. Further appeals ensued, and in the autumn of 1306 Hoton travelled to the curia to secure from Clement V (*r.* 1305–14) his restoration—secured in October 1307—at an alleged price of 1000 marks to the papal coffers. Hoton died at Poitiers on 9 January 1308.

In the estimation of the Durham chronicler Robert Graystanes, Hoton was a well-educated man, eloquent, and of good presence. At his first confrontation with Bishop Bek in January 1286 he had declared: 'I say nothing to your prejudice, only to preserve the state of my office and the ancient custom of my house. I do not aspire to any worldly dignity' (*Durham Annals*, 66). It was his misfortune to be matched against an even more determined churchman. His lawsuits, by making it necessary to raise loans from foreign bankers, were a heavy drain on the priory's revenue, and their memory was a deterrent against future disputes with the bishops. The papal ordinance 'Debent', defining numbers for episcopal visitations, was incorporated into the *Extravagantes* of the canon law.

C. M. FRASER

Sources F. Barlow, ed., *Durham annals and documents of the thirteenth century*, SurtS, 155 (1945), 66–7, 69–76, 82 · *Records of Antony Bek … 1283–1311*, ed. C. M. Fraser, SurtS, 162 (1953), 30–31, 34, 59–78, 83–5, 86–7, 100–01, 113–20, 139, 149–51, 182, 188, 192, 204–8 · *Historiae Dunelmensis scriptores tres: Gaufridus de Coldingham, Robertus de Graystanes, et Willielmus de Chambre*, ed. J. Raine, SurtS, 9 (1839), 70–89 · bursars' accounts, 1293, U. Durham L., archives and special collections, Durham dean and chapter muniments · bursars' accounts, 1306, U. Durham L., archives and special collections, Durham dean and chapter muniments · register I, U. Durham L., archives and special collections, Durham dean and chapter muniments, fol. 57v. · C. M. Fraser, *A history of Antony Bek* (1957), 44–7, 122–75, 219: see esp. 150, no. 1 · R. B. Dobson, *Durham Priory, 1400–1450*, Cambridge Studies in Medieval Life and Thought, 3rd ser., 6 (1973), 212, 342–4

Archives Durham Cath. CL, register I, fol. 57v

Hotspur. *See* Percy, Sir Henry (1364–1403).

Hotten, John Camden (1832–1873), publisher and writer, was born at 45 St John's Square, Clerkenwell, London, on 12 September 1832, the son of William Hotten of Probus, Cornwall, a master carpenter who was variously described as an undertaker and a builder, and his wife, Maria, *née* Cowling, of Roche, Cornwall. John Camden Hotten's original middle name was William and it is not clear when or why he adopted the name Camden.

In 1846 Hotten was apprenticed to the antiquary, author, publisher, and bookseller John Petheram of 71 Chancery Lane, London. He did not complete his time with Petheram (Mark Twain suggested that he was caught selling some of Petheram's books on his own account) and he left for North America with his brother in 1848. He seems to have tried his hand at many jobs while in the USA including coal mining and journalism. He was probably back in Britain by 1853 and was acting as some form of travelling salesman. A diary he left from this period shows him unhappy in his home life and agonized by worries about his spiritual and physical health, the latter problem being associated with occasional drinking binges. By mid-1855 he had set up a bookselling and publishing business in London—possibly having taken over Messrs Cockburn and Campbell—at 151B Piccadilly (he later moved to larger premises at 74–5 Piccadilly), publishing his first recorded pamphlet in 1856. On 14 September 1867 he married Charlotte Stringer (d. 1888), daughter of William Stringer, designer. They had three daughters, two of whom survived to adulthood.

Hotten was frantically busy as a bookseller, publisher, journalist, author, controversialist, and general textual entrepreneur. His range of publishing interests was wide, and included comic books (such as W. S. Gilbert's *Bab Ballads*, 1868), 'How to' books on conjuring tricks (1871) and stamp collecting (1864), collections of political speeches (Bright's, 1869, Disraeli's, 1870), and dictionaries. His particular strengths lay in illustrated books (he was a pioneer in the use of chromolithography); in producing historical facsimiles and works of popular antiquarian history (such

as *The History of Signboards*, 1866); and in local and family history, where he offered a full ancestor-tracing service under the title St James' Heraldic Office. In literature he published works by European writers such as Balzac (1860), Baudelaire (1869), and de la Barca (1870), and was responsible for promoting (at low prices between 1s. and 2s. 6d) a number of American writers in the British market including Artemus Ward, J. R. Lowell, Bret Harte, O. W. Holmes, Walt Whitman, and Mark Twain.

Not all these books were authorized editions but, as no copyright agreement then existed between the UK and the USA, these publications were not illegal. However, Hotten was frequently tempted to intervene in his publications and Twain and others reasonably objected to seeing their texts amended or added to others they had not written. On other occasions Hotten was more clearly on the wrong side of the law. In 1862 Tennyson took Hotten to chancery over the republication of suppressed poems originally published in the 1830s—and won. This may not have stopped Hotten selling *Poems MDCCCXXX / MDCCCXXXIII* under the counter. Hotten was a natural risk-taker: he published or republished books on phallic worship (1869) and aphrodisiacs (1869); he had a particular line in flagellation literature, which ranged from *A History of the Rod* (1870) to a collection of mostly eighteenth-century flagellation pamphlets under the general title of Library Illustrative of Social Progress (1873). There is some evidence that he also dealt in pornographic paintings and photographs and operated a small circulating library of pornographic works available to a select mailing list.

Hotten the publisher was also capable of nobler projects: he published Swinburne's *Poems and Ballads* (1866) when its original publisher, Moxon, got cold feet and, despite worsening relations with the poet, went on to produce a number of Swinburne's other works, including *William Blake: a Critical Essay* (1868), which was illustrated by hand-coloured lithographs. Hotten was also the first publisher to reprint an entire work by Blake, *The Marriage of Heaven and Hell* (1867), since the poet's death. Hotten's interest in radical Romantic poets was also expressed in a planned three-volume (finally four) edition of Shelley's *Poetry and Prose* (1871–5), and in 1872 he published MacCarthy's ground-breaking *Shelley's Early Life from Original Sources*, the first to use the spy-reports in the Public Record Office. Hotten's journalistic training made him a great occasional publisher, and he produced a flurry of cheap books and pamphlets in response to the Franco-Prussian War and the subsequent invasion scares over the period 1870–72. He was able to publish biographies of Macaulay, Thackeray, and Dickens, each within a month of the respective author's death, writing the first two himself.

As an author Hotten was diverse and prolific, his works including *A Dictionary of Modern Slang, Cant and Vulgar Words* (1859), *A Hand-Book to the Topography and Family History* (1863), *The History of Signboards* (with Larwood) (1866), *Abyssinia and its People* (1867), *Literary Copyright* (1871), *The original lists of persons of quality … and others who went from Great Britain to the American plantations, 1600–1700* [1873], and *The Golden Treasury of Thought* (1874). In addition he contributed articles on literary news to the *Literary Gazette* (1862), *The Parthenon* (1862–3), and the *London Review* (1863–4). Hotten was a man of furious energy and indestructible enthusiasm, often working for twelve hours and more a day. He managed to alienate many of the writers he dealt with, and was always regarded with suspicion by other publishers. Nevertheless he was a great publishing innovator—for instance, the first to issue complete paperback editions of novels at 6*d.* (Hotten's Library of World-Wide Authors) as early as 1866.

Hotten's last year was made miserable by ill health, a feckless brother-in-law, and a strong sense that his chief clerk, Andrew Chatto, was negotiating behind his back. He died on 14 June 1873 at his home, 4 Maitland Park Villas, Haverstock Hill, Hampstead, London, of an intestinal canal embolism and was buried in Highgate cemetery. He died intestate. His widow sold the business as a going concern to Chatto and his sleeping partner W. E. Windus for the substantial sum of £25,000.   SIMON ELIOT

Sources S. Eliot, '"Hotten, rotten, forgotten"?: an apologia for a general publisher', *Book History* (2000), 61–93 · *Mark Twain's letters*, ed. L. Salamo and H. E. Smith, 5 (1997) · D. Ganzel, 'Samuel Clemens and John Camden Hotten', *The Library*, 5th ser., 20 (Sept 1965), 230–42 · O. Warner, introduction, *A century of writers, 1855–1955*, ed. D. M. Low and others (1955) · D. Welland, *Mark Twain in England* (1978)

Archives Bodl. Oxf., bills and corresp. with Sir Thomas Phillips · U. Edin. L., corresp. with James Halliwell-Phillips · U. Reading L., Chatto and Windus archive

Wealth at death under £20,000: administration, 4 July 1873, *CGPLA Eng. & Wales*

Hottentot Venus, the. *See* Baartman, Sara (1777×88–1815/16).

Houblon, Sir James (*bap.* 1629, *d.* 1700). *See under* Houblon, Sir John (1632–1712).

Houblon, Sir John (1632–1712), merchant, was born on 13 March 1632, the third son in the family of ten sons and three daughters of James Houblon (1592–1682), merchant, and his wife Marie du Quesne (or Ducane). He became more eminent than any of his nine brothers, four of whom were also prosperous merchants and two of whom served on the directorate of the Bank of England.

The Houblons were descendants of a largely protestant, French-speaking (Walloon) family centred in Lille, and although Sir John's father was born and bred in London, he retained close ties with the French protestant church in Threadneedle Street, of which he was an elder. As a leading citizen, and member of the Merchant Adventurers' Company, he was well placed to establish his numerous sons in London's overseas commerce. John, like most of his brothers, specialized in trade to Portugal, as well as with Spain, Italy, and the Mediterranean. In 1669, for example, he imported oil from Italy, wine from Spain, and canvas and linens from France, while exporting large amounts of English cloth to Portugal and re-exporting some of the canvas to Virginia. Four of his merchant brothers followed an identical pattern and, as Pepys observed, the five were as notable for their mutual

Sir John Houblon (1632–1712), by R. Williams (after John Closterman, 1695–6)

affection as for their evident prosperity. Like most of London's trading community, they were to gain handsomely from England's neutrality during the Franco-Dutch conflicts of 1674–8, and their returns from Spain, largely in silver, were profitably sold on to the East India Company, in which they held shares.

John Houblon became a member of the Grocers' Company, in which he served as warden in 1682 and master in 1690–91. In 1688 he was chosen as common councilman for the Broad Street ward and on 17 September 1689 he began his long tenure as alderman for the Cornhill ward. The political orientation of the Houblons was comparatively discreet but undoubtedly whig during the Exclusion crisis of 1678–81. John's election as a sheriff for the City of London at midsummer in the post-revolution year of 1689 was significant, and on 29 October 1689 he was knighted by William III. In 1692 and 1693 he was a whig candidate for the mayoralty, which he was reluctant to assume, but under royal pressure he was finally chosen lord mayor on 28 September 1695.

Regardless of his political sympathies, John Houblon had long been useful to the government as an adviser on commercial and financial matters. Serving on the directorate of the powerful Levant Company in 1691–5, he petitioned vigorously during the Nine Years' War for the naval protection of the Anglo-Portuguese trade in which he and his brothers were leading participants and on 30 January 1694 he was commissioned as a lord of the Admiralty, an appointment rarely given to mere merchants, which he held until 1699. His reputation for acumen and great wealth also made him a natural choice, by ballots of the subscribers, first as a director and then as first governor of the new Bank of England which received its charter on 27 July 1694. Sir John, who had subscribed £10,000 to the flotation, was thus deeply involved in financing the most difficult period of the Nine Years' War and on 5 December 1696 he attended the House of Commons to render account for the bank's funding operations. His two-year term as governor was extended into 1697 and in 1994, to mark the tercentenary of the bank's foundation, his portrait was embodied in the design of a new £50 note. In 1702 he was appointed as a commissioner for navy victualling and on 16 March 1704 he was chosen by the House of Lords as one of the parliamentary commissioners of accounts. He also served as a director of the New East India Company set up in 1698 to rival the largely tory Old East India Company.

In July 1660 John Houblon married Mary (d. 1732), daughter of Isaac Jurin (or Jurion), a London merchant of Flemish protestant origin. They had five sons and six daughters, but only two sons survived their father and they had no heirs. The family lived in some style in their mansion off Threadneedle Street, adjoining their parish church of St Christopher-le-Stocks, on the site later occupied by the Bank of England. In October 1694 Sir John had secured the bank's transfer of its offices from the Mercers' Company premises to those of his own company, the Grocers, where it remained until 1734. He also acquired a country house at High Ongar in Essex. He played little part in the activities of the French protestant church, but served as a trustee for funds set up to support French refugees in linen manufacture at Ipswich. Sir John died suddenly on 10 January 1712 at his London home and was buried at St Christopher-le-Stocks on 18 January 1712.

His elder brother, **Sir James Houblon** (bap. 1629, d. 1700), merchant, baptized on 26 July 1629, at St Mary Woolchurch, London, was the second son of James and Marie and shared in the family's Iberian trading interests, while also holding directorships in the East India Company and Levant Company. He was of even more moderate whig sympathies than John and was a very reluctant candidate for election as a member of parliament for the City in 1690. In September 1692, however, after much service as a London common councilman (1675–83, 1688–90, and 1691–2) he became alderman for the Aldersgate ward and was knighted shortly after. He joined his brother John on the first directorate of the Bank of England and made valuable contributions of skill, knowledge, and money to the funding of the Nine Years' War. Selected as a commissioner of accounts in April 1694 he held responsibility to parliament for the scrutiny of government expenditure and, with his brother John, gave forceful advice on the protection of English overseas trade. In July 1698, after much prompting, he stood successfully for election as one of the members of parliament for the City of London, but he was already a sick man and was unable to make any mark in the House of Commons. He died on 25 October 1700 and was buried at St Benet Paul's Wharf, where on 11 May 1658 he had married Sarah Wynne. His will recognized his attachment to the French protestant church, and to the poor of those London and Essex parishes in which he had houses. Of his two sons, Wynne and James, and his two daughters, Catherine and Elizabeth, only Elizabeth was married, but she failed to produce heirs.

H. G. ROSEVEARE

Sources A. A. Houblon, *The Houblon family: its story and times*, 1 (1907) · J. R. Woodhead, *The rulers of London, 1660–1689* (1965) · A. B. Beaven, ed., *The aldermen of the City of London, temp. Henry III–*[1912], 1 (1908) · 'Houblon, Sir James (1629–1700)', HoP, *Commons* [draft] · *Letters and the second diary of Samuel Pepys*, ed. R. G. Howarth (1932) · Pepys, *Diary* · N. Luttrell, *A brief historical relation of state affairs from September 1678 to April 1714*, 6 vols. (1857) · J. Clapham, *The Bank of England: a history*, 1 (1944) · P. G. M. Dickson, *The financial revolution in England: a study in the development of public credit, 1688–1756* (1967) · H. E. S. Fisher, *The Portugal trade: a study of Anglo-Portuguese commerce, 1700–1770* (1971) · H. Horwitz, *Parliament, policy and politics in the reign of William III* (1977) · J. M. S. Brooke and A. W. C. Hallen, eds., *The transcript of the registers of … St Mary Woolnoth and St Mary Woolnoth Haw … 1538 to 1760* (1886) · E. Freshfield, ed., *The register book of the parish of St Christopher le Stocks*, 3 vols. in 1 (1882), vol. 2, p. 62 · R. Gwynn, ed., *Minutes of the consistory of the French church of London, Threadneedle Street, 1679–1692*, Huguenot Society of Great Britain and Ireland, 58 (1994), 61, 311, 347 · G. S. De Krey, *A fractured society: the politics of London in the first age of party, 1688–1715* (1985) · *Markets and merchants of the late seventeenth century: the Marescoe-David letters, 1668–1680*, ed. H. Roseveare, British Academy, Records of Social and Economic History, new ser., 12 (1987)

Archives priv. coll. | CLRO, repertories of the court of aldermen · PRO, Colonial Office MSS, CO 388, 389 · PRO, chancery masters' exhibits, C 114/64–78 · PRO, state papers domestic, SP 29

Likenesses I. Whood, oils, Bank of England, London · R. Williams, mezzotint (after J. Closterman, 1695–6), BM, NPG [*see illus.*] · portraits, priv. coll.

Wealth at death property; minor bequests: will, proved 1/2/1712, PRO, PROB 11/525, sig. 31 · over £100,000

Hough, John (1651–1743), college head and bishop of Worcester, was the son of John Hough, citizen of London (but of Cheshire descent), and Margaret Byrche, daughter of John Byrche of Leacroft, Staffordshire, born in Middlesex on 12 April 1651; it was probably his baptism recorded thirteen days later as a haberdashers son at St Lawrence Jewry, London. Schooled perhaps at Birmingham or (more probably) Walsall, he became a demy of Magdalen College, Oxford, in November 1669, graduated BA in 1673, and obtained a fellowship, took holy orders, and proceeded MA in the three successive years.

Hough became domestic chaplain to James Butler, duke of Ormond, after the duke passed through Oxford to Ireland in 1677. But in 1679 Hough was still at Oxford, his rooms being searched (ironically enough, in view of his later role) for incriminating letters relating to the Popish Plot. More characteristically he is said to have preached a sermon in Dublin in October 1682 that led 'popish lords' to threaten that he would 'never have any preferment in Ireland or in England' (Macray, 391). The expected benefits to a lord lieutenant's chaplain did elude him, but in 1686 he obtained a Worcester prebend, a living at Tempsford, Bedfordshire, and the degree of BD.

John Hough (1651–1743), by Sir Godfrey Kneller, c.1700

Hough came to prominence when the president of Magdalen, Henry Clerke, died on 31 March 1687. James II directed the fellows to elect Anthony Farmer, a Roman Catholic, statutorily ineligible as unconnected with the foundation, and whose reputation offered at least some material for exaggerated polemical attack. The fellows, encouraged by the visitor, Peter Mews, bishop of Winchester, requested another nominee from the crown but, when the statutory fortnight for the election expired, none the less elected Hough on 15 April by eleven votes to two. Mews admitted him the following day. His particular recommendation, being a relative 'academic nonentity' (Beddard, 941), was his connection with Ormond, from whom the fellows persistently sought support, as chancellor of the university. They hoped, unavailingly, that Ormond could repeat his intervention in repelling Catholic intruders from the Charterhouse. Hough, with legal advice from his maternal uncle, Serjeant Edward Byrche, led in carrying 'resistance to extremes' (Beddard, 943).

A delegation of fellows (excluding Hough), summoned before the court of high commission at Westminster on 22 June, was told that the election was void; on the same day the university defiantly made 'President' Hough DD. Abandoning Farmer, James ordered the fellows on 14 August to elect Samuel Parker, bishop of Oxford, and appeared in Oxford on 4 September to abuse them for failing to do so. William Penn came to advise submission; Hough demurred, fearing that after Magdalen 'the papists … will have the rest' of the university (Bloxam, 105). Continuing obstinacy brought a special visitation of the college by Thomas Cartwright, bishop of Chester, Sir Robert Wright, and Sir Thomas Jenner. Hough set the example for all but one of the fellows in submitting to this so far as law

and the college statutes allowed—which was, in his view, not at all, as the commission bypassed the college's own visitor and in June he had been arbitrarily deprived, unheard. On 22 October 1687 Hough's name was struck from the college books; he appealed to 'the king in his courts of justice' (Bloxam, 136), fruitlessly if whiggishly preferring the common law. Jenner punned, 'Do not think to huff us, sir' (Macaulay, 2.105), and the bystanders' reaction caused Hough to be bound over for £2000 into king's bench for inciting a riot. On 25 October Parker was declared president and the lodgings broken open, as Hough had retained the keys.

The other fellows declined to improve their submission and, still harping on their statutes, were expelled the following month; first Hough and then the rest were declared incapable of ecclesiastical preferment, but clearly received financial backing. Hough managed to get himself discharged in king's bench, Wright negligently failing to block this as James ordered. Hough remained in London with Edward Byrche during the winter of 1687–8 but, having the reputation of being 'a centre of correspondence' with 'disaffected' notables (Bloxam, 239), thought it more discreet to retire to Worcester, where he remained undisturbed in his prebend and where he preached in June 1688. In October James belatedly conceded that the fellows might return; they had apparently already been confident enough to agree presentations to college livings. Bishop Mews delayed a few days, but Hough's restoration was accomplished on 25 October 1688, the anniversary of Parker's intrusion. This justified a story that Emilia, countess of Ossory (Ormond's daughter-in-law) had told him then, 'be of good courage, 'tis but twelve months to this day twelve-month' (Macray, 413). Clearly not impoverished the president celebrated his restoration with a dinner, annually emulated since in the college.

Hough avenged the intrusion of Bishop Parker by becoming bishop of Oxford—consecrated by six bishops in May 1690 owing to the default of the nonjuring Archbishop Sancroft—with the Magdalen presidency *in commendam*. He repaired the president's lodgings, gave £1000 for Magdalen's new buildings, and refurbished the bishop's house at Cuddesdon. His divided attention ironically let Magdalen become a haunt of Jacobites. Translated to Lichfield and Coventry in August 1699, he finally resigned the Magdalen presidency in March 1701, not until then performing regular ordinations in his diocese. In May 1702 he married a Staffordshire lady, Lettice Lee (1659–1722), *née* Fisher, widow of Sir Charles Lee.

Most agree that 'all that really distinguished his career is confined to the days of 1687 and 1688' (Macray, 383); or, to put it more positively, 'Bishop Hough seems to have contented himself with the proofs which he had before given of his patriotism' (Wilmot, ix) and avoided political partisanship and theological controversy to the point that even royal commands could barely bring him to publish sermons. In the jaundiced conversations of Thomas Hearne, Hough was noted as 'a nice carver' and nothing heard 'either of his learning or piety' (*Remarks*, 5.169). But to George Lyttelton, holding up Hough as a model resident bishop, his characteristics were 'a decent hospitality and a charity void of ostentation' and modest religious moderation (Wilmot, 71). The epicureanism Hearne implied was in any case restricted by medical problems, causing Hans Sloane to prohibit the reluctant Hough pepper (BL, Sloane MS 4076, fol. 3), though 'strong beer and sugar' (Nash, 2.clxiv) as a panacea may have been his own idea.

Hough's iconic status caused him to be produced for politically appropriate set piece sermons, such as the *Sermon Preached before the … Parliament* (1701) against Rome and the *Sermon Preached before the Queen* (1705) against 'arbitrary power'. Based perhaps on his early experience, Hough was put on the 1690 committee for Church of Ireland appointments, and was also for some years a mainstay of the Society for the Propagation of the Gospel in Foreign Parts. The limitations of his whiggery appeared when he allegedly told Robert Spencer, earl of Sunderland, with extreme tactlessness, that he preferred an honest papist to an opportunist convert to protestantism. It was, however, unsurprising that he should fear Roman Catholics more than dissenters and so (at least from 1703) was active in the Lords against the occasional conformity and schism bills. The 'childish disgusts' of disorganized dissenters could not, he explained, compare with Rome's 'indefatigable industry and restless malice, firmly combined under a despotic power' (Russell, 16–17). By high-churchmen, presumably, he was 'called fanatick in my own diocese' about 1705 (Jones, 767) owing to this stance.

Richard Smalbroke alleged that Hough was offered the archbishopric of Canterbury in 1715, but felt too 'modest' (and, probably, infirm) for its 'perplexing difficulties' (Smalbroke, 20). As Thomas Tenison's chaplain Smalbroke might have known; but, as William Wake's appointment was both rapid and expected, such a proposal cannot have got far. Instead, in September 1717, Hough followed William Lloyd in moving from Lichfield to Worcester. An indefatigable repairer, already active at Eccleshall, Staffordshire, he spent £7000 on the episcopal palaces of Worcester, Hartlebury, and Grimley, and gave £1000 for All Saints' Church, Worcester. In 1729, he declared, 'I will see town no more' (Wilmot, 196); his increasingly conscientious residence was substantially a function of infirmity. Hough died at Hartlebury Castle on 8 May 1743, according to his chaplain of an 'epidemical cold' (Macray, 401). He was buried in Worcester Cathedral. A monument by L. F. Roubiliac showed him facing James II's commissioners in Magdalen hall—still the high point of his career.   JULIAN LOCK

Sources J. Wilmot, *The life of the Rev. John Hough, DD* (1812) · A. Macintyre, 'The college, King James II and the revolution, 1687–8', *Magdalen College and the crown: essays for the tercentenary of the restoration of the college, 1688*, ed. L. Brockliss, G. Harriss, and A. Macintyre (1988) · J. R. Bloxam, ed., *Magdalen College and James II, 1686–1688: a series of documents*, OHS, 6 (1886) · W. D. Macray, 'Table-talk and papers of Bishop Hough, 1703–1743', *Collectanea: second series*, ed. M. Burrows, OHS, 16 (1890), 381–416 · [R. Smalbroke], *Some account of the Right Reverend John Hough* (1743) · W. Russell, 'Memoir', *Sermons and charges by the Right Reverend John Hough, DD* (1821) · *Remarks and collections of Thomas Hearne*, ed. C. E. Doble and others, 11 vols., OHS, 2, 7, 13, 34, 42–3, 48, 50, 65, 67, 72 (1885–1921) · R. A. Beddard,

'James II and the Catholic challenge', *Hist. U. Oxf.* 4: *17th-cent. Oxf.*, 907–54 · E. H. Pearce, *Hartlebury Castle* (1926) · S. Shaw, *The history and antiquities of Staffordshire*, 1 (1798) · T. Nash, *Collections for the history of Worcestershire*, 2 (1782) · *The diary of Thomas Cartwright, bishop of Chester*, ed. J. Hunter, CS, 22 (1843), 87–92 · *The London diaries of William Nicolson, bishop of Carlisle, 1702–1718*, ed. C. Jones and G. Holmes (1985) · F. G. James, 'The bishops in politics, 1688–1714', *Conflict in Stuart England*, ed. W. A. Aiken and B. D. Henning (1960), 227–57 · C. Jones, 'Debates in the House of Lords on "the church in danger", 1705, and on Dr Sacheverell's impeachment, 1710', *HJ*, 19 (1976), 759–71 · N. Sykes, *William Wake, archbishop of Canterbury*, 2 vols. (1957) · W. Wake, correspondence, Christ Church Oxf., Wake MSS 4, 6–8, 10, 17, 20–23 · BL, Sloane MS 4076 · Oxford episcopal register, Oxfordshire Archives, MS Oxf. dioc. d. 106 · episcopal register, Lichfield, Staffs. RO, LRJO B/A/1/19 · T. B. Macaulay, *The history of England from the accession of James II*, new edn, 3 vols. (1906), vol. 2, pp. 95–108 · R. O'Day and F. Heal, *Princes and paupers in the English church* (1981) · Worcester episcopal register, Worcs. RO, BA 2648/11 (i) · battels books, 1696–1704, Magd. Oxf., archives, BB/3 · A. W. Hughes Clarke, ed., *The register of St Lawrence Jewry, London*, 1, Harleian Society, registers, 70 (1940), 54 · G. E. Cokayne and E. A. Fry, eds., *Calendar of marriage licences issued by the faculty office, 1632–1714*, British RS, 33 (1905), 192 · E. O. Browne and J. W. Willis Bund, eds., *Register of Worcester Cathedral, 1693–1811*, Worcestershire Parish Register Society, 1 (1913), 52 · will, PRO, PROB 11/726, fol. 324

Archives Oxon. RO, Oxfordshire Archives, register, Oxf. dioc. MS d. 106 · Staffs. RO, register, LJRO B/A/1/19 · Worcs. RO, register, BA 2648/11 (i) | BL, letter to Lord Digby, Add. MS 42590 · BL, letters to John Ellis, Add. MSS 28884, 28927, 28940 · BL, letters to the earl of Hardwicke, Add. MSS 35586, 35587 · BL, letters to Mrs Knightley, Add. MS 9828 · BL, letters to Hans Sloane, MSS 4043, 4046, 4048, 4059, 4076 · Bodl. Oxf., letter to Arthur Charlett, Tanner MS 22 · Christ Church Oxf., letters to Archbishop Wake · LPL, letters, MSS 933, 1373, 2457, 3152 · LPL, Society for the Propagation of the Gospel MSS · Welbeck Abbey, Worksop, Nottinghamshire, Portland MSS, corresp. with duchess of Newcastle

Likenesses R. Williams, mezzotint, c.1690 (after J. Riley), BM, NPG; repro. in J. F. Kerslake, *Early Georgian portraits in the National Portrait Gallery* (1977), pl. 413 · S. Digby, watercolour miniature, c.1695–1720, NPG; repro. in Wilmot, *Life*, frontispiece · G. Kneller, oils, c.1700, LPL [*see illus.*] · J. Faber senior, mezzotint, 1715, BM, NPG; repro. in J. Kerslake, *Early Georgian portraits in the National Portrait Gallery* (1977), pl. 414 · J. Richardson, drawing, c.1720, Magd. Oxf.; repro. in *Magdalen College and the crown* (1988), frontispiece · attrib. E. Seaman, portrait, c.1720, Bodl. Oxf. · attrib. J. Dyer, oils, 1734, Magd. Oxf.; copy, bishop's palace, Lichfield · J. Dyer, portrait, 1736, Hartlebury Castle, Worcestershire · T. White, bust, c.1738–1742, All Saints Church, Worcester · J. Faber junior, mezzotint, c.1742 (after J. Dyer, 1736), BM, NPG; repro. in J. F. Kerslake, *Early Georgian portraits in the National Portrait Gallery* (1977), pl. 416 · L. F. Roubiliac, funerary bas-relief, 1746, Worcester Cathedral; repro. in *Magdalen College and the crown* (1988), pl. 2 · G. Kneller, oils, second version, copy, Hartlebury Castle, Worcestershire

Wealth at death legacies of £756 plus £5 to each servant (number unspecified); annuities of £50; loan of £1000 converted into gift: will, PRO, PROB 11/726, fol. 324 · kept £1000 in cash in case of charitable application; Oxford income conventionally est. £600, Lichfield £1400, Worcester up to £3000: O'Day and Heal, *Princes and paupers*

Houghton. For this title name *see* Milnes, Richard Monckton, first Baron Houghton (1809–1885).

Houghton, Adam of (*d.* 1389), bishop of St David's and chancellor of England, was born at Caerforiog, Whitchurch, Pembrokeshire, though his name shows him to have been of English origin. Educated at Oxford, he had taken the degree of DCL by 1340. He may be the Adam de Houton, clerk of Oxford, charged with wounding Jo. le

Blake of Tadyngton in 1338. He was concerned with Geoffrey Scrope in a disagreement with the university over elections in June 1344. On 20 June 1376 he was one of the commissioners employed to settle a dispute between the university and the faculty of laws.

Houghton was admitted precentor of St David's on 26 December 1339, and between then and 1358 he acquired a number of preferments, but gave them all up when he became a bishop. Having become king's clerk by 1352 and been admitted advocate at the court of arches, on 18 July 1355, he was engaged on business for the king in France in 1360 and again in 1361. On 20 September 1361 he was papally provided to the see of St David's, and was consecrated bishop at St Mary's, Southwark, by William Evendon, bishop of Winchester.

As a supporter of the court Houghton was a trier of petitions in every parliament down to 1377. Probably through the influence of John of Gaunt, he was appointed chancellor of England on 11 April 1377. In April of the same year he headed the commission sent to negotiate peace with France, but on account of Edward III's death he was recalled. He was resworn chancellor on 26 June 1377 and held the office until 29 October 1378. In his addresses to parliament, Houghton made somewhat ludicrous use of biblical texts. In 1380 he was employed in negotiations for the marriage of Richard II with Anne of Bohemia.

Five sets of Houghton's statutes—published in 1365, 1368, 1379, 1380, and 1384—survive in the statute book of St David's (BL, Harley MS 6280) and are mainly concerned with economic conditions in his diocese and the state of clerical residence there. He established the cathedral school and endowed the choristers, and is also reputed to have erected the vicars' college. His chief foundation was the fine college of St Mary, which he, in conjunction with John of Gaunt, established in 1365, and handsomely endowed. Its main object was to strengthen the number of clerks and choristers resident at St David's. Houghton was also responsible for the cloisters which connect the college with the cathedral.

Between the years 1379 and 1382 Houghton was involved with William Nicoll, prebendary of Llanddewi-brefi, in a lengthy lawsuit at the Roman curia. As a result, according to a curious tradition surviving at St David's, Houghton was excommunicated by Pope Clement VI (in fact probably the anti-pope Clement VII, r. 1378–94) and in return excommunicated the pope. This episode was said by the eighteenth-century antiquary Yardley to be 'shew'd in the paintings of the windows of his college' (Yardley, 57). Houghton died at St David's on 13 February 1389 and was buried in the chapel of his college under a large tomb, since destroyed. His will, dated 8 February 1389, was proved on 23 May 1389.   GLANMOR WILLIAMS

Sources E. Yardley, *Menevia sacra*, ed. F. Green (1927) · W. B. Jones and E. A. Freeman, *The history and antiquities of St David's* (1856) · Emden, *Oxf.* · *Fasti Angl.*, *1300–1541*, [Welsh dioceses] · W. Stubbs, *Registrum sacrum Anglicanum*, 2nd edn (1897) · *RotP* · Rymer, *Foedera* · G. Williams, *The Welsh church from conquest to Reformation*, rev. edn (1976) · J. R. L. Highfield, 'The English hierarchy in the reign of Edward III', *TRHS*, 5th ser., 6 (1956), 115–38 · Tout, *Admin. hist.* · J. Campbell, *Lives of the lord chancellors*, 7 vols. (1845–7)
Archives BL, Harley MS 6280
Wealth at death see Emden, *Oxf.*, 2.973

Houghton, Arthur Boyd (1836–1875), painter and illustrator, was born on 13 March 1836 at Kotagiri Hill Station in the Nilgiris of Madras, India, the fourth son of John Michael Houghton (1797–1874), a commander in the East India Company's marine, and his wife, Sophia Elizabeth Renshaw (1805–1888), the daughter of the customs master of Bombay. Poor sight caused by the loss of his right eye in childhood failed to discourage his ambition to be a painter. On leaving school in 1852 at the age of sixteen, however, Houghton was enrolled at St Bartholomew's Hospital medical school in London. But his parents' hopes that he would follow a surgeon's career were short-lived: in 1853 he began preparatory studies at Leigh's General Practical School of Art in Newman Street, Holborn, where the Paris-trained James Mathews Leigh prepared candidates for further training at the Royal Academy Schools. Houghton entered the Royal Academy Schools in 1854, but after three years failed to be accepted by the painting school. He completed his studies at Leigh's and its corollary, the Artists' Society or 'the Langham'.

This body offered life classes, with both clothed and nude models, lectures, and a wardrobe of historical costume—facilities not then available even in the Royal Academy Schools. Here, with older artists such as Charles Keene, Houghton learned the art of meeting deadlines, interpreting set weekly genre or literary subjects. He grew a bushy, Bengal cavalry-style beard and sported a black eyepatch and began portraying scenes of London life: such paintings as *Punch & Judy* (1860; Tate collection), *Volunteers* (1860; Tate collection), and *Holborn in 1861* (priv. coll.) made a significant contribution to Victorian narrative art. On 26 February 1861 he married Susan Elizabeth (1841–1864), the daughter of Thomas Gronow, domestic chaplain to the earl of Lisburne; she is an elusive figure whose haunting beauty Houghton immortalized in an illustration for *The Family* in 1861 and numerous magazine plates. Three years later, on 13 July 1864, Susan Houghton died of pyaemia (blood poisoning) after giving birth to their third child, an irreparable loss that drove Houghton to drink. He turned to illustration as a means of supporting his three children.

It was probably Keene, then at the start of his humorous reporting for *Punch*, who came to Houghton's rescue and introduced the grief-stricken widower to his former employer, the master engraver J. W. Whymper. Under Whymper's tutelage Houghton evolved an innovative technique. Before the introduction of photomechanical techniques of reproduction, drawings were painstakingly transferred to type-high woodblocks; Houghton's, however, were reproduced with comparative freshness, as he drew in pen and ink on the polished boxwood block, which was thinly coated with Chinese white to resemble paper. Thus every line engraved was an exact facsimile of his combination of thick and thin brush strokes and crosshatched pen strokes. Like Keene he had learned much from the masterly illustrations for *Frederick the Great* (1843) by the innovative German illustrator Adolf Von Menzel. An equally important influence on his style was the work of the Japanese masters Utamaro and Hiroshige, whose block prints were first shown in England at the London Exhibition of 1862.

Houghton's success in overcoming the limitations of wood-engraving immediately brought his work to the attention of the influential Dalziel brothers, who dominated illustrated publishing. Although they were not the only talented engravers of their day—Joseph Swain, Edmund Evans, W. J. Linton, and Whymper were of the same calibre—the Dalziels were unique in acting also as art directors, designers, printers, and publishers of both books and periodicals. This package proved attractive to young publishing entrepreneurs such as Alexander Strahan, Fredrick Warne, and William Luson Thomas, as it enabled them to maintain a steady stream of profitable publications aimed at an expanding middle-class reading public. Until 1864 Houghton found illustration a natural and remunerative corollary to his painting, and his early work for the periodical *Good Words* includes some of the finest examples of Victorian illustration. His output of more than a thousand published illustrations appeared in monthly magazines, weekly reviews or news magazines, and books. Houghton's lyrical designs for the Warne edition of the *Arabian Nights* (1863) and the wryly humorous illustrations for the same publisher's edition of *Don Quixote* (1866) remain masterpieces of Victorian book illustration. His draughtsmanship was bold and inventive and his mastery of visual effects has been compared to that of Gustave Doré: Forrest Reid commented that his naturalism was 'modified by a temperament … which inclined him to seek the bizarre and fantastic even in ordinary life' (Reid, 187). The complex and rather disturbing presentation of children in Houghton's illustrations to *Home Thoughts and Home Scenes* (1865) hints at depths beneath these scenes of domestic comfort in a manner characteristic of the most intriguing of his images.

It was in the pages of the weekly *Graphic*, launched by William Luson Thomas in December 1869, that Houghton grew to full stature not only as a 'special artist' (artist-reporter) but, with his chronicle of a seven-month trip to America from October 1869 to April 1870, as a sophisticated observer of modern life. From the moment Houghton began his journey he conveyed the romance and excitement of travel: his portrayals of the embarkation at Liverpool in the driving rain, the voyage across the Atlantic, and the cavernous steerage crowded with emigrants are vivid, even weird. He found New York a city of violent and exotic contrasts: he had arrived during Grant's first term as president, which coincided with the heyday of robber barons such as Jim Fisk and political fixers such as Boss Tweed. Yet he was attracted by the sheer vitality of the city. He paid a graceful tribute to American femininity in *Ladies' Window at the New York Post Office* (which appeared in *The Graphic* of 23 April 1870) and caught the flamboyant luxury of *Barbers' Saloon at the Fifth Avenue Hotel* (16 April 1870). Another powerful image, *New York Veils* (26 March 1870), portrayed a disabled civil war veteran begging in Fifth Avenue from a pair of wealthy widows in mourning.

Houghton travelled on to Boston, where he depicted an old-fashioned snowy New England winter (30 April 1870). From Boston he proceeded to the Shaker commune at Lebanon Springs, near the boundary of Massachusetts and New York, and devoted some of his best designs to the portrayal of their simple and austere way of life. The Wild West was even more to his taste: 'Off to the plains', he wrote, before leaving on a three-day buffalo hunt with the young Buffalo Bill Cody, 'is nothing less than inspiring, this thought of leaving civilisation all behind' (*The Graphic*, 5 Aug 1871, 135–6). He also stayed in a Pawnee village (illustrated in *The Graphic* of 28 July 1870) and paid a visit to the Mormon utopia at Salt Lake City (2 September 1871), newly accessible because of the recently completed Union Pacific Railway. Houghton's 'Graphic America' created a sensation on both sides of the Atlantic. American readers protested at the presentation of the shady side of New York in such images as *New York Police* (26 March 1870) and *Tammany Democratic Procession in New York* (26 March 1870). But it was not only the glitter and the gaucherie of New York that Houghton pricked with his rapier-like pen: in his 'Sketches in London', printed in *The Graphic* between 1869 and 1872, he turned his sharp satire against his native capital.

The war between France and Germany in 1870–71, especially its bloody aftermath, the Paris commune, was Houghton's next reporting assignment for *The Graphic*. Plunged into the midst of a ferocious civil war, he found the commune a test of his own political dissent. 'Paris under the Commune' appeared but sporadically, with illustrations relatively few in number. None the less, *A Barricade in Paris* (3 April 1871), *Womens' Club at the Boule Noir* (13 May 1871), and *The Commune, or, Death* (10 June 1871) rank among the most chillingly authoritative images of that holocaust.

Houghton has been described as 'arguably the greatest member of the Idyllic group' (Goldman, 126), a school of sixties illustrators—including Fred Walker, George Pinwell, Robert Barnes, and J. W. North—who exhibited a fresh interest in everyday life but with a profound sense of its innate poetry. This fascination with current events was particularly apparent in Houghton's work for *The Graphic*. Like all members of the group, he was influenced by Pre-Raphaelite ideas and style: Sacheverell Sitwell described him as 'a lesser, or unconscious Pre-Raphaelite' (*Narrative Pictures*, 1937, 87), and there are traces of Ford Madox Brown and Millais in his scenes of London life and of his wife and children and touches of Holman Hunt in his oriental-cum-biblical scenes. But his later work was much removed from the medievalizing tendencies of Rossetti and his disciples and exhibits a pervasive satirical and even fantastical influence which can be traced to William Hogarth. Houghton was clearly responsive to the pictorial moralists who had inspired the previous generation of illustrators, most especially George Cruikshank. Van Gogh recognized that Houghton was part of this British tradition of satirical yet impassioned social comment, coloured by a tinge of the phantasmagorical. 'He was', he wrote to his brother Theo, 'somewhat weird and mysterious like Goya. In the same way, quite Goya-like, he also treated the American subjects, but then all at once there are some that by a wonderful soberness remind one of [the French etcher of Parisian scenes Charles] Meryon' (*The Letters of Vincent Van Gogh to his Brother, 1872–1886*, 1927–9, 2.74). Houghton's work is well represented in the Tate collection, the Victoria and Albert Museum, and Kenwood House, and the print room of the British Museum holds the unique Dalziel collection of proofs of his book and magazine illustrations. In America, the Museum of Fine Arts in Boston and the Fogg Art Museum at Harvard hold fine collections of his work.

As was the case with some of his fellow illustrators of the 1860s—Matthew Lawless, George Pinwell, and Fred Walker—Houghton's life was tragically short. He died at the age of thirty-nine of cirrhosis, at his home, 162 King Henry's Road, Hampstead, London, on 25 November 1875, and was buried on 27 November in Paddington old cemetery, Kilburn. It is always a matter of conjecture whether or not an artist who dies young, or before his prime, would have justified the promise of his earlier career. In Houghton, the promise and achievement were crammed into the short space of little more than a decade.

PAUL HOGARTH

Sources P. Hogarth, *Arthur Boyd Houghton: introduction and checklist* (1975) · P. Hogarth, *Arthur Boyd Houghton* (1981) · P. Hogarth, *The artist as reporter* (1986) · L. Housman, *Arthur Boyd Houghton* (1896) · H. Quilter, 'Some graphic artists: Arthur Boyd Houghton', *Universal Review*, 1 (1888), 99 · E. J. Sullivan, 'Arthur Boyd Houghton', *Print Collector's Quarterly*, 10 (1923), 94–122, 125–48 · private information (2004) [S. C. H. Davis] · *Art Journal*, 37 (1875), 47 · W. M. Rossetti, *The Academy* (4 Dec 1875), 586 · *Fun* (11 Dec 1875), 239 · *Concordia* (4 Dec 1875), 510 · *Hampstead & Highgate Express* (27 Nov 1875), 47 · BL OIOC · P. Hogarth, *Artists on horseback: the old West in illustrated journalism, 1857–1900* (1972) · F. Reid, *Illustrators of the sixties* (1928) · P. Goldman, *Victorian illustration: the Pre-Raphaelites, the idyllic school and the high Victorians* (1996) · G. White, *English illustration, 'the sixties': 1855–70* (1897); repr. (1970) · [G. Dalziel and E. Dalziel], *The brothers Dalziel: a record of fifty years' work … 1840–1890* (1901) · G. N. Ray, *The illustrator and the book in England from 1790 to 1914* (1976) · d. cert. · Burke, *Peerage*

Likenesses G. Du Maurier, portrait, repro. in *Punch* (24 Oct 1868) · A. B. Houghton, group portrait, self-portrait (with his family), CUL; repro. in N. Mcleod, ed., *Good Words*, 3 (1862), p. 721 · A. B. Houghton, self-portrait, repro. in *The Argosy*, 1 (1866), frontispiece

Wealth at death under £3000: probate, 23 Feb 1876, CGPLA Eng. & Wales

Houghton, Daniel Francis (1740–1791), traveller in Africa, was born in Ireland, the son of William Houghton. He was commissioned in 1759 in the 69th regiment of foot, and retired in 1778 with the rank of captain, having been on a mission to Morocco in 1772 when stationed in Gibraltar. Heavily in debt, he left for India in 1779 to take employment as an engineer. On the way, the commander of the fleet with whom he travelled captured Goree Island, off the west African coast, from the French. Houghton joined the occupying garrison and held various civilian posts including town-major. He also visited the Gambia River with a view to moving there to trade. In 1781 he became entangled in a dispute between two rival governors, was dismissed, and returned to London. Already a widower, on 20 December 1783 he married Philippa Evelyn, whose considerable fortune was immediately seized by his creditors.

Having failed to interest the government in schemes to exploit the economic potential of the Gambia, in 1790 Houghton approached the committee of the Association for Promoting the Discovery of the Interior of Africa, founded in 1788 (styling himself misleadingly 'Fort-Major', implying it was his military rank). He proposed to go out for them, via the Gambia, to find the reputed cities of 'Houssa and Tombuctoo' and trace the still unknown course of the Niger. He saw the expedition partly as his own commercial venture, and submitted a modest estimate (£260), which the committee gladly accepted. He arrived in November 1790 and equipped himself with an interpreter, a horse, and five asses to carry his trading stock, proposing to travel up the north bank, about 200 miles, to the kingdom of Wuli. But, having heard that the locally established traders, fearing his competition, were plotting with their African wives to have him killed, he took the less frequented south bank, crossing back eventually to Wuli where he was welcomed at Medina by King Jata. He wrote enthusiastically to his wife that the king had given him land for a trading fort where one could live for £10 a year, and make trading profits of 'upwards of eight hundred per cent' (cited in Hallett, 132).

Then misfortune struck: fire broke out in Medina and most of Houghton's trading stock, as well as his personal belongings, were destroyed. His interpreter disappeared with his horse and three asses, and a trade gun exploded in his hands, wounding him in the face and arm. But he was sustained by 'a natural intrepidity of character that seems inaccessible to fear, and an easy flow of constitutional good humour, that even the roughest accidents of life have no power to subdue' (Hallett, 137). Undaunted, he set off for Timbuktu and reached the kingdom of Bondu where the king's son appropriated more of his trade goods. He then moved on to visit the more friendly king of Bambuk. By now the heavy rains had set in, impeding his movements and bringing him down with a fever from which, however, he quickly recovered. He exchanged his two asses for a horse, converted his remaining goods into more portable gold dust, and started out again on 24 July accompanied by an elderly trader who promised to take him to Timbuktu and bring him safely back to the Gambia.

Houghton's experiences thus far were detailed in letters to the secretary of the association. On 1 September he sent a pencilled note from Simbing, in the Moorish kingdom of Ludamar, to a British trader in the Gambia saying he was in good health. The rest of his story was pieced together by Mungo Park, who visited Simbing six years later. He had diverted his journey northwards into country under the influence of desert Moors whose hostility to Europeans Park was himself to experience. His companions refused to venture into Moorish country and left him alone. He then agreed with some Moorish merchants to take him on his journey, but, once underway, they robbed him of all he possessed. He made his way on foot to Tarra, a Moorish settlement, where he was refused food:

> Whether he actually perished of hunger, or was murdered outright by the savage Mahomedans, is not certainly known; his body was dragged into the woods, and I was shown at a distance, the spot where his remains were left to perish. (Park, 103–4)

By 1794 Mrs Houghton and her three children were in the king's bench prison for debt. The association, which had already given her financial support, added a further £300, and obtained a pension of £30 a year from the government. Houghton's contribution to geographical knowledge was inevitably limited, and overshadowed by Park's, but he remains an engaging and intrepid figure.

CHRISTOPHER FYFE

Sources R. Hallett, *Records of the African Association, 1788–1831* (1964) · PRO, CO 267/18, 19, 20 · *GM*, 1st ser., 64 (1794), 482–3 · M. Park, *Travels* (1799) · *IGI*

Archives Lancs. RO, letters to his wife concerning his travels and domestic affairs · PRO, CO 267/18, 19, 20

Wealth at death lost in debt: Hallett, *Records of the African Association*, 139–40

Houghton, Henry Hall- (1823–1889), Church of England clergyman, son of Jeremiah Houghton, and his wife, Hannah Hall, was born at Dublin on 10 December 1823. He was educated first at Sherborne School, and afterwards obtained a close scholarship at Pembroke College, Oxford. He graduated BA in 1845, and MA in 1848. He was ordained deacon in 1849, and priest in 1850. Until 1852 he served the curacy of St Peter's, Cheltenham, but from that year ill health compelled him to refrain from active work. In 1871, on the death of his uncle, John Hall, honorary canon of Bristol since 1846, he succeeded to the estate of Melmerby, Cumberland, and changed his name to Hall-Houghton. The work of his life was the endeavour to promote the accurate study of holy scripture. In conjunction with Canon Hall, a graduate of St Edmund Hall, which was associated with the evangelical party in the university, he founded at Oxford in 1868, 1870, and 1871 the Canon Hall and the Hall-Houghton prizes for a knowledge of the Greek Testament, the Septuagint, and the Syriac versions, the latter at the suggestion of Robert Payne Smith. To the Church Missionary Society he gave in all a sum of £4500 to promote the systematic study of the Bible in the north of India, west Africa, north-west America, and New Zealand. In 1875 Hall-Houghton married Mary Henrietta, daughter of the Revd John Dawson Hull. He died at Melmerby Hall on 4 September 1889.

A. R. BUCKLAND, rev. M. C. CURTHOYS

Sources *Record* (20 Sept 1889) · *Church Missionary Intelligencer*, 40 (Nov 1889) · J. S. Reynolds, *The evangelicals at Oxford, 1735–1871: a record of an unchronicled movement*, [2nd edn] (1975), 142 · Boase, *Mod. Eng. biog.* · *CGPLA Eng. & Wales* (1889)

Wealth at death £32,462 3s. 2d.: probate, 8 Oct 1889, *CGPLA Eng. & Wales*

Houghton, John of (d. 1246), ecclesiastic, was successively archdeacon of Bedford and of Northampton in the medieval diocese of Lincoln. While nothing is known for certain of his family or early life, he must have had a university education since he was consistently accorded the title of master. He was recognized as a skilful canon lawyer and advocate by September 1214, when he took the case of the abbot-elect in a disputed election at Bury St Edmunds. He is next found in the entourage of Hugh of Wells, bishop of Lincoln, whom he accompanied to Rome for the Fourth Lateran Council (November 1215). Made archdeacon of Bedford by Hugh in 1218 (between 12 June and 2 December), he was at once heavily involved in instituting parsons, ordaining vicarages, holding chapters of the clergy in each of his rural deaneries, and presiding over his court in Bedford. So assiduous were he and his official in their work that complaints were made in royal courts, but the archdeacon's jurisdiction was upheld. By January 1224 he had been recommended for service to the king as a royal emissary, and during the siege of Bedford Castle in the summer of that year he was entrusted with negotiations with its lord, Falkes de Bréauté. After the castle fell to the king's forces, the archdeacon was charged with its dismantling, and he was also sent to Rome to defend, before the pope, the siege and Bréauté's disgrace. In 1225 he was appointed to two prestigious embassies, besides serving as a justice of assize in Bedford and collector of the tax of a fifteenth in the borough of Dunstable.

But thereafter Houghton eschewed such secular employments, evidently preferring clerical pursuits. In January 1226 at a council called to meet in Westminster by a papal nuncio, the archdeacon was chosen by the other prelates to be their spokesman. In 1228–9 he went to Rome, as a representative of the bishops of the province of Canterbury appealing against a metropolitan election made without their participation. The election was indeed quashed, and, apparently at the archdeacon's suggestion, his fellow canon Richard Grant, the chancellor of Lincoln, was named archbishop instead. During the same stay in Rome the archdeacon also successfully represented the dean of Lincoln in an action brought by a cardinal. Promoted to the archdeaconry of Northampton in 1231 (between 9 September and 27 December), he was often appointed by Pope Gregory IX (r. 1227–41) a judge-delegate in great and vexed causes, a clear testimony to his skill as a mediator. When Bishop Hugh died in 1235 the archdeacon was one of the executors of his will, and when Robert Grosseteste was consecrated bishop the archdeacon was not infrequently in his company. But this ceased to be true after November 1236, and for his last decade little is known of the archdeacon's activities. He died in 1246, some time after 17 June. 'Snatched up by an unexpected death', according to Matthew Paris, he died intestate, leaving a great fortune of 5000 marks in money, about thirty cups made of gold and silver, and an infinite number of jewels (Paris, 4.552).

FRED A. CAZEL, JR.

Sources Paris, *Chron.* · *Ann. mon.* · H. R. Luard, ed., *Flores historiarum*, 3 vols., Rolls Series, 95 (1890) · C. W. Foster and K. Major, eds., *The registrum antiquissimum of the cathedral church of*

Lincoln, 10 vols. in 12, Lincoln RS, 27–9, 32, 34, 41–2, 46, 51, 62, 67–8 (1931–73) · W. P. W. Phillimore and others, eds., *Rotuli Hugonis de Welles, episcopi Lincolniensis*, 3 vols., CYS, 1, 3–4 (1907–9) · F. N. Davis, ed., *Rotuli Roberti Grosseteste, episcopi Lincolniensis*, CYS, 10 (1913) · A. W. Gibbons, ed., *Liber antiquus de ordinationibus vicariarum tempore Hugonis Wells, Lincolniensis episcopi, 1209–1235* (1888) · Chancery records

Wealth at death 5000 marks; thirty cups of gold and silver; an infinite number of gems: Paris, *Chron.*

Houghton, John [St John Houghton] (**1486/7–1535**), prior of the London Charterhouse and martyr, was born in Essex. His parents apparently belonged to the local gentry but cannot be identified. According to a fellow monk of the London Charterhouse, Maurice Chauncy, Houghton studied at the University of Cambridge, taking BA, LLB and BTh degrees, but little certain reference to him can be found in the extant university records. While Chauncy gives an eyewitness account of the events at the London Charterhouse, writing a decade later, his statements about matters outside his immediate ken must be treated with caution. Apparently Houghton's parents wished him to marry, but he left home and lived in concealment with a secular priest until he himself was ordained, presumably in 1511. The date of his ordination cannot, however, be traced in the extant episcopal registers. He entered the London Charterhouse some years later, where he was professed in 1515. In 1523 he was sacristan and in 1526 procurator before being transferred to the Charterhouse of Beauvale in Nottinghamshire as prior in 1531. He was elected unanimously prior of the London Charterhouse in November 1531 and appointed visitor of the English province in 1532.

In May 1534 the peace of the community was rudely shattered by the arrival of royal commissioners instructed to obtain oaths from religious communities under the Act of Succession passed earlier that year whereby Katherine of Aragon's daughter, Mary, was to be excluded in favour of Anne Boleyn's daughter, Elizabeth. Thus Henry VIII's marriage to Katherine was to be regarded as *de facto* annulled, and that with Anne Boleyn as valid. The sympathies of the English Carthusians and many monasteries certainly lay with Katherine. Thus Houghton pleaded that he and his community should be exempted from taking the oath, as they had dedicated their lives to God and did not occupy themselves with worldly affairs. The commissioners thereupon arrested both Houghton and his procurator, Humphrey Middlemore, and sent them to the Tower. By the end of the month John Stokesley, bishop of London, and other divines had persuaded them that the required oath was consistent with the Catholic faith and, on swearing, though with reservations, they were thus released and returned to the Charterhouse. The community only agreed to take the oath, again with reservations, after considerable procrastination, and when the presence of armed guards made it obvious what the consequences of refusal would be.

The respite was brief, for in the spring of 1535 it became clear that the community would be required to swear to the Act of Supremacy of late 1534, whereby Henry VIII was to be acknowledged as supreme head of the church in England, under pain of high treason. The London Carthusians prepared themselves for the hour of trial with special masses and general confessions before Houghton, Augustine Webster, the prior of Axholme in Lincolnshire, and Robert Lawrence, the prior of Beauvale, sought an audience with Thomas Cromwell, where they pleaded to be exempted from taking the oath. They were promptly sent to the Tower, where they were soon joined by the Brigittine monk Richard Reynolds of Syon Abbey. On 26 April the three Carthusians were interrogated by Thomas Cromwell and the council. Houghton took notes of the proceedings, sending copies to John Fisher, bishop of Rochester, and the London Charterhouse. Tried by a special commission on 28–9 April, they were sentenced to death, pressure probably having been brought to bear on the jury. The three Carthusians and Richard Reynolds, all wearing their religious habits, and a secular priest, John Hale, vicar of Isleworth, were hanged, drawn, and quartered before a large crowd at Tyburn on 4 May 1535. They met their fate with serenity and courage, Houghton (who was forty-eight years old) declaring on the scaffold: 'Our holy mother the Church has decreed otherwise than the king and parliament have decreed. I am therefore bound in conscience and am ready and willing to suffer every kind of torture rather than deny a doctrine of the Church' (Hendriks, 153). One of Houghton's arms was fixed to the gatehouse of the London Charterhouse, but fifteen members of the community refused all blandishments and threats, preferring death to submission. Five died on the scaffold and the other ten were starved to death in Newgate prison.

Houghton was beatified by Pope Leo XIII on 29 December 1886 and canonized on 25 October 1970, as one of the forty martyrs of England and Wales. His sermons, if ever collected, are no longer extant, but a letter to the vicar of the Cologne Charterhouse, Theodore Loer, dated 23 July 1532, concerning the acquisition of the printed works of Denys the Carthusian, was printed by Hendriks, together with a further letter by John, prior of Beauvale, dated 22 July in an unspecified year, which may well be from Houghton's hand. Meticulous and austere in his observance, Chauncy notes that Houghton 'was slight of stature, elegant in appearance, shy in look, modest in manner, sweet in speech, chaste in body, humble in heart, amiable and beloved by all' (Chauncy, *History of the Sufferings*, 21). He certainly guided his community with admirable acumen, for not all its members were secure in their vocations—Thomas Salter, George Norton, Nicholas Rawlins, John Darley, and Andrew Borde were all clearly monastic misfits—but he inspired most of his monks to a heroism unequalled in any other English monastery of the time.

JAMES HOGG

Sources Pseudo-Erasmus, *Expositio fidelis de morte Th. Mori et quorundam aliorum insigniorum virorum in Anglia* (1535) · T. Petreius, *Bibliotheca Cartusiana, sive, Illustrium sacri Cartusiensis ordinis scriptorum catalogus* (1609), 194–5 · J. Pits, *Relationum historicarum de rebus Anglicis*, ed. [W. Bishop] (Paris, 1619), 724 · P. de Gembloux, *Londres et Grenoble: Henri VIII et les chartreux, Mignard et les supplices* (1838) · Cooper, *Ath. Cantab.*, 1.52 · J. A. Froude, *History of England*, new edn, 12 vols. (1870–75), vol. 2, pp. 363–82 · *LP Henry VIII*, 7, nos.

728, 1046; 8, nos. 566, 609, 661, 675, 726, 898, 901, 904, 932 · R. Challoner, *Della vita e della gloriosa morte di multi sacerdoti e laici occisi in odio della fide Cattolica nell'Inghilterra* (1883) · Gillow, *Lit. biog. hist.*, 3.416 · M. Chauncy, 'Opusculum RP Mauritii Chauncy et de beatis martyribus Anglicis ordinis Carthusiensis, Joanne Houghton et sociis eius', *Analecta Bollandiana*, 6 (1887), 35–51 · J. Morris, *The pictures of the English College at Rome* (1887) · M. Chauncy, *Historia aliquot martyrum Anglorum maxime octodecim Cartusianorum sub rege Henrico octavo ob fidei confessionem et summi pontificis jura vindicanda interemptorum*, 1888 (1550) · *Analecta Juris Pontificii*, 27 (1888), 64 [decree of beatification, 1886] · L. Hendriks, *The London Charterhouse: its monks and its martyrs* (1889) · M. Chauncy, *History of the sufferings of eighteen Carthusians in England* (1890) · V.-M. Doreau, *Henri VIII et les martyrs de la Chartreuse de Londres* (1890) · B. Camm, *The martyrs of the London Charterhouse* (1893) · B. van Ortroy, ed., 'De BB. martyribus Carthusiensibus in Anglia', *Analecta Bollandiana*, 14 (1895), 268–83 · B. van Ortroy, ed., 'M. Chauncy: martyrum monachorum Carthusianorum in Anglia passio minor', *Analecta Bollandiana*, 22 (1903), 51–78 · B. Camm, ed., *Lives of the English martyrs declared blessed by Pope Leo XIII in 1886 and 1895*, 1 (1904) · Venn, *Alum. Cant.*, 1/2.413 · J. Gairdner, *Lollardy and the Reformation in England*, 1 (1908), 420–505 · E. M. Thompson, *The Carthusian order in England* (1930), 371ff. · D. B. Christie, *While the world revolves: being the life and martyrdom of Blessed John Houghton Carthusian monk and martyr* (1932) · D. Mathew and G. Mathew, *The Reformation and the contemplative life: a study of the conflict between the Carthusians and the state* (1934) · M. Chauncy, *The passion and martyrdom of the holy English Carthusian fathers: the short narration*, ed. G. W. S. Curtis (1935) · P. de Toth, *La certosa di Londra e i suoi martiri nella persecuzione di Enrico VIII* (1936) · D. Knowles [M. C. Knowles], *The religious orders in England*, 3 (1959), 222ff. · D. Knowles, *Saints and scholars* (1962), ch. 21 · *Biblioteca sanctorum*, 12 vols. (1961–9), vol. 3, pp. 1140–42 · L. Whatmore, *Blessed Carthusian martyrs* (1983) · *New Catholic encyclopedia*, 18 vols. (1967–89) · 'Decretum de martyrio Joannis Houghton et sociorum qui ob professionem fidei Catholicae saec. XVI–XVII sanguinem fuderunt', *Acta Apostolicae Sedis*, 62 (1970), 555–60 · A. Baglioni, 'Memorie Toscane dei Martiri inglesi', *Revista Diocesana ufficiale di Grosseto, Abbazia delle Tre Fontane in Toscana, e diocesi di Sovana Pitigliana* (May 1971), 416–20 · L. E. Whatmore, 'The Carthusians under King Henry the Eighth', *Analecta Cartusiana*, 109 (1983) · P. Nissen, 'Een schilderij van de marteldood der Londense Kartuizers in 1535 in het Gemeentelijk Museum van Roermond', *De Maasgouw*, 103 (1984), 49–59 · E. Dubois, 'La résistance spirituelle des martyrs anglais des XVIe et XVIIe siècles devant les exigences de l'autorité royale', *Les résistances spirituelles: actes de la Xe rencontre religieuse tenue à Fontevraud, 2–4 octobre 1986* (1987), 63–76 · W. Beutler, 'Vicente Carducho in El Paular', *Analecta Cartusiana*, 130/12 (1997), 238–9, 248 · J. Hogg, 'The pre-reformation priors of the Provincia Angliae', *Analecta Cartusiana*, new ser., 1 (1989), 25–59, particularly 27–8 and n. 90 · J. C. H. Aveling, 'John Houghton', *Dictionnaire d'histoire et de géographie ecclésiastiques*, ed. A. Baudrillart and others (Paris, 1912–)

Archives Archives of the Grande Chartreuse, MSS, etc. · Bibliothèque Nationale, Paris, MSS, etc. · Charterhouse of Parkminster, Sussex, MSS, etc. · GL, MSS, etc. · PRO, MSS, etc.

Likenesses V. Carducho, two portraits (for the charterhouse of El Paular) · S. Cotán, portrait (for the charterhouse of Granada) · F. de Zurbarán, portrait (for the charterhouse of Jerez de la Frontera) · portrait, charterhouse of Trisulti, Italy · portrait, St Hugh's Charterhouse, Parkminster, Sussex · portrait, English College, Rome

Houghton, John (1645–1705), pharmacist and author, was born in Waltham Cross and baptized on 21 July 1645 at Cheshunt, Hertfordshire, one of at least two sons and three daughters of Roger Haughton or Houghton, an embroiderer, perhaps employed at the nearby royal residence of Theobalds. He was briefly at Corpus Christi College, Cambridge, before being apprenticed to Nathaniel

Upton, apothecary and master of the pest house in Finsbury Fields. He long retained a memory of the dreadful plague year and the concomitant desolation of the City. He was a member of the Society of Apothecaries by 1672 and later sat on its court of assistants.

On 11 November 1687 Houghton married Elizabeth Claget of Greenwich. Throughout his working life he lived in the commercial heart of the City of London, first by the Ship tavern in St Bartholomew Lane, then, by 1703, at the Golden Fleece on the corner of Little Eastcheap and Gracechurch Street. Here he kept an apothecary's shop and dealt in such exotic overseas produce as coffee, chocolate, and spices. His brother—perhaps Henry (b. 1637)—was a merchant trading with Virginia, and he clearly moved in mercantile and banking circles.

Houghton's first publication was a pamphlet advocating free trade, entitled *England's Great Happiness*. Anonymous on its first appearance in 1677, a second edition that year bore his name, and possibly brought him to the notice of Robert Hooke, who proposed him to the Royal Society, to which he was elected in January 1680. Henceforth he always appended FRS to his name, and in turn brought other merchants into the society, though, as they contributed little to its proceedings, accusations that he thereby lowered the tone of the membership may have been justified. Houghton contributed regularly to discussions and was delegated to collect arrears of subscriptions, serving as one of the society's auditors during the 1680s. His frequent donations to the society's repository consisted principally of foreign natural history specimens.

Houghton was recruited as a member of the society's revived georgical (agricultural) committee. Thus encouraged, he began his best-known works, *A Collection of Letters for the Improvement of Husbandry and Trade*, which appeared at monthly intervals from September 1681 to 1683 (though the final numbers emerged from the press only in 1685). Each issue consisted of Houghton's lengthy editorial, plus one or more letters, covering all aspects of agriculture and land improvement and occasionally venturing into matters of commerce or popular science and technology; they dealt with matters then under active discussion by progressive agriculturalists. Houghton was the first to remark on the cultivation of the potato as a field crop, just beginning at that time. His practice was to send the letters free of charge to those who agreed to supply him in return with local prices and news. His correspondents included many small farmers, countrywomen, rural merchants, and husbandmen such as John Worlidge, besides his fellow members of the Royal Society, among them John Evelyn, John Flamsteed, Edmond Halley, and Robert Plot.

After a short delay Houghton began a second series, *A Collection for Improvement of Agriculture and Trade*, issued weekly as a single folio sheet, price 2*d*., from March 1692 to September 1703. Each number consisted of a brief article by Houghton, backed by commercial information of a most diverse nature. Constrained by the limits of his page, he included selections from a round-up of current prices, not simply of such agricultural products as grains, hay, manure, wool, livestock, and carcases, but taking in coal, tallow, glass, metals and sundry manufactures, imports and exports, movements of shipping, and 'actions'; the last was his Anglicization of a Dutch word, namely prices of East India, Africa, and Hudson's Bay companies stock, foreign exchange rates and bullion—effectively the earliest stock exchange figures.

Houghton's first advertisement, for the chocolate that he sold, filled a space at the end of an issue of 1693. In later years he included a growing number and variety of such notices, offering, besides his own pharmaceutical merchandise, a bewildering diversity of goods—brimstone, sago, coffee, spectacles and telescopes, even such specialities as manuscript sermons and advowsons—and extending to book reviews. Eventually he was acting as agent for those in London and the provinces wishing to let or rent property and hire domestic servants. To accommodate the growing number of such notices, he added from time to time a second leaf, at no extra charge. Presumably he found his own business increased thereby, for at last he bade his readers farewell with the explanation:

> But truly, since (beside my trade of an *apothecary* wherein I have always been, and still am, diligent) I have fallen to the selling of *Coffee, Tea and Chocolate* in some considerable degree. I cannot without inconvenience to my private Affairs, which must not be neglected, spare time to carry on this History as well as I would do.   (no. 583 of 24 Sept 1703)

Over the years Houghton's respected authors had covered virtually every aspect of farming and land management, and the sustained interest in his *Letters* led to their reissue in 1728. He died intestate in 1705, his widow being granted administration of his estate in November that year.   ANITA MCCONNELL

Sources D. T. O'Rourke, 'John Houghton, 1645–1705, journalist, apothecary and FRS', *Pharmaceutical Historian*, 9/1 (1979), 1–2 · G. E. Fussell, 'John Houghton', *N&Q*, 148 (1925), 345–6 · D. McDonald, *Agricultural writers from Sir Walter of Henley to Arthur Young, 1200–1800* (1908) · J. Donaldson, *Agricultural biography* (1854), 36 · J. E. T. Rogers, *A history of agriculture and prices in England*, 5 (1887), 22–3, 236–54 · C. H. Cooper, *Memorials of Cambridge*, 1 (1860), 154 · J. Houghton, *A collection of letters for the improvement of husbandry and trade*, 2 vols. (1681–3) · T. Birch, *The history of the Royal Society of London*, 4 vols. (1756–7), vol. 4 · GL, Society of Apothecaries' MSS, 8294, 8208/1 · J. Houghton, *A collection for improvement of husbandry and trade*, 20 vols. (1692–1703) · parish register (baptisms), Cheshunt, Hertfordshire, 21 July 1645 · parish register (marriages), St Stephen's, Coleman Street, London, 11 Nov 1687

Houghton, Joseph (*c*.1885–*c*.1945), trade unionist, was born in England of unknown parentage. Little is known of him until he came north to Scotland some time in the early 1900s. He worked in the leather industry in the manufacture of footwear and represented the National Union of Boot and Shoe Operatives as delegate to Glasgow Trades Council (GTC), and the Scottish Trades Union Congress (STUC). Houghton was to become a leading political activist within the council; he was elected to the parliamentary committee of the GTC in 1907 and to the trades disputes committee the following year. As an active trade unionist he argued continually for workers' rights. As an active socialist he tirelessly promoted any campaign which would challenge the conditions of poverty experienced by the working classes on Clydeside and elsewhere.

In 1910—still representing the boot and shoe operatives—Houghton denounced the 'scandalous sentences' passed against the former dockers' organizer Jim Larkin, of the National Union of Dock Labourers (NUDL). Larkin had been accused by James Sexton, leader of the NUDL, of attempting to defraud the union. Houghton testified to Larkin's honesty and integrity but he was nevertheless found guilty and imprisoned for twelve months. When shortly afterwards the Glasgow dockers finally decided to leave the NUDL, James Kessack approached the GTC for assistance in encouraging men 'back into the union', and in December 1910 a ten-man committee, which included Joseph Houghton, was set up to help reform Glasgow dockers. By January 1911, however, the Glasgow docks branch of the NUDL was closed down and within six months the men were reorganized into a new union, the Scottish Union of Dock Labourers (SUDL). Houghton played a leading role in this development and in 1911 was elected general secretary of the SUDL.

During the labour unrest between 1910 and 1914 Houghton was to become closely associated with the London activists Tom Mann and Ben Tillett, the French syndicalist Madame Sorgue of the Confédération Générale du Travail, and Captain Edward Tupper of the seamen's union, as well as other socialist and industrial activists in Scotland, including Kessack and James Keir Hardie. By 1916 Houghton was a member of the parliamentary committee of the STUC and was office bearer on that committee between 1917 and 1919. He was the Clyde district secretary and executive council member to the National Transport Workers' Federation (NTWF) and a fervent supporter of the Triple Industrial Alliance. He served on several wartime governmental bodies, and in 1919 gave evidence on behalf of the Glasgow dockers to the transport workers' court of inquiry—where he worked closely with Ernest Bevin. It was at this inquiry that he stated he was the only Englishman among the Scots and Irish who made up the dock labour force at Glasgow.

Houghton remained leader of the SUDL until the membership (reluctantly) transferred to the Transport and General Workers' Union (TGWU) in 1923. During that time he witnessed the membership of the SUDL double from 5000 to 10,000 and extended to cover other workers—most notably female munitions workers at Nobel's chemical factory at Ardeer in Ayrshire. In 1923 Houghton became docks secretary of the TGWU in Scotland, a position he held until his retirement in 1941. During that time he remained active in Scotland and represented the TGWU at the Trades Union Congress. He was brought out of retirement briefly in 1942, but his activities thereafter are unknown. It is probable, but not certain, that he died in the 1940s.   WILLIAM KENEFICK

Sources K. Coates and T. Topham, *The making of the Transport and General Workers Union: the emergence of the labour movement, 1870–1922*, 1 (1991), pt 2 · E. L. Taplin, *The dockers' union: a study of the*

National Union of Dock Labourers, 1889–1922 (1985) • W. Kenefick, *Ardrossan, the key to the Clyde: a case study of the Ardrossan dock strike, 1912–1913* (1993) • W. Kenefick, 'The struggle for control: the importance of the great unrest at Glasgow harbour, 1911–1912', *The roots of red Clydeside? Labour unrest in the west of Scotland, 1910–1914*, ed. W. Kenefick and A. McIvor (1996), 129–52 • W. Kenefick, 'The impact of the past upon the present: the experience of the Clydeside dock labour force, c.1850–1914', PhD diss., University of Strathclyde, 1995 • 'Enquiry into the wages and conditions of employment of dock and waterside labourers', *Parl. papers* (1920), vol. 5, Cmd 936; vol. 24, Cmd 937 • Glasgow Trades Council annual reports and executive minutes, Mitchell L., Glas. • National Union of Dock Labourers (occasional) annual reports, Mitchell L., Glas., S.F. 331. 8811 3871 SCO • Scottish Trade Union Congress annual reports • Scottish Union of Dock Labourers Executive minutes and annual reports, Mitchell L., Glas., S.F. 331. 8811 3871 SCO • Scottish Union of Dock Labourers returns to the Registrar of Friendly Societies, Scotland, NA Scot., FS 10.3. • Transport and General Workers Union Area 7 branch (Scotland) executive and area minutes, Mitchell L., Glas., TU F331 88 TRA. MS C.372254 • *Glasgow Herald* • *Forward* • *Daily Record* • *Daily Mail*

Likenesses photograph, 1920–29, repro. in *TGWU publication* • photograph, 1922, repro. in STUC annual reports, Parliamentary Committee

Houghton, Margaret (*fl.* 1441). *See under* Women traders and artisans in London (*act. c.*1200–*c.*1500).

Houghton, Sir Robert (1548–1624), judge, was born at Gunthorpe, Norfolk, on 3 August 1548, the third son of John Houghton of Gunthorpe and his wife, Agnes, the daughter of Robert Playford of Brinton. Entering Lincoln's Inn on 11 March 1569 Houghton was called to the bar on 10 February 1577, and in the early part of his career was particularly active in his native East Anglia. Having served from 1585 as its steward, Houghton was elected MP for Norwich in 1593 and appointed recorder in 1595. He also acted as counsel for King's Lynn in the 1590s and was made a justice of the peace for Norfolk in 1593. Meanwhile at Lincoln's Inn he was advanced to the bench in 1589, served as Lent reader in 1591 and 1600, and was appointed treasurer in 1599. He became a serjeant-at-law in 1603.

On being knighted and made a justice of the king's bench in 1613, Houghton resigned the recordership of Norwich, pledging his future good offices to the city and noting that, as recorder, he had always tried 'to advance truth and do right to everyone' (HoP, *Commons, 1558–1603*, 2.344). Described by Sir Francis Bacon as 'a soft man' (*DNB*) when he was required in January 1615 to give a separate extra-judicial opinion for the guidance of the crown in *Peacham's case*, Houghton at first demurred on the ground of inexperience, but ultimately consented; he also acted with the majority of judges in the case of *Commendams*, promising under pressure from James I to take heed of royal wishes even in cases before the courts where the king's own interests were involved. Houghton died on 6 February 1624 at his chambers in Serjeants' Inn. Sir Richard Hutton, who was present at his death, described him as a learned and religious judge, a grave and temperate man of profound judgement and approved honesty, who was much beloved by all. He was buried in St Dunstan-in-the-West, where his widow, Mary, daughter of Robert Rychers of Wrotham, Kent, erected a monument to his memory; this was destroyed in the Second World War. He

left a life interest to his house in Norwich and his manor of Lessy in Suffolk to his wife, with the remainder of these and his other landholdings to his eldest son, Francis.

CHRISTOPHER W. BROOKS

Sources DNB • HoP, *Commons, 1558–1603*, 2.344 • will, PRO, PROB 11/143, fols. 219r–220 • J. R. Tanner, ed., *Constitutional documents of the reign of James I* (1961) • *The diary of Sir Richard Hutton, 1614–1639*, ed. W. R. Prest, SeldS, suppl. ser., 9 (1991) • A. Hassell Smith, *County and court: government and politics in Norfolk, 1558–1603* (1974) • Baker, *Serjeants*

Archives University of Chicago, Joseph Regenstein Library, case papers

Likenesses effigy, Shelton, Norfolk; repro. in Baker, *Serjeants*, 519

Wealth at death moderately wealthy; manor of Lessy, Suffolk; plus lands and tenements in Norfolk; £333 bequeathed to wife: PRO, PROB 11/143, fols. 219r–220

Houghton, (William) Stanley (1881–1913), playwright, was born at 1 Amy Villas, Doveston Road, Ashton upon Mersey, Cheshire, on 22 February 1881, the only son and second child of John Hartley Houghton, a Manchester cloth merchant, and his wife, Lucy Mary Darbyshire. Educated at Bowdon College, Cheshire, and Manchester grammar school, in 1897 he began work in his father's warehouse. From 1897 to 1912 the selling of 'grey cloth' occupied him eight hours a day. He was, however, an enthusiastic and dedicated amateur actor and a keen observer of human nature, and from 1900 he devoted himself to playmaking and acting: in 1905–6 he was unpaid drama critic for the *Manchester City News*. Between August 1905 and April 1913 he contributed seventeen 'back-page' articles and more than a hundred theatrical notices and literary reviews to the *Manchester Guardian*. Although he had written a number of unpublished plays, his first productions were *The Intrigues* (Athenaeum Society, Manchester, 19 October 1906) and *The Reckoning* (Queen's Theatre, London, 22 July 1907). His public career as a playwright, however, began with the performance of *The Dear Departed* (Gaiety Theatre, Manchester, 2 November 1908).

Harold Brighouse's edition of Houghton's *Works* (1914) gives everything which is accessible in print. It omits all the early experiments (that is, those before 1908) except *The Old Testament and the New* (1907/8; Gaiety Theatre, Manchester, 22 June 1914); the rest are still in manuscript form and none of these has been professionally acted. Of the plays written in and after 1908, Brighouse omits only three: *Ginger* (written 1910; performed 19 July 1913), and a sketch and a play, *Pearls* (20 December 1912) and *Trust the People* (6 February 1913), which were written, with *Phipps* (19 November 1912), on Arthur Bourchier's commission in 1912. These three have never been printed. All the plays written from 1908 onward, except *Marriages in the Making* (1909), have been performed on the public stage. *Hindle Wakes*, Houghton's most successful play, was first produced at the Aldwych Theatre, London, on 16 June 1912 by A. E. F. Horniman's company at the invitation of the Stage Society; the earlier of the acted plays had their premières at the Manchester Gaiety Theatre—*The Dear Departed* on 2 November 1908, *Independent Means* on 30 August 1909, *The*

Younger Generation and *The Master of the House* on 21 November and 26 September 1910 respectively, and *Fancy-Free* on 6 November 1911.

Houghton's dramatic cleverness is most obvious in his theatrical craftsmanship and facility with dialogue. At the outset he divined the method most suited to his range of interests, and from *The Dear Departed* little but adaptation to larger issues was necessary. Learning, through the experiments in social problem writing and the fashioning of theatrical situation in *Independent Means* and *Marriages in the Making*, he attained almost complete technical mastery in *The Younger Generation* which he later perfected, especially in the first act of *Hindle Wakes*. In the intervening plays his cleverness is indebted to the influence of writers such as Shaw, Wilde, and St John Hankin. Yet he was much more than a competent artisan: mere technique is inadequate to account for the structural harmony of person, setting, incident, and idiom which gives to the first act of *Hindle Wakes* the relentless inevitability of fine drama.

Houghton was influenced strongly by Ibsen: but he differs from other English writers in that, apart from *Independent Means*, he wrote no propagandist plays. Disinterest in social and political problems freed his dramatic action from their constraint. Like Ibsen, he was led to concern himself with a narrow society, the nexus of which he saw in a simple convention; for Houghton, the simpler the better. He showed it purely in its human aspect before it had been resolved into a sociological problem. If the end of a play provides no solution which a sociologist would accept, it is partly because he lacked Ibsen's penetrating imagination, but also because he preferred an issue too elemental for solution: the conflict between youth and age.

The attempt of the Gaiety Theatre to rear a local drama inspired Houghton to his best use of the Ibsenite tradition. It limited him to material dramatically similar to Ibsen's, and it involved such preoccupation with manners as to exclude problematic abstractions. It diverted the Ibsen tradition towards comedy, but circumstances corrected the bias. The Manchester school of dramatists might caricature Lancashire for a London audience; but in Manchester it had to present a more realistic depiction. *The Dear Departed* is local only in its manners, customs, and speech. *The Younger Generation* claims to depict a local creed, but as contempt for the creed creates all the fun of the piece, its professors have only a limited humanity. *Hindle Wakes* is in the main so truly local that it is universal; its interest is in human nature as it manifests itself in Lancashire. It has glaring faults, and the whole is certainly less than the part. But its two old men are great figures, for, as Houghton created them, his sympathy got the better of his prejudices and cleverness. His reputation largely rests on this single play, the most successful example of the Edwardian 'Manchester school' of playwriting and identified especially with Annie Horniman's work at the Gaiety Theatre. His contribution was that he gave English dramatic writing an authentic Lancashire voice which became recognized internationally.

By the autumn of 1912 the success of *Hindle Wakes* had enabled Houghton to pursue a full-time career as a dramatist, and he left Manchester for London. He rapidly became part of London's dramatic and literary culture and was much in demand by theatre managers such as Arthur Bourchier and Charles Hawtrey. He decided, however, to detach himself from these pressures and in 1913 he settled in Paris, where he wrote the extant six chapters of his novel, *Life*. In the summer he contracted a viral pneumonia at Venice and was brought back an invalid to Manchester. Stanley Houghton died, unmarried, of meningitis at his home, 2 Athol Road, Whalley Range, Withington, south Manchester, on 11 December 1913 and was cremated on 13 December at the Manchester crematorium. In February 1915 a memorial tablet was unveiled in the Manchester Reference Library.

VICTOR EMELJANOW

Sources P. Mortimer, 'W. Stanley Houghton: an introduction and bibliography', *Modern Drama*, 3/28 (Sept 1985), 474–89 • *The works of Stanley Houghton*, ed. H. Brighouse, 3 vols. (1914) • R. Pogson, *Miss Horniman and the Gaiety Theatre, Manchester* (1952) • S. Gooddie, *Annie Horniman: a pioneer in the theatre* (1990) • D. Scott, *Men of letters* (1917) • *Manchester Guardian* (11 Dec 1913) • *The Era* (20 Dec 1913) • b. cert. • d. cert. • *CGPLA Eng. & Wales* (1914)

Archives Salford City Archives, corresp., literary MSS, and papers • University of Salford Library, literary MSS, contracts, photographs of productions, papers | JRL, letters to Allan Monkhouse

Likenesses photograph, repro. in *Manchester Guardian* • photograph, repro. in *The Era* • photograph, repro. in H. Brighouse, ed., *Works of Stanley Houghton*, frontispiece

Wealth at death £5488 14s. 5d.: probate, 7 Feb 1914, *CGPLA Eng. & Wales*

Houghton, Sir William Frederick (1909–1971), educational administrator, was born on 30 November 1909 at 27 Rutland Street, Oldham, Lancashire, son of Arthur Houghton, travelling salesman for a vinegar manufacturer, and his wife, Annie, *née* Cocker. It is not recorded where he attended school. In 1928 he matriculated at Christ's College, Cambridge, where he gained a second class in part one (1930) and a first class in part two (1931) of the historical tripos.

After graduating in 1931 Houghton spent four years (1932–6) as a schoolmaster, first at Methodist college, Belfast, and then at Wirral grammar school, Cheshire. Just before he left teaching, his fictional work *Greeks and Romans* (1935) was published. He married on 31 December 1935, at the Baptist chapel in King Street, Oldham, Mary Wimpenny Newton (*b.* 1909), daughter of Frederick Schofield Newton, an Oldham waste dealer.

In 1936 the newly married couple moved to east Suffolk where Houghton had been appointed as assistant secretary to the education committee. He took to educational administration and made rapid progress. A post as deputy director of education in west Sussex followed in 1938 and from 1941 to 1947 he was chief education officer in Darlington. Two deputy education officer posts in larger local education authorities came next: the first in Birmingham from 1947 to 1952 and the second with London county council (LCC) from 1952 to 1956.

With senior experience in five different local education

authorities, Houghton was an obvious candidate for promotion to the most influential and prestigious educational administration post in Britain: the position of LCC education officer, to which he was appointed when it became vacant in 1956. Father of two sons, of whom one predeceased his father and the other became a teacher, he made his home in London and remained at the helm of its education for the rest of his life. Only Sir Robert Blair, who led education in London from 1904 to 1924, served longer. When the LCC was abolished in 1965, to be replaced by the inner London education authority (ILEA), Houghton became ILEA's first education officer and oversaw the smooth transition from one system to the other.

Houghton was renowned in ILEA for his approachability and practical 'northern' common sense. He made tireless visits to schools, irrespective of other commitments, during which he invariably took time and trouble to talk to pupils and teachers informally. Another strength was his ability to see things from a teacher's point of view. Under him a new education welfare service was set up in London. He also led the imaginative establishment in the ILEA area of a network of local teachers' centres at which teachers from different schools could meet and undergo in-service training. The acquisition and development of a residential in-service training centre at Stoke D'Abernon, near Leatherhead, in Surrey, was another innovation which took place under Houghton's leadership. He served on a number of national and international bodies and, early in 1971, led an ILEA team which went to Hong Kong to advise on the colony's education service.

Beyond education Houghton pursued interests in reading, theatre, sport, and travel. He became an honorary fellow of the College of Preceptors in 1965 and was granted an honorary doctorate by the University of Surrey in 1968. In 1967 he was knighted for services to education. He suffered a stroke after attending a meeting of the Home Office committee on adopted children and died from a 'cerebro-vascular accident' at Whittington Hospital, Islington, London, on 16 November 1971. He had planned to take early retirement at the end of 1971.

SUSAN ELKIN

Sources *Times Educational Supplement* (19 Nov 1971) · *The Times* (17 Nov 1971) · R. Aldrich and P. Gordon, *Dictionary of British educationists* (1989) · WWW · b. cert. · m. cert. · d. cert. · CUL, department of manuscripts and university archives · archives, Christ's Hospital, Horsham · S. Maclure, *A history of education in London, 1870–1990* (1990) · A. S. Williams, P. Ivin, and C. Morse, *The children of London: attendance and welfare at school, 1870–1990* (2001)
Archives JRL, letters to the *Manchester Guardian*
Wealth at death £17,019: probate, 8 Feb 1972, CGPLA Eng. & Wales

Houghton, William Narcissus [*name in religion* Hyacinth] (**1736–1823**), Dominican friar, born in 1736 in the hundred of West Derby, Lancashire, was descended from the Hoghtons of Hoghton Tower in the same county. He entered the order of Preachers (Dominicans) at Brussels on 15 October 1753. Professed as a friar in October 1754, he studied in the Low Countries at Louvain and the English Dominican College at Bornhem near Antwerp. He was ordained priest at Ghent in 1760, having held the office of prefect of studies

at Bornhem from 1758. He remained as prefect until 1762, when he returned to serve on the English mission, first at Hexham, an English Dominican mission since about 1635, and then at Stonecroft, a Northumberland mission sponsored by the recusant Gibson family, where he served for nine years. In January 1775 he returned to Bornhem where he was elected prior, and then successively appointed subprior and procurator of the convent. In March 1779 he was assigned to the English Dominican College at Louvain as professor of philosophy. Within a year he had offended the university authorities by promoting the defence of some of the theories of Descartes and Newton in theses submitted by his Dominican pupils fathers Vincent Bowyer, Benedict Atkinson, and Ceslaus Fenwick. All three died in the order. Fenwick later accompanied his nephew, Edward Dominic Fenwick, first bishop of Cincinnati, and other American friars from Bornhem to establish the order in the United States. The legislation of Joseph II, designed to apply some of the rational principles of the Enlightenment to ecclesiastical life, was currently in force in the Southern Netherlands.

Houghton found himself embroiled in a larger conflict than he realized. It was thought prudent for him to return to England in October 1780 to act as chaplain to the mission based at Fairhurst Hall, near Wigan, the seat of the Nelson family, where he was to remain for much of the remainder of his life. He had been honoured with the title of preacher-general in 1771 and in 1786 was promoted to the degree of master in sacred theology.

Houghton had keen literary and scholarly interests, and was a competent poet. In 1801 he founded the first Catholic periodical to appear in England: the *Catholic Magazine and Reflector*, published by the London firm of Keating, Brown, and Keating. Houghton served as its editor, and wrote many of the articles and some of the poetry it featured. However, the journal closed after six months: the Roman Catholic community proved too small and too scattered to sustain its circulation. Houghton was described by one contemporary as a tall and athletic man, but a very slovenly dresser. Father Houghton died at Fairhurst on 3 January 1823 and was buried at Windleshaw, Lancashire.

ALLAN WHITE

Sources MI profession register, English Dominican Archives, 87–8 · Gillow, *Lit. biog. hist.* · D. A. Bellenger, ed., *English and Welsh priests, 1558–1800* (1984), 73 · W. Gumbley, *Obituary notices of the English Dominicans from 1555 to 1952* (1955)

Houlding, John (**1833?–1902**), brewer and football club sponsor, was born in Tenterden Street, off Scotland Road, Liverpool, probably in 1833, the year his father, Thomas Houlding, established himself there as a cow keeper and dairyman. His parents came from Lancashire farming stock.

Educated at the Church of England school in Bond Street, Houlding spent a year at Liverpool College before taking a job as office boy in a firm of shipbrokers, although only eleven and a half years old. Over the next two years he made good progress, but his father's cows were stricken by cattle disease and when only three remained John had to give up his job to look after them while his father took better-paid work in a brewery. Houlding later worked as a porter at the Liverpool Exchange until his father helped him obtain a position as labourer and drayman at a brewer's in Soho Street delivering beer to public houses for £1 a week. This lasted for about four years when the brewer employed by the firm left and John Houlding was appointed in his place in January 1856. A rent-free house went with the job, and marriage soon followed, on 20 July of the same year, together with a pay increase of 5s. a week. His wife was Jane Lowe, a farmer's daughter, with whom he had a son and a daughter. He joined the St Anne's Building Society and at the end of the year had saved his first £12. In 1864 Houlding had saved his first £100 and bought a public house followed by a second in 1869. By this time he had taken over the administration of the brewery and become its manager on a salary of £200 a year. By 1870 Houlding had accumulated capital to the extent of £900 and in 1871 he went into business on his own buying a piece of land in Tynemouth Street, Breck Road, and converting it into a brewery. He only had one employee at first but good profits were made from the start.

Houlding lived and worked in Everton, a rapidly growing working-class suburb containing an occasionally combustible mixture of Liverpool-born and English, Irish, and Welsh immigrants and it was Everton which supported his public career. This began in 1872 when he was appointed chairman of the Everton branch of the Conservative Association. The following year he was elected the representative for Everton on the west Derby board of guardians of which he was later chairman in 1878 and 1887. He joined the Everton burial board in 1876 and was chairman from 1880 for twenty years. Houlding won the Everton and Kirkdale ward in the city council elections of 1884, was elected alderman in 1895, became a JP in 1897 and lord mayor of Liverpool in 1897-8. He was the first president of what became the Mersey Quay and Railway Carters' Union, a freemason, Orangeman, churchman, and philanthropist being among the initiators of the annual dinner for the aged poor.

Houlding was interested in sport, playing cricket and swimming in his younger days, and it was as the benefactor of the Everton Football Club that he became best known. He became the club's president in 1882 and managed the move to a ground in Anfield Road which the football club rented from him. Football became very popular in the 1880s as both a recreative and a spectator sport and therefore important as a market for brewers. The club agreed that as their income rose so would Houlding's rent, but the membership later felt that he was making too much money out of it. His role in the drink trade also upset some of them. Houlding found his vision for the commercial development of the club challenged by groups within the membership who differed from him ideologically, politically, and socially. In 1892 he gave the club notice to quit the Anfield Road ground and Everton moved to the other side of Stanley Park and built a new stadium in Goodison Road. Undaunted, Houlding created a new club from scratch and called it Liverpool. Not only

did it obtain a place in the second division of the Football League but it won the championship without losing a match in 1893-4. His shrewdest move was to persuade Tom Watson to transfer from Sunderland and become club secretary with full responsibility for the playing side, an early example of what would later be called a football manager. Liverpool won the first of their Division One championships in 1900-01 under Houlding's chairmanship.

Houlding was a popular figure, particularly in Everton, and was often referred to as 'King John', a nickname affectionate rather than critical. Contemporaries attributed his success to a combination of hard work, determination, a powerful physique, and intelligence. A Liverpool newspaper judged that his popularity was due 'to his intimate acquaintance through experience of the condition and requirement of the working classes, absence of any pride of position and a daily readiness to help in any undertaking from a school room concert to a Parliamentary deputation' (*Liverpool Review*, 26 May 1888). Houlding was a 'parochial patriot' (Waller, 63), who may have lost the chance to stand for parliament because important local Conservatives thought him insufficiently polished. In later years he became a good French scholar and travelled widely on the continent. He died in France at the Pension Thomson, Cimiez, Nice, on 17 March 1902. He was buried next to his wife in Everton cemetery, Fazakerley, on 21 March 1902, when large crowds turned out to see the cortège pass.   TONY MASON

Sources P. J. Waller, *Democracy and sectarianism: a political and social history of Liverpool, 1868–1939* (1981) · T. Mason, 'The Blues and the Reds', *Transactions of the Historic Society of Lancashire and Cheshire*, 134 (1984), 107–28 · *Liverpool Courier* (18 March 1902) · *Liverpool Courier* (20 March 1902) · *Liverpool Courier* (22 March 1902) · *Liverpool Courier* (25 March 1902) · *Liverpool Daily Post* (18 March 1902) · *Liverpool Daily Post* (22 March 1902) · *Liverpool Mercury* (22 March 1902) · *Liverpool Review* (7 Oct 1882) · *Liverpool Review* (14 Oct 1882) · *Liverpool Review* (26 May 1888) · *Liverpool Review* (19 March 1892) · *Liverpool Review* (24 May 1892) · *Liverpool Review* (13 Nov 1897) · *The Porcupine* (22 March 1902) · *The Porcupine* (29 March 1902) · m. cert. · D. Kennedy, 'The split of Everton football club, 1892: the creation of distinct patterns of boardroom formation at Everton and Liverpool football club companies', unpubd paper, 2002

Likenesses oils, c.1887; formerly Brougham Terrace, West Derby board of guardians · Messrs Brown, Barns & Bell, photographs, c.1890–1900 · Messrs Brown, Barns & Bell, photograph, repro. in *The Porcupine* (22 March 1902) · portrait, repro. in *Portraits of Mayors and Lord Mayors of Liverpool*, 1

Wealth at death £44,946 7s. 10d.: probate, 10 May 1902, CGPLA Eng. & Wales

Houldsworth, Sir Hubert Stanley, first baronet (1889–1956), coal industry manager and industrialist, was born at Heckmondwike, Yorkshire, on 20 April 1889, the only child of Albert Edward Houldsworth (d. 1896), drysalter, and his wife, Susannah Buckley (d. 1947). He was educated at Heckmondwike grammar school and at Leeds University where he graduated BSc with first-class honours in physics in 1911, MSc in 1912, and DSc in 1925; he also joined the staff there in 1916. In addition, he fulfilled a boyhood ambition by reading for the bar and was called by Lincoln's Inn in 1926. He married in 1919 Hilda Frances,

Sir Hubert Stanley Houldsworth, first baronet (1889–1956), by Walter Stoneman, 1945

daughter of Joseph Clegg, of Heckmondwike. They had one son.

An able barrister, with a strong sense of humour, Houldsworth's practice on the north-eastern circuit steadily increased, and by the early 1930s his long association with the mining industry had begun. After 1931 he was occupied mainly with his brief as standing counsel for the midland district executive board of colliery owners which, under the act of 1930, fixed a standard tonnage for each colliery. If an owner were aggrieved at the output decided upon for his colliery he could appeal to independent arbitration. Most owners did.

Control of selling was introduced in 1935 and from 1936 until 1942 Houldsworth, who took silk in 1937, was independent chairman of the committee of the midland scheme which administered these selling provisions. At the start of the war he was appointed joint coal supplies officer for the midland (amalgamated) district and unobtrusively exercised great influence on the national administration of the government scheme of control of coal supplies. In 1942 he became regional controller for south and west Yorkshire and in 1944 he took over as controller-general of the Ministry of Fuel and Power.

In 1945 Houldsworth returned to the bar but when the mines were nationalized the following year he became chairman of the east midland division of the National Coal Board, which covered the coalfields of Nottinghamshire, Derby, and Leicester—relatively low-cost areas with good labour relations. He knew the division intimately and threw himself with energy and skill into building up its organization and securing increased productivity and lower costs. He soon realized the need for increased mechanization. Successful though he was in the division, he resented the control exercised by the National Coal Board.

He accepted a measure of overall financial control; but it was his view, openly expressed, that in other respects the divisional boards should be autonomous.

In 1951 Houldsworth became chairman of the National Coal Board. His predecessor, Lord Hyndley, had built up an organization for the nationalized industry; a national plan for the reconstruction of the collieries had been prepared. It was Houldsworth's task, tackled with his customary zeal, to secure the rapid modernization of the industry. In the process he failed to secure the whole-hearted agreement of all his colleagues on the national board, and had uneasy relations with some of his senior officials. One of his most charitable colleagues, Sir Geoffrey Vickers, said that 'whereas Hyndley conducted cabinet government, Houldsworth's style was presidential' (Ashworth, 192).

In particular, Houldsworth wanted the divisions to introduce more mechanization; he appreciated the need for improved management; and he strove for better labour relations. But he still believed in divisional autonomy and on 22 October 1953 a general directive was issued to divisional chairmen and heads of departments at headquarters firmly laying down the policy of *primus inter pares*.

Public comment on the need to review the organization of the National Coal Board caused the formation of an independent advisory committee in December 1953 under Alexander Fleck. In its report published in February 1955 the committee approved the main structure of the board's organization but considered that it was too half-hearted in seeing that the divisions carried out the policies it laid down. It recommended that the general directive of October 1953 be withdrawn and reissued emphasizing the authority of the board. Most of the committee's recommendations were adopted but its report was a blow to Houldsworth, criticizing, as it did so strongly, the policy he had consistently advocated. Nevertheless, his dedication to the industry was unimpaired. He continued his travels throughout the length and breadth of the coalfields.

Throughout his life Houldsworth was passionately interested in the cause of education. He became chairman of the board of governors of Heckmondwike School, and continued his long association with Leeds University. From 1949 until his death Houldsworth was pro-chancellor of the university. He was a lifelong Liberal, and in 1929 unsuccessfully contested the parliamentary constituency of Pudsey and Otley. Houldsworth received an honorary LLD from Leeds (1951) and from Nottingham (1953). He was knighted in 1944 and created a baronet in January 1956.

Houldsworth ignored the warning of a slight heart attack in 1955, and died suddenly on 1 February 1956 at his London flat, 6 Stone Buildings, Lincoln's Inn. He was survived by his wife, and his son succeeded as second baronet. An obituary in *The Times* described him as a near-perfect example of a self-made man. Praising his great humanity and popularity in the midlands and the north, it described him as 'a physicist of standing, an ardent educationalist, but above all … he excelled as public servant and administrator, especially in his work with the coal industry' (*The Times*, 2 Feb 1956).

R. J. MOFFAT, *rev.* ROBERT BROWN

Sources B. Supple, *The political economy of decline: 1913–1946* (1987), vol. 4 of *The history of the British coal industry* (1984–93) · W. Ashworth and M. Pegg, *The nationalized industry: 1946–1982* (1986), vol. 5 of *The history of the British coal industry* (1984–93) · private information (1971) · *CGPLA Eng. & Wales* (1956) · *The Times* (2 Feb 1956), 12 · *WWW* · C. G. Down, 'Houldsworth, Sir Hubert Stanley', *DBB* · d. cert. · d. cert. [Albert Edward Houldsworth]
Likenesses W. Stoneman, photograph, 1945, NPG [*see illus.*] · G. Kelly, oils, *c.*1953, U. Leeds
Wealth at death £18,208 8s. 2d.: probate, 7 May 1956, *CGPLA Eng. & Wales*

Houldsworth, Margaret Marshall (1839–1909), educationist and philanthropist, was born in Manchester on 14 September 1839, only daughter of Henry Houldsworth (1797–1868), a cotton manufacturer, of Coltness and his second wife, Marianne (*d.* 1865), daughter of James Burt from Chorlton, near Manchester. Her grandfather, also named Henry Houldsworth, and great-uncle, Thomas Houldsworth, founded a flourishing cotton-spinning business in Manchester. The family also opened a mill in Glasgow before diversifying into the coal and iron industries in Lanarkshire.

Little is known of Margaret Houldsworth's early life but the evidence suggests that it was spent in Manchester, first at the family residence at Ardwick Green and then Oak Hill, Cheetham Hill, with her brothers Walter (1845–1903) and Arthur (1847–1890). When her great-uncle Thomas Houldsworth died in 1852 and her grandfather, Henry, died in 1853 her father, now in his sixties, was freed from the restrictions of a sometimes difficult working relationship with his uncle. He went on to expand the cotton mills in Manchester, was involved in the partnership of the Coltness Iron Company, and became the new laird of the Coltness estate in Lanarkshire, where the family settled. After the deaths of her parents Margaret Houldsworth lived with her brother Arthur at Springfield House, Polton, near Lasswade in Midlothian.

Margaret Houldsworth's move to the east of Scotland led to her involvement in the movement for promoting women's education. In April 1871 she joined the Edinburgh Ladies' Educational Association (ELEA), an association set up in 1867 to further the cause of higher education of women with a view to gaining admission to the universities. She was on the executive of the association in 1876. After the death in 1877 of Mary Crudelius, the pioneering secretary of the association, and its reconstitution as the Edinburgh Association for the University Education of Women, Margaret Houldsworth became the vice-president. Once the work of the association was completed, when women were admitted to the Scottish universities in 1892, she was one of the main instigators in the setting up of Masson Hall, a hall of residence for women students at Edinburgh University.

From 1872 Margaret Houldsworth was a member of the Edinburgh Ladies' Debating Society, which brought

Margaret Marshall Houldsworth (1839–1909), by unknown photographer

together many of the women who led the Scottish campaigns for women's suffrage and education in the second half of the nineteenth century. With Sarah Siddons Mair, the founder of the debating society and member of the ELEA, and two other members of the association, Ann Dundas and Mary Jane Urquhart, she helped to set up in 1876 the St George's Hall oral and correspondence classes to prepare girls for local examinations. The inadequacy of training for women teachers led the hall committee to set up St George's Training College in 1886. The need for women teachers to have practical experience in an appropriate setting and the desire to set up a school modelled on the Girls' Public Day School Company saw the foundation in 1888 of St George's School for Girls. At the centre of this new venture were the founding pioneers of Margaret Houldsworth, Sarah Siddons Mair, and Miss Urquhart.

As a comparatively wealthy woman in a family whose male members were steeped in entrepreneurial and business acumen, Margaret Houldsworth was able to provide practical, and particularly financial, help for the women's causes she promoted. She took a much less public role than some. Sarah Mair noted: 'she was very quiet and unassuming, very shy and diffident—the heart of the enterprise—but I could never persuade her to speak' (Welsh, 38). She supported other causes including the Edinburgh National Society for Women's Suffrage, the

Edinburgh Hospital and Dispensary for women and children, and the Scottish Central Bureau for the Employment of Women. Margaret Houldsworth died on 29 October 1909 at 3 Ainslie Place, Edinburgh, where she had lived for the previous twenty years. She was buried at Cambusnethan cemetery.   SHEILA HAMILTON

Sources N. Shepley, *Women of independent mind: St George's School, Edinburgh, and the campaign for women's education, 1888–1988* (1988) • L. M. Rae, *Ladies in debate, being a history of the Ladies' Edinburgh Debating Society, 1865–1935* (1936) • B. W. Welsh, *After the dawn: a record of the pioneer work in Edinburgh for the higher education of women* (1939) • U. Edin. L., special collections division, Edinburgh Association for the University Education of Women MSS, GEN 1877 • E. J. B. Watson, *Edinburgh Association for the University Education of Women, 1867–1967* (1967) • S. Hamilton, 'Women and the Scottish universities, *circa* 1869–1939: a social history', PhD diss., U. Edin., 1987 • W. H. Macleod and H. H. Houldsworth, *The beginnings of the Houldsworths of Coltness* (1937) • *St George's Chronicle*, 48 (Nov 1909) • Burke, *Peerage* (1907) • Burke, *Peerage* (1970) • J. L. Carvell, *The Coltness Iron Company* (1948) • M. Williams and D. A. Farnie, *Cotton mills in Greater Manchester* (1992) • *Manchester Directories* • *Edinburgh Directories* • census returns for Manchester, 1851; for Lasswade, 1871 • d. cert.
Archives U. Edin., Masson Hall MSS, Da 64 MAS • U. Edin. L., Edinburgh Association for the University Education of Women MSS, GEN 1877
Likenesses photographs, St George's School for Girls, Edinburgh [see illus.]
Wealth at death £88,014 5s. 7d.: confirmation, 7 Dec 1909, *CCI* • £1370 18s.: additional estate, 11 June 1910, *CCI*

Houldsworth, **Sir William Henry**, first baronet (1834–1917), cotton industrialist and politician, was born on 20 August 1834 at Ardwick, Manchester, the fourth son of Henry Houldsworth (1797–1868), cotton spinner, and his first wife, Helen, daughter of James Hamilton of Glasgow and his wife, Ann. He was educated at Mr Jackson's school, Broughton, and in 1852 matriculated at St Andrews University. On 20 August 1862 Houldsworth married Elisabeth Graham Crum (d. 1923), daughter of Walter Crum FRS, calico printer; they had three daughters and two surviving sons.

Houldsworth's early business life was spent in the family's fine-cotton spinning mills in central Manchester. Then, having taken over the firm, he conducted an unusual experiment in community building: he erected two new mills in 1865 and 1872 at Reddish, near Stockport, around which were added over the next twenty years some houses and a school, together with a working men's club, a parsonage, and a church (the work of Alfred Waterhouse and a reflection of Houldsworth's deeply felt high-church sentiments). As a community Houldsworth's scheme was at best a limited success, but his firm now led Manchester's fine-spinning trade, employing more than 1000 workers and owning some 296,000 spindles.

Entrepreneurial prominence proved a vital asset to Houldsworth's political ambitions. For, although abandoning his father's dissenting Liberalism, he followed other Anglican cotton masters in seeking to create a working-class base for toryism in Manchester. As president of its Conservative Association, he did much to reorganize the party locally. He stood for parliament unsuccessfully in 1880 before winning a Manchester seat

at a by-election in 1883; thereafter he held Manchester North-West from 1885 until 1906. Although his advocacy of a democratic national organization proved fruitless, his contribution to the growing tory ascendancy in Lancashire was suitably recognized by a baronetcy in 1887.

Within parliament Houldsworth proved a capable advocate of local and national concerns, the chief of which became monetary reform. For, believing that the bimetallic standard offered the most eligible remedy for the widely perceived 'depression' in British industry in the 1880s, Houldsworth participated in a vigorous nationwide campaign, energizing the Manchester Bimetallic League (based on the old Anti-Corn Law model), speaking volubly, and writing expertly on this exotic theme. In 1892 he was the most avid bimetallist among the British delegation to the Brussels International Monetary Conference. Houldsworth also represented Britain at the Berlin Labour Conference of 1890 and, as one of the most widely respected businessmen within the Conservative Party, he was often spoken of as a potential minister of commerce. Interestingly, after 1903 Houldsworth became one of the minority of cotton magnates ready to lend his name to Chamberlain's tariff reform campaign; this entailed bitter local controversy and his own retirement from active politics in 1906. Closely involved with the National Conservative Temperance Union and the Church of England Temperance Society, Houldsworth also pursued the cause of sobriety with a vigour unusual in the tory party.

Politics had not in any way diminished Houldsworth's business enthusiasm. Beyond his cotton interests, he reorganized the affairs of his family's Scottish ironworks and coalmines in the early twentieth century. But above all, in 1898 he led what resulted in the most successful early merger in the English cotton industry, from which the Fine Spinners and Doublers Association was formed and of which his own firm was the largest founder member. Even if the creative energies lay elsewhere, Houldsworth's masterly business diplomacy contributed much to the success of this business venture, which on his retirement as chairman in 1908 was Britain's largest manufacturing company with more than 30,000 employees.

Popular, shrewd, kindly, and energetic, Houldsworth also served on the Lancashire county council, the Manchester chamber of commerce, the Manchester diocesan board of education, and the court of Manchester University, which made him an honorary LLD. He was granted the freedom of the city of Manchester in 1905. In his later years he moved from his Cheshire home at Norbury Booth's Hall to his Coodham estate near Kilmarnock in Scotland, where he had erected a fine chapel, embellished with windows by F. J. Shields. Here he continued to enjoy organ playing as well as golf, fishing, and shooting. Houldsworth's Lancashire links were now largely severed, as his sons had turned towards Scottish acres and Highland regiments.

Houldsworth died on 18 April 1917 at Coodham, and he was interred three days later in the burial-ground on the estate. He was also commemorated by a clock tower within the Houldsworth conservation area set up in Stockport in the 1980s. A. C. HOWE

Sources A. C. Howe, 'Houldsworth, Sir William Henry', *DBB* · W. H. Macleod and H. H. Houldsworth, *The beginnings of the Houldsworths of Coltness* (1937) · *The Fine Cotton Spinners' and Doublers' Association Limited: a survey of the Association and its historical setting* (privately printed, Manchester, 1909) · J. L. Carrel, *The Coltness Iron Co.* (1948) · *The Bimetallist*, 1–6 (1895–1900) · *Annual Report* [Church of England Temperance Society] (1887–1906) · P. F. Clarke, *Lancashire and the new liberalism* (1971) · *Manchester Guardian* (19 April 1917) · *Manchester Weekly Times* (21 April 1917) · *Kilmarnock Standard* (21 April 1917) · *Kilmarnock Herald* (20 April 1917) · *Stockport Advertiser* (20 April 1917) · *The Times* (24 April 1917) · *WWW* · *CGPLA Eng. & Wales* (1918) · Burke, *Peerage* · parish register, St Thomas's, 1740–1876, Man. CL, Manchester Archives and Local Studies [baptism] **Archives** Bodl. Oxf., corresp. with Sir William Harcourt · Courtauld's, Coventry, Fine Cotton Spinners' and Doublers' Association records · GL, Gibbs MSS · Hatfield House, Hertfordshire, Salisbury MSS **Likenesses** Ape [C. Pellegrini], cartoon, repro. in *VF* (3 Oct 1885) · photograph, repro. in E. Gaskell, *Lancashire leaders: social and political* (1908) **Wealth at death** £467,489 17s. 5d.: probate, 12 Jan 1918, *CGPLA Eng. & Wales*

Houling [Howling], **John** (1543/4–1599), Jesuit, was born in Wexford in 1543 or 1544. Little is known of his early life. He was already a priest when he entered the Society of Jesus at Rome in 1583. He is known to have been in Spain and Portugal in the late 1570s and early 1580s. Hogan's account of 'Father John Howling' in his *Distinguished Irishmen of the Sixteenth Century* notes that he was at Alcalá de Henares in 1577, and in Galicia in 1580 in connection with a pilgrimage to the shrine of St James of Compostela. In February 1583 Houling was at Lisbon prior to going to Rome and joining the Society of Jesus. Some time before 1583 he had also returned to Dublin and had met bishops and priests at the house of the redoubtable Mrs Margaret Ball, who was twice imprisoned for the profession of her beliefs, the second time by her son, Walter, mayor of Dublin; she died in prison in 1584 and was beatified in 1989.

After his Jesuit noviceship at Arona, in the province of Milan, Houling exercised his ministry at Genoa. In 1589 he was sent to Lisbon to replace another Irish Jesuit, Robert Rochford, who had died there the previous year. Rochford had ministered to the merchants and the sailors who frequented the port. Soon Houling met with poor students arriving from Ireland or living precariously in the city and anxious to study for the priesthood. By questing for alms for their support he was able to meet their immediate and most pressing needs: food, clothing, and lodging adequate for study and religious exercises. But royal recognition and support were necessary to assure stability for the work. With the influential assistance of a Portuguese Jesuit, Pedro Fonseca, the royal approval was secured and the Irish College, Lisbon, came into being on 1 February 1593.

Houling himself never became rector of the college he did so much to found. The reason for this is not clear. It may just have been that the time required for such a task would conflict with his special mission among sailors, traders, and refugees from the Elizabethan persecution.

He seems to have been effective in his mission. A number of Irishmen were said to have returned to religious practice and 120 Englishmen to have been converted to Catholicism as a result of their contact with him. He died during an outbreak of plague in Lisbon in 1599 and was buried there. The precise date of his death is not clear. Hogan mentions November and 31 December, but the Portuguese Jesuit provincial catalogues give 7 March 1599.

In spite of his busy years at Lisbon, Houling managed to compile a small work which entitles him to be regarded as the precursor of the modern Irish martyrologists. The work, entitled 'Perbreve compendium', is significant for the author's personal acquaintance with many of those whose lives he records. It was printed from a manuscript at Salamanca by Cardinal Moran in *Spicilegium Ossoriense*, 1.82ff., and sketches briefly the life and death of eleven bishops, ten priests, thirty-three laymen, and two women who suffered for their religious beliefs.

THOMAS J. MORRISSEY

Sources P. Ó Fionnagáin, *The Jesuit missions to Ireland in the sixteenth century* (privately printed, Dublin, [n.d., c.1975]) · P. F. Moran, ed., *Spicilegium Ossoriense*, 3 vols. (1874–84) · E. Hogan, *Distinguished Irishmen of the sixteenth century* (1894), 28–47 · E. Hogan, ed., *Ibernia Ignatiana, seu, Ibernorum Societatis Jesu patrum monumenta* (1880) · Irish Jesuit Archives, 35 Lower Leeson Street, Dublin

Houlton, Robert (*b. c.*1739, *d.* in or after 1816), playwright and journalist, was the son of the Revd Robert Houlton of Milton, Clevedon, Somerset. On 24 July 1755 he matriculated at Corpus Christi College, Oxford, but in 1757 he was chosen a demy of Magdalen College. He graduated BA on 27 April 1759, MA on 21 April 1762. He resigned his demyship in 1765, and shortly afterwards married.

In 1767 Houlton's father published a sermon entitled *The Practice of Inoculation Justified*, dedicated to Daniel Sutton, a surgeon who had improved the method of inoculation, and announced in the appendix *A Volume of Miscellaneous Poetry*, to be issued by his son, but nothing further is known of the volume. Sutton the surgeon seems to have instructed the younger Houlton in his method of inoculation, and Houlton went to Ireland in 1768 to practise it. By way of advertising himself, he published *Indisputable Facts Relative to the Suttonian Art of Inoculation* (1768). In 1770 Houlton was admitted to an *ad eundem* degree of MA in Trinity College, Dublin, and was subsequently admitted MB. To eke out an income, he engaged in dramatic writing and journalism, and supplied many librettos for the Dublin operatic stage.

In the spring of 1792 Houlton returned to London, and was soon afterwards appointed editor of the *Morning Herald*. Ill health compelled him to resign this post after about a year, and after a long and expensive illness he was committed to the Fleet prison for debt in 1795. In January 1796 Dr Routh, president of Magdalen College, sent him some financial assistance in answer to his appeal. With the aid of James Hook, who composed the music, Houlton brought out at Drury Lane Theatre on 21 October 1800 his comic opera called *Wilmore Castle*, which was apparently an attempt to 'revive Old English Opera' (*Thespian Dictionary*). After running for five nights it was withdrawn in response to what Houlton described as an organized attack. In protest, he published a pamphlet entitled *A Review of the Musical Drama of the Theatre Royal, Drury Lane, for … 1797–1800* (1801). Nothing is known of Houlton after this time, although he does appear in Watkins's and Shoberl's *Biographical Dictionary of the Living Authors of Great Britain and Ireland* (1816).

GORDON GOODWIN, rev. MEGAN A. STEPHAN

Sources Foster, *Alum. Oxon.* • J. R. Bloxam, *A register of the presidents, fellows … of Saint Mary Magdalen College*, 8 vols. (1853–85), vol. 6, pp. 304–8 • *The thespian dictionary, or, Dramatic biography of the present age*, 2nd edn (1805) • D. J. O'Donoghue, *The poets of Ireland: a biographical dictionary with bibliographical particulars*, 1 vol. in 3 pts (1892–3) • T. Gilliland, *The dramatic mirror, containing the history of the stage from the earliest period, to the present time*, 2 vols. (1808) • D. E. Baker, *Biographia dramatica, or, A companion to the playhouse*, rev. I. Reed, new edn, rev. S. Jones, 3 vols. in 4 (1812) • [J. Watkins and F. Shoberl], *A biographical dictionary of the living authors of Great Britain and Ireland* (1816) • Watt, *Bibl. Brit.*

Hourani, Albert Habib (1915–1993), author and university teacher, was born on 31 March 1915 in Didsbury, south Manchester, the fifth of the six children of Fadlo Hourani (1871–1960), a textile exporter, and his wife, Soumaiya (1881–1943), daughter of the Revd Yuakim and Khazma Racy. His parents were both born in Marj 'Ayyun in what is now south Lebanon and his father emigrated to England in 1891.

Hourani was educated at a primary school founded by his father and at Mill Hill School. He won a scholarship to Magdalen College, Oxford, in 1933 where he obtained a first in philosophy, politics, and economics. After graduation in 1936 he used a small grant from the college to visit Lebanon where he obtained a job teaching British and Middle Eastern history at the American University of Beirut.

Returning home in 1939, Hourani was recruited to the newly organized Foreign Office research department run by Arnold Toynbee and Hamilton Gibb. He was sent to the Middle East in 1942 on a mission which culminated in his official report, 'Great Britain and Arab nationalism' (1943). In 1943 he became assistant adviser on Arab affairs to the British minister of state resident in Cairo, writing a series of papers which later formed part of his first two books, *Syria and Lebanon: a Political Essay* (1946) and *Minorities in the Arab World* (1947). The ambivalence which he felt towards the Arab nationalism of that period and his firsthand experience of the key role played by influential urban families in Arab politics remained important themes throughout his scholarly life.

In November 1945 Hourani joined the Jerusalem section of the Arab office, which had been set up to promote the Palestine Arab case. He testified with great skill before the Anglo-American committee of inquiry in February 1946. He did similar work for the Arab office in London from May 1946 to June 1947 before resigning on the grounds that he found this type of political propaganda uncongenial.

At the encouragement of Hamilton Gibb, Hourani returned to Oxford in early 1948 as a research fellow at Magdalen College and then, in 1951, as the university's first lecturer in the modern history of the Middle East. He continued to write on contemporary Middle Eastern affairs in articles and reviews which were sometimes sharply critical of what he took to be ill-informed official prejudice about the Arab people, notably his 'The decline of the West in the Middle East' (*International Affairs*, 1953). But after one last trenchant piece looking at the Suez affair from the perspective of declining imperial power, 'The Middle East and the crisis of 1956' (1958), he deliberately confined himself to historical themes and, in particular, to the impact of modern Europe on certain leading Arab thinkers, published as *Arabic Thought in the Liberal Age* (1962). This was a pioneering work which opened up many new areas for academic research.

In the early 1950s Hourani converted to Roman Catholicism. In February 1955 he married Christine Mary Odile Wegg-Prosser (*b.* 1914), an antiques restorer; they had one daughter, Susanna (*b.* 1956). Hourani moved to St Antony's College, Oxford, in 1958 as the second director of its newly created Middle East Centre. He was immediately drawn into an energetic period of institution building, using the government funds recommended by the Hayter committee report to place modern Middle Eastern studies on a firm basis with the establishment of eight new posts. The intelligent guidance which he exercised over this whole process, the intellectual frameworks he established for examining what was still a fledgeling field, and his patient supervision of a growing number of graduate students soon made Oxford one of the premier Middle East centres in the world. Of particular importance were his ability to open up the older, orientalist, approach to insights from the work of the important social scientists he encountered during two visits to the University of Chicago in 1962 and 1963 and to reach out to European scholars, particularly in France and Germany. First fruits of this can be seen in his influential article 'The politics of the notables' (1966), and in his leadership of the Oxford Near East History Group and its series of international symposia beginning with 'The Islamic city' (1965).

Hourani resigned as director of the St Antony's Middle East Centre in 1971 and as university reader in Middle East history in 1980. This gave him more time to write and also to do what he enjoyed best, teaching and advising graduate students in Britain, the United States (particularly at Harvard), and Europe. He remained unusually open to the ideas of his younger colleagues and was always willing to share his own thoughts with them. At first meeting, many seemed in awe of a man who acted with a dignified old-fashioned courtesy and who was so knowledgeable and well read. But they were soon put at their ease by his warmth and interest and by the skill with which he and his wife, Odile, were able to make visitors feel welcome and at home.

Hourani published two collections of essays, *Europe and the Middle East* (1980) and *The Emergence of the Middle East* (1981). These contain many of the seminal works by which he was best known, notably 'Islam and the philosophers of history' in which he sets out several themes later developed by Edward Said in *Orientalism* (1979), 'Ideologies of the mountain and city: reflections on the Lebanese civil war', and his very personal memoir, 'H. A. R. Gibb: the vocation of an orientalist'.

It was a source of much discomfort to Hourani that he was unable to complete a major work on the Arab provinces of the Ottoman empire which had been commissioned in the 1950s. Nevertheless, he eventually found a satisfactory way of writing general history based on an emphasis on the central importance of notable politics and the agro-city, first unveiled as a research agenda in 1976, and then used to structure his highly successful *A History of the Arab Peoples* (1991).

Hourani was appointed CBE in 1980. He and his wife moved to London in 1984. In 1988 he delivered the Tanner lectures at Cambridge University, later published as *Islam in European Thought* (1991). He took obvious pleasure in the enthusiastic reception accorded to *A History of the Arab Peoples*, which appeared at a time of great public interest in the Middle East during the Gulf crisis of 1990–91. He continued to write and meet students until two days before his death in the John Radcliffe Hospital, Oxford, on 17 January 1993. He was cremated at Oxford crematorium on 25 January. ROGER OWEN

Sources N. E. Gallagher, *Approaches to the history of the Middle East: interviews with Middle East historians* (1994) · T. Naff, ed., *Paths to the Middle East: ten scholars look back* (1993) · private information (2004) [Cecil Hourani and Mrs Odile Hourani] · personal knowledge (2004) · M. Wilson, 'A bibliography of Albert Hourani's published works', *Problems of the modern Middle East in historical perspective: essays in honour of Albert Hourani*, ed. J. P. Spagnolo (1992), 287–306 · The Arab Studies Society, Jerusalem, Musa Alami files

Likenesses photograph, St Ant. Oxf., Middle East Centre

Wealth at death £101,910: probate, 10 June 1993, *CGPLA Eng. & Wales*

House, (Arthur) Humphry (1908–1955), literary scholar, was born at Sevenoaks, Kent, on 22 May 1908, the second son of William Harold House, solicitor, and his wife, Eleanor Clara Neve. A scholar of Repton School and Hertford College, Oxford, he took a first in *literae humaniores* in 1929 and in 1930 a second in modern history. After a year's teaching at Repton he was ordained deacon in the Church of England in 1931 and was elected fellow, lecturer in English, and chaplain at Wadham College, Oxford; but during 1932 he felt unable to take priest's orders, so resigned his fellowship and retired into lay life. On 21 December 1933 House married Madeline Edith (*b.* 1903/4), daughter of Henry Pitman Church, company director; they had two daughters and one son. Before and during the early years of the marriage House was conducting an affair with Elizabeth *Bowen (1899–1973), herself married to Alan Cameron. From October 1933 he spent two years as assistant lecturer in classics and English at University College, Exeter, and then sailed for Calcutta, where he was first professor of English at the Presidency College and then lecturer in English at the university.

In 1938 House returned to England and in 1940 was elected a William Noble fellow in the University of Liverpool, but before long he was called up as a trooper in the Royal Armoured Corps. He was later commissioned and held a number of staff appointments until 1945, when he was invalided out with the rank of major. He always said that he had begun to learn how to organize paper not in any university, but at the Staff College at Camberley.

From 1947 to 1949 House was director of English studies at Peterhouse, Cambridge, and during those years he gave many talks on the Third Programme of the BBC. In 1948 he was appointed university lecturer in English literature at Oxford, and in 1950 was elected to a senior research fellowship at Wadham.

From early years House concentrated on nineteenth-century England—not only its literature, but its history, economics, manners, and particularly its religion—believing that only in a synthesis of all these could the truth be found. His method was to analyse a work of literature minutely, as a classical scholar would, but always to interpret it in the light of the larger context. Despite the subtlety of his approach he was never afraid to be simple and direct. The first published fruits of his method, and of the breadth of his learning, appeared in his edition of *The Note-Books and Papers of Gerard Manley Hopkins* (1937), which, with its massive organization and wide-ranging notes, was immediately recognized as an indispensable source for the study of that poet and his work.

House then turned his attention to Dickens, whose fame had hitherto been supported mainly by enthusiastic amateurs. There was no adequate biography or collection of letters, no satisfactory edition of the novels, and few critical studies based on a thorough knowledge of the period. House set about changing all that: his book *The Dickens World* (1941) was the first serious attempt to examine the novels in the light of the times in which they were written; a second edition was issued in 1971. He later began to collect, date, and annotate every Dickens letter that could be traced; and he helped in launching the first critically annotated edition of the novels. The two last projects were completed by others, but House was a prime mover.

In 1953 House published *Coleridge*, an expanded version of the Clark lectures given at Cambridge in 1951–2. Here his power of precise detail, biographical and literary, combined with humanity and vision to analyse those aspects of Coleridge's genius which made him inescapably the poet he was. In this book House was able to make effective use of quotations from Coleridge's notebooks which had not before been printed. After his death two posthumous books appeared: *All in Due Time* (1955), a collection of his essays, reviews, and broadcast talks; and *Aristotle's 'Poetics'* (1956), a course of Oxford lectures, revised and introduced by Colin Hardie, which had had a revolutionary success in the English school when first given in 1952.

House's pupils—schoolboys, undergraduates, and graduates—thought him the most inspiring teacher they had ever known, and it is as a teacher-critic-scholar that he would have liked to be remembered. Of all his teaching he gained most satisfaction from the lectures on the nineteenth century which he gave to graduate students during his final years at Oxford—the culmination and reward, he felt, of twenty years of work and reading.

Like Matthew Arnold, House knew a great deal about

schools and universities, language and literature, and from this solid base his critical and creative perception took wing. For him scholarship involved discovering a writer's intention, which inevitably led to a minute study of the writer's life and personality and of the society in which he lived. House had an unusual sense of the past, of its remoteness, and at the same time of its relevance to the present. His writing was economical, and his criticism had an absolute directness and seriousness which brought it close to its living subject. He was the most imaginative of pedants, the most flexible of perfectionists. No one could be long in House's presence without becoming aware of his intellectual stature and deep integrity. To strangers he might at first seem formidable—as in one sense he was—but closer knowledge soon disclosed his warmth, humour, kindliness, and generosity.

At the time of his sudden death from thrombosis at his home, 61 Bateman Street, Cambridge, on 14 February 1955, House was deeply engaged in editing Dickens's letters. His notes on them might well have proved his greatest monument, for his gift as a writer was to apply the severity of his scholarship to himself and to distil it into deceptively simple annotations. He was survived by his wife and three children. Madeline House, 'a remarkably exact, erudite and nice woman' (Hart-Davis, 7), took over the organization of her late husband's papers. She saw through to publication a revised edition of *The Note-Books and Papers of Gerard Manley Hopkins*; this was completed by Graham Storey and appeared in 1959 as *The Journals and Papers of Gerard Manley Hopkins*. She was also one of the general editors, with Graham Storey, of *The Letters of Charles Dickens* (12 vols., 1965–2002). Her husband's biography of Gerard Manley Hopkins's early life, well advanced when he died, was never finished.

RUPERT HART-DAVIS, rev. MARK POTTLE

Sources *The Times* (17 Feb 1955), 10e · *The Times* (24 Feb 1955), 10e · *The Lyttelton Hart-Davis letters: correspondence of George Lyttelton and Rupert Hart-Davis*, ed. R. Hart-Davis, 1 (1978) · personal knowledge (1971) · private information (1971) · m. cert. · d. cert.
Archives BL, corresp. with Society of Authors, Add. MS 63267
Wealth at death £9426 10s. 9d.: probate, 28 July 1955, *CGPLA Eng. & Wales*

House, John [Jack] (1906–1991), journalist and writer, was born on 16 May 1906 at 13 Deerpark Gardens, Tollcross (subsumed in 1912 into the city of Glasgow), the eldest of eight children born to English parents, John House, a company secretary, and his wife, Georgina Tindle Thomson; his upbringing was solidly middle-class. He attended Whitehill secondary school in Dennistoun, where he formed ambitions to become an author, actor, or artist. However, he finally acceded to his father's demand that he train to be an accountant. This, though, was not to his taste, and by 1928 he was working as a reporter and feature writer on the *Glasgow Citizen* newspaper.

The first major feature by House covered one of John Logie Baird's demonstrations of his new television technology at Glasgow University. He later recalled that the journalistic corps attending thought that this innovation, though interesting, would not amount to much. House

also covered many major news events in the city, including the Glen cinema fire of 31 December 1928 in which eighty children died. He continued to work as a journalist on Glasgow's evening newspapers—*The Citizen*, the *Evening Times*, and *The News*—and also in light entertainment for the BBC. In the 1930s House's interest in the theatre resulted in the publication of *Eight Plays for Wolf Cubs*. This passion never left him, and later in life he acted with the Scottish National Players. In the Second World War he served as lance-corporal in the Gordon Highlanders before moving to the army cinematographic unit. Here he worked as a scriptwriter for propaganda films alongside, among others, Peter Ustinov and David Niven.

After the war House returned to Glasgow and to journalism and, increasingly, to book publication. His knowledge of his home city (and its surrounding areas) was encyclopaedic, and he had huge affection for the place. This, combined with his lively and infectious writing style, meant that he published prolifically in the thirty years following the end of the war. In a period when Glasgow was better known for its poverty, grime, sectarianism, and violence, in books such as *The Heart of Glasgow* (rev. edn 1965) and *Glasgow Old and New* (1974) Jack House enthusiastically championed the character of Glasgow's people as well as the city's history, culture, and architecture. Indeed, he recounted that, on showing John Betjeman round Glasgow, the poet exclaimed that this was 'the greatest Victorian city in the world' (*Heart of Glasgow*, 20). Key to his success was his willingness to spin a yarn. Although he treated facts as 'sacred', he also maintained that 'if there's a good story I'm going to tell it, whether there's an iota of factual evidence or not' (ibid., 27). Thus, in *Heart of Glasgow*, he described the city's foundation by St Mungo in the style of a medieval romance. Another key was drink; in the same book he did not flinch from relating the various ways, both ingenious and highly dangerous, that Glasgow's drunks had found to remain inebriated despite abject poverty. House was not, however, censorious; he spent a lot of time in the many bars around Glasgow's city centre, and the liveliness he found here informed his writing as much as it cemented his popularity.

Together with Moray McLaren, a friend from Edinburgh, House formed the All Saints Club. Consisting of 100 members split evenly between Edinbrovians and Glaswegians, this was formed for the purposes of keeping the old feud between the two cities going. Although the rivalry among the All Saints was friendly (House thought it remarkable that 'in a country as small as Scotland you should find two such completely divergent towns less than fifty miles apart') there was the occasional edge; the difference between Glasgow and Edinburgh, he once told the lord provost of Edinburgh, 'is that Edinburgh has culture for 3 weeks of the year while Glasgow has culture for fifty-two' (*Heart of Glasgow*, 17).

Jack House was not sentimental about Glasgow, however, and retained a fascination from his earlier journalistic days for crime, particularly murder. In *Square Mile of Murder* (1961) he explored four murders which occurred in the west end of the city, including the case of Oscar Slater, who was wrongly convicted of murder. In the four cases he examined he found a common thread to be a concern for respectability at the expense of honesty.

Though his writing was seldom overtly political House was a member of the Liberal Party, and stood unsuccessfully for the Liberals at the Glasgow Woodside by-election of 1963. Throughout the 1960s and 1970s he was heavily involved in campaigning against the building of the M8 motorway through the centre of the city, which destroyed, among other places, much of the Anderston and Charing Cross areas. He was prescient in the early 1970s in describing the peripheral estates of Easterhouse, Castlemilk, and Drumchapel as slums of the future. About this time he was worried that Glasgow was losing its 'city-state' feel, and expressed a nostalgia for the town that he thought had been disappearing since the last tram ran in 1962. House married a fellow journalist, Jessie Bennet Millar (d. 1974). There were no children from the marriage.

House continued writing into his later years. In 1981 he published his first novel, *The House on the Hill*, an adaptation of the successful Scottish Television series of the same name. His last, and fifty-fourth, book, *Music Hall Memories*, was published to celebrate his eightieth birthday in 1986. During the 1980s he continued to write a column for the Glasgow *Evening Times*, 'Ask Jack', in which he answered questions from readers (on which often rested a wager) about people, places, and events in Glasgow's history. In 1988 he was awarded the St Mungo medal by the city council in honour of his services to Glasgow. He died in the Western Infirmary, Glasgow, on 11 April 1991 after a short illness.

Despite a faintly ludicrous appearance, with buck teeth and a lazy eye, House was a memorable figure. His enduring legacy, according to fellow journalist, Jack McLean, was to have defended Glasgow's working-class culture at a time when the city was perceived by many to be beyond the pale. There was some irony in his being born technically outside Glasgow, of English parentage, and into a middle-class milieu, but the respect for him among the city's people was genuine.   JOHN McMANUS

Sources J. House, *Heart of Glasgow*, rev. edn (1965) · *Glasgow Herald* (12 April 1991) · *The Scotsman* (12 April 1991) · *Evening Times* (12 April 1991) · b. cert. · d. cert.

Household, Geoffrey Edward West (1900–1988), novelist, was born on 30 November 1900 in Clifton, a suburb of Bristol, the son of Horace West Household (1870–1954), secretary of education for Gloucestershire, and his wife, Lucy Beatrice Noton (1870–1955). Household's grandfather had inherited an estate in Norfolk, but this had to be sold following the agricultural depression of the 1870s. His father qualified as a barrister and then took up a career in education. Household was educated at Durnford preparatory school, and at Clifton College. He then went to Magdalen College, Oxford, where in 1922 he took a first in English. He had no particular ambition, and might easily have followed his father into the civil service; instead, through a Magdalen connection, he joined the Ottoman

Bank and was sent to Bucharest. So began twenty-five years of almost uninterrupted residence abroad.

Bucharest was the making of Household. Thanks to the very favourable exchange rate he could live like a prince on £400 a year. The callow former public schoolboy became a discriminating hedonist, well versed in the pleasures of the table and the bed. About banking he was less enthusiastic, so that when, in 1926, he had to choose between his job and Elisaveta (Betty) Kopelanoff, the Americanized Russian émigrée he would later marry, he chose Betty. But neither party relished domesticity, and it was not until 1935, five years after they were married, that they began, 'reluctantly', to cohabit (Household, 93). They were divorced in 1942. From 1926 to 1929 Household sold bananas in Spain for Elders and Fyffes. He fell in love with the Basque country and its 'noble' inhabitants but could not persuade Betty to settle there ('Lives and times of Geoffrey Household'). Instead he joined her in the United States, in Los Angeles, reckoning that there would be jobs to spare in Hollywood now that the talkies had arrived. But nobody made him an offer, so he followed Betty to New York, arriving just as the stock market crashed. Reduced to living off bread and bananas, he landed a job writing entries for a children's encyclopaedia. He did this and similar tasks for two years until, tiring of hack writing and bathtub gin, he returned to England. There followed four peripatetic years in Europe, the Near East, and South America as a traveller in printing inks. Then in 1935, with an advance from the Atlantic Monthly Press, to whom he had sent a long short story, he began work on his first novel, *The Third Hour*. This was followed by a book of short stories and then, in September 1939, came *Rogue Male*, the spare, tense thriller that put Household firmly and forever on the map.

A passionate believer in European civilization, Household blamed Hitler personally for perverting it. 'The man had to be dealt with, and I began to think how much I would like to kill him' (*The Times*, 7 Oct 1988). This is the departure point for *Rogue Male*, in which a laconic English sportsman sets out to bag 'the biggest game on earth' (G. Household, *Rogue Male*, 1973 edn, 7–8), only to be hunted down in his turn. Reviewers were enthusiastic, but Household was too preoccupied to register more than a 'detached pleasure' (Household, 211) in what they said. He was back in Bucharest, attached to a section of the British military mission, whose task was to blow up the Romanian oil wells if and when the Germans invaded. But in June 1940 the increasingly pro-axis Romanians got wind of the section's plan and it had to be aborted. Three months later, after various central European adventures, Household arrived in Cairo. There he joined field security—'the only branch of Intelligence in which a free-lance could enjoy the care and companionship of a unit under his own command' (Household, 121)—and was almost immediately sent with his section to Greece.

In his autobiography, *Against the Wind*, Household admitted that it was not simply the urge to have a crack at Hitler that impelled him to join the special reserve of officers during Munich week. Like many others who had just missed the First World War, he had a 'burning curiosity' (Household, 99) to know what it was like to be under fire. His curiosity was satisfied in April 1941 during the Greek débâcle, from which he managed to extricate his men 'naked, but reasonably unashamed' (*The Times* 7 Oct 1988). He then served in Palestine, Syria, and Iraq, rising to the rank of lieutenant-colonel and being mentioned in dispatches.

Household returned from the war with a family. In 1942 he married Ilona Maria Judith Zsoldos-Gutmán (*b.* 1914), a Hungarian he had met in Jerusalem, and by 1945 they had a son and a daughter (a second daughter was born in 1953). Providing for his dependants proved a struggle until, reluctantly (for he disliked the brutality of the genre), he wrote two further thrillers, *A Rough Shoot* and its sequel, *A Time to Kill*. Rather more to his taste were picaresque novels of suspense such as *The Lives and Times of Bernado Brown*, whose hero 'is in trouble with everyone and yet is not what is commonly called a criminal' ('Lives and times of Geoffrey Household'). He felt most at home with the short story, and said he would prefer to be judged by collections like *Tales of Adventurers* and *Sabres in the Sand* than by any of his novels.

Household had always intended to settle in the country, but was unable to leave London permanently until 1957, when he and Ilona moved from Chiswick to Buckinghamshire. There, every morning, he would write between 700 and 1000 words in pencil, knock off for lunch, garden in the afternoon, and then type up the morning's work between tea and dinner. Apart from his family, his writing, and his garden, he took pleasure in animals, especially cats, log fires, good food and wine, and reading history and biography. He loathed mediocrity and bureaucracy in equal measure, and when, in 1970, it looked as if a third London airport might be built nearby, put his saboteur's skills at the disposal of the local resistance movement.

Household once described himself as 'an Englishman with no national prejudices', but in *Against the Wind* he admitted to being 'at bottom far more typical of my countrymen than it pleases me to think' (Household, 71, 131). With his lean frame, deep, fruity voice, pink cheeks, and bristling moustache, he had ex-officer written all over him. He published his last novel in 1988, and died shortly afterwards from heart failure on 4 October 1988 at Wardington House, Banbury, Oxfordshire; after a funeral service at St James's Church, Newbottle, his remains were cremated in Oxford crematorium on 11 October.

MICHAEL BARBER

Sources G. Household, *Against the wind* (1958) • *The Times* (7 Oct 1988) • 'Lives and times of Geoffrey Household', *Books and Bookmen* (May 1973) • private information (2004) [family]
Archives Indiana University, Bloomington, Lilly Library, literary papers
Wealth at death under £70,000: probate, 2 Aug 1990, *CGPLA Eng. & Wales*

Housman, Alfred Edward (1859–1936), poet and classical scholar, was born on 26 March 1859 at Valley House, Fockbury, a hamlet near Bromsgrove, Worcestershire, the first

Alfred Edward Housman (1859–1936), by Francis Dodd, 1926

of the seven children (born within the space of ten years) of Edward Housman (1831–1894), solicitor, and his wife, Sarah Jane (1828–1871), daughter of the Revd John Williams, rector of Woodchester, Gloucestershire. Shortly afterwards the family moved to Perry Hall, Bromsgrove (later a hotel), where Housman spent his childhood. Of his siblings, Laurence *Housman (1865–1959) became a successful writer and his brother's literary executor, while Clemence Annie *Housman was a noted illustrator and suffragette campaigner. Though he came to be popularly associated with the neighbouring county of Shropshire, Housman insisted that he did not know Shropshire well and freely admitted that his poems contained topographical errors: the fact that in his early years 'its hills were our western horizon' (letter to Maurice Pollet, 5 Feb 1933, *Letters*) qualified it as a territory that dreams are made of.

Childhood and schooling A happy childhood was terminated by the death of Housman's mother, after a long illness, on his twelfth birthday. Towards the end of his life he told Pollet that he 'became a deist at thirteen and an atheist at twenty-one' and that reading Lemprière's *Classical Dictionary* from the age of eight 'attached my affections to paganism' (*Letters*, 328). His father subsequently married a cousin, Lucy Housman (on 26 June 1873), and Housman quickly formed a good relationship with his stepmother, as is evident from his earliest surviving letter, written to her during a visit to London (probably his first) in January 1875. Following his second marriage Edward Housman moved back to Fockbury, settling at Fockbury House (also known as Clock House), Catshill. After receiving his first lessons from a governess, Housman attended a dame-school in Bromsgrove, winning a scholarship to Bromsgrove School in July 1870. Under Herbert Millington, headmaster from 1873 and an enthusiastic teacher of Latin and Greek, he was groomed for an Oxford classical scholarship. Unsuccessful at his first attempt, he was awarded a scholarship at St John's College in June 1877 and went into residence in October.

Oxford and the civil service In two different though possibly related ways Housman's time at Oxford profoundly affected his subsequent life. It began promisingly: in his second term he was among the top six candidates for the Hertford scholarship and in 1879 was placed third in the competition for the Newdigate prize, as well as obtaining a first class in honours moderations. There were, however, symptoms of an intellectual self-assurance hazardously verging on arrogance: after attending one lecture given by Benjamin Jowett, regius professor of Greek, he declined to waste his time on another, and he spoke contemptuously of the classical attainments of his college tutors. The passion for accurate learning and the unconcealed, and often gleeful, scorn for those who failed to live up to the highest standards—attributes that proved to be characteristic of the mature scholar—were already evident in the undergraduate. In practical terms, his disrespect for his mentors and for the official course of study led him to pursue private enthusiasms, specifically the text of Propertius, when he should have been reading the philosophers and historians assigned in the Greats syllabus.

At some stage Housman fell in love with Moses Jackson, a college contemporary who had come up with a science scholarship, and whose interests were athletic rather than literary. This love—intense, lifelong, and seemingly unrequited—came to exert a deep influence on Housman's poetry, as well as on his personal life. In his fourth year he moved out of college and shared rooms with Jackson and another friend, Alfred Pollard (later a distinguished bibliographer), in a house, now demolished, in St Giles'. His infatuation with Jackson may well have led him further to neglect the prescribed studies, and the outcome was as uncompromising as it was startling to those who knew him: in the finals examinations that began on 27 May 1881 the examiners had no choice but to fail him outright. In October he returned to Oxford for one term in order to satisfy the residence requirement for a pass degree: he was successful in the examination the following summer but waited ten years before proceeding to the degree.

At the end of 1881 Housman returned to Bromsgrove to prepare for the civil service entrance examination, held in June. His success led to the offer of a post in Dublin, which he declined; a clerkship in the Patent Office in London, at an annual salary of £100, proved less unattractive, for Moses Jackson was already employed in the same institution, though in a considerably less humble capacity than Housman was now to fill. He promptly found lodgings at 15 Northumberland Place, Bayswater, and began a ten-year period of servitude as a higher division clerk in the trade marks registry. Early in the following year he moved to 82 Talbot Road, Bayswater (where he is now commemorated by a plaque), sharing a home with Moses and his younger brother Adalbert, a classics student at University College. Adalbert, the 'A.J.J.' of poem 42 in *More Poems*, died of typhoid fever in 1892 at the age of twenty-seven. There is no evidence to support the suggestion that Housman formed a romantic, and perhaps a sexual, relationship with Adalbert, though it is by no means impossible. What is known is that towards the end of 1885 Housman left the shared home in dramatic circumstances (he disappeared for a week) and did not return. In 1887 Moses Jackson took up a teaching position in India, and in later years his meetings with Housman were very infrequent. After quitting the Jacksons and spending a brief period in lodgings at 39 Northumberland Place, Bayswater, Housman moved to Byron Cottage, 17 North Road, Highgate (the site of another commemorative plaque), where he remained for nineteen years. When in 1905 his landlady moved to 1 Yarborough Villas, Pinner, Middlesex, he moved with her.

The classical scholar Very soon after settling in London Housman had begun to work in the evenings in the British Museum Library, and as early as 1882 had begun to publish in important journals a series of papers on textual criticism, at this stage working on both Greek and Latin authors. On 11 December 1885 he offered Macmillan his edition of Propertius: the offer was declined and the edition never published, but by 1892 he had twenty-five papers to his credit. On the strength of this record he applied in April 1892 to University College, London, where chairs of Latin and Greek had been advertised, expressing an interest in both, with a preference for the Latin chair. His letter of application noted, perhaps uniquely, that he had 'failed to obtain honours in the Final School of Literae Humaniores', and added, pointedly, that for the past ten years 'the study of the Classics has been the chief occupation of my leisure'; he enclosed a printed booklet containing seventeen testimonials from some of the most distinguished classical scholars of the day. He was offered the chair of Latin on 24 May and took up his duties in the autumn.

For nearly nineteen years Housman served University College well, contributing to its administration and its social life, as well as being responsible, at first almost single-handedly, for the teaching of Latin, and playing a significant role in improving the college's academic reputation, at a low ebb on his arrival. He formed particularly happy relationships with W. P. Ker, who had become professor of English in 1889, and Arthur Platt, who became professor of Greek in 1894. Housman was active in the college literary society, delivering witty addresses on various English poets. A very early example of his skill as a public speaker is the introductory lecture delivered on 3 October 1892 (published 1937).

A *Shropshire Lad* and public acclaim From 1897 Housman frequently took holidays on the continent, especially in France and Italy, where he was able to indulge his enthusiasm for ecclesiastical architecture and fine food and wine.

Despite a heavy burden of teaching, most of it at an elementary level, he continued his researches, producing during his years in Gower Street not only a number of learned papers, but also editions of Ovid (1894) and Juvenal (1905; 2nd edn, 1931), as well as the first instalment of his edition of Manilius (1903), dedicated to Jackson. But the most celebrated as well as the most inexplicable production of this period was his collection of sixty-three lyrics, *A Shropshire Lad* (1896). In the important letter to Pollet already cited Housman states that his 'most prolific period' as a poet was 'the first five months of 1895' (*Letters*, 329), and it is striking that this period coincided with the arrest, trials, and imprisonment of Oscar Wilde, who was sentenced on 25 May and was the unnamed subject of one of Housman's most compelling poems (*Additional Poems*, 18). Originally titled *Poems by Terence Hearsay*, the volume was refused by Macmillan, but published by Kegan Paul in March 1896 at Housman's expense. A second edition, in September 1898, was issued by another publisher, Grant Richards, who became a close friend. Though not an instant success, the little volume gradually won a large audience through the universality of its dominant themes (nature, love, war, and death) and the directness of its language and rhythms. In a period of war, uneasy peace, and rapid social change, Housman was one of the most familiar and most highly regarded of the poets of his time. His celebration of landscapes and a rural life distinctively and traditionally English contributed to his poetry's appeal.

By that time Housman had moved from London to Cambridge, where he spent the remainder of his life. The chair of Latin there fell vacant in December 1910, and in the following month Housman accepted the post (shortly afterwards renamed the Kennedy professorship), as well as a fellowship at Trinity College, while his old Oxford college, St John's, elected him to an honorary fellowship on 1 May. He took up residence in Cambridge in May and, after living briefly in lodgings at 32 Panton Street, moved into rooms in a distant corner of Trinity (Whewell's Court, K staircase). His inaugural lecture, published only in 1969 (as *The Confines of Criticism*), was given promptly on 9 May and judged 'brilliant' by its audience. During the next quarter of a century, and almost until the day of his death, Housman lectured on textual criticism and pursued studies that resulted in a large body of articles, as well as an edition of Lucan (1926; 2nd edn, 1927), and the remaining four books of the astronomer–poet Manilius (completed 1930). The latter, a task in which his predecessors included Scaliger and Bentley, was conceived by its editor as his monument.

While Housman enjoyed the conveniences, and especially the gastronomic delights, available to a bachelor don in the period, his rooms were spartan and his devotion to his work unremitting. Although addicted to solitary walks, and with a reputation for unapproachability, he could also be convivial, and had a considerable reputation as a raconteur and an after-dinner speaker. He continued until very near the end of his life to travel to France for holidays, one Paris restaurant naming a dish after him (*barbue Housman*). It seems likely that these visits also provided opportunities for homosexual adventures. In his later years he took great pleasure in making his journeys to Paris by aeroplane.

The growing popularity of *A Shropshire Lad* produced many enquiries concerning a successor—all firmly discouraged by Housman, who affected pride in his own poetic 'barrenness', until, towards the end of 1920, he displayed a sudden interest in publishing a further volume. The result was the defiantly titled *Last Poems*, published on 19 October 1922 to considerable acclaim: a leader in *The Times* was devoted to its author on the day of publication, and 21,000 copies had been printed by the end of year. The impetus for its publication was perhaps provided by the knowledge that Moses Jackson, now retired and living in Vancouver, was suffering from stomach cancer. On the day of publication a copy was dispatched to Jackson, who died on 14 January 1923. Despite its title, *Last Poems* was supplemented by the posthumous *More Poems* (1936), selected, 'by his permission, not by his wish' (preface), by Laurence Housman, and by the 'Additional Poems' included in Laurence's *A.E.H.* (1937). Published in the same year as T. S. Eliot's *The Waste Land*, *Last Poems* remains resolutely traditional in subject matter and style, reflecting a pastoral England that moved rapidly towards extinction during Housman's lifetime. However, the poems' distinctive blend of lapidary phrasing, musicality (there is considerable variety and subtlety in the handling of metrical forms), and sentiments evoking a universal response guaranteed him a continuing public. On Housman's own admission, his poetic manner owes less to the mainstream traditions of Victorian or Georgian verse than to the border ballads, Shakespeare's songs, and Heine.

Later years and reputation It was as poet rather than as classical scholar that Housman, in his later years, enjoyed considerable fame, but attempts to turn the conversation towards his poetry were discouraged, sometimes peremptorily, and honorary degrees from a number of universities (including, twice, Oxford) were all declined, as was, in 1929, the Order of Merit. Although unwilling to accept the Clark lectureship at Cambridge, he delivered the Leslie Stephen lecture in 1933: the result was *The Name and Nature of Poetry*, which includes some unexpectedly personal reflections on poetic composition, as well as a thinly veiled attack on the new Cambridge critics, and was in printed form a best-seller. By this time, though still carrying out his academic duties, Housman was a tired and ailing man. Only a week before his death he gave the first two lectures advertised for the Easter term of 1936, but was too weak to continue. He died from myocarditis in the Evelyn Nursing Home, Trumpington Road, Cambridge, on 30 April 1936, and on 25 July his ashes were interred against the north wall of St Laurence's, Ludlow, Shropshire. On 22 March 1985 a statue was unveiled at Bromsgrove in his honour, and in 1996 a memorial was housed in Poets' Corner, Westminster Abbey. Housman is the central character in Tom Stoppard's play *The Invention of Love* (1997).

Slight of build, precise of speech, and conservative in

dress, Housman acquired a reputation for dryness and even severity of manner that represented only one aspect of a complex nature. Notorious for withering sarcasms, employed to admirable effect in his castigation of incompetent fellow editors, he also possessed a strong sense of fun and was a gifted writer of comic verse and parodies. His letters have an epigrammatic wit and an unfailing elegance of phrasing. While making no secret of his unwillingness to suffer fools gladly, he was capable of lasting friendships with such diverse figures as Grant Richards, Gilbert Murray, William Rothenstein, and Witter Bynner.

Housman would probably have wished to be remembered primarily as a textual editor in the great tradition of Bentley and Porson—and he retains an awed respect among classical scholars—but the poems whose authorship he was not eager to acknowledge have achieved a more widespread and more enduring fame. They continue to find readers worldwide and have been a source of inspiration for many composers. At the same time Housman merits recognition as a prose stylist in the tradition of Dr Johnson and as an epigrammatist in that of Oscar Wilde. NORMAN PAGE

Sources *The letters of A. E. Housman*, ed. H. Maas (1971) · N. Page, *A. E. Housman: a critical biography* (1983) · A. S. F. Gow, *A. E. Housman: a sketch* (1936) · L. Housman, *A. E. H.* (1937) · P. Withers, *A buried life* (1940) · G. Richards, *Housman, 1897–1936* (1941) · L. Housman, *The unexpected years* (1937) · *CGPLA Eng. & Wales* (1936) · b. cert. · d. cert. **Archives** BL, diaries, Add. MSS 45861, 54349 · Bodl. Oxf., corresp. with Society for the Protection of Science and Learning · Bryn Mawr College Library, Pennsylvania, corresp., diaries, and papers · Col. U., Rare Book and Manuscript Library, corresp. and literary MSS · CUL, lecture notes · FM Cam., MS poems and corresp. · Indiana University, Bloomington, Lilly Library, MSS and letters · L. Cong., poetical notebooks and papers · Ransom HRC, MSS and papers · UCL, letters to his stepmother · University of Illinois, Urbana-Champaign, letters | BL, corresp. mainly with E. H. Blakeney, Add. MS 48980 · BL, corresp. with The Richards Press, Add. MSS 44923–44924 · BL, letters to F. M. Cornford, Add. MS 58427 · BL, literary MSS · Bodl. Oxf., corresp. with Robert Bridges · Bodl. Oxf., letters to Gilbert Murray · CUL, letters to Sir Sydney Roberts · Harvard U., Houghton L., letters to Witter Bynner · Harvard U., Houghton L., letters to Sir William Rothenstein · NL Scot., letters to Richards and Ashbourne families · Somerville College, Oxford, letters to Percy Withers and family · Trinity Cam., letters to his sister, Katherine Symons · U. St Andr. L., letters to Sir D'Arcy Wentworth Thompson · UCL, letters to Mildred Platt | FILM BFI NFTVA, *Poetry in motion*, Channel 4, 13 June 1990 **Likenesses** W. Rothenstein, chalk drawing, *c.*1903, Man. City Gall. · W. Rothenstein, chalk drawing, 1906, NPG · H. Lamb, pencil drawing, 1909, Trinity Cam. · E. O. Hoppé, print, *c.*1911, NPG · T. Spicer-Simson, plasticine medallion, *c.*1922, NPG · F. Dodd, drawing, 1926, St John's College, Oxford · F. Dodd, pencil drawing, 1926, NPG [*see illus.*] · R. E. Gleadowe, pencil drawing, 1926, Trinity Cam. · statue, 1985, Bromsgrove, Worcestershire · F. Dodd, pencil drawing, UCL · W. Rothenstein, chalk drawing, Trinity Cam. **Wealth at death** £7969 14*s.* 9*d.*: resworn probate, 4 Aug 1936, *CGPLA Eng. & Wales*

Housman, Clemence Annie (1861–1955), illustrator and suffragette, was born on 23 November 1861 at Bromsgrove (her birth registered, nameless, as 'female'), the third child and first daughter of Edward Housman (1831–1894), a solicitor, and his wife, Sarah Jane Williams (1828–1871). Her eldest brother was the poet A. E. *Housman (1859–

1936). Clemence was educated at home by a governess. By her early twenties she was undertaking much of her father's clerical work; a second brother, Laurence *Housman, recorded that she 'was, for two or three years, the expert who worked out all the Income tax calculations for half the County of Worcestershire' (L. Housman, 94). Her mother died when she was nine, charging her with special responsibility for Laurence, four years her junior. Indeed Laurence Housman records in his autobiography that it was only in order to look after him in London that Clemence was eventually 'released from the Victorian bonds of home' (ibid., 104).

In 1883, having been left a small legacy, Clemence Housman went with Laurence to London and trained as a wood-engraver at the City and Guilds South London Technical Art School at Kennington, and at the Millers' Lane City and Guilds School in South Lambeth. After a year away from home, Clemence was very nearly recalled in order to provide domestic support for her stepmother and younger siblings. She did, however, 'claim a return to freedom' (L. Housman, 110) after inheriting another legacy. The brother and sister lived for fourteen years in Marloes Road in Kensington and then, in 1903, settled in Pembroke Cottages, Edwardes Square, which they took over from the artist William Rothenstein. Clemence Housman gained employment as a wood-engraver, at first providing illustrations for such weekly illustrated papers as *The Graphic* and the *Illustrated London News*. Then, as wood-engraving was superseded by photomechanical 'process' engraving for commercial work, she began to work for such fine private presses as C. R. Ashbee's Essex House Press and James Guthrie's Peartree Press. She also published two novels of Christian allegory. The first, *The Were-Wolf*, was written to entertain her fellow students in the engraving class at Kennington and was first published in *Atalanta*, and then in 1896, illustrated by Laurence Housman, by John Lane at the Bodley Head. The second, *The Unknown Sea*, was published by Duckworth in 1898. She based her third novel, *The Life of Sir Aglovale de Galis* (1905), on a story, teased out of Malory's *Morte d'Arthur*, of a knight who put truth above honour. Laurence Housman, not one to underestimate his own talent, always considered Clemence the finer literary artist and in 1954 arranged for the publication by Cape of a new edition of *Sir Aglovale*. The only other of her publications to be traced is a short story, 'The Drawn Arrow', published in *31 Stories by Thirty and One Authors*, edited by Ernest Rhys and C. A. Dawson Scott and published by D. Appleton & Co. (New York) in 1923.

In 1908 Clemence Housman subscribed to the militant suffragist Women's Social and Political Union and in 1909 was a co-founder of the Suffrage Atelier, which described itself as 'An Arts and Crafts Society Working for the Enfranchisement of Women'. Laurence Housman described her as the atelier's 'chief worker' (L. Housman, 274) and the studio in the Housmans' garden became a centre of banner making. Clemence Housman worked on three banners designed by her brother: the 'Prison to citizenship' banner for the Kensington WSPU in 1908; that for the Hampstead branch of the Church League for Women's

Suffrage (now in the Museum of London); and that for the United Suffragists in 1914. She also made a banner (1913), now lost, for the Conservative and Unionist Women's Franchise Association, and may have worked on those of the Oxford Graduates, the Women's Tax Resistance League, and the Actresses' Franchise League. She was kept busy repairing banners damaged in use.

In 1910 Clemence Housman became a member of the committee of the Tax Resistance League, doubtless inspired to follow this particular form of protest by her youthful involvement with income tax forms. On 30 September 1911 she was the first woman arrested for following that society's precepts; she had for eighteen months refused to pay inhabited house duty. Her reward was a prison sentence with all its attendant publicity. A photograph of her arrest appeared in the *Evening Standard* and the Tax Resistance League organized a procession and demonstration to protest against her imprisonment. She was released after a week, no reason being given, and did not pay her debt until she received the right to vote in 1918. After Mrs Pankhurst's statue was unveiled in Victoria Gardens in 1930, Clemence Housman for many years supplied it with flowers. She and Laurence were, from before the First World War, close friends of Roger and Sarah Bancroft Clark, both parties sharing an interest in women's suffrage and pacifism. In 1924 the Housmans moved to Street, home of the Clarks' family shoemaking business. Clemence Housman's relationship with her brother Laurence remained intense throughout her life. In her last years she declined into senility, suffering a severe stroke in 1953, and was cared for assiduously by her brother and by Roger and Sarah Clark. She died on 6 December 1955 at Mount Avalon, Glastonbury, having suffered a further stroke, and was buried at Smallcombe cemetery outside Bath, alongside her brother Robert (*d*. 1905) and her sister Kate (*d*. 1945).   ELIZABETH CRAWFORD

Sources Street Public Library, Somerset, Housman MSS · J. Pugh, *Bromsgrove and the Housmans* (1975) · L. Housman, *The unexpected years* (1937) · L. Tickner, *The spectacle of women: imagery of the suffrage campaign, 1907–14* (1987) · S. S. Holton, *Suffrage days: stories from the women's suffrage movement* (1996) · P. Lovell, *Quaker inheritance, 1871–1961: a portrait of Roger Clark of Street based on his own writings and correspondence* (1970) · K. L. Mix, 'Laurence, Clemence and Votes for women', *Housman Society Journal*, 2 (1975), 42–52 · H. S. Housman, 'The Housman banners', *Housman Society Journal*, 18 (1992), 39–47; 19 (1993), 39–50 · b. cert. · d. cert.
Archives Bromsgrove Library, corresp. and papers · Street Public Library, Somerset, papers, incl. letters of Laurence Housman and Clemence Housman—to each other and to Roger Clark and Sarah Clark | Street Public Library, Somerset, letters to Roger Clark and Sarah Clark · Street Public Library, Somerset, letters to Laurence Housman
Likenesses A. Graham, pastel drawing, Street Public Library, Somerset
Wealth at death £9121 0s. 6d.: probate, 14 May 1956, *CGPLA Eng. & Wales*

Housman, Laurence (1865–1959), writer and artist, was born on 18 July 1865 at Perry Hall, Bromsgrove, Worcestershire. His father, Edward Housman (1831–1894), a solicitor practising in Bromsgrove, was emphatically tory. Housman's mother, Sarah Jane Williams (1828–1871), died

Laurence Housman (1865–1959), by Howard Coster, 1937

when he was five years old, leaving her five sons (Laurence, Alfred Edward *Housman, the scholar and poet, Robert, Basil, and Herbert) and two daughters (Clemence *Housman and Kate) in their father's care. The children were brought up at Perry Hall, Bromsgrove, the family home belonging to John Adams, Edward Housman's great-uncle. They were educated by a governess, Miss Milward. After Edward's second marriage, to his cousin Lucy Housman, the family moved to nearby Fockbury House, Catshill. Laurence, like each of his brothers, won a scholarship to be educated as a day boy at Bromsgrove School. Financial constraints limited his further education, although his elder brother Alfred attended Oxford University. On Edward Housman's insistence, Laurence sat the Oxford and Cambridge local entrance examination: the father had no intention of supporting a university education, but agreed that, if Laurence passed, he could go to art school in London. On having this condition explained to him, the examiner, Dr Spooner, passed Laurence Housman on the spot.

Housman's schooldays made a lasting impression. He later compared the oppressive experiences of bullying and fagging with the subjugation of colonized countries under imperialism. The rigidly conservative political and religious influences of his childhood provoked a rebellious response and at eighteen years of age he broke away from his father's control. Assisted by a legacy of £500 each, he and Clemence moved to London in November 1883. They found lodgings at 36 Camberwell New Road.

Clemence had been working long hours as a clerk for her father, but found that her skills flourished in the field of wood-engraving for James Guthrie at the Pear Tree Press. Like Laurence, Clemence was a writer as well as an artist, publishing books such as *The Were-Wolf* (1896), *The Unknown Sea* (1898), and *The Life of Sir Aglovale de Galis* (1905). Housman studied at the Arts and Crafts School, and at Miller's Lane City and Guilds Art School, South Lambeth. His first work was in the field of illustration, but he eventually exhibited in spaces such as the Baillie Gallery, the Fine Art Society, and the New English Art Club. He wrote for Harry Quilter's *Universal Review* and as art critic for the *Manchester Guardian*, an association which lasted for sixteen years: he dealt with controversies such as the Chantrey bequest and the statues by Jacob Epstein on the British Medical Association building. He also contributed to the *Yellow Book*, and published his poetry in two volumes, *Green Arras* (1896) and *Spikenard* (1898). In the course of his literary and artistic career Housman came to know Charles Ricketts, Charles Channon, and Oscar Wilde. Rodney Engen's study (1983) provides a comprehensive list of his artwork and writings.

In 1900 the anonymous publication of *An Englishwoman's Love Letters* caused a furore and brought Housman £2000. His nativity play *Bethlehem* was given an impressive production in 1902 by Edward Gordon Craig. It faced numerous difficulties, however, ranging from the artistic—Craig's disregard for the integrity of Joseph Moorat's accompanying music—to the practical, where the sacks of straw representing sheep were deemed to be a fire hazard. Although the production was run at a financial loss to Housman, he recalls the episode with good humour in his autobiography.

In 1906 Housman's collaboration with Harley Granville Barker on a pierrot play, *Prunella*, produced at the Court Theatre, led to an extended dramatic career. Housman's *Pains and Penalties*, a play about Queen Caroline, wife to George IV, was refused a licence by the lord chamberlain. It was produced without licence by Edith Craig for a private performance for members of the Pioneer Players society in 1911, challenging the powers of the lord chamberlain. In the context of an increasingly forceful campaign against the Theatre Licensing Act, a Caroline Society was founded after the performance and members of the audience were invited to join. *Pains and Penalties* also appropriated the figure of Queen Caroline for the women's suffrage cause in its representation of a woman refused entry at Westminster. Housman was an ordinary member of the Pioneer Players from 1911 to 1914.

Housman was committed to the women's suffrage movement. He was a founder member of the Men's League for Women's Suffrage, an indefatigable public speaker, and a writer of pamphlets, articles, and plays. He translated *Lysistrata*, produced at Gertrude Kingston's Little Theatre instead of the banned *Pains and Penalties*. The satirical form attracted Housman, as demonstrated by his play *Alice in Ganderland*, and his later novels *John of Jingalo* (1912), *Trimblerigg* (1924), and *The Life of HRH the Duke of Flamborough* (1928).

Laurence and Clemence Housman moved to 1 Pembroke Cottages, Edwardes Square, Kensington, London, in 1902. This became the headquarters of the Suffrage Atelier, a society which produced banners and artwork for the movement. Housman took part in the Hyde Park demonstration of 1908. In July 1910 he collaborated with Edith Craig on the design of one section of a Women's Social and Political Union (WSPU) demonstration. Prominent in the campaign to resist the census in 1911, he published advice on strategies for protesting in the Women's Freedom League's newspaper, *The Vote*. Clemence Housman was imprisoned in October 1911 during another campaign of passive resistance in support of women's enfranchisement: tax resistance. Housman was disgusted by the sexual discrimination in favour of male supporters of women's suffrage, as his arrest for protesting against the forcible feeding of hunger-striking suffragists, unlike that of the female protesters, did not result in imprisonment. However, objecting to its later arson campaign, he parted company with the WSPU and was a founder member of the United Suffragists in 1914.

Housman was fearless in public commitment to controversial campaigns. He was an active member of the British Society for the Study of Sex Psychology and the Order of Chaeronea, and the First World War found him writing for Sylvia Pankhurst's *Workers' Dreadnought* and in support of Indian independence. In 1919 he joined the Independent Labour Party and prison reform and international peace became pressing issues for him. He resigned from the Franchise Club in protest against its anti-German stance. In 1916 Housman visited the United States with C. R. Ashbee and G. Lowes Dickinson on a lecture tour in support of the League of Nations. In 1920 he returned to the United States, visiting Sing Sing prison in New York state where Mott Osborne had been running an experiment in self-government under the Mutual Welfare League.

Some of Housman's plays, popular with amateurs, were given fund-raising performances for charities; however, he deplored the insidious exploitation of the author perpetrated through the assumption that fees for performance would be waived. The representation of heroes, public figures, and role models preoccupied him in his later plays, collected as the *Little Plays of St Francis* (1922) and *Victoria regina* (1934). The Queen Victoria plays were performed privately at the Gate Theatre in 1935, and publicly in 1937 at the Lyric Theatre, after the lord chamberlain had granted a licence. The topicality of the performances in the summer of the coronation brought Housman some £15,000. In the same year he published his autobiography, *The Unexpected Years*, which is of interest in its representations of his upbringing, and the cultural and political milieu of his times in London, but reticent on his homosexuality.

Housman's beliefs found a home in Quakerism after the First World War. He wrote for *The Ploughshare*, a Quaker publication. However, it was not until 1952 that he joined the Society of Friends in Street, Somerset. He and Clemence had moved to Street in 1924 and had made close friends of Quakers Sarah and Roger Clark. It was an environment which suited the siblings in their later years. Clemence Housman's death in 1955 left Laurence bereft of a beloved companion. He died on 20 February 1959 in Butleigh Hospital in Glastonbury, Somerset.

KATHARINE COCKIN

Sources L. Housman, *The unexpected years* (1937) · R. Engen, *Laurence Housman* (1983) · S. S. Holton, *Suffrage days: stories from the women's suffrage movement* (1996) · L. Tickner, *The spectacle of women: imagery of the suffrage campaign, 1907–14* (1987) · J. Hunt, 'Laurence Housman, the younger brother', *Housman Society Journal*, 16 (1990), 6–19 · K. L. Mix, 'Laurence, Clemence and votes for women', *Housman Society Journal*, 2 (1975), 42–52
Archives BL, introduction to the diaries of A. E. Housman, Add. MS 45861 · BL, corresp. with Society of Authors, Add. MSS 63268–63273, *passim* · Bryn Mawr College Library, Pennsylvania, corresp., memoirs, and papers · CUL, letters to Royal Society of Literature · Hunt. L., letters · JRL, letters to *Manchester Guardian* · L. Cong., corresp. · Ransom HRC, corresp. and literary MSS · Street Public Library, Somerset, corresp. and literary MSS · U. Reading L., corresp. · University of Iowa Libraries, Iowa City, corresp. and MSS | BL, corresp. with Sir Sydney Cockerell, Add. MS 52726 · BL, letters to Ellen Coleman, Add. MS 59898 · BL, corresp. with Macmillans, Add. MS 55010 · Bodl. Oxf., letters to Gilbert Murray · Bodl. Oxf., letters to Lady Piercy · Bodl. Oxf., letters to Lord Ponsonby · Bodl. Oxf., letters to Evelyn Sharp · Bodl. Oxf., corresp. with Sidgwick and Jackson · Bromsgrove Library, Worcestershire, letters to Ethel Mannin; letters to Reginald Reynolds · Col. U., Rare Book and Manuscript Library, letters to Cyril Clemens · CUL, letters to Ida Northcote · King's AC Cam., letters to C. R. Ashbee and Janet Ashbee · LPL, corresp. with H. R. L. Sheppard · McMaster University Library, Hamilton, Ontario, letters to Frank Russell · Ransom HRC, corresp. with John Lane · Street Public Library, Somerset, letters to Roger Clark and Sarah Clark · Trinity Cam., letters to S. F. Gow · U. Reading, corresp. with Jonathan Cape; letters to Chatto and Windus · U. Southampton L., letters to Bournemouth Poetry Society · U. Warwick Mod. RC, letters to Victor Gollancz · Women's Library, London, letters to Ruth Cavendish-Bentinck · Worcs. RO, letters to Sir Edward Elgar |SOUND BL NSA, recorded talk
Likenesses W. Rothenstein, lithograph, 1898, Bradford City Art Gallery, NPG · photograph, 1911, Museum of London · A. Miller, wooden bust, *c*.1924, NPG · P. Tanqueray, photograph, *c*.1930–1939, NPG · H. Coster, photographs, 1936–50, NPG [*see illus.*] · portrait, Religious Society of Friends meeting house, Street, Somerset
Wealth at death £4367 18*s*. 5*d*.: probate, 30 July 1959, *CGPLA Eng. & Wales*

Housman, Robert (1759–1838), Church of England clergyman, born at Skerton, near Lancaster, on 25 February 1759, was the son of Robert Housman, a maltster. He was educated at the Lancaster Free Grammar School. At the age of fourteen he was apprenticed to a local surgeon, but against his father's wishes turned his attention to the church, and in 1780 went to Cambridge as a sizar at St John's College. He took deacon's orders in October 1781, and served a curacy at Gargrave, Yorkshire. On returning to Cambridge he was ordained priest on 26 October 1783, and became intimate with Charles Simeon and Henry Venn, friendships which firmly established his evangelical view of religion. He graduated BA in 1784, and did not proceed beyond that degree. He officiated as curate at St John's, Lancaster, in 1785–6, but his evangelical emphases did not commend themselves to his congregation. In 1786 he became curate at Langton, Leicestershire, and in 1787–

8 and again in 1790 he was curate to the Revd Thomas Robinson of St Mary's, Leicester, while also holding curacies at Markfield (1788–*c*.1791) and Foston, both near Leicester, as well as a lectureship at St Martin's, Leicester in 1792. During his time in the Leicester area he married, first, in 1785, a Miss Audley, who died in the following winter, and secondly, on 24 September 1788, Jane Adams (*d*. 1837) of Langton, author of a popular tract called *The History of Susan Ward* (1817). In 1795 he finally settled at Lancaster, where he built a new church (St Anne's), of which he remained incumbent until his resignation in 1836. At first he met with much opposition on account of his evangelical teachings, though he ultimately became one of the most influential clergymen of the district, and was known as 'the evangelist of Lancaster'. He instituted weekly lectures, conducted Sunday evening prayer meetings to his last years, ran a benevolent society, was active in the work of the Bible Society, and introduced hymn-singing in his services, much to the disapproval of his bishop. Doctrinally, he was a moderate Calvinist, unwilling to dogmatize about predestination, and rejecting the ideas both of Christian perfection and premillenarianism. His writings include *A Sermon Preached at Lancaster* (1786), which aroused local controversy; *The Pastoral Visitor*, in sixteen numbers (1816–19), the last of which, on the deity of Christ, incurred a charge of Sabellianism; and *Sermons Preached in St Anne's Chapel, Lancaster* (1836). There are also seventeen sermons in the *Life and Remains* (1841).

Housman died at Woodside, near Liverpool, on 22 April 1838, and was buried at Skerton. There is a memorial inscription in St Anne's, Lancaster. Housman's second wife had predeceased him on 27 January 1837.

C. W. SUTTON, *rev.* ARTHUR POLLARD

Sources R. F. Housman, *The life and remains of the Rev. Robert Housman* (1841) · Venn, *Alum. Cant.*
Likenesses S. W. Reynolds, mezzotint, pubd 1822 (after J. Lonsdale), NPG; repro. in Housman, *Life and remains*

Houston, Dame Fanny Lucy (1857–1936), adventuress, was born on 8 April 1857 at Kennington, fourth daughter of Thomas Radmall, box-maker, and his wife, Maria Isabella Clarke. A juvenile actress known as Poppy Radmall, she eloped at the age of sixteen to Paris with the brewer Frederick Gretton (1840–1882), who abandoned his wife. Mrs Gretton, as she became known, was a beautiful young coquette, with direct, impudent speech and a tiny waist, who became expert in Parisian fashions and manners. During their riotous partnership Gretton gave her many gifts, before bequeathing her £6000 a year for life. On 3 September 1883, pretending to be aged nineteen, she married Theodore Francis Brinckman or Broadhead (1862–1937), afterwards third baronet. They separated years before their divorce (1895) but remained friendly. On 1 March 1901 she married (very quietly, posing as an invalid widow, which enabled the ceremony to occur in church without the bigoted demonstrations that disgraced Brinckman's remarriage) George Frederick William Byron, ninth Baron Byron (1855–1917). A bankrupt since 1899, Red-Nosed George was a cipher in her hands and lived in her house on Hampstead Heath. During the First

Dame Fanny Lucy Houston (1857–1936), by Bassano, c.1909–10

World War she opened a rest home for nurses who had served at the front, and was created DBE in 1917.

Having been a suffragette, patrolling Hampstead Heath in her carriage and haranguing holidaymakers, Lady Byron developed post-war obsessions with Prussians, communists, and socialists. She anathematized Woodrow Wilson and his fourteen points but extolled Mussolini. About 1921 she met a hard, ruthless, unpleasant bachelor, Sir Robert Paterson Houston, first baronet (1853–1926), a Liverpool shipowner and a sectarian Conservative MP. Several of his friends, notably Lord Birkenhead, warned him against Lady Byron: her response was to send such wild denunciations of Birkenhead to Stanley Baldwin that the latter asked the police to investigate her eccentricities. After a long, wily campaign she married Houston in December 1924, and they settled as tax exiles in Jersey. Throughout his brief marriage Houston suffered mental disorders. She accused his friends of trying to poison him and tasted all his food. When he showed her his will leaving her £1 million, she tore it in half and threw it on the floor, declaring 'If I'm only worth a million, then I'm worth nothing at all' (Day, 44).

Houston died in April 1926 somewhat mysteriously, on board his 1600 ton steam yacht *Liberty*, having (by a will dated 19 January 1926) bequeathed four-fifths of his £7 million fortune to his wife, whose 'wonderful intuition on two occasions saved my life when the doctors despaired of it' (*The Times*, 21 April 1926). His widow immediately became deranged by paranoia and religious delusions, was decreed unfit to manage her own affairs, and

restrained. After several months she escaped from Jersey on the *Liberty*. Until Houston's death it was little known that Channel Islands residents were exempt from mainland fiscal controls. In 1927 Lady Houston had secret, flirtatious meetings at the Treasury with Winston Churchill, whom she adulated as an anti-Bolshevik, and agreed to pay the exchequer £1.6 million without admitting legal liability for death duties.

Having achieved her apotheosis as a financial adventuress, Lady Houston embarked upon noisy and gleeful political adventures. She abominated Ramsay MacDonald, whom she vilified both in print and by such stunts as ordering that *Liberty* blaze at night with 8 foot high lights reading 'To hell with the traitor Macdonald' (1932). During 1933 she disrupted nine by-elections by financing demagogic rumpuses against National Government candidates and bought the *Saturday Review*, which she transformed into a mouthpiece of high tory chauvinism: she was herself a frequent and emotional contributor. As part of her longing to see Britain supreme everywhere she donated £100,000 to enable a British team to compete for the Schneider aviation trophy (1931) and gave large gifts to the Navy League. In order to counteract the National Government's proposed scuttle from India she funded the Houston-Mount Everest aeronautical expedition of 1933. The 1935 general election was enlivened by an expensive campaign of her pamphlets, placards, and slogans. Her influence waned as her eccentricity became more offensive.

A fresh-air fiend and nudist, Lady Houston claimed prophetic powers and made much of her Sibylline dreams. In later life she made a vulgar fetish of the Union Jack, taking red, white, and blue as her racing colours and for her clothes. Her strident, sometimes incoherent, letters were, however, always written on purple or blue notepaper in violet ink. On her increasingly rare outings she carried a gigantic shabby handbag crammed with bank notes, jewels, documents, and miscellanea. Pestered by begging letters and importunate tricksters she was surrounded by obsequiousness. Implacable in her hatreds she was also insatiable in her kindness. She translated her Latin motto as 'Whoever hits me I hit back—harder.'

Heartbroken by the abdication of Edward VIII, Lady Houston stopped eating, and died of myocardial degeneration on 29 December 1936, at Byron Cottage, Hampstead. She was buried in St Marylebone cemetery, East Finchley, on 4 January 1937. All her property was bequeathed informally to a friend; a legal will was never found.

RICHARD DAVENPORT-HINES

Sources *The Times* (31 Dec 1936) · *The Times* (5 Jan 1937) · *Daily Telegraph* (31 Dec 1936) · *News Chronicle* (31 Dec 1936) · *The Spectator* (1 Jan 1937) · *National Review*, 108 (1937), 167–8 · J. W. Day, *Lady Houston, DBE: the woman who won the war* (1958) · H. W. Allen, *Lucy Houston, DBE, 'One of the few'* (1947) · CUL, Baldwin MSS [vol. 159, fols. 213–25] · J. Campbell, *F. E. Smith, first earl of Birkenhead* (1983), 98, 718–19 · [F. W. F. Smith, earl of Birkenhead], *F. E.: the life of F. E. Smith, first earl of Birkenhead* (1959), 71–3 · J. Charmley, *Lord Lloyd and the decline of the British empire* (1987), 188–92 · C. C. Owen, 'The greatest brewery in the world': a history of Bass, Ratcliff & Gretton, Derbyshire RS, 29 (1992), 100 · T. R. Gourvish and R. G. Wilson, *The British brewing* industry, 1830–1980 (1994), 222, 224 • will of Frederick Gretton, 26 Aug 1882, Principal Registry of the Family Division, London • *The Times* (29 April 1895) • *The Times* (30 April 1895) • *The Times* (8 May 1895) • *The Times* (14 May 1895) • Burke, *Gen. GB* • GEC, *Peerage* • d. cert.

Archives CAC Cam., Churchill MSS, Lloyd MSS • CUL, Baldwin MSS • PRO, MacDonald MSS

Likenesses photographs, *c.*1875–1925, repro. in Day, *Lady Houston*, frontispiece and facing p. 30 • Bassano, photograph, *c.*1909–1910, NPG [*see illus.*] • photograph, 1931, Keystone Photo Agency • photographs, 1931, Central Press Photo Agency • H. J. Thaddeus, portrait

Wealth at death £1,528,083 12s. 6d.: administration with will, 5 April 1937, *CGPLA Eng. & Wales*

Houston, John (1802–1845), anatomist, born in the north of Ireland, was the eldest son of a Presbyterian minister and was brought up by his uncle Joseph Taylor, physician to the forces. In 1819 he was apprenticed in Dublin to John Shekleton, a young anatomist and founder of the Dublin College of Surgeons' Museum. On Shekleton's premature death in 1824 Houston succeeded him as curator of the museum; he held the office until 1841, and the collection was greatly improved by him. In 1834 he published a catalogue of the normal preparations, and in 1840 one of the pathological. He was also demonstrator of anatomy to the students at the College of Surgeons for a time after 1824. In 1826 he graduated MD at Edinburgh. In 1832 he was elected surgeon to the new City of Dublin Hospital, and in 1837 lecturer on surgery at the Park Street school of medicine, the rich museum of which he catalogued in 1843. He was medical officer to several institutions in Dublin, and carried on a private practice in York Street.

Houston was one of the first to introduce the microscope in Dublin medicine. He was interested in the work of J. Muller and read a paper on 'The microscopic pathology of cancer' to the Surgical Society of Ireland in May 1844 which was published in the *Dublin Medical Press* in the same year. Houston wrote that

> up to the date of my resignation of the curatorship of the Museum of this College (1841), microscopic pathology was not much appreciated or cultivated … But since that period, I have taken every opportunity of making myself acquainted with the microscopic characters of morbid growths. (Widdess, 64–5)

Houston contributed to the medical journals of Dublin, Edinburgh, and London, and to the transactions of societies. Many of his papers were descriptions of anatomical and pathological specimens; others were surgical. In a paper on the mucous membrane of the rectum he described a condition which led to controversy. The rectal 'valves' were named after him. He also published 'On the structure and mechanism of the tongue of the chameleon', in the *Transactions of the Royal Irish Academy* (1828), illustrated from his own drawings, a treatise on *Dropsy* (1842), and a pamphlet on *The Mode of Treatment in Fever* (1844). Houston died at Dalkey on 30 July 1845 from disease of the brain which began while he was delivering a clinical lecture in the previous April.

CHARLES CREIGHTON, *rev.* MICHAEL BEVAN

Sources J. D. H. Widdess, *An account of the schools of surgery, Royal College of Surgeons, Dublin, 1789–1948* (1949) • J. S. Crone, *A concise dictionary of Irish biography*, rev. edn (1937) • R. G. Butcher, 'Memoir', *Dublin Quarterly Journal of Medical Science*, new ser., 2 (1846), 294–302 [incl. analysis of Houston's writings]

Likenesses oils, Royal College of Surgeons in Ireland, Dublin; repro. in Widdess, *Account of the schools of surgery*

Houston, Renée [*real name* Caterina Rita Murphy Gribbin] (1902–1980), actress, was born on 24 July 1902 at 55 Grahame Street, Johnstone, Renfrewshire, one of at least two daughters of James Gribbin (1876–1939), then a spirit salesman, and his wife, Elizabeth Houston (1875–1942). She later gave her maiden forenames as Katerina Valorita. Her parents, who billed themselves as James Houston and Company, became a well-known touring variety act combining comedy and song; the children lived with their grandmother in the small farming community of Carntyne, near Glasgow, where Renée Houston, as she was known from a child, attended the local convent school. By 1914 she had developed her own act, filling in for an absent comedian in the Fyfe and Fyfe Company. She described her three years with them as her 'theatrical education' (Houston, 21), playing a variety of roles, developing the coloratura voice she inherited from her mother, and learning Scottish dancing and ballet.

When her parents become ill on tour Renée replaced them with a double act she invented with her sister Billie. The Houston Sisters established themselves with comedy grounded in sibling rivalry, Billie playing the boy; they combined meticulous attention to detail, including furniture scaled up to make them look like toddlers, with almost tangible on-stage rapport that gave them improvisatory flair. They were both sharply observational about working-class Scottish life and childhood, and sexually magnetic. In 1926 they appeared at the royal command performance, and they were still successful when Billie retired owing to ill health in 1935. In 1923 Houston was married for the first time, her husband being George Balharrie; they adopted two sons but the marriage ended in divorce and on 28 November 1932 she married Patrick de Lacy Aherne (*b.* 1900/01), a film actor. They had a son and a daughter but that marriage, too, ended in divorce, in 1948. On 7 August that year she married the actor Donald Stewart (1909/10–1974).

After the retirement of her sister, Houston subsequently developed an act with Donald Stewart. They performed in revue and pantomime, and in the first production of the 1959 play *Roar Like a Dove*, subsequently a Houston trademark; she was to play in six different productions. Her film career took off after the war and she played in several distinguished British films, in comedies such as *The Belles of St Trinian's* (1957), *Watch it, Sailor* (1961), and *Twice Round the Daffodils* (1961), and in dramas such as *The Horse's Mouth* (1959), *A Town Like Alice* (1956), and *Time without Pity* (1957). She also worked several times with the director Roman Polanski, notably on the experimental *Repulsion* in 1965, and was an occasional member of the informal company of British comic actors who appeared

Renée Houston (1902–1980), by Anthony Buckley, 1938 [in the film *A Girl Must Live*; second from left, with (left to right) Margaret Lockwood, Hugh Sinclair, and Lilli Palmer]

in the Carry On series, in *Carry on Cabby* (1963), *Carry on Spying* (1964), and *Carry on at your Convenience* (1971). In 1963, while continuing with stage, film, and television work, she began a radio career in *Petticoat Line*, a lighter version of *The Brains Trust* in which a female panel discussed listeners' questions. The show made good use of her talent for the spontaneous and her ability to interact with panellists such as Barbara Cartland and Rachel Heyhoe Flint to generate lively and controversial discussion. She worked on the show for more than ten years and became closely identified with it.

While she never attained star status, Houston's talents are evident even in small and unrewarding roles. In *Carry on at your Convenience*, for example, she plays a strike-breaking mother who spanks her shop steward son. The role is often awkwardly written but she gives it a consistency largely absent from the script, making effortless transitions between screaming abuse and vamping her lodger with curdled charm. Her Scottish timbre freed her from the cut-glass diction that enfeebled many of her generation—she was never typecast. Her looks were distinctive and her face mobile, seeming to become raddled or seductive within moments.

It was not surprising that Houston continued working until her death from pneumonia at St Peter's Hospital, Chertsey, on 9 February 1980. One of her proudest boasts was that she had been 'christened' as a clown by the great Coco, one of the few women thus honoured. She published her autobiography, *Don't Fence me in*, in 1974. It pays extensive tribute to Donald Stewart and to her sister Billie. FRANCES GRAY

Sources R. Houston, *Don't fence me in* (1974) · S. Palmer, *British film actors' credits, 1895–1987* (1988) · *The Times* (2 Nov 1980) · b. cert. · m. certs. · d. cert.
Archives FILM BFI NFTVA, current affairs footage · BFI NFTVA, performance footage |SOUND BL NSA, documentary recordings · BL NSA, performance recordings
Likenesses double portrait, photograph, 1927 (with B. Houston), Hult. Arch. · two photographs, 1927, Hult. Arch. · photograph, 1935, Hult. Arch. · A. Buckley, photograph, 1938, NPG [*see illus.*] ·

group portraits, photographs, *c.*1944, Hult. Arch. · photographs, repro. in Houston, *Don't fence me in* · photographs, BFI, Hult. Arch.

Houston, Richard (1721/2–1775), engraver, was born in Dublin, possibly one of the numerous children of Richard Houston, baker (d. 1730/31?), whose widow, Rachel, received a grant from the corporation to help her to support the family. He was apprenticed to John Brooks as a draughtsman and mezzotint-engraver, James Macardell, Richard Purcell, and Charles Spooner being among his fellow pupils. He learned to draw under West in the Dublin Society Schools. Houston moved to London in 1746 with Brooks, who published their portrait of Sir John Vandeput in 1750. He established himself in premises identified as 'next the Golden Lion, Charing Cross' or 'near Drummonds at Charing Cross', from where he published several portraits of newsworthy figures including William Pitt and the king of Prussia, and several strong mezzotints after Rembrandt. For others he engraved a series of portraits of racehorses.

Undoubtedly talented, Houston was also, as Horace Walpole put it succinctly, 'idle, capricious and extravagant' (*Anecdotes of Painting*, 211–15) and he proved incapable of sustaining a career as an independent engraver–publisher. He found himself in debt to the printseller Robert Sayer, who is said to have had him imprisoned in the Fleet so that he would know where to find him. He did some very mundane work for Sayer and other printsellers and his reputation suffered in consequence, notably when in 1761 the newspapers exposed his part in the production of a portrait supposedly showing Princess Charlotte, recently engaged to George III, after a miniature by Houston. What the publisher did not advertise was that Houston's miniature had depicted Penelope Pitt and his print was the recently published plate of that lady with a new title. However, Sayer also employed Houston to engrave some of his most ambitious publications, notably *The Marquis of Granby* (1769) and *The Death of Wolfe* (1772) after Penny, portraits of the king and queen after Zoffany (1772), and *The Syndics* after Rembrandt (1775). This, Houston's finest plate, was published just before his death in Hatton Street, London, on 4 August 1775.

TIMOTHY CLAYTON and ANITA McCONNELL

Sources D. Alexander, 'Richard Houston', *The dictionary of art*, ed. J. Turner (1996) · Redgrave, *Artists* · Bryan, *Painters* (1886–9) · J. C. Smith, *British mezzotinto portraits*, 2 (1879), 644–702 · W. G. Strickland, *A dictionary of Irish artists*, 2 vols. (1913); repr. with introduction by T. J. Snoddy (1989), vol. 1, pp. 526–7 · *Anecdotes of painting in England, 1760–1795 … collected by Horace Walpole*, ed. F. W. Hilles and P. B. Daghlian (1937), 211–15

Houston, William. See Houstoun, William (*c.*1704–1733).

Houston, Sir William, first baronet (1766–1842), army officer, was born on 10 August 1766, of Scottish descent, and entered the army as an ensign in the 31st foot on 18 July 1781. He became a lieutenant of an independent company in 1782, and captain of the 19th foot in 1785. After serving in the West Indies, at Gibraltar, and at home, he became a major in 1794, and commanded the 19th in Flanders under the duke of York.

Houston was appointed a lieutenant-colonel in the 84th

foot in 1795, and after transferring to the 58th foot he commanded that regiment at the capture of Minorca in 1798, in the Mediterranean in 1800, and in the expedition to Egypt in 1801. The 58th was heavily involved on the British left at the battle of Abu Qir on 20 March. Houston subsequently commanded a brigade at the capture of Rosetta and Cairo and during the siege of Alexandria. He received the second-class decoration of the Turkish order of the Crescent. He next held brigade commands in Malta, at Brighton, and in the Walcheren expedition of 1809. On his return to Brighton he was made a major-general. On 5 November 1808 he married Lady Jane (d. 1 June 1833), daughter of James Maitland, seventh earl of Lauderdale, and the widow of Samuel Long; they had two sons.

Houston commanded the 7th division in the Peninsula from 10 January 1811, and was present with it at the battle of Fuentes d'Oñoro and the attack on San Christobal, Badajoz, before being invalided home in the autumn of 1811. He subsequently commanded the south-western district, and though he applied for re-employment in Spain, Wellington was unable to provide a vacancy. Houston was made KCB in January 1815, and served as lieutenant-governor of Gibraltar from 8 April 1831 to 28 February 1835.

Houston was GCB (1831) and GCH (1827). He was created a baronet by William IV in 1836 and became a full general in 1837. He was colonel of the 4th garrison battalion and the 20th foot respectively. Houston died at Bromley Hill, Kent, on 8 April 1842, and was buried at Carshalton, Surrey.　　　H. M. CHICHESTER, rev. S. KINROSS

Sources GM, 2nd ser., 18 (1842) · The dispatches of … the duke of Wellington … from 1799 to 1818, ed. J. Gurwood, 4: Peninsula, 1790–1813 (1835) · Fortescue, Brit. army, vols. 8–9 · Burke, Peerage (1840) · J. Haydn, The book of dignities: containing rolls of the official personages of the British empire (1851) · T. C. W. Blanning, The French revolutionary wars, 1787–1802 (1996) · R. Muir, Britain and the defeat of Napoleon, 1807–1815 (1996)
Likenesses W. Theed junior, bust, Royal Military Academy, Sandhurst, Camberley, Surrey

Houston [née Jesse; other married name Fraser], **Matilda Charlotte** (1815–1892), novelist and travel writer, was the daughter of Edward *Jesse (1780–1868), writer on natural history and surveyor of royal parks and palaces, and his wife, Matilda, the daughter of Sir John Morris. Later enquiries of relatives in Wiltshire purportedly revealed a link to the Jessés of Languedoc, who had emigrated to England in the sixteenth century. Matilda Jesse had one sister and a brother, John Heneage *Jesse (bap. 1809, d. 1874), historical writer. As a girl she lived in Molesey in Windsor Forest, but when she was eight years old the family moved to a rented house in Hampton. She was educated at home by a Welsh governess 'whom she loathed for not allowing her to read novels' (Blain, Clements & Grundy, Feminist comp., 542). She became engaged at the age of sixteen to the Revd Lionel Fraser, a grandson of Charlotte Smith's sister. They married shortly afterwards, and had one son, but her husband died only a year after their wedding, and Matilda Fraser returned to her family in Hampton.

About 1842 Matilda Fraser married Captain William Houstoun of the 10th hussars, and about five years later the couple took over from Lord Sligo an 80,000 acre estate at Black Lake, Connaught, co. Mayo. About one hundred families worked the land, which was in disarray after Lord Sligo had evicted most of his original tenants when the famine rendered them unable to pay the rents. Twenty Years in the Wild West, or, Life in Connaught (1879) recounts this period in Matilda Houstoun's life, and she also wrote her best-known novel, Recommended to Mercy (1862), while living in Ireland. Her later memoir, A Woman's Memories of Well-Known Men (2 vols., 1883), was dedicated to Richard Sheridan, grandson of Richard Brinsley Sheridan, who was a close friend of her brother, and to Caroline Norton, his sister, whom Houstoun knew. Although this account, which contains as much biographical information as is known, describes her acquaintance with figures such as Wordsworth, Disraeli, Sir William Follett, and John Wilson Croker, it also describes her residence in Mayo as a 'growing ill effect'. She felt very isolated there, and she was thrilled when her husband bought a yacht, The Dolphin, from Lord Grosvenor, and the family set out for a nine-month tour of the West Indies and the Gulf of Mexico. She wrote about her adventures in Texas and the Gulf of Mexico (2 vols., 1844) and Hesperos, or, Travels in the West (2 vols., 1850). The latter is a series of letters covering the journey from Liverpool to Massachusetts, and describing New York, Pennsylvania, Maryland, and Washington, DC. Always opinionated, Houstoun describes American women as 'Free' in their public behaviour, and is particularly interested in the lives of the Irish in America, and in the condition of enslaved blacks on the plantations which she visited in Louisiana and Mississippi.

Houstoun published novels between 1862 and 1891, and these often focus on the perilous life of the single woman. Recommended to Mercy was in its fourth edition by 1863, although she states in her memoir that she had been warned that Mudie would not accept this story of free love for his circulating libraries, as it was 'one which mothers would not permit their daughters to read' (Houstoun, 143). In this tale, Helen Langton and Philip Thornleigh are lovers, but the heroine rejects his offer of marriage, choosing instead to live with him during his India posting for five years. Thornleigh is tricked into marriage on his return to England, and Helen is left to fend for herself with a compromised sexual reputation; she is forced to move about when her past becomes known. When Philip dies, he leaves his considerable estate to Helen, and she establishes a home for prostitutes and abandoned women. In addition to this philanthropic activity, in the complicated, melodramatic sub-plot she devotes herself to ensuring that Philip's children regain their inheritance, which she is glad to sign over once their mother is cleared of bigamy charges. Another of her novels, The Poor of the Period, or, Leaves from a Loiterer's Diary (1884), is dedicated to George Eliot. This book contains twenty-two narratives of incidents of hardship in the lives of servants, tenant families, and fallen women as told to a first-person observer narrator. Her Records of a Stormy Life (1888) is a semi-autobiographical novel describing the fate of a lively girl who marries a reckless army colonel, and who loses, through loneliness and worry, her spirit and moral courage. In 1889 Houstoun produced *Only a Woman's Life; by One who Saved It*, which details her work on behalf of Francis Stallard, a woman tried for infanticide in 1877.

Houstoun died of a cerebral haemorrhage in her house at 16 Gloucester Street, London, on 14 April 1892. Predeceased by her second husband, she was survived by her son, George Houstoun. BEVERLY E. SCHNELLER

Sources M. Houstoun, *A woman's memories of well-known men*, 2 vols. (1883) • S. Mitchell, *Fallen angel: chastity, class and women's reading, 1835–1880* • H. Black, *Notable women authors of the day* (1906) • Blain, Clements & Grundy, *Feminist comp.* • d. cert.
Likenesses H. Black, drawing, repro. in *Ladies Pictorial* (24 Jan 1891)
Wealth at death £979 11s. 6d.: probate, 12 May 1892, CGPLA Eng. & Wales

Houstoun, William (*c*.1704–1733), botanist, may have come from a Scottish landed family in Renfrewshire; he entered St Andrews University in February 1719. The next certain date is that he entered Leiden University in October 1727 and in two years took a degree in physic under Boerhaave, though he did not take a Leiden doctorate. Experiments which he performed on animal respiration, in conjunction with Van Swieten, described in the *Philosophical Transactions*, were a product of this Dutch interlude and point to his emergence as an accomplished experimentalist. From Leiden he moved on to study in Paris, where in 1728 he had gained election to the Académie Royale des Sciences. Plant specimens of his from the Isle of Sheppey testify to an interest in field botany and to his presence next in England in the summer of 1729. In 1730 he also drew up a list (now among the Sloane papers) of plants in the Jardin du Roi in Paris. That same year found him a surgeon in the service of the South Sea Company and collecting plants extensively in Jamaica, Cuba, and neighbouring parts of the mainland. Though that activity was ended by shipwreck near Vera Cruz, most of his belongings were rescued, and quantities of seeds and dried specimens had earlier been safely transmitted to Sir Hans Sloane and Philip Miller. Houstoun had also provided Sloane with an account of the Indian method of making cochineal, and tantalized him with the promise of roots of the mysterious Mexican drug-plant jalap (though they were to prove to be of the wrong species).

By the autumn of 1731 Houstoun had returned to England, where he was the guest of Miller at several meetings of the Royal Society (he was elected a fellow in January 1733). In 1732 he appears to have obtained the degree of MD from his original university, St Andrews. That October, doubtless at the instance of Sloane, he was commissioned by a number of wealthy botanists and cultivators of exotics, in conjunction with the Georgia trustees, to make a three-year return voyage to the West Indies, at a salary of £200 a year. He was instructed to sail by way of Madeira, where he was to study wine-making and procure vine cuttings; on reaching Jamaica he was, in co-operation with the South Sea Company, to visit the Spanish colonies at Cartagena, Porto Bello, Campeche, and Vera Cruz;

finally, after returning to Jamaica, he was to proceed to Georgia and oversee the laying out of a public garden and nursery in Savannah.

This ambitious plan was, however, only half completed when Houstoun died in Jamaica, on 14 August 1733, from either the heat (Pulteney) or, more probably, tuberculosis (Gronovius, in Linné). He was buried at Kingston the next day. Some of his collections had fortunately been shipped to Charles Town and others were safely in Jamaica. All of these, together with his manuscripts and drawings, were bequeathed to Miller, from whom the majority passed in 1774 to Banks and so to the British Museum. Many of the specimens are of great importance, as they formed the basis of new species described by Miller in his *Gardeners Dictionary*. Also, on the strength of duplicates given to him by Miller on his London visit in 1736, Linnaeus adopted and published many of the working names (such as *Buddleja*) which Houstoun coined for the novelties he encountered. Alive to this importance, in 1781 Banks paid for the catalogue left by Houstoun of what he had collected to be printed and given a wide circulation, under the title *Reliquiae Houstoniae*.

More than seventy-five new plant species were introduced to Europe through Houstoun's efforts, though few of those are still in cultivation. A genus *Houstonia* was named in his honour by Gronovius. G. S. BOULGER, rev. D. E. ALLEN

Sources R. P. Stearns, *Science in the British colonies of America* (1970), 327–30 • J. Britten and J. E. Dandy, eds., *The Sloane herbarium* (1958), 139–40 • R. Pulteney, *Historical and biographical sketches of the progress of botany in England*, 2 (1790), 231–4 • E. D. Johnston, *The Houstons of Georgia* (1950), chap. 11 • B. Henrey, *British botanical and horticultural literature before 1800*, 2 (1975), 175–7 • W. B. Hemsley, 'A sketch of the botanical exploration of Mexico and Central America', *Biologia Centrali-Americana: botany*, ed. F. D. Godman and O. Salvin, 4 (1887), 118–19 • R. W. Innes Smith, *English-speaking students of medicine at the University of Leyden* (1932), 121 • R. P. Stearns, 'Colonial fellows of the Royal Society of London, 1661–1788', *Osiris*, 8 (1948), 73–121, esp. 96 • A. M. Coats, *The quest for plants* (1969), 332–3 • J. Britten and E. G. Baker, 'Houstoun's Central American leguminosae', *Journal of Botany, British and Foreign*, 35 (1897), 225–34 • C. von Linné, *Caroli Linnæi … bibliotheca botanica recensens libros plus mille de plantis huc usque editos*, new edn (Halle an der Saale, 1747) • *GM*, 1st ser., 3 (1733), 662 • election certificate, RS
Archives Institute of Jamaica for the Encouragement of Literature, Science and Art, West Indies, MSS, drawings, and specimens of Jamaican plants • San Francisco, California, specimens | NHM, Banksian MSS 67–69 • NHM, botanical catalogues • U. Cam., department of plant sciences, specimens • U. Oxf., department of plant sciences, specimens

Houthuesen, Albert [*formerly* Albertus Antonius Johannes Houthuesen] (**1903–1979**), painter, was born on 3 October 1903 in Albert Cuypstraat, Amsterdam, the eldest of the four children of Jean Charles Pierre Houthuesen (1878–1911), a pianist and artist, and his wife, Elizabeth, *née* Wedemeyer. Following the unexpected death of their father, in 1912 the Houthuesen children moved with their mother to London, settling at Constantine Road, Hampstead. Desperately poor, and unable to speak English, Houthuesen left school at the age of fourteen to work in a variety of menial jobs. He attended evening classes in art at St Martin's School of Art, and his spare time was spent drawing in the British Museum and the National Gallery. In 1922, aged nineteen, he became a British citizen, and in 1923 his paintings were recommended to William Rothenstein who offered him a scholarship to the Royal College of Art, of which he was the director. This began a lifelong friendship with the Rothenstein family, particularly with Sir John Rothenstein, who became Houthuesen's foremost supporter.

While studying at the Royal College from 1923 until 1927, Houthuesen met the painter Catherine Dean (d. 1983). They were married in 1931 and settled at 20 Abbey Gardens, moving in 1938 to a studio flat at 37B Greville Road, St John's Wood. The couple had no children. Unable to make a living through selling his own work, Houthuesen gave evening classes in painting. For three decades until 1961 he endured poverty and neglect, making a very occasional sale and receiving a few portrait commissions. His subjects included scenes of London life and sketches made on Hampstead Heath. He first visited Trelogan in north Wales in 1932, staying for a month in a cottage to which he and Catherine returned annually until 1940. Here he was greatly inspired by the people and landscape: his portraits and drawings of Welsh miners and farmers are among his finest work.

It was, however, as a painter of the sea that Houthuesen was later recognized, and his first interpretations of violent waves lashing against jagged rocks date from the 1930s, when he also visited the coasts of Sussex and Devon. Rejected by the army as medically unfit, he worked as a tracer in the technical drawing office of the London and North Eastern Railway Company in Doncaster, Yorkshire. During his absence from London over forty oil paintings stored in a neighbour's cellar were destroyed beyond repair by damp. The effect of this calamity, combined with the tedium of tracing engine designs for the railway company, led to a nervous breakdown. Houthuesen returned to London at the end of the war and met a family of Russian clowns who inspired him to work on a series of studies of clowns, a theme he continued to explore until his death. In 1952 he and Catherine settled permanently at 5 Love Walk, Camberwell, never leaving London again. His expressionist, sometimes violent, colourful paintings of the imagined sea dominated his prodigious artistic output, which remained unseen outside a small circle until 1961 when he had his first one-man exhibition, at the Reid Gallery, Cork Street, London. Houthuesen was fifty-nine years old, and although his work was virtually unknown to private collectors of art, three of his paintings, including *Crown of Thorns* (1939–40), were by then in the collection of the Tate Gallery, London, two (*Grain Barrels* and *The Collier*) in the Sheffield City Art Galleries collection, and others in museums in Nottingham, Leeds, and Carlisle. During the 1960s a series of exhibitions in London brought him both critical acclaim and income through sales. His second exhibition at the Reid Gallery was in 1963; the Mercury Gallery then mounted five exhibitions between 1967 and 1977. Despite the recognition he received during his final decade, Houthuesen continued to be dogged by ill health, which at times made it impossible for him to paint. He died at his home in Camberwell on 20 October 1979.

JAMES HUNTINGTON-WHITELEY

Sources J. Rothenstein, *Modern English painters*, 3: *Wood to Hockney* (1974) • R. Nathanson, *Walk to the moon: the story of Albert Houthuesen* (1990) • J. Rothenstein, *Albert Houthuesen: an appreciation* (1969) [exhibition catalogue, Mercury Gallery, London] • J. Rothenstein, *British art since 1900* (1962) • J. Rothenstein, *Autobiography*, 3: *Time's thievish progress* (1970), 100–03

Archives Tate collection, letters to John Rothenstein | FILM BBC, Omnibus profile, *Walk to the moon*

Wealth at death £124,049: probate, 12 March 1980, *CGPLA Eng. & Wales*

Houton, John de. *See* Houghton, John of (d. 1246).

Hoveden, John. *See* Howden, John of (fl. 1268/9–1275).

Hoveden, Roger of. *See* Howden, Roger of (d. 1201/2).

Hovell, William Hilton (1786–1875). *See under* Hume, Hamilton (1797–1873).

Hovenden, Robert (1544–1614), college head, was the eldest son of William Hoveden or Hovenden of Canterbury. He was educated at Oxford, was elected a fellow of All Souls College in 1565, graduated BA in the following year, and proceeded MA in 1570. He became chaplain to Matthew Parker, archbishop of Canterbury, and from 1571 to his death held the prebend of Clifton in the diocese of Lincoln. On 12 November 1571 he succeeded Richard Barber as warden of All Souls College. In 1575 he supplicated for the degree of BTh, and for that of DTh in 1580; he was admitted to both degrees in 1581. Papal authority was the subject of his inception disputations, made at a time when the university was more concerned with the defence of protestantism against Roman Catholicism than with debate among various protestant views. In 1582 he became vice-chancellor of the university and in 1582/3 instituted a new visitation of the independent academic halls with the aim of tightening discipline. From 1580 to his death he held the prebend of Henstridge in the diocese of Bath and Wells and the third prebend in the archdiocese of Canterbury.

Hovenden became warden of All Souls while the college was striving to preserve the statuary in the chapel from demolition, but in December 1573 the orders of the commissioners in the matter were too pressing to be any longer disobeyed. After an early crisis he had far more success in his attempts to improve the management of college estates. In or about 1569 the college had leased some woodland in Middlesex to Hovenden's brother Christopher on terms which were disadvantageous to it. Two years later the lease was surrendered, but the affair was noticed at court at a time when the crown and courtiers were for their own profit increasingly interfering in the affairs of Oxford colleges. In 1587 a letter was sent on behalf of Elizabeth I calling on the college to make a lease of the same woodland on similar terms to Lady Jane Stafford, a royal favourite. Hovenden resisted although the queen herself offered the warden £100 if he would accommodate her wishes. This was easier to resist than the letter from William Cecil, Baron Burghley, which charged him with nepotism and with negligence in granting the lease to his brother without first having a proper survey made. Hovenden replied pleading lack of time and resistance by fellows to the expenditure of a survey. In the end he was able to withstand the pressure being put on him, but he learned his lesson and a comprehensive programme of survey mapping and recovery of land lost through poor management began shortly thereafter. The result was the Hovenden maps (now in the college's library), some 100 estate maps drawn on vellum and exhibiting a very high standard of accuracy and detail and considerable aesthetic judgement. Most are attributable to the surveyors Thomas Clerke and Thomas Langdon, or both, though after 1605, when the college was trying to cut down on its expenditure, Hovenden resorted to using fellows to do at least some of the survey work. The late Elizabethan period witnessed a remarkable flowering of estate surveying and mapping, but Hovenden was one of the earliest fully to recognize the value of maps in estate management, and the maps he commissioned are among the finest of their period.

The maps enabled the college to manage its assets more rigorously. Hovenden succeeded in recovering the rectory of Stanton Harcourt, Oxfordshire, which had been granted to it by Cardinal Reginald Pole, archbishop of Canterbury, but resumed by the crown on the accession of Elizabeth. He also completed the warden's lodgings, which had been begun about fifteen years before, enlarged the grounds of the college by adding the site of the house known as The Rose, where there was a famous well, rearranged the old library, providing it with a splendid plaster ceiling, introduced a better system of keeping the college books and accounts, and put in order and catalogued the archives. An oak cabinet in the college bears his name written in his own hand.

Hovenden rigorously upheld his authority within the college and with the aid of the visitor Edmund Grindal, archbishop of Canterbury, he compelled fellows who wanted to practise law or medicine in London to vacate their fellowships. He carefully scrutinized claims to fellowships on the grounds of founders' kin. The principal alteration which Hovenden made in the constitution of the college was the admission of poor scholars (*servientes*), of whom there were thirty-one in 1612, though they were discontinued during the Commonwealth. In 1571 he decreed that each probationer must present to the college a piece of plate or 20s. This led to a steady increase in the college's collection of secular plate.

Hovenden married Katherine, eldest daughter of Thomas Powys of Abingdon, Berkshire. He was the first married warden of the college and panelled the new warden's lodgings to make them more comfortable for himself and his wife. Elizabeth Hovenden, who married Edward Chaloner, second son of Sir Thomas Chaloner of Steeple Claydon, Buckinghamshire, was once thought to have been their daughter. She was in fact the daughter of George, Robert's brother.

Hovenden wrote a manuscript life of Henry Chichele,

archbishop of Canterbury, the founder of All Souls College, which was used by Sir Arthur Duck in his life of the primate (1617), and compiled a register of the wardens and fellows of the college. He died on 25 March 1614 and was buried in the college chapel. His wife survived him.

Hovenden had two younger brothers. Christopher (1559–1610) was a fellow of All Souls College (1575–81), a member of the Middle Temple, and rector of Stanton Harcourt by presentation of All Souls. He was buried at Stanton Harcourt in 1610, having married Margery Powys, sister of the warden's wife. The warden erected a monument over his grave. The second brother, George (1562–1625), was rector of Harrietsham, Kent, another living in the gift of All Souls, of which he was a fellow (1581–90). He held the tenth prebend in the diocese of Canterbury from 1609 until his death at Oxford on 24 October 1625.

ELIZABETH BAIGENT

Sources *Hist. U. Oxf.* 3: *Colleg. univ.* • *Fasti Angl., 1541–1857,* [Canterbury] • *Fasti Angl., 1541–1857,* [Bath and Wells] • *Fasti Angl., 1541–1857,* [Lincoln] • C. T. Martin, *Catalogue of the archives in the muniment room of All Souls' College* (1877) • P. Eden, 'Three Elizabethan estate surveyors: Peter Kempe, Thomas Clerke and Thomas Langdon', *English map making, 1500–1650,* ed. S. Tyacke (1983), 68–84 • Foster, *Alum. Oxon.* • M. W. Beresford, *History on the ground: six studies in maps and landscapes* (1957); rev. edn (1984) • F. W. Steer and others, *Dictionary of land surveyors and local map-makers of Great Britain and Ireland, 1530–1850,* ed. P. Eden, 2nd edn, ed. S. Bendall, 2 vols. (1997) • D. H. Fletcher, *The emergence of estate maps* (1995) • *DNB* • will, PRO, PROB 11/124, sig. 84 • private information (2004) [J. Simmonds]
Likenesses stone bust on monument, 1664, All Souls Oxf. • J. Cheere, bust, All Souls Oxf.

How, Elizabeth (d. 1692). *See under* Salem witches and their accusers (*act.* 1692).

How, John (d. 1571), organ builder, was probably the son of the John Hewe who in 1485 was paid 13s. 9d. for work relating to the organ in the lady chapel at York Minster, and who received the freedom of the city four years later. The younger John How, who also tuned and repaired the minster's instruments in 1531 and 1536, has been identified with the John 'Heweson' made free of the city in the 1540s, which has led to speculation that the family originated from York. The Hows' workshop was 'at the sign of the Organe Pype' in the London parish of St Stephen Walbrook, where John junior was churchwarden in 1535–6, as his father had been before him. After the latter's death in 1519, How appears to have entered into partnership with John Clynmowe, or Clymmowe, and in 1526 they contracted to build a new organ for Holy Trinity, Coventry, for £30. In 1531–2 Eton College acquired a new instrument from 'Clymmo and his brother', from which it may be inferred that one partner had married the sister of the other.

When the London guild of organ makers was dissolved in 1531, the city gave How permission to transfer to the Skinners', an appropriate move given the use organ builders made of animal hides. It was as a member of this company that he signed a tuning contract with the church of St Andrew Hubbard in 1534, according to which he received an annuity of 12*d*. for maintaining its instrument. How made similar agreements with other city churches, though his annual fee, which was presumably based on the number and size of the organs, varied enormously. Thus from 1539 to 1554 St Mary Woolnoth paid him just 4*d*. a year, while at St Dunstan-in-the-West his charges increased from 12*d*. to 2*s*. to 3*s*. 4*d*. over the same period. Altogether he is known to have built or repaired over thirty organs, and there may have been others of which there is now no record. At the height of his career he exercised a virtual monopoly over his craft, and created the most extensive business of any organ builder in England before the Commonwealth.

By 1548 How's son Thomas was assisting him in his work. However, the various Edwardian injunctions against the use of florid polyphony and organs in church spelt financial ruin for the family, and it may have been for this reason that in 1551 How sold his house to the parish, though he continued to live there as a tenant. This arrangement remained in effect until the death of his widow, Anne, in 1585. The Marian restoration of traditional religion may have revived How's fortunes, but several references to him in the 1560s, when London's organs were again dismantled, confirm his decline into poverty. From 1563 his parish paid him an annual stipend of 52*s*., probably as sexton, and certain churches pensioned him off at his full fee for the last two or three years of his life. He is sometimes referred to as 'Goodman' or 'Father' How, doubtless in recognition of his age and to distinguish him from his son. How and his family may have harboured Catholic sympathies, for on 23 April 1561 Thomas was examined before the lord mayor of London on suspicion of recusancy, and admitted that he had not received communion since Queen Elizabeth's accession. How died apparently without leaving a will and was buried at St Stephen Walbrook on 20 March 1571.   DAVID MATEER

Sources parish register, St Stephen Walbrook, GL, MS 8319/1 · churchwardens' accounts, St Andrew Hubbard, GL, MS 1279/2 · churchwardens' accounts, St Dunstan-in-the-West, GL, MS 2968/1 · churchwardens' accounts, St Stephen Walbrook, GL, MS 593/1, 593/2 · churchwardens' accounts, St Mary Woolnoth, GL, MS 1002/1A · S. Bicknell, *The history of the English organ* (1996) · H. Baillie, 'Some biographical notes on English church musicians, chiefly working in London (1485–1569)', *Royal Musical Association Research Chronicle*, 2 (1962), 18–57 · A. Freeman, 'Records of British organ builders, 940–1660', *The dictionary of organs and organists*, ed. F. W. Thornsby, 2nd edn (1921), 7–62, 1st ser. · A. Freeman, 'Father Howe, an old-time maker of organs', *MT*, 62 (1921), 633–41 · S. Bicknell, 'Howe: English family of organ builders', *New Grove*, 2nd edn · A. Smith, 'Parish church musicians in England in the reign of Elizabeth I (1558–1603): an annotated register', *Royal Musical Association Research Chronicle*, 4 (1964), 42–92 · W. L. Sumner, *The organ*, 4th edn (1973) · D. Owen, ed., *A history of Lincoln Minster* (1994)

How, John (*c*.1657–1719), bookseller and printer, was the son of Mary How. Little is known of How's heritage but the printer Job How was probably a brother, possibly a twin. John was bound as an apprentice on 3 June 1672 to the London bookseller and printer Benjamin Harris; the indenture recorded his mother as a widow of London. Job was bound on the same day to a different London printer. It appears that How was not trained as a printer, although this is at odds with his later criticism of those who print without serving an apprenticeship. Where book imprints lack a forename, it is difficult to distinguish John from Job, but before 1699 How probably worked primarily as a bookseller rather than as a printer; John Dunton notes in 1705 that How 'was a Bookseller for many Years, and now follows the Trade of Printing' (Dunton, 297). John and Job may have had some sort of business relationship, as they produced at least three works together.

How's first publications appeared in 1680, during which year he was based successively in Mutton Court, Maiden Lane, and at the Seven Stars in Sweetings, or Swithins, Alley to the east of the Royal Exchange in Cornhill, London. By the following year he had moved the Seven Stars to the south-west corner of the Exchange itself. By 1683, however, his imprints place him to the north of Bishopsgate, and in 1684 his sign was given as the Coach and Horses.

At some time before 1686 How married Katherine, with whom he had at least three children: Job, Rachel, and Susannah. How then disappears from the records for over a decade, a gap which may be attributable to his political sympathies as a whig; Dunton claims that How had been 'a great Sufferer in King *James's* Reign, and has had the FATE of being a Traveller' (Dunton, 298). How's re-entry into the book trade in 1696 was inaugurated by work jointly printed with Job, John Seller's *History of England*, and from 1697 until at least 1702 he was based in Ram-Head-Inn-Yard in Fenchurch Street. In 1700 he became quite active, printing at least ten original or subsequent editions of works by Edward Ward.

During his career How commissioned or printed several weekly and bi-weekly newspapers, usually satirical and pointedly anti-Catholic. His first two publications were such periodicals: *Mercurius Publicus*, printed for How from 28 February to 18 March 1680, and the *Catholick Intelligence*, which survived only a little longer, from 1 March to 29 March 1680. On his return to the trade How printed the *Weekly Comedy* from 17 May 1699 to 12 July of the same year. His most contentious periodical was *The Observator*, a publication commissioned by the whig pamphleteer John Tutchin, printed by How, and sold by the bookseller Benjamin Bragg; it first appeared in April 1702 and was at times associated with Daniel Defoe. In 1703 How's connection with it resulted in a proclamation by Queen Anne for his apprehension along with that of Tutchin and Bragg. Although *The Observator* ran until 1712, How is associated with it only until 1704, perhaps falling victim to Tutchin's tendency to quarrel with political allies as well as opponents. Dunton specifically cites How's involvement with *The Observator* as evidence of his awareness of developing trends in the book trade: How, 'being a great Projector … is like to encrease a pace' (Dunton, 298).

By 1707 How had moved to Talbot Court, Gracechurch Street, where in 1709 he produced one of his final printings, his own pamphlet entitled *Some Thoughts on the Present State of Printing and Bookselling*. His text is an invective against wealthy printers who pirate texts and freely vend their wares 'because they are rich' (How, 4). He concludes with twelve proposals for securing and protecting copyright laws. The pamphlet is dated 28 November, four months prior to parliamentary approval of the Copyright Act of 1710. How's pamphlet must have been an irritation, both for the printers to whom he alludes and for those directly named. The proposals were essentially conservative, however, and failed to address two of the most controversial issues connected to the emerging copyright laws: time limits on a printer or publisher's right to print a particular text, and the developing debate over who is entitled to literary property rights.

How was buried at St Benet Gracechurch, London, on 16 September 1719. Dunton describes him as 'Generous and Franck, and speaks what he thinks; which … has given him an Honest Character' (Dunton, 297). His will, dated 6 September 1719, was proved on 20 September 1720. A year after his death financial pressures led his widow to put the printing house up for sale.   MARY P. ANDERSON

Sources ESTC, accessed 18 March 2001 · H. R. Plomer and others, A dictionary of the printers and booksellers who were at work in England, Scotland, and Ireland from 1668 to 1725 (1922); repr. (1968) · M. Treadwell, 'London printers and printing houses in 1705', Publishing History, 7 (1980), 5–44 · J. How, Some thoughts on the present state of printing and bookselling (1709) · D. F. McKenzie, ed., Stationers' Company apprentices, [2]: 1641–1700 (1974) · Wing, STC · J. Dunton, The life and errors of John Dunton … written by himself (1705) · The Observator (1 April 1702–6 Dec 1704) · Catholick Intelligence, or, Infallible News (1–28 March 1680) · Mercurius Publicus (21 Feb–18 March 1680) · M. Rose, Authors and owners: the invention of copyright (1993) · S. H. Steinberg, Five hundred years of printing (1959) · DNB · private information (2004) [M. Treadwell, Trent University, Canada]

How, William (1620–1656), physician and botanist, was born in London, the son of William How. He entered Merchant Taylors' School, London, on 11 December 1632 and proceeded in 1637 to St John's College, Oxford, where he studied medicine. In 1641 he graduated BA, advancing to MA in 1645. On leaving Oxford during the English civil war he joined the royal forces and was made captain of a troop of horse. When the conflict ended How began a medical practice at St Laurence Lane, City of London, and later moved to Milk Street, Cheapside. By then he was involved in botanical studies and appears to have spent his leisure time in search of plants, chiefly in southern England and the midlands, though he did visit Dublin. He had a number of botanical correspondents and may have known Thomas Johnson, an apothecary who had a physic garden at Snow Hill, Holborn, and Christopher Merrett. By this time he was firmly established as a physician and had married Elizabeth, daughter (or granddaughter) of the immigrant from France, Mathias De L'Obel (1538–1616), author of several botanical works.

In 1650 How published anonymously a slim octavo volume entitled Phytologia Britannica, natales exhibens indigenarum stirpium sponte emergentium. Although this was one of the earliest studies on the plants of the British Isles, it was based on the two volumes of Thomas Johnson's Mercurius Botanicus (1634 and 1641), Johnson's records being rearranged in alphabetical order with additional records by How and his associates. The identity of the author of Phytologia was revealed by Merrett in his Pinax rerum

naturalium Britannicarum (1666). A great admirer of De L'Obel's work, How in 1655 edited and published Matthias de Lobel stirpium illustrationes. Although this was a mere fragment of a much larger work planned by De L'Obel, How used the book to make a vituperative attack on the classification employed by the deceased London apothecary John Parkinson (d. 1650), author of Theatrum botanicum (1640).

How died at Milk Street, Cheapside, London, on 31 August 1656 and at his own request was buried beside his mother in the churchyard of St Margaret's, Westminster. He was survived by his wife. His personal interleaved copy of Phytologia, containing annotations in his hand written between 1650 and 1656, was acquired by John Goodyer (1592–1664) of Mapledurham, Hampshire, who bequeathed it to Magdalen College, Oxford.

B. D. JACKSON, rev. D. H. KENT

Sources R. T. Gunther, Early British botanists and their gardens (1922) · R. Pulteney, Historical and biographical sketches of the progress of botany in England, 1 (1790), 164–72 · G. C. Druce, The flora of Berkshire (1897), ci · Wood, Ath. Oxon.
Archives Beds. & Luton ARS, accounts of his life · Magd. Oxf., botanical notes

How, William Walsham (1823–1897), bishop of Wakefield, was born on 13 December 1823 at College Hill, St Chad's parish, Shrewsbury. He was eldest son of William Wybergh How (d. 1862), who belonged to an old Cumberland family and practised at Shrewsbury as a solicitor, and his first wife, Frances Jane, daughter of Thomas Maynard of Wokingham. She died when her two sons were infants; they were brought up by their father's second wife, the only daughter of Samuel Allsopp of Burton upon Trent. He was educated at Shrewsbury School, and went into residence at Wadham College, Oxford, in the summer term of 1841. He was Goodridge exhibitioner at his college in 1842, and Warner exhibitioner 1842–3. He graduated BA in the university with third-class honours in literae humaniores in 1845, and he proceeded MA in 1847.

How then passed through the theological course at Durham University, was ordained deacon in December 1846, and became curate at St George's, Kidderminster, under Thomas Legh Claughton, afterwards bishop of St Albans, from whom he received an excellent training for his ministerial work. He was ordained priest in December 1847, and in 1848, for family reasons, returned to Shrewsbury, where he acted as curate in the parish of Holy Cross. On 6 November 1849 he married Frances Ann, daughter of Henry Douglas, rector of Salwarpe and residentiary canon of Durham.

In 1851 How became rector of Whittington in Shropshire, and remained there, an exemplary parish priest, for twenty-eight years. From 1852 until 1870 he was a diocesan inspector of education. In 1854 he was appointed rural dean of Oswestry, in 1860 honorary canon of St Asaph, in 1868 proctor for the clergy in convocation, and in the same year select preacher at Oxford. Although not a disciple of the Tractarians, he acknowledged their beneficial influence in the parishes, and in an important speech on

William Walsham How (1823–1897), by Samuel Alexander Walker

church ceremonial, at the church congress of 1867, restated the Catholicity of the Anglican church.

How soon became known as a devotional writer, an efficient conductor of parochial missions, quiet days, and retreats, and a congress speaker. His *Daily Family Prayers for Churchmen*, which he published in 1852, soon after becoming rector of Whittington, was his earliest contribution to devotional literature and instantly secured a general circulation which it enjoyed for fully thirty years.

How's growing reputation led to a long series of offers of preferment, both in the colonies and at home, but he was in no haste to abandon his parochial labour in the country. He was offered and declined the bishoprics of Natal (1867), New Zealand (1868), Montreal (1869), Cape Town (1873), and Jamaica (1878), besides a canonry (with superintendence of home mission work) at Winchester (1878), and the livings of Brighton (1870), All Saints, Margaret Street (1873), and Windsor, with a readership to Queen Victoria (1878). The first offer he accepted was that of suffragan to the bishop of London, with episcopal supervision of east London. He had to assume the title of bishop of Bedford, because the only titles which could then be used by suffragan-bishops were those specified in the Suffragan-Bishop Act of Henry VIII. That act had fallen into abeyance since the early years of the seventeenth century, and had been revived only in 1870, when the first two suffragan-bishops, Henry Mackenzie, bishop-suffragan of Nottingham, and Edward Parry, bishop-suffragan of Dover, were appointed.

How was consecrated on St James's day, 1879, and on the following day was instituted to the living of St Andrew Undershaft, which supplied the income for the bishop, and a prebendal stall in St Paul's Cathedral; in the same year he was created DD by the archbishop of Canterbury, and on 15 June 1886 by Oxford University. He lived at Stainforth House, Upper Clapton, which was generously put at his disposal by the owner, and became, as a co-worker said, 'the leader of an east London crusade'. Exploiting the general feeling that the spiritual destitution of east London was appalling, he obtained assistance from all quarters. His first policy was 'to fill up the gaps in the ministry, both clerical and lay' (How, 155), and for this purpose he founded an east London church fund, which met with a ready response. The Princess Christian showed the deepest sympathy with his work. He secured pulpits and drawing-room meetings in the rich West End to help the poor East, and awakened an interest in the subject in rich watering-places such as Brighton, Tunbridge Wells, and Eastbourne, and also in the public schools and universities. In 1884 he was appointed a member of the royal commission on the housing of the working classes, chaired by Charles Dilke. Being recognized as a spiritual force, he attracted all spiritually minded people round him, and especially the clergy and laity in his own diocese. A teetotaler and supporter of the Church of England Temperance Society, he preached on two occasions to the Salvation Army (1883 and 1885). He received his clergy daily at Clapton, visited them at their own homes, and spent every available Sunday with one or other of them. But perhaps the work he loved best was that among children. There was no title that he valued more than that of 'the Children's Bishop', which was popularly accorded him, and no one of his compositions that he wrote with greater zest than his volume of sermons to children. His wife shared in this work, taking a particular interest in 'purity' missions, and she was a strong supporter of the Girls' Friendly Society. She founded a home in Walthamstow for the rescue of young prostitutes.

The bishop of London appointed in 1885, Frederick Temple, was less willing than his predecessor to allow How a free rein in east London. Temple's assertion of authority, followed by the death of How's wife, on 28 August 1887, probably influenced How's decision when, in 1888, he accepted the offer of the new bishopric of Wakefield. He soon became as great a power in the north as he had been in the south. He met, perhaps, with more troubles in his new sphere than in his old. His tendency to promote high-churchmen created ill-feeling in Yorkshire, and an appeal which he promoted in 1889 to raise £50,000 to build new churches in this industrial diocese produced a disappointing result. The building of a modest house for the bishop in Wakefield became the subject of an unpleasant public row, local critics wanting their bishop to be accommodated (against How's wishes) in a grander edifice. He moved into the house, Bishopsgarth, in 1893, having in 1890 declined Salisbury's offer of the see of Durham. He preferred to complete his reorganization of the Wakefield diocese, and did not wish to leave in an atmosphere of acrimony. His effort to mediate in the coal strike, in 1893, was a failure. He was an outspoken critic of indecent or irreligious literature, publicly declaring in a letter to the *Yorkshire Post* (8 June 1896) that he had thrown his copy of Thomas Hardy's *Jude the Obscure* into the fire in disgust. How died during his August holiday at Dhulough Lodge, Killary Bay, co. Mayo, in the west of Ireland, on 10 August 1897. He was buried at Whittington, and the enlargement of Wakefield Cathedral was decided upon as a fitting memorial to him. He left a family of five sons and one daughter.

How was a keen fisherman, an accomplished botanist, and a most popular writer, both in prose and verse. His writings include *Plain Words*, four series of admirable short sermons, the first of which appeared in 1859 and passed through more than fifty editions; several other volumes of sermons, published at various times; a *Commentary on the Four Gospels* for SPCK, begun in 1863 and finished in 1868, which had a sale of nearly 300,000; *Pastor in parochiâ* (1868; 5th edn 1872) and *Pastoral Work* (1883), which also had a very large sale; *Manual for the Holy Communion* (SPCK, 1868), of which some 700,000 copies were sold; and *Daily Family Prayers* (1852; 4th edn 1872), which was very widely used. In 1854 he published, in conjunction with the Revd T. B. Morrell, a compilation of *Psalms and Hymns*; he was one of the original compilers of *Church Hymns*, brought out by SPCK in 1871, and Frances Carey Brock's *Children's Hymn Book* (1881) was published under his revision. His own original hymns were very popular. He is now best remembered for his hymn 'For all the saints who from their labours rest', sung to Vaughan Williams's fine tune.   J. H. OVERTON, *rev.* M. C. CURTHOYS

Sources F. D. How, *Bishop Walsham How: a memoir* (1899) · private information (1901) · personal knowledge (1901) · O. Chadwick, *The Victorian church*, 2 (1970) · E. F. Hatfield, *The poets of the church: a series of biographical sketches of hymn writers* (1884)
Archives BL, letters to Royal Literary Fund, loan 96 · Bodl. Oxf., letters to E. H. Bickersteth · LPL, corresp. with Frederick Temple; letters and papers on alleged ritualistic practices · NL Wales, letters to Louisa Lloyd · W. Yorks. AS, Wakefield, corresp.
Likenesses E. Taylor, oils, 1879; presented to How by the clergy of St Asaph diocese, 1879 · H. L. Norris, oils, 1897, Wadham College, Oxford · J. N. Forsyth, marble statue, exh. 1902, Wakefield Cathedral · C. Butterworth, woodcut, BM · S. A. Walker, photograph, NPG [*see illus.*]
Wealth at death £72,574 13s. 3d.: probate, 30 Oct 1897, CGPLA Eng. & Wales

Howard. For this title name *see* individual entries under Howard; *see also* Anne, Lady Howard (1475–1511) [*see under* Howard, Thomas, third duke of Norfolk (1473–1554)]; Griffin, John Griffin, fourth Baron Howard de Walden and first Baron Braybrooke (1719–1797); Ellis, Charles Augustus, sixth Baron Howard de Walden and second Baron Seaford (1799–1868); Ellis, Thomas Evelyn Scott-, eighth Baron Howard de Walden (1880–1946).

Howard [*née* Tilney], **Agnes, duchess of Norfolk** (*b.* in or before **1477**, *d.* **1545**), noblewoman, was the daughter of Hugh Tilney of Skirbeck and Boston, Lincolnshire; her mother, as the daughter of Walter Tailboys, came of an important Lincolnshire family. Agnes's brother Philip was a servant of Thomas *Howard, then earl of Surrey (1443–1524), and on 17 August 1497, barely four months after the death of the first countess, Agnes was dispensed to marry the earl, to whom she was related in the second degree. The marriage took place on 8 November. It is a measure of Howard's success in restoring his family's fortune, imperilled by his and his father's support for Richard III, that he was prepared to marry a woman with hardly any dowry—but also perhaps a tribute to her attraction for him. She had five sons, among them Lord Thomas *Howard (three also died young), and eight daughters (four of whom died young). She outlived her husband, who became duke of Norfolk in 1514 and died in 1524, by twenty years and in this time maintained large households at Horsham and Lambeth, bringing up the children of relatives and affinity, among whom was Katherine Howard. The cousins shared a dormitory with the upper servants, and they were brought up to be attractive marriage prospects, having lessons in music but not in the classics. Her charges were not neglected by Agnes, but she was preoccupied with the running of the household and allowed them considerable freedom, only reacting sharply when she found out about their misconduct.

Norfolk's leading position among the English nobility was reflected in his wife's and widow's role at court. She was godmother to Princess Mary, and was with the little princess when in 1520 she delighted visitors from France with her accomplishments. In 1528 Cardinal Wolsey received recipes for medicines from her, with a letter blaming poor housekeeping in her stepson Norfolk's house for the prevalence of the sweating sickness there, perhaps a hint that she did not get on with Elizabeth Howard, the third duke's wife. She was a patron of John Skelton, which is the only evidence of her cultural tastes, though one that may well have had political overtones. She was the first lady of the queen's household after the king's sister, according to the ordinances issued at Eltham in 1526 for the reform of the royal household. Despite her disapproval of the royal divorce proceedings, her high status and relationship to Anne Boleyn (her step-granddaughter) ensured that she remained in this exalted position—it explains her prominence at the St Matthias day feast of 1533 when Henry displayed his bride's rich plate; her precedence in the coronation procession, where she bore Anne Boleyn's train; and her carrying the infant Elizabeth at her baptism, when she acted as her godmother. Lord William Howard and Norfolk both asked Cromwell to intercede on their behalf with her. She may only rarely have been at court, but this did not mean that she could be discounted.

When another step-granddaughter, Katherine Howard,

caught the eye of the king, the dowager duchess did her utmost to sing her praises. However, when the truth emerged about Katherine's extra-marital affairs, it also became clear that the dowager knew about her behaviour. She was well aware of her liaisons with members of the households at Horsham and Lambeth (Henry Manox and Francis Dereham). She once 'beat' her, but failed to control her. Later, she had even encouraged Katherine to promote Dereham. In a bid to cover all this up, she had opened coffers belonging to Dereham and destroyed letters. Agnes Howard did not give in to interrogation easily, but was put under continuous pressure to reveal more about Katherine and also the whereabouts of her own fortune, so that she became 'so meshed and tangled ... that she might not wind out again' (*LP Henry VIII*, vol. 16, no. 1411). Her indictment was brought forward because it was feared that the strain would be too much for her, and that the confiscation of her goods would be endangered. She was convicted of misprision of treason and imprisoned in the Tower in January 1542, but pardoned early in May. She died in 1545, aged at least sixty-eight, and was buried on 31 May in Thetford Abbey; but on 13 October her remains were removed to Lambeth church, Surrey, as she had directed in her will. By 1546 most of her lands (she had a considerable jointure of twelve manors in Suffolk, Surrey, Essex, and Lincolnshire, and a further twelve in Sussex) had been regained by her stepson.

CATHARINE DAVIES

Sources *LP Henry VIII* • L. B. Smith, *A Tudor tragedy: the life and times of Catherine Howard* (1961) • R. Virgoe, 'The recovery of the Howards in East Anglia, 1485–1529', *Wealth and power in Tudor England: essays presented to S. T. Bindoff*, ed. E. W. Ives, R. J. Knecht, and J. J. Scarisbrick (1978), 1–20 • A. Plowden, *Tudor women* (1979) • GEC, *Peerage*, new edn, 9.615 • G. Walker, *John Skelton and the politics of the 1520s* (1988), 60 • D. M. Head, *The ebbs and flows of fortune: the life of Thomas Howard, third duke of Norfolk* (1995), 272

Archives Arundel Castle, Sussex, Arundel papers • BL, state papers relating to Henry VIII • PRO, state papers relating to Henry VIII

Howard, Sir Albert (1873–1947), agricultural botanist, was born on 8 December 1873 at Bishop's Castle, Shropshire, the fourth child of Richard Howard (*bap.* 1833, *d.* 1893), farmer, and his wife, Ann Kilvert. As a child Howard worked on the family farm, an experience which affected his later attitude to agricultural science, making him critical of what he termed 'the laboratory hermit'. From Wellington College, Telford, he went in 1893 to the Royal College of Science, South Kensington, where he took his associateship in chemistry with first-class honours. On entering St John's College, Cambridge, in 1896, he specialized in biological subjects. In 1897 he was first in all England in the Cambridge agricultural diploma and the following year he was placed second in all England in the national diploma in agriculture.

In 1899 Howard was awarded first-class honours in the natural sciences tripos and took up his first post, at Harrison College, Barbados. He was soon appointed mycologist and agricultural lecturer to the newly formed imperial department of agriculture for the West Indies. Influenced by the Cambridge botanist Marshall Ward, Howard was already developing the idea which became central to his view of plant disease, that parasites are less likely to attack plants which are healthy. In 1902 he joined the staff of the South-Eastern Agricultural College at Wye, in Kent, where his work on hops proved of great value to growers. He never really settled at Wye, and in 1905 accepted the post of imperial economic botanist to the government of India. Also that year he married Gabrielle Louise Caroline Matthaei (1876–1930), sometime fellow of Newnham College, Cambridge, who had produced outstanding work on plant respiration.

Albert and Gabrielle Howard became known as the Sidney and Beatrice Webb of India, their planning and research being invariably a joint effort, and in 1913 Gabrielle was appointed second imperial economic botanist to the government of India. From 1905 until 1924 the Howards ran the experiment station at Pusa, carrying out research on many crops, notably wheat and cotton, and from 1912 to 1919 they were responsible for the fruit experiment station at Quetta. They based their work on holistic principles, as far as possible studying the plant in its context of ecological relationships. Howard greatly respected Asian agriculture, believing that it had lessons to teach the West about keeping soils fertile and crops healthy in difficult conditions. In 1914 Howard was appointed companion in the Order of the Indian Empire and helped establish the Indian Science Congress, of which he was elected president in 1926.

Howard's dissatisfaction with the fragmented nature of agricultural research resulted in the creation of the Institute of Plant Industry at Indore. He and Gabrielle oversaw its planning and construction, which began in 1924. They were convinced that the health of plants was a function of soil fertility, and thought that food grown in humus-rich soil was likely to promote animal and human health. They gradually developed the Indore process of composting, which adapted oriental methods to Indian conditions.

Gabrielle died suddenly in 1930 and Howard decided to leave India. He wanted to convey the lessons of the Indore process to Indian cultivators, and *The Waste Products of Agriculture* (1931), written with his colleague Y. D. Wad, was intended as his final contribution to agricultural science. He returned to England in 1931 and also that year married Louise Ernestine Matthaei (1880–1969) [*see* Howard, Louise Ernestine], who supported his work with the same dedication as her sister Gabrielle had shown. Howard was knighted in 1934. During the 1930s he travelled widely, advising cultivators in Asia, Africa, and Europe on adapting the Indore process to their circumstances; his expertise helped save the Costa Rican coffee industry from collapse.

A pugnacious critic of chemical sprays and fertilizers, Howard spoke at many venues. From 1936 onwards he advised and wrote for the *New English Weekly*, a journal which enthusiastically promoted organic husbandry. In 1939 he and the nutritionist Sir Robert McCarrison launched the Cheshire doctors' *Medical Testament* on agriculture and health. In *An Agricultural Testament* (1940), Howard reviewed the achievements of the Indore process. His converts included Lady Eve Balfour and the horticulturist Lawrence Hills. Despite being a chief source of inspiration for the founding of the Soil Association in 1946, Howard refused to join, unhappy at its scientific work's being subject to control by laymen. He edited his own quarterly journal, *Soil and Health* (1946–8).

Howard's views on agriculture were underpinned by a religious faith in a natural order whose limits could not be exceeded with impunity. Possessed of an amiable brutality in debate, he commanded the respect of opponents for his sincere championing of humus. *Farming and Gardening for Health or Disease* (1945) gives the best summary of his ideas and practice. He died of a heart attack at his home, 14 Liskeard Gardens, Blackheath, London, on 20 October 1947; his funeral service was held at Honor Oak crematorium three days later. He had no children.

PHILIP CONFORD

Sources *Soil and Health* [memorial number] (spring 1948) · L. E. Howard, *Sir Albert Howard in India* (1953) · A. Howard, *Farming and gardening for health or disease* (1945) · V. M. Hamilton, 'Sir Albert Howard', *Organic Gardening* (Dec 1947), 14–21 · E. J. Russell, *Nature*, 160 (1947), 741–2 · *WWW, 1941–50* · *The Times* (9 Nov 1905) · *The Times* (21 Aug 1930) · *The Times* (28 Aug 1931) · *The Times* (21 Oct 1947) · *The Times* (22 Oct 1947) · private information (2004) [St John Cam.] · *Fertiliser and Feeding Stuffs Journal* (5 Nov 1947), 643 · Shrops. RRC, Howard family records · *CGPLA Eng. & Wales* (1948) · *DNB* · d. cert.
Likenesses portrait, repro. in L. J. Picton, *Thoughts on feeding* (1946), facing p. 31
Wealth at death £33,807 16s. 8d.: probate, 23 Jan 1948, *CGPLA Eng. & Wales*

Howard [*née* Dacre], **Anne, countess of Arundel** (1557–1630), noblewoman and priest harbourer, was born in Carlisle on 1 March 1557, the eldest daughter of Thomas Dacre, fifth Lord Dacre of Gilsland (1526?–1566), and his second wife, Elizabeth (d. 1567), daughter of Sir James Leybourn of Cunswick, Westmorland. Her brother, George, sometimes called Francis, was born in 1562, then two sisters followed: Mary, born in 1563, and Elizabeth, born in 1564. Her father died two years later, and in January 1567 her mother became the third wife of Thomas *Howard, fourth duke of Norfolk (d. 1572). Within a year she died in childbirth.

Upbringing and marriage The children's upbringing was largely in the hands of their grandmother, Lady Mounteagle, formerly married to Sir James Leybourn. She was responsible for the children of her two daughters, Anne, the elder, who married the son of her second husband, and the younger, Elizabeth. Lady Mounteagle was a devout Catholic, and in her care the children were instructed by a Catholic priest. Lady Montague, sister of Lord Dacre, was also a member of this Catholic group, whose influence was balanced by the presence in the duke's household of his sister, Lady Westmorland, a fervent protestant. Following a visit to Oxford in 1568 the duke introduced Gregory Martin as tutor, although after the great Norfolk house at Kenninghall was closed in 1570 Martin left for the continent and was ordained as a Catholic priest in 1573. A protestant tutor took his place. As a child Anne showed no inclination to follow the Catholicism of her grandmother and mother.

Anne Howard [Dacre], **countess of Arundel** (1557–1630), by Wenceslaus Hollar (after Lucas Vorsterman, c.1626)

After much difficulty the duke obtained the wardship of the four Dacre children. He planned that George should marry Margaret, daughter of his second wife, Margaret Audley, and that the three girls should marry his three sons: Philip, his heir, son of Mary Fitzalan, daughter of Henry, earl of Arundel; and Thomas and William, sons of Margaret Audley. George, who had succeeded as Lord Dacre, was killed in 1569 by a fall from a vaulting horse, a wooden structure designed to teach young riders to leap on to their mounts. Margaret Howard, a particular favourite of Anne, married instead Robert Sackville, Lord Buckhurst, later earl of Dorset. The three girls duly married the three sons of the duke.

Anne was first married to Philip *Howard (1557–1595) in a ceremony in 1569, when both were twelve. It was repeated two years later after they had reached the age of consent and the duke, then a prisoner in the Tower, had made a bargain with the earl of Arundel that a portion of his inheritance would be advanced to Philip, held in trust until he was twenty-five. Styled earl of Surrey, Philip would succeed to the title of earl of Arundel. Anne, coheir with her sister Elizabeth, inherited extensive Dacre lands, including the estates of Gilsland and Greystoke, nine baronies, and manors in many counties.

The duke showed himself a fond father to the children, and one of his last letters, directed to all of them in January 1572, when he daily expected execution, expresses his love and deep concern for Philip and Anne. He urges

Philip to 'love and make much of your wife', speaking of her as 'endued with so great towardness in resolve and good qualities and in person comparable with the best sort'. When he writes to her directly, he calls her his 'well-beloved Nann, that hath been as dear to me as if you had been mine own daughter', committing to her care his only daughter, Margaret (Williams, 239, 243–4).

Domestic problems Norfolk's fears that Philip would prove unworthy were justified all too soon. After some years at Cambridge, where his conduct was as reprehensible as that of any young irresponsible nobleman, he presented himself at court, striving to gain the favour of the queen. Meanwhile Anne was entirely neglected. Unsettling moves, from Audley End to Arundel House, London, to Nonsuch, with occasional visits to the Charterhouse, then known as Howard House, occurred frequently for many years. By the early 1580s she was at Arundel Castle in Sussex, and there she was converted to Catholicism, received by a Marian priest to whom she was brought by one of Philip Howard's servants, Richard Bayly. Lady Margaret Sackville also became a Catholic about this time. Philip showed no displeasure; out of favour at court and hurt by the apparent coldness of the queen, he returned to the country and joined his wife. The queen, however, expressed strong disapproval, and ordered Anne to the house of Sir Thomas Shirley at Wiston, Sussex, where her first child, Elizabeth, was born in 1583. She was forced to remain there for about a year, writing pitifully to Sir Francis Walsingham on 10 June 1584 for release from 'my unfortunate estate' (copy, Arundel Castle Archives, MD 2734).

Towards the end of 1584 Philip was converted to Roman Catholicism by the Jesuit William Weston. The queen's suspicions led to his house arrest, and when her fears were confirmed in 1585 on his attempt to escape to France, he was captured at sea and committed to the Tower. He was tried in Star Chamber and condemned to indefinite imprisonment, with a fine of £10,000. From this time the queen's behaviour towards both Philip and Anne was spiteful and mean. Refused permission to live in London, Anne rented a house in Romford, Essex. On 7 July 1585 her son, Thomas *Howard, the future fourteenth earl of Arundel, was born in the parsonage of Finchingfield, Essex, a house that had been granted to the third duke of Norfolk by Henry VIII. Philip was told that the child was another daughter, and although he discovered that he had a son, he never saw the child or his wife again.

Poverty and widowhood After Philip's imprisonment, and on the urging of Thomas Morgan, her agent in France, Mary, queen of Scots, wrote to Anne to praise the constancy in religion the Howards showed. She expressed her willingness to act in order to secure the release of the earl 'who is so dear to me', but was afraid that her motives would be wrongly interpreted. She enclosed letters addressed to her friends in Scotland, and asked Anne to forward them through her 'friends and servants upon the borders' and to receive answers, a correspondence that was to be secret (Walter, 2.256). There were letters also to

Lord Henry Howard, Philip's uncle, and to Lady Cobham. She could apparently rely upon a close friendship with Anne, whom she addressed as 'cousin', for she asked her to purchase silks or velvets sufficient for two gowns for Lady Cobham, leaving the gift to Anne's discretion. The letter was to be delivered by means of the French ambassador, and replies sent by the same route. At this time of such tension it would have been most unwise if Anne had allowed herself to be enmeshed in Mary's political machinations.

In 1588 Anne was living in a wing of Arundel House, for which she paid a lease of £30 a year. When Queen Elizabeth wished to visit Somerset House, next door to the property, Anne was required to vacate it.

Philip's ordeal was intensified when he was accused of arranging a mass to be said on behalf of the Spanish forces at the time of the Armada. He was tried for treason and condemned to death. Execution was postponed, but his close imprisonment continued until his death on 19 October 1595, not without suspicion of poison. His lands and those of his wife were attainted. Arundel House was searched, and most of the furniture carried away. For some time Anne took refuge in small houses, one in Spitalfields and one in Acton. Reduced to a meagre £8 pension a week, irregularly received, she sold jewels to pay her remaining servants and, deprived of her coach, she was forced to walk. Her state seemed to her like penury. Her grandson William Howard, writing the life of his father, describes the difficulties she suffered:

> all her estate beinge taken from her, and a very small allowance allowed her, hardly enough to kepe her selfe and children, much lesse to bee able to give her sonne such breedinge, as was fitte for a personne of his qualety, during the Queenes rayne.   (Hervey, appx 3, 463)

Religious devotion, material recovery Throughout these years the countess called upon the services of Catholic priests. Martin Array, a seminary priest, was her chaplain until his arrest in June 1586 and banishment a month later. Within a few months the Jesuit Robert Southwell entered her household. He acted also as spiritual adviser to the earl, with whom he exchanged letters, the basis of the lengthy prose study *An Epistle of Comfort*. The volume was printed on a press set up in one of the countess's houses, probably that in Spitalfields, where the Jesuit John Gerard saw it in 1588. Southwell understood the difficulties faced by the countess in establishing a religious life. For her he wrote 'A shorte rule of good life', a simple statement of faith and a guide to everyday living. It is a directive for a devout laywoman of high rank and, like the Ignatian *Spiritual Exercises*, is a flexible outline, expressed in the first person, to be enlarged according to changing circumstances. The countess followed the 'Rule' for the rest of her life.

In 1592 Southwell was captured after he had left the comparative security of the countess's house. She tried to alleviate the conditions in which he was held by sending him books and necessaries through his sister, Mary Bannister. He was executed on 21 February 1595, a few months before Philip Howard died. The countess's hopes for her children had to be abandoned. In 1598 her daughter, Elizabeth, died of tuberculosis. As he grew older, she was forced to relinquish the direction of Thomas's education. An early biographer states that he attended Westminster School, and passed on to Cambridge, after which he travelled abroad.

The possessions that should have come to Anne after the death of her husband were withheld. In her financial affairs she was guided by her steward, Robert Spiller, who served her for more than forty years before his death in 1615. When he first undertook the task, she had debts of £14,000 as a result of her husband's free-spending at court. She eventually had to pay £10,000 for lands designated as her jointure. In 1599 and again in 1602 she sold lands in order to secure an income. In 1601 John Hobart, a Norfolk man and an agent for the marquess of Winchester, tried to arrange a loan for the countess and her brother-in-law Lord William Howard so that they might make composition to the queen for Lord Dacre's lands. The baronies of Gilsland and Greystoke finally became her property by an instruction given to the attorney-general, probably in 1603. In 1607 she recovered Arundel House, although forced to pay £4000 to Charles Howard, earl of Nottingham, who had claimed it quite unjustifiably.

As she regained the property due to her as her inheritance and her jointure, Anne was also able to secure a place in society for her son. At the new year's festivities in 1606 both the countess and Thomas made gifts of £20 to the king, who responded with a gift of 30 ounces of 'guilt plate'. That summer Thomas married Aletheia, youngest daughter and coheir of Gilbert Talbot, seventh earl of Shrewsbury, a match brokered by John Hobart, who proposed it to the countess of Shrewsbury.

Pillar of Catholicism Anne's admiration for the Society of Jesus was shown in 1612 when she made a gift of £2500 to the Jesuit Richard Blount, then serving in England. She hoped that the sum would be invested and the interest compounded until she died, but the money was mishandled and lost. An even more significant gift was made in 1621, when she founded the tertianship in Ghent. If ever England again embraced Catholicism, the house was to move to Carlisle, where she was born. For the last fourteen years before her death the countess maintained a Jesuit priest who wrote accounts of her life and that of the earl. 'The life of the right honourable and vertuouse lady, the Lady Anne late countesse of Arundell and Surrey' has an intimacy that could arise only after many years' observation. The manuscript work is clearly a compilation of reminiscences, some of which represent her attempts to recall early stages in her life, while others record the day-to-day life in her household, when she practised a disciplined and practical piety. Events are overlaid with the emotions that remained with the countess, as in the account 'Of the Queen's hatred towards Her' ('Life of ... the Lady Anne', chap. 6) and in her thankfulness that Southwell came to live with her as the result of a misunderstanding, admitted some years afterwards 'in pleasant

discourse' (ibid., chap. 7). The death of the earl was followed by a period of intense mourning and of physical suffering, when, against the advice of Lady Montague, she took a vow of chastity, regularly renewed. The writer admires her for her 'vertuous, modest and discreet' behaviour, and notes that 'altho there wanted not many that did not much care for her naturally speaking, yet none were ever hear'd to speak one evil word of her' (ibid., chap. 8).

The account is made up of frequent anecdotes, including the story of the plan Anne made to rescue George Blackwell, the arch-priest, when he had hidden for three days in a house that was closely watched. She not only provided a substantial bribe for the officer in charge, but sent him a venison pie every year on twelfth night, the anniversary. Not unexpectedly, she was deeply hurt by her son's submission to the Church of England. The explanation given by her biographer is that 'partly through fear, partly through desire of the King's favour (meeting with some bad counsellors) he accommodated himself by degrees to the times more than he ought to have done'. In no way did she change her affection for him, but 'I and others' heard her say that she would welcome the news of his death if 'she might have good hopes of his salvation' ('Life of ... the Lady Anne', chap. 12). She was indeed able to rejoice at the deaths of those who died in the old faith. When her eldest grandson, James, died in 1623 of smallpox in Ghent, reconciled by John Gerard, she felt that his good death was a sign of God's approval of the Jesuit house she had founded there, and similarly when her grandson Charles died in her care aged about seven, she was said to have exclaimed aloud of her joy that he had gone to heaven (ibid.).

Last years In advanced age Anne spent much of the day in attendance in the chapel and in other religious observances. She oversaw the preparation of medicines and dressings, and many came to her seeking treatment. She had obtained a relic, a bone from one of Southwell's feet, and was said to effect cures by its powers. (At her death it was left to Richard Blount, the Jesuit provincial.) She was extremely generous, giving alms to all kinds of people in need, distributing food three times a week, sometimes to 'well nigh a Hundred', and paying pensions, and also (remembering her northern origins) supplying a quantity of woollen cloth from her northern estates and providing a salary for a schoolmaster in Cumberland. She made great occasions of the birthdays of her three great-grandchildren. When the eldest was three, shortly before her death, she entertained 'almost eight score poor Children', giving each a herring pie (since it was Lent) and three pennies ('Life of ... the Lady Anne', chap. 10).

The admiration expressed by Anne's biographer extends to her appearance. Those who knew her when she was young reported that she was fair and beautiful, and she still retained a fresh colour. She was tall, and towards the end of her life was 'something corpulent', a state that might have set off her grace and dignity, but she would do nothing out of vanity. She wore simple black gowns of inexpensive material, with a piece of religious jewellery on festival occasions. The rather unperceptive chaplain found it hard to see that she ever made any change, 'the new being so like the old in all respects' ('Life of … the Lady Anne', chap. 17). He records that a portrait was sent to Philip III of Spain and was hung in the Escorial (ibid., chap. 16), but it can no longer be found. When she was sixty-nine, drawings were made by Lucas Vorsterman: one is preserved in the British Museum, and another was later engraved by Wenceslaus Hollar, of which several copies survive.

During the period when her biographer lived with her the countess moved four times. For the last two years of her life she was at the manor house at Shifnal, Shropshire. She appears to have had such confidence in her chaplain that he was present at the making of her will, and he records that having had the usual legacies to her family and close friends written out for her, she wrote in her own hand a number of particular bequests. After more than six months' decline she became so weak that she could no longer attend chapel. She was visited by Thomas Howard and his wife and children, and by others to whom the reader is told—with perhaps a touch of irony—she gave her last advice and counsel. She died quietly at Shifnal on 13 April 1630 and was buried in the Fitzalan Chapel, Arundel Castle.

Assessment The countess's biographer finished his work on 15 June 1635, meticulously recording the years, months, and days after her death. Two manuscript copies are preserved at Arundel Castle. The earlier, in octavo, probably dates from the mid-seventeenth century and includes material omitted from the other copy in quarto. A printed version, with many abridgements, was edited by the duke of Norfolk in 1857. The manuscripts vary so much in details of style that the biography may have been written originally in Latin, to be sent to Rome.

Although the work is hagiography, from it there emerges a vivid picture of a woman of extraordinary strength and endurance, recalling the past and re-creating in the present a useful, busy, and ordered life out of the public eye. Other sources reveal how watchful she was over her son and his family, whose fluctuating fortunes continued to bring her anxiety. She worked so diligently to recover her lands that it was said at her death that she left Thomas Howard an income of £6000. In her faith she was greatly sustained by the directive prepared for her by Robert Southwell. She was indeed an exemplar of a Catholic woman of rank whose piety and charity helped to keep Catholicism alive in England.

NANCY POLLARD BROWN

Sources 'The life of the right honourable and virtuoseus lady, the Lady Anne late countesse of Arundell and Surrey', octavo MS, Arundel Castle archives, West Sussex · R. Southwell, 'A shorte rule of good life', Gon. & Caius Cam., MS 218/233 [collated with other MSS] · J. H. Pollen and W. MacMahon, eds., *The Ven. Philip Howard, earl of Arundel, 1557–1595: English martyrs*, Catholic RS, 21 (1919) · N. Williams, *Thomas Howard, fourth duke of Norfolk* (1964) · M. F. S. Hervey, *The life, correspondence and collections of Thomas Howard, earl of Arundel* (1921) · Duke of Norfolk, ed., *The lives of Philip Howard, earl of Arundel, and of Anne Dacres, his wife* (1857) · D. Howarth, *Lord Arundel and his circle* (1985) · J. Morris, ed., *The troubles of our Catholic forefathers related by themselves*, 1–2 (1872–5) · *Robert Southwell, S. J.: two letters and 'Short rules of a good life'*, ed. N. P. Brown (1973), xxvi–

xxxvii · N. P. Brown, 'Robert Southwell: the mission of the written word', *The reckoned expense: Edmund Campion and the early English Jesuits*, ed. T. M. McCoog (1996), 193–213 · M. A. Tierney, *The history and antiquities of … Arundel* (1834) · *CSP dom.*, 1603–10; 1627–8 · *John Gerard: the autobiography of an Elizabethan*, trans. P. Caraman (1951) · *William Weston: the autobiography of an Elizabethan*, trans. P. Caraman (1955) · W. J. Walter, *Mary queen of Scots*, 2 (1840), 256 · *STC, 1475–1640* · A. F. Allison and D. M. Rogers, eds., *The contemporary printed literature of the English Counter-Reformation between 1558 and 1640*, 2 vols. (1989–94) · Bodl. Oxf., MS Tanner 286, fol. 36
Archives Arundel Castle archives, West Sussex, autograph corresp. and copies of letters · Arundel Castle archives, West Sussex, manuscript biography, 1635 | Coll. Arms, Talbot MSS, corresp.
Likenesses L. Vorsterman, drawing, c.1627, BM · W. Hollar, etching (after drawing by L. Vorsterman, c.1626), BM, NPG [*see illus.*] · stained-glass window, Arundel Cathedral, West Sussex
Wealth at death reportedly left son income of £6000

Howard, Bernard Edward, twelfth duke of Norfolk (1765–1842), aristocrat, born at Sheffield on 21 November 1765, was the eldest son of Henry Howard (1713–1787) of Glossop, Derbyshire, land agent and wine merchant, and Juliana (d. 1808), second daughter of Sir William Molyneux, bt, of Wellow, Nottinghamshire. He was educated at the English College at Douai; in 1799 he was elected FRS, and FSA in 1812. He married, on 24 April 1789, Lady Elizabeth Belasyse (1770–1819), daughter of Henry, second earl of Fauconberg; they had one son. Lady Elizabeth had been an unwilling party to the marriage, and in May 1794 Howard divorced her for adultery with the Hon. Richard Bingham, later second earl of Lucan. Lady Elizabeth married Bingham on 26 May 1794, but separated from him in 1804. She died, from cancer, in Paris, on 24 March 1819. Reports of Norfolk's remarriage in 1823 were unfounded.

On 16 December 1815 Howard succeeded his third cousin, Charles *Howard, eleventh duke, as twelfth duke of Norfolk. Unlike his predecessor he was a Roman Catholic, but by act of parliament passed on 24 June 1824, he was allowed to act as earl marshal. He was made a councillor of the University of London in 1825, took his seat in the House of Lords after the Roman Catholic Relief Bill of 1829, was sworn of the privy council in 1830, and was appointed KG in 1834. A whig, he steadily supported the Reform Bill. He died at Norfolk House, St James's Square, London, on 19 March 1842, and was buried at Arundel. He was succeeded by his son, Henry Charles *Howard, thirteenth duke. W. A. J. ARCHBOLD, rev. K. D. REYNOLDS

Sources GEC, *Peerage* · J. M. Robinson, *The dukes of Norfolk* (1982) · *GM*, 1st ser., 93/1 (1823), 368
Archives Arundel Castle, West Sussex, archives, corresp., and papers | Bodl. Oxf., corresp. with John Charles Brooke · W. Sussex RO, letters to duke of Richmond
Likenesses T. Gainsborough, oils, c.1788, Arundel Castle, West Sussex · H. Pickersgill, exh. RA 1830, Arundel Castle, West Sussex · J. Francis, marble bust, 1842, Arundel Castle, West Sussex · J. Doyle, pen and chalk drawing, BM · F. P. Stephanoff, watercolour painting, V&A

Howard, Bernard Marmaduke Fitzalan-, sixteenth duke of Norfolk (1908–1975), courtier, was born at Arundel Castle on 30 May 1908, the only son (there were also three daughters) of Henry Fitzalan-*Howard, fifteenth

Bernard Marmaduke Fitzalan-Howard, sixteenth duke of
Norfolk (1908–1975), by Elliott & Fry, 1952

duke of Norfolk (1847–1917), and his second wife, Gwendolen Mary Constable-Maxwell (1877–1945), daughter of
Marmaduke Francis, eleventh Lord Herries of Terregles,
and heir of that Scottish title. He succeeded to the dukedom in 1917, his half-brother from a previous marriage
having died in 1902. He was educated privately and at the
Oratory School, Birmingham.

The young duke, whose hereditary duties as earl marshal were performed until 1929 by his uncle, Viscount Fitz-
Alan of Derwent, was commissioned into the 4th (territorial) battalion of the Royal Sussex regiment early in 1928,
but at the end of that year transferred to the Royal Horse
Guards, with whom he was not happy. He returned gladly
to the Sussex regiment in 1934, rising to the rank of major
and serving in France and at Dunkirk in 1940. He succeeded his mother as thirteenth Lord Herries of Terregles
in 1945. His interests were emphatically those of a
countryman; he loved hunting, shooting, racing, and
cricket, and in 1936 became master of the Holderness
hunt. He was sworn of the privy council in 1936. He married on 27 January 1937 the Hon. Lavinia Mary Strutt [see
below]; they had four daughters, the eldest of whom succeeded to the Scottish barony of Herries. In 1938 he sold
Norfolk House on the corner of St James's Square,
London.

The duke's apprenticeship in official duties came with
the funeral of George V (1936), followed by the coronation
of George VI, initially planned for Edward VIII. He rapidly

demonstrated that he would stand no nonsense from anybody in ensuring the precise and punctual performance of
majestic ceremonial. Later in 1937 he was appointed a
knight of the Garter, at an unusually early age. His experience was put to good use in 1953 at the coronation of Elizabeth II, which the duke managed with magisterial authority and expertise. On this occasion he coped skilfully with
the introduction into Westminster Abbey of television, to
which he was initially opposed. His hereditary position
also made him responsible for the College of Arms and its
officers, in whom he took a consistent interest and with
whose aid he regulated two other great state occasions,
the (long prepared) funeral of Sir Winston Churchill in
1965 and the investiture of the prince of Wales at Caernarfon in 1969, where the size of the budget and the weather
both gave grounds for apprehension.

Norfolk was a lifelong devotee of the turf and made his
mark both as an administrator and as an owner and
breeder of horses. He became a member of the Jockey
Club in 1933 and served as steward from 1966 to 1968; in
addition he was vice-chairman of the Turf Board (1965–8),
where he took a traditionalist attitude to the problems of
modern racing. Nothing gave him greater pleasure than
his position as the queen's representative at Ascot (1945–
72); the victory of Ragstone, trained and bred at Arundel,
in the Ascot gold cup of 1974 was a fine climax to his career. Another sporting enthusiasm was cricket. Not only
did he welcome visiting teams with an opening game in
the park at Arundel but he took a team to tour the West
Indies in 1956–7, playing occasionally himself; then in
1962–3 he acted as manager of the English team to Australia, bringing his bluff common sense to bear on the problems of the tour. It was an unusual role for the senior duke
of England.

In Sussex, Norfolk played his proper part. He was mayor
of Arundel in 1935–6 and lord lieutenant of the county
from 1949 to 1974, as well as sitting on the county council.
From 1941 to 1945 he served as parliamentary secretary to
the Ministry of Agriculture in the coalition government,
putting his robust knowledge of farming to the public
good, but his heart was not in politics. In parallel with
these official duties went his position as a spokesman for
the Roman Catholic laity of England. As a chairman he
was terse and efficient; in general his attitude was conservative and he did not welcome the alterations in language
and ritual of the Second Vatican Council. In 1970 he participated in the canonization of the forty martyrs, who
included his ancestor St Philip Howard (1557–1595), and
was received by Pope Paul VI. His local experience also led
him to be a powerful and ardent advocate of the Territorial Army; in 1956–9 he was chairman of the Territorial
Army council.

The duke of Norfolk was happier in the countryside
than in the metropolis; but his potent sense of duty drove
him to undertake a broad variety of tasks, some hereditary, some of obligation, but also many of inclination. His
often unmoving face concealed a considerable sense of
humour and power of anecdote. In his old-fashioned way

he was a grandee by birth, a countryman by inclination, and a good man who did his duty. He was appointed GCVO (1946), GBE (1968), and received the Royal Victorian Chain (1953). He died at Arundel Park House, which he had himself built in the grounds of Arundel Castle, on 31 January 1975. He was succeeded in the dukedom by his cousin, Miles Francis Stapleton Fitzalan-Howard, Baron Beaumont and Howard of Glossop (1915–2002).

Norfolk's wife, **Lavinia Mary Fitzalan-Howard** [née Strutt], duchess of Norfolk (1916–1995), racehorse owner and breeder, was born on 22 March 1916 at Kingston Hall, Nottingham, the only daughter of Algernon Henry Strutt, third Baron Belper (1883–1956), and his first wife, Eva Isabel Marian, née Bruce (1892–1987), the third daughter of Henry Campbell Bruce, second Baron Aberdare. In 1922 her parents divorced, and in 1924 her mother married (Albert Edward) Harry (Meyer Archibald) Primrose, Lord Dalmeny (1882–1974), who in 1929 became sixth earl of Rosebery. He was a keen cricketer, racehorse owner, sometime steward of the Jockey Club, and master of the fashionable Whaddon Chase hunt. His stepdaughter (who was educated at Abbot's Hill, near Hemel Hempstead, Hertfordshire) rode his horses with the Whaddon Chase and in point-to-point races with her distinctive colours and, until the Disney Corporation intervened claiming copyright, a large Mickey Mouse on her jersey. Following her marriage to the duke of Norfolk she did not convert to Roman Catholicism, but their daughters were brought up as Catholics. She entered fully into the duke's public life and sporting interests, especially horse breeding and racing. At the coronation of 1937 she was one of the four duchesses who held the canopy over the queen at her annointing, and in 1953 she took the part of the queen in rehearsals at Westminster Abbey for the coronation. After her husband's death she continued to live at Arundel Park, and to breed and race horses with notable success: Moon Madness won the St Leger in 1986, and Sheriff's Star won the coronation cup at Epsom in 1989. The duchess was the first woman steward at Goodwood (1975–95). From 1975 to 1990 she was lord lieutenant of West Sussex, the first woman lord lieutenant, and she had numerous local and charitable engagements: she estimated that she was involved with some 150 charities. In 1971 she was made a CBE and in 1990 the first non-royal lady companion of the Garter. According to one obituarist she was 'a formidable character: a true county lady of few words and all of them very much to the point' (*Daily Telegraph*, 12 Dec 1995). She died at Arundel Park, Arundel, Sussex, on 10 December 1995, and was survived by her four daughters.

MICHAEL MACLAGAN, *rev.*

Sources *The Times* (1 Feb 1975) · *The Times* (3 Feb 1975) · *The Times* (11 Feb 1975) · personal knowledge (1986) · private information (1986) · E. Longford, *Elizabeth R: a biography* (1983) · GEC, *Peerage* · Burke, *Peerage* (1999) · *WWW* · *The Times* (12 Dec 1995) · *Daily Telegraph* (12 Dec 1995) · *The Independent* (12 Dec 1995) · *Daily Telegraph* (13 Dec 1995) · *CGPLA Eng. & Wales* (1975) · *CGPLA Eng. & Wales* (1996)
Archives Arundel Castle, West Sussex, confidential papers and papers relating to activities as Earl Marshall · priv. coll., MSS |

Bodl. Oxf., corresp. with Lord Wooton | FILM BFI NFTVA, documentary footage · BFI NFTVA, news footage
Likenesses Elliott & Fry, photograph, 1952, NPG [*see illus.*]
Wealth at death £3,536,537: probate, 16 May 1975, *CGPLA Eng. & Wales* · £4,117,746—Lavinia Mary Fitzalan-Howard, duchess of Norfolk: probate, 1996, *CGPLA Eng. & Wales*

Howard [née Bollin; *other married names* Alpenny, Blanchard], **Caroline Cadette** (*b.* 1821, *d.* in or after 1901), businesswoman and promoter of emigration and employment for women, was born on 3 August 1821, in Richmond, Surrey, the daughter of Charles Bollin, a plumber, and his wife, Ann. On 1 August 1843, in St Pancras Church, London, she married William Morris Alpenny, an artist. The marriage was apparently an unhappy one, and she fled to Ireland in the 1850s, where she leased a large dairy farm, part of which she devoted to the fledgeling flax-growing industry. The fates of her first husband and a possible daughter from the marriage are unknown. She used the prosperous flax farm to provide training and employment for women and children, and, inspired by Caroline Chisholm's famous emigration schemes to Australia, encouraged young Irish women to emigrate to New Zealand.

By the 1860s Caroline Alpenny had returned to London, where she joined forces with Maria Rye and a small coterie of women attempting to create new employment and emigration opportunities for mainly middle-class women. In 1862 she accompanied a shipload of young women to Dunedin, New Zealand, where she remained until 1872 and was active in voluntary work assisting female immigrants and related business pursuits. For eight years she operated an employment register office, mainly for female servants but occasionally for male workers. She enjoyed a reputation for reliability among employers as well as immigrant workers, and became well known in the colony for her public lectures on cultural matters and her reports for the local press on the labour market. While in Dunedin she married Dr George Richard Howard, a chemist, on 26 December 1867; after his death in April 1872 she returned to London, with laudatory testimonials from Dunedin notables and a gift of £50.

Early in 1873 the New Zealand agent-general appointed Mrs Howard as a recruiting agent, an appointment which was short-lived. She was charged with persuading a larger number of Irish single women to emigrate to New Zealand, and, like many of her predecessors, became embroiled in controversy when she was driven to recruit from workhouses some women whose qualifications and character did not suit the colonists who paid their fares. Her dismissal followed the arrival in Dunedin of the *Asia* from Cork with 200 immigrants, including thirty-seven single women. Undeterred, however, she continued to work as a recruiting agent from 1875 for the Queensland and other Australian governments, combining this employment with a prominent role in the variety of voluntary female emigration societies which sprang up in the 1870s and 1880s. With Viscountess Strangford she established the Women's Emigration Society, the Colonial

Emigration Society, and, at their own cost, the Northern Branch and Home in Portman Square, essentially a hostel and training school for intending female emigrants. She also operated the Loan Fund for Educated Gentlewomen. Under her pen name, Carina, she was a regular contributor on emigration for the women's magazines the *Woman's Gazette* and *Work and Leisure*.

In London, on 11 June 1874, Mrs Howard married her third husband, Edward Litt Laman *Blanchard (1820–1889), a playwright and theatre critic; the match was the revival of an early romance, and, on his part at least, the result of some twenty years of unrequited love. He named his co-written play of 1888, *Carina: a Comic Operatic Romance*, after her. After his death on 4 September 1889 the Drury Lane Theatre gave a benefit performance for her, in which her emigration career was recalled in verse form. In 1890 her emigration work was recognized with the grant of a civil-list pension of £50 a year. The date and place of her death are unknown, but in 1901 she was living at 44 Stanwick Mansions, Fulham.   A. JAMES HAMMERTON

Sources E. A. Pratt, *Pioneer women in Victoria's reign* (1897) · C. J. MacDonald, 'Howard, Caroline Cadette', *DNZB*, vol. 1 · *The life and reminiscences of E. L. Blanchard, with notes from the diary of Wm. Blanchard*, ed. C. W. Scott and C. Howard, 2 vols. (1891) · A. J. Hammerton, *Emigrant gentlewomen: genteel poverty and female emigration, 1830–1914* (1979) · U. Monk, *New horizons: a hundred years of women's migration* (1963) · C. J. MacDonald, 'Single women as immigrant settlers in New Zealand, 1853–1871', PhD diss., University of Auckland, 1986 · R. P. Davis, *Irish issues in New Zealand politics* (1974) · census returns, 1901

Howard, Charles, second Baron Howard of Effingham and first earl of Nottingham (1536–1624), naval commander, was the eldest son of William *Howard, first Baron Howard of Effingham (*c*.1510–1573), and his second wife, Margaret (*d*. 1581), daughter of Sir Thomas Gamage. His early years are obscure. He spent some time in the household of his uncle Thomas *Howard, third duke of Norfolk, where he may have acquired his enduring enthusiasm for the hunt and similar gentlemanly pursuits. Before 1552 he was sent to live at the household of the Huguenot leader, the *vidame* of Chartres, but his father was petitioning the privy council in that year to have him return to England. He may have accompanied his father to Calais during the latter's tenure as lord deputy and governor of the town (October 1552–December 1553). Following William's further appointment as lord admiral in March 1554, Charles sailed under his command in an English fleet of twenty-eight ships, intended to prevent the interception of Prince Philip by French naval forces as he voyaged to England to marry Queen Mary. Charles did not sail with the English fleet when his father escorted Philip to Flanders in August 1555, because William, it was said, 'dare(d) not adventure his sonne to the seas' (*APC*, 5.339). However, he may have been in the fleet which patrolled the channel and transported the earl of Pembroke's expeditionary force in 1557 during the brief Anglo-French war. The most lasting benefit of these early experiences may have been in providing an implicit association of

Charles Howard, second Baron Howard of Effingham and first earl of Nottingham (1536–1624), by Daniel Mytens, *c*.1620

Howard with matters nautical in the mind of his cousin Elizabeth, queen from November 1558.

Courtier and diplomat With Elizabeth's accession Howard reaped the benefits of his father's support for her during the dangerous years of her half-sister's reign. Of a similar age to the new monarch and physically personable, he enjoyed her friendship and confidence, and became one of her closest male companions. Accompanying his father to the peace negotiations which concluded with the treaty of Câteau-Cambrésis in 1559, Howard personally brought word of its ratification to Elizabeth. This episode may have led to his appointment in the same year as the queen's emissary to the French court, to convey her good wishes and hopes for the recovery of the injured Henri II. Arriving too late in Paris, Howard was the first English diplomat to congratulate François II and his queen, Mary Stuart, on their accession, a task which, given their known antipathy to English interests, was perhaps more delicate than had been envisaged for him. Howard appears to have made a favourable impression, though this might have paled somewhat had Mary known that he was simultaneously organizing the safe passage of her potential successor to the Scottish throne, the earl of Arran, from Geneva to England.

For the next few years Howard's role at the English court was relatively discreet. He became keeper of the queen's house at Oatlands in 1562, and acquired Chievely rectory in Berkshire, with further lands in Northamptonshire. While useful tokens of favour, such gifts were not sufficient to support a young man of high aspirations. However, his marriage in 1563 to Katherine Carey (d. 1603), eldest daughter of Lord Hunsdon, the queen's second cousin and her most intimate female companion, reinforced his already-close ties with his monarch and ensured that his name was not lost among competing claims for advancement. Nevertheless, his progress was steady rather than remarkable. He was elected to parliament for Surrey in December 1562, and appears to have applied himself to the role dutifully, if never assiduously. His first substantial appointment did not arise until the northern rising of 1569, when he persuaded Ambrose Dudley, earl of Warwick, to give him employment as general of the horse in the army that was to relieve the hard-pressed English forces in the north. The rising was over before the army saw any fighting. Nevertheless, Howard subsequently did useful service in confiscating the properties of the defeated Northumberland and, importantly, acting as the queen's rent-collector thereupon.

In 1570 Howard received his first naval appointment, as joint commander of the English fleet that was to shadow and screen the Spanish ships carrying Philip's bride-to-be, Anne of Austria, to Spain. However, it is almost certain that his co-commander William Winter enjoyed effective command of the ships, while Howard provided the courtly presence intended to give some credibility to the fiction that the English fleet had a purely diplomatic function. Richard Hakluyt, who dedicated the 1598 edition of *Principal Navigations* to Howard, later credited him with forcing the larger Spanish fleet to give the salute to the English ships upon this occasion, but the anecdote appears either to have been the deliberate fiction of an author intending to flatter his patron, or the misreporting of a similar incident involving Howard's father, William, in 1554. Knighted some time following this service, Howard performed the duties of lord chamberlain as surrogate for his cousin, the earl of Sussex, during the latter's illness in 1574–5. As the son of Sussex's predecessor in that role (William Howard had held the office from 1558 almost until his death in 1573), Charles was already familiar with its duties, and appears to have discharged them efficiently. In April 1575 he was admitted to the Order of the Garter, filling a vacancy created almost three years earlier by the execution of another Howard, the fourth duke of Norfolk.

For the next eight years Howard added little to his offices and duties. He assembled the fleet that carried the duc d'Anjou back to France in February 1582, and appears to have had a brief diplomatic mission to Ireland later in the same year; otherwise he remained a relatively discreet presence at court. However, the death of Sussex in 1583

provided an opening which Howard had proved himself well qualified to fill. On 1 January 1584 he was appointed lord chamberlain and, less than a week later, a privy councillor. In the previous autumn he had rekindled his association with naval matters—most pertinently with naval administration—when he chaired a commission to investigate charges against the treasurer of the navy, John Hawkins. This, and previous duties associated with the queen's ships, may have brought Howard most readily to mind when a further vacancy, created by the death of the earl of Lincoln, arose in January 1585. In May of that year he succeeded to yet another office formerly enjoyed by his father, and one with which his name was to be indelibly associated.

Lord admiral of England As the commander of England's only standing military resource and the principal judicial authority over English seas and English subjects at sea, the lord admiral exercised far more than a ceremonial function. Nevertheless, Howard's was much less a 'professional' office than in later centuries. Relevant experience may have been a factor in his appointment, but he was hardly a seaman. Rather, it was his close personal relationship with the queen, and the association of previous generations of his family with the post, that made him the first choice to succeed Lincoln. His first duty as lord admiral was both weighty and poignant. He was appointed as a commissioner for the trial of Mary Stuart and, according to the secretary and diplomat William Davison, urged the extreme solution to that most abiding problem of Elizabeth's reign. The claim, made by Davison in his testimony from the Tower (BL, Cotton MS Titus C VII, fol. 48), cannot be verified, however, and upon other evidence appears to be unjust. Howard is known to have displayed a measure of calculating ruthlessness upon only one occasion—the trial of his great rival Essex—and the story may have been intended to dilute Davison's own culpability. Nevertheless, Mary's execution undoubtedly brought closer the conflict that was to advance Howard's career from a degree of distinction to outright glory.

On 21 December 1587, with war against Spain a reality in all but its declaration, Howard received a commission to concentrate and command the English naval forces against the anticipated assault upon England. Readily admitting his own lack of experience as a wartime leader, he almost immediately surrounded himself with expert councillors—Drake, Hawkins, Frobisher, and Thomas Fenner—and, more nepotistically, his nephew Lord Sheffield and cousin Lord Thomas Howard. All of these men urged him to carry the conflict to the Spanish coast, to destroy the Spanish fleet as it concentrated. Though originally sharing the queen's preference for keeping both the western approaches and the narrow seas guarded, Howard came to agree strongly with their views. However, Elizabeth—tormented by the probability that to miss the Armada at sea would be to lose the war—refused to allow this in the early months of 1588. Even as the Armada was reported to be at sea, she acquiesced only so far as to allow the now-combined fleet to 'ply up and down in some indifferent place' between England and the Spanish coast

(PRO, SP 12/211, fol. 8). When he managed to put to sea against contrary winds, Howard obeyed her instructions, though spreading his ships as thinly as possible between the Scillies and Ushant, hoping to catch sight of the approaching enemy. An imposed strategy, poor intelligence, and enduring foul weather (which kept the fleet in Plymouth harbour for several weeks during June and July) reduced Howard to alternating moods of frustration and despondency. The tenor of his correspondence to Burghley, Walsingham, and even to the queen herself (whom he regarded as insufficiently sensitive to her danger) became increasingly intemperate; on 23 June, recounting his difficulties, he wrote to her: 'For the love of Jesus Christ, Madam, awake thoroughly, and see the villainous treasons round about you' (PRO, SP 12/211, fol. 50). Nevertheless, he provided a calming influence upon Drake and others, and took an active role in the difficult task of prising victualling moneys from Lord Burghley to keep his fleet in being during a period when the potential for large-scale desertions among the ships' crews was substantial.

Criticized by Elizabeth for not doing enough to anticipate enemy intentions, Howard in fact acted with great dispatch upon discovering that the Armada was off the Scillies. During the evening of 20 July 1588 he had his fleet warp out of Plymouth, and by dawn of the following day had crossed the path of the advancing Spanish ships to steal the weather gauge. Thereafter, obsessed with preventing the enemy from landing upon English soil, Howard's only strategy was to keep the Armada from attempting it. If this was a failure of imagination on his part, it was one that he shared with his subordinates. The coming battle did not develop beyond a series of localized, if vicious, brawls, a reflection of the fact that its overall scale was entirely beyond the experience or understanding of any who took part in it. Nevertheless, the actions off Portland Bill (23 July) and the Isle of Wight (25 July), if inconclusive, were successful from the English perspective in driving the Spanish ships away from what were considered to be potential landfalls. Thereafter, the failure of the Armada, still intact, to effect a liaison with Parma's invasion army proved fatal for Spanish prospects of imposing a settlement upon England. On the morning of 29 July, following the flight of the Armada from the threat of English fireships at Calais, Howard announced his intention of leading his ships against the Spanish flagship, *San Martin*. However, he was distracted into sending the *Ark Royal's* longboats to take the beached galleass *San Lorenzo*, and Drake's *de facto* assumption of his commander's role in the first hour of fighting has since brought much criticism of the lord admiral. Corbett implied that this was the moment at which he relinquished the moral right of leadership to Drake. In fact Howard was subsequently praised by Sir William Winter—undoubtedly the most experienced English commander in fleet actions—for supporting his men during the assault on the *San Lorenzo* and re-engaging the Armada promptly thereafter. Nevertheless, Howard was sensitive to potential criticism, and probably urged the drafting of the 'Relation of the proceedings', the only semi-official

English account of the campaign (BL, Cotton MS Julius F, x, fols. 111–17), to forestall it.

Following the battle off Gravelines, the English fleet followed the Armada northwards, though now almost entirely lacking powder and shot. In Howard's own words, 'we put on a brag countenance and gave them chase' (PRO, SP 12/214, fol. 42). He was obliged subsequently to justify his decision to break off the chase near the Firth of Forth, but in reality his ships had no ability to re-engage the enemy. It may be argued that Howard's greatest service was performed in the aftermath of the campaign. Following the English fleet's scattered return to port, Elizabeth effectively abjured any responsibility for her mariners' welfare, and an epidemic of typhus, originating in the *Elizabeth Jonas*, swept through her ships. At Dover, Howard took an aggressive role in securing victuals for his starving men and arranging more sanitary accommodation onshore, while urging that the fleet be kept in existence to counter the continuing threat from an enemy whose fate was not yet understood. Neither effort was popular with his parsimonious monarch, but Howard persisted: paying for fresh wine and beer from his own pocket when he knew that there could be no possibility of reimbursement; selling his personal plate to buy clothing for the men; and even requisitioning part of the booty Drake had taken from the captured *Rosario* to feed his mariners— 'and had it not been mere necessity, I would not have touched (it); but if I had not some to have bestowed upon some poor and miserable men, I should have wished myself out of the world' (PRO, SP 12/215, fol. 59). His final correspondence of the campaign, written as he prepared to return to court, reflected his continuing efforts on behalf of his charges: 'and if men should not be cared for better than to let them starve and die miserably, we should very hardly get men to serve … but before God, I had rather have never penny in the world than they should lack' (PRO, SP 12/215, fol. 66). If Howard's willingness to endure personal hardship on their behalf was somewhat overstated, it is to his credit that he made an attempt to keep their plight before his queen long beyond the point at which she had made her indifference clear.

In the years immediately following the campaign Howard saw little active service at sea, though vessels financed or owned by him took part in several privateering voyages organized by others. The rigours of a life in near-constant attendance at court, and more mundane matters arising from the exercise of admiralty jurisdiction—particularly his right to tenth-shares of prize cargoes—provided his habitual employments. The principal naval efforts in the period 1589–94 consisted of semi-private expeditions to intercept that elusive golden prize, the Spanish plate fleets of Tierra Firme and New Spain; none required the intervention of the lord admiral, other than in disputes regarding good or bad prizes taken. Briefly Howard was mooted as leader of the naval expedition that would carry Sir John Norreys's relieving army to Brest in 1594, but the eventual scale of the operation required a less august appointment, and Martin Frobisher was chosen instead. Nor did Howard have any involvement in the disastrous

Drake/Hawkins voyage to the Panama isthmus in 1595, which, as a project strongly urged by Drake and Essex, he probably regarded as an unwelcome diversion of resources. In 1596, however, he was to play a leading role in that year's major English effort against Spain.

The Cadiz expedition, 1596 English plans for an assault upon targets on the Spanish mainland had been developing since autumn 1595. A mood of optimism that the war could be forced to a satisfactory conclusion (if not won), bolstered by early—and inaccurate—reports that Drake and Hawkins were making good progress in their West Indies expedition, appears to have enthused even the cautious spirit of the queen. Howard, perhaps hoping for a final opportunity for glory and—more importantly—for plunder, led arguments in the privy council for the scheme. Preparations commenced in great secrecy in October, and the form of the expedition was first elucidated in January 1596 in a note by Robert Cecil, Howard's closest ally in the council. This envisaged a force of 5000 soldiers and 4500 mariners, supplied for up to five months, which would assault and sack unspecified targets on the Spanish mainland (in fact Cadiz was already the intended, if unstated prize). Command would be shared by Howard and Essex, generals at sea and upon land respectively, who were also to bear part of the costs of securing private vessels to accompany the fleet. At the end of March, news of the siege of Calais by Spanish forces threw these preparations into confusion. Essex was ordered to use the assembling fleet and men as a relieving force, and the commission which authorized this task omitted Howard's name. Thinking himself both slighted and superseded, the lord admiral reacted furiously and wrote an extremely imprudent letter to the queen, in which he claimed pettishly: 'I am yoused but as the druge' (Hatfield House, Cecil MS 40/6). Wisely, his friend Robert Cecil withheld it from Elizabeth's eyes.

Despite Essex's almost frantic efforts, Calais fell before the expedition could sail. The attack upon Cadiz had now acquired a sense of urgency and—for Howard—an opportunity to redeem the slur upon his honour. The expedition sailed on 3 June 1596, and from the start was hampered by the clashing, fragile egos of its commanders. Claims and counter-claims of precedence and perceived affronts undermined the effectiveness of the assault upon Cadiz. Though the town was easily taken, the citadel held out, and considerable merchant shipping in the harbour was allowed to escape and then burn before it could be recaptured. Pillaging was disorganized, and little booty found its way into official English coffers. Essex then expressed an intention of holding the town while ships returned to England to reinforce him. Howard objected to this, on the reasonable grounds that such a strategy formed no part of their instructions. He also vetoed Essex's subsequent plans to attack the port of Lagos and to make an attempt upon the incoming plate fleets. Subsequently criticized for excessive caution (not least by the queen herself, once she understood how modest the return had been upon her investment), Howard was in fact acting prudently in curbing plans which took no account of the parlous state of the English fleet's supplies by the time of its evacuation of Cadiz. Moreover, both in military and psychological terms the expedition had been a spectacular success, humiliating Philip and further disheartening his many creditors, though the knighting *en masse* of every senior officer in the English force by Howard and Essex at Cadiz somewhat overesteemed their achievement.

Earl of Nottingham As Elizabeth recovered from her disappointment, she came to appreciate Howard's service during the expedition. In October 1597 he was created earl of Nottingham. Claiming descent through the female line from the title's original holder, John Mowbray, he became at a stroke the second peer of the realm (allowing precedence only to Oxford). The honour incensed Essex, who felt slighted until the queen placated him with the curious trifle of an earl marshaldom, thus restoring his precedence. In 1598 the two men worked relatively effectively together to organize the kingdom's defences against a much exaggerated threat of Spanish invasion. In mid-1599 it was Nottingham alone, responding to a similar peril, who was given responsibility for the kingdom's defences, being appointed 'Lord Lieutenant-General of all England'—an unprecedentedly powerful commission which he discharged with appropriate gravitas, if little active service. This was Nottingham's final military role, though he continued to perform duties commensurate with his exalted station. In February 1601 he was a commissioner at the trial of his former rival Essex, and following the earl marshal's execution he took on some of the responsibilities of that office. With the fall of the last in a succession of younger favourites, Elizabeth appears to have transferred her affections to the reliable Nottingham once more. As she lay dying in March 1603 it was to him that she finally confirmed her successor, James VI of Scotland, enabling her old friend to continue the family tradition of cultivating a new sovereign's gratitude. In May 1604 Nottingham led a spectacular embassy to Spain to ratify the peace treaty which ended the Anglo-Spanish war. As one who understood precisely how to play the grandee, he was shown great respect and affection by Philip III, son of his old enemy.

Following his return to England, Nottingham was involved in considering the proposed union of England and Scotland, in judging the conspirators in the Gunpowder Plot, and, as its now-senior companion, in reviewing the statutes and articles of the Order of the Garter. His final active role as lord admiral was to escort the newly married Princess Elizabeth (the future 'winter queen' of Bohemia) to Flushing in February 1613. The rise of Buckingham briefly threatened a reprise of Nottingham's old feud with Essex but, beset by increasing pressures to address endemic corruptions within the navy (for which his own nepotism and laxity provided great encouragement), and sensitive to his advancing years, the lord admiral wisely avoided confrontation. With good grace he sold his office to Buckingham in 1619 for £3000 and an annuity of £1000. From then until his death Nottingham wholly retired from public life, but continued to relish the role of the kingdom's most distinguished magnate, entertaining on a scale that did justice to the vastness of his prestige if not his wealth—which, though substantial, lessened significantly in his final years. Active until his final illness, he died on 14 December 1624, at Haling, Surrey. He was buried four days later in the family vault in Reigate church.

With his first wife, Katherine, Nottingham had two sons, William, who died in 1615, and Charles, who succeeded as second earl of Nottingham, and three daughters. Katherine's death in February 1603 was a severe blow to her husband, and was said also to have hastened the death of her old friend and confidante Queen Elizabeth. Nottingham married his second wife, Lady Margaret Stewart (*d.* 1639), daughter of James Stewart, second earl of Moray, in 1604; they had a surviving son, Charles, who succeeded his childless half-brother as third earl of Nottingham in 1642. With his death in 1681 the title became extinct.

Appreciation Even during his lifetime Charles Howard's name commanded respect rather than genuine admiration. Subsequent appreciations have done little to revise the balance. Blood alone had brought him favour at court; thereafter, the offices he acquired reflected the need for a trusted, rather than an innately talented, holder. His role during the Armada campaign—as chief executive to men whose habitual business was that of fighting at sea—reflected this trust. In time of war the lord admiral was expected to be less an absolute leader than a conduit between such men and their sovereign, whose intentions and preoccupations were often wholly antipathetic. In reconciling these fundamental dissonances Nottingham fulfilled his role admirably, though he also tested his queen's patience by exhibiting a strong concern for the welfare of the common mariner. Accused of excessive caution upon several occasions—most notably during the 1596 Cadiz expedition—it was rather the case that he was unwilling to acquiesce in the judgement of less circumspect men whose failures might have rebounded poorly upon his own reputation.

Personable, vain, brave, courtly, prodigiously nepotistic, and acutely sensitive to perceived assaults upon his dignity, Nottingham was an exemplar of the Elizabethan courtier, notwithstanding his reputed distaste for the breed. His clashes with Essex, particularly upon points of precedence, were probably inevitable given the uncomfortable coincidence of their conceits, though his relationship with Ralegh, an earlier favourite of the queen, remained amicable. Burghley and his son Robert Cecil were probably his closest political allies, though his father-in-law Hunsdon provided much support during his early career. In later years Nottingham's cupidity, nurtured by his family's constant struggle to live up to its putative station in society, was increasingly apparent in the manner in which he chased his lord admiral's perquisites. The nature of the office, which remained a medieval sinecure, undoubtedly encouraged his behaviour. It was probably Nottingham's eminence that saved him from accusations of personal corruption during the latter

phase of his stewardship of the navy—and also, perhaps, the protective colouration of a court that itself had come to be an exemplar of venality. To allow Nottingham a final, if somewhat worn, mitigation, he was kind to dogs. Indeed, he became one of the kingdom's foremost breeders of spaniels, and continued to hunt enthusiastically, even into his final illness. JAMES MCDERMOTT

Sources PRO, SP/12 · J. K. Laughton, ed., *State papers relating to the defeat of the Spanish Armada, anno 1588*, 2 vols., Navy RS, 1–2 (1894) · R. W. Kenny, *Elizabeth's admiral: the political career of Charles Howard, earl of Nottingham, 1536–1624* (1970) · *The naval tracts of Sir William Monson*, ed. M. Oppenheim, 5 vols., Navy RS, 22–3, 43, 45, 47 (1902–14) · M. Oppenheim, *A history of the administration of the Royal Navy* (1896) · *APC, 1554–6, 1586–98* · declared accounts of the navy, PRO, E351/2221–2230 · correspondence of the admiralty court, BL, Add. MSS 12505, 15208 · R. Hakluyt, *The principal navigations, voyages, traffiques and discoveries of the English nation*, 2nd edn, 3 vols. (1598–1600); repr. 12 vols., Hakluyt Society, extra ser., 1–12 (1903–5), vol. 4 · D. M. Loades, *The Tudor navy* (1992) · J. S. Corbett, *Drake and the Tudor navy*, 2 vols. (1898) · R. B. Wernham, *Before the Armada: the growth of English foreign policy, 1485–1588* (1966) · R. B. Wernham, *After the Armada: Elizabethan England and the struggle for western Europe, 1588–1595* (1984) · R. B. Wernham, *The return of the armadas: the last years of the Elizabethan war against Spain, 1595–1603* (1994) · K. R. Andrews, *Elizabethan privateering* (1964) · C. Martin and G. Parker, *The Spanish Armada*, 2nd edn (1999) · M. J. Rodriguez-Saldago and S. Adams, *England, Spain and the Gran Armada, 1585–1604* (1991) · testimony of Wm. Davison, BL, Cotton MS, Titus C VII, fol. 48 · Hatfield House, Hertfordshire, Cecil MS 40/6 · A. F. Kinney, ed., *Elizabethan backgrounds: historical documents of the age of Elizabeth I* (1990) · inquisition post mortem, PRO, C 142/471/69

Archives BL, political corresp., Harley MSS · Bodl. Oxf., papers relating to suppression of piracy, etc. · East Kent Archives Centre, Dover, account of Embassy to Spain · Hatfield House, Hertfordshire, letters and papers | BL, corresp. of the admiralty court, Add. MSS 12505, 15208 · BL, letters to Sir Julius Caesar, Add. MSS 12504–12508, 15208, *passim* · CKS, corresp. with Lionel Cranfield · PRO, declared accounts of the navy, E 351/2221–2230, *passim*

Likenesses T. Cockson, line engraving, *c.*1596–1603, BM · oils, *c.*1600, Knole, Kent, BM, NPG; version, BM; NPG?; Royal Collection · group portrait, oils, 1604 (*The Somerset House conference, 1604*), NPG · N. Hilliard, miniature, 1605, NMM · D. Mytens, oils, *c.*1620, NMM [*see illus.*] · portrait, *c.*1625, NPG · M. Gheeraerts, group portrait, etching (*Procession of Garter knights, 1576*), BM · S. de Passe, line engraving (after unknown artist, *c.*1600), BM, NPG · W. Rogers, line engraving, BM, NPG; repro. in W. Segar, *Honor, military and civill* (1602) · oils (after type of *c.*1602), NPG

Wealth at death see inquisition post mortem, PRO, C 142/471/69

Howard, Charles, first earl of Carlisle (1628–1685), army officer and politician, was born on 4 February 1628, the second son and eventual heir of Sir William Howard (*c.*1602–1643), of Naworth, Cumberland, and Mary (*bap.* 1602, *d.* 1638), eldest daughter of William Eure, fourth Baron Eure. His father was a grandson of Lord William *Howard (1563–1640). Raised as a Roman Catholic, in 1646 he was charged with having borne arms for the king, largely on the grounds of having resisted capture by a parliamentarian force during the civil war. He was cleared of his delinquency by ordinance of parliament and on payment of a fine of £4000. Lady Halkett, who visited Naworth in 1649, gave particulars of Howard's household in her *Autobiography*. In December 1645 he had married Anne Howard (*d.* 1696), daughter of Edward, first Baron Howard of Escrick.

In 1650 Howard was appointed high sheriff of Cumberland. Though professing to be a supporter of the Commonwealth, his known loyalist predilections led to several charges of disaffection being brought against him before the commissioners for sequestrations in Cumberland in the beginning of 1650. His explanation seems to have satisfied the council of state (25 March 1650), and in the following May directions were sent him respecting the trial and punishment of certain witches whom he professed to have discovered in Cumberland. Sir Arthur Hesilrige was, however, instructed to sift the charges thoroughly and report the result. Howard bought for his residence Carlisle Castle, a crown revenue, and became governor of the town. At the battle of Worcester in 1651 he distinguished himself on the parliamentarian side.

> Captain Howard of Naward, captain of the life guards to his excellency, has received divers sore wounds, and Major Pocher, but both with hope of life, and some few others. Captain Howard did interpose very happily at a place of much danger, where he gave the enemy (though with his personal smarts) a very seasonable check, when our foot, for want of horse, were hard put to it.   (Cary, 2.363)

In 1653 Howard sat as MP for Westmorland in Barebone's Parliament, and on 14 July in the same year was appointed a member of the council of state, and placed on various committees. He appears to have been nominated to the assembly partly in acknowledgement of his advanced puritan connections, as a member of George Cokayne's St Pancras, Soper Lane, congregation; and partly in respect of his greater gentry background. In November he was reappointed to the council of state. In 1654 and 1656 he represented Cumberland in parliament. Cromwell dispatched him to the north in April 1654 to check the inroads of the Scots. He was also to check horse-racing and prevent all meetings of papists or disaffected persons. At that time he was captain of the lord protector's bodyguard. When Colonel Rich was deprived of his regiment in January 1655 its command was given to Colonel Howard. In March 1655, being then colonel of a regiment of horse, he was nominated a councillor of state for Scotland, and in the ensuing April was appointed a commissioner of oyer and terminer to try the rebels in the insurrection in Yorkshire, Northumberland, and Durham. He became deputy major-general of Cumberland, Northumberland, and Westmorland in October 1655. In December 1657 he was summoned to Cromwell's 'other house', the protector having conferred upon him the titles of Lord Gilsland and Viscount Howard of Morpeth on 21 July of that year. By his titles he received one of the two hereditary peerages conferred by Oliver Cromwell.

In April 1659 Howard urged Richard Cromwell to act with vigour against the army leaders, and offered, if the protector would consent, to take the responsibility of arresting Lambert, Desborough, Fleetwood, and Vane; but his advice was rejected, and he was deprived of his regiment on Richard's fall. For a time imprisoned, he was released on parole in August 1659, but on 21 September he was rearrested and sent to the Tower on a charge of high treason, being suspected of complicity with Sir George

Booth's insurrection. He was set free without trial, and on 3 April 1660 was elected to the Convention for Cumberland. Within months of the Restoration, Howard had been appointed as a privy councillor, *custos rotulorum* of Essex, and lord lieutenant of Cumberland and Westmorland. He was not reappointed to the governorship of Carlisle, that post being conferred on his old enemy Sir Philip Musgrave in December 1660. On 20 April 1661 (no recognition being made of his Cromwellian honours) he was created Baron Dacre of Gillesland, Viscount Howard of Morpeth, and earl of Carlisle. On 18 June following he was constituted vice-admiral of Northumberland, Cumberland, and Durham, and became joint commissioner for office of earl marshal on 27 May 1662. From 20 July 1663 to December 1664 he was ambassador-extraordinary to Russia, Sweden, and Denmark. He was appointed captain of a troop of horse on 30 June 1666, captain in Prince Rupert's regiment of horse on 13 June 1667, and on the 20th of the same month lieutenant-general of the forces and joint commander-in-chief of the militia of the four northernmost counties. On 29 November 1668 he was sent as ambassador-extraordinary with the Garter to Charles XI of Sweden. With the earl's approval, Guy Miège, one of Carlisle's attendants, wrote an account of these embassies, which was published in English and French in 1669.

Carlisle succeeded to the lord lieutenancy of Durham on 18 April 1672, colonel of a regiment of foot on 22 January 1673, and deputy earl marshal of England in June. From 25 September 1677 to April 1681 he was governor of Jamaica. On 1 March 1678 he was reappointed governor of Carlisle. An ally of Shaftesbury for a time, Carlisle himself moved in 1674 the exclusion from the succession of any member of the royal family who married a Catholic, but he opposed such a course by 1684. He died on 24 February 1685 at Castle Howard in Cumberland, and was buried on 12 March in York Minster, where there is a monument to his memory. He was survived by his wife, with whom he had three sons—Edward, who succeeded him, Frederick Christian (d. 1684), and Charles (d. 1670)—and three daughters.   GORDON GOODWIN, rev. SEAN KELSEY

Sources GEC, *Peerage*, 3.33–4; 4.615 · A. Woolrych, *Commonwealth to protectorate* (1982), 201, 420 · M. W. Helms and E. Cruickshanks, 'Howard, Charles', HoP, *Commons, 1660–90*, 2.588–91 · A. Swatland, *The House of Lords in the reign of Charles II* (1996) · A. Collins, *The peerage of England: containing a genealogical and historical account of all the peers of England* · IGI · H. Cary, ed., *Memorials of the great civil war in England from 1646 to 1652*, 2 vols. (1842) · will, PRO, PROB 11/380, fol. 27r · A. Davies, *Dictionary of British portraiture*, 1 (1979), 20

Archives BL, corresp. and papers, Sloane MSS 2723–2724 · BL, Yorkshire estate papers, Add. MS 32163 | BL, Lansdowne MS DCCCXXI · Cumbria AS, Kendal, corresp. with Daniel Fleming and others · NRA, priv. coll., letters to Robert Atkins, Kendal

Likenesses A. Blooteling, line engraving, BM, NPG; repro. in Guillim, *Heraldry* (1679) · W. Faithorne, line engraving, BM, NPG; repro. in G. Miège, *A relation of three embassies from his sacred majesty Charles II* (1669) · G. Kneller, oils, Castle Howard, Yorkshire · enamel miniature · oils (probably when colonel of Cromwell's lifeguards); formerly at Naworth, Cumbria, in 1891 · oils; formerly in town hall, Carlisle, Cumbria

Wealth at death disposed of (unvalued) real estate in Cumberland and Somerset, and 'remaining term' of £1000 annuity granted by Charles II: will, PRO, PROB 11/380, fol. 27r

Howard, Charles (1630–1713), landowner and natural philosopher, was born on 13 September 1630, the fourth son in the family of nine sons and three daughters of Henry Frederick *Howard, fifteenth earl of Arundel (1608–1652), and his wife, Lady Elizabeth Stuart (d. 1674), daughter of Esmé, earl of March and later third duke of Lennox.

In the late 1640s and early 1650s Howard spent time in France and the Netherlands. In 1652, on the death of his father, he inherited the estate of Deepdene, near Dorking, Surrey, and thereafter he devoted much effort to its beautification, constructing an elaborate Italianate garden of the kind popular in seventeenth-century England, with terraces landscaped on a U-shaped hillside, and with appendages including a laboratory. The garden was admired by John Evelyn in 1655, while John Aubrey gave a lengthy illustrated account of the estate in his *Perambulation of Surrey* (1673). The remains of Howard's landscaping are still to be seen at Deepdene; a further surviving relic of his horticultural activities there is provided by his herbarium, dated 1660, now at Arundel Castle. In the 1650s Howard evidently also developed an interest in industrial practices, and on 27 October 1660 he applied for a patent for a new method of tanning, the subject of a printed broadsheet, *Brief Directions how to Tanne Leather According to a New Invention* [n.d.].

On 24 December 1662 Howard was elected a fellow of the Royal Society; he almost immediately began to participate in its proceedings, taking a special interest in agrarian and technological matters. Various of the committees on such topics that the society instituted in 1663 and 1664 met at his lodgings at Arundel House, notably the agricultural or georgical committee. Howard's own contribution to the latter particularly concerned kitchen gardens and winter greens. In addition, a paper by him on the cultivation of saffron was published in the society's *Philosophical Transactions* in 1678 (a paper on his novel tanning technique had appeared there in 1674). In 1678 he applied for a patent for a new way of processing flax, which may have been related to investigations of this topic made under the society's auspices in the 1660s.

In the early 1680s Howard was twice involved in the public arena. In 1681 he was the victim of blackmail involving Titus Oates. More importantly, Howard engaged in protracted litigation against his brother, Henry *Howard, sixth duke of Norfolk, concerning the estate of Greystoke in Cumberland. His father had provided for this property to pass to Charles if his brother inherited the earldom of Arundel; but when this occurred in 1677 Henry refused to give up the estate, and Charles took the case to chancery, in 1682 obtaining a celebrated decision in his favour by Heneage Finch, first earl of Nottingham. This was challenged by his brother, however, and reversed by the lord keeper, Francis North, first Baron Guilford; the case continued after Henry's death and the succession to the dukedom of Charles's nephew, Henry. The issue was finally

resolved in Charles's favour in the House of Lords in June 1685.

In his later years Howard seems increasingly to have retired from public life. His attendance at the Royal Society dwindled after the early 1670s, and he evidently divided his time between London and Deepdene, devoting himself to horticultural, alchemical, and other pursuits. His wife, Mary, daughter of George Tattershall of Finchampstead, Berkshire, whom he had married in the early 1660s, died on 7 November 1695, and Howard himself died on 31 March 1713; both were buried in Dorking church. As laid down in the will that he had made on 29 April 1696, revising an earlier one dated 13 July 1685, in which his wife had been named as his sole heir, Howard's estates were inherited by his only surviving child, Henry Charles Howard (b. 18 Oct 1668); from him they descended to his son, Charles *Howard, who became tenth duke of Norfolk in 1777. MICHAEL HUNTER, rev.

Sources H. Howard, *Indications of the memorials of the Howard family* (1834), 39, 46–7 · *Lord Nottingham's chancery cases*, ed. D. E. C. Yale, 2 vols., SeldS, 73, 79 (1957–61) · D. Mercer, 'The Deepdene, Dorking', *Surrey Archaeological Collections*, 71 (1977), 111–38, esp. 114–15 · M. Hunter, *The Royal Society and its fellows, 1660–1700: the morphology of an early scientific institution*, 2nd edn (1994), 158–9 · M. Hunter, *Establishing the new science: the experience of the early Royal Society* (1989), 73–121 · H. K. S. Causton, *The Howard papers* (1862), 365–78 · Arundel Castle archives, West Sussex · J. M. Robinson, *The dukes of Norfolk*, rev. edn (1995)

Howard, Charles, third earl of Carlisle (1669–1738), politician and landowner, was born at Naworth, near Carlisle, the eldest son of Edward, second earl of Carlisle (c.1646–1692), and his wife, Elizabeth (1646–1696), the daughter of Sir William Uvedale of Wickham, Hampshire, and the widow of Sir William Berkeley. He was educated at Morpeth grammar school, then in 1688 embarked on a grand tour which lasted three years and took him to the Netherlands, the German states, and Italy. Before his departure Howard, then Viscount Morpeth, had married (25 July 1688) the thirteen-year-old Lady Anne Capel, the daughter of the first earl of Essex. He represented Morpeth in parliament from 1690 until 23 April 1692, when, on his father's death, he became the third earl. He was soon afterwards appointed to three regional offices: governor of Carlisle Castle (1 March 1693, a position he held until his death), lord lieutenant of Cumberland and Westmorland (28 June 1694, which he held to 29 April 1712), and vice-admiral of Cumberland. A staunch whig and anti-Jacobite, Carlisle used his local standing to influence the result of the 1695 general election in Cumberland and Westmorland, often to the annoyance of neighbouring landed families. In the same year he moved to the family's London residence, Carlisle House, at 20A Soho Square, which became a base for his forays into the capital's political and cultural society. His support for the whig cause put him in favour with William III, and on 23 June 1700 he was appointed gentleman of the king's bedchamber with an annual salary of £1000. On 19 June the following year he became a privy councillor; he also served as deputy earl marshal of England (8 May 1701–26 August 1706) and first lord of the Treasury (30 December 1701–6 May 1702).

Charles Howard, third earl of Carlisle (1669–1738), by William Aikman, 1729

Carlisle's ambitions were not in these years limited to political appointment. In 1698 he visited the village of Henderskelfe, near York, which became the site of a new family seat, Castle Howard, designed by his friend and fellow Kit-Cat Club member Sir John Vanbrugh. The house was intended to reflect the importance of the Howard family past and present while also further impressing a monarch interested in architectural projects. Built at what was a considerable expense for a relatively minor peer, it was financed through a combination of revenue from land, loans, and the third earl's successes at the gaming table (this last providing almost one-third of his annual income).

Although he was appointed as a commissioner for the union with Scotland (10 April 1706), Carlisle's political career began to falter under Queen Anne. After her death he served as one of the lords justices of Great Britain until the arrival of George I from Hanover in 1714. In October of the same year he was reappointed lord lieutenant of Cumberland and Westmorland (which office he held until his death), and between 23 May and 11 October 1715 he served for a second time as first lord of the Treasury. Carlisle held

a number of other offices under the first two Hanoverians: constable of the Tower of London (16 October 1715–29 December 1722), lord lieutenant of the Tower Hamlets (12 July 1717 to December 1722), constable of Windsor Castle and warden of the forest (1 June 1723 to May 1730), and master of the foxhounds (May 1730). Few of these offices would have satisfied him earlier in his career, but now plagued by gout he was increasingly content to spend more time in seclusion at Castle Howard. He died at Bath on 1 May 1738 and was buried at the parish church of Bulmer, near York, on 14 May. His body was moved on 28 June 1745 to the mausoleum at Castle Howard. He was survived by his five children, two sons and three daughters, including the poet Anne *Ingram, and his wife who, noted for her charity work, died aged seventy-eight on 14 October 1752.

The title passed to his eldest son, **Henry Howard**, fourth earl of Carlisle (1694–1758), politician and landowner, who was educated at Eton College and Trinity College, Cambridge, where he matriculated on 2 May 1711. On his return from the grand tour he was elected in 1715 for the family seat of Morpeth, which he held until he inherited the earldom in 1738. Two years after becoming an MP he married (27 November 1717) Lady Frances, the daughter of Charles Spencer, third earl of Sunderland; the marriage produced five children—three sons and two daughters. He supported his father-in-law during the whig schism and became an opponent of the Walpole government in the 1720s and 1730s, when he called for a reduction in the size of the standing army. He made several unsuccessful attempts to gain office after Walpole's fall, which came a few months before the death of his wife, on 27 July 1742. He married again, on 8 June 1743, this time to Isabella (1721–1795), the daughter of William Byron, fourth Baron Byron. He was made a KG in 1756. He died on 3 September 1758 and was buried at Castle Howard. The title passed to his one remaining son, Frederick *Howard, fifth earl of Carlisle. His wife, who later married Sir William Musgrave, died on 22 January 1795.

PHILIP CARTER

Sources GEC, *Peerage*, new edn · R. R. Sedgwick, 'Howard, Henry', HoP, *Commons* · C. S. Smith, *The building of Castle Howard* (1990)
Archives Castle Howard, Yorkshire, corresp. and papers · Cumbria AS, Carlisle, admiralty corresp. | BL, MSS collection [Henry Howard] · CUL, letters to Sir Robert Walpole · Cumbria AS, Kendal, corresp. with Sir Daniel Fleming
Likenesses G. Kneller, oils, c.1700–1710, NPG · W. Aikman, oils, 1729, Castle Howard, Yorkshire [see illus.] · photograph (Henry Howard; after M. Dahl, c.1715), Courtauld Inst.

Howard, Sir Charles (c.1696–1765), army officer, was the second son of Charles *Howard, third earl of Carlisle (1669–1738), and Anne (1674/5–1752), daughter of Arthur Capel, third earl of Essex. He entered the army in 1715 as an ensign in the 2nd (Coldstream) foot guards. In 1717 he was promoted to captain in the 16th foot but soon transferred to the 9th dragoons, before returning to the Coldstream Guards as captain (and lieutenant-colonel), 21 April 1719. He was appointed groom of the bedchamber to the king in 1724, lieutenant-governor of Carlisle in 1725, and colonel and aide-de-camp to the king in 1734.

Howard sat as MP for Carlisle in his family's interest from 1727 until 1761 and was a firm supporter of the government. In 1738 he became colonel of the 19th foot, now the Yorkshire regiment, which he held until transferred to the present 3rd dragoon guards in 1748. The 19th, then wearing grass-green facings, acquired its still familiar sobriquet of the Green Howards in 1744, upon joining the army in Flanders, in order to distinguish it from the 3rd regiment of foot, then commanded by Field Marshal Sir George Howard, thereafter known by the epithet the Buffs. Howard was promoted to the rank of brigadier-general in 1742 and major-general in 1743, and commanded a brigade at Dettingen and at Fontenoy, where he received four wounds, and afterwards under George Wade and William, duke of Cumberland during the Jacobite rising of 1745–6. He commanded the British infantry at the battles of Val and Roucoux in 1746 and was made KB on 2 May 1749. As the new colonel of the 3rd dragoons, he was a member of the board, set up by order of the king in May 1749, to consider amendments to the standard cavalry drill. He was made governor of Carlisle on 24 July of that year. In 1752 the king granted him the governorships of Forts George and Augustus. In 1760 he replaced General Richard Onslow, who had taken ill, as president of the court martial on Lord George Sackville. He stood for Carlisle in the election of 1761, but withdrew when it became likely the seat would be contested. He attained the rank of general in March 1765, and died at Bath, unmarried, on 26 August 1765. He was buried in the family vault at Castle Howard, Yorkshire. His will made provision for a natural son, William Howard, then a captain in the army.

H. M. CHICHESTER, rev. JONATHAN SPAIN

Sources A. N. Newman, 'Howard, Hon. Sir Charles', HoP, *Commons, 1754–90* · R. R. Sedgwick, 'Howard, Hon. Charles', HoP, *Commons, 1715–54* · Burke, *Peerage* (1999) · C. Dalton, *George the First's army, 1714–1727*, 2 vols. (1910–12) · *The manuscripts of the earl of Carlisle*, HMC, 42 (1897) · M. L. Ferrar, *A history of the services of the 19th regiment* (1911) · J. A. Houlding, *Fit for service: the training of the British army, 1715–1795* (1981) · P. Mackesy, *The coward of Minden: the affair of Lord George Sackville* (1979) · PRO, PROB 11/911–298
Archives Bucks. RLSS, corresp. and papers | Castle Howard, Yorkshire, letters to third and fourth earls of Carlisle
Likenesses oils, repro. in Ferrar, *History of the services of the 19th regiment*

Howard, Charles, tenth duke of Norfolk (1720–1786), landowner and writer, was born on 1 December 1720, the posthumous son of Henry Charles Howard (d. 1720), of Deepdene, Surrey, and Greystoke, Cumberland, and his wife, Mary, the daughter and coheir of John Aylward, a London merchant and banker, originally from co. Waterford. His father, a nephew of Thomas Howard, fifth duke of Norfolk, and Henry Howard, sixth duke, had been a devout Roman Catholic and had frustrated negotiations between Bishop Thomas Strickland and Secretary of State James Craggs in 1719 that sought toleration for Roman Catholics in England. Howard was educated on the continent. He was probably still at school when, on the death of his elder brother Henry, he succeeded to the Deepdene

estate, near Dorking, as well as to the more substantial lands and castle at Greystoke. On 8 November 1739, at Worksop Manor, the seat of his second cousin Edward Howard, ninth duke of Norfolk, he married Catherine (1718–1784), the daughter of John Brockholes, of Claughton, Lancashire. They had one child, Charles *Howard, later eleventh duke of Norfolk.

Howard led a quiet existence at Deepdene, improving his house and gardens. His first pamphlet was published in 1763 and was a statement claiming on behalf of himself and his sister Frances a share in the estate of their mother's cousin in France, Michel Toublet. This was followed by three more works: *Considerations on the Penal Laws against Roman Catholics in England and the New-Acquired Colonies in America* (1764), *Thoughts, Essays and Maxims, Chiefly Religious and Political* (1768), and *Historical Anecdotes of some of the Howard Family* (1769). The last two were influenced by the death of Edward Howard, a nephew of the duke of Norfolk, which left Charles Howard as heir to the dukedom. His publications and impending inheritance probably contributed to his election as FSA on 14 January 1768 and FRS on 24 March 1768. But they did not impress Horace Walpole, who regarded Howard as a plagiarist on the grounds of the extensive quotation from his *Catalogue of the Royal and Noble Authors of England* that Howard used to fill out his account of the poet earl of Surrey in the *Historical Anecdotes*. In a letter to Horace Mann, dated 27 February 1770, Walpole characterized Howard as 'a drunken old mad fellow' (Walpole, *Corr.*, 23.194) who attended a masquerade ball dressed as a cardinal. Howard's irreverent attitude towards his Catholic faith—he described himself as 'a whig Papist—a monster in nature' (Robinson, 166)—contributed to his lasting reputation for 'eccentric manners and more eccentric habits' (Tierney, 2.569).

Howard succeeded to the dukedom on 20 September 1777. He took little part in public life beyond signing the petition to the crown in 1778 that led to the Catholic Relief Act. However, he did secure a private act of parliament in 1783 that attached the revenues of the ducal estate in Westminster to the restoration of Arundel Castle, which helped establish it as the principal residence of the dukes of Norfolk. His wife died on 21 November 1784, and he followed, 'of drink' (Robinson, 171), on 31 August 1786, at his London home, Norfolk House, St James's Square, Westminster. He was buried on 7 September 1786 alongside his father at Dorking.

GORDON GOODWIN, rev. MATTHEW KILBURN

Sources J. M. Robinson, *The dukes of Norfolk* (1982) · Walpole, *Corr.* · G. Brenan and E. P. Statham, *The house of Howard*, 2 (1907), 627–8 · M. A. Tierney, *The history and antiquities of the castle and town of Arundel*, 2 (1834), 566–71 · H. K. S. Causton, *The Howard papers: with a biographical pedigree and criticism* [1862] · C. Howard, *Historical anecdotes of some of the Howard family* (1769) · C. Butler, *Historical memoirs respecting the English, Irish, and Scottish Catholics, from the Reformation to the present time*, 2nd edn, 4 (1821), 261–8 · GEC, *Peerage*, new edn · will, PRO, PROB 11/1146, sig. 485 · *Collins peerage of England: genealogical, biographical and historical*, ed. E. Brydges, 9 vols. (1812), vol. 1, p. 141 · *A catalogue of the royal and noble authors of England, Scotland and Ireland … by the late Horatio Walpole*, ed. T. Park, 4 (1806), 328–31
Archives Arundel Castle, West Sussex, papers; family and estate MSS | Bodl. Oxf., corresp. with John Brooke

Likenesses R. E. Pine, oils, exh. RA 1784, Arundel Castle, West Sussex; repro. in Robinson, *Dukes of Norfolk* · British school, miniature, Arundel Castle, West Sussex · oils, Arundel Castle, West Sussex

Wealth at death see will, PRO, PROB 11/1146, sig. 485

Howard, Charles, eleventh duke of Norfolk (1746–1815), politician, born on 14 or 15 March 1746, was the only son of Charles *Howard, tenth duke of Norfolk (1720–1786), landowner, and Catherine (1718–1784), daughter of John Brockholes of Claughton, Lancashire. He was educated by Roman Catholic tutors at Greystoke Castle, Cumberland, and in France, where he spent much of his youth. On 1 August 1767 at Dublin he married Marian (d. 1768), daughter and heir of John Coppinger of Ballyvolane, co. Cork, and Elizabeth Moore of Drogheda. She died in childbirth on 28 May 1768 and Howard married on 2 April 1771 Frances Fitzroy-*Scudamore (1750–1820) [see under Scudamore family], daughter and heir of Charles Fitzroy-Scudamore of Holme Lacey and Frances Scudamore, divorced wife of Henry Somerset, third duke of Beaufort. His second wife became mentally unstable soon after their marriage and was certified a lunatic. Howard had several relationships with other women, including the actress Charlotte *Tidswell. Mary Gibbon, a relative of the historian Edward Gibbon, became established as his semi-official mistress. They had six children, including Matthew Charles Howard Gibbon (1796–1873) and Edward Howard Howard-Gibbon (1799–1849), both of whom became heralds. Howard, who was styled the earl of Surrey from 1777, was elected FRS in 1767 and FSA in 1779, becoming president of the Society of Arts in 1794.

At the time of the anti-Catholic Gordon riots in 1780 Surrey conformed to the Church of England, and at the general election that year he was elected, with the duke of Portland's support, as MP for Carlisle, a borough whose freemen he had encouraged to shake off the influence of the Lowther family. In parliament he voted against North's administration and he joined Fox in actively opposing the conduct of the Anglo-American War and in speaking in favour of parliamentary reform. He turned down Shelburne's offer of the post of ambassador to the United States in December 1782 and continued to support Fox during the coalition with North, in which he held office as a Treasury lord. In spite of voting for Pitt's 1783 motion for parliamentary reform, Surrey proved to be 'a great borough monger': he was elected for Carlisle, Arundel, and Hereford in 1784 and wielded influence at Gloucester (Brooke, 645). He was appointed deputy lieutenant of Sussex in 1781, earl marshal of England in 1782, and lord lieutenant of the West Riding of Yorkshire in 1782. He also became colonel of the 1st West Yorkshire militia regiment in 1784.

On the death of his father on 31 August 1786 Surrey succeeded to the peerage and was subsequently appointed high steward of Hereford in 1790, recorder of Gloucester in 1792, and colonel in the army during service in 1794. At a great political dinner, attended by some 2000 people, that was held at the Crown and Anchor tavern in Arundel Street, Strand, on 24 January 1798, the duke gave a toast to 'Our sovereign's health—the majesty of the people' (GEC, *Peerage*, 9.634). The king, highly offended, stripped him of his lord lieutenancy and colonelcy, the news reaching Norfolk on 31 January when he was entertaining his friend the prince of Wales at Norfolk House, St James's Square, London. He was later consoled for the loss of these dignities by being made colonel of the Sussex regiment of militia in 1806 and lord lieutenant of Sussex in 1807. Lord Liverpool tried in vain to secure the duke's support for his administration by an offer of the Garter.

Norfolk was a 'large, muscular, and clumsy, though active' man, whose figure and habitual slovenliness of dress were often caricatured by Gillray (*Memoirs of … Wraxall*, 3.361). He wore his hair short and renounced powder except when attending court. He was celebrated for his conviviality and, together with the prince of Wales, was the first to bring into fashion late hours of dining. His servants used to wash him in his drunken stupors as he detested soap and water when sober. Despite his personal eccentricities, he lived in great splendour, spent vast sums on Arundel Castle, and bought books and pictures. He was deeply interested in everything that illustrated the history of his own family and was always ready to assist anyone named Howard who claimed the remotest kinship. He encouraged the production of works on local antiquities, such as John Duncumb's *Collections towards the History and Antiquities of the County of Hereford* and James Dallaway's *History of the Western Division of the County of Sussex*.

Norfolk died at Norfolk House on 16 December 1815 and was buried on 23 December at Dorking, Surrey, where his first wife was buried. He was survived by his second wife who died on 22 October 1820 at Holme Lacey, where she was buried. There were no surviving children from either marriage and the title passed to his cousin, Bernard Edward Howard (1765–1842).

GORDON GOODWIN, rev. S. J. SKEDD

Sources GEC, *Peerage* · J. Brooke, 'Howard, Charles, earl of Surrey', HoP, *Commons, 1754–90* · *The historical and the posthumous memoirs of Sir Nathaniel William Wraxall, 1772–1784*, ed. H. B. Wheatley, 5 vols. (1884) · H. Lonsdale, *The worthies of Cumberland*, 3 (1872), 57–64 · GM, 1st ser., 85/2 (1815), 631–2 · GM, 1st ser., 86/1 (1816), 65–7, 104 · J. M. Robinson, *The dukes of Norfolk* (1982)

Archives Arundel Castle, West Sussex, corresp. and papers | Bodl. Oxf., corresp. with John Charles Brooke · NRA, priv. coll., corresp. with first wife, Marian Coppinger, and letters to H. Howard of Corby · U. Nott. L., letters to third duke of Portland

Likenesses J. Sayers, cartoon, etching, pubd 14 May 1782, NPG · T. Gainsborough, portrait, 1783 · T. Gainsborough, oils, c.1784–1786, Arundel Castle, West Sussex · R. Dighton, cartoon, coloured etching, pubd 1796, BM, NPG · T. Lawrence, oils, 1799, Arundel Castle, West Sussex · J. Hoppner, portrait, 1800 · T. Williamson, stipple, pubd 1813 (after W. C. Ross), BM, NPG · J. Lonsdale, oils, 1815, Arundel Castle, West Sussex · D. Gardner, pastel drawing, BM; unfinished · stipple (after J. Hoppner), BM, NPG

Howard, Charles James Stanley, tenth earl of Carlisle (1867–1912). *See under* Howard, George James, ninth earl of Carlisle (1843–1911).

Howard, Dame (Rosemary) Christian (1916–1999), churchwoman and ecumenist, was born on 5 September

1916 at 32 Chester Square, Belgravia, London, the elder daughter and eldest of the five children of Geoffrey William Algernon Howard (1877–1935), politician and landowner, and his wife, the Hon. (Ethel) Christian, *née* Methuen (1889–1932), elder daughter of Paul Sanford *Methuen, third Baron Methuen of Corsham, army officer. Her father, the fifth son of George James *Howard, ninth earl of Carlisle, was Liberal MP for Eskdale (1906–10), Westbury (1911–18), and Luton (1923–4). She was educated at home and at Westbourne House School, Folkestone, and in Florence and Paris. Her first major task was to take over, at the age of nineteen, the running of Castle Howard, following the death of her father (all of whose elder brothers had died in early manhood). In 1940 she played a leading part in rescuing family treasures when much of the house was destroyed by a disastrous fire.

During the late 1930s Christian Howard studied for the London University certificate of religious knowledge, tutored by Michael Ramsey, the future archbishop of Canterbury. She obtained the certificate in 1939. In 1943 she gained a first in the Lambeth diploma of theology, and the inter-diocesan certificate which equipped her for professional lay work in the Church of England. She taught at Chichester high school for two years, returning then to York to work in the diocese as a licensed lay worker. From 1947 to 1972 she served as secretary of the diocesan board of women's work, continuing until 1979 to be secretary to the re-formed and renamed board of lay ministry, with its wider remit. This involved pastoral work and training, and membership of other diocesan committees. From 1960 to 1970 she was an elected lay member for York of the church assembly, and from 1970 to 1985 of the general synod. In 1961 and 1968 she was a delegate to the World Council of Churches assembly, becoming first a member and then the first woman vice-moderator of the faith and order commission of the World Council of Churches. She also served on the executive of the British Council of Churches. From 1978 to 1982 she was a member of the Churches' Council for Covenanting. In 1979 she became a vice-moderator of the newly formed movement for the ordination of women. She was appointed by Archbishop Donald Coggan a lay canon provincial of York Minster in 1969, and in 1979 was awarded a Lambeth MA. In 1986 she was made DBE.

Christian Howard's major contribution to the life of the Church of England was through her tireless work in the struggle to develop women's ministry and to achieve the ordination of women as priests through a positive vote of the general synod. After many years of reports and debates on this subject it was she who, in 1968, led the church assembly to see that they could make no sense of women's ministry until a decision had been reached on women in holy orders (deacons) and in the priesthood. It was characteristic of her to be able to propel the assembly into facing up to the real issue. At that time she was already a force to be reckoned with, an able speaker with an astute and penetrating mind, who could think on her feet and make a telling contribution at the end of a debate.

Although Christian Howard had this recognized ability for demolishing earlier arguments with devastating clarity and skill, she was deeply respected for fairness and generosity of understanding. This led, after many years of circular debate and discussion, to her being asked, in 1971, to produce a survey of the current state of opinion about the ordination of women. Her magisterial, even-handed, and lucid report, published in 1972, provided background information for the synod and, with her supplement in 1978 and her further report in 1984, she wrote three important documents which dealt with theological questions, tradition, biblical evidence, social considerations, the Anglican communion, ecumenical evidence, and much else besides. To these documents the general synod and other church members turned in the years leading up to debates in 1975, 1978, and 1984.

Christian Howard was unusual in being both a judicious document writer and also a campaigner, inheriting her stance perhaps from her paternal grandmother, Rosalind Frances *Howard, countess of Carlisle, a leading figure in the women's suffrage movement. 'A suffrag*ist*, you know', she would say 'not a suffrag*ette*, but she still had a house burned down for her pains' (private information). With her brilliant blue eyes, her ready understanding, and her great enjoyment of people and life, she made true friends in the very varied settings in which she found herself. Her humour, together with her clarity of mind and her acute political sense—'I am a political animal', she would say (private information)—made her unusually good company. Even her occasional explosions on committees could be seen as part and parcel of an intense commitment to achieving a change for the better in the Church of England, but achieving it in the way she felt to be right. This was illustrated in the opening paragraph of her first report (1972):

> In asking: 'Can a woman be ordained to the priesthood?' we are dealing not with a woman's question, but a church question. Our answer must be determined not primarily by what is good for women, but what is good for the Church. And consequently, 'What is the will of God?' 'What will further the Gospel?'

Christian Howard's interests outside the church included active support for the Liberal Party, later Liberal Democrats, and the Girl Guide movement, as well as a great love for her garden and for woodwork. Her travels abroad, especially to Sweden, enriched her experience of women's ministry. She never married. She died of cardiac failure at the District Hospital, York, on 22 April 1999, the funeral taking place in the Castle Howard chapel on 29 April. By her special request half her ashes were placed in the Castle Howard mausoleum and the other half placed in the cemetery at Coneysthorpe, her nearby home.

MARGARET WEBSTER

Sources M. Webster, *A new strength, a new song* (1994) · *Daily Telegraph* (26 April 1999) · *The Times* (23 April 1999) · *The Independent* (26 April 1999) · *The Guardian* (26 April 1999) · *Reports of Proceedings* [of the Church Assembly and the General Synod] (Nov 1962); (Feb 1967); (July 1973); (Nov 1978); (July 1979); (July 1980); (Nov 1982);

(Nov 1984) · J. Field-Bibb, *Women towards priesthood: ministerial politics and feminist praxis* (1991) · *WWW* · Burke, *Peerage* · private information (2004) · personal knowledge (2004) · b. cert. · d. cert. · *CGPLA Eng. & Wales* (1999)

Archives Borth. Inst., papers · Women's Library, London, papers relating to campaign for ordination of women | Church of England Record Centre, London, papers from British Council of Churches · Church of England Record Centre, London, papers from general synod · Church of England Record Centre, London, papers on ordination of women · Church of England Record Centre, London, papers on guide and scout movement · Church of England Record Centre, London, papers on York board of women's work

Likenesses photograph, 1972, repro. in *Daily Telegraph* · photograph, 1979, repro. in *The Independent* · photograph, repro. in *The Times* · photograph, repro. in *The Guardian*

Wealth at death under £200,000—gross; under £200,000—net: probate, 18 Aug 1999, *CGPLA Eng. & Wales*

Howard [*married name* Parker], **Constance Mildred** (1910–2000), embroiderer and textile artist, was born on 8 December 1910 at 26 Albany Road, Abington, Northampton, the eldest among the three daughters of Arthur Howard, an elementary schoolmaster, and his wife and first cousin, Mildred Annie Abbott. She recalled that her father 'drew like an angel' (*The Independent*, 28 July 2000), and from the age of ten she attended weekly classes at Northampton School of Art. When she was fourteen she won a scholarship to attend art school full time, and in 1931 she won a free scholarship to the Royal College of Art (RCA); the local education authority refused her a subsistence grant, considering that it was pointless to fund the studies of a woman who would probably marry. She had to borrow money to take up her place at the school.

At the RCA, the shy and hard-working Howard studied engraving and book illustration under Edward Bawden and Eric Ravilious, producing some impressive white-line wood-engraving. She also attended Edward Johnston's calligraphy classes and Kathleen Harris's classes in embroidery. 'I hated embroidery when I was young because I didn't realise its creative possibilities', she recalled (Brown, 22). She went on to take a teaching qualification at the college in 1935; her first post was at Cardiff School of Art, where she set up a course in dress design. In Cardiff she joined a circle of artists patronized by the director of the National Museum of Wales, David Baxendall, but 'was so lonely … that in my free time I did embroidery' (Howard, 4). She moved to Kingston School of Art, where she spent the Second World War. At Kingston she and her students embroidered maps for the RAF, which were then photographed; this technique apparently produced results of great clarity. But she produced no other embroidery in this period. On 15 December 1945 she married the sculptor Harold Wilson Parker (1895/6–1980), with whom she had a daughter, Charlotte.

Howard gave up teaching for a time following her marriage, and began to exhibit imaginative embroidered pictures at the Arts and Crafts Exhibition Society. In 1947 she exhibited in the 'Pictures for Schools' exhibitions orchestrated by Nan Youngman. That same year she returned to teaching, part-time, at Goldsmiths' College, London, where she set up embroidery classes for young artists training to be teachers. Her success was such that by 1953

a department of embroidery was established in the school of art at Goldsmiths', and Howard became its head in 1958. Early students recalled the contrast between her teaching and the comparative conservatism of the college's sculpture and painting departments. She herself later recalled initial hostility to her department: 'Most of the men didn't agree with embroidery at all; they used to be terribly rude too … it wasn't supposed to be there—it was a Fine Art School' ('"Waves"', 12). In 1964 the course became a main subject for the diploma in art and design and was expanded to include printed, woven, and knitted textiles: the yearly shows of her students' degree work drew wide audiences from among those interested in innovative textile art.

In 1950 Constance Howard was commissioned by F. H. K. Henrion to produce a hanging for the country pavilion of the South Bank exhibition for the Festival of Britain. The stumpwork narrative hanging, *The Country Wife* (measuring 18½ ft x 13½ ft), depicted the varied activities of the National Federation of Women's Institutes (NFWI), and was designed by Howard and executed with the assistance of her students (including the future fashion designer Mary Quant) and craftswomen from the women's institutes: after the festival it was given to the NFWI, and it hangs at their residential college, Denman College, in Oxfordshire. Howard's embroidery in the 1950s was heraldic and figurative, demonstrating an interest in popular art as well as Scandinavian and Russian illustration. Her early work was characterized by a lively disjunction of line and colour, influenced perhaps by the art of Paul Klee and Joan Miró; her 'strikingly linear work' also shows the imprint of her early training as a wood-engraver (Benn, 268). During the 1960s she moved towards abstraction, and by the 1980s she was creating completely abstract panels using a wrapping technique of her own invention.

A superb technician herself, Howard emphasized the importance of ideas in embroidery: 'embroidery should have an art basis if it is to have any lasting impact. All students should draw … Stitches and textures without purpose become boring', she observed (Howard, 43). None the less, she conveyed her comprehensive knowledge of technique in a number of books. *Design for Embroidery from Traditional English Sources* (1956) coincided with her first solo exhibition, at the Crafts Centre, Hay Hill, and was followed by (among others) *Inspiration for Embroidery* (1966), *Embroidery and Colour* (1976), *The Constance Howard Book of Stitches* (1979), and her majestic four-volume *Twentieth-Century Embroidery in Great Britain* (1981–6). Howard retired from Goldsmiths' in 1975 and was appointed MBE for services to embroidery. She continued to write and teach in Britain, North America, Australia, and New Zealand, gaining a devoted following among embroiderers of all levels of skill and experience.

Constance Howard had eclectic tastes, with special interests in theatrical costume, millinery, and *haute couture*, cherishing a special fondness for the work of the Spanish couturier Balenciaga. Personally she dressed strikingly, with great elegance, her clothes set off by her carefully arranged hair, which was dyed a vivid shade of green: her choice long pre-dated the punk fashion for peacock-hued heads—for many years before purpose-made dyes became available she used lithographers' ink. Her voice was soft, and she spoke rapidly, with enthusiasm and humour. She died from cancer on 2 July 2000 in Wilton Nursing Home in Hindhead, Surrey. She was the pre-eminent teacher and advocate of the art of embroidery of the second half of the twentieth century; examples of her work are to be found in Northampton Art Gallery, Lincoln Cathedral, Eton College, the Victoria and Albert Museum, and Makerere University, Kampala. She was a fellow of the Society of Designer Craftsmen, and a member of the Costume Society, the Art Workers' Guild, and the Embroiderers' Guild. In 1980 the Constance Howard Textile Resource and Research Centre was opened at Goldsmiths' College, and in October 2000 an exhibition of the work of the textiles department at Goldsmiths' since its inception, 'Waves', was dedicated to her memory.

TANYA HARROD

Sources *The Independent* (28 July 2000) · *The Guardian* (20 July 2000) · *Constance Howard, Christine Risley, Eirian Short*, Goldsmiths' College (1985) [exhibition catalogue, Goldsmiths' College, Nov–Dec 1985] · T. Harrod, *The crafts in Britain in the twentieth century* (New Haven, CT, 1999) · BL NSA, NLSC · C. Howard, 'A personal account', *Embroidery*, 24/2 (1973), 40–43 · E. Benn, 'Tribute to Constance', *The World of Embroidery*, 51 (2000), 68–9 · '"Waves": Goldsmiths' glorious fifty years', *Workbox*, 67 (Feb–March 2001), 12–13 · P. Brown, 'Constance Howard: a colourful life', *Stitch*, no. 1 (2000), 22–3 · *Waves: fifty years of textiles at Goldsmiths*, Creative Exhibition Ltd (2000)
Likenesses photograph, repro. in *The Guardian* · photograph, repro. in *The Independent*
Wealth at death £682,340: probate, 13 Oct 2000, *CGPLA Eng. & Wales*

Howard, David (1839–1916), chemical manufacturer, was born in Tottenham, Middlesex, the third of four sons (there were no daughters) of Robert Howard, chemical manufacturer, of Stratford, London. He studied at the Royal College of Chemistry, London, under A. W. von Hofmann, and in 1860 joined as a partner the well-established chemical manufacturing business founded by his grandfather, Luke Howard, in 1807. This firm began by manufacturing fine chemicals, especially the anti-malarial drug quinine and its derivatives, for the pharmaceutical industry. David Howard's uncle, J. E. Howard, did much original research on the chemistry of cinchona alkaloids, and he himself pursued the same line of enquiry. He became an acknowledged authority in this field, publishing a number of papers in the *Journal of the Chemical Society* from 1871. On 4 May 1865 he married Anna Dora (*b*. 1843/4), daughter of John Jowitt of Leeds. They had two sons, both of whom became directors of Howards & Sons, the family firm.

During the nineteenth century quinine was the firm's most profitable product, though it also manufactured many other fine chemicals, including cocaine, ether, borax, and citric acid. In 1888, the year in which the Kodak camera was launched, the Howards acquired Hopkin and Williams, of Wandsworth, who made photographic chemicals. Around the turn of the century, manufacture

began to be concentrated at a new site in Ilford. In 1903 David Howard succeeded his father as chairman and there followed a period of rapid growth. In 1905 the firm acquired an interest in Bowmans of Warrington, making chemicals for the brewing industry, and in 1914 Thorium Ltd was established to make thorium nitrate for gas mantles. Two years later aspirin manufacture was commenced.

Howard's lifelong interest in chemistry and the chemical industry was not limited to manufacture. He served on the council of the Chemical Society and was president of the Society of Chemical Industry (1886–7) and of the Institute of Chemistry (1903–6). He was much concerned with strict honesty in business transactions and was closely involved in the agitation that led to the passing of the Prevention of Corruption Act in 1900: he was subsequently chairman of the Bribery and Secret Commissions Prevention League, set up to give effect to the provisions of the act. He also served as deputy lieutenant for the county of Essex.

Howard maintained an active interest in his company to the end of his long life. He died suddenly on 14 November 1916 at Snaresbrook railway station while travelling from his home at Devon House, Buckhurst Hill, Essex, to the Ilford factory. TREVOR I. WILLIAMS, *rev.*

Sources *Journal of the Society of Chemical Industry*, 35 (1916), 1144 · *Journal of the Society of Chemical Industry* (July 1931), 55 [jubilee number] · RS Friends, Lond., archives · m. cert. · d. cert.
Wealth at death £100,465 7s. 4d.: probate, 11 April 1917, *CGPLA Eng. & Wales*

Howard, Sir Ebenezer (1850–1928), founder of the garden city movement, was born at 62 Fore Street in the City of London on 29 January 1850, the third child and only son of Ebenezer Howard, confectioner, who owned several shops in and near the City, and his wife, Ann Tow, of Colsterworth, Lincolnshire. He was educated from the age of four to the age of fifteen at private boarding-schools, first at Sudbury, Suffolk, then at Cheshunt, Hertfordshire, and finally at Ipswich. After leaving school, he earned his living as a clerk in the City of London, obtaining a varied experience in the offices of a firm of stockbrokers, a firm of merchants, and two firms of solicitors. He taught himself shorthand in his spare time. After sending him a verbatim transcript of one of his sermons, Howard was employed for a short period as private secretary by Dr Joseph Parker, the renowned Congregational preacher (afterwards of the City Temple, Holborn), whose charismatic personality exercised a considerable influence on Howard.

Late in 1871, with two companions of his own age, Howard sailed for New York. They made their way to the midwestern state of Nebraska, appropriately to Howard county, where they arrived in March 1872. They took a 160 acre plot and attempted homestead farming, but the enterprise failed after one winter, and Howard went to Chicago, where he joined the firm of Ely, Burnham, and Bartlett, official stenographers to the law courts. The city

Sir Ebenezer Howard (1850–1928), by E. Housden, *c.*1908

was rebuilding itself after a serious fire in 1871, and its suburbs were spreading westwards. The extensive public parks then being projected and laid out gave the name 'garden city', a term not lost on Howard. His intellectual horizons broadened through friendship with Alonzo Griffin, a Quaker, who introduced him to the writings of Ralph Waldo Emerson, Nathaniel Hawthorne, J. R. Lowell, and Walt Whitman. He met Cora Richmond, a 'spiritualist medium', and studied Tom Paine's *The Age of Reason* and Benjamin Ward Richardson's *Hygeia, or, The City of Health*, both of which profoundly influenced him. He became a freethinker, although he continued to attend the Congregational church.

After returning to Britain in 1876, Howard joined Gurney & Sons, the official parliamentary reporters, as a shorthand writer: he carried on his own business as shorthand writer in the law courts, for a few years in partnership with William Treadwell, and later on his own, until his retirement in 1920. On 30 August 1879 Howard married Elizabeth Ann (Lizzie), daughter of Thomas Bills, a prosperous innkeeper of Nuneaton, Warwickshire. Within seven years they had one son and three daughters; a fifth child died in infancy, which undermined Lizzie's health, although she indefatigably and loyally assisted Howard's work. The Howards lived in Dulwich, then on the southern suburban fringe of London, later in Stoke Newington and Stamford Hill, to the north. Howard had an inquisitive, inventive turn of mind, and began work on a variable spacing mechanism for typewriters, which he offered to Remingtons, and visited the United States in 1884 and again in 1886, but the deal was not closed as he

regarded their offer of £250 for a half-share in the patent as derisory. His interest in typewriters remained to the end of his life. Late in 1879 Howard joined the Zetetical Society, a philosophical and sociological debating group, whose membership included George Bernard Shaw (with whom Howard remained associated until his death) and Sidney Webb, founder of Fabian socialism. In February 1880 Howard presented a paper on spiritualism, a topic which had fascinated him since making the acquaintance of Mrs Richmond.

In 1889 Howard read Edward Bellamy's *Looking Backward*, which had been published in America the previous year. This book describes the experiences of a Bostonian who falls into a trance and wakes up in the year 2000 to find the United States transformed into an ideal community by technological advance and state monopoly capitalism. Howard read the book straight through at a sitting and, as he later wrote, 'realised as never before, the splendid possibilities of a new civilisation, based on service to the community, and not on self-interest … I determined to take such part as I could … in helping to bring a new civilisation into being' (Macfadyen, 20). As a first step he persuaded William Reeves, a radical Fleet Street publisher, to bring out an English edition, but only by offering to take the first 100 copies. *Looking Backward* acted as catalyst for Howard's drafting *Tomorrow: a Peaceful Path to Real Reform*. During its long gestation, other influences made their mark: *Fields, Factories and Workshops*, by the Russian anarchist Peter Kropotkin, and *Progress and Poverty*, by the American Henry George, in which land nationalization was proposed. Howard had been aware of the latter since George's well-attended lectures in London in 1882. He acknowledged three sources which helped define his 'unique combination of proposals': the organized migration of population, as formulated by Edward Gibbon Wakefield and Professor Alfred Marshall, the system of land tenure proposed by Thomas Spence (a Quaker radical from Newcastle upon Tyne), with a modification by Herbert Spencer, and the ideal model city of *Victoria*, by James Silk Buckingham. Systematic decentralization of London's population had been advocated by monarchs in the sixteenth century, and as a compulsory policy by William Cobbett, but Howard firmly linked it to the development of new settlements. Howard circulated drafts of his book among friends, with the title 'The master key', while his ideal settlement progressed from 'Unionville' to 'Rurisville', then 'Garden City'. Swan Sonnenschein eventually published *Tomorrow: a Peaceful Path to Real Reform* in October 1898, with the inducement of a £50 donation to Howard from George Dickman, managing director in Britain for the Kodak Company. The book was republished in 1902 under the title *Garden Cities of Tomorrow*, by which it has subsequently become better known.

Howard's objective was to find a remedy for overcrowded and unhealthy conditions in the fast-growing industrial cities, and the accompanying rural depopulation and agricultural depression. He believed access to the countryside to be necessary for the complete physical and social development of humankind. It was no longer acceptable for urban development to be left to the minimally regulated private enterprise of landowners and industrialists. In taking evidence for royal commissions, Howard had been impressed by the unanimity of opinion of labour and capital over the failure of the city to provide decent housing and working conditions. Howard's solution was to provide a new form of settlement as a vehicle for radical social and environmental reform. He proposed the development of new towns, not for individual or corporate profit, but for the benefit of the whole community. These, the garden cities, were to be both residential and industrial, well planned, of limited size and population, and surrounded by a permanent rural belt, integrating the best aspects of town and country. Each garden city was to be self-contained, and built on land purchased by trustees, and used as an asset, against which the cost of development would be raised. The value of the land would increase, and periodic revaluation of the plots leased to individuals would reap the benefit for the community, with dividends to shareholders in the enterprise limited to 5 per cent. Howard envisaged that an urban cluster of garden cities, the 'Social City', would develop in the longer term, with a population of 250,000, in six garden cities of 32,000 each, and a central city of 58,000, all linked by rapid transit. Industrial development would eliminate pollution through the introduction of electricity as the major source of energy.

In 1899 Howard formed the Garden City Association to press for implementation of a garden city as a practical exemplar for others to follow. The movement was greatly assisted through the recruitment of Thomas Adams, a young Scottish surveyor, as secretary to the association, and Ralph Neville, an eminent lawyer and Liberal politician, as chairman. Widespread interest was fostered through international conferences, hosted by George Cadbury at Bournville in 1901, and W. H. Lever at Port Sunlight in 1902. These model industrial villages also demonstrated the benefits of enlightened design of working-class housing. In July 1902, the Garden City Pioneer Company was constituted, with Howard as managing director, to find a suitable site for the first garden city, and in summer 1903 a site at Letchworth, Hertfordshire, was acquired. Development, promoted by First Garden City Ltd, registered on 1 September 1903, began early in 1904, on the basis of a master plan by Barry Parker and Raymond Unwin, selected through a limited competition. Howard's concept was modified in detail, though his general principles were maintained. Sites were leased for ninety-nine years, without interim revaluations, and growth was initially slow. The outstanding mortgage on the site, and the high cost of infrastructure were further handicaps; the first dividend, of 1 per cent, was not paid until 1913, and the cumulative dividend arrears were not paid off until 1946. The population rose to 10,212 in 1917 and to 20,321 in 1951, before achieving Howard's target of 32,000 in the late 1980s.

Lizzie Howard died in the late autumn of 1904. Howard moved to a house in Norton Way South, Letchworth, part of a group designed by Parker and Unwin. On 25 March 1907 he remarried; his second wife, Edith Annie (*b.* 1864/5), a 42-year-old spinster daughter of William Knight Hayward, farmer, of Highfield House, Wellingore, Lincoln, survived him. The marriage was unsuccessful, and Howard left for a while to live alone in the Homesgarth co-operative flats, Sollershott East, Letchworth, which he had founded in 1911.

The aftermath of the First World War brought government involvement with the provision of working-class housing, through grants made to local authorities under the 1919 Housing Act. Disappointed at the lack of commitment to the building of new self-contained communities by state or private enterprise, in 1919 Howard learned that a suitable site at Welwyn, Hertfordshire, 15 miles south of Letchworth, was about to be sold by auction. He raised £5000 from friends, attended the sale, and successfully bid for the land. Second Garden City Ltd was formed to take over and develop the estate. In twelve years, on the basis of a master plan by Louis de Soissons, Welwyn Garden City became a flourishing town of nearly 10,000 residents.

Garden Cities of Tomorrow was translated into many languages, and societies for the promotion of garden cities were established throughout Europe and in the United States of America. In 1913 Howard founded the International Garden Cities Association: he was its president until his death. His study of Esperanto, the international language, was intended to foster co-operation and understanding. Howard travelled widely in the 1920s, and returned to America in 1925, in the company of Parker and Unwin, for the International Garden Cities Association conference held in New York. Howard's ideas were extensively updated and modified during the twentieth century, with the growth of motor traffic, and Radburn, New Jersey, designed by Henry Wright and Clarence Stein, which pioneered the separation of pedestrians and motor vehicles, was begun in 1928, the year of his death. In Britain, through the efforts of Patrick Abercrombie, F. J. Osborn, and Raymond Unwin, the royal commission on the distribution of the industrial population reported in 1940 in favour of planned decentralization of London to a ring of garden cities. This was more precisely defined in Abercrombie's *Greater London Plan, 1944*, and enacted as a state reconstruction programme by the post-war Labour government, through the New Towns Act of 1946. This in effect fulfilled Howard's strategic objective, first proposed almost fifty years before in 'The future of London', the final chapter of *Tomorrow*.

Howard remained a poor man all his life, receiving little monetary return from his directorships at Letchworth and Welwyn. He was devoid of personal ambition, but had a remarkable gift of inspiring other people. Being absolutely convinced of the rightness of his ideas, he was driven by an ardent enthusiasm. Neither a professional town planner nor a financier, he convinced town planners and financiers of the practical soundness of his ideas, but readily accepted their expertise in carrying his concepts into practice. George Bernard Shaw aptly characterized Howard as 'one of those heroic simpletons who do big things whilst our prominent worldlings are explaining why they are Utopian and impossible. And of course it is they who will make money out of his work' (G. B. Shaw to A. C. Howard, 25 May 1928, Howard MSS, Hertfordshire County RO). Public recognition came late in life: he was appointed OBE in 1924 and knighted in 1927. Howard's public work and his profession allowed him little leisure for other interests. As a young man he enjoyed watching cricket at Kennington Oval. In later life he was a fair chess player. During his final years Howard divided his time between a projected third garden city, and developing his phonoplayer, a shorthand typewriter, of which proto-types were made. Early in 1928 Howard's health began to fail, and by mid-March he was confined to a sofa at his home at 5 Guessens Road, Welwyn Garden City; Mrs Howard slept upstairs in the only bed. Visitors were kept at bay, and he died, at home, in a neglected state on 1 May 1928. His funeral was held at the Free Church in Letchworth, and he was buried on 4 May in the cemetery on Icknield Way. His height was about 5 feet 5 inches, his hair and complexion fair, and his eyes blue and animated. A memorial tablet was installed in Howard Park, Letchworth, in 1930, and a plain brick memorial in Howardsgate, Welwyn Garden City. This was replaced in July 1964 by a bronze plaque by James Woodford RA, set flat in a cobbled surround, with a portrait relief, and inscribed 'His vision and practical idealism profoundly affected town planning throughout the world'.   MERVYN MILLER

Sources DNB · R. Beevers, *The garden city utopia: a critical biography of Ebenezer Howard* (1988) · D. Macfadyen, *Sir Ebenezer Howard and the town planning movement* (1933) · F. J. Osborn, 'Sir Ebenezer Howard: the evolution of his ideas', *Town Planning Review*, 21/3 (1950), 221–35 · S. Burder, *Visionaries and planners* (1990) · S. Burder, 'Ebenezer Howard: the genesis of a town planning movement', *Journal of the American Institute of Planners*, 35/6 (1969), 390–97 · W. A. Eden, 'Ebenezer Howard and the garden city movement', *Town Planning Review*, 19/3–4 (1947), 123–43 · J. Moss-Eccardt, *Ebenezer Howard, 1850–1928* (1973) · M. Miller, *Letchworth: the first garden city* (1989) · M. de Soissons, *Welwyn Garden City: a town designed for healthy living* (1988) · *The Times* (2 May 1928) · *Letchworth Citizen* (4 May 1928) · *Letchworth Citizen* (11 May 1928) · *Welwyn News* (4 May 1928) · *Welwyn News* (11 May 1928) · *Garden Cities and Town Planning*, 18/5 (1928), 101–3, 109–13 · CGPLA Eng. & Wales (1928)
Archives Herts. ALS, corresp. and papers | Welwyn Garden City Library, corresp. and papers of Frederic Osborn relating to Howard, incl. corresp. with him | FILM First Garden City Heritage Museum, Letchworth, Hertfordshire, *The life of Ebenezer Howard*
Likenesses E. Housden, photograph, c.1908, First Garden City Heritage Museum, Letchworth, Hertfordshire [*see illus.*] · S. Pryse, oils, 1912, First Garden City Heritage Museum, Letchworth, Hertfordshire · I. Young, bust, 1927, First Garden City Heritage Museum, Letchworth, Hertfordshire · photographs, First Garden City Heritage Museum, Letchworth, Hertfordshire · photographs, Town and Country Planning Association
Wealth at death £788 14s. 1d.: probate, 25 June 1928, CGPLA Eng. & Wales

Howard, Edmund Bernard Fitzalan- [*formerly* Lord Edmund Talbot], **first Viscount FitzAlan of Derwent** (1855–1947), politician, was born in London on 1 June 1855, the third son of Henry Granville Howard (later Fitzalan-*Howard), earl of Arundel, politician, who became fourteenth duke of Norfolk (1815–1860), and his

wife, Augusta Mary Minna Catherine (1821–1886), daughter of Edmund *Lyons, first Baron Lyons. He was educated at the Oratory School, Birmingham. In July 1876, in accordance with the will of Bertram Arthur Talbot, seventeenth earl of Shrewsbury, which made him a major beneficiary, he assumed the surname Talbot, and was until 1921 styled Lord Edmund Talbot. He served as a regular soldier and became lieutenant-colonel of the 11th hussars, and he was an active sportsman, but determined early on a political career. Service in the Second South African War, when he was deputy assistant adjutant-general under Lord Roberts, awarded the DSO, and among the first to enter besieged Kimberley, was an interlude in a mainly political life.

Talbot married on 5 August 1879 Mary Caroline Bertie (d. 1938), daughter of Montagu Arthur Bertie, Lord Norreys, later seventh earl of Abingdon. Lady Edmund Talbot became a formidable political wife, ever attentive to her husband's interests, and they shared an interest in settlement work. They had one son and one daughter. Talbot was defeated as Conservative candidate at Burnley in 1880, and in 1885 and 1886 by A. J. Mundella in the Brightside division of Sheffield, both safe Liberal seats. The Howards owned land in Sheffield, and also in south-west Sussex, where Talbot was returned unopposed at a by-election in 1894. Conservatives won about two-thirds of the vote in this Chichester constituency, so Talbot easily held it until promoted to the Lords in 1921.

Talbot found his political *métier* in June 1905, when he was appointed a Conservative whip. Ned Talbot remained in the whips' room until 1921, as Unionist chief whip in the turbulent years 1913–21, and joint parliamentary secretary to the Treasury from May 1915. His appointment as chief whip in 1913, when his predecessor went to the Lords as earl of Crawford, was a key decision: Crawford thought Talbot would be 'as good as could be desired', and six months later noted that 'my old friend Ned Talbot seems to be carrying out his duties with faultless and unwearied skill' (*Crawford Papers*, 306, 315). Another whip, William Bridgeman, had confidently predicted that 'we shall get on well with Ned Talbot, but I fear his health may not stand it for long' (*Modernisation*, 70). Talbot's health was indeed fragile, and he sometimes missed key occasions, such as the beginning of the parliamentary session in 1918. Increasingly he resented being taken for granted in a mainly invisible role, but was too good to be easily replaced. Robert Sanders, who served with him from 1911, noted in 1920 that 'the fact of his being such a good whip stands in the way of his preferment' (*Real Old Tory Politics*, 123). His eventual move in 1921 was therefore a key tactical error by the new party leader Austen Chamberlain, and it is unlikely that Chamberlain would have lost control in October 1922 if Talbot had still been there.

Before the First World War, Talbot was the orchestrator of the Unionists' final parliamentary campaigns against Irish home rule, a member of the shadow cabinet, and one of the channels through which attempts to settle the Irish issue by compromise were made, and the government assured of Unionist support in any war against Germany.

He was especially close to Bonar Law: their thinking was in step through the convoluted coalition politics of 1915–16. This was a significant factor in the Conservatives remaining behind Law in the December 1916 crisis which replaced Asquith by Lloyd George. When the new government was formed, Talbot was at Law's elbow as he manoeuvred senior Conservatives such as Balfour into ministerial posts. During the Lloyd George coalition Talbot was one of the inner core of ministers invited to key tactical meetings: his assessment of what tory MPs would stand for was generally heeded. He was, for example, crucial in May 1918 in getting Conservative MPs to back the government during debates on General Maurice's accusations of deception by Lloyd George, arguing clear-headedly that the facts were less significant than the war effort, since Lloyd George was 'necessary to the cause of the alliance' (*Real Old Tory Politics*, 104). His final duty as whip was to manage Austen Chamberlain's succession to the party leadership when Bonar Law retired in March 1921. He chaired the party meeting with great skill and, as Lord Selborne noted, 'squelched' proponents of other candidates in a way that made voting unnecessary (Boyce, 226). He received a 'great ovation' at the end (*Real Old Tory Politics*, 150).

The Government of Ireland Act (1920) made it possible for a Roman Catholic to be viceroy of Ireland, and, with civil war rampant, Lloyd George asked Talbot to take the post. Though anxious to exchange offices, he had already turned down the War Office and the Air Ministry, and was not attracted to this offer; Lady Edmund was even less happy that he accept such a dangerous posting. A sense of duty was, however, central to Talbot's make-up, and for that reason he accepted. When his old army friend Sir Henry Wilson asked, 'How could you do such a thing? How could you?' Talbot succinctly replied, 'Because I was brought up in cherry breeches, not with a green coat', his words not only contrasting his old regiment's uniform with Wilson's rifle brigade, but hinting that a refusal to serve would have been cowardly. Robert Sanders, who thought that 'Edmund's taking his new post is heroic', added that he 'has the feeling that the honour of his regiment is involved' (*Real Old Tory Politics*, 150, 154). Talbot was appointed viceroy on 2 April 1921 and sworn in on 2 May, created Viscount FitzAlan to enhance his prestige, and reverted to the family name Fitzalan-Howard. Winston Churchill wrote that 'devotion to public duty alone inspired him to undertake so melancholy a task' (*DNB*).

FitzAlan was neither the first nor the last chief whip to be asked by British governments to manage Irish disorder, on the basis that demonstrable tact and firmness in the lobbies might somehow transfer to Dublin or Belfast. On no occasion has this proved to be the case, and, even though FitzAlan as a Catholic offered additional hope that he might bridge both communities, events were too far gone to give him much chance of success. For, as a nationalist Irishman remarked, a Catholic viceroy was no more welcome than 'a new Catholic hangman' (*DNB*). FitzAlan, who had been sharply critical of the government's coercive Irish policies, now found himself running a detested

military government. In spite of lifelong Unionist convictions, he came rapidly to the conclusion that the only alternative to unacceptable military repression was compromise with Sinn Féin. He was therefore one of the architects of the 'truce of God' which the king offered in June 1921, and supportive of the Irish treaty negotiated by November. He was not over-optimistic, however, and Sanders recorded in August that he 'thinks well of Griffith and hopes for the best from Collins' (*Real Old Tory Politics*, 160). The Irish viceroyalty, to which FitzAlan had been appointed, ceased to exist, and in December 1922 he was replaced by Tim Healy in the Irish Free State and the duke of Abercorn as governor of Northern Ireland. He remained close to George V, and was granted in 1924 Cumberland Lodge in Windsor Great Park as a grace-and-favour residence after the land on which stood his own Derwent Hall in Derbyshire had been acquired for a reservoir project.

FitzAlan did not seek office again, but attended regularly in the Lords, and took special interest in the reform of the house when opportunity seemed to present itself in 1927. He also retained wider political interest, opposing the Government of India Bill (1935), and in 1936 joining in deputations to Baldwin of what Austen Chamberlain called 'old stagers' to offer views on the abdication crisis and the slowness of rearmament. He seems to have come belatedly to admire Baldwin, whose confirmation as party leader he had declined to propose in 1924 since 'he thought him so unfit for the leadership that he could not do it' (*Austen Chamberlain Diary*, 249, 513).

FitzAlan was a profoundly religious man who held his Catholic faith with robust simplicity. During the minority of his nephew Bertram Marmaduke Fitzalan-Howard, the sixteenth duke of Norfolk, he was the leading Roman Catholic layman, and deputy earl marshal of England. He was president of the Catholic Union of Great Britain, and an intimate of cardinals Vaughan and Hinsley, to whom he offered 'a clear, sharp candour' (*The Times*, 19 May 1947). His good-humoured representation of the Catholic viewpoint helped reduce prejudice against Catholics in public life, and he himself received signal honours. He was sworn of the privy council in 1918, appointed GCVO in 1919, and a knight of the Garter in 1925.

FitzAlan was not an intellectual. The arts meant little to him, and, being gregarious, he preferred conversation to reading. Yet he had wide experience, and was a shrewd but charitable judge of human nature. His personal popularity, even enhanced by a certain brusqueness, was rooted in acknowledged integrity and a sense of duty, kindliness, and a homely sense of humour. 'Short, stocky, and erect, he remained a soldier to the last' (*DNB*), and, though often in poor health, only in the last few years did his sight and hearing fail. He died on 18 May 1947 at Cumberland Lodge, succeeded in the viscountcy by his son, and was buried at Arundel.   JOHN RAMSDEN

Sources DNB · *The Times* (19 May 1947) · *WWW, 1941–50* · GEC, *Peerage* · *Real old tory politics: the political diaries of Robert Sanders, Lord Bayford, 1910–35*, ed. J. Ramsden (1984) · *The modernisation of conservative politics: the diaries and letters of William Bridgeman, 1904–1935*, ed. P. Williamson (1988) · *The Crawford papers: the journals of David Lindsay, twenty-seventh earl of Crawford … 1892–1940*, ed. J. Vincent (1984) · G. Boyce, *Englishmen and Irish troubles: British opinion and making Irish policy, 1918–1922* (1972) · M. Cowling, *The impact of labour, 1920–24* (1971) · R. J. Q. Adams, *Bonar Law* (1999) · *The Austen Chamberlain diary letters: the correspondence of Sir Austen Chamberlain with his sisters Hilda and Ida, 1916–1937*, ed. R. C. Self, CS, 5th ser., 5 (1995) · *The crisis of British unionism: the domestic political papers of the second earl of Selborne, 1885–1922*, ed. G. Boyce (1987) · J. Ramsden, *The age of Balfour and Baldwin, 1902–1940* (1978)

Archives Arundel Castle, West Sussex, family corresp. | BL, letters to Lady Austin-Lee, Add. MS 46766 · Bodl. Oxf., letters to Lord Hanworth · HLRO, corresp. with Lloyd George on Irish affairs · NA Scot., corresp. with A. J. Balfour about ownership of *Morning Post* · Nuffield Oxf., corresp. with Lord Cherwell · PRO, corresp. with Lord Midleton, PRO 30/67 | FILM BFI NFTVA, current affairs footage; documentary footage; news footage

Likenesses W. Stoneman, two photographs, 1921–43, NPG · O. Birley, oils, 1932, Arundel Castle, West Sussex

Wealth at death £69,777 4s. 2d.: probate, 1947

Howard, Sir Edward (1476/7–1513), naval commander, was the second son of Thomas *Howard, second duke of Norfolk (1443–1524), and his first wife, Elizabeth Tilney (d. 1497).

Education and early life Edward's father was wounded fighting for Richard III at Bosworth, and was subsequently deprived of his title of earl of Surrey and imprisoned. These circumstances must have severely disrupted the lives of Edward, his mother, and his elder brother, Thomas *Howard, the future third duke, but no details are known of his upbringing and education. Thomas was restored to the earldom of Surrey in 1489, although he was not yet allowed to inherit his father's duchy of Norfolk, and thereafter Edward would have been trained in the manner appropriate to a nobleman's son of that period; that is to say, given a basic education by a tutor, and instructed in the courtly and martial arts. His military apprenticeship seems to have begun in 1492, when at the age of fifteen he served under Sir Edward Poynings at the reduction of Sluys. It is unlikely that he would have been allowed to take part in the fighting, and opportunities for active service under Henry VII were not numerous. However, in 1497 the earl of Surrey was given a major command against Scotland, and took both his sons with him. There was no serious fighting, but he found a pretext to knight both of them while they were in the north, and the younger man seems to have made an impression as a jouster, if not as a soldier. His appointment as Henry VIII's standard-bearer on 20 May 1509, when he was over thirty, and his appearance in a prominent role in the coronation tournament, suggests that he had been selected as a suitable companion for the young duke of York before his accession, but there is no tangible evidence of their relationship.

How and when Howard acquired any expertise in seafaring is not known, but between June and August 1511 he was paid over £600 to fit out ships 'for the fast and sure condyteing of the merchant aventurers' (Spont, ix). A subsequent tradition, recorded in circumstantial detail both by Holinshed and the 'Ballad of Andrew Barton', claims that, in the course of these 'wafting' operations, he and

his brother Thomas encountered and defeated the Scottish adventurer Andrew Barton, and captured his ships. There is no direct contemporary evidence for this victory, but two Scottish ships, the *Lion* and the *Jenett of Purwyn*, were certainly taken at about that time, and James IV complained to King Henry about the loss of the former. The Howards, and particularly Edward, were thereafter regarded as suitable for high naval command.

War with France, 1512 Soon after the outbreak of war with France in April 1512, Edward Howard was appointed admiral of the fleet that Henry VIII sent out to keep the seas between Brest and the Thames estuary. He was given the command of eighteen ships, and his extremely detailed instructions survive. The terms of these instructions, and of the indenture that accompanied them, meant that the whole force of 3000 men was treated as Howard's private retinue. John Dawtrey, the customer of Southampton, was appointed treasurer for the expedition under Howard, and £6000 was paid into his account in prest.

Howard set out about the end of April, and initially spent about two weeks at sea, seizing and plundering vessels of various nationalities on the pretext that they were carrying French cargoes. There was a good deal of diplomatic fall-out from these activities, but Louis XII was taken completely by surprise, and could assemble no war fleet in time to take effective countermeasures. At the beginning of June, Henry sent an army under the marquess of Dorset, believing that Ferdinand of Aragon intended a campaign into southern France which would have given the English a chance to recover control of Guyenne. Howard and his fleet, now augmented by two or three other large royal warships, escorted him as far as Brittany, the agreement being that the English would keep the seas to the north and east of Finistère, and the Spaniards to the south and west. Having done his duty by Dorset, Howard then turned his forces against the Breton coast, making a number of destructive raids on Conquet and Crozon.

During June and July 1512 Howard effectively controlled the channel, capturing, it was claimed, over sixty vessels. The French responded in two ways: by sending out their own privateers in large numbers, and by slowly assembling a war fleet of twenty-two vessels. The fact that only five of these belonged to Louis partly explains the different speeds of mobilization. At the beginning of August, when Howard had returned to Portsmouth to revictual, news reached him that the French fleet was assembling at Brest. So far there had been no serious fighting at sea, but Howard took this to be a challenge, and construed his instructions to mean that he should seek battle. As most admirals spent their energies trying to avoid battle, this was an unorthodox approach, and took the French commanders by surprise. Although the English retained the initiative, the battle itself was indecisive, being famous mostly for the mutual destruction of the *Regent* and the *Cordelière*, the largest ships on each side, which were lost when the *Cordelière*'s magazine exploded. Although not in any sense defeated, the French broke off the action and retreated, leaving Howard free to resume his depredations on the Breton coast. Henry VIII was pleased, both with his admiral's success and with his attitude. On 10 October he granted him an annuity of 100 marks for his good service, and the reversion of the office of lord admiral, currently held by the earl of Oxford. The Spanish fleet, promised for April, eventually turned up in September, and went home three months later, having done precisely nothing.

Campaigning and death at sea, 1513 Louis learned one lesson immediately from the failure of his fleet at Brest. No sooner did he understand what had happened than he sent for the veteran galley commander Prégent de Bidoux, who brought six of his ships north from the Mediterranean in the late autumn of 1512. These galleys were not ideal for operations in northern waters because of their light construction, but for coastal and harbour defence they could be very valuable, particularly when they were armed (as these were) with forward firing basilisks, or heavy guns. The French seemed determined to take the initiative in 1513, and had a sizeable fleet mobilized by the end of March, in addition to the galleys. An early descent on the English coast may have been planned, but if so it was frustrated by the spring weather. Henry's fleet was also ready by the middle of March, and was larger than that which had been deployed in the previous year.

On 10 March 1513 the earl of Oxford died, and Howard's reversion of the office of lord admiral became effective. On 19 March he sailed from the Thames, but did not reach Plymouth until 5 April because of the adverse winds. Most of his correspondence at this time relates to delays and frustrations over victualling, and five days later he decided (very unwisely as it turned out) to wait no longer for his supply ships. Although the French had ships at sea, they did not challenge his advance, but retreated into Brest, a manoeuvre that Howard mistakenly attributed to timidity. Several eyewitnesses have left a detailed record of what followed. Having lost one ship on a hidden rock, and not having the benefit of local pilots, Howard decided against a frontal assault on the main French fleet, which was moored under the guns of the fortress. On the other hand, being critically short of provisions, he could not sustain even a short blockade. A few exploratory landings gave his soldiers something to do, but produced no tangible results. Then on 22 April he was attacked by Bidoux's galleys, whose heavy guns inflicted severe damage, sinking one ship. Howard decided upon a swift action to take out the galleys which, if successful, would give him some tangible and honourable achievement should he be forced to retreat. Unfortunately, Bidoux had a secure and well-defended anchorage a little further along the coast and Howard had no large galleys, only the small boats known as row-barges. Nevertheless, leaving his great ships on station off Brest harbour, on 25 April 1513 Howard attacked Bidoux's position with all the boats he could muster.

Being a man of great panache, and with more courage than discretion, Howard led the attack upon his opponent's flagship in person. For whatever reason—and the contemporary accounts are somewhat conflicting—he was not adequately supported, and died the same day by being forced over the side of the galley and drowned by the weight of his armour. Before this happened he was observed to take off the silver whistle which was the lord admiral's badge of office, and hurl it into the sea. Both his body and his whistle were found three days later, and delivered to Bidoux at Conquet. The latter sent his armour as a trophy to Princess Claude, the king's daughter, and his whistle to Queen Anne.

As soon as news of Howard's death was confirmed (it was at first thought that he had been taken prisoner), the English fleet, now completely out of provisions, retreated to Plymouth on 30 April. When Sir Thomas Howard arrived on 4 May to take over his brother's command, he found the fleet utterly demoralized and most of the soldiers missing. Further operations were for the time being out of the question, but the French made no serious attempt to follow up their advantage; Louis almost immediately demobilized the ships from Normandy. Howard's death was more an emotional shock than a serious military set-back, and the contemporary dismay was out of all proportion to the real scale of the reverse. At the end of June, Henry VIII landed at Calais, and launched a brief but successful campaign which resulted in the capture of Tournai and Thérouanne. In July the Scots declared war, and James IV sent a squadron of ships to join the French fleet. However, his army was heavily defeated and James himself killed at the battle of Flodden on 9 September. The French mobilized a large fleet to intercept Henry on his return from Picardy in October 1513, but it was scattered by storms and achieved nothing. These were the last significant military operations and in March of 1514 a truce was agreed.

Character and reputation On balance 1513 had been a successful year for English arms, and the death of Sir Edward Howard made very little difference. It is impossible to say whether he made a good lord admiral, since he held the post for only six weeks or so. Dashing captains do not always make fine commanders, but his record of command during 1512 suggests a man of energy, commitment, and authority. He could be described as an innovative naval commander, but his fate suggests a serious lack of tactical awareness. He was elected a knight of the Garter in 1513, but died before he could be installed.

Howard's fame depends more upon the accidents of record survival than it does upon his actual achievement: a great deal of his own correspondence relating to the campaigns of these two years survives, together with accounts and other contemporary documents. Apart from these, not much is known about Howard. The date of his birth can be determined only approximately. He married at some point during 1505, his wife being Alice (d. 1518), daughter and heir of William Lovel, Lord Morley, and Eleanor, Baroness Morley, and widow of Sir William Parker. Alice held the barony of Morley in her own right, and was ten or twelve years older than Howard. From the fact that he wrote to her from shipboard during his campaigns, it may be surmised that their relationship was a good one, but there were no children. However, when he wrote his will in January 1513 (in anticipation of a dangerous campaign) Howard provided for two bastard sons, both of whom were clearly under age, without naming them. One of these he commended to the care of the king, and left him 'my bark called the Genett'; the other he commended to 'my special trusty friend', Charles Brandon, and left him 100 marks (Nicolas, 516). It is recorded that Prégent de Bidoux had his body embalmed, but it is not known where he bestowed it. When Howard's wife came to make her will in December 1518, she provided for a tomb to be built for her late husband in Brittany, so presumably he remained close to where he had fallen. As a younger son whose father did not die until 1524, he appears to have held only the manor of Morley in Norfolk, which he willed to his stepson Henry Parker once his widow's life interest had expired. DAVID LOADES

Sources GEC, *Peerage* · N. H. Nicolas, ed., *Testamenta vetusta: being illustrations from wills*, 2 vols. (1826) · *LP Henry VIII*, vol. 1 · A. Spont, ed., *Letters and papers relating to the war with France, 1512–1513*, Navy RS, 10 (1897) · Rymer, *Foedera*, 1st edn · PRO, E101/61/12 · PRO, E351/210

Howard, Edward, first Baron Howard of Escrick (d. 1675), politician, was the seventh son of Thomas *Howard, first earl of Suffolk (1561–1626), and his second wife, Katherine (b. in or after 1564, d. 1638) [see Howard, Katherine, countess of Suffolk], widow of Lord Robert Rich and daughter of Sir Henry *Knyvet (Knyvett) of Charlton, Wiltshire. As one of a number of younger sons, Howard's early years were passed in obscurity: his exact birth date and the details of his education remain unknown. His first appearance on the public stage came at Prince Charles's investiture as prince of Wales in November 1616, when Howard became a knight of the Bath. With his own family's political fortunes in eclipse, and possessing little more than the reversion of his mother's property at Escrick, Yorkshire, Howard sought a patron and found one in the king's favourite, George Villiers, first duke of Buckingham. On 30 November 1623 he married one of the duke's legion of poorly endowed relations: Mary Boteler (d. 1634), the fifth daughter of Sir John (later first Baron) Boteler of Brantfield, and his wife, Elizabeth, who was Buckingham's sister. Marriage to the favourite's niece brought its rewards: Howard was returned to the parliament of 1624 as member for Calne, Wiltshire, and in 1628 for Hertford. Clarendon later claimed that Howard had 'his whole dependence' upon Buckingham, 'and being absolutely governed by him, was made by him a baron' (Clarendon, *Hist. rebellion*, 1.392). On 12 April 1628 Howard was created Baron Howard of Escrick. But the murder of his patron appears to have left him without a link to the court and the subsequent death of his wife in January 1634 added to his woes.

Although granted the farm of the Greenwax in March 1639, along with his brother the earl of Berkshire, Howard's stance towards the court became increasingly hostile. In February 1639 he promised to attend the king at York as he prepared to face the Scottish threat, but his activity in the Short Parliament, where he consistently supported the opposition, marked him as one of the king's more persistent critics. In August 1640 he and Lord Mandeville presented Charles with a petition calling for redress of grievances and a peaceful settlement with the Scots. In 1641 parliament named Howard as one of a committee charged with observing the king's Scottish negotiations. He had, Clarendon declared, 'now delivered himself up body and soul to be disposed of by that party which appeared most averse and obnoxious to the Court and the Government' (Clarendon, *Hist. rebellion*, 1.392). In May 1642 he delivered parliament's declaration supporting Sir John Hotham in his confrontation with the king at Hull. When Charles ordered him to carry his own answer back Howard refused, provoking an angry royal response.

With the outbreak of the civil war Howard's path was clear: he sided with parliament. His wartime role was limited to his work on committees and in the House of Lords. The occupation of his Yorkshire lands by the royalists forced him to live on parliament's charity and his own sharp practices. But the king's defeat and Howard's steadfastness in parliament's cause created opportunities for him. He was, from November 1642, a member of the committee for the advance of money, frequently chairing its sessions. He sat on the Derby House committee in 1648. He was one of only three peers who joined the Commons following the abolition of the Lords in 1649, serving as MP for Carlisle from 5 May 1649. He joined the council of state in 1650, and played a significant role in the government's work, serving on the ordnance committee and the committee charged with the disposition of Charles I's goods.

But it was Howard's role as a member of the committee for compounding and for the advance of money where he made the most notable impact. One witness asserted that the committees would have dissolved without Howard's constant attendance, and that his efforts had saved the state hundreds of thousands of pounds. The records indicate that he was a ubiquitous presence in this work. The encomium was, however, one of the few Howard received. It seems clear that he used his position at the heart of the government's finances to enrich himself and oppress his enemies. In 1645 he prevailed upon his colleagues to grant him a lease of Wallingford House in London at far below its true value, turning out its then tenant (who paid a much larger rent), the earl of Rutland. Howard also charged creditors with delinquency in order to avoid his debts: for example in 1645 he secured the cancellation of a £300 tailor's bill, and in 1649 he swindled a Cheapside silk mercer of £60 in the same way.

In 1650 Howard went too far, and Major-General Harrison accused him of accepting bribes from sequestrated royalists. He was convicted, expelled from parliament and the council of state, fined £10,000 (which he never paid), and jailed in the Tower for a year. By 1655 he managed to secure command of Colonel Rich's regiment of horse, though he had no other post of significance under Cromwell thereafter. A final attempt to revive his political fortunes was his election to the Commons for Yorkshire in

April 1660. But the Restoration left him thoroughly discredited and he retired to private life; he died in London on 24 April 1675. He was buried on 5 May at St Mary Savoy, Strand, and was succeeded by his son Thomas, then, in 1678, by his more famous second son, William *Howard, third Baron Howard of Escrick, a Cromwellian trooper, Baptist preacher, and conspirator. VICTOR STATER

Sources GEC, *Peerage* · M. A. E. Green, ed., *Calendar of the proceedings of the committee for advance of money, 1642–1656*, 1, PRO (1888) · M. A. E. Green, ed., *Calendar of the proceedings of the committee for compounding … 1643–1660*, 1, PRO (1889) · *CSP dom.*, 1638–9; 1641–3; 1648–50; 1655; 1659–60 · Clarendon, *Hist. rebellion*, 1.392
Archives PRO, committee for compounding MSS, SP 23 · PRO, committee for the advance of money MSS, SP 19 · PRO, council of state MSS, SP 18 · PRO, Derby House committee MSS, SP 21

Howard, Edward (*bap.* 1624, *d.* 1712), playwright, was baptized at St Martin-in-the-Fields, London, on 2 November 1624, the fifth son of Thomas Howard, first earl of Berkshire (1587–1669), and Elizabeth (*d.* 1672), daughter of William Cecil, second earl of Exeter. He was brother of Sir Robert *Howard (1626–1698) and cousin of James *Howard (*c.*1640–1669), both playwrights.

Howard married first Anne (*fl.* 1648–1655) and second Lucy (Monk or Monck) in or before 1677. He appears to have had no children, with either of his wives (Howard, 281–3).

Howard's works suffered at the hands of contemporary critics. His heroic poem *The British Princes* (1669) was ridiculed by the earl of Rochester among others; Howard himself was caricatured as Poet Ninny in Shadwell's *Sullen Lovers* (1668); and his plays proved rather unsuccessful. *The Usurper*, a tragedy probably first staged at the Theatre Royal on 2 January 1664, was a scarcely veiled attack on the regicides. Pepys, who went to see it on 2 December 1668, judged it 'a pretty good play, in all but what is designed to resemble Cromwell and Hugh Peters, which is mighty silly' (Pepys, 9.381). *The London Gentleman* and *The Change of Crownes* were entered in the Stationers' register on 7 August 1667. The former was probably neither published nor acted. The latter remained unprinted until 1949, having been suppressed soon after what was probably its first performance on 15 April 1667 by order of Charles II, who resented the actor John Lacy's (ad libbed) abuse of the court in the part of Asinello. As a result Lacy suffered a short period of imprisonment and was congratulated by Howard on his release, whereupon:

> Lacy cursed him as that it was the fault of his nonsensical play that was the cause of his ill usage. Mr Howard did give him some reply, to which Lacy [answered] him, that he was more a fool than a poet; upon which Howard did give him a blow on the face with his glove; on which Lacy, having a cane in his hand, did give him a blow over the pate. (Van Lennep, 107)

The Womens Conquest, a comedy performed at Lincoln's Inn Fields in or before 1670, was ridiculed in Buckingham's *The Rehearsal*. Partly based on Ben Jonson, *The Six Days Adventure, or, The New Utopia*, possibly first performed at the same theatre on 6 March 1671, was also demolished by the critics. In the words of one satirist:

> thy play's
> Laugh'd at by the box, pit, gallery, nay stage
> And grown the nauseous grievance of this age!
> (Lord, 341)

Howard's last and mediocre venture into drama was *The Man of Newmarket*, performed at Drury Lane in March 1678.

Together with William Richards, Howard on 24 April 1671 brought a claim for £183 against one Thomas Crosse. In 1678 he sold the manor of Erchfont, Wiltshire, until then his seat of residence, to William Pynsent. On 15 November 1683 the petition of Edward Howard of Berkshire, 'praying his Majesty to bestow some future subsistence on him', was referred to the lords of the Treasury (*CSP dom.*, 1683–4, 91). In December 1684 he was accordingly granted a pension of £200 to commence from October 1683. He was still receiving this pension at Michaelmas 1692. His will, in which he is described as 'until recently of New Windsor', is dated 26 May 1710; it was proved by his widow, Lucy, the sole beneficiary and executor, on 19 December 1712. J. P. VANDER MOTTEN

Sources H. S. H. [H. S. Howard], 'The dramatist sons of Thomas, earl of Berkshire', *N&Q*, 187 (1944), 281–3 · H. J. Oliver, *Sir Robert Howard (1626–1698): a critical biography* (1963) · will, PRO, PROB 11/530, sig. 237 · J. A. Winn, *John Dryden and his world* (1987) · Pepys, *Diary*, vol. 8–9 · W. Van Lennep and others, eds., *The London stage, 1660–1800*, pt 1: *1660–1700* (1965) · G. de F. Lord and others, eds., *Poems on affairs of state: Augustan satirical verse, 1660–1714*, 7 vols. (1963–75), vol. 1 · *CSP dom.*, 1683–5 · J. Milhous and R. D. Hume, eds., *A register of English theatrical documents, 1660–1737*, 1 (1991) · *DNB*
Wealth at death unspecified estate, both real and personal: will, PRO, PROB 11/530, sig. 237

Howard, Edward (*bap.* 1793, *d.* 1841), novelist, was baptized on 20 March 1793 in Reading, where he was probably born. His mother was almost certainly Elizabeth Bellasis (*d.* 1819), who had been forced to marry Bernard Edward *Howard (1765–1842), heir of the eleventh duke of Norfolk, and who was pregnant when she eloped with her childhood sweetheart, Richard Bingham (1764–1839), heir of the first Lord Lucan. Howard was never acknowledged, but brought up by foster parents in Lambeth. He attended three schools, and met the Marryat family through Kerval's school, Sydenham.

In 1808 Howard joined the HMS *Aurora* and served at least two years. He left the service a lieutenant, but with permanently damaged hearing and internal bleeding. His novels and short stories drew on his naval experiences. About 1815 Howard had a windfall which he invested in a firm of gunpowder merchants. He was the only member of the partnership to keep his good name in their 1817 bankruptcy.

Howard married a daughter of William Williams in 1823, and they had a daughter and two sons. Howard was variously employed in teaching, painting, and writing while his wife kept a school, until in 1833 Frederick Marryat made him sub-editor of his *Metropolitan Magazine*. The semi-autobiographical *Life of a Sub-Editor* was first serialized there in 1834. It was broken off in 1836, but published whole with a fictional ending as *Rattlin, the Reefer* that year, in which he also became editor of the *Magazine*. Only

Marryat's name, as 'editor', appeared on the title-page of the novel, which was extremely successful. Its hero, Ralph Rattlin, is abandoned in Reading as a child, and is brought up in working-class London. He eventually goes to sea, and his first-person narrative effectively combines conventional elements of nautical action and humour with powerful criticism of extreme disciplinary methods used on board ship; his graphic descriptions of instances of flogging are particularly horrible. On Rattlin's return to England, his true identity is revealed to be that of Sir Ralph Rathelin. Howard's next novel, *The Old Commodore* (1837), was less popular; none of Howard's subsequent nautical novels repeated *Rattlin*'s success.

In 1838 Howard's first wife died, and he remarried on 4 March 1839. Ann Roper Williams, the daughter of David Williams, was twenty-two and devoted to her clever husband. Another daughter was born in 1840. Howard died at 12 Gravel Lane, London, on 30 December 1841, of internal haemorrhaging. His *Sir Henry Morgan, the Buccaneer* (1842) was published posthumously and critically acclaimed. His widow later married Octavian Blewitt.

JESSICA HININGS

Sources A. P. Howse, 'The life and works of Edward Howard, novelist', MA diss., King's Lond., 1956 · E. Howard, *Rattlin the reefer*, another edn, ed. A. Howse (1971) · *GM*, 2nd ser., 18 (1842) · *New Monthly Magazine*, new ser., 54 (1838), 560–2 · review, *New Monthly Magazine*, new ser., 64 (1842), 438–41 · *N&Q*, 7th ser., 8 (1889), 58 · *N&Q*, 8th ser., 1–4 (1892–3) · Burke, *Peerage* · *The Athenaeum* (8 Jan 1842), 41 · *Rattlin, the reefer*, ed. F. Marryat (1897) · *Annual Register* (1842) · *IGI* · m. cert. · d. cert.
Likenesses Freeman, engraving (after Osgood), repro. in *New Monthly Magazine*, 64
Wealth at death £100: administration, PRO, PROB 6/218, fol. 272

Howard, Edward Charles (1774–1816), chemist, was born on 28 May 1774 at Darnell Hall, near Sheffield, the youngest of three sons of Henry Howard of Glossop (1713–1787), estate manager to his relative, the ninth duke of Norfolk, and his wife, Juliana (d. 1808), daughter of Sir William Molyneux, bt. He traced his descent from the family of Henry Frederick Howard, fifteenth earl of Arundel, and his wife, Elizabeth Stuart, a cousin of King James I. His eldest brother, Bernard Edward *Howard (1765–1842), succeeded as twelfth duke of Norfolk. Howard and his brothers were educated at the English College of the Benedictines at Douai (1783–8). Having no claim, as a younger son, to title and estates, Howard chose a scientific career and became an accomplished chemist and chemical engineer. His choice of profession may have owed something to hereditary influences: his ancestors Charles Howard (1630–1713), and Philip (1730–1810), of the Corby line of Howards, were both actively engaged in scientific pursuits, and four successive dukes of Norfolk were admitted to the Royal Society.

Howard was elected a fellow of the Royal Society in 1799 and was awarded its coveted Copley medal in 1800, for his discovery of the highly explosive mercury fulminate, which subsequently proved to be the ideal detonator for conventional explosives. Joining the newly established Royal Institution in 1800, he was appointed almost immediately to its permanent chemistry committee. In 1804 he served on a committee of the Royal Society charged with adjudicating the dispute between W. H. Wollaston and R. Chenevix concerning the nature of the metal palladium. In 1802 Howard adduced decisive chemical and mineralogical evidence supporting the extraterrestrial origin of meteorites, until then a controversial subject. Thereafter he turned his attention to chemical technology, introducing radical improvements at all stages of sugar manufacturing, but especially by his novel steam-heated vacuum vessel, which replaced the pans heated over open fires, hitherto used in evaporating sugar syrups to the point of crystallization. By this and other inventions he obtained a superior product, and eliminated the notorious fire-hazards of sugar-houses, that had attracted exceptionally high insurance premiums. Howard disclosed and protected the fruits of his long efforts in three detailed patents, 3607 of 1812, 3754 of 1813, and 3831 of 1814. Rather than accept an offer of £40,000 for surrendering his patent rights, he licensed his process to manufacturers, deriving an income that was said to exceed £30,000 a year by 1816, the year of his death.

In 1799 Howard installed his private laboratory at 6 Doughty Street, Bloomsbury, where he remained for three years, moving thereafter to Westbourne Green, Bayswater. He married in 1804, at St Leonard, Shoreditch, Elizabeth (1772–1810), daughter of William Maycock. Of their three children, the only son, Edward Giles (1805–1840), held a commission in the Life Guards, and was the father of Cardinal Edward Henry Howard (1829–1892). From 1813 Howard occupied a town house in Nottingham Place, Marylebone, where he died suddenly on 27 September 1816, aged forty-two, of an apoplexy, apparently brought on by his having spent an excessively long time in an overheated drying-room of a sugar refinery. He was buried in the cemetery of St Pancras Old Church, the resting place of his wife and of his ancestor Esmé Howard (1645–1728); the graves were obliterated when most of the burial-ground fell victim to railway extensions in 1868.

FREDERICK KURZER

Sources F. Kurzer, 'The life and work of Edward Charles Howard', *Annals of Science*, 56 (1999), 113–41 · D. W. Sears, 'Edward Charles Howard and an early British contribution to meteorites', *Journal of the British Astronomical Association*, 86 (1975–6), 133–9 · N. Deerr, *The history of sugar*, 2 vols. (1949–50), vol. 2, p. 599 · E. O. von Lippmann, 'Zum 100-jährigen Jubiläum des Vacuum Apparats', *Abhandlungen und Vorträge zur Geschichte der Naturwissenschaften*, 2 (Leipzig, 1913), 395–438 · G. Brenan and E. P. Statham, *The house of Howard*, 2 vols. (1907) · E. H. Burton and T. L. Williams, eds., *The Douai College diaries, third, fourth and fifth, 1598–1654*, 1–2, Catholic RS, 10–11 (1911) · E. H. Burton and E. Nolan, *The Douay College diaries: the seventh diary, 1715–1778*, Catholic RS, 28 (1928) · *GM*, 1st ser., 86/2 (1816), 380 · *Laity's Directory* (1817)
Likenesses J. F. Skill, J. Gilbert, W. and E. Walker, pencil and wash drawing, c.1857–1862 (*Men of Science living in 1807–8*; after bronze medal), NPG · W. Walker and G. Zobel, group portrait, composite engraving, 1862 (after *Men of science living in 1807–8*), NPG · attrib. J. Hayes, bronze medal; now lost · two portraits (after Walker and Zobel), repro. in Deerr, *History of sugar*, 551

Wealth at death income from licensing of manufacturing process said to be in excess of £30,000 p.a.; plus property: Deerr, *History*, vol. 2, p. 560

Howard, Edward George Fitzalan- [*formerly* Lord Edward Howard], **first Baron Howard of Glossop** (1818–1883), politician, was the second son of Henry Charles *Howard, thirteenth duke of Norfolk (1791–1856), and his wife, Lady Charlotte Sophia Leveson-Gower (1788–1870), the eldest daughter of George Granville Leveson-Gower, first duke of Sutherland. He was born on 20 January 1818 at Norfolk House, St James's Square, London, and, though a Catholic by birth, finished his education at Trinity College, Cambridge. On the death, on 16 March 1842, of his grandfather, Bernard Edward *Howard, twelfth duke of Norfolk, his father succeeded to the titles and estates, and Howard became known as Lord Edward Howard. That year, at his father's suggestion, he and his brothers took the additional surname of Fitzalan. He was portrayed as Lord Vere by Disraeli in 1844 in *Coningsby*. He was a Liberal in politics, and in July 1846, when the first Russell administration came into power, he was appointed vice-chamberlain to the queen and sworn a privy councillor, retaining his office until March 1852. After unsuccessfully contesting Shoreham at the general election of 1847, Fitzalan-Howard was returned in 1848 as MP for Horsham. From 1853 to 1868 he was MP for Arundel, but was rejected by that constituency in the general election of 1868. On 9 December 1869 Gladstone created him a peer of the United Kingdom as Baron Howard of Glossop. Howard rendered signal service to the cause of Roman Catholic primary education. From 1869 to 1877 he was chairman of the Catholic Poor Schools Committee, in succession to the Hon. Charles Langdale. As chairman of the committee he set on foot the Catholic Education Crisis Fund, not only subscribing £5000 to it himself, but securing £10,000 from his nephew the fifteenth duke of Norfolk, and another £10,000 from his son-in-law the marquess of Bute. 70,000 scholars were thus added to the Roman Catholic schools in England at a cost of at least £350,000. During the eight years' minority of his nephew the fifteenth duke of Norfolk (1860–68), he presided over the College of Arms as deputy earl marshal. In 1871 Howard bought from James Robert Hope-Scott, for nearly £40,000, his highland estate at Dorlin, near Loch Shiel, Inverness-shire.

Howard married, first, on 22 July 1851, Augusta Talbot (d. 1862), the only daughter (and the heir to a fortune of £80,000) of George Henry Talbot, half-brother of John, sixteenth earl of Shrewsbury; and second, on 16 July 1863, Winifred Mary (d. 1909), the third daughter of the Catholic convert Ambrose Phillipps De Lisle, of Garendon Park and Grace Dieu Manor in Leicestershire. He and his first wife, who died on 3 July 1862, had two sons, Charles Bernard Talbot, who died in 1861, aged nine, and Francis Edward, who succeeded as second baron, and five daughters. Howard died, after a long illness, on 1 December 1883 at his London house, 19 Rutland Gate, Knightsbridge, and was buried at Hadfield, Derbyshire. His second wife died of influenza at Felixstowe on 7 December 1909.

CHARLES KENT, *rev.* H. C. G. MATTHEW

Sources *The Tablet* (8 Dec 1883), 882 · *The Times* (8 Dec 1883) · GEC, *Peerage*
Archives Arundel Castle archives, Sussex, family corresp.
Wealth at death £118,325 5s. 5d.: probate, 27 March 1884, *CGPLA Eng. & Wales*

Howard, Edward Henry (1829–1892), cardinal, was born at Nottingham on 13 February 1829, the eldest son of Edward Gyles Howard (1805–1840), nephew of the twelfth duke of Norfolk, and Frances Anne, eldest daughter of George Robert Heneage of Hainton Hall, Lincolnshire. After education at Oscott College, he served briefly as an officer in the 2nd Life Guards, in which capacity he headed the duke of Wellington's funeral procession in 1852. After studying theology at the Accademia Ecclesiastica in Rome, he was ordained priest by Cardinal Wiseman in the English College on 8 December 1854, and attached himself to the service of Pius IX. He learned Arabic, Coptic, Hindustani, and Russian, and became an accomplished linguist. For about a year he was employed in India in connection with the Anglo-Portuguese dispute over the territorial jurisdiction of the see of Goa, but the rest of his ecclesiastical career was spent in Rome.

Howard's graceful and dignified bearing was an adornment to St Peter's, where he held the office of archpriest's vicar. He was consecrated archbishop of Neocaesarea *in partibus infidelium* in 1872, and made coadjutor-bishop of Frascati, an office which he retained for only a few weeks. He was created a cardinal-priest by Pius IX on 12 March 1877, the titular church assigned to him being that of St John and St Paul on the Coelian Hill, and on 24 March 1878 was appointed protector of the English College in Rome—to which he afterwards bequeathed his magnificent library. In December 1881 he was nominated archpriest of the basilica of St Peter, and in that capacity also became prefect of the congregation in charge of the building. In the spring of 1884 he was made a cardinal-bishop by Leo XIII and translated to the suburbican see of Frascati. After becoming seriously ill in 1887, he was taken to England in the spring of the following year. He died on 16 September 1892 at Hatch Beauchamp, Brighton, and was buried at Arundel on 1 October. Howard was every inch (his coffin measured 7 ft 6 in.) the princely prelate, well suited to his ceremonial duties, but exercised little influence on Roman policy.

THOMPSON COOPER, *rev.* G. MARTIN MURPHY

Sources J. M. Robinson, *The dukes of Norfolk* (1982) · M. Bence-Jones, *The Catholic families* (1992) · L. E. O. Charlton, *The recollections of a Northumbrian lady* (1949) · *The Oscotian*, 2nd ser. (1888), 47 · *The Standard* (17 Sept 1892) · *The Tablet* (24 Sept 1892), 481 · *The Times* (17 Nov 1892) · *ILN* (24 Sept 1892), 390 · E. S. Purcell, *Life of Cardinal Manning*, 2 (1895), 2.20
Archives English College, Rome, corresp. and papers
Likenesses J. Story, oils, 1884, Arundel Castle, Sussex · oils, Chirk Castle and Garden, Denbighshire · oils, English College, Rome · portrait, repro. in *The Oscotian*
Wealth at death £57,158 1s. 1d.: resworn probate, Jan 1894, *CGPLA Eng. & Wales* (1892)

Howard [*née* Stafford], **Elizabeth, duchess of Norfolk** (1497–1558), noblewoman, was the eldest daughter of Edward *Stafford, third duke of Buckingham (1478–

1521)—and so a descendant of Edward III—and Eleanor (*d.* 1530), eldest daughter of Henry *Percy, fourth earl of Northumberland (*c.*1449–1489). She was educated at home and betrothed to her father's ward Ralph *Neville, fourth earl of Westmorland. She later wrote, '[H]e and I had loved together two year, and … I had married [him] before Christmas', if the widowed Thomas *Howard (1473–1554), the earl of Surrey's heir, had not made vigorous suit to her father (*LP Henry VIII*, 12/2, no. 976). They were married in 1513, when Howard received her dowry of 2000 marks and she was promised an annual jointure of 500 marks, an undertaking that was not kept. She had entered court in 1509 as lady-in-waiting to Katherine of Aragon, whose devoted friend she became and remained. She was also, she later asserted, a dutiful and devoted wife: 'I was daily waiter in the Court sixteen years together, when he hath been from me more than a year on the King's wars' (ibid., 12/2, no. 143). She accompanied her husband to Ireland, where he served in 1520–22, and as late as 1524, when he became third duke of Norfolk, they appeared to be bonded by mutual love and loyalty.

In 1527, however, Norfolk took a mistress, Elizabeth Holland, the daughter of his private secretary. The duchess described 'Bess' as a harlot, a drab and 'a churl's daughter', who was but 'washer of my nursery' for eight years (ibid., 12/2, no. 143; Harris, *Edward Stafford*, 63). Bess Holland's family was, however, of gentry stock and she became one of the ladies-in-waiting to Anne Boleyn, with whom the duchess had a quarrel of her own, due to Anne's insistence that Elizabeth Howard's daughter Mary should marry Henry VIII's illegitimate son Henry Fitzroy. All this doubtless reinforced the duchess's loyalty to Katherine of Aragon during the long annulment crisis. In 1531 she was exiled from court, 'because she spoke too freely, and declared herself more than they liked for the Queen' (*LP Henry VIII*, 5, no. 238), and two years later she refused to attend Anne's coronation.

During the 1530s Lady Norfolk's marriage collapsed. In March 1534 the duke 'locked me up in a chamber, [and] took away my jewels and apparel' (*LP Henry VIII*, 12/2, no. 976). She was then moved to Redbourne, Hertfordshire, where she lived apart and, as she complained, in a state of virtual imprisonment with a meagre annual allowance of only £200. Despite Norfolk's offers of material awards and the return of her jewels and clothes, she refused to agree to a divorce. Instead, in a series of letters to Thomas Cromwell between 1535 and 1539, she aired her grievances and sought a fair financial arrangement. Three times she wrote how women of the household had bound her, pummelled her, and sat on her breast until she spat blood. She also made the claim, uncorroborated and strenuously denied by Norfolk, that while she was in labour with their daughter Mary in 1519, he had dragged her by her hair out of bed and around the house, wounding her in the head with his dagger. Her publicly aired complaints and accusations isolated her from her eldest son and her daughter, while her brother Henry *Stafford condemned her for her 'wild language' and her 'sensual and wilful mind' (ibid., 6, nos. 474–5).

In the 1540s Elizabeth Howard was reconciled to her brother. But Norfolk remained with his mistress, and when he was accused of treason in December 1546 the duchess and her rival were both living in his house at Kenninghall near Thetford, and were taken into custody together. Elizabeth Howard subsequently gave evidence against the duke, and after his attainder her apparel at Kenninghall was restored to her—at the time of her arrest she had little in the way of valuables, 'all being very bare and her jewels sold to pay her debts' (*LP Henry VIII*, 21/2, no. 548). When Mary Tudor became queen in 1553 Lady Norfolk was also, at last, restored to the court, accompanying the queen into London on 3 August, and bearing her train at her coronation. She was not named in the will of her husband when he died on 25 August 1554. Elizabeth died on 30 November 1558 and was buried in the Howard chapel, Lambeth. Her brother Henry wrote her epitaph:

> Thou wast to me, both far and near,
> A Mother, sister, a friend most dear.
> (Sessions, 61)

Three of her children survived childhood: Henry *Howard, styled earl of Surrey; Thomas, Viscount Bindon; and Mary *Fitzroy, duchess of Richmond.

MICHAEL A. R. GRAVES

Sources B. J. Harris, *Edward Stafford, third duke of Buckingham* (1986) · B. J. Harris, 'Marriage sixteenth century style: Elizabeth Stafford and the third duke of Norfolk', *Journal of Social History*, 15/2 (1981), 371–82 · D. M. Head, *The ebbs and flows of fortune: the life of Thomas Howard, third duke of Norfolk* (1995) · W. A. Sessions, *Henry Howard, the poet earl of Surrey: a life* (1999) · C. Rawcliffe, *The Staffords, earls of Stafford and dukes of Buckingham, 1394–1521*, Cambridge Studies in Medieval Life and Thought, 3rd ser., 11 (1978) · M. J. Tucker, *The life of Thomas Howard, earl of Surrey and second duke of Norfolk, 1443–1524* (1964) · *LP Henry VIII*, 5, no. 238; 6, nos. 474–5; 12/2, nos. 143, 976; 21/2, no. 548 · R. M. Warnicke, *The rise and fall of Anne Boleyn* (1989) · BL, Cotton MS Titus B.i, fol. 383c · *GM*, 2nd ser., 23 (1845), 259–67 · GEC, *Peerage*, new edn, 9.619–20
Likenesses double portrait, tomb effigy (with her husband), Framlingham church, Suffolk

Howard, Esme William, first Baron Howard of Penrith

(1863–1939), diplomatist, was born at Greystoke Castle, Cumberland, on 15 September 1863, the youngest child in the family of four sons and two daughters of Henry Howard (1802–1875), landowner, of Greystoke Castle and Thornbury Castle, Gloucestershire, and his wife, Charlotte Caroline Georgiana (1823–1896), eldest daughter of Henry Hawes Long, of Hampton Lodge, Surrey. Educated at school in Farnborough and then at Harrow School, he was given the option of entering Cambridge University, but chose a diplomatic career. After two years in Europe improving his languages—he was a gifted linguist—he entered the Foreign Office by competitive examination in April 1885. Before taking a foreign posting, he was seconded to Dublin to assist his brother-in-law, Henry Howard Molyneux Herbert, fourth earl of Carnarvon, who was lord lieutenant of Ireland. For six months he was exposed to the perplexing Irish question, experience that enabled him, when he began his diplomatic career, the

Esme William Howard, first Baron Howard of Penrith (1863–1939), by Walter Stoneman, 1918

better to grasp both the difficulties of imperial governance and the empire's importance in Britain's position as the only global power. Over the next five years he was apprenticed in diplomacy as third secretary at the embassy at Rome (from January 1886 to June 1888) and then as private secretary to Sir Edward Malet, the ambassador at Berlin (until December 1890). He excelled in his work but, tiring of diplomacy and wanting to do more for Britain and the empire, he left the diplomatic service in April 1892.

For the next eleven years Howard aspired to give substance to what he called the 'two great ideas at present in embryo in England' (McKercher, 14): imperial federation and state socialism. He explored Amazon jungles, the Caribbean, and southern and north Africa, helped establish a rubber plantation in Tobago, ran unsuccessfully as a Liberal candidate supporting Irish home rule at Worcester in 1892, worked for Charles Booth's enquiry into the 'Life and labour of the people of London', served as a private secretary to the foreign secretary, Lord Kimberley (1894–5), and fought with the imperial yeomanry in the Second South African War, during which he was captured and escaped. Most importantly in this period, he married on 17 November 1898 an Italian noblewoman, Donna (Maria) Isabella Giovanna Teresa Gioacchina Giustiniani-Bandini (1867–1963), fifth surviving daughter of Sigismondo Niccolo Venanzio Gaetano Francisco Giustiniani-Bandini, Prince Giustiniani-Bandini and eighth earl of Newburgh. They had five sons: Esme (1903–1926), Francis (1905–1999),

Hubert (b. 1907), Edmund (b. 1909), and Henry (1913–1977). Howard converted to Roman Catholicism before his marriage.

At the beginning of 1903, thirty-nine years old and with a young family, Howard needed full-time employment, especially since he had bought out his rubber plantation partners. Accordingly he returned to diplomacy, obtaining at the instigation of his old friend Sir Francis Bertie, British ambassador in Italy, the post of honorary second secretary at the embassy in Rome. From this vantage point he had the good luck to be able to help to smooth the visit of Edward VII to Pope Leo XIII in April, and this diluted Foreign Office objections to welcoming back a person who had earlier resigned. He was then assigned as British consul-general (from July 1903 to November 1906) in Crete, a Turkish province, and a problematic posting as the island's Hellenic majority wanted union with Greece. An uprising by Greek nationalists in 1895–6 had seen Britain, France, Russia, and Italy take control of Cretan affairs in the sultan's name; in 1905 a second uprising occurred. Howard proved central to its resolution—an education in the 'Eastern question'—whereby British interests remained undiminished. He was rewarded with appointment as CVO and CMG in 1906 (he had already been made MVO in 1904), and with promotion as counsellor in the Washington embassy, a post he held from November 1906 to October 1908. This posting was followed by his selection as consul-general in Hungary (until January 1911) and minister to Switzerland (until May 1913). At Washington, Budapest, and Bern, he added to his firsthand knowledge about the diplomatic problems confronting Britain: the growing strength of the United States, the delicacy of the continental balance of power, the strategic importance of the Anglo-French and Anglo-Russian ententes, and the aggressiveness of German external policies. His handling of every issue that confronted him between 1903 and 1913 impressed his Foreign Office superiors, both the foreign secretaries, Lord Lansdowne and Sir Edward Grey, and key officials, including Sir Charles Hardinge and Sir Eyre Crowe. He shared prevailing Foreign Office views that Britain had no permanent friends or enemies, only permanent interests, and that those interests were best protected by the balance of power, the two ententes, and British financial and military strength.

In May 1913 Howard became minister at Stockholm, remaining there until August 1918. Sweden's government and society were both pro-German and anti-Russian, a situation that produced major political problems after the First World War broke out in August 1914. Sweden chose neutrality, despite Britain's blockade imposed against the central powers. Stockholm threatened to disrupt allied supply of tsarist Russia if Swedish–German trade was hampered. Until mid-1917, while ensuring the strongest possible blockade against Germany, Howard balanced successfully between Stockholm and London. Sweden's hand was weakened when revolution drove Russia from the war. Howard's work then expanded as he endeavoured to ensure post-war British strength in the Baltic by promoting the creation of an anti-Bolshevik Finland. He was appointed KCMG in 1916 and KCB in 1919.

Howard next served as a member of the British delegation to the Paris peace conference from January to July 1919. At Paris he was tasked in particular with helping to re-establish Poland. He advocated a large Poland, though David Lloyd George, the British premier, wanted a smaller state to improve British post-war relations with both Germany and Bolshevik Russia. Howard saw a robust Poland as essential to the post-war balance in eastern Europe and the Baltic; and he was one of the architects of the 'Polish corridor', the strip of territory that connected Poland to the Baltic while cutting off East Prussia from the rest of Germany.

Ultimately pushed aside by Lloyd George—as were many professional diplomats at Paris—Howard became ambassador at Madrid in September 1919, an appointment engineered by his Foreign Office benefactors. Privately critical of Spanish political corruption, he none the less sought to assure British influence in Spain with the same diplomatic technique that had won respect in Stockholm: balancing between his host and home governments. Until September 1923, when the authoritarian military regime of General Francisco Prima de Rivera seized power, Howard impressed on London the need to support Spain's crumbling position in its Moroccan colony against French inroads. A simple matter of realpolitik, this policy was necessary to maintain the western Mediterranean balance of power. Concurrently, he played a pivotal role in negotiating an Anglo-Spanish commercial treaty, fundamental to reviving war-damaged British trade. He was promoted GCMG in 1923.

Expecting to retire at the end of his Spanish posting in February 1924, Howard was suddenly asked by the foreign secretary, Lord Curzon, to transfer to Washington, to succeed Sir Auckland Geddes as ambassador. Curzon wanted an experienced diplomat at the embassy, an increasingly difficult post given trade, naval, and war debt questions. Howard accepted, and his time in Washington proved the pinnacle of his career. In his first three years in America he grasped the importance of domestic factors in shaping American foreign policy. Although the war debt and trade issues quickly faded into obscurity, the emotive naval question hindered good Anglo-American relations. Tied to the failure of the Geneva naval conference in 1927 and slow progress in League of Nations arms limitation discussions, Washington's demand for full naval equality with Britain, and British resistance, poisoned Anglo-American relations. For his last three years Howard worked to re-establish a positive British image with the American government and within congressional and public opinion. He also convinced two British governments—a Conservative one in power until June 1929 and its Labour successor—that the Americans wanted only paper parity, and that they would never build to treaty levels. His advice was important during Prime Minister Ramsay MacDonald's American visit in autumn 1929 and the subsequent ending of Anglo-American naval rivalry at the London naval conference in 1930. Howard (who was promoted GCB in 1928)

retired in February 1930 and from a thankful government received a hereditary peerage, as the first Baron Howard of Penrith.

Howard's diplomatic achievements derived from his personal qualities tied to a grasp of what he once called 'the grammar of foreign affairs' (Howard to E. S. Howard, 18 March 1913, Howard MSS, DHW4/Family/13). Not insular or tied to old ways of doing things, he willingly grasped new ideas and technologies, such as radio speeches. Possessing charm and grace that enabled him to win powerful friends within the countries he served, he never lost sight of defending and extending Britain's interests. Tying empathy with his hosts to an icy realpolitik that served his country and empire, he was one of Britain's great diplomats of the twentieth century. In 1935–6 he published his memoirs, *The Theatre of Life*, in two volumes. He died at his home, Ridgecoombe, Hindhead, Surrey, on 1 August 1939, and was survived by his wife and four of their sons. He was succeeded as second baron by his second son, Francis.

B. J. C. McKercher

Sources DNB · *The Times* (2 Aug 1939) · Lord Howard of Penrith, *The theatre of life*, 2 vols. (1935–6) · Cumbria AS, Carlisle, Howard papers · PRO, FO 371 series · B. J. C. McKercher, *Esme Howard: a diplomatic biography* (1989) · WWW · Burke, *Peerage* · FO List (–1930) · CGPLA Eng. & Wales (1939)
Archives Cumbria AS, Carlisle, MSS, corresp., and papers | Bodl. Oxf., letters, mainly to James Bryce · Bodl. Oxf., corresp. with Gilbert Murray · CAC Cam., corresp. with Cecil Spring-Rice · CUL, corresp. with Lord Hardinge · HLRO, corresp. with David Lloyd George · NA Scot., eleventh marquess of Lothian MSS · PRO, FO 371 series
Likenesses W. Stoneman, two photographs, 1918–31, NPG [see illus.] · H. Harris Brown, portrait, priv. coll. · photograph, repro. in McKercher, *Esme Howard*, frontispiece
Wealth at death £11,704 2s.: resworn probate, 15 Jan 1940, CGPLA Eng. & Wales (1939)

Howard [*married names* Devereux, Carr], **Frances, countess of Somerset** (1590–1632), courtier, was born on 31 May 1590, the daughter of Thomas *Howard, first earl of Suffolk (1561–1626), and his second wife, Katherine Knyvett (*b*. in or after 1564, *d*. 1638) [*see* Howard, Katherine]. On 5 January 1606 she married Robert *Devereux, third earl of Essex (1591–1646), son of the late queen's disgraced favourite. The match was political, intended to unite the Howard family, now re-established at court in spite of their continuing Catholic tendencies, with the son of their old enemy, but as both a personal and political relationship the marriage was a disaster. Because of the couple's youth, sexual intercourse was postponed for three years while the earl travelled abroad, but on his return Essex proved unable to consummate the marriage. Although the physical or emotional causes of his impotence can only be guessed, the political and dynastic implications were grave. The relationship deteriorated and, probably some time in 1611 or 1612, the countess became romantically involved with Robert *Carr, Viscount Rochester (1585/6?–1645), favourite of James I. Her family may have encouraged the relationship, for an alliance with Carr would significantly increase the Howards' access to and political influence with the king.

In May 1613, with the support of her family and the king

Frances Howard, countess of Somerset (1590–1632), by Simon de Passe

and the grudging co-operation of Essex and his friends, Countess Frances petitioned for an annulment of her marriage. Her case was heard before a special ecclesiastical commission. The complaint alleged that Essex was incapable of sexual intercourse with his wife, though it formally recognized his claim to have no such problem with other women. A succession of witnesses, mostly servants, testified to the couple's attempts at consummation during the requisite three years. A panel of matrons inspected the countess and found her capable of intercourse but still a virgin. Despite the collusion between the two parties, the nullity ran into difficulties. The claim that Essex was impotent only with his wife had been designed to save the earl's reputation, but created a legal problem. How was such selective impotence to be explained? One option was to blame 'maleficium' (witchcraft), but that explanation raised more questions than it answered and was eventually discarded. In the summer of 1613 the opposition of the archbishop of Canterbury, George Abbot, and several other commissioners stalled the proceedings, but the king intervened, adding enough pliable new commissioners to secure a majority for the annulment. The nullity was granted on 25 September 1613, with its final sentence remaining vague about the sources of the earl's impotence. Three months later, on 26 December, Countess Frances married Robert Carr, newly created earl of Somerset, in a lavish court wedding. Allied by marriage with the favourite, the Howards stood at the pinnacle of court power.

The nullity caused widespread scandal. Refusing to believe that Essex was impotent, malicious wits portrayed the countess as the sexual villain, alleging that she had betrayed Essex, rebuffed his advances, and tricked the matrons who attested to her virginity. 'A mayde, a wyfe, a Countesse and a whore', one poet dubbed her (Bodl. Oxf., MS Ashmole 38, fol. 116r); another mocked:

Theare was at Court a ladye of late
That none could enter shee was soe streight
But now with use shee's growne so wide
Theare is a passage for a Carre to ride.
(Bodl. Oxf., MS Malone 19, fol. 74v)

Countess Frances survived the nullity scandal but during the summer of 1613, while the nullity hung in the balance, she set the course that would eventually destroy her.

Ten days before the nullity was granted Sir Thomas Overbury died in the Tower of London. Overbury, Carr's friend and adviser, had assisted the favourite's earliest dalliances with the countess by composing his love letters. But Overbury fiercely opposed anything more than dalliance and was especially hostile to a possible political *rapprochement* between the favourite and the Howards. Overbury's attitude alienated his friend: at the very least, Carr acquiesced in Overbury's imprisonment for contempt in April 1613 and then collaborated with Frances's great-uncle, the earl of Northampton, to manipulate Overbury into accepting closer political ties with the Howards. The countess, however, sought deadlier revenge. Overbury had maligned her, and he seemed a permanent threat to her chances of marrying Carr. She resolved to kill him. With the help of her friend Anne Turner and a small group of accomplices, the countess tried repeatedly to have Overbury poisoned. He lingered into September 1613 before being finished off with a poisoned enema.

For nearly two years most people assumed Overbury had died a natural death but in summer 1615 Sir Gervase Elwes, lieutenant of the Tower, admitted he had known of—and, he claimed, thwarted—a plot to kill Overbury. Elwes's confession was exploited by courtiers hostile to Somerset and the Howards. Elwes had named Richard Weston, Overbury's keeper, as the attempted poisoner, and during his interrogations in late September 1615 Weston implicated Anne Turner and Countess Frances. At the ensuing trials of Weston and his accomplices, prosecutors and judges publicly proclaimed the countess's guilt, and she quickly became the most vilified of the Overbury murderers. Bitter libels, following the prosecutors' lead, depicted her as a witch and a whore, a sexually promiscuous, murderous, syphilitic sorceress who had used love magic to seduce the king's favourite, wax images to cripple Essex's manhood, and cruel poisons to kill the virtuous Overbury. In an age peculiarly anxious about transgressive women, Frances Howard became the most troubling of all.

Imprisoned since October, the earl and countess were eventually indicted in January 1616. Alone of all the accused, Countess Frances confessed before trial and pleaded guilty before the court of the lord high steward in May 1616. The king cited her confession and penitence as reason to spare her life and in July 1616 granted her a pardon. Somerset, who did not confess, was also spared, but not immediately pardoned. The two remained prisoners in the Tower for a further five and a half years. Upon their release in January 1622, they retired into semi-obscurity with their daughter, Anne, who had been born in custody late in 1615.

Frances Howard died at Chiswick on 23 August 1632, probably of ovarian or uterine cancer, and was buried on 27 August at her family's seat at Saffron Walden. Some contemporaries, convinced of her moral malignancy, assumed her sexual organs had rotted as providential punishment for her sins. William Larkin's portrait of the countess, dressed in an exquisitely elaborate ruff and daringly low-cut dress, hangs at Woburn Abbey. Some claim to detect malice in her eyes and carnal promise in her exposed breasts, but their suppositions say little about Larkin's art. The painting is a compelling document of Jacobean aristocratic taste in clothes and portraiture, and a vivid testament to the countess's beauty, but it reveals little of Frances Howard's heart.   ALASTAIR BELLANY

Sources *State trials*, 2.785–850, 911–1034 · GEC, *Peerage*, new edn · *The letters of John Chamberlain*, ed. N. E. McClure, 1 (1939), 446–80; 2 (1939), 421 · Earl of Northampton, letters to Viscount Rochester, 1613–14, CUL, MS Dd.3.63 · *Memorials of affairs of state in the reigns of Q. Elizabeth and K. James I, collected (chiefly) from the original papers of … Sir Ralph Winwood*, ed. E. Sawyer, 3 vols. (1725), vol. 3, pp. 478–9 · verse libels on the Essex nullity, 1613–14, Bodl. Oxf., MS Ashmole 38, fol. 116r · verse libels on the Essex nullity, 1613–14, Bodl. Oxf., MS Malone 19, fol. 74v · verse libel on the countess of Somerset, 1615, BL, Sloane MS 1792, fols. 2v–4r · confession of Sir Gervase Elwes, PRO, SP 14/81/86 · S. D'Ewes, autobiography, BL, Harleian MS 646, fol. 27r · autopsy on Frances Howard, 24 Aug 1632, BL, Add. MS 46189, fol. 29r · D. Lindley, *The trials of Frances Howard: fact and fiction at the court of King James* (1993) · R. C. Strong, 'William Larkin: icons of splendour', *The Tudor and Stuart monarchy: pageantry, painting, iconography*, 3 (1998) · A. M. Hind, *Engraving in England in the sixteenth and seventeenth centuries*, 2 (1955), 191, 268–9
Likenesses oils, 1600–25, Audley End House, Essex · W. Larkin, oils, *c*.1614, Woburn Abbey, Bedfordshire; version attrib. W. Larkin, *c*.1615, NPG · R. Elstrack, engraving, *c*.1614–1616 · S. de Passe, line engraving, BM, NPG [*see illus.*]

Howard, Francis, fifth Baron Howard of Effingham (*bap.* 1643, *d.* 1695)

colonial governor, was baptized on 17 September 1643 at St Nicholas, Great Bookham, Surrey, the eldest son and heir of Sir Charles Howard, baronet (*d.* 1673), of the manor of Eastwick, near Great Bookham, and his wife, Frances, daughter of Sir George Courthope of Whiligh in Ticehurst, Surrey. Born into an Anglican branch of the many-limbed Howard family, he matriculated from Magdalen College, Oxford, on 2 August 1661 but never graduated. He married on 8 July 1673 Philadelphia (*bap.* 1654, *d.* 1685), daughter of Sir Thomas Pelham, baronet, of Sussex; the couple had eight children but only three survived childhood. After the death of his father in 1673 he became both a deputy lord lieutenant and a JP for Surrey. He might have remained an obscure country gentleman for the rest of his days but for the death in 1681 of his cousin Charles Howard, third earl of Nottingham and fourth Baron Howard of Effingham, leaving him heir to the barony. Succeeding to the title provided little by way of additional income or estates, though it raised the visibility of the new Lord Howard at court. His

Francis Howard, fifth Baron Howard of Effingham (*bap.* 1643, *d.* 1695), school of Sir Godfrey Kneller

kinsmen Henry Howard, sixth duke of Norfolk, and Henry Mordaunt, earl of Peterborough, introduced him to the duke of York and William Blathwayt, and by their contrivance Charles II named him to replace Thomas Culpeper, second Baron Culpeper of Thoresway, as governor of Virginia.

Howard rejoiced at his appointment. Not only would he serve his king, but he got a salary of £2000, plus numerous other perquisites and potential rewards. The financial considerations were especially important given his need to support a large household. With one young daughter and an aunt he left the remainder of his family behind, to join him once Philadelphia recovered from the birth of her eighth child, and set sail for Jamestown late in November 1683, big with expectations of how he would faithfully and rigorously execute the king's instructions.

Having arrived in Virginia in February 1684, Howard was determined to succeed in his royal commission to end the colony's position of near autonomy. His resolution to prevail was the singular quality that distinguished him from his predecessors. By establishing himself as the bestower of all offices he manipulated local politics and decreased the power of established gentry families. He also sought to control law-making in the colony, and greatly reduced the power and role of the colonial legislature, the general assembly, by vetoing its legislation, issuing his own proclamations, and eventually dissolving the assembly of 1685-6. While many colonists saw his reforms as a threat to their well-being, Howard's steadfastness in restoring the royal prerogative ensured him the steady support of Charles II, James II, and William and Mary, and even the Virginians appreciated his role in negotiating a peace treaty with the Iroquois. Not even the devastating death of his wife in 1685 reduced Howard's tenacity in carrying out his commission from his royal masters.

Poor health finally forced Howard back to England in February 1689; he had suffered throughout his life with kidney stones. He arrived knowing that King James no longer sat upon the throne and that his Virginia enemies were lobbying for his dismissal. With the support of the crown and the privy council he easily brushed aside the attempt to replace him and was pleased when William and Mary reappointed him in February 1690. His physical condition and a new wife, Susannah (c.1650-1726), widow of Philip Harbord, and daughter of Sir Henry Felton, baronet, argued against a speedy return to Virginia. In the end he acquiesced in the naming of a lieutenant governor, Francis Nicholson, who served for two years before Howard resigned in 1692. He lived his final years in obscurity before dying in London on 30 March 1695. He was buried near his first wife in St Peter and St Paul, Lingfield, Surrey, on 5 April, and was survived by his second wife, who died in 1726.

Howard governed Virginia at a critical point in its history. He compelled its leading inhabitants to become more accepting of the conception of empire that the later Stuarts sought to impose on England's oldest American dominion during the last quarter of the seventeenth century. Leaving the colony more firmly under royal control than it had been when he became its governor was his mark and his significance. WARREN M. BILLINGS

Sources T. J. Wertenbaker, *Virginia under the Stuarts, 1607-1688* (1915) • W. M. Billings, J. E. Selby, and T. W. Tate, *Colonial Virginia: a history* (1986) • W. M. Billings, ed., *The papers of Francis Howard, Baron Howard of Effingham* (1989) • W. M. Billings, *Virginia's viceroy, their majesties governor and captain-general of Virginia: Francis Howard, Baron Howard of Effingham* (1991) • GEC, *Peerage* • Foster, *Alum. Oxon.* • D. A. Meyers, 'Howard, Francis', *ANB*
Archives L. Cong., corresp. and papers
Likenesses school of G. Kneller, two portraits, Virginia Historical Society, Richmond [*see illus.*]

Howard, Frank (1805-1866), history and portrait painter, was born in Poland Street, London, the son of the painter Henry *Howard (1769-1847) and his wife, Jane, daughter of Philip Reinagle, also a painter. After schooling at Ely, Cambridgeshire, he studied with his father and at the Royal Academy Schools, and then worked as an assistant to Sir Thomas Lawrence. Following Lawrence's death in 1830 he made small-scale portraits and designed objects in gold and silver. He exhibited at the British Institution from 1824 to 1846 and was a frequent contributor to Royal Academy exhibitions from 1825 to 1833, showing there again in 1839, 1842, and 1846. He also exhibited at the Society (later Royal Society) of British Artists in Suffolk Street in London. As well as portraiture, he favoured tragic, romantic, or melodramatic scenes from Shakespeare and the Bible. Between 1827 and 1833 he published *The Spirit of the Plays of Shakespeare*, a five-volume folio of outline drawings.

About 1842 Howard moved to Liverpool, where he struggled to earn a living as a painter, drawing teacher, lecturer on art, and theatre critic for a local paper. To the Fine Arts Commission's first competition, in 1843, for designs for frescoes to decorate the houses of parliament in the new Palace of Westminster, he submitted three chalk cartoons, including *Una Coming to Seek the Assistance of Gloriana*, an allegory from Spenser's *Faerie Queene* of reformed religion seeking the aid of England, which won one of the extra prizes of £100. He also entered the contests of 1845 and 1847, when his *Night Surprise of Cardiff Castle by Ivor Bach* was poorly received.

Howard's books of art instruction, several of which went through multiple editions, include *The Sketcher's Manual: Colour as a Means of Art* (1838), *The Science of Drawing* (1839), and *Imitative Art* (1840). He served as editor for his father's *Course of Lectures on Painting* (1848), for which he wrote a not-uncritical memoir which leaves the impression of a strong-willed and self-assured son. In addition he made lithographic illustrations for Sir William C. Harris's *Portraits of Game and Wild Animals of Southern Africa* (1840) and for *The Ten Cartoons* (1844), which included his winning submission to the houses of parliament competition of the previous year. He also edited James Byres's folio *Hypogaei, or, Sepulchral Caverns of Tarquinia* (1842) and furnished designs for church and memorial windows for *The St Helen's Crown Glass Company's Trade Book of Patterns for Ornamental Window Glass* (1850). In later years he suffered severe financial hardship, and he died of paralysis in the Royal Infirmary, Mount Pleasant, Liverpool, on 30 June 1866. LUCY OAKLEY

Sources Redgrave, *Artists* • *Art Journal*, 28 (1866), 286 • GM, 4th ser., 2 (1866), 280 • d. cert. • DNB • Graves, *Brit. Inst.* • Graves, *RA exhibitors*

Howard, Frederick, fifth earl of Carlisle (1748-1825), politician and diplomat, was born on 28 May 1748, the youngest and only surviving son of Henry *Howard, fourth earl of Carlisle (1694-1758), politician and landowner [*see under* Howard, Charles, third earl of Carlisle], and his second wife, Isabella (1721-1795), the daughter of William Byron, fourth Lord Byron.

Education and early career Styled Lord Morpeth in his early life, he succeeded as fifth earl of Carlisle on his father's death on 4 September 1758. He was educated at Eton College by a private tutor, the Revd Jeffrey Elkins, and became the friend of Charles James Fox and Earl Fitzwilliam. In 1764 he entered King's College, Cambridge, with Elkins in attendance, but he left after only a year without taking a degree. After embarking on the grand tour he was awarded the green ribbon of the Order of the Thistle on 23

Frederick Howard, fifth earl of Carlisle (1748–1825), by Sir Joshua Reynolds, 1769

December 1767, but spent most of his time on the continent with Fox, drinking, gambling, and carousing. By this time his mother had remarried, and Sir William Musgrave became Carlisle's stepfather. The marriage soon descended into acrimony, and Carlisle later claimed that his home life had been ruined by domestic disagreements.

Carlisle returned to England in 1769, just as his mother's marriage was ending, and took his seat in the House of Lords on 9 January 1770. Initially he had little interest in politics, and his weaknesses as a speaker contributed to his indifference. On 22 March 1770 he married Lady Margaret Caroline Leveson-Gower (1753–1824), the sixteen-year-old daughter of Granville Leveson-*Gower, second Earl Gower, later first marquess of Stafford (1721–1803), and his second wife, Louisa Egerton (1723–1761); they had four sons and three daughters. Their youngest child, Henry Edward John *Howard, became dean of Lichfield in 1833. This marriage was of great political importance and gave Carlisle an important connection to cabinet; in the 1770s Gower was far more politically influential than Fox in Carlisle's political development. Continuing his life of dissipation, Carlisle developed a reputation as a rake and steadily lost large amounts of money at the gaming table.

His mistresses included Frances *Villiers, countess of Jersey. As he also acted as guarantor for Fox's loans, his debts mounted steadily, and he was forced to retire to Castle Howard to wait for his rents so that he could pay his creditors. Carlisle always fancied himself as a poet of some repute, although he had little genuine ability, and he published his first collection in 1773, which consisted of two poems, 'Ode … upon the Death of Mr Gray' and 'For the Monument of a Favourite Spaniel'. This ran to three editions in the same year, and was reprinted in Dublin in 1781.

As he approached his thirtieth birthday Carlisle began to develop diplomatic ambitions, and he resolved to abandon his extravagances; he was appointed treasurer of the household on 13 June 1777 and was sworn of the privy council. The first major test of his abilities was on 22 February 1778, when he was surprisingly named the head of a peace mission sent to America to negotiate with the colonists and attempt to find a solution to the crisis. William Eden was also named one of the commissioners, and in many ways led the mission; he developed an effective relationship with Carlisle, constantly pushing him in the right direction, and was a crucial adviser in the years ahead. The commissioners sailed for America in April but were unable to find a formula that would appeal to the continental congress. The reserved and taciturn Carlisle was not ideally suited to diplomatic work, and he was embroiled in controversy on 3 October when he issued a manifesto which criticized the influence of the French and insisted defiantly that Britain would fight to the end. The marquis de Lafayette was enraged and challenged Carlisle to a duel, but he declined, declaring that he was responsible only to his king and country, and not to any individual.

On his return to England in December 1778, after the failure of the mission, Carlisle resigned his post as treasurer of the household. Eden began to press George III for Carlisle's promotion, having recognized that it would assist his own rise, and published *Four Letters to the Earl of Carlisle* in 1779 on Irish and British matters. Because of this Carlisle was named president of the Board of Trade on 6 November 1779, replacing Lord George Germaine. Carlisle and Eden again made an effective combination and displayed great commercial abilities in what was normally an unimportant office.

Ireland On 9 February 1780 Carlisle was named lord lieutenant of the East Riding of Yorkshire, and he was handed his most serious challenge at the end of the year, when he was appointed lord lieutenant for Ireland on 29 November; he was sworn in at Dublin on 23 December. His chief secretary was William Eden, for he had refused to accept the office unless his trusted aide accompanied him. Carlisle was convinced that the Irish loved a colourful court and brought a lavish entourage with him to Dublin; the press admired his 'pomp and show' and dubbed him 'Lord Red-heels' (Duncan, 105). Again, Carlisle's superior and aloof manner created some problems, and his pride alienated some Irish politicians; John Beresford, for example, found him rather 'stiff and distant' (26 Jan 1781, *Correspondence*, 1.156), while the *Dublin Evening Post* referred to his 'freezing reserve' (23 Jan 1781). However, Eden's cunning and congenial attitude helped compensate for these deficiencies. Both men recognized the challenge facing the administration in Ireland and were determined to restore the crown's authority. Carlisle was sympathetic to the volunteers, and this may have contributed to their peaceful disposition in 1781. He was confident that 'good government' would be restored in Ireland (Kelly, 277), and to this end dismissed Judge Richard Power for prolonged absences. He also pressurized John Hely-Hutchinson, one of the more troublesome parliamentarians, to give a promise of complete support. The new approach of the administration brought dividends, and Henry Flood travelled to Dublin to offer his support. Carlisle told him bluntly that, as he profited from offices of the crown, he had to give decisive support. However, by the end of the year Carlisle had grown tired of Flood's 'double conduct', and resolved to relieve him of his office as vice-treasurer. At the opening of parliament on 9 October Flood made a speech hostile to government, and the following month Carlisle wrote to Lord Hillsborough, secretary of state for the southern department, recommending that he should be dismissed from office. In a skilful political manoeuvre, Carlisle detached two influential MPs, Denis Daly and Barry Yelverton, from the opposition at this time, thereby compensating for the loss of Flood. Carlisle was rightly proud of the 'broad-bottom' of his administration (*Carlisle MSS*, 534). One notable achievement of his viceroyalty was the introduction of the preliminaries to the founding of the Bank of Ireland.

In late December 1781 Carlisle recognized the growing demands in the country for greater political responsibility and, anticipating a possible demand for legislative independence, urged the British government for permission to address 'the chief subjects of popular ferment' (PRO, state papers, 63/480, fols. 10–13). He wanted to introduce an annual mutiny bill, a habeas corpus act, a measure of Catholic relief, a solution to the Portuguese trade dispute and the Marine Bill, and a modification of Poynings' law. In the spring of 1782 Flood began to agitate for constitutional reform, but Carlisle worked to outflank him at every turn. Yelverton's bill to modify Poynings' law received much support in the Commons, and Carlisle advised the British government to return it unaltered; he also recommended an immediate repeal of the Declaratory Act. This would have transformed the Anglo-Irish relationship, and would have placed the Irish administration in a rare position of strength, but events soon displaced Carlisle's ambitions. On 14 March Lord North's long ministry collapsed, and when a new ministry was formed Carlisle was removed as lord lieutenant for the East Riding. Furious, he tendered his resignation as lord lieutenant for Ireland, but the decision had already been taken to replace him with the duke of Portland. However, on 11 May, in a conciliatory gesture from the crown, he was appointed lord steward of the household. When Lord Shelburne introduced his Irish resolutions in the House of Lords on 17 May Carlisle spoke approvingly of them and took the opportunity to praise the loyalty of the volunteers during his time in Ireland, especially for offering their services if the country was attacked. But he resigned his office in the following year when Shelburne's administration signed a peace treaty with America; he was upset that the terms were not more favourable to the crown. He was briefly lord privy seal in the Fox–North coalition (2 April–23 December 1783) but was removed when William Pitt the younger took office as prime minister. During this period he published a five-act tragedy in verse, *The Father's Revenge*, which won praise from Samuel Johnson for its realistic characters and sentiments. Even the normally critical Horace Walpole said that it had great merit and praised the language and imagery.

In opposition After joining with Fox in opposition to Pitt's ministry, Carlisle took a prominent stand against the government during the regency crisis of 1788–9. He disapproved of any restrictions placed on the powers of the regent, but the recovery of the king resolved the question. The French Revolution disturbed him, and he gradually broke with Fox on that issue. In 1792 he supported the Alien Act, to monitor and spy on foreigners, and the following year he backed the government in the war with France. As a reward for this support he was invested with the Order of the Garter on 12 June 1793. Increasingly he spoke in the Lords in favour of the repressive policies of the Pitt administration, and he defended the suspension of habeas corpus in May 1794. With the rising in Ireland in May 1798 he recognized the dangers facing the country. In August he warned his old friend Eden, now Lord Auckland, that the country 'was a ship on fire' (30 Aug 1798, *Journal and Correspondence of … Auckland*, 4.52) and that it should either be extinguished or cast adrift. The government introduced a legislative union to solve the Irish crisis, and he gave it a qualified support in the Lords; on 26 February 1799 he was reappointed lord lieutenant of the East Riding. In 1800 he published another five-act tragedy, *The Stepmother*, which he revised for a new edition in 1812. In 1801 a complete collection of his work was published as *The Tragedies and Poems of Frederick, Earl of Carlisle*. This was his last major publication, although he also wrote *Thoughts upon the Present Condition of the Stage, and upon the Construction of a New Theatre* in 1808, and privately printed some *Miscellanies* in 1820.

Guardian to Lord Byron Despite Carlisle's enthusiastic forays into print, he achieved lasting literary fame only through the works of his ward, Lord Byron. Through the intervention of John Hanson, he was made the guardian of the eleven-year-old Byron in 1799 and reluctantly accepted the responsibility. Their relationship was coloured initially by the antagonism between Carlisle and Byron's mother; he quickly tired of her tantrums and capricious nature, although he nevertheless secured her an annual pension of £300 from the civil list. Carlisle had more time for Byron's half-sister, Augusta Byron, and she spent much time at Castle Howard; she made many attempts to build a relationship between Carlisle and her half-brother and succeeded in bringing about a temporary rapprochement. Carlisle maintained a discreet, but protective, eye over Byron and interfered as little as possible; in 1805 he allowed his ward to choose for himself between Oxford and Cambridge universities. In 1807 Byron was desperate to be introduced to the House of Lords, and in the preface to his first edition of his collection *Hours of Idleness* he included a note that Carlisle's works 'have long received the meed of public applause, to which by their intrinsic worth, they were well entitled'. He followed this by dedicating the second edition to 'The right honourable Frederick, earl of Carlisle' and signed it 'his obliging ward and affectionate kinsman'. The following year *Poems Original and Translated* was also published with an identical dedication. It was only in January 1809 that Byron was able to enter the Lords; he had to present proof of his birth and ancestry, and was enraged that Carlisle had not done enough to smooth his way. This marked a break with his guardian, and he removed the flattering couplet

> On one alone Apollo deigns to smile
> And crowns a new Roscommon in Carlisle

from the second edition of his *English Bards and Scotch Reviewers*, which was then being published, and replaced it with

> No muse will cheer with renovating smile
> The paralytic puling of Carlisle

as well as the acerbic attack

> who forgives the senior's ceaseless verse
> Whose hair grows hoary as his rhymes grow worse?

and dismissed him as a 'Lord, rhymester, petit-maitre, and pamphleteer' (lines 725–40). Carlisle had not withheld information from the lord chancellor, as Byron had suspected, and was hurt by his treatment in print; he was wounded by his ward's 'vulgar malignity' (Castle Howard archives), but Byron dismissed him as 'a silly old man' (*Byron's Letters and Journals*, 1.256). Even in 1814 Byron was still bitter about his treatment, and, despite some efforts by Lord Holland at a reconciliation, he insisted that he would not 'concede to the devil!—to a man who used me ill!' (ibid., 4.73). However, he included an apology in the third canto of his *Childe Harold's Pilgrimage*, after the death of Carlisle's son, Frederick Howard, at Waterloo.

Final years and significance Although he withdrew gradually from public life, Carlisle occasionally spoke in the House of Lords on issues that were close to him. In 1811 he criticized any attempts to restrict the power of the prince of Wales, when a regency was formally declared. He also opposed the Corn Bill in March 1815 and entered a protest in the journals against it. It was his final intervention in parliament. He had suffered from neuralgia since having an operation on his cheek in 1798. He died at Castle Howard on 4 September 1825 and was buried in the mausoleum there. His wife had predeceased him, on 27 January 1824, and he was succeeded by his eldest son, George *Howard (1773–1848), politician, as sixth earl of Carlisle.

Carlisle was never an influential politician. He had weak judgement and foolishly attempted to pursue an independent line in parliament. Bringing a certain naïvety to politics, he often underestimated the complexities of issues and was never able to apply himself to becoming a man of business. Perhaps his greatest work was done in the 1790s, when he supported Pitt in government and worked for the establishment of a strong national government. Despite some ability as a conciliator, he was too proud and reserved for his own good, and his inability to understand the dynamics of politics often cost him dearly.   P. M. GEOGHEGAN

Sources A. I. M. Duncan, 'The life and public career of Frederick Howard, fifth earl of Carlisle', DPhil diss., U. Oxf., 1981 · *The manuscripts of the earl of Carlisle*, HMC, 42 (1897) · A. P. W. Malcomson, *John Foster: the politics of the Anglo-Irish ascendancy* (1978) · A. C. Kavanaugh, *John Fitzgibbon, earl of Clare* (1997) · J. Kelly, *Henry Flood: patriots and politics in eighteenth-century Ireland* (1998) · E. A. Smith, *Whig principles and party politics: Earl Fitzwilliam and the whig party, 1748–1833* (1975) · A. Valentine, *Lord North*, 2 vols. (1967) · GEC, *Peerage* · *The journal and correspondence of William, Lord Auckland*, ed. [G. Hogge], 4 vols. (1861–2) · *The correspondence of the Right Hon. John Beresford, illustrative of the last thirty years of the Irish parliament*, ed. W. Beresford, 2 vols. (1854) · *Byron's letters and journals*, ed. L. A. Marchand, 1 (1973); 4 (1975) · G. O'Brien, *Anglo-Irish politics in the age of Grattan and Pitt* (c.1987) · E. M. Johnston, *Great Britain and Ireland, 1760–1800* (1963)

Archives Castle Howard, North Yorkshire, corresp. and papers · York City Archives, estate corresp. | Beds. & Luton ARS, corresp. with Lord Grantham · BL, corresp. with Lord Auckland and Lord Hillsborough, Add. MSS 34415–34460, *passim* · BL, letters to T. Granville, Add. MS 42058 · BL, letters to Lord Granville, Add. MS 58992 · BL, corresp. with W. Huskisson, Add. MSS 38734–38737 · NL Scot., letters to duchess of Sutherland · NMM, letters to T. Lewis · PRO, state papers · PRO, letters to marquess of Stafford, PRO 30/29 · Sheff. Arch., corresp. with Earl Fitzwilliam

Likenesses J. Reynolds, oils, 1757–8, Castle Howard, North Yorkshire · J. B. Greuze, oils, 1768, Buccleuch estates, Selkirk · J. Reynolds, oils, 1769, Castle Howard, North Yorkshire [*see illus.*] · J. Reynolds, oils, 1769–70, Castle Howard, North Yorkshire · H. D. Hamilton, crayon drawing, 1772, Castle Howard, North Yorkshire · G. Romney, oils, 1781, King's Cam. · F. Wheatley, group portrait, 1781 (with his family), Castle Howard, North Yorkshire · R. Cosway, pencil drawing, Castle Howard, North Yorkshire · J. Hoppner, oils, Castle Howard, North Yorkshire · J. Jackson, oils, Castle Howard, North Yorkshire · J. Nollekens, marble bust, Castle Howard, North Yorkshire

Howard, Sir George (*b.* before 1523, *d.* 1580), soldier and courtier, was the third son of Lord Edmund Howard (1478–1539) and his first wife, Joyce or Jocasta (*d. c.*1530), daughter and coheir of Sir Richard Culpeper of Oxenhoath, Kent, and widow of Sir Ralph Legh, under-sheriff of London. He was born into the great Howard clan: Thomas *Howard, third duke of Norfolk (1473–1554), was his uncle and Katherine Howard [*see* Katherine (1518x24–1542)] was his sister. But his father was a wastrel, who squandered his wife's inheritance and then had to flee abroad to avoid his creditors; she died leaving several small children, who were probably brought up in the household of his grandmother Agnes *Howard, the dowager duchess. Lord Edmund sought help from Thomas Cromwell, who arranged his appointment as comptroller of Calais in 1530, but he nevertheless died engulfed in debts in 1539.

When Katherine Howard married the king in 1540, her brothers prospered too. George was first given apparel, and then a pension of 100 marks and lands which had belonged to the Benedictine nunnery of Wilton, and which he later sold for £800. He and his brother Charles also had a licence to import 1000 tuns of Gascon wine and Toulouse woad. The grants came temporarily to an end after Katherine's disgrace and execution in 1542, but Howard nevertheless made a good career for himself. He probably campaigned in France in 1544, and was certainly a captain at Boulogne in 1546; he was also made an equerry of the stable to Henry VIII. He bore the standard at Pinkie in 1547, for which he was knighted at Roxburgh by the duke of Somerset, to whom, in 1548, he signed a letter about that year's campaign. He was initially selected to take charge of the young nobles who were being sent to France to guarantee the 1550 peace treaty and was subsequently appointed master of the henchmen, an office he held between 1550 and 1553. In 1551 he was sent by Northumberland on a Garter embassy to Henri II of France.

Howard played an active role in the court entertainments of three Tudor monarchs. He took part in the 1547 coronation jousts and again in the Christmas jousts of 1551–2. Later that year he appears to have suggested to the council that the theme of a court masque at Christmas might be a debate between Mars and Venus, but to have been horrified when his idea was taken up! In the event he left 'the hole Device' to the 'deskression' of George Ferrers, the lord of misrule that year, 'whow his better abull to Dow hit then I cane thinke hit or wryt hit' (Anglo, 312). He did, however, act as master of the horse to the lord of misrule.

On the death of Edward VI Howard at first joined Northumberland's force which set out to take Mary prisoner, but he quarrelled with Northumberland's son, the earl of Warwick, and rode off to join Mary with fifty horse. On 25 July 1553 Mary temporarily suspended him as master of the henchmen, but the following January granted him an annuity of £200 in deference to the good opinion she had come to hold of him, and because of his services to Henry VIII and Edward VI. Later that year he was sent with his uncle Norfolk to deal with Wyatt's rebellion, for which he was awarded a further £100.

In 1554 Howard was appointed a carver in the household of Philip of Spain, but the king subsequently dismissed all English nominees. Howard was then sent on a mission to the emperor, bearing condolences on the death of Queen Juana, the nominal queen of Spain. In 1555 he joined with an unnamed Spanish noble as challenger in a splendid joust at Westminster where King Philip may have been one of the answerers. However, at the end of the year he nearly came to blows in the Commons with Sir Edward Hastings, who was promoting the bill to force religious exiles to return to England on pain of losing their land, and he clearly welcomed the accession of Elizabeth, whose coronation he predictably honoured in the tiltyard. He was made master of the armoury in 1560 and was granted seven patents of concealed religious lands about the same time. He was also granted a thirty-year lease of lands at Kidbrooke in Kent, became a JP in that county in 1562, and was declared 'of sound religion' by Archbishop Parker in 1564. Furthermore, he became steward of crown

lands at Greenwich, Blackheath, and Deptford. By 1570 he was a gentleman usher in the privy chamber.

Howard first sat in parliament for Devizes in 1547 and then for Rochester in 1555, Winchelsea in 1558, Newton (Lancashire) in 1559, and Reigate in 1563. His friend and distant kinsman Sir Thomas Cheyne, lord warden of the Cinque Ports, was almost certainly responsible for his election to Winchelsea and Rochester, where, surprisingly, he was one of many members who opposed a government bill (not identified).

Apparently Howard never married. The exact date of his death is not known but a privy seal docquet book records both a payment to him as master of the armoury in May 1580 and the appointment of his successor in the following month. No will has yet been found.

PATRICIA HYDE

Sources HoP, Commons, 1509–58, 2.399–401 · HoP, Commons, 1558–1603, 2.346 · G. Brenan and E. P. Statham, The house of Howard, 2 vols. (1907), vol.1, pp. 242–4, vol. 2, pp. 341–4 · will of John Legh, PRO, PROB 11/21, fol. 113v · Literary remains of King Edward the Sixth, ed. J. G. Nichols, 2 vols., Roxburghe Club, 75 (1857) · S. Anglo, Spectacle, pageantry, and early Tudor policy (1969); repr. (1989) · CSP Spain, 1553 · The diary of Henry Machyn, citizen and merchant-taylor of London, from AD 1550 to AD 1563, ed. J. G. Nichols, CS, 42 (1848) · A. Weir, The six wives of Henry VIII (1992) · J. G. Nichols, ed., The chronicle of Queen Jane, and of two years of Queen Mary, CS, old ser., 48 (1850) · A. Fraser, The six wives of Henry VIII (1992) · E. K. Chambers, Sir Henry Lee (1936), 109 · E. K. Chambers, The Elizabethan stage, rev. edn, 4 vols. (1951), vol. 3, p. 399 · LP Henry VIII, vols. 16–21 · P. T. J. Morgan, 'The government of Calais, 1485–1558', DPhil diss., U. Oxf., 1966, 296 · N. Williams, Thomas Howard, fourth duke of Norfolk (1964), 39 · privy seal docquet book, PRO, indexer to various classes, IND 6743

Howard, Sir George (bap. 1718, d. 1796), army officer and politician, was baptized at Great Bookham, Surrey, on 20 June 1718, the eldest son of Lieutenant-General Thomas Howard (1684–1753) of Great Bookham, and his wife, Mary, the youngest daughter of William *Moreton, bishop of Meath, and his second wife, Mary. His father, a nephew of Francis, fifth Baron Howard of Effingham, probably entered the army in April 1703. During the War of the Spanish Succession he was taken prisoner at Almanza in 1707 and again at Brihuega in 1710. He was colonel of the 24th foot from 1717 to 1737 and of the 3rd foot (known as the Buffs, to distinguish it from the Green Howards, commanded by his kinsman Sir Charles Howard) from 1737 to 1749.

George Howard was made an ensign in the 24th foot in 1725, when he was still a child. He was educated at Westminster School from 1729 and matriculated at Christ Church, Oxford, in 1735. He joined the 24th foot in 1736 as a lieutenant and was promoted captain the following year. He transferred to the 3rd foot in 1739, two years after his father had done, and was made lieutenant-colonel of the regiment in April 1744. He commanded the Buffs at Fontenoy, Falkirk, and Culloden. In the pacification of the highlands his regiment gained a reputation for harshness. After returning to Flanders later in 1746 he commanded the regiment at Val (Lauffeldt). On 16 February 1747 he married Lady Lucy Wentworth (d. 1771), the sister and coheir of William, fourth earl of Strafford. His father retired in 1749, and on 21 August Howard was appointed full colonel of the Buffs in his place. He purchased a Georgian mansion, Stoke Place, near Stoke Poges, Buckinghamshire, about 1750, together with a surrounding estate, and added two wings between 1750 and 1770. The architect Stiff Leadbetter was employed in building works in 1765–6, and the grounds, together with a large lake, were laid out by Capability Brown between 1765 and 1767.

Howard appears to have been on the home staff, under General Sir John Ligonier, during the early part of the Seven Years' War, but he took part in the Rochefort expedition of 1757. He was promoted major-general in January 1758 and lieutenant-general in 1760. From 1760 to 1762 he commanded a brigade under John Manners, marquess of Granby, in Germany, at Warburg, the relief of Wesel, and elsewhere. In September 1762 he signed the convention of Bruncker Muhl with the French general Guerchy. For his distinguished service he was given a sword, set with jewels, by Prince Ferdinand of Brunswick, together with the prince's portrait. He transferred to the colonelcy of the 7th dragoons in 1763.

Howard sat in the House of Commons for Lostwithiel from 1761 to 1766. He vacated his seat to take up the appointment of governor of Minorca between 1766 and 1768, after which he returned to the Commons as MP for Stamford (1768–96). He was governor of Chelsea Hospital from 1768 until 1795. In 1773 he was granted an honorary doctorate by Oxford University, and in 1774 he was made KB. Following the death of his first wife on 27 April 1771, on 21 May 1776 he married Elizabeth (d. 1791), the daughter of Peter Beckford, speaker in the Jamaican assembly, and the sister of William Beckford of Fonthill Abbey, MP and lord mayor of London. She was previously married to his kinsman Thomas Howard, second earl of Effingham (d. 1763).

Howard was promoted to the rank of general in 1777, and he transferred to the colonelcy of the 1st dragoon guards in 1779. As an MP he was a supporter of the crown and spoke mainly on matters of military administration rather than policy, though in 1783 he voted against Shelburne's peace terms. Nathaniel Wraxall thought that he was appointed commander-in-chief on the resignation of Henry Seymour Conway in 1784, but the office actually remained vacant until Jeffrey, first Baron Amherst, was reappointed in 1794. In 1793 Howard was promoted to the rank of field marshal, and in July 1795 was sworn of the privy council. He was governor of Jersey from 1795 until his death.

Sir Nathaniel Wraxall wrote that Howard 'was a man universally esteemed, highly bred and a gallant soldier: but … he owed his military Elevation and Employment, more perhaps to Royal Favour, than to any distinguished talents of professional services' (Wraxall, 618). He died at his home in Grosvenor Square, London, on 16 July 1796, after a long and painful illness, and was buried in the family vault at Great Bookham, Surrey. He had no children with his second wife, Elizabeth, who died in 1791. Anne,

the only surviving daughter and heir from his first marriage, married General Richard *Vyse [see under Vyse, Richard William Howard] and died on 2 August 1784, shortly after giving birth to his grandson and heir, Richard William Howard *Vyse (1784–1853). The Howard-Vyses maintained the family's strong associations with the military into the twentieth century.   JONATHAN SPAIN

Sources J. Brooke, 'Howard, George', HoP, *Commons, 1754–90* · GEC, *Peerage* · Burke, *Peerage* · Burke, *Gen. GB* · Colvin, *Archs.* · W. A. Shaw, *The knights of England*, 2 vols. (1905) · *Buckinghamshire*, Pevsner (1994) · C. Dalton, *George the First's army, 1714–1727*, 2 vols. (1910–12) · C. Dalton, ed., *English army lists and commission registers, 1661–1714*, 5 (1902); 6 (1904) · C. T. Atkinson, *The history of the south Wales borderers, 1914–1918* (1931) · C. R. B. Knight, *Historical record of the Buffs, east Kent regiment (3rd foot): 1704–1914*, 1: 1704–1814 (1935) · N. W. Wraxall, *Historical memoirs of my own time*, ed. R. Askham (1904) · *N&Q*, 146 (1924), 216 · J. Britton, *Graphical and literary illustrations of Fonthill Abbey, Wiltshire, with heraldic and genealogical notices of the Beckford family* (1823) · Foster, *Alum. Oxon.* · *Old Westminsters* · *The Times* (18 July 1796), 3a

Archives Bucks. RLSS, commissions, corresp., and papers | BL, Hardwicke MSS · BL, letters to first earl of Liverpool, Add. MSS 38306–38309 · BL, corresp. with duke of Newcastle, Add. MS 32693, fol. 430 · Chatsworth House, Derbyshire, letters to fourth duke of Devonshire

Likenesses J. Watson, mezzotint (after J. Reynolds), BM, NPG; repro. in Knight, *Historical record*, vol. 2, facing p. 182, pl. 6

Howard, George, sixth earl of Carlisle (1773–1848), politician, was born in London on 17 September 1773, the eldest son of Frederick *Howard, fifth earl of Carlisle (1748–1825), and his wife, Margaret Caroline Leveson-Gower (1753–1824). His younger brothers included Henry Edward John *Howard (1795–1868). He was styled Viscount Morpeth from his birth until 1825, when he succeeded his father in the earldom. Educated at Raikes's school, Neasden, and at Eton College, he matriculated on 19 October 1790 from Christ Church, Oxford, where he graduated MA on 30 June 1792 and was made DCL on 18 June 1799. He was a contemporary of George Canning in his school and university days.

In 1794 Morpeth's father deserted Charles James Fox and, along with the majority of whigs, transferred his support to Pitt's government. Morpeth was returned for the family borough of Morpeth, Northumberland, at a by-election in January 1795, and continued to sit for that borough until October 1806. William Huskisson, under-secretary at war, was his colleague in the representation of Morpeth from 1796 to 1802. At the general election in November 1806 Morpeth was returned for the county of Cumberland, where his father had an estate. He was elected together with John Lowther, a member of the most powerful tory family in the county. He sat for Cumberland until 1820.

Morpeth made several literary contributions to *The Anti-Jacobin* in the later 1790s. In the House of Commons he moved the address at the opening of the new parliament in October 1796. In May 1797 he spoke against Fox's motion for the repeal of the Treason and Sedition Acts. From July to September of that year he was one of the main aides to James Harris, first earl of Malmesbury, on a fruitless mission to seek peace terms with France. In the

Commons in February 1799 he warmly defended Pitt's policy of parliamentary union with Ireland. This, he declared over-optimistically, 'would, if effected, extinguish all religious feuds and party animosities and distinctions' (Cobbett, *Parl. hist.*, 34.501–2). Morpeth had thus made quite a notable start as a parliamentary speaker, and he continued on occasion to show that he could be eloquent in that role. But he took little further part in debate during his remaining forty-three years in parliament. What was noted as his exceedingly retiring disposition and his extreme sensitivity towards criticism probably accounted for this. During his last seventeen years in parliament he made no contribution to the debates. This may have been partly explained by the ill health which troubled him from 1830.

Despite his comparative silence in debates, he proved to be a useful minister in various governments, both as Viscount Morpeth and later as earl of Carlisle. In 1804, when Pitt formed his second ministry, Morpeth was moving into association with Fox. This was partly a result of his marriage, on 21 March 1801, to Lady Georgiana Dorothy Cavendish (1783–1858), eldest daughter of William Cavendish, fifth duke of Devonshire, a close ally of Fox. Six sons and six daughters, including Harriet Elizabeth Georgiana Leveson-*Gower, were the abundant fruit of this union. When the 'ministry of all the talents', led by Grenville and Fox, was formed in February 1806, Morpeth was sworn of the privy council and became a commissioner for the affairs of India. In October of that year he was sent on an abortive mission to Berlin to seek an alliance with Prussia against Napoleon. He resigned his post at the India board when the duke of Portland's tory ministry was formed in March 1807.

In February 1812 Morpeth brought forward a motion on the state of Ireland, and in his speech advocated 'a sincere and cordial conciliation with the Catholics' (*Hansard 1*, 21.494–500, 669). But his motion was defeated. In December 1819 he spoke in favour of the Seditious Meetings Prevention Bill introduced by Lord Liverpool's tory government. This speech was not appreciated by the whigs in his constituency, who returned another candidate (J. C. Curwen) at the general election in March 1820. Morpeth retired from the poll at an early stage, and did not return to parliament until, after his father's death (4 September 1825), he took his seat in the Lords as earl of Carlisle on 21 March 1826. In November 1824 he was appointed, through the influence of his old friend Canning, lord lieutenant of the East Riding of Yorkshire. He retained this office until 1847, when he was succeeded in it by his eldest son, George William Frederick *Howard, Viscount Morpeth and later seventh earl of Carlisle.

On 18 May 1827, as part of a contentious compact between Canning (now prime minister) and some of the whigs, Carlisle became chief commissioner of woods and forests with a seat in the cabinet. Carlisle played a considerable part in arranging this alliance, which caused an acrimonious split among the whigs and proved very uncomfortable for Canning, though it did keep him in office until he died in August. In July of the same year Carlisle became lord privy seal, and continued in that position, under Canning and then Goderich, until the latter resigned in January 1828.

Carlisle returned to the cabinet, without portfolio, when Lord Grey's whig ministry was formed in November 1830. On Lord Ripon's resignation from the ministry in June 1834, Carlisle resumed his old post of lord privy seal. The government was dissolved in the following month, and, owing to ill health, Carlisle virtually retired from political life. He received the Order of the Garter on 17 March 1837, and in the following year became a trustee of the British Museum. He died at his main residence, Castle Howard, near Malton in Yorkshire, on 7 October 1848, and was buried in the mausoleum in the park.

IAN MACHIN

Sources DNB · GEC, *Peerage* · GM, 2nd ser., 30 (1848), 537–8 · J. M. Collinge, 'Howard, George, sixth earl of Carlisle', HoP, *Commons* · J. Ehrman, *The younger Pitt, 3: The consuming struggle* (1996) · *Diaries and correspondence of James Harris, first earl of Malmesbury*, ed. third earl of Malmesbury [J. H. Harris], 4 vols. (1844) · A. Aspinall, ed., *The formation of Canning's ministry, February to August 1827*, CS, 3rd ser., 59 (1937) · *The later correspondence of George III*, ed. A. Aspinall, 5 vols. (1962–70) · *Three Howard sisters: selections from the writings of Lady Caroline Lascelles, Lady Dover, and Countess Gower, 1825 to 1833*, ed. Maud, Lady Leconfield, rev. J. Gore (1955) · M. Roberts, *The whig party, 1807–12* (1939) · G. I. T. Machin, *The Catholic question in English politics, 1820 to 1830* (1964) · Foster, *Alum. Oxon.*

Archives Castle Howard, near Malton, Yorkshire, corresp. and papers · U. Durham L., estate corresp. and papers | BL, corresp. with Lord and Lady Holland, Add. MSS 51577–51583 · BL, letters to Lord Morley, Add. MS 48226 · Harewood House, near Leeds, Harewood MSS · NL Ire., corresp. with Thomas Wyse · PRO, letters to Lord Grenville, PRO 30/29 · PRO, Leveson-Gower MSS · U. Durham L., letters to second Earl Grey

Likenesses J. Jackson, double portrait, oils, *c*.1808 (with his son, George), Castle Howard, Malton, Yorkshire · J. Jackson, oils, *c*.1815–1820, Castle Howard, Malton, Yorkshire · T. Lawrence, oils, after 1825 (finished by Tomlinson), Castle Howard, Malton, Yorkshire · H. Edridge, pencil drawing, Castle Howard, Malton, Yorkshire · T. Trotter, line engraving (after J. Reynolds, 1786), BM, NPG; repro. in *Catalogue of the exhibition of old masters* (1878), no. 372 · double portrait, engraving (with son, Viscount Morpeth; after J. Jackson), repro. in W. Jerdan, *National portrait gallery of illustrious and eminent personages*, 3 (1831)

Howard, George Anthony Geoffrey, Baron Howard of Henderskelfe (1920–1984), landowner and chairman of the BBC, was born on 22 May 1920 at 32 Chester Square, London, the second of three sons of the Hon. Geoffrey William Algernon Howard (1877–1935) and his wife, Ethel Christian Methuen (1889–1932). His father was the fifth son of the ninth earl of Carlisle; his mother, the daughter of the third Baron Methuen.

Howard was educated at Eton College and spent a year at Balliol College, Oxford, before being commissioned in the Green Howards in 1940. Attached to the Indian army with the rank of major, he saw service in India, and in Burma, where he was wounded. His elder and younger brother were both killed in action in 1944, and it was upon Howard that the duty of managing the family estates in the post-war years accordingly devolved.

Castle Howard had been completed for the third earl of

Carlisle in 1714. More than two centuries later, the stewardship of Vanbrugh's great pile presented problems of nightmare proportions. The upkeep of a large agricultural estate and the care of a great art collection both made heavy calls on family resources, and these were further strained by the need to restore the ravages caused by a fire in 1940; most of the south front had been destroyed, and the great dome, with its Pellegrini frescoes, had come crashing to the ground. Ably assisted by his wife—he was married on 11 May 1949 to Lady Cecilia Blanche Geneviève FitzRoy (1922–1974), daughter of the eighth duke of Grafton, with whom he would have four sons—Howard conducted a doughty holding operation. Eventually, when the burden became too great, responsibility for the preservation of the fabric passed to Castle Howard Estates Ltd.

Family responsibilities did not stand in the way of public service. Howard was active in the affairs of the National Trust and was a member of the National Parks Commission. He served as president of the Country Landowners' Association from 1969 to 1971 and from 1974 to 1977 he was chairman of the Meat and Livestock Commission. He was also chairman of the Royal College of Art.

Howard became a governor of the BBC in February 1972, and although he had served as 'senior ordinary governor' there was general surprise when he was appointed to succeed Sir Michael Swann as chairman in 1980—he was believed to have lobbied his friend William Whitelaw, who as home secretary in Margaret Thatcher's administration had an important say in the matter. 'I knew that something had happened,' Swann said. 'When George came to tell me he was to be my successor, he had grown to twice his normal size' (Milne, 81).

That must have been a memorable sight, because in his prime Howard was a man of massive girth. He had a gargantuan appetite and smoked incessantly. He had a weakness for silk suits and vividly coloured shirts and ties; when taking his ease, he favoured more exotic attire, often sporting a kaftan—one of his favourites was silver, with a huge red bird embroidered across his chest. He was fond of the company of young women (he had been widowed in 1974); if they were would-be broadcasters, he was shameless in attempting to advance their interests with members of BBC staff.

Howard regarded the BBC very much as a personal fiefdom, and announced from the start that he intended to adopt a 'high profile'. He travelled extensively overseas, sometimes on business that would have been better conducted by a senior official more familiar with the issues involved. 'Would you like to see a picture of my place in England?' he enquired amiably during a lull in the conversation at a banquet in Beijing, and unfolded a glossy brochure with a panoramic view of Castle Howard. 'Is it all yours?' asked his wide-eyed Chinese neighbour (private information). The chatelain of one of England's stateliest homes had distinctly grand ideas about how he should be accommodated during these frequent peregrinations at public expense. In Venice for the prix Italia, only the Cipriani would do; on another occasion, he and his director-general were booked in at the sumptuously appointed Bel Air in Los Angeles. 'I don't like cottage hotels,' he rasped (Milne, 81).

Howard did not take a conventional view of how the affairs of the board of governors should be conducted, and could be both mischievous and manipulative—a marked contrast to the subtle, relaxed style to which the board had become accustomed during the tenure of the pipe-smoking Michael Swann. Stuart Young, Howard's successor as chairman, later told the director-general that it was at Howard's instigation that William Rees-Mogg, newly appointed as vice-chairman, had made an ill-informed attack, at his very first board meeting, on BBC management practices (Milne, 82).

Howard could point to a number of solid achievements, for all that. It was, for instance, greatly to his credit and to the BBC's advantage (the director-general at the time was Ian Trethowan) that together they persuaded the government to abandon annual negotiations over the licence fee and agree to a three-year settlement.

Howard's most important initiative as chairman was to put his weight behind an architectural competition for a new BBC building on the site of the Langham Hotel opposite Broadcasting House. The winner was Norman Foster. His team produced a brilliantly imaginative design which would have enhanced the reputation of the BBC as a discerning patron of the arts; it would also have done much to rescue John Nash's beautiful All Souls, Langham Place, marooned at the top of Regent Street amid much undistinguished post-war building. After Howard's departure in 1983, men of narrower vision—and possibly less extravagant tastes—decreed that it would cost too much. The national instrument of broadcasting opted instead to buy the site of a greyhound stadium at White City, and built a totally undistinguished new office block in the wastes of London W12.

As chairmen of the BBC often do, even when they have ostensibly been sent in 'to sort the place out', Howard developed an intense loyalty to the corporation. This was well demonstrated on the occasion he and Alasdair Milne were invited to meet the Conservative backbench media committee. It was during the Falklands War, and an edition of the *Panorama* programme had explored the views of those who had reservations about British policy. Howard and Milne were given a roasting, and the temperature was not lowered by what Milne later described as 'George's occasional tendency to perform like a great Whig grandee addressing his retainers' (Milne, 92). As they left, a young tory MP approached and said, 'You, sir, are a traitor.' Howard, sweating freely and with thoughts only for the glass of whisky promised by Willie Whitelaw, jabbed a finger at him and growled, 'Stuff you!' (ibid.).

For the last year and a half of his chairmanship Howard was a very sick man, and he did not long survive his retirement. He was created a life peer, and took the title of Baron Howard of Henderskelfe—the original name of the site on which Castle Howard now stands. In February 1984 he was appointed chairman of the Museums and Galleries Commission, but he was to serve for only a few months.

He died at Castle Howard from heart failure on 27 November 1984 and was buried in the family mausoleum there on 30 November. IAN McINTYRE

Sources A. Milne, *DG: the memoirs of a British broadcaster* (1988) · personal knowledge (2004) · private information (2004) · *The Times* (28 Nov 1984) · *WWW* · b. cert. · m. cert. · d. cert. · *Debrett's Peerage*
Archives SOUND BL NSA, performance recording
Wealth at death £25,781,615: probate, 17 June 1986, *CGPLA Eng. & Wales*

Howard, George James, ninth earl of Carlisle (1843–1911), artist and politician, was born at 56 Park Street, London, on 12 August 1843, the only son of the Hon. Charles Wentworth George Howard (1814–1879), and his wife, Mary Priscilla Harriett Parke (1822–1843), second daughter of James Parke, Baron Wensleydale. His father was the fifth son of George *Howard, sixth earl of Carlisle (1773–1848), and MP for East Cumberland, and his father's eldest brother was the statesman George William Frederick Howard, seventh earl of Carlisle (1802–1864). He was educated at Eton College, and at Trinity College, Cambridge, where in 1861 he attended a private course of lectures on history by Charles Kingsley; he graduated BA in 1865. On the death of his father in 1879, he was elected Liberal MP for East Cumberland and lost the seat in 1880, but regained it in 1881. In 1885 he opposed Gladstone's Home Rule Bill for Ireland, joining the Liberal Unionists, and when the constituency of East Cumberland was replaced by the single seat of North Cumberland he declined to stand in the election of 1886. He succeeded his uncle, William George Howard (1808–1889), the invalid and bachelor eighth earl of Carlisle, in 1889, at which time he inherited the Howard estates in Cumberland, Northumberland, and north Yorkshire totalling 78,000 acres.

On 4 October 1864 Howard married Rosalind Frances Stanley (1845–1921) [see Howard, Rosalind Frances], youngest daughter of Edward John Stanley, second Lord Stanley of Alderley, who became a strong advocate for the temperance and women's suffrage movements. They had six sons, three of whom predeceased their father, and five daughters, one of whom died in infancy. As a married couple they moved among artistic circles in London, and made frequent visits to Europe. Already, as a young man, Howard professed his desire to become an artist rather than pursue a political career, as his family wished, and later, after succeeding to the Carlisle title, he increasingly left the management of the family estates to his wife in order to devote himself to painting. In 1865 he had travelled to Italy where he studied painting under Giovanni Costa, and on his return to London he continued his artistic training at the Kensington School of Art and with the painter J. M. Leigh at Heatherley's Art School. His circle of artist friends included Frederic Leighton, Ford Madox Brown, William Holman Hunt, Val Prinsep, Edward Lear, Alphonse Legros, George Frederic Watts, Dante Gabriel Rossetti, and Edward Poynter; he sketched intimate pencil portraits of many of his fellow artists. Howard formed an especially close friendship with Edward Burne-Jones, under whom he studied initially and from whom he later purchased numerous pictures. Burne-Jones's late masterpiece *Arthur in Avalon*, begun in the 1880s, was originally commissioned as a fresco for Naworth Castle in Cumberland, but realizing the artist's devotion to the composition Howard relinquished his claim upon the picture and accepted another in lieu of the money he had already paid. Rosalind Howard and Georgiana Burne-Jones also formed a close attachment.

In 1867 Howard and his wife commissioned Philip Webb, the leading Queen Anne architect, to build a London home for them at 1 Palace Green, Kensington. Completed two years later, the interiors were decorated by Morris & Co. and included a frieze illustrating the story of Cupid and Psyche designed by Burne-Jones and completed by Walter Crane. Morris and his family, like Burne-Jones's, were close friends of the Howard family. Both men were commissioned repeatedly to supply furnishings, textiles, and paintings for the other Howard homes, Castle Howard in north Yorkshire and Naworth Castle in Cumberland. Howard made several portrait sketches of both men and their families during their visits to Cumberland. Webb was also commissioned by the Howard family to build St Martin's Church (1874–8), Brampton, Cumberland, and the church was furnished with stained glass by Morris and Burne-Jones. Howard befriended and supported many artists throughout his life, including the sculptors Jules Dalou (during his exile in England from 1879 to 1899), George Cowell, and Edgar Boehm, who executed Burne-Jones's designs for a bas-relief of Flodden field for Naworth Castle.

Repeated visits abroad, to Italy and Egypt especially, but also to India, South Africa, and the West Indies, supplied the impetus for much of Howard's landscape painting, though he never ceased to paint the countryside in Cumberland, Yorkshire, and Northumberland. He exhibited oils and watercolours regularly at the Grosvenor Gallery in London between 1877 and 1887. In 1882, together with W. B. Richmond, M. R. Corbet, and others, he founded the Etruscan school of painting: this group of Italian and English artists, of whom Giovanni Costa was the acknowledged leader, drew inspiration for their lyrical landscapes from Italian scenery and its mythical, historical, and literary associations. From 1881 until his death Howard sat on the board of trustees of the National Gallery, eventually becoming chairman. He was involved in the founding of the Tate Gallery, and was a member of the Society for the Protection of Ancient Buildings. He also sat on committees for the National Gallery of New South Wales and the South African Fine Art Gallery, and was also involved in establishing funds and memorials following the deaths of Ruskin, Burne-Jones, and Holman Hunt. Noting his philanthropy, Philip Webb described him as 'a constitutional caretaker of precious things' (Castle Howard archives, J22/64). In 1885 Howard advised Gladstone over the offer of a baronetcy to Watts, which the artist declined, and between 1905 and 1911 he sat on the committee which decided on the historical murals for the House of Lords.

From the late 1880s onwards Lord Carlisle began to sell a number of items from the collections assembled by his ancestors at Castle Howard. These included pictures by Canaletto and his contemporaries, a series of drawings by François Clouet, and a collection of gems which was sold to the British Museum. Further sales of individual pictures to dealers such as Martin Colnaghi, George Donaldson, and Joseph Duveen continued until his death. He negotiated with the National Gallery to sell Mabuse's *Adoration of the Kings* (*c.*1510–*c.*1512), the single most important picture in the collection, at less than the market price in lieu of death duties. He also left instructions that the trustees of the gallery should have eleven paintings of their choice from Castle Howard. He continued painting until his sudden death from heart failure at his daughter's residence at Bracklands, Hindhead, near Haslemere, Surrey, on 16 April 1911. He was buried on 20 April at Lanercost Priory, near Naworth Castle, Cumberland. His wife survived him. One of his last works was a series of designs to illustrate a children's songbook which he published in 1910; the frontispiece is a self-portrait with him presenting the book to his children.

Carlisle was succeeded by his son **Charles James Stanley Howard**, Viscount Morpeth and tenth earl of Carlisle (1867–1912), politician. Born at 122 Park Street, London, on 8 March 1867, he was educated at Rugby School and at Balliol College, Oxford. He became Viscount Morpeth in 1889. On 17 April 1894 he married Rhoda Ankaret (*b.* 1867), daughter of Colonel Paget Walter L'Estrange; the couple had one son and three daughters. He was captain in the 3rd battalion Border regiment of militia, with which he served in South Africa in 1902. An active member of the London school board (1894–1902), he contested without success in the Unionist interest Chester-le-Street, the Hexham division of Northumberland, and Gateshead. He was Unionist MP for South Birmingham from 1904 to 1911, and from 1910 was one of the parliamentary whips for his party. His health was already failing when he succeeded to the earldom in 1911, and he died at 105 Eaton Place, London, on 20 January 1912. He was buried at Lanercost Priory, near Naworth Castle, on 24 January.

CHRISTOPHER RIDGWAY

Sources V. Surtees, *The artist and the autocrat: George and Rosalind Howard, earl and countess of Carlisle* (1988) · Castle Howard, Yorkshire, Castle Howard archives, J22 and J23 · C. Newall, *The Etruscans: painters of the Italian landscape, 1850–1900* (1989) [exhibition catalogue, Stoke-on-Trent City Museum and Art Gallery, 1989] · GEC, *Peerage* [G. J. Howard and C. J. S. Howard] · *DNB* · b. cert. · m. cert. · d. cert. · d. cert. [Charles James Stanley Howard] · *CGPLA Eng. & Wales* (1911–12)
Archives Castle Howard, Yorkshire, corresp. and papers · U. Durham L., estate papers relating to Northumberland and Cumberland | BL, letters to W. E. Gladstone, Add. MSS 44346–44787, *passim* · Bodl. Oxf., corresp. with Sir William Harcourt and Lewis Harcourt · Bodl. Oxf., corresp. with Gilbert Murray · U. Glas. L., letters to D. S. MacColl
Likenesses G. F. Watts, oils, *c.*1866, Castle Howard, Yorkshire · W. B. Richmond, oils, 1880, Castle Howard, Yorkshire · H. T. Wells, crayon drawing, 1893, Castle Howard, Yorkshire · G. Sephton, oils, 1898, Castle Howard, Yorkshire · G. C. Beresford, photographs, 1903, NPG · C. Holroyd, watercolour, 1907, Castle Howard, Yorkshire
Wealth at death £97,151 17s. 5d.: probate, 14 June 1911, *CGPLA Eng. & Wales* · £58,937 15s. 4d.—Charles James Stanley Howard: probate, 27 Feb 1912, *CGPLA Eng. & Wales*

Howard, George William Frederick, seventh earl of Carlisle (1802–1864), politician, was born in Hill Street, Berkeley Square, London, on 18 April 1802, the eldest child in a family of six sons and six daughters of George *Howard, sixth earl of Carlisle (1773–1848), and his wife, Georgiana Dorothy Howard *née* Cavendish (1783–1858), daughter of the fifth duke of Devonshire. He was educated at Eton College before matriculating at Christ Church, Oxford, on 15 October 1819. In 1821 he won the university prizes for Latin and English verse. He obtained a first class in classics in the following year, and graduated BA in 1823 and MA four years later. In September 1825, when his father became earl of Carlisle, he acquired the courtesy title of Viscount Morpeth by which he was known until he succeeded his father in the earldom in 1848.

In 1826 Morpeth accompanied his maternal uncle, the sixth duke of Devonshire, on a mission to St Petersburg to attend the coronation of Tsar Nicholas I. While abroad he was returned unopposed as a whig in the general election of June 1826 for his family borough of Morpeth, Northumberland. He had initially entered the lists for the large constituency of Yorkshire in this election, but withdrew his candidature on the grounds of youth and inexperience.

Morpeth's early efforts in parliament showed his interest in promoting religious equality. He held to this aim without surrendering any of his loyal, basically broad-church Anglicanism. This was accompanied by marked personal devotion, showing an inclination to evangelicalism in some respects, more especially to incarnationalism and premillennialism. He had also a firm wish to maintain the Church of England as an establishment. Later he showed that his toleration did not extend to Tractarianism, which he denounced in some parliamentary speeches. In his maiden speech, on 5 March 1827, he seconded Sir Francis Burdett's motion for Catholic emancipation, and in April 1830 he spoke in favour of Robert Grant's motion for leave to introduce a bill for Jewish relief. At the general election in August 1830 Morpeth was returned for Yorkshire at the head of the poll, and in March 1831 he extolled the Reform Bill as 'a safe, wise, honest, and glorious measure' (*Hansard 3*, 2, 1831, 1217–20).

Morpeth was returned unopposed for Yorkshire in the general election in May 1831, and for the new constituency of the West Riding in the first post-reform general election in December 1832. He was returned for the West Riding in three subsequent elections, two of which were contested, but was narrowly defeated in the general election of July 1841. In 1833, amid controversy surrounding the campaign for a ten-hour day for all factory workers, he introduced a compromise bill on the factory question. The move was unsuccessful, but it antagonized the Ten Hours campaigners and caused Richard Oastler to stigmatize him as 'the sleek and oily Morpeth' (Southgate, 146). After

George William Frederick Howard, seventh earl of Carlisle (1802–1864), by T. Cranfield

this, Morpeth continued to be an object of suspicion to the Ten Hours campaigners.

In February 1835 Morpeth proposed an amendment to the address, and this was carried against Peel's Conservative government. On the formation of Lord Melbourne's second ministry in April that year, he was admitted to the privy council and appointed chief secretary for Ireland, commencing a lengthy and intimate acquaintance with the affairs of that country. He already had a reputation as a sympathizer with Irish claims for reform. During his difficult chief secretaryship, which he held for six years, he showed marked reforming and debating ability, carrying Irish tithe, poor-law, and municipal reform bills through parliament after long and gruelling struggles. The contentious tithe question was the subject of several reforming bills from 1834. Morpeth failed to carry tithe commutation bills in 1835, 1836, and 1837, mainly because they included the appropriation of Church of Ireland revenues. But in 1838 he carried a much amended tithe bill which did not contain appropriation. The dropping of the rancorous appropriation issue was seen as an olive branch, in return for which the House of Lords might pass Irish poor-law and municipal councils bills. The Irish poor relief question was by no means without dispute but it proved easier to settle than tithes. Morpeth helped to

carry a bill in 1838 which applied to Ireland similar provisions to those of the contentious Poor Law Amendment Act of 1834 for England and Wales (including workhouses). Efforts to settle the municipal government issue, however, rivalled the tithe in intricacy and difficulty, and took five years to succeed. A bill of 1835 was dropped. One of 1836 was lost through opposition in the Lords, as was another in 1838–9. Finally a bill establishing elective councils on a partial basis was passed in 1840 after heavy amendment by the Lords. Thus Morpeth and his whig colleagues carried their Irish reform programme only to a limited extent.

In attempting to carry government policy Morpeth was tactful and fairly successful in his relations with O'Connell's repealers, with whom the whigs were allied from 1835. He exerted himself to execute the policies initiated by his under-secretary, Thomas Drummond, a zealous reformer with whom he worked closely and effectively. Morpeth entered the cabinet in February 1839, but lost his seat for the West Riding at the general election in 1841 and did not return to parliament until 1846.

During a year spent in North America, Morpeth was nominated as a candidate for the city of Dublin at a by-election in January 1842, but narrowly lost the contest to a Conservative. In a by-election for the West Riding in February 1846, however, he was returned unopposed. After the fall of Peel's ministry in June that year, Morpeth was appointed (on 7 July) to Lord John Russell's cabinet as chief commissioner of woods and forests (a position his father had held in 1827). On 22 July 1847 he succeeded his father as lord lieutenant of the East Riding of Yorkshire, and in the general election in August he was again returned unopposed for the West Riding (this time along with Richard Cobden). After an unsuccessful attempt at public health reform in 1847, Morpeth reintroduced his Public Health Bill in February 1848, and after a struggle this became law by the end of the parliamentary session. Considered a weak and inadequate measure by the later standards of state intervention, it was original and ground-breaking if not very decisive or far-reaching.

Morpeth became the seventh earl of Carlisle in October 1848 on the death of his father, and took his seat in the Lords in the following February. Carlisle was made chancellor of the duchy of Lancaster on 6 March 1850, remaining in the cabinet. He left his post when Russell's ministry resigned in February 1852, and was disappointed not to receive office in the Peelite–Liberal coalition which came to power in December. In consequence of this he believed that he had failed in politics. He was installed as lord rector of Marischal College, Aberdeen, in March 1853, and spent most of the next twelve months travelling on the continent.

In February 1855 Carlisle was invested with the Order of the Garter and was appointed lord lieutenant of Ireland by the new Liberal premier, Lord Palmerston. As Irish viceroy he had reached the summit of his public career. He filled this important office for most of the remainder of his life, leaving it only between February 1858 and June 1859 when Palmerston was out of office. In Ireland, Carlisle's periods as lord lieutenant were a time of continuing political tension, and there was marked Conservative encroachment on the Liberals' electoral position. But there was comparatively little direct political threat or action. The Irish Independent Party dwindled into a small and disparate number of individuals by 1857. A motion in favour of the disestablishment and disendowment of the Church of Ireland was defeated in the House of Commons in May 1856, and the issue was not raised again in parliament until 1868. Fenian threats to the regime were in the wings, but did not materialize in the form of rebellion until 1867. Nor did the constitutional movement for Irish reform become effectively organized again until 1864. During Carlisle's periods of viceregal office, therefore, the turbulence was either dying or in the making, rather than being active in the open. He experienced something of a lull before a storm, and attained a fair degree of popularity through his expansive social behaviour (which included wearing an enormous bunch of shamrock on St Patrick's day) and his encouragement of agricultural and industrial improvements.

Ill health compelled Carlisle to retire from the lord lieutenancy in October 1864, after he had presided at the Shakespeare tercentenary at Stratford upon Avon in the preceding April. He died at his main residence, Castle Howard, near Malton, Yorkshire, on 5 December 1864, and was buried in the family mausoleum in the park. He had never married, and was succeeded in the earldom by his brother, the Hon. and Revd William George Howard, rector of Londesborough, Yorkshire, a living belonging to his cousin the duke of Devonshire.

Carlisle's main role was that of an effective though not a foremost Liberal politician and reformer over a very wide range of questions in both Britain and Ireland. He was intellectually very able and had strong literary and theological interests, whose depth was revealed by the extracts from his journals privately printed after his death. He published a good deal of poetry, a play (*The Last of the Greeks, or, The Fall of Constantinople*) in 1828, speeches, pamphlets, lectures on literary figures, and his own travel diaries. His *Lectures and Addresses in Aid of Popular Education*, published in 1852, indicates a deep concern with this subject. He gave it much practical help by assisting the establishment of mechanics' institutes, founding a reformatory on his estate at Castle Howard, and supervising the village schools on his land. He had an attractive but not a forceful personality, and was a notably fluent speaker.

IAN MACHIN

Sources D. D. Olien, *Morpeth: a Victorian public career* (1983) · B. Hilton, 'Whiggery, religion and social reform: the case of Lord Morpeth', *HJ*, 37 (1994), 829–59 · *Extracts from journals kept by George Howard, earl of Carlisle: selected by his sister*, ed. C. Lascelles (privately printed, London, c.1864) · I. Newbould, *Whiggery and reform, 1830–41* (1990) · J. Prest, *Lord John Russell* (1972) · J. T. Ward, *The factory movement, 1830–1855* (1962) · D. Southgate, *The passing of the whigs, 1832–1886* (1962) · A. D. Macintyre, *The Liberator: Daniel O'Connell and the Irish party, 1830–1847* (1965) · O. MacDonagh, *The emancipist: Daniel O'Connell, 1830–47* (1989) · R. Brent, *Liberal Anglican politics: whiggery, religion, and reform, 1830–1841* (1987) · G. I. T. Machin, *Politics and the churches in Great Britain, 1832 to 1868* (1977) · *Three Howard sisters:* selections from the writings of Lady Caroline Lascelles, Lady Dover, and Countess Gower, 1825 to 1833, ed. Maud, Lady Leconfield, rev. J. Gore (1955) · G. I. T. Machin, *The Catholic question in English politics, 1820 to 1830* (1964) · *DNB* · Burke, *Peerage*

Archives Castle Howard, Malton, Yorkshire, corresp. and papers incl. diary | BL, corresp. with Lord Broughton, Add. MSS 47226–47228 · BL, corresp. with W. E. Gladstone, Add. MSS 44356–44403 · BL, corresp. with Lord Holland, Add. MSS 51583, 52010 · Bodl. Oxf., corresp. with fourth earl of Clarendon · Borth. Inst., corresp. with Sir Charles Wood · Chatsworth House, Derbyshire, letters to dukes of Devonshire · NA Scot., letters to second Lord Panmure · NRA, priv. coll., letters to Harriett, duchess of Sutherland · PRO, letters to Earl Granville, PRO 30/29 · PRO, corresp. with Lord John Russell, PRO 30/22 · St Deiniol's Library, Hawarden, letters to duke of Newcastle · U. Durham L., Grey MSS · U. Southampton L., corresp. with Lord Palmerston · UCL, corresp. with Edwin Chadwick · W. Sussex RO, letters to duke of Richmond

Likenesses drawings, 1818–c.1853, Castle Howard, Malton, Yorkshire · D. Wilkie, group portrait, oils, 1837 (*The Queen presiding after her first council*), Royal Collection · C. R. Leslie, group portrait, oils, 1838 (*Queen Victoria receiving the sacrament at her coronation*), Royal Collection · C. Moore, marble bust, 1839, NG Ire. · T. H. Carrick, miniature on marble, exh. RA 1843?, Castle Howard, Malton, Yorkshire · F. Holl, stipple and line print, after 1854 (after G. Richmond), NG Ire. · J. H. Foley, bronze statue, 1870, Phoenix Park, Dublin · J. H. Foley, statue, 1870, Brampton Moat, Carlisle · J. H. Foley, statue, 1870, Carlisle · T. Cranfield, photograph, NPG [*see illus.*] · J. Doyle, caricatures, drawings, BM · J. H. Foley, bust, town hall, Morpeth, Northumberland · J. H. Foley, two busts, Castle Howard, Malton, Yorkshire · G. Hayter, group portrait, oils (*The House of Commons, 1833*), NPG · F. Holl, engraving, Castle Howard, Malton, Yorkshire · F. C. Lewis, stipple (after J. Slater), BM, NPG · J. Partridge, group portrait, oils (*The Fine Arts Commissioners, 1846*), NPG · J. Partridge, oils, Castle Howard, Malton, Yorkshire · D. J. Pound, stipple and line print (after photograph by Mayall), NPG · C. Scott, oils (after photograph), Castle Howard, Malton, Yorkshire · S. C. Smith, oils, Dublin Castle · oils, Eton · watercolour, Castle Howard, Malton, Yorkshire · wood-engraving, NG Ire.; repro. in *ILN* (13 Feb 1864)

Wealth at death under £160,000: resworn probate, June 1868, *CGPLA Eng. & Wales*

Howard, Gorges Edmond (1715–1786), writer and lawyer, the son of Francis Howard, a captain of dragoons, and his wife, Elizabeth Jackson, was born at Coleraine, co. Londonderry, on 28 August 1715. Howard was educated at the Dublin school of Thomas Sheridan, the most famous in Ireland at the time, and apparently entered Trinity College, Dublin. His name is not included, however, in surviving lists of matriculands or graduates, suggesting that any stay there was brief. Howard himself admitted that depressed circumstances frustrated his hopes of being elected to a fellowship. Instead he was obliged to take an apprenticeship with an attorney practising in the Dublin exchequer court. This calling he exchanged briefly for that of a soldier in General Otway's foot regiment. But within a year Howard had returned to the trade of attorney, in which he flourished. Thanks in part to connections acquired through marriage into the office-holding dynasty of Parry, he secured agencies and briefs from the landed in Ireland. He also received official preferment. In 1743 Howard was appointed solicitor for the king's rents in Ireland. He also held an established post in the quit rent office. Soon he was legal counsel for the revenue commission in Dublin, registrar to the trustees for the creditors of the failed Burton's Bank, and registrar and treasurer of an act (which he had helped to promote) to improve thoroughfares in central Dublin. Howard's familiarity with the legal side of the revenue system led him to write twelve voluminous treatises on the functioning and faults of the exchequer and revenue service and the law courts. In these works he also pressed for the reform of his own trade of attorney, particularly by controlling entry more strictly and so reducing numbers. His strictures did not stop him being chosen as president of the Society of Attorneys in Dublin. His growing familiarity with the jurisdiction of the court of chancery resulted in manuals which would guide novices through its arcane processes.

Howard's expertise and experience secured him a profitable practice which by 1765, when he retired, he valued at £1600 p.a. They also commended him to successive Irish administrations. During the political crisis in 1753 over how the surplus revenue should be spent, he wrote *A Short Account*. Seen as a defence of a beleaguered court, it led its author to be dubbed 'a mercenary court scribbler' (Howard, 1.xxxiii). Aggrieved MPs identified Howard closely with the unpopular vice-regal regime and blocked a proposed salary increase of £300. However, his usefulness to successive lords lieutenant, and his willingness to support them, eventually earned greater rewards. After 1772 Lord Harcourt made him solicitor for the revenue of Ireland, reckoned to be worth a yearly £1200.

Howard, as well as supporting the English administration in Ireland, promoted the physical improvement of the city of Dublin. These services led to his being made free of the senior Dublin guild of merchants in 1766. In the controversies in the corporation of Dublin over whether or not to reinstate a wider and participatory franchise, he backed municipal oligarchy and regretted the growth of populism. He was also involved in several collective enterprises for material and moral improvement. In 1766 he became a member of the Dublin Society. In addition he pressed for statutory relief of the Irish Catholics, particularly to allow them to take leases on lands for longer than thirty-one years. However, the bill for this purpose, which he had drafted in 1761, was suppressed in England. In the same cause he collected and published legal cases relating to the property rights of the Catholic community. Grateful Catholics presented him with a silver epergne inscribed 'for his candour and humanity in endeavouring to obtain a relaxation of the Popery laws' (Howard, 1.lii).

Howard, notwithstanding his professional standing and secure income, aspired to something more. He harboured higher literary ambitions. Since youth he had written verse and plays. The former ploddingly celebrated his contemporaries. The latter included *The Siege of Tamor*, which celebrated early Irish resistance to Danish invaders. A similar theme of true liberty challenged but preserved animated *Almeyda*. Neither succeeded, although he entreated his acquaintance Edmund Burke to help have them staged. Burke apparently shared the generally low opinion of their merits, and failed to respond to the Irish patriotism of *The Siege of Tamor*. Howard's persistence made him the butt of Dublin satirists. One, Robert Jephson, published a collection of spurious letters purportedly written by the earnest Howard. Even Howard's *Collection of Apothegms and Maxims for the Good Conduct of Life*, published in Dublin in 1767, proved ponderous rather than pithy or witty. Although he had hoped to achieve lasting fame for his literary inventions, which also included *The Life of Man*, Howard's enduring legacy is in his detailed analyses of law, revenue, and administrative practice in mid-eighteenth-century Ireland. Howard died in Dublin in June 1786.   TOBY BARNARD

Sources G. E. Howard, *The miscellaneous works, in verse and prose*, 3 vols. (1782) · establishment book of Irish revenue, 1747, PRO, CUST 20/115 · F. P. Lock, *Edmund Burke*, 1 (1998) · W. N. Osborough, 'Catholics, land and the popery acts of Anne', *Endurance and emergence: Catholics in Ireland in the eighteenth century*, ed. T. Power and K. Whelan (1990) · minute books, Royal Dublin Society
Archives Sheff. Arch., letters to Edmund Burke
Likenesses line engraving (aged sixty-three), BM, NPG · line engraving, satirical sketch (*Candid appeal by G. E. Howard*), BM
Wealth at death £60,000: D. E. Baker, *Biographia dramatica, or, A companion to the playhouse*, rev. J. Reed, new edn, rev. S. Jones, 3 vols. in 4 (1812)

Howard [née Hobart; *other married name* Berkeley], **Henrietta, countess of Suffolk** (*c*.1688–1767), mistress of George II and architectural patron, was the third daughter of Sir Henry Hobart, fourth baronet (1657/8–1698), of Blickling, Norfolk, and his wife, Elizabeth (*d*. 1701), the daughter and coheir of Joseph Maynard of Clifton Reynes, Buckinghamshire. John *Hobart, later first earl of Buckinghamshire (1693–1756), was her younger brother. Following the death of her mother her upbringing, and that of her sisters, was entrusted to her step-great-grandmother Mary, *née* Upton, the widow of Sir John Maynard (1604–1690) and the second wife of Henry Howard, fifth earl of Suffolk. All the Hobart children had inherited part of Sir John Maynard's wealth, although his complex will was the subject of litigation in chancery. None the less, Henrietta displayed finances that were sufficiently sound to attract Charles Howard (1675–1733), Lord Suffolk's third son from his first marriage, a captain in Lord Cutts's regiment of dragoons. They married on 2 March 1706 at St Benet Paul's Wharf, London.

A few days before her marriage Henrietta protected her fortune, the value of which was unknown to her but estimated at £6000, by placing £4000 in trust with her uncle John Hobart and Dr James Wellwood, thereby guaranteeing a small income for her personal use. This precaution proved necessary. In June 1706 Howard sold his commission for £700, and a cycle began which Mrs Howard, bred to expect more from the life of a gentlewoman, found excessively degrading. After a year of marriage she gave birth to a son, Henry, on 1 January 1707, but the couple increasingly lived apart, Mrs Howard in Berkshire while her husband stayed in London, until bailiffs seized their property and they were forced to move in with Lord Suffolk. Suffolk expelled his son and daughter-in-law when Howard was unable to pay their board, and the couple then lived in lodgings in St Martin's Street, London, under the name of Smith. Howard was frequently absent for long periods, and when with his wife subjected her to physical and verbal abuse. Mrs Howard's attempts to

Henrietta Howard, countess of Suffolk (*c*.1688–1767), attrib. Charles Jervas

restore their fortunes involved negotiations with her husband's creditors in the City, pawning her few valuables, and selling her hair. What money she raised was usually spent by Howard, until, probably in 1713, she retained enough for them to travel to Hanover and seek favour in the electoral court. Mrs Howard won the approval of the dowager electress Sophia and probably also of the electoral princess Caroline. Following the accession of Sophia's son as George I of Great Britain on 1 August 1714, Mrs Howard returned to London with the royal party, and about 26 October 1714 was appointed woman of the bedchamber to Caroline, by then princess of Wales. Her husband became a groom of the bedchamber to George I, placing them in separate households, although they shared apartments in St James's Palace.

Mrs Howard enjoyed the social and intellectual opportunities of the princess's circle, where she befriended Alexander Pope, John Gay, John Arbuthnot, and Jonathan Swift, among others, but she continued to be harassed by her husband, who wished to borrow money from the princess's courtiers. In a memorandum of 29 August 1716 she reasoned with herself that her husband's brutality and neglect meant that he had invalidated the marriage contract, and so 'I must believe I am free' (BL, Add. MS 22627, fol. 13), but that social conventions would make it difficult for her to leave him. In November 1717, however, George I expelled the prince and princess of Wales from St James's Palace, and Mrs Howard followed them to their new home at Leicester House. She was then told by Charles Howard that he no longer considered her his wife. He retained control of their son.

It was probably soon after this that Mrs Howard became the mistress of the prince of Wales, afterwards *George II (1683–1760). The nature of their relationship was such that Lord Hervey later wrote that many courtiers doubted George II 'ever having entered into any commerce with her, that he might not innocently have had with his daughter' (Hervey, 1.41), but Hervey confirmed that the two did have a sexual relationship, with the support of Caroline, who knew that Mrs Howard's advice would

never be preferred over her own. None the less she was taken up by the brothers John Campbell, second duke of Argyll, and Archibald Campbell, earl of Ilay, in the belief that she would have influence with the prince. On their advice she invested in the Mississippi scheme promoted on the Paris stock exchange by John Law, and may well have lost money. In 1723 the prince settled £11,500 worth of South Sea stock on her, with Argyll, Ilay, and Robert Britiffe, a lawyer whose sister was the wife of Mrs Howard's brother Sir John Hobart, as her trustees.

Her financial settlement allowed Mrs Howard to express her interest in architecture and develop an identity separate from her husband and from the prince and princess of Wales. John Gay found a plan of a projected house in her apartments at Richmond in July 1723. Through Lord Ilay, she bought 25½ acres along the River Thames at Twickenham in 1724, which became the setting for her Palladian villa, Marble Hill House. The first design for the house may have been by Colen Campbell, to whose third volume of *Vitruvius Britannicus* Mrs Howard was a subscriber, but it was Roger Morris who was contracted to build the house in June 1724; he was probably advised on design by Henry, Lord Herbert, later ninth earl of Pembroke. Pope and Allen, Lord Bathurst, contributed to the design of the gardens, but they were principally realized by Charles Bridgeman. The house was not finished until 1728 or 1729, and during 1727 work seems to have stopped altogether. This may have been because Charles Howard, encouraged by George I, was attempting a reconciliation with Mrs Howard which would have entailed her departure from the princess's service and her retirement to the country; the king probably saw her as one of the ties that connected the prince of Wales to the opposition. For several weeks in spring 1727 she lived in fear of kidnapping after Howard procured a warrant for her arrest. The death of George I in June 1727 made Mrs Howard's position safer, and her husband was bought off by an annuity of £1200, paid by Mrs Howard but largely provided by the new king. For the 1727 coronation she managed Queen Caroline's clothes and jewellery, and later reminisced to Horace Walpole of her economy. The document effecting her separation from her husband was signed on 29 February 1728.

Jonathan Swift had assumed in verse and in correspondence that Mrs Howard would abandon Marble Hill on the accession of George II, but she did not relish her place as a servant to Queen Caroline, where her labours both physical and social were aggravated by her deafness. Her husband became ninth earl of Suffolk in 1731, and consequently she became of too high a rank to continue as a woman of the bedchamber. Her new office, mistress of the robes, left her with a reduced obligation to the queen, but with a higher salary, which relieved her of the apprehension that she would have to sell Marble Hill and allowed her to spend more time there. She continued to attend court and maintained her relationship with the king, although George II 'seemed to look upon a mistress rather as a necessary appurtenance to his grandeur as a prince than an addition to his pleasures as a man' (Hervey,

1.42), and, to the disappointment of her admirers, her political influence with the king was minimal. Marble Hill allowed her to entertain friends such as Pope and Gay who were unsympathetic towards the court, although her unwillingness to break with the king and queen alienated Swift, whose attempts to gain royal patronage for himself and for Mary Barber through Lady Suffolk had not been as successful as he had wished. Other regular visitors included the opposition politician George *Berkeley (1693?–1746) and Charles Mordaunt, third earl of Peterborough, with whom for several years she conducted a written discussion on love, although she seems to have kept their affair a theoretical one.

Lady Suffolk shared the interest in rational religion of her fellow courtier Mary, Lady Hervey. Peterborough hailed Lady Suffolk in verse as 'O wonderful creature! a woman of reason!' (*Letters to and from Henrietta*, 1.xlvii), paying tribute to her as a woman who could make her own way in a man's world. The praise that Peterborough and her literary friends heaped upon her went unappreciated by George II, who was annoyed by 'her constant opposition to all his measures' and 'her wearying him with her perpetual contradiction' (Hervey, 2.382). The end of their relationship came in 1734. His visits to her, which had once been nightly, became less regular, and in October, after she returned from a six-week visit to Bath, the king ignored her. In November she resigned from her position as mistress of the robes following a difficult interview with the queen, who accused her of overreacting to the king's behaviour and of surrendering to manipulation by opposition politicians. Gossips speculated that she had departed for political reasons—she was often in the company of the opposition whig Richard Temple, first Viscount Cobham, and it was rumoured, incorrectly, that she was having an affair with Henry St John, first Viscount Bolingbroke—but the main cause was that the king had found her less attractive with age, reportedly describing her as 'an old, dull, deaf, peevish beast' (Hervey, 2.600–01). Pope lamented her resignation as the end of the intellectual court that had gathered around Caroline when princess of Wales.

The earl of Suffolk had died on 28 September 1733, so Lady Suffolk's hard-won liberty was no longer under threat. She married George Berkeley at Cranford, Middlesex, on 26 June 1735, and, aside from visits to friends and continental Europe, the two divided their time between Marble Hill and her new town house at 15 Savile Row, where she commissioned Morris, advised by Pembroke, to model the external features. Assisted by Berkeley, with whom she enjoyed a close and emotionally satisfying relationship until his death on 29 October 1746, she continued to extend the Marble Hill estate and make changes to the house, including the construction of a cottage where her extensive porcelain collection could be displayed. She bought paintings for the house, but they were not many and dominated by architectural studies. She continued to keep up with changes in taste, and employed Matthew Brettingham the elder to make alterations to Marble Hill in 1750–51. It has been argued that she was the first woman significantly to encroach 'upon the gentlemanly pursuits of a connoisseur' (Bryant, 6). She had little contact with her son, Henry, tenth earl of Suffolk, who died childless in 1745, but took a large share of the responsibility for the upbringing of John and Dorothy Hobart, her brother's children from his first marriage. John *Hobart, who became second earl of Buckinghamshire in 1756, sought her advice on matters ranging from the design of a fireplace to how to conduct himself at court; she took part in the management of his domestic political interests following his appointment as ambassador to Russia in 1762, and represented his private concerns about the posting to the ministry.

In later life Lady Suffolk was befriended by Horace Walpole, who shared her interest in architecture and contributed towards the Gothic farm at Marble Hill, called the priory of St Hubert, whose chief designer was Richard Bentley; according to Walpole, two of the towers were designed by Lady Suffolk herself. Walpole made notes of their conversations for their anecdotes and for their information on the politics of his youth. Her closest male friend in her later years was probably William Chetwynd, third Viscount Chetwynd, who was with her when she died at Marble Hill on 26 July 1767. According to Walpole, her later years had seen a struggle to keep out of debt, which she had hidden from most of her friends. She left Marble Hill to her nephew Lord Buckinghamshire, a legacy of £500 to a goddaughter, and also a few small legacies, but the bulk of her estate passed to her great-niece Henrietta Gertrude Hotham (1753–1816), the daughter of her niece Lady Dorothy Hobart, who had married Charles Hotham, elder brother of William, first Baron Hotham. Henrietta Hotham had lived with Lady Suffolk for several years, and inherited Marble Hill in 1793. The estate was sold by the Hobart family in 1824, and in 1902 was bought by London county council to save it from development. The council opened the house and grounds to the public in 1903; the house was restored to a close approximation of its appearance in Lady Suffolk's day in 1965–6, and passed into the care of English Heritage in 1986.

MATTHEW KILBURN

Sources M. P. G. Draper and W. A. Eden, *Marble Hill House and its owners* (1970) · 'Original letters written by various persons of distinction to Henrietta Hobart, countess of Suffolk', BL, Add. MSS 22625–22629 · J. Bryant, *Mrs Howard: a woman of reason* (1988) [exhibition catalogue, Marble Hill House, 14 June 1988–30 September 1988] · John, Lord Hervey, *Some materials towards memoirs of the reign of King George II*, ed. R. Sedgwick, 3 vols. (1931) · *Letters to and from Henrietta, countess of Suffolk, and her second husband the Hon. George Berkeley, from 1712 to 1767*, ed. J. W. Croker, 2 vols. (1824) · Walpole, *Corr.* · *Reminiscences written by Mr Horace Walpole in 1788*, ed. P. Toynbee (1924) · *Report on the manuscripts of the marquess of Lothian*, HMC, 62 (1905) · *The correspondence of Alexander Pope*, ed. G. Sherburn, 5 vols. (1956) · *The correspondence of Jonathan Swift*, ed. H. Williams, 5 vols. (1963–5) · *Manuscripts of the earl of Egmont: diary of Viscount Percival, afterwards first earl of Egmont*, 3 vols., HMC, 63 (1920–23) · *The manuscripts of J. B. Fortescue*, 10 vols., HMC, 30 (1892–1927), vol. 1 · *The manuscripts of the House of Lords*, new ser., 12 vols. (1900–77), vol. 8, pp. 363–4 · GEC, *Peerage*, new edn, 11.473–5 · *IGI*

Archives BL, corresp. and papers, Add. MSS 22625–22629 · Hunt. L., corresp. | Norfolk RO, Kerr MSS, accounts and papers

Likenesses attrib. M. Dahl, oils, c.1715–1725, Blickling Hall, Norfolk · portraits, c.1724–c.1820, repro. in Bryant, *Mrs Howard* · T. Gibson, oils, c.1730, Blickling Hall, Norfolk · B. Lens, gouache on ivory, c.1730, priv. coll. · C. Philips, group portrait, oils, 1730 (*A tea party at Lord Harrington's house*), Yale U. CBA · C. Philips, oils, c.1735, priv. coll. · J. Heath, stipple, pubd 1798, BM, NPG; repro. in *Works of Lord Orford* (1798) · stipple, pubd 1824 (after M. Dahl), BM, NPG · J. Faber junior, mezzotint (after J. Peters), NPG · G. P. Harding, watercolour and pencil drawing (after C. Jervas), Marble Hill House, London · J. Harris, engraving (after T. Gibson, c.1820), NPG; repro. in *Letters*, ed. Croker, frontispiece · attrib. C. Jervas, oils, priv. coll. [*see illus.*]

Wealth at death est. maximum £20,000: *DNB*; will, PRO, PROB 11/933, sig. 390

Howard, Henry, styled earl of Surrey (1516/17–1547), poet and soldier, was born in 1516 or 1517, the eldest son of Lord Thomas *Howard, third duke of Norfolk (1473–1554), and his second wife, Elizabeth Stafford (d. 1558). He was the grandson of the second duke of Norfolk, victor of the battle of Flodden, and of Edward Stafford, third duke of Buckingham, who was executed for treason in 1521. For part of his early childhood Henry Howard lived in Ireland, where his father was sent as lord lieutenant in 1520–21. Upon the death of his Howard grandfather in 1524 Lord Henry Howard, who was never a peer, became known as the earl of Surrey. During his boyhood the Howard household moved between the family mansions at Lambeth and Tendring Hall in Stoke by Nayland, Suffolk, in the summers and Hunsdon in Hertfordshire for the winters. In 1526–7 the household was living at the ducal castle at Framlingham, Suffolk. By 1529, when the duke visited Butley Priory with his son, Henry Howard had a personal retinue of twenty-four men.

Early service at court Educated in the humanist schoolroom by tutors whose names are unknown, Surrey was trained to that virtue consisting in action and public service which humanists taught was true nobility. In December 1529 the duke of Norfolk showed the imperial ambassador a letter which his son had written in elegant Latin, and delighted that he had made a good start in virtue. Then, or later, the earl learned modern languages as well as Latin. In March 1543 John Clerke, dedicating his translation from French of the narrative *Lamant mal traicte de samye* to the earl, praised him for his great efforts in translating from Latin and Italian as well as from Spanish and French. The earl was trained also in the skills and ideals of chivalry and, so his father planned, was ready to become tutor and guide to King Henry VIII's illegitimate son Henry Fitzroy, duke of Richmond, and thereby to hold influence close to the throne. Surrey became companion to Richmond, and later remembered poetically the years 1530–32 spent 'with a kinges soon' at Windsor 'in greater feast then Priams sonnes of Troye', a world of chivalry and unclouded, equal friendship (*Howard: Poems*, 27, ll. 3–4). At the end of 1529 the duke of Norfolk was envisaging a marriage between Surrey and Princess Mary, a match which Anne Boleyn, Surrey's first cousin, at first advanced but soon turned against. In February 1532 Norfolk suddenly contracted Surrey in marriage to Lady Frances de Vere (d. 1577), daughter of the fifteenth earl of Oxford. They were formally married in the spring of 1533, although neither

Henry Howard, earl of Surrey (1516/17–1547), by unknown artist, c.1546

was yet old enough to cohabit. It may have been upon the occasion of his marriage that Surrey sat to Hans Holbein for the first of five portraits. In this portrait drawing Holbein recorded a striking asymmetry in the earl's features and a cast in his right eye.

In October 1532 Surrey, with Richmond, accompanied Henry VIII and Anne Boleyn to Calais for their meeting with François I of France. Among the entourage was Sir Thomas Wyatt, Surrey's poetical mentor. Surrey attended upon Henry to Boulogne. Richmond and Surrey stayed behind in France as pledges for the treaty, in the entourage of the dauphin and his brothers. The spring of 1533 they spent at Fontainebleau. The poets whom Surrey met there, and the works of art of the French and Italian Renaissance which he encountered, were crucial in the making of the poet earl. In the summer of 1533 Surrey and Richmond travelled south to Provence with the French king, visiting Avignon. In September they returned to Calais, to England, and to separate lives. Richmond married Lady Mary Howard, Surrey's sister, in November 1533, and Surrey went to live with his wife. The Howard alliances with the royal family were prodigious and dangerous. In May 1536 Surrey deputized for his father, the earl marshal, at the trials of his first cousins Queen Anne and Viscount Rochford. Two months later Lord Thomas Howard, his half-uncle, was sent to the Tower for the *lèse-majesté* of contracting a clandestine marriage with the king's niece, Lady Margaret Douglas, and there he died in 1537. In July 1536 the death of Richmond left Surrey isolated in his princely eminence. He was distraught and undermined for much of the following year.

The outbreak of the Lincolnshire rising in October 1536 gave Surrey his first military command. In the crisis of rebellion, the Howards were given conflicting orders; initially, Norfolk was commanded to remain to secure East

Anglia while Surrey was sent north with as many horse as he could raise; but on 11 October the duke, now appointed marshal of the army, was begging that Surrey be allowed to accompany him. On 15 October Surrey, who was at Cambridge mustering Howard forces out of Norfolk and Suffolk, received and disregarded the council's orders to stay his troops. During the Pilgrimage of Grace Norfolk's policy of conciliation rather than engagement with the vastly superior rebel force raised suspicions concerning the Howards' allegiance. In February 1537 a Norfolk fiddler sang a ballad about the rising which questioned the earl's loyalties, and claimed that he had sung it before Surrey at Cambridge and Thetford Abbey. Surrey returned south, but in the spring of 1537 rejoined his father, who had returned to the north as lieutenant. In May Norfolk denied rumours that he had summoned Surrey, without the king's knowledge, in order to train him to serve as his deputy.

In the Tower between April and June 1537, Lord Darcy sought to incriminate Surrey as a sympathizer of the pilgrim cause. The earl was in Kenninghall in early July with his countess, suffering the kind of physical and mental collapse that afflicted him in time of crisis. At court in late July or early August he fought an accuser, whose identity and charges are now unknown, perhaps to defend himself and his family honour against the accusations of disloyalty. Instead of the penalty of the loss of a hand—an unbearable loss for a soldier—Surrey was sent to live confined at Windsor Castle. In Surrey's sonnet 'When Windesor walles' and in his elegy 'So crewell prison' the speakers attest from a real time and place to the suicidal despair of remembering happy in unhappy times, and lament the loss of 'fredome', in the double sense of blood nobility and lack of constraint:

Thus I alone, where all my fredome grew,
In pryson pyne with bondage and restraynt.
(*Howard: Poems*, 27, ll. 51-2)

The poet mourned his friend Richmond—'wher is my noble fere'—and their 'rakhell [unconsidered] life' (ibid., 27, l. 46; 26, l. 8). It was in custody at Windsor, so his sister recalled, that Surrey's resentment grew against the new men at court whom he saw as inimical to the old nobility. Thereafter he assumed the role of guardian of honour and defender of true nobility, and began to be notorious for the extremity of his pride. By November 1537 he was restored to primacy at court, and was a principal mourner in the funeral procession of Jane Seymour. Yet he was ambivalent about service at court and daily waiting there. The speaker in his poem 'To dearely had I bought my grene and youthfull yeres' avoided the court: 'And seldom though I come in court among the rest' (ibid., 18, l. 3).

From the late 1530s Surrey was given offices in East Anglia: in 1538 he was appointed commissioner of sewers in Norfolk, and in 1539 made steward for the duchy of Lancaster's lands in Norfolk, Suffolk, and Cambridgeshire. In 1539 he was employed to organize the defence of Norfolk against threatened invasion. Early in that year there was talk of sending Surrey into Cleves to assist in arranging

the marriage treaty between Henry VIII and Anne of Cleves. At the May day tournament in 1540 he rode as Queen Anne's chief defender. On St George's day 1541 the earl was elected knight of the Order of the Garter, and in May he was installed at St George's Chapel, Windsor. This was the culmination of honour, but the Howards were again endangered by their royal alliances and by their hostility to the new families at court whom they perceived as a threat. In December 1541 Surrey attended the trial of his cousin Queen Katherine Howard and witnessed her execution in February 1542. In his beast fable 'Eache beast can chuse his feere' he lamented the tragedies which had befallen the Howards, and he fictionalized his ambivalent friendship with the Seymours. The white lion (the Howard heraldic lion, argent) reproaches the white wolf (the Stanhope heraldic wolf: Anne, Viscountess Beauchamp) for her public refusal to dance with him. Surrey parodied his own famous pride through the prancing of the lion, but there was deadly seriousness in his contrast between the nobility of the lion and the viciousness of the wolf. The lion vowed revenge:

I shall be glad to feede on that
that wold have fed on me.
(Hughey, 1.78, l. 68)

Surrey inhabited a range of voices in his poetry—of the Petrarchan lover, of neo-classical restraint, of the avenging prophet—and the predicaments of his speakers often seemed to be his own. Real people and places spurred his poetic invention. His verse, which revealed his own preoccupations and ventured upon matters where, after the Treason Act of 1534, it was only safe to be silent, circulated in manuscript in court circles where the beliefs of the earl were matters of concern and controversy. It is in his poetry that his religious beliefs are clearest. Although Surrey had been brought up in the traditional religion, in the household of his father who was a leading opponent of the 'new learning', at some point and through some agency unknown, he abandoned his father's faith. Early in 1539 there were hopes among evangelicals that the earl would be firmly won to their faith, and in October–December he dined fifteen times at Beauchamplace, the household of Edward Seymour, Viscount Beauchamp, and his wife, where an evangelical coterie gathered. Sir Thomas Wyatt addressed the proem to his paraphrase of Psalm 37 to 'Mine Earl', apparently meaning Surrey. This psalm, with its theme of the prosperity of the wicked and ambitious, may have had a special appeal to Surrey, whose coruscating hatred of 'th'outrageous' and their 'blind prosperity' recurs in his own biblical paraphrases and in his later actions (*Sir Thomas Wyatt: the Complete Poems*, poems CCLXVI–CCLXVII). That dedication was not unrequited. Shortly after Wyatt's death in October 1542 Surrey published (although anonymously) an elegy which celebrated the virtues of the disgraced poet, and declared his loss in ways which were evangelical and prophetic. This was a remarkable tribute by a noble to a commoner and to the life of poetry. Surrey's commemoration of Wyatt's psalm paraphrases as 'witnesse of faith that never shall be ded' (*Howard: Poems*, 28, l. 35) was testimony not only to Wyatt's evangelical faith but also to his own. In the sonnet 'The Great Macedon' Surrey again venerated Wyatt, but also dared to warn that his psalms hold up a 'myrrour clere' where rulers may see 'The bitter frewte of false concupiscense' and the consequences of their tyranny for the whole people (ibid., 31).

In July 1542 Surrey was imprisoned in the Fleet, ostensibly for challenging John à Leigh to a duel. He admitted his youthful recklessness and promised amendment. But the offence concerned more than the challenge to revenge his own quarrel, for he wrote four years later of being charged with matters concerning his allegiance, and of his narrow escape then despite his innocence. What the charge of disloyalty was is unknown, but à Leigh had been charged with treasonable association with Cardinal Pole. Later Edmund Knyvet, Surrey's first cousin, accused him of retaining a servant who had been in Italy with Pole, and of keeping Pasquil, an Italian who was reputedly a spy, as a jester. Surrey's fascination with Italy, which he never visited, was political as well as artistic. On 7 August he was released on sureties, and he accompanied his father on the expedition into Scotland in October 1542. There he watched the burning of Kelso.

In the winter of 1542–3 Surrey, returned from the wars in Scotland, was lodging in the house of Mistress Millicent Arundell in St Lawrence Jewry in London, and there he with his friends and dependants provocatively broke the Lenten fast. About Candlemas, 2 February, the traditional time for misrule, Surrey, with Sir Thomas Wyatt the younger, William Pickering, and their friends and servants ran wild through the city, breaking the windows of churches and grand city houses with their stone bows, and throwing stones at the whores of the Bankside stews. Surrey was at first repentant, but from the Fleet he wrote in outraged self-defence an oration, 'London, hast thow accused me' (*Howard: Poems*, 33), a satire which was later revived as evidence against him. The night of misrule he justified as a warning to the citizens of London, sunk in their seven deadly sins, in idolatry and spiritual blindness, of their impending doom. It was Surrey himself who appeared as the righteous reformer—'wrested to wrathe in fervent zeale' (ibid., 33, l. 48)—and the agent of divine wrath. Through this prophetic persona he mockingly presented his vandalism as the inscrutable warning to a corrupt and heedless society. The evangelical campaign against London's vice that spring may have incited the challenge from Surrey and his friends. Surrey wrote often of 'reckless youth' and the 'rakhell [unconsidered] life'; reckless and 'rakhell' in the double sense of imprudent and careless of his own danger or of public opinion. Prudence did not always accord with his honour.

Military command In October 1543 Henry VIII sent Surrey to aid Emperor Charles in his campaign in northern France, hoping that he would acquire the experience in war which would make him the true heir of his ancestors. On 4 October Surrey joined the English forces at the siege of Landrecy. Upon Surrey's taking leave in November, the emperor sent a letter praising his noble heart and his talents. Later there were rumours that Surrey was 'the Emperor's man', and that at Landrecy he had 'entered into intelligence with divers great captains' (Thomas, 73–4). Surrey returned to England, and was present at the chapter of the Order of the Garter at Hampton Court on Christmas eve, and again on St George's day 1544 at Greenwich. On the visit of the duke of Najera, Charles V's emissary, in February 1544 Surrey was his guide, and at the end of May he was sent with a large retinue to meet the duke of Albuquerque. About this time he was created cupbearer to the king.

In June 1544 Surrey was appointed marshal of the army sent to capture Montreuil. He carried news to the king at the English camp at Boulogne and there witnessed the city's fall on 11 September. On 19 September he was wounded during a failed attempt to storm Montreuil. At the town gate, believing himself to be dying, he entrusted his will to his squire, Thomas Clere, but it was Clere who received the wound or contracted the illness which killed him six months later. To Clere Surrey addressed an elegy, adapted from a Virgilian epitaph, identifying Clere with the Howard family and celebrating their companionship in arms. Surrey recovered from his own injury sufficiently to attend a council of war on 26 September and to evacuate the retreating army to Calais. He attended the St George's day chapter of the Order of the Garter at St James's, but was rarely at court that spring. Then, and earlier, he was building, at ruinous expense, Surrey House at Mount Surrey, a mansion in a commanding position on a hill outside Norwich. In mid-July 1545 the earl was in attendance upon the king as he inspected his navy in the Solent for its readiness against a French invasion. On 21 July Surrey went as emissary to Lord Admiral Dudley aboard the *Harry Grace à Dieu* to learn his thinking concerning an attack upon the French fleet. That summer he was sent to command the vanguard of the army to defend Boulogne. By 9 August 1545 he had marshalled 5000 men, and on 15 August he sailed to Calais to gather a further 3000. In early September he was appointed lieutenant-general of the king on sea and land for all England's continental possessions.

Through the autumn and winter of 1545 Surrey encouraged the king in his desire for further conquest in France, against the prudential advice of the privy council which urged the ceding of Boulogne. Norfolk wrote on 27 September, warning his son not to persuade the king unduly to defend Boulogne, and by early November was so fearful of the financial ruin of the realm that he believed that Surrey should be removed from command. News of the earl's reckless chivalry reached Henry VIII, who was angered by the risks he took. But by December 1545 Surrey's general strategy of preventing the reinforcement of the French fortress of Chatillon, which threatened the harbour of Boulogne and the supply of the English garrison, was working. On 4 December French troops were ambushed, and on 7 December the English thwarted an attempt to supply Chatillon and laid plans for its capture. However, on 7 January 1546 at St Étienne Surrey suffered an ignominious and portentous defeat. The best and bravest captains were killed, and the unpaid, underfed, mutinous troops fled downhill, disobeying the earl's orders for them to turn and fight. Dishonoured, Surrey called upon Sir John Bridges to help him fall upon his sword. After this defeat Surrey lost in reputation, and was convinced that the king had withdrawn his favour. Later it was alleged that he had had the opportunity to capture Hardelot Castle but had neglected it. 'Amiddes the hylles in base Bullayn', he grew depressed and disaffected and, as he wrote in a sonnet reminiscent of one of Wyatt's, 'restlesse to remayn' (*Howard: Poems*, 10, ll. 12–13). His command failing, his personal debts mounting as he expended money which would not be recompensed, his request for his wife and family to join him denied, he believed that the French campaign would overwhelm him.

From Boulogne, it seems, Surrey wrote two poems in female voice, transposing his own characteristic sense of isolation and abandonment into lamentations by women parted from their lovers. He explored the 'wofull plight, and sorowes great' of his wife separated from her 'lord and love', dreaming of his return (*Howard: Poems*, 24, ll. 8–9) and, in 'O happy dames', the thoughts of a woman waiting for her lover to come across the sea: 'Lo, what a mariner love hath made me!' (ibid., 23, l. 28). By the time of this separation Surrey and his countess had four children: Thomas *Howard, future duke of Norfolk, who was born on 10 March 1538, and for whom Surrey had his nativity cast; Jane, who married Charles Neville, earl of Westmorland; Henry *Howard, later earl of Northampton; and Catherine, who married Henry, Lord Berkeley. These children had as their tutor at Kenninghall the Dutch humanist Hadrianus Junius. A fifth child, Margaret, who married Henry, Lord Scrope of Bolton, was born after her father's death. It was perhaps to his first son that Surrey addressed his translation of Horace *Odes*, ii.10, 'Of thy lyfe, Thomas', urging the golden mean which Surrey himself sought but often failed to follow (ibid., 39).

On 19 February 1546 Sir William Paget sent Surrey the news that the earl of Hertford would replace him as lieutenant-general, and with it advice that he should demote himself to some 'place of honour' where he might restore his reputation. A week later Surrey was named captain of the rearward. On 21 March the privy council summoned him home for, ominously, the king had received reports of treachery, of irregularities and mismanagement regarding victuals and munitions. The earl left France, believing that he would return. He arrived at court on 27 March, when he had a cold reception and was denied access to the king. On 3 April the council of Boulogne was ordered to investigate Surrey's accounts, which he had left unsettled. Yet in recognition of his service in France he was granted the reversion and rent of the estates and buildings of Wymondham Priory, Norfolk.

Last months Returned to court after military disgrace, and under investigation for mismanagement, Surrey was isolated and vulnerable. It may have been then, as Henry VIII abandoned his imperial ambitions in France along with his noble commander, that Surrey wrote of Sardanapulus,

the standard exemplum of the vice of intemperance, and perhaps a figure of his own king, in his sonnet 'Th'Assyryans king' (*Howard: Poems*, 32). Contention surrounded the regency which would follow Henry VIII's death, and controversy about the Howards' part in it, first voiced in 1543, recurred. In a bitter dispute with Sir George Blage in the spring of 1546 Surrey insisted that the Howards had the strongest claim to control the protectorate, but Blage believed that their attachment to traditional religion disqualified them. Although Surrey had been suspected of Lutheranism, his evangelical friends now believed that he had reverted to the old faith. He knew that some suspected him for setting up an altar in Boulogne. In his paraphrase of Psalm 73, and in its prologue dedicated to Blage, the theme of faltering faith recurs, and Surrey writes of a crisis of faith engendered by despair (ibid., 49, 37). In the summer of 1546 the protestant martyr Anne Askew borrowed from Surrey's paraphrase of Ecclesiastes, chapter 3, for a ballad she wrote in Newgate, and followed him in inventing a figure of tyranny and persecution; 'a blody beast' enthroned, 'that drounke the giltles blode' (ibid., 45, l. 46).

Seeking political alliance to safeguard his family's position, in June 1546 Norfolk proposed marriages between the Howards and Seymours. But Surrey had turned against the earl of Hertford and his brother, Sir Thomas Seymour, and had a grander alliance planned for his sister. The earl, who had warned princes of 'the bitter frewte of false concupiscense' (*Howard: Poems*, 31, l. 11), suggested that she become the royal mistress and use her influence to advance her friends. At enmity with her brother, and appalled by his scheme, she related it to the earl's friends that August, and they distanced themselves from him. On 12 July John Dudley received a letter full of dark sayings from Surrey, and the privy council again censured the earl. On 21 August, at the reception of the admiral of France, Surrey was in attendance upon the king in the foremost rank: the last time that he was in public favour.

On 2 December 1546 Richard Southwell came forward with evidence against Surrey and challenged his fidelity. Surrey was arrested and held at Ely Place. Upon the promise of immunity two gentlemen revealed a conspiracy. On 12 December Surrey, long accustomed to riding with a retinue, was led on foot through the city streets to the Tower. Urgent searches for evidence against him were made in the Howard household at Kenninghall and elsewhere, and the earl and his intimates were interrogated. The questions concerned his determination for the rule of the prince; his procuring his sister to be the royal mistress; his slandering of the royal council; and his plans to flee the realm. On 15 and 16 December news was sent to English ambassadors abroad and to foreign ambassadors in London of the Howards' schemes to murder the council and take control of the prince. Yet none of these charges were brought against the earl.

On 31 December 1546 a commission was sent to inquire into treason in Norfolk; on 1 January 1547 a precept was issued to summon a grand jury to try the earl. That jury on

7 January found a true bill against Surrey under the Treason Act (28 Hen. VIII c.7, section 12); the sole charge, that he had on 7 October 1546 at Kenninghall displayed in his own heraldry the royal arms and insignia, with three labels silver, thereby threatening the king's title to the throne and the prince's inheritance. In August 1545 Surrey had consulted the Garter king of arms at Lambeth about his right to bear the arms of Brotherton and St Edward the Confessor and Anjou and Mowbray quartered, and insisted that he would bear them. Surrey's sister deposed that he had reassumed the arms of their attainted Stafford grandfather. The earl had claimed, so his servant deposed, that King Edward the Confessor gave the arms of England to his predecessors. A claim to an inheritance of the Saxon kings was a threat to the Tudor heirs of William the Conqueror. Surrey never denied bearing Edward the Confessor's arms, but claimed it—justly— as a hitherto unchallenged right, immemorially borne by his ancestors, the dukes of Norfolk. A painting in which he was portrayed leaning against a broken pillar formed part of the charges against the earl. Surrey was depicted thus, at the age of twenty-nine, in a remarkable portrait thought to be by G. Scrots or Stretes, painted in 1545 or 1546. The earl appears from under a grotesque archway, similar to those he had seen at François I's gallery at Fontainebleau, flanked by figures holding shields which bear the arms of Brotherton and of Thomas of Woodstock, both of which he was entitled to bear. Lord Chancellor Wriothesley, who composed the interrogatories and framed the charges against Surrey, knew the ineluctability of the heraldic charge: once the heralds had declared against Surrey there was no defence. Surrey never confessed. At his trial—before a common inquest, not peers— at the Guildhall on 13 January he pleaded not guilty and defended himself throughout a whole day. The records of the trial are now lost, but from evidence recorded by Lord Herbert of Cherbury it is clear that charges were brought and evidence given which concerned overt conspiracy as well as the usurpation of the royal arms.

In the Tower, Surrey understood the new political order. His paraphrases of Psalms 73, 88, and 55, the prayers of the psalmist abandoned and betrayed, thinking upon death and judgment, reflect his own predicament and seem to have been written during his last imprisonment. The paraphrases of Psalms 73 and 88 are prefaced by verse epistles to Sir George Blage and Sir Anthony Denny, leading figures in the group at court which held influence over the dying king. Surrey, who had written often of friendship, now saw his friends 'forced, for my greater greif, from me their face to hyde' (*Howard: Poems*, 48, l. 44). In Psalm 55, in a passage of invention, Surrey understood that 'It was a frendly foo … my guyde, that trapped me' (ibid., 50, ll. 22–3). He was destroyed by a league of former friends to whom he had confided his religious beliefs, his secrets, and his plans. Complicity with the Howards, who were too close to the throne, was dangerous. Promised indemnity or reward, Surrey's intimates—his sister, Richard Southwell, Edward Warner, Edmund Knyvet, Gawain Carew, Edward Rogers, and others—deposed against him.

In the psalm paraphrases Surrey again revealed his evangelical faith. On 19 January 1547 he went to the block at Tower Hill. His body was first buried at All Hallows Barking, but was moved to St Michael's Church, Framlingham, Suffolk, in 1614 by his son Henry, earl of Northampton.

The poet earl Surrey's motto, inscribed in his last portrait, was *Sat superest* ('Enough survives'). He sought in his chivalry, in royal service, in his self-depiction in his portraiture, in his building, and above all in his poetry, to make his life an image of his honour. In a passage of invention rather than translation in his paraphrase of Ecclesiastes, chapter 2, he wrote 'By princely acts thus strave I still to make my fame indure' (*Howard: Poems*, 44, l. 12). At some time and place unknown Surrey translated books 2 and 4 of Virgil's *Aeneid* and, in finding a verse form worthy of the elevated vision of classical epic, invented a vernacular form, without rhyme, which could emulate dactylic hexameter. English blank verse is Surrey's discovery. His translation may owe to the Italian translation of the *Aeneid* in *versi sciolti* (unrhymed decasyllables) by several authors, published in Venice from 1539, and is certainly influenced by Gawain Douglas's translation of 1513, but the creation of English heroic line is his own. The inspiration of Aeneas, left alone in blazing Troy, upon the earl who wrote in his last poem of

> that blood that hath so oft bene shed
> For Britannes sake
> (ibid., 38, ll. 16–17)

seems clear.

Surrey left a political and poetical legacy for those who recognized his great talent and promise while regretting, or doubting, his treason. Sir John Cheke pronounced an unnamed and disgraced contemporary poet, who can only have been Surrey, as 'worthie Chawcers mate' (Hughey, 1.282, l. 10). George Cavendish was the first of those who lamented the fall of:

> So noble a yong man
> of wyt and excellence … condempned
> for so small offence.
> (Cavendish, ll. 1194–5)

About 1554 Surrey's *Fourth Boke of Virgill*, one of the 'monumentes of that noble wyt of hys', was published by John Day for William Awen (*Surrey's Fourth Boke of Virgill*, ed. H. Hartman, 1933, 3). Richard Tottel published *Songes and Sonettes by the Ryght Honorable Lorde Henry Haward Late Earle of Surrey, and other* in 1557, especially commending the 'honorable stile of the noble earle of Surrey' (*Tottel's Miscellany*, 1.2). Thomas Sackville saluted Surrey's 'glistering fame' and 'his proud ryme that thunders in the aier' (*Complaint of Henrie Duke of Buckingham*, ed. M. Hearsey, 1936). Sir Philip Sidney found in Surrey's poetry 'manie thinges tasting of noble birth and worthy of a noble mind' (*A Defence of Poetry*, ed. J. van Dorsten, 1966, 64), and for William Camden Surrey's nobility of birth and mind were one. In 1589 George Puttenham saluted Surrey, with Thomas Wyatt, as the 'two chieftaines' of 'a new company of courtly makers' who, emulating Italian poets, were the 'first reformers of our English meetre and stile' (*The Arte of English Poesie*, in E. Arber, *English Reprints*, 1870, 74). By this time their works had reached far beyond the courtly audience for whom they were first written: circulating as broadside ballads, parodied, and bowdlerized as moralistic verse.

For all their popularity in their own century, the works of both poets entered into genteel obscurity in the next. Wyatt and Surrey were more closely associated after death than they had been in life; the one often judged at the expense of the other. By the early eighteenth century Surrey's reputation transcended Wyatt's, for in the neoclassical age his poetry was judged to show greater prosodic decorum. In *Windsor Forest* Alexander Pope praised 'noble *Surrey*', '*Surrey*, the *Granville* of a former Age'. Thomas Warton recognized Surrey's particular importance as 'the first English classical poet' (*History of English Poetry*, 1781, section xxxviii). A century of editorial neglect followed the Revd George Frederick Nott's great edition of Surrey's work of 1815, and in the twentieth century Wyatt's reputation eclipsed Surrey's. Surrey himself had venerated Wyatt as the master who 'taught what might be sayd in ryme' (*Howard: Poems*, 28, l. 13), but he himself was the first poet in English to explore what might be said without rhyme.   SUSAN BRIGDEN

Sources Henry Howard, earl of Surrey: poems, ed. E. Jones (1964) · The works of Henry Howard, earl of Surrey, and of Sir Thomas Wyatt the elder, ed. G. F. Nott, 2 vols. (1815) · Tottel's miscellany (1557–1587), ed. H. E. Rollins, 2 vols. (1966) · Sir Thomas Wyatt: the complete poems, ed. R. A. Rebholz (1975) · LP Henry VIII · State papers published under … Henry VIII, 11 vols. (1830–52) · APC, 1542–7 · CSP Spain · State trials, vol. 1 · Edward, Lord Herbert of Cherbury, The life and raigne of King Henry the Eighth (1649) · R. Hughey, ed., The Arundel Harington manuscript of Tudor poetry, 2 vols. (1960) · G. Cavendish, Metrical visions, ed. A. S. G. Edwards (1980) · W. Thomas, The pilgrim, ed. J. A. Froude (1861) · E. Bapst, Deux gentilshommes-poètes de la cour de Henry VIII (Paris, 1891) · S. Brigden, 'Henry Howard, earl of Surrey, and the "conjured league"', HJ, 37 (1994), 507–37 · E. Casady, Henry Howard, earl of Surrey (1938) · M. B. Davies, 'Surrey at Boulogne', Huntington Library Quarterly, 23 (1960) · S. M. Foley, 'The honorable style of Henry Howard, earl of Surrey: a critical reading of Surrey's poetry', PhD diss., Yale U., 1979 · O. B. Hardison, Prosody and purpose in the English Renaissance (1989) · H. A. Mason, Humanism and poetry in the early Tudor period (1959) · W. A. Sessions, Henry Howard, the poet earl of Surrey: a life (1999) · R. Zim, English metrical psalms: poetry as praise and prayer, 1535–1601 (1987)
Archives BL, Cotton MS Titus B ii · BL, Harley MSS 78, 283 · BL, Stowe MS 396 · Bodl. Oxf., MS Jesus 74 · PRO, SP 1
Likenesses Holbein or his school, chalk drawing, c.1540, Morgan L. · H. Holbein the younger, oils, c.1542, Museu de Arte de São Paulo, Brazil · oils, c.1546, NPG [see illus.] · E. Scriven, stipple, pubd 1817 (after painting attrib. H. Holbein the younger), BM, NPG · H. Holbein, three chalk drawings, Royal Collection · G. Scrots or Stretes, oils, NPG · oils (after type of, c.1546), Arundel Castle, West Sussex; versions, Knole, Kent

Howard, Henry, earl of Northampton (1540–1614), courtier, administrator, and author, was born on 24 February 1540 at Shottesham, Norfolk, the second son of Henry *Howard, styled earl of Surrey (1516/17–1547), poet and courtier, and his wife, Lady Frances de Vere (1517–1577), daughter of John de Vere, fifteenth earl of Oxford.

Education and early years In 1547 Surrey was attainted and executed for treason. His father, the third duke of Norfolk, escaped the block only by the death of Henry VIII the night before the scheduled execution, but remained in

Henry Howard, earl of Northampton (1540–1614), by Nicholas Stone, 1615

the Tower. After the catastrophic fall of the Howard family, Surrey's children (including Thomas *Howard, the future fourth duke) were placed in 1548 in the guardianship of their aunt, Mary, duchess of Richmond, who appointed John Foxe the martyrologist as their tutor. The distinguished humanist Hadrianus Junius also instructed the two boys. Later Henry Howard recalled that he had been brought up 'from a child' (*CSP dom.*, 1611–18, 214) in the lodge at Greenwich Park, which he regarded as his original home. After the accession of Mary I in 1553 he was placed as a page in the household of the staunch Marian Catholic John White, bishop of Lincoln and after 1556 of Winchester. He remained there until 1558. These adolescent years were probably crucial in forming his religious outlook, which accommodated inner commitment to the Roman Catholic church with a later acceptance of the need for outward conformity to the worship of the Church of England. In this he followed the pattern set by his grandfather Norfolk, a conservative who conformed under Henry VIII.

Howard was restored in blood on 8 May 1559, an act of parliament reversing the family's earlier attainder and disgrace. At Queen Elizabeth's expense he was educated at King's College, Cambridge, where he studied the classics and graduated MA in 1566; he also read civil law at Trinity Hall. He incorporated MA at Oxford in 1568, but remained at Cambridge as reader in rhetoric until at least 1569, the only nobleman to teach at either university in the Tudor and early Stuart periods.

In the agitation following Elizabeth's papal excommunication, Howard was arrested in 1571 under suspicion of involvement in his elder brother Norfolk's aspirations for the hand of Mary, queen of Scots. He returned to partial favour after his brother's execution in 1572 but remained linked to a group of Catholic gentlemen, several of them with French connections, who sought to advance the interests of the Scottish queen and improve the lot of English Catholics. He came under suspicion again in 1574 and 1581; in September 1583, suspected of involvement in the Throckmorton plot, he suffered miserable conditions of imprisonment in the Fleet prison, and in July 1585 he was confined to Sir Nicholas Bacon's house in Suffolk. In all he was arrested and imprisoned five times. By the 1580s he was in secret correspondence with the queen of Scots (who did not trust him with anything of importance) while between 1582 and 1584 the Spanish ambassador Mendoza paid him a substantial pension for regular information from Elizabeth's court. He attended the Chapel Royal but was widely regarded as a Catholic. He wrote regularly to Burghley protesting his fidelity, and after Mary's execution in 1587 made repeated entreaties to be allowed to offer some naval service against the expected Spanish invasion.

For most of the years after 1572 Howard depended on the hospitality of his nephews, and on a small annual allowance of £50 from his sister Catherine, Lady Berkeley. He spent much of his time writing a series of treatises by which he vainly hoped to enter royal service.

The return to favour By 1595 Howard was attaching himself to the young favourite, the earl of Essex, acting as his adviser, occasional secretary, and man of business. Between 1596 and 1599 he became very close to Essex, usually the first admitted to his chamber and 'by his bedside in the morning' (Hammer, 287). As a result he was brought in 1597 into Elizabeth's presence, which led to the grant of an annual pension of £200. Essex in December 1597 extorted from Elizabeth the office of earl marshal, traditionally the arbiter of honours bestowed by the crown and also the overseer of the heralds. Both men were obsessed with noble honour, and Howard set to work to produce for Essex a lengthy tract on the earl marshalship. He drew on his late brother's attempts to reform the office of arms as well as his own researches. He argued for much tighter supervision of the heralds' grants, violently attacking the inflation of honours in which the heralds collaborated for financial gain. Howard saw their acceptance of social mobility as a debasement of the whole system of gentility and urged the implementation of Norfolk's orders of 1568, including the calling in of all arms granted without the earl marshal's consent. Howard's antiquarian researches, aimed at formulating a policy for the favourite, established the pattern he followed throughout his subsequent career. The assault on merchants and others deemed unworthy of arms also pointed to his lifelong belief in the innate superiority of ancient families and his failure to understand or sympathize with the economic vitality and fluidity of late Elizabethan and

early Stuart society. Howard saw noble birth as the essential foundation on which rested all hierarchy and authority; in his static world, the gentrification of the upstart could lead only to disorder.

Initially enthralled by the glamorous and martial young nobleman who had brought him back to court, Howard gradually began to mistrust Essex's political judgement. He urged him to adopt a less impassioned approach to the struggle for patronage and power, which was making too many enemies. He became increasingly convinced that the favourite was dangerously mismanaging his relationship with the queen. Howard was also alienated by Essex's refusal after the Azores expedition to support his nephew Lord Thomas Howard, son of the late duke of Norfolk. By September 1599 the earl's other followers regarded Howard as 'a newter' (Hammer, 287) rather than a supporter. From 1598 Howard was carefully cultivating his contacts with Sir Robert Cecil, as well as consolidating his place in royal favour. In September 1600 he was at the palace of Oatlands, where Elizabeth demonstrated her regard by ordering his bed to be removed from the tented accommodation into the council chamber.

Collaboration with Robert Cecil, 1601–1611 Howard played no part in Essex's revolt in 1601, and immediately after it moved smoothly to the victorious Cecil faction at court. The question of the English succession was at the forefront of Anglo-Scottish politics, and Howard's trump card was his already-established contact with James VI of Scotland, who from at least 1598 was corresponding with Essex as his strongest English supporter. In May 1601 Cecil entered into a secret correspondence with the king, who recommended Howard to him as 'long approved and trusty' (Akrigg, 179). The three men formed an alliance to ensure the smooth transfer of power after the death of Elizabeth, and Howard frequently acted as the go-between, conveying James's letters to Cecil to avoid the greater dangers of discovery that might arise if regular letters were sent directly by the king to the secretary. Intent on securing a monopoly of the king's future favours for himself and Cecil, Howard constantly warned James against other English courtiers, particularly Cobham and Ralegh. The king occasionally grew tired of his 'ample Asiatic and endless volumes' (Akrigg, 190), but the secret correspondence cemented Howard's place at the centre of Anglo-Scottish politics. He had succeeded in making himself indispensable to both James and Cecil.

The outward sign of his acceptance by the regime came in 1601 when Howard was placed on a commission of noblemen attempting to reform long-standing abuses in the heralds' office. After his tract for Essex on the earl marshalship in 1597, he was known for challenging the heralds' claims to give arms without supervision. Some of the heralds themselves deplored the debasement of the dignity, and suggested Howard as a commissioner. His passionate concern for status and honour led him to devote considerable amounts of time and effort, both between 1601 and 1603 (when the commission was dissolved by the death of Elizabeth), and again after 1606, to attempts to reform the heralds' more dubious practices, but without much practical result.

James succeeded unopposed to the English throne in March 1603. On hearing the news of Elizabeth's death he sent from Scotland the first token of his regard, a jewel of three stones which Howard cherished until 1614 when he bequeathed it to his nephew Thomas. Howard rode north to meet the king at Newcastle, thereafter accompanying him south and reporting back to Cecil. On 4 May 1603, at Cecil's mansion of Theobalds in Hertfordshire, the king appointed Howard to the privy council along with Lord Thomas, and on 16 May granted him the precedence due to the son of a duke. On 6 January 1604 Howard was made constable of Dover Castle and lord warden of the Cinque Ports—positions which he held to his death. On 4 February 1604 he became to his gratification a joint commissioner for the office of earl marshal, a post renewed in 1605. On 13 March 1604, at the Tower, he was created baron of Marnhull, Dorset, and earl of Northampton.

The way was now open for Northampton to sit in the House of Lords in the parliament which met on 19 March 1604. He made his first speech a week later, with a lengthy oration on the bill recognizing James's title to the English throne. He lavished praise on the new king, noting his care to employ the noblest-born in the highest offices, and thanking him for the restoration of the house of Howard. Using his long training as a rhetorician, Northampton made considerable efforts to support James's project for the union between England and Scotland, the crucial issue of the session. He urged the adoption of the contentious name 'Great Britain'. Although Northampton tended to regard the House of Commons with some disdain, he proved one of the most assiduous parliamentarians on the privy council, named to a large number of committees and attending fifty-seven out of seventy-one sittings.

As a further token of the king's confidence, Northampton was one of the five principal commissioners appointed to treat with Spain in the negotiations which began in May 1604. He was the only recorded commissioner to speak apart from Cecil, who led the negotiations which brought the Armada war formally to a close with the peace treaty of London. Northampton spoke forcefully in favour of English merchants' claims to trade openly with the East and West Indies, as they had done illicitly but lucratively during the war years. Briefed by Sir Robert Cotton, who emerged as his most devoted aide and researcher, Northampton cited precedents for freedom of trade and freedom of the seas, using legalistic and historical arguments to rebut the claim of Spain (which incorporated Portugal in 1580) to a monopoly of all the Indies by the right of first discovery. He was effective, in that both sides agreed eventually to omit the issue rather than pressing it to the point at which the talks nearly broke down.

As lord warden of the Cinque Ports Northampton was at the forefront of the ceremonies welcoming the constable of Castile, who arrived to conclude the treaty in August 1604. He reported proudly to James that the constable had treated him with outstanding courtesy from his first arrival at Gravesend, as well as commenting sympathetically on his earlier sufferings and his fidelity to the cause of Mary, queen of Scots. Northampton found such an encounter with a Spanish grandee profoundly satisfying to his self-esteem. A great banquet concluded the diplomatic efforts, but a more lasting memorial was the splendid group portrait of the English and Spanish commissioners, probably by Pantoja de la Cruz and now in the National Portrait Gallery. The first painting of its kind in English art, *The Somerset House Conference* depicts the negotiating table, covered with a fine Turkey carpet and lit by a great window opening into a verdant courtyard. Despite its almost photographic realism, the picture was a fiction, depicting the constable (who had not been present at the discussions) at the head of the Spanish delegation. Northampton sits on Cecil's right hand, his sharp dark features and wispy beard emphasized by his white ruff and black tunic. Second only to the secretary at the forefront of the English side of the table, he half-hides a small wad of papers that may represent his forceful speech arguing for the freedom of the Indies trade.

The political alliance between Cecil and Northampton, begun in the anxious months leading to James's accession, was steadily consolidated between 1603 and 1605. It was hardly a friendship, but despite numerous strains it survived until at least 1611, and contributed significantly to the effectiveness and cohesion of the privy council. Northampton often attended Star Chamber and the House of Lords when Cecil, now earl of Salisbury, was unable to be present. His skill as an orator stood him in good stead in both places, and he was perceived by suitors and lesser officials as the most powerful privy councillor after Salisbury himself.

As a further sign of royal favour Northampton was installed as a knight of the Garter on 16 May 1605, just after being made steward of Greenwich Park, where he began to improve the old lodge to create for himself an imposing country house. Title, high office, and fortune had come at last; but at the age of sixty-five, Northampton's character was still governed by his years in hated obscurity. He remained fawning, obsequious, and ambiguous in both religion and sexuality, earning the unflattering popular epithet of 'his Majesty's earwig' (Croft, 278). The king regarded him, together with Salisbury and Thomas Howard, now earl of Suffolk, as his three most senior privy councillors, jocularly labelling them 'a trinity of knaves' (Akrigg, 257), but also taunted Northampton for his belief in transubstantiation and his constantly predictable flattery. The king commented repeatedly on his 'black and coal-faced' appearance (ibid.). More seriously, at some point about 1605 the king twice wrote angrily to him, accusing him of misliking the two young princes Henry and Charles, and of 'innate hatred to me and all Scotland for my cause'. James threatened to pay him back 'for your often cruel and malicious speeches against Baby Charles and his honest father' (ibid., 250, 254). The episode remains obscure, and may reflect only a passing irritation, but if the king even briefly believed that Northampton had shown some hostility to Scots in general and the Scottish royal family in particular, it may help to explain why he never gave Northampton major office. In 1608, as Salisbury added lord treasurer to his existing posts of secretary of state and master of the wards, Northampton received merely the hollow administrative title of lord privy seal. In this capacity he oversaw the privy seal office and, nominally, the court of requests, although no lord privy seal appears to have sat with the masters of requests who acted as judges of the court. The office gave him a formal honour but few additional powers and little patronage, while the privy seal clerks fought a rearguard action against his attempts to collect his proper fees.

After 1603 Northampton was in a position to exercise influence at court, and to extend his power in the localities through his position as lord warden of the Cinque Ports in Kent, and using his East Anglian lands. He developed a formidable loyalty to his followers, particularly in the Cinque Ports, where he cherished his role. In addition, he systematically rewarded his Howard family connections; active client gentry from Kent, Norfolk, and Suffolk; and also numerous former followers of the earl of Essex. In this way Northampton worked to maintain vital links between court and country, as well as helping to reintegrate several disaffected Essexians back into the fabric of political life. One striking example was the Roman Catholic Roger Manners, fifth earl of Rutland, who as a young man had been a devoted follower of Essex. Between 1608 and 1614 Rutland repaid his political debt to his new patron with a series of new year gifts of lavish silver and gilt basins and ewers curiously wrought to resemble a snail, a mermaid, and Bacchus and Ceres. From a surviving example, these were among the most fantastic works produced by Jacobean silversmiths. Northampton also acted discreetly as a patron of many other recusants or Roman Catholic sympathizers, provided they were loyalists and not ideologues. His clients, like the members of his household, were well-born, politically active, and religiously conservative.

The discovery of the Gunpowder Plot revived the menace of recusant treachery just as Northampton had secured a senior place in government. He was one of the four privy councillors at Whitehall on 26 October 1605 to whom Lord Monteagle handed the mysterious letter warning of a conspiracy. His own conformity was not in doubt, for after James's accession he regularly attended the Chapel Royal as a member of the king's train, and in September 1604 he served on the commission to expel Jesuits and seminary priests. Yet the plot was potentially a severe embarrassment, if not worse. It was a gesture of confidence on James's part to name Northampton to the commission of investigation that was immediately set up. Subsequently he made an effective speech at the plotters' trial in January 1606, and was also prominent as an orator two months later when Henry Garnet, superior of the English Jesuits, was tried for his involvement with the conspirators. Northampton was the author of most of the

government's main statement of its case against the plotters, *A True and Perfect Relation*. He was named again to a commission to banish Jesuits in 1610. By his conspicuous support of the regime during and immediately after the plot, and by his sedulous court conformity, Northampton worked successfully to allay any fears the king might harbour about his political and religious reliability.

Northampton was also active in the parliamentary session of 1606–7, when he again urged the acceptance of the revised plans for the union and sought advice from Cotton on detailed aspects such as the proposal of free trade for the Scots. In May 1607 merchants' grievances came to the forefront. English traders to the re-opened Spanish markets were frequently harassed by local officials and unable to obtain redress from the notoriously slow central courts in Madrid. By 1606 irritation in mercantile circles had reached such a height that there were calls for the reissue of letters of marque, to allow complainants to recoup their losses by seizing Spanish vessels. This would have threatened the peace agreement of 1604, and Salisbury and Northampton jointly fought off the Commons committee by emphasizing that matters of high foreign policy were for the king and his privy council, not for the House of Commons. Northampton also shrewdly emphasized that retaliation might provoke Spain to take more severe measures that would prove very costly to English trade.

In parliament Northampton often defended the efforts of the king's government to curb abuses. He showed his commitment to administrative reform in investigations into the expenditures of the royal household, purveyance, the ecclesiastical courts, the ordnance office, and most importantly the navy. In 1608, heading a commission of fifteen members, he conferred repeatedly with his advisers, personally inspected naval yards, and examined numerous witnesses, among them naval officers alienated by the corruption and incompetence of their superiors. Assisted by Cotton, he wrote an extensive report detailing corrupt practices and subsequently drew up a book of ordinances for the navy. Accused of 'spleen' (Peck, *Northampton*, 155) by fellow courtiers and those whose interests were threatened, Northampton had no hesitation in exposing the managerial inadequacies of his cousin, the elderly Lord Admiral Nottingham. The Howard interest at court was not a cohesive one. The fact that virtually nothing was done was the fault of the king, who took no serious action. Northampton revived the navy commission in 1613 but with even less success.

The commission of 1608 formed part of the general programme of financial reform that culminated in Salisbury's proposals for the 'great contract' of 1610. The nineteenth-century view that Northampton constantly tried to undermine Salisbury is no longer tenable; in 1610 he actively backed the lord treasurer's initiative both in the Lords and in conferences with the Commons. Moreover his usual rhetoric, which tended to exalt the Lords and denigrate the Commons, was significantly modified for the occasion: Northampton went out of his way to emphasize the need for co-operation and negotiation between the two houses. He served as envoy between the

Lords and the Commons and from the king to both. As in earlier sessions he also shouldered much of the heavy workload of overseeing private bills and attending committees, relieving Salisbury to concentrate on the burdensome task of leading the discussions on the contract. There are indications in his private papers that Northampton thought some of the proposals too sweeping, and he had no personal affection for Salisbury, but in public he was a loyal and effective privy council spokesman. He did not hesitate, however, to underline the risks of not concluding the bargain that Salisbury offered. The king might then be forced to press his subjects with more onerous financial burdens. 'Whilst we hold monarchy we must maintain the monarch', he warned (Foster, 1.35–6; 2.55). Even in the autumn session, when the contract was effectively dead, Northampton continued to urge the voting of subsidies by invoking the spectre of war and the need for national unity; in an emergency it might not be feasible to call a parliament. He was deeply aware that relations between the king and his subjects were at a turning point.

Northampton and the rise of Carr The later years of Northampton's political pre-eminence were shaped by the emergence after 1611 of Sir Robert Carr, the young Scottish courtier of whom the king became publicly enamoured. Created Viscount Rochester in March 1611, he attracted a growing number of clients seeking his favour. Thereafter Northampton gradually moved away from Salisbury, just as he had distanced himself from Essex, and began to cultivate Carr, increasingly the centre of patronage at court. As Salisbury fell seriously ill in 1611–12, Carr's control steadily strengthened, and James placed him on the privy council only weeks after Salisbury's death in May 1612. Northampton had already urged James to elevate Carr and he immediately manoeuvred to become the younger man's guide and informant, sending him a stream of letters that outlined and explained the business transacted by the privy council when Carr was absent attending James.

After May 1612 Northampton also took over control of the day-to-day business of government, arranging the council's agenda and carrying on an extensive correspondence with Carr and Sir Thomas Lake, who usually acted as secretary to the king on his hunting expeditions. Foreign and domestic policy came before the privy council, but the most important issue was still finance. James did not replace Salisbury, instead placing the treasury in the hands of six commissioners led by Northampton. Although it was widely expected that the senior office would come to him after a thorough investigation of the state of the revenues, the king did not dissolve the commission until shortly after Northampton's death, when he appointed Suffolk as lord treasurer. Whatever James's reasons for withholding the prestigious title, Northampton conscientiously undertook a heavy workload in addition to his duties as a privy councillor. He attempted to curb expenditures, seeking to cut down the costs of the royal household and restrain the king's bounty in free gifts and pensions. He also made efforts to increase

income, carefully investigating potential money-making projects such as the domestic manufacture of alum and schemes for the tighter control of the crown's landed revenues. In his efforts he was again assisted by Cotton, who provided him with massive information on medieval and later precedents.

These measures were only marginally successful, but Northampton achieved more when he turned after 1612 to the London merchant Lionel Cranfield, who became his chief adviser on economic and financial matters. Using information provided by Cranfield, Northampton succeeded in delaying the renewal of the grant of the lucrative great farm of the customs. Writing to the king, he blackened the character of the previous lord treasurers Dorset and Salisbury by alleging that they had negligently, or fraudulently, drawn up the contract more in the interest of the customs farmers than of the crown. Cranfield meanwhile analysed the terms of the farm, providing ammunition for Northampton, whereupon the farmers were forced to increase their offer of rent. The wine and silk farms came under similar scrutiny. Playing rival syndicates of merchants off against one another, Northampton and Cranfield improved the royal revenues from the farms of the customs. Furthermore, from September 1613 Cranfield administered a new form of customs duty which he had personally devised, an additional imposition on goods imported and exported by alien merchants.

The alliance with his city informants also allowed Northampton to act decisively in another area. In 1612 a trade boycott of English cloth was launched by the Archduke Albert in the southern Low Countries. In the summer of 1613 the privy council realized that its legal protests were getting nowhere, and instead adopted Cranfield's advice to threaten a counter-boycott, since the archduke and his subjects profited from the trade far more than the English. The tough new response based on the economic realities of the situation forced the archduke to negotiate. Northampton took pride in bringing Cranfield into the king's service. The merchant was granted arms and knighted in 1613; there could be no doubt that the statistical information provided for Northampton by his London contacts had been used to great effect. Cranfield was launched on a career that was to culminate in the office of lord treasurer denied to his patron.

By 1613 Northampton had reached the pinnacle of his power and prestige. No longer in the shadow of Salisbury, he was the single most influential privy councillor and in constant contact with Carr, who largely monopolized the king's favour. Carr himself, however, was deeply dependent on his old friend and mentor Sir Thomas Overbury. Yet by spring 1612 he had fallen in love with Frances Howard, Northampton's great-niece. Northampton saw her adulterous liaison with Carr as a way of strengthening Howard dominance at court. He manoeuvred to obtain a divorce for Frances from her husband, the young earl of Essex, son of his Elizabethan patron. He wrote letters to Carr that were full of almost sadistic sexual innuendo, encouraging the favourite in his pursuit of Frances. As Overbury strongly opposed the match, Northampton conspired to confine him to the Tower, cut off from Carr. There in September 1613 Overbury died. Carr was created earl of Somerset, and in December 1613 he and Frances were married. Northampton presented them with £1500 in plate together with an elaborate sword for the groom which he had commissioned at a cost of £566.

The letters to Carr underline again what was already apparent in Northampton's attacks on the customs farmers, his desire retrospectively to undermine the reputation of Salisbury. Northampton revealed how bitterly he had resented Salisbury's success in monopolizing political power. He complained of 'the little lord's … tossing and transposing' of state papers, making 'his own cabinet the treasury of the state's whole evidence, (which no man ever either durst before his time attempt nor in his time reprove)' (Peck, *Northampton*, 86). He also wrote with savage enjoyment to James I that Salisbury had assuredly joined his former mistress Queen Elizabeth 'by an extreeme whotte fieres side'—the fires of Hell (PRO, SP 14/71/3).

By the winter of 1614, however, Northampton was failing in health, and on 22 February he attended his last privy council meeting, which met for his convenience at Northampton House, in Charing Cross. It was widely known that his control over business was beginning to slip, particularly as his nephew Suffolk had formed an increasingly effective alliance with the favourite, now married to Suffolk's daughter. Ever since May 1612 there had been talk of another parliament to solve the financial crisis, and in July 1613 the privy council held lengthy but inconclusive discussions. The king hoped that a French match for his son Prince Charles might solve his problems by producing a large dowry. Northampton, who always emphasized the need to prepare carefully for a parliament, was convinced that the recent failure of the Irish parliament showed that an English one would have no better success. However, by February 1614 Northampton was incapacitated by illness, just at the time when French domestic difficulties halted the marriage negotiations. Thereupon Suffolk and Somerset, who were both pressing for a parliament, obtained the king's reluctant consent.

The failure of the Addled Parliament has long been blamed on Northampton, who was alleged to have planted an inflammatory, anti-Scots speech in the Commons knowing that it would enrage the king. He led a strong faction on the privy council that argued for a Spanish match rather than a French one, and in February 1614 he was secretly received back into the Roman Catholic church by a priest sent by the Spanish ambassador Sarmiento (the future count of Gondomar). If the parliament failed to provide desperately needed funds, James would have little alternative but to turn to Philip III in the hope of a large Spanish dowry. However, although some contemporary observers believed that Northampton was indeed implicated in wrecking the session with this political scenario in view, the evidence is at best circumstantial. He played no part in the parliament itself, remaining an invalid at his home in Greenwich, and Hoskyns's anti-Scots speech was merely the last straw which broke James's forbearance, not the main cause of the dissolution that took place on 7 June.

Nevertheless it seems clear that Northampton was far from displeased by the addling of the parliament. James, greatly agitated, came to Greenwich on 4 June 1614 to consult with him before deciding to dissolve, and less than an hour later Northampton wrote a full account of their meeting and sent it to Sarmiento. His letter included the assurance that his advice to the king was 'in keeping with the good of Christianity and the advantage and service of Spain' (Loomie, 2.38–9). On 8 June the king returned to Westminster to summon his privy council for an emergency session. Northampton likewise came from Greenwich by coach, at the head of a procession of forty horse described by at least one contemporary as a triumph. The very public return to London perhaps signalled an intention to re-enter politics after his illness, but Northampton was unlucky. Within a week it was deemed necessary to operate on the tumour on his thigh that had incapacitated him since February. A fatal gangrene resulted, although Northampton did not recognize the hopelessness of his situation until Sir Robert Cotton told him to make his will. Two days later, on 16 June 1614, Northampton died, unmarried, at his Charing Cross house, and all his honours became extinct.

The will began with a carefully phrased statement that he died 'a member of the Catholicke and Apostolike Churche, saying with Saint Jerome "In qua fide puer natus fui in eadem senex morior"' (GEC, *Peerage*, 9.676–7). The quotation from the Nicene creed was entirely acceptable to the Church of England, and when Northampton was born in 1540 England was already separated from papal jurisdiction. His reception into the Roman Catholic church earlier in the year remained a secret. Nevertheless it was noted that his lying-in-state, surrounded by candles, and his elaborate funeral procession all smacked of popery. There were constant rumours that he had received extreme unction. The corpse was carried to Dover, where later in June, as lord warden of the Cinque Ports, he was buried in the chapel; a grand monumental effigy and tomb were designed and executed by the royal master mason Nicholas Stone.

The pre-eminence of the Howards at court was not much affected, for Suffolk succeeded to the lord treasurership in July while his son-in-law Somerset remained secure in James's favour. All this began to change after September 1614 with the rise of George Villiers, later duke of Buckingham, and even worse, with the unravelling a year later of the Overbury scandal. It emerged that Frances Howard, countess of Somerset, had been deeply implicated in a plot to poison Overbury during his imprisonment, and in November 1615 Sir Gervase Elwes, lieutenant of the Tower, was tried for murder. This was sensational enough but was followed in 1616 by the trial of Frances and her husband, from whom James had withdrawn his protection. In Elwes's trial Northampton's letters to Somerset were read out, and the prosecution lawyer Lawrence

Hyde baldly stated that Northampton had plotted Overbury's death. This was widely accepted as true but, although Northampton had obviously hated Overbury, the evidence for his involvement in the poison conspiracy was unclear. However, the salaciousness and voyeurism of the carefully selected passages read out from the letters shocked their hearers, as the prosecution intended them to do. Lord Chief Justice Coke described them as 'beastly and bawdy', while one hearer commented that 'it would turn chaste blood into water to hear the unchaste and unclean phrases' (Somerset, 278–9). Northampton was not there to defend himself and, although in his lifetime he was never involved in sexual scandal, the damage done to his reputation has been permanent.

Finances and fortune At his death Northampton may have been worth as much as £80,000, although he was also in debt for £6000. It was estimated that his yearly landed income amounted to over £3000, about average for a peer but in his case built up remarkably quickly since 1603, when the Stuart succession restored the Howard fortunes. James regranted jointly to Northampton and Suffolk a substantial part of the family lands which had come to the crown by the previous attainders, and in 1604 they reached a settlement dividing the grants between them. Northampton steadily added to his East Anglian lands by purchase but took no interest in their administration, remaining focused on the court, his Charing Cross townhouse, and his residence in Greenwich Park.

From March 1608 Northampton enjoyed a monopoly of both imported and domestically manufactured starch, making a large profit until complaints in the 1610 parliament led to the revocation of the grant. By way of compensation James in 1612 granted him an annual pension of £3000 and a lump sum of £6000. The landed revenues and the starch patent were the principal props of Northampton's fortune. In addition he was granted some lucrative wardships, including that of his great-nephew George, Lord Berkeley, grandson of his sister Catherine whose generosity had sustained him years earlier. In a striking display of meanness, Northampton listed the wardship as part of his estate worth £1500, and his executors forced the Berkeley family to pay up.

Northampton also benefited from payments made to him to secure his influence. The most notable was his Spanish pension after 1604, when he began to receive about £1000 annually as well as occasional gifts of cash and jewels. He frequented the Spanish embassy on an almost daily basis and the pension must have increased the strongly pro-Spanish tendency of his conciliar advice. However, it was often in arrears, and may have been less important to him than the ill-documented profits which he seems likely to have made from his association with the great London merchants such as Swinnerton and Cranfield who advised him on the customs farms.

By 1605 Northampton had purchased property in St Martin-in-the-Fields, pulling down tenements to build a great mansion fronting on the Strand with gardens stretching down to the river. He continued to buy up surrounding properties to extend his estate. In addition he steadily expanded his holdings in Greenwich and its royal park. These houses were lavishly furnished with tapestries, paintings, books, and other moveables. Northampton owned no fewer than five portraits of Mary, queen of Scots, and items of elaborate jewellery for himself were on order at the goldsmiths or awaiting collection when he died. He also bought maps of Rome, Amsterdam, and Antwerp as well as Speed's large map of England, Scotland, and Ireland. He owned two of the globes developed by Emery Molyneux (d. 1598) to assist the English search for the north-west passage—one terrestrial and the other celestial, covered with green taffeta curtains. His collection of clocks and watches included a timepiece embedded in a representation of St George and the dragon, symbols of the Garter.

The bulk of Northampton's estate was left to his great-nephew the earl of Arundel, titular head of the Howard family, but the Charing Cross house went to his nephew Suffolk. It was later renamed Northumberland House, and the famous depiction of it by Canaletto is proof of its grandeur. Yet Northampton also spent a substantial amount in establishing three almshouses—in Kent, Norfolk, and Shropshire—an old-fashioned type of philanthropy that harked back to the corrodies of the monastic system that had existed in England before 1540. In his will Northampton carefully ensured the survival of his almshouses. A flatterer to the last, he also left a silver cup to James, engraved with the words *detur dignissimo* ('let it be given to the worthiest').

Treatises Northampton left another enduring legacy, of an intellectual rather than material kind. His treatises form perhaps the most remarkable body of writings completed by any early Stuart politician with the exception of Sir Francis Bacon. His first known work, a tract on natural philosophy, was completed at Trinity Hall in August 1569 and dedicated to his sister Catherine; it contains a significant reference to 'that most excellent work of the Count of Castiglione called the Courtier' (Peck, *Mental World*, 150), indicating that he had not given up hope of a career at court. He continued to write throughout Elizabeth's reign, choosing the subjects carefully to underscore his political reliability and orthodoxy, and adorning his work with the elaborate apparatus of Renaissance scholarship. He frequently aimed to reinforce the regime's propaganda, in 1574 entering the debate between Thomas Cartwright and John Whitgift by publishing a defence of the bishops against the attacks of Cartwright and the presbyterians. About 1576 he praised the queen (and distanced himself from the fate of his brother) in the unpublished 'Regina fortunata'. In 1580 his *Answer* responded to Stubbes's *Gaping Gulf* opposing the Anjou match, and attacked 'the importunate tattlings of these peevish Puritans' (Peck, *Northampton*, 12). The tract argued that as the queen could not marry at home for fear of discontenting her nobility (a shrewd thrust at Leicester, the leading patron of puritanism), she should opt for the French alliance that might also produce an heir to the English throne. Some time in the 1580s he also wrote 'A dutiful defence of the lawful regiment of women', acting upon a suggestion probably made by Lord Burghley that he should refute Knox's much earlier tract deploring the 'monstrous regiment'. It was presented to the queen in 1590. He wrote out and presented to Burghley a book of his own Latin prayers, and later sent similar examples of his work to Burghley's political heir, Robert Cecil.

In a further attempt to attract the patronage of leading privy councillors, Howard published *A Defensative Against the Poyson of Supposed Prophesies* (1583), dedicated to Walsingham. A curious work, it argued that 'prophecies of wicked men are a kind of science which was never grafted by our heavenly Father' (Peck, *Northampton*, 220). He emphasized his own religious orthodoxy while apparently aiming at the magico-philosophical circles of Richard Harvey and John Dee. Numerous lesser works circulated in manuscript, including his translation of the advices left by Charles V to his son Philip II, a testament for princes widely studied in late sixteenth-century Europe, which he prefaced with a dedicatory epistle to Elizabeth. Howard actively collected materials for other treatises, including an unfinished one on royal power which made extensive use of Jean Bodin, whose political philosophy he admired; it refuted the anti-monarchical arguments associated with James VI's hated tutor, the political theorist George Buchanan. Internal evidence suggests that the manuscript dates from the 1580s, and it may have been intended as a first attempt to ingratiate himself with the young king of Scots, who effectively emerged from his minority about 1585.

Insofar as Howard did not regain royal favour, the treatises failed in their immediate purpose, but they marked him out as a nobleman of extensive learning and high culture, anxious to dissociate himself from political troublemakers and worthy of better employment. After the execution of Mary, queen of Scots, in 1587 the Elizabethan regime could in any case feel more secure, while Howard was left with no option but to accommodate himself to Elizabeth as best he could. He continued to offer advice on current issues, including some draft considerations on the beneficial aspects of a plantation of Ireland, a theme he returned to in 1607–9. The wide-ranging literary efforts of the years before 1603 laid a basis for much of his later work as a privy councillor.

Throughout his life Northampton kept up the contacts with antiquaries and academics which distinguished his early years. He was not a member of the recently established Society of Antiquaries but he moved in the same intellectual circles and repeatedly drew on their ideas. The most significant of his later publications was *The true and perfect relation of the whole proceedings against the late most barbarous traitors, Garnet, a Jesuite, and his confederats*, which emerged in late 1606. The volume presented the government's case against both the gunpowder plotters and Henry Garnet, who had heard the confession of one of them but not divulged it. The core of the treatise was a long dissertation on the papal usurpation of temporal power, with a history of political conspiracies involving the Jesuits (whom James particularly disliked). Northampton was the author but Sir Robert Cotton made a significant contribution, supplying the historical evidence which provided the framework for the central argument that the papal claim to temporal power was not scriptural but a novelty dating from the reign of Gregory VII. Cotton also edited the numerous drafts and encouraged Northampton not to push too fast. The king was delighted with the final version, ordering it to be translated into French, Latin, and Italian and sent to the other rulers of Europe. The strategy of using a known crypto-Catholic as the author of the official statement on the plot and its aftermath helped to underscore the point that the plotters were abhorrent to their own co-religionists, whose political loyalty had not wavered in 1605. At the same time it was a tribute to Northampton's stature as a polemicist, earned by years of similar but unrewarded literary diligence under Elizabeth.

His reputation for exceptional learning helped Northampton to become high steward of Oxford in 1609, and chancellor of Cambridge in June 1612 after the death of Salisbury, although the latter university briefly offended the king by passing over the young Prince Charles as an alternative candidate. The last tract that Northampton composed was written in the autumn of 1613, just before his health began to fail. Designed to accompany the royal proclamation against private challenges and combats, issued on 4 February 1614, it was written in the king's name. James detested duelling, but the treatise also reflected Northampton's own long-standing anxieties. From 1613 a campaign against duelling was under way, led by Northampton and enforced in Star Chamber and the court of the earl marshal. He also collected extensive information on the code and practice of duelling, imported from France and Spain. The proclamation was triggered by several duels involving courtiers, the most notorious being one between Lord Henry Howard, brother of Frances, and the earl of Essex, the husband whom she was divorcing.

Northampton recognized that it was not enough to ban duels. Instead he proposed alternative remedies to provide satisfaction for those who believed their honour and reputation had been traduced. The commissioners for the earl marshalship, together with the lords lieutenant in the counties, would hear cases, and heavy punishments would be inflicted on those who disobeyed their attempts at conciliation. Potential duellers were exhorted to remember the king's interest in the lives of his subjects. The treatise exemplified Northampton's passion for social order, while marking a radical departure from many current notions of honour, which embraced private combats with an often deadly enthusiasm. Moreover the common lawyers were increasingly averse to the earl marshal's jurisdiction, already seen as an objectionable and irregular aspect of the royal prerogative. There was little hope that the extensive system proposed by Northampton could ever be translated into reality; not surprisingly neither the proclamation nor the treatise succeeded in ending the plague of duelling. Yet the tract was in many ways strikingly enlightened, and its composition, only a few months before Northampton's death, when he was still burdened with privy council business, underlined the seriousness of his concern. It marked the worthy culmination of a literary career begun in 1569 as a young don at Cambridge.

Northampton's reputation was often under attack in his own lifetime and shortly afterwards, but the first scholarly biography of him, published in 1982, presents a more balanced assessment. The many objectionable features of his character and actions cannot be denied, but these must be set against his breadth of scholarly interests, his innovative use of a wide circle of antiquarian and mercantile advisers, and his administrative efforts between 1603 and 1614. He wrestled with a system of monarchical rule that was steadily deteriorating, and many of his initiatives bore little fruit. Northampton spent too much time on his obsessions with noble blood, rank, and arms. Yet he worked tirelessly for the monarch whose accession to the throne had brought him out of obscurity and revived the fortunes of the Howards. It was his tragedy that he was given no opportunity to contribute to English government until he was in his sixties. The long years he spent in the political wilderness before 1603 deeply embittered him, and the consequent atrophying of so many talents and energies must be counted a considerable loss to the regimes of both Queen Elizabeth and King James.

PAULINE CROFT

Sources GEC, *Peerage*, new edn, 9.674–7 · L. L. Peck, *Northampton: patronage and policy at the court of James I* (1982) · L. L. Peck, *The mental world of the Jacobean court* (1991) · *Letters of King James VI & I*, ed. G. P. V. Akrigg (1984) · *The letters of John Chamberlain*, ed. N. E. McClure, 2 vols. (1939) · P. E. J. Hammer, *The polarisation of Elizabethan politics: the political career of Robert Devereux, 2nd earl of Essex, 1585–1597* (1999) · E. R. Foster, ed., *Proceedings in parliament, 1610*, 2 vols. (1966) · A. Somerset, *Unnatural murder: poison at the court of James I* (1997) · A. J. Loomie, ed., *Spain and the Jacobean Catholics*, 2 vols., Catholic RS, 64, 68 (1973–8) · P. Croft, 'Libels, popular literacy and public opinion in early modern England', *Historical Research*, 68 (1995), 266–85 · M. Jansson, ed., *Proceedings in parliament, 1614* (*House of Commons*) (1988) · E. P. Shirley, 'An inventory of the effects of Henry Howard, K. G. … with a transcript of his will', *Archaeologia*, 42 (1869), 437–78 · *CSP dom.*, 1601–18

Archives Arundel Castle, Sussex, papers · BL, papers · BL, treatises, Add. MSS 12513, 12515; Egerton MS 944 · BL, tract answering Knox's attack on women, Add. MS 64123 · Bodl. Oxf., treatise on natural philosophy · CUL, letters, mainly relating to Essex divorce · U. Durham, commonplace books · U. Glas., translation of Charles V's discourse on his abdication | PRO, state papers, SP 12, SP 14

Likenesses follower of H. Custodis, oils, 1594, Mercers' Company, London · group portrait, oils, 1604 (*The Somerset House Conference*, 1604), NPG · attrib. J. Belkamp, oils, before 1605, Knole, Kent · oils, after 1605 (with Garter George), Petworth House, Sussex · portrait, 1606, priv. coll. · N. Stone, effigy, 1615, Trinity Hospital, Greenwich [*see illus.*]

Wealth at death approx. £80,000: Peck, *Northampton*, 64, 76

Howard, Henry, sixth duke of Norfolk (1628–1684), nobleman, was born on 12 July 1628 at Arundel House in the Strand, London, the second son of Henry Frederick *Howard, Lord Maltravers and later fifteenth earl of Arundel (1608–1652), and his wife, Lady Elizabeth Stuart (*d.* 1674), daughter of Esmé *Stuart, third duke of Lennox,

and Katharine Clifton. Details of his early life and education are uncertain, but he may have shared in the studies of his elder brother, Thomas (1627–1677), at Utrecht, and by about 1643 or 1644 he had joined his grandfather Thomas *Howard, fourteenth earl of Arundel (1585–1646), at Padua. From 1645 the younger Thomas was incarcerated there as a lunatic, and it was Henry Howard who, with his father, accompanied the fourteenth earl's body back to England after his death in September 1646.

On the death of his father on 17 April 1652 Howard became *de facto* head of a family burdened by debts arising from its royalism and Catholicism. Shortly before 21 October that year he married Lady Anne Somerset (1631–1662), daughter of Edward *Somerset, second marquess of Worcester, and his first wife, Elizabeth Dormer. They had two sons, Henry *Howard, later seventh duke of Norfolk (1655–1701), and Thomas, and three daughters.

In 1660 parliament passed a bill to revive the dukedom of Norfolk, ostensibly for Thomas Howard, technically now sixteenth earl of Arundel, but really for his younger brother Henry. Moves in 1674 and 1677 to bring the former back to England, amid claims that he was not really insane, were unsuccessful, and Thomas finally died in Padua in December 1677, allowing Henry to succeed as sixth duke. In the meantime, Howard had been created Baron Howard of Castle Rising on 27 March 1669 and earl of Norwich and earl marshal on 19 October 1672. He had compounded for, or refinanced, many of his grandfather's debts, giving him an income said to be £25,000 a year, although he complained that much of the property was tied up in entails during his brother's lifetime. His younger brothers and sisters in turn accused him of mismanaging family moneys, denying them their due, and using his privilege as a peer to protect himself from legal action.

John Evelyn thought Howard had great abilities and a smooth tongue, but little judgement. He allowed his priests to steal books from his magnificent library. In an attempt to preserve it Evelyn persuaded him to give much of it to the Royal Society, of which Howard became a fellow on 28 November 1666. In 1668 he gave many of the marbles accumulated by his grandfather to Oxford University, where he was made a DCL on 5 June. Like his grandfather, he travelled widely, visiting Vienna and Constantinople in 1665, and going at some point to India. He had a little house at Prinzenhof in the Low Countries and in England built lavishly but (in Evelyn's view) unwisely. He spent £10,000 on a palace at Weybridge (on a 'miserable sandy site'), completed in 1678, and at least £30,000 on the Duke's Palace at Norwich in a 'dunghole place', too cramped and close to the river, so that the cellars flooded (Evelyn, 3.592–3; *Portland MSS*, 2.270). This was begun about 1671, but although the outside was completed in 1681, the inside was never finished. Howard entertained there sumptuously, however, erecting temporary accommodation in order to keep open house for the visit of the king and queen in September 1671.

Howard was a Roman Catholic, but no bigot, asking no more than that the laws against Catholics should not be enforced. His religion debarred him from playing a part in public life appropriate to his rank and wealth, and he complained of being 'so useless a drone in my own country' (*Finch MSS*, 1.368). He considered conversion, but thought that, as head of the family, it would be unbecoming to change, although his son Henry did so. None the less, he was not without either office or influence. From 1663 to 1673 he was high steward of Guildford, he was ambassador to Morocco in 1669, and after the Restoration he was a major figure in Norfolk. Norwich looked to him for assistance at court, rang the bells when he was made a peer, and accepted his nominee as town clerk. He was an important electoral patron, controlling both seats at Castle Rising and at least one at Aldeburgh; he also had a considerable interest at Thetford and Arundel. A variety of suitors, Catholic and protestant, sought his patronage and assistance, ranging from humble revenue officials to the former queen of Bohemia. Despite his violent temper, he was on good terms with a wide variety of people: in 1669 he asked the bishop of Norwich and his wife if there was anything they would like him to bring back from Morocco. When Norfolk became deeply divided politically in the wake of the 1675 by-election Howard took a more partisan role. The leader of the church party, Robert Paston, earl of Yarmouth, relied heavily on Howard's 'interest' in the city and the county. But his religion made him vulnerable and the Popish Plot destroyed his influence: he refused to endorse any parliamentary candidates in February 1679 on the grounds that it would do them more harm than good, and then went abroad.

After the death of his wife, Anne, in 1662, Howard had according to Evelyn fallen into 'base and vicious courses' (Evelyn, 3.592–3, 4.128), keeping as his mistress an actress, Jane (*d.* 1693), daughter of Robert Bickerton, gentleman of the king's wine cellar, and his wife, Anne Hester. Although he had promised he would never marry her, their marriage was announced on 23 January 1678, soon after his succession to the dukedom of Norfolk. They had four sons and three daughters. In 1679 Norfolk became embroiled in a property dispute with his eldest son, Henry, by this time earl of Arundel, who took advantage of his father's absence abroad to promote a bill in the Lords to vest the ducal estates in trustees in order to pay their debts and provide for his children.

By the time Norfolk returned to England in 1681 his influence in his home county had been eclipsed by that of his protestant son Arundel, who became lord lieutenant on Yarmouth's death in March 1683. Norfolk died at Arundel House on 13 January 1684 and was buried at Arundel Castle; his heart was deposited at the convent of St Elizabeth in Bruges. His widow, who subsequently married Thomas Maxwell (*d.* 1693), a quartermaster-general in the army, died at Rotherham, one of the estates she had received by the duke's will, on 28 August 1693, aged forty-nine, and was buried at Arundel. JOHN MILLER

Sources J. M. Robinson, *The dukes of Norfolk* (1982) · Evelyn, *Diary* · T. Browne, *Works*, ed. S. Wilkin, 4 vols. (1836) · E. A. Kent, 'The houses of the dukes of Norfolk in Norwich', *Norfolk Archaeology*, 24 (1930–32), 73–87, esp. 80–85 · R. H. Hill, ed., 'The correspondence

of Thomas Corie, town clerk of Norwich, 1664–1687', *Norfolk Record Society*, 27 (1956), 7–58 · J. T. Evans, *Seventeenth-century Norwich* (1979) · C. Robbins, 'Election correspondence of Sir John Holland of Quidenham', *Norfolk Archaeology*, 30 (1947–52), 130–39 · M. A. Tierney, *The history and antiquities of the castle and town of Arundel*, 2 vols. (1834) · *JHC*, 9 (1667–87), 385–417 · *JHL*, 11 (1660–66), 184–90 · *JHL*, 13 (1675–81), 80, 549, 572–93 · *Ninth report*, 2, HMC, 8 (1884), 60–101 · *The manuscripts of the House of Lords*, 4 vols., HMC, 17 (1887–94), vol. 1, pp. 137–41 · GEC, *Peerage* · *The manuscripts of his grace the duke of Portland*, 10 vols., HMC, 29 (1891–1931), vol. 2 · *Report on the manuscripts of Allan George Finch*, 5 vols., HMC, 71 (1913–2003), vol. 1

Archives Arundel Castle, West Sussex, papers · BL, letters, Add. MSS 18744, 27447 · Bodl. Oxf., letters | Leics. RO, corresp. with earl of Winchelsea · U. Nott. L., 1676, letters to first and second dukes of Newcastle

Likenesses A. Hannemann, oils, 1660, Arundel Castle, Sussex · J. M. Wright, portrait, *c.*1663–1665, NPG · P. Lely, oils, 1677, Arundel Castle, Sussex · G. Kneller, portrait (after Lely; after J. M. Wright, 1677), Arundel Castle, Sussex · J. M. Wright, portrait, Powis Castle · T. Wyck, oils, Arundel Castle, Sussex · oils, Arundel Castle, Sussex

Howard, Henry, seventh duke of Norfolk (1655–1701), politician, was born on 11 January 1655, the son of Henry *Howard, sixth duke of Norfolk (1628–1684), and his wife, Lady Anne Somerset (1631–1662), elder daughter of Edward *Somerset, second marquess of Worcester. He attended Magdalen College, Oxford, for one whole year, without matriculating and possibly subsequently to his being created MA at the age of thirteen on 5 June 1668 but before February 1671. He married, on 8 August 1677, Lady Mary Mordaunt (1658/9–1705) [see Howard, Mary, duchess of Norfolk], the daughter of Henry *Mordaunt, second earl of Peterborough, and his wife, Penelope O'Brien, daughter of the earl of Thomond. From 1678, after his father succeeded to the dukedom, Howard was styled earl of Arundel, but was summoned to parliament on 27 January 1678 as Baron Mowbray.

Reared a Catholic, Arundel briefly withdrew from parliament after refusing the tests prescribed by the 'act for disabling papists from sitting in either house of parliament' of November 1678. By April 1679, however, he had taken the oaths of allegiance and supremacy and subscribed to the declaration against transubstantiation, and thus resumed his seat. The sincerity of his conversion to protestantism is not determinable, but Sir John Reresby reported in 1688 that he found Howard 'firm to the Protestant religion' (*Memoirs of Sir John Reresby*, 505). Arundel was made steward of the honorable artillery company (20 April 1682); constable of Windsor Castle and warden of the forest and parks (December 1682); lord lieutenant of Berkshire and Surrey (December 1683) and of Norfolk (1683); high steward of Lynn, and of Norwich Cathedral (1684). On 13 January 1684 he succeeded to the dukedom of Norfolk, and on 1 September he was created DCL at Oxford. He served in 1685 as the chief butler at the coronation of James II, and became the first knight of the Garter instituted in the new reign (22 July 1685). As earl marshal of England he held marshal's courts between 1687 and 1689.

Norfolk's conversion to protestantism did not prevent him from faithfully serving James II. Court agents counted

Henry Howard, seventh duke of Norfolk (1655–1701), by
William Sherwin, 1687 (after John Riley)

upon him to deliver votes in the scheme for packing parliaments in 1687–8, and to use his powers as lord lieutenant to obtain information about popular attitudes to the declaration of indulgence. He was not one of the signatories of the 1688 invitation to William, prince of Orange, but he may have been among the lords and bishops who petitioned James to call a free parliament on 17 November 1688. It was in the free parliament which James had reluctantly promised that Norfolk declared his hopes to rest for securing the 'laws, liberties, and protestant religion' when, on 1 December 1688, he marched the militia into Norwich market place and 'perceiving great numbers of common people gathering together, called them to him, and told them, he desired they would not take occasion to commit any disorder or outrage, but go quietly to their homes'. One week later, however, he announced at King's Lynn that he (and the militia) would support William, whereupon 'tradesmen, seamen, and *mobile* generally put orange ribbons on their hats, echoing Huzzas to the Prince of Orange and the Duke of Norfolk' (*State Tracts*, 2.437–9).

Thanks to this timely change of allegiance Norfolk retained his honours and offices, serving as earl marshal and chief butler in the coronation of William and Mary just as he had previously done for James II. He likewise continued in his three lord lieutenancies and as constable of Windsor Castle. In addition he was made a gentleman of the king's bedchamber and member of the privy council (14 February 1689), and became colonel of a regiment of foot (16 March 1689). On 25 March 1690 he was granted a pension of £3000 per annum 'for good and noble services by him performed', and was further honoured with the titles of captain-general of the honorable artillery company of London during the king's absence (3 June to September 1690), commissioner of appeal for prizes of war (1694), commissioner of Greenwich Hospital (20 February 1695), colonel in the Berkshire, Norwich, Surrey, and Southwark regiments of militia (1697), commissioner of appeal in Admiralty cases (1697), captain of the first troop of Surrey horse militia (1697), and ranger of Windsor Forest (1700–01). In 1691 he attended William III to the Netherlands.

These honours and offices did Norfolk less material good than one might imagine. At the time of his death, for example, he was owed £12,000 in arrears in salary as governor of Windsor Castle. His financial circumstances were strained. The protracted legal proceedings begun in 1682 by Charles Howard, his uncle, against his father and himself concerning the title to the manor of Greystoke were finally settled by parliament in 1685, after many reversals, to the plaintiff's advantage, leaving Norfolk to pay seven and a half years of back rent to Charles Howard as well as the costs of the case. His unfulfilled obligations with respect to the marriage portion of his aunt, Lady Elizabeth Macdonnel, put further pressure on his resources. To make matters worse the refusal of his wife, Mary Mordaunt, to relinquish her life interest in Castle Rising and other manors settled upon her at her marriage by his father prevented him from selling those estates to raise necessary cash. If Mary's account can be believed it was this financial predicament, rather than the adultery that he discovered her committing in 1685 with John Germain, which led him to seek an almost unprecedented act of divorce from the House of Lords.

Norfolk first introduced a bill to divorce his wife in the House of Lords in 1692. It was one of the first of such parliamentary divorces which (unlike divorces *a mensa et toro* granted by ecclesiastical courts) conferred on the injured party the right to remarry. It was also the most publicized and politicized case of its kind, with accounts of the Lords' proceedings and related trials circulating in print and manuscript. Some observers, like Gilbert Burnet, denounced opponents of the bill as papists and Jacobites, and pointed out that unless the duke were allowed to divorce and remarry, his large estates would fall into Catholic hands. But the duke attracted little public sympathy. When he sued his wife's lover (later husband), John Germain, in the king's bench in 1692 the jury awarded him only 100 marks rather than the £100,000 damages he had requested. John Evelyn, although a family friend, characterized Norfolk as a 'dissolute protestant' (Evelyn, 5.394). When the duke went to Norwich in 1696 openly flaunting his mistress, Mrs Lane, the assize ball that he tried to throw was boycotted by the respectable of the city so that, Humphrey Prideaux observed, 'he failed of his main purpose, which was to entertain himselfe with the ladys'. 'All that have any reguard to their reputations', he concluded, 'think it scandalous to accept his invitations' (Thompson,

184). These circumstances explain why parliament narrowly failed to pass the bill the first time it was introduced, and again in 1693. Norfolk did finally succeed, first in persuading his wife to allow him to sell Castle Rising and other properties in 1695, and ultimately in obtaining a parliamentary act of divorce in 1700. But even his triumph brought liabilities, as he was ordered by parliament to repay to his wife the £10,000 he had received with her marriage portion. Before he was able to do so, however, he died of an apoplectic fit on 2 April 1701 at his London home, Norfolk House, St James's Square, Westminster. He was buried at Arundel, Sussex, six days later and the Norfolk title fell into the Catholic hands of his nephew, Thomas Howard (1683–1732). RACHEL WEIL

Sources Evelyn, *Diary* · GEC, *Peerage* · *A vindication of her grace Mary dutchess of Norfolk* (1693) · *The proceedings upon the bill of divorce between his grace the duke of Norfolk and the Lady Mary Mordaunt* (1700) · *State tracts: being a farther collection of several choice treatises relating to the government, from the year 1660 to 1689* (1692) · *The arguments of the right honorable, the late Lord Chancellor Nottingham, upon which he made the decree in the cause between the honorable Charles Howard, esq; plaintiff; Henry, late duke of Norfolk, Henry Lord Mowbrey his son, etc.* (1685) · *Memoirs of Sir John Reresby*, ed. A. Browning (1936) · N. Luttrell, *A brief historical relation of state affairs from September 1678 to April 1714*, 6 vols. (1857) · *The duke of Norfolk's case, or, The doctrine of perpetuities fully set forth and explained* (1688) · H. K. S. Causton, *The Howard papers: with a biographical pedigree and criticism* [1862] · J. R. Jones, *The revolution of 1688 in England* (1972) · C. Howard, *Historical anecdotes of some of the Howard family* (1769) · J. M. Robinson, *The dukes of Norfolk* (1982) · F. W. Steer, ed., *The Arundel Castle archives*, 4 vols. (1968–80) · G. Duckett, ed., *Penal laws and Test Act*, 2 vols. (1882–3) · *Bishop Burnet's History* · L. Stone, *Road to divorce: England, 1530–1987* (1990) · W. D. Macray, *A register of the members of St Mary Magdalen College, Oxford*, 8 vols. (1894–1915), vol. 4, p. 26 · Foster, *Alum. Oxon.* · *Letters of Humphrey Prideaux … to John Ellis*, ed. E. M. Thompson, CS, new ser., 15 (1875)
Archives Arundel Castle, West Sussex, papers
Likenesses W. Sherwin, engraving, 1687 (after J. Riley), AM Oxf. [*see illus.*] · possibly G. P. Harding, pen-and-ink, and wash drawing, NPG · S. Verelst, oils, Arundel Castle, West Sussex · oils, Arundel Castle, West Sussex

Howard, Henry [*alias* Henry Paston] **(1684–1720),** Roman Catholic priest, born on 10 December 1684, was the second son of Lord Thomas Howard (*d.* 1689) of Worksop and his wife, Elizabeth Marie (*d.* 1732), daughter of Sir John Saville of Copley, Yorkshire, and therefore grandson of Henry, sixth duke of Norfolk, and great-nephew of Cardinal Philip Howard. He entered the English College at Douai, where he assumed the name Paston, and studied with his brothers Thomas, Edward, and Philip. Thomas and Edward Howard afterwards became successively eighth and ninth dukes of Norfolk. There he was first noticed as defending universal philosophy in July 1704. He was listed as a divine for the academic year 1704–5. On 7 September 1706 he took the mission oath, on 16 December he received minor orders at Cambrai, and at Advent 1709, probably on 21 December, was ordained priest. He had passed with praise, it was afterwards asserted, through the courses of philosophy and theology.

In 1710 Howard joined the Pères de la Doctrine Chrétienne at Paris, at the time when the Jansenist controversy was raging there. The English Jesuits were strongly orthodox, and they persuaded Howard to move in the same year (May 1710) to the college of St Gregory, Paris. Here he resided until at least 1715, when he was visited by the duke of Norfolk and a party of family, but left without taking a degree. He returned to England on the mission, and is said, while living at Buckingham House, to have effected many conversions. For a time he worked in Lancashire, and in 1716 he was denounced as a 'popish priest' by Thomas Ford of Liverpool (Estcourt and Payne, 89). In April 1717 he signed two testimonials to and in favour of the vicar apostolic.

By 1719 Bishop Bonaventure Giffard, the ageing vicar apostolic of the London district, thought it wise to petition Rome for a coadjutor, and asked for Henry Howard. Giffard described him in a letter to Lawrence Mayes, an influential priest in Rome, as 'this most excellent person', and continued:

> His humility is so great that he applies himself wholely to the poorest sort of person … He frequently visits them in their poor cellars; he instructs them with incredible zeal, and the poorest and most abandoned by others are the objects of his care. (Hemphill, 67–8)

Giffard referred to his solid judgement, inoffensive temper, and his talent in preaching.

On 2 October 1720 Howard was appointed coadjutor to Bishop Giffard, with the title of bishop of Utica *in partibus*. He died, however, of a fever caught while visiting the poor, before his consecration, on 22 November 1720, and was buried at St Andrew's, Holborn, from Bedford Court on 26 November, but two days later his body was taken to Arundel Castle, accompanied by several brothers including the ninth duke of Norfolk. He was reburied there in the old family vault, under the lady chapel, in the Fitzalan chapel. 'Such charity,' said Bishop Giffard, 'such piety, has not been seen in our land of a long time' (Gillow, *Lit. biog. hist.*, 3.427).

W. A. J. ARCHBOLD, *rev.* TIMOTHY J. McCANN

Sources G. Anstruther, *The seminary priests*, 3 (1976), 105 · 'The register book of St Gregory's College, Paris, 1667–1786', *Miscellanea, XI*, Catholic RS, 19 (1917), 93–160 · E. H. Burton and E. Nolan, *The Douai College diaries: the seventh diary, 1715–1778*, Catholic RS, 28 (1928) · *The letter book of Lewis Sabran*, ed. G. Holt, Catholic RS, 62 (1971) · P. R. Harris, ed., *Douai College documents, 1639–1794*, Catholic RS, 63 (1972) · E. E. Estcourt and J. O. Payne, eds., *The English Catholic nonjurors of 1715*, [8 vols.] (1886) · Gillow, *Lit. biog. hist.*, 3.426–7 · B. Hemphill, *The early vicars apostolic of England, 1685–1750* (1954), 52, 53, 59, 67–8 · M. A. Tierney, *The history and antiquities of the castle and town of Arundel*, 2 vols. (1834) · Westm. DA · Burke, *Peerage* (1980)
Archives Arundel Castle, West Sussex, archives · Westm. DA
Likenesses portrait (Henry Howard?); formerly at Greystoke, 1891

Howard, Henry, fourth earl of Carlisle (1694–1758). *See under* Howard, Charles, third earl of Carlisle (1669–1738).

Howard, Henry, twelfth earl of Suffolk and fifth earl of Berkshire (1739–1779), politician, was born on 10 or 16 May 1739, the eldest son of William Howard, styled Viscount Andover (*bap.* 1714, *d.* 1756), politician, and his wife, Mary (1717–1803), the second daughter of Heneage Finch, second earl of Aylesford, and his second wife, Mary Fisher. He was educated at Eton College from 1748 and entered

Henry Howard, twelfth earl of Suffolk and fifth earl of Berkshire (1739–1779), by Sir Joshua Reynolds, 1780 [replica; original, 1778]

Magdalen College, Oxford, in 1757; he graduated MA in 1759 and DCL in 1761. Styled Viscount Andover after his father's death on 15 July 1756, he succeeded his grandfather as earl of Suffolk and Berkshire on 21 March 1757, when he inherited the main family estate of Charlton, Wiltshire, as well as others in Staffordshire and Westmorland. On 25 May 1764 he married Lady Maria Trevor (1744–1767), the eldest daughter of Robert Hampden-*Trevor, first Viscount Hampden, and his wife, Constantia de Huybert. She died in childbirth on 8 February 1767, and more than ten years later, on 14 August 1777, he married his cousin Charlotte (1754–1828), the eldest daughter of his uncle Heneage Finch, third earl of Aylesford, and his wife, Charlotte Seymour. Their two sons both died in infancy.

From 1760 Suffolk, a year younger than George III himself, was much in favour at the royal court. He was bearer of the sword at the coronation and was invited to a very select ball at court in November 1761. It is not clear why in 1762 he allowed himself to be put forward for the chancellorship of Oxford University against the government candidate Lord Litchfield, being the candidate of the supposed whig interest in that traditionally tory stronghold; his youth was an obvious objection, and a widespread view was that his candidature came twenty years too soon. He did not stand a poll. Suffolk's inclination in national politics was to support government. His maiden speech in the Lords, on 9 December 1762, was in favour of the terms of what would be the peace of Paris. In 1763 he was given the court post of deputy earl marshal. He seconded the Lords address on 24 November 1763 and spoke often in

support of George Grenville's ministry. His political loyalty was transferred to Grenville, and on that minister's dismissal in July 1765 Suffolk decided to resign his court post; however, he was persuaded to remain in office under Lord Rockingham. He nevertheless, so he told Grenville, informed the king of 'the total impossibility of my supporting any measures contrary to those which had been adopted by my friends and connections' (*Additional Grenville Papers*, 303). On 29 October he was replaced by a Rockinghamite peer. American policy was what Suffolk had in mind, and he was always to be a hardliner on that issue. In the parliamentary session of 1765–6 he took a leading role in criticizing the policy that led to repeal of the Stamp Act. On 17 December 1765 he proposed a Lords denunciation of colonial resistance, and on 14 January 1766 he was one of only two peers to criticize the rather ambiguous address. It was Suffolk who on 29 January drew up a list of opposition resolutions for the Lords, and who on 4 February actually carried one, by sixty-three votes to sixty, 'requiring' compensation to be paid by colonial rioters. In the Lords debate of 11 March on the repeal of the Stamp Act he replied to the argument that the Lords should agree with the Commons by haughtily declaring that the house constituted 'the hereditary Council of this Kingdom, not subject to the caprice of interested electors' (Thomas, *British Politics*, 244–5).

Suffolk was never at ease in opposition, and in 1766 he vainly asked Grenville not to oppose the new Chatham ministry. But by March 1767 he was urging Grenville to construct an opposition alliance to oppose what he deemed to be the weak ministerial policy on America, and he spoke in several debates as part of such an alliance. His health was already deteriorating, and he was often absent from Westminster during the later 1760s, when there is little evidence of his parliamentary or other political activity. This semi-retirement paradoxically ended on Grenville's death in November 1770. His rank and parliamentary prominence led Suffolk to stand forth as his successor, and it was with the earl that the prime minister, Lord North, negotiated the accession of Grenvillites to the administration. In January 1771 Suffolk was offered the northern secretaryship, though 'a young man of thirty-two, totally unpractised in business, pompous, ignorant, and of no parts', as Horace Walpole scathingly wrote. 'The young Earl answered with modesty, that as he could not speak French, he was incapable of treating with foreign ministers, nor was he conversant in business: he wished for some high office, but not that of Secretary' (Walpole, *Memoirs*, 4.173). He was appointed lord privy seal, but few Grenvillites followed his leadership. Four months later, in June, he succeeded the deceased Lord Halifax as northern secretary.

Suffolk, who entirely lacked diplomatic and administrative experience and was dogged by ill health, owed his cabinet post to Lord North's desire to strengthen his ministry in parliament. Walpole noted in 1771 that, 'though young, he is all over gout' (*Letters of Horace Walpole*, 8.1). Yet contrary to contemporary expectation, and belying his historical reputation, he pulled his weight in the ministry.

In parliament he was a frequent speaker, especially on America as the colonial crisis deteriorated into war. He was prominent also in cabinet. It was Suffolk who suggested the 1774 general election, to pre-empt any colonial influence. He early pressed for the recall of the soft-line General Gage from America, he advocated the arrest of Benjamin Franklin before he left Britain, he ordered the prosecution of radical John Horne Tooke for a seditious libel about Lexington, and he temporarily took charge of the American department in 1775 when the American secretary, Dartmouth, proved unwilling to conduct the war. But while Suffolk never relaxed his opinion on America, northern Europe was his departmental concern, and here he performed his duties with pragmatic competence, ever on the lookout for allies. His personal preference was for a renewal of the Austrian alliance that had ended in 1756. But the logic of the first partition of Poland in 1772, described by an indifferent Suffolk as 'this curious transaction' (Scott, 179), was that a reconciliation with France seemed the only viable option. In 1773 Suffolk finally abandoned the decade-long search for a Russian alliance. But he always disapproved of a rapprochement with France, and on the outbreak of the American War of Independence in 1775 conceived the idea of hiring 20,000 Russian soldiers, commenting to his under-secretary William Eden that they would be 'charming visitors at New York, and [would] civilize that part of America wonderfully' (ibid., 218). Catherine II refused, angry at Russia's being treated on a par with Hesse, whence Suffolk obtained the soldiers in 1776. In the wider diplomatic sphere Suffolk, anxious to avoid a European war until the American rebellion was crushed, now pragmatically sought to appease France and Spain, contrary to the view of the southern secretary, Weymouth. Supported by George III and Lord North, Suffolk overruled Weymouth in a successful attempt to keep Spain and France apart. When France alone entered the war in 1778, Suffolk sought to construct a diversionary war front in Europe and approached the other three great powers, Austria, Prussia, and Russia, even suggesting in April 1778 a Prussian alliance that would reconstruct the successful scenario of the Seven Years' War. But he was knocking on closed doors: no one wanted Britain as an ally or to fight France.

By now Suffolk's health had given way. In 1777 Walpole wrote of his new second wife, 'she cannot complain of being made a nurse, for he could have no other reason for marrying her, she is so plain' (*Letters of Horace Walpole*, 10.92). On 7 April 1778, the same day that Chatham collapsed in the Lords, Suffolk spoke 'with every symptom of debility, repeated his own phrases, could not recollect his own ideas' (ibid., 10.214). By January 1779 he was unable to perform his official duties, and his death on 7 March at Bath merely prevented his long-rumoured resignation. He was not yet forty. He was buried at Charlton, Wiltshire, on 20 March. PETER D. G. THOMAS

Sources P. Lawson, *George Grenville: a political life* (1984) · H. M. Scott, *British foreign policy in the age of the American revolution* (1990) · P. D. G. Thomas, *British politics and the Stamp Act crisis: the first phase of the American revolution, 1763–1767* (1975) · P. D. G. Thomas, *Tea party to independence: the third phase of the American Revolution, 1773–1776* (1991) · *The Grenville papers: being the correspondence of Richard Grenville … and … George Grenville*, ed. W. J. Smith, 4 vols. (1852–3) · *Additional Grenville papers, 1763–1765*, ed. J. R. G. Tomlinson (1962) · *The letters of Horace Walpole, fourth earl of Orford*, ed. P. Toynbee, 16 vols. (1903–5); suppl., 3 vols. (1918–25) · H. Walpole, *Memoirs of the reign of King George the Third*, ed. G. F. R. Barker, 4 vols. (1894) · *Hist. U. Oxf.* 5: *18th-cent. Oxf.* · GEC, *Peerage*
Archives BL, corresp. with R. Cunning, William Eden, etc., Egerton MSS 2700–2706, Add. MSS 34412–34460 · BL, corresp. with George Grenville, Add. MS 57816 · BL, corresp. with Sir Robert Keith, Add. MSS 35503–35545 · NMM, Sandwich MSS · NRA, priv. coll., letters to Charles, ninth Lord Cathcart
Likenesses A. Ramsay, oils, *c*.1758, Eton College, Berkshire · J. Reynolds, oils, 1780 (after original, 1778); Sothebys, 18 Nov 1987, lot 44 [*see illus.*] · J. Reynolds, oils, Charlton, Wiltshire

Howard, Henry (**1757–1842**), landowner and antiquary, was born at Corby Castle, Cumberland, on 2 July 1757, the eldest son of Philip Howard (1730–1810) of Corby Castle, religious writer, and Anne, daughter of Henry Witham of Cliff, Yorkshire. His was a Roman Catholic family: his father wrote a *Scriptural History of the Earth and of Mankind* (1797) and published an address to the Anglican episcopacy on the Test Act in 1801. Henry Howard was educated at the college of the English Benedictines at Douai, and for a short time in 1774 studied at the University of Paris. On 17 December 1774 he entered the Theresian Academy in Vienna, where he became a friend of Montecuculi and Marsigli. He left Vienna in September 1777 but, failing to obtain permission to serve in the English army, he travelled for a time with his parents.

Howard studied at Strasbourg for two to three years where he lived with his parents and often visited Cardinal Rohan. Both the governor, M. de la Salle, and General Wurmser treated him well. The latter tried to persuade him to accept a commission in the Austrian service but he refused, still hoping to obtain a commission in the English army. In 1782 he went with Prince Christian of Hesse-Darmstadt to the camp at Prague. In 1784 an attempt by the earl of Surrey to have him admitted into the German detachment of the Duke of York's failed.

The next year Howard retired to Corby to spend the rest of his life as a country gentleman and antiquary. On 4 or 26 November 1788 he married Maria (*d*. 1789), third daughter and coheir of Andrew Archer, last Lord Archer of Umberslade (1736–1778), and his wife, Sarah West (1741–1801). She died on 9 November 1789 giving birth to their only child, a daughter, who also died. The monument by Nollekens erected to her memory in Wetheral church, Cumberland, is the subject of a sonnet by Wordsworth. Howard's second wife, whom he married on 18 March 1793, was Catherine Mary (*d*. 1849), the second daughter of Sir Richard Neave, bt, of Dagnam Park, Essex. They had two sons and three daughters. His wife kept extensive journals and had her *Reminiscences*, of the years 1836 to 1838, printed privately in four volumes for her children.

In politics Howard was a whig; he signed the petition in favour of parliamentary reform and continually advocated the repeal of the penal laws against Roman Catholics. In 1795 he was made captain in the 1st York militia, serving for a time in Ireland. In 1802 he raised the Edenside rangers, and in 1803 the Cumberland rangers; for the latter regiment he wrote a small work on the drill of light infantry. In later life he was a friend and correspondent of Louis Philippe. In 1832 he became high sheriff of Cumberland.

His main published works were *Remarks on the Erroneous Opinions Entertained Respecting the Catholic Religion* (1825) and *Indications of Memorials … of Persons of the Howard Family* (1834). He was a fellow of the Society of Antiquaries and contributed papers to *Archaeologia* in 1800 and 1803. He also helped other historians in their work; these included Dr Lingard and Miss Strickland. Howard died at Corby Castle on 1 March 1842; he bequeathed the estates left to him by Charles, eleventh duke of Norfolk, to Charles John Howard, Viscount Andover, and to his eldest son, Philip Henry Howard.

W. A. J. ARCHBOLD, rev. J. A. MARCHAND

Sources GM, 2nd ser., 17 (1842), 437–8 · GEC, *Peerage* · Gillow, *Lit. biog. hist.*, 1.437 · IGI · GM, 1st ser., 59 (1789), 1057 · will, PRO, PROB 11/1965, sig. 479
Archives Arundel Castle, West Sussex, papers · priv. coll., corresp. | Bodl. Oxf., corresp. with Sir Thomas Phillipps · UCL, letters to James Brougham
Likenesses C. Turner, mezzotint (after J. A. Oliver, 1839), BM
Wealth at death estate and property left to him by Charles, duke of Norfolk; bequethed to Hon. Charles John Howard (Lord Viscount Andover) and his own eldest son Philip Henry Howard; bequethed £200 each to rest of children; personal estate to wife: will, PRO, PROB 11/1965, sig. 479

Howard, Henry (1769–1847), portrait and history painter, was born in London on 31 January 1769, the son of a coach-builder in Wardour Street. He received his elementary education at a school at Hounslow, and in 1786, aged seventeen, became a pupil of the painter Philip Reinagle. In 1788 he entered the Royal Academy Schools, where in 1790 he gained the first silver medal for the best drawing from the life, and the gold medal for historical painting for *Caractacus Recognising the Dead Body of his Son*.

Howard left London in March 1791, and travelled to Italy via France and Switzerland. He took with him a letter of introduction from Sir Joshua Reynolds to Lord Hervey, then British minister at Florence, in which Sir Joshua said of his *Caractacus* that 'it was the opinion of the Academicians that his picture was the best that had been presented to the Academy ever since its foundation' (Ingamells, 527). At Rome he met Flaxman and John Deare, and joined them in a diligent study of sculpture. In 1792 he painted the *Dream of Cain* (exh. RA, 1794) and sent it to England in competition for the travelling studentship of the Royal Academy, without success. In 1793 he applied, from Rome, for an annuity from the Royal Academy. Reinagle spoke in his favour, describing his former pupil as an 'ingenious young man & of gentleman like manners' (Farington, *Diary*, 9 Nov 1793) who sought the academy's support following the bankruptcy of his father. The painter Edmund Garvey, below whom Howard lived in the strada Georgiana in Rome, was also impressed with the young painter's character, and spoke 'warmly in favour of … his ability & character' (ibid.). In 1794 Howard returned home via

Vienna and Dresden. On his return he instructed Reinagle's daughter, Jane (b. 1780), in drawing, having 'known her from an infant state' (ibid., 24 April 1811). They married about 1803 and had four daughters and three sons.

In 1795 Howard sent three small pictures and a portrait, and in 1796 a finished sketch from Milton's *Paradise Lost*, *The Planets Drawing Light from the Sun*, and other works to the Royal Academy. He made some designs for Sharpe's *British Essayists*, Du Roveray's edition of Pope's translation of Homer, and other books, and he painted some of his own designs on the vases made at Wedgwood's pottery. In 1799 he began a series of drawings of English ancient sculpture for engravings published by the Dilettanti Society. He made further drawings of sculpture for the collector Charles Townley and the sculptor John Flaxman in 1800 and 1801 respectively, and later for the Society of Engravers. His drawings in Indian ink and chalk were highly finished.

In 1800 Howard exhibited *Eve* and *The Dream of the Red Cross Knight* at the Royal Academy and was elected an associate a year later. He continued to exhibit there until his death in 1847, being elected a full academician in 1808. His diploma work was *The Four Angels Loosed from the Great River Euphrates*. Other exhibited works included *Love Animating the Statue of Pygmalion* (exh. RA, 1802; V&A) and *Sabrina*, shown in 1805, the first of a series of pictures from Milton's *Comus*, which furnished him with subjects almost to the end of his career. In 1809 he exhibited *Christ Blessing Young Children*, which later formed the altarpiece at St Luke's, Berwick Street, London. He also showed a number of works relating to Shakespeare, for example *Titania* (exh. RA, 1809); *Caliban Teased by the Spirits of Prospero* (exh. RA, 1822); and *Shakespeare Nursed in the Lap of Fancy* (exh. RA, 1831; Sir John Soane's Museum, London). One of his most important patrons was Lord Egremont, for whom Howard painted *The Apotheosis of the Princess Charlotte* in 1818 and who later bought a number of other works, including *Lear and Cordelia* (exh. RA, 1820; Sir John Soane's Museum, London), *Study of Beech Trees at Knowle Park* (exh. RA, 1820), and *The House of Morpheus, Hylas Carried off by the Nymphs* (exh. RA, 1826).

In 1806 Howard moved to 5 Newman Street, the former residence of the sculptor Thomas Banks, and lived there until the end of his life. He became secretary of the Royal Academy in 1811 and in 1833 was appointed professor of painting; his lectures were published by his son Frank in 1848.

Howard also painted a number of decorative works. In 1805 he was commissioned by a Mr Hibbert to paint an extensive frieze representing the story of Cupid and Psyche and in 1814, on the occasion of the visit to London of the allied sovereigns, he painted the large transparencies for the Temple of Concord erected in Hyde Park (assisted by Stothard, Hilton, and others). In 1835 he adapted an earlier exhibited work, *Solar System* (exh. RA, 1823) for the ceiling of the duchess of Sutherland's boudoir at Stafford House, followed in 1835 by subjects drawn from the Pandora myth and in 1837 by a modification of Guido's *Aurora* for ceilings at the Soane Museum. Howard took part unsuccessfully in the Westminster Hall competition of 1842. He continued to exhibit, but with rapidly failing powers, until 1847, when he sent to Westminster Hall a second cartoon, *Satyrs Finding a Sleeping Cyclops*.

Howard died at George Street, St Michael, Oxford, on 5 October 1847 of paralysis and general decay, leaving three sons: Frank *Howard (1805–1866), also a history and portrait painter; William, advocate-general in Bombay, killed while hunting in 1862; and Edward Irvine, founder of the *Bombay Quarterly*, killed in a railway accident in 1868. Howard was never a popular artist. His early works were his best, and many of them were engraved for the *Literary Souvenir*, *The Keepsake*, *The Gem*, and other annuals. Sir John Soane's Museum and the National Portrait Gallery, London, possess a number of his works.

R. E. GRAVES, *rev.* DEBORAH GRAHAM-VERNON

Sources H. Howard, *A course of lectures on painting*, ed. F. Howard (1848) · J. Ingamells, ed., *A dictionary of British and Irish travellers in Italy, 1701–1800* (1997) · Farington, *Diary* · *The Athenaeum* (9 Oct 1847) · *The Art Union* (1847), 378 · *The Times* (9 Oct 1847) · S. C. Hutchison, *The history of the Royal Academy, 1768–1968* (1968) · Graves, *RA exhibitors* · will, PRO, PROB 11/2063, sig. 778 · d. cert.
Likenesses A. E. Chalon, group portrait, pen, ink, and watercolour (*Students at the British Institution, 1805*), BM · G. Dance, drawing, RA · J. Flaxman, plaster bust, Sir John Soane's Museum, London

Howard, Henry Charles, thirteenth duke of Norfolk (1791–1856), politician, the only son of Bernard Edward *Howard, twelfth duke of Norfolk (1765–1842), and his wife, Elizabeth Belasyse (1770–1819), third daughter of Henry, the second and last Earl Fauconberg, was born on 12 August 1791 in George Street, Hanover Square, London. Three years after his birth his parents were divorced, in May 1794, by act of parliament, and his mother then married her lover, the Hon. Richard Bingham, later second earl of Lucan. On 27 December 1814 Howard married Lady Charlotte Leveson-Gower (1788–1870), the eldest daughter of George Granville, first duke of Sutherland, KG. She was a lady of the bedchamber from 1842. His father had succeeded to the title and estates of the dukedom of Norfolk on the death, on 16 December 1815, of his cousin Charles, the eleventh duke, and Howard, as heir, was styled (1815–42) earl of Arundel and Surrey.

On the passing of the Act of Catholic Emancipation in April 1829, the earl was the first Roman Catholic since the Reformation to take the oaths and his seat in the House of Commons. He sat as MP for Horsham from 1829 to 1832, Hurst, the sitting member, having resigned in 1829 to give him the opportunity. He was elected in 1832, in 1835, and in 1837 as member for the western division of Sussex. In politics he was a staunch whig. From July 1837 to June 1841 he was treasurer of the queen's household in Melbourne's ministry. In August 1841 he was summoned to the House of Lords as Baron Maltravers.

When his father died, on 16 March 1842, Howard succeeded to the dukedom, and during Russell's premiership was master of the horse (July 1846 to February 1852). On 4 May 1848 he was created a knight of the Garter, and, under Aberdeen's ministry, was lord steward of the household (4 January 1853 to 10 January 1854). Holding that 'ultramontane opinions are totally incompatible with allegiance to our Sovereign and with our constitution' (Machin, 219), he supported Russell's Ecclesiastical Titles Bill, but never formally renounced his faith, though he built Anglican schools on his estates. On his deathbed he was reconciled by Canon Tierney to the Roman Catholic religion, a fact recorded on his coffin plate. Known as 'old Pepper and Potatoes', Norfolk was more pompously ducal than the other Howards, and he had a reputation for arrogance; Thomas Creevey found him 'odious'. He expanded Arundel Castle and developed New Glossop. He was also at one time president of the Royal Botanic Society of London. He died at Arundel Castle on 18 February 1856, and was buried in the family vault in the parish church at Arundel on 26 February.

Norfolk had three sons, Henry Granville Fitzalan-*Howard, his heir and successor, Edward George Fitzalan-*Howard, afterwards Baron Howard of Glossop, and Lord Bernard Thomas Howard, born on 30 December 1825, who died during his travels in the East at Cairo on 21 December 1846; and two daughters, Lady Mary Charlotte, married in 1849 to Thomas Henry, fourth Lord Foley, and Lady Adeliza Matilda, married in October 1855 to Lord George John Manners, third son of the fifth duke of Rutland. CHARLES KENT, *rev.* H. C. G. MATTHEW

Sources GEC, *Peerage* · *The Times* (19 Feb 1856) · J. M. Robinson, *The dukes of Norfolk* (1982) · G. I. T. Machin, *Politics and the churches in Great Britain, 1832 to 1868* (1977)
Archives Arundel Castle, West Sussex, corresp. and papers | W. Sussex RO, letters to duke of Richmond
Likenesses H. J. Stewart, pencil and watercolour drawing, 1849, Scot. NPG · attrib. J. O. Archer, oils, Arundel Castle, Sussex · D. Dalbey, oils, Arundel Castle, Sussex · G. Hayter, group portrait, oils (*The House of Commons, 1833*), NPG · G. Hayter, oils (as a page at the coronation of George IV), Arundel Castle, Sussex

Howard, Henry Edward John (1795–1868), dean of Lichfield, the youngest child of Frederick *Howard, fifth earl of Carlisle (1748–1825), and his wife, Margaret Caroline Leveson-Gower (1753–1824), and brother of George *Howard, sixth earl of Carlisle, was born at Castle Howard, Yorkshire, on 14 December 1795, and entered at Eton College in 1805. He matriculated from Christ Church, Oxford, in 1814, graduated BA in 1818, MA in 1822, BD in 1834, and DD in 1838. In 1820 he was ordained deacon and priest, and in 1822 appointed succentor of York Cathedral, with the prebendal stall of Holme attached. He held the living of Slingsby, Yorkshire, in the gift of his father, from 1823 to 1833. On 13 July 1824 he married Henrietta Elizabeth, sixth daughter of Ichabod Wright of Mapperley Hall, Nottinghamshire. They had five sons and five daughters.

Howard became dean of Lichfield and rector of Tatenhill, Staffordshire (a preferment worth £1524 a year with a residence), on 27 November 1833, and in the following year he also obtained the rectory of Donington, Shropshire, worth £1000 per annum. He took part in, and contributed largely to, the restoration of Lichfield Cathedral (1842–3), undertaken at the instigation of the banker Richard Greene. The establishment of the Lichfield Diocesan Training School, afterwards united to that at Saltley, as well as of the Theological College, owed much to his efforts. He was a scholarly cleric, who published translations from the Latin poet Claudian (1823, 1854) and of Old Testament books (1855–7). Howard died, after many years of physical infirmity, at his home, Donington rectory on 8 October 1868. A memorial effigy was placed in Lichfield Cathedral.   G. C. BOASE, *rev.* M. C. CURTHOYS

Sources *The Guardian* (14 Oct 1868) · *ILN* (17 Oct 1868), 386 · *VCH Staffordshire*, vol. 14 · J. Burke, *The portrait gallery of distinguished females*, 2 vols. (1833), 2.99–100
Likenesses effigy, Lichfield Cathedral
Wealth at death under £60,000: resworn probate, April 1869, *CGPLA Eng. & Wales*

Howard, Henry Fitzalan-, fifteenth duke of Norfolk (1847–1917), courtier, born at Carlton House Terrace, London, on 27 December 1847, was the eldest son of Henry Granville Fitzalan-*Howard, fourteenth duke (1815–1860), and his wife, Augusta (1821–1886), younger daughter of the first Baron Lyons. Edmund Bernard Fitzalan-*Howard, first Viscount FitzAlan of Derwent (1855–1947), was a younger brother. In 1860, at the age of thirteen, he succeeded his father. In that year he was sent to the Oratory School, Edgbaston, Birmingham, where John Henry Newman was endeavouring to imbue the sons of English Roman Catholics with the English public-school tradition. At the age of seventeen the duke was sent abroad to travel. He stayed for a long time at Constantinople with his uncle, Richard Bickerton Pemell *Lyons, Earl Lyons, to whose formative influence he owed much.

Norfolk married twice. On 21 November 1877, at the Brompton Oratory, he married Lady Flora Paulyna Hetty Barbara Abney-Hastings (1854–1887), daughter of Charles Frederick, first Baron Donington. She died on 11 April 1887 having had an only son who died in 1902. The duke married his second wife, Gwendolen Mary (1877–1945), elder daughter of Marmaduke, eleventh Lord Herries, on 15 February 1904 at Everingham, Yorkshire. She succeeded to her father's Scottish lordship of parliament in 1908. They had a son and three daughters.

While still a young man the duke began his long career of work on behalf of his co-religionists. His judgement was active and independent to a degree which must have tried the patience of great prelates and others in authority. Their arguments, except on matters of doctrine, were always subjected to his searching criticism, in spite of his regard for the individuals with whom the arguments originated.

Politically, he was a pronounced unionist and he was postmaster-general from 1895 to 1900. He balanced his unionism with substantial donations to Roman Catholic schools and churches in Ireland. He resigned from Salisbury's government in order to volunteer for active service, as an officer of the imperial yeomanry, in the Second South African War. He remained active in the House of Lords, but never again held ministerial office. He was the first mayor of Westminster in 1899; he was mayor of Sheffield in 1895, and first lord mayor of that city in 1896. The parks and recreation grounds which he gave to Sheffield covered 160 acres and were valued at £150,000. He was one of the founders of the University of Sheffield, and its first chancellor (1904).

Throughout his life the duke of Norfolk was in close relations with the Vatican, and he had dealings with four successive popes. In 1887 he was sent by Queen Victoria as a special envoy to Pope Leo XIII, reciprocating a visit from a papal envoy to her jubilee celebrations. His influence was credited with gaining the cardinal's hat for John Henry Newman in 1897. He several times entertained papal nuncios who came on missions to this country. He liked such duties, though he was sufficiently British to find entertaining eminent foreigners rather irksome. He was intensely interested in public ceremonials, both civil and ecclesiastical, and his hereditary office of earl marshal was for him no sinecure. Despite his Roman Catholicism, he found himself arranging Anglican ceremonies. He managed the funerals of Gladstone and Victoria. At the coronation of Edward VII in 1902 he revived many historical practices which had fallen into disuse. Both on this occasion and at the coronation of George V in 1911, he collaborated happily with the Anglican bishops. Despite his enthusiasm he struggled with his administrative duties as earl marshal. Following the funeral of his father, George V commented that the duke was 'a charming, honourable, straightforward little gentleman, no better in the world. But as a man of business he is absolutely impossible' (Rose, 77).

Norfolk's careful attention to detail is illustrated by the architectural works for which he assumed responsibility. He was a great builder, passionately devoted to the Gothic style. His first church was that of Our Lady and St Philip Neri at Arundel, of which Joseph Aloysius Hansom was the architect. As the duke's taste developed, he cultivated an earlier and severer style; he preferred the great church of St John the Baptist at Norwich to any of his other buildings. He became more and more independent of his architects, and during years of mourning and bereavement he found a constant solace in working out his own designs. All his buildings boast stained glass of high quality, but especially the exquisite little chapel which he built at Arundel Castle. The duke died from gastric influenza at Norfolk House, London, on 11 February 1917, and was buried at Arundel. He was succeeded by his son, Bernard Marmaduke Fitzalan-*Howard (1908–1975).

[ANON.], *rev.* K. D. REYNOLDS

Sources GEC, *Peerage* · E. R. Norman, *The English Catholic church in the nineteenth century* (1984) · *The Times* (12 Feb 1917) · K. Rose, *King George V* (1983) · W. R. Kuhn, *Democratic royalism: the transformation of the British monarchy, 1861–1914* (1996)
Archives Arundel Castle, West Sussex, corresp. and papers · Sheff. Arch., corresp. and papers relating to Sheffield estates | BL, corresp. with W. E. Gladstone, Add. MSS 44421–44783, *passim* · BL, corresp. with Arthur James Balfour, Add. MS 49821, *passim* · CUL, corresp. with Lord Hardinge · NL Ire., corresp. with William Monsell, first Baron Emly · priv. coll., letters to Edwin de Lisle · U. St Andr. L., corresp. with Wilfrid Ward
Likenesses E. Moore, oils, 1897, Arundel Castle, West Sussex · E. O. Ford, statue, 1900, City Hall, Sheffield · P. de Laszlo, oils, 1908, Arundel Castle, West Sussex · Elliott & Fry, photograph, NPG; repro. in *Our conservative and unionist statesmen* (1896–7), vol. 2 · J. Russell & Sons, photograph, NPG · Spy [L. Ward], caricature,

chromolithograph, NPG; repro. in *VF* (1 Oct 1881) • Walery, photograph, NPG

Wealth at death under £300,000: probate, 19 May 1917, *CGPLA Eng. & Wales*

Howard, Henry Frederick, fifteenth earl of Arundel, fifth earl of Surrey, and second earl of Norfolk (1608–1652), nobleman, was born at Arundel Castle, Sussex, on 15 August 1608, the second but eldest surviving son of Thomas *Howard, fourteenth earl of Arundel (1585–1646), and his wife, Lady Alathea Talbot (*d.* 1654), third daughter and coheir of Gilbert *Talbot, seventh earl of Shrewsbury. The godson of Queen Anne, Howard was made KB at the creation of Charles, prince of Wales, on 3 November 1616, after which he was educated on the continent; in 1624 he was at St John's College, Cambridge. He succeeded to the courtesy title of Lord Maltravers on the death of his elder brother in 1624. On 7 March 1626 he married Lady Elizabeth Stuart (*d.* 1674), eldest daughter of Esmé *Stuart, third duke of Lennox. The match was arranged without the knowledge of the king, who had intended that the bride, his own ward and kinswoman, should marry Archibald, Lord Lorne. Arundel was committed to the Tower and the couple were confined at Lambeth under the supervision of Archbishop Abbot.

Howard was elected MP for Arundel, Sussex, in 1628 and, although probably more interested in the family's art collection than in politics, assumed office commensurate with his status as heir to the premier earldom in England. He was a gentleman of the privy chamber, member of the high commission, and joint lord lieutenant of Northumberland, Cumberland and Westmorland, Sussex and Surrey, and Norfolk. His friendship with the earl of Ormond, and his concern to recover ancestral lands in Ireland, probably lay behind his election to the Irish parliament as MP for Callan in 1634 and his nomination as an Irish privy councillor in the same year. From 1636 he also served as deputy to his father as earl marshal of England.

Howard strove to raise troops for the king during the first bishops' war, and was returned MP for Arundel in the Short Parliament of 1640. He was elevated to the Lords as Baron Mowbray on 21 March 1640. During the Long Parliament he absented himself during the vote on the attainder of Strafford and caused a minor stir in July 1641 when an altercation with Philip Herbert, fourth earl of Pembroke, at a parliamentary committee ended in blows and the committal of both men to the Tower. He was a vocal supporter of the king's interest in early 1642, not least over the militia, and by June had joined Charles at York, where he proved willing both to lend money and to implement the commission of array. He subsequently fought at Edgehill, served on the council of war at Oxford, and held the post of governor of Arundel Castle, although his letters reveal a sense of gloom regarding both the war and the prospects of a peaceful settlement. The illness of his father took him to Padua in 1645 and he stayed with him until his father's death on 4 October 1646, when he succeeded as fifteenth earl of Arundel, fifth earl of Surrey, second earl of Norfolk, and earl marshal of England. Returning to England he found his estates sequestered, on

account of delinquency and recusancy; the sequestration was not lifted until late 1648, upon payment of a fine of £6000. Ongoing suspicions regarding Arundel's religion and royalist activity, however, ensured that his dispute with the government continued and that his estates were sequestered again in 1651. Neither this matter nor the bitter familial row over the inheritance of the estate was settled in his lifetime. He died in London, at Arundel House in the Strand, on 17 April 1652 and was buried at Arundel Castle. He had nine sons and three daughters, including his mentally ill eldest son, Thomas (1627–1677), who was restored to the dukedom of Norfolk in December 1660, though he never returned to England; Henry *Howard (1628–1684), his second son, was sixth duke of Norfolk, his third son, Philip *Howard, the future cardinal, and his fourth son, Charles *Howard, a landowner and natural philosopher.   GORDON GOODWIN, *rev.* J. T. PEACEY

Sources GEC, *Peerage* • *CSP dom.*, 1631–50 • M. F. S. Hervey, *The life, correspondence and collections of Thomas Howard, earl of Arundel* (1921) • *JHL*, 4 (1628–42), 234, 236, 509, 622, 627 • M. A. E. Green, ed., *Calendar of the proceedings of the committee for compounding … 1643–1660*, 1, PRO (1889), 295, 620, 645; 4 (1892), 2461 • Clarendon, *Hist. rebellion*, 1.345; 2.186, 540; 3.287–8 • *CSP Ire.*, 1633–47 • H. Howard, letters to W. Petty and MSS, BL, Add. MS 15970, fols. 7, 8, 10, 14, 16, 17, 23, 65, 67 • Arundel Castle MSS, MD1249 • BL, Harley MS 6852, fols. 37, 85, 92, 117, 204, 233 • *Calendar of the manuscripts of the marquess of Ormonde*, new ser., 8 vols., HMC, 36 (1902–20), vol. 1, pp. 26–9, 36

Archives Arundel Castle, West Sussex, papers | BL, letters to William Petty and papers, Add. MS 15970

Likenesses A. Van Dyck, portrait, *c.*1632–1640, Arundel Castle, West Sussex; repro. in Hervey, *Life, correspondence and collections*, 334 • P. Lombart, line engravings (after A. Van Dyck), BM, NPG

Howard, Henry Granville Fitzalan-, fourteenth duke of Norfolk (1815–1860), Roman Catholic layman and politician, the eldest of the three sons of Henry Charles *Howard, thirteenth duke (1791–1856), and his wife, Charlotte Leveson-Gower (1788–1870), eldest daughter of George Granville, first duke of Sutherland, was born Henry Granville Howard on 7 November 1815 in Great Stanhope Street, London, and baptized a Roman Catholic. Known to his family as Fitz (from his courtesy title, Lord Fitzalan), he was educated privately and at Trinity College, Cambridge, but did not take a degree. Afterwards he entered the Life Guards as a cornet, eventually retiring as captain. Fitzalan was elected MP for Arundel at the general election of 1837, a seat he held in the whig interest for fourteen years. He fell in love with a Miss Pitt, of whom very little is known; they never married and his father suggested he take a trip abroad to forget her. While travelling in Greece during the autumn of 1838 he became seriously ill at Athens, and recuperated at the British embassy there. On 19 June 1839 he married Augusta Marie Minna Catherine (1821–1886), younger daughter of Admiral Sir Edmund Lyons, the ambassador at Athens. They had three sons, one of whom, Philip Thomas (1853–1855), died in infancy, and eight daughters. His eldest son, Henry Fitzalan-*Howard (1847–1917), succeeded him as fifteenth duke, and his eldest daughter married the parliamentary barrister J. R. Hope-Scott (1812–1873).

Soon after his marriage Fitzalan met the Catholic writer

Henry Granville Fitzalan-Howard, fourteenth duke of Norfolk (1815–1860), by unknown artist

and politician Count de Montalembert in Paris. The friendship that resulted was the most important of his early life. Until then he had been only nominally Catholic; now he threw himself into the French Catholic revival of the 1840s, attending mass at Notre Dame, and listening to the sermons of Père Lacordaire and Père de Ravignon. 'You must look upon me as a convert', he told Montalembert. For his part Montalembert considered Fitzalan 'the most pious layman of our times' (Montalembert, 770).

This 'conversion' determined Fitzalan's life's work. He became earl of Arundel and Surrey on the death of his grandfather Bernard Howard, twelfth duke of Norfolk, in March 1842 (taking the additional surname Fitzalan soon afterwards), and spoke infrequently in the Commons, but invariably on Catholic themes. He also published *A Few Remarks on the Social and Political Condition of British Catholics* (1847), *Letter to J. P. Plumptre, M.P. on the Bull 'In coenâ domini'* (1848), and *Observations on Diplomatic Relations with Rome* (1848). The views which he expressed in parliament were unexceptional—he supported the Maynooth grant, chaplains in workhouses, and the Irish poor—but eccentricity occasionally broke through. In 1847, deploring his countrymen's anti-Catholicism, he 'delighted in the idea that when they were most disturbed it was religious feeling by which they were excited' (*Hansard 3*, 91, 1847, 1056). This pleasure was tempered in 1850 when Lord John Russell introduced the Ecclesiastical Titles Bill. His father, the thirteenth duke, strongly supported the bill as safeguarding 'the spiritual independence of the nation' (Robinson,

201), whereas he opposed it as 'the beginning of a persecution' (*Hansard 3*, 114, 1851, 1331). The breach between them was serious, even threatening the duke's health. When the bill became law he resigned his seat as representative of the family borough, and was at once returned as member for the city of Limerick, its representative, John O'Connell (one of the sons of the Daniel O'Connell), retiring in his favour. On the dissolution of parliament in July 1852 he finally retired from the House of Commons. He took his seat in the House of Lords as duke of Norfolk on the death of his father in February 1856. In the same year Augusta, his wife, became a Catholic. Disapproval of Lord Palmerston's policy led him to decline the prime minister's offer of the Order of the Garter.

Norfolk's faith had two wellsprings. One was the early intimacy with Montalembert, from whom he derived an acute sense of Europe's Catholic past. The vanished simplicity of master and servant holding a common faith greatly appealed to him. In later years greater influence was exerted by John Henry Newman and Frederick Faber. Faber—who acted as his confessor—considered him a near saint. With his wife he devoted much of his time and wealth to charity on a vast scale. 'There is not a form of want', Cardinal Wiseman noted, 'or a peculiar application of alms which has not received his relief or co-operation' (*The Times*, 4 Dec 1860). Diffident, ascetic, indifferent to fashionable opinion, he achieved much as a philanthropist, less as a politician. His fortune, Montalembert recalled, was 'used only for the service of God and of the poor' (Montalembert, 766). It was the Catholic poor who had most cause to give thanks for his brief life. Norfolk died of liver disease at Arundel Castle on 25 November 1860, aged forty-five, and was buried in the chapel there on 6 December. His widow survived him by more than twenty-five years, dying on 22 March 1886.

DERMOT QUINN

Sources Montalembert, 'Le duc de Norfolk', *Le Correspondant* (Dec 1860), 766–76 · J. M. Robinson, *The dukes of Norfolk* (1982) · *Hansard 3* (1841), vol. 57; (1846), vol. 86; (1847), vols. 90–91; (1848), vol. 96; (1851), vol. 114 · M. Bence-Jones, *The Catholic families* (1992) · *GM*, 3rd ser., 10 (1861) · *The Times* (27 Nov 1860)
Archives Arundel Castle, Sussex, corresp. and memoranda | Brompton Oratory, London, corresp. with the oratory · W. Sussex RO, letters to duke of Richmond
Likenesses J. Francis, marble bust, 1845, Arundel Castle, West Sussex · J. Partridge, oils, 1862, Arundel Castle, West Sussex; photographic reproduction, Courtauld Inst. · M. Noble, marble effigy on tomb, Fitzalan Chapel, Arundel Castle, West Sussex · W. C. Ross, miniature, Arundel Castle, West Sussex · H. Smith, oils, Arundel Castle, West Sussex · group portrait, miniature (with wife and children), Arundel Castle, West Sussex; repro. in Robinson, *Dukes of Norfolk* · oils, Arundel Castle, West Sussex [*see illus.*]
Wealth at death under £90,000: probate, 2 Jan 1861, *CGPLA Eng. & Wales*

Howard, Hugh (1675–1738), portrait painter and art collector, was born on 7 February 1675 in Dublin, the eldest son of the six children of Ralph *Howard (1638–1710), doctor and regius professor of physic at the University of Dublin, and his wife, Catherine Sotheby (*fl. c.*1655–1714). In 1688 the family left for England, their estates in Shelton, co. Wicklow, having been taken following the revolution.

Hugh Howard (1675–1738), by John Faber junior, 1737 (after Michael Dahl, 1723)

In 1697 Howard accompanied Thomas Herbert, eighth earl of Pembroke and ambassador to the treaty of Ryswyck, to the Netherlands. He travelled to Italy, where he was resident in Rome from 1697 to 1700 and studied under Carlo Maratti. A portrait drawing of the master by his pupil (Courtauld Inst.) is among his earliest works, as are many of the twenty-two drawings after old masters in the British Museum.

Howard returned to Dublin in 1700 but soon settled in London, where he set up a portrait-painting practice. Although they were reasonably successful, his remaining works are unremarkable examples in the tradition of Sir Godfrey Kneller. In 1708 the poet Matthew Prior wrote 'To Mr Howard: an Ode' to mark his appreciation of a now lost portrait of his mistress, Anne Durham. This was published in *Poems on Several Occasions* (1709), for which Howard designed the frontispiece. In 1710 his father died, and Howard returned to Ireland as heir to the estate at Shelton. On his return to London in 1711 he attended Kneller's academy in Great Queen Street. He also painted the second of two portraits of Sir Justinian Isham (priv. coll.), the first having been deemed an unsatisfactory likeness by the sitter's father. From this date onwards references to other works are rare.

In 1714 Howard married Thomasine Langston (*d.* 1728), a wealthy heiress, and through his patron, William, second duke of Devonshire, was appointed keeper of the papers and records of state. He was able to retire from painting and devote himself to virtu, acting as artistic adviser to the rich and powerful, by whom, according to Vertue, he was known as the Oracle. Jonathan Richardson the

younger, however, described him as 'muzzy headed', and alleged that, with 'polite knowledge', he managed to disguise his 'extreme ignorance and illiteracy' (Richardson, 1.336). In 1726 he was made paymaster-general of the royal works, a post which he declared was 'more profitable with less trouble of attendance' (letter to William Howard, 21 May 1726; NL Ire., Wicklow papers). He was able to build up an important collection of drawings, prints, books, and medals, knowledge of which is based on two sales by his descendants at Sothebys in 1873 and 1874. Highlights of the collection included Albrecht Dürer's *Head of a Young Man* and a sheet of studies by Michelangelo. In 1728 Howard inherited part of the library of the lord chancellor, James West, from his brother William. He bequeathed his collection to another brother, Robert, bishop of Elphin, by whom it descended to the earls of Wicklow. Howard died at his house in Pall Mall on 17 March 1738, worth £40,000, and was buried in Richmond church, Surrey.

EMMA LAUZE

Sources M. Wynne, 'Hugh Howard: Irish portrait painter', *Apollo*, 90 (1969), 314–17 · Vertue, *Note books*, 2.24; 3.69, 83; 6.168 · F. Lugt, *Les marques de collections de dessins et d'estampes* (Amsterdam, 1921); repr. (The Hague, 1956) · H. Walpole, *Anecdotes of painting in England*, ed. R. Wornum, new edn, 3 vols. (1849); repr. (1876) · A. Poetz, 'Howard, Hugh', *The dictionary of art*, ed. J. Turner (1996) · *DNB* · Waterhouse, *18c painters* · E. Waterhouse, *Painting in Britain, 1530–1790*, 5th edn (1994) · T. Pears, *The discovery of painting* (1988) · W. T. Whitley, *Artists and their friends in England, 1700–1799*, 2 vols. (1928) · J. Richardson, *Richardsoniana, or, Occasional reflections on the moral nature of men* (1776) · A. Crookshank and the Knight of Glin [D. Fitzgerald], eds., *Irish portraits, 1660–1860* (1969) [exhibition catalogue, Dublin, London, and Belfast, 14 Aug 1969 – 9 March 1970] · *GM*, 1st ser., 8 (1738), 165 · will, PRO, PROB 11/688, sig. 94

Archives NL Ire., corresp. | NL Ire., Wicklow papers, corresp.

Likenesses J. Faber junior, mezzotint, 1737 (after M. Dahl, 1723), BM, NPG [*see illus.*] · woodcut, repro. in Walpole, *Anecdotes of painting*, ed. Wornum, 2 (1876), 246

Wealth at death £40,000 plus £1500 p.a. from estate in Ireland: will, PRO, PROB 11/688, sig. 94; Vertue, *Note books*, 3.83

Howard, James, **third earl of Suffolk** (1619–1689), nobleman, born on 23 December 1619, was the eldest son of Theophilus *Howard, second earl of Suffolk (1584–1640), and his wife, Lady Elizabeth Home (1599/1600–1633), daughter and coheir of George Home, earl of Dunbar, and his wife, Elizabeth Gordon. He was baptized on 10 February 1620 with James I and the first duke of Buckingham as his godfathers. At the coronation of Charles I on 2 February 1626 he was created KB. In February 1639 Howard joined the king at York as leader of a troop of horse for the campaign against the Scots. Having on 3 June 1640 succeeded his father as earl of Suffolk, on 16 June he was sworn joint lord lieutenant of that county. He married, on 1 December 1640, Lady Susanna Rich [*see* Howard, Susanna, countess of Suffolk (1627–1649)], daughter of Henry *Rich, first earl of Holland (*bap.* 1590, *d.* 1649), and his wife, Isabella Cope; they had one daughter, Essex.

On 5 March 1642 parliament nominated Lord Suffolk sole lord lieutenant of Suffolk and he subsequently sided with parliament in the civil war, although he took no active military role. On 28 December 1643 he received but ignored a summons to attend the king's parliament at

Oxford, and was one of the few peers who sat, if intermittently, in the House of Lords throughout the war, serving on a number of commissions in the years 1645 to 1648. On 7 July he was appointed joint commissioner from parliament to the king at Newcastle. However, in September 1647, acting on a report from the committee of safety, the Commons impeached Suffolk, together with six other peers, of high treason. The House of Lords ordered his arrest on 14 October but, when the Commons failed to substantiate their charges, in June 1648 the proceedings were dropped and he was freed.

Suffolk's first wife, Susanna, died on 19 May 1649 at Kensington, and shortly after 19 February 1651 he married Barbara (*bap.* 1622, *d.* 1681), widow of Richard Wenman and daughter of Sir Edward *Villiers (*c.*1585–1626), with whom he had a daughter, Elizabeth (*b.* 1656). Suffolk became high steward of Ipswich on 8 September 1653, but otherwise kept a low political profile during the interregnum, thus retaining his estates intact. He supported the Restoration and was appointed lord lieutenant of Suffolk and of Cambridgeshire on 25 July 1660. From 18 to 23 April 1661 he acted as earl marshal of England for the coronation of Charles II, and on 4 March 1665 was made gentleman of the bedchamber, while his wife, Barbara, became groom of the stole to Queen Catherine. In 1661 he became colonel of the Suffolk regiment of militia horse, and it was in this capacity that he mobilized and took personal command of the forces which repelled an assault by 2000 Dutch troops near Felixstowe on 3 July 1667. In 1666 he agreed to sell his vast palace at Audley End to Charles II for £50,000, while retaining the bulk of the estate, and in March 1667 was himself appointed keeper of the king's new house. However, although Suffolk was in 1673 appointed joint commissioner for the office of earl marshal and in 1678 colonel commandant to three regiments of the Cambridgeshire militia, he gradually drifted towards the country opposition. Considered by some observers 'a Whig in politics' (GEC, *Peerage*, 12.468), he voted for the second Exclusion Bill on 15 November 1680, and in February 1681 was discharged from the lord lieutenancy of Suffolk and Cambridgeshire, and from attendance in the king's bedchamber.

Suffolk's second wife, Barbara, died of 'apoplexy' on 13 December 1681. About 10 June 1682 he married, as his third wife, the twenty-two-year-old Lady Anne (1659/60–1720), daughter of Robert *Montagu, third earl of Manchester (*bap.* 1634, *d.* 1683) [see under Montagu, Edward], and his wife, Anne Yelverton. Although there were no children from this marriage, she was a devoted companion and nurse in Suffolk's declining years. Increasingly afflicted by gout and other infirmities during the 1680s, he died at Great Chesterford, Essex, on 7 January 1689, and was buried ten days later at Walden. He was succeeded as earl of Suffolk by his brother George Howard (*c.*1625–1691), while his barony of Howard de Walden went eventually to the descendants of his daughters, Essex, who had married Edward Griffin, the future Jacobite peer, in 1667, and Elizabeth, who married Sir Thomas Felton.

RICHARD MINTA DUNN

Sources GEC, *Peerage*, new edn, vol. 12/1 · DNB · CSP dom., 1660–61; 1665–7; 1680–81 · W. Addison, *Audley End* (1953) · J. Rushworth, *Historical collections*, new edn, 7–8 (1721) · C. H. Firth and R. S. Rait, eds., *Acts and ordinances of the interregnum, 1642–1660*, 1–2 (1911) · N. Luttrell, *A brief historical relation of state affairs from September 1678 to April 1714*, 1 (1857); repr. (1969) · *JHL*, 9 (1646–7)
Archives Essex RO, Chelmsford, manorial court and estate records | BL, corresp. relating to work as lord lieutenant of Suffolk, Add. MS 21048 · BL, letters to Lord Essex, Stowe MSS 200–210, *passim*
Likenesses E. Seeman, oils (after unknown portrait at Dingley, Northamptonshire), Audley End House, Essex
Wealth at death £6558 p.a.: Addison, *Audley End*

Howard, James (*c.*1640–1669), playwright, was the eighth son of Thomas Howard and Werburge, daughter of James Kirkhoven, lord of Henfleet, Holland, and grandson of Theophilus *Howard, second earl of Suffolk (1584–1640), and Elizabeth (*d.* 1633), daughter of the earl of Dunbar. He was the second cousin of Sir Robert *Howard (1626–1698) and Edward *Howard (*bap.* 1624, *d.* 1712), both playwrights, and of Lady Elizabeth, wife of John Dryden. He may have been the James Howard who, before March 1667, married Charlotte Jemima Henrietta Maria (1652–1684), later countess of Yarmouth, illegitimate daughter of Charles II and Elizabeth Killigrew (1622–1681), who was the sister of the dramatist and theatrical manager Thomas Killigrew (1612–1683). As of the early years of the Restoration, James Howard appears to have been connected with the Killigrews: on 13 August 1661 Sir William Morice, secretary of state, issued a warrant for Howard's imprisonment, together with Sir Robert Howard, Philip Howard, Sir Robert Killigrew, and Henry Killigrew. A week later the five prisoners were discharged. Howard probably died in July 1669, leaving a daughter, Stuarta Howard (*d.* 1706), a maid of honour to Queen Mary. His widow, Charlotte, later petitioned the king, asking for payment of the pension granted on 18 March 1667 'to her and her husband for their joint lives and the life of the survivor, of which since his death she has had no benefit' (*CSP dom.*, addenda, 1660–85, 344).

Howard was the author of two plays, both of which were important links in the development of Restoration comedy. Published in 1674 but performed at the Theatre Royal as early as 30 July 1663, *The English Mounsieur* combined the gay couple pattern (in the characters of Lady Wealthy and the extravagant rake Welbred) with systematic anti-French satire in the character of Frenchlove, a whining fop. Pepys saw it performed on 8 December 1666, 29 October 1667, and 7 April 1668; on the first occasion, he was 'mightily pleased with the play' and with Nell Gwyn in the part of Wealthy (Pepys, 7.401). If performed in May 1665 (as has been suspected), *All Mistaken, or, The Mad Couple* was another prototype, which may have served as an example for such double plot tragicomedies as Dryden's *Secret Love* and *Marriage-à-la-mode*. Philidor and Mirida, the gay couple, were played by Gwyn and Charles Hart in the December 1667 production. According to the prompter John Downes, Howard was also the author of a tragicomic adaptation of *Romeo and Juliet* (performed at Lincoln's Inn Fields in 1663–4), in which the couple were preserved alive, 'so that when the Tragedy was Reviv'd again, 'twas Play'd Alternately, Tragical one Day, and Tragicomical another; for several Days together' (Downes, 53).

J. P. VANDER MOTTEN

Sources J. L. Chester, ed., *The marriage, baptismal, and burial registers of the collegiate church or abbey of St Peter, Westminster*, Harleian Society, 10 (1876) • CSP dom., addenda, 1660–85 • Burke, *Peerage* • J. Howard, *The English mounsieur: a comedy* (1674); repr. with introduction by R. D. Hume (1977) • W. Van Lennep and others, eds., *The London stage, 1660–1800*, pt 1: 1660–1700 (1965) • H. J. Oliver, *Sir Robert Howard (1626–1698): a critical biography* (1963) • Pepys, *Diary*, vol. 7 • J. A. Winn, *John Dryden and his world* (1987) • J. Downes, *Roscius Anglicanus*, ed. J. Milhous and R. D. Hume, new edn (1987) • R. D. Hume, 'Dryden, James Howard, and the date of *All mistaken*', *Philological Quarterly*, 51 (1972), 422–9 • J. R. Sutherland, 'The date of James Howard's *All mistaken, or, the mad couple*', N&Q, 209 (1964), 339–40 • E. Seaton, 'Two Restoration plays', TLS (18 Oct 1934), 715 • G. Brennan and H. Phillips Statham, *The house of Howard*, 2 vols. (1907)

Howard, James (1821–1889), agriculturist and manufacturer of agricultural implements, was born on 16 October 1821, the eldest son of John Howard, maker of agricultural implements, of Bedford. He was educated at Bedford School, and as a boy he also gained much practical knowledge of agriculture from visiting his grandfather at Priory Farm, near Bedford.

Howard joined his father's business about 1837. He had a special interest in ploughs and designed new types of iron plough which were much lighter than others then available. In 1841 he won the first prize at the Liverpool meeting of the Royal Agricultural Society of England. In 1842 he was equally successful at the Bristol meeting. These successes and the continuing improvements he was making to ploughs brought increased business to John Howard & Son and established the firm as one of the leading British plough makers.

In 1850 John Howard retired from the business; James Howard became senior partner and was joined by his younger brother Frederick. The firm was now styled James and Frederick Howard. Frederick's talents were in financial and commercial organization; James continued to direct production and technical development, registering some seventy patents in his own name for various improvements in agricultural machinery. In 1856 the building of the firm's new Britannia ironworks began at Bedford, with the shops and principal details all carefully planned by Howard himself. The firm continued to expand as a maker of ploughs and cultivating implements, and by 1860 sales of ploughs had risen to about 6000 a year, with substantial exports to eastern Europe and Russia, India, Australia, and South Africa. Attempts to diversify the range of products were not always successful, however. Corn-harvesting machinery was tried, but quickly given up because competition from other manufacturers was intense. Howard persevered with the system of steam cultivation devised by William Smith, of Woolston, in the 1850s. He continued to market it and develop it long after the success of Fowler's system had captured the market.

On 9 September 1846 Howard married Mahala Wenden (*d.* 1888), daughter of P. Thompson of St Osyth and Brook House, Great Bentley, Essex; they had two sons and three daughters. Howard was always a practical agriculturist. In 1862 he bought the Clapham Park estate from the earl of Ashburnham, and farmed it in a scientific manner. Howard was especially successful in the breeding of large white Yorkshire pigs, shire horses, and shorthorn cattle. He built a new house for himself on the estate, and it was completed in 1873. He also had housing of good standard built for the labourers on the estate.

Howard was the first man in Bedfordshire to enrol himself as a volunteer. He formed a company of his own workmen. This became the 9th Bedfordshire rifles, of which he was long the captain. He was elected mayor of Bedford in 1863 and again in 1864. He continued to serve on the town council, and was an alderman in 1879 and 1880. He carried out many local improvements, and to him is due the institution of the Bedfordshire county school for the sons of farmers; he and the duke of Bedford contributed much of the capital for this school. He also promoted the improvement of Bedford's water supply and sewerage systems, and was elected to the new Bedfordshire county council only the week before his death. He was a justice of the peace for Bedfordshire and a deputy lieutenant, and he was high sheriff of the county from 1878 to 1879.

Howard was the Liberal representative in parliament for Bedford from 1868 to 1874 and for Bedfordshire from 1880 to 1885. In the House of Commons he quickly became known as the leading champion of tenants' rights and an authority on all agricultural questions. In 1873, in association with Mr Clare Sewell Read, he brought forward his Landlord and Tenant Bill, but the measure was dropped because he was ill at the time of the second reading. He endeavoured, without much success, to amend the agricultural holdings bills of 1875 and 1883. Another cause that he promoted in parliament was the reform of the law on patent, upon which he was a great expert. Howard also served as chairman of the Bedford and Northampton Railway. He was a member of the Reform Club and the National Liberal Club.

Howard was one of the founders of the Farmers' Alliance in 1879, and was elected to be its president. He was instrumental in the erection in 1861–2 of the Agricultural Hall, London, and was for long a director. He was a founder and the inaugural vice-president of the Agricultural Engineers' Association; later he became its president. He was a member of the council of the Royal Agricultural Society of England in 1857–61 and again in 1878–89. He was a president of the London Farmers' Club, he actively supported the Bedfordshire Agricultural Society, and he was a corresponding member of several foreign societies. He was also a prolific writer, and contributed many articles to journals and daily newspapers on agricultural and political questions.

Towards the close of the Franco-Prussian War, Howard originated a fund for the relief of French peasant farmers whose fields had been devastated; £50,000 was raised, and expended principally in seed. The French government passed a vote of thanks to him. In 1878 Howard was made a chevalier of the Légion d'honneur in recognition of his services as one of the English commissioners of the Paris Exhibition.

Howard died suddenly in the Midland Hotel, St Pancras, London, on 25 January 1889; he was buried on 30 January in Clapham churchyard, Bedford.

GORDON GOODWIN, rev. JONATHAN BROWN

Sources 'Men of mark', *Implement and Machinery Review*, 8 (1881–2), 4423–4 · *Implement and Machinery Review*, 14 (1888–9), 11473, 11647–8 · *The Engineer*, 67 (1889), 90 · *The Engineer*, 30 (1870), 187–8 · *Bedfordshire Times* (26 Jan 1889) · *Bedford Bee* (11 June 1879) · R. Trow-Smith, *Power on the land: a centenary history of the Agricultural Engineers Association, 1875–1975* (1975)
Archives Beds. & Luton ARS, business papers | BL, letters to W. E. Gladstone, Add. MSS 44459–44481
Likenesses photograph, repro. in *Implement and Machinery Review*, 11647
Wealth at death £82,702 11s. 4d.: probate, 6 May 1889, *CGPLA Eng. & Wales*

Howard, John, first duke of Norfolk (d. 1485), soldier and member of parliament, was the only son and heir of Robert Howard (d. 1436) and Margaret (d. 1459), daughter of Thomas (I) Mowbray, first duke of Norfolk (d. 1399), and eventual coheir of John (VII) Mowbray, duke of Norfolk (d. 1476). His date of birth is not known, but his mother was still single in 1421 and his own eldest son, Thomas, was born in 1443, so it is reasonable to suppose that he was born in the mid-1420s. His place of birth is also unknown, but in 1437 on the death of his grandfather, Sir John Howard, he inherited a small estate at Stoke by Nayland in Suffolk, which had been the inheritance of his grandmother, Alice Tendring. This was to be his home until he was created duke of Norfolk, the first of his family to hold that title.

Howard married twice. His first wife, whom he married between about 1440 and 1442, was Catherine, the daughter of William, styled Lord Moleyns, and Margery Whalesborough. Catherine died on 3 November 1465, leaving six children: Thomas, earl of Surrey; Nicholas (d. c.1468); Isabel, who married Sir Robert Mortimer; Anne, the wife of Sir Edmund Gorges; Margaret, who married Sir John Wyndham; and Jane, the wife of John Tymperley. Howard's second wife, Margaret (d. 1494), whom he married in January 1467, was the daughter of Sir John Chedworth and the widow of Nicholas Wyfold (d. 1456), mayor of London, and of John Norris, esquire (d. 1466). With Margaret, Howard had a daughter, Catherine, who married John Bourchier, Lord Berners.

Like his father before him, Howard entered the household of the duke of Norfolk, serving his cousin, John (VI) Mowbray (d. 1461), and was thus involved in the factional struggles in East Anglia in the 1450s between Norfolk and William de la Pole, duke of Suffolk. Howard (described as of Framlingham, the Norfolk seat) was named in numerous indictments for misdemeanours, such as breaking closes and hunting on de la Pole land, and in 1453 he was involved in an unsuccessful lawsuit with the duchess of Suffolk, Alice Chaucer, over manors belonging to the barony of Kerdiston which Howard claimed in right of his grandmother. During the 1450s Howard held several local

offices. He was first elected to parliament in 1449 for Suffolk and in 1453, 1455, and 1461 was involved in three disputed elections for which evidence survives. At one point when things were not going his way he was described as 'as wode as a wilde bullok' (Gairdner, 3.39). According to Tudor historians, he also took part in Lord Lisle's expedition to Guienne, which culminated in the defeat at Castillon on 17 July 1453.

In 1461 Howard led the duke of Norfolk's contingent to fight for Edward IV at Towton and immediately reaped the rewards for such service. He was knighted at Edward's coronation, appointed sheriff of the joint shrievalty of Norfolk and Suffolk, constable of Norwich and Colchester castles, and entered the royal household as a king's carver. It was the start of a service to the house of York which was to last for the rest of his life. By 1467 he was being referred to as a knight of the body and in September 1468 was appointed treasurer of the household, an office he held only until Edward lost his throne in 1470; but before that, at some time between 29 December 1469 and 12 February 1470, Edward created Howard a baron.

Howard's royal service during the first decade of Edward's reign was largely military. In 1462 and 1463 he was part of the Yorkist force besieging the three great Northumberland castles of Alnwick, Bamburgh, and Dunstanburgh, still in Lancastrian hands, and then in 1464 he campaigned against Lancastrian rebels in Denbighshire, based in Norfolk's castle of Holt, of which he was constable. Later in 1464 Howard led his own force to join the king in the last campaign against the Lancastrians in the north. In 1467 he deputized for his cousin Norfolk as earl marshal at the most splendid tournament of the age when Antoine, count of La Roche, the Bastard of Burgundy, jousted against the queen's brother, Anthony, Lord Scales, and spent 300 marks of his own money. In the same year came his first appointment as a royal envoy. Edward sent a high-powered embassy to Burgundy to negotiate the marriage of his sister Margaret with Charles, duke of Burgundy, and a much less impressive one to France, where Louis XI was trying to tempt him away from the Burgundian alliance. It consisted of Howard, Sir Richard Tunstall, and Thomas Langton, and despite the inauspicious occasion the three seem to have impressed both Louis and Edward, for they went on to become some of the most senior and trusted envoys of the English crown. It was at about this time that Howard was made a member of the king's council. In 1468 he formed part of the entourage which escorted Margaret to Burgundy for her marriage.

By this time, Howard was a wealthy man. From the nucleus of land round Stoke by Nayland he had built up an estate which consisted of some sixteen manors, seven of them a royal grant in 1462, two held of his cousin Norfolk, and three of another cousin, Elizabeth Howard, countess of Oxford, heir of their grandfather, Sir John Howard, and his first wife, Margaret Plaiz. The others he may have purchased, possibly at the time of his marriage to Catherine Moleyns, in the early 1440s. From his own memoranda and other surviving accounts it is clear that Howard took a considerable interest in the day-to-day management of his estates and was a careful and efficient administrator. From 1463 he bought or was granted a number of other manors including six forfeited by the earl of Oxford, son of his cousin Elizabeth. Before his elevation to the dukedom his income from lands alone was probably about £800 per annum; to this must be added his income from offices and commerce. By 1467 he was rich enough to be owed £1000 by his impoverished cousin, Norfolk.

In the first half of Edward IV's reign Howard's influence was largely local. He was appointed to the benches of Norfolk and Suffolk and other local commissions from the early 1450s and served as sheriff in 1461. Between 1449 and 1467 he represented Suffolk in three parliaments, and Norfolk in one. Until the death of Norfolk in 1476 Howard remained a retainer and a member of his council, but increasingly in the late 1460s and more particularly after 1471 his abilities and the trust reposed in him by the king, coupled with his increasing wealth and influence, led to his becoming the crown's principal supporter in East Anglia. Of the four magnates who should have been the natural leaders in East Anglia, the dukes of Norfolk and Suffolk were political nonentities, Anthony, Lord Scales, was always at court, and the earl of Oxford in exile.

Howard was one of the greatest shipowners of the fifteenth century. Over a period of years he owned at least ten, and possibly twelve, ships, of which six were big enough to be engaged in foreign trade and their voyages can be traced in his own accounts or in customs records. The first volume of Howard's financial memoranda is dominated by the payments for a ship being built at Dunwich, a project which had some financial backing from the crown; he noted that 'the king owes me £30 for money laid down for the carvel' (Crawford, pt 2, 86). The 80 ton *Edward*, as she was christened, cost between £150 and £200 to build and several of her voyages are documented in the memoranda. Howard's ships were chartered for trading voyages, used to convoy smaller ships as protection from enemy shipping or pirates, and supplied to the crown to form part of a royal fleet, often commanded by Howard himself. His connection with the sea seems to have been an early one. He was appointed to commissions dealing with naval matters before the accession of Edward IV and before 1464 was appointed deputy admiral for Norfolk and Suffolk. In 1468 he was responsible for assembling and victualling the east coast contingent of a fleet to be commanded by Lord Scales. In 1470 he was himself in command of a fleet patrolling the channel, and on 2 July he was appointed deputy lieutenant of Calais.

Howard did not follow Edward IV into exile. As a newly created baron he received his first summons to parliament in October 1470 during the readeption of Henry VI. On Edward's return he took a contingent of men to fight for him at Barnet. He was re-appointed to his Calais post and in the early 1470s he spent a considerable amount of time there. In 1473, crossing back to Calais on his way to Bruges to settle Burgundy's commercial differences with England before their joint attack on France

could begin, Howard's ship was attacked by three Hanse ships and driven onto the sands. Sixteen of his servants were killed and he only escaped himself by taking to a small boat. When the planned invasion took place, Howard provided 20 men-at-arms and 200 archers and then played a major part in the diplomatic manoeuvring that led to the treaty of Amiens. He remained with Louis as a hostage while the English army retired back across the channel. At this point he became personally known to the French chronicler Philippe de Commines, who commented that the English did not conduct their negotiations with the cunning of the French, but proceeded with more ingenuousness and straightforwardness, and yet, he added, care should be taken not to affront them, for it was dangerous to meddle with them. This generalization tallies with what is known of Howard's character. Like a number of leading English councillors Howard benefited financially from the peace, receiving a pension of 1200 crowns from Louis as well as other money and plate. He continued to be one of Edward's most trusted envoys for the rest of the reign. In 1481 he led a successful naval expedition against Scotland, burning shipping in the Firth of Forth, and his memoranda detail all the personal possessions he regarded as essential to take with him for his comfort. A major land campaign led by the duke of Gloucester was intended to coincide with Howard's naval attack but was postponed until the following year.

On the death of Edward IV in 1483 Howard was not a natural supporter of the queen and her family and had been associated on a number of occasions with the late king's brother, Richard, duke of Gloucester. Gloucester ensured Howard's support for his usurpation by creating him duke of Norfolk and earl marshal on 28 June 1483, two days after he seized the throne. Howard and his cousin, William, Lord Berkeley, were the legal coheirs through their mothers to the Mowbray lands. On the death of the last Mowbray duke in 1476 his only child and heir, Anne, had been swiftly married to the king's younger son, Richard, duke of York, but had died in 1481 while still a child. The legal rights of Anne's coheirs had been set aside by two acts of parliament in favour of York, who had been created duke of Norfolk. Berkeley had received generous compensation for his loss but Howard had not. Richard III's creation set aside both York's new dukedom and the acts of parliament and took place before there was any suggestion that York or his brother, Edward V, were dead. Berkeley received the Mowbray lands in the midlands and the earldom of Nottingham, while Howard received the East Anglian estates and others in Surrey and Sussex. Richard III also bestowed on Howard an additional grant of lands and the offices of chief steward of the duchy of Lancaster south of the Trent (13 May 1483) and admiral of England (25 July 1483). In return Howard remained loyal to the usurper, defending London successfully for him during Buckingham's rebellion. He spent comparatively little time at court, preferring to be at home in East Anglia where his deepest loyalties lay, but he joined the king at Nottingham to receive ambassadors from Scotland in

1484. When Henry Tudor landed in Wales he mustered 1000 men to fight for the king at Bosworth on 22 August 1485. The night before the battle Howard was warned:

Jack of Norfolke, be not to bolde
For Dykon thy maister is bought and solde,

but for the sake of his oath and his honour he would not desert the king (Hall, 419). Although by this time he was about sixty years old, Howard himself commanded the van of the army, which for most of the battle was the only part of it to engage the enemy, led by the earl of Oxford. Howard was killed shortly before Richard III launched his desperate personal attack on the future Henry VII. His body was carried home to be buried at Thetford Priory, the customary burial place of the dukes of Norfolk. Both he and his son, Thomas *Howard, earl of Surrey, were attainted by Henry VII's first parliament. Surrey was eventually restored as second duke of Norfolk.

Howard was an extremely versatile royal servant; as a soldier, administrator, and diplomat he had few equals among his contemporaries. His loyalty to the house of York was total and if he supported Richard's usurpation out of self-interest, he defended it to the end.

ANNE CRAWFORD

Sources A. Crawford, ed., *Howard household books* (1992) · *The Paston letters, AD 1422–1509*, ed. J. Gairdner, new edn, 6 vols. (1904) · P. de Commynes, *Mémoires*, ed. J. Calmette and G. Durville, 3 vols. (Paris, 1924–5) · A. Crawford, 'The Mowbray inheritance', *Richard III: crown and people*, ed. J. Petre (1985), 79–85 · R. Virgoe, 'Three Suffolk parliamentary elections of the mid-fifteenth century', *BIHR*, 39 (1966), 185–96 · *The manuscripts of the duke of Leeds*, HMC, 22 (1888), 95 · [E. Hall], *The union of the two noble and illustre famelies of Lancastre and Yorke*, ed. [R. Grafton] (1548) · PRO · Chancery records **Archives** Arundel Castle, papers, MS G1/3 · BL, Add. MS 46349 · Norfolk RO, household accounts, etc. | BL, Add. charter 16559 · BL, Add. MS 34889, fol. 59 · Norfolk RO, Norfolk and Norwich Archaeological Society MSS · Raynham Hall, Norfolk, Townshend MSS, box 125 **Likenesses** oils, *c.*1580–1599 (John Howard?), Arundel Castle, West Sussex; version, Royal Collection · stained glass, repro. in J. Dalloway, *A history of the western division of the county of Sussex; rape of Bramber*, 2/2 (1815–30) **Wealth at death** one of the richest peers in the kingdom: BL, Add. charter 16559

Howard, John (1726?–1790), philanthropist, was born in either Hackney or Enfield, probably on 2 September 1726. It is not certain that the inscription on his monument in St Paul's Cathedral, which gives Hackney as his place of birth, is correct. His father, John Howard (d. 1742), had acquired a modest fortune as partner in an upholstery and carpet business in Long Lane, Smithfield. Little is known about his mother (*née* Cholmley), who died in his infancy.

Early life and career Howard was a sickly child and was nursed by a cottager at Cardington, near Bedford, where his father had a small estate and where, in adult life, Howard settled. He was later sent, it is not clear at what age, to a school run by John Worsley, a strict dissenter whose religious views were those of Howard's Calvinist father, but whose pedagogic abilities were questionable. Here Howard remained seven years and, according to John Aikin, his friend, editorial assistant, and biographer, Howard later complained that he was taught very little. Certainly

John Howard (1726?–1790), by Thomas Holloway, *c.*1788

he did not acquire great knowledge of spelling, grammar, or foreign languages. After a short period at the academy of Mr Eames in Newington Green, Howard was apprenticed to the firm of Newnham and Shepley, wholesale grocers, of Watling Street, London. He did not like the business, but his father considered it would teach him method and industry.

In September 1742 his father died and left Howard and his sister each a substantial inheritance, part of which Howard used to obtain release from his indentures. He went on a tour of France and Italy. His health remained poor and on his return he lived in lodgings in Stoke Newington, where he was cared for by his landlady, Sarah Loidore (or Lardeau), whom he married in 1752; they had no children. Twice his age and also in poor health, Sarah died on 10 November 1755 and was buried in St Mary's, Whitechapel. Soon after, Howard set out for Lisbon, which had been devastated by the recent earthquake. But his ship, the *Hanover*, was captured by a French privateer, and the crew, Howard, and his fellow passengers were taken prisoner. In a dungeon at Brest Howard experienced some of the privations that inspired his life's work. Released on parole, he petitioned the commissioners of sick and wounded seamen and an exchange of the prisoners in the prisons in which he had been confined was arranged.

In 1756 Howard moved to Cardington, where he sought to improve the condition of his estate and his tenants' well being. He had most of the houses in the village pulled down and rebuilt, providing each cottage with a fenced kitchen garden. He organized the children's elementary education, and provided stocks of materials for the employment of the poor. He also supervised his tenants' moral condition. He made it a requirement that they attend divine service and abstain from public houses and such popular amusements as cock- and prize-fighting. Howard also took some interest in meteorological observation: in May 1756 he was elected fellow of the Royal Society and on three occasions subsequently communicated his recordings of temperatures.

On 25 April 1758 Howard married Henrietta Leeds (d. 1765), daughter of Edward *Leeds of Croxton, Cambridgeshire, serjeant-at-law. His second wife was his equal in age and social standing, but he secured her pre-marital agreement to the proposition 'that to prevent altercations about those little matters which he had observed to be the chief grounds of uneasiness in families, he should always decide' (Brown, 55). Soon after her marriage Henrietta sold some of her jewellery and placed the proceeds in a 'charity purse', consecrated to the wants of the poor. Henrietta also suffered poor health, and after their marriage Howard purchased for £7000 a house and small estate at Watcombe, near Lymington, in the hope that the New Forest climate would better suit her. It did not, and after three or four years they returned to Cardington. Here, on 31 March 1765, Henrietta died, shortly after giving birth to their only child, John, known as Jack.

Howard himself continued in poor health. In late 1766 he spent two months taking the waters at Bath, and in 1770, while at Hotwells, Bristol, he was overcome by a combination of gout and fever which laid him low for nine months. He nevertheless travelled a great deal. In 1767 he went for two months to the Netherlands with his brother-in-law Edward Leeds. In 1769 he went, alone, for the better part of a year to Italy via the Netherlands and France, returning via Geneva, Germany, and the Netherlands, a country to which he had by now formed a strong attachment because of its orderliness and religious liberty. On his return he visited Wales, the west of England, and the Channel Islands. When at home he spent a good deal of time with his young son, believing it vital that he be inured to the habits of obedience and hardiness. He took him to the meeting-house in Bedford, and visitors to Cardington observed that Howard was often alone with his son in the garden. When Jack was four, however, he was sent to a boarding-school at Cheshunt and thereafter to various schools. When Howard was away from home Jack stayed during school holidays with his aunt in London.

Penal reformer On 8 February 1773 Howard was appointed high sheriff of Bedfordshire, though he had not served as a magistrate. As a dissenter, he accepted office in spite of the Test Act: no legal action was taken against him though he failed to conform. Among his duties he was keeper of the county gaol. Unlike many sheriffs of his day he did not delegate the task but attended to it assiduously. He found that prisoners acquitted at trial, or whose cases did not advance, were not released by the court but, unless they paid fees levied on them by the gaoler and others, were 'dragged back to gaol and locked up again till they should pay' (State of Prisons, 1–2). This outrageous practice was lawful. Howard proposed to the justices that the gaoler be paid a salary in lieu of fees, an arrangement which prevailed in the houses of correction established under the poor law. The justices demanded a precedent for imposing this burden on the ratepayers. This led Howard to visit and look into the organization of gaols in neighbouring counties. He found no precedent and no change was made at Bedford prison during his lifetime. But he uncovered many other penal abuses which he resolved further to look into and record. He was particularly concerned by the incidence of gaol fever and smallpox, from which, he observed, many prisoners died. Thus began his gruelling tours of inspection of prisons, bridewells, houses of correction, and hospitals, in Britain and on the continent, to which he devoted most of the remaining seventeen years of his life.

Howard allied himself with other penal reformers. In 1774 he gave evidence to the House of Commons in committee in support of a bill requiring that prisoners be set free if acquitted, their gaol discharge fees to be paid by the county (14 Geo. III c. 20). He was afterwards called to the bar of the house to receive thanks for 'the humanity and zeal which have led him to visit the several gaols of this kingdom, and to communicate to the house the interesting observations he has made on that subject' (JHC, 34.535). He arranged at his own expense for copies of this act, and another providing for medical attention and hygiene in prisons (14 Geo. III c. 59), to be sent to the keeper of every county gaol in England. One of the sponsors of these bills was Howard's second cousin, Samuel Whitbread the elder, MP for Bedford.

By summer 1774 Howard had visited almost every county gaol in England and Wales and embarked on a survey of city and town gaols and houses of correction. This work was briefly interrupted in October 1774 when in the general election he stood alongside Whitbread as an opposition candidate for Bedford borough. They both lost but petitioned against their defeat, successfully so in the case of Whitbread. Howard never subsequently sought elected office. He resumed his journeys, visited many gaols in England now for the second time, and in 1775 travelled to Scotland, Ireland, France, the Netherlands, Flanders, and Germany. On his return he embarked on his second general survey of English gaols, which he completed at the end of 1776. He planned to publish his findings, but put off the venture until satisfied that the survey was complete and he had comparative data and good practices to report. In May 1776 he went again to France, Switzerland, Germany, and the Netherlands, revisiting institutions whose regimes he later commended. At the beginning of 1777 he decided he was ready to go into print. He went to Warrington, where his surgeon friend John Aikin and trusted printer William Eyres lived. Here he spent three months collaboratively editing his notes and personally seeing the final text through the press. The State of the Prisons in England and Wales, with Preliminary Observations, and an Account of some Foreign Prisons was published in 1777, Howard fixing the price so low as to ensure a wide distribution, but failing to cover the printing costs. He gave away many copies to persons of note.

From *The State of the Prisons* and his correspondence, it is possible to trace the prodigious single-minded industry represented by Howard's second survey. Between autumn 1775 and his retirement in January 1777 he undertook some 350 visits to approximately 230 different institutions. Some prisons, particularly the major sites in London, he visited two or three times. Having set out from Bedford in November 1775 he journeyed through the midlands, the Welsh borders, and the south-west. Cutting back through the midlands he passed close by Cardington but did not go home, travelling clockwise through the north country and then down to East Anglia. Not until mid-February 1776 did he return to Cardington, and during the three days he was at home he was at Bedford county gaol on two successive days before setting out again for the south-east and the metropolis. In May 1776 he went again to the continent, travelling through Switzerland, Germany, and the Netherlands after spending three weeks in Paris: he revisited some prisons and acquainted himself with others. On his return he spent part of August and September at Cardington before going again to East Anglia and London. He was almost constantly on the road, in England and Wales generally with his groom, John Prole, travelling on horseback, upwards of 40 miles a day. He stayed in modest inns. When abroad he initially travelled alone, by public conveyance, though in later years he was accompanied by a servant and used his own chaise. He did not always gain immediate access to prisons overseas, but he was persistent, and from his accounts it appears that he always prevailed. Once, at Toulon, he disguised himself as a fashionable Parisian to gain entry, and in later years he travelled as a physician. At home he developed a technique of generously tipping compliant ostlers so as to ensure that his demanding schedule was achieved: unhelpful servants witnessed their expected reward being distributed as alms.

Proposed reforms The places of confinement that Howard visited were seldom purpose-built. They were rooms in ancient fortresses or city gateways, cellars or stables behind the keeper's house, a few rooms in a domestic house or municipal building. Some gaols were privately owned. Only in the major cities, particularly London, were there purpose-built prisons accommodating many prisoners. Because most prisons were small, with populations fluctuating between infrequent gaol deliveries, the task of managing them was seldom full-time. Gaolers were generally police functionaries or tradesmen, their incomes derived from exploitative fees and the entrepreneurial provision of services. These often included the provision of a tap for the sale of alcohol. This situation, Howard argued, 'doth notoriously promote and increase the very vices it was designed to suppress' (*State of Prisons*, 10). In the introduction to *The State of the Prisons* he briefly summarized these abuses and recommended improvements, including the ground plan of a model county gaol. The remainder of the substantial text comprised a detailed description of approximately 300 places of confinement, their physical layout and capacity, their regime, the names of their officers and terms of employment,

their occupation when visited, and the fees levied on their prisoners. In this unprecedented survey Howard advanced no new principles. He emphasized that many of the abuses he described were contrary to law. He also drew on established legal and other reforming opinion, including the works of William Eden, Sir William Blackstone, and recent translations of Cesare Beccaria. Howard's seminal contribution was that he provided the systematic evidence which demonstrated the extent of the poor standard of gaol management, and thus provided a powerful case for reform. His recommendations urged that new purpose-built gaols be constructed, close by the courts they served, and that these buildings be well lit and ventilated, incorporate running water and sewerage, and have separate sleeping cells for each prisoner as well as day rooms for different classes of prisoners, thereby preventing the indiscriminate mixing of debtors and criminals, men and women, young and old. He also recommended that gaols be separate from houses of correction, the function of the latter, he argued, being the improvement of the inmates. For each establishment there should be appointed a paid gaoler, surgeon or apothecary, and chaplain, none of whom should have a pecuniary interest in their charges. There should be no fees: food and water should be provided for prisoners according to a dietary scale and there should be no sale of alcohol. The daily routine should be regulated. Sentenced prisoners should have to work and the unsentenced given the possibility of voluntary work. Divine service should be held on Sundays.

In 1778 Howard gave evidence to the House of Commons in committee, regarding the use of hulks for the temporary detention of convicts following the suspension of transportation necessitated by the outbreak in 1775 of the American War of Independence. He had found conditions on the hulks gravely wanting. He collaborated with Blackstone and Eden to draft an act (19 Geo. III c. 74) whereby two large penitentiaries, one for men and one for women, were to be built in the London area. Howard returned to the continent in April 1778 to gather more material on practices there, particularly the models provided by the Netherlands and Flanders. He went also to Germany, Bohemia, Italy, Switzerland, and France. The Penitentiary Act provided for the appointment of three commissioners to oversee the plan, two of whom were Howard and his friend John Fothergill. But progress was slow and the commissioners could not agree on the choice of sites. Following Fothergill's death, Howard resigned in January 1781.

Reputation and final years Howard was an eccentric and zealot but not a religious bigot. An Independent himself, both his wives were Anglican, and with them Howard attended churches and chapels, a choice he gave his Cardington tenants. He was puritanical and obsessively sought out God's predestined purpose for him. Even during the grand tours of his youth, his pleasure was tinged with guilt. When in Turin in 1769, he wrote in his journal: 'Oh, why should Vanity and Folly Pictures and Baubles or even the stupendious mountains beautiful Hills or rich

Vallies which ere long will all be consumed engross the thoughts of a Candidate for an eternal everlasting Kingdom' (Brown, 79). He became a teetotaller and vegetarian, frugal in his habits and plain in his dress. He rose regularly at 3 a.m. to work, and when conversing sometimes sat with a watch on his knee so that he could terminate the exchange at the time he had fixed in advance. He was blunt in his opinions and during his travels did not shrink from criticizing the local arrangements for which the leaders to whom he was everywhere introduced were responsible. He became a celebrity but would not tolerate adulation. In 1786–7 he put a stop to a subscription to erect a statue of him, and he never sat for a portrait. He was courageous: the dangers of contagion in the institutions he visited were great and on several occasions he caught fevers from which he almost died. His contribution to penal reform was singular. *The State of the Prisons* seems no more than a tedious catalogue, but as Jeremy Bentham, who visited Howard in 1778, observed:

> his book is a model for method and for the sort of style which is competent for his subject. He carries his plan with him in his head. He is set down at the door of a prison, makes enquiries under a certain number of heads which exhaust the subject, does his business and drives off again to another. His thoughts, his conversation, his writings are confined to this one subject. (*Correspondence of Jeremy Bentham*, 2.106)

Sir Samuel Romilly, who acknowledged Howard's influence, later agreed:

> It is not a book of great literary merit: but it has a merit infinitely superior; it is one of those works which have been rare in all ages of the world—being written with a view only to the good of mankind. (*Memoirs of … Romilly*, 1.169–70)

A century later Howard was to be lauded as a father to social science.

In the final decade of his life Howard repeated and broadened his surveys both in Britain and on the continent. An appendix to, and further enlarged editions of, his work were published plus a pamphlet, translated from the French, on the Bastille. In 1781 a seven-month tour abroad included Scandinavia, Russia, and Poland. In 1782–3 he surveyed again most of the British Isles and spent six months in western Europe, including Spain and Portugal. He painstakingly added up the distance he had travelled, 42,033 miles since he first embarked on the work. In 1782 he gave evidence to the Irish House of Commons on the state of Irish gaols and was awarded an honorary LLD by Trinity College, Dublin. In 1785 he began the final phase of his life's work, journeying for fifteen months throughout western and southern Europe inspecting Lazarettos for the treatment of plague victims. The result of this work, *An Account of the Principal Lazarettos in Europe, with Various Papers Relative to the Plague*, was published at Warrington in 1789. He now settled all his affairs, apparently not expecting to return, and went again to the continent; after journeying through the Netherlands, Germany, and Poland, he died of fever on 20 January 1790 at Kherson in southern Russia, where he was buried. A memorial was erected to him there. His death was announced in the *London Gazette* (1790, 174), a unique honour for a civilian, and his statue,

the first to be admitted to the cathedral, was erected by public subscription in St Paul's.

Much has been made of the charge, first levelled in an obituary in the *Gentleman's Magazine* (1790), and thereafter vigorously contested, that Howard was a cruel father, ultimately responsible for his son's insanity. A parallel has since been drawn between Jack's condition and the madness which many prisoners, isolated within the 'separate' regimes of the model prisons in the nineteenth century, later suffered. Howard was undoubtedly a stern disciplinarian. When Jack was young Howard provided demonstrations for his guests of his obedience: if instructed, Jack would walk shoeless over rough ground or sit motionless without speaking, and Howard is said to have claimed that Jack would put his hand in the fire if told to. Howard's closest admirers admitted that his treatment of his son inspired fear rather than affection. But it seems certain that Howard neither approved of nor used corporal punishment, and his decision not to send Jack to Eton reflected not meanness or neglect but his opinion that the school was not a fit moral environment. After Howard's sister died in August 1777, leaving him her house in Great Ormond Street, London, Howard spent time with Jack during school holidays and the lad accompanied his father on one or two journeys before being sent, with disastrous delinquent consequences, to university first in Edinburgh and then in Cambridge. John Howard the younger was sent to an asylum in 1789 and died, insane, at Cardington in 1799. The estate he had inherited from his father passed to Samuel Whitbread the younger. The Howard League for Penal Reform, founded in 1866, perpetuates John Howard's name and cause. **ROD MORGAN**

Sources J. Howard, *The state of prisons in England and Wales* (1777) · J. Aikin, *A view of the character and public services of the late John Howard* (1792) · J. B. Brown, *Memoirs of the public and private life of John Howard, the philanthropist* (1818) · J. Field, *The life of John Howard* (1850) · *GM*, 1st ser., 60 (1790), 277 · *Correspondence of John Howard, the philanthropist*, ed. J. Field (1855) · H. Dixon, *John Howard and the prison-world of Europe* (1850) · L. Baumgartner, 'John Howard (1726–1790), hospital and prison reformer: a bibliography', *Bulletin of the History of Medicine*, 7 (1939), 486–626 · L. Radzinowicz, *A history of English criminal law and its administration from 1750*, 1: *The movement for reform* (1948) · W. Eden, *Principles of penal law* (1771) · W. Blackstone, *Commentaries on the laws of England*, 4 vols. (1765–9) · M. Ignatieff, *A just measure of pain: the penitentiary in the industrial revolution, 1750–1850* (1978) · E. Stockdale, *A study of Bedford prison, 1660–1877* (1977) · S. McConville, *A history of English prison administration*, 1: *1750–1877* (1981) · D. L. Howard, *John Howard: prison reformer* (1958) · S. Webb and B. Webb, *English local government*, 6: *English prisons under local government* (1922) · *The correspondence of Jeremy Bentham*, ed. T. Sprigge and others, [11 vols.] (1968–), in *The collected works of Jeremy Bentham* · S. Romilly, *Memoirs of the life of Sir Samuel Romilly*, 3 vols. (1840)

Archives Beds. & Luton ARS, papers relating to estate after his death · Hist. Soc. Penn., papers relating to him | Beds. & Luton ARS, letters to T. A. Leach · Beds. & Luton ARS, letters to John Prole · BL, letters to William Seward, Add. MSS 5409, 5418 · Bodl. Oxf., corresp. and papers · priv. coll., corresp. with Samuel Whitbread

Likenesses line engraving, pubd 1787 (after M. Davis), BM · T. Holloway, chalk drawing, c.1788, BM [*see illus.*] · T. Cook, line engraving, pubd 1790 (after Brown), BM, NPG · J. Bacon, sculpture, St Paul's Cathedral, London · M. Brown, oils, NPG · D. Martin, oils,

Dean Orphanage, Edinburgh · T. Prattent, line engraving, BM, NPG; repro. in *European Magazine* (1786)

Howard, John (1753–1799), mathematician, was born at Fort George garrison, near Inverness, the son of Ralph Howard, a private soldier. He was brought up by relatives in Carlisle. Apprenticed at fourteen to his uncle, a cork cutter, who treated him harshly, he ran away to sea; he afterwards worked as carpenter, and as a flax dresser.

Howard spent his limited leisure in study, then resolved 'to teach himself by instructing others' (Franklin, 145) and opened a school near Carlisle. His mathematical proficiency attracted the attention of Bishop Edmund Law, who secured his entry to Carlisle grammar school, with the prospect of entering the church. Howard's liaison with a young woman led him to abandon that scheme, and in 1780 he set up school in Carlisle. Two years later he became steward to Law's son John, newly appointed bishop of Clonfert. In Ireland he benefited from his employer's library and conceived the plan of his future *Treatise*. An 'unfortunate marriage' in 1786 ended his four-year stewardship.

In 1786 Howard returned to Carlisle, where he continued to work as a schoolteacher until 1794. From 1788 until his death he frequently contributed to both the *Ladies' Diary* and the *Gentleman's Diary*. In the latter in 1791 he gave an elegant solution to his own problem of constructing a spherical triangle, given the base, an adjacent angle, and the sum of the other two, which was much admired. He surveyed the nearby town of Whitehaven for the 1790 map.

Howard moved in 1794 to Newcastle upon Tyne, where he rented the schoolhouse built by Charles Hutton in Westgate Street and gained a good standing as a teacher. Among his pupils was William Armstrong. In 1795 Howard read a paper to the Literary and Philosophical Society entitled 'The common balance'; two years later he contested a paper of Armstrong's, 'On imaginary quantities in algebra', the discussion continuing over several meetings.

Howard's reputation as a mathematician rests mainly on his *Treatise on Spherical Geometry* (1798). The book filled a gap in existing texts, and was praised for its 'arrangement, perspicuity of demonstration, and extension of theory' (*Analytical Review*, 287). The list of subscribers has 544 names. Soon after the work appeared Howard's health failed. He died, aged forty-six, on 26 March 1799 at The Leazes, Newcastle, and was buried in St John's churchyard.

Besides his mathematical abilities, Howard was something of a versifier, and was humorous, satirical, and convivial. His memorialist, Franklin, who knew him personally, saw him as 'an indefatigable scholar, a sincere friend and a placable enemy' (Franklin, 146).

R. E. ANDERSON, rev. RUTH WALLIS

Sources Franklin, 'Memoirs of the late Mr John Howard', *The Satellite*, 6 (1800), 143–7 · E. Mackenzie, *A descriptive and historical account of the town and county of Newcastle upon Tyne*, 2 (1827), 465–6 · 'A treatise on spherical geometry', *Analytical Review*, 1 (1799), 287–8

[review] · M. A. Richardson, ed., *The local historian's table book … historical division*, 5 vols. (1841–6), vol. 2, p. 410

Howard, John Eliot (1807–1883), quinologist, was born on 11 December 1807 at Plaistow, Essex, the youngest of three children of Luke *Howard (1772–1864), meteorologist and chemist, and his wife, Mariabella, *née* Eliot (1769–1852). Both parents were members of the Society of Friends. With the exception of two years at Josiah Forster's school, Howard was educated at home. Apprenticed to his father's chemical business at Stratford in 1823, he was made a partner of the firm in 1828. In 1830 he married Maria (1807–1892), daughter of William D. Crewdson of Kendal. The couple moved into a substantial house in Tottenham, Middlesex, where they had five daughters and four sons.

As early as 1827 Howard showed interest in what would prove to be his life's work: the extraction of the anti-malaria drug quinine from the bark of the *Cinchona* (*cinchonaceae*) genus of South American tree. His first paper, a report on the collection of cinchona in the British Museum made by the Spanish botanist José Pavón (1754–1840), was published in 1852. In the following year Howard joined the Pharmaceutical Society, and in 1857 the Linnean Society. In 1858 he purchased Pavón's manuscript 'Nueva Quinologia' and his specimens of cinchona. Howard employed a botanical artist and published the well-received *Illustrations of the 'Nueva Quinologia' of Pavon … and Observations on the Barks Described* in 1862. Howard's second major work, *The Quinology of the East Indian Plantations* (1869–76), was the result of his examination of the bark of all the forms of cinchona introduced into India from the Andes by Clements Markham, Richard Spruce, and Robert Mackenzie Cross. For this Howard received the thanks of her majesty's government in 1873. In 1874 his citation for election as a fellow of the Royal Society recognized the importance of his work: 'the name of Mr Howard is inseparably connected with his lifelong investigation respecting the identification and chemistry of the cinchona' (Kirkwood and Lloyd, 1).

Howard took considerable interest in gardening, and especially in hybridization as bearing upon cultivated cinchonas, and he was the author of numerous scientific papers, chiefly on quinine. He also gave addresses on both science and revelation at the Victoria Institute, of which he was a vice-president. Howard and his wife were both deeply religious and had been raised as Quakers. In 1836 they resigned from the Society of Friends and became Baptists. Howard published several religious tracts and was instrumental in establishing the Brook Street Chapel, Tottenham. He died at his house, Lord's Meade, Tottenham, on 22 November 1883, and was buried in Tottenham cemetery. The genus *Howardia* of the *Cinchonaceae* was posthumously dedicated to him.

G. S. BOULGER, rev. MAX SATCHELL

Sources J. H. Kirkwood and C. H. Lloyd, *John Eliot Howard: a budget of his papers on his life and work* (1995) · *Proceedings of the Linnean Society* (1883–4), 35 · *The record of the Royal Society of London*, 4th edn (1940) · *CGPLA Eng. & Wales* (1883)

Archives NHM, MSS · Royal Pharmaceutical Society of Great Britain, London, papers relating to cinchona
Wealth at death £43,548 7s. 5d.: probate, 1884

Howard [née Knyvett; *other married name* Rich], **Katherine**, **countess of Suffolk** (*b*. in or after **1564**, *d*. **1638**), courtier, was the eldest child of Sir Henry *Knyvet (Knyvett) (1537?–1598) of Charlton, Wiltshire, MP, and his first wife, Elizabeth Stumpe (*d*. 1585), daughter of Sir James Stumpe, knight, of Malmesbury, Wiltshire. Katherine's first husband was Richard Rich, eldest son of Robert, second Baron Rich; he died some time before 27 February 1581. In or before 1583 she married, as his second wife, Lord Thomas *Howard (1561–1626), second son of Thomas *Howard, fourth duke of Norfolk (1538–1572). He was created earl of Suffolk on 21 May 1603, and was privy councillor (4 May 1603), lord chamberlain of the king's household (4 May 1603–10 July 1614), and lord treasurer (11 July 1614–20 July 1618). She had no children with her first husband; with her second, she had twelve—eight sons, including Theophilus *Howard, and four daughters, including the notorious Frances *Howard, countess of Essex and Somerset (1590–1632).

In April 1597 Katherine Howard was reported to be in competition for a prospective place in Queen Elizabeth's bedchamber: she was eventually sworn of the privy chamber on 12 September 1599. In the new reign the countess (as she now was) undoubtedly owed her posts in the household of Anne of Denmark, consort of James VI and I, as lady of the privy chamber and keeper of the jewels (which she held from 1603 to about 1608), to the influence of her husband and of her close friend, Robert Cecil, first earl of Salisbury, secretary of state and later lord treasurer to James I. She danced in two of the queen's six masques, Samuel Daniel's *The Vision of the Twelve Goddesses* (8 January 1604) and Ben Jonson's *The Masque of Blackness* (6 January 1605). The influence of Suffolk and Salisbury is also apparent in the joint authority she was given (shared with Salisbury's favourite niece, Elizabeth, countess of Derby) over the privy lodgings at Greenwich in April 1605 after Queen Anne had given birth to Princess Mary there. The princess was given into the care of Lady Suffolk's uncle, Thomas *Knyvett (1545/6–1622), and his wife. The countess may have been given the same authority for the birth of Princess Sophia in June 1606, as she was on hand to be her godmother before the infant died the following day (Rimbault, 170).

Apart from securing her official posts, the countess's activities at court were also shaped by her relationship with Suffolk and Salisbury. Beautiful, avaricious, unscrupulous, and ultimately corrupt, Lady Suffolk wielded a measure of power through these relationships which she exploited for financial gain. An attack of smallpox in 1619 destroyed the beauty which she had also used to advantage: Lady Anne Clifford recalled that the attack 'spoiled that good face of hers which had brought to others much misery & to herself greatness which ended with much unhappiness' (K. O. Acheson, ed., *The Diary of Anne Clifford, 1616–1619: a Critical Edition*, 1995, 100).

Contemporary libels alleged that Lady Suffolk had an adulterous sexual relationship with Salisbury (Croft, 58–60). Whatever the nature of their association, their relationship and the role she played as a go-between with successive Spanish ambassadors made her useful both to Salisbury and to Spain. Though the services of herself and her husband were not considered by the ambassador Juan de Taxis in 1604 'to be so great', he believed her demands for gifts of jewels and money totalling £6000, and a pension of 4000 ducats (approximately £1100), should be satisfied on the basis of her influence with Salisbury (Loomie, *Toleration*, 53). Taxis was also convinced that she was a Roman Catholic 'although not in public' (ibid.). She was assigned the code-name Roldan and continued to receive a pension even after Salisbury's death (BL, Add. MS 31111, fol. 45).

After her husband was appointed lord treasurer Lady Suffolk took advantage of his position to extort kickbacks from suitors. Sir John Finet reported in great detail to Salisbury's son, the second earl, the nature and extent of her activities, as revealed in the Suffolks' trial in Star Chamber in 1619. In one instance, 'to be spared a bond of £500' a citizen gave £83 and a sable muff to the countess (*Salisbury MSS*, 22.99). In another she was given £1900 for her favour to procure the security of one Turner's debt of £20,000 from the farmers of the custom (ibid., 103). She was aided in her activities by Sir John Bingley, an exchequer official. Contemporary sympathies were with her husband who was reportedly 'more pitied than condemned', while the countess was 'more condemned than pitied' (*CSP dom.*, *1619–23*, 93). The Suffolks were convicted and fined £30,000 (later reduced to £7000), and both husband and wife were imprisoned in the Tower for ten days.

Besides acting on her own behalf, the countess of Suffolk also forwarded the interests of others: in 1618 she was reported to be supporting Lord Hollis (with Lady Hatton) in his bid for the post of comptroller of the king's household (*Letters of John Chamberlain*, 2.128). Although deprived of her power base at court after 1619, the countess continued to solicit on behalf of other people—for a gentlewoman who had been in Queen Anne's service and for her granddaughter Elizabeth Howard. In January 1626 she wrote to a Dr Collins 'to support the candidature of Sir Robert Naunton and Sir John Cooke as Members [of parliament] for the University' of Cambridge (*First Report*, HMC, appx, 68), of which her husband was chancellor. Lady Suffolk was still living on 19 August 1638 but died before 12 September. Her second son, Thomas, earl of Berkshire, inherited the Wiltshire estates which had passed to her on her father's death in 1598. Lady Suffolk and her daughter, the countess of Somerset, together probably contributed more than any other women to the debauched reputation of the Jacobean court. HELEN PAYNE

Sources J. G. Nichols, ed., *The topographer and genealogist*, 3 vols. (1846–58) · P. Croft, 'The reputation of Robert Cecil: libels, political opinion and popular awareness in the early seventeenth century', *TRHS*, 6th ser., 1 (1991), 43–69 · A. J. Loomie, 'Sir Robert Cecil and the Spanish embassy', *BIHR*, 42 (1969), 30–57 · A. J. Loomie, *Toleration and diplomacy: the religious issues in Anglo-Spanish relations, 1603–05* (1963), 53 · 'Transcripts of state papers, 1603–25, made by S. R. Gardiner, from originals at Simancas and Venice', BL, Add. MS

31111, fol. 45 · HoP, *Commons, 1558–1603* · H. Sydney and others, *Letters and memorials of state*, ed. A. Collins, 2 vols. (1746) · *Calendar of the manuscripts of the most hon. the marquis of Salisbury*, 24 vols., HMC, 9 (1883–1976) · L. L. Peck, *Court patronage and corruption in early Stuart England* (1990); new edn (1993) · receiver-general's account for Queen Anne, June 1603–Sept 1604, PRO, LR 6/154/9 [no foliation] · receiver-general's account for Queen Anne, 1607–8, Duchy of Cornwall Office, London, DCO rolls series box 122A [no foliation] · PRO, state papers domestic, James I and Charles I, SP14, SP16 · GEC, *Peerage*, new edn · First report, HMC, 1/1 (1870); repr. (1874), appx · *The manuscripts of the Earl Cowper*, 3 vols., HMC, 23 (1888–9), vol. 2, p. 182 · administrations, PRO, PROB 6/16, fol. 206r; PROB 6/17, fol. 82r · *VCH Wiltshire* · S. R. Gardiner, *History of England from the accession of James I to the outbreak of the civil war*, 10 vols. (1883–4) · *The letters of John Chamberlain*, ed. N. E. McClure, 2 vols. (1939) · E. F. Rimbault, ed., *The old cheque-book, or book of remembrance, of the Chapel Royal, from 1561 to 1744*, CS, new ser., 3 (1872) · S. Daniel, *The true description of a royal masque* (1604) · *The works of Ben Jonson*, ed. W. Gifford, new edn, 9 vols. (1875) · *DNB* · PRO, state papers (Holland), SP84 · LPL, MS 3201, fol. 257v
Likenesses W. Larkin, oils, *c*.1614–1618, Ranger's House, Blackheath, Greenwich
Wealth at death Wiltshire estates to second son: letters of administration, given 21 Sept 1638, PRO, PROB 6/16, fol. 206r; PROB 6/17, fol. 82r; Nichols, ed., *Topographer*, vol. 1, p. 470; *VCH Wiltshire*, vol. 14, p. 41

Howard, Kenneth Alexander, first earl of Effingham (1767–1845), army officer, was born on 29 November 1767 at Tower House, Arundel, Sussex, the only child of Captain Henry Howard of Tower House and his second wife, Maria (*d*. 29 Jan 1826), the second daughter and coheir of Kenneth Mackenzie, Viscount Fortrose, the eldest son of William, fifth earl of Seaforth. He was descended from Sir William Howard of Lingfield (*d*. 1600), who was the second son of William Howard, first Baron Howard of Effingham (a title created in 1554).

After acting as page of honour to George III, Howard became an ensign in the Coldstream Guards on 21 April 1786. He served with his regiment in Flanders between February 1793 and May 1795, being wounded at St Amand on 8 May 1793. He was promoted lieutenant and captain on 25 April 1793 (acting as adjutant of his regiment from December 1793 to December 1797); became a captain-lieutenant and lieutenant-colonel on 30 December 1797; and became brigade-major to the foot guards on 17 April 1798. In this last capacity he served during the Irish uprising of 1798 and was present during every action of the duke of York's expedition to Holland in 1799.

Howard was appointed a captain and lieutenant-colonel on 25 July 1799. He served as deputy inspector-general, inspector-general, and commandant of the depot of the foreign troops in the British service. He resigned the latter office on being appointed colonel and aide-de-camp to the king on 1 January 1805. He became second major of his regiment on 4 August 1808, and a major-general on 25 July 1810. Howard married Lady Charlotte Primrose (*b*. 27 Aug 1776), daughter of Neil Primrose, third earl of Rosebery, on 27 May 1800 at St George's, Hanover Square, London. They had five sons and four daughters.

In January 1811, Howard joined the army in the Peninsula as Sir William Erskine's successor as commander of a brigade of the 1st division. In the following July he was

Kenneth Alexander Howard, first earl of Effingham (1767–1845), attrib. Archer James Oliver, *c*.1800

transferred to the 2nd division, which he commanded as senior officer under Lord Hill until August 1812. In November of that year he was selected to command the 1st brigade of guards in the 1st division. He assumed command of the division from Sir John Hope for a period after June 1813, during which time it crossed the Bidassoa (7 October), and again at Bayonne in April 1814 after Sir John was captured. Howard was specially commended for gallantry in Lord Hill's dispatches after the battles of Arroyo de Molinos (28 October 1811), and Almaraz (19 May 1812), for which he was thanked by the government (*Dispatches*, 8.381–3, 388; 9.184–5). He received the medal and one clasp for his part in the battle of Vitoria (21 June 1813) and the passage of the Nive (9–10 November 1813).

At the end of the war Howard was appointed lieutenant-governor of Portsmouth, with command of the south-western district. This position prevented him from joining the army in Belgium, but after Waterloo he was given command of the 1st division, occupying Paris, with the local rank of lieutenant-general. Howard's third cousin, Richard Howard, fourth earl of Effingham, died on 11 December 1816, and Howard succeeded as eleventh Baron Howard of Effingham, taking his seat in the House of Lords on 30 May 1817 (*JHL*, 51.243). He resigned his command at Portsmouth on account of his promotion to the official rank of lieutenant-general on 12 August 1819. On 24 October 1816 he had been appointed colonel of the 70th regiment, from which, on 30 January 1832, he was transferred to the colonelcy of the 3rd (Buffs), and on 10 January 1837 he became a full general. He was created a KCB on 5 January 1815, and a GCB on 17 March 1820. He was also made a knight of the Portuguese order of the Tower and Sword.

Howard took no prominent part in politics, but acted generally with the whig party, and in 1820 and 1834 he seconded the address at the opening of the session (*Hansard 2*, 1, 1820, 17; *Hansard 3*, 21, 1834, 8). In July 1821 he acted as deputy earl marshal of England for the coronation of George IV. It is said that during the ceremony in Westminster Hall his horse, which had been hired from Astley's circus, displayed a tendency to rear rather than back, and had to be ignominiously pulled out by its tail.

On 27 January 1837 the earldom of Effingham was revived in Howard's favour. He took his seat as earl in the House of Lords on 21 April 1837 (*JHL*, 69.215). Howard died at Brighton on 13 February 1845, and was buried in the family vault at All Saints' Church, Rotherham, Yorkshire, where a monument was erected in his memory. A memorial tablet to him was placed in the guards' chapel, Wellington barracks, London. His eldest son, Henry (1806–1894), succeeded him. His wife, Charlotte, married again on 30 April 1858. Her second husband was Thomas Holmes, a scripture reader from Brighton. She died on 17 September 1864.   G. F. R. BARKER, *rev.* S. KINROSS

Sources GEC, *Peerage* · Fortescue, *Brit. army*, vols. 8–10 · J. Haydn, *The book of dignities: containing rolls of the official personages of the British empire* (1851) · W. F. P. Napier, *History of the war in the Peninsula and in the south of France*, 3 vols. (1882) · *The dispatches of … the duke of Wellington … from 1799 to 1818*, ed. J. Gurwood, 7–9 (1837) · *Supplementary dispatches … of Field Marshal Arthur, duke of Wellington, K.G.*, ed. A. R. Wellesley, second duke of Wellington, 7–8, 10, 13–14 (1860–72) · *JHL*, 51 (1817–18) · *JHL*, 69 (1837) · J. Philippart, ed., *The royal military calendar*, 1 (1815) · *The Times* (17 Feb 1845) · *GM*, 2nd ser., 23 (1845) · *Annual Register* (1845) · R. Muir, *Britain and the defeat of Napoleon, 1807–1815* (1996)
Archives NL Scot., letters to Sir Thomas Graham · priv. coll., letters to Lord Rosebery
Likenesses attrib. A. J. Oliver, oils, *c.*1800, priv. coll. [*see illus.*] · G. Hayter, group portrait, 1820–23 (*The trial of Queen Caroline, 1820*), NPG · G. Nayler, portrait, 1839 (*Ceremonial of the coronation of George IV*) · Tidy, watercolour, priv. coll.
Wealth at death under £120,000: GEC, *Peerage*

Howard, Lavinia Mary Fitzalan-, duchess of Norfolk (1916–1995). *See under* Howard, Bernard Marmaduke Fitzalan-, sixteenth duke of Norfolk (1908–1975).

Howard, Leonard (1698/9–1767), Church of England clergyman and writer, was first a clerk in the Post Office. In 1728 he published some absurd *Verses on the Recovery of the Lord Townshend*, inscribed to Sir Robert Walpole; they were annexed to a poem on William III. He took orders, was awarded an MA, possibly by a Scottish university, and was DD by 1745. From 1732 he was vicar of Bishops Tawton, Devonshire. In 1742 he was curate of the parishes of St John, Southwark, and St Botolph, Aldersgate, and chaplain to the prince of Wales. In 1745 he became lecturer of St Magnus the Martyr, London Bridge, and of St James Garlickhythe. On 18 July 1749 he was presented by the crown to the rectory of St George the Martyr, Southwark, which he held with the lecturerships of St Magnus and of St Margaret's, New Fish Street Hill. He subsequently was appointed chaplain to the princess dowager of Wales. He was a popular preacher and, although not a model pastor, he was a favourite with his parishioners. His extravagant ways frequently led to his imprisonment in the king's bench, where he was dubbed poet laureate, and he sometimes obtained money as subscriptions to books which he pretended to have in hand.

Howard's best-known work is *A collection of letters from the original manuscripts of many princes, great personages and statesmen, together with some curious and scarce tracts and pieces of antiquity* (1753). At the back of the last page is a list of the contents of a second volume which was in preparation, but which never appeared. To another edition, in two volumes, are added *Memoirs of the Unfortunate Prince Anthony the First of Portugal, and the Oeconomy of High-Life* (1756). Besides several sermons and miscellaneous works in prose and verse, Howard also published *The Newest Manual of Private Devotions*, in three parts (1745, 1753, 1760); *The Royal Bible, or, A Complete Body of Christian Divinity* (1761); and *The Book of Common Prayer … Illustrated and Explained by a Full … Paraphrase* (1761). He also revised the *New Companion for the Festivals and Fasts of the Church of England* (1761). Howard's literary thefts were to lead to much disgrace, to which he refers in the prefaces to his *Newest Manual* and *Collection of Letters*. Howard died on 21 December 1767, aged sixty-eight, and was buried underneath the communion table in St George the Martyr, Southwark, London.

GORDON GOODWIN, *rev.* J. A. MARCHAND

Sources Hennessy, 'Devon Incumbents: List of Incumbents, 1456–1894 for Parishes in the Diocese of Exeter', MS, West Country Studies Library, Exeter · *GM*, 1st ser., 37 (1767), 611 · O. Manning and W. Bray, *The history and antiquities of the county of Surrey*, 3 (1814), 641
Likenesses Bellamy, etching, BM · J. Goldar, line engraving, NPG · Proud, line engraving, NPG · portrait, repro. in L. Howard, *Miscellaneous pieces in prose and verse* (1765)

Howard, Leslie [*real name* Leslie Howard Steiner] (1893–1943), actor and film director, was born at 31 Westbourne Road, Forest Hill, London, on 3 April 1893. He was the eldest son of Ferdinand Steiner, a stockbroker's clerk, and his wife, Lilian Blumberg. He was educated locally in Dulwich and he then became a bank clerk. At the outbreak of the First World War in 1914 he enlisted and was a second lieutenant in the Northamptonshire yeomanry from March 1915 until May 1916, when he resigned his commission. On 3 March 1916 he married Ruth Evelyn, daughter of Henry William Martin, laundry manager, of Colchester. They had a son and a daughter. During his army service an early interest in theatricals increased, and on returning to civilian life he sought a professional engagement, adopted the name by which he was known henceforth, and made his first appearance as a professional actor in 1917, touring the provinces in the part of Jerry in *Peg o' my Heart* by J. Hartley Manners. He made his first appearance in London at the New Theatre, on 14 February 1918, in the small part of Ronald Herrick in the 'idyll of suburbia' *The Freaks* by Sir Arthur Pinero. Howard continued to act in London until the summer of 1920, appearing notably in Gladys Unger's *Our Mr Hepplewhite*, A. A. Milne's *Mr Pim Passes by*, and Gertrude E. Jennings's *The Young Person in Pink*. He then

Leslie Howard (1893–1943), by Fred Daniels, 1942

went to the United States, first appearing in New York at the Henry Miller Theatre in November 1920 in *Just Suppose*. He continued to act in America until 1926, appearing successfully in a variety of plays, notably as Henry in *Outward Bound*, and as Napier Harpenden in *The Green Hat*. He returned to London for a short engagement in 1926, but went back to New York to play in *Her Cardboard Lover*, and in *Escape* by John Galsworthy. Subsequently he divided his time between New York and London. He played Peter Standish in *Berkeley Square* in both cities. His only other performance of note in London was at the Lyric Theatre in October 1933 when he appeared as Shakespeare in *This Side Idolatry*. He played the leading part, Alan Squier, in *The Petrified Forest*, which he presented with Gilbert Miller in 1935 at the Broadhurst Theatre, New York, and in November 1936 he appeared as Hamlet at the Imperial Theatre, New York, in his own production which, however, proved somewhat of a disappointment.

Thereafter Howard devoted his talents to films, both as actor and director, and it was in this medium—in which he first appeared, in *Outward Bound*, in 1930—that he gained full recognition. As a film actor he made notable successes in *Smilin' through* (1932); *Berkeley Square* (1933); *The Scarlet Pimpernel* (1934); *The Petrified Forest* (1936); *Pygmalion* (1938), of which he was co-director; *Gone with the Wind* (1939), in which he starred opposite Vivien Leigh as the ineffectual, gentlemanly Ashley Wilkes; *49th Parallel* (1941), a war film; and many others. After the outbreak of war in 1939 he took to production and was part-producer of some of the best British war films: in *Pimpernel Smith* (1941) and *The First of the Few* (1942) he also played the leading part, and he was a raconteur in *The Gentle Sex* (1943), a story of the ATS. A film about the nursing profession, *The*

Lamp Still Burns (1943), was released after his death. The unescorted passenger aeroplane in which he was returning from a visit to Spain and Portugal under the auspices of the British Council was shot down by the enemy on 1 June 1943.

Leslie Howard was a polished actor, quiet in his method, with a certain wistfulness that added to his natural charm of manner and intelligence. His voice was charming, gracious, and beautifully modulated. In private life he was of a rather shy and retiring nature, but he was extremely popular.
J. PARKER, *rev.* K. D. REYNOLDS

Sources J. Parker, ed., *Who's who in the theatre*, 6th edn (1930) • L. Halliwell, *The filmgoer's companion*, 5th edn (1976) • L. R. Howard, *A quite remarkable father* (1960) • personal knowledge (1959) • private information (1959) • b. cert. • m. cert.
Likenesses photographs, 1927–41, Hult. Arch. • R. G. Eves, oils, c.1937, NPG • F. W. Daniels, photograph, 1942, NPG [*see illus.*] • R. G. Eves, oils, Huddersfield Art Gallery • R. G. Eves, oils, Garr. Club • photograph (after R. G. Eves), NPG • photographs, Theatre Museum, London • postcards, Theatre Museum, London

Howard, Lizzie. *See* Haryett, Elizabeth Ann, countess of Beauregard in the French nobility (*bap.* 1823?, *d.* 1865).

Howard [*née* Matthaei], **Louise Ernestine**, Lady Howard (1880–1969), international civil servant and advocate of organic husbandry, was born on 26 December 1880 at 10 Priory Grove, Kensington, London, the youngest daughter in a family of three girls and a boy of Carl Hermann Ernst Matthaei, commission merchant, and his wife, Louise Henriette Elizabeth Sueur, musician. Of German, French, and Swiss stock, she was educated at South Hampstead high school and at Newnham College, Cambridge, where, in addition to several scholarships and prizes, she obtained firsts in both parts of the classical tripos (1903 and 1904), followed by a research fellowship. In later years she would acknowledge to Leonard and Virginia Woolf how she had been inspired at Cambridge by the teaching of the socialist and feminist Janet Case. In 1909 she became lecturer and director of studies in classics at Newnham, where she gained a reputation as a rigorous but stimulating and sympathetic teacher. In 1918 she published *Studies in Greek Tragedy*, focusing on the role of tragic accident.

Soon after the outbreak of the First World War, Louise Matthaei testified to her idealistic internationalism in a brief essay, *The Lover of the Nations* (1915), in which she pleaded for some attempt at a loving understanding of Germany, and for encouragement for the liberals and radicals in its universities. In a subsequent essay, 'Selfish states and moral individuals', published in the international suffragist periodical *Ius Suffragii* on 1 October 1915, she urged the necessity for contemporaries to purge themselves of collective paranoia. Such views did not recommend themselves to a Cambridge that 'had become a hospital and a camp' (E. M. Forster, *Goldsworthy Lowes Dickinson*, 1934, 163). Anti-German feeling caused the half-German Louise Matthaei to leave her university post, and in 1918 she became an assistant to Leonard Woolf on his *International Review*. After publishing her pro-Spartacist study *Germany in Revolution* in 1920, she joined the agricultural section of the International Labour Organization in Geneva, having successfully sat the competitive examination. In 1924 she was promoted chief of the agricultural section and in 1935 her huge overview, *Labour in Agriculture, an International Survey*, was published by Oxford University Press. During the 1930s and 1940s she expended much energy helping German refugees from Nazism.

In 1931 Louise Matthaei married Albert *Howard (1873–1947), economic botanist to the government of India, and the widower of her elder sister Gabrielle (d. 1930), who had also been a botanist. He was the son of Richard Howard, a Shropshire farmer, and was knighted for his services to the government of India in 1934. Like her sister before her, she devoted herself to furthering her husband's work. He was a passionate campaigner against the use of chemicals to restore fertility to the depleted soils of the world, being a doughty champion of organic methods instead. He argued that the plant should be studied together with its environment as a single unit and that mankind should respect the traditional wisdom gained from the trial and error of generations of peasants the world over. Together the Howards brought out *Farming and Gardening for Health or Disease* in 1945, and in 1947 Louise Howard published *The Earth's Green Carpet*, which foreshadowed the later ecological movement's central concerns, with its chapters on 'Soil fertility and human health', 'The wheel of life', 'The growth of the plant', and 'The retreat of the forest'. Louise Howard's hope for a world without frontiers fused with her advocacy of 'a free exchange between the nations of the direct and indirect products of sunlight' (and of a fertile soil) as the birthright of all races (*Earth's Green Carpet*, 9). After her husband's death in 1947 she published *Sir Albert Howard in India* (1953) and co-founded the Albert Howard Foundation, which in 1953 merged with the Soil Association, of which she became honorary life vice-president.

To all three of her careers, as classics don, international civil servant, and advocate of organic husbandry, Louise Matthaei Howard brought wide social sympathies, a highly cultivated mind, and a large measure of dry humour. She died at her home, 14 Blackheath Park, Blackheath, London, on 11 March 1969. She had no children.

SYBIL OLDFIELD

Sources L. E. Howard, *Sir Albert Howard in India* (1953) · 'Mother Earth', *Journal of the Soil Association* (Oct 1953) · *Newnham College Roll Letter* (1970) · *The letters of Virginia Woolf*, ed. N. Nicolson, 2 (1976) · *The diary of Virginia Woolf*, ed. A. O. Bell and A. McNeillie, 1 (1977) · L. E. Howard, *The earth's green carpet* (1947) · *The Times* (13 March 1969) · *CGPLA Eng. & Wales* (1970) · d. cert. · b. cert. · WWW
Likenesses group portrait, photograph, c.1906, Newnham College, Cambridge · H. Wrightson, photograph, c.1940, repro. in 'Mother Earth'
Wealth at death £64,622: probate, 30 July 1970, *CGPLA Eng. & Wales*

Howard, Luke (1621–1699), Quaker activist and writer, was born at Dover on 18 October 1621, the son of Robert Howard (c.1580–1625), a shoemaker, and his wife, Susanna. His mother married a butcher when Luke was eight, but when he came to decide on his future occupation 'something in my Conscience … stirred against Evil, and made me dislike a Butcher's Life and Trade' (Howard, 4), and he chose to follow in his late father's trade. He was apprenticed at the age of fourteen to a shoemaker, and for a time was a strict conformist to the Church of England. He later recalled, however, that his master 'began to enquire after Religion, and went amongst such as separated from the Publick Worship, and began to make more Conscience of Religion than he had done; the which then opened a Door to me' (ibid.). His seven-year term completed, Howard went to London and joined John Goodwin's Independent congregation at Coleman Street.

At the outbreak of the civil war Howard had hoped to join the parliamentarian army but failed to get enrolled; he later rejoiced that this failure had saved him from shedding human blood. He then took service with the garrison in Dover Castle, and there refused to sing psalms in 'rhyme and meter' (Howard, 6). The chaplain preached against him, and Samuel Fisher (1605–1665), the future Quaker, reasoned with him, but was himself convinced of Howard's viewpoint.

In his journal Howard relates that, after becoming successively a Brownist, presbyterian, and Independent, he joined the Baptists, and journeyed to London to be 'dipped' by William Kiffin on a December day 'when ice was in the water' (Howard, 8). In turn he shifted from the Particular Baptism of Kiffin to General Baptism, rejecting the 'dark stuff' of Calvinist election as 'God's Witness in my own Conscience arose and opened my Understanding, and I then saw Man's Destruction to be of himself, and not of the Lord' (ibid., 9). Howard found his first wife among the Baptists: Anne Stevens (d. 1665) of Canterbury, whom he described as 'the first baptised person in Kent', and whom he married some time after 1644 (ibid., 34). They had at least two children: Luke (1645/6–1667) and Robert (1647/8–1665). He became disillusioned with the Baptists, coming to see the very act of baptism as a merely worldly form. Following this, Howard says, 'I gave myself up to a seeking state again, and became as dead to all forms' (ibid., 11).

In March 1655 Howard again went to London and was converted to Quakerism by William Caton and John Stubbs. In his journal Howard discusses how he adapted to Quaker customs and habits, saying, 'And then as to my whole life and course thereof, I had all to learn again … both eating and drinking, and wearing apparel, and talking, and buying, and selling; yea, all to be made new' (Howard, 24–5). Howard notes that he was the 'first receiver of Friends' in Kent (ibid., 34). Following his convincement he was frequently in trouble for interrupting ministers in church services, noting that he 'was moved to go to the priest, and bear a testimony for God in time of their preaching' (ibid., 30). He also recounts how he sometimes fasted for long periods of time, unknown to all but his wife, feeling as well after seven or eight days as he did at the outset.

Through Howard's work Quaker numbers increased at Dover, and the movement attracted many Baptists, the cause of much controversy between the two groups. Howard was largely responsible for the conversion to Quakerism of the Leveller John Lilburne, who was imprisoned in Dover Castle, where the Quaker visited him many times, Lilburne becoming fully convinced in 1656 and describing Howard as his 'indeared, spiritual and faithful friend' (*Resurrection of John Lilburne*, 5).

At the Restoration Howard himself was imprisoned in Dover Castle for three months. In June 1661 he was committed to Westgate prison in Canterbury for five days, and in the July following was sent to Dover Castle for about sixteen months 'because we could not forbear meetings' (Howard, 28). On 30 January 1684 he was taken, along with seven others, from a meeting and imprisoned in the same dungeon for fifty-one weeks.

Following the death of his first wife, Anne, Howard married Elizabeth Loper (*d.* 1714) on 17 July 1666. Together they had at least two sons, Luke (*b.* 1669) and Solomon (1672–1694). Mary Howard (*d.* 1719) who married John Knott, a shoemaker, may have been a daughter. Howard was held in high esteem by leading London Quakers, for a testimony from the second day morning meeting, signed by William Penn, George Whitehead, and others, described him as 'of an exemplary christian conversation, and of a good report among his friends and neighbours, and beloved of them for his just and upright dealing' ('A testimony concerning … Luke Howard'). He was evidently a leading Quaker in Kent, for the 1672 yearly meeting minutes show that he was the recipient of books for his county. In relation to local meetings, he wrote in his journal that since becoming a Quaker,

> I never had liberty in Dover to omit one meeting; except by sickness or lameness kept away, but outward business I have been constrained to make bow to the Lord, and the meeting, and the time as much as I could, and not to miss one, unto this day. (Howard, 33)

Howard wrote a number of tracts, many of which are found in *Love and Truth in Plainness Manifested*. Some of these are replies to Baptists, such as *A Looking Glass for the Baptists* (1673) and *The Seat of the Scorner Thrown Down* (1673); in the latter Howard explains why he left the Baptists, and more generally discusses ideas such as the Quaker notion of the 'inner light' and their views on baptism. He also wrote *The Devil's Bow Unstringed* (1659), a reply to the non-conformist divine Thomas Danson, and testimonies to leading Quakers, namely 'A testimony concerning Samuel Fisher', in Samuel Fisher's *The Testimony of Truth Exalted* (1679), and 'A testimony concerning George Fox', in George Fox's *Gospel Truth Demonstrated* (1706). Luke Howard died on 7 October 1699 and was buried on 13 October 1699, presumably at Dover.   CAROLINE L. LEACHMAN

Sources L. Howard, 'A short journal of Luke Howard', in L. Howard, *Love and truth in plainness manifested* (1704) [1697] · J. Smith, ed., *A descriptive catalogue of Friends' books*, 1 (1867), 978–80 · *The resurrection of John Lilburne, now a prisoner in Dover-castle … in these following lines, penned by himself*, 2nd edn (1656) [with added appendix] · P. Gregg, *Free-born John: a biography of John Lilburne* (1961) · 'A testimony concerning our dear Friend and brother Luke Howard', L. Howard, *Love and truth in plainness manifested* (1704) · yearly meeting minutes, 1668–93, RS Friends, Lond., 1.4 · digest registers (marriages and burials to 1837), RS Friends, Lond. [Kent quarterly meeting] · 'Dictionary of Quaker biography', RS Friends, Lond. [card index] · L. V. Hodgkin, *The shoemaker of Dover: Luke Howard, 1621–1699* (1943)
Archives RS Friends, Lond., Swarthmore MSS, vol. 3, MS vol. 354

Howard, Luke (1772–1864), manufacturing chemist and meteorologist, was born on 28 November 1772 in London, one of the several children of Robert Howard (1738–1812) and his wife, Elizabeth Leatham (1742–1816) of Pontefract. His father was a wealthy tin plate manufacturer and the chief agent for introducing the Argand lamp into Britain. From 1780 to 1787 Howard was educated at a Quaker grammar school in Burford, Oxfordshire. The headmaster was Thomas Huntley, whose teaching methods involved flogging pupils who did not learn quickly enough. The result, according to Howard, was that he learned more Latin than he was able to forget, but little science or mathematics—a loss he felt deeply and which was probably responsible for a continuing modesty regarding his own scientific opinions. He did, however, claim an inborn capacity for observation.

On leaving school Howard served a seven-year apprenticeship in pharmacy under Ollive Sims of Stockport; he returned to London and joined a firm of druggists in Bishopsgate during 1794. An attempt to set up independently in Fleet Street was unsuccessful, but in 1798 he went into partnership with William Allen, another Quaker, who owned the Plough Court pharmacy, Lombard Street, Howard taking charge of the firm's laboratory at Plaistow, Essex. The partnership was dissolved after seven years, and Howard moved the laboratory to Stratford where he built it into a thriving business, supplying chemicals to industry and pharmaceuticals to retail pharmacists. He also provided pure ether to his friend and fellow Quaker John Dalton for his experiments.

Howard never published anything on chemistry, observing that it was his trade—he lived in the practice of chemistry as an art, not to impart it as a science—and that it was necessary to maintain trade secrecy. He noted that his true penchant was for meteorology, and he also studied botany and geology.

Howard married Mariabella (1769–1852), daughter of John and Mary Eliot, in London, on 7 December 1796. They had eight children (four sons, four daughters); one son died in infancy. Mariabella published three books between 1827 and 1850: *Hints on the Improvement of Day Schools* (1827), *The Young Servants' Own Book* (1828), and *Boys' Own Book* (1850). The family lived first at Plaistow, moving to Tottenham in 1812, and spent time at their country home near Ackworth, Yorkshire. Their sons Robert Howard and John Eliot *Howard took over the family firm in 1830. There was more than a hint of brilliance in the line. Among their direct descendants were Thomas Hodgkin, the historian, Paul Waterhouse, the architect, Margery Fry, the prison reformer, and the Labour politician R. H. S. Crossman.

Luke Howard (1772–1864), by John Opie?

Howard and Allen both joined the Askesian Society, a philosophical group that met fortnightly during 1796–1806. Howard also presented a paper on pollens to the Linnean Society in 1800, and began a register of meteorological observations the following year, these being published in *The Athenaeum*, 1807–9. Doubtless the Linnaean classification system made an impression, and during the Askesian's 1802–3 session Howard presented a paper on the classification of clouds, later published as 'On the modification of clouds, and on the principles of their production, suspension and destruction' (*Philosophical Magazine*, 16, 1803). Lamarck had devised a classification system in 1802 but Howard's proved the more durable, and was the basis of the international system.

Using the Latin terminology *stratus*, *cumulus*, *cirrus*, and *nimbus*, Howard defined three groups: simple modifications (cirrus, cumulus, stratus); intermediate modifications (cirro-cumulus, cirro-stratus); and compound modifications (cumulo-stratus, cumulo-cirro-stratus vel nimbus). The system gave evidence of his keen observational powers in differentiating the fundamental cloud forms of heaped (cumulus), layered (stratus), and fibrous (cirrus), even though his knowledge of their mode of formation was rudimentary.

Howard's series of meteorological observations was also maintained and in 1818–20, using the data obtained, he published *The Climate of London* (2 vols.), updating it with a second edition in 1833. This was the first book in English on urban climatology, and it introduced new thinking on atmospheric electricity and the causes of rain. He also expounded his theories in seven lectures during 1817 (not published until 1837), a later edition (1843)

being dedicated to Dalton, and he investigated the possibility of lunar influence on weather. Election as FRS came in 1821.

Meanwhile Johann Wolfgang von Goethe, himself interested in meteorology, had seen a translation of Howard's 1803 paper. Goethe was enchanted by the descriptive classification system, praising its terminology as 'bestowing form on the formless, and a system of ordered change in a boundless world' (Slater, 120), and responded with a lyrical poem, *Howard's Ehrengedächtnis*, in celebration. Most of this was published in 1817, but Goethe later added three introductory strophes. He was intrigued by the personality of the younger man, to whom he referred as 'our Master', and sought a biographical sketch through an intermediary, Johann Huttner, in 1822. After some hesitation Howard supplied this himself. Goethe was overjoyed but the two never met, nor did they correspond directly.

About 1810 Howard made a series of watercolour sketches of clouds, a series which later came into the ownership of the Royal Meteorological Society. His classification scheme may have become known to more famous artists. Claims that he influenced Constable and Turner are controversial, but the former's study of skyscapes in the 1820s followed soon after publication of *The Climate of London*, which included a description of the scheme, and there is evidence that Constable was aware of Howard's work.

A deeply religious man, Howard held strongly to Quaker traditions of service and humility: he wrote tracts upholding the Quaker way of life, and became a minister in 1815. His father was a founder member of the British and Foreign Bible Society, serving on its first committee, and Howard followed him on to the committee, besides becoming engaged in campaigns aimed at the improvement of society. He and Allen were involved in the antislave trade movement at the turn of the century, and later Howard joined the campaign to raise support for relieving distress in Germany, following the fighting across Europe and defeat of Napoleon at Leipzig, becoming joint secretary (with W. H. Marten) of the organizing London committee. This held its first meeting on 27 January 1814 and the sums raised were remarkable: £4000 was subscribed before the meeting, with £112,000 obtained by 18 October, and reports claimed £300,000 as a final total. For this service he and Marten were awarded gold rings and Meissen vases by the kings of Prussia and Saxony, and received the freedom of the city of Magdeburg. However, despite some contrary accounts, the balance of evidence appears to show that Howard did not visit Germany in that year. In 1816 Howard did travel to Germany, as a member of a delegation from the London based Quaker meeting for sufferings to Quaker groups there. Distribution of relief did not, apparently, form part of this visit, which was merely to meet the German Friends.

In subsequent years Howard became involved in controversies which terminated his membership of both the British and Foreign Bible Society and the Society of Friends. He came into conflict with the British and Foreign Bible Society in a dispute over the Apocrypha, which he sought to clarify by translating several of the Apocryphal books into English from the Latin Vulgate, and he resigned from this society in 1825. A more far-reaching split followed in the next decade. In 1835 Isaac Crewdson published *A Beacon to the Society of Friends*, which had an evangelical message and challenged Quaker thinking. Howard supported Crewdson and resigned from the society in 1836. The Beaconites supported the Quaker way of life and duty, but held to the revealed word of God in the scriptures, and called for acceptance of baptism and the Lord's supper. During the period 1833–7 he edited *The Yorkshireman*, a Quaker magazine, and used its pages to argue the Beaconite cause. The only other dissenting sect in Britain accepting baptism and the Lord's supper, while rejecting an ordained priesthood, was the Plymouth Brethren, which Howard, Crewdson, and a number of other Friends now joined, and Howard was baptized by Crewdson on 7 June 1837. The following year he published an appeal against a sentence of disownment passed upon a member by the Society of Friends.

Two significant scientific publications were to follow. In 1842 Howard produced an essay based on observations made at London (1807–23) and Ackworth (1824–41), in which he proposed an eighteen-year cycle of weather. This was, perhaps, a little hopeful, but his last major work, *Barometrographia* (1847), gave a series of curves of the variation of the barometer, with large circular diagrams representing its changes with other particulars of weather, and incorporating the position of the moon. Appended were papers presented by Howard to the Royal Society. The publication was described by Napier Shaw as 'a book of some magnificence' (N. Shaw, *Manual of Meteorology*, 1932, 1.133).

After the death of his wife Howard spent his later years with his eldest son, Robert, at Bruce Grove, Tottenham, where he died on 21 March 1864. He was buried at Winchmore Hill.   JIM BURTON

Sources A. W. Slater, 'Luke Howard, FRS, and his relations with Goethe', *Notes and Records of the Royal Society*, 27 (1972–3), 119–40 · B. J. R. Blench, 'Luke Howard and his contribution to meteorology', *Weather*, 18 (1963), 83–92 · D. F. S. Scott, ed., *Luke Howard, 1772–1864* (1972) · S. Godman, 'Father of British meteorology', *The Times* (21 March 1964) · J. A. Day and F. H. Ludlam, 'Luke Howard and his clouds', *Weather*, 27 (1972), 448–61 · 'Dictionary of Quaker biography', RS Friends, Lond. [card index] · D. F. S. Scott, 'Luke Howard and Goethe', *Durham University Journal*, 45/3 (1953), 94–103 · J. A. Kington, 'A century of cloud classification', *Weather*, 24 (1969), 84–9 · R. M. Jones, *The later periods of Quakerism*, 2 vols. (1921) · E. F. Howard, 'Goethe and Luke Howard FRS', *Friends' Quarterly Examiner*, 66 (1932), 221–8 · D. F. S. Scott, *Some English correspondents of Goethe* (1949) · CUL, Bible Society Archives · d. cert.
Archives LMA, corresp. and papers · Meteorological Office, Bracknell, Berkshire, National Metereological Library and Archive, meteorological journals and observations · RS · RS Friends, Lond., corresp. and papers · Sci. Mus., corresp. and papers · Wellcome L., corresp. and papers
Likenesses J. Opie?, oils, Royal Meteorological Society, Bracknell [*see illus.*]
Wealth at death under £14,000: probate, 7 April 1864, *CGPLA Eng. & Wales*

Howard, Mary. *See* Fitzroy, Mary, duchess of Richmond (*c.*1519–1555?).

Howard [*née* Fitzalan], **Mary, duchess of Norfolk** (1539/40–1557), noblewoman, was the third child of Henry *Fitzalan, twelfth earl of Arundel (*d.* 1580), and his first wife, Katherine, daughter of Thomas Grey, second marquess of Dorset. Jane *Lumley (1537–1578) was her sister and Henry, Lord Maltravers (1538–1556), was her brother. In or about 1554 Mary married, as his first wife, Thomas *Howard, fourth duke of Norfolk (1538–1572), and in June 1557 she gave birth to their only son, Philip *Howard (*d.* 1595), who succeeded in her right to the earldom of Arundel. She died, probably at Arundel House, London, from complications arising from the labour on 25 August, and was buried in St Clements without Temple Bar on 1 September 1557. Mary is mainly remembered for her classical learning, the result of her father's care to educate all of his children. Arundel's impressive library was the means by which some examples of Mary's work were preserved, as they (together with the works of her siblings) were kept together with the main collection, which passed into royal ownership in 1609 and now forms part of the British Library. BL, Royal MSS 12 A.i–iv, comprise four collections of *sententiae*, from Greek and English sources, translated by Mary into Latin and dedicated as new year's gifts to her father. Two were written before her marriage and two afterwards, the final one being a joint effort with her stepbrother John Ratcliffe; these works evidence an enduring personal and intellectual relationship with the highly cultured family circle into which she was born.   STEPHANIE HODGSON-WRIGHT

Sources *DNB* · 'The life of Henrye Fitzallen', BL, Royal MS 17 A.ix · J. H. Pollen and W. McMahon, eds., *The Ven. Philip Howard, earl of Arundel, 1557–1595* (1919) · BL, Royal MSS 12 A.i–iv · S. Jayne and F. S. Johnson, eds., *The Lumley Library: the catalogue of 1609* (1956)

Howard [*née* Mordaunt; *other married name* Germain], **Mary, duchess of Norfolk** (1658/9–1705), noblewoman and divorcee, was the only daughter and heir of Henry *Mordaunt, second earl of Peterborough (*bap.* 1623, *d.* 1697), and his wife, Lady Penelope (*c.*1622–1702), daughter of Barnabas *O'Brien, sixth earl of Thomond. Her mother later served as groom of the stole to Mary of Modena.

As a member of Charles II's court Lady Mary Mordaunt played Psecas in Thomas Crowne's masque of 1675, 'Calisto'. On 8 August 1677 she married Henry *Howard (1655–1701), who became earl of Arundel in 1678 and seventh duke of Norfolk in 1684. Owing to the differences in their religion (he was a Catholic at the time, she a protestant, though their positions were later reversed) the wedding was private. As Lady Arundel she was lady of the bedchamber to Queen Catherine of Braganza. Like many women of the Restoration court she was the object of obscene satirical poetry. Her name was linked in particular to that of Charles Talbot, duke of Shrewsbury, which caused her to have a semi-publicized quarrel with Betty Felton over his affections.

In 1685 Mary, now duchess of Norfolk, was taken to France by her husband. The duke, who had conformed to the Church of England in 1679, left her in a convent, where she was required to convert to Catholicism. Although he may have been spurred to part with her by the discovery of her adultery she later maintained that the duke was moved by financial necessity, 'to ease him in his charge and part; he frequently declaring, that when he should be more easy in his fortunes they should live together' (*A True Account of the Proceedings*, 10). The separation, however, proved permanent. When the duchess returned to England in 1686 she took up residence at her estate at Drayton, Northamptonshire, and sued the duke for alimony of £400 a year, which he had promised in 1685 but never paid. She left England again in 1688, but returned again when her father (who had been imprisoned in the Tower after the revolution of 1688) fell ill. This time she took up residence in 'Fox-hall' (Vauxhall) under the assumed name of Lady Bateman, later explaining that she needed to remain incognito because she 'had at that time nothing to live upon', and 'not able to appear in a condition answerable to her quality' felt bound to retrench her expenses (*A True Account of the Proceedings*, 21).

In January 1692 the duke of Norfolk introduced the first of what were to be three bills in parliament to allow him to divorce his wife and remarry. A string of witnesses, mostly servants, attested before the House of Lords to the duchess's keeping company in 1685 and again in 1691 with the Dutch adventurer Sir John *Germain (1650–1718). Divorces by act of parliament were at the time almost unprecedented and sparked a highly politicized debate over the relationship of church and state and the unreformed character of English canon law (which in contrast to continental protestantism permitted only separation from bed and board rather than full divorce).

The duchess of Norfolk mounted a vigorous defence in parliament. She drew attention to the irregular nature of the proceedings which, she said, violated Magna Carta and her rights as an English subject by creating new laws arbitrarily, she emphasized her status as a noblewoman descended from an ancient family, she threatened to prove the duke guilty of adultery, she pointed to the unfairness of making her 'prove a negative' of events that had happened so long ago, and she contended that the divorce proceeding was an attempt by the duke to pressure her into relinquishing her interest in Castle Rising, Norfolk, and other estates so that he could sell them to rescue his ailing fortunes. Her use of the press is especially striking. In response to 'libellous pamphlets' she published in 1692 *A True Account of the Proceedings* (printed again in 1693 as *A Vindication of her Grace Mary Dutchess of Norfolk*), a long tract which interspersed summaries of testimony with observations attacking the credibility of the duke's plebeian witnesses. Still conscious of maintaining a wifely image the duchess explained that she had initially intended to release her pamphlet after the Lords rejected the duke's first bill in February 1692, but had suspended publication 'that there might be no offence to the Duke'. Given, however, that the duke had tried again with a suit in king's bench against John Germain and another bill for divorce in 1693, 'it now may not be thought impertinent for this true account to appear to the world' (*True Account*,

advertisement). The jury in king's bench had found Germain guilty of criminal conversation with the duchess, but awarded her husband in damages a derisory 100 marks (£66) rather than the £10,000 that he had sought. Although the duke was unable to obtain the passage of his second bill the duchess was persuaded in April 1694 'after long agitation' to convey to him the use of the manor of Castle Rising and her interest in 'a considerable part' of the manor of Sheffield in Yorkshire, 'it being condicible to their respective quiets and ease' (*The Case of Mary Dutchess of Norfolk*).

In December 1696 the duchess was called to testify before the House of Lords regarding the behaviour of her cousin Charles *Mordaunt, earl of Monmouth, during the attainder proceedings against the Jacobite Sir John Fenwick. Monmouth had apparently used the duchess as a conduit to convey advice to her friend, Mary, Lady Fenwick, to the effect that her husband should save himself by accusing prominent members of William III's government of Jacobite plotting. Whether the duchess wished like Mary Fenwick to expose Monmouth's intrigues, or whether she simply could not avoid testifying, is unclear. James Vernon, under-secretary of state, who certainly relished Monmouth's embarrassment, praised the duchess's performance: 'she behaved herself with great prudence and address; she appeared to be an unwilling witness, and yet left little room to suspect her sincerity' (*Letters Illustrative*, 1.140). The result, in any case, was that Monmouth was humiliated, and blamed the duchess's malice. The duchess was also embarrassed in the proceedings by testimony that she had tried to recruit a widow, Mrs Norton, to discredit George Porter, the chief witness against Fenwick, by charging him with the murder of her husband.

The antagonism between the duchess of Norfolk and her cousin Charles, who had succeeded her father as earl of Peterborough in 1697, was further inflamed by a legal dispute over the manor of Drayton and other properties. Peterborough's enmity may well have contributed to the reversal of her fortunes when the duke of Norfolk once more brought a bill for divorce in February 1700. A new raft of witnesses came forth to prove her adultery, some of whom claimed to have been sent abroad by Germain to prevent their testifying in 1692. The duke also emphasized the danger of his estate's falling into the hands of his Catholic collateral heirs, or of Germain's not-yet-conceived bastard children begotten on the duchess, should he not be allowed to remarry. This time the bill passed both houses, although with the proviso that the duke pay the duchess back her £10,000 marriage portion.

The duke died in April the following year, and five months later Mary married Sir John Germain, baronet: the licence, dated 15 September 1701, was made out in the names of Lady Mary Mordaunt, spinster, and Sir John Germain, baronet (the title he had held since 1698). She died on 17 November 1705, aged forty-six, at her estate at Lowick, Northamptonshire, and was buried in the parish church there five days later. She had settled Drayton and other Mordaunt family property (according to one estimate worth £70,000) on her second husband: despite legal challenges by Peterborough he retained them until his death in 1718, when they passed to his second wife, Lady Elizabeth *Germain, *née* Berkeley.   RACHEL WEIL

Sources *The proceedings before the House of Lords between the duke and dutchess of Norfolk* (1692) · *A true account of the proceedings before the House of Lords from January 7 1691 to February 17 following … occasioned by two libellous pamphlets* (1692) [Also published as *A vindication of her grace Mary dutchess of Norfolk*, 1693] · *The proceedings upon a bill of divorce between his grace the duke of Norfolk and the Lady Mary Mordaunt* (1700) · *The tryal between Henry duke of Norfolk and John Jermaine, defendant* (1692) · 'Case of divorce', in papers of Roger North, BL, Add. MS 32523, fols. 42–6 · J. H. Wilson, *Court satires of the Restoration* (1976) · *Charles earl of Peterborow appellant. Sir John Jermaine, and Lady Mary Mordaunt his wife, respondants. The appellant's case* (1702) · R. Weil, *Political passions: gender, the family and political argument in England, 1680–1714* (1999) · L. Stone, *Road to divorce: England, 1530–1987* (1990) · E. Boswell, *The Restoration court stage (1660–1702): with a particular account of the production of 'Calisto'* (1932) · *Letters illustrative of the reign of William III from 1696 to 1708 addressed to the duke of Shrewsbury by James Vernon*, ed. G. P. R. James, 3 vols. (1841) · *JHL*, 16 (1696–1701) [Dec 1696; Jan 1697] · GEC, *Peerage*

Howard [*née* Shireburne], **Mary**, **duchess of Norfolk** (**1692–1754**), Jacobite sympathizer and landowner, was born on 22 November 1692 at Bedford Row, Bloomsbury, the second daughter and third child of Sir Nicholas Shireburne (1658–1717) and Catherine Charleton (*d.* 1728). She was baptized Maria Windforda Francesca, but was always known as Mary. She was raised at the family seat of Stonyhurst Hall, Lancashire, at a time when the wealth of the Shireburnes, carefully amassed through the acquisition of large estates and the pursuit of the woollen trade, was being confidently exhibited through massive building schemes and ostentatious charity. As children, neither she nor her siblings enjoyed good health. Her sister, Isabel, had died in 1688, and when Mary began to sicken in the spring of 1698, her father showed no hesitation in sending her to seek a cure at the exiled Jacobite court of St Germain. During her seven-month stay she was touched for the king's evil by James II and came under the care of his personal physician, Sir William Waldegrave. Though the touching made for good propaganda, and was used both to emphasize Sir Nicholas's continued refusal to acknowledge the legitimacy of the English government and his faith in the quasi-divine properties of the fallen Stuart dynasty, Waldegrave's practical assistance in saving the girl's life was promptly rewarded with the gift of a gold watch, worth in excess of £26. On her return home on 12 December 1698 Mary was consigned once again to the relative obscurity of the nursery and the schoolroom until the tragic death of her brother, Richard Francis (1693–1702), after eating poisonous berries, robbed her family of their only male heir and transformed her own dynastic importance and social standing.

As the future recipient of valuable estates and properties in Lancashire, the West Riding of Yorkshire, and the Isle of Man, her wealth, religion, and politics made Shireburne extremely eligible for marriage into the declining English circle of great Jacobite and Roman Catholic families. Accordingly, she was betrothed to Thomas Howard, eighth duke of Norfolk (1683–1732), and even though the penal laws prohibited a public wedding, the dinner that followed it at Shireburne House in St James's Square (26 May 1709) was the occasion for enormous expense and display. The princely sum of more than £668 spent on gilt plate as part of her dowry, and '£350 in part for my daughter's weding cloathes' (Shireburne and Weld papers), attests to the desire of Sir Nicholas to maintain a prominent position in noble society, even though a role in public life was denied him on account of his faith.

The young couple spent much of the remainder of the year at Stonyhurst, before returning to the Howard estates in the spring of 1710. Bitter disputes between the duke and the corporation of Norwich led to his abandonment, and eventual demolition, of his palatial property there, and he subsequently settled with the duchess at Worksop Manor in Nottinghamshire. However, there is little to indicate that the pair were ever particularly close, and Mary maintained a peripatetic existence, travelling between her residences in the north and the midlands. It is conceivable that a breach occurred between husband and wife in 1715–16 over the duke's willingness to acknowledge the legitimacy of the Hanoverian succession after the failure of the Jacobite rising. Even though this was done in order to save his brother's life, the duchess remained scornful of the attempted rapprochement. She was also hostile towards her husband's attempts in 1719 to engineer a concordat between the pope, the Hanoverian government, and the Roman Catholic community in England. While it is possible that Mary's continued opposition to any such scheme might have proved decisive in eroding support for it within the ducal household, it seems certain that it was her lobbying which ensured that considerable funds were diverted from the Howard estates to help finance the Jacobite cause on the continent. The transference of these moneys served to implicate the duke in an abortive Jacobite plot of 1722. Arrested at Bath, the duke was quickly conveyed to the Tower of London, where he was held prisoner for the next six months. However, the general lack of hard evidence against him ensured that he was eventually released on bail, having given assurances of his future good conduct.

An active supporter and patron of the Society of Jesus, the duchess was instrumental in securing appointments for Jesuit priests within her household, effectively overruling the duke's preference for Franciscans. In 1725 she brought Father Thomas Lawson SJ, the former almoner to Mary of Modena and confessor to James II, back from exile to serve as her personal chaplain. Thereafter, it would seem that the duke and duchess lived increasingly separate lives, and the premature death of her husband on 23 December 1732 permitted her to retire to the house of her kinsman Peregrine Widdrington (1692–1748) in Chiswick, Middlesex. Though there can be no doubt that she embarked upon a sexual relationship with Widdrington, it is not known whether the couple were formally contracted in marriage. Thus, although her remarriage was announced in the pages of the *Gentleman's Magazine*

(November 1733), Mary's silence on this matter in her own, otherwise meticulous, correspondence and her failure to record any allusion to her relationship with Widdrington in the inscription for his funerary monument would seem to attest quite strongly to a common-law partnership. Certainly, her failure either to acknowledge or disown a morganatic marriage led to the severance of her friendship with Father Lawson and to a cooling of her regard for the Jesuit order.

The duchess spent the remainder of her life overseeing the careful management of her northern estates, combining a sense of paternalism to her favoured tenants with an unflinching hardness towards outside interference and towards any who were judged unworthy of her protection. Though still committed to the Jacobite cause, to which she provided some financial support, she does not appear to have played a role in the rising of 1745. As befitted the last of her line, she devoted considerable energy to the raising of monuments commemorating departed members of the Shireburne family; these not only recorded their commitment to Roman Catholicism but also celebrated the perils that they had been forced to endure as the result of their devotion to the Stuart cause. She died at Preston on 25 September 1754, and was buried beside Peregrine Widdrington in the Shireburne chapel of All Hallows Church, Great Mitton, Lancashire, on 20 October. According to local tradition her coffin was borne on its last journey, across the fell tops, by her own servants and retainers. Having died without children, her property and estates were bequeathed to the family of her aunt Elizabeth, through whom they devolved upon successive generations of the Welds of Lulworth until 1794.

JOHN CALLOW

Sources J. Gerard, *Stonyhurst College* (1894) • F. J. A. Skeet, 'The eighth duchess of Norfolk', *Stonyhurst Magazine*, 256–8 (1925), 71–4, 117–21, 173–5 • F. J. A. Skeet, *Stuart papers, pictures, relics … in the collection of Miss Maria Widdrington* (1930) • H. Howard, *Indications of memorials, monuments … of the Howard family* [1834–6] • S. Hibbert Ware, *Lancashire memorials of the rebellion*, 2 pts in 1, Chetham Society, 5 (1845) • G. Brenan and E. P. Statham, *The house of Howard*, 2 vols. (1907) • F. W. Steer, ed., *The Arundel Castle archives*, 4 vols. (1968–80), vol. 1 • G. Gruggen and J. Keating, *Stonyhurst* (1901) • H. Chadwick, *St Omers to Stonyhurst* (1962) • C. D. Sherborn, *A history of the family of Sherborn* (1901) • parish register, Great Mitton, All Hallows Church, 20 Oct 1754, Lancs. RO, PR 3031: acc. 4232 [burial] • Lancs. RO, Shireburne and Weld papers, DDSt • Arundel Castle archives, West Sussex, T. 70 • Stonyhurst College archives, Shireburne box file B; E/2/4/4, 1, 5, 9 and e; E/2/6, 9, codicils to will of 8 Aug 1750, 12 March 1753, 13 March 1753, 23 Aug 1754

Archives Lancs. RO, Shireburne and Weld papers, incl. accounts for Mary's wedding to the duke of Norfolk and corresp. relating to his imprisonment in the Tower • Stonyhurst College, Lancashire, corresp. and estate records | Arundel Castle, Sussex, archives, letters and papers, letter to kinswoman 'Mrs Howard'; will and codicils; other Shireburne wills • Lancs. RO, Great Mitton parish register, incl. details of duchess's table, acc. 4232.8, PR 3031: acc. 4232

Likenesses W. Maxwell-Stuart, watercolour, *c*.1707–1720 (after earlier portrait), Stonyhurst College, Lancashire; copy, Lulworth Castle • oils, *c*.1709–1730, Stonyhurst College, Lancashire

Wealth at death Stonyhurst Hall; estates at Blackburn, Ormskirk, Isle of Man; Bailey Hall; property in Preston and Mitton: Arundel Castle archives, T. 70; Stonyhurst College, Lancashire,

archives: Shireburne box file B; E/2/4/4, 1, 5, 9 and e; E/2/6, 9, codicils to will of 8 Aug 1750, 12 March 1753, 13 March 1753, 23 Aug 1754

Howard [*née* Blount], **Mary**, duchess of Norfolk (1701/2–1773), noblewoman, was the second daughter of Edward Blount, of Blagdon, Devon, and his wife, Anne, daughter of Sir John Guise, second baronet. The Blounts were a prominent Catholic family; Mary's brother Edward was a patron of Alexander Pope, and they were distantly related to Pope's close friends Martha and Teresa Blount.

On 26 November 1727 Mary Blount married Lord Edward Howard (1686–1777), younger brother and heir to Thomas Howard, eighth duke of Norfolk. Edward Howard had been tried for treason after serving in the Jacobite forces in Scotland during the 1715 rising, but had been acquitted when no witnesses could be found to testify against him. The eighth duke of Norfolk had been imprisoned in the Tower of London in 1722 on suspicion of involvement in a Jacobite conspiracy; the eighth duke's duchess, Mary *Howard, *née* Shireburne, was a determined opponent of any *rapprochement* between English Catholics and the protestant succession and an enthusiastic financial supporter of the Jacobite cause. The realignment of the dukes of Norfolk away from a Jacobite identity and towards accommodation with the whig establishment, despite their Catholicism, was to a great extent Mary Blount's achievement.

Edward Howard succeeded as ninth duke of Norfolk in December 1732; he and his duchess presented themselves at court to George II in January 1733, where, according to the duke's kinswoman Anne Ingram, Viscountess Irwin:

> The Duchess, who is a sensible woman, and must act the man where talking is necessary, behaved much to her credit; she assured the Queen, though she and the Duke were of different religion, they had as much duty and regard for the King as any of his subjects, and should be glad of every occasion that gave èm opportunity to show it … the Duke and Duchess of Norfolk are both such bigots, it was not expected they would give this open declaration of quitting the interest of the Pretender. (*Carlisle MSS*, 96)

During the breach between George II and Frederick, prince of Wales, between 1737 and 1742, the Norfolks sided with Frederick by allowing him to live in Norfolk House, their London residence in St James's Square. However, in February 1742 Horace Walpole was able to report that 'At night the royal family were all at the Duchess of Norfolk's' (Walpole, *Corr.*, 17.337) where she held a masquerade to celebrate the reconciliation between Frederick and George II. Charles Butler, writing in 1821, thought that her ease at entertaining both Catholic and protestant nobility and gentry encouraged the protestant ruling élite to lose their suspicion of Roman Catholics, and he also named the duchess as an early employer of William Murray, subsequently lord chief justice and earl of Mansfield, who became known in his judicial career for his reluctance to enforce the penal laws against Catholics.

Frederick left Norfolk House in 1742, and the Norfolks, with the duchess taking the lead, began work on a new house on the same site, designed by Matthew Brettingham the elder. It was not completed until February

1756, when it was hailed by Horace Walpole as 'a scene of magnificence and taste. The tapestry, the embroidered bed, the illumination, the glasses, the lightness and novelty of the ornaments, and the ceilings, are delightful' (Walpole, *Corr.*, 37.438). The duchess was an accomplished needlewoman, and many of her chair covers survive at Arundel Castle, the Norfolks' Sussex residence, which they rarely used. She regularly solicited patronage from the duke of Newcastle, on one occasion chastising Newcastle for doubting the integrity of one of her clients: 'I am sure you will doe me the Justice to be assured that I am incapable of becoming a Sollicitor in a Cause that appeared to me doubtful' (duchess of Norfolk to duke of Newcastle, BL, Add. MS 32879, fol. 122; Chalus, 120–21). Following the accession of George III and the consequent political realignments, members of old corps families, as well as George II's children Princess Amelia and Prince William, duke of Cumberland, regularly attended the duchess's Wednesday evening balls in the winter of 1760–61.

The duchess also took part in the replacement of her husband's favourite residence, Worksop Manor, Nottinghamshire. The old house had been remodelled over two decades by the duke, but was destroyed by fire in 1761. The duchess supervised the design of the new house, by James Paine. The house was intended to make a square block of four fronts, each 300 feet in length, and the interior featured *trompe l'œil* painting by a Dutch artist patronized by the duchess, Theodore de Bruyn. The duchess herself was the architect of a Gothic farm at Worksop, prior to the destruction of the first house, and the menagerie at Worksop. The new house expressed the Norfolks' dynastic confidence, but the duchess ordered work to end when the duke's nephew and heir, Edward Howard, died of measles in 1767, rather than allow the completed house to pass with the dukedom and most of the estates to a distant cousin, Charles Howard, eventually tenth duke of Norfolk, of whom the Norfolks knew little.

The duchess of Norfolk died, childless, on 27 May 1773 at the age of seventy-one, and was buried at Arundel, Sussex. Horace Walpole called her 'my Lord Duchess' (Walpole, *Corr.*, 37.572), a term that backhandedly acknowledged her contribution to rehabilitating the Howard dukes of Norfolk as part of the mainstream of aristocratic and political society, and thus making it more possible for élite Catholics to participate in public life, despite continuing legal disabilities.   MATTHEW KILBURN

Sources J. M. Robinson, *The dukes of Norfolk* (1983) · C. Butler, *Historical memoirs respecting the English, Irish, and Scottish Catholics, from the Reformation, to the present time*, 2 (1819) · *The manuscripts of the earl of Carlisle*, HMC, 42 (1897) · E. H. Chalus, 'Women in English political life, 1754–1790', DPhil diss., U. Oxf., 1997 · Walpole, *Corr.* · *Report on the Laing manuscripts*, 2, HMC, 72 (1925) · *Report on the manuscripts of the late Reginald Rawdon Hastings*, 4 vols., HMC, 78 (1928–47), vol. 3 · G. Brenan and E. P. Statham, *The house of Howard*, 2 vols. (1907)

Archives BL, corresp. with duke of Newcastle, Add. MSS 32699, 32703, 32710, 32730, 32735, 32850, 32879, 32880, 32898, 32916, 32917, 32918, 32921, 32922, 32930, 32945

Likenesses J. Vanderbank, double portrait, oils, 1732 (with her husband), repro. in Robinson, *Dukes of Norfolk*, 153; priv. coll.

Howard, Mary. *See* Scott, Mary (*bap.* 1703, *d.* 1744).

Howard, Philip [St Philip Howard], **thirteenth earl of Arundel** (1557–1595), magnate and alleged traitor, was born on 28 June 1557 at Arundel House, the Strand, London, the only child of Thomas *Howard, fourth duke of Norfolk (1538–1572), nobleman and courtier, and his first wife, Mary *Howard, *née* Fitzalan (1539/40–1557), noblewoman, second daughter and coheir of Henry *Fitzalan, twelfth earl of Arundel (1512–1580), magnate, and his first wife, Katharine. As heir to the dukedom of Norfolk, he was known by the courtesy title earl of Surrey. He was baptized on 2 July 1557 in the Chapel Royal at Whitehall Palace, in the presence of his godfathers, Philip of Spain (after whom he was named) and the lord chancellor, Nicholas Heath, archbishop of York, and of his godmother, Elizabeth *Howard, *née* Stafford, dowager duchess of Norfolk (1497–1558), noblewoman. His mother died from complications arising from labour on 25 August 1557 at Arundel House.

Early years and education, 1557–1580 Norfolk's subsequent marriages increased the Howard ties with other leading families, creating a great matrix of wealth and property. In 1558 or 1559 he married Margaret (1540–1564), first daughter and heir of Thomas Audley, Baron Audley of Walden, and his second wife, Elizabeth, and widow of Lord Henry Dudley. Norfolk and his wife had two sons, Thomas *Howard, first earl of Suffolk (1561–1626), naval officer and administrator, and Lord William *Howard (1563–1640), nobleman and antiquary, and three daughters, including Margaret or Meg (*d.* 1591), who married Robert *Sackville, second earl of Dorset (1560/61–1609). On 29 January 1567 Norfolk married his third wife, Elizabeth (*d.* 1567), daughter of Sir James Leybourne of Cunswick, Westmorland, and his second wife, Helen, and widow of Thomas Dacre, fourth Baron Dacre of Gilsland (*b.* in or before 1527, *d.* 1566). She died on 4 September, and Norfolk secured the wardship of his four stepchildren. Surrey was first married to Anne *Howard, *née* Dacre (1557–1630), noblewoman and priest harbourer, the eldest of the three daughters, in 1569, when both were twelve. The marriage was solemnized some time after June 1571 once both children had reached fourteen, the age of full consent.

After his father's execution for treason on 2 June 1572, Philip Howard (having lost his courtesy title), who was allowed to retain much of the family property, travelled between various family residences, including Kenninghall in Norfolk and Audley End in Essex. He then spent about two years at St John's College, Cambridge, and proceeded MA in November 1576. After university he took up residence at court, for he wished to win Elizabeth I's favour. While he lived at Howard House in London, spending great sums of money in playing the part of a courtier, his wife remained neglected in the country. He was unsuccessful in his pursuit of royal patronage, perhaps because he was very tall and had a swarthy complexion, which the queen might have found unpleasing, or because he had many enemies at court. His spendthrift and sycophantic

Philip Howard [St Philip Howard], **thirteenth earl of Arundel** (1557–1595), by unknown artist

behaviour offended his grandfather, Arundel, and his aunt, Jane *Lumley, *née* Fitzalan, Lady Lumley (1537–1578), the translator. They were angered that, during Elizabeth's progress through East Anglia in August 1578, first at Kenninghall and then at Mount Surrey outside Norwich, Howard:

> Wasted a great part of that Estate which was left him, by profused expences of great Summs of money in diverse Tiltings & Tourneys made upon the anniversary dayes of the Queen's Coronation to please her, and at the entertainment of Certain great Embassadors, and also by the entertaining of the Queen her self.   (Fitzalan-Howard, 7)

He became deeply indebted (owing at least £14,000) and was forced to sell some of his own and his wife's properties. He left court in disgrace and returned to the country and his wife.

The earldom of Arundel, 1580–1585 Life changed dramatically for Howard with Arundel's death on 24 February 1580, for it was then that he succeeded to the earldom of Arundel *jure matris*. His title to the earldom was questioned, the matter being brought before the privy council, and Howard was not restored in blood until March 1581. His uncle, John *Lumley, Baron Lumley (*c.*1533–1609), collector and conspirator, made over his life interest in the castle and honour of Arundel, Sussex, to him on 24 February 1580. He now possessed extensive estates in Sussex, as well as two London residences, Howard House and Arundel House, and the extensive family inheritance. His wife, as

coheir to the Dacre lands, had already brought the estates of Gilsland and Greystoke in Cumberland, nine baronies, manors in several counties, and a house at Romford, Essex, to their union. Howard took the Fitzalan arms only on 28 May 1580 and was summoned to parliament as earl of Arundel on 16 January 1581, being restored in blood by statute on 15 March and taking his seat in the House of Lords on 11 April. Arundel and his wife set up their household together, and their only son, Thomas *Howard, fourteenth earl of Arundel (1585–1646), art collector and politician, was born at Finchingfield, Essex, on 7 July 1585. The couple also had a daughter, Elizabeth Howard (1583–1598).

The countess of Arundel was a 'woman of strong character and religious disposition' (*DNB*). During the early 1580s, while living at Arundel Castle, she converted to Roman Catholicism. She openly professed her beliefs, and the queen committed her for a year to the care of Sir Thomas Shirley at Wiston, Sussex, during which time her first child, Elizabeth, was born in 1583. Arundel later claimed to have begun favouring his wife's faith after Edmund Campion's disputations with Church of England divines in September 1581. For three years he kept his wavering beliefs from Elizabeth, but drew attention to himself for his failure to condemn his wife's religious convictions. On 24 December 1583 Sir Walter Mildmay and Henry Carey, first Baron Hunsdon, questioned him about harbouring the Jesuit Thomas Heywood. Arundel later claimed that he was then commanded by the queen to keep to his house until April 1584. On 30 September 1584 the Jesuit William Weston formally received him into the Roman Catholic church at Arundel Castle. Arundel still kept his beliefs from Elizabeth, though his conscience weighed increasingly upon him, forcing him to forgo at least one sermon in Westminster Abbey and another in the Chapel Royal at Greenwich Palace, Kent. Unable to endure the pressures being brought to bear on recusants, he planned to flee abroad. So secret were his plans that he did not inform his wife, who was pregnant with his heir. He did not see his wife or children again.

In April 1585 Arundel's ship departed from Littlehampton in Sussex, but was boarded as soon as it entered the English Channel by 'one Keloway, Captain of a little Ship of War, who pretended himself to be a Pirate' (Pollen and MacMahon, 109). Arundel was immediately conducted to the Tower of London by Sir George Carey, the son of his arch-enemy and interrogator, Hunsdon, and committed on 25 April. Before fleeing, Arundel wrote a letter to Elizabeth between 11 and 14 April, explaining his actions and left it with his half-sister, Lady Margaret Sackville. In this letter he depicted himself as a loving servant shunned by his queen and unable to defend himself by reason of her suspicions and 'mislike' of him, based only upon his adherence to 'that Religion which your Majesty doth detest & of which you are most jealous & doubtfull' (BL, Harley MS 787, fols. 46*r*–49*v*). Claiming to have been insulted and frightened by his months of house arrest, Arundel reflected on the fate of his father, and of his grandfather and great-grandfather (Henry Howard, earl of

Surrey, and Thomas Howard, third duke of Norfolk, respectively), as well as the implications of a new act making it high treason to entertain a priest. Concluding that he had to choose between loyalty to Elizabeth and religious conscience, Arundel explained that he had decided to forsake the comforts of friends, family, and property, and to 'live without danger of my Conscience, without offence to your Majesty, without this servile abjection to mine enemies, & without the dayly peril to my life' (ibid.).

Trial, imprisonment, and death, 1585–1595 Arundel was arraigned before the court of Star Chamber on charges of being a Roman Catholic, fleeing from England without the queen's leave, intriguing with William Allen and Robert Persons, and claiming title to the dukedom of Norfolk. In May 1586 he was fined £10,000 and imprisoned during Elizabeth's pleasure. A more definitive charge was brought against him in 1588 after William Bennet, a fellow Roman Catholic imprisoned in the Tower, was tortured and confessed that Arundel had moved him to say a secret mass on behalf of the Spanish Armada. Arundel was brought to trial and attainted on 14 April 1589. All his honours became forfeit and he was condemned to death, but the sentence was never carried out. The regime's attitude towards him was coloured by the virulent anti-Catholic mood in the wake of the bond of association (1584) and by unease at the wealth and power of the Howards.

Arundel's wife and children lived on a pension of £8 a week in a wing of Arundel House at the mercy of the queen and Hunsdon, now lord chamberlain. Some time after the attainder, the countess of Arundel moved into two smaller houses, one in Spitalfields and the other in Acton, Middlesex, where her family retained the services of Roman Catholic priests. Arundel spent his time in the Tower in pious exercises, translating various works, including one by Johann Justus as *An Epistle of Jesus Christ to the Faithful Soule* (1595). He left in manuscript three treatises 'of the excellency and utility of virtue' (*Fourth Report*, HMC, 372). He was afforded few comforts during his imprisonment and his health suffered. Believing that he was dying, Arundel wrote to the queen in August 1595 to ask that he might see his wife and children, as she had once promised him. She replied that if he would only attend the services of the Church of England, he would be restored to all his former honours and returned to his family. Stubborn to the end, Arundel died in the Tower on 15 October, rumoured to have been poisoned by his cook. He was buried on 22 October in the chapel of St Peter ad Vincula in the Tower, his coffin wrapped in just 3 yards of black cloth. His total funeral expenses amounted to less than £5. Some years later his remains were conveyed to West Horsley, Surrey, thence to Arundel Castle in 1624, and finally, in 1971, to the Roman Catholic cathedral in Arundel. His will, made shortly before his attainder, was kept private. His half-brother, Lord William Howard, and his brother-in-law, Sackville, were named his executors

and were to receive £3000. The will authorized the sale of Castle Rising in Norfolk to pay Arundel's debts and to provide a portion of £2000 for his daughter and another for one of his sisters. He left all his household goods to his wife and wished that her debts be paid before all others. Kenninghall went to his son, and various legacies were left to family and friends, as well as £20 each to the poor of London and Dr Martin. None of these instructions was carried out. Lord William Howard attempted to have the properties affected by his half-brother's attainder regranted to other members of the family, but without success. Most of Arundel's property, including his wife's jointure estates, went to the crown. The countess inherited her husband's debts and was forced to sell land to honour them and to safeguard her small income. Her jointure was restored after Elizabeth's death in 1603. Arundel's estates were granted to his heir, Thomas Howard, after he was restored in blood by act of parliament as fourteenth earl of Arundel on 18 April 1604. Elizabeth Howard died unmarried of tuberculosis in 1598, but in September 1606 the dowager countess of Arundel was able to marry her son to Alathea (*d.* 1654), third daughter and coheir of Gilbert Talbot, seventh earl of Shrewsbury, and his wife, Mary. The dowager countess died of old age at Shifnal in Shropshire on 13 April 1630 and was buried in the Fitzalan Chapel in Arundel Castle.

Most of the work on Arundel is hagiographical. A Jesuit priest, whose identity is now unknown and who was supported for the last fourteen years of her life by the dowager countess of Arundel, wrote accounts of the lives of Arundel and his wife. Roman Catholics generally celebrate Arundel for his behaviour while a prisoner and the ultimate sacrifice he made for his religious beliefs. Much is made by his admirers of the Latin inscription carved into the wall of his octagonal room in the Tower, 'quanto plus afflictionis pro Christo in hoc saeculo, tanto plus gloriae cum Christo in futuro' ('the more affliction we endure for Christ in this world, the more glory we shall obtain with Christ in the next'). Arundel was named the Venerable Philip Howard, earl of Arundel, in 1886, beatified by Pius XI in 1929, and canonized along with thirty-nine English martyrs by Paul VI on 25 October 1970 as a witness of Christ and an example of the Roman Catholic faith.

J. G. ELZINGA

Sources J. H. Pollen and W. MacMahon, eds., *The Ven. Philip Howard, earl of Arundel, 1557–1595: English martyrs*, Catholic RS, 21 (1919) · H. G. Fitzalan-Howard, *The lives of Philip Howard, earl of Arundel, and of Anne Dacre, his wife* (1857) · JHL · M. A. Tierney, *History and antiquities of the castle and town of Arundel* (1834) · Cooper, *Ath. Cantab.*, 2.187–91 · J. Nichols, ed., *The progresses and public processions of Queen Elizabeth*, 3 vols. (1823), 2.130–31, 198 · A. C. Kerr, *The life of the Venerable Philip Howard, earl of Arundel and Surrey* (1926) · GEC, *Peerage* · BL, Lansdowne MS 94, fol. 188r; Lansdowne MS 79, fol. 74r · *Fourth report*, HMC, 3 (1874)

Archives Arundel Castle, West Sussex, papers · BL, Add. MSS 15891, 41499, 48016, 48029, 48032 · BL, Cotton MS Julius F. vi; Cotton MS Titus B. ii · BL, Lansdowne MSS 46, 55, 59, 79, 94, 95, 106 · BL, Stowe MS 164 · CUL, letters · Gon. & Caius Cam., letters · Suffolk RO, estate papers, HD 1453 | BL, Egerton MS 2074 · BL, Lansdowne MSS, xlv.n.84 · BL, Add. MS 15891 · Bodl. Oxf., Tanner MSS, letters • Bodl. Oxf., Ashmole MS 829, vii, 3 fols. 219–223 [copy] • Norfolk House, original deeds and bonds relating to castle and honour of Arundel • priv. coll., MS, Yelverton XXXVIII

Likenesses engraving, pubd 1808 (after miniature by I. Oliver), BM • portrait, exh. 1890 (as child), Arundel Castle, West Sussex; repro. in *Venerable Philip Howard*, ed. Pollen and MacMahon, facing p. 18 • J. Thomson, stipple (after F. Zucchero), BM; repro. in E. Lodge, *Portraits of illustrious persons of Great Britain* (1825) • L. Vorsterman, line engraving, BM • F. Zucchero, oils • engraving (as a youth; after portrait at Arundel Castle), repro. in *Venerable Philip Howard*, ed. Pollen and MacMahon, facing p. 98 • oils, Arundel Castle, West Sussex [*see illus.*] • portrait (when in the Tower), repro. in *Venerable Philip Howard*, ed. Pollen and MacMahon, frontispiece; priv. coll. • portrait (as a youth), Arundel Castle, West Sussex

Wealth at death burial suggests extreme poverty; owed substantial debts 1584–5; 1585 debt was £17,977 plus £4666 interest p.a.: BL, Lansdowne MS xlv.n.84

Howard, Philip [*name in religion* Thomas] (**1629–1694**), prior of Bornhem and cardinal, was born on 21 September 1629 at Arundel House, London, the third son of Henry Frederick *Howard, fifteenth earl of Arundel (1608–1652), and his wife, Elizabeth Stuart (*d.* 1674), the daughter of the third duke of Lennox. He was raised by his paternal grandfather, Thomas *Howard, fourteenth earl of Arundel (1585–1646), a convert to protestantism, and his Catholic grandmother, Alethea Talbot (*d.* 1654), the daughter of the earl of Shrewsbury. Philip Howard and his brothers, baptized protestants, were entered on 4 July 1640 at St John's College, Cambridge, where they remained less than a year before accompanying their grandparents to the continent, where they studied at the University of Utrecht. In 1642 Philip and his elder brother Henry *Howard (1628–1684), later sixth duke of Norfolk, were received into the Roman Catholic church at Antwerp. In 1644 the fourteenth earl, who was renowned as an art collector, took his eldest grandson and Philip with him on an extended tour of Italy, possibly to remove them from the influence of their grandmother. In Milan in Holy Week 1645 Philip Howard encountered John Baptist Hackett, a cosmopolitan Irish Dominican who had distinguished himself in philosophical and theological studies in Spain and who was now teaching in Italy. He planted the seeds of Philip's Dominican vocation. Philip left Milan for Piacenza but returned in June, meeting Hackett again and, under his influence, joined the Dominican order at Cremona on 28 June 1645.

The earl of Arundel, fearing the effect of these events in England, reacted angrily to Philip Howard's action and began a furious correspondence with Rome to free him from his attachment. The matter reached the pope's attention and Howard was taken into the custody of Cardinal Monti, archbishop of Milan, until his vocation could be tested. In the face of serious questioning Howard remained firm in his resolve, even writing directly to the pope to put his case on 29 July 1645. The pope summoned him to Rome, where he was first lodged in the Dominican convent of San Sisto. He was then transferred to the care of the Oratorians, where he remained obstinate, and, after a personal meeting with the pope, he was allowed to

Philip Howard (1629–1694), by Jan van der Bruggen (after François Duchatel)

return to San Sisto to complete his noviciate. On 19 October he made his profession as a Dominican friar in the Dominican church of San Clemente.

Howard then studied for four years at the Dominican convent of La Sanita in Naples. In June 1650, passing through Rome on his way to Rennes to complete his studies, he submitted a petition to the Dominican general chapter proposing the foundation of a priory on the continent for the training of English, Scottish, and Irish friars for the mission. He was to realize this scheme himself in later years. He was ordained priest in Rennes in 1652. In January 1654 he was in Antwerp and then spent some time in England from where he wrote to Rome in October 1654 asking that Thomas Catchmay be appointed Dominican vicar-general in England. In November Howard wrote asking that English Dominicans be given permission to celebrate the Roman rather than the Dominican rite and that those who refused be compelled to adopt it. The master granted the first request but denied the second. He also asked the Congregatio de Propaganda Fide if faculties to function as a missionary could be granted to superiors of institutions rather than to individual priests directly. This would enable greater discipline to be exerted by legitimate superiors over their subjects. The request was refused. In January 1656 he wrote to Rome asking that Vincent Torre, an English friar who had entered the order in Brittany, be given leave to address the forthcoming general chapter on the needs of England. He also requested permission to establish a noviciate in England. Both requests were denied, although in November of the same year he wrote pressing once more the case for a continental house for the training of English friars. During this time he was not the superior of the English Dominicans but exerted considerable influence because of his drive and family connections.

In spring 1657 Howard set out for Rome and on the way realized his dream of an English Dominican foundation in the purchase of a monastery at Bornhem near Antwerp. The convent was transferred from the Williamite monks to the English Dominicans, who took up residence on 17 April 1657 with Howard appointed the first prior on 15 December. This house was to act as refuge, school, and seminary for the province for the next century and a half. While in exile Howard, along with his uncles, William, Viscount Stafford, and Ludovic d'Aubigny, supported the future Charles II, hoping for toleration of Catholicism at the Restoration. In early 1659 Howard took part in an unspecified and unsuccessful political mission to England. After the Restoration he and d'Aubigny were much involved in the marriage negotiations of Charles II with Catherine of Braganza. At the same time Howard was working for the establishment of a Dominican monastery of nuns in Flanders. In April 1660 his niece Antonia Howard entered the monastery of Tempsche near Bornhem. On 10 June 1661 she began the English Dominican monastery of Vilvorde, which was to transfer to Brussels in 1669. Howard also tried to add to the English Dominican patrimony by persuading the Lower German province to surrender their priory at Douai to him but was never to achieve this ambition.

On 24 July 1661 Howard was appointed vicar-general of the English Dominicans and in January 1662 was promoted a master of sacred theology during a visit to Bornhem. The arrival of Queen Catherine of Braganza in May the same year gave him scope to increase his influence. His uncle d'Aubigny was a favourite of the king and was created grand almoner to the new queen while Howard was appointed one of her principal chaplains. Catherine expressed her satisfaction with Howard's services in a letter to the master of the order in September 1663. On the death of Lord d'Aubigny, Howard succeeded him as grand almoner on 3 January 1665. The terms of the queen's marriage settlement stipulated that her principal chaplain should be in episcopal orders. Some had hoped that d'Aubigny, who died just before news of his promotion to the cardinalate reached him, would exercise authority over the queen's chaplains but also as ordinary of the English Catholic church. His premature death prevented the realization of this project.

The English chapter, which saw itself as the residual body governing English Catholicism, continued to petition for a bishop who would hold ordinary jurisdiction and not the powers of vicar apostolic. They believed a vicar apostolic would enjoy a limiting dependence on the papacy which would give encouragement to the anti-Romanism of English public life. Rome suspected the English chapter of Blackloism (the ideas associated with Thomas White alias Blacklo) and an undue acceptance of civil authority which savoured of compromise. The religious orders were unwilling to see the full restoration of ordinary episcopal jurisdiction since it would limit their own freedom of action. It was against this background that Howard was first proposed as bishop in England. Although some reservations were expressed about his intellectual and pastoral qualifications for the position, his family associations, his involvement in the court and acquaintance with the king, as well as his Dominican vocation, which distinguished him from the Jesuit and secular priest party, made him a reasonable choice. In 1668 John Leyburn, secretary of the English chapter proposed Howard as bishop to his colleagues, who tepidly endorsed it. The Holy See was reluctant to make the appointment without the consent of the king, who refused to give a firm opinion lest he further encourage anti-Catholic sentiment.

The election of Pope Clement X in April 1670 was to affect decisively Howard's career. The new pope's secretary of state, Cardinal Paoluzzi-Altieri, maintained John Baptist Hackett as his confessor and confidant. From this time Hackett is also found acting as Howard's Roman agent. In September 1670 Propaganda Fide proposed Howard's appointment as bishop in England, but did not finalize the nature of his jurisdiction. The appointment was kept a strict secret, while opinion was sounded out in England. When news reached the chapter they expressed their dissatisfaction with it and their opposition continued. In May 1672 Howard was named bishop of Helenopolis *in partibus infidelium* but the appointment was never rendered effective since on 24 August the pope was informed that the king, owing to domestic political reasons, had asked for its suspension.

On 3 February 1675 a proclamation was issued expelling all Catholic priests from England by 25 March. Howard determined to withdraw temporarily from England, and with letters of commendation from the king and queen, he boarded one of the navy yachts at Dover on 23 March and set sail for Flanders. He resumed his priorship at Bornhem, where, on 27 May 1675, he heard of his nomination as cardinal by Pope Clement X with the title of Santa Cecilia in Trastevere, which he retained until he exchanged it for that of Santa Maria sopra Minerva in 1679. In Rome Howard found himself without friends and short of money. He remained grand almoner until 1682, but the salary was rarely if ever paid. He received no support from his own country and refused benefices from other sovereigns lest they expect services in return. He relied on the meagre sum the papacy offered him, although in 1683 he received 1600 crowns on benefices in Portugal. Nevertheless, he continued to work for the Catholic church in England and served on the congregations of Propaganda Fide, Rites, and the short-lived Relics. He was also able to obtain the church and conventual buildings of Sts John and Paul on the Coelian hill for the English Dominicans in June 1677.

In 1678 correspondence belonging to Edward Coleman, secretary to the duke of York, was seized and used as evidence of a Catholic conspiracy. Ten of the letters were from Howard, written between his arrival in Rome in 1676 and the summer of 1677. Most of them refer to the factionalism of the English church and the cardinal's economic affairs. He also wrote of his involvement in the marriage of the duke of York and Mary of Modena and claimed that his dispatch of Thomas White, an English Dominican resident in Rome, had facilitated the marriage, which had been in doubt owing to the uncertainty of the duke's religious allegiance. According to the earl of Peterborough it was Howard who performed the marriage ceremony. In 1679 Howard and the remaining Dominicans working in England were all cited as conspirators in the Popish Plot. Oates alleged that a number of them were to be made bishops, with Howard himself to serve as archbishop of Canterbury. Howard, along with other friars, was charged with high treason.

In March 1680 Howard's appointment as cardinal protector of England and Scotland involved him more deeply in the affairs of the English church, as well as in the government of its seminaries and religious houses abroad. In 1685 the English College, Rome, and his own adjoining palace were completed according to the designs of Legenda and Fontana. His relations with the Benedictines were not always good as they attempted to curtail his influence with the duke of York and also accused him of Jansenism. Howard was out of sympathy with Peter Talbot, the archbishop of Dublin, and his supporters, whose intrigues around the duke of York he regarded as deeply dangerous to the Catholic cause. In effect the priests and religious competing for power around the duke were struggling for supremacy in what they believed would one day be a royal court. Howard's consistent advice was for caution and discretion in the conduct of religious affairs in public life. He also opposed the Blackloist tendencies on the English chapter represented by John Sergeant.

James II's accession was welcomed in Rome and appeared to open the way for the appointment of bishops for England. In September 1685 John Leyburn, the former leader of the anti-Blackloist party on the English chapter, was appointed vicar apostolic. Leyburn had gone to Rome to act as Howard's auditor when he received the red hat and his appointment was a gesture of confidence in Howard's policies. King James proved unwilling to share that confidence. He was uncompromising in his determination to act as a Catholic monarch and was intent on exercising the same rights as his fellow sovereigns, despite the papal preference for caution and discretion. In 1685 Howard entertained affably Bishop Burnet, who reported that the cardinal's advice to England was always 'for slow, calm, and moderate courses'. He lamented that violent courses would probably be followed and maintained that these were very much not the counsel of the Roman authorities.

In April 1686 the earl of Castlemaine, the husband of one of Charles II's mistresses, was reluctantly received as ambassador to the Holy See. Castlemaine renewed the request first made by James in 1676 for a red hat for Queen Mary's brother, Rinaldo d'Este, and also that one of his chaplains and advisers, Edward Petre, a Jesuit, be raised to the episcopate with jurisdiction in the royal household. Howard loyally raised these issues with the pope. The pope held firm on not making Petre a bishop, but in September 1686 made d'Este a cardinal. James II then proposed d'Este as ambassador to Rome with a substantial salary. When this proved unacceptable James asked that he serve as co-protector of England. From the end of 1687 James effectively lost confidence in Howard and ignored him. English agents were instructed to deal through Cardinal d'Este, although the Holy See still recognized Howard as the true protector. Significantly, when news of James's fall reached Rome in January 1689 the Holy See dealt directly with d'Este. Perhaps as a consolation Howard was given the lucrative office of archpriest of Santa Maria Maggiore. James's accession and continual attempts to exercise ecclesiastical prerogatives, even after his deposition, led to the gradual eclipse of Cardinal Howard. His humiliation at the hands of a dynasty he had served loyally was ascribed, by his allies, to the Jesuit influence in James's circle and the king's displeasure at Howard's not securing a red hat for Rinaldo d'Este sooner.

Cardinal Howard died at his palace in Rome on 17 June 1694 and was buried next day in the choir of the church of the Minerva under a plain white marble slab inscribed with the Howard coat of arms. He had been the principal instrument in the restoration of the English Dominican province, had re-established the English Dominican contemplative nuns, but had failed to see his church achieve that measure of toleration and acceptance by his fellow countrymen that he had longed and worked for.

ALLAN WHITE

Sources W. Gumbley, *Obituary notices of the English Dominicans from 1555 to 1952* (1955), 47 · R. Palmer, *The life of Philip Thomas Howard* (1867) · Gillow, *Lit. biog. hist.*, 3.442–51 · G. Anstruther, 'Cardinal Howard and the English court, 1658–94', *Archivum Fratrum Praedicatorum*, 28 (1958), 315–61 · G. Anstruther, 'The vocation of Philip Howard', *Blackfriars*, 39 (1958), 156–69, 211–24 · G. Anstruther, 'The English Dominicans in Rome', *Archivum Fratrum Praedicatorum*, 29 (1959), 168–99 · *Dominicana*, Catholic RS, 25 (1925) · G. Anstruther, *A hundred homeless years: English Dominicans, 1558–1658* (1958) · W. M. Brady, *The episcopal succession in England, Scotland, and Ireland, AD 1400 to 1875*, 3 (1877), iii, 105, 107, 109–14, 118–21, 124, 127–39, 283 · G. Anstruther, unpublished MS biography of Cardinal Howard, Edinburgh Archives of the English Dominican Province · J. M. Robinson, *The dukes of Norfolk* (1982) · *Bishop Burnet's History* · *A collection of letters and writings relating to the horrid Popish Plot printed from the originals in the hands of George Treby* (1681), 78–91

Archives Archivio Vaticano, Vatican City, letters and documents relating to him · Archivio Vaticano, Vatican City, Archive of Propaganda Fide, letters and documents relating to him · Arundel Castle, Sussex, corresp. · BL, executor's accounts, Add. MS 38652 · English Dominican Province Archive, Carisbrooke · Westm. DA

Likenesses Veslierhout, portrait, 1688 · J. van der Bruggen, engraving (after F. Duchatel), NPG [*see illus.*] · G. Hamerani, bronze medal, BM · attrib. C. Maratti?, oils, Arundel Castle, West Sussex · H. Noblin, line engraving, BM, NPG · miniature, oils on copper, NPG; version, Arundel Castle, West Sussex · oils, Blackfriars, Edinburgh · oils, priv. coll. · oils, Bodl. Oxf. · portrait, Arundel Castle,

West Sussex • portrait, Wardour Castle, Wiltshire • portrait, English College, Rome, Italy

Howard, Ralph (1638–1710), physician, was the only son of John Howard (*d.* 1643), of Shelton, co. Wicklow, Ireland, and his wife, Dorothea Hasels (*d.* 1684). He was educated at the University of Dublin, and proceeded MD in 1667.

Howard succeeded John Margetson in 1670 as regius professor of physic at Dublin, and held the chair until his death. He left Ireland for England in 1688 when war broke out, and was attainted by James II's parliament in 1689, while his estate in co. Wicklow was handed over to one Hacket, who entertained James at Shelton after the battle of the Boyne. Howard subsequently returned to Dublin and recovered his property. He married on 16 July 1668 Catherine (*fl.* *c.*1655–1714), eldest daughter of Roger Sotheby, MP for Wicklow city, and with her had three sons— Hugh *Howard (1675–1738), Robert *Howard (1683–1740), father of Ralph Howard (1726/7–1789), and William Howard, MP for Dublin city from 1727 until his death in the next year—and three daughters. He died on 8 August 1710.   WILLIAM REYNELL, *rev.* PATRICK WALLIS

Sources J. L. McCracken, *The Irish parliament in the eighteenth century* (1971) • Burtchaell & Sadleir, *Alum. Dubl.*, 2nd edn

Howard, Ralph, first Viscount Wicklow (1726/7–1789). *See under* Howard, Robert (1683–1740).

Howard, Richard Baron (1807–1848), physician, the sixth son of Charles Howard of Hull and his wife, Mary Baron of Manchester, was born at Melbourne Farm in the East Riding of Yorkshire, on 18 October 1807. He was educated at Northallerton, and in 1823 he moved to Edinburgh, where he obtained a surgeon's diploma. In 1829 he became a licentiate of the Society of Apothecaries of London, and took the degree of MD at Edinburgh. From 1829 to 1833 he was physician's clerk in the Manchester Infirmary, though in 1831 an illness saw Howard himself become a patient in the Manchester Fever Hospital. From 1833 until February 1838 he acted as medical officer at the Manchester workhouse, subsequently holding the office of physician to the Ardwick and Ancoats Dispensary in the same town. Illness interrupted his career once again in April 1834, when he suffered an attack of rheumatic fever.

During these years Howard's work had been mainly among the poor, and his deep interest in their condition led him in 1839 to publish *An inquiry into the morbid effects of deficiency of food, chiefly with reference to their occurrence amongst the destitute poor*. In the following year, at the invitation of the poor-law commissioners, he wrote 'A report upon the prevalence of disease arising from contagion, malaria, and certain other physical causes amongst the labouring classes in Manchester'; this appeared in the *Sanitary Inquiry in England* (1840). In 1842 he wrote on the same subject in Joseph Adshead's pamphlet on the state of the working classes in Manchester. In the same year, on being appointed physician to the infirmary, he printed *An Address Delivered to the Pupils*. Howard's other appointments were those of physician at Haydock Lodge Lunatic Asylum and lecturer at the Manchester College of Medicine. He had extensive connections with the scientific societies of the town, where he was highly esteemed as a lecturer, practitioner, and philanthropist. Howard died at his father's house at York on 9 April 1848, after a painful illness, and was buried in the neighbouring cemetery.

C. W. SUTTON, *rev.* MICHAEL BEVAN

Sources GM, 2nd ser., 30 (1848), 323–5 • M. C. H. Hibbert Ware, *The life and correspondence of the late Samuel Hibbert Ware* (1882), 451

Howard, Sir Robert (1584/5–1653), adulterer and royalist adherent, was the fifth son of Thomas *Howard, first earl of Suffolk (1561–1626), and his wife, Katherine (*b.* in or after 1564, *d.* 1638), daughter of Sir Henry Knyvet and formerly wife of Richard Rich [*see* Howard, Katherine, countess of Suffolk]. Robert was the uncle of his namesake Sir Robert *Howard (1626–1698), the historian and poet, and the brother of Theophilus *Howard, second earl of Suffolk (1584–1640), and Edward *Howard, first Baron Howard of Escrick (*d.* 1675). He and his younger brother William (1600–1672) were made knights of the Bath on 4 November 1616, when Prince Charles, afterwards Charles I, was created prince of Wales. At the death of an elder brother, Sir Charles Howard of Clun, in connection with whose estate he was granted letters of administration on 21 June 1626, Howard succeeded to the property of Clun Castle, Shropshire, as heir of the entail under the settlement of his great-uncle Charles *Howard, first earl of Nottingham.

In 1624 Howard became notorious through his intrigue with Frances Villiers, Viscountess Purbeck (1600/01–1645), the daughter of Sir Edward Coke. She had been forced in September 1617 at the age of sixteen into a marriage with Sir John Villiers (from 1619 Viscount Purbeck), brother of the royal favourite George Villiers, earl (and by 1623 duke) of Buckingham. After living some time apart from her husband she was privately delivered, on 19 October 1624, of a son, Robert, who was baptized at St Giles Cripplegate under the name of Robert Wright; Howard was the child's reputed father.

Buckingham had the pair cited before the court of high commission on 19 February 1625. Howard was committed a close prisoner to the Fleet prison when he refused to answer questions on oath, but was probably quickly released when he claimed the privileges of an MP. He was publicly excommunicated at Paul's Cross on 23 March 1625 for continuing to refuse to answer, but he appears to have been pardoned at the coronation of Charles I. Lady Purbeck was sentenced to a fine of 500 marks, to be imprisoned during the pleasure of high commission, and to do penance at the Savoy. She evaded the penalties by escaping to France. When the storm was over she returned to England. On the allegation that she then lived with Howard at his house in Shropshire, and had other children with him, high commission proceedings were afterwards renewed. In April 1635 Howard, for not producing Lady Purbeck as ordered, was again committed a close prisoner to the Fleet, without use of pen, ink, or paper for three months. He was then enjoined to keep from her company, and released on giving a bond for

£2000 and finding a surety in £1500 for his personal appearance within twenty-four hours if called upon.

Howard was returned to parliament as member for the borough of Bishops Castle, Shropshire, on 21 January 1624 and was re-elected in 1625, 1626, 1628, and to both the Short and Long parliaments in 1640. At the opening of the last parliament in 1640 the star-chamber proceedings were brought before the House of Commons on a question of privilege. The proceedings against him were declared illegal. A sum of £1000 was voted to Howard in compensation for false imprisonment, and a fine of £500 was imposed on Archbishop Laud, the president of the high commission court, and one of £250 on each of his legal assistants, Sir Henry Marten and Sir Edward Lambe. Laud complains in his memoirs that he had to sell some of his plate to pay the fine. Viscountess Purbeck died in 1645.

In 1642 Howard was expelled from the House of Commons for executing the king's commission of array. He attended the royal summons to the parliament at Oxford in the following year. His name does not appear in the list of officers of the royal army in 1642 in the Bodleian Library but he is said to have commanded a regiment of dragoons, and was governor of Bridgnorth Castle when it surrendered to the parliamentarian forces on 26 April 1646. His estates were sequestered, for which he had to pay £952 in compensation on recovery. Special arrangements were made by the Rump Parliament for the sale of some of his lands for payment of his fine and debts.

In 1648 Howard married Catherine, daughter of Henry Nevill, seventh Baron Abergavenny, with whom he had two sons and a daughter. Howard died, aged sixty-eight, on 22 April 1653, and was buried at Clun. His widow, as guardian of their elder son, Henry, filed a petition on 7 July 1663 against the second reading of a bill to confirm the Rump's sale of Sir Robert's estate to pay his debts. She later married John Berry of Ludlow, Shropshire. Howard's son Robert, though recognized by Purbeck as his son and heir, later renounced both the name of Villiers—instead adopting the surname of his wife's family and becoming Robert *Danvers—and the title.

H. M. CHICHESTER, rev. SEAN KELSEY

Sources Keeler, Long Parliament, 61, 223 · H. K. S. Causton, The Howard papers (1862), 524–9 · F. E. Paget, Some records of the Ashtead estate, and of its Howard possessors (1873), 57n. · E. Peacock, ed., The army lists of the roundheads and cavaliers (1863) · JHL, 4 (1628–42) · JHC, 2 (1640–42) · CSP dom., 1623–35 · GEC, Peerage, new edn, 10.684–7
Wealth at death estate assessed at £295 p.a. for purposes of compounding: Keeler, Long Parliament

Howard, Sir Robert (1626–1698), playwright and politician, was born in January 1626, the sixth son of Thomas Howard, first earl of Berkshire (1587–1669), and Elizabeth (d. 1672), daughter of William Cecil, second earl of Exeter; he was the brother of Edward *Howard (bap. 1624, d. 1712) and second cousin of James *Howard (c.1640–1669), both playwrights. Little is known of Howard's life prior to the Restoration. According to Anthony Wood, he entered Magdalen College, Oxford, about 1641. The son of a family actively engaged in the defence of the royalist cause, Howard was knighted for gallantry in action at the battle of

Sir Robert Howard (1626–1698), by Robert White, pubd 1692 (after Sir Godfrey Kneller, c.1685–90)

Cropredy Bridge, on 29 June 1644. On 1 February 1645 he married Anne, daughter of Sir Richard Kingsmill of Malhanger, with whom he had six children, only one of whom, Thomas (1651–1701), survived his father. About the time of his wife's death, in 1657 or 1658, in an arrangement advantageous both to the state and to himself, Sir Robert obtained for his father the renewal of the lease of the post fines and the greenwax, first granted the old earl by Charles I in 1625. His royalist sympathies, however, caused him to be arrested and imprisoned at Windsor Castle in 1658.

After the Restoration Sir Robert collected an impressive number of lucrative offices and profitable grants, which soon made him a wealthy man and a prominent figure in the government. In June 1660 he was appointed serjeant-painter to the king; in the same month Lord Chancellor Clarendon made him clerk of the patents in chancery, an office worth £3000 a year. The former position he surrendered on 28 February 1663; he sold the latter in 1664 or 1665 for almost £3000. In October 1660 Howard was made a member of the committee for the recovery of concealed lands, and in November he was commissioned as colonel of a regiment of infantry in the Hampshire militia. First returned to parliament for Stockbridge, Hampshire, in

May 1661, Howard served as an influential MP almost uninterruptedly until his death. Despite his unfailing attempts to obtain supply for the king, he first made his mark opposing the royal prerogative in the debates on the Poll Bill in December 1666. One of the leaders of the country-based opposition, Howard introduced a famous 'Proviso', that empowered a parliamentary committee to examine the expenditure of the money raised for the naval war against the Dutch. In October 1667, in alliance with Buckingham's anti-Clarendonian party, Howard vociferously agitated for the chancellor's impeachment. And in April 1668 he played a prominent part in the impeachment of Sir William Penn, charged with the embezzlement of goods 'out of the East India Prizes' (Evelyn, 3.508).

Howard's turbulent private life and his boastful manner, meanwhile, won him great notoriety. On 10 August 1665 he married Lady Honoria O'Brien, daughter of the earl of Thomond and the wealthy widow of Sir Francis Englefield; she was more than ten years Sir Robert's senior. The manor of Wootton Bassett, Wiltshire, left to Honoria by her husband, became Howard's new seat of residence. The marriage soon proved a failure. By early 1667 Honoria was petitioning the king 'for relief from the ill usage of her husband' and in April 1668 she complained to the Commons that 'her Husband would allow her nothing, though she was worth to him £40,000' (Oliver, 127–8). By an arrangement reached in October 1670, Sir Robert agreed to the payment of £8240 for his wife's undisturbed use. When he sold the manor for £36,000 in April 1676, he paid her another £8000. In her will dated 6 September of the same year, Lady Honoria left her second husband 1s. By then, he had become known as Sir Positive At-All, the arrogant and foolish knight meant to caricature him in Shadwell's *Sullen Lovers* (May 1668).

In the first decade of the Restoration, Howard combined his political career with that of a successful dramatist and critic. Howard's *Poems* (1660) contains his comedy *The Blind Lady*, although there is no indication that it was performed at this time. Under the terms of the agreement with the earl of Bedford drawn up on 20 December 1661, and of a further agreement dated 28 January 1662, Howard, Thomas Killigrew, and a group of eight actors became shareholders in the Theatre Royal, Bridges Street. In addition to being the scene designer for this theatre in 1663, Howard became the literary collaborator, and subsequent opponent, of John Dryden, who married Howard's sister Elizabeth in December 1663. *The Committee*, a political comedy first performed in November 1662, proved the most enduringly popular of Howard's plays; *The Indian Queen*, a rhymed heroic play co-authored with Dryden and first performed in January 1664, provided one of the topics in the literary quarrel between the two men, the effect of rhyme in drama. Dryden introduced Howard in his *Essay of Dramatic Poesy* (1668), assigning to Crites Howard's arguments against rhyme as developed in the preface to *Four New Plays* (*The Surprisal, The Committee, The Vestal Virgin, The Indian Queen*) (1665). *The Great Favourite, or, The Duke of Lerma*, premièred on 20 February 1668, is his

most powerful drama. The play's unmistakable attack on the exiled Clarendon helped to intensify the caustic nature of the quarrel. *The Country Gentleman*, written in collaboration with the duke of Buckingham, was prepared for production in early 1669 but suppressed before its première. Long thought to be lost, it was rediscovered in 1973. Featuring Sir William Coventry as the scheming Sir Cautious Trouble-all, this satirical comedy sheds light on Howard's political position as an opponent of the court party's 'caballing' practices.

Howard's own dealings were not beyond reproach. In March 1669 he was made to surrender the patent for the greenwax, after complaints about the farmers' abuse of their power. Such temporary set-backs did not obstruct the steady progress of his political career. Between November and December 1670 he submitted several proposals for the farming of the customs at £600,000 a year. In October 1671 he succeeded Sir George Downing as secretary to the Treasury and in March 1673 was granted the posts of writer of tallies in the exchequer and auditor of the receipt. The latter position, worth about £3000, he held until his death. Already in 1672 he was financially secure enough to lend £9000 to the crown in support of the war against the Dutch. Although in later years fiercely opposed to Catholic domination of English policy, Howard in the spring session of parliament in 1673 spoke against removing Roman Catholics from their military posts. Despite differences between himself and Treasurer Danby, involving suspicions of mismanagement of funds in the exchequer, Howard in 1674 and 1675 continued to add to his extensive collection of government posts: on 12 June 1675, he was appointed deputy lieutenant of Wiltshire and on 19 October following he was granted the office of keeper of the royal game. As a member of the new parliament of 1679, in which he represented Castle Rising, Norfolk, he took part in the proceedings and the pamphlet war against Danby, accusing the treasurer of incompetence and fraud. In 1680 Howard bought the manor of Ashtead, Surrey, from Henry Howard, duke of Norfolk.

About this time, probably before June 1680, Howard married his third wife, Mary Uphill (*b.* 1652x62). Mary's ill health forced the couple to spend time alternately at Ashtead and Tunbridge Wells. In the summer of 1682, while they were on their way to 'the Bath', Mary died 'in a Convulsion' according to the *London Mercury* (Oliver, 249–50).

Under James II, Howard helped bring about the revolution that put William of Orange on the throne. He served in William's first parliament, contending in the Commons on 22 January 1689 that James II had in effect 'abdicated the government' (Oliver, 256). Several years later Howard was to sign the 'Association of 1698', an agreement to defend William against the Jacobites. As in the past, Howard tried to strike a balance between his royalist sympathies and his belief in the rights of parliament. In February 1689 the king appointed him to the privy council, the crowning achievement of his political career.

Howard's final years were taken up with both professional and literary concerns. Late in 1694 he helped Betterton and his actors to procure a licence for the new theatre at Lincoln's Inn Fields; and in 1695 he renewed his friendship with John Dryden. Meanwhile, he had published his *History of the Reigns of Edward and Richard II* (1690), involving him in the ongoing controversy concerning the divine right of kings, and *The History of Religion* (1694), an anti-Catholic tract. On 26 February 1693 he contracted his fourth marriage, to Anabella Dives (*d.* 1728), an eighteen-year-old maid of honour. The marriage did not alter his son Thomas's rights to the Ashtead estate. In June 1694 father and son subscribed £18,000 to the newly erected Bank of England, and as late as 1697 Sir Robert, continuing in his office as auditor, was still working on currency reform. In his will, dated 26 May 1697, he made Anabella his sole executor and beneficiary of all his possessions. Howard died on 3 September 1698 and was buried on 8 September in Westminster Abbey.

J. P. Vander Motten

Sources H. J. Oliver, *Sir Robert Howard (1626–1698): a critical biography* (1963) • Evelyn, *Diary*, vols. 3–4 • P. H. Hardacre, 'Clarendon, Sir Robert Howard, and chancery office-holding at the Restoration', *Huntington Library Quarterly*, 38 (1974–5), 207–14 • J. A. Winn, *John Dryden and his world* (1987) • J. Milhous and R. D. Hume, eds., *A register of English theatrical documents, 1660–1737*, 1 (1991) • Wood, *Ath. Oxon.*, new edn, 4.594 • J. Orrell, 'A new witness of the Restoration stage', *Theatre Research International*, new ser., 2 (1976), 16–28 • R. Howard and G. Villiers, *The country gentleman: a 'lost play' and its background*, ed. A. H. Scouten and R. D. Hume (1976) • W. Van Lennep and others, eds., *The London stage, 1660–1800*, pt 1: *1660–1700* (1965) • J. L. Chester, ed., *The marriage, baptismal, and burial registers of the collegiate church or abbey of St Peter, Westminster*, Harleian Society, 10 (1876)
Archives Bodl. Oxf., exchequer papers
Likenesses R. White, line engraving (after G. Kneller, *c.*1685–1690), BM, NPG; repro. in R. Howard, *Five new plays*, 2nd edn (1692), frontispiece [*see illus.*]
Wealth at death bequest to widow est. £40,000: N. Luttrell, *Brief historical relation of state affairs from September 1678 to April 1714*, 6 vols. (1857), vol. 4, pp. 423–4

Howard, Robert (1683–1740), Church of Ireland bishop of Elphin, was born in Dublin, the second son of Ralph *Howard (1638–1710), a leading physician in Dublin, and Katherine, daughter of Roger Sotheby, MP for Wicklow. By birth and kinship a member of the office-holding, clerical, and academic élites of later seventeenth-century Dublin, he was related to the Dopping and Molyneux dynasties. One brother, Hugh *Howard (1675–1738), painter, connoisseur, and collector, throve in Hanoverian London; another, William Howard, was elected to the Irish parliament for Dublin in 1727. After attending Mr Jones's school in Dublin, Robert Howard entered Trinity College, Dublin, in 1697, graduated BA in 1701, and was made MA in 1703. Also in 1703 he was elected to a fellowship of his college. In 1705 he was ordained in the diocese of Meath. He soon won the favourable opinion of his seniors in the university and in the Church of Ireland, notably Archbishop King. In 1712 he was appointed to a prebend in St Patrick's Cathedral, Dublin, of which in 1722 he became precentor and chancellor. He had parochial cures in Dublin, first at

the new church of St Anne between 1707 and 1721, next at St Bride's from 1717 to 1722, and finally at St Werburgh's between 1723 and 1727, and these duties were readily combined with college business.

Howard's reputation as a calm and dexterous man of affairs, as well as his staunch whiggery, brought him a large role in the negotiations which followed the Hanoverian accession. Trinity College cleansed itself of any Jacobite stains, and secured the resignation of Provost Pratt and the installation of the prince of Wales as its chancellor. These delicate missions took Howard to England in 1715 and 1716, but probably stopped him from making a projected tour of France and Italy. During these visits he usefully extended his acquaintance within the English church and universities. In Dublin he was in demand as a reliable preacher on state occasions, such as the fast day to deflect a plague from Ireland in 1721 and on 23 October 1722. These and other occasional sermons were printed. Regarded as a favourite of Archbishop King and so a member of the Irish interest among the clergy, he had to wait longer than his talents merited for higher preferment. In 1722 he was named as dean of Ardagh, essentially a sinecure. On 19 March 1727 he was consecrated bishop of Killala. On 13 January 1730 he was translated to the richer and more accessible see of Elphin.

A suave politician, fluent preacher, and able administrator, Howard furthered philanthropic and practical ventures aimed at strengthening the protestant interest, both in his dioceses and in the House of Lords. Left £750 by his father in 1710, he inherited from his elder brother, William, extensive lands, mainly in co. Wicklow around what subsequently became known as Shelton Abbey, to which he added by his own purchases and thanks to his marriage in 1724 to Patience Boleyn (*d.* 1764). She was the daughter and heir of Godfrey Boleyn of Fennor, co. Meath, and his wife, Mary, daughter of Edward Singleton.

During summer residences at Elphin, Howard rebuilt the episcopal palace, financed schools, oversaw church- and road-building and encouraged the linen industry. In Dublin he took credit for several bills designed to assist the established church, including one against clandestine marriages. In his publications he supported the programme of protestant schools and revealed a continuing worry about the resilience of international popery and the disaffection of Irish Catholics. He followed Archbishop King in speculating on the theological problem of the origin of evil. In 1707 he had been drawn into the revived Dublin Philosophical Society, and he remained close to a cultivated circle of Dublin graduates, whom, through his brother Hugh, he supplied with books, medals, paintings, and engravings. Something of this cultivation passed to his eldest son, **Ralph Howard**, first Viscount Wicklow (1726/7–1789), politician, who inherited the family estate on the death of Robert Howard on 3 April 1740.

Ralph Howard, who was educated at Trinity College, Dublin, became sheriff of co. Wicklow in 1749 and of co. Carlow in 1754. He married Alice (1736/7–1807), daughter and sole heir of William and Isabella Forward of Castle

Forward, co. Donegal, on 11 August 1755. He was elected to the Irish parliament in 1761 and 1768 as MP for both co. Wicklow and the borough of St Johnstown, and in May 1770 he was sworn of the Irish privy council. On 12 July 1776 he was created Baron Clonmore of Clonmore Castle, co. Carlow, and on 23 June 1785 was promoted to be Viscount Wicklow. He died on 26 June 1789 at Rutland Square, Dublin, and his widow was created countess of Wicklow in her own right on 20 December 1793. Following her death on 7 March 1807, the eldest of their eight children, Robert Howard, succeeded as second earl of Wicklow; he had earlier sat as a representative peer in the united parliament of 1801.   TOBY BARNARD

Sources NL Ire., Howard (Wicklow) MSS, PC 222, 223, 225, 227 · calendar of Howard MSS, NL Ire., MS 12149 · Howard accounts, NL Ire., MS 8390 · will, NL Ire., PC 351 (1) · R. Howard, unpublished sermons, NL Ire., MS 7238 · W. King, correspondence, TCD, Lyons collection, MSS 1995–2008 · W. Wake, correspondence, Christ Church Oxf., Wake MSS 12–14 · Burtchaell & Sadleir, *Alum. Dubl.* · H. J. Lawlor, *The fasti of St Patrick's, Dublin* (1930), 65, 131 · J. B. Leslie, succession list for Dublin, Representative Church Body Library, MS 61/2/4/1 · *Catalogue of the choice collection … formed by Hugh Howard* (12 Dec 1873) [sale catalogue, Sothebys, London] · GEC, *Peerage* · *DNB* · E. B. Fryde and others, eds., *Handbook of British chronology*, 3rd edn, Royal Historical Society Guides and Handbooks, 2 (1986)
Archives NL Ire., corresp. | TCD, corresp. with Archbishop William King
Likenesses J. Brooks, mezzotint (after portrait by M. Dahl), BM

Howard, Robin Jared Stanley (1924–1989), patron of ballet and the performing arts, was born in Mayfair, London, on 17 May 1924, the son of Sir Arthur Jared Palmer Howard and Lady Lorna Baldwin (d. 1989). His paternal great-grandfather was Donald Alexander Smith, first Lord Strathcona, the railway magnate and high commissioner for Canada; his mother was the daughter of Stanley *Baldwin. His family had a tradition of public service and, through his mother, involvement in the arts. The eldest of four children, Howard was educated at St Aubyn's School, Rottingdean, and Eton College. He served with distinction as a lieutenant in the Scots Guards and was severely wounded in Holland in 1945, losing both legs. At Trinity College, Cambridge, he read law after the war; he went to the Inner Temple and was called to the bar, but never practised. Among other business ventures, he bought a modest hotel in London at Queen's Gate, Kensington, which he turned into the Gore Hotel; there he put to good use his enthusiasm for good wine, and the hotel became a centre of gastronomic excellence. In 1953 he launched the Elizabethan Room at the Gore, and was the first to succeed with a 'period' restaurant; in 1964 he organized a significant exhibition, 'Shakespeare's England', there.

Appalled at the 1954 Soviet invasion of Hungary, Howard volunteered to help the United Nations Association and was asked to form the Hungarian department dealing with refugees and displaced persons. For eight years, until 1963, he was honorary director of their international service department. Throughout his life he contributed to humanitarian causes. His lasting importance was for securing and fostering the development of contemporary dance in Britain. In spite of his disability, Howard loved dance. He became a regular at ballet performances at Covent Garden but his enthusiasm was waning when the Martha Graham Company first appeared in London in 1954. He was one of the few who then appreciated that Graham's choreography 'genuinely spoke to every part of you on many levels'. When in 1963 Graham was returning to Europe, Howard promoted her return to Britain; 'There was no fool prepared to lose a lot of money on it' (*The Times*, 14 June 1989). This time Graham was widely acclaimed, and Howard was enthusiastically encouraged in his plans to make American contemporary dance available—most notably by Dame Marie Rambert. In time, to support dance, he sold his hotels: The Gore, Gravetye Manor at East Grinstead, and the Yard Arm Club, Victoria Embankment; his collections of antique cars, art, ceramics, Ballets Russes material, and early printed books including copies of the first four folios of Shakespeare. In 1966 he founded the Contemporary Dance Trust (originally Contemporary Ballet Trust) of which, in 1988, he became life president, having guided all its activities since its foundation. In *Ballet Review* (fall 1989) after Howard's death, Charles Reinhart (director of the American Dance Festival) noted that he was the first person to treat modern dancers and choreographers as first-class citizens.

Howard's original aim was simple: to train dancers whom someone else would form into a company; but, having provided scholarships for gifted dancers to train in America, he found they were being employed there, so he set up a London school from which an embryonic company quickly emerged. Howard claimed that his aim was not to transplant American modern dance to Britain but to develop a native style appropriate to the bodies and outlook of British people, to its climate and culture. He considered Graham technique the most developed and successfully sought Graham's permission to set up a school based on it. He then invited Robert Cohan, one of Graham's dancers, to lead and develop his dancers. Contemporary Dance Trust became an umbrella for the school, London Contemporary Dance Theatre (1969–94); for the Place Theatre, initially to show home-grown talent, which has become the foremost venue for new and experimental dance in London; as well as for numerous other dance activities including outreach programmes to educate new audiences.

Strong-willed, tenacious, and determined, Howard was a large, bearded man whose plan for the trust was to 'be of service to and through dance'. In spite of promoting his own companies, he favoured differing approaches to dance and frequently supported rival dance organizations. In addition to funding and supporting visits by the American companies of Martha Graham, Paul Taylor, Twyla Tharp, and Merce Cunningham to Britain, he enabled Ballet Rambert to reactivate their creativity in 1966, and sponsored Norman McDowell's London Dance Theatre. Companies ranging from Richard Alston's Strider to Kim Brandstrup's Arc benefited from his support and encouragement.

A man without ego, Robin Howard was justly awarded the 1975 Queen Elizabeth II coronation award of the Royal

Academy of Dancing for outstanding services to ballet; he was made CBE in the 1976 new year's honours and an honorary DLitt of the University of Kent in 1987. He was a man of high ideals, a real patron of the arts (supporting fine art and music as well as dance) prepared to invest all his considerable wealth in developing contemporary dance not only for its own sake but as a means of promoting international harmony.

Howard died, unmarried, of a heart attack at University College Hospital, London, on 11 June 1989. He had been taken ill in Helsinki immediately after he had been elected president of the dance committee of the International Theatre Institute. JANE PRITCHARD

Sources D. Blake, 'As Robin Howard's dream comes true', *The Stage* (21 Nov 1974) • M. Clarke and C. Crisp, *London Contemporary Dance Theatre: the first 21 years* (1987) • C. Colvin, 'O lucky man', *Evening News* (9 Dec 1977) • A. Kisselgoff, 'Britain's adventurous patron of modern dance', *New York Times* (26 June 1977) • J. Percival, 'Meet Robin Howard', *Dance Magazine* (March 1967), 22–3, 86 • S. Seddon, 'Master of the one per cent', *Sunday Times*, 20/11 • *Financial Times* (14 June 1989) • *The Times* (14 June 1989) • *The Times* (1 July 1989) • *The Independent* (15 June 1989) • *The Guardian* (19 June 1989) • J. Anderson, 'Pioneering Graham technique in British dance', *New York Times* (14 Aug 1989) • R. Cohan, 'Obituary: Robin Howard', *Dancing Magazine* (Dec 1989), 30, 32 • F. Mason, P. Taylor, C. Reinhart, and T. Tharp, 'Robin Howard (1924–1989)', *Ballet Review* (autumn 1989), 75–80

Archives Theatre Museum, London, Contemporary Dance Trust archive | SOUND NYPL, Dance Collection, oral interview

Likenesses A. Crickmay, photographs, Theatre Museum, London

Rosalind Frances Howard, countess of Carlisle (1845–1921), by George Howard, ninth earl of Carlisle, 1868

Howard [née Stanley], **Rosalind Frances**, countess of Carlisle (1845–1921), promoter of women's political rights and of temperance reform, was born on 20 February 1845, probably at Alderley, Cheshire. She was the youngest daughter of Edward John *Stanley, second Baron Stanley of Alderley (1802–1869), who between 1855 and 1866 held office as president of the Board of Trade and postmaster-general. Her mother, Henrietta Maria *Stanley (1807–1895), eldest daughter of a former Jacobite peer, Henry Augustus Dillon-Lee, thirteenth Viscount Dillon, was one of the founders of Girton College, Cambridge.

Educated at home by private tuition, Rosalind Stanley married on 4 October 1864 George James *Howard (1843–1911), a landscape painter in the Pre-Raphaelite tradition and a friend of Sir Edward Burne-Jones and William Morris. During the following two decades they had a family of six sons and five daughters. The Howards' house at Palace Green, Kensington, became a meeting-place for Liberal politicians; George Howard was Liberal MP for East Cumberland from 1879.

In contrast with her moderate husband, Rosalind Howard moved beyond the whig heritage to the radical left. She denounced W. E. Gladstone's occupation of Egypt and advocated women's suffrage. When criticized, she said that 'fanatics have done a lot of the world's work, and I don't mind being classed with the fanatics' (Roberts, ix). The Liberal Party schism over home rule further divided the family. George Howard followed his cousin the duke of Devonshire into Liberal Unionism. His wife was fervently for home rule. Except for their dislike of alcoholic drink, George and Rosalind Howard agreed on little, and for the rest of their married life they were estranged both personally and politically. Much of the time she withdrew to their country houses, Castle Howard in Yorkshire and her favourite home, Naworth Castle in Cumberland.

Although often complaining of ill health, Rosalind Howard found scope for her organizational abilities in the temperance movement, in Liberal Party women's associations, in local government, and in the management of the extensive family estates. By the end of the 1880s she had the advantage of the title of countess—in 1889 her husband became ninth earl of Carlisle—and wealth. Although as a young woman she had canvassed in elections for her father-in-law and husband, she had avoided the impropriety of speaking in public. In 1891, however, an official of the United Kingdom Alliance persuaded her to address a drawing-room meeting for women on behalf of temperance, and she went on to become an effective platform speaker. It was on committees that she excelled. She was persuasive with small groups, a generous supporter of her colleagues, and knowledgeable.

Rosalind Howard was a prominent figure in the temperance movement. She took the pledge in 1881 and in the following year began temperance work on her Cumberland estates, where she made teetotalism a condition of tenancy and closed down public houses. She became a vice-president of the United Kingdom Alliance and in 1892 president of the North of England Temperance League. She acquired her principal office in 1903, when she was elected president of the National British Women's Temperance Association, a position she retained until her death. Ironically she was an agnostic, while most members were Methodists or belonged to other devoutly evangelical groups, and until her election she, like other aristocratic hostesses, had served her guests wine. The anecdote that she poured the contents of the wine cellar of Castle Howard down the drain is an exaggeration; she merely disposed of some spoiled hock. Her daughter Lady Cecilia Roberts (d. 1947) succeeded her as president of the British women.

Lady Carlisle's election helped her shore up the crumbling advanced temperance party. In the early 1900s veteran reformers such as her predecessor Lady Henry Somerset and T. P. Whittaker argued that prohibition by direct local veto plebiscites stood no chance of parliamentary enactment, conceded the necessity for compensation for licence holders who lost their livelihoods because of a change in public policy, and wanted to experiment with non-commercial 'disinterested' management of the retail trade on the model of Scandinavia. Lady Carlisle fiercely resisted this shift in temperance thinking. She also lent her aristocratic prestige to the World's Woman's Christian Temperance Association, as president from 1906 to her death.

In the years before the First World War Lady Carlisle was closely allied with a small group of Liberal MPs: her son Geoffrey Howard (1877–1935), her son-in-law Charles Henry Roberts (1865–1959), her secretary Leif Jones, later Lord Rhayader, and her neighbour Sir Wilfrid Lawson, the long-standing president of the United Kingdom Alliance. When Lawson died in 1906, Jones became the new alliance president. In her diehard policies Lady Carlisle also had the support of the Good Templar fraternal order but declined invitations to join this predominantly working-class and lower middle-class organization.

Lady Carlisle organized many women's local Liberal associations that affiliated with the Women's Liberal Federation, of which she was a member from 1890. She succeeded in persuading the federation to support women's suffrage on the same terms as men, a position that drove anti-suffrage women to start a rival organization, the National Women's Liberal Association. Lady Carlisle was president of the federation from 1894 to 1902 and from 1906 to 1915. Recognizing the danger for Liberals of accepting enfranchisement limited to propertied women, she insisted that all women whose husbands could vote be enfranchised. She was concerned to ensure that the federation did not jeopardize the election prospects of Liberal candidates, rejected the feminist women's charter, and repudiated the violent tactics of the Pankhurst suffragettes.

Lady Carlisle was an active member of district councils in the north: Brampton in Cumberland from 1895 and Malton in Yorkshire from 1898. She worked to improve housing, education, and social conditions.

Although Lady Carlisle had opposed the Second South African War and was committed to international arbitration, she hated German militarism and had no doubts as to the rightfulness of the British cause in the First World War. By this time her political influence had waned. The temperance movement was divided and in decline, as was the Liberal Party. Lady Carlisle supported Asquith in the wartime Liberal schism despite his lack of enthusiasm for prohibition and opposed Lloyd George's proposal for the wartime nationalization of the drink trade.

Lady Carlisle's husband died in 1911, and by this time her autocratic style had alienated many of her children and friends. When they were young she humiliated her daughters at any hint of flirting, and she quarrelled bitterly with her tory eldest son, Lord Morpeth (who died in 1912). For several years she did not speak to her daughter Dorothy after she had married Francis Henley (later sixth Baron Henley), in part because he was a brewer. This daughter said that Lady Carlisle, tyrannical in private life, appeared at her best in the public sphere.

Lady Carlisle defined radicalism as 'unselfishness applied to politics' (Roberts, xii). She was an élitist who distrusted the wisdom of a working-class democracy, but she worked hard to improve ordinary people's lives. Respectful of talent, she accepted middle-class sons-in-law with little money, notably the classicist and League of Nations advocate Gilbert Murray, who married her eldest daughter, Mary Henrietta.

Lady Carlisle died at her London home, 13 Kensington Palace Gardens, on 12 August 1921. She was cremated at Golders Green crematorium on 16 August and her ashes were interred in her husband's grave at Lanercost Priory, Cumberland, on 18 August. Her casket was accidentally left on a train by her son Geoffrey, the chief mourner, but was fortunately returned by the railway authorities. Her husband had left her most of the family property for life, with discretionary authority to divide it among their children at her death. When she died, her surviving children regarded her will as unfair and by agreement redivided their inheritance.   DAVID M. FAHEY

Sources D. H. E. Henley, *Rosalind Howard, countess of Carlisle* (1958); repr. (1959) · C. Roberts, *The radical countess: the history of the life of Rosalind, countess of Carlisle* (1962) · V. Surtees, *The artist and the autocrat: George and Rosalind Howard, earl and countess of Carlisle* (1988) · L. L. Shiman, *Women and leadership in nineteenth-century England* (1992) · *Liberal Year Book* (1916), 7 · CGPLA Eng. & Wales (1922) · M. Barrow, 'Teetotal feminists: temperance leadership and the campaign for women's suffrage', *A suffrage reader: charting directions in British suffrage history*, ed. C. Eustance and others (2000)

Archives Castle Howard, Yorkshire, corresp. and papers | Bodl. Oxf., corresp. with Gilbert Murray and Lady Mary Murray · U. Durham, department of palaeography, ninth earl of Carlisle MSS

Likenesses G. Howard, ninth earl of Carlisle, drawing, 1868, NPG [*see illus.*] · D. G. Rossetti, chalk drawing, 1870, AM Oxf. · W. B. Richmond, oils, 1880, Castle Howard, North Yorkshire

Wealth at death £180,406 9s. 7d.: probate, 5 April 1922, CGPLA Eng. & Wales

Howard, Samuel (1710–1782), organist and composer, was a chorister of the Chapel Royal under Dr William Croft, and had further instruction from J. C. Pepusch. He sang tenor in the chorus for Handel from 1732 to 1735, and became an organist in London at St Clement Danes,

Strand, and St Bride's, Fleet Street. He wrote a little church music, including the hymn tune 'St Bride', which continued in use in *Hymns Ancient and Modern Revised* throughout the twentieth century, and a fine anthem, 'This is the day which the Lord hath made', for soloists, chorus, and full orchestra, which was published after his death (1792). It was probably his doctoral exercise: he graduated MusD from King's College, Cambridge, in 1769. He assisted William Boyce in the preparation of his anthology of cathedral music (1760–73). Most of his output, however, was secular. His early works in this genre have been much praised. They included the incidental music for the Drury Lane pantomime *The Amorous Goddess* (1744); *New Grove* considers the overture 'outstanding', and comments that the vocal score was republished in 1785, although the pantomime had never been revived. He also wrote two new songs for Arne's pastiche *Love in a Village* (1762). He wrote many other single songs for Vauxhall Gardens, but his later works lacked the merits of the earlier compositions. Howard died on 13 July 1782 at his house in Norfolk Street, Strand. His obituarist remarked on his great personal charity: 'He was ever ready to relieve distress, to anticipate the demands of friendship, and to prevent the necessities of his acquaintance' (*GM*).

L. M. MIDDLETON, rev. K. D. REYNOLDS

Sources *New Grove* · Grove, *Dict. mus.* (1927) · Venn, *Alum. Cant.* · *GM*, 1st ser., 52 (1782), 359

Howard [née Rich], **Susanna, countess of Suffolk** (1627–1649), exemplar of godly life, was born in the spring of 1627, the second daughter of Henry *Rich, first earl of Holland (*bap.* 1590, *d.* 1649), and Isabella (*d.* 1655), daughter of Sir Walter *Cope (1553?–1614) of Kensington, Middlesex, and Dorothy, née Greville (*d.* 1638). She was clever, with an enquiring mind and a natural gift for languages, sciences, music, and theology, as well as drawing and needlework. She probably met the poets in the circle around Henrietta Maria through her father's links with it, and came to love religious poetry, especially George Herbert's, saying that if there were no more copies of *The Temple* she would not sell hers for several hundred pounds. These poems and parts of the Bible she learned by heart, and it was claimed that she could write out a sermon almost word for word the next day.

At Kensington on 1 December 1640 Lady Susanna married James *Howard, third earl of Suffolk (1619–1689). As he had just inherited a debt of £132,000 from his father their union was doubtless intended to improve the Suffolk finances. They lived at the family mansion of Audley End, near Saffron Walden, Essex. Their first child, Lady Essex Howard, was born in 1641 and soon followed by a son, Lord James. When the death of their next son, unbaptized, in January 1644 was succeeded in May by that of Lord James, the countess was devastated. According to Samuel Clark she alleviated her grief by singing psalms until she had ceased crying and submitted to the will of God. Subsequently another child was born.

The countess was very devout. She was zealous in prayer and worship, and careful in self-examination before holy

communion. Dr Edward Rainbowe, the family chaplain, described her in his funeral sermon as sanctified by the Holy Spirit 'whose Image sat bright and Glorious on her Soul, and did shine through all her Conversation' (Rainbowe, 11). She was seen as equable, cheerful, unaffected, loyal, forgiving, generous-minded, and indulgent when servants made mistakes, regarding them as humbler friends. Only profanity and scurrility angered her. Compassionate, she often visited poor people, feeding the starving, giving medicine to the sick and mentally ill, spiritual counsel to the doubting, and praying for them. She studied theology critically, yet accepting scriptural authority, and read six chapters of the Bible daily, using Diodates' notes. According to Samuel Clark, who included her in his exemplary lives, she dressed always in black, both as suiting her serious disposition and regarding the biblical admonition that women should be concerned with spiritual rather than outward adornment. The copy of her portrait at Audley End shows her wearing neither lace nor a necklace, although a Samuel Cooper miniature depicts her serious but with a string of pearls.

The family was only marginally affected by the first civil war, as Suffolk merely participated as a parliamentary representative in peace negotiations with the king in 1646; only when he was accused of treason by the Commons in September 1647 was he temporarily endangered and imprisoned. In 1648 Lady Susanna thought herself again pregnant but her 'labour' revealed no living child. Following her adored father's capture and subsequent condemnation for his part in the second civil war she was able to support him before his execution, on 9 March 1649, but her disease, possibly pituitary gland malfunction, finally affected her brain, although she had lucid intervals. She died at Kensington on 19 May 1649, aged just twenty-two, and was buried at Saffron Walden parish church ten days later.   ELIZABETH ALLEN

Sources S. Clark [S. Clarke], *The lives of sundry eminent persons in this later age* (1683), 209–15 · E. Rainbowe, *A sermon preached at Walden in Essex* (1649), 11–12, 15–19 · GEC, *Peerage* · L. Stone, *The crisis of the aristocracy, 1558–1641* (1965), 140, 358–9, 428, 435, 442, 462 · F. N. MacNamara and A. Story-Maskelyne, eds., *The parish register of Kensington, co. Middlesex, from AD 1539 to AD 1675*, Harleian Society, register section, 16 (1890), 18, 21, 30, 70–71, 118, 120, 125 · *The letters of John Chamberlain*, ed. N. E. McClure, 2 (1939), 537, 552, 571, 625 · [T. Birch and R. F. Williams], eds., *The court and times of Charles the First*, 1 (1848), 451; 2 (1849), 261 · L. Stone, *Family and fortune* (1973), 289 · parish register, Saffron Walden, Essex RO, D/P 192/1/2 · *CSP dom., 1641–3*, 337; *1645–7*, 454, 570 · *JHL*, 9 (1646–7), 667 · H. Howard, *Indications of memorials, paintings, etc. … of persons of the Howard family* (1834), 55 · *DNB* · E. Thomson, 'Poetry and the court of Charles I', DPhil diss., U. Oxf., 1989, 16 · R. J. B. Walker, *Audley End: catalogue of pictures in the state rooms*, 4th edn (1973), 13

Likenesses S. Cooper, miniature, *c.*1649, Audley End House, Essex · E. Zeeman, portrait, 18th cent. (after A. Van Dyck?), Audley End House, Essex

Howard, Theophilus, second earl of Suffolk (1584–1640), courtier and politician, was the eldest son of Thomas *Howard, first earl of Suffolk (1561–1626), lord treasurer from 1614 to 1618, and his second wife, Katherine *Howard, countess of Suffolk (*b.* in or after 1564, *d.* 1638); she was the daughter of Sir Henry *Knyvet and widow of Richard Rich (d. in or before 1581). Theophilus Howard was baptized on 13 August 1584 at Saffron Walden, Essex. He matriculated at Magdalene College, Cambridge, in 1598, but did not graduate; he was created MA at Cambridge in 1605, a degree incorporated at Oxford the same year when he accompanied James I on a visit there. He was admitted to Gray's Inn in March 1606.

His father's prominence at court ensured Howard's success there; he was a constant presence at masques and jousts, and in 1610 his performance at a tilt in honour of Henry, prince of Wales, won him high praise: 'the Lord Walden [his courtesy title] carried away the reputation for bravery that day' (Nichols, 2.361). In 1605 he was appointed lieutenant of the band of gentlemen pensioners and in 1606 he received the joint stewardship of several royal manors in Wales. Along with other prominent courtiers, he had an interest in colonization; in 1609 he became a member of the council of the Virginia Company and in 1612 was a charter member of the North-West Passage Company. He represented the Essex borough of Maldon in the parliament of 1604–10 from 1605 until February 1610, when he was summoned to the Lords as Baron Howard of Walden during his father's life. In the same year he served as a volunteer at the siege of Juliers, where he was challenged to a duel by Lord Herbert of Cherbury after a drunken quarrel. The authorities prevented the fight, which did nothing to hinder Howard's advance at court.

In 1611 Walden became keeper of the Tower of Greenwich and in 1614 he was promoted to captain of the gentlemen pensioners. Probably as a result of his marriage in March 1612 to Lady Elizabeth Home (c.1599–1633), a daughter of George *Home, earl of Dunbar, a power on the borders, he served from 1614 to 1639 as lord lieutenant of the counties of Cumberland, Westmorland, and Northumberland. In 1618 he was one of the signatories to a petition to King James deploring the creation of baronets.

Though he survived the scandal which in 1616 engulfed his sister Frances *Howard, countess of Essex and Somerset (1590–1632), Walden's career received a blow with his father's fall from power in 1619, when he lost his captaincy of the gentlemen pensioners. His period out of favour was relatively brief, however, thanks to his friendship with Buckingham, who stood godfather to Walden's child in January 1620. In the same month he resumed his command of the gentlemen pensioners. In 1621, pursuing his father's enemy Francis Bacon, he proposed to the House of Lords that Bacon be stripped of his peerage—a suggestion that went unheeded. His close connections to Buckingham ensured that he would remain a force at court. Following his father's death in 1626 Walden became earl of Suffolk and won a seat in the privy council as well as the lieutenancies of Dorset, Suffolk, and Cambridgeshire. As a lieutenant and privy councillor he worked hard to forward collections of the forced loan in the country. John Clayworth told Lord Montagu of Boughton that Suffolk's seat on the council was the result of the king's need for reliable peers to press the loan forward. In 1627 Suffolk became high steward of Ipswich and was awarded the Order of the Garter. In 1628, along with the king, he stood

as godfather to Buckingham's son and heir. In July 1628 Buckingham resigned his place as warden of the Cinque Ports in Suffolk's favour, and the earl was also appointed constable of Dover Castle. At some point before 1637 he became custos rotulorum of Essex.

The duke of Buckingham's assassination marked a turning point for Suffolk. The loss of his friend and patron was important, but also significant were his declining health and desperate financial plight. He was always extravagant—in 1623, for example, he lost £1500 at bowls in a single day—and debts inherited from his father as well as his own threatened to devour his estate. His career as a courtier won him many offices and honours but only hindered him in his struggle for solvency. Despite an annual income of over £10,000 debts mounted steadily, reaching a total of over £130,000 by 1640. Although he continued as an active lord warden through the 1630s, a post which brought in about £1700 a year, in 1635 Suffolk gave up his court offices. In 1636 he petitioned for relief from his debts to the crown—debts which were more than outweighed by the unpaid balance of a privy seal grant—but his plea was denied. Unable to maintain his father's massive home at Audley End he retired to another family estate at Lulworth Castle, Dorset, where he devoted his time to his garden. His hopes to marry an heiress after the death in 1633 of his first wife were in vain, and he was forced to sell land worth more than £36,000 to stave off ruin. The king's need for an active lord lieutenant in the northern counties in the midst of the Scottish crisis led to his resignation of his northern lieutenancies in 1639. His last political appointment was as a commissioner of regency, in March 1639, though it seems doubtful, given the state of his health, that he was active. He died on 3 June 1640 aged fifty-five, at Suffolk House in London; he was buried at Saffron Walden a week later. He was succeeded as third earl by his son James *Howard (1619–1689). VICTOR STATER

Sources GEC, Peerage · J. Nichols, The progresses, processions, and magnificent festivities of King James I, his royal consort, family and court, 1 (1828), 555; 2 (1828), 108, 175, 186, 361, 629, 714, 759 · L. Stone, Family and fortune: studies in aristocratic finance in the sixteenth and seventeenth centuries (1973), 270–91 · The autobiography of Edward, Lord Herbert of Cherbury, ed. S. L. Lee (1886), 116–24, 326–32 · R. Lockyer, Buckingham: the life and political career of George Villiers, first duke of Buckingham, 1592–1628 (1981), 64, 371–2, 419, 448 · S. R. Gardiner, History of England from the accession of James I to the outbreak of the civil war, 4 (1883), 103; 6 (1884), 256; repr. (1965) · Report on the manuscripts of his grace the duke of Buccleuch and Queensberry ... preserved at Montagu House, 3 vols. in 4, HMC, 45 (1899–1926), vol. 3, p. 315 · The manuscripts of the Earl Cowper, 3 vols., HMC, 23 (1888–9), vol. 2, pp. 123–4 · Report on manuscripts in various collections, 8 vols., HMC, 55 (1901–14), vol. 5, pp. 119–20 · Venn, Alum. Cant.
Archives BL, papers as warden of the Cinque Ports, Egerton MS 2584 · CUL, accounts, Add. MS 7094
Likenesses B. Rebecca, oils, 1750–75 (after drawing), Audley End House, Essex; copy, nineteenth century, Ranger's House, London · painting, oils, 1800–99, Ranger's House, London
Wealth at death est. more than £130,000 in debt: Stone, Family and fortune

Howard, Thomas, second duke of Norfolk (1443–1524), magnate and soldier, was the eldest son of John *Howard

(d. 1485), a kinsman of the Mowbray dukes of Norfolk and first Howard duke, and Catherine (d. 1465), daughter of William, Lord Moleyns. He was probably born at Tendring Hall, Stoke by Nayland, Suffolk, and educated at home and at Thetford grammar school. His upbringing was chivalric in character and modelled on his father's career as a soldier and gentleman.

Early career and marriage Little is known of Howard's early life; he was in his twenties when he entered royal service between 1466 and 1469 as a henchman to Edward IV. At some point before the autumn of 1471 he was at the court of Charles the Bold, duke of Burgundy. When Edward was driven to the Low Countries by the earl of Warwick, Howard took sanctuary at St Joan's Church, Colchester. He was badly wounded fighting for Edward at Barnet in April 1471, but recovered to be appointed an esquire of the body and continued in close personal attendance on Edward IV until 1477.

On 30 April 1472 Howard married Elizabeth, daughter of Sir Frederick Tilney and widow of Humphrey Bourchier, who had been killed at Barnet, and took up residence at her manor of Ashwellthorpe, Norfolk. The marriage was a blow to the Pastons, as they had sought her hand, and it marked the growing status of the Howards in East Anglia. Howard had with Elizabeth three sons and two daughters who lived to maturity; the eldest son, Thomas *Howard, born in 1473, succeeded as earl of Surrey and third duke of Norfolk. In 1475 Howard accompanied Edward IV to France, witnessed the treaty signed at Picquigny, and was granted a French pension. Until the end of Edward's reign he served as a justice of the peace for Norfolk and as sheriff of Norfolk and Suffolk; he was a member of parliament for Norfolk in 1477 and again, after a disputed election, in 1483. He was knighted on 14 January 1478 at the marriage of the king's second son, Richard, newly created duke of York and Norfolk, and Anne Mowbray, heir to the last Mowbray duke of Norfolk. This marriage extinguished the Howards' faint claim to lands and titles of their Mowbray kinsmen, and it may have determined their role in the events that followed.

Relations with Richard III Despite taking ceremonial roles in Edward IV's funeral the Howards supported the usurpation of Richard, duke of Gloucester, and reaped handsome rewards for their service. They were intimates of Richard in the weeks preceding his coronation; Thomas Howard helped to arrest Lord Hastings at the Tower of London on 13 June, and he and his father may have participated in the murder of Edward V and Richard, duke of York and Norfolk, an act from which they had much to gain (Sutton and Hammond, 26). Richard saw the Howards as being among his most important supporters, for, on 28 June, John was created duke of Norfolk and Thomas earl of Surrey; both were granted lands and Thomas Howard an annuity of £1000. Norfolk acquired the bulk of the former Mowbray lands in East Anglia, Sussex, and Surrey, as well as forfeited estates from Lord Rivers and the earl of Oxford, which established him as the greatest landed baron in the south-east of England. Surrey was sworn of the council and elected to the Order of the Garter. At Richard's coronation Surrey bore the sword of state and served as steward at the coronation feast, entering Westminster Hall on horseback. That autumn Norfolk and Surrey demonstrated their loyalty by suppressing the rebellion of Henry Stafford, duke of Buckingham, which led to the latter's execution. Both Howards remained close to Richard throughout his brief reign. Interestingly, Thomas Howard's funeral monument, which bore a lengthy autobiographical inscription, glossed over this period, blandly asserting that the Howards 'both served the said King Richard truly as his subjects during his life, lying at home in their own countries and keeping honorable houses' (Weever, 835).

When Henry Tudor challenged for the throne, the Howards came to Richard's defence. Norfolk was slain and Surrey wounded and taken prisoner at Bosworth on 22 August 1485 as Henry VII claimed the crown. Surrey was attainted in Henry's first parliament and, stripped of titles and lands, languished in the Tower of London for three years. Offered escape during the rebellion of the earl of Lincoln in 1487, Thomas Howard refused, perhaps convincing Henry of his loyalty. In May 1489 he was restored as earl of Surrey, although most of his lands were withheld, and sent north to quell rebellion in Yorkshire. Having shown his value to the new regime Surrey continued in the north as king's lieutenant until 1499, residing at Sheriff Hutton Castle, Yorkshire. In 1497 he repelled an attack on Norham Castle by James IV of Scotland in support of the pretender Perkin Warbeck and followed with a raid into Scotland to seize Ayton Castle. However, Henry sought peace rather than war with Scotland, and Surrey concluded a truce and began negotiations for the marriage of James IV to Henry's daughter Margaret.

Second marriage, 1497, and continental diplomacy In April 1497 Surrey's wife, Elizabeth, died, and he married Agnes Tilney (d. 1545) [see Howard, Agnes, duchess of Norfolk], a cousin of Elizabeth, on 8 November 1497. This marriage produced six surviving children, including the naval commander William *Howard; through his five sons and six daughters, Howard had marital ties to most of the leading English families. Having demonstrated beyond doubt his loyalty and usefulness as a soldier and administrator, Surrey was recalled to court in 1499 and accompanied Henry VII on a state visit to France the next year. In 1501 he was sworn of the council and, on 16 June, made lord treasurer. Along with Richard Fox, lord privy seal, and William Warham, the chancellor, Surrey became part of Henry's executive triumvirate. As Surrey proved his loyalty, he steadily recovered lands once held by his father, mainly in East Anglia, and until 1513 he continued to accumulate lands and consolidate his holdings in the region. By 1500 his East Anglian lands alone had a net value of over £600 a year, and after the death of the dowager duchess of Norfolk in November 1506 he gained other, mainly East Anglian, lands, with an additional net value of some £600 a year.

Surrey took an active role in diplomacy, including the 1501 negotiations for Katherine of Aragon's marriage to

Prince Arthur, and also supervised Arthur's funeral in April 1502. In 1503 he conducted Princess Margaret to Scotland for her wedding to James IV. Despite their past battles James and Surrey got along splendidly as fellow chivalrous knights, and Surrey left Scotland laden with gifts—much to Margaret's chagrin, since her new husband seemed to prefer Surrey's company to her own. Surrey had accompanied Henry VII to Calais in 1500 to meet Philippe, duke of Burgundy, and went to Flanders in 1507 to seek a marriage between Philippe's son and heir, the future Charles V, and Henry's second daughter, Mary. The marriage was agreed upon in 1508 with Surrey leading negotiations with the emperor Maximilian in Antwerp, although the wedding never took place.

Serving Henry VIII At Henry VII's death in April 1509 Surrey was an executor of the king's will and played a prominent role in his funeral and in the coronation of Henry VIII, when he served as earl marshal, an office which was later granted for life. Surrey sought to become the young king's leading minister, but by 1511 Thomas Wolsey had emerged as the dominant figure at court, and this led Surrey, after a final attempt to retain his position in September 1511, to a reconciliation with Wolsey and an acceptance of his supremacy. The main point of contention was foreign policy. Surrey had joined Fox and Thomas Ruthal in March 1510 in signing an Anglo-French truce, but Wolsey, sensing Henry's ambition, sought a policy of war. Surrey led the negotiations with Ferdinand of Spain which bound England to attack France in the spring of 1512, and his sons Edward (killed at sea in 1513) and Thomas served as Henry's admirals in a series of engagements along the channel. Surrey went north to muster soldiers and inspect defences for an invasion of France in 1513 which he expected to lead.

Defeating the Scots on Flodden Field, 1513 Instead Surrey was left behind when Henry departed for Calais on 30 June 1513. Perhaps the king did not want the old soldier at his elbow during his first campaign; certainly Wolsey was happy to have his rival out of the way. Yet while Henry played at war in France, Surrey won his family's and one of his kingdom's greatest victories. Henry had hardly left the realm when James IV launched an invasion. Surrey, with the aid of his sons Thomas and Edmund and such nobles as Henry had left behind, scraped together an army and met James's much larger force near Flodden on 9 September 1513. Surrey, low on supplies and unable to delay the confrontation, boldly divided his forces and took the fight to James in a series of flanking attacks which, combined with superior English weapons in the longbow and bill, threw the Scots into confusion. In a battle lasting from 4 p.m. until nightfall the Scots may have lost as many as 10,000 men, most in the confused last stages of the battle, and King James was killed. While Henry fought the meaningless battle of the Spurs and seized Tournai and Thérouanne, Surrey sent his master the blood-soaked coat of a king and won great popular renown.

Howard was rewarded for his service on 1 February 1514 when he was created duke of Norfolk and his son Thomas

was made earl of Surrey, each with grants of land and annuities. All of Norfolk's new lands lay outside East Anglia, with thirty manors scattered across the realm from Kent to Nottinghamshire. The Howard arms were augmented in honour of Flodden with an escutcheon bearing the lion of Scotland pierced through the mouth with an arrow. The new duke of Norfolk held a major role in affairs, and in 1514 he joined Wolsey and Fox in negotiations for the marriage of Princess Mary to Louis XII of France. Norfolk and his family led the grand party which escorted Mary to France for the wedding in the autumn. Norfolk again irritated a princess to please a king by clearing Mary's court of her English servants, which had the further effect of displacing many handpicked by Wolsey.

Final years, death, and reputation Despite his disappointment at being eclipsed by Wolsey, who was made cardinal in November 1514, Norfolk continued as a courtier and diplomat and on 1 May 1517 led a private army of 1300 retainers into London to suppress the 'evil May day' riots. This episode not only reconfirmed Howard's value as a soldier but also showed the private power of a Tudor magnate. The greatest such figure was Edward Stafford, duke of Buckingham, and when in May 1521 Henry determined to destroy the duke, Norfolk had the painful duty of presiding over the trial as lord high steward—he pronounced the sentence of death with tears streaming down his face.

By the spring of 1522, nearing eighty years of age and in failing health, Norfolk withdrew from court. In December 1522 he resigned as treasurer in favour of his son and, after attending the opening of parliament in April 1523, retired to his ducal castle at Framlingham in Suffolk. He died there on 21 May 1524. His funeral and burial on 22 June at the Cluniac priory at Thetford were spectacular and enormously expensive, costing over £1300 and including a procession of 400 hooded men bearing torches and an elaborate bier surmounted with 100 wax effigies and 700 candles. This was befitting the richest and most powerful peer in England. At the interment, a sermon on the text 'Behold the lion of the tribe of Judah triumphs' (Revelation 5: 5) so terrified the congregation that the mourners fled the church. Norfolk left an estate worth £4500 per annum and, according to his funeral monument, when he died 'he could not be asked one groat for his debt, nor for restitution to any person' (Weever, 835).

Norfolk was a man of intense determination and courage, cautious when he was able but reckless, as at Flodden, when he needed to be. His role in the usurpation of Richard III raises questions about his character, but he was otherwise staunchly devoted to the crown. His personal and family pride is evident from his funeral and the beginning of his will, dated 31 May 1520, in which he referred to himself in the plural—'We Thomas, Duke of Norfolk'. To judge from an engraving based on a lost brass, he was small and spare in person, with a long face, straight fair hair worn long, and an aquiline nose. He was a faithful conventional Catholic who endowed churches and supported religious foundations. It may have been well that he died when he did, for it is doubtful he could have given even the reluctant assent his son did to the changes of the English Reformation. Howard was one of the last English feudal barons, a man who made his career by his sword and his counsel to his king and who reaped all the rewards and fame one might so seek. Polydore Vergil described Howard as *vir prudentia, gravitate et constantia praeditus* ('a man endowed with prudence, dignity, and firmness'). It still seems a fitting epitaph.   DAVID M. HEAD

Sources M. Tucker, *The life of Thomas Howard, earl of Surrey and second duke of Norfolk, 1443–1524* (1964) • D. M. Head, *The ebbs and flows of fortune: the life of Thomas Howard, third duke of Norfolk* (1995) • J. Weever, *Ancient funerall monuments* (1631), 834–40 • *Hall's chronicle*, ed. H. Ellis (1809) • J. Gairdner, ed., *Letters and papers illustrative of the reigns of Richard III and Henry VII*, 2 vols., Rolls Series, 24 (1861–3) • *LP Henry VIII* • A. F. Sutton and P. W. Hammond, eds., *The coronation of Richard III: the extant documents* (1983) • M. J. Bennett, *The battle of Bosworth* (1985) • R. Virgoe, 'The recovery of the Howards in East Anglia, 1485–1529', *Wealth and power in Tudor England: essays presented to S. T. Bindoff*, ed. E. W. Ives, R. J. Knecht, and J. J. Scarisbrick (1978) • *The Anglica historia of Polydore Vergil, AD 1485–1537*, ed. and trans. D. Hay, CS, 3rd ser., 74 (1950) • J. M. Robinson, *The dukes of Norfolk* (1982)

Archives Arundel Castle, Sussex, papers | PRO, SP series • PRO, tellers' rolls, E 405

Likenesses engraving (after brass sculpture at Lambeth, now lost), repro. in Bennett, *Battle of Bosworth* • oils (possibly posthumous), Arundel Castle, Sussex

Wealth at death £4500 p.a.: Virgoe, 'Recovery of the Howards'

Thomas Howard, third duke of Norfolk (1473–1554), by Hans Holbein the younger, *c*.1539–40

Howard, Thomas, third duke of Norfolk (1473–1554),

magnate and soldier, was the eldest son of Thomas *Howard, second duke of Norfolk (1443–1524), and his first wife, Elizabeth (*d*. 1497), the daughter of Sir Frederick Tilney of Ashwellthorpe Hall, Norfolk, and widow of Sir Humphrey Bourchier.

Early years and political rise The Howards were under a political shadow in the early years of Henry VII's reign. Thomas Howard's father and grandfather had prospered under the Yorkist kings, and both fought for Richard III at Bosworth. Thus his own marriage on 4 February 1495 to Anne [**Anne**, Lady Howard (1475–1511)], the fourth surviving daughter of *Edward IV and thus King Henry's sister-in-law, represented an important step in his family's rehabilitation. As a young child Anne had been intended for Philip, the only son of Archduke Maximilian and Edward IV's niece Marie. The marriage was in negotiation by July 1479 and was agreed by treaties in the following year, despite Edward's determination to give no dowry with his daughter. But the match fell through when Edward's foreign policy collapsed in 1482. One of the princesses whose safety Richard III guaranteed on 1 March 1484, Anne took part in court ceremonies after 1485, though her own and her sisters' claims to a share of the Yorkist inheritance made them a potential embarrassment to the new dynasty. On 1 July 1510 Henry VIII made Anne and her husband a grant of lands in several counties in compensation for her rights, but limited its descent to the heirs of her body. In the event, the four children of the marriage all died young, and Anne had no surviving issue when she herself died in November or December 1511.

Meanwhile Thomas Howard had continued his progress into royal favour. In 1497 he served first against the Cornish rebels and then, in September, against the Scots, in the latter instance under the command of his own father, who knighted him on 30 September. In April 1510, following the accession of Henry VIII, he was made a knight of the Garter, and he was often employed as a soldier. On 22 May 1512 he was appointed lieutenant-general (under the second marquess of Dorset) of an army sent to Spain to co-operate with Ferdinand of Aragon in an Anglo-Spanish invasion of southern France. Lack of Spanish support caused the expedition to return home. On 4 May 1513 Howard became lord admiral (an office he held until 1525), and on 9 September he was prominent in the defeat of the Scots at the battle of Flodden. The English army was commanded by Sir Thomas's father, the earl of Surrey, who appointed his son to lead the vanguard. As the two armies moved to face each other Thomas sent a provocative message to King James IV concerning Andrew Barton, a Scottish sea captain whom Howard and his brother Sir Edward *Howard had killed in a sea fight in 1511. Sir Thomas called Barton a pirate and declared that he was there to justify his death. He also warned that he would take no prisoner except the king, because he himself expected no mercy from the Scots. On 9 September the English army manoeuvred itself between James's forces and Scotland. Sir Thomas then led the vanguard ahead of the rest of the army and his own artillery, in the process exposing himself to the much larger Scottish forces, positioned above him on Branxton Hill. Fortunately for his son and vanguard, Surrey brought up the rest of the army in time. Thomas Ruthal, bishop of Durham, reported afterwards that in the ensuing battle and crushing defeat of the Scots, 'Surrey, and my Lord Howard, the admiral, his son, behaved nobly' (*LP Henry VIII*, 1/2, no. 2283).

Sir Thomas's loyalty and service brought their reward. When his father was created duke of Norfolk on 1 February 1514 he resigned the earldom of Surrey in favour of his eldest son. It is clear that the latter did not merely succeed to his father's earldom. According to letters patent issued on the same day, he was created 'as Earl of Surrey, for life, with annuity of £20', and received a grant, also for life, of two castles and eighteen manors in Lincolnshire. This was '[i]n consideration of the timely assistance he rendered his father … at the battle of Branxton, 9 Sept. last. This creation is made on surrender by the said Duke … of the title of Earl of Surrey' (*LP Henry VIII*, 1/2, no. 2684 (2)). In the third session of Henry VIII's second parliament (23 January – 4 March 1514) a grace act, in the form of a petition bearing the royal sign manual, confirmed the letters patent. The preamble stated that the king, by his 'most noble and habundaunt grace' and '[i]n consideration of the true and feithfull service of your said Suppliant done unto your Highnes, hath made and creatid your said Suppliaunt Erle of Surrey' (*Statutes of the Realm*, 11 vols., 1810–28, 3.99).

Surrey continued to serve the king in a variety of ways. He escorted Henry's sister Mary to France for her marriage in September 1514. In 1517 he led soldiers into London to quell the May day riots, whereupon the rioting apprentices 'scattered by sudden fright, just like sheep at the sight of the wolf' (*Anglica historia*, 245). Royal trust also brought promotion to positions of responsibility in the government: in particular he became a member of the king's council (before May 1516), while on 4 December 1522 he was made lord treasurer, when his aged father resigned the office. He remained treasurer until 12 December 1546. He was also one of Henry VIII's close companions, with daily livery and lodging at court.

Royal service, 1520–1525 Early in 1513 Sir Thomas Howard took as his second wife the fifteen-year-old Elizabeth (1497–1558), daughter of Edward Stafford, third duke of Buckingham, and Eleanor Percy, daughter of the fourth earl of Northumberland [*see* Howard, Elizabeth]. On 10 March 1520, as earl of Surrey, he was appointed lord lieutenant of Ireland, possibly because Henry VIII or Wolsey wanted him out of the way while his father-in-law was arrested, tried, convicted, and, on 17 May 1521, executed for treason. He disapproved of the change in royal policy whereby Ireland was to be pacified by friendship rather than force, being of the opinion that 'this londe will never be broght to dew obeysaunce but only with compulsion and conqwest' (Head, 57). After eighteen months of attempts to reconcile the Fitzgeralds and the Butlers and repeated requests for money and manpower he secured his recall late in 1521 because he was ill with dysentery. But in June 1522 he acted as admiral in escorting the emperor Charles V back from England to northern Spain. He then raided Brittany, sacked Morlaix, and sailed home laden with booty. In August and September 1522 he led an Anglo-Burgundian force from Calais through northern France on an expensive and destructive march which served no military purpose and which had to be abandoned in October as winter approached. Nevertheless the poet John Skelton sang his praises:

> … the good Erle of Surray
> The Frenche men he doth fray.
> And vexeth them day by day
> With all the power he may.
> …
> Of chivalry he is the floure:
> Our lorde be his soccoure!
> (Walker, 26)

In 1523 Surrey was appointed warden-general of the Scottish marches and also (on 26 February) lieutenant-general of the army against Scotland. During the summer he ravaged parts of southern Scotland, then when the duke of Albany marched south late in October and besieged Wark Castle, Surrey moved to its relief and Albany hurriedly retreated. Skelton praised 'our stronge captaine' in a poem commissioned by Wolsey (ibid., 29–30). Surrey himself had reported a few weeks earlier feeling 'decayed in body, as well as worn out in purse, by these four years, during which he has been continually in the wars' (*LP Henry VIII*, 3/2, no. 3384).

On 21 May 1524 Surrey succeeded his father as third duke of Norfolk; his title as earl of Surrey then passed to his son. Although he served again on the Scottish borders later in the year, eventually he was allowed to retire to his Norfolk home of Kenninghall. He was there on 1 April 1525, when he reported his early efforts to raise money due to the government from the so-called 'amicable grant'. This new exaction soon prompted an uprising, however, centred on Lavenham, Sudbury, and Hadleigh but extending into much of East Anglia, and Norfolk, along with the duke of Suffolk, was soon diverted from collecting the levy to trying to control popular resistance to it. They acted swiftly in raising troops, but Norfolk, unlike his fellow duke (and in contrast with his own policy in Ireland), preferred to resolve the crisis by negotiations rather than by force. Ultimately the two men proceeded with tact and skill, and 'so wysely handeled themselfes, that the commons were appeised' (Hall, fol. 141v). They also obtained the rebels' public submission to the king's authority. Wolsey gave thanks for their pains and their diplomatic and restrained conduct, for which, he said, they deserved high praise from the king. John Foxe, too, later wrote of their 'wisdom and gentleness' (*Acts and Monuments*, 4.590).

Norfolk and Wolsey, 1516–1530 According to Polydore Vergil and Herbert of Cherbury (and also some more recent historians), the political ascendancy of Cardinal Wolsey in the king's counsels aroused the hostility and opposition of the Howards. This does not in fact appear to have been true of Surrey's father, who as the Venetian ambassador observed was very intimate with the cardinal. Surrey himself, however, was more ambitious, and was also possessed of a violent temper and quick to take offence. He did not respond calmly when, on 31 May 1516, with the marquess of Dorset and Baron Abergavenny, he was expelled from the council, on Wolsey's orders, for breaching the laws against armed retainers. When his father died in 1524 and Surrey became duke of Norfolk and accordingly more prominent politically, his liking for war, and for the honour, glory, and rewards it could bring, was frustrated by Wolsey's preference for diplomacy as the main instrument of foreign policy. This feeling was shared by Charles Brandon, duke of Suffolk. The two men were not intimate friends or firm allies, but they were alike in their suspicion, sometimes even hostility, towards the ecclesiastical power which Wolsey personified.

In 1525 Norfolk was appointed a commissioner for peace negotiations with France. Although he later received a pension from François I, at this time the duke was a pensioner of Charles V, and Wolsey's preference for Anglo-French amity clashed with Norfolk's pro-imperial position. Relations had earlier worsened when in 1523 Wolsey secured the reversion to the duke of Suffolk of the office of earl marshal on the death of Norfolk's father, and when the duke of Richmond replaced Norfolk himself as admiral in 1525. Pushed aside from the centre of affairs, Norfolk spent much time away from court in 1525–7 and 1528. His differences with Wolsey had a public airing in spring 1527 when duke and cardinal had a heated exchange over foreign policy in the king's presence. By this time, however, Norfolk's political fortunes were reviving as he became increasingly involved in the politics surrounding the annulment of Henry VIII's first marriage, especially as the chosen successor to Katherine of Aragon was Norfolk's niece Anne Boleyn. He was the king's obedient servant, sometimes to Wolsey's discomfort as the cardinal's efforts to secure an annulment failed. By 1529 matters of state were being increasingly handled by the two dukes and the Boleyns, who together pressed Henry to remove Wolsey. In July the king chose Norfolk and Suffolk to demand a judgment from the legatine court, where Wolsey sat as one of the two judges of his marriage; in October the king sent them to obtain the great seal from Wolsey; and early in 1530 it was Norfolk who directed the cardinal to retire to York. When the duke visited Wolsey during his fall from power, they embraced, dined together courteously, and afterwards 'continued in consultation a certain season' (Cavendish, 117–20). Nevertheless he remained nervous that his capricious king might recall Wolsey. On 6 February 1530 the imperial ambassador Eustace Chapuys reported that Norfolk 'began to swear very loudly that rather than suffer this he would eat him up alive' (LP Henry VIII, 4/3, no. 6199). He need not have worried, however, for the following November the cardinal was arrested on a charge of treason, though he died on his way south to stand trial.

Norfolk benefited from Wolsey's fall. In November 1530 the Venetian ambassador Lodovico Falieri reported that the king 'makes use of him in all negotiations more than any other person … and every employment devolves to him' (CSP Venice, 1527–33, 294–5). He became the leading councillor, thwarted Suffolk's attempt to become lord chancellor, and was a warm friend of Henry's choice for that office, Sir Thomas More. In particular he dutifully served Henry VIII in his search for divorce and remarriage. In 1531 and 1533 he attempted, unsuccessfully, to obtain Katherine's submission. He was described to Charles V in 1532 'as a man who willingly takes trouble in this matter, but would suffer anything for the sake of ruling' (LP Henry VIII, 5, no. 1059).

The 1530s: competing with Cromwell Although Norfolk remained conservative in religion and consistently hostile to the reformed faith, swearing that he neither had nor would ever read the scriptures, he adopted an anticlerical stance in public. He criticized the clergy's wealth and privileges, and in January 1531 and February 1532, according to Chapuys, he denied papal jurisdiction in matrimonial and all other causes except heresy. But he had no new strategy to offer Henry VIII and saw papal consent as the only answer to the king's dilemma, even though he expatiated to Chapuys on the English king's imperial status, with its implicit rejection of papal sovereignty. It was this line which Thomas Cromwell subsequently followed in order to resolve Henry's marital problems and earn his unrivalled favour. Meanwhile, Norfolk's failure to achieve a solution by putting pressure on the papacy caused his relations with his niece to deteriorate. Anne Boleyn's pregnancy in 1533 finally sidelined Norfolk and led to the adoption of an internal English solution for the divorce.

During and after the lengthy annulment crisis, Norfolk profited handsomely from his loyalty and prominence in royal service, even though he had the temerity to beat the king at bowls and so win £21 from him in 1532. He was created earl marshal on 28 May 1533, and a knight of the French order of St Michel at a meeting between Henry VIII and François I in 1532. He received grants of monastic lands in Norfolk and Suffolk and he had the opportunity to purchase other East Anglian estates. Meanwhile the king employed him on diplomatic service in 1533, on a futile embassy to France to meet François I and Pope Clement VII. He was also one of Henry's more experienced and realistic advisers on Ireland, though his influence on Irish affairs declined as Thomas Cromwell, with whom he disagreed in council in 1533–4, rose in the king's favour and confidence. This simply reflected his diminishing role in government during the time of Cromwell's predominance. Nevertheless his services were still needed, and as lord steward, for the occasion he presided at the trials of Lord Dacre in June 1534 and of his niece Anne Boleyn, Viscount Rochford, and others in May 1536.

When the Pilgrimage of Grace broke out in Lincolnshire and the north late in 1536, Norfolk cited an old Latin text on the rights of the earl marshal as justification for his taking command of the king's forces, though in the end he shared it with the fourth earl of Shrewsbury. In fact his dealings with the pilgrims in Yorkshire do more than anything else to show Norfolk's stature, for it is hardly an exaggeration to say that for a few weeks late in 1536 the future of the Tudor dynasty lay in his hands. Having grasped the unprecedented scale of the crisis, he perceived, as King Henry did not, that it was not one which could be resolved by force. His basic honesty may be doubted, since he begged Henry to 'take in gode part what so ever promes I shall make unto the rebells (if any suche I shall by th'advyse of others make) for sewerly I shall observe no part theroff' (Dodds and Dodds, 1.259). Nevertheless he assured the pilgrim leaders of his good faith, and for several weeks applied himself, ultimately successfully, to persuading the rebels to disperse, on promise of a pardon and of a parliament which would consider their grievances. But when further rebellions erupted in January 1537 he carried out a policy of brutal retribution and supervised executions in five northern counties. Religious conservative though he was, he later reflected that if loyal preachers 'had been continually in these parts instructing the unlearned [people], no such follies would have been attempted' (LP Henry VIII, 12/1, no. 1158). His hope that the pilgrimage 'will ultimately work the ruin and destruction of his competitor and enemy, Cromwell' was not realized (CSP Spain, 1536–8, 268). He even had cause to be grateful to Cromwell when, in 1537, the minister helped him to obtain former monastic property. Norfolk was also still active and honoured at court: in 1537 he was godfather to Prince Edward and a commissioner for Queen Jane Seymour's funeral; he was granted Clerkenwell nunnery in 1539; and with Suffolk he attended Anne of Cleves on her arrival in England at the end of 1539.

By then Norfolk was presenting an increasingly serious challenge to Thomas Cromwell and the reformed faith. In 1539 Henry VIII sought from parliament an end to diversity in religious opinion and some kind of statutory declaration on doctrine. On 5 May the House of Lords responded by appointing a committee which represented wide-ranging opinions. Although Norfolk was not a member of the committee, it was he who on 16 May reported to the Lords on its lack of progress. As the committee had failed to reach any conclusions he presented six conservative articles of religion for consideration, as the basis for discussion which might lead to religious unity and the drafting of a penal statute to punish those who would not conform. Whether Norfolk was encouraging, even manoeuvring, the king in a conservative direction, or simply promoting the wishes of a conservative monarch, is not clear. Then on 20 May, five days before Whitsunday recess, Norfolk proposed to the house a week-long prorogation. Ostensibly intended to provide members with time to contemplate the grant of appropriate supply to the king for his good governance, reformation, and defence of the kingdom, in fact the interval gave Norfolk and the other conservatives time to promote their cause. When parliament reconvened, on 30 May, the six articles and accompanying penalties for failure to conform were enacted into law, and on 28 June received the royal assent. Although Thomas Cromwell was vicegerent and Norfolk had not been on the parliamentary committee, the duke seems to have scored a victory over the reformists.

The fall of Cromwell: political resurgence The tensions between Norfolk and Cromwell had already been given public expression on 29 June 1539, when the two dukes and Cromwell dined with the king as guests of Archbishop Cranmer. They fell to heated discussion about Wolsey, during which Cromwell charged Norfolk with disloyalty and the latter called the lord privy seal a liar. Thereafter their rivalry and hostility could not be concealed. Cromwell's initiative and organization of Henry's marriage to Anne of Cleves played into Norfolk's hands. The king was disillusioned when he met the uninspiring princess in January 1540, enabling Norfolk to promote his niece Katherine Howard [see Katherine (1518x24–1542)] as a desirable replacement later in the year. At the same time Cromwell's position was weakened by his protection of religious reformers. Although Norfolk failed to secure an Anglo-French alliance when he went on a diplomatic mission to Paris in February, 1540 marked a decisive upward turn in his fortunes. His greatest triumph came on 10 June, when Cromwell was arrested in the council chamber on charges of high treason. Norfolk himself, 'after reproaching him with some villanies, tore the St George from his neck' (CSP Spain, 1538–42, 540). The subsequent charges against Cromwell and the phrasing of the act of attainder also suggest the duke's handiwork.

On 9 July 1540 Henry's marriage to Anne of Cleves was annulled, leaving him free to remarry. On 28 July Thomas Cromwell was executed, and on the same day Norfolk's niece Katherine became the king's fifth wife. The marriage brought significant benefits. Norfolk enjoyed political prominence, royal favour, and material rewards. However, the Howards' ascendancy was brief. Katherine's pre-marital sexual indiscretions and her alleged adultery with Thomas Culpeper were exposed and revealed to the king. His wrath turned on to the Howard family, members of whom were accused of concealing the young queen's misconduct. On 15 December 1541 Norfolk wrote an abject letter to the king, in which he deserted his implicated relatives, figuratively prostrated himself, and earnestly hoped that Henry's gentle heart would not be ill disposed towards one who never had a thought which might cause discontent in his royal master. These were the words of an experienced, self-interested courtier. Queen Katherine was condemned by act of attainder and executed on 13 February 1542. By then, as the French ambassador Marillac wrote on 17 January, Norfolk had escaped punishment and had been received back in court 'apparently in his full former credit and authority' (LP Henry VIII, 17, no. 34).

The 1540s: struggling for position Renewed outbreaks of war helped Norfolk to secure his position. On 29 January 1541 he was appointed lieutenant-general north of the Trent, and in August 1542 captain-general against the Scots. In October he burnt and pillaged the Scottish borderlands without meeting serious resistance. His military reputation and apparent sympathies with France caused the imperial ambassador to write on 21 November 1542 that 'The Duke being too much of a Frenchman, I am afraid he will perhaps do us harm and spoil our game' (CSP Spain, 1542–3, 182). However, diplomatic positions often reflected court rivalries rather than genuine preferences for an imperial or a French alliance, and it has been suggested that in the early 1540s 'Norfolk's pro-French stance was as much the result of his opposition to Cromwell as attributable to any real affection for the French', just as 'the thwarting of the duke and his pro-French influence was a cornerstone of the lord privy seal's policy' (Head, 193, 167). Nevertheless his receipt of a French pension (handsomely increased in 1532) had encouraged Norfolk to support the continuance of Henry VIII's pro-French position in the 1530s, and he was a natural choice for a secret diplomatic mission to the French court in February 1540 in an attempt to detach King François from Charles V. He also held intermittent talks with the French ambassador Marillac over a six-month period in 1541. Henry VIII, however, was turning increasingly towards an Anglo-imperial alliance and a renewal of war with France, so that by 1542 Norfolk's desire for agreement with France left him increasingly isolated in the privy council. His relatively unrewarding northern campaign against the Scots that year, moreover, harmed his reputation, causing him to regard war against the French as a means of restoring his prestige and political place. Indeed, it was Norfolk who in June 1543 declared war on France in King Henry's name and was appointed lieutenant-general of the army. During the campaign of May–October 1544 he besieged Montreuil, while Henry himself captured Boulogne before returning home. Henry had never, however, made it clear what he expected Norfolk to achieve. The duke repeatedly lamented his lack of provisions and munitions, and having raised the siege of Montreuil and left Boulogne garrisoned, he withdrew to Calais. He was a realist about Boulogne who 'certainly knoweth the realm of England not possible to bear the charges' of defending that town for long (*LP Henry VIII*, 20/2, no. 738). For his withdrawal he received a stinging rebuke from the king who none the less appointed him captain-general of the army raised in East Anglia in 1545 to resist an anticipated French invasion.

Politically Norfolk lost ground during the king's last years. The increasingly influential Edward Seymour, earl of Hertford, and Queen Katherine Parr both favoured the reformed faith, whereas the duke remained staunchly conservative and hostile to 'stirrers-up of heresy' (*CSP Spain*, 1545–6, 555–6). An attempt by Norfolk, Bishop Gardiner, and other conservatives to secure Archbishop Cranmer's arrest in 1543 was unsuccessful. Hertford, established by 1544–5 as Henry's leading general, rose steadily in royal favour and Norfolk's proposal for a marriage alliance between Howards and Seymours came to nothing.

The fall of the Howards, 1546–1547 In an increasingly tense political climate, in 1546 the Seymours and William Paget sought to manipulate the king against the conservatives, especially the Howards and Stephen Gardiner. Although by the end of 1546 Henry VIII was increasingly ill and vulnerable, he continued to exercise a degree of control as the rival politicians sought his support. Against this dangerous background Norfolk attempted to safeguard his interests with further proposals for an alliance with the Seymours, through the marriage of his widowed daughter Mary to Hertford's brother Thomas, but his efforts were fatally undermined by the conduct of his heir, Henry

*Howard, styled earl of Surrey (1516/17–1547). Surrey's provocative and arrogant conduct had alienated many; his adoption of armorial bearings, which quartered the royal arms, seemed to signal monarchic ambitions. On 12 December Surrey and his father were arrested and sent to the Tower. Next day Norfolk wrote to the king pleading his innocence and offering his lands to Henry as a mark of his loyalty. He begged 'that he may know what is laid to his charge and have some word of comfort from his Majesty', and also wrote to the privy council, asking 'that he meet his accusers face to face before the King or else before the Council' (*LP Henry VIII*, 21/2, nos. 540, 554). The duke received no 'word of comfort' from the king, however, and gambling on a restoration to favour if he confessed all, on 12 January 1547 he made his submission:

> I have offended the King in opening his secret counsels at divers times to sundry persons to the peril of his Highness and disappointing of his affairs. Likewise I have concealed high treason, in keeping secret the false acts of my son, Henry earl of Surrey, in using the arms of St. Edward the Confessor, which pertain only to kings. (ibid., no. 696)

Norfolk requested that his estates go to Prince Edward and the king decided to keep them, except for certain properties in Sussex and Kent.

None of Norfolk's hopes was realized. In Henry's last days he received no mercy. His family, including his estranged wife, his daughter the duchess of Richmond, and his mistress, Elizabeth Holland [*see below*], all gave evidence against him. On 27 January 1547 he was attainted by statute, without trial. The assent of the dying king was given by royal commissioners, who were authorized by letters patent signed by the dry stamp. It was rumoured that he would die the next day. Odet de Selve, the French ambassador, reported to François I on 31 January that the duke had been secretly beheaded on the previous day. In fact his execution was not carried out, because after the king's death on 28 January the council decided to avoid bloodshed at the beginning of a new reign. Norfolk's estates were plundered by the ruling clique in Edward VI's reign. His receiving lands worth £1626 10s. per annum from Queen Mary indicates the extent of his losses under her brother.

Survival and revival, 1547–1554 Norfolk stayed in the Tower throughout the reign of Edward VI. His daughter the duchess of Richmond made persistent efforts to obtain his release, and even had the bishops of Lincoln, Rochester, and St David's, evangelicals to a man, sent to minister to him on Christmas eve 1549. But if this was an attempt to win his compliance with religious reform it failed, and he remained in the Tower until the accession of Mary Tudor, who released and pardoned him in August 1553. He was resworn a privy councillor, and as lord high steward he presided at the trial of the duke of Northumberland on 18 August. As earl marshal he bore the crown at Mary's coronation on 1 October and as steward, assisted by his young heir Thomas *Howard (1538–1572), Surrey's eldest son, the aged duke supervised the coronation banquet. Later that year, in response to his petition, Mary's first parliament nullified his attainder.

Norfolk's last service to the crown was given against Sir Thomas Wyatt's rising in January 1554. Having been appointed lieutenant-general, he led a force which included 500 Londoners against Wyatt at Rochester. At Rochester Bridge, however, the Londoners changed sides and the royal commanders hastily retreated, 'both void of men and victory, leaving behind them both six pieces of ordnance, and treasure' (Acts and Monuments, 6.543). Norfolk was clearly now in fragile health—a contemporary described him as 'by long imprisonment diswanted from the knowledge of our malicious World' (Loades, Conspiracies, 60 n. 1)—and he died at Kenninghall on 25 August 1554 and was buried at St Michael's Church, Framlingham, Suffolk. He was survived by only two of his children, both from his second marriage: Thomas, created Viscount Howard of Bindon in 1559, and Mary *Fitzroy, widow of the duke of Richmond. His property passed into the crown's hands during the minority of his grandson and heir.

Norfolk the man In 1531 the Venetian ambassador had described the 58-year-old duke as 'small and spare in person, and his hair black'. In contrast, the Holbein portrait, painted when Norfolk was about sixty-seven, masks his slightness of figure with the symbols of status, office, power, and honour. He is clad in silk, satin, and ermine; the golden George of a knight of the Garter hangs from his neck; and he bears in one hand the white staff of the lord treasurer, and in the other the gold baton of the earl marshal. The ambassador thought him a 'prudent, liberal, affable and astute' man who 'associates with everybody' (CSP Venice, 1527–33, 295). Chapuys, after an evening as Norfolk's guest in 1529, attested that he was sociable, even gregarious, but always to a purpose, because he was driven by an appetite for prestige, position, and power. His wife, Elizabeth, observed that he could dissemble, appearing as amicable to his enemy as to his friend. She was one of those best qualified to pronounce on his unreliability, their married life, apparently mutually affectionate at first, having been overshadowed when in 1527 the duke took a mistress. Elizabeth Howard became increasingly isolated, the more so as she formally separated from her husband in the 1530s. She claimed to have suffered physical maltreatment at the hands of Norfolk and members of the ducal household, and when the duke was charged with treason at the end of 1546, she gave evidence against him. Not surprisingly, perhaps, he left her nothing in his will.

The woman who thus came between the duke and duchess of Norfolk was **Elizabeth Holland** (d. 1547/8), also known as Bess Holland, who was the daughter of the duke's secretary and household treasurer. At the time her liaison with Norfolk began she was one of Anne Boleyn's attendants. He installed her in the Howard household, thereby deepening his estrangement from his wife, but when he and his son fell from grace in 1546–7, Bess looked after her own interests. Under cross-examination she reported damaging statements by the duke: that the king 'loved him [Norfolk] not because he was too much lov'd in his country', and that Henry was sickly and could not last

long (Herbert, 627). Her jewellery, new house, and estate were seized, but were later restored as reward for her co-operation. She married Henry Reppes, an East Anglian JP and landowner, and became pregnant in 1547, but she died after childbirth, before April 1548.

The third duke of Norfolk was a powerful regional magnate, the controller of parliamentary boroughs in Norfolk and Sussex, and the wealthiest English peer. He was a skilful gambler, not only in court politics, where he was above all a survivor, but also at cards and dice, on one occasion winning £45 from Henry VIII. Like many contemporaries he was publicly loyal and ingratiating, but underneath he was unscrupulous, guileful, and ruthlessly ambitious. His representation by Nigel Davenport in the 1966 film of Robert Bolt's A Man for All Seasons, as a model of hearty straightforwardness, was probably true to Norfolk's public persona, but did not hint at his darker qualities. His personal acquaintances, his relations, and above all the king's protesting or rebellious subjects could all have borne witness to his capacity for violence, even brutality. His considerable pride, however, was not matched by his ability, in which he was much inferior to both Wolsey and Cromwell. On the other hand he was no mere philistine, for he 'was fluent in French, knew the Burgundian world of romance, and was quite literary in his way' (Sessions, 74). Norfolk reputedly saved Cardinal College at Oxford from dissolution after Wolsey's fall, and on 8 September 1540 he was appointed steward of Cambridge University. His surviving buildings, too, shed light on Norfolk's taste. With an income of about £3000 per annum from land in 1546 he could afford the best, and seems to have aspired to have it. At Framlingham he had the chancel of the parish church pulled down and replaced by a substantial extension, primarily to house family tombs, notably that of his son-in-law, Henry Fitzroy, duke of Richmond. His own handsome memorial was also placed there. But the work was still unfinished in 1549, and may not have been completed by the third duke. In the late 1520s the latter was building what John Leland referred to as a fine new house at Kenninghall. Recorded by the antiquary Francis Blomefield as H-shaped, 'having a porter's lodge, and all things else in the grandest manner' (Blomefield, 1.215), after Norfolk's attainder it made an appropriate residence for Princess Mary. But except for a single service wing it was demolished in the mid-seventeenth century.

MICHAEL A. R. GRAVES

Sources GEC, Peerage, 9.615–20 · D. M. Head, The ebbs and flows of fortune: the life of Thomas Howard, third duke of Norfolk (1995) · W. A. Sessions, Henry Howard, the poet earl of Surrey: a life (1999) · M. J. Tucker, The life of Thomas Howard, earl of Surrey and second duke of Norfolk, 1443–1524 (1964) · LP Henry VIII, vols. 1–21 · CSP Spain, 1509–58 · G. Walker, John Skelton and the politics of the 1520s (1988) · Edward, Lord Herbert of Cherbury, The life and raigne of King Henry the Eighth (1649) · The Anglica historia of Polydore Vergil, AD 1485–1537, ed. and trans. D. Hay, CS, 3rd ser., 74 (1950) · J. S. Block, Factional politics and the English Reformation, 1520–1540 (1993) · [E. Hall], The union of the two noble and illustre famelies of Lancastre and Yorke, ed. [R. Grafton] (1550) · G. W. Bernard, ed., The Tudor nobility (1992) · N. Williams, Thomas Howard, fourth duke of Norfolk (1964) · DNB · G. Cavendish, The life and death of Cardinal Wolsey, ed. R. S. Sylvester and D. P. Harding (1962) · G. W. Bernard, War, taxation, and rebellion in early Tudor

England (1986) · *The acts and monuments of John Foxe*, ed. J. Pratt, [new edn], 8 vols. in 16 (1853–70), vols. 4–6 · D. MacCulloch, ed., *The reign of Henry VIII: politics, policy and piety* (1995) · N. Williams, *Henry VIII and his court* (1971) · *CSP Venice, 1520–54* · M. H. Dodds and R. Dodds, *The Pilgrimage of Grace, 1536–1537, and the Exeter conspiracy, 1538*, 2 vols. (1915) · F. Blomefield and C. Parkin, *An essay towards a topographical history of the county of Norfolk*, [2nd edn], 11 vols. (1805–10) · J. Ridgard, ed., *Medieval Framlingham: select documents, 1270–1524*, Suffolk Records Society, 27 (1985) · Exchequer, king's remembrancer, lay subsidy rolls, PRO, E 179/69/49, m. 1 · *Suffolk*, Pevsner (1974) · *Norfolk: south and west*, Pevsner (1999) · *John Leland's itinerary: travels in Tudor England*, ed. J. Chandler (1993) · D. M. Loades, *Two Tudor conspiracies* (1965) · D. Loades, *The reign of Mary Tudor: politics, government and religion in England, 1553–58*, 2nd edn (1991) · 'The letters of Richard Scudamore to Sir Philip Holby, September 1549 – March 1555', ed. M. Dowling, *Camden miscellany, XXX*, CS, 4th ser., 39 (1990) · C. Ross, *Edward IV*, new edn (1975) · T. B. Pugh, 'Henry VII and the English nobility', *The Tudor nobility*, ed. G. W. Bernard (1992), 49–110 · 'Lady Anne Howard', *GM*, 2nd ser., 23 (1845), 147–52

Archives Arundel Castle, West Sussex, corresp. and papers · BL, political corresp., Add. MSS 32646–32654 · Holkham Hall, Norfolk, account of his possessions · U. Cal., Berkeley, Bancroft Library, household account book | BL, Cotton MSS, corresp. with Thomas Wolsey · BL, corresp. with Lord Dacre, etc., Add. MS 24965 · BL, Harley MSS, corresp.

Likenesses H. Holbein the younger, oils, *c*.1539–1540, Royal Collection [*see illus.*] · H. Holbein the younger, oils, second version, Arundel Castle, West Sussex · double portrait, tomb effigy (with his wife), Framlingham church, Suffolk

Wealth at death fifty-six manors, thirty-seven advowsons; other extensive estates

Howard, Lord Thomas (*c*.1512–1537), courtier, was the second son of Thomas *Howard, second duke of Norfolk (1443–1524), and of his second wife, Agnes *Howard (*née* Tilney) (*d*. 1545), daughter of Sir Hugh Tilney of Boston, Lincolnshire. He was thus half-brother to Thomas *Howard the third duke. Nothing is known of his early life, except that the antiquary John Leland, who was roughly five years Howard's senior, acted in some capacity as companion or tutor during his childhood.

Howard first appeared at court in 1533 for the marriage of his niece Anne Boleyn to the king, and was one of the bearers of the canopy at Princess Elizabeth's baptism. After this he was often found at court, where he was associated with a Howard group that gathered there. It was thus that he met Lady Margaret *Douglas (1515–1578), the daughter of Henry VIII's sister, Margaret, and half-sister to James V of Scotland. BL Add. MS 17492, an anthology of mostly amorous verses emanating from this circle, contains a number of poems by either Thomas or Margaret. By the end of 1535 they had fallen in love and they agreed to marry early in 1536.

The fall of Anne Boleyn in May that year was the backdrop to the discovery of their contract. The bastardization of Princess Elizabeth as well as Mary meant that until the king could produce another heir, the Lady Margaret could claim precedence in the succession. Her secret marriage to a member of the leading noble house of England was therefore politically dangerous. Although there are hints that the king had encouraged their courtship the year before, he had certainly not sanctioned a marriage contract. When this was discovered, early in July 1536, the couple were arrested and imprisoned in the Tower of London.

On the morning of 18 July 1536 a bill of attainder against Howard passed both houses of parliament, and later in the day parliament was dissolved. The act of attainder accused Lord Thomas of having been 'ledde and seduced by the Devyll not havyng God afore his eyes, not regardyng his duetye of Allegeaunce that he oweth to have borne to the Kyng oure and his most dread Sovereign Lorde' and stated that 'yt is vehemently suspected and presumed malicyously and trayterously myndyng and imagynyng to putt dyvisyon in this Realme. And to interrupt ympedyte and lett the seid Succession of the Crowne contrary to the lymytacyon therof mencyoned in the sayd acte' (*Statutes of the Realm*, 3.680). The act went on to sentence Howard to death and forbid the marriage of any member of the king's family without his permission.

The sentence of death was never carried out, but Howard remained in the Tower for the rest of his life, even though Lady Margaret Douglas had renounced his love by the end of the year. There is a tradition that he was poisoned, but in reality he caught a fatal sickness in the wretched conditions of the Tower. He died on 31 October 1537 and his body was given to his mother, the dowager duchess, to be buried 'without pomp' (*LP Henry VIII*, vol. 12/2, no. 1013). He was interred at Thetford Abbey.

MICHAEL RIORDAN

Sources D. M. Head, '"Beying ledde and seduced by the Devyll": the attainder of Lord Thomas Howard and the Tudor law of treason', *Sixteenth Century Journal*, 13/4 (1982), 3–16 · *LP Henry VIII*, vols. 6–12 · C. Wriothesley, *A chronicle of England during the reigns of the Tudors from AD 1485 to 1559*, ed. W. D. Hamilton, 1, CS, new ser., 11 (1875) · A. Luders and others, eds., *Statutes of the realm*, 11 vols. in 12, RC (1810–28), vol. 3 · D. M. Head, *The ebbs and flows of fortune* (1995) · S. E. Lehmberg, *The later parliaments of Henry VIII, 1536–1547* (1977) · R. Southall, *The courtly maker* (1964) · *The works of Henry Howard, earl of Surrey, and of Sir Thomas Wyatt, the elder*, ed. G. F. Nott, 2 vols. (1815–16) · R. C. Harrier, *The canon of Sir Thomas Wyatt's poetry* (1975) · GEC, *Peerage*, new edn, 9.612–20 · *DNB* · E. W. Ives, *Anne Boleyn* (1986)

Howard, Thomas, fourth duke of Norfolk (1538–1572), nobleman and courtier, was born at Kenninghall Palace, Norfolk, on 10 March 1538, the eldest son and heir of Henry *Howard, styled earl of Surrey (1516/17–1547), and Frances (1517–1577), daughter of John de Vere, earl of Oxford.

Early years and education When his father was executed in 1547 Howard was taken from his mother and placed in the custody first of Sir John Williams at Rycote near Thame and then, in 1548, of his aunt Mary Fitzroy, duchess of Richmond, at Reigate Castle. Thomas Howard's first tutor, Hadrianus Junius, a scholar of European reputation, left the family service in 1547. His successor, appointed by the duchess of Richmond in 1548, was the protestant martyrologist John Foxe. The influence which Foxe had on the future duke of Norfolk and his brothers and sisters, who were also in the duchess's care, cannot be determined, but it is certain that Thomas Howard had a lifelong respect for his tutor, who was present when he died, a professed protestant. It was therefore with regret that at the accession of Mary I in 1553 he lost the services of Foxe, who was dis-

Thomas Howard, fourth duke of Norfolk (1538–1572), by Hans Eworth, 1563

missed and went into exile. The aged duke of Norfolk, who had been attainted in January 1547 but, unlike his son Henry, earl of Surrey, had not been executed, was released from imprisonment in the Tower of London. He was restored to the office of earl marshal and as such officiated at Mary's coronation on 1 October 1553. Afterwards, as lord high steward, he presided at the coronation banquet. In both offices he was assisted by Thomas Howard, his grandson. Thomas was made a knight of the Bath on 29 September 1553. Then, in Mary's first parliament (October–December 1553), Norfolk's statutory attainder was declared void, thereby entitling him to the dukedom, while Thomas and any future heirs were restored in blood and he was recognized as rightful earl of Surrey.

Norfolk assigned the further education of his fifteen-year-old heir to the devout Roman Catholic John White, successively bishop of Lincoln and Winchester. Despite a succession of tutors Thomas professed himself 'ashamed of my unskilfulness' in Latin, and early in the next reign he had to ask Secretary Cecil to negotiate with the Spanish ambassador 'because his own Latin tongue was not ready' (*CSP for.*, 1563, 26). Such shortcomings were no impediment to a great peer. In July 1554 he became first gentleman of the chamber to Mary's consort, King Philip, and in November he was with them at the opening of parliament.

The young duke in Mary's reign, 1554–1558 On 25 August 1554 his grandfather died and Thomas duly inherited his title as fourth duke of Norfolk and his hereditary office of earl marshal. As he was a minor, however, his extensive

estates including fifty-six manors were held by the crown until he came of age. When, on or before 30 March 1555, the seventeen-year-old duke married Mary Fitzalan [*see* Howard, Mary (1539/40–1557)], daughter and heir of Henry, twelfth earl of Arundel, he did so with permission from the queen, whose ward he was. The marriage added Arundel Castle and other Fitzalan estates in Sussex to the Howard properties. When Mary's fourth parliament met in October 1555 a private bill was introduced empowering him, by the advice of the lord chancellor, the earl of Arundel, and the bishop of Ely to sell, grant, and lease lands during his minority. Its purpose was to enable him to maintain his wife, but it was countered in the Commons by patentees of lands acquired from the late duke during his attainder. When they exhibited a bill of their own for assurance of their lands Norfolk came to the house with four serjeants-at-law and 'required his bill to be furthered; and declared the speciall poynts of his bill and then departed out' (*JHC*, 1.43). The Commons sent a delegation 'to shew hym, that the house wolde consider the case' (ibid.), and the bill duly became law.

The young duke's life was spent in public service, ceremonial duties, attendance and activities at court, and the enlargement of his Norwich residence. As earl marshal he was also responsible for the College of Arms, which he reorganized and for which, in 1555, he obtained a new royal charter of incorporation. Offices multiplied: he was, for example, elected high steward of Cambridge and Great Yarmouth in 1554; and in 1558 he was appointed lord lieutenant of Norfolk and Suffolk. On 28 June 1557 his young wife gave birth to a son, Philip *Howard, who was named after his godfather Philip of Spain and who would become earl of Arundel in 1580. The duchess, however, did not recover from the birth and on 25 August she died. In 1558 the queen too fell mortally ill. On 16 October she commanded Norfolk and other peers to repair to the court in order to advise on 'great and urgent affaires' (PRO, SP 11/14, fol. 2). Shortly afterwards, on 5 November, he received his first parliamentary writ of summons. He was recorded as present on seven of the nine sittings of the Lords in a session suddenly terminated by Mary's death on 17 November. By then Norfolk's lawyer had spent months in Rome negotiating for a papal dispensation which would allow him to marry his cousin Margaret Dudley (1540–1564). She was the eighteen-year-old widow of Lord Henry Dudley and sole heir of Thomas, Lord Audley of Walden. With the accession of the protestant Queen Elizabeth, Norfolk proceeded to marry Margaret Dudley without papal dispensation. In Elizabeth's first parliament, 1559, his marriage received statutory ratification. Margaret brought a rich inheritance, including Audley End in Essex, into the Howard family.

Premier peer during Elizabeth's early years, 1558–1568 As he grew up Norfolk had experienced a succession of changes in religion, receiving instruction from first Foxe and then White. He proved adaptable to yet another change with the establishment of the Elizabethan church in 1559. Although there is no evidence that he was an enthusiastic godly protestant, he remained loyal to the new church. In his last days he wrote to his children 'to spend some time in reading of the Scriptures, for therein is the whole comfort of man's life … And upon my blessing beware of blind papistry, which brings nothing but bondage to men's consciences' (Williams, 242). As a protestant, a loyalist, and England's premier peer he had a prominent part to play in national life. In his capacity as earl marshal he supervised Mary's funeral rites in December 1558 and Elizabeth's coronation on 15 January 1559; he took part in the tiltyard jousting next day; and in the first Elizabethan parliament, 25 January – 8 May, he was present on forty-eight of the fifty-four business days for which attendance is recorded and was appointed to five bill committees. Norfolk was also the recipient of honours and awards. He was elected knight of the Garter on 24 April 1559, and he was admitted to Gray's Inn on 28 December 1561 and the freedom of the city of London in January 1562. He received the degree of MA at Cambridge University on 10 August 1564, and at Oxford University on 19 April 1568. With Robert Dudley, earl of Leicester, he was installed as a knight of the French order of St Michael on 24 January 1566. As husband of Lord Audley's heir he also became patron of Magdalene College, Cambridge, to which, in 1564, he promised an annual grant of £40 for the completion of its quadrangle.

In the first decade of Elizabeth's reign the duke was also a regional prince. Norfolk was his 'country' and, according to Camden, 'when he was in his Tennis court at Norwich, he thought himselfe in a manner equall with some Kings' (Camden, *Historie*, 130). He conducted himself in regal manner. He was the protector and patron of an East Anglian gentry network. In 1562 three earls, other peers, and many knights and ladies lodged at his Norwich palace and were sumptuously entertained. Three years later he came to Norwich's economic assistance when he obtained letters patent admitting Walloon and Dutch cloth and arras makers. In London he enlarged the Charterhouse, renamed Howard House, after purchasing it from Lord North in 1564. In spite of his exalted status, Norfolk derived great pleasure from time spent with his family and in the Howard homes, especially Kenninghall. He experienced intense grief on the deaths of his first wife, Mary, and, fewer than seven years later, his second wife, Margaret. Even in happier times he displayed a marked preference for the country over the court, and he was reluctant to accept his first military responsibility when it came in 1559.

Elizabeth's mother was the second duke of Norfolk's granddaughter and she expected her cousin, England's only duke, to be prominent in her service. When the government began its attempt to remove the French political and military presence from Scotland in 1559 Norfolk was offered the position of lieutenant-general of the north. His reluctance was political as well as personal. He believed that security against the French would be more effectively achieved by the queen's marriage to Archduke Charles of Austria than by military intervention in Scotland. He finally accepted, however, and arrived in Newcastle in early January 1560. His tasks were the defence of Berwick and a military alliance with the Scottish lords of

the congregation directed against the French regency. Although, on 27 February 1560, it was Norfolk who signed a military pact with the Scots, his role was 'a showy but circumscribed one' (MacCaffrey, 91). He was accompanied by experienced diplomats and councillors; though organizing supplies he played no part in the military operations, and the treaty of Edinburgh, which in July 1560 removed the French from Scotland, was negotiated by Sir William Cecil and Nicholas Wotton.

Throughout the Scottish venture Norfolk displayed what were to prove characteristic qualities of changeability, half-heartedness, and suggestibility. He had originally opposed the whole Scottish venture and Cecil, its promoter. He was, however, flattered by his appointment as lieutenant-general and so became Cecil's political ally. He was frequently very critical of others involved in the venture. His letters, carefully recorded in a personal entry book while he was in the north, revealed feelings of harassment, a desire 'to fynysshe this warr nowe begonne' (*State Papers and Letters of Sir Ralph Sadler*, 1.721), and to get away from the far north, because 'this country and I can ill agree' (Williams, 63). At the same time there were frequent whispered criticisms that he was incompetent, disloyal, or anxious to prolong the conflict for personal advantage. There is, however, no reason to doubt Norfolk's sincerity when he repeatedly proclaimed his loyalty and sense of duty in his letters south.

In August 1560 Norfolk returned to the court. On Shrove Tuesday 1562 he jousted before the queen, who, in November of that year, appointed him privy councillor. In August 1564 he was in attendance when she visited Cambridge. During the 1560s he jostled for place and favour with William Cecil, and especially with the royal favourite Robert Dudley, who was made a privy councillor at the same time as Norfolk and created earl of Leicester in 1564. The rivalry between Norfolk and Leicester was intensified and complicated by their attitudes to the queen's marriage. The duke was implacably opposed to Leicester's aspirations to marry her, and supported the Austrian archduke's suit. In March 1564 they reputedly quarrelled in the presence of Elizabeth, who ordered them to resolve their differences. The event, or at least the form in which it supposedly occurred, may have been apocryphal. In any case some form of rapprochement between them occurred, for on 2 December Norfolk informed Cecil that in accordance with his advice he had written a letter of thanks to Leicester for some service rendered. He also expressed his friendship for Cecil, declared his devotion to the queen, and, typically, at the same time complained that 'her Hyenes hardlye thynkes enye Thynge well bestowyd apon me, be yt never so small' (Haynes and Murdin, 442). In 1566 Norfolk personally guaranteed that Leicester's interests would be safeguarded and successfully pressed him to support the Austrian Habsburg marriage suit, but their relationship continued to be a volatile one.

The related issues of marriage and succession, which tended to focus such court rivalries during the 1560s, became a central concern in the two sessions of the 1563–7 parliament. Norfolk, as earl marshal, was present at the opening and closing ceremonies, took his seat in the upper house, and was patron of eighteen borough seats in the Commons for the counties of Norfolk and Suffolk. In 1563 he attended the Lords on forty-nine of the fifty-seven recorded business sittings and was appointed to three bill committees. He was present in 1566–7 on only two-thirds of business sessions, but he was chairman of a committee to scrutinize a mining patents bill and he was named to three others. Furthermore in 1566–7 he became actively involved in the parliamentary agitation concerning the marriage and succession. As the prospect of royal marriage lessened, so a settlement of the succession grew in importance. Once again there was division: Norfolk favoured Katherine Grey and Leicester the Scottish queen, Mary Stuart—but there was a widespread desire for a solution. In the privy council on 12 October Norfolk sought the queen's co-operation; and twice he was a vocal member of parliamentary deputations to her, for which he received an angry royal rebuff.

During the 1560s Norfolk also experienced anguish in his personal life. His second wife, a devout protestant, died on 10 January 1564, three weeks after childbirth. The children of the marriage were Thomas *Howard, Lord Howard de Walden and later earl of Suffolk (1561–1626); three daughters, including Meg (later wife of the second earl of Dorset); and Lord William *Howard (1563–1640). On 29 January 1567 he married Elizabeth, *née* Leybourne, widow of Thomas, Lord Dacre of Gilsland, and mother of four children, George, Anne, Mary, and Elizabeth, but on 4 September she died in childbirth. Norfolk obtained a grant of the wardship of her children and schemed to absorb the Dacre inheritance into the Howard estate by a series of marriages between his children and stepchildren. Mary died young; so did George, Lord Dacre, who in May 1569 was crushed when a wooden vaulting horse fell on top of him. Nevertheless Norfolk proceeded with the scheme whereby Anne and Elizabeth became coheirs of Dacre estates and wives of his sons Philip and William. When their uncle, Leonard Dacre, asserted his claim to the estates as male heir, the case was heard not, as was usual, in the court of the earl marshal, Norfolk's own special jurisdiction, but by a special commission. The commissioners swiftly concluded in Norfolk's favour and so Howard influence was extended into the far north of England.

Initiation of the Norfolk–Mary Stuart marriage match, 1568–1569

Mary, queen of Scots, fled to England in May 1568. By then Norfolk, the wealthiest and most eligible peer of the realm, had been a widower for more than eight months. When Elizabeth was persuaded by her privy council to examine the Scots' charges against Mary Stuart, he, the earl of Sussex, and Sir Ralph Sadler, were appointed to meet the earl of Moray (Murray) at York in October, together with those named by the deposed Scottish queen and the Scottish regent. Until then Norfolk's focus had been the Austrian archduke's suit for Elizabeth's hand.

When his opinion was sought by the queen in 1567 he responded favourably but, as he wrote to Sussex in December, he was censured at court for this. Although he persisted in this sentiment, as indicated in a letter to Cecil on 'this 14th of cold April 1568' (*Salisbury MSS*, 1.355, no. 1170), it was no longer a possibility. Furthermore, as the prospects of Elizabeth's marriage faded Lady Katherine Grey died (February 1567), while her sister Mary had been in disgrace since 1564. Mary Stuart's position and claim as Elizabeth's successor were thereby strengthened.

One central concern of the York investigation into the Scottish queen's disagreements with her subjects was the extent to which Mary had been involved in the murder of her second husband, Henry, Lord Darnley. Norfolk appears to have been convinced, for some time at least, that she was culpable. Then, on 3 November 1568, Elizabeth notified him that the hearing, before an enlarged commission including Leicester and Cecil, had been transferred to London. The duke was required to inspect and report on the condition of the Berwick fortifications and garrison and the general state of the Scottish marches before journeying south to London. The seed of his ruin and death had already been sown when, during his time in York, he went hawking with Maitland of Lethington, one of the Scottish regent's commissioners. It was Maitland who suggested that a marriage between Scotland's deposed queen and England's pre-eminent noble could revive her fortunes, advance his, and resolve current Anglo-Scottish problems. This was not the first time that he had been considered as a possible consort. In December 1564 Elizabeth herself had forwarded the names of Norfolk, Leicester, and Darnley as suitable husbands, and in 1565 Maitland had recommended the duke as his preferred choice. In 1568, however, the circumstances were critically different. Mary was a deposed monarch, accused of murder and adultery, and Elizabeth was not consulted.

In the politics of intrigue and conspiracy which characterized the crisis years of Elizabeth's reign, 1568–72, Norfolk's role is at times difficult to detect, and his motives, obscured by a contradictory mixture of confidence and uncertainty, loyalty and ambition, are capable of conflicting interpretations. At times they are even impossible to determine. The problem is magnified by the double motives, shifting alignments, and calculated self-interest of most of those involved in the extended crisis. Nevertheless, there are some consistent traits in his behaviour during these years. He was susceptible to persuasion and easily influenced by others, among whom were both protestants—Maitland, the earls of Moray and Leicester—and Catholics, including his father-in-law Henry, earl of Arundel, the conspirator Ridolfi, Mary Stuart, and her ambassador, John Leslie, bishop of Ross. Norfolk proved to be incapable of acknowledging and confessing his errors, and he made repeated protestations of loyalty to the queen. He certainly had no calculated intention to commit treason.

Maitland's suggestion of a marriage appealed to Norfolk on several admittedly unrealistic counts. Mary could then be restored to the Scottish throne without imperilling

Elizabeth; in due course the English queen would recognize her as rightful successor; and one day he would be king consort throughout the British Isles. During the Westminster conference on Mary, in December 1568, Norfolk also had a clandestine meeting with Moray in Hampton Court Park at which the proposed marriage was discussed. What happened in the following weeks is unclear, because of the continuous intrigues among both Scottish and English politicians and the conflicting reports and rumours. It does seem clear, however, that despite his knowledge of the casket letters, which provided evidence of her adultery and her complicity in her husband's murder, by early 1569 Norfolk was determined to marry a woman whom he had never met. The extent of Queen Elizabeth's knowledge of developments is also uncertain, although in November 1568 she did enquire about rumours which she had heard. He reportedly answered that 'he did not only mislyke of suche Spechees, but also of suche a Mariadg'. According to a damning indictment of Norfolk's conduct, written by Secretary Cecil a year later,

> Although he had spoken with the Quenes Majesty, and had so ernestly myslyked both the Speche of Mariadg, and the Mariadg it self … he did directly, with other Lords, prosequute the Marriadg indede with the Quene of Scotts; not makyng the Quenes Majesty prive therof. (Haynes and Murdin, 574)

Norfolk, Queen Elizabeth, and the marriage match, 1569 At this point the marriage manoeuvrings became linked to the growing and widespread aristocratic hostility and resistance to Cecil. Both disgruntled protestant courtiers, such as Leicester and Pembroke, and Catholics, such as Arundel, Northumberland, and Westmorland, sought not only personal advancement but national security. This required improved Anglo-Spanish relations, which had recently deteriorated owing to the devoutly anti-Catholic Cecil's provocative actions, and settlement of the succession. Catholic nobles, especially in the north, favoured a Mary–Norfolk marriage, which would protect their faith and provide a secure succession. There developed a court conspiracy to remove Cecil, but in February 1569 the queen intervened to prevent it. The conspirators had engaged Norfolk's support, because he regarded Cecil's hostility to Mary as a major obstacle, but by May 1569 he had resumed his former friendly relations with the secretary. Leicester, Arundel, and Pembroke, foiled in their attempt to unseat Cecil, turned to promotion of the Mary–Norfolk marriage. Norfolk was now increasingly led by the various designs of Maitland, Moray, and the Scottish go-between, the bishop of Ross, by Leicester, Pembroke, and their go-between, Sir Nicholas Throckmorton, and by Mary through Ross. The problems and obstacles were numerous: Mary's abdication, adultery, complicity in murder, and her current marriage to the earl of Bothwell; the attitude of the Scots to her restoration; and Cecil's implacable hostility. There was also the crucial question, how would Elizabeth respond?

Increasingly Norfolk, who remained protestant and, as he saw it, a loyal subject, depended on the words and actions of others. Often they failed to confide in him, especially as some of the plans involved collaboration with Spain and even the liberation of Mary Stuart by force. Some of the northern nobles, who favoured the use of force, were hostile towards the duke and sympathetic to Leonard Dacre, who had lost the lawsuit over the family inheritance. In June 1569 Mary responded to the approaches of Leicester and others by giving her consent to a marriage match, but she asked the same question which perplexed Norfolk: how was Elizabeth's consent to be obtained? This was the crucial problem which caused everyone, not just Norfolk, to procrastinate. He looked to Moray in Scotland for action, writing to him on 1 July that he could not 'with honour proceed further till such time as he should remove all stumbling-blocks to more apparent proceedings' (Haynes and Murdin, 520). The Scottish regent, however, no longer approved of the marriage scheme and later that month he secured the defeat of an attempt to end Mary's marriage to Bothwell. In England, Leicester, who had previously stressed the need for the public marriage proposal to come from Scotland, agreed to approach the queen on his behalf. He insisted, however, that care must be taken to choose the most favourable opportunity. At a meeting of the privy council in late July from which Cecil was absent, there was overwhelming support for the proposition that Mary should be freed if she married an English nobleman. Even with this conciliar endorsement, however, neither Leicester nor Norfolk made a move.

On 5 August the duke went on progress with Elizabeth and the court in order to keep in touch with Leicester and prompt him to action. He also failed to respond to prompting from the queen; when they dined alone at her invitation and, at the end of the meal, 'she gave him a nip, saying "that she would wish me to take good head to my pillow … I was abashed at Her Majesty's speech", Norfolk confessed, "but I thought it not fit time nor place there to trouble her"' (Williams, 157). Finally it was Leicester who nervously seized the initiative. At the residence of the earl of Southampton at Titchfield he was smitten with a genuine or tactical ailment and besought the queen to visit him. There he gave a detailed account of the marriage scheme, with which she angrily confronted Norfolk later the same day 'commanding him to free himselfe of it, for the fidelity and loyalty sake which he ought to beare unto his Sovereign' (Camden, *Annales*, 212). From then on he was shunned at court, from which he withdrew without leave on 15 September 1569 and journeyed to London, visiting Pembroke *en route* to discuss the situation.

Norfolk's fall from favour, 1569–1570 The queen, alarmed by the possibility of attempts to liberate Mary or of armed insurrection, especially in the north where Catholic nobles looked to Norfolk for a signal, ordered him to return to the court, now housed at Windsor. When, on 22 September, he learned from Leicester that he would probably be sent to the Tower, he panicked and fled to Kenninghall in Norfolk. From there he advised Cecil that he was incapacitated by a fit of the ague, but promised to journey to court within a few days. He also wrote to the queen, swearing that he had declared everything to her and 'some of your Counsell; nor ever had any Intencion otherwyse to deale, then as I might obtayne your Highnes's favour to doo'. Next day (25 September), however, she ordered his return without delay or excuse, adding ominously that she 'never intended in Thought to ministre any thyng to yow, but as you shuld in Truth deserve' (Haynes and Murdin, 528–9). While *en route* for the court he sent an urgent dispatch to the northern earls not to rebel, 'for if they did, it should cost him his head' (Williams, 165).

On his arrival at St Albans on 2 October 1569 the duke was taken to Paul Wentworth's house at Burnham. There he was held a prisoner in the custody of Sir Henry Neville until 8 October, when he was transferred to the Tower, shortly before the northern uprising. His imprisonment prompted the publication of Thomas Norton's *A Discourse Touching the Pretended Match*, which questioned the presumption of a subject 'to seeke to match with a Competitor of this crowne without making his Soveraigne first privie thereof' (Graves, 162–3). Norfolk had known of the various schemes to liberate Mary and to raise rebellion on her behalf, but he had not been enthusiastic about them, while the battle over the Dacre inheritance had widened the gap between the protestant duke and the Catholic northerners. On 3 December 1569 he wrote to Elizabeth protesting that he had not been in league with the northern insurgents. Although a trial was contemplated Cecil showed the queen that his offences did not amount to a breach of existing treason statute laws. Unbeknown to them, however, Norfolk continued to correspond secretly in cipher with Mary Stuart. She affirmed her love and devotion, faithful to death, and he sent her rings at Christmas and at midsummer 1570. At almost the same time, 23 June, he was allowed to draft a voluntary written submission in which he acknowledged his error, craved the queen's forgiveness, and bound himself by his bond of allegiance to her 'never to deale in that Cause of Mariage of the Quene of Scottes, nor in any other Cause belonginge to her, but as your Majestie shall commaund me' (Haynes and Murdin, 597–8). In July he also sent hearty thanks to Cecil 'for your faythfull and fryndlye dealing on my Behalf, whereof, I assure you, I will not be forgetfull' (ibid., 596). On 3 August 1570 he was duly released from the Tower, where plague had occurred, but he was not allowed to return to Kenninghall, which he would never see again. Instead he was placed under virtual house arrest in his London residence, Howard House, where he passed his time in the supervision of its enlargement and embellishment.

Involvement in treasonable conspiracy During his enforced residence in Howard House the duke took no part in public life: so, in the parliament of April–May 1571, the earl of Worcester deputized for him as earl marshal, although he still secured the return of a dozen Commons members for Norfolk and Sussex boroughs. For a while after his release from the Tower he acted more cautiously towards Mary Stuart and was more circumspect about contact with her. Nevertheless he did not observe the promises made in his

submission to Elizabeth, who had emphatically registered her hostility to any association between them, especially a marriage match. Furthermore, in 1571 the susceptible duke was drawn into conspiracy, because he and others continued to believe that such a marriage was both possible and desirable.

Early in 1571 Mary began to seek a solution to her problems outside England. Roberto Ridolfi, an energetic and imaginative Florentine banker, who had already been in Walsingham's custody for his implication in the events of 1569, acted as papal agent and intermediary between Mary, her agent, the bishop of Ross, her English supporters, and Spain. An extensive, overmanned, and vulnerable conspiratorial network, including the servants of the principal participants, planned the release of the Scottish queen, her marriage to the duke, and, with Spanish military assistance, Elizabeth's removal in favour of Mary and the restoration of Catholicism in England. The success of the plan required Norfolk's approval and involvement. An initial approach by the bishop of Ross, forwarding ciphered letters from Mary, failed to secure his support. However, Norfolk reluctantly agreed to meet Ridolfi, as a result of which he gave verbal approval to the request for Spanish military assistance. His name was also subscribed to letters to the pope, Philip II, and the duke of Alva, Philip's commander in the Netherlands.

The Ridolfi plot was exposed more as a result of a series of accidents than of deliberate official investigation. Servants of Mary's agent, the bishop of Ross, and of Norfolk did not prove adept at avoiding suspicion and detection as they travelled with ciphered letters and money for their supporters. On about 12 April 1571 Charles Bailly, Ross's servant, was caught with letters for him at Dover. Then, on 29 August, Norfolk's secretaries William Barker and Robert Higford entrusted to Thomas Browne, a Shrewsbury draper, what purported to be a bag of silver coin for delivery to Laurence Bannister, one of the duke's officials in the north of England. Browne grew suspicious of the bag's weight, opened it, and discovered £600 in gold from the French ambassador and destined for Scotland on Mary's behalf. It also contained ciphered letters. Because he knew that Norfolk was under suspicion Browne reported his find to Cecil, now Lord Burghley. Higford and Barker were examined, the letters were partly deciphered, and a search for the cipher key at Howard House uncovered a ciphered letter from Mary Stuart hidden under a doormat. From this point the duke's failure to honour his submission was revealed and his complicity in a wider treasonable conspiracy was established.

Norfolk's servants were arrested and interrogated and confessions were extracted from them by threats or application of torture. Sir Thomas Smith and Thomas Wilson were sent to confront Norfolk, who claimed that the £600 was for his own private purposes. The deciphered letter, however, proved that he was lying. Unaware of his servants' confessions or the survival of letters which, contrary to his instructions, had not been burnt, he denied the charges against him. On 7 September the queen's warrant for conveying him to the Tower arrived. Thereupon the duke admitted a degree of involvement in the transmission of money and correspondence to Mary's Scottish supporters, before he was taken through London to the Tower. A servant of the Spanish ambassador reported that those who witnessed this were vocal in Norfolk's favour. Guerau de Spes, the ambassador, referred to 'this popularity of his amongst the common people'. He observed that 'the concourse of people was so large and the shouts so general that a very little more and he would have been liberated' (*CSP Spain*, 1509–25, 335).

In the following weeks the duke and his servants were subjected to repeated examinations which, together with his confessions, confirmed his disloyalty to Elizabeth, the breach of his own submission to her, and his complicity in conspiracy. They also provided the evidence to prepare the indictment and proceed against him at law. Care was taken to cultivate public opinion in preparation for the trial. Whether or not there was justice in Thomas Norton's scornful explanation of the duke's favour with the commonalty, that it was due to 'a kinde of familiaritie used towardes them in publike sport, as in shoting and cockefightes' (Norton, fol. Avv), he was undoubtedly popular. On 12 October Recorder Fleetwood of the city of London delivered an oration in the Guildhall to its governors and 'a great multitude of other Citizens'. In it he described the recent 'great and daungerous conspiracies' and (without naming Norfolk) called for the condign punishment of those who sought 'to avaunce any singular person now apprehended by her Majesties authoritie for most just causes' (Fleetwood, sigs. A2–A4, B4–B2, B4–C1).

Indictment and trial for treason In December 1571 a comprehensive indictment was found against the duke in Middlesex for

> having conspired and imagined to deprive the queen of her crown and dignity, and compassed to excite sedition, to cause great slaughter amongst the queen's lieges, to levy war and rebellion against the queen, to subvert the government, to change and alter the pure religion established in the kingdom, and to bring in strangers and aliens to invade the realm, and to carry on a bitter war against the queen. (Cooper, *Ath. Cantab.*, 1.305)

He was brought to trial by his peers in Westminster Hall on 16 January 1572. His request for legal counsel was disallowed on the grounds that it was not permissible in cases of high treason. Three charges of treason were then summarized by Serjeant Nicholas Barham from the lengthy indictment to which he had pleaded not guilty: that he practised to deprive the queen of her crown and life and thereby 'to alter the whole state of government of this realm'; that he had succoured the English rebels who fled after the failed northern rising of 1569; and that he had given assistance to the queen's Scottish enemies (*State trials*, 1.968). The first of these, upon which Barham focused, was the principal treason. It concerned in particular Norfolk's pursuit of the marriage project. As Barham told the peers who were the duke's judges, 'He … that will marry a wife that layeth claime to a Kingdome, doth likewise affect the same Kingdome' (Camden, *Annales*, 289).

The government case was thoroughly prepared and the charges were supported with documentary proof, the written confessions of the bishop of Ross, his servant Bailly, the duke's secretaries, and other servants, and his own admissions. Furthermore, as was usual in a treason trial, the accused was not able to question his accusers, he did not receive a copy of the indictment, and he had to contest with a team of skilled professional lawyers. At first, however, Norfolk assumed an air of aristocratic disdain in his responses to the mounting evidence against him. It was reinforced by what appeared to be a disbelief that the greatest noble in the land, scion of an ancient family, could be treated in this way. Indeed this sense of immunity was a recurrent though not consistent feature of his disloyal conduct from the time of the commission at York in 1568. He was also dismissive of the evidence against him because of the inferiority of those who provided it. The bishop of Ross, for example, 'is a Scot' and Barker 'is not of credit'. Counsel responded that 'You may not stand upon your honour and difference of degree, and thereby limit how far they are to be credited' (*State trials*, 1.978, 1019, 1022). Gradually, as the trial proceeded, the duke's haughty demeanour gave way to defensiveness and then resignation. At its end he was convicted of high treason, condemned to death, and returned to the Tower to await execution.

Last months and execution Norfolk, however, passed more than four months awaiting execution because of the queen's reluctance to authorize it. Warrants were repeatedly signed and then cancelled. Meanwhile he wrote letters to her, in which he still endeavoured to persuade her of his loyalty, and to his children, in which he belatedly offered the wisdom of experience:

> Beware of the court, except it be to do your prince service, and that as near as you can in the meanest degree; for place hath no certainty, either a man by following thereof hath too much to worldly pomp, which in the end throws him down headlong, or else he lieth there unsatisfied. (Williams, 241–2)

He also reaffirmed his religious position because

> perchance you may heretofore heard, or perchance hereafter shall hear, false bruits that I was a papist. But trust unto it, I never since I knew what religion meant, I thank God, was of other mind than now you shall hear that I die in. (ibid.)

On 26 January 1572 Norfolk was ceremonially degraded from the Order of the Garter, when his banner of arms, mantles, helm, and crest were cast into the ditch of Windsor Castle. Thereafter he passed his time in organizing his affairs, writing to his servants, especially his steward William Dyx to whom he sent a copy of the New Testament, and receiving visits from Alexander Nowell, dean of St Paul's. Then, on 8 May, parliament assembled. It had been called by a reluctant queen, under pressure to act against Mary Stuart. The House of Commons used the opportunity to agitate relentlessly for the death of the man who had striven to marry her and to advance her cause. Elizabeth finally yielded to pressure, perhaps in the hope that, by sacrificing Thomas Howard to the wolves, she could spare a fellow queen. According to an anonymous eyewitness, '[S]trait after vii acloke' on the morning of 2 June, and accompanied by Dean Nowell and his old tutor John Foxe, Norfolk addressed the crowd from the scaffold on Tower Hill. Despite attempts to cut him short he acknowledged his faults, but denied the most serious accusations, reaffirmed his protestantism, 'telleth how gratiously he is bounde to the Queen's Majestie for the mercie which of her self she hath shewed [and] wissheth her long continuance to the maintenance of religion' (Hartley, 1.332–3). He was beheaded and buried in the chapel of St Peter ad Vincula in the Tower.

Victim or villain? Thomas Howard was a man of contrasts and this helps to explain the diversity of opinions about his culpability or innocence. On the one hand, there was the public image of the handsome and mannered outdoor aristocrat, the lover of field sports and tennis, and a responsible, paternal 'king in his country'. On the other there was the socially powerful but personally weak magnate who practised dissimulation, lacked the courage to be honest with his queen, allowed himself to be exploited by others, and failed to learn the lessons of experience. He was also a man of ambition, in pursuit of which he imperilled both monarch and realm. William Camden wondered at the contrast and apparent contradiction:

> Divers of the wiser sort ... passed their censures diversly, some from an apprehension they had of great feare and danger [which] might have ensued, had hee survived; others, commiserating the case of one so nobly borne, so gentle by nature, so comely of personage, of so manly an aspect, so compleat in all parts, to perish so pittyously. (Camden, *Annales*, 300)

Norfolk's conduct raised doubts about his religious loyalties, which were certainly questioned by some of his contemporaries. Thomas Norton itemized reasons for believing that 'he should not be setled in religion': that his son was educated by a Roman Catholic, that he put his trust in 'the chiefest Papistes of this realme', that his last marriage was 'with a Papist', and that there was 'this pretended match' to Mary Stuart (Norton, sig. A3). As the House of Commons pressed for Norfolk's execution in 1572 many members echoed Norton's views about the duke's religious disloyalty. Their position was reinforced by the information given to a joint parliamentary committee by the queen's learned counsel. It was natural for members to be convinced of Norfolk's attachment to Catholicism when 'The Pope writt ii lettres, one to the Queen of Scots and one to the Duke in cyphre, promisyng ayde' in order to achieve the objectives of the Ridolfi conspiracy (Hartley, 1.270–72). This highlights, however, the contradictions and inconsistencies of Norfolk's character and career. He stoutly and consistently professed his protestantism, not only to his queen but also privately to his family, and even to the point of death.

Norfolk's political conduct is also open to question and criticism. To some extent he was led on and then deserted by confederates, and there is some justification for the way he projected himself as the instrument and victim of others' ambition. Nevertheless his own lack of foresight, his capacity for deceit, his aristocratic aloofness, and his sense of immunity all contributed to his fall. Furthermore

he persisted in denials of treason, even when charges against him had been substantially proved. While he was not an enemy of queen or kingdom, when he failed to observe his submission of 1570 and when he tacitly accepted aspects of the Ridolfi conspiracy he was guilty of disloyal, even treasonable, conduct.

MICHAEL A. R. GRAVES

Sources N. Williams, *Thomas Howard, fourth duke of Norfolk* (1964) · GEC, *Peerage*, new edn, 9.620–23 · *A collection of state papers ... left by William Cecil, Lord Burghley*, ed. S. Haynes and W. Murdin, 2 vols. (1740–59) · *Calendar of the manuscripts of the most hon. the marquis of Salisbury*, 1–2, HMC, 9 (1883–8) · W. T. MacCaffrey, *The shaping of the Elizabethan regime: Elizabethan politics, 1558–1572* (1968) · *State trials*, 1.957–1050 · W. Camden, *Annales: the true and royall history of the famous Empresse Elizabeth*, trans. A. Darcie (1625) · W. Camden, *The historie of the most renowned and victorious princesse Elizabeth*, trans. R. N. [R. Norton] (1630) · Cooper, *Ath. Cantab.*, 1.302–5 · *JHL*, 1 (1509–77), 492–727 · C. Hamshere, 'The Ridolfi plot, 1571', *History Today*, 26 (1976), 32–9 · BL, Lansdowne MSS 4.37; 8.44; 9.64; 11.78; 17.94; 58.24 · M. A. R. Graves, *Thomas Norton: the parliament man* (1994) · T. E. Hartley, ed., *Proceedings in the parliaments of Elizabeth I*, 1 (1981) · T. Norton, *A discourse touching the pretended match betwene the duke of Norfolke and the queene of Scottes* (1569) · W. Fleetwood, *The effect of the declaration made in the Guildhall by M. recorder of London, concerning the late attemptes of the quenes majesties evill, seditious, and disobedient subjectes* (1571) · HoP, *Commons, 1558–1603* · F. Edwards, *The marvellous chance: Thomas Howard, fourth duke of Norfolk, and the Ridolphi plot, 1570–1572* (1968) · D. E. Rhodes, 'A party at Norwich in 1562', *Norfolk Archaeology*, 37 (1978–80), 116–20 · *The state papers and letters of Sir Ralph Sadler*, ed. A. Clifford, 2 vols. (1809) · *CSP Spain, 1568–79*

Archives Arundel Castle, Sussex, corresp. and papers · BL, Harley MSS, papers · BL, Cotton MSS, corresp. and papers

Likenesses oils, 1550–75 (after S. van der Meulen), Audley End House, Essex · H. Eworth, oils, 1563, priv. coll. [*see illus.*] · attrib. S. van der Meulen, portrait, 1565, priv. coll. · L. de Heere, pencil and black chalk drawing, *c*.1569, repro. in Edwards, *Marvellous chance*, frontispiece · J. Houbraken, line engraving, pubd 1735 (after the English school, *c*.1560), NG Ire. · C. Turner, mezzotint, pubd 1810 (after H. Holbein junior), NPG · attrib. J. Belkamp, oils (after type, *c*.1563), Knole, Kent · R. Elstrack, line engraving, BM · B. Rebecca, oils (after type by S. van der Meulen?, *c*.1565), Audley End House, Essex · oils (posthumous), Audley End House, Essex · portrait, priv. coll. · portrait, Royal Collection · watercolour drawing, NPG

Howard, Thomas, first earl of Suffolk (1561–1626), naval officer and administrator, was born on 24 August 1561, the elder son of Thomas *Howard, fourth duke of Norfolk (1538–1572), and his second wife, Margaret Dudley, Lady Dudley (1540–1564), daughter and heir of Thomas *Audley, Baron Audley of Walden.

Early years and education On his mother's death on 10 January 1564 Howard inherited the estate of Saffron Walden and other properties of his maternal grandfather. He apparently spent a short time at St John's College, Cambridge, was later granted honorific admission to Gray's Inn on 2 February 1598, then in 1605 was created MA at Cambridge and subsequently incorporated at Oxford.

Writing to his children from the Tower in January 1572, the duke of Norfolk commented 'Tom, you have ever from your infancy been given to be stubborn' (GEC, *Peerage*, 12(1), 465n.), but urged the boy to consider marrying his stepsister Mary Dacre (1563–1578), second of the three daughters and coheirs of Elizabeth Leybourne, the duke's

Thomas Howard, first earl of Suffolk (1561–1626), by unknown artist, 1598

third wife, and her previous husband Thomas, fourth Lord Dacre of Gilsland. The marriage took place before 9 May 1577 but Mary died childless in April 1578 at Walden. In or before 1583 Howard married another heiress, Katherine (b. in or after 1564, d. 1638), widow of Richard Rich and eldest daughter and coheir of Sir Henry Knyvett of Charlton, Wiltshire, and Elizabeth, daughter and heir of Sir James Stumpe of Bromham, Wiltshire [see Howard, Katherine, countess of Suffolk]. Katherine was a noted beauty widely suspected of loose morals; the couple had at least seven sons, including the politician Edward *Howard, and four daughters, the youngest of whom died of pleurisy in 1609.

Service under Elizabeth Howard was restored in blood as Lord Thomas Howard in December 1584. He captained the *Golden Lion* in the fleet fending off the Spanish Armada and after the decisive attack on Calais was knighted on the *Ark* on 26 July 1588 by his cousin Charles Howard, Lord Howard of Effingham. In 1591 he commanded the expedition which hoped to capture the Spanish treasure fleet; all his ships prudently retreated when heavily outnumbered,

except the *Revenge* under Sir Richard Grenville, with fatal consequences. As vice-admiral Howard took a leading part in the largely successful Cadiz expedition of 1596. The queen was fond of her 'good Thomas' (*CSP dom.*, 1595–7, 453) and he was elected knight of the Garter in April 1597. In June he sailed as vice-admiral of the fleet on the 'Islands voyage' to the Azores, an expensive failure to which he had contributed large sums of his own money. In autumn 1597 he fell dangerously ill and as a possibly final mark of honour Elizabeth summoned him as Lord Howard de Walden to the parliament which opened on 24 October. He survived but was unable to be present in the Lords until January 1598. In April 1598 he became lord lieutenant of Cambridgeshire and the Isle of Ely, in recognition of his estates in East Anglia. He commanded the defensive fleet in the Downs in the summer of 1599 and was appointed constable of the Tower of London on 13 February 1601, as an additional security measure after Essex's revolt. On 19 February he was one of the commission of peers who tried the earls of Essex and Southampton, and he was also present on 25 February 1601 at Essex's execution.

Throughout the 1590s Howard participated in privateering ventures, often alongside Sir Robert Cecil, but never achieved the lucrative captures for which he hoped. Howard was sworn high steward of Cambridge University in February 1601, when Cecil succeeded Essex as chancellor, and continued in the post until 1614. His friendship with Cecil proved useful in the tense closing years of the reign, and on 28 December 1602 he became acting lord chamberlain of the royal household, a key post. Elizabeth visited him at the Charterhouse, his grand London home which had formerly belonged to his father, and was lavishly entertained there in January 1603.

Service under James I It is possible that Howard was one of the still-unidentified correspondents drawn by his uncle Lord Henry *Howard and Cecil into the secret circle preparing for the accession of James VI and I. As the queen lay dying the privy council invited Howard together with two other noblemen, the earl of Northumberland and Lord Cobham, to reinforce their deliberations. Howard was immediately favoured by the new king, who at Berwick on his way south on 6 April 1603 appointed him lord chamberlain of the household in place of the ailing Lord Hunsdon, and on the following day made him a privy councillor. Howard greeted the king at Theobalds, Cecil's country mansion, and after the royal arrival in London was visited by him at the Charterhouse in May. On 21 July 1603 Howard was created earl of Suffolk, and was appointed one of the commissioners for making knights of the Bath at the coronation of the king and queen on 25 July. Between February 1604 and February 1618 he also served as a joint commissioner for the office of earl marshal, and became lord lieutenant of Suffolk in 1605.

Tassis, the Spanish ambassador sent to England in 1604 to negotiate the treaty ending the Armada war, thought Suffolk sufficiently amenable to the cause of peace to be worth rewarding with a gift. However, the countess of Suffolk, whom Tassis considered a Roman Catholic sympathizer, was so valuable as an informant and adviser that she easily topped his potential pension list. Cecil, whose mistress she was widely assumed to be, excused her greed, telling the Spanish ambassador that the Suffolks were desperately in need of money and that he shared the Spanish pension with them. All the indications suggest that Suffolk was far less pro-Spanish and pro-Catholic than his countess. In 1603 and again in 1618 he acted as a commissioner for the banishing of Jesuits and seminary priests, and he bitterly resented allegations that he had urged the king to enter an alliance with Spain. Nevertheless the countess was generally perceived as the stronger character in matters of politics, religion, and family finance.

By autumn 1605 Salisbury, Lord Henry Howard (now earl of Northampton), Edward Somerset, fourth earl of Worcester, and Suffolk had emerged as the king's most trusted privy councillors. On 26 October 1605 they were about to sit down to supper together at Whitehall when Lord Monteagle arrived with the anonymous letter obscurely warning of the Gunpowder Plot. On 4 November, Suffolk as lord chamberlain conducted a tour of inspection of the palace of Westminster to ensure that all was ready for the state opening of parliament the next day. He spotted a large pile of brushwood; the king instructed Suffolk's brother-in-law, Sir Thomas *Knyvett, keeper of the palace, to investigate further, and the barrels of gunpowder were found. Subsequently Suffolk was one of the commissioners who investigated the conspiracy, then on 27 January 1606 tried the plotters. In November 1605 he also succeeded the disgraced earl of Northumberland, suspected of involvement in the plot, as captain of the king's band of gentlemen pensioners, handing the office over to his eldest son, Theophilus *Howard, in July 1614.

James twitted Salisbury, Northampton, and Suffolk as his 'trinity of knaves' and teased the fair-haired 'honest big Suffolk' (Letters of King James VI and I, 234, 250, 257) both for his girth and for his wife's morals. Yet at the same time the king thought him loyal and reliable. The families of Howard and Cecil were further linked by the marriage in December 1608 of Salisbury's son and heir William with Catharine, Suffolk's third daughter. Whatever his relationship with Lady Suffolk, in his will Salisbury praised the sincerity, constancy, honour, and virtue of his close friend, with whom he had counted it a great felicity to exchange his dearest thoughts. After Salisbury's death in 1612 the king entrusted the treasury to four commissioners of whom Suffolk was one. The following year Suffolk supported his eldest daughter, Frances *Howard, a court beauty like her mother, in her desire to divorce Robert *Devereux, third earl of Essex, to whom she had been married in January 1606. She wished instead to marry the Scottish royal favourite Sir Robert *Carr. A genial father, Suffolk cannot have been indifferent to the prospect of further promotion that the alliance would bring, although he disliked Carr. Frances married Carr, newly created earl of Somerset, in December 1613. On 8 July 1614 Suffolk succeeded his late cousin Northampton as chancellor of Cambridge, and on 11 July became lord treasurer. In an oblique criticism of Salisbury, the king told Suffolk that he 'made him Treasurer for his fidelity and integrity,

not for his Greek and Latin, his epigrams and orations' (Letters of John Chamberlain, 1.548). As Somerset at once succeeded his father-in-law as lord chamberlain, the extended Suffolk family now dominated the court, and in March 1615 Suffolk entertained the king lavishly at Cambridge, staying at St John's while his countess held receptions at Magdalene, founded by Suffolk's grandfather Lord Audley.

The time of glory was to be short. By August 1615 James was deeply attracted to George Villiers, the future duke of Buckingham, and during the summer progress the king learned that Sir Thomas Overbury, lately a prisoner in the Tower, had almost certainly been poisoned. It emerged that Frances Howard and probably also her husband were deeply implicated. Found guilty of murder in May 1616, they were freed in January 1622 but never returned to court. James accused Suffolk of assisting Somerset in seeking to suppress the early investigation of the scandal, but he continued as lord treasurer and even attempted to help his imprisoned son-in-law by proffering an advantageous financial settlement. However, the enmity felt by both Suffolk and his wife towards the new favourite Buckingham led them to try to supplant him by another handsome young man, 'tricking and prancking him up' (Letters of John Chamberlain, 2.144) to attract the king's attention. This ploy succeeded only in kindling Buckingham's anger, and in summer 1618 he made sure that James became aware of allegations that creditors owed money by the crown found themselves badgered by Lady Suffolk. A large bribe to her was necessary before they were able to obtain payment from the exchequer. Enquiries were mounted and Suffolk was suspended from the lord treasurership, then dismissed on 19 July 1619. Since January 1619 he had been pleading ill health in an attempt to avoid a trial, while the countess suffered an attack of smallpox which destroyed her famous looks. Suffolk also submitted privately to the king. All these delaying efforts failed and in October 1619 he and his wife, together with their crony the exchequer official Sir John Bingley, were prosecuted for corruption in the court of Star Chamber, under five headings: fraud in jewels, indirect dealing concerning the ordnance, abuse in the alum works, misemployment of the king's treasure, and extortion upon the subject. Named a commissioner in May 1616 for the surrender of Flushing and Brill, the cautionary towns returned to the Dutch, Suffolk was accused of retaining for years in his own hands the sum of £3000 received as part-payment to the crown, together with moneys intended for Ireland. In addition the countess and Bingley bargained with creditors, barring access to the lord treasurer unless they were rewarded. Sir Francis Bacon, prosecuting, compared Lady Suffolk to a shopwife with Bingley as her apprentice, touting for custom. After an eleven-day hearing that attracted wide attention, on 13 November 1619 they were found guilty on all counts, fined £30,000, and sentenced to be imprisoned at the king's pleasure.

After only ten days in the Tower of London the couple were released, and at once applied to Buckingham to intercede for them, but Suffolk angered James afresh by placing his lands in the hands of trustees and removing all the furniture from his houses in a blatant attempt to avoid any seizure of his property. The king even threatened a further Star Chamber case for fraudulent conveyance. Buckingham, once convinced that the Howard interest at court had been comprehensively destroyed, intervened to arrange an audience, and in February 1620 Suffolk was allowed to kiss the king's hands. Subsequently the fine was remitted, apart from £7000 which James demanded in order to pay the debts of a Scottish courtier, Lord Haddington, and in 1623 a marriage was arranged between Suffolk's seventh son and the daughter of a Buckingham client. Suffolk never returned to high office, but was active in the House of Lords in 1621, as well as serving as a commissioner for ecclesiastical causes in 1620 and again in January 1625. He retained until his death the chancellorship of Cambridge, and was reappointed by Charles I in 1625 to the offices of lord lieutenant of Suffolk, of Cambridgeshire and Ely, and of Dorset (held from 1613).

Finances and final years Despite his bluff seafaring manner, Suffolk proved one of the most extravagant courtiers at the extravagant Jacobean court. In Elizabeth's reign his costly naval ventures brought him near to bankruptcy, and he borrowed heavily despite some help from the queen and a grant of the customs on gold and silver thread imported from Venice. He was saved from financial disaster by the accession of James, which brought him valuable court office, including board and lodging, together with the regrant of part of the sequestered Howard estates. Suffolk at once bought land, enhancing his properties in East Anglia. A series of customs farms between 1604 and 1613, including that on currants, also helped redeem his finances, while he and his sons further benefited from the deaths of various relatives. His uncle Northampton in 1614 bequeathed him Charing Cross, his luxurious London mansion, to replace the Charterhouse, which Suffolk was forced to sell in 1611. Thereafter Suffolk's promotion to the lord treasurership led to another series of lucrative deals with, and cheap loans from, the customs farmers. There can be no doubt that his tenure of the lord treasurership greatly worsened the pervasive corruption of the Jacobean court, with its subordination of the royal finances to private gain and the consequent alienation of public and parliamentary opinion. Yet none of this was enough to stave off bankruptcy, and by 1618 Suffolk owed £40,000 in bonds and mortgages.

The prime causes of his indebtedness have been described as 'excessive building and excessive children' (Stone, 282). Audley End in Essex, begun in 1603 and completed in 1616, was easily the largest private house in England. Suffolk told the king that including all the furniture it had cost him £200,000, and although the sum seems exaggerated, the upkeep rapidly proved too great for the family. Undeterred, after inheriting Northampton's palatial townhouse he added a capacious new wing fronting the Thames. In addition Lady Suffolk built Charlton Park, a handsome brick mansion with striking similarities to Robert Cecil's Hatfield, on her inherited Knyvett estates

near Malmesbury. Their second son was settled there by 1620.

The eleven children were inevitably expensive to bring up and marry off. Upholding the high social profile of his family, Suffolk lavishly provided for their numerous appearances in masques, running at tilt, and other court entertainments. He was also generous in sacrificing his short-term income to enhance the long-term financial prospects of his offspring, ensuring that they all made advantageous matches. He settled substantial sums on his sons to match their brides' landed estates, while three of his daughters were at enormous cost married to the most prominent members of the court nobility. The result was that Suffolk was never able to clear his heavy debts and his heir was left seriously encumbered with accumulated financial problems.

Suffolk died at his Charing Cross house on 28 May 1626 and was buried on 4 June in Saffron Walden parish church in the Howard vault. His widow survived in obscurity until 1638.   PAULINE CROFT

Sources GEC, *Peerage*, new edn, vol. 12/1 · *CSP dom., 1588–1626* · *Calendar of the manuscripts of the most hon. the marquis of Salisbury*, 24 vols., HMC, 9 (1883–1976), vols. 8–22 · *The letters of John Chamberlain*, ed. N. E. McClure, 2 vols. (1939) · *Letters of King James VI & I*, ed. G. P. V. Akrigg (1984) · K. R. Andrews, *Elizabethan privateering* (1964) · Bodl. Oxf., MS Ashmole 1729, fols. 62–74 · A. J. Loomie, 'Sir Robert Cecil and the Spanish embassy', *BIHR*, 42 (1969), 30–57 · L. Stone, *Family and fortune: studies in aristocratic finance in the sixteenth and seventeenth centuries* (1973)
Archives Bodl. Oxf., corresp. and papers | CKS, corresp. with Lionel Cranfield
Likenesses portrait, 1598, Ranger's House, Blackheath [*see illus.*] · attrib. J. Belkamp, oils, c.1614 (with Garter George), Knole, Kent · R. Elstrack, line engraving, c.1614, BM, NPG · style of D. Mytens, oils, 1617 (*Tho. Howard earle of Suffolk ld treasurer of England*), NMM; repro. in *Concise catalogue of oil paintings in the National Maritime Museum* (1988) · oils, 1617, NMM · T. Blood, stipple (after F. Zuccaro), BM, NPG; repro. in E. Lodge, *Portraits of illustrious personages in Great Britain* · oils (with Lesser George; after type of c.1605), NPG
Wealth at death estate heavily encumbered at death: Stone, *Family and fortune*

Howard, Thomas, fourteenth earl of Arundel, fourth earl of Surrey, and first earl of Norfolk (1585–1646), art collector and politician, was born at Finchingfield, Essex, on 7 July 1585, the only son of Philip *Howard, thirteenth earl of Arundel (1557–1595), and his wife, Anne Dacre [see Howard, Anne, countess of Arundel (1557–1630)], daughter and coheir of Thomas, Lord Dacre. He was grandson to Thomas *Howard, fourth duke of Norfolk, executed for treason in 1572. Both parents were Roman Catholics, regarded with suspicion by the government, and shortly after his son's birth Philip was imprisoned in the Tower of London, where he died ten years later, after being convicted of treason in 1589. This meant the loss of the Arundel title and confiscation of his property, including that brought to him by his wife.

Early life and young adulthood The young Thomas Howard, known in his youth by the courtesy title of Lord Maltravers, therefore grew up in greatly straitened circumstances under the influence of an embittered mother. From earliest childhood he was taught that the titles and properties

Thomas Howard, fourteenth earl of Arundel, fourth earl of Surrey, and first earl of Norfolk (1585–1646), by Sir Peter Paul Rubens, 1629

that were his birthright, as heir to the greatest noble family in England, had been taken from him through two corrupt judicial sentences. This upbringing left a permanent imprint on his character, giving him a fierce pride in his ancestry, an intense desire to recover everything that his father and grandfather had lost, and an aloof and prickly demeanour that contemporaries variously interpreted as nobility or arrogance. Despite its animus, the earl of Clarendon's pen portrait suggests the effects of a lonely and bereaved childhood on Arundel's mature personality:

> He was a man supercilious and proud, who lived always within himself and to himself … so that he seemed to live as it were in another nation, his house being a place to which all men resorted who resorted to no other place; strangers, or such who affected to look like strangers. (Clarendon, *Hist. rebellion*, 1.69)

But this haughtiness was tempered by a sense of his responsibility as England's premier nobleman, voracious curiosity about foreign cultures, and generosity towards people who shared his enthusiasms and won his trust.

According to an early biographer the young Maltravers was educated at Westminster School, where he would have studied under William Camden, before proceeding to Trinity College, Cambridge, and rounding out his education by a tour of the continent (Hervey, 34). Although the loss of Westminster's records makes this account impossible to verify, it seems plausible and would help explain Arundel's lifelong interest in antiquarian pursuits

and later patronage of other Westminster scholars, notably Sir Robert Cotton and John Selden. As a young man he also fell under the influence of Gilbert *Talbot, seventh earl of Shrewsbury, whose daughter Alathea (*d.* 1654) he married in September 1606. Shrewsbury was an early collector of paintings, who passed on his enthusiasm to both his daughter and his son-in-law.

By the outset of James I's reign the Howard family had begun to recover from its disastrous loss of royal favour, chiefly through the careers of Maltravers's uncles, Henry *Howard, first earl of Northampton, and Charles *Howard, first earl of Nottingham. The success of these relatives was something of a mixed blessing, since they acquired from the crown many properties that had once belonged to the senior Howard line. But it did facilitate Thomas's restoration in blood by act of parliament on 14 April 1604, which brought the restoration of his father's title, as well as his entry into the court, where despite a disappointing début as a jouster on 5 March 1606 his standing steadily improved. On 17 July 1607 the king and the earl of Salisbury stood godfather at the baptism of his first son, James. The following year he regained possession of Arundel House on the Strand from Nottingham, reportedly for £4000. About this time he joined the circle around Henry, prince of Wales, after whom he named a second son, born on 15 August 1608. He participated in 'Prince Henry's barriers', a joust embellished with verse by Ben Jonson and scenery designed by Inigo Jones (January 1610), and was installed as knight of the Garter, along with Prince Charles and the royal favourite Robert Carr, earl of Somerset, in May 1611. A year later he and his wife entertained Prince Henry and Prince Charles with a May day banquet at their suburban mansion in Highgate.

First trips abroad and formation of the collection Arundel's participation in Prince Henry's court brought him into contact with immigrant artists like Constaninio de Servi and Saloman de Caus, as well as other young aristocrats interested in continental European cultures. His own fascination with the arts flourished in this environment, giving him a reputation as an expert. In March 1610 Sir David Murray told Salisbury that if he was unable to attend court with the paintings he had just acquired, 'you may send my Lord of Arundel as deputy to set forth the praise of your pictures' (*Salisbury MSS*, 24 vols., 1883–1976, 21.39). By this time Arundel was also patronizing antiquaries, including Cotton, with whom he formed a lifelong friendship, and John Hayward, whom he retained to compile a history of the Howard family (BL, Cotton MS Julius CIII, fol. 204).

In July 1612 Arundel obtained a licence to travel abroad for six months to seek a cure for his consumption. He departed for Spa in the Spanish Netherlands, probably stopping along the way to visit the duke of Aerschot's picture collection in Brussels. He met the painter Hendrik van Balen and, through him, Peter Paul Rubens, to whom he sat for a now lost portrait. In September he proceeded to Padua, where he learned of Prince Henry's death, which had occurred on 6 November. He returned to London remaining long enough to carry the sword of state during the wedding of Princess Elizabeth to the elector palatine in February 1613 and participate in the celebratory jousts, but in April he obtained a licence to return to the continent with his wife for three years for reasons of health.

The Arundels set out as part of the official entourage escorting the elector and Elizabeth on their journey through the Netherlands to Heidelberg, where they arrived on 7 June. After a week's stay Arundel and his wife departed with the duke of Lennox for Strasbourg, then headed south through Basel to Milan. Their party included Prince Henry's former surveyor Inigo Jones, who had not yet distinguished himself as an architect but who did speak Italian and was already acquainted with northern Italy. Experiences shared on this trip, which were fundamental in educating both Jones and Arundel in Italian visual culture, cemented a lifelong relationship between them. After a quick visit to Parma, abruptly terminated when the Spanish governor failed to pay him the respect he believed due to his rank, Arundel took up residence near the hot springs of Albano, a few miles outside Padua.

Arundel interrupted his cure to fulfil the diplomatic assignment of conveying James I's respect and support to the government of Venice, which had recently emerged from a serious dispute with the papacy. This mission assured him a lavish reception, by a welcoming party that included Gregorio Barbarigo, a cultivated and well-read follower of Paolo Sarpi, whose family had bought up the contents of Titian's studio after the artist's death. Barbarigo arranged a *feste di gentildonne* to conclude the earl's visit and must have educated him in the city's rich artistic culture. Arundel's connections with Venetian nobles probably also facilitated Jones's introduction to the architect Scamozzi and his inspection of Palladian villas in the Veneto. The earl himself quickly began acquiring paintings and patronizing Venetian artists. In September he wrote to Cotton, 'if you could pick out some story of my ancestors, which would do well in painting, I pray send me it in writing' (BL, Cotton MS Julius CIII, fol. 205).

That same month Arundel may have made a brief trip to Mantua to pay James's respects to its newly installed duke, before departing for Florence by way of Bologna. He then proceeded to Siena, where he took up residence in a monastery with his wife to perfect their Italian. In the winter he left Alathea behind to visit Rome, where he stayed several months, probably with the leading art patron Vincenzo Giustiani, who gained him permission to conduct an archaeological dig in the Forum and contrived to have ancient statues placed where he would uncover them. With these 'discoveries' Arundel began the collection of classical statues and inscriptions which he installed in the galleries and gardens of Arundel House. In March the earl and his wife visited Naples, before returning north at a leisurely pace through Florence, where Duke Cosimo gave them a lavish reception, and Genoa.

Although Arundel returned to Venice to complete some sort of transaction with Scamozzi the couple had still not resumed residence at Albano in July when they received news that Northampton had died, leaving them most of his estate, including a large house in Greenwich and land worth £3000 a year. They returned home to take up this inheritance, arriving by January 1615 after delays caused by a magnificent reception at the duke of Savoy's court in Turin and a further bout of illness. Arundel commissioned a tomb for his uncle from Nicholas Stone and Isaac James, which included sculpted representations of the cardinal virtues that may have been influenced by the Roman statues he had brought back from Italy. His finances were further improved in May 1616 when Shrewsbury died, leaving Alathea half his estate. Arundel had now assembled most of the resources that ultimately gave him an income estimated by Lawrence Stone at over £13,000 per annum, making him one of the three wealthiest peers in England on the eve of the civil war.

This wealth allowed the earl to set about improving Arundel House, where he commissioned Jones to build or remodel a gallery for his collection, as well as his new mansion in Greenwich and a suburban retreat in Highgate. He also continued acquiring art. His reputation as a collector led Sir Dudley Carleton to seek him out in 1616, when he needed to dispose of a number of ancient marbles and modern paintings acquired in Venice for the earl of Somerset just before that favourite's precipitous fall. Carleton gave Arundel a large sculpted head of Jupiter in an attempt to interest him in his other sculptures and may also, as a further inducement, have commissioned Daniel Mytens's portraits of the earl and countess before idealized representations of the new gallery at Arundel House. Although Arundel declined to buy Carleton's statues he soon acquired them anyway, as a gift from the purchaser, his cousin Lord Ros.

Despite a devastating set-back in January 1617, when several prize paintings perished in a fire that consumed the Greenwich house, the collection continued to expand. In building it Arundel consolidated and enlarged the network of contacts with foreign artists, dealers, and other collectors that he had begun to form on his travels. Unlike other Jacobean aristocrats he rarely purchased entire collections for lump-sum payments, preferring instead to drive hard bargains for works that especially interested him. This required unusually good intelligence of foreign art markets. Like other courtiers he frequently used English diplomats and professional dealers as intermediaries, but he also recruited his own purchasing agents—notably William Gage, John Markham, and William Petty. Markham went to Asia Minor in search of antiquities and was replaced after his death in 1624 by Petty, who spent years scouring the Ottoman Levant for finds, travelling with Greek fishermen, collaborating with King Charles's ambassador in Constantinople, Sir Thomas Roe, and outmanoeuvring other collectors.

Relationships with artists and scholars Arundel stood out among early Stuart collectors not only for the size and quality of his collection but for the depth of his intellectual interest in the arts, the range of his personal links with other collectors and artists, and the scale of his efforts to promote knowledge of visual culture. He almost certainly played a pivotal role in recruiting Anthony Van

Dyck to England, both for his initial visit in 1620 and later in 1633. In Italy Arundel gathered a library of treatises on painting and architecture surpassing any then available in England, and after returning home he patronized scholars who wrote on subjects relating to art. These included Henry Peacham, whose influential manual, *The Complete Gentleman*, helped to disseminate a new ideal of gentility encompassing knowledge of art, and John Selden, whose *Marmora Arundeliana* (1628), analysing classical inscriptions in the earl's collection, deeply impressed Rubens. Another antiquary who enjoyed Arundel's patronage was Francis Junius (François du Jon), who transferred to his household from that of Bishop Samuel Harsnett and served him as a secretary responsible for correspondence with foreign scholars and collectors. Junius first acquired a scholarly reputation for his pioneering studies of Anglo-Saxon and ancient Germanic languages, but in the 1630s, with the encouragement of the earl and countess, he embarked on new studies of the arts in classical antiquity that culminated in the publication of *De pictura veterum*, translated as *The Paintings of the Ancients* (1638).

Peacham and Junius viewed painting as an extension of wider cultural and intellectual pursuits, including history, poetry, antiquarian research, and the empirical study of nature. This attitude reflected Arundel's own outlook. Unlike collectors such as the duke of Buckingham, who acquired works purely for purposes of display, the earl valued even mutilated artefacts and rough sketches for what they revealed about the artistic process. He acquired fragments of ancient sculptures and what may have been the best collection of drawings by major Renaissance artists ever assembled, including over 600 by Leonardo da Vinci alone. His interests extended to medallions and carved gemstones, which were regarded in the period as invaluable sources of antiquarian information. He exchanged gemstones with Rubens and in 1637 paid the Venetian dealer Daniel Nys £10,000 for a collection that had reputedly belonged to the dukes of Mantua. Clarendon asserted that Arundel was never able to understand the ancient artefacts he collected, but this seems unlikely in light of the expert advice at his disposal. An undated note by him survives requesting Cotton and a Mr James (or Jones?) to 'come hither this morning to go along with me to see some excellent medals which I saw yesterday' (BL, Cotton MS Julius CIII, fol. 209).

Arundel's interests were not limited to visual culture, however. He encouraged James Ussher to pursue his projected ecclesiastical history of Great Britain, employed Camden to draw up pedigrees for him, and enjoyed a friendship with his Norfolk neighbour the antiquary Sir Henry Spelman. From an early age he collected books and manuscripts. In 1636, while passing through Nuremberg on the way back from a mission to Vienna, he bought a major portion of the great Prickheymer collection, including manuscripts illuminated by Dürer. Arundel's role as a bibliophile and the range of his scholarly interests are hard to appreciate today because his library has been dispersed—most of the manuscripts are in the British Library, while the books have been scattered among public and private collections, where many now lie untraced—but it is clear that he possessed one of the greatest libraries in the British Isles, probably totalling over 3000 volumes.

Political career, 1615–1640 After his return from Italy in 1615 Arundel began to play a more important role in the affairs of the royal court, despite rumours that his visit to Rome had involved inappropriate contacts with papal enemies of the king. He was sworn of the privy council in July 1616 and appointed to the commission charged with overseeing the creation of Prince Charles as prince of Wales later that year. On Christmas day he removed a major impediment to his political career by receiving communion in the Church of England. The next year he accompanied King James on a progress to Edinburgh, where he was sworn of the Scottish privy council; on the journey home he made a detour to visit Ireland and was named to the council in Dublin as well. That autumn Arundel supported Sir Dudley Carleton in the competition to succeed Sir Ralph Winwood as secretary of state. During January 1618 rumours circulated that Arundel would soon be made a duke, along with the king's cousin Lennox and the new favourite Buckingham. In the event he was the only one of the three not to receive the predicted elevation, possibly because he refused a new creation that would have placed him below Buckingham in precedence, holding out for a restoration of the title forfeited in 1572. Arundel was also rumoured to be a leading candidate for the treasurership in November 1619, although he was again disappointed.

Arundel was given many lesser responsibilities, however, such as appointments to a commission to discover the value of fines, heriots, perquisites, and offices at court, and to the council for the plantation of New England. About this time he also began to play a leading role on the commission for buildings that James I set up to enforce crown regulations governing construction in London. This responsibility, which Arundel continued to fulfil until the outbreak of the civil war, involved him in major projects such as building the new Banqueting House in 1620 and renovating St Paul's Cathedral, as well as in an unsuccessful effort to build a classical amphitheatre in London and many lesser attempts at improving the quality of the capital's housing stock. In the parliament of 1621 Arundel presided over the Lords committee that heard evidence against Francis Bacon after his impeachment on charges of bribery. After Bacon's dismissal he served, between 3 May and 10 July, as a commissioner for the great seal. He also took an active part in debates on the case of the monopolist Sir Giles Mompesson, trying to prevent the implication of Buckingham, whose favour he was then cultivating. When Sir Henry Yelverton openly accused Buckingham in the Commons of procuring patents of monopoly, Arundel moved to have the speech declared a dishonour to the king and argued against giving Yelverton the opportunity to explain his words to the Lords. This led to a testy exchange with Robert Spencer,

Lord Spencer of Wormleighton, in which Arundel asserted that his own ancestors had been peers while his antagonist's were still herding sheep. He was briefly incarcerated in the Tower of London by order of the house for refusing to apologize to Spencer for this outburst, where he was consoled by visits from Buckingham and several of the favourite's friends.

In late summer 1621 Arundel received a coveted appointment as earl marshal—an ancient office previously held by his family, vacant since the execution in 1601 of the last incumbent, the second earl of Essex—which had jurisdiction over the heralds and all matters relating to honour. The king also awarded him a salary of £2000 per annum. Arundel had previously been appointed in 1616 to a commission charged with exercising the earl marshal's functions and had temporarily filled the post for ceremonial purposes during Charles's installation as prince of Wales in 1616 and in the procession opening the 1621 parliament. Lord Keeper Williams objected to the resurrection of the earl marshal's authority, since it was vaguely defined and 'impossible to be limited', but James overruled him and also granted Arundel the right to restore the ancient court of chivalry, over which the marshal and the high constable of England had once presided. This court encountered opposition from common lawyers, who saw it as an irregular tribunal. In 1630 it was attacked by the judges of the king's bench, led by Sir William Jones but including Sir Nicholas Hyde, uncle of Edward, the future earl of Clarendon. Arundel again prevailed but the issue resurfaced in the Short Parliament, with Edward Hyde leading the opposition, before being resolved when the Long Parliament abolished the marshal's jurisdiction.

Arundel's standing at court reached a new pinnacle in spring 1623. In April he received the constable's staff, making him the senior privy councillor in honorific terms, while in June he gained a more substantive appointment to the newly formed inner or 'cabinet' council charged with advising the king on sensitive issues relating to the Spanish match. The earl's inclusion in this group reflected both the continuing favour of Buckingham towards him and his own sympathies with the pro-Spanish orientation of royal policy and the greater measure of toleration for English Catholics that a marriage treaty would have entailed. Despite his outward conformity to the Church of England, Arundel remained sympathetic to his former co-religionists. In July 1621 he had joined with Buckingham and John, Lord Digby, in offering assurances to Gondomar that English Catholics would not be harmed in retaliation for Spain's involvement in the Palatinate crisis in Germany (Archivo General, Simancas, Libro 374, 2 vii 1621). In the same year he had also been among the first to congratulate the earl of Northumberland after his release from the Tower of London for alleged complicity in the gunpowder treason, and was dining with him the next day when the Spanish ambassador dropped by. Unfortunately the collapse of the Spanish match in the autumn of 1623 set Arundel on a collision course with the duke of Buckingham and, in effect,

Charles, prince of Wales. In November he opposed Buckingham's proposal to break off negotiations with Madrid and by the end of the year was absenting himself from council meetings, as rumours circulated that he would soon be arrested. In January John Chamberlain listed him as one of five staunch supporters of the match in the cabinet council, which was now badly split. By then the earl was co-operating with the Spanish ambassador in efforts to undermine royal confidence in the favourite. In June it was rumoured that James had secretly met the Spanish ambassador at Arundel House.

So long as James lived it remained possible that Spain's supporters might regain the upper hand at court. Charles's accession in 1625 removed this hope and seems to have encouraged Arundel to become involved in parliamentary manoeuvres against Buckingham. His protégé Cotton began collecting precedents for punishing corrupt ministers of the crown, and three days after the dissolution of the 1625 parliament the earl of Kellie and Sir Arthur Ingram both reported rumours that Arundel—along with the earl of Pembroke, Lord Keeper Williams, and Archbishop Abbot—would be questioned over their roles in the session. The first overt sign of royal displeasure came in February 1626, following the coronation ceremonies, when Charles avoided the lavish reception Arundel had arranged for him in Cotton's riverside garden. A short time later the king gained an excuse to strike back more effectively, when Arundel's eldest surviving son eloped with the daughter of the third duke of Lennox, thwarting royal plans to marry her to Lord Lorne. Arundel was blamed for his son's transgression and was sequestered from the council and placed under arrest, preventing him from attending the Lords and voting his five proxies. The peers immediately protested against the arrest of one of their members during a session and on 26 May voted not to consider any other business until Arundel was permitted to take his seat. Although Charles gave way he imposed further restraints on the earl's liberty after the parliament's dissolution. These were fully rescinded only in March 1628, after Buckingham decided to appease former enemies before the start of a new parliament. The duke therefore arranged for Arundel to be received back into favour and restored to the council.

Arundel played a conciliatory role in the debates of 1628, arguing unsuccessfully for the insertion of a clause saving the king's prerogative in the petition of right. In the following year he was named a commissioner to negotiate peace with Spain and a member of the council's sub-committee charged with negotiations with France. The Spanish negotiations brought him into agreeable contact with Rubens, who arrived as Philip IV's agent in June 1629 and wasted little time in visiting Arundel's galleries. Three Rubens portraits of the earl, now in the National Gallery and National Portrait Gallery in London and the Isabella Stewart Gardner Museum in Boston, have been ascribed to this period. In 1632 Charles chose Arundel to travel to The Hague bearing an invitation to his sister, Elizabeth of Bohemia, for her to reside in England pending the restoration of her recently deceased husband's hereditary dominion of the Palatinate, which had been occupied by Spanish, Bavarian, and imperial troops. She refused but did permit him to escort her sons, Charles Louis and Rupert, to London. The following year the earl accompanied the king on his progress to Edinburgh.

Early in 1636 Charles's ambassador to the Holy Roman empire, John Taylor, reported that the Habsburgs were ready to reach a peace settlement that would involve the restoration of the Palatinate to Charles's nephew, Charles Louis. Arundel was named as extraordinary ambassador with instructions to gauge the accuracy of this assessment and commence negotiations if it proved true. His record of sympathy for Habsburg interests, together with his previous friendly relations with Elizabeth of Bohemia going back to her marriage in 1613, probably recommended him for the post, as a man who might hope to win the confidence of both sides. Although privately expressing scepticism about his chances of success, Arundel set off at the head of a splendid entourage that included Sir John Borough, an expert on international law whom he had earlier appointed a herald, Francis Windebanke the younger, son of the secretary of state, and William Harvey, the discoverer of the circulation of the blood. After stopping at The Hague to brief Elizabeth of Bohemia on the scope of his mission, he proceeded south through a devastated countryside to Nuremberg, where he met Taylor, before proceeding on to Linz, for his first audience with the emperor. Much to his annoyance Arundel's forceful demands for a restitution of the Palatinate met with evasive responses. He was further embarrassed when it became clear, from discussions with Spanish as well as imperial diplomats, that he had not been fully briefed on secret negotiations by English diplomats in Madrid which had encouraged the Habsburgs to believe that Charles would offer them an offensive and defensive alliance in exchange for the restoration of his nephew, a concession Arundel's instructions expressly forbade him from making. His patience exhausted and his delicate sense of honour offended, Arundel began hinting in his dispatches that he wished to be recalled. He finally concluded his embassy in November, arriving in London about the new year. His diplomatic failure convinced him of the need for strong action against Habsburg interests, a stance that brought him into alliance with the earl of Holland, a consistent advocate of pro-French policies on the council, and Elizabeth's own followers. However, delays in concluding an alliance treaty with France and growing problems in Scotland soon ruled out England's re-entry into the Thirty Years' War.

The recruitment of Hollar and van der Borcht and Arundel's patronage of prints Although Arundel's mission to Vienna was a diplomatic failure, it did bring opportunities to inspect artistic treasures along his route and to make new acquisitions. The bishop of Wesburg presented him with a Dürer *Virgin and Child*, the king of Hungary with several volumes of drawings, and the duke of Neuburg and the commander of French troops besieging Koblenz with further gifts of art. His most significant acquisitions were two artists: the engraver Wenceslaus Hollar, who presented

himself in Cologne in 1636, and Henry van der Borcht the younger, whom the earl recruited while passing through Frankfurt. Hollar produced a series of drawings of territories traversed by Arundel's party, which he later engraved. Following his patron to London, he resided in Arundel House, although he also won the king's patronage. Van der Borcht was the talented son of an artist and collector. Arundel sent him to William Petty in Italy, who was instructed to train the young man to 'see and observe paintings and designs well, that he might be fit another day to take our pictures and collections of designs at Arundel House' (Springell, 100 n. 53). In 1637, with his apprenticeship completed, van der Borcht rejoined Arundel in England. Along with Hollar and Lucas Voesterman, he was thereafter employed producing etchings and engravings of works in the earl's collection.

Until this period England had lagged well behind France and the Spanish Netherlands in the use of print media to disseminate high-quality reproductions of important works of art, and Arundel was the first patron to make a sustained effort to close this gap. In one area—the reproduction of drawings and sketches—his artists were of pioneering importance in a European context. Arundel's patronage of etching and engraving may have been motivated in part by a desire to enhance his reputation as a collector, but it also served the advancement of knowledge of art.

Last years Despite his disillusionment with the Habsburgs in 1636, Arundel continued to be identified with Catholic interests at court in the years preceding the civil war. He and his wife developed a close relationship with the papal envoy George Conn, aiding his efforts to persuade Prince Rupert that converting to Rome would provide the best means of recovering his family's lost inheritance. Conn complained of the earl's reluctance to exert himself in the cause but remained in close contact with him as the crisis in Scotland developed. Arundel's appointment to lead the forces against the northern kingdom in 1639 was therefore perceived by many as another sign of growing popish influence, especially when Arundel tactlessly borrowed the papal representative's coach to drive to a meeting with the king. By April 1639 Arundel had emerged as one of the leading hardliners on the council in his attitude towards the Scots, and one of Charles's most trusted advisers. He helped devise a highly controversial army oath, conceived as a substitute for the 1606 oath of allegiance, which removed all direct references to Catholic assertions of papal supremacy while implicitly condemning Calvinist resistance theory. Lord Brooke and Lord Saye and Sele were imprisoned when they refused to take it.

Hollar commemorated his patron's command of the campaign against Scotland with an engraved equestrian portrait of Arundel, briefly sold by the Strand bookseller Thomas Walkley, who had previously published the Caroline masques. The earl must have been disappointed by the inconclusive results of the war, however. Probably for this reason, he became absorbed after his return by a scheme to colonize the island of Madagascar. He had earlier promoted this project in 1636 as an outlet for the energies of Prince Rupert, much to the horror of Elizabeth of Bohemia, who likened it to the adventures of Don Quixote. Arundel and his wife now took it up on their own behalf, obtaining a royal licence to move to the island and commissioning a double portrait by Van Dyck, showing them seated next to a large globe, with the earl pointing to Madagascar with his finger. The scheme soon evaporated, however, perhaps because of Arundel's deteriorating health. Bad health may also explain why he was not asked to play a role in the second campaign against Scotland in 1640. Following the truce he was appointed commander of the king's forces south of the Trent, as well as steward of the household, in which capacity he presided over the trial of Thomas Wentworth, earl of Strafford. Although his relations with the king's embattled minister had long been strained, he voted against the attainder.

After Charles failed to act on a petition by eighteen peers to restore Arundel as duke of Norfolk, the earl resigned as steward and asked leave to travel. Charles appointed him and his wife to escort the queen's mother, Marie de' Medici, back to the continent after her expensive visit to London. The countess soon grew impatient at Marie's delays and left for The Hague on her own, but Arundel waited dutifully until he could escort Marie to Flushing in September. He returned the next month to join the commission that negotiated the marriage of Princess Mary to William of Orange, then left again to accompany the couple to the Netherlands in May 1642. He then took up residence in Antwerp, avoiding direct involvement in the civil war. He made his royalist sympathies clear, however, by contributing an eventual £54,000 to the king's cause, which provoked parliament into seizing jewels he had left behind in England and confiscating his estates in 1643. In June 1644, belatedly and only partially, the king restored the Norfolk title to Arundel, as earl rather than duke, a creation which served to ensure that the title would remain with the Howards and not be granted away to another family, but which seems to have given the earl little or no satisfaction.

Arundel continued to live in exile for the few remaining years of his life, separated from his wife, with whom his relationship had deteriorated, thanks in part to her embarrassing involvement in Catholic proselytizing during the late 1630s. He moved from Antwerp to Padua, where he entertained John Evelyn in July 1645, showing him his gardens and giving him written suggestions on what to see elsewhere in Italy. Arundel's undiminished interest in art and architecture is shown by a paper of 'Remembrances at Vicenza' drawn up during this period, concerning the newly built villas, art collections, and other sights he had seen in that city, as well as in Verona and Milan. But having been cut off from his English revenues, he was now forced to sell off parts of his collection to obtain money on which to live.

Arundel's life was further saddened by the entry of his grandson, Philip *Howard, into a Dominican monastery.

Although Arundel quietly reconverted to Catholicism during his final years, his religious ardour seems always to have remained cool, and the renunciation of secular life by a young man who stood to inherit his lands and titles and carry on the Howard line made him physically ill. After another visit on Easter Monday 1646, Evelyn left him bedridden and 'in tears upon … the crosses had befallen his illustrious family', the 'unkindness of his countess', and 'the misery of his country' (Evelyn, 2.479). Arundel died in Padua on 24 September / 4 October 1646. His body was taken back to England for burial in the Fitzalan chapel at Arundel Castle, except for his heart and entrails, which were interred at St Anthony's basilica at Padua. He was succeeded as earl by his second, but eldest surviving, son, Henry Frederick *Howard.

Concluding remarks Termed by Horace Walpole 'the father of vertue in England', Arundel has interested twentieth-century scholars chiefly for his pioneering role as a collector and patron of the arts. He certainly deserves his reputation in this sphere, even if gaps in the evidence make it difficult to evaluate the precise extent of his contributions. An inventory of his paintings drawn up after his death, in 1655, omits a number of important works he is known to have possessed, while also referring to numerous paintings that are now impossible to trace. It is therefore difficult to know just how important the collection was in its prime, although it was certainly distinguished. At the time of his death Arundel possessed over 600 paintings, including 40 attributed to Holbein, 37 to Titian, 26 to Parmigiano, 17 to Giorgione, 16 to Dürer, and 13 each to Raphael and Brueghel. Even allowing for false attributions, this was undoubtedly one of the greatest aristocratic collections in Europe. It was also an unusually varied one, displaying, in addition to the usual Caroline taste for Venetian art and other major Italian schools, a strong interest in northern painting. Moreover, as David Jaffe has remarked, paintings once owned by Arundel that can now be identified very often turn out still to be regarded as important.

Arundel's influence on the artists he patronized is even more difficult to measure since it involved face-to-face encounters that left almost no traces in the documentary record. He must have had many conversations with Rubens during the artist's embassy to London in 1629 but since these have gone unrecorded it is possible only to speculate about whether they discussed plans for the Banqueting House ceiling or other matters relating to the iconography of the Caroline court. It is highly suggestive that Van Dyck's first portrait of Arundel, painted about 1620, shows unusually strong Venetian influences for this stage in the artist's career. Circumstantial evidence indicates that Van Dyck may have first toured Venetian territories in the entourage of the countess of Arundel in 1621, compiling a sketchbook dominated by copies of Titian canvases as he did so. But in the absence of fuller documentation it is impossible to be certain how far Arundel nurtured the affinity for Titian that Van Dyck developed after his first departure from England in 1621. Even the earl's relationship with Inigo Jones, the most significant and enduring of all his ties to an important artist, has left frustratingly scant documentation. It is known that Jones continued to advise Arundel about paintings after their return from Italy in 1614/15; that they worked together on the commission for buildings and other projects for more than twenty years; and that the architect borrowed manuscripts from the library of Arundel's other protégé, Robert Cotton. There is even evidence of their travelling together to Ware in the autumn of 1618 to feast on ripe grapes and peaches, but the content of their many conversations during more than a quarter-century of friendship will always remain somewhat mysterious. What can be said with confidence is that between his return from Italy and the eve of the civil war, Arundel was at once the most knowledgeable and energetic noble collector and patron of the arts at the Stuart court, and the one who appears to have enjoyed the broadest range of personal contacts with important artists and scholars interested in artistic subjects, both in England and abroad. His influence must have been substantial, even if now difficult to pin down.

At the same time, viewing Arundel as a pioneer of connoisseurship can be limiting and distorting, by obscuring other facets to his complex personality, especially his fierce pride in his ancestry and commitment to honour values. Historians have discussed his role as a leading aristocratic opponent of Buckingham, but his activities as earl marshal, his opposition to the sale of offices at the start of Charles's reign, and his persistent efforts to revive sumptuary legislation in Caroline parliaments have attracted only passing notice. Yet Arundel's preoccupation with genealogy and titles of nobility was not only central to his own personality but an important clue to his place in the wider culture of his period. These values link him to other Stuart peers and gentry, to the antiquaries he patronized, such as Cotton, Selden, and John Spelman, and to aristocratic values embedded in the cultures of seventeenth-century Italy and classical antiquity.

Arundel's career transcends modern concepts of taste and connoisseurship, revealing an eclectic range of interests characteristic of the early seventeenth century. His fascination with strange and exotic lands is shown not only by the Madagascar project of the late 1630s but by his earlier involvement in 1620 in a scheme to colonize the Amazon basin, his curiosity about Irish antiquities whose discovery Wentworth reported from Dublin, and his keen desire 'to possess something of Persia', which led him to persuade Charles to send an artist on an embassy to that country 'to make drawings of everything rare' (Hervey, 401). The items in his collection engraved by Hollar included not only paintings and drawings but butterflies and animal pelts. Arundel's borrowings from Sir Robert Cotton's library were equally varied, including an inventory of tapestries owned by Henry VIII, a list of statutes of the Order of the Garter, 'a meditation of the state of England … by the lord Burghley in his hand', and a volume of 400 printed maps (BL, Harley MS 6018, fol. 148).

The papal envoy George Conn thought Arundel's cultural interests made him less effective in affairs of state, yet Arundel had a long and often eventful career in Stuart politics, including nearly twenty-five years on the privy council, an active role in several sessions of parliament, the important embassy to Germany in 1636, and a brief, if ultimately fruitless, period as one of the main architects of Charles's war with Scotland. His contacts with scholars, artists, and European collectors often helped him deal with political affairs. His work on the commission for buildings and his role as earl marshal, which required researches into genealogy, heraldry, and court ceremonies, provide obvious examples. The scholar most closely associated with Arundel's political career was Sir Robert Cotton, who helped him vet projects by other scholars who wanted his help in gaining the attention of the council and supplied him with precedents for schemes to enhance crown revenues. Arundel nominated Cotton to a seat in the parliament of 1625, relied on his expertise in the campaign against Buckingham, and probably encouraged him to write *The Condition in which the Kingdome now Standeth* in 1628. The extent of John Selden's relations with the earl is less clear, but the two probably collaborated repeatedly during parliamentary sessions in the late 1620s. It is suggestive that, while imprisoned on suspicion of sedition in 1629, Selden was consoled by a visit from William Petty, who took along several old manuscripts for his perusal.

Arundel's range of cultural and political interests is best understood within the context of an international aristocratic society of the early seventeenth century in which antiquarian scholarship and art collecting had become intertwined with diplomacy and high politics. He was a thoroughly cosmopolitan figure who spoke Italian fluently, enjoyed travelling abroad, and sent some of his sons to be educated at Padua rather than Oxford or Cambridge. Yet his cosmopolitanism never precluded strong attachment to his native country and its traditions. Although he filled his houses with classical and modern art, Arundel was also praised by his first biographer for being 'sumptuous in his plate and household stuff, and full of state and magnificence' in the manner of the ancient English nobility. The papal envoy Gregorio Panzani described a banquet at Arundel House where he was entertained by Countess Alathea's Italian conversation and by seeing the earl's volumes of drawings by Michelangelo and Raphael, as well as by English country dances and comedies. Hollar's engraving of the earl's favourite country retreat at Albury, Surrey, shows a traditional timber house set in a very English landscape. Only toward the end of his life did his weariness with a deteriorating political situation and disappointment over Charles's failure to restore the ducal title forfeited in 1572 lead Arundel into voluntary exile. Even then he probably always intended to return home some day, as he was about to do when death overtook him. The perspectives of later historians have tended to separate 'the father of vertue in England' from the proud peer who revived the court of chivalry and fought to restore the political pre-eminence of the kingdom's ancient titled families, but for Arundel himself, the two roles were not only compatible but complementary.

R. MALCOLM SMUTS

Sources M. F. S. Hervey, *The life, correspondence and collections of Thomas Howard, earl of Arundel, 'father of vertu in England'* (1921) [repr. 1969] · D. Howarth, *Lord Arundel and his circle* (New Haven, 1985) · F. Springell, *Connoisseur and diplomat: the earl of Arundel's embassy to Germany in 1636 as recounted in William Crowne's diary, the earl's letters and other contemporary sources with a catalogue of the topographical drawings made on the journey by Wenceslaus Hollar* (1963) · D. Jaffe and others, 'The earl and countess of Arundel: Renaissance collectors', *Apollo*, 144 (Aug 1996), 3–35 · D. Scarisbrick, 'The Arundel gem cabinet', *Apollo*, 144 (Aug 1996), 45–56 · A. F. Kolb, 'The Arundels' printmakers: four approaches to the reproduction of drawings', *Apollo*, 144 (Aug 1996), 57–62 · J. Fletcher, 'The Arundels in the Veneto', *Apollo*, 144 (Aug 1996), 63–9 · D. Howarth, 'The patronage and collection of Alatheia, countess of Arundel, 1606–54', *Journal of the History of Collections*, 10 (1998), 125–37 · K. Sharpe, 'The earl of Arundel, his circle and the opposition to the duke of Buckingham, 1618–1628', *Faction and parliament*, ed. K. Sharpe (1978), 1–42 · *DNB* · *GEC, Peerage* · *CSP dom.*, *1603–46* · state papers, James I and Charles I, PRO, SP/14, SP/16 · L. Levy Peck, 'Uncovering the Arundel Library at the Royal Society: changing meanings of science and the fate of the Norfolk donation', *Notes and Records of the Royal Society*, 52 (1998), 3–24 · K. Sharpe, *Sir Robert Cotton, 1586–1631: history and politics in early modern England* (1979) · K. Sharpe, *The personal rule of Charles I* (1992) · Clarendon, *Hist. rebellion* · Edward Walker's life of Arundel, BL, Harley MS 6272 · papers from Arundel's mission to Germany in 1636, PRO, SP 80/9–10 · BL, Cotton MS Julius C III · corresp., 1617–32, Arundel Castle archives, West Sussex · *The letters of John Chamberlain*, ed. N. E. McClure, 2 vols. (1939) · loans of Cotton's manuscripts, BL, Harley MS 6018 · F. du Jon, *The painting of the ancients* (1638) · transcripts of dispatches of Gregorio Panzani, PRO, PRO 31/9 · transcripts of dispatches of George Conn, BL, Add. MS 15390 · Sir Dudley Carleton's correspondence with William Trumbull from Venice in 1613, BL, Trumbull MSS, vol. 15 · Evelyn, *Diary* · M. Jansson and W. B. Bidwell, eds., *Proceedings in parliament, 1625* (1987) · M. F. Keeler, M. J. Cole, and W. B. Bidwell, eds., *Lords proceedings, 1628* (1983) · T. Cogswell, *The blessed revolution: English politics and the coming of war, 1621–1624* (1989) · C. M. Hibbard, *Charles I and the Popish Plot* (1983) · J. M. Robinson, *The dukes of Norfolk* (1982) · *Calendar of the manuscripts of the most hon. the marquess of Salisbury*, 21, HMC, 9 (1970)

Archives Arundel Castle, West Sussex, corresp. and papers · BL, Arundel MSS · Coll. Arms, historic and heraldic collections · PRO, SP 80/9–10 · Westm. DA, list of jewels | BL, letters to Sir Julius Caesar, letters to William Petty, and papers, Add. MS 15970

Likenesses portrait, *c.*1610, Arundel Castle, West Sussex · oils, *c.*1612, Buccleuch estates, Selkirk · D. Mytens, oils, *c.*1618, Arundel Castle, West Sussex · D. Mytens, oils, *c.*1618 (with Alathea Talbot), Arundel Castle, West Sussex · A. Van Dyck, portrait, *c.*1620, J. Paul Getty Museum, Malibu, California · P. P. Rubens, oils, 1629/30, Isabella Stewart Gardner Museum, Boston · P. P. Rubens, oils, 1629, NPG [see illus.] · P. P. Rubens, ink and chalk sketch, *c.*1629–1630, AM Oxf. · P. P. Rubens, oils, 1629–30, National Gallery, London · A. Van Dyck, oils, *c.*1635–1636, Arundel Castle, West Sussex · W. Hollar, etching, 1639, BM · A. Van Dyck, group portrait, oils, *c.*1639 (*The Madagascar Portrait*), Arundel Castle, West Sussex · W. Hollar, etching, *c.*1646 (after C. Schut), NPG · J. Basire, line engraving, 1743 (after A. Van Dyck), NPG · J. Houbraken, line engraving, pubd 1763 (after P. P. Rubens), BM, NPG · R. Dumbarton, mezzotint, pubd 1813 (after A. Van Dyck), NPG · P. W. Tomkins, stipple, pubd 1818 (after A. Van Dyck), BM, NPG · W. Sharp, line engraving, pubd 1823 (after A. Van Dyck), NPG · L. Vosterman, line engraving, pubd 1823 (after A. Van Dyck), BM, NPG · S. de Passe, line engraving (after a portrait by 'M. Miereveldt', *c.*1612), BM · A. Van Dyck, chalk sketch, BM · group portrait (after type by P. Frujthiers, *c.*1642), Arundel Castle, West Sussex · pen, ink, and watercolour, NPG · photograph (after A. Van Dyck), NPG

Howard, Trevor [*real name* Trevor Wallace Howard-Smith] (1913–1988), actor, was born in Cliftonville, Kent, on 29

Trevor Howard (1913–1988), by Cornel Lucas, 1950

September 1913, the only son and elder child of Arthur John Howard-Smith, who worked as Ceylon representative for Lloyd's of London, and his Canadian wife, Mabel Grey Wallace, nurse. Until he was five he lived in Colombo, Ceylon, but then travelled with his mother until the age of eight, when he was sent to school at Clifton College, Bristol. He was an isolated child and when neither of his parents returned to England holidays were spent either in seaside bed-and-breakfast accommodation or in the home of one of the housemasters. At school Howard was not strongly academic and it was sport that caught his interest, particularly boxing and cricket. The latter became one of the great loves of his life, together with jazz. Towards the end of his school career he started visiting the local theatre, and he left Clifton to become an actor, getting into the Royal Academy of Dramatic Art (RADA) without any previous stage experience.

Howard's first paid work was in the play *Revolt in a Reformatory* (1934), before he left RADA in 1935 to take small roles. That year he was spotted by a Paramount studio talent scout but turned down the offer of film work in favour of a career in theatre. This decision seemed justified when, in 1936, he was invited to join the Stratford Memorial Theatre and, in London, given the role of one of the students in *French without Tears* by Terence Rattigan, which ran for two years. He returned to Stratford in 1939. At the outbreak of war he decided to enlist, but both the army and the Royal Air Force rejected him. However, in 1940, after working at the Colchester repertory theatre, he was called up into the Royal Corps of Signals, airborne division, becoming a second lieutenant before he was invalided out in 1943. The stories of Howard's war heroism were fabricated, without his consent, for publicity purposes.

Howard moved back to the theatre in *The Recruiting Officer* (1943), where he met the actress Helen Cherry, daughter of William Cherry, retired army officer, and his wife, Annie Nall; they married in 1944. They had no children. A short part in one of the best British war films, *The Way Ahead* (1944), provided a springboard into cinema. This was followed by *The Way to the Stars* (1945), which led to the role for which Howard became best known, the doctor in *Brief Encounter* (1945), in which his co-star was Celia Johnson. Directed by David Lean, the film won an award at the Cannes festival and considerable critical acclaim for Howard. Next came two successful Frank Launder and Sidney Gilliat thrillers, *I See a Dark Stranger* (1945) and *Green for Danger* (1946), followed by *They Made me a Fugitive* (1947), in which the roots of British realism in cinema can be traced. In 1947 he was invited by Laurence Olivier to play Petruchio in an Old Vic production of *The Taming of the Shrew*. Despite *The Times* declaring 'We can remember no better Petruchio', the opportunity of working again with David Lean, in *The Passionate Friends* (1948), drew Howard back to film and, although he had a solid reputation as a theatre actor, his dislike of long runs, and the attractions of travel afforded by film, made him concentrate on cinema from this point.

Howard's film reputation was secured in *The Third Man* (1949). He played the character type with which he became most associated, the British military officer, but his capabilities were stretched by his role in this story of post-war Vienna by Graham Greene. Howard had a certain notoriety as a hellraiser, based on his drinking capacity. Under the influence of alcohol he could embark on celebrated exploits, one of which led to his arrest in Vienna, for impersonating an officer. Despite his drinking, however, he always remained reliable and professional, never allowing alcohol to affect his work.

During the 1950s, while often eliciting good notices for his work, Howard frequently appeared in flawed films like *Odette* (1950) and *An Outcast of the Islands* (1951). An exception was *The Heart of the Matter* (1953), another Graham Greene story, in which he produced his best screen performance. Such opportunities were rare, even though he shifted into the American market. In 1958 he received the best actor award from the British Film Academy for his performance in *The Key*, but this film, too, failed to meet his high standards.

Although *Sons and Lovers* (1960), for which Howard received an Oscar nomination for his performance as the father, and *Mutiny on the Bounty* (1962), in which he worked with Marlon Brando, enabled him to move away from playing military stereotypes, *Von Ryan's Express* (1965) and *The Long Duel* (1967), with Yul Brynner, saw a return to playing officer figures. Even the role of the pugnacious Cardigan in *The Charge of the Light Brigade* (1968) revisited military territory, and in this uneven yet innovative film Howard gave a fine performance. Working with Brando and Brynner proved frustrating experiences, leaving him with

a mistrust of Hollywood. After the 1960s cinema gave him fewer opportunities to display his ability. His performance as the cynical priest in Lean's *Ryan's Daughter* (1971) is one of the most memorable in this over-long film, but for much of the 1970s he was increasingly relegated to cameo appearances in films such as *Ludwig* (1973) or disappointing movies such as *Persecution* (1974) and *Conduct Unbecoming* (1975). However, in 1978 he played a choric-narrator figure in *Stevie* with Glenda Jackson, an experience he found satisfying.

In television Howard began to find more substantial roles. In 1962 he played Lovborg in *Hedda Gabler* with Ingrid Bergman, and in 1963 won an Emmy award as Disraeli in *The Invincible Mr Disraeli*. In the 1970s he was acclaimed for his playing of an abbot in *Catholics* (1973) and in 1975 he received an Emmy nomination for his role as Abbé Faria in a television version of *The Count of Monte Cristo*. The decade ended with him reunited with Celia Johnson, giving a moving performance in the nostalgic *Staying on* (1980), written by Paul Scott.

The 1980s saw a resurgence of Howard as a film actor. The exhilarating role of a Cheyenne Indian in *Windwalker* (1980) revitalized his acting. However, as was the case with *Sir Henry at Rawlinson End* (1980), a low-budget black and white film, this impressive movie never reached a wide audience. He continued with cameo roles, including Judge Broomfield in *Gandhi* (1982). His final films were *White Mischief* and *The Old Jest*, both released in 1988. Howard did not abandon the theatre altogether in 1947, returning to the stage on occasion, most notably as Lopakhin in *The Cherry Orchard* (1954) and the captain in *The Father* (1964). His last appearance on the British stage was in *Waltz of the Toreadors* in 1974.

Howard made seventy-four films. He embodied the traditional Englishman: his tight-lipped features and quiet, well-bred speaking voice caught the mood of post-war Britain while, in later years, his craggy face and gravelly voice animated the crusty character roles he played. He lacked the looks and physique to be an archetypal male hero, and his tall frame suited military roles. He failed to fulfil his potential, for he rarely played the lead roles he deserved. Supporting some of the most notable names in the world of cinema, he often received the highest critical acclaim. Howard died on 7 January 1988, at Bushey Hospital in Hertfordshire, of bronchitis complicated by jaundice.   LIB TAYLOR, rev.

Sources M. Munn, *Trevor Howard: the man and his films* (1989) · V. Knight, *Trevor Howard: a gentleman and a player* (1986) · *The Times* (8 Jan 1988) · *The Guardian* (8 Jan 1988) · *The Observer* (10 Jan 1988) · *CGPLA Eng. & Wales* (1988) · private information (1996) · T. Pettigrew, *Trevor Howard: a personal biography* (2001)

Likenesses photographs, 1945–74, Hult. Arch. · C. Lucas, photograph, 1950, NPG [*see illus.*]

Wealth at death £3,024,130: probate, 23 June 1988, *CGPLA Eng. & Wales*

Howard, Walter Hope Long (1759–1830/31), peerage claimant, was born on 10 May 1759 and baptized on 10 June at St Anne's, Soho, the son of William Howard (1724/5–1777) and his wife, Catherine Tidcomb or Titcombe (*bap.*

1725, *d.* 1778), the daughter of Hope Long Tidcomb and his wife, Elizabeth. One E. M. S., probably James Dallaway, secretary to the duke of Norfolk as earl marshal, wrote in 1816 that 'His grand-father was certainly considered as a country gentleman; but his father was in very reduced circumstances' (*GM*), supposedly descended from an illegitimate son of a Howard earl of Suffolk who had been settled on an estate in Westmorland. According to his son, William Howard had been acknowledged as a relative by Edward Howard, ninth duke of Norfolk; Norfolk had supported William Howard financially and paid for Walter Howard's education at the English College at St Omer. Howard does not appear in the published register, although it is acknowledged to be incomplete. He was later withdrawn from St Omer as he was a protestant, but in 1773 Norfolk arranged for him to be placed with a wine merchant, Mr Searle, at Oporto; he is mentioned as living there in Norfolk's will. Howard returned to Britain some time after the deaths of the duke and his father, having received a disabling wound. Norfolk left him an annuity drawn from £1500 in old South Sea annuities, the whole sum to be handed over when he should 'enter into or engage in on his own Account any reputable Business of Employment' (PRO, PROB 11/1035, fol. 313v). He seems to have lived on the annuity after his return from Portugal, and Charles, tenth duke, may have continued the allowance made to his father. During this period, possibly on 16 October 1786 at St James's, Piccadilly, he married Jane Martin (*b.* 1760), 'of Gateside, in Northumberland' (Causton, 428), who was probably the Jane, daughter of William Martine, baptized at Castle Garth Presbyterian Church, Newcastle upon Tyne, on 24 January 1760.

In 1793 Howard found himself seriously in debt and applied to Charles, eleventh duke of Norfolk, for assistance. On 21 December 1795 Norfolk released Howard from debtors' prison and settled him and his wife on a property at Ewood in Surrey. However, before doing so Norfolk had requested that the heralds investigate Howard's relationship to the ducal line; they had been unable to prove a connection, and so Norfolk ordered that Howard take the name of Smith. Howard returned to London to complain, but Norfolk refused to see him and excluded him from the property at Ewood.

Howard now devoted himself to the correction of the College of Arms pedigree of the ducal family and the resumption of the Ewood property. His obsession led him to question the right of Bernard Edward Howard, of Glossop, Derbyshire, to be presumptive heir to the dukedom. He wrote to Lord Chancellor Eldon in 1805 and even attempted to address the House of Lords. Howard's campaign attracted attention from the press, and he gained the nickname the Heir of Poverty. His cause was not helped when it was taken up by Thomas Christopher Banks, the proprietor of the so-called Dormant Peerage Office. Banks wrote two pamphlets inspired by the case— *An Analysis of the Genealogical History of the Family of Howard* (1812) and *Ecce homo: the Mysterious Heir, or, Who is Mr Walter Howard?* (1815)—both of which implied that Howard, not the eleventh duke of Norfolk, was the rightful holder of the titles. Banks helped Howard draw up a petition, which was presented to the prince regent on 25 April 1812; Howard then waylaid the prince in Pall Mall on 12 May, for which he apologized in another letter. He was taken into custody on presenting himself at Norfolk House. Following his accession, Bernard Edward, twelfth duke of Norfolk, restored Howard's annuity, and Howard lived on that until his death in 1830 or 1831.

The interest of the press and mischief makers in Howard's cause weakened when the debauched eleventh duke of Norfolk died, but his claims remained of antiquarian interest. H. Kent Staple Causton, the son of Banks's publisher, acquired Howard's correspondence and collection of notes on the Howard family from his widow, and in 1862 published *The Howard Papers*, an exhaustively footnoted history of the Howard family. Causton used John Hodgson's *History of Northumberland* to show that Howard's father, William Howard, was probably the William Howard who in 1750 had sold the estate of Overacres and lordships of Redesdale and Harbottle to Hugh Percy, second earl of Northumberland. According to Hodgson, this Howard was a descendant of Lord William Howard of Naworth, Cumberland, younger son of the fourth duke of Norfolk. Alternatively, in *Notes and Queries* (6th ser., 1, 1880) W. S. Ellis argued that he was a descendant of Theophilus, second earl of Suffolk, through a previously unnoticed but recorded son, confirming to some degree James Dallaway's hypothesis of 1816. However, according to the Northumberland antiquary Spearman, whose mother had known the family, William Howard of Overacres, 'who did not conduct himself as became his descent' (*Proceedings of the Society of Antiquaries of Newcastle upon Tyne*, 2nd ser., 3, 1887–8, 319), had died at about the time the estate was sold in 1750. A more far-fetched account of Howard's origins appeared in Walter Chitty's *All the Blood of All the Howards* (1906), which argued that Howard's father was born in Lambeth in 1725, the son of the ninth duke of Norfolk by a concealed Anglican marriage. More credibly, it suggested that Howard's mother, Catherine Tidcomb, was the great-granddaughter of Hope Long of South Wraxall in Devon, with a potential claim on the Long estates, explaining Howard's unusual forenames.

GORDON GOODWIN, *rev.* MATTHEW KILBURN

Sources H. K. S. Causton, *The Howard papers: with a biographical pedigree and criticism* [1862] · *GM*, 1st ser., 86/1 (1816), 104 · J. Hodgson, *A history of Northumberland*, 3 pts in 7 vols. (1820–58), pt 2, vol. 1, pp. 80–82 · T. C. Banks, *Ecce homo: the mysterious heir, or, Who is Mr Walter Howard?* (1815) · T. C. Banks, *An analysis of the genealogical history of the family of Howard … erroneously attributed to be vested in the dukedom of Norfolk* (1812) · W. Chitty, *All the blood of all the Howards, with a little of other people's* (1906) · PRO, PROB 11/1035, fols. 308r–314v [will of Edward Howard, ninth duke of Norfolk] · *N&Q*, 6th ser., 1 (1880), 342–3 · IGI

Howard, Sir William [William of Wiggenhall] (*b.* in or before **1255**, *d.* **1308**), justice, was probably born at Wiggenhall in Norfolk. There seems to be no contemporary evidence to support the later tradition that made him the son of one John Howard and his wife, Lucy Germund. Between 1276 and 1279 he received a number of appointments to act as the attorney of Norfolk litigants in the common bench. By the mid-1280s he was in practice as a serjeant and is known to have acted in the Essex eyre of 1285, the Norfolk eyre of 1286, and the Wiltshire eyre of 1289. His first known appearance as a common-bench serjeant was in Trinity term 1290. When the eyre circuits resumed in June 1292, Howard offered his services to clients in the eyres of the southern circuit. The reports show him as among the most active serjeants on that circuit. He resumed practice in the common bench in Hilary term 1294 and can then be traced appearing for clients in almost every term until Easter term 1297.

Howard's first appointment as a regular justice came in June 1293 when he and John Batesford were appointed as assize justices in the seven northern counties. Between 1293 and 1297 he seems to have fitted his assize work into the vacations between eyre and common-bench sessions. Howard ceased acting as an assize justice on his appointment as a fifth, additional, justice of the common bench in October 1297. The final concords show him sitting in the court every term until Trinity term 1308. The reports, however, appear to indicate that he was absent from the court in Trinity and Michaelmas terms 1302, in Trinity term 1305, and in Hilary and Easter terms 1306. Other evidence confirms that he and two of his colleagues were absent from the court (then at York) while attending a session of parliament in London in Trinity term 1302, and suggest that his later absences in 1305 and 1306 were connected with his work as a trailbaston justice. He was also absent from the court for much, if not all, of Easter and Trinity terms 1307 while leading a trailbaston circuit. The reports also show an active and capable judge, well able to hold his own with successive chief justices (Mettingham and Hengham) and his very able colleague William Bereford.

Howard was twice married. His first wife, Alice, is said to have been the daughter of Robert of Ufford. His second wife, also named Alice, is said to have been the daughter of John Fitton of Wiggenhall and had previously been married to Simon Constable of Burton Constable in Yorkshire, who had died in prison in 1294 while refusing to plead on a number of criminal charges, including that of poisoning his first wife. Alice was successful in obtaining her dower from Constable's lands, although there was also a rival second wife, Katherine of Weelsby. Howard seems to have married Alice between 1297 and 1300, by which date he had been knighted. His son and heir, John, was almost certainly a child of his first marriage, and this may also have been the case with his second son, William. Howard's traceable property acquisitions were all concentrated in Norfolk, in or close to his home village, his connection with which led to his being sometimes known as William of Wiggenhall. They included the manor of East Winch, which he appears to have acquired through his second wife's first marriage to Simon Constable; it was at East Winch, in a chapel on the south side of the chancel, that he was buried. Howard seems to have died shortly before 24 August 1308, when he was replaced as an assize justice and recorded as deceased. PAUL BRAND

Sources *Chancery records* · published and unpublished law reports of the reign of Edward I · court of common pleas, feet of fines, PRO, CP 25/1 · Common bench plea rolls, PRO, CP 40 · G. Brenan and E. P. Statham, *The house of Howard*, 1 (1907)

Howard, William, first Baron Howard of Effingham (*c.*1510–1573), naval commander, was the fourth son of Thomas *Howard, second duke of Norfolk (1443–1524), and his second wife, Agnes Tilney (*d.* 1545). Educated at Trinity Hall, Cambridge, Lord William was brought to court immediately thereafter, where he appears to have made an early and favourable impression. In 1531 Henry VIII entrusted him with an embassy to the Scottish court, though its precise purpose remains obscure. He accompanied Henry to Boulogne for his meeting with François I in October 1532, and in May of the following year acted as earl marshal for his absent half-brother Thomas *Howard, third duke of Norfolk, in the ceremonies which culminated in Anne Boleyn's coronation. In February 1534 he travelled to Scotland once more to present the young James V with the Order of the Garter; twelve months later, accompanied by the bishop of St Asaph, he returned there with an entourage of sixty men to persuade James to go to England to be invested as duke of York. During his embassy Howard appears to have been shown great favour by the queen mother, Margaret Tudor, though he was unsuccessful in the clandestine task of urging her and James to shake off the pope's authority and seize the church's lands in Scotland. The matter came to the attention of Scottish bishops faithful to Rome, who promptly offered James an annuity of £3000 to stay out of England.

Howard married twice. His first wife was Katherine (*d.* 1535), daughter of John Boughton of Tuddington, Bedfordshire, with whom he had a daughter, Agnes. Second, in 1535, he married Margaret (*d.* 1581), daughter of Sir Thomas Gamage of Coety, Glamorgan, with whom he had two sons: Charles *Howard (1536–1624), who succeeded him as second Lord Howard of Effingham, and William.

In June 1535, with the duke of Norfolk, Sir William Fitzwilliam, and the bishop of Ely, Howard was part of an embassy to France to hold secret negotiations with the French admiral Philippe de Shabot. He returned to France in 1537; while there he received word from Thomas Cromwell that Jane Seymour had died, and was asked to report on suitable candidates to be Henry VIII's fourth wife. Howard may have been among those who met and subsequently recommended Anne of Cleves for that precarious honour. He was one of a guard of notables appointed to welcome her to England in 1539, though he seems not to have been harmed by the king's subsequent disappointment regarding her physical attributes. More seriously, while on a subsequent embassy to France in 1541, he was recalled to face trial for misprision of treason for seeking to conceal the adulteries of his niece Katherine Howard. King Henry, who almost certainly regarded Howard as innocent of anything more than kinship with the executed queen, pardoned him immediately following his conviction.

In 1544 Howard was with the army of the earl of Hertford at the siege of Edinburgh, during which he was

William Howard, first Baron Howard of Effingham (c.1510–1573), after Hans Eworth?, 1558

slightly wounded in the face. In July of the same year he accompanied Henry VIII to the siege of Boulogne. His earliest experience of command at sea, however, is obscure. Two of his half-brothers, Sir Edward *Howard (d. 1513) and Lord Thomas Howard, had been lord admirals, though at a time when William was too young to be employed by them. His first known role dates from 27 May 1545, when the king's council sent letters to Reigate ordering Howard to 'repayre to serve uppon the sees', with ten retainers of his choosing (*APC*, 1.171). Further orders in council during the year show him to have been patrolling the channel in the ship *Great Venetian*, during which he detained a number of foreign vessels; and in May 1546 he transported £12,000 to pay the English army at Calais. In discharging these duties, he was referred to as 'vice-admiral' to the lord admiral, Viscount Lisle. Lisle gave overall command of the English fleet to Howard in May 1546 when he joined the negotiations for the peace treaty of Cercamp.

Though not directly implicated, Howard was undoubtedly harmed by the fall of his nephew Henry *Howard, styled earl of Surrey, in 1547. Howard escaped punishment, but his family connections now made him ineligible to succeed Lisle, and in February 1547 Hertford's brother Lord Seymour of Sudeley was appointed lord admiral. However, though previously associated with the religiously conservative party against the reformist faction, Howard was not excluded from the new court. During Warwick's coup against the Somerset administration in October 1549, he was described as 'lord Marshall of the kinges oste', and was an influential ally of his former admiral (PRO, SP 10/9/24). Warwick's gratitude brought Howard several properties, including the manor of Effingham, Surrey, in 1551. In the following year Warwick (now duke of Northumberland) had him appointed lord deputy and governor of Calais, at a time when England and France seemed dangerously close to war once more.

With the death of Edward VI and fall of Northumberland in July and August 1553 Howard again applied his loyalties shrewdly. He held Calais for Mary against Jane Grey's supporters, and in January 1554 he formally met the Spanish ambassadors upon their arrival at London for negotiations on the proposed marriage of Mary and Philip, heir to the Spanish throne. When Wyatt advanced upon London in the same month, Howard, Pembroke, and Clinton took the lead in raising the militia in the city's defence. It was rumoured that on 4 February 1554 Howard attempted to parley with Wyatt at London Bridge. Three days later he played the decisive role in preventing Wyatt from entering the city when he held Ludgate against the advancing rebels, a check which led directly to Wyatt's surrender some hours later. Though subsequently of the eclipsed 'secular' grouping that briefly attempted to prevent Gardiner's re-establishment of papal influence in England, Howard was not discarded by Mary. A privy councillor since 3 January 1554, on 11 March he was ennobled as Baron Howard of Effingham, and nine days later received a patent as lord admiral (he had been discharging the duties of the office for almost four months), replacing the protestant Clinton.

In April 1554 Howard put to sea with a fleet of twenty-eight ships, ostensibly to protect channel trade and arrest pirates. In fact, his principal task was to prevent the interception of Philip by hostile French forces during his voyage to England to marry Mary. The lord admiral met the imperial fleet at the Needles, and obliged it to dip its colours to the queen's flag, an act motivated more by frustration at Philip's tardiness than by patriotic fervour, as was later implied. In May 1555 he was appointed to bear news to Charles V of the happy birth of an heir to Philip and Mary; poignantly, the sex of the child and date of birth were left blank in the premature passport which authorized his voyage. Three months later he escorted the disappointed Philip to Flanders, and, in 1557, during the Anglo-French war, his fleet transported the earl of Pembroke's expeditionary force to Calais. These duties were Howard's only substantial contribution to naval operations, and his influence upon other aspects of admiralty administration appears to have been negligible. His grip upon the office was always tenuous; though never considered disloyal by the queen, his consistent and courageous support for the right of succession of his great-niece the princess Elizabeth made him, while lord admiral, a potential threat to the Marian counter-reformation. Though he appears to have retained Mary's trust, his patent was revoked in February 1558 in favour of the now contrite Clinton. The immediate reason for his removal may have been the fall of Calais the previous month (though the navy had no part in that débâcle), or possibly his attendance as a mourner at the funeral of Anne of Cleves on 3 August 1557, a gesture that was undoubtedly regarded as provocative by Mary. As compensation for his loss, Howard was appointed lord chamberlain and provided with an annuity of 200 marks, predated to September 1557.

The accession of Elizabeth in November 1558 saw Howard's confirmation in the office of lord chamberlain. He received few other overt rewards for his support of her cause, though his retention as head of the royal household undoubtedly reflected the new queen's need to have her true friends close to her. From its first meeting on 20 November he was a member of her privy council, and her trust was further reflected in his appointment as one of the English negotiators for the treaty of Cateau Cambrésis at the beginning of 1559. His embassy to the French court in May was personally expensive, as he complained to Sir William Cecil, but a substantial present of silver plate from Henri II provided some compensation. As Elizabeth's rule stabilized, however, Howard's role in government became increasingly passive. A near constant attendee at privy council meetings during the 1560s, his duties were consequential but unspectacular, a reflection in part of his loyal but reticent character. As lord chamberlain, he was necessarily in frequent attendance upon the peripatetic queen, and the onerous requirements of his office, as much as growing ill health, appear to have been responsible for his gradual withdrawal from active political life. Council orders record minor collateral duties discharged by him, though these were increasingly of an honorific nature.

By the latter part of 1572 Howard's health had deteriorated to the point at which he could not discharge the duties of lord chamberlain. Recognizing this, Elizabeth appointed his nephew the earl of Sussex as his replacement and gave Howard the post of lord privy seal, a potentially lucrative but physically sedentary office. According to Holinshed (the only authority), Howard died at Hampton Court on 12 January 1573, and was buried at Reigate church. His survival in various offices during several antipathetic regimes has since encouraged the suggestion that he possessed the elastic principles of a *politique*. In fact, his record reflected considerable consistency of conviction. He remained a Henrician 'catholic', both spiritually pragmatic and politically conservative. In so far as he possessed any strong beliefs, they were directed to preserving the order of succession as determined by his old friend Henry VIII. He was a dutiful administrator, though not gifted; the imperial naval commander La Capelle, writing in 1555, regarded him as an incompetent lord admiral who had no effective control over his men.

Though he was a scion of one of the kingdom's most powerful families, Howard's estate was not that of a magnate. His correspondence contains several references to his relative poverty, even as late as 1567. Allocated modest properties by Mary and a pension from Prince Philip (which, like many similar awards, seems never to have been paid), his tenure as lord admiral was too brief for him to benefit greatly from the droits and tenths due from prize cargoes taken in the Anglo-French war of 1557–8. Warwick's gifts to him were more substantial but expensive to maintain; and while Elizabeth's favour was unstinting, Howard failed to transmute it into sufficient income to support a lifestyle commensurate with his dignity. To his son Charles he bequeathed lands worth some £300 per year, as well as properties of an unspecified value to his wife.   JAMES McDERMOTT

Sources APC, 1542–70 · CSP for., 1564–5; 1577–8 · LP Henry VIII, vols. 20–21 · R. Lindsay, *The history of Scotland from 21 February 1436 to March 1565, to which is added a continuation by another hand till August 1604* (1728) · J. Bain, ed., *The Hamilton papers: letters and papers illustrating the political relations of England and Scotland in the XVIth century*, 2 vols., Scottish RO, 12 (1890–92) · J. G. Nichols, ed., *The chronicle of Calais*, CS, 35 (1846) · *The diary of Henry Machyn, citizen and merchant-taylor of London, from AD 1550 to AD 1563*, ed. J. G. Nichols, CS, 42 (1848) · J. G. Nichols, ed., *The chronicle of Queen Jane, and of two years of Queen Mary*, CS, old ser., 48 (1850) · *Holinshed's chronicles of England, Scotland and Ireland*, ed. H. Ellis, 6 vols. (1807–8) · D. M. Loades, *The reign of Mary Tudor: politics, government and religion in England, 1553–58* (1979) · D. M. Loades, *The Tudor navy* (1992) · *The naval tracts of Sir William Monson*, ed. M. Oppenheim, 5 vols., Navy RS, 22–3, 43, 45, 47 (1902–14) · M. Oppenheim, *A history of the administration of the Royal Navy* (1896) · R. W. Kenny, *Elizabeth's admiral: the political career of Charles Howard, earl of Nottingham, 1536–1624* (1970) · R. M. Warnicke, *The rise and fall of Anne Boleyn* (1989) · M. B. Pulman, *The Elizabethan privy council in the 1570s* (1971)

Likenesses after H. Eworth?, portrait, 1558; Christies, 11 October 1957, lot 16 [*see illus.*] · W. Fiux, engraving, 1558 · J. Ogborne, line engraving, pubd 1774 (after H. E.), BM, NPG

Wealth at death bequeathed lands and property worth approx. £300 p.a. or more

Howard, Lord William (1563–1640), antiquary and landowner, was born at Audley End, Essex, on 19 December 1563, the younger son of Thomas *Howard, fourth duke of Norfolk (1538–1572), and his second wife, Margaret (1540–1564), only daughter and heir Thomas, Lord Audley of Walden and widow of Lord Henry Dudley. Howard's mother died shortly after his birth and he was brought up at Audley End with his elder brothers, Philip *Howard, later thirteenth earl of Arundel, and Thomas *Howard, later first earl of Suffolk. Both William and Thomas were tutored for a time in 1568–9 by Gregory Martin, a Catholic who resigned his fellowship at St John's College, Oxford, on 16 December 1568 to take up the post, and who fled to Douai in 1569 or 1570.

Marriage and a contested inheritance Norfolk's third wife, Elizabeth Leybourne (d. 1567), was the widow of Thomas, fourth Baron Dacre, with whom she had a son, George, who died in 1569, and three daughters, who became coheirs of the extensive Dacre estates in northern England. Norfolk's plan was to marry his three sons, Philip, Thomas, and William, to the three daughters, by now his wards, and they were duly betrothed in 1569, although the Dacre heiress designed for Thomas died after only one year of marriage in 1578. In 1572, following the execution of his father, William and Thomas were committed to the care of his elder half-brother Philip, and the guardianship of William Cecil, Lord Burghley. However, as planned by his father, on 28 October 1577 William duly married Elizabeth Dacre (1564–1639). They had at least seven sons and three daughters.

About 1577 Howard entered St John's College, Cambridge, probably shortly after his elder brother Thomas. William may have been the Mr Howard who gave a piece of plate to the college in 1575 or 1576. Both brothers seem also to have been tutored there by George Laughton, a fellow of King's College, Cambridge, and, unlike Martin, a protestant, who complained that William was 'slower of perception and to my great wonder, weaker in retaining what he has perceived' (Pollen and MacMahon, 18) than Thomas. William's arms are painted in the college's 'Liber memorialis' in recognition of a gift to the college, possibly the £100 he gave for the acquisition of books in 1629.

During the early 1580s Howard and his wife lived at Mount-Pleasant, Enfield Chase, Middlesex, and at Arundel House in London. Their first child, Philip, was born on 6 December 1581. During the 1580s Howard began to embrace Catholicism openly, probably due to the influence of his brother Philip, with whom he was incarcerated in the Tower of London in 1583 and again in 1585–6. As early as 1583 there were references to mass being celebrated at Howard's house in London, and he was to remain an ardent Catholic throughout his life. In 1584 the Howards' less secure position at court encouraged Francis Dacre, fourth son of the third Baron Dacre, in his efforts to claim the family estates. Similarly the earl of Leicester appears to have turned one of the Howards' local agents, Gerard Lowther (who was married to a Dudley), against the family and encouraged him to pursue a royal claim to the Dacre inheritance on the grounds that it was forfeit to the crown. In 1585 Elizabeth I duly sequestrated the estates, thereby adding to the litigation between the Howard brothers and the Dacre girls' uncles. Nor was the conflict confined to Cumberland: in 1587 both William and his brother Philip were arguing with Francis Dacre over Henderskelfe Castle in Yorkshire, eventually to become the site of Castle Howard. Howard responded to the Dacre and Lowther threats by building allegiances with his tenants, sometimes extending patronage to reiving families. During the 1590s the power vacuum created by Dacre's self-exile in Spain and Howard's absence in the south allowed members of the Lowther family to obtain local offices at the expense of Howard protégés.

Antiquary and collector Throughout the 1580s Howard began to associate with leading antiquaries, book collectors, and scholars. During his second period in the Tower, Howard was joined by the antiquary Nicholas Roscarrock, who may have provided him with an entrée into erudite circles. By 1587 Howard was acquiring important manuscripts, such as a copy of Ranulf Higden's *Polychronicon* from Bath Abbey, and by 1589 his collecting was in full swing with no less than eleven medieval manuscripts bearing inscriptions with that date joining his collection, and the years between 1587 and 1595 saw him acquire at least twenty-six significant medieval manuscripts. Altogether he accumulated a very significant library of manuscripts and printed books, now dispersed, which contained at least 128 medieval manuscripts, at least twenty-one of which came from identifiable British monastic libraries. The Durham antiquary William

Claxton refers to contacts between Howard and the London antiquary John Stow, and five of Howard's manuscripts bear Stow's annotations. John Dee was another source of manuscripts for Howard, four volumes having moved from Dee to Howard between 1589 and 1607. Howard also acquired manuscripts from members of the circle which had surrounded Matthew Parker during the 1560s and 1570s, indicating contact with Parker's son John, with John Twyne, with the London merchants William and Christopher Carye, and with the Kentish antiquary William Lambarde. James Ussher visited Naworth (Howard's seat in Cumberland from at least 1604) to consult the *Magna tabula* from Glastonbury Abbey some time before 1639. When the duke of Buckingham proposed the revival of the Society of Antiquaries in 1617 Howard's reputation was such that his name was found at the head of a list of 'persons of proven worth, fit to keep up, and celebrate' (Gough, xvi).

A significant facet of Howard's manuscript collecting was his penchant for illuminated books. A number of these—such as the Howard-Fitton psalter and the Luttrell psalter, both now in the British Library—he inherited from Howard or Arundel sources. Others, such as the De Lisle and the Eadui psalters (British Library), he acquired either through the book trade or through his contacts with other antiquaries. In 1592 Howard published an edition of the *Chronicon ex chronicis* of John of Worcester, thought at the time to be by Florence of Worcester. His edition was dedicated to Burghley and taken from a manuscript borrowed from William Lambarde and now in Trinity College, Dublin. The text was printed in London by Thomas Dawson for the stationer Richard Watkins, and was reprinted for the benefit of continental scholars in Frankfurt in 1601 together with the *Flores historiarum* of Matthew of Westminster.

In 1599 William Camden undertook a great northern antiquarian tour in the company of Sir Robert Cotton, and the two men were entertained at Naworth by Howard, who acted as their host and guide. Camden referred to him in the *Britannia* as 'a singular lover of venerable antiquity and learned with all' (Camden, 783), as Howard had copied inscriptions for him for inclusion in later editions of *Britannia*. Howard introduced the two men to Hadrian's Wall and other remains of Roman Britain, and attempted to convey Roman inscribed stones to Cotton in 1608. Howard owned a number of properties which included sections of the wall and other Roman remains, and gathered many Roman inscribed stones at Naworth, now mostly dispersed, but seen by numerous eighteenth-century visitors such as William Stukeley, Thomas Pennant, and John Horsley. Cotton and Howard formed a close friendship, with numerous loans of manuscripts taking place between them. Howard's daughter Margaret married Cotton's son Thomas about 1620.

Naworth Castle and the borders In 1601 Queen Elizabeth relented and allowed Howard's wife and the widowed Lady Arundel to buy back the forfeited Dacre lands; this was confirmed by letters patent of 19 December 1601. Howard's share included Naworth Castle, although it is not clear when he took possession of the Dacre estates. In 1602 he repurchased the barony of Gilsland from the crown. He was probably in residence at Naworth by 1604 and in 1607 Francis Dacre abandoned his claims to the property. In the 1607 edition of *Britannia*, Camden reported that Howard was involved in repairing Naworth Castle. One of the two great towers at Naworth is known as Lord William's tower, in which he housed his library in a room decorated with an ornate ceiling brought there from the Dacre castle at Kirkoswald, and statuary and part of a panelled screen brought from the ruins of Lanercost Priory, situated less than a mile to the north and closely associated with the Dacre family. In 1608 Howard was regranted the sequestered lands of his father. Howard was thus able to gather around him at Naworth a small community of like-minded individuals. One such was Roscarrock, who had joined the Naworth circle by 1607, the close friendship between the two symbolized in the Langdale rosary, an important piece of late medieval English jewellery with later beads inscribed for both men. Another significant artefact owned by Howard was the Howard grace cup, now in the Victoria and Albert Museum, arguably the finest piece of English renaissance silverware, and acquired by Howard from the estate of his uncle of Northampton, who also left him £2000 in recompense for the manor of Clun, which Howard's father had originally intended for him.

Howard was unable to play a full role in the politics of his day because of his religion. As James I noted in 1606, 'notwithstanding the infinite trust I had in the faithfulness of his brother [Thomas, earl of Suffolk] and uncle [Henry, earl of Northampton], yet I durst never bestow any preferment upon him in my days only because of his religion and devotion to the Jesuits' (Peck, 55). In both 1608 and 1616 there are references to Naworth being a refuge of religious conservatism presided over by Howard and his Benedictine chaplain, Augustine Hungate. Nevertheless, from his base at Naworth, Howard began to assert himself in the north-west, assisted by a policy of maximizing his estate revenues. This manifested itself in strong seigniorial leadership, Howard playing a key part in the pacification of the Cumberland borders, stamping out reiving, enforcing local justice, and even attempting to establish a unified policy on both sides of the border. Any opposition to his actions on the grounds of religion foundered on the protection offered by the king. Indeed, in 1616 recusancy proceedings were quashed by royal command. He was assisted in this by the influence at court of his relatives, first his uncle Henry *Howard, earl of Northampton (d. 1614), and his brother Suffolk (until his disgrace in 1618), and then his nephew Thomas *Howard, fourteenth earl of Arundel (who had succeeded Philip in 1595). The peak period of his influence in border politics followed the death of the earl of Dunbar in 1611, but gradually, in the 1620s and 1630s, the balance of local power shifted to the Cliffords.

Despite the importance of his life at Naworth, Howard continued to make frequent visits to London, to judge from references to expenses there in his household books.

When there he stayed in Arundel House, which had passed to his elder brother Philip, but which from 1607 was the property of Thomas Howard, fourteenth earl of Arundel. Howard also visited other parts of Britain, his accounts referring to purchases of old books made in Worcester in 1628.

Howard's wife died on 9 October 1639 and Howard himself died on 7 October 1640, in the ancient Dacre stronghold of Greystoke, Cumberland, to which he had fled fearing the incursions of the Scottish army at the more vulnerable Naworth. He was buried in Greystoke church on 9 October. He left ten children, his son William appearing to be his principal heir, although much of his library passed to his nephew, the second earl of Arundel.

RICHARD OVENDEN and STUART HANDLEY

Sources [G. Ornsby], ed., *Selections of the household books of the Lord William Howard of Naworth Castle*, SurtS, 68 (1878) · H. Howard, *Indications of memorials, monuments, paintings, and engravings of persons of the Howard family* (1834–6) · D. Mathew, 'The library at Naworth', *For Hilaire Belloc*, ed. D. Woodruff (1942), 117–30 · *Nicholas Roscarrock's lives of the saints: Cornwall and Devon*, ed. N. Orme, Devon and Cornwall RS, new ser., 35 (1992) · H. S. Reinmuth, 'Lord William Howard (1563–1640) and his Catholic associations', *Recusant History*, 12 (1973–4), 226–34 · G. Worsley, 'Naworth Castle, Cumberland', *Country Life* (12 Feb 1987), 74–9; (26 Feb 1987), 88–91 · C. G. C. Tite, 'Lost stolen or strayed? a survey of manuscripts formerly in the Cotton Library', *Sir Robert Cotton as collector: essays on an early Stuart courtier and his legacy*, ed. C. J. Wright (1997), 262–306 · D. Howarth, 'Sir Robert Cotton and the commemoration of famous men', *Sir Robert Cotton as collector: essays on an early Stuart courtier and his legacy*, ed. C. J. Wright (1997), 40–67 · K. Sharpe, *Sir Robert Cotton, 1586–1631: history and politics in early modern England* (1979) · N. Williams, *Thomas Howard, fourth duke of Norfolk* (1964) · R. T. Spence, 'The pacification of the Cumberland borders, 1593–1628', *Northern History*, 13 (1977), 59–160 · J. A. Hilton, 'The Cumbrian Catholics', *Northern History*, 16 (1980), 40–58 · J. H. Pollen and W. MacMahon, eds., *The Ven. Philip Howard, earl of Arundel, 1557–1595: English martyrs*, Catholic RS, 21 (1919) · Venn, *Alum. Cant.* · IGI · GEC, *Peerage* · S. J. Watts and S. J. Watts, *From border to middle shire, Northumberland, 1586–1625* (1975) · H. S. Reinmuth, 'Border society in transition', *Early Stuart studies: essays in honour of David Harris Wilson*, ed. H. S. Reinmuth (1970), 231–50 · P. Williams, 'The northern borderland under the early Stuarts', *Historical essays, 1600–1750, presented to David Ogg* (1963), 1–17 · L. L. Peck, *Northampton: patronage and policy at the court of James I* (1982) · B. Dietz, 'Louther, Gerard (i)', 'Louther, Gerard (ii)', HoP, *Commons, 1558–1603* · J. C. Henderson, 'Dacre, Francis', HoP, *Commons, 1558–1603* · W. Camden, *Britain, or, A chorographical description* (1610) · R. Gough, 'Introduction, containing an historical account of the origin and establishment of the Society of Antiquaries', *Archaeologia*, 1 (1770), xvi

Archives Castle Howard, Yorkshire, corresp. and accounts · U. Durham, Howard of Naworth books · U. Durham, Howard of Naworth estate MSS | Arundel Castle, Sussex, letters to earl of Arundel · BL, Arundel MSS 29, 150 · Coll. Arms, Arundel MSS · Cumbria AS, Carlisle, Aglionby MSS · Cumbria AS, Carlisle, Howard of Naworth MSS

Likenesses C. Janssens, portrait, oils, c.1630, Naworth Castle, Cumbria · W. K. Ashford, lithograph (after C. Johnson), BM, NPG; repro. in Howard, *Indications of memorials*

Howard, William, Viscount Stafford (1612–1680), nobleman, was born on 30 November 1612, the fifth son of Thomas *Howard, fourteenth earl of Arundel (1585–1646), courtier and art collector, and his wife, Lady Alathea (d. 1654), daughter of Gilbert *Talbot, seventh earl of Shrewsbury. His grandfather Philip *Howard, thirteenth earl of

Arundel, had been imprisoned as a Roman Catholic under Queen Elizabeth I and died in the Tower of London, but his father converted to the Church of England in 1616. William's education was ostensibly Anglican, but at home he was doubtless exposed to Catholic influences, especially from his mother. In 1620 he was placed in the household of Samuel Harsnett, bishop of Norwich and an anti-Catholic controversialist, to be educated. Henry Peacham was one of his tutors in Norwich and dedicated his work *The Complete Gentleman*, published in 1622, to him. In 1624, at the age of eleven, Howard went as a gentleman commoner to St John's College, Cambridge, but he took no degree. He was made a knight of the Bath at Charles I's coronation in 1626. He is listed as an ecclesiastical commissioner in 1633, which argues for continued conformity to the established church. He already seems to have been bitten by the collector's bug, like his father, and in 1633 he wrote to William Petty who was in Venice buying books and works of art for his father, 'I pray if you meet with any thing that is good … buy it for me' (Hervey, 338–9). He accompanied his father on an embassy to the Holy Roman empire in April 1636, and the following year acted as part of the escort when the elector palatine went to the Netherlands.

By a marriage licence granted by the bishop of London on 11 October 1637, Howard married Mary (1620/21–1694), daughter of Edward Stafford and sister of Henry, fifth (or fourteenth) Baron Stafford. The Staffords were Roman Catholics and the marriage was conducted by a Catholic priest on 12 October with the connivance of the bridegroom's mother, to the embarrassment of Howard's conformist father. The fifth Baron Stafford, who had been a ward in the Arundel household, died shortly afterwards, leaving his property to his sister, and the Howards, with royal support, secured the title for the newly-weds. The last male Stafford, Roger, a cousin, who was of a 'very mean and obscure condition' (GEC, *Peerage*, vol. 12, pt 1, 188), surrendered the barony to the crown in return for a payment of £800, and on 12 September 1640 William and Mary Howard were created Baron and Baroness Stafford. Two months later, on 11 November, Lord Stafford took a step up in the peerage, being created Viscount Stafford. The Staffords eventually had three sons and six daughters.

As political tensions in England heightened Stafford, his wife, and their newborn baby went abroad, leaving in August 1641 for the Low Countries. Based largely at Antwerp, he was free to practise Catholicism, and was close to his parents, the earl and countess of Arundel, who too left England. In 1646 and 1647 he was permitted by parliament to return with his wife to England. In 1649 Stafford's estate was sequestered, and later compounded for his recusancy and royalism. At his trial in 1680 Stafford claimed he went abroad 'thinking that my presence might rather prejudice' the king 'than serve him'. But, he said, he 'was not satisfied in my conscience to see my king in so much disorder and I not endeavouring to serve him what I could, to free him from his troubles', and hence 'I did come to England, and served his majesty faithfully and loyally as long

as he lived' (*State trials*, 7.1359). There is at present no evidence to provide further details of what services he performed for Charles I. During the interregnum he travelled quite often to and from England and the Low Countries. In 1649 and 1650 he visited Rome. In 1652 he was in the Palatinate and was arrested and imprisoned for a year in Heidelberg. According to one report he was imprisoned for immorality; writing half a century later, Bishop Burnet said vaguely he 'had been guilty of great vices in his youth, which had almost proved fatal to him' (*Burnet's History*, 2.269), and this has been held to refer to this incident, although the matter is disputed. While he was in prison, Stafford's friends and relations made strenuous efforts to secure his release, and it was finally due to the intervention of a certain Padre Saria that he was freed. The death of his father in 1646 and of his mother in 1654 precipitated family quarrels over inheritance, especially between Stafford and his elder brother's family. In 1656 he was briefly imprisoned again, this time for his father's debts in the Netherlands.

With the Restoration in 1660 Stafford was restored to his property and resumed his seat in the House of Lords. Although he was by no means a major political figure, some of his Howard relatives held places at court, notably his nephew Philip *Howard, one of Catherine of Braganza's Roman Catholic chaplains and later a cardinal. He himself played a small role in the intricate affairs of the Restoration state. He tried to use his influence to secure the removal of the anti-Catholic penal laws. Stafford first broached the matter with the king at the time when Charles II made the declaration of Breda shortly before the Restoration, and offered to raise £100,000 among Catholics in order to buy toleration. In 1675 he approached the earl of Shaftesbury and discussed toleration for Catholics with him, offering to gain the support of James, duke of York, for a dissolution of the Cavalier Parliament in return for some concessions. He was willing at this time, as were other Catholic peers, to take the oath of allegiance. Stafford's efforts seem to have been desultory and he was not a leading figure among the Catholics. Neither was he close to the royal family, feeling resentful that the king did not favour him more, and having no strong links with the duke of York. He had many aristocratic diversions to occupy him. He became a fellow of the Royal Society in 1665 and was elected in 1672 to the society's council. Stafford county, Virginia, may have been named after Stafford, who apparently patronized a group of Catholic colonists in the colony. He continued to travel abroad. A magnificent portrait by Van Dyck shows the young Stafford perhaps haughty, but also cagey and defensive in his suit of armour. According to John Evelyn, 'he was not a man beloved, especially of his own family' (*Diary of John Evelyn*, 2.65). He suffered from an irrational fear of roses.

In 1678 Titus Oates and other informants implicated Stafford in the Popish Plot. He gave himself up to the authorities and, along with four other Catholic peers similarly accused, was imprisoned in the Tower of London on

31 October 1678. In the spring of 1679 preparations for the trial of the five lords reached an advanced stage, but they were saved when Charles prorogued parliament. A mood of scepticism about the plot developed and it looked as though Stafford and his fellow accused had escaped. But in 1680, with parliament again in session, the whig exclusionists felt it was in their interests to stir up anti-Catholic feeling, and on 30 November Stafford was put on trial. The process was one of impeachment—indeed it was the only successful impeachment in the reign of Charles II. Stafford was tried by the Lords on the accusations of the Commons in a great show trial staged, in the presence of the king himself, in Westminster Hall. It has been asked why Stafford was singled out, alone of the Catholic peers, for this treatment. Some commentators have alleged his general unpopularity; others his reputation for timidity, which led his accusers to think he might break down, or defend himself weakly. A more straightforward reason is that the prosecution felt it had more evidence to bring against him than the other peers. Moreover, no one could say at the time of his trial that the other Catholic lords would not later have been put on trial.

The case against Stafford was based on the evidence of Oates and another veteran of earlier trials, Stephen Dugdale. Oates said that he had seen a document from the pope naming a series of highly placed English conspirators and conferring on them positions in the expected Catholic restoration; among those named was Stafford, who was to be paymaster of a papal army. Dugdale swore that Stafford had attempted to suborn him into assassinating the king while Stafford had been visiting Lord Aston, Dugdale's employer. Much turned on whether Dugdale and Stafford had been alone together, which may have been the case on 21 September 1678, the day of a local foot race which Dugdale attended in the company of one of Stafford's servants. A third witness, a certain Edward Turberville, alleged that he had visited Stafford when he was staying in Paris and had also been encouraged to kill Charles II. Turberville at first named a year for this plot which was impossible, but then adopted another one more consistent with Stafford's defence. This meagre evidence was topped and tailed with the usual mythology of papal pretensions and Catholic turpitude. Stafford's family connection with another of those accused by Oates, Cardinal Howard, cannot have helped his case. Stafford was taken ill during the trial but conducted a defence unaided which according to some observers was good and according to others was not. He brought witnesses to undermine the evidence of his accusers, and he questioned the legal basis of the prosecution. He also made very fulsome declarations of his loyalty to the king, and rejected wholeheartedly the Catholic doctrines of papal political power. He was convicted on 7 December by a majority of 55 to 31 and sentenced to the barbarous punishment of traitors, which the king commuted to beheading. Stafford protested his innocence to the end, appearing before the House of Lords after his conviction to give a somewhat incoherent account of his political activities

under the Restoration, the purpose of which seems to have been to underline how innocuous they were. Stafford was executed at Tower Hill on 29 December 1680. He is usually said to have been buried the same day in the chapel of St Peter ad Vincula in the Tower, but at least one report stated that his body was returned to his relations.

After he had witnessed the execution Sir John Reresby dined with Lord Halifax and both agreed that there would soon be another civil war. It was forty years since the impeachment of Lord Strafford, a trial over which the present victim's father had presided. But history was not repeating itself; some months later the king took decisive action in dissolving the third Exclusion Parliament and the tide turned against the whigs, ensuring that Charles II would save the succession for his brother. The accession of James II led to the restoration of the title to Stafford's widow (who was created countess of Stafford in 1688 and died on 13 January 1694), but it was not until 1824 that Stafford's attainder was reversed, removing, in the words of the then prime minister, Lord Liverpool, 'the greatest blot in our history' (S. N. D., 225). PETER HOLMES

Sources DNB · GEC, Peerage · S. N. D., Sir William Howard, Viscount Stafford (1929) · Gillow, Lit. biog. hist. · M. F. S. Hervey, The life, correspondence and collections of Thomas Howard, earl of Arundel (1921) · Memoirs of Sir John Reresby, ed. A. Browning (1936), 205–9, 330 · The Nicholas papers, ed. G. F. Warner, 4 vols., CS, new ser., 40, 50, 57, 3rd ser., 31 (1886–1920), vol. 2, pp. 298, 311–12; vol. 3, pp. 247, 252 · Diary of John Evelyn, ed. W. Bray, new edn, ed. H. B. Wheatley, 4 vols. (1906), vol. 2, pp. 307–8; vol. 3, pp. 26, 57–66 · J. Kenyon, The Popish Plot (1972) · J. Miller, Popery and politics in England, 1660–88 (1973), 33, 96, 141, 175–6 · C. Dodd [H. Tootell], The church history of England, from the year 1500, to the year 1688, 3 (1742), 242–7 · Burnet's History of my own time, ed. O. Airy, new edn, 2 (1900), 165–6, 268–78 · Calendar of the Clarendon state papers preserved in the Bodleian Library, 1: To Jan 1649, ed. O. Ogle and W. H. Bliss (1872), 390; 2: 1649–1654, ed. W. D. Macray (1869), 154, 222, 263, 276 · Report on the manuscripts of Allan George Finch, 5 vols., HMC, 71 (1913–2003), vol. 2, pp. 94, 102 · The manuscripts of the Earl Cowper, 3 vols., HMC, 23 (1888–9), vol. 2, pp. 161, 290 · Clarendon, Hist. rebellion, 6.6; 7.369 · Stafford's memoires, or, A brief impartial account of the birth and quality, imprisonment ... of William, late Lord Viscount Stafford (1681) · W. Howard, A pattern of Christian loyalty (1634) · State trials, 7.1213–575 · The manuscripts of the House of Lords, 4 vols., HMC, 17 (1887–94), vol. 1, pp. 23–45, 222, 292–3 · The manuscripts of the House of Lords, new ser., 12 vols. (1900–77), vol. 11, pp. 342–4 · JHL, 4 (1628–42), 84, 86; 8 (1645–6), 384; 9 (1646–7), 327; 11 (1660–66), 79; 13 (1675–81), 270, 698 · R. North, Examen (1740), 215–20 · H. Foley, ed., Records of the English province of the Society of Jesus, 7 vols. in 8 (1875–83), vol. 5, pp. 26, 27n., 43n., 83, 96, 107, 432, 827, 839 · R. Challoner, Memoirs of missionary priests, ed. J. H. Pollen, rev. edn (1924), 569–74 · Venn, Alum. Cant. · G. Sitwell, 'Leander Jones's mission to England', Recusant History, 5 (1959–60), 132–83 · W. K. L. Webb, 'Thomas Preston O. S. B., alias Roger Widdrington', Biographical Studies, 2 (1954), 216–68 · The manuscripts of Lord Kenyon, HMC, 35 (1894), 104–5, 122–4 · M. A. E. Green, ed., Calendar of the proceedings of the committee for compounding ... 1643–1660, 5 vols., PRO (1889–92); repr. (1967) · CSP dom., 1654, 442; 1655, 142, 581; 1650, 273; 1657–8, 550; 1659–60, 572 · T. Birch, History of Royal Society, 4 vols. (1756–7) · Thurloe, State papers, 4.355; 6.436

Archives Arundel Castle, West Sussex, papers · Costessey Park, Norfolk, Jerningham MSS · HLRO, impeachment and trial · Westm. DA, personal and family papers

Likenesses E. Luttrell, mezzotint, BM · A. Van Dyck, portrait, Cardiff Castle; version, Marquis of Bute · engraving (after A. Van Dyck), repro. in Ludge, Portraits, vol. 6 · miniature, priv. coll. · oils (after A. Van Dyck), Arundel Castle, West Sussex · portrait, St Augustine's Priory, Newton Abbot · portraits, repro. in S. N. D., *Sir William Howard* · watercolour miniature (after unknown portrait, *c*.1670), NPG

Howard, William, third Baron Howard of Escrick

(*c*.1630–1694), conspirator, was the second son of Edward *Howard, first Baron Howard of Escrick (*d*. 1675), and Mary (*d*. 1634), daughter of John Boteler, first Baron Boteler of Brantfield. After attending Corpus Christi College, Cambridge, where he matriculated in 1646, he moved to Lincoln's Inn in 1648 and was called to the bar in 1654. Dismissed from Cromwell's life guards early in 1656 because of his Leveller views, Howard, a Baptist, visited the exiled court at Bruges later that year, but he failed to obtain the £2000 he sought from Charles in return for securing Leveller support. Betrayed, possibly by John Wildman, Howard was arrested three times in the months following his return. He received monetary support from Sir Edward Hyde, with whom he corresponded using the aliases Richard Collins and John Fisher. Charles expressed his confidence in Howard's integrity in October 1658, and the following year wanted him to foster dissension among the troops and incite opposition to Richard Cromwell. In the summer of 1659 Howard spread the word that Charles, if restored, would indulge tender consciences. The government ordered his arrest in January 1660, but in the changing political climate he won the seat for Winchelsea in the Convention, probably owing to William Ashburnham's assistance. Howard served on only one committee, to preserve the Forest of Dean. For his service to the exiled court Clarendon gave him £500, and Howard and his younger brother, Sir Cecil, also received £1500, payable from smuggling fines and forfeitures, for secret service. He served as commissioner of oyer and terminer for the home circuit in July 1660 and as an assessment commissioner for Westminster from 1661 to 1663. He subsequently profited from the sale of several baronetcies.

On 21 July 1661 Howard married Frances Bridgeman (1645/6–1716), daughter of Sir James Bridgeman of Whitley, Yorkshire, with whom he had four sons and two daughters. When the Baptist printer Francis Smith was arrested on suspicion of issuing *Mirabilis annus*, an allegedly seditious book of prodigies, the government had Howard attempt to obtain his confession. He was apparently experiencing financial difficulties by 1665, when he unsuccessfully sued the keeper of the king's bench prison for £900 after the latter failed to return prisoners to the exchequer in a timely fashion. In July 1665 he moved to Ireland to practise law, enjoying the benefits of a king's counsellor at Charles's request. Jailed for debt, he borrowed from a client, the earl of Meath, and then, to avoid repayment, took refuge at Whitehall as a gentleman of the privy chamber. From late June to October he was incarcerated in the Tower for suspected seditious activity, after which he went to the Netherlands and served as a double agent during the Third Anglo-Dutch War. Following the death of his older brother, Thomas (*b*. 1625), on 24 August 1678, he succeeded to the peerage, but the estate had been sold ten years earlier.

Howard endorsed Titus Oates's allegations of a popish plot and was one of the most outspoken 'opposition' peers, being among those who petitioned Charles in December 1679 to permit parliament to convene the following month. An ally of Shaftesbury and a member of the Green Ribbon Club, he became embroiled in charges and countercharges of sedition. In November 1680 he helped convict his own Catholic relative, Viscount Stafford, of treason. With two footmen he assaulted an informer in April 1681, and the victim repaid him by accusing him of seditious language. Falsely charged with having written *The True Englishman*, which accused Charles of arbitrary rule, he was arrested on 11 June. In the king's bench he protested his innocence, and, with Algernon Sidney's assistance, persuaded the government to drop the case in the absence of credible witnesses. In July the state went after him again, this time when William Carr, the English consul in the Netherlands, accused him of treasonable conduct in the recent war, but once again the case was eventually dropped. By December, in self-defence, Howard, Essex, Sir Patience Ward, and others were compiling evidence against the fabricators of the alleged presbyterian plot. During the spring of 1682 Howard participated in the whig dinner parties that discussed the forthcoming London shrieval elections. In October he first learned about plans for an insurrection to pressure Charles to exclude his brother from the succession. Shaftesbury asked him to lead an uprising in Essex, but he demurred until he could consult other peers. He served as an intermediary between Monmouth and Shaftesbury, and following the latter's death he participated in the so-called council of six with Monmouth, Sidney, Essex, Lord William Russell, and John Hampden. Through his association with the attorney Robert West he knew about schemes to assassinate Charles and James. The government arrested Howard on 8 July 1683: magistrates found him hiding in a cupboard behind a chimney. Although Charles reportedly thought Howard 'soe ill a man that he would not hang the worst dog he had on his Evidence' (committee minutes, House of Lords, 22 Nov 1689), in fact he believed the substance of Howard's charges following Monmouth's private confession. The government used Howard to testify against Russell, Sidney, and Hampden. Pardoned on 2 October 1683, he testified at the trial of Henry Booth, Lord Delamere, in January 1686. In 1689 he was among the supporters of William in determining the constitutional settlement. A 'little crooked', misshapen man (*CSP dom.*, 1672, 302), Howard was praised by Clarendon as 'a person of very extraordinary parts, sharpness of wit, readiness and volubility of tongue' (*Clarendon State Papers*, 6.78). Howard died in April 1694, probably in York, and was buried at York Minster on the 24th. Aged seventy, his widow was interred at Richmond, Surrey, on 24 December 1716.   RICHARD L. GREAVES

Sources PRO, SP 29/417, 29/428, 29/432 · *CSP dom.*, 1659–60, 326; 1661–2, 87, 158, 175, 203, 288, 327; 1663–4, 9, 45; 1665–6, 151, 154; 1668–9, 647; 1672, 284, 302; 1679–80, 296; 1680–81; July–Sept 1683 · *Calendar of the Clarendon state papers preserved in the Bodleian Library*, 4: 1657–1660, ed. F. J. Routledge (1932) · BL, Add. MS 38847 · [T. Sprat],

Copies of the informations and original papers relating to the proof of the horrid conspiracy against the late king, his present majesty and the government (1685) • *Calendar of the manuscripts of the marquess of Ormonde*, new ser., 8 vols., HMC, 36 (1902–20), vols. 6–7 • R. L. Greaves, *Secrets of the kingdom: British radicals from the Popish Plot to the revolution of 1688–89* (1992) • Clarendon, *Hist. rebellion*, vol. 6 • M. W. Helms and B. D. Henning, 'Howard, Hon. William', HoP, *Commons, 1660–90*, 2.605–6 • GEC, *Peerage*, new edn, 6.586–7 • K. H. D. Haley, *William of Orange and the English opposition, 1672–4* (1953) • *CSP Ire.*, 1663–5, 611

Likenesses G. Bower, silver medal, BM • G. P. Harding, wash drawing (after unknown artist), Scot. NPG

Howarth, Charles (1814–1868), co-operative movement activist, was born on 9 February 1814 in Rochdale, Lancashire, the son of George Howarth and his wife, Susan (*née* Bamford). Little is known of Howarth's early life and education, but while in his teens he was drawn to socialism and influenced by the ideas of Robert Owen. An Owenite project of self-employment among flannel weavers in Rochdale was established in 1829, followed in 1830 by the First Rochdale Co-operative Store. It is unclear how long the latter survived and whether it was through this venture or a successor that Howarth became associated with co-operation. He was, however, linked with a store trading at 15 Toad Lane between 1833 and 1835.

On 5 April 1835 Howarth married Ann Chadwick, and in the years to 1862 they had four sons and five daughters. Howarth secured relatively well-paid employment as a warper at Hoyle's cotton mill on Oldham Road, Rochdale, and was recorded as living nearby in 1841 and 1851. He remained an active Owenite as a member of the no. 24 branch of the Rational Society from its foundation in 1838 until 1845. During the early 1840s Howarth was also locally prominent in agitation for the Ten Hours Act, being sent as a delegate to lobby parliament. He is, however, most associated with the revival of co-operative trading in Rochdale.

At the first formal meeting of the Rochdale Equitable Pioneers Society [*see* Rochdale Pioneers] on 11 August 1844 Howarth was appointed as one of three trustees. He was also chiefly responsible for drafting the society's rules. These reflected not only immediate concerns about wage rates and malpractice by shopkeepers but also radical causes then current in Rochdale. The project attracted disillusioned Chartists, and the planned temperance hotel suggests the involvement of teetotallers; but it was pre-eminently Owenite in stamp, and its aims included industrial and agricultural self-employment and the development of a co-operative colony. Howarth indeed drew upon existing Owenite sources, notably the model rules presented at the 1832 Co-operative Congress and those governing the Rational Association Sick and Burial Society of Manchester. He also included provisions for the conduct of co-operative storekeeping which have been seen as laying foundations for successful consumers' co-operation. Claims made for the originality of this constitutional development cannot, however, be substantiated. Dividend on purchase, for example, was known from at least the 1820s and was more widely discussed in the 1830s and 1840s than some historians have credited. It is unlikely that Howarth independently reinvented the 'divi'.

Howarth's rules were, however, the basis for the development of the Rochdale Equitable Pioneers Society, which started trading on 21 December 1844. Howarth acted as president of the society during 1845 and as secretary for several periods. In 1850 Howarth drafted rules for a co-operative corn mill society being established in Rochdale, and became its first secretary, and in 1854 he was a promoter of the Rochdale Co-operative Manufacturing Society. Howarth also contributed to the wider extension of co-operation. In 1856 he was a delegate at a conference in Rochdale which considered developing a wholesaling operation co-owned and funded by several consumers' co-operatives. Howarth was also involved in campaigning for the amendment of the Industrial and Provident Societies Act to allow such co-operative federation. The passage of new legislation in 1862 enabled the foundation of the North of England Co-operative Wholesale Society of which Howarth was a leading promoter, serving on its management committee until October 1866.

During the late 1850s Howarth moved some 3 miles to Heywood. By 1859 he was auditor for the Heywood Co-operative Society. He was also manufacturing washing soda and bleach which were sometimes purchased by the Co-operative Wholesale Society—a potential conflict of interest which led to his departure from its committee. Howarth was, however, a founder of the Co-operative Insurance Company in 1867, remaining a director until his death.

Howarth's death on 25 June 1868 at his home, 28 Wilton Street, Heywood, was attributed to asthma. He was buried five days later at Heywood cemetery. Howarth was probably not well off in his later years, having left his work as a warper during the mid-1860s. On his death the Co-operative Wholesale Society granted £20 to Howarth's wife who, with five of their children, survived him.

MARTIN PURVIS

Sources G. D. H. Cole, *A century of co-operation* (1945) • G. J. Holyoake, *Self-help by the people: the history of the Rochdale Pioneers, 1844–1892*, 10th edn (1900) • W. H. Brown, *Heywood's co-operative centenary, 1850–1950* (1950) • H. F. Bing and J. Saville, 'Howarth, Charles', *DLB*, vol. 1 • private information (2004) [Mrs Dorothy Greaves, Toad Lane Co-operative Museum, Rochdale] • W. Robertson, 'Rochdale: the birthplace of modern co-operation', *Handbook of the annual co-operative congress* (1892) • D. J. Doyle, 'Rochdale and the origins of the Rochdale Society of Equitable Pioneers', DPhil diss., St John's University, New York, 1972 • A. Bonner, *British co-operation: the history, principles, and organisation of the British co-operative movement*, rev. edn (1970) • P. Redfern, *The story of the C.W.S., 1863–1913* (1913) • *Weekly Free Press* (25 April 1829) • *Weekly Free Press* (13 Nov 1830) • *Rochdale Observer* (4 July 1868) • parish records (marriage), St Chad's, Rochdale, 5 April 1835

Archives Man. CL, Manchester Archives and Local Studies, papers relating to the Rochdale Equitable Pioneers Society, minute book of board meetings and general meetings, MF 870 [microfilm] • Rochdale Public Library, local history collection, Rochdale Equitable Pioneers Society, minute book, C/CO-OP/1 1/1/1

Likenesses photograph, *c.*1845, Rochdale Pioneers Museum, Rochdale • group portrait, photograph, 1865 (with Rochdale Pioneers), Rochdale Pioneers Museum, Rochdale; *see illus. in* Rochdale Pioneers (*act.* 1844) • group portrait, photograph, 1865 (with Rochdale Pioneers), Rochdale Public Library, Rochdale, local history collection

Howarth, John Aubrey Conway [Jack] (1896–1984), actor, was born at 96 Mitchell Street, Rochdale, on 19 February 1896, son of the comedian Richard (Bert) Howarth and his wife, Amelia Townsend. He was educated at the local board council school, which was also attended by Gracie Fields at the time, and became a circus-lover after a visit to Rochdale by Buffalo Bill in 1904. He found his first taste of show business when he sold programmes in the auditorium at the Theatre Royal, Rochdale, where his father performed, before making his acting début at the age of twelve by playing children's roles with Churchill's Minstrels at the Happy Valley, Llandudno.

During the First World War he served with the Lancashire Fusiliers in France, then transferred to the bantams, a regiment for those under 5 feet 4 inches tall, but was demobilized after just six weeks on being classified unfit. For the rest of the war he ran a small cinema. Then he returned to the theatre as a member of Leslie Henson's touring company, before working as a stage director and actor for the actor–writer–producer Hamilton Deane on the original British productions of *Dracula* and *Frankenstein*. He made his London West End début in the first play, in 1927. After meeting the actress Sarah Elizabeth (Betty) Murgatroyd, daughter of John Murgatroyd, who appeared in both productions on tour, he married her in Hull on 25 July 1929 between a matinée and an evening performance of *Frankenstein*. They had a son, John. In 1935 he started his own theatre company in Colwyn Bay, and during the Second World War took most of the male roles there himself because too few men were available.

After the war Howarth was cast as Mr Maggs, odd-job man and husband of the charwoman, in the BBC radio serial *Mrs Dale's Diary* when it began in 1948, and stayed for twelve years until the character was killed off. He was also in early episodes of the legendary radio comedy series *The Clitheroe Kid*, which started in 1957 and featured the Lancashire comedian Jimmy Clitheroe as an eternal naughty schoolboy. Among dozens of television programmes in which he appeared, he played the pigeon-fancying grandfather in the 1956 ITV comedy series *My Sister and I*, which starred Dinah Lee and Jane Taylor as two sisters with the capacity to think alike. He also acted Alderman Joseph Helliwell in J. B. Priestley's *When we are Married* (1951), the Pedlar in *The Secret Garden* (1952), a cricketer in *The Pickwick Papers* (1952), a waiter in *Vanity Fair* (1956), Mr Briggs in *Champion Road*, a publican in *The Man who Made Keys* (1959), and Uncle Fred in the Armchair Theatre production *Honeymoon Postponed* (1961).

During Howarth's long career he took roles in eighteen films, most notably that of the clogmaker Tubby Wadlow in director David Lean's acclaimed screen version of *Hobson's Choice* (1953; originally a 1915 stage play by Harold Brighouse), starring Charles Laughton in the story of a Lancashire cobbler and his eldest daughter, who sets up a business in competition with him. The actor had played the same role on television three years earlier. His other films included *Cure for Love* (1949), *The Man in the White Suit* (1951), *Lady in the Fog* (1952, released in the USA as *Scotland Yard Inspector*), and *Professor Tim* (1957). 'I've appeared in a lot of films I'd like to forget', he once said, 'but they keep turning up on television on Sunday afternoons' (*Television Today*, 5 April 1984).

Then he joined *Coronation Street* as Albert Tatlock when the ITV serial set in the north of England began, appearing from its first episode on 9 December 1960. The widowed uncle of Ken Barlow's first wife-to-be, Valerie, the grumpy skinflint famous for his cloth cap and cadging of rums in the Rovers Return was often seen with his fellow pensioners Ena Sharples, Minnie Caldwell, and Martha Longhurst, forever talking of the past and only grudgingly coming to terms with changing times. As Uncle Albert, the actor immortalized a generation who had fought through two world wars and wondered at the lack of respect he and others received from the young for keeping their country free from fascism. Howarth wore a false moustache to play the role and, for all of his twenty-three years and most of 1322 episodes, the same suit—a dark grey, three-piece, woollen, single-breasted outfit—which was a feat included in the children's television programme *First Post* during a look behind the scenes at Granada Television. Only on very special occasions did Albert sport a newer suit. The actor was one of just two chosen to meet the queen backstage when the *Coronation Street* cast performed a sketch at the Palace Theatre, Manchester, during her silver jubilee celebrations in 1977. On screen he also appeared in the film version of Bill Naughton's stage play *Spring and Port Wine* (1970).

Howarth was made an MBE in the 1983 new year's honours list for his charity work, most notably as a vice-president of the Stars Organization for Spastics. The last of *Coronation Street*'s original pensioners, he was last seen on screen on 25 January 1984 and died of renal failure and pneumonia at Llandudno General Hospital two months later, on 31 March 1984. A memorial service was held at the actors' church, St Paul's, Covent Garden, London, on 19 June 1984.   ANTHONY HAYWARD

Sources A. Hayward and D. Hayward, *TV unforgettables* (1993) · *The Times* (2 April 1984) · *Television Today* (5 April 1984) · *Daily Mirror* (3 Nov 1983) · SIFT database, BFI National Library · b. cert. · m. cert. · d. cert.
Likenesses photographs, Hult. Arch.
Wealth at death £61,488: probate, 17 July 1984, *CGPLA Eng. & Wales*

Howarth, Thomas Edward Brodie (1914–1988), schoolmaster and historian, was born on 21 October 1914 in Rutherglen, Lanarkshire, the elder son (there were no daughters) of Frank Fielding Howarth, director of an insurance company, and his wife, Edith Brodie. From Rugby School he won a scholarship to Clare College, Cambridge, where he achieved firsts in both parts of the history tripos (1935 and 1936). His forte was teaching. He taught briefly at Canford School, Dorset, then at Winchester College (1938–9), but then came the Second World War. He enlisted immediately, was commissioned in the King's (Liverpool) regiment, reaching the rank of brigade major, and in February 1945 joined the personal staff of Field

Marshal Bernard Montgomery. A significant friendship began. He wrote, 'After the first soul-stripping scrutiny which he [Montgomery] imposed on anybody crossing his path, he was to treat me with consistent kindness and consideration for the next twenty-five years'. He emerged from the war with an MC (1945) and returned to Winchester. In 1948 he was appointed headmaster of King Edward's School, Birmingham. He was instrumental in raising the school's academic standards, but he lacked the patience to deal with an oppressive governing body, and in 1952 was back at Winchester as second master. The accusation that he had run away from an important job stung him.

The second master of Winchester is housemaster of the scholars, and they needed a sympathetic and inspiring pastor. Howarth, delighting in the company of intelligent young people, proved just that. One pupil described 'the taut wiry figure, keen eye, broad forehead, listening curled up in his chair, coiled for action with a mind never still, stabbing at words'. His wit was liberally spiced with gossip, and outrageous statements were uttered with a nasal intonation imitated by generations of his pupils, accompanied by great gusts of laughter. It was very exciting to be taught by him, and his courses on the French Revolution and nineteenth-century France were particularly memorable.

In 1962 Howarth was appointed high master of St Paul's School in London. His achievement there was the transplanting of the school from its gaunt Hammersmith setting to a superb site in Barnes. He never pandered to the confused but impassioned values of the 'revolting students' of the late 1960s. He left the detailed management of the school to people with less imagination than himself. He was uninterested in the minutiae of headmastering, preferring a more public life, as a member of the Public Schools Commission (1966) and then, in 1969, chairman of the Headmasters' Conference.

These roles enabled Howarth to assert his views. He wrote that his experiences on the commission 'convinced me that the reformers are determined to sacrifice scholarship and a great many values which I regard as essential to a civilised community on the altar of a totally unattainable egalitarianism'. These values included a passionate commitment to meritocracy, together with active opposition to social élitism, and he expounded them, unfashionable as they were at the time, in a Public Schools Commission minority report.

Howarth left St Paul's in 1973 to become senior tutor of Magdalene College, Cambridge. Here he used his numerous contacts to good effect, lifting the quality while broadening the range of the college's entry. In 1980 he was invited to become headmaster of Campion International School in Athens, and briefed to sort out massive administrative problems. He left it in much better order in 1982, and spent his remaining years in London, enjoying a sociable life and writing copiously. His published works included *Citizen-King* (1961), a biography of Louis Philippe, his most successful contribution to scholarship; a sharp

polemic, *Culture, Anarchy and the Public Schools* (1969); *Cambridge between Two Wars* (1978), in which he stopped short of naming Anthony Blunt as the 'fourth man' only after taking legal advice; and *Prospect and Reality: Great Britain, 1945–1955* (1985). He also edited a collection of reminiscences, *Monty at Close Quarters* (1985). He was a governor of several schools, including his own old school, Rugby, and was an active trustee of the Imperial War Museum (1964–79).

In 1943 Howarth married Margaret, daughter of Norman Teakle, businessman. Sadly his wife became afflicted with mental illness, to a degree that made separation in the early 1960s unavoidable. There were three sons and a daughter of the marriage. The eldest son, Alan, was a Conservative, and later Labour, politician; he was parliamentary under-secretary of state responsible for higher education when the government decided, in January 1992, to support the new edition of *Dictionary of National Biography*.

In an abundant and energetic life, Howarth made his mark as teacher, scholar, soldier, writer, housemaster, headmaster, and bon viveur. Yet he often seemed a solitary figure, rarely relaxed, grieved by the problems of his marriage, and in 1977 by the death from cancer in his twenties of his second son, Peter. He sometimes concealed his consequent unease behind a barrier of intellectual arrogance and less than charitable judgements. Much more often, however, he was a most warm-hearted man, delightful company, exulting in the success of his children, a patient and faithful friend, and a champion of excellence who achieved it himself, most especially as a teacher. He died of motor neurone disease in London on 6 May 1988 (his home was 112A Elgin Crescent, Notting Hill) and he was buried in Winchester.

PATRICK HUTTON, *rev.*

Sources WWW · *The Times* (11 May 1988) · *The Times* (29 June 1988) · personal knowledge (1996) · private information (1996, 2004) [Alan Howarth, son] · CGPLA *Eng. & Wales* (1988)
Likenesses J. Gilroy, portrait, oils, St Paul's School
Wealth at death £304,637: probate, 25 Oct 1988, CGPLA *Eng. & Wales*

Howden. For this title name *see* Caradoc, John Francis, first Baron Howden (1762–1839); Caradoc, John Hobart, second Baron Howden (1799–1873).

Howden, James (1832–1913), marine and general engineer, was born on 29 February 1832 in Prestonpans, East Lothian, the son of James Howden and his wife, Catherine Adams. His father was a market gardener and his early schooling was received in Prestonpans parish school. In 1847 he made his way to Glasgow by boat, on the Forth and Clyde Canal. Whether he chose the boat over the train for reasons of preference or of economy is not certain but it soon became clear that his lifelong career interest was to be in boats rather than trains.

On arrival in Glasgow, Howden took up an engineering apprenticeship with James Gray & Co.—a firm with an established reputation for stationary engines. His talents for technical drawing were considerable and even before his formal apprenticeship was concluded he was promoted to the position of chief draughtsman. This did not satisfy a man of his ambitions, and almost as soon as his apprenticeship was completed he sought alternative employment, before setting up on his own account in 1854, aged only twenty-two, as a consulting engineer and designer. He had already taken out a patent for rivet making and had sold the rights to a Birmingham company. Nevertheless his early career was not a great success and he had to supplement his income by teaching mechanical drawing in the Glasgow School of Art.

Howden's first major contract came in 1859 from Hendersons for the Anchor Line's ship *Ailsa Craig*. The order was for compound engines and water tube boilers, of Howden's own design, using steam at 100 lb pressure. This was a considerable advance on existing technology. Although he did not win every race to invent new technologies it is clear that Howden's inventive genius placed him in the forefront of several developments which were to establish Clydeside's reputation as a world leader in shipbuilding and related activities.

In 1862, in partnership with James Mathie, Howden purchased land at Scotland Street on the south side of Glasgow, and established the firm of James Howden & Co. to manufacture engines and boilers. Shipbuilding was later added to the firm's activities, although the work of hull building was contracted out. A shortage of working capital presented problems but it did not ultimately inhibit the long-term growth of the firm. This success was undoubtedly due to Howden's growing list of patent rights, which cover almost the whole field of engineering and boilermaking. Although he spent a great deal of his time at the drawing board and in experimentation, Howden did not neglect the all-important sales dimension of his business; and he established a wide network of acquaintances in the Glasgow business community. He soon numbered many of the world's leading shipping lines among his customers.

The invention for which Howden is best remembered, and which added so much to his fortune, was the forced-draught system for boilers. He had begun to experiment with this in 1862 but it was not until the 1880s that he perfected it by utilizing waste gases to heat the air used in the combustion chamber. The effect of this was to provide a more efficient combustion process at varying speeds, using any quality of steam coal. The resulting improvements in efficiency and cost reduction were considerable. The system was soon in widespread use and the company's energies were devoted almost entirely to its promotion. Howden himself devoted much of his time to establishing connections with shipbuilders and shipowners of note in most parts of the world. Several ships equipped with the forced-draught system in their boilers subsequently won the Blue Riband for the fastest Atlantic crossing.

Howden was fully aware of the dangers of relying too much on one product, and despite the success of the forced-draught system he continued to design new engines. By 1900 his company was busy making high-speed engines of the enclosed, forced-lubrication type, which were used chiefly for generating electricity. This was followed by the Howden Zoelly impulse type of steam turbine, which the firm supplied to many municipalities, including an installation for the corporation of Manchester. Not only was this a new technology for Howden but it also involved a new marketing strategy in selling to local authorities throughout the country. At the time of Howden's death in 1913 his company was busy experimenting with land-based applications for the forced-draught system and with diesel engines, which were to revolutionize the shipping industry in the inter-war years.

Howden's restless spirit did not always produce marketable products, however. In 1904 he became involved with another large Glasgow company, James Finlay & Co., in a process for curing tea. In the early stages of development Howden recruited a scientist from Glasgow University and set him up in a laboratory, but despite the best efforts of the men of science and business, the process could not be turned into a commercial success. Another of his business interests was a marble quarry in Greece, for which he used his business contacts to raise capital. In 1912 he raised capital among his friends for the St Helena Whaling Company. In 1912 he was involved in secret work for the Admiralty, for whom he made a recoilless gun using a non-explosive (pneumatic) propellant. He had the vision to see how useful this type of gun would be on aeroplanes, but the experiment was not a success.

Howden was a public figure and participated vigorously in debates in the various professional bodies of which he was a member. These included the Institution of Engineers and Shipbuilders in Scotland, the Institution of Naval Architects, and the Institution of Civil Engineers, to whose journals he contributed many articles. An active churchman, Howden was a member of the kirk session of Wellington United Free Church. He also contributed largely, but privately, to various charitable and religious causes including Barnardo's Homes, missionary activities, and Indian orphans. A member of the Merchants' House of Glasgow and of the Incorporation of Hammermen, Howden was also a JP for the city of Glasgow. His political convictions were with the Liberal Party until Gladstone introduced the Home Rule Bill, whereupon he became a Unionist, but he did not take any active public part in politics. He was married first to Helen Burgess Adams, and then to Allison Moffat Hay, with whom he had two sons and a daughter. Both of his wives predeceased him. His principal residence was at 2 Princes Terrace, Dowanhill, Glasgow.

Howden was one of that enterprising group of engineers whose inventive genius and flair for business transformed the Scottish economy in the second half of the nineteenth century. Tenacious and outspoken in his views, Howden spent his working life in Glasgow, where he died on 21 November 1913.   CHARLES W. MUNN

Sources J. Howden, *The Howden system of forced draught* (1896) · J. Howden, *The screw propeller controversy* (1906) · d. cert. · *DSBB* ·

letter-book of James Howden, Howden plc Archives, Glasgow • 'An outline of Victorian achievement', *Howden Quarterly*, 39 (1959) • *The Scotsman* (22 Nov 1913) • *CGPLA Eng. & Wales* (1914)

Archives Howden plc Archives, Glasgow, letter-book

Wealth at death £388,251 13s. 11d.: confirmation, 22 June 1914, *CCI*

Howden, John of (*fl.* 1268/9–1275), religious poet, was a chaplain of Queen Eleanor, mother of Edward I. His name appears in documents of 1268–9 and another of 1275; in colophons to some of the poems he is named *magister*, but this may not be significant. Howden is in the East Riding of Yorkshire, and Stone has shown that, for metrical reasons, the poet's name must be pronounced 'Howden' rather than the traditional 'Hoveden' (Houeden). He is probably, as Russell suggested, to be identified with the John of Howden who in 1275 was given a prebend at Bridgnorth, Shropshire (in the royal gift); two persons of this name were alive at the beginning of the fourteenth century; one of them became abbot of Sawley, Yorkshire.

John of Howden has sometimes been identified with a John of London, a skilled astrologer of saintly character who was a prebendary of the collegiate church of Howden and was buried there in 1275. A. J. Taylor identified this man with John of Melton, a founder prebendary of Howden, but this identification depends entirely on Bale, who in his *Index* cites a manuscript of Alfred of Beverley; in fact the continuation of Alfred of Beverley in Paris, Bibliothèque Nationale, MS Lat. 4126, does not contain Bale's quotation, which is suspiciously similar in its wording to the continuation of William of Newburgh (minus Bale's words about the poems). In any case, the dates are too tight, if he witnessed a document in 1275 and died in the same year. Further, the collegiate church at Howden was not founded until 1265, and it is unlikely that John would have taken his name from that place as early as 1268–9. Above all, neither the Lanercost chronicle nor the continuation to William of Newburgh, both of which record the death and burial of the Howden prebendary, mentions that he wrote poems.

The poet's principal works are in Latin. *Philomena* (edited by C. Blume) consists of 1131 quatrains on the passion of Christ in an extremely affective and repetitive style, powerful for its striking images. This was influenced by Walter of Wimborne's *Marie carmina*, and a section of it was utilized by Stephen Deverell, monk of Glastonbury, in a poem on ingratitude. Its influence is also seen in Richard Rolle's *Incendium amoris* and *Melos amoris*.

The remaining Latin poems were edited by F. J. E. Raby. *Canticum amoris* (deficient, in 239½ stanzas) closely parallels the *Philomena* in style, content, and metre, and may be an adaptation or early draft of it. *Cythara* has 150 stanzas in a different metre, but uses the same themes and ideas. *Quinquaginta cantica* (723 quatrains of twelve-syllable lines) is in a deliberately difficult style. *Quindecim gaudia*, *Viola*, and *Quinquaginta salutationes* are on the Virgin Mary, and *Lira* and *O mira creatura* are short poems on God's power.

John himself loosely recast the *Philomena* in French verse as the *Rossignos* ('Nightingale'), dedicated to Eleanor,

some time after 1272. The Middle English *Meditations on the Life and Passion of Christ* is loosely based on the *Philomena*.

Some works have been wrongly credited to him. Another nightingale poem, *Philomena previa temporis ameni*, is the work of John Pecham, archbishop of Canterbury. The cosmological poem *Scribo sed ut merear* (occasionally attributed to Howden because it mentions a nightingale) is by Grosseteste or a student of his. Although the *Speculum laicorum* remains anonymous, it is certainly not Howden's, since internal allusions place it later. A florilegium *De beneficiis Dei ex Bernardo* remains untraced. The astronomical *Practica chilindri*, edited by Brock, is ascribed in the manuscript to 'magister Johannes de Houeden astrologus'; the example of Chaucer shows that there is nothing incompatible between poetry and technical astronomy, but, as discussed above, the astronomer John of London, if distinct from the poet, may be a better candidate for this work.   A. G. RIGG

Sources J. C. Russell, 'Dictionary of writers of thirteenth century England', *BIHR*, special suppl., 3 (1936) [whole issue], esp. 65–8 • *Poems of John of Hoveden*, ed. F. J. E. Raby, SurtS, 154 (1939), xi–xviii, and appx by A. J. Taylor, 270 • A. G. Rigg, *A history of Anglo-Latin literature, 1066–1422* (1992), 208–15 • L. W. Stone, 'Jean de Howden: poète anglo-normand du XIIIe siècle', *Romania*, 69 (1946–7), 469–519 • *CPR*, 1266–72, 189, 258, 338; 1272–81, 103; 1301–7, 259, 337 • Bale, *Cat.*, 430–1 • Bale, *Index*, 220–1 • *Johannis de Hovedene Philomena*, ed. C. Blume (Leipzig, 1930) • J. Hoveden, 'Practica chilindri, or, The working of the cylinder', ed. E. Brock, *Essays on Chaucer: his words and works*, 2 (1874), 53–81 • *Calendar of the charter rolls*, 6 vols., PRO (1903–27), vol. 2, p. 189 • *CClR*, 1302–7, 458, 521 • R. Howlett, ed., *Chronicles of the reigns of Stephen, Henry II, and Richard I*, 2, Rolls Series, 82 (1885), 571–2

Howden, John (*fl.* 1499–1527), bishop of Sodor and Man, is first recorded in 1499 as a Dominican friar at the order's York convent, where he was ordained subdeacon in that year. He had moved to the Oxford convent by 1508, where, being described as having studied logic, philosophy, and theology for twelve years, he received the degrees of BTh in 1508 and DTh in 1510. He was incorporated at Cambridge in 1513–14. By 1510 he was prior of the Oxford convent and appears to have stayed in that post until at least 1514. In 1515 he was left 20s. in the will of William Bessels, esquire. By 1518 he was prior of the London convent and is listed in the accounts of the fifth earl of Northumberland, where, in 1521–2 as Hugh Done, he received a fee of 66s. 8d. (*LP Henry VIII*, 4/2, no. 3380(8)). He seems to have remained as prior of the London convent until 1527. He had been made bishop of Sodor and Man by papal provision on 19 June 1523, although there is no record of any instrument to allow him to hold the priory in conjunction with the diocese.

It is not known whether Howden visited or lived in his diocese, although, if he did live there, this might explain why so little is known about him. Alternatively, he may have remained in the London convent until 1527. He continued to receive a fee from the earl of Northumberland, at least for a while, being paid £10 3s. 4d. as bishop of Man in 1524–5. Nor is it known when he died, although a date between 1527 and 1530, when his see was reported to be vacant, seems likely. Sodor and Man remained vacant until 1546, when the bishopric was granted to Henry Man.   D. G. NEWCOMBE

Sources M. Bateson, ed., *Grace book B*, 2 (1905) · Emden, *Oxf.*, 4.301 · A. B. Emden, *A survey of Dominicans in England* (1967) · *LP Henry VIII*, vol. 4/2 · A. J. Moore, *Diocesan histories: Sodor and Man* (1893) · *VCH Oxfordshire*, vol. 2 · *VCH London*, vol. 1 · W. G. Searle, ed., *Grace book Γ* (1908)

Howden [Hoveden], **Roger of** (*d.* 1201/2), chronicler, succeeded his father, Robert, in or before 1174, as parson of Howden, a township in the East Riding of Yorkshire. The church, in the gift of the prior and convent of Durham, was a jurisdictional peculiar of the bishop of Durham, who also held the large manor on which the church was situated. Howden must, however, have been often absent from his Yorkshire living, for, probably shortly before 1174, he became a clerk at the court of Henry II, where he was based until after the king's death in 1189. During this long period of royal service the chronicler undertook several important tasks on behalf of Henry II. In 1174 he went on a diplomatic mission to Galloway; in 1175 he was concerned with the arrangements for elections to a number of vacant English monasteries; in 1185, 1187, and 1189 he acted as an itinerant justice of the forest.

After Henry II's death Howden ceased to be directly involved in royal affairs and joined the service of Hugh du Puiset, bishop of Durham (1153–95). In the short term, however, he retained significant diplomatic and administrative responsibilities since, in a period of just nine months at the end of 1189 and the beginning of 1190, he was sent to persuade Pope Clement III to release the bishop of Durham from his crusading vow, performed another tour as an itinerant justice of the forest, and travelled, at least partly on du Puiset's behalf, to join Richard I's journey to the third crusade at Marseilles where he was, perhaps, already in the company of those other men from the East Riding with whom he attested a grant of land at Hessle to the Temple of the Lord during the siege of Acre. In August 1191 Howden left Palestine, to resume his contacts with Hugh du Puiset, for whom he undertook a diplomatic mission to Normandy in 1194 and at whose deathbed he was present in 1195. At this stage of his career the chronicler was much more regularly resident in his parish and it was this tie with Howden that kept him in touch, during the last six or seven years of his life, with Hugh's successor, Philip of Poitou (1197–1208), and other influential East Riding landlords such as Robert of Thornham.

It is now generally accepted that Howden wrote two chronicles, the *Gesta Henrici II Benedicti abbatis* and the *Chronica*. The *Gesta*, whose longer title simply indicates that BL, Cotton MS Julius A.xi, in which it appears, was part of the library of Benedict, abbot of Peterborough from 1177 to 1193, consists of annals covering the years from 1169 to 1192, which were drafted and revised throughout that period of the author's life during which he was in closest contact with the royal court. It is not surprising, therefore, that in the *Gesta* the chronicler writes authoritatively about the king and the governmental machine from the point of view of a well-informed royal servant, who was eager to impart detailed information in relation to such matters as judicial reforms, the royal itinerary, and diplomatic exchanges. There are even occasions upon which the *Gesta* parades not only the knowledge, but also the frustrations, of a committed bureaucrat when, for example, it ascribes the failure in 1186 of the negotiations about the possible marriage of Henry II's niece to the king of Hungary, to the English king's dilatory behaviour towards envoys whose questions went unanswered 'from day to day, as was his custom' (*Gesta … Benedicti*, 1.346).

By the time Howden was completing the final edition of his *Gesta*, in or shortly after 1192, he had already embarked on his *Chronica*, a compilation upon which he was to work until his death. The *Chronica* covers the history of England from the time of Bede to 1201. To 1148 it is principally based on the *Historia post Bedam*, a mid-twelfth-century text, probably from Durham, made up of extracts from the *Historia regum*, attributed to Symeon of Durham, and the *Historia Anglorum* of Henry of Huntingdon. From 1148 to 1169 the *Chronica*'s main source is a text associated with the chronicle of Melrose. And from 1169 to 1192 it is based on Howden's own *Gesta*, to which the author then added contemporaneously drafted annals, covering the period from 1192 to 1201, which were produced in the period in which, having left the service of the king, he was based in Yorkshire.

Some of the differences between the *Gesta* and the *Chronica* are matters of editorial approach. Howden did not, for example, maintain in the *Chronica* his practice, developed in the *Gesta*, of ending annals with a summary of the year. Other differences are, however, the direct result of the different contexts in which the two works were written. In the *Chronica*, for instance, Howden abbreviates a significant proportion of the *Gesta*'s administrative material, while giving greater prominence to such events as the death of Hugh du Puiset at Howden in 1195, and King John's frantic search for hidden treasure at Corbridge which led, in 1201, to the discovery of nothing more than certain stones 'marked with bronze, lead and iron' (*Chronica … Hovedene*, 4.157).

The earliest surviving manuscript of the *Gesta* is BL, Cotton MS Julius A.xi, which contains the text of the annals to 1177. This manuscript probably reflects very closely the first formal version of the work. It is, however, an 'official' copy and is, therefore, quite different in character from the earliest surviving manuscripts of the *Chronica*, BL, Royal MS 14 C.ii, and Bodl. Oxf., MS Laud 582. These latter manuscripts jointly make up a text, produced between 1199 and 1201 or 1202, which represents an attempt at the compilation of an authoritative version which, however, degenerates into a working copy. It is all the more interesting because it is, in part, an autograph, and therefore yields a particularly valuable insight into the *modus operandi* of a medieval chronicler. It is the recent investigation of this *modus operandi*, through the detailed analysis of both the structure and the content of his writings, that has led to a significant modification of what had become the standard view of Howden's historiographical approach. The chronicler used to be seen as a trimmer, as a rather dull and inaccurate transcriber of official documents. It is now clear, however, that there is little sign of trimming in his discussion of issues that involve those by whom he was employed and even less indication of editorial carelessness. Apparent inconsistencies in the texts of Henry II's assizes, for instance, are in fact impressive evidence for Howden's concern with factual detail as well as for the dynamism of Angevin judicial reform.

DAVID CORNER

Sources W. Stubbs, ed., *Gesta regis Henrici secundi Benedicti abbatis: the chronicle of the reigns of Henry II and Richard I, AD 1169–1192*, 2 vols., Rolls Series, 49 (1867) · *Chronica magistri Rogeri de Hovedene*, ed. W. Stubbs, 4 vols., Rolls Series, 51 (1868–71) · D. Corner, 'The earliest surviving manuscripts of Roger of Howden's *Chronicle*', *EngHR*, 98 (1983), 297–310 · D. Corner, 'The *Gesta regis Henrici secundi* and *Chronica* of Roger, parson of Howden', *BIHR*, 56 (1983), 126–44 · A. Gransden, *Historical writing in England*, 1 (1974) · F. Barlow, 'Roger of Howden', *EngHR*, 65 (1950), 352–60 · D. M. Stenton, 'Roger of Howden and Benedict', *EngHR*, 68 (1953), 574–82 · D. J. Corner, 'The texts of Henry II's assizes', *Law-making and law-makers in British history*, ed. A. Harding, Royal Historical Society Studies in History, 22 (1980), 7–20
Archives BL, Cotton MS Julius A.xi · BL, Royal MS 14 C.ii · Bodl. Oxf., MS Laud 582

Howe. *See also* How.

Howe, Sir Assheton Gore Curzon- (1850–1911), naval officer, born at Gopsall, Leicestershire, on 10 August 1850, was the ninth son of Richard William Penn Howe, first Earl Howe of the second creation (1796–1870), being the second son of his second wife, Anne (*d.* 23 July 1877), second daughter of Admiral Sir John Gore. He was a great-grandson of Richard Howe, first Earl Howe, the great admiral, whose daughter and heir, Sophia Charlotte, Baroness Howe, married Penn, eldest son of Assheton Curzon, first Viscount Curzon. Curzon-Howe entered the navy on board the *Britannia* in December 1863, and from 1868 to 1871 served in the frigate *Galatea*, captain the duke of Edinburgh, which went round the world during that commission. He was promoted sub-lieutenant on 18 March 1870, and served on the *Bellerophon* in the channel squadron. His commission as lieutenant was dated 18 September 1872, and in November 1873 he was appointed to the sloop *Eclipse* on the North American station. A year later he was transferred to the *Bellerophon*, flagship on the same station, and in February 1876 was appointed to the *Sultan* in the Mediterranean, commanded by the duke of Edinburgh, whom two years later he followed into the *Black Prince*.

In July 1879 the *Bacchante* was commissioned by Captain Lord Charles Scott for a cruise round the world, and to give Albert Edward, duke of Clarence, and the prince of Wales, afterwards King George V, their sea training as cadets. Curzon-Howe was chosen to be her first lieutenant, and was directly responsible for the seamanship instruction of the princes. On the return of the ship to England he was promoted commander on 31 August 1882.

In January 1883 Curzon-Howe became executive officer of the *Sultan* in the channel squadron, and two years later was appointed in the same capacity to the *Raleigh*, flagship

on the Cape station. In July 1886 he was given the command of the royal yacht *Osborne*, from which on 6 January 1888 he was promoted captain. Shortly afterwards Curzon-Howe commissioned the *Boadicea* for the East India station, where, in August 1888, she relieved the *Bacchante* as flagship of Sir Edmund Fremantle. As flag captain and chief of the staff he took part in the Vitu (Witu, Kenya) expedition of October 1890, for which he received the CB. Curzon-Howe married on 25 February 1892 Alice Ann (*d.* 5 Nov 1948), eldest daughter of General Sir John Cowell PC KCB, master of her majesty's household. They had two sons and three daughters. Their eldest daughter, Victoria Alexandrina, to whom Queen Victoria was godmother, died at Malta on 3 February 1910.

From August 1891 he served for a year at the Admiralty as assistant director of naval intelligence, and then went to the North American station in command of the *Cleopatra*, and as commodore during the Newfoundland fishing season. In this ship he was present at Bluefields, Nicaragua, during the disturbances of 1894, and by his prompt action in landing a party of seamen and marines averted a civil war. In January 1896 he was created CMG for his services in Newfoundland, and in the same month became flag captain to Rear-Admiral A. T. Dale in the *Revenge*, flagship of the flying squadron which was put in commission shortly after the publication in January 1896 of the Kaiser's telegram to Kruger; this congratulated Kruger on the defeat of the Jameson raid, a gesture perceived by the British as a hostile intervention in their imperial affairs. In April 1897 he was appointed to command the training ship *Britannia* at Dartmouth, and afterwards, from February 1900, he commanded the battleship *Ocean* on the China station. In July 1899 Curzon-Howe was appointed an aide-de-camp to Queen Victoria, and held this post until promoted to flag rank on 23 July 1901.

In June 1902 he hoisted his flag in the *Magnificent* as second in command in the channel, and from that time his employment was practically continuous. In June 1903 he became second in command on the China station with his flag in the *Albion*. On 30 June 1905 he was appointed KCB, and on 12 September he was promoted vice-admiral. In the December following he returned to the Channel Fleet, now greatly enlarged, as second in command, with his flag on board the *Caesar*. In February 1907 he was appointed commander-in-chief of the Atlantic Fleet, whence in November 1908 he was transferred in the same capacity, but with acting rank as admiral, to the Mediterranean, his flagship during both commands being the *Exmouth*. The disastrous earthquake at Messina in December 1908 called the commander-in-chief with part of his squadron to aid in the relief work, and the crisis which accompanied the revolution in Turkey made the Mediterranean for the time the centre of concern. On 2 January 1909 he was advanced to admiral, and in July received the GCVO. He was relieved in April 1910, and immediately hoisted his flag on the *Victory* as commander-in-chief at Portsmouth.

Curzon-Howe died suddenly at Admiralty House, Portsmouth, on 1 March 1911 and was buried with naval honours at Highcliffe, near Christchurch. A memorial tablet was placed in Portsmouth Dockyard church. 'Holding strong opinions on some points, he constantly stood aloof from all controversies of public character. Few flag-officers who have held such important appointments have ever been so little in the public eye as he' (*The Times*). This reflected a solid career, undistinguished by any particular contribution.

L. G. C. LAUGHTON, rev. ANDREW LAMBERT

Sources *The Times* (2 March 1911) · *WWW, 1897–1915* · Burke, *Peerage* (1959) · Kelly, *Handbk* (1893) · *CGPLA Eng. & Wales* (1911)
Archives NMM, papers
Wealth at death £21,985 19s. 3d.: resworn probate, 19 May 1911, *CGPLA Eng. & Wales*

Howe, Charles (1661–1742), devotional writer, was born in Casy Compton, Gloucestershire, the third son of John Grobham Howe (1625–1679) of Langar, Nottinghamshire, and Annabella Scrope (1630/31–1704), the illegitimate daughter of Emanuel *Scrope, earl of Sunderland (1584–1630), and his servant Martha Jeanes. Howe matriculated at Christ Church, Oxford, on 14 May 1677, and spent much of his youth at Charles II's court. About 1686 he is said to have gone abroad with an unidentified relative who was an ambassador of James II's. After the ambassador's death Howe successfully managed the embassy business, but declined to accept the office permanently. On his return he married Elianor Dering (1665–1696), widow of Sir Henry Dering (d. 1688), and only child of Sir William Pargiter of Greatworth, Northamptonshire, and Elianor Guise of Elmore, Gloucestershire. They had three sons and three daughters, all of whom predeceased their mother except Leonora Maria (d. 1720), who married Peter Bathurst of Clarendon Park, Wiltshire. Elianor Howe died on 25 July 1696 and was buried in Greatworth church, where she is commemorated in an inscription written by her husband.

Howe lived in seclusion as a widower and devoted himself to religious meditation. His *Devout Meditations, or, A Collection of Thoughts upon Religious and Philosophical Subjects* was first published posthumously and anonymously in 1751 together with an admiring preface by Edward Young, author of *Night Thoughts*. Later editions were edited by Dr George MacAulay, who married Howe's granddaughter Leonora Bathurst. Howe died on 17 February 1742 and was buried in the same vault as his wife and children at Greatworth church. He left his property in Greatworth and Weedon Pinckney, Northamptonshire, to his granddaughter Leonora Bathurst, 100 guineas to his other granddaughter Frances Cooper, and about £150 to friends and to charity.

B. H. BLACKER, rev. ADAM JACOB LEVIN

Sources G. Baker, *The history and antiquities of the county of Northampton*, 1 (1822–30), 508–11 · J. Bridges, *The history and antiquities of Northamptonshire*, ed. P. Whalley, 1 (1791), 124–7, 184, 202 · GEC, *Peerage* · *Collins peerage of England: genealogical, biographical and historical*, ed. E. Brydges, 9 vols. (1812), vol. 8, pp. 137–9 · Foster, *Alum. Oxon.* · IGI · B. H. Blacker, ed., *Gloucestershire Notes and Queries*, 2 (1884), 469–71, 555–7 · *GM*, 1st ser., 46 (1776), 249 · *GM*, 1st ser., 64 (1794), 700 · will, proved, 12 April 1742, PRO, PROB 11/717, sig. 118, proved 12 April 1742

Wealth at death over £250; plus property in Greatworth and Weedon Pinckney, Northamptonshire: will, PRO, PROB 11/717, sig. 118

Howe, (Mary Sophia) Charlotte [née Sophia Charlotte Mary von Kielmansegg], **Viscountess Howe** (1703–1782), politician, was born on 23 September 1703 NS, probably in Hanover. She was the eldest daughter and second child of Sophia Charlotte von *Kielmansegg, later countess of Darlington and Leinster (1675–1725), and her husband, Johann Adolf, Baron von Kielmansegg (d. 1717), deputy master of the horse to the elector of Hanover, later George I. Her mother's high status at the Hanoverian court resulted from the acknowledgement that she was the illegitimate daughter of Elector Ernst August and Clara von Meysenbug, Countess von Platen und Hallermund. The family moved to England with George I in 1714.

On 8 August 1719 Sophia Charlotte Mary married Emanuel Scrope Howe, second Viscount Howe (1698/9–1735). Lord Howe's uncle, also Emanuel Scrope Howe, had been English minister to Hanover in 1706–9, as well as the husband of Prince Rupert of the Rhine's illegitimate daughter Ruperta. The Howe family was thus already known to the Hanoverian nobility. Lady Howe's close relations with the royal family encouraged gossip in Britain that her mother was a mistress of George I and that she was the king's daughter, but this interpretation of the relationship was generally rejected by twentieth-century historians. At some point after her marriage the order of her baptismal names was changed, probably in order to emphasize Charlotte.

Lady Howe brought a marriage portion of £5000 and an annuity of £1500 per year. In addition George I settled a pension from the Irish revenues of £750 per annum on the couple, later raised to £1250. This helped relieve pressure on the family estate at Langar in Nottinghamshire and supported the family's attempts to extend their political patronage in the county. The couple had ten children, among whom were George Augustus *Howe, Richard *Howe, and William *Howe, all prominent commanders and successively viscounts Howe, and Caroline, who was later closely involved with the attempted American peace negotiations of her brothers in 1777–8.

Lady Howe travelled to Barbados after her husband's appointment as governor in 1732, as she is listed as a witness to the codicil to his will executed at Barbados on 24 May 1734. Following her husband's death his sister Mary, dowager countess of Pembroke, lobbied for Lady Howe to be appointed lady of the bedchamber to Augusta, princess of Wales; she was eventually appointed in 1745, perhaps as a consequence of the political alliance between the Howe family and the Pelhams in Nottinghamshire.

Lady Howe assumed the role of manager of the Howe family's political interests in Nottingham. Although the Howe family supported the Pelham administration its plans came into conflict with those of Thomas Pelham-Holles, duke of Newcastle, who was recorder of the borough. Lady Howe's tactic was to adopt the position of champion of the corporation against powerful outsiders. In 1758, following the death of the third Viscount Howe at

(Mary Sophia) Charlotte Howe, Viscountess Howe (1703–1782), attrib. Enoch Seeman, 1719

the battle of Ticonderoga, Newcastle proposed that her next son, Richard, fourth viscount, take the seat. John Plumptre, who had earlier been Newcastle's choice as whig member for Nottingham but had been manoeuvred out of the seat by the Howes, would be compensated with Richard Howe's seat at Dartmouth. Instead, Lady Howe accepted a petition from the corporation asking that Lieutenant-Colonel William Howe be their representative, and so ensured that the family would still hold two seats in the Commons. Lady Howe declared her youngest son's candidacy in a newspaper advertisement that aroused comment both for being an open political intervention by a woman—it was signed 'Charlotte Howe'—and for brazenly playing the patriot card. It was reprinted in the *Annual Register* (1758, 73).

As the influence of the Smith banking family in Nottingham politics grew after the 1758 election, that of the Howe family diminished. Lady Howe's energies were employed in her life at court, where her position as lady of the bedchamber gave her some influence over access to the princess dowager. She entertained her nephews Frederick and Charles von Kielmansegg on their visit to England in 1761–2, and made at least two visits to Germany, once in 1763, and another accompanying the princess dowager in 1770. She remained an active participant in court life well into old age, appearing in the same circles as Horace Walpole and Lady Mary Coke, and defending the actions of her

family against criticism during the American War of Independence. Lady Howe died on 13 June 1782 at her home in Albemarle Street, London, and was buried on 23 June at Langar.   MATTHEW KILBURN

Sources BL, Add. MS 32883, fols. 186, 197, 220, 246, 308, 452 · BL, Add. MS 32874, fol. 187 · L. B. Namier, *The structure of politics at the accession of George III* (1960), 91–5 · *Annual Register* (1758), 72–3 · R. Hatton, *George I: elector and king* (1978) · Erich, grafen von Kielmansegg, ed., *Familien-Chronik der Herren, Freiherren und Grafen von Kielmansegg*, another edn (Vienna, 1910) · F. von Kielmansegg, *Diary of a journey to England in the years 1761–1762*, trans. Countess Kielmansegge [S. P. Kielmansegg] (1902) · Walpole, *Corr.*, 31.180, 187; 32.326 · John, Lord Hervey, *Some materials towards memoirs of the reign of King George II*, ed. R. Sedgwick, 3 (1931), 849–50 · GEC, *Peerage*, new edn, 4.80–81; 6.596–7; 14.236 · J. Lodge, *The peerage of Ireland*, rev. M. Archdall, rev. edn, 5 (1789), 85–6 · *Collins peerage of England: genealogical, biographical and historical*, ed. E. Brydges, 9 vols. (1812), vol. 8, p. 164

Archives BL, duke of Newcastle's corresp.

Likenesses attrib. E. Seeman, portrait, 1719, priv. coll. [*see illus.*] · G. Kneller, portrait, repro. in von Kielmansegge, *Diary*, facing p. 54

Wealth at death pension of £1250 p.a. on Irish revenues: will, PRO, PROB 11/1093

Howe, Clarence Decatur (1886–1960), politician and engineer in Canada, was born on 15 January 1886 in Waltham, Massachusetts, the first child and only son of William Clarence Howe, a builder, and his wife, Mary Emma Hastings. His parents were of New England stock, and Howe attended the local high school and the Massachusetts Institute of Technology, where he received his BSc in civil engineering in 1906. He joined the engineering faculty of Dalhousie University in Halifax, Nova Scotia, in 1908, and remained there for five years.

In 1913 Howe became a British subject and accepted a post as chief engineer with the Canadian government's board of grain commissioners. His task was to site, design, and build grain elevators, a skill he took with him into his private engineering firm, C. D. Howe & Co., at Port Arthur, Ontario, in 1916. In that year he married, on 16 September, Alice Martha Worcester (*b.* 1889), daughter of a successful consulting engineer in Boston, Massachusetts, with whom he had worked from 1905 to 1908; they had two sons and three daughters. The First World War created a huge demand for Canadian wheat, and Howe's company's first elevator at Port Arthur made money. So did the superbly designed elevators Howe built across the Canadian prairies for the Alberta and Saskatchewan wheat pools after the war. His reputation in his field was high, and in 1935 he ran for the Liberal Party in the federal general election.

Elected member of parliament for Port Arthur, Howe instantly joined the cabinet of W. L. Mackenzie King as minister of railways and canals and minister of marine. He quickly brought the two departments into the Department of Transport and made his mark. Howe established the Canadian Broadcasting Corporation, an arm's-length government agency, in 1935, to replace the feeble commission created by the previous government. He began Trans-Canada Airlines as a crown corporation in 1937, and his reputation for tough, business-minded efficiency began to develop.

The beginning of the Second World War saw Howe's responsibilities increase. In 1940 King made him minister of munitions and supply, in charge of mobilizing the industrial war effort. Howe brought 'dollar-a-year' men from business to Ottawa to work without pay in running the economic war effort. No one doubted that, as the actual executive head of his department, Howe would make all the key decisions. None the less, he delegated power freely to those he trusted, he created crown corporations to produce everything from wood veneers to artificial rubber, and he administered critical agreements with the United States to allocate supplies and production. He served as the Canadian representative to the combined production and resources board and made many trips to the United Kingdom to co-ordinate production and supply matters. In December 1940 a U-boat torpedoed his ship and he was rescued from a lifeboat by a merchantman that disobeyed orders and turned back to pick up survivors.

In 1944, as Canada prepared itself for an expected postwar depression, King made Howe the minister of reconstruction in addition to his other duties, and CD, as he was universally called, laid the groundwork for the industrial reconversion of Canadian industry. The government was beginning to put together a package of social welfare policies, and Howe was cool to this. But staunch advocate of free enterprise that he was, Howe could adapt. His deputy minister, the economist W. A. Mackintosh, once bemoaned the difficulties in 'bouncing ideas off Mr. Howe's battleship steel headpiece' (Granatstein, 166). None the less, Howe agreed in 1945 to present a white paper to parliament that declared itself for Keynesian policies and pronounced full employment a national goal. His department controlled more than $3 billion in assets, and he gave substantial sums to manufacturing firms to help them re-tool to produce civilian goods. Moreover, he presided over the cancellation of war contracts, the liquidation of war surpluses, and the lifting of wartime controls on labour movement. Many of the crown corporations he had established were sold off, sometimes at fire-sale prices if the buyers pledged to create permanent jobs. There were complaints and disturbances aplenty, but Canada's reconstruction process was none the less very smoothly handled. The resulting post-war economic boom was not all Howe's doing, but his fingerprints were all over the economy. In 1946 he became an imperial privy councillor.

Shortly before he retired as prime minister, King made Howe his minister of trade and commerce, a critical post at a time when Canada (like every other country) was short of American dollars. Howe took charge of Canadian efforts to sell goods to European Recovery Program nations, and he prevented Canada from suffering the worst effects of the dollar shortage. He supported Canada's push for multilateral tariff reductions as the key to the dominion's (and the world's) post-war prosperity, and he supported the secret attempt to negotiate a customs union between Canada and the United States in 1947–8. He hoped, after King stopped the talks, that his successor might move them forward once more. When Louis St Laurent, King's 'Quebec lieutenant', became prime minister late in 1948, Howe was his senior English-speaking minister, the key Liberal fund-raiser, a man already being called the 'minister of everything' for his pervasive influence on government economic policy. But St Laurent never found the time right for free trade with the Americans, and the idea disappeared for a generation.

After the start of the Korean War and the Canadian decision to send troops to Europe for NATO service, Howe added the portfolio of minister of defence production to his already burdensome duties. Given a virtually free hand by his prime minister, Howe led the dominion into the production of modern jet fighter interceptors and engines and a wide range of military equipment intended for the Canadian forces and NATO allies. American investment poured over the border, buoying mining and industrial production and creating jobs, and Howe welcomed the influx. The booming economy, though troubled by inflation, rolled on, making the decade after the Second World War the golden age of Canadian prosperity.

Elected time after time in his Port Arthur constituency, Howe sat on the front benches for twenty-two years. The Liberals were 'the government party', an invulnerable national coalition that used an able public service to generate ideas. By 1956, however, the perceived governmental arrogance was offending more and more Canadians, and Howe, who wanted to see a US-controlled natural gas pipeline built from Alberta to eastern Canadian markets, rode roughshod over parliament in his efforts to get the bill passed. The riotous scenes in the House of Commons were all but unparalleled, and Howe's personal reputation for authoritarian behaviour did not help. His critics damned the American-born Howe as too pro-American, a slur that in a newly nationalist and still pro-British Canada carried some weight. The bill passed, but the government lost the 1957 election to John Diefenbaker's Progressive Conservative Party. Howe himself lost his own seat to a social democratic schoolteacher, Douglas Fisher.

Howe left politics after his defeat and after moving to Montreal, Quebec, went into business full-time and built up a substantial fortune. He joined the boards of fourteen companies and became chairman of Ogilvie Brothers, a large flour miller, and Price Brothers, a pulp and paper company controlled by Lord Beaverbrook. He also became chancellor of Dalhousie University and a board member at the Massachusetts Institute of Technology.

Howe had as much influence on Canada's economic development in the twentieth century as any single person. Utterly fearless and unafraid to use the fullest range of government powers to get done what needed to be done when it needed to be done, he ironically—for a capitalist free enterpriser—developed the government's use of the crown corporation into an art form. His strong personality, his decisiveness, and his ability to attract good men and to keep them working for him, made him into the indispensable minister in wartime and post-war Canada.

His no-nonsense, take-no-prisoners style, however, played into the hands of his critics in parliament and the media, and Howe came to personify Liberal arrogance. This was unfair, but by 1957 CD had become a political liability for his party. There was scant gratitude in Canadian politics or public life.

Howe died of a heart attack in Montreal on 31 December 1960 and was buried at the Mount Royal cemetery in Montreal on 4 January 1961. He was survived by his wife.

J. L. GRANATSTEIN

Sources R. Bothwell and W. Kilbourn, *C.D. Howe: a biography* (1979) • L. Roberts, *C.D.: the life and times of Clarence Decatur Howe* (Toronto, 1957) • J. W. Pickersgill, ed., *The Mackenzie King record*, 4 vols. (1960–70) • J. L. Granatstein, *The Ottawa men: the civil service mandarins, 1935–1957* (1982) • www.worcesterfamily.com
Archives NA Canada | FILM BFI NFTVA, news footage
Likenesses R. Watt, oils, Dalhousie University, Halifax, Nova Scotia
Wealth at death $1 million valuation of assets; est. $2 million market value: Bothwell and Kilbourn, *C.D. Howe*

Howe, Emanuel Scrope (*c.*1663–1709), diplomat, was the fourth son of John Grobham Howe (1625–1679), of Langar, Nottinghamshire, and Annabella (1630/31–1704), illegitimate daughter of Emanuel *Scrope, first earl of Sunderland (1584–1630), and his servant Martha Jeanes. Little is known of Howe's early life, but he came to prominence when, together with his brother John Grobham *Howe (1657–1722), known as Jack, he supported the revolution of 1688 and was rewarded with an army commission as a captain in the foot guards and a household post as groom of the bedchamber. He followed a military career during the Nine Years' War, being wounded at the siege of Namur in 1695. In late November 1695 there was talk that he had married Ruperta (1673–1740), the illegitimate daughter of Prince *Rupert (1619–1682) and Margaret *Hughes (*d.* 1719). Howe purchased the colonelcy of the 15th foot in November 1695, which he retained until his death. In November 1699 he became the keeper of the royal forests of Alice Holt and Woolmer in Hampshire.

In the general election of January 1701 Howe stood at Wigan, but was defeated, but in the following election, in December of the same year, he was returned for Morpeth. In June 1702, following the accession of Queen Anne, Howe was named a commissioner of prizes, a post which he retained until 1705. He was again returned for Morpeth at the general election of 1702. In the Commons he was a whig who supported the court. He was made a brigadier-general in 1704 and in the following year was appointed envoy-extraordinary to Hanover. He was still keen to acquire a seat in the Commons, and was indeed elected for Wigan, although he was to be absent for most of the parliament. Howe arrived at Hanover in October 1705, where his main task was to keep the electorate firm to the alliance against Louis XIV, and at the same time keep an eye on tory intrigues at the electoral court.

The presence in Hanover of Frances Bard, also known as Lady Bellamont, who claimed to have gone through a marriage ceremony with Prince Rupert, with whom she had a son, no doubt added to the intrigue at the court. Unfortunately so did Howe's wife, niece of the electress through her father. She entered into some indiscreet correspondence with the duchess of Marlborough which related the uneasiness of the electoral family concerning the Bill of Naturalization, and later the elector's willingness to accept command of the allied forces in Flanders if Marlborough went to Italy. In summer 1706 Howe was made a major-general, and a diplomatic move to Berlin was being considered for him, although the duke of Marlborough objected because of 'his want of dexterity for so tricking a court'. Lord Godolphin felt that Howe had his advantages as he 'will have no whimsies of his own, but be sure to follow your directions'. In the event, Howe remained where he was even though Marlborough thought 'he certainly can never be easy nor do her Majesty any service where he is' (Snyder, 1.636).

Ill health, particularly gout, made Howe think about a post in England in 1707, but a suggestion that he become comptroller of the army accounts was rejected as he was reluctant to see a fall in his income. He did however pay a visit to England in 1707, and in September he opined that he would not mind moving from Hanover to the Netherlands. He was back in Hanover before the end of the year. In May 1708 he was ill, so that it was thought unlikely that he could accompany the elector on campaign, but he was promoted to lieutenant-general at the beginning of 1709. Howe returned to England again in May 1709, where he died on 26 September 1709. In his will he left £4000 in bank stock to his daughter Sophia (a maid of honour to Princess Caroline while princess of Wales, and the subject of a society scandal involving Anthony Lowther), his tithes at St Neots, Huntingdonshire, to his son William, and the remainder of his estate to his son Emanuel.

STUART HANDLEY

Sources 'Howe, Emanuel Scrope', HoP, *Commons, 1690–1715* [draft] • J. J. Howard and F. A. Crisp, eds., *Visitation of England and Wales: notes*, 14 vols. (privately printed, London, 1896–1921), vol. 13, pp. 96, 105 • *The Marlborough–Godolphin correspondence*, ed. H. L. Snyder, 3 vols. (1975) • C. Dalton, ed., *English army lists and commission registers, 1661–1714*, 2 (1894), 230; 3 (1896), 42; 5 (1902), 16 • D. B. Horn, ed., *British diplomatic representatives, 1689–1789*, CS, 3rd ser., 46 (1932), 50 • J. F. Chance, 'A Jacobite at the court of Hanover', *EngHR*, 11 (1896), 528–30 • *The Lexington papers*, ed. H. Manners Sutton (1851), 151 • PRO, PROB 11/511, sig. 232 • J. C. Sainty and R. Bucholz, eds., *Officials of the royal household, 1660–1837*, 1: *Department of the lord chamberlain and associated offices* (1997), 124 • *The letters and dispatches of John Churchill, first duke of Marlborough, from 1702 to 1712*, ed. G. Murray, 5 vols. (1845) • J. Macpherson, ed., *Original papers: containing the secret history of Great Britain*, 2 vols. (1775), vol. 2, p. 37
Archives BL, Blenheim papers, letters • BL, diplomatic reports, Add. MSS 7075, 21551, 37407 • BL, diplomatic reports, Stowe MS 222 • PRO, diplomatic reports
Likenesses C. Sherwin, stipple (after P. Lely), BM, NPG; repro. in G. Bromley, *Collection of original royal letters* (1787)

Howe, George (1654/5–1710), physician, was the eldest of the four sons (there was one daughter) of John *Howe (1630–1705), nonconformist minister, and Katherine (*c.*1630–1697), daughter of George *Hughes (1603/4–1667), a nonconformist minister of Plymouth. He entered Glasgow University in 1671 and graduated MA in 1673. He later entered Leiden University, where he is described in the register for 8 September 1677 as 'Georgius Howe, Scotus', a student of physic aged twenty-two. He graduated MD at Leiden in 1679. Howe became a licentiate of the Royal College of Physicians, London, on 30 September 1679, fellow in 1687, and censor in 1707. He is described in the annals of the college under 22 March 1710 as 'an industrious and eminent practiser of physic'. For his opposition to the planned dispensary of the College of Physicians, Howe was mocked under the guise of Querpo by Sir Samuel Garth in his poem *The Dispensary*:

> His sire's pretended pious steps he treads,
> And where the doctor fails the saint succeeds,

Howe attended William III in his final illness and was present at the post-mortem in 1700.

Howe married Laetitia, daughter of Philip *Foley (*bap.* 1648, *d.* 1716) [*see under* Foley family] of Prestwood, Staffordshire (the licence was dated 21 February 1693); they had two sons, John and Philip, both of whom had died without children by 1729. Howe died suddenly of apoplexy on 22 March 1710 while walking in the Poultry, London, and was buried in the same vault as his father in All Hallows Church, Bread Street.

CHARLES CREIGHTON, rev. PATRICK WALLIS

Sources R. W. Innes Smith, *English-speaking students of medicine at the University of Leyden* (1932) · N. Luttrell, *A brief historical relation of state affairs from September 1678 to April 1714*, 6 (1857), 560 · H. Rogers, *The life and character of John Howe* (1836) · J. F. Senna, *The best natured man: Sir Samuel Garth, physician and poet* (1986) · Munk, *Roll* · annals, RCP Lond.

Howe, George Augustus, third Viscount Howe (1724?–1758), army officer, was the second but eldest surviving son of Emanuel Scrope Howe, second Viscount Howe (1698/9–1735), and his wife, (Mary Sophia) Charlotte *Howe (1703–1782), daughter of Sophia Charlotte von *Kielmansegg, countess of Darlington and Leinster, illegitimate half-sister of George I. Like his younger brothers Richard *Howe, Earl Howe, and William *Howe, fifth Viscount Howe, the third viscount left his mark upon a crucial era for Anglo-American relations. Educated at Westminster School and Eton College, Howe succeeded his father in the Irish peerage in 1735, and was returned as member of parliament for Nottingham on 30 June 1747. He was re-elected in April 1754, retaining the seat until his death. Howe entered the 1st foot guards as an ensign in March 1745; during 1747 he served as aide-de-camp to the duke of Cumberland in Flanders. On 1 May 1749 he was appointed lieutenant-colonel and captain; on 25 February 1757 Howe attained the rank of colonel, and was placed in command of the 3rd battalion 60th foot or Royal American regiment. He arrived at Halifax, Nova Scotia, in July along with reinforcements for the aborted assault on Louisbourg. On 28 September Howe was appointed colonel of the 55th foot, and swiftly earned a reputation as a vigorous and diligent officer: in November, when French and Native Americans raided the frontier settlement of German Flats, he was picked to lead the belated relief column. Howe received the local rank of brigadier-general in North America on 29 December.

For the campaigning season of 1758 Pitt nominated Howe second-in-command to Major-General James Abercromby in the force ordered to capture Ticonderoga and Crown Point from the French, and thus open the route by Lake Champlain for the invasion of Canada; he trusted that Howe's energy would compensate for Abercromby's sluggishness. Pitt's faith was not misplaced. Throughout the 'American army' Howe was celebrated 'for his robust soldier-like constitution, his bold enterprising spirit, and every other military accomplishment' (*Scots Magazine*, 442). In a war where relations between British officers and their colonial counterparts were frequently strained, Howe's personal charm won him the esteem of Americans of all ranks. As one colonist recalled, Howe's character proved so appealing 'that every soldier in the army had a personal attachment to him' (*Memoirs of Rufus Putnam*, 23).

Howe was keen to learn the unfamiliar techniques of American wilderness warfare and strove to adapt his men to local conditions by modifying their clothing and equipment; in this he led by example, 'going himself to the brook and washing his own linen' (*New Hampshire Gazette*, 7 July 1758). On 5 July 1758 the Anglo-American army proceeded down Lake George, and by nightfall had disembarked at Sabbath Day Point. Early next morning Howe probed inland to find a practicable route to Fort Ticonderoga. At Trout Brook, 2 miles from the outlet of the lake, Howe's command encountered a French detachment. During the ensuing skirmish Howe was shot through the heart and died instantly. Despite enduring legends that he was buried on the spot, Howe's body was in fact transported to Albany, and eventually interred in St Peter's Church.

Howe's death undermined the morale of the army and its commander. Abercromby acknowledged the widespread 'Grief and Consternation' occasioned by Howe's fall (*Correspondence of William Pitt*, 1.298); on 8 July his own unimaginative frontal assault upon the French position was repulsed with heavy casualties. Whether or not Howe would have avoided this disaster, or fulfilled the potential suggested by his short life must remain matters for speculation; what is beyond dispute is the lasting impression he left upon contemporaries on both sides of the Atlantic. Throughout the British army his death was viewed as a catastrophe: to James Wolfe, Howe was 'the very best officer in the King's service' and his loss was 'one of the greatest that could befall the nation' (Willson, 385). Howe's unusual popularity in America was underlined in moving fashion by the unprecedented action of the colony of Massachusetts in erecting a monument to his memory in Westminster Abbey. A bachelor, Howe was succeeded, as fourth viscount, by his brother Richard.

STEPHEN BRUMWELL

Sources T. Mante, *The history of the late war in North America and the islands of the West Indies, including the campaigns of MDCCLXIII and MDCCLXIV against his majesty's Indian enemies* (1772) · *Correspondence of William Pitt, when secretary of state, with colonial governors and military and naval commissioners in America*, ed. G. S. Kimball, 2 vols. (1906); repr. (1969) · R. Rogers, *The journals of Major Robert Rogers, containing an account of the several excursions he made under the generals* who commanded upon the continent of North America, during the late war (1765) • P. Pouchot, *Memoirs on the late war in North America between France and England*, ed. B. L. Dunnigan, trans. M. Cardy (1994) • *The life and letters of James Wolfe*, ed. H. B. Willson (1909) • E. B. O'Callaghan and B. Fernow, eds. and trans., *Documents relative to the colonial history of the state of New York*, 15 vols. (1853–87), vol. 10 • A. Grant, *Memoirs of an American lady*, 2 vols. (1808) • *The memoirs of Rufus Putnam*, ed. R. Buell (1903) • *New Hampshire Gazette* (7 July 1758) • *Scots Magazine*, 20 (1758), 442 • *GM*, 1st ser., 17 (1747), 45, 103 • *GM*, 1st ser., 28 (1758), 463 • J. Brooke, 'Howe, George Augustus', HoP, *Commons*, 1754–90 • R. R. Sedgwick, 'Howe, George Augustus', HoP, *Commons*, 1754–90

Archives U. Mich., Clements L., papers | BL, Newcastle MSS
Likenesses engraving, repro. in J. Entick, *The general history of the late war* (1763–4), vol. 3, opposite p. 209

Howe, Henry (1812–1896), actor, whose real name was Henry Howe Hutchinson, was born of Quaker parents in Norwich on 31 March 1812. His father would not hear of his becoming an actor, so he ran away from home at the age of nineteen to join a travelling company. After some experiments as an amateur under the name Halsingham, he made his début at the Royal Victoria in London in October 1834 as Rashleigh Osbaldistone in an adaptation of *Rob Roy*. At East End and suburban theatres he played Antonio in *The Merchant of Venice* and Tressel in *Richard III*, and at the Strand, under J. W. Hammond in 1837, he was Winkle in a piece called *Pickwick*. Many years later he played Mr Pickwick in James Albery's play at the Lyceum. Also in 1837 he acted with W. C. Macready at Covent Garden. On the occasion of Macready's farewell in 1839 Howe played Mark Antony to the latter's Julius Caesar.

Howe then joined the Haymarket under Benjamin Webster, and remained there without a break in his engagement for the almost unprecedented term of forty years. Among his innumerable original parts were Brandon in G. W. Lovell's *Look before you Leap* (October 1846), Ernest de Fonblanche in *The Roused Lion* (November 1847), and Lord Arden in Lovell's *The Wife's Secret* (January 1848). His other characters included Lord Towneley in Vanbrugh's *The Provoked Husband*, Archer in Farquhar's *The Beaux' Stratagem*, Benedick, Joseph Surface, Sir Anthony Absolute, Sir Peter Teazle, Malvolio, Jaques, and Macduff. He used to state that there were pieces in which, during his gradual rise, he had played every male part, from the lowest to the highest. In 1879 he left the Haymarket for the Vaudeville, and took Henry Irving's role of Digby Grant in a revival of Albery's *Two Roses*. In December 1881, as Mr Furnival in the same piece, he appeared under Irving at the Lyceum, with which his closing years were connected. Here he played characters such as Old Capulet, the Duke in *Measure for Measure*, Burgomaster in *Faust*, and very many others. He went with Irving to America, and he died in Cincinnati, Ohio, on 9 March 1896. Affectionately known as 'Daddy' Howe, he was a thoroughly conscientious actor, and a worthy and amiable man, whose one delight was to cultivate his garden at Isleworth. His son, Henry A. Hutchinson Howe (1832/3–1894), was a music and theatre critic for the *Morning Advertiser*.

JOSEPH KNIGHT, *rev.* NILANJANA BANERJI

Sources C. E. Pascoe, ed., *The dramatic list*, 2nd edn (1880) • *Era Almanack and Annual* (1897) • E. Reid and H. Compton, eds., *The dramatic peerage* [1891]; rev. edn [1892] • P. Hartnoll, ed., *The Oxford companion to the theatre* (1951); 2nd edn (1957); 3rd edn (1967) • Hall, *Dramatic ports*. • *The Player* (12 May 1860) • *The life and reminiscences of E. L. Blanchard, with notes from the diary of Wm. Blanchard*, ed. C. W. Scott and C. Howard, 2 vols. (1891) • C. W. Scott, *From 'The bells' to 'King Arthur': a critical record of the first-night productions at the Lyceum Theatre from 1871 to 1895* (1896) • J. Knight, *Theatrical notes* (1893)
Likenesses prints, Harvard TC
Wealth at death £1672 1s. 0d.: probate, 27 July 1896, CGPLA Eng. & Wales

Howe, James (1780–1836), animal and portrait painter, was born on 30 August 1780 at Skirling in Peeblesshire, the second of four children of William Howe (d. 1796), a parish minister, and his second wife. Howe attended the parish school and developed an interest in art at an early age. He was sent in 1795 to Edinburgh, where he was apprenticed to the Nories, well-known house-painters and interior decorators. His earliest surviving painting is *Boy on a Pony* (Biggar Museum Trust), and this reflects his interest in the subject matter that was to dominate his work.

Howe worked for (possibly Peter) Marshall, the Edinburgh pioneer of panoramas, and in 1805 was listed in the Edinburgh postal directory as a portrait painter. In 1807 he painted a banner for the Biggar Whipman Society (Biggar Museum Trust), and from 1808 exhibited with the Society of Artists in Edinburgh. Howe's work attracted the attention of David Steuart Erskine, eleventh earl of Buchan, who commissioned him to paint a series of portraits of centenarians for posterity.

With Buchan's support Howe travelled to London with letters of introduction to allow him to paint the horses in King George III's stables. The earl believed that he was 'a second Stubbs in embryo', but the artist did not receive the acclaim in London that his patron had anticipated (Irwin and Irwin, 192). Howe returned to Scotland, where he pursued a successful career painting animals, and received commissions from the nobility and gentry to record their prize cattle and favourite horses and dogs. His work also embraced portraits of huntsmen, gamekeepers, and grooms, and one of his most famous pictures, *Hawking at Barochan* (1815; priv. coll.), was engraved as a mezzotint by Charles Turner in 1834. It was an extremely popular print in Victorian times. In 1815 Howe visited Waterloo, possibly accompanied by his pupil William Kidd (1796–1863), and on his return to Edinburgh produced a large panorama painting of the battle which was exhibited in the capital and in Glasgow. He also painted a panorama of the victory at Quatre Bras.

Howe came to be regarded as Scotland's leading animal painter and some of his drawings of horses and cattle were engraved by W. H. Lizars and published in Howe's *Life of the Horse* (1824), his pioneering *The Breeds of our Different Domestic Animals Engraved from Portraits and Painted from Life* (1829–31) under the patronage of the Highland Society of Scotland, and in *Portraits of Horses and Prize Cattle* (1832). Howe was a prolific artist and had a sense of humour which was reflected in many of his comical drawings of animals and scenes from rural life. Examples of these are in Aberdeen Art Gallery and Museums; Dundee Art Galleries and Museums; the National Gallery of Scotland, Edinburgh, and Edinburgh City Libraries.

Howe's most famous and successful paintings were produced in the 1820s. As a child he had been entranced by the annual fairs in his place of birth. Two views of *Skirling Fair* (priv. colls.), one showing the highland cattle on the drove road, the other the parade of stallions, capture the bustle and excitement of the day.

A. D. Cameron described two styles in Howe's work. The earlier, for portraits and animals, was 'careful and professionally competent, bringing out [their] character and distinguishing features' (Cameron, 78–9). The second 'lively' style can be seen in his paintings of fairs and 'drawings for fun', which showed a marked 'return to his natural way of drawing and painting. Done with great economy of line and capacity to occupy the available space' (ibid.). As a man, he has been described as 'improvident, irresolute and unstable, saved by his friends and patrons', and his lifestyle resulted in him suffering poor health for a number of years (McEwan, 284). In 1836 he returned to Skirling for the good of his health but died there at Townhead Farm, apparently unmarried, on 11 July 1836, and was buried in Skirling churchyard. Further examples of Howe's works are held in Glasgow Art Gallery and Museum; the Scottish National Portrait Gallery, Edinburgh; and Perth Museum and Art Gallery.   GEORGE FAIRFULL SMITH

Sources A. D. Cameron, *The man who loved to draw horses: James Howe, 1780–1836* (1986) · 'Howe, the animal-painter', *Chambers' Edinburgh Journal* (3 Nov 1838), 323–4 · D. Irwin and F. Irwin, *Scottish painters at home and abroad, 1700–1900* (1975) · J. R. Brotchie, 'James Howe', *Scottish Arts Review*, 4/1 (1952), 24–5 · J. L. Caw, *Scottish painting past and present, 1620–1908* (1908) · P. J. M. McEwan, *Dictionary of Scottish art and architecture* (1994) · H. Smailes, *The concise catalogue of the Scottish National Portrait Gallery* (1990) · Irving, *Scots.* · DNB
Likenesses T. S. Good, oils, Scot. NPG · J. Howe, self-portrait, pencil drawing, Scot. NPG

Howe, John (1630–1705), Presbyterian minister, was born at Loughborough, Leicestershire, on 17 May 1630 and baptized there six days later, the son of John How, Church of England clergyman, and his wife, Anne.

Early life and career, 1630–1660 Howe's father was curate to John Browne, rector of Loughborough, from 1628 until November 1634, when he was suspended from the ministry, imprisoned, and fined for praying publicly 'that the young prince, meaning Prince Charles, might not be brought up in popery' (*CSP dom.*, 1634–5, 314, 318, 550). In the following year the family settled in Ireland. They narrowly escaped harm in the rising of 1641 and soon afterwards returned to England, probably settling in Winwick, Lancashire, where Howe attended the grammar school of Ralph Gorse.

Howe was admitted on 19 May 1647 as a sizar at Christ's College, Cambridge, where his tutor was the puritan Henry Field. At Christ's he came under the influence of the Cambridge Platonists Ralph Cudworth and Henry More, but claims that Howe himself is to be numbered among the Cambridge Platonists are mistaken. His lifelong friendship with More, a love of Platonist writings, an

John Howe (1630–1705), after Sir Godfrey Kneller, 1690s

abstract and rarefied spirituality, and a shared commitment to 'moderation' are sufficient to account for the 'Platonick tincture' which Calamy rightly says runs throughout his writings, but his doctrinal commitment to Calvinism firmly set him apart from the movement (Calamy, *Memoirs*, 7).

On 20 October 1648 Howe was admitted as a Bible clerk at Brasenose College, Oxford, where he graduated BA on 18 January 1650. Later that year he was elected chaplain at Magdalen College, where at first he avoided the 'church meeting' of the president, Thomas Goodwin, judging that its distinguishing peculiarities would exclude him. Goodwin admitted him on 'catholick terms' (Calamy, *Memoirs*, 11). Howe graduated MA on 9 July 1652 and was a fellow of Magdalen until his marriage three years later. It was probably also in 1652 that he received Presbyterian ordination from Charles Herle, once prolocutor of the Westminster assembly and at that time rector of Winwick, and the curates of the four chapelries of Winwick.

In 1654 Howe was appointed to the perpetual curacy of Great Torrington in Devon, a donative of Christ Church, Oxford, where the first of his many endeavours at promoting visible union among Christians met with real although short-lived success. Though accused of ill temper by Thomas Larkham, vicar of Tavistock, Howe brought together the Independents and Presbyterians who had gone their separate ways in the time of the previous minister, Lewis Stucley. He also established a meeting for ministers of differing persuasions, perhaps one of the seven subdivisional meetings of the 'association of Presbyterian ministers of the county of Devon', opened to Independents in May 1656. He formed a friendship with

George *Hughes, vicar of St Andrew's, Plymouth, a leading Presbyterian in the county and a prime mover in establishing the Devon association, with whom he conducted a weekly correspondence in Latin. On 1 March 1655 he married Hughes's daughter Katherine (c.1630–1697). They had five children: George *Howe, James, John, Obadiah, and Philippa.

In 1656, through the influence of his friend the MP Thomas Boon, Howe came to the attention of Oliver Cromwell and became the protector's domestic chaplain with responsibility for 'the setting up of the worship and discipline of Christ in this family' (corresp. of Richard Baxter, DWL, MS 59, 6.232). He played little part in affairs of state but gained a reputation for impartiality, unselfishness, latitude, and no little courage. His counsel helped the clergyman and church historian Thomas Fuller through the examination of the 'triers'; his influence with Cromwell won favours for Seth Ward, later bishop of Salisbury, and he caused a stir by his forthright repudiation in a sermon before Cromwell of the notion (to which Cromwell was inclined) that subjective impressions received during prayer might serve as a guarantee that the request made in prayer would be granted.

Howe's correspondence with Baxter at this time confirms that he was already vigorous in his pursuit of greater union between Presbyterians and Independents and had a truly eirenical spirit. He made suggestions to Cromwell for furthering such a union, but these came to nothing. He found his work in Cromwell's house uncongenial both because he met with little success in it and because he longed to be back with his flock in Great Torrington, who were asking Howe to return having failed to agree upon a successor to him. By the time a compromise had been negotiated, by which Howe was to spend three months of the year in Devon, Cromwell had died. After attending the Savoy conference, which produced a confession of faith for Independent churches, as an observer in September 1658, Howe went back to the south-west for some months. He returned in the spring to fill a lectureship at St Margaret's, Westminster, and to serve as domestic chaplain to Richard Cromwell, whose reputation he afterwards consistently defended and who came to visit him shortly before Howe's death. A few weeks later, in May 1659, Cromwell was deposed and Howe returned once more to Great Torrington.

Restoration and ejection, 1660–1670 Howe continued at Great Torrington until the summer of 1662, disturbed only by charges of seditious preaching which were easily rebutted before the mayor on 14 November 1660 and at the spring assize in 1661. On 24 August 1662, when, in Howe's words, 'many ... lights were in one day put under a bushel', he was ejected from his charge (*Works*, ed. J. P. Hewlett, 1848, 3.425). The question as to why Howe did not conform vexed at least two friends of his who became bishops, Seth Ward and John Wilkins. To Ward, Howe explained that the requirement of re-ordination 'hurt his understanding' since nothing could have two beginnings (Calamy, *Memoirs*, 39). When Wilkins expressed surprise to Howe that a person of his known latitude should have

not conformed, Howe explained that it was this very latitude which kept him a nonconformist. He could not belong to a church which established 'terms of communion narrower than Christ made' (*Principles of the Oracles of God*, pt 1, lecture 11). He viewed conformity to the settlement of 1662 as a form of sectarianism.

Howe spent the next seven years in the south-west of England, preaching mostly in private homes. Reference is made to him in the 1665 episcopal returns as 'Mr. John Howe A.M. inhabiting in great Torrington who behaves himselfe peaceably', and he was one of twelve nonconformist ministers in Devon to take the Oxford oath (G. Lyon Turner, *Original Records of Early Nonconformity under Persecution and Indulgence*, 1911–14, 1.308, 409). In 1666 he took the oath required by the Five Mile Act (1665) and enjoyed relative freedom to continue his occasional and itinerant ministry in the houses of the gentry.

In 1668 Howe's first major work, *The Blessedness of the Righteous*, was published. An exposition of the content and mode of that 'transformative knowledge' of God which inwardly renews human beings, it is Howe's most Platonist work. In his preface Baxter, who later described Howe as 'a very Learned, judicious, godly man, of no Faction, but of Catholick, healing Principles, and of excellent ministerial Abilities', was already writing of Howe's 'famed worth' (*Reliquiae Baxterianae*, 97).

In 1670 Howe, frustrated at the limitations under which he endeavoured to minister and also in some financial difficulty, accepted the invitation of John, second Viscount Massareene of Antrim, to serve as his personal chaplain, moving to Ireland early in 1671. While in Ireland he preached in the parish church each Sunday afternoon with the approval of both the diocesan bishop and the archbishop of Armagh, James Margetson. He took an active part in the weekly Presbyterian 'Antrim meeting', taught with Thomas Gowan at a training school for Presbyterians in 1675, and wrote two of his greatest works, the devotional treatise *Delighting in God* (1674) and the anti-atheist natural theology *The Living Temple, Part One* (1675).

London nonconformist ministry, 1675–1689 In September 1675 Lazarus Seaman, pastor of the Presbyterian congregation which met at Haberdashers' Hall, Staining Lane, Cheapside, London, died, and Howe was invited to join Thomas Jacombe as the co-pastor. He travelled to London in December and decided to remain. Assisted successively by Daniel Bull, John Shower, Daniel Williams, Thomas Reynolds, and John Spademan, Howe ministered to this congregation until his death.

The early years of Howe's London pastorate brought him to prominence among the dissenters. He was appointed as one of the Merchants' lecturers after the death of the Presbyterian Thomas Manton in 1677, and he became more widely known still following the publication of his essay *God's Prescience* (1677). Written in response to a query from Robert Boyle, this was one of the most theologically acute of Howe's writings and dealt with the asymmetry between God's predetermination of good on the one hand and evil on the other. Misread as compromising Calvinism, the work was attacked by the strict Calvinists

Thomas Danson and Theophilus Gale, the latter describing Howe as a 'new methodist' (*The Court of the Gentiles*, pt 4, bk 2, 1677, 522–3). The poet Andrew Marvell defended Howe, but on the grounds of the reasonableness and Christian demeanour of the book, and this did not prevent, and may even in some minds have confirmed, the perception that Howe had shifted from the standard Calvinist understanding of these matters. Anthony Wood later mistakenly labelled Howe a 'great and strict Arminian' (Wood, *Ath. Oxon.*, new edn, 1813–20, 4.589).

Howe's status as one of the leaders of the nonconformists was confirmed in 1680 when, during one of the periodic spells of *rapprochement* between the Anglicans and the dissenters, it was to him, rather than to Baxter or Bates, that Bishop William Lloyd first went in order to discuss terms of comprehension. In the same year Howe defended dissenters from Dean Edward Stillingfleet's charge of schism, made in a sermon of 11 May 1680 and published as *The Mischief of Separation*. Stillingfleet was grateful for the manner of Howe's response, which, he wrote, showed him to be 'more like a Well-disposed Gentleman than like a Divine' (*The Unreasonableness of Separation*, 1680, lxii). Howe's gracious rebuke of Dean Tillotson's Erastianism in 1680 was equally well received.

Pressure upon the nonconformists intensified between 1681 and 1685. Unable to engage in public ministry and in poor health, Howe published more in this period than any other in his life, notably his *Union among Protestants* and *Redeemer's Tears*. In 1682 his assistant Daniel Bull was disgraced for adultery, and in the same year he preached Margaret Baxter's funeral sermon. Late in 1682 and early in 1683 one of his meetings was broken up, eight members were arrested, and Howe was fined for holding a conventicle. By 1685 he wrote that 'the anger and jealousies of such as I never had a disposition to offend, have of later times occasioned persons of my circumstances very seldom to walk the streets' (Calamy, *Memoirs*, 115). In August 1685 he was invited to accompany Philip, fourth Baron Wharton, to the continent and reluctantly agreed. His congregation knew nothing of the plan until Howe wrote to them from overseas.

Wharton and Howe travelled for a year before Howe settled in Utrecht. There he ran a boarding house, helped local students prepare for disputations, and preached regularly in the English church as well as in his own home. It was while in Holland that he made the acquaintance of Gilbert Burnet, Sir John Thompson, later Lord Haversham, and William, prince of Orange. On 11 May 1687, five weeks after James II had issued his first declaration of indulgence, Howe gladly returned to England. Having been urged by William not to fall in with James's wishes to win over the dissenters, he then stood firm with Baxter and Bates in discouraging any address of thanks to the king for the indulgence. He conferred with Sir John Swynfen, Richard Hampden, and Robert Harley in September 1687 and, despite being personally interviewed by James on at least one occasion, refused to be drawn into approval of his schemes. Howe later wrote of the 'arts and insinuations … used with us to draw us into a concurrence with

designs tending to the prejudice of the nation', but again in May 1688 and once more in October of that year the pressure which James brought to bear on Howe and others failed to move them (Howe, *The Case of the Protestant Dissenters*, 1689, Q3). On 5 November 1688 William landed in England, and just seven weeks later James fled the country. With both Baxter and Bates unwell, Howe was recognized as the leader of the dissenters, and on 2 January 1689, having been formally introduced by lords Wharton, Devonshire, and Wiltshire, he gave a speech of welcome and loyalty to William on behalf of the Presbyterians and Independents. Early in 1689 Howe was working for comprehension, but he was satisfied with the toleration granted in May of that year. In his *Humble Requests to both Conformists and Dissenters* (1689), he pleaded with both conformists and dissenters to join a spirit of tolerance to the legal toleration which now existed.

Last years, 1690–1705 With hopes for comprehension at an end, closer union between the Presbyterians and the Independents was sought, and Howe played a leading part in the two initiatives intended to bring this about. These were the establishment in 1689 of the Common Fund for the support of needy nonconformist ministers and the training of new ones, and, in 1691, the Happy Union of the London Presbyterian and Independent ministers themselves under certain 'heads of agreement'. Howe was one of the ministers chosen to manage the Common Fund, undertook the survey of needy ministers in four counties, pledged the largest annual subscription recorded, and was largely responsible for drawing up the 'heads of agreement'. But even as he wrote of the eradication of the distinction between Presbyterian and Independent and rejoiced with others at the 'two sticks made one' (Ezekiel, 37: 16–20) the seeds of disunion had already been sown. A spark of controversy was created when Howe and eleven others injudiciously signed a certificate of genuineness prefixed to some sermons of Tobias Crisp published for the first time in 1690. This was taken by some as approval of the antinomianism of the sermons, and the spark was fanned into a flame by Richard Baxter, Thomas Cole, Isaac Chauncy, Nathaniel Mather, and Daniel Williams. That controversy was the ruin of the Happy Union despite several efforts by Howe to save it. The Common Fund divided in 1693; in the following year Williams's exclusion from the Merchants' lecture led to the withdrawal of Howe, Alsop, and Bates, who refused 'to be tied to any party so as to abandon all others' (Calamy, *Memoirs*, 196). A new lecture was formed at Salters' Hall, but although Howe continued to enjoy close personal ties with Matthew Mead, the leader of the largely congregational group which stayed at Pinners' Hall, the episode signalled the breakdown of his efforts for union and was a bitter disappointment to him. In striving to prevent the breach he had published *The carnality of Christian Contention*, encapsulating his previous writings on ecclesiology.

In 1694 Howe declined to take part in the public ordination of Calamy, oversaw the removal of his congregation to a new meeting place in Silver Street, Wood Street, and played a minor part in the Trinitarian controversy. Increasingly assuming the role of an elder statesman of nonconformity, he ministered to his own congregation, published frequently, wrote prefaces for others, preached funeral sermons, and was consulted on various matters of church order and on the suitability of pastoral candidates. In 1697 his wife, Katherine, died and in the same year he married Margaret (d. 1743), whose parentage is unknown.

In 1701 Daniel Defoe reissued his tract *The Occasional Conformity of Dissenters in Cases of Preferment* of 1698 with a preface addressed to Howe, challenging him to denounce or defend the practice of occasionally conforming in order to qualify for civic office. Sir Thomas Abney, the new lord mayor and a member of Howe's congregation, practised occasional conformity. Howe was an enthusiastic supporter of the 'healing custom' of dissenters periodically taking the sacrament in the Church of England in order 'to testify they decline it not as no church', and he deeply resented Defoe's charges that the practice arose from self-interest, hypocrisy, or inconsistency (Howe, *Works*, ed. J. P. Hewlett, 1848, 3.544). Howe's response contained the most vigorous polemic he published and cogently restated his principled catholicism.

Howe then 'began to be weary of living' (Calamy, *Memoirs*, 223). In 1705, just a few days before his death, he endorsed Calamy's scheme of non-synodical Presbyterianism. After a short final illness he died, 'being at last quite worn out', on Monday 2 April 1705 in London and was buried on 6 April at All Hallows, Bread Street, London (ibid., 227). On the next Sunday, 8 April, Howe's funeral sermon was preached by his colleague John Spademan.

Writings and Reputation Howe was an extremely prolific writer, publishing, in addition to those mentioned above, some twenty-eight other works. Almost 200 further lectures and sermons were published posthumously and, after Calamy's edition of his collected works of 1724, several more multi-volume editions were published in the nineteenth century. Howe's writings have a consistent seriousness of tone; there are passages of sustained irony in his polemic but he is never frivolous. At once capable of relentless logic and deep feeling, he reveals an otherworldly fervour, and the abstraction of his writings is only rarely relieved by the metaphors, illustrations, and biblical examples which mark the writings of the more popular puritan divines. Fewer than two dozen letters are extant, and almost no other manuscripts; on his deathbed Howe had ordered his son George to destroy the 'multitude of small volumes ... of the large memorials he had collected of the material passages of his own life and of the times wherein he lived', thereby depriving posterity of the materials necessary for the composition of a critical biography (letter from George Howe to George Hughes in Calamy, *Memoirs*, 228).

Calamy described Howe as 'very tall and exceeding graceful' with 'a good presence and a piercing but pleasant eye' (Calamy, *Memoirs*, 234). He was also a man of high principle and intense seriousness, elevation of mind and a

studied moderation, calm reasonableness, Christian charity, personal dignity, and depth. Contemporaries and commentators have positioned Howe variously on the theological and ecclesiastical spectrum of his day, assessing him as the last of the puritans on the one hand and as a dissenting, liberalizing latitudinarian on the other. Howe is rather to be regarded as one of the leaders of early nonconformity and a major representative of the distinct, moderate Presbyterian, Baxterian middle-way Calvinists who, sensitive to the charges of the anti-Calvinists, emphasized reasonableness, moderation, and catholicity while remaining faithful to what they perceived as Calvinist orthodoxy. His eirenic spirit, profound and extensive writings, wide-ranging connections, and thirty-year-long career as a London minister combined to make Howe one of England's most influential religious figures of the late seventeenth century and won him a breadth of respect given to very few others in his divided generation.

DAVID P. FIELD

Sources E. Calamy, *Memoirs of the life of the late Revd John Howe* (1724) · *An abridgment of Mr. Baxter's History of his life and times*, ed. E. Calamy (1702) · E. Calamy, ed., *An abridgment of Mr. Baxter's history of his life and times, with an account of the ministers, &c., who were ejected after the Restauration of King Charles II*, 2nd edn, 2 vols. (1713) · E. Calamy, *A continuation of the account of the ministers ... who were ejected and silenced after the Restoration in 1660*, 2 vols. (1727) · *Reliquiae Baxterianae, or, Mr Richard Baxter's narrative of the most memorable passages of his life and times*, ed. M. Sylvester, 1 vol. in 3 pts (1696) · DNB · R. Baxter, correspondence, DWL, MS 59 [6 vols.] · DWL, Howe MS 24.16–20, 28.113–114 · CSP dom., 1634–5, 1657–60, 1676–7, 1682–4 · D. P. Field, '"Rigide Calvinisme in a Softer Dresse": the moderate Presbyterianism of John Howe (1630–1705)', PhD diss., U. Cam., 1993 · A. Gordon, ed., *Freedom after ejection: a review (1690–1692) of presbyterian and congregational nonconformity in England and Wales* (1917) · E. Calamy, *An historical account of my own life*, 2 vols. (1731) · *Calamy rev.* · *Calendar of the correspondence of Richard Baxter*, ed. N. H. Keeble and G. F. Nuttall, 2 vols. (1991) · H. Rogers, *The life and character of John Howe*, 2nd edn (1862) · R. F. Horton, *John Howe* (1905) · A. B. Grosart, *Representative nonconformists* (1879) · J. R. Jones, *The revolution 1688 in England* (1972) · D. R. Lacey, *Dissent and parliamentary politics in England, 1661–1689* (1969) · J. I. Packer, 'The redemption and restoration of man in the thought of Richard Baxter', DPhil diss., U. Oxf., 1954 · *Calendar of the correspondence of Philip Doddridge*, ed. G. F. Nuttall, HMC, JP 26 (1979), 173

Archives DWL, sermons and papers · Harris Man. Oxf., sermons

Likenesses oils, 1690–99 (after G. Kneller), NPG [*see illus.*] · oils, c.1690–1700, DWL · J. Closterman, oils, 1702, Christ's College, Cambridge · R. White, line engraving, 1702, BM, NPG; repro. in J. Howe, *The living temple, part two* (1702) · Adlard, engraving, NPG · Bidley, engraving, NPG · J. Caldwell, engraving, NPG · J. Cochran, engraving, NPG · S. J. Freeman, engraving, NPG · W. Holl, engraving, NPG · Trotter, engraving, NPG

Howe, John, fourth Baron Chedworth (1754–1804), eccentric, was born on 22 August 1754, the second and only surviving child of the Revd Thomas Howe (1716–1776), rector of Great Wishford and Kingston Deverill, Wiltshire, and his wife, Frances (1722–1778), daughter of Thomas White of Tattingstone Place, Suffolk. His father was the third son of John Howe, first Baron Chedworth (d. 1742).

Educated at Harrow School, Howe matriculated at Queen's College, Oxford, on 29 October 1772 and left after three years' residence without taking a degree. Following his father's death he moved with his mother to Ipswich to be near her family; she died in 1778. In 1781—on the death of his uncle, Henry Frederick Howe, third Baron Chedworth—he succeeded to the title and estates, but continued to live in Suffolk and took no interest in Stowell Park, the family seat in Gloucestershire.

Chedworth's reputation as an eccentric began with the contrast between his prominent social position and his appearance—he was described by contemporaries as a very strange looking man, awkward and ungainly, 'an odd fox', 'very singular, and negligent in his dress' (*Two Actions*, 15). This singularity often gave rise to social difficulties, as when in 1780 he was famously turned away from Tiptree militia camp by a sentry under orders not to let in any 'mean looking person' (*Letters from the Late Lord Chedworth*, vii).

Many of Chedworth's dealings were characterized by unworldliness. He lived exceedingly modestly, and for many years failed to notice that he was being systematically defrauded by his steward—almost £60,000 was eventually recovered by his solicitor. He rejected fashionable society, frequented theatres and racecourses, and scandalized his social equals by haunting the parlour of The Griffen Inn at Ipswich and the green room of the Theatre Royal, Norwich. Chedworth's *Notes upon some of the Obscure Passages in Shakespeare's Plays*, published posthumously in 1805, demonstrated the seriousness of his interest in the theatre.

There are suggestions of sexual ambivalence: despite Chedworth's many women friends—actresses, milliners, and innkeepers' daughters—and his professions of despair at losing one of them to another man (related in *Letters from the Late Lord Chedworth*, 19.34–5), he never married, and was publicly accused of homosexual behaviour in an incident at Epsom races in 1781. Chedworth refused to defend his honour by duelling; instead, in a case which caused much excitement, he successfully sued for damages—but the episode exacerbated his dislike of society.

Chedworth's eccentricities possibly accentuated his reputation as a man of principle. An obituarist described him as being 'of a very religious cast of mind' (*GM*, 1st ser, 74/2, 1804, 1242) and much attached to the establishment in church and state, while his epitaph noted his devotion to the revolutionary settlement of 1688. *A charge delivered to the grand jury at the general quarter sessions of the peace for the county of Suffolk*, in 1793, which he delivered as chairman of the sessions, made a plea for reason in the face of the hysteria generated by the terror in France. He was noted for his shrewdness: Thurlow maintained that Chedworth 'understood the laws of his country better than any country magistrate in the kingdom' (Glyde, 'Biographical sketch'). His accurate recording of the proceedings against Warren Hastings was taken as authoritative by his fellow peers. Though he never owned horses or betted, he was a member of the Jockey Club and was much respected at Newmarket where it was said that nobody could out-calculate him.

Howe died at his home in Brook Street, Ipswich, on 29 October 1804, 'after three months illness during which he was invisible to his friends' (*GM*, 1st ser, 74/2, 1804, 1242) and was buried on 2 November in St Matthew's Church, Ipswich. There were no heirs and the barony became extinct. His will caused a sensation, and sealed his reputation for eccentricity, since he left nearly £300,000 which, after modest bequests to three cousins, was divided between numerous friends and acquaintances, many of them actors and actresses. £15,000 was left to the woman he had hoped to marry, £3000 to 'that Illustrious Statesman and true patriot the Honorable Charles James Fox' (will, PRO PROB 11/1417, fol. 173v), and £4000 to a cheesemonger on the quay with whom he played whist and with whose wife he enjoyed conversing. His family failed to have the will overturned on the grounds of insanity. His estate at Stowell Park, where he never lived, was sold in 1811 to Sir William Scott, the judge, later Baron Stowell.

M. ST JOHN PARKER

Sources *GM*, 1st ser., 74 (1804), 1242–4; 76 (1806), 672, 1201–7 · *Letters from the late Lord Chedworth to the Revd Thomas Crompton, 1780–1795* (1828) · *Two actions between John Howe esq. and George Lewis Dive esq. tried by a special jury before Lord Mansfield at the assizes holden at Croydon on Wednesday 15 August 1781* (1781) · Silverpen [J. Glyde], 'Biographical sketch of Lord Chedworth and autograph letter', manuscripts and cuttings from series Suffolk Worthies and Persons of Note in East Anglia no. 24, Suffolk RO, Ipswich, HD 467 · 'Lord Chedworth and his celebrated will', *Glyde's official directory* (1887), 187–93 · R. Miller, 'Profile of an English eccentric', *Suffolk Fair* (Nov 1985) · F. Haslewood, ed., *The monumental inscriptions in the parish of St Matthew, Ipswich, Suffolk* (1884), 16, 273 · John Howe, Lord Chedworth, *A charge delivered to the grand jury at the general quarter sessions of the peace for the county of Suffolk holden by adjournment at Ipswich on Friday January 18 1793* (1793) · B. Burke, *A genealogical history of the dormant, abeyant, forfeited and extinct peerages of the British empire*, new edn (1883) · GEC, *Peerage*, new edn, 3.157 · Foster, *Alum. Oxon.* · parish registers, Wiltshire, St Edmund's, Salisbury, 27 Sept 1754 [baptism] · will, PRO, PROB 11/1417, sig. 778

Likenesses G. Rowe, lithograph, 1804 (after pencil sketch by Penon?), Suffolk RO, Ipswich, HD480/29, fol. 80 · Penon?, pencil sketch, Suffolk RO, Ipswich, HD480/29, fol. 79

Wealth at death approx. £300,000; Stowell Park and estates sold for £268,635; other income and property, incl. Brook St, Ipswich: *GM*, 2 July 1811, vol. 81, pt 2, p. 80; will, PRO, PROB 11/1417, sig. 778

Howe [How], **John Grobham** [Jack] (1657–1722), politician, was born on 9 February 1657, the second of the four sons (there were also five daughters) of John Grobham Howe (1625–1679) of Langar, Nottinghamshire, a politician who represented Gloucestershire during the Cromwellian and Cavalier parliaments. His mother was Annabella (1630/31–1704), the third and youngest illegitimate daughter and coheir of Emanuel *Scrope, first earl of Sunderland, who upon her legitimization in 1663 became Lady Annabella.

The place and manner of Howe's education are unknown, but as a young man he attached himself to the court of Charles II, where he soon drew attention as 'a young amorous spark' (H. Sidney, *Diary of the Times of Charles II*, 1843, 100). His rakish exploits culminated in 1678 in his openly boasting of an affair with the duchess of Richmond. This was proved false, and he was banished from the royal precincts. Subsequently, after taking up the pen, he entertained London society with a series of biting lampoons, while at the same time he himself, on account of his own dalliances, was often the object of satiric comment. In 1683, by a licence of 30 April, he married Mary (*bap.* 1656, *d.* 1699), the recently widowed wife of Sir Edward Morgan, third baronet, of Llantarnam Abbey, Monmouthshire, and daughter and coheir of Humphrey Baskerville of Pontrilas, Kentchurch, Herefordshire. It was an advantageous match which brought him landed wealth and the means to establish himself as a gentleman in his own right. The Howes subsequently had a son, Howe's heir John (later first Lord Chedworth), and a daughter.

In 1689 Howe entered the Convention Parliament for Cirencester, and almost immediately gained recognition as a frequent and intrepid speaker. His support for the revolution, which was distinctly whiggish in tone, was promptly rewarded with his appointment as vice-chamberlain of Queen Mary's household and to the lesser post of keeper of Pall Mall. He was not uncritical, however, of the newly appointed chief ministers, especially lords Carmarthen and Halifax, who had been associated with James II's regime and who, in Howe's opinion, had thus rendered themselves unfit for office under William III. Neither did he show any sign of restraint in the early sessions of the 1690 parliament. In March 1692, at the end of a session which had seen his energetic participation in the opposition attacks on the ministry for mishandling the naval campaign against the French, Howe was dismissed from his offices. Although his removal was variously attributed to his irreligion, his womanizing, and his alleged bawdiness in the queen's presence, his lack of commitment to the court in the Commons was certainly the major factor.

In the years that followed Howe grew in stature as a formidable opponent of the government. It has been assumed that he promptly shed his whig principles and became a tory, but, although he associated himself with tory leaders such as Sir Edward Seymour and Sir Christopher Musgrave, he was in essence a powerful 'country' spokesman, subjecting all aspects of government policy to his own brand of hard-hitting, quickfire rhetoric. His invective, especially that which he poured upon 'court corruption', was often felt to contain a strong personal edge, and left a distinct impression of disappointed and self-interested motive. He gained a reputation for unpredictability, extremity, and impulsiveness, of 'daring to say what he pleases' (J. Macky, *Memoirs of the Secret Services of J. Macky*, 1733, 118); and not infrequently taxed the patience of MPs with his habit of addressing his observations to them seemingly upon everything that came under discussion.

Howe even opposed the government in 1696 over its impeachment of Sir John Fenwick, the chief conspirator in the assassination plot to kill the king, finding this a particularly appropriate issue over which to dramatize the distance between himself and the court, although there was never any serious suggestion that he was a Jacobite sympathizer. His efforts to stir up trouble could often appear foolish and ill-considered. At other times his initiatives were more constructive, as on those occasions when he introduced or helped to promote measures to regulate elections and to reduce the numbers of placemen in the Commons.

At the election in 1698, having lost favour with the electors at Cirencester, Howe was elected knight of the shire for Gloucestershire. Over the next two years he made erratic efforts to establish his own platform in the country opposition, but not infrequently clashed with tory chiefs, particularly Robert Harley, who was endeavouring to unify whig and tory opponents in a campaign to oust the junto ministers. His exclusion from office at the close of 1700, when the ministry was reconstructed along tory lines, only worsened his deep personal sense of grievance. When the second partition treaty was debated in March 1701, he injudiciously likened the king to one of three robbers who had combined to rob the house of a sick man, a widely reported remark which gave him celebrity status in France and was long remembered in political circles at home as one of the most scurrilous reflections ever heard publicly against the king.

The torrent of public abuse to which Howe was subjected as a result of this tactlessness led to his defeat in the election of December 1701. After the death of William III in March 1702, however, he was quick to make his court to Queen Anne, and on 21 April he was sworn of the privy council. He made great show of not wanting an office of profit under the new tory ministry, yet soon became irritated with Godolphin's failure to offer something suitable. In the summer election of that year he performed the unusual feat of standing for four constituencies: Gloucestershire, Gloucester, Bodmin, and Newton. After recovering his Gloucestershire seat, he soon proved himself a dutiful court tory and in December 1702 was made joint paymaster of the forces. In the light of his much vaunted antipathy to offices and pensions, this, to his detractors, appeared only to confirm earlier intimations of a shallowness of purpose and an unprincipled nature.

Howe lost his seat in the 1705 election, and made no subsequent attempt to re-enter parliament. He continued to perform his official duties as joint paymaster with a punctiliousness which impressed many, and though plagued by worsening ill health he was not removed from the post until 1714. In the latter years of Queen Anne's reign he was venerated as 'a true patriot' who had obtained office 'not by flattery, but by freedom of speech in parliament' (Atkyns, 367). He died at his country seat, Stowell, Gloucestershire, on 11 June 1722, and was buried at Stowell church three days later. A. A. HANHAM

Sources 'Howe, John Grobham', HoP, *Commons, 1690–1715* [draft] · B. D. Henning, 'Howe, John Grobham II', HoP, *Commons, 1660–90* · IGI · J. J. Howard and F. A. Crisp, eds., *Visitation of England and Wales: notes*, 14 vols. (privately printed, London, 1896–1921), vol. 13, pp. 96, 103 · R. Atkyns, *The ancient and present state of Glostershire*, 2 pts in 1 (1712)

Archives BL, letters to Lord Nottingham, Add. MS 29588

Howe, Joseph (1804–1873), journalist and politician in Canada, was born on 13 December 1804 at the Northwest Arm, Halifax, Nova Scotia, the only son of John Howe (1754–1835), postmaster-general and king's printer of the

Joseph Howe (1804–1873), by T. & R. Annan & Sons, pubd 1914

maritimes, and his second wife, Mary Edes. His father was a Massachusetts loyalist who apparently instilled in the boy a deep reverence for the British empire. The family was of modest means, and Howe was largely self-educated. At the age of thirteen he began to work in his father's printing office, but since his older half-brother was to inherit the business he had to carve out a career for himself as a journalist and publisher. Early in 1827 he became co-owner of the *Weekly Chronicle*, which he renamed *The Acadian*, but in December he sold his share and became the sole proprietor of *The Novascotian*, which he turned into the most influential newspaper in Nova Scotia. He wrote most of *The Novascotian* himself, including lengthy descriptions of his travels across the colony— *Eastern Rambles* (1828), *Western Rambles* (1829), and *Letters from the Interior* (1832)—and the occasional poem. He also acted as the paper's parliamentary correspondent and legal reporter. Between 1829 and 1836 he published, often at a loss, such works as Beamish Murdoch's *Epitome of the Laws of Nova Scotia* and Thomas Chandler Haliburton's *An Historical and Statistical Account of Nova Scotia* and *The Clock-maker*, and he was in great demand as a public speaker (he gave, for example, the inaugural address to the mechanics' institute in Halifax in 1832). On 2 February 1828 Howe married Catherine Susan Ann McNab (*b.* 1807), with whom he had ten children (he also had at least one illegitimate child); their home in Halifax became an informal meeting place for the town's small literary community. Throughout his life Howe wrote numerous public letters, speeches, and addresses, many of which were published in a two-volume edition, *The Speeches and Public Letters of Joseph Howe* (1858). Shortly after his death a collection of his *Poems and Essays* (1874) was published by his fourth son,

Sydenham Howe. Howe was undoubtedly a minor literary figure, but he is now seen as an influence seminal in the evolution of an indigenous Canadian literature, and most of his publications have been reissued in modern editions.

Initially Howe, like his father, leaned towards the moderate Conservative side in politics, but in the 1830s he became increasingly critical of the Nova Scotia government and in 1835 published a letter accusing the Halifax magistrates of corruption, whereupon he was brought to trial for libel. He pleaded his own case and in an eloquent address lasting for six and a half hours defended the freedom of the press. Although clearly guilty, he was acquitted by a sympathetic jury. The trial established his leadership of the reformers and in 1836 he was elected to the assembly for the county of Halifax. The following year he was the author of the twelve resolutions passed by the assembly calling for a reform of the colony's institutions, including the radical measure of an elective upper chamber. In 1838 he travelled to London to present the assembly's grievances to the Colonial Office and then embarked on a tour of the British Isles and the continent. On his voyage home in 1839 he read Lord Durham's report and was convinced by its analysis. Later that year he addressed a series of public letters to the secretary of state for the colonies, Lord John Russell, demanding that the colonies be given responsible government. On his return he also fought a duel with John Halliburton, the son of the chief justice. When Lieutenant-Governor Sir Colin Campbell refused to introduce responsible government, in 1840 Howe supported an address to the crown calling for Campbell's removal, and Lord John Russell sent the governor-general, Charles Poulett Thomson, to Halifax to create a government supported by the assembly. Thomson persuaded Howe to enter into a coalition with the Conservatives, led by James W. Johnston, but Howe was unable to carry all of the Reformers into the coalition.

In 1841 Howe sold *The Novascotian*. He served as speaker of the assembly in 1841 and as collector of excise at Halifax in 1842. But the coalition was an uneasy one. In 1843 Howe annoyed Johnston by speaking out against grants to denominational colleges, and after the election that year the Conservatives formed a clear majority in the assembly and demanded a dominant role in the coalition. In December 1843 Howe and two other Reformers resigned from the executive council and rejoined the Reform Party. From May 1844 to April 1845 Howe was the editor of both *The Novascotian* and the *Morning Chronicle*, and he helped the Reformers win a majority in the election of 1847. This time he refused to listen to the Colonial Office's plea for another coalition, and in February 1848 the Reformers took office as a party. Nova Scotia thus became the first colony in the British empire in which responsible government was fully put into effect.

Although it was James Boyle Uniacke rather than Howe who headed the Reform Party, Howe was a figure of great influence, and he became provincial secretary. An early advocate of provincial railways, he oversaw the completion of railways linking Halifax with Windsor and Truro, though he unsuccessfully sought to persuade the British government to grant an imperial loan for an intercolonial railway from Halifax to Quebec City. Railways occupied so much of his time that in 1854 he resigned as provincial secretary to serve as chief commissioner of the province's bipartisan railway board. In 1855 he became a figure of controversy when he assisted the British government in recruiting American volunteers to fight in the Crimean War, and he was forced to flee from the United States for fear of being arrested for breaking America's neutrality laws. On his return he was defeated in the general election of 1855 by a young doctor named Charles Tupper, who was rebuilding the Conservative Party. Howe contributed to Tupper's success. Although not a man of deep religious convictions and a believer in freedom of religion, Howe had been brought up as a protestant (his father had belonged to the Sandemanians, a minor branch of New England puritanism) and he was increasingly critical of the Irish Catholic press for gloating over British reverses in the Crimea. Unable to hold his tongue, he antagonized the Catholic Liberals, who deserted the party and brought the Conservatives to power in 1856. Howe resigned as railway commissioner and considered forming a protestant alliance, but in the end he stood as a Liberal in the election of 1859, in which the party ran a thinly disguised anti-Catholic campaign and was rewarded with a small majority in the assembly. Howe again became provincial secretary and in August 1860 succeeded William Young as head of the government. His majority was a precarious one, and in the election of 1863 his party suffered overwhelming defeat and he lost his own seat.

Howe now concentrated on the office of imperial fisheries commissioner, to which he had been appointed in December 1862, and he was unable to attend the Charlottetown conference in September 1864. He also missed the Quebec conference in October, where the delegates worked out a detailed scheme for confederation. The Quebec Resolutions aroused considerable opposition in Nova Scotia, and Howe gradually emerged as the head of a diverse coalition of anti-confederates. In the 'Botheration letters', initially published anonymously in the *Morning Chronicle*, Howe spelt out his objections to a union which he feared would be dominated by the Canadians, would undermine his efforts at a larger imperial federation, and would create a federal union which would be unworkable. Historians have long debated the sincerity of Howe's opposition to union, pointing out that he had earlier spoken favourably of the idea of colonial union. Certainly he was motivated by a loathing for his old adversary, Charles Tupper, who led the pro-confederates, and he found particularly objectionable Tupper's refusal to allow the people of Nova Scotia to be consulted in an election. He also sincerely believed that confederation on the basis of the Quebec Resolutions would lead to the economic ruin of Nova Scotia. And a large number of Nova Scotians agreed with him. Although Howe could not prevent the assembly from passing a resolution in favour of confederation, he headed a delegation to London from July 1866 to May 1867 to lobby against the union. He published

a paper entitled *Confederation Considered in Relation to the Interests of the Empire* (1866), but he was unable to persuade the British government that confederation was antithetical to the interests of the empire and so had to sit helplessly in the imperial parliament, noting with disdain that only ten peers were present when the House of Lords gave final approval to the British North America Act. He returned to Nova Scotia to head the repeal movement. In the federal election of 1867 Tupper was the only pro-confederate elected in Nova Scotia while the repealers, led by Howe, swept the rest of the province. Howe then led a repeal delegation to London in 1868, but it soon became apparent that repeal had no chance of success, and in January 1869 he reached an agreement with the federal administration of Sir John A. Macdonald under which, in return for a slightly larger financial grant from Ottawa and a few other minor concessions to Nova Scotia, he entered the cabinet as president of the council. Howe's decision bitterly divided the repeal movement, many of whom viewed him as a turncoat. In November 1869 he became secretary of state in the Macdonald government and presided over the entry of Manitoba into confederation, but his health was rapidly deteriorating. So was his enthusiasm for the empire. All his life he had supported the imperial connection but, disillusioned by the failure of the imperial government to respond to Nova Scotia's concerns and by what he saw as its failure to safeguard Canadian interests in the negotiations leading to the treaty of Washington, in 1872, much to the annoyance of Macdonald, he publicly complained that, if Britain would not live up to its obligations, Canadians must work out their own national destiny. In this sense the Nova Scotian imperialist had indeed become a Canadian nationalist. But by this time Howe was a spent force. In May 1873 he became lieutenant-governor of Nova Scotia, but held the office for only three weeks before his death, at Government House in Halifax on 1 June.

A man of inordinate talent, Howe also had an inordinate ego. Within Nova Scotia he has become almost a mythical figure, the quintessential Liberal, the leader in the struggle for responsible government, and the defender of Nova Scotia's right to self-determination in 1866–7. He was a populist who fought for colonial self-government, but his Liberalism was of the mid-nineteenth-century variety, limited by a deep suspicion of Roman Catholicism and by a desire to restrict voting rights to men of property. A self-educated and self-made man, he fought against the power of entrenched élites and the privileges of the established church, but he also sought status and financial security for himself, and once in power abused patronage as flagrantly as his opponents. Excessively sensitive to criticism, he did not work well with others. In 1840 he disrupted the reform movement by entering the short-lived coalition and then in 1843 disrupted the coalition by returning to the reformers; in 1856 he split the Liberal Party by his vehement anti-Catholicism, which drove the Catholic Liberals into the Conservative Party and the Liberals into opposition; and in 1866 he refused to support the Liberal leadership, which was committed to confederation, and headed the repeal movement, which he abandoned in 1869 when he entered the federal government. To contemporaries Howe was a wild card whose behaviour was unpredictable. There can be no doubt of his enormous popular influence as a journalist and his skill as a public orator, and no doubt also of his love for his native province and the British empire. But he was committed to a vision of Nova Scotia's future greatness that was increasingly unrealistic, and he could not see, as Tupper did, that if the province was to evolve into a modern industrial economy it could do so only as part of Canada. He was also committed to a vision of Nova Scotia's significance to the empire which was increasingly unrealistic, as he himself seems to have recognized at the end of his career.

PHILLIP BUCKNER

Sources J. M. Beck, 'Howe, Joseph', *DCB*, vol. 10 · J. M. Beck, *Joseph Howe*, 2 vols. (1982–3) · P. A. Buckner, 'Canadian biography and the search for Joseph Howe', *Acadiensis*, 14 (1984), 105–16 · J. A. Roy, *Joseph Howe: a study in achievement and frustration* (1935) · D. C. Harvey, *The heart of Howe* (1939) · J. Howe, *Western and eastern rambles: travel sketches of Nova Scotia*, ed. M. G. Parks (1973) · *The speeches and public letters of Joseph Howe*, ed. J. A. Chisolm, 2 vols. (1909) · J. Howe, *Poems and essays*, ed. M. G. Parks (1973) · *My dear Susan Ann: letters of Joseph Howe to his wife*, ed. M. G. Parks (1985) · P. A. Buckner and J. G. Reid, eds., *The Atlantic region to confederation: a history* (1994) · J. W. Longley, *Joseph Howe* (1909)
Archives Harvard U., Houghton L., corresp. and papers · NA Canada, corresp. and papers | BL, corresp. with Sir J. G. Le Marchant, Egerton MS 2972 · Bodl. Oxf., corresp. with Sir John Fiennes Crampton · NA Canada, George Johnson MSS
Likenesses T. & R. Annan & Sons, engraving, pubd 1914, NPG [*see illus.*] · daguerreotype, Nova Scotia Museum, Halifax, Canada · lithograph, Nova Scotia Museum, Halifax, Canada

Howe, Josias (*bap.* 1612, *d.* 1701), Church of England clergyman and poet, the elder son of Thomas Howe (*b.* 1567/8), rector of Grendon Underwood, Buckinghamshire, was baptized there on 29 March 1612. He was elected scholar of Trinity College, Oxford, on 12 June 1632, and graduated BA on 18 June 1634, the year that his brother Richard matriculated at Christ Church, Oxford. He proceeded MA in 1638. On 26 May 1637 he was chosen fellow of his college at the insistence of Bishop Walter Curll.

A sermon on Psalm 4:7, 'Thou hast put gladnesse', which Howe delivered before the king at Christ Church, was, it is said, ordered by Charles to be printed at Oxford in 1644. Only thirty copies are supposed to have been printed, in haste and without a title-page. Thomas Hearne, whose copy is in Bodley's library, claimed that Howe 'told his friends that if ever he printed any sermon it should be in red Letters' (Hearne, 2.669). The sermon, of which only this copy survives, was printed by Henry Hall in double pica italic in red, presumably (and apparently the point of the Hearne anecdote) to match Leonard Lichfield's publication of the epistles of Ignatius for James Ussher at Oxford the same year. Howe's preaching before the court at Oxford was much admired and on 10 July 1646 he was created BD. Howe was removed from his fellowship by the parliamentary visitors in 1648 for 'non-appearance', but was restored in 1660 as senior fellow, and died in college on 28 August 1701. He was buried in September in the college chapel.

From about 1642 Howe was an acquaintance of John Aubrey, furnishing him with anecdotes of the parish constable at Grendon, who was allegedly the model for Shakespeare's Dogberry, about his contemporary at college Sir John Denham (1615–1669), 'the dreamingst young fellow' (*Brief Lives*, 91), and of the drunken Bishop Richard Corbett and his chaplain Lushington enjoying themselves in the cellars. As a minor poet Howe contributed any number of congratulatory verses to the university collections offered at the births of James, duke of York (1633), Princess Anne (1637), Princess Catherine (1639), and Prince Henry (1640), for the safe return of the king from Scotland (1641), and for the queen's safety upon her going into exile (1643). He also wrote commendatory pieces to preface Thomas Randolph's *Poems with the Muses Looking Glasses* (1638) and to pay tribute to the poet William Cartwright (*d.* 1643), whose *Comedies, Tragicomedies, with other Poems* appeared in 1651. In the latter his eighty-line poem is little match for the pieces by the likes of Henry Vaughan, Izaak Walton, John Fell, or even the Cambridge friends John Finch and Thomas Baines. In none of his poetry does he rise above the mundane.

NICHOLAS W. S. CRANFIELD

Sources F. Madan, *Oxford books: a bibliography of printed works*, 3 vols. (1895–1931); repr. (1964) · T. Hearne, *Works*, 4 vols. (1810) · *Aubrey's Brief lives*, ed. O. L. Dick (1949) · [J. Walker and P. Bliss], eds., *Letters written by eminent persons in the seventeenth and eighteenth centuries*, 2 vols. (1813) · Wood, *Ath. Oxon.: Fasti*, new edn · Wood, *Ath. Oxon.*, new edn · Foster, *Alum. Oxon.* · H. E. D. Blakiston, *Trinity College* (1898) · *IGI* · M. Burrows, ed., *The register of the visitors of the University of Oxford, from AD 1647 to AD 1658*, CS, new ser., 29 (1881) · tombstone, Trinity College chapel, Oxford

Howe, Michael (1787–1818), bushranger, was born at Pontefract, Yorkshire, the son of Thomas Howe and his wife, Elizabeth. After serving for two years on board a Hull merchantman, and acquiring a reputation at home as a poacher, he deserted to join the Royal Navy and in 1806 joined the army, but again deserted. He was tried at York in 1811 for highway robbery, and was sentenced to seven years' transportation. On his arrival in Van Diemen's Land he was assigned to a settler, from whom he ran away into the bush, and became the leader of a band of twenty-nine convict escapers and army deserters. With them, and accompanied by his devoted Aborigine companion, Black Mary, he terrorized settlers, killing some, wounding others, and forcing many to help him.

In 1814 many of Howe's band deserted to take advantage of an amnesty, but he gathered a new band and continued his activities, styling himself Lieutenant-Governor of the Woods after Lieutenant-Governor Davey's attempts to use martial law to quash the gang failed. Internal rivalry in the gang and the offer of a pardon led Howe to give himself up in 1817, but hearing a false rumour that his pardon had been refused he escaped again. At last a reward of 100 guineas was placed on his head, with a free pardon and passage to England if required.

Howe's position became desperate. A party of three men, bent on obtaining the hundred guineas, tracked him, overtook him at his hut on the Shannon River on 21 October 1818, and endeavoured to take him prisoner. After a desperate resistance he was killed by a blow from the butt-end of a musket. His body was buried there but his head was cut off and carried into Hobart Town. In his knapsack was found a pocket book, in which he had written with blood notes of forebodings and dreams, and a list of Yorkshire flowers which he hoped to grow if he made good his escape.

In 1818 Thomas Wells published in Hobart Town *Michael Howe: the Last and Worst of the Bushrangers*, the first work of general literature printed in Australia and as such a much prized collectors' item.

J. K. LAUGHTON, rev. ELIZABETH BAIGENT

Sources T. E. Wells, *Michael Howe* (1818) · J. Bonwick, *The bushrangers* (1967) · AusDB · *A bloodthirsty banditti of wretches: information on oath relating to Michael Howe and others between 1814 and 1818*, Texts from Historical Records of Australia, 3rd ser., 2 (1985) · [F. Watson], ed., *Historical records of Australia*, 3rd ser., 2 (1921) · L. Robson, *A history of Tasmania*, 1: *Van Diemen's Land from the earliest times to 1855* (1983)

Howe, Obadiah (1615/16–1683), Church of England clergyman and author, was born in Leicestershire, the son of William Howe, vicar of Tattershall, Lincolnshire. The ejected minister John Howe (1630–1705) was his nephew. Obadiah matriculated at Magdalen Hall, Oxford, on 11 May 1632 aged sixteen, graduated BA on 23 October 1635, and proceeded MA on 26 May 1638. Shortly before the battle of Winceby in October 1643 parliamentary forces under the earl of Manchester were quartered at nearby Stickney in Lincolnshire. Howe may already have been rector of this living; it was certainly sequestrated to him from Anthony Peniston before February 1647, when Peniston's wife petitioned the county committee for a fifth of the profits. On 12 June Howe was ordered to pay, but he resisted, arguing that his predecessor had acquired another living worth over £30 and could well afford to support his own family. The outcome is unknown. It was as minister of Stickney that Howe issued *The Universalist Examined and Convicted* (1648), in answer to a free-grace tract. He evidently thought of himself as a defender of orthodoxy and was alarmed by the religious ferment of the day: 'Such daily births of pamphlets to and fro can be no less to the people then the winds are to the waves, make them crowd into new storms' ('To the Christian reader', preface to *The Universalist Examined and Convicted*, sig. A2).

In 1651 Howe removed to Horncastle, where he carried out to the letter the provisions for publishing 'contracts of matrimony' set out in the act of 24 August 1653. In 1655 he issued *The Pagan Preacher Silenced*, which defended limited atonement against the famous John Goodwin. In his *Triumviri* (1658) Goodwin accused Howe of traducing the remonstrants as incendiaries, remarking caustically that he was 'in my opinion, a man of considerable parts and learning, and yet (I believe) much more considerable in his own' (preface to the reader, *Triumviri*, sig. o). Horncastle parish register records Howe as having officiated at a marriage on 15 March 1658, but that year he moved to the parish of Gedney, Lincolnshire. Robert Rich, the sequestrated vicar, was restored to Gedney in 1660. But

already Howe had been able to secure the prestigious vicarage of Boston. He held on to this living after the Restoration, and became conspicuous for loyalty to the new order. In 1663 he issued *God and the Magistrate*, the published version of a sermon preached in Lincoln Cathedral before the assize judges and the high sheriff, Sir Edward Dymocke. In this he argued that 'When the magistrate commands, its not man in the magistrate, but God in the magistrate that obligeth: he hath God's power, and because God's power binds, a magistrates doth also' (p. 23). But he also stressed the importance of judging the facts impartially. On 9 July 1674 Howe was awarded the degrees of bachelor and doctor of divinity at Oxford. He remained vicar of Boston until his death on 27 February 1683, and was buried in the church.

STEPHEN WRIGHT

Sources *Walker rev.* · Foster, *Alum. Oxon.* · Wood, *Ath. Oxon.*, new edn, vol. 4 · J. Swaby, 'Walker, Matthews, and the sufferings of the Lincolnshire clergy', *Lincolnshire History and Archaeology*, 19 (1984), 89–92 · BL, Add. MS 15671 · J. Hudson, ed., *The second register book of the parish of Horncastle* (1896) · J. Goodwin, *Triumviri* (1658) · P. Thompson, *History of Boston* (1856) · J. Vicars, *Gods arke overtopping the worlds waves, or, The third part of the 'Parliamentary Chronicle'* (1645) · T. Cox, *Magna Britannia et Hibernia*, 6 vols. (1720–31), vol. 2

Howe, Richard, Earl Howe (1726–1799), naval officer, was born in London on 19 March 1726, the second son of an Irish peer, Emanuel Scrope Howe, second Viscount Howe (1698/9–1735), and (Mary Sophia) Charlotte *Howe (1703–1782), daughter of Baron von Kielmansegg, deputy master of the horse to George I when elector of Hanover. Howe appears in the Westminster School lists as admitted in November 1732, and leaving the next year. The assumption has been made that he went to Eton College, for his three brothers did so and later in life he subscribed to *Musae Etonenses*, but there is no direct documentary evidence that he went there. On his lieutenant's passing certificate it is stated that he spent four years in this period serving on a 'merchant ship, the Thames, William Merchant, master', which indicates that he went to sea in 1735.

Early career On 16 July 1739 Howe was entered into the *Pearl* (40 guns, Captain Edward Legge) and sailed on 23 July with Edward Vernon's squadron to Lisbon. He was mustered until 3 November 1739, but not again until 10 March 1740. When Legge transferred to the *Severn* (50 guns) Howe went with him, having joined on 2 July 1740; the ship sailed on 18 September 1740, as part of George Anson's squadron, to attack Spanish colonies in the Pacific but it failed to weather Cape Horn and came home via Barbados, reaching England in April 1742. Howe then joined the *Burford* (70 guns, Captain Franklin Lushington), which went to the West Indies under Charles Knowles's squadron, and he was present at the unsuccessful attacks on Spanish bases on the South American mainland. The first was on La Guayra on 18 February 1743, when Lushington was killed. On 10 March he was moved by Knowles into his own ship, the *Suffolk* (70 guns), where he again saw action in the attack on Porto Cabello in late April. On 10 July he went to the *Eltham* (44 guns) as acting lieutenant, but on 8

Richard Howe, Earl Howe (1726–1799), by John Singleton
Copley, *c.*1790

October he again joined the *Suffolk* as midshipman. He passed his lieutenant's examination on 24 May 1744 and was transferred by Knowles the next day to the bomb vessel *Comet*, commanded by Richard Tyrrell and, from 28 June, by Clark Gayton. After another year's service in the West Indies the ship was paid off in August 1745. Howe was confirmed as lieutenant on 8 August 1744.

Howe next served for a short time in Vernon's flagship, *Royal George* (100 guns), appointed on 12 August 1745, after which he was given command of the newly built sloop *Baltimore* on 5 November; thereafter he cruised in waters off the west of Scotland in operations against the Jacobites. On 3 May 1746 the *Baltimore* and the *Greyhound* (20 guns) came upon two large French privateers, of 32 and 34 guns, in a loch in the Sound of Arisaig but, because of the superior weight of French fire, the British ships had to break off the attack and Howe was wounded in the head. Prior to this he had been made post captain, and appointed to the *Triton* (24 guns) on 10 April 1746, in which he cruised and escorted a convoy to Lisbon. There he transferred to the *Ripon* (60 guns), since her captain was unwell, and he sailed in March 1747 to the west coast of Africa, arriving on 19 May and putting himself under the orders of Captain Ormond Tomson of the *Poole* (44 guns). Though he lost men from fever it was an uneventful cruise up and down the Guinea coast, inspecting slaving posts and resolving a dispute between British and Dutch merchants. Howe then went to Barbados to join Knowles, arriving on 23 January 1748. On 29 October Knowles transferred Howe, then aged twenty-two, to the *Cornwall* (70 guns) to be his flag-captain, and the ship was paid off in July 1749.

Howe used his connections to secure commands in the years of peace. In March 1751 he was appointed to the *Glory* (44 guns) and again went to the west coast of Africa. He then crossed to the West Indies, calling at Barbados and

Jamaica, and arrived back at Spithead in April 1752. On 3 June he commissioned the *Dolphin* (24 guns), cruising in the Mediterranean from October of that year to August 1754; a description of this quiet period is stylishly described in *Augustus Hervey's Journal*, the work of a captain on the same station, in which Howe is particularly mentioned in various professional disagreements with Hervey.

The Seven Years' War On 20 January 1755 Howe was appointed to the *Dunkirk* (60 guns) and sailed with Edward Boscawen to North America. On 7 June the British found the French fleet in the fog off the mouth of the St Lawrence River. On 10 June the *Dunkirk*, coming up with the *Alcide*, fired the first shots of the Seven Years' War; the French ship, being unprepared, was quickly overcome. This was the first time that Howe came to significant public notice, since, in view of deteriorating relations with France, the country was waiting for something to happen. Leaving Holburne to blockade Louisbourg, Boscawen returned to England, as did Howe and the *Dunkirk*.

As one of the most promising captains Howe, still only thirty, was to spend almost all of the war in the Channel Fleet. During the summer of 1756, under the command of Edward Hawke, Howe, still in the *Dunkirk*, commanded a small squadron in the Channel Islands, cruising against enemy privateers and merchant ships, and this he did effectively. His first task was to remove a small French force which had occupied the Isle de Chaussey and which was threatening Guernsey and Jersey. At the end of the year he returned to Plymouth to refit. By the spring of the following year Howe was again cruising in the channel in the *Dunkirk*, and on 10 June, with the *Lancaster*, he chased and easily overwhelmed the *Comte de Gramont*, a 36-gun privateer from Bayonne. On 2 July he and his ship's company took over the *Magnanime* (74 guns), and on 10 September they left Spithead in Hawke's fleet of sixteen ships of the line and fifty transports for the expedition against Rochefort. Howe distinguished himself early when the *Magnanime* alone anchored within 60 yards of the fort of the Isle d'Aix, holding his fire until anchored and reducing the fort with a thirty-five-minute bombardment of such ferocity that it excited comment from his fellow officers, including even Captain George Rodney. In theory, it was foolhardy; in fact, Howe calculated that the discipline and expertise of the artillery in an isolated fort would be weak. It was an impressive display which added to his growing reputation. The rest of the expedition was a failure, with naval and army commanders at variance; the army withdrew and the fleet put back to Spithead.

During 1758 William Pitt persevered with the strategy of raids against the French coast. The first was against St Malo, when Howe was selected by Pitt and Anson to be made commodore of transports for the land expedition. This commission caused Hawke to think that he had been in part superseded, and he struck his flag without orders; but this was a misunderstanding with Anson at the Admiralty and Hawke bore no grudge against the young commodore. Anson was forced to assume command of the fleet. Howe moved into the smaller *Essex* (64 guns) to command four small ships of the line, several frigates, sloops, and bomb vessels, and the transports. He sailed on 1 June, with Robert Duff as his second in command, while the commander of the army was the duke of Marlborough and Lord George Sackville was second in command. It was not a happy team. Although a successful landing was made they found St Malo too well fortified to be captured without a siege, though much shipping was burnt. The troops were re-embarked at Cancale on 11 and 12 June. After an initial attempt at Cherbourg on 29 June, spoiled by an onshore wind, the fleet returned to Spithead. Another attempt, this time with Lieutenant-General Thomas Bligh in command of the troops, sailed on 30 July. The troops met little resistance, due to fire from the ships. On 8 August Cherbourg was occupied and the harbour and piers demolished very thoroughly; on 15 and 16 August the troops were re-embarked and the fleet returned to Portland. Howe, anxious to try St Malo again, eventually got away on 31 August. The landing was made to the west of the Rance River, its strong tides making it impossible to cross and onshore winds soon making the fleet's position untenable; Bligh therefore had to march his troops to the new anchorage at St Cas, pressed by strong French forces under the duc d'Aiguillon. Although the majority of the troops were taken off the guards brigade took heavy casualties, while four naval captains in command of the flatboats were taken prisoner. Howe himself led the boats inshore for the last evacuation; naval casualties were light. There were no further expeditions against the French coast until 1761.

1759 saw Howe, now back in the *Magnanime*, in the remorseless blockading of Brest and the French coast under Hawke and searching for the French fleet; this led eventually to the pursuit of the French fleet under Maréchal de Conflans, in gale-force winds into Quiberon Bay in the late afternoon of 20 November. The fast-sailing *Magnanime* was the leading ship and forced the *Heros* to surrender at 4.30, but Howe did not put a prize crew aboard because of the dangerous seas; the *Heros* was wrecked the next day, trying to enter the harbour at Croisic, and was later burnt by the British. For the next two years Howe was on the coast of France, often at Quiberon Bay, keeping up the blockade, and was commodore of the Basque Roads, watching the French at Rochefort. In June 1762 the duke of York, on appointment as rear-admiral, hoisted his flag on board the *Princess Amelia* (80 guns), with Howe as his flag-captain, serving under Hawke and then, in the autumn, under the younger Sir Charles Hardy. On the signing of the peace in February 1763 the fleet was paid off and Commodore Howe struck his broad pennant.

Early political career From this point Howe's life and career reached a more expansive stage. On 23 May 1757, while at sea, he had been returned unopposed for the government as MP for Dartmouth, which seat he held for twenty-five years until he went to the upper house on 20 April 1782. On 16 February 1758, at Tamerton Foliot, near Plymouth, he had married Mary Hartopp (*bap.* 1732, *d.* 1800), daughter of the governor of Plymouth; she inherited a

considerable fortune on the death of her father on 2 April 1759. On 6 July 1758 Howe had succeeded to the viscountcy, his elder brother having been killed at the battle of Ticonderoga, and was now the fourth Viscount Howe. After a notably successful war he now had considerable wealth and it was time for him to pursue a political career. Although in the late 1760s he voted regularly with the Chatham and Grafton administrations he remained characteristically independent in his political views. He was appointed to the Board of Admiralty by Grenville on 20 April 1763 (and was there until 31 July 1765), with Lord Sandwich as first lord. Soon after the change of government the Rockingham administration made Howe treasurer of the navy, from which post he resigned at the end of April 1766. Pitt, whom Howe much admired, restored him to the post three months later and he continued until Pitt, by then Lord Chatham, went into opposition in January 1770. From this appointment Howe must have gained considerable wealth; for instance, the last ship's book from the period of his treasurership was 'made up' eight years later in 1778, and in 1780 he still had over £18,000 of government money on his own account. This was the system just before it was to be reformed; Howe was no worse nor better, in spite of the opinions of Victorian apologists, than anyone else who held the sinecure.

The potential trouble with Spain over the Falkland Islands brought Howe the promise of further service. He was made rear-admiral on 18 October 1770, and on 26 November Hawke, as one of his last acts as first lord, appointed him commander-in-chief, Mediterranean, over the heads of many older admirals, though the mobilization was short-lived. It was otherwise a quiet period, in which Howe spoke frequently in parliament on naval matters. On 9 February 1773 he presented the petition of the naval captains on half-pay but generally he was classed by political managers as a 'friend to government'.

North America The period in the early part of the American War of Independence when Howe was commander-in-chief in North America, was then and is still the most controversial of his long career. For most of his command his younger brother Major-General Sir William *Howe commanded the army in the colonies. Much has been written of their combined approach to hostilities, torn between conciliation and aggression, and the extent to which they exceeded or ignored instructions. What is without question is that their relations with Lord North's government were never less than complicated and that the Howe family had long connections with the colonists. Howe certainly met Benjamin Franklin when the latter was in London in late 1774 and became involved in the negotiations then and in early 1775, putting himself forward to the government as a peace commissioner. The circumstances in which Howe was appointed did not bode well. He was made vice-admiral on 7 December 1775 and on the same day Admiral Sir Charles Saunders died, vacating a sinecured lieutenant-generalship of marines worth £1200 a year. Howe claimed that Lord North had promised it to him but by then North had forgotten and had given it to Sir Hugh Palliser, Lord Sandwich's nomination. At this slight Howe threatened to resign 'all his employments'. North immediately apologized but could find no other way of mollifying Howe; after protracted negotiations, brokered in their last stages by the king, on 5 February 1776 Howe was appointed commander-in-chief of the North American station, with powers to negotiate with the colonists. It was a popular measure in the country.

Having unsuccessfully tried to get his powers as peace commissioner widened, though many considered them wide enough already, Howe left for North America on 11 May 1776 in the *Eagle* (64 guns). He had instructions from the government to pursue the war as aggressively as possible, both by supporting army operations and by blockading the long North American coast, in order to prevent the colonists from obtaining war supplies from France and the Netherlands; since Sandwich's orders lacked absolute clarity Howe had to decide which of these priorities came first. He arrived off Halifax on 23 June, and by 12 July he was at New York, to support the army on Staten Island. He immediately tried to conciliate the colonists and to contact George Washington but diplomatic niceties over the form of address enabled Washington to decline receiving Howe's letter. Howe had arrived just after the Declaration of Independence and the Americans had little room for manoeuvre; in short he had too little to offer and had arrived too late. On 22 August the British army moved against New York, supported by the navy, landing on Long Island, where they outmanoeuvred the continental army and trapped them in their fortifications on the Brooklyn Heights; seven days later Washington removed all his army from Long Island. Further conciliatory talks on 11 September at Staten Island failed and General Howe then advanced to take New York.

Howe supported the army's further successes, which lasted until the end of 1776 with the reverses of Trenton and Princeton. He was in the meantime having to balance which ships should support the army, either by moving troops or by providing static defence, and which should implement the coastal blockade. He did not have enough ships to undertake both tasks properly but it is also true that he gave greater priority than he might have done to supporting the army. During 1776 his command averaged seventy ships, of which only two were ships of the line, and though the average went up during the next year it was never enough. The need to protect with warships places of strategic importance, such as the St Lawrence, Halifax, Newport, and New York, together with the need to send replacement ships to England, Halifax, or the West Indies, owing to the lack of careening wharfs and dockyards in America, reduced the force blockading the American coast. At any one time there were gaps in the blockading ring around the coast; there seems to have been little cover north of Cape Cod during Howe's command, while during the winter of 1776–7 no British cruisers were watching Charles Town and Savannah. By contrast the blockade of the middle colonies during the same period was virtually absolute, resulting in depressed American morale and crippling trade. Baltimore, for instance, was forced to put an embargo on all outgoing

shipping. Between 10 March and 31 December 1776 Howe's ships took 140 American ships and recaptured twenty-six British vessels. However, continental frigates and privateers did break out and during the whole of 1776 they captured 347 British vessels, including several loaded ordnance storeships and six troop transports. More important to the course of the war as a whole, the flow of munitions was not stopped. Before Christmas 1776 the Americans had imported more than 80 per cent of all the powder that they consumed during the first two and a half years of the war.

In spite of the fact that the British army had been relatively successful in 1776, 1777 was to be the year in which the British failed. The blockade was even less effective, the French supporting the American effort with more vigour, both financially and through the use of their ports on the Atlantic coast, and it was during this year that continental frigates began to make real inroads into British shipping in European waters. By now naval failure had become a central political issue in London. After New Jersey was abandoned early in the year, following the defeat at Trenton, the army could not rely on supplies other than from England. With General John Burgoyne coming down the Hudson from Canada, General Howe decided to take Philadelphia, transporting his troops by sea. After a long delay waiting for supplies from England, on 23 July 14,000 troops in 267 ships left New York for Philadelphia. The expedition made slow progress; Lord Howe did not arrive in the *Delaware* until 6 October. Both Howes, making decisions together, acted indecisively in the campaign and it did not go well. Although the *Delaware* was eventually forced by 23 November it was not without the loss of a new 64-gun ship, the *Augusta*. Philadelphia was captured but it did not affect the course of the war. On 31 October Howe heard of the surrender of Burgoyne at Saratoga, and the entire nature of the war had changed; both general and admiral asked to be relieved of their commands.

The winter of 1777–8 was spent in a state of inactivity, waiting for orders from London. The blockade continued to prove ineffective and still the emphasis was on supporting the army; on 9 March 1778, for instance, forty-four of the ninety-two warships under Howe's command were employed in defending the British positions. On 21 April the first intelligence reports reached New York about the possibility of war with France, and General Howe was ordered home. On 8 May news came of the Franco-American alliance and of the Carlisle commission coming from London to talk with the Americans; Philadelphia was to be evacuated and a force was to be sent to seize St Lucia, to reinforce Halifax and the Floridas, and to return ships and troops to England. Lord Howe received permission to quit his command for reasons of ill health and to return to England. Philadelphia was evacuated on 18 June.

Howe was leaving the Delaware River for New York when, on 29 June, he first had warning from the Admiralty that a French fleet under D'Estaing had orders to sail for North America. Howe had fifteen ships at his disposal, only seven of the line, and all of them poorly manned. He immediately placed cruisers along the American coast and stationed troops on Sandy Hook itself. By 5 July he learned that the French were off the Chesapeake, and on 11 July D'Estaing appeared off Sandy Hook with eleven ships of the line. For ten days only a mile or so separated the fleets, with the dunes of Sandy Hook between them, but D'Estaing's heavier ships had deeper draughts and he decided not to attempt the bar. On 22 July he sailed to the south. On 30 July the first damaged ships from Vice-Admiral John Byron's relieving squadron, which had been hit by storms, limped into New York and it was clear to Howe that the French naval superiority remained.

Having anticipated and headed off the superior fleet Howe played a defensive game with D'Estaing. The French had in fact doubled back to the north, to Rhode Island, where the American army surrounded Newport. Howe had worked out D'Estaing's destination, refitted his fleet, and arrived off Rhode Island on 9 August. The next day D'Estaing gave chase and Howe retreated to the south, his ships trying to weather the French; but on 11 August a severe gale struck both fleets, which had to disperse. D'Estaing returned to Boston, where Howe again discovered him on 1 September, but he found the French defensive position too strong. He again returned to New York, where he finally found six more ships from Byron's squadron, under Rear-Admiral Hyde Parker, which had been repaired in Halifax. He considered the naval situation now under control, decided finally to hand over his command to Gambier, and sailed for England on 26 September, reaching St Helens on 25 October.

Howe in parliament   Howe, now fifty-two and at the height of his powers, was not to have an active command for three and a half years, during which time he lived at Porter's Lodge, near St Albans, attending parliament frequently. With his brother he immediately defended his conduct in America in the House of Commons and eventually demanded a parliamentary investigation, which began on 29 April 1779. It continued, without any real conclusion, until parliament adjourned on 29 June. In the meantime the weak position of Sandwich as first lord, under pressure from all sides, made the king and Lord North think of Howe as a possible replacement. On 4 February 1779 North negotiated with him but he laid down impossible, though unspecified, conditions; it is difficult to see how he could have imagined himself in a cabinet with Lord George Germain (formerly Sackville), with whom he is supposed never to have spoken since the joint expedition in 1758. Yet Howe was again approached by the government at the end of February. From this point his speeches in the house became increasingly bitter, and he voted with the opposition; though he was no friend to Keppel, he took an active anti-government part in the Keppel–Palliser affair. For instance he made an important contribution on 8 March to the debate on Charles James Fox's motion of censure against the Admiralty. When North's government finally fell in March 1782 the Rockingham ministry appointed Howe commander-in-chief of the Channel Fleet on 2 April, a full admiral on 8 April, and

a British peer on 20 April 1782. Together with the appointment of his brother as lieutenant-general of the ordnance this was Howe's price to the new ministry.

The relief of Gibraltar   On the same day, 20 April 1782, Howe hoisted his flag on the *Victory* (100 guns) at Spithead and on 8 May he received orders to watch the Dutch fleet off the Texel. Two days later he sailed for the North Sea with only nine ships of the line and several warships, although by 25 May he had returned to Spithead, leaving eight ships of the line under Sir James Lockhart Ross. He then turned his attentions to the threat of the combined Franco-Spanish fleet, which he learned on 5 July was now at Brest, and to the task of ensuring that a West Indies convoy could be safely escorted home. With twenty-five of the line he met the combined fleet of thirty-six. While the French and Spanish formed a line of battle fleet Howe sailed between the Isles of Scilly and Land's End, trying to get to windward, and in the night the two fleets parted. He missed the convoy, which arrived safely anyway, and the enemy fleet left the western approaches; this was an embarrassment to the new administration, even though the Franco-Spanish fleet accomplished nothing. On 9 August Howe received orders to return to Spithead to prepare the fleet for the expedition to relieve Gibraltar and, though there was the Dutch threat to the Baltic convoys, this concern melted away when intelligence arrived in England that the Dutch fleet was back in the Texel. On 30 August the Admiralty began to issue instructions for the resupply of Gibraltar, and on 11 September the Channel Fleet—thirty-five of the line, the supply ships for Gibraltar, and three trade convoys—left Spithead. Winds from the south delayed progress so that it did not arrive off Cape St Vincent until 9 October. This timing was fortunate for Howe for the next day a storm scattered the combined fleet under Cordova, forcing them out of Gibraltar Bay; the British convoy came in unopposed, although most of the storeships were swept past by the current into the Mediterranean. Howe sent the storeships to an anchorage off the African coast. On 13 October the Channel Fleet was 50 miles off the Spanish coast in the Mediterranean but a shift of wind from the east, again fortunate, gave them the opportunity of getting into Rosa Bay. The storeships followed soon and quickly discharged their cargoes. Gibraltar had been again relieved. Although the Franco-Spanish fleet came into contact again when Howe left Gibraltar on 19 October, and though the next day there was some desultory, long-range fire between them, Howe decided to withdraw and return to England. He arrived at St Helens on 14 November. It was the last major operation of the Channel Fleet in this war.

Howe as first lord of the Admiralty   On 30 January 1783 Howe was appointed first lord of the Admiralty. He resigned soon afterwards, on 10 April, and Keppel was again first lord. However, Howe again took up the post on 31 December and held it for five years, until his resignation on 16 July 1788. His years in political charge of the navy were not distinguished personally, although much was achieved by the navy as a whole in the building and maintenance of the fleet after the American War of Independence. There were no particular naval crises, save for concern over the high level of French naval expenditure. Howe was hindered by both personality conflicts and limitations in his political skills, both of which caused his isolation within the government and his lack of interest in any matter in the political world that did not concern the navy. His relations with his cabinet colleagues ranged from detestation of the overbearing duke of Richmond, master-general of the ordnance, to considerable distance from William Pitt the younger himself. The stormy relationship with Richmond came to a climax over the proposals in the Fortifications Bill in February 1786, which was defeated by the narrowest of margins, thus leading to almost open warfare between the Admiralty and the Ordnance offices.

Howe's most serious continuous breach, however, was with the controller of the navy, Charles Middleton, who since 1778 had established a formidable administrative reputation in the post. The gulf between the two men is best illustrated by the way in which Pitt worked round Howe, dealing with questions of naval reform and finance directly with Middleton at the Navy Office. Middleton had long been used to being consulted on appointments but soon after taking office Howe appointed a joint surveyor without any reference to him. Relations were immediately soured and contact became almost non-existent. Other squabbles followed, in particular a surprise visit by the first lord to Portsmouth Dockyard in September 1784, during which Howe found many faults. This was a direct invasion of the controller's territory. Nevertheless the navy estimates remained high and the debt was brought under control, the fleet was maintained at a high level, and there was investment at Gibraltar and at the West Indies bases; at the end of the decade the navy was significantly more prepared for war than it had been at any time in the eighteenth century. Even so the evidence remains strong that these achievements were more in spite of than because of Howe. It was due to Pitt's concern for security, for which the government provided a high level of funds, that the prime minister trusted Middleton to see that improvements would be carried out efficiently.

Howe's close and impenetrable personality also contributed to his other great difficulty as first lord, namely the mismatch between the promotions available and the number of officers who expected advancement. The same problem faced Lord Sandwich in the late 1770s. Howe's restrictions on promotion in the brevet of 1787 provoked an outcry, as well as personal attacks on him in the press and in caricatures that stressed his close relationship with the king. In January and February 1788 there were three stormy debates in both houses. Howe's position was difficult; he took what he saw as the common-sense view of the situation but he lacked the political touch to deal with the situation: 'he assured their Lordships that patronage was not so desirable as might be imagined, and that he was sure, out of twenty candidates for an appointment, to disappoint nineteen, and by no means certain of pleasing the twentieth' (Barrow, 182). Though he survived these attacks it was not long afterwards that he resigned, on the question of Charles Middleton's promotion to rear-admiral. Howe's case was strong for no controller of the navy had held any rank more senior than that of a captain. Howe felt that he was not supported in this argument by Pitt and left office in July 1788. His departure was not regretted by his political colleagues, who were uncomfortable that the man responsible for the largest-spending department of state had distanced himself for five years from the centre of government. Middleton, as rear-admiral, continued as controller but he resigned two years later, when Pitt refused to support the extensive naval reform for which Middleton had worked so hard during the 1780s. Had Howe and Middleton managed to work together it might have been a brilliant period, and their failure to do so must be seen as a lost opportunity. For his service, however, Howe was created Earl Howe and Baron Howe of Langar on 19 August 1788.

Commander-in-chief, Channel Fleet After eighteen months of what Howe called 'rural dissipation' (Barrow, 203) he was again called to active service. At the start of the Nootka Sound confrontation with Spain in June 1790 he was appointed commander-in-chief of the Channel Fleet. He was now sixty-four and troubled by gout, and for the next five years he was at sea for long periods. He was given the rank of temporary admiral of the fleet and flew the union flag, which had not been done since the early part of the century and was seen as a particular compliment. Howe had six flag officers under him: Samuel Barrington, Samuel and Alexander Hood, John Jervis, Richard Bickerton, and William Hotham. Howe, with the *Queen Charlotte* (100 guns) as his flagship, left Spithead on 17 August with a fleet of thirty-five ships of the line. The fleet cruised for under a month, fruitlessly looking for the Spanish fleet and exercising endlessly; it anchored at Spithead on 14 September. Once the crisis had been resolved Howe was ordered to strike his flag, in December, whereafter he was inactive for the next eighteen months and visited Bath, trying to find relief from what he called 'gouty infirmity' (ibid., 209). On the death of Lord Rodney in May 1792 Howe was appointed vice-admiral of England.

With relations with France deteriorating, on 1 February 1793 Howe was again appointed commander-in-chief of the Channel Fleet, although it was not until the end of May that the fleet was ready for him to take up command. He again hoisted the union flag, on board the *Queen Charlotte*. On 23 July he sailed from St Helens with twenty-three ships of the line and Vice-Admiral Thomas Graves and Alexander Hood as his flag officers. The fleet then started the long blockade of the French fleet at Brest, although Howe did not believe in the close blockade favoured by his old commander Lord Hawke. In the worst of the winter weather Howe's cautious nature led him to a policy of 'open blockade'; he left only frigates to watch the French port and withdrew the main fleet to Torbay and to Spithead. As a result there was little action, for which he was much criticized, until the spring of 1794, when the channel squadron combined the task of escorting the East and West Indies and Newfoundland convoys out of the western approaches, together with intercepting the incoming

French grain convoy. Under Admiral Vanstabel this convoy was gathering at Chesapeake Bay and was desperately needed by the Paris authorities, for the city was short of food. Howe sailed on 2 May from Spithead with thirty-two of the line and, having detached eight ships off the Lizard to escort the outgoing convoy, went to Brest to discover that the French fleet was still there. He then stood to the westward hoping to find the grain convoy, leaving Rear-Admiral George Montagu with six ships to cruise between Cape Ortegal and the latitude of Belle Isle. Howe returned from his westward cruise to Brest on 19 May to find that the French fleet of twenty-six ships of the line, under Villaret-Joyeuse, had escaped. Howe searched for both convoy and fleet until 28 May, when 400 miles west of Ushant, in very fresh weather, the French fleet was seen to windward. Villaret-Joyeuse's main objective was to lead the British fleet away from the grain convoy. With both fleets close-hauled, to try to get to windward of each other, Howe pursued the French for nearly two days. A thick mist then came down on both fleets when they were very close. For a further two days, in thick weather, the fleets sailed to the west.

The 'glorious first of June' On 1 June 1794, with the weather moderating to a stiff breeze and the visibility clear, the French were 4 miles to leeward of the British fleet and Howe was able to choose his moment. He formed his line with care; each British vessel was to cut through under the stern of its opposite number. In the event only seven ships broke through the line, while the remainder hauled up to windward and opened fire. The fight became very general and fierce, with the *Queen Charlotte* in the thick of it. All ships, setting maximum canvas in a strong breeze, suffered heavy damage to masts and spars, and each ship's manouverability depended upon the seamanship and teamwork of the crews; several ships on both sides were totally dismasted. The French, not as trained and as experienced as the British, were inferior in both seamanship and gunnery; several French ships took very heavy casualties. Allowing for prisoners, British killed and wounded amounted to 1148, while French losses were estimated to be over 7000; the *Vengeur de Peuple* (74 guns) sank in the course of the battle. In less than an hour after the close action began Howe reported:

> the French Admiral engaged by the Queen Charlotte crowded off; and was followed by most of the ships in his van, in condition to carry sail after him: leaving with us, about ten or twelve of his crippled or totally dismasted ships exclusive of one sunk in the engagement. (Marcus, 36)

However, several of the French ships managed to sail back to their main fleet under their spritsails, and three were taken in tow by French frigates. Failure to follow up such a clear-cut victory was to blight Howe's reputation, especially among the next generation of fleet commanders; his order to recall the *Thunderer* (74 guns) and the *Queen* (74 guns) when they were just about to take possession of two of the dismasted ships was particularly remembered. Howe's age and health after several days of unremitting strain must have inhibited effort at this late stage; he is said to have been on deck almost continuously for five days. In the meantime Montagu failed to find the convoy and put back into Plymouth, thus missing Vanstabel and the grain convoy, who with great skill had steered south and had come up the French coast through the Raz du Sein into Brest.

Though a great strategic opportunity had been missed by the British fleet the 'glorious first of June' was a considerable tactical and psychological victory, and the British public saw it as such. There was general rejoicing. Howe returned to Spithead on 9 June with his six prizes; on 24 June the king presented him with a diamond-hilted sword on board *Queen Charlotte*, a scene celebrated by Henry Briggs's painting in the Greenwich Hospital collection. The king also promised Howe the Order of the Garter, which caused a long misunderstanding with Pitt, who had promised the vacant one elsewhere; Howe eventually received it on 2 June 1797. There was discord too over those captains mentioned in his dispatches, and Howe once again found himself unpopular with a large section of his fellow officers; in his first dispatch after the battle he omitted an honourable mention of a number of captains, and there was much ill feeling. Despite the exonerating circumstances presented in Barrow's biography this episode showed Howe's political incapacity. Besides, the responsiveness of several ships to signals and their general performance was below the standard that Howe expected, and one captain, Anthony James Pye Molloy of the *Caesar* (74 guns), mentioned by Howe in an unfavourable light, demanded a court martial. He was dismissed his ship.

Howe's last years in service Though by now Howe was asking to be relieved of his post neither the king nor Pitt wanted him to go, and on 22 August he left St Helens with a fleet of thirty-seven British and five Portuguese ships of the line, cruising between Ushant and the Isles of Scilly until the end of October, when he took shelter in Torbay. By the end of November the fleet was back in Spithead. Howe spent the winter ashore, but in February 1795, on receiving news that the French fleet was at sea, he set out again. It was then that he had a lucky escape; while the fleet sheltered in Torbay on 13 and 14 February, with thirty-six ships, the gale swung round to south-east. Nine ships parted their cables and were fortunately brought up again; it is claimed by some that the experience, in which Howe faced the prospect of losing British naval superiority in an afternoon, finally broke his nerve. After a short cruise, in which he saw the outward bound convoys off safely, he finally came ashore. Even so he nominally held command of the fleet while ashore for the next two years, with Alexander Hood (now Viscount Bridport) reporting to him, a scarcely satisfactory arrangement which added to the friction that already existed between the two men. Howe was onshore, inactive and still troubled by gout, during the rest of 1795, and was nominally commander-in-chief until May 1797. On 12 March 1796 he was appointed admiral of the fleet, and on the same day he was appointed general of marines; he resigned unwillingly the honorary rank of vice-admiral of England. In the following month he presided over the court martial of

Admiral Sir William Cornwallis at Portsmouth, a tricky subordination issue that needed Howe's seniority; the verdict went with the admiral rather than with the Admiralty. It was Howe's last official service.

Howe and the Spithead mutiny Howe was again at Bath when in early March 1797 he received eleven petitions for more pay from the fleet. Although he made informal enquiries as to whether this was a serious matter he was inclined to disregard them and, significantly, he did not send this information to Bridport on board the flagship *Royal George* (100 guns) at Spithead. It was not until 22 March that he went to London to present them to Lord Spencer, the first lord of the Admiralty, by which time the situation had deteriorated. By 7 May there had been some bloodshed, unpopular officers were sent ashore, and the fleet was in open mutiny. After hesitation on the part of the government and a short debate in the House of Lords, in which Howe spoke briefly and which worsened the situation at Spithead, a bill for a supplementary estimate to pay the men was brought forward, as well as a royal pardon for the mutineers. It was at the request of the king that Howe was sent down to talk to the men, without any official powers, for he had finally had his resignation accepted some days before. On 11 May Howe arrived at Portsmouth and was rowed out immediately to the *Royal George* to win round the confidence of the seamen. Through the following days he visited every ship, explaining the Admiralty's position and taking opinion on the wording of the final pardon. On 13 May, on board the guardship *Royal William* (84 guns), he received petitions from all the ships on individual grievances against oppressive officers. He had little alternative but to agree to the dismissal of fifty-nine officers and warrant officers, including one admiral and four captains. Once the second royal pardon had arrived from London the mutiny at Spithead was over and Howe was the focus of the reconciliation. A month late Bridport put to sea with the Channel Fleet. The mutiny at the Nore had yet to happen.

Death and assessment After two more years living in the country, though still not in health, Lord Howe died in London, at his home in Grafton Street, on 5 August 1799, having been persuaded to try 'electricity', the fashionable remedy for gout. His wife survived him, dying just over a year later on 9 August 1800. Howe was buried at the parish church in Langar, Nottinghamshire. His achievements in fifty-nine years of active service in the navy were prodigious and must put him in the first rank of any of the naval commanders of any age. Beyond his actions and his honours, however, his career spanned a period in which the navy was growing fast and its increased size needed regulation and system; the officer corps became a professional body and required leadership and example. No one was more influential in this process than Howe, in particular in the improvement of command and control of fleets. From the days when he first commanded squadrons and flotillas in the Seven Years' War he grappled with the problem of signals and the traditional fighting instructions. At that time some of the systems and conventions

were hopelessly outmoded; some instructions had to be conveyed by a combination of flags and hauling of sails up and down, while ships were instructed to give way to ships commanded by a more senior officer. Howe worked doggedly on these systems and by the time of the American War of Independence he had worked out a far more effective system, which he expected his captains to obey promptly. In 1790 he issued his final development, a numerical system, upon which the more sophisticated naval signalling developments of the Napoleonic Wars based. These systems were constantly improved and the management of fleets became more precise.

Howe's restless mind dwelt on every detail, described by his only biographer as 'his precision in minute matters' (Barrow, 314–15). There was no room in the eighteenth-century navy for an aristocratic disinterest in technical detail, and Howe's concern and interest in the condition of his ship and in the welfare of his men were influential. Those who served under him were notably loyal; he was an early exponent of the divisional system, and his 'captain's order book' kept in the *Magnanime* from 1759 was one of the first attempts to bring system to the management of the officers and crew on board a ship of the line. His concern led him to the conclusion that the close blockade off Brest under Hawke was wearing on ships and men to the point of ineffectiveness. 'From his own knowledge', he said in parliament during the American War of Independence, he knew 'that a station off Brest was a dangerous situation, and should never be taken but upon great emergencies' (Cobbett, *Parl. hist.*, 20, col. 202). At various times he was much criticized for his readiness to use Torbay, and it is ironic that this anchorage nearly caused his undoing in the final winter of his active career.

Neither popularity nor public opinion was ever a priority with Howe, either as a sea officer, administrator, or politician. Indeed he was completely devoid of the political arts, partly due to an inarticulacy, both written and verbal, remarkable in one who achieved so much. Though ever a favourite of the king he had very few lasting friendships with his brother officers and certainly not politicians. To those who did not know him well he was distant and difficult; nevertheless a friend could write that 'There was a shyness and awkwardness in Lord Howe's manner which made him apparently difficult of approach, and gave him a character of austerity which did not belong to him' (Bourchier, 12). Yet he sought office, both from ambition and because of a need for money. For some years he was not trusted and it took the brothers Howe a long time to live down the lack of success and the contradictions in their American command. Horace Walpole's blistering words reflected a general view:

> [they] had accepted the American command against their principles, and against all their inclinations but one of interest, who had conducted it treacherously as many thought, impotently as everyone knew, who had returned hostile to the Ministries, yet so far from joining Opposition, had distressed it by counteracting it. (H. Walpole, *The Last Journals*, 2 vols., 1910, 2.429)

Certainly Howe, with his great grasp of detail, had no capacity for political strategy or sagacity, nor probably did he feel that it would have been honourable to possess those qualities. For one thing, however, there was universal and automatic respect, and that was his courage. Two examples will suffice: first, his stunning bombardment of the fort on the Isle d'Aix in 1756 from the range of 60 yards, when, as he slowly approached through the French gunfire, he made his crew lie down on the deck so that only he and the pilot were standing. Second, when the brash Augustus Hervey published a criticism of Howe's tactics after the relief of Gibraltar in 1782 Howe challenged him to a duel; the two men, both nearer sixty than fifty, met, with their seconds, and the unfortunate Hervey made a humiliating apology. Howe was ever a formidable enemy.   ROGER KNIGHT

Sources J. Barrow, *The life of Richard, Earl Howe* (1838) · I. D. Gruber, *The Howe brothers and the American Revolution* (Chapel Hill, NC, 1972) · J. Brooke, 'Howe, Richard', HoP, *Commons, 1754–90*, vols. 1–2 · R. Knight, 'Richard, Earl Howe, 1726–1799', *Precursors of Nelson: British admirals of the eighteenth century*, ed. P. Le Fevre and R. Harding (2000), 279–99 · N. A. M. Rodger, *The wooden world: an anatomy of the Georgian navy* (1986) · D. Syrett, *The Royal Navy in American waters, 1775–1783* (1989) · D. Syrett, *The Royal Navy in European waters during the American revolutionary war* (1998) · D. A. Baugh, 'The politics of British naval failure, 1775–1777', *American Neptune*, 52 (1992), 221–46 · J. Ehrman, *The younger Pitt*, 3 vols. (1969–96) · G. J. Marcus, *A naval history of England*, 2: *The age of Nelson* (1971) · A. French, ed., *The Earl and Countess Howe by Gainsborough: a bicentenary exhibition* (1988) · J. E. Talbott, *The pen and ink sailor: Charles Middleton and the king's navy, 1778–1813* (1998) · J. S. Corbett, ed., *Signals and instructions, 1776–1794*, Navy RS, 35 [1909] · A. Pearsall, 'Naval aspects of the landings on the French coast, 1758', *The naval miscellany*, 5, Navy RS, 125 (1984) · J. Knox Laughton, 'Earl Howe K.G.', in J. Knox Laughton, *From Howard to Nelson: twelve sailors* (1899) · B. Tunstall, *Naval warfare in the age of sail: the evolution of fighting tactics, 1650–1815*, ed. N. Tracy (1990) · G. E. Manwaring and B. Dobrée, *The floating republic: an account of the mutinies at Spithead and the Nore in 1797* (1935); repr. (1966) · *The parliamentary register, or, History of the proceedings and debates of the House of Commons*, 16–17 (1780); 1–14 (1780–84) · Cobbett, *Parl. hist.*, vol. 20 · R. F. Mackay, *Admiral Hawke* (1965) · P. Mackesy, *The war for America, 1775–1783* (1964) · N. A. M. Rodger, *The insatiable earl: a life of John Montagu, fourth earl of Sandwich* (1993) · [earl of Bristol], *Augustus Hervey's journal*, ed. D. Erskine (1953) · *Memoir of the life of Admiral Sir Edward Codrington: with selections from his public and private correspondence*, ed. J. B. Bourchier, 2 vols. (1873) · T. S. Anderson, *The command of the Howe brothers during the American revolution* (1936) · B. Lavery, ed., *Shipboard life and organisation, 1731–1815*, Navy RS, 138 (1998) · J. Brooke, *The Chatham administration, 1766–1768* (1956) · P. L. C. Webb, 'The rebuilding and repair of the fleet, 1783–1793', *BIHR*, 50 (1977), 194–209 · *The Hawke papers: a selection, 1743–1771*, ed. R. F. Mackay, Navy RS, 129 (1990) · M. Acerra and J. Meyer, *Marines et revolution* (1988) · D. Syrett, 'A check list of Admiral Lord Howe's manuscripts in United States archives and libraries', *Mariner's Mirror*, 67 (1981), 273–84 · *An address to the rt hon. the first lord commissioner of the admiralty upon the visible decreasing spirit, splendour, and discipline of the navy* (1787) · will, PRO, PROB 11/1328 · monument, St Paul's Cathedral, London · private information (2004) · lieutenant's passing certificates, PRO, ADM 6/36 · confirmed commissions, PRO, ADM 6/16 · pay book, 14 April 1739–25 Feb 1743, PRO, ADM 33/372 · muster book of the *Pearl*, June 1739–April 1740, PRO, ADM 36/2403 · captain's log of the *Comet*, PRO, ADM 51/152 · captain's log of the *Ripon*, PRO, ADM 51/786 · captain's log of the *Dunkirk*, PRO, ADM 51/287 · master's log of the *Dunkirk*, PRO, ADM 52/838 · log of the *Baltimore* sloop, NMM, ADM/L/B/7

Archives NMM, corresp. and papers; signal books · U. Mich., Clements L., corresp. and papers | Beds. & Luton ARS, corresp. with Lord Grantham · BL, corresp. with Lord Bridport, Add. MSS 35193–35197 · BL, letters to Sir Frederick Haldimand, Add. MS 21709 · BL, letters to Sir Henry Martin, Add. MS 41364 · CKS, corresp. with Lord and Lady Altamont · Hunt. L., letters to Sir Roger Curtis · NMM, letters to Lord Hood · NMM, corresp. with Sir Charles Middleton · NMM, letters to Lord Sandwich · PRO, Admiralty papers · PRO, letters to William Pitt, second earl of Chatham, PRO 30/8 · Royal Arch., letters to George III · U. Hull, Brynmor Jones L., letters to Lord Hotham · U. Mich., Clements L., corresp. with Sir Henry Clinton · U. Mich., Clements L., corresp. with Lord George Germain · U. Mich., Clements L., corresp. with William Pitt · U. Nott. L., letters to second duke of Newcastle · University of Virginia, Charlottesville, corresp. with Sir A. S. Hamond · Yale U., Beinecke L., orders to Sir John Duckworth [copies]
Likenesses J. S. Copley, oils, *c*.1790, NMM [*see illus.*] · M. Brown, oils, 1794 (*The glorious first of June, 1794; Lord Howe on the deck of the Queen Charlotte*), NMM · H. P. Briggs, portrait (*George III presenting a sword on board the Queen Charlotte, 26 June 1794*), NMM · J. Flaxman, statue on monument, St Paul's Cathedral, London · J. Flaxman, wax sculpture, NPG · Gainsborough Dupont, oils, Trinity House, London · H. Singleton, oils, NPG · J. de Vaere, medallion, BM
Wealth at death very considerable: will, PRO, PROB 11/1328

Howe, Robert (1732–1786), politician and revolutionary army officer in America, was born on the rice plantation belonging to his father, Job Howe (*d.* 1748), in New Hanover county, North Carolina, beside the Cape Fear River. His family was a branch of the distinguished Howe family of England; his grandfather went to Carolina with the colony of Sir John Yeamans in 1665, and was connected by ties of blood and marriage to half a dozen or more wealthy English families who owned large plantations near the mouth of the river. Howe's mother's name is not known. She may have been Job's first wife, Martha Jones, daughter of Chief Justice Frederick Jones, or his second wife, Elizabeth Watters, daughter of a prominent planter. Both women died young. The former is more probable, however, as relations between Robert and the younger children of his father sometimes seemed strained. Job Howe married a third time, and some of these children may have been from that marriage.

Information on Robert Howe's education is traditional and circumstantial, as documentation may have been lost when his house was destroyed by the British army in 1781. Local reports said that his father sent him as a youth to England, where he studied for two years, and that he then travelled in Europe. He returned shortly before his father died in 1748. Contemporaries commented on his fine command of the English language, his knowledge of literature, especially Shakespeare, and his ability as a military engineer. His genteel manners and social skills—he was fond of dancing and entertaining—were said to have made him welcome in the best society. Howe's earliest participation in politics apparently was in 1756, when at the age of twenty-four he became a justice of the peace in Bladen county, North Carolina, where his family owned a large plantation. He also participated in other manly activities, conferred with Lord Adam Gordon (a military officer and member of parliament) when he called on Governor William Tryon in 1765, and was cited by Tryon for his service in the French and Indian War. Except for brief intervals, Howe represented either Bladen or Brunswick county in the North Carolina House of Commons from 1760 until 1775, which were years of significant legislative activity.

Crown officials at the beginning of this period held Howe in high regard for his support and advice, but as their demands on the colonists became more dictatorial and their disregard for what the colonists considered their 'rights as Englishmen' grew, Americans began to think of themselves as their own masters.

By 1763 Bob Howe, as he was called, had his own rice plantation inherited from his father at the site of Yeamans's earlier settlement. His residence, adjacent to Orton plantation, was a large three-storey building on a brick or stone foundation. He perhaps felt less kindly towards England than he had previously. The precise date of Howe's marriage to Sarah Grange has not been found, but they were the parents of three children, Ann, Mary, and Robert, before 15 September 1772. On that date they declared they could not live happily together, and Howe conveyed property to Sarah's brothers to provide for her support. The separation appears to have been mutually agreeable.

Fort Johnston, guarding the mouth of the Cape Fear River, was completed in 1749 near Howe's plantation, and he became commandant during the years 1766–7 and 1769–73. Multiple office-holding was not unusual, and Howe was commissioned captain and chief baron of the exchequer on 30 June 1767.

In 1768 anticipation of military experience probably began to occupy Howe's thoughts; as major of brigade with the rank of colonel, he was a member of Governor Tryon's force on his expedition to the North Carolina backcountry during the regulator troubles in 1768, as well as in 1771 on the expedition to Alamance. The role he played in the three North Carolina provincial congresses held in 1774 and 1775 made real military action more certain. Among other steps, these meetings, at which Howe was a delegate from Brunswick county, fully launched the revolutionary movement by calling for a declaration of independence by all of the American colonies. This was the first time such a call was made.

As the crisis of events foretold the coming of active warfare, Howe became a member of the committee of safety and supervised the collection of supplies. Following the exchange of gunfire between colonists and British regulars in Massachusetts in April 1775, North Carolina recruited troops, and Howe was named colonel of the 2nd regiment of the continental line. With his troops he marched into Virginia and assumed command of the forces that captured Norfolk. Having been appointed brigadier-general of the continental army by the continental congress on 1 March 1776, he was ordered to South Carolina and put in charge of that state's militia for service under Major-General Charles Lee. When Lee was ordered elsewhere, Howe was left in command of the troops then in that state and in Georgia. On 20 October 1777 he was promoted to major-general, the only commander from the southernmost states to hold that rank.

Georgia and South Carolina resented the leadership of a North Carolinian and declined to support him, contributing to the loss of Savannah. Howe was court-martialled and completely exonerated. He retained the confidence and friendship of his peers from General George Washington downward. In fact, Howe was sent to join Washington's army along the Hudson River. A shortage of artillery pieces and the absence of ammunition, entrenching tools, wagons, and provisions, however, made it impossible for him to be effective there. Howe was then made commandant at Fort West Point, and in 1780 served on the court martial of the British major John Andre, for spying. Through Washington's intervention and with the use of troops, Howe resolved the mutiny that spread among troops from New Jersey and Pennsylvania in 1783.

After the war Howe returned to Kendall, one of his plantations near his birthplace. Congress in 1785 engaged him to define the western boundary with the American Indians, and in 1786 he was elected to the state legislature. *En route* for Fayetteville for that session, he became ill and died, on 14 December 1786, at the home of an old friend, General Thomas Clark, in Bladen county, North Carolina. The exact place of his burial is not certain, but tradition has it at Grange Farm, where Howe had lived as a young planter. It is likely that his body was returned to Kendall and interred in the family cemetery there.

WILLIAM S. POWELL

Sources C. E. Bennett and D. R. Lennon, *A quest for glory: Major General Robert Howe and the American revolution* (1991) · W. L. Saunders and W. Clark, eds., *The colonial records of North Carolina*, 30 vols. (1886–1907), vols 6–18, 20, 22 · J. D. Bellamy, 'General Robert Howe', *North Carolina Booklet*, 7/3 (Jan 1908) · C. C. Davis, *Revolution's godchild* (1970) · H. F. Rankin, *The North Carolina continentals* (1971) · S. B. Weeks, 'Robert Howe', draft biography for *Biographical History of North Carolina*, vol. 9, Duke U., Perkins L. · L. Van L. Naisawald, 'Military career of Robert Howe', MA diss., University of North Carolina, 1948 · *Virginia Gazette* (Oct 1775–Dec 1776) · *The correspondence of William Tryon and other selected papers*, ed. W. S. Powell, 2 vols. (Raleigh, NC, 1980–81) · W. S. Powell, J. K. Huhta, and T. J. Farnham, eds., *The regulators of North Carolina: a documentary history, 1759–1776* (1971)

Archives North Carolina State Archives, Raleigh, papers · University of North Carolina, Chapel Hill, Southern Historical Collection, papers

Howe, Scrope, first Viscount Howe (1648–1713), politician, was born in November 1648, the eldest son of John Grobham Howe (1625–1679) and Annabella Scrope (1630/31–1704), natural daughter of Emanuel *Scrope, earl of Sunderland. His father represented Gloucestershire in the Cavalier Parliament; his mother, a substantial heiress, was legitimized by royal warrant on 1 June 1663. Scrope Howe's siblings surviving infancy included three brothers—John Grobham *Howe, Charles *Howe, and Emanuel Scrope *Howe—as well as five sisters. He was knighted on 11 March 1663, granted a courtesy MA degree by Christ Church, Oxford, on 8 September 1665, and created Baron Glenawly and Viscount Howe in the Irish peerage on 16 May 1701.

Howe married, first, Lady Anne Manners, sixth daughter of John *Manners, eighth earl of Rutland, after they eloped, on 20 April 1672. Anne was born in London about

1655 and died before 1698. Their son, Charles Scrope, died young, but two daughters, Annabella and Margaret, survived into adulthood. Howe married, second, Juliana Alington, daughter of William, third Baron Alington, in July 1698. She was baptized at Horseheath, Cambridgeshire, on 30 October 1665 and died on 10 September 1747. They had three daughters—Mary, Judith, and Anne—and a son, Emanuel Scrope.

Although a newcomer to Nottinghamshire, Scrope Howe's father had made an advantageous marriage which brought him an estate of some 10,000 acres in the northwestern corner of the Vale of Belvoir. Centred on the manor at Langar, it provided an ample base from which Scrope Howe was able to launch a political career, beginning with his return to the House of Commons as one of the knights of the shire in a 1673 by-election. Howe early gravitated toward the nascent whig party, and had become associated with the leadership by the time of the exclusion crisis. He was, for instance, the person designated by the Commons to carry up the impeachment of Lord Stafford to the House of Lords in December 1678, and in July 1680 he joined the earl of Shaftesbury, lords Cavendish and Russell, and a half dozen other prominent whigs in an unsuccessful attempt to use the Middlesex grand jury as a forum in which to present the duke of York as a Catholic recusant.

A supporter of the duke of Monmouth during exclusion, Howe remained active in his behalf even after the dissolution of the Oxford parliament. The revelations of the Rye House plot rapidly transformed the political landscape, however, and at the Nottingham assizes in July 1683 Howe carefully 'associated himselfe wth … the Loyal Gentlemen cursing my Ld of Shaftsbury that ever he was borne' (John Millington to marquess of Halifax, 3 July 1683, Halifax correspondence). By this conversion of expediency Howe hoped to extricate himself from a charge of having made some highly intemperate remarks about the government, but affidavits had already been taken and his weapons were seized shortly thereafter. On 23 January 1685 Howe appeared before the king's bench to answer an indictment growing out of the affair, but all charges were dropped the following day after he admitted fault and apologized to the king and his brother. Even so, Howe was pressured into withdrawing as a candidate during the election later that spring to the first and only parliament of James II's reign.

Too shrewd to have been caught up in the Monmouth rebellion, Howe's political sympathies made him a natural target for recruitment into a movement focused on the prospects of William of Orange. He and two of his brothers first met with the prince's emissary Dykvelt in 1686, and he was later drawn into active engagement in the conspiracy against James II by William Cavendish, an ally of exclusion days and now earl of Devonshire, and Henry Compton, bishop of London. So it was that on 17 November 1688, less than two weeks after William landed at Torbay, Howe, accompanied by two other gentlemen and about sixteen followers, 'well horst & all in Armes rod up the Long row towards Derby to meet the Earl of Devon[shire]' (intelligence from Burton, Derby, and Nottingham, 21 Nov [1688], BL, Add. MS 41805, fol. 245). In an act of considerable personal bravery, Howe numbered among only a handful of leading members of the midlands gentry, whig or tory, to declare openly for the prince of Orange and a free parliament. But Nottingham was suddenly transformed the first week in December from centre of rebellion to place of refuge for Princess Anne, who fled there in the company of the bishop of London. Howe and the men he raised were then incorporated into a larger force assembled to escort Anne to Oxford and ultimately back to London.

In the Convention Parliament Howe voted in favour of declaring the throne vacant and designating William and Mary as joint sovereigns. Thereafter he remained a constant supporter of the whig interest, but not a player of much consequence on the national scene. William III rewarded Howe's loyalty by appointing him comptroller of the excise in 1693, a position he exploited thoroughly before selling it off in 1710; but the king did not think him qualified for a special posting to The Hague he subsequently sought. After the dissolution of parliament in July 1698, Howe failed to regain a seat in the Commons until the autumn of 1710, a rare whig victory in a tight local contest. Howe died at Langar Hall, Nottinghamshire, on 26 January 1713 and was buried in the parish church there.

DAVID HOSFORD

Sources Thoroton's history of Nottinghamshire, ed. J. Throsby, 3 vols. (1797), vol. 1 · D. H. Hosford, Nottingham, nobles and the north: aspects of the revolution of 1688 (1976) · J. Redington, ed., Calendar of Treasury papers, 6 vols., PRO (1868–89) · W. A. Shaw, ed., Calendar of treasury books, 8–10, PRO (1923–35); 19 (1938) · CSP dom., 1684–5; 1690–92 · The manuscripts of his grace the duke of Portland, 10 vols., HMC, 29 (1891–1931), vols. 3, 10 · The manuscripts of Lord Kenyon, HMC, 35 (1894) · Report on the manuscripts of his grace the duke of Buccleuch and Queensberry … preserved at Montagu House, 3 vols. in 4, HMC, 45 (1899–1926), vol. 2/2 · N. Luttrell, A brief historical relation of state affairs from September 1678 to April 1714, 6 vols. (1857) · A. C. Wood, 'The revolution in the north of England', Transactions of the Thoroton Society, 44 (1940), 72–104 · G. N. B. Huskinson, 'The Howe family and Langar Hall, 1650–1800', Transactions of the Thoroton Society, 56 (1952), 54–9 · E. Hughes, Studies in administration and finance (1934) · HoP, Commons, 1660–90 · GEC, Peerage · 'Ent'ring book', DWL, Morrice MS Q · BL, Add. MS 41805 [various newsletters and reports] · Lefleming newsletters, Bodl. Oxf., MS Don. c.39 · BL, Spencer MSS, Halifax correspondence, Box C6
Archives Bodl. Oxf., account book

Howe, William. See How, William (1620–1656).

Howe, William, fifth Viscount Howe (1729–1814), army officer, was born on 10 August 1729, the third surviving son of Emanuel Scrope Howe, second Viscount Howe (1698/9–1735), politician and colonial governor, and his wife, (Mary Sophia) Charlotte *Howe (1703–1782), daughter of Johann Adolf, Baron von Kielmansegg, and his wife, Sophia Charlotte, countess of Darlington, illegitimate half-sister of George I.

Howe entered the British army in 1746, a seventeen-year-old cornet of dragoons with many advantages. He was not a handsome or engaging young man. His features were heavy, his complexion swarthy—his brothers and sisters called him the Savage (Gruber, *The Howe Brothers*, 57)—and his nature taciturn. But he was impressively tall and athletic, with the intelligence and desire to learn his profession and an aptitude for leading men. Just as important, he had the support of wealthy and powerful relations. Although his father had lived extravagantly and died before William was six, his family retained its ancestral seat at Langar, an estate of 10,000 fertile acres southeast of Nottingham; and his mother had an independent income of more than £2250 per year as well as the support of the royal family. She was able to educate William with tutors and four years at Eton College (1742–6), and to see that he advanced as rapidly in the army as his talent would allow. He could also depend on his brothers to provide examples of distinguished military service: George Augustus *Howe, third Viscount Howe, an officer in the 1st foot guards, would be one of the most admired British soldiers in America when killed at Ticonderoga in 1758; and Richard *Howe, later Earl Howe, was already in 1746 the captain of a warship and on his way to becoming a celebrated naval officer.

With such advantages, Howe soon developed a successful career in the army. He gained repeated promotions while serving with his regiment in Flanders at the end of the War of the Austrian Succession, and in Scotland and Ireland during ensuing years of peace: from cornet and lieutenant in the 15th dragoons (1746–9), to captain-lieutenant and captain in the 20th foot (1750–56), to major in the 60th foot (1756–7), and lieutenant-colonel in the 58th foot (1757–62). By 1758, when he took the 58th regiment to North America for the Seven Years' War, he was widely respected as a knowledgeable and conscientious officer. During the subsequent conquest of Canada, 1758–60, he proved a brave and skilful commander, winning praise especially for leading the advance guard to the Plains of Abraham and precipitating the decisive battle for Quebec in 1759. He further distinguished himself in the expeditions that captured Montreal in 1760, Belle Île on the coast of Brittany in 1761, and Havana, Cuba, in 1762.

In the decade between the Seven Years' War and the American War of Independence, Howe's career continued to flourish. He sometimes attended parliament (as an independent member for Nottingham, 1758–80), and on 2 June 1765 he married Frances Conolly (*c*.1742–1817), daughter of Thomas Conolly of Castletown, co. Kildare, from a prominent Anglo-Irish family. But Howe got more satisfaction from the army than from politics or domestic life (he did not have children). He became colonel of ever more prestigious infantry regiments: the 58th (1762–4), the 46th (1764–75), and the 23rd (1775–86). He obtained the lieutenant-governorship of the Isle of Wight (1768–95), and he was promoted to major-general in 1772. On the eve of the Anglo-American War he was one of the most active and esteemed officers in the army. He kept his regiment 'as fit for Service as any in H[is] M[ajesty's] A[rmy]' (regimental review, 15 May 1775, PRO, WO 27/35); he regularly and meticulously inspected other regiments; and in the late summer of 1774 commanded seven companies of light infantry for six weeks of intensive training on Salisbury Plain and a special demonstration for George III at Richmond. No wonder that during the following winter when the king sought a talented general to serve as second in command of his forces in North America—to help put down the rebellion there—he chose Howe.

Howe accepted the command even though he knew he would be serving in circumstances that were sure to be as painful for him as they were difficult for Britain. He had a deep affection for American colonists, especially the people of Massachusetts who had been his comrades during the Seven Years' War and who had honoured his brother, George Augustus, with a memorial in Westminster Abbey. He had also been publicly critical of British efforts to punish the people of Massachusetts for having resisted imperial taxes. Yet in January 1775 he let friends in the government know that he would accept appointment as second in command of the British army at Boston. He offered to go to America in hopes of succeeding General Thomas Gage as commander-in-chief and of promoting a reconciliation between mother country and colonies. He was to be sorely disappointed. By the time he reached Boston, on 25 May 1775, the colonists had fought British troops at Lexington and Concord and surrounded their army in Boston. Howe had hoped to make peace; instead he found himself attacking entrenched rebel forces in the battle of Bunker Hill. That costly battle persuaded the British government to recall Gage and forced Howe to put aside temporarily any thought of negotiating an end to the imperial crisis. At about this time Howe took a Mrs Joshua Loring (*née* Lloyd), from Boston, as his mistress, but she seems to have had no influence on his decisions or wider career. By October when he succeeded Gage as commander-in-chief, Howe had decided to take his army to New York city to seek the decisive battle that he now believed 'the most effectual Means to terminate this expensive War' (quoted in Gruber, *The Howe Brothers*, 83).

After reaching New York in late June 1776, Howe changed his plans. He did so in part because the rebels were strongly entrenched around New York city and in part because his brother, Admiral Richard, Lord Howe, arrived on 12 July to revive hopes for peace. The Howes were now peace commissioners as well as commanders-in-chief. Although General Howe doubted that the colonists, who had just declared their independence, would be attracted by the terms he and his brother could offer, he agreed to modify his strategy to promote a negotiated settlement—and reduce the risk of casualties. For nearly five months he gave up opportunities for a decisive battle while executing a series of manoeuvres that produced limited victories at Long Island, Kip's Bay, White Plains, and Fort Washington and that gradually forced the rebels to withdraw from Long Island, Manhattan, and much of New Jersey. After each limited victory, the Howes made overtures to the continental congress or the American people; but not until December did these overtures, sustained by seemingly inexorable British advances, begin to succeed. Then while some 5000 colonists were accepting offers of pardon, rebel forces surprised British detachments at Trenton and Princeton. These small victories restored American morale, forced the British to withdraw from all save eastern New Jersey, and ruined the Howes' hopes for peace. Once again General Howe conceded he would need a decisive battle to end the rebellion.

But Howe—now Sir William Howe in recognition of his victory at Long Island—did not pursue a decisive battle or any other strategic goal consistently in 1777; and he deliberately ignored the government's plans for the campaign. He knew that the government, disgusted with his cautious manoeuvres and conciliatory efforts in 1776, expected him to crush the rebellion in 1777—specifically to co-operate along the Hudson River with British forces advancing south from Canada in operations designed to draw the continental army into a decisive battle. He also knew that a decisive battle might be the only way to end the rebellion. Yet, stung by defeats at Trenton and Princeton, he remained determined to show that he had not been mistaken in trying to appeal to the American people in 1776. To satisfy these conflicting intentions, he shifted from one strategy to another during the campaign of 1777 and never co-operated as the government intended with the army advancing from Canada. He opened the campaign in June trying to engage the continental army in New Jersey. That failing, he embarked his army for the Chesapeake so as to manoeuvre the rebels out of Philadelphia, recover Pennsylvania as a haven for loyalists, and forestall any prospect of using his own forces on the Hudson. Once he discovered that Pennsylvanians were not so loyal as he hoped, he again sought a decisive battle. Although he did win a significant victory at Brandywine on 11 September, he did not pursue or destroy the American forces; and he devoted nearly all that remained of the campaign to securing Philadelphia. Howe's shifting strategies not only spared the continental army and contributed to the loss of the Canadian army at Saratoga in October, but also encouraged France to enter the war on the side of the rebels.

Even before the campaign of 1777 ended Howe was determined to go home and confront his critics. Knowing that the government was dissatisfied with his conduct of the war and feeling vulnerable to criticism, he asked to resign. While he awaited a reply—through the winter and spring of 1778–he refused to undertake further offensive operations. In late May he was at last able to turn over his command to Sir Henry Clinton and sail for England. He arrived home on 1 July to find that although the king received him 'very graciously', the ministry blamed him for failing to end the rebellion (Gruber, The Howe Brothers, 326). When the ministry refused to acknowledge his services, he and his brother (who returned home on 25 October) joined the opposition in parliament and asked for an inquiry into their commands. They had little chance of persuading the House of Commons to thank them or to censure the ministry; but for two months (22 April – 30 June 1779) they presented their case and examined witnesses. In these parliamentary hearings and in more than two dozen pamphlets—including Sir William Howe's Narrative (1780)—the Howes and the government sought to justify themselves and blame one another for the continuation of the American rebellion.

Although Sir William left parliament in 1780 and never again led British forces in battle, he remained active and successful in the army. Once his enemies had fallen from political power, he was sworn of the privy council (1782), and became lieutenant-general of the ordnance (1782–1804) and colonel of the 19th dragoons (from 1786 until his death). In 1790, when Britain and Spain quarrelled over trading rights in the Pacific (the Nootka Sound controversy), he was nominated to command in the event of war. During the French Revolutionary Wars he was promoted to general, and was given command of forces training in the north and then in the east of England (1793–5). Even after age and illness began to limit his military duties, he held the lucrative governorships of Berwick (1795–1808) and Plymouth (from 1808 until his death). Following the death of his brother Richard, Earl Howe on 5 August 1799, he succeeded as fifth Viscount Howe in the peerage of Ireland. He died at Plymouth on 12 July 1814 and was buried at Twickenham on 22 July.

Howe was an accomplished soldier. In more than half a century of service he proved himself a knowledgeable and meticulous officer and a skilful commander. Yet because he did not end the American rebellion when it seemed most vulnerable he was widely criticized, and historians have continued to puzzle over his failure. It is now clear that he was not the victim of instructions that required him to combine force and persuasion, of cautiously conventional strategic thinking, of his own lethargy, or even of a rebellion too well established to be ended by force. Rather, he failed because he persisted in trying to make peace when empowered to make war. His efforts were especially destructive of the British government's plans for ending the rebellion because he had the skill and reputation to place him beyond the government's direction or recall until an army had been lost and the Anglo-American War had become a world war.

Ira D. Gruber

Sources I. D. Gruber, The Howe brothers and the American Revolution (Chapel Hill, NC, 1972) · T. S. Anderson, The command of the Howe brothers during the American revolution (1936) · B. Partridge, Sir Billy Howe (1932) · I. D. Gruber, 'George III chooses a commander in chief', Arms and independence: the military character of the American Revolution, ed. R. Hoffman and R. J. Albert (1984), 166–90 · I. D. Gruber, 'British strategy: the theory and practice of eighteenth-century warfare', Reconsiderations on the revolutionary war, ed. D. Higginbotham (1978), 14–31 · M. A. Jones, 'Sir William Howe: conventional strategist', George Washington's opponents, ed. G. A. Billias (1969), 39–72 · DNB · J. R. Alden, General Gage in America (1948) · Army List (1759) · Army List (1763) · Army List (1772) · Army List (1775) · Army List (1786) · Army List (1798) · GEC, Peerage, new edn, 6.598–9 · L. B. Namier and J. Brooke, 'Howe, Hon. William', HoP, Commons, 1754–90 · R. R. Sedgwick, 'Howe, Emanuel Scrope', HoP, Commons, 1715–54 · R. R. Sedgwick, 'Howe, George Augustus', HoP, Commons, 1715–54 · The journal of Nicholas Cresswell, 1774–1777 (1924), 229 · G. N. B. Huskinson, 'The Howe family and Langar Hall, 1650–1800', Transactions of the Thoroton Society, 56 (1952), 54–9

Archives PRO, Colonial Office MSS, CO 5/91–6, 5/117, 180 • PRO, corresp. and papers as commander-in-chief in the American colonies, PRO 30/55 • Royal Artillery Institution, Woolwich, London, order book • U. Mich., Clements L., orderly book • University of West Virginia, Morgantown, order book | Alnwick Castle, Northumberland, Percy MSS • BL, corresp. with General Haldimand, Add. MSS 21807–21808 • Bodl. Oxf., Thomas Villiers, letters • Hunt. L., letters to Sir George Pocock • NA Scot., letters to Sir Alexander Hope • U. Mich., Clements L., Germain, Knox, Gage, Clinton, Howe, and Wedderburn MSS • Althorp, Northamptonshire, Spencer MSS • Heinde, Hildesheim, Kielmansegge MSS

Likenesses Corbutt, mezzotint, pubd 1777, BM, NPG • H. B. Hall, engraving, 1872, repro. in Partridge, *Sir Billy Howe*, following p. 34 • J. Rogers, engraving (after print, 1777), repro. in Jones, 'Sir William Howe', following p. 78 • B. West, group portrait (*Death of Wolfe*) • engraving (after Cobbett, 1777), repro. in Partridge, *Sir Billy Howe*, frontispiece • portrait, repro. in Anderson, *Command*, frontispiece

Wealth at death left wife £36,648 in 3 per cent annuities as well as his real estate, personal effects, and plate (none appraised); left servants a total of £1900 in separate bequests: will, PRO, PROB 11/1558, fols. 403–4

Howel ab Edwin. *See* Hywel ab Edwin (*d.* 1044).

Howel ab Ieuav. *See* Hywel ab Ieuaf (*d.* 985).

Howel ab Owain Gwynedd. *See* Hywel ab Owain Gwynedd (*d.* 1170).

Howel [Hywel], **Harri** (*b. c.*1610, *d.* in or after **1671**), Welsh-language poet, was the son of Howel ap Siôn Ieuan of the parish of Dolgellau in Merioneth, who was also a poet. A section of mountain pasture on the boundary of the parishes of Dolgellau and Llanfachraeth called Ffridd Harri Howel may well be a memorial of the poet and an indication that he was a farmer, and therefore not a full-time professional poet. The earliest date appended to a poem by Howel is 1627, and the latest is 1671.

Some fifty-five poems by Howel have been preserved in Welsh manuscripts. A few of these are single *englynion* (four-line stanzas), and most of the remainder are poems addressed to members of families in north Wales. Howel addressed poems to some well-known patrons, such as the Nannau family of Nannau in Merioneth, the Thelwalls of Plas-y-ward in Denbighshire, and the Miltons (Miltwniaid) of Gwenynog in Denbighshire, but he composed more poems to members of the Prys family of Llwyn Ynn and Cerddinen in Denbighshire than to any other. His elegy to Siôn Prys of Llwyn Ynn appears to have been his most popular poem. He composed some poems to clerics, the most eminent among them being Dr John Davies of Mallwyd, Merioneth (for example NL Wales, MS 529, fol. 421b). All poems addressed to living persons or in memory of the dead contain, after the fashion of traditional Welsh poets of the seventeenth century, detailed references to pedigrees and members of the family, and to any public offices held. If there are gaps in Howel's knowledge of a family's pedigree he excuses himself by saying:

> I could not cope with naming
> Her extensive pedigree.
> (NL Wales, Llanstephan MS 123, fol. 476)

One detail in Llanstephan MS 124 (fols. 647 ff.) in the colophon of an elegy to Siôn Bodwrda of Bodwrda in the Llŷn peninsula who died in December 1647, stating that Howel composed the poem in April 1648, may have some significance in relation to the custom of presenting poems to families. His ode on the death of Huw Nannau, 1647, contains an example of every one of the twenty-four metres of the traditional Welsh poetic craft.

Howel composed two 'love' poems; one is a *cywydd* to a girl complaining of the suffering that her love has brought him, and the other a poem to a girl who had scorned a suppliant. In the whole of this body of poetry there is hardly one line which displays anything except a mechanical ability to compose in *cynghanedd*.

GWYN THOMAS

Sources *DWB*

Howel [Howell], **Thomas** (*c.*1480–1537), merchant and philanthropist, was the son of John Howel, a prosperous and well-established merchant of Bristol, and his wife, Alice, who subsequently married Sir Thomas Morgan of Pen-coed, Monmouthshire. His father's family seems originally to have come from Monmouthshire. Born and bred in Bristol, Howel went to Spain about 1502 as an apprentice to Hugh Elyot, a merchant of Bristol. Howel married Joanna Christian, who proved to be an admirable wife and business associate to him. By 1507 he had moved to London and become a freeman of the Drapers' Company, and in 1512 he enlisted the interest of William Roche, warden of that company. In 1514 he was retained by the earl of Surrey for military service in France. He joined the livery of the Drapers' Company in 1517 and in 1527 became its junior warden.

By this time, Howel had long been a very successful and wealthy merchant engaged in Anglo-Spanish commercial exchanges. He traded in fine cloths of all kinds which he exported to Spain and in return imported oil, alum, iron, raisins, and wine. He stated in June 1528 that he had been in Spain on and off for about twenty-six years, and in that year he took up permanent residence in Seville. He left his wife to look after his affairs in London; she died in 1529. One of the most interesting remains of Howel's activities as a merchant is the remarkable ledger he kept. Deposited with the Drapers' Company during his lifetime and preserved in Drapers' Hall ever since, it is of unique interest for two reasons: for the light it sheds on Anglo-Spanish trade during the early Tudor period, and as the earliest surviving English example of double-entry bookkeeping.

Howel's health was failing by 1536, when he drew up his third and final will, and he died and was buried in Seville the following year. Under the terms of his will he left by far the biggest sixteenth-century charitable endowment for marriage subsidies. Having no children, Howel bequeathed 12,000 ducats in gold to his company to be employed in the purchase of land so as to raise 400 ducats a year to provide marriage portions for deserving Welsh maidens, with an indicated preference for orphan girls of his own lineage. Although many benefited from the bequest, it also gave rise to much controversy and litigation. Finally, the report of the fourth Charity Commission of 1837 dealt with Howell's Trust among other charities. A private act of parliament (1853) provided for a scheme to regulate Howell's Charity. In 1860 two girls' schools, each known as Howell's School, were established, one at Llandaff and the other at Denbigh. They have since become two of the best-known schools in Wales.

GLANMOR WILLIAMS

Sources T. Falconer, *The charity of Thomas Howell, A. D. 1540* (1860) · J. E. McCann, *Thomas Howell and the school at Llandaff* (1972) · A. H. Johnson, *The history of the Worshipful Company of the Drapers of London*, 5 vols. (1914–22) · W. K. Jordan, *The charities of London, 1480–1660: the aspirations and achievements of the urban society* (1960) · G. Connell-Smith, 'The ledger of Thomas Howell', *Economic History Review*, 2nd ser., 3 (1950–51), 363–70 · will, PRO, PROB 11/31, sig. 24
Archives Drapers' Hall, London, Thomas Howell's ledger
Wealth at death left by far the biggest sixteenth-century charitable endowment for marriage subsidies

Howell. *See also* Howel, Hywel.

Howell, Charles Augustus (1840?–1890), artists' agent and rogue, was born on 10 March, probably in 1840, in Oporto, Portugal, the youngest of the six children of Alfred William Howell, an English drawing master and wine merchant, and Dona Enriqueta Amelia de Souza De Rosa Coehlo. Through his mother's distinguished Portuguese family Howell claimed to have inherited the red ribbon of the order of Christ. Renowned during his lifetime principally as a prodigious liar and gifted raconteur, Howell's historical importance lies in his varied dealings with members of the Victorian art world, notably John Ruskin, Dante Gabriel Rossetti, Charles Algernon Swinburne, and James McNeill Whistler. 'He had the gift of intimacy,' Whistler said, observing that 'it was easier to get involved with Howell than to get rid of him' (Pennell and Pennell, *Whistler Journal*, 59).

Little is known about Howell's early years, though he seems to have assisted his father in the wine trade until, at the age of sixteen, he went to England to live with his uncle, who was vicar of Darlington. There he gained employment with the Stockton and Darlington Railway and made the acquaintance of the Italian revolutionary Felice Orsini (1819–1858); because of some involvement—probably innocent—with the Orsini conspiracy, Howell was compelled to leave the country in 1858, returning only in 1865. The intervening years he spent, according to various reports, diving for treasure off the coast of Portugal, becoming a sheikh of an Arab tribe in Morocco, and serving as an attaché to the Portuguese embassy in Rome. Upon returning to England, Howell lived at 3 York Villas in Brixton with his aunt and his cousin Frances Kate (Kitty) Howell (*d.* 1888), whom he married on 21 August 1867; their daughter, Rosalind Blanche Catherine, was born on 20 March 1877.

By the end of 1865 Howell had become Ruskin's secretary, almoner, and confidant, producing skilful facsimiles of works of art, serving as intermediary in Ruskin's ill-fated liaison with Rose La Touche, and settling in Fulham to keep up the spirits of Edward Burne-Jones, Ruskin's protégé. Howell's association with Ruskin ended in 1870, for reasons that remain obscure. Howell and Ruskin had met through Dante Gabriel Rossetti, who was for a time Howell's intimate friend. It was Howell who, in 1869, managed the exhumation of Rossetti's poems from the grave of his wife, Elizabeth Siddal: no one else, Rossetti said, 'could well have been entrusted with such a trying task' (Angeli, 139–40). Also through Rossetti, Howell met Swinburne, who unwisely employed him to negotiate with his publisher John Camden Hotten, and met Whistler, who relied on him through a period of financial crisis to take on debts, manage his affairs, and help prepare his lawsuit against Ruskin, which went to court in 1878.

At Chaldon House, his exquisitely furnished residence at North End Road, Fulham, Howell established himself as an art expert and interior decorator. One of his clients, George Howard, later ninth earl of Carlisle, commended his 'wonderful skill in the discovery of pretty things' (Cline, 7). He also possessed keen business instincts, and as a dealer in fine arts helped foster the Victorian taste for Chinese porcelain and Japanese prints and elevated the value of contemporary art, especially works by Rossetti, Burne-Jones, Ford Madox Brown, Frederick Sandys, and G. F. Watts. According to William Michael Rossetti, Howell was 'rich in versatile resource and in attractive personal qualities' (Rossetti, 81). He appears in Theodore Watts-Dunton's *Aylwin* (1898) as De Castro, 'a professional anecdote-monger of extraordinary brilliancy, a raconteur of the very first order', with the bearing of a gentleman and a face revealing 'power and intelligence'. Endowed with tremendous personal charm, Howell founded his dealings with artists in friendships that inevitably foundered through evidence of his dishonesty and double-dealing. Rossetti characterized him in a limerick as

A Portuguese person called Howell,
  Who lays on his lies with a trowel,

and Graham Robertson observed that he attracted 'portable property'—pictures, furnishings, bric-a-brac—as a magnet attracts steel (Robertson, 187). Skilled in winning confidence and notoriously unprincipled, Howell is also suspected of having engaged in (or at least contemplated) blackmail, which may account for Georgiana Burne-Jones's chilling dismissal of her husband's former intimate as 'a stranger to all that our life meant' (Burne-Jones, 1.294).

In 1878 Howell was forced by the extension of the railway lines to leave Chaldon House and persuaded a court to award him substantial compensatory damages. He lived the rest of his life at 91 Southampton Row and at Old Danner, a house by the sea at Selsey Bill, Sussex, where he is said to have entertained the local children with stories and games and played the part of a distinguished personage. He had become involved in 1873 with the artist Rosa Corder (1853–1893), with whom he is alleged to have supplied spurious Rossettis and other forgeries for the art market; their daughter, Beatrice Ellen Howell (whom Howell referred to in his will as his niece), was born about 1883. Howell's death was reported more than once—'It is believed by his own agency', according to G. C. Williamson, 'in order that he might hear what was to be said' (Williamson, 150), and also to afford an occasion for a sale, to which his former acquaintances flocked in fruitless hope of recovering their long-lost possessions. His actual demise was consequently met with disbelief: it took place on 24 April 1890, at Home Hospital, 16 Fitzroy Square, after a long illness, probably tuberculosis. A lurid story arose—apparently without foundation, but befitting Howell's predilection for mendacity—that he was discovered in a gutter outside a Chelsea pub with his throat cut and a ten-shilling piece clenched between his teeth. He was buried in the Brompton cemetery.

LINDA MERRILL

Sources H. R. Angeli, *Pre-Raphaelite twilight: the story of Charles Augustus Howell* (1954) · G. Burne-Jones, *Memorials of Edward Burne-Jones*, 2 vols. (1904); repr. (1993) · *The Owl and the Rossettis: letters of Charles A. Howell and Dante Gabriel, Christina and William Michael Rossetti*, ed. C. L. Cline (1978) · E. Robins Pennell and J. Pennell, *The life of James McNeill Whistler*, 2 vols. (1908) · E. R. Pennell and J. Pennell, *The Whistler journal* (1921) · W. G. Robertson, *Time was: the reminiscences of W. Graham Robertson*, pbk edn (1981) · W. M. Rossetti, *Dante Gabriel Rossetti as designer and writer* (1889) · G. C. Williamson, *Murray Marks and his friends: a tribute of regard* (1919) · m. cert. · d. cert.
Archives JRL, corresp. · Ransom HRC | U. Glas., Whistler MSS
Likenesses F. Sandys, coloured chalk drawing, 1882, AM Oxf.
Wealth at death £3072 6s. 11d.: resworn probate, May 1891, CGPLA Eng. & Wales (1890)

Howell, David [*pseud.* Llawdden] (1831–1903), dean of St David's, was born on 16 August 1831, at Tre-os, Llan-gan, in Glamorgan, son of John Howell (*d.* 1880), farmer and Calvinistic Methodist elder. His mother was an invalid and he was brought up mainly by his grandmother, Mary Griffiths of Tynycaeau, a churchwoman. At the age of fifteen he returned to his father's home, which was now at Bryn Cwtyn, near Pen-coed. He was educated at the Eagle School, Cowbridge, and Merthyr preparatory school. Persuaded by the Revd John Griffiths, later archdeacon of Neath, he entered the Anglican ministry, passing through the Llandaff Diocesan Institute at Abergavenny. He was ordained deacon in 1855 and priest in 1856. He served as a curate at Neath before his appointment in 1857 as secretary for Wales to the Church Pastoral Aid Society. He was vicar of Pwllheli (1861–4), and of St John's, Cardiff (1864–75). He endeavoured to adapt the structure of the church to the needs of a rapidly growing community, and raised £30,000 for the purpose. In 1875 he was elected a member of the first Cardiff school board. In this year he became vicar of Wrexham, where he remained until 1891, when he moved to the neighbouring vicarage of Gresford. At Wrexham, as at Cardiff, he greatly extended the activities of the church. He received the degree of BD from the archbishop of Canterbury in 1878, was appointed prebendary of Meliden and honorary canon of St Asaph in 1885, and became archdeacon of Wrexham in 1889.

Howell's gifts, temperament, and his family connections fitted him to become a mediating influence between the church and Welsh nonconformity. He was well versed in Welsh literature, particularly its hymnology, and was sympathetic to Welsh national movements, though party politics did not interest him, and after 1875 he held aloof from political disputes. He was a gifted orator, powerful not only in the pulpit but also on the eisteddfod platform, where he was known by the bardic name of Llawdden and

renowned for his *englynion*. He brought the evangelical temper and the Methodist fervour into all his church work. Yet his 'churchmanship though always broad was never really vague' (*The Times*, 16 Jan 1903). His pastoral work was thorough, and he was a believer in the voluntary school system. Among his published works was a study of foreign missionaries (1879), as well as regular contributions to Welsh periodicals.

Howell married Anne Powell of Pen-coed; they had four surviving sons, of whom the youngest, William Tudor Howell, was Conservative MP for the Denbigh boroughs from 1895 to 1900. In 1897 Howell was appointed dean of St David's, a post regarded as a form of unofficial retirement. The restoration of the lady chapel in the cathedral showed that he had not lost his zest for work. He died on 15 January 1903 at St David's, and was buried in the chapel of St Nicholas in the cathedral.

J. E. LLOYD, rev. ROBERT V. SMITH

Sources DWB · R. Ellis, *Doniau a daniwyd* (1957) · H. T. Evans, *A bibliography of Welsh hymnology to 1960* (1972) · *Y Geninen*, 21 (1903), 151–6 · J. Vyrnwy Morgan, ed., *Welsh religious leaders in the Victorian era* (1905) · *The Times* (16 Jan 1903)
Archives NL Wales, letters to D. S. Evans
Wealth at death £10,160 4s. 11d.: probate, 27 Feb 1903, CGPLA Eng. & Wales

Howell, Denis Herbert, Baron Howell (1923–1998), politician, was born on 4 September 1923 at 115 Guildford Street, Birmingham—a back-to-back house—the middle of the three children of Herbert Howell (*d.* 1961), an engineer's fitter, and his wife, Bertha Amelia Watkins. Political awareness came early: his first memory was of sitting on his father's knee at a general strike meeting in 1926. So too did his devotion to football, and to Aston Villa Football Club in particular. He left Handsworth grammar school, in Birmingham, at fifteen and started work as an office boy. Rejected for military service, he served as a fire-watcher and in the Home Guard throughout the Second World War, and began refereeing football matches for the Birmingham Sunday League in 1942. In 1951 he graduated as a linesman in the Football League, and was a Football Association referee from 1956 until 1966.

Howell was active from an early age in the Clerical and Administrative Workers' Union—he was president, from 1971 to 1989, of its expanded successor, the Association of Professional, Executive, Clerical and Computer Staff (APEX)—and in 1942 he joined the Labour Party. He was elected to Birmingham city council at twenty-three, and four years later, in 1950, was elected to the important post of secretary of the Labour group. This experience was his training ground as one of the most effective operators in British politics of his generation. He contested the unwinnable King's Norton parliamentary seat in 1951, won Birmingham All Saints in 1955, and lost it by twenty votes in 1959. On 20 August 1955 he married Brenda Marjorie Willson (*b.* 1928/9), with whom he had three sons and a daughter. He found great pleasure and support in his family: 'I find the fellowship and affection of the family to be an indispensable part of my public life' (Howell, 85). Out of parliament, and with characteristic resilience, he creating the conditions for the Commonwealth games in Edinburgh in 1970. In 1969 he was moved from the Department of Education to be minister of state at the Ministry of Housing and Local Government, but carried his portfolio as minister of sport with him, 'the first man in history to take a Ministry with him when he moves' (ibid., 199).

Howell sat on the opposition front benches between 1970 and 1974, and was inevitably reappointed minister for sport when Labour returned to office in 1974. Shortly after the election an IRA car bomb was planted at his Birmingham home; his wife and youngest son narrowly escaped death or injury. Sport now came under the Department of the Environment. Here he gained a reputation as a different kind of rain-maker. In the notoriously dry summer of 1976 James Callaghan appointed him minister for drought. The legend quickly grew up that just as he appealed for restraint in the use of water it began to rain, and continued to do so for most of a month. In fact the rains did not arrive for ten days, beginning in Yorkshire just as Howell ceremonially turned on an emergency standpipe.

Back in opposition Howell energetically opposed Margaret Thatcher's ban on British athletes competing at the Moscow Olympic games in 1980, following the Soviet invasion of Afghanistan. He raised funds to send a British team, bolstered Dennis Follows, the wavering chairman of the British Olympic Association, and forcefully expressed the view that the Olympic games were beyond politics. The military forces of the west were unable to interpose themselves between the USSR and Afghanistan; Howell and his supporters would not accept that 'our freedoms must be defended by Olympic sport' (Howell, 293). The depleted British team won twenty-one medals; Howell was awarded the Olympic order silver medal by the International Olympic Committee Congress.

Denis Howell retired from the House of Commons in 1992, after two major heart operations and the tragic death in a car crash of his youngest son, David, in 1986. He took a life peerage as, inevitably, Baron Howell, of Aston Manor in the city of Birmingham. His last great campaign was an unsuccessful attempt to bring the 1992 Olympics to the city to which he always owed his greatest allegiance. He published his autobiography in 1990, under the apt title *Made in Birmingham*. Lord Howell collapsed after making a speech at a dinner in support of Cancer Research at Birmingham, and died from heart disease in Solihull Hospital on 19 April 1998. His public funeral took place on 24 April at St Paul's Church, Birmingham, where many tributes were paid to the man known in his own city as Mr Brum. TAM DALYELL

Denis Herbert Howell, Baron Howell (1923–1998), by Godfrey Argent, 1968

founded his own public relations company and became a founding member of the Campaign for Democratic Socialism, the Gaitskellite organization formed to counter the left-wing unilateralists in the Labour Party. The connections he formed at this time helped to get him the Labour nomination for the 1961 by-election at Birmingham Small Heath, which he held for the next thirty-one years. He thus had a power-base in the party; Harold Wilson, from a different political stable, could never ignore Howell.

On Labour's victory in 1964 Harold Wilson appointed Howell the country's first minister for sport, as a parliamentary under-secretary at the Department of Education, but did not want to give him a budget because 'the country's broke' (Howell, 142). Howell, no respecter of persons and the least deferential of men, reminded the prime minister that Britain was to host the 1966 world cup and would need funds. Howell got his budget—and his prestige was mightily, if irrationally, enhanced by England's winning the tournament. Howell—sometimes a bully and cajoler, always active—became one of Whitehall's most effective ministers. In the teeth of civil service opposition he set up the Sports Council. He appointed an important enquiry, under Sir Norman Chester, of Nuffield College, Oxford, into Association Football (1966–8). A committed opponent of apartheid, especially in sport, he shamed the MCC into cancelling their 1968–9 tour of South Africa on account of the racial problems surrounding the Worcestershire and England cricketer Basil D'Oliveira, which marked the beginning of the long sporting boycott of South Africa. He was a tower of strength in

Sources D. Howell, *Made in Birmingham* (1990) · *The Times* (20 April 1998) · *The Independent* (20 April 1998) · *Daily Telegraph* (20 April 1998) · *The Guardian* (20 April 1998) · *WWW* · personal knowledge (2004) · private information (2004) · *Birmingham Post* (20–21 April 1998) · *Birmingham Post* (25 April 1998) · b. cert. · m. cert. · d. cert. **Likenesses** photograph, 1966, repro. in *The Independent* · G. Argent, photograph, 1968, NPG [*see illus.*] · photographs, 1969–

80, Hult. Arch. · photograph, 1976, repro. in *The Times* · photograph, 1989, repro. in *Daily Telegraph* · photograph, repro. in *The Guardian* · photographs, repro. in Howell, *Made in Birmingham*

Howell, Dorothy Gertrude (1898–1982), composer and pianist, was born on 25 February 1898 in Handsworth, Birmingham, the daughter of Charles Edward Howell (1855–1932) and his wife, Viola Rosetta Feeny (1862–1942). Dorothy's father worked as an ironmaster in Birmingham; he was a self-taught pianist and was for a time organist and choirmaster at Handsworth church. Her mother was the daughter of Alfred Feeny, the arts and music critic of the *Birmingham Post*. She had three brothers and two elder sisters. Her eldest brother, Charles, was a very talented violinist; he was killed in action during the First World War. The family were Roman Catholic, and Dorothy's younger brother Clifford had much to do with the working-out of the form of the English mass after the Second Vatican Council.

They were a musical family, and Dorothy Howell received lessons and encouragement from an early age. One of the first examples of her compositional work is a set of six pieces for piano, printed in 1911 when she was thirteen. Educated at convents in Birmingham, and also in Belgium, she went on to study with John McEwen and Tobias Matthay at the Royal Academy of Music. She was a gifted pianist and composer, and much of her work was subsequently written for this instrument, most notably the piano concerto, which was premièred in 1923 at the Queen's Hall, London, with herself as soloist. Howell first gained recognition, however, in 1919, when her symphonic poem *Lamia* was premièred at the BBC Proms by Sir Henry Wood, the work being performed four more times that same season and again at the Proms in 1920, 1921, and 1926. Her orchestral overture *The Rock* was premièred at the last night of the Proms in 1928.

Dorothy Howell's style is essentially romantic, often drawing on nature and landscape for inspiration. The music is tonal, coloured by rich harmonies and chromaticism. Her output covered the whole range of instrumental, vocal, and choral genres. An early piece, her *Phantasy* for violin and piano, won the Cobbett prize in 1921. Her music for the stage included *Christmas Eve* (1922) and *Sanctity* (1938), and among her significant orchestral works were *Two Dances* (1920), *Danse grotesque* (1919), *Three Divertissements* (1940?), *Fanfare* (1930?), *Humoresque* (1921), and a symphony. Her notable chamber works included piano sonatas (1916 and 1955), a string quartet (1919), and a violin sonata (1947), as well as a work for piano, *Spindrift* (1920), and *The Moorings* for violin and piano (1925).

From 1924 to 1970 Dorothy Howell was professor of harmony and counterpoint at the Royal Academy of Music, having been elected a fellow in 1928. In 1971 she was elected a member of the Royal Philharmonic Society. She was also a professor at the Tobias Matthay Pianoforte School. Having spent the early part of her career in London, she moved during the Second World War to Letchworth in Hertfordshire, where she lived with her parents,

commuting to London when necessary. During this time she served in the Women's Land Army. Dorothy Howell was a founder member of the Society of St Gregory, and her church music includes several masses—both Latin and English—as well as motets and psalm settings. In her later years she had connections with both Ampleforth and Stanbrook abbeys. Howell wrote a mass in English for Ampleforth and seven pieces for Stanbrook, and gave the copyright and the manuscripts to the abbey; these pieces include a mass, responsorial chants and psalms, and an alleluia written for a celebration of the dedication of the church. Owing partly to illness, the majority of her later works were small-scale pieces for piano, voice, or ensemble. In her late forties Dorothy Howell was diagnosed with cancer, and although she survived many more years, her later life was clouded by periods of depression. She moved to Malvern Wells and eventually to a nursing home nearby, Perrins House, 28 Moorlands Road, Malvern. Howell died there on 12 January 1982 and was buried on 30 March at St Wulstan's Church, Little Malvern, Worcestershire, directly next to the grave of Edward Elgar, which she herself had tended. She was unmarried.

CELIA MIKE

Sources C. Mike, 'The life and works of Dorothy Howell', BMus diss., U. Aberdeen, 1990 · E. Kuhe, 'A girl musician: Miss Dorothy Howell', *Lady's Pictorial* (4 Oct 1919) · D. Cox, *The Henry Wood Proms* (1980) · private information (2004) [family diaries and records] · *CGPLA Eng. & Wales* (1982) · C. Mike, 'Howell, Dorothy', *The new Grove dictionary of women composers*, ed. J. A. Sadie and R. Samuel (1994) · C. Mike, 'Dorothy Howell', *British Music*, 14 (1992), 48–58
Archives Dorothy Howell Trust, 63 High Street, Bewdley, Worcestershire, diaries and letters
Wealth at death under £25,000: probate, 15 April 1982, *CGPLA Eng. & Wales*

Howell, Francis (1624/5–1680), college head, was the son of Thomas Howell of Gwinear, Cornwall. He attended Oxford University, matriculating at the age of seventeen as a commoner at Exeter College on 24 July 1642. He graduated MA on 14 April 1648 and was a fellow and Greek reader from 1648 to 1658. He was appointed a proctor of the university in 1652, and was Whyte professor of moral philosophy from 1654 to 1657; he acted as an assistant to the commissioners for approving parish ministers in Oxfordshire in 1654.

In April 1652 a visitation of the university was held, but was terminated before completion on the orders of the Rump. Howell, by now a fellow of Magdalen College, was named with John Owen and others to the Independent-dominated visitation which succeeded it. Howell was a friend of Thomas Goodwin, and a supporter of the religious Independency underpinned by the Cromwellian political dispensation. It was with the support of John Owen that Howell was appointed principal of Jesus College in 1657 in preference to Seth Ward, a more conservative figure backed by the deposed former principal Francis Mansell and, according to Wood, a majority of the fellows. Howell had to live beside two deposed principals, Mansell and his intruded successor, Jonathan Roberts, both of whom remained resident at the college. He is reported to have brought order to the college's finances.

On 1 August 1660 Mansell was restored by the commissioners to his position as principal of Jesus College. Howell remained in residence for some months but then moved to London. His days of privilege and prominence were over. In the capital he became co-pastor with John Collins of an Independent church which met in Paved Alley, Lime Street, and also acted as a lecturer at Pinner's Hall, establishing a reputation as 'a man mighty in the scriptures' (Calamy, *Abridgement*, 2.838). He died, unmarried, at Bethnal Green on 10 March 1680 and was buried at Artillery Yard, Bunhill Fields, in the City of London.

STEPHEN WRIGHT

Sources B. Worden, 'Cromwellian Oxford', *Hist. U. Oxf. 4: 17th-cent. Oxf.*, 733–72 · *Calamy rev.* · E. Calamy, ed., *An abridgement of Mr. Baxter's history of his life and times, with an account of the ministers, &c., who were ejected after the Restauration of King Charles II*, 2nd edn, 2 vols. (1713) · Wood, *Ath. Oxon.: Fasti* (1820), 111

Howell, George (1833–1910), politician and writer, was born on 5 October 1833 in Wrington, Somerset, the eldest of the eight children of Edwin John Howell (1809–1868) and Mary Welsh (1806–1891). He had four brothers and three sisters. Edwin Howell, a mason like his father before him, became a self-employed subcontractor for railway bridges and waterworks in Somerset and Monmouthshire. Financial reversals and a ruinous lawsuit against a defaulting contractor reduced the family to penury, so that George Howell's formal education was sporadic and rudimentary, ending before he was twelve. At eight he began working as a ploughboy, later assisting his father as a mortar boy. In 1847 he was apprenticed to a Wrington shoemaker. Largely self-taught, he was to become a voracious reader, notably of religious tracts and radical periodicals. After enrolling in a local Chartist group in 1848, he underwent conversion to Wesleyan Methodism and taught at Sunday school.

When his apprenticeship ended in 1851, Howell moved first to Weston-super-Mare and then to Bristol, where he was employed as a shoemaker and participated in a Methodist improvement society and the local YMCA. Once his parents moved to Bristol in 1853, Howell was prevailed upon to return to the building trade, although as a bricklayer rather than a mason. Arriving in London in 1855, he found it difficult at first to obtain journeyman's wages, but by 1859 he had risen to deputy foreman. His early piety was tempered by an emerging political consciousness spurred by acquaintance with former Chartists and political exiles, including Mazzini, Kossuth, and Marx. In 1856 Howell married Dorcas Taviner (1834–1897), the daughter of a Wiltshire farmer. She died an alcoholic. Their only son, George Washington Taviner Howell, born in 1859, died at the age of twenty-one.

The nine-hours dispute in the building trades from 1859 to 1862, a watershed in Victorian labour history, prompted Howell to join the London order of the Operative Bricklayers' Society and brought him into contact with

George Howell (1833–1910), by James Russell & Sons, 1887

the dominant London trade unionists: William Allan, Robert Applegarth, Edwin Coulson, George Odger, and George Potter. A member of the bricklayers' strike committee, Howell helped to reorganize his own union on amalgamated principles and launched the *Operative Bricklayers' Society Trade Circular* in 1861. His increasing prominence threatened Coulson's domination of the union, and his endorsement of greater working-class political involvement clashed with his rival's focus on industrial issues. He failed to displace Coulson from the secretaryship, and his systematic effort to undermine Coulson's authority widened a breach which led to Howell's eventual resignation from the London order. His involvement in the strike committee also prompted London builders to blacklist him, necessitating a removal to Surrey from 1862 until 1864, when he returned as a foreman with a former employer, a position he retained until he abandoned bricklaying for radical politics in 1865.

Elected to the executive of the London Trades Council in May 1861, Howell was promptly named as secretary, serving in that capacity until July 1862 when ill health and Coulson's enmity forced him to resign. It was his duty as secretary to respond to the fraternal greetings of the General Neapolitan Society of Working Men and to affirm the solidarity of the London Trades Council with Italian nationalists. During his absence from London he remained politically active and was instrumental in establishing the trade unionists' Manhood Suffrage and Vote by Ballot Association. He spoke at the St James's Hall meeting on 26 March 1863 in support of the Unionist cause in the American Civil War and was a member of the National

League for the Independence of Poland in 1863, the Garibaldi Reception Committee in 1864, and the International Working Men's Association from 1864 to 1869. These activities, fostering links between politically ambitious London working men and middle-class reformers, prepared the way for Howell to become secretary of the Reform League from 1865 to 1869. The league was the first national organization to mobilize urban artisans for franchise reform since the Chartist campaign a generation earlier. As its only full-time, salaried functionary, Howell was responsible for keeping financial records, corresponding with branches, fund-raising, organizing deputations and demonstrations, and starting new branches around the country. While the league did not determine the content or progress of the second Reform Bill, it did foment orderly agitation and curtail the disruptive potential of the working-class movement. After the suffrage was extended in 1867, Howell tied the Reform League more closely to the Liberal Party in order to secure those reforms, such as the ballot and trade union legalization, awaiting parliamentary action. During the 1868 general election he administered a special fund to mobilize new working-class voters on behalf of Liberal candidates in marginal constituencies. His management of the fund, little of which subsidized working-class candidacies, evoked criticism from more radical contemporaries and some later historians, who regarded him as unprincipled and opportunist.

Howell's administrative expertise and familiarity with Liberal politicians generated career opportunities, none of which, however, brought him the financial rewards he might have anticipated. In 1869 he launched an abortive Liberal Registration and Election Agency with funds provided mainly by Samuel Morley and James Stansfeld. He was closely involved with the futile effort of the Labour Representation League to devise an arrangement whereby Liberals would endorse working-class candidates in selected boroughs in return for league support for official Liberals elsewhere. Between 1868 and 1874 Walter Morrison hired him as paid secretary of the Representative Reform Association, which advocated proportional representation; he was also paid secretary of the Plimsoll and Seamen's Fund Committee from 1873 to 1875 and financial agent for the Land Tenure Reform Association. In addition he chaired the Working Men's Committee for Promoting the Separation of Church and State and served on the councils of both the National Education League and the Liberation Society. In 1870–71 Howell launched the Adelphi Permanent Building Society to provide money to enable workers to purchase homes, but he lacked sufficient business acumen and capital to make the venture profitable.

Howell, who retained close links with the London union leaders known as the junta, attended the Birmingham trades union congress in 1869 as unofficial representative of the Conference of Amalgamated Trades. In 1871 he emerged as secretary of the parliamentary committee of the TUC and used his office to promote the repeal of the Master and Servant Act and the Criminal Law Amendment Act of 1871. Despite widespread disapproval of his penchant for private lobbying and his readiness to make concessions, Howell personified the parliamentary committee and guided the TUC during his five-year stint as secretary. Pragmatic and cautious, he repudiated militant tactics, his accommodating methods reflecting a conviction that compromise was the only way to elicit support from influential politicians.

After retiring from the TUC, Howell never again attained his former eminence in radical and trade union politics. He had become a labour statesman whose participation was welcomed but whose influence was limited. Lacking opportunities to achieve middle-class status, he remained rooted in the world of labour. He served successively as secretary of London school board election committees and as parliamentary agent of the Women's Suffrage Committee but failed to obtain an appointment as a school or factory inspector. Unable to secure regular employment, he turned increasingly to writing as a source of income, contributing to the labour journal the *Bee-Hive* in the 1870s and publishing *A Handy Book of the Labour Laws*, a guide to recent legislation, in 1876. The favourable response to its publication encouraged him to write an interpretive study of trade unionism, *The Conflicts of Capital and Labour* (1878). He also served as London business agent for a Manchester coal merchant and, in 1881, briefly edited the labour weekly *Common Good*.

The Liberal Party was slow to recognize Howell's loyalty, and he made a series of unsuccessful attempts to enter parliament. In Aylesbury in 1868, hampered by lack of funds, he finished third in the poll. In 1871 Liberal officials persuaded him to withdraw during a Norwich by-election rather than risk splitting the Liberal vote. In 1874 he again came in third in Aylesbury, despite financial support from prominent Liberals like Samuel Morley. He contested Stafford as the official Liberal upon the death of trade unionist MP Alexander MacDonald in 1881 but lost in a straight fight with the tory candidate. In 1885 he was finally elected for the new constituency of North-East Bethnal Green and held the seat until 1895, when he was defeated by the Indian politician M. M. Bhownaggree. A typical 'Lib–Lab' MP, he advocated legislation to improve seamen's conditions and sponsored a bill to exempt trade union provident funds from income tax but refrained from assuming an independent role as a labour spokesman.

While in parliament Howell continued to rely on journalism for his livelihood, although he was also briefly employed by the National Home Reading Union. His controversial *Trade Unionism New and Old* (1891) extolled amalgamated craft union policies and criticized the socialist agenda of the more militant new unionists. After 1895 he withdrew entirely from political life, devoting himself to writing. His biography of Ernest Jones, serialized in the *Newcastle Weekly Chronicle* in 1898, never appeared in book form. His final work, *Labour Legislation, Labour Movements and Labour Leaders* (1902), traced the progress of the working classes in the nineteenth century with particular emphasis on the events and leaders with whom he had been involved. In 1897 Robert Applegarth organized a testimonial fund of £1650 to provide Howell with an annuity. In 1904, after he was stricken with partial blindness, another public subscription was devised to purchase his library, including the papers of the Reform League, which was presented to the Bishopsgate Institute in London. In July 1906 he was granted a civil-list pension of £50 per annum.

Howell's contribution to the Victorian labour movement was primarily as an administrator and professional bureaucrat rather than as a popular leader. His success in working-class politics turned him into an organizational entrepreneur who used pressure group activity as the means to his own career advancement. Deferential to middle-class politicians, he was none the less an articulate exponent of working-class interests as he perceived them. He sought piecemeal reforms through conciliation and in alliance with the more enlightened political leaders. Discovering in the principles of Gladstonian Liberalism a reflection of his own values, he never outgrew the cautious radicalism of his early years and opposed the creation of an independent Labour Party. His personal quest for respectability was only partially realized since financial security and public recognition continued to elude him. In his last years he was discredited as an anachronism, an apologist for Liberalism whose reputation never revived. Apart from two years in Surrey, Howell lived in London from 1855 to 1910, mainly in Kennington and in Shepherd's Bush, where he died (of Bright's disease and cardiac failure) on 16 September 1910. His burial at Nunhead cemetery was attended by prominent trade unionists and Labour leaders.   F. M. LEVENTHAL

James Howell (1594?–1666), by Claude Mellan and Abraham Bosse, pubd 1641

Sources F. M. Leventhal, *Respectable radical: George Howell and Victorian working class politics* (1971) · R. Harrison, *Before the socialists: studies in labour and politics, 1861–1881* (1965) · G. Howell, *Labour legislation, labour movements and labour leaders* (1902) · A. Watson, 'George Howell', *The Millgate Monthly*, 3 (1908), 665–71 · E. F. Biagini, *Liberty, retrenchment and reform: popular liberalism in the age of Gladstone, 1860–1880* (1992) · W. J. Davis, *The British Trades Union Congress* (1910) · A. D. Bell, 'Administration and finance of the Reform League, 1865–67', *International Review of Social History*, 10 (1965), 385–409 · d. cert. · memoir

Archives Bishopsgate Institute, London, corresp., diaries, papers · Labour History Archive and Study Centre, Manchester, corresp. and papers | Co-operative Union, Holyoake House, Manchester, Co-operative Union archive, letters to George Jacob Holyoake

Likenesses J. Russell & Sons, photograph, 1887, NPG [*see illus.*] · G. A. Holmes, oils, Bishopsgate Institute, London · Mrs H. White, oils, Bishopsgate Institute, London

Wealth at death £210 8s. 10d.: probate, 28 Sept 1910, *CGPLA Eng. & Wales*

Howell, Gillian Margaret (1927–2000). *See under* Howell, William Gough (1922–1974).

Howell, James (1594?–1666), historian and political writer, was born at Llangamarch, Brecknockshire, the second son and fourth child of Thomas Howell (*d.* 1632) and his wife, who was a daughter of James David Powell of Buallt. Howell claimed to have fourteen siblings but the pedigree in BL, MS Harl. 4181, p. 258 lists only three sisters and three

brothers, who include Thomas *Howell, bishop of Bristol. The pedigree traces the family back to Tudwal Glôff (*fl.* 878), son of Rhodri the Great. Howell's father was curate of Llangamarch and later rector of Cynwyl and Aber-nant, Carmarthenshire, until his death in 1632. Although Howell's admiration of his clerical father emerges from a letter to the bishop of St David's, Theophilus Field, in 1632 his relations with his more successful brother were not close. Howell may have been aware that Thomas had been obliged to apologize to Sir Francis Windebank on behalf of his over-eager younger brother for James's having 'lately broken in upon you, soe farre beyond the bounds of common modesty' (*CSP dom.*, 1635–6, 204, 2 Feb 1636; Howell, 655).

Education and early career Howell matriculated on 16 June 1610, as James Howells of Carmarthenshire, at Jesus College, Oxford, the college of choice for Welshmen. There he was tutored by Francis Mansell and also attracted the attention of Sir Eubule Thelwall. A loyalty to Oxford emerges from his later writings, suggesting that his university experience was a happy one. After taking his BA in 1613 Howell initially found employment through Sir Robert Mansell, uncle of his former tutor and steward of a glass factory in Broad Street, London. In 1616 the owners of the factory sent Howell abroad in search of materials and of workmen under a warrant for three years' travel issued by the privy council. The first part of his widely read *Epistolae Ho-elianae: Familiar Letters* (a series of epistolary volumes assembled and mainly written while Howell was imprisoned in the Fleet during the 1640s) offers a retrospective account of his travels together with his opinions on the peoples and places he encountered along the way. During this period he appears to have become a proficient linguist, and this too would bear fruit in some of his later writings, for instance in his suggestion that English orthography be reformed along phonetic lines in order to eliminate superfluous letters such as the 'u' in 'colour' (Howell, 510).

On returning to England in 1622 Howell gave up his position in the glass factory. After an unsuccessful suit to join Sir John Ayres's embassy to Constantinople he briefly found employment as tutor to the sons of Lord Savage, a Catholic. Later the same year he returned to France with another young charge, Richard Altham (son of Baron Altham), of whom he spoke fondly (Howell, 109). Having made himself ill by overstudiousness while on this foray abroad Howell was attended on his return to London by Dr William Harvey. At the end of the year he was sent on a mission to Spain and Sardinia to negotiate the release of an impounded English vessel. Howell remained in Madrid in 1623–4 during the negotiations over the Spanish match, and it was on this expedition that he initiated a connection with John Digby, earl of Bristol, which would continue into the next decade (Howell to Bristol, 23 April 1630, BL, Add. MS 5947, fol. 155) and, more significantly, with Sir Kenelm Digby, who arrived in Madrid in 1623. Howell and Kenelm Digby shared an interest in natural philosophy and medicine; Digby eventually claimed Howell as one of the first beneficiaries of his 'sympathetic powder', which he applied to a wound Howell had received on his hand while intervening in a duel (Digby, 6–10). On returning to England in 1624 Howell sought preferment from the duke of Buckingham but was denied, mainly because of his connection with the Digbys (Howell, 239). A suggestion that he go back to Italy as an agent to Charles I failed to materialize because Howell apparently set the price for his services too high. He was however recognized by the court as a useful informer (Howell to Edward Conway, January 1626, PRO, SP 16/19/100).

The late 1620s saw Howell attached to a series of noble masters. As secretary to Emanuel, Lord Scrope, later earl of Sunderland, who was president of the council of the north, Howell resided in York. He was elected to the parliament of 1628 as member for Richmond, Yorkshire. Howell remained with Scrope after his replacement as president by Sir Thomas Wentworth, who promised Howell the reversion to the next attorney's place at York. Howell, who disliked provincial life, elected to sell this just as a place came open, in 1629 (Howell, 106, 373, 443); he nevertheless appreciated Wentworth's gesture. Regret over the future earl of Strafford's fate at the hands of the Long Parliament emerges from one of his wartime political works, *Dodona's Grove* (pt 2, 1650).

Sunderland died in 1630 and little is heard of Howell until shortly before his own father's death in 1632. In that year he went abroad once more, this time accompanying Robert Sidney, earl of Leicester, on an embassy to Denmark, for which Howell arranged the travel plans (Howell, 650; *CSP dom.*, 1631–3, 382, 390, 409, 412). He kept a brief Latin 'diarium' of the journey (Bodl. Oxf., MS Rawl. C. 354, fols. 1–43). On his return to London with Leicester in March 1633 Howell spent his time in the company of literary figures such as Ben Jonson, while corresponding with others such as Edward, Lord Herbert of Cherbury. When Jonson died in 1637 Howell sent an elegy to Brian Duppa, who included it in his tribute to the poet, *Jonsonus virbius*.

Once again pursuing royal employment Howell proposed the establishment of an office for the registration of foreigners living in England, who were to be reported by churchwardens to a 'consul'; this was clearly another attempt to create a position for himself (Bodl. Oxf., MS Bankes 6, fols. 57–8, 65–6, undated proposals). Howell also travelled anew at this time (he went to Orléans for a few weeks in 1635) and wrote news letters to crown officials, such as Sir Francis Windebank and Wentworth, now lord deputy in Ireland. Howell visited Wentworth in Dublin in 1639, just before the latter's return to England as earl of Strafford. It was probably through Strafford's patronage that Howell received a reversion to a clerkship of the council (PRO, SP 16/245/33; Howell, 656–7). On being sworn in to the clerkship at Nottingham in 1642, however, he discovered that the place vacated by Sir Edward Nicholas had in fact been filled by Sir John Jacob. Howell was offered the next vacancy but the immediate advent of the civil war rendered this an empty promise (Howell, 657, 667).

Early writings and moral outlook In the face of further disappointment Howell began his literary career in earnest in 1640 with the political allegory *Dendrologia: Dodona's Grove, or, The Vocall Forest*, an account of events since 1603; on travelling to France in that year he took with him his own French translation of the book, which was published at Paris. On 1 January 1642 he presented the king with a printed poem, *The Vote*, as a new year's gift. This was followed soon after by publication of Howell's *Instructions for Forreine Travel* (1642), dedicated to Prince Charles; containing useful information on France, Spain, and Italy, this would be reissued in 1650 with additions pertaining to the Levant and Turkey. Most of his writings over the next few years, however, fall into two different categories: the several editions of *Familiar Letters* published in the 1640s and 1650s but also a number of political tracts in which he attempted to steer a safe course between royalist and parliamentarian alternatives.

Howell was a voracious if undiscriminating reader who drew material for his letters and other writings from authors as various as Aristotle and Suarez, Machiavelli and Giovanni Botero. He eschewed deep learning, preferring to make 'useful application of it in common discourse' (Howell, 413, 526). A great deal of what Howell says concerning human nature and politics derives from an outlook first formulated by the later Roman stoics (especially Epictetus, Seneca, and Marcus Aurelius) and adapted to post-Tridentine Christianity by the great Flemish scholar Justus Lipsius amid the religious warfare of the later sixteenth century. Howell's circle of friends included several stoically minded individuals such as Digby and Jonson. Howell was well acquainted with two ancient stoic texts, the writings of the emperor Marcus Aurelius and the *Noctes Atticae* of Aulus Gellius.

In *Familiar Letters* Howell adopts a stance of Christian resignation towards his own fate and towards the apparent madness that had beset England. Both there and in *The Vision*, a short dialogue between Soul and Body (probably written in the late 1640s and published in the winter of 1651–2), Howell suggests that the task of the virtuous citizen is to harness the passions that arise from bodily humours and turn them to good use. 'As long as there are men, there must be malignant humours, there must be vices, and vicissitudes of things', he commented in one letter. 'As long as the world wheels round, there must be tossings and tumblings, distractions and troubles, and bad times must be recompens'd with better' (Howell, 354).

Much of Howell's wartime writing had been concerned with political issues such as the proper relation of king to parliament. Yet he was no secularist, and he saw the civil war as fundamentally a religious struggle which had generated secondary political and constitutional issues, rather than the other way around. He aimed his sharpest prose darts at sectaries and Presbyterians rather than at lawyers and members of parliament. Writing to the moderate churchman Daniel Featley in 1644 he expressed the view that 'These times (more's the pity) labour with the same disease that France did during the League'. This made it all the worse for England since, in Howell's view, strife over religion was at once the most foolish and the most terrible form of human conflict. As he wrote near the end of the war:

> Difference in opinion, no more than a differing complexion, can be cause enough for me to hate any. A differing fancy is no more to one than a differing face … If I have a fair opinion, tho' another have a hard-favour'd one, yet it shall not break that common league of humanity which should be betwixt rational creatures, provided he corresponds with me in the general offices of morality and civil uprightness. (Howell, 553)

Although priding himself on loyalty to friends and allies Howell was dogged throughout the second half of his life by accusations of time-serving and lukewarmness, which produced frequent apologies and defences; a letter to the king, dated 3 September 1644, expresses Howell's concern that 'among divers things which go abroad under my name reflecting upon the times there are some which are not so well taken; your Majesty being inform'd that they discover a spirit of indifferency, and lukewarmness in the author' (Howell, 488–9). The charge of faint loyalty was all the more irritating since Howell saw himself as a martyr to the royalist cause. On a visit to London early in 1643 he was arrested in his chambers, his books were seized, and he was imprisoned in the Fleet. There he remained for eight years, on his account purely for his allegiance to the king, but more likely because of the insolvency to which he confesses in *Familiar Letters*. He hoped to 'o'ercome all these pressures, survive my debts, and surmount my

enemies' but despite modest literary success his failure to obtain the clerkship, and the fall of former allies like Windebank and Strafford, had left him close to ruin. It was this period of confinement that forced Howell into an intense period of writing, for both financial and political reasons. The works that he published over the next seven years, and in particular the early editions of *Familiar Letters*, were calculated to earn some income but also to explain his peculiar version of moderate, pacifist royalism (Howell, 355, 367, 369, 374; J. Howell, 'Upon himself, having bin buried alive for many years in the prison of the Fleet, by the state or Long Parliament for his loyalty', in *Poems upon Divers Emergent Occasions*, 1664, 62; *CSP dom.*, 1660–61, 12).

Almost immediately after his imprisonment Howell was forced into a defence of parliamentary privilege in order to deflect William Prynne's charge that he was 'no friend to Parliaments, but a malignant' (Prynne, 42). Prynne based his objections on a few mildly anti-parliamentary remarks Howell had made in *Dodona's Grove* in 1640. In 1644 Howell issued from the Fleet a series of tracts intended to present a carefully worded, moderate position and at the same time to urge a general return to reason. Among them *England's Teares* consists of a series of laments from England to the City of London, in which are elaborated the very themes of conscience and loyalty that he would work out more abstractly in *The Vision* a few years later.

In *The Preheminence and Pedigree of Parlement* (1644) Howell endeavoured to fend off the charge that he was a malignant by showing himself respectful of parliamentary traditions and privileges. In substance and style this work is reminiscent of earlier writings by John Selden and Sir Robert Cotton, both of whose works Howell would eventually edit. In an undated manuscript letter to John Selden, Howell sent several of his works to the great lawyer, praising the latter's 'universality of knowledge' (BL, MS Harl. 7003, fol. 374; *Cottoni Posthuma: Divers Choice Pieces of that Renowned Antiquary Sir Robert Cotton*, ed. J. Howell, 1651). Howell's defence of parliamentary and especially aristocratic privilege was influenced by Selden's *Priviledges of the Baronage of England* (1642), and he would later publish an English edition of Selden's *Mare clausum*. In the *Preheminence* Howell assumes the perspective of the parliamentarian, and ascribes most of what is good in English law, including Magna Carta, to the influence of parliament. He avers that it is the great strength of England and her monarchy that she maintains such an institution, in contrast to other realms; it is parliament that makes the king rule over free men, not slaves, and through which he may remedy their grievances. No one who loves England can be antagonistic to parliament's role as a legislature.

Howell's two-part dialogue entitled *Casuall Discourses, and Interlocutions betwixt Patricius and Peregrin* was largely concerned with the events of 1641–2. A complete version of this tract, revised by Howell in the late 1650s, would not appear until 1661, when it was reprinted, complete with a 1642 imprint, in a collection of his works entitled *Twelve Severall Treatises*. As Patricius notes, the very discourse in which he and his friend are engaged 'was stopp'd in the press by the tyranny of the times, and not suffer'd to see open light till now' (J. Howell, 'Casuall discourses', in *Twelve Severall Treatises*, 1661, 119). Peregrine, a traveller, asks Patricius, a nobleman, to explain the causes of current distempers. Patricius replies that just as there appear from time to time storm clouds to disrupt the weather and monsters to violate nature, so even within the most well-balanced kingdom there are those with rotten hearts. This number embraces the English Presbyterians who stirred up the London populace, and the barbarous Irish rebels. It also includes the preachers who incited rebellion in Scotland where 'the woman [sic] and baser sort of mechaniks threw stooles and stones at the bishops heads' when the liturgy was read; dislike of the Scots as quixotic trouble-makers is a recurring theme of Howell's work. Perhaps conscious of his own equivocation on matters of principle he preferred ties of personal loyalty, expressing a profound distaste for persons who betrayed their friends and benefactors. In a letter allegedly written in 1644 and first published four years later, to his remote kinsman Philip, earl of Pembroke, Howell chided the former lord chamberlain for putting personal conviction ahead of his oaths to the king.

By the time Howell's letter to Pembroke appeared in print the first civil war had been fought and the country was settling in for two tense years of tortuous negotiation and diplomacy between king, army, parliament, and the Scots. Howell had once cited approvingly the proverb that 'the spectator oft-times sees more than the gamester'; a prisoner still, he played upon his non-involvement in the war in order to encourage all parties to come to terms. In a short pamphlet entitled *Down-Right Dealing, or, The Despised Protestant Speaking Plain English*, he continued to present himself as an impartial observer of events rather than a partisan. The central theme of this tract was that the war had done little to resolve the tensions of 1642; Howell's intent was not to nurture further faction or discontent but to appeal to King Charles to come to terms with his enemies, and to the parliamentarians and army leaders to surrender fine points of religious conviction in the interests of a lasting settlement.

Howell's career during the interregnum Such pacifism was, of course, unsuccessful. It is evident from works first published anonymously in 1648 and 1649, and later reprinted by Howell, that he regarded the imprisonment, trial, and execution of the king as acts of an arbitrary and tyrannical government, driven by a base mob. Although no evidence survives that he actively sought employment by the Rump regime, neither did he refuse it. He participated, probably as an interpreter, in a case against the Spanish ambassador brought to the council of state in 1649 (*CSP dom.*, 1649–50, 178, 9 June 1649); two years later he translated, at the council's prompting, Agustín de Hierro's Spanish account of the trial of the assassins of the republic's ambassador Anthony Ascham (1651). It is likely that Howell took the engagement (the prerequisite for any state employment). He reiterated his loyalty to the

Long Parliament in the second part of *Dodona's Grove* (1650), a work that described the opening months of that body and included the attainder of Rhodophil (his allegorical figure for Strafford), and declared himself bound to submit to parliamentary authority in church or state.

Released on bail from the Fleet some time in 1650 and adjusting to the prospect of life in a republic Howell dedicated to the Rump his 1651 survey of the history and government of Venice. Ostensibly a plea to all Christian nations to come to Venice's aid in her hour of need, it is difficult to see this as anything other than an attempt to impress the 'most noble senators' of England, the Rump MPs, by drawing parallels between the two republics. 'England hath reson to affect Venice more than any other, for in point of security ther is much resemblance between them, being both seated in the sea, who is their best protector' (J. Howell, *S.P.Q.V: a Survay of the Signorie of Venice, of her Admired Policy and Method of Government*, 1651, sig. B1r). The book casts further light on Howell's belief that a reassertion of aristocratic influence, of the kind that characterized Venetian government, would be necessary in the new Commonwealth if its descent into the chaos of a popular state was to be arrested.

Although no remuneration from the government was forthcoming Howell wrote to the council of state at some point after the start of the First Anglo-Dutch War in 1652, proposing that in view of the devolution of government from monarchy to republic he should update Selden's 1635 treatise *Mare clausum* in order to sustain the claims Selden had advanced for England's dominion over the near seas. In that year there appeared an English translation of Selden by Marchamont Nedham under the title *Of the Dominion, or Ownership of the Sea, Two Books*. This was published by William Dugard by appointment of the council of state, which suggests that Howell had simply put his bid in too late. Not to be outdone he would eventually reissue Nedham's translation in 1663 under the title *Mare clausum: the Right and Dominion of the Sea, in Two Books*. Having been robbed of this opportunity by a man whom he regarded as the lowest form of turncoat, Howell had the satisfaction of replacing Nedham's anti-Stuart preface with Selden's original dedication to Charles I, along with an advertisement by himself denouncing Nedham as 'one no way affected to our ancient and happy government of monarchy, who was also an immediate servant to our usurping states'; he cleverly defended the faithfulness of the Nedham translation (and thus escaped the labour of correcting it) on the grounds that in 1652 Selden had still been alive and Nedham would not have had the nerve to 'abuse his writings to his face' (BL, Add. MS 32093, fol. 370; Howell, 661).

Most of Howell's writing following his release from prison in 1650 or 1651 was literary rather than political. His publications over the next few years included *Londinopolis* (1657), an account of the city's history and major sites of interest; various books on grammar, orthography, and proverbs; numerous translations from French and Italian; and his *Lexicon tetraglotton* (1660), a dictionary in four languages. The publication of this work was supported by Bulstrode Whitelocke, a frequent correspondent and reader of Howell's works from 1654 until the Restoration (*Diary of Bulstrode Whitelocke*, 50).

The dispersal of the Rump and the advent of the protectorate required both further comment and still another reversal of direction on Howell's part, this time towards a limited hereditary monarchy. In 1654 he completed a partial edition of the notebooks of Sir John Finet, Charles I's master of the ceremonies, a book which he would publish two years later as further encouragement to Cromwell in the establishment of a quasi-monarchical court. He also reprinted, under the title *Some of Mr Howell's Minor Works* (1654), several tracts previously issued anonymously in 1648–9, including *The Instruments of a King*, which dealt with the nature of royal sovereignty. A year later, in 1655, Howell dedicated to Cromwell *Som Sober Inspections Made into the Cariage and Consults of the Late Long Parlement*, a devastating attack on the regime that he had applauded three years earlier and on its failure to contain the thirst for novelty rampant among the 'mechanick' populace. Despite Cromwell's prominent role in the execution of the king Howell flatters him as a champion of liberty and property and as an opponent of the tyranny of a perpetual parliament. Sir William Dugdale gleefully recommended that a friend read Howell's newly published work:

> wherein, cogging up [the] protector (for to him he dedicates it) with some superlative language for destroying that monster (as he calls it) [he] hath taken the boldness to speak more truth, barefaced, than any man that hath wrote since they sate; nor doth he spare the Scot and Presbyterian. (*Fifth Report*, HMC, 176)

Howell placed his faith in the protector because he had now lost confidence in the ability of the peerage to restore order. His sense of the aristocracy's eclipse is conveyed in verses, also published in 1654, which Howell penned to commemorate the death of his friend Edward Sackville, earl of Dorset, who had died two years previously (*Ah, Ha; Tumulus, Thalamus: Two Counter-Poems*, 1653).

The death of Cromwell, on 3 September 1658, and the return of the Rump the following May provided a further reminder of the lack of constitutional stability. With many minds already running towards the return of the old regime Howell issued one final political plea, entitled *A brief admonition of some of the inconveniences of all the three most famous governments known to the world: with their comparisons together* (1659). Once more Howell presented himself as a moderate, appealing to common sense, compromise, and charity rather than to rigid principles and partisanship.

Final years With the return of the king Howell, now in his mid-sixties, tried again to achieve the rewards of office that had eluded him for nearly four decades. One by one he made a series of proposals for his employment, each of which was in turn denied: that he assume the long-promised clerkship of the council; that he be appointed secretary to the commission for the regulation of trade; and that he become tutor, by virtue of his linguistic skills, to the queen, Catherine of Braganza (*CSP dom.*, 1660–61, 12,

288; *1661–2*, 37). Howell was not the only former royalist to have such requests rebuffed. Within a year of the Restoration many of Charles II's most faithful adherents were to be bitterly disappointed by their failure to achieve the rewards of loyalty. Many had lost estates and other personal property, suffered exile or imprisonment, and now sought recompense if not advancement. Against this they saw former roundheads being favoured, an indemnity being offered to virtually every subject other than regicides and certain other excepted persons, and former grandees like Monck—belated converts to royalism—growing rich. Howell attempted to address this issue in *A Cordial for the Cavaliers*, published by Henry Marsh in the summer of 1661. The dedication is dated 20 July 1661, only a few days after Howell's futile application to Clarendon (11 July) for the position of tutor to the queen (*CSP dom.*, 1661–2, 37). Addressing himself to the 'worthy and deserving gentlemen' who felt themselves aggrieved by their lack of royal reward Howell urges the cavaliers to be patient, citing his own case as an example of loyalism made its own reward. At least one former cavalier, Sir Roger L'Estrange, was quick to respond to the *Cordial*, in *A caveat to the cavaliers, or, An antidote against mistaken cordials: dedicated to the author of 'A cordial for the cavaliers'* (1661), wherein the future surveyor of the press accused Howell of collaboration first with the Rump and then with Cromwell. As he had done nearly two decades earlier with Prynne, but from an ironically opposite perspective, Howell was once more obliged to defend his own perceived lack of principles, in *Som sober inspections made into those ingredients that went to the composition of a late cordial … for the satisfaction of som, who misapprehended the author* (1661). When L'Estrange replied with *A Modest Plea both for the Caveat, and the Author of It*, further ridiculing Howell's interregnum activities, the author prudently declined to contribute further to the controversy.

It was probably only after this exchange had begun that Howell finally achieved his reward. Clarendon doubtless recognized Howell's potential as a polemicist on behalf of national reconciliation, and Howell also had other old friends at court, such as Secretary Sir Edward Nicholas and Sir Philip Warwick. Consequently Howell was offered a gift of £200 and the position of historiographer royal, which (once again) Howell himself had proposed be created, at a stipend of £100 per year. Other European courts had appointed such officers since the Renaissance but the position was new to England. Howell produced very little in the five years that remained of his life beyond reprints of his earlier tracts and some further tracts on behalf of the government. These included an unprinted work defending the retention of Cromwellian colonial conquests such as Jamaica and Dunkirk, and, when royal policy changed in 1662 and Dunkirk was sold back to the French, another short work in defence of that sale, later revised and published as *A Discours of Dunkirk* (1664). Once more Howell's remarkable ability to contradict his earlier opinions at short notice stood him in good stead. In 1664 he published the *Proedria Basilikē: a discourse concerning the precedency of kings*, engraved with portraits of Charles II and the author, a tract arguing that the English monarchy had as long a claim to antiquity and authority as other European monarchies.

Howell's last non-political work, *Poems on Severall Choice and Various Subjects*, was edited by Payne Fisher in 1663 and reissued under a different title the following year. Howell died in the parish of St Andrew's, Holborn, and was buried on 3 November 1666 outside the Temple Church. A monument of Howell's design was erected in the Temple Church at a cost of £30. In his will, dated 8 October 1666 and proved 18 February 1667, he left small bequests to his brother Howell Howell, his surviving sisters 'Gwin' and 'Roberta-ap-Rice', and to his landlady. He also left small amounts to three children of his brother Thomas. Another nephew, Henry Howell, was appointed his executor.

Howell has not had a modern biographer but his many works in verse and prose were the fruit of a significant literary life stretching from the end of England's Renaissance to the very different age ushered in with the Restoration. Howell's career and thought have never been fully appreciated. While most of his political works lacked the depth of learning or acuity of intellect of the treatises of major contemporary thinkers such as Selden or Hobbes they are significant statements of the moderate royalist position throughout the 1640s and 1650s. In religious and political terms Howell's fellows were the likes of the earl of Dorset, the minister and future historian Clarendon, and, on the other side, Selden himself. His linguistic abilities were not limited to foreign tongues but can be seen in miscellaneous books such as his edition of English proverbs *Paroimiographia* (1659). There is no question, however, that his greatest literary achievement lies in *Familiar Letters*. These have been praised by admirers from Anthony Wood, who thought Howell had 'a singular command of his pen whether in verse or in prose', to Thomas Warton a century later, and to Thackeray, who made *Familiar Letters*, together with Montaigne's *Essais*, his bedside book. Many observers, from Wood himself to the Victorian historian S. R. Gardiner, have pointed out the chronological inaccuracies in the letters, and scholars have been wise not to rely on them as evidence for the dates of events. While many of them may have been based on earlier letters that Howell either recalled from memory or had at hand in the Fleet, most were very likely invented by him during his confinement. Since the convention of familiar letter-writing in print was well established, however, it would be wrong to presume that Howell wished to fool his readers. The letters themselves contain so many very obvious chronological and factual clues to their later composition as to suggest that Howell never intended to have them read as genuine correspondence; like so much of his writing they represent a concerted attempt to fashion a public self and to support himself in so doing, making him one of the earliest English writers to have earned his living almost solely from the proceeds of his pen.

D. R. WOOLF

Sources D. R. Woolf, 'Conscience, constancy and ambition in the career and writings of James Howell', *Public duty and private conscience in seventeenth-century England*, ed. J. Morrill, P. Slack, and D. Woolf (1993), 243–78 · G. F. Warner, 'Two letters of James Howell', *EngHR*, 9 (1894), 127–30 · K. Digby, *A late discourse made in a solemn assembly of nobles and learned men at Montpellier in France* (1658) · Wood, *Ath. Oxon.*, new edn · J. Howell, *Epistolae Ho-elianae*, ed. J. Jacobs, 2 vols. (1890–92) · G. E. B. Eyre, ed., *A transcript of the registers of the Worshipful Company of Stationers from 1640 to 1708*, 3 vols. (1913–14) · G. Coleridge, 'The letters of James Howell', *Contemporary Review*, 172 (1947), 368–71 · *DNB* · undated proposals for registry of foreigners, Bodl. Oxf., MS Bankes 6, fols. 57–8, 65–6 · D. Hay, 'The historiographers royal in England and Scotland', *SHR*, 30 (1951), 15–29 · R. L'Estrange, *A caveat to the cavaliers* (1661) · W. Prynne, *The popish royall favourite* (1643) · W. H. Vann, *Notes on the writings of James Howell* (1924) · J. Reilly, 'A Jacobean chatterbox', in J. Reilly, *Of books and men* (1942), 237–44 · V. M. Hirst, 'The authenticity of James Howell's *Familiar letters*', *Modern Language Review*, 54 (1959), 558–61 · D. L. Smith, *Constitutional royalism and the search for settlement, c. 1640–1649* (1994) · M. Nutkiewicz, 'A rapporteur of the English civil war: the courtly politics of James Howell (1594?–1666)', *Canadian Journal of History*, 25 (1990), 21–40 · *The diary of Bulstrode Whitelocke, 1605–1675*, ed. R. Spalding, British Academy, Records of Social and Economic History, new ser., 13 (1990) · P. Seaward, 'A Restoration publicist: James Howell and the earl of Clarendon', *Historical Research*, 61 (1988), 123–31 · J. W. Stoye, *English travellers abroad, 1604–1667*, rev. edn (1989) · *Fifth report*, HMC, 4 (1876) · Bodl. Oxf., MS Rawl. C. 354, fols. 1–43 [Howell's *diarium*] · Howell to Edward Conway, Jan 1626, PRO, SP 16/19/100 · PRO, SP 16/245/33 · BL, MS Harl. 7003, fol. 374 · BL, Add. MS 32093, fol. 370

Archives Bodl. Oxf., MS Rawl. C. 354 | Bodl. Oxf., MS Bankes 6, fols. 57–8, 65–6

Likenesses C. Mellan and A. Bosse, line engraving, pubd 1641, BM, NPG; repro. in J. Howell, *Dendrologia: Dodona's grove*, French edn [*see illus.*] · W. Marshall, line engraving, BM, NPG; repro. in Howell, *Epistolae Ho-elianae*, ed. Jacobs · engraving, repro. in Howell, *Epistolae Ho-elianae*, ed. Jacobs · engraving, repro. in J. Howell, *Proedria basilikē* (1664)

Wealth at death £67 to various people: will, Howell, *Epistolae Ho-elianae*, ed. Jacobs, 669–70

Howell, John (1670/71–1708), singer, the son of John Howell, was one of the boy choristers of Westminster Abbey at James II's coronation in April 1685 and was a lay vicar in the choir there from 1691. In March 1697 he was appointed to the royal private musick, with livery payments backdated to 1689. He sang in the Chapel Royal choir from August 1691 and also became a vicar-choral at St Paul's Cathedral in 1697. Henry Purcell wrote 'High countertenor for Mr. Howel' (Bodl. Oxf., MS Mus. C. 26) against the upper line of the duet 'Hark each tree' in his 1692 ode for St Cecilia's day. Howell's voice was about a third higher than the generality of Purcell's countertenors, and the composer gave him solos in his 1693 ode for Queen Mary's birthday, in his ode on the birthday of the duke of Gloucester (1695), and almost certainly in his 1694 birthday ode for the queen. Thomas Brown draws a satirical picture of ladies attending St Paul's 'for the sake of the *musick* and *long perukes* … while *H—ll* was a-stretching his lungs in order to maintain a long white wig, and a hackney-coach' (*Works*, 18). On 2 April 1706 at St Bride's, Fleet Street, Howell married a widow, Katherine Ent, probably *née* Bathurst (*b*. 1662). He died on 15 or 16 July 1708 and was buried in the south aisle of St Paul's Cathedral, where his memorial tablet states that he died in his thirty-eighth year. In his will he left £5 each for mourning to his father, his brother William, and his three sisters Bridget, Elizabeth, and Sarah, and the bulk of his estate to his 'deare and loveing Wife Katherine', whom he made his sole executor. OLIVE BALDWIN and THELMA WILSON

Sources A. Ashbee, ed., *Records of English court music*, 2 (1987) · A. Ashbee, ed., *Records of English court music*, 5 (1991) · A. Ashbee and J. Harley, eds., *The cheque books of the Chapel Royal*, 2 vols. (2000) · F. B. Zimmerman, *Henry Purcell, 1659–1695: an analytical catalogue of his music* (1963) · H. Purcell, 'Hail bright, Cecilia', Bodl. Oxf., MS Mus. C.26 · *The works of Mr Thomas Brown*, ed. J. Drake, 9th edn, 3 (1760) · F. Sandford, *The history of the coronation of James II* (1687) · A. Ashbee and D. Lasocki, eds., *A biographical dictionary of English court musicians, 1485–1714*, 1 (1998) · *LondG* (2 Jan 1699) · will, PRO, PROB 11/504, sig. 251 · memorial tablet, St Paul's Cathedral
Wealth at death see will, PRO, PROB 11/504, sig. 251

Howell, John [Ioan ab Hywel] (1774–1830), Welsh-language poet and literary editor, also known as Ioan ab Hywel, the Welsh form of his name, was born at Abergwili, Carmarthenshire, where he received very little schooling. He was apprenticed to a weaver, but soon joined the Carmarthenshire militia, where his musical talent led him to be employed in the band as fife-major. He served with his regiment in Ireland in 1799, and rejoined it on re-embodiment in 1803. He used his leisure time in a process of self-education, and was discharged as regimental schoolmaster on 24 July 1815, while the regiment was at Bristol. He then became master of the national school at Llandovery, Carmarthenshire, where he lived, with few intermissions, until his death.

At Llandovery, Howell produced much poetry, which he sent to various eisteddfods. These were models of metric correctness and appropriate diction, but they lacked fire or subtle imagery. His most important work was as an editor rather than a poet; in 1824 he brought out at Carmarthen by subscription a volume entitled *Blodau Dyfed*, containing selections from the compositions of eighteenth- and nineteenth-century bards of the district, including some productions of his own. A 'good example of the local-anthology type of publication', Howell's anthology remains a useful source for information on the history of Welsh literature, particularly with regard to the provincial eisteddfods (*DWB*). John Howell died on 18 November 1830 at Llandovery, and was buried beside the porch of Llandingad church.

H. M. CHICHESTER, *rev.* M. CLARE LOUGHLIN-CHOW

Sources DWB · R. Williams, *Enwogion Cymru: a biographical dictionary of eminent Welshmen* (1852) · M. Stephens, ed., *The Oxford companion to the literature of Wales* (1986)

Howell, John (1788–1863), writer and inventor, was born at Old Lauriston, Edinburgh, the son of James Howell. He was apprenticed to a bookbinder, but afterwards was an assistant to Robert Kinnear, bookseller, in Frederick Street, Edinburgh, and subsequently spent five years with the firm of Stevenson, printers to the university, where he is said to have made improvements in the art of stereotyping. On 24 August 1808, he married Jane Duncan. He next returned to his trade of bookbinding at a workshop in Thistle Street, where he invented the 'plough' for cutting

edges. Sir Walter Scott was among those who patronized his business.

Howell had some success as an editor and writer. He published *An Essay on the War-Galleys of the Ancients* (1826), *The Life and Adventures of Alexander Selkirk* (1829), and *The Life of Alexander Alexander* (1830). He also edited the *Journal of a Soldier of the 71st Regiment, 1806–1815*, and *The Life of John Nichol, the Mariner*. He contributed several stories to John Mackay Wilson's *Tales of the Borders* (1835–40).

Howell later opened a shop as curiosity dealer and china and picture repairer at 22 Frederick Street, where the sign over the door described him as a 'Polyartist and dealer in curiosities, old coins, china, carvings etc.'. Though Howell had considerable skill in repairing china and old furniture, the shop was not very successful, and he moved his business to 110 Rose Street.

Howell, described as 'A very singular, eccentric person, possessed of a considerable amount of information on many subjects with a turn for mechanics, invention' (*N&Q*, 3rd ser., 3, 78), was a well-known character in Edinburgh. On one occasion he attempted to use a flying machine he had built in what are now Princes Street Gardens, but broke one of his legs by falling on a pile of stones. At another time, having made, at considerable expense, a model in the shape of a fish, he entered the machine, tried to swim in a pool on the Water of Leith, and was nearly drowned—it took nearly half an hour to revive him. He was more successful as an amateur doctor where he developed a salve for ringworm, and dentist: he introduced the manufacture of Pompeian plates (a type of false teeth).

Towards the end of his life, and in ill health, Howell fell on hard times and was an out-pensioner of Trinity Hospital, Edinburgh. He died in Edinburgh on 4 April 1863.

A. P. WOOLRICH

Sources DNB · *The Scotsman* (6 April 1863) · *N&Q*, 3rd ser., 2–3 (1862–3); 4th ser., 2 (1868) · *Staffordshire Advertiser* (18 April 1863) · IGI
Archives NL Scot., MSS, Acc. 5779 · NL Scot., MSS 19738–19739

Howell, Laurence (c.1664–1720), nonjuring Church of England clergyman, was born at Deptford, Kent, the son of John Howell. He was educated at Colfe's School, Lewisham, where he was a foundation scholar. He matriculated in 1681 from Jesus College, Cambridge, whence he graduated BA in 1684 and MA in 1688. A zealous member of the nonjuror party, he was ordained deacon in London on 22 September 1706 but refused to take the oath of abjuration, which the lord mayor tendered to him in 1708. After that date Howell seems to have been a part of the nonjuring communion. On 2 October 1712 he was ordained priest by George Hickes, the nonjuring bishop-suffragan of Thetford, at Samuel Grascome's oratory at St Andrew's, Holborn.

At the time of the revolution of 1688 Howell was master of the school at Epping and curate of Eastwick, Hertfordshire. In 1708 he published the first of three volumes of his *Synopsis canonum*, a Latin record of the Greek and Latin ecumenical and provincial councils. Howell sought to dedicate the first volume to the earl of Salisbury, who refused the honour, feeling it undesirable to patronize a nonjuror.

The second volume appeared in 1710 but publication of the third volume was delayed by a fire at the printers in 1712 which destroyed the manuscript; Howell rewrote the third volume, finally publishing it in 1715. A prolific writer, he also published an attack on the papacy, entitled *The view of the pontificate, from its supposed beginning to the end of the Council of Trent, A.D. 1563* (1712), and the popular three-volume *A Complete History of the Bible* (1725), which was revised and augmented in 1807 by George Burder. He also published the *Orthodox communicant, by way of meditation on the order for administration of the Lord's supper or holy communion, according to the liturgy of the Church of England* in 1721. His miscellaneous collections for a history of the University of Cambridge are in the Bodleian Library (MS Rawlinson B. 281).

The claim by John Disney that Howell composed the speech of the Jacobite William Paul that was delivered on the gallows in 1716 is incorrect, as Thomas Deacon has been shown to be its author. Howell, however, was a committed Jacobite and authored a pamphlet printed for private circulation entitled *The Case of Schism in the Church of England Truly Stated*, which led to his arrest in 1716 on the charge of treason after a thousand copies of the pamphlet had been discovered at his house in Bull Head Court, Jewin Street. All his papers were seized, including his 'Letter of orders' and a copy of a work entitled 'The form of absolution and reception of converts'. The printer of the *Case of Schism*, Redmayne, was tried and sentenced to pay a fine of £500 and serve a prison term of five years. Howell was then tried at the Old Bailey on 28 February 1717 before the lord mayor and justices Powys and Dormer. The jury found him guilty, and two days afterwards he was sentenced to stand in the pillory, pay a fine of £500, and serve a prison sentence of three years without bail. The court also ordered that he find four sureties of £500 each and have himself bound for £1000. As a final indignity the court ordered that he be stripped of his clerical gown and be twice whipped, which he protested on the ground that he was a clergyman. The court responded that Howell was a disgrace to the ministry of the Church of England and that he had no right to wear the gown, as his ordination by the nonjuring bishop of Thetford, George Hickes, was illegal; accordingly by the court's direction the common executioner roughly pulled his gown off his back. A few days later, however, on his humble petition to the king, the corporal punishment was remitted.

The pamphlet that led to Howell's arrest was not dissimilar to the writings of other nonjurors, including Charles Leslie and John Kettlewell, who had written in support of the nonjuror separation from the Church of England and of the Stuart cause. Written after the accession of George I the pamphlet denounced the new king as a usurper and declared that the Church of England was in schism, as it had separated from the true church after the deprivation of Archbishop William Sancroft in 1689. It therefore followed that all subsequent actions of the Church of England were illegal and uncanonical, making the nonjuring church the only true Church of England. The severity of Howell's sentence may have stemmed, as

Mark Noble suggested, from the Jacobites and nonjurors having become 'extremely daring and troublesome' (Noble, 3.154). The government, in turn, found it necessary to crack down on them 'in order to check their progress, and counteract the effect their violence might otherwise have on the body of the people' (ibid.). Whatever the case Howell's political involvements probably cut short a productive career in the church and as a writer. He did not survive his detention in Newgate prison and died there on 19 July 1720.   ROBERT D. CORNWALL

Sources Venn, *Alum. Cant.* · *A biographical history of England, from the revolution to the end of George I's reign: being a continuation of the Rev. J. Granger's work*, ed. M. Noble, 3 vols. (1806) · Nichols, *Lit. anecdotes* · J. H. Overton, *The nonjurors: their lives, principles, and writings* (1902) · *N&Q*, 3rd ser., 1 (1862), 312 · *Remarks and collections of Thomas Hearne*, ed. C. E. Doble and others, 2, OHS, 7 (1886), 125 · G. Burder, *A complete history of the holy Bible*, 2 vols. (1807) · Allibone, *Dict.* · A. Chalmers, ed., *The general biographical dictionary*, new edn, 13 (1814), 270–72 · *DNB* · J. Disney, *Memoirs of the life and writings of Arthur Ashley Sykes* (1785), 33–4
Archives BL, Add. MS 5871, fol. 66 | Bodl. Oxf., MS Rawl.
Likenesses G. Vandergucht, line engraving, NPG

Howell, Thomas (*fl.* 1560–1581), poet, refers to himself as a native of Dunster in Somerset, a seaside location that is reflected in the maritime imagery of many of his poems and a locality which provided the dialect for one of his poems, 'Mine owne zweet Ione'. From an autobiographical poem, 'When each wight wonted is, to take by nature rest', it seems that despite being well-born and well-educated, Howell soon lost his parents' inheritance. He consequently took up service in the household of the sixth earl of Shrewsbury, George Talbot, and dedicated his first collection of poems, *The Arbor of Amitie*, published by Henry Denham in 1568, to Talbot's daughter-in-law, Lady Anne Talbot (*née* Herbert). Howell was keen to insist on his status of 'gentleman', however, an inscription that appeared on the title-pages of his first two collections, the first being *The Arbor of Amitie*; the second, *Newe Sonets and Pretie Pamphlets*, was printed by Thomas Colwell in 1570 and probably in 1575, and dedicated to Howell's 'approued Freinde Maister Henry Lassels Gentilman' (sig. A2r). Howell's collections are presented as coterie pieces, miscellanies of poems written to and from friends, among whom the most frequent correspondent is John Keeper, a fellow Somerset man and student of Hart Hall, Oxford.

On the marriage of Katherine Talbot to Henry Herbert, the second earl of Pembroke, in 1563, Howell appears to have passed with her into the Herbert household at Wilton, where another Somerset poet, Samuel Daniel, would also find employment in the 1580s and where Howell mentions writing much of his third and final collection of poems, *H. his Devises, for his Owne Exercise, and his Friends Pleasure* (published by W. How for Henry Jackson in 1581), dedicated to the influential patron Mary Sidney, sister of Sir Philip Sidney, who became Pembroke's third wife on the death of Katherine in 1577. Much of the work is written under Katherine's auspices, however, including a set of new year's poems, addressed in acrostics to her and her two sisters: Lady Mary, wife of Sir George Savile, and Lady Grace, married to the heir of Sir George Cavendish. The fourth poem in the sequence is written to 'The Ladi Speke', of a Somerset family. This work holds what is believed to be the first reference to Sidney's *Arcadia* (then probably circulating at Wilton in manuscript form). In the poem 'Written to a most Excellent Booke, Full of Rare Invention', Howell praises the work for 'such pithe in filed phrase' and urges its publication (T. Howell, *H. his Devises*, 1581, sig. E4*v*). Howell casts himself as a victim. The emblem placed on the title-page of his *Devises* reads 'Who suffers, wins', and besides lovers' complaints and ballads with classical themes (staple in the period), his collections abound in poems bemoaning the fickleness of friends, the vagaries of service, and financial hardship.

Although condemned by nineteenth-century critics, Howell was popular enough among contemporaries for some of his poems to be set to music, and several of his poems were included in Thomas Proctor's *Gorgious Gallery of Gallant Inventions* (1578). In the twentieth century E. W. Pomeroy credits Howell with being 'a minor link between the traditions of Surrey and Sidney' (Pomeroy, *The Elizabethan Miscellany*, 1973, 13), and J. Buxton declares that 'though undistinguished, [his poetry] is not wholly without grace' (Buxton, *Sir Philip Sidney and the English Renaissance*, 1987, 136). The dedicatory epistles of his second two collections show a wit and inventiveness often lacking in the genre, and flashes of Sidney-like idiom as, in 1570, he begs excuse for 'these trifling toyes' and 'fond phansies' (Howell, *Newe Sonets*, 1570, sig. A1*v*).

Howell seems to have remained unmarried. Certainly in 1568 he states that

> by proofe these rules of mariage,
> I doe not surely know.
> (Howell, *Arbor of Amitie*, 1568, 15)

He disappears from view after 1581, possibly dying from the illness which forms the subject of a pair of poems written by Keeper and himself towards the end of his *Devises*.

Also ascribed to Howell is *The Fable of Ovid Treting of Narcissus* by T. H., published by T. Hackette in 1560, which uses the myth as warning of the transience of mortal things.

CATHY SHRANK

Sources *Howell's devises, 1581*, ed. W. Raleigh (1906) · *The poems of Thomas Howell*, ed. A. B. Grosart (1879) · M. E. Lamb, *Gender and authorship in the Sidney circle* (1990) · M. P. Hannay, *Philip's phoenix: Mary Sidney, countess of Pembroke* (1990) · E. Brydges, *The British bibliographer*, 4 vols. (1810–14), vol. 1 · J. Ritson, *Bibliographia poetica* (1802) · W. T. Lowndes, *The bibliographer's manual of English literature*, ed. H. G. Bohn, [new edn], 6 vols. (1864) · W. C. Hazlitt, *Hand-book to the popular, poetical and dramatic literature of Great Britain* (1867) · E. H. Fellowes, ed., *English madrigal verse, 1588–1632*, 3rd edn, rev. F. W. Sternfeld and D. Greer (1967)

Howell, Thomas (1588–1650), bishop of Bristol, was born at Cefn Bryn, Llangamarch, Brecknockshire, the third child and eldest son of Thomas Howell (*d.* 1632), curate of Llangamarch and later of Aber-nant in Carmarthenshire, and his wife, whose name is unknown, a daughter of James David Powell; he was the elder brother of James *Howell (1594?–1666). He matriculated at Jesus College, Oxford, on 20 November 1607, graduating BA on 20 February 1609 and proceeding MA on 9 July 1612, and BD and DD on 5 or 8 July 1630.

Having been ordained Howell quickly became well known as a preacher, and was appointed a royal chaplain by Charles I. He also received the rectory of West Horsley, near Guildford in Surrey, and was presented by the king to the rectory of St Stephen Walbrook, London, on 13 April 1635. Howell's appointment occasioned a brief dispute between the crown, the parishioners of St Stephen's, and the impropriators, the Grocers' Company, when the parishioners objected to the choice of Howell because of his refusal to reside in the parish. Their selection of an alternative candidate for the vacant curacy, Thomas Saxby, provoked an angry response from the king, who elicited Saxby's resignation and the formal election of Howell. Howell was appointed by the king to a canonry of Windsor on 15 November 1636, and on the promotion of Henry King to the see of Chichester, received from the crown on 25 March 1642 the sinecure rectory of Fulham. By then Howell was married to Honor Bromfield (*d.* 1650) of Chalcroft, Hampshire; the couple had five daughters and six sons, including John, later a London merchant, Thomas, later fellow of New College, Oxford, George, later rector of Buckland, Surrey, and Arthur, a London merchant who experienced a period as a slave in Turkey.

Although regarded 'by many as a puritanical preacher' (Wood, 4.804), Howell was early marked out for attack by parliament, being charged with delinquency and called to the bar of the Commons on 19 March 1642 to answer allegations that he had criticized parliament and voiced support for the king. He was driven from his various livings, resigning St Stephen's in 1641, and being sequestered for non-residence at West Horsley before July 1644. On the death in June 1644 of Thomas Westfield, bishop of Bristol, Howell was selected by Charles I to succeed Westfield in that important stronghold, just recovered to the royal cause. He was consecrated by Archbishop James Ussher of Armagh in August 1644—the last bishop consecrated in England for sixteen years. Howell's episcopate was short and disastrous: Bristol was surrendered to Fairfax by Prince Rupert on 10 September 1645 and all the royalist clergy were violently ejected.

Howell's whereabouts between 1645 and 1650 are unknown, but according to his will, he leased a property at Frogmore, Windsor, so it is possible he resided there for a time, with his in-laws in Hampshire, or, most probably, in Bristol. A letter sent by Howell to a brother in March 1650 describes the recent death of his wife while in childbirth and his fear of imminent eviction, and it is possible that this combination of events contributed to his own death some time between 20 March and 22 April 1650. He was buried in Bristol Cathedral alongside his wife, his memorial simply bearing the word 'Expergiscar' ('I shall awake'). Shortly before his death, in December 1649, Howell had been successful in lifting a sequestration order against his property in Berkshire, but despite this breakthrough he appears to have died in comparative poverty. By the terms of his will he left the Frogmore farm and £30 each to his ten youngest children, but took care to appoint Henry Hammond the trustee of a charitable fund designed to support the family after his death. Hammond later estimated Howell's total income at death to have been no more than £30 per annum. Hammond's efforts at collecting money from sympathetic royalists appear to have been unsuccessful, and after living for a time with their guardian, Howell's nephew, Richard Phillips, the children became separated when they were divided among various friends and family.

Howell is described by Lloyd as 'a person of great clearness, candour, solidness, sweetness, and eloquence, with an insight into state affairs, as well as those of his own office' (Lloyd, 522). Of his preaching Fuller writes: 'His sermons, like the waters of Siloah, softly gliding on with a smooth stream, his matter, with a lawful and laudable felony, did steal secretly the hearts of the hearers' (Fuller, 3.515). Howell has been loosely credited with the publication of a funeral sermon, in 1623, but it would appear unlikely that the author was the future bishop.

GEOFFREY BROWELL

Sources Wood, *Ath. Oxon.*, new edn, vols. 3–4 · *Fasti Angl.* (Hardy), 1.216–17 · *Walker rev.*, 1 · will, PRO, PROB 10/715, PROB 11/211/52 · T. Howell, letter to his brother, 11 March 1650, Bodl. Oxf., MS Rawl. 93, fol. 373 · N. Pocock, ed., 'Illustrations of the state of the church during the Great Rebellion', *The theologian and ecclesiastic*, 7 (1849), 49–148 · Foster, *Alum. Oxon.* · Pedigree of Howell family, BL, Harleian MS 4181, fol. 131v · Fuller, *Worthies* (1840), 3.515 · D. Lloyd, *Memoires of the lives … of those … personages that suffered … for the protestant religion* (1668), 522 · J. Howell, *Epistolae Ho-elianae*, ed. A. Repplier, 2 vols. (1907) · Grocers' Company court minutes, 1616–39, GL, MS 11588, vol. 3, fols. 546–7 · S. Bond, ed., *The chapter acts of the dean and canons of Windsor: 1430, 1523–1672* (1966) · Signet Office books, PRO, SO 3/12 Nov 1638 – Dec 1644 · *JHC*, 2 (1640–42), 478, 486 · *CSP dom.*, 1635–6, 204 · *Lords' Journals*, 1645–6, 379 · *IGI*

Archives Bodl. Oxf., letters to his brother, 93 fol. 373 · St George's Chapel, Windsor, MSS, IV B6 [Howell's transcript]

Wealth at death over £300; plus farm approx. £30 p.a.; also plate: will, PRO, PROB 10/715; 11/211/52

Howell, Thomas Bayly (1767–1815), legal writer, was born in Jamaica on 6 September 1767, the son of John Howell (d. 1802), who purchased Prinknash Park, near Gloucester, in 1770, and his wife, Elizabeth Charlotte, widow of Isaac Grove, barrister, and daughter and heir of John Demetress, one of the assistant judges of Jamaica. He was in residence at Christ Church, Oxford, as a gentleman commoner from 1784 to 1787, but did not graduate. In 1782 he was admitted to Lincoln's Inn, and was called to the bar on 12 June 1790. He married Lucy Anne, youngest daughter and coheir of Robert Long, on 24 May 1790. They had a son and at least one daughter. On his father's death (2 November 1802), Howell succeeded to the Prinknash estate.

When in 1808 William Cobbett projected a new edition of the *State Trials*, he secured Howell as editor. Howell carried the work from the first volume (1809) to the twenty-first (1814), taking over from Cobbett as proprietor in 1811. The remaining twelve volumes were edited by his son, Thomas Jones Howell [*see below*]. Together they succeeded in arranging and co-ordinating the untidy mass of information left by previous editors, thus providing a collection of all the important criminal and constitutional cases

with a bearing on public law. Howell was made a fellow of the Royal Society in 1804 and was also a fellow of the Society of Antiquaries. He died at Prinknash Park, on 13 April 1815.

Thomas Jones Howell (1793–1858), legal writer, was born on 24 December 1793. Admitted in 1814 to Lincoln's Inn, he was called to the bar on 15 May 1822. On 4 September 1817 he married Susanna Maria (*d.* 15 Oct 1842), eldest surviving daughter of Alexander Macleod, of Harris, Inverness; they had seven sons and three daughters. Thomas Howell took over from his father the editing of the *State Trials*, completing the series with twelve volumes in as many years (vols. 22–33, 1815–26). He became judge-advocate and judge of the vice-admiralty court at Gibraltar in 1822; he was secretary to the commissioners of colonial inquiry in 1830, commissioner for West Indian relief in 1832, and inspector of factories in 1833. He sold Prinknash Park in 1842, and on 6 August 1851 married Ellen, daughter of Thomas Ffooks, a solicitor. He died at 6 Eaton Place West, London, on 4 June 1858, his second wife surviving him. His eldest son, William Charles Howell, studied at Brasenose College, Oxford, and was vicar of Holy Trinity, Tottenham, from 1861 to 1904.

GORDON GOODWIN, *rev.* JONATHAN HARRIS

Sources Burke, *Gen. GB* · W. P. Baildon, ed., *The records of the Honorable Society of Lincoln's Inn: admissions*, 1 (1896), 502 · W. P. Baildon, ed., *The records of the Honorable Society of Lincoln's Inn: the black books*, 4 (1902), 240, 249 · Foster, *Alum. Oxon.* · *GM*, 1st ser., 62 (1792), 765 · *GM*, 1st ser., 85/1 (1815), 472 · *GM*, 3rd ser., 5 (1858), 93 · Holdsworth, *Eng. law*, 12.128–30 · L. Melville [L. S. Benjamin], *The life and letters of William Cobbett in England and America*, 1 (1913), 241; 2 (1913), 20–25 · G. Spater, *William Cobbett: the poor man's friend*, 1 (1982), 170–71, 254 · J. W. Wallace, *The reporters*, 4th edn (1882), 64–9 · Boase, *Mod. Eng. biog.* · m. cert.

Wealth at death under £16,000; Thomas Jones Howell: will, 1858

Howell, Thomas Jones (1793–1858). *See under* Howell, Thomas Bayly (1767–1815).

Howell, William (1631/2–1683), historian and civil lawyer, was the son of Robert Howell of Walkeringham, Nottinghamshire, who died when William was still young. He matriculated aged sixteen at Magdalene College, Cambridge, at Easter 1648, graduated BA in 1651 and MA in 1655, and became a fellow of the college. On 25 November 1664 he was created DCL, which degree was incorporated at Oxford on 6 July 1676. He was tutor to John Sheffield, third earl of Mulgrave and later first duke of Buckingham and Normanby. Howell was admitted an advocate of Doctors' Commons on 4 February 1678 and subsequently became chancellor of the diocese of Lincoln. He married on 3 August 1678 Mary Ashfield of St Giles-in-the-Fields, London.

Howell was a substantial but under-appreciated historical writer of the Restoration, in the tradition of world history writing that included Sir Walter Ralegh's *History of the World* (1614), then the most popular work of its kind in English, but which ended before the birth of Christ. Howell's most widely read work, which clearly borrows from

Ralegh, was *An institution of general history … from the beginning of the world till the monarchy of Constantine the Great*. This first appeared in 1661 and then in several subsequent editions. He abridged it into Latin as *Gulielmi Hoeli, LL.D. Elementa historiae* for the use of Mulgrave and other young men in 1671, wishing to 'reduce History into such a form, as might resemble that of a compleat Art or Science, and prove inviting to young students' (*Elements of History*, 1700 edn, sig. A6v). The *Elementa*, translated into English as *Elements of History* in 1700, covers the same period as the *Institution*, but without the elaborate marginal notes and without quotations from his sources.

Howell had always intended to publish a second part of the *Institution*, covering western and eastern Christendom after Constantine, and refers to this second part in his *Elementa*. It was unpublished at Howell's death in 1683, but in 1685 his widow, Mary, had it published, complete with her own dedicatory epistle to James II. That the continuation was Howell's own work is further attested in a preface by Bishop Henry Compton and others; that Howell counted among his friends both the future Williamite Compton and the Catholic sympathizer Mulgrave testifies to his middling position in religious matters.

Borrowing from Reformation chronological writing, Howell organized his book according to the principle of synchronism, making it easy for a reader following his account of one kingdom or empire to grasp contemporary events that occurred elsewhere. Howell's *Institution* was perhaps the most readily accessible history of the world published in the Restoration, appealing to a growing readership for comprehensive histories that provided a straightforward summary of events since the creation. The Hertfordshire gentlewoman Sarah Cowper, for instance, epitomized it in 1686 for the benefit of her daughter-in-law, Judith (S. Cowper, 'History of the world', Herts RO, D/EP F.41); much later Edward Gibbon, whose *Decline and Fall* covers some of the same ground, thought it useful (Gibbon, 42). Howell also published anonymously the *Medulla historiae Anglicanae: being a comprehensive history of the lives and reigns of the monarchs of England* (1679 and several subsequent editions in duodecimo and octavo format). Like the *Elementa*, this was a history intended less for the scholarly world, or even for the audience of the *Institution*, but rather for those 'whose humour or leisure will not permit them to turn over larger volumes' (*Medulla*, 1724 edn, author's preface, sig. A6r). Wood declared that 'only report makes Dr Howell the author' but was prepared to accept this attribution, as did subsequent readers and editors. Later recensions, such as the elaborately illustrated eighth edition of 1724, wherein his account was brought up to the reign of Queen Anne, appear under Howell's name. William Nicolson thought highly of the *Medulla*, deeming it 'done with that great judgment, that it deserves a place among the best of our writers on this subject' (Nicolson, 198).

Howell should not be confused with the ecclesiastical author William Howell (1656–1714), author of the much-reprinted *The Common Prayer Book the Best Companion*.

Wood, who heard this latter Howell preach in Oxford (Wood, *Ath. Oxon.*, 1.xciii, 4.787), clearly recognized the two authors as distinct. D. R. WOOLF

Sources Venn, *Alum. Cant.* · DNB · Wood, *Ath. Oxon.*, vols. 1, 4 · E. Gibbon, *Memoirs of my life*, ed. G. A. Bonnard (1966) · W. Nicolson, *The English historical library*, 3 pts (1696–9) · parish register, London, St Mary Magdalen, Old Fish Street, GL, 3 Aug 1678 [marriage]

Howell, William (1655/6–1714), Church of England clergyman, was the son of William Howell, a tailor of Oxford, who is termed *pauper* ('poor') in the register of Wadham College, Oxford, where William matriculated as a servitor on 19 May 1670, aged fourteen. Howell moved shortly afterwards to New Inn Hall, where he graduated BA on 20 January 1674 and proceeded MA on 17 October 1676. He took holy orders and over his career served in several Oxfordshire parishes. He was rector of Wilcote in Oxfordshire from 1680 to 1683, vicar of North Leigh from 1680 to 1684, and vicar of Pyrton from 1702 until his death. He was also schoolmaster and curate of Ewelme from at least 1688 and it was here that his wife, Lydia, died on 24 November 1700. Howell died on 20 January 1714 and was buried at Ewelme three days later. There is a memorial to him in the church.

Howell was a popular devotional writer, producing collections from the Book of Common Prayer, selections from scripture as aids to personal conduct in *The Word of God the Best Guide* (1689), and a small pamphlet of prayers for private use, *Prayers in the Closet* (1689). He published two sermons given to the University of Oxford. One, printed in 1711, was dedicated to Ulrich Roche, Lord Viscount Fermoy, who had been his pupil and whom he claimed he had successfully converted to protestantism. Another, printed in 1712 and licensed by William Lancaster, formerly vice-chancellor of the university, reveals Howell's high-church beliefs. In it he declared that it was lawful for the church to demand conformity in indifferent things. He accused those that would not conform on these grounds of being schismatics. Howell cited the disciplinarian schemes for church government produced by presbyterians during the civil war as evidence that even the dissenters conceded the need for uniformity and obedience. EDWARD VALLANCE

Sources Foster, *Alum. Oxon.* · DNB · *Parochial collections made by Anthony à Wood and Richard Rawlinson*, ed. F. N. Davis, 2, Oxfordshire RS, 4 (1922), 140 · I. Green, *Print and protestantism in early modern England* (2000) · administration, PRO, PROB 6/90, fol. 26v · Wood, *Ath. Oxon.*, new edn, 4.787 · Wood, *Ath. Oxon.: Fasti* (1820), 334, 354

Howell, William Gough [Bill] (1922–1974), architect, was born in London on 5 February 1922, the younger child and only son of Charles Gough Howell, a barrister of Welsh descent, and his Australian wife, Sidney Gretchen Innes-Noad. In 1926 Howell's father joined the colonial legal service; he subsequently served in Kenya, Fiji, Malaya, and Singapore, where he became attorney-general. He was taken prisoner by the Japanese when Singapore fell and died in a prison camp in Formosa (Taiwan). William Howell, at school at Marlborough College, was visiting his family in Singapore at the outbreak of the Second World War and was unable to get back to Britain until Christmas

1939. After one more term at Marlborough he joined the Royal Air Force, where he served first at the radar establishment at Stanmore and then in the Middle East as a navigator in night fighters. He was awarded the DFC in 1943. After the war he embarked on a career in architecture, which he studied first at Cambridge (where he was at Gonville and Caius College) and then at the Architectural Association school in London. On 10 August 1951 he married a fellow student, Gillian Margaret (Jill) Sarson [see below]. They had three sons and one daughter. He qualified in 1952, having joined the architects' department of the London county council (LCC). In the post-war era the architectural profession was becoming deeply concerned with integrating building programmes with social needs, an aim in which the LCC took the lead, most notably in schools and housing. Howell was one of the group of young architects responsible for the LCC's Alton West estate at Roehampton, one of its most admired and progressive housing projects. His experience at the LCC coloured his later approach to architecture and to its proper role in the community.

In 1956 Howell left the LCC to practise architecture privately and to teach at the Regent Street Polytechnic in London. In 1959 he and three other architects, who had been his colleagues at the LCC, set up the partnership of Howell, Killick, Partridge, and Amis. They entered the competition for Churchill College, Cambridge, held in that year, and theirs was one of four designs chosen for the final stage; although they were not the eventual winners their participation brought them a number of commissions for university buildings. These included buildings at Oxford, for St Anne's and St Antony's colleges, and at Cambridge, for Downing and Darwin colleges and the University Centre, as well as for buildings at Birmingham and Reading universities. The work at Cambridge was Howell's particular concern: its style was uncompromisingly modern, characterized by a vigorous use of precast concrete, but he showed sensitivity about the relation of new buildings to old in his sympathetic addition of a new combination room to Downing College, completed in 1970. Others of the firm's projects in which Howell played the leading part were a group of unusual houses for visiting mathematicians at Warwick University and an arts centre for Christ's Hospital, Horsham.

In 1973 Howell was appointed to the chair of architecture at Cambridge, where he became a fellow of Caius, but he had had only a little over a year to establish himself there when he died. He had shown promise of becoming a highly successful professor and a useful influence on Cambridge architecture. Although relaxed and sociable, Howell had strong convictions and the ability to express them persuasively. His stocky figure, bushy moustache, and genial personality were familiar on many architectural occasions, for he gave much to the profession besides his buildings and his teaching. He was active at the periodical conferences of the Congrès Internationaux d'Architecture Moderne, notably those at Aix-en-Provence in 1953 and Dubrovnik in 1955. He served on the council of

the Royal Institute of British Architects and was vice-president in 1965–7. He was elected ARA in 1974.

Outside architecture Howell's varied interests and pursuits included rugby football, riding, and the history of the First World War. His collection of First World War memorabilia was the source of a book, *Popular Arts of the First World War*, published in 1972, which he compiled in collaboration with Barbara Jones. Another interest in his last years was his family's weekend home near Savernake Forest, originally a Victorian Methodist chapel, which he converted with zest and wit. On 29 November 1974 he was killed in a car accident near Leighton Buzzard, Bedfordshire, at the age of fifty-two.

Howell's wife, **Gillian Margaret** [Jill] **Howell** (1927–2000), architect, was born on 3 November 1927 at Multan, in the western Punjab, the daughter of Colonel Edward Vipan Sarson, commandant at the Royal Artillery training centre, and his Norwegian wife, Dagny. She was educated at the Royal School, Bath, and then the Architectural Association School in London. She and Howell met during a school excursion to the Bryn-mawr rubber factory in south Wales, then considered an outstanding example of modern architecture. From the mid-1950s, they lived in one of the terrace of houses they built in Hampstead to Le Corbusier's design concepts. Jill worked alongside her husband in the LCC's housing department, and then formed her own architectural practice with Jean Elrington. After Howell's death she continued to teach in the university school of architecture in Cambridge, where she both enjoyed and contributed to the social life of the Cambridge student and artistic community. She took over Howell's role as a governor of Marlborough College and advised on its building projects, and was involved with the built environment of Fen Ditton and its surrounding area. In 1995 she married (John) Michael (Mike) Watt, a retired company secretary. She died of cancer at her home, Fen Ditton Hall, on 2 May 2000, and was survived by her second husband.

JEFFREY RICHARDS, *rev.* CATHERINE GORDON

Sources M. Emanuel, ed., *Contemporary architects* (1994), 456–9 · *RIBA Journal*, 82 (Jan 1975), 14 · *Architects' Journal* (11 Dec 1974), 1363 · S. Cantacuzino, *ArchR*, 157 (1975), 124 · personal knowledge (1986) · private information (1986) · *CGPLA Eng. & Wales* (1975) · *The Independent* (22 May 2000) · d. cert. [Gillian Margaret Howell]

Archives RIBA, RIBA nomination papers

Likenesses portrait, repro. in *RIBA Journal*, 14

Wealth at death £199,712: probate, 23 Oct 1975, *CGPLA Eng. & Wales*

Howells, Herbert Norman (1892–1983), composer, was born on 17 October 1892 at High Street, Lydney, Gloucestershire, the youngest of the eight children of Oliver Howells (1854–1919), painter and decorator, and his wife, Elizabeth Burgham (1856–1946). His parents were both natives of Gloucestershire from the Forest of Dean, and this border country was to remain a source of inspiration to Howells throughout his life.

Howells attended the dame-school in Lydney (1896–8) and progressed to the Church of England elementary

Herbert Norman Howells (1892–1983), by Howard Morgan, 1978

school (1889–1905) whence he won a scholarship to Lydney grammar school (1905–9). Howells's first piano lessons were taken with his eldest sister, Florence, after which he went to Herbert Brewer at Gloucester Cathedral. At about this time (1905) Oliver Howells was declared bankrupt. The family's resulting impoverishment and their treatment by local people had a serious effect on the young Howells, something from which he never fully recovered.

Howells did not much like Brewer's teaching at first, but a mutual respect developed which led, in 1909, to Howells's becoming an articled pupil at the cathedral. This now defunct position gave a valuable training in the art of church music and full musical tuition. Howells was apprenticed with Ivor Gurney and Ivor Novello. Gurney became Howells's closest friend for some years, and they spent days together walking the Gloucestershire countryside and talking of music and English literature, about which they were both passionate and knowledgeable.

In 1910 Howells witnessed the first performance of Vaughan Williams's *Fantasia on a Theme by Thomas Tallis* at the Three Choirs meeting in Gloucester, singling it out as the seminal musical event in his life. Two years later he won a scholarship to study composition with Charles Villiers Stanford at the Royal College of Music. His other teachers included Hubert Parry and Charles Wood. During his student days Howells was seen as the outstanding talent of his generation. Principal among his works at this time were the first piano concerto (1914), the orchestral suite *The B's* (1914), *Lady Audrey's Suite* for string quartet

(1915), the piano quartet in A minor (1916), and the 'Phantasy' string quartet (1916–17).

The onset of Graves' disease in 1916 left Howells with a life expectancy of only six months and he was given radium treatment, then largely untested. He visited St Thomas's Hospital twice a week for the next two years and this eventually restored his health. Despite being ill Howells left the Royal College of Music to take up his first full-time appointment as assistant organist at Salisbury Cathedral in 1917. This was very short-lived owing to the nature of his illness and six months later, after relinquishing his post at Salisbury, he was awarded a three-year grant by the Carnegie Trust to help Richard Terry at Westminster Cathedral editing Tudor church music. In all these things Howells was very fortunate in having powerful friends to speak for him. The First World War was still raging and Howells, who had not been enlisted because of his health, felt the need to immerse himself in as much editorial work and composition as his frail constitution would allow: two violin sonatas (1917); the *Elegy* for viola solo, string orchestra, and string quartet (1917), written in memory of fellow student Francis Purcell Warren; the *Rhapsodic Quintet* for clarinet and strings (1919); and the three *Carol-Anthems* (1918–20) were among the outstanding music written at this time.

In 1920 Howells married Dorothy Dawe (1891–1975) and joined the teaching staff at the Royal College of Music. It marked the end of that period when he was able to devote himself freely to composition. From now on he concentrated on his onerous teaching schedule, an increasing commitment to adjudication at local music festivals, and work as an examiner for the associated board of the Royal Schools of Music. In 1925 he was commissioned by the Royal Philharmonic Society to write a piano concerto in which the soloist was Harold Samuel and the conductor Malcolm Sargent. The first performance of the work at the Queen's Hall became a *cause célèbre* as it was greeted by shouts of disapproval from a critic in the audience. It also signalled the onset of a debilitating insecurity (never far beneath the surface). He achieved rehabilitation, such as it was, through his first book of clavichord pieces, *Lambert's Clavichord*, inspired by a beautiful instrument made by Herbert Lambert. In taking his inspiration from music of the Tudor period without compromising his own style, Howells found a voice which he could use with confidence and which was also entirely new.

Herbert and Dorothy Howells had two children, Ursula, later to become a distinguished actress, and Michael, who died in 1935 of poliomyelitis. This bereavement was the single most powerful influence of Howells's life. *Hymnus paradisi*, widely acknowledged as Howells's towering achievement, was written in the boy's memory shortly after his death but not performed until 1950 in Gloucester. Almost all the significant music which followed was in some way connected to Michael, some overtly as in the slow movement of the *Concerto for String Orchestra* (1938), but mostly by implication.

A period as acting organist of St John's College, Cambridge (1941–5), rekindled Howells's interest in church music, and he began his remarkable series of works for the Anglican church which include the *Collegium regale* settings (1944–5), the 'Gloucester' service (1946), and the 'St Paul's' service (1951). These and many other canticle settings, anthems, and motets demonstrated Howells's intuitive affinity with the medium of the small-scale choir, with or without organ, in the surroundings of a great stone building. His early exposure to music in Gloucester Cathedral found its natural outlet in these works, which represent the single greatest contribution to music for the Anglican church of the twentieth century, and the principal achievement of his maturity.

The two great choral–orchestral works which Howells wrote later in his life, the *Missa Sabrinensis* (1954) and *Stabat mater* (1965), succinctly sum up the two opposing and problematical sides of the Howells equation. On one hand the extreme complexity, the concentration on a single mood, and the huge forces involved make the works unapproachable for all but the most expert; but on the other, the drama, scale, and unique voice with which Howells speaks marks him out as one of the century's great visionaries. These works, and others like them, show Howells not as the miniaturist for which he is often mistaken, but as a composer on the very grandest scale capable of huge spans and vast contrapuntal schemes. They deserve to be more widely known.

Howells was director of music at St Paul's Girls' School (1936–62); King Edward professor of music at London University (1954–64); master of the Worshipful Company of Musicians (1959); president of the Incorporated Society of Musicians (1952), and of the Royal College of Organists (1958–9). He was appointed CBE in 1953 and CH in 1972. He was a DMus at Oxford (1937), and had honorary degrees from Cambridge (1961) and both the Royal Academy and Royal College of Music. He was elected an honorary fellow of the Queen's College, Oxford, in 1977. Howells died on 23 February 1983 at the Cintra Nursing Home, 7 Gwendolen Avenue, Putney, London. He was cremated at Putney Vale on 2 March, and his ashes were placed in the north aisle of Westminster Abbey at a service of thanksgiving on 3 June alongside those of friends, colleagues, and mentors, including Parry and Stanford: a roll call of those who gave English music a new identity for the twentieth century. PAUL SPICER

Sources C. Palmer, *Herbert Howells: a centenary celebration* (1992) • P. Spicer, *Herbert Howells* (1998) • personal knowledge (2004) • private information (2004) • *CGPLA Eng. & Wales* (1983) • d. cert.
Archives Royal College of Music, London | SOUND BL NSA, *Composer's portrait*, M75 W • BL NSA, documentary recording • BL NSA, 'Echoes of a lifetime', T5237 BW BD1 • BL NSA, 'Herbert Howells: a 90th birthday tribute', T5318/9 BW BD1 • BL NSA, *Music weekly*, BBC Radio 3, 6 Nov 1977, M5927/R • BL NSA, oral history interview • BL NSA, 'Out of the deep: a portrait of Herbert Howells', BBC Radio 3, 16 Oct 1992, H749/1 • BL NSA, performance recordings • BL NSA, recorded talk • BL NSA, *Talking about music*, 296, 1LP0205115 S2 BD2 BBC TRANSC
Likenesses W. Rothenstein, sanguine drawing, 1919, Royal College of Music, London • H. Lambert, photogravure photograph, c.1922, NPG • B. Treuberg, plaster bust, 1965, Royal College of Music, London • B. Moore, two pencil drawings, 1972, Royal College of Music, London • R. Walker, oils, 1972, Royal College of

Music, London • L. Boden, oils, 1974, Royal College of Music, London • H. Morgan, oils, 1978, NPG [*see illus.*]
Wealth at death £73,482: probate, 8 Aug 1983, *CGPLA Eng. & Wales*

Howels [Howells], **William** (1778–1832), Church of England clergyman, the eldest of the twelve children of Samuel Howells, a substantial farmer, was born in September 1778 at Llwynhelyg, near Cowbridge, in Glamorgan. After some years' study under Dr Williams, the master of the local school, he was sent to train for the law, but disliked it and returned home to study under the Revd John Walters, the lexicographer. In April 1800 he went to Wadham College, Oxford, and left about 1803 without a degree, having suffered ill health, and after serving for a while as a sub-librarian in the Bodleian Library. At Oxford he came under Baptist influences, and attended the local Baptist chapel. He was also approached by Roman Catholics, to whom he developed an unshakeable aversion.

None the less, after a reported romantic disappointment, Howels was ordained by Richard Watson, bishop of Llandaff, in June 1804, to the curacy of Llan-gan, Glamorgan. Both he and his vicar, David Jones, occasioned some complaint by preaching at Methodist chapels. In 1812 Howels became curate to William Goode (d. 1816) in the united parishes of St Andrew by the Wardrobe and St Ann Blackfriars, London, but, as in Glamorgan, the taint of Methodism proved an obstacle to further promotion. In 1817 he became lessee of the episcopal chapel in Long Acre, where he gradually gathered together an appreciative audience. His strongly evangelical sermons (of which several editions were published after his death) were widely popular, and his self-denying life, despite his eccentricities, gave no handle to his enemies.

Howels was widely regarded as a Calvinistic Methodist. He had been shocked by early contact with learned free-willers at Oxford and uneducated ones in Glamorgan, but inveighed equally against theories of predestinate reprobation. He always professed adherence to the established church, an identification no doubt reinforced in the course of his 1828–9 campaign of prayer and petition against Catholic emancipation. He was a strong opponent of the Irvingite (Catholic Apostolic) church.

Howels died in London on 18 November 1832 of bronchial inflammation, no doubt aggravated by his inability to give up smoking. As he remarked on his deathbed, 'The soul too has its air-tubes, and they are choked by sin' (*Evangelical Magazine*, 8). He was buried in a vault under Holy Trinity Church, Cloudesley Square, Islington; in the church itself a tablet was placed to his memory.

W. A. J. ARCHBOLD, *rev.* JULIAN LOCK

Sources H. Melvill, *A sermon preached at Long Acre Episcopal Chapel on Sunday, Nov. 25, 1832: on the occasion of the death of the Reverend William Howels, M.A.* [sic], *minister of that chapel* (1832) • *Remains of … William Howels*, ed. W. P. Moore, 2nd edn (1852), preface • C. Bowdler, 'Memoir', in W. Howels, *Sermons*, 2 vols. (1834) • 'Memoir of the late Rev. William Howels', *Evangelical Magazine and Missionary Chronicle*, new ser., 11 (1833), 1–9 • *The Record* (19 Nov 1832) • J. Evans, *Biographical dictionary of ministers and preachers of the Welsh Calvinistic Methodist body* (1907), 124–7 • T. R. Roberts, *Eminent Welshmen: a short biographical dictionary* (1908), 173–4 • Allibone, *Dict.* • E. Morgan, *A brief*

memoir of the late W. Howels, minister of Long Acre Chapel, London (1854)
Likenesses engraving, repro. in Morgan, *Brief memoir*
Wealth at death estate to Church Missionary Society: Melvill, *A sermon*; *Evangelical Magazine and Missionary Chronicle*

Howerd, Frankie [*real name* Francis Alick Howard] (1917–1992), comedian, was born in York on 6 March 1917, the elder son and eldest of three children of Francis Alfred William Howard, soldier and tutor in the army education corps, and his wife, Edith Florence, *née* Morrison. When Frankie was born his father was a private in the 1st (Royal) Dragoons. In 1920 he was posted to Woolwich barracks and he set up home in Eltham, London—coincidentally the place where Bob Hope, another major comic talent, was born in 1903. After a spell in the army education corps Howard senior's health deteriorated and he was invalided out of the army when Frankie was in his teens. At the age of eleven Frankie won a scholarship to Shooters Hill grammar school, where his best subject was mathematics. At the age of thirteen he became a Sunday school teacher at the local church of St Barnabas. Later he joined the church dramatic society and he appeared in an amateur production of *Tilly of Bloomsbury*, his stage début. This led him to apply for a place at the Royal Academy of Dramatic Art, but he failed the audition and took a series of undemanding clerical jobs, spending his evenings appearing with local concert parties, and in talent shows where his hesitant, stumbling manner was not appreciated. It was not the sort of stumbling that subsequently made him famous, but was born of nerves and shyness.

In 1940 Frankie was called up and he served in the Royal Artillery. Stationed at Shoeburyness, Essex, he became, at last, a popular entertainer much appreciated by his fellow servicemen and women, and he honed the mixture of banter, insult, and denigration that later became his trademark. In 1943 he joined a civilian concert party called the Co-oddments, touring the Southend-on-Sea area. It was here that he met the two women—Vere Roper and Blanche Moore, both pianists—who became in turn his much maligned, allegedly deaf accompanist, and the butt of his humour. Next he was posted to Germany and, after some false starts (failed auditions with humourless officers), he attracted the attention of Major Richard Stone, who in the post-war years was to become a leading theatrical agent. He liked Frankie's routine and sent him off with a concert party to entertain the troops. It was at this time that he adapted his surname to Howerd 'to be different'.

Demobbed in 1946 Howerd appeared at the Stage Door Canteen in Piccadilly Circus, a venue that in the later stages of the Second World War was a popular meeting-place for allied troops. Here, at a concert, he was a success and he was spotted by a theatrical agent, Stanley 'Scruffy' Dale. Dale's boss, Jack Payne, an astute impresario, duly put Howerd under contract. Dale arranged an audition for the BBC radio comedy and music show *Variety Bandbox*, and on 3 December 1946 the nation heard Frankie Howerd on the wireless for the first time; he became that rarest of creatures, a star overnight. By 1947 he was one of the most

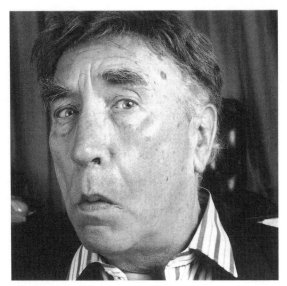

Frankie Howerd (1917–1992), by Vincent Gillett

popular entertainers in the country, broadcasting regularly and touring the music-halls, often with Max Bygraves, a contemporary from a similar background. Jack Payne's ingenious manipulation of contracts made sure that Howerd received only a small percentage of his actual fee. In 1957, after a protracted court case, Howerd won both money and freedom from Payne. Stanley Dale had, by this time, left Payne, and he became Howerd's personal manager. Their fortunes soared.

By 1951, joined by Eric Sykes, the writer chiefly responsible for Howerd's radio scripts, Howerd and Dale formed F. Howerd Scripts Ltd, which later blossomed as Associated London Scripts (the directors were Dale, Howerd, Sykes, and the writers Ray Galton and Alan Simpson, Johnny Speight, Tony Hancock, and Spike Milligan). Dale, with a technique similar to that of Payne, managed to pocket a large sum of money to which he was not entitled; he was ejected from Associated London Scripts and faded from the story. Howerd's success continued and he had many triumphs, including the radio show *Frankie's Bandbox* (1961), and films, principally *The Runaway Bus* (1954), *The Lady Killers* (1955), *The Great St Trinian's Train Robbery* (1966), *Carry on Doctor* (1968), and *Up Pompeii* (1970). His television successes included *The Howerd Crowd* (1952, script by Eric Sykes), *Nuts in May* (1953, script by Galton and Simpson), and, most importantly for Howerd, *That Was The Week That Was* (1962, script by Galton, Simpson, and Speight). Most memorable was the long running *Up Pompeii* (script by Talbot Rothwell). On stage he had success in the revue *Pardon my French* (1953), the farce *Charlie's Aunt* (1955), as Bottom in *A Midsummer Night's Dream* at the Old Vic (1956), and in the musical *A Funny Thing Happened on the Way to the Forum* (1964–5). On Howerd's way to the forum there were hiccups. Molière's *School for Wives* (1957) was not a success, and a musical, *Mr Venus*, folded after only seventeen performances in 1958. Worse was to come: a situation comedy, *Frankly Howerd* (1959), was a flop; a television version of *Twenty Questions* (1961) also failed; and by 1962 the top bosses of the BBC, both radio and television, felt that Howerd was finished. But in 1962 help was at hand. Peter Cook, seeing Howerd at the *London Evening Standard* drama awards, where he was doing a spot, invited him to appear at his recently opened nightclub The Establishment. This led to Howerd's being given a spot on *That Was The Week That Was*, with such topical remarks as 'David Frost—you know, the one who has his hair on backwards', and 'Robin Day—hasn't he got cruel glasses'. This one television appearance had Howerd back at the top, and he was never to suffer the agonies of failing so badly again.

Personally, Howerd could be charming or acerbic as the mood took him, kindness itself or bitingly sarcastic. He was not above inviting himself to friends' homes for lunch or dinner, but he entertained lavishly when on occasion he pushed the boat out. He was conspicuously untidy in appearance and wore a revolting toupee, to which he never referred. Howerd's speciality was the conversational innuendo—a constant banter addressed to the camera or to individual members of the audience—whose content was much less smutty than its tone. Frankie Howerd never married; he died in hospital of heart failure on 19 April 1992, surrounded by friends and family. He was buried in the churchyard of St Gregory's Church, Weare, Somerset, on 29 April. He was one of the most outstanding comedians of his day and he brought originality and flair to many of his performances.　　　　　　　　BARRY TOOK

Sources B. Took, *Star turns* (1992) · F. Howerd, *On the way I lost it* (1976) · personal knowledge (2004) · private information (2004) · *The Times* (20 April 1992) · *The Independent* (20 April 1992) · b. cert. · W. Hall, *Titter ye not! the life of Frankie Howerd* (1992) · *The Times* (30 April 1992)

Likenesses photographs, 1949–90, Hult. Arch. · V. Gillett, photograph, NPG [*see illus.*] · photograph, repro. in *The Times* · photograph, repro. in *The Independent* · photographs, repro. in Howerd, *On the way I lost it* · photographs, repro. in Took, *Star turns* · photographs, repro. in Hall, *Titter ye not!*

Wealth at death £1,327,198: probate, 13 July 1992, *CGPLA Eng. & Wales*

Howes, Edmund (*fl.* 1602–1631), chronicler, is of uncertain family background, education, and early career, but by 1602 he was living in London and calling himself a 'gentleman'. He continued the work of John Stow, extending his *Abridgement of the English Chronicle* (1607) and *Annales, or, A Generall Chronicle of England*. There is some indication that he shared Stow's links with the great companies and the office-holders of the City of London. Howes tells us in his preface to the *Abridgement* that he began to work on Stow's material in 1602, three years before the latter's death. When Stow died, Howes tried to find someone else to take on the task of writing a chronicle of the years since Stow's last edition, but failed. Some told him that this work would bring poverty, backbiting, and perhaps 'capitall displesaure'. Others said that the work must be one of flattery in order to avoid scandal. Nevertheless, Howes told the lord mayor and court of aldermen that he would do the work. He ended his preface with an encomium of London and an expression of confidence that

with the protection of the City and of 'Honourable Superiors' he would be safe from danger. He published an edition of Stow's *Annales* with a continuation in 1615, and continued his extension of Stow's work up to his last edition of the *Annales* in 1631.

Howes states that he was encouraged in his work by Archbishop Whitgift, the pre-eminent exponent of Anglican orthodoxy, and in a list of acknowledgements of 1631 he also thanks archbishops Bancroft and Abbott, besides such other eminent bishops as Lancelot Andrewes. He may have felt anxious on the matter of religion because Stow had been suspected of recusancy. Political figures on the list included Sir Thomas Egerton, chancellor of England; Robert, earl of Salisbury, lord high treasurer; Viscount Fenton; and Sir Edward Coke. He also acknowledged the antiquaries Sir Robert Cotton, William Camden, and Abraham Hartwell, though his own work is not noticeably antiquarian in style.

Evidence that Howes was well connected and was perhaps himself a political figure comes from his letter of 1630 written to Edward Nicholas, secretary to the Admiralty, giving an account of a conversation he had had with Robert Pye, auditor of the receipt of the exchequer, saying that he had assured Pye of Nicholas's integrity. The letter presumes a high degree of influence with an important official. A manuscript in the British Library in Howes's hand, apparently used in preparing the 1631 *Annales*, includes far greater detail than the printed book. Howes's continuation of the *Abridgement* includes a mix of elements. Odd events such as the birth of lion cubs in the Tower of London and the discovery of a whale's dead body far up the Thames estuary, in which one might see omens or the hand of God, contrast with lengthy discussions on important political events such as the Gunpowder Plot, the creation of the East India Company, and news from Virginia, where Stow had chronicled the history of English efforts at colonization from 1584 to his date of writing. The king's contacts with guilds receive much attention, and Howes includes further foreign elements, among them a very brief history of the republic of Venice. Where Stow had appended accounts of Oxford and Cambridge universities to the *Annales*, Howes added one on 'the University of London', that is, the inns of court and other institutions of higher learning, written by Sir George Buck.

　　　　　　　　　　　　　　　　　CHRISTINA DECOURSEY

Sources B. L. Beer, *Tudor England observed: the world of John Stow* (1998) · *CSP dom.*, 1629–31, 416 [letter to Edward Nicholas, secretary to the Admiralty, 1630] · *N&Q*, 6 (1852), 199–200

Howes, Edward (*fl.* 1632–1659), mathematician, of unknown parentage, studied law at Inner Temple, probably under Emanuel Downing, with whom he lodged in Fleet Street, London. He was a close friend and frequent correspondent of John Winthrop, first when Winthrop was still living at Groton, Suffolk, and later when he was governor of Massachusetts. In 1632, writing from Inner Temple, he sent Winthrop a tract which he had printed, entitled *Of the Circumference of the Earth, or, A Treatise of the North West Passage*, claiming that a north-west passage to the Pacific was probably to be found at about 40° N, rather than at 60° N or 70° N as generally supposed. After Winthrop's departure for New England, Howes regularly sent him news and packets of books, copied out useful recipes for the colonists, and in 1635 intimated that he would send Winthrop one of the magnetic 'engines … that will sympathise at a distance' ('Letters of Edward Howes', 25 Aug 1635), perhaps a means of remagnetizing compass needles. In exchange he asked Winthrop to send him some furs to line his winter coat.

In 1640 Howes informed Winthrop that his parents were both alive and well, and that he and his wife were as yet childless. By 1644 he was a master in the Ratcliffe Free School; at this time he was urging Winthrop to acquire some land in Boston, where he might set up a school for the colonists' children, but although he several times alluded to his intention of emigrating to New England, he never did so.

Howes had presumably taken holy orders, for he was described as rector of Goldhanger, Essex, when he published his *Short Arithmetick, or, The Old and Tedious Way of Numbers Reduced to a New and Briefe Method* (1659). This text dealt effectively with the practical instruction; Howes referred to the theoretical part's being finished and ready for publication, if desired, but this did not happen. The circumstances of Howes's later years remain obscure.

R. E. ANDERSON, rev. ANITA MCCONNELL

Sources R. C. Winthrop, ed., *Life and letters of John Winthrop*, 2nd edn, 2 vols. (Boston, 1869), vol. 1, p. 20 · *The Winthrop papers* (Boston, 1846), 226–301 · 'Letters of Edward Howes', *Collections of the Massachusetts Historical Society*, 4th ser., 6 (1863), 467–513 · E. Howes, *Short arithmetick, or, The old and tedious way of numbers reduced to a new and briefe method* (1659)

Howes, Francis (1776–1844), classical scholar, was born at Morningthorpe, Norfolk, on 29 February 1776, the fourth surviving son of the Revd Thomas Howes (1732–1796) of Morningthorpe, successively rector of Fritton and Illington, Norfolk, and Susan (b. 1736), daughter of Francis Longe of Spixworth in the same county. Howes was descended from a minor gentry family who had lived in the Wymondham area since the middle ages. His eldest surviving brother, John (1758–1787), entered Gray's Inn but died young. Two other brothers, Thomas (1770–1848) and George (1772–1855), took holy orders, the latter taking over Spixworth, a family living. One of their six sisters, Margaret, married Edward Hawkins, and was mother of Edward Hawkins, provost of Oriel. Their cousin Thomas Howes (1729–1814) had previously been rector of Morningthorpe.

Francis Howes was educated at Norwich grammar school under Dr Samuel Parr. He entered Trinity College, Cambridge, in 1794, graduated BA in 1798 as eleventh wrangler, and proceeded MA in 1804. In 1799 and 1800 he obtained the members' prize. His chief college friend was John Williams, the judge, who subsequently made him an allowance of £100 per annum. Howes is said to have 'married early' (*DNB*) but in fact was of full age, having married Sarah (1773–1863), daughter of Christopher Smithson, in St Nicholas Chapel, King's Lynn, on 23 March 1802. It is probable that his family disapproved of the match; the late father of his bride had been a member of St John's College, Cambridge—but as a cook, not a fellow (*Universal British Directory*, 2, c.1792, 493). Their sons were Thomas George (b. 1807), later rector of Belton, Suffolk; John (1808–1837), parish clerk; and Charles (1813–1880), fellow and chaplain of Dulwich College. Three of their six daughters married clergymen.

Howes had been ordained deacon on 21 December 1800 and priest on 9 August 1801. He was appointed vicar of Shillington, Bedfordshire, in 1801, a position which he held until 1816. He appears not to have lived there: his sons were baptized in Acle, Norfolk, from where his first books were dated. He was also vicar of Wickham Skeith, Suffolk, from 1809 until his death (including Wickham Market until 1827), and rector of Buckenham (with Hassingham), Norfolk, from 1811 to 1814. In 1814 he moved to St George Colegate, Norwich, as parish chaplain, a position which he held until 1831, and was appointed vicar of Bawburgh, Norfolk, remaining in this post until 1829. But in 1815 he was appointed a minor canon of Norwich Cathedral and moved to the close, where he lived for the rest of his life. He received the rectories of Alderford (in 1820) and Framingham Pigot (in 1829), both in Norfolk, and retained them until his death. The diocese of Norwich was notorious for pluralism and absentee clergy, but the bishop, Henry Bathurst, always pointed out that the majority of parishes were small and produced a low income.

Some translations from Latin into English verse were printed privately for Howes in 1801 and included in his *Miscellaneous Poetical Translations* (1806). His translation of *The Satires of A. Persius Flaccus* (1809) was unsuccessful. Although he claimed that his translation of Horace's *Satires* was 'shortly' to be published, *The Epodes and Secular Ode of Horace* did not appear until 1841 and *The First Book of Horace's Satires* in 1842; both were privately printed in Norwich. Only after his death did his son Charles publish his father's *The Epodes, Satires, and Epistles of Horace* (1845) on which his reputation rests. The latter was commended by John Conington as:

> very good, unforced, idiomatic, felicitous … I should be glad if any notice which I may be fortunate enough to attract should … extend to a predecesor who, if he had published a few years earlier, when translations were of more account, could scarcely have failed to rank high among the cultivators of this branch of literature. (Conington, xxii–xxiii)

Howes, who composed epitaphs for monuments in Norwich Cathedral, spent his last years transcribing the diary of his eccentric but cultured neighbour Sylas Neville (1741–1840), though nothing extensive was published for over a century (*Diary of Sylas Neville*, xiv). Howes died at the close, Norwich, on 26 March 1844 and was buried in the west cloister of the cathedral near his son John. His widow died on 3 January 1863.   K. A. MANLEY

Sources family pedigrees, Norfolk RO · Venn, *Alum. Cant.* · D. Turner, *List of Norfolk benefices* (1847) · R. G. Wilson, 'The cathedral in the Georgian period, 1720–1840', *Norwich Cathedral: church, city and diocese, 1096–1996*, ed. I. Atherton and others (1996), 578–611, esp. 591 · J. Conington, *The satires, epistles, and art of poetry of Horace,*

4th edn (1874), xi, xxii–xxiii • *The diary of Sylas Neville, 1767–1788*, ed. B. Cozens-Hardy (1950), xiv

Archives Norfolk RO, family papers

Howes, Frank Stewart (1891–1974), music critic and author, was born on 2 April 1891 at 13 Cobden Crescent, Oxford, the elder child and only son of George Howes (1866–1949), a grocer and amateur singer of Oxford, and his wife, Grace Selina Phipps (1866–1949). He was educated at Oxford high school, then at St John's College, Oxford (1910–14). He obtained third classes in classical honour moderations and *literae humaniores*, rowed for his college at Henley, and sang in the chorus in performances of Beethoven's *Fidelio* and Weber's *Der Freischütz* conducted by Hugh Allen. He became a schoolmaster, served a brief prison sentence during the First World War as a pacifist conscientious objector, and then went to the Royal College of Music (1920–22), attending the criticism class run by H. C. Colles. In 1925 he joined Colles as a music critic on *The Times*, and he succeeded to the principal post on Colles's death in 1943. On 18 September 1929 Howes married Barbara Mildred (1902–1998), daughter of John Tidd Pratt, a solicitor of Newark-on-Trent, and niece of the warden of Wadham; they had three daughters and one son.

Howes's first book, *The Borderland of Music and Psychology* (1926), and his editing of what became the *Journal of the English Folk Dance and Song Society* (1927–45) indicated the cast of his mind, in which speculation was rooted in the soil of his native country. His *A Key to Opera* (with P. Hope-Wallace, 1939) revealed another enthusiasm. In his *Full Orchestra* (1942, a revised edition of which appeared posthumously in 1976) his experience as a lecturer together with his lively, lucid prose produced a popular success.

Howes taught history of music and criticism at the Royal College of Music from 1938 to 1970, during the war coming up from his family retreat, an old mill house near Standlake, where the River Windrush flows into the Thames. When he took over at *The Times* in 1943, readers were jaded, and both newsprint and music were in short supply. With vigour and assurance he directed the post-war expansion. He approved the anonymity then in force—though his own views and style were recognizable enough—as an aid to objective, responsible criticism without personal display. Though no longer a Congregationalist but a secular humanist, Howes maintained Colles's support for church music. He insisted on a wide coverage in the paper, so that débuts and amateur events were reported as well as major national occasions. He retained *The Times*'s weekly music article, valuing the chance to expand on a remote or a topical point, and was once delighted to be complimented simply on the range of his subjects. He refused to look at scores in advance or to attend dress rehearsals, and liked writing his notice on the night, believing that the pressure made for immediacy and allowed no opportunity for outside influence.

Howes threw his considerable weight behind such causes as opera in English (he himself knew no modern languages), the founding of Musica Britannica, and the building of the Royal Festival Hall; *The Times*'s coverage of the Festival of Britain was reprinted in *Musical Britain, 1951*. His authority and urbane common sense made him much in demand on committees: he was president of the Royal Musical Association (1948–58) and chairman of the Musicians' Benevolent Fund (1938–56) and of the English Folk Dance and Song Society (1932–46), and also served on the Arts Council and the British Council and held responsibilities in the BBC, the British Institute of Recorded Sound, and the Music in Hospitals. He gave the Cramb lectures at Glasgow University in 1947 and 1952, and the first Crees lectures (1950) for the Royal College of Music. He was created CBE in 1954; he was an honorary fellow of the Royal College of Music and honorary member of the Royal Academy of Music, and an honorary freeman of the Worshipful Company of Musicians.

In spite of these commitments, Howes's early *William Byrd* (1928) was followed by the valuable and substantial studies *The Music of Ralph Vaughan Williams* (1954) and *The Music of William Walton* (1965; revised, 1974). Though his approach was on the whole analytical, he was always concerned to uncover the thoughts behind the sound, to relate music and ethics, to consider symbolism and aesthetics. These ideas he set out in *Man, Mind and Music* (1948). His wide sympathies extended notably to Benjamin Britten, but less to Igor Stravinsky and hardly at all to Arnold Schoenberg and his school, but his strong intellect and professional curiosity enabled him to write stimulatingly about music he disliked, and only occasionally could he be provoked into bluntness. His probity and good humour were respected even by those who might disagree with his taste.

Howes retired from *The Times* in 1960, and out of his study beside the murmuring mill-race came *The Cheltenham Festival* (1965), published while he was chairman of that festival, and *Oxford Concerts: a Jubilee Record* (1969). During these years he wrote his autobiography: a record of the changes in his world and vignettes of notable people he knew as well as a personal testament, it remains in typescript in the British Library. His major works, summarizing his life's interest, were *The English Musical Renaissance* (1966), an overview of a period he had largely lived through, and *Folkmusic of Britain—and Beyond* (1969). He contributed many notices to the *Dictionary of National Biography*.

Howes was a deeply emotional but self-reliant man, for whom music was one of the humanities. He was a trenchant speaker who enjoyed great occasions; but was as happy among his family and close friends on his river bank. There in the end he suffered from cancer. Howes died at the Radcliffe Infirmary, Oxford, on 28 September 1974. He was cremated at Oxford crematorium on 2 October 1974, and his ashes were interred at St Lawrence, Combe, Oxfordshire.   DIANA MCVEAGH

Sources personal knowledge (2004) • private information (2004) [Barbara Howes, widow; family] • F. S. Howes, autobiography, priv. coll. • *CGPLA Eng. & Wales* (1974)

Archives priv. coll., autobiography | BL, corresp. with Society of Authors, Add. MS 63274 | SOUND BL NSA, performance recordings
Likenesses photograph, 1960–1969?, priv. coll.

Howes, John (*fl.* **1772–1793**), miniature and enamel painter, of whose parents nothing is known, entered the Royal Academy Schools on 28 June 1770 and gained the academy's silver medal in 1772. He is principally known as an exhibitor of portraits and of other subjects in enamel at the Royal Academy from 1772 to 1793. He occasionally exhibited miniatures and latterly a few historical pictures. In 1777 he painted and exhibited a medallion portrait in enamel of David Garrick from a drawing by G. B. Cipriani, which was presented to the actor by the Incorporated Society of Actors of Drury Lane Theatre, of which he was perpetual president. This miniature was loaned to a special exhibition at the South Kensington Museum in 1862. Graves recorded Walpole's comment that the likeness was 'very bad and unlike' (Graves, *RA exhibitors*, 4.175). L. H. CUST, *rev.* ANNETTE PEACH

Sources D. Foskett, *Miniatures: dictionary and guide* (1987) · S. C. Hutchison, 'The Royal Academy Schools, 1768–1830', *Walpole Society*, 38 (1960–62), 123–91, esp. 135 · B. S. Long, *British miniaturists* (1929) · G. C. Williamson, *The history of portrait miniatures*, 1 (1904), 147, 188; 2 (1904), 58 · Graves, *RA exhibitors* · Science and Art Department of the Committee of Council on Education, *Catalogue of the special exhibition of works of art of the mediaeval, Renaissance and modern periods, on loan at the South Kensington Museum, June 1862* (1862), p. 212

Howes, Thomas (1728–1814), historian and religious controversialist, was born at Thorndon, Suffolk, and was baptized at All Saints' Church there on 19 October 1728. He was the only son of Thomas Howes (1698–1773), clergyman, and his wife, Elizabeth, daughter of John Colman of Hindringham, Norfolk. He matriculated at Clare College, Cambridge, in 1743, graduating BA in 1746. Howes served in the army before entering the church. He was ordained priest at Norwich in 1756, and was rector of Illington, Norfolk (1756–87), of Morningthorpe (1756–71), and of Thorndon (1771–1814). He ordinarily resided in Norwich, where he became acquainted with Samuel Parr, with whom he afterwards corresponded.

Howes was of a retiring, bookish nature and appears to have mixed very little with the Norwich intelligentsia. His *Critical Observations on Books, Antient and Modern* commenced publication in 1776. Until 1783 Howes published a numbered part each year; these formed the first two volumes of the work. 'Number I' was miscellaneous in nature, but 'Number II' and subsequent parts were largely concerned with Howes's favourite subject of 'the Principles of Antient Chronology': he wanted to explain 'doubtful and contested passages in the Jewish Scriptures by means of a more accurate system of prophane chronology' (Howes, 2.110). His treatment of the subject was increasingly systematic. While these recondite researches went largely unnoticed by Howes's contemporaries, the appearance of Joseph Priestley's controversial *History of the Corruptions of Christianity* in 1782 led Howes to believe that he could contribute to a topic of more general interest. For several years he suspended his chronological

researches in favour of a study of the unitarian question. The first product of this was *A Discourse on the Abuse of the Talent of Disputation in Religion* (1784), published separately and as the first part of 'Number IX' of *Critical Observations*. Howes argued, against Priestley, that the early Gnostic sects had not understood Jesus's 'humanity' as extending throughout his life but rather believed that, at his baptism, 'an union was formed between the pre-existent divinity of the Christ or Savior and the humanity of Jesus; which was dissolved again … before his passion' (Howes, 3.14). Howes promised a full discussion of the subject in the fourth volume of *Critical Observations* (the third was intended to complete his chronological system). Parr reviewed the *Discourse* favourably in the *Monthly Review*, taking the opportunity to endorse *Critical Observations*: 'We are happy … in this opportunity of informing our Readers, that for acuteness of reasoning, and depth of erudition, the criticisms of Mr. Howes deserve to be ranked in the highest class of literary publications' (71.319). *Critical Observations* gained further publicity when Priestley responded to the *Discourse* in his *Importance and Extent of Free Inquiry in Matters of Religion* (1785).

From this period the bibliographical history of *Critical Observations* is complicated. Because of the topical nature of the unitarian question Howes published the fourth volume in three instalments (1785, 1787, 1795), respectively the remainder of 'Number IX', an 'Appendix', and 'Number X', before the bulk of the third volume had appeared. He then returned to his chronological enquiries and published the third volume in five instalments (1788, 1791, 1800, 1805, 1807), respectively an 'Appendix', 'Illustrations of the Appendix', and 'Number XI' to 'Number XIII'. Very few surviving copies are complete. The parts published in 1785 and 1787 brought Howes a brief celebrity. The first was answered by Priestley in his *Letters to Dr. Horsley, Part III* (1786), Priestley mixing flattery with his criticisms, as he wished to establish Howes as his principal trinitarian antagonist. The second was answered by Priestley in his *Defences of Unitarianism for the Year 1787* (1788), Priestley now adopting a more contemptuous tone. At this stage Howes does seem to have felt that he was being hurried into arguments that were not fully defensible, hence the long delay before the completion of volume 4. Priestley characteristically represented Howes's retreat from the controversy as a victory for the unitarian cause.

Apart from the publication of *Critical Observations* Howes appears to have lived a retired and entirely uneventful life. He died unmarried, in St Giles's parish, Norwich, on 29 September 1814, and was buried at All Saints' Church, Thorndon, on 6 October. DAVID CHANDLER

Sources T. Howes, *Critical observations on books, antient and modern* (1776–1807) · Venn, *Alum. Cant.* · *DNB* · parish register, Thorndon, Suffolk [baptism, burial] · *Norfolk Chronicle and Norwich Gazette* (1 Oct 1814) · *GM*, 1st ser., 84/2 (1814), 404 · *IGI* · Sudbury induction book, Suffolk RO, MS E14/5/1 · *The works of Samuel Parr … with memoirs of his life and writings*, ed. J. Johnstone, 8 vols. (1828) · D. Chandler, 'A bibliographical history of Thomas Howes' *Critical observations* (1776–1807) and his dispute with Joseph Priestley', *Studies in Bibliography*, 54 (2001)

Howes, Thomas George Bond (1853–1905), zoologist, was born on 7 September 1853 at 4 High Street, St Mary Newington, Surrey, the eldest son of Thomas Johnson Howes, hosier, and his wife, Augusta Mary, daughter of George Augustus Bond, a captain in the East India Company's service. Privately educated, he was introduced to Thomas Huxley in 1874 as a good draughtsman and keen naturalist. He assisted Huxley in the development of practical instruction in biology at the Normal School of Science and the Royal School of Mines at Kensington, London. In 1880 he was appointed demonstrator of biology at the latter institution. The following year Howes married Annie, daughter of James Watkins. They had one daughter.

In 1885 Howes was made an assistant professor of zoology at the Normal School of Science, and in 1895 was appointed first professor of zoology at the Royal College of Science, South Kensington, a position he held for the rest of his life.

Howes excelled as a teacher; the thoroughness of the biology courses at South Kensington was largely due to his knowledge and zeal. He devoted much time and energy to founding or extending the work of societies that promoted natural knowledge, and he occupied a responsible position on most of the London societies. At the Belfast meeting of the British Association in 1902 Howes was president of section D (zoology). His skill as a draughtsman was great, and the work by which he is best known to students, *Atlas of Elementary Biology* (1885), was entirely illustrated from his own drawings; the zoological part was revised as *Atlas of Elementary Zootomy* (1902). Another well-known textbook, Huxley and Martin's *Elementary Biology* (1875), was issued in a revised form by Howes and Dukinfield Scott in 1888.

As an investigator, Howes dealt chiefly with the comparative anatomy of the Vertebrata, to the knowledge of which he made many contributions, the most important being an account written with H. H. Swinnerton of the development of the skeleton of the rare Norfolk Island reptile, *Sphenodon* (*Transactions of the Zoological Society*, 1901). He was elected FRS in 1897, LLD at St Andrews in 1898, and DSc at Manchester in 1899. He died at his home, Ingledene, Barrowgate Road, Chiswick, on 4 February 1905, survived by his wife.   F. W. GAMBLE, *rev.* V. M. QUIRKE

Sources T. R. R. S., *PRS*, 79B (1907), xxxi–xxxiv · *Nature*, 71 (1904–5), 419–20 · *Proceedings of the Linnean Society of London*, 117th session (1904–5), 34–9 · private information (1912) · b. cert.
Archives ICL, letters to Leonard Huxley · Royal Entomological Society of London, corresp. with Herbert Druce
Likenesses Maull & Fox, portrait, RS
Wealth at death £1522 19s. 6d.: probate, 13 March 1905, *CGPLA Eng. & Wales*

Howey, (Rose) Elsie Neville (1884–1963), suffragette, was born at Finningley, Nottinghamshire, on 1 December 1884, the daughter of Thomas Howey (b. 1851/2), rector of Finningley, and his wife, Emily Gertrude (*née* Oldfield). Following Thomas Howey's death, the family moved to the Malvern area which remained Elsie's home for life. Although details of her childhood are sparse, Elsie was educated to a good standard, and in 1902 enrolled in St Andrews University for a standard arts degree course, taking classes in English, French, and German. For unspecified reasons she did not complete her studies, but left in 1904 to travel to Germany. Here 'she first had occasion to realise women's position' and determined to work to improve it (*Votes for Women*, 18 June 1908).

In December 1907 Elsie encountered the Women's Social and Political Union (WSPU) campaigning in a by-election at Ross. With her mother and elder sister Marie she joined the union. Both Howey girls embraced militant tactics and were arrested and gaoled in February 1908 when, with other suffragettes, they hid inside a pantechnicon and were 'delivered' into the House of Commons. For Elsie this marked the beginning of a dedicated WSPU career. She soon joined a group of young 'freelance militants' undertaking daring independent actions for the cause. A loyal and popular suffragette, she was motivated as much by friendship as political conviction. In January 1910 when Lady Constance Lytton, disguised as a working-class woman, was arrested and forcibly fed in Walton gaol, Elsie broke the governor's windows and was also gaoled in order that Lady Constance should not suffer alone. Constance Lytton felt this made Elsie the 'most dear one of our members' (C. Lytton and J. Warton, *Prisons and Prisoners: some Personal Experiences*, 1914, 247). Elsie also drew sympathy from less expected quarters. In December 1912, when she was gaoled for two months for giving a false fire alarm, seventy-five 'working men and farmers' from Malvern wrote to their MP demanding a reduced punishment for their 'much loved' local suffragette (*The Suffragette*, 27 Dec 1912).

Although an active militant, Elsie did not eschew the more mundane sides of WSPU work. Early in 1909 she responded to a call for 'young women with private means' to work as honorary WSPU organizers for a year. Supported financially and morally by her mother, Elsie spent the next year working in Plymouth and Torquay where she helped to establish a suffragette presence. She also achieved national recognition that year when she headed a WSPU demonstration through London dressed as Joan of Arc, in a full set of armour, 'astride a great white charger' (Pankhurst, *Suffragette Movement*, 367).

From 1910 Elsie was 'in the vanguard' of militancy (*The Suffragette*, 3 Jan 1913). She underwent at least six imprisonments. This hides the full extent of her daring as she was skilled at escaping arrest. In September 1909 with two others she climbed into Lympne Castle, Kent, where the prime minister was staying, and demanded 'votes for women' through the dining-room window while the Asquiths dined. The suffragettes escaped via an adjacent canal. On the occasions that she was arrested, Elsie demonstrated total dedication to her cause, undergoing several hunger strikes and enduring forcible feeding. Her final imprisonment was in December 1912. This time she was released early following a prolonged hunger strike which prompted questions in parliament, although the anonymous friend who paid her fine was too late to prevent forcible feeding from breaking most of Elsie's teeth.

Tired and ill, Elsie vanished from public life when militancy ended in 1914. She remained in Malvern but followed no career, and never fully recovered from the sacrifices she made in the name of the WSPU. She died on 13 March 1963 at the Court House Nursing Home, Court Road, Malvern, from chronic pyloric stenosis, almost certainly connected to her numerous forcible feedings. Aside from about £2000 in personal legacies, she left the residue of her £23,000 estate to the English Theosophical Trust. She gave instructions in her will for cremation and the scattering of her ashes, requesting 'that no funeral service of any kind shall be held for me'. Her cremation took place at Worcester. KRISTA COWMAN

Sources R. Fulford, *Votes for women: the story of a struggle* (1957) · *Votes for Women* (18 June 1908) · *Votes for Women* (11 Feb 1909) · *The Suffragette* (27 Dec 1912) · *The Suffragette* (3 Jan 1913) · *The Suffragette* (17 Jan 1913) · U. St Andr. L. · A. Morley and L. Stanley, *The life and death of Emily Wilding Davison* (1988) · A. Raeburn, *The militant suffragettes* (1973) · A. J. R., ed., *The suffrage annual and women's who's who* (1913) · S. Pankhurst, *The suffragette* (1911) · E. S. Pankhurst, *The suffragette movement: an intimate account of persons and ideals* (1931); repr. (1977) · b. cert. · d. cert. · will · Foster, *Alum. Oxon.* · *Malvern Gazette* (15 March 1963) · *CGPLA Eng. & Wales* (1963)
Likenesses photograph, *c.*1913, repro. in *The Suffragette* (17 Jan 1913) · photograph (as Jeanne d'Arc), repro. in Pankhurst, *Suffragette* · photographs (engaged in Women's Social and Political Union activities), Museum of London, Suffragette Fellowship Collection; repro. in D. Atkinson, *The suffragettes in pictures* (1996)
Wealth at death £22,964 10s. 6d.: probate, 13 May 1963, *CGPLA Eng. & Wales*

Howgill, Francis (1618?–1669), Quaker activist, was born probably in 1618, in the small village of Todthorne, near Grayrigg, Westmorland. His father was possibly a yeoman, though nothing else of his parentage is known. One near-contemporary record of Quaker preaching, though, does seem to indicate that Francis had a sister; most biographers assume that the reference is to Mary Howgill, who was a well-known Quaker minister. However, the Mary Howgill who addressed Oliver Cromwell, travelled to Ireland, was imprisoned in Lancaster, and achieved a notorious reputation for 'ministering confusion' was probably not the same Mary Howgill said to have been a spinster resident in Over Kellet, Lancashire. None the less, despite the difficulties involved in establishing Mary's background, and thereby either proving or disproving the sibling connection, there are certainly parallels between Francis's and Mary's Quaker experiences in that both addressed Cromwell and both ministered in Ireland.

Francis's account of his life before Quakerism (given in *The Inheritance of Jacob*, 1656) is so much concerned with describing religion that the details about his education, family, and occupation can only be inferred. He does not make much explicit mention of his family, though the fact that the twelve-year-old Howgill decided to follow the 'strictest' religion indicates, perhaps, that he had been brought up to be sober-minded (p. 5). He chooses to depict his childhood as a spiritually isolating time, but feeling like an outsider did not prevent him from pursuing a relatively conventional religious career; he appears, for instance, to have been university-educated, although his name does not appear in the registers of either Oxford or

Cambridge. Howgill had flirted with the Independents and the Baptists, finding much love but little wisdom in their company, but by 1652 he had established himself as a minister in Colton. He may have made his living farming and tailoring in addition to drawing upon the tithe that he was entitled to take from his parishioners. In 1652, however, he and a fellow local minister John Audland both converted to Quakerism after having been cross-questioned by George Fox, the Quaker leader who set himself up as a rival to the incumbents by preaching from a grassy knoll nearby. Howgill was quick to recognize Fox's wisdom, but he was less spiritually ready to embrace the full implications of Quakerism. *The Inheritance of Jacob* is indeed subtly different from many other Quaker autobiographies in that it is expansive about the doubts and insecurities occurring after the first 'convincement'. It is perhaps unsurprising that Howgill's theological disputes were many; he could even parody anti-Quaker attitudes, writing a tongue-in-cheek call for the righteous repression of 'blasphemous doctrines' (*Mistery Babylon*, 1659, 14).

Fox's conversion of an established minister was a significant one for the nascent movement; Howgill soon left his home and family to travel as a Quaker preacher. He had been a respectable social figure—'[a] great Acquaintance with the highest Sorts of Priests'—but this did not put him outside the law which dealt harshly with Quakers (Howgill, *The Dawnings*, sig. D1v). When in January 1653 the Quaker James Nayler was tried for blasphemy in Appleby, Howgill purposely went there in an expression of support. Brought before the bench himself but unprepared to show deference to the judges by doffing his hat, Howgill enraged authority figures. They proceeded to burn his hat, accusing him of being an enemy to 'Ministry and Magistracy', and imprisoned him for five months (Besse, 2.3).

Howgill then joined with the Quaker Edward Burrough, who was his companion in Bristol (1654), London (1654), and Ireland (1655–6). The work in London was particularly demanding because high emotions were soon roused at the large Quaker meetings, as Howgill's frequent letters show. Caught up in the fervour, Howgill once tried, unsuccessfully, to heal a lame boy. Sometimes the letters show him despairing of making an impact, and, indeed, he later viewed the great fire of 1666 as an act of divine retribution for London's ungodliness. But being near the centre of political power also enabled Howgill to address the man of 'subtlety and deceit'—Cromwell (Braithwaite, 445). Howgill and Burrough ministered throughout Ireland in the winter of 1655–6, leaving Nayler in London but upon their banishment from Ireland in 1656 by Henry Cromwell, they returned to a now divided London. Howgill was critical of Nayler's ministry and supporters long before Nayler notoriously re-enacted Christ's entry into Jerusalem in October, which led to his conviction for blasphemy. Though a critic of Nayler, Howgill believed that the Bible could be literally interpreted, and endorsed going 'naked as a sign' (*A Woe Against the Magistrates, Priests, and People of Kendall*, 1654, 1).

The little that can be extracted from contemporary letters about Howgill's personal life presents a man who prioritized his spiritual commitments. Dorothy Howgill, his wife and the mother of at least one child, died in March 1656. After the events in London subsided, Howgill went through a relatively quiet period, which may have reflected his changing domestic circumstances. He was travelling again in Scotland by 1657, and turning up on the list of names of those imprisoned in London in 1661, so his children must have been cared for by someone other than himself. Howgill certainly remarried, but very little is known about his second wife. She may have been from Newcastle, and she gave birth to a child, Henry, on 27 September 1665; but her name is unknown, as is the date of their union. She is referred to, if at all, within her prescribed role as mother and wife; Francis does not name her when writing of the 'sufficient dowry and portion' she brought to the marriage, although this—in a letter to his daughter Abigail—was presumably thought unnecessary information (*The Dawnings*, sig. g3v). Abigail had other sisters (who are also unnamed) and at least two brothers—Thomas and Henry.

Howgill's fortunes changed again when the Commonwealth, which he had supported, was overthrown. In one of his most passionate tracts, Howgill wrote as though addressing himself to the nation, incredulously observing that they had 'Chosen Madness for thy Crown' (*One Warning More*, 1660, 3). His pessimism seems only to have deepened with time. Burrough died in 1663, which was a cause of deep regret, and Howgill was himself found guilty of *praemunire* at Appleby in 1663 after refusing to swear the oath of allegiance. This sentence being passed, he was imprisoned for life. In 1665 he showed that he no longer believed in an eventual Quaker triumph over adversity, resignedly committing himself to suffering 'though the day be dark and gloomy' (*A General Epistle*, 1665, 13). He grew sick through an unspecified illness while in prison in Appleby, dying on 11 February 1669; he was buried on 20 February in Westmorland. Fox commemorated Howgill's suffering, writing, and ministry in the collection of his works (published in 1676 as *The Dawnings of the Gospel-Day*), though the testimony does not seem to show that Howgill had much charisma. However, as this eloquent Quaker once observed, faith meant being 'less in words, and more in action' (*An Information*, 1659, 5). By the time of his death, Howgill had contributed significantly to the growth of the Quaker movement, and he played no small part in its development. CATIE GILL

Sources 'A. R. Barklay MSS', *Journal of the Friends' Historical Society*, 33 (1936), 55–64 · 'A. R. Barklay MSS', *Journal of the Friends' Historical Society*, 46 (1954), 78–91 · E. Backhouse and T. Backhouse, *Biographical memoirs*, 1 (1854) · J. Besse, *A collection of the sufferings of the people called Quakers*, 2 vols. (1753) · W. C. Braithwaite, *The beginnings of Quakerism*, ed. H. J. Cadbury, 2nd edn (1955); repr. (1981) · E. Brockbank, *Edward Burrough: a wrestler for the truth* (1949) · K. Carroll, 'Quakerism in the Cromwellian army', *Journal of the Friends' Historical Society*, 54 (1976–82), 135–54 · 'Dictionary of Quaker biography', RS Friends, Lond. [card index] · R. Foxton, *'Hear the word of the Lord': a critical and bibliographical study of Quaker women's writing* (Melbourne, 1994) · P. Kilroy, *Protestant dissent and controversy in Ireland, 1660–1714* (Cork, 1994) · S. Kite, 'Francis Howgill', *Quaker biographies*, 2 (Philadelphia, 1909) · G. Nuttall, *Early Quaker letters* (1952) · N. Penney, *The first publishers of truth* (1907) · *The journal of George Fox*, ed. N. Penney, 2 vols. (1911) · N. Penney, *Extracts from the state papers* (1913) · Quaker register of births, marriages, and burials, RS Friends, Lond. · J. Smith, *A descriptive catalogue of Friends' books*, 2 vols. (1867) · F. Howgill, *The dawnings of the gospel-day* (1676) · F. Howgill, *The inheritance of Jacob* (1656)
Archives RS Friends, Lond., corresp. and material | RS Friends, Lond., Barklay MS · RS Friends, Lond., Swarthmore MS

Howgill, William (*fl.* 1794–1810), organist and composer, was an organist in Whitehaven in 1794, and some years later, probably in 1810, moved to London. His works include *An original anthem & two voluntaries for the organ or piano forte, with a selection of thirty-eight … psalm tunes* (1800?); *A sonata for the grand piano forte with flute and violoncello accompaniments, with an introductory prelude by G. F. Handel* (1805?); *Purcell's or the Welsh Ground with one Hundred Variations for the Grand Pianoforte* (1810?); and *Four voluntaries, part of the 3rd chapter of the Wisdom of Solomon for three voices, and six favourite psalm tunes, with an accompaniment for the organ* (1825?). R. F. SHARP, *rev.* DAVID J. GOLBY

Sources F.-J. Fétis, *Biographie universelle des musiciens, et bibliographie générale de la musique*, 2nd edn, 3 (Paris, 1862), 375 · W. H. Husk, 'Howgill, William', Grove, *Dict. mus.* (1954)

Howgrave, Francis (*fl.* 1724–1726). *See under* Peck, Francis (1692–1743).

Howick. For this title name *see* Baring, (Charles) Evelyn, first Baron Howick of Glendale (1903–1973).

Howie, John (1735–1793), historian and biographer, was born on 14 November 1735 at Lochgoin in the parish of Fenwick, Ayrshire, the son of John Howie, a farmer. The family traced its origins to three French Albigensian brothers named Huet, who fled to Scotland in the twelfth century to escape religious persecution. One of them, Howie's ancestor, settled at Lochgoin; his descendants still lived there in the nineteenth century. During the episcopal regime in the Church of Scotland, Howie's grandparents and great-grandparents suffered persecution as Cameronians or covenanters, who remained true to the outlawed Scottish Presbyterian religious tradition. Their farm was plundered by government forces, their property was confiscated, and they were declared rebels and had to flee to the mountains. The persecutions ended immediately after the revolution of 1688.

His father having died about a year after his birth, Howie was taken in by his maternal grandparents, who farmed at Blackshill in Kilmarnock, Ayrshire. There he received a basic education, first at his uncle's school at Whirlhall, and later at the school kept by Adam Millar at Horsehill. On reaching adulthood he took over the ancestral farm at Lochgoin. Howie's first wife, Jean Lindsay, died in 1761 or 1762, shortly after the marriage, leaving an infant son. In 1766 Howie married his cousin Janet Howie, and the couple had five sons and three daughters.

Howie's second wife and his neighbours were critical of his interests in religious history and biography, believing they caused him to neglect his farm work. His studies took the form of research into the lives of noted Scottish protestant reformers and covenanting martyrs, reflecting his commitment to his family's covenanting tradition. The chief product of his labours was *Biographia Scotiana*, commonly known as *Scots Worthies*, which was first published by subscription in 1775 by the evangelical Glasgow printer and bookseller John Bryce, who remained Howie's primary publisher. It was a series of biographies of Scots who had been prominent on the Presbyterian or covenanting side during the Scottish religious struggles. An enlarged second edition appeared in 1781–2, with an appendix (which also appeared separately in 1781) covering the lives and, in many cases, unpleasant deaths of the reformers' chief persecutors, including kings and bishops. *Scots Worthies* continued to be reprinted long after Howie's death, though nineteenth-century editions usually omitted the provocative appendix. Howie also published on other religious topics, including church patronage, which he condemned, and the Lord's supper. In 1780 he edited an edition of Michael Shields's history of the Church of Scotland from 1681 to 1691, *Faithful Contendings Displayed*, which appeared along with a work by James Guthrie and a collection of sermons by the reformers. Howie is also purported to have edited an edition of Andrew Clarkson's *Plain Reasons for Dissenting*, which outlined the covenanting view of civil government.

Howie's collection of more than 100 books and numerous manuscripts relating to covenanting history was dispersed after his death. He also possessed memorabilia of the covenanting struggle, including a sword, a battle flag, and a bible that had belonged to the covenanting leader Captain John Paton. Having always been in poor health, Howie died at Lochgoin on 5 January 1793, after a long illness, and was buried in Fenwick churchyard among his ancestors. He was survived by his second wife. Three years later his son James Howie of Lochgoin published Howie's autobiographical *Memoirs*. ALEXANDER DU TOIT

Sources W. M'Gavin, preface, in J. Howie, *Biographia Scoticana, or, A brief historical account of the most eminent Scots worthies*, ed. W. M'Gavin, new edn (1827), xi–xxiii · W. H. Carslaw, preface, in J. Howie, *The Scots worthies*, ed. W. H. Carslaw, [new edn] (1870), ix–xv · 'Biographical sketch of John Howie', J. Howie, *The Scots worthies*, ed. J. Howie, [new edn] (1844), vii–xii; repr. (1876) · J. Howie, *Biographia Scoticana, or, A brief historical account of the lives, characters, and memorable transactions of the most eminent Scots worthies*, 2nd edn (1781–2), appx, 1–62 · W. Anderson, *The Scottish nation*, 2 (1868), 500 · Irving, *Scots.*, 221 · *Memoirs of … JH* (1796) · W. J. Couper, 'John Howie of Lochgoin and Fenwick', *Records of the Scottish Church History Society*, 6 (1936–8), 55–65 · M. Grant, 'Howie, John', *DSCHT*
Archives U. Glas. L., papers relating to the Covenanters

Howie, Robert (*d.* 1641×7), theologian and college head, was born in Aberdeen, the son of Thomas Howie, a merchant burgess. After early education at the grammar school of New Aberdeen he entered King's College, University of Aberdeen, from which he graduated MA, probably in 1584. Along with his fellow student John Johnston (*c.*1565–1611) he matriculated at the University of Rostock, in what is now Germany, in August 1584. A year later Howie went to the newly founded *Hochschule*, or *Gymnasium Illustre*, in Herborn to study theology under the

reformed theologian Caspar Olivian, and biblical languages and exegesis under Johannes Piscator. Both scholars made a profound impression on the young man, which was most evident in his adoption and subsequent exposition of covenant or federal theology. With the help of Johannes Pincier, professor of medicine, he also edited from the manuscript, which he had brought with him from Aberdeen, George Buchanan's unfinished *Sphaera*, published in Herborn in 1586 by Corvinus.

In May 1588 Howie matriculated at the University of Basel, where before the end of the month he was exhibiting his ability in theology by publicly defending theses set out by J. J. Grynaeus. In subsequent years he did so regularly. In addition, in 1590 he provided theses for disputations in which others were the respondents. In the following year he published a short but important tractate entitled *De reconciliatione hominis cum Deo*, his only printed theological work. Early in 1591 Howie, reunited with his friend Johnston, set out for Scotland. On 31 October Howie was appointed assistant to David Cunningham, the senior minister of Aberdeen, and in 1592 he became one of the ministers of the city. At this time Howie supported the officially recognized presbyterian form of church government set out in the act of parliament of June 1592. In 1593 he was the obvious local choice for the principalship of the newly founded Marischal College in New Aberdeen, and to him must be given much of the credit for the successful launching of this new academic venture, which mirrored so much that had happened in Germany and in protestant areas of France. Along with his teaching responsibilities in philosophy—not theology, which he would have preferred—he continued to exercise his pastoral ministry and to take his place in the courts of the church. Both his ministry and his diligence on behalf of the college won him popular public and civic recognition and in 1597 he was so highly thought of that he was invited to become one of the ministers of Edinburgh. He declined, but in 1598 accepted election by the general assembly as minister of Dundee.

By 1597, however, Howie had begun to change his views on church government, in particular on what he had previously branded, when writing of the Church of England to friends on the continent, as 'the tyranny of pseudo-bishops' (*Letters of Johnston and Howie*, 310, l. 24). From 1598 to 1605 he aligned himself with the royal policy of extending episcopal power in the church. At the same time he began to take a leading part, if not, according to his opponents, the leading part, on behalf of the city's guilds, in an attempt to reform the civic administration of Dundee. His opponents declared him to be a man of a hot and vehement humour and of a contentious disposition who had put himself at the head of a faction. In 1604 he resisted attempts of the ecclesiastical provincial synod to discipline him for his political activity, or, as many supposed, to depose him from the ministry. Disregarding prohibitions from the privy council, he travelled widely, even to London, on behalf of the reform party among the citizens. Finally the privy council, maintaining him to be the author and fountain of the disordered state of the burgh, in July 1605 forbade him from performing any public function and excluded him from living in Dundee for the rest of his life.

Howie was translated to the parish of Keith in Banffshire in 1606, and was appointed constant moderator of the local presbytery. Removal from Dundee did not, however, lead to his exclusion from ecclesiastical events: within a year he had recovered favour. In September 1606 he attended a meeting in Hampton Court summoned by the king to discuss the ecclesiastical affairs of Scotland. Howie was now unmistakably on the side of the bishops and had no hesitation in condemning those presbyterian ministers who had attempted to thwart royal policy. On 9 March 1607 the king chose Howie, 'a most meitt and sufficient person, both in respect of his lyf and literature' (*Letters of Johnston and Howie*, 352, l. 13f.), as a permanent replacement for the ejected presbyterian leader Andrew Melville, as principal of St Mary's College, St Andrews. At first Howie refused to accept the office, concerned that the royal commissioners visiting the university had, contrary to the king's instructions, made the appointment dependent on the king's pleasure. The privy council peremptorily ordered him to accept, which he was obliged to do. However, he petitioned the king in August and craved full and formal confirmation. He claimed that he was devoted to the task set before him, but acknowledged that it was 'a wark full of difficultie and invy' and that he had been committed to 'the hazard of most violent tempestis' (*Letters of Johnston and Howie*, 326f.).

Howie, inducted on 27 July 1607, could not have relished being made the successor to Andrew Melville in what had been one of the bulwarks of the presbyterian polity, nor could he have found much satisfaction in being placed over the head of his former close friend and student companion John Johnston, who since 1591 had been second master in the college and had expected to succeed Melville. However, Howie did not take the oath of office until 15 March 1611, by which time Johnston was terminally ill. Howie's open defence of the superiority of bishops over presbyteries was resented by many in St Andrews, but he was not deterred from supporting the royal ecclesiastical policy. In 1610 he was appointed to the court of high commission and was in that year a member of the general assembly held in Glasgow at which the presbyterian polity of the church was effectively curtailed and the episcopal office restored.

From 1610 to 1638 Howie regularly attended the courts of the church and was frequently made a member of commissions charged with carrying through a variety of matters furthering the royal policy. Such action displeased many. At the general assembly in Montrose in 1616 he was appointed one of the revisers, and has subsequently been regarded as one of the principal authors of a new confession of faith, which reflects the contemporary reformed orthodoxy and in its teaching on the sacrament of the Lord's supper is in line with Howie's manuscript work, 'Accuratus de coenae domini tractatus' (St Andrews University Library, MSS BV 8 24 H7).

Howie also took a prominent part in both the general administration of St Andrews University, for a time as rector, and in furthering a number of changes which the new chancellor, Archbishop George Gledstanes, pandering to the king, wished to bring about. One of the most significant of these was the creation of a common university library, another was the revival of formal graduation ceremonies, and in particular the awarding of doctorates in divinity 'to encourage our ignorant cleargie in learning' (Cant, 68f.). As dean of the faculty of divinity and principal of the theological college, Howie, along with the heads of the other two colleges, was made a DD at a ceremony held on 29 July 1616 directed by the king's emissary, John Young, dean of Winchester. The royal confidence in Howie was reflected in the king's plans to have St Andrews as 'the principall fountayne of religion and good letters in Scotland' (Cant, 70f.). On demitting office as rector he delivered an *oratio*, 'De fundatoribus academiae et collegiorum in universitate Andreapolitana' (1617), which has to be seen as the earliest attempt to sketch the history and development of the university. For King James's visit to St Andrews in July of that year Howie's primary official duty was to act as the president at a theological disputation held in the king's honour, for which he provided theses setting out the royal power in matters ecclesiastical.

Howie's success as principal is reflected in steady matriculations and significant numbers of visiting students from the continent. His level of commitment, to St Mary's College in particular, is seen in the administrative documents in his own hand. To Howie must also be given full credit for gracefully remodelling the buildings of his college to which he added an 'attractively arcaded north building' (Cant, 77). Although this was removed in the nineteenth century there is built into the east frontage of the west building a fine carving of Howie's coat of arms, his monogram, and the date 1621, when the rebuilding took place.

In 1618 Howie was one of a royal commission appointed to carry out a visitation of the Aberdeen colleges, which led to the revitalization of university education there by Bishop Patrick Forbes. In 1624 provision for a chair of divinity at Marischal College was offered by Patrick Copland, one of Howie's former students there and a staunch upholder of reformed orthodoxy. Efforts were made at this time both by Copland and the town council to recall Howie to Aberdeen, but he decided to remain in St Andrews.

As Charles I's ecclesiastical policy in Scotland unfolded Howie's ardour for episcopacy began to cool, as did that of his three university colleagues. He went along with the decision of the general assembly in Glasgow in 1638 to rid the church of bishops and he himself signed the covenant and remained in his office as principal of St Mary's College, but following complaints in 1641 from Samuel Rutherford, then professor of divinity, over misappropriation of funds, Howie was forced to resign. When Howie's demission came before the general assembly for confirmation, Alexander Henderson, the prime architect of the national covenant and one of the leaders of the presbyterian cause, described as Howie's 'good friend', acted with commendable charity. He so guided the matter that 'with ane great deall of commendation to the old man, ... it was voyced that his dismission should be rendered to him [and] that he should all his life tyme enjoy his full rent and honour, without any diminution' (*Letters and Journals of Robert Baillie*, 1.361).

Howie died without leaving a will some time between 1641 and 1647. The disposal of his 'guids and geir' was registered on 25 September 1652. He had married, probably while he was still in Aberdeen at Marischal College, Jean Skene, daughter of Andrew Skene of Anchorie, a burgess of Aberdeen in 1598, who predeceased him. He was survived by his eldest son, Robert, who had been made a burgess of Aberdeen on 11 August 1624, and a daughter, Margaret, who married Andrew Lamont, a former St Andrews student and subsequently minister at Markinch, Fife. JAMES K. CAMERON

Sources *Letters of John Johnston, c.1565–1611 and Robert Howie, c.1565–c.1645*, ed. J. K. Cameron (1963) · R. Lippe, ed., *Selections from Wodrow's biographical collections: divines of the north-east of Scotland*, New Spalding Club, 5 (1890) · *Acts of the general assembly of the Church of Scotland, 1638–1842* (1843) · *The letters and journals of Robert Baillie*, ed. D. Laing, 3 vols. (1841–2) · T. Thomson, ed., *Acts and proceedings of the general assemblies of the Kirk of Scotland*, 3 pts, Bannatyne Club, 81 (1839–45) · D. Calderwood, *The history of the Kirk of Scotland*, ed. T. Thomson and D. Laing, 8 vols., Wodrow Society, 7 (1842–9), vols. 5–6, 8 · R. G. Cant, *The University of St Andrews: a short history*, 3rd edn (1992) · J. Stuart, ed., *Extracts from the council register of the burgh of Aberdeen*, 2: *1570–1625*, Spalding Club, 19 (1848) · P. J. Anderson and J. F. K. Johnstone, eds., *Fasti academiae Mariscallanae Aberdonensis: selections from the records of the Marischal College and University, MDXCIII–MDCCCLX*, 3 vols., New Spalding Club, 4, 18–19 (1889–98) · *Fasti Scot.*, new edn · G. D. Henderson, *The founding of Marischal College Aberdeen* (1947) · *The autobiography and diary of Mr James Melvill*, ed. R. Pitcairn, Wodrow Society (1842) · F. J. Grant, *St Andrews Testaments, 1549–1800*, Scottish RS (1902), 170

Archives U. St Andr., 'Accuratus de coenae domini tractatus' · U. St Andr., 'De fundatoribus academiae, et colleciorum in universitate Andreapolitana', 1617

Wealth at death 'guids and geir': Grant, *St Andrews Testaments*

Howison, John (1797–1859), writer and surgeon, was born on 10 May 1797 in Edinburgh, third and youngest child of William Howison, financial writer, and his wife, Janet Bogle. He was the brother of William *Howison (*b.* 1796?). From 1818 to 1820 Howison travelled in Quebec and Ontario, Canada, and practised medicine in St Catharines, Ontario. His *Sketches of Upper Canada, domestic, local, and characteristic: to which are added, practical details for the information of emigrants of every class* (1821) was an immediate success and is one of the best documentary sources for pioneer life in Canada. It went into three editions, and was translated into German. The first edition was reprinted in 1965 and 1970.

In 1820 Howison left Canada via the United States, and in 1822 he went to Bombay as an assistant surgeon with the East India Company. He published eight short stories in *Blackwood's Edinburgh Magazine* at this time, two of which were later republished in *Nimmo's Popular Tales* (1858). He was stationed in Poona in 1825, and belonged to the literary society there. Descriptions of the life of the foreign colony in Bombay and a journey through the Deccan with Major-General Sir Lionel Smith can be found in Howison's *Foreign Scenes and Travelling Recreations* (1825); this work also contains an account of Cuba which continues to interest French and Hispanic historians. His *Tales of the Colonies* (1830) consists of Gothic stories set in the West Indies. Howison became a member of the Bombay branch of the Royal Asiatic Society, and served as vice-president in 1832. He demonstrated that he was more than an author of light travel works and fiction with his unjustly neglected *European Colonies ... Viewed in their Social, Moral, and Physical Condition* (1834). In this, his most ambitious work, Howison's analysis ranges over Africa, India, the Caribbean, and the Arctic. In 1835 the East India Company promoted him to the post of full surgeon.

Howison's sketch of 'the Bengal assistant-surgeon, with his fists in his pockets, and habited in a dress half military, half civilian' on promenade at the Cape of Good Hope is probably a self-portrait (J. Howison, *Foreign Scenes*, 1825, 2.216). He seems never again to have experienced the 'freedom ... independence ... and ... joyousness, connected with' Canada (J. Howison, *Sketches*, 1821, 263), and certainly India presented 'a succession of struggles against personal inconveniences and bodily uneasiness' (*Foreign Scenes*, 2.74). He concluded that those who pursue 'foreign adventure' lose 'in contentment and serenity what they gain in wealth and knowledge of the world' (ibid., 2.115). Howison retired in 1842 and died on 8 February 1859 at his home, 1 Pelham Place, Brompton, London.

BONNIE SHANNON McMULLEN

Sources E. Waterston and J. J. Talmon, 'Howison, John', *DCB*, vol. 8 · D. G. Crawford, ed., *Roll of the Indian Medical Service, 1615–1930* (1930) · *East-India Register and Directory (1820–42)* · *GM*, 3rd ser., 6 (1859) · J. P. Merritt, *Biography of the Hon. W. H. Merritt, M.P., of Loncoln, district of Niagara* (1875) · 'Howison's Canada', *Blackwood*, 10 (1821), 537–45 · J. J. Talmon, 'Candid pioneer', *Canadian Literature*, 36 (spring 1968), 98–100 · review of *Sketches of Upper Canada*, *EdinR*, 37 (1822), 249–68 · 'European colonies', *The Athenaeum* (21 June 1834), 470–71 · 'European colonies', *The Athenaeum* (9 Aug 1834), 585–7 · *Journal of the Royal Asiatic Society*, 1 (1834) · M. Guicharnaud-Tollis, *Regards sur Cuba au XIXe siècle: témoignages européens* (Paris, 1996) · G. M. Craig, *Early travellers in the Canadas, 1791–1867* (1955) · d. cert.

Archives NL Scot., Blackwood MSS, letters

Wealth at death under £8000: will, Principal Registry of the Family Division, London, 1859, *CGPLA Eng. & Wales*

Howison, William (*b.* 1796?), writer, was born in Edinburgh, the son of William Howison, financial writer, and his wife, Janet Bogle. He was the brother of John *Howison (1797–1859). His boyhood ballad, 'Polydore', was published in Walter Scott's *Edinburgh Annual Review for 1810* (3/2, 1812, 178–83) and republished as 'The Robber Polydore' in a revised version in Joanna Baillie's *Collection of Poems* (1823, 178–83). The 'sedentary' and unworldly Howison, who visited Scott in 1811, was described by him as 'a thin hectic youth with an eye of dark fire' (*Letters*, 8.54). In 1817 Howison published *Fragments and Fictions*, a fictitious translation from the French of 'Jean Pococurante de Peudemots'. In *Blackwood's Magazine*, John Wilson celebrated its 'elegant style' and 'lively and exquisite wit' (3.47).

Howison's friend J. G. Lockhart praised the book, 'a perfect bijou', and its author's 'inward strength' and 'commanding intellect' in *Peter's Letters to his Kinsfolk* (Lockhart, 138–43).

In March 1818 Howison initiated the 'Time's Magic Lanthern' series in *Blackwood's Edinburgh Magazine*, and continued as a contributor until June 1822, writing on literature, music, and art. The December 1818 'Essay on the Lake school of poetry, no. II, "On the habits of thought, inculcated by Wordsworth"', formerly credited to John Wilson (Christopher North), is now thought to be Howison's (*Blackwood*, 4, 1818, 257–63). He describes himself in the 'Prospective letter concerning poetry' of September 1821 as 'a young poet wishing to distinguish, by new literary exploits, the reign of George the Fourth' but 'still doubtful whether to write in verse or prose' (*Blackwood*, 55, 1821, 125). In his last *Blackwood's* review, signed Peu-de-Mots, he complains of his confinement to one page for his review of *The Fortunes of Nigel* (11, 734), and a letter to Blackwood confirms his impatience with this format. By this time, Howison had 'turnd metaphysician full fifty fathom deep' (*Letters*, 7.59). His 1822 *Essay on the sentiments of attraction, adaptation, and variety to which are added, a key to the mythology of the ancients; and Europe's likeness to the human spirit* was 'not a bag of nuts ready crackd', in Scott's opinion (ibid.). Scott was dismayed by Howison's appearance in 1821—'a thin consumptive looking man bent double with study' wearing 'immense green spectacles' (ibid., 7.54). He subsequently wrote *The Grammar of Infinite Forms* (1823), *The Contest of the Twelve Nations* (1826), and the supplementary *Philosophical Tables* (1829). In the judgement of R. P. Gillies, Howison was 'a man of real genius' whose 'excessive fastidiousness' prevented the realization of his potential (Gillies, 50). BONNIE SHANNON McMULLEN

Sources *The letters of Sir Walter Scott*, ed. H. J. C. Grierson and others, centenary edn, 12 vols. (1932–79), vols. 2, 7–8 · E. Waterston and J. J. Talmon, 'Howison, John', *DCB*, vol. 8 · A. L. Strout, *A bibliography of articles in Blackwood's Magazine … 1817–1825* (1959) · A. L. Strout, 'The authorship of articles in *Blackwood's Magazine*, nos. xvii–xxiv (Aug 1818–Mar 1819)', *The Library*, 5th ser., 11 (1956), 187–201 · B. M. Murray, 'The authorship of some unidentified or disputed articles in *Blackwood's Magazine*', *Studies in Scottish Literature*, 4 (1966–7), 146 · [J. G. Lockhart], *Peter's letters to his kinsfolk*, 2nd edn, 3 vols. (1819) · [J. Wilson], 'Extracts from M. de Peudemots', *Blackwood*, 3 (1818), 46–50 · R. P. Gillies, *Memoirs of a literary veteran*, 3 vols. (1851) · 'An essay on the sentiments of attraction, adaptation, and variety', *Blackwood*, 9 (1821), 393–7 · J. G. Lockhart, *Memoirs of the life of Sir Walter Scott*, 7 vols. (1837–8) · J. Galt, *The letters of John Galt from the Blackwood papers in the National Library of Scotland*, ed. G. S. Beasley (1951) · *Post Office annual directory of Edinburgh, Leith, and Newhaven* (1826)
Archives NL Scot., letters

Howison [Howieson], **William** (1798–1850), engraver, was born at Edinburgh, the son of a local carver and gilder. He was educated at George Heriot's Hospital, and on leaving that institution was apprenticed to an engraver named (Andrew?) Wilson. He never received any formal instruction in drawing beyond that which he acquired during the period of his apprenticeship, after which he worked for the engravers Daniel and William Henry Lizars and was employed chiefly in the production of small plates. Some of these were after David Octavius Hill, secretary of the Royal Scottish Academy, and it was through Hill's introduction that Howison received his first important commission, to engrave *The Curlers* after the Scottish genre painter Sir George Harvey, sometime president of the Royal Scottish Academy, which was published by Gambart. The merits of this engraving led to his election in 1838 as ARSA, the only instance of such an honour having been conferred on an engraver. It was through further plates after genre scenes by Harvey, and his engraving of *The Polish Exiles*, after Sir William Allan, president of the Royal Scottish Academy, that Howison's reputation was established. These works consisted of large, highly finished line engravings: Howison is not known to have used any mixed method of engraving. He produced portrait, figure, and landscape engravings, chiefly after contemporary works. At the time of his death he was engaged upon *The First Letter from the Emigrants*, after Thomas Faed RA, for the Association for the Promotion of the Fine Arts in Scotland. He died at 8 Frederick Street, Edinburgh, on 20 December 1850, and was buried in the Greyfriars churchyard, leaving a widow and three children.

R. E. GRAVES, *rev.* ASIA HAUT

Sources B. Hunnisett, *An illustrated dictionary of British steel engravers*, new edn (1989) · R. K. Engen, *Dictionary of Victorian engravers, print publishers and their works* (1979) · Anderson, *Scot. nat.* · Redgrave, *Artists* · Bryan, *Painters* (1866); (1886–9) · Irving, *Scots.* · *Art Journal*, 13 (1851), 44 · P. J. M. McEwan, *Dictionary of Scottish art and architecture* (1994) · J. C. Guy, 'Edinburgh engravers', *Book of the Old Edinburgh Club*, 9 (1916), 91–5

Howitt, Alfred William (1830–1908), anthropologist, born on 17 April 1830 at Nottingham, was the eldest son in a family of three sons and two daughters to survive infancy of William *Howitt (1792–1879) and his wife, Mary Botham [*see* Howitt, Mary (1799–1888)], writers. After home instruction at Nottingham and Esher, his parents in 1840 took their children to Heidelberg to continue their education. They returned in 1843, and lived in London at Clapham (1843–8) and then St John's Wood (1848–52), while Alfred attended University College School. In 1852 William Howitt with his sons Alfred and Herbert Charlton, went to Australia, partly to visit William's brother Godfrey, who had practised medicine at Melbourne since 1840. After two years' wandering in Australia hoping to improve family fortunes, William and Herbert Charlton returned to Britain, leaving Alfred behind.

Alfred first farmed land belonging to his uncle at Caulfield, near Melbourne, and then took to cattle-droving. He soon acquired the reputation of an able, careful, and fearless bushman. In 1859 he explored the pastoral potential of the Lake Eyre region for a Melbourne syndicate. He briefly managed Mount Napier station, near Hamilton, Victoria, before his appointment as leader of a prospecting party by the Victorian government in 1860. He found gold in mountainous Gippsland, where, following his advice, the goldfields on the Crooked, Dargo, and Wentworth rivers were opened.

On 18 June 1861 Howitt was appointed leader of the expedition in search of the explorers Robert O'Hara Burke and William John Wills, who had disappeared on an expedition to the Gulf of Carpentaria. He was absent from Melbourne from 14 July to 28 November 1861, advancing rapidly despite the difficulties of travel, and rescued the one survivor of the Burke and Wills expedition (John King) on Cooper Creek. Howitt again visited Cooper Creek the following year and arrived back in Melbourne with the remains of Burke and Wills on 28 December 1862. For these services he was appointed police magistrate and warden of the goldfields in Gippsland. He held these posts from 1863 until 1889. He married on 18 August 1864 Maria Liney (d. 1902), daughter of Benjamin Boothby, judge of the South Australian supreme court. They had two sons and three daughters.

During the expedition of 1862 Howitt became interested in the customs of the Dieri people about Cooper Creek. In Gippsland he came into close touch with the Kurnai people, a number of whom he employed on his Bairnsdale farm. They adopted him as a member and admitted him to their secret ceremonies. He thus went beyond any other European in his study of the social organization of Australian Aboriginal people. He also designed several complex questionnaires to record the observations of others who had studied Aboriginal life, and he sifted and arranged the information thus gained with extraordinary care.

Lorimer Fison recruited Howitt in 1872 in his investigations into social organization under the influence of the evolutionary theories of Lewis Henry Morgan. Together the two friends published *Kamilaroi and Kurnai* (1880). It embodied the results of their enquiries and reflections on group marriage and relationship and marriage by elopement, with much incidental information concerning Gippsland society.

Following Morgan's death, Howitt established a postal friendship with the Oxford anthropologist E. B. Tylor. Tylor prompted several of Howitt's investigations and introduced his papers at the Royal Anthropological Institute (RAI). During 1883 and 1884 he published seven papers, two jointly with Fison. Howitt travelled hundreds of miles on horseback annually and used opportunities while on circuit as a magistrate to collect data. Befriending many Aboriginal men and some women, he used his influence to revive traditional ceremonies, which he attended and described. The first was held near Bega, southern New South Wales, in 1883, and Tylor read his account of the intricate ceremonies to the RAI later that year. Early in 1884 a further ceremony was held in Gippsland and another was planned. Missionaries became alarmed at Howitt's revival of 'pagan rituals', and successfully lobbied the government to prevent the third ceremony.

Howitt was a competent geologist. He pioneered the use in Australia of thin-section petrology and chemical analysis on rocks. His studies of the Devonian series in Gippsland remain basic papers. He also collected extensively among Gippsland flora, and his memoir 'Eucalypts of Gippsland', published in the *Transactions of the Royal Society of Victoria* for 1889, was a significant study. In it he emphasized the ecological importance of the Aboriginal practice of fire management, one of the first scientists to do so.

In 1889 Howitt left Gippsland to become secretary of mines in Victoria, and in 1896 he was appointed commissioner of audit, a member of the public service board, and a council member of the University of Melbourne. He retired from the public service at the end of 1901, but remained active in public life. He served in 1903 on a royal commission which examined sites for the future seat of commonwealth government, and chaired the 1905–6 royal commission on the Victorian coal industry.

In Melbourne during the 1890s Howitt and Fison were both appointed fellows of the newly established Queen's College, at the university. They associated there with Walter Baldwin Spencer, the youthful professor of biology. They proved instrumental in encouraging Spencer's anthropological interests, and Spencer and Francis James Gillen dedicated their first book, *The Native Tribes of Central Australia*, to Howitt and Fison. In his turn, Spencer assisted Howitt to finalize his long-awaited book, published in 1904 as *The Native Tribes of South East Australia*.

It may fairly be claimed that Fison and Howitt were pioneers of the new anthropology, and that by their researches into the organization of the human family they gave the study direction, even though their evolutionist model was soon outmoded. Lewis Henry Morgan, in his great book on the *Systems of Consanguinity and Affinity of the Human Family* (1869), had led the way, but they went on their own lines further than he, notably in regard to systems of marriage and relationship among Aboriginal Australians. His major contributions to Australian anthropology, botany, and geology, his distinguished success as an explorer and public servant, combine to rank Howitt as a polymath meriting greater recognition in his adopted country.

After his retirement Howitt lived chiefly at Metung, Gippsland, in the enjoyment of widespread recognition as an ethnologist. He died at Bairnsdale on 7 March 1908.

E. F. IM THURN, rev. D. J. MULVANEY

Sources M. H. Walker, *Come wind, come weather: a biography of Alfred Howitt* (1971) · D. J. Mulvaney, 'The anthropologist as tribal elder', *Mankind*, 7 (1970), 205–17 · D. J. Mulvaney and J. H. Calaby, *So much that is new: Baldwin Spencer, 1860–1929* (1985) · W. E. H. Stanner, 'Howitt, Alfred William', *AusDB*, vol. 4 · W. B. Spencer, *The Victorian naturalist*, 24 (1908)
Archives Museum of Victoria, Melbourne · State Library of Victoria, Melbourne, La Trobe manuscript collection | U. Oxf., Pitt Rivers Museum, letters to Sir W. B. Spencer
Likenesses T. Roberts, portrait, 1902, Monash University, Victoria, Melbourne, Australia, Howitt Hall · C. Sumner, bas-relief, Melbourne, Australia, Burke and Wills monument

Howitt [*married name* Watts], **Anna Mary** (1824–1884), painter and writer, was born into a Quaker family in Nottingham on 15 January 1824, the eldest of the five surviving children of William *Howitt (1792–1879) and Mary Botham (1799–1888) [see Howitt, Mary], both hardworking writers who founded *Howitt's Journal of Literature and Popular Progress* which espoused the causes of peace, free trade, and civil liberty. In 1846 they went bankrupt, so, although

Anna Mary Howitt grew up in a cultured household, with introductions to many literary figures such as Elizabeth Barrett Browning, Elizabeth Gaskell, and Anna Jameson, the family's finances were precarious and she always had to support herself by writing journal articles and books. Howitt showed precocious talent, which was encouraged by the painter Margaret Gillies, a family friend; at fifteen, her drawings were used to illustrate her mother's book *Hymns and Fireside Verses* (1839). In 1846 she attended Henry Sass's Art School in London, one of the few places where women could receive first-class tuition. When her parents could no longer afford the fees, the principal, Francis Cary, allowed her to continue because he was so impressed with her talent. Her fellow students included Eliza Fox (married name Bridell), Holman Hunt, Dante Gabriel Rossetti, and Thomas Woolner. Howitt became engaged to marry Edward Bateman, a decorative designer and illustrator who worked with the architect and designer Owen Jones, and also became friends with the Pre-Raphaelite Brotherhood [*see also* Pre-Raphaelite women artists].

As women were not allowed to study at the Royal Academy Schools, in 1850 Howitt and another woman artist, Jane Benham (married name Hay), went to Munich to study informally under Wilhelm von Kaulbach. She wrote articles about Munich life and society published variously in the *Ladies Companion*, *Household Words*, and the *Athenaeum*, later collected in her book *An Art-Student in Munich* (1853) together with more material about her two-year apprenticeship. She also wrote two serialized stories, 'The School of Life', whose protagonists were two young male artists, which appeared in the *Illustrated Magazine of Art* (1853–4) with her own illustrations and was published in book form in 1856, and 'Sisters in Art', which appeared in the *Illustrated Exhibitor* (1853). The latter elaborated the professional aspirations of the Langham Place feminists, whose leader was her close friend the landscape painter Barbara Leigh Smith (married name Bodichon). She contributed a poem to *The Victoria regia* (1861), a book designed to exhibit the skills of the women compositors in the press set up as one of the Langham Place initiatives, and contributed in 1862 to the *English Woman's Journal* (the Langham Place periodical).

Howitt broke off her engagement to Bateman in August 1853, after he had travelled to Australia to seek his fortune in goldmining. Following her return from Munich she joined D. G. Rossetti's Folio club together with Barbara Leigh Smith. In 1854 she made her exhibition début at the National Institution (also known as the Free Exhibition) with *Margaret Returning from the Fountain*, a picture inspired by Goethe's *Faust*. Her diptych, called *The Lady* (oil on canvas, each 30 x 25 cm) in response to Shelley's poem 'The Sensitive Plant', was exhibited at the National Institution in 1855. Howitt's paintings were often called 'strongminded' by critics, as, for example, *The Castaway* (exh. RA, 1855), a painting of a woman who had fallen into prostitution. This was purchased by the Pre-Raphaelite patron Thomas Fairburn, who lent it to the 'Art Treasures' exhibition of 1857 in Manchester.

Howitt was connected with feminist activism primarily through her friendship with Barbara Leigh Smith and in 1856 was involved with collecting the signatures of women for Leigh Smith's petition to parliament urging the reform of the Married Women's Property Acts. Leigh Smith posed more than once as a model for Howitt. When she was commissioned by the philanthropist Angela Burdett-Coutts to paint a picture of Beatrice and Dante, the red-haired Barbara was her unlikely choice to model for the medieval Italian heroine. It seems as if Barbara in some sense represented Beatrice—'she who makes blessed'—in the symbolic rather than the physical sense. Barbara Leigh Smith was more aptly the model for a large-scale historical oil painting, *Boadicea*, inspired by Tennyson's poem, which was exhibited at the Crystal Palace in 1856. This was rejected by the Royal Academy, and when Ruskin sent her a letter criticizing it and, it seems, rejecting the feminist iconography, Howitt suffered a nervous breakdown. In 1857, when Barbara Leigh Smith married Eugène Bodichon, a resident of Algiers, Howitt had another, more serious breakdown. She destroyed her paintings and determined never to exhibit again. Consequently her only extant original drawing is one of D. G. Rossetti's pupil and model Elizabeth Siddal, whom she drew in 1854 (pencil on paper; priv. coll.). The only subsequent exhibition of her work as a painter after 1856 was *From a Window*, exhibited by the Society of Female Artists in 1858.

In 1859 Howitt was baptized in St Michael's Church, Highgate, as a preliminary to marrying a childhood friend, Alaric Alfred Watts (*b.* 1823/4), an official in the revenue office. He held literary ambitions and he shared with his wife a belief in spiritualism. After their marriage on 18 October 1859 she produced only 'spirit-drawings' in vermilion ink, which arose out of trance-like states, although she continued to produce illustrations for her mother's books. There are some indications that it was a *mariage blanc*. From 1870 the couple lived at 19 Cheyne Walk, Chelsea. She published *Pioneers of the Spiritual Reformation* (1883) which consisted of biographical sketches of Dr Justinus Kerner and of her father, William Howitt, but the purpose of which was as an apologia for spiritualism, mesmerism, and associated phenomena. Together with her husband she wrote *Aurora: a Volume of Verse* (1884) in which she eschews personal ambition in favour of spiritual salvation. That same year Anna Mary Watts died suddenly of diphtheria at Mayr-am-Hof, Dietenheim, on 23 July during a visit to her mother in the Austrian Tyrol. Her mother had been received into the Catholic church in 1882, and she arranged for her daughter to be buried in the Roman Catholic cemetery in Dietenheim.

PAM HIRSCH

Sources A. L. Beaky, 'The letters of Anna Mary Howitt to Barbara Leigh Smith Bodichon', PhD diss., Columbia University, 1974 · M. Howitt, *An autobiography*, ed. M. Howitt, another edn (1891) · C. R. Woodring, *Victorian sampler: William and Mary Howitt* (Kansas, 1952) · A. Lee, *Laurels and rosemary* (1955) · P. Hirsch, *Barbara Leigh Smith Bodichon: feminist, artist and rebel* (1998) · J. Marsh and P. G. Nunn, *Women artists and the Pre-Raphaelite movement* (1989) · P. Gerrish Nunn, ed., *Canvassing: recollections by six Victorian women artists*

(1986) · J. Marsh and P. G. Nunn, *Pre-Raphaelite women artists* (1997) [exhibition catalogue, Manchester, Birmingham, and Southampton, 22 Nov 1997 – 2 Aug 1998] · A. M. H. Watts, 'A contribution towards the history of spirit-art', *Light: a journal of psychical, occult, and mystical research*, 9 (13 April 1889), 176–7 · *Autobiographical notes of the life of William Bell Scott: and notices of his artistic and poetic circle of friends, 1830 to 1882*, ed. W. Minto, 2 vols. (1892) · Graves, *Artists*, 3rd edn · m. cert.

Likenesses D. G. Rossetti, caricature, repro. in *Journal of Pre-Raphaelite and Aesthetic Studies* (1989)

Howitt, Sir Harold Gibson (1886–1969), accountant, was born at Nottingham on 5 October 1886, the second son of Arthur Gibson Howitt, printer and lithographer, and his wife, Elizabeth Archer. He was educated at Uppingham and retained an active interest in the school throughout his life, becoming chairman of the trustees (1949–67). In 1904 he was articled to W. R. Hamilton, chartered accountant, of Nottingham, qualifying in 1909 and joining W. B. Peat & Co. (later Peat, Marwick, Mitchell & Co.) in London in the same year. In 1911 he accepted a partnership in their Middlesbrough office and remained a partner until his retirement in 1961.

Howitt was always a believer in hard work and physical fitness. As a young man he played rugby for Midland Counties and Harlequins, and throughout his life he treated holidays as an opportunity for vigorous physical exercise. His energy, and a taste for adventure, were early called into play when in 1910, in the first of two professional visits to the Donets coal basin in southern Russia, he reached the Vagliano anthracite collieries, after stowing away on a goods train, to find the miners on strike and the place in chaos. He stayed for three months, paid the wages with money brought in under Cossack guard, and got the place working again.

On 4 August 1914 Howitt left his office in Middlesbrough and joined the 4th battalion, the Green Howards; he served throughout the war, mainly in France, but for a short period in Egypt and Palestine, and was appointed to the DSO and awarded the MC, being mentioned in dispatches four times. In a renowned exploit in March 1918, borrowed by John Buchan for his novel *Mr. Standfast*, he was captured during the German advance at St Quentin; he observed and was impressed by his captors' preparations for the next move, broke free from his guards and, after running back part of the way in the glare of a burning dump, regained the British lines, having discovered where he was after hearing in the darkness a familiar British oath. Howitt married in 1917 Dorothy Wentworth (*d.* 1968), daughter of William Henry Radford, of Sherwood, Nottingham; they had one son and three daughters.

In 1919 Howitt returned to Peats, in their London office, where he remained for the rest of his working life. Within a few months he had embarked on the long series of public commissions and inquiries which were the outstanding feature of his career. Beginning with the commission on Southern Rhodesia (1919–20), chaired by Viscount Cave, he dealt with major valuation problems, several of

them in colonial territories, culminating with the committee on the financial structure of the Colonial Development Corporation (1959). From 1932, when he was appointed to the reorganization commission on pigs and pig products, he was prominent in agricultural inquiries, and even found time to run a small farm of his own. He was involved in fixing the compensation due to several nationalized industries at home and abroad: coal (1946), Argentine Railways (1947), Anglo-Iranian Oil (1951), and Cable and Wireless (1956). He was also concerned with cost control questions, from Lord Bridgeman's committee on the British Legion (1930) to the British Transport Commission (1957), and he rendered distinguished service on the Air Council throughout the Second World War. This main wartime duty he managed to combine with being chairman and deputy chairman of British Overseas Airways Corporation (1943–8), a member of the council of the Navy, Army, and Air Force Institutes (1940–46), chairman of the Building Materials Board, and financial adviser to the Ministry of Works (1943–5). He was an effective and lucid speaker, a patient and courteous negotiator, always charming and friendly.

In the long list of Howitt's services the best known was his membership, with Lord Cohen and Sir Dennis Robertson, of the original Council on Prices, Productivity and Incomes (1957–9), popularly known as 'the three wise men', the forerunner in the search for a national incomes policy. With some reluctance, Howitt himself came to the conclusion that attempts to regulate the industrial economy were the price of full employment and the existence of powerful associations of labour and employers.

Howitt was a member of the council of the Institute of Chartered Accountants in England and Wales in 1932–61, its president in 1945–6, and president of the International Congress of Accountants in London in 1952. After his retirement from practice he wrote the *History of the Institute of Chartered Accountants in England and Wales, 1880–1965* (1966).

Howitt's charitable activities, often concerned with financial matters, were many, and were often directed to the needs of young people. He was a member of the council of Toynbee Hall (1922–51) and of the United Services Trustees (1946–66), and was master of the Merchant Taylors' Company in coronation year 1953. Howitt was knighted in 1937 and appointed GBE in 1946; he became a magistrate in Hampstead in 1942 and was chairman of its bench in 1950–58; he was also an honorary DCL of Oxford (1953) and honorary LLD of Nottingham (1958).

At the time of his death, Howitt was living at 1 Cressy House, Queens Ride, Barnes, London. He died at 8 Queens Ride, on 30 November 1969. His son, A. W. Howitt, became a senior executive partner in Peat, Marwick, Mitchell & Co., management consultants.   WALTER TAPLIN, *rev.*

Sources T. A. Wise, *Peat, Marwick, Mitchell & Co.: 85 years* (1982), 17, 19 · *The Times* (2 Dec 1969), 12 f–g · *The Times* (19 Dec 1969), 10c [memorial service] · *The Accountant* (4 Dec 1969), 757, 783 · *WWW* · d. cert.

Likenesses F. O. Salisbury, oils, Institute of Chartered Accountants in England and Wales, London · photograph, repro. in H. G. Howitt, *History of the Institute of Chartered Accountants in England and*

Wales, 1880–1965 (1966), following p. 146 · photograph, repro. in *The Accountant*, 783

Howitt [*née* Botham], **Mary** (1799–1888), writer and translator, was born on 12 March 1799 at Coleford, Gloucestershire, the second child of Samuel Botham (1758–1823), a land surveyor, and Anne Wood (1764–1848). She and her elder sister, Anna, were brought up in Uttoxeter, Staffordshire, according to strict Quaker principles; permitted few books, they made up their own stories and verses. A servant's stories had a powerful influence upon their imagination, but eventually they were sent to school at first locally, then in Croydon (1809), and later in Sheffield (1810–12). Thereafter, they studied not very systematically at home.

In 1818 Mary met William *Howitt (1792–1879), a writer and also a Quaker, who shared her enthusiasm for natural history and literature. They married at Uttoxeter on 16 April 1821, and settled in Nottingham. During the first dozen years of her marriage Mary had nine pregnancies, but only three children were to survive infancy: Anna Mary *Howitt (1824–1884), Alfred William *Howitt (1830–1908), and Claude Middleton (1833–1844). Married life also broadened her literary experience: she read widely and published poems in annuals and magazines. Two joint collections of verses appeared, *The Forest Minstrel* (1823) and *The Desolation of Eyam* (1827). In 1834 she published both *Sketches of Natural History* and the more ambitious *The Seven Temptations*. Devastated by a negative review, she based *Wood Leighton* (1836) on stories she knew from Uttoxeter.

On moving to Esher in 1836, the Howitts plunged into new work and a second phase of parenthood (Herbert Charlton (1838–1863), and Margaret Anastasia (1839–1930)). In 1839 Mary Howitt published *Hymns and Fireside Verses*, and succeeded L. E. L. as editor of the *Drawing Room Scrapbook*, earning £150 p.a. for providing poems for the publisher's engravings. At this time she and William grew increasingly uncomfortable as members of the Society of Friends. In 1840, attracted by the reputation of German education, they moved to Heidelberg. Mary Howitt undertook a series of *Tales for the People and their Children*, designed to promote middle-class virtues among working-class families. She also began the translations that secured her contemporary fame: eighteen volumes of the Swedish novelist Frederika Bremer (1842–1863) and a number of translations of Hans Christian Andersen.

After returning to England in 1843, Mary Howitt was grieved by the death of her son Claude, and felt some guilt that she had not completely neglected her writing to tend to him. Working at the dining-room table, so that she could be interrupted by any pressing needs of the household, she continued to write her children's books, including *My Own Story* (1845). Her literary interests took her into society, and her religious quest led her to the Unitarian chapel. In 1847 the Howitts formally left the Society of Friends, and began a period of experiments in spiritualism. *Ballads and other Poems* (1847) was the fruit of her life-long love of old ballads; in the same year, she published *The Children's Year*, a chronicle of her youngest children. Meanwhile, the bankruptcy of *Howitt's Journal*, which had

run to three volumes between 1847 and 1848, was a severe blow to a couple whose only income came from writing, but observers remarked upon her excellent management of both family and literary work. Her translations of Andersen earned little, but the Bremer books were sufficiently popular to be pirated, and she eventually wrote, edited, or translated over 100 titles.

From 1852 to 1854, while her husband and sons travelled to Australia, Mary Howitt and her daughters pursued their political and artistic interests in London. The support of women's rights by so unthreatening a figure as Mary was particularly welcomed by moderates. Spiritualism and work comforted her when Anna Mary suffered a breakdown and Charlton drowned exploring New Zealand. In 1870 the Howitts began to spend winters in Italy and summers in the Tyrol. By this time spiritualism had lost its appeal, and Mary was attracted to Roman Catholicism. After William's death in 1879, she was granted a civil-list pension of £100 in her own right. Baptized into the Catholic church in 1883, she died at via Gregoriana 38, Rome, on 30 January 1888, and by special permission she was buried beside her husband in the Monte Testaccio cemetery, Rome. Her *Autobiography* was edited by her daughter Margaret and published posthumously in 1889.

Susan Drain

Sources M. Howitt, ed., *Mary Howitt: an autobiography*, 2 vols. (1889) · M. Howitt, *My own story* (1845) · C. Woodring, *Victorian samplers: William and Mary Howitt* (1952) · J. Dunicliff, *Mary Howitt: another lost Victorian writer* (1992) · A. Lee, *Laurels and rosemary: the life of William and Mary Howitt* (1955) · A. Lee, *In their several generations* (1956) · Society of Friends, *Biographical catalogue* (1888) · J. Britten, 'Mary Howitt', *The Month*, 43/289 (July 1888), 339–51 · B. R. Parkes, 'Mary Howitt', *In a walled garden* (1895), 78–99 · 'Illustrious women of our time', *Godey's Lady's Book*, 45 (1852), 320–22 · S. J. Hale, *A cyclopaedia of female biography* (1857) [BBA 128: 184–6] · A. H. Japp, 'Mary Howitt', *The poets and the poetry of the century*, ed. A. H. Miles, 7 (1898), 81–6

Archives Boston PL, corresp. and MSS · Heanor Library, collection · Hunt. L., corresp. · NL Scot., corresp. and literary MSS · Nottingham Central Library, articles and books · Notts. Arch., corresp. · U. Nott. L., family and literary corresp. | BL, letters to Royal Literary Fund, loan 96 · Girton Cam., letters to Bessie Rayner Parkes · Harvard U., Houghton L., letters to Eliza Meteyard · JRL, letters to Gaskell and Mrs Gaskell · Notts. Arch., letters to W. C. Bennett · U. Nott. L., letters to Eliza Oldham | FILM Hunt. L., corresp.

Likenesses J. B. Hunt, stipple, pubd 1852 (after T. J. Hughes), BM, NPG · M. Gillies, double portrait, miniature (with her husband), Castle Art Gallery, Nottingham · A. Harral, woodcut (after M. Gillies), NPG · portrait, repro. in *Hale's Woman's Record* (1855) · portrait, repro. in *The Graphic* (18 Feb 1888) · portrait, repro. in Society of Friends, *Biographical catalogue* · two portraits, repro. in Howitt, ed., *Mary Howitt*

Howitt, Richard (1799–1869), poet, was born on 23 February 1799 at Heanor in Derbyshire, the son of Thomas Howitt (*b.* 1763), a mine superintendent, and Phoebe Tantum, a herbalist. William *Howitt (1792–1879) was his brother. He spent his earlier years as a druggist in Nottingham, for an initial year in partnership with his brother William, but then from 1823 on his own account. He was an ardent lover of literature and his shop—'quite as much of a Parnassium as a pharmacy' (Hall, 308)—served as a focal point for a circle of 'Sherwood poets' and other local writers, including Robert Millhouse, Thomas Miller, Spencer T. Hall, and Jane Holmes (later Jerram). His own poems—many of which appeared first in *Tait's Edinburgh Magazine* and W. Dearden's *Miscellany*—were collected into *Antediluvian Sketches* (1830) and *The Gipsy King and other Poems* (1840). In August 1839 Richard Howitt, in company with his brother Godfrey, emigrated to Australia, but he returned in 1844, and published his experiences in *Impressions of Australia felix* (1845), which some regarded as the 'most reliable description of Australian life at that date' (*AusDB*, 4.435).

Suffering from illness and consequent depression, Howitt retired to Edingley, Nottinghamshire, where he ultimately found peace and contentment in poetry and in kind attentions to his poorer neighbours. In 1865 he survived, like Charles Dickens, the great Staplehurst railway disaster and he published in 1868 a final volume of verse, *Wasp's Honey*. He died unmarried at Edingley on 5 February 1869, and was buried in the Quaker burial-ground at Mansfield. Alfred Tennyson praised his 'truthful, earnest, kindly, poetical temperament' (*Letters*, 234).

RONALD BAYNE, rev. PETER MANDLER

Sources C. R. Woodring, *Victorian samplers: William and Mary Howitt* (1952) · A. M. Howitt, 'Richard Howitt', *The Reliquary*, 10 (1869), 209–16 · A. M. Howitt, 'Richard Howitt', *The Reliquary*, 11 (1870), 17–22, 103–8, 141–4 · A. Lee, *Laurels and rosemary: the life of William and Mary Howitt* (1955) · S. T. Hall, *Biographical sketches of remarkable people* (1873) · *The letters of Alfred Lord Tennyson*, ed. C. Y. Lang and E. F. Shannon, 1: *1821–1850* (1982) · *AusDB*, 4.435 · Boase, *Mod. Eng. biog.* · Allibone, *Dict.*
Archives BL, letters to Royal Literary Fund, loan 96
Wealth at death under £100: probate, 9 March 1869, *CGPLA Eng. & Wales*

Howitt, Samuel (1756/7–1823), painter and etcher, is traditionally said to be a member of an old Nottinghamshire Quaker family, although details of his birth and parentage are unknown. He is first recorded as having a property at Chigwell, in Essex, and living as a gentleman of means—a keen sportsman, hunter, rider, and angler. A self-taught artist, he turned professional when financial difficulties forced him to earn a living. He drew on his enthusiasm and knowledge as a sportsman and produced sporting and natural history paintings, etchings, and illustrations. He sometimes worked in oils but more frequently in watercolours, and he was an accomplished etcher, signing his work 'Howitt' or 'S. Howitt', sometimes with the date. His earliest exhibits at the Incorporated Society of Artists, in 1783, were three 'stained drawings' of hunting scenes; he continued to exhibit, at the Royal Academy and elsewhere, until 1815. He also illustrated many sporting and zoological books, including *Miscellaneous Etchings of Animals* (1803), *Oriental Field Sports* (1807), *Aesop's Fables* (1811), and *The British Sportsman* (1812). His watercolours and prints are represented in various collections, including the Victoria and Albert Museum, the British Museum, and the Tate collection.

Howitt married Elizabeth Rowlandson on 2 October 1779. They had three children—Elizabeth, William, and Maria—but had separated by the time that Howitt died.

His wife was Thomas Rowlandson's sister, and Howitt and Rowlandson were friends as well as brothers-in-law. Howitt's early watercolour style has similarities to Rowlandson's, but Howitt developed a more individual style as his career as a sporting artist progressed. He seems to have had an innate capacity for drawing animals, from commonplace hare and deer to exotic species that he studied in menageries. He was an animated draughtsman, and his drawings of hunts and sporting events have a fluidity and excitement fitting to the subject.

Howitt was reputed to be somewhat unsteady and lively:

> somewhat of a spoiled child—a wayward genius—of a congenial soul, and vivacious impulses, a trifle too given to yield to careless convivial company, or the allurements which the hour might hold forth, oblivious of sober consequences to follow. (Grego, 50)

He seems to have lived in London from 1793, apart from a short period when he gave an address as Richmond, Yorkshire. He returned to London, however, and lived and worked there until his death, at his home, 103 Chalton Street, Somers Town, between 9 February 1823, the date of his will, and his burial at St Pancras Old Church on 21 February.

RUTH COHEN

Sources *DNB* · J. Baskett and D. Snelgrove, *English drawings and watercolours, 1550–1850, in the collection of Mr and Mrs Paul Mellon*, New York (1972) · F. Siltzer, *The story of British sporting prints* (1929), 160–65 · Redgrave, *Artists*, 227 · *The reminiscences of Henry Angelo*, ed. H. Lavers Smith, 2 (1904), 256–60 · J. Grego, *Rowlandson the caricaturist* (1886), 1.50 · Graves, *RA exhibitors*, 3.175 · Graves, *Soc. Artists*, 124–5 · J. Gilbey, 'Samuel Howitt: sporting artist', *Apollo*, 63 (1956), 25–6 · P. Goldman, *Sporting life: an anthology of British sporting prints* (1983) · will, PRO, PROB 11/1667, sig. 147 · parish register, St Pancras Old Church, 21 Feb 1823 [burial] · parish register, St James's, Piccadilly, 2 Oct 1779 [marriage]

Howitt, William (1792–1879), writer, was born on 18 December 1792 in Heanor, Derbyshire, the fourth of seven sons of Thomas Howitt (*b.* 1763), a mine superintendent, and his wife, Phoebe, *née* Tantum, a herbalist. William and his brothers were reared as members of the Society of Friends, countrymen, and book lovers. After spells at Ackworth and Tamworth schools, and with a vague ambition to study pharmacy or medicine, William was apprenticed by his father to a Quaker cabinet-maker in Mansfield. His imagination was captured there more by the romance of Newstead Abbey and Sherwood Forest than by the challenges of the trade, and on the road home to Heanor in 1813 he shredded his indentures and cast them to the winds. Working for a time on an elder brother's farm, he began to write and publish in local journals (sometimes under the pen-name Wilfred Wender). His contributions consisted of poetry and topographical prose, variously inspired by Byron, Scott, Percy's *Reliques*, and Washington Irving. In 1818 he met Mary (1799–1888) [*see* Howitt, Mary], daughter of Samuel and Ann Botham of Uttoxeter, and they were married on 16 April 1821.

Howitt practised as a chemist for a few months in Hanley and then, from 1822, in Nottingham, where he set up shop with his brother Richard *Howitt (1799–1869), close to their physician brother Godfrey. The following

William Howitt (1792–1879), after Thomas Frank Heaphy

year William and Mary established their own premises at Newcastle Street and Timber Hill, on the edge of the largest market place in England, partly to make room for an expanding family: Anna Mary *Howitt (1824–1884), Charles Botham (1826–1828), Alfred William *Howitt (1830–1908), and Claude Middleton (1833–1844). Working separately and collaboratively, 'the second William and Mary' began to build a reputation as milk-and-water Romantic poets now publishing in London and in midland outlets. Around their hearth gathered the circle of Sherwood poets that included Richard Howitt, Robert Millhouse, and Thomas Miller. One of their earliest metropolitan connections was the annual-editor Alaric Watts, who negotiated their first major book contract with Colburn and Bentley for *The Book of the Seasons* (1831), a characteristic blend of poetry and natural history that went through seventeen editions. The Watts family became lifelong friends and Alaric's son later married the Howitts' daughter Anna Mary.

Howitt's pantheistic poetry was already attracting suspicion among stricter members of the Society of Friends, and he gave them further cause for concern in his growing engagement with radical reform politics. From 1833 he wrote a series of articles (mostly in *Tait's Edinburgh Magazine*) critical of Quaker detachment from the modern world and calling for a greater emphasis on pure faith than on scripture; these culminated in his entries on the Quakers for the seventh and eighth editions of the *Encyclopaedia Britannica*. His *Popular History of Priestcraft* (1833) became a standard work for plebeian advocates of church

disestablishment. In 1835 Nottingham elected Howitt an alderman, and he hosted Daniel O'Connell at a public dinner in the city. But local politics were too confining for Howitt and in autumn 1836 he uprooted his family and moved to Esher, on the Surrey fringe of London, for an initially precarious career as a writer. In addition to political articles for Joseph Hume's *Constitutional*, broadsides against the enslaved condition of the Indian people, and a history of parliamentary reform, Howitt published lighter material in a wide array of English and Scottish magazines and annuals, and three highly influential books that form a piece: *The Rural Life of England* (1838), *The Boy's Country-Book* (1839), and *Visits to Remarkable Places* (2 vols., 1840, 1842). These works hymn the delights of the old English countryside in the manner of Cobbett, but are generally more optimistic and less nostalgic, taking tradition as the foundation on which a democratic modernity could be built, rather than as a land of lost content. Among the distinctive features of these volumes was their vigorous promotion of popular tourism, by foot and by rail. All of this literary activity was successful enough at least to support two more children, Herbert Charlton (*b.* 1838) and Margaret (Meggie; *b.* 1839).

The Howitts spent the early 1840s in Heidelberg, to advance the education of the older children and to experiment in new literary fields, experimentation which yielded a stream of original works and translations on German literary and social life. On their return to England in April 1843, they settled in Clapton, closer to the centre of London, where their home, The Elms, became a meeting-place for German exiles, American anti-slavery agitators, domestic radicals, feminists, painters, poets, and particularly Unitarians (among whose number the Howitts now effectively considered themselves). Scandinavian visitors were also welcome, as Mary (with William's mostly uncredited assistance) had embarked on translations in those languages, which led to their jointly written history *The Literature and Romance of Northern Europe* (1852).

Aiming to turn his interests in radical politics and popular literature to some profit, Howitt bought a half-share in John Saunders's *People's Journal* in April 1846, and then launched his own 1½d. weekly, *Howitt's Journal*, in May 1847. The disastrous outcome was a judgment against him in chancery in May 1847 for nearly £4000 in Saunders's debt; bankruptcy followed in December 1848, by which date *Howitt's Journal* had already folded. In its brief life it had clocked up a respectable circulation of 30,000 on a bland but timely diet of popular uplift; posterity remembers it chiefly as the medium for the first publications of Elizabeth Gaskell, whom Howitt had met through his Unitarian contacts. Howitt also secured for Gaskell her first book contract, but his close interest in dirty commercial considerations earned him some contempt in more elevated quarters. Robert Browning warned Elizabeth Barrett against any connection with the Howitts: 'Come out from among them my soul, neither be thou a partaker of their habitations!' (R. Browning to E. Barrett, 1 May 1846, in *The Brownings' Correspondence*, ed. P. Kelley and S. Lewis, vol. 12, 1994, 292). Unfortunately, Howitt had employed his financial acumen less effectively on his own family's account, and after the bankruptcy they moved to more modest quarters in St John's Wood. There they returned to scraping a living; several editions of *Homes and Haunts of the most Eminent British Poets* (1847) may have brought some financial relief. Howitt became a regular contributor to Dickens's *Household Words* and an active promoter of co-operation.

In June 1852 Howitt went to Australia, in the company of his sons Alfred and Charlton and the writer R. H. Horne. He spent two years there, visiting his brother Godfrey (who had settled in Melbourne), panning for gold, and exploring the bush for literary material. The result was little gold but five books: *Land, Labour, and Gold, or, Two Years in Victoria* (1855), best-known under its subtitle, remains a valuable document of boom-time Australia. When Howitt returned to England in late 1854, Alfred stayed behind and became celebrated as an adventurer and serious investigator into Aboriginal life and culture.

Howitt rejoined Mary, now settled in Highgate, where they resumed their literary activities and developed a new circle of friends among the Pre-Raphaelite painters. He wrote frequently for the popular publisher John Cassell, including the bulk of *Cassell's Illustrated History of England* (1856–64), said to have sold 100,000 penny numbers a week. But the Howitts were ageing and growing eccentric. They had been badly affected by the death of their son Claude in 1844, and this was reinforced by the drowning of Charlton in New Zealand in 1863. Veering away from Unitarianism, they became avid spiritualists—William was one of the leading spiritualist journalists of the 1860s and flirted with the Swedenborgians and yet more exotic creeds.

Armed with a civil-list pension of £140, granted in 1865, the Howitts left England for good in 1870. For the rest of their life together, they alternated between summers in the south Tyrol and winters in Rome, accompanied by their daughter Meggie and the American sculptor Margaret Foley. Their minds were fixed firmly on the afterlife, but while his wife ultimately converted to Catholicism, Howitt remained attached to the simplicity and pure spirituality of his Quaker youth. Howitt was writing a life of George Fox at the time of his death, on 3 March 1879, at via Sistina 86, Rome. He was buried in the protestant cemetery near Rome. The 180 books which the Howitts produced between them have not worn well, but in his own day Howitt's blend of history, topography, spirituality, and democratic politics was immensely popular. A contemporary riddle asked, 'What authors do you think of first when you see a burning library? Dickens, Howitt Burns!' PETER MANDLER

Sources C. R. Woodring, *Victorian samplers: William and Mary Howitt* (1952) · A. Lee, *Laurels and rosemary: the life of William and Mary Howitt* (1955) · *Mary Howitt: an autobiography*, ed. M. Howitt, 2 vols. (1889) · S. J. Butlin, 'Introduction', in W. Howitt, *Land, labour, and gold, or, Two years in Victoria* (1972) · S. T. Hall, *Biographical sketches of remarkable people* (1873) · J. S. Uglow, *Elizabeth Gaskell: a habit of stories* (1993)

Archives Boston PL, corresp. and papers · Derbys. RO, papers · Nottingham Central Library · State Library of Victoria, Melbourne, autobiography | BL, letters to Royal Literary Fund, loan 96 · U. Nott. L., letters to William Oldham
Likenesses G. Frampton, bronze monument, 1902 (*William and Mary Howitt*), City of Nottingham Art Gallery · M. Gillies, miniature, oils (*William and Mary Howitt*), Castle Art Gallery, Nottingham · oils (after T. F. Heaphy), Castle Museum and Art Gallery, Nottingham [*see illus.*] · wood-engraving, NPG; repro. in *ILN* (1879)

Howland, Richard (*bap.* 1540, *d.* 1600), bishop of Peterborough, was the son of John Howland, gentleman, of London, and Anne Greenway of Cley, Norfolk, and was baptized at Newport Pond, near Saffron Walden in Essex on 26 September 1540. Admitted a pensioner at Christ's College, Cambridge, on 18 March 1558, he graduated BA in 1561 and is said to have migrated to St John's. He was elected a fellow of Peterhouse on 11 November 1562 and proceeded MA in 1564, being incorporated at Oxford in 1567. He was presented to the substantial rectory of Stathern in Leicestershire by the college in 1569 but remained in his fellowship at Cambridge, where he took the degree of BTh in 1570. In the following year he was among those younger dons who signed the unsuccessful petition to Lord Burghley requesting that the presbyterian Thomas Cartwright, Lady Margaret professor of divinity, be allowed to return to Cambridge after his expulsion.

That Howland was a committed supporter of presbyterian views at this time seems unlikely, as he soon engaged in vigorous debate with the puritans in the university, and following a sermon in October 1573 gained the confidence of Burghley, who was chancellor of the university. He was instituted to the rectory of Sibson in Huntingdonshire in 1573, which he continued to hold until his death, and in the same year was made a chaplain to Burghley. In 1576, through Burghley's influence, he was appointed master of Magdalene College, then on the verge of bankruptcy. He proved an astute administrator and when John Whitgift became bishop of Worcester in 1577 he recommended Howland to be his successor as master of Trinity. The queen had already chosen John Still for the mastership so it was arranged that Howland, being 'a man of gravity and moderation, and of neither party or faction' (Strype, 1.153) should follow Still as master of St John's, a college with a history of disruption and discord consequent upon differing views about church discipline between puritans and defenders of episcopacy among the fellowship.

Howland's administrative skills were employed in giving effect to a new body of statutes designed to settle the differences within the college, and indeed during his mastership the college remained relatively quiescent, more so than under most of the other Elizabethan masters. He was a major figure in the university, serving as vice-chancellor in 1577–8. As head of the institution he waited on the queen during her visit to Audley End, making an oration and presenting her with a Greek Testament and a pair of gloves on behalf of the university on 27 July 1578. He served as vice-chancellor again in 1583–4, by when his old friend and mentor Whitgift had become archbishop of Canterbury. Whitgift considered Howland to be episcopal material and recommended him for some of the sees vacant in 1584, or failing those for the deanery of Peterborough. Burghley, whose views of Howland's capacities were not as high as Whitgift's, advised the deanery but Elizabeth, while not following the archbishop's recommendations, regarded him as worth more than that, promoting him to the bishopric of Peterborough on Scambler's translation to Norwich. Howland was consecrated by the archbishop at Lambeth on 7 February 1585.

Peterborough was not a wealthy see and it was agreed that Howland should retain the mastership of St John's for the immediate future, especially as the appointment of a successor was likely to revive the factional disputes within the college. Burghley had lent his support to the puritan William Whitaker, then a fellow of Trinity, but this had not been well received by the fellowship. Nor would Whitaker have been Howland's preferred successor, but pressured by his patron he agreed to press Whitaker's cause with the fellowship. The opponents of Whitaker were determined to obstruct his appointment if they could, with the result that a stalemate between Burghley and the fellowship delayed Whitaker's election until February 1587, Howland trying to keep the governance of the college on course while also entering on his new responsibilities in the meantime.

When Howland was finally able to leave Cambridge he received Burghley's permission to take with him to Peterborough some younger well-born members of the college, including the earl of Southampton, for health and recreation during the summer months. On entering his new diocese the bishop found a vigorous puritan contingent among the parochial clergy, many of whom had refused to subscribe to Whitgift's three articles at their first formulation in 1583. Compromise followed and despite the region's reputation for nonconformity only one cleric was deprived in 1584. Thereafter, however, Peterborough diocese emerged as one of the principal, and perhaps the greatest, centre of provincial puritan activity and the home of the clerical conferences, by means of which puritan clergy attempted to graft a presbyterian form of discipline onto the parochial structure. Between 1588 and 1591 a number of the local leadership were prosecuted before the high commission in the greatest confrontation between the puritans and the establishment during Elizabeth's reign. These prosecutions aroused opposition among godly members of parliament, the most celebrated individual case being that of Robert Cawdry, rector of South Luffenham, whose refusal to take the *ex officio* oath was taken up by the common lawyers as part of their attack on the church courts. Cawdry was deprived in 1588 but refused to leave the parsonage and was once again convicted of nonconformity and of reading the satirical pamphlets of Martin Marprelate, whose scurrilous pen had lampooned Howland among other bishops. Cawdry's patron in the living was none other than Burghley, Howland's patron also, and it is significant that it was left to the bishop to appoint a successor to the deprived incumbent, Burghley failing to act in the matter.

Faced with widespread support for puritanism among the clergy and the laity of the diocese Howland's capacity for vigorous action against nonconformity was limited, and his episcopate remained troubled by sporadic confrontations which made little impact on the support the puritans enjoyed, though after the prosecutions of 1588–91 both sides avoided large-scale confrontation. In addition to puritan nonconformity the diocese also contained pockets of committed Catholic recusancy, most particularly near Oundle where the Tresham family estates were found. In dealing with the Catholics, Howland was prepared to go further than many of his episcopal colleagues and to enlist the support of the puritan clergy, even encouraging meetings rather like the illegal conferences to reinforce the protestant message in the most recalcitrant Catholic area. Faced with such intractable problems on both sides of the theological divide and struggling with the finances of a poorly endowed see whose income had been further diminished by his predecessor, it is not surprising that Howland sought further promotion. Always sure of Whitgift's backing, Howland considered that he was favoured for the archbishopric of York by the president and council of the north in 1594, but may have overestimated the strength of their support. Nothing came of his hopes, Burghley declining to act on his behalf.

Howland's most public role as bishop was on 1 August 1587 when he presided over the funeral of the executed Mary, queen of Scots, who was buried in his cathedral, and it was in the same cathedral that Howland himself was buried, in an obscure grave without any memorial, having died unmarried in his palace at Castor on 23 June 1600, in debt to the crown. A middle-ranking figure in the Elizabethan church, Howland was said to have been 'a very learned and worthy man' (Strype, 2.213). His administrative skills served the church well in a faction-ridden college and a difficult diocese, but his retiring nature, reflected in his funeral arrangements, ensured that further promotion evaded his grasp.   WILLIAM JOSEPH SHEILS

Sources W. J. Sheils, *The puritans in the diocese of Peterborough, 1558–1610*, Northamptonshire RS, 30 (1979) · P. Lake, *Moderate puritans and the Elizabethan church* (1982) · F. Heal, *Of prelates and princes: a study of the economic and social position of the Tudor episcopate* (1980) · Cooper, *Ath. Cantab.*, 2.287–8 · Venn, *Alum. Cant.*, 1/2.419 · H. C. Porter, *Reformation and reaction in Tudor Cambridge* (1958) · J. Strype, *The life and acts of John Whitgift*, new edn, 3 vols. (1822) · S. Gunton, *The history of the church of Peterburgh*, ed. S. Patrick (1686)
Wealth at death in debt to crown: Heal, *Of prelates and princes*, 290–91

Howland, Sir William Pearce (1811–1907), businessman and politician in Canada, was born at Pawling, New York, on 29 May 1811, the son of Jonathan Howland, a descendant of Henry Howland, a Quaker who migrated to New England in 1621, and his wife, Lydia Pearce. After attending the local school and Kinderhook Academy, Kinderhook, New York, he went in 1830 to Upper Canada, where he found work in a general store at Cooksville (Mississauga). While he was working with his brothers Peleg, Frederick Aiken, and later Henry Stark, his business interests grew rapidly, until by the later 1850s he was one of the wealthiest millers in Upper Canada and owned several stores, grain concerns, and lumbering, rafting, and potash manufacturing operations, as well as other industries in the townships of Toronto and Chinguacosy. On 12 July 1843 he married Marianne (Mary Anne) Blyth (Blythe; *d.* 1860), the widow of David Webb, with whom he had a daughter and two sons.

Shortly after the union of the Canadas, Howland, until then an American, took out citizenship and entered politics. His American origins predisposed him to become a Reformer and, drawn from the Toronto professional and business élite, he gravitated into the ranks of the moderate Reformers led by George Brown. In the election of 1857–8 Howland was elected to parliament representing York West. The manoeuvring which followed the election and which deprived the Reformers of power convinced Brown and Howland that a radical restructuring of the legislative union was needed, and in 1859 both became founder members of the Constitutional Reform Association.

In the 1860s Howland's business interests became increasingly concentrated in Toronto, where he served as the president of the board of trade from 1859 to 1862 and where he was active in insurance and banking. Widowed in 1860, on 21 November 1865 he married Susanna Julia Shrewsbury (*d.* 1886), herself the widow of Captain Philip Hunt. After being re-elected in York West in 1861, Howland served as minister of finance (1862–3), receivergeneral (1863–4), and postmaster-general (1864–6), and again as minister of finance (1866–7). He was one of three delegates from Upper Canada at the London conference of 1866–7 which framed the British North America Act which determined the form of the Canadian confederation. Divorced from the main body of the Reformers who followed George Brown's leadership and withdrew their support from the coalition government headed by John A. Macdonald, Howland became minister of internal revenue in the first Canadian cabinet in 1867, but, increasingly politically isolated and suffering from ill health, he retired from politics in 1868. He was immediately appointed lieutenant-governor of Ontario and continued to be active in business and particularly in the promotion of railways. He retired as lieutenant-governor in 1873. He was appointed CB on 1 July 1867 and KCMG in May 1879. Widowed again in 1886, on 15 August 1895 he married Elizabeth Mary Rattray, the widow of James Bethune QC, but they soon separated. He died at Toronto on 1 January 1907 and was buried there. Howland, and to a far lesser extent his two sons, both of whom were mayors of Toronto, were important figures in Ontario's and particularly Toronto's business communities at a formative period, and Howland himself was a pragmatic and successful reforming politician.   ELIZABETH BAIGENT

Sources R. B. Fleming, 'Howland, Sir William Pearce', *DCB*, vol. 13 · *DNB* · *The Times* (3 Jan 1907)
Archives Public Archives of Ontario, Toronto
Likenesses M. Peel, bust; formerly in the Normal school, Toronto, Canada, 1912 · oils; formerly at Government House, Ottawa, Canada, 1912 · oils; formerly in the National Club, Toronto, Canada, 1912
Wealth at death wealthy

Howlet, John. *See* Howlett, John (*c*.1548–1589).

Howlett, Bartholomew (1767–1827), draughtsman and landscape engraver, was born in Louth, Lincolnshire, and was baptized on 5 July 1767 at Gainsborough, the son of Bartholomew Howlett (*b.* 1739) and his first wife, Judith. He was apprenticed in London to the engraver James Heath, and afterwards lived in the Blackfriars area of London. In 1801 he published *A Selection of Views of the County of Lincoln*, with numerous engravings after works by Thomas Girtin, James Bourne, and others. A second edition appeared in 1805. In 1803 he exhibited his own illustration *Gate of White Friars at Stamford, Lincolnshire* at the Royal Academy; from 1807 he contributed to John Britton's *Architectural Antiquities of Great Britain* and from 1808 to Robert Wilkinson's *Londina illustrata*. He engraved the six plates for George Anderson's *Plan and Views of the Abbey Royal of St Denys* (1812), and contributed to Charles Frost's *Notices of … the Town and Port of Hull* (1827). Throughout his career he produced topographical plates for *Gentleman's Magazine* and other periodicals.

On moving to Clapham in 1816, then still a rural village south of London, Howlett issued proposals for 'A topographical account of Clapham, in the county of Surrey, illustrated by engravings', which were to have been made from his own drawings, but only one number, consisting merely of three plates, was published. His manuscript material for this work passed into Mr Tyton's Surrey collection. In 1826 Howlett made a series of drawings during the demolition of the Royal Hospital and the collegiate church of St Katharine by the Tower, for the construction of a new dock. These passed into the hands of Mr Nichols. Howlett's major contribution to antiquarianism was, however, the thousand or more drawings he made of the original seals of monastic and religious houses for his friend and patron John Caley FRS FSA, keeper of the records in the augmentation office.

Howlett became destitute in his old age; at his death on 18 December 1827 at Newington (probably Newington Butts, Surrey, rather than Newington, Middlesex) moves were made to obtain relief for his widow from the committees of the literary and artists' funds.

L. H. CUST, rev. MARY GUYATT

Sources Bryan, *Painters* (1903–5), 3.78 · Redgrave, *Artists*, 2nd edn, 227 · Graves, *RA exhibitors*, 175 · W. Upcott, *A bibliographical account of the principal works relating to English topography*, 3 vols. (1818); repr. with introduction by J. Simmons (1978), entries 559, 898 · *N&Q*, 1 (1849–50), 321 · *N&Q*, 7 (1853), 69 · *N&Q*, 5th ser., 9 (1878), 488 · *New Monthly Magazine*, new ser., 24 (1828), 271 · *GM*, 1st ser., 98/1 (1828), 277
Wealth at death minimal: *DNB*

Howlett [Howlet], **John** (*c*.1548–1589), Jesuit, was born in the county of Rutland. He entered Exeter College, Oxford, in 1564 and became a fellow of that college on graduating BA in June 1566. Soon after graduating MA in November 1569 he obtained permission to travel to Rome, but went no further than Flanders, where in 1570 he entered the English College at Douai as a student of theology, along with Edmund Campion and Gregory Martin. In May 1571 he was received into the Society of Jesus at Louvain, and took his first vows at St Omer in January 1574. In March

1576 he was posted to the Jesuit province of Upper (that is, southern) Germany, as a teacher of the humanities, and from 1582 to 1587 he was prefect of studies at the newly founded college in Fribourg, Switzerland. Howlett's name was subscribed to the preface of the *Brief Discourse Contayning Certain Reasons why Catholiques Refuse to Goe to Church*, published by Robert Persons soon after his arrival in England in 1580, but although his name became associated with the work, he had no part in its composition. In 1587 he was appointed to the Jesuit mission in Transylvania, within the jurisdiction of the Polish province, but never reached his destination. Instead he became professor of scholastic theology in the college at Vilna, Lithuania, where he died on 14 September 1589.

G. MARTIN MURPHY

Sources T. M. McCoog, *English and Welsh Jesuits, 1555–1650*, 2, Catholic RS, 75 (1995), 212 · L. Lukács, *Catalogus personarum et officiorum provinciae Austriae S. J.*, 1 (1978), 466, 695 · A. de Backer and others, *Bibliothèque de la Compagnie de Jésus*, new edn, 4, ed. C. Sommervogel (Brussels, 1893), 492 · A. F. Allison and D. M. Rogers, eds., *The contemporary printed literature of the English Counter-Reformation between 1558 and 1640*, 2 (1994), 121, no. 613 · L. Grzebień, *Encyklopedia wiedzy o jezuitach na ziemiach Polski i Litwy, 1564–1995* (Krakow, 1996), 223 · Foster, *Alum. Oxon.* · T. F. Knox and others, eds., *The first and second diaries of the English College, Douay* (1878), 4

Howlett, John (1731–1804), economist and writer on the poor, was the son of John Howlett of Bedworth, Warwickshire. Educated at the University of Oxford, he matriculated from St Edmund Hall in 1749, gaining his BA from St John's College in 1755. He later obtained the degrees MA (1795) and BD (1796) from St John's. In 1782 Howlett was given the parish of Great Dunmow, Essex, by the bishop of London. In 1786 he also acquired the nearby living of Badow, furnishing him with an ample income to support his correspondence, writing, and travels, including a tour of France in 1787. Little is known of his whereabouts and activities between university and his first publications in 1781, which show him to have been living in Maidstone.

Most of Howlett's writings concentrated on the well-being of the poor, an issue for which he was well equipped as an able statistician and demographer, and inclined to see in a broader compass than many of his contemporaries. Heated debates took place in the pre-census era over the population of England and this was the subject of Howlett's first writings. In *An Essay on the Population of England and Wales* (1780), the philosopher and demographer Richard Price famously made the case that England and Wales were experiencing depopulation, and his views, shared by a number of other pessimists, found a wide audience. Howlett responded with *An Examination of Dr. Price's Essay on the Population of England and Wales* in 1781. This argued to the contrary that the population of England and Wales had doubled since 1688 and was expanding at a quickening pace to the benefit of the rural poor. One of the principal factors was the changing pattern of land usage, especially through the intensification of commercial agriculture, enclosures, the progressive loss of common rights, and the engrossing of small farms. Howlett believed that resistance to change was motivated by sentiment and irrational argument, which he sought to dismiss in a 1787 pamphlet with a wide range of evidence on population trends. The title of this essay is a summary of its main argument: *Enclosures, a cause of improved agriculture, or plenty and cheapness of provisions, of population and of both private and national wealth*. A widespread network of correspondents in England, Wales, and beyond meant that Howlett was not short of data and that regional differences could be factored into his estimates and explanations. In 1786 he published an essay on the population of Ireland.

Alongside the issue of enclosure Howlett was concerned by the manner in which food price rises had from the 1750s eroded the real wages and living standards of the rural poor. Here too he favoured commercial modernity and liberal free trade against those who called for the reinstatement of medieval marketing laws and price controls. Howlett was an admirer of the work of Adam Smith, and his circle included others influenced by the economic thought of the Scottish Enlightenment. Between the 1780s and his death he corresponded with the agricultural reformer Arthur Young and contributed several letters to the latter's *Annals of Agriculture*. Although Howlett had taken a generally benign view of the economic trends which led to the growth of a landless class of agricultural wage labourers in the late eighteenth century, his optimism was not facile. The desperate circumstances and threatened famine of the mid-1790s led him to argue in support of a minimum wage and some sort of compensation for the loss of the commons, views set out in his *An Examination of Mr Pitt's Speech … Relative to the Condition of the Poor* (1798). He was engaged in writing a report on the county of Essex for the board of agriculture at the time of his death, while visiting Bath, on 29 February 1804. It is not known whether he married or had children.

R. D. SHELDON

Sources DNB · Foster, *Alum. Oxon.* · GM, 1st ser., 74 (1804), 282 · J. Howlett, *An enquiry into the influence which enclosures have had upon the population of England* (1786) · J. Howlett, *Dispersion of the gloomy apprehensions* (1797)
Archives BL, letters in files of association for protecting liberty and property from republicans and levellers, Add. MS 16920, fol. 7 · BL, letters to Arthur Young, Add. MS 35126, fols. 193, 409

Howlett, Robert (1830–1858), photographer, was the son of the Revd Robert Howlett, Church of England clergyman, of Longham, Norfolk. He only comes to notice three years before his premature death in 1858; nothing is known of his mother, early life, education, or training. During his brief career he produced some of the most significant photographs of the period, most notably his portrait, *Isambard Kingdom Brunel and the Launching Chains of the Great Eastern*, made during the closing months of 1857.

Although he is known to have taken photographs as early as 1852, Howlett first came to notice working as a photographer for the Photographic Institution in New Bond Street, London. Established by Joseph Cundall and Phillip Delamotte in 1853, the Photographic Institution quickly became the leading establishment for the commercial promotion of photography through exhibitions, publications, and commissions. It may be presumed that Howlett joined the company after Delamotte left to take up his appointment as professor of drawing at King's College, London.

1856—the year in which Howlett is first mentioned in the photographic press—was extremely busy for him: during the course of the year he sent prints to the annual exhibitions of photographic societies in London, Manchester, and Norwich. Among the work he submitted were two landscape studies, *In the Valley of the Mole, Mickleham* and *Box Hill, Surrey*, which are likely to have been taken the previous year. In the same year he undertook the first of a number of commissions for Queen Victoria and Prince Albert, who regularly called upon the services of the Photographic Institution. Apart from copying the works of Raphael for Prince Albert's comprehensive art historical study, Howlett also made a series of notable portraits of soldiers who had distinguished themselves during the Crimean War. These were exhibited the following year at the Photographic Society of London's annual exhibition under the title *Crimean Heroes* and are now frequently confused with the series taken by Joseph Cundall. Despite the ascendancy of photography there were growing fears about the stability and permanence of prints, many of which were showing signs of premature fading. It is within this context that Howlett published *On the various methods of printing photographic pictures upon paper with suggestions for their preservation* (1856).

In common with many other London establishments the Photographic Institution also operated a studio where Howlett made a significant number of portraits. Doubtless through Cundall's intimate connections within the world of publishing and fine art, a number of the most eminent artists of the day came to be photographed. Howlett's portraits of W. P. Frith, F. R. Pickersgill, J. C. Horsley, and Thomas Webster were among a larger group exhibited at the Art Treasures Exhibition in Manchester in 1857. It was Frith who commissioned Howlett to photograph crowd scenes at the 1856 Derby from the roof of a cab for use as preliminary studies for his 1858 painting *Derby Day*.

Howlett's most memorable series of photographs, and ones which are now regarded as epitomizing the spirit of Victorian engineering and endeavour, are those he made of the steamship the *Great Eastern*. The vessel was designed by Isambard Kingdom Brunel and built by Messrs Scott, Russell & Co. at Millwall, on the banks of the Thames. The single largest engineering enterprise of the period, its protracted launch nearly defeated everyone involved, including Brunel, whose posture, gaze, and muddied clothes transmit the sense of difficulty and impending failure in Howlett's portrait. Paradoxically, this portrait has since assumed iconic status, standing as it now does for all that was heroic and noble during the Victorian period.

Robert Howlett died, unmarried, of a fever on 2 December 1858 at his lodgings at 10 Bedford Place, Campden Hill, Kensington, London. It was thought by colleagues that his untimely death had been brought about by the fatal combination of overwork and his imprudent use of poisonous photographical chemicals.　　　　ROGER TAYLOR

Sources G. Seiberling and C. Bloor, *Amateurs, photography, and the mid-Victorian imagination* (1986) • Mr Hardwick, *Journal of the Photographic Society*, 5 (1858–9), 111–12 • A. Hamber, *A higher branch of the arts* (1996) • R. Taylor, 'Critical moments: British photographic exhibitions, 1839–1865', data base, priv. coll. • d. cert. • *CGPLA Eng. & Wales* (1859)
Likenesses photograph, V&A
Wealth at death under £1500: administration, 22 Jan 1859, *CGPLA Eng. & Wales*

Howlett, Samuel Burt (1794–1874), surveyor and inventor of scientific instruments, the only son of Samuel Howlett of Gracechurch Street, London, was born on 10 July 1794. After leaving school at thirteen, he secured, through the influence of an uncle with military connections, an apprenticeship with the royal military surveyors and draughtsmen. He became a cadet on 20 August 1808 and each day attended the drawing-room of the Tower of London where he learned plan drawing. He excelled in mathematics and technical drawing and also read widely on religious, artistic, and professional subjects. On becoming a third-class draughtsman in 1811 he was sent into the field and, having been supervised for a brief period, was left to survey single-handed parts of Berkshire and Wiltshire for the Ordnance Survey. This practice was then customary and it accounts for much of the variation in the early Ordnance Survey maps. In 1824 he was appointed assistant and in 1830 chief military surveyor and draughtsman to the Board of Ordnance. In 1826 he exhibited at the Royal Academy and in 1828 published a *Treatise on Perspective*. As inspector of scientific instruments for the war department he made many improvements in the mountain barometer and stadiometer (an instrument for judging distances), and invented an anemometer and also a method of construction which was widely adopted for large drawing-boards, with compensations for moisture and temperature. His descriptions of new instruments and improved techniques were published in the *Professional Papers of the Royal Engineers*. Howlett was deeply religious and from the time he was a young man was much occupied in promoting church schools and relieving poverty. He retired at the age of seventy-one and died at his home, Pulham House, Palace Grove, Bromley, Kent, on 24 January 1874. He is best remembered for his pocket book which he maintained during his service on the Ordnance Survey; he later wrote up his notes into a memoir which gives a unique insight into the life of an early ordnance surveyor and shows him to have been highly conscientious and professional. Nothing is known of his marriage save that two sons and one daughter survived him.

ELIZABETH BAIGENT

Sources W. A. Seymour, ed., *A history of the Ordnance Survey* (1980) • J. B. Harley and Y. O'Donoghue, introduction, in *The old series ordnance survey maps of England and Wales*, Ordnance Survey, 3: *South-central England (Hampshire and the Isle of Wight and parts of Berkshire, Dorset, Somerset, Surrey, Sussex and Wiltshire)* (1981), vii–liv • *DNB* • *CGPLA Eng. & Wales* (1874)
Archives priv. coll. • U. Durham L., corresp. and papers

Wealth at death under £3000: probate, 20 June 1874, *CGPLA Eng. & Wales*

Howley, Henry (1775?–1803), Irish nationalist, who engaged in the rebellion of 1798 and Robert Emmet's abortive Dublin city coup in 1803, is variously reported to have hailed from Roscrea, co. Tipperary, and more generally from co. Kildare. An evidently enterprising man, he evaded the authorities in the aftermath of the 1798 insurrection and resumed his career as a carpenter.

In early March 1803 Howley was contacted by Emmet's main Kildare organizer, Michael Quigley, who persuaded him to sign a lease on a Thomas Street premises for use as an illegal arms depot in Dublin. Howley subsequently procured large quantities of timber for the plotters and became one of their chief pike makers. When the plans for the rising were advanced because of fear of discovery, Howley formed part of the rebel group led by Emmet on Thomas Street on 23 July 1803. He was then entrusted with the vital task of bringing hired coaches to the vicinity of the depot so that they could be used in the storming of nearby Dublin Castle. Howley was engaged on this mission when he chanced upon a fracas between an unarmed Kildare insurgent and a soldier on Bridgefoot Street and felt compelled to intervene. Howley shot and killed Colonel Lyde Brown of the 21st regiment and thereby scuppered the coach plan, a reverse to which Emmet attributed the failure of the rising.

With many others Howley went into hiding on the night of the 23rd but his refuge was betrayed by Pat Finnerty, who led a police patrol to his city workplace. Rather than surrender, Howley fatally shot one Hanlon, keeper of the tower in Dublin Castle, but was soon afterwards apprehended in a hayloft on Pool Street. Tried at Green Street court house on 27 September 1803, Howley admitted killing Colonel Brown and was publicly executed the following day.   RUÁN O'DONNELL

Sources H. Landreth, *The pursuit of Robert Emmet* (1949) · R. R. Madden, *The United Irishmen: their lives and times*, 3rd ser., vol. 3 (1846), 339–54, 366, 381–2 · R. O'Donnell, *Aftermath: post-rebellion insurgency in Wicklow, 1799–1803* (2000) · 1803, PRO, Home Office, 100/115/4 [information of Michael Quigley] · *DNB*
Likenesses P. Maguire, stipple (after pencil drawing by J. Petrie, 1803), NG Ire.

Howley, Richard Joseph (1871–1955), transport company director, was born on 9 July 1871 at Rich Hill, co. Limerick, the son of Lieutenant-Colonel John Howley, deputy lieutenant. He was educated at Oscott College, the Jesuit establishment near Birmingham, and at the University of Dublin. He trained as an engineer, and joined the British Electric Traction company in that capacity in August 1899.

Howley moved to executive duties and became joint manager (with C. H. Dade) in 1912, and was appointed to the board in 1923 with responsibility for administration. He succeeded the founder, Emile Garcke, as chief executive in 1929, and became deputy chairman in 1930. When J. S. Austin retired in 1942, Howley took over the chairmanship, which he handed in 1946 to H. C. Drayton. He remained on the board until 1953. During much of this time he served as chairman or on the board of several subsidiary companies, notably the Birmingham and Midland Motor Omnibus company ('Midland Red'). He played a significant part in the diversification of BET from power generation and traction to become the parent of a large group of bus companies, with interests extending into non-transport activities.

In his public life Howley was a member of the tramways committee of the Board of Trade, and afterwards served from 1917 to 1919 on the railways priority committee. In 1919 he was a founder member of the Institute of Transport. In his evidence to the royal commission on transport (1929–31) he made his mark on the future of the bus industry. The commission was examining a draft bill produced by a Ministry of Transport committee on the licensing and regulation of public service vehicles, under the chairmanship of Sir Henry Percy Maybury (1864–1943). Howley's evidence led the commission to modify Maybury's draft bill so as to set up *ad hoc* regional licensing authorities, rather than give the powers to county and county borough councils. Nevertheless his submissions did not neglect the interests of his company, nor those of the larger firms in the bus industry.

Howley was a quiet man, who never married, but he was noted for his singleness of purpose. He took over as chairman of BET when a long-standing partnership with the Tilling group was breaking up, and he had little sympathy with the policies of Sir J. F. Heaton, Tilling's chairman. This difference of opinion was reflected in the decision of the board under Drayton's chairmanship not to sell BET bus companies to the British Transport Commission in 1948. Howley's influence, both on BET and on the statutory control of the British bus industry, remained significant in the late twentieth century.

Howley was appointed CBE in 1919, for his war work, and he was awarded the Road Transport (Passenger) Medal of the Institute of Transport in 1924. He died on 2 April 1955 at his home 49 Hallam Street, Marylebone, London, leaving £230,710 gross.   JOHN HIBBS

Sources R. Fulford, *Five decades of BET: the story of the British Electric Traction Company, Limited* (privately printed, London, 1946) · R. Fulford, *The sixth decade, 1946–1956* (1956) · *Modern Transport* (11 July 1955) · A. S. T. Griffith-Boscawen, *Minutes of evidence taken before the royal commission on transport*, 3 vols. (1929–30), vol. 2 · J. Hibbs, 'Howley, Richard Joseph', *DBB* · *The Times* (22 April 1955), 15d · *CGPLA Eng. & Wales* (1955)
Archives Tramway Museum Society, Crich, Matlock, Derbyshire, BET MSS
Likenesses photograph, repro. in Fulford, *Five decades of BET*, facing p. 72
Wealth at death £230,710 11s. 1d.: probate, 21 April 1955, *CGPLA Eng. & Wales*

Howley, William (1766–1848), archbishop of Canterbury, the only son of William Howley, vicar of Bishop's Sutton and Ropley, and his wife, Mary, daughter of John Gauntlett, a Winchester wine merchant, was born at Ropley, Hampshire, on 12 February 1766. He was elected a scholar

William Howley (1766–1848), by Sir Thomas Lawrence, 1816

at Winchester College and entered New College, Oxford, in 1783 as a scholar. He graduated BA in 1787 and MA in 1791, and was elected fellow and tutor. While at New College he served as tutor to the hereditary prince of Orange, later William II of the Netherlands. In 1792 he became domestic chaplain to the marquess of Abercorn, who played a vital role in forwarding his career. In 1794 he was elected fellow of Winchester College, and was appointed vicar of Bishop's Sutton in 1796 in succession to his late father. He became vicar of Andover on 22 January 1802, and on 23 May 1811 vicar of Bradford Peverell, both Winchester College livings. Howley married Mary Frances (d. 1860), eldest daughter of John Belli of Southampton, of the East India Company service, on 29 August 1805; they had two sons and three daughters. In 1804 he had been made canon of Christ Church, Oxford, and in 1809 was appointed regius professor of divinity there. He was offered the see of London by the prime minister, Lord Liverpool, in August 1813 after the death of John Randolph. He was consecrated on 10 October 1813 at Lambeth Palace.

Howley was a high-churchman, whose theological outlook was influenced by the writings of the Caroline divines and later writers such as Daniel Waterland. On his arrival in London he made common cause with those of like theological mind, especially members of the Hackney Phalanx of high-churchmen, including Joshua and Archdeacon J. J. Watson. The dining club Nobody's Friends was the centre of this nexus. His primary charge, published in 1814, contained an attack on unitarians, which drew a

response from Thomas Belsham. All Howley's major ecclesiastical appointees were high-churchmen. His name is particularly associated with that of Charles James Blomfield, whom he appointed to a lucrative City living and as archdeacon of Colchester, and who was his successor as bishop of London.

At London, Howley was concerned with clerical nonresidence. He was a keen supporter of the educational work of the National Society for Promoting the Education of the Poor in the Principles of the Established Church and of the Society for the Promotion of Christian Knowledge. He encouraged the work of the Church Building Commissioners and the Incorporated Church Building Society. Howley was a conservative in politics. In 1820 he had supported the bill of pains and penalties against Queen Caroline from a 'moral, constitutional and religious point of view' (*Parliamentary Debates*, new ser., 3, 1711). At the same time, he was bitterly criticized in the press for saying that the king could do no wrong morally or physically. This was a distortion of his private view that, constitutionally speaking, the king could do no wrong morally or politically (*GM*, 2nd ser., 29, 1848, 427).

Howley's translation to Canterbury in July 1828 after the death of Charles Manners Sutton was widely anticipated. Wellington fought shy of appointing him because of his strong opposition to Catholic emancipation, but there were few other feasible candidates. Howley strongly opposed the repeal of the Test and Corporation Acts in 1828, whereby nonconformists had been barred from holding certain public offices. He spoke against Catholic emancipation in April 1829, but was defeated. He also spoke against the second reading of the Reform Bill in October 1831, though it passed in 1832. His opposition to all three bills stemmed from his loyalty to a view of the interdependence of church and state typical of the divines who had influenced him. Howley was the only prelate to speak against the Reform Bill in 1831. However, the bishops were acutely aware of their uncomfortable position and wanted a settlement earnestly. The bill was defeated by forty-one votes, twenty-one of which were episcopal. Had the bishops voted in favour, the bill would have passed, and they were vilified in the country for 'defeating' it. In 1832, on the bill's return to the House of Lords, they offered negligible resistance. Also in 1831, however, Howley introduced three ecclesiastical bills in the Lords—only one of which, on augmentations, passed—which anticipated the reforms of the rest of the decade.

Howley played an influential part in the development of the Ecclesiastical Commission in the 1830s and 1840s. Although wary of the need for reform he became convinced that it was imperative for the church to reform itself on its own terms, rather than wait for an unfriendly government to do so. He became increasingly persuaded that the church must redistribute some of its historic resources to provide more church space in the expanding urban and industrial areas. His willingness to encroach on the historic resources of cathedrals caused outrage among some of his former allies when he introduced the

Deans and Chapters Bill in the Lords in 1840 with a vigorous defence of the need of the Church of England to accept change.

Howley's archiepiscopate saw the genesis and expansion of the Oxford Movement. As a high-churchman he welcomed the restatement of that position on matters of church–state relations, the importance of the apostolic succession, and baptismal regeneration, to name the most important shibboleths of high-churchmen. His immediate circle included those such as Benjamin Harrison, who were personally close to the leading Tractarians. Howley and his associates lost sympathy with the Tractarians from the late 1830s onwards, when they seemed to many to be encouraging crypto-Roman Catholicism and later when ritual observance came more to the fore. He was horrified by the anti-Reformation sentiments of R. H. Froude's *Remains* (1838) and by what he regarded as the casuistry of Newman's Tract 90 (1841).

Throughout the 1840s Howley furthered the work of the Ecclesiastical Commission. He was instrumental in tightening the rules on clerical discipline, although several bishops complained that their prerogatives were infringed. He supported the fledgeling theological colleges and the setting up of chairs in pastoral theology and ecclesiastical history at Oxford. He was intensely suspicious of Lord John Russell's suggestions for the provision of secular education, and in July 1839 successfully moved a series of six resolutions denouncing them (*Parliamentary Debates*, 3rd ser., 48, 1234–55). Although declining in health throughout the 1840s (he nearly died of cholera in 1842), he produced his *Letter Addressed to the Clergy and Laity of his Province* (1845), which urged moderation in matters of liturgical innovation and rubrical observance. He published little beyond his charges to the clergy, a few of his sermons, and *An Inquiry into the Authority of the Coronation Oath* (1844). Contemporaries reckoned him a fine classical scholar, though he never ventured into authorship; Hugh James Rose, his domestic chaplain, even considered him the best scholar that he had met.

Howley's reputation is slighter than it might have been because of the attacks on him by contemporary politicians and on account of his poor public speaking. He is known for being the last archbishop to wear a wig and the last regularly to dine in state at Lambeth, but such caricatures often omit to mention that he ceased such practices while archbishop. His reputation also suffered at the hands of the more intemperate Tractarians. Nevertheless, as a senior bishop for thirty-five years he exercised considerable influence at court, in parliament, and in the church's counsels. Howley died at Lambeth Palace on 11 February 1848, the day before his eighty-second birthday, and was buried at Addington, Croydon.

J. R. GARRARD

Sources B. Harrison, *The remembrance of a departed guide and ruler in the church of God* (1848) · J. R. Garrard, 'William Howley (1766–1848): bishop of London, 1813–28, archbishop of Canterbury, 1828–48', DPhil diss., U. Oxf., 1992 · *GM*, 2nd ser., 30 (1848), 426–8 · *The Times* (12 Feb 1848) · *The Times* (21 Feb 1848) · *ILN* (19 Feb 1848) · *Fasti Angl.* (Hardy), 1.31; 2.306, 526, 530; 3.511 · T. F. Kirby, *Winchester scholars: a list of the wardens, fellows, and scholars of … Winchester College* (1888) · Foster, *Alum. Oxon.* · G. F. A. Best, *Temporal pillars: Queen Anne's bounty, the ecclesiastical commissioners, and the Church of England* (1964)

Archives Bodl. Oxf., papers · LPL, corresp. and papers; corresp. and papers as bishop of London | BL, corresp. with Lord Aberdeen · BL, corresp. with W. E. Gladstone, Add. MSS 44356–44364 · BL, corresp. with second earl of Liverpool, Add. MSS 38254–38323 · BL, corresp. with Sir Robert Peel, Add. MSS 40266–40596 · CUL, letters to Sir George Arthur · LPL, Fulham MSS; Kingsmill MSS, corresp. with Lord John Russell · Lpool RO, letters to Lord Stanley · NL Scot., letters to John Lee · PRO, corresp. with Lord John Russell, PRO 30/22 · U. Durham, corresp. with second Earl Grey

Likenesses T. Lawrence, oils, 1816, Winchester College [*see illus.*] · W. Owen, mezzotint, pubd 1818 (after S. W. Reynolds), NPG · W. Owen, oils, exh. RA 1818, Fulham Palace, London · F. Chantrey, marble bust, 1821, Canterbury Cathedral · W. Owen, oils, c.1823–1825, NPG · S. F. Diez, pencil and ink drawing, 1841, Scot. NPG · T. Lawrence, mezzotint, pubd 1845 (after J. R. Jackson), NPG · F. Chantrey, bust, priv. coll. · J. Doyle, caricatures, pen-and-pencil sketches, BM · G. Hayter, group portrait, oils (*The House of Commons, 1833*), NPG · C. R. Leslie, portrait, priv. coll. · M. A. Shee, oils, LPL · R. Westmacott junior, effigy, Canterbury Cathedral

Wealth at death under £120,000: GM, 428

Howson, George (1886–1936), founder of the British Legion Poppy Factory, was born on 7 September 1886 at the rectory in Overton, Flintshire, the youngest in the family of four sons (the eldest of whom died in infancy) and one daughter of George John Howson (1854–1943), rector of Overton, and his wife, Ethel, daughter of Thomas Dealtry, vicar of Maidstone. At his christening his mother gave him a second forename, Arthur, which he did not like and never used. Descended from generations of churchmen on both sides—his paternal grandfather, John Saul Howson, was dean of Chester; his maternal great-grandfather, Thomas Dealtry, was bishop of Madras—Howson derived from this upbringing a strong sense of service. His eldest brother, Roger, followed his father, first to Haileybury, then to Cambridge, and later became librarian at Columbia University, New York; the next brother, Geoffrey, also went to Haileybury, and thence into the Indian army, serving in both world wars. George was educated at Loretto School, Musselburgh, and at Heriot-Watt Engineering College, Edinburgh, which formed his practical outlook.

George Howson became assistant manager at the Melalap rubber estate in British North Borneo from 1909. As vicar of Christ Church, Salford, Howson's father had known several directors of the Manchester Rubber Co., who leased the estate and aimed to exploit the rising demand for tyres. Howson's Borneo experiences were testing. The isolation necessitated self-reliance and improvisation. Machinery had to be maintained and adapted to the task by the man on the spot. Chinese and Javanese contract labourers made a rough workforce. Howson, who confronted more than one disturbance, had little respect for the arbitrariness of his superior, a Dutchman, who was murdered in 1914.

At that time Howson was in England on sick leave, his health weakened by malaria, dysentery, and jaundice; he was preparing to return to Borneo when European war broke out. In September he joined, as a second lieutenant, the 11th service battalion of the Hampshire regiment. He served throughout the war: at the Somme, Messines, Passchendaele, Cambrai, and in the retreat and final offensive in 1918. At Pilckem Ridge on 31 July 1917 Howson's unit was undertaking road repairs during persistent shelling. Howson, by then a captain, won the MC for 'splendid work encouraging his men and refusing to go back', despite a shrapnel wound in one arm. Howson was promoted major and remained on the army list until May 1920. On 10 September 1918 at St Paul's, Onslow Square, London, he married Jessie (b. 1883/4), daughter of William Gibson of Melbourne, a Scottish-Australian department-store magnate. Jessie had been studying art at Munich before the war and there met Howson's sister, Joan, also a student, who later established a stained-glass factory at Putney which provided windows for the chapter house of Westminster Abbey. Howson's marriage brought personal happiness and financial independence: Jessie inherited great wealth upon her father's death on 5 November 1918.

After the war Howson became the founding chairman of the Disabled Society: among his co-founders was Major J. B. B. Cohen MP, who lost both legs at Ypres in 1917. They lobbied the government to improve the quality of artificial limbs, publishing their own guide. Howson's engineering expertise was invaluable; so was his recognition that the disabled faced demoralization as well as hardship unless they secured employment. Armistice day 1921 saw the first poppy day appeal, sponsored by the British Legion. Symbolizing the slaughter of the Flanders battle-fields, the fabricated poppies were initially imported from France, where they were made by war victims' families. British demand outstripped French supply, and the legion was obliged to turn to domestic artificial-flower manufacturers, a trade notorious for sweated labour. Howson persuaded the legion to contract the Disabled Society to supply the 1922 armistice day appeal. Given six months to deliver, Howson wrote to his parents on 14 May 1922:

> it is a large responsibility and will be very difficult. If the experiment is successful it will be the start of an industry to employ 150 disabled men. I do not think it can be a great success but it is worth trying. I consider the attempt ought to be made if only to give the disabled their chance. I have to find a factory tomorrow and interview men. (Royal British Legion Poppy Factory archive)

Howson started production in a former collar factory off the Old Kent Road on 8 June 1922 with a workforce of five disabled men. He had not only to acquire knowledge of the artificial-flower trade but to compete, while paying full male wages, against other manufacturers who employed low-waged girls. His practical genius for ergonomics enabled him to adapt tasks to suit his workforce's restricted capacities. Over forty disabled former servicemen were employed within a month, and they produced their first million poppies within two months. By 1924, 185 people were employed, whose average disability was between 60 and 70 per cent. Preference was given to the most disabled and to those with dependants; yet the more Howson employed, the longer grew the waiting-list of applicants. In November 1924, when 27 million poppies had been produced, the prince of Wales made the first royal visit to the factory. Howson understood the value of such publicity and exploited a court connection with Lady Cynthia Colville, daughter of the marquess of Crewe, made when Howson's father was vicar of Crewe. Howson also cultivated the president of the British Legion, Earl Haig: their sons attended Stowe School, and when Haig died he left Howson his dispatch case.

In 1925 the Disabled Society merged with the British Legion. The poppy factory became a limited company, with Howson as its chairman, moving in 1926 to new premises, an old brewery on Petersham Road, Richmond, where it remains still. The purchase was made possible only by Howson's donation of family money. The modern factory and accommodation for disabled workers and their families, built under Howson's direction, stand as monuments to his philanthropy and enterprise. This was recognized by the British Legion in 1930, when it stated that its ability to assist all former servicemen, fit as well as disabled, depended on the annual poppy day collection. Howson also struck the public imagination in 1928 by devising the field of remembrance service at Westminster Abbey, thereafter the central ceremony in the annual homage the nation pays to its war dead. Remembrance crosses and wreaths became major items in the factory's production, in addition to the poppies.

Howson had never been in good health since Borneo. Addiction to strong Turkish cigarettes did not improve it. These he bought 10,000 at a time, and those that survived his last purchase malingered, according to his children, into the 1950s. What politics he had were of the Baldwin Conservative hue, and more by temperament than reflection. He was a straightforward patriot, who sighed when Britain went off the gold standard, believing this to mark the end of empire. Above all, he was a man of action. His deepest hatred was for indulgent idleness. The custodial use of the wealth he enjoyed through his marriage was exemplary. The man of action was also a man of natural sensitivity towards suffering. He never patronized the disabled but restored in them a zest for life and work. In public and in private Howson showed the same inventiveness and fun. At Hyde Cottage, Hambleden, his home near Henley-on-Thames, he rigged up a flying fox between trees across the lawn to amuse his children. During his final illness, on being moved from the family town house in Kensington to a nursing home, he asked the ambulance to make a detour via the poppy factory. Some 365 disabled veterans were then producing 29 million poppies annually. They evacuated the workshops to salute Howson who gathered strength to sit up and lead the singing of 'Old Soldiers Never Die' and his own version of a popular ditty, 'It Ain't Goin' to Pain No More'. He told the foreman, 'Remember, if I peg out, I go in the factory van', and as the ambulance set off, he struck up the singing of 'Are We Downhearted?' (The Times, 30 November 1936). He died on 28 November 1936 at 5 The Boltons, South Kensington, of cancer of the pancreas; the interment at Hambleden was conducted by his father, then archdeacon and canon emeritus of Liverpool. George Howson was survived by his wife and four children, the eldest of whom, his only son, Peter (b. 1919), became a government minister in Australia.   PHILIP WALLER

Sources archives, Royal British Legion Poppy Factory, Richmond, Surrey · private information (1993) · b. cert. · m. cert. · d. cert. · Venn, *Alum. Cant.* · C. T. Atkinson, *Regimental history: the royal Hampshire regiment*, 2: 1914–1918 (1952)

Wealth at death £70 7s. 2d.: probate, 11 Jan 1937, *CGPLA Eng. & Wales*

Howson, John (1556/7–1632), bishop of Durham, was born in the London parish of St Bride. The identity of his parents is unknown. He was educated at St Paul's School and Christ Church, Oxford, where he was elected a member of the governing body, that is a fellow, in 1577. He was admitted BA on 12 November 1578 and proceeded MA on 3 March 1582, but nothing certain is known of him during the next fifteen years, except that he presented a book to Christ Church Library in 1587, and another in 1588, suggesting that he remained in Oxford. He was licensed to preach on 23 July 1597 and within a year had preached twice at Paul's Cross, on Matthew 21: 12–13, inveighing against the buying and selling of spiritual promotions. Both sermons (4 December 1597 and 21 May 1598) were subsequently printed. He took the degrees of BD and DD together on 17 December 1601. In his doctoral exercise he argued whether marriage was a sacrament, whether adultery constituted grounds for divorce, and whether it was possible to make a second marriage after divorce on the grounds of adultery. The third tenet was later published as *Uxore dismissa propter fornicationem aliam non licet superinducere* (1602) and answered by Thomas Pie the following year (*Epistola ad ornatissimum virum D. Joannem Housonum, qua dogma eius novum & admirabile de Judaeoruum divortiis refutatur*, 1603). In 1606 Howson reprinted an expanded version of his first piece with an added letter to John Rainolds, the president of Corpus Christi College, about the controversy.

Howson was installed a prebendary of Hereford Cathedral on 15 July 1587 (he resigned in 1603) and as a prebendary of Exeter on 29 May 1592. On 7 July 1598 he became vicar of Bampton and chaplain to the queen. A week later Elizabeth presented him to the next vacant prebendal stall at Christ Church, which resulted in his obtaining the second stall there, on 15 May 1601, six weeks after he had become vicar of Great Milton. Later that year, on 16 August, he married Jane Floyd, a former parishioner from Bampton, with whom he had several children, including at least three sons and also two daughters, named in his will as Anne Farnaby and Melicent Cleaver.

On 15 July 1602 Howson was nominated vice-chancellor of the University of Oxford. His accession day sermon before the university defended the use of ceremony and the keeping of festivals. In giving precedence to liturgy over preaching he caused grave offence, as he himself admitted to the chancellor of the university, Lord Buckhurst, and he was attacked by representatives of the godly

John Howson (1556/7–1632), by unknown artist, 1631

in Oxford. According to John Chamberlain, Howson was accused of preaching 'false doctrine'. He responded by suspending Henry Airay, provost of Queen's College and a leading advocate of the primacy of the sermon, from preaching, and also by appealing to the privy council. After examination in London his adversaries were forced to submit, and before his year of office ended Howson promulgated articles intended to control the licensing of preachers in Oxford. In 1608 he was appointed rector of Brightwell, Oxfordshire, settling to live there comfortably and providing a pew for his wife and family. On 8 May 1610 he was among the divines nominated original fellows of Chelsea College.

Pulpit war broke out again in Oxford in the early 1610s. William Laud, then president of St John's College, was censured for his attack on Robert Abbot, brother of Archbishop George Abbot, and Howson was criticized for condemning the Genevan biblical annotations. Both men were summoned to court to answer for their views before the king and the archbishop. On 10 June 1615 Howson publicly defended his views at Greenwich. He admitted that he 'preached not soe often, as some others against the papists, because in my tyme there were never above 3 or 4 att once, that were suspected of popery' ('Answers', 330), and was cleared. Laud too was acquitted. Six years after the trial James himself ordered Howson to print his Oxford sermons of 1616, on Luke 12: 41–2, pleased no doubt at their conformist tenor. The addresses attack Catholicism in setting out to prove that St Peter had no monarchical authority over the other apostles, while also criticizing the 'puritan democracie' of presbyterianism, and denouncing its adherents as 'Schismatickes in Religion who affect statizing and cantonizing in the Commonwealth' (*Certaine Sermons*, 92–3).

In the summer of 1618 Howson was appointed bishop of Oxford; the instruction to elect was issued at Westminster on 28 July 1618, and Archbishop Abbot confirmed the appointment on 7 May 1619. Howson was consecrated two days later, and enthroned by proxy on the 22nd. He found his small diocese in parlous condition. His extensive articles (for 1619, 1622, and 1628: no triennial visitation took place in 1625) derive from Neile's Coventry articles of 1610 (and ultimately from Bancroft, 1598–1604) but he was further concerned to emphasize catechizing as a preparation for confirmation and the proper use of the Book of Common Prayer. Anxious to reintroduce regular confirmation, and to encourage local clergy to prepare their younger parishioners for it, Howson caused his chaplain Edward Boughen to preach at his primary visitation (27 September 1619) on the antiquity and significance of the rite.

Howson continued to be involved in theological controversy. In the summer of 1625 he, together with Laud and John Buckeridge, bishop of Rochester, assured the duke of Buckingham that Richard Montagu, who was charged with holding Arminian views (akin to those of his three defenders), was a 'very good scholar and right honest man; a man every way able to do God, his Majesty, and the Church of England, great service' (*Works of … Laud*, 6.246). Two years later Howson was called upon to adjudicate when Richard Sibthorp's Northampton assize sermon 'Apostolic obedience' (on Romans 13: 9) was censured by Archbishop Abbot. The latter's refusal to license it for press made it a test case, but by the end of the summer the archbishop's political isolation was complete. He was suspended and Howson, with Laud, now bishop of Bath and Wells, Buckeridge, Richard Neile of Durham, and George Montaigne of London, formed the five-man commission that exercised metropolitical authority. The experience that Howson now gained of exercising a commission of appointment in matters of granting faculties, dispensations, petitions, and absolutions for the archdiocese stood him in good stead, and on 4 July 1628 he was preferred to Durham as successor to Neile, who had been translated to Winchester. In the same month Laud was advanced to London and Richard Montagu nominated for Chichester.

Howson's time at Durham was neither straightforward, largely because his style differed substantially from that of his predecessor, nor particularly happy. He should have found his chapter congenial to work alongside. Richard Hunt was dean, while Richard Neile's half-brother, Robert Newell, Augustine Lindsell, Eleazor Duncon, John Cosin, and Gabriel Clarke were all canons. The orders for his primary visitation of the cathedral, however, and especially his changes to cathedral worship, insisting as he had in his Oxford diocesan visitations on the full use of the Book of Common Prayer without abridgement, proved as unpopular with the canons as with parishes. In January 1631 Lindsell and Cosin, who came from the same theological stable as Howson, wrote to Eleazor Duncon, serving as Neile's chaplain at Winchester, to bring him up to date with the

alleged 'abuses' (PRO, SP 16/182/61). Howson complained somewhat bitterly to Laud that he had only changed the liturgy for the best and that he was neither stubborn, baseminded, nor attempting to cause deliberate difficulty. In the end it was the king who intervened to silence Howson and make him desist from his attacks on Cosin.

Howson faced other difficulties. Perhaps in 1629 Sir Henry Marten, dean of arches, petitioned the king for the restitution of clerical fines which, he alleged, Howson had improperly obtained from the clergy for a pretended visitation in Oxford, 'when none was executed or intended' (PRO, SP 16/154/22). This may explain the 'missing' visitation of 1625. Howson responded that like all bishops he was commanded by the king to reside in his diocese and that he would only answer such charges in York. In fact he spent much of that summer in London. Archbishop Abbot observed, perhaps maliciously, that Howson had further compounded his wrongdoing in that he 'most unseemly lieth at an inn' (PRO, SP 16/153/40).

Howson's arrival in Durham also coincided with, or occasioned, an outburst by Peter Smart, a canon since 1610. On 27 July 1628 Smart, who had been at school with Richard Neile, preached against the 'altar' as a 'damnable idol'. In the same sermon, according to Cosin, he also denounced those who bowed towards it as 'spiritual fornicators' (*Correspondence of John Cosin*, 1.xxii, 144–5). Printed later that year as *The Vanitie and Downefall of Superstitious Popish Ceremonies*, this was by no means Smart's first attack on ceremonialism, but it made his position in the chapter untenable, and although he continued to attend every meeting until 14 January 1630 he was degraded on 18 November that year by the high commission 'ab omni gradu et dignitate clericali'. Smart continued to assert his right to sit, and although Howson had been certain that he had no right to suspend one of the canons, he was prevailed upon by Viscount Wentworth, the lord president of the north, to advance one of the latter's household, Dr Thomas Carr, to the vacant stall, in place of his own kinsman and a possible royal candidate. Howson candidly admitted that he pitied Smart, trusting his offers of future conformity and suspecting that so many innovations in the liturgy 'superstitiously urged' had finally driven him to unacceptable actions (PRO, SP 16/174/64). At about the same time Howson was faced with the threat of a metropolitical visitation. He complained to Laud that Archbishop Harsnett had no such authority and that the people of Durham recognized only 'God, King and St Cuthbert' (PRO, SP 16/162/32, 33). Thomas Crosfield reported at Michaelmas that Harsnett had excommunicated Howson for denying his spiritual jurisdiction in Durham.

John Howson died on 6 February 1632, aged seventy-five. Contrary to the express instructions of his will—drawn up on 11 September 1629—he was not buried in his old church at Brightwell, as he had hoped 'if God shall call mee in the Southerne Partes', nor in the cathedral church at Durham (his chosen resting place if he died in the north), but in St Paul's Cathedral in London (PRO, PROB, 11/161, fol. 188r–v). An uninscribed marble slab covered his grave. His personal estate was small and he appointed his widow as his sole executor, 'not doubting of her care for the education of our children'. To those who were married or aged over twenty-one he gave £5 apiece and he settled £50 on each of his two grandchildren, provided they reached the age of seven.

NICHOLAS W. S. CRANFIELD

Sources J. Howson, *Certaine sermons made in Oxford, 1616* (1622) · J. Howson, *A sermon preached at St Maries in Oxford* (1603) · 'John Howson's answer to Archbishop Abbot's accusations at his "trial" before James I', ed. N. W. S. Cranfield and K. Fincham, *Camden miscellany, XXIX, CS*, 4th ser., 34 (1987) · *Reg. Oxf.* · PRO, SP 12/287/28; 14/80/113; 14/80/124; 14/98/42*; 16/109/3*; 16/182/61;1 6/186/97; 16/187/16; 16/134/22; 16/153/40; 16/154/95; 16/174/9; 16/174/64; 16/162/32, 33 · will, PRO, PROB 11/161, fol. 188 · Oxford, dean and chapter MS i.b.1, fol. 94 · Bodl. Oxf., MS Tanner 70 · *The works of the most reverend father in God, William Laud*, 6, ed. J. Bliss (1857) · *The correspondence of John Cosin D.D., lord bishop of Durham*, ed. [G. Ornsby], 1, SurtS, 52 (1869) · W. H. D. Longstaffe, ed., *The acts of the high commission court within the diocese of Durham*, SurtS, 34 (1858) · K. Fincham, ed., *Visitation articles and injunctions of the early Stuart church*, 1 (1994) · J. Le Neve, *Fasti ecclesiae anglicanae* (1716) · Foster, *Alum. Oxon.* · J. Ingamells, *The English episcopal portrait, 1559–1835: a catalogue* (privately printed, London, 1981) · Queen's College, Oxford, MS Reg. 380, fol. 52 · chancery, patent rolls, PRO, C66/1484 · Wood, *Ath. Oxon.*, new edn, 2.517–19 · N. Tyacke, *Anti-Calvinists: the rise of English Arminianism, c.1590–1640* (1987) · K. Fincham, *Prelate as pastor: the episcopate of James I* (1990) · *Hist. U. Oxf.* 3: *Colleg. univ.* · C. M. Dent, *Protestant reformers in Elizabethan Oxford* (1983)

Archives PRO, SP 14/80/113

Likenesses oils, 1631, Christ Church Oxf. [*see illus.*] · M. Droeshout, line engraving, *c*.1632 (after unknown artist, 1631), BM, NPG · oils, second version, Auckland Castle, co. Durham

Wealth at death see will, PRO, PROB 11/161, fol. 188*r–v*

Howson, John Saul (1816–1885), biblical scholar and dean of Chester, was born on 5 May 1816 at Giggleswick in Craven, Yorkshire, the son of the Revd John Howson, for a long time second master of Giggleswick grammar school. John Saul became a pupil in his father's school, and at the age of seventeen entered Trinity College, Cambridge. There he made lifelong friendships with G. E. Lynch Cotton, the future bishop of Calcutta, W. J. Conybeare, and T. Whytehead of St John's. Howson graduated BA in 1837, obtaining a wranglership and a double first-class honours in the classical tripos. He proceeded to an MA in 1841 and a DD in 1861. He won the members' Latin essay prize two years in succession (1837 and 1838), and was Norrisian prizeman in 1841. He then acted as tutor to the marquess of Sligo and subsequently to the marquess of Lorne.

In 1845 Howson became senior classical master at the Liverpool Collegiate Institution (Liverpool College from 1864). He was ordained deacon in 1845, and priest in 1846. He left Liverpool for a short time to become tutor to the third duke of Sutherland, but returned again in 1849 to become principal of the Liverpool Collegiate Institution, upon the resignation of W. J. Conybeare, a post which he held until 1865. He was a successful manager and also helped to establish a college for girls in Liverpool on the same principles.

During his time in Liverpool he married Mary Cropper, daughter of John Cropper of Dingle Bank. They had three sons and two daughters who survived him. During this

period he also wrote in collaboration with W. J. Conybeare, the work for which he is best known, *The Life and Epistles of St Paul* (2 vols., 1852). Most of the work, including the historical, geographical, and archaeological sections for which it was most praised, were Howson's contribution. The book went through many nineteenth-century editions and continued to be respected by twentieth-century theologians. In 1862 he delivered the Hulsean lectures on the character of St Paul at the University of Cambridge. In 1866 Bishop Harold Browne of Ely, who had recently appointed him his examining chaplain, presented him to the vicarage of St Peter, Wisbech. He left Wisbech in 1867 on being nominated dean of Chester.

During his eighteen years at Chester, Howson devoted his energy to projects concerned with both the cathedral and the city. He found Chester Cathedral in a state of decay and in some parts in danger of total collapse. Howson immediately commenced the Sunday-evening services in the long-disused nave. The work of restoration, which had already begun, he continued and carried through with vigour. The cathedral was reopened on 25 January 1872, after an expenditure of nearly £100,000, most of which had been raised through his own efforts. Work continued for the decoration and completion of the interior and exterior, and Howson published a historical and architectural guide to the building, as well as *Chester as it was* (1872). In addition, he worked to restore the King's School, also reorganizing it as an institution open to all creeds and ranks, and also the Queen's School, for the higher education of girls. He contributed greatly to the building and organizing of a new museum, and took a keen interest in the school of art, of which he acted as president for many years. He gave serious attention to the gambling at race week in Chester, and Charles Kingsley, then canon of Chester, contributed to the papers Howson published on the subject. Despite Howson's prejudice against broad-churchmen, he and Kingsley were on very cordial terms during Kingsley's three years' stay as canon at Chester. Howson took an active part in the convocation of York especially in opposing the retention of the Athanasian creed in the public services of the church.

Howson was a frequent preacher in the university pulpits of Cambridge and Oxford, and at St Paul's Cathedral and Westminster Abbey. He was also active at the meetings of the church congress. In 1861 he contributed an article in the *Quarterly Review*, 'Deaconesses in the Church of England', reissued as *The Official Help of Women in Parochial Work and in Charitable Institutions* (1862), which, along with his speech to the church congress at York in 1866, helped to promote the revival of a ministry of women in the church. He also travelled abroad a good deal, and visited the United States twice, in 1871 and 1880. Having established his scholarly reputation though his lectures and best-known work on St Paul, he continued to write on New Testament subjects, contributing to commentary editions such as Speaker's Commentary (1881) and Schaff's Popular Commentary (1880) as well as Smith's *Dictionary of the Bible*. He was also an occasional contributor to the *Quarterly Review* and he published devotional works and many separate sermons. Howson died at Bournemouth on 15 December 1885. He was buried in the cloister garth of Chester Cathedral on 19 December where his wife, who survived him by only a few days, was also buried.

Howson was regarded for his unaffected simplicity and honesty. His sympathies were broadly evangelical rather than high-church, but he was open-minded in his church views and contributed to the *Transactions* of the Cambridge Camden Society as well as denouncing the eastward position of the celebrant at consecration. He was a sound scholar, an extensive reader, and a prolific writer. While not an eloquent preacher, his sermons were always interesting. EDMUND VENABLES, *rev.* JOANNA HAWKE

Sources *The Guardian* (Dec 1885) · *The Times* (Dec 1885) · G. J. H., 'A short biographical sketch', in J. S. Howson, *The diaconate of women in the Anglican church* (1886), xiii–xxvii · L. C. Sanders, *Celebrities of the century: being a dictionary of men and women of the nineteenth century* (1887) · P. Schaff and S. M. Jackson, *Encyclopedia of living divines and Christian workers of all denominations in Europe and America: being a supplement to Schaff-Herzog encyclopedia of religious knowledge* (1887) · Boase, *Mod. Eng. biog.* · personal knowledge (1891) · private information (1891)

Archives BL, letters to W. E. Gladstone, Add. MSS 44389–44762 · Durham Cath. CL, letters to J. B. Lightfoot

Likenesses G. A. Richmond, oils, exh. RA 1878, Liverpool College · Elliott & Fry, carte-de-visite, NPG · Lock & Whitfield, woodburytype photograph, NPG; repro. in T. Cooper, *Men of mark: a gallery of contemporary portraits* (1882) · R. T., wood-engraving, NPG; repro. in *ILN*, 87 (26 Dec 1885), 667 · R. & E. Taylor, print (after photograph by Elliott & Fry), NPG · R. & E. Taylor, woodcut, NPG; repro. in *Day of Rest* (7 June 1873)

Wealth at death £11,252 13s. 0d.: administration with will, 1 Feb 1886, *CGPLA Eng. & Wales*

Howth. For this title name *see* St Lawrence, Robert, second Baron Howth (1435?–1486); St Lawrence, Nicholas, third Baron Howth (*d.* 1526); St Lawrence, Christopher, seventh Baron Howth (*d.* 1589); St Lawrence, Nicholas, eighth Baron Howth (*d.* 1607) [*see under* St Lawrence, Christopher, seventh Baron Howth (*d.* 1589)]; St Lawrence, Christopher, ninth Baron Howth (*d.* 1619).

Hoy, Thomas (*b.* 1659, *d.* in or after 1721), physician, born on 12 December 1659, was the son of Clement Hoy of London. He was admitted into Merchant Taylors' School, London, in 1672, and was elected a probationary fellow of St John's College, Oxford, in 1675. He graduated BA in 1680, MA in 1684, MB in 1686, and MD in 1689. He was admitted a candidate of the Royal College of Physicians in 1693 and appointed regius professor of physic at Oxford in 1698. Thomas Hearne (1678–1735), whose opinion of 'a ranck low church whigg' is not likely to be impartial, says that he owed his appointment to the influence of William Gibbons with Lord Somers, and that he scandalously neglected the duties of his office. Hoy was released from his office by royal dispensation in 1717. At some time about this date he left Britain for Jamaica. Before this he appears to have practised as a physician in Warwick, but in 1698 John Evelyn, writing from Wotton, speaks of Hoy as 'a very learned, curious, and ingenious person, and our neighbour in Surrey'. The date of Hoy's death is unknown, although he was still living in Jamaica in 1721, when he

Thomas Hoy (*b.* 1659, *d.* in or after 1721), by Thomas Forster, 1696

issued a power of attorney for the surrender of his professorship. He contributed to the translations of Plutarch's *Morals* (1684), of Cornelius Nepos (1684), and of Suetonius's *Life of Tiberius* (1689), and he also published two essays, 'Ovid de arte amandi, or, The art of love, book i' and 'Hero and Leander of Musaeus from the Greek' (1682), as well as a poem, *Agathocles, the Sicilian Usurper* (1683). C. J. ROBINSON, *rev.* MICHAEL BEVAN

Sources Munk, *Roll* · Wood, *Ath. Oxon.* · Bodl. Oxf., MS Rawl. 533 · T. Hearne, *A collection of curious discourses*, 1 (1771), 230, 322 · *The diary of John Evelyn* · *Hist. U. Oxf.* 5: *18th-cent. Oxf.*, 702 · PRO, Specification Roll 2, nos. 5 and 6 · *CPR*, 3548, no. 27 · SP domestic, George I, bundle 30, no. 46

Likenesses T. Forster, miniature, 1696, RCP Lond. [*see illus.*]

Hoyland, Francis (1727–1786), poet, was born at Castle Howard, Yorkshire, the son of James Hoyland. He was educated at Halifax grammar school, and on 18 June 1744 matriculated at Magdalene College, Cambridge, where he graduated BA in 1749. Soon afterwards he seems to have made a voyage to the West Indies for the sake of his health (see his 'Ode to Sleep').

Hoyland was ordained deacon in 1751 and entered the priesthood in 1753. In 1769 he became the rector of Little Oakley, Northamptonshire, and in 1774 became the vicar of Weekley in the same county. Hoyland was a friend of the poet William Mason (1724–1797) and was introduced, probably by Mason, to Horace Walpole, who exerted himself on Hoyland's behalf, and printed his poems at the Strawberry Hill press in 1769. Mason, along with Richard Stonehewer, also seems to have assisted in securing Hoyland the living of Weekley. From his own works and from letters between Mason and Walpole, it may be gathered that Hoyland struggled with recurring bouts of physical and mental illness, was married with four children, and was poor. In 1769 illness prevented him from accepting an offer of a living in South Carolina. He died in 1786.

Hoyland's poetical output was small. His first collection of poems appeared in 1763. Two of the five poems printed in the Strawberry Hill edition of his poems, which underwent two impressions, were from this collection. In 1783 his *Odes* appeared. Hoyland's complete poems were reprinted twice in the early nineteenth century.

W. A. J. ARCHBOLD, *rev.* JEFFREY HERRLE

Sources Venn, *Alum. Cant.* · Walpole, *Corr.*, vol. 28 · F. Hoyland, *Poems* (1769) · private information (1891)
Wealth at death some degree of poverty: Walpole, *Corr.*, vol. 28

Hoyland, John (1750–1831), writer on Gypsy culture, is variously designated as 'of Sheffield, Yorkshire', and as 'formerly of York', although details of his parentage and upbringing are unknown, aside from his being a Quaker. It was, however, in the counties of Northampton, Bedford, and Hertford that he began, in 1814, his study of Gypsy communities. For a time he was 'disunited' from the Quakers, possibly on account of his having fallen in love with 'a black-eyed gipsy girl' (*N&Q*, 2nd ser., 5.386), though James Simson's claim that Hoyland 'married the gipsy girl' (Simson, 380n.) is unfounded. Hoyland's will records that he was married to a woman named Elizabeth, who survived him. In 1812 he published, anonymously, his *Epitome of the History of the World from the Creation to the Advent of the Messiah*, which appeared in its third edition as *The Fulfilment of Scripture Prophecy* (1823). A euhemeristic work, it identifies Elijah as the prototype of Phaeton, Jephtha's daughter of Iphigenia. Hoyland's *Historical Survey of the Customs, Habits, and Present State of the Gypsies*, which was published in York in 1816, was drawn extensively from Matthew Raper's translation of Heinrich Moritz Grellmann's *Historischer versuch über die Zigeuner* (1787). Hoyland died in Northampton, where his will shows him to have been resident, on 30 August 1831.

F. H. GROOME, *rev.* PHILIP CARTER

Sources J. Simson, *A history of the Gipsies* (1865) · *Annual Register* (1831), 257 · will, PRO, PROB 11/1795, fols. 329r–329v · J. Smith, ed., *A descriptive catalogue of Friends' books*, suppl. (1893)

Hoyland, John (1783–1827), organist and composer, was the son of a Sheffield cutler. He showed talent for music as a child and, due to financial hardship, eventually turned to teaching. In 1808 he succeeded his former teacher, William Mather, as organist of St James's, Sheffield, and eleven years later moved to Louth, Lincolnshire, where he taught and was appointed organist of the parish church. Hoyland composed several anthems and sacred pieces in addition to piano studies and songs. He was perhaps best known for his setting of Psalm 150 and a version of 'The Land o' the Leal'. He died on 18 January 1827, leaving at least one daughter and a son, William, who served as organist of Louth parish church from 1829 until his death on 1 November 1857.

R. F. SHARP, *rev.* DAVID J. GOLBY

Sources W. H. Husk, 'Hoyland, John', Grove, *Dict. mus.* (1878–90) · private information (1891)

Hoyle, Edmond (1671/2–1769), writer on card games, is said to have been a barrister by profession (Chambers, 282). In 1741 he was living in Queen Square, London, and gave lessons on whist playing. He also circulated a manuscript handbook, which developed into his famous and popular *Short Treatise on the Game of Whist*, first printed in 1742, 'for which he received from the publisher the sum of £1000' (ibid.). In the early editions the author offers for a guinea to disclose the secret of his 'artificial memory which does not take off your Attention from your Game'. Hoyle was often referred to by his contemporaries. An amusing skit, *The Humours of Whist* (1743), satirized the teacher and his pupils, and alluded to the dismay of sharpers who saw their secrets revealed to the general reading public. A supposed female correspondent, who had had problems with her game, wrote to *The Rambler* on 8 May 1750 that 'Mr. Hoyle, when he had not given me above forty lessons, said, I was one of his best scholars'. Hoyle and his teaching were also spoken of in the *Gentleman's Magazine* (*GM*, 1st ser., 25, 1755, 75), in Henry Fielding's *Tom Jones* (bk 13, ch. 5), in Alexander Thomson's poem 'Whist' (1792), and in Byron's 'Don Juan' (1821).

Hoyle was the first to write scientifically on whist, or indeed any card game. He was a careless editor, but possessed a vigorous and original writing style. He seems to have profited by the experience of the best players of the day, and introduced many improvements in his successive editions. The *Short Treatise* was entered at Stationers' Hall on 17 November 1742 by the author, as sole proprietor of the copyright. The high price of 1 guinea gave rise to many piracies, which started to appear from 1743, if not earlier. Hoyle's own second edition (1743), with additions, was sold at 2s. 'in a neat pocket size'. From then until his death numerous editions appeared. Of particular interest are the fourth edition (1743), in which the laws of the game were reduced to twenty-four, remaining so until the twelfth edition; the eighth edition (1748), where thirteen new cases were added, together with the treatises on quadrille, piquet, and backgammon; and the ninth edition (1748), in which the title appeared as *The Accurate Gamester's Companion*. A French translation, *Le jeu de whist de M. Hoyle*, was published in 1763. A bibliographical account of the early editions can be found in Julian Marshall's contributions to *Notes and Queries* (7th ser., vols. 7, 8, 9). For many years every genuine copy of the *Short Treatise* bore the qualifying statement 'No copies of this book are genuine but what are signed by Edmond Hoyle and Thomas Osborne'. In the fifteenth edition the signature is reproduced from a woodblock. Hoyle's laws of 1760, revised by members of White's and Saunders's clubs, were the standard rules for whist until 1864, when they were superseded by the code drawn up by the Arlington and Portland clubs. Other works by Hoyle include 'short treatises' on backgammon (1743), piquet (1744), quadrille (1745), and brag (1751), and *An essay towards making the doctrine of chances easy to those who understand vulgar arithmetick* only (1754); *An Essay towards Making the Game of Chess Easily Learned* appeared in 1761.

Hoyle died on 29 August 1769 at Welbeck Street, Cavendish Square, London aged ninety-seven, and was buried in Marylebone churchyard. His will, dated 26 September 1761, was proved in London on 6 September 1769; the executors were his sister Eleanor, a spinster, and Robert Crispin (*N&Q*, 7th ser., 8, 481–2). The house in Queen Square was left to his sister, along with an annuity to his niece Fanny, after his sister's death. Since Eleanor Hoyle is described as a spinster, he presumably had a brother, although no reference has been found to one. No authentic portrait is known; the picture by Hogarth, exhibited at the Crystal Palace in 1870, represents a Yorkshire Hoyle.

After his death, Hoyle's name became synonymous with any book on card games: an *American Hoyle* appeared in 1860, and *The Standard Hoyle, a Complete Guide upon All Games of Chance* came out in New York in 1887. In London, G. F. Pardon's edited collection, *Hoyle's Games Modernized*, was published in three editions between 1863 and 1872, and has since been reissued on a number of occasions in the twentieth century.

H. R. TEDDER, *rev.* HEATHER SHORE

Sources H. Jones, 'Whist', *Encyclopaedia Britannica*, 9th edn (1875–89) · J. Marshall, 'Books on gaming', *N&Q*, 7th ser., 7 (1889), 481–2 · *N&Q*, 7th ser., 8 (1889), 3, 42, 83, 144, 201, 262, 343, 404, 482 · *N&Q*, 7th ser., 9 (1890), 24, 142 · Cavendish [H. Jones], *The laws and principles of whist stated and explained*, 18th edn (1889) · R. Chambers, ed., *The book of days: a miscellany of popular antiquities in connection with the calendar*, 2 vols. (1863–4) · W. Pole, *The philosophy of whist*, 2nd edn (1884) · *GM*, 1st ser., 25 (1755), 75 · *GM*, 1st ser., 39 (1769), 463

Hoyle, John (d. 1797?), author, produced a dictionary of musical terms, *Dictionarium musica; Being a Complete Dictionary or Treasury of Music* (1770). It was republished, as *A Dictionary of Music*, in 1790 and 1791. Although pretending to be an original work, it was in fact an abridgement of James Grassineau's *A Musical Dictionary* (1740), itself a translation with additions and alterations of Sebastien de Brossard's *Dictionnaire de musique* (1703). Hoyle, a Yorkshireman, is said to have died in 1797.

R. F. SHARP, *rev.* K. D. REYNOLDS

Sources W. H. Husk, 'Hoyle, John', Grove, *Dict. mus.* (1927) · Allibone, *Dict.*

Hoyle, Joshua (d. 1654), college head, was born in Sowerby, near Halifax, Yorkshire, one of at least six children, although his parents are unknown. After spending some time at Magdalen College, Oxford, he went to Trinity College, Dublin, where he graduated BA in 1610, became a fellow in 1617, proceeded MA in 1618, succeeded James Ussher as professor of divinity in 1623, and proceeded BD in 1625. In Dublin he was apparently indefatigable, covering the whole Bible in daily lectures over fifteen years, spending another decade of lectures on the New Testament, lecturing weekly on theological controversies (particularly Bellarmine), and preaching three times on Sundays and often twice on holy days. As time went on he

became 'the most persistent critic of Arminian innovations' at Trinity (Ford, 218–19). He had a prolonged conflict with William Bedell, provost of the college from 1627 to 1634, over the latter's desire to minimize the differences between the churches of England and Ireland and the Church of Rome, and later complained of William Chappell, Bedell's successor installed in 1637, that he had suggested priests should not be subject to the secular power.

In 1640, having finished his series of lectures on Bellarmine, Hoyle belatedly entered a controversy over the doctrine of the real presence which dated from Archbishop Ussher's publications of the 1620s. As he explained in the epistle to the reader in his *A Rejoynder to Master Malone's Reply Concerning Real Presence* (1641), dedicated to Ussher, although he continued to be very busy, and his adversary a mere 'pratling, trifling Jesuite', he could not have chosen a better time to 'put forth of a Booke against the Church of Rome than this present'; he commended his auditors, in the words of 'Dr Holland of Oxford', 'to love God, and hate the Pope'.

With the outbreak of the Irish rising later that year Hoyle fled to England, and became vicar of Stepney, Middlesex. Anthony Wood's contention that his congregation found his sermons 'too scholastical' (Wood, 3.382) is given some plausibility by the fact that Jeremiah Burroughs and William Greenhill both preached there regularly during his incumbency, but he made sufficient impression on the House of Commons for them to appoint him on 18 February 1643 to the living of Sturminster Marshall, Dorset, although he was sanctioned to continue minister at Stepney in August 1645. A member from 1643 of the Westminster assembly, he was a regular attender, a member of the first committee, and a prominent speaker on the presbyterian wing.

At Laud's trial Hoyle gave evidence against the archbishop, bearing witness to the corruption of Trinity College by the popish and Arminian errors Laud and his agents had introduced. In his *Jehojadahs Justice Against Mattan, Baals Priest, or, The Covenanters Justice Against Idolaters* (1645), a sermon preached in response to 'a Speech utter'd upon Tower Hill'—evidently although not explicitly identified as Laud's on the scaffold—Hoyle made a robust defence of the covenant and of 'Mattan's' (unmistakably the archbishop's) death sentence. His mood of thankfulness and message of perseverance is clear throughout, from the optimism of 'how do the deeds of darkness vanish' in his dedication to Serjeant John Wild to the exultant rhetoric of his conclusion. Laud would:

> no more play the Beast against the Lamb, nor set up superstition above worship … He shall no more give libertie to prophane the Sabbath; nor set up May-poles as his pillars … He shall no more set up Candlesticks, and put down Catechising … nor tolerate playes, and suppress christian libertie in private communion for fasting.

Above all, he would 'no more remove [faithful pastors] from their Congregations' or 'seduce the Kings of the earth; nor delude great ones; nor overawe the Judges; nor terrifie the Counsellor ... He shall no more sow sedition, set kingdomes on fire, raise warre' (*Jehojadahs Justice*, 12).

In 1648, having been already employed by the parliamentary committee for the reformation of Oxford University, Hoyle was appointed master of University College and regius professor of divinity. In his inaugural addresses as professor he spoke 'in glowing terms' (*Hist. U. Oxf.* 4: *17th-cent. Oxf.*, 597) of one of his illustrious predecessors, John Prideaux, and showed some of the latter's energy in his support for Chancellor John Owen's campaign against Socinianism and anti-trinitarianism in the university, but seems to have made little impression on his college. Wood depicts a bookish, unworldly man lacking in judgement, but Hoyle's lack of success may equally well have been due to divisions within the college and to its weak financial state.

In his will, drawn up on 24 October 1654, Hoyle expressed a fervent faith. Along with small bequests to his three brothers, Johnathan, Joseph, and Joachim, and a larger one to his servant William Bottalion, and rings to his overseers Henry Wilkinson, principal of Magdalen Hall, and John Palmer, warden of All Souls, he left a copy of 'the learned bible that is now a printing' to University College Library (PRO, PROB 11/241, p. 16). He had apparently neither wife nor children as the residue of the estate was to be shared between his sisters and executors Anne and Elizabeth Hoyle. He died at the college on 6 December and was buried, as he had desired, 'under the Communion table' in the college chapel, but (if Wood is correct) his request that Wilkinson preach the funeral sermon was not honoured, Edward Terry, a fellow of University College, officiating instead.   VIVIENNE LARMINIE

Sources Foster, *Alum. Oxon.* · Burtchaell & Sadleir, *Alum. Dubl.*, 2nd edn · J. Hoyle, *A rejoynder to Master Malone's reply* (1641) · Wood, *Ath. Oxon.*, new edn, 3.382–3 · A. Ford, *The protestant Reformation in Ireland, 1590–1641*, 2nd edn (1997), 182, 218–19 · R. S. Paul, *The assembly of the Lord: politics and religion in the Westminster assembly and the 'Grand debate'* (1985) · *Hist. U. Oxf.* 4: *17th-cent. Oxf.*, 597, 754, 765 · M. Burrows, ed., *The register of the visitors of the University of Oxford, from AD 1647 to AD 1658*, CS, new ser., 29 (1881), 492, 557 · PRO, PROB 11/241, p. 16 · *Walker rev.*, 58

Hoyle, Thomas (*bap.* 1587, *d.* 1650), politician, was baptized at St Martin's, Micklegate, York, on 29 January 1587, the eldest son of Thomas Hoyle (*d.* 1607), clothier, of Slaithwaite, Yorkshire, and his wife, Elizabeth. He came from a line of godly but otherwise unremarkable Pennine clothiers. Apprenticed to a York merchant and future mayor, he took up residence in his master's parish of St Martin, Micklegate, and in 1611 married Elizabeth Maskew (1592–1639), the daughter of a wealthy civic office-holder. His success in commerce won him promotion to the aldermanic bench in 1626, and in 1628 he and Sir Arthur Ingram defeated Sir Thomas Savile—a political rival of Sir Thomas Wentworth (the future earl of Strafford)—to represent the city at Westminster. Hoyle was on close terms with Wentworth by 1631, when he was described as 'a person that honours W[entworth] and one that W[entworth] loves' (Bodl. Oxf., MS Firth b.2, fol. 183).

Hoyle was a prominent figure among the York godly. His mayoralty in 1632 was marked by efforts to set the city's poor on work, and he was instrumental in establishing St Martin's, Micklegate, as a bastion of 'painful' protestantism. He installed his private chaplain, the trenchantly Calvinist John Birchill, as parish incumbent, and settled the advowson upon a group of godly trustees, one of whom, the puritan divine William Gouge, had been closely involved with the London feoffees for impropriations. Birchill held regular conventicles and prayer meetings, through which Hoyle and his equally pious wife acquired a wide circle of godly friends and admirers. When Archbishop John Neile cracked down on the York puritans during the 1630s Hoyle was one of his principal targets and was proceeded against in the church courts for a variety of nonconformist offences. He and two of his fellow aldermen were snubbed by Laud himself in 1636, when they attempted to explain their defiance of Neile to the privy council. Hoyle's hostility to Laudianism probably alienated him from Strafford, and in the elections to the Long Parliament the York freemen rejected two of Strafford's candidates in favour of Hoyle and his fellow godly alderman, Sir William Allenson.

Although named to several committees concerning the grievances of the personal rule, Hoyle apparently played no part in the attack on the Laudian bishops or the king's 'evil counsellors'. After investing £450 as an Irish adventurer in March 1642 he withdrew to York, where he remained until the city fell prey to cavalier mobs in the autumn. Back at Westminster he joined those urging the vigorous prosecution of the war, and in December declared that unless the earl of Essex acted more decisively the kingdom would be ruined (BL, Harleian MS 164, fol. 243). His committee appointments and contributions in debate suggest that he favoured all-out war against the king. He also emerged as a leading figure in the administration of the excise, customs, and the navy, and was an active member of the committees for revenue and compounding. In 1644 he was appointed treasurer remembrancer in the exchequer (worth £1200 per annum), allegedly for his services to the war party (C. Walker, 'The history of Independency', 14 Sept 1648, 142, BL, E463/19).

Hoyle testified against Laud at the archbishop's trial in 1644, but though described as a 'deep Presbyterian' (*Autobiography of Mrs Alice Thornton*, ed. C. Jackson, SurtS 62, 1875, 210) showed no liking for the *jure divino* church discipline of the Scots. By 1647 he was firmly aligned with the political Independents, and during 1648 gravitated towards the more radical wing of that faction. In September 1648 he pronounced it 'utterly unsafe and dangerous' (*Parliamentary or Constitutional History of England*, 24 vols., 2nd edn, 1762–3, 17.435) for parliament to make peace with the king, and in October presented a petition from Yorkshire demanding that Charles be brought to justice. He retained his seat at Pride's Purge, but apparently withdrew from the house until the autumn of 1649 and had no hand in the king's trial. He had been named to only eight committees in the Rump before the first anniversary of the regicide, 30 January 1650, when he hanged himself at

Broad Sanctuary, his Westminster lodgings. He was buried two days later in St Margaret's, Westminster.

The timing of Hoyle's suicide suggests that the regicide had troubled him deeply—despite his non-involvement in the trial—and inevitably led to rumours that he died of a guilty conscience. However, the untimely demise of all thirteen of his children with his first wife, and one of his two sons with his second wife, Susanna (d. 1668), whom he had married by 1643, may also explain his lapse into 'excessive melancholy' (Jackson, 146) in 1649. He died intestate, and, despite allegations that he profited handsomely from office (D. Holles, 'Memoirs of Denzil, Lord Holles', ed. F. Maseres, *Select Tracts Relating to the Civil Wars in England*, 2 vols., 1815, 1.268), made no major land purchases during the 1640s. His only surviving child, John Hoyle, was Aphra Benn's lover, and was described as an 'atheist, a sodomite professed, a corrupter of youth and a blasphemer of Christ' (A. Goreau, *Reconstructing Aphra: a Social Biography of Aphra Benn*, 1980, 206).

DAVID SCOTT

Sources D. Scott, 'Hoyle, Thomas', HoP, *Commons* [draft] · C. Cross, 'A man of conscience in seventeenth-century urban politics: Alderman Hoyle of York', *Public duty and private conscience in seventeenth-century England*, ed. J. Morrill, P. Slack, and D. Woolf (1993), 205–24 · R. H. Skaife, 'Civic officials of York', York City Library, MS 2, fols. 395–7 · *JHC*, 1–6 (1547–1651) · J. H. Turner, ed., *Yorkshire Genealogist*, 2 (1890), 250–52 · J. Snow, 'The life of Master John Shaw', *Yorkshire diaries and autobiographies*, ed. C. Jackson, [1], 121–62, SurtS, 65 (1877), esp. 145–6 · R. Marchant, *The puritans and the church courts in the diocese of York, 1560–1642* (1960), 76–8, 81, 86–7, 321, 323 · *JHL*, 4–9 (1628–47) · *Mercurius Pragmaticus*, 23 (29 Aug–5 Sept 1648), sig. Ff [Thomason tract E 462(8)]; 36–7 (5–7 Dec 1648), sig. Ccc3 [E 476(2)]; 14 (17–24 July 1649), pl. 2, sig. o4 [E 565(21)] · York House books, York City Archives · C. H. Firth and R. S. Rait, eds., *Acts and ordinances of the interregnum, 1642–1660*, 3 vols. (1911) · Keeler, *Long Parliament*, 224–5 · overseers' acts, St Margaret's, 1644–5, City Westm. AC, E158 · 'The Rebells Warning-piece', 19 Feb 1650, BL, E 593/13, p. 6 · A. M. Burke, ed., *Memorials of St Margaret's Church, Westminster* (1914), 624

Archives BL, Harley MSS 164, fol. 243; 165, fol. 267 · BL, Thomason tracts, esp. E 116/9, E 462/8, E 463/18, 19, E 476/2, E 565/21, E 593/13, 669 f.6/44, 669 f.12/103 · PRO, papers of the committee for revenue, SP 28/269, *passim* | Bodl. Oxf., Strafford MSS, MS Firth b. 2, fol. 183

Wealth at death property in York; land in Wakefield; manor house at Colton, near York: Scott, 'Hoyle, Thomas'

Hoyle, William (1831–1886), temperance reformer, the fourth child of poor parents, was born in the valley of Rossendale, Lancashire. He started work in a cotton mill at eight years of age, educated himself, and, by constant labour, succeeded in 1851 in starting a business as a cotton spinner in partnership with his father, at Brooksbottom, near Bury, Lancashire. In 1859 he married, and moved to Tottington, where a large mill was built.

When his business was established Hoyle threw himself with great energy into the temperance movement. In 1869 he published a pamphlet by 'A Cotton Manufacturer' entitled *An Inquiry into the Long-Continued Depression in the Cotton Trade*, which, revised and enlarged into a book, was published in 1871 as *Our National Resources, and how they are Wasted*. This volume made Hoyle at once a recognized authority on the statistics of the drink question. The 'people's edition' of 1873 sold 60,000 copies within four months, making it the most successful educational publishing venture of the United Kingdom Alliance. Hoyle followed it up with many short publications, and with an annual letter to *The Times* on the 'drink bill' of successive years. In 1876 appeared *Crime in England and Wales in the Nineteenth Century*, in which Hoyle attributed the rising crime rate to intemperance, a problem which could be solved, he asserted, only by significantly reducing the number of liquor outlets.

Hoyle was an ardent supporter of the policy and proceeding of the United Kingdom Alliance, contributing to it financially and serving on its executive for a number of years. He interested himself also in the introduction into England of Good Templarism, and was an active Wesleyan Methodist throughout his life. He died on 26 February 1886 at the Alliance Hotel in Southport, Lancashire, and was survived by his wife, Alice, and an unmarried daughter, Hannah.

RONALD BAYNE, *rev.* MARK CLEMENT

Sources P. T. Winskill, *Temperance standard bearers of the nineteenth century: a biographical and statistical temperance dictionary*, 2 (1898) · A. E. Dingle, *The campaign for prohibition in Victorian England: the United Kingdom Alliance, 1872–1895* (1980) · B. Harrison, *Drink and the Victorians: the temperance question in England, 1815–1872* (1971) · *Manchester Guardian* (1 March 1886) · *Temperance Record* (4 March 1886) · CGPLA Eng. & Wales (1886)

Wealth at death £9304 8s. 1d.: probate, 2 June 1886, CGPLA Eng. & Wales

Hozier, Sir Henry Montague (1838–1907), army officer and business administrator, was born on 20 March 1838, at St Enoch's Hall, Bothwell, Lanarkshire, fifth son of James Hozier (1791–1878), landowner and barrister, later of Newlands, Glasgow, and Mauldslie Castle, Lanarkshire, and his wife, Catherine Margaret (d. 1870), daughter of Sir William Fielden, first baronet. The eldest of his four brothers was created Baron Newlands (1898). He was educated at Rugby School, Edinburgh Academy, and the Royal Military Academy at Woolwich. He joined the Royal Artillery (1856) and saw action in the Second Opium War (1860) before transferring to the 2nd Life Guards (1863). After passing out of the staff college at the head of the list, he compiled four War Office manuals on topics such as the equipment of cavalry and staff corps (1863–5).

Hozier was present at the Prussian-Danish War (1864) and Austro-Prussian War (1866), acting in the latter as correspondent of *The Times*. While serving as assistant military secretary to Lord Napier of Magdala on the Abyssinian expedition (1867), he was again engaged by *The Times* as a war correspondent: this necessitated complicated telegraphic arrangements which proved the grounding of his later expertise in international communications. Aged only thirty-two he was appointed controller at Aldershot with the rank of honorary lieutenant-colonel (1870). After the outbreak of the Franco-Prussian War he served as assistant military attaché at German army headquarters (1870–71) and received the Iron Cross. His reputation as a highly educated modern soldier with an authoritative knowledge of strategy and technology was strengthened by his military writings, including *The Seven Weeks' War* (1867), *The British Expedition to Abyssinia* (1869), and *The Franco-Prussian War* (1870–72). He later worked at the War Office reaching the rank of colonel in the 3rd dragoon guards, and seemed marked for high promotion, but abruptly abandoned soldiering as a career. His first marriage, of which he suppressed all details, is presumed to have ended in divorce about this time: he had married Eleanor Elizabeth Lyon (*b. c.*1850), daughter of James Lyon of Woolavington, Sussex, on 6 August 1868. The circumstances doubtless obliged him to resign his commission.

In 1874 Hozier became secretary of Lloyd's. This society was only indirectly concerned with the insurance business, which was transacted by its members individually, but was responsible for superintending agents and collecting marine intelligence globally. Hozier immediately reorganized its management, and continuously proved his efficiency as an administrator. His system of paying cargo claims at foreign ports facilitated an expansion of business after 1886. By the 1890s he had established 40 coastal signal stations in Britain and 118 overseas that were either controlled by or allied to Lloyd's. This superior intelligence system confirmed the society as the centre of world shipping news. Hozier swiftly recognized the possibilities of Marconi's wireless telegraphy in 1897, and together with Neville Maskelyn developed his own automatic wireless beacon, which underwent trials in 1900. Its results, however, were unimpressive: he tried to sell his interest to Marconi, to whom Lloyd's awarded a contract for ten wireless signalling stations in 1901. Disputes between Hozier, Marconi, and the British government persisted until his retirement from Lloyd's in 1906.

Hozier was autocratic, energetic, resourceful, and shrewd. His appearance was imposing and martial, though latterly he looked old for his age. For some years he was honorary colonel of the 3rd Kent volunteer artillery. *The Invasions of England* (1876) and *The Russo-Turkish War* (1877–9) were his more important later books. He unsuccessfully contested Woolwich as Liberal parliamentary candidate (1885), but rejected Gladstone's Irish policy and became a Liberal Unionist. As a freemason he became senior grand deacon of England, founder of the Lutine Lodge at Lloyd's, and member of the grand lodge of the Scotland, Westminster, and household brigade lodges. He was created CB (1897) and KCB (1903).

Hozier married second, on 28 September 1878, at Cortachy Castle, Scotland, Lady Blanche Henrietta Ogilvy (1852–1925), daughter of the seventh earl of Airlie and his wife, Henrietta Blanche Stanley, daughter of the second Baron Stanley of Alderley. They had one son and three daughters, including Clementine, Baroness Spencer-*Churchill. Hozier parted from his wife in 1891, and afterwards evinced bitterness towards her, leaving her family to finance her and her children. He died of pyaemia on 28 February 1907 in Panama, where he was buried on 1 March in the foreign cemetery.

RICHARD DAVENPORT-HINES

Sources *The Times* (2 March 1907) · *ILN* (9 March 1907), 364 · *The Athenaeum* (6 July 1867), 9–10 · *The Athenaeum* (13 Nov 1869), 620–21 · D. E. W. Gibb, *Lloyd's of London: a study in individualism* (1957) · C. Wright and C. E. Fayle, *A history of Lloyd's from the founding of Lloyd's Coffee House to the present day* (1928) · *The Times* (12 Aug 1867) · *The Times* (15 Aug 1867) · *The Times* (25 May 1871) · *The Times* (2 Feb 1877) · *The Times* (13 Feb 1877) · *The Times* (17 July 1879) · *The Times* (30 Aug 1884) · *The Times* (26 May 1888) · E. H. C. M. Bell, *Life and letters of C. F. Moberley Bell* (1927), 28–9 · M. Soames, *Clementine Churchill* (1979) · parish register (birth), Bothwell, Scotland, 20 March 1838 · parish register (baptism), Bothwell, Scotland, 20 April 1838 · m. cert., Scotland · m. cert., Eleanor Elizabeth Lyon · *IGI* · census returns, 1881

Archives Lloyds TSB, London, TSB archives

Likenesses photograph, *c.*1905, repro. in *ILN*

Wealth at death £15,049 16*s.* 5*d.*: Scottish probate sealed in London, 25 June 1907, *CCI* · £558 11*s.* 6*d.*: additional estate, 15 Feb 1912, *CCI*

Hubback [*née* Spielman], **Eva Marian** (1886–1949), social reformer and feminist, was born at 23 Oxford Square, London, on 13 April 1886, the second child and elder daughter in the family of two daughters and two sons of Sir Meyer Adam Spielman (1856–1936), stockbroker (later inspector of Home Office schools), and his wife, Gertrude Emily (1864–1949), daughter of George Raphael, banker. After St Felix School, Southwold, Eva persuaded her parents to allow her to go up to Newnham College, Cambridge, in October 1905. This was the formative time of her life intellectually—she took a first in part two of the economics tripos in 1908—and emotionally, through enduring friendships formed. Her circle included Rupert Brooke, Dudley Ward, the Olivier sisters, Dorothy Layton, Ka Cox, and Shena Potter.

In 1911, after voluntary social work for the London county council and for the suffragists, Eva Spielman married Francis William Hubback, son of John Hubback, corn merchant of Liverpool. He had been a Cambridge friend and was then lecturing in classics and economic history at Manchester University. She shared his love of strenuous holidays by the sea and in the mountains, and retained it throughout life. Two daughters and a son were born to them before Bill was killed on the western front in February 1917. Eva Hubback taught economics briefly at Newnham in 1916–17 before becoming parliamentary secretary to the suffragists, in 1919 transformed into the National Union of Societies for Equal Citizenship. She rapidly mastered the art of lobbying, working on all legislation concerning women and children, from franchise reform to divorce law. Her organizational flair complemented the charisma of Eleanor Rathbone in the campaign for family allowances.

In 1927 Eva succeeded Barbara Wootton as principal of Morley College, which provided non-vocational adult education in Lambeth. She secured new buildings; and her recruitment of distinguished lecturers and performers from many spheres brought intellectual excitement and cultural richness. Morley became well known for its music (Sir Michael Tippett), its theatre and ballet (Rupert Doone), and its art (Eric Ravilious and Edward Bawden). Morley took up her evenings but daytime was given to voluntary work. Her initiatives led to the creation in 1930 of the Townswomen's Guilds, the founding, with Sir Ernest Simon, of the Association for Education in Citizenship

Eva Marian Hubback (1886–1949), by Robin Adler

(1934), and the launching of the Children's Minimum Committee (1936) to campaign for better standards of care and nutrition. She became a JP in 1939 and a London county council Labour councillor in 1946. Her work for the Eugenics Society and the Family Planning Association gave her a keen interest in population issues. Many considered she should have been a member of the royal commission on population (1946–9), but she did give evidence and published her widely read *The Population of Britain* in 1947. Perhaps her very strengths, her enthusiasm and drive for so many causes, led to inadequate public recognition of her work. Illness and death came suddenly: it was as if, over many years, she had simply worn herself out. Eva Hubback died at Edgware General Hospital, Edgware, Middlesex, on 15 July 1949.

GILLIAN SUTHERLAND, *rev.*

Sources Newnham College, Cambridge, archive · D. Hopkinson, *Family inheritance: a life of Eva Hubback* (1954) · D. Hopkinson, *The incense-tree: an autobiography* (1968) · B. Harrison, *Prudent revolutionaries: portraits of British feminists between the wars* (1987) · private information (1993) · *CGPLA Eng. & Wales* (1949)

Archives London Metropolitan University, draft articles and papers

Likenesses R. Adler, photograph, repro. in D. Hopkinson, *Family inheritance*, frontispiece [*see illus.*]

Wealth at death £19,702 0s. 1d.: probate, 23 Sept 1949, *CGPLA Eng. & Wales*

Hubbard, John Gellibrand, first Baron Addington (1805–1889), merchant and fiscal reformer, was born on 21 March 1805, the eldest son of John Hubbard (d. 1847), a Russia merchant of Stratford Grove, Essex, and his wife, Marian (d. 1851), daughter of John Morgan of Bramfield Place, Hertfordshire. He was educated privately and, from 1816, at a school in Bordeaux. In 1821 he entered his father's firm in the City of London. On 19 May 1837 he married Maria Margaret, the eldest daughter of William John Napier, eighth Lord Napier, with whom he had five sons and four daughters.

The Hubbard business consisted of two interlocking partnerships, J. Hubbard & Co. in London and W. E. Hubbard & Co. of St Petersburg. The London partnership acted as the agent and banker for the family's interests in Russia, where his brother William Egerton Hubbard (1812–1883) was the senior partner until he settled in Sussex in 1843. The main interests in Russia were the Petroffsky and Spassky cotton spinning and weaving companies formed in 1842 and 1869, and the Schlusselberg calico printing company formed in 1864, which were eventually united as the Anglo-Russian Cotton Factories Ltd in 1897. The print works were very profitable between 1866 and 1880, but the return was subsequently modest, before declining into losses as a result of over-expansion, low-quality production, involvement in distribution, and a need to borrow. The London firm also had a modest business accepting bills on Russian houses.

John Gellibrand Hubbard was, according to his nephew Egerton, 'most arbitrary and sometimes inconsistent in his business dealings' (Guildhall Library, MS 10364, Egerton Hubbard to Stuart Rendel, 6 Feb 1900) and he 'never encouraged much independent thought' (ibid., Hubbard to Rendel, 9 April 1901). Stuart Rendel (who married a niece of Hubbard) criticized him for 'the generous but totally mistaken idea' that the factories in Russia could sustain the firms and support future generations of Hubbards; their management was left to 'a set of cousins' who brought in no new capital or business talents, and treated them simply as a form of outdoor relief (ibid., Rendel to Hubbard, 23 Aug 1911). The business was not in a strong position when it was handed over to Hubbard's youngest son Evelyn (1852–1934) and William's son Egerton (d. 1918). They were pathetically incapable and inept, suffering from a self-confessed 'obtuse stupidity' (ibid., Hubbard to Rendel, 15 Feb 1913).

By 1899 the Hubbard enterprise was in serious difficulties, and it fell to Rendel to provide financial assistance and to goad Evelyn and Egerton into some sense, with scant success. They were, as Rendel complained, 'incapable of regarding [the Russian factories] in any other way than as the milch cow of the firm' (Guildhall Library, MS 10364, Rendel to Egerton, 11 Dec 1911), in order to preserve their comfortable lifestyle and status in the City; the firm, he felt, did not deserve to be rescued, but he did wish to preserve the honour of the family name, and was activated by 'pity for your victims in your family' (ibid., Rendel to Egerton Hubbard, 14 Feb 1913). But the problems arose not only because of the culpable stupidity of the sons, but also because 'the two old brothers left their officers in a difficult situation' (ibid., Henry Gladstone to S. Rendel, 14 Feb 1913).

John Gellibrand and William Hubbard made the mistake of appointing Evelyn and Egerton as their sole executors after their deaths, so leaving them open to a conflict of interests between their desire both to continue the firm and to protect the interests of other members of the family. The firms in London and Russia did not have adequate capital, and withdrawal of money to pay bequests to members of the family would make the survival of the business problematical. John Gellibrand Hubbard, like his brother, left his 'capital very evenly distributed over a very large family' (Guildhall Library, MS 10364, Egerton Hubbard to Rendel, 20 July 1899), and in 1889 the beneficiaries of his will agreed to deposit their money in the business and not to withdraw it without the firm's consent. 'My father certainly believed absolutely in his Russian business', claimed Evelyn; 'it was his central interest, he put all he had into it, and never took anything out that he could avoid' (ibid., Evelyn Hubbard to Rendel, 20 Feb 1900). This was a convenient position for him to adopt, and Rendel believed that Evelyn was misinterpreting his father's will. Indeed, a few months after John Gellibrand Hubbard's death a settlement came to light which he had drawn up in 1871 without informing his trustees. This seemed to require the withdrawal of money from the firm for the benefit of those family members who were not directly involved in the business. Evelyn convinced himself it was not legally binding, but the courts ruled otherwise in 1900 and the business was thrown into confusion. The failure of John Gellibrand Hubbard to provide adequate safeguards for other beneficiaries of his will ultimately brought the whole family to ruin.

Hubbard was elected a director of the Bank of England in 1838, and was chairman of the Public Works Loan Commission from 1853 until his death. He was elected Conservative member for Buckingham in 1859, and held the seat until 1868. In 1874 he became one of the members for the City of London, until he was raised to the peerage as Baron Addington in 1887. His main political interest—indeed obsession—was reform of the income tax which he believed to be inequitable between income arising spontaneously from existing property, and profits earned from trades and professions. The 'spontaneous' income was secured by an underlying investment, so that 90 per cent was available for spending and only 10 per cent needed to be saved. By contrast, persons in receipt of earned incomes needed to save in order to provide security in retirement and for their dependants, so that only 60 per cent was available for consumption. An equitable tax system should therefore, he argued, impose tax on the earnings of trades and professions at two-thirds the rate on incomes derived from invested property. Such a change would, in his view, 'present the fewest discouragements to the exercise of industry and to the accumulation of capital', and ensure that the income tax fell equally on the various classes of the community (J. G. Hubbard, *How should an Income Tax be Levied?*, 1852, 4). His greatest success was securing the appointment of a select committee on income and property tax in 1861 under his chairmanship, but his draft report was not accepted by the committee.

He did have a posthumous triumph in 1907 when the chancellor of the exchequer (H. H. Asquith) introduced the principle of differentiation between earned and unearned income. He was also interested in issues relating to coinage, and spoke on ecclesiastical issues. Although he was a high-churchman, who built and endowed St Alban the Martyr in Holborn, he protested to the bishop of London about the ritualistic practices of the incumbent, Alexander Mackonochie.

Hubbard's father had started to purchase land, and he followed suit: he owned 2576 acres with a gross annual value of £4887 (Bateman, 231) which passed to his eldest son in entail. Hubbard died at his home, Addington Manor, Buckinghamshire, on 28 August 1889, and was buried in Addington parish churchyard.

MARTIN DAUNTON

Sources M. J. Daunton, 'Inheritance and succession in the City of London in the nineteenth century', *Business History*, 30 (1988), 269–86 · J. Bateman, *The great landowners of Great Britain and Ireland*, 4th edn (1883), 231 · 'Select committee on … income and property tax', *Parl. papers* (1861), 7.1, no. 503; 7.339, no. 503-I · *DNB* [see also 'Hubbard, Louisa Maria'] · *DWB* [Stuart Rendel entry] · *Debrett's Peerage* · *WWW*, 1929–40 [Evelyn Hubbard] · GL, MS 10364, files 1, 2 · d. cert.
Archives GL | Balliol Oxf., corresp. with David Urquhart · BL, corresp. with W. E. Gladstone, Add. MS 44095 · Bodl. Oxf., letters to Benjamin Disraeli · Hunt. L., letters to Grenville family · LPL, corresp. with E. W. Benson · LPL, corresp. with A. C. Tait
Likenesses J. R. Jackson, stipple and line engraving (aged sixty-five; after G. Richmond), Bank of England, London · Spy [L. Ward], cartoon, repro. in *VF* (4 Oct 1884)
Wealth at death £111,985 6s. 1d.: probate, 26 Feb 1890, *CGPLA Eng. & Wales*

Hubbard, Louisa Maria (1836–1906), promoter of employment for women and journal editor, was born on 8 March 1836 in St Petersburg, Russia, the eldest of four sons and three daughters of William Egerton Hubbard (1812–1883), merchant, younger brother of John Gellibrand *Hubbard, first Baron Addington, and Louisa Ellen Baldock, daughter of Captain William Baldock.

In 1843 the family returned to England, settling at Leonardslee, near Horsham, Sussex, where Louisa Hubbard was privately educated and where she spent most of the rest of her life. Freed from the necessity of earning her own living, she spent most of her life campaigning to widen the opportunities available to women who were required to work. She described her mission: 'I gradually drifted into the position of wishing to champion the cause of the unmarried woman, and from the first I refused to apologise for her existence' (Pratt, 3).

Louisa Hubbard's first task was the encouragement of the deaconess movement and she published in 1871 a pamphlet: *Anglican Deaconesses: is there No Place for Women in the System?* Seeking to give practical help to the order of deaconesses she established 'assistance meetings', thereby bringing together 'an active body of ladies who took up the movement with much zeal and were able to help it in many different ways' (Pratt, 10).

The 1870 Education Act stimulated the demand for

Louisa Maria Hubbard (1836–1906), by unknown photographer

elementary school teachers thereby creating an alternative source of employment for large numbers of women. Louisa Hubbard encouraged the professionalization of teaching by helping to establish Otter College, a teacher training college for women which opened in Chichester in 1873. She also published works encouraging teaching and education: *Work for Ladies in Elementary Schools* (1872), *Why should I Send my Child to School* (1878), and *A Few Words to the Mothers of Little Children* (1880).

Louisa Hubbard believed that the most effective way to help women was to provide information on the opportunities open to them. Accordingly, between 1869 and 1878 she compiled *A Guide to All Institutions for the Benefit of Women*. Convinced that this was not enough, in 1875 she started, and edited, two publications: *The Handbook of Women's Work*, renamed in 1880 *The Englishwoman's Year-book*, and the *Women's Gazette*, a monthly magazine later called *Work and Leisure*. These were pioneering publications which did much to remove the stigma attached to existing professions as well as to publicize new areas of women's work, and were pivotal in bringing about changes in the position of women.

Articles and correspondence appearing in these publications spawned a variety of schemes, movements, societies, and institutions, all designed to widen opportunities available to women. For example, between 1875 and 1878 a series of articles entitled 'Nursing as a career for educated women' for the first time made information on this profession available to women. Other new employment opportunities such as gardening, massage, and typewriting were also advocated. The Working Ladies Guild was formed by Lady Mary Fielding as a result of a letter in the first issue of the *Women's Gazette*; an article entitled 'Cooperation of governesses' led to the creation of the Teachers' Guild in February 1884. Other organizations set up as a result of articles in Louisa Hubbard's publications included the United British Women's Emigration Association, the Matrons' Aid or Trained Midwives Registration Society (which became in 1886 the Midwives' Institute and Trained Nurses Club), and the Church of England Women's Help Society.

Keen that the provision of suitable accommodation for working gentlewomen be extended, Louisa Hubbard supported the The Ladies' Dwellings Company Ltd which was set up in 1887 and began conversion work on Sloane Gardens House in Lower Sloane Street, London. She also provided the financial backing for the Gentlewomen's Employment Club, established in October 1889 and run by J. Adèle Younghusband.

Louisa Hubbard was particularly influential in her role of widening opportunities open to women because she was an enabler who brought together from her wide range of contacts women who shared views or interests on particular subjects. Her role in the establishment of the National Union of Women Workers, formed in 1895 after her suggestion that the various strands of philanthropic work undertaken by women should be co-ordinated, illustrates her effectiveness as a provider of ideas which others could take forward.

Louisa Hubbard never married. In her spare time she pursued her interests of landscape painting and horse-riding. Her other publications include: *The Beautiful House and Enchanted Garden* (1885), *Where to Spend a Holiday* (1887), and 'Statistics of women's work', in *Woman's Mission* (1893), edited by Angela Burdett-Coutts.

In 1893 Louisa Hubbard's health collapsed and she was forced to give up most of her work; *Work and Leisure* ceased publication and Emily Janes took over as editor of *The Englishwoman's Yearbook*. In 1899 a stroke partially paralysed her while on holiday in the Tyrol in Austria and she remained in Austria until her death at the Hotel Austria, Gries bei Bozen, on 25 November 1906.

SERENA KELLY

Sources E. A. Pratt, *A woman's work for women* (1893) · *The Times* (1 Dec 1906) · O. Banks, *The biographical dictionary of British feminists*, 1 (1985) · Burke, *Peerage*
Likenesses photograph, repro. in Pratt, *A woman's work for women*, frontispiece [*see illus.*]
Wealth at death £2675 11s. 6d.: probate, 7 Jan 1907, CGPLA Eng. & Wales

Hubbard, William (1621/2–1704), minister in America and historian, was the second son of William Hubbard (1594–1670), husbandman, of Tendring, Essex, and his wife,

Judith, daughter of John Knapp and Martha Blosse of Ipswich, Suffolk. His father and mother, with their six children, emigrated to New England in 1635, settling in Ipswich, Massachusetts. The father prospered as a husbandman, accumulating several parcels of land before moving to Boston in 1662.

Hubbard graduated from Harvard College in 1642, a member of that institution's first graduating class. In 1646 he married Margaret, daughter of Nathaniel *Rogers, minister of Ipswich; they had three children. In 1656, soon after the death of his father-in-law, Hubbard entered the ministry and was ordained teacher by Rogers's Congregational church in Ipswich in 1658, an affiliation he maintained until his retirement from the ministry in 1703.

Hubbard's career as a published writer began late in life. In 1676, amid the turmoil of King Philip's War, he was invited to deliver the annual election-day sermon by the general court. Countering the gloomy predictions of some of his contemporaries, Hubbard urged church and state officials to adopt a moderate, tolerant, and optimistic point of view toward events. The sermon was published later that year by order of the general court. The same tone of moderate and tolerant—though still orthodox puritan—rationalism infuses Hubbard's other published works: several sermons, *Narrative of the Troubles with the Indians in New-England* (1677)—a history of King Philip's War—*A General History of New England from the Discovery to MDCLXXX* (1678–82), and his jointly authored petition in 1703 to clear formally the names of all who had been accused of witchcraft in Salem in 1692.

In 1694, his first wife having died, Hubbard married Mary Pearce. Like many ministers in colonial New England, Hubbard struggled financially for most of his adult life. He defaulted on several loans in the 1670s and 1680s, and upon his death on 14 September 1704 he left his wife, who was childless, indigent. The town of Ipswich granted her a life pension in 1710.   STEPHEN CARL ARCH

Sources 'Genealogical memoir of the family of Rev. Nathaniel Rogers', *New England Historical and Genealogical Register*, 6 (1851), 105–52 · C. K. Shipton, *Sibley's Harvard graduates: biographical sketches of graduates of Harvard University*, 17 vols. (1873–1975), vol. 1, pp. 54–63 · A. MacPhail, 'William Hubbard', *American colonial writers, 1606–1734*, ed. E. Elliott, DLitB, 24 (1984), 164–72 · J. Eliot, 'Ecclesiastical history of Massachusetts [pt 2]', *Collections of the Massachusetts Historical Society*, 10 (1809), 1–37, esp. 32–3 · S. G. Drake, *Result of some researches among the British archives for information relative to the founders of New England* (1860), 39 · S. G. Drake, 'Life of the author', in W. Hubbard, *The history of the Indian wars in New England*, ed. S. G. Drake (1865), xix–xxxi · *DNB* · W. C. Metcalfe, ed., *The visitations of Suffolk* (1882), 149

Wealth at death probably indigent: MacPhail, 'William Hubbard'; Shipton, *Sibley's Harvard graduates*; Drake, *Result*

Hubberthorne, Richard (*bap.* 1628, *d.* 1662), Quaker activist, was baptized at Warton, Lancashire, on 8 June 1628. His yeoman father, John, and his mother, Jane, may have been involved with rural protests (Jane refused to pay tithes); however, they prospered by maintaining a reputation for honesty and 'uprightnesse' in their dealings with others (Hubberthorne, sig. a1r). Two other children are known to have been born to the couple: Ellinyr (1616–1666) and Jane (1621–1647); Richard was certainly the only son.

Richard Hubberthorne joined Cromwell's army when he was about twenty, becoming a veteran of Dunbar and Worcester where more than a military apprenticeship was served. He wrote idealistically of the soldiers' aims to defend the liberties of parliament and the people against monarchical tyranny, and he was a champion of 'the good old cause' until the Commonwealth's collapse, in 1659. Hubberthorne's religious loyalty to the Quakers began in 1652, when he chanced to hear George Fox preach. These spiritual changes were so affecting that a witness records that Hubberthorne appeared to be 'passing out of the body' (Hubberthorne, sig. a1r). Once secure in his conversion, however, the former soldier increasingly took a more pacifistic stance as a Quaker minister and polemicist. Indeed, he signed the Quakers' 'peace testimony' in 1661, an affirmation of the movement's pacifism; Hubberthorne thereby became a spokesperson for peaceable measures, rather than conflict.

Throughout the 1650s Hubberthorne travelled extensively and suffered intermittently. The Quaker Edward Burrough states that Hubberthorne journeyed through 'most of the Counties of this Nation' (Hubberthorne, sig. a1v). Cheshire (1653), Oxford (1654), East Anglia (1654), London (1655), and Cornwall (1656) were among the places that he visited, and he suffered for preaching and refusing to remove his hat in the presence of so-called superiors. Suffering, however, only increased his political commitment: one tract of his, written from Cambridge prison, criticizes those who 'are rich, who live at ease [...] you live upon the labours of the poor' (*The Immediate Call*, 1654, 4–5). However, Hubberthorne seems to have been so pleasant a person as even to attract occasional praise from his opponents: Adam Martindale acknowledged Hubberthorne was the 'most rationall, calme-spirited man of his judgement that I was ever publickly engaged against' (Brockbank, 76).

Hubberthorne did not survive long after the restoration of the monarchy, dying in prison; yet, ironically, during an interview with the king in June 1660, he had secured the promise that 'you shall none of you suffer ... so long as you live peaceably' (*Something that Lately Passed*, 1660, 5). Hubberthorne's account of this meeting shows Charles as responsive to the call for religious toleration. However, Hubberthorne himself was arrested during a period of intense persecution while attending a meeting in London in 1662. Once inside Newgate, Hubberthorne soon became ill. He had, in any case, a frail physique: George Whitehead, a close companion to Hubberthorne in East Anglia, contrasted his friend's 'solid spirit' with his weak body and voice (Hubberthorne, sig. a3v). Hubberthorne's final illness lasted about ten days, and he died on 17 August 1662; the coroner held it to be a natural death. Hubberthorne was a man seemingly of a gentle disposition that endeared him to many; George Fox described him 'as Innocent a man as liveth on the Earth' (Hubberthorne, sig. a3r).   CATIE GILL

Sources J. Besse, *A collection of the sufferings of the people called Quakers*, 2 vols. (1753) · E. Brockbank, *Richard Hubberthorne of Yealand: yeoman, soldier, Quaker, 1628–1662* (1929) · R. Hubberthorne, *A collection of the several books* (1663) · L. Ingle, 'Richard Hubberthorne and history: the crisis of 1659', *Journal of the Friends' Historical Society*, 56 (1990–93), 189–200 · R. Moore, *The light in their consciences: early Quakers in Britain, 1646–1666* (University Park, PA, 2000) · N. Penney, ed., *The first publishers of truth* (1907) · *The journal of George Fox*, ed. N. Penney, 2 vols. (1911) · J. Smith, *A descriptive catalogue of Friends' books*, 2 vols. (1867) · J. Tomkins, *Piety promoted*, 1 (1812)
Archives RS Friends, Lond.

Hubbock, William (1560–1631), Church of England clergyman, was born in co. Durham of unknown parentage. After matriculating at Magdalen Hall, Oxford, in April 1580, aged nineteen, he graduated BA in 1581, then moved to Corpus Christi College where he became probationer fellow in February 1582 and proceeded MA in 1585. Hubbock's translation of William Whitaker's *Ad rationes decem Edmundi Campion* (1581), presumably composed at this period, survives in manuscript as Crymes MS 837, item 3, in the Bodleian Library in Oxford. About 1588 Hubbock sought, and apparently obtained, the patronage of the lord treasurer, Lord Burghley, but in March 1590 he fell foul of Archbishop Whitgift's drive for clerical conformity following the appearance of the Marprelate tracts. Cited before the high commission for attacking Whitgift's three articles during a sermon, he appealed to Burghley and to Sir Francis Knollys. Whitgift rebuffed their attempts to intercede on Hubbock's behalf, and after refusing to subscribe or enter bonds not to preach or come within 10 miles of Oxford, Hubbock was imprisoned. When he received the commissioners' decree Burghley forwarded it to Knollys, whose angry response (31 March) gave new impetus to his campaign against Whitgift and *jure divino* episcopacy.

Hubbock, incarcerated for six months and deprived of his fellowship, summarized his offensive sermon and added a brief account of his troubles which survives in manuscript (BL, Add. MS 48064, fols. 148–51). He retained Burghley's goodwill, in March 1594 obtaining the royal chaplaincy of St Peter ad Vincula within the Tower of London and the following July confidently petitioning Michael Hickes, Burghley's secretary, for repairs to his lodgings in the Tower. In 1595 Hubbock published *An Apologie of Infants*, a sermon arguing that those unbaptized at death 'by God's election may be saved'. Having been appointed lecturer at St Botolph, Aldgate, on 6 February 1597, in August 1598 he apparently arranged for Eusebius Paget to succeed him when he accepted the crown living of Nailstone, Leicestershire.

When James I visited the Tower in March 1604 on his way to open parliament and revive coronation festivities postponed by plague in 1603, Hubbock delivered a Latin address on the subject of the 'union of the kingdomes', later published in English 'by his highnesse special command' as *An Oration Gratulatory to ... James of England* (1604). An anti-Catholic work, *Great Brittaines resurrection, or, The parliaments passing bell: Against the tryumphing of the papists*, appeared in 1606. A petition about 1609 for the constable's lodgings in the Tower met with opposition from Sir William Waad, its lieutenant, who claimed that when in Leicestershire Hubbock provided 'lewd substitutes' in the chapel.

Hubbock was twice married. Nothing is known about his first wife, whom he married in the early 1590s. His second, who also predeceased him, was Mrs Moore at the time of their marriage, and may have been divorced since her husband was apparently still living in 1631. After his exchange with Waad he seems to have lived a settled and prosperous life. The duke of Buckingham's expedition to the Île de Ré probably prompted the publication in 1627 of his *A Prayer used in Private*, originally conceived as a supplication for the 'prosperous successe' of a voyage to 'Cales' in 1596. In Hubbock's will, dated 20 July 1631, he requested burial by his pulpit in the Tower; the bulk of his estate went to the third of four surviving sons, Simon, and his daughter, Susan. Hubbock died, at the Tower, within days and, despite their brothers' attempt to challenge the will, Simon and Susan on 3 August secured probate as joint executors. BRETT USHER

Sources W. Hubbock to Burghley, 1588?, BL, Lansdowne MS 99, fol. 62 · F. Knollys to Burghley, 29 March 1590, BL, Lansdowne MS 68, fol. 173 · F. Knollys to Burghley, 31 March 1590, BL, Lansdowne MS 64, fol. 32 · W. Hubbock to M. Hickes, 12 July 1594, BL, Lansdowne MS 77, fol. 135 · BL, Lansdowne MS 445, fol. 43*v* · Hubbock, sermon, 1590, and summary of his troubles, BL, Add. MS 48064 fols. 148–51 · GL, MS 9234/6, fols. 97*r*, 107*v*; 9234/7, fols. 122*r*, 135*v* · J. Strype, *The life and acts of John Whitgift*, new edn, 3 vols. (1822), vol. 2, pp. 32–4 · J. Nichols, *The progresses, processions, and magnificent festivities of King James I, his royal consort, family and court*, 1 (1828), 325 · W. Waad, report, *c*.1609, PRO, SP 14/51/7 · Wood, *Ath. Oxon.*, new edn, 1.752–3 · Venn, *Alum. Cant.* · PRO, PROB 11/160, fols. 208–9 · G. Hennessy, *Novum repertorium ecclesiasticum parochiale Londinense, or, London diocesan clergy succession from the earliest time to the year 1898* (1898), 373 · P. S. Seaver, *The puritan lectureships: the politics of religious dissent, 1560–1662* (1970), 136, 359 · P. Collinson, *The Elizabethan puritan movement* (1967), 405, 446 · C. M. Dent, *Protestant reformers in Elizabethan Oxford* (1983), 149–50 · W. D. J. C. Thompson, *Studies in the reformation* (1980), 120 · will of spouse, 1631
Archives BL, copy of 1590 sermon and his troubles, Add. MS | BL, letters to Burghley and M. Hickes, Lansdowne MSS
Wealth at death approx. £1500–£2000; plus property: will, PRO, PROB 11/160, fols. 208–9

Hubert, Sir Francis (1568?–1629), poet, was the son of Edward Hubert, a wealthy and well-connected landowner of Birchanger, Essex, who became receiver-general to Edward de Vere, seventeenth earl of Oxford (to whom he was related through the marriage of the earl's nephew to his sister), and one of the six clerks of chancery. Edward's first wife, Francis's mother, was a member of the Southall family; his second wife, Eleanor, was the daughter of Sir John Fortescue, keeper of the wardrobe and subsequently chancellor of the exchequer; her uncle, Sir Thomas Bromley, became lord chancellor and undoubtedly helped advance Edward's legal career. Mellor suggests that as a boy Francis may have served as a page in Oxford's household (*Poems*, xii). At about age fifteen he matriculated at Hart Hall, Oxford (5 June 1584), where he was a contemporary of John Donne but apparently took no degree; three years later he was admitted to Lincoln's Inn (16 October 1587). Between 1590 and 1592 Hubert returned from

London to Essex, living until 1597 or later at Stansted Mountfitchet, an estate which his father had acquired and which became his country residence. In 1592 he married Elizabeth (*bap.* 1568), daughter of Thomas Leventhorpe of Albury, Hertfordshire, through whom he became part heir of Albury Manor, his interest in which he later sold to Richard Frank, husband of one of Elizabeth's sisters. They had twelve children: six were baptized in the church of Stansted Mountfitchet; three others were probably born in London. About 1599, in a speculative venture, Hubert lent £30 to one John Davies, owner of the *Margaret and John*, a trading and privateering ship, but was apparently cheated of his investment. Between 23 January and 23 August 1601 he was knighted, having succeeded his father as one of the six clerks of chancery, a post which he retained for about two years. Thereafter, his fortunes waned. By 1603 he was back in Essex as one of the justices of the peace, but in 1604 he was outlawed, probably for debt. As his wealth diminished Hubert involved himself in an arrangement with Sir Edward Coke, the attorney-general, concerning property that had once belonged to Sir Edmund Baynham, one of the pardoned conspirators in the Essex rising of 1601. Coke, in order to avoid a business transaction with a proclaimed traitor, and acting as guardian for his prospective daughter-in-law, Meriel Wheatley, wished to purchase the property through Hubert, who agreed to buy and then resell it to him. When Coke reneged on the agreement (perhaps because of Baynham's association with the gunpowder plotters whom he was bringing to justice in 1604–5), Hubert tried unsuccessfully to find another buyer but ended by selling to Coke at a greatly reduced price, thus suffering a severe loss. His reverses continuing, he was ultimately forced to sell all his Essex properties to Sir Thomas Middleton, retired lord mayor of London, for £16,000 in settlement of his debts.

In 1628 and 1629 Hubert published *The historie of Edward the Second … together with the fatall down-fall of his two unfortunate favorites Gaveston and Spencer*. This moralistic narrative of 664 stanzas in rhyme royal is in the tradition of the *Mirror for Magistrates* with borrowings from Michael Drayton's *Piers Gaveston* (1594) and elements of heavy-handed satire on royal favouritism. Hubert originally composed it between 1597 and 1600, but publication under Elizabeth was officially suppressed because of its politically dangerous topic, the deposition of an English monarch, after which (according to the stationer Lawrence Chapman) Hubert kept it 'for a long time charily … as a Jewell in his secret Cabinet' (*Egypts Favorite*, sig. A3v). Nevertheless the poem, which proved popular, circulated widely: six manuscripts plus a fragment survive in the British and Bodleian libraries (*Poems*, 280). When an unauthorized version was published anonymously in 1628, Hubert hurriedly rewrote and expanded the poem, inducing his friend Chapman to publish the authentic version a year later with a dedication to his brother Richard. In addition to correcting many misprints, Hubert's revisions (including deletions of passages potentially offensive to Buckingham and Laud) were intended to negate the possible imputation of disloyalty to Charles I. Hubert's 'second Worke', as Chapman calls it, *Egypts Favorite, the Historie of Joseph*, was published posthumously in 1631. This biblical paraphrase, based on Genesis and written in quatrains, consists of four cantos (with a continuation of the fourth) and a final section narrating Jacob's 'Progresse into the Land of Goshen'. It was entered in the Stationers' register on 10 February 1631 but could have been written at any time between the late 1590s and Hubert's death. Mellor believes it 'was composed by sections over a considerable period' and that the fourth canto dates from about 1605 after Hubert had surrendered his chancery clerkship (*Poems*, 327–9). Hubert's additional writings are presumably lost; Chapman mentions 'diverse other Workes … excellently well composed' that comprise 'a chiefe ornament of [the poet's] owne private Librarie' (*Egypts Favorite*, sig. A3v).

Hubert passed his declining years in a small house in London and was buried in December 1629 in St Andrew's, Holborn. The tablet that marked his grave was destroyed with most of the church during the Second World War.

CHARLES R. FORKER

Sources *The poems of Sir Francis Hubert*, ed. B. Mellor (1961) · H. Nearing, *English historical poetry, 1599–1641* (Philadelphia, 1945) · E. Brydges, *Restituta, or, Titles, extracts, and characters of old books in English literature*, 4 vols. (1814–16), vol. 1, pp. 93–106 · IGI · DNB
Archives BL, Harley MSS · Bodl. Oxf.
Wealth at death poor: *Poems*, ed. Mellor

Hubert, Robert (*c.*1640–1666). *See under* Farriner, Thomas (1615/16?–1670).

Hübschmann, Kurt Heinrich. *See* Hutton, Kurt (1893–1960).

Huby, Marmaduke (*c.*1439–1526), abbot of Fountains, probably came from the Huby family of York, who had been associated with the Cistercian house of Fountains from the thirteenth century. In 1519 he described himself as aged eighty, and in 1523 as having been professed sixty years before. By 1482 he was serving as bursar to Abbot John Darnton, and as his proctor in his role as one of the commissioners in England of the abbot of Cîteaux. His known activities in these earlier years foreshadow the main lines of his later career. He was engaged in the collection of the yearly subsidy due from English and Welsh abbeys to the mother house of their order at Cîteaux, and even attempted to arrange for the export of lead to provide utensils for use at the general chapter. He also conducted visitations of the Welsh monasteries. He worked for the restoration to the order of Scarborough church, given by Richard I for the expenses of the general chapter, and for the establishment of a Cistercian college at Oxford. He made the first of several attempts, in the face of opposition from some abbots, to obtain governmental permission for a visit to England by the abbot of Cîteaux—this was the great reformer Jean de Cirey, of whose work Huby's own may be seen as an insular reflection.

Huby was elected abbot of Fountains in 1495. During his abbacy the number of professed monks rose from twenty-two to fifty-two. He embarked on an ambitious building programme, marked most notably by the great tower at the end of the north transept of the church, but also by the doubling in size of the abbot's quarters and the extension of the infirmary. He commissioned a new cartulary and had new rentals made after local inquests. This attention to the abbey's material prosperity was complemented by concern for the spiritual life, even beyond the cloister. He built or rebuilt several chapels in the West Riding, including that of St Michael overlooking the abbey, and the chapel of the Blessed Virgin on the site of St Wilfrid's original church at Ripon; this last is a practical expression of his pride in the north and in local saints, also evident in his letters. His position in northern society was reflected in his frequent appointment to commissions of the peace, for the last time in August 1525.

For most of his time as abbot Huby continued to be one of the commissioners of the abbot of Cîteaux, and he commented himself on the tremendous labour, worry, and expense that this caused him. He acted as joint president of several chapters of the province. He was instrumental in the foundation of St Bernard's College, Oxford, for which he sought to organize a book collection in 1495 and to raise a subsidy in 1496; twenty years later he saw the completion of the hall and chapel. In 1496 he conducted another visitation of Wales and deposed the abbot of Strata Marcella, Montgomeryshire. In 1497 his intervention in the troubled affairs of Furness was less successful, bringing him initially into disfavour with the English government and causing him long-term problems when his candidate for the abbacy proved utterly unsatisfactory. Huby faced many obstacles in his quest for reform. Most serious was the multiplication of commissioners, whose number seems to have doubled; in addition he appears to have been frequently frustrated by the resentment of his colleague, the abbot of Stratford Langthorne. Huby was also constantly concerned by the efforts of English bishops, and especially of Archbishop John Morton (d. 1500), to undermine the exemption of the order, a situation worsened by the complicity of some abbots and their readiness to resort to secular jurisdiction. He complained, too, of the growing habit of petitioning the papal court for dispensations for individual monks. Unfortunately, none of his letters between 1500 and 1517 are extant, but afterwards the old problems still plagued him. He again reported the efforts of some abbots to throw off the authority of Cîteaux, and suggested that Cardinal Wolsey should be admitted into confraternity in order to win his support for the order's immunity.

Huby's main aim was the maintenance of the unity of the order and uniformity of observance, and although his building programme and his concern for university provision conflicted with the early prohibitions of ostentation and learning, he was remarkably successful in his advocacy of the Cistercian tradition. His easy relationship with Henry VII, and later with Thomas Wolsey, did much to protect its position. He was certainly the outstanding English Cistercian of his age, attracting praise from most of his contemporaries, and his career is one that suggests that the monastic order in England was not, in the seventy years before the dissolution, either as lax or as irrelevant as has sometimes been suggested.

Huby died, a very old man, in 1526, before 24 September. His grave is not marked, but he was probably buried beneath the chapter house floor of Fountains. His arms (a shield charged with a mitre enfiled with a pastoral staff, with the initials M. H.) and monogram appear frequently on the buildings that he raised.

CHRISTOPHER HARPER-BILL

Sources C. H. Talbot, ed., *Letters from the English abbots to the chapter at Cîteaux, 1442–1521*, CS, 4th ser., 4 (1967) · J. R. Walbran, ed., *Memorials of the abbey of St Mary of Fountains*, 1, SurtS, 42 (1863) · C. H. Talbot, 'Marmaduke Huby, abbot of Fountains (1495–1526)', *Analecta Sacri Ordinis Cisterciensis*, 20 (1964), 165–84 · D. Knowles [M. C. Knowles], *The religious orders in England*, 3 (1959), 35–8 · W. H. St J. Hope, 'Fountains Abbey', *Yorkshire Archaeological Journal*, 15 (1898–1900), 269–402 · *CPR, 1494–1509* · *LP Henry VIII*, vols. 1, 3–4
Archives BL, Add. MS 18276

Hucheon [Huchown] **of the Awle Ryale** (*fl.* 14th cent.), author of several alliterative verses, has long been considered an important fourteenth-century Scottish poet. However, the evidence for this must be considered questionable. Hucheon owes his literary reputation to Andrew Wyntoun, who, writing about 1420, praised him as 'cunnand … in literature' and credited him with three works: *The Gest of Arthure*, *The Awyntre of Gawane*, and *The Pistil of Suet Susane* ('Original Chronicle', 4.23). These have been most plausibly identified as the non-rhyming *Morte Arthure*, *The Awntyres of Arthure at the Terne Wathelyne*, and *The Pistil of Susan* respectively. The first two of these works form part of the Arthurian cycle, while the third is based on the biblical story of Susanna and the elders. Numerous theories have also been propounded concerning Hucheon's authorship of other works, and practically every anonymous alliterative verse in either English or Scots has at one time or another been ascribed to him.

Speculation concerning Hucheon's identity has been equally intense. He is, perhaps, most commonly taken to be the Ayrshire knight Sir Hugh *Eglinton (d. 1376), mentioned by William Dunbar in his 'Lament for the Makaris', written between 1505 and 1508. Dunbar also refers to one 'Clerk of Tranent' as the author of 'The Anteris of Gaurane', suggesting either that there were two such works in existence or, more likely, that the authorship of the poem was open to question (there is no good reason to link Eglinton with the mysterious 'Clerk'). Wyntoun's designation 'of the Awle Ryale' (rendered in one manuscript as 'Auld Ryall') has proved just as contentious. Although it has usually been taken as a vernacular corruption of *aula regis*, this is by no means certain, and it cannot be considered proof that Hucheon was—like Eglinton—attached to the royal court. F. J. Amours has argued that Dunbar's 'gude Syr Hew' was not the fourteenth-century lord of that name but a cleric, possibly the chaplain of Dumbarton. Other proposals have included John Hucheon, a Kentish squire, a Northumbrian named Hugo de Aula of 'Ryhull' (either Ryal or Ryle), and a member of Oriel College, Oxford. What is clear is that if Hucheon was the author of the three works most credibly attributed to him, he was not a Scot. Recent scholarship suggests that *The Awntyres of Arthure at the Terne Wathelyne* and *The Pistil of Susan* are of English provenance, most probably deriving from the north or north-west of the country. This may help explain Hucheon's otherwise surprising omission from Dunbar's famous catalogue of Scottish 'makars'.

Because of the fragmentary nature of the evidence, Hucheon's canon and his identity remain highly elusive. Indeed, most modern scholars have abandoned what has become a largely sterile, at times ludicrous, debate. Nevertheless, Wyntoun's enigmatic references provide an important glimpse into the little understood literary culture of fourteenth-century Scotland, pointing to both the prominence of Arthurian romance within this tradition and the community of interest which extended north and south of the Anglo-Scottish border.   C. EDINGTON

Sources The 'Original chronicle' of Andrew of Wyntoun, ed. F. J. Amours, 6 vols., STS, 1st ser., 50, 53–4, 56–7, 63 (1903–14) • W. Geddie, *A bibliography of Middle Scots poets, with an introduction on the history of their reputations*, STS, 61 (1912) • F. J. Amours, ed., *Scottish alliterative poems in riming stanzas*, 2 vols., STS, 27 (1897); 38 (1897) • G. Neilson, 'Huchown of the Awle Ryale', the alliterative poet: a historical criticism of fourteenth century poems ascribed to Sir Hugh of Eglintoun (1902) • S. O. Andrew, 'Huchoun's works', *Review of English Studies*, 5 (1929), 12–21 • A. Miskimin, ed., *Susannah: an alliterative poem of the fourteenth century* (1969) • R. Hanna III, ed., *The awntyrs off Arthure at the terre Wathelyn: an edition based on Bodleian library MS Douce 324* (1974) • *William Dunbar: poems*, ed. J. Kinsley (1958) • *The poems of William Dunbar*, ed. J. Kinsley (1979) • *Morte Arthure, edited from Robert Thornton's MS in the library of Lincoln Cathedral*, ed. G. G. Perry, EETS, 8 (1865)

Huckell, John (*bap.* 1729, *d.* 1771), poet, son of Thomas Huckell (*d.* 1741), burgess of Stratford upon Avon, was baptized at Stratford, on 29 December 1729. His mother, whose name is unknown, died in December 1756. He studied at the grammar school of Stratford, matriculated at Magdalen Hall, Oxford, on 8 April 1747 and proceeded BA on 11 March 1751. He was presented to the curacy of Hounslow in Middlesex and to the chapel standing on the confines of two parishes, Heston and Isleworth. He resided at Isleworth.

Huckell's chief work, *Avon*, first appeared in 1758, printed 'in an elegant manner by the celebrated Baskerville', as claimed in the work's preface. It was reprinted in Stratford in 1811. Though *Avon* garnered generally positive reviews from contemporary critics and portions of it were reprinted in the *Gentleman's Magazine* and in Dodsley's *Annual Register* that year, it gained equal, or perhaps greater, attention as an early specimen of John Baskerville's typesetting. 'Avon is nothing but a Type', Thomas Gray remarked (letter to William Mason, 11 Aug 1758). Huckell reportedly wrote several songs for the 1769 Shakespeare Jubilee in Stratford, of which only his 'Epistle to David Garrick' survives. He died at Isleworth on 12 September 1771, and was buried there on 20 September.

     FRANCIS WATT, *rev.* JEFFREY HERRLE

Sources R. B. Wheeler, 'Biographical memoir of the Rev. John Huckell', *GM*, 1st ser., 83/1 (1813), 212–13 • *N&Q*, 2nd ser., 6 (1858), 91–2 • Foster, *Alum. Oxon.* • *Correspondence of Thomas Gray*, ed. P. Toynbee and L. Whibley, 2 (1935), 579–81 • J. Huckell, *Avon* (1758) • *GM*, 1st ser., 28 (1758), 282 • *GM*, 1st ser., 41 (1771), 427 • *Monthly Review*, 19 (1758), 272–6
Archives Bodl. Oxf., Malone Add. MS 36 b. 1 • NL Wales, letters to Mrs Baker

Huddart, James (1847–1901), shipowner, was born at Whitehaven, Cumberland, on 22 February 1847, the son of William Huddart, shipbuilder, of Whitehaven, and his wife, Frances Lindow. He was educated at St Bees College.

In 1860 Huddart went to Australia, where he joined the shipping firm of his uncle, Captain Peter Huddart of Geelong, Victoria, and received a commercial training. In 1866 his uncle left Australia, and Huddart took charge of the firm, then engaged in the coal trade between Geelong and Newcastle (New South Wales). On 1 September 1869 he married Lois Elizabeth, daughter of James Ingham of Ballarat, consulting engineer. He and his wife had three sons and a daughter. The youngest son, Midshipman Cymbeline A. E. Huddart of HMS *Doris*, was killed in the battle of Graspan in the Second South African War (25 November 1899), and was posthumously awarded the conspicuous service cross.

In 1876 Huddart was one of the founding partners of Huddart, Parker & Co., an intercolonial steamship line. In 1889 it became a limited liability company, Huddart Parker Proprietary Ltd, with a capital of £300,000. It grew to be one of Australia's leading shipping lines, with a fleet of modern steamers built in Britain. As it expanded, through Huddart's drive, the company came into conflict with several other major lines, particularly Union Steamship, with whom it fought several freight wars. In 1887 he returned to Britain, where he organized a new and improved passenger service between Australia and New Zealand. He was chairman of the Employers' Union during the Australian maritime strike in 1890.

One of Huddart's major objectives in the later years of his career was to establish the 'All Red Route'—a series of fast steamship lines which, with the help of the Canadian Pacific Railway, would link New Zealand, Australia, and Canada to Great Britain, and keep within the empire a large amount of trade which was being carried across foreign countries. He began work to this end in 1893 by starting a fast line of steamers, the Canadian–Australian Royal Mail Steamship Line, which ran between Sydney and Vancouver. The Canadian government voted a grant of £25,000 a year for the first ten years, and the government of New South Wales £10,000 per annum for three years. The co-operation of the Canadian Pacific Railway was secured, and the New Zealand government belatedly offered £7500 per annum.

The next step was a fast line between Canada and the UK. At Huddart's instigation a conference among all the colonies concerned was held at Ottawa in 1894. The project was an ambitious one, involving high quality steamships and requiring a large capital and it was determined that Great Britain should be asked to contribute a grant towards the service. Joseph Chamberlain, the colonial secretary, welcomed the scheme, but called for tenders, which were submitted in 1896 by Huddart and by the Allan Line. However, the scheme did not come to fruition, and in 1897 Huddart was forced to give up the project after sinking his private fortune in order to maintain it. He died on 27 February 1901 at his house, 2 Chatsworth Gardens, Southcliff, Eastbourne. He was buried in Ocklynge cemetery, Eastbourne, and was survived by his wife.

A. B. WHITE, *rev.* SIMON VILLE

Sources G. A. Hardwick, 'The centenary of Huddart Parker', *Royal Australian Historical Society Journal and Proceedings*, 63 (1977–8), 184–96 · *Huddart Parker Limited, 1876–1926*, Huddart Parker Ltd ([Melbourne], [1926]) · G. McLean, *The southern octopus: the rise of a shipping empire* (1990) · *The Times* (1 March 1901) · *The Times* (4 March 1901) · *Sydney Morning Herald* (1 March 1901) · *Sydney Mail* (9 March 1901) · private information (1912) · N. L. McKellar, *From Derby Round to Burke Town: the A.U.S.N. story* (1977) · *CGPLA Eng. & Wales* (1901) **Archives** USS Co. Archives, Wellington, New Zealand, Union Steamship Company MSS **Wealth at death** £181 11s. 5d.: probate, 13 July 1901, *CGPLA Eng. & Wales*

Huddart, Joseph (1741–1816), hydrographer and engineer, was born on 11 January 1741 at Allonby, Cumberland, the only child of William Huddart (1704–1762), farmer and shoemaker, and his wife, Rachel. Huddart attended school in Allonby under the local clergyman, a well-educated man who introduced him to astronomy. He showed particular ability in mathematics and practical mechanics, building a working model of flour milling machinery and, using Mungo Murray's *Treatise on Ship-Building* as his only guide, a detailed model of a 74-gun ship. His parents lived a simple life but Joseph had the advantage of wider contacts and support through a prosperous paternal uncle in London and friendship with the local landowning family, the Senhouses.

Huddart's seafaring career began in local fishing vessels in 1756 when his father and others set up a herring curing business. In his twenties he commanded coasting brigs in the cured fish and coal trades and then built, evidently largely with his own hands, the brig *Patience*, launched at Maryport in 1768. He was a part-owner and commanded her on several voyages to North America, earning a reputation as a fine navigator. He made his first voyage in East India Company service as fourth officer of the *York* (1773–5) at the instigation of the shipowner Sir Richard Hotham, his uncle's son-in-law. Between 1778 and 1788 he completed four further voyages to the East as commander of the East India Company ship *Royal Admiral*.

Throughout his time at sea Huddart drew charts and collected hydrographic information. His charts of Sumatra, the Cape of Good Hope, the Strait of Gaspar, and the approaches to Canton (Guangzhou) were published by Robert Sayer, who also commissioned a chart of the Irish Sea from him. He made an important series of observations fixing positions on the west coast of India and improved the sailing directions for the route to the East. He had a reputation as an extremely accurate observer of geographical positions and was quick to adopt the latest survey techniques.

On 16 July 1762 Huddart married Elizabeth Johnston, the daughter of a local landowner. Three of their five sons survived infancy but only one outlived him. His wife died

Joseph Huddart (1741–1816), by John Hoppner, in or before 1801

in 1786. On retirement from the sea Huddart took up residence in London, where he mixed with the scientific establishment of the day and, still full of vigour, applied his skills to a wide range of activities. His East India Company service had left him comfortably off and he was able to offer his services free, as he did in 1789 when he charted the west coast of Scotland for the British Society of Fisheries.

In 1790 Huddart surveyed Hasboro' Gat off the Norfolk coast for Trinity House and in 1791 was elected an elder brother of the corporation. For the next twenty years he was active in the designs and placing of new lighthouses, for which he prepared surveys, wrote sailing directions, and personally supervised building work. He was elected a fellow of the Royal Society in 1791, with sponsors headed by Alexander Dalrymple and James Rennell. His early paper on colour blindness had been read at the society in 1777 and in 1796 he contributed a paper on refraction.

Huddart became a prominent figure in the field of harbour engineering, to which he brought the experience of a practical seaman. In 1786 his opinion was sought on improving Maryport harbour and he was soon frequently consulted on similar projects. In 1794 he was elected to the Society of Civil Engineers and dined regularly with the leading members of the new young profession. Harbours and docks that he advised on included Whitehaven, Hull, Boston, Swansea, Portsmouth, Leith, Dublin, Woolwich, and Sheerness. On many of these he worked with John Rennie who evidently respected his opinion on marine work. In 1804 he arbitrated between rival schemes proposed for the Eau Brinck Cut on the River Great Ouse. He played a leading part in the construction of the London and East India docks. As a director of the London Dock Company he was jointly responsible with Robert Mylne and Rennie for the engineers' report of 1801 which laid down the general scheme of the docks. He was also a director of the East India Dock Company and served on both boards until shortly before his death.

Huddart had firsthand experience of the weakness of rope cables laid up in the traditional way and applied his mechanical inventiveness to designing rope-making machinery which strengthened the rope by adjusting the relative lengths of the strands so that all took an equal strain. In 1793 he took out the first of five patents connected with cordage manufacture and in 1800 with three others formed the partnership of Huddart & Co. to manufacture rope by his patent process. His machinery was described as among the finest of the time. The venture was a commercial success and made him a wealthy man.

Huddart found time for two other lifelong interests, experimental naval architecture and astronomy. With the aim of improving the speed of ships he conducted numerous experiments on the effect of friction on the motion of bodies in fluids. He built experimental vessels to test his theories but died before he could publish the results. He set up an astronomical observatory at his house in Highbury. He had a workshop with a forge and himself designed and constructed the ironwork for the fine 5 foot equatorial telescope he installed.

Captain Huddart, as he was always known, was described as a tall, upright, kind man of simple habits, who smoked a pipe. He combined intellectual understanding of mathematical theory with powers of patient investigation and practical skills, a combination which enabled him to excel in remarkably diverse fields. Although relatively little known to subsequent generations his contemporaries considered him an outstanding hydrographer and among the greatest engineers of the day. Huddart died at home at 12 Highbury Terrace, Highbury, Middlesex, on 19 August 1816 of a dropsy, of unknown underlying cause, and was buried in St Martin-in-the-Fields.　　　　SUSANNA FISHER

Sources J. Huddart, *Memoir of the late Captain Joseph Huddart* (1821) · W. Cotton, *A brief memoir of the late Captn. Joseph Huddart, FRS, and an account of his inventions in the manufacture of cordage* (1855) · W. Huddart, *Unpathed waters* (1989) · S. Fisher, 'Capt. Joseph Huddart's survey of the west coast of Scotland, 1789', *Scottish Geographical Magazine*, 107 (1991), 47–51 · log books of HEIC ships *York* and *Royal Admiral*, 1773–88, BL OIOC · minute books of East India and London Dock Companies, 1800–1816, Port of London Authority · J. Huddart, harbour reports, 1786–1804 · Cumbria AS, Carlisle, Senhouse papers · NL Scot., Rennie MSS · parish records, Bromfield, Cumbria AS · *The Times* (30 Aug 1816) · *GM*, 1st ser., 86/2 (1816) · J. Huddart, *Remarks on patent registered cordage* (1807) · J. Huddart, *On the improvement in manufacturing of cordage* (1804) · will, PRO, PROB 11/1583, IR 26/678, fol. 707

Archives BL, charts

Likenesses portrait on glass, 1785, priv. coll. · G. Dupont, group portrait, 1794 (with the Elder Brethren of Trinity House), Trinity House · J. Hoppner, oils, in or before 1801, priv. coll.; Christies, 19 Nov 1965, lot 63 [*see illus.*] · J. Stow, line engraving, pubd 1801 (after J. Hoppner), BM, NPG, RS · F. J. Skill, J. Gilbert, W. and E. Walker, group portrait, pencil and wash drawing, 1857–62 (*Men of science living in 1807–08*), NPG · Fontano, marble relief on memorial tablet, Christ Church, Allonby · J. Hoppner, portrait, second version, Inst. CE · engraving (after J. Hoppner), RS · oils (after J. Hoppner), Royal Institution of South Wales, Swansea · portrait, RS

Wealth at death under £60,000; also 7000 acres in Caernarvonshire: PRO, death duty registers IR 26/678, fol. 707

Huddesford, George (*bap.* 1749, *d.* 1809), satiric poet, was baptized at St Mary Magdalen Church, Oxford, on 7 December 1749, the youngest son of George Huddesford DD (1698/9–1776), president of Trinity College, Oxford, and his wife, Elizabeth. William *Huddesford (*bap.* 1732, *d.* 1772) was his elder brother. George Huddesford became a scholar of Winchester College in 1764, and matriculated at Trinity College, Oxford, on 15 January 1768. On 8 May 1769 he was elected a scholar of New College, Oxford, where he graduated BA in 1779 and MA in 1780. He became a fellow on 8 May 1771, but vacated his fellowship soon afterwards, when he married impulsively in August 1772. A note against his name in a list of the members of the college adds: *Amatricem Londini juvenile amore correptus præpropere duxit* ('he married his girlfriend hastily in London, carried away by youthful passion'; *Poems of John Bampfylde*, 20). After Oxford Huddesford studied painting, and was a pupil of Sir Joshua Reynolds. By 1775 he had exhibited three pictures at the Royal Academy exhibition. In 1778 Reynolds painted Mrs Huddesford, and Huddesford then commissioned a double portrait of himself and John Bampfylde. This painting, entitled *Portraits of Two Gentlemen*, is described in Cook's *Popular Handbook* as 'A charming portrait of two young connoisseurs of the time ... shown as kindred spirits, brought together by their common love of the arts' (Cook, 2.247).

Huddesford was already developing his literary skills, and his first literary production was *Warley, a Satire*, published anonymously in 1778, which ridiculed the military reviews at Warley in Essex. As it was dedicated to Reynolds, it soon came to the attention of his friends. Fanny Burney called it 'This vile Poem' (*Letters*, 3.193) and was much distressed at its revelation of her authorship of *Evelina* and its use of Samuel Johnson's private description of her as 'dear little Burney' (ibid., 193 n.). Huddesford also edited and was the principal contributor to *Salmagundi: a Miscellaneous Combination of Original Poetry* published anonymously in 1791, which was followed by an attack on French politics in *Topsy Turvy: with Anecdotes and Observations Illustrative of the Present Government of France*, published anonymously in 1793. Other works include: *Bubble and squeak: a gallimaufry of British beef with the chopp'd cabbage of Gallic philosophy and radical reform* (published anonymously, 1799); *Crambe repetita, a Second Course of Bubble and Squeak* (published anonymously, 1799); and *Les champignons du diable, or, Imperial Mushrooms* (1805). A collected edition of his works appeared in two volumes in 1801. Huddesford subsequently published two satires on the Middlesex election in 1802 and the duke of Northumberland's neutrality, the second of which was entitled *Wood and Stone, or, A Dialogue between a Wooden Duke and Stone Lion*. In 1804 he edited a volume of poems written by boys who were his contemporaries at Winchester, which he called the

George Huddesford (*bap.* 1749, *d.* 1809), by Sir Joshua Reynolds, 1778 [left, with John Codrington Warwick Bampfylde]

Wiccamical Chaplet. He is also credited with the authorship of 'Bonaparte: an Heroic Ballad'.

With many influential connections in the church Huddesford eventually took holy orders. He became vicar of Loxley in Warwickshire on 21 October 1803, and was incumbent of Sir George Wheler's chapel, Spital Square, London. He died in London in November 1809.

W. P. COURTNEY, *rev.* S. C. BUSHELL

Sources *GM*, 1st ser., 79 (1809), 1238 · *The poems of John Bampfylde*, ed. R. Lonsdale (1988), 20–21 · *The early journals and letters of Fanny Burney*, ed. L. E. Troide, 3: *The Streatham years, part 1, 1778–1779* (1994), 193 n., 210, 218–19, 221, 224 · Foster, *Alum. Oxon.* · C. R. Leslie and T. Taylor, *Life and times of Sir Joshua Reynolds*, 2 (1865), 126, 224, 228 · *N&Q*, 6th ser., 11 (1885), 148 · *N&Q*, 6th ser., 11 (1885), 198 · E. T. Cook, *A popular handbook to the National Gallery*, 8th edn, 2 (1912), 247–8 · *English Illustrated Magazine*, 8 (1890–91), 72, 92 · T. F. Kirby, *Winchester scholars: a list of the wardens, fellows, and scholars of … Winchester College* (1888), 259 · J. Peshall, *Antient and present state of the city of Oxford* (1708), 228
Likenesses J. Reynolds, double portrait, oils, 1778 (with J. C. W. Bampfylde), Tate collection [*see illus.*] · W. B. Gardner, engraving (after J. Reynolds), repro. in *English Illustrated Magazine*, 72 · G. Huddesford, self-portrait, oils, New College, Oxford · attrib. J. Miller, group portrait (as Sancho Panza in *Don Quixote*), Trinity College, Oxford

Huddesford, William (*bap.* 1732, *d.* 1772), museum curator, was baptized on 15 August 1732 at St Mary Magdalen, Oxford, the eldest son of George Huddesford (1698/9–1776), president of Trinity College, Oxford, and his first wife, whose family origins are uncertain. His youngest half-brother, George *Huddesford (*bap.* 1749, *d.* 1809), achieved distinction as a poet. William attended Abingdon School under Thomas Woods and on 20 October 1749

matriculated from Trinity College, Oxford, where he was elected scholar in 1750 and fellow in 1757. He graduated BA in 1753, MA in 1756, and BD in 1757. In 1758 he was ordained and served as curate in his father's living of Garsington, near Oxford: in 1761 he was appointed vicar of Bishop's Tachbrook, Warwickshire, a living in his uncle's gift. He served as university proctor in 1765.

In 1755, at twenty-three, Huddesford succeeded his father as keeper of the Ashmolean Museum. Previous eighteenth-century keepers had been notoriously casual in the discharge of their duties, and by 1755 the museum was regarded as a mere assemblage of curiosities, subject to casual plunderings. Huddesford aimed to restore the Ashmolean's reputation as a centre for scientific teaching and research, in accordance with the founders' intentions. He worked vigorously and persistently to this end, recommencing the classification of the collections, the compilation of catalogues, and the keeping of records, and, in addition, corresponding with enquirers; he also took full advantage of the visitors' permission 'to remove the decay'd and trifling things which will show the valuable ones in a much better light' (MS Ashmole 1822, fol. vii). Among the 'decay'd' objects condemned in this clearance were two dodos—some fragments of which, however, survived to find a home in the University Museum, where they inspired an episode in *Alice in Wonderland*.

In the early stages of his work Huddesford cautiously sought advice and approval from scholars such as William Borlase, Smart Lethieullier, and Emanuel Mendes da Costa, with whom he corresponded and whose collections he studied. The scale of his improvements to the museum was evident from a letter da Costa wrote in 1758 expressing his delight at seeing the Lhuyd collection of fossils, '(before so vilely neglected) so well arranged and order'd, as they now are by you' (MS Ashmole 1822, fol. lvi). Huddesford's interest in fossils seems, in fact, to have been motivated more by a passion for order than by any particular scientific bent, and while his work on the collections was of subsequent assistance to later scholars he was not himself concerned with speculations about the significance of the fossils which he arranged. His reforms secured not only the admiration of the learned but also, more importantly, a resumption in benefactions to the Ashmolean. However, the museum seems to have become less popular with the general public, since receipts from admissions fell during Huddesford's keepership.

In 1760 Huddesford published, at his own expense, a major revision of Edward Lhuyd's catalogue of his collection, *Lithophylacii Britannici ichnographia*; Lhuyd had been keeper between 1691 and 1709, and his work on fossils had contributed largely to the early reputation of the Ashmolean. Ten years later, in 1770, Huddesford brought out a revision of Martin Lister's catalogue of sea-shells, *Historia sive synopsis methodica conchyliorum*, again based on material in the Ashmolean; he gave the new edition an index based on the Linnaean system, in addition to the one which Lister had devised. Out of modesty Huddesford declined to claim authorship of these two works of scholarship, but together they made a significant contribution to the development of scientific methodology.

The contents of the Ashmolean at this time included manuscripts, and Edward Lhuyd was a noted antiquary as well as a naturalist. Huddesford's immersion in Lhuyd's interests led him to compose or edit biographical studies of several antiquaries, including Lhuyd himself, John Leland, and Thomas Hearne, but he disclaimed any special antiquarian expertise and rejected an offer of election to the Society of Antiquaries. In 1761 he published a catalogue of the manuscripts of the Oxford antiquarian and memorialist Anthony Wood, *Catalogus librorum manuscriptum vivi clarissimi Antonii a Wood*, of whom he wrote a brief biography which appeared in Bliss's 1813 edition of *Athenae Oxonienses*. Fellow-feeling was evident in his remark 'The examination and digesting of the records, … consisting of various donations, purchases, assignments, leases, all of these, perhaps, lying in confusion and disorder, require a large portion of time and industry' (Wood, *Ath. Oxon.*, 1.135).

If the routines of curatorship inhibited Huddesford's scholarly aspirations, so his taste for connoisseurship was restrained by his conscientiousness in discharging parish, college, and university responsibilities. As he wrote ruefully in a letter of 1769, he could fancy himself 'an Antiquarian and a Connoisseur; but, for some time to come, my work will be to prove that two and two makes four, and to dun poor innocent children for their battells' (*Letters*, 143). His sense of humour survived these pressures, however, and he was valued by his friends for his whimsical letters and for such gentle literary excursions as his *Address to the Freemen and other Inhabitants of the City of Oxford* (1764), a mild satire on the city's lighting problems.

After 1770 Huddesford's health seems to have been weak, and in February 1772 he wrote 'I have gone through a great deal of pain, and some sharp operations' (*Letters*, 147). He died suddenly at Coventry on 6 October 1772, of a 'scorbutic humour … upon his brain' (ibid., 151), and was buried close to the south wall of the chancel at St Mary's, Garsington. 'He had many works in eye' (Nichols, *Lit. anecdotes*, 8.600) at the time of his death and left some manuscript remains, together with a modest fortune invested in government funds.   M. ST JOHN PARKER

Sources letters to William Huddesford, 1755–72, Bodl. Oxf., MS Ashmole 1822 · *Letters between Rev. James Granger … and many of the most eminent literary men of his time*, ed. J. P. Malcom (1805), 136–51 · R. F. Ovenell, *The Ashmolean Museum, 1683–1894* (1986) · Nichols, *Lit. anecdotes*, 5.291, 296; 8.600 · Nichols, *Illustrations*, 3.667; 4.456–80; 6.473 · Wood, *Ath. Oxon.*, new edn, 1.135–8 · A. MacGregor, ed., *Tradescant's rarities: essays on the foundation of the Ashmolean Museum* (1983) · A. G. MacGregor and A. J. Turner, 'The Ashmolean Museum', *Hist. U. Oxf.* 5: *18th-cent. Oxf.*, 639–58 · M. E. Jahn, 'The Ashmolean Museum and the Lhuyd collections', *Journal of the Society of the Bibliography of Natural History*, 4 (1962–8) · K. C. Davies and J. Hull, *The zoological collection of the Oxford University Museum* (1976) · *An address to the freemen and other inhabitants of the city of Oxford* (1764) · parish register, 15/8/1732, Oxford, St Mary Magdalen [baptism] · *Jackson's Oxford Journal* (10 Oct 1772) · will, PRO, PROB 11/982, fols. 277v–281r · *DNB* · Foster, *Alum. Oxon.*

Archives BL, notes and papers, Add. MS 22596 · Bodl. Oxf., corresp., MS Ashmole 1822 | BL, corresp. with Emanuel Mendes da Costa, Add. MS 28538 · Bodl. Oxf., letters to Samuel Pegge, MSS Eng. letters d.43

Wealth at death £1283 invested in 3 per cent consolidated stock: will, PRO, PROB 11/982, fols. 277v–281r

Huddleston, Sir Hubert Jervoise (1880–1950), army officer and colonial administrator, was born at Thurston, Suffolk, on 20 January 1880, the second son of Thomas Jervoise Huddleston (1841/2–1885), of Little Haugh, Norton, Suffolk, who had a distinguished career at Eton College and Christ Church, Oxford. His mother, Laura Josselyn, was a sister of Colonel F. Josselyn, chief constable of Bedford.

Huddleston was educated at Bedford School and Felsted School (1892–7). Determined to join the army, he enlisted in the Coldstream Guards in 1898 and in 1900 was drafted to the 2nd battalion and sent to South Africa. In May 1900 he was commissioned second lieutenant in the Dorsetshire regiment (lieutenant November 1901). He was mentioned in dispatches. From 1903 to 1908 he served with the West African frontier force, and in 1909, with the rank of captain (April 1909), he went to the Sudan. At first he was employed in administration in the turbulent district of the Nuba mountains, but at his own request he joined the 10th Sudanese battalion, Egyptian army, and took part, in 1910 and 1914, in punitive expeditions in the same area (MC 1914).

After the outbreak of the First World War Huddleston commanded the Egyptian army camel corps, one of its finest units, and played a leading part in the 1916 Darfur campaign. Following years of friction with the Sudan government, in 1915 Ali Dinar, sultan of the old slaving state of Darfur—an autonomous tributary state, since the reconquest unvisited by Sudan officials, west of the Kordofan administrative frontier and adjoining French territory—had renounced allegiance to the Sudan. Sir Reginald Wingate (governor-general, 1899–1916) decided to conquer Darfur. In 1916 he sent a force commanded by Lieutenant-Colonel P. V. Kelly—with three aeroplanes borrowed from the general officer commanding, Egypt—which invaded Darfur, defeated the sultan's army, and captured his capital, al-Fasher, on 23 May 1916. Huddleston, sent to establish a post at Dibbis, took the initiative, followed Ali Dinar into the far south, and on 6 November led the dawn attack in which Ali Dinar was killed. This ended the campaign, and at the close of 1916 Huddleston temporarily left the Egyptian army and commanded a brigade during the campaign of Sir Edmund Allenby in Palestine. Huddleston was appointed DSO in 1917 after the Darfur campaign and CMG in 1918 after the Palestine campaign. He held staff appointments in Iraq and Persia, and in 1922 was back in Egypt where disturbances had broken out. He rejoined the Egyptian army in 1923 as chief staff officer and adjutant-general under Sir Lee Stack, the sirdar and governor-general of the Sudan. When Stack was murdered in Cairo in November 1924 Huddleston enforced the evacuation of the Sudan by Egyptian troops and suppressed the Egyptian-instigated mutiny in Khartoum of the 11th Sudanese battalion: when they refused to obey he ordered his contingent of Argyll and Sutherland High-landers to open fire. In 1925 the Sudanese and Arab units were reorganized as the Sudan defence force with Huddleston, who was appointed CB (1925), as its first commandant (kaid el 'amm) with the local rank of major-general. He held this post, and that of general officer commanding, Sudan, until 1930. The Sudanese called him 'the hyena with white feet' (Hanes, 250) because of his penchant for night marches and white spats. As a member of the governor-general's council during this period he became familiar with political and administrative problems. In 1928 Huddleston married Constance Eila, daughter of the late Frederick Hugh Mackenzie Corbet, advocate-general of Madras; they had one daughter.

In late 1930 Huddleston left the Sudan to command the 14th infantry brigade. He was promoted major-general in 1933, and from 1934 to 1938 commanded districts in India. He was then placed on retired pay and appointed lieutenant-governor of the Royal Hospital, Chelsea, but he was recalled to active service in 1940 and became general officer commanding, Northern Ireland district. In late 1940 he was appointed governor-general of the Sudan, under threat of an Italian invasion from Eritrea, until the British victory at Keren (15 March 1941). Probably no better appointment could have been made, for he was honoured and respected throughout the Sudan. For seven years he held this post, countering Egyptian claims and intrigues, and maintaining with determination the rights of the Sudanese to eventual self-government. With Douglas Newbold (civil secretary 1939–45) he established a nominated advisory council of the northern Sudan, inaugurated in May 1944, but it failed to satisfy the northern politicians. Huddleston shared the Sudan political service belief, reinforced by his own experience in 1924, that the Sudanese should be advanced to eventual independence and the Egyptians, whom he considered despotic and corrupt, should be excluded. He publicly pronounced in favour of Sudanese independence in April 1946. In 1946 Ernest Bevin and the Foreign Office were attempting to gain a military alliance with Egypt to underpin British strategy in the Middle East. So the Attlee government decided to formally recognize Egyptian sovereignty over the Sudan, and this was embodied in the Sidqui–Bevin protocol (October 1946), viewed by Huddleston and others in the Sudan as a betrayal. By his stubborn rearguard action, insisting on Sudanese self-determination, he contributed to the 1947 failure of the Anglo-Egyptian negotiations. He had a key role in securing Sudanese independence, but insufficiently addressed the crucial long-term problem of safeguarding the peoples of the southern Sudan from exploitation and repression by the northern Sudanese.

Huddleston was promoted KCMG in 1940, and appointed GBE in 1946; he was colonel of the Dorsetshire regiment from 1933 to 1946. In March 1947 he 'resigned'. In fact he wanted to continue but was in effect dismissed. Bevin wanted him to be given 'at least a barony' (Hanes, 267) to show his 'retirement' was not in disgrace, but Attlee refused anything more than GCMG (1947). In 1948 he

was chairman of the Old Felstedian dinner. He died of cancer at his home, 7 Cleveland Row, St James's, London, on 2 October 1950, and was survived by Lady Huddleston. One of the last imperial proconsuls, Huddleston had a commanding personality. His main characteristics were his 'straightness and simplicity, his strength of character and courage …; his modesty and kindness … with a whimsical sense of humour, brought affection. He was a great reader with a variegated store of knowledge' (DNB).

ROGER T. STEARN

Sources DNB · war office records, PRO · G. MacMunn and C. Falls, Military operations: Egypt and Palestine, 3 vols., History of the Great War (1928–30) · private information (1959) · personal knowledge (1959) [DNB] · WWW · Burke, Peerage (1949) · W. T. Hanes III, 'Sir Hubert Huddleston and the independence of the Sudan', Journal of Imperial and Commonwealth History, 20 (1992), 248–73 · P. M. Holt, A modern history of the Sudan (1972) · R. Wingate, Wingate of the Sudan: the life and times of General Sir Reginald Wingate (1955) · Foster, Alum. Oxon. · C. Chittock and others, eds., Alumni Felstedienses: being a list of boys entered at Felsted School, April 1890 – September 1950, 7th edn (1951) · Hart's Army List (1913)
Wealth at death £49,345 3s. 8d.: probate, 28 Dec 1950, CGPLA Eng. & Wales

Huddleston, John (1608–1698), Benedictine monk, was born at Farington Hall, Leyland, Lancashire, in April 1608, the second son of Joseph Huddleston of Farington Hall and Hutton John, Greystoke, Cumberland, and his wife, Eleanor Sisson, second daughter of Cuthbert Sisson of Kirkbarrow, Westmorland, 'impoverished by persecution and the care of 11 children'. He was educated in humanities at Blencow grammar school, Cumberland, 'under a heretical teacher'. He then returned home and later lived in London and Yorkshire 'at his parents' whim'. Aged nineteen he studied in the class of syntax at the Jesuit college at St Omer on the advice of his priest uncle. In 1632 he began to study philosophy and theology at the English College, Rome, in preparation for ordination, although Dodd maintained that he studied, and was ordained, at the English College, Douai.

After being ordained a secular priest Huddleston returned to England in May 1639. He served as chaplain to a number of Catholic families, including the Prestons of the manor, Furness, between 1639 and 1645, Danby Hall, or Grove House, in Wensleydale (seat of the Thornboroughs), and the Ingelbys of west Yorkshire, before returning to the manor in 1648 and remaining there until early 1651. Later that year he became chaplain to the Whitgreaves at Moseley House in Staffordshire. At Moseley he acted as tutor to young gentlemen, and it was there that he met the future Charles II, who went there disguised as a peasant after his defeat at the battle of Worcester on 3 September 1651. Huddleston was in constant attendance on Charles during this time, sheltering him in his chamber and guarding him from his opponents, and when in danger hiding him in the house's priest's hole. During the royal residence Huddleston stationed his pupils at the garret windows as sentinels. In return Charles promised to remember his good services when he became king. About 1653, perhaps influenced by his Benedictine uncle Richard Huddleston (1583–1655), Huddleston was professed on

John Huddleston (1608–1698), by Jacob Huysmans, 1685

the English mission as a Benedictine monk, probably for the abbey of Lambspring, near Hildesheim. He took the name Denis or Dionysius, and was granted nine years' seniority. Both he and his family were to remain generous benefactors of Lambspring. An educational bursary for the Huddleston family was established there in 1684.

At the restoration of the monarchy the king fulfilled his promise by inviting Huddleston to join the court at Somerset House, where he enjoyed the protection of the queen-dowager. In 1661, at the Benedictine general chapter, he was elected to the cathedral priorship of Worcester. Between 1664 and 1685 he officiated at marriages in the chapels royal in St James's Palace and Somerset House. On Henrietta Maria's death in 1669 he became chaplain to Queen Catherine of Braganza and a member of her household, with a salary of £100 and a pension of a similar amount. During some of this time he lived with the Benedictine Thomas Vincent Sadler in a house called Amsterdam Court in Oxford, where he met Anthony Wood, who succeeded in persuading him to write up his experiences during Charles II's escape. On account of his service to the king after the battle of Worcester he was specifically exempted from the terms of the statute of 27 Elizabeth, aimed at Catholic priests, which was revived on 20 November 1678 in the aftermath of the anti-popery scare prompted by Titus Oates. He achieved some notoriety when he was brought through the queen's backstairs by the duke of York to the deathbed of Charles II on 5 February 1685. At the king's request, because he had been 'so instrumental in his preservation in the tree and now hopes he would preserve his soul', he heard the dying king's confession, administered extreme unction and the viaticum, and reconciled him to the Catholic church.

At the accession of James II in 1685 Huddleston became superintendent of the chapel of Somerset House and was deputed by the Benedictine general chapter to inform the king of its proceedings and to await the royal orders. During a royal progress of James, he was in charge of preparations at Bath Abbey for the ceremony of touching for the king's evil, and there preached a proselytizing sermon. In James's reign a number of his court sermons were published, and he edited in 1688 Richard Huddleston's *Short and Plain Way to the Faith and Church*, which had been circulating in manuscript for some years and had impressed Charles II, who had found the manuscript lying on the chaplain's table at Moseley. To this he annexed the papers of Charles II 'found in his Closet upon his Decease', and his own account of the king's deathbed conversion. The papers revealed the king's Catholic sympathies over many years, and caused some controversy since their authenticity was disputed.

On her retirement to Portugal in 1692 Catherine of Braganza put Huddleston into the care of the recent Catholic convert, Lord Feversham, who went up to the leads of the roof and found him alone and quite senile, though he was able to make his will, dated 30 January 1693. He died at Somerset House 'in senectute bona' in late September 1698. The royal confidence he enjoyed for so long brought Huddleston some fame and he became the model for Father John Ingoldsby in Richard Barham's nineteenth-century romantic work *The Ingoldsby Legends.*

GEOFFREY SCOTT

Sources D. Lunn, *The English Benedictines, 1540–1688* (1980) · A. Kenny, 'John Huddleston', *Biographical Studies*, 1 (1951–2), 168–88, 253–60 · G. Anstruther, 'Abstracts of wills—IV', *London Recusant*, 5/1 (1975), 4 · J. Gillow, ed., 'The Huddleston obituaries', *Miscellanea, I,* Catholic RS, 1 (1905), 123–32 · J. P. Smith, ed., *The Lancashire registers,* 3, Catholic RS, 20 (1916) · J. S. Hansom and J. Gillow, 'Catholic registers of Danby, West Witton and Leyburn, Yorkshire, 1742–1840, with notes of the Scrope family, 1663–1754', *Miscellanea, VIII,* Catholic RS, 13 (1913), 227–87, esp. 233 · Gillow, *Lit. biog. hist.,* 3.463–5 · 'Catholic chapels in Staffordshire', *The Catholic Magazine,* 5, no. 41 (June 1834), 391–3 · J. C. M. Weale, ed., *Registers of the Catholic chapels royal and of the Portuguese embassy chapel, 1662–1829,* Catholic RS, 38 (1941) · A. Kenny, ed., *The responsa scholarum of the English College, Rome,* 2, Catholic RS, 55 (1963) · B. Weldon, 'Memorials', Douai Abbey, Woolhampton, Berkshire, English Benedictine Congregation Archives, 1.373–80, 2.530–34, 4.2, 5.321 · C. Dodd [H. Tootell], *The church history of England, from the year 1500, to the year 1688,* 3 (1742), 490

Archives Douai Abbey, Woolhampton, Berkshire, B. Weldon, 'Memorials'

Likenesses J. Huysmans, oils, 1685, priv. coll. [*see illus.*] · Keating, Brown & Co., engraving, repro. in *Laity's Directory* (1816) · oils (after type by J. Huysmans, 1685), Ampleforth College, York

Wealth at death see will, Anstruther, 'Abstracts of wills—IV'

Huddleston [*alias* Dormer, Shirley], **John** (1636–1700), Jesuit, was born on 27 December 1636 in the village of Clavering, Essex, the son of Sir Robert Huddleston. He was brought up in London until the age of twelve. In 1649 he was sent to the English College, St Omer, where he remained until he entered the English College, Rome, on 9 September 1655 under the alias Shirley. He left Rome to join the noviciate at Bonn in 1656, was probably ordained in 1669 and was at the English College in Liège in 1670–72.

He left for the English mission in 1673 and lived in the College of St Thomas (1673-4), the College of St Ignatius (1674-5), and the College of St Hugh (1676-8). In 1678 he was serving on the mission at Blyborough in Lincolnshire. He published *A New Plot* (1679) defending the martyrs of the Popish Plot, and wrote *A Brief Instruction Touching the Oath of Allegiance* directed against the oath. He appears in Paris in 1681-2 and at Liège in 1683. He returned to England, to the College of St Hugh, in 1684. James II had a great regard for him and appointed him one of the royal preachers at the court of St James. Several of his sermons between 1686 and 1688 were published, including a call to repentance in *A Sermon of Judgement* (1688) and *Rebellion Arraign'd* (1688), preached on the anniversary of the execution of Charles I and condemning the use of religion as a justification for rebellion. On the outbreak of the revolution in 1688 he escaped to the continent and was chosen rector of the college at Liège on 4 November 1689. His government of the college was criticized and he left Liège on 23 April 1691 and returned to England, living mostly in the College of St Ignatius, covering the London district. His *Usury Explain'd, or, Conscience Quieted in the Case of Putting out Mony at Interest* (1695-6), published under the name Philopenes, may have been written against Bishop James Smith's treatise on the subject and was condemned by the Holy Office in 1703. He died in London on 16 January 1700.

THOMPSON COOPER, *rev.* RUTH JORDAN

Sources Gillow, *Lit. biog. hist.*, 3.460-62 • G. Holt, *The English Jesuits, 1650-1829: a biographical dictionary*, Catholic RS, 70 (1984) • D. A. Bellenger, ed., *English and Welsh priests, 1558-1800* (1984) • G. Holt, *St Omers and Bruges colleges, 1593-1773: a biographical dictionary*, Catholic RS, 69 (1979), 87 • T. H. Clancy, *English Catholic books, 1641-1700: a bibliography*, rev. edn (1996), 84-5 • G. Oliver, *Collections towards illustrating the biographies of the Scotch, English and Irish members of the Society of Jesus*, 2nd edn (1845), 267 • T. H. Clancy, *A literary history of the English Jesuits: a century of books, 1615-1714* (1996)
Archives Kirk biographical collections, no. 16

Huddleston, Sir John Walter (1815-1890), judge, eldest son of Thomas Huddleston, captain in the merchant service, and his wife, Alethea, daughter of H. Hichens of St Ives, Cornwall, was born in Dublin on 8 September 1815. He was educated in Ireland, and matriculated at Trinity College, Dublin, on 5 January 1835. He did not graduate and after some time spent as usher in a school in England, he entered Gray's Inn on 18 April 1836, and was called to the bar by that society on 7 May 1839. He went on the Oxford circuit, and attended the Worcester and Staffordshire sessions. He also practised at the Middlesex sessions, where he chiefly argued poor-law cases, and at the Old Bailey. There and on circuit he gradually acquired an extensive criminal practice. He appeared for the prosecution in the trial of William Palmer, 'the Rugeley poisoner', in May 1856 and was engaged in many other *causes célèbres*, in which he distinguished himself in cross-examination, and by the lucidity with which he presented his points to the jury. He took silk in 1857, and was elected a bencher of his inn, of which he was treasurer in 1859 and 1868.

After unsuccessfully contesting several constituencies, he was elected Conservative MP for Canterbury in 1865. Unseated at the election of 1868, he contested Norwich

unsuccessfully in 1870, and successfully in 1874. On 18 December 1872 he married Lady Diana de Vere Beauclerk (*d.* 1905), daughter of William Aubrey de Vere Beauclerk, ninth duke of St Albans.

Huddleston was judge-advocate of the fleet from 1865 to 1875, when, on 22 February, he was called to the degree of serjeant-at-law, raised to the bench of the Common Pleas, and knighted. On 12 May he was transferred to the exchequer. On the passing of the Judicature Act of 1875 the court of exchequer became the Exchequer Division of the High Court of justice, and it was decided that the style of baron of the exchequer should lapse on the death of the existing holders of the title. Huddleston's patent was the last issued, and he was accustomed on that account to call himself 'the last of the barons'. On the consolidation of the Exchequer with the Queen's Bench Division in 1880, he became a judge of the latter division, still, however, retaining the style of baron. It was thought by his contemporaries that he was greater as an advocate than as a judge. During the last ten years of his life he suffered from a chronic and painful disease, and heavy cases severely tried his health. He died at his town house, 43 Ennismore Gardens, South Kensington, on 5 December 1890, and was cremated at Brookwood cemetery, Woking, on 12 December.

Huddleston was an accomplished man, and well read in French literature. He also spoke French with ease and grace: in 1868, as the representative of the English bar, he made a speech in Paris over the bier of the great French advocate Pierre Antoine Berryer. Huddleston was also a lively conversationalist, a lover of the theatre, and an authority on horse-racing.

J. M. RIGG, *rev.* ERIC METCALFE

Sources *WWBMP*, vol. 1 • Boase, *Mod. Eng. biog.* • *The Times* (6 Dec 1890) • *The Times* (9 Dec 1890) • *The Times* (12 Dec 1890) • *Law Times* (20 Dec 1890) • *Men of the time* (1879) • C. Shaw, *Inns of court calendar*, 2 vols. (1877-8) • *Annual Register* (1848) • *Chronicle* (1860), 39 • *Law reports: appeal cases*, 12 (1887), xvii • *Hansard 3* (1853) • Burke, *Peerage* • W. Ballantine, *Some experiences of a barrister's life*, new edn (1890), 29
Likenesses S. Evans, sketch, 1877, NPG • H. W. Petherick, etching, 1884, NPG • F. Holl, oils, 1888, NPG • Lock & Whitfield, woodburytype photograph, NPG; repro. in T. Cooper, *Men of mark: a gallery of contemporary portraits* (1876) • Walery, photograph, NPG • oils, Harvard U., law library • portrait, repro. in *Pump Court* (1884), 135 • portrait, repro. in *The Graphic* (13 Dec 1890), 667 • portrait, repro. in *ILN*, 66 (1875), 229 • two portraits, Royal Courts of Justice, Judge's common room
Wealth at death £64,330 12s. 7d.: resworn probate, June 1891, CGPLA Eng. & Wales

Huddleston [Hudleston], **Richard** (1583-1655), Benedictine monk, was born at Farington Hall, Leyland, Lancashire, the youngest son of Andrew Huddleston, esquire, and his wife, Mary, third daughter of Cuthbert Hutton of Hutton John, Greystoke, Cumberland. He was educated by the future Catholic martyr, Thomas Somers (*d.* 1610), who was executed alongside the Benedictine John Roberts, and was taught in the house of the earl of Westmorland and by the English Jesuits at St Omer. He entered the English College, Douai, on 6 March 1599 and was sent to Rome in September 1601. He entered the English College on 21 October

1601 but returned ill to Douai on 22 April 1606. He was in Lancashire as a mission priest by March 1610 but about 1613 he was professed as a monk of Montecassino, perhaps while still in England (Lunn, 159). Certainly by 1619 he was again active on the English mission where he was a noted proselytizer. He 'laboured incessantly in his vocation and exerted his talents in preaching, teaching, disputing and reducing his strayed countrymen to the fold of Christ' (Allanson, 1.143). He was particularly successful as a converter of the aristocratic families 'such as the Irelands, Watertons, Middletons, Trappes, Thimblelyes in Yorkshire, the Prestons, Andertons, Downss, Straffords, Sherburns, Inglebyes in Lancashire' as well as 'numberless others of all states and conditions' (ibid.).

Huddleston was the author of *A Short and Plain Way to the Faith and Church*, which Charles II read in manuscript when hiding at Moseley House after his defeat at Worcester. When it was published posthumously in London in 1688 (reprinted in Dublin the same year) by his nephew and fellow Benedictine John Huddleston it included an account of the king's escape and conversion. He was also the author of a short life of the Catholic divine Richard Bristow included in volume 3 of Bristow's *Motiva* (1616). Huddleston died at Stockeld Park, Ilkley, Yorkshire, the seat of the Middletons, on 26 November 1655.

THOMPSON COOPER, *rev.* DOMINIC AIDAN BELLENGER

Sources A. Allanson, 'Biography of the English Benedictines', 2 vols., 1850, Downside Abbey · D. Lunn, *The English Benedictines, 1540–1688* (1980) · G. Anstruther, *The seminary priests*, 2 (1975) · T. H. Clancy, *English Catholic books, 1641–1700: a bibliography* [1974]

Huddleston, Robert (1814–1887), poet, was born at Moneyreagh, co. Down, the son of a small farmer. Few details can be ascertained concerning his upbringing and early life. His marital status is uncertain: though he frequently adopts the persona of the young (or not so young) suitor, at least one semi-autobiographical poem, 'Epistle to Mr John Pettigrew', mentions an 'auld guid dame' (*Poems and Songs on Different Subjects*, 51). He had little formal schooling, having attended a local school in Moneyreagh for only a few years, and is at pains to point out that he is no scholar and that standard literary English is not his natural medium: 'I can neither read Hebrew, Greek, Latin, or French. Thank my stars, I can read English a kind of a way, but to write it correctly, I fear, I would blunder' (ibid., x). Far from this proving an impediment, he professes to prefer 'the common-place illiterate school learning of a mere homely peasant' to the attainments of 'highly educated gentlemen' (*Poems and Songs on Rural Subjects*, iv). Thus his work possesses the eccentricity characteristic of the autodidact.

From the early 1840s Huddleston began to contribute poems to local newspapers and periodicals. In 1843 he issued a florid prospectus and began to solicit subscriptions. His first volume, *A Collection of Poems and Songs on Rural Subjects*, appeared the following year, but a disagreement with his publisher over the printing costs followed, when some subscribers defaulted. Undaunted, he saw a second volume through the press in 1846, *A Collection of Poems and Songs on Different Subjects*. This too met with a lukewarm reception. Disillusioned by the fact that his poetic genius had not been recognized, he turned his attentions to prose, planning to rival William Carleton as a great Ulster novelist. He was following the example of the Larne poet James McHenry (1785–1845), who had published successful novels in Philadelphia before returning to Belfast. In 1860 Huddleston issued a prospectus for a work entitled *The Adventures of Hughey Funny, or, The many Tales of Love*, but once again quarrelled with his publisher. He turned again to poetry and contributed a few poems in the *Ulster Magazine* (1860–63), but much of his work after 1846 remains unpublished.

According to J. Hewitt, Huddleston was one of the last folk-bards of Ulster (Hewitt, 54). He was a strong defender of the use of vernacular Ulster Scots, which he termed 'Ulster Irish' (*Poems and Songs on Rural Subjects*, ix). He was equally vehement in his rejection of the charge of imitating Robert Burns. Never one to exercise false modesty, he believed that Burns was overestimated to the same degree that Huddleston was underestimated. 'Though I may not be a Robert Burns to the lowland Scottish peasantry, let me hope, at least, that I shall one day be a Robert Huddleston to the Ulster Irish' (*Poems and Songs on Different Subjects*, xi). His uncompromising use of Ulster Scots, together with an equally uncompromising political radicalism, made it difficult for him to publish his work. Nevertheless, he was acclaimed by David Herbison and his local fellow bards as the 'Bard of Moneyrea', in which place he died on 15 February 1887, still lamenting his literary obscurity.

IVAN HERBISON

Sources Huddleston MSS, Ulster Folk and Transport Museum, Cultra Manor, Holywood, co. Down · R. Huddleston, preface, *A collection of poems and songs on rural subjects* (1844) · R. Huddleston, preface, *A collection of poems and songs on different subjects*, 2 (1846) · J. Hewitt, *Rhyming weavers and other country poets of Antrim and Down* (1974) · J. R. R. Adams, 'A rural bard, his printers and his public: Robert Huddleston of Moneyrea', *Linen Hall Review*, 3–4/9 (1992), 9–11 · J. R. Boyd, 'The Bard of Moneyrea: Robert Huddleston (1814–1887)', *Ullans*, 1 (1993), 30–33 · J. R. Boyd, 'The Bard of Moneyrea: Robert Huddleston (1814–1887)', *Ullans*, 2 (1994), 32–4 · I. Herbison, *The rest is silence: some remarks on the disappearance of Ulster-Scots poetry* (1996) · B. Walker, 'Country letters: some correspondence of Ulster poets of the nineteenth century', *An uncommon bookman: essays in memory of J. R. R. Adams*, ed. J. Gray and W. McCann (1996), 119–39 · P. Walsh, 'In search of the rhyming weavers', *Causeway*, 4/3 (1996), 40–44 · d. cert.
Archives Ulster Folk and Transport Museum, Cultra Manor, Holywood, co. Down, papers
Wealth at death £357 8s.: probate, 11 March 1887, *CGPLA Ire.*

Huddleston, (Ernest Urban) Trevor (1913–1998), archbishop of the Indian Ocean and member of the Community of the Resurrection, was born on 15 June 1913 in Golders Green, Middlesex, the younger child and only son of Captain Sir Ernest Whiteside Huddleston (1874–1959), naval officer with the Royal Indian Marine, and his first wife, Elsie (d. 1931), daughter of John Barlow-Smith, of Buenos Aires. Huddleston's mother was from a prominent Anglo-Argentinian family; his father was at the time of his birth commander of Bombay dockyard, later rising to become deputy director and officiating director of the Royal Indian Marine, before retiring in 1925. He was later

(Ernest Urban) Trevor Huddleston (1913–1998), by Godfrey Argent, 1969

an adviser to the government of India on naval and shipping matters, for which he received his knighthood in 1939. His enforced absence in India during and after the First World War meant that Huddleston did not meet his father until he was nearly seven years old; his mother was also frequently absent in India, so he and his sister, Elsie Barbara (*b.* 1910), were largely brought up by their maternal aunt Charlotte Dawson Robinson in Golders Green.

Education and vocation Huddleston was a true child of the Anglo-Catholic movement in the Church of England. He attended St Michael's, Golders Green, as server from the age of four. At seven he went to Tenterden Hall preparatory school in Hendon, where he was confirmed in 1925. After four years at Lancing College, he went to Christ Church, Oxford, in 1931. There his tutors included Keith Feiling, Patrick Gordon Walker, and J. C. Masterman. He graduated with a second-class degree in modern history in 1934.

Huddleston appears never to have deviated from his total commitment to the high Anglicanism in which he was brought up, but unlike some other Oxford-educated high-church clerics he learned that you cannot love the invisible God unless you find Him in 'the brother whom you have seen' (Denniston, 6). After Christ Church he went to Wells Theological College where he was gradually drawn to the monastic life—specifically the Community of the Resurrection, based at Mirfield in the West Riding of Yorkshire. A senior colleague there directed Huddleston to the parish of St Mark's, Swindon, a powerhouse of Anglo-Catholicism and a great training ground for its young priests. In 1936 he was ordained deacon and in 1937 he was made a priest. Two years later he was at Mirfield as

a novice, and in 1941 he was professed as a full member of the Community of the Resurrection, taking the threefold vows of poverty, chastity, and obedience.

Huddleston felt no call towards pacifism and hoped to be called on to serve as an army chaplain, as had several of his Mirfield contemporaries. But what turned out to be a greater challenge to his faith and courage as well as to his vows was the decision of his superior, Father Raymond Raynes [*see* Raynes, Richard Elliott], to appoint him in November 1943 as priest-in-charge of the Sophiatown and Orlando Anglican missions, in the diocese of Johannesburg. Raynes, who had been provincial in South Africa prior to his return to Mirfield as superior, was looking for someone who would eventually succeed him in overseeing the community's many commitments, educational as well as pastoral and ecclesiastical, in southern Africa. In Huddleston he identified the man.

South Africa During the years before the nationalists came to power in South Africa in 1948 the Community of the Resurrection's stance on human rights for all and for racial justice there was unequivocal but localized. Huddleston's own early encounters with the African, Indian, and coloured families of Sophiatown and Orlando brought out in him the *saeva indignatio* at the sufferings and indignities of his parishioners which was to inspire and determine the course of the rest of his life. He was soon caught up in official and unofficial protests against discriminatory government legislation. His unique contribution to these was fuelled by a personal passion to oppose evil and fight for dignity and fairness for the non-whites among whom he ministered. Nelson Mandela said in 1998 that 'Father Huddleston walked alone at all hours of the night where few of us were prepared to go. His fearlessness won him the support of everyone. No-one, not the gangster, tsotsi, or pickpocket would touch him' (Mandela, message to memorial service, 29 July 1998).

Huddleston had come to realize by 1948 that institutionalized racism—which after 1948 was to find its full expression in the nationalists' policy of apartheid—was incompatible with the gospel. His calling was pastoral, his commitment was to care for the souls and lives of his people. In addition to his responsibilities as a priest he was expected to trace husbands, wives, brothers, and sisters and other family members who were arrested because of a violation of the pass laws or some other infringement of discriminatory legislation. Many of his parishioners were already caught up in a vortex of petty crime, gangsterism, and alcoholism. His mission was to rescue them, knowing that each individual was a child of God, filled with enduring vitality and great gifts. He was awakened to the plight of the urban black people of South Africa who lived every hour with danger. He identified apartheid as an intolerable evil, a crime against humanity, a demonic power that violated the image of God in people. His Sophiatown years taught what it meant to love and hate, passionately.

Huddleston was made provincial of the Community of the Resurrection in South Africa in 1949. Nevertheless the fact that the institutional Anglican church was reluctant to provide him with the kind of support he hoped for elicited his despair and led to open clashes with other clergy, not least Geoffrey Clayton, archbishop of Cape Town from 1949 to 1957, who regarded Huddleston's views and actions, especially in relation to the Bantu Education Act, as excessive. Huddleston was convinced that this act was the most iniquitous of all apartheid laws, systematically destroying the potential and therefore the image of God in innocent children. One of his worst moments was when Oliver Tambo, then a graduate of St Peter's College, Rosettenville, and a regular worshipper at the church of Christ the King in Sophiatown, was served with a banning order under the Suppression of Communism Act.

On 24 October 1955 it was announced that Huddleston was to be recalled to Mirfield. Oliver Tambo wept at the news. But Huddleston by then had completed a book on his African experiences, *Naught for your Comfort*, published in London and New York in May the next year. He had written it out, chapter by chapter, in longhand, with virtually no crossings out, and it, or a typed version, was smuggled out of the country just a day before the police raided his home and took away some of his papers. In his book Huddleston concentrated on those still growing aspects of apartheid legislation and practice which robbed the urban black people he served of any rights—whether to education, health, employment, or self-respect. He blamed himself bitterly for having achieved so little while in South Africa, so entrenched were Pretoria's policies with the white electorate and so slow were Europeans, Americans, and the Soviet Union to oppose them actively until as late as 1976. Nevertheless the sharply focused power and even beauty of his writing communicated strongly to a wide, mainly young readership in Europe, the Commonwealth, and the USA. The little he felt he had achieved was greatly supplemented by the effect of his book on many readers; some later became influential in politics and world affairs.

Huddleston's actual achievement by 1956 was more complicated. Indeed, that year might have marked the end of his most creative time. He had become a prohibited immigrant from the land he loved. Albeit a famous and easily identifiable author, a global celebrity, he had no ascertainable future. Speculation about the reasons for his recall mounted, but no conclusive answer was forthcoming from the words and actions of his superior—to whom he gave unquestioning but reluctant obedience.

Mirfield and Masasi After a hectic publicity tour of the USA Huddleston attempted to settle down as novice guardian at Mirfield. There he was besieged by requests to recount his African experiences. He longed to be allowed to speak, not about himself or South Africa, but about the gospel. His frequent absences rendered him a poor pastor to the novices. In 1958 a new superior transferred him to the London priory as prior, to help his new public persona and perhaps to help create a personal pastoral role for some of those who sought him out. But Africa called him incessantly and in 1960 he returned there to serve as bishop of Masasi, in the south-west of Tanganyika. Before he left London, on 26 June 1959, together with his close friend Julius Nyerere, soon to become first prime minister and then first president of Tanganyika, he addressed the founding meeting of the Anti-Apartheid Movement, convened in response to an international appeal by the president of the African National Congress, Chief Albert Luthuli, for a boycott of South African goods.

Tanganyika became independent in 1961, a republic in 1962, and was merged with Zanzibar to form Tanzania in 1964. Huddleston's years there proved a total contrast to the decade that preceded them. Though sometimes profoundly depressed, he discovered a role within the infant democracy of his adopted country to aid Nyerere's programme of Arusha (self-reliance). He also raised money for hospitals, enhanced the role and standing of local clergy, learned Swahili, encouraged the development of education away from traditional missionary values towards preparation for a secular life, albeit with little opportunity for bright pupils to build career opportunities in the poor developing world—and ended close to despair. He thought of applying for Tanzanian citizenship but was gently dissuaded by Nyerere. Though again he felt he had failed, his achievement in Masasi was subsequently recognized as creative and valuable, and the legacy he left was not forgotten.

Stepney and the Indian Ocean In 1968 Huddleston returned to England to serve as suffragan bishop of Stepney in the East End of London. Here he again responded strongly to new challenges, and found a new cause in opposing a rising tide of racism in many parts of the country. He loved East Enders of all races and ages, and exercised episcopal oversight over a remarkable body of clergy and laypeople, including social workers, local politicians, and community leaders. His personal life was enhanced by seeing friends both old and new.

Africa still lingered in Huddleston's heart and he was persuaded not to give up his Stepney job only by Nyerere, who told him he must stay in England as the British voice of the 'third world'. Nevertheless, after nearly a decade and under circumstances which remain unclear, he again left England in 1978, when elected bishop of Mauritius and (shortly afterwards) archbishop of the Indian Ocean.

By this time Huddleston was famous, controversial, forthright, intolerant of opposition, sometimes dictatorial. At sixty-five, having been insulin dependent for many years, he showed signs of deteriorating health, which, it was said, ruled him out for a top position (mooted by some in 1974) within the Church of England. It was while in Mauritius that he was elected president of the Anti-Apartheid Movement, a move which gave more meaning and purpose to his remaining years than would any upward movement within the Church of England's hierarchy.

The province of the Indian Ocean comprised the Seychelles and Madagascar as well as Mauritius. It had little cultural or political cohesion, and within its area Christians were a small minority. Undaunted, Huddleston carried out his new duties with vigour and panache. He learned to preach in French and Creole, though he could not master Malagasy. He also promoted inter-faith understanding and co-operation throughout the region and beyond. Early in 1980 he developed serious eye problems, requiring emergency treatment in London. But he was soon back in Mauritius, making new friendships and new connections. His retirement from Mauritius in 1983 followed shortly after a magnificent inter-faith convention there, at the end of which delegates dedicated themselves to the cause of inter-faith understanding that he espoused.

The Anti-Apartheid Movement Since 1976, the year of the Soweto uprisings against the forcible introduction of Afrikaans as the medium of instruction in non-white schools, Huddleston had worked closely with the Anti-Apartheid Movement in Britain, and related groups throughout the world. He was elected president of the Anti-Apartheid Movement while still archbishop of the Indian Ocean, in 1981, in succession to Bishop Ambrose Reeves. (He had been a vice-president since 1969.) To this movement he dedicated the rest of his life. He also served as chairman of the International Defence and Aid Fund for Southern Africa from 1983.

The struggle against apartheid was a long-drawn-out process, and Huddleston and his colleagues became increasingly disillusioned by the British government's prevarications. 'Apartheid is a challenge to the conscience of the whole world, and it is a challenge which the West consistently refuses to meet', he told a Cambridge congregation in 1988. Nevertheless, under Huddleston's leadership, the Anti-Apartheid Movement made an enormous impact on British public opinion. In June 1984 the movement organized a massive protest against the visit of President P. W. Botha to Britain on the eve of which Huddleston led a delegation in a tense meeting with the prime minister, Margaret Thatcher. In November 1985 the Anti-Apartheid Movement protested against the government's anti-sanctions stance at the Nassau conference summit. In June 1986 Huddleston shared with Thabo Mbeki the platform for an Anti-Apartheid Movement march and festival attended by 250,000 to demand Nelson Mandela's release. The Nelson Mandela 'Freedom at 70' campaign in 1988 was initiated by Huddleston and included a seven-hour pop concert in Wembley stadium, broadcast to an audience of one billion worldwide, followed by a rally in Hyde Park of over 200,000. The movement also organized numerous, smaller-scale and often local, protests, meetings, and vigils. Huddleston led delegations to meet successive British foreign secretaries and other government ministers on a range of issues relating to southern Africa, but his greatest contribution to the success of the Anti-Apartheid Movement was probably addressing many hundreds of meetings throughout Britain. He also travelled extensively, addressing the United Nations general assembly in 1982, and touring the 'frontline states' (Botswana, Mozambique, Tanzania, Zambia,

Zimbabwe) in 1984. In the same year he delivered a worldwide petition to the United Nations calling for the unconditional release of Mandela, and also visited India, New Zealand, and Australia, meeting their respective prime ministers. In subsequent years he addressed meetings in numerous countries. He also found time to serve as president of the National Peace Council and provost of Selly Oak colleges, both from 1983 until his death.

The part played by Huddleston's increasing ill health in the 1990s is difficult to judge. While he delighted in the victory over apartheid for which he, and many thousands of others, had struggled for over forty years, he felt frustrated by the politicking of Pretoria's transitional regime, the doublespeak of British diplomats and government ministers, and even the conditional forgiveness offered to some of the perpetrators of apartheid by its leading surviving victims. Apartheid was not dead, he claimed in 1994, and he said what he felt to be true. But his increasingly intemperate language may have affected his credibility, and this may have been partly due to his worsening diabetic condition. To this his eye problems, his falls, his pain, and stress all contributed—not helped by his rigorous determination to drive himself hard when his presence was required. Only his undeviating attention to his daily routines of intercessory prayer and worship kept him sane and kept his demons at bay.

Huddleston's South African citizenship was restored to him in 1994, enabling him to vote, in South Africa House, London, in the general elections on 26 April. He then returned to Johannesburg in a highly charged, but ultimately successful, visit, which included participation in Mandela's inauguration as president at Pretoria on 10 May. At his friend Abdul Minty's suggestion Huddleston wrote a short book about this visit. He intended to return permanently to South Africa, but left again after only a few months.

Huddleston's final years were marked by worsening health and by a number of falls involving broken limbs. He was also becoming short-tempered and irascible, and found settling down at Mirfield, or indeed anywhere else, difficult. Honours were bestowed—including ten honorary doctorates, and in 1995 the Indira Gandhi memorial prize. He was gazetted KCMG in the new year's honours list in 1998, and was invested at Buckingham Palace on 24 March 1998. He died less than a month later, on 20 April 1998, at Mirfield. A packed Westminster Abbey was the scene of an electrifying memorial service on 29 July 1998, the high point of which was a trumpet solo lament from the pulpit by Hugh Masekela, the famous musician whose career Huddleston had launched in 1955 by giving him a trumpet. On 30 January 2000, at the direction of President Mandela, his ashes were interred at the east end of the church of Christ the King, in Sophiatown, South Africa.

No account of Huddleston's life and work would be complete without reference to his remarkable gift for giving and receiving loving friendship. By way of contrast to the rigours of his spiritual and public life, his friends—male and female, old and young, white, coloured, and black, pious and otherwise—formed a rich web of comfort and delight, bringing a measure of completion to his complex personality. His friendships once made never faded, and extended to the spouses and children and grandchildren of those on whom his light shone.

ROBIN DENNISTON

Sources T. Huddleston, *Naught for your comfort* (1956) · D. D. Honoré, ed., *Trevor Huddleston: essays on his life and work* (1988) · *From protest to challenge: a documentary history of African politics in South Africa, 1882–1964*, 3, ed. T. Karis and G. M. Gerhart (1977) · A. Sampson, *Drum: a venture into the new Africa* (1956) · C. Villa-Vincencio, *Trapped in apartheid: a socio-theological history of the English-speaking churches* (1988) · C. Villa-Vincencio, 'Father Trevor Huddleston: a tribute', *Journal of Theology for Southern Africa* (1998) · R. Denniston, *Trevor Huddleston: a life* (1999) · D. Mattera, *Memory is the weapon* (1987) · N. Mosley, *The life of Raymond Raynes* (1961) · A. Wilkinson, *The Community of the Resurrection: a centenary history* (1992) · *The Times* (21 April 1998) · *The Independent* (21 April 1998) · *Daily Telegraph* (21 April 1998) · *The Guardian* (21 April 1998) · WWW · personal knowledge (2004) · private information (2004)

Archives Bodl. RH, corresp. relating to Africa Bureau · Bodl. RH, corresp. and papers | Borth. Inst., corresp. with Patrick Durcan · U. Durham L., letters to Lord Howick of Glendale

Likenesses group photograph, 1960 (with Orthodox Russian churchmen), Hult. Arch. · G. Argent, photograph, 1969, NPG [*see illus.*] · portrait, 1992 · S. Eason, photograph, 1993, Hult. Arch. · N. Sharp, portrait, NPG · photograph, repro. in *The Times* · photograph, repro. in *The Independent* · photograph, repro. in *Daily Telegraph* · photograph, repro. in *The Guardian* · photographs, Bodl. RH, Huddleston papers · photographs, repro. in Denniston, *Trevor Huddleston*

Wealth at death £100: probate, 27 Aug 1998, *CGPLA Eng. & Wales*

Hudleston [*formerly* Simpson], **Wilfrid Hudleston** (1828–1909), naturalist and geologist, was born on 2 June 1828 at St Martin, Coney Street, York, the eldest son of John Simpson (*d.* 1867), a Knaresborough physician, and his wife, Elizabeth Ward, the heir of the Hudlestons of Cumberland through her mother, Eleanor Hudleston. After early education at St Peter's School, York, Wilfrid Hudleston Simpson moved to Uppingham School and subsequently entered St John's College, Cambridge. Following his BA graduation, in 1850, he began reading law and was called to the bar in 1853, but never practised.

At Cambridge a youthful interest in ornithology led to an association with Alfred Newton and participation in expeditions to Northumberland, Cumberland, and north-west Ireland. The 1850s were spent on other bird collecting expeditions to Scandinavia (1855), Algeria (1857), Greece and Turkey (1859–60), and Switzerland (1861). In 1862–7 Simpson studied the natural sciences, initially at Edinburgh, and subsequently at the Royal School of Chemistry in London. A chance meeting with Marshall Hall at Chamonix in 1866 and the influence of Professor John Morris persuaded him to pursue geology rather than chemistry. In 1867 his family assumed the surname of Hudleston by royal licence, and inherited the estates of his mother's family.

Hudleston was elected a fellow of the Geological Society in 1867, served on council for five terms until his death, was secretary in 1869–90 and president from 1892 to 1894. He was also very active with the Geologists' Association, which he joined in 1871; he was secretary from 1874 to 1877 and president (1881–3), and his inclination for field

studies resulted in his writing numerous accounts of its excursions. Early papers on the Yorkshire oolites (1873–8) and *Corallian Rocks of England* (1877), the first major work on the subject, published with his friend J. F. Blake, established Hudleston's geological reputation. He was also one of the editors of the *Geological Magazine* in 1886–1901. Among other offices, he was president of the Mineralogical Society (1881–3), and of section C (geology) of the British Association for its meeting in Bristol, 1898. All his presidential addresses were succinct reviews that made a significant contribution to their subject. In 1894 he evaluated the work of the Geological Society, a task which had the potential to upset many egos, and which Hudleston himself compared to 'a man trying to lift up a beehive' (Hudleston, 142). However, he accomplished the appraisal with such perfect judgement that others believed it should be repeated every decade. He was also active in a number of other smaller scientific societies. Apparently he fulfilled his duties as a landowner and magistrate in Dorset and the West Riding with the same thoroughness.

Hudleston's publications in the early 1880s either described the geology of particular districts, satisfied his own predilection for 'chemical geology' (Woodward, *PRS*, viii), or were concerned with palaeontological descriptions. His monographs and papers on Mesozoic gastropoda, often based on his own collection, are still the only significant British work in this field. Although he was awarded the Geological Society's Wollaston medal in 1897 for his valuable contributions to all aspects of geology, particular reference was made to the value of his Palaeontographical Society monograph *The Inferior Oolite Gasteropoda* (1897). Later, Hudleston's knowledge of Jurassic faunas, together with evidence from east African geology, disproved theories on the marine origin of the Lake Tanganyika mollusca (1904). An interest in marine mollusca had prompted a joint venture with Henry Woodward and C. E. Robinson during 1886 and 1887, to study their ecology in the English Channel. Later, in 1893, Hudleston was one of the ten founder members of the Malacological Society. Shortly before his death he provided the site and capital for the establishment of the Dove Marine Biological Laboratory at Cullercoats, Northumberland.

Private resources allowed Hudleston to indulge his varied scientific interests: 'He stood out as one of the few left of "a good old school", men of fortune, who … did no amateurish work … and turned attention … to questions of importance … in the advancement of science' (Watts, 136). His professional contemporaries all attested to the untiring energy that was seen in his official service for many scientific societies. The list of his publications indicates his diverse interests and overall capability. Hudleston amassed a fossil collection that, apart from confirming his meticulous curation, was probably unsurpassed at that time for recording the precise provenance of its specimens. Together with an extensive field knowledge, it allowed him to make a significant contribution to British Jurassic palaeontology especially through his papers (1880–81), monographs (1887–97), and contribution to the

Catalogue of British Jurassic Gasteropoda (1892). His acute critical facility and geological insight often enabled him to interpret difficult strata, for example in the north-west highlands and in India.

Hudleston did not marry until late in life, although he had two illegitimate children (William and Florence Herbert) with Emma Tuck (otherwise Emma Herbert or Emma Rix). In 1890 he married Rose Matilda Heywood, second daughter of William Heywood Benson of Little Thorpe, Ripon. She accompanied him to India in 1895, when they visited the north-west frontier, crossed the Punjab, and reached the eastern end of the Salt range. A keen sportsman, in 1897 Hudleston bought the East Stoke estate in Dorset for the shooting. Tall, spare, and strongly built, Hudleston enjoyed good health throughout his life. His last years were spent at West Holme, near Wareham, where he died on 29 January 1909 after suffering a heart attack on returning from a walk.   R. J. CLEEVELY

Sources [H. Woodward], 'Eminent living geologists: Wilfrid Hudleston Hudleston', *Geological Magazine*, new ser., 5th decade, 1 (1904), 431–8 · W. J. Sollas, *Quarterly Journal of the Geological Society*, 65 (1909), lxi–lxiii · W. W. Watts, 'The jubilee of the Geologists' Association', *Proceedings of the Geologists' Association*, 21 (1910), 119–49 · A. Bernie, 'The inaugural chairman: W. H. Hudleston', *Bulletin of the Malacological Society of London*, 23 (Aug 1994), 10–11 · H. W. [H. Woodward], *PRS*, 81B (1909), vi–x · *Mineralogical Magazine*, 15 (1908–10), 265 · *Geological Magazine*, new ser., 5th decade, 6 (1909), 143–4 · H. S. Torrens, 'Wilfred H. Hudleston', *Geological Curator*, 2 (1977–80), 510, 513 · W. H. Hudleston, *Quarterly Journal of the Geological Society*, 49 (1893), 142 · Venn, *Alum. Cant.*

Archives Bristol City Museum and Art Gallery · GS Lond. · Hunterian Museum and Art Gallery, Glasgow · priv. coll. · U. Cam., Sedgwick Museum of Earth Sciences

Likenesses Maull & Fox, photograph, GS Lond., Portrait Album, vol. 6, p. 43 · photograph, repro. in Woodward, 'Eminent living geologists' · portrait, repro. in Woodward, 'Eminent living geologists'

Wealth at death £160,903 6s. 10d.: resworn probate, 3 April 1909, CGPLA Eng. & Wales

Hudson, Charles (1828–1865), mountaineer, was born on 4 October 1828 in Ripon, Yorkshire, the only son of Joshua Hudson, gentleman, and his wife Jane, *née* Abbott. He had two older sisters. He was educated at St Peter's School, York, under the Revd William Hey, who recalled Hudson as intellectually undistinguished, but exercising influence over others on account of his athleticism. G. F. Browne certainly remembered him as 'our very best athlete' (*Recollections of a Bishop*, 1915, 104–5), capable of a 21 foot long-jump in ordinary boots; on a walking tour in what is now Cumbria in 1845 he averaged 27 miles daily. He was admitted pensioner at St John's College, Cambridge, in March 1847, and elected scholar in 1850, taking his BA in 1851, and proceeding MA in 1854. In 1851 Hudson stroked the college eight to head of the river, won the fours and pairs (in a boat fitted with a special rudder to compensate for Hudson's superior strength), and rowed a dead heat in the sculls. In the same year he travelled to Switzerland for the first time, and he spent the winters of 1851–2 and 1852–3 in Geneva. Here his 'distinguished and polite manners gained him admission to all the fashionable houses' (P. Chaix), where he enjoyed dancing until

Charles Hudson (1828–1865), by unknown photographer

the small hours. Hudson became a keen if unsuccessful chamois hunter, and acquired a taste for alpinism, climbing minor peaks and experimenting with a bivouac in an improvised sleeping bag at over 7000 feet and at −13 °F in February 1853. Between 24 and 25 March 1853 he walked from Bionassay to Geneva and back within twenty-four hours, a round trip of 86 miles.

Hudson was ordained deacon on 18 December 1853, taking priest's orders the following year. He seems to have undergone an evangelical conversion: the secularity of his journals from the early 1850s contrasts with his later pattern of private devotions (even during climbs) and the extreme piety of letters surviving from the 1860s. Frequently taking pupils, he would request their relatives to join him in daily prayer for them at a pre-arranged hour. Hudson assisted the Revd J. Prior at Kirklington, and volunteered as a chaplain to the Army Works Corps in the Crimea, where he spent the winter of 1854–5. After the fall of Sevastopol he crossed Armenia with the unfulfilled intention of climbing Mount Ararat. Hudson was curate of St Mary's, Bridgnorth, from 1856 to 1857, and in 1860 became vicar of Skillington, Lincolnshire. His climbing campaigns in the later 1850s led to his election to the Alpine Club in 1859 (sitting on its council 1863–5) and as a fellow of the Royal Geographical Society (1865): Leslie Stephen described Hudson as 'the strongest and most active mountaineer I have ever met', and, although much more experienced on snow than on rock, he was widely regarded as having talent and stamina unmatched except perhaps by Whymper. In 1855 he participated in the first ascent of the highest summit of Monte Rosa and the first guideless ascent of Mont Blanc (important in breaking the stranglehold of the Chamonix cartel), an experience recounted with E. S. Kennedy in *Where there's a Will there's a Way* (1856).

In 1865 Hudson travelled to Switzerland with a former pupil, D. R. Hadow. After pioneering a new route on the Aiguille Verte and taking Hadow up Mont Blanc, Hudson planned an assault on the Matterhorn with Hadow and the guide Michel Croz. Joined by Lord Francis Douglas, his guides the Taugweilders, and Edward Whymper, the party successfully achieved the first ascent on 14 July 1865. Early in the descent, however, Croz, Douglas, Hadow, and Hudson plunged to their deaths: the initial cause of the accident is unknown. Hudson's horribly mutilated remains were identifiable only from his wallet and a letter to his wife, Emily Antoinette, daughter of Major Charles Mylne of the Bombay army, whom he had married in Paris on 26 June 1862 and with whom he had two children; she lived at least until 1917. He was buried in the village churchyard at Zermatt; in 1913 he was reinterred in the English church there. ARTHUR BURNS

Sources J. McCormick, *A sad holiday*, 3rd edn (1865) • A. L. Mumm, *The Alpine Club register*, 1 (1923), 160–62 • C. Hudson and E. S. Kennedy, *Where there's a will there's a way: an ascent of Mont Blanc by a new route and without guides*, 2nd edn (1856) • J. P. Farrar, 'Days of long ago: Charles Hudson, the prototype of the mountaineer of today', *Alpine Journal*, 32 (1918–19), 2–36 • Venn, *Alum. Cant.* • Boase, *Mod. Eng. biog.* • D. F. O. Dangar and T. S. Blakeney, 'A word for Whymper: a reply to Sir Arnold Lunn', *Alpine Journal*, 71 (1966) • L. Stephen, 'In memoriam: John Birkbeck', *Alpine Journal*, 15 (1890–91), 279 • P. Chaix, letter, *The Times* (1 Aug 1865) • R. W. Clark, *The day the rope broke: the story of a great Victorian tragedy* (1965)

Archives Alpine Club, London, journals | Alpine Club, London, corresp. with G. W. Young, B48 • BL, corresp. with J. McCormick, Add. MSS 63102

Likenesses photograph, after 1853, repro. in R. Clark, *The Victorian mountaineers* (1953) • engraving, 1855, repro. in Hudson and Kennedy, *Where there's a will there's a way* • photograph, repro. in *Alpine Journal*, 32 (1918), no. 217, frontispiece • photograph, priv. coll. [*see illus.*]

Wealth at death under £5000: probate, 23 Aug 1865, *CGPLA Eng. & Wales*

Hudson, Charles Thomas (1828–1903), naturalist, was born at Brompton, London, on 11 March 1828, and baptized on 10 August 1828 at St Mary's, Lambeth. He was the third of five sons of John Corrie Hudson (1795–1879), chief clerk of the legacy duty office, and Emily (1794–1868), daughter of James Hebard, of Ewell, Surrey. Hudson's father was an advanced radical in his youth, and friend of William Godwin, the Shelleys, Charles Lamb, and William Hazlitt; but in later life his opinions changed. Hudson himself was educated at Kensington grammar school and The Grange, Sunderland. He excelled at music and drawing and as a young man wrote and composed songs. He was compelled by family circumstances to earn his living by teaching at an early age, first at Glasgow and than at the Royal Institution, Liverpool. It was largely through his

own efforts that he was able in 1848 to go to St John's College, Cambridge, where he graduated as fifteenth wrangler in 1852, proceeding MA in 1855 and LLD in 1866.

After leaving Cambridge, Hudson became second master of Bristol grammar school on 25 July 1852, and on 30 March 1855 was appointed headmaster. On 19 June 1855 he married Mary Ann (*b.* 1831/2), daughter of William Bullock Tibbits of Braunston, Northamptonshire, with whom he had one daughter, Florence. On 24 June 1858, at Clifton, he married Louisa Maria Fiott, daughter of Freelove Hammond, of the Inner Temple; Hudson and his second wife had four sons and five daughters. He resigned his post at Bristol grammar school in 1860, and in 1861 opened a private school at Manilla Hall, Clifton, formerly the residence of Sir William Draper, which he ran until 1881. Subsequently he resided at 6 Royal York Crescent, Clifton, until 1891 when he moved to Dawlish, Devon. In 1899 he moved to Shanklin on the Isle of Wight.

Hudson was a born naturalist who devoted his leisure to microscopical research, in particular the study of the Rotifera. His first printed paper was on *Rhinops vitrea* in the *Annals and Magazine of Natural History* for 1869. This was followed by numerous papers in the *Microscopical Journal* and the *Quarterly Journal of Microscopical Science*, describing new genera and species of Rotifera, of which *Pedalion mirum* was a noteworthy discovery. A list of these papers is given in the *Journal of the Royal Microscopical Society* (1904).

He was elected fellow of the Royal Microscopical Society in 1872, was president from 1888 to 1890, and an honorary fellow from 1901 until his death. With the assistance of the marine zoologist Philip Henry Gosse he published in 1886–7 *The Rotifera, or, Wheel-animalculae*. In recognition of this, the standard monograph on the subject, he was elected FRS in 1889. John Lubbock, first Baron Avebury, remarked (in his *Pleasures of Life*, chap. 9.) that Hudson's charming introduction to this work showed that the true naturalist was no mere dry collector.

Hudson's natural gift for drawing found expression not only in the beautiful illustrations of *The Rotifera*, but also in the talks on natural history that he gave during his later years, chiefly at public schools, which he illustrated with ingenious coloured transparencies of his own making. Hudson died at his home, Hillside, Clarence Road, Shanklin, Isle of Wight, on 24 October 1903, and was buried at Shanklin. On 25 April 1921 the original drawings of *The Rotifera* were presented to the Royal Society by the executors of Florence, his daughter (Royal Society MS 132).

C. L. KINGSFORD, *rev.* YOLANDA FOOTE

Sources personal knowledge (1912) • private information (1912) • *Men and women of the time* (1899) • *Journal of the Royal Microscopical Society* (1904), 48–9 • *BL cat.* • Venn, *Alum. Cant.* • IGI • *CGPLA Eng. & Wales* (1903) • d. cert. • m. cert.

Archives BL, letters of and relating to him, Add. MS 63102

Wealth at death £6771 18s. 5d.: probate, 3 Dec 1903, *CGPLA Eng. & Wales*

Hudson, Edward Burgess (1854–1936), magazine printer and publisher, was born in November 1854, the son of John Francis Daniel Hudson, printer. The family was descended from modest landowners in Cumberland, but

Hudson's grandfather had moved to London, made money as a merchant, and then established the family printing business of Hudson and Kearns, with premises in Southwark Street. At the time of Hudson's birth his father was head of the firm and had recently purchased a 'gloomy mansion' (Maude, 58) near Hyde Park. Together with his several brothers and sisters, Edward grew up in this house surrounded by his father's collections of antiques, and although he appears to have been largely uneducated his 'instinctive appreciation of beauty' (Hussey, 96) was surely fostered in the family home. Indeed, long after his parents' death Hudson continued to live there with his sickly brother, Henry, and his two unmarried sisters. It was not until he reached middle age that he eventually moved, to 15 Queen Anne's Gate. There, in an early eighteenth-century house which he is said to have coveted throughout his youth, he began to indulge his own lifelong love of collecting art and furniture, making every room 'like a picture' (Strong, 18).

Little is known about Hudson's early life, except that his passion for open-air pursuits such as walking and cycling began in childhood. Capable and ambitious, he had been articled to a solicitor at the age of fifteen and within two years had become chief conveyancing clerk. However, he evidently disliked the profession and by the age of twenty-one, after a stint as a 'printer's traveller' (Edwards, 334), he persuaded his father to let him take over the family business. There he quickly emerged as a shrewd businessman and under his direction Hudson and Kearns went from strength to strength. In the 1870s they had simply been a busy company printing a diverse range of books, mostly for other publishers. By the early 1890s Hudson's interest in recent advances in the technology of blockmaking and half-tone printing had led the firm to expand into the booming field of illustrated magazine publishing.

This entrepreneurial scheme came about after Hudson's first contact with Lord Riddell (1865–1934), chairman of the *News of the World*, and Sir George Newnes (1851–1910), the publishing magnate who had made his fortune with the enormously popular magazine *Tit Bits*, launched in the early 1880s. Hudson's first magazines, produced from his London offices at 10–11 Southampton Street in partnership with the firm of George Newnes Ltd, were *Famous Cricketers*, the *Navy and Army Illustrated*, and *Racing Illustrated*. On 8 January 1897 the company merged the ailing *Racing Illustrated* with a new magazine, *Country Life Illustrated*, which focused on sport, country pursuits, and the social side of land ownership. Importantly, this first number also included an article on Baddesley Clinton in Warwickshire, *Country Life*'s first weekly portrait of a country house. The magazine prospered financially from the beginning, thanks in part to its success in attracting advertising from estate agents in a rapidly growing country-house market. By 1902 the business had so expanded that Hudson commissioned the young and charismatic architect Edwin Lutyens to design suitably imposing offices in London's Covent Garden, and by 1905 he had bought out George Newnes and established Country Life Ltd.

Although he did not write for the magazine and was never its editor, Hudson always exerted his authority over *Country Life*'s contents, style, and policy. Its distinctive appearance and regular features evolved over the next few years as a combined result of his fiercely critical eye and his remarkable success in assembling a band of expert advisers and contributors. Despite his early investment in 'the finest pictorial printing machinery obtainable' (Strong, 19), when *Country Life* was first launched there was no specialist photographer on the staff and many of the images were bought in from elsewhere. In 1898 Hudson met Charles Latham (d. 1909), one of Britain's finest architectural photographers, who helped to define the magazine's unique style with his perfectly balanced pictures of country house interiors—combining a romantic feeling for atmosphere with documentary clarity.

In 1899 Hudson met Gertrude Jekyll (1843–1932), an established figure in the gardening world, who edited a gardening magazine for him in 1900–01 and contributed a 'Garden notes' column to *Country Life* for the next thirty years. It was she who had introduced him to Lutyens, who, though he 'ragged Hudson unmercifully' (Edwards, 333), quickly became a dear friend whom Hudson loved like a son. Hudson took great pains to promote Lutyens's career in the pages of *Country Life*. In 1931, when he accompanied him to India for the inauguration of New Delhi, Hudson was said to have been 'on the verge of tears … from emotion and pride' (Maude, 59). It was through Lutyens that Hudson's own artistic tastes found expression in his succession of country homes: first at a new house, the 'arts and crafts' Deanery Garden (1899) in Sonning, Berkshire; then in the romantic restoration of the ruined sixteenth-century Lindisfarne Castle (1902) on Holy Island; and lastly at the timber-framed Sussex manor of Plumpton Place (1927–8), which Lutyens turned into an 'enchanted place' (Pevsner), complete with moat and lake.

Lutyens benefited from—and may have influenced—the increasing professionalism of the magazine's architectural journalism, which became a central part of its identity under the guidance of its architectural editor H. Avray Tipping, whose articles on historic houses first appeared in 1906, and Sir Lawrence Weaver, who concentrated on new buildings. Hudson attracted equally distinguished writers, including Percy Macquoid and Margaret Jourdain, for articles on furniture and other antiques. These contributors also helped to author books published by *Country Life*, in a venture originally set up by Hudson to recycle photographs commissioned for the magazine; among its most ambitious productions were the three-volume *Dictionary of Furniture* (1924–7), by Macquoid and Ralph Edwards, and Tipping's nine-volume *English Homes* (1920–37).

Described by several contemporaries as gruff, difficult, boring, and tongue-tied, Hudson had a fondness for Lutyens and his young family—he was a devoted godfather to Lutyens's daughter Ursula—which revealed a more affectionate and tender side to his character. Although he was always nervous and reticent in company, he hosted regular Monday luncheons at Queen Anne's Gate, where contributors to *Country Life* were entertained alongside such guests as Lytton Strachey or Guilhermina Suggia, the renowned Italian cellist by whom Hudson was 'starstruck' (Edwards, 335). His reputation received its greatest social recognition when he was visited at Lindisfarne Castle by the prince and princess of Wales in 1908. Although he must have been somewhat lonely, he took great solace in his love of music, collecting fine objects, driving in the countryside, playing golf, and spending time with his few intimate friends. On 2 May 1929, at the age of seventy-four, he married Ellen Gertrude Woolrich (*b.* 1876/7), who edited the magazine *Homes and Gardens*, another of Hudson's creations. On 17 September 1936 Hudson died at his London home in Queen Anne's Gate, and his funeral took place nearby on 28 September at Christ Church, Lancaster Gate. It is likely that following his death his wife disposed of his personal papers, since none has come to light.

Country Life was Hudson's finest creation and the greatest love of his life. He continued to supervise its publication until he retired, a few years before his death, confident in the knowledge that the magazine would outlive him. It succeeded with both readers and advertisers thanks to the immense and enduring popular appeal of his personal ideal of the civilized life: an architecturally distinguished house in unspoilt countryside, furnished with choice collections of paintings and furniture, and set in a beautiful garden.   CLIVE ASLET

Sources R. Edwards, 'Percy Macquoid and others', *Apollo*, 99 (1974), 332–9 • D. Bank and A. Esposito, eds., *British biographical index*, 4 vols. (1990) • H. Friedrichs, *The life of Sir George Newnes, bart* (1911) • M. Hall, 'How beautiful they stand', *Country Life* (16 Jan 1997), 91–5 • C. Hussey, 'Edward Hudson: an appreciation', *Country Life*, 80 (1936), 318–19 • C. Hussey, *The life of Sir Edwin Lutyens* (1950) • P. Maude, 'Portrait of a perfectionist: Edward Hudson, the founder of *Country Life'*, *Country Life*, 141 (1967), 58–60 • 'Mr Edward Hudson: an appreciation', *The Times* (23 Sept 1936) • M. Lutyens, *Edwin Lutyens* (1980) • *Country Life*, 80 (1936), 317 • *The Times* (26 Sept 1936) • *The letters of Edwin Lutyens to his wife Lady Emily*, ed. C. Percy and J. Ridley (1985) • Pevsner • *The Post Office London directory* (1902) • R. Strong, *Country Life, 1897–1997: the English Arcadia* (1996) • *WWW* • *CGPLA Eng. & Wales* (1937) • P. Mandler, *The fall and rise of the stately home* (1997) • C. Aslet, *The last country houses* (1982) • m. cert. • d. cert.
Likenesses photograph, repro. in *Country Life* (12 Jan 1987), 58
Wealth at death £82,070 13s. 2d.: probate, 24 Feb 1937, *CGPLA Eng. & Wales*

Hudson, George (*d.* 1672/3), composer and musician, first appears when he was sworn by warrant of 3 December 1641 into the next but one vacancy among the lutes and voices at the royal court, but the dissolution of the establishment in 1642 foiled this opportunity. He is named among 'able masters for voyce or viol' in John Playford's *A Musicall Banquet* (1651). In 1656 he composed some of the music for William Davenant's *The First Dayes Entertainment at Rutland House* and his *Siege of Rhodes*. Either George or Richard Hudson (*c.*1617–1668)—probably his brother, a court violinist—was the Mr Hudson who made music with Samuel Pepys in January 1660. In midsummer that year George was appointed to two posts as composer for and practice of (i.e. rehearser of) the violins at £200 and £42

George Hudson (*d.* 1672/3), by unknown artist

15s. 10d. respectively. He shared direction of the group with Matthew Locke, although John Banister later creamed off a select band of twelve players.

Records show that late payments of his salary caused Hudson financial difficulties in the 1660s, although he always supported Richard Hudson's family, who were poor. Hudson played a full part in the affairs of the Corporation of Musick of Westminster, acting as warden on occasion. The reversion of his court places was promised to Pelham Humfrey and Thomas Purcell in January 1672, perhaps an indication that he was then in poor health.

Anthony Wood remarked that Hudson was 'excellent at the lyra-viol and hath improved it by his excellent inventions' (Bodl. Oxf., MS Wood D 19(4), fol. 71r). A consort featuring the instrument and twenty-three solos are extant, together with more than fifty light dances in two and three parts arranged as suites. Presumably these are skeleton versions of music written for the court violin band. Hudson died having made his nuncupative will (describing himself as of St Martin-in-the-Fields) at Greenwich on 10 December 1672; the will was proved on 17 February 1673.   ANDREW ASHBEE

Sources J. Hawkins, *A general history of the science and practice of music*, new edn, 3 vols. (1853); repr. in 2 vols. (1963) • R. Poole, 'The Oxford music school and the collection of portraits formerly preserved there', *Musical Antiquary*, 4 (1912–13), 143–59 [repr. 1968] • Pepys, *Diary*, vol. 7 • G. Dodd, *Thematic index of music for viols* (1980–) • A. Ashbee, ed., *Records of English court music*, 1 (1986) • A. Ashbee, ed., *Records of English court music*, 5 (1991) • A. Ashbee, ed., *Records of English court music*, 8 (1995) • P. Holman, *Four and twenty fiddlers: the violin at the English court, 1540–1690*, new edn (1993) • A. Ashbee and D. Lasocki, eds., *A biographical dictionary of English court musicians, 1485–1714*, 2 vols. (1998) • M. Reed, 'A footnote to the history of English music: the will and probate inventory of George Hudson', *Music Review*, 41 (Aug 1980), 169–71 • will, PRO, PROB 11/341, q. 20
Likenesses oils, U. Oxf., faculty of music [*see illus.*]
Wealth at death £11 15s. 4d.; £1188 10s. 3d. owed to him: inventory, Reed, 'Footnote to the history of English music'

Hudson, George [*called* the Railway King] (**1800–1871**), railway promoter and fraudster, was born in March 1800 at Howsham, about 12 miles north-east of York, the fifth son of a farmer who died in 1806. He went to local schools and in 1815 was apprenticed to Bell and Nicholson, a firm of drapers in College Street, York. When his apprenticeship was complete he received a share in the business. Bell

George Hudson [the Railway King] (**1800–1871**), by Sir Francis Grant, 1846

retired and the firm became Nicholson and Hudson. In 1821 he married Elizabeth Nicholson, who was the daughter of one of the partners in the firm and five years older than he was. Four of their children survived into adulthood: George, who was called to the bar and became an inspector of factories; John, who entered the army and was killed in the Indian mutiny; William, who became a doctor; and Anne, who married a Polish count, Count Suminski.

The Railway King In 1827, already a wealthy man, Hudson received a legacy of £30,000 from a great-uncle, Matthew Bottrill. This money enabled him to establish himself in the political and social life of York. He became treasurer of the local tory party at the time of the election following the Reform Bill of 1832, and in 1833 he took a leading part in the establishment of the York Union Banking Company. In 1835 Hudson was elected to the newly reformed York city council and in November of 1837 he became lord mayor. He entertained lavishly and was re-elected in the following year, although he was not strictly eligible to stand.

In 1833 Hudson attended a meeting in which the construction of a railway from York to link up with the Leeds to Selby line was proposed. He subsequently subscribed for 500 shares and was the largest shareholder. An act of parliament was obtained in 1837 and Hudson became chairman of the company, known as the York and North Midland Railway Company, with George Stephenson as the engineer.

In 1841 he persuaded the shareholders in eight railway companies engaged, so far unsuccessfully, in building a line from York to Newcastle, to join together to build the section of the line from Darlington to Newcastle and an act of parliament was obtained in 1842 for that purpose. In the same year he obtained control of the North Midland Leeds to Derby line and this was followed by the merger of the Birmingham and Derby and the Midland Counties companies with his own. By 1844 he controlled over 1000 miles of railway and was dubbed the Railway King but his 'kingdom' lacked any direct line into London. He, together with George Stephenson, had long planned a line into London from the midlands, and when the Great Northern line from London through Peterborough to York was proposed he made determined and often unscrupulous efforts to block the scheme, unsuccessfully, the act for the line being passed in June of 1846.

Early in 1844 William Gladstone, then president of the Board of Trade, prompted by the large number of railway bills then coming before parliament and alarmed at the intense competition between rival companies, set up a House of Commons committee of inquiry into the railways. This was seen by many railway proprietors as the beginning of state control and a campaign of opposition was headed by Hudson. He had a private meeting with Gladstone and compromise terms were agreed which removed any immediate prospect of railway nationalization.

By this time Hudson was very wealthy, with several estates in Yorkshire, including the Londesborough estate of some 12,000 acres, bought from the duke of Devonshire for £470,000, partly with the aim of blocking a possible competitor from building a line from York to Hull. He bought Newby Park from Earl de Grey in October of 1845 and also owned a large mansion, Albert House, in Knightsbridge. In 1846 he outlined plans for thirty-two parliamentary bills for railway projects costing a total of £10,000,000. In July of that year Queen Victoria travelled to Cambridge to attend the installation of Prince Albert as chancellor of the university in a special train provided by Hudson. In the same month he was returned as member of parliament in the tory interest for Sunderland. This was the high point of his career. His companies controlled over a quarter of the railways then built in England, with lines from Bristol to Newcastle, and branches to Scarborough, Hull, Leeds, Nottingham, and Rugby, together with the Eastern Counties line from London to Colchester and to Ely.

Sharp practices exposed Hudson gained many admirers through the skill with which he manipulated share prices, but he also made many enemies because of his arrogant and domineering manner and the lax way in which he reported on the finances of his companies, although in this he was by no means unique, since standards of accounting and audit were generally undemanding at that time. He also cut costs ruthlessly, and was much criticized for this when an accident at Romford in July of 1846 revealed that the staff of the Eastern Counties Railway, of which he had become chairman in the previous October, lacked experience, and were poorly paid and grossly overworked.

In June of 1846, in spite of all that Hudson could do, the act for the Great Northern line became law. His railway monopoly was increasingly threatened with isolation, particularly after the amalgamation which created the Caledonian Railway, with the prospect of a west coast line to Glasgow, and the formation of the London and North Western Railway with its line from London to Liverpool. The years 1846 and 1847 were marked by severe depression. Railway shareholders found it difficult to meet the calls made upon them and dividends had to be reduced. In August of 1848 he was compelled to repay nearly £400,000 to the banks, and when this news began to leak out the prices of railway shares fell sharply. In 1849 he was increasingly criticized by irate shareholders. At a meeting of the shareholders of his York, Newcastle, and Berwick Railway Company it was revealed that the company had bought shares at artificially inflated prices in another of Hudson's companies and that Hudson himself had been the owner of the shares. A committee of inquiry was set up, in spite of Hudson's attempts to prevent it. A meeting of Eastern Counties shareholders was equally turbulent and another committee of inquiry into his management of affairs was set up. When the findings of these two committees were published Hudson lost all credibility. Dividends had been paid out of capital; figures of traffic, revenue, and expenditure had been manipulated. He was compelled to resign from many of his company directorships and to repay large sums of money which he was deemed to have misappropriated. Money withdrawn from the York, Newcastle, and Berwick Railway Company in order to pay contractors had got no further than his personal bank account, for example.

Hudson remained a member of parliament, however, being returned for Sunderland in 1847 and again in 1852. This meant that he could not be arrested for debt while the House of Commons was in session, but in between sessions he went to France and Spain in order to evade his creditors. He was compelled to sell his landed estates, his Knightsbridge mansion was leased to the French ambassador, and his name was removed from the roll of aldermen at York. By May 1849 where he once had been adulated he was now execrated, although *The Times*, often one of his severest critics, did write of him on 10 April 1849 that the system itself was to blame:

> a system without rule, without order, without even a definite morality … He had to do everything out of his own head, and among lesser problems to discover the ethics of railway speculation and management … Mr Hudson's position was not only new to himself, but absolutely a new thing in the world altogether.

In June of 1850 the Sunderland Dock was opened amid scenes of jubilation. This was Hudson's last triumph. He was re-elected member of parliament for Sunderland in 1857, but the dock company was beginning to fail and he lost his seat at the general election of 1859. He now retired permanently to France to avoid his creditors.

Final years Hudson returned to England in 1865, by now largely forgotten by the public, in order to fight the general election for a seat at Whitby, to which he had been nominated as a tory candidate by some of his remaining admirers. Just before the election Hudson was arrested at the suit of one of his creditors and imprisoned at York, where he remained for three months. His creditors relented, not least because he had no resources left with which to satisfy them; and he still retained sufficient friends and admirers to raise a subscription with which to buy him an annuity of £600 per annum. With this he went to live with his wife in a small house at 87 Churton Street, London. His debts were finally compounded and he was slowly re-accepted into society. He was even re-elected chairman of the smoking room of the Carlton Club. However, Hudson was taken ill in York in the December of 1871 and returned to London, where he died at home in Churton Street from angina on 14 December. He was survived by his wife. His coffin was, fittingly, taken by train to York and he was buried at Scrayingham, Yorkshire, less than 3 miles from the place of his birth. As the funeral cortège passed through York on the morning of 21 December the shops were closed and the great bell of the minster was tolled.

In his prime Hudson was a short, stocky man, with sharp, piercing eyes. As a public speaker his personal magnetism made up for his grammatical solecisms and his broad Yorkshire accent. He could be ruthless and domineering but he was also capable of acts of great personal generosity. His obituarist in *The Times* (16 December 1871) gave a balanced assessment:

> The world which blindly trusted him, which cringed to him and flattered him avenged itself by excessive and savage reprobation … It is impossible to deny that he did great things to develop the railway system in the North of England. He was a man who united largeness of view with wonderful speculative courage. He went in for bigger things than any one else. He took away people's breath at first, but he soon succeeded in persuading them that the larger the project and the bolder the scheme, the more likely it was to pay. He showed his confidence by investing more largely than anyone else.

On 25 December 1871, however, *The Times* also commented, 'the main charge against him was proved. He did "cook accounts"'.　　　　　　　　　　MICHAEL REED

Sources R. S. Lambert, *The railway king … a study of George Hudson and the business morals of his time* (1934) · D. Mountfield, *The railway barons* (1979) · A. J. Peacock and D. Joy, *George Hudson of York* (1971) · *The Times* (10 April 1849) · *The Times* (16 Dec 1871) · *The Times* (25 Dec 1871) · B. J. Bailey, *George Hudson: the rise and fall of the Railway King* (1995) · *DNB*

Archives PRO, corresp. with George Leeman, RAIL 1155/15

Likenesses I. Andrews, oils, 1845, priv. coll.; repro. in Peacock and Joy, *George Hudson*, cover · caricature, lithograph, pubd 1845, NPG · F. Grant, oils, 1846, Mansion House, York [*see illus.*] · F. Frith, silhouettes, NPG · F. Frith, watercolour, NPG

Wealth at death bankrupt

Hudson, Henry (*d.* 1611), explorer, was almost certainly a native of London, although nothing is known of his antecedents or early life. A Henry Hudson (or Herdson), skinner, alderman of Aldersgate ward until his death in December 1555 (Beaven, 1.4), may have been a relative, but this cannot be determined. Hudson is said to have been an employee of the Russia Company before the first of his known voyages; surviving accounts thereof refer to him as 'master' rather than captain, a distinction that indicates that he was a pilot by profession, though no details of his early career survive.

Into northern waters On 19 April 1607 Hudson was one of twelve men and boys (including his son John) to take communion at St Ethelburga, Bishopsgate, before embarking upon a voyage, sponsored by the Russia Company, to discover a transpolar route to the Far East. The scheme, first mooted in the 1520s by the Bristol merchants Robert Thorne and Roger Barlowe was resurrected following failures to find a route via anticipated north-west or north-east passages. In the small bark *Hopeful* (sometimes referred to also as *Hopewell*) Hudson and his mariners departed from Gravesend on 1 May and passed northwards via the Shetland Islands to the eastern coast of Greenland, which they sighted on 13 June at a latitude of about 68° N. For several days they followed the coast and reached 73° N, but pack ice diverted them northeastwards thereafter. By 27 June the *Hopeful* was off Newland (Svalbad). Attempts to pass further northwards in the following weeks were frustrated by ice; after a brief landing at Whale's Bay, North East Land, and reaching 82° N at sea the following day, Hudson turned the *Hopeful* about, with the ostensible intention of returning to England. However, his subsequent discovery of Hudson's Tutches (Jan Mayen Island) on the return passage suggests that he may have thought to seek an alternative, north-west passage, before hunger and his men's pale enthusiasm compelled him to turn his course due south. The *Hopeful* entered the Thames on 16 September 1607.

A direct northern route had been proved impossible (though Hudson's report of the abundance of whales in waters about Svalbad promised some compensation); the Russia Company therefore decided to resurrect its search for a north-eastern passage. On 22 April 1608, again in the *Hopeful*, Hudson and fourteen mariners departed from St Katharine's Dock, London, to follow up the previously unsuccessful navigations of Sir Hugh Willoughby and Stephen Borough. An uneventful voyage via the Norwegian coastline brought the *Hopeful* into the Barents Sea, though her crew were not, apparently, untouched by the effects of bad beer *en route* (on June 15 two mariners sighted a mermaid and described her in lascivious detail). The coast of Novaya Zemlya was sighted on 26 June. However, the contrast between the temperate nature of the land and the continuing prevalence of impassable pack ice at sea immediately convinced Hudson that further progress eastwards was probably impossible at any time of year; accordingly, he decided to retrace his route. Once past the Lofoten islands off the Atlantic coast of Norway,

he set a westerly course—again, it seems, with the intention of testing a north-western route to the East. The reaction of the *Hopeful*'s crew was more forcible than in the previous year, and in his journal Hudson later confirmed a near mutiny by unconvincingly denying it: 'I gave my companie [that is, his backers] a certificate under my hand, of my free and willing returne, without perswasion or force of any one or more of them' (Purchas, 13.332). Faced with this threat of insurrection, Hudson had abandoned any further reconnaissance, and set the *Hopeful*'s course for England, which she reached on 26 August 1608.

On Dutch East India Company service The Russia Company's enthusiasm for any further exploratory voyages was by now exhausted, but the Dutch East India Company remained keen to find a route to the East beyond potential Spanish or Portuguese interference. Accordingly, its representatives invited Hudson to Amsterdam late in 1608, and on 8 January 1609 commissioned him to make a further attempt to force a north-eastern passage via Novaya Zemlya (though they also specifically ordered him not to attempt to find its western equivalent). Hudson appears to have entered into this agreement with absolutely no intention of passing eastwards; his experiences of the previous two years had inclined his attention entirely to prospects for the obvious alternative—a north-west passage. With a crew of sixteen, in the ship *Halve Maen* ('Half Moon') of some 120 tons burden, he departed from Amsterdam on 25 March 1609. Initially he followed the expected route; but on 21 May, after one half-hearted attempt to round Norway's North Cape against contrary winds, he set his course to the west. The Dutch historian van Meteren later suggested (without offering corroborating evidence) that the Dutch element of the crew had refused to pass further east (Johnson, 128); but Hudson's known predilections required little coercion in this respect.

On 9 July, after a slow Atlantic crossing during which Hudson attempted to find 'Busse Island', supposedly discovered during Martin Frobisher's voyage of 1578, the *Halve Maen* made contact with French fishing vessels off the Newfoundland Grand Banks. Three days later she reached the coast of Nova Scotia. Thereafter she passed on to the coast of Maine and turned southwards. On 17 July a brief landing brought a parley with Indians, who spoke some French and told Hudson of gold, silver, and copper mines nearby. Subsequent contacts with the local population were cautiously friendly and trade was initiated; however, constantly (if erroneously) fearing treachery, the Anglo-Dutch voyagers pre-empted their putative peril by robbing an Indian settlement on 25 July and fleeing precipitously to sea thereafter. They touched briefly upon Cape Cod, but then lost contact with the American coast for two weeks; however, on 18 August the *Halve Maen* entered the mouth of Chesapeake Bay. Hudson correctly identified this although, curiously, he did not attempt to seek out the new English colony at Jamestown. Almost immediately the ship stood out to sea to weather storms before turning northwards. Delaware Bay was entered on

2 August, but again no landing was made there. Moving further to the north, the *Halve Maen* reached New York Bay on 3 September and anchored.

The following day Hudson and his mariners had the first in an intensive series of encounters with Indians of the region. These were very friendly but inveterately light-fingered, and from the start the potential for conflict was apparent. Two days later, having passed through the Ver-razano Narrows into the Hudson River, an Anglo-Dutch reconnaissance party was attacked by Indians in two canoes and one of their number was slain. However, this may have been a raiding party, as other Indians who visited the *Halve Maen* in the following days seemed not to know of the encounter.

The obvious riches of the region, minutely observed in the later account of the voyage written by the master's mate, Robert Juet (Purchas, 13.364, 368–9), inclined Hudson to explore the interior. In the following ten days the *Halve Maen* moved up the Hudson River as far as the pres-ent site of Albany, encountering several more friendly tribes. On their return passage downriver, however, they killed an Indian who tried to steal some trifle from the ship, and mutilated another. A minor battle followed, with two further Indian deaths. The affray encouraged the Europeans to end their explorations and make for home; nevertheless, they departed with uniformly positive impressions of the land and its bounties, and with a name—the Indian Manna-Hata—for the large island at the lower extremity of the Hudson River (ibid., 3.372).

The *Halve Maen* made an uneventful eastern passage across the Atlantic, but returned to England, rather than the Netherlands, on 7 November 1609. The ship and her Dutch crew, together with Hudson's journals (which had been pored over in the meantime by curious Englishmen), were sent on to Amsterdam some seven months later.

With *Discovery* to Hudson Bay Though Hudson expressed himself willing to make a further north-western explor-ation under the aegis of his former Dutch employers, it was a new English syndicate of some twenty-four merch-ants, gentlemen, and parliamentarians—the nucleus of the future North-West Passage Company—who now financed an attempt to realize his goal under a legitimate commission, rather than by the somewhat devious means he had employed previously. On 17 April he sailed with a crew of twenty-two (including his son John once more) in the ship *Discovery*. Having explored the American coastline southwards from about 44° N in 1609, Hudson realized that the north-west passage—if it existed—must lie fur-ther north. Accordingly, the *Discovery* crossed the Atlantic at approximately 65° N, making contact with the Green-land coast on 4 June. Moving southwards and crossing Davis Strait, the *Discovery* rounded Resolution Island a month later and entered what would become known as Hudson Strait, retracing the route of Martin Frobisher and George Weymouth, who had entered this passage in 1578 and 1602 respectively.

The timing of subsequent events is obscure; Hudson's journal, following its 3 August entry (at roughly which time the *Discovery* emerged from the strait into Hudson

Bay), was deliberately destroyed by the men who would become its author's executioners. The great prevalence of ice, experienced at every stage of their passage into the bay, caused even Hudson to fall into despair, as was later reported by a survivor, Abacuk Prickett. For three months, forced ever southwards by this barrier, the Englishmen slowly penetrated the great bay, or 'labyrinth', as Prickett gloomily termed it, touching occasionally upon its east-ern shores. By 10 November the expedition was frozen in at the southernmost point of James Bay, where the *Discov-ery* was hauled aground. Initially the men were relatively comfortable; with almost six months' provisions, and their diet supplemented by partridges and fish caught locally, they passed the harsh winter without fatalities. However, a general air of discontent, caused in large part by Hudson's peremptory manner of dealing with what he considered to be occasions of insubordination, was exacerbated when supplies began to fail from May 1611. Hudson also appears gradually to have fallen into an abject lethargy, creating a vacuum of authority when firm leadership was required. In early June the division of their final provisions degenerated into a free-for-all between the men, with lockers ransacked thereafter to find imagined caches of bread. Hudson did nothing to prevent this disorder. Eventually one of the crew, Henry Greene, spoke to several of his disaffected crewmates, urging them to join him in a mutiny. The most enthusiastic of his supporters was Robert Juet, who had been hired once more for this voyage but then dismissed as master's mate by Hudson. On the morning of 22 June, as ice began to break up in the bay, they surprised and seized those who had refused to join them; Henry Hudson, his son John, and six others were placed into the *Discovery*'s small shallop and towed behind the ship into open water. There, they were cast adrift.

The mutineers sailed north, returning to 'Cape Digges' at the entrance to Hudson Bay, where they had observed a great prevalence of fowl in the previous year. Landing to replenish their dwindling stores on 28 July, they encoun-tered an Inuit party. The meeting was friendly, and the two groups agreed to trade the following day. However, the Inuit appear to have been an uncharacteristically aggressive group; their subsequent meeting was in fact an ambush, in which four Englishmen—including Greene—were slain. The survivors fled back to their ship and set a course for Ireland. In the return passage Robert Juet died of malnutrition, though his near starving shipmates made the coast of Galway in September 1611, and from there, by stages, went to London.

The surviving mutineers made depositions to the admir-alty court, and it was suggested initially by the masters of Trinity House that all should be hanged (Johnson, 196); but legal proceedings were not commenced for some five years thereafter. In the meantime, the unsentimental adventurers of the North-West Passage Company used the men's expertise in subsequent voyages to Hudson Bay (one of them, Robert Bylot, Juet's replacement as master in 1610–11, made several further voyages to find a north-west passage). When, in 1616, four of the crew (including

Abacuk Pickett) were tried for murder, they successfully argued that they had mutinied only to avert starvation, and that the conveniently dead Greene and Juet had been their ringleaders. The accused were found not guilty in February 1618.

No trace of Hudson, his son, or the other abandoned unfortunates was ever found. Though their fate was a cruel one, it had been brought on in large part by Hudson's intemperate and unpredictable nature. This weakness of character apart, he had proved himself a competent, perhaps even a gifted, navigator, though—ironically—he was responsible for the discovery of none of the features that were to be named in his honour. Portentously, his growing obsession with finding a north-west passage to the East, and his failure to appreciate the concerns of his men, had been responsible for two near mutinies before the fatal insurrection of 1611.

Little is known of Hudson's family. His wife, with whom he had at least three sons, including the unfortunate John, was said to have been named Katherine.

JAMES MCDERMOTT

Sources S. Purchas, Hakluytus posthumus, or, Purchas his pilgrimes, bk 13 (1625); repr. Hakluyt Society, extra ser., 26 (1906), vol. 13 · D. S. Johnson, Charting the sea of darkness: the four voyages of Henry Hudson (Camden, Maine, 1993) · G. M. Asher, ed., Henry Hudson the navigator, Hakluyt Society, 1st ser. (1856) · W. Foster, England's quest of Eastern trade (1933) · D. W. Waters, The art of navigation in Elizabethan and early Stuart times (1958) · T. K. Rabb, Enterprise and empire: merchant and gentry investment in the expansion of England, 1575–1630 (1967) · A. B. Beaven, ed., The aldermen of the City of London, temp. Henry III–[1912], 1 (1908)
Likenesses P. van Somer, oils, 1620, City of New York Public Collection

Hudson, Henry (*fl.* 1782–1792), mezzotint engraver, is known to have been in London and Surrey at the end of the eighteenth century. Nothing else is known except that a relative, W. Hudson, worked alongside him for a time. Redgrave suggests that he died abroad. His earliest known work, a portrait of Sir William Hamilton after Sir Joshua Reynolds, which he published himself from 13 Great Russell Street, Bloomsbury, is dated 1782. In 1786 he published a portrait of the antiquary John Henniker after a painting by George Romney, and another entitled *Music* after a painting by the Revd Matthew William Peters. The latter depicted the daughters of the bishop of Peterborough, Frances and Emma Hinchcliffe. In 1787 Hudson engraved William Tate's portrait of Andrew Wilkinson, captain and sportsman, publishing it at Petersham, Surrey. His print of Lemuel Francis Abbott's portrait of Vice-Admiral Robert Roddam was published at 116 Holborn, in 1789. In 1790 he published an engraving of Mather Brown's portrait of George, Viscount Macartney, and in 1792 he published the same artist's portrait of Alexander Wedderburn, Lord Loughborough. Hudson's portrait of Joseph Planta, librarian at the British Museum, was published in 1791, after a painting by George Engleheart. Other paintings engraved by Hudson were John Hoppner's *A Rescue from an Alligator* of 1786, George Morland's *Industry* and *Idleness* of 1790, and *David and Bathsheba* after Valerio Castelli. All these painters were his contemporaries, but he also engraved *Belshazzar's*

Feast after Rembrandt. Examples of his work are held by the British Museum, the National Portrait Gallery, and the Victoria and Albert Museum.

MARY GUYATT

Sources J. C. Smith, British mezzotinto portraits, 2 (1879), 703–8 · T. Dodd, History of English engravers, BL, Add. MS 33402, fol. 120 · Redgrave, Artists, 2nd edn, 228 · Bryan, Painters (1903–5), 3.82

Hudson, Hilda Phoebe (1881–1965), mathematician, was born on 11 June 1881 in Cambridge, one of the four children of William Henry Hudson (1836–1916), fellow of St John's College, Cambridge, later professor of mathematics at King's College and Queen's College, Harley Street, London, and his wife, Mary (1843–1882), daughter of Robert Turnbull of Hackness, Yorkshire. Mary Hudson died when Hilda was still an infant, and her father had a strong influence on his children's early life; three of them became mathematicians. Indeed, Hudson's first publication, a simplified proof in Euclidian geometry, appeared in *Nature* in 1891 when she was ten.

Hudson entered Newnham College, Cambridge, from Clapham high school with a Gilchrist scholarship in 1900 and took both parts of the mathematical tripos (bracketed with the seventh wrangler, 1903; first class (division three) in part two, 1904). After a year at the University of Berlin she returned to Newnham as lecturer in mathematics (1905–10). A Newnham associate's research fellowship (1910–13) enabled her to spend a year at Bryn Mawr College, USA; she was also awarded MA, and in 1913 ScD, degrees by Trinity College, Dublin. She then became lecturer at West Ham Technical Institute where she prepared students for London University degrees. Although inspiring to the mathematically gifted, she was not an especially successful teacher.

In 1917 Hudson took a wartime civil service post, heading an Air Ministry subdivision doing aeronautical engineering research. Her work on the application of mathematical modelling to aircraft design was pioneering, and a tribute to her versatility. She continued this line of research with Parnell & Co. of Bristol until 1921, and then retired from salaried work to write the treatise for which she is remembered, *Cremona Transformations in Plane and Space* (1927).

Although she published several papers in applied mathematics (1917–20) and a well-received monograph, *Ruler and Compasses* (1916), most of Hudson's work was in the area of pure mathematics concerned with algebraic surfaces and plane curves. Cremona transformation, an analytical technique for studying the geometry of these, was her special interest. Though now displaced by powerful tools of abstract algebra, it was then a subject of considerable activity. Her exceptional geometrical intuition led her by basically elementary methods to solutions of quite difficult problems (reported in seventeen articles, 1911–29), and her much-quoted treatise, the culmination of nearly two decades of scholarly work, presented a unified account of the major elements of the field, supplemented with an extensive annotated bibliography.

A small woman, light of step and bright-eyed behind thick-lensed glasses, Hilda Hudson enjoyed hockey and swimming when young. Her life was simple, almost austere, though she had many friends. She never married. Deeply religious, she sought to unite her intellectual with her spiritual concerns, and increasingly found in mathematics an unending revelation of the glory of God. She was long a supporter of the Student Christian Movement, and honorary finance secretary of its auxiliary movement in 1927–39. As a distinguished mathematician she was one of the few women of her time to serve on the council of the London Mathematical Society, and in 1919 she was appointed OBE for her war work. Early onset of severe arthritis left Hilda Hudson progressively more disabled; latterly she moved into the Anglican St Mary's Convent and Nursing Home in Chiswick, where she died on 26 November 1965, at the age of eighty-four.

MARY R. S. CREESE

Sources M. D. K., 'Hilda Phoebe Hudson, 1881–1965', *Newnham College Roll Letter* (1966), 53–4 · J. G. Semple, *Bulletin of the London Mathematical Society*, 1 (1969), 357–9 · [A. B. White and others], eds., *Newnham College register, 1871–1971*, 2nd edn, 1 (1979), 10, 58 [Mary Turnbull] · Venn, *Alum. Cant.* [Ronald Hudson and William Henry Hudson] · students in residence ledger, 1898–1906, Newnham College, Cambridge, archive · *Proceedings of the London Mathematical Society*, 2nd ser., 17–24 (1918–26) · d. cert. · private information (2004) · *The Times* (30 Nov 1965)
Wealth at death £32,815: probate, 30 March 1966, *CGPLA Eng. & Wales*

Hudson, Sir James (1810–1885), diplomatist, was born in London, the eighth child of Harrington Hudson of Bessingby Hall, Bridlington, Yorkshire, and his wife, Lady Anne (d. 1826), daughter of the first Marquess Townshend and his second wife, Anne Montgomery. He was educated at Rugby School (1823–5) and Westminster School (1825–6) and in Italy (1826–9), at or near Florence. He was appointed clerk to the lord chamberlain in 1830, he was gentleman usher to Queen Adelaide in 1831, 1834, 1836, and 1837, and assistant to William IV's private secretary, Sir Herbert Taylor, from 1830 to 1837. In 1834, following William IV's dismissal of Lord Melbourne's whig government, Hudson was sent to summon home Sir Robert Peel from Italy so that Peel could form a tory administration. In 1835 Hudson was involved in an anti-Russian propaganda campaign instigated by Lord Palmerston. Shortly afterwards he was sent by Palmerston to the Near East, to report on the Circassian war against Russia.

After William IV's death Palmerston made Hudson secretary of legation at Washington (1838). He was appointed in the same capacity to The Hague in 1843 and to Rio de Janeiro in 1845. In June 1850 he was appointed minister of legation at Rio (by Palmerston) after nearly four years as chargé d'affaires. He was active in the suppression of the Brazilian slave trade, for which he was made CB in March 1851. In September 1851 Palmerston offered Hudson a new mission in Italy, consisting of Rome and Florence combined, commenting, 'you have successfully combated the Black Slave Trade in bodies, we now want you to come to Europe to help us to combat the White Slave Trade in minds' (Fleming, 4). The offer was subsequently withdrawn and he was appointed minister of legation at Turin in January 1852.

An Italophile, Hudson supported the cause of Italian independence and became closely associated with the policies of Cavour. In 1855 he was made KCB for his part in securing the Piedmontese alliance in the Crimea. Favoured by the whig leadership, Hudson was distrusted by the tories. His identification with the Italian liberal-nationalist movement prompted Malmesbury to describe him in April 1859 as 'more Italian than the Italians themselves, and he lives almost entirely with the ultras of that cause' (Malmesbury, 475). Malmesbury had determined to sack Hudson, but the tory government fell in June 1859 and Hudson remained minister at Turin for another four years, becoming in 1861 the first British minister to the kingdom of Italy. He was made GCB in 1863 and retired in August that year, amid press speculation that Lord John Russell had forced him from office to make way for Russell's brother-in-law Henry Elliot. The controversy was revived in 1868 and 1885. Hudson lived in retirement in Italy, where he figured prominently in a number of major commercial and financial ventures and was a noted amateur art dealer and collector. He married his long-time partner, Eugenia Vanotti, shortly before his death. He died at the Hôtel d'Angleterre, Strasbourg, on 20 September 1885 from cancer of the tongue, and was buried in Florence.

N. E. CARTER

Sources N. Carter, 'Sir James Hudson, British diplomacy and the Italian question, February 1858–June 1861', PhD diss., U. Wales, Cardiff, 1994 · F. Curato, ed., *Le relazioni diplomatiche tra la Gran Bretagna ed il regno di Sardegna, 1852–56: Il carteggio diplomatico di Sir James Hudson* (1956) · G. Elliot, *Sir James Hudson and Earl Russell* (1886) · J. Fleming, 'Art dealing in the Risorgimento [pt 1]', *Burlington Magazine*, 115 (1973), 4–16 · A. Clarke, 'Cavour e Hudson, 1855–60', *Miscellanea Cavouriana* (1964), 212–49 · C. de Cugis, ed., *England and Italy a century ago: a new turn in economic relations*, 2 vols. (1967–8) [exhibition catalogue, Milan, 9–17 Oct 1965] · J. H. Harris [third earl of Malmesbury], *Memoirs of an ex-minister: an autobiography*, new edn (1885) · L. Bethell, *The abolition of the Brazilian slave trade* (1970) · F. Curato, 'Alcune lettere inedite di Sir James Hudson a patrioti Italiani', *Archivio Storico Italiano* (1968), 465–77 · N Blakiston, 'Carteggio Hudson-Russell (Gennaio–Marzo 1861)', *Archivio Storico Italiano* (1961), 362–86 · Burke, *Peerage* (1939)
Archives Balliol Oxf., corresp. with David Urquhart · BL, letters to A. Panizzi, Add. MSS 36717–36727 · BL, letters to Sir A. Layard, Add. MSS 38986–39120 · BL, corresp. with W. E. Gladstone, Add. MSS 44234–44251 · Hants. RO, corresp. with third earl of Malmesbury · PRO, corresp. with Lord John Russell · PRO, corresp. with Odo Russell, FO 918 · U. Durham L., letters to Viscount Ponsonby · U. Southampton L., corresp. with Palmerston
Likenesses E. Gordigiani, portrait, 1872, Museo Nazionale del Risorgimento, Turin, Italy · Ape [C. Pellegrini], caricature, watercolour study, V&A · Ape [C. Pellegrini], chromolithograph caricature, NPG; repro. in *VF* (26 Sept 1874) · photograph, BM
Wealth at death £4439 6s. 1d.: resworn probate, March 1886, *CGPLA Eng. & Wales* (1885)

Hudson, Jeffery (1619–1682), dwarf, was born at Oakham, Rutland, the son of John Hudson, a butcher employed by the duke of Buckingham. Although both parents were of normal stature, Jeffery developed as a perfectly proportioned dwarf, who was barely 18 inches in height by about the age of eight, when his father presented him to the duchess of Buckingham. She immediately took the dwarf into her service and not long afterwards introduced him to Charles I and Henrietta Maria by having him emerge

Jeffery Hudson (1619–1682), by Daniel Mytens, c.1630

from a cold baked pie during a feast given in their honour. Hudson quickly joined the queen's household, adopting her religion and becoming a Roman Catholic by at least 1636. He reportedly became the boon companion of her monkey, Pug, with whom he is shown in a Van Dyck portrait of Henrietta Maria now in the National Gallery, Washington.

Another portrait, by Daniel Mytens, showing Hudson holding the leash of a large dog, alludes to his participation in court hunts. He also danced in several court masques: as Tom Thumb in Jonson's *Fortunate Isles* (1625), a prince from Hell in the same author's *Chlorida* (1631), and 'a little Swiss who played the wag' in William Davenant's *Salmacida Spolia* (1640). Fuller tells of another appearance in a lost antimasque, in which a porter at the court named William Evans, who was 7½ feet tall, pulled a loaf of bread from one pocket and Hudson, instead of a piece of cheese, from another. Hudson and Evans are pictured together in a print of 1636, along with Thomas Parr (d. 1635), who was reputedly 152 years old, as the smallest, tallest, and oldest men in the world.

In 1630 Hudson was captured by Dunkirk pirates on his return voyage from the court of France, where he had been sent to procure a midwife to assist at the birth of the future Charles II. News of this misadventure moved the queen to tears and, according to the Venetian ambassador, upset the court more than if it had lost an entire fleet (*CSP Venice*, vols. 22, 316). Fortunately he was soon released, although £2500 in jewels and presents from Marie de' Medici to her daughter said to be worth £5000 were never recovered. The incident inspired a mock epic, *Jeffreidos*, by Davenant, printed in 1638. Among other episodes this relates the dwarf's combat with a turkeycock that tried to eat him. Hudson also received the dedication of a tiny book on the virtues of smallness, *The New-Yeeres Gift: Presented at Court from the Lady Parvula to … Little Jefferie* (1636; re-issued 1638).

Despite his small stature Hudson took an interest in military affairs, joining the earls of Warwick and Northampton during the siege of Breda in 1637. He had returned to England by 1640, when he contributed to the bedding ceremony following the marriage of William of Orange to the king's daughter Mary, by producing a large pair of shears with which to cut stitches of the nightgown into which she had been sewn. He accompanied Henrietta Maria at her departure for the Netherlands in early 1642, but returned to England and, according to Thomas Fuller, took command of a troop of horse in the king's army. He was with the queen in the late spring and early summer of 1644, as she made her way from Oxford to Exeter, and then in disguise to Falmouth and safety in France as the forces of parliament closed in around her.

Three months later Hudson issued a challenge to the brother of William Crofts, the captain of the queen's guard, perhaps out of frustration at the teasing to which he was subjected by the cavaliers gathered at her court in exile. The weapons chosen were pistols on horseback. Crofts showed up armed only with a giant squirt with which to 'extinguish' little Hudson and his powder, but the dwarf managed to elude the liquid barrage and shot his opponent fatally in the head. The queen successfully interceded with Mazarin to spare him the death penalty for murder, but was obliged to banish him from her household. While leaving France by sea he was captured by Barbary pirates and sold into slavery. His freedom was finally purchased, possibly by the second duke of Buckingham and his wife, who provided him with a pension when he returned to England. During his captivity he grew to about 3 ft 9 ins., which he attributed to his harsh treatment at the hands of the Turks.

In 1679 Hudson made his way to London, apparently in the hope of again winning employment at court. Instead he arrived just in time to be imprisoned for suspected complicity in the Popish Plot. He was eventually released and received payments from the king's secret service fund for unspecified services, of £50 in June 1680 and £20 in April 1681. He died in 1682. His waistcoat, breeches, and stockings survive in the Ashmolean Museum, Oxford.

R. MALCOLM SMUTS

Sources DNB · J. Southworth, *Fools and jesters at the English court* (1998), chap. 16 · Fuller, *Worthies* (1662), 2.348–9 · J. Wright, *The history and antiquities of the county of Rutland* (1684), 105 · W. Lithgow, *A true and experimentall discourse upon the last siege of Breda* (1637), 45 · GM, 1st ser., 2 (1732), 1120 · H. Walpole, *Anecdotes of painting in England*, ed. R. Wornum, new edn, 3 vols. (1849); repr. (1876) · W. Davenant, *Shorter poems, and songs from the plays and masques*, ed.

A. M. Gibbs (1972), 37–43 • Master Slater, *The new-yeeres gift: presented at court from the Lady Parvula to the Lord Minimus* (commonly called Little *Jefferie*) (1636) • E. Hamilton, *Henrietta Maria* (New York, 1976)

Likenesses D. Mytens, oils, *c.*1630, Royal Collection [*see illus.*] • D. Mytens, group portrait, oils, *c.*1630–1632 (*Charles I and Henrietta Maria departing for the chase*), Royal Collection • A. Van Dyck, oils, *c.*1633–1635 (*Henrietta Maria with her dwarf Sir Jeffery Hudson*), National Gallery of Art, Washington, DC • engraving, repro. in Master Slater, *New-yeeres gift* • group portrait, engraving, BL

Hudson, John (1662–1719), librarian and classical scholar, was born at Wythop, in the parish of Brigham, near Cockermouth, Cumberland, the son of James Hudson. His mother may have been Alice Hudson, whose will was proved in December 1690. No more is known about his family background than that he was educated in grammar by Mr Jerom Hechsteller of the same parish. In 1676 he was admitted as a servitor at the Queen's College, Oxford, and then elected a taberdar. He studied under Thomas Crosthwaite and graduated BA on 5 July 1681 and MA on 12 February 1684. He received his degrees of BD and DD on 5 June 1701, but made no career in the church. He became a fellow of University College on 29 March 1686. Working as a tutor of the college, he printed for his students Beveridge's *Introductio ad chronologiam* (1691), among a few other works, at Leonard Lichfield's Oxford press. Throughout his career Hudson worked closely with Arthur Charlett, who had been elected master of University College (with Hudson's support) in 1692 and who was an influential delegate of the Oxford University Press. Hudson's *Velleius paterculus*, printed together with *Annales Velleiani* by the nonjuror Henry Dodwell (1693; reprinted with additional notes in 1711) was Charlett's new year's gift to the college. In 1698 Hudson failed to get the Greek professorship, which instead went to Humphrey Hody through the political influence of Gilbert Burnet; Burnet emphasized Hody's loyalty, whereas Hudson was known to be a Jacobite. The experience may have caused Hudson to moderate his Jacobitism in future years.

On 11 April 1701 Hudson was elected librarian of the Bodleian Library on the resignation of Thomas Hyde. He chose as his assistant and later second librarian the industrious student Thomas Hearne, the Oxford antiquary. Hudson was a 'considerable bookman' (Philip, *Bodleian*, 72) who corresponded with scholars and librarians at home, such as Thomas Smith and Sir Hans Sloane, as well as with those abroad like Perizonius and Zacagnius. He collaborated with Hearne on several projects to expand the Bodleian collections in difficult times: financially the library was in a bad state, and there was no deposit system owing to the lapse of the Licensing Act in 1695 (renewed in 1710). Hudson donated some 600 books himself and successfully approached authors and booksellers to send presentation copies. Lists of books to be procured for the library are among Hearne's papers. Hearne's *Reliquiae Bodleianae* (1703) was also planned as an attempt to draw attention to the Bodleian as a repository for private collections.

Hudson intended to publish a new catalogue of books, based on earlier plans. Modifying Vice-Chancellor Roger Mander's initial plan, Hudson wished to amalgamate Hyde's 1674 catalogue, by then fully revised by Hearne, and Hearne's 'Appendix' and to publish this Bodleian catalogue under his own name. To this end, he hired an assistant, Moses Williams, to transcribe the catalogue for publication in six volumes. Proposals and a specimen were published in 1714, but Hudson subsequently gave priority to his classical editing. Charlett maintained his interest in the project, and after renewed efforts by Hudson's successors Joseph Bowles and Robert Fysher, the new catalogue was published in 1738.

Despite Hudson's enthusiasm for books, he had a reputation as a negligent if not incapable librarian. The librarian Humfrey Wanley, previously an assistant at the Bodleian, commented contemptuously on Hudson's lack of knowledge about the collections, especially when Hudson failed to locate the recent acquisition of Edward Bernard's books and manuscripts. Hudson was much interested in the business aspect of book production and bookselling. He was closely involved with other scholars' projects, such as David Gregory's *Euclid* (1703) and Hearne's early classical editions: he financed *Eutropius* (1703), *Justin* (1705), and an edition of Pliny the younger (1703), and urged Hearne to publish new editions of Livy (1708) and Cicero. He sold Bodleian duplicates as well as his own publications and Theatre Press books from his library study. In 1713 he purchased, with two of his friends, the whole stock in the press warehouse for £751.

Contemporary critics commented that Hudson, nicknamed the Bookseller, confused his book business with his responsibilities as librarian. Among these critics were the biblical scholar John Mill, the German traveller Z. C. von Uffenbach, visiting the Bodleian in 1710, and Thomas Hearne. Von Uffenbach's caustic description of Hudson's book dealing and his neglect of the library may have been influenced by his talks with the assistant Hearne. As much as the young Hearne had praised Hudson's scholarship, their collaboration as classical editors had come to an end after *Livy* (1708). Their friendship seriously deteriorated through personal and political quarrels which led to the nonjuror and Jacobite Hearne being dismissed as second librarian in 1716. The estrangement caused most of the bitterly negative characterization of Hudson in Hearne's diaries. An anecdote from Thomas Warton (Milton, *Poems*, 1785), concerning the removal about 1720 of Milton's presentation copies from the Bodleian shelves to be sold as duplicates, is without foundation.

Hudson enjoyed an active career as a 'conscientious' classical scholar (Clarke, 528) and was responsible for editions of Thucydides (1696), Dionysius of Halicarnassus (1704), and Dionysius Longinus (1710), and other works. He was involved with many Oxford projects, among them Thomas Smith's edition of St Ignatius (1709), and together with Hearne he assisted his Cambridge friend Joshua Barnes in the latter's edition of Homer's works (1711). Hudson is especially remembered today as the editor of the Greek geographers, for which he enlisted Henry Dodwell's scholarly co-operation. The impressive *Geographiae veteris scriptores Graeci minores* was published in four volumes between 1698 and 1712.

On 2 April 1710 Hudson married Margaret (*bap.* 1686, *d.* 1731), widow of Robert Knapp, a barrister at the Inner Temple and a commoner of University College, and only daughter of Sir Robert Harrison, alderman and mercer of Oxford. Their daughter, Margaret, was born on 24 July 1711. In that year Hudson refused the principalship of Gloucester Hall and on 14 June resigned the fellowship of University College. He was elected principal of St Mary Hall and installed on 16 January 1713, through the interest of John Radcliffe. Hudson had the lodgings of the principal built. In 1714 John Ayliffe's *Antient and Present State of the University of Oxford* printed an account of the Bodleian Library contributed by Hudson. Hudson's last edition, *Flavii Josephi opera*, was published posthumously by his friend Anthony Hall in 1720. Hudson died of dropsy in Oxford on 27 November 1719, and he was buried on 30 November in the chancel of the university church of St Mary the Virgin, Oxford. He left the first choice of his books to University College.

THEODOR HARMSEN

Sources Bodl. Oxf., MSS Rawl. D. 316, D. 732; MS Rawl. letters 7; MS Ballard 17; MS Lister 37; MS Locke c. 24 · J. Hudson, correspondence, Bodl. Oxf., MSS Smith 50, 63 · T. Hearne, correspondence, Bodl. Oxf., MSS Rawlinson K (Hearne–Smith) · corresp., BL · *Remarks and collections of Thomas Hearne*, ed. C. E. Doble and others, 11 vols., OHS, 2, 7, 13, 34, 42–3, 48, 50, 65, 67, 72 (1885–1921) · W. D. Macray, *Annals of the Bodleian Library, Oxford*, 2nd edn (1890); facs. edn (1984), 169–93 · Wood, *Ath. Oxon.*, new edn, 4.451–60 · T. Harmsen, 'Bodleian imbroglios, politics and personalities, 1701–1716: Thomas Hearne, Arthur Charlett and John Hudson', *Neophilologus*, 82/1 (1998), 149–68 · T. H. B. M. Harmsen, *Antiquarianism in the Augustan age: Thomas Hearne, 1678–1735* (2000) · H. Carter, *A history of the Oxford University Press*, 1: *To the year 1780* (1975), 151, 241; appx · I. Philip, *The Bodleian Library in the seventeenth and eighteenth centuries* (1983), chap. 4 · M. L. Clarke, 'Classical studies', *Hist. U. Oxf.* 5: *18th-cent. Oxf.*, 513–34 · *Letters of Humfrey Wanley: palaeographer, Anglo-Saxonist, librarian, 1672–1726*, ed. P. L. Heyworth (1989), 74, 162, 185, 240, 253, 318 · S. Gibson and J. Johnson, eds., *The first minute book of the delegates of the Oxford University Press, 1668–1756* (1943), 38–9, 41, 75 · P. Simpson, *Proof-reading in the sixteenth, seventeenth and eighteenth centuries* (1935); repr. (1970) · I. G. Philip, 'Libraries and the University Press', *Hist. U. Oxf.* 5: *18th-cent. Oxf.*, 725–54 · J. E. B. Mayor, *Cambridge under Queen Anne* (1911), 379, 386 · J. Ayliffe, *The antient and present state of the University of Oxford*, 2 vols. (1714), vol. 2, pp. 457–66 · Foster, *Alum. Oxon.* · P. Bayle and others, *A general dictionary, historical and critical*, 6 (1738), 299–302 · J. R. Magrath, *The Queen's College*, 2 (1921), 62 · W. Hutchinson, *The history of the county of Cumberland*, 2 (1794), 229–30 · M. Clapinson and T. D. Rogers, *Summary catalogue of post-medieval manuscripts in the Bodleian Library, Oxford* (1991) · F. Madan and others, *A summary catalogue of Western manuscripts in the Bodleian Library at Oxford*, 7 vols. (1895–1953) · *DNB* · will, proven in deanery of Copeland, 22 Dec 1690, Cumbria AS [Alice Hudson, widow of Wythop]

Archives Bodl. Oxf., papers · Bodl. Oxf., 'Indices auctorum a variis scriptoribus vel citatorum vel etiam laudatorum', Rawl. MS misc. 350 · Bodl. Oxf., biographical information, MS Rawl. J fol. 3. 317, MS Rawl. 4°2. 251, 7.363 | BL, notes relating to A. Beverland, Add. MS 4221 · BL, letters to P. Desmaizeaux, Add. MS 4284. 88–92 · BL, letters to W. Kennett, J. G. Graeve, F. Rostgaard, C. Neville, M. Lequien, Add. MSS 4275–4277 · BL, letters to Sir Hans Sloane, Sloane MSS 4038–4043 · BL, letter to Wanley, loan MS 29/255 · BL, letters, Harley MS 3781, 191–212 · BL, loan 29 · Bodl. Oxf., corresp. with Thomas Smith · Bodl. Oxf., Ballard MSS · Bodl. Oxf., MSS Hearne diaries · Bodl. Oxf., MSS Rawl. lett.

Likenesses S. Gribelin, line engraving (after W. Sonmans), BM · W. Sonmans, oils, Bodl. Oxf.

Wealth at death see *Remarks*, ed. Doble and others

Hudson, John (1795–1869), agriculturist, was born at Grimston, Norfolk; little is known about his early life, but in 1822 he and his father took on the tenancy of Lodge Farm (788 acres) and of Manor (or Lower) Farm (653 acres), at Castle Acre, Norfolk, from Thomas William Coke of Holkham. He soon became a leading figure in the second generation of improving farmers on the Holkham estate.

1822 was a time of agricultural depression and the previous tenant of Lodge Farm (Mr Purdey) had sold up for the benefit of creditors in that year. The farms were said to be in poor condition and had been refused by three previous prospective tenants. Yields were no more than 20 bushels of wheat and 24 bushels of barley per acre. The root crops grown had not enabled the outgoing tenant of Lodge Farm to winter more than 10 bullocks (Jenkins, 460–74).

The background of the Hudsons is obscure, but they must have had plenty of capital. This they immediately put to use in improving the farms. According to the 1851 census John's wife, Anne Rebecca, was three years his junior and born in Warham, Norfolk, possibly the daughter of a Holkham tenant there. The Revd Armstrong, writing in 1856, described Hudson as a 'princely yeoman of Norfolk' and was told that he had been a postilion to Mr Hammard (landowner of West Acre, Norfolk), 'in which capacity he had saved £100. He married a widow of Lynn by whom he had accession to a fortune, became Lord Leicester's tenant at Castle Acre and is now worth £100,000' (Armstrong, 63). Hudson managed both farms until his father's death in 1840. Manor Farm was then run by executors until his son, Thomas, took over in 1857; Thomas Hudson remained there until his death in 1903.

John Hudson's immediate task in 1822 was to improve the fertility of the farms, which he undertook in two ways. First he followed the traditional method of increasing stocking rates to produce more manure, which involved the expenditure of between £2000 and £3000 per annum on oil cake and other artificial feeds. He thus doubled the number of animals kept and claimed that by feeding sliced turnips and oil cake to his sheep in the fields he had increased the output of the land by a third. By 1850 there were 2500 sheep and 150 bullocks on the two farms; in 1822 there had been only 400 sheep and 40 bullocks. Second, he spent £800 to £1000 per annum on the new artificial manures such as superphosphates and guano. As a result of this extremely high investment he claimed that the barley crop had nearly doubled. In 1843 he told R. N. Bacon, author of *The Agriculture of Norfolk*, published that year, that 'with more capital and more skill, this country might be an exporting rather than importing country' (Norfolk RO, MS 4363).

In spite of the large quantities of artificial fertilizers being used, Hudson preferred to farm by the four-course rotation system which he was said to practise 'with the greatest skill and liberality' (Jenkins, 460–74). William Keary, the Holkham agent, noted in 1851 that the farm was almost weed-free and 'that such lands produce this enormous bulk of roots and corn is truly astonishing and proves indisputably the high condition of the farm and the skill of the tenant' (Holkham MS, Keary's report).

Hudson was also interested in mechanization. By 1843 he had erected a steam engine to drive a threshing machine and grind oil cake. Such machines were unusual in Norfolk, a county far away from coal supplies and where cheap labour was plentiful. By 1850 he had two steam engines on his farm, one stationary and one portable, as well as one threshing machine worked by horsepower. In 1866 he bought his own steam plough to overcome the need to hire steam tackle (Jenkins).

It was Hudson's methods of 'high farming' and his enthusiasm for and promotion of this high-input, high-output system that made him famous. By 1842 he was a member of the recently formed Royal Agricultural Society of England and at that time he was portrayed in a painting of the society's meeting at Bristol. In 1850 he wrote an essay for the Royal Agricultural Society's farm prize competition and it was published that year. In it he described himself as having spent 'a life devoted to practical farming' (Hudson, 282–7). He was in addition the first chairman of the Farmers' Club in London in 1842–3, and a member of the club's tenants' rights committee in 1846.

Hudson died on 26 July 1869 at The Beeches, Cirencester, Gloucestershire. He was survived by his wife. An obituary in the *Journal of the Royal Agricultural Society* described him as 'one of the first exponents and chief illustrators of the principles and practice of high farming'. Lodge Farm was then run by executors until 1878, when it was re-let.

SUSANNA WADE MARTINS

Sources S. Wade Martins, *A great estate at work: the Holkham estate and its inhabitants in the nineteenth century* (1980), 114–19 · H. M. Jenkins, 'Lodge Farm, Castle Acre', *Journal of the Royal Agricultural Society of England*, 2nd ser., 5 (1869), 460–74 · Norfolk RO, MS 4363 MFRO 12–13 · J. Caird, *English agriculture in 1850–51* (1852), 165, 168 · Holkham MS, Keary's report and the letter books, Holkham Hall, Norfolk · J. Hudson, 'A plan for farm buildings', *Journal of the Royal Agricultural Society of England*, 11 (1850), 282–7 · B. Almack, 'On the agriculture of Norfolk', *Journal of the Royal Agricultural Society of England*, 5 (1845), 321–57 · D. J. M. Armstrong, ed., *Armstrong's Norfolk diary*, 63 · census returns, 1851 · CGPLA Eng. & Wales (1869)
Likenesses portrait, 1842, Royal Agricultural Society of England, Warwickshire · bas-relief on monument (to T. W. Coke; with his son), Holkham park, Holkham · oils, Royal Agricultural Society of England, Warwickshire
Wealth at death under £25,000: probate, 15 Sept 1869, *CGPLA Eng. & Wales*

Hudson, Sir John (1833–1893), army officer, was the eldest son of Captain John Hudson RN (1796–1869), and his first wife, Emily (d. 9 Oct 1844), only child of Revd Patrick Keith, rector of Ruckinge and Stalisfield in Kent. He was educated at the Royal Naval School, New Cross, and became ensign by purchase in the 64th (2nd Staffordshire) regiment on 22 April 1853. He was promoted lieutenant on 9 March 1855 and served as adjutant to his regiment throughout the Persian campaign of 1856–7. He was present at the storm and capture of Rishahr, the surrender of Bushehr, the night attack and battle of Khushab, and the bombardment of Muhammarah.

At the time of the Indian mutiny Hudson was serving as regimental adjutant in Bengal and the North-Western Provinces. He was present in 1857 with Sir Henry Havelock's column in the actions at Fatehpur (12 July), Aong (15 July), Pandu Nadi (15 July), Cawnpore (16 July), Unao (29 July), Basiratganj (29 July), and Bithur (16 August). He was deputy assistant adjutant-general on Havelock's staff during the advance to Lucknow, and was mentioned in dispatches. He then served as adjutant of the 64th foot during the defence of Cawnpore, and was present at the defeat of the Gwalior mutineers, at the actions of Kali Nadi (2 January 1858) and Kanker (17 April), and at the capture of Bareilly (May). He was then attached to Brigadier Taylor's brigade as brigade major in the actions at Burnai, Muhamdi, and Shahabad. For his services he was promoted captain in the 43rd (Monmouthshire) light infantry on 23 July 1858, and was allowed a year's service for Lucknow.

On 7 April 1859, at Allahabad, Hudson married Isabel Muir, daughter of Major-General Charles Frederick Havelock (d. 14 May 1868) of the Ottoman army and niece of Sir Henry Havelock; she survived her husband. He was appointed assistant adjutant-general of the division at Lahore on 26 July 1861, and on 22 March 1864 he received the brevet rank of major. In the Abyssinian expedition (1867–8) he was second in command of the 21st Bengal native infantry and was mentioned in dispatches. He received the brevet rank of lieutenant-colonel on 13 June 1870, and on 11 April 1873 attained the regimental rank of major. On 1 October 1877 he obtained the brevet rank of colonel.

On 10 August 1878 Hudson was appointed commandant of the 28th Bengal native infantry, with which he served throughout the Anglo-Afghan War of 1878–80. He was present during the operations in the Khost valley, including the action at Matun, and was twice mentioned in dispatches. He was with Sir Frederick Roberts's division in the advance on Kabul in 1879, and with Brigadier-General Herbert Macpherson's brigade in the rear-guard at Charasia on 6 October 1879. During the operations around Kabul in December he commanded the outpost at Lataband, and was mentioned in dispatches for sallying out and dispersing a hostile force which threatened to invest the garrison. He attained the regimental rank of lieutenant-colonel on 22 April 1879 and on 22 February 1881 was made CB. He commanded the British troops occupying the Khyber Pass from January 1881 until they were withdrawn.

In 1885 Hudson commanded the Indian contingent in the Sudan campaign, with the rank of brigadier-general, for which he was made KCB on 25 August 1885. On his return to India he commanded the Rohilkhand brigade of the Bengal army from 1886 to 1888 and attained the rank of major-general on 2 August 1887. From 1888 to 1889 he was in command of the Quetta division of the Indian army, and from 1889 to 1892 commanded the Allahabad division of the Bengal army. On 13 January 1892 he became a lieutenant-general. Early in 1893 he was appointed commander-in-chief in Bombay. He was killed at Poona on 9 June 1893 by a fall from his horse, and was buried there on the following day.

E. I. CARLYLE, rev. ALEX MAY

Sources *Army List* · *Indian Army List* · *The Times* (10 June 1893) · *The Times* (12 June 1893) · G. H. Hunt, *Outram and Havelock's Persian campaign* (1858) · J. C. Pollock, *The life of Havelock of Lucknow* (1957) · C. Hibbert, *The great mutiny, India, 1857* (1978) · B. Robson, *The road to Kabul: the Second Afghan War, 1878–1881* (1986) · Lord Roberts [F. S. Roberts], *Forty-one years in India*, 2 vols. (1897) · Boase, *Mod. Eng. biog.*

Likenesses portrait, repro. in *ILN* (17 June 1893)

Wealth at death £165 16s. 6d.: probate, 1894, *CGPLA Eng. & Wales*

Hudson, (Arthur) Kenneth (1916–1999), industrial archaeologist and museologist, was born on 4 July 1916 at 12 Lushington Road, Harlesden, Middlesex, the son of Arthur Leonard Hudson, an insurance official, and his wife, Edith Mary, *née* May. He was educated at the John Lyon's School, Harrow on the Hill, and in 1935 went to University College, London, from which he graduated BA in English in 1938. On 23 June 1938 he married Hope Edith Agnes Symons (*b.* 1916/17), a teacher; they had a son and two daughters. Hudson spent the war as a noncombatant, serving with the Friends' Ambulance Unit and as an army education officer.

After a brief post-war spell in Germany engaged on educational work for the Foreign Office, Hudson joined the adult education department of Bristol University in 1947, leaving in 1954 to become a radio talks producer and later the first Bristol-based industrial correspondent for the BBC. In 1966 he was appointed by Bristol College of Science and Technology (later Bath University of Technology, now the University of Bath) to found the university's educational television service.

But it was in the fields of industrial archaeology, in which he was an early pioneer and populist, and later museums, that Hudson made his name. In 1961 he was commissioned by the publisher John Baker to write on industrial archaeology, a subject which Hudson virtually invented. The term had first appeared in print in 1955; Hudson's *Industrial Archaeology: an Introduction*, published with the active support of the Council for British Archaeology in 1963, was the first general work on the subject. H. J. Habakkuk, in the introduction, offered the cautionary and prophetic warning that 'This essay is a foray into the debatable borderland between history, technology and economics': it was the beginning of a new and fruitful way of examining recent history. Among Hudson's other books on the subject were *The Industrial Archaeology of Southern England* (1965), *A Guide to the Industrial Archaeology of Europe* (1971), *The Archaeology of Industry* (1976), and *World Industrial Archaeology* (1979). He was the founder of the *Journal of Industrial Archaeology* and served as its first editor, from 1964 to 1968. *Industrial Archaeology Review*, published by the Association for Industrial Archaeology, is its direct descendant.

Hudson left the university in 1972 to become a freelance writer and broadcaster. By then he had become increasingly interested in museums. The first tangible expressions of this were his involvement as a judge for the museum of the year awards, launched by National Heritage in Britain in 1972, and the publication of the monumental *Directory of Museums* (1975, 1981, and 1985), in collaboration with Ann Nicholls. In 1976, after an approach

(Arthur) Kenneth Hudson (1916–1999), by Theo Richmond

by National Heritage, the European Cultural Foundation offered a grant to set up a similar award scheme in Europe, and Hudson took on the task of creating the new international body that would accomplish it. The first European museum of the year awards (EMYA), under the auspices of the Council of Europe and sponsored by IBM, were made in 1977. From then until his death, Hudson, with the support throughout of Nicholls, managed the scheme. He brought together the organizing committee and panels of judges, set out a rational and practicable way of proceeding, and instructed them on what criteria to apply and how to categorize the results. He raised the sponsorship (and when this was no longer forthcoming kept things going anyway), devised the presentation ceremonies, and, in 1996, secured the patronage of Queen Fabiola of Belgium. In 1997 the European Museum Forum was set up, with Hudson at the helm, to administer both the awards and the associated publications and workshops.

These arrangements suited Hudson's temperament to perfection. A compulsive traveller, and fluent in most European languages (he readily admitted to being less than proficient in Greek and Finnish), he visited literally hundreds of museums throughout Europe, scrutinizing entries, encouraging the diffident, and from time to time castigating those who paid scant attention to the needs of their visitors. His heart was always with the underdog, those museums that had succeeded in the face of adversity, with minimal funding or in the teeth of political or bureaucratic opposition. And what he saw as the self-serving arrogance of art museums he viewed with a circumspection bordering on outright hostility.

Hudson published prolifically on museums for more than twenty years, titles including *A Social History of Museums* (1975), *The Cambridge Guide to the Museums of Britain and Ireland* (with Ann Nicholls) (1987, 1989), *1992: prayer or promise? The opportunities for Britain's museums and the people who work in them* (1990), *The Cambridge Guide to the Museums of Europe* (with Ann Nicholls) (1991), and *Museums: Treasures or Tools?* (1992). In 1989 he was awarded the Council of Europe medal of honour in recognition of his advocacy for the cause of museums across Europe, and in 1993 he was made an honorary fellow of the Museums Association. He had been elected FSA in 1967 and was appointed OBE in 1997. He died from cancer on the way to Shepton Mallet Community Hospital on 28 December 1999, and was buried in Ditcheat, Somerset, on 6 January 2000.

Hudson's eclecticism and journalistic flair, his passionately expressed views, his enthusiasms, and his driving energy (he wrote more than fifty books) took him from industrial archaeology, via feminism, shipwrecks, and the history of pawnbroking to the uses of English and the social history of air travel. But it was his unrelenting but always well-intentioned stirring of the world of museums that marked his main contribution to the cultural life of Britain and of Europe.   NEIL COSSONS

Sources *European Museum Forum*, 6 (summer 2000) · *The Times* (1 Feb 2000) · J. Letts, *The Independent* (24 Jan 2000) · R. M. Vogel, *Society for Industrial Archeology Newsletter*, 29 (spring 2000), 16 · M. M. Rix, 'Industrial archaeology', *The Amateur Historian*, 2 (1955), 225–9 · *The Guardian* (21 March 2000) · b. cert. · m. cert. · d. cert.
Likenesses T. Richmond, photograph, priv. coll. [*see illus.*] · photograph, repro. in *The Guardian* · photograph, repro. in *The Independent*

Hudson, Mary (*d.* 1801), organist, was the daughter of the composer Robert *Hudson (1732–1815). She was elected organist of St Olave, Hart Street, London, on 20 December 1781, at an annual salary of 25 guineas, and held the post until her death. From some point in the 1790s she was also organist at St Gregory, Old Fish Street. She composed several hymn tunes, and a setting for five voices of a translation of the epitaph on Purcell's gravestone, beginning 'Applaud so great a guest!'. The hymn tune 'Llandaff' is attributed to both Mary Hudson and her father. She died in London on 28 March 1801.

R. F. SHARP, *rev.* K. D. REYNOLDS

Sources W. H. Husk, 'Hudson, Robert', Grove, *Dict. mus.* (1927) · Brown & Stratton, *Brit. mus.* · vestry minutes, St Olave's, Hart Street, London · J. Love, *Scottish church music* (1891)

Hudson, Michael (1605–1648), Church of England clergyman and royalist agent, was born in Penrith, Cumberland. He went up to Queen's College, Oxford, as 'a poor child', matriculated on 1 February 1622, proceeded BA on 15 February 1626, and took his MA on 29 January 1629. In college he and his brother were friends and contemporaries of the diarist Thomas Crosfield, who had become a fellow in October 1627. Hudson was among four fellows admitted at the next election, 30 October 1630, alongside the logician Christopher Airay. Although Crosfield knew his friend as 'Sir Hudson' (*Diary*, 3), there is no evidence that he came from a landed family; David Lloyd's portrait of him as a 'gentleman of great parts, and greater courage' is coloured by hagiography (D. Lloyd, *Memoirs*, 1668, 624). As a fellow of Queen's, Hudson seems also to have been tutor to Prince Charles. He was granted a licence to marry Elizabeth Pollard, daughter of Colonel Lewis Pollard of Nuneham Courtenay, Oxfordshire, in April 1633, a woman at least ten years his junior. No date is recorded for their marriage but he and Elizabeth had several children by the

early 1640s although they increasingly lived apart. Hudson was presented to the rectory of Wirksworth in Derbyshire, in 1633, and to Uffington, Lincolnshire, in December 1638. In 1640 Market Bosworth, Leicestershire, and Greetham, Lincolnshire, and, by the king's gift, the mastership of St John's Hospital in Lutterworth were added to his clerical portfolio. As the living at Uffington was worth £140–£160 per annum, and that of Market Bosworth some £300–£400, Hudson enjoyed a substantial income. (He is not to be confused with his Corpus Christi College, Cambridge, contemporary and namesake, whose career involved holding at various times, the livings of West Deeping, Lincolnshire, Witching in Kent, and Irthlingborough, Northamptonshire, and who was prebend at Lincoln in 1633–6.)

At the outbreak of the civil wars Hudson joined the royalists after the battle of Edgehill and shortly afterwards moved to Oxford to be with the king. By royal order he was granted the degree of DD on 21 February 1643, and about the same time he became one of the king's chaplains. The king, who 'usually called him *his plain dealing chaplain*, because he told him his mind, when others would or durst not' (Wood, *Ath. Oxon.*, 3.233), thought well enough of him to make him scout master to the royal army in the north under the marquess of Newcastle, a position he held until 1644. Not surprisingly these court offices and royal deployments took him away from his parochial duties and he was denounced for non-residency. On 20 January 1645 he was ejected by the earl of Manchester from the living at Uffington, on the evidence of four witnesses. The five charges against him, as well as three years' non-residency, claimed that he had only preached once a quarter. He was regarded as a notorious malignant who was constantly at Belvoir and other royal garrisons. Since Thomas South was also deprived of Uffington at the same date it is unclear when Hudson had ceased to minister there, but his family had stayed on in the rectory and his sister looked after South, an unmarried cleric. South in his own evidence claimed that he had obtained the rectory from Hudson 'for a good summe of money' (*Walker rev.*, 257) and possibly in part-exchange for that of Kings Cliffe, Northamptonshire, rated at £300 per annum.

Some time in the summer of 1645 Hudson moved to London, to the White Hart tavern in Southwark, where he remained for nine months, dressed 'in the habit of a scoller then in grey suite with a black casocke' (*Portland MSS*, 1.370) before returning to Oxford in the spring of 1646. During the king's abortive first attempt to entrust his person to the Scots, Hudson may have been involved in the discussions with the French envoy Montreuil and in the attempt to bring 500 of the Scots horse to Market Harborough to meet the king. Certainly the king later chose Hudson and John Ashburnham on 27 April 1646 to conduct him in disguise away from Oxford and the tightening stranglehold of the parliamentary armies of Fairfax and Whalley. He later described 'the prodigious preposture and confusion which reigneth in your Majesties Dominions, where servants ride on horse-back and princes walk on foot' (M. Hudson, *The Divine Right of Government*, 1647, sig. A2r). Their movements, bringing the king eventually to the Scottish army at Newark and continuing north to the Tyne, were regularly reported to parliament by Miles Corbett and Valentine Watson.

Although he evaded capture in Newcastle, when parliament sent a serjeant-at-arms to require his attendance in the house (23 May 1646), Hudson failed to reach France, on 6 June being denounced at Sandwich by Colonel Pitman, who had met him at Rochester. The Scots disavowed his claim that he had fully intended to bring the king to parliament. As to the king's intentions, Hudson allegedly revealed that 'the king would yeelde the militia and Ireland, but the Bishops lands the bishops had soe satisfied his scruples he could not yeelde' (*Portland MSS*, 1.371). Brought back to London House he was further examined by a committee of parliament and detained on 18 June. Five months later he escaped; he rejoined his royal master in Newcastle before the end of November, representing himself apparently as an agent for a general uprising. Charles accredited him for the purpose and Hudson wrote to Major-General Rowland Laugharne to offer such assistance. Laugharne turned the papers over to parliament and Hudson was recaptured at Hull on 19 December 1646 and imprisoned in the Tower.

In prison Hudson wrote a royalist defence, *The Divine Right of Government; Naturall and Politique*, as an attack on the parliamentary attempts to limit the king's power and 'the Phansyed State-Principles supereminencing *Salutem Populi* above the Kings Honour' (*The Divine Right*, title page). While he admitted that 'conscience was above all regal power and authority' (ibid., sig. A3r) he asserted that monarchy was the more perfect form of government, appealing to the scriptural precedent of Melchizedek to establish that kings and priests antedate lawgivers. He is also credited with the anonymous pamphlet, *The Royall and Royallist Plea*, published in the same year on another press, which accused those who sought to abandon monarchy and settle the government in the two houses of parliament.

In 1648 Hudson contrived to leave the Tower, allegedly in disguise with a basket of apples on his head although it was claimed that he had been released on compassionate health grounds. In Lincolnshire he raised a loyalist force hoping to win over the gentry of Norfolk and Northamptonshire. Although he took Crowland Abbey he was rapidly outmanoeuvred at Woodcroft Castle, at Etton in the soke of Peterborough. The parliamentarians who besieged him there fought him through the house and out on to the leads, a scene vividly recounted by Walter Scott in *Woodstock*, describing the death of Dr Rochecliffe. Although the details of Hudson's actual death in the moat on 6 June 1648 owe more to later royalist hagiography than historical truth, his fanatical generosity in support of his king is not to be underestimated. He was buried at Denton in Northamptonshire.

NICHOLAS W. S. CRANFIELD

Sources Foster, *Alum. Oxon.* · *The manuscripts of his grace the duke of Portland*, 10 vols., HMC, 29 (1891–1931), vol. 1 · F. Peck, ed., *Desiderata curiosa*, 2 (1735), bk 9 · T. Hearne, *Chronicon, sive annales prioratis de Dunstaple* (1733) · H. Cary, ed., *Memorials of the great civil war in England from 1646 to 1652*, 2 vols. (1842) · H. I. Longden, *Northamptonshire and Rutland clergy from 1500*, ed. P. I. King and others, 16 vols. in 6, Northamptonshire RS (1938–52), vol. 7 and addendum · *Walker rev.* · *The diary of Thomas Crosfield*, ed. F. S. Boas (1935) · J. L. Chester and G. J. Armytage, eds., *Allegations for marriage licences issued from the faculty office of the archbishop of Canterbury at London, 1543 to 1869*, Harleian Society, 24 (1886) · Wood, *Ath. Oxon.*, new edn, 3.233

Hudson, Robert (*d.* 1596), poet and musician, was associated with the court of King James VI of Scotland, and a musician of James's Chapel Royal. At the formation of 'the kingis hous' on 10 March 1568, Hudson was listed as one of the 'violaris', along with Thomas Hudson, James Hudson, and William Hudson, very probably all of the same family, and their servant William Fullartoun. The Hudsons, with Robert Hudson among them, appear to have been present in Scotland in 1565 at the wedding of Mary, queen of Scots, and Lord Darnley; there appear to have been five members of the group at that time and they are also referred to as 'sangistaris', or singers. It has been argued at least since David Irving's *Scottish Poetry* (1861) that they were English in origin, and indeed entries in the exchequer rolls of Scotland refer to them as 'Inglis violaris, servandis to his majestie'. No music is directly attributed to Robert Hudson. He was appointed treasurer of the Chapel Royal in 1587, and served until about 1593.

In the court of James VI, Robert Hudson was also a member of the 'Castalian' circle of courtier–poets which also included Thomas Hudson and Alexander Montgomerie, and although few of his poems have survived, he seems to have been active and recognized as a poet, especially during the 1580s. He is likely to be the R. H. who writes a commendatory sonnet to King James's translation of Du Bartas's work, *Essayes of a Prentise in the Divine Art of Poesie* (1584), and is possibly the R. H. whose dedicatory sonnet appears in Sylvester's translation of Du Bartas. A sonnet written by Hudson as an epitaph to Richard Maitland (*d.* 1586) survives (printed in Pinkerton, 2.351). A further commendatory sonnet by Hudson is prefixed to the manuscript of William Fowler's translation of *Triumphs of Petrarke* (1587), alongside poems by Thomas Hudson and King James, among others. Hudson is also the addressee of a number of poems from that circle of Scottish poets, including a small group of sonnets written by Alexander Montgomerie. Montgomerie begins by addressing Hudson as 'my best belovit brother of the band', and by describing his love for the king, apparently in an attempt to promote himself at court. In the course of this appeal, he also praises Hudson's poetic skill, his 'Homers style, thy Petrarks high invent'. The final poem of this series, however, apparently written by one 'Christen Lyndesay' (which may be a pseudonym of Montgomerie's), complains of Montgomerie's distress at Hudson's faltering friendship. Hudson is also the addressee of an anonymous and incomplete poem found in a manuscript with others by William Fowler (Hawthornden MS xiii, fol. 15r; printed in Fowler, 3.cli), although probably not in Fowler's hand. He is possibly the 'olde crucked Robert' to whom King James refers in a poem about the writers of his court (*New*

Poems, 41); his lameness may also be described in Montgomerie's poems addressed to him, in the form of an allusion to Vulcan. He died in 1596.

CHRISTOPHER BURLINSON

Sources H. M. Shire, *Song, dance and poetry at the court of Scotland under King James VI*, ed. K. Elliott (1969) · *Thomas Hudson's Historie of Judith*, ed. J. Craigie, STS, 3rd ser., 14 (1941) · *Report on the manuscripts of Lord Polwarth*, 5, HMC, 67 (1961) · D. Irving, *The history of Scottish poetry*, ed. J. A. Carlyle (1861) · D. Irving, *The lives of the Scotish poets*, 2 vols. (1804) · *The poems of Alexander Montgomerie*, ed. J. Cranstoun, STS, 7 (1887) · J. Pinkerton, *Ancient Scottish poems*, 2 vols. (1786) · *The works of William Fowler*, ed. H. W. Meikle, J. Craigie, and J. Purves, 3 vols., STS, new ser., 6 (1914), STS, 3rd ser., 7, 13 (1936–40) · C. Rogers, *History of the Chapel Royal of Scotland* (1882) · BL, Add. MS 24488, fol. 411 · *New poems by James I of England from a hitherto unpublished manuscript (Add. 24195) in the British Museum*, ed. A. F. Westcott (New York, 1911)

Hudson, Robert (1732–1815), composer and singer, was born in London on 25 February 1732. Possessed of a good tenor voice, he sang at concerts in the Ranelagh and Marylebone Gardens. In 1755 he was elected assistant organist to St Mildred, Bread Street, and in the following year was appointed vicar-choral of St Paul's Cathedral. He was created a gentleman of the Chapel Royal in 1758, and became almoner and master of the children at St Paul's in 1773, retaining these latter posts for twenty years. He was also music master at Christ's Hospital. He took the MusB at Cambridge in 1784, and was admitted a fellow-commoner of Trinity College. His compositions include a cathedral service, several chants and hymn tunes, and *The Myrtle* (1767), a collection of songs in three books. His daughter, Mary *Hudson (d. 1801), was also an organist. Robert Hudson died at Eton on 19 December 1815 and was buried in St Paul's Cathedral.

R. F. SHARP, *rev.* K. D. REYNOLDS

Sources W. H. Husk, 'Hudson, Robert', *New Grove* · 'Hudson, Robert', Grove, *Dict. mus.* (1927) · Venn, *Alum. Cant.*

Hudson, Sir Robert Arundell (1864–1927), political organizer, was born at Lapworth, Warwickshire, on 30 August 1864, the eldest son of Robert Hudson of Lapworth, and his wife, Jessie, daughter of John Kynoch of Peterhead. He was a delicate boy, and his education at Ludlow grammar school was cut short at the age of sixteen, when he was sent to South Africa for his health. A year later (1881) he was placed in an office in Birmingham, where it is supposed that he came under the spell of Bright and Chamberlain. In 1882 he obtained a post in the National Liberal Federation, founded in Birmingham five years earlier. Hudson quickly attracted the notice of the secretary, Francis Schnadhorst, and was appointed assistant secretary in 1886, in which year, as a result of the defection of Chamberlain, and therefore of Birmingham, on the home rule question, the offices of the federation were transferred to London. In 1889 Hudson married Ada (d. 1895), daughter of Henry Hammerton of Coventry; they had one daughter, Dorothy.

In London Hudson was closely associated with the more radical Liberals, notably Sir Arthur H. D. Acland, who in 1892 became vice-president of the committee of the council on education, Thomas Edward Ellis, later chief whip,

Sir Robert Arundell Hudson (1864–1927), by Elliott & Fry

and J. A. Spender, afterwards editor of the *Westminster Gazette*. Hudson had a share with these men in planning the social legislation advocated by Gladstone in the Newcastle programme of 1891. Succeeding Schnadhorst in 1893 he became secretary both of the federation and of the Liberal Central Association. These institutions had offices under one roof in Parliament Street, and their joint secretary was the link between the confidential organization of the parliamentary party and the autonomous machine which represented the Liberalism of the constituencies. In this capacity Hudson was influential in guiding the party through the many troubles of the next twelve years and in reforming the party's organization. He worked particularly closely with Herbert Gladstone, who became chief whip in 1899, and successive presidents of the federation, Robert Spence Watson and Augustine Birrell. Although himself a staunch member of the Church of England, Hudson came to be regarded as keeper of the nonconformist conscience. After the Liberal triumph of 1906 the labour of years was recognized; Hudson was hailed as the 'organizer of victory', and was knighted. The Liberal organization maintained its efficiency in power, as the two elections of 1910 showed.

In 1914 Hudson offered his services to the Red Cross, and became chairman of the joint finance committee of the British Red Cross Society and the order of St John of Jerusalem. This brought him into co-operation with Lord Northcliffe whose widow, Mary Elizabeth Harmsworth, daughter of Robert Milner of Kidlington, Oxfordshire, he married in 1923. She had been active in the Red Cross and was a lady of grace of the order of St John of Jerusalem. It also made him responsible for the *Times* fund for the British Red Cross, and so ultimately for the collection and administration of nearly £17 million subscribed to relieve the sick and wounded. In 1916 he was offered high office by Lloyd George, an offer which he at once refused. In 1918 he was created GBE and made a member of the Légion d'honneur.

On returning to party politics in 1919 Hudson continued to act, as secretary of the Central Liberal Association, with the independent Liberals under Asquith; but not even he could make bricks without straw, and on 21 January 1927 he resigned. He lived latterly at Hill Hall, Theydon Mount, Essex.

Both in his political work before the war, and in his war work, Hudson's success was complete. In 1906 it was officially declared that in twenty-five years of political work he had made 'countless friends and no enemies'. For the Red Cross he earned the reputation of an irresistible beggar and an impeccable administrator. He was a man of great energy and practical ability. One of the secrets of his political success was his extraordinary knowledge of the persons and local conditions in every constituency. An acute observer wrote that he had 'more common sense and a shrewder judgement of men than any one I ever met'. But by general consent the greatness of his achievement was due less to his intellectual powers than to his qualities of character; to a rare union of strength and sweetness, which found expression in his keen, hard features, lit up by an unforgettable smile. He was a man of varied interests: religion, philanthropy, sport, travel, and society all had a share in his time. The number of his friends and acquaintance was enormous. But it did not seem possible to exhaust his sympathy or his inventive kindliness. Hudson died at 25 Park Crescent, London, on 25 November 1927, survived by his daughter and his second wife.   R. W. CHAPMAN, *rev.* H. C. G. MATTHEW

Sources J. A. Spender, *Sir Robert Hudson* (1930) · T. O. Lloyd, 'The whip as paymaster: Herbert Gladstone and party organization', *EngHR*, 89 (1974), 785–813 · M. W. Hart, 'The decline of the liberal party in parliament and in the constituencies, 1914–1931', DPhil diss., U. Oxf., 1982 · personal knowledge (1937) · *CGPLA Eng. & Wales* (1928)
Archives BL, corresp. with Lord Gladstone, Add. MS 46475 · BL, corresp. with Lord Northcliffe, Add. MS 62169 · Bodl. Oxf., corresp. with Herbert Asquith · Bodl. Oxf., letters to Sir William Harcourt and Lewis Harcourt · Bodl. Oxf., corresp. with Sir Donald Maclean · King's AC Cam., letters to E. F. Bulmer · NL Ire., letters to J. F. X. O'Brien · NL Scot., corresp. with Lord Rosebery · NL Wales, letters to T. E. Ellis and his wife
Likenesses W. Stoneman, photograph, 1919, NPG · Elliott & Fry, photograph, NPG [*see illus.*]
Wealth at death £23,765 9s. 10d.: resworn probate, 11 Jan 1928, *CGPLA Eng. & Wales*

Hudson, Robert George Spencer (1895–1965), geologist and palaeontologist, was born at Rugby, Warwickshire, on 17 November 1895, eldest of four sons and the six children of Robert Spencer Hudson, carpenter and joiner, and later mayor and first freeman of Rugby, and his wife, Annie Wilhelmina, *née* Goble, of Bicester, Oxfordshire.

Hudson was educated in Rugby, at St Matthew's School (1899–1908) and the lower school of Lawrence Sheriffe (1908–13). He then spent a year as a student teacher at Elborow Boys' School and in 1914 entered St Paul's Training College for teachers at Cheltenham. In the First World War, he saw active service in France as a machine-gunner in the Royal Warwickshire regiment, and received a severe facial wound that resulted in his being invalided back to England and discharged from the army. After the war, he entered University College, London, to read geology. He had a successful undergraduate career during which he was secretary and then president of the Greenough Club, and received the London University geology scholarship (1919) and the college's Morris prize. He graduated BSc with first-class honours in 1920. In 1923 he married Dorothy Wayman, daughter of Edward James Pocock Francis, gentleman of London. The three children of this marriage, one son and two daughters, all entered the teaching profession. The couple separated in 1932 and the marriage was dissolved in 1944.

After graduation Hudson was appointed a part-time demonstrator in geology at University College, London, a post which he held for two years and which he combined with postgraduate research. Hudson made a study of the Yoredale rocks in north-west Yorkshire—this formed the basis of his thesis for his MSc (London), which he obtained in 1922. This work was to mark the beginning of his association with the geology of the Carboniferous rocks of Yorkshire, an association which was to last for a quarter of a century.

In 1922 Hudson joined the department of geology at the University of Leeds where he was, successively, assistant lecturer, lecturer (1927), and professor (1939). He resigned the chair in 1940 and remained at Leeds until 1942 as research fellow. From his earliest days in Leeds, he identified himself with Yorkshire rather than with his birthplace, a regional identity which was to persist throughout his adult life. His ability as a teacher was quickly recognized and he established a remarkable rapport with his students who assisted him in many of his projects, collecting suites of fossils from particular areas and breaking many hundreds of feet of drill-hole core, materials on which his many palaeontological publications were based.

Hudson became involved in caving and potholing, serving on the organizing committee and later the council of the British Speleological Association. Later, when in Iraq, he explored some of the more spectacular potholes in the Zagros Mountains. Although involved in many activities outside his teaching and research commitments he still found time to deliver evening lectures to the Workers' Educational Association in Leeds and, after the outbreak of war, he assisted the commissioner for civil defence in the north-western region from 1940 to 1942.

In 1942 Hudson left Leeds University to become a consultant geologist, retained by a number of companies engaged in oil exploration on the Carboniferous rocks in Yorkshire and contiguous counties. It was perhaps inevitable that he should become involved in petroleum geology, for much of his work on the palaeogeography and palaeoenvironment of the Carboniferous rocks, although of academic importance, was also of significant relevance in the interpretation of oil sources, traps, and reservoirs at a time when interest in Britain's onshore oil prospects was developing.

In February 1946 Hudson was appointed to the staff of the Iraq Petroleum Company as geologist and macropalaeontologist and for the next six years he was to take an active part in fieldwork, mapping, collecting fossils, and interpreting structures in the Middle East, from north Iraq to south-west Arabia. He entered into these new duties with tremendous enthusiasm and although initially agreeing to spend eight months in the area, he extended this to a year, returning to London in February 1947. Although engaged in applied economic geology he had not yet abandoned academic commitments and from 1947 to 1958 he was an honorary lecturer in geology at University College, London, serving on the geology board of studies of the University of London in the years following. In 1958 he became an honorary research associate at University College, and from then until 1961 he continued to publish papers on corals, brachiopods, and stromatoporoids from the Mesozoic of the Middle East. In 1960 he was appointed to a research fellowship at Trinity College, Dublin, where his former student W. D. Gill, held the chair of geology. In 1961 Hudson himself was appointed to the chair of geology and mineralogy, a position which he held until his death.

From 1923 to 1950 Hudson published some eighty-seven papers dealing with Carboniferous stratigraphy and palaeontology of the midlands and north of England. He was editor of the *Transactions of the Leeds Geological Association* (1927–40) and the *Proceedings of the Yorkshire Geological Society* (1934–47). Between 1953 and 1961 he published twenty-four papers dealing with the Permian and Mesozoic palaeontology and stratigraphy of the Middle East. From 1964 to his death he returned once again to his first interest, the Dinantian, and in collaboration with postgraduates and colleagues he wrote five papers dealing with the stratigraphy and palaeontology of the Lower Carboniferous of Ireland.

Hudson made important contributions to the palaeontology, stratigraphy, and palaeogeography of the Carboniferous of the north of England and the Mesozoic of the Middle East. His palaeontological work embraced the Lower Carboniferous rugose corals, and he erected the genera *Rhopalolasma*, *Cravenia*, *Hettonia*, and *Rylstonia* (the last three names deriving from Yorkshire place-names). He described the ontological development of many rugose genera; introduced the term *rhopaloid septum* and, in the siliceous sponges, erected the genus *Erythrospongia*. In his work on Mesozoic stromatoporoids from the Middle East he erected the genus *Actostroma* from the Jurassic of Israel and the genus *Steinerina* for a Jurassic hydroid.

Hudson, known affectionately as Hud, was a burly man with a ruggedly handsome face, clipped moustache, and candid grey eyes. Although of more than average height, this was masked by his stocky build. His left jaw was marked by a bullet wound dating from the First World War. His irrepressible enthusiasm and often unorthodox views made him excellent company. He recounted with animated and unfeigned gusto his field experiences in the Middle East. His sense of values was simple; geology occupied the pre-eminent position and material things, and his own personal comfort, came very low on the scale. He was a superb teacher, teaching by example rather than by precept. Even in his last years he was usually to be found in his department up to midnight on most evenings, during both term and vacation. However, he could be indiscreet, and in academic politics he was patently guileless, not to say naïve. Following his separation from his first wife in 1932 Hudson lived, for about ten years, with Irene May Kirby Blackburn; they had five daughters. In 1947 he married Jane Naden, daughter of Cecil Philip Airey. The couple later had three sons and a daughter.

Hudson was active in national and local geological societies. In 1921 he was elected a fellow of the Geological Society of London, and was its vice-president from 1955 to 1956; he was awarded the Wollaston fund in 1931 and the Murchison medal in 1958. He served on the council of the Yorkshire Geological Society, and was its president from 1940 to 1942. From 1939 to 1944 he was secretary of section C of the British Association. When the Palaeontological Association was formed in 1957 he was invited to become its first president. He was president of the Liverpool Geological Society in 1960. In 1961 he was elected a fellow of the Royal Society and in 1962 became a member of the Royal Irish Academy and a fellow of University College, London. In 1964 he became president of the Irish Geological Association and at the time of his death, on 29 December 1965, at Sir Patrick Duns Hospital, Dublin, he was serving his second term in that office. His ashes were scattered at Malham Tarn on the Yorkshire moors. After his death the Royal Dublin Society published the Hudson Memorial Numbers in 1966—which consisted of four papers of which Hudson and his colleagues at Trinity College, Dublin, were co-authors—together with an appreciation and a bibliography. That same year a bell was dedicated to his memory in St Mary's Church, Headley, Surrey. Several fossils were named for him, including the Namurian goniatite genus *Hudsonoceras* by E. W. J. Moore in 1946.   J. S. JACKSON, *rev.* PATRICK N. WYSE JACKSON

Sources C. J. Stubblefield, *Memoirs FRS*, 12 (1966), 321–33 · J. S. Jackson, 'Robert George Spencer Hudson, 1895–1965', *Scientific Proceedings of the Royal Dublin Society*, series A, 2 (1966), i–ix · K. C. Dunham, 'Professor R. G. S. Hudson, F. R. S., M. R. I. A.', *Irish Naturalists' Journal*, 15 (1966), 215–17 · P. W. Jackson, ed., *In marble halls: geology in Trinity College Dublin* (1994) · W. H. C. Ramsbottom, 'Robert George Spencer Hudson', *Proceedings of the Yorkshire Geological Society*, 35 (1966), 450–51 · W. D. Gill, 'Robert George Spencer Hudson', *Proceedings of the Geological Society of London*, 1636 (1965–6), 201–2 · personal knowledge (2004)

Archives BGS, fossil collection · NHM, corresp. and papers relating to the Palaeontological Association · NHM, fossil collection · TCD, department of geology · U. Leeds, fossil collection | U. Glas., corresp. with T. N. George

Likenesses W. Bird, photograph, *c.*1960, TCD

Wealth at death £4689: probate, 29 Sept 1966, *CGPLA Eng. & Wales*

Hudson, Robert Spear, first Viscount Hudson (1886–1957), politician, was born in London on 15 December 1886. He was the eldest son of Robert William Hudson (1856–1937), of Villa Paloma, Monaco, and later high sheriff of Buckinghamshire, who had sold the family business of soap manufacture as soon as he succeeded to it, and his first wife, Gerda Frances Marion Bushell (d. 1932), only daughter of Robert Johnson, of Liverpool. Educated at Eton College and at Magdalen College, Oxford, where he obtained a second class in modern history in 1909, Hudson entered the diplomatic service in 1911 and was posted successively to St Petersburg, Washington, Athens, and Paris, becoming a first secretary in 1920. On 1 December 1918 he married Hannah (d. 1969), daughter of Philip Synge Physick Randolph, of Philadelphia. They had one son.

In 1923 Hudson resigned as a diplomat in order to stand for parliament as Conservative candidate for the Whitehaven division of Cumberland. He was unsuccessful in this first attempt, but was elected the following year in the same constituency, which he represented until 1929. In 1931 he again entered parliament, as member for Southport, a seat which he retained until his elevation to a viscountcy in 1952. In recognition of his services to the area Southport conferred on him the honorary freedom of the borough.

From 1931 to 1935 Hudson was parliamentary secretary to the Ministry of Labour. He publicly opposed the government's centralization of services for the unemployed through the Unemployment Assistance Board, with Neville Chamberlain calling his actions 'positively disloyal' (Lowe, 176). He was moved soon after to be, from 1935 to 1936, minister of pensions, and from 1936 to 1937 parliamentary secretary to the Ministry of Health. Then followed nearly four years (1937–40) as secretary of the department of overseas trade and a brief spell (April–May 1940) as minister of shipping. In these offices he established a reputation for competence and hard work. He took a particular interest in the organization of the British Industries Fair and other activities for the promotion of British overseas trade—activities which at that time were thought to clash with the interests of farmers and the protection of agricultural prices.

It was with some apprehension therefore that the agricultural world received the news of Hudson's appointment in 1940 by Churchill as minister of agriculture and fisheries, particularly as he was taking the place of Sir Reginald Dorman-Smith, who was a popular past president of the National Farmers' Union with firsthand knowledge of farming problems. In fact Hudson was judged an outstanding success in this post. With a determination, as Lord Winterton commented, 'to see that farmers and landowners alike used every acre of soil to help keep the nation from starvation' (Winterton, 272), Hudson and his junior minister, Tom Williams, undertook a massive organizational and publicity task. Through guaranteed prices and markets for most goods, and the development of a nationwide network of decentralized county and district committees involving local farmers themselves in the monitoring of land use, farming output was increased greatly. The acreage in England and Wales of wheat, for example, was by 1944 increased by 82 per cent, potatoes by 116 per cent, sugar beet by 24 per cent, and the total area under tillage by nearly 4.75 million acres (69 per cent).

For householders, simple 'dig for victory' leaflets were widely distributed and the *In your Garden* radio broadcasts were popular with a large audience. Hudson was also supportive of a range of other innovations. Regarding the Women's Land Army, formed to fill labour shortages in agricultural areas, Vita Sackville-West said that it 'can have had no kinder or more co-operative friend than the Minister of Agriculture, Mr Robert Hudson' (Foreman, 96).

But Hudson also faced difficult challenges. It was apparent that guaranteed prices for farm produce had been set at too high a level in the early period of the war to encourage the use of all, even perhaps unviable, land. When farm workers received wage rises in 1942 and 1943 Hudson refused to increase these guaranteed prices; a 'storm of angry meetings and speeches followed which Hudson, not the most tactful of men, was unable to pacify' (Calder, 425). Some concessions were made by the government. But early in 1944 anger among farmers against Hudson found an outlet in their support for the left-wing Common Wealth candidate who was victorious in a by-election at Skipton, in the Yorkshire dales. Despite these conflicts, Hudson, in the view of Winterton and many others, 'was by far the best of Ministers of Agriculture in either war' (Winterton, 272).

Hudson remained in office until the Labour government was elected in 1945. He was sworn of the privy council in 1938 and made a CH in 1944. He had become personally interested in the problems of practical agriculture and purchased a farm in Wiltshire where he established a successful Friesian herd. In 1954–5 he was president of the British Friesian Society, and he served on the council of the Royal Agricultural Society. He also became chairman of the board of governors of the Imperial Institute and Britain's representative on the United Nations Trusteeship Council. He also embarked on farming in Southern Rhodesia and it was during a visit there that he died, on 2 February 1957, at Charter estate, Beatrice, near Salisbury.

WILLIAM GAVIN, rev. MARC BRODIE

Sources *The Times* (4 Feb 1957) · *The Times* (6–7 Feb 1957) · *The Times* (11–12 Feb 1957) · *Farmers' Weekly* (8 Feb 1957) · D. N. Chester, ed., *Lessons of the British war economy* (1951) · K. A. H. Murray, *Agriculture* (1955) · personal knowledge (1971) · GEC, *Peerage* · Burke, *Peerage* (1959) · S. Foreman, *Loaves and fishes: an illustrated history of the ministry of agriculture, fisheries, and food, 1889–1989* (1989) · R. Lowe, *Adjusting to democracy: the role of the ministry of labour in British politics, 1916–1939* (1986) · A. Calder, *The people's war: Britain, 1939–1945* (1969) · E. T. Winterton, *Orders of the day* (1953) · J. Ramsden, *The age of Churchill and Eden, 1940–1957* (1995) · P. Addison, *Churchill on the home front, 1900–1955* (1992) · *WWW* · *CGPLA Eng. & Wales* (1957)

Archives FILM BFI NFTVA, news footage · IWM FVA, news footage

Likenesses H. Coster, photographs, 1930–39, NPG · W. Stoneman, photograph, 1935, NPG · photograph, repro. in *The Times* (4 Feb 1957) · photograph, repro. in Foreman, *Loaves and fishes*

Wealth at death £140,797 14s. 0d.: probate, 6 Aug 1957, *CGPLA Eng. & Wales*

Hudson, Stephen. *See* Schiff, Sydney Alfred (1868–1944).

Hudson, Thomas (*d.* in or before **1605**), musician and poet, was probably a native of the north of England, possibly Yorkshire. He spent most of his adulthood and professional life in Scotland as a musician and first appears in the list of 'violaris' in the service of James VI in 1567: 'Mekill [that is, "muckle" or "big"] Thomas Hudsone, Robert Hudsone, James Hudsone, William Hudsone, and William Fullartoun their servand' [*see* Hudson, Robert (*d.* 1596)]. The Hudsons in all likelihood were brothers, and James Craigie concludes from Thomas's appearance at the head of various lists that he was the eldest; he was certainly the highest paid, which suggests 'that he was the most important of them as a musician' (Craigie, x). An entry dated 1578 in the *Register of the Privy Seal* runs:

> Ane letter makand Thomas, Robert, James and William Hudsounis, Musicianis, oure soverane lordis domestick servandis and gevand to thame the zeirlie fie undir written, That is to say, the said Thomas the sowme of Thre scoir poundis, and ilk ane of the uther three fiftie poundis money of this realme. (ibid., xiii)

The Hudsons were clearly valued performers from then on, as payments totalling £210 Scots are recorded between 1579 and 1595. All their names reappear in 'The Estait of the King's Hous' for 1584 and 1590, with particulars as to salary and liveries. Thomas Hudson was installed master of the Chapel Royal on 5 June 1586, his appointment being ratified by two acts of parliament dated respectively 1587 and 1592. This office was intended to fulfil the terms of a 1579 act of the Scottish parliament that called for the establishment of 'sang sculis' (Craigie, xv). Craigie conjectures that Hudson's appointment also marked a move from presbyterianism to episcopacy, in line with James's vision as embodied in the Black Acts of 1584. Craigie offers a third factor in Hudson's appointment, that it constituted the raising of a layman to an ecclesiastical office—and at a salary (£200 Scots) that was twice that paid previously to the cantor, his pre-Reformation precursor, and the same as that accorded to college principals (ibid., xvi–xvii).

Hudson's chief work is *The historie of Judith in forme of a poeme, penned in French by the noble poet, G. Salust, lord of Bartas, Englished by Tho. Hudson* (1584). It was probably suggested by the king, to whom Hudson dedicates it and who supplied a commendatory sonnet that alludes to Hudson's Englishness:

> Though a straunger yet he lovde so dere
> This Realme and me, so as he spoilde his avvne.
> (Craigie, x)

It runs fluently and the number of verses is limited to that of the original text. Hudson's version was reissued in London in 1608 with the later editions of Josuah Sylvester's translation of Bartas's work, and again in 1613, alone. His 'Englishing' of Bartas is significant as the work of an expatriate Englishman earning his living in Scotland but William Drummond of Hawthornden much preferred Sylvester's translation, a rendering that Ben Jonson

thought 'was not well done' (*Notes of Ben Jonson's Conversations*, 51). Hudson is one of the contributors to *England's Parnassus* (1600), and Ritson and Irving are agreed in identifying him with the T. H. who contributed a sonnet to James VI's *Essays of a Prentise* (1585). Both Hudson's *Historie of Judith* and James's *Essays of a Prentise* were published by the same Scottish-based English printer, Thomas Vautroullier. The sole surviving correspondence from Hudson is a letter written in 1587 to Archibald Douglas, who was then in London, requesting a copy of *Common Places* (1583), an English translation of the work of Peter Martyr.

From January 1594 Hudson received a life pension of £110 Scots, and ten months later this was supplemented by a grant of 500 merks a year, also for life. Craigie conjectures that Hudson was dead by 1605. His name drops from the records in 1595, when there is an entry on payment in the exchequer rolls of Scotland. Craigie's claim is supported by the fact that John Gib was appointed to the Chapel Royal in February 1605. Hudson had a wife and children, mentioned in a lawsuit with Thomas Kay of Crail in Fife but not named; no details are known beyond a bare reference to 'bairns'. In 'The Return from Parnassus' (played at Cambridge in 1606) Hudson and Henry Lock (or Lok) are advised to let their 'books lie in some old nooks amongst old boots and shoes', to avoid the satirist's censure. Thomas Hawkins hastily inferred (*The Origin of the English Drama*, 3 vols., 1773, 2.214) that Hudson and Lok were the Bavius and Maevius of their age. Hudson's efforts are never contemptible, and Sir John Harington (in his notes to *Orlando Furioso*, bk 35) characterizes the *Historie of Judith* as written in 'verie good and sweet English verse'.

T. W. BAYNE, *rev.* WILLY MALEY

Sources BL, Add. MS 24488, p. 411 · J. Ritson, *Bibliographia poetica* (1802) · D. Irving, *The lives of the Scotish poets*, 2 vols. (1804) · *Notes of Ben Jonson's conversations with William Drummond*, ed. D. Laing (1842) · J. Craigie, 'The life of Thomas Hudson', in *Thomas Hudson's Historie of Judith*, ed. J. Craigie, STS, 3rd ser., 14 (1941), ix–xx

Hudson, Thomas (*bap.* **1701**, *d.* **1779**), portrait painter and art collector, was a native of Devon. He was probably the son of James Hudson (*d.* 1704) of Exeter, a victualler, and his wife, Anne, who was baptized George Hudson at the church of St Mary Major, Exeter, on 8 December 1701. According to George Vertue he was 'learnt of' the London artist Jonathan Richardson (Vertue, *Note books*, 3.66) and had married Richardson's daughter Mary (1700–1769) by 1725, when their first child, Ann Elizabeth (1725–1737), was baptized. Two other children, Mary (*b.* 1728) and Henry (*b.* 1729), died in infancy. Richardson made a portrait of Hudson, a drawing in red chalk (British Museum), at some time during the 1720s.

Until Richardson's retirement in 1740 Hudson painted portraits primarily in the west country, including Devon and Bath. His earliest portraits are documented in the accounts of the Courtenay family of Devon for 1728 (manuscript, priv. coll.). His early work imitates Richardson's in composition and technique. On Richardson's retirement Hudson gained a number of his master's clients and became more prominent in London. Described

Thomas Hudson (*bap.* 1701, *d.* 1779), by Joseph Wright of Derby, *c.*1751

by Vertue in 1742 as 'a good ingenious man really of great merrit' (Vertue, *Note books*, 3.111), Hudson increased his patronage by hiring the Flemish artist Joseph van Aken as his drapery painter, a successful collaboration first mentioned by Vertue in 1743. His work soon showed the influence of portraits by Anthony Van Dyck.

During his career Hudson painted at least 400 portraits, about eighty of which were engraved. Sitters included members of the aristocracy, landed gentry, political leaders, Anglican clergy, and popular figures in music and the theatre. He was one of England's most employed portraitists in the 1740s and 1750s. Among his best-known portraits are *Theodore Jacobsen* (1746; Thomas Coram Foundation for Children, London), *Lady Mary Andover* (1746; Ranger's House, Blackheath, London), *Benn's Club of Aldermen* (1752; Goldsmiths' Company, London), *Charles Spencer, Third Duke of Marlborough, and his Family* (*c.*1755; Blenheim Palace, Oxfordshire), and two portraits of George Frideric Handel (1748–9; Staats- und Universitätsbibliothek, Hamburg; and 1756; NPG).

Some of Hudson's compositions may have been influenced by a trip in 1748 to France, Holland, and Flanders. By this time he had begun to form a collection of paintings, drawings, prints, and sculpture by other artists. His collection stamp, TH, is found on numerous old master drawings. Hudson continued to employ drapery painters after van Aken's death in 1749. A rapid trip to Rome in 1752 did not dramatically alter his work. Hudson's success attracted apprentices, among them Joshua Reynolds (1740–43), Joseph Wright of Derby (1751–3 and 1756–7), and John

Hamilton Mortimer (1757). After the mid-1750s, when Reynolds began to receive commissions from Hudson's patrons, a rivalry developed that has adversely coloured subsequent opinions of Hudson.

Although Hudson exhibited with the Society of Artists in 1761 and 1766 he was receiving fewer commissions by this time, and he retired to his villa in Twickenham. In 1770, after the death of his first wife, he married Mary Fynes (1702–1783). Hudson died at Twickenham on 26 January 1779. His will, dated 25 October 1776, names his second wife and members of the May and Carpenter families of Exeter among the legatees. Although Horace Walpole stated that 'the better taste introduced by Sir Joshua Reynolds put an end to Hudson's reign' (Walpole, 4.124) an unidentified writer in the *St James's Chronicle, or, British Evening Post* for 13 January 1781, wrote that 'Hudson was no bad Colourist, and was one of those Limners who gave an easy, if not a graceful, Attitude to the human Figure'. His collection was dispersed in 1779 and 1785, in three important sales.   ELLEN G. MILES

Sources E. G. Miles and J. Simon, *Thomas Hudson, 1701–1779, portrait painter and collector: a bicentenary exhibition* (1979) • E. G. Miles, 'Thomas Hudson (1701–1779): portraitist to the British establishment', PhD diss., Yale U., 1976 • H. Walpole, *Anecdotes of painting in England ... collected by the late George Vertue, and now digested and published*, 3rd edn, 4 (1782) • Vertue, *Note books*, vol. 3 • J. Simon, ed., *Handel: a celebration of his life and times, 1685–1759* (1985) • J. Boundy, 'Two youthful west country sitters to Hudson', *Apollo*, 123 (1986), 90–91 • will, PRO, PROB 11/1050, fols. 58v–6or

Archives BM, engravings, after Hudson • Courtauld Inst., photographs • NPG, photographs

Likenesses J. Richardson, chalk drawing, *c.*1725–1730, BM; copy, V&A • J. Wright of Derby, drawing, *c.*1751, Derby Museum and Art Gallery [*see illus.*] • H. Adlard, engraving (after drawing by P. Sandby, 1764), repro. in *Arnold's Magazine of the Fine Arts* (1833)

Wealth at death villa in Twickenham; paintings; prints; furniture; models; casts; chinaware; jewellery: will, PRO, PROB 11/1050, fols. 58v–6or

Hudson, William (*c.*1577–1635), barrister and writer, was probably a native of Kent; nothing is known of his parents, early education, and first marriage, save for the names of his children. He was admitted to Gray's Inn in 1601 and called to the bar in 1605, was 'ancient' by seniority in 1622, and as Lent reader was called to the bench in 1625. In 1594 he had become a clerk to one of the three attorneys in Star Chamber, and in 1604 had succeeded to an attorneyship there. Even before quitting the office in the spring of 1608 he had already begun to practise as a barrister in Star Chamber. He quickly became the pre-eminent leader of the specialized sub-bar there, the fifty-four barristers (out of a total of some 1250) who signed pleadings in 40 per cent of the nearly 8000 cases in 1603–25. Hudson signed in 16 per cent of the cases—almost 900 cases, nearly evenly divided between prosecution and defence—between 1608 and 1625; each of the two counsel who came closest to him attained only about two-thirds of his caseload. Moreover, Hudson was the master of special pleading, adept at dashing a case before it could proceed to the proof stage. He was often retained merely to prevent the other side from enjoying his services, as relators suing by the attorney-general indicated: during the attorney-generalship of Sir Thomas Coventrye (1621–5), Hudson signed jointly with him almost a quarter of his informations. Increasingly the court turned to Hudson when he was 'at bar' (and his caseload determined that he was seldom absent) to instruct it in procedural matters. As advocate, not only did he have an unparalleled knowledge of procedure, but he was quick and direct in responding to challenges from the other side, precise and economical in construing the evidence, and very concise in his submissions, avoiding grandiloquence, which he clearly detested and for which he tacitly condemned Francis Bacon.

Lord Chancellor Bacon was the target of the faintly veiled opprobrium repeatedly directed at 'the old chancellor' in Hudson's treatise on the Star Chamber, written in 1621 with subsequent additions in some copies of the manuscript version. Hudson meant to instruct Bacon's successor, John Williams, bishop of Lincoln, who received the great seal in July 1621, in Star Chamber's procedural and substantive law. His didactic end was to urge Williams to return to the sound practices of the court under Thomas Egerton, Lord Ellesmere, in 1596–1617, that 'most reverend and learned lord chancellor' (Hudson, 95). Hudson obliquely taxed Bacon with creating unnecessary offices in the court, favouring some counsel (especially his numerous relatives) over others, presiding in the court with orotundity and glib wittiness rather than with appropriate dignity, encouraging procedural deceleration with attendant delay and expense to the litigants, and in at least one notorious case (*Attorney-General v. Alien Merchants*) perpetrating a palpable miscarriage of justice. Hudson argued that the court must be returned to its 'antient course', as it had been under Ellesmere, if it was not only to do justice commensurate with its 'antiquity' and 'dignity' but defend itself against those who disparaged it, challenged its jurisdiction, and denied its privileges. Chief among these was Sir Edward Coke, who unlike Bacon enjoyed Hudson's respect, though he was no longer on the bench or a privy councillor in Star Chamber, simply because of the esteem in which lawyers and laity alike held him. The court was in danger.

Hudson's apprehension about the peril to the court was premature but no less prescient. His politics were clearly 'court'. His close work with Coventrye when attorney-general carried over into great respect for him as lord keeper after 1625. Hudson opened for the attorney-general *pro rege* in the prosecution of William Prynne for *Histriomastix* in 1634, and his accustomed rhetorical spareness and precision had a sharp edge in suggesting Prynne's libel bordered on advocating tyrannicide (Harvard U., Houghton L., Eng. MS 1359, fols. 23v–25). Hudson's closest friend at Gray's Inn and overseer of his will was Chief Justice Sir John Finch, who epitomized the court lawyer and to whom he bequeathed his 'great cabinett' out 'of my love and respect' in expectation that Finch would settle differences among the legatees without suit at law (will, fol. 58). One of Hudson's two trustees was John Lightfoot of Gray's, his protégé and successor to his practice and his papers, who would defend Strafford and was a notable royalist. The preamble to Hudson's will

is conventionally Anglican, lending credence to the notion that Hudson was among those 'antipathetic to the puritan cause' (Prest, 215).

Hudson wore his allegiance on the sleeve of his gown, and his treatise was clearly a labour of love in defence of an institution that he had made peculiarly his own. It was also a remarkable vade-mecum to practise in the court. Though not printed until 1792 by Francis Hargrave from two defective manuscripts, it was widely distributed in manuscript in the 1620s and 1630s. Some two score manuscripts exist in major libraries on both sides of the Atlantic, eighteen in the British Library alone (Guy, 78), and in private hands. The most accurate extant version, BL, Harley MS 1226, was given to Chief Justice Sir John Finch by Hudson's son and heir. Contemporaries recognized the treatise as authoritative, thanks to Hudson's pre-eminence at the court's bar. But even a decade before his call, as a clerk to a Star Chamber attorney young Hudson had been asked by the lord keeper and others his opinion on procedural matters (Barnes, 'Mr Hudson's Star Chamber', 288). Behind the treatise lay the assiduous collection of cases from reports, extracts from the court's order and decree books, notes of precedents, and a contemporary treatise by Isaac Cotton gathered together in BL, Lansdowne MS 639.

Hudson's practice inhibited much other activity. He was not a justice of the peace in Middlesex. He was one of a dozen counsel in the 1624 commission to abate nuisances of building in Middlesex and liberties—understandably since the builders were prosecuted in Star Chamber. While he was assiduous in his duties at Gray's, his only office was as dean of the chapel in 1630–31. He appears to have written nothing else. His Lent reading of 1625 has not been found; it may be speculated that it was on 3 Hen. VIII c. 1, *Act pro camera stellata* (1487).

Hudson amassed a sizeable fortune, worth about £500 per annum, entirely by practice and shrewd investment in real estate and secured loans. He preferred a diversified range of realty held by socage and customary rather than superior tenures, along with leasehold property and other chattels primarily in Middlesex and the environs of London, including his house in Hosier Lane, Smithfield, a short walk from his commodious chambers in Gray's Inn hard by the Star Chamber office, with lesser holdings in Lincolnshire, Staffordshire, Herefordshire, and Oxfordshire. His country seat was a modest house at Muswell Hill, Hornsey and Tottenham parish, Middlesex. He had bought and already settled on his son and heir, Christopher, the manor and messuage of Mareham on the Hill, Lincolnshire (Lindsey), and he left the bulk of his estate to Christopher after the death of his second wife, Anne, widow of William Stodderd, a London skinner, whom he had married on 3 April 1613; there were apparently no children of this marriage. His three other sons were dealt with at best slightly; his second son, William, was left 20s. to buy a ring, Hudson 'having already given him more then I could well spare' (will). In expectation of death he was as precise and focused as he had been in the practice of his profession in life. Hudson died, probably at Muswell

Hill, in December 1635, spared from seeing the disaster that overtook 'his' court in 1641. His treatise is his monument, and that of the court. THOMAS G. BARNES

Sources Hudson's law collection, BL, Lansdowne MS 639 · Hudson's treatise on star chamber, BL, Harley MS 1226 · will, PRO, PROB 11/170, sig. 8, fols. 57-58v · star chamber proceedings, 1603–25, PRO, STAC 8 · MS pension book, Gray's Inn, London, fols. 273, 277-8, 325v, 326, 329v, 333v, 339v, 350v, 351, 355, 361v, 365, 369, 371v, 372v, 374, 375, 377v, 383v, 390 · W. Hudson, 'A treatise of the court of star chamber', *Collectanea juridica*, ed. F. Hargrave, 2 (1792) · T. G. Barnes, 'Mr. Hudson's star chamber', *Tudor rule and revolution: essays for G. R. Elton from his American friends*, ed. D. Guth and J. W. McKenna (Cambridge, 1982), 285–308 · J. A. Guy, *The court of star chamber and its records to the reign of Elizabeth I*, Public Record Office Handbooks, 21 (1985), 78–80 · T. G. Barnes, 'A Cheshire seductress, precedent, and a "Sore blow" to star chamber', *On the laws and customs of England: essays in honor of Samuel E. Thorne*, ed. M. S. Arnold and others (Chapel Hill, 1981), 359–82 · W. R. Prest, *The inns of court under Elizabeth I and the early Stuarts, 1590–1640* (1972), 215 · T. Allen, *The history of the county of Lincoln*, 2 (1834), 9 · J. L. Chester and G. J. Armytage, eds., *Allegations for marriage licences issued by the bishop of London*, 2, Harleian Society, 26 (1887), 19 · W. R. Douthwaite, *Gray's Inn, its history associations* (1886), 68
Archives BL, reports, extracts, etc. collected by Hudson, Lansdowne MS 639
Wealth at death moderately wealthy; landed in Middlesex and Lincolnshire (Lindsey); incidental lands elsewhere; roughly £500 p.a. value: will, PRO, PROB 11/170, sig. 8, fols. 57-58v

Hudson, William (1730x32–1793), botanist, was born at the White Lion inn, Kendal, which was kept by his father. He was educated at Kendal grammar school, and apprenticed to a London apothecary. While an apprentice, he obtained the prize for botany given by the Apothecaries' Company, a copy of Ray's *Synopsis*. From 1757 to 1758 he was resident sub-librarian of the British Museum, and his studies in the Sloane herbarium enabled him to adapt the Linnaean nomenclature to the plants described by Ray far more accurately than did Sir John Hill in his *Flora Britannica* of 1760. In 1761 he was elected a fellow of the Royal Society, and in the following year appeared the first edition of his *Flora Anglica*, which, according to Pulteney and Sir J. E. Smith, marked the establishment of Linnaean principles of botany in England. At the time of its publication Hudson was practising as an apothecary in Panton Street, Haymarket. One of his neighbours there, Benjamin Stillingfleet, is credited both with introducing him to the Linnaean system and with writing the preface to *Flora Anglica*. The publication of this work gave Hudson considerable reputation as a botanist.

From 1765 to 1771 Hudson acted as *praefectus horti* and botanical demonstrator to the Apothecaries' Company at Chelsea. A considerably enlarged edition of the *Flora* appeared in 1778 and a third edition in 1798. In 1783 his house in Panton Street took fire, his collections of insects and many of his plants were destroyed, and those present narrowly escaped with their lives. What materials he had assembled for a *Fauna Britannica* were consumed in the blaze. Hudson retired to Jermyn Street, where he lived with the daughter (and her husband) of the apothecary to whom he had been apprenticed and whose practice he had assumed. In 1791 he joined the newly established Linnean Society. He died in Jermyn Street from paralysis

on 23 May 1793 and was buried at St James's Church, Piccadilly. He bequeathed the remains of his herbarium to the Apothecaries' Company, and some of his specimens became part of the collections at the Natural History Museum and at Kew. Linnaeus gave the name *Hudsonia* to a North American genus of Cistaceae.

G. S. BOULGER, *rev.* P. E. KELL

Sources R. Pulteney, *Historical and biographical sketches of the progress of botany in England*, 2 (1790), 351–2 · H. Field, *Memoirs of the botanic garden at Chelsea belonging to the Society of Apothecaries of London*, rev. R. H. Semple (1878), 88–93 · B. Henrey, *British botanical and horticultural literature before 1800*, 3 (1975), 110–11 · *GM*, 1st ser., 63 (1793), 485 · Nichols, *Lit. anecdotes*, 8.695 · C. Nicholson, *The annals of Kendal* (1832), 245
Archives RS
Likenesses engraving, Linn. Soc.

Hudson, William Henry (1841–1922), author and naturalist, was born on 4 August 1841 on a small ranch, Los Vientecinco Ombúes, near Quilmes in Buenos Aires province, a sovereign state of the Argentine confederation. He was the fourth child of Daniel Hudson (1804–1868), a farmer, and his wife, Caroline Augusta Kimble (1804–1859), both American citizens from New England who emigrated to South America in the 1830s. Brought up on the family's ranch, Las Acacias, in the Chascomús district south of Buenos Aires, without curb or rein except those on his own horse, Hudson ran wild in a wild and not infrequently strife-torn land, associating with neighbouring settlers and their gaucho herdsmen who were a law unto themselves. He had a passion for the wildlife of the pampas, particularly its birds on which he early became an authority.

The little formal education Hudson received was imparted by three successive, unreliable, live-in tutors, two of whom were incompetent—a potential handicap indeed for one who, many years later, would be pronounced 'unsurpassed as an English writer on Nature' (*The Times*, 19 Aug 1922). But at fifteen, following an attack of typhus, Hudson discovered the solace and pleasure of good reading. Later in his teens rheumatic fever, brought on by overexertion and exposure on a cattle drive, almost killed him. Its aftermath, organic heart disease and an acute sense of his own mortality, dogged him for the rest of his life.

Between 1866 and 1869 Hudson collected birds' skins for the Smithsonian Institution in the United States. In 1870 he became a corresponding member of the Zoological Society of London, and by a letter published in its *Proceedings* persuaded Charles Darwin to correct a misleading statement in his *Origin of Species* about pampas woodpeckers. Although an 'evolutionist' Hudson did not believe 'natural selection' to be the sole and sufficient cause of biological change. He spent 1871 observing birds in the valley of the River Negro in Patagonia where he discovered a new species of tyrant bird, subsequently named *Cnipolegus hudsoni*.

Hudson became disillusioned by what he saw as the effect on the pampas's ecosystem caused by the large-scale immigration of bird-eating Italians. On 1 April 1874

William Henry Hudson (1841–1922), by Elliott & Fry

he took passage on the Royal Mail steamer *Ebro* for England, his self-styled 'spiritual country' (W. H. Hudson, *Afoot in England*, 1909, 271). Unsuccessful in obtaining employment as a naturalist, he elected to write; but during the first ten years of his residence in England his only published work comprised nine articles in popular journals and four in the Zoological Society's *Proceedings*.

On 18 May 1876, at St Matthew's Church, Bayswater, London, Hudson married Emily Wingrave, a former professional singer, daughter of John Hanmer Wingrave, a senior civil servant. While a companionable marriage, it was no love match, and despite their fondness for children the couple had none. A discrepancy between her age in the marriage register (thirty-six) and the death register (eighty-five), together with her husband's belief in 1920 that she was almost 100, suggests that she adjusted her age according to circumstances.

For ten years the Hudsons lived, first in Leinster Square, London, then in nearby Southwick Crescent, in dwellings conducted by Emily as boarding-houses. But the failure of both businesses drove them into rented rooms at 5 Myrtle Terrace, Ravenscourt Park, where they lived in genteel poverty on what she earned by giving private music lessons and the little he made by writing. Finally, in the autumn of 1888, they moved into a substantial three-storey house Emily had inherited at 40 St Luke's Road, Bayswater, in which Hudson had lodged during his bachelor days. They retained a few rooms for themselves and let the remainder as flats, the rents from which paid the interest on the mortgage. Despite Hudson's dislike of it and the district in which it was located, Tower House, as it was called, remained his home base for the rest of his life.

Hudson's first two books—works of fiction published in 1885 and 1887 respectively—were commercial failures; but a donation of £40 from the Royal Society enabled him to contribute significantly to the two-volume *Argentine Ornithology* (1888–9) by Dr P. L. Sclater, secretary of the Zoological Society. In 1892 he achieved his first individual success with a collection of 'open-air' essays, *The Naturalist in La Plata*. During that year the dismal failure of his novel *Fan* convinced him that the essay was his most appropriate literary form, a conviction confirmed in 1893 by the success of his *Idle Days in Patagonia*. Until 1892, when he managed to afford to spend a few weeks in Berkshire collecting material for his first English nature book, his visits to the English countryside had been few and brief. A subsequent commission to write a popular reference book of British birds took him to Northumberland; in 1899 he tramped the Sussex downs, which resulted in his celebrated *Nature in Downland* (1900).

In June 1900 Hudson became a naturalized British subject, and on 9 August 1901 he was awarded a civil-list pension of £150 per year 'in recognition of the originality of his writings on Natural History' (*Parl. papers*, 1902, 55.133). For the next ten years, until his wife's decline in health, this regular income—voluntarily surrendered in 1921—enabled him to ramble the southern counties observing all forms of plant and animal life, and also the countryfolk. More importantly, during this period he acquired the subject material for, and wrote, some of his finest rural classics, notably *Hampshire Days* (1903), *The Land's End* (1908), *Afoot in England* (1909), and *A Shepherd's Life* (1910).

But despite his declared preference for natural history and factual rural subjects, Hudson did not abandon fiction. *Green Mansions* (1904), his romance set in a forest in Venezuela, achieved substantial sales, particularly in the United States where it was made into a motion picture by Metro-Goldwyn-Mayer in 1959. Revised editions of his first novels were successful: *The Purple Land* (1904), an action-packed picaresque tale set in nineteenth-century Uruguay and liberally spiced with humour; and *A Crystal Age* (1906), a romance of a future in which the human sex drive is dormant, each community being sustained by a single breeding pair. In *El ombú* (1902), later published in the USA under the more descriptive title of *Tales of the Pampas* (1916), Hudson demonstrated his competence as a short-story writer, the title-story of this collection being hailed as 'a work of genius' (*Letters*, 1). His children's book, *A Little Boy Lost* (1905), is a delightful blend of fact and fantasy containing echoes of his own South American boyhood sensitively narrated in his autobiographical *Far Away and Long Ago* (1918).

Hudson's appearance was impressive. He was 6 feet 3 inches tall, though a little stooped, with long muscular limbs and large well-shaped hands, a sallow complexion, abundant brown hair which had turned grey in later years, a short beard and an untrimmed moustache which almost hid his mouth, brown eyes, and a prominent nose which looked as though it might have been broken. Invariably he wore a tailcoat with pockets in the tails, matching trousers and waistcoat, a high stiff collar, and a tie. His intolerance of class boundaries and an ability to encourage others to talk while he listened attentively enabled him to establish a rapport with people of the rural working class about whom he wrote much and among whom he made many friends. When he was out of London and away from his literary companions he chose to stay in cottages and farmhouses where he could be privy to the life of the community.

Hudson's collected works, issued in 1922–3, fill twenty-four volumes; but despite the extent and variety of his *œuvre* he was not a dedicated writer. Although writing was his livelihood, he regarded it more as a product of his vocation—the gleanings of a 'field naturalist' whom he defined as 'an observer of everything he sees from a man to an ant or a plant' (W. H. Hudson, *A Hind in Richmond Park*, 1922, 334). It also enabled him to satisfy his innate desire to share with others some of the wonders he had seen in nature. His carefully crafted and precise prose has a poetic quality which appeals to the senses as much as its meaning does to the intellect. His achievement in both occupations was recognized, first, by a fellowship of the Zoological Society of London in 1898, and secondly, by an honorary fellowship of the Royal Society of Literature in 1912.

Birds, the subject of such works as *Adventures among Birds* (1913) and *Birds in Town and Village* (1919), continued to be Hudson's speciality, occasionally to be rivalled by an interest in snakes. For thirty-one years, mainly through the Royal Society for the Protection of Birds, of which he was a councillor, he campaigned vigorously for wild bird conservation, eventually being cited as one of its principal British champions.

Hudson had a great affection for old village churches and cathedrals and would often attend and participate in their services; but although brought up in his mother's traditional protestant New England faith, he belonged to no religious denomination. The 'kindly light' of his favourite hymn was the light of his lifelong mistress, Nature, with whom he essayed to coalesce in a process he called 'animism' and defined as 'the mind's projection of itself into nature' (*Idle Days*, 119). Nature and religion were synonymous; and although he held to the continuity of life, he disbelieved in personal salvation.

In August 1911 Hudson's wife Emily became a partial invalid, ostensibly from neurasthenia. Two and a half years later, with little likelihood of her recovering, he moved her into lodgings in Worthing, Sussex, where, with a nurse–companion to care for her, she remained until her death from a cerebral haemorrhage on 19 March 1921. Hudson continued to live in London; and although periodically incapacitated by his injured heart, he visited her frequently. From 1917 he spent his winters in Cornwall, lodging at 23 North Parade, Penzance. Throughout this entire period he continued to write; but his inability to ramble the countryside, as he had done formerly, compelled him to resort, for much of his material, to old field notebooks and to his essays already published in periodicals.

On the morning of 18 August 1922, at his home in 40 St Luke's Road, London, Hudson died of heart failure in his sleep. In accordance with instructions contained in his will his body was taken to Sussex and interred alongside Emily's under the fourth pine tree in a row of seventeen in Worthing's old Broadwater cemetery at Southfarm Road. In Hyde Park in London on 19 May 1925 Stanley Baldwin, the prime minister, unveiled a memorial to him, a stone panel sculpted by Jacob Epstein and set in a bird sanctuary. In Argentina, where half a dozen of his books are esteemed for their portrayal of the pampas before the advent of crop farming and the demise of the gauchos as a discrete social group, his birthplace was transformed into a museum and ecological park named after him, the Parque ecológico cultural Guillermo Enrique Hudson.

With the exception of a few personal bequests amounting to £510, Hudson left his entire estate, valued at some £8225, to the Royal Society for the Protection of Birds for the purpose of providing village schools with illustrated pamphlets and leaflets intended to instil and foster a love of wild birds. He wanted no biography to be written about him, and he left instructions for his executors to destroy most of his notebooks and papers.

DENNIS SHRUBSALL

Sources W. H. Hudson, *Far away and long ago* (1918) · D. Shrubsall, 'W. H. Hudson's English country rambles: a chronology derived mainly from his published and unpublished correspondence', *English Literature in Transition, 1880–1920*, 33 (1990), 64–83 · J. R. Payne, *W. H. Hudson: a bibliography* (1977) · D. Shrubsall, 'Updating W. H. Hudson's bibliography [2 pts]', *English Literature in Transition, 1880–1920*, 31 (1988), 186–8, 437–44 · M. Roberts, *W. H. Hudson: a portrait* (1924) · W. H. Hudson, *Letters on the ornithology of Buenos Ayres*, ed. D. R. Dewar (1951) · *Birds of a feather: unpublished letters of W. H. Hudson*, ed. D. Shrubsall (1981) · S. J. Looker, ed., *William Henry Hudson: a tribute by various writers* (1947) · W. H. Hudson, *Idle days in Patagonia* (1893) · *Letters from W. H. Hudson to Edward Garnett*, ed. E. Garnett (1925) · m. cert. · d. cert. · d. cert. [Emily Hudson] · *Vital records of Marblehead, Massachusetts, to the end of the year 1849, 1: Births* (1903) · J. Sutherland, *The Longman companion to Victorian fiction* (1988)
Archives Dartmouth College, Hanover, New Hampshire, corresp. and papers · Man. CL, Manchester Archives and Local Studies, corresp. and papers · New York University, Elmer Holmes Bobst Library · NYPL, Berg collection · Ransom HRC, literary papers · Royal Society for the Protection of Birds, Sandy, Bedfordshire · Smithsonian Institution, Washington, DC · U. Mich., special collections library, corresp. and papers · U. Oxf., Edward Grey Institute of Field Ornithology · W. Sussex RO · Zoological Society of London | Forbes Magazine, New York, corresp. with John Galsworthy · Harvard U., Houghton L., corresp. with Sir William Rothenstein
Likenesses T. Spicer-Simson, plasticine medallion, *c.*1922, NPG · W. Rothenstein, oils, 1965, NPG · F. Brooks, oils (after photograph), Royal Society for the Protection of Birds, Sandy, Bedfordshire · Elliott & Fry, photograph, NPG [*see illus.*] · E. Williams, photograph, priv. coll.; repro. in D. Shrubsall, *W. H. Hudson: writer and naturalist* (1978), pl. 15 · photograph, Royal Society for the Protection of Birds, Sandy, Bedfordshire
Wealth at death £8225 7s. 2d.: probate, 11 Nov 1922, *CGPLA Eng. & Wales*

Hueffer, Francis (1845–1889), music critic, was born on 22 May 1845 in Münster, where his father held various municipal offices. After school in Münster, he studied philology and music in Leipzig (1866) and Berlin (1867–9). He took the degree of PhD at Göttingen in July 1869, writing his dissertation on the troubadour Guillem de Cabestanh. This was published in Berlin in 1869. In the same year Hueffer moved to London and began writing for journals, including *The Academy* (for which he served as assistant editor), the *Fortnightly Review*, the *Musical World*, and the *North British Review*. The publication of *Richard Wagner and the Music of the Future* (1874, reprinted from the *Fortnightly Review*) attracted much attention. He also edited the *New Quarterly Magazine* and began writing for *The Times*, succeeding J. W. Davison as music critic in 1879. His study *The Troubadours: a History of Provençal Life and Literature in the Middle Ages* (1878) led to his election to the 'Félibrige', and he lectured on the subject at the Royal Institution in 1880. He was naturalized in January 1882.

Hueffer edited a series of biographies, the Great Musicians, and contributed to the opening volume, *Richard Wagner* (1881). He wrote the librettos for Alexander Mackenzie's *Colomba* (1883) and *The Troubadour* (1886, originally entitled *Guillem le troubadour*, based on Cabestanh), and for F. H. Cowen's cantata *The Sleeping Beauty*; he also made a skilful translation of Verdi's *Otello* (1887), making as much use of Shakespeare's original as he could. He was correspondent of *Le Ménestrel*, and wrote articles in Grove's *Dictionary of Music and Musicians*, Mendel's *Musikalisches Conversations-Lexicon*, and the ninth edition of the *Encyclopaedia Britannica*. His other works include a very serviceable translation of the correspondence between Wagner and Liszt (1888) and *Half a Century of Music in England: 1837–1887* (1889), which dates the revival of English music from the accession of Queen Victoria and with it the reversal of the Hanoverian lack of interest, especially through her patronage of Mendelssohn. Hueffer was one of the first critics to draw the attention of the English to Wagner, Liszt, and Berlioz. Although he wrote in a language not his own, he filled posts of great responsibility with success, and he exerted an elevating influence on the art of his time. In 1872 he married Catherine (1850–1927), the younger daughter of the painter Ford Madox *Brown. He died after a short illness on 19 January 1889, and was buried on 24 January at St Pancras cemetery, East Finchley.　　　　J. A. F. MAITLAND, rev. JOHN WARRACK

Sources Grove, *Dict. mus.* · *New Grove* · personal knowledge (1891) · F. Howes, *The English musical renaissance* (1966) · E. Ripert, *Le Félibrige* (1924) · *CGPLA Eng. & Wales* (1889)
Likenesses R. T., wood-engraving, NPG; repro. in *ILN* (2 Feb 1889), 135 · portrait, repro. in T. Baker, ed., *A biographical dictionary of musicians* (1900), 286
Wealth at death £2521 19s. 10d.: probate, 3 Sept 1889, *CGPLA Eng. & Wales*

Hueffer, Oliver Franz (1876–1931), writer, was born on 9 January 1876 at 5 Fairlawn Villas, Merton, Surrey, the second of the three children of Francis *Hueffer (1845–1889), a free-thinking émigré German musicologist and author who Anglicized his name from Franz Hüffer, and his wife, Catherine (1850–1927), daughter of the Pre-Raphaelite painters Ford Madox *Brown (1821–1893) and his second wife, Matilda (Emma) Hill (1829–1890). Francis Hueffer had come to England in 1869 and was for a decade the music critic of *The Times*. Oliver's elder brother, Ford Hermann, was the writer later known as Ford Madox Hueffer, and eventually (from 1919) Ford Madox *Ford (1873–1939). Oliver too incorporated Madox into his name, publishing mainly as Oliver Madox Hueffer.

Oliver, like his brother, went first to an advanced boarding school in Folkestone run by German émigrés, the Praetoriuses. Then both boys attended University College School (in Gower Street, London), Oliver from 1888 to 1892. In 1889, after the sudden death of their father, the boys were sent to live with Madox Brown, whom they adored.

Ford recalled Madox Brown's pride in the 'genius' of his talented grandchildren, and his delight that Oliver was that rarer being, a 'mad genius' (Ford, 251). He was extravagant, theatrical, charming, entertaining, and ingeniously irresponsible, particularly where facts, money, or women were concerned. The dash he cuts in the diaries and memoirs of his circle is of a person of gusto, caprice, and hilarity; someone always larger than life. He moved in a cloud of exaggeration, rumour, and pranks.

Hueffer tried acting, and in September 1895 was given a small part in *Romeo and Juliet*, starring Mrs Patrick Campbell. But his stage presence turned out as anarchic as it was untheatrical. Ford said he 'ran through the careers of Man About Town, Army Officer, Actor, Stockbroker, Painter, Author and, under the auspices of the father of one of his fiancées, that of valise manufacturer' (Ford, 251). Oliver went to Rome in 1893, hoping to be employed by a wealthy Hüffer uncle, and where he was said to have had an audience with the pope. He also considered becoming a barrister, or even a tobacco trader. However, he gave his 'rank or profession' as 'gentleman' when, on 2 March 1897, at Kippington, near Sevenoaks, Kent, he married the violinist Zoe Pyne (1867–1938), daughter of James Kendrick Pyne, who had been the organist in Manchester town hall when Ford Madox Brown painted its frescoes. The couple lived in Chelsea.

Hueffer had begun to write: first plays, later novels; six of his novels were written under the pseudonym Jane Wardle of which *The Lord of Latimer Street* (1907) was one of the most successful. He also wrote journalism and books of reminiscence and cultural observation (*French France*, 1929, was particularly well received). He specialized in portraying artists, vagabonds, burglars, and outcasts. His style is versatile and fluent; often light and entertaining, with touches of Dickensian comic realism. His pleasure in straining the credibility of his plots results in facetiousness. His personal vivacity and wit is thinner on the page than in life, and his work is little read now.

In 1903 Hueffer was hired by the *Manchester Guardian* to write 'a daily "miscellany" column, "shorts", special articles, drama criticism, personals, and a London letter'

(Troy, 173). This was the beginning of a decade of journalism. In 1906 he wrote for *Tribune*. He was Paris correspondent for *The Times*, and covered the Mexican revolution for the *Daily Express*, beginning in 1910. That May he and four other journalists were arrested by Mexican secret police. He also said he wrote for the *New York Sun*, and was a correspondent during the Balkans campaign of 1912–13 and at the start of the First World War.

It was said that Hueffer 'went wrong' before the war. He appears to have squandered the Pyne family fortunes in an 'unfortunate investment'. In July 1911 he was cited as co-respondent in the divorce case of the actress Elaine Inescourt and John Wightman. By 1915 he was living with the novelist and journalist Muriel Harris (1879–1975), who also worked for the *Manchester Guardian*. She continued to use her own name professionally, but later 'told a friend that they were married in the United States because "circumstances" prevented them from marrying in England. It is not clear whether Hueffer was ever legally divorced from Pyne' (Troy, 176).

In October 1915 Hueffer got a commission in the 10th battalion of the East Surrey regiment; he was wounded in the shoulder at Thiepval in September 1916, during the battle of the Somme. He was invalided home, but in February 1918 he was transferred to the 3rd battalion of the Suffolk regiment with the temporary rank of lieutenant, and returned to France to serve as a railway transport officer. He was gazetted out of the army in February 1919. In the 1920s Hueffer and Harris lived in France. On 21 June 1931, after 'an exceptionally good dinner', he is said to have exclaimed 'I've never felt better in my life', and died of a heart attack, aged fifty-four, in West Lavington, Midhurst, Sussex (Saunders, 2.383). He was cremated at Golders Green on 25 June.   MAX SAUNDERS

Sources M. Troy, 'Oliver Madox Hueffer', *Late-Victorian and Edwardian British novelists: second series*, ed. G. M. Johnson, DLitB, 197 (1999) · B. Johnson, ed., *Tea and anarchy* (1989) · *Olive and Stepniak: the Bloomsbury diary of Olive Garnett, 1893–1895*, ed. B. C. Johnson (1993) · F. M. Ford, *It was the nightingale* (1934) · J. M. Soskice, *Chapters from childhood* (1921) · *The Times* (24 June 1931), 18 · M. Saunders, *Ford Madox Ford*, 2 vols. (1996) · R. Skinner, 'A notable family: Oliver Madox Hueffer', *The Scotsman* (27 June 1931), 18 · b. cert. · d. cert.
Archives HLRO, Stow Hill papers · JRL, letters to *Manchester Guardian*
Likenesses photographs, repro. in Saunders, *Ford Madox Ford*

Hues, Robert (1553–1632), mathematician and geographer, was born at Little Hereford, Herefordshire, of unknown parentage. He matriculated at Brasenose College, Oxford, in 1571. Wood recounts that on arrival he was 'only a poor scholar or servitor … he continued for some time a very sober and serious servant … but being sensible of the loss of time which he sustained there by constant attendance, he transferred himself to St Mary's Hall' (Wood, *Ath. Oxon.*, 2.534). Displaying notable proficiency in Greek, he obtained his BA degree in 1578. Many of his lifelong friendships began at Oxford. He probably met Thomas Harriot and Walter Warner at the popular mathematics lectures given by Thomas Allen of Gloucester Hall. All four were later associated with Henry Percy, ninth earl of Northumberland. Another friend was the geographer Richard Hakluyt, then regent master of Christ Church, who drew Hues into Ralegh's circle of navigators and explorers in the 1580s.

There is unsubstantiated evidence that after completing his degree Hues was held in the Tower and then went abroad. His interest now centred on geography and mathematics, and an undated reference shows that he personally made observations of compass variations off the coast of Newfoundland, challenging the accepted values. He may have gone on one of the many fishing trips to the area, or he may have taken part in the 1585 Virginia voyage organized by Ralegh and led by Richard Grenville, when one of the ships sailed home via Newfoundland. Hues's friendship with Thomas Cavendish may date from this period, when both were involved with Ralegh's school of navigation and were tutored by Harriot. Between 1586 and 1588 Hues circumnavigated the world with Cavendish, 'purposely for taking the true Latitude of places', according to an anonymous seventeenth-century report (Bodl. Oxf., MS Rawl. B 158). He may also have been the author of the short account of the voyage by 'NH' published by Hakluyt in his *Principal Voyages* (1589).

In 1589 Hues served with Edward Wright on a voyage to the Azores, and in 1591 he again travelled with Cavendish on a prospective second circumnavigation. Cavendish died in the attempt, but Hues returned to England with John Davis in 1593. In the south Atlantic he had made astronomical observations of the Southern Cross and other southern hemisphere stars, and added new observations on compass variation at the equator and in southern waters. On his return Hues incorporated his findings in a treatise, *Tractatus de globis et eorum usu* (1594). Dedicated to Ralegh, it was intended to encourage the use of practical astronomical navigation by English seamen, and was published to accompany and elucidate the terrestrial and celestial globes made by Emery Molyneux two years earlier. The treatise circulated widely; it was translated into Dutch in 1597, 1611, and 1613, into German in 1613, but not into English until 1638.

Hues continued his connection with Ralegh in the 1590s, and may be the 'Hewes' recorded as dining regularly with Northumberland in 1591. Thereafter he was a servant of Thomas Grey, last Baron Grey of Wilton (d. 1614). From 1604, when Grey was imprisoned in the Tower for his part in the Bye plot against James I, he requested that Hues should be allowed to visit him; in fact Hues was permitted to remain in the Tower with Grey. Although Grey was interested in scientific matters, there is no evidence that Hues took part in experiments with him, or that he was one of the 'three magi' (including Harriot and Warner) who were supposed to have participated in such feats with Northumberland, similarly incarcerated from 1605 to 1621.

Hues only began to be 'attendant upon th'aforesaid Earle of Northumberland for matters of learning' (Shirley, 577) in 1616. Until Northumberland's death in 1632 he received £40 annually. He tutored Algernon Percy, Northumberland's son, at Oxford, where Percy matriculated at Christ Church in 1617, and in 1622–3 Hues was paid to tutor Henry Percy, a younger son. During this time Hues lived at Christ Church, but may have occasionally visited Northumberland at Petworth, Sussex, and Syon House, London, where on one occasion Hues and Warner discussed the reflection of bodies.

Hues passed the remainder of his life in Oxford, discussing mathematics and related topics with those of similar mind. Another task was to price Harriot's books and other items for sale to the new Bodleian Library, under the terms of Harriot's will. Hues and Warner were also jointly charged with assisting Harriot's executor, Nicholas Torporley, in the preparation of Harriot's mathematical papers for publication. Hues died, unmarried, on 24 May 1632 in Stone House, St Aldates, the house of John Smith, cook at Christ Church, opposite the Blue Boar. He made numerous small bequests to friends, one of £20 to his 'kinswoman' Mary Holly, who has not been traced, and 20 nobles to each of her three sisters. He was buried at Christ Church Cathedral.   SUSAN M. MAXWELL

Sources J. W. Shirley, *Thomas Harriot: a biography* (1983) · *Reg. Oxf.*, 2.27 · M. Feingold, *The mathematicians' apprenticeship: science, universities and society in England, 1560–1640* (1984) · [C. B. Heberden], ed., *Brasenose College register, 1509–1909*, 2 vols., OHS, 55 (1909) · Foster, *Alum. Oxon.* · Wood, *Ath. Oxon.*, new edn, 2.534–5 · G. Brenan, *A history of the house of Percy*, ed. W. A. Lindsay, 2 (1902) · D. B. Quinn and J. W. Shirley, 'A contemporary list of Hariot references', *Renaissance Quarterly*, 22/1 (1969), 9–26 · G. Batho, 'Thomas Harriot and the Northumberland household', *Durham Thomas Harriot Seminar occasional paper*, 1 (1983) · will, PRO, PROB 11/163, sig. 30 · *Calendar of the manuscripts of the most hon. the marquis of Salisbury*, 7–17, HMC, 9 (1899–1938) · J. Hutchinson, *Herefordshire biographies* (1890) · Bodl. Oxf., MS Rawl. B. 158 · R. Hues, *Tractatus de globis et eorum usu* (1594) · memorial brass, Christ Church Oxf.

Huet, Thomas (*d.* 1591), biblical translator, was probably a native of Brecknockshire and in 1544 was a member of Corpus Christi College, Cambridge (though probably not the Huet who took his BA in 1562). He became master of the college of the Holy Trinity at Pontefract, and when it was dissolved received a pension, which he was still in receipt of in 1555. Huet was a close associate of leading protestants during Edward's reign, yet survived unscathed under Mary, and even obtained further preferment. He continued to prosper under Elizabeth. He received a number of benefices between 1559 and 1565, including the rectories of Cefnllys and Llanbadarn Fawr in Radnorshire and the prebends of Llanbadarn Trefeglwys and Ystrad in Cardiganshire and of Llandegla in Radnorshire. From 1562 to 1588 he was precentor of St David's Cathedral. Described in the bishop's return (1569) as 'professor of divinity' and 'learned in ecclesiastical laws', he was accused by the diocesan treasurer of having kept the chapter's seals and thus being able to lease estates for his own profit.

Huet was a strong protestant. He signed the Thirty-Nine Articles in the convocation of 1562–3, and in 1571 dismissed the cathedral sexton at St David's for concealing popish mass books; these books he publicly burned. Richard Davies, bishop of St David's, recommended him in 1565 for the bishopric of Bangor, but he failed to secure it, though supported at first by archbishop Parker. As Parker calls him Doctor Huett, he probably at some time proceeded to the degree of DD. Huet was married, although no details of his wife are known. Their daughter married James Vychan, a gentleman of Pembrokeshire.

Huet was called upon (apparently in 1566) by Richard Davies to assist in the Welsh translation of the New Testament (1567). He co-operated with Davies and the Welsh scholar William Salesbury, and was particularly responsible for the translation of the book of Revelation. Huet tended to sacrifice strict accuracy for fluency and his version is characterized by its natural, contemporary language which both reveals his own south-western Welsh dialect and also avoids archaisms, Latinizations, and rhetorical features.

Huet died at Tŷ Mawr, Llysdinam, Brecknockshire, on 19 August 1591, and was buried in the chancel of Llanafan Fawr church, in the same county.

BRYNLEY F. ROBERTS

Sources Venn, *Alum. Cant.* · D. R. Thomas, *The life and work of Bishop Davies and William Salesbury* (1902) · G. Williams, *Welsh Reformation essays* (1967) · G. Williams, *Wales and the Reformation* (1997) · G. Williams, *Bywyd ac amserau'r Esgob Richard Davies* (1953) · I. Thomas, ed. and trans., *Y Testament Newydd Cymraeg, 1551–1620* (1988) · T. Jones, *History of Brecknockshire* (1909), 2.227 · *DWB* · *DNB*

Hugeburc [Huneburc] (*fl.* 760–780), Benedictine nun and hagiographer, spent many years at the double monastery of Heidenheim in Germany; she was also known as Huneburc. She was the author of the lives of Willibald and of his brother Winnebald, composed between 778 and 780, and is the first known Englishwoman to have written a full-length literary work. Her identity as the author of the lives was discovered only in 1931 by Bernhard Bischoff; her name was concealed in cipher between the two lives in their oldest manuscript (Munich, Bayerische Staatsbibliothek, MS Clm 1086), written about 800. Hugeburc was related in some degree to the two brothers, 'a humble relative' she writes, and to their sister Walburg, but nothing else is known of her except the sketchy information given in her writings.

Walburg became abbess of Heidenheim in succession to her brother Winnebald, who had founded it as a monastery in 752. When Walburg inherited Heidenheim, it had to become a double monastery and she brought a group of nuns with her to form the only such institution on the continent founded by the Anglo-Saxon mission. Hugeburc may already have been in Germany with Walburg; it seems likely that both women had been summoned to Germany by Boniface at an earlier date. Hugeburc remarks that she came to Heidenheim immediately after Winnebald's death in 761; she witnessed some of the post-mortem miracles which she records in his life.

Willibald, visiting his sister's monastery, dictated parts of his so-called *Hodoeporicon* (an account of his life and, most notably, his travels in the Holy Land in the 730s) to

Hugeburc on Tuesday 23 June 778. Despite opposition within the monastery, but with the encouragement of Walburg, Hugeburc determined to record the known facts of Willibald's life, fearing lest the verbatim account she had recorded should be lost. Although professing herself inhibited by her sex from writing the lives of the venerable bishop and his brother, she was fired by the importance of the task she set herself. The *Hodoeporicon*'s English translator remarks that 'one can sense her intense curiosity to discover all about the places Willibald had visited' (Talbot, 152). Hugeburc's style is ambitious, with 'exuberantly crammed, complex periods, enhanced by rare words and phrases ... bizarre cases and case-endings, tenses and verb-forms' (Dronke, 33), using Sedulius's prelude to his *Carmen paschale* as a source for certain phrases, borrowing motifs from the life of St Boniface, and adapting a riddle of Aldhelm's. The report that Willibald gave of his travels and the accounts of the miracles of Winnebald are textually distinct, indicating that here Hugeburc was drawing on oral reports and eyewitness accounts. Her style has been compared to that of Hrotsvitha, the later German monastic writer.   CAROLYNE LARRINGTON

Sources E. Gottschaller, *Hugeburc von Heidenheim: philologische Untersuchungen zu den Heiligenbiographien einer Nonne des achten Jahrhunderts* (1973) · B. Bischoff, 'Wer ist die Nonne von Heidenheim?', *Studien und Mitteilungen zur Geschichte des Benediktiner Ordens*, 49 (1931), 387ff. · C. H. Talbot, ed. and trans., *The Anglo-Saxon missionaries in Germany* (1954) · A. Bauch, ed. and trans., *Quellen zur Geschichte der Diözese Eichstätt*, 1: *Biographien der Gründungszeit* (Eichstätt, 1962) · P. Dronke, *Women writers of the middle ages* (1984) · Hugeburc, 'Vitae Willibaldi et Wynnebaldi', [*Supplementa tomorum I–XII, pars III*], ed. O. Holder-Egger, MGH Scriptores [folio], 15/1 (Stuttgart, 1887), 80–117
Archives Bayerische Staatsbibliothek, Munich, clm 1086

Hügel, Friedrich Maria Aloys François Charles von, Baron von Hügel in the nobility of the Holy Roman empire (1852–1925), philosopher and theologian, was born at Florence on 5 May 1852, the elder son of Carl Alexander Anselm, Baron von Hügel (1795–1870), naturalist and traveller, and of Elizabeth Farquharson, daughter of General Francis Farquharson and niece of Sir James Outram. Carl von Hügel was born into a Rhineland family, and after a military career with the Austrian army against Napoleon he entered diplomatic service; he was Austrian ambassador to Tuscany in 1852, when Friedrich (the eldest of three children) was born. The young Friedrich lived in Florence until he was eight, and then in Brussels (where his father was Austrian minister) until he was fifteen. Consequently he never had regular schooling and never attended university. In childhood he was taught by an Anglican governess, and for seven years tutored by a German Lutheran pastor; he then had the Catholic historian and diplomat Alfred von Reumont as supervisor of his studies. His mother was originally a Presbyterian, but converted to Roman Catholicism, in which faith Friedrich was brought up. After Carl von Hügel's retirement in 1867 the family settled at Torquay. There Friedrich continued to be tutored at home, in part by William Pengelly, a

Friedrich Maria Aloys François Charles von Hügel, Baron von Hügel in the nobility of the Holy Roman empire (1852–1925), by F. A. Swaine

schoolteacher and scientist of wide interests, who lectured on geology and anthropology; Pengelly contributed to Friedrich's lifelong interest in geology. His younger brother, Anatole, became an anthropologist and the first director of the Museum of Archaeology and Ethnology at Cambridge in 1883; in later years Friedrich often visited him at Cambridge.

In 1870 von Hügel suffered an attack of typhus, which permanently impaired his hearing and led eventually to deafness; he was always nervous and frail in health. Following a religious and moral crisis (which he himself recorded) he was guided by the Dutch Dominican Raymond Hocking in Vienna.

In 1873 von Hügel married Mary Catherine, daughter of Sidney Herbert, first Lord Herbert of Lea, and sister of the thirteenth earl of Pembroke. They had three daughters, the eldest of whom, Gertrude (who married Count Salomei), died in 1915. It had been she who most closely shared von Hügel's interests, and he felt her loss severely. From 1876 he made his home in London, living from 1876 to 1903 at Hampstead, and from 1903 to 1925 at 13 Vicarage Gate, Kensington. For some years, winters were spent abroad (for his wife's delicate health as much as his own), and most often they stayed in Rome. In a letter of 1903 to Clement Webb he wrote that: 'since those early years it has been England that has been my home, except for nine winters spent in Rome, a summer in Westphalia, and two short visits to Jena, Heidelberg, and Würzburg, and one (further) visit to the Tyrol. And an English wife and British-born daughters of course strengthened these ties' (Bedoyère, 21).

There were many friends on the continent, including Henri Huvelin (1838–1910), a much respected spiritual director who guided von Hügel in Paris and was strongly influential throughout his life. Huvelin published nothing in his lifetime, but many of his conferences of spiritual direction were written down and published after his death. Von Hügel's *Selected Letters* (58ff.) includes notes of Huvelin's advice made by the baron at thirty-four and kept as spiritual guides, and his *Eternal Life* (1912) is in part a tribute to Huvelin. Von Hügel said he 'owed infinitely much' to Huvelin, and he expressed the same indebtedness to William George Ward, the Roman Catholic convert, philosopher, and theologian. In 1897 von Hügel began his lifelong friendship with the Jesuit George Tyrrell, with whom he frequently discussed biblical criticism and mysticism. Also in 1897 von Hügel delivered a paper before the Catholic International Scientific Congress at Fribourg, Switzerland, 'The historical method and the documents of the Hexateuch', and he followed this with a privately printed pamphlet on biblical inspiration (1901) and contributions on biblical topics for the *Bulletin Critique*, edited by Louis Duchesne. In 1904 von Hügel co-founded the London Society for the Study of Religion, a discussion group that became a notable society of largely Catholic scholars and included Arthur Balfour; von Hügel's later collections, *Essays and Addresses on the Philosophy of Religion* (1921, 1926), include addresses to the society as well as other essays and papers. Through his attendance at international conferences and his relations with other scholars, von Hügel developed friendships with a number of protestant scholars. He was particularly close to Rudolf Eucken and Ernst Troeltsch (1865–1923), whose early death on the eve of a visit to England arranged by von Hügel was a deeply felt blow. Later friends (such as Bernard Holland and Clement C. J. Webb) shared an interest in philosophy or mysticism. Von Hügel was a strong and influential link between French and German scholars and English colleagues in several fields.

Von Hügel's correspondence (still uncollected) is vital to understanding his own development and his place at the storm centre of the modernist theological movement. He supported and contributed to the modernist review *Il Rinnovamento* (1907–9) and corresponded with nearly all of those who figured in the movement. The modernist movement attacked the intellectualism of scholastic theology and favoured the adoption of biblical criticism and a teleological view of church history, tendencies which deviated from orthodox Roman Catholic positions. Together with other views (not all accepted or advocated by the movement), modernism was condemned by Pope Pius X in his decree *Lamentabili* (1907) and the encyclical *Pascendi* (1907).

Following the issue of these decrees Alfred Loisy, the prominent modernist biblical scholar, was excommunicated in 1908, as was Tyrrell. Von Hügel, who had never sought the ecclesiastical imprimatur for his writings, was not censured; he was never named, and he escaped the excommunication imposed on Loisy and Tyrrell although he had been closely associated with both of them, and was generally thought of as the father of modernism. Doubtless this was due in large part to his social position and to the great respect in which he was held by so many scholars and notables outside the Roman Catholic church. Von Hügel, however, did not modify his views or his essential position, and his *Encyclopaedia Britannica* article on the fourth gospel (11th edn, 1910) was published three years after the papal edicts on modernism. He remained publicly faithful to free scientific and historical investigation, and staunchly loyal to friends who suffered under the ecclesiastical censures; he continued to support *Il Rinnovamento*, lamenting the enforced cessation of its publication.

Von Hügel's major publications are an early work, *The Mystical Element of Religion as Studied in St. Catherine of Genoa and her Friends* (2 vols., 1908), and *The Reality of God*, intended for the Gifford Lectures in 1924–6, edited by E. G. Gardner, and published posthumously in 1931. This work reveals how his religious and philosophical thought continued to develop; in it he argues that eternal life is not restricted to the hereafter, but is part of man's earthly existence (anticipating much in the thought of Garrigou-Lagrange's *Les trois âges de la vie intérieure* (1941) concerning the indwelling of the Holy Ghost).

Naturalized as a British subject in 1914 von Hügel was given an honorary LLD by St Andrews in 1919, and to this Scottish university he bequeathed his library and many of his papers. In 1920 he received an honorary DD from Oxford University. His always frail health deteriorated, and he was unable to deliver the Gifford Lectures in 1924. He died at home in Kensington, on 27 January 1925, and was buried near Downside Abbey at Stratton on the Fosse near Bath, next to the graves of his mother and his sister, Pauline, who had died in 1901 at the age of forty-five.

Many notices in newspapers and reviews testified to von Hügel's remarkable place in the thoughts and affections of the scholarly and religious world. Abbot Cuthbert Butler remarked on 'the powerful intellect, the acute, massive, highly trained metaphysical mind, compelling attention by the manifest value of the message delivered' (von Hügel, *Selected Letters*, 49). Von Hügel's influence, especially in matters of religious thought and in the philosophy of religion, was widely felt in Europe—even more so than in England—and Evelyn Underhill was but one notable disciple. Von Hügel's personality charged his writings, which were markedly Germanic earlier in his career but became increasingly direct and simple, and his listeners and readers alike felt the power of his passion for communion with God. Abbot Butler described how he would sit in church, 'the great deep eyes fixed on the Tabernacle, the whole being wrapt in an absorption of prayer, devotion, contemplation', and added: 'Those who have not seen him so know only half the man' (von Hügel, *Selected Letters*, 49). He was always concerned with the reality of God, and tried to share that conviction with those for whom he served as a spiritual director through his count-less letters, through conferences, and through his writ-ings. He insisted on the necessity of sensory stimulation in every human activity, not excluding the religious.

R. J. SCHOECK

Sources DNB · M. de la Bedoyère, *The life of Baron von Hügel* (1952) · F. von Hügel, *Selected letters*, ed. B. Holland (1927) · F. von Hügel, *Letters … to a niece*, ed. G. Greene (1928) · A. A. Cock, 'Friedrich von Hügel and his work', *Speculum religionis* (1929), 195–213 · J. J. Heaney, 'The enigma of the later von Hügel', *Heythrop Journal*, 6/2 (April 1965), 145–59 · R. Marlé, *Au coeur de la crise moderniste: lettres de M. Blondel, H. Bremond, Fr. von Hügel, A. Loisy* (1960) · *Autobiography and life of George Tyrrell*, ed. M. D. Petre, 2 vols. (1912) · A. F. Loisy, *Mémoires pour servir à l'histoire religieuse de notre temps*, 3 vols. (Paris, 1930–31) · N. J. Abercrombie, *The life and work of Edmund Bishop* (1959)
Archives LPL, letters to *Church Quarterly Review* · U. St Andr. L., corresp., diaries, and notes | Bibliothèque Nationale, Paris, Alfred Loisy MSS · Birmingham Oratory, letters to J. H. Newman and Ignatius Ryder · BL, letters to Maud Petre, Add. MSS 45361–45362 · BL, corresp. with George Tyrrell, Add. MSS 44929–44933 · Bodl. Oxf., letters to Percy Gardner · Bodl. Oxf., letters to Francis Marvin · Borth. Inst., corresp. with Lord Halifax · Downside Abbey, near Bath, Edmund Bishop MSS · U. St Andr. L., letters to the sisters Banks, booksellers in Oxford · U. St Andr. L., corresp. with Al Lilley · U. St Andr. L., letters to Wilfrid Ward
Likenesses F. A. Swaine, photograph, repro. in von Hügel, *Selected letters* [*see illus.*] · photographs, repro. in de la Bedoyère, *Life of Baron von Hügel*
Wealth at death £5749 7s. 6d.: administration with will, 21 April 1925, *CGPLA Eng. & Wales*

Hugessen, Edward Hugessen Knatchbull-, first Baron Brabourne (1829–1893), politician, was the eldest son of Sir Edward *Knatchbull, ninth baronet (1781–1849), of Mersham Hatch, Kent, where he was born on 29 April 1829. His mother, Fanny Catherine, daughter of Edward Knight of Godmersham Park, Kent, was a niece of Jane Austen. Knatchbull went to Eton College in 1844, and matriculated at Magdalen College, Oxford, on 9 July 1847. He graduated BA in 1851, and proceeded MA in 1854. His father died on 24 May 1849, having stated in his will his desire that his son should add to his surname the name Hugessen, after the testator's mother, Mary, daughter and coheir of William Western Hugessen of Provender, Kent. This was done by royal licence.

At the general election of 1857 Knatchbull-Hugessen was elected for Sandwich as a Liberal, with Lord Clarence Paget for a colleague. His maiden speech in the House of Commons was made on 21 April 1858 in support of the abolition of church rates. When Palmerston on 30 June 1859 formed his second administration he included Knatchbull-Hugessen in it as a lord of the Treasury (that is, as a whip). This office he filled until 1866, when he became under-secretary for the Home Office. In Gladstone's first administration, formed on 9 December 1868, Knatchbull-Hugessen returned to the under-secretaryship for the Home Office. In 1871 he became under-secretary for the colonies. On 24 March 1873 he was sworn of the privy council. He left office when Gladstone resigned on 13 February 1874. He moved away from Liberalism, especially on church questions and the establishment of the Church of England. He was not included in Gladstone's second

Edward Hugessen Knatchbull-Hugessen, first Baron Brabourne (1829–1893), by Camille Silvy, 1861

administration, which was formed on 28 April 1880, but on 24 March in that year he had been created Baron Brabourne. Shortly after becoming a peer he became a Conservative and joined the Carlton Club. He was chairman of the East Kent quarter sessions and deputy chairman of the South-Eastern Railway.

Brabourne was twice married, first, on 19 October 1852, to Anna Maria Elizabeth (d. May 1889), younger daughter of the Revd Marcus Richard Southwell, vicar of St Stephen's, Hertfordshire, and his wife, Cecilia Jane; this marriage produced two sons and two daughters. His second marriage was on 3 June 1890, at Maxwelton Chapel, Glencairn, to Ethel Mary (d. 1929), third daughter of Colonel George Gustavus Walker of Crawfordton, Dumfriesshire, and his wife, Anne Murray, née Lennock, the marriage producing two daughters.

Before and after his elevation to the peerage Brabourne was an energetic author, chiefly known for numerous stories for children. He was also a book collector. His library, which was sold by auction in May 1892, 'abounded in topographical works, scarcely any English county being unrepresented', and the sum realized was over £2000. After the death of his mother on 24 December 1882, in her ninetieth year, Brabourne became possessor of ninety-four letters written by his great-aunt, Jane Austen, to her elder sister, Cassandra. At the close of 1884 he published these letters in two volumes, with introductory and critical remarks, which were mainly notable for their diffuse irrelevance.

Brabourne wrote original fairy stories, the first of his many volumes being *Stories for my Children* (1869). Its opening tale, 'Puss Cat Mew', was later a favourite of J. R. R. Tolkien and may have provided some of the inspiration for characters in Tolkien's *The Lord of the Rings*. Brabourne claimed Hans Christian Andersen as his model, but his stories, though sometimes attractive, lack Andersen's skill and are 'often long-winded, macabre, and sadistic' (Carpenter and Prichard, 298). Brabourne also published a lecture on Oliver Cromwell (1877) and *Facts and Fictions in Irish History* (1886), attacking Gladstone. He died on 6 February 1893 at Smeeth Paddocks, and was buried at Smeeth, Kent, three days later.

W. F. RAE, *rev.* H. C. G. MATTHEW

Sources *The Times* (7 Feb 1893), 9 • *Annual Register* (1893) • Gladstone, *Diaries* • H. Carpenter and M. Prichard, *The Oxford companion to children's literature* (1984) • Burke, *Peerage*
Archives CKS, corresp., diaries, and papers | BL, corresp. with W. E. Gladstone, Add. MS 44111 • King's AC Cam., letters to Oscar Browning • LPL, letters to A. C. Tait
Likenesses C. Silvy, photograph, 1861, NPG [*see illus.*] • Ape [C. Pellegrini], chromolithograph caricature, NPG; repro. in *VF* (11 June 1870) • H. von Herkomer, oils, Maidstone county hall
Wealth at death £13,800 12s. 7d.: probate, 11 May 1893, *CGPLA Eng. & Wales*

Hugessen, Sir Hughe Montgomery Knatchbull- (1886–1971), diplomatist, was born on 26 March 1886 in London, the elder son in a family of two sons and one daughter of the Revd Reginald Bridges Knatchbull-Hugessen (1831–1911), rector of Mersham, Kent, and his second wife, Rachel Mary (d. 1929), daughter of Admiral Sir Alexander Leslie Montgomery, third baronet, of The Hall, Donegal. He had one half-brother and four half-sisters from his father's first marriage, to Maria (d. 1880), daughter of the Revd Tatton Brockman, of Beachborough, near Hythe. Knatchbull-Hugessen (or Snatch, as he was often known) was educated at Eton College and at Balliol College, Oxford, from which he graduated with a third in modern history in 1907. He then entered the Foreign Office in October 1908. On 16 July 1912 he married Mary (d. 1978), oldest daughter of Brigadier-General Sir Robert Gordon-Gilmour, first baronet. They had one son, Norton Reginald (1913–1941), and two daughters, Elisabeth (1915–1957) and Alethea (b. 1918).

Apart from a brief stint in Constantinople, Knatchbull-Hugessen's early career was spent in London. During the First World War he was attached to the Foreign Office's contraband department, and he attended the Versailles peace conference in 1919 as a second secretary. He was promoted first secretary and transferred to The Hague in November 1919; he then served in Paris, from January 1923, and in Brussels, from May 1926. Up to this point Knatchbull-Hugessen had met many of the characteristic problems of diplomatic work: serious crises, particularly in Paris during the French occupation of the Ruhr, and

Sir Hughe Montgomery Knatchbull-Hugessen (1886–1971), by Rembrandt, 1934–6

heavy loads of important but routine work. His April 1930 posting as minister to the Baltic states, however, yielded the new and testing experience of serving at three legations (Riga, Tallinn, and Kaunas) simultaneously. When his one colleague who possessed some knowledge of local affairs was sent to the Soviet Union almost immediately on his arrival, he was driven to protest by sending to the Foreign Office a highly amusing but deeply felt parody of the definition of the Trinity recorded in the Athanasian creed. Assistance quickly arrived.

In November 1934 Knatchbull-Hugessen was, unexpectedly to him, sent as minister to Persia and, brief as it proved to be, it was perhaps his favourite posting. The problems of the mission were serious, Anglo-Persian relations being difficult in themselves and complicated by differences between London and New Delhi, but he was enchanted by the country and its people. If Persia was difficult but pleasant, China, to which he was sent as ambassador in succession to Sir Alexander Cadogan in September 1936, was both difficult and, as the war with Japan broke out in August 1937, increasingly unpleasant. For Knatchbull-Hugessen the unpleasantness was highly personal. While travelling to Shanghai where fighting had broken out, inevitably involving the British community, his car, though clearly marked with union flags, was strafed by a Japanese plane, and he was severely wounded, bullets passing right through him, close to his spine. After a year-long convalescence he recovered, but in later life his injuries increasingly disabled him and he became confined to a wheelchair. During his convalescence, Knatchbull-Hugessen was given temporary employment as one of three diplomatic service members of the departmental committee appointed to consider the amalgamation of the diplomatic and consular services; he opposed amalgamation, and was deputed by his two colleagues to send a private letter to Cadogan (now permanent under-secretary) giving the 'social' argument against amalgamation, which was deemed too sensitive to include in their minority report.

Following his recovery, Knatchbull-Hugessen was appointed ambassador to Turkey in February 1939. He remained there until September 1944, and thus entered the most significant phase of his career. The outbreak of war in 1939 and the dire emergencies of 1940 and 1941 made the support of Turkey, whether as benevolent neutral or fighting ally, of profound importance to Britain and her friends. Knatchbull-Hugessen's view both at the time and in retrospect was that, despite the obvious hopes of the allies that Turkey would join the war and their occasional direct efforts to persuade her to do so, particularly in 1943, her most practically useful role was as a non-participant. He never thought that there was a risk, as during the First World War, that she might join the German side, though he constantly counteracted the efforts of the German ambassador, Franz von Papen, to persuade her to do so, and he recognized the force of Turkish arguments that they were insufficiently prepared to face the inevitable air attacks that Germany would launch if they joined the allies. He also understood their reluctance to join a conflict in which their own interests were unlikely to be paramount in the minds of more powerful combatants such as the USSR. His understanding of Turkish opinions and his unusually close personal relations with individual Turks were certainly a major contribution to the generally successful conduct of Anglo-Turkish relations of the war period. Eventually Turkey did join the war in February 1945, and Knatchbull-Hugessen always believed that she might have done so earlier, had it not been for maladroit handling of the Turks by Eden at the Cairo conference.

Knatchbull-Hugessen's final posting was as ambassador to Belgium and minister to Luxembourg in September 1944. He arrived just as Belgium was being liberated by allied forces and initially there was some potential unrest, particularly in Brussels, which he was able to help restrain by rapid communication with the American command. He had become an admirer of the Belgians when he served in Brussels in the 1920s and watched with pleasure as the country recovered quickly from the German occupation. He retired in November 1947 and returned to his family's Kentish origins to live near Canterbury.

Knatchbull-Hugessen's retirement was overshadowed by the consequences of what became known as the 'Cicero' affair. During his time at Ankara a security lapse had occurred which allowed his Albanian butler, Elyesa *Bazna, to gain access to and photograph highly secret documents. Despite the security clearance given to the butler on appointment, he sold these documents to the German embassy during the period November 1943 to February 1944. As the American diplomat Charles Thayer later commented,

The first place where secrets are guarded is in the chancellery safe. When Sir Hughe Knatchbull-Hugessen … left the keys to his safe in his trousers pocket, it was an invitation to his astute valet, known as Cicero, to filch and sell his secrets to the Germans. Needless to say, this lapse on the part of a popular and able diplomat made him the laughing-stock of the profession.   (Thayer, 237–8)

An inquiry eventually found that Knatchbull-Hugessen had been responsible for the lapse, and he was reprimanded. What was almost worse from his point of view was that highly sensationalized versions of the story emerged after the war, particularly the film *Five Fingers* (1952), based on the memoir of the German commercial attaché and spymaster Ludwig Carl Moyzisch, in which he was lampooned and the notion that the stolen material had contained the details of the Normandy landings was dramatically asserted. It subsequently emerged that this last embellishment was not true, though other highly sensitive material was obtained, and the Germans generally failed to make use of the information they had paid for. Knatchbull-Hugessen never accepted blame for the leak, but what made him particularly distressed was that he was not allowed by the Foreign Office to rebut even patently ridiculous orchestrations of the story. He loyally honoured the prohibition, but he never ceased to try to find ways of publicizing a more accurate account, and probably did not feel the force of the argument that if the matter was opened up at all, it might have led to a fairer assessment, but that it would also have led to a public assertion of the blame that the inquiry had assigned to him personally. For this reason many of his friends and former colleagues connived, as he felt, at the policy of asking him to remain silent.

Knatchbull-Hugessen was particularly gifted at human relations. He inspired great affection both because of his genuine concern for others and because of his ready and at times subversive wit, occasionally recorded in the form of highly skilful comic verse. He was also a talented artist and was more than able to provide excellent illustrations for his own autobiography. He was appointed CMG in 1920 and advanced to KCMG in 1936. He died at his home, the Red House, Barham, Canterbury, on 21 March 1971; he was survived by his wife and one daughter, Alethea.

RICHARD LANGHORNE

Sources H. M. Knatchbull-Hugessen, *Diplomat in peace and war* (1949) · H. M. Knatchbull-Hugessen, *Kentish family* (1960) · personal knowledge (2004) · private information (2004) · *The Times* (23 March 1971) · *WWW* · Burke, *Peerage* · L. C. Moyzisch, *Operation Cicero* (1950) · F. von Papen, *Memoirs* (1953) · E. Bazna and H. Nogly, *I was Cicero*, trans. E. Mosbacher (1962) · C. Thayer, *Diplomat* (1960) · D. C. M. Platt, *The Cinderella service: British consuls since 1825* (1971) · *DNB*

Archives CAC Cam., corresp. and diaries · CKS, notebooks on family history · PRO, corresp., FO 800 | BL, corresp. with P. V. Emrys-Evans, Add. MS 58238

Likenesses Rembrandt, photograph, 1934–6, NPG [*see illus.*] · W. Stoneman, photograph, 1936, NPG · A. Verheyen, portrait, 1947, repro. in Knatchbull-Hugessen, *Diplomat*, frontispiece

Wealth at death £31,792: probate, 5 July 1971, *CGPLA Eng. & Wales*

Hugford, Ferdinando Enrico (1695–1771). *See under* Hugford, Ignazio Enrico (1702/3–1778).

Hugford, Ignazio Enrico (1702/3–1778), painter and picture collector and dealer, was born in Pisa, the son of Ignazio Hugford (*b. c.*1675), an English Catholic clockmaker who had emigrated to Tuscany, and his wife, Bridget Radcliffe. He studied painting with Antonio Domenico Gabbiani between 1719 and 1726. Although he is now better known as a picture collector and dealer, in the 1730s he painted a number of altarpieces for Florentine churches. He was elected to the Accademia del Disegno in Florence in 1729, where he served as principal from 1762 to 1772; in 1761 he became an honorary member of the Accademia Clementina in Bologna.

In 1729 Hugford and his brother Cosimo are recorded as major lenders to the exhibition in honour of St Luke at SS Annunziata in Florence; he contributed to subsequent exhibitions at the church in 1737 and 1767. In 1762 he published the biography of his master, Gabbiani, and five years later he contributed to the sixth edition of Vasari's *Vite* (1767–72) with Tommaso Gentili and Giovanni Francesco de Giudici. He was also a collaborator in the production of *Elogie e Rittratti* (1769–75), a book that includes prints from many of his drawings. Such published works helped to inspire confidence in his knowledge as a picture dealer. Presumably there were many paintings that passed through his hands, although most is known about those that were in his possession at his death. His connoisseurship was highly regarded; he sold drawings, at that time attributed to Holbein, to Sir Horace Walpole, through the agency of Sir Horace Mann. He also offered paintings to the antiquarian Giovanni Ludovico Bianconi, who had been commissioned by Augustus III to purchase artworks in Italy for his collection in Dresden. Bianconi rejected two canvases by Luti, and in 1757 Hugford sold them to the dealer William Kent, who in turn sold them to Sir Nathaniel Curzon for his collection at Kedleston Hall, Derbyshire, where they remain. He was not above selling paintings with spurious attributions and occasionally tampered with the pictures to the extent that they should be regarded as fakes. For instance he painted a 'duocento' *Madonna* for S. Maria at Imprunta and there is evidence that a so-called Filippino Lippi self-portrait may also be by him. None the less he was hospitable to artists visiting Florence and a generous teacher; he helped to launch successful careers for both Giovanni Battista Cipriani and Francesco Bartolozzi in London.

For the last twelve years of his life Hugford was confined to a chair by arthritis. Following his death, in Florence on 16 August 1778 at the age of seventy-five, his executors sold part of his collection of paintings and 3100 drawings to Grand Duke Pietro Leopoldo I, holdings that eventually became part of the collections of the Uffizi Gallery in Florence.

Ferdinando Enrico Hugford (1695–1771), elder brother of Ignazio, was born in Florence on 19 April 1695 and entered the monastery of Vallombrosa on 27 April 1711. In 1732 he was transferred to S. Reparata at Marradi, where he learned to make scagliola, an imitation marble. In 1743 he became abbot of Vallombrosa and in 1759 he was persuaded by the grand duke to take a pupil, Lamberto Gori, who had been taught by Ignazio Hugford. A little later Don Pietro Belloni and Don Torello Mannini were taught the technique by Don Enrico. Ferdinando Hugford died in Florence on 1 February 1771, while visiting his brother. He is buried at Vallombrosa.   HUGH BELSEY

Sources J. Fleming, 'The Hugfords of Florence', *Connoisseur*, 136 (1955), 106–10, 197–206 · B. Cole and U. Middeldorf, 'Masaccio, Lippi, or Hugford?', *Burlington Magazine*, 113/2 (Sept 1971), 500–07 · R. Smith, 'Filippino Lippi and Ignazio Hugford', *Burlington Magazine*, 114/1 (April 1972), 244 · F. Lui, 'Un "oltremontano" a Firenze: Ignazio Enrico Hugford, pittore, storiografo, collezionista', *Gazzetta Antiquaria* (1994), 62–7 · M. Chiarini, 'Inediti del settecento Fiorentino: Antonio Domenico Gabbiani, Ignazio Hugford, Gian Domenico Ferretti', *Scritti di storia dell'arte in Onore di Ugo Procacci*, 2 vols. (1977), 2.586–9 · F. B. Salvadori, 'La esposizione d'arte a Firenze, 1674–1769', *Mitteilungen des Kunsthistorisches Institutes in Florenz* (1974), 33, 150–51 · F. B. Salvadori, 'Ignazio Enrico Hugford collectionneur de portraits', *Gazette des Beaux-Arts* (Nov 1983), 165–8 · F. B. Salvadori, 'Ignazio Hugford collezionista con la vocazione di mercante', *Annali della Scuola Normale Superiore di Pisa. Classe di lettere e filosofia* (1983), 1025–56 · G. Perini, 'Dresden and the Italian art market in the eighteenth century: Ignazio Hugford and Giovanni Ludovic Bianconi', *Burlington Magazine*, 135 (1993), 550–59 · F. Russell, 'William Kent and the Kedleston Lutis', *Burlington Magazine*, 135 (1993), 828 · L. T. Tomasi and A. Tosi, 'Enrico Hugford e la "Galleria delle scagliole" a Vallombrosa', *Arista, Critica dell'arte in Toscana* (1991), 90–103 · J. Cook, 'Masters of the art of scagliola', *Country Life* (29 Sept 1994), 84–8 · *Gazzetta Toscana* (21 Aug 1778), 135–6
Likenesses A. D. Gabbiani, portrait, drawing, *c.*1720, Uffizi, Gabinetto Disegni e Stampe · G. Fratellini, chalk drawing, BM · I. E. Hugford, self-portrait, oils, Uffizi Gallery, Florence

Huggarde, Miles (*fl.* 1533–1557), poet and religious polemicist, was described by his contemporaries as a hosier who lived and traded in Pudding Lane in the city of London (*Acts and Monuments*, 7.111, 759). Much of his life is shrouded in obscurity: the identity of his parents and the date and place of his birth are unknown. He lacked a formal education and may have been largely self-taught: Wood states that Huggarde was: 'The first trader or mechanic to appear in print for the Catholic cause [...] that had not received any monastical or academical breeding' (Wood, *Ath. Oxon.*, 1.301).

The earliest recorded incidents involving Huggarde describe his participation in the prosecution of London protestants for heresy: they demonstrate an abhorrence of religious nonconformity that also formed a central theme in his writings. In May–June 1543 he acted as a prosecution witness against the evangelical preacher Robert Wisdom during Wisdom's trial for heresy before the privy council. Wisdom's account of the proceedings denounces Huggarde's zeal in persecuting him. Naming him three times Wisdom writes of Huggarde that 'accordyng to his name he hath swynyshly accused me' (Strype, 2.465–8). That this was not an isolated incident is attested by the preacher Robert Crowley who in 1548 accused Huggarde of complicity in the execution of every protestant who had been burned at Smithfield between 1533 and 1546: 'from the tyme of John Frith to the death of Anne Askew' (R. Crowley, *A Confutation of the Mishapen Aunswer to the Ballade*, 1548, sig. A4v–5r).

The tolerance shown to protestantism after Edward VI's accession compelled Huggarde to find means other than heresy prosecutions with which to defend Catholic orthodoxy. His first work of religious polemic was a defence of the Catholic eucharistic doctrine of transubstantiation. He wrote *An Aunswer to the Ballad called the Abuse of ye Blessed Sacrament* (*c*.1547) in reply to a Sacramentarian ballad of the same year. The answer was swiftly suppressed and its author examined by the privy council. Crowley published a confutation of the book in 1548, while the London gospeller Luke Shepherd warned his readers to beware of what he sarcastically called Huggarde's 'clarkely aunswer' in defence of the mass (Shepherd, *A Pore Helpe*, 1548?, sig. A7r–v). Huggarde's *Assault of the Sacrament of the Altar* met with similar treatment. Finally published in 1554, the *Assault* had originally been written in 1549 but not published, as the title-page explains, since 'heresie then raigning it could take no place'.

Not until the accession of Mary did Huggarde's fortunes begin to revive. Appointed hosier to the queen (25 November 1553) he was paid a daily wage and a shilling every quarter. From this date he began to describe himself in his writings as 'servant to the queen's most excellente majesty', and all his subsequent works, save two, were dedicated to her. Huggarde was a prolific and extremely effective propagandist for the Catholic cause during the pamphlet war of 1553–8 between the Marian authorities and the English protestant community in exile. Throughout 1554–7 he composed six tracts in verse and one in prose. His most accomplished and influential work was *The Displaying of the Protestants* (1556), a prose satire on the religious practices of the English reformers; it describes, without pity, the burnings of the protestant martyrs under Mary that had begun the year before. The *Displaying* ran through two editions, the second, augmented version (July 1556) being published only one month after the first. It provoked angry replies from a number of protestant writers, most notably John Plough, Dr Lawrence Humphrey, and William Heth. However, Huggarde was well known to his protestant enemies before the publication of the *Displaying*. A treasonous tract, falsely claiming Huggarde's authorship, had been published by his protestant antagonists at Wesel in 1555, presumably with the intention of impugning his standing with Mary's government. In July of the same year he was a guest in Bonner's episcopal residence in London where, as Foxe relates, he met the Essex gentleman and future martyr Thomas Haukes, whom he engaged in disputation concerning the scriptural authority for paedo-baptism. Upon learning of Huggarde's identity Haukes refused to discuss scriptural matters with an unlearned artisan, exclaiming 'Ye can better skill to eate a pudding and make a hose than in Scrypture eyther to answere or oppose' (*Acts and Monuments*, 7.111).

Huggarde was still alive in 1557 when he presented a manuscript of his last substantial work, 'A Mirroure of Myserie' (Hunt., HM 121) to Queen Mary. Nothing more is known of him after this time; he left no will and the date and place of his death are unknown.   C. BRADSHAW

Sources *The acts and monuments of John Foxe*, ed. S. R. Cattley, 8 vols. (1837–41), vol. 7 · J. Strype, *Ecclesiastical memorials*, 3 vols. (1822) · J. W. Martin, 'Miles Hogarde: artisan and aspiring author', *Religious radicals in Tudor England* (1989), 83–105 · Wood, *Ath. Oxon.*, new edn · S. Bailey, 'Robert Wisdom under persecution, 1541–1543', *Journal of Ecclesiastical History*, 2 (1951), 180–89 · *CPR*, 1553–4 · J. N. King, *English Reformation literature: the Tudor origins of the protestant tradition* (1982) · T. Warton, *The history of English poetry*, new edn, ed. W. C. Hazlitt, 4 vols. (1871)

Huggins, Edward (1755?–1829), plantation owner, was probably the son of Edward Huggins (*c*.1708–*c*.1758) of the island of Nevis in the West Indies, and his wife, Elizabeth, née Kelly (*d*. 1818). Educated on the island, he became an overseer before setting himself up as a successful planter.

Huggins had a reputation for cruelty dating from his time as an overseer. In the publicity surrounding his subsequent trial it was alleged, among other things, that he had shot a slave and then burnt the body and the hut into which it had been thrown. It was also claimed that he used iron collars armed with spikes as punishments. Because of his reputation it was only on the second attempt, in 1808, that Huggins persuaded the family of John Pretor *Pinney to sell him their Nevis estate, Mountravers. Huggins put in charge of it his son Peter, one of five children of his marriage to Frances (1751/2–1837), whom one source describes as being a good planter and businessman, but 'always hysterical' about slavery (Pares, 154). It was alleged at the time that in the six months after the Huggins family took possession of the estate nine slaves died of unnatural causes. The slaves, used to more liberal and humane treatment, resisted the new manager's methods both by running away and by refusing to work. On 23 January 1810, in response to this resistance, Huggins ordered the public flogging of thirty-two slaves, including at least ten women. According to testimony at Huggins's trial, the first slave was whipped for fifteen minutes, five slaves received over 100 lashes each, and four others over 200 each, including a woman who received 291; although this number of lashes was not illegal it contravened the local custom of a maximum of thirty-nine lashes. Three magistrates were present, including a doctor, but no one intervened. One of the women, Fanny, died five months later.

People on the island were divided on the issue. After the island's assembly had condemned the punishment, Huggins was tried for cruelty on 1 May 1810. He was acquitted in what Governor Hugh Elliot described as a 'perversion of human feeling' in the face of 'incontrovertible evidence' (African Institution, 5th report, 78–80). By contrast, the printer of the *St Christopher Gazette* was fined £15 for printing the assembly's resolution of condemnation.

James Webbe Tobin, brother of Rear-Admiral George Tobin, led the public opposition to Huggins on Nevis and publicized the case in Britain through the African Institution. He presented evidence to the governor that the judge, prosecution, and some of the jury were in various ways connected, or indebted, to Huggins. One resident of the island observed about the jury before the trial that there were ten for Huggins and two against. A similar story was told of the coroner's jury, which found that the dead slave had died of natural causes.

The government took little action in this case, but Governor Elliot deplored the state of justice in the Leeward Islands, and was prompted to intervene in the case of Arthur Hodge of Tortola, who was tried and hanged for numerous acts of outrageous cruelty. Members of the Huggins family were involved in other trials. In 1812 Edward Huggins junior was convicted of manslaughter for shooting dead a young slave outside his yard. In 1817 his father was again on trial for cruelty, this time for forcing a driver to cartwhip members of his own family. Again he was acquitted. However, the publicity surrounding all these cases helped to sway public opinion in Britain against slavery. The outrages strengthened the case for abolition by demonstrating that laws which aimed to protect slaves did not necessarily do so.

Having, reputedly, survived five attempts on his life, Huggins died on Nevis on 3 June 1829, in an accidental fall from his gig, and was buried in the island church of St George, Gingerland.　　　　　　　　　　　DAVID SMALL

Sources R. Pares, *A West India fortune* (1950) · PRO, Colonial Office MSS, CO 152/96, 98, 100, 105, 106, CO 239/3, 4, 30 · T. Southey, *Chronological history of the West Indies*, 3 (1827) · L. J. Ragatz, *The fall of the planter class in the British Caribbean, 1763–1833* (1928) · will, PRO, PROB 11/1770 · T. J. Cottle, *A plain statement of the motives which gave rise to the public punishment of several negroes* (1811) · J. W. Tobin, *J. W. Tobin's reply to Mr Cottle's pamphlet* (1812) · 'Case in Nevis, 1817', *Political tracts* (1817) · 'The Huggins family of Nevis, 1677–1777', Nevis Historical and Conservation Society · NL Scot., Minto MS 13058 · *Fifth report of the directors of the African Institution* (1811) · letters from Charles Pinney, 1829, University of Bristol, Pinney MSS, Box O · V. L. Oliver, *Monumental inscriptions of the British West Indies* (1927)
Archives Nevis Historical and Conservation Society, West Indies | NL Scot., Minto MS 13058 · PRO, CO 152/96, 98, 100, 105, 106, CO 239/3, 4, 30 · University of Bristol, Pinney MSS
Wealth at death £11,850 left to grandchildren; plus at least nine plantations and approx. 900 slaves; other land on Nevis left to children: will, 1830, PRO, PROB 11/1770

Huggins, Godfrey Martin, first Viscount Malvern (1883–1971), prime minister of Southern Rhodesia, was born on 6 July 1883 at Dane Cottage, Knoll Road, Bexley, Kent, the eldest son and second in the family of four sons and three daughters of Godfrey Huggins, a member of the London stock exchange and son of a brewer, and his wife, Emily Blest, a Woolwich innkeeper. Huggins was educated at Brunswick House preparatory school, Hove, Sutherland House, Folkestone, and Malvern College. From an early age he suffered from a serious ear disease which surgery was unable to remedy. The condition heightened his developing interest in medicine, however, and he subsequently studied at St Thomas's Hospital, London, qualifying as a physician and surgeon (MRCS and LRCP, 1906, FRCS, 1908). In 1908 he became house surgeon at St

Godfrey Martin Huggins, first Viscount Malvern (1883–1971), by Howard Coster, 1937

Thomas's, and later at Great Ormond Street Hospital for Sick Children.

Southern Rhodesia His ageing father's finances were scant and Huggins, aspiring to a gentlemanly lifestyle, needed to make money quickly. He accepted a locumship in Salisbury, Southern Rhodesia, where good doctors were scarce and he could earn five times his London salary. Highly regarded by the settlers, he soon built up a lucrative private practice and gained experience in public medicine as schools doctor and adviser to the government and municipality on European and African health, and he did much to promote the modernization of medical and sanitation facilities. As a young unmarried doctor and a skilled horseman, he was also a great social success, becoming prominent in the Salisbury shooting, hunting, and polo-playing set. Membership of the Southern Rhodesia Volunteers and the Sons of England Patriotic and Benevolent Society provided further social and professional introductions. In 1912 Huggins displayed political leadership by echoing settler opinion in a dispute over the siting of a hospital, which drew on wider settler animosity towards the ruling British South Africa Company.

At the outbreak of the First World War Huggins immediately joined the Royal Army Medical Corps, seeing service in England, Malta, Gallipoli, and France. Demobilized in 1917, with his patriotism reaffirmed, he had no doubts about the necessity of the conflict. Indeed, he regarded the war as 'a gigantic surgical refresher course' (Gann and

Gelfand, 45), publishing his authoritative *Amputation Stumps: their Care and After-Treatment* (1918), as well as articles in the *South African Medical Journal* and *The Lancet*. On returning to Rhodesia he distinguished himself in tackling the influenza epidemic, acquiring his own medical practice which expanded rapidly. By his late thirties he was earning £8000 a year, enough to pay his family's debts and acquire a house for his parents and two sisters in Salisbury. He decided to specialize in surgery, which he continued to practise until 1950. On 21 November 1921 he married Blanche Elizabeth (1886/7–1976), daughter of James Slatter, a physician, of Pietermaritzburg, and stepdaughter of Major Thomas Power, a retired member of the South African constabulary, and later a Salisbury accountant. Two sons were born of this lifelong marriage.

Post-war Southern Rhodesia was in a state of political agitation, as the expiry of the British South Africa Company's charter was imminent. Late in 1919 Huggins's growing prominence was recognized when, during a threatened police strike against the company over pay, he was elected president of the Salisbury branch of the Comrades of the Great War Association, which pledged itself willing to police the town in an emergency. In the 1922 referendum, when the settlers were offered a choice between incorporation in the Union of South Africa as a fifth province and responsible government, Huggins supported union, a course advocated by the British Conservative Party in the interests of strengthening Smuts and pro-British Afrikaners in the Union, while his wife Blanche championed the separatist cause, reflecting her staunchly British Natal background, with its fears of the political dominance of republican-minded poorer Afrikaners. Both, nevertheless, agreed to abstain from the vote. When Sir Charles Coghlan's Responsible Government Association won, Huggins decided to support it when it entered government as the Rhodesia Party. In 1924 he was elected to the legislative assembly for the middle-class constituency of Salisbury North. At this time he shared the widespread settler belief in the absolute necessity of white supremacy. In 1925, when asked whether Africans should have the same right of progress as Europeans, he replied 'Yes, as long as it is harmless' (Palmer, 230 n. 3). His developing political reputation could be seen in his chairmanship of the White Rhodesia Association, supported by the main political parties, which sought to accelerate the immigration of large numbers of Europeans of all classes in order to transform the colony into a true 'white man's country'. The association's ultimate objective, the so-called 'twin pyramid' policy, was a segregated society in which all labour, including unskilled work and primary production in the European sector, would be done by whites. The African sector would be similarly self-sufficient, accommodating all strata, including black professionals, who would occupy positions of authority. Racial conflict would thus be avoided by lack of economic and political competition between the two sectors. Such views might have been regarded as radical or eccentric, but Huggins's defence of them in the legislative assembly gave them a weighty respectability.

Prime minister In 1931, during the world slump, the government decided to cut civil service salaries. Huggins's vote was critical and he cast it in favour of the measure, arguing that he was bound to support the general policy of the government, but then he immediately left the party in protest. Elected leader of the opposition Reform Party in the following year, he became prime minister in 1933. After a period of party instability, elements of the Reform Party and Rhodesia Party formed the United Party under Huggins's leadership, winning an overwhelming majority in the 1934 general election. This marked for him the beginning of twenty-three unbroken years of political power, a record unparalleled in the British empire since the days of Walpole. As Churchill later told Commonwealth prime ministers: 'He probably knows more about running a cabinet than all of us put together, with the exception of Smuts' (*Rhodesia Herald*, 10 May 1971). His parliamentary style was assured. He would remove his hearing aid when members widely recognized as bores rose to speak, in order to abbreviate their contributions. His auricular disability could also prove a disadvantage. When, for example, he reviewed a mass gathering of cadets and their parents at a camp in Gwelo in 1950, he was heard to remark loudly: 'They'll make excellent cannon fodder for the next war' (private information, Hummel to Lowry, 31 Aug 1985). Shrewd, humorous, highly intelligent, if pragmatic and unintellectual, he used his common touch to great advantage in his dealings with the egalitarian-minded settler electorate, without sharing, crucially, their habitual sense of cultural and social inferiority in negotiations with Whitehall. He believed that Rhodesia needed those who 'had fagged at school and had been flogged at school, people who knew how to command and obey and knew how to command their black labourers' (Gann and Gelfand, 70). He always spoke without a trace of a Rhodesian accent and referred to England as 'home'. From the outset he developed a decisive skill in appearing hardline to local voters while reluctantly recognizing the need to mollify metropolitan opinion.

Two overriding issues dominated Huggins's premiership: the economic and political relationship between the African majority and the European minority within the colony; and the colony's wider regional relationships. In keeping with his earlier views, in 1933 he, together with the chief native commissioner, contemplated sending all 'advanced natives' to Northern Rhodesia, which would relieve Southern Rhodesia of 'the embarrassing necessity to consider native interests' (Palmer, 230 n. 4). With the colony's economy in a slump, he supported the introduction of the Industrial Conciliation Act (1934) which effectively discriminated in favour of white artisans. A Cold Storage Commission was established to assist agriculture, while European school attendance to the age of fifteen was made compulsory in an effort to combat white poverty. In public he maintained a strongly segregationist position, famously likening the Europeans to 'an island of white in a sea of black, with the artisan and the tradesman forming the shores and the professional classes the highlands in the centre'. If the African were 'to be allowed to erode away the shores and attack the highlands … [then] the leaven of civilisation would be removed from the country, and the black man would inevitably revert to a barbarism worse than anything before' (Blake, 228). Privately, he had begun to realize the futility of segregation. White labour was too costly, and mass immigration would dilute the social structure of the colony and create a class of poor whites, large numbers of whom would almost certainly be Afrikaner republicans, whom he abhorred. In an era when the 'racial problem' (as distinct from the 'native problem') largely meant Afrikaner impoverishment, Huggins's political outlook resembled that of a Victorian doctor who knew what was best for his ill-equipped patients.

War and its aftermath The war of 1939–45 and its immediate aftermath were central to the transformation of Huggins's political vision. The colony's economy improved, boosted not least by the need for Southern Rhodesian coal for smelting Northern Rhodesian copper and by the requirement for base metals caused by British rearmament. The outbreak of strikes on the strategically vital copperbelt, orchestrated by a bizarre alliance of communists and Afrikaner nationalists, highlighted the political perils of white labour, and Huggins had no hesitation in providing military force for their suppression. Against his staunchly tory instincts, he sanctioned state intervention in the creation of an Iron and Steel Commission (1942), an Industrial Development Commission (1944), an Electricity Supply Commission, and the nationalization of Rhodesia railways. He reluctantly accepted that post-war attitudes towards colonialism would be altered by the political ideals of the Atlantic charter, even suggesting that whites and blacks were blood brothers differentiated only by history, climate, and environment, rather than innate characteristics. He passed in 1941 a new Land Apportionment Act further restricting African urbanization, while forcing European employers to provide better African housing. No longer a convinced segregationist, he believed that the harsher aspects of the act were temporarily necessary to reassure the electorate. The wartime concession of the permanence of African townships represented a tacit acceptance of the structural interdependence of black and white. In 1946 he appointed Sir Edgar Whitehead, a believer in a racially composite economy, as minister of finance. In 1948, with serious African strikes in Bulawayo and Salisbury, ended by a combination of police action and judicious negotiation, he conceded that a proletariat was emerging that happened to be black. On the other hand, he was always sensitive to the need to carry the white electorate. He only barely survived the general election of 1946, which underlined further for him the need not to appear weak. After the war, since only 136 Africans out of 6000 potential voters had bothered to register, he toyed with preventing further African acquisition of the franchise and providing for African representation by nominated European MPs, an idea which Whitehall would almost certainly have rejected. Nevertheless, he had emerged from the war as a KCMG (1941), a CH

(1944), and a privy councillor (1947), and with renewed respect, both in Southern Rhodesia and in Britain.

The war had highlighted the colony's wider connections. Militarily it came under the regional command of South Africa, but economically and politically the conflict greatly strengthened co-operation with Northern Rhodesia, and Huggins sought to build on these achievements. He shared the ambition of many Southern Rhodesians for a straightforward amalgamation with their mineral-rich namesakes but, as the Bledisloe commission of 1939 had revealed, Whitehall was determined to protect Northern Rhodesia from Southern Rhodesian native policy. Huggins had long disdained the achievement of dominion status for Southern Rhodesia, a policy advocated by the parliamentary opposition, which he felt would be at the cost of a lucrative northern expansion. He realized that the British government would only concede a federation encompassing the differing native policies of the two Rhodesias and Nyasaland, and he thought that the push for dominion status should be delayed until this was achieved.

Huggins thus played a central role in the negotiations leading to the creation of the Federation of Rhodesia and Nyasaland in 1953, which he hoped would prove a loyal imperial buffer between African nationalism to the north and Afrikaner republicanism and rigid apartheid to the south. Although administratively complicated, economically it appeared to be an immediate success. Secondary industries and European immigration boomed. In place of segregation Huggins now advocated 'partnership' between white and black, revealingly likening it to the unequal relationship between rider and horse. He had powerful friends in the British Conservative Party and relied on his personal Commonwealth contacts, since Southern Rhodesia had been admitted as a privilege to conferences of dominion premiers since the 1930s. Like his friend Jan Smuts his racial ideology was pragmatic rather than definitive. He accepted reluctantly the reality of African political ambitions. He championed the hydroelectric dam at Kariba and the multi-racial university college at Salisbury (whose medical school would be named after him), both prestigious federal projects. He was raised to the peerage in 1955 as first Viscount Malvern of Rhodesia and of Bexley, thus combining his old school, his adopted country, and his birthplace. Honorary doctorates were awarded by the universities of Oxford, Witwatersrand, London, and Rhodes. Nevertheless, he now recognized that metropolitan support was no longer resolute. Anticipating the sentiment behind the unilateral declaration of independence (UDI) of 1965, he told the federal assembly in 1956:

> We have complete control of our own Defence Force. I only hope we shall not have to use it as the North American colonies had to use theirs, because we are dealing with a stupid government in the United Kingdom.   (Richmond, 57)

He was succeeded as prime minister by Sir Roy Welensky on 1 November 1956, coincidentally the launch date of the ill-fated Anglo-French attack on Suez.

Final decade   In retirement, with what appeared to be successive British capitulations to African nationalism, Huggins's world began to disintegrate. In the early 1960s he privately cautioned Whitehead, the Southern Rhodesian prime minister and a former cabinet colleague, against moving too fast for the white electorate. He witnessed the dissolution of the federation which he had done so much to promote, but he strongly opposed UDI, arguing that Britain only had the power of veto and could never initiate change. Southern Rhodesia, he argued, already had effective dominion status. Only if Britain broke the convention of non-intervention and appeared as an aggressor should UDI be contemplated. While they 'kept to the law and the constitution', he declared, 'the cry of "one man, one vote" could not be imposed' (*Rhodesia Herald*, 10 May 1971). No Rhodesian Front premier, he believed, except Winston Field, understood the benefits of the existing constitution, certainly not Ian Smith, whom he regarded as an unsophisticated 'farm-boy from Selukwe' (Blake, 361). Smith ought to have been more patient, but in declaring UDI in 1965 he had 'exchanged the substance for the shadow' of power. Huggins deplored Harold Wilson's decision in 1964 to revoke unilaterally the custom of allowing Rhodesia to attend Commonwealth conferences, as well as his involvement of the United Nations in the crisis, thus changing a 'family squabble into an international one' (*Rhodesia Herald*, 21 Jan 1969). His outlook had altered considerably, however, as he conceded to Lord Blake that 'Rhodesia is a black man's country. People used to talk about "the native problem". What they ought to talk about now is "the European problem"' (Blake, 227).

Huggins remained a convinced monarchist to the end. When in 1969, their conditional loyalty now unrequited, Smith's government replaced the union flag, presaging a republic, he denounced the new flag as 'pagan' (*The Times*, 10 May 1971). He died at his farm, The Craig, Highlands, near Salisbury, on 8 May 1971. His son John Godfrey Huggins (*b*. 1922) succeeded to the viscountcy. With UDI presenting issues of legality, the family declined a state burial, opting instead for a national funeral, which took place on 12 May. The British government felt politically unable to send a representative, but from Canada Queen Elizabeth sent a telegram paying tribute to his loyal service to three successive sovereigns. His tory friend Lord Salisbury aptly described him as a master of pragmatism, 'a tactic that exasperated some of his colleagues, but perfectly suited the temperament of the times' (*Rhodesia Herald*, 10 May 1971). He was cremated at Warren Hills, and his ashes were interred in the Anglican cathedral church of St Mary, Salisbury, on 14 May 1971. He was survived by his wife, who died on 30 July 1976.   DONAL LOWRY

Sources   *The Times* (10 May 1971) · *Rhodesia Herald* (10–13 May 1971) · *Bulawayo Chronicle* · *Africa Daily News* · *Central African Examiner* · *Debates of the legislative assembly, Southern Rhodesia* (1924–53) · *Debates of the federal assembly, Rhodesia and Nyasaland* (1953–6) · R. Blake, *A history of Rhodesia* (1978) · T. Bull, ed., *Rhodesian perspective* (1967) · F. Clements, *Rhodesia: the course to collision* (1969) · T. Creighton, *Southern Rhodesia and the Central African Federation: the anatomy of partnership* (1960) · L. H. Gann and M. Gelfand, *Huggins of Rhodesia: the man and his country* (1964) · M. Gelfand, *A non-racial island of learning: a history of the University College of Rhodesia from its inception to 1966* (1978) · J. Greenfield, *Testimony of a Rhodesian federal* (1977) · R. Gray, *The two nations: aspects of the development of race relations in the Federation of the Rhodesias and Nyasaland* (1960) · I. Hancock, *White liberals, moderates and radicals in Rhodesia, 1953–1980* (1984) · H. Holderness, *Lost chance: Southern Rhodesia, 1945–58* (1985) · P. Joyce, *Anatomy of a rebel: Smith of Rhodesia, a biography* (1974) · P. Keatley, *The politics of partnership: the Federation of Rhodesia and Nyasaland* (1963) · C. Leys, *European politics in Southern Rhodesia* (1959) · D. Lowry, '"Shame upon 'Little England' while 'Greater England' stands"! Southern Rhodesia and the imperial idea', *The round table, the empire/commonwealth and British foreign policy*, ed. A. Bosco and A. May (1997) · P. Murphy, *Party politics and decolonization: the conservative party and British colonial policy in tropical Africa, 1951–1964* (1995) · R. Palmer, *Land and racial domination in Rhodesia* (1977) · C. Palley, *The constitutional history and law of Southern Rhodesia, 1888–1965, with special reference to imperial control* (1966) · A. H. Richmond, *The colour problem: a study of race relations* (1961) · A. R. W. Stumbles, *Some recollections of a Rhodesian speaker* (1980) · D. Taylor, *The Rhodesian: the life of Sir Roy Welensky* (1955) · R. Tredgold, *The Rhodesia that was my life* (1968) · L. Vambe, *From Rhodesia to Zimbabwe* (1976) · R. Welensky, *Welensky's 4000 days: the life and death of the Federation of Rhodesia and Nyasaland* (1964) · H. I. Wetherell, 'N. H. Wilson: populism in Rhodesian politics', *Rhodesian History*, 6 (1975), 53–76 · J. R. T. Wood, *The Welensky papers: a history of the Federation of Rhodesia and Nyasaland* (1983) · private information (2004) [letter, Prof. H. C. Hummel to Dr D. Lowry, 31 Aug 1985] · b. cert. · Burke, *Peerage*

Archives   Bodl. Oxf., corresp. and papers · Bodl. Oxf., corresp. and papers relating to Federation · National Archives of Zimbabwe, Harare, corresp. and papers | Bodl. RH, corresp. with Michael Blundell, etc. · Bodl. RH, papers of Sir Robert Tredgold · Bodl. RH, corresp. with Sir Roy Welensky · Bodl. RH, papers of Sir Edgar Whitehead · Bodl. RH, corresp. with L. G. Curtis · University of Cape Town Library, corresp. with C. J. Sibbett

Likenesses   H. Coster, photograph, 1937, NPG [*see illus.*] · group photograph, 1952, Hult. Arch.

Huggins [*née* Murray], **Margaret Lindsay**, Lady Huggins (1848–1915), astronomical spectroscopist and photographer, was born on 14 August 1848 at 23 Longford Terrace, Monkstown, co. Dublin, the second of the three children of John Majoribanks Murray (1822–1893), a solicitor, and his first wife, Helen Lindsay (1826–1857), the daughter of Robert Lindsay of Tiree, Scotland. Though John Murray had lived in Ireland since early childhood, he was of Scottish ancestry and received his education at Edinburgh Academy. Anecdotal sources credit Margaret's paternal grandfather, Robert Murray, chief officer of the Provincial Bank of Ireland in Dublin, with inspiring her interest in the stars during their many evening walks following the untimely death of her mother. She reportedly attended a private boarding-school in Brighton. As a young woman she developed considerable skill both as an illustrator and a photographer, which she ably employed in artistic and scientific projects throughout her life. In *A Sketch of the Life of Sir William Huggins* (1936), C. E. Mills and C. F. Brooke recount that she was first introduced to her future husband, the amateur astronomer and pioneer spectroscopist William *Huggins (1824–1910), in London by mutual friends. Thanks to the mediation of the instrument maker Howard Grubb (1844–1931), the two met again in Dublin during Huggins's visits to inspect Grubb's progress on the construction of a new telescope for the former's observatory located in his residence at 90 Upper Tulse Hill Road,

Lambeth, London. The couple were married on 8 September 1875, in the parish church at Monkstown.

Acquaintances have suggested that Lady Huggins, as she became in 1897 when her husband was created KCB, had, from an early age, developed an interest in spectroscopy, even constructing her own spectroscope guided by an anonymous article in a popular periodical. Some have romantically, but erroneously, claimed that Sir William was the author of the article in question. However she came by her interest and knowledge of spectroscopy, following her marriage Margaret Huggins became involved in the work of the observatory. Her presence changed both the kind of work done at Tulse Hill and its organization. In particular, photography appeared as a new method of recording what had previously been purely visual spectroscopic observations. Although published articles about the early photographic accomplishments at Tulse Hill make no mention of her, evidence gleaned from the observatory's notebook entries, for which she assumed responsibility in March 1876, points to Margaret Huggins as a major impetus behind the establishment of her husband's successful programme of astronomical photography.

From the start Margaret Huggins exhibited a strong interest in experimental design—improving and adapting both instruments and methods used at Tulse Hill to the new photographic tasks at hand. In June 1876 she described and illustrated her plan for a camera to convert the telescope previously dedicated to visual observation into one suitable for photography. She devoted months to experimentation with different types of photographic plates and designed a sighting-tube to ensure the alignment of the spectroscope with the telescope. Working as a team, the Hugginses moved quickly to the forefront of spectroscopic astrophotography, learning photography's limitations and moulding its capabilities to their agenda, which included photographing the spectra of stars, comets, and nebulae, and perfecting a method of photographing the solar corona without an eclipse.

Margaret Huggins appreciated the importance of spectroscopic information to the diligent observer. Photographs of a celestial object may expose the body's outward form to scientific scrutiny, but, 'if we can get good spectra', she wrote, 'we should have the soul' (M. L. Huggins, notebook 2, 4 Dec 1888, Margaret Clapp Library, Wellesley College). In 1888 the Hugginses focused their attention on the spectrum of the Orion nebula (M42) to determine the nature of the so-called chief nebular line, a green emission line that William had been the first to observe some years earlier in the spectra of several nebulae. His claim that it represented a new element was disputed, and it was with the hope of resolving this controversy in their favour that the Hugginses observed and photographed M42's spectrum between October 1888 and April 1889. These difficult observations, which required repeated direct comparison of the spectrum generated by burning magnesium against that produced by the faint nebula, formed the basis of the first of William's scientific papers on which Margaret Huggins appeared as co-author

and serve as a benchmark in their relationship (W. Huggins and M. L. Huggins, 'On the spectrum'). Their course of investigation, with Margaret Huggins and her husband alternating as observer and apparatus tender, confirmed their belief that the nebular line, though near that of magnesium, was nevertheless distinct from it. At the outset of the research effort Margaret Huggins noted the need for 'photographs of the complete neb[ular] spectrum and … the [magnesium] lines … on the same plates' in order 'not to have to depend on eye observations in anything so difficult and important' (M. L. Huggins, notebook 2, 24 Oct 1888, Margaret Clapp Library, Wellesley College). One week after their only satisfactory photograph had been obtained Margaret Huggins made the alarming discovery that their specially calibrated comparison apparatus was slightly misaligned, but their anxiety subsided as continued investigation lent welcome support to their preliminary findings.

Margaret Huggins was co-author and illustrator of most of her husband's later published scientific papers. Her many and varied interests are evident in her own publications, which included a monograph on the master violin maker Giovanni Paulo Maggini (1892), articles on the armillary sphere and the astrolabe in the eleventh edition of *Encyclopaedia Britannica*, and articles in *Astronomy and Astrophysics*, *Astrophysical Journal*, and *Popular Astronomy*, among others. She assisted her husband in the editing and illustration of both *An Atlas of Representative Stellar Spectra from λ4870 to λ3300* (1899) and *The Scientific Papers of Sir William Huggins* (1909).

Margaret Huggins was active in the British Astronomical Association from its inception in 1890. In 1903 she was elected to honorary fellowship in the Royal Astronomical Society. In that same year, immediately following the visit of Pierre and Marie Curie to London, the Hugginses instigated an entirely new line of research, namely photographing the spectrum of radium.

Following the death of her husband on 12 May 1910, Lady Huggins began work on a personal memoir of their life and work together. Although she was unable to see this project to completion, she was untiring in her efforts to ensure the accuracy of such accounts written by others in his memory. In 1913 she moved to 8 More's Garden, Cheyne Walk, Chelsea, where she died on 24 March 1915 after a long illness. Her ashes were laid beside those of her husband in Golders Green crematorium, Middlesex. The couple had no children. Lady Huggins bequeathed a number of scientific instruments and personal effects to Wellesley College, Wellesley, Massachusetts. This bequest included the six bound observatory notebooks she and her husband kept throughout their long observing careers.

BARBARA J. BECKER

Sources B. J. Becker, 'Eclecticism, opportunism, and the evolution of a new research agenda: William and Margaret Huggins and the origins of astrophysics', PhD diss., Johns Hopkins University, 1993 · B. J. Becker, 'Dispelling the myth of the able assistant: Margaret and William Huggins at work in the Tulse Hill observatory', *Creative couples in the sciences*, ed. H. Pycior and others (1996), 98–111 · M. T. Brück and I. Elliott, 'The family background of Lady Huggins (Margaret Lindsay Huggins)', *Irish Astronomical Journal*, 20

(1991–2), 210–11 · C. E. Mills and C. F. Brooke, *A sketch of the life of Sir William Huggins* (1936) · W. Huggins and M. L. Huggins, observatory notebooks, Wellesley College, Wellesley, Massachusetts, USA, Margaret Clapp Library · M. L. Huggins, 'Teach me how to name the ... light', *Astrophysical Journal*, 8 (1898), 54 · W. Huggins and M. L. Huggins, 'On the spectrum, visible and photographic, of the Great Nebula in Orion', *PRS*, 46 (1889), 40–60 · W. Huggins and Lady Huggins, *An atlas of representative stellar spectra from λ4870 to λ3300: together with ... a short history of the observatory and its work* (1899) · *The scientific papers of Sir William Huggins*, ed. W. Huggins and M. L. Huggins (1909) · d. cert. · private information (2004)

Archives Wellesley College, Massachusetts, Clapp Library | California Institute of Technology, Pasadena, Hale MSS · RS, Larmor MSS · U. Cal., Santa Cruz, Lick Observatory, Mary Lea Shane archives

Likenesses black and white photograph, Wellesley College, Massachusetts, Whitin Observatory · oils, RAS

Wealth at death £12,586—incl. bequests of £1000 to Bedford College for Women; £500 for erection of memorial to William Huggins in St Paul's Cathedral; £1000 to City of London School; £300 for completion of biography of William Huggins; many objets d'art, scientific instruments, and other artefacts were given to Wellesley College, incl. the observatory notebooks kept by both William and Margaret Huggins: *Nature* (6 May 1915)

Huggins, Samuel (1811–1885), architect and writer, was born at Deal in Kent but grew up in Liverpool, the son of Samuel Huggins and his wife, Elisabeth. He resided in Liverpool most of his life, although he lived in Chester from 1861 to 1865 with his brother the animal painter William *Huggins (1820–1884). In 1846 he began practice as an architect, but built little. He defended the classical style against the attacks of Ruskin and published *The Course and Current of Architecture, with a Chart of the History of Architecture* (1863). He joined the Liverpool Architectural Society in 1849, and was president from 1856 to 1858. He read papers before the society opposing the proposed restoration of Chester Cathedral (1868), and 'On so-called restorations of our cathedral and abbey churches' (1871), which led to the formation of the Society for the Protection of Ancient Buildings. In 1872 his catalogue of Liverpool Free Public Library was published. Huggins died, apparently unmarried, at Christleton, where he lived, near Chester, on 10 January 1885. His portrait was painted by his brother William. ALBERT NICHOLSON, *rev.* VALERIE SCOTT

Sources *The Builder*, 48 (1885), 129, 182 · M. Brooks, *John Ruskin and Victorian architecture* (1987) · *Dir. Brit. archs.* · *CGPLA Eng. & Wales* (1885)

Archives Lpool RO, index to the Holt MSS and related papers

Likenesses W. Huggins, portrait

Wealth at death £663 7s. 6d.: probate, 6 Feb 1885, *CGPLA Eng. & Wales*

Huggins, William (bap. 1696, d. 1761), translator, was baptized on 9 January 1696 at St Mildred Poultry, in London, the son of John Huggins (1655–1745), solicitor and warden of the Fleet prison from 1713 to 1728 and subject to a government investigation, together with Thomas Bambridge, because of his mismanagement of the prison. Intended for holy orders, William Huggins matriculated at Magdalen College, Oxford, on 16 August 1712, proceeded BA on 23 June 1716, MA on 20 April 1719, and became fellow in 1722. He abandoned the intention to take orders, and on 27 October 1721 was made wardrobe

keeper and keeper of the private lodgings at Hampton Court.

On 20 December 1722 Huggins married Anne, daughter of William Tilson of the Dower House, Hampton Court. He resigned his fellowship the following July. They had three daughters: Anna Maria (d. 1793), Jane, and Maria Anna (d. 1783). After the death of his father Huggins spent most of his time at his country house, Headley Park, Hampshire.

Through his father, who was close to Sir James Thornhill, Huggins became a close friend of William Hogarth. They were both members of the Academy of Ancient Music: their names appear in the subscription lists for the years 1728 and 1730. About the same time Huggins was writing librettos for oratorios and in 1733 he wrote *Judith, an Oratorio or Sacred Drama*, the music being composed by William Defesch. It was performed on 16 February at Lincoln's Inn Fields and according to J. Ireland, 'when the *Jewish heroine* had made her theatrical *debut*, and so effectually smote *Holofernes*, "As to sever, / His head from his great trunk for ever, and for ever", the audience compelled her to make her exit' (Ireland, 2.526–30). Hogarth illustrated the performance in *A Chorus of Singers*, which he used as a subscription ticket for *A Midnight Modern Conversation*. He also designed the frontispiece for the publication showing Judith about to cut off Holofernes's head.

In 1755 Huggins published his first translation from Italian, *Sonnets by John Baptist Felix Zappi, Selected and Translated by the Translator of Ariosto*. The copy in the Dyce collection contains a manuscript dedication signed by Temple Henry Croker, who called himself the editor. According to Edward Payson Morton, the translator might have asked Croker's help in order to get subscriptions and to write 'diplomatic dedications' (Morton, 202). In the same year Huggins's translation of *Orlando Furioso* was published by Croker, again calling himself editor, who also contributed some cantos. Huggins's name first appeared on the title-page of an edition of 1757, but he was clearly the chief contributor. Of Croker's part of the work Huggins issued a corrected version in pamphlet form in 1758; he also collaborated with the Italian critic Giuseppe Baretti on the translation, but they later became estranged. Huggins's *stanze* are an interesting exception within the British tradition in being 'as near the original as possible' (ix). This occasioned Marshall's criticism for lack of clarity for 'playing havoc with English grammar' (Marshall, 34). In its own times the translation was praised by the *Critical Review* (July 1757, 83).

In 1756 Huggins was involved in a literary dispute concerning Thomas Warton's disparagement of Ariosto in his *Observations on Spenser's Faerie Queen* (1756). Huggins's *Observer Observ'd* (1756) amounts to an indignant answer to Warton's attack, 'done by a person, totally a stranger to the language of the Original, who form'd his judgment from a nominal translation' (Huggins, *Observer Observ'd*, 17). The controversy occasioned Dr Johnson's remark: 'Huggins has ball without powder, and Warton powder without ball' (Boswell, *Life*, 2.338). At his death Huggins left in manuscript a tragedy, a farce, and a complete translation of the *Divine Comedy*. This would have been the first complete English translation of the poem. During his lifetime Huggins published only a specimen of twenty-one lines in the *British Magazine* (1760, 266). A letter from Hogarth of 24 June 1760 reveals that the translation was finished by then. In his will, dated 26 May 1761, Huggins left instructions for his translation to be published by the Revd Mr Thomas Monkhouse, fellow of Queen's College, Oxford, but his request was not fulfilled and the manuscript went missing. Huggins died on 2 July 1761 at Nether Wallop, Hampshire, at the residence of his son-in-law, Thomas Gatehouse. ANTONELLA BRAIDA

Sources will, PRO, PROB 11/867, sig. 252 · IGI [London marriage licences] · J. R. Bloxam, *A register of the presidents, fellows … of Saint Mary Magdalen College*, 8 vols. (1853–85), vol. 3, pp. 185–6 · *GM*, 1st ser., 31 (1761), 334 · L. F. Powell, 'William Huggins and Tobias Smollet', *Modern Philology*, 34 (1936–7), 179–92 · E. P. Morton, 'An eighteenth-century translation of Ariosto', *Modern Language Notes*, 20 (1905), 199–202 · J. Ireland, *Hogarth illustrated*, 2 (1791), 526–30 · *Critical Review*, 4 (1757), 83 · *Giuseppe Baretti: epistolario*, ed. L. Piccioni, 1 (Bari, 1936), 100–07 · Boswell, *Life*, 1.255; 2.338 · L. Collison-Morley, *Giuseppe Baretti* (1909), 91–6 · R. Marshall, *Italy in English literature, 1755–1815* (1934), 34 · P. Toynbee, *Dante Studies* (1921), 285–9 · D. E. Baker, *Biographia dramatica, or, A companion to the playhouse*, rev. I. Reed, new edn, 1 (1782), appx, 483 · Nichols, *Lit. anecdotes*, 3.686 · Nichols, *Illustrations*, 3.601 · BL, MS Eg. Ch. 7836 · R. Paulson, *Hogarth*, 1 (1991), 188; 2 (1992), 62–3 · Cobbett, *Parl. hist.*, 8.706–53
Archives Adderbury Manor, Banbury, Oxfordshire, MSS
Likenesses T. Major, line engraving, 1760 (after W. Hogarth), BM · W. Hogarth, portrait, priv. coll.
Wealth at death owned Headley Park, Hampshire; manor of Chinnor, Oxfordshire, left to Dr James Murgrave and daughter Jane; left daughter Maria Anna one annuity of £240; also 'tax purchased' a farm in parish of Nether Wallop, leaving tithes to Mr James Phipps and John Gatehouse; also remaining lands in Middlesex, Surrey, Sussex, Dorset, Westmorland, Kent, and Southampton: will, PRO, PROB 11/867, fols. 110r–115r

Huggins, William (1820–1884), animal painter, was born on 13 May 1820 in Liverpool, the son of Samuel Huggins and his wife, Elisabeth. He was the younger brother of the architect Samuel *Huggins (1811–1885), and the brother of Anna Huggins (*fl*. 1854–1862) and Sarah Huggins (*fl*. 1853–1865), who both painted flowers, fruit, game, and landscapes, and exhibited at the Liverpool Academy and the Liverpool Society of Fine Arts. William was taught drawing at the mechanics' institute in Liverpool and at the age of fifteen won a prize there for an ambitious design, *Adam's Vision of the Death of Abel*.

Huggins spent many hours making life studies at the Liverpool zoological gardens. He was specially fascinated by the lions and tigers of Wombwell's travelling menagerie, and these he sketched whenever the opportunity allowed. His drawings in chalk and pencil, often on grey paper, displayed fine draughtsmanship; he worked equally well with watercolours and later oils. He never saw big cats in their natural environment and in consequence his backgrounds were understated. Their subtlety, however, served to focus all attention on the powerful depiction of the animals themselves. The influence of George Stubbs, which Huggins readily acknowledged, may be seen in an early painting of two pumas. As well as big cats, Huggins painted farmyard animals and was particularly successful with his drawings of donkeys and groups of cattle. Sentimental works, such as *Faithful Friends*, earned him the epithet the Liverpool Landseer, which he resented. When one of his patrons tried to pay him a compliment by comparing him to Landseer, Huggins allegedly responded: 'Landseer! If I had had Landseer through my hands for six months I could have made a man of him' (Marillier, 151).

About 1845 Huggins became disappointed with the response to his purely animal studies and for a short time diverged into works with grandiose biblical and literary themes. One of the best known is *Fight between an Eagle and a Serpent*, illustrating a passage from Shelley's *The Revolt of Islam*. However, these narrative works were not well received. Huggins was, however, a highly versatile artist, equally adept at landscape, architectural drawing, and portraiture. His portraits ranged from the small crayon and chalk heads of friends, to studies of large equestrian groups. A fine example of the latter is the painting of the master of Holcombe hunt, Mr T. Gorton, with a leash of hounds. Huggins was also skilled in painting ceramics and glass and was a collector of fine china.

In mid-career Huggins developed the highly individual technique that characterized some of his best work. Having first drawn a pencil outline on smooth white millboard he then glazed in oils 'very strongly and richly with transparent colours' (Marillier, 145). This allowed the white background to show through, creating a luminous effect. Huggins delighted in the translucency and proceeded to experiment with brilliant colours, which he fully anticipated would dull with time. The approach was not, however, universally admired. Some thought his colouring crude and inaccurate, and a purple donkey attracted particular criticism: 'No other animal painter of the school found in old Nature so many hues, or made so much allowance for the deepening tone given to dried paint by time' (Sparrow, 216). This mellowing effect was already apparent when Huggins's works were favourably assessed by H. C. Marillier some twenty years after the artist's death.

Huggins first exhibited at the Royal Academy in 1842 with *Androcles and the Lion*, and was a regular exhibitor until shortly before his death. His connection with the Liverpool Academy began when he attended as a student in the life class. He was elected an associate in 1847 and a member in 1850. His active connection ceased in 1856. He also sent works to exhibitions at Manchester, Dublin, Edinburgh, and Glasgow.

In 1861 Huggins moved to Chester, where he lived with his brother. It was presumably under the latter's influence that he took up architectural drawing, and he painted many views of the city. He developed a particular liking for its red sandstone, which featured prominently in his later work. In 1876 he left Chester for Betws-y-Coed, where he painted landscapes, including *The Fairy Glen*, exhibited in Liverpool in 1877. He later settled in the village of Christleton, Cheshire, where he died on 25 February 1884.

In his last years he suffered partial paralysis, which eventually stopped him from painting. Of less than average height, with a florid complexion, Huggins had unusually long hair and dressed somewhat shabbily. He was good-natured and helped friends who were in financial straits, despite often facing difficulties himself. But he could also be shy and prickly.

ALBERT NICHOLSON, *rev.* MARK POTTLE

Sources H. C. Marillier, *The Liverpool school of painters* (1904) · W. Huggins, *William Huggins of Liverpool* (1966) · *The Athenaeum* (1884), 317–18 · W. S. Sparrow, *British sporting artists from Barlow to Herring* (1965) · E. Morris and E. Roberts, *The Liverpool Academy and other exhibitions of contemporary art in Liverpool, 1774–1867* (1998) · J. C. Morley, *Biographical notes on some Liverpool artists* (1890) · Bryan, *Painters* (1886–9) · W. Huggins, *The menagerie of William Huggins* (1984) · *The Times* (8 Nov 1966), 11e · *The Times* (8 Dec 1966), 18g · *The Times* (8 April 1967), 12e · Wood, *Vic. painters*, 2nd edn · d. cert.
Likenesses W. Huggins, self-portrait, oils, c.1841, Walker Art Gallery, Liverpool
Wealth at death £1623 5s.: administration, 30 May 1884, *CGPLA Eng. & Wales*

Huggins, Sir William (1824–1910), astronomer, was born on 7 February 1824 in the parish of St Peter, Cornhill, London, the only child of William Thomas Huggins (1780?–1856), a silk mercer and linen draper, and his wife, Lucy Miller (1786?–1868), a native of Peterborough. He attended the City of London School from 1837 to 1839, then until 1842 was tutored privately.

In 1843 Huggins acquired a small telescope. He formalized his interest in scientific matters in 1852 by becoming a fellow of the Royal Microscopical Society. In 1853 he purchased a 5 inch Dollond equatorial, and in 1854 he was elected a fellow of the Royal Astronomical Society (RAS). Soon afterwards he sold the family business and moved to Tulse Hill, a London suburb where he found both the time and the darkened skies necessary to pursue astronomy. Huggins had a substantial observatory building constructed at his home, and in 1856 acquired a notebook in which to record his observations. Although his first brief and sporadic entries described subjects common to casual observers, he soon undertook more systematic research through the guidance and encouragement of expert amateurs, notably William Rutter Dawes (1799–1868) of Haddenham, from whom, in 1858, he purchased an 8 inch object glass made by Alvan Clark of Cambridge, Massachusetts; this he had mounted in an equatorial, clock-driven instrument by Thomas Cooke of York.

Pioneering celestial spectroscopy Huggins's rise to prominence coincided with the successful adaptation of the spectroscope to new astronomical purposes following the announcement in 1859 by the German scientists Gustav Kirchhoff (1828–1887) and Robert Bunsen (1811–1899) of their interpretation of Fraunhofer's lines. Their suggestion that these perplexing dark interruptions in the otherwise continuous solar spectrum betrayed the sun's terrestrial chemical make-up stimulated much interest and discussion in Britain, especially among analytic chemists such as Huggins's friend and neighbour William Allen Miller (1817–1870). Miller, professor of chemistry at King's

Sir William Huggins (1824–1910), by John Collier, 1905 [replica]

College, London, was an experienced spectroscopist and photographer whom Huggins later credited as both the source of his introduction to spectrum analysis and the catalyst for his later efforts to discover the chemical composition of the heavenly bodies. The intrusion of chemical instruments and research goals into the observatory required major alterations to the traditional organization of astronomical work and workspace. With Miller, Huggins perfected a spectroscope which, attached to his telescope, brought the prominent spectral lines of the brighter stars into view. Huggins's star spectroscope enabled astronomers to ask new questions and undertake new mensuration, and ultimately altered the boundaries of acceptable astronomical research. He was recognized by contemporaries as a principal founder of this new science of celestial spectroscopy.

Direct visual comparison of stellar spectra against those produced by known terrestrial elements was hindered by the lack of standard and precise spectrum maps. To rectify that, in 1863 Huggins embarked on an extensive examination of metallic spectra, making important improvements in instrument design and research methodology. As an independent observer he tested the spectroscope's analytic power on his choice of a variety of celestial objects. Thus in 1864 his research shifted from stars to nebulae in the hope that the spectroscope would resolve the many unanswered questions about their nature. It was a bold initiative which ultimately propelled Huggins to a position of prestige and authority among his fellow astronomers. He selected a bright planetary nebula (37 H. IV. Draconis) as his first object, fully expecting to find that it differed from a star not so much in terms of composition but in its temperature and density. He was astonished to find a bright line spectrum unlike that of any known terrestrial element. The spectra of other planetary nebulae showed similar characteristics, leading him to conclude that they were not only gaseous in nature but represented a class of truly unique celestial bodies. Huggins's announcement captured his colleagues' imagination and heightened their awareness of the potential of spectrum analysis to generate new knowledge about the heavens. In June 1865 he was elected to fellowship in the Royal Society, and in February 1867 he and Miller were jointly awarded the RAS gold medal for their collaborative research on nebular spectra.

Celestial spectroscopy developed rapidly in a wide range of directions. No one knew which would prove most fruitful. Huggins therefore explored a variety of subjects in innovative and technically challenging ways. In May 1866 he became the first to analyse the spectrum of a nova (T Coronae). Months later he examined solar prominences, devising methods to observe them without an eclipse. He investigated the chemical composition of meteors, looked for reported changes in lunar surface features, and pioneered the use of a thermopile to measure the heat reaching earth from the moon and brighter stars. Although each of these projects met with mixed success, the attempts reveal much about his willingness to pursue risky projects to establish himself in the forefront of the new astronomy.

Huggins is renowned for his development of a spectroscopic method to determine a star's motion in the line of sight, begun in 1867. Although astronomers routinely measured the motion of stars across the field of view, they lacked visual cues for determining stellar motion towards or away from earth. Huggins believed that this information could be gained by observing an individual line in a star's spectrum alongside its counterpart in the spectrum of a known terrestrial element. As with the change in pitch that Christian Doppler (1803–1853) predicted would be heard emanating from a moving source of sound, Huggins reasoned that any lack of coincidence in the two lines' positions would be due to their sources' relative motion. He received encouragement from the physicist James Clerk Maxwell (1831–1879), along with a warning to expect the observed differences to be extremely small. Armed with new and more precise instruments, Huggins relied solely on direct visual observations of the bright star Sirius in February 1868; he compared the prominent Fraunhofer F line in the star's spectrum to that of a laboratory hydrogen spark, but obtained occasionally conflicting results. To reduce alignment error he designed an improved arrangement for throwing the light of the comparison spark into the telescopic view. He concluded that, despite some inconsistencies, Sirius appeared to be receding from the earth at a speed of 29.4 miles per second (the modern assignation is 5 miles per second towards the earth). In announcing his result Huggins expressed satisfaction that he had resolved the instrumental problems and stressed the care he had taken. He invoked Maxwell's

name to underscore the theoretical soundness of his conclusions. His tone was one of confidence and spirited adventure. Indeed, arguably his greatest contribution to the successful introduction of this new method into astronomical research lay in his persuasion of his contemporaries that he had, in fact, accomplished what he claimed despite the overwhelming mensurational and interpretive difficulties the method entailed. Although few understood the physical theory, and although implementing his method was largely beyond the resources and ability of many of his fellow amateurs, celestial mechanicians such as those at the Royal Observatory, Greenwich, recognized, and later took up, its potential as an aid to charting the heavens. By giving astronomy an elegant and reliable research tool of broad utility, Huggins became recognized as the one upon whom even the astronomer royal, George Biddell Airy (1801–1892), could rely for advice on spectroscopic matters.

Funding: obligations and status However, the highly refractive train of prisms that facilitated Huggins's line-of-sight investigations impaired his nebular work. Because of the limited light-gathering capability of his 8 inch telescope, the feeble light of a nebula faded to invisibility when subjected to his spectroscope's dispersive power. The influential director of the Armagh observatory, Thomas Romney Robinson (1792–1882), desiring to advance the cause of celestial spectroscopy, persuaded the Royal Society to finance for £2000 the construction of instruments for Huggins's use. Huggins enlarged his observatory in November 1870 to accommodate a pair of fine telescopes by Howard Grubb of Dublin—one a 15 inch refractor and the other an 18 inch reflector—which could be mounted interchangeably on the equatorial base. Although the accompanying spectroscopes were not yet complete, the telescopes were ready for visual observations in February 1871. (In 1882 the instrument was modified to incorporate two independent declination axes so that both telescopes could be mounted and used simultaneously.)

The arrival of Huggins's Great Grubb Equatorial marked a turning point in his career. No longer independent of institutional expectations or constraints, he was now custodian of state-of-the-art telescopes paid for with funds appropriated by the Royal Society, and so directly answerable to criticism of his choice of observational problems, his methods, even his diligence in the use of these coveted instruments. During the protracted debate regarding state funds for research which split the RAS in 1872, there was criticism of awarding limited resources to private individuals, such as Huggins, who could further their own personal research goals instead of those in the national interest. To critics, Huggins exemplified the inadequacy and inefficiency of relying on individuals to carry out the essential work of the new astronomy.

For Huggins the trust which custody of the Royal Society's instruments represented imposed an overwhelming obligation to use them. He found the new work exhausting. No doubt he had planned to rely on Miller's skilled assistance, but Miller died unexpectedly in September

1870, just months before Grubb installed the new instruments. Huggins also needed to incorporate photography to maintain his pioneering role. His need for an assistant, preferably one familiar with the techniques of photography, combined with his sense of frugality may have encouraged him to commit to a greater change in his personal life. On 8 September 1875 he married Margaret Lindsay Murray (1848–1915) [*see* Huggins, Margaret Lindsay] of Monkstown, on Dublin Bay, Ireland, a woman with skills and sufficient astronomical interest in whom he found a lifelong and devoted companion as well as a capable collaborator. They had no children. Margaret's presence changed both the kind of work done at the Tulse Hill observatory and its organization. Her entries in the observatory notebooks clearly reveal her initiative in problem selection, instrument design, methodological approach, and data interpretation. More importantly, they point to her as the impetus behind the establishment of Huggins's successful programme of photographic research. Her long hours of skilled guiding produced a sharpness in the definition of the photographs which was difficult to surpass for spectra only half an inch in length.

Solar research Because he is remembered principally as a pioneer in the field of stellar and nebular spectroscopy, Huggins's forays into solar research are less well known; indeed, they are conspicuously missing from his retrospective account. He played a significant role in resolving the so-called willow-leaves controversy in 1864, and in 1866 was the first to develop both spectroscopic and nonspectroscopic methods for rendering solar prominences visible without an eclipse. In 1870 he led an eclipse expedition to observe the solar corona's spectrum, for which task he designed a sophisticated automatic recorder, but inclement weather left him empty-handed. His interest revived in 1882 when he viewed a recent eclipse photograph showing the light of the coronal spectrum to be strongest in the violet. Eager to provide solar observers with a reliable means of routinely recording coronal phenomena, Huggins and his wife developed a unique method for photographing the corona whenever the sun was visible, first using violet glass as a filter, and later relying on selective sensitivity in photographic emulsions. They pursued this project enthusiastically for over a decade, during which time Huggins successfully petitioned the Royal Society to have the method tested in locations free of atmospheric obscuration. Some of the photographs thus obtained appeared to show the general form of the solar corona.

In 1885 Huggins gave two major addresses on the corona, including the Royal Society's Bakerian lecture, in which he described the method he and his wife had devised for observing the corona without an eclipse, giving particular attention to the many precautions taken to prevent the appearance of false effects. He emphasized the persuasive weight of the numbers of successful plates obtained, their corroboration by experts, and the tests in progress. He speculated on the nature of the corona, drawing attention to the analogous appearance of its structural features to the glowing streamers seen in comets' tails,

suggesting that high electrical potential at the level of the photosphere could account for both the movement and the glow of oppositely charged material far above the sun's surface. In 1886 Étienne Leopold Trouvelot (1827–1895), of the Meudon observatory in France, reported that he, too, had seen the corona without an eclipse. Despite this news, critics of Huggins's method abounded and further tests of the method proved inconclusive. By the time Bernard Lyot (1897–1952) took the first successful photograph of the solar corona without an eclipse in 1930, few remembered Huggins's earlier work. Nevertheless, his pioneering efforts contributed to the emerging discipline of solar research, the useful questions being asked about the solar atmosphere, the type and form of evidence considered as conclusive, and the direction in which solar observation was taken by the growing international network of solar observers.

Nebular theory In 1887 the Hugginses began their search for the cause of the principal emission lines in nebular spectra, an exciting subject, though contentious because of the rich variety of nebular theories then vying for observational confirmation. Their conclusion that the lines derived from the glowing gas of some heretofore unknown element contradicted that of Norman Lockyer (1836–1920), who claimed they were produced by the magnesium in incandescent swarms of colliding meteorites. The rancorous controversy which ensued taxed Huggins's rhetorical skills. By advocating his method of gathering evidence and, hence, his interpretation of it, he contributed much towards refining and defining standards of proof within the maturing science of celestial spectroscopy.

In 1892 Huggins had the opportunity to subject the light of another nova (T Aurigae) to spectrum analysis. With his wife he conducted an exhaustive and exhausting study of the nova's spectrum. Understanding of the physical mechanisms at work in such events had not improved since T Coronae in 1866, nevertheless celestial spectroscopy and photography had greatly enriched the astronomer's methodological and interpretive potential. Alert now for any tell-tale signs of stellar motion in the line of sight, or spectral signatures betraying the presence of some new and as yet undiscovered element, the Hugginses, like all other astronomers for whom these methods had now become routine, looked at T Aurigae with new eyes.

In the final decade of his life, as direct telescopic observations became increasingly difficult for him, Huggins found other ways to advertise the investigative power of the spectroscope and to promote its use in astronomy as well as in other sciences. In 1899 he and his wife published *An Atlas of Representative Stellar Spectra*, a volume aimed at establishing Huggins as the pre-eminent authority in the field of stellar spectroscopy, and disseminating the spectrographic evidence gathered at Tulse Hill in support of his views on the chemical and physical nature of stars and their probable evolution. In 1903 they embarked on a long-term spectroscopic study of the newly discovered element radium. In 1908, no longer able to make routine use of the instruments entrusted to his care for nearly four decades, Huggins recommended their transfer to enhance H. F. Newall's work at the Cambridge University observatory, where they remained until 1954. In 1909 the Hugginses published *The Scientific Papers of Sir William Huggins*, an edited collection of previously published documents organized topically and accompanied by new interpretive commentary.

Huggins was an active member, and served as president, of the Royal Astronomical Society (1876–8), the British Association for the Advancement of Science (1891), and the Royal Society (1900–05). He received honorary degrees from the universities of Cambridge (1870), Oxford (1871), Edinburgh (1871), Dublin (1886), St Andrews (1893), and various foreign countries, and he received the Royal Society's royal (1866), Rumford (1880), and Copley (1898) medals. In 1885 he joined the ranks of those elect few in the history of the RAS to be honoured with a second gold medal. The emperor of Brazil, Pedro II, bestowed on him the order of the Rose (1871). The Académie des Sciences in Paris awarded him the Lalande prize (1882), the Valz prize (1883), and the Janssen gold medal (1888), and he received the Draper medal (1901) from the National Academy of Sciences in Washington, DC. In addition he held honorary or foreign membership in numerous national learned societies, including the Académie des Sciences de l'Institut National de France, Paris; the Reale Accademia dei Lincei; the royal academies of Berlin and Göttingen; the Royal Irish Academy; the royal societies of Edinburgh, Sweden, Denmark, and the Netherlands; the National Academy of Sciences, Washington, DC; the American Philosophical Society, Philadelphia; and the American Academy of Arts and Sciences, Boston.

Huggins was created a KCB by Queen Victoria in 1897 and was among the first twelve individuals awarded the prestigious Order of Merit by Edward VII in 1902. He died on 12 May 1910 of heart failure following surgery. He was cremated and his ashes placed in Golders Green crematorium, Middlesex. He was survived by his wife and collaborator of thirty-four years, who bequeathed a number of his scientific instruments as well as six bound observatory notebooks to Wellesley College, Wellesley, Massachusetts. She also established a scholarship in her husband's name at the City of London School.

BARBARA J. BECKER

Sources B. J. Becker, 'Eclecticism, opportunism, and the evolution of a new research agenda: William and Margaret Huggins and the origins of astrophysics', PhD diss., Johns Hopkins University, 1993 · B. J. Becker, 'Dispelling the myth of the able assistant: Margaret and William Huggins at work in the Tulse Hill observatory', *Creative couples in the sciences*, ed. H. Pycior and others (1996), 98–111 · C. E. Mills and C. F. Brooke, *A sketch of the life of Sir William Huggins* (1936) · W. Huggins and M. L. Huggins, observatory notebooks, Wellesley College, Wellesley, Massachusetts, USA, Margaret Clapp Library · W. Huggins, 'The new astronomy', *Nineteenth Century*, 41 (1897), 907–29 · W. Huggins and Lady Huggins, *An atlas of representative stellar spectra from λ4870 to λ3300: together with … a short history of the observatory and its work* (1899) · *The scientific papers of Sir William Huggins*, ed. W. Huggins and M. L. Huggins (1909) · PRO, RG4/4226 · m. cert. · d. cert. · census returns, 1841, 1851, 1861, 1871

Archives RAS, corresp. and papers · RS, corresp. · South African Astronomical Observatory, Cape Town, archives · Wellesley College, Massachusetts, Clapp Library, letters, observatory notebooks, scientific instruments, objets d'art | Air Force Research Laboratories, Cambridge, Massachusetts, letters to Lord Rayleigh · Bodl. Oxf., letters to Sir Henry Wentworth Acland · California Institute of Technology, Pasadena, archives, corresp. with George Hale · CUL, corresp. with Sir George Stokes and T. R. Robinson · Dartmouth College, Hanover, New Hampshire, C. A. Young MSS · Hunt. L., G. E. Hale MSS · ICL, letters to S. P. Thompson · NYPL, J. Draper MSS · RS, corresp. with Sir J. F. W. Herschel · RS, J. Larmor MSS · U. Cal., Santa Cruz, Lick Observatory, Mary Lea Shane archives, E. Holden MSS · University of Exeter, J. N. Lockyer MSS · W. Sussex RO, letters to Sir Alfred Kempe · Yale U., D. Todd MSS **Likenesses** photograph, c.1900, Hult. Arch. · J. Collier, oils, 1905, RS · J. Collier, oils, second version, 1905, NPG [see illus.] · Spy [L. Ward], caricature chromolithograph, NPG; repro. in *VF* (9 April 1903) · H. J. Whitlock, carte-de-visite, NPG · oils, RAS **Wealth at death** £6920 3s. 5d.: probate, 15 July 1910, CGPLA Eng. & Wales

Huggins, William John (1781–1845), marine painter, of whose parents nothing is known, reputedly began life as a sailor in the East India Company, but his only known voyage was from December 1812 to August 1814, to Bombay and China, when he was listed for wages as 'ordinary seaman' while serving as steward to Captain Thomas Buchanan on the company ship *Perseverance*. Unless the 'ordinary' rating reflects the circumstance of a man no longer fit to do an able seaman's duty, he may never have been one, although he clearly knew his subject. A painting of the frigate *Phoenix* (36 guns), under Captain W. H. Webley (later Webley-Parry), convoying seventeen ships including the *Perseverance* home from Madras in 1814, was reputed in the Webley-Parry family to have been his first picture, and they lent it to the Royal Naval Exhibition at Chelsea in 1891 (catalogue no. 566). By 1817, when Huggins first exhibited at the Royal Academy (at the British Institution from 1825), he had settled in London at 36 Leadenhall Street (no. 105 from 1823 or 1824), near East India House. Here he remained for the rest of his life, specializing in portraits of East India vessels for captains, owners, and others, and similar shipping and naval subjects, including in watercolours. He appears to have had some early help from Thomas Duncan (c.1779–1841), a ship decorator, print colourist, and art teacher whose son, Edward Duncan (1803–1882), a member of the Old Watercolour Society, subsequently collaborated with him as a lithographer. Edward reproduced about 150 of Huggins's works, acquired skill as a marine painter from him, and in 1834 married his eldest daughter, Berthia (1809–1884). Huggins and Duncan—a better artist—also occasionally painted pictures together, such as one of Indiamen in the China Sea, now in the National Maritime Museum, Greenwich, which is signed by both. Huggins's Eastern sketches provided authentic backgrounds to his work, although he is also likely to have used other people's. He was a competent ship portraitist with a distinctive smooth finish to his oils and rather silvery, muted colour, and his work provides an important record of the shipping of his time. However, although prolific and popular with a maritime audience, 'Uggins' was thus summarily dismissed in 1856 by Ruskin in his *Harbours of England* (Ruskin, 16), and Redgrave characterized his works as 'tame in design, skies bad in colour, seas thin and poor' (Redgrave, 228). Turner, whom Ruskin was defending from seamen's derogatory comparisons, none the less partly used his pictures of whalers, owned by their joint patron the whale-oil merchant Elhanan Bicknell, as the basis of his own, about 1845. Aesthetic critics notwithstanding, on 20 September 1830 Huggins was appointed marine painter to William IV (the 'sailor king'), who according to Redgrave 'esteemed his work rather for its correctness than its art' and commissioned three large paintings of the battle of Trafalgar from him. The first two were shown publicly at Exeter Hall in 1834, the third at the British Institution in 1837: all remain in the Royal Collection. His works still often appear in the market, fetching substantial prices from collectors, and there are twenty-six in the National Maritime Museum. This also holds drawings, watercolours, prints, and two ship portraits by James Miller Huggins (*bap.* 1807), who was his son and pupil; he exhibited at the Society of British Artists, 1826–30, once at the British Institution in 1842, and was still working in 1865. He and another son, John W. Huggins (*bap.* 1809), also etched a number of Huggins's shipping studies published between 1824 and 1833 (later gathered in bound form as 'Huggins' Marine Sketches', n.d.). Huggins died on 19 May 1845, aged sixty-four. A letter of 1951 in the National Maritime Museum, London, suggests family papers were carelessly destroyed. Huggins and his wife, Berthia (a name also spelt Berthier), had three other daughters, Elizabeth Mary (*bap.* 1813), Amelia, later Gibbs (*bap.* 1817), and Sarah Christiana (*bap.* 1821). His will, dated 1841 and proved on 12 August 1845, made them his beneficiaries, appointing the last two and his widow as executors, with directions to 'sell by public auction all my sketches drawings and paintings', but retaining his stock of engraved plates to reissue for joint benefit. Neither his daughter Berthia nor his sons are mentioned.   PIETER VAN DER MERWE

Sources DNB · W. Gilbey, *Animal painters of England*, 3 (1911), 11 [Edward Duncan] · *Perseverance* log and pay ledger, 1812–14, India RO · P. Bicknell, 'Turner's *The whale ship*: a missing link?', *Turner Studies*, 5/2 (1985), 20–23 · J. Ruskin, *Harbours of England* (1856), 16 · Redgrave, *Artists*, 228 · O. Millar, *The later Georgian pictures in the collection of her majesty the queen*, 1 (1969), 56 · *Royal naval exhibition*, [another edn] (1891) [exhibition catalogue, Chelsea, London, 1891] · E. H. H. Archibald, *The dictionary of sea painters of Europe and America*, 3rd edn (2000) · notes in picture files, NMM [incl. copy of letter from Mrs Joan Pamm, descendant, 5 Sept 1951] · 'Household index' of appointments, Royal Arch. · Graves, *RA exhibitors* · Graves, *Brit. Inst.* · will, PRO, PROB 11/2022, sig. 641 · *IGI* · J. Johnson, ed., *Works exhibited at the Royal Society of British Artists, 1824–1893, and the New English Art Club, 1888–1917*, 2 vols. (1975) · 'Huggins' marine sketches', [n.d.], NMM [bound copy]

Hugh. *See* Grandmesnil, Hugh de (*d.* 1098); Montgomery, Hugh de, second earl of Shrewsbury (*d.* 1098); Avranches, Hugh d', first earl of Chester (*d.* 1101); Wells, Hugh of (*d.* 1235).

Hugh [Hugues d'Amiens] (*d.* **1164**), abbot of Reading and archbishop of Rouen, was also variously known as Hugues

d'Amiens, Hugues de Ribemont, and Hugues de Ste Marguerite. Ribemont (Aisne) lies to the north of Laon, close to St Quentin; another Ribemont (Somme) lies between Amiens and Boves. Osbert de Clare calls him Hugues de Ste Marguerite, but this connection is obscure. Hugh's mother's name was Héceline, and he may have been connected with the Boves family in the Amiennois; he is known to have held lands in the Pas-de-Calais. He was a relative of Guillaume Talvas (*d.* 1172), count of Ponthieu, north-west of Amiens, and also of Matthieu, who became prior of the Cluniac house of St Martin-des-Champs, Paris, and later cardinal-bishop of Albano.

Hugh's identification with the poet Hugues d'Amiens is secure, along with his authorship of a number of early poems on religious subjects (including one on the Pentateuch), as well as a tract on the origin of the human soul and original sin. Of Matthieu, Hugh wrote that France had given birth to them both, that both were educated at Laon, and wore the garment of Christ at Cluny. At the cathedral school of Laon, Hugh would have been taught the scriptures by the brothers Anselm and Raoul. He became a monk of Cluny after 1099 and before 1113, one of an élite which included, besides Matthieu, Gilbert Foliot (*d.* 1187), Henry de Blois (*d.* 1171), and Peter the Venerable. Peter, later abbot of Cluny, once described any letter received from Hugh as a sparkling jewel. Abbot Pons made Hugh prior of St Martial at Limoges *c.*1113; in 1120 he became prior of St Pancras at Lewes, also a Cluniac house, where Osbert de Clare, monk of Westminster, wished he could join him. From 15 April 1123 to September 1130 Hugh was first abbot of Reading, founded by Henry I between 1121 and 1125. The abbey's responsibilities included praying for the soul of the king's son who had drowned at sea in November 1120. The monks—200 in number according to Orderic Vitalis—were drawn from Cluny and Lewes. Reading was a model of reform: its possessions were held by the abbot and the convent in common and there were no knights' fees.

By summer 1126 Hugh had written six books of *Dialogues* in which he and Matthieu discuss theological subjects. Between 1130 and 1134 (and after Matthieu had become a cardinal in October 1126), Hugh revised the work and added a seventh book preceded by a letter. The work resembles the systematic collections of theological questions then associated pre-eminently with the school of Laon. Hugh has been suggested as the author of a spirited reply, written *c.*1127–8, to Bernard, abbot of Clairvaux, the champion of the new Cistercian order of monks and a critic of the well-endowed Cluniac way of life. The writer shows an equally brilliant command of the weapons of satirical exaggeration and humorous invective. According to Osbert de Clare, Hugh—'a man of venerable life … liberally educated in human and divine learning' (Clare, 67)—introduced to Reading the feast of the immaculate conception of the Virgin Mary at the king's request.

On 30 April 1128 Pope Honorius II (*r.* 1124–30) summoned Hugh to work in the papal curia; following protests by the king and the monks Hugh returned to Reading in 1129. Honorius required him to negotiate over arrears of

'Peter's pence', and to settle the rate for future annual payments. Before 21 November Hugh was elected to the archbishopric of Rouen. He apparently left England with the king on 8 September 1130; his consecration took place at Rouen on 14 September. Bernard of Clairvaux wrote a letter of encouragement. Hugh took the side of Pope Innocent II (r. 1130–43) against his rival Anacletus, and received Innocent in 1131 at Rouen, where he was joined by Bernard who sought the support of Henry I for Innocent. Hugh rejoined the pope at the Council of Rheims in the same year, bringing him letters in which the king of England gave recognition. Henry was incensed by Hugh's refusal to consecrate as bishop of Bayeux the king's grandson Richard, bastard son of Robert, earl of Gloucester (d. 1147). This difficulty was surmounted by a papal dispensation. Hugh attended the Council of Pisa (1135), and on its conclusion remained in Italy. Complaints were made about this absence too, and Hugh returned, in time to attend the king, and to give him absolution, before his death on 1 December 1135 at Lyons-la-Forêt.

Hugh was a staunch supporter of King Stephen, and joined his court in England in 1136. At the legatine council at Winchester, summoned by Bishop Henry of Winchester (29 August 1139), Hugh defended the king's seizure of the castles of the bishops of Salisbury, Lincoln, and Ely. After Stephen's capture at Lincoln in February 1141 he and a group of Norman magnates unsuccessfully offered England and Normandy to Stephen's brother Theobald, who refused. Between 1141 and 1144 Hugh wrote letters to the Londoners expressing his satisfaction at their support of Stephen. He continued to recognize Stephen until 1144, when Rouen fell to Count Geoffrey of Anjou. Thereafter Hugh supported Geoffrey and the latter's son Henry.

Hugh played a large part in the administration of the duchy. He was a vigorous metropolitan who developed the archdeaconries, although he held no known provincial synods. He strove to obtain written professions of obedience from the abbots in his diocese, and thereby again displeased Henry I. For a brief while in 1148 Hugh excommunicated his kinsman Count Guillaume Talvas and Count William's son John, in the course of a dispute involving the abbey of Troarn. Among his achievements was the foundation of the abbey of St Martin at Aumale in 1130, and the settlement of a number of disputes between abbeys, including one involving Furness, which had held out against the absorption of the order of Savigny into the order of Cîteaux.

As archbishop, Hugh continued to write. He produced in 1142 or a little later, for his suffragan Arnulf, bishop of Lisieux (d. 1181), a Commentary on Genesis 1–3. He also wrote Against Heretics in Brittany between late 1145 and Easter 1147, on the prompting of Cardinal Alberic. In the course of a mission he undertook in Brittany, Hugh and Alberic, then legate, celebrated together the feast of the saints Donatian and Rogatian at Nantes in May 1145, when they also observed a comet over the Atlantic. In 1147 Hugh attended the Council of Paris where Gilbert de la Porrée, bishop of Poitiers, was accused of error concerning the Trinity. Hugh attacked his teaching in a work On Catholic

faith [the apostles' creed] and the Lord's prayer, written between 1155 and 1159 for Gilles his nephew, archdeacon of Rouen. In March 1152 he took part in the assembly at Beaugency where the marriage between Louis VII of France and Eleanor of Aquitaine was annulled. His Treatise on Memory, written between 1160 and 1164, explains the content of religious faith which should always be kept in mind; in the preface, addressed to a certain Philip, Hugh writes of his old age. He also wrote a life of St Adiutor, a monk of Tiron. On 2 November 1160 he officiated at the wedding of Henry, the young son of Henry II, and Marguerite, daughter of Louis VII, at Neubourg.

One of Hugh's last acts was to write in 1164 to the bishops and abbots in Normandy to ask for support for Alexander III (r. 1159–81) following the election of a rival pope, Paschal III. The Archdeacon Lambert wrote to the French king to inform him of this and of Hugh's last moments. He died about 10 November 1164, and was buried in the cathedral at Rouen where an epitaph was placed, composed by Arnulf of Lisieux. Robert de Torigni wrote that he had governed his church honeste et viriliter ('honourably and vigorously'; Chronica Roberti de Torigneio in Chronicles, ed. Howlett, vol. 4). His successor, Archbishop Rotrou, gave two volumes of Hugh's writings to the cathedral. About eighteen letters, and numerous acts, survive.

DAVID LUSCOMBE

Sources T. G. Waldman, 'Hugh "of Amiens", archbishop of Rouen (1130–64)', DPhil diss., U. Oxf., 1970 [incl. edn of Hugh's acta and letters] · Hugo Rothomagensis, Patrologia Latina, 192 (1855), 1117–1352 · P. Hébert, 'Un archévêque de Rouen au XIIe siècle: Hugues III d'Amiens, 1130–1164', Revue des Questions Historiques, 64 (1898), 325–71 · D. Van den Eynde, 'Nouvelles précisions chronologiques sur quelques ouvrages théologiques du XIIe siècle', Franciscan Studies, 13 (1953), 71–118 · J. Huemer, Zur Geschichte der mittelateinischen Dichtung: Hugonis Ambianensis sive Ribemontensis opuscula (1880), 37–40 · F. Lecomte, 'Un commentaire scripturaire du XIIe siècle: le Tractatus in hexaemeron de Hugues d'Amiens, archévêque de Rouen, 1130–1164', Archives d'Histoire Doctrinale et Littéraire du Moyen Âge, 25 (1958), 227–94 · A. Wilmart, 'Un riposte de l'ancien monachisme au manifeste de S. Bernard', Revue Bénédictine, 46 (1934), 296–344 · C. H. Talbot, 'The date and author of the Riposte', Petrus Venerabilis, 1156–1956, ed. G. Constable and J. Kritzeck, Studia Anselmiana, 40 (1956), 72–80 · 'Hugues d'Amiens, archévêque de Reims [sic]', Histoire littéraire de la France, ed. P. Paris, 12 (1869), 647–67 [with an account of Hugh's writings] · Gallia Christiana in provincias ecclesiasticas distributa, 11, ed. P. Henri and J. Taschereau (1759), cols. 43–8 · Osbert de Clare, Letters, ed. E. W. Williamson (1929), letters 1, 7 · R. Manselli, 'Per la storia dell'eresia', Bollettino dell'Istituto Storico Italiano per il Medio Evo, 67 (1955), 235–44 · Ordericus Vitalis, Eccl. hist., 6.448–9 · R. Howlett, ed., Chronicles of the reigns of Stephen, Henry II, and Richard I, 4, Rolls Series, 82 (1889), 223 · D. Knowles, C. N. L. Brooke, and V. C. M. London, eds., The heads of religious houses, England and Wales, 1: 940–1216 (1972)

Likenesses recumbent sculpted figure on top of tomb, Rouen Cathedral; repro. in Waldman, 'Hugh "of Amiens"', following p. 164

Hugh [Hugh of Cyfeiliog], **fifth earl of Chester** (1147–1181), magnate, was the son of *Ranulf (II), fourth earl of Chester, and his wife, *Matilda, daughter of *Robert, earl of Gloucester, the illegitimate son of Henry I. He is sometimes called Hugh of Cyfeiliog (Meirionydd), because, according to a late writer, he was born in that district of

Wales. His father died on 16 December 1153, when Hugh was still under age. His inheritance, on both sides of the channel, included the hereditary viscountcies of Avranches, Bessin, and Val de Vire, the honours of St Sever and Briquessart, and the Chester earldom together with its associated honours in England and Wales, making the earl one of the greatest of all Anglo-Norman landholders. Hugh came of age in 1162, when he took seisin of his lands and received his title. He was present in 1163 at Dover for Henry II's renewal of the Flemish money fief, and also attended the Council of Clarendon in January 1164. He failed to make a return to the English survey of knight's fees in 1166, and later apparently went unassessed under the 1168 aid taken for the marriage of the king's daughter.

Hugh joined the rebellion of Henry II's sons in 1173. Aided by Ralph de Fougères he utilized his great influence in the north-eastern marches of Brittany to incite the Bretons to revolt. Henry II dispatched an army of Brabant mercenaries against them. The rebels were defeated in a battle, and on 20 August were shut up in the castle of Dol, which they had captured by fraud not long before. On 23 August, Henry II arrived to conduct the siege in person. Hugh and his comrades had no provisions, and were therefore forced to surrender on 26 August on a promise that their lives and limbs would be saved. Eighty knights surrendered with them. Hugh was treated leniently by Henry, and was confined at Falaise, where the earl and countess of Leicester were also soon brought as prisoners. When Henry II returned to England he took the two earls with him. They were conveyed from Barfleur to Southampton on 8 July 1174. Hugh was probably afterwards imprisoned at Devizes. On 8 August, however, he was taken back from Portsmouth to Barfleur, when Henry II returned to Normandy. He was now imprisoned at Caen, and from there removed to Falaise. He was admitted to terms with Henry before the general peace, and witnessed the treaty of Falaise on 11 October.

Hugh seems to have remained some time longer without restoration. At last, at the Council of Northampton on 13 January 1177, he received grant of the lands on both sides of the channel which he had held fifteen days before the war broke out. In March he witnessed Henry II's award in the dispute between Alfonso IX, king of Castile, and Sancho V, king of Navarre. In May, at the Council of Windsor, Henry restored to him his castles, and required him to go to Ireland, along with William fitz Audelin and others, to prepare the way for the king's son. But no great grants of Irish land were conferred on him, and he took no prominent part in the Irish campaigns. Nevertheless, Chester's increased trade with Ireland amply profited the earldom in years to come.

Hugh's liberality to the church was not as great as that of his predecessors. He granted some lands in the Wirral to the abbey of St Werburgh, Chester, and made other special gifts to Stanlow Priory, St Mary's, Coventry, and the nuns of Bullington and Greenfield priories. He also confirmed his mother's grants to her foundation of Augustinian canons at Calke, Derbyshire, and those of his father to

his convent of the Benedictine nuns of St Mary's, Chester. In 1171 he confirmed the grants of Ranulf to the abbey of St Stephen in the diocese of Bayeux. More substantial were his grants of Belchford church to Trentham Priory, and of Combe in Gloucestershire to the abbey of Bordesley, Warwickshire.

Hugh married in 1169 Bertrada, the daughter of Simon, count of Évreux. Hugh died at Leek in Staffordshire on 30 June 1181. He was buried next to his father on the south side of the chapter house of St Werburgh's, Chester, now the cathedral. His only legitimate son, *Ranulf (III), succeeded him as earl of Chester. He and his wife also had four daughters, who became, on their brother's death, coheirs of the Chester earldom. They were: Maud, who married David, earl of Huntingdon, and became the mother of John the Scot, earl of Chester from 1232 to 1237, on whose death the line of Hugh d'Avranches became extinct; Mabel, who married William d'Aubigny, earl of Arundel (d. 1221); Agnes, the wife of William Ferrers, earl of Derby; and Hawise, who married Robert de Quincy (d. 1217), son of Saer de Quincy, earl of Winchester. Hugh was also the father of several bastards, including Pagan, lord of Milton; Roger; Amice, who married Ralph Mainwaring, county justice of Chester; and another daughter, who married Richard Bacon, the founder of Rocester Abbey.

T. F. TOUT, rev. THOMAS K. KEEFE

Sources G. Barraclough, ed., *The charters of the Anglo-Norman earls of Chester, c.1071–1237*, Lancashire and Cheshire RS, 126 (1988), 140–96 • R. C. Christie, ed. and trans., *Annales Cestrienses, or, Chronicle of the abbey of S. Werburg at Chester*, Lancashire and Cheshire RS, 14 (1887), 19, 28 • T. A. Heslop, 'The seals of the twelfth-century earls of Chester', *Journal of the Chester Archaeological Society*, 71 (1991) [G. Barraclough issue, *The earldom of Chester and its charters*, ed. A. T. Thacker] • J. Tait, ed., *The chartulary or register of the abbey of St Werburgh, Chester*, Chetham Society, 82 (1923) • W. Stubbs, ed., *Gesta regis Henrici secundi Benedicti abbatis: the chronicle of the reigns of Henry II and Richard I, AD 1169–1192*, 2 vols., Rolls Series, 49 (1867), 1.161, 277 • *Chronica magistri Rogeri de Hovedene*, ed. W. Stubbs, 2, Rolls Series, 51 (1869), 51, 118 • R. Howlett, ed., *Chronicles of the reigns of Stephen, Henry II, and Richard I*, 1, Rolls Series, 82 (1884) • *Jordan Fantosme's chronicle*, ed. and trans. R. C. Johnston (1981), 12–18 • Ralph de Diceto, 'Ymagines historiarum', *Radulfi de Diceto ... opera historica*, ed. W. Stubbs, 1: 1148–79, Rolls Series, 68 (1876), 378 • G. Barraclough, *The earldom and county palatinate of Chester* (1953) • G. Ormerod, *The history of the county palatine and city of Chester*, 2nd edn, ed. T. Helsby, 1 (1882), 29 • T. K. Keefe, 'King Henry II and the earls: the pipe roll evidence', *Albion*, 13 (1981), 191–222 • M. T. Flanagan, *Irish society, Anglo-Norman settlers, Angevin kingship: interactions in Ireland in the late twelfth century* (1989), 75, 144, 168, 291 • T. K. Keefe, *Feudal assessments and the political community under Henry II and his sons* (1983) • *English historical documents*, 2nd edn, 2, ed. D. C. Douglas and G. W. Greenaway (1981), 449, 767 • *Pipe rolls, 20 Henry II*, 21 • W. Dugdale, *The baronage of England*, 2 vols. (1675–6) • L. Delisle and others, eds., *Recueil des actes de Henri II, roi d'Angleterre et duc de Normandie, concernant les provinces françaises et les affaires de France*, 4 vols. (Paris, 1909–27), vol. 1, p. 380; vol. 2, p. 23 • T. Stapleton, ed., *Magni rotuli scaccarii Normanniae sub regibus Angliae*, 2 vols., Society of Antiquaries of London Occasional Papers (1840–44) • H. Hall, ed., *The Red Book of the Exchequer*, 3 vols., Rolls Series, 99 (1896) • J. W. Alexander, *Ranulf of Chester: a relic of the Conquest* (1983)
Likenesses seal, repro. in Ormerod, *History of the county palatine*, 1.32

Hugh Candidus [Hugh Albus] (*c*.1095–*c*.1160), Benedictine monk and chronicler, wrote a history of Peterborough

Abbey from its first foundation to the mid-twelfth century. His work, which survives entirely in texts incorporated in thirteenth-century cartularies, was edited and continued by later monks of the house, first anonymously shortly after his death, then by Robert of Swaffham in the mid-thirteenth century, and finally by Walter of Whittlesey in the early fourteenth century. Information on Hugh's life comes from his chronicle. He was the younger brother of Reinald Spiritus, who served as sacrist for more than thirty years, and he records Reinald and Abbot Ernulf (1107–14) as his first teachers. He gained his name Hugh the White (Hugh Albus or Hugh Candidus) 'because he was white and of fair countenance' (*Chronicle of Hugh Candidus*, 95). While still a boy he fell very ill; his symptoms, which included recurrent severe haemorrhaging, are consistent with the presence of a peptic ulcer that healed. He gives eyewitness accounts of important events in the history of the monastery. The earliest of these was the burning of the church in 1116; when this was reconsecrated by Alexander, bishop of Lincoln (d. 1148), in Lent 1140, Hugh kissed and washed the right arm of St Oswald (d. 642), the most precious of the relics of the house. In 1149 he was one of the monks who went north with Prior Richard, after the latter's election as abbot of Whitby.

In Hugh's chronicle the senior monks provide the continuity as abbots come and go. Himself appointed subprior in the time of Abbot Martin of Bec (1133–55), he was reappointed to this office by Abbot William de Waterville (1155–75), and died during William's abbacy. As the senior member of the community in 1155 he presided over the election, and he gives interesting details of the deliberations both at Peterborough and at the royal court at Oxford. The elect came from one of the families that held land from the abbey in the soke of Peterborough; and it is likely that Hugh himself came from this milieu. The abbatial election of 1155 concludes also the final version (E) of the Anglo-Saxon Chronicle, which is a Peterborough text after 1121. The Latin chronicle of Hugh Candidus and the E text of the Anglo-Saxon Chronicle are contemporary and are closely related. Hugh occasionally makes use of E, but more often the two texts make independent use of a common set of materials. It is to Hugh that credit was given for collecting these, by his first editor. Among the materials were a set of narrative charters from the early twelfth century, which he may also have written. He occurs as witness to one of these, a charter of Robert de Torpel, dated 1147.

Hugh's chronicle opens with the first monks coming to Medeshamstede (the name of the original foundation), 'a very paradise on earth granted to them by God' (*Chronicle of Hugh Candidus*, 6); and it uses charters to establish the names of the earliest abbots and of early daughter houses. It tells of the refoundation of the monastery in 966, after the viking invasions; and how before the conquest it grew in wealth, so that it was called 'the golden borough' (ibid., 66). Much of this, in Hugh's view, was dissipated in the aftermath of the conquest in 1066. The advent of the first Norman abbot, with his grasping relations, and the subsequent rebellion of Hereward, are vividly described. He was highly selective in the events that he chose to treat

during his own lifetime. He could say much in a phrase, as of the civil war of Stephen's reign, when 'the land was awash with young men', but was reluctant to say more on this, 'for many have written much thereon' (ibid., 104–5). Hugh's writings never stray far from the monastery, its fabric, and its endowment, and the saints who watched over it. The later editions kept his work current within the monastery, and it had some circulation outside it. An Anglo-Norman translation of the first edition, *La geste de Burc*, survives from the late thirteenth or early fourteenth century. Hugh's chronicle was first published by Joseph Sparke in 1723, as part of his *Historiae Anglicanae scriptores variae*. Another edition of the Latin text, along with the Anglo-Norman *Geste de Burc*, was published in 1949 by W. T. Mellows, who had earlier produced an English translation in 1941. EDMUND KING

Sources *The chronicle of Hugh Candidus, a monk of Peterborough*, ed. W. T. Mellows (1949) [Lat. text; also prints and trans. *La geste de Burc*, ed. A. Bell] · *The Peterborough Chronicle of Hugh Candidus*, trans. C. Mellows and W. T. Mellows, 2nd edn (1966) · C. Clark, ed., *The Peterborough Chronicle, 1070–1154*, 2nd edn (1970) · A. Gransden, *Historical writing in England*, 1 (1974) · private information (2004) · E. King, *Peterborough Abbey, 1086–1310: a study in the land market* (1973)

Hugh of Abernethy (d. 1291). *See under* Abernethy family (*per. c.*1260–*c.*1465).

Hugh of Lincoln [St Hugh of Lincoln, Hugh of Avalon] (1140?–1200), bishop of Lincoln, was the son of Guillaume d'Avalon, a Burgundian aristocrat, and Anne, daughter of the lord of Theys. He was probably born at Avalon near Grenoble.

Upbringing and early years in England As a boy Hugh was educated by the Augustinian canons at their house of Villarbenoît on the River Isère, which his father joined shortly after his mother died. Hugh himself was professed as a canon at the age of fifteen, and in his early twenties assumed pastoral office as deacon in the parish of St Maximin. Feeling a vocation to the Carthusians, when he visited the Grande Chartreuse in the diocese of Grenoble, he joined them aged twenty-three, and after ten years he became procurator (similar to a bursarship) for six years. In 1179 Hugh came to England as prior of Henry II's new Carthusian foundation of Witham in Somerset, after it had been in danger of collapse through poor administration. It is not improbable that Henry II's motivation was partly further expiation for Thomas Becket's martyrdom, since 1179 was also the year in which Louis VII of France made a pilgrimage to Becket's shrine at Canterbury, whither Henry II accompanied him.

One problem at Witham had been the peasant holdings and their occupants who remained on the site. By a generous arrangement, and with the king's money, Hugh bought them out, and, having purchased their hovels, said to the king with a smile, 'See, my lord king, how I, a poor stranger, have enriched you in your own land with many houses' (Eynsham, 1.62). Henry remarked with amusement on the boldness of the foreigner. The coming of Hugh to England reflects the scope of Henry II's Angevin empire, for he was chosen by the advice of the count of

Maurienne, near Grenoble, with whom the king had earlier been in negotiations about the marriage of his youngest son, John. Hugh's dealings with the king over the material requirements of Witham, were so tactful and good-humoured, and so won Henry II's affection, that, according to Hugh's biographer, Adam of Eynsham, the belief spread that he was the king's natural son, which evidence rules out but which seemed reinforced by a physical resemblance between the two men.

In his period as prior of Witham Hugh frequently rebuked the king for his sins, particularly in drawing the revenues of long-vacant bishoprics and abbacies, and in denying free elections of bishops and abbots to the churches. In the case of his own election to the bishopric of Lincoln, Adam says that 'God had the heart of the king in his hand and inclined it to his will' (Eynsham, 1.93)—for a change, it seems. Hugh, however, refused to accept his election as valid unless made in the Lincoln chapter; the canons were so impressed to hear this that they elected him with apparent unanimity. That was not yet enough, for Hugh then insisted that he needed the consent of his still lawful superior, the prior of Chartreuse, to whom a delegation had to be sent. He was consecrated bishop in St Katherine's Chapel, Westminster Abbey, on 21 September 1186. The first detail that his biographer gives of his pontificate concerns a huge and ferocious swan on the bishop's manor of Stow, Lincolnshire, who became tame only in the bishop's presence and was his special pet—an anecdote reminiscent of the long tradition in Christian hagiography whereby saints demonstrated their harmony with God by their harmony with nature.

Bishop of Lincoln: worldly concerns By no means all of Hugh's activities were of a spiritual character, and inevitably he was frequently involved in public affairs. An early dispute with Henry II over Hugh's excommunication of a royal forester did not prevent Hugh either from attending the Council of Geddington in February 1188, at which plans were made for the king's crusade, or his being sent to France in the summer of that year as an ambassador to King Philip Augustus. Present at Richard I's coronation on 3 September 1189, Hugh attended the Council of Pipewell shortly afterwards, when provision was made for the government of England while the king was absent on crusade. In 1191 he opposed the justiciar, William de Longchamp (d. 1197), following the latter's mistreatment of Archbishop Geoffrey of York (d. 1212), but in the following year was commissioned by the pope to annul the sentence of excommunication which Geoffrey had pronounced upon the bishop of Durham. In 1194 he was himself one of the ecclesiastics who excommunicated the king's brother, the rebellious Count John. In the same year he agreed to pay £2000 to Richard I in settlement of royal claims to a yearly tribute from his diocese. He frequently acted as a papal judge-delegate, although he resented having to do so. He accompanied Archbishop Hubert Walter (d. 1205) on at least one provincial visitation, and in 1198 was the colleague of the archbishop and Abbot Samson of Bury St

Edmunds (d. 1211) in removing secular canons from Coventry Cathedral and reinstating monks.

In the context of his secular activities, it is not surprising that after the swan, the next point his biographer should stress about Hugh as bishop is his search for influential clerical assistants. This was indeed an important matter on account of the growing complexity of canon law and diocesan administration in the twelfth century, and as a foreigner it was not easy for him to know the field. On application to Baldwin, archbishop of Canterbury (d. 1190), he secured Master Robert of Bedford and Master Roger of Rolleston (the latter would later become dean of Lincoln), as well, no doubt, as others. A bishop could reward his clerks most conveniently by collating them to canonries in his cathedral. Here, according to his biographer, Hugh adopted what in his day was an exceptionally rigorous stance, by insisting that canons should treat their positions as ones of pastoral care, and should actually reside at Lincoln. He refused canonries to distinguished clerics, one a Parisian master, if they would not reside. The evidence of Hugh's surviving *acta*, or charters, 224 of them in all, supports Adam of Eynsham's observations, showing his benefactions of the Lincolnshire churches of Glentham, Scredington, and Wellingore (among others) to the common fund of the cathedral for the support of the resident canons. These 224 documents can be only a tiny proportion of those actually issued in Hugh's name and they provide disappointingly thin evidence for his diocesan activities. But they show the normal emphasis of the time to provide adequately for resident priests in parish churches, and they also show him raising money for the building work of the cathedral, for which he employed a brilliant architect, Geoffrey de Noyers. 'St Hugh's choir' at Lincoln is a *chef-d'œuvre* of early English Gothic architecture. The success of Hugh as a pastor in his diocese is all the more remarkable in view of the evidence that he was not fluent in English, albeit French was at this time the lingua franca of the upper classes.

Bishop of Lincoln: diocesan concerns Even in a period generally conscientious in this respect, Hugh participated actively in the government of his diocese. His synodal decrees, preserved in the chronicle known as *Gesta Henrici secundi*, and the only such to survive from the twelfth century, are mainly concerned with the regulation of the clergy. He once suspended a priest and sequestered his benefice for naïvely celebrating an illegal, under-age marriage; he enquired carefully into the religious practice of the laity in such matters as divination, and he followed his predecessors in having an organization of penitentiaries who oversaw the practice of confession and penance; for instance the prior of Huntingdon had this responsibility in his region. He was notably favourable to the full participation of the laity in the life of the church, not least women; he sometimes invited devout matrons and widows to eat at his table. In relation to his clergy he was hospitable and kept a light touch. Gerald of Wales, who knew the bishop from his residence at Lincoln in the

1190s, tells in his *Gemma ecclesiastica* of an occasion when Hugh attended mass in a parish church, and the priest started to say several gospels (for it seems that the offerings were increased if the laity heard their favourite gospel); the bishop said good-humouredly, 'What will this priest say to-morrow who has poured out everything he knew to-day!' (*Gir. Camb. opera*, 2.129). Hugh modelled his conduct as bishop (and indeed as prior of Witham) on the precepts of Pope Gregory the Great, whose *Pastoral Care* he clearly admired. This will explain his principle of individual discernment and differentiation, of being strict with one priest while treating another with latitude, and why so much is made of his rebuking the powerful, not least the Angevin kings. Above all it explains the stress laid upon his annual return to Witham while he was bishop, to refresh himself amid his external activities by sharing in the inner life of reading and meditation there. His early life is presented as a constant struggle against carnal lusts which were eventually to be cured by experience of a vision; this nicely replicates in essence the story of the holy man Equitius of Valeria told in Gregory's *Dialogues*.

The fact that the bishop of Lincoln had the largest diocese in England and one of the richest, and that he owed the king homage for his temporalities, did not necessarily make him a central political figure. Bishop Robert de Chesney (*d.* 1166) had more or less avoided the pyrotechnics of the Becket era by immersing himself in his diocese. But Hugh had too strong a sense of his mission in the world, and of his duty to protect the interests of his church, to avoid the limelight. Early in his episcopate he excommunicated Geoffrey, the king's chief forester, for oppressing the tenants of the church of Lincoln, thus arousing Henry II's wrath in much the same way that Thomas Becket had done earlier. Unlike the humourless Becket, however, Hugh had the detachment and relaxation to seek out the king, make a highly effective joke to tease him out of his sullenness, and renew his peace with him. Hugh's relations with Richard I were seldom easy, owing to the latter's financial exactions, which afflicted the clergy as well as the laity. In 1197 he provoked the king's fury when his opposition to demands for knights' service overseas led to refusal of such service by the entire English church, and although he became reconciled to Richard when he visited him in Normandy, two years later the temporalities of his diocese were seized when Hugh rejected a demand that twelve canons of Lincoln should act as royal agents abroad at their own expense. The boldness—*franchise*, it has been called—that enabled Hugh to deal with kings as their critic, but also as their support (there is the famous story of how, in the course of their dispute in 1197, he physically shook Richard I until the king agreed to give him the kiss of peace), derived partly from his much emphasized status as a foreigner, which seemed in a sense to put him above the fray, but even more from his reputation for sanctity. The holy man's curse was feared by exchequer officials and others, and when at the request of Hubert Walter, chief justiciar and archbishop of Canterbury, Hugh's lead in refusing in 1197 to make a contribution to Richard I's war effort in France (to the detriment of the rights of his church) was followed by Herbert Poor, bishop of Salisbury (*d.* 1217), it was the latter who bore the brunt of the king's government's anger.

Biographical themes and spiritual choices The principal biographer of Hugh was a monk, his chaplain, Adam, of the Black-monks' monastery of Eynsham. His *Magna vita*, elicited by the Carthusians of Witham, was completed soon after 1212. Gerald of Wales added a brief life to his *Life of St Remigius* and wrote a fuller one before 1220, which contained accounts of miracles at Hugh's tomb. After Hugh's canonization in 1220 a metrical life was written, possibly by Henry d'Avranches (*d.* 1262/3). Gerald and *The Metrical Life of St Hugh of Lincoln* both contain some independent material, but it is on Adam of Eynsham that the modern biographer must principally depend. That Adam was well informed there is no doubt. Equally it must be admitted that he brought his own perceptions to the work, not least in emphasizing Hugh's close links with the black monks in general, and with Eynsham in particular, over which Hugh had mounted a successful legal struggle to establish his right of patronage and abbatial appointment against Richard I. There is no reason to think, however, that there was any significant gap between Adam's perceptions and those of Hugh himself, a point that may be illustrated through three important facets of Hugh's life.

First, the early part of the *Magna vita* presents Hugh's life as a series of moral dilemmas: should he obey his Augustinian superior or should he answer the call of God to the Carthusian vocation, a *mira perplexitas* indeed; should he desire to be a priest or bishop, or not; should he go to Witham as prior, particularly if he had not yet totally mastered his carnal temptations? As regards the second of these dilemmas, the Carthusian way of life was obviously one of seclusion and meditation, but it did not shun all aspects of community, and it took seriously spiritual duty to those in the outside world. 'Isolated but not solitary' is a true characterization. Prior Guy (I) wrote in his Carthusian *Meditations*, 'If for whatever reason you lose the will to save one man, no matter whom, you cut off a limb from Christ's body' (H. Leyser, 17). Thus several Carthusians became bishops in France; but the fact that there remained a dilemma for them of choosing between the contemplative and active lives is demonstrated by Hugh's desiring the prior of Chartreuse to resolve that dilemma for him at Lincoln. This problem is presented by Adam in very similar terms to those of Pope Gregory the Great's writings. Like Gregory, Hugh specially revered St Martin, the fourth-century monk and bishop, who also spoke boldly to rulers. Gregory was clearly a central author among the fathers in the reading of both saint and biographer; Hugh attached importance to learning and was an exceptionally quick reader.

Second, the *Magna vita* presents Hugh's religious culture not only in terms of his personal sanctity, but also as a nodal point between black monks and white monks, that is, between traditional Benedictines and Cistercians. As

prior of Witham he happily accepted the lavishly ornamented Winchester Bible from Henry II but returned it at
once to the monks of St Swithun's, Winchester, when he
learned to his horror that the king had commandeered it
from them without his knowledge. Thus he in no way
shared the Cistercian opposition to expensive art. Moreover he admonished Benedictine abbots not to be stricter
than their own rule required in imposing abstinence from
meat. His interest in relics—his gruesome theft of a relic
of St Mary Magdalen from Fécamp, for instance, or his
having a tooth of St Benedict set in his episcopal ring by
his goldsmith—fits into the same context, for the Cistercians did not trouble so much with relics. On the other
hand, apart from his actual visits to Cîteaux and Clairvaux, the transcription of his visions (which unfortunately have not survived) fits better into a Cistercian context, as does his concern with the vocational aspects of lay
life, considering the Cistercian emphasis on vocation generally. Adam himself may perhaps be regarded as one of
those many black monks who were more or less influenced by Cistercian modes of thinking in the twelfth century.

Third, Hugh's personal connections with the theology
schools of Paris are clearly evident in the *Magna vita*, as are
the concepts particularly of the contemporary Parisian
school of Peter the Chanter. That school emphasized the
central sacramental life of the church (Hugh himself confessed weekly), and lay participation in it, as did Hugh. It
was in favour of curbing the secular activities of the
clergy, as was Hugh, who once remarked that he would
obey Hubert Walter as his archbishop, but not as chief justiciar; and if the *Magna vita* does not convey the emphasis
on prompt burial and worthy funeral rites which are to be
found in Hugh, this strong feature of Hugh's interests has
the general marks of Parisian moral earnestness and concern for the poor. Not mentioned by name in the *Magna
vita* is William de Montibus (*d.* 1213), a former Parisian
master, who, though not of the school of Peter the
Chanter, was a similar theologian and his contemporary,
and who became under Hugh first a canon, then chancellor, of Lincoln Cathedral. A favourite of Hugh, as Gerald of
Wales says, he must have been one of the principal medi-
ators of Parisian ideas to Hugh as bishop. It is known, not
from Adam of Eynsham indeed, but from contemporary
Bury St Edmunds, for instance, that several black monks
had themselves been educated at Paris. The influence of
Parisian theology, therefore, is likely to have been another
common factor between Hugh himself and Adam his
biographer.

Death, burial, and cult Hugh took part in Richard I's
funeral on 11 April 1199 at Fontevrault, and was present at
John's coronation in Westminster Abbey on 27 May following. In the following year he visited Grenoble and the
Grande Chartreuse, to which he attracted crowds. However, on the journey back he fell ill, and though he
returned to England he died in the Old Temple, London
(where the bishops of Lincoln had a house), on 16 November 1200, not long after a cursory interview with John, at
which he seems to have made little effort to conceal his

low opinion of the king. His body was transported back to
Lincoln, in what is represented as a triumphant, miraculous progress of four days, and was buried on 23 November near the altar of St John the Baptist on the north side
of the cathedral (exactly where is the subject of modern
detective scholarship). Miracles afterwards occurred at his
tomb, and he was canonized by Pope Honorius III in 1220.
In 1280 two new shrines were set up, one for the saint's
head in a splendid reliquary, the other for his bodily
remains. The latter was apparently placed, with a pyram-
idal canopy, in the altar screen behind the high altar in the
'angel choir', then newly built to accommodate it. When
this shrine was destroyed in 1540, the remains of St Hugh
were removed to a less prestigious place in the east end of
the cathedral. In 1886 St Hugh's Hall (later St Hugh's College), Oxford, was founded in his memory by Dorothy
Wordsworth, daughter of another bishop of Lincoln.

HENRY MAYR-HARTING

Sources Adam of Eynsham, *Magna vita sancti Hugonis / The life of
Saint Hugh of Lincoln*, ed. D. L. Douie and D. H. Farmer, 2 vols., OMT
(1961–2) · D. M. Smith, ed., *Lincoln, 1186–1206*, English Episcopal
Acta, 4 (1986) · *Gir. Camb. opera*, 2, 7 · D. H. Farmer, *St Hugh of Lincoln*
(1985) · H. Leyser, 'Hugh the Carthusian', *Saint Hugh of Lincoln*, ed.
H. Mayr-Harting (1987), 1–18 · D. M. Smith, 'Hugh's administration
of the diocese of Lincoln', *Saint Hugh of Lincoln*, ed. H. Mayr-Harting
(1987), 19–47 · K. J. Leyser, 'The Angevin kings and the holy man',
Saint Hugh of Lincoln, ed. H. Mayr-Harting (1987), 49–73 · D. H.
Farmer, 'The cult and canonization of St Hugh', *Saint Hugh of Lincoln*, ed. H. Mayr-Harting (1987), 75–87 · D. A. Stocker, 'The mystery
of the shrines of St Hugh', *Saint Hugh of Lincoln*, ed. H. Mayr-Harting
(1987), 89–124 · R. Loomis, 'Giraldus de Barri's homage to Hugh of
Avalon', *De cella in seculum*, ed. M. Sargent (1989) · H. E. J. Cowdrey,
'Hugh of Avalon, Carthusian and bishop', *De cella in seculum*, ed.
M. Sargent (1989) · J. Goering, *William de Montibus (c.1140–1213): the
schools and the literature of pastoral care*, Pontifical Institute of Medieval Studies: Texts and Studies, 108 (1992) · *The metrical life of St Hugh
of Lincoln*, ed. C. Garton (1986) · N. Pevsner, *The choir of Lincoln Cathedral: an interpretation*, Charlton Lectures on Art (1963) · W. Stubbs,
ed., *Gesta regis Henrici secundi Benedicti abbatis: the chronicle of the
reigns of Henry II and Richard I*, AD 1169–1192, 2 vols., Rolls Series, 49
(1867), 1.357
Likenesses seal, BL; Birch, *Seals*, 1705

Hugh of Lincoln [St Hugh of Lincoln, Little St Hugh]
(*c.*1246–1255), supposed victim of crucifixion, was the son
of Beatrice of Lincoln. He is known as Little St Hugh to distinguish him from St Hugh, bishop of Lincoln (1140?–
1200). His death, in all probability accidental, and most
likely on 27 August 1255, was the catalyst for the accusation of ritual murder aimed at the Jewish community of
Lincoln. The first accusation of this kind in England
appeared in 1144 in Norwich, where a description of a non-
existent Jewish ritual involving a mock crucifixion was
provided by a converted Jew named Theobald, and connected with the death of a child, William of Norwich
(1132/3–1144).

Popular accounts indicate that Hugh's mother was told
by her neighbours that the boy had been seen 'playing
with some Jewish boys of his own age, and going into the
house of a Jew' (Paris, 5.517). Hugh's body was reportedly
found in a well or pit inside the house of this Lincoln Jew,
Copin (or Jopin). Versions of the story differ on the length
of time that Hugh was held captive before his supposed

sacrifice: one asserts that he was held for ten days (ibid.), while Jews gathered from 'all the cities of England' to take part. Another maintains that Hugh was kept prisoner for twenty-six days (*Ann. mon.*, 1.341). Copin was immediately accused and seized by those present when Hugh's body was discovered in the well: Beatrice, the bailiffs of Lincoln, and assorted neighbours. These 'witnesses' included John of Lexington (d. 1257), who first raised the question of ritual murder in conjunction with Hugh's death, possibly through familiarity with the incident concerning William of Norwich. He induced Copin to confess and to describe how the ritual murder had taken place, promising to protect him from torture and execution in return. Matthew Paris's account indicates that Copin, in dire circumstances, not only confessed his own involvement but further implicated the rest of the Jews of England as well as of Lincoln, stating that 'nearly all the Jews in England agreed to the death of this boy', which involved scourging, crowning with thorns, and crucifixion (Paris, 5.519). Hugh's body was then, Copin stated, disembowelled in order to perform various magic arts.

This confession, extracted from a man attempting to save his own life, resulted in a series of persecutions levied against the Jews of Lincoln and throughout England. Copin, contrary to John of Lexington's promises, was executed on the king's order by being 'tied to a horse's tail and dragged to the gallows' (ibid.). Eighteen other Jews were hanged in London in connection with Hugh's reported ritual murder, and ninety-one others were imprisoned in the Tower of London. They persuaded the Franciscans (ibid., 5.546) or the Dominicans (*Ann. mon.*, 1.346) to plead their case, but in vain. The imprisoned Jews were released on 15 May 1255, only after a huge sum was paid to Richard, earl of Cornwall, to plead on their behalf.

Popular accounts ascribed many miracles to Hugh's body: Copin purportedly swore that the grave the Jews dug threw the corpse back out, and that even the well could not conceal it; another story tells how a blind woman regained her vision after bathing her eyes in the water from the well where Hugh's remains were discovered. His assumed martyrdom was the inspiration for a French ballad, and continued in later times to be a popular subject for ballad poetry. Hugh's death and its association with martyrdom and miracle caused the clergy of Lincoln to have the body interred in Lincoln Cathedral in 1255, and his tale remained the focus of literary and historical speculation and controversial opinion long after his still unknown, but likely circumstantial demise.

HAIDEE J. LORREY

Sources *Ann. mon.*, vols. 1–2 • Paris, *Chron.*, vol. 5 • Rymer, *Foedera*, vol. 1 • *Chancery records* • T. Stapleton, ed., *De antiquis legibus liber: cronica majorum et vicecomitum Londoniarum*, CS, 34 (1846) • G. Chaucer, 'The prioress's tale', *Canterbury Tales* • F. Midiel, *Hughes de Lincoln* (1834) • F. J. Child, ed., *The English and Scottish popular ballads* (1883–98); repr. 5 vols in 3 (1965), vols. 3–5 • [T. Percy], ed., *Reliques of ancient English poetry*, 2nd edn, 3 vols. (1767) • J. Jacobs, 'Little St Hugh of Lincoln', *Jewish ideals and other essays* (1896), 192–224 • F. Hill, *Medieval Lincoln* (1965) • A. Hume, *St Hugh of Lincoln* (1849) [on the various versions of the ballad.] • G. I. Langmuir, 'The knight's tale of young Hugh of Lincoln', *Speculum*, 47 (1972), 459–82
Likenesses Lethieullier, drawing (after thirteenth-century sculpture), repro. in C. Anderson, *Lincoln pocket guide*, 3rd edn (1892), pl. 4

Hugh the Chanter [Hugh the Chantor, Hugh Sottovagina] (d. c.1140), historian, may have had family origins in Flanders or Picardy, a suggestion supported by the other name by which he was known, Sottovagina (Sottewain in the vernacular), evidently a nickname meaning 'foolish (or absurd) scabbard'. It was an unusual name, which Hugh shared with a number of individuals associated with York. Thomas Sottovagina and his brother Ernulf, for instance, both York canons, occurring from the 1120s to the 1150s, may have been Hugh's nephews or sons. Hugh's place and date of birth are, however, unknown. The text of his history of the church of York (which survives in one manuscript copy, in the early fourteenth-century *Magnum registrum album* (MS L2/1) of York Minster Library) does not bear his name, but he is identified as its author by the Digby chronicle of the archbishops of York, written soon after 1140. The chronicler acknowledged his own debt to Hugh, whom he described as 'an admirable man, worthy of remembrance' and 'a man of venerable age and happy urbanity' (Raine, 2.355).

Hugh's history, covering the period from 1070 to 1127, is an account of the primacy dispute between the churches of York and Canterbury, which centred on the demands by the southern archbishops that those of York make written profession of obedience. The way in which he refers to the cathedral chapter makes it clear that Hugh was a canon from the time of Archbishop Thomas (II; 1109–14), and he may have been collated c.1108. Until 1114 some aspects of Hugh's account are confused and misleading, but from that date, and thus for the main body of the book, Hugh was writing as an eyewitness. He was probably with Archbishop Thurstan (1114–40) in 1119 and 1120, years for which he was able to give details of dates and places of events and meetings. His narrative therefore, although partisan, is generally well informed. At the very end of the work Hugh states its purpose, that posterity might forgive those who professed obedience to Canterbury, and imitate those who maintained York's independence, notably the book's central character, Thurstan. He suggests that the book might have been entitled 'The man set free' because it demonstrated how Thurstan brought the church of York back to its ancient freedom. The history shows Hugh to have been a skilful and lively writer. It is his only surviving historical work, but Richard of Hexham quotes two lines from an account by Hugh of the battle of the Standard, which took place near Northallerton on 22 August 1138, and Hugh was also the author of a set of versified moral precepts, dealing with themes such as tyranny and government, wealth and poverty.

The date at which Hugh became archdeacon and precentor is not known. As canon of York he was a frequent witness to charters issued by the archbishop and others, and was attesting *acta* as precentor by 1133; however he is not likely to have held that office before *c*.1125. His occurrences as archdeacon are not easy to establish, since there was a slightly earlier archdeacon of York also named Hugh. It is therefore not certain which of these, for instance, accompanied Archbishop Thurstan to St Mary's Abbey, York, in October 1132 when a number of monks seceded to found Fountains Abbey. Hugh's archidiaconal title is either simply 'archdeacon' or 'archdeacon of the church of York', but it is probable that the archdeaconry which he held was that of Cleveland. As precentor and archdeacon Hugh issued a charter addressed to Prior Roger and the convent of Durham, which cannot be later than 1137. This survives in its original (Durham Cath. CL, Charter 2.4 Ebor.6), with Hugh's seal attached. Hugh was still alive in August 1138, at the time of the battle of the Standard, but had been succeeded as precentor by William d'Eu before January 1140. The *Liber vitae* of Durham Cathedral priory records the commemoration of an archdeacon Hugh on 4 July. If this was the obit of Hugh the Chanter, then his death occurred on 4 July 1139. However, there exists a poem written by Hugh, monk of Pontefract, which contains strong verbal echoes of the history of Hugh the Chanter. It is therefore possible that Hugh the Chanter and Hugh the monk of Pontefract were one and the same, and that Hugh did not die in office, but retired to Pontefract with Archbishop Thurstan in 1140.

JANET BURTON

Sources *Hugh the Chanter: the history of the church of York, 1066–1127*, ed. and trans. C. Johnson, rev. edn, rev. M. Brett, C. N. L. Brooke, and M. Winterbottom, OMT (1990) · J. E. Burton, ed., *York, 1070–1154*, English Episcopal Acta, 5 (1988) · C. T. Clay, 'The early precentors and chancellors of York', *Yorkshire Archaeological Journal*, 35 (1940–43), 116–38 · C. T. Clay, 'Notes on the early archdeacons in the church of York', *Yorkshire Archaeological Journal*, 36 (1944–7), 269–87 · J. Raine, ed., *The historians of the church of York and its archbishops*, 3 vols., Rolls Series, 71 (1879–94) · D. Nicholl, *Thurstan: archbishop of York, 1114–1140* (1964) · R. M. T. Hill and C. N. L. Brooke, 'From 627 until the early thirteenth century', *A history of York Minster*, ed. G. E. Aylmer and R. Cant (1977), 1–43 · R. Hexham, 'De gestis regis Stephani et de bello standardi', *Chronicles of the reigns of Stephen, Henry II, and Richard I*, ed. R. Howlett, 3, Rolls Series, 82 (1886), 163 · T. Wright, ed., *The Anglo-Latin satirical poets and epigrammatists of the twelfth century*, 2, Rolls Series, 59 (1872), 2.219–29 · [J. Stevenson], ed., *Liber vitae ecclesiae Dunelmensis*, SurtS, 13 (1841), 144

Archives BL, MS Cotton Vitellius A xii, fols. 133–135*v* · Bodl. Oxf., MS Digby 65, fol. 11 · Durham Cath. CL, Charter 2.4, Ebor. 6 · York Minster, MS L2/1, fols. 1–32

Hughe, William (*d.* 1549), theologian, was born in Yorkshire. He may be the William Hewys who was an usher at Magdalen School, Oxford, between 1540 and 1546. Hewys was admitted BA by 1540, and incorporated MA on 11 July 1543. Alternatively, he may have taken his MA from Corpus Christi College, Oxford, in 1543. About 1548 Hughe was admitted to Christ Church as a theologian. More importantly, however, by 1546 or earlier he had apparently become chaplain to Lady Denny, the wife of Sir Anthony Denny, a leading courtier and supporter of religious reform; it was this association which gave rise to his brief literary career. *The Troubled Mans Medicine*, a devotional tract explaining God's purpose in allowing suffering, was printed in 1546, and reprinted in 1559 and 1567. The first part, apparently written before his association with the Denny household, is largely a showcase for his humanist education. The second part is dedicated to Lady Denny and opens with Hughe rejoicing to have found 'so benigne and vertuous a maistres' (Hughe, pt 2, sig. A1*v*). It is again heavy with classical allusion, although when he borrowed—and garbled—a section from Erasmus's *Preparation to Deathe* he allowed it to pass as his own composition. Traces of protestant sympathies in the first part become a clearer bias in the second when he discusses justification in evangelical terms. Even these moderate sentiments were probably only publishable because of Denny's patronage. That patronage apparently led Hughe further into court circles: John Bale (who praises his erudition) records that he wrote a treatise on infant baptism, dedicated to Queen Katherine Parr. He also translated a treatise on the eucharist arguing (in measured terms) that Christ's presence in the elements should be interpreted figuratively; published in 1548, this went through six editions by 1623. Hughe died from a ruptured blood vessel at Christ Church shortly before Michaelmas 1549.

ALEC RYRIE

Sources W. Hughe, *The troubled mans medicine* (1546) · Bale, *Cat.* · Emden, *Oxf.*, 4.287 · Wood, *Ath. Oxon.*, 1st edn · *The boke of Barthram priest intreating of the bodye and bloude of Christ*, trans. W. Hughe (1548) · D. Erasmus, *Preparation to deathe* (1538), sigs. F6*r*–7*v*

Hughes, Alice Mary (1857–1939), photographer, was born on 3 August 1857 at 11 Kensington Park Terrace North in London. She was the daughter of the painter Edward *Hughes (1832–1908) and his first wife, Mary Ann Sherratt (*née* Pewtner). Her mother died when Alice Hughes was seven, and her father remarried two years later, by which time Hughes's two elder siblings had also died. She did not warm to her stepmother, Kate (*née* Margetts), nor to her three half-siblings. She did however find an ally in her step-grandmother, 'a woman of strong character who had found life difficult and faced it bravely' (Hughes, 30–31).

Hughes went to boarding-school in Edenbridge in Kent and then in Brussels. While she was in Europe her stepmother died and she was summoned home to become the housekeeper, hostess, secretary, and companion of her demanding father. Their unconventional relationship, which she called 'my romance', was documented in her 1923 memoir, *My Father and I* (Hughes, 260).

In the late 1870s Edward Hughes turned from painting subject pictures to the exclusive production of society portraits. When he found that he required a record of his works his daughter suggested that she take up photography. After a course of private lessons from Howard Farmer at the Regent Street Polytechnic School of Photography, Hughes had a large 20 by 16 inch camera made for her with which she photographed her father's paintings. She soon began, however, to make portrait compositions directly from her father's sitters, and in 1891 she opened a photographic portrait studio at 52 Gower Street, one of the two linked houses that she shared with her father.

In order not to compromise her aesthetic preferences, Hughes only photographed women and children and always used natural light. She also used an extremely narrow repertoire of backdrops (said to be eight in total) and of props, including the trunk of an oak tree and both natural and artificial flowers, to create a flattering idyll in which to pose her sitters. Having persuaded Princess Alexandra to wear a ruffled fichu, or lace shawl, when the future queen first sat to her c.1889 (photograph at University of Texas, Austin), Hughes significantly contributed to the vogue for being photographed in 'picturesque' dress inspired by the portraits of Reynolds and Gainsborough. By fusing the conventions of society portraiture with the cool, monochromatic tones of the platinum print Hughes created a new and distinctive style of photographic portraiture.

By the mid-1890s Alice Hughes was the leading society photographer in London. Her photographs regularly appeared in all the society journals and, by the end of the decade, she had a virtual monopoly on the cover of *Country Life*. In 1902 she and her father acted as Queen Alexandra's official portraitists at the coronation of Edward VII (her photograph is now held by the University of Texas, Austin). She remained a favourite photographer of the royal family despite also photographing two of the king's mistresses, Alice Keppel (c.1898, untraced) and the countess of Warwick (c.1900; NPG). Her portrait of the duchess of York (later Queen Mary) in 1905 became the official portrait when the duke acceded to the throne as George V in 1910 (NPG).

In 1908 Edward Hughes died and his daughter was left bereft. Three years later she sold her photographic business, including her stock of over 50,000 negatives, to her rivals Speaight & Son of Bond Street. The terms of the contract barred her from practising as a photographer in most European capitals. Berlin was one exception and, in an ill-timed move, she set up a portrait studio there in early 1914. When the outbreak of war later that year obliged her to flee Germany, Hughes was forced to leave her equipment and possessions behind.

In 1915 Hughes bought back her right to practise in London and opened a new studio at 104 Ebury Street, Pimlico. Despite some setbacks she managed to establish herself as a favoured photographer of wealthy families visiting the capital from the provinces and from overseas. By the early 1920s she was collaborating with Sir Charles Forbes in his experiments to produce an affordable process of colour photography.

In her seventies Hughes was described as 'Small and slight and dainty as the most exquisite china figure: with little grey head held proudly, and mouth and chin denoting an unswerving resolution' (Coury, 13). Hughes had become, as her father had before her, a symbol of a bygone age. She retired in 1933 to the south coast and died, unmarried, on 4 April 1939 at the age of eighty-one in Worthing Hospital, Sussex.   JULIET HACKING

Sources A. Hughes, *My father and I* (1923) · T. Pepper, *High society: photographs, 1897–1914* (1998) · 'Miss Alice Hughes', *British Journal of Photography* (14 April 1933), 201 · L. A. Coury, 'Royalty faces a woman's camera', *The Queen* (25 March 1931), 13–15 · 'An interesting amalgamation', *Amateur Photographer and Photographic News* (3 Jan 1911), 4 · H. Vickers, 'Mothers and cupids', *Country Life* (14 July 1994), 74–7 · *The Times* (10 April 1939) · *DNB* · b. cert. · d. cert.
Archives NPG, photographs · PRO, photographs · Ransom HRC
Likenesses E. Hughes, oils, repro. in Hughes, *My father and I*
Wealth at death £72 1s. 0d.: resworn probate, 5 July 1939, *CGPLA Eng. & Wales*

Hughes, Amy Sarah (1856–1923), nursing administrator, born on 24 February 1856, was the daughter of Arthur Horsley Hughes, vicar of Holy Trinity Church, Darlington, co. Durham, and his wife, Sarah Hughes. She was educated at Darlington and South Norwood, and trained as a nurse at St Thomas's Hospital, London, between 1884 and 1885. Amy Hughes took up district nursing on completing her hospital training. Her first post, which included her district training, was with London's Metropolitan and National District Nursing Association. After fifteen months there, and three more with Kensington's association, she worked with associations in Westminster for one year and in Chelsea for three. She was Chelsea's superintendent during her final year there, before moving on to a similar post at the Metropolitan's much bigger Bloomsbury establishment in 1891; she left this in 1895 to become superintendent at Bolton's poor-law workhouse, with special responsibility for organizing nurses' training at its infirmary. Before returning to district nursing in 1902 she served for some time as superintendent of the Nurses' Co-operation, a large private nurses' organization.

The post that Amy Hughes took up in 1902 was with the Queen Victoria's Jubilee Institute for Nurses, as its superintendent of county nursing associations. Founded in 1887, the institute promoted voluntary district nursing associations and co-ordinated their work through a form of affiliation that provided for nurses' training, supervision, and inspection. Nurses in the higher of the two grades in the institute's system were registered on its 'queen's roll' and known as queen's nurses. The metropolitan association was in the forefront of the movement that led to the establishment of the institute, and its nurses' home was the first one approved by the institute for queen's nurses' training. The other associations with which Amy Hughes had worked were also affiliated to the institute, and her name was one of the earliest on the queen's roll.

Following Amy Hughes's resignation from district nursing in 1895 the institute expressed its regret and noted her aptitude for organization and training in the queen's roll. The roll's comments on nurses' careers are notably candid, and the post that she took up with the institute in 1902 was exceptionally demanding. It entailed implementing new arrangements for accommodating rural district nursing within a system that was designed primarily with regard to urban experience: earlier adaptations had presented intractable problems. Her success led to her appointment as the institute's general superintendent in 1905, a post which she held until her retirement in 1917.

Further recognition of Amy Hughes's administrative flair came with a request for her help in organizing district nursing in Australia, and as a result she spent six months there in 1910. Her work as the institute's chief officer included much by way of representing it to organizations with related interests, and by publishing articles that reflected wider concerns than the immediacies of district nursing. The Queen's Institute's practice of recruiting fully trained nurses for further training in district work gave Amy Hughes an extensive knowledge of national variations in training and certification, of the diversity of practice, and of the problems of access to the larger training schools, which she put to good use in her formidable evidence to the parliamentary select committee on the registration of nurses, 1904–5. Her advocacy in 1908 of written examinations for queen's nurses rested in part on the argument that their selection needed to have some reference to their capacity for career development as well as for practical nursing. The chapter on district nursing that she provided for *Women in the Medical, Nursing and Allied Professions* (a careers handbook published in 1914 by the Women's Employment Publishing Company) explained how district nursing could extend to other domiciliary services. Nevertheless, her most notable contribution to women's occupational history, aside from district nursing, was to midwifery—a calling distinctly separate from nursing, but one for which queen's nurses were often trained. She joined the Midwives Institute in 1892 at the height of its campaign for midwives' statutory accreditation, achieved in the Midwives Act of 1902. This was not a conclusive victory, and Amy Hughes continued to be active in promoting midwives' interests, serving as the Midwives Institute's president from 1911 to 1919, two years beyond her retirement from the Queen Victoria's Jubilee Institute. She had been honoured as a lady of grace of the order of St John of Jerusalem, as well as having been presented with the queen's nurses' highest award, their gold badge, in 1906. She retained the connections that she had established with numerous organizations related to her profession and its associated interests, as well as with the Queen Victoria's and the Midwives institutes. Although her activities after retirement were constrained by failing health, she was elected to Westminster city council in the two successive municipal elections of 1919 and 1922, representing Victoria ward and serving on the council's housing, public health, and maternity and child welfare committees. She was still in office at the time of her death, on 6 September 1923, at the Ewell Grove Nursing Home, Ewell, Surrey; she was buried at the west cemetery, Darlington, on 14 September. She was unmarried.

By the mid-1930s district nursing was available to almost the whole population of England and Wales, mostly by more than 7000 nurses working in connection with what was by then known as the Queen's Institute of District Nursing. Amy Hughes had taken over at a critical point in the institute's development, and it was under her energetic and farsighted superintendence that the system stabilized, then more than doubled its coverage, and never looked back.								ENID FOX

Sources queen's roll, Wellcome L., Queen's Nursing Institute archives · obituary file, Wellcome L., Queen's Nursing Institute archives · *Nursing Notes and Midwives Chronicle* (Oct 1923) · B. Cowell and D. Wainwright, *Behind the blue door: the history of the Royal College of Midwives, 1881–1981* (1981) · M. Stocks, *A hundred years of district nursing* (1960) · E. N. Fox, 'District nursing and the work of district nursing associations in England and Wales, 1900–48', PhD diss., U. Lond., 1993 · *Nursing Times* (15 Sept 1923) · d. cert. · 'Select committee on the registration of nurses', *Parl. papers* (1904), 6.701, no. 281; (1905), 7.733, no. 263 · Westminster City Council minutes, 1919–23, City Westm. AC
Archives London Metropolitan University, Metropolitan District Nursing Association archives · PRO, Queen's Nursing Institute files on affiliates · Wellcome L., Queen's Nursing Institute archives
Wealth at death £1251 3s. 3d.: probate, 5 April 1924, CGPLA Eng. & Wales

Hughes, Arthur (1832–1915), painter, was born on 27 January 1832, probably at 7 Dover Street, Mayfair, Westminster, the third son of Edward Hughes (*c*.1788–1865), of Dover Street, and his wife, Amy (*b. c*.1792). His father, who was from a family in Oswestry, Shropshire, had apparently inherited a modest estate and at some point had become a London hotel-keeper. His only other known siblings were William Hughes (1815–1893) and the younger Edward Hughes (*b.* 1828). He was educated at Archbishop Tenison's Grammar School in Castle Street, Long Acre, London, and showed such early artistic talent that he was allowed to enter the Government School of Design at Somerset House in 1846, where he studied under Alfred Stevens, and then the Royal Academy Schools, in which he enrolled on 17 December 1847. Two years later he won a silver medal for drawing from the antique, and in the same year, still only seventeen, his oil painting *Musidora* (City of Birmingham Museum and Art Gallery) was hung in the Royal Academy summer exhibition.

A *Self-Portrait* of 1851 (National Portrait Gallery, London) confirms a later memory of Hughes's appearance recorded by William Michael Rossetti: 'His face, giving evidence of his Welsh parentage, was singularly bright and taking—dark, abundant hair, vivid eyes, good features, and ruddy cheeks which earned him among his fellow-students the nickname of "Cherry"' (Rossetti, 1.146). Through Walter Howell Deverell and Alexander Munro, Hughes became aware of the early work of the Pre-Raphaelite Brotherhood and could claim to have been directly inspired by reading its magazine, *The Germ*, the four issues of which appeared in the early months of 1850. Munro introduced him in 1851 to Ford Madox Brown and Dante Gabriel Rossetti, and he met John Everett Millais on varnishing day at the Royal Academy exhibition in 1852; there, by coincidence, both artists were showing paintings of *Ophelia*. (Hughes's is now in the collections of Manchester City Galleries.)

Hughes makes no appearance in the pages of the Pre-Raphaelites' journal, but there is ample evidence, for instance from the diaries of George Price Boyce, that he slipped easily into the Pre-Raphaelite social circle. He modelled for the head of *The Proscribed Royalist* (priv. coll.) in Millais's painting of 1853 and was discovered by Boyce working in Rossetti's studio in 1854. Since 1852 he had been sharing rooms and a studio with Munro at 6 Upper Belgrave Place, Pimlico, London, where he had also brought his wife, Tryphena Foord (c.1828–1921), the fourth child of Robert and Ann Foord, of Maidstone, Kent. They had been courting since 1850 and were married in Trinity Church, Maidstone, on 26 November 1855.

The joint illustration with Rossetti to *The Music Master* (1855), a book of poems by William Allingham, was a great success, and Hughes was recruited to participate in the Pre-Raphaelites' exhibition at Russell Place in London in June 1857, and in Rossetti's scheme for the decoration of the Oxford Union Society in the same summer. He was also a founder member of the Hogarth Club in 1858. John Ruskin, whom he had known since 1855, began to commend his annual exhibits at the Royal Academy in *Academy Notes*, particularly admiring *April Love* (bought by William Morris; now in the Tate collection) in 1856, *The Nativity* (City of Birmingham Museum and Art Gallery) in 1858, and *The King's Orchard* (priv. coll.) in 1859. As the originators of the movement ceased to exhibit together regularly in the later 1850s, Hughes's work became the focus of public scrutiny of the mature Pre-Raphaelite style, his combination of naturalistic detail and a trademark use of brilliant green and purple eventually falling foul of the critics. His acknowledged masterpiece, *The Long Engagement* (City of Birmingham Museum and Art Gallery), begun in 1853 but completed and shown at the Royal Academy only in 1859, received but lukewarm praise.

The birth of two children—Arthur (Arty) Foord on 7 October 1856 and Amy on 15 December 1857—precipitated a move to Buckland Terrace, Maidstone, in the summer of 1858. From there the Hughes family moved to Ivy Cottage, Staines, Middlesex, in 1860, then again in the spring of 1863 to 12 Oberstein Road, Wandsworth, London. Another daughter, Agnes, had been born on 17 November 1859, and twins followed on 26 August 1861, though the boy, Edwin, died at the age of six months; the girl, Emily, survived to outlive all her siblings, dying at the age of eighty-seven in 1949. A last child, Godfrey, was born on 14 October 1865.

Not at all discouraged by adverse criticism, Hughes declared himself busy with 'ever so many things' in a letter of December 1861 to Pauline, Lady Trevelyan. He had found additional patrons in another of Ruskin's friends, Ellen Heaton; in the industrialist James Leathart of Newcastle upon Tyne; and in the Brighton wine merchant John Hamilton Trist (1811–1891). The purchase by Trist of two paintings, *Silver and Gold* and *The Font* (both priv. coll.), enabled Hughes to make his only substantial trip abroad, in the spring of 1863, when he travelled to Venice in the company of his old friend Munro.

In 1859 Hughes had met the fantasy writer George MacDonald, an immediate friendship leading to the illustration of a great deal of MacDonald's work, beginning with *Dealings with the Fairies*. These designs, made in 1862, attracted the attention of Lewis Carroll, who also became a family friend and who took photographs of Hughes and his daughters in October 1863. An unexpected commission for designs to Tennyson's *Enoch Arden* in an edition of 1865 proved hugely popular and established Hughes as one of the foremost illustrators of the day. His simple

command of line and sometimes startling imagination perfectly complemented MacDonald's stories, for which he produced a host of illustrations in the magazine *Good Words for the Young*, beginning with the best of their collaborations, *At the Back of the North Wind* (1868–70). This was followed by perhaps his best-known work in this field, the forty-three designs for the first illustrated edition of Thomas Hughes's *Tom Brown's School Days*, published in 1869, though even this success was surpassed by the universal critical acclaim for his delightful illustrations to *Sing Song* (1871), a book of nursery poems by Christina Rossetti. A further set of designs for the same author's Christmas book, *Speaking Likenesses* (1874), was less successful, and Hughes would return to illustration only at the turn of the century, with further work for books by George MacDonald's children Lilia (*Babies' Classics*, 1903–4) and Greville (*The Magic Crook*, 1911; *Trystie's Quest*, 1912; and *Jack and Jill*, 1913).

As a painter, Hughes was faring less well. His regular patrons now bought little, and he received generally poor reviews for the kind of idealized rural and domestic genre paintings which he now favoured, such as *The Mower* (exh. RA, 1865; priv. coll.) and *L'enfant perdu* (exh. RA, 1867; priv. coll.). Works such as *A Birthday Picnic* (exh. RA, 1867; Forbes Magazine collection) reinforced his reputation as a painter of children, but otherwise it was his misfortune to be damned with faint praise. A cruelly candid account of his work by William Michael Rossetti declared him to be 'one of those artists who reach, before youth has passed, to as high a point of development as they are destined for' (*Portfolio*, 1870, 114). It is much to his credit that Hughes soldiered on, producing such major paintings in the 1870s as *The Lady of Shalott* (exh. RA, 1873) and *The Convent Boat* (c.1873–4; priv. coll.). The sale of both these to Trist's brother George made possible a trip to Brittany in September 1874, which inspired the oils *Vouée au blanc* (1875) and *The Sluggard* (1876; Art Gallery, Rochdale).

By this time financial difficulties had already led Hughes and his family to give up another house, at Windsor Lodge, Putney, London (occupied from 1865 to 1869), in favour of a smaller dwelling at 2 Finborough Road, off the Fulham Road in West Brompton. In 1875 Hughes inherited from his godmother Wandle Bank, a riverside house in Wallington, Surrey, where his neighbour was the novelist William Hale White, whose son Jack married Agnes Hughes in 1891. This became the family home from 1878 until again its upkeep proved too much, prompting a final move in 1891 to East Side House on Kew Green.

Hughes's reputation, still founded on his Pre-Raphaelite paintings of twenty years before, dwindled in the 1880s and 1890s, though he continued to submit paintings both to the Royal Academy and to the Grosvenor Gallery in London and its rival and successor, the New Gallery. His frequent disappointments and occasional triumphs (such as *The Heavenly Stair*, c.1887–8; exh. RA, 1888; Russell-Cotes Art Gallery and Museum, Bournemouth) are documented—vividly and often with surprising good humour, as Hughes was a lively correspondent—in letters to William Bell Scott and Alice Boyd (1825–1897), with whom he stayed several times at their Pre-Raphaelite stronghold, Penkill Castle in Ayrshire. To supplement his income he served from 1886 as examiner for the national School of Art system, based at South Kensington in London. Relief from this tedious work came in frequent trips to Devon (visiting his protégé Albert Goodwin) and Cornwall, often in the company of his sons Arty and Godfrey; these jaunts produced a body of little-known but engagingly fresh landscapes, forming the bulk of his only important one-man exhibition, held at The Fine Art Society in the summer of 1900. Sadly, Hughes became a regular attender of funerals, including in 1896 those of his old friends Millais and Morris, and in 1910 of William Holman Hunt, at which he was a pall bearer.

Only a few significant paintings were undertaken after 1900, but Hughes still persevered with submissions to the Royal Academy, such as *The Rescue* (exh. 1908; priv. coll.), even though hope of election as an associate had long faded. He was greatly cheered when a new patron, Harry Bolus, engineered the purchase in 1904 of his finest late religious painting, *The Door of Mercy* (c.1892–3; exh. RA, 1893), for the University of Cape Town in South Africa. Awarded a civil-list pension in 1912, his last years were clouded by the deaths of his nephew, the painter Edward Robert Hughes (1851–1914), and his daughter Amy, whose son had been killed in action at the beginning of the First World War. Hughes himself died on 22 December 1915 at his home, East Side House, Kew Green, and was buried on 31 December in Richmond cemetery. He was survived by his wife.

Obituaries, including that in *The Times* (23 December 1915), called him 'the last Pre-Raphaelite', which moved Robert Ross to point out tactfully, in the *Burlington Magazine*, that both Henry Wallis (who died in 1916) and William Michael Rossetti (who survived until 1919) were then still alive. Of that close-knit circle Hughes was, however, the last who could be said to have remained steadfast to the original Pre-Raphaelite ideals, and who was unique in having maintained so many friendships throughout his life. Modest but determined, he was universally liked, as William Michael Rossetti testified:

> If I had to pick out from amid my once numerous acquaintances of the male sex, the sweetest and most ingenuous nature of all, the least carking and querulous, and the freest from 'envy, hatred and malice, and all uncharitableness', I should probably find myself bound to select Mr. Hughes. (Rossetti, 1.147)

STEPHEN WILDMAN

Sources L. Roberts, ed., *Arthur Hughes, his life and works: a catalogue raisonné* (1997) [incl. biographical introduction by S. Wildman] • 'Mr A. Hughes: last of the Pre-Raphaelites', *The Times* (23 Dec 1915) • DNB • *Memorial exhibition of some of the works of the late Arthur Hughes* (1916) [exhibition catalogue, Walkers Galleries, London, Oct 1916; incl. preface by A. Goodwin] • L. Cowan, *Arthur Hughes: Pre-Raphaelite painter* (1971) [exhibition catalogue, NMG Wales, 5–24 Oct 1971, and Leighton House, London, 3–23 Dec 1971] • W. E. Fredeman, *A Pre-Raphaelite gazette: the Penkill letters of Arthur Hughes to William Bell Scott and Alice Boyd, 1886–97* (1967) • R. Gibson, 'Arthur Hughes: Arthurian and related subjects of the early 1860s', *Burlington Magazine*, 112 (1970), 451–6 • J. G. Millais, *The life and letters of Sir John Everett Millais*, 2 vols. (1899) • W. M. Rossetti, *Some reminiscences*, 2 vols. (1906) • *The diaries of George Price Boyce*, ed. V. Surtees (1980) • [L. Parris], ed., *The Pre-Raphaelites* (1984) [exhibition catalogue, Tate Gallery, London, 7 March – 28 May 1984] • m. cert. • d. cert. • private information (2004) [friends, family] • register, 1847, RA, Royal Academy Schools • *Richmond and Twickenham Times* (1 Jan 1916) • IGI

Archives Tate collection, corresp. and papers | Bodl. Oxf., letters to F. G. Stephens • U. Newcastle, Trevelyan MSS • University of British Columbia Library, letters to Alice Boyd and William Bell Scott • University of British Columbia Library, letters to James Leathart • University of Illinois, Urbana-Champaign, Allingham MSS

Likenesses S. Lane, oils, c.1837, Tate Collection • A. Hughes, self-portrait, oils, c.1849, Birmingham Museums and Art Gallery • A. Hughes, self-portrait, oils, 1851, NPG • J. E. Millais, pencil drawing study, 1853 (for *The proscribed royalist*), RA • possibly by W. & D. Downey, photograph, 1860–69, NPG • L. Carroll, photograph, 1863 (with daughter Agnes), Tate Collection • F. Dodd, etching, 1907, Birmingham Museums and Art Gallery • F. Dodd, drypoint, BM

Wealth at death £6037 19s. 5d.: probate, 29 March 1916, CGPLA Eng. & Wales

Hughes, Charles (1746/7–1797), equestrian and circus proprietor, about whose early life nothing is known, first came to notice as an accomplished rider performing at Philip Astley's British Riding School, Westminster Bridge Road, London, from June 1771 until 1772. During this time he performed with Astley's company before George III at Richmond Gardens, and was invited to France by the French ambassador. Hughes was said to have been a handsome man of great strength but of rather irritable temper. He opened his own riding school near Blackfriars Bridge on Easter Monday 1772, riding with his wife, a Miss Tomlinson, and his sister, who was romantically named Sobieska Clementina, a variation on the name of the consort of the Jacobite claimant James Edward Stuart. Playbills state that Hughes vaulted backwards and forwards over three horses then over a single horse forty times without stopping. In the same year he published *The Complete Horseman*, a manual of equestrianism. Astley was outraged and from then on he and Hughes were fierce rivals, seeking to disparage and outdo each other at every turn. Also in 1773 Hughes toured Hungary and France with his wife and sister, and returned with an Italian company to his British Horse Academy. The next year both Hughes's and Astley's establishments were forced to close because they had no licences for music and dancing. Hughes then went abroad, visiting France, Sardinia, Naples, Spain, Portugal, Germany, and Morocco. Astley meanwhile received permission to continue his performances and in 1775 he reopened his show as the Amphitheatre Riding-House.

In 1782 Hughes, in association with Charles Dibdin the elder, opened the Royal Circus and Equestrian Philharmonic Academy at Blackfriars Road, St George's Fields, on land owned by a Colonel West. This large building, 'inside very handsome, commodious, and neat' (Disher, 41), included a stage as well as the arena. Part of the building was run as the Equestrian Coffee House by Charles Tomlinson, Hughes's brother-in-law. At the opening on 2 November 1782 more than half the people attempting to enter had to be turned away. The authorities again acted promptly to close the rival establishments, but both resumed performances in open defiance of the law.

Hughes, 'having exclusive management of the equestrian department was always acting contrary to the system of management which Mr Dibdin had laid down' (*Memoirs of J. Decastro*, 120). At the Surrey sessions in January 1783 Hughes won the legal right to perform and his circus reopened for a season on 15 March 1783.

Quarrels between Hughes and his theatrical partners, and Lady West, the site's proprietor, led to the gradual decline of the circus. By 1793 Hughes had lost interest and on the recommendation of Sir John Dick accepted an invitation to buy stallions and mares at Newmarket and elsewhere for Count Orlov, a favourite of Catherine the Great. Hughes accompanied the racehorses to St Petersburg, taking a troupe of performers and circus horses with him. He made a favourable impression on Catherine, who ordered imperial circuses to be built at St Petersburg and Moscow. Hughes broke horses and taught the English style of riding to members of Catherine's court, but returned to England on the news that an order for the ground rent on his Royal Circus had been made against him; he sold his stud of circus horses to the empress at a good profit before leaving.

In the winter of 1793 Hughes procured horses, hounds, and foxes for a hunt in the Christmas pantomime at Covent Garden. After numerous struggles he regained possession of the Royal Circus, renovated it, and in 1794 advertised his troupe as 'lately returned from Russia', but achieved little success. Again, Hughes offended the magistrates and lost his licence, which in October 1796 was granted instead to James and George Jones. Charles Hughes felt the loss so severely that he gave way to despair and died on 7 December 1797 aged fifty. He was buried on 13 December in St George the Martyr's churchyard, Southwark.

JOHN M. TURNER

Sources *The memoirs of J. Decastro, comedian*, ed. R. Humphreys (1824) • T. Frost, *Circus life and circus celebrities* (1875) • R. Toole-Stott, *Circus and allied arts: a world bibliography, 1500–1970*, limited edn, 4 (1971) • M. W. Disher, *Greatest show on earth: as performed for over a century at Astley's (afterwards Sanger's) Royal Amphitheatre of Arts* (1937) • R. Manning-Sanders, *The English circus* (1952) • A. H. Saxon, *The life and art of Andrew Ducrow* (1978) • A. H. Saxon, *Enter foot and horse* (1968) • G. Speaight, *A history of the circus* (1980) • parish register (burial), 13 Dec 1797, Southwark, St George the Martyr

Hughes, David (1561?–1610), founder of Beaumaris Free Grammar School, Anglesey, was born in a cottage on the land of Glan-y-gors farm in the parish of Llantrisant near Llannerch-y-medd in Anglesey. His parentage is unknown, and there is conflicting evidence as to his year of birth and his education. Anthony Wood believed that Hughes studied at Cambridge. However, Foster states that a David Hews of Caernarfon matriculated as a commoner of Hart Hall, Oxford, on 20 December 1577, aged sixteen; and that after studying at Magdalen he was admitted to Gray's Inn on 28 January 1583. This would suggest that Hughes had left Llantrisant for Caernarvonshire, where he had family in the Llŷn peninsula, before he went to Oxford. At Gray's Inn, Hughes made friends with Sir Robert Southwell and Robert Cecil, both of them 'specially admitted' in 1580. Then he moved to East Anglia, probably

through the good offices of an Anglesey man, Owen Hughes, who had settled in Norfolk, and also of David Hughes's own nephew William Prichard, who was in Sir Robert Southwell's service at Woodrising.

David Hughes was a copyholder of the manor of Woodrising in 1596, and shortly afterwards was appointed steward of the same manor, the lord of which was Sir Robert Southwell. His new-found affluence and the needs of his countrymen in Anglesey for an education motivated him to consider setting up a school. He secured the co-operation of Sir William Jones (1566–1640) of Castellmarch in Llŷn, MP for the borough of Beaumaris in the parliament of 1597. Jones's wife, Margaret (*d.* 1609), was related to Hughes. On the death of Rowland Thickins, owner of a large tannery near the castle ditch in Beaumaris, William Jones persuaded Thickins's son to sell the new 'burke house' to David Hughes for £20 and took possession of the premises on 23 December 1602. The premises were then altered and enlarged and opened as a school in 1603. During Hughes's lifetime the school was conducted by himself through an agent, John ap Rees ap Williams of Pentraeth in Anglesey. The agent received the rents and paid the salaries of the master and usher, the boys paying no fees during Hughes's lifetime. This, however, changed after his death, with the boys in the upper school paying 5*s.* a year to the headmaster and the usher receiving half that amount.

Hughes made his will on 30 December 1609, and it is full of valuable details. He desired to be buried near to the grave of his nephew William Prichard (*d.* 1592) in the church of Woodrising. Hughes appointed seven trustees, namely William Rowlands, Sir Richard Bulkeley, a friend of Queen Elizabeth, and four Anglesey landowners, Pierce Lloyd, Hugh Wood, Rowland ap Harry Wynn, and William Lewis. He also insisted that the master and the usher should be graduates of Oxford University and unmarried (reinforcing the arguments that he was a bachelor and an Oxford graduate). Also he made provision for the establishment of an almshouse at Llannerch-y-medd. In actual fact it was erected near Beaumaris in 1613. Provision was made to help the very poor of Llantrisant and district in the will.

Richard Llwyd (1752–1835; the Bard of Snowdon), an old pupil of Beaumaris School, was instrumental in 1804–7 in raising money for a monumental tablet in St Mary's Church, Beaumaris, to David Hughes. Llwyd was a bibliophile, but slipped up with one detail on his inscription on the tablet: 'He was interred at Woodrising, Norfolk 13 February 1609'. It should have been 1610, as Hughes's will and his executors, George Pagrave of Thurston and Alexander Duke of Woodrising, would have testified. The exact date of his death is not known, however.

D. BEN REES

Sources E. M. Jones, 'The free school of Beaumaris', *Transactions of the Anglesey Antiquarian Society and Field Club* (1922), 36–46 • D. A. Pretty, *Two centuries of Anglesey schools, 1700–1902* (1977), 254 • R. Parry, *Enwogion Môn* (1877), 59–67 • J. Morgan, *David Hughes, founder of Beaumaris free grammar school: his times and charity* (1892), 1–32 • A. D. Carr, 'The free grammar school of Beaumaris', *Transactions of the Anglesey Antiquarian Society and Field Club* (1962), 1–22 •

J. Williams, *David Hughes, M.A., and his free grammar school at Beaumaris* (1864); later edn, ed. V. Bowen (1933), vol. 4, p. 30 · *DWB* · NL Wales, MS 1527E [Kinmel MS 27] · Foster, *Alum. Oxon.*
Archives NL Wales
Wealth at death see will, Parry, *Enwogion Môn*, 60–66

Hughes, David (1813–1872), Congregational minister and writer, was born at Cefn-uchaf, Llanddeiniolen, Caernarvonshire, on 21 June 1813, the son of Hugh and Anne Hughes. He became a member of Bethel Independent Church at an early age, and complied with the request of the congregation to begin preaching in 1832. He studied at Hackney College, and reputedly graduated at Glasgow University (though his name is not on its roll of graduates). He was ordained on 14 September 1841, and became pastor of two small congregations in Denbighshire, namely St George and Moelfre. In 1845 he moved to St Asaph, where he became part editor of the *Beirniadur*, and projected his chief work, *Geiriadur Ysgrythyrol a Duwinyddol* (*A Scriptural and Theological Dictionary*), which was completed in 1852. In July 1846 Hughes took over the Welsh Independent church at Great Jackson Street, Manchester, before moving shortly afterwards in May 1847 to keep a school at Bangor, where he remained for nine years. During this period he continued preaching and regularly contributed to the Welsh press. On 1 November 1855 he resumed his ministerial work, at Saron, Tredegar, in Monmouthshire, and remained there until his death on 3 June 1872 at his house in Prospect Place, Georgetown, Tredegar; he was buried at Cefn Golau cemetery, Tredegar. His wife, Jane, survived him.

Hughes was a large contributor to *Y Gwyddoniadur* (*The Welsh Encyclopaedia*), and edited and enlarged Thomas Edwards's English and Welsh dictionary. He began, with the author's sanction, a Welsh edition of T. H. Horne's *Introduction to the Critical Study and Knowledge of the Holy Scriptures*, but it was not completed.

R. M. J. JONES, rev. MARI A. WILLIAMS

Sources *Y Geninen*, 8 (1890), 49–54 · *DWB* · T. Lewis, ed., *Geiriadur Ysgrythyrol a Duwinyddol* (1879), 151–2 · *CGPLA Eng. & Wales* (1872)
Archives U. Wales, Bangor
Wealth at death under £600: administration, 29 June 1872, *CGPLA Eng. & Wales*

Hughes, David Edward (1831–1900), teacher and telegraph engineer, was born on 16 May 1831 at Corwen, near Bala, Merioneth, or in Holborn, London, the second son in the family of three sons and one daughter of David Hughes, and grandson of Robert Hughes, bootmaker, of London and Bala. About 1838 the family emigrated to North America, eventually settling at St David's Farm, Rockingham county, Virginia, and David received his education at a college in Bardstown, Kentucky. At an early age he displayed a talent for music and in 1850 became professor of music at the Presbyterian Female Seminary (later the Roseland Academy). His great interest in experimental science also enabled him to teach natural philosophy, and it was during this period that the idea of his type printing telegraph occurred to him. Charles Wheatstone had exhibited a type printer in 1841, and the first practical machine, invented by House, was adopted by the

David Edward Hughes (1831–1900), by unknown photographer, 1890s

American Telegraph Company in 1847. House's machine used a series of electrical pulses to print every letter, whereas Hughes proposed to synchronize the transmitting and receiving type wheels of his machine and to use the electric current only once for each letter printed. In 1852 Hughes resigned his position and then spent two years perfecting his instrument, which he completed in 1855 and patented (no. 14917) the following year, when it was adopted by the American Telegraph Company. Improved patents were later taken out in America in 1859 and other countries including Britain in 1858 and 1863. In 1857 Hughes brought his invention to Britain but it was not well received, so he proceeded to France, where it was purchased by the government in 1860 and widely installed. During the next ten years it was adopted by most European countries (including Britain) and Hughes received many decorations and honours. He also became a director of the British Electric Telegraph Company.

Other projects followed, including experiments on the use of oil as a cable insulator, patented in 1859, and studies on lightning conductors (1864) and the problem of induction in telegraph wires (1868). In 1872, while resident in Paris, Hughes was elected a foreign member of the Society of Telegraph Engineers (later the Institution of Electrical Engineers), and about 1877 he settled in London at 94, and later 108, Great Portland Street, where he devoted much of his time to experimental electrical work. Most of his apparatus was homemade, and he often used pill boxes, nails, sealing wax, bonnet wire, knitting needles, and tumblers to produce his cells, galvanometers, and other instruments.

The telephone, although improved by Bell in 1876, was

still unsatisfactory until the invention of the microphone in 1878. This was almost simultaneously discovered by Lüdtge, who obtained a German patent, and by Hughes, who refused to patent it and generously gave it to the world of science. It owes its action to the variation of electrical resistance when the loose contact between two conductors is affected by sound waves. In early experiments Hughes found that three nails in an 'H' formation and in contact with metallic powder could be used as a simple microphone, but later he discovered that mercury-impregnated charcoal or carbon used as a conductor produced a better sound quality. In May 1879 Hughes exhibited to the Royal Society a new induction balance in which a telephone replaced the galvanometer and current rectifier in the balance designed by the Italian physicist Riccardo Felici. This new balance could be used for detecting metals and, with some adaptation, as an audiometer for testing human hearing. In 1880 he was elected a fellow of the Royal Society, and in 1885 received the society's royal medal for research in electricity and magnetism, especially for the microphone and induction balance. He became an ordinary member of the Society of Telegraph Engineers in 1879, and was successively a council member (1880), vice-president (1882), and president (1886).

During 1879, Hughes, when trying to trace what he first thought was a faulty circuit, discovered the existence of electromagnetic waves and the means to detect them. Unfortunately the members of the Royal Society who witnessed his demonstrations were unimpressed; the early experiments were not made public, and it was left for Hertz to demonstrate the existence of such waves in 1887, for Branly to reinvent a detector in 1891, and for Marconi to combine the two into a system of wireless telegraphy in 1896.

In 1889 Hughes was elected a manager, and in 1891 a vice-president, of the Royal Institution. In 1896 the Society of Arts conferred the Albert medal on him (presented by the prince of Wales in 1897) for his numerous inventions, especially the printing telegraph and the microphone. Hughes spent many years improving telegraph systems and wrote many papers on electricity and magnetism. His discoveries and inventions were greatly admired and his highly successful printing telegraph made him a wealthy man. Today, though, he will probably be remembered mainly for his microphone, which, as his obituarist in *Nature* reported, could cause 'the footsteps of a house-fly to resound like the tread of an elephant' (p. 326).

In stature Hughes was slightly below average height and fair, with wavy hair and a walrus moustache. He was a genial and charming man of simple tastes and often the life and soul of the party at the regular lunches he attended with his friends. He married Anna (d. 1920), the daughter of Dr Thomas Chadbourne. In later years Hughes began to be troubled with paralysis following a fall, and he died at his home, 40 Langham Street, Marylebone, London, on 22 January 1900, after an attack of influenza. He was interred in the Lebanon catacombs at Highgate old (west) cemetery on 27 January. Leaving no children and having provided for his wife and relatives, he bequeathed some £400,000

to four London hospitals, £1000 to the Royal Institution, and £12,000 in total to the Royal Society, Académie des Sciences, Institution of Electrical Engineers, and the Société Internationale des Electriciens, for the foundation of scholarships and prizes for work in physical science.

C. H. LEES, *rev.* CHRISTOPHER F. LINDSEY

Sources J. O. Marsh, ed., letters and papers of David Edward Hughes, 1980, RS, microfilm archive for Victorian technology · J. O. Marsh and R. G. Roberts, 'David Edward Hughes: inventor, engineer and scientist', *Proceedings of the Institution of Electrical Engineers*, 126 (1979), 929–35 · G. B. Brown, 'David Edward Hughes, FRS, 1831–1900', *Notes and Records of the Royal Society*, 34 (1979–80), 227–39 · S. Evershed, 'The life and work of David Hughes', *Journal of the Institution of Electrical Engineers*, 69 (1931), 1245–50 · J. Munro, 'The late Prof. Hughes', *Electrical Review*, 46 (2 Feb 1900), 185–7 · *The Electrician* (26 Jan 1900) · *ILN* (10 Feb 1900) · *Journal of the Institution of Electrical Engineers*, 29 (1900), 951–4 · *Journal of the Society of Arts*, 48 (1899–1900), 211 · *Nature*, 61 (1899–1900), 325–6 · *The Times* (24 Jan 1900) · W. De La Rue, 'Prof. D. E. Hughes (Royal medal)', *Royal Society medal claims, 1873–1909* · 'Albert medal', *Journal of the Society of Arts*, 44 (1895–6), 676 · 'Albert medal', *Journal of the Society of Arts*, 45 (1896–7), 227 · *The Times* (9 March 1900) · Inst. EE · census returns, 1881, 1901 · Highgate cemetery records · F. Greenaway, ed., *The archives of the Royal Institution of Great Britain in facsimile: minutes of manager's meetings, 1799–1900*, 1 (1971) · J. J. Fahie, *A history of wireless telegraphy, 1838–1899* (1899) · D. E. Hughes, patents, 1858–63 · D. E. Hughes, USA patents, 1856 · D. E. Hughes, USA patents, 1859 · parish register, Holborn, St Andrew's, 18 June 1829 [birth]

Archives BL, notebooks of experiments and lectures, Add. MSS 40161–40163, 40641–40648 · NL Wales, papers [microfiche] · RS, letters and MSS · Sci. Mus. | Inst. EE, corresp. with John Joseph Fahie · Inst. EE, corresp. with William Henry Preece

Likenesses photograph, 1890–99, Sci. Mus. [*see illus.*] · A. Delzers, engraving, Inst. EE · Elliott & Fry, photograph, Inst. EE · International Telecommunications Union (Geneva), photograph (after engraving), Sci. Mus. · Maull & Fox, two photographs, RS · A. Stroh, photograph (after engraving), Inst. EE · glass slide, Inst. EE · photograph, Sci. Mus. · two engravings, Inst. EE · two photographs, Inst. EE

Wealth at death £469,419 11s. 9d.: resworn probate, March 1901, CGPLA Eng. & Wales (1900)

Hughes, Sir Edward (c.1720–1794), naval officer, was born in Hertfordshire. He entered the navy on 4 January 1735 in the *Dunkirk* (60 guns), with Captain Digby Dent, commodore on the Jamaica station. From the *Dunkirk* he was moved in September 1736 to the *Kinsale* (32 guns) on the same station, and in July 1738 to the *Diamond* (50 guns, Captain Knowles), in which he was present at the reduction of Porto Bello in November 1739.

In February 1740 Hughes was moved into the *Burford* (70 guns), Admiral Vernon's flagship, and on 25 August he was promoted lieutenant of the fireship *Cumberland* serving in the West Indies. On 6 March 1741 he was transferred to the *Suffolk* (70 guns, Captain Davers), and took part in the unsuccessful operations against Cartagena in March and April 1741. In June he was appointed to the *Dunkirk*, and in her witnessed the action off Toulon on 11 February 1744, but took no part in it, the *Dunkirk* being in the rear of the fleet under the immediate command of Richard Lestock. In the following August Hughes was moved into the *Stirling Castle* (70 guns), and in October 1745 into the *Marlborough* (90 guns), still in the western Mediterranean, in which in 1746 he returned to England. In June 1747 he

Sir Edward Hughes (*c*.1720–1794), by Sir Joshua Reynolds, 1786–7

joined the *Warwick* (60 guns) as a supernumerary for a passage to North America and the West Indies. On the way the *Warwick*, in company with the *Lark* (44 guns), met the Spanish ship *Glorioso* (70 guns). After a sharp engagement the *Warwick*, unsupported by the *Lark*, was disabled, and the *Glorioso* escaped. John Crookshanks, captain of the *Lark*, was condemned by court martial for his conduct; Hughes was promoted to the vacancy on 6 February 1748, and commanded the *Lark* in North America and the West Indies until July 1750.

For the next five years Hughes was on half pay but on 28 January 1756 he commissioned the *Deal Castle* (20 guns), after which she cruised in the Channel Islands. In January 1757 he commanded the *Prince George* (90 guns) but in June he moved to the *Somerset* (64 guns); Hughes joined Vice-Admiral Holburne at Halifax on 6 September and remained there until 5 April 1758 when the *Somerset* formed part of the fleet under Admiral Edward Boscawen at the capture of Louisbourg. She was, however, back at Spithead in November. In February 1759 Hughes set off again for Halifax, and in June he left for Quebec under Vice-Admiral Charles Saunders; the *Somerset* played her part in the capture of the city, and afterwards Saunders hoisted his flag in her and sailed for England with part of the fleet. After hearing that the French were at sea, he hastened to assist Admiral Hawke off Brest, but was too late to take part in the battle of Quiberon Bay. In May 1760 the *Somerset* went to the Mediterranean with Saunders, who on 27 September 1762 moved Hughes into his own ship, the *Blenheim* (90 guns), in which he returned to England in April 1763. After another spell of half pay Hughes recommissioned the *Somerset* in January 1771, and commanded her as a guardship, first at Chatham and, after June 1771, at Plymouth. In September 1773 Hughes was appointed commander-in-chief in the East Indies, as commodore in the *Salisbury* (50 guns). In India he spent an uneventful though watchful three years, in which the French increased their military and diplomatic strength. Up to this point Hughes's career had been unremarkable, though he was dependable and was notable for his care for his crew. He left Bombay in October 1777 and reached Spithead on 14 May 1778, having been promoted rear-admiral of the blue on 23 January 1778.

In July Hughes was again appointed commander-in-chief in the East Indies, though he did not sail until 7 March 1779. He was in the meantime created a knight of the Bath (late 1778), apparently in fulfilment of a condition made by Hughes on his returning to the East Indies at the request of the East India Company. When he finally put to sea he had under his command a squadron of six ships of the line, including his own flagship, the *Superb* (74 guns), and with these on the way out he had no difficulty in dispossessing the French, who had lately seized on the English settlement of Goree in west Africa. His squadron reached Madras in January 1780. At first Hughes's force was far in excess of anything the enemy could muster in eastern waters, but by September 1780 he had received intelligence of substantial French reinforcements. On 26 September he was advanced to be vice-admiral of the blue.

In December 1780 Hughes destroyed at Mangalore a number of armed vessels fitted out by Haidar Ali, who was by then attacking East India Company territory. In November 1781, after receiving intelligence of the war with the Netherlands, he co-operated with the troops under Sir Hector Munro in attacking Negapatam. Then, taking some 500 soldiers on his ships, he went to Trincomalee (Ceylon), where he arrived on the evening of 4 January 1782. Unable to offer effective resistance, the town and the lower fort were occupied on the night of 5 January 1782, the Dutch retreating to Fort Osnaburg on a commanding eminence. Preparations were immediately made for an assault on this fort, and on 9 January Hughes sent in a formal summons. It was refused, and the place was taken by force two days later. Hughes provided for its defence and returned to Madras, where he anchored on 8 February. Here he was joined a few days later by three ships newly arrived from England, and, having received intelligence of the presence of a superior French force on the coast, he took up a defensive position under the batteries.

On 16 February the French squadron under Suffren came in sight, but regarding the British position as unassailable, he made sail to the south. Suffren was immediately followed by Hughes, who during the night slipped past him, and on the morning of 17 February captured a number of the merchantmen in convoy and a transport laden with military stores. Suffren hastened to the rescue, while Hughes, having secured his prizes, prepared to defend them. But the fitful wind made his line irregular, and at about four o'clock in the afternoon the French attacked his rear division, which held its own in a very severe struggle, centring on the *Superb* and *Exeter* until a favourable shift in the wind permitted the four ships of the van to come to its relief. On this Suffren drew off to reform his line, and lost the advantage. During the night the fleets separated; both had sustained considerable casualties and damage. The French drew back to Pondicherry and the British went to Trincomalee to refit. In the meantime Cuddalore fell to the French army, allowing Suffren an east coast port for supplies without which he could not have remained on the east coast.

Hughes then returned to Madras, and was carrying back to Trincomalee a strong reinforcement for the garrison and a quantity of stores when, approaching his port on 9 April, he again fell in with the French fleet. This time he had the advantage of the wind, but being anxious to land his cargo before engaging, and with weak and sickly crews, he went on, in a light and variable wind, and allowed the enemy to take the weather gauge; by 12 April Hughes found himself on a lee shore, with Suffren outside preparing to engage. This he did at about two o'clock, in a manner contrary to all experience, and concentrating his attack on the British centre, placed it for a time in a position of great danger. The battle raged with exceptional severity round the *Superb* and *Monmouth*, the latter being wrecked with heavy losses. At about four o'clock Hughes made the signal to wear, and in reforming his line succeeded in placing the *Monmouth* in comparative safety to leeward. The fight then continued on more equal terms for a further one and a half hours until, in a rain-squall, the fleets separated, and anchored for the night off the islet of Providien. British casualties then totalled 137 killed and 430 wounded; the French 139 killed and 351 wounded.

Both fleets then anchored for some days to make repairs, though on 18 April Suffren set sail hoping to tempt Hughes to battle. The British squadron, however, proceeded to Trincomalee. It was now that Suffren proposed an arrangement for the exchange of prisoners, which Hughes declined, alleging that he did not have the authority. However, as the commander-in-chief on a distant station with considerable discretionary power, it is not improbable that he judged the exchange would be more to the advantage of the French, whose resources, at such a distance from their base at Mauritius, were very limited. Suffren seems to have regarded this as the real reason, and forthwith handed his prisoners, numbering 60 officers and 400 men, over to Haidar Ali, who treated them with great cruelty.

Hughes had meanwhile refitted his fleet at Trincomalee with difficulty; his men were at half strength and the ships lacked naval stores. By the end of June he had taken up a position before Negapatam, which he understood the French were preparing to attack by land and sea. He was still there when the French fleet came in sight on 5 July, and Suffren proposed to attack him at anchor. As he was standing in, however, one of his ships was partially dismasted in a squall; in the resulting delay Hughes weighed, but would not be tempted seaward in case he gave an opportunity to the French to get between him and the shore, and so land the troops which they had on board. The next morning, 6 July, on Suffren again standing in, Hughes, having the advantage of the wind, made the signal to engage van to van, line to line, in a dispersed attack along the whole line, and the result was indecisive. After a fierce exchange of over two hours' duration, a sudden shift of wind threw both lines into confusion; and so they separated, the damage on each side being fairly equal. The British took up their former position off Negapatam, and the French, unable to effect their proposed landing, carried their troops back to Cuddalore.

On 1 August the French sailed for Ceylon, while Hughes lay at Madras refitting. He was informed by the governor, Lord Macartney, that the French had left Cuddalore and sailed to the south; Hughes answered that he was not responsible to the governor for the management of the fleet. It was not until 19 August that one of his own frigates, the *Coventry*, confirmed the news of the French departure. Then, indeed, Hughes realized that Trincomalee might be in danger, and he put to sea on the following day, with unfavourable winds. Not until the evening of 2 September was he off the port. It had fallen to the French two days before, and the next morning, when Hughes was standing in towards the mouth of the harbour, he was shocked to see the French flag suddenly hoisted. He necessarily drew back, and Suffren, who now had fifteen ships against Hughes's twelve, at once followed, hoping to complete his victory by the destruction of the British fleet. His orders repeated the tactics which had proved so formidable on 17 February and 12 April. Once again the whole of Suffren's superiority was to be directed against the British rear, leaving a barely equal force to hold the van in check. After a desultory action of three hours, however, the fleets separated, the French making their way back to Trincomalee, and the British to Madras. On 15 November a storm swept over the Tellicherry Roads and forced them to sea. The *Superb* was lost and all ships were more or less damaged; Hughes shifted his flag to the *Sultan*, and by slow degrees the fleet gathered together at Bombay. Here it was reinforced by a squadron of four ships brought out from Britain by Sir Richard Bickerton, and when, after an extensive and much needed refit, Hughes later returned to the east coast, he had, for the first time, a numerical superiority to the French, and was able in June 1783 to co-operate with the army in the siege of Cuddalore. On 14 June the French fleet appeared in the offing, and on 17 June succeeded in passing inside the British and establishing a free communication with the shore. The French ships were very short-handed, and took on board some 1200 men from the garrison, before engaging the British fleet outside. On 20 June the two enemies again met; but though Suffren had the position to windward, and though he had, before leaving Trincomalee, given out a detailed order for concentrating his attack on the British rear, he countermanded these orders, which resulted in a dispersed attack along the whole line. The result was the useless slaughter of 100 men on each side, but the advantage remained with the French. Hughes raised the blockade and withdrew to Madras, where he soon received news of the peace.

So ended one of the few periods in which two fleets fought five battles within little more than a year (four of them within seven months) with no very clear advantage on either side. Suffren's role has been more celebrated than that of Hughes, although by no means all historians feel that the French admiral is entitled to the credit afforded him either at the time or since. Hughes was mindful of the fact that a serious defeat at any time during 1781–2 would probably have meant the loss of India, and this led him to take few risks. His logistical problem, greater than Suffren's, who was supplied by Dutch allies, together with the poor health of his men, called for great determination. No less determination was needed in dealing with the interference of Lord Macartney and the Madras council. Hughes's conduct can be said to have fulfilled the words of Sir Hugh Palliser in 1773, recommending Hughes for the command: 'he will not wander out of the path that may be prescribed to him to follow any schemes or whim of his own, nor never will study how to find fault with his orders but always how he may best execute them for his Majesty's service' (Palliser to Lord Sandwich, 11 Aug 1773, NMM, MS SAN/F/4/80).

At the end of the war Hughes returned to England, arriving at Spithead on 16 May 1785. He held no further command, but was promoted admiral of the blue on 1 February 1793. He acquired in India a considerable fortune from prize money with which he purchased estates in Hertfordshire, Surrey, and Essex, but he did not flaunt his wealth. In the 1780s he granted the impecunious Sandwich huge, unsecured loans. Hughes died at Luxborough House near Chigwell, Essex, on 17 February 1794. His wife, Ruth Ball, eldest daughter of Sir Charles Gould Morgan, and widow of Captain Ball, naval officer, later married Samuel Humfrey of Penydarren Place, Glamorgan. She died at West Hatch, Essex, on 30 September 1800.

As Hughes's marriage was childless his wealth passed to the son of Ruth Ball's son by her first marriage. **Edward Hughes Ball Hughes** [called Golden Ball] (1799–1863), naval officer, was a hedonist who was educated at Eton College and entered Trinity College, Cambridge, on 20 June 1815. On 7 August 1819 Ball took the additional name of Hughes after inheriting a fortune of £40,000 p.a. from Admiral Edward Hughes. In 1823 he married Miss Mercandotti, a celebrated Spanish dancer. Said to be 'one of the spendthrift dandies of the Regency period' (*N&Q*, 5th ser., 10, 1878, 455), Hughes lost £45,000 in one night gambling at Wattier's Club, Piccadilly, London. He later moved to St Germain-en-Laye, near Paris, where he died on 10 March 1863.   J. K. LAUGHTON, *rev.* ROGER KNIGHT

Sources PRO, ADM 7/733–760 · NMM, MS SAN/F/4, 34 · NMM, ADM/L/S/444, L/L/31, L/S/328, L/S/353 · H. W. Richmond, *The navy in India, 1763–1783* (1931) · J. Charnock, ed., *Biographia navalis*, 6 vols. (1794–8) · *The private papers of John, earl of Sandwich*, ed. G. R. Barnes and J. H. Owen, 4 vols., Navy RS, 69, 71, 75, 78 (1932–8) · N. A. M. Rodger, *The insatiable earl: a life of John Montagu, fourth earl of Sandwich* (1993) · N. A. M. Rodger, *The wooden world: an anatomy of the Georgian navy* (1986) · *The correspondence of King George the Third from 1760 to December 1783*, ed. J. Fortescue, 6 vols. (1927–8) · *Memoirs of William Hickey*, ed. P. Quennell (1960) · R. Cavaliero, *Admiral Satan: the life and campaigns of Suffren* (1994) · F. Caron, *La guerre incomprise ou le mythe de Suffren* (1996) · B. Tunstall, *Naval warfare in the age of sail: the evolution of fighting tactics, 1650–1815*, ed. N. Tracy (1990) · *GM*, 1st ser., 70 (1800), 1008 · *GM*, 3rd ser., 14 (1863), 533–4 · *GM*, 1st ser., 63 (1793), 478 · *CGPLA Eng. & Wales* (1863) [Edward Hughes Ball Hughes] · Venn, *Alum. Cant.*

Archives Admiralty Library, London, letter-book · BL OIOC, Home misc. series, corresp. relating to India · BL OIOC, journal, MS Eur. F 27–29 · National Archives of India, New Delhi, official papers · PRO, journal, logs, letter- and order books, ADM 7 | BL, corresp. with Warren Hastings, Add. MSS 29134–29167, *passim* · Bodl. Oxf., corresp. with Lord Macartney · Duke U., Perkins L., corresp. with Lord Macartney · NL Scot., corresp. with James Stuart · NMM, letters to Lord Sandwich · priv. coll., corresp. with Norman Macleod

Likenesses V. B. Siries, oils, 1761, NMM · gouache, *c.*1783, BL OIOC · J. Reynolds, oils, 1786–7, NMM [*see illus.*] · attrib. W. Beechey, portrait, National Art Museum, Wellington, New Zealand · attrib. G. Stuart, portrait, John Herron Art Museum, Indianapolis, Indiana

Wealth at death under £30,000; estates in Hertfordshire, Surrey, and Essex; Edward Hughes Ball Hughes: will, 14 July 1863, PRO, PROB 11/1241, *CGPLA Eng. & Wales*

Hughes, Edward (1832–1908), portrait painter, was born on 14 September 1832 at Myddelton Square, Pentonville, London, the son of George Hughes (*fl.* 1813–1858), painter and exhibitor at the Royal Academy, and his wife, Mary Lucas. From his father and John Pye, the engraver of Turner's pictures, Hughes received his earliest training in art. In December 1846 he was admitted to the Royal Academy Schools, and in 1847, at the age of fourteen, was awarded a silver medal from the Royal Society of Arts for a chalk drawing. His precocious ability rapidly developed, and in that same year Hughes's earliest painting, *The First Primer*, won distinction at the Royal Academy exhibition. A more ambitious subject, *Nourmahal's Dream; Light of the Harem*, from Thomas Moore's *Lalla Rookh*, was hung the following year.

From 1855 to 1876 Hughes was regularly represented at the academy by subject pictures, which he afterwards abandoned for the more remunerative work of portraiture. He exhibited portraits exclusively at the Royal Academy from 1878 to 1884, after which, the *Art Journal* noted, 'he rather prided himself on not having contributed' (*Art Journal*, 1908, 223). The most noteworthy were those of Miss Louisa Parnell and Dr Lightfoot, bishop of Durham. 'Very many artists,' Millais is reported to have said, 'can paint a portrait of a man, but very few can paint a portrait of a lady, and Edward Hughes is one of those few' (ibid.). Hughes, who made a study of portraiture from Sir Joshua Reynolds onwards to the modern French school, devoted his technical skill chiefly to an idealistic treatment of his sitters. His popularity steadily increased, and in 1886 his whole-length painting of Miss Jeannie Chamberlain, exhibited at Agnew's Galleries, brought him important commissions.

In 1895 Hughes received his first royal commission. He painted a whole-length seated portrait of Queen Mary when duchess of York (Royal Collection). Of Queen Alexandra, Hughes painted four portraits, the most notable being that of her in her coronation robes, which was hung in the state rooms at Buckingham Palace (Royal Collection). It was engraved by E. L. Haynes, and replicas were executed for the king of Denmark and the Durbar Hall at Patiala, India. For this painting Hughes was awarded the artists' gold medal, a private decoration given by the monarch. Several other members of the royal family sat to Hughes, including the princess royal, the Princess Victoria, the prince of Wales, his brother Prince Albert, and his sister Princess Mary (Royal Collection). His earliest portrait of Queen Alexandra, those of Queen Mary, Lady Naylor Leyland, and seven others were reproduced in photogravure in *The Book of Beauty* (1896).

Hughes's later work was confined entirely to portraits of ladies and children. The countess of Leven and Melville, Mrs William James, and Mrs Miller Mundy were painted in full length with their children. The group of the earl and countess of Minto's three daughters, painted in 1905, was Hughes's largest picture. Hughes's many American sitters included Jean Reid, daughter of Whitelaw Reid, American ambassador in London from 1904. This portrait was included in the exhibition of Hughes's work at the Mount Street Galleries, which opened in the week of the artist's death.

On 15 January 1851 Hughes married Mary Ann Sherratt Pewtner (*c*.1832–1864/5); following her early death Hughes remarried on 5 February 1867. His second wife, Kate Ellen Margetts, also predeceased him, but a third possible marriage was abandoned just days before the ceremony was due to take place in Yorkshire, when Hughes was persuaded that the marriage would cut his future bride off from friends and family. His daughter Alice *Hughes (1857–1939), a highly respected portrait photographer, lived with him until his death, taking care of his business affairs, as her mother, Mary, had done; they communicated throughout the day via a speaking tube that ran from his studio to hers. She described her father as 'a man of intense inner refinement … sensitive to atmosphere and easily affected by his surroundings. He was shy and reserved … always self-possessed and master of himself. He was extremely active and restless' (Hughes, 57). Hughes died of bronchitis on 14 May 1908 at his home, 52 Gower Street, London, and was buried at Highgate cemetery on 19 May.　　J. D. MILNER, *rev.* MARK POTTLE

Sources *Art Journal* (1908) · *The Times* (16 May 1908) · J. Johnson and A. Greutzner, *The dictionary of British artists, 1880–1940* (1976), vol. 5 of *Dictionary of British art* · B. Stewart and M. Cutten, *The dictionary of portrait painters in Britain up to 1920* (1997) · F. Harcourt Williamson, ed., *The book of beauty* (1896) · Graves, *RA exhibitors* · private information (1912) [Charlotte Knollys; Alice Hughes, daughter] · A. Hughes, *My father and I* (1923) · *IGI* · m. cert. [Kate Ellen Margetts] · m. cert. [Mary Ann Sherratt Pewtner]

Likenesses E. Hughes, self-portrait; known to be in possession of his daughter, 1908

Wealth at death £4355: probate, 29 May 1908, *CGPLA Eng. & Wales*

Hughes, Edward David (1906–1963), physical organic chemist, was born on 18 June 1906 at Ynysgain Bach, a farm near Cricieth, Caernarvonshire, the ninth and last child of Hugh Hughes, farmer, and his wife, Ann Roberts. The Welsh-speaking family was close-knit, convivial, and ambitious. As a youth Ted, as he was always known, helped on the family farm where he acquired a lifelong love of animals that in later years led him to breed and race greyhounds, a passion he picked up from his wife's family. His increasingly portly figure and taciturn friendliness were to become as familiar to touts and tipsters of the track, who knew him as 'the Prof.', as to the less racy denizens of academic chemistry.

Hughes entered Llanystumdwy elementary school in 1911 and then moved on to Portmadoc grammar school, where he was greatly encouraged in his studies by the head science teacher, W. J. Hughes, who groomed him for university. In 1924 he entered University College, Bangor, and was awarded the BSc degree with first-class honours in chemistry in 1927. His original intention was to become a teacher, but early experience convinced him that classroom instruction was not his forte. In 1928 he elected to repay his grant to the Board of Education rather than enter schoolteaching. By then he had started research, under H. B. Watson, on prototropy, a subject of great interest to the head of department, Professor K. J. P. Orton, who stimulated Hughes's interest in mechanistic organic chemistry, a field he was to espouse for the rest of his life. One of the examiners for his PhD in 1930 was Christopher K. Ingold, and thus began a 33-year-long partnership that was to end only with Hughes's death. Ingold was already an established figure when Hughes joined him at University College, London (UCL), in 1930 as a postdoctoral fellow. In 1932 Hughes obtained the degree of MSc and in 1936 DSc of the University of London. He was awarded the Meldola medal of the Royal Institute of Chemistry in 1936 and appointed a lecturer at UCL in 1937. In 1934 he married Ray Fortune Christina, a linguist and pianist, daughter of the Revd Ll. Davies, of Brecon; their only child, Carol Anthea, was born five years later.

On the outbreak of war in 1939 the chemistry department of UCL was evacuated to Aberystwyth and Bangor, Hughes and Ingold going to the former. When in 1943 the chair of chemistry at Bangor became vacant, Hughes was appointed and at the end of the war organized the rapid rebuilding of his department. During his five years at Bangor he extended the work on substitution and elimination reactions he had begun in London and also initiated work on isotope separation, with a view to using isotopes as indicators of mechanisms. He paid frequent visits to UCL where collaborative research was continued with Ingold and his students. In 1948 he was appointed to a second chemistry chair at UCL, becoming deputy head in

1957. In 1949 he was elected a fellow of the Royal Society and in 1954 a fellow of UCL.

Together Hughes and Ingold fashioned what later came to be called the 'electronic theory of the English school'. This qualitative theory was to dominate the interpretation of organic chemistry in the period 1935 to 1950 and many of its ideas, nomenclature, and notation have become permanent features of chemistry. The central problem was to elucidate how the electron-pair nature of the chemical bond, first proposed by G. N. Lewis in 1916, could illuminate the paths by which one organic molecule is converted into another. The detailed mechanisms by which one chemical structure changes into another were elusive and speculative, but Hughes showed how chemical kinetics, the study of the rates at which the concentrations of various substrates change with respect to time and temperature, could be exploited to provide an experimental macroscopic reflection of the speculative microscopic mechanism. While Ingold had a brilliant ratiocinative mind he was not a born experimenter. By contrast, the less subtle Hughes had an extraordinary talent for ferreting out the experimental rate laws and kinetic data. Furthermore, he was able to transfer this talent, temporarily at least, to a long line of research students.

The partnership between Hughes and Ingold is perhaps unique in the history of chemistry. Together they wrote, or rather published, since Ingold did the bulk of the writing, over 140 papers ranging over much of mechanistic organic chemistry. Inevitably Hughes lived somewhat in the shadow of the more versatile and brilliant Ingold. Nevertheless, he was much in demand as a chairman of scientific committees because of his expeditious handling of business. He served on many committees of the Chemical Society, and was honorary secretary in 1950–56 and vice-president in 1959–60. He also served UCL as chairman of the Ramsay advisory council. When Ingold retired in 1960, Hughes succeeded him as head of department, but he had not long to live; he died of cancer in University College Hospital, London, on 30 June 1963.

DEREK A. DAVENPORT

Sources C. K. Ingold, *Memoirs FRS*, 10 (1964), 147–82 · *DNB* · K. Leffek, *Sir Christopher Ingold: a major prophet of organic chemistry* (1996) · C. K. Ingold, *Chemistry and Industry* (18 Jan 1964), 96–8 · C. W. Shoppee, *Memoirs FRS*, 18 (1972), 349–411 [obit. of C. K. Ingold] · *CGPLA Eng. & Wales* (1963)

Likenesses portrait, repro. in Ingold, *Memoirs FRS* · portrait, repro. in Leffek, *Sir Christopher Ingold* · portrait, repro. in Ingold, *Chemistry and Industry*

Wealth at death £18,445 5s. 4d.: administration, 14 Oct 1963, *CGPLA Eng. & Wales*

Hughes, Edward Hughes Ball (1799–1863). *See under* Hughes, Sir Edward (c.1720–1794).

Hughes, Edward James [Ted] (1930–1998), poet and writer, was born on 17 August 1930 at 1 Aspinall Street, Mytholmroyd, West Yorkshire, the youngest of the three children of William Henry Hughes (1894–1981), joiner, and his wife, Edith Farrar (1898–1969), a tailor. The Farrars

Edward James Hughes (1930–1998), by Henri Cartier-Bresson, 1971

traced their ancestry back through the father of Nicholas Ferrer, founder of the religious community of Little Gidding, to William de Ferrières, who came over with William the Conqueror. On the Hughes side there was certainly Irish and possibly Spanish or Moorish blood. But Hughes's immediate forebears were descended from farmers and hand-loom weavers from the poor slopes of the Pennines, forced by the industrial revolution down into the mills of the Calder valley. The valley was the main link between the woollen towns of Yorkshire and the cotton towns of Lancashire. It was so narrow in places that the river, the canal, the railway, and the trunk road could only get past the mills and houses, pubs, chapels, and graveyards, by weaving over and under each other. Hughes's earliest memories were of being in a 'shadow-trap'.

Childhood and education In Hughes's childhood his maternal grandmother's family was still farming at Hathershelf. Otherwise, most of the family for two or three generations had worked in some capacity in the local woollen and clothing industries. Two of his uncles, Walter and Tom Farrar, were the prosperous owners of a clothing factory. William Hughes could have become a professional footballer, but chose to become a joiner. At the age of twenty he was one of 30,000 young men to join the Lancashire Fusiliers, of whom 13,642 were to be listed killed. William Hughes was awarded the DCM 'for conspicuous courage and great leadership' at Ypres. Uncle Walter had been wounded, and William saved from death by the pay-book in his breast pocket. The imagination of the growing Hughes was shadowed by fearful images of trench warfare, images which were not difficult to match with the harsh images of nature struggling to survive and sometimes failing on the exposed moors.

Nevertheless Hughes had a happy childhood. A few yards away from Aspinall Street was the canal where the local children would fish for loach. Hughes and his friends would explore the nearby woods, or climb through fields towards the exhilaration of the moor with its heather and bilberries and curlews and wide horizons (the same moor which a few miles further north becomes the Brontë country). Though the Calder may have been 'the hardest worked river in England', most of its tributary valleys were beautiful and unspoiled. Edith Hughes loved walking, and took her children at every opportunity to picnic, and swim in the pools. There were shopping trips to Halifax where Ted would choose another lead animal for his collection. Best of all were the paradisal hunting and camping trips with his brother Gerald, ten years older, his guide to the secret magical places.

Hughes attended Burnley Road School in Mytholmroyd until 1937, when the family moved to Mexborough, a grimy mining town in south Yorkshire, where his father had bought a newsagent's and tobacconist's shop. There Hughes attended Schofield Street junior school. The move marked the end of the close relationship between the brothers, Gerald becoming an assistant gamekeeper in Devon for a year, then serving in the RAF during the war, and subsequently emigrating to Australia. Hughes often wondered in later life whether it would have been better to emulate his brother than to follow the literary life.

It was not so easy to escape from Mexborough, but Hughes soon discovered Manor Farm, on the Don at Old Denaby, which he came to know 'better than any place on earth'. His first animal poem, 'The Thought Fox', and his first story, 'The Rain Horse', were both memories of encounters there. At about thirteen his new friend John Wholey introduced Hughes to the Crookhill estate above Conisborough, where his father was head gardener and gamekeeper and a fount of knowledge on flora and fauna. There was an idyllic pond with huge pike. Hughes soon became part of the family, often staying with them over the weekend. Sometimes Ted went off for hours by himself with a book or pencil and paper. He would read poems or passages of Greek drama to Edna, John's older sister. The two boys cycled all over south Yorkshire fishing and shooting. Fishing became, for Hughes, a religious activity, a way of connecting his own life to a larger non-human life. It was also a perfect metaphor for the poetic act, drawing unknown life out of the darkness into the light of consciousness.

At eleven Hughes had discovered Henry Williamson's *Tarka the Otter* in the library of Mexborough grammar school, and this became his bible for two years. Hughes's introduction to poetry came not so much from school as from native American war songs chanted to him by his brother. His own earliest poems were Kiplingesque ballads about Zulus or the Wild West or complaints about having to study when he could have been shooting or fishing. After Gerald's departure Hughes's older sister Olwyn became his mentor. She was very well versed in poetry. When Miss McLeod, his first form English teacher, praised his writing, Hughes's mother bought him a whole second-hand library of classic poets, including the Warwick Shakespeare. Hughes discovered folk-tales for himself. His favourite teachers, Pauline Mayne and John Fisher, fostered his creative writing, and Mayne later introduced him to Hopkins and Eliot. He received Robert Graves's *The White Goddess* as a gift from Fisher. By the age of sixteen he had no thought of becoming anything but a poet.

In 1948 Hughes won an open exhibition to Pembroke College, Cambridge (as a 'dark horse' on the strength of his poems), but before he could take it up he had to serve as a national serviceman for two years. For most of the time he was a radio mechanic at a remote radar station at Fylingdales in north Yorkshire, where he had little to do but read Shakespeare and Yeats until he knew them almost by heart. By the time he got to Cambridge his 'sacred canon' was fixed: Chaucer, Shakespeare, Marlowe, Blake, Wordsworth, Keats, Coleridge, Hopkins, Yeats, Eliot; but Cambridge English alienated him. He felt that analytical criticism and the elevation of great writers to a higher plane than common mortals stifled the imaginative creativity of the students. He later referred to 'the terrible, suffocating, maternal octopus' of the English poetic tradition, and the difficulty of making one's own voice heard 'against that choir' (Hughes, *Winter Pollen*, 1994, 193). In his second year he dreamed that he was visited by a scorched and bleeding fox the size of a man, which said to him 'You're killing us':

> I connected the fox's command to my own ideas about Eng. Lit., & the effect of the Cambridge blend of pseudo-critical terminology and social rancour on creative spirit, and from that moment abandoned my efforts to adapt myself. I might say, that I had as much talent for Leavis-style dismantling of texts as anyone else, I even had a special bent for it—nearly a sadistic streak there,—but it seemed to me not only a foolish game, but deeply destructive of myself.　(Sagar, 46)

Hughes decided to change from reading English to archaeology and anthropology. His knowledge in these fields fed directly into his poetry, and in the lean years of the 1960s he was able to support himself and his children partly by reviewing books in these subjects regularly in the weekly magazines. Some of these books, such as Mircea Eliade's *Shamanism*, deeply and permanently affected him.

Hughes graduated in 1954. In that same year he published his first poem (other than in his school magazine), 'The Little Boys and the Seasons' (under the pseudonym Daniel Hearing), in *Granta*, and also wrote the first of the poems which appeared in *The Hawk in the Rain* (1957). Hughes lived partly in Rugby Street, London, and partly in Cambridge and tried a number of jobs including rose gardener, night-watchman, dishwasher at the cafeteria in London Zoo, and reader for J. Arthur Rank.

First marriage and early success Hughes and a group of his friends, Lucas Myers, Daniel Huws, David Ross, and Daniel Weissbort, decided to launch their own poetry magazine, the *St Botolph's Review* (named after the former rectory where Myers resided and which the rest regarded as their spiritual home). The first issue contained four poems by Hughes. A 23-year-old Fulbright scholar from Northampton, Massachusetts, Sylvia *Plath (1932–1963), was at Newnham College. She read the first and only issue of the review, memorized some of the poems by Myers and Hughes, and attended the party celebrating the launch of the review at Falcon Yard on 26 February 1956 with the express intention of meeting them. There was a strong immediate attraction between Plath and Hughes. Their second meeting did not take place until 23 March, when Plath visited Hughes in London on her way to Paris. She stayed with Hughes on her return three weeks later. They were married by special licence of the archbishop of Canterbury at St George the Martyr's Church, Bloomsbury, on 16 June (a date chosen because it is James Joyce's Bloomsday). Hughes did not learn until later the full story of Plath's psychological history, the suicide attempts, hospitalization, and electroconvulsive therapy she later wrote about in her novel *The Bell Jar* (1963). He was unprepared for her sudden mood swings and irrational outbursts. At the best times he felt their love bonded them 'into a single animal, a single soul' ('Flounders'); at the worst 'each of us was the stake impaling the other' ('9 Willow Street'). The vicissitudes of their relationship were recorded at the time in Plath's journals, and decades later in Hughes's *Birthday Letters* (1998).

The honeymoon began by showing Paris to Sylvia's mother, Aurelia. Then, with only a rucksack and typewriter, they set off for Spain. On their return they lived at 55 Eltisley Avenue, Cambridge. Hughes taught English and drama at a local secondary modern school. In August Hughes took Plath to meet his parents, who had returned to the Calder valley to live at Heptonstall Slack. In Cambridge, Plath, who believed that her husband's poetry was the most rich and powerful since that of Yeats and Dylan Thomas, had typed out almost all his poems and submitted them, as *The Hawk in the Rain*, to a competition for a first book of poems being run by the Poetry Centre of the Young Men's and Young Women's Hebrew Association of New York. In February 1957 the judges, W. H. Auden, Stephen Spender, and Marianne Moore, awarded the first prize—publication by Harper and Row—to Hughes. Marianne Moore wrote: 'Hughes' talent is unmistakable, the work has focus, is aglow with feeling, with conscience; sensibility is awake, embodied in appropriate diction' (introduction to the US edition). When the book was published in September, the reviews were almost unanimously enthusiastic. Hughes described his poems as bulletins from the battle between vitality and death. The book was as original in style as in content. Hughes rejected the Latinate and courtly iamb in favour of bludgeoning trochees and spondees. The strong alliteration, onomatopoeia, and hyperbole gave his poems an impact not heard in English verse since the demise of Middle English. Sylvia Plath ordered the poems so that the book began with the arresting lines:

> I drown in the drumming ploughland, I drag up
> Heel after heel from the swallowing of the earth's mouth,
> From clay that clutches my each step to the ankle
> With the habit of the dogged grave ...

The reviewers welcomed *The Hawk in the Rain* as a release from what Charles Tomlinson called the 'failure of nerve' of those poets represented in *New Lines* (1956) who had had enough of the big themes and had chosen to restrict themselves to ordinary events in ordinary language. Hughes, on the other hand, was 'all for opening negotiations with whatever happened to be out there' (Faas, 201). The book won a Somerset Maugham award.

Poetry, 1957–1963 In June 1957 the Hugheses went to the USA, where Plath had obtained a teaching post at her old college, Smith College, Northampton, Massachusetts. Here Hughes met W. S. and Dido Merwin, and the sculptor and engraver Leonard Baskin, who later worked with Hughes on several books and who talked to him about the Hebrew mystical tradition. In the following year he taught briefly at the University of Massachusetts at Amherst, and gave a reading at Harvard. In June the Hugheses rented a flat in Boston. Plath, suffering from writer's block and depression, began to see her psychiatrist again. In April 1959 Hughes was awarded a Guggenheim scholarship which eventually enabled him to escape from an exile of which he was becoming weary. But before that they toured North America by car, and spent eleven weeks at the Yaddo artists' colony at Saratoga Springs, New York. There Hughes finished his second volume of poems, *Lupercal* (1960), and worked with the Chinese composer Chou Weng-Chung on a libretto for *The Tibetan Book of the Dead*.

After his return to England at the end of the year Hughes wrote poems later published in *Wodwo* (1967) or *Recklings* (1966), and several unpublished radio plays. In February 1960 the Hugheses, with help from the Merwins who lived nearby, found and furnished a cramped apartment at 3 Chalcot Square, Primrose Hill, London. On 1 April Frieda Rebecca Hughes was born there. Hughes and Plath shared the childminding, with Plath writing in the morning and Hughes in the afternoon. *Lupercal* had been published two weeks earlier and won the Hawthornden prize. Here Hughes took further his attempt to come to terms with the apparent violence of nature—'Terrifying are the attent sleek thrushes on the lawn'—drawing increasingly on myth. The reviews were largely favourable, but the media had found a label to stick on Hughes—'animal poet'. Of course he did have the ability to conjure up the vital distinctiveness of any creature, but it was not widely recognized that animals were for him 'a symbolic language which is also the language of my whole life' (*Paris Review*, 81). Animals bellowed the evidence that humans wrapped in sophistries. Hughes could also enter into the spirit of plants and landscapes so that they too became part of that language.

Like Blake and Yeats, Hughes fully recognized the dangers of scientific rationalism and the limitations of Christianity. Like them he believed that imagination had the capacity to heal the disastrous dualistic split in the human psyche, to embrace both inner and outer worlds, to unify male and female, body and spirit. He saw it as essentially holistic, biocentric, a religious or visionary faculty, and part of the essential survival gear of the race. He believed that poetry is a language for perceiving connections, relationships, systems, wholes, for escaping the tyranny of the ego and of received ideas. Hughes therefore sought to open himself to alternative modes of knowledge such as astrology (which he often used to determine the publication dates of his books), Tibetan Buddhism, Sufism, shamanism, and the hermetic sciences—alchemy, Rosicrucianism, Cabbala. Some of his works have a hidden (or, in the case of *Cave Birds*, 1975, overt) alchemical structure.

In 1961 Hughes simplified some of the exercises he had been using with Plath to release her true poetic voice (concentration techniques and dreams) as a series of radio talks for schools, later collected as *Poetry in the Making* (1967). These perfectly pitched talks had a huge impact on the teaching of creative writing in schools. Hughes made many other broadcasts for schools, and, though public appearances were often an ordeal for him, gave a great many readings in schools, inspiring generations of children with a love of poetry. He also judged many competitions for children's writing, and (with his friend Seamus Heaney) edited two school anthologies, *The Rattle Bag* (1982) and *The School Bag* (1997). Roger McGough described Hughes as 'our greatest ambassador for poetry'.

While Hughes was at the BBC being interviewed by Moira Doolan, the producer of the *Poetry in the Making* series, Plath, in a jealous rage (he was half an hour late), destroyed all his work in progress. When a second child was on the way, they needed a larger home. They hoped that in the west country they would be able to live more cheaply and quietly. They found Court Green, a large cottage with some medieval walls, a courtyard, and an orchard, next to the village church at North Tawton near Dartmoor.

In her first months at Court Green, Plath seemed very happy; but her poems became more and more doom-laden as she found her 'Ariel' voice. Nicholas Farrar Hughes was born there on 17 January 1962. Among the visitors to Court Green the following spring were David and Assia Wevill. Assia (1927–1969; former married name Lipsey) was a darkly attractive German-born Jew, whom Sylvia saw as a rival. When Plath discovered in July that she and Hughes were indeed having an affair, she ordered him to leave. In November Plath decided to rent a flat in Fitzroy Street, London, for the winter. There Hughes visited her regularly and babysat for her. He felt that things were moving towards a reconciliation. In the coldest winter for years Plath succumbed to serious depression, and on 11 February 1963 gassed herself.

Hughes returned to Court Green with Olwyn looking after the children. He responded to the death of Sylvia Plath with two agonized poems, 'The Howling of Wolves' and 'Song of a Rat', after which he lapsed into a poetic silence for three years. He supported his family by broadcasting (including several plays for children), reviewing in the weeklies, and with a large award from the Abraham Woursell Foundation at the University of Vienna. He began to write critical essays, on Keith Douglas, Isaac Bashevis Singer, Vasco Popa.

Writings for children Though many of Hughes's works for children grew out of the stories he told his own children and nonsense poems he wrote for them, he evidently had a vocation for writing for children, since his earliest children's poems (*Meet my Folks!*, 1961) and stories (*How the Whale Became*, 1963) were written before the birth of Frieda, and he continued to write for children long after his own were grown up. *How the Whale Became* was clearly inspired by Kipling's *Just So Stories*. But in two subsequent collections of creation stories, *Tales of the Early World* (1988) and *The Dream Fighter* (1995), he made the genre his own. Its flexibility allowed for comic tales of God's bungling, the tragic plight of the bee which must spend its life gathering more and more sweetness from the flowers to counter the sadness in its veins from the demon's tears of which it had been made, the anti-racist satire of the polar bear's absurd prejudice in favour of whiteness. In 1967 Hughes wrote the most popular of all his works for children, *The Iron Man* (1968), subsequently made into both a rock opera by Pete Townshend (1993) and an animated film, *The Iron Giant* (1999). The story is Hughes's attempt to counter such false myths as St George and the dragon, where the hero's task is simply to destroy what he does not understand or feels threatened by. Hogarth, the boy hero of the story, persuades the iron man to use his strength for constructive purposes, and the iron man in turn transforms the energies of the demonic dragon to creative ends. In the sequel, *The Iron Woman* (1993), Hughes passionately attacks the sacrilege of pollution.

Hughes's poems for children began with the nonsense of *Meet my Folks!* (1961) and *The Earth Owl and other Moon People* (1963) but gradually acquired the sacramental vision of *Season Songs* (1975), *Under the North Star* (1981), and *What is the Truth?* (1984). Hughes's works for children cannot be clearly separated from his adult works. *Season Songs*, for example, though not written specifically for children, was designed to remain 'within hearing' of young readers.

Most of Hughes's plays for children began as radio plays for schools. They infuse traditional material with his typical transforming power. In *Orpheus* he clearly used the myth to help him come to terms with the loss of Sylvia Plath, but could permit himself to envisage reunion with her spirit only in a work for children. Hughes tried to make all his works for children 'upbeat', giving them strength and confidence to tackle the trials of life. In his works for adults, on the other hand, there are no wishful solutions—'everything must be paid for'.

Poetry, 1966–1979 When he began to write adult verse again, in 1966, Hughes's poems had shed the rhetoric, the 'masculine persuasive force' of his earlier work, for a new, moving simplicity, partly influenced by such eastern European poets as Popa and Janos Pilinszky, by Lorca's idea of the *duende*, and by Buddhism. In 1966 he published *Recklings* and in 1967 *Wodwo*—a large collection of poems, stories, and a play (*The Wound*)—which he described as a single adventure, 'a descent into destruction' (Faas, 205).

Ted and Assia worked together translating Yehuda Amichai. Their daughter, Alexandra Tatiana Elise ('Shura') Wevill, was born in March 1965, and in October that year Assia and Shura moved to Court Green. In the following spring Hughes took them to Ireland for several months. His parents stayed at Court Green, where he thought the milder weather would do his mother good, but by the time he returned she was too ill to move. His parents were never able to accept Assia, who was obliged for many months to care for four adults (one bedridden) and three children. Early in 1968 she returned to London, where, though Hughes visited her as often as he could, she became very depressed.

During these years Hughes was active in the organization of international poetry festivals to combat what he felt to be the insularity of English poetry. In 1965 he and Daniel Weissbort launched *Modern Poetry in Translation*. Hughes also served on the literature panel of the Arts Council.

In 1966 Hughes had begun to write some poems to accompany Leonard Baskin's drawings of crows. The project grew into a folk epic, *The Life and Songs of the Crow*, a prose quest narrative to be studded with hundreds of poems. Crow is initially a Trickster, mischievously or inadvertently making creation go wrong. Then he begins his largely unconscious quest to discover who made him and for what purpose. It is a search for his own mother, whom he encounters frequently, but never recognizes, since he projects onto her the monstrous images generated by his own split psyche. He tries to kill her. But gradually he develops a conscience and the desire to become a man. He recapitulates most of the errors of western man. Eventually he is helped by an Inuit shaman to understand the way things are. The intention was that he would ultimately pay for his crimes and reach the Happy Land where his bride (his transfigured victim) awaits him.

In March 1969 Hughes gave his first televised reading in Manchester. From there he and Assia went house-hunting on Tyneside. Hughes then returned to Devon, where the news reached him that on her return to London, Assia had gassed herself and their daughter on 25 March. He could not proceed with the resolution of the Crow story, but published the darkest poems from the first two-thirds of the story 'in memory of Assia and Shura'. *Crow: from the Life and Songs of the Crow* (1970) had a huge impact, provoking both admiration and horror, but was widely misunderstood because of the absence of the prose context and the ending. Crow's quest was completed in *Cave Birds*.

The publication of *Crow* provided another opportunity for hostile critics to renew their charge that Hughes was the high priest of a cult of violence. Fay Godwin's much published photographs of Hughes looking bleak in a leather jacket reinforced the public perception of him as craggy and unapproachable. He was, of course, large and imposing, in presence as well as physique, but it was shyness, not aggression, which masked, for those who did not know him, his essential gentleness and generosity.

Hughes's mother died in May 1969. On 19 August 1970 Hughes married Carol Ann Orchard (*b*. 1947/8), a nurse at Exeter General Hospital, and the daughter of Herbert John Orchard, a Devon farmer. In September 1969 Hughes had bought a mill owner's house, Lumb Bank, at Heptonstall Slack. Hughes, Carol, and the children lived there for a time, but it proved too cold and damp and they decided to return to Court Green. After Hughes had spent a considerable amount on the renovation of Lumb Bank it was leased in 1975 to the Arvon Foundation. Hughes was subsequently enormously supportive of Arvon's creative writing courses. In 1971 Hughes, Olwyn (who had been acting as Hughes's agent since 1965), and Keith Gossop founded the Rainbow Press, which published fine limited editions of nine of Hughes's books over the next decade. Also in that year Hughes wrote the introduction to *A Choice of Shakespeare's Verse* in which he first sketched his idea of the 'tragic equation' from which his Shakespeare book later developed.

Hughes's relationship with Peter Brook had begun with his adaptation of Seneca's *Oedipus* for Brook's 1968 National Theatre production, with John Gielgud as Oedipus. The summer of 1971 was spent in Persia with Peter Brook's company working on *Orghast* (written in a synthetic language designed to be universally understood) for the Shiraz festival. In Persia, Hughes also wrote *Prometheus on his Crag* (1973), which he described as 'a numb poem about numbness', but in which Prometheus eventually comes to terms with the vulture which torments him and transforms it into the midwife of his reborn self. He declined Brook's invitation to join the company in Africa, but provided him with about a hundred scenarios to use on the tour. Some of these were inspired by the Sufi classic *The Conference of the Birds*.

In 1972, as an investment for the children of the profits from Plath's novel *The Bell Jar*, and in the hope of tempting his brother Gerald to return home, Hughes bought Moortown, a 95 acre farm, where, together with Carol and her father, he bred sheep and South Devon cattle. After the death of Jack Orchard in 1976 the stock had to be sold, but the farming experience had produced many poems published in *Season Songs* (1975) and *Moortown* (1979). These poems, together with *Adam and the Sacred Nine* (1979), reaffirmed Hughes's vision of spirit grounded in the world of mud and blood.

At the Ilkley literature festival in 1975 Hughes read from two major new works, *Cave Birds* and *Gaudete* (1977). *Cave Birds* enacts an alchemical purgation, resurrection, and wedding. At the beginning the protagonist is a gross cockerel 'ridiculous with cocky pride' ('Six Young Men'). He dies, and his spirit, now a crow, is hauled before a bird court in the underworld for correction. Stripped to the bone, he and his former victim, now his bride, reassemble each other in the lovely poem 'Bride and Groom Lie Hidden for Three Days'.

Gaudete ('Rejoice!') started out as a film script but developed into an ambitious work, drawing heavily on folklore, myth, and, particularly, Wolfram's *Parzival*. Lumb, an Anglican minister, is abducted by spirits who confront him with the task of curing the stricken goddess in the underworld. They replace him in his parish with a substitute whose priapic energies disrupt the bourgeois world. Hughes's original intention had been to tell the stories of both Lumbs, but the experiences of the real Lumb were finally distilled into a series of forty-five short and mysterious prayers based on the Dravidian *vacanas*. These deeply felt poems are among Hughes's finest. Lumb prays to be enlisted, alongside the loyal grass-blade, the sleek blackbird, and the grim badger (jaw-strake shattered by the diggers' spade) as one of the goddess's warriors:

Let your home
Be my home. Your people
My people.

These dense and difficult works were closely followed by *Remains of Elmet* (1979) in which Hughes, responding to Fay Godwin's photographs, returned to his roots and evoked the spirit of the Calder valley. He could not regret that the moors, into which so many lives were ploughed like manure, were now breaking free from the harness of men. The image of stone returning to the earth is one of many images for the restoration to nature of her own, the healing and rededication of the holy elements before man can approach them again with clean hands, with respect and humility, and for purposes more natural, sane, and worthily human than the enslavement of body and spirit which had characterized industrialism and its supporting protestantism.

Recognition In spite of his reference to collaboration as 'like running a three-legged race', much of Hughes's finest work was in this form: *Cave Birds* with Leonard Baskin, *Remains of Elmet* with Fay Godwin, and *River* (1983) with another photographer, Peter Keen. In *Three Books* (1993) Hughes produced revised versions of these works closer to what he might have written without collaborators.

Hughes's work had an extraordinarily fertilizing effect on the work of other poets, especially the young, artists, and musicians. Exhibitions of works of art inspired by Hughes were staged at the Victoria and Albert Museum in 1979 and Manchester Art Gallery in 1980. His work of the 1970s and early 1980s brought him a long way from the sometimes bludgeoning poetry of the 1950s and the bleak verse of the 1960s, to poems of air and light almost purged of self.

Hughes was awarded the OBE in 1977. In the 1970s and 1980s he gave up a great deal of his time to judging poetry competitions, and gave many readings, especially to schoolchildren. His distinctive, deliberate voice, giving full value to every cadence and nuance of a poem, inspired many listeners to a love of poetry. However, at readings in Australia in 1976 and the USA in 1977 he was heckled by radical feminists accusing him of the murder of Sylvia Plath. Feminists later defaced Plath's gravestone in Heptonstall cemetery, repeatedly removing the name Hughes. The administration of the Plath estate became a millstone to Hughes, and he later gave the Plath copyright to their children.

Frieda Hughes was now becoming a successful painter and poet in Australia, and Nicholas, having graduated from Oxford with a degree in zoology, had become a specialist in freshwater biology. Hughes joined him in Kenya, Iceland, and Alaska. Hughes also made frequent fishing trips, particularly to Scotland, Ireland, and British Columbia. Drawing on these and on his intimate knowledge of his local rivers, the Taw and the Torridge, Hughes wrote *River* (1983):

But water will go on
Issuing from heaven
In dumbness uttering spirit brightness
Through its broken mouth.

Several of the best poems are hymns to Hughes's sacred fish, the heroic salmon.

In December 1984 Hughes was appointed to succeed John Betjeman as poet laureate. The appointment startled the literary world, but many felt, especially after the almost immediate publication of his first laureate poem, 'Rain Charm for the Duchy', that Hughes could transform the office and become virtually the national shaman. These hopes soon faded as the subsequent laureate poems turned out to be mainly arcane tributes to members of the royal family.

Late works In spite of the demands of the laureateship, Hughes continued to give much of his time to working for various charities, answering at length most of the many letters he received, especially from children, and making constructive comments on poems which were sent to him. His letters make wonderful reading, whether they are about his work in progress, other writing, the spirit of place, or more personal and mundane matters.

After Hughes reviewed Max Nicholson's *The Environmental Revolution* in 1970, environmental and ecological concerns came to figure more and more centrally both in his poems and in his life, and led to his working for such organizations as the Atlantic Salmon Trust, Farms for City Children, and the Sacred Earth Drama Trust (which he founded). He won the admiration and friendship of Prince Charles. This aspect of Hughes's work inspired the aerial ballet which was to be the central feature at the Millennium Dome.

Hughes spent the first three months of 1983 writing a long and intense essay on Leonard Baskin, 'The Hanged Man and the Dragonfly', which is essentially a statement of faith in the therapeutic function of art. It was the beginning of a decade in which most of Hughes's energies went into prose, especially *Shakespeare and the Goddess of Complete Being* (1992) and his essays on Eliot and Coleridge, collected with the best of his earlier prose in *Winter Pollen* (1994).

Shakespeare and the Goddess of Complete Being was a colossal undertaking, the culmination of a lifetime's absorption in Shakespeare. He aimed to demonstrate that there exists a paradigm or 'tragic equation' deriving initially from 'Venus and Adonis', which expresses the most profound aspects of Shakespeare's creative psyche and dramatic method, and which can be found behind almost every mature work. The book was received with such virulence by the academic Shakespeare scholars that it seemed these reviewers were more interested in jealously protecting their territory than in exploring Shakespeare's imaginative processes; it was as though an upstart crow had suddenly surpassed them all. Other reviewers were more enthusiastic, one claiming that Hughes was the first adequate reader that Shakespeare had ever had.

Most of the poems Hughes had written between 1983 and 1989 were collected in *Wolfwatching* (1990), which included several poems about his family. Though Hughes had written most of *Birthday Letters* (1998) by 1994, he felt that it would have been kinder to himself had he written and published that poetic account of his relationship with Sylvia Plath much earlier. He also believed that devoting so much of his energies to prose for several years (a defection from the demands of poetry) had destroyed his immune system and made him vulnerable to the cancer which was diagnosed in 1997. In that year Hughes sold most of his vast collection of his own manuscripts to Emory University in the United States.

Hughes's *New Selected Poems* (1995) contained sixteen poems about Sylvia Plath and Assia Wevill which passed unnoticed, so that the publication of eighty-eight poems about Sylvia Plath in *Birthday Letters* came as a shock to most readers, who had assumed that Hughes would maintain to the end his silence on the subject of his relationship with Plath. Here all his reservations about 'confessional' poetry were dropped. Sales were enormous. Most of the anticipated opposition melted away before the candour and vulnerability of the poems. They revealed that both Hughes and Plath had believed that the release of Plath's demon into her poetry would be therapeutic. But that demon, assuming the form of her dead father, had proved more than they could cope with.

Apart from *Birthday Letters*, Hughes's energies in his last years went mainly into 'translations' (he usually worked from literal translations) and work for the theatre: versions of Wedekind's *Spring Awakening* (1995), Lorca's *Blood Wedding* (1996), Racine's *Phèdre* (1998), Aeschylus's *The Oresteia*, and Euripides's *Alcestis* (1999). He also spent a good deal of time recording many of his own works, Eliot's poems, and the whole of his anthology *By Heart* (1997).

In 1998 *Birthday Letters* won the Forward, T. S. Eliot, Whitbread, South Bank, and book of the year prizes. *Tales from Ovid* (1997) also won several awards. *The Oresteia* was prepared for production at the National Theatre, and *Tales from Ovid* was adapted by the Royal Shakespeare Company.

In October 1998 Hughes received the Order of Merit from the queen at Buckingham Palace. Just two weeks later, on 28 October, Hughes died from cancer of the colon in the London Bridge Hospital. He was buried at St Peter's Church, North Tawton, on 3 November. A memorial service, attended by Queen Elizabeth, the queen mother, and the prince of Wales, was held at Westminster Abbey on 14 May 1999.   KEITH SAGAR

Sources personal knowledge (2004) · private information (2004) [Olwyn Hughes, Carol Hughes, John Wholey] · E. Faas, *Ted Hughes: the unaccommodated universe* (1986) · *Paris Review* (spring 1995) · A. Skea, 'Timeline', in K. Sagar, *The laughter of foxes: a study of Ted Hughes* (2000) · C. Fraser, 'Reshaping the past: the personal poetry of Ted Hughes', PhD diss., University of New England, Australia, 1998 · E. Feinstein, *Ted Hughes: the life of a poet* (2001) · A. Stevenson, *Bitter flame: a life of Sylvia Plath* (1989) · b. cert. · m. certs. · d. cert. · K. Sagar and S. Tabor, *Ted Hughes: a bibliography, 1946–1995* (1998)
Archives Col. U., Rare Book and Manuscript Library, corresp. and proofs · Emory University, Atlanta, Georgia, Robert W. Woodruff Library, papers · U. Lpool, letters and papers relating to Seneca's *Oedipus*, literary MSS · University of Victoria, British Columbia, McPherson Library, corresp. and literary MSS | BL, letters to Keith Sagar, Dep. 10003 · BL, letters to Ann Skea | FILM BFI NFTVA, 'Ted Hughes: in his own words', Channel 4, 24 Dec 1998 · BFI NFTVA, *Close up*, BBC 2, 25 Dec 1998 | SOUND BBC WAC · BL NSA
Likenesses R. McKenna, photograph, 1959 (with Sylvia Plath), NPG; *see illus. in* Plath, Sylvia (1932–1963) · H. Cartier-Bresson, photograph, 1971, NPG [*see illus.*] · L. Baskin, ink and wash, 1972, priv. coll. · L. Baskin, fibreglass relief, 1978, priv. coll. · photographs, Hult. Arch.
Wealth at death £1,417,560 gross; £1,196,737 net: administration with will, 1999, *CGPLA Eng. & Wales*

Hughes, Elizabeth Phillips (1851–1925), college head and promoter of education in Wales, was born in Carmarthen on 22 June 1851, the eldest of three daughters and second of five children of John Hughes (1817–1897), a surgeon, and his wife, Anne (d. 1900), the daughter of Philip Phillips. Elizabeth's great-grandfather Samuel Levi Phillips was one of the founders of the banks in Haverfordwest and Milford Haven, and converted from Judaism to Christianity, changing his surname from Levi to Phillips. Her father was prominent in the civic life of Carmarthen as medical officer of health, chairman of the school board and board of guardians, and president of the literary and scientific institute. Her elder brother, Hugh Price *Hughes, became an eminent Methodist preacher.

Little that is definite is known of Elizabeth's early years, except that she was said to have found learning difficult as a child and that she was sent to a private school, Hope House, in Taunton. Like her sister Frances Emily *Hughes, she broke away from the family tradition of Methodism and became an Anglican. She came to the attention of Dorothea Beale, and taught at Cheltenham Ladies' College from 1877 until 1881. There she acquired the qualifications that took her in 1881 to Newnham College, Cambridge, where she got a first in the moral science tripos in 1884, and a second in history in 1885; she also helped to form the Association of Assistant Mistresses.

On going down from Newnham, Elizabeth Hughes was appointed as the first principal of Cambridge Training College, formed by a committee including Frances Buss, Sophie Bryant, and Anne Jemima Clough with the purpose of training university women to teach in girls' secondary schools. In 1949, when the college became a recognized institution of the University of Cambridge, it was renamed Hughes Hall in her honour. The college opened with fourteen students, in cramped premises, in October 1885. Elizabeth Hughes was responsible at first for most of the teaching, and had no assistant except a resident housekeeper. By 1898 the college had been incorporated as a limited liability company; it had acquired new premises, a large lecture hall, a library of 3000 books, a museum, and a gymnasium. There was an academic staff of three besides the principal, and the nucleus of a picture collection acquired by her during her extensive travels. In her forceful evidence to the royal commission on secondary education (Bryce commission) in June 1894, she asserted the value of a theoretical knowledge of teaching and her ideal of a trained profession. She wanted men and women teachers trained together, as well as those seeking to teach in elementary and secondary schools. Her undated pamphlet *The Education of the Majority* included a plea for middle schools for boys and girls between the ages of twelve and sixteen.

Elizabeth Hughes was also a leading figure in education in Wales, and was an advocate of a national educational system. At the Liverpool national eisteddfod in 1884 she won a prize for her essay 'The higher education of girls in Wales', and during a conference of the Cymmrodion Society on education, in 1888, she urged that in any system of Welsh secondary education equal provision should be made for girls and boys. In 1887 she addressed the first meeting of the Association for Promoting the Education of Girls in Wales, of which she became secretary in 1898. She was the only woman member of the committee which drafted the charter for the University of Wales (1893) which, unlike Oxford and Cambridge, placed men and women on an equal footing as regards admission to degrees. In 1894, as a crown nominee, she became one of only six women on the university's court of governors. In her pamphlet *The Educational Future of Wales* (1894) she argued for the democratic principle of education for all, and the Christian principle of excluding none on the grounds of gender or creed.

In 1899 Elizabeth Hughes resigned as principal of the Cambridge college, pleading ill health, and went to live with her younger brother, Colonel John Arthur Hughes (1860–1938), in Barry. She had a private income. She travelled round the world, paid two visits to the United States, and for a time in 1902 taught English in Japan. She was much in demand as a speaker at educational conferences. In 1903, at the conference of the National Union of Women Workers, she criticized the exclusion of women from membership of county councils. She was subsequently co-opted to the Glamorgan county education committee. In 1914 she helped to establish the training college for women teachers in Barry; she also formed the Twentieth Century Club for women in the town. She organized the first Red Cross women's camp, and during the First World War was commandant of a voluntary aid detachment hospital in Glamorgan, for which she was appointed MBE. She received an honorary LLD from the University of Wales in 1920 for her services to Welsh education. She developed an interest in Welsh literature, and

took the bardic name of Merch Myrddin as a reminder of her birthplace. In spite of her fears for her health, she was remarkably energetic (she climbed the Matterhorn at the age of forty-eight). Elizabeth Hughes died at Penrheol, 2 Park Road, Barry, Glamorgan, on 19 December 1925. In appearance, she was described as 'rather short, rotund, and plain' (E. V. Hughes, 68). A medallion in Hughes Hall portrays her with short hair, an aquiline nose, and a determined chin. She was unmarried.   G. H. L. LE MAY, *rev.*

Sources E. V. Hughes, 'A saint and his progeny', *Carmarthenshire Historian*, 7 (1971), 46–68 · M. V. Hughes, *A London girl of the eighties* (1936) · M. Bottrall, *Hughes Hall, 1885–1985* (1985) · *DWB* · W. G. Evans, *Education and female emancipation: the Welsh experience, 1847–1914* (1990)
Likenesses plaster medallion, 1899?, Hughes Hall, Cambridge
Wealth at death £5139 10s. 2d.: probate, 19 Jan 1926, *CGPLA Eng. & Wales*

Hughes, Ezekiel (1766–1849), settler in America, was born at Cwm Carnedd Uchaf, Llanbrynmair, Montgomeryshire, on 22 August 1766, the second son of Richard Hughes (1734/5–1815), freehold farmer, and his wife, Ann Jones. Hughes received some education at Shrewsbury, and in May 1786 he was bound apprentice to John Tibbot, a clock- and watchmaker at Newtown, Montgomeryshire. After completing his apprenticeship in 1789, Hughes established his own clock-making business at Machynlleth. It was during this period that he came under the influence of the republican and radical William Jones (1726–1795) of Llangadfan. Inspired by Jones's dream of establishing a new Welsh community in a land free from religious, social, and political oppression, Hughes, together with his cousin Edward Bebb, George Roberts (1769–1853)—the younger brother of the Revd John Roberts (1767–1834)— and others, decided to emigrate to America. In mid-July 1795 they led a small party of emigrants from Llanbrynmair and walked to Carmarthen, from where they sailed to Bristol. On 6 August they left Bristol and sailed in the *Maria* for Philadelphia, where they arrived on 25 October. After spending the winter in the city, Hughes and Edward Bebb set off in April 1796 on the long trail to the River Ohio. Within three months they had reached Fort Washington, now known as Cincinnati, a town which Hughes estimated to be 'as large as Machynlleth (a town in Wales of about 800 inhabitants)' (Peate, 'Ezekiel Hughes's autobiography', 133). There, near the Miami River, Hughes and Edward Bebb (whose son William Bebb became governor of Ohio) bought 100 acres of land, which they began to cultivate. In September 1802 Hughes returned to Wales and in May 1803 married Margaret Bebb of Brynaerau, Llanbrynmair. The couple returned to America, but within less than a year Margaret died, and was buried in the first grave to be opened at Berea. In 1808 Hughes married Mary Ewing, a native of Pennsylvania, and they had nine children.

Hughes undertook many important public and official roles in his adopted country. In 1805 the governor of Ohio appointed him and two others to plan and construct a new road from the mouth of the Miami River to the town of Hamilton, and the following year he was appointed the first justice of the peace in the district. As the years went by he bought a great deal of land which he leased at reasonable rates to his tenants. Hughes also generously supported the religious life of the district. He played an instrumental role in the establishment of the Welsh Congregational chapel at Paddy's Run in 1803, some 10 miles from his home. In 1828 he became a member at Berea, a Presbyterian chapel which was erected in 1822 upon land which he himself donated. William Henry Harrison, who later became president of the USA, attended the same class as Hughes at Berea Sunday school, and the two became great personal friends. As well as helping to build the chapel, Hughes was largely responsible for supporting the work of the ministry.

Despite suffering a serious fall in 1820 which left him lame, Hughes continued to serve his church and his community for many years. He was an extremely popular man who was fondly remembered by his tenants and by the dozens of Welsh emigrant families whom he warmly welcomed to the area. He died on 2 September 1849 at Miami, Ohio, and was buried the following day at Berea cemetery. At his funeral he was described as 'a friend of the poor, a true patriot, and a loyal Christian' (*Y Cenhadwr Americanaidd*, Dec 1849). The tale of his eventful journey from Llanbrynmair to Ohio was fictionalized by W. Ambrose Bebb (1894–1955) in the novel *Dial y tir* ('The land's revenge'), published in 1945.

MARI A. WILLIAMS

Sources 'Biographical sketch: Ezekiel Hughes', *The Cambrian* (May–June 1882), 108–12 · NL Wales, MS 9260 A · NL Wales, MS 491 E, fol. 20 · *DWB* · J. E. Lloyd, R. T. Jenkins, and W. L. Davies, eds., *Y bywgraffiadur Cymreig hyd 1940* (1953) · *Y Cenhadwr Americanaidd* (Dec 1849) · *Y Cronicl* (Feb 1850) · I. C. Peate, 'Ezekiel Hughes's autobiography', *Montgomeryshire Collections*, 70 (1982), 131–3 · I. C. Peate, 'John Tibbot, clock and watch maker', *Montgomeryshire Collections*, 48 (1943–4), 176–85 · I. C. Peate, *Clock and watch makers in Wales* (1975) · G. A. Williams, *The search for Beulah Land: the Welsh and the Atlantic revolution* (1980) · C. Taylor, 'Paddy's Run: a Welsh community in Ohio', *Welsh History Review / Cylchgrawn Hanes Cymru*, 11 (1982–3), 302–16 · non-parochial registers, PRO, RG4 4068
Archives NL Wales
Likenesses carte-de-visite (after print), NL Wales · engraving, repro. in 'Biographical sketch: Ezekiel Hughes'

Hughes [*married name* Webb-Peploe], **Frances Emily** (1855–1927), principal of a women's university hall of residence, was born on 14 April 1855, one of the five children to survive infancy of John Hughes (1817–1897), surgeon, of Carmarthen, and his wife, Anne Phillips (*d.* 1900). Frances's eldest brother, Hugh Price *Hughes, became an eminent Wesleyan minister, and her elder sister, Elizabeth Phillips *Hughes, was appointed first principal of the Cambridge Training College for Women Teachers in 1885. Both she and Frances became Anglicans. It is possible that she was educated at Hope House, Taunton (like her sister), and went on to the North London Collegiate School.

Frances Hughes's significance arises from the controversy surrounding her role as lady principal of the women's hall of residence at Bangor. The University College of North Wales, Bangor, had been founded in 1884,

and from the start had been co-educational. The establishment of women's halls, providing a healthy, studious environment and allaying parental fears about unsupervised boarding-houses, was seen as an integral part of the development of women's education at the time. The North London Collegiate School promised a supply of students to Bangor on condition that a women's hall was established, and an independent limited company was formed to provide a hall, opened in 1886, of which Frances was appointed lady principal. The college registrar noted it was 'something in her favour that she is the sister of Miss Hughes of Cambridge' (W. C. Davies to D. Davies, 25 July 1886, Dilys Glynne Jones MSS). Frances was responsible for supervising female residents and ensuring a family environment. She took her pastoral role seriously, asserting that 'The College deals with character and conduct; the Hall, if it is to fulfil its aim, must deal also with moral tone' (F. Hughes, letter, *The Times*, 1 May 1893). In 1887 about one half of the fifty-eight registered students were women, some of them 'ladies of position … whose very presence gives tone to the classes' (W. C. Davies to D. Davies, 7 Dec 1887, Dilys Glynne Jones MSS). Balancing the requirements of the ladies of 'class', while avoiding 'pauperizing the Welsh girls', was a difficult task, and soon tensions were evident.

Rules prohibited hall students from visiting those living out in lodgings, and restricted out-students visiting the hall. In 1892 Frances spoke in confidence to Mrs Elspeth Rhys, the wife of Professor Rhys, the Celtic scholar of Jesus College, Oxford, expressing concerns that their daughter had been keeping company with an older student, Miss Violet Osborn, who had left the hall to take up residence in town. Violet had apparently claimed that one of the 'young professors' had 'treated her with familiarity', quoting Elspeth Rhys as an authority on the professor's reputation in such matters (F. Hughes, letter, *The Times*, 1 May 1893). But Frances questioned Violet's veracity, reliability, and intentions. This soon became the talking point of the university. Male members of staff rushed to defend the honour of Miss Osborn, and friends in high places were contacted. At a meeting of the governing committee of the hall Frances was pressed to reveal the basis of her concern but, once again, words uttered 'in the strictest confidence' soon became public property. A senate committee appointed to inquire into the matter concluded that 'charges of untruthfulness, lack of decorum, and impurity of mind' (special report of the senate enquiry laid before council, 21 Dec 1892, University of Wales, Bangor, Archives) were without foundation, and that 'Miss Osborn's conduct and character had been those of a refined and honorable woman' (ibid.). The university senate resolved that unless Frances Hughes was dismissed or resigned the university would withdraw recognition from the hall. The hall committee refused, the university withheld the licence, and the hall was perforce wound up.

The 'Bangor dispute' had received widespread publicity, elicited numerous letters to *The Times*, questions in parliament, calls for a public inquiry, and led to two libel cases.

Frances Hughes won £350 in damages from the *Weekly Dispatch*, but in cross-examination it was alleged that she favoured Anglicans over nonconformists, and this led to counter-claims of religious and political bigotry, in turn denied by the college authorities. Although the actual divisions were not clearly drawn, for there were churchmen and nonconformists on both sides of the controversy, the case provided ammunition deployed in the House of Lords by the Welsh bishops in opposing the University of Wales charter. In Frances's opinion 'the two professors'—her most senior opponents—had taken advantage of sectarian and political bias against her. Hugh Price Hughes was angered that 'in the heated political and ecclesiastical atmosphere' then prevailing in north Wales, rumours were fomented, and that his sister, 'a patriotic Welshwoman', had suffered for being an episcopalian and a conservative (H. P. Hughes, letter, *North Wales Chronicle*, 22 April 1893).

Frances's supporters believed that she had suffered 'a grave injustice', and even her opponents conceded she was a woman of courage and intellect. Her aim was to see women enter higher education on an equal footing with men, but at the same time retaining their 'womanliness'. In a letter to *The Times* (1 May 1893) she wrote that she

> felt that sometimes during the student days of women the softer and essentially womanly side of life, is somewhat neglected, and my one hope when I came to Bangor was to round off the earnest student life of my girls with the softening influence of home life.

Of the two professors one, Edward Vernon Arnold, married Violet Osborn in 1894, and the other, Keri Evans, resigned his academic post following continued rumours of 'impropriety'.

Frances Hughes left Bangor in the autumn of 1893, and on 6 February 1895 married the Revd Francis Hanmer Webb-Peploe (1867/8–1944), who was twelve years her junior; he was the son of the Revd Hanmer William Webb-Peploe and his wife, Frances Emily Lush. Frances was to spend the rest of her life as the wife of an Anglican clergyman. She died at Christ Church vicarage, Cheltenham, on 12 February 1927.   PAMELA F. MICHAEL

Sources W. G. Evans, 'A Victorian cause célèbre', *Planet*, 102 (1993–4), 80–86 · J. G. Williams, *The University College of North Wales: foundations 1884–1927* (1985) · W. G. Evans, *Education and female emancipation: the Welsh experience, 1847–1914* (1990) · T. Richards, *Atgofion Cardi* (1960) · *The Times* (28 April–26 May 1893) · *The Times* (26 Aug 1893) · *The Times* (12 May 1927) · *North Wales Chronicle* · *Liverpool Mercury* · *Cambrian News* · *Educational Review* (June 1893) · H. R. Reichel, *The Bangor controversy: a statement of facts* (1893) · student records, U. Wales, Bangor, MS 16444 · college minutes, U. Wales, Bangor · E. V. Jones, 'A saint and his progeny', *Carmarthen Journal*, 8 (1971) · D. P. Hughes, *The life of Hugh Price Hughes* (1904) · Crockford · Venn, *Alum. Cant.* · U. Wales, Bangor, Dilys Glynne Jones MSS · staff record, U. Wales, Bangor

Wealth at death £5304 2*s*. 8*d*.: resworn probate, 6 May 1927, *CGPLA Eng. & Wales*

Hughes, Francis (1666/7–1744), singer, appears to have made his stage début as a countertenor at Drury Lane theatre early in 1700, when he sang music by Daniel Purcell in John Oldmixon's dramatic opera *The Grove*. During the next five years he sang in plays and entr'acte entertainments at Drury Lane and performed in concerts at the theatre and in Hampstead Wells, York Buildings, and other venues. In January 1705 he created the hero, Ormondo, in the first all-sung English opera in the Italian style, Thomas Clayton's *Arsinoe*, which was very popular for two seasons. In his preface to *Arsinoe*, Clayton claimed that the singers were 'the Best that were to be found in England'. Hughes went on to sing Turnus in the première of the English adaptation of Giovanni Bononcini's *Camilla* (30 March 1706) and King Henry II in Clayton's unsuccessful *Rosamond* (4 March 1707). However, in the revival of *Camilla* in 1707 he lost his role to the recently arrived Italian castrato Valentini, who sang the part in Italian. For the pasticcio opera *Thomyris* (1 April 1707), Valentini and Hughes appear to have alternated the leading role of Orontes, each singing in his own language, but from autumn 1707 the part was monopolized by Valentini and Hughes's operatic career came to an end. He continued to perform English stage music at Drury Lane until January 1708, when, by the lord chamberlain's decree, all singers and musicians were transferred to the Haymarket theatre, where only operas were to be performed.

Hughes then left the stage, and sang in the Chapel Royal from 1 July 1708. He joined the choir of St Paul's Cathedral in September 1708 and became a lay vicar at Westminster Abbey in 1715. He retained all three positions until his death. Handel wrote for Hughes in the 1713 ode for the birthday of Queen Anne, the Utrecht Te Deum and Jubilate (1714), and several anthems, including those for George II's coronation (1727). He was probably the 'Hues' who was accused of 'Assaulting & refusing his Ldp Entrance into the Choir' for a public rehearsal of the coronation music (Burrows, 473). On 1 October 1730 Hughes was given a second place at the Chapel Royal, because of 'his extraordinary skill in singing, & his great usefulness to the Choir in the performance of verse Anthems' (Ashbee and Harley, 1.222). He then sang there all year, rather than for the usual half-year, and was the first singer to be employed in this way. John Hawkins noted that Hughes, with his 'very strong counter-tenor voice, could with ease break a drinking-glass' (Hawkins, 217). In 1742 Hughes was excused attendance at the Chapel Royal on account of his poor health. He died on 16 March 1744, aged seventy-seven, and was buried, as he had requested in his will, in the cloisters of Westminster Abbey, on 21 March.

OLIVE BALDWIN and THELMA WILSON

Sources W. Van Lennep and others, eds., *The London stage, 1660–1800*, pt 1: *1660–1700* (1965) · E. L. Avery, ed., *The London stage, 1660–1800*, pt 2: *1700–1729* (1960) · A. Ashbee, ed., *Records of English court music*, 2 (1987) · A. Ashbee, ed., *Records of English court music*, 5 (1991) · A. Ashbee and J. Harley, eds., *The cheque books of the Chapel Royal*, 2 vols. (2000) · M. Tilmouth, 'A calendar of references to music in newspapers published in London and the provinces (1660–1719)', *Royal Musical Association Research Chronicle*, 1 (1961), i–vii, 1–107 · D. Hunter, *Opera and song books published in England, 1703–1726* (1997) · B. Baselt, *Thematisch-systematisches Verzeichnis* (1984), vol. 2 of *Händel-Handbuch*, ed. W. Eisen and M. Eisen (1978–85) · D. Burrows, 'Handel and the 1727 coronation', *MT*, 118 (1977), 469–73 · O. E. Deutsch, *Dokumente zu Leben und Schaffen* (1985), vol. 4 of *Händel-Handbuch*, ed. W. Eisel and M. Eisel (1978–85) · J. Hawkins, *A general* *history of the science and practice of music*, 5 (1776) · Burney, *Hist. mus.*, vol. 4 · A. Ashbee and D. Lasocki, eds., *A biographical dictionary of English court musicians, 1485–1714*, 1 (1998) · T. Clayton, preface, in P. A. Motteux, *Arsinoe, queen of Cyprus: an opera, after the Italian manner, all sung* (1705) · J. Milhous and R. D. Hume, eds., *Vice Chamberlain Coke's theatrical papers, 1706–1715* (1982) · J. L. Chester, ed., *The marriage, baptismal, and burial registers of the collegiate church or abbey of St Peter, Westminster*, Harleian Society, 10 (1876) · will, PRO, PROB 11/732, sig. 72

Wealth at death see will, PRO, PROB 11/732, sig. 72

Hughes, George (1603/4–1667), clergyman and ejected minister, was born in Southwark. He matriculated from Corpus Christi College, Oxford, on 28 June 1620, aged sixteen, and after graduating BA on 19 February 1623 he became a fellow of Pembroke College and proceeded MA on 23 June 1625. He held curacies near Oxford before becoming a lecturer at All Hallows, Bread Street, London, in 1628. He proceeded BD in 1633 but was suspended by Laud in 1636, accused of stealing his neighbour's flock, of refusing to use the sign of the cross in baptism, and of not bowing to the altar. He contemplated emigrating but was persuaded to stay by John Dodd, rector of Fawsley, who obtained a chaplaincy for him with Lord Brooke at Warwick Castle. While there he married a daughter of a former sheriff of Coventry, whose family name was Packstone. In 1638 he was presented to the living of Tavistock by the earl of Bedford, who also made him his chaplain. Hughes instituted a lecture there as well as being vicar.

During the first civil war, while Exeter was held by the parliamentarians, Hughes was one of the puritans drawn in to preach in the city. He did so in July 1643, when the city was under siege, and on its surrender to Prince Maurice in September withdrew with the defeated forces, although his wife had recently died in Exeter and was buried there. He was elected vicar of Plymouth on 21 October 1643 and instituted on 3 February 1644 by a commission acting on behalf of the absent Bishop Ralph Brownrigg; sixteen years later, at the Restoration, this secured his position against another claimant. During the siege of Plymouth in 1644 Hughes prepared for publication extracts of his sermons, drawn together into *A Dry Rod Blooming* 'to be both a remedy against present pressures, and an Antidote against the malignity of future troubles of the flesh'. His vicarage was obviously severely damaged during the siege as he resigned the property to the corporation in 1646 for an annuity of £200. His work on Genesis and part of Exodus (eventually printed in 1672) gives some idea of his weighty sermons on Sunday mornings. On 26 May 1647 he preached before the Commons on their fast day.

Hughes was active in drawing together the ministers in Devon. In 1648 he organized and wrote *The Joint Testimonie of the Ministers of Devon* and was the first of its seventy-four signatories. It included 'a brief Confutation of the Errors, Heresies and Blasphemies of these times' and supported the solemn league and covenant. In 1655 he was the prime mover, with Thomas Ford, in organizing the Exeter assembly, which drew together ministers regardless of their particular persuasion. At the first general assembly on 18 October 1655 they divided themselves into four divisions to meet every quarter in their own areas and to divide further into smaller groups meeting every six weeks. The west Devon area meeting was held at Hughes's house. He was the moderator of the next assembly in May 1656, yet managed to maintain friendships with Anglicans both then and after the Restoration. In 1659 he refused to read the warrant declaring the Booth rebels traitors.

Hughes retained his living of St Andrew, Plymouth, in 1660, owing to the manner of his institution, and was among those suggested by Richard Baxter for a bishopric. However, the following year his second wife, Rebecca Upton, died, and in 1662, when he failed to give the assent to the Book of Common Prayer required by the Act of Uniformity, he was ejected. He continued to preach and was so popular that when the people attending the bishop's visitation at Totnes in 1663 heard that Hughes was in town they left the bishop to accompany Hughes. In 1665 Hughes and Thomas Martin, his brother-in-law and assistant at Plymouth, were arrested as 'sometime publique now private perverters in this Towne' (Calamy, *Abridgement*, 2). Both were imprisoned on St Nicholas Island for nine months in such severe conditions that Hughes developed dropsy and scurvy. He was offered his liberty on the security of £2000 and an undertaking not to live within 20 miles of Plymouth. The security was paid by his friends without his knowledge and so he was released. He lived in Kingsbridge until his death on 3 July 1667, attended by a young ejected minister, John Quick, who left an account of him. He was survived by his children from his first marriage—a son, Obadiah (*d*. 1704), later a nonconformist preacher, and two daughters, one married to John Howe, the ejected minister. Hughes was buried in Kingsbridge.

MARY WOLFFE

Sources Calamy rev. · E. Calamy, ed., *An abridgement of Mr. Baxter's history of his life and times, with an account of the ministers, &c., who were ejected after the Restauration of King Charles II*, 2nd edn, 2 vols. (1713) · P. S. Seaver, *The puritan lectureships: the politics of religious dissent, 1560–1662* (1970) · *The nonconformist's memorial … originally written by … Edmund Calamy*, ed. S. Palmer, [3rd edn], 2 (1802) · R. N. Worth, 'Puritanism in Devon and the Exeter assembly', *Report and Transactions of the Devonshire Association*, 9 (1877), 250–91 · J. I. Dredge, 'A few sheaves of Devon bibliography, pt 1', *Report and Transactions of the Devonshire Association*, 21 (1889), 498–548 · E. Calamy, *A continuation of the account of the ministers … who were ejected and silenced after the Restoration in 1660*, 2 vols. (1727) · A. Brockett, *Nonconformity in Exeter, 1650–1875* (1962) · Wood, *Ath. Oxon.*, new edn · Foster, *Alum. Oxon.* · R. S. Paul, *The assembly of the Lord: politics and religion in the Westminster assembly and the 'Grand debate'* (1985) · I. Gowers, 'The clergy in Devon, 1641–62', *Tudor and Stuart Devon … essays presented to Joyce Youings*, ed. T. Gray, M. Rowe, and A. Erskine (1992), 200–26 · M. Stoyle, *From deliverance to destruction: rebellion and civil war in an English city* (1996) · S. K. Roberts, *Recovery and restoration in an English county: Devon local administration, 1646–1670* (1985) · *Calendar of the correspondence of Richard Baxter*, ed. N. H. Keeble and G. F. Nuttall, 2 vols. (1991) · I. Gower, 'Puritanism in the county of Devon, 1570 to 1641', MA diss., University of Exeter, 1970

Likenesses J. Caldwell, line engraving, NPG

Wealth at death tenancy of ninety-nine years in house in Plymouth; bequest of £100 to daughter; two bequests of £20, one of £30, and £10 for poor of Plymouth: will

Hughes, Goronwy [Ronw] **Moelwyn** (1897–1955), lawyer and politician, was born in Llwyn Onn, Cardigan, on 6 October 1897. Baptized Goronwy, he was always known as Ronw. A Welsh-speaker, he was the eldest of the six children of the Revd Dr John Gruffydd Moelwyn Hughes (1866–1944), a former moderator of the Welsh Presbyterian church, and his wife, Anna Maria Lewis. After attending council schools in Cardigan, he entered University College Wales, Aberystwyth, where his studies were interrupted by the First World War. While serving with the West Yorkshire regiment he was wounded in 1916. He transferred to the Royal Flying Corps and served as a pilot (1917–19). After the war he returned to Aberystwyth and graduated BA, before going on to Downing College, Cambridge, where he graduated LLB, obtained first-class honours in the law tripos, and won the chancellor's gold medal in English law. He joined the Inner Temple and was called to the bar in 1922.

Moelwyn Hughes practised on the northern circuit, where his reputation in transport and commercial law grew rapidly (he once successfully represented Billy Butlin in litigation over property which subsequently became the Pwllheli holiday camp). He also lectured in international law at the London School of Economics and in commercial law for the Law Society, and was an examiner for the Council of Legal Education and for London University. He wrote extensively, and edited the seventh edition of Lord Birkenhead's *International Law* (1928), as well as contributing the sections on agency, bills of exchange, money, and moneylending to the 1931–5 edition of *Halsbury's Laws of England*. He also wrote jointly with Dingle Foot a standard work on rail and road traffic legislation. This ensured the continued demand for his services at hearings of various transport tribunals. On 11 May 1929 he married Louise Mary (Lulu; 1902–1973), the only child of (Frederick) Arthur *Greer, lord justice of appeal. They had two sons and one daughter.

Brought up in the Welsh radical tradition (he was active in the Fabian Society in his earlier days), Moelwyn Hughes unsuccessfully contested two general elections for the Liberal Party: at West Rhondda in 1929 and at Southport in 1931. He joined the Labour Party in November 1934 and stood unsuccessfully as its candidate for Cardiganshire in 1935. He was, however, elected unopposed at a by-election at Carmarthen in March 1941 and held the seat until his defeat by a Liberal at the general election in 1945. He made a modest contribution to parliamentary proceedings during those war years, inquiring, for example, about school funding under Rab Butler's Education Act 1944 and condemning excessive costs in undefended divorce proceedings. He returned to parliament for North Islington in 1950 but retired owing to ill health in the autumn of 1951. There had been speculation whether he might have become one of the law officers in 1950 (he had worked with Sir Hartley Shawcross on war crimes prosecutions) but events surrounding one of the public offices he held suggest that this would have been unlikely. During his first spell as an MP he was appointed king's counsel (1943)

and during his second he was made a bencher of his inn (1950).

Outside parliament during the momentous years of the first Attlee government, Moelwyn Hughes was none the less extremely active in public affairs. He was chairman of the Greater London water inquiry (1947), special assistant commissioner for Wales under the Local Government Boundary Commission (1946–9), and recorder of Bolton (1946–53). The latter no doubt prompted his appointment as commissioner for inquiry into the Burnden Park, Bolton, football disaster in 1946, when thirty-three spectators were crushed to death by the sheer pressure of numbers in the stadium. In analysing the circumstances, which in many respects uncannily rehearsed the Hillsborough disaster in 1989, Moelwyn Hughes's report attributed the tragedy to the unanticipated size of the crowd (85,000 as against the expected 50,000), the admission of too many spectators to the fatal enclosure, unauthorized entries, and, perhaps crucially, the lack of machinery to ensure proper co-operation between police and club (since turnstile officials and keys were not readily available). Bolton Wanderers Football Club itself was not blamed but the club felt a great deal of remorse. Anticipating the post-Hillsborough disaster legislation, Moelwyn Hughes recommended that football grounds be made subject to safety licensing and that a centralized system at each ground be installed to count the number of spectators present. No legislation followed, merely an inadequate system of voluntary licensing for all grounds of at least 10,000 capacity.

As chairman of the cotton manufacturing commission from 1946 to 1949 Moelwyn Hughes was aware of the need to improve industrial productivity. To this end he suggested that where factories could demonstrate that redeployment had occurred, incentive payment schemes (which the official papers called the 'Moelwyn Hughes system') might be introduced. They would replace the industry-wide uniform price list legally enforceable by orders issued under the Cotton Manufacturing Industry (Temporary Provisions) Act 1934 to prevent undercutting by employers. The scheme anticipated the later growth of plant-level bargaining.

From April 1946 to 31 January 1950 Moelwyn Hughes chaired the Catering Wages Commission. His resignation from that body dovetailed with his campaigning as Labour Party candidate for North Islington at the general election of February 1950. However, the timing hides the controversy which would undoubtedly have precipitated his resignation in any case. The sixth report of the commission, published in December 1949, had criticized what it considered to be inadequate government steps to support and encourage the dollar-earning potential of the British tourist industry, pointing to the absence of what later generations would call 'joined-up government'. The report quoted from correspondence passing, among others, between the president of the Board of Trade, Harold Wilson, and the commission, and appeared to suggest that the government had ignored the commission's recommendations. A number of ministers, including Wilson and George Isaacs, the minister of labour, took exception to what they claimed was a breach of confidence in publishing the correspondence, and Isaacs wrote to Moelwyn Hughes condemning his alleged indiscretion. It was an accusation which hurt him deeply and, more importantly, which he vehemently rejected. One department, he insisted, was aware that the correspondence, drafted in formal style, would be published and none was marked private and confidential. On his resignation, the ministry press release announcing his departure gave no hint of the dispute. His replacement pro tem was Sir John Forster, president of the industrial court.

Moelwyn Hughes was also a member of the Rushcliffe committee on legal aid and advice, appointed in 1944, which unanimously recommended a publicly funded system of legal aid. The principle was eventually adopted in the Legal Aid and Advice Act 1949. Both the Society of Labour Lawyers and the Haldane Society of Socialist Lawyers, of which he had been a prominent member, presented to the inquiry evidence which did not fundamentally challenge the role of private legal practice, although they favoured wider lay involvement in the administration of the scheme than eventually obtained.

Moelwyn Hughes accepted a range of appointments in the public service, where his professional skills could be displayed and where he could bring forward fresh ideas; his useful and thoughtful analysis of the Bolton disaster of 1946 was again cited, many years after his death, in the unfortunate circumstances following the Hillsborough, Heysel, and Bradford City football disasters involving English fans in the 1980s. He died at 6 Heather Gardens, Golders Green, Middlesex, of heart failure, on 1 November 1955, and was cremated three days later at Golders Green crematorium.   G. R. RUBIN

Sources *The Times* (15 Sept 1950) · *The Times* (2 Nov 1955) · *WWW* · PRO, BT 64/1249 · PRO, LAB 10/801 · S. Inglis, *The football grounds of Great Britain* (1987) · PRO, ED 34/3 · *WWBMP*, vol. 4 · R. I. Morgan, 'The introduction of civil legal aid in England and Wales, 1914–1949', *Twentieth Century British History*, 5 (1994), 38–76 · P. Scraton, *Hillsborough: the truth* (1999) · private information (2004) [family] · b. cert. · m. cert. · d. cert.
Wealth at death £1437 14s. 1d.: probate, 1955

Hughes, Griffith (*bap.* 1707, *d.* 1758?), Church of England clergyman and naturalist, was baptized on 29 April 1707 in Tywyn, Merioneth, the son of Edward Hughes and Bridget, his wife. He matriculated at St John's College, Oxford, in May 1729. Following a recommendation to the Society for the Propagation of the Gospel of his suitability for missionary work, he left St John's in 1732 without taking his degree and was ordained priest. From 1732 to 1736 he was an Anglican missionary in the scattered, rural community of Radnor, Pennsylvania. From 1736 to 1748, and possibly nominally into the 1750s, he was rector of St Lucy's, Barbados. Each tenure was marked by differences of opinion with the congregation and also coincided with the preparation of a book for publication. For the Welsh immigrants of Pennsylvania, Hughes produced in 1735 an edition of Welsh devotional meditations, a reprint with additions of John Morgan's *Myfyrdodau bucheddol ar y*

pedwar peth diweddaf, originally published in London in 1714. This was the fourth Welsh book published in America.

In Barbados, Hughes developed the idea of publishing a book on the island's natural history. In 1743 he visited London with the intention of promoting this work and ingratiated himself with the leading scientists of the day, men such as Sir Hans Sloane and Martin Folkes. Before returning home, he had arranged for the leading artist George Dionysius Ehret to prepare plates for his book. Because his plan was both interesting and ambitious, on Hughes's return to England in 1748 he was elected a fellow of the Royal Society as well as receiving his BA and MA degrees from his old college.

The Natural History of Barbados, a lavish production in folio, with coloured plates and a most impressive list of about a thousand subscribers (with Hughes as publisher/author), appeared in the spring of 1750. It was not well received among his fellow scientists, and was described as lacking in both accuracy and scholarship. Thenceforward, Griffith Hughes disappeared from prominence. His name disappeared from the list of fellows of the Royal Society in 1758, and it is assumed that he died in that year.

RAYMOND B. DAVIES

Sources F. J. Dallett jun., 'Griffith Hughes dissected', *Journal of the Barbados Museum and Historical Society*, 23/1 (1955), 3–29 · E. M. Shilstone, 'Rev. Griffith Hughes', *Journal of the Barbados Museum and Historical Society*, 19/3 (1952), 102–6 · W. Williams, 'More about the first three Welsh books printed in America', *National Library of Wales Journal*, 3 (1943–4), 19–22 · J. Clement, 'Griffith Hughes: S.P.G. missionary to Pennsylvania and famous 18th century naturalist', *Historical Magazine of the Protestant Episcopal Church*, 17 (1948), 151–63 · 'The natural history of Barbados in ten books, by the Reverend Mr Griffith Hughes, rector of St Lucy's parish in the said island, F.R.S.', *Monthly Review*, 3 (1750), 197–206 [review] · *DWB* · R. P. Stearns, 'Colonial fellows of the Royal Society of London, 1661–1788', *Osiris*, 8 (1948), 73–121 · Tywyn, bishop's transcripts, 1695–1713, NL Wales
Archives Society for the Propagation of the Gospel, London, letters [transcripts in L. Cong.] | NHM, letters to Hans Sloane
Likenesses line engraving, repro. in G. Hughes, *The natural history of Barbados* (1750)

Hughes, Henry (*b.* 1602/3, *d.* in or after 1650), physician and poet, was the son of Andrew Hughes of Wilsborough, Kent, and graduated BA from St John's College, Oxford, in 1623, aged twenty. According to Evans 'he became Doctor of Physic to the Prince Elector [Charles Lewis, elector palatine], ran away from his wife, Katherine, to Holland in 1642, and returned, perhaps with Queen Henrietta Maria, in 1643' (Evans, 222). Some of these details are confirmed in a letter written by Hughes to Sir Richard Browne, English resident in Paris, towards the end of 1644 in which he claims he has 'bin labouringe three yeares to get to the King but cannot handsomely as I would'. In trying to render the king service

> I had provided six Horse and armes but I was betraid and they seaz'd on, myselfe committed prisoner; but by vertue of a Paper I had (wch stilde me Prince Electors Physitian in ordinary) I got leave to goe to the Hague, where I remaine, expecting some good Occasion to carry me over. (BL, Add. MS 15858)

He offers to join the force which the queen was intending to send across to assist the royal cause 'if you can whisper a Command for me out of my Lord Jermins Eare. I have many Freinds theare will second you, my Lady Denbigh especially'.

It is difficult to work out quite what this signifies with regard to Hughes's serving the queen, bearing in mind his poem *On the Queen's Landing at Burlington* (22 February 1643) which seems to have been written as an eyewitness. He was back in England in 1649, however, for in October he was arrested in connection with some trouble in Essex but soon released. In January 1650 he was again being held in custody as a 'recusant and delinquent'. Matters relating to his deceased wife Katherine's estate came up before the committee for advance of money in March and April the same year, by which time (or soon after) he was said to be in The Hague. In all probability he died there, perhaps soon after, since he never seems to have returned to England or to have had further dealings with Henry Lawes, who set many of his lyrics to music. If he had still been alive he might well have contributed commendatory verses to one or more of Lawes's books of *Ayres and Dialogues*, published in 1653, 1655, and 1658.

Hughes was named as author of five lyrics in Lawes's second book of airs, and thirty-one in the third. Some are found in manuscript copies, one or two were published in miscellanies like *Wit's Interpreter* (1655) and *Sportive Wit* (1656), while others were misattributed—'I prithee send me back my heart', for example, came out in Sir John Suckling's *Last Remains* (1659); a few have been anthologized in modern times, for example in J. Wardroper's *Love and Drollery* (1969). On the whole they adopt the conventional idioms of Platonic love poetry—mildly ironic addresses to Chloris (Henrietta Maria), gently sentimental complaints of Amintor (Charles I)—deftly handled and delicately expressed in regular, well-shaped verse. It would not be going too far to say that as a lyric poet in this vein he stands comparison with Waller and other 'cavalier poets'.   IAN SPINK

Sources W. M. Evans, *Henry Lawes, musician and friend of poets* (1941) · I. Spink, *Henry Lawes: cavalier songwriter* (2000), 82–6 · Foster, *Alum. Oxon.* · M. A. E. Green, ed., *Calendar of the proceedings of the committee for advance of money, 1642–1656*, 2–3, PRO (1888), 1151, 1194

Hughes, Henry George (1810–1872), judge, was born in Capel Street, Dublin, on 22 August 1810, the eldest son of James Hughes, solicitor, of Dublin, and his wife, Margaret, *née* Morton, the daughter of Trevor Stannus Morton, a Dublin solicitor. He was taught at a private school in Jervis Street, Dublin, and on 17 October 1825 he entered Trinity College, Dublin, where he did not take a degree. In Hilary term 1830 he was admitted a student of the King's Inns, Dublin, and on 14 June 1832 he entered Gray's Inn, London; he was called to the Irish bar in Michaelmas term 1834. In 1836 he married Sarah Isabella L'Estrange; they had two daughters.

Hughes devoted himself almost exclusively to the chancery courts, and in 1837 he published *Practice at the Court of Chancery, Ireland*. He soon built up an extensive practice and became an expert on the then complex details of

chancery procedure. In 1844 he took silk, and as a leader of his circuit he continued to enjoy a very large practice, especially in the rolls court. In 1850 Lord John Russell appointed him solicitor-general for Ireland, an office which Hughes held until the fall of the ministry in 1852. The Ecclesiastical Titles Act, a protest against what were felt by some to be the outrageous claims of the newly re-established Catholic hierarchy of England and Wales, was passed during this time. Although a Roman Catholic, Hughes brought his children up as protestants. His commitment to non-denominational education and his connections with the government, combined with what was seen by some as his apostasy, made him unpopular among some fellow Catholics. He nevertheless received the support of the Roman Catholic bishop and clergy when he (unsuccessfully) contested Cavan in 1855. In 1856 he was elected MP for Longford, but he failed to be re-elected in 1857. In 1858 he was again solicitor-general for Ireland in Lord Palmerston's administration, and in 1859, on the return of Lord Palmerston to power, Hughes was appointed a baron of the court of exchequer in succession to Baron Richards.

Hughes was a rare example of a chancery lawyer who also made a successful common-law judge. He continued as a member of the court of exchequer until his death in Bray, co. Wicklow, on 22 July 1872 and he was buried in Dean's Grange cemetery, Dublin.

J. D. FITZGERALD, *rev.* SINÉAD AGNEW

Sources F. E. Ball, *The judges in Ireland, 1221–1921*, 2 (1926), 296–7, 304, 330, 362–3 · Burtchaell & Sadleir, *Alum. Dubl.*, 2nd edn · Boase, *Mod. Eng. biog.* · J. S. Crone, *A concise dictionary of Irish biography*, rev. edn (1937), 99 · *Annual Register* (1872), 158 · E. Lucas, *The life of Frederick Lucas MP* (1886), 2.197 · J. Foster, *The register of admissions to Gray's Inn, 1521–1889, together with the register of marriages in Gray's Inn chapel, 1695–1754* (privately printed, London, 1889) · Allibone, *Dict.* · *Irish Law Times and Solicitors' Journal* (27 July 1872), 404
Wealth at death under £8000: probate, 16 Aug 1872, *CGPLA Ire.*

Hughes, Herbert Delauney [Billy] (1914–1995), adult educationist and politician, was born on 7 September 1914 at 47 The Mall, Swindon, Wiltshire, the only child of Arthur Percy Hughes, secondary school teacher, and his wife, Maggie Ellen Delauney, former elementary school headteacher. When he was six the family moved to Bakewell, Derbyshire, because of Hughes's ill health. After being taught at home until the age of eleven, he attended Bakewell grammar school and then was a boarder at Manchester Warehousemen's and Clerks' Orphans School at Cheadle Hulme, Cheshire. With a county major and a state scholarship he entered Balliol College, Oxford, in 1933 and graduated with a second-class degree in modern history in 1936. In 1935 he was chair of the Oxford University Labour Club. During this time he was a member of G. D. H. Cole's circle, helped with soup kitchens in Oxford for hunger marchers from south Wales, and later took part in demonstrations in the Rhondda.

From Oxford, Billy Hughes went to Manchester University to train as a secondary school teacher, but he moved to London after only one term to take up the post of assistant secretary of the New Fabian Research Bureau (NFRB) which had been set up by G. D. H. Cole in 1931 to prepare viable plans for the implementation of Labour Party policies in the form of books and research pamphlets. When the NFRB united with the Fabian Society in 1938 Hughes became organizing secretary, editing the bureau's journal and pamphlets and servicing research committees.

In London, Hughes worked with John Parker, MP for Dagenham and secretary of the NFRB, and served as a member of Lambeth borough council. He also got to know Parker's sister (Winifred) Beryl (1912/1913–1995), whom he married on 25 September 1937. The marriage lasted until she died in 1995; there were no children.

From 1942 to 1945 Hughes served with the Royal Artillery, taking part in the invasion of Normandy in 1944. In the following year while his unit was camped on the Dutch–German border he learned that he had been nominated as the Labour candidate for the Wolverhampton West constituency. As the constituency's MP from 1945 to 1950 he served as parliamentary private secretary to Ellen Wilkinson, minister of education. The Education Act of 1944 was being implemented at this time; despite postwar economic difficulties, schools were rebuilt, emergency measures for the supply of teachers were introduced, the school-leaving age was raised to fifteen, and a beginning was made to provide a secondary education for all children. Ellen Wilkinson (whose personal secretary Beryl had been between 1937 and 1941) died in 1947; she was long mourned by both Billy and Beryl Hughes. Billy stayed in the Ministry of Education for another year, after which he became parliamentary private secretary to Michael Stewart, then financial secretary to the War Office. Here his work was largely concerned with parliamentary committees on colonial development and welfare.

In the general election of 1950 Hughes defended a redistributed constituency against Enoch Powell, the Conservative Party candidate, losing by 600 votes. Later that year the post of principal of Ruskin College, Oxford, became vacant on the sudden resignation of Lionel Elvin to take up a position with UNESCO. Ruskin College was (and is) an independent college, with strong associations with the labour movement and trade unions, which prepared working-class men and women to undertake responsible leadership in their organizations and communities. R. H. Tawney and G. D. H. Cole were academic advisers to the college, and it was Cole who suggested that Hughes apply for the position. The interview panel included Tawney and Cole and he was appointed at a salary of £1000 per annum.

The years of Hughes's principalship from 1950 to 1979 were successful if difficult. Informality was his style of leadership, and this quality characterized college teaching. He was an accessible principal who continued to teach, in particular taking responsibility for courses on politics, public speaking, and trade union studies. In 1950 Ruskin was in danger of becoming a backwater. Finance was a constant problem for the college and its students, and Hughes worked hard on both fronts. The Ministry of Education grant to the college was increased in 1951, and

in the 1960s he persuaded the education department to agree to a 50 per cent grant for the development of new buildings; this in turn led to an increase in student numbers and a broadening of the courses on offer. He worked through the Trades Union Congress to encourage trade unions to provide scholarships for their members to pursue Ruskin courses. For much of the time student grants from local education authorities were discretionary, but in 1974 the Department of Education and Science, following a recommendation of the Russell committee on education (1973), made these grants mandatory for students at Ruskin and similar residential adult colleges. During the 1970s, while the two-year University of Oxford special diploma in social studies remained, students increasingly opted for college-validated diplomas in labour studies, history, literature, and development studies. During the same period the history workshop of socialist and feminist historians was established at the college. In October 1976 the prime minister, James Callaghan, inaugurated a national debate on educational standards while laying the foundation stone of the Steve Biko building at the college's Headington site.

As student numbers increased Hughes put special effort into obtaining funding for overseas students. By the time of his retirement one-tenth of the 180 students at the college were from overseas, in particular from Africa, to which he had a strong commitment. Tom Mboya was a former Ruskin student and Hughes helped greatly in establishing and developing Kivukoni College in Tanzania. In later years, as chair of the Webb memorial trust (funded from the sale for £1 million of Beatrice Webb House, at Holmbury St Mary, Surrey), he encouraged students from eastern and central Europe to attend Ruskin as Webb fellows.

During his time at Ruskin and in retirement Hughes was actively involved in educational committees and agencies. These included the Workers' Educational Association (as vice-president and president), the Russell committee on adult education (1969–73), the advisory council for adult and continuing education, the Fabian Society, the National Institute of Adult and Continuing Education, and the Civil Service Arbitration Tribunal. His work at the college and his active involvement with bodies related to the education of adults was his life. He regretted the official neglect of adult education, and that England was still educationally two nations and would remain so until schools and further and higher education institutions were integrated to provide for the whole population in a comprehensive system of continuing education. Hughes survived his wife by four months, dying at his home, the Manor House at Merton, Bicester, on 15 November 1995.

BILL BAILEY

Sources [H. D. Hughes], autobiographical manuscript, Ruskin College, Oxford, archives · *The Times* (28 Nov 1995) · B. Harrison, 'Oxford and the labour movement', *Twentieth Century British History*, 2 (1991), 226–71 · H. Pollins, *The history of Ruskin College* (1984) · K. O. Morgan, *Labour people: leaders and lieutenants, Hardie to Kinnock* (1987), 107–18 · J. Parker, *Father to the house* (1982) · *Adults Learning*, 7 (Jan 1996), 126–7 · b. cert. · m. cert. · d. cert.

Archives Bodl. RH, corresp. relating to colonial issues · Ruskin College, Oxford, MSS relating to adult education and industrial relations, handwritten autobiographical MS, and notes of speeches and articles

Likenesses photographs (with Ruskin College students and staff), Ruskin College, Oxford

Wealth at death £461,586: probate, 5 June 1996, *CGPLA Eng. & Wales*

Hughes, Hugh (1693–1776), Welsh-language poet, was born on 1 August 1693 at Llwydiarth Esgob (also called Y Foel) in the parish of Llandyfrydog near Llannerch-y-medd in Anglesey, the eldest son of Hugh Hughes (*d.* 1727/1728), carpenter and farmer, and Margaret Parry (*fl.* 1673–1710). On 5 May 1719 Hughes married Ann (1698–1759), daughter of Edward Jones, tenant farmer of Rhydyrarian in the parish of Llanfihangel Ysgeifiog, and on his father's death inherited the ancestral home and small estate. There he was able to live in a gentlemanly manner and enjoy the usual privileges of a lesser country squire. Between 1720 and 1739 they had eight children, of whom four of the sons eventually settled as farmers in Anglesey.

About 150 of Hughes's poetic compositions survive, none of which can be dated before 1728, when he was actively involved in the lively poetic activities which characterized Anglesey during the second quarter of the eighteenth century; the greater part of his poems remains unedited and unpublished. He was greatly influenced by Lewis Morris (1701–1765), becoming an active member of his circle, accepting him as his poetic master, and always striving for his acclaim. He was equally proficient in free-metre and strict-metre prosody. Many of his free-metre poems, which were intended to be sung, are devoted to religious topics, including carols composed regularly to celebrate Christmas. He also emulated Lewis Morris in his fondness for composing poems containing a series of *tribannau*.

In his strict-metre poems Hughes restricted himself to the two most popular metres of his contemporaries— *englyn* and *cywydd*—being as prolific in the latter measure as any of his contemporaries and submitting much of his work to Lewis Morris for correction and approval. Among his *cywyddau*, forty-five in number, there are several elegies which include one each to three of the four Morris brothers—Siôn in 1741, William in 1763, and Lewis in 1765. Other *cywyddau* were composed on the loss of Minorca in 1756, on the sad state of Britain in 1757, and to three members of the royal family between 1760 and 1765. In 1756 he composed 'Cywydd annerch' to Goronwy Owen (1723–1769), which prompted the latter's famous response, and another in the following year in praise of the Honourable Society of Cymmrodorion, which led to his being elected a corresponding member. On the death of Lewis Morris in 1765 Hugh Hughes seems to have lost interest almost completely in composing poetry. But because of his close attachment to Lewis Morris and his solid commitment to the art of Welsh poetry for the greater part of his life Hugh Hughes must be regarded as an integral part of the classical awakening in Wales in the eighteenth century.

Hughes also developed more than a general interest in various aspects of the history and antiquities of Anglesey, which included the pedigrees of the gentry and the history of the churches. In his library there were at least two early manuscripts of Welsh poetry. Three manuscripts in his own hand have survived: Ashby 49 (University of Wales, Bangor), Wynnstay 8 (NL Wales), which is a collection of his poetry with a preface intended for publication, and another, in a private collection, containing pedigrees and notes on antiquities.

Some of Hughes's poems were published during his lifetime: a poem criticizing the Methodists was appended to *Ymddiddanion cyfeillgar rhwng gŵr o Eglwys Loegr, ac ymneillduwr* (1752); four free-metre poems were printed separately at Shrewsbury; one carol was printed in *Blodeugerdd Cymry* (1759); one in *Dewisol ganiadau* (1759); several in *Diddanwch teuluaidd* (1763); and finally eleven of his carols appeared in *Diddanwch i'w feddiannydd: neu ganiadau defosionol* (1773). During the latter part of his life he also translated two works from the English: *Deial Ahaz, wedi ei hysprydoli* (1773) from *The Dial of Ahaz Spiritualized* by David Tucker, and *Rheolau bywyd dynol* (1774) from *The Oeconomy of Human Life* by Philip Dormer Stanhope.

Hughes buried his wife on 25 January 1759 and by 1766 seems to have moved to Mynydd-y-gof-du at Holyhead, where his son David was a tenant farmer. He died on 6 April 1776 and was buried at Holyhead parish church on 10 April. His will, dated 27 February 1776, is extant.

DAFYDD WYN WILIAM

Sources H. Hughes, U. Wales, MS Ashby 49 · H. Hughes, NL Wales, Wynnstay 8 · J. H. Davies, *A bibliography of Welsh ballads* (1911) · E. Rees, *Libri Walliae* (1987), vols. 1 and 2

Hughes, Hugh [*pseud.* Cristion] (1790–1863), painter and engraver, was born at Pwll-y-gwichiad, near Llandudno. He was the son of Thomas Hughes and his wife, Jane Williams, and was baptized at Llandudno on 20 February 1790. His parents died while he was young and he was educated by his maternal grandfather, Hugh Williams, of Meddiant Farm, Llansanffraid Glan Conwy, Denbighshire. Hughes was apprenticed to an engraver at Liverpool and later moved to London where he learned to paint in oils. The earliest known example of his work is a portrait (dated 1812) of the Revd John Evans (1723–1817) of Bala, Merioneth, which was engraved in the *Drysorfa* (vol. 3). Between 1819 and 1822 he worked at Meddiant Farm on a volume of wood-engravings entitled *Beauties of Cambria* (1823) which was published by subscription and which became his best-known work. All the views were engraved by himself, fifty-eight from his own drawings. His engraving style has been compared to that of Thomas Bewick. His treatment of natural objects was realistic, minute, and laborious, and his foliage always graceful. Four of these 'singularly beautiful wood engravings' are reproduced in Chatto (Chatto, 538–40).

Hughes was a religious and political radical and in 1828 he signed a petition in favour of the passing of the Catholic Emancipation Bill. As a result he was expelled from the London section of the Welsh Calvinistic body to which he belonged. He complained publicly about this intolerant behaviour, producing pamphlets and letters to *Seren Gomer* (1828–30). His efforts were rewarded by a move towards political free speech among Welsh Calvinists, but he was not reinstated as a member of the denomination. He later joined the independents, and later the Plymouth Brethren. In 1832 he wrote about church issues under the pseudonym Cristion, often taking issue with the Revd Evan Evans (Ieuan Glan Geirionydd).

Hughes exhibited in London between 1827 and 1854 with four pictures at the British Institution and six at the Society of British Artists. Titles include *Flowers*, *The Minas Bridge, North Wales*, and *Falls of Helygog*. He also made many lithographs of Welsh scenery and caricatures of the commissioners of education sent down to Wales (1846–7). Several of his sketches were published, including a map of north Wales entitled *Dame Venedotia*, one of Pitt's Head near Beddgelert, and others of the neighbourhood of Snowdon. Many other examples of his work remain in country houses about Caernarfon.

In the 1820s Hughes also published works on Welsh antiquities; his lectures delivered before the London Cymmrodorion in 1831; *Y Papur Newydd Cymreig* (1836; a Welsh newspaper), wrongly ascribed to another in *Cardiff Eisteddfod Transactions*; *The Genteelers*, a political pamphlet; *Yr eglwys yn yr awyr*, an essay in *Traethodydd* (1853); and edited three volumes of sermons by his father-in-law, David Charles. The volume published in 1846 contains a memoir. He also planned a reprint of the *Brut* in twenty numbers, but only one appeared.

Hughes died at Great Malvern on 11 March 1863, and was buried in the cemetery there. After 1828 he had married Sarah, daughter of the Revd David Charles of Carmarthen. They had three children, all of whom died young. Mrs Hughes died at Aberystwyth on 28 December 1873.

R. M. J. JONES, rev. CHLOE JOHNSON

Sources Graves, *Artists* · W. Chatto, J. Jackson, and H. G. Bohn, *A treatise on wood-engraving*, 2nd edn (1861), 538–40 · R. K. Engen, *Dictionary of Victorian wood engravers* (1985) · T. M. Rees, *Welsh painters, engravers, sculptors* (1527–1911) (1912) · CGPLA Eng. & Wales (1863) · private information (1891)
Archives NL Wales, journals of tours in Wales
Likenesses H. Hughes, group portrait (with his wife and child), priv. coll.
Wealth at death under £450: probate, 19 Sept 1863, CGPLA Eng. & Wales

Hughes, Hugh [*pseud.* Tegai] (1805–1864), poet and Congregational minister, was born at the village of Cilgeraint, Llandygái, Caernarvonshire, the son of Thomas Hughes and his wife, Barbara Owen. The family soon moved to nearby Tre-garth, where his father served as a deacon at the Independent church at Cororion and was district president of the British and Foreign Bible Society. Hughes received all his early education at Sunday school, but was taught the rules of Welsh grammar and poetry by Gutyn Peris, a slate quarryman with whom he worked for some years. He married Jane Parry from Llandygái on 24 August 1827, and they had five children.

In 1834 Hughes joined the Cymreigyddion Society at Bethesda, where his interest in and knowledge of Welsh poetry and literature deepened. When the Independent church, to which his family belonged, was closed, Hughes joined the Wesleyan Methodists, but subsequently returned to the Independents, and became well known in the district as a powerful preacher. In October 1847 he took up ministerial charges at Rhos-lan, Tabor, and Llanystumdwy in Eifionydd, Caernarvonshire. In 1849 he moved to the Welsh chapel at Jackson Street, Manchester, but due to poor health he returned to north Wales to farm at Pant Ifan, Llanrug, Caernarvonshire. In 1853 he returned to the ministry, and was ordained minister at Capel Helyg, Chwilog, and Aber-erch in Eifionydd. During this time, he established a printing press at Pwllheli and began publishing *Yr Arweinydd* (*The Leader*), a penny monthly which he edited for many years. In 1859 he moved to Aberdâr, Glamorgan, where he took charge of the new church at Bethel. Here he was extremely successful and soon gathered a large congregation.

Hughes was one of the most productive Welsh writers of his day, contributing largely to contemporary Welsh-language magazines and journals. He was also a much respected poet who competed frequently and successfully at eisteddfods, with his mainly theological and biographical compositions. In later years he became well known as an adjudicator and critic. A collection of his poetry, *Bwrdd y bardd*, appeared in print in 1839 and many other works were published in various Welsh-language journals and newspapers. His studies in Welsh grammar were also well received, and his *Gramadeg athronyddol* (1841) was reputed to have been the best-selling Welsh grammar of its time.

In October 1863 Hughes suffered a stroke which left him ailing. He never fully recovered and on 4 December 1864 he fell ill while delivering a sermon at Bethel. He died on 8 December at Cwmdare, Aberdâr, and was buried at the new cemetery, Aberdâr, on 12 December. He died a poor man, having lost money through his publications; a testimonial raised during his final year through public subscription was presented to his wife after his death.

MARI A. WILLIAMS

Sources J. T. Jones, *Geiriadur bywgraffyddol o enwogion Cymru*, 1 (1867) · G. T. Roberts, 'Hugh Hughes (Tegai) a'r Wesleaid', *Bathafarn*, 9 (1954), 5–17 · T. Rees and J. Thomas, *Hanes eglwysi annibynol Cymru*, 2 (1872) · DWB · T. R. Roberts, *Eminent Welshmen: a short biographical dictionary* (1908), 180 · D. Griffith, 'Beirdd a barddoniaeth Gymreig y bedwaredd ganrif ar bymtheg', *Y Traethodydd*, 58 (1903), 295–9 · Hwfa Môn, 'Tegai', *Y Geninen*, 5 (1887), 264–5 · Hwfa Môn, 'Tegai', *Y Geninen*, 7 (1889), 100–02, 179–83 · *Y Dysgedydd* (Jan 1865), 34–5
Archives NL Wales | NL Wales, Cymreigyddion Y Fenni MSS
Likenesses J. E. James, carte-de-visite, NL Wales · engraving, NL Wales · photograph, repro. in Roberts, *Dictionary of eminent Welshmen*

Hughes, Hugh Price (1847–1902), Wesleyan Methodist minister, was born on 8 February 1847 at 10 King Street, Carmarthen, to John Hughes (1817–1897), surgeon, and his wife, Anne, *née* Phillips (d. 1900). Educated at Carmarthen grammar school and Thistleboon boarding-school, Mumbles, near Swansea, Hughes was a frail child. At thirteen he was converted to Christ under the influence of the preaching of visiting Cornish fishermen, and a year later he began preaching himself. In 1865 he entered Richmond College to train for the ministry, graduating from London University with a BA in 1869.

Hughes's subsequent stationing by the conference to

Hugh Price Hughes (1847–1902), by W. & D. Downey, pubd 1890

the Dover circuit proved to be formative. His first sermon, 'What think ye of Christ?', saw eighteen people converted, much to his surprise. Similarly, his rather conservative social views were transformed through his association with the radical Welshman Alderman Rees. Rees took him to hear Josephine Butler campaign for the abolition of the Contagious Diseases Acts. The meeting reduced Hughes to tears, and as a result he became actively involved in agitation for repeal. In 1872 he moved from Dover to Brighton where, on 20 August 1873, he married Mary Katherine [**Mary Katherine Hughes** (1853–1948)], daughter of the Richmond College governor, Alfred Barrett (d. 1897). Together they were to have four children, Arnold, Bernard, Gwendolen, and Dorothea.

Just before Hughes departed from Brighton in 1875 a holiness convention was held in the town under the leadership of Robert and Hannah Pearsall Smith. Hughes recognized their teaching as a restatement of part of Wesley's understanding of 'entire sanctification'. During the convention he also had a significant experience of God dealing with his personal ambitions. In the circuit appointments that followed, Tottenham (1875) and Dulwich (1878), Hughes completed the requirements for the degree of MA of London University. However, it was at Oxford (1881) that his developing social conscience received its intellectual underpinning through becoming a student and friend of the philosopher T. H. Green, whose

emphasis on altruism, self-sacrifice, and the abandonment of self-sufficiency for the fulfilment of social and political obligations caught Hughes's imagination. Furthermore, as Green's ethic of altruism was grounded in the belief that the spring of all ethical action is the human need for religious self-realization, Hughes found a philosophical means to express his understanding of Christian perfection.

In 1884 Hughes returned to London as the minister at Brixton Hill, launching the *Methodist Times* as a new denominational weekly in 1885. The following year saw him appointed superintendent of the new West London Mission, which commenced in October 1887. Together with Hughes's evangelistic preaching the mission ran thrift societies, a labour bureau, a poor man's lawyer, a soup kitchen, two dispensaries, a rescue home, various recreational and literary clubs, and a hospice for the terminally ill. Katherine (as she was known) was active alongside her husband, pioneering an early form of deaconess service in the Sisters of the People. These single women lived in a community under her supervision and offered humanitarian aid to the poor, including a crèche for working mothers. This dual emphasis on evangelism and social concern typified the Forward Movement within Wesleyanism. This was an unconstituted grass-roots movement for which Hughes was the unofficial leader and spokesman through his editorials in the *Methodist Times*. Hughes wrote, 'Christ came to save the nation as well as the individual … it is an essential feature of His mission to reconstruct human society on the basis of justice and love' (H. P. Hughes, *Social Christianity*, 1889, viii).

In appraising Hughes's life many have concentrated exclusively on the pioneering social dimension of his ministry. Seen in isolation this creates an unbalanced picture. Analysis of his four books of collected sermons and the editorial columns he wrote each week for the *Methodist Times* reveals the spiritual frame of reference that was primary to his understanding and motivation. He constructed an experiential theology, based on Wesley's doctrine of entire sanctification and the need for 'baptism in the Holy Spirit', which he applied to the quest for personal and 'social holiness'. From this base he engaged with all forms of contemporary thought and agitated for social and political change. He fought for improvements in recreation, sanitation, housing, and medical services, and advocated prison reform, child welfare legislation, and the emancipation of women. With other nonconformists, he also campaigned for the moral integrity of political leaders. This was particularly difficult for him when, in 1890, the Irish home-rule leader, Parnell, was implicated in a notorious divorce case. Having previously supported Parnell, he only reluctantly withdrew his support on the ground that 'what is morally wrong can never be politically right' (D. P. Hughes, 353).

While his loyalty to Wesleyanism was unquestionable, Hughes argued strongly for denominational reconstruction (for example, through the admission of women to the representative session of conference) and free church unity. The latter was generated by increasing nonconformist co-operation and the developing nonconformist conscience. This conviction placed him in leadership at the church unity conference at Grindelwald in 1892, and as the first president of the National Council of the Evangelical Free Churches in 1896. A firm defender of the orthodoxy of the apostles' creed, he urged the exclusion of Unitarians from the Free Church Council.

In 1898 Hughes was elected president of the Wesleyan conference, indicating the high regard in which he was held by his peers. During the Second South African War he was an outspoken champion of the imperialist cause. Increasing ill health due to overwork plagued his final years. He collapsed and died at his home, 8 Taviton Street, Gordon Square, London, on 17 November 1902. A funeral at Wesley's chapel, City Road, was followed by burial at Highgate cemetery on 21 November. His widow continued her work at the West London Mission after his death, and was appointed CBE in 1938. She died on 13 January 1948.

ROGER STANDING

Sources D. P. Hughes, *The life of Hugh Price Hughes* (1907) • A. Walters, *Hugh Price Hughes: pioneer and reformer* (1907) • K. P. Hughes, *The story of my life* (1945) • editorials, *Methodist Times* (1885–1902) • J. G. Mantle, *Hugh Price Hughes* (1902) • P. S. Bagwell, *Outcast London* (1987) • J. A. Robinson, *Hugh Price Hughes as we knew him* (1902) • J. Kent, 'Hugh Price Hughes and the nonconformist conscience', *Essays in modern English church history: in memory of Norman Sykes*, ed. G. V. Bennett and J. D. Walsh (1966), 181–205 • R. Standing, 'The relationship between evangelicalism and the social gospel, 1875–1914', MPhil diss., University of Manchester, 1992 • M. Vicinus, *Independent women: work and community for single women, 1850–1920* (1985) • *CGPLA Eng. & Wales* (1948) [Mary Katherine Hughes]
Archives JRL, Methodist Archives and Research Centre
Likenesses W. & D. Downey, woodburytype photograph, NPG; repro. in W. Downey and D. Downey, *The cabinet portrait gallery*, 1 (1890) [*see illus.*] • portrait, repro. in Hughes, *Life* • portrait (Mary Katherine Hughes), repro. in Hughes, *Story of my life*
Wealth at death £5373 13*s.* 8*d.*: probate, 18 May 1903, *CGPLA Eng. & Wales* • £10,755 2*s.* 8*d.*—Mary Katherine Hughes: probate, 25 June 1948, *CGPLA Eng. & Wales*

Hughes, Jabez (1684/5–1731), translator, was the younger son of John Hughes (*d.* 1715), clerk in the Hand-in-Hand Fire Office, Snow Hill, London, and his wife, Anne Burgess, of Wiltshire; his brother was the playwright John *Hughes (1678?–1720). It is not known where he was educated, but his brother attended a dissenting academy in London. Hughes and his wife, Sarah, had one daughter.

From 1710 or earlier, Hughes was employed as a deputy in the clerks' and apprentices' duty office under John Montague; later he moved to a similar position in the stamp office under William Thompson. He combined his responsibilities with scholarly and literary interests. His first work to appear in print was *An Ode on the Incarnation* (1709), sixteen pindaric stanzas published anonymously, to a reissue of which was appended *The True State of Mortality*, 'By T. R.', according to the title-page, seven pages of couplet verse on Job 5: 7. He then wrote *On November 4, 1712: the anniversary of the birth of his late majesty, King William the third, of glorious memory* ([1712]), reprinted three years later as *Verses on November the 4th*. Neither work promised much, but Hughes soon found his métier in literary translation.

The rape of Proserpine, from Claudian, in three books: with the story of Sextus and Erichtho, from Lucan's Pharsalia, book 6 (1714), a slim, elegant octavo, demonstrated his abilities in verse (a second edition, corrected and enlarged with notes, appeared in 1723). He also turned his hand to prose: *The Lives of the XII. Cæsars* (1717), an annotated, illustrated duodecimo dedicated to John Duncombe, and reprinted in 1726, was the first eighteenth-century English version of Suetonius. And attributed to Hughes in the catalogue of the Bodleian Library is a translation of Bernard Le Bovier de Fontenelle's 'A discourse concerning the antients and moderns', appended to the fifth edition of John Glanvill's rendering of Fontenelle's *Conversations with a Lady, on the Plurality of Worlds* (Dublin, 1728). (The text added to the fourth edition, London, 1719, however, appears to be identical.)

Hughes's brother died on 17 February 1720. Jabez sent Alexander Pope a copy of his brother's play *The Siege of Damascus*, a tragedy which opened on the night John Hughes died (he learned of the success of the première on his deathbed) and for which Pope had agreed to compose the prologue. In return, Pope sent to Hughes—who may have been living at his mother's home in Red Lyon Street, Holborn—the final volume of *The Iliad*, completing the set with which his brother had been presented. Hughes further published *Verses Occasion'd by Reading Mr Dryden's Fables* (1721), an eight-page octavo written, the author said, *c.*1707 and dedicated to John Sheffield, duke of Buckinghamshire, who died three or four days before the eventual publication. He also translated episodes from Horace, Statius, and Ovid, and passages of Greek, including Theocritus— specimens not printed in his lifetime. And he is said to have contributed a number of anonymous translations of Cervantes to the second edition of Samuel Croxall's *A Select Collection of Novels* (1729); many of those renderings, however, are also to be found in the first edition (1720–21). As the prefaces to his translations demonstrate, Hughes was a thoughtful classical scholar. In addition he was discerningly well read: echoes of Milton's blank verse, and the diction of John Philips, for example, and Dryden, may be heard in his work.

Following a six-month illness, Hughes died of consumption on 17 January 1731. He was forty-six. He thus did not live to see the discovery of his thoroughgoing fraud. Seven months after his death, Henry Cartwright, receiver of the stamp duties, informed the ministry that Hughes had embezzled £4000 of public receipts, misappropriation which he seems to have begun in August 1729. Cartwright sought, and in May 1732 was granted, the crown's assistance in prosecuting Hughes's estate. In November 1733 Cartwright, who was liable for his deputy's malpractice, further petitioned to be relieved of the debts he had incurred, a matter which was referred to the stamp commissioners. They, in turn, in May 1734, asked John Willes, the newly appointed attorney-general, to investigate. Willes reported on the affair in March 1736; included in his deliberations was an affidavit sworn by Sarah Hughes, the chief clerk's widow. The posthumous appearance of Hughes's *Miscellanies in Verse and Prose* (1737), edited by William Duncombe, the husband of Hughes's sister Elizabeth, and published for the benefit of his widow, was a consequence of the affair; 'The Publication has been so long delay'd by several Accidents needless to be mentioned', Duncombe stonewalls ('To the reader', sig. A4r). (Nichols further states that the dedication to Gertrude Russell, duchess of Bedford, subscribed by Sarah Hughes, was in fact written by the Revd John Copping, dean of Clogher.) The volume was reissued in 1741 as *Claudian the Poet, his Elegant History of Rufinus*.) Hughes's widow finally accompanied the wife of the Hon. Robert Byng, governor of Barbados, to the Caribbean, presumably in 1739, when Byng took up his appointment. She died there in 1740.

JONATHAN PRITCHARD

Sources [G. Jacob], *The poetical register, or, The lives and characters of all the English poets*, 2 (1723), 85 · J. Duncombe, ed., *Letters, by several eminent persons deceased*, 2nd edn, 3 vols. (1773), vol. 1, p. 160 · *DNB* · D. F. Foxon, ed., *English verse, 1701–1750: a catalogue of separately printed poems with notes on contemporary collected editions*, 2 vols. (1975), vol. 1, p. 364 · W. A. Shaw, ed., *Calendar of treasury books and papers, 1731–1734, preserved in her majesty's Public Record Office*, PRO (1898), 91–2, 110, 150, 227, 277, 284, 411, 453, 550 · W. A. Shaw, ed., *Calendar of treasury books and papers, 1735–1738, preserved in her majesty's Public Record Office*, PRO (1900), 163 · W. A. Shaw, ed., *Calendar of treasury books, 25/2*, PRO (1961), 245, 608 · Nichols, *Lit. anecdotes*, 8.266, 268 · J. Hughes, foreword, in *The works of John Dryden*, ed. W. Scott, rev. G. Saintsbury, 18 (1893), 237–8 · J. Poyer, *The history of Barbados, from the first discovery of the island, in the year 1605, till the accession of Lord Seaforth, 1801* (1808); repr. (1971), 292

Hughes, James [*pseud.* Iago Trichrug] (**1779–1844**), Welsh Calvinistic Methodist minister, was born at Neuadd-ddu, in the parish of Ciliau Aeron, at the foot of Trichrug Mountain, Cardiganshire, on 3 July 1779. After being educated locally, he became an apprentice blacksmith, and at the age of twenty-one settled at Deptford, Kent, where he played a key role in establishing a Welsh Calvinistic Methodist church. He seceded for a while but in 1805 he returned under the influence of the Revd John Elias, and joined the Wilderness Row Chapel, London, becoming a deacon in 1809. About 1807 he married Martha Griffiths (d. 1863); they had no children. In 1810 he began preaching and was ordained at Llangeitho in 1816. In 1823 his church built a new chapel at Jewin Crescent, London, and he became its minister. During his period as minister he became involved in some of the Methodist doctrinal discussions, particularly regarding the 'buying of the blessings'. In 1828 he became embroiled in a fierce public debate with members of his congregation and the denomination, regarding the emancipation of the Catholics, which he vehemently opposed. Despite this he remained minister at Jewin Crescent until his death, which took place at Stringers Row, Rotherhithe, London, on 2 November 1844. He was buried at Bunhill Fields on the 11th.

Hughes was a frequent contributor to Welsh periodicals and was a well-known hymn writer and poet, known by his bardic name, Iago Trichrug, derived from his birthplace. He was noted for his religious translations and commentaries, particularly his 'Bible expositor', which he began in 1829, and left uncompleted at his death.

R. M. J. JONES, *rev.* MARI A. WILLIAMS

Sources G. M. Roberts, *Y ddinas gadarn: hanes eglwys Jewin Llundain* (1974) · J. E. Davies, *James Hughes: sef cyfrol goffa* (1911) · J. Thickens, *Y Drysorfa*, 79 (1909), 161–4 · *DWB* · J. T. Jones, *Geiriadur bywgraffyddol o enwogion Cymru*, 1 (1867)
Archives NL Wales, Bala College papers
Likenesses photograph, *c*.1823–1844, repro. in Roberts, *Ddinas gadarn*, pl. 5 · photograph, *c*.1823–1844, repro. in Davies, *James Hughes*, pl. 1 · J. Thompson, engraving (after J. R. Wildman, *c*.1830), repro. in P. Lord, *Hugh Hughes Arlunydd Gwlad* (1995), 157

Hughes, Joan Lily Amelia (**1918–1993**), airwoman, was born on 28 April 1918 at Eversley, Glengall Road, Woodford, Essex, the only daughter of Arthur Edward Hughes, a braid manufacturer, and his wife, Lily Amelia Lekeup. She had one older brother. Growing up in the golden era of aviation in the 1920s and early 1930s, Joan Hughes was bitten by the flying bug at an early age. So determined was she to become a pilot that at fifteen her parents allowed her, together with her brother, to have flying lessons once a week at the East Anglian Aero Club, at a cost of £2 10s. per hour. She was soon flying solo, but an accident in which a sixteen-year-old boy was killed resulted in a legal limit of seventeen years for solo flying being imposed. This temporarily halted Joan's ambitions but in 1935 she obtained her pilot's licence.

Joan Hughes obtained her first job as a flying instructor at Chigwell Flying Club and, but for the war, a club flying instructor is probably what she would have remained. The formation of the Civil Air Guard (CAG) in October 1938, providing cheap subsidized flying for anyone of either sex between the ages of eighteen and fifty, resulted in hundreds of applications from many who could not otherwise obtain a pilot's licence. This provided more work for flying clubs and their instructors. At the outbreak of war Hughes was instructing in the women's corps of the CAG at Romford, Essex, and had accrued over 500 flying hours. She was one of a small band of women instructors who then applied to join the Air Transport Auxiliary (ATA). Composed of older men and those not considered fit for combat activities with the RAF, it was not deemed a suitable organization for those fit and active young women with hundreds of hours of flying experience. However, as a result of the persistence of Pauline *Gower and lobbying from these women, it was eventually agreed that a small pool of women based at Hatfield could be formed to ferry De Havilland Tiger Moths from factories to storage units dispersed around the UK.

In January 1940 Joan Hughes became the youngest of the first eight selected by Pauline Gower for what was at the time considered merely an experiment. For much of her time in the ATA she worked as an instructor, initially on Tiger Moths and Miles Magisters. By the end of hostilities she and ten of her contemporaries were flying four-engined aircraft and Joan herself was instructing both sexes at the Advanced Flying Training School (AFTS) at White Waltham. She was the only woman instructor on all types of aircraft (including Oxfords, Harvards, Hudsons, and Wellingtons), with the exception of seaplanes and four-engined types.

Hughes served in the ATA for six years, until December 1945, never losing an aircraft, though she did have one or two hair-raising experiences. The first occurred when she was ferrying a Hurricane from Silloth to Hatfield in August 1941. After take-off she was unable to move the selector lever in order to raise the undercarriage. Aware that these first Hurricane flights by women were attracting undue attention and fearing that if she returned to complain it might be thought that she lacked the stature and strength to cope, she used her foot to move the lever. The undercarriage retracted but the lever would not return to neutral. Arriving at Finningley to refuel, she could lower neither the undercarriage nor the flaps since both worked off the same lever. After orbiting for some time she had no alternative but to make a flapless belly-landing. Oblivious of her personal safety, she was mainly worried about what the accident committee would say and the effect it would have on women's capabilities to fly Hurricanes. In the event the aircraft slid smoothly over the grass, the only damage a bent propeller. Happily, Hughes was exonerated by the accident committee. Much later, in March 1943, she was on a conversion course on the Stirling four-engined bomber at Stradishall when, on her second take-off, a tyre went flat and the aircraft ran off the runway—confirming the expectations of onlookers who were sure that a slip of a girl would never be able to keep a large aircraft like the Stirling straight. However, she progressed with the course and ferried her first Stirling four days later on 4 April. With the end of hostilities Joan returned to civilian flying as a flying instructor at the West London Flying Club at White Waltham, where her wartime colleague Margot Gore was chief flying instructor. Here she taught many Air Training Corps cadets who became RAF pilots. After Margot left, Joan succeeded her for a brief period as chief instructor but administration was not her style and she moved on to the British Airways Flying Club at Booker in 1961.

It was during her Booker years that Hughes's reputation and ability to fly almost anything made her a natural film stunt pilot. She coached Kenneth More for his role as Douglas Bader in the film *Reach for the Sky* (1956). When a lightweight was needed to fly the tiny replica 1909 Santos-Dumont Demoiselle, Hughes undertook the flying sequences for *Those Magnificent Men in their Flying Machines* in 1965. She also flew replicas of First World War German aircraft in simulated dog-fights for *The Blue Max* (1966). Her most notable flying episode in films was as a stand-in pilot for Lady Penelope in the 1968 film version of the television series *Thunderbirds*. The storyline led her to obtain permission to land a Tiger Moth biplane on a motorway near High Wycombe, taxi under the bridge, and take off again. In the event, she flew under the bridge and found herself on seven charges of dangerous flying at Buckinghamshire quarter sessions. In court she pleaded that in her judgement turbulent weather made it safer to fly straight through. After a three-day hearing she was acquitted on all charges.

Joan Hughes retired after fifty years of flying with 11,800 hours in her log book, 10,000 of which were spent instructing. On retirement she moved from Wargrave to Somerset. She returned to White Waltham in 1991 for the unveiling by Prince Michael of Kent of Roderick Lovesay's painting *Tribute to Women Aviators*, in which she was one of the twelve women pilots depicted. She was appointed MBE in 1945 for her wartime service in the ATA. In 1954 she finally gained her wings from the RAF. She was awarded the British Women Pilots Association's most prestigious trophy, the Jean Lennox Bird jade vase, in 1962. The Royal Aero Club of Great Britain awarded her the bronze medal in 1967 for outstanding service to aviation in every sphere. She died of cancer on 16 August 1993 at Musgrave Park Hospital, Taunton, and was cremated.

ENID deBOIS

Sources L. Curtis, *The forgotten pilots: a story of the Air Transport Auxiliary, 1939–45* (1971) · private information (2004) [John Coleman, producer, *The forgotten pilots*, BBC, 1984] · IWM FVA · IWM SA · *The Guardian* (25 Sept 1993) · CGPLA Eng. & Wales (1993) · b. cert. · d. cert. · *The forgotten pilots*, BBC documentary film, 1984
Archives FILM IWM FVA, *The forgotten pilots*, BBC documentary | SOUND IWM, interview, 1984
Likenesses R. Lovesay, group portrait, 1991 (*A tribute to Women Aviators*), priv. coll.
Wealth at death under £125,000: probate, 16 Sept 1993, CGPLA Eng. & Wales

Hughes, John. *See* Owen, Hugh (1615–1686).

Hughes, John (1678?–1720), writer and librettist, was born probably on 29 January 1678 at Marlborough, Wiltshire, the eldest child of John Hughes (*d.* 1715), who was later a clerk in the Hand-in-Hand Fire Insurance Office, Snow Hill, London, and Anne, daughter of Isaac Burgess of Wiltshire. Hughes was descended from well-educated, middle-class puritans, a background that influenced his politics and literary outlook. His grandfather William Hughes (1619–1688) followed the life of a dissenting teacher and preacher after the Act of Uniformity in 1662.

Hughes's younger brother was the poet Jabez *Hughes (1684/5–1731). His only sister, Elizabeth (*c.*1692–1736), married William *Duncombe on 1 September 1726, and their son was the Revd John Duncombe. William and John Duncombe posthumously edited Hughes's poetry and correspondence.

Hughes's early education was in dissenting schools in London. In 1692 or more probably 1693 he entered an academy run by the Independent divine Thomas Rowe, probably in Little Britain, London, where he was a contemporary of Isaac Watts. After leaving Rowe's academy about November 1697, Hughes did not enter the ministry and probably soon thereafter conformed.

From his earliest years Hughes 'was led with an equal Ardor to the pursuit of the Sister Arts of Poetry, Drawing, and Musick' (Jacob, 80). By November 1697 he had a tragedy, *Amalasont, Queen of the Goths, or, Vice Destroys Itself* (1697), ready for the stage, which may have been produced some time before 1700. A proficient violinist, about 1700 he joined the weekly private concerts organized by Thomas Britton, the musical 'small-coal man'. His musical and poetic skills led him to write poems for musical setting.

Probably some time after 1706 Hughes obtained a place in the Office of Ordnance, and shortly afterwards some form of patronage from Thomas, earl (later marquess) of Wharton. When Wharton was appointed lord lieutenant of Ireland in 1708 he offered Hughes a place in his entourage; however, on the hopes of other patronage that never materialized, Hughes declined and lost the chance of preferment. Probably after the whigs returned to power in 1714 he became secretary to several commissions for strengthening the fortifications of royal harbours. In 1717 Earl Cowper, the lord chancellor, appointed Hughes secretary to the commissions of the peace in the court of chancery, which gave him financial security for the remainder of his life; during his last years, Hughes had a warm friendship with the earl and countess.

Hughes's poems, primarily lyric, draw on diverse traditions and verse forms and exemplify the often contradictory nature of Augustan verse, but generally avoid sharp wit or satire. His poetic reputation was established with a series of ambitious and inflated panegyrics: *The Triumph of Peace* (1698), *The Court of Neptune, Occasioned by King William's Return from Holland in 1699* (1700), and *The House of Nassau: A Pindarick Ode* (1702). They express a dissenting whig's celebration of William III and whig ideals, and he probably entertained hopes that they would secure him political favour.

Less Augustan and more pre-Romantic is 'A Thought in a Garden' (1704), a poem of rural retirement that is Hughes's most attractive and refreshing lyric. Two religious odes, *An Ode to the Creator of the World* (1712) and *The Ecstasy* (1720), in their enthusiasm and rapture are only vaguely Christian.

Without a clerical career, and apparently failing to gain patronage through his panegyric verse, Hughes turned to providing booksellers with modern editions of English writers and translations of classical and continental authors. His translations include Euripides, Horace, Lucan, Pindar, Boileau, Boccalini, Molière, Fontenelle, and Vertot. He began compiling *A Complete History of England* (1706), the third volume of which was written by White Kennett, after whom the history is usually named. His extremely popular translation *Letters of Abelard and Heloise* (1713) was the basis for Pope's poem *Eloisa to Abelard* (1717). His largest undertaking was a six-volume edition of Edmund Spenser's works (1715), the first critical edition of Spenser. His new acting version of *Hamlet*, prepared for Robert Wilks, held the stage from 1718 until Garrick's version of 1763.

Probably through his connections with whig lords, his publisher Jacob Tonson, and the Kit-Cat Club, Hughes was drawn into the Steele–Addison circle, and from 1709 to 1712 wrote for *The Tatler* and its successors. Attributions are often uncertain, but Hughes contributed to at least three numbers of *The Tatler*, seventeen of *The Spectator*, and to number 37 of *The Guardian*. His contributions (about one-third of the essays) to Sir Richard Blackmore's *Lay-Monk* (1713–14) provide a leavening of humour to the otherwise solemn essays.

Fundamentally, Hughes believed that literature cannot be divorced from morality and that it has a primary function to present a clear moral. But his specific criticism—

more appreciative than analytical or theoretical—touched a wide range of topics and put him in the vanguard of new directions of eighteenth-century taste.

In the preface to his *Works* of Spenser, Hughes resolved the problem of *The Faerie Queene* (that is, although popular, it was incorrect as an epic) by arguing that it should be understood as an allegory; and he sanctions the simplicity and Englishness of Spenser's pastorals against critics who wanted a more elevated, classical pastoral style. In *Lay-Monk* essays, he champions the new sentimental comedy (no. 9) and, using sensational psychology, accounts for the pleasure of descriptive poetry in terms of immediacy and vividness (no. 39). In *The Guardian* (no. 37), using a psychological approach to character and audience, he answers Thomas Rymer's intemperate attack on Shakespeare's *Othello*.

Hughes's most original and important poetic contribution was his role in the campaign for dramatic and vocal music in English. Here Hughes's practical musical and poetic skills made him the most qualified librettist of his day. 'Nothing is more necessary', Hughes asserted, 'than that the Words shou'd be understood, without which the End of *Vocal Musick* is lost' ('Preface', J. C. Pepusch, *Six English Cantatas*, 1710). To counteract the dominance of opera sung in Italian, he wrote English texts for odes, cantatas, and an opera for which he provided 'a sort of Verse, in regular Measures, purposely fitted for Musick' which would forge 'a better Correspondence … between the two Sister Arts' of poetry and music (ibid.).

Hughes's first major lyric poem, *An Ode in Praise of Musick*, was set by Philip Hart and performed at Stationers' Hall in 1703. About this time he began writing cantata texts for John Christopher Pepusch (*Six English Cantatas*), followed by texts for Nicola Haym, Daniel Purcell, John Ernst Galliard, and George Frideric Handel (*Venus and Adonis*). Along with Pope and Gay, he contributed to the libretto to Handel's *Acis and Galatea* (1718).

At Steele's request Hughes adapted for the new Italian style Dryden's *Alexander's Feast* (1711), which was set by Thomas Clayton for a concert series promoted by Steele in the York Buildings. His severe criticisms of Clayton's setting in a subsequent letter to Steele reveal the sophistication of Hughes's musical knowledge. His masque *Apollo and Daphne* (1716), set by Pepusch, was part of Steele's new campaign at Drury Lane to offer an alternative to Italian opera.

Hughes's major libretto was *Calypso and Telemachus* (1712), based on an episode from Fénelon's *Les aventures de Télémaque*, and set by Galliard, which Hughes offered as an 'Essay for the Improvement of Theatrical Musick in the *English* Language' (preface). This English opera apparently aroused the ire of 'the whole *Italian* band', and the Italianophile lord chamberlain, the duke of Shrewsbury, 'designed to sink it' by forcing withdrawal of the subscription and opening 'the House at the lowest Prices, or not at all' (Duncombe, xviii).

Hughes's tragedy *The Siege of Damascus* (1720), originally planned for the 1716–17 season, was a popular and critical success; it held a place in the repertory for the remainder of the century and is the work by which he was most remembered as a poet. It combines classical, heroic, and Shakespearian features, but the basis for its popularity was its prevailing sentimental tone.

In weak health since childhood, Hughes died, unmarried, in London of tuberculosis on 17 February 1720, the night of the première of his play *The Siege of Damascus*; he was buried in the vault under the chancel of St Andrew's, Holborn. Richard Steele provided a eulogy in *The Theatre* (no. 15, 20 February 1720). Hughes left an estate above £500.

Although Pope concurred with Swift's assessment that Hughes was 'among the *mediocribus* in prose as well as verse' (A. Pope, *Correspondence*, ed. G. Sherburn, 1956, 3.492, 508), he was a versatile writer whose literary works and criticism made varied contributions to developments in early eighteenth-century literature and taste.

THOMAS N. MCGEARY

Sources DNB • N. M. Shea, 'John Hughes, Augustan: a critical study of his works', PhD diss., U. Cal., Los Angeles, 1969 • G. Jacob, *An historical account of the lives and writings of our most considerable English poets* (1720), 80–85, 327 • *Letters by several eminent persons deceased. Including the correspondence of John Hughes, esq.*, ed. J. Duncombe, 2nd edn with additions, 3 vols. (1773) • W. Duncombe, 'An account of the life and writings of John Hughes, esq.', in J. Hughes, *Poems on several occasions. With some select essays in prose*, ed. W. Duncombe, 2 vols. (1735), 1.i–xxxvii • J. Campbell, 'John Hughes', *Biographia Britannica, or, The lives of the most eminent persons who have flourished in Great Britain and Ireland*, 4 (1757), 2697–709 • P. E. Roberts, 'John Hughes and his patron, Lord Cowper: some unpublished correspondence', *N&Q*, 220 (1975), 353–7 • H. T. Swedenberg, *The theory of the epic in England, 1650–1800* (1944), 71–3 • S. Johnson, *Lives of the English poets*, ed. G. B. Hill, [new edn], 2 (1905), 159–66 • J. Loftis, *Steele at Drury Lane* (1952) • J. M. Knapp, 'A forgotten chapter in English eighteenth-century opera', *Music and Letters*, 42 (1961), 4–16 • W. J. Burling, 'British plays, 1697–1737: premieres, datings, attributions, and publication information', *Studies in Bibliography*, 43 (1990), 164–82 • *The nonconformist's memorial … originally written by … Edmund Calamy*, ed. S. Palmer, [3rd edn], 3 (1803), 365–6 • W. J. Burling, 'John Hughes', *Restoration and eighteenth-century dramatists: second series*, ed. P. R. Backscheider, DLitB, 84 (1989), 227–33 • *The correspondence of Richard Steele*, ed. R. Blanchard (1941); repr. (1968) • R. Steele and J. Addison, *The Spectator*, ed. D. Bond, 5 vols. (1965) • D. F. Bond, ed., *The Tatler*, 3 vols. (1987) • R. Steele, *The Theatre*, ed. J. Loftis (1962) • R. M. Myers, *Handel, Dryden, and Milton. Being a series of observations on the poems of Dryden and Milton, as alter'd and adapted by various hands, and set to musick by Mr Handel* (1956) • D. C. Sutton, *Location register of English literary manuscripts and letters, eighteenth and nineteenth centuries*, 2 vols. (1995) • *Engraved Brit. ports.*
Archives BL, corresp., Add. MS | Herts. ALS, letters to first Earl Cowper • Yale U., Beinecke L., corresp. with Samuel Say
Likenesses J. Richardson, oils?, 1714 • G. Kneller, oils, 1718; Christies, 16 Oct 1953, lot 62 • B. Arlaud, miniature?, before 1719 • J. Richardson, drawing, graphite on vellum, 1736 (after J. Richardson, 1714), BM • P. Audinet, engraving (after G. Kneller, 1718) • J. Caldwell, engraving (after G. Kneller, 1718) • Cook, engraving (after G. Kneller) • E. Finden, engraving (after G. Kneller, 1718) • J. Hopwood, engraving (after G. Kneller, 1718) • G. Kneller, oils? • C. Knight, engraving (after G. Kneller, 1718) • Rivers, engraving (after G. Kneller) • Smith & Bye, engraving (after G. Kneller, 1718) • G. Vandergucht, line engraving (after G. Kneller, 1718), BM, NPG; repro. in Hughes, *Poems* • bust in plaster of paris • engraving (after G. Kneller, 1718)
Wealth at death over £500: J. Spence, *Observations*, ed. J. M. Osborn, 2 vols. (1966), vol. 1, p. 212

Hughes, John (1776–1843), Wesleyan Methodist minister and antiquary, the third child of William Hughes, a hatter, and his second wife, Elizabeth, daughter of John and Gwenllian Thomas of Lanyewan and sister of John Thomas, vicar of Caerleon, was born on 18 May 1776 at Brecon. He was educated at Christ College Grammar School at Brecon. Although his relatives were Anglican he joined the Methodists following a visit by John Wesley to Brecon in 1790. From 1796 he itinerated as a minister, and was appointed to the Welsh-speaking mission in north Wales under Owen Davies in 1800. He served at Ruthin and Caernarfon, before returning to English-language work in Liverpool and Carmarthen. Following a disagreement with Welsh Methodists, he subsequently itinerated mostly in the border counties of Cheshire, Staffordshire, and Herefordshire, though retaining an interest in the Welsh work. In 1811 he married Esther, eldest daughter of Edward Clarke of Knutsford.

Despite his lack of spoken fluency in the Welsh language Hughes became a prolific writer of pamphlets, sermons, commentaries, and works in Welsh. His *Horae Britannicae, or, Studies in Ancient British History*, published in two volumes (1818–19), and the *Essay on the Ancient and Present State of the Welsh Language* (1822) were important contributions to Welsh antiquarianism. He was an enthusiastic supporter of eisteddfod, compiled a Welsh hymn book, *Diferion y cysegr*, in 1802, contributed regularly to *Yr Eurgrawn*, and started a Welsh translation of Thomas Coke's *Commentaries*. He is commemorated as one of the founders of Welsh-speaking Methodism. In 1832 Hughes became a supernumerary, and retired to Knutsford in Cheshire, where he died on 15 May 1843.

TIM MACQUIBAN

Sources W. Hill, *An alphabetical arrangement of all the Wesleyan-Methodist ministers, missionaries, and preachers*, rev. J. P. Haswell, 9th edn (1862) • *Minutes of the Methodist conference* • DWB • N. B. Harmon, ed., *The encyclopedia of world Methodism*, 2 vols. (1974) • *Wesleyan Methodist Magazine*, 70 (1847), 209 • DNB
Archives NL Wales, journal and papers

Hughes, John (1787–1860), Church of England clergyman, second son of John Hughes, mayor of Aberystwyth and JP, and his wife, Mary, third daughter of James Evans, was born on 8 June 1787 at Llwyn Glas, Llanfihangel Geneu'r Glyn, near Aberystwyth. After attending the grammar school of Ystradmeurig, he became classical master at a large school at Putney, Surrey, where he remained about eighteen months. He returned to Wales and was ordained on 13 January 1811 by Bishop Cleaver at a private ordination in the cathedral of St Asaph. He was curate first for six years at Llandrillo-yn-Rhos, near Conwy, and from about 1817 at Foleshill, near Coventry. He married Jane Foulkes (1790–1826) in 1817; they had six children.

At Foleshill, Hughes became very popular; but when the vicar died, in 1822, Lord Chancellor Eldon, the patron, refused the petition of the parishioners to bestow the living on him, because of his evangelical opinions. Hughes therefore left, and settled at Deddington, near Oxford. Here again his fame as a preacher soon filled the church, and students from Oxford, including John Henry Newman, were among his hearers. He became perpetual curate of St Michael's, Aberystwyth, on 16 May 1827, and vicar of Llanbadarn Fawr in June 1834, with a prebendal stall in the church of Brecon. On 1 May 1828 he married his second wife, Laura Anne Poole (1794–1847). In 1859 Bishop Connop Thirlwall gave him the archdeaconry of Cardigan. In the course of that year he visited eighty parishes, preaching in each and establishing his reputation as one of Wales's strongest and most popular preachers.

Hughes was active in the movement to reform the Anglican church in Wales, particularly in the field of building reconstruction. The great demographic changes, which were occurring throughout much of Wales as a result of industrialization, combined with the decrepit condition of a considerable number of Welsh church buildings, meant this task was an essential part of any movement to revitalize Welsh Anglicanism. This spirit was witnessed in his own parish of Aberystwyth, where St Michael's Church was built, in no small part due to the constant efforts of Hughes himself. He was also a tireless supporter and fund-raiser for the Bible Society. He published extensively, particularly translations into Welsh of religious tracts and explanations. His most important English works include *Esther and her People* (1832), *Ruth and her Kindred* (1839), and *The Self-Searcher* (1848). He died on 1 November 1860 at Llanbadarn Fawr vicarage, near Aberystwyth.

R. M. J. Jones, *rev.* Robert V. Smith

Sources *DWB* · J. Ross, *A light upon the road: Archdeacon John Hughes of Aberystwyth, 1787–1860* (1989) · R. Hughes, 'Memoir of the author's life by his son', in *Sermons by the late Ven. J. Hughes* (1864) · *CGPLA Eng. & Wales* (1860) · IGI
Wealth at death under £7000: probate, 20 Dec 1860, *CGPLA Eng. & Wales*

Hughes, John (1790–1857), author, born on 2 January 1790, was the only child of Thomas Hughes DD, clerk of the closet to George III and George IV, vicar of Uffington, Berkshire, and canon of St Paul's Cathedral, and his wife, Mary Anne, daughter of the Revd George Watts, vicar of Uffington. 'Clever, active Mrs Hughes' (Lockhart, 524) was an early friend of Sir Walter Scott, whom she visited with her husband in 1824. Hughes was educated at Westminster School and at Oriel College, Oxford, where he graduated BA in 1812 and MA in 1815. He gained the prize for Latin verse and was the author of the macaronic Oriel grace-cup song, 'Exultet mater Oriel'. About 1820 he went to live at Uffington, and on 14 December 1820 he married, as his second wife, Margaret Elizabeth (1797–1887), second daughter of Thomas Wilkinson, of Stokesley Hall, Yorkshire: they had six sons and one daughter, the workhouse and school inspector and philanthropist Jane Elizabeth *Senior. Their second son, Thomas *Hughes, was the author of *Tom Brown's Schooldays*.

Hughes was a good scholar and linguist, a clever draughtsman and wood-carver. His chief publications were *An Itinerary of Provence and the Rhone*, with etchings by the author (1822) and an edition of *The Boscobel Tracts* (1830). He wrote much for magazines under the name 'Buller of Brasenose' and was celebrated in 'Christopher

in the Tent' in John Wilson's *Noctes Ambrosianae* (5 vols., 1855). On the death of his father in 1833 Hughes moved to Donnington Priory, Berkshire. He died at 7 The Boltons, West Brompton, London, on 13 December 1857.

W. W. Wroth, *rev.* Elizabeth Baigent

Sources J. G. Lockhart, *Memoirs of the life of Sir Walter Scott*, [new edn] (1845) · *N&Q*, 3rd ser., 3 (1863), 66 · *GM*, 3rd ser., 4 (1858), 225 · T. Hughes, *Memoir of a brother* (1873) · M. R. Mitford, *Recollections of a literary life*, new edn (1859) · Allibone, *Dict.* · Ward, *Men of the reign* · Burke, *Gen. GB* · *DNB* · Boase, *Mod. Eng. biog.*
Archives NL Scot., letters to Blackwoods

Hughes, John (1796–1860), Calvinistic Methodist minister, was born at Adwy'r-clawdd, near Wrexham, on 11 February 1796, son of Hugh Hughes (1763–1850) and his wife, Mary Davies, only child of Edward Davies of Adwy. He was the younger brother of Richard Hughes (1794–1871), founder of the publishing house of Hughes & Son, Wrexham, who published all his major works. Hughes's father was a carpenter, and Hughes himself followed the same trade until he was nineteen. Educated at the Sunday school, he joined the Calvinistic Methodist church at Adwy in 1810, and three years later began preaching. On 13 September 1815 he opened a school at Cross Street, near Hope, Flintshire, but in August 1817 he went to school himself to learn Latin and Greek. After a time he opened a new school called the Fairford Academy at Wrexham; it became renowned as a centre which prepared many young men for the pulpit in the absence of an established Welsh Methodist seminary. In February 1821 he was authorized as regular preacher to visit all parts of Wales, and in 1822 he preached before the Methodist Association. On 17 June 1829 he was ordained by the North Wales Association meeting at Bala. In 1834, owing to bad health, he gave up his school, and became a flour merchant, in partnership with a brother. In 1838 he went to Liverpool, attained considerable eminence there as a preacher, and became co-pastor with Henry Rees of the Welsh Calvinistic churches of Liverpool.

Hughes was twice married. His first wife, Mary Anne Jones, whom he married in June 1820, died on 26 March 1827. He married his second wife, Grace (1798–1860), in June 1833. He had five sons and seven daughters. He died on a visit to Abergele, Denbighshire, on 8 August 1860.

Hughes's influence coincided with a crucial period for Welsh nonconformity and was important in ending the political conservatism of nonconformist denominations and, especially, in achieving the divorce of the Methodists from the Anglican church. He published extensively, his main work being *Hanes Methodistiaeth Cymru* in three volumes (1851, 1854, 1856). Although the analysis contained in this work is weak and the volumes contain many inaccuracies, the work remains an important factual account of the development of Welsh Methodism, especially the personalities involved, and offers a vivid insight into early Methodist beliefs and preoccupations. In addition to this work, he published numerous theological tracts, particularly on the history of religion, and several works for religious education including translations into Welsh.

R. M. J. Jones, *rev.* Robert V. Smith

Sources DWB · R. Edwards, *Buchdraeth y diweddar Barchedig John Hughes* (1864) · E. Francis, *Marwnadau i'r diweddar Barchedig John Hughes, Mount Street, Liverpool: yr hwn a fu farw Awst 8, 1860* (1860) · *CGPLA Eng. & Wales* (1861)
Archives NL Wales, letters to Lewis Edwards
Wealth at death under £1500: probate, 5 Feb 1861, *CGPLA Eng. & Wales*

Hughes, John (*c*.1816–1889), ironmaster and engineer, was born at Merthyr Tudful, Glamorgan, the son of John Hughes, engineer. Although his family origins are obscure, his father was employed at the Cyfarthfa ironworks in Merthyr Tudful and, later, at the Victoria works in Ebbw Vale, Monmouthshire. According to tradition, Hughes joined his father, learning his trade at both works. By the early 1840s he held a senior position at the Uskside engineering works at Newport.

The Uskside works had grown from a small smithy in 1827 into a foundry specializing in ships' equipment such as anchors and chains. Hughes is variously described as proprietor, manager, and director of the works. Whatever his position, his time at Uskside was actively spent in consolidating both his personal and professional life. On 27 October 1844, at St Paul's Church, St Woolos, Newport, Monmouthshire, Hughes married Elizabeth (*d*. 1880), daughter of William Lewis. His wife's family were associated with the Tredegar Arms, adjoining the Uskside foundry and supplying its workers with beer. John and Elizabeth Hughes lived at 36 Church Street, near the works. Their eight children, six boys and two girls, were all born at home in Newport between 1846 and 1858. During the same period, Hughes developed the Uskside works, and patented a number of inventions in armaments and armour plating.

In 1859 the family moved to London. Through his marine engineering and armament experience Hughes obtained a senior position with the Millwall Engineering and Shipbuilding Company on Thameside, and later he became a director of the company. The firm won the British Admiralty's 1864 trials of armour plating for 'ironclads' with the Millwall shield, and John Hughes's reputation was secured. It was this that attracted the attention of the Russian government. Hughes was invited to St Petersburg to discuss the possibility of plating the naval fortress at Kronstadt. The negotiations soon developed into a proposal that Hughes should establish a metallurgical plant somewhere in Russia. Geological surveys had already indicated the mineral riches of the Donbass coal basin in southern Ukraine. Although previous attempts at industrial development in the area had not met with success, Hughes decided, after a tour of inspection, to take up the challenge. He bought a concession for building a full-cycle metallurgical plant and rail-producing factory based on local Donbass materials from Prince Sergey Kochubey, and negotiated for land, mineral rights, and contracts. Hughes signed a formal agreement with the Russian government in 1868, and the New Russia Company Limited was registered in London on 3 July 1869, with a capital of £300,000. Hughes's professional prestige attracted a number of prominent industrialists, including Sir Daniel

John Hughes (*c*.1816–1889), by unknown photographer

Gooch, Thomas Brassey, father and son, and Joseph Whitworth, whose names among his seventeen original shareholders helped to raise the necessary capital for his enterprise.

The site Hughes had chosen for the factory lay on the open steppe, about 75 kilometres north of the nearest port. All the equipment needed to establish an ironworks had to be hauled by bullocks across the steppe from Taganrog, on the Sea of Azov. In the summer of 1870 Hughes arrived with about a hundred specialist ironworkers and miners, mostly recruited from the industrial valleys of south Wales. Within eight months, on 24 April 1871, the first blast furnace had been commissioned, despite an unusually severe winter and a cholera epidemic. Regular production of iron began in January 1872. The Russian government provided initial subsidies and relaxed import duties, although minimum production levels and commencement dates had been set for the mines and furnaces. Hughes and his men overcame the early difficulties, and by 1880 were able to produce daily the agreed weekly quota of iron. The surrounding area was able to provide the works with all the necessary raw materials except specialized labour. Hughes therefore imported a small core of expert workers from south Wales, but local labourers were also recruited and trained; nevertheless, the company continued to employ British workers in senior positions until 1917. The company's works were known familiarly by the name of the founder, a testament to his forceful personality. The 'Hughes factory' gave its name to the settlement which grew up in its shadow. Hughes and his family lived in Hughesovka (Yuzovka) from 1870; four of his sons helped to establish and run the works, and a number of his grandchildren were born in the town.

A contemporary account describes John Hughes as 'an open-faced, clear-eyed, bluff and handsome man, with laughter as well as command in the tones of his voice' (obituary, quoted in Bowen). He was an industrial entrepreneur of the old school with a firm belief in the values of hard work, honesty, and hands-on management. He shared his workers' discomforts during the first winter at the site, and later is described visiting their homes to celebrate a wedding or to greet a new baby. In 1879 Hughes wrote from London to the minister of domains expressing his fears that an outbreak of plague could spread to Hughesovka: 'I have impressed on the workmen in our employ to abstain from drinking vodka … and also to avoid eating a large amount of cucumbers and melons and especially unripe fruit' (Central State Historical Archives, St Petersburg, F.37, op.53, d.746, p.297). He established hospitals, a fire brigade, and a police force in his town and took a personal interest in the health and general behaviour of his workforce.

John Hughes died on 29 June 1889 of a stroke while on business in St Petersburg. His body was returned to London for interment, beside his wife, in the family plot at Norwood cemetery. The town and the works which bore his name continued to expand under his sons' leadership, becoming one of the largest industrial enterprises in the Russian empire, until by 1917 the registered capital of the New Russia Company stood at £2.5 million. After the revolution of that year the majority of the company's foreign employees left the country, although the works survived and prospered under new management and a new name. The town of Hughesovka became Stalino in 1924, and adopted the name Donetsk in 1961. It remained one of the largest industrial centres in Ukraine. The New Russia Company was formally liquidated in 1970.

When he founded the New Russia Company, Hughes was a successful businessman in his fifties. In contrast to most foreign industrialists in Russia he cut his links with his British business interests and established his home in his adopted country. The likelihood of large profits was undoubtedly a major motivation, together with the technological challenge presented by building a new industry from the ground. His cautious, sure development of the company and paternalistic concern for his workers suggest a longer-term commitment to the creation of a stable industrial base in the Donbass, and a dynastic vision for the town which bore his name. SUSAN EDWARDS

Sources T. H. Friedgut, *Iuzovkaand revolution*, 2 vols. (1994) · S. Edwards, *Hughesovka: a Welsh enterprise in imperial Russia* (1992) · E. G. Bowen, *John Hughes (Yuzovka)* (1978) · I. A. Gonimov, *Staraia Yuzovka* (1967)
Archives Central State Historical Archive, St Petersburg, Russia · Glamorgan RO, Cardiff, Hughesovka Research Archive
Likenesses photograph, Donetsk Oblast Historical-Geographical Museum, Ukraine [*see illus.*]
Wealth at death £90,550 4s. 6d.: probate, 26 July 1889, *CGPLA Eng. & Wales*

Hughes, John [*pseud.* Ceiriog] (**1832–1887**), poet, was born on 25 September 1832 at Pen-y-bryn, Llanarmon, Dyffryn Ceiriog, Denbighshire, the youngest of the eight children of Richard Hughes (*d.* 1859), farmer, and his wife, Phoebe Evans (1796–1884). After a rudimentary education in the local school at Nant-y-glog, where he showed an early interest in English and Welsh literature, he worked grudgingly on his father's farm until 1848, when he was apprenticed to a printer in Oswestry. Not finding that work to his liking either, by the beginning of 1849 he was in Manchester with hopes of setting himself up as a grocer, but he found employment as a railway agent at the London Road goods station with responsibility eventually for some fifty clerks. He married Annie Catherine Roberts (1838/9–1931), a chemist's daughter, on 22 February 1861, and they had four children.

In Manchester, where Hughes found congenial company among fellow exiles in Welsh societies, he was prompted to write lyrics of a kind associated with Robert Burns, Thomas Moore, Beranger, and John Greenleaf Whittier. His success saw him labelled the Burns of Wales, but it has rightly been said that he lacked Burns's uncompromising readiness to engage life in full. Adopted by his compatriots as their advocate, Ceiriog denied his undoubted talents as a satirist and writer of nonsense verse revealed in his many contributions to some Welsh weeklies, and in particular in *Y Punch Cymraeg* ('The Welsh Punch'), which appeared intermittently between 1858 and 1864. He thought this denial necessary in order better to fulfil his 1860s role as serious advocate of Welsh pride and patriotism. Hughes built on the early success of 'Myfanwy Fychan' and 'Alun Mabon' to make himself 'a necessity' for a people short on self-belief and yearning for recognition as an 'imperial asset'.

As a poet, Ceiriog became a national figure following the eventful Llangollen eisteddfod of 1858, when his *rhieingerdd* (literally 'love poem') 'Myfanwy Fychan o Gastell Dinas Bran' was seen as a vindication of Welsh womanhood, sadly tarnished by the vilification of the three government-appointed commissioners who published their reports on the educational wants of Wales in 1847. Ceiriog's riposte to 'the treachery of the blue books', further strengthened by his prize-winning pastoral 'Alun Mabon' at the first official national eisteddfod, held at Aberdâr in 1861, made him something of a national comforter, and his first collection of poems, *Oriau'r hwyr* ('The Evening Hours'), published in 1860, was into its fifth edition by 1872 and reputed to have sold 25,000 copies. His popularity had assumed Tennysonian proportions in Wales. *Oriau'r bore* ('The Morning Hours') followed in 1862, *Cant o ganeuon* ('A Hundred Songs') in 1863, and *Y bardd a'r cerddor* ('The Poet and the Musician') in 1864.

In 1865 Ceiriog returned to mid-Wales to work for the Cambrian Railway Company as stationmaster at Llanidloes. An unspecified disagreement saw him move in 1870 to Tywyn in Merioneth, and by 1872 he had moved to Caersŵs in Montgomeryshire, where he was employed by the Van Railway Company to manage the 6 mile single line which served the Van Copper works. That venture having failed by the end of the 1870s, Ceiriog was to live out the rest of his life managing a ghost train for a mere pittance. His literary productivity also fell, although during this period he wrote *Oriau eraill* ('Other Hours') in 1868, *Oriau's haf* ('The Summer Hours') in 1876, and *Yr oriau olaf* ('The

Last Hours'), published posthumously in 1888. He also collected and published *Gemau'r adroddwr* ('Gems for Recitation') in 1865, and collaborated with the musician Brinley Richards to publish *The Songs of Wales* in 1873—a best-selling edition of traditional Welsh melodies, for some fifty of which Ceiriog wrote Welsh words in tune with the spirit of Victorian Wales.

Hughes had returned to Wales a poet of unprecedented popularity with high hopes of ascending in the social scale and yet lived to regret his return, pining for Manchester *bonhomie*, as man and poet, to his dying day. His failure and subsequent disillusionment saw him resort to drink; he died at his home, Carnedd Villa, in Caersŵs, of liver failure, on 23 April 1887, and was buried on 26 April in the cemetery of Llanwnnog church, near Caersŵs.

Ceiriog's coming coincided with the emergence of Wales as 'the land of song' and he rode to huge popularity on the backs of concert artistes who were in increasing demand from the 1860s onwards. Their repertoire included bourgeois parlour versions of traditional melodies for which Ceiriog composed winning words, and his exposition of his craft in *Y bardd a'r cerddor* shows that his shortcomings as a musician were compensated for by his instinctive sense of a melody's character and his sure aim at Welsh sentiments. Rooted in the exile's *hiraeth* for home—a *hiraeth* which was the tilth of popular nineteenth-century art on both sides of the Atlantic—Ceiriog evoked the natural beauty and richness of Wales, the virtue and valour of its people, and the pride of its past, leaving behind him in poems such as 'Y garreg wen', 'Cân yr arad goch', 'Bugail Aberdyfi', 'Aros mae'r mynyddau mawr', 'Nant y mynydd', 'Yn iach iti Gymru', 'Pe cawn i hon', 'Dros y garreg', and 'Bugail yr hafod' a legacy of song whose appeal remains undiminished.

HYWEL TEIFI EDWARDS

Sources I. Foulkes, *John Ceiriog Hughes: ei fywyd, ei athrylith, a'i waith* (1887) · S. Lewis, *Ceiriog* (1929) · H. T. Edwards, *Ceiriog* (1987) · E. G. Millward, *Cenedl o bobl ddewrion* (1991) · D. G. Jones, 'Ceiriog (1832–87)', *Gwŷr llên y bedwaredd ganrif ar bymtheg a'u cefndir*, ed. D. Morgan (1968), 199–213 · W. J. Gruffydd, *Ceiriog* (1939) · J. Lloyd-Jones, ed., *Caneuon Ceiriog: detholiad* (1925) · d. cert. **Archives** NL Wales, corresp. and papers · NL Wales, MS vol. of old Welsh melodies | NL Wales, letters to A. J. Brereton **Likenesses** photographs, 1860, NL Wales · J. Thomas, photograph, *c*.1865–1870, NL Wales · J. Thomas, photograph, 1884 (with Eos Môn), NL Wales · wood-engraving, repro. in Lloyd-Jones, ed., *Caneuon Ceiriog* **Wealth at death** £96 18*s*.: probate, 8 July 1887, *CGPLA Eng. & Wales*

Hughes, John [*called* Glanystwyth] (**1842–1902**), Wesleyan Methodist minister and editor, son of John Hughes (1815–1843), a butcher, and Jane, his wife, was born on 15 April 1842, at Cwm Magwr Isaf, in the village of Cnwch-coch, parish of Llanfihangel-y-Creuddyn, Cardiganshire. Left an orphan at an early age, he received some education at Llanfihangel-y-Creuddyn national school (*c*.1850–1854), and found employment first as a farmworker and afterwards as a lead miner. In 1863 he became a slate quarryman at Blaenau Ffestiniog where his interest in literary and theological questions made him a leader among his

fellow workers, and he was designated a Wesleyan lay preacher. Resolving to enter the ministry, he passed a brief period of preparation at Jasper House, Aberystwyth, in 1866–7, and was accepted by his connexion in 1867. In 1867 he began his work as a minister in south Wales and laboured at Treherbert (1867), Mountain Ash (1868), and Cardiff (1869) before moving further north to Tre'r-ddôl (1872), Trefeglwys (1873), Machynlleth (1876), Coed-poeth (1878), Caernarfon (1881), and Llanrhaeadr-ym-Mochnant (1884). In 1886 he went to London, returning to Wales in 1889 to minister at Rhyl. His last two ministries were at Manchester (1891) and Mount Zion, Liverpool (1894–7).

In 1897 Hughes was appointed Welsh connexional editor, and superintendent of the Welsh Wesleyan bookroom at Bangor. He took an active part in the affairs of his connexion, and was largely responsible for the establishment of an annual general assembly for north and south Wales. In 1901 he received the degree of DD from the South Western University, Georgetown, Texas. On 12 March 1873, at the Wesley Chapel, Charles Street in Cardiff, he married Emily, daughter of the Revd Henry Wilcox, with whom he had four sons and two daughters. He died at Isfryn, Bangor, on 24 February 1902 and was buried at Glanadda cemetery, Bangor; his wife survived him. One of his sons, Henry Maldwyn Hughes BA DD, was a Wesleyan Methodist minister and co-author of his father's biography (1904).

Hughes, best known by his bardic name of Glanystwyth, was respected as a preacher and as a writer of Welsh prose and verse. He edited *Y Winllan* from 1874 to 1876, *Y Gwyliedydd* newspaper in 1890, and *Yr Eurgrawn Wesleyaidd* from 1897 to 1902. He published many religious commentaries and was well known as a hymn writer. He was also a highly regarded eisteddfod bard.

J. E. LLOYD, rev. MARI A. WILLIAMS

Sources D. G. Jones and H. M. Hughes, *Cofiant Glanystwyth: sef bywyd y diweddar Barch* (1904) · *Yr Eurgrawn*, 94 (1902) [memorial issue] · *DWB* · *CGPLA Eng. & Wales* (1902) · m. cert. **Archives** NL Wales, diary **Likenesses** photographs, *c*.1874–1897, repro. in Jones and Hughes, *Cofiant Glanystwyth* **Wealth at death** £1071 9*s*. 7*d*.: probate, 17 April 1902, *CGPLA Eng. & Wales*

Hughes, Joseph (**1769–1833**), Baptist minister, was born on 1 January 1769 at Hand Court, Holborn, one of five surviving children of Thomas Hughes, an admirer of George Whitefield, and his wife, Sarah, *née* Brier, a Baptist. Six siblings had died before Joseph was born, and for health reasons he spent his infancy with a nurse at Enfield Chase. On returning home, he was taught by a Mrs Hudson. Mature for his age, extremely serious, and with strong religious leanings, he became known as 'a boy who could preach'. The family was not well off, and Hughes's father died when he was ten, but his mother's charitable activities brought them some prosperous connections.

In 1778 Hughes became a boarding pupil with Mr Smalley, Congregational minister in Darwen, Lancashire, moving in 1780 to the free school at nearby Rivington. Back in London in 1784 he was baptized by Dr Samuel

Stennett, pastor of the Baptist church at Little Wild Street. Through Stennett's influence he went later that year as a Ward scholar to the Bristol Baptist Academy, transferring to King's College, Aberdeen, in 1787. In Aberdeen, though dissatisfied with his own academic progress, Hughes founded one of Scotland's first Sunday schools. He graduated MA in March 1790, spent a session at Edinburgh University, then walked back to Aberdeen. On his return to London in 1791 the Little Wild Street Church recognized his calling to the ministry. Hughes's London friends had been seeking out a suitable position, and in July 1791 he became classical tutor at Bristol Baptist Academy and temporary assistant to Caleb Evans, pastor of Bristol's Broadmead Baptist Church.

The following month Caleb Evans died, and for more than eighteen months Hughes had sole charge of church and academy. In Bristol he became acquainted with Hannah More and the poets Samuel Taylor Coleridge and Joseph Cottle, and in 1793 he married Hester Rolph (1763/4–1839), a local solicitor's daughter. The couple had two surviving sons. When the Broadmead church appointed John Ryland as pastor Hughes stayed on as his assistant, but some thought his preaching style too stiff and his sermons insufficiently evangelical. Continuing dissatisfaction prompted his removal to Battersea in July 1796, to a chapel part owned by a member of Little Wild Street. A church was formed there in June 1797, and the congregation swelled. Tall, slightly stooping, with cultivated manners, and always anxious to express himself precisely, Hughes was at home in literary circles in Clapham and elsewhere. While never a popular preacher, he drew a sophisticated audience.

In 1798 Hughes co-founded the Surrey Mission Society, energetically canvassing support for its work of village evangelism, and in 1799 he helped form the Religious Tract Society, dedicated to circulating pure Christian literature. The society's first secretary (a title which he held until his death), he wrote several of its early tracts, edited others, and compiled an address to the public on the society's behalf. It was as the 'father' of the British and Foreign Bible Society, founded in 1804 to distribute Bibles worldwide, that Hughes became best-known, however. The idea of the society is widely attributed to him, and he developed it in a paper later published as *The excellence of the holy scriptures an argument for their more general dispersion at home and abroad*. As one of its joint secretaries from 1804 to 1833, Hughes helped the society weather some early controversies. He also travelled widely, pressing the society's claims, nurturing auxiliary bodies, and overseeing a massive expansion in its operations.

Hughes remained pastor at Battersea until his death, resisting suggestions that he should move as supporters moved away and the congregation dwindled. His few publications consist mainly of sermons, though he was much in demand as an editor. Abstemious in his personal habits, he became a generous (often anonymous) benefactor, especially of educational institutions. He was awarded an honorary DD by Brown University, Rhode Island, in 1811 and by Yale College, Connecticut, in 1821, but wished to keep both honours secret. Always sensitive, his home life was scarred by his eldest son's suicide about 1827. Hughes himself died in Battersea on 3 October 1833, having cut short a Bible Society tour because of an infection of the foot. He was buried at Bunhill Fields.

ROSEMARY CHADWICK

Sources J. Leifchild, *Memoir of the late Rev. Joseph Hughes, AM* (1835) · W. Canton, *A history of the British and Foreign Bible Society*, 2 (1904) · J. Sheppard, *A discourse occasioned by the death of Rev. Joseph Hughes, AM* (1833) · F. H. Gale, *Battersea Chapel, 1797–1897: a centenary record* (1897) · C. S. Hall and H. Mowvley, *Tradition and challenge: the story of Broadmead Baptist Church, Bristol, from 1685 to 1991* (1991) · J. Owen, *The history of the origin and first ten years of the British and Foreign Bible Society* (1816) · G. Browne, *The history of the British and Foreign Bible Society, from its institution in 1804 to the close of its jubilee in 1854*, 1 (1859)
Archives CUL, Bible Society MSS
Wealth at death left £555 in individual bequests; plus est. £120 p.a. in annuities: will, 1833, PRO, PROB 11/1822

Hughes, Joshua (1807–1889), bishop of St Asaph, was born on 7 October 1807 at Nevern, Pembrokeshire, the son of Caleb Hughes, a miller, and his wife, Magdalen. He was educated at Cardigan and Ystradmeurig grammar schools, and at St David's College, Lampeter (1828–30), where he was placed in the first class in the examinations every year, and where he gained prizes for Latin and Welsh essays. Hughes entered the ministry of the Church of England, as did two of his brothers, being ordained deacon in 1830, and priest in 1831. In 1832 he married Margaret (*d.* 1899), daughter of Sir Thomas McKenny and widow of Captain Gun. There were three sons and five daughters of the marriage. One son, Thomas McKenny *Hughes, became professor of geology at Cambridge; another, Joshua Pritchard Hughes, became bishop of Llandaff.

Hughes's first curacy was at Aberystwyth, and he then served at St David's, Carmarthen, before becoming vicar of Abergwili, near Carmarthen, in 1837. At Abergwili he worked closely with Bishop Thirlwall, whose episcopal residence was in the parish and whose influence left its mark upon his character. In 1846 Hughes was presented to the vicarage of Llandingad, otherwise known as Llandovery. During his long tenure of the parish he laboured with conspicuous evangelical zeal, as he had done at Abergwili. He often rode 25 miles on Sundays in order to conduct four services in his parish. His bishop made him rural dean, and his fellow clergy elected him to convocation in 1857. In 1867 he took his BD degree at Lampeter.

In 1870, W. E. Gladstone, seeking a Welsh-speaking bishop, and after consulting Connop Thirlwall, offered the vacant bishopric of St Asaph to Hughes. Gladstone may have been misled by an error in a clerical directory into thinking that Hughes was a Cambridge BA. The appointment was criticized by some, including some clergy in St Asaph diocese, because Hughes was not a university graduate, was practically unknown outside Wales, and had had exclusively parochial experience. As G. Hartwell Jones commented: 'The moral of the story seems to be that alumni of Oxford and Cambridge are in Wales, as elsewhere, more at their ease than alumni of Lampeter and better able to command obedience in exalted spiritual spheres' (Jones, 51–2).

Hughes's tenure of the see, however, soon justified the choice. He ruled his diocese with vigour and impartiality, setting up new boards and committees to assist him in its administration. Exacting a high standard from candidates for holy orders, and strenuously upholding the prerogatives of the church, he strove none the less to cultivate friendly relations with nonconformists. He was especially noted for the effectiveness of his confirmation addresses. He favoured moderate measures of church reform, laboured hard, as the first Welsh-speaking bishop of the diocese since 1727, to secure Welsh-speaking clergy for Welsh and bilingual parishes, and promoted the provision of services in Welsh for Welsh residents in English towns. He was one of the first as well as warmest supporters of the movement for promoting higher education in Wales, initially hoping that St David's College, preferably moved from Lampeter to Brecon, would become the centre of a Welsh university. He was the author of several charges, sermons, and pamphlets.

In August 1888 Hughes was struck with paralysis while staying at Crieff in Perthshire. He never rallied, and was unable to sign a deed of resignation from the see. He died at the Drummond Arms Hotel, Crieff, on 21 January 1889 and was buried at St Asaph Cathedral, Flintshire, on 25 January.   A. R. BUCKLAND, *rev.* D. T. W. PRICE

Sources *Yr Haul* (March 1889), 66–9 · *The Times* (22 Jan 1889) · *The Times* (26 Jan 1889) · D. R. Thomas, *Esgobaeth Llanelwy: the history of the diocese of St Asaph*, rev. edn, 1 (1908), 242 · J. Vyrnwy Morgan, ed., *Welsh religious leaders in the Victorian era* (1905), 53–7 · T. R. Roberts, *Eminent Welshmen: a short biographical dictionary* (1908), 189 · G. H. Jones, *A Celt looks at the world* (1946), 51–2 · tutor's register, U. Wales, Lampeter · Gladstone, *Diaries*
Archives NL Wales, corresp. and papers | BL, corresp. with W. E. Gladstone, Add. MSS 44425–44499 · LPL, letters to A.C. Tait
Likenesses photograph, repro. in Thomas, *Esgobaeth Llanelwy*, 193 · photograph, repro. in Morgan, *Welsh religious leaders*, 53

Hughes, Lewis (*b. c.*1570, *d.* in or after 1646), Church of England clergyman, was probably the Lewis Hughes resident in St Sepulchre's parish, London, on 17 November 1594, when he married Katherine Cornewall (*d.* 1625) of Foster Lane. By 1600 Hughes was rector of St Helen, Bishopsgate. In November 1602 he became embroiled in controversy when he supported Mary Glover, a servant in his parish, who accused a gentlewoman, Elizabeth Jackson, of bewitchment. The bishop of London and the College of Physicians doubted Glover's claim, but Hughes forced a trial, at which Jackson was found guilty. A month later Hughes and four other ministers exorcized Glover's demon, prompting the bishop to imprison Hughes and deprive him of his place at St Helen's.

Hughes vanishes from the record until 18 March 1614, when he contracted with the Virginia Company to serve as minister in Bermuda for three years. Leaving his wife in London, he reached the island in the spring of 1614. His *Letter Sent into England from the Summer Ilands* (1615) presents Bermuda as a paradise reserved by God for the English nation. To Hughes, the island's miraculous discovery by Sir George Somers and the abundant food, fertile soil,

healthy climate, and natural defences of the colony proved that the Almighty was favourably disposed towards the colonial venture. Accordingly, he warned potential emigrants to 'leave their sins behinde them and come hither as it were into a new world, to lead a new life' (Hughes, *Letter*, B4). During a famine in 1615 he dutifully remained with a group of mostly 'hartlesse and lazie' settlers so that they would not 'starve in body and soule together'. As he 'pine[d] away to skinne and bone', he witnessed a just God cull the 'lazie-starvinge-crue' (Hughes, *Privie Council*, A3; Craven, 80). Mr Lewes, as he was known, was esteemed by his congregation for such devotion; in 1616 they rose against acting governor John Mansfield, who had gaoled him for mutiny and exiled him to a small island, and forced his release.

In 1617 Hughes embarked on a radical restructuring of public worship in Bermuda. In a letter to his puritan patron Sir Nathaniel Rich he admitted, 'The book of common praier, I use it not at all', preferring 'A Manner of Publicke Worship', a liturgy of his own devising (Ives, 10, 337–46). Following the Presbyterian form, he had four elders elected to lead the church in St George's. He frequently criticized Governor Daniel Tucker from his pulpit, confident that, as the colony's sole minister, he was safe from dismissal. In 1618 he penned a description of the island and a doctrine on the sabbath, which were printed together three years later as *A Plaine and True Relation of the Goodnes of God towards the Summer Ilands*. Unlike other promotional tracts, the works were addressed to settlers in Bermuda rather than potential English backers, reminding them of God's many blessings and exhorting them to lead virtuous lives.

Hughes was a close friend of the colony's third governor, Nathaniel Butler, who in 1620 introduced into Bermuda the Genevan liturgy used in the Channel Islands. He preached at the opening of the island's first elected assembly in August 1620 and played no small part in keeping its disgruntled members tractable. In October 1620 he returned to England to recruit additional ministers and present colonists' grievances to the Bermuda Company but found himself attacked in court for his unorthodox liturgy. He returned to Bermuda in the autumn of 1621 and was one of four councillors who took over the government when Butler departed. In November 1622 a hostile faction within the Bermuda Company led by Sir Edwin Sandys displaced Hughes and sent four new ministers to the island. A 'lamentable letter' from his 'miserable, weake, and sicke' wife in England prompted his return in early 1623. He spent the next two years suing the company for back wages and ultimately appealed to the privy council for justice.

Hughes's post-Bermuda career is obscure. He was probably the man who in 1628 was dismissed from 'preaching in the Gaol of the White Lion', Southwark, by the bishop of Winchester. Certainly in 1640 he published *The Covenant of Grace*, a tiny book in question and answer format which described itself as having been 'set forth for the benefit of the Inhabitants of the Summer Ilands'. It included examples of providential lightning strikes against named church buildings, a feature repeated in a number of his other works.

Also in 1640 appeared *Certaine Grievances Well Worthy the Serious Consideration of … Parliament*. Although published anonymously, later editions, some with variant titles, were attributed to 'Lewes Hewes' and repudiated the first edition as unauthorized. The work attacked the prayer book as 'full of popish errours', denouncing the use of the Apocrypha and responses in worship, and the form of both baptism and the Lord's supper. By the third edition of 1641 he found room to include his earlier suffering at the hands of Bancroft over the Glover case, and ended his pamphlet by widening his attack to episcopacy, claiming 'every Bishop of the Church of *England* is an Antichrist' (L. Hewes, *Certaine Grievances*, 1641, 40). Five editions seem to have appeared in 1640–42, followed by other short, providentialist works, *A Looking-Glasse for All True Hearted Christians* (1642) and *Signes from Heaven* (1642). *The Errors of the Common Catechism* (1645), repeating the charges of *Certaine Grievances*, described its author as rector of Westbourne, Sussex. He does indeed seem to have been the 'godly and orthodox' Lewis Hughes associated with the living by parliament's committee for plundered ministers. In a petition of 1646 he claimed to have resided and preached there. It is not clear whether he ended his days there, though perhaps more likely than that he was the Lewis Hughes reported as preaching in Machynlleth, Montgomeryshire, in 1647.

Hughes laboured for nine years in the 'Vineyard of the Lord', as he called Bermuda, and during its formative years imparted a puritan cast to the colonial church. With Governor Butler, he worked to build social stability in the fledgeling settlement. Although snubbed by an ungrateful Bermuda Company and persecuted as a dissenter in England, he emerged as a prolific author in the early 1640s before retiring to the land of his birth. Hughes has been called one of the first American authors and 'the first Puritan minister of prominence in the English colonies' (Craven, 64, 85).   MICHAEL J. JARVIS

Sources G. W. Cole, 'Lewis Hughes, the militant minister of the Bermudas and his printed works', *American Antiquarian Society Proceedings*, 37 (1927), 247–311 • W. F. Craven, 'Lewis Hughes' *Plaine and true relation of the goodnes of God towards the Sommer ilands*', *William and Mary College Quarterly*, 2nd ser., 17 (1937), 56–89 • V. A. Ives, ed., *The Rich papers: letters from Bermuda, 1615–1646* (1984) • [N. Butler?], *The historye of the Bermudaes or Summer Islands*, ed. J. H. Lefroy, Hakluyt Society, 1st ser., 65 (1882) • L. Hughes, *To the right honourable lords of his majesties privie council* [n.d., 1625?] • L. Hughes, *A letter, sent into England from the Summer ilands* (1615) • J. H. Lefroy, *Memorials of the discovery and early settlement of the Bermudas or Somers Islands*, 2 vols. (1878–9) • G. Shipley, 'Turbulent times, troubled isles: the rise and development of puritanism in Bermuda and the Bahamas, 1609–1684', ThD diss., Westminster Seminary, 1989 • M. Jarvis, '"In the eye of all trade": maritime revolution and the transformation of Bermudian society, 1612–1800', PhD diss., College of William and Mary, 1998 • *Walker rev.* • Venn, *Alum. Cant.*

Hughes, Margaret [Peg] (*d.* 1719), actress and royal mistress, is of unknown origins, but as her brother had the same surname it is unlikely that she ever married. It is possible that Margaret Hughes was among the first group of actresses to join the King's Company of players after the Restoration. John Downes, prompter for the Duke of York's Company, later listed her among the members of the King's Company who had opened the New Theatre in Drury Lane on 8 April 1663, and recalled that she had subsequently played Desdemona in *Othello*, the first recorded performance by an actress in that role. On the other hand, she does not appear in the lord chamberlain's lists of players from autumn 1663 to February 1668. The first contemporary notice of Hughes may be that of the diarist Samuel Pepys, who on 7 May 1668 went backstage after a performance of *The Virgin Martyr* and stole a kiss from an actress named 'Pegg' whom he described as 'newly come', recently a mistress of Sir Charles *Sedley (*bap.* 1639, *d.* 1701) and 'a mighty pretty woman, and seems, but is not, modest' (Pepys, *Diary*, 9.189). She was the first actress to play Theodosia in John Dryden's *Evening's Love, or, The Mock Astrologer*, which premiered on 22 June 1668, and thereafter her progress in court society was rapid.

Having played Panura in Fletcher's *Island Princess* in November 1668, St Catherine in Dryden's *Tyrannic Love* in June 1669, and, from January to August 1669, also taken the role of Angellina in a revival of Shirley's *The Sisters*, Margaret left the stage at the end of the year in order to set up home with Prince *Rupert (1619–1682), cousin of Charles II. How and when she met the prince are uncertain. According to Anthony Hamilton's *Memoirs of the Count de Grammont*, she was with the count on a summer visit to Tunbridge Wells in 1668 when she made the acquaintance of Prince Rupert. The old soldier's hamfisted attempts at wooing her caused great amusement to Charles II and his courtiers; for the 'impertinent gipsy' initially refused Rupert's offers of money and gifts, preferring instead to 'sell her favours at a dearer rate'. This unexpected rejection 'caused the poor prince to act a part [as a suitor] so unnatural that he no longer appeared like the same person', but paid dividends as Margaret gradually assumed the role of Rupert's 'only mistress' and effectively 'brought down and greatly subdued his natural fierceness' (Hauck, 346; Hamilton, 306). When or even if the supposed events occurred is unclear. Rupert showed largesse towards her family, and employed at least one of her brothers in his household. Unfortunately in June 1670 'Mr. Hues … servant to [the] P[rince]' became embroiled in a quarrel with one of the king's retainers over which of the royal mistresses, Margaret Hughes or Nell Gwyn, was 'the handsomer now att Windsor'. In the ensuing struggle, insults flew, swords were drawn, and Hughes was killed (*Rutland MSS*, 2.17).

Installed in a lavishly furnished mansion at Hammersmith, later known as Brandenburg House, Margaret gave birth to a daughter in 1673, christened Ruperta. The solidity of the couple's relationship caused some anxiety, both dynastic and financial, to Rupert's youngest sister, the electress Sophia of Hanover. In the summer of 1674 Sophia complained bitterly to her husband that Margaret was in high favour with the court at Windsor and that she seemed certain to gain possession of those family jewels which had once belonged to Elizabeth, the 'winter queen' of Bohemia. Furthermore, in 1679, when the Danish ambassador praised Margaret Hughes's charm and reported her to be among the most virtuous women of the English court, the electress sourly reflected that that would have been no great praise (Scott, 363–4).

Margaret returned to the stage in 1676 as a member of the Duke of York's Company, based at the Dorset Garden Theatre. Over the course of that year she played Mirva in Settle's *Ibrahim*; Octavia in Ravenscroft's *The Wrangling Lovers*; Mrs Moneylove in Rawlins's *Tom Essence*; Gerana in *Pastor Fido*; Charmion in Sedley's version of *Antony and Cleopatra*; Valeria in Aphra Behn's *The Rover*; Cordelia in D'Urfey's *The Fond Husband*; and Leonora in *The French Conjurer*. After the 1676–7 season, however, she retired from acting altogether in order to devote her attentions to her daughter, and to Rupert, whose health was already beginning to fail. The prince was bedridden in 1680 and took to using an invalid chair. There is no truth in Warburton's rather prudish assertion that he latterly 'appears to have seen little of Mrs. Hughes … and to have been still less under her influence' (Warburton, 3.512). On 18 August 1682 Rupert wrote to the electress Sophia that Margaret 'took great care of me during my illness and I am obliged to her for many things'. He also revealed something of his domestic life, adding 'as for the little one [Ruperta], she cannot resemble me, [for] she is turning into the prettiest creature. She already rules the whole house and sometimes argues with her mother, which makes us all laugh' (Hauck, 302–3).

On 27 November 1682, two days before his death, Rupert signed his will, which provided handsomely for Margaret and their daughter. Margaret was to receive all of Rupert's money, plate, English estates, and investments, and the prince listed in detail some of the personal estate she was to have: the string of pearls which had once belonged to the winter queen; his diamonds; and all of his tapestries, gold stucco work, and hangings. He was at pains to point out that he had already given her a large cabinet worth an estimated £8000 and that this was now her own property. The earl of Craven was appointed executor and trustee of the estate, and it was left in no doubt that Margaret and Ruperta were to be the chief beneficiaries, while a former mistress, Francesca Bard, was pointedly excluded and their son, Dudley Bard, was left only Rupert's house at Rhenen and the hypothetical proceeds from the moneys owed to him by the emperor and the elector palatine.

From his deathbed the prince made a last request to Charles II that a marriage be contracted between Ruperta and Lord Burford, son of Nell Gwyn and the king. This, however, was refused. Concerned that his daughter should make an advantageous match, Rupert stipulated in his will that she should be 'dutiful and obedient to her mother, and not … dispose herself in marriage, without her consent, and the advise of the … earl of Craven' (Hauck, 351; Warburton, 3.558–60). Ruperta subsequently married Brigadier-General Emanuel Scrope *Howe, a prominent whig, soldier, and diplomat, and brother of the first Viscount Howe.

Rupert's corpse was accompanied to the grave on 6 December 1682 by a party which included a 'Mr. Hughes—

Gentleman', probably another brother or kinsman to Margaret (Warburton, 3.557). Within a few months Craven had already paid out £6000 each to her and her daughter, and had sold one of the most valuable items—the pearl necklace—to Nell Gwyn for £4520 in an attempt to clear household debts. According to one satire Margaret then set about gambling 'away the large estate given you by the good old gentleman [that is, Rupert]' (Genest, *Eng. Stage*, 1.386), but little is known of her later life. She eventually moved to Eltham in Kent. She died there on, or shortly before, 1 October 1719, and was buried at Lee, Kent, on 15 October. On 2 November 1719 her sister Judith Hawley was granted administration of her estate.　　　JOHN CALLOW

Sources Highfill, Burnim & Langhans, *BDA*, 8.24–7 · Pepys, *Diary*, vol. 9 · J. Downes, *Roscius Anglicanus, or, An historical review of the stage* (1708) · K. Hauck, *Die Briefe der Kinder des Winterkönigs* (1908) · J. H. Wilson, 'Pepys and Peg Hughes', *N&Q*, 201 (1956), 428–9 · *The manuscripts of his grace the duke of Rutland*, 4 vols., HMC, 24 (1888–1905), vol. 2, p. 17 · Genest, *Eng. stage*, 1.386–7 · P. Cunningham, 'Margaret Hughes, the mistress of Prince Rupert', *N&Q*, 2nd ser., 3 (1857), 6–7 · *Memoirs of Prince Rupert and the cavaliers including their private correspondence*, ed. E. Warburton, 3 vols. (1849), vol. 3 · T. Brown, Capt. Ayloff, and H. Barker, *Letters from the dead to the living* (1702); (1703) · E. Scott, *Rupert, prince palatine* (1899) · A. Hamilton, *Memoirs of the count de Grammont*, ed. and trans. H. Walpole and Mrs Jameson (1911) · P. Morrah, *Prince Rupert of the Rhine* (1976) · *Diary and letters of John Evelyn*, ed. W. Bray, 2nd edn (1819); repr. (1871) · *Memoirs of Sophia, electress of Hanover*, ed. and trans. H. Forester (1888) · *Briefwechsel der herzogin Sophie von Hanover*, ed. E. Bodeman (Leipzig, 1885) · PRO, LC5/138, fol. 71; 5/62, fols. 1, 107; 5/138, fol. 271 · *Letters to and from Henrietta countess of Suffolk*, ed. J. W. Croker, 2 vols. (1824)

Archives BL, household accounts, Add. MS 29767 · Hammersmith and Fulham Archives and Local History Centre, London, papers

Likenesses Lely, oils, 1670–74, priv. coll. · Bocquet & Schneker, engraving, pubd 1792 · Lely, oils, 1866–9, Tate collection · S. Cooper, engraving, repro. in *La Belle Assemblée* (1819) · E. Scriven, engraving, repro. in A. Hamilton, *Mémoirs du comte de Grammont*, new edn, 2 vols. (1811) · R. Williams, mezzotint (after P. Lely), BM, NPG · oils, priv. coll.

Hughes, Marian Rebecca (1817–1912), Anglican nun, was born on 14 January 1817 at Shenington, Gloucestershire, the youngest of the three children of the Revd Robert Edward Hughes (*d.* 1846), rector of Shenington, and his wife, Martha Pyner (1786–*c.*1852). She had a brother, Robert, and a sister, Fanny.

Marian Hughes is distinguished as being the first woman to take religious vows in the Church of England since the Reformation. The idea of reintroducing Sisters of Mercy within the Church of England had first been suggested by E. B. Pusey in 1839 but it was not until 1845 that the sisterhood at 17 Park Village West began its life. Meanwhile, after reading an essay by Newman, Marian Hughes had resolved to become a Sister of Mercy. She became acquainted with the Revd Charles Seager (1808–1878), a friend of Pusey and of her cousin the Revd Thomas Chamberlain, vicar of St Thomas's, Oxford, and from them she learned that there were no Anglican sisterhoods.

Despite this, Marian Hughes took the three vows of poverty, chastity, and obedience privately before Pusey at Seager's home early in the morning of Trinity Sunday (6

June) 1841. She then went to St Mary's Church and received holy communion from Newman. Kneeling beside her was Pusey's daughter, Lucy, who was receiving her first holy communion. That night Marian Hughes wrote: 'This day Trinity Sunday 1841, was I enrolled one of Christ's Virgins, espoused to Him and made His handmaid. … Written by me in the 24th year of my life at 12 o'clock at night on my knees' (Hughes, MS diary). Family ties prevented Marian from forming a sisterhood or from joining Park Village but she played an important advisory role in these formative years. Thus a few months after making her vows she accompanied Seager and his wife to Normandy, where she visited several religious orders and studied their rules and constitutions. On returning home she helped Pusey draw up the Park Village rule and also advised Lydia Sellon (1821–1876), who was planning her sisterhood at Devonport.

After Robert Hughes's death in 1846 Marian's brother became rector of Shenington and Marian stayed there to keep house. Following his marriage in 1849 she and her mother moved to Oxford and lived in Chamberlain's parish, where there was much work to be done among the poor. On 10 December 1849 Bishop Samuel Wilberforce formally sanctioned the foundation of a sisterhood, but it was not until after her move to a house in St John's Street in 1851 and her mother's death shortly afterwards that it assumed the character of a religious community. The Society of the Holy and Undivided Trinity (not to be confused with Lydia Sellon's Society of the Most Holy Trinity) had as its object service of the poor, sick, and needy. Within a few years it ran a number of schools and an orphanage, besides carrying out parish work in the Jericho district of Oxford; in 1854 the sisterhood displayed great heroism in the cholera epidemic. The rule and habit, formulated by Mother Marian, were based on those of the French Ursulines, and the magnificent new convent erected in 1866–8 along the Woodstock Road (later St Antony's College) was known for its austerity.

Mother Marian Hughes died on 7 May 1912 at the convent, having remained mother superior until her death. She was buried on 9 May in St Sepulchre's cemetery, Walton Street, Oxford, following a requiem in the convent chapel. A large number of clergy and lay people joined in the funeral procession, which was headed by girls from the orphanage carrying flowers, with twenty-four sisters following the bier.

Mother Marian was described in *The Times* as: 'a woman of great force of character, great capacity for organisation and government, and remarkable energy'. The church newspaper *The Guardian* paid similar tribute to her strength of character, and to her 'deep devotion of life', adding that 'she died as she had lived—in prayer'. Canon Henry Scott Holland remarked that: 'She never let her wonderful past imprison her … and was always a most delightful companion and friend' (*Oxford Magazine*). Her later years had been spent within the convent where she loved to reminisce about Pusey, Newman, and Keble; but while the past may not have imprisoned her, deafness certainly did. Hindsight might question the wisdom of retaining the office of mother superior all those years, but her real achievement lay in that vast act of faith made on Trinity Sunday 1841 when she stood completely alone in the Church of England under the vows she had made—and which she kept for seventy-one years.

VALERIE BONHAM

Sources M. Hughes, diary, 1841–52, Pusey Oxf., Society of the Holy and Undivided Trinity · *Oxford Journal Illustrated* (15 May 1912) · *The Times* (11 May 1912) · *The Guardian* (1912?) · *Church Times* (17 May 1912) · *Oxford Magazine* (16 May 1912) · *Oxford Times* (11 May 1912) · P. F. Anson, *The call of the cloister: religious communities and kindred bodies in the Anglican communion*, 2nd edn (1964) · A. M. Allchin, *The silent rebellion* (1958) · T. J. Williams, *The Park Village sisterhood* (1965) · d. cert.

Archives Pusey Oxf., corresp. and papers

Likenesses photograph (in old age), Society of the Holy and Undivided Trinity Archives, Pusey Oxf.

Wealth at death £1356 15s. 7d.: administration with will, 5 June 1912, CGPLA Eng. & Wales

Hughes, Mary (1860–1941), social worker, was born on 29 February 1860 at 80 Park Street, Mayfair, London, the youngest of the nine children (four daughters and five sons) of the Christian socialist Thomas *Hughes (1822–1896), author of *Tom Brown's Schooldays*, and his wife, Anne Frances Ford (c.1826–1910). The social interventionist Jane Elizabeth Senior (Mrs Nassau Senior) was her paternal aunt. She was educated by governesses at home. From the age of twenty-three she kept house for her uncle John Hughes, vicar of Longcot, Berkshire, where she became a poor-law guardian and district councillor.

In 1896 Mary Hughes moved to the East End of London as an unofficial, voluntary parish worker at St Jude's, Commercial Road, Whitechapel, where her sister Lilian was the wife of the vicar, the Revd Henry Carter. There she began her real life's work of sharing—and trying to shoulder—the troubles of the most afflicted, despairing people in London. She went into the slum dwellings, the workhouses, the doss houses, the lock wards (where sufferers from venereal disease were treated), and the infirmary, growing more and more at one in solidarity with the outcast. To the respectable world it seemed that she became ever more careless of herself and her surroundings—especially after she lost her sister and brother-in-law through the sinking of the *Titanic*. In 1915 she moved into the community settlement Kingsley Hall in Bow. She lived on bread and margarine and vegetables with a very little cheese, and always refused a fire, declaring 'Indignation keeps me warm!' 'For thirty years she had no new clothes, no holiday and no proper bed' (Pyper, 26). In 1917 she was made a JP for the Tower division, Shoreditch, sitting on rates and educational cases, sometimes being moved to tears by the tragedy behind the cases, and herself paying the fines the law demanded.

In 1918 Mary Hughes was accepted into the Society of Friends. She moved back to Whitechapel and became a poor-law guardian and regular visitor at the children's home and poor-law infirmary. Every day the unemployed would knock on the door of her two-room flat in Blackwall Buildings asking if she knew of any work available. In 1928 she moved to a converted pub at 71 Vallance Road,

Whitechapel, which she renamed the Dew Drop Inn and offered as a social centre and refuge for the homeless of the neighbourhood. Predictably, the poorest were also verminous, and it was said of Mary Hughes that 'Her lice were her glory'. She called herself a communist, acquiring the nickname Comrade, and took part in the marches of London's unemployed, no matter how threatening or how threatened they were by mounted police. 'She was always there', wrote Father Groser (Hobhouse, 114). When Gandhi visited Kingsley Hall in 1931 he asked to see her. She died in the East End at St Peter's Hospital, Whitechapel, on 2 April 1941, a lifelong pacifist appalled by those Christians in Britain calling for retaliation against the German blitz. George Lansbury wrote: 'Our frail humanity only produces a Mary Hughes once in a century' (ibid., 92).

SYBIL OLDFIELD

Sources R. Hobhouse, *Mary Hughes: her life for the dispossessed* (1949) · H. Pyper, *Mary Hughes: a friend to all in need* (1985) · *The Friend* (11 April 1941) · d. cert.
Likenesses photograph, repro. in Hobhouse, *Mary Hughes*, frontispiece
Wealth at death £9387 13s. 8d.: probate, 25 June 1941, CGPLA Eng. & Wales

Hughes, Mary Katherine (1853–1948). *See under* Hughes, Hugh Price (1847–1902).

Hughes [*née* Thomas], **Mary Vivian** [Molly] (1866–1956), writer, was born in Epping Forest, Essex, the daughter of Tom Edward Williams Thomas (*d.* 1879), stockbroker, and his wife, Mary Vivian (*d.* 1890). No birth certificate has been located. Molly Thomas had four much-loved brothers, and in the first of her four autobiographical volumes—*A London Child of the Seventies* (1934)—she describes their happy childhood in Canonbury. With an insight, rare among adults, into how children think, she recalls childhood's attractions at a time when families were larger and recreations simpler and family-centred. Educated at home until aged twelve, she then went to a nearby girls' school, and at sixteen to North London Collegiate School for Girls. Happy and well taught there, she none the less perceptively criticized in her memoirs the school's strict discipline under Frances Buss. This happy phase of Molly Thomas's life ended with her beloved father's sudden death in 1879. In one of her occasional autobiographical divergences from the truth, she ascribes it to 'a fatal accident'; in reality he killed himself, by falling under a train at Barnes, possibly to respect family sensitivities after a financial or personal scandal.

Census night on 3–4 April 1881 revealed at 1 Canonbury Park a houseful of eleven, all twenty-one or younger except for Mary Thomas, then allegedly fifty. Together with three of the five Thomas children there were seven others, presumably visitors or servants. In her historical (and covertly autobiographical) novel *Vivians* (1935) Molly Thomas united her affection for Cornwall with her growing interest in her mother's background. In her second overtly autobiographical volume—*A London Girl of the Eighties* (1936)—Molly Thomas describes how she and her resilient mother, financially hard-pressed, moved about the country together while her brothers dispersed. Dark

haired, with a high forehead and rather protruding eyes, she lacked her mother's striking looks. After teacher training at the Cambridge Training College for Women in 1885–6 she taught briefly in Darlington and then in a Kensington girls' day school, while at the same studying for a BA. *A London Girl* ably portrays from the inside the pioneering and experimental mood of the woman teacher's life in a late-Victorian secondary school for girls. It also elaborates upon what she saw as the old-fashioned habits of rural Wales, whence came Arthur Edward Hughes—close friend of her brother Charles, who had died young. Son of the late Robert Hughes, a land agent, Arthur was teaching mathematics in Bedford to fund his two younger brothers into medicine and the church before training as a barrister; at twenty-one Molly became engaged to him. The volume ends with the death on 1 May 1890 after a short illness of Mary Thomas, as much Molly Thomas's friend and companion as her mother.

Her third autobiographical volume—*A London Home of the Nineties* (1937)—begins with Molly Thomas resuming her studies with difficulty, and passing her final examination for the BA in autumn 1890. She had already impressed several women influential in the educational world, and was chosen to set up the new teacher-training department of Bedford College, London. Beginning work there in January 1892 she seems to have shown initiative and imagination. Her third autobiographical volume lacks the charm and cohesion of the first two because it is less firmly focused on the Thomas family and is disrupted by what amounts to a travel diary of her visit to an educational conference in Chicago in 1893. On 10 July 1897 her career at Bedford College ended when she married Arthur Hughes at St Andrew's Church, Holborn, and moved to a flat in Ladbroke Grove, where they lived for seven years. While as a young woman she had helped to open up women's career opportunities, her feminism did not extend to repudiating domesticity and motherhood, both of which she now embraced with enthusiasm. Their first child, Bronwen, born in 1898, died a year later but was followed by three sons. The Hughes family moved to Barnet, where Molly Hughes's public life dwindled to occasionally reviewing books for an educational periodical.

At this point her memoirs descend into a rather humdrum north London outer-suburbanity, and this is the tone deliberately adopted in her *A London Family Between the Wars* (1940), written at a time when the war's outcome was utterly uncertain. The book begins with another tragedy, the death of Arthur Hughes in February 1918, run over by a tram in the blackout. 'I was crazy with grief', she recalled twenty-two years later (*A London Family*, 1), and for the rest of her life she longed to be reunited with him. With her three sons at school, this personal tragedy was compounded by money worries. Her life of unmoneyed and unconventional intellectualism was now perforce confirmed. She moved to Cuffley, Hertfordshire, in 1920 and her memoirs would have been rounded off logically if their fourth volume had focused on bringing up her boys, thereby returning to her initial theme of childhood. Instead she chose to focus on the small change of outer-suburban existence, commenting on the quaintness of her surroundings and presenting a somewhat quirky image of herself. Her book combines a lack of introspection—surprising given her deep but undiscussed Anglican faith—with what is if anything an over-detailed account of daily life. Outside events scarcely impinge on her domesticated narrative, except for the general strike, which she unhesitatingly opposed.

After her husband's death Molly Hughes had to resume a career, returning to teaching; she eventually became an inspector for the University of London and for the Board of Education. In the latter role she was observant, critical when necessary, but constructively so, and as one schoolteacher recalled, 'she had a fine sense of humour and fun and her laugh was infectious' (J. A. Leishman, *The Times*, 15 June 1956). By the mid-1930s she found herself living alone, relishing her work but also friends, gossip, and the rural enjoyments of Cuffley, together with visits from her boys, outings in their cars, and occasional concerts. Her equable guidebook for Englishmen, *About England* (1927), reflects her interest in literature, history, and topography, together with her observant and affectionately conventional but somewhat surprised and amused response to the world around her. In her *America's England* (1930) she adapted her history and topography with the American visitor in mind. Again in *London at Home* (1931) and *The City Saints: a Guide to Churches in the City of London* (1932) she elaborated upon parts of earlier publications, seizing the opportunity to express her enthusiasm for the curiosities of the London streets and for the people in them; in *The City Saints* she drew together her topographical and religious enthusiasms. Her *Hidden Interests in the Bible* (1932) follows her earlier line in textbooks, whether on Latin or on religious subjects, and shows a very close knowledge of its subject, which it seeks to illuminate by bringing out its literary and historical dimensions. The seriousness of her religious preoccupations resurfaced in her *Scripture Teaching Today* (1939), a practical manual for teachers of the subject.

Meanwhile *A London Child* had brought her a large fan mail, and many of her correspondents became family friends; among them were the American poet H. D. and the author Bryher, with whom she corresponded regularly. For a short time after the war she lived with her youngest son, Arthur, in Dublin, but her eyesight and memory were by then failing, and the pressures on the Dublin family made it seem sensible for her to spend her last days with her second son, Barnholt, in South Africa. There she went in 1948, and it was at Saalen Rest Home, Bromley, Johannesburg, South Africa, that she died on 29 May 1956.

It is for her four autobiographical volumes—the first three republished as a single-volume trilogy, *A London Family, 1870–1900* (1991)—that Molly Hughes will be remembered. 'We were just an ordinary, suburban, Victorian family', she says in her preface, 'undistinguished ourselves and unacquainted with distinguished people'. No less valuable for that, these volumes were closely observant, and drew upon occasional documents that she had preserved but also upon diaries, though she does not quote them directly. She emerges as a common-sensical, liberal-minded young woman, fond of children, who became an imaginative teacher. Inheriting her mother's zest for life and sense of fun, she reveals almost incidentally how constricting were late-Victorian restraints on women's freedom of movement, let alone on women's career opportunities. She experienced sadness enough in her young life—the first two of her four volumes each being separated from their successors by the death of a much loved parent, the fourth beginning with her husband's sudden death; furthermore, two of her four brothers died young, as did her daughter. Yet she tended not to dwell on these or other difficulties, and her determined middle-aged cheerfulness amid the small change of suburban domestication bestows on her quietly understated memoirs a nostalgic tone—even, for one hostile reviewer, a 'rose-tinted blandness' (Mary Brennan, *Glasgow Herald*, 28 July 1981). This domesticated, rural, and traditionalist tone helps to explain the wide readership her memoirs enjoyed during the disturbingly fast-changing decades in Britain from the 1940s. Yet when the memoirs were first published they helped to provide the more balanced and sympathetic view of the Victorians that was then much needed; the second volume appeared, after all, in the same year as G. M. Young's *Portrait of an Age*. Furthermore, in their quiet preoccupation with the ordinary and the commonplace, the memoirs provide a salutary balance to historical writing that is always at risk of being over-preoccupied with the self-advertising and the unusual.

BRIAN HARRISON

Sources *The Times* (5 June 1956) · letters, *The Times* (15 June 1956) · private information (2004) · m. cert. · census returns, 1881 · Venn, *Alum. Cant.* [Arthur Edward Hughes]
Likenesses photographs, priv. coll.
Wealth at death £2615 15s. 11d.: South African probate sealed in England, 13 March 1957, *CGPLA Eng. & Wales*

Hughes, Obadiah (1695–1751), Presbyterian minister, was born in Canterbury and baptized on 23 September 1696 at Guildhall Street Chapel, Canterbury, the son of George Hughes (d. 1719) and his wife, Mary. His father was the minister of the chapel. There were three further Presbyterian ministers in the family—his grandfather, Obadiah, his brother, John (d. 1729), and John's son, also Obadiah, who took the family connection with the Presbyterian ministry into the next generation. Little is known of his early education, except that between about 1705 and 1710 it was undertaken in Canterbury, probably by his father, and is believed to have been completed in Scotland. He was educated for the ministry under John Jennings at Kibworth dissenting academy. About 1715 or 1716 Hughes became private chaplain to Mrs Delicia Woolf at Kensington. In 1719 he voted with the non-subscribing ministers in the Salters' Hall debate and the following year he became assistant minister to Joshua Oldfield at Maid Lane Chapel, Southwark. Hughes soon revived a declining congregation and became sole pastor in 1729.

Hughes's marriage on 2 March 1727 to his former patron Delicia Deacle (*née* Roberts; *first married name* Woolf; *bap.*

1680, *d.* 1749), the widow of John Deacle and daughter of Sir Gabriel and Mary Roberts, gave him a secure income; there were no children, although they adopted his wife's niece, Delicia Fryer, daughter of Sir John Fryer, who brought with her a considerable fortune. 'Having the advantage of an ample Fortune, it rather quickened than abated his Diligence in his beloved Work' (Allen, 27). In December 1728, along with five other London dissenting ministers, he was made DD by King's College, Aberdeen.

Hughes was above all a preacher and minister to a gathered congregation: 'To preach the Gospel he considered the noblest work in the world. … His public discourses were of a plain, scriptural and evangelical nature' (Wilson, 4.101). In theology he appears to have been a moderate Calvinist. By 1740 he had become one of the leading and most influential Presbyterian ministers of his day. He was secretary of the Presbyterian Board from 1738 to 1750 and a Salters' Hall lecturer from 1746. His published output was meagre, mainly consisting of funeral sermons. A benevolent man and highly respected, he had a reputation for deep seriousness. 'His Gravity and Seriousness of Spirit were so remarkable, that I believe a light and frothy Word was never heard to drop from his lips' (Allen, 32).

In 1743 Hughes became minister of Princes Street Chapel, Westminster, a position he retained until his death. He died quite suddenly on 10 December 1751 at Aldermanbury, in the City of London, after a long decline, though carrying on an active ministry to the end. He was buried on 17 December 1751 with his wife in the chancel of the nearby St Martin Outwich Church, 'there to rot and sleep together until the great resurrection day' (will, 1751). ALAN RUSTON

Sources W. Wilson, *The history and antiquities of the dissenting churches and meeting houses in London, Westminster and Southwark*, 4 vols. (1808–14), vol. 4, pp. 96–102 · J. Allen, *A sermon on occasion of the death of Obadiah Hughes* (1752), 27–32 · IGI · H. McLachlan, *English education under the Test Acts: being the history of the nonconformist academies, 1662–1820* (1931), 141 · will, PRO, PROB 11/791/334 · burial register, St Martin Outwich, GL, MS 6837 · minutes, senatus meeting, University and King's College, Aberdeen, 23 Dec 1728, U. Aberdeen, archives · E. Calamy, *An historical account of my own life, with some reflections on the times I have lived in, 1671–1731*, ed. J. T. Rutt, 1 (1829), 437, 514 · *Protestant Dissenter's Magazine*, 6 (1799), 14 · GM, 1st ser., 21 (1751), 752 · *Calendar of the correspondence of Philip Doddridge*, ed. G. F. Nuttall, HMC, JP 26 (1979), 519, 1149, 1216, 1570 · DNB · C. Surman, index of dissenting ministers, DWL · parish register, St Olave, 2 March 1727, GL, MS 17818 [marriage]
Archives DWL, letter, MS 12. 107 (208)
Wealth at death see will, 20 Dec 1751, PRO, PROB 11/791/334

Hughes, Patrick Cairns [Spike] (**1908–1987**), musician and writer, was born at 445 Cockfosters Road, Enfield, Middlesex, on 19 October 1908, the son of the Irish music critic and composer Herbert Hughes (1882–1937) and his wife, Lilian Florence Peploe Meacham, a Harley Street psychiatrist then enjoying her third marriage. As Spike Hughes recounted in his amusing, discerning, and detailed autobiographies, *Opening Bars* (1946) and *Second Movement* (1951), his father never had much time for him beyond providing the financial support for his erratic career up to the age of sixteen, and most of his early and much travelled youth was spent in the company of his mother. His father, a founder of the Irish Folksong Society, had published his *Irish Country Songs* just after Patrick's birth, and Patrick was always proud of the dedication to him.

Hughes's longest period of sustained education was at the Perse School in Cambridge, but otherwise much of his knowledge was self-taught in various parts of Europe, notably in Boulogne and in Sicily and various parts of mainland Italy, including Venice and Florence. The formal musical training he received came from studies with the composer Egon Wellesz in Vienna, from 1923 to 1925. Like many composers before him, he learned most from copying the craft of other people's scores, having particular admiration for the varied arts of Mozart, Puccini, and Wagner. During his time in Vienna he started on his career as a music critic by sending fitful notices of musical happenings in the city to *The Times* in London. His first completed musical composition was a setting of 'Who is Sylvia?'

In 1926 Hughes lived for a while in Cambridge and there he wrote a cello sonata, which was performed in London, and the incidental music for two Cambridge productions: in 1926 *Love for Love* by William Congreve and in 1927 *The Player Queen* by W. B. Yeats. About 1927 he began to find an increasing fascination in the world of jazz, being first thoroughly stirred by hearing the Blackbirds, an all-black revue pit orchestra, and then by hearing the 'Bessie Smith-like' singing of Edith Wilson, whom he preferred to the more studied Florence Mills. He began to play the double bass in various small neo-jazz groups, including the Night Watchmen (1929–30). At this time he acquired the lasting forename Spike, which he assumed was an allusion to the bottom end of his chosen instrument, but which he later found to be a matey naval name for all the Hughes clan.

Hughes formed his own jazz group in 1930; it played at the Café de Paris in London and recorded at the Chenil Galleries for Decca as the Decca-Dents (a slight contortion of the originally intended name Deccadents), and received most encouraging reviews in *Melody Maker* and elsewhere. He became a house arranger for Decca, as well as continuing to record and to build a reputation abroad, which resulted in a tour of the Netherlands. Having been offered a job in the orchestra pit for C. B. Cochran's *The 1931 Revue*, he found himself orchestrating the score, which involved him in his first contact with Noël Coward via 'Half-Caste Woman', and the production of a score for a ballet based on Pergolesi which led to the writing of the ballet *High Yellow*, successfully performed at the Savoy Theatre in 1932 with Alicia Markova as its star. Spike Hughes's very individual jazz compositions were often distinguished by distinctive, often rather Irish-sounding tunes; others, as in his *A Harlem Symphony*, owed something to his admiration for the music of Duke Ellington. He toured with the Jack Hylton orchestra (1931–2), which recorded his best-known jazz piece, 'Six Bells Stampede', in 1932. The high spot of his jazz career came in 1933, when he went to America to lead a recording orchestra including such jazz luminaries as Coleman Hawkins, Benny Carter, Red Allen, Dicky Wells, Choo Berry, and Sidney Catlett; this made minor masterpieces of such distinctive pieces as 'Nocturne', 'Pastoral', 'Arabesque', and 'Donegal Cradle Song', which show a distant kinship with the writings of Herbert Hughes. The apex of Hughes's activities as an arranger came when he was employed to score the whole of Noël Coward's revue *Words and Music* and ended up as conductor for the show as well.

Spike Hughes's achievements as a musician and composer were interesting and highly individual, while his writings as a jazz record reviewer for *Melody Maker* (1931–44) were very influential and did much to instil a proper understanding of jazz in Britain. He took over from a legacy of suspicion of (even prejudice against) black jazz, revelled in the 'art vs. music' debate under the pseudonym Mike, and was particularly eloquent and effective in his appreciation and approval of the work of Duke Ellington. From 1933 to 1936 he was also music critic of the *Daily Herald* and was becoming increasingly involved in the world of classical music and his old love of opera. He returned to the subject of jazz in *The Times* (1957–67). Hughes was married, and he and his wife, Charmian Joyce Hughes, lived at Broyle Gate Farm House, Ringmer, near Lewes, Sussex.

Hughes is remembered by many as a regular broadcaster on many fields of classical and light music, and he became a skilful exponent of the radio and later of television. His first radio plays were heard in 1936, and he wrote incidental music for a radio production of Ferenc Molnar's *The Swan* in 1937. His opera *Cinderella* received an early BBC television production in 1938. A later opera, *St Patrick's Day* (derived from R. B. Sheridan), was broadcast in 1947; and his musical *Frankie and Johnny* was televised in 1950. During the Second World War he worked for the BBC German service and often broadcast on *Children's Hour*. He wrote a number of books on music with a popular slant, the earliest, *Nights at the Opera* (1948), and the best-known, *Great Opera Houses* (1956), reflecting his lifelong interest in opera and based on his personal experiences of most of these works. There were also readable individual studies including *Famous Mozart Operas* (1957), *Famous Puccini Operas* (1959), *Famous Verdi Operas* (1968), and *The Toscanini Legacy* (1959). He had a long association with Glyndebourne, whose productions he had first reviewed in 1934, and he wrote its history in 1965.

In 1954 Hughes produced the amusingly illustrated *The Art of Coarse Cricket: a Study of its Principles, Tradition and Practice*. He subsequently developed it into a genre, writing similarly titled books covering travel (1957), gardening (1968), bridge (1970), cookery (1971), entertaining (1972), and language (1974). In these books, as in all his writings, he displayed a wicked sense of humour and a satirical view of the world and its contrived labours. The subtitle of the gardening book ('The care and feeding of slugs') gives a good flavour of the jocular tone, which went down well with readers.

Spike Hughes was a wonderfully entertaining companion and a loyal supporter of what he most appreciated—the art of such masters as Duke Ellington, Arturo Toscanini, and Bruno Walter, and jazz and opera in general. He died of heart failure on 2 February 1987 at the Royal Sussex County Hospital, Brighton. At the time of his death Hughes was working on a new encyclopaedia of opera. He was survived by his wife.   PETER GAMMOND

Sources S. Hughes, *Opening bars* (1946) [autobiography] · S. Hughes, *Second movement* (1951) [autobiography] · b. cert. · d. cert. · *The Times* (5 Feb 1987) · *New Grove*, 2nd edn · J. Chilton, *Who's who of British jazz* (1997) · J. Godbolt, *A history of jazz in Britain* (1984) · *CGPLA Eng. & Wales* (1987) · M. Tucker, *The Duke Ellington reader* (1994) · I. Carr, D. Fairweather, and B. Priestley, *Jazz: the rough guide*, 2nd edn (2000)

Wealth at death under £40,000: probate, 30 March 1987, *CGPLA Eng. & Wales*

Hughes, Richard (*c*.1565–1619), poet and courtier, was born in Cefnllanfair, Llanbedrog, Caernarvonshire, the second son of Huw ap Rhisiart ap Dafydd (*d*. 1590) and Annest (*d*. 1592), daughter of Robert ap Hywel, Saethon. His father, a well-known poet and patron of bards, probably taught his son the basics of *cynghanedd* (a combination of alliteration and internal rhyme), but Richard was more proficient in the freer metres becoming popular in the sixteenth century. As far as is known he received no formal education and probably followed his father into the army. His second cousin, John Salesbury, of Rug and Bachymbyd, was a recruiter for the retinue of the earl of Essex, and Hughes was in the latter's service by the late 1590s. He was appointed one of Queen Elizabeth's footmen on 21 December 1599 but maintained contacts with Captain Salesbury; through him he became associated with the Essex rebellion. Before 11 February 1601 Hughes was interrogated about a meeting with Salesbury and other conspirators on the eve of the uprising (7 February) but he cleared himself of involvement or foreknowledge, and kept his post as footman. His appointment was confirmed by James I, and he received the customary issue of red velvet for new uniforms for James's coronation. One of his elegists states that he remained in the king's service until his death (in 1619).

The few other known details must be garnered mostly from Hughes's poetry. He visited his family in Llŷn, and several risqué *englynion* (quatrains in strict *cynghanedd*) reflect tavern life, probably in the borough of Pwllheli, where they owned property. Two itinerant poet–heralds based in Oswestry, father and son, Rhys and Siôn Cain, were friends; Hughes wrote admiringly of Rhys but satirized his son in *englynion* to avenge a satire (now lost) on himself. Siôn Cain also wrote a charming *cywydd* (a series of seven-syllable rhyming couplets in full *cynghanedd*) addressed to Hughes and his nephew, Huw Bodwrda, on an occasion when both were ill. Another poet, Rhisiard Phylip, composed a *cywydd* asking Hughes for a bow and arrows for Huw Llwyd, Cynfal, which depicts scenes of hunting on the hills of Ardudwy and the shores of Llŷn. Hughes composed thanksgiving *englynion* for the foiling of the Gunpowder Plot, and he contributed the last of the laudatory tributes at the beginning of *Coryat's Crudities* (1611); Hughes's was one of two Welsh examples and was commented on jocularly by Thomas Coryate in his introduction. This connection and other tenuous, but cumulatively significant, references indicate that Hughes was on the fringes of a courtly, literary circle which included Ben Jonson, John Donne, Hugh Holland, Michael Drayton, and many others. Hughes himself is best-known for his lyrical love poetry in rhythmic accentual metres, and in these he has been seen as breaking new ground in Welsh verse.

Hughes's will, signed on 6 February 1619, was proved on 3 May by his younger brother, John. Two poets composed elegies to him; a formal *cywydd* by Gruffydd Phylip states that Hughes was buried with his ancestors in Llanbedrog church; the other, *englynion* by a personal friend, Hugh Roberts, is a more intimate poem. Neither wife nor child is ever mentioned.   NESTA LLOYD

Sources N. Lloyd, ed., *Ffwtman hoff: cerddi Richard Hughes, Cefnllanfair* (1998) · N. Lloyd, 'Richard Hughes, Cefnllanfair: courtier and poet', *Transactions of the Caernarvonshire Historical Society*, 58 (1997), 47–67 · J. H. Davies, ed., *Caniadau yn y mesurau rhyddion* (1905), 21–4 · J. H. Davies, *Carolau gan Richard Hughes* (1900) · M. Fardd [J. Jones], *Cynfeirdd Lleyn, 1500–1800* (1905), 203–18 · T. H. Parry-Williams, *Canu rhydd cynnar* (1932) · scattered references in public records, e.g. CSPD wardrobe accounts, LC 5/37, 292 · *Calendar of the manuscripts of the most hon. the marquis of Salisbury*, 24 vols., HMC, 9 (1883–1976), esp. vols. 11, 14, *passim*

Wealth at death bequests of £106 13s. 4d. and £113, and £5 each to three sisters; lands to elder brother, residue to younger brother: will

Hughes, Sir Richard, second baronet (*b.* in or before **1723**, *d.* **1812**), naval officer, was the eldest son of Sir Richard Hughes, first baronet (*d.* 1780), and Joanne, daughter of William Collyer. Richard's father, like his grandfather, also Richard (*d.* 1756), served as a commissioner of the navy at Portsmouth. In 1739 he was entered at the Royal Naval Academy at Portsmouth, and three years later he joined the *Feversham*, commanded by his father. On 1 April 1745, while acting lieutenant of the *Burford* in the Mediterranean, he passed his lieutenant's examination, and was declared in the certificate to be 'upwards of 21'. The next day he was promoted lieutenant of the *Stirling Castle* by Vice-Admiral William Rowley, and he continued serving in her until the peace.

In 1752 Hughes was appointed to the *Advice*, going to the West Indies with the broad pennant of Commodore Thomas Pye; in her he lost his sight in one eye when it was accidentally pierced by a table fork. He was promoted commander of the *Spy* on 6 February 1756 and was posted to the *Hind* on 10 November.

In January 1758 Hughes was appointed to the *Active*, one of the squadron employed during the summer on the coast of France under Commodore Richard Howe, and in February 1759 he was transferred to the *Falmouth*, one of the ships sent under Rear-Admiral Samuel Cornish to join Vice-Admiral Thomas Pocock in the East Indies. In the following January he was moved into the *York*, and in her he participated in the reduction of Pondicherry in 1760–61. He was shortly afterwards obliged by ill health to return to England, and in November 1761 he was appointed to the *Portland*, for service on the home station; in her, in the following summer, he carried the earl of Buckinghamshire, as ambassador to Russia, to Kronstadt. In April 1763 he was transferred to the frigate *Boreas* for occasional service,

including that of convoying troops to Goree in the spring of 1766.

Hughes commanded the guardship *Firm* at Plymouth from May 1767 to May 1770, and the guardship *Worcester* at Portsmouth from January 1771 to January 1774. Three years later he was appointed to the *Centaur*, and in June 1778 he was sent out in the storeship *Pacific* as resident commissioner of the navy at Halifax, and also, in express terms, 'commander-in-chief of his Majesty's ships and vessels which shall from time to time be at Halifax, when there shall be no flag officer or senior officer present'. During his thirty-five months as resident commissioner (he returned to England in August 1781) Hughes made one important contribution. He concluded the first contract let in the colony of Nova Scotia to supply masts, yards, and bowsprits for the home yards. It occurred at a moment of acute shortage of larger masts in England, occasioned by the disruption of American supply in 1775 and the increased difficulties with the Baltic supply from 1778 onwards. The Navy Board initially was highly sceptical about the likely quality—an attitude which the first samples sent them seemed to justify—yet by the war's end the navy had become dependent on Nova Scotia masts, and thereafter on those of New Brunswick.

On 26 September 1780 Hughes was promoted rear-admiral of the blue; in the previous April he had succeeded to the baronetcy, on the death of his father. In 1781 he was commander-in-chief of the squadron in the downs, and in 1782, with his flag in the *Princess Amelia*, he commanded a division in the Grand Fleet under Lord Howe at the relief of Gibraltar, and the encounter with the allies off Cape Spartel. He was afterwards sent to the West Indies to reinforce Admiral Hugh Pigot, and on Pigot's returning to England he remained as commander-in-chief, with his flag in the *Leander*, and afterwards in the *Adamant*, the larger ships being ordered home.

Hughes's period of command was marked by two incidents of interest, mainly from their connection with the career of Horatio Nelson. In 1785 Hughes, on the representations of the merchants, had been induced to waive the enforcement of the navigation laws with respect to vessels of the United States trading in the West Indies. But Nelson pointed out to him that the suspension of the act exceeded his legal power, and Hughes, accepting Nelson's view, was afterwards thanked by the Treasury for his action, to the annoyance of Nelson who, aware of his own heavy-handed approach to the issue, emerged as Hughes's critic. The second incident arose out of Hughes's giving Captain John Moutray, the naval commissioner at Antigua, an order to act as commander-in-chief of the ships there in the absence of a senior officer. It seems likely that Hughes—who was almost certainly on half pay at Halifax—was misled by the extent of his own responsibilities into giving Moutray the authority to act in this capacity. Nelson for one refused to obey it, thus drawing on himself an official admonition.

Hughes appears to have been an amiable, easy-tempered man, whose talent for French enabled him to produce a translation of *The Spectator*.

In the summer of 1786 Hughes returned to England, and in 1789, again in the *Adamant*, he went out as commander-in-chief at Halifax, a position from which he returned in May 1792. He had experienced a quiet command concerned principally with unavailing attempts to thwart illegal trade with New England. His one innovation related to the mails. At first his dispatches were routed through New York, which meant that in winter mail to England might take as long as five months to reach its destination. His solution, in the absence of available merchant shipping, was to use his naval schooners. The onset of war with France in 1793 obliged the postmaster-general thereafter to send British mails directly to Halifax.

Hughes, who had become a vice-admiral on 21 September 1790, became admiral on 12 September 1794, but he had no further service. He had married Jane, daughter of William Sloane of South Stoneham, Hampshire, the nephew of Sir Hans Sloane; the couple had two sons and two daughters. Hughes died on 5 January 1812 whereupon the baronetcy passed to his younger brother Robert, rector of Frimley St Mary in Suffolk.

J. K. LAUGHTON, rev. JULIAN GWYN

Sources J. Gwyn, 'The Halifax naval yard, mast contractors and wood merchants', *Northern Mariner*, 11 (Jan 2001) • P. Webb, 'British squadrons in North American waters, 1783–1793', *Northern Mariner*, 5 (April 1995), 19–34 • J. Gwyn, 'The culture of work: in the Halifax naval yard before 1820', *Nova Scotia Historical Society, Journal* 2 (1999) • *Nelson's letters from the Leeward Islands*, ed. G. Rawson (1953) • GEC, *Baronetage*

Archives PRO, ADM 1/492; 11/2471; 1/491 | BL, corresp. with Frederic Haldimand, Add. MSS 21734, 21809 • NMM, letters to Lord Sandwich • PRO, ADM 1/492; 11/2471; 1/491 • PRO, corresp. with Sir H. Clinton, PRO 30/55 • University of Virginia, Charlottesville, Hamond papers

Hughes, Richard Arthur Warren (1900–1976), novelist and playwright, was born on 19 April 1900 at Beeching, St Marys Road, Oatlands, Walton-on-Thames, Surrey, the second son and third child of Arthur Hughes (1861–1906), who was employed in the Public Record Office, and his wife, Louisa Grace Warren (1870–1950), daughter of Ernest Warren; both his brother and sister had died by the time he was two. Although the family had lived in England since the sixteenth century, *Debrett's Peerage* traces its ancestry through Elystan Glodrydd (*c*.940–1010) to Beli Mawr, king of the Britons during the time of Julius Caesar, and Hughes therefore considered himself a Welshman. Educated at local preparatory schools, he is said to have dictated poems to his mother before he had learned to write. He visited Wales for the first time at the age of eight and made up his mind to live there; and, as a schoolboy at Charterhouse (1911–17), he felt homesick not for Surrey but for the land of his ancestors. Eight years later he used his pocket money to rent a cottage known as Ysgol Fach, on the estate of Maes-y-neuadd (then a mansion; later a hotel) near Talsarnau in Merioneth, close to Robert Graves's house at Harlech, and it became the home to which he returned during school holidays and later from Oxford.

After spending the last few months of the war at an army training school, Hughes entered Oriel College, Oxford, in January 1919, quickly fell under the spell of T. E. Lawrence, began publishing poems in various magazines, and was introduced into literary society. His university career was crowned by the critical acclaim accorded to his first play, *The Sisters' Tragedy*, performed in John Masefield's garden in January 1922—the year of his graduation with a fourth-class degree—then at the Little Theatre in Oxford, and published two years later. Also in 1922 his first book of poems appeared, under the title *Gipsy-Night*, published by the Golden Cockerel Press. While still at Oxford he began travelling as a way of countering the strain of creative writing and, within a week of graduating, he was sailing a boat down the Danube and dabbling dangerously in Balkan politics; thus began a wanderlust and taste for adventure which he was to indulge for the rest of his active life. Back in Wales by 1923, and living at Garreg Fawr, a cottage near Croesor, Merioneth, which his mother had bought, he became involved in the campaign for a Welsh national theatre led by Lord Howard de Walden Evelyn Scott-Ellis, founded the Portmadoc Players (against much local opposition), and wrote *A Comedy of Good and Evil* (1924), perhaps his best play, and *Danger* (1924), which became the first play to be broadcast by radio, on 15 January 1924. He then abandoned drama and cleared his decks with the publication of *Plays* (1924), *Confessio juvenis: Collected Poems* (1926), and a volume of short stories, *A Moment of Time* (1926).

Hughes's first novel, *A High Wind in Jamaica* (1929; published in the USA as *The Innocent Voyage*), begun on Capodistria (Koper) in the Adriatic in 1925 and finished near New Preston, Connecticut, in 1928, was an immediate bestseller. It tells the story of a group of English children captured but befriended by pirates during a voyage to England in the 1860s, the most remarkable of whom is Emily Bas-Thornton, a child on the verge of womanhood, whose psychology is brilliantly explored in a manner owing something to the theories of Darwin and Freud. The novel examines some of the confusions and absurdities to which conventional assumptions about the nature of good and evil sometimes lead. It also seeks to explode, by means of irony, the Romantic literary tradition of the child as essentially innocent, which had become decadent in the popular Victorian novel. It was made into a film in 1965.

Shortly after the publication of his first novel, Hughes went to live in Morocco to escape the attention which it had brought him. He bought a house in the kasbah of old Tangier for two donkey-loads of silver—the first Christian to own property in the quarter since the reign of Charles II; the best of his writing about Morocco, his favourite country after Wales, was collected under the title *In the Lap of Atlas* (1979). On his return to Britain in 1932 he married, on 8 January, the landscape painter Frances Catharine Ruth Bazley (1905–1985), granddaughter of Sir Thomas Sebastian Bazley, second baronet (*b.* 1829), of Hatherop Castle, Gloucestershire. They made their first home at the dilapidated Old Hall in Stiffkey, Norfolk, and then, in 1934, in a Georgian house abutting Laugharne Castle, on the Towy estuary in Carmarthenshire, where he was appointed to the honorary office of petty constable; they had two sons and three daughters. It was there, too, that Hughes (known in the family as Diccon) wrote his second novel, *In Hazard* (1938), based on the true story of a steamship caught by a hurricane in the Caribbean, in which the storm is a symbol of the world war about to begin. From 1940 to 1945 he served as a civilian in the Admiralty and then, in 1946, after two winters at Lyulp's Tower on Ullswater in the Lake District, went with his family to live at Môr Edrin, a large house at Talsarnau overlooking the Dwyryd estuary opposite Portmeirion, which was to be his home for the rest of his life. He became an active member of the Church in Wales and received the honorary degree of DLitt from the University of Wales in 1956. In 1969 he was elected to membership of the American Academy of Arts and Letters, and delivered the Blashfield address under the title 'Fiction as truth'.

During the 1950s Hughes collaborated with J. D. Scott in writing *The Administration of War Production* (1955), a volume in the official History of the Second World War, reviewed books for the *Sunday Times*, and wrote a series of screenplays, mostly for Ealing Studios. Appointed Gresham professor of rhetoric at the University of London in 1954, he lectured there on the art of fiction before resigning his post in order to devote himself to his *magnum opus*, to which he gave the title *The Human Predicament*. Of this ambitious work, conceived as an exploration of the social, political, economic, and moral forces which shaped Europe from the Munich *putsch* of 9 November 1923 to the defeat of Nazi Germany in 1945, only two volumes were published: *The Fox in the Attic* (1961) and *The Wooden Shepherdess* (1973); twelve chapters of a third volume were written but they remain unpublished. The action takes place in Wales, England, Germany, the United States, and Morocco, and fictitious characters rub shoulders with historical figures, most notably the upper-class Welshman Augustine Penry-Herbert, cast as 'the superfluous man' of Russian literature who embodies the moral and intellectual uncertainties of his class and generation, and Adolf Hitler, whose depiction as Uncle 'Dolph is a convincingly chilling portrait of unmitigated evil at its most commonplace. Hughes, who wrote slowly and meticulously and was much given to procrastination and redrafting, regarded his work on this *roman-fleuve* as 'a race between the publisher and the undertaker' (Stephens, 270); if the latter won, at least he had been able to put together a collection of charming stories for children, *The Wonder-Dog*, which was published in the year after his death. Another posthumous volume, *Fiction as Truth*, a selection of his miscellaneous literary writings, appeared in 1983 under the editorship of Richard Poole.

Richard Hughes had been suffering from leukaemia, and died of a heart attack at Môr Edrin on 28 April 1976; he was buried in the churchyard at nearby Llanfihangel-y-traethau, where he had been churchwarden. A service of thanksgiving for his life was held at St Martin-in-the-Fields, London, on 10 June 1976; the address was given by Father Peter Levi, of the Society of Jesus, and the blessing by the archbishop of Wales. MEIC STEPHENS

Sources P. Thomas, *Richard Hughes*, Writers of Wales (1973) · R. Poole, *Richard Hughes, novelist* (1986) · B. Humfrey, 'Richard Hughes', *British novelists, 1930–1959*, ed. B. Oldsey, DLitB, 15/1 (1983), 186–94 · 'Hughes, Richard', *The Oxford companion to the literature of Wales*, ed. M. Stephens (1986) · P. Morgan, *The art of Richard Hughes: a study of the novels* (1993) · P. Hughes, *Richard Hughes: author, father* (1984) · R. Poole, ed., *Fiction as truth: selected literary writings* (1983) · J. Harris and E. J. Davies, *A bibliographical guide to twenty-four modern Anglo-Welsh writers* (1994) · R. P. Graves, *Richard Hughes: a biography* (1994) · b. cert. · d. cert. · Burke, *Peerage* · Debrett's *Peerage* · personal knowledge (2004)
Archives BBC WAC · NL Wales, corresp. · U. Reading L., corresp. | SOUND NL Wales, BBC Wales Archives
Likenesses S. Morse-Brown, oils, 1938, NMG Wales · R. Sheppard, drawing, 1974, NMG Wales · A. John, portrait, priv. coll.
Wealth at death £19,991: probate, 30 Sept 1976, CGPLA Eng. & Wales

Hughes, Robert [*pseud.* Robin Ddu yr Ail o Fôn] (1743/4–1785), poet, was born at Ceint Bach in the parish of Penmynydd, Anglesey. After receiving a good education under the care of Ellis Thomas, vicar of Llanfair Mathafarn Eithaf, he served as schoolmaster in various villages in Anglesey, and afterwards spent twenty years in London as barrister's clerk. Ultimately his health failed and he returned to Wales, acting as schoolmaster at Caernarfon.

In assuming the bardic name Robin Ddu yr Ail o Fôn (the Second Robin from Anglesey—the first being a mid-fifteenth-century poet renowned for his prophetic verse and pro-Lancastrian sentiments in the years preceding the battle of Bosworth) Robert Hughes followed in the footsteps of other contemporary Anglesey poets connected with the eighteenth-century literary revival in Wales. Likewise, his chosen medium was the *cynghanedd* and strict metres, especially the *englyn*, which figures prominently among his 110 or so extant poems. These are mostly occasional pieces to friends and acquaintances, together with some love songs, some in a satirical and ribald vein. His works survive in three eighteenth-century manuscripts, and are, interestingly, copied in order of composition. Although these date from his seventh to his fortieth year, the majority belong to a period of approximately nine years prior to his departure for London, which saw the suspension of his poetic activity, only briefly revived in his last years. Hughes died of consumption at Caernarfon on 27 February 1785, aged forty-one, and was buried on 4 March in Heneglwys churchyard, near Llangefni, Anglesey. His wife survived him. The Gwyneddigion Society funded a monument to his memory.

Robert Hughes is commemorated as one of the founders of the Gwyneddigion; he was its secretary and treasurer for three years, and was its president in 1778. He assisted in the collecting of Dafydd ap Gwilym's poems, and his works serve as testimony to the influence of another Anglesey poet, Goronwy Owen. More importantly, he is credited with conveying to Dafydd Ddu Eryri and others Goronwy's literary ideals, which would subsequently colour the compositions of the Gwyneddigion-sponsored eisteddfodau. R. M. J. JONES, *rev.* A. CYNFAEL LAKE

Sources G. T. Roberts, 'Robin Ddu yr Ail o Fôn', *BBCS*, 6 (1931–3), 1–24, 231–52 · G. T. Roberts, 'Robin Ddu yr Ail o Fôn', *BBCS*, 7 (1933–5), 260–69 · NL Wales, MSS 3060 D, 4550 B · BL, Add. MS 14993 · J. E.

Lloyd, R. T. Jenkins, and W. L. Davies, eds., *Y bywgraffiadur Cymreig hyd 1940* (1953) · *DWB* · R. Williams, *Enwogion Cymru: a biographical dictionary of eminent Welshmen* (1852) · bishop's transcripts, Heneglwys, Anglesey, NL Wales

Archives BL, Add. MS 14993 · NL Wales, poetry and MSS
Likenesses stipple, NL Wales, MS 4550 B, 87

Hughes, Robert Ball (1806–1868), sculptor, was born in London on 19 January 1806, probably the son of Captain Ball RN, whose mother's second husband was Admiral Sir Edward Hughes, and whose son Edward, the admiral's heir, assumed the surname of Hughes in 1819. From 1818 Robert worked for seven years in the studio of the sculptor Edward Hodges Baily in London. He entered the Royal Academy Schools in September 1818 and was awarded their silver medal in 1819 and 1822; in 1823 he gained the gold medal for a bas-relief, *Pandora Brought by Mercury to Epimetheus*, which was exhibited at the academy in the following year. In 1825 he exhibited a statue of Achilles, in 1826 busts of the duke of Sussex and duke of Wellington, and in 1828 *A Shepherd Boy*.

Hughes and his wife, Eliza, left England in 1829 and spent the rest of their lives in the United States, mainly in New York city, Philadelphia, and Boston. His most important works—some neo-classical, others more naturalistic—were the marble statue of Alexander Hamilton, secretary of the treasury, for the merchants' exchange, New York city, destroyed by fire in 1835; the statue of the mathematician and astronomer Nathaniel Bowditch, the first bronze statue to be cast in the United States (replaced by another cast in 1886), erected in Mount Auburn cemetery, Cambridge, Massachusetts; the high-relief marble monument to Bishop John H. Hobart in Trinity Church, New York; and a marble bust of the painter John Trumbull, now in Yale University Art Gallery, New Haven, Connecticut. He also did well-known busts of the writer Washington Irving and John Marshall, chief justice of the United States, and executed plaster groups inspired by novels, including *Uncle Toby and the Widow Wadman* and *Little Nell*. In 1851 he sent to the Great Exhibition in London a statue of Oliver Twist.

In spite of some early successes, Hughes's life in the United States was not an easy one and he was forced to earn his living by working in a number of media. He designed cameo wax portraits (considered to be among the finest of the period), coins for the United States mint, and sketches in burnt wood. It is not clear why his work was not more successful at a time when many commissions were available. He is regarded by many critics as a transitional figure between those sculptors who emigrated to the United States and such eminent native-born Americans as Horatio Greenough and Hiram Powers. The Boston Athenaeum, the Boston Public Library, and the Pennsylvania Academy of the Fine Arts in Philadelphia own examples of his work. He died in either Boston or Dorchester, Massachusetts, on 5 March 1868.

F. M. O'DONOGHUE, *rev.* RICHARD M. DUNN

Sources W. Craven, *Sculpture in America* (1968) · A. Adams, 'Hughes, Robert Ball', *DAB* · R. Gunnis, *Dictionary of British sculptors, 1660–1851*, new edn (1968) · inventories of American painting and sculpture, www.Siris.si.edu [Smithsonian American Art Museum, Research and Scholars Center], 23 Feb 1998 · W. Breen, *Walter Breen's Complete encyclopedia of US and colonial coins* (Garden City, NY, 1988), 285–7 · E. S. Bolton, *Dictionary of wax modelers* (1973) · L. Taft, *The history of American sculpture* (1924) · S. C. Hutchison, 'The Royal Academy Schools, 1768–1830', *Walpole Society*, 38 (1960–62), 123–91, esp. 172

Hughes, Sir Samuel (1853–1921), army officer and politician in Canada, was born on 8 January 1853 at Darlington, Durham county, Upper Canada, the son of John Hughes, an Irish immigrant teacher from co. Tyrone, and his wife, Caroline Laughlin, a Canadian of mixed Huguenot and Irish extraction. The Hughes family was fiercely loyalist and active in the Orange order, as was Samuel throughout his life.

Hughes excelled at running and lacrosse in his youth, and served as a militia volunteer during the Fenian raids of 1870, the start of a lifelong interest in military affairs. He was gazetted lieutenant-colonel in the militia in 1897 and was a major-general by 1912. He started teaching at the age of sixteen and earned a first-class teacher's certificate from the Toronto normal school. An early marriage in 1872 to one of his students, Caroline Preston, the daughter of a prominent local family, ended with her death in 1874. The following year Hughes married Mary Burk, the daughter of Harvey William Burk, a local farmer and MP for West Durham. She survived him, and had with him a son, Garnett, and two daughters, Roby and Aileen. Hughes received an honours degree in modern languages from the University of Toronto in 1880, and taught English literature and history from 1875 to 1885; he then bought and became editor of the *Lindsay Warder*, a Conservative paper in southern Ontario. Personal ambition and a desire for power led him into politics, and in 1892 he was elected MP for Victoria county, a seat he held until his death.

Hughes was enormously successful as a constituency politician, where hard work, wit, and charm endeared him to the electorate. He was a staunch believer in Anglo-Saxon values, temperance, and a protestant God. Not surprisingly, he was also an imperialist, although recent historians have pointed out that Hughes's brand of imperialism was also a kind of Canadian nationalism. Hughes and many of his contemporaries believed that Canada, with its potential for growth and its unsullied, hard-working frontier people, would rule the British empire by the end of the twentieth century.

The notion that colonial frontiersmen were superior to the indolent and corrupted inhabitants of modern Britain—and French Canada—shaped Hughes's public career. In 1899 he was among those who badgered Sir Wilfrid Laurier's government into sending a contingent to the Second South African War. Although only a militia officer, Hughes assumed he should command the contingent, and argued with General Sir E. T. H. Hutton, general officer commanding (GOC) the Canadian militia, over the issue. When Hutton denied him not only command but even a place in the force, Hughes went to South Africa on his own. There he convinced senior British officers to grant him a commission. After a brief stint as a supply and transport officer he joined the Orange River campaigns as an intelligence and scout officer.

Hughes proved himself fearless in battle, a superb tactician, an excellent leader, and an unruly subordinate. His reckless but successful leadership of scouting parties earned him notoriety, and his quick action may have saved Lieutenant-General Sir Charles Warren's force at Faber's Put in 1900. Hughes's letters home—many of which were published—were boastful of his own exploits and sharply critical of British officers and their conduct of the war. This might have been tolerated. But when Warren approached the last great Boer commando under Piet de Villiers in June 1900 expecting it to surrender, Hughes impetuously bungled the operation. With Warren still two days' march behind, Hughes hid his eighteen scouts on the veld and rode alone into de Villiers's camp, vastly exaggerated the size of his force, and suggested that the several hundred Boers surrender to him. Most did. But de Villiers and about fifty stalwarts rode off. The prize had escaped, Warren was furious, and Hughes was sent home. Rather typically, Hughes never forgave or forgot his dismissal by British regular officers, nor their failure to award him the two VCs he thought he deserved.

Hughes was one of the few Conservatives to sit throughout their fifteen years in opposition, and by 1911 he was of sufficient seniority to be made minister of the militia by the new prime minister, Sir Robert Borden. He did much between 1911 and 1914 to reform the Canadian militia. The Second South African War had confirmed his belief that hard-riding and straight-shooting frontiersmen were a match for any European force. As a result he feuded constantly with the British GOC and downplayed the importance of the regular army. His uncompromising protestant Orange background also made it all but impossible for Hughes to deal equitably with French Canadians on militia issues, such as their demands for distinctive uniforms and use of their own language.

On the eve of the First World War, Hughes also modernized the militia's equipment, among other things adopting a new service rifle designed and manufactured by his friend Sir Charles Ross. With a powerful breech mechanism and a high velocity bullet, the Ross rifle was ideal for sniping on the veld of South Africa. But it jammed when heated by rapid fire and was quickly discarded by Canadian troops when they began fighting in France in 1915.

Hughes was responsible for the remarkable expansion of Canada's army during the first years of the First World War. True to form, he threw out the GOC's mobilization plans, sent the regular battalions off to garrison duty, and called upon his friends, prominent Canadians, and ordinary civilians to raise battalions and fill their ranks. These he hurled overseas pell-mell, while creating an unwieldy and grossly inflated establishment in Canada and Britain. Recruitment in Quebec he mismanaged entirely, and his inability to engage French Canadians in the war effort was one of his great failures. In the end he 'raised' some 248 battalions for the Canadian expeditionary force, although only some fifty served at the front. Hughes made all the

decisions; nothing was delegated. In 1915 he was knighted for his work. However, by 1916 his mismanagement of the war effort led to pressure from many fronts, not least the army in the field, to impose some system on the lumbering bureaucracy and protect an emerging professional field force from the minister's nepotism. Hughes, of course, could not see the problem, and Borden dismissed him from the cabinet in November 1916.

Vain, ill-tempered, and never one to forgive a slight, Hughes remained a thorn in the side of the government until his death from pernicious anaemia at Lindsay, Ontario, on 24 August 1921.   MARC MILNER

Sources R. G. Haycock, *Sam Hughes: the public career of a controversial Canadian, 1885–1916* (1986) · *DNB*
Archives NRA, priv. coll. | Bodl. Oxf., corresp. with Louis Harcourt · HLRO, corresp. with Lord Beaverbrook · NA Canada, minister of militia's MSS · PRO, corresp. with Lord Kitchener, PRO 30/57; WO 159
Likenesses J. Russell & Sons, photograph, NPG

Hughes, Stephen (1622?–1688), nonconformist minister and publisher, was born in Carmarthen, the second son of John Hughes (more traditionally John ap Hugh ap William ap Rhisiart), a puritan silk merchant in comfortable circumstances, who was an alderman and twice mayor of Carmarthen (1650 and 1660, the year of his death), and his wife, Elizabeth Bevan, daughter of Dafydd, a tanner who was himself an alderman and mayor of Carmarthen in 1631 and 1642. Stephen's elder brother, John, was mayor in 1659.

Hughes was probably educated at Queen Elizabeth's Grammar School, Carmarthen, and from about 1653 he was minister at Merthyr, Carmarthenshire. He removed to Meidrim in 1655 where, loyal to Cromwell and an approver in Carmarthenshire, he ministered until he was ejected in 1661. He returned to his father's house in Carmarthen and was imprisoned for a short period, but on his marriage (after 1655) to an affluent lady (possibly called Catherine) of Swansea, who shared his religious zeal, he moved to that town, where he lived for the rest of his life.

Hughes continued to minister to a number of dissenting churches in Carmarthenshire in spite of the constraints of the penal laws, avoiding persecution and imprisonment. Hughes was a popular and effective preacher. A moderate puritan and a peaceable man of generous spirit, he was highly regarded and was friendly with many Anglicans. His role in setting up schools in the 1660s to teach children and adults to read Welsh, his pastoral and preaching ministry, and the churches which he established earned for him the popular title the Apostle of Carmarthenshire, and there is no doubt that he laid the foundations of dissent in south-west Wales.

Like other dissenters Hughes had realized early in his career the advantages of the permanence of print as a source of continuing and renewed edification, notwithstanding the fervour of the spoken word. But he had also seen that if ordinary folk were to benefit from their reading, the books provided should appeal both in content and in style. Hughes began his literary mission with his collections of the poems of the Revd Rees Prichard, 'the Old

Vicar', whose homely moralizing and instructional verses were circulating in manuscript and orally. Hughes, assisted by Henry Maurice and Iaco ab Dewi, compiled an edited collection, the first part of which was published in 1659; a second part, now lost, appeared soon after. He returned to this task some ten years later, publishing the third part of Prichard's poems in 1670, and the four parts as a single volume in 1672.

Henceforth until his death in 1688 Hughes worked closely with Thomas Gouge, Charles Edwards, and others to publish or to reissue a large number of translations of popular English religious works, some under the aegis of the Welsh Trust but others at considerable personal cost, involving extended visits to London to supervise printing and proof-reading during the years of his active pastoral ministry. Hughes edited many of these works, adapting, paraphrasing, and revising them so that they might better meet the needs of his intended readership. He often included in his books the Welsh alphabet and provided glossaries or marginal notes which gave south Wales equivalents for north Wales words or vice versa. A new edition of Rees Prichard's poems appeared in 1681, under the title by which it has been known ever since, *Cannwyll y Cymru*. This book, fourteen editions of which appeared between 1658 and 1730, became one of the most popular works of Welsh piety ever: Hughes is responsible for the form in which Prichard's poems have been known, and his is the credit for giving these verses such currency, especially in south Wales.

Hughes's major concern was that the Bible in Welsh should be more generally available. He promoted the publication of the New Testament in 1672 but was acutely conscious that the publishing of the Bible would require substantial capital. Some £2000 was raised and in 1677–8 the co-operation of Hughes, Gouge, and Edwards enabled a corrected version of the Welsh Bible to be published on good paper and in larger, improved type. Eight thousand copies were published to be sold for 4s. 2d., and 1000 were distributed free.

In 1672 Hughes also brought out a composite volume, *Catechism Mr Perkins*, which contained in addition to William Perkins's *Catechism*, *Sail y grefydd Gristnogol* (Evan Roberts's translation of Perkins's *The Foundation of Christian Religion*), *Rhodfa feunyddiol y Christion* (Richard Jones's translation of Henry Oasland's *Christian's Daily Walk*), and *Amdo neu amwisc i babyddiaeth* (Jones's translation of Richard Baxter's *A Winding Sheet for Popery*). This was followed in 1677 by other composite volumes: *Tryssor i'r Cymru*, containing translations of works by Arthur Dent, Oliver Thomas, and Richard Baxter, and *Cyfarwydd-deb i'r anghyfarwydd*, translations of works by Baxter (*Call to the Unconverted*, translated by Richard Jones as *Galwad i'r annychweledig*) and others. Hughes himself translated Francis Peraud's *Adroddiad cywir o'r pethau ar a wnaeth ac a ddwedodd ysbryd aflan ym Mascon yn Burgundy* (1681) and published Robert Holland's *Dau Gymro yn taring yn bell o'u gwlad* (1681), two contemporary accounts of, and warnings against, the wiles of witchcraft and evil spirits. Hughes assisted Charles Edwards in the 1682 publication of *Llwybr*

hyffordd … i'r nefoedd (Arthur Dent's *The Plain Man's Pathway to Heaven*).

Hughes published at his own cost Henry Evans's *Cynghorion tad i'w fab* (1682), moralizing verses in the style of Rees Prichard, but his other most important publication was the translation which he and three others (unnamed but probably including Charles Edwards and less certainly Iaco ab Dewi) produced of Bunyan's *Pilgrim's Progress*, *Taith neu siwrnai y pererin*. Hughes bore the greatest burden of translating, and the book, published after his death in 1688, reveals him to be a fluent, confident translator.

Hughes did not claim to be knowledgeable in the Welsh literary tradition, and he was motivated more by his religious fervour and personal love of books than by a deep regard for Welsh literature. Nevertheless, his work on the 1677 edition of the Bible reveals both his scholarship and his familiarity with the standards of Welsh writing. He was himself an effective writer, and some of his comments show that he was not without concern for the well-being of the Welsh language. His efforts to create a literate Welsh peasantry and his success in providing the Bible and other books in Welsh for them were important factors in safeguarding the language in the face of the Anglicizing influences of puritanism and of the Welsh Trust, and contributed to the revival of Welsh literary culture in the eighteenth century.

Hughes died in Swansea on 16 June 1688. He was buried at St John's Church, Swansea, two days later.

BRYNLEY F. ROBERTS

Sources G. J. Williams, 'Stephen Hughes a'i gyfnod', *Y Cofiadur*, 4 (1926), 5–44 · G. H. Jenkins, 'Apostol Sir Gaerfyrddin: Stephen Hughes, *c*.1622–1688', *Cadw tŷ mewn cwmwl tystion: ysgrifau hanesyddol ar grefydd a diwylliant* (1990), 1–28 · G. H. Jenkins, '"A lleufer dyn yw llyfr da": Stephen Hughes a'i hoff awduron', *Agweddau ar dwf piwritaniaeth yng Nghymru yn yr ail ganrif ar bymtheg*, ed. J. G. Jones (1992), 203–27 · T. Shankland, 'Stephen Hughes', *Y Beirniad*, 2 (1912), 175–85 · N. Lloyd, *Cerddi'r ficer: detholiad o gerddi Rhys Prichard* (1994), xv–xx · J. Ballinger, *The Bible in Wales: a study in the history of the Welsh people* (1906), 33–9 · J. D. Owen, *Stephen Hughes* (1912)

Wealth at death £30: will, 1688, NL Wales; Jenkins, 'Apostol Sir Gaerfyrddin', n. 101

Hughes, Sir Thomas (*fl.* 1571–1623), lawyer and playwright, a native of Cheshire, matriculated at Queens' College, Cambridge, in November 1571, and proceeded BA (1575/6) and MA (1579). From 1576 until 1582 he was a fellow of Queens'. In 1579 he was admitted to Gray's Inn where he was an active lifetime member: he became a barrister in 1585, a reader in 1606, and dean of the chapel in 1618. His career was not without incident: he was accused of robbery by a fellow templar in 1590, and in the same year that he was knighted, 1619, he was briefly incarcerated in the Fleet prison for having given some erroneous legal advice. Hughes was married; there is a reference to a legitimate son in the Gray's Inn pension book but nothing more is known of his family. The last reference to Hughes appeared in the pension book in 1623.

Hughes had the chief share in the authorship of *The Misfortunes of Arthur, Reduced into Tragical Notes by T.H.*, a play performed before Queen Elizabeth at Greenwich on 8 February 1588, by members of Gray's Inn (it was published that year with the title *Certaine Devises and Shewes Presented to her Majestie by the Gentlemen of Grayes-Inne*). Among others, Francis Bacon helped to arrange the play's dumbshows. Like the earlier inns of court play *Gorboduc*, *The Misfortunes* may well have had a contemporary political message for the queen—in this case, concerning the recent execution of Mary, queen of Scots—but on the surface what is noteworthy is Hughes's setting of Seneca's classical form and melodramatic material (adultery, incest, mutual slaughter of father and son, often directly translated from the *Thyestes*) in the romance world of King Arthur's Britain.   P. J. FINKELPEARL

Sources [T. Hughes], 'The misfortunes of Arthur, reduced into tragical notes by T. H.', 1587, BM [Robert Robinson, b.l., 8vo; also at Hunt. L. and Harvard] • *DNB* • Venn, *Alum. Cant.* • J. Ramel, 'Biographical notices on the authors of *The misfortunes of Arthur* (1588)', *N&Q*, 212 (1967), 461–7 • [T. Hughes], 'The misfortunes of Arthur', *Early English classical tragedies*, ed. J. Cunliffe (1912), 217–342 [with critical introduction] • [T. Hughes], *The misfortunes of Arthur: a critical old-spelling edition*, ed. B. J. Corrigan (1992) [with critical introduction] • J. W. Cunliffe, *The influence of Seneca on Elizabethan tragedy* (1925) • D. Bevington, *Tudor drama and politics* (1968) • A. W. Green, *The inns of court and early English drama* (1931) • I. Ribner, *The English history play in the age of Shakespeare* (1957) • J. Merriman, *The flower of kings: a study of the Arthur legend in England between 1485 and 1835* (1973)

Hughes, Thomas (1822–1896), social reformer and children's writer, was born at Uffington, Berkshire, of which parish his paternal grandfather was vicar, on 20 October 1822, the second of the six sons of John *Hughes (1790–1857), author, and his second wife, Margaret Elizabeth Wilkinson (1797–1887). Jane Elizabeth *Senior (1828–1877) was his only sister.

Early years, Rugby School, and Oxford In 1833 the family moved from Uffington to Donnington Priory, near Newbury, Berkshire. Hughes was educated first at a private school near Twyford, Hampshire (1830–33), and then, in February 1834, was sent with his elder brother, George (1821–1872), to Rugby School. Hughes's father had known the headmaster, Thomas *Arnold (1795–1842), at Oriel College, Oxford, although he did not share either Arnold's political or his theological liberalism. Hughes later described the school as 'a very rough, not to say brutal place when I went there, but much mended during those years'. This was the reform which was to make Rugby world-famous; its essential characteristic was that the older boys were given responsibility for disciplining the younger, in an atmosphere of moral earnestness and self-questioning.

George Hughes distinguished himself at Rugby, but Thomas Hughes, though he rose to be captain of the cricket team, did not excel academically: a contemporary, the classical scholar John Conington (1825–1869), wittily recalled him as 'on the whole very like Tom Brown, only not so intellectual' (Kilbracken, x n.). As cricket captain he made an innovation which anticipated his later work, by inviting on to the playing fields the local boys who previously had been chased off. However, he later said that the

Thomas Hughes (1822–1896), by Julia Margaret Cameron, 1865

'most marked characteristic' of his generation of Rugby boys was 'the feeling that in school and close we were in training for a big fight—were in fact already engaged in it—a fight which would last all our lives, and try all our powers, physical, intellectual, and moral, to the utmost' (Hughes, *Fifty Years Ago*, 1891, 5). Hughes went to Oriel College, Oxford, in February 1842. There he rowed enthusiastically, and did not try to work for an honours degree. His tutors were A. H. Clough (1819–1861), whose fag he had been at Rugby, and James Fraser (1818–1885), later an ally in the co-operative movement, of whom he published a biography in 1887. During his second year, in August 1843, Hughes became engaged to his sister's friend Anne Frances Ford (c.1826–1910), daughter of the Revd Dr James Ford (d. 1877), prebendary of Exeter, and his wife, Frances Nagle, and niece of the Hispanophile Richard Ford (1796–1858). After some opposition they were married on 17 August 1847.

Chartism and working men's education Meanwhile Hughes had come down from Oxford, taken rooms in Lincoln's Inn, and begun to read for the bar. The period between his engagement and his marriage was a crucial one, which saw the political conversion which shaped the rest of his life. While still at Oxford he had travelled, in the long vacation of 1844, to Scotland and the north, and become convinced of the need to repeal the corn laws; at about the same time he read A. P. Stanley's biography of Arnold (1844), and was influenced by his former master's ideas on political reform. He started to attend the services of another liberal theologian, the Lincoln's Inn chaplain

F. D. Maurice (1805–1872), who encouraged young students to discuss social questions and to work among the poor. On 10 April 1848, as the Chartists rallied on Kennington Common, Hughes, though he had some sympathy with them, was acting as a special constable while Maurice, Charles Kingsley (1819–1875), and J. M. Ludlow (1821–1911) had the famous meeting which resulted in the appearance in May of the first number of *Politics for the People* and the foundation of the Christian socialist movement. It is said that when it was proposed that Hughes should join somebody protested, 'We are not going to start a cricket club', but he was soon a member of the group, which also included the chemist Charles Mansfield (1819–1855), George Robinson—then Lord Goderich and later marquess of Ripon (1827–1909)—and Edward Vansittart Neale (1810–1892). *Politics for the People* soon ceased publication, but it was followed by the *Christian Socialist* newspaper and the *Journal of Association*, the latter edited by Hughes in 1852. After Maurice's departure from King's College, London, the group founded, in 1854, the Working Men's College, one of its most lasting achievements. Hughes taught some law and Bible classes at various times, but his real success was in teaching boxing. He succeeded as its principal after Maurice's death and served from 1872 to 1883. A keen supporter of the volunteer movement during the war scare of the late 1850s, Hughes commanded the working men's corps, which was reviewed by the queen in June 1860, and he helped to found the Working Men's Club and Institute Union in 1862.

It appeared to the Christian socialists that the exploitation of the workers could be alleviated if instead of producing goods for middlemen they formed co-operatives to deal directly with consumers. The Society for Promoting Working Men's Associations was founded in 1850. Hughes devoted a great deal of energy to the encouragement of such co-operatives, and the successive failures of many enterprises he was interested in never eradicated his lifelong faith in them. He did not welcome the later dominance of consumer co-operatives, which increasingly flourished under the leadership of J. T. W. Mitchell (1828–1895), through which the poor could wield their collective buying power to obtain cheap and reliable goods. He published much on the subject, and campaigned for statutory change. His *History of the Working Tailors' Association* (1850) was one of the series Tracts on Christian Socialism. *A Manual for Co-Operators* (1881), which he wrote with Neale, was criticized by G. J. Holyoake (1817–1906) for making religion too central to co-operation. He was associated with R. A. Slaney (1792–1862) in the campaign to secure the Industrial and Provident Societies Act of 1852, which made it easier to set up co-operatives. After his election to parliament he played an important part in achieving other improvements in their legal status, such as that enabling them to be limited companies, and to invest more than £200 in one another.

Trade unions Hughes also figures in the history of British trade unionism. In 1858 he was made secretary of a committee of the Social Science Association to investigate strikes; out of this work came his *Account of the Lock out of Engineers in 1851–2* (1860). He was involved in the strike of master builders in 1860, and became associated with those trade unionists, such as George Howell (1833–1910), who sought to increase the political influence of working men. In 1865, with Howell's support, he was elected as Liberal MP for Lambeth. He became a member of the Reform League and, later, of the parliamentary committee of the Trades Union Congress. With Frederic Harrison (1831–1923) he gave his professional help to the campaign to improve the status of trade unions, in particular to give legal protection to their funds. He edited a translation, by his brother-in-law Nassau John Senior (1822–1891), of the comte de Paris's *Associations ouvrières en Angleterre* (1869). He sat on the royal commission on trade unions of 1867–8 which had been set up to investigate trade union intimidation, and, with Harrison and the second earl of Lichfield (1825–1892), signed the minority, pro-union, report. He was also employed as a government arbitrator in various industrial disputes.

Tom Brown In 1856 Hughes began to write a story with the idea of thus explaining to his eldest son, Maurice, then about eight, about school life. *Tom Brown's School Days* (first edition thus, later editions often vary to *Schooldays* or *School-Days*) was published on 24 April 1857, and by the standards of the time was a best-seller, having sold 28,000 copies by the end of 1862 and gone through fifty-three editions by 1892. Nor did the fact of its being about an English public school prevent it from circulating widely in America and Europe well into the twentieth century. The first of three film adaptations appeared in 1916, and television versions have twice been made by the BBC, the latest in 1981. It was published anonymously, but Hughes was soon known to be its author; whatever his later achievements, it was always his claim to fame.

The book is significant in the history of nineteenth-century public schools, as a celebration of their ethos which reached an enormous public. In particular, it was Hughes's version of Rugby which created the popular idea of Arnold's work there, though it was often objected that the book gave a limited representation of that work, especially by placing so little emphasis on intellectual as opposed to physical and moral development. But caution should be exercised in reading *Tom Brown's School Days* in the light of the later history of public schools. Although Hughes gave currency to the idea that competitive games were essential to the public-school spirit (an idea which would have very much surprised Dr Arnold), he himself frequently protested in later years against the excesses of the late Victorian cult of sport. He noted in his *Memoir of a Brother* that the 'machinery of games gets every year more elaborate' (p. 96), whereas in his day at Rugby the boys had rolled and watered the cricket pitch themselves. In *The Manliness of Christ* he commented: 'Athleticism is a good thing if kept in its place, but it has come to be very much overpraised and over-valued amongst us' (p. 24).

In fact, whatever the novel's influence on the servants of late Victorian imperialism, it belongs with the condition-of-England novels of the 1840s and 1850s, with their message of the urgent need for reform from within. Its popularity must be linked to its powerful structuring myth in which Rugby School is England, and the experience of the boy, learning self-reliance so that authority may be delegated to him, symbolizes the experience of the man of the governing class. By the end this becomes explicit: 'Perhaps ours is the only little corner of the British Empire which is thoroughly, wisely, and strongly ruled just now' (*Tom Brown's School Days*, 1857, 395). Tom Brown is born to the landed gentry, and grows up in the Berkshire countryside knowing the land and people intimately. He will inherit the duties of this station. The novel's opening paragraphs constitute one of the great evocations of Englishness. From this pre-industrial idyll he is transferred to Rugby, to experience the perils and temptations of the world. These include the political instability caused by misrule and tyranny, figured in the rebellion of the fags against the fifth form. Tom's schooldays thus enable him to experience the problems of society from the points of view both of the underdog and of the ruling class: his friend East is 'always a people's man—for the fags, and against constituted authorities' (ibid., 403). Vivid scenes of the trouncing of bullies, and the glories of the cricket and football fields, enliven the narrative, which also has much emphasis on boxing, for Hughes believed passionately in the healthiness and manliness of a fair fight.

Other writings and activities The early chapters of *Tom Brown's School Days* describe in nostalgic detail the traditional festivals of rural Berkshire, which brought all ranks of society together to compete in backswording, running, and fighting. This Carlylean and Kingsleyesque fantasy of an organic society cemented by physical activity is the main theme of Hughes's second novel, *The Scouring of the White Horse, or, The Long Vacation Ramble of a London Clerk* (1859), in which a go-getting lower-middle-class townee sees the ancient festival of the scouring of the white horse of Uffington, and realizes that squires are not all oppressors of the poor and that the past has something to teach the present. A trite plot is made the vehicle for a good deal of second-hand folklore and local history. The book looks forward to Hughes's idiosyncratic biography *Alfred the Great* (1869), which seeks in the career of the Anglo-Saxon king a Carlylean hero and remedy for modern problems. Nor did Hughes's third, last, and in some ways most ambitious, three-volume novel, *Tom Brown at Oxford* (1862), ever approach either the sales or the power of his first. Again, it draws largely on first-hand experience. Tom finds Oxford snobbish and money-worshipping, and he is there exposed to several temptations, of which extravagance and sex are more powerfully presented than unbelief and Tractarianism. A sub-plot, in which his childhood friend Harry Winburn is victimized by cruel landlords and prosecuted for poaching, completes the hero's political conversion; as the narrator disingenuously observes: 'the great Harry Winburn problem … for him had now fairly swelled into the condition-of-England problem' (3.36). The book is an attempt to depict the intellectual and political progress of a young

man, in this case towards Christian socialism via Carlyle's *Past and Present*. Perhaps this was rather old-fashioned by 1862; it has more in common with J. H. Newman's *Loss and Gain* (1848), J. A. Froude's *The Nemesis of Faith* (1849), and Charles Kingsley's *Alton Locke* (1850) than with the sensation fiction of the early 1860s. What charm the book still possesses derives from its dense description of the manners and customs of Oxford of the 1840s.

Hughes was called to the bar in 1847, three months after his marriage, and—despite the distractions of his work for the Christian socialists, for the co-operative movement, as an MP, and as a writer—built up a fair practice, being appointed QC in 1869. Probably the wide range of his enthusiasms prevented his achieving great success either as a barrister or as a politician. These included plans for the regulation of weights and measures, life insurance for the poor, profit sharing by employees, public housing, parish councils, Sunday closing, and opposition to the enclosure of public lands. His writing career embraced fields just as diverse, including, as well as the books discussed, *Religio laici* (1861), a personal credo, and *Memoir of a Brother* (1873), a strangely inarticulate biography of George Hughes, a high tory, who never played any part in public life or fulfilled his early promise. One other cause taken up by Hughes which deserves mention was the struggle, in 1865, by him and others on the Jamaica Committee to impeach the governor of Jamaica, Edward John Eyre (1815–1901), for racist atrocities.

During the 1860s ebbing sympathy with trade union demands began to distance Hughes from his old Reform League allies like Howell and Harrison. This was exacerbated by the sectarian controversy over the Education Act of 1870, because Hughes had associated himself with the established church in the shape of the National Education Union and thus found himself in alliance with many Conservatives. Matters came to a head when he accepted an appointment to the royal commission on trade unions in 1874, although the parliamentary committee of the Trades Union Congress had, with his agreement, opposed the setting up of the commission. He compounded his offence by signing its report of February 1875. It was the more significant that he lost the support of the labour wing of the Liberal Party, because some of his opinions were unpopular in other quarters: his Anglicanism was offensive to nonconformists and secularists, as was his belief in co-operation to shopkeepers. In 1868 he had been elected MP for Frome, having had differences with his Lambeth constituents. But he failed to be elected as Liberal MP for Marylebone in 1874. In 1878–9 an attempt to be selected for Salisbury was unsuccessful partly because of opposition from the tradesmen's Anti-Co-operative Society.

The United States One of Hughes's most lasting enthusiasms was for America. His lectures on the slavery issue to the Working Men's College were published as a supplement to Ludlow's *A Sketch of the History of the United States* (1862). On the outbreak of the American Civil War he was a staunch public supporter of the North and a member of the Emancipation Society, which published his *The Cause* of Freedom: which is its Champion in America, the North or the South? (1863). Perhaps because of this, as well as of the fame of Tom Brown's School Days, he was heartily welcomed on his first visit to Canada and America in 1870, and became friends with James Russell Lowell (1819–1891), whose poetry he had long admired. In 1880 he became involved in a project to found a co-operative settlement in Tennessee to be populated by English public schoolboys who found no opportunities at home. One of those who took part was his younger brother William Hastings Hughes (1834–1907), who described it as 'indeed the last of the many castles in Spain which he had, always with some high and unselfish object in view, helped to build during his life' (W. H. Hughes, 2). By 1882 it was evident that the project had failed, though it struggled on for a few years. Some of the buildings at Rugby, Tennessee, still exist, but as a co-operative enterprise it was given up in 1891.

Final years Hughes had invested more than he could afford to lose, about £7000, and he sought an appointment, which he was given in July 1882, as a county court judge. This brought an end to his involvement in politics, and a move to Chester. He resigned from the Co-operative Union. His work as a judge seems to have been congenial to him although, according to John Telford, 'his rough and ready justice became a byword for constant reversal on appeal' (Telford, 10). During the 1880s he wrote four more biographies, including Daniel Macmillan (1882) and David Livingstone (1889). He built himself a house called Uffington, at Dee Hills Park, Chester, to which he moved in October 1885. He died of congestion of the lungs at the Royal Crescent Hotel, 101 Marine Parade, Brighton, on his way to Europe for his health, on 22 March 1896.

Three of Hughes's nine children predeceased him: the eldest, Maurice, who died in 1859; Evie, who died in his arms in December 1856 of scarlet fever as Tom Brown's School Days was being written; and Jack, who died of paralysis in 1888. The three sons and three daughters who survived him included two sons who emigrated to America; Lilian (Lily) Carter, who died on the SS Titanic in April 1912; and the Quaker social worker Mary *Hughes (1860–1941).

Hughes's life and work are commemorated in several places. There is still a Hughes Library in Rugby, Tennessee, a statue by Brock still stands in front of the Rugby School Library, and a portrait by Lowes Dickinson still hangs in the library of the Working Men's College. The statue, like his tombstone in Woodvale cemetery, Brighton, where he was buried on 25 March 1896, bears an inscription from 1 Corinthians 16: 3, 'Quit you like men: be strong'.

CHARLOTTE MITCHELL

Sources E. C. Mack and W. H. G. Armytage, Thomas Hughes: the life of the author of 'Tom Brown's Schooldays' (1952) • E. Trory, Truth against the world: the life and times of Thomas Hughes, author of 'Tom Brown's School Days' (1993) • private information (2004) [Sir Brinsley Ford] • G. J. Worth, Thomas Hughes (1984) • Lord Kilbracken [J. A. Godley], introduction, in T. Hughes, Tom Brown's school days (1913) • W. H. Hughes, The true story of Rugby (1972) • J. Telford, introduction, in T. Hughes, Tom Brown's school days (1913) • J. Richards, Happiest days: the public schools in English fiction (1988) • I. Quigly, The heirs of Tom Brown: the English school story (1982) •

N. Vance, The sinews of the spirit: the idea of Christian manliness in Victorian literature and religious thought (1985) • T. Hughes, Tom Brown's school days (1913)
Archives Hunt. L. • Working Men's College, Crowndale Road, London | Bishopsgate Institute, London, letters to George Howell • BL, letters to the Macmillans, George Cruik, the marquess of Ripon, etc., Add. MSS 54917, 43547–43549 • Bodl. Oxf., corresp. with Sir William Harcourt • Co-operative Union, Holyoake House, Manchester, letters to G. J. Holyoake • CUL, letters to J. M. Ludlow and others • Halifax Central Library, letters to George Thomson • Princeton University Library, Parrish collection • Tennessee State Library, Rugby MSS
Likenesses attrib. A. C. Sterling, print, 1853, NPG • L. Dickinson, oils, exh. RA 1859, Rugby School, Warwickshire; replica, Oriel College, Oxford • J. M. Cameron, albumen print, 1865, NPG [see illus.] • J. E. Boehm, plaster statuette, 1871, NPG • S. P. Hall, pencil drawing, 1889, NG Ire. • T. Brock, memorial statue, Rugby School • A. Cecioni, chromolithograph caricature, NPG; repro. in VF (8 June 1872) • L. Dickinson, portrait, Working Men's College, Crowndale Road, London • Elliott & Fry, carte-de-visite, NPG; repro. in VF (8 June 1872) • W. H. Hunt, group portrait, oils (London Bridge on the night of the marriage of the prince and princess of Wales, 1863), AM Oxf. • W. Jeffrey, cartes-de-visite, NPG • Lock & Whitfield, woodburytype photograph, NPG; repro. in T. Cooper, Men of mark: a gallery of contemporary portraits (1880) • J. Watkins, carte-de-visite, NPG • G. F. Watts, oils, Watts Gallery, Compton, Surrey • H. Weigall, oils, Inner Temple, London
Wealth at death £12,483 9s. 10d.: resworn probate, May 1897, CGPLA Eng. & Wales (1896)

Hughes, Thomas John [pseud. Adfyfr] (1853–1927), journalist, was born in Bridgend, Glamorgan, the son of the Revd Thomas Hughes of Miskin, Llantrisant, Glamorgan. He rose to prominence in October 1886 when he published under the pseudonym Adfyfr the first of three essays on the political condition of Wales in the Liberal Daily News (on the land question on 12 October 1886, the established church on 27 October 1886, and education on 16 November 1886). These essays appeared as Neglected Wales (1887), the first of a series of pamphlets published by the South Wales Liberal Federation. Third in the series was his Landlordism in Wales (1887), an indictment of the power of landowners and the 'politico-ecclesiastical alliance in Wales', endorsed in an appendix by Stuart Rendel, Liberal MP for Montgomeryshire (1880–94) and president of the North Wales Liberal Federation. Privately, however, Rendel and other Welsh Liberal leaders disapproved of Adfyfr's overblown political style and sought to marginalize his influence within Welsh Liberalism. A pamphlet entitled The Welsh Magistracy also appeared under the name Adfyfr. Between January 1888 and May 1889 he was the founding editor of the bilingual Liberal nationalist monthly Cymru Fydd, and in June 1890 was delegated to represent the North and South Wales Liberal Federations on the general committee of the National Liberal Federation.

In declining health from the early 1890s, Adfyfr turned to newspaper journalism, becoming south Wales correspondent of the Daily News and the Manchester Guardian, papers which he praised for having 'substantially assisted the Principality to speak its deep-seated convictions in English' (Cymru Fydd, 1/3, 1888, 126). He was also for more than forty years before his death Pontypridd and Rhondda reporter for the South Wales Daily News, and served for a time as its sub-editor. He augmented his income by acting as a private secretary to Alfred Thomas, Liberal MP for East Glamorgan (1885–1910), and as an official shorthand writer in the bankruptcy court and public inquiries. He was a practising Calvinistic Methodist, and helped establish the St David's Calvinistic Methodist Church, Gelliwastad Road, Pontypridd. He resisted on grounds of ill health Lord Rhondda's inducements to return to active political life during the First World War, and devoted his final years to newspaper reporting and shorthand writing. He died of heart disease at Pontypridd on 24 October 1927, leaving a widow, six sons, and six daughters. He was buried at Glyntaf cemetery, Pontypridd, on 28 October 1927.

ALED G. JONES

Sources *Pontypridd Observer* (29 Oct 1927) · *Pontypridd Observer* (5 Nov 1927) · *South Wales News* (25 Oct 1927) · minute book, North Wales Liberal Federation, 1 July 1890 · NL Wales, Glansevern I, 200, 419, 463 · NL Wales, MSS 19451D/274, 19451D/286, 21171D

Hughes, Thomas McKenny (1832–1917), geologist, speliologist, and archaeologist, was born in December 1832, in Aberystwyth, one of the family of three sons and five daughters of the Revd Joshua *Hughes (1807–1889), afterwards bishop of St Asaph, and his wife, Margaret (*d.* 1899), widow of Captain Gun, and daughter of Sir Thomas McKenny, first baronet, lawyer, lord mayor of Dublin, and a notable fighter for Catholic emancipation. From Llandovery College (Carmarthenshire), Hughes won a scholarship to Trinity College, Cambridge, whence he graduated BA in 1857, and proceeded MA in 1867. He had a brief career as a diplomatist in Rome in 1860–61, first as secretary to the consul, Charles Newton, and later as acting consul. Newton, who later became keeper of Greek and Roman antiquities at the British Museum, inspired in McKenny Hughes an interest in archaeology which lasted all his life. Together they carried out many archaeological expeditions in the area.

While at Cambridge, McKenny Hughes had attended the lectures of Professor Adam Sedgwick, and he continued his geological interests with fieldwork in Italy in 1860. In 1861 he accepted an invitation from Sir Roderick Murchison to join the geological survey. Between 1861 and 1865 he developed his interests in stratigraphy of the Chalk and in Pleistocene and recent deposits in the Medway valley, and in 1865–6 he worked on drift gravels in the St Albans and Hertford areas. He was transferred to the Lake District in 1866, and worked in Westmorland, Cumberland, and the Yorkshire dales until 1873, living for much of the survey in Sedbergh. In this period, he began his work on Lower Palaeozoic stratigraphy, concentrating on the areas of Kirkby Lonsdale, Sedbergh, Dent, Shap, and Kendal, Bowness, and Tebay. During these years he was entertained by the Revd George Frederick Weston, canon of Carlisle, at Crosby Ravensworth—he was later to marry Weston's daughter, Mary Caroline (1860–1916).

McKenny Hughes began a regular correspondence with Sir Charles Lyell, who was then working on the revision of his *Elements of Geology* and on *The Student's Elements of Geology*. The debate, aroused by McKenny Hughes's fieldwork, which broke new ground in the understanding of the mountain limestone country, and in particular the connection between Upper and Lower Silurian, Coniston Flags, Upper Red Conglomerate, and Millstone Grit, was of considerable importance and caused Lyell to revise several sections. Lyell and McKenny Hughes went on many geological expeditions together, including, in 1872, an extended tour of various caves of archaeological interest in the Dordogne valley, and the famous cave at Aurignac described later by Edouard Lartet.

McKenny Hughes and Lyell became firm friends, and Lyell subsequently supported McKenny Hughes as a candidate for the Woodwardian chair in geology at Cambridge, to which he was appointed in 1873 (succeeding Adam Sedgwick). Between them they held the chair in geology for ninety-nine years, until Hughes's death in 1917. The growth in the teaching of natural science, caused by the introduction of the Cambridge natural science tripos in 1851, had led to extensive redevelopments by the university on both the north and the south sides of Downing Street. McKenny Hughes planned a new geological museum on the south side to provide more space for the geological collections and better classrooms, and as a memorial to his predecessor. He contrived, by patience and persuasion, to plan and complete the new museum. Despite pressure from the department of zoology to merge and rearrange the exhibits McKenny Hughes succeeded in retaining the geological exhibits, with the stratigraphical arrangement which he regarded as vital to their true understanding. Over one hundred years later they remain much as he planned them. The museum was designed between 1904 and 1911 by the famous architect T. G. Jackson (1835–1924). It was opened by Edward VII and Queen Alexandra.

During his years at Cambridge, McKenny Hughes gathered about him a staff of distinction, which included Edward Tawney, Alfred Harker, J. E. Marr, Henry Woods, F. R. C. Reed, and Gertrude L. Elles. Under his leadership the school of geology spawned a long list of well-known geologists who served in universities, geological surveys, and museums in Britain, India, South Africa, and other countries. McKenny Hughes continued his own fieldwork on Lower Palaeozoic rocks, caves, and drift deposits in Wales, and in north Yorkshire (where he took his students every year), and made many contributions to archaeology in the Cambridge area. He was elected as fellow of the Geological Society in 1862, and fellow of the Royal Society in 1889, and was made a chevalier of the Italian order of SS Maurizio e Lazzaro. In 1891 he was awarded the Lyell medal of the Geological Society.

McKenny Hughes was a popular and gregarious man. In 1882, when university professors were permitted to marry, he returned, at the age of fifty, to Crosby Ravensworth to seek the hand of Mary Caroline Weston. She was a keen amateur archaeologist, a botanist, and a distinguished artist, and under his tuition she became a valuable geologist. Following their marriage, the couple travelled together on field excursions, and worked on the

Pleistocene deposits, and on excavations in the Cambridge area. They both attended the International Geological Congress of 1891 in the USA, where they were part of a small group which visited the national parks of North America, including the Grand Canyon, into which descent was made from the north rim. Much of the journey was made on horseback, through territory still under Native American occupation. They subsequently attended the International Geological Congress in Russia in 1897, visiting sites in the Caucasus and Georgia, returning via Sevastopol, Odessa, Constantinople, Athens, Pompeii, and Rome. In the more remote areas they were accompanied by an armed guard. They had three sons: Tom, an architect (the eldest, killed in 1918 while carrying out aerial reconnaissance behind enemy lines in France), George, clerk to the Worshipful Company of Goldsmiths, and Alfred, an entomologist. McKenny Hughes died at his home, Ravensworth, Brooklands Avenue, Cambridge, on 9 June 1917, and was buried in Cambridge three days later. His published works and articles included, with J. W. Clarke, *The Life and Letters of Adam Sedgwick* (1890) and, with Mary Caroline Hughes, *Cambridgeshire* (1909).

JANE FAWCETT

Sources 'Eminent living geologists. Extracts from the *Geological Magazine*', *Geological Magazine*, new ser., 5th decade, 3 (1906), 1–13 · private information (2004) · *The Times* (11 June 1917), 10 · *Geological Magazine*, new ser., 6th decade, 4 (1917), 334–5 · *Nature*, 99 (1917), 326–7 · E. B. Bailey, *Geological survey of Great Britain* (1952)
Archives CUL, corresp. and papers · CUL, family and scientific corresp. and papers | Cambs. AS, Cambridge, papers · CUL, papers relating to Adam Sedgwick · U. Cam., Sedgwick Museum of Earth Sciences, corresp. and papers
Likenesses photographs, priv. coll.
Wealth at death £9275 13s. 1d.: probate, 29 Aug 1917, *CGPLA Eng. & Wales*

Hughes, Thomas Rowland (1903–1949), novelist and poet, was born on 17 April 1903 at 13 Goodman Street, Llanberis, Caernarvonshire, the son of William Hughes, a slate quarryman, and his wife, Mary Owen, and the younger brother of Euronwy. After being educated at Ysgol Elfennol Dolbadarn, Llanberis, and Ysgol Sir Brynrefail (1915–20), he attended the University College of North Wales, Bangor (1921–6), where he gained first-class honours in English. After obtaining a teacher's diploma (again with a first) he took up a post at the County School for Boys, Aberdâr, Glamorgan, where he taught English and Welsh for two years. He gained the degree of MA from the University of Wales in 1928 for his thesis 'The melancholy element in English poetry from Widsith to Chaucer'. In the same year he was awarded a University of Wales scholarship to undertake another research project at Jesus College, Oxford, and in 1931 was awarded the degree of BLitt for a thesis entitled 'The *London Magazine* from 1820 to 1829'. From 1930 to 1934 he was lecturer in English and Welsh at Coleg Harlech, an adult education college in Merioneth. He married (Margaret) Eirene Williams on 26 August 1933. They had met at Oxford, where she was studying for a diploma in education, and she was a practising teacher until their marriage. They had no children. From 1934 to 1935 he was warden of another adult education establishment, the Mary Ward Settlement, in London, and was at the same time director of the Tavistock Little Theatre. He was then appointed programmes producer with the BBC in Cardiff, where he remained until 1945.

Hughes first came to literary prominence as a poet, winning the chair at the Machynlleth national eisteddfod in 1937 and repeating the feat at the 1940 national eisteddfod. His only collection of poems was published in 1948 under the title *Cân neu ddwy*. He also published a popular version of world-famous stories, *Storïau mawr y byd* (1936), and some plays, including *Y ffordd* (1945), but his main contribution to Welsh literature was his five novels. He embarked on these as an attempt to escape the constraints his multiple sclerosis placed on him. The first, *O law i law* (1943), is largely based on a recollection of things past, and is a wistful glance at the slate quarrying background of his upbringing and the warm neighbourliness of that society, with its nonconformist culture. *William Jones* (1944) begins as a comic prose epic featuring a henpecked husband who leaves north Wales for the coalmining south. Despite the comic elements, this develops into a more serious depiction of life in south Wales in the thirties, although it does not succeed in delving deeply into the social ills of the time. His next novel, *Yr ogof* (1945), takes a biblical theme, and focuses on the conversion of Joseph of Arimathea. *Chwalfa* (1946) is undoubtedly his most ambitious and most successful novel. It is based on the great strike in the Penrhyn slate quarry in Bethesda, Caernarvonshire, during the years 1900–03. The story follows the gradual disintegration of one family as a result of the social upheaval caused by the strike. The heroic suffering of a close-knit community is conveyed and, despite the fact that the battle is eventually lost, the novel ends on a note of stoicism. The author's last novel was *Y cychwyn* (1947), the first and only part of what was conceived as a trilogy. It tends to tread familiar ground and does not add much to the novelist's stature. All the novels have been translated into English, and *Yr ogof* has also appeared in Swedish and Norwegian.

The University of Wales made Hughes a DLitt *honoris causa* in 1948. His last years were plagued by multiple sclerosis, and he died on 24 October 1949 in Cardiff Royal Infirmary and was buried in Cathays cemetery, Cardiff. Thomas Rowland Hughes was hailed by critics as 'the second Daniel Owen' when his novels first appeared. In recent years critical opinion has not been so generous, and his work is compared less favourably with that of such contemporaries as Kate Roberts and Caradog Prichard.

JOHN ROWLANDS

Sources E. Rees, *T. Rowland Hughes: cofiant* (1968) · J. Rowlands, *T. Rowland Hughes* (1975) · W. G. Lewis, ed., *Bro a bywyd: T. Rowland Hughes, 1903–1949* (1990) · m. cert.
Archives Angorfa Museum, Llanberis, Gwynedd · Coleg Harlech, Gwynedd · U. Wales, Bangor
Likenesses D. Bell, oils, NMG Wales
Wealth at death £5639 6s. 7d.: probate, 30 Jan 1950, *CGPLA Eng. & Wales*

Hughes, Thomas Smart (1786–1847), historian, was born at Nuneaton, Warwickshire, on 25 August 1786, the eldest surviving son of Hugh Hughes, curate of Nuneaton and rector of Hardwick, Northamptonshire. He received his early education from the Revd J. S. Cobbold, first at Nuneaton grammar school and afterwards as a private pupil at Wilby in Suffolk. In 1801 he was sent to Shrewsbury School, then under the headmastership of Dr Samuel Butler (1774–1839), and in October 1803 was entered as a pensioner at St John's College, Cambridge. His university career was distinguished. Besides college prizes he gained the Browne medals for the Latin ode 'Mors Nelsoni' in 1806 and for the Greek ode 'In obitum Gulielmi Pitt' in 1807. He graduated BA in 1809 as fourteenth senior optime, and proceeded MA in 1811 and BD in 1818. He obtained the members' prize for the Latin essay in 1809 and 1810. The latter essay, a discussion of the merits of Cicero and Clarendon, was printed in volume 17 of the *Classical Journal* in 1818.

In 1809 Hughes was appointed to an assistant mastership at Harrow School, under Dr George Butler, but he found the position irksome and returned to Cambridge in 1811. In the same year he was elected to a foundation fellowship at St John's, and in December 1812 accepted the post of travelling tutor to Robert Townley Parker of Cuerden Hall, Lancashire. During a tour of about two years he visited Spain, Italy, Sicily, Greece, and Albania. The result of his observations he published as *Travels in Sicily, Greece, and Albania* in 1820; the work was illustrated with plates from the drawings of C. R. Cockerell.

In September 1815 Hughes was ordained deacon. He was appointed assistant tutor at his college, but immediately resigned and accepted a fellowship and tutorship at Trinity Hall, thus materially injuring his prospects. In 1817 he accepted a fellowship at Emmanuel College, was elected junior proctor, and won the Seatonian prize for his poem on 'Belshazzar's Feast'; his verses inspired John Martin's painting on that subject. In 1819 he was ordained priest and was appointed by Dr Herbert Marsh, bishop of Peterborough, his domestic and examining chaplain. Hughes, however, remained at Emmanuel, where he became dean and Greek lecturer. In 1822 he published *An address to the people of England in the cause of the Greeks, occasioned by the late inhuman massacres in the Isle of Scio*, and in 1823 *Considerations upon the Greek revolution, with a vindication of the author's 'Address' … from the attacks of C. B. Sheridan*. At Christmas 1822 he was appointed Christian advocate.

On his marriage in April 1823 to Ann Maria Forster, the daughter of the Revd John Forster of Great Yarmouth, Hughes became curate at Chesterton, but two years later he returned to Cambridge, where he lived until about a year before his death. His activities were mainly literary, although he sometimes took some clerical duty. He was one of the first examiners for the new classical tripos of 1824, an office that he again filled in 1826 and 1828. In February 1827 he was collated by Bishop Herbert Marsh to a prebendal stall at Peterborough. In the same year he was an unsuccessful candidate for the headmastership of Rugby School. In 1830 he undertook an edition of the writings of some of the great divines of the English church, with a biographical memoir of each writer, and a summary in the form of an analysis prefixed to each of their works; twenty-two volumes of this collection appeared. Earlier he had been greatly interested in the critical analysis, interpretation, and defence of St Paul's Epistles, and had published various articles on the subject between 1824 and 1828. In 1832 he was presented by the dean and chapter of Peterborough to the rectory of Fiskerton, Lincolnshire, and in the same year succeeded to the family living of Hardwick. His chief work, the continuation of the *History of England* from the accession of George III by David Hume and Tobias Smollett, was undertaken in 1834, at the request of the London printer of classical works A. J. Valpy. A third edition appeared in 1846. Hughes considered other projects, such as an English edition of Strabo's *Geography* in conjunction with Dr John Lee and a Mr Akerman, and a compilation of commentaries on the Bible; but he did not live to execute them. In May 1846 he was presented to the perpetual curacy of Edgware, Middlesex, by Lee, but he died there the following year, on 11 August 1847. He was survived by his wife, who died on 5 April 1890, and his son Thomas Fiott Hughes. His literary and artistic collections were sold by Sothebys in January and February 1848. His *Essay on the Political System of Europe … with a Memoir and Portrait* was published posthumously in 1855.   GORDON GOODWIN, rev. NILANJANA BANERJI

Sources *GM*, 2nd ser., 29 (1848), 310–11 · Venn, *Alum. Cant.* · 'Memoir', T. S. Hughes, *An essay on the political system of Europe* (1855)

Archives BL, corresp. with Samuel Butler, Add. MSS 34583–34590

Likenesses G. R. Lewis, pencil drawing, 1822, V&A · portrait, repro. in Hughes, *Essay on the political system of Europe*

Hughes, William (c.1535–1600), bishop of St Asaph, was the son of Huw ap Cynfrig ap Tudur ap Gruffydd Gymro, rector of St George's in the diocese of St Asaph (1548/9–53), and Gwenllian ferch John Fychan ap John of the Pigot family of Llansannan. Noted as born in Caernarvonshire, most of his family connections were east of the Conwy where several of the benefices he later held were located. No evidence supports Wood's claim that Hughes studied at Oxford before moving to Cambridge. He matriculated as a sizar of Queens' College, Cambridge, on 12 November 1554 and was admitted BA in 1557. Thereafter he progressed rapidly, being elected fellow of Christ's College in 1557 and graduating MA from Christ's in 1560 and BTh in 1565. He became chaplain to the duke of Norfolk and was elected Lady Margaret preacher during 1565. Hughes's views may have been coloured by his Marian background, although he did not oppose the settlement of 1559. He was drawn into the theological debate in Cambridge during the 1560s over the *descensus* article, after delivering a sermon at Leicester in the spring of 1567 in which he promulgated his belief in Christ's spatial descent into hell, a view that antagonized his radical, Calvinist audience. The town's burgesses' complaint to the university, demanding Hughes's removal as preacher for unsound doctrine, led to a protracted dispute in 1567 relating more to the powers of the university against the intrusion of higher authority than to doctrine. Hughes remained intransigent, refusing to accept discipline by university delegates whom he considered theologically biased against him. The issue was intensified when Leicester burgesses petitioned the puritan earl of Leicester to champion their cause at court. The final outcome of the procedural compromise, brokered by William Cecil, allowing the university to deal with the matter, is not known, but Hughes was refused grace to proceed to DTh because of his opinions.

The duke of Norfolk's patronage secured Hughes's survival. Leicester refrained from pressing too hard against Norfolk's protégé and both became instrumental in Hughes's rehabilitation. With doors closed at Cambridge, Oxford (where Leicester was chancellor) accepted him and on 19 April 1568 he was incorporated BTh. Hughes then ceased to be Norfolk's chaplain, but on 1 October 1568, through the duke's influence, he was instituted to the living of Dennington in Suffolk, which he held until 3 December 1573. Pressure from the duke won Hughes a conditional grace to proceed DTh, provided that he publicly recanted his unsound views on the *descensus* article. He did so and received the doctorate by July 1570. His recantation may have drawn him closer to the earl of Leicester, through whose territorial links and influence in north Wales he gained the bishopric of St Asaph. He was consecrated at Lambeth Chapel on 13 December 1573. Leicester may also have been instrumental in his eventual restoration at Cambridge on 2 July 1575, when he was incorporated DTh.

Hughes remained a controversial figure as bishop. He was, *ex officio*, a member of the council in the marches of Wales, but did not take an active part in its affairs. Strype contended that Richard Davies referred unfavourably to him in a letter to Cecil in 1566 relating to the vacant see of Llandaff, but that was more likely a reference to Hugh Jones, the elected bishop. Archbishop Parker, however, a participant in the Cambridge controversy, entered a cautionary note against Hughes's appointment to St Asaph in 1573, and later historians have condemned him as an unworthy, self-seeking pluralist, guilty of mismanaging and fleecing his see. This view is based on an anonymous denunciation of him in February 1587, 'A discoverie of the present estate of the byshoppricke of St. Asaphe', charging him with gross malpractices, chief among which was pluralism in that he held *in commendam* the archdeaconry and a total of twenty-two livings, seven of them without cure, valued at over £1000. The problem was compounded by the thirteen livings held by absentees, seven collated by Hughes. The charges are not totally unfounded. At the time of his appointment Parker gave him faculty to hold the archdeaconry and other livings to the value of £150 a year *in commendam*, but this was a recognition of the poverty of the diocese and followed established practice in all Welsh sees to supplement a meagre episcopal income. The number held by Hughes may seem inordinately large, and he held a further two livings not mentioned in the report. But, excluding those that were part of the archdeaconry, he held only one living *in commendam* throughout his episcopate, namely Llysfaen, to which he had been first instituted in 1567; others, such as Mallwyd, were held for only a few weeks. It has also been suggested that the value given to the livings in the 'Discoverie' is unduly exaggerated.

Detailed charges were also made of Hughes's alienation of church property by leasing, sometimes to his own family, and increasing involvement in the land market for personal gain. The granting of leases cannot be denied, nor that he was involved in legal disputes over ecclesiastical rights and properties, but a far lower than average 13 per cent of the property of the diocese had been impropriated by 1603. The imprudence that is suggested in his lending to John Edwards of Chirk, a gentleman of notorious Catholic sympathies, £700 to meet mortgage interest payments reflects the report's conservatism in fiscal matters. It was argued, however, that such transactions resulted not only in the decay of pastoral care in terms of clerical hospitality and poor relief, but also of spiritual care, with only three named as resident preachers in the diocese. Further charges were that administrative neglect led to a large increase in the number of recusants in the diocese and financial impropriety in the administration of the consistory court. Hughes's deficiencies have, in particular, been held to be the basis of John Penry's censure in 1587 of the established church in Wales for its failure to preach and evangelize.

Such condemnation seems unduly harsh. Hughes's appointment as a native Welshman was hailed by compatriots, and his residence in the diocese for twenty-seven years firmly consolidated the Elizabethan church there despite Catholic and puritan challenges in areas such as Wrexham. His concern for the needs of his flock is revealed in a case brought against him in 1585 for refusing to institute an Englishman who could not serve monoglot Welsh parishioners as rector of Whittington. He also responded to efforts to improve clergy quality and promote preaching. By 1592, 45 of the 144 clergy in the diocese were graduate preachers, and although only 8 clergymen held a degree in divinity, 54 were graduates. Hughes himself was praised as a learned preacher by contemporary poets, as was his dean, Thomas Banks, singled out as an unfit absentee by the 'Discoverie' but praised in verse for hospitality and lively preaching. Recusancy was also addressed by Hughes. Although his report of 1577 to Whitgift, that none in his diocese neglected to come to church, and the complaint of 1587 both suggest tolerance, there is no doubt of his zeal in securing the Elizabethan settlement during the 1590s by regularly presenting recusants of all social degrees to the courts of great sessions. He also attacked superstition, being pivotal in a witchcraft prosecution of 1594 involving his kinswoman Jane Conway, mother of Robert and Henry Holland.

Hughes was praised by Welsh poets for his mastery of common and canon law, his classical and linguistic learning, and his encouragement of historical debate; he also fostered Welsh culture through his patronage of poets including William Cynwal, William Llŷn, and Siôn Tudur. This and his learning in divinity placed him in a unique position to supervise the work of translating the scriptures into Welsh undertaken by William Morgan and published in 1588. Hughes presented Morgan to several livings in his diocese between 1575 and 1588, including Llanrhaeadr-ym-Mochnant where he was resident. In the dedication to his Bible, Morgan openly acknowledged Hughes's assistance by lending books and examining the work in progress. Hughes also supported Morgan in parochial disputes (1589–92).

Although Hughes was in 1595 recommended for translation to Exeter, he remained at St Asaph until his death at Diserth on 18 November 1600; he was buried in the cathedral choir in an unmarked grave the following day. His will of 14 November 1600 mirrored the tensions in his life between concerns for promoting the Anglican faith and the prosperity of his family. He bequeathed £20 and his books towards building a library at St Asaph and £5 towards the repair of the cathedral church. Three other parishes held *in commendam* and St George's were also granted bequests to repair the fabric of their churches. A reversionary gift to establish a free school at St Asaph was contingent on the default of issue from his heirs. He left a widow, Luce Knowsley (d. 1636), with whom he had had a son, William, and a daughter, Anne, wife of Thomas Mostyn of Rhyd and his sole heir. Since she already had two living children when her father died the educational bequest failed. Hughes was succeeded as bishop by William Morgan. NIA M. W. POWELL

Sources D. R. Thomas, *Esgobaeth Llanelwy: the history of the diocese of St Asaph*, rev. edn, 3 vols. (1908–13) • D. R. Thomas, ed., 'A discoverie of the present estate of the byshoppricke of St. Asaphe', *Archaeologia Cambrensis*, 5th ser., 1 (1884), 53–8 • *Willis' survey of St Asaph, considerably enlarged and brought down to the present time*, ed. E. Edwards, 2 vols. (1801) • W. P. Griffith, 'William Hughes and the descensus controversy of 1567', *BBCS*, 34 (1987), 185–99 • J. G. Jones, 'Thomas Davies and William Hughes: two Reformation bishops of St Asaph', *BBCS*, 29 (1980–82), 320–35 • W. P. Griffith, *Learning, law and religion: higher education and Welsh society, c.1540–1640* (1996), 113, 223, 249–50, 303–18 • *DWB*, 392–3 • Foster, *Alum. Oxon.* • Venn, *Alum. Cant.*, 1/2.428 • Wood, *Ath. Oxon.*, new edn, 1.615; 2.844 • Wood, *Ath. Oxon.: Fasti* (1815), 182–4 • J. Strype, *Annals of the Reformation and establishment of religion … during Queen Elizabeth's happy reign*, 2nd edn, 2 (1725), 293–4, appx, pp. 62–4; 3 (1725), 467 • F. O. White, *Lives of the Elizabethan bishops of the Anglican church* (1898), 196–8 • F. Godwin, *De praesulibus Angliae commentarius* (1616), 664 • B. Willis, *A survey of the cathedral church of St Asaph* (1720) • G. M. Griffith, 'Bishop William Hughes and his bequests to St Asaph, 1600', *National Library of Wales Journal*, 6 (1949–50), 303–4 • PRO, C 3/97/36 • PRO, SP 12/118/18 • NL Wales, SA/BR/1, 73r, 66, 69–70 • NL Wales, SA/MB/21, 1–22 • NL Wales, SA/Misc./835–839 • NL Wales, Welsh church commission papers, B/10/139; B/10/139/649 • great sessions, NL Wales, 4/8–11, esp. 4/9/4/8–10, 12–13, 33–35, 55–56, 94 • NL Wales, Thorne deeds and documents 160 • NL Wales, Puleston 1041 • NL Wales, Mostyn 145, 91 • NL Wales, Peniarth (28), DG49 • NL Wales, Peniarth 128, 172 • NL Wales, Peniarth 287, 636 • NL Wales, Peniarth 135, 406 • NL Wales, Peniarth 139ii, 191 • U. Wales, Bangor, Mostyn MS 2727 • Cooper, *Ath. Cantab.*, 2.1586–609, 289–90 • J. Peile, *Biographical register of Christ's College, 1505–1905, and of the earlier foundation, God's House, 1448–1505*, ed. [J. A. Venn], 1 (1910), 52 • *Reg. Oxf.*, 1.270 • *CSP dom.*, 1597, p. 257, no. 46 [incorrectly calendared as 1596] • C. Davies, *Rhagymadroddion a chyflwyniadau Lladin, 1551–1632* (1980), 70 • *Heraldic visitations of Wales and part of the marches … by*

Lewys Dwnn, ed. S. R. Meyrick, 2 vols. (1846), 299 • G. Williams, *Wales and the Reformation* (1997) • *Correspondence of Matthew Parker*, ed. J. Bruce and T. T. Perowne, Parker Society, 42 (1853), 446 • J. Strype, *The life and acts of Matthew Parker* (1711), 459 • P. Williams, *The council in the marches of Wales under Elizabeth I* (1958) • N. M. W. Powell, 'Dr William Morgan and his parishioners at Llanrhaeadr ym Mochnant', *Transactions of the Caernarvonshire Historical Society*, 49 (1988), 87–115
Wealth at death see will, 14 Nov 1600, NL Wales, SA/Misc./835–839

Hughes, William (1587/8–1663?), translator and compiler of legal works, was the eldest son of Reginald Hughes (d. 1616), a citizen of London and member of the Fishmongers' Company, and his wife, Margaret. Hughes matriculated at St Alban Hall, Oxford, on 18 January 1605, aged seventeen, and was admitted to Gray's Inn on 7 November 1606. There is no date for his call to the bar, but he was made an ancient on 7 June 1627, and on 14 March 1628 his son, also William, was admitted to the inn.

Hughes was more of a translator and compiler of legal works than a reporter of cases in the strictest sense. His first published work was *The Parson's Law* (1641). On 25 September 1645 the Stationers' Company records an entry for *The Mirror of Justice … Translated out of the Old French into English by William Hughes of Gray's Inn*. Other works followed in the 1650s, including *Reports of Certain Cases … Reviewed … by … Justice Godbolt*, published by Hughes in 1652. *The Commentaries upon Original Writs*, which produced the original writs from the books, duly edited, was published in 1655. *An Exact Abridgement of Public Acts*, covering 1640–56, appeared in 1657, and in 1659 he produced *The Declarations and Other Pleadings* in Coke's reports.

Hughes continued to publish after the Restoration. *The Grand Abridgement of the Law Continued*, a three-volume collection of the principal case and points of the common law of England, appeared in 1660–63. In 1663 *An Exact Abridgement of All the Statutes in Force*, a comparative work of the sixteenth to eighteenth years of Charles I, and the twelfth to fourteenth of Charles II, was published, as was *Gregories Moot-Book … much Inlarged by William Hughes. An Exact Abridgement in England of the Cases Reported by Sir F. Moore*, collected by Hughes, was published in 1665.

The date of death of William Hughes is unknown, but is conjectured to be 1663. STUART HANDLEY

Sources J. Foster, *Register of admissions to Gray's Inn, 1521–1881* (privately printed, London, 1887), 118, 184 • Foster, *Alum. Oxon.* • R. J. Fletcher, ed., *The pension book of Gray's Inn*, 1 (1901), 276 • PRO, PROB 11/128, sig. 77 [will of R. Hughes, father] • G. E. B. Eyre, ed., *A transcript of the registers of the Worshipful Company of Stationers from 1640 to 1708*, 3 vols. (1913–14) • J. G. Marvin, *Legal bibliography, or, A thesaurus of American, English, Irish and Scotch law books* (1847), 402–3 • Holdsworth, *Eng. law*, 4.313; 11.307

Hughes, William (d. 1683), horticultural writer, worked on board a pirate ship in the West Indies, and then visited, among other places, Barbados, St Kitts, Hispaniola, Jamaica, and Florida. After his return, about 1652, he worked, probably as a gardener, for the dowager Viscountess Conway at Ragley in Warwickshire. While working there he published *The Complete Vineyard, or, A Most Excellent Way for the Planting of Vines* (1665). A third edition appeared in 1683. He later produced *The Flower-Garden Enlarged* (1671), with a third and final edition in 1683, and *The American Physitian, or, A Treatise of Roots, Plants, Trees … Growing in the English Plantations in America*, in which he describes West Indian plants. Hughes died in 1683.

B. D. JACKSON, rev. ANNE PIMLOTT BAKER

Sources Desmond, *Botanists* · G. A. Pritzel, ed., *Thesaurus literaturae botanicae omnium gentium* (Leipzig, 1851) · *DNB*

Hughes, William (1718/19–1798), writer on music and Church of England clergyman, was the son of William Hughes (d. 1768), who was made minor canon of Worcester Cathedral in 1718 and in 1721 was presented to the vicarage of Old Sodbury, Gloucestershire, which he held until his death. The younger William Hughes matriculated at Merton College, Oxford, on 15 November 1737, aged eighteen, graduated BA in 1742, and subsequently proceeded MA. He also was admitted a minor canon of Worcester Cathedral on 25 November 1741, an appointment he held for more than forty years. In 1757 he resigned the rectory of Bredicote and the curacy of St Clement's, Worcester, and on 6 December was presented by the chapter to the vicarage of St Peter's, also in that city.

Hughes's interests extended to music, and while he did not publish any compositions his *Remarks upon Church Music, to which are Added Several Observations on Mr. Handel's Oratorios* (Worcester, 1763) enjoyed some popularity. He also published sermons, including *On the Efficacy and Importance of Music*, preached at the Three Choirs Meeting (13 September 1749), and *A Discourse in Favour of the Abolition of Slavery in the British West Indies*, preached in Ware, Hertfordshire (1788). His cheerful disposition made him a great favourite in Worcester. According to a contemporary:

> Great was his genius, small his preferment. The Oracle of a coffee-house, he wished not to shine in a more exalted sphere. He laughed through life, and his face made others laugh too; not that it was particularly comic, but ludicrously serious.

Hughes died at Leominster, in Herefordshire, on 31 July 1798, according to the *Gentleman's Magazine*, although *The State of the Bishopric of Worcester*, compiled by Richard Hurd, nephew and namesake of the bishop, gives the date as 9 August. He had bequeathed his estate to Worcester Infirmary.

R. F. SHARP, rev. DAVID J. GOLBY

Sources *GM*, 1st ser., 68 (1798), 725 · M. Ransome, ed., *The state of the bishopric of Worcester, 1782–1808*, Worcestershire Historical Society, new ser., 6 (1968), 158, 224 · Foster, *Alum. Oxon.* · J. Chambers, *Biographical illustrations of Worcestershire* (1820), 469 · private information (1891, 2004) [bishop of Peterborough]
Wealth at death estate bequeathed to Worcester Infirmary: *GM*

Hughes, William (1793–1825), wood-engraver, was born in Liverpool. He was taught to engrave by Henry Hole, who had been a pupil of Thomas Bewick. The influence of Thurston Thompson's wood-engravings is also observable in Hughes's work, which was always carefully executed, but sometimes dry in manner; Linton declared him 'an excellent engraver' (Linton, 187). Hughes was especially gifted at representing architectural subjects. His first wood-engravings of buildings appeared in Matthew Gregson's *Fragments … of Lancashire* (c.1816); among the most impressive were his cuts of Clitheroe Castle after C. Barber and of Lathom House after G. Cuitt. Later Hughes produced vignettes for John Rutter's *Delineations of Fonthill* (1823), and the author praised all the artists employed for their 'zeal and ability' (preface, x). In Richard Thomson's *Chronicles of London Bridge* (1827) there are further wood-engravings by the artist.

Hughes was also invited to furnish engravings for three great works on the history of printing. For Thomas Frognall Dibdin's *Bibliographical Decameron* (3 vols., 1817) he engraved illustrations after Hans Sebald Beham's work in Coverdale's Bible of 1535, as well as copies of two illustrations from Hans Holbein's *Histories of the Old Testament*, which Dibdin described as 'beautiful specimens' and worthy of 'the approbation of the skilful' (preface, iii). John Johnson's *Typographia* (2 vols., 1824) included several wood-engravings by Hughes, such as a portrait of William Caxton and the frontispiece of the first volume showing the interior of a chapel adorned with banners and shields of the Roxburghe Club, to which the author drew attention in the preface (p. vii). The two endpieces in William Young Ottley's *History of Engraving* (2 vols., 1816), showing the printer's motto and device, are also by Hughes.

Between 1819 and 1822 Hughes worked in collaboration with the celebrated printer Charles Whittingham the elder, in London. As Whittingham and Hughes, of 12 Staining Lane, the firm produced the enormous Chiswick Press edition of *British Poets* (1822), comprising 100 volumes. Later, in 1834, Whittingham published an edition of James Puckle's *The Club* which, in line with an earlier edition of 1817, reproduced three comic headpieces—'Gamester', 'Knave', and 'Projector'—and five tailpieces by Hughes. On two occasions the engraver reproduced humorous vignettes by George Cruikshank: in Whittingham's 1824 edition of Washington Irving's *Knickerbocker's History of New York* as well as in John Wight's *Mornings at Bow Street* (1824). He also supplied amusing images for an edition of *The Genuine Poetical Remains of Samuel Butler* (posthumously published in 1827), including 'Repartees between Cat and Puss at a Caterwauling, in the Modern Heroic Way'. He usually signed his work 'W Hughes, Sc' or used a monogram.

Hughes died young, on 11 February 1825, in Lambeth, London; the precise cause of his death is unknown. The British Museum and the Victoria and Albert Museum, London, preserve examples of his work.

SUSANNA AVERY-QUASH

Sources *DNB* · W. J. Linton, *The masters of wood-engraving* (1889), 187 · W. Chatto, J. Jackson, and H. G. Bohn, *A treatise on wood-engraving*, 2nd edn (1861), 538 · R. K. Engen, *Dictionary of Victorian wood engravers* (1985) · Thieme & Becker, *Allgemeines Lexikon*, vol. 18 · Redgrave, *Artists* · Bryan, *Painters* (1903–5) · Bénézit, *Dict.* · C. Le Blanc, *Manuel de l'amateur d'estampes*, 4 vols. (Paris, 1854–89) · F. Bruillot, *Dictionnaire des monogrammes, marques figurées, lettres* *initiales, noms abrégés etc. avec lesquels les peintres, dessinateurs, graveurs et sculpteurs ont designés leur noms*, 3 vols. (1832–4)

Hughes, William (1803–1861), writer on law and angling, was born at the vicarage, Maker, Cornwall, on 2 March 1803, the fourth son of Sir Robert Hughes, third baronet (1740–1814), rector of Frimley St Mary and Weston, Suffolk, and curate of Maker, and his second wife, Bethia, daughter of Thomas Hiscutt. He was the nephew of Admiral Sir Richard Hughes. He was admitted to Gray's Inn on 10 May 1828 and called to the bar on 11 June 1833. He practised as a conveyancer on the western circuit, where he was also auditor of the poor-law union district of Cornwall and Devon. He married Jane Caroline, daughter of Edward Knapman of Bideford, with whom he had five children.

Hughes wrote a number of handbooks on the law of property, a guide for making wills, and two novels. Under the pseudonym Piscator, he also wrote on angling and the cooking of fish. He died at Millbay Grove, Plymouth, on 20 August 1861 and was buried at Plymouth and Devonport cemetery. G. C. BOASE, *rev.* JONATHAN HARRIS

Sources Boase & Courtney, *Bibl. Corn.*, 1.258 • J. Foster, *The register of admissions to Gray's Inn, 1521–1889, together with the register of marriages in Gray's Inn chapel, 1695–1754* (privately printed, London, 1889), 436

Hughes, William (1818–1876), geographer, was born in Middlesex. Nothing is known of his parentage, early life, or education, though it seems probable that he had no education beyond school. On his election to the fellowship of the Royal Geographical Society on 26 November 1838 he was an engraver of 9 Wharton Street, Pentonville, London. He continued to trade as an engraver, printer, and map seller, but it is as a pioneer of geographical education that he is best remembered. An early teaching appointment was as professor at an (unidentified) college of engineers, but his most influential appointment came in 1840 when he became lecturer at St John's College, Battersea. At this newly established pioneering college which used the methods of Pestalozzi to train poor boys to be teachers in schools for the poor, Hughes taught geography and cartography. His own inclinations to teach by explanation rather than rote learning and to follow the scientific German school of geography were mirrored in the attitude of the school's founder, James Kay-Shuttleworth, who drew inspiration from progressive developments throughout Europe.

While at Battersea Hughes published his first major work, *Principles of Mathematical Geography* (1843), a treatise on the construction of maps, which ran to three editions in English and one in Urdu for use by civil engineering students in India. He also continued his engraving and map business and, from 1841 to 1843, worked three days a week in the British Museum, cataloguing maps and charts. He expounded his teaching methods in *Remarks on Geography … Chiefly with Reference to the Principles upon which it should be Taught in Normal Schools* (1847) and a textbook, *A Manual of Geography* (1852; reissued 1864).

In 1853 Hughes was appointed to teach geography at the Church of England Metropolitan Training College, Highbury, but was less successful there. He began, possibly in 1858, to teach evening classes at King's College, London, and his success here and his publications, which now included *Classbook of Modern Geography* (1859), led to his appointment as first professor of geography at the college in 1864, to teach day-boys, 'riotous hobbledehoys sent by parental compulsion' (Hughes, in Vaughan, 49), and evening classes for serious, eager, older students, many of whom were teachers. From 1863 Hughes was also professor at Queen's College, Harley Street, a women's college. His textbooks were by now used in many leading public schools as well as national schools, and contemporaries found them eminently readable. Unlike most geography textbooks which simply gave lists to be memorized, Hughes sought to help students understand the nature and distribution of phenomena. His methodological writings and lectures stressed the scientific nature of geography, its links with the natural and physical sciences, and his belief that an understanding of physical geography could unify the physical and human, pure and applied, aspects of the subject. He felt that students must be able to draw maps to understand the character of great natural features and thus come to revere the natural world. Through his books for young children, such as *A Child's First Book of Geography* (1854), he hoped to excite children's wonder at and interest in studying the world around them. Believing that maps could captivate children's imagination, Hughes published educational maps, wrote the text for a Philips schoolroom map of 1859, and helped produce a map jigsaw puzzle. Despite his publishing success he died in modest circumstances on 21 May 1876 at Adelaide Road, Hampstead, leaving less than £1500. He was survived by a widow, Susanna, and two daughters of whom no more is known.

Unquestionably a pioneer of geographical education, Hughes foreshadowed rather than shared in the main developments in British scientific geography. His death before John Scott Keltie's 1886 report, which revolutionized British geography, combined with lack of money and education, which cut him off from developments in German geography, led to the obscurity from which he was deservedly rescued in the late twentieth century.

ELIZABETH BAIGENT

Sources J. E. Vaughan, 'William Hughes, 1818–1876', *Geographers: biobibliographical studies*, 9, ed. T. W. Freeman (1985), 47–53 • T. W. Freeman, *A hundred years of geography* (1961) • R. Alcock, *Proceedings* [Royal Geographical Society], 21 (1876–7), 429–30 • J. Kay-Shuttleworth, *Four periods of public education* (1862) • W. H. Parker, *Mackinder: geography as an aid to statecraft* (1982)
Archives BM, official papers • RGS
Wealth at death under £1500: Vaughan, 'William Hughes'

Hughes, William (1856–1924), missionary and teacher, was born on Tu Hwnt i'r Afon farm at Rhoslan, near Criccieth, Caernarvonshire, and trained as a minister at Llangollen Baptist College. In 1882 the Baptist Missionary Society accepted him for service in the Congo, five years after Europeans had identified the massive Congo river system. Spiritual progress was slow, with the first conversion in

1886, the year in which Hughes returned to Britain. Leaving neither a martyr's grave in tropical Africa nor philological publications such as those of W. Holman Bentley, Hughes made a different impact on Africa.

Sick, nursed by two stalwart Africans, Hughes reached Liverpool in September 1886, settling in Colwyn Bay, where they gave public lectures. Appointed a local pastor, Hughes's African ambitions led to the formation of the Congo Training Institute in 1889. His idea was simple: instead of sending white missionaries to Africa, Africans would be brought to Britain. In a firmly Christian society, with training from local professionals—as carpenters, printers, tailors, nurses, pharmacists—students would become practical leaders. The explorer Henry Stanley spoke in support of the institute in June 1891, and his employer, King Leopold of the Belgians, became the institute's patron that July. Subscriptions rose fivefold between 1889 and 1891, and Hughes relinquished his pastorates. The institute had a new building by 1890; his *Dark Africa: and the Way out* was published in 1892.

Initially Congo-centred, the institute soon attracted students from Cameroon, Nigeria, Sierra Leone, Liberia, and the United States. Sir Samuel Lewis, the British-trained lawyer of Sierra Leone (and the first African knight), joined the board; Nigerian churchman Mojola Agbebi visited Colwyn Bay and organized financial aid from Africa. Financial support was largely from within Wales, with Mr I. McPherson, a black resident of Newport, the most successful adult collector in 1895–6. By 1899 over £2000 was collected annually. Students moved on—Paul Gabasie Daniels to a lifetime of orphanage administration in Charleston, South Carolina; D. D. T. Jabavu to university and then a career in 'native education' in South Africa. Joseph Morford from Tennessee went to Nigeria; Kwesi Quainoo and Ishmael Pratt studied medicine at Edinburgh, with the value of Hughes's ideas seen in the fact that Pratt's tailoring skills acquired at the institute supported him during his studies. Ayodeji Oyejola graduated in medicine in 1906; Akinsanya Oluwale qualified as a medical officer at Liverpool; one Nigerian became a carpenter and another the director of education in Abeokuta.

By 1903 over twenty students were training with local citizens and living in Colwyn Bay. This was noted in the district's guidebooks, and holidaymakers made donations and purchased photographs taken by Frederick Bond who, with student help, printed other promotional material. Hughes's successes were public: in 1908 he was a guarantor and then honorary secretary of the national eisteddfod of 1910. Privately there were great sadnesses. His daughter Edith died, aged six months, in March 1893; his wife, Catherine (Katie), *née* Hughes, died aged thirty-three on 20 August 1894; and his eldest daughter (also Katie) died, aged twenty-two, in May 1909. The cemetery at Old Colwyn also had four African graves by 1909.

Far removed from the Baptist Missionary Society's ideas, Hughes had developed a practical scheme of black uplift. The young men and women who passed through his institute could hardly fail to be impressed by the practical Christianity of his helpers, and of supporters such as the Boys' Brigade lads camping nearby in mid-1899, who gave over £6 to the work. The students met Britons of all walks of life, at institute garden parties, at work, or as guests in local homes.

The birth of a child to a local minister's daughter, fathered by John Franklin from Grenada, led to scandalmongering in Horatio Bottomley's *John Bull* in December 1911, attacking Hughes's scheme. Hughes foolishly sued Bottomley for libel. The litigious and astute Bottomley argued his own case; Hughes, who had difficulties explaining both the finances of the institute and its achievements, lost and was declared bankrupt in mid-1912. The institute closed; Hughes died of heart disease at 12 Waen Terrace, Conwy, on 28 January 1924 and was buried in Old Colwyn cemetery. Franklin's son was brought up by his mother in Liverpool, where he worked as a seaman, having visits from his 'uncle' who, decades later, was revealed to have been his loving father.

Hughes's contribution to development continued for decades, as his students (there were over eighty) worked with their people. Part of his legacy was the independent Baptist church of the once-German Cameroon, led by Africans who had been his friends and students. He himself, although estranged from mainstream missionary contacts, remained recognized in north Wales as a man of achievement.   JEFFREY GREEN

Sources L. M. Jones and I. Wynne Jones, *H. M. Stanley and Wales* (1972) · *African Times* [London] (Nov 1895), 167 · *African Times* [London] (July 1896), 107 · *African Times* [London] (Sept 1896), 139 · *African Times* [London] (April 1897), 55 · *African Times* [London] (June 1899), 87 · H. King, 'Mojola Agbebi: Nigerian Church leader', *Under the imperial carpet*, ed. R. E. Lotz and I. Pegg (1986) · African Institute annual reports, U. Wales, Bangor · African Institute annual reports, NL Wales · W. Hughes, *Dark Africa: and the way out* (1892) · H. King, 'Cooperation in contextualization', *Journal of Religion in Africa*, 16/1 (1986), 2–21 · *North Wales Herald* (12 June 1912) · private information (2004) [I. Wynne Jones, C. Dalton, H. King] · d. cert. · d. cert. [Catherine Hughes]

Archives NL Wales, African Institute annual reports · U. Wales, Bangor, African Institute annual reports

Likenesses photographs, repro. in Hughes, *Dark Africa*

Hughes, William Little (1822–1887), translator and civil servant, was born in Dublin, the son of William Hughes and his wife, Margaret, *née* Acheson. As a young man he settled in Paris, becoming a clerk in the foreign press department of the ministry of the interior about 1857 and remaining in that post until his death. He translated a number of English and American works into French, beginning with two of Dickens's novels: *Hard Times* (*Les temps difficiles*, 1857) and *Little Dorrit* (*La petite Dorrit*, 1858). These translations, which were published soon after the appearance of the novels in English, were prepared under the supervision of Paul Lorain as part of a contract Dickens had made with Hachette, the leading French publishing house, for the translation of eleven of his novels. Other English fiction translated by Hughes included Bulwer Lytton's *Devereux* (1859) and Thackeray's *Yellowplush Papers* (*Mémoires d'un valet de pied*, 1859). Among his translations of American literature were a collection of Edgar Allan Poe's stories (1862), John Habberton's *Helen's Babies* (1879), and Mark Twain's *Tom Sawyer* (1884) and *Huckleberry Finn* (1886). A notable piece of non-fiction was Faraday's lecture entitled *The Chemical History of a Candle* (*L'histoire d'une chandelle*, 1865). Hughes also published a few translations of minor works under the pseudonym of W. O'Gorman. Besides translating, Hughes's principal literary activity lay in collecting works in all languages on Shakespeare. He died in Paris on 5 January 1887.

DONALD HAWES

Sources DNB · J. S. Crone, *A concise dictionary of Irish biography*, rev. edn (1937) · J. Mistler, *La Librairie Hachette* (1964) · F. Delattre, *Dickens et la France* (1927) · *Annual Register* (1887) · Boase, *Mod. Eng. biog.* · *The letters of Charles Dickens*, ed. M. House, G. Storey, and others, 8 (1995)

Hughes, William Morris (1862–1952), prime minister of Australia, was born in London on 25 September 1862. His father, William Hughes, was a carpenter of north Welsh artisan stock and his mother, Jane Morris, was from a Montgomeryshire farming family. His mother died in 1869, and until 1874 Hughes lived with an aunt at Llandudno and attended the grammar school there; he was then admitted to St Stephen's School, Westminster, where he remained first as pupil then as pupil-teacher until 1884, when he migrated to Queensland. For two years he wandered the back country taking odd jobs, until employment on a coastal ship brought him in 1886 to Sydney. After further casual employment, including that of a stage extra in *Henry V*, he married in 1886 Elizabeth Cutts (d. 1906), said to have been his landlady's daughter, and settled in a small shop with living accommodation in Balmain, a dockside slum area. They had seven children.

Trade unionist and politician Hughes then became active in the growing labour movement. He was employed in 1893 as an organizer for the newly created Political Organisation of Trade Unions and Labor Electoral Leagues, and he advocated the subjection of parliamentary Labor representatives to control by the annual conference, the central executive, and a majority in the parliamentary caucus—ironical having regard to his later quarrel with the Labor 'machine'. In 1894 he was elected as Labor Party member for the Lang electorate in Sydney, which included his dockside home, and rapidly rose to prominence in parliament and in the outside labour organizations; he held Lang with increasing majorities at elections in 1895 and 1898. In parliament he was especially prominent in pushing through measures for 6 p.m. closing of shops and for old-age pensions.

Hughes was disappointed when Labor failed to get any of its representatives elected to the decisive federal conventions of 1897–8, and his opposition to the federal scheme hardened when in 1899 G. H. Reid failed to get the draft constitution modified as Labor wished, especially on the senate's powers. He accordingly became one of the main public opponents of federalism at the plebiscite of 1899, but the required majority for bringing New South Wales into federation was eventually obtained. Hughes then transferred to the federal sphere; at the first election

William Morris Hughes (1862–1952), by George Lambert, 1927

for the commonwealth house of representatives in 1901 he was elected for West Sydney, which included his old state electorate.

The Hughes who now emerged on the federal stage, and soon became and long remained a dominating influence there, had already moved far in personal life and political views from the poverty-stricken doctrinaire found in the scanty records of his life from 1884 to 1893. Payment of members was adopted in New South Wales in 1888 and written into the federal constitution, and although the expenses involved in being a member and the demands of a rapidly increasing family left little over, he never again suffered the grinding poverty and insecurity of earlier years. He was short, slightly built, stooped, with an engagingly ugly face and big ears, a gift to cartoonists but correspondingly soon familiar to the nation as Billy. Ill health which had contributed to his migration from England had been made chronic by his early hardships in Australia; dyspepsia and bad hearing plagued the rest of his life, although he soon learned to use the hearing aid as a weapon to avoid inconvenient questions or obtain time for a reply. Immense energy and drive largely overcame these handicaps, although ill health contributed to the surprising lapses in political judgement which marred his career after 1915. Throughout the 1890s he both studied and practised public speaking, read for the bar (to which he was admitted in 1903), and developed a capacity for fluent writing as well as speaking. At his best Hughes was a superb orator, using by turns a rollicking humour, satire, scathing invective, and emotional rhetoric, but with great clarity and directness where these were required. His small figure became transformed by flailing arms and stamping legs into the embodiment of persuasion or domination. In 1911 he married Mary Ethel, the daughter of Thomas Campbell, a grazier of Burrandong, New South Wales. She was appointed GBE in 1922. They had a daughter.

The lessons in political realism learned in the New South Wales parliament were reinforced by Hughes's experience of industrial warfare. In 1899 he reorganized and became secretary of the Sydney Wharf Labourers' Union, a position he held until 1915. In 1902 he created an Australia-wide Waterside Workers' Federation and became its first president, and later he procured its first award in the newly created commonwealth court of conciliation and arbitration. Hughes fought vigorously for the interests of this and other trade unions, but did so increasingly from the point of view of a tactician out to secure optimum gains in wages and conditions for a minimum loss through strikes and the antagonizing of public and even employer opinion.

Minister and prime minister Until Alfred Deakin fused the non-Labor parties in 1909, Labor held the balance of power, and for two short periods itself held office; Hughes was minister for external affairs in the government of J. C. Watson in 1904 and attorney-general in the first government of Andrew Fisher in 1908–9. He became a principal Labor speaker on most subjects and delivered masterpieces of invective against those who incurred his party's wrath, notably in the 1909 debates on Deakin's final decision to remove the Fisher government and join the conservatives. Hughes's main constructive activities in this period concerned maritime legislation and defence. In 1904 he became chairman of a royal commission investigating a proposed federal code of navigation law, and in 1907 he visited Britain for a conference on the relation of such legislation to the imperial Merchant Shipping Acts; legislation based on his recommendations was ultimately passed in 1913. He adopted, and persuaded first his party and then the Deakin government of 1909 to adopt, the principle of compulsory military training for male citizens, with obligation to serve only within Australia, as the foundation of Australian military defence policy.

Labor swept the polls in 1910, and Hughes was attorney-general in the second Fisher government, which held office until 1913. Besides his heavy involvement in the legal and constitutional aspects of government, including unsuccessful attempts at procuring constitutional amendment by referendum in 1911 and 1913, he became the main government spokesman on nearly all matters of difficulty. The constructive achievements with which he was associated included the creation of a commonwealth bank and a commonwealth note issue, the extension of commonwealth social services, and the introduction of a federal land tax.

The Fisher government was defeated at the election of 1913, but so narrowly that its opponents soon obtained a 'deadlock' double dissolution. War broke out immediately before polling day, and Hughes vied with Fisher in pledging the complete support of the Labor Party for the

British war effort. Hughes had formed and led organizations interested in Australian defence from 1905 on, and during his visit to Britain in 1907 had attracted attention by his vehement support for a strong defence policy. Without the authority of his party, he now proposed that the election be postponed and a political truce proclaimed for the duration of the war so that all effort should be concentrated on its conduct. Constitutional difficulties prevented this, but Hughes's attitude began the break between himself and the left wing of the Labor movement. At the election Labor was returned with large majorities in both houses, and Hughes again became attorney-general under Fisher. Fisher retired from politics in October 1915 and Hughes succeeded him as party leader and prime minister, while remaining attorney-general. Although he was not wholly inattentive to Labor's social aims, he concentrated throughout this period on war problems, particularly on the dissolution of German economic interests and influences in Australia and on vesting the relevant enterprises in Australian concerns.

Military preoccupations In March 1916 Hughes arrived in Britain to consult with the Asquith administration on military and economic policy and attracted widespread attention in vigorous, patriotic speeches advocating a total war effort and a war aim of completely crushing the central powers, militarily and economically. Asquith was compelled to make him a delegate to the Paris economic conference in June, where his fire-eating policy pleased Clemenceau. He visited the Australian troops and acquired the sobriquet the Little Digger. He also negotiated contracts for the sale of Australia's wheat, wool, and other primary products, and to ensure their shipment founded the Australian Commonwealth Shipping Line by purchasing fifteen cargo vessels. Attempts were made to induce him to remain in England, with suggestions that he should be given a Commons and a cabinet seat, but he returned to Australia in July.

Hughes was now convinced that voluntary recruitment was insufficient and that conscription for overseas service, already mooted by leaders of the opposition Liberal Party, had become necessary. However, he knew that resistance to such a policy was widespread in the labour movement, and accordingly on his return to Australia he toured the capitals, making patriotic public speeches on the one hand and on the other endeavouring in private to persuade Labor Party and trade-union leaders to back his judgement about conscription. The Labor Party's parliamentary caucus in Melbourne by majority approved a compromise proposal for putting the conscription issue to the electors at a plebiscite, but even the legislation for this was opposed in parliament by a Labor minority and caused the resignation of a senior minister, and further resignations occurred when Hughes attempted to employ the plebiscite as a means of checking on 'draft-dodgers' under a home service call-up. The plebiscite held in October resulted in a narrow majority against conscription, and in November the caucus rebelled against the leadership of Hughes; anticipating a vote against him, Hughes on 14 November led twenty-four followers out of the

Labor Party and formed a government from their number depending upon the benevolent support of the Liberals.

Hughes wished to create a 'national labour' party to support him, but it became evident that the task of organizing a mass basis for a new party was beyond his resources, and the Liberal Party leaders were not prepared indefinitely to support a rump government, so the National Labor group merged with the Liberals to form the Nationalist Party, with Hughes as prime minister and attorney-general. At a general election in 1917 Hughes led the Nationalists to an overwhelming victory in both houses, and he continued as prime minister until 1923. He himself was returned for the Bendigo seat in Victoria. In November 1917 Hughes pledged himself to resign if conscription were not approved, and did so when a second plebiscite failed by a larger majority, but when it became obvious that no other leader could form a government he again became prime minister and was able to concentrate on the war and its aftermath.

Hughes went to Britain in June 1918 and remained until August 1919, pressing Australia's claims in the peace settlement. He was a member of the British delegation to the Paris conference in 1919, and was influential, with Sir Robert Borden and J. C. Smuts, in procuring the separate recognition of the dominions in the form of the peace treaty and their separate membership of the League of Nations. Hughes had no confidence in Woodrow Wilson, or his fourteen points, or in the League of Nations; he favoured a harsh peace and wanted outright annexation of German territories near Australian shores and heavy reparations. He settled for the C-class mandate system and the rejection of Japanese attempts to write a racial equality clause into the league covenant. On his return Hughes received a thunderous popular welcome, and the Nationalist Party scored another triumph at the elections of 1919. He again visited Britain in 1921 for the Imperial Conference, and he favoured renewal of the Anglo-Japanese treaty, but he accepted the American proposals which led to the Washington naval conference.

Interwar political activities From 1920 onwards Hughes's position in the Nationalist Party became increasingly precarious because the powerful conservative wing of the party and the newly created Country Party distrusted him. While he had come to seem a conservative to his former Labor colleagues, he still seemed a dangerous socialist to many of his new political colleagues. Hughes regarded government enterprise and intervention in economic affairs as natural and proper if undertaken in the national interest, and he had become increasingly overbearing and secretive, and in the opinion of many Nationalists inefficient, in his way of conducting such affairs. He also continued to favour—and did throughout his life—expansion of federal power. The farmers objected to his handling of primary produce marketing because he sought to stabilize food prices by government controls when in the post-war inflation a free market would have brought them higher returns, and there was a strong state-right element among his followers. The opposition to him reached a climax when, after the election of December 1922, the Nationalist majority was so reduced that they had to seek a coalition with the Country Party; that party, in particular its leader, Earle Page, declined to support a government led by Hughes. Accordingly he was induced to resign the prime ministership and the Nationalist leadership in favour of S. M. Bruce, who became prime minister on 9 February 1923.

At the election of 1922 Hughes again moved his constituency, from Bendigo to North Sydney. In 1920 admirers had presented him with £25,000 in recognition of his war services, and from now until 1928 he led a relatively quiet back-bencher's existence, but through 1928–9 he became increasingly critical of the Bruce–Page government, particularly of the way it handled industrial disputes. In 1929 he and three other Nationalists voted with the Labor Party to defeat the government on its proposal to remove the commonwealth from the greater part of the field of industrial arbitration. Thus was Hughes revenged for the shabby treatment accorded him in 1923.

Hughes tried to form a new party, called the Australian Party, for the ensuing general election, but his efforts failed. The Labor Party obtained a majority in the representatives, but, between its own dissensions and a hostile senate, it achieved little and in 1931 split into three, one group combining with the Nationalists to form the United Australia Party (UAP). Hughes played only a minor part in the disputes about depression financial policy which were the main cause of these crises. In 1931 he joined the UAP, which under J. A. Lyons scored a decisive electoral victory; right-wing antagonism to Hughes because of his destructive activities in 1929 prevented his immediate appointment as a minister, but in 1932 he represented Australia at a League of Nations assembly, and in 1934 he became minister for repatriation and health in the Lyons government.

From 1934 until 1943 Hughes played a leading part in the UAP, and he was a minister almost continuously until 1941. In 1939 R. G. Menzies narrowly defeated him for the succession to the UAP leadership on the death of Lyons; he was deputy leader until October 1941, when Menzies resigned from leadership and Hughes succeeded him, but their roles were again reversed in 1943. In 1944 Menzies transformed the UAP into the Liberal Party, of which Hughes became a back-bench member. He was minister for health and repatriation from 1934 until 1937, with a brief break in 1935–6 when he was compelled to resign for a few months because he published a book, *Australia and War Today*, which contained views on the Italo-Abyssinian dispute at odds with the policy of the Lyons government. From 1937 until 1939 he was minister for external affairs; thereafter he was attorney-general (1939–41) and minister for industry (1939–40) and navy (1940–41). Under the Labor government of John Curtin from 1941 until 1944 he was a member of the war advisory council. Throughout these years Hughes's experience was highly valued by governments, and his manner of imparting it much mellowed. However, he adhered uncompromisingly to his distrust of international organization and his belief in a strong, independent Australian defence force. His vigorous exposition of these views grated somewhat on all the major parties in the period after 1935 when the public and governments were against rapid rearmament and hoped that appeasement policies would succeed, but his insistence contributed to the important defence measures which were begun, especially after 1938. As attorney-general after 1939 he was responsible for ferreting out enemy agencies and banned the Communist Party in its anti-war phase, but he incurred little of the distrust with which he had been regarded on the political left in the first war.

Final years After 1944 Hughes receded into the political background. At the redistribution in 1949 he chose the Bradfield division, part of his former seat. He had now become a legend in his own lifetime, much sought after as a raconteur and public speaker, and cheered by the marchers on each Anzac day as he stood in Martin Place, Sydney, as he had done since 1920. He died at Lindfield on 28 October 1952, still a member of the house of representatives and the last sitting survivor from the first commonwealth parliament. One hundred thousand people attended his state funeral in Sydney.

Hughes had a prose style almost as lively as his speaking style, and his two volumes of memoirs, *Crusts and Crusades* (1947) and *Policies and Potentates* (1950), while unreliable in detail, convey excellently the atmosphere of many episodes in his earlier career. He also published *The Case for Labor* (1910), a selection from articles under that title which appeared in the Sydney *Daily Telegraph*; *The Splendid Adventure* (1929); and *The Price of Peace* (1934). He was sworn of both the Canadian and United Kingdom privy councils in 1916, took silk in 1919, and was made a CH in 1941.

GEOFFREY SAWER, rev.

Sources L. F. Fitzhardinge, *William Morris Hughes* (1964) · W. F. Whyte, *William Morris Hughes* (1957) · F. C. Browne, *They called him Billy* (1946) · G. Sawer, *Australian federal politics and law*, 2 vols. (1956–63) · private information (1971) **Archives** HLRO, letters to David Lloyd George · NL Aus., corresp. with Alfred Deakin · NL Aus., corresp. with Viscount Novar | FILM BFI NFTVA, documentary footage; news footage **Likenesses** F. D. Wood, plaster head, 1919, IWM; version, terracotta?, Art Gallery of New South Wales, Sydney, Australia · J. Guthrie, oils, *c*.1919–1921 (study for *Statesmen of World War I*), Scot. NPG · J. Guthrie, group portrait, oils, *c*.1924–1930 (*Statesmen of World War I*), NPG · G. Lambert, oils, 1927, King's Hall, Parliament House, Canberra, Australia [*see illus.*] · F. D. Wood, bronze bust, King's Hall, Parliament House, Canberra, Australia · cartoons, repro. in D. Low, *The Billy book: Hughes abroad* (Sydney, 1918)

Hugo of Bury St Edmunds. *See* Bury St Edmunds, Hugo of (*fl. c.*1130–*c.*1150).

Hugo, Thomas (1820–1876), antiquary and print collector, the eldest son of Charles Hugo (1784/1785–1860), surgeon to the 1st Somerset militia, was born in Taunton, Somerset. He entered Worcester College, Oxford, in 1839, graduating BA in 1842. He was ordained priest by the bishop of Chester in 1843 and served as curate in several Lancashire parishes (Walton-le-Dale, 1842–4; Childwall, 1844–6; and Bury, 1846–50) and as vicar of Halliwell (1850–51). There his zealous propagation of extreme high-church views antagonized both patron and bishop, and he moved to London, where he held the post of curate at St Botolph without Bishopsgate from 1851 to 1858.

While in Lancashire in 1850 Hugo became an associate member of the British Archaeological Association; his first antiquarian publications appeared in their journal and related to finds in that county. In 1853 he was elected one of the three secretaries of the association, only to be removed the following year as unfit for office after a bitter argument with the treasurer, Thomas Pettigrew, and the Baptist minister W. H. Black. He then joined the Archaeological Institute and several of his papers were printed in its *Archaeological Journal* between 1855 and 1859. In 1853 Hugo secured election to three learned societies, the Society of Antiquaries of London, the Linnean Society, and the Royal Society of Literature, on whose council he sat from 1855 to 1873. In 1855 Hugo helped to found the London and Middlesex Archaeological Society, chairing the provisional committee, and the inaugural meeting, which established the society, and publishing many articles in its *Transactions*. Sir Thomas Phillipps withdrew his support for the society because Hugo had apparently declared a wish to see the monasteries restored.

Hugo made several communications at the meetings of the Society of Antiquaries. One paper read in 1859 on his collection of badges worn by medieval pilgrims was issued in *Archaeologia* and showed more discrimination than his evidence the previous year in the celebrated case concerning forged medallions, *Eastwood v. The Athenaeum*. Then he stated, without being able to give any reason, that he believed that the forgeries by Billy Smith and Charley Eaton, later known as 'Billys and Charleys', were genuine antiquities. Apart from London, Hugo's greatest antiquarian interest was the medieval church history of his native county of Somerset. He contributed many papers to the county archaeological society's proceedings between 1856 and 1868, and his most substantial historical work was *The Medieval Nunneries of Somerset* (1867).

Hugo is best known as a collector of Bewick wood-engravings. However, although still widely quoted by antiquarian booksellers, Hugo's *The Bewick Collector* of 1866, with its supplement of 1868, is a mine of inaccuracy, put together by an omniverous collector whose enthusiasm, as in other areas of his life, overwhelmed his judgement. The occasional doubts expressed as to the authenticity of some of the material he assembled were put forward reluctantly. Hugo scoured the premises of printing offices and the stock of booksellers across the country, claiming in 1866, with a blithe disregard of his mere forty-six years of age, to have been pursuing the Bewick brothers for upwards of sixty years. In Newcastle he relied heavily on William Garret, a one-time foreman and general manager to the bookseller Emerson Charnley, as a source for not always dependable information, and for material for his collecting passion. In 1870 Hugo published impressions from his collection of original wood-engravings in his *Bewick's woodcuts, impressions of upwards of two thousand wood-blocks, engraved for the most part, by Thomas and John Bewick of Newcastle-on-Tyne*; 100 copies of this publication, in large folio, appeared. Less than half of the cuts could be considered to be from the Bewick workshop, and very many fewer directly from the master's hand, but it is a remarkable assembly of otherwise valuable material. The blocks, books, and printed ephemera were unfortunately dispersed at auction after Hugo's death.

In church matters Hugo described himself as a ritualist and an admirer of Dr E. B. Pusey; at the time of his death he was a member of the council of the English Church Union. A powerful and popular preacher and hymn writer, several of his sermons and hymns were published in his lifetime and after his death in the memorial volume *Miscellaneous Papers* (1878). His views were too extreme to gain preferment in the Church of England, and he frequently quarrelled with his vestries. In 1858 he was appointed perpetual curate of the impoverished and short-lived district chapel of All Saints within the parish of St Botolph without Bishopsgate. On 15 September 1863 he married the widow Agnes Jane Harkness (c.1812–1881), who was born in Jamaica, the daughter of George Buchanan. They lived in Clapton until he was able to exchange his benefice for the rectory of West Hackney in 1868. While in Hackney Hugo compiled a lengthy *Calendar of Records … of West Hackney* (1872), having found them in a poor condition in the church.

In his later years Hugo became interested in the controversy over vivisection. He wrote several sermons and pamphlets against cruelty to animals and was one of the first members of the International Association for the Total Suppression of Vivisection, founded in 1876 and later absorbed into the National Anti-Vivisection Society. Hugo was said to have suffered from a long-standing disease, and died at the rectory on 31 December 1876 after a short illness. He was buried at Highgate cemetery on 6 January 1877. His Bewick collection was sold at Sothebys on 8 and 9 August 1877 in 674 lots. Also included in the sale were the early churchwardens' accounts for St Botolph without Bishopsgate, which were returned to the parish after a complaint in the *City Press* (4 August 1877). His widow died on 11 October 1881.

BERNARD NURSE and IAIN BAIN

Sources T. Hugo, *Miscellaneous papers* (1878), introduction · *Men of the time* (1875), 561–2 · F. Ouvry, 'Presidential address', *Proceedings of the Society of Antiquaries of London*, 2nd ser., 7 (1876–8), 199–200 · F. T. Bussey, *Some notes on West Hackney church, 1824–1924* (1924) · R. Halliday, 'The Billy and Charley forgeries', *Antique Collecting*, 18 (June 1984), 46–9 · T. Pettigrew, *Letter to the members of the British Archaeological Association on the conduct of the Rev. Thos. Hugo FSA* (1855) · P. Levine, *The amateur and the professional* (1986) · Foster, *Alum. Oxon.*, 1715–1886, 2.710 · *London and Provincial Medical Directory* (1861), 1013 · T. Hugo, *Walks around Bishopsgate* (1857) [Bishopsgate Institute, London, copy with additional material] · certificate of ordination, 16 July 1843, GL, MS 10189/2, part 2, fol. 373 · 'Another sale of Bewick's woodcuts', *Printing Times and Lithographer* (15 Sept 1877) · m. cert.
Archives BL, corresp. and papers, Add. MSS 30277–30300 · Som. ARS, MS notes, press cuttings, etc. | Bodl. Oxf., corresp. with Sir Thomas Phillipps · Newcastle Central Library, Pease collection
Likenesses J. S.?, wood-engraving, BM; repro. in *Transactions of the London and Middlesex Archaeological Society*, 5 (1876–81), facing p. 183 · photograph, Bishopsgate Institute, London; repro. in Hugo, *Walks*
Wealth at death under £4000: probate, 27 Feb 1877, *CGPLA Eng. & Wales*

Huicke, Robert (d. 1580/81), physician, was born in Berkshire, and educated at Oxford, where he was admitted BA in 1529, and MA in February 1533, and was elected fellow of Merton College in 1530. On 10 March 1535 he became principal of St Alban's Hall, but his critical views of contemporary scholars lost him this position and he was never reinstated, despite a petition to Cromwell on 13 September 1535 by the members of the hall. In 1536 he became a fellow of the College of Physicians, and proceeded MD at Cambridge in 1538. He was censor of the College of Physicians in 1541, 1556, 1557, 1558, and 1559; was named an elect in 1550; was president in 1551, 1552, and 1564, and consiliarius in 1553, 1559, 1560, and 1561. He was physician to Henry VIII and Katherine Parr, and was also a witness to her will.

In 1546 Huicke sought a divorce from his wife, Elizabeth. John Croke, who tried the suit, gave sentence in favour of Mrs Huicke; her husband thereupon appealed to the privy council. Examinations were made at Greenwich on 11 and 12 May 1546. The Lords, after hearing both of them face to face, wrote to Secretary Petre, to say that 'we never in all our liefes harde matter that more pitied us: so much crueltie and circumvencion in the man, so little cause ministered by the woman' (Munk).

Edward VI, by letters patent dated 4 July 1550, appointed Huicke his physician-extraordinary, with the annual stipend of £50. He was also one of the physicians to Queen Elizabeth. On 28 February 1562 the sub-warden and fellows of Merton College addressed a letter to Sir William Cecil in favour of Huicke's appointment as warden of that house. In November 1564 he became a member of the Inner Temple. He took part in the Physic Act kept at Cambridge on 7 August 1564, 'her majesty merrily jesting with him when he desired her licence'. He also disputed in the Physic Act before the queen at Oxford on 5 September 1566, and on the following day was incorporated MD in that university. He was subsequently appointed chief physician to the queen, who in 1570 granted him a mansion called White Webbs House, in Enfield, Middlesex.

By 1575 Huicke had apparently got rid of his wife, for on 2 November he obtained a general licence to marry Mary Woodcocke, spinster, of the city of London; he was then resident in St Martin-in-the-Fields. Huicke died at his house in Charing Cross. His will, dated 27 August 1580, was proved on 17 April 1581 (PRO, PROB 11/63/13). He requested to be buried in the chancel of Harlington church, Middlesex. His wife survived him, together with two daughters, Atalanta, married to William Chetwynde, and Elizabeth. He is the author of 'Poemata ad R. Eliz.', preserved in the British Library (Royal MS 12.A.xxxviii). Huicke bequeathed all his lands and tenements to Merton College, conditional on his daughter Atalanta dying childless.　　GORDON GOODWIN, rev. RACHEL E. DAVIES

Sources Cooper, *Ath. Cantab.*, 1.554–5 · Munk, *Roll* · will, PRO, PROB 11/33, sig. 17 [Roger Chaloner, 1550] · private information (1891) · Emden, *Oxf.*

Huish, Alexander (1595–1668), Church of England clergyman and biblical scholar, was born in the parish of St Cuthbert, Wells, Somerset, one of at least three sons of

Edward Huish (d. 1624?), notary and deputy registrar of the diocese of Bath and Wells. In 1598 his father was promoted to registrar, a grant reissued for three lives in 1619 and duly transferred to Alexander's brother James Huish (d. 1639); assisted by their extensive kinship network across the diocese, the Huishes 'seem to have been the bishops' and chancellors' chief [resident] men of business' (Stieg, 173). On the evidence of a later poem, one of Alexander's enduring childhood memories was of the accidental uncovering in the cathedral of an Easter sepulchre (rapidly destroyed on the orders of the dean).

Alexander Huish entered Magdalen Hall, Oxford, in 1609, but transferred in 1613 to become one of the first scholars of the newly founded Wadham College. On 10 February 1614 he graduated BA, being one of the first from the college to obtain that degree. On 27 June that year he was recommended by the founder, Dorothy Wadham, for election to a fellowship, to which he was admitted on 30 June 1615; he subsequently held various college offices. He proceeded MA on 17 December 1616. In 1619 he produced an edition of John Flavel's *Tractatus de demonstratione methodicus & polemicus*, and in 1626 he published, in three parts, his own *Lectures upon the Lords Prayer*.

According to a narrative which Huish supplied to Bishop William Piers in the mid-1630s, it was while he was spending Christmas 1627 at Wells with his brother James that the latter, then acting registrar, first encouraged him to seek the vacant living of Beckington, Somerset. While Huish returned to Oxford, James continued to press his claims on the patron, John Webb, who reluctantly agreed to prefer Alexander from among several competing candidates. Huish was inducted as rector on 15 March 1627, proceeded BD on 2 June, and was appointed a prebendary of Wedmore Secunda in Wells Cathedral on 26 October; he was licensed to preach on 11 December and inducted for a second time to Beckington on 21 December 1628. He resigned his fellowship on 28 June 1629, and some time afterwards married Deborah Brian, a widow with two sons, Thomas and Robert. However, in February 1630 Webb took offence when Huish refused to let his daughter act as a godmother on the grounds that she had not yet received communion. 'Hence grew the malice', claimed Huish, which subsequently thwarted his ministry, 'for not content to discountenance me by all means he could, he added many threats withall' (Robinson, 'Documents of the Laudian period', 207).

In time James Huish's efforts to extract from Webb repayment of a loan became bound up with charges that Alexander had obtained the living through James by simony. The situation was further exacerbated by Bishop Piers's campaign to enforce William Laud's archiepiscopal orders of 1634. In a statement of 21 December 1635 Huish, described by Piers in forwarding it to Laud as 'a learned man, a good preacher and very well affected to the governement and rites of the church' (Robinson, 'Documents of the Laudian period', 199–200), put forward his personal conviction of the convenience, decency, and reverence entailed in repositioning the communion table at the east end of the chancel at Beckington. James Wheeler

and John Fry, the churchwardens, being, as Peter Heylin put it, 'rich, well-backed and disaffected to the service … determined otherwise' (ibid., 183). Having ignored a consistory court order to appear and comply, they were excommunicated on 6 October 1635. With the support of John Ashe, son of the lord of the manor, the churchwardens appealed to the court of arches and the case became a *cause célèbre*, continuing for several years and provoking near riots locally. With James Huish as 'chief orchestrator' (Stieg, 300) for the Laudians, it was a hard-fought campaign on both sides and made a major contribution to the polarization of opinion. Meanwhile, on 6 February 1638, Huish was instituted additionally to the rectory of Hornblotton, also in Somerset, a living in the gift of the lord keeper.

The advent of the Long Parliament brought petitions against Huish's 'innovations', and he was named in articles against Bishop Piers. On 12 December 1640 he was sent for as a delinquent by parliamentary order, but he was allowed bail on 4 January. According to John Walker, during the following years he was forced regularly to move from place to place; he was imprisoned for a time in the village of Chalfield, Wiltshire, and his son was expelled from Wadham College. His wife, Deborah, was granted a fifth from both his livings in December 1646, and he compounded for delinquency in 1649. However, it was not until 1650 that he was finally dispossessed of his living at Beckington.

Probably in 1653 Huish was approached by Dr Brian Walton to collaborate with him and other biblical scholars and experts in oriental languages in the production of the London polyglot Bible, one of the most significant productions of biblical criticism in the seventeenth century. Huish was assiduous in this task, making a significant contribution. He lent his expertise to both the Vulgate Latin and Septuagint Greek texts, and acted as one of the four correctors of the work at press. He also collated the Alexandrian manuscript to a degree of excellence praised by Richard Bentley, and his work benefited later scholars such as Grabe and Mill. In the sixth volume of the polyglot Bible there is a Greek hymn with a Latin version by Huish.

Following his involvement in the polyglot Bible, Huish agreed to work with Samuel Clarke and Edmund Castell on the latter's project, a heptaglot lexicon in Hebrew, Chaldee, Syriac, Samaritan, Ethiopic, Persian, and Arabic. The work, however, was beset with difficulties. Clarke pulled out in 1658 and Huish appears to have followed suit after the Restoration. In 1660 he published *Musa ruralis*, poems in Latin and English celebrating the return of Charles Stuart to the English throne. Huish recovered both his livings and also, on 12 September 1660, received the prebend of Whitelackington in Wells Cathedral. An unpublished volume of his Latin poems dated 1667 contained verses in praise of Wells, epitaphs from the tombs of its bishops, and some comment on the state of the cathedral in his youth.

Huish died on 15 April 1668. He divided his estate between his wife, Deborah, his sons, Alexander and

James, and his daughters, Anne, Deborah, and Margaret, the last of whom was married to Thomas Milbourne, a London printer. It was to his daughters that he left the predominant portion of his library. He was buried at either Beckington or Hornblotton.   NICHOLAS KEENE

Sources J. A. Robinson, ed., 'Documents of the Laudian period', *Collectanea II*, ed. T. F. Palmer, Somerset RS, 43 (1928), 177–218 · M. Stieg, *Laud's laboratory: the diocese of Bath and Wells in the early seventeenth century* (1982) · Foster, *Alum. Oxon.* · J. A. Robinson, 'The effigy of "John de Middleton" at Wells', *Proceedings of the Somersetshire Archaeological and Natural History Society*, 71 (1925), 77–83 · will, PRO, PROB 11/327, sig. 82 · *Walker rev.*, 315 · H. J. Todd, *Memoirs of the life and writings of the Right Rev. Brian Walton*, 2 vols. (1821) · *CSP dom.*, *1660* · G. J. Toomer, *Eastern wisedome and learning: the study of Arabic in seventeenth-century England* (1996) · Wood, *Ath. Oxon.* · J. Prince, *Danmonii orientales illustres, or, The worthies of Devon*, 2nd edn (1810) · *DNB* · Som. ARS

Archives Bodl. Oxf., lectures and translations

Wealth at death see will, PRO, PROB 11/327, sig. 82

Huish, Mark (1808–1867), railway manager, was born on 9 March 1808 at Nottingham, the elder son of Mark Huish, a hosier, and Eliza, the daughter of John Gainsford of Worksop. His father was for many years deputy lieutenant of Nottinghamshire, and a staunch member of the congregation of the Church of Protestant Dissenters in High Pavement, Nottingham. Mark was educated in the classical tradition at Mr Taylor's school in Castle Gate.

In 1823 Huish became a cadet in the East India Company army, and in the following year ensign with the 67th regiment, Bengal native infantry in Calcutta. Promoted to lieutenant with the newly created 6th extra regiment (later known as the 74th) in 1825, he was personal escort to Lord Amherst, the governor-general of Bengal from 1826 to 1830, and then spent five years at Chittagong as quartermaster and acting interpreter for the regiment. All this provided an invaluable, if somewhat arduous, training in administrative management, at a time when there were few training grounds for managers. In 1834 he returned to England on leave, and although promoted to captain in his absence he showed no inclination to return to India. Finding himself in Liverpool at the time of the 'railway mania' he looked for work in the industry, and in 1837 he was appointed to the post of secretary of the Glasgow, Paisley and Greenock Railway, with a salary of £200 p.a.

Within a decade Huish progressed from modest official of a minor railway in Scotland to the highly paid chief executive of the largest company in the world in 1846. This astonishing rise demonstrated the opportunities which the railways in their pioneering stage provided for ambitious, energetic, and charismatic figures. Four years in Scotland gave him a thorough grounding in railway management at a formative stage; then in 1841 he was approached by the Grand Junction Railway, which was dissatisfied with its existing managers and was looking for both a competent administrator, and a skilful negotiator with other companies. On returning to Liverpool, Huish became secretary and general manager, and was plunged into, and clearly relished the cut and thrust of, English railway politics. He engineered the merger with the Liverpool and Manchester Railway in 1845, and also that with

Mark Huish (1808–1867), by William Henry Mote, pubd 1848 (after Abraham Wivell)

the London and Birmingham in the following year which created the London and North Western Railway (LNWR), a giant company, which formed a continuous route from London (Euston) to Birmingham, Liverpool, and Manchester. Huish was a natural choice to lead its executive as general manager. His salary of £2000 p.a. made him the supreme railway manager of his day. In the late 1840s and 1850s he was the lion of railway diplomacy.

Huish's managerial abilities were notable, making him one of the leading railway executives of the nineteenth century. Known for his interest in rail safety, cost accounting, and financial management, he contributed to key debates about freight traffic management, permanent way costing, and telegraphic communication. He was, above all, a highly skilled traffic manager, who established the early railway cartels, dominated by LNWR. A master strategist of 'railway diplomacy' he found it difficult to delegate and became the scapegoat for the collapse of his cartel agreements in 1857. His Achilles' heel was undoubtedly an unscrupulous and often crude, bullying approach to business dealings. However, his manoeuvring and tendency to ride roughshod over officials of minor companies, and directors of major ones, finally caught up with him. He was forced to resign in November 1858 after a directorial coup led by Richard Moon, Edward Tootal, and George Carr Glyn. He then retired to the Isle of Wight, where he acted as a director of the Isle of Wight Railway, and chairman of two non-railway concerns, the Clifton Suspension Bridge Company and the Electric and International Telegraph Company. A somewhat disgraced figure in the 1860s, he nevertheless acted as arbitrator in a number of inter-railway disputes, and gave evidence to the royal commission on railways in 1867. He died on 18 January 1867 at his home, Combe Wood, Bonchurch, Isle of Wight, and was buried in St Boniface's graveyard there. He was survived by his wife, Margaret, but nothing else is known about his family life.

While recent scholarship has placed Huish in his context—that of traffic manager in the pioneering stage of railway development—closer inspection reveals a thoughtful executive who contributed much to a broader understanding of the challenges of railway management. He was the general manager *par excellence* of the early railway age, who demonstrated managerial capitalism at the proto-corporate stage of Britain's history.

TERRY GOURVISH

Sources T. R. Gourvish, *Mark Huish and the London–North Western Railway* (1972) · T. R. Gourvish, 'Captain Mark Huish: a pioneer in the development of railway management', *Business History*, 12 (1970), 46–58 · *PICE*, 27 (1867–8), 600–02 · *ILN* (4 Dec 1858) · d. cert. · *CGPLA Eng. & Wales* (1867)
Archives BL OIOC, East India MSS · NA Scot., Glasgow, Paisley, and Greenock Railway MSS · PRO, Grand Junction and London and North Western Railway MSS
Likenesses W. H. Mote, stipple, pubd 1848 (after A. Wivell), NPG [*see illus.*] · photograph, British Railways Board, London
Wealth at death under £40,000: administration with will, 9 March 1867, *CGPLA Eng. & Wales*

Huish, Robert (1777–1850), apiculturist and writer, son of Mark Huish of Nottingham, was born in the city and baptized at High Pavement Presbyterian Chapel there. After studying at Frankfurt am Main, where he acquired a good knowledge of German and French, he spent time in central Europe, Scandinavia, and Russia.

Huish's wide-ranging literary output covered natural history, current and historical topics, romances, and poetry. He is best remembered, however, for his books on bees and beekeeping; he was well read on the subject, and had considerable first-hand experience in both England and Scotland. He also maintained an extensive European correspondence on beekeeping.

Huish drew on his experience and on his reading for *A Treatise on the Nature, Economy, and Practical Management of Bees* (1815). This book is a valuable addition to early nineteenth-century apicultural literature. Three further editions followed, in 1817, 1842, and 1844, each with additional material. The first two editions included six very clear fold-out plates showing the various types of hive in use at that time.

As honorary secretary of the short-lived British Apiarian Society, Huish published in 1819 two pamphlets, *Rules of the British Apiarian Society* and *Instructions for Using the Huish Hive* (a second edition of which followed in 1822). *The Cottager's Manual*, first published in 1820, followed by editions in 1821 and 1832, was a month-by-month instructional booklet based upon a chapter extracted from *A Treatise*.

As Huish built up a considerable popular readership he became dogmatically involved in a war of words with those who accepted the ideas of the eminent Swiss apicultural scientist Francis Huber. In the 1844 edition of *A Treatise* he set out in tabular form the thirty-four 'errors' of Huber. This tabulation shows how far Huber advanced scientific apiculture, whereas Huish, for all his technical skill, failed to make full observations and to interpret his observations correctly. He also assumed that his own conclusions, based on a single hive, were 'normal' for all colonies of bees. However, despite its faults, *A Treatise* offers a good insight into both British and European beekeeping in the opening decades of the nineteenth century.

Until his death Huish wrote an influential beekeeping column for the monthly journal *Gardener, Florist and Apiculturist*. He died in Camberwell, Surrey, in April 1850; he was survived by his wife, Maria Petty Huish, who administered his estate.

KARL SHOWLER

Sources J. P. Harding and others, *British bee books: a bibliography, 1500–1976* (1979) · H. J. O. Walker, *Catalogue of bee books* (1929) · R. Huish, *A treatise on the nature, economy, and practical management of bees* (1844) · *N&Q*, 176 (1939), 102–3
Likenesses R. Page, stipple, pubd 1820 (after R. Drummond), BM, NPG · Brain, stipple, pubd 1842 (after drawing by D. Wilkie), repro. in Huish, *Bees: their natural history and general management*, 4th edn (1844)

Hulbert, Charles (1778–1857), writer, son of Thomas Hulbert (d. 1805), a soldier, of Hulbert Green, near Cheadle, Cheshire, and his wife, Anne, née Mottishead (d. 1783), was born at Manchester on 18 February 1778, and was educated at the grammar school of Halton, Cheshire. After learning cotton-weaving he became manager, at the age of twenty-two, of a large calico-print works at Middleton, near Manchester, and subsequently began business with his elder brother at Swinton, also near Manchester. In 1803, in partnership with others, he leased some large factories at Coleham, near Shrewsbury. In 1805 he married Anna, daughter of Thomas Wood, proprietor of the *Shrewsbury Chronicle*. He underwent a religious conversion and entered ardently into Sunday school and religious work, conducting classes and services at the factory. He even applied, but unsuccessfully, for ordination in the church. At the request of W. Wilberforce and the Hon. H. G. Bennet, in 1808 he drew up a report on the management of factories, as an answer to a charge made in parliament that manufactories were hotbeds of vice. Soon afterwards he declined a tempting offer to remove to St Petersburg, made to him, it is said, by an agent of the emperor of Russia. In 1813 his business as a cotton manufacturer having fallen off, he opened a bookshop and printing office at Shrewsbury, where he published the *Salopian Magazine* (1815–17), and printed many small books, the majority of a religious or antiquarian nature and written by himself. In 1827 he built a house at Hadnall, near Shrewsbury, which he called Providence Grove, and here he continued to print and publish his writings. This house burnt down, and his large library was destroyed, on 7 January 1839; but he was enabled, by a public subscription and a grant from the Royal Literary Fund, to rebuild his residence and to purchase an annuity. He composed his autobiographical *Memoirs of Seventy Years of an Eventful Life* (published 1848–52); an abridged version appeared in 1857. He died at Providence Grove on 7 October 1857, and was buried at Hadnall.

Charles Augustus Hulbert (1805–1888), Church of England clergyman, was his eldest son. He was born at Coleham, near Shrewsbury, on 31 December 1805, and was educated at Shrewsbury School and at Sidney Sussex College, Cambridge. He graduated BA in 1834, and MA in 1837; he was curate of St Mary's, Islington, 1834–9, perpetual curate of Slaithwaite, Yorkshire, 1839–67, and vicar of Almondbury, near Huddersfield, 1867–88. He was mainly instrumental in the restoration of Almondbury church. In 1866 he was collated honorary canon of Ripon. He published several books of a religious nature. He died unmarried on 5 March 1888 at the vicarage, Almondbury.

C. W. SUTTON, rev. ANITA MCCONNELL

Sources C. Hulbert, *Memoirs of seventy years of an eventful life* (privately printed, Providence Grove, 1852) · C. A. Hulbert, *Obituary of C. Hulbert*, 2nd edn (1860) · *CGPLA Eng. & Wales* (1888) [Charles Augustus Hulbert] · d. cert. [C. A. Hulbert] · Venn, *Alum. Cant.*
Likenesses engraving, repro. in Hulbert, *Memoirs*, frontispiece
Wealth at death £2092 10s. 6d.—Charles Augustus Hulbert: probate, 19 May 1888, *CGPLA Eng. & Wales*

Hulbert, Charles Augustus (1805–1888). *See under* Hulbert, Charles (1778–1857).

Hulbert, Claude Noel (1900–1964), actor, was born on 25 December 1900 at 732 Fulham Road, London, the younger son of Henry Harper Hulbert, physician and surgeon, and his wife, Lilian Mary Hinchliffe. From early childhood Claude displayed droll qualities in family theatricals. He was educated in London at Freherne House preparatory school and Victoria Tutorial College before following his actor brother, John Norman (Jack) *Hulbert, to Gonville and Caius College, Cambridge, in October 1918. Hulbert resided for nine terms but did not take a degree. However, he rowed for his college and attended some lectures on moral science. Frances Partridge, a contemporary, wrote that 'Beside some dedicated swots sat the unexpected figure of Claude Hulbert—who couldn't help looking funny even during a lecture on Hegel' (Partridge, 66).

Hulbert spent rather more time as leading comic in the Footlights Dramatic Club, with which he made quite a success in *His Little Trip*, a special matinée at the Strand Theatre, London, on 18 June 1920. In the same year Hulbert made his professional début at the Alhambra, Bradford. He subsequently played several music-halls with his sister-in-law Cicely *Courtneidge, learning to 'put over' his naturally diffident personality. Off-stage a sweet-natured, simple, happy man, on 11 February 1924 he married Enid Trevor (b. 1899/1900), daughter of Colonel Philip Christian Trevor, a well-known sports correspondent. They had two daughters, Jill and Jacqueline.

Hulbert appeared in London in the revue *Fantasia* (1921) then made a success in *Primrose* (1924), a musical comedy by George Grossmith and Guy Bolton, with music by George Gershwin. This led to a string of musical comedy roles from 1925 to 1930: in *Sunny*, *Oh Kay*, *Song of the Sea*, and *Follow a Star*, among other shows. Hulbert became well known for playing gentlemanly dimwits and was hailed as a remarkable eccentric dancer, doing roll-overs and, seemingly, walking on his head. As early as 1926 *Punch* described him as 'that great artist' who stopped the show *Kid Boots* with a routine of his own devising, 'Ballet de bain', which involved taking an imaginary bath to music. Although he was no singer, Hulbert's few recordings from

these shows have considerable charm, notably Jerome Kern's wistful *Two Little Bluebirds* and a hilariously polite English rendition of George Gershwin's pastiche gospel song *Clap yo' Hands*.

In 1930 Hulbert left the stage for nine years to concentrate on the two coming media—wireless and the talkies. Having already made his film début in Alfred Hitchcock's *Champagne* (1928) he played in innumerable cheapskate 'quota quickies' or programme fillers. He also appeared in film versions of three of Ben Travers's farces, including *A Night Like This* (1931) and *Thark* (1932). His quiet, understated style in these suited the screen better than that of the stagey star players. More noteworthy was the spoof Drummond thriller *Bulldog Jack*, with Ralph Richardson as villain and Fay Wray the heroine. Hulbert as his brother Jack's inept assistant had some delightful comic moments in lurid sequences below the British Museum and on the tube.

Hulbert's film career continued during and after the Second World War, notably in three Ealing pictures—*Sailors Three* (1940), *The Ghost of St Michael's* (1941), and *My Learned Friend* (1943)—in the last two as a foil to the irascible Will Hay. Few could forget the closing sequence of the third and best film when, bizarrely disguised as beefeaters, Hay and Hulbert hang from Big Ben's minute hand in an effort to prevent a concealed bomb from exploding. Hay shrieks 'Stop the clock!' Hulbert, mildly reproachful, says 'You can't stop Big Ben old boy—people set their watches by it.'

It might seem odd that a visual, acrobatic comedian should make a success on the wireless but Hulbert's sensitive voice, apparent spontaneity, and excitable, nervous stutter proved immediately popular. His interest in radio's possibilities is clear in his surprisingly serious book *Learn to Write for Broadcasting* (1932). Often heard with his off-stage wife, Enid Trevor—domineering on the air, devoted in real life—he remained a radio favourite until well after the war, writing much of his own material. The Hulberts were also early television stars.

In 1939 Claude returned to the London stage in *Worth a Million*, a farce. Subsequent West End engagements included *Panama Hattie* (1943), a Cole Porter musical in which Claude played a deadpan butler; *The Wizard of Oz* (1946), playing the Cowardly Lion; and the revue *Sauce Tartare* (1949). In the 1950s Claude's theatrical career dwindled a little. He toured in several mediocre farces and was a guest star in various repertory theatres, where his generous good humour and sure-fire technique impressed many younger actors. Legend has it that his devoted Enid would occasionally prompt him—whispering through canvas fireplaces. Happily his last West End appearance—in Frederick Lonsdale's creaking country house comedy *Let them Eat Cake* (at the Strand in 1959)—was one of his most successful. With only a handful of lines—among an all-star cast—his bemused Lord Plynne, gently popping up at inopportune moments, stole both the show and its notices.

The Wodehousean silly ass role has surely never had a

more endearing exponent than Claude Hulbert—all flustered, well-meaning earnestness with an inspired touch of pure fantasy. He was blessed with a wonderfully comic appearance—resembling a startled hare with his moonstruck eyes, jug ears, and projecting upper lip. His slim body retained into middle age the agility of a dancer.

Lacking the driving command of his brother, Jack, and too often working with feeble scripts and unimaginative directors, Claude Hulbert never quite developed into a major star but in second-lead parts could be uniquely, exquisitely funny. He died on 23 January 1964 in a hospital at Sydney, Australia, while on a world cruise with his wife and daughter Jackie undertaken to restore his failing health.   JONATHAN CECIL

Sources F. Gaye, ed., *Who's who in the theatre*, 14th edn (1967) · *Who's who in broadcasting* (1933) · personal knowledge (2004) · private information (2004) [Betty Astell] · J. Hulbert, *The little woman's always right* (1975) · C. Courtneidge, *Cicely* (1953) · F. Partridge, *Memories* (1981) · b. cert. · m. cert. · *The Times* (24 Jan 1964) · *CGPLA Eng. & Wales* (1964)
Likenesses photographs, 1926–47, Hult. Arch.
Wealth at death £4336: probate, 12 June 1964, *CGPLA Eng. & Wales*

Hulbert, John Norman [Jack] (1892–1978), actor and theatre producer, was born in Ely, Cambridgeshire, on 24 April 1892, the elder son (there were no daughters) of Henry Harper Hulbert MRCS LRCP and his wife, Lilian Mary Hinchliffe. His younger brother, Claude Noel *Hulbert, also achieved prominence as an actor. He was educated at Westminster School, and Gonville and Caius College, Cambridge. He decided as a schoolboy to earn his living as an actor, and this early decision was actively encouraged by his father's enthusiasm for the theatre. Later, indeed, Dr Hulbert forsook the medical profession and gave up his practice in order to lecture on voice production to stage aspirants. Meanwhile, father and son regularly visited the London theatres, seated usually in the gallery on a Saturday night, and earnestly discussed the acting techniques and personalities (as projected on the stage) of the players. Charles Hawtrey and Gerald Du Maurier were their particular favourites.

Although at the end he managed to scramble into a degree during his three years at Cambridge (he used to refer to them as the best years in his life) Jack Hulbert spent his days and nights on any university or local theatre stage that was offered—except when he was rowing. In his last year he was secretary of the Caius boat club, and on one memorable afternoon was tried as bow in the university boat. For the Amateur Dramatic Club and the Marlowe Society he played as many diverse parts as were offered—from Anthony Absolute to Sir Toby Belch. In his second year, at the local theatre in a privately sponsored production, he acted the title part, which was played in London by Charles Hawtrey, in the comedy *Jack Straw* by W. Somerset Maugham. In his last term, for 'The Footlights' revue of May week 1913, he wrote most of the sketches, produced, and played the leading part, achieving a personal success which led, in the following week, to a special matinée at the Queen's Theatre in London. It was

Hulbert's father who had arranged this venture, and among the London theatre managers invited was Robert Courtneidge. Courtneidge at once engaged Hulbert on a three-year contract, and to go into immediate rehearsal to play opposite his twenty-year-old daughter, Cicely, at the Shaftesbury Theatre. And so began a sixty-five year partnership perhaps unique in theatrical annals.

Hulbert married (Esmeralda) Cicely *Courtneidge (1893–1980) in 1916, before serving for two years (1917–19) in the Army Service Corps. The stage careers of Hulbert and his wife were so interlinked that they are described together in the article on Cicely Courtneidge. After their successes on the London stage during the 1920s, Hulbert concentrated exclusively on acting for the cinema between 1931 and 1938.

One of Hulbert's earliest films, made at the old Gaumont-British studios, and directed by Victor Saville, was an English translation from the German, renamed *Sunshine Susie*, with the German actress Renate Muller in love with Owen Nares, the manager of a Viennese bank, of which Hulbert was the hall porter. With the director's delighted approval, Hulbert played this apparently incongruous role in his musical comedy manner of breezy good humour, in amusing contrast to the delicate 'legitimate' technique of Nares, an actor whom Hulbert greatly admired. The film, in spite of its German origin, was refreshingly and unmistakably English, and proved an immediate success, first in London and then throughout the country.

There followed for Hulbert a succession of films in which he starred. These films were in a sense the culmination of his stage career in the musical comedy world of the 1920s and 1930s, to which he really belonged. Their titles, which were typical of his stage and screen personality, are significant: *Jack's the Boy* (1932), *Jack Ahoy* (1934), *Bulldog Jack* (1935), and *Jack-of-All-Trades* (1936). Tall, fair, and angular, Hulbert had a chin which protruded with an amiable resolution. His dancing may have lacked the technical and rhythmic precision of a Fred Astaire or Jack Buchanan but it had a quality of impromptu ease in its variations.

As a producer of plays, and particularly of musical comedies, Hulbert not only was ingenious and competent but had the gift of getting into his shows a vitality and movement on the part of his choruses that could only have been obtained by a perfectionist—as indeed he was, in everything that concerned him in the theatre as actor, producer, trainer of choruses, and author. He had the reputation in the profession, and particularly among the choruses he trained, of being a genial slave-driver, but the discipline he called for and inspired was mitigated by his understanding, good humour, and the certain knowledge that he never spared himself.

Hulbert was a man of many interests and hobbies, among them farming. He owned and worked a farm for many years at Essendon, in Hertfordshire, and (in his own words) escaped there whenever he reasonably could. Among his interests was geology. Samuel Pepys was one of his historical heroes, and during Hulbert's not infrequent visits to Cambridge when on tour he usually found time to include a visit to the Pepys Library in Magdalene College.

Jack Hulbert died at his home, 18A Charles Street, Westminster, London, on 25 March 1978; he was survived by his wife and their only child, a daughter.

D. PEPYS-WHITELEY, rev.

Sources *Daily Telegraph* (27 March 1978) · *The Times* (4 April 1978) · C. Courtneidge, *Cicely* (1953) · J. Hulbert, *The little woman's always right* (1975) · personal knowledge (1986) · d. cert.
Archives FILM BFI NFTVA, documentary footage · BFI NFTVA, news footage · BFI NFTVA, performance footage | SOUND BL NSA, performance recording
Likenesses photographs, 1916–54, Hult. Arch.
Wealth at death £19,667: probate, 11 Aug 1978, *CGPLA Eng. & Wales*

Hulett, Charles (1700?–1735), actor, was born in Russell Street, Bloomsbury, London, the son of John Hulett, said to have been a yeoman of the guard, warden of the Tower, and steward to the earl of Northampton. He was apprenticed in the house of the publisher and bookseller Edmund Curll, where, according to W. R. Chetwood, he recited heroics in the kitchen at night with chairs as characters. While playing Alexander in Nathaniel Lee's *The Rival Queens* he demolished a chair. When Curll asked what the noise was, the cook replied, 'Nothing, sir, but that Alexander has kill'd Clytus' (Chetwood, 171). This persuaded Curll to allow his apprentice to try his luck in the theatre.

Hulett may have been employed at Lincoln's Inn Fields as early as autumn 1719, for he received benefits on 21 May 1720 and 9 May 1721. He is not noticed in the bills until he played Lenox in *Macbeth* on 26 October 1721. He participated in the series of Shakespeare revivals occasioned by the defection from Drury Lane of Lacy Ryan and James Quin; the latter was then the leading young star of the London stage. Hulett's roles included Lucius in Ravenscroft's adaptation of *Titus Andronicus*, Casca in *Julius Caesar*, Kent in *King Lear*, and Achilles in Dryden's *Troilus and Cressida*. He played little comedy, but appeared as secondary figures in many of the heroic dramas which still held the stage: Hottman in Thomas Southerne's *Oroonoko*, Hannibal in James Thomson's *Sophonisba*, and Polyperchon, then Cassander, in *The Rival Queens*. Working in Quin's shadow, he played no leads, which provoked his old master to accuse the manager, John Rich, of 'wanting to keep under hatches that improving Young Fellow *Charles Hulett*' (Curll, 11).

Like other actors of his time, Hulett sometimes performed at fairground booths when the playhouses were closed in August. After Bartholomew fair in 1727, he may have left London, but returned to play such leading parts as Macheath in *The Beggar's Opera* by John Gay and the title roles in *Oroonoko* and *Hurlothrumbo* by Samuel Johnson at the Haymarket in 1729. He did not settle at a London playhouse again until 1732, when he appeared as Falstaff in *Henry IV* at Goodman's Fields on 2 October. Thereafter he played there regularly, sustaining such parts as Falstaff and Henry VIII, which accorded better with the 'Mountain of Flesh he is loaded with' (Chetwood, 173) than heroes

or lovers; nevertheless, his last appearance was as Pierre in *Venice Preserv'd* on 3 October 1735.

Little is known of Hulett's private life. The parish register at St Paul's, Covent Garden, records the burial of James, son of Charles 'Hulit', on 8 March 1726; and Henrietta-Maria, the daughter of Charles and Mary 'Hewlet', was baptized at St Clement Danes on 8 March 1727. His widow and child received a benefit at Goodman's Fields on 19 November 1735. Several accounts confirm the manner of his death: as a prank to startle a colleague at a rehearsal, he pronounced a tremendous 'hem', which burst a blood-vessel in his throat. He died of haemorrhage on 8 October 1735 and was buried at St Mary's, Whitechapel.

ALAN HUGHES

Sources Highfill, Burnim & Langhans, *BDA* · E. L. Avery, ed., *The London stage, 1660–1800*, pt 2: *1700–1729* (1960) · A. H. Scouten, ed., *The London stage, 1660–1800*, pt 3: *1729–1747* (1961) · B. R. Schneider, *Index to 'The London stage, 1660–1800'* (1979) · W. R. Chetwood, *A general history of the stage, from its origin in Greece to the present time* (1749) · T. Davies, *Dramatic miscellanies*, 3 vols. (1784) · W. C. Russell, *Representative actors* [1888] · [E. Curll], *The life of that eminent comedian Robert Wilks, esq.* (1733)

Hulett, James (d. 1771), engraver, was active from at least 1740. He lived in London, and was extensively employed on book illustrations. These include plates for D. de Coetlogon's *Dictionary of Arts and Sciences* (1745), portraits of the earl of Essex and Lord Fairfax for Francis Peck's *Memoirs of the Life and Actions of Oliver Cromwell* (1740), and illustrations to one of the editions of Henry Fielding's *Joseph Andrews*. He engraved *Hampton Court Bridge* after a drawing by Canaletto, which was published by Robert Sayer in 1754. Hulett also contributed a portrait of Mary II, after George Kneller, to William Rider's *A New History of England* (1761–1764?). He lived in Red Lion Street, Clerkenwell, and died there in January 1771.

L. H. CUST, rev. ANNE PUETZ

Sources Redgrave, *Artists* · Thieme & Becker, *Allgemeines Lexikon* · T. Dodd, 'History of English engravers', BL, Add. MS 33402 · *Engraved Brit. ports.*, 6.635 · M. Liversidge and J. Farrington, eds., *Canaletto and England* (1993), 95 [exhibition catalogue, Birmingham Gas Hall Exhibition Gallery, Birmingham, 14 Oct 1993 – 9 Jan 1994] · Bryan, *Painters* (1886–9) · Bénézit, *Dict.*, 3rd edn

Hulke, John Whitaker (1830–1895), surgeon, fourth son of William Hulke, surgeon, was born on 6 November 1830 at Deal, Kent. From 1843 to 1845 he attended the Moravian college in Neuwied, where he gained a good knowledge of the German language while also studying natural history and geology. Hulke returned to England in 1846 and attended King's College School in 1846–7, and in 1849 he entered the medical department of King's College, London. During this time he served as a dresser at King's College Hospital to Sir William Bowman, whose collected papers he later edited with J. Burdon-Sanderson. Hulke was admitted a member of the Royal College of Surgeons on 16 July 1852, but soon returned to Deal, where he acted as assistant to his father and attended the duke of Wellington during his fatal illness in September 1852. Hulke subsequently became house surgeon to Sir William Fergusson at King's College Hospital.

In 1855 Hulke served on the medical staff of the general

hospital in the Crimea, and in March of that year he joined the staff of the English hospital at Smyrna. In September 1855 Hulke left Smyrna for Sevastopol, where he spent the winter of 1855–6. He then returned to England, and was elected a fellow of the Royal College of Surgeons on 23 May 1857. For a short time he was a tutor at King's College Hospital, where he was elected assistant surgeon in 1857, for a term of five years. In 1858 he married Julia Grace, daughter of Samuel Ridley; there were no children.

In the same year as his marriage Hulke was elected assistant surgeon at the Royal London Ophthalmic Hospital, Moorfields; he became full surgeon there in 1868 and consulting surgeon in 1890. At the Royal College of Surgeons, Hulke filled in succession every office open to him. In 1859 he won the college's Jacksonian prize with an essay on the morbid changes of the retina. He was appointed Arris and Gale lecturer on anatomy and physiology (1868–71), an examiner on the board of anatomy and physiology (1876–80), and a member of the court (1880–89) and the dental board (1883–9). He also served as a member of the council (1881–95), vice-president (1888 and 1891), Bradshaw lecturer ('On fractures and dislocations of the vertebral column', in 1891), and president (1893–5); his Hunterian oration, 'John Hunter the biologist', was read for him on 14 February 1895, while he lay dying of pneumonia.

Hulke was elected a fellow of the Royal Society in 1867, and served on the council of the Royal Society in 1879–80 and again in 1888–9. Elected a member of the Geological Society in 1868, he became its president from 1882 to 1884, and in 1887 he was presented with the Wollaston medal, the greatest honour of the society. In 1891 he was appointed foreign secretary, a position he held until he died.

In February 1862 Hulke was elected an honorary fellow of King's College, and in 1878 he became a corresponding member of the Academy of Natural Sciences, Philadelphia. In 1884 he became an honorary member of the Cambridge Philosophical Society and from 1883 to 1885 he was president of the Pathological Society of London. In 1886–7 he was president of the Ophthalmological Society of the United Kingdom, and in 1893–4 he was president of the Clinical Society.

Hulke died at his home at 10 Old Burlington Street, London, on 19 February 1895, and was buried in the cemetery at Deal. He was survived by his wife. During his lifetime Hulke had been an early supporter of aseptic methods. He was highly skilled in ophthalmic surgery and pathology, and to a certain extent he was a pioneer in cerebral surgery, wise enough to identify and practise surgical techniques that he considered would stand the test of time.

D'A. POWER, rev. JEFFREY S. REZNICK

Sources *The Lancet* (23 Feb 1895) · *BMJ* (23 Feb 1895), 451–3 · J. B. S. [J. B. Sanderson] and E. T. N., *PRS*, 58 (1895), xlix-liii · personal knowledge (1901) · private information (1901) · *CGPLA Eng. & Wales* (1895) · *DNB*
Archives Elgin Museum, Elgin, letters to George Gordon
Likenesses H. J. Brooks, group portrait, oils (*Council of the Royal College of Surgeons of England of 1884–85*), RCS Eng. · pen drawing, repro. in *Middlesex Hospital Journal*, 1 (1897) · pen drawing, repro. in *Lancet*

Wealth at death £8018 4s. 8d.: probate, 10 April 1895, *CGPLA Eng. & Wales*

Hull, (James) Alan (1945–1995), popular singer and songwriter, was born on 20 February 1945 at 68 Sutton's Dwellings, Benwell, Newcastle upon Tyne, the home of his father, Anthony Hull, who was unemployed, his mother, Sarah (Sally), née Broadbent, and his elder sister Moira. He attended Rutherford Grammar School, Newcastle. He was given a guitar at the age of twelve and wrote his first song soon afterwards. As a teenager he became lead guitarist in several amateur rock groups, one of which, the Chosen Few, recorded for Pye Records in 1965.

At twenty-one Hull began training as a psychiatric nurse at St Nicholas's Hospital, Newcastle, where he met Patricia Sharp (known as Pat; b. 1940/41). They were married on 22 August 1966, and had three daughters. During this period he wrote several of his most memorable songs, including 'Lady Eleanor' and 'We can Swing Together', and in 1973 a book of poems based on his experiences there, *The Mocking Horse*, was published by Spice Box Books. He left nursing in 1969 to concentrate on performing his songs and organized a folk club at the Rex Hotel, Whitley Bay. During 1969 he composed more than fifty songs while working as a window cleaner. Among those who appeared at his club was the local folk-rock group Brethren, with whom he teamed up.

The group signed a recording contract with the London-based Charisma Records, owned by Tony Stratton-Smith, and were renamed Lindisfarne by John Anthony, the producer of their first album, *Nicely out of Tune* (1970). This contained seven songs composed by Hull, including the psychedelic 'Clear White Light'. Bob Dylan was a primary influence on Hull's songwriting and Dylan's former producer Bob Johnston was brought in from the United States to produce the next album, *Fog on the Tyne* (1971). The title-song was to become Hull's best-known composition, a singalong number with which Lindisfarne would end each concert. The song's status as a modern Geordie anthem was underlined in 1990, when the group re-recorded it with locally born soccer star Paul Gascoigne.

During 1971 Lindisfarne had top ten hits with 'Meet me on the Corner', composed by group member Rod Clements, and Hull's 'Lady Eleanor', inspired by Edgar Allan Poe. Hull again wrote most of the songs for the group's third album, *Dingly Dell* (1972). Among these were 'All Fall Down', 'Bring Down the Government', and 'Poor Old Ireland'. Lindisfarne performed extensively in Europe, North America, and the Far East; the pressure of touring contributed largely to the group's dissolution in 1974. Hull had meanwhile made the solo album *Pipedream* (1973), which included 'Money Game', a sharp expression of his disillusionment with the music industry. He also composed the music for, and acted in, *Squire*, a 1975 BBC television play by the Newcastle writer Tom Pickard.

In 1976 the original members of Lindisfarne reunited for what would turn out to be the first of many Christmas concerts at Newcastle City Hall. The group toured occasionally and also recorded many new Alan Hull songs, including 'Run for Home', an international hit in 1978, and 'Dedicated Hound', an attack on music journalists. In 1983 Conservative members of parliament denounced his song 'Malvinas Melody', 'a criticism of war as a solution to disputes', whose title referred to the Falklands conflict of the previous year. Lindisfarne remained a vehicle for Hull's songs throughout the 1980s, and his final album with the group, *Elvis Lives on the Moon* (1993), included two of his most potent political commentaries, 'Day of the Jackal' and 'Mother Russia'.

Hull also made solo recordings as well as collaborating with Pickard in 1986 on *Heads Held High*, a musical show commemorating the fiftieth anniversary of the Jarrow march. This reflected his lifelong commitment to socialism; for a time he was secretary of his local constituency Labour Party. He performed in Blackpool to coincide with the Labour Party conference in 1990 and played at numerous benefit concerts for striking or redundant miners and shipyard workers.

Alan Hull died of a heart attack at the General Hospital, North Shields, Northumberland, on 17 November 1995 and his ashes were scattered at the mouth of the River Tyne. His final composition, 'We can Make It', a celebration of northern working-class resilience, appeared on a posthumously released album, *Statues and Liberties*. This was completed by his musical collaborators, who included his son-in-law Dave Denholm.   DAVE LAING

Sources C. Groom and J. Revell, 'Lindisfarne', *Record Collector*, 198 (Feb 1996) • P. Hardy and D. Laing, *Faber companion to 20th century popular music* (1995) • D. A. Hill, *Fog on the Tyne: the official history of Lindisfarne* (1998) • S. Jones, 'Cat o' Tyne tales', *Rock 'n' Reel*, 154 (April 1996) • *The Times* (20 Nov 1995) • *The Independent* (20 Nov 1995) • b. cert. • m. cert. • d. cert. • www.lindisfarne.de [official Lindisfarne website]

Likenesses photograph, www.lindisfarne.de, 4 Oct 2002 • photograph, www.geordie-roots.org.uk/james_alan_hull.htm, 4 Oct 2002

Hull [*née* Henderson], **Edith Maud** [*pseud.* E. M. Hull; *known as* Edith Maud Winstanley] (1880–1947), writer, was born at 28 Marlborough Hill, London, on 16 August 1880, the only daughter of James Henderson, a Liverpool shipowner, and his Canadian wife, Katharine (Katie) Thorne, formerly Sancton. Little is known of Edith's early life, except that she made a visit to Algeria, most probably the inspiration for her novels set in north Africa, with a female friend. In the early 1900s she married Percy Winstanley Hull (b. 1869), who was eleven years older than her. The couple settled in Hazelwood, Derbyshire, at The Knowle, the Hull family estate, and the second largest private home in the district (Smith, 34). Percy's father was William Winstanley *Hull (1794–1873), liturgical writer and hymnologist; Percy became a gentleman farmer and a breeder of prize-winning pigs. While he was away serving in the First World War, Edith wrote her first novel, *The Sheik*, merely as a personal distraction from her isolation.

Published in 1919, *The Sheik* was an immediate *succès de scandale*, going through 108 British impressions before 1923. In America its huge popularity was fuelled by the Hollywood mogul Jesse Lasky's risky decision to make a film version using, in the lead role, the little-known Rudolph Valentino, who came to epitomize the male romantic lover. Eventually 125 million people saw the film, making it the most popular of the age (although it has been suggested that Hull did not reap the financial rewards of her book because of unfortunate contracts). *The Sheik* generated catch-phrases (such as 'Shriek for the sheik will seek you too') and popular songs, notably 'The Sheik of Araby'; it gave a new connotation of seducer to the word 'sheik'.

This first novel by a reticent, provincial Englishwoman had become not only a huge best-seller but also a cultural phenomenon, despite being reviled by the few reviewers who did not consider it altogether beneath their contempt: 'Poisonously salacious in conception', decried the *Literary Review* in a typical response (quoted in Raub, 126). Yet it was salaciousness purveyed within the safe realm of romantic fantasy that accounts for the impact of *The Sheik*. On the surface the plot is rather flimsy: Diana Mayo, a cold but spirited young girl with a quality of boyishness, takes a month-long trek into the Sahara desert. On the second day she is captured by Arabs, and their sheikh, Ahmed Ben Hassan, transports her to his luxurious tent where he rapes her. For several weeks the sheikh forces himself on her, breaking her will, until her fear and hatred of him are swamped by passionate love. When a vile rival sheikh abducts her and attempts to assault her, Ahmed rescues her. Wounded in the effort and now realizing his love for her, Ahmed is so ashamed of his previous behaviour that he feels he must renounce Diana and return her to England. She implores him to let her stay with him, fails, and attempts to shoot herself. Ahmed deflects the bullet, and confesses his love, and the couple embrace as the novel closes. It is conveniently revealed that Ahmed is actually not an Arab but the son of a cruel English aristocrat and a Spanish woman, thus rendering the supposed sheikh a perfect matrimonial prospect.

This novel did not initiate the so-called desert romance, as some have claimed, but rather drew on the tradition of female nineteenth-century British travellers, and probably on the scandalous life of Jane Digby, a divorced aristocrat who married Sheikh Medjouel al-Mesrab (Bettinotti and Truel, 186–7). In fiction the most famous precedent was *The Garden of Allah* (1904) by the decadent novelist Robert Hichens, also a runaway best-seller. Elinor Glyn's *Three Weeks* (1907), which advocated that a 'woman will stand almost anything from a passionate lover', also provided a model for the seduction scenes. Hull's viewpoint is similar, but the originality of *The Sheik* lies in its merging of villain and hero in the figure of the sheikh and even more strikingly in the heroine's response to the villain's brutal caresses; Diana the victim becomes an equal sexual partner, and neither she nor her villain lover is punished for their extramarital liaison. *The Sheik* also subverts traditional romance, in that the passionate couple have no plan to marry or return to the safe, civilized world.

The Sheik spawned numerous imitations through the 1920s. Hull herself brought out a sequel, *Sons of the Sheik* (1925), also filmed with Rudolph Valentino, as well as a handful of other romances in the same vein, including *The*

Shadow of the East (1921), *The Desert Healer* (1923), *The Lion Tamer* (1928), and *The Captive of Sahara* (1931). None of the others achieved the success of *The Sheik*; *Sons of the Sheik*, as the title suggests, follows the lives of Diana's and Ahmed Ben Hassan's less virile sons, and it plummets from melodrama into sentimentality.

Despite the popularity of her work, Hull shunned publicity. She frequently travelled abroad to America, India, and Europe, and was away from Derby when the film of *The Sheik* premiered there in 1923. In her *Camping in the Sahara* (1926) she recounts her voyage to Algeria in the early 1920s, which she undertook with her daughter and only child, Cecil, who took the photographs illustrating the book. In it Edith conveys her admiration for the stern yet just leadership of the chieftains she encountered; the admiration was obviously reciprocated since she earned the title 'friend of the Arabs', which thrilled her. Cecil (so named because the Hulls had wanted a boy) was equally fearless on this rather daring journey. During the Second World War she served as an army colonel and later as chief commander of the Auxiliary Territorial Service stationed at Leicester; she was awarded an OBE. Edith herself took her part in the war, serving as local representative of the Soldiers', Sailors' and Airmen's Families Association.

During her lifetime Hull's novels were translated into fourteen languages, but for reasons unknown she ceased publishing in 1939; her final novel was *The Forest of Terrible Things*. Eight years later, on 11 February 1947, she died after a short illness at her home, Holmeside, in Hazelwood, the town where she had quietly lived for most of her life. She was buried at Hazelwood church on 14 February 1947. E. M. Hull has been described as a modest, gentle, clever woman, and a hard-working professional author who guarded her privacy (*Derbyshire Advertiser*). A photograph taken in her later years reveals a woman with a serious, even careworn expression, perhaps conveyed by hooded eyes behind rather severe wire-rimmed glasses. Her hair is pinned into a roll and her face is squarish, with just the suggestion of a dimple in her chin, and there is nothing in this glimpse of her that evokes the author of wildly popular, racy desert romances.

Despite their flaws, including purple prose and melodramatic plotting, Hull's novels have had a lasting power, as is evidenced by the recent reprint of five of them and a resurgence of critical interest in her. Feminist scholars such as Patricia Raub have argued that *The Sheik* can be seen as a precursor of the Harlequin romances which became popular in the late 1950s, with its portrayal of a woman who gains power over her love (Barbara Cartland, the queen of Harlequin romances, abridged several of Hull's novels). While contemporary audiences may find the sado-masochism, racism, and sexism of *The Sheik* unpalatable, Hull's open exploration of female desire from a woman's perspective, and her depiction of sexual experience as the basis for identity, can be seen within a wider context of liberalized sexuality.

GEORGE MALCOLM JOHNSON

Sources P. Raub, 'Issues of passion and power in E. M. Hull's *The Sheik*', *Women's Studies*, 21 (1992), 119–28 • S. Wintle, '*The Sheik*: what can be made of a daydream', *Women, a Cultural Review*, 7 (1996), 291–302 • J. Bettinotti and M. F. Truel, 'Lust and dust: desert fabula in romances and media', *Paradoxa: Studies in World Literary Genres*, 3/1–2 (1997), 184–94 • R. Anderson, 'E(dith) M(aude) Hull', *Twentieth-century romance and historical writers*, ed. L. Henderson, 2nd edn (1990), 340–41 • R. Anderson, *The purple heart throbs: the sub-literature of love* (1974) • V. Smith, 'The great lover and the desert queen', *Evening Telegraph* [Derby] (31 July 2000) • K. Saunders, 'New introduction', in E. M. Hull, *The Sheik* (1996), v–xi • *Derbyshire Advertiser* (14 Feb 1947)

Likenesses photograph, 1947, repro. in *Derbyshire Advertiser* • drawing, 2000, repro. in Smith, 'The great lover', 34

Wealth at death £34,510 1s. 6d.: probate, 1947, *CGPLA Eng. & Wales*

Hull, Edward (1829–1917), geologist, was born in Antrim town on 21 May 1829, the eldest son of the Revd John Dawson Hull (*c*.1801–1886). He attended schools in Edgeworthstown, co. Longford, and Lucan, co. Dublin. In April 1846 he entered Trinity College, Dublin, from where he was awarded a diploma in engineering in 1849, a BA in 1850, and a master's degree in engineering in 1871. He joined the Geological Survey of Great Britain under Sir Henry Thomas De la Beche (1796–1855) on 1 April 1850, and was trained in north Wales by Joseph Beete Jukes (1811–1869). His early survey duties took him into Cheshire, Gloucestershire, Oxfordshire, Shropshire, and Worcestershire, while between 1860 and 1867 he was responsible for mapping the south Lancashire coalfield. On 4 August 1857 he married Mary Catherine Henrietta (*d*. 1901), daughter of Charles Turner Cooke of Cheltenham. They had two sons and four daughters, one of whom was Eleanor Hull (1860–1935), historian and founder of the Irish Texts Society.

Some of Hull's early mapping was adjudged to be grossly inadequate, and about 1854 he came close to dismissal. However, his work improved somewhat and his career began to prosper when Sir Roderick Impey Murchison (1792–1871) succeeded De la Beche as director in 1855. Hull's cousin was married to Murchison's sister. When the geological survey of Scotland was organized in 1867, Hull became its district surveyor under Archibald Geikie (1835–1924), and he mapped in the Lanarkshire coalfield. In April 1869 Murchison sent him to Dublin to take charge of the Irish survey during the illness of Jukes, who was now that survey's director. Following Jukes's death, Hull became the Irish director in October 1869.

In Ireland, Hull persisted with the sound methods devised by Jukes, and between 1869 and 1890 he supervised the preparation of the eighty-five sheets necessary to complete the survey's one-inch geological map of Ireland. For this achievement he deserves great credit (he himself had hoped for a knighthood), but many of his numerous personal publications are marred by superficiality in field examination and by sweeping generalization. For far too long he clung to belief in a glacial submergence, he sought to impose a tripartite division upon the Pleistocene deposits of Britain and Ireland, and in the south of Ireland he thought he had found solutions to problems which for long had baffled far more talented geologists. His survey revision of the geology of southern

Ireland (1878–81) was a disaster which later had to be expunged from the one-inch sheets involved. Among Hull's many books the three most significant are, arguably, *The Coal-Fields of Great Britain* (five edns 1861 to 1905), *A Treatise on the Building and Ornamental Stones of Great Britain and Foreign Countries* (1872), and *Contributions to the Physical History of the British Isles* (1882), the last of which pioneered the genre of the palaeogeographical atlas.

While Irish director, Hull sometimes obtained permission to act as a private consultant, and in this capacity he visited Hungary in 1873 and the USA in 1890. In 1883–4 he led an expedition to the Wadi Araba on behalf of the Palestine Exploration Fund, with Horatio Herbert Kitchener as a member of his party. Hull was elected to the Royal Society in June 1867, was professor of geology in the Royal College of Science for Ireland in 1869–90, and president of the Royal Geological Society of Ireland (1873–5), but he was never elected a member of the Royal Irish Academy. He received an honorary LLD from the University of Glasgow in 1879, and the Murchison medal of the Geological Society of London in 1890.

Hull retired from the survey on 30 September 1890. The following year he left Dublin to live in London, where he served as a consultant, mostly in the area of water-supply, and engaged himself in the affairs of the Victoria Institute. He died of bronchitis at his home, 14 Stanley Gardens, Kensington, London, on 18 October 1917. A hardworking man of shallow intellect, who was often the butt of his colleagues' ridicule, Hull's years in Dublin were sullied by his notorious feud with George Henry *Kinahan (1829–1908), the survey's district surveyor. Kinahan believed himself to have been Jukes's rightful successor as director, and Hull's fussiness and petulance in the position only served to exacerbate the situation.

GORDON L. HERRIES DAVIES

Sources E. Hull, *Reminiscences of a strenuous life* (1910) • archives, Geological Survey of Ireland, Dublin • G. L. Herries Davies, *North from the Hook: 150 years of the Geological Survey of Ireland* (1995) • A. Harker, *Quarterly Journal of the Geological Society*, 74 (1918), liv • *Geological Magazine*, new ser., 6th decade, 4 (1917), 553–5 • *Irish Naturalist*, 27 (1918), 17 • m. cert. • d. cert.

Archives Geological Survey of Ireland, Dublin • U. Edin. | CUL, letters to Sir George Stokes • U. Edin. L., corresp. with Sir Charles Lyell

Likenesses photographs, repro. in Hull, *Reminiscences of a strenuous life* • photographs, BGS

Wealth at death £11,916 15s. 4d.: probate, 1 Feb 1918, CGPLA Eng. & Wales

Hull [*née* Malet], **Eleanor, Lady Hull** (*c.*1394–1460), translator, was the only child of Sir John Malet of Enmore, Somerset (*d.* before 1395), retainer of John of Gaunt, duke of Lancaster, and of his wife, Joan (*c.*1370–1426), daughter of Sir John Hylle of Exeter (*d.* 1426), sister of Robert Hylle (compiler of the so-called Hylle cartulary) and subsequently the wife of, in turn, Simon Michell, John Luttrell, and William Cornu. Before 1413 Eleanor married Sir John Hull (*d. c.*1420), retainer of John of Gaunt and ambassador to Castile for Henry IV and Henry V, and had a son, Edward (*c.*1410–1453). Unlike her mother she did not remarry after her husband's death.

Like her father, husband, and son, Eleanor served the house of Lancaster. In 1417 she was granted 50 marks per annum as servant of Queen Joan, second wife of Henry IV; the grant was renewed in 1420 and 1423, and granted her jointly with her son in 1444 and 1451. In 1444 she and her son travelled to France for the proxy marriage of Henry VI and Margaret of Anjou. She was indirectly connected with the foundation of Syon Abbey as she is said to have brought Thomas Fishbourne, later its first confessor-general, to the attention of its founder, Henry V. She was more closely associated with the abbey of St Albans, to whose confraternity she was admitted in February 1417 and to whom she and her family made frequent gifts. Most notably she and her spiritual and legal adviser Roger Huswyf presented the abbey with a copy of Nicholas de Lyre's *Postillae* (now CUL, MSS Dd.7.7–10) in 1457. After her husband's death she was by 1427 living from time to time at Sopwell Priory, a Benedictine nunnery dependent on St Albans: she was temporarily absent when the priory was attacked by the robber William Wawe and his gang, *quaerentes Elienoram Hull* ('seeking Eleanor Hull'; *Annales … Amundesham*, 1.11). It was probably during this period that she made her translations. In 1436 she was listed with an annual income of £86 in the national return under the county of Hertfordshire, where Sopwell and St Albans are situated. Her son, Sir Edward, was killed at the battle of Castillon in 1453; his will appointed her as his executor. By 1458 she had retired to the Benedictine priory at Cannington, Somerset, where in the will made 'with her own hand' (Maxwell-Lyte and Dawes, 352) she requested to be buried. She probably died in December 1460, since her will was proved on 2 January 1461.

Two translations from the French extant in CUL, MS Kk.1.6, a commentary on the penitential psalms, *The Seven Psalms*, and a collection of prayers and meditations, are attributed to Eleanor Hull by the manuscript's compiler, Richard Fox, *procurator*, or steward, of St Albans (*d.* 1454). She could read Latin as well as French (she bequeathed her breviary, psalter, and Latin Bible to Huswyf), and both read and write English. No doubt as an heiress she was educated at home with more than usual care, possibly under the influence of her maternal uncle Robert Hylle. As the first woman translator from French into English whose name is known she is indicative of the level of culture that some fifteenth-century laywomen of the gentry class achieved. Although she was devout, learned, and alive to her secular responsibilities, the neglect of her by subsequent historians is equally significant.

ALEXANDRA BARRATT

Sources *Annales monasterii S. Albani a Johanne Amundesham*, ed. H. T. Riley, 2 vols., pt 5 of *Chronica monasterii S. Albani*, Rolls Series, 28 (1870–71) • *CPR, 1416–22*, 304; *1446–52*, 429–30 • *CClR, 1441–7*, 428 • *CEPR letters*, 6.346 • BL, Cotton MS, Nero D.vii, fols. 141–2 • H. C. Maxwell-Lyte and M. C. B. Dawes, eds., *The register of Thomas Bekynton, bishop of Bath and Wells, 1443–1465*, 1, Somerset RS, 49 (1934), 352–3 [will] • R. W. Dunning, ed., *The Hylle cartulary*, Somerset RS, 68 (1968) • H. L. Gray, 'Incomes from land in England in 1436', *EngHR*, 49 (1934), 607–39, esp. 634 • BL, Add. MS 23938, fols. 5, 13v • H. C. Maxwell-Lyte, *Historical notes on some Somerset manors*, Somerset RS, extra ser. (1931), 273–4 • L. T. Smith, ed., *Expeditions to Prussia and the*

Holy Land made by Henry, earl of Derby, CS, new ser., 52 (1894) • *The seven psalms*, ed. A. Barratt, EETS, old ser. 307 (1995) • S. Armitage-Smith, *John of Gaunt* (1904)
Archives CUL, MS Kk.1.6 • University of Illinois, MS 80
Likenesses drawing, BL, Cotton MS Nero D.vii, fol. 141
Wealth at death property at Cannington: will, Maxwell-Lyte and Dawes, eds., *Register of Thomas Bekynton*

Hull, John (1624–1683), goldsmith and merchant in America, was born in 1624, about 18 December according to his later diary, in Market Harborough, Leicestershire, the son of Robert Hull (*d.* 1666), blacksmith, and his wife, Elizabeth (*d.* 1646), the widow of Paul Storer. Educated at the grammar school in Market Harborough, he completed his education at the first Boston School after his family had emigrated to the colony in 1635. Apprenticed to his half-brother Richard Storer, a London-trained goldsmith, Hull began his own business in 1645, and in 1647 he married Judith (1626–1695), daughter of Edmund Quincey. They had five children, although only one, Hannah (1657–1717), reached maturity, and later married Samuel Sewall, the famous diarist and a future judge at the Salem witch trials of 1692. Deeply religious, Hull was granted membership (a prerequisite for citizenship of the colony) in the Revd John Cotton's church in October 1648. Unlike his father, however, who had been briefly disfranchised after the antinomian crisis of 1636–7, Hull remained deeply orthodox and supported the banishment of both Quakers and Baptists from the colony.

Hull's business benefited greatly from the commercial expansion of Massachusetts in the 1640s, and in May 1652 the general court authorized a mint, appointing Hull the mint-master. In June 1652 he took into partnership Robert Sanderson. Their shillings remained in circulation until the outbreak of the American War of Independence and though their designs often changed, from a willow tree to an oak tree and then pine tree designs, their coins were always dated 1652. Their commission, up to 1*s*. 7*d*. per 20*s*. coined, was larger than received by any royal mint in Europe, and it laid the basis for Hull's extensive, if often exaggerated, wealth. From their mint next to Hull's house on Great Street the partnership produced some of the finest early silver work, noted for its proportion and balance, in New England. The partnership also apprenticed some of the most notable later goldsmiths in Massachusetts: Jeremiah Drummer, Daniel Quincey, and Timothy Dwight.

Some of Hull's profits were invested in land. As well as properties in Boston and Braintree, he was one of five speculators who secured the Pettiquampscut purchase from the Narragansett in Rhode Island in 1657, a 12 square mile land grant near South Kingston. In 1659 he purchased another 1000 acres near Boxford, Massachusetts. He also developed a flourishing provision and lumber trade to the West Indies and, through family contacts in London, an extensive import–export trade to England and Europe. His letter-book between 1671 and 1683 mentions over fifty ships, fifteen of which he either owned or had part ownership in. Hull's busy career prompted him to sell his share of the mint to his partner, Sanderson, in 1675.

From Hull's appointment as corporal in the militia in 1648, he maintained a lifelong commitment to service, joining the ancient and Honourable Artillery Company in 1660, and becoming its captain in 1675. Elected a Boston selectman in 1657, he became the town treasurer in 1658, a position he occupied for a decade. In 1661 he was part of the mission sent to London to defend Massachusetts's charter from royal encroachment. The mission was only partially successful, but Hull, as a leading Boston magistrate, continued to champion the Bible commonwealth and was vocal in his opposition to Charles II's navigation policy, especially the Plantation Duty Act of 1673.

Elected a deputy in 1671, Hull became a member of the colony's general court and served as treasurer on the committee which conducted the near disastrous war with the Wampanoags, King Philip's War, 1675–6. Becoming treasurer of Massachusetts in 1676, he used his own resources to support the war effort but was never adequately repaid by the colony during his lifetime. Appointed an assistant of the general court in 1680, his health began to fail, and on 1 October 1683 he died intestate, with Massachusetts still owing him an estimated £2125. His funeral was held in the Old South Church, Boston, where he had been a charter member, and he was buried on 5 October 1683 in the Granary burying-ground. An important figure in the early years of Massachusetts, the Bible commonwealth did not long survive him; the charter, which had been amended in 1662, was vacated by Charles II in 1684. Hull's wife outlived him, dying in 1695.   RORY T. CORNISH

Sources S. E. Morison, *Builders of the Bay Colony*, 2nd edn (1958) • H. F. Clarke, *John Hull: a builder of the Bay Colony* (1940) • S. Crosby, *Early coins in America* (1875) • 'The diaries of John Hull, mint-master and treasurer of the colony of Massachusetts Bay', ed. S. Haven, *Archaeologia Americana: Transactions and Collections of the American Antiquarian Society*, 3 (1857) • J. M. Sosin, *English America and the Restoration monarchy of Charles II* (1980) • B. Bailyn, *The New England merchants in the seventeenth century* (1955) • G. W. R. Ward, 'Hull, John', *ANB*
Archives American Antiquarian Society, Worcester, Massachusetts, public and private diaries and his letter-book • New England Historic Genealogical Society, Boston, account books | Mass. Hist. Soc., Samuel Sewan's diary

Hull, John (1764–1843), physician and botanist, was born at Poulton, Lancashire, and was possibly a kinsman of Richard Hull, a Lancashire surgeon. In May 1792 he graduated as MD at Leiden, his dissertation being 'De catharticis'. He settled in Manchester, where he practised especially as an accoucheur, and became physician to the lying-in hospital. Between 1798 and 1801 he published several papers in defence of the caesarean operation, including *A Defence of the Cesarean Operation … Addressed to Mr W. Simmons* (1799). He also communicated a case of quintuplets to Gilbert Blane, a report on which appeared in the *Philosophical Transactions of the Royal Society* (77, 1787, 344–58). In 1834 Hull was a founder member, and first president, of the Manchester Medical Society.

Hull also studied botany. He published in 1799 a *British Flora* (2 vols.), which reached a second edition in 1808, and two volumes on the *Elements of Botany* in 1800. He became a fellow of the Linnean Society in 1810. In 1819 he became a licentiate of the Royal College of Physicians, having been

John Hull (1764–1843), by Henry Cousins, 1808 (after Joseph Allen)

an extra-licentiate since 1806. He died at his eldest son's house in Tavistock Square, London, on 17 March 1843. His son William Winstanley *Hull (1794–1873) is noticed separately. G. S. BOULGER, rev. MICHAEL BEVAN

Sources Munk, *Roll* · E. M. Brockbank, *A centenary history of the Manchester Medical Society* (1934) · Desmond, *Botanists* · P. J. Wallis and R. V. Wallis, *Eighteenth century medics*, 2nd edn (1988)
Likenesses H. Cousins, mezzotint, 1808 (after J. Allen), Wellcome L. [*see illus.*] · D. Lucas, mezzotint (after D. H. Parry), Wellcome L. · portrait, repro. in Brockbank, *Centenary history*

Hull, Sir Richard Amyatt (1907–1989), army officer, was born on 7 May 1907 in Cosham, Hampshire, the only son and youngest of three children of Major-General Sir Charles Patrick Amyatt Hull, late of the Royal Scots Fusiliers, of Beacon Downe, Pinhoe, near Exeter, Devon, and his wife, Muriel Helen, daughter of Richard Reid Dobell, businessman, of Beauvoir, Quebec, and Vancouver, Canada. He was educated at Charterhouse School and at Trinity College, Cambridge, where he took a pass degree. At Cambridge he was a close friend of Peter Scott, the naturalist, and it was there that he began to develop his great interest in wildlife and country sports.

Hull was commissioned as a university entrant into the 17th/21st lancers in 1928 and went with the regiment to Egypt in 1930. It was then still horsed. Hull, who in any case lacked the money for expensive mounts, was a competent rather than enthusiastic horseman, but acquired a reputation as a polo umpire. His knowledge of the rules and firmness in applying them were paralleled by the attention to detail, energy, and integrity he showed in his professional life, qualities which underlay his successful career and brought him early promotion to captain and appointment as adjutant when the regiment moved to India in 1933.

In 1934 Hull married Antoinette Mary, only child of Francis Labouchère de Rougemont, of the Bank of Egypt. They had two daughters and a son, and were a couple noted for their devotion.

Hull was a student at the Staff College, Quetta, in 1938–9, while the regiment was undergoing mechanization, a change which the forward-looking Hull strongly supported, and then supervised the return home of the regimental families in 1939. His efficiency in so doing brought him an appointment in the staff duties branch of the War Office, and promotion to lieutenant-colonel, but he soon chose to drop a rank and return to the 17th/21st as a squadron leader. He became commanding officer in 1941.

In 1942 Hull was promoted colonel and given command of Blade Force, an all-arms group based on the 17th/21st, which had the mission during the north African landings of November 1942 of advancing from Algiers to capture Tunis. The force covered the 350 miles in two days but was thwarted 15 miles from the city when German reinforcements secured it first. For the dash he had shown and his bravery under fire Hull was appointed to the DSO (1943) and promoted brigadier to command 12th infantry and then 26th armoured brigade during the Tunisian campaign.

After another spell at the War Office, Hull was promoted major-general and given command of 1st armoured division in Italy in 1944. Its role was to outflank the Gothic Line on the Adriatic shore and lead a break-out into the plain of the Po. At Coriano on 5 September, however, its armoured brigade met heavy German resistance and was checked. Controversy surrounds this episode; terrain and weather were on the side of the enemy but Hull has also been criticized for his tactical dispositions.

This did not halt Hull's progress. His formidable abilities as a staff officer had been recognized and, after commanding 5th infantry division, he embarked on a long ascent of all the key staff appointments, interspersed with several important commands. He was commandant of the Staff College, Camberley (1946–8), director of staff duties, War Office (1948–50), chief army instructor, Imperial Defence College (1950–52), and chief of staff, Middle East land forces (1953–4). As lieutenant-general he then succeeded to the command of the British troops in Egypt and supervised the difficult evacuation from the canal zone in 1955–6.

On his return Hull became deputy chief of the Imperial General Staff (1956–8) and was at once embroiled in the series of defence reductions, imposed by Britain's shrinking world role and financial difficulties, that were to dominate the rest of his service career. He first chaired a committee whose task was to determine the future size of the army and, though he unsuccessfully opposed the army's reduction to a strength of 165,000, his doubts about its ability to meet its commitments with those numbers were proved right and the figure was later fixed at 185,000. He oversaw the abolition of national service in 1957, and the regimental amalgamations that resulted, but succeeded in sparing several threatened regiments. The shape of the army for the next thirty years was largely determined by his guidance.

Promoted general in 1958, Hull was commander-in-chief, Far East land forces (1958–61), but then returned to the Ministry of Defence as chief of the Imperial General Staff (1961–5; 'imperial' was dropped in 1964 and so he was the last holder of the office), and then chief of the defence staff (1965–7), in succession to the second holder of that office, Earl Mountbatten of Burma. In these posts he was responsible for the army's part in such operations as the deterrence of the Iraqi attack on Kuwait in 1961, 'confrontation' with Indonesia in Malaysia, the suppression of the east African revolts, and the defeat of the Nasserist rising in the Radfan province of the Aden protectorate.

Hull's bitterest battles, however, were fought in Whitehall after he became chief of the defence staff in July 1965. During his term of office Britain withdrew from Singapore and Aden and was challenged by revolt in Rhodesia. At home, he found the navy and air force locked in conflict over the funding of air power, while Denis Healey, an imperious defence secretary, demanded budgetary sacrifices by all services. Hull, whose professional feelings for Mountbatten had amounted to loathing, was too upright to allow that to influence his arbitration of the dispute between the air marshals and the admirals. He perceived that the large carriers the navy wanted would cost too much and threw his weight behind the decision to spend available funds for the purchase of American aircraft for the Royal Air Force as a means of providing Britain with long-range strike capability. The small carriers that provided the Royal Navy with its later air support were the product of that chiefs of staff committee's decision.

Hull was promoted field marshal on appointment as chief of the defence staff. On retirement in 1967 he became a director of Whitbreads (1967–76) and rationalized business in its western division. He held many state, army, and charitable appointments, including those of constable of the Tower of London (1970–75), deputy lieutenant of Devon (1973–8), high sheriff (1975), and lord lieutenant (1978–82). He was president of the Army Benevolent Fund (1968–71), and was made an honorary LLD by Exeter University in 1965. Appointed CB in 1945, he was advanced to KCB in 1956 and GCB in 1961. He became a knight of the Garter in 1980.

Hull typified a certain sort of regular cavalry officer of his generation. A devout but undemonstrative Christian, a devoted husband and father, whose temperament often prevented him from disclosing his affections, a loyal friend to brother officers who won his favour, a devotee of regimental tradition, he was happiest shooting or fly-fishing, two sports at which he excelled, and in his garden, where he knew the Latin, English, and Devon name of every plant. He was tall and of impressive bearing, with grave features. Hull died on 17 September 1989, of cancer, at his home, Beacon Downe, Pinhoe, near Exeter, which

he had rebuilt after wartime bombing, was given a state funeral at Windsor, and was buried in the graveyard of the local church where he had regularly worshipped.

JOHN KEEGAN, rev.

Sources W. Jackson and Lord Bramall, *The chiefs: the story of the United Kingdom chiefs of staff* (1992) · *The Independent* (20 Sept 1989) · *The Times* (19 Sept 1989) · private information (1996)
Likenesses D. Miller, group photograph, 1964, Hult. Arch.
Wealth at death £831,822: probate, 15 March 1990, CGPLA Eng. & Wales

Hull, Thomas (1728–1808), actor and playwright, was born in London in the house in the Strand where his father, whose identity is otherwise unknown, practised as an apothecary. According to the *Biographia dramatica*, Hull was educated for some time at Charterhouse School and had been intended for the church, but he rejected that vocation and also failed as an apothecary. He appeared as an actor at the Smock Alley Theatre, Dublin, for the 1753–4 season and then played at Bath from 1754 until 1758. The Bath engagement ended controversially: Hull accused the theatre owner, John Palmer, of reneging on an agreement that Hull should manage the theatre from 1757, on a three-year contract with escalating rewards, and of ousting him from the theatre without a benefit. Some indication of Hull's plight may be gleaned from the fact that he ended his pamphlet of complaint with an advertisement for apothecary's wares 'at the *lowest Prices*' (Highfill, Burnim & Langhans, *BDA*, 3.34).

Hull first appeared in London at Covent Garden on 5 October 1759. He subsequently enjoyed a long London career in secondary roles, interspersed with summers of provincial theatrical appearances and management in, for example, Birmingham, Bristol, Margate, and Brighton. He married the actress Anna Maria Morrison at an unknown date between 1764 and 1766. They appear to have had at least one child (a Master Hull was in the company at Bristol in 1769 when Thomas and Anna Maria Hull were there).

In an acting career of more than fifty years Hull played well over 200 characters and missed only one performance, as a result of illness. In London he started in roles such as Renault in Thomas Otway's *Venice Preserv'd*, Horatio in *Hamlet*, Antonio in *The Merchant of Venice*, and Pinchwife in William Wycherley's *The Country Wife*. He stayed at Covent Garden as an actor until 28 December 1807, and was acting manager from 1775 to 1781. With few exceptions, such as Prospero and Angelo, which he took over in 1776–7 when he was manager, he continued to play significant parts but was seldom the motor of the action. He was the epitome of a sound company man and, as his early problems at Bath suggest, concerned with professional conditions of service; in 1765 he was one of the prime movers in the establishment of the Covent Garden Theatrical Fund to provide a pension fund for old or ill actors and actresses.

According to Francis Gentleman (1770), Hull was 'very capable of supporting paternal characters with propriety and feeling' and was well suited for the 'graver parts of comedy', since 'declamation and paternal tenderness are his style, not love nor fire'; he was 'better calculated for exhibiting amiable and tender feelings, than any which border on gloomy and sanguinary designs' and 'had nature given him executive requisites equal to his judgment and assiduity, he would have been a capital pillar of the stage'. Francis Godolphin Waldron in 1795 suggested that it was time he retired, noting that he 'has long enjoyed a respectable rank in the theatrical world in personating old trusty *Stewards* and parts that require an apparent honest sincerity of expression', but, as Genest noted, 'he stayed on the stage until he was quite worn out'.

As a writer, Hull was a 'respectable' (Baker), if undistinguished, practitioner of most of the eighteenth century's theatrical genres. None of his dramatic works long survived him in the repertory, and several were written as novelties for his own or others' benefits—for example, a version of *Timon of Athens*, adapted from that by Shadwell, for his own benefit in 1768, or *Iphigenia, or, The Victim*, an adaptation of Abel Boyer's *Achilles*, itself a translation of Racine, for Mrs Barry's benefit in 1778. He adapted *The Comedy of Errors* twice, once as *The Twins* and once under Shakespeare's title, and turned Beaumont's and Fletcher's *The Beggar's Bush* into a comic opera, *The Royal Merchant* (with music by Thomas Linley, 1767). *The Perplexities*, originally staged in 1767 on the same bill as his *The Fairy Favour*, a masque to music by J. C. Bach, was one of Hull's more successful pieces. A mediocre if competent adaptation of Samuel Tuke's *Adventures of Five Hours*, the play is 'a chaos of balconies, cloaks, rapiers and dark lanterns' (*Biographia dramatica*), deploying a range of love–honour conflicts in a Spanish setting with a familiar cast of jealous brothers and spirited young women, mistaken identities, and hidden doors. Hull's popular tragedy *Henry II, or, The Fall of Rosamund*, adapted from William Hawkins's play of 1749, was staged in an early version at Birmingham in 1761 and revised at the suggestion of Hull's friend the poet William Shenstone. Although Joseph Knight suggested in the *Dictionary of National Biography* that the play 'could rank with most tragedies of the day', it is a sentimental small-cast tragedy in which affairs of state are little more than period colour, and the verse, at best competent, is haunted by the thinnest Shakespearian overtones mediated through Dryden and Rowe. Hull also achieved success with a patriotic afterpiece, *The Spaniards Dismayed, or, True Blue Forever*, also known as *True Blue, or, The Press Gang*, adapted from Henry Carey's *Nancy*, first staged in 1776. His non-dramatic works include the novel *The History of Sir William Harrington* (1771–97), which was translated into both French and German.

Hull's wife died on 23 October 1805, and he himself died on 22 April 1808, at his house near Dean's Yard, Westminster. Both were buried in the churchyard of St Margaret, Westminster.   TREVOR R. GRIFFITHS

Sources D. E. Baker, *Biographia dramatica, or, A companion to the playhouse*, rev. I. Reed, new edn, rev. S. Jones, 3 vols. in 4 (1812) • [F. G. Waldron], *Candid and impartial strictures on the performers belonging to Drury-Lane, Covent-Garden, and the Haymarket theatres* (1795) • F. Gentleman, *The dramatic censor, or, Critical companion*, 2 vols. (1770) • Highfill, Burnim & Langhans, *BDA* • Genest, *Eng. stage* • G. W. Stone, ed., *The London stage, 1660–1800*, pt 4: *1747–1776* (1962) • C. B. Hogan, ed., *The London stage, 1660–1800*, pt 5: *1776–1800* (1968)
Archives Yale U., Beinecke L., 'Shenstone's walks' | Hunt. L., Larpent MSS
Likenesses J. Zoffany, group portrait, 1765 • Finlayson, engraving, 1768 (after J. Zoffany, 1765) • Grignion, engraving, 1775 (after T. Parkinson) • Pollard, engraving, 1777 (after J. Roberts) • M. Brown, group portrait, oils, exh. RA 1787 (in *The gamester*), Garr. Club • Leney, engraving, 1791 (after S. De Wilde) • Leney, engraving, 1797 (after Graham) • G. Dance, pencil drawing, 1799, NPG • S. De Wilde, oils (as Jarvis in *The gamester*), Garr. Club, NPG • J. Graham, oils, Garr. Club • T. Parkinson, portrait, BM • J. Roberts, portrait • oils, NPG • prints, BM, NPG

Hull, William (1820–1880), landscape painter, was born on 6 May 1820 at Graffham in Huntingdonshire, the son of a small farmer who moved soon after his son's birth to Keysoe, Bedfordshire, and then to the nearby village of Pertenhall. There, in the village school, William received his early education; afterwards he went for three years to Ockbrook, near Derby, to be educated as a minister at the Moravian Settlement, where he had a few lessons in drawing from two Germans named Petersen and Hassé. After spending a year at the settlement at Wellhouse, near Mirfield, Yorkshire, as student and assistant, he went in 1838 to the Moravian establishment at Grace Hill, near Ballymena in Ireland, where he made many sketches. He spent five weeks in London in 1840, studying the works of art in the British Museum.

Acknowledging that he did not have a vocation for the ministry, Hull gave up his position at Grace Hill and moved to Manchester, where his father was a missionary. He became a clerk in the printing and lithographic works of Bradshaw and Blacklock and studied at the school of design there for a short time. From 1841 to 1844 he travelled in France, Germany, and the Low Countries as tutor to the two sons of a Mr Janvrin, a merchant of St Helier in Jersey, and took every opportunity of continuing his study of art. He returned to Manchester in 1844, and on 7 July 1847 married Mary Elizabeth Newling, the daughter of Joshua Newling, a draper. Three years later he was partially paralysed by a stroke which also left him deaf, and then, in 1861, his wife died while they were staying in Wales. Childless and lame, Hull was regarded by his friends as a 'somewhat lonely but genial-minded man' (Letherbrow, 'William Hull in the lake country', 33).

From 1844, when he contributed two pictures to the exhibition at the Royal Manchester Institution, Hull devoted himself entirely to painting and sketching. During his career he produced careful watercolours of objects of interest and rural beauty in almost every county in England. His works in black and white and sepia were highly regarded by his contemporaries for their skill, although John Ruskin advised him to introduce more colour; more recently he has been noted for his detailed fruit and flower pieces. The prince consort acquired a couple of Hull's watercolours on a visit to Manchester in 1857, and his views of Oxford and Cambridge and his illustrations to *Charles Dickens and Rochester* (engraved by his friend Robert Langton, the author of the book) were also popular. Hull drew some of the illustrations to J. P. Earwaker's *East Cheshire, Past and Present* (1877–81), and his drawings of the mill at Ambleside and Wythburn church were reproduced in autotype. He etched several plates, some of which appeared as illustrations to books, and he contributed an article on taste to *Bradshaw's Magazine* in 1842–3. After his death, reproductions of his drawings were published, with extracts from his letters, in *The Portfolio* in 1886 and 1887. These notes expressed his delight in the landscape of the Lake District, which he first saw in 1854, and which he described to his associates in the Letherbrow Club, a private literary and artistic society in Manchester. In 1870 he moved permanently to the Lake District. In *The Portfolio* of 1886 Thomas Letherbrow described his friend's affection for this dramatic landscape, which he linked to the artist's admiration for Wordsworth.

Despite his residence in the Lake District, Hull continued to contribute to artistic society as a member of the Manchester Academy of Fine Arts, and he also took some part in its management; he exhibited there regularly and studied in its life class. He exhibited at the regular exhibitions of the Royal Manchester Institution and at the black and white exhibitions held there from 1877 to 1880. He died at Rydal, Westmorland, on 15 March 1880, and was buried in the churchyard at Grasmere.

ALBERT NICHOLSON, *rev.* SUZANNE FAGENCE COOPER

Sources T. Letherbrow, 'William Hull', *The Portfolio*, 17 (1886), 15–17 • T. Letherbrow, 'William Hull in the lake country', *The Portfolio*, 18 (1887), 33 • W. Hull, 'My winter quarters', *The Portfolio*, 17 (1886), 19–22 • W. Hill, 'Letters from the English lakes', *The Portfolio*, 18 (1887), 35, 113, 195, 216 • Wood, *Vic. painters*, 3rd edn • Mallalieu, *Watercolour artists* • Bryan, *Painters* • *Papers of the Manchester Literary Club*, 6 (1880) • *Manchester City News* (27 March 1880) • m. cert.
Wealth at death under £800: probate, 24 April 1880, *CGPLA Eng. & Wales*

Hull, William Winstanley (1794–1873), liturgical writer and hymnologist, born at Blackburn, Lancashire, on 15 March 1794, was the son of John *Hull MD (1764–1843). After attending Manchester and Macclesfield grammar schools, he was for a time a pupil of John Dawson of Sedbergh, the mathematician. He was sent to Brasenose College, Oxford, in 1811; obtained a first class in classics at Michaelmas, 1814; spent some months abroad, and was elected a fellow of his college in 1816. He was called to the bar at Lincoln's Inn on 16 June 1820, and in the same year vacated his fellowship on his marriage (27 December 1820) at Manchester Cathedral to Frances Wilson. But he was always interested in Oxford affairs, and maintained throughout his life his intimacy with his Oxford friends Richard Whately, Sir John Taylor Coleridge, and Thomas Arnold. Many of Arnold's letters to him appear in A. P. Stanley's *Life of Arnold*. He gave up his practice at the chancery bar in 1846, and left London for Tickwood, near Wenlock, Shropshire.

Hull oscillated between broad churchmanship and tory evangelicalism. He was especially interested in liturgical reform. In 1828 he published *An inquiry concerning the means and expedience of proposing and making any changes in the canons, articles, and liturgy, or in any of the laws affecting the interests of the Church of England*, followed in 1831 by a learned pamphlet advocating the disuse of the Athanasian creed. A petition seeking the revision of the liturgy was drawn up by Hull and his brother, the Revd John Hull, and presented to the House of Lords by Archbishop Whately on 26 May 1840. Perhaps the most interesting of his liturgical researches is the 'Inquiry after the original Books of Common Prayer' in his *Occasional Papers on Church Matters* (1848); his search for the manuscript of the prayer-book of 1662 led to A. P. Stanley's discovery of it at Westminster Hall. Hull opposed the Tractarian movement, and actively supported R. D. Hampden, defending him in a pamphlet issued in 1836. But his *The Month of January: Oxford* (1845) (which reached a second edition), strongly opposed the degradation of W. G. Ward. In certain respects a high tory and ultra-protestant, Hull joined Sir Robert Inglis's committee formed in 1829 to oppose the return of Robert Peel as MP for Oxford University, and a pamphlet he wrote in 1829 opposed the admission of Roman Catholics or Jews to parliament.

Hull was an early pioneer in the cause of improved hymnology, and published anonymously in 1827 and 1832 two books of original prayers and hymns, republished under his name in 1852 as *A Collection of Prayers for Household Use, with some Hymns and Other Poems*.

During the last years of his life at The Knowle, Hazelwood, Derbyshire, Hull actively supported Lord Ebury's movement for liturgical reform. Following the death of his first wife he married, on 11 September 1850, Frances, the daughter of George Rowe, a solicitor. After her death he married, on 4 July 1861, Eliza Matilda, the daughter of Sydenham Good, also a solicitor. He had a family with each wife. He died at The Knowle on 28 August 1873. His third wife survived him.

W. A. GREENHILL, *rev.* H. C. G. MATTHEW

Sources Boase, *Mod. Eng. biog.* • J. F. Smith, ed., *The admission register of the Manchester School, with some notes of the more distinguished scholars*, 3/1, Chetham Society, 93 (1874), 37; 3/2, Chetham Society, 94 (1874), 289 • private information (1891) • *CGPLA Eng. & Wales* (1873) • m. certs. • IGI
Archives Brasenose College, Oxford, 'On the advantages resulting to a clergyman from a knowledge of civil law'
Wealth at death under £5000: probate, 26 Sept 1873, *CGPLA Eng. & Wales*

Hullah, John Pyke (1812–1884), music teacher and composer, was born in Worcester on 27 June 1812. His father, apparently descended from a Huguenot family, was a native of Yorkshire, but lived in London from the early years of the century. Hullah seems to have inherited his musical gifts chiefly from his mother, who had been a pupil of the organist and composer John Danby. After attending private schools, including one in Brixton, he became in 1829 a pupil of William Horsley, with whom he studied the piano, vocal music, and composition. In 1833 he entered the Royal Academy of Music, where he was taught singing by Domenico Crivelli. Two years later he met Charles Dickens (through his sister, Fanny Dickens, also a pupil of Crivelli). Hullah's comic opera *The Village Coquettes*, set to words by Dickens, was produced at St

John Pyke Hullah (1812–1884), by Ernest Edwards, pubd 1865

James's Theatre on 5 December 1836, and ran for sixty nights with great success. Much of the music was burnt in a fire at the Edinburgh theatre soon after it first opened there (a version was published in 1933). In 1837 Hullah became organist of Croydon church. About this time he composed several songs and a madrigal, 'Wake now my Love' (printed in *Vocal Scores* in 1847), which was performed at the Madrigal Society's meeting. On 11 November 1837 *The Barbers of Bassora* (words by Maddison Morton) was produced at Covent Garden, and on 17 May 1838, at the same theatre, *The Outpost*, Hullah's last attempt at dramatic music. Both were unsuccessful. Having learned of Joseph Mainzer's public singing classes in Paris in 1837 from an article by H. F. Chorley in *The Athenaeum*, in 1839 he went, with Chorley, to Paris to investigate the Mainzer system; finding the classes discontinued, they attended G. L. B. Wilhem's rival classes.

With James Kay (later Sir James Kay-Shuttleworth), secretary to the committee of council on education, Hullah began on 18 February 1840 a class based on Wilhem's model at the recently opened Normal School for Schoolmasters at Battersea. Kay, keen to introduce continental teaching methods into England, commissioned Hullah to prepare an English version of Wilhem's *Manuel Musical* (1836), which was published in 1841 as *Wilhem's Method of Teaching Singing Adapted to English Use*. In February 1841, after improving his knowledge of the system by another visit to Paris, Hullah formed, with government support obtained by Kay, his immensely successful 'singing school for school masters and school mistresses' at Exeter Hall, London. Later in the same year the system was started in

Manchester under Hullah's direction. The widespread popularity of the classes, with 400 teachers attending weekly, resulted in classes for the general public. In July 1842 the number of persons attending was calculated to be fifty thousand. Classes were also held at some of the great public schools, among them Eton, Winchester, and the Charterhouse. Often the teachers were Hullah's disciples. He was professor of vocal music at King's College, London, from 1844 to 1874, and also at Queen's College and Bedford College. In fact, in June 1847 he took a prominent role in the foundation of Queen's College in Harley Street, the first establishment in the country for the higher education of women. Later in the year he went again to Paris, and in October 1849 his classes began to meet in St Martin's Hall, Long Acre, which was built especially for the purpose. It was formally opened on 11 February 1850, and in 1854 Hullah took up residence there. He also lectured on vocal music at the Working Men's College, founded in 1854 by F. D. Maurice, a theologian and close friend who shared Hullah's connection with the Christian socialist movement, a significant factor in his teaching philosophy. In 1858 Hullah succeeded Horsley as organist at the Charterhouse (a post which he retained until his death). Some of his most successful songs were written at this time; several of them remained popular for a century. 'Three Fishers Went Sailing' (1857) and 'O that we two were a-Maying' (1862), to words by Charles Kingsley, another Christian socialist, are the most notable examples. Besides the work connected with the hall, which included the organization of historical and other concerts, Hullah also found time to take part in the controversy concerning musical pitch, and used his influence to promote the adoption by the Society of Arts of C at 528 Hz. On 26 August 1860 St Martin's Hall was burnt to the ground, an event which had serious financial consequences for Hullah.

Hullah's series of lectures on the history of modern music was delivered at the Royal Institution early in 1861 (published in 1862). In 1864 he lectured at Edinburgh, but the following year he failed in his candidature for the Reid professorship of music, owing to the casting vote of the rector of the university, W. E. Gladstone, which was given for Herbert Oakeley. In 1866 and 1867 Hullah conducted the Philharmonic concerts in Edinburgh, and in the latter year he received a medal at the Paris Universal Exhibition. In 1869 he was elected to the committee of management of the Royal Academy of Music, and from 1870 to 1873 conducted the academy concerts. In March 1872 he was appointed by the committee of the council on education as the first inspector of music in training colleges for the United Kingdom. Having taught in six London teacher training colleges, he was the natural choice for the post. The reports drawn up by him in 1873, 1877, and 1880 are notable for the fairness with which they deal with systems different to his own. His own system was in fact flawed on account of the sol-fa names' being fixed in the key of C. John Curwen's tonic sol-fa method used a movable *doh* but initially lacked government support. Although

Hullah's method was still used in the training of teachers, the tonic sol-fa method was ultimately successful.

In 1876 Hullah received the degree of doctor of laws from Edinburgh University. In 1878 he read a paper on music education at a meeting of the Social Science Association in Cheltenham, and in the same year he went abroad in order to report on the condition of music education in continental schools. The report is quoted in his wife's memoir of him (1886), which expands on the small portion of autobiography that he had begun to compile. Hullah was married twice, first, on 20 December 1838 to a Miss Foster who died in 1862, and second, in December 1865, to Frances, the only daughter of Lieutenant-Colonel G. F. Rosser.

In addition to numerous original songs, Hullah produced arrangements, collections, hymnals, and psalters. His editorial work also included important collections of early choral and vocal music, such as *Part Music, Sacred and Secular* (1842–5). Among his many essays, papers, and musical textbooks were *A Grammar of Vocal Music* (1843), *The Duty and Advantage of Learning to Sing* (1846), *A Grammar of Musical Harmony* (1852, 2nd edn 1872), *A Grammar of Counterpoint* (1864), *The Cultivation of the Speaking Voice* (1870), *Time and Tune in the Elementary School* (1874, rev. 1880 as *Hullah's Method of Teaching Singing*), and *Music in the House* (1877).

Early in 1880 Hullah had a stroke, although he was able to resume his work later in that year. He suffered another stroke in November 1883, and died at his home at Grosvenor Mansions, Victoria Street, Westminster, on 21 February 1884. He was buried at Kensal Green cemetery on 26 February.

Hullah was convinced that 'music contained within it a moral force which could refine and cultivate individuals and encourage a sense of value and worth within the community' (Cox, 8), and complemented this with a belief in 'the musical superiority of the working classes; the importance of nurture as opposed to nature; the need for music to be identified as part of a liberal education' (ibid., 14). Despite the failings of his own system, he secured a place for music in the school curriculum in Britain, greatly influencing amateur music in the process, and so is assured of his position as 'the fountain head of music education in the nineteenth century' (ibid., 8).

J. A. F. MAITLAND, *rev.* DAVID J. GOLBY

Sources G. Cox, *A history of music education in England, 1872–1928* (1993) · B. Rainbow, *The land without music: musical education in England, 1800–1860* (1967) · B. Rainbow, 'Hullah, John (Pyke)', *New Grove* · [F. Hullah], *Life of John Hullah* (1886) · C. Ehrlich, *The music profession in Britain since the eighteenth century: a social history* (1985) · P. A. Scholes, *The mirror of music, 1844–1944: a century of musical life in Britain as reflected in the pages of the Musical Times*, 2 vols. (1947) · *CGPLA Eng. & Wales* (1884)

Likenesses W. B. Richmond, pencil, 1859, repro. in Rainbow, *Land without music*, facing p. 128 · R. Bowen, portrait, 1881–2; formerly in the possession of Mrs Severn Walker of Malvern Wells, 1891 · Butterworth & Heath, woodcut, BM; repro. in *Leisure Hour* (1876) · E. Edwards, photograph, NPG; repro. in *Portraits of men of eminence*, 3 (1865) [see illus.] · pencil drawing ('from the *Graphic* on the occasion of his death'), repro. in Scholes, *Mirror of music*, 16

Wealth at death £8642 10s. 3d.: probate, 24 April 1884, *CGPLA Eng. & Wales*

Hullmandel, Charles Joseph (1789–1850), lithographer, was born on 15 June 1789 in Queen Street, Mayfair, Westminster, one of the two children of Nicolas-Joseph Hüllmandel (1756–1823), a German composer and keyboard performer, and Camille-Aurore Ducazan, niece of the receiver-general of France. His parents left France on the eve of the revolution and settled in London. By 1816 he was living with his father at 51 Great Marlborough Street, where, late in 1818 or early 1819, he set up a lithographic press. This remained his home and the principal address of his firm, though he also occupied no. 49 from around 1829 to the mid-1840s.

After a private education and training as an artist in Paris, Hullmandel travelled extensively on the continent making drawings. Some of his Italian sketches were later developed as lithographs or paintings. Few of his drawings or paintings can be traced, though he exhibited at the Royal Academy, the British Institution, and elsewhere between 1816 and 1826. On returning from one of his continental tours in 1817 he met the inventor of lithography, Senefelder, in Munich. This experience seems to have changed the direction of his life and, back in London, he began drawing on stone and, later, printing from it. His first lithograph, undated, is preserved in an album of his experiments in the St Bride Printing Library, London. His earliest published lithographs, a set of *Twenty-Four Views of Italy* (1818), were drawn on stone by him and printed at the press of Moser and Harris in Somers Town, London, but were published from Great Marlborough Street. He seems to have taken advantage of this publication to make himself familiar with lithographic printing, and soon afterwards he set up a press in his own home.

From that point Hullmandel's professional life was devoted to lithography. With the guidance of F. Delpech and G. Engelmann in France, he soon became a capable lithographic draughtsman and a successful printer. One of his most important early publications was *Britannia delineata* (1822–3), which he worked on as a draughtsman with James Duffield Harding, Samuel Prout, and William Westall, in addition to printing all the lithographs. By this time he had established himself as the finest lithographic printer in Britain.

By example and through his writing Hullmandel managed to inspire confidence among artists in a process that up until then had been regarded in Britain as unreliable. Among the many artists who had their lithographs printed at his press were Thomas Shotter Boys, Théodore Géricault, Harding, Richard Lane, Edward Lear, Prout, George Scharf, and James Ward. Initially Hullmandel worked as a lithographic draughtsman, making his own drawings on stone and translating those of others; as his firm grew he acted more as a proprietor and manager, and in this role he turned his own artistic experience to commercial advantage. His efforts to publicize lithography, and thereby his own activities, began with two books: a translation of the French manual of A. Raucourt de Charleville, *Manual of Lithography* (1820), and his own *Art of*

Charles Joseph Hullmandel (1789–1850), by G. B. Black, 1851

Drawing on Stone (1824). The latter was extremely influential and ran to two further editions (1833, 1835). Most of the major improvements made to lithography in Britain in the 1820s and 1830s can be attributed to Hullmandel, and in this period he was also the most prolific printer of pictorial lithographs in the country.

In the 1820s, aided by Michael Faraday as technical consultant and Harding as specialist lithographic draughtsman, Hullmandel developed ways of producing and preparing crayon-drawn lithographs so that they could withstand edition printing, and he also devised chemical methods of treating the stone that allowed corrections to be made to a drawing once printing had begun. In the mid-1830s, in co-operation with Harding, he pioneered methods of creating tonal effects on stone using a variety of techniques (stump, reserving lights with gum arabic, rubbing down tones with coarse cloth) that were taken up for the tint stones of tinted lithography, especially in skies. These developments put him at the forefront of European lithography. In the same period he printed colour plates for G. A. Hoskins's *Travels in Ethiopia* (1835), which were the first real colour lithographs to be published in Britain. His experiments in rendering tones and colour printing were put to good use in one of the major lithographic achievements of the middle of the nineteenth century, Boys's *Picturesque Architecture in Paris …* (1839), which he printed and probably masterminded technically. His final improvement to lithography was lithotint, which he patented in 1840. This was a technically exacting process which allowed artists to work on stone with washes of diluted ink much as they could on

paper. Though not widely used, it had one major application in Harding's *The Park and the Forest* (1841). In the 1840s Hullmandel's firm lost its leading edge and faced strong competition from other lithographic houses. Around 1843 he went into partnership with Joseph Fowell Walton, to whom he left the lease on his premises in Great Marlborough Street, his patent rights, and his share in the business. The imprint Hullmandel and Walton continued in use for about a decade after his death.

Hullmandel remained a bachelor and lived with his sister, (Adelaide Charlotte) Evelina (*d.* 1839), and his manager, the flower painter Valentine Bartholomew (1799–1879), until the two married in 1827. In the 1840s he also had, at different times, two modest country houses in Fulham. A lithographed portrait shows him as a serious and somewhat dour figure, though other evidence points to a gregarious and generous character who enjoyed the company of people from the worlds of science, music, and the visual arts, including Faraday, Manuel del Popolo Vicente Garcia, Lear, Maria Felíciá Malibran, and J. M. W. Turner. What is known about his business activities suggests that he was meticulous and put great demands on himself and others; obituary notices stress his honour and integrity. He died suddenly at Great Marlborough Street of a brain haemorrhage on 15 November 1850 and was buried in Highgate cemetery on 21 November.

MICHAEL TWYMAN

Sources M. Twyman, 'Charles Joseph Hullmandel: lithographic printer extraordinary', *Lasting impressions*, ed. P. Gilmour (1988), 42–90, 362–7 · M. Twyman, *Lithography, 1800–1850* (1970) · J. R. Abbey, *Travel in aquatint and lithography, 1770–1860*, 2 vols. (1956–7) · *Expositor*, 8 (21 Dec 1850), 114 · *Art Journal*, 13 (1851), 30 · R. Benton, 'Hüllmandel, Nicolas-Joseph', *New Grove* · W. S. Williams, 'On lithography', *Transactions of the Society for the Encouragement of Arts, Manufactures, and Commerce* (1847–8), 226–50 · *Library of the Fine Arts*, 1 (1831), 44–58 · *Library of the Fine Arts*, 1 (1831), 201–16 · M. Twyman, *A directory of London lithographic printers, 1800–1850* (1976) · Graves, *Artists* · Graves, *Brit. Inst.* · Thieme & Becker, *Allgemeines Lexikon* · records, Highgate cemetery, London

Archives Archives Office of Tasmania, invoice, CS01/910/19174 · Kingston Lacy, Dorset · Linn. Soc., invoices · St Bride Institute, London, St Bride Printing Library, collection of proof impressions and experiments in lithography | Lpool RO, corresp. with Gregson

Likenesses G. B. Black, lithograph, 1851, AM Oxf., BM [*see illus.*] · wood-engraving, repro. in *Expositor*

Hullock, Sir John (1767–1829), judge, was born on 3 April 1767, the son of Timothy Hullock (*d.* 1805), master weaver and proprietor of a timber yard at Barnard Castle, co. Durham, and his wife, of whom little is known. Early in his career he is thought to have been articled to an attorney at Stokesley in the North Riding. Subsequently, on the advice of a well-known barrister of the time, 'Jack' Lee, who was a friend of his uncle's, he decided to seek his fortune at the bar. Having been admitted a student of Gray's Inn on 7 May 1788, he became a pupil of George Sowley Holroyd, afterwards a justice of the king's bench. In 1792 he published *The Law of Costs* (2 vols.), a second edition of which, with considerable additions, appeared from a London press in 1810.

On being called to the bar in May 1794, Hullock joined

the northern circuit and gradually acquired a considerable practice. He served as recorder of Berwick for several years until he was made a serjeant-at-law on 18 June 1816. He was involved in the prosecutions against Henry Hunt and Andrew Hardie in 1820, despite objections that he was not qualified to appear. On the resignation of Sir George Wood, he was appointed a baron of the exchequer and took his seat on the bench for the first time on 16 April 1823. He was knighted on 21 April 1823. After holding the office of judge for little more than six years he was seized with a sudden illness while on circuit, and died of cholera at Abingdon on 31 July 1829. He was buried in the family vault at Barnard Castle. He was survived by his wife, who died on 18 November 1852.

Hullock was regarded as a sound and industrious lawyer, and was widely valued as a humane and charitable man who once saved a fellow attorney from professional disgrace. During the conduct of one of his cases as a barrister, Hullock was instructed not to produce a certain document. However, ignoring the warning, he produced it only to find that it had been forged by his client's attorney. Judge Bayley ordered that the deed be impounded; however, Hullock asked for leave to inspect it and, upon being given it, put it back in his bag. During Bayley's subsequent absence to consult on measures to be taken, Hullock destroyed the document and saved the attorney, who escaped.   G. F. R. BARKER, rev. SINÉAD AGNEW

Sources Foss, *Judges* • H. J. Rose, *A new general biographical dictionary*, ed. H. J. Rose and T. Wright, 12 vols. (1853) • *Annual Biography and Obituary*, 14 (1830), 308–11 • *N&Q*, 7th ser., 8 (1889), 48, 197 • *Annual Register* (1829), 239 • J. Foster, *The register of admissions to Gray's Inn, 1521–1889, together with the register of marriages in Gray's Inn chapel, 1695–1754* (privately printed, London, 1889), 393 • *GM*, 1st ser., 99/2 (1829) • *GM*, 2nd ser., 39 (1853), 106 • *Law Magazine*, 2 (1829), 708–10 • E. Mackenzie and M. Ross, *An historical, topographical, and descriptive view of the county palatine of Durham*, 2 (1834), 242–3 • W. R. Douthwaite, *Gray's Inn: its history and associations* (1886), 441 • *LondG* (22 April 1823), 651 • Allibone, *Dict.*

Likenesses portrait, Gray's Inn, London

Hulls [Hull], **Jonathan** (*bap.* **1699**, *d.* **1758**), mechanical inventor, was born at Hanging Aston and baptized in Blockley parish church, Gloucestershire, on 17 December 1699. His parents, Thomas Hull, or Hulls, and Mary, had two other children, Thomas and Sarah. Hulls inherited mechanical skills from his weaver father and displayed a youthful aptitude for repairing neighbours' clocks. He attended Campden grammar school, earning a reputation as a diligent mathematician and skilled technician. By 1719 he had already married Anne, daughter of Stephen and Rebecca Davis of Broad Campden; they had at least one daughter. On 7 April 1730 he leased from the countess of Gainsborough some 60 acres of farmland and a house at Broad Campden, where he lived for the rest of his life.

Hulls is remembered principally for having patented the application of the atmospheric steam engine to marine propulsion. A communication from M. de Quet on mechanical propulsion of ships, published in 1734 in volume 6 of the abridgement of *Philosophical Transactions of the Royal Society*, may have spurred Hulls to attempt to apply the Newcomen engine for this purpose. The means to do

so eluded him until a neighbour at nearby Batsford Park, Mr Freeman, contributed about £160 to finance a patent application, granted to Hulls on 21 December 1736. As was required by the grant, Hulls published within three months *A description and draught of a new-invented machine for carrying vessels or ships out of or into any harbour, port or river against wind and tide or in a calm.* He proposed a stern-wheeled paddle towboat carrying a boiler coupled to a vertical steam cylinder. Atmospheric pressure depressed a piston towards the bottom of the cylinder when the steam beneath it was suddenly condensed. Through a linkage of ropes over pulleys, this movement turned an adjacent layshaft and simultaneously raised a counterweight, the subsequent descent of which reversed the rotation of the layshaft as fresh steam was admitted beneath the piston. Friction ratchets on the layshaft converted this alternating motion to continuous rotation of the adjacent paddleshaft mounted on a framework over the stern. When the water was sufficiently shallow, Hulls proposed to employ a pair of mechanical quanting poles operated by the same alternating motion.

No conclusive evidence has survived to substantiate the tradition that Hulls experimented with such a vessel on the Avon at Evesham. Had his pamphlet provoked serious trial of his scheme history would certainly have noted it, but the intermittent motion of the Newcomen engine made it fundamentally unsuitable for continuous propulsion, whether on land or water. Hulls's only subsequent patent, applied for in 1753, describes an apparatus for detecting counterfeit coins by their specific gravity, and an improvement in the logarithmic scale. An example of the apparatus in the Science Museum illustrates Hulls's ingenuity in perfecting a mechanism little bigger than a penknife.

In his will dated 17 May 1758, Hulls described himself as a yeoman. He died less than a month later at the house in Broad Campden where he had spent virtually all his adult life but the exact date of his death and his burial place are not known, nor is any memorial. A portrait commissioned for a stateroom in the RMS *Queen Mary* (1936) credited Hulls as inventor of the steamboat, as did a late nineteenth-century portrait formerly in the London headquarters of the Institute of Marine Engineers. It would be fairer to remember Hulls as an early patentee of the principle of steam propulsion for ships, rather than as a practical exponent of that technology, which was achieved only after James Watt's introduction of the separate condenser and other improvements after 1769.

J. C. ROBINSON

Sources P. C. Rushen, *History and antiquities of Chipping Camden in the county of Gloucester* (1899) • L. G. Hulls, 'Jonathan Hulls and his steamboat', *Journal of Naval Engineering*, 6 (1953), 92–102 • L. G. Hulls, 'Jonathan Hulls and his steamboat: an engineering enigma', *The Edgar Allen News*, 30 (1952), 42–3 • J. H. Hulls, 'Introduction of steam navigation', *Transactions of the Institute of Marine Engineers* (1906) • R. Stuart [R. S. Meikleham], *Historical and descriptive anecdotes of steam-engines, and of their inventors and improvers*, 2 vols. (1829) • B. Woodcroft, *Origins and progress of steam navigation* (1848) • J. Fincham, *A history of naval architecture* (1857) • C. Matschoss, *Die*

Entwicklung der Dampfmaschine (1908) • W. S. Lindsay, *History of merchant shipping and ancient commerce*, 4 vols. (1874–6) • R. A. Fletcher, *Steamships and their story* (1910) • E. C. Smith, *A short history of naval and marine engineering* (1937) • G. H. Preble, *History of the origin and development of steam navigation* (1883) • J. Hulls, *A description and draught of a new-invented machine for carrying vessels … out of or into any harbour … against wind and tide or in a calm* (1737)

Likenesses W. T. Fry, stipple, BM, NPG • portrait, *Queen Mary*, Long Beach, California, stateroom

Hulme, Frederick Edward (1841–1909), naturalist and artist, was born at Hanley, Staffordshire, on either 29 (his own claim) or 30 (according to his birth certificate) March 1841, the only son of Frederick William *Hulme (1816–1884), landscape painter, and his wife, Caroline Jackson. In 1844 the family moved to London, where Hulme later attended the Western Grammar School in Brompton and, from his seventeenth year, studied art in South Kensington. On 5 March 1866 he married Emily, daughter of John Napper of Henfield, Sussex. The couple had two sons and two daughters; the elder son, Frank Howell Hulme, became dean of Bloemfontein, Orange Free State.

In 1870 Hulme was appointed art and drawing master at Marlborough College. He was also a keen amateur naturalist (he had been elected FLS in 1869) and, while at Marlborough, began publication of his *Familiar Wild Flowers*, the work for which he became best known. Copiously illustrated with coloured plates from his own drawings, a ninth volume was completed just before his death and the whole work was later reissued serially. He also produced several botanically orientated textbooks for art students, and furnished illustrations for Shirley Hibberd's *Familiar Garden Flowers* (1879) and F. G. Heath's *Sylvan Spring* (1880). Hulme also had strong antiquarian interests (he was elected FSA in 1872) and wrote *The Town, College and Neighbourhood of Marlborough* (1881).

Hulme left Marlborough in 1883 and, in 1885, was appointed lecturer to the Architectural Association in London. In the following year he joined King's College as professor of geometrical drawing (from 1896 professor of freehand and geometrical drawing). He also served for a number of years as examiner to the Department of Science and Art and the London chamber of commerce. However, he still found time to write on natural history and antiquarian subjects; his later works included *The History, Principles and Practice of Heraldry* (1891; edn 1897), *The History of Symbolism in Christian Art* (1891; rev. edn 1899), *Butterflies and Moths of the Countryside* (1903), and *Familiar Swiss Flowers* (1908).

Hulme died at his home, Newark, Kew Gardens Road, Kew, on 11 April 1909 and was buried at Brookwood, Surrey. He was survived by his wife and four children.

PETER OSBORNE

Sources *DNB* • *WWW* • b. cert. • m. cert. • *CGPLA Eng. & Wales* (1909) • G. W. De Lisle and H. W. Simpkinson, eds., *Marlborough College register, from 1843 to 1889 inclusive*, 3rd edn (1890) • private information (2004)

Wealth at death £3049 13s. 7d.: probate, 6 May 1909, *CGPLA Eng. & Wales*

Hulme, Frederick William (1816–1884), landscape painter, was born at Swinton, Yorkshire, on 22 October 1816. His early training was with his mother, a painter on porcelain. He first exhibited at the Birmingham Academy in 1841, where he showed a landscape; with very rare exceptions thereafter, his contributions were invariably landscapes. Fresh in colour and carefully drawn, they resembled the works of William Shayer and Thomas Creswick.

In 1844 Hulme went to London, where he worked as a draughtsman engraving for magazines such as the *Art Journal*, and for books, including S. C. Hall's *Book of South Wales* (1861) and the *Poetical Works of E. A. Poe* (1853). He specialized in scenes of Surrey and Wales, paying many visits to Betws-y-coed, Caernarvonshire; some of his best-known works are views in that neighbourhood. He occasionally worked on pictures in conjunction with other artists, including Henry Brittan Willis. He had a large practice as a teacher of drawing and painting, and he published *A Graduated Series of Drawing Copies on Landscape Subjects for Use of Schools* (1850). Hulme was a frequent exhibitor at the British Institution (1845–62), the Royal Manchester Institution (from 1845), the Royal Academy (1852–84), and at smaller galleries. Hulme was married to Caroline Jackson, with whom he had one son, the naturalist and artist Frederick Edward *Hulme. He died at his home, 8 St Albans Road, Kensington, London, on 14 November 1884.

ALBERT NICHOLSON, rev. ROMITA RAY

Sources *The Athenaeum* (22 Nov 1884), 666 • R. K. Engen, *Dictionary of Victorian wood engravers* (1985) • Wood, *Vic. painters*, 3rd edn • Bryan, *Painters* (1877) • *CGPLA Eng. & Wales* (1885)

Wealth at death £3149 12s. 1d.: probate, 10 Jan 1885, *CGPLA Eng. & Wales*

Hulme, Nathaniel (1732–1807), physician and natural philosopher, was born on 17 June 1732 at Hulme Thorp, near Halifax, Yorkshire. After serving his apprenticeship with his brother Joseph, a medical practitioner at Halifax, he proceeded to Guy's Hospital, London, and in 1755 joined the navy as surgeon's mate. Being stationed at Leith after the peace of 1763 he attended the medical classes at Edinburgh, and graduated MD there in 1765; his thesis was '*De scorbuto*', his naval experience having brought him into contact with scurvy. After moving to London he commenced practice in Hatton Garden, and in May 1768 published *Libellus de natura, causa, curationque scorbuti*, an expansion of his thesis with an appendix in English, setting out how every sailor in the navy could be supplied with orange or lemon juice as an antiscorbutic at a cost of 3 farthings per day. Unfortunately, he added a postscript accepting the new idea that any fermentation yielding 'fixed air' (carbon dioxide) would be equally effective.

On the founding of the General Dispensary for the Relief of the Poor, Hulme was elected its first physician. He was also physician to the City of London Lying-in Hospital, a position not tenable by an accoucheur. His *Treatise on the Puerperal Fever* (1772) was the outcome of his experience there. On 17 March 1774 he was elected physician to the Charterhouse by the interest of Lord Sandwich, first lord of the Admiralty, and moved to Charterhouse Square, where he lived until his death. At the same time he joined the Royal College of Physicians, but never became a fellow.

In 1777 Hulme gave an 'Oratio de re medica' before the Medical Society, with the description of the case of a Charterhouse pensioner, aged seventy-three, in whom he had succeeded in breaking up a stone within the bladder by the following prescription: fifteen grains of salt of tartar (potassium carbonate) in 3 ounces of pure water, four times a day, followed immediately by a draught of water containing twenty drops of weak spirit of vitriol (sulphuric acid), in order to induce the release of fixed air. The alleged result was that hundreds of fragments of calculus came away for several weeks, and the patient remained in good health a year later. The same remedy was advocated by him in the following year (1778) also for scurvy, gout, and worms, in a quarto pamphlet *A Safe and Easy Remedy Proposed for the Relief of Stone and Gravel, the Scurvy, Gout, etc.*, with an appendix on a method of impregnating water with fixed air, by simple mixture only, without the assistance of a complicated machine. In 1787 he received a gold medal from the Medical Society of Paris for an essay on sclerosis of the cellular tissue in the new born. He was elected FRS in 1794, and contributed two papers, 'Experiments and observations on the light which is spontaneously emitted from various bodies', to the *Philosophical Transactions* in 1800 and 1801 (vols. 90 and 91), and to *A Journal of Natural Philosophy* (vol. 4 and ser. 2, vol. 2) in 1800 and 1802. He found that the luminescence of the tissues of dead fish required the presence of oxygen, being extinguished in atmospheres of hydrogen, nitrogen, or carbon dioxide. It was also reversibly inhibited by freezing and strong salt solutions and irreversibly by boiling. Hulme was a fellow of the Society of Antiquaries, and contributed to *Archaeologia* (14, 1803) 'Account of a brick brought from the site of Ancient Babylon'. He died on 28 March 1807 as a result of a fall from the roof of his house, to which he had ascended to observe the damage done to the chimneys by a hurricane. He was buried as he had requested, in the burial-ground of the Charterhouse. The *Gentleman's Magazine* gives the text of his last prayer as an evidence of his piety.

CHARLES CREIGHTON, *rev.* KENNETH J. CARPENTER

Sources N. Hulme, *A proposal for preventing scurvy in the British navy* (1768) · [Clarke], *The Georgian era: memoirs of the most eminent persons*, 2 (1833) · Munk, *Roll* · *GM*, 1st ser., 77 (1807), 487–8 · P. J. Wallis and R. V. Wallis, *Eighteenth century medics*, 2nd edn (1988)

Likenesses N. Branwhite, group portrait, stipple, pubd 1801 (after S. Medley), BM · aquatint, silhouette, 1801, Wellcome L. · S. Medley, group portrait (*Institutions of the Medical Society of London*) · stipple, BM

Hulme, Thomas Ernest (1883–1917), philosopher and poet, was born on 16 September 1883 at Gratton, Horton, Staffordshire, the eldest of two sons and one daughter of Thomas Hulme (1853–1933), a gentleman farmer who later went into the ceramic transfer business, and his wife, Mary Young. He attended Newcastle High School for Boys (1894–1902), where he won many of the school's mathematics and science prizes and was elected 'whip' of

Thomas Ernest Hulme (1883–1917), by unknown photographer, 1914

the debating society. Admitted to St John's College, Cambridge, on an open mathematics exhibition in 1902, he became rebellious and was sent down two years later for idleness and a surfeit of pranks. The mock funeral organized by his friends in farewell was so large and rowdy that news of it reached *The Tatler* in London (1904). He enrolled at University College, London, but left in 1906 without a degree and set sail for a stay of several months in Canada, where he began jotting down his thoughts on the nature of truth, knowledge, the world, and language. Published after his death, these notes, known as 'Cinders', together present a nominalistic view of the world as a plurality which no single theory can comprehend. In the spring of 1907 he returned to England, but soon crossed to Brussels where he taught English for a year and worked on his 'Notes on language and style'. A collection of jottings like 'Cinders', they present a similar view of the world: all theories are toys, language is not equivalent to reality, a writer's beliefs reflect his prejudices rather than universal truth—though in 'Notes' these themes are applied to language and style.

When Hulme returned home to London in 1908, he joined a group of enthusiasts known as the Poets' Club and soon was calling for a new beginning in English poetry; he wanted an 'impressionistic' verse not bound by the old rules of metre. Early in 1909 he formed his own group of like-minded poets, which included F. S. Flint and the young American Ezra Pound, who acknowledged his debt to Hulme when he launched his imagist movement and published Hulme's 'Complete Poetical Works' (five short, gem-like poems) as an appendix to his own book *Ripostes* (1912).

In mid-1909 the second period of Hulme's intellectual life began with a more serious study of philosophy. Convinced that Henri Bergson provided a way out of the nightmare of nineteenth-century materialism and mechanism, he began a three-year stint of writing and lecturing about Bergson. He also translated into English Bergson's *Introduction à la métaphysique* (1912).

But even as Hulme was busy explaining and defending Bergson, he became interested (1911) in political theory. Hulme described himself as a tory, but he was not much interested in day-to-day politics. Instead, he began to write about the philosophical issues: the nature of man, the idea of progress, the difference between theory and practice, and the emotional and non-rational character of political belief. He pointed to Georges Sorel and to the group of contemporary French writers known as *L'Action française*. What he liked was their opposition to 'romanticism'; and in 1911, on his way to or from the Fourth International Philosophical Congress in Bologna, which he covered for the magazine *Nature* and the London weekly the *New Age*, he met Pierre Lasserre, a leading member of *L'Action française*, who endeavoured to prove to him that Bergson was nothing but 'the last disguise of romanticism', and that, if applied to politics, Bergson's theory of real time would mean a continual progress for mankind—an idea Hulme opposed.

Unable to reconcile his own political beliefs with Bergson's philosophy, Hulme ceased writing about Bergson in 1912 and began to work out his own philosophical position, which drew a sharp distinction between two ways of regarding the nature of man, namely the 'romantic' and the 'classical'. In *A Tory Philosophy* (1912) he described the classical as based on a belief that man is by nature limited and incapable of attaining any kind of perfection. Only through discipline could he achieve anything of value. The romantic view, Hulme said, was the opposite: it asserted man was naturally good and that whatever he accomplished was by the breaking of rules. One or other of these two attitudes lay, Hulme maintained, behind opinions on every subject, from politics to art. The romantic and classical temperaments as reflected in poetry is the subject of what is probably his best-known work, the 1912 lecture 'Romanticism and classicism' (first published posthumously in *Speculations*, 1924). Readmitted to Cambridge in the spring of 1912, owing largely to a letter from Bergson, Hulme fled to Germany that summer to avoid prosecution by an enraged don whose sixteen-year-old daughter had received letters from Hulme while she was at school at Roedean. During his German trip (1912–13) he became interested in the visual arts through the work of the art theorist Wilhelm Worringer. Hulme came to think of the avant-garde art of pre-war England as heralding the breakup of the humanistic attitude which, taking man as the centre of all things, had dominated thinking since the Renaissance. Thus he began to publicize the work of such contemporary artists as Jacob Epstein (who sculpted Hulme) and David Bomberg, whose hard-edged style seemed to point to a classical renewal. He also translated into English Sorel's *Réflexions sur la violence* (1914).

When war broke out in August 1914 Hulme enlisted in the army as a private and in December was sent to the western front. In April 1915 he was sent home wounded and did not return to the fighting until March 1916 when, through the help of Sir Edward Marsh, he was granted a commission as temporary second lieutenant in the Royal Marine Artillery. While at home he published a long series of 'War notes', some of which revolved round his opposition to the pacifists of the day, including Bertrand Russell, with whom he debated in the *Cambridge Magazine*. He also wrote what would be his final and most important pages, called simply 'A notebook' when published in the *New Age* in 1915–16 (posthumously retitled 'Humanism and the religious attitude' in 1924). Here he synthesized what he had thought his way through during the past decade: ideas on discontinuity and 'cinders'; his theory that beliefs and convictions are based on unconscious assumptions about the world; the difference between the romantic and classical views of man; and most important, perhaps, his belief in the existence of original sin. Though closely related to views he had expressed earlier on romanticism and classicism, he now went further. The realization that there is nothing wonderful in man was, he said, a necessary preparation for the religious attitude, but, by itself, led only to a rejection of romanticism and the adoption of the classical attitude. The religious attitude required further that one recognize a separation between the material world and the world of ethics and religion. Perfection belonged only to the divine and could not be legitimately introduced on the human plane. All philosophies since the Renaissance shared a 'family resemblance' in that they failed to see the chasm between the organic world and the worlds of ethics and religious values. Hulme claimed they all accepted an unconscious humanism, in which man was viewed as naturally good, a reservoir of possibility. He himself believed 'the religious conception of ultimate values to be right, the humanist wrong'. And he predicted that the religious attitude, which had prevailed in the Egyptian and Byzantine empires and during the middle ages in western Europe, would come back in some form to replace the humanistic attitude of his own day.

Hulme was a large man, with an open, genial face. From 1911 until the war he presided over a weekly salon which nearly everyone in London who was connected with the arts seems at one time or another to have attended. He was remembered as a brilliant Johnsonian talker, with a ranging curiosity and dominating personality which drew out the opinions of others and stimulated debate. Though he was known for his energetic pursuit of young women and had long friendships with Ethel Kibblewhite and artist Kate Lechmere (1887–1976), he never married. He was killed in action near Nieuport in Flanders on 26 September 1917 and was buried in Koksijde military cemetery in

Belgium. He published no book of his own during his lifetime; nor did his writings become the basis for any philosophical school. Despite this, he held a small but definite place in twentieth-century intellectual life and letters, particularly as forerunner in the movement towards a 'new classicism'. Such diverse thinkers as Ramiro de Maeztu, I. A. Richards, V. A. Demant, J. G. Crowther, and Iris Murdoch all commented on his importance. T. S. Eliot, in *Criterion*, went so far as to describe him as 'the forerunner of a new attitude of mind, which should be the twentieth-century mind, if the twentieth century is to have a mind of its own'. KAREN CSENGERI

Sources *The collected writings of T. E. Hulme*, ed. K. Csengeri (1994) • K. Csengeri, 'The life and works of T. E. Hulme', PhD diss., U. Mich., 1985 • 'Introduction', T. E. Hulme, *Speculations*, ed. H. Read (1924) • M. Roberts, *T. E. Hulme* (1938) • Crites [T. S. Eliot], 'A commentary', *Criterion*, 2/7 (1924), 231–5 • E. Pound, *Ripostes* (1912) • private information (2004) • F. S. Flint, 'The Ripostes of Ezra Pound with "The complete poetical works of T. E. Hulme"', *Poetry and Drama*, 1 (March 1913), 60–62 • *Cambridge Magazine*, 5/12–17 (1916) • *The Tatler* (30 March 1904), 513 • *Fire-Fly* [Magazine of Newcastle high school] (1894–1902) • *Staffordshire Sentinel* (9 June 1913) • *Evening Sentinel* (31 Aug 1933) • d. cert. • b. cert. • R. de Maeztu, *Authority light and function in the light of the war* (1916) • I. A. Richards, 'Review of *Speculations*', *Mind*, new ser., 33 (1924), 469–70 • V. A. Demant, *The religious prospect* (1939) • J. G. Crowther, *The social relations of science* (1941) • I. Murdoch, 'T. S. Eliot as a moralist', *T. S. Eliot: a symposium for his seventieth birthday*, ed. N. Braybrooke (1958) • parish records (baptism), 4 Nov 1883, St Michael's, Horton, Staffordshire

Archives Harvard U., Houghton L. • Ransom HRC, corresp. • U. Hull, Brynmor Jones L., letters and papers • University of Keele, papers | Cornell University, Wyndham Lewis corresp. • Indiana University, Bloomington, corresp. with Richard Carle • McMaster University, Hamilton, Ontario, corresp. with Frank Ogden • NYPL, Henry W. and Albert A. Berg collection, corresp. with Edward Margh • Ransom HRC, Flint collection, corresp.

Likenesses photograph, 1914, Hult. Arch. [*see illus.*] • two photographs, 1914–17, U. Texas • J. Epstein, bust, 1916, probably priv. coll.

Hulme, William (*bap.* **1631**, *d.* **1691**), benefactor of Hulme's Charity, was baptized at St Peter, Bolton, Lancashire, on 23 March 1631, the only son of William Hulme (*d.* 1637) of Hulme Hall, Reddish, near Prestwich, Lancashire, and his wife, Christian (*d.* 1633), daughter of Richard Banaster of Oakenbottom in the same county. On his father's death Hulme's uncle John Hulme became his guardian until he came of age. Because of family connections it is plausibly conjectured that Hulme was educated at Manchester grammar school, though the claim that this is confirmed by the fact that he was a trustee of the school from 1685 is incorrect, owing to a confusion with another William Hulme of Droylsden. In 1648 some of his property was sequestered for royalist 'delinquency'. Almost certainly he was the William Hulme matriculated at Brasenose College, Oxford, on 20 February 1649 and admitted to Gray's Inn, London, on 17 May 1650. There is no evidence that he graduated or was called to the bar and it is likely that, as for other men of his class, his enrolment was for social rather than professional reasons. On 2 August 1653 he married Elizabeth (*d.* 1700), daughter of Ralph Robinson of Kearsley, at Prestwich. The marriage brought him an

estate and mansion where he afterwards resided. At Kearsley he also bought land and built a house, the income from which was paid to the minister of Ringley, where he attended church. Hulme's only son, Banaster, was born in 1658 but died while at Manchester grammar school in 1673. Though it has been surmised that Hulme increased his income by mercantile pursuits, there is no evidence for this and it is likely that he lived the life of a country gentleman. He also held minor offices in the court leet of Manchester and became a JP. According to the dissenting minister Oliver Heywood, who said that William Hulme was his 'old schoolfellow', Banaster's death left Elizabeth Hulme 'almost distracted with excessive grief'. He added that Hulme:

> hath been somewhat debauched, though of late much reformed, yet exceeding devoted to conformity, the first work he did after he was justice of peace, was sending good Mr Wood [probably James Wood, former curate of Allerton] to Lancaster gaol for preaching. He hath said of my brother's [brother-in-law's] Hulton's house, which is his, that he had rather see it afire than have it hold a conventicle. (*Autobiography*, 1.355)

Given Heywood's puritanical morality, 'debauchery' should probably not be taken too literally. William Hulme died, probably in Manchester, in 1691 and was buried on 29 October in the then Hulme chapel in Manchester collegiate church.

Hulme is significant less for his sparsely recorded career than for the subsequent use of his estates in Reddish, Kearsley, and Manchester. By his will dated 24 October 1691 most of his property was left to his wife for her lifetime and after her death to trustees and their heirs. The income was to support four poor bachelors of arts of Brasenose College for four years after graduation. They were to be nominated by the warden of Manchester collegiate church and the rectors of Prestwich and Bury. The trustees agreed to restrict nominees to sons of Lancashire clergy. Friends after Hulme's death said he was concerned that poor Lancashire men were unable to stay at university after graduation and therefore were inadequately equipped for the ministry. His will may have been intended to remedy this but if so it was drawn up hastily just before his death and no such purpose was specified. As the trust's income increased, partly from profitable use of building leases, the number of Hulme exhibitions was increased and in 1814 a lectureship in divinity was established at Brasenose. From 1827 the trust was empowered to purchase Anglican benefices, eventually twenty-eight in all, twenty-one being in Lancashire, and in 1839 the income of these benefices was augmented. There followed a prolonged public controversy over what critics regarded as misuse of the trust for such purposes. In 1881 the charity commissioners, while allowing the Anglican benefices to be retained, empowered the trustees to found schools in Manchester, Oldham, and Bury and a hall of residence in Owens College (then the only constituent college of the University of Manchester) for Anglican students. Grants were later made to Manchester High School for Girls, Manchester grammar school, and other halls in the university, while scholarships to Brasenose from the three Hulme schools were added to the original college exhibitions.   HENRY D. RACK

Sources [T. Nicklin], *William Hulme, 1631–91, founder and benefactor* (1931) • K. P. Thompson, 'History of William Hulme's Grammar School', 1976, Man. CL • *The Rev. Oliver Heywood … his autobiography, diaries, anecdote and event books*, ed. J. H. Turner, 1 (1881), 355 • G. H. Swindells, 'William Hulme the founder', *Manchester City News* (1890), 2–8 • A. A. Mumford, *The Manchester grammar school, 1515–1915* (1919), 116–18 • J. Booker, *A history of the ancient chapels of Didsbury and Chorlton, in Manchester parish*, Chetham Society, 42 (1857), 213–19 • H. Brierley, ed., *Registers of parish church of Prestbury, 1603–88*, Lancashire Parish Register Society, 34 (1909) • *IGI*

Wealth at death minor legacies; estate to wife for lifetime and after her death to trustees; value of lands in trust in 1710 £212 5s. 11d.: Nicklin, *William Hulme*, 15–17

Huloet [Howlet], **Richard** (*fl.* 1552), lexicographer, was, according to John Bale, who cited John Day as his source, probably born in Wisbech, Cambridgeshire. A Howlet family was certainly established there by the mid-fifteenth century. Practically no details of his life are known. There is no record of a university education, though this seems likely, Bale describing him as 'in bonis literis foeliciter educatus' (Bale, *Cat.*, 753). He may have been taught by William Lilly at Colet's school in London, since in his published writings he calls Lilly 'preceptor meus Lillius' (Huloet, sig. Aair). His *Abcedarium Anglico-Latinum* was published in 1552 under the Latinized name Huloetus, which has given rise to Huloet, the form of the surname most often used since. The work was printed by William Riddell, probably for John Day, whose device appears on the title-page. The *Abcedarium* is an English–Latin dictionary intended for teaching, as its title suggests, in the tradition of works such as the *Promptorium parvulorum, sive clericum* of c.1440 and the *Catholicon Anglicum*, which suggests that Huloet may have been a teacher. The *Abcedarium* is dedicated to the lord chancellor, Thomas Goodrich, the bishop of Ely. The only subsequent edition, greatly altered by John Higgins and published in 1572, was dedicated by Higgins to the merchant Sir George Peckham; in the absence of a modern edition a facsimile version is available.

This was the first new such dictionary published in the sixteenth century. Its compilation was perhaps prompted by the sustained popularity of the *Promptorium parvulorum* early in the century, but it was immediately superseded by John Withals's successful *Shorte Dictionarie for Yonge Begynners* published in 1553. Peter Levens mentions the work of 'Maister Howlet' in the dedication of his *Manipulus vocabulorum* of 1570 (Levens, sig. [para] 4r). Huloet's is the more learned work, providing some grammatical information and translations of quotations, and includes both proper names and explanations of the letters of the alphabet. The structure of its entries is borrowed from a French–English dictionary by Robert Stephanus, while many of the entries are adapted from Sir Thomas Elyot's *Bibliotheca*, as revised by Thomas Cooper in 1548. Latin synonyms of the English headwords are copiously provided, and the headwords themselves are often entire phrases or even lengthy comments, suggesting that the dictionary was compiled, as was usual, by inverting the entries of Latin–English dictionaries.

    R. W. McCONCHIE

Sources DNB • Bale, *Cat.* • Bale, *Index* • G. Stein, *The English dictionary before Cawdrey* (1985) • De W. T. Starnes, *Renaissance dictionaries: English–Latin and Latin–English* (1954) • De W. T. Starnes and G. E. Noyes, *The English dictionary from Cawdrey to Johnson, 1604–1755*, new edn, ed. G. Stein (1991) • P. Levens, *Manipulus vocabulorum: a rhyming dictionary of the English language by Peter Levins* (1570), ed. H. B. Wheatley (1867) • R. Huloet, *Abcedarium Anglico-Latinum pro tyrunculis* (1552) • H. B. Wheatley, preface, in S. J. H. Herrtage, *Catholicon Anglicum, an English–Latin wordbook* (1882), i–xii • S. J. H. Herrtage, *Catholicon Anglicum, an English–Latin wordbook* (1882) • E. G. Duff, *A century of the English book trade* (1905); repr. (1948) • F. B. Williams, *Index of dedications and commendatory verses in English books before 1641* (1962) • R. W. McConchie, 'Richard Huloet, right or wrong?', *N&Q*, 245 (2000), 26–7 • De W. T. Starnes, 'Richard Huloet's *Abcedarium*: a study in English–Latin lexicography', *Studies in Philology*, 48 (1951), 717–37

Hulsbergh [Hulsberg], **Henry** (*d.* 1729), engraver, was born in Amsterdam but was in London by 1709 when he engraved a frontispiece to Bulstrode Whitelocke's *Memorial of English Affairs*. The following year he produced a bird's-eye view of Portsmouth and Gosport, the first of several views of ports published by Robert Hulton and Thomas Taylor. He went on to engrave a number of copies of French prints and other foreign models for leading printsellers, including copies of the Raphael cartoons for Henry Overton and a large set of the four elements for Thomas Bowles. However, Hulsbergh's speciality was architecture. Plates such as *The North Prospect of the Cathedral Church of St Paul's*, engraved for Thomas Bowles, caught the eye of the printseller Joseph Smith, who was organizing the production of *Vitruvius Britannicus*, the great collection of elevations and plans of the most distinguished modern British buildings begun in 1714. In the first volume (1715) none of the plates was signed, but Hulsbergh put his name to all of the elevations in the second and third volumes (1717, 1725) and he probably also engraved the stylistically similar first group of plates. The consistent lucidity of this great series of architectural prints owes much to Hulsbergh's abilities as an engraver. He was also responsible for many of the private plates made after drawings by leading architects for distribution among potential sponsors of various building projects. These included prints of All Souls College, Oxford, after Nicholas Hawksmoor; King's College, Cambridge, after James Gibbs; and St Philip's, Birmingham, after Thomas Archer. From about 1724 Hulsbergh was engaged with Hawksmoor on a project for collecting plates of Sir Christopher Wren's public works. He had engraved at least nine of these before he suffered a 'paraletic fitt' that left him 'intirely incapable of business' (Vertue, *Note books*, 3.38–9). During an illness lasting two years or more he was supported by the Lutheran church in the Savoy, of which he had been warden, '& by the brethren of a Dutch Box-club' (Vertue, *Note books*, 3.38–9). He died in May 1729 and was buried in the Savoy by the Lutheran church. Examples of his work are in the Bodleian Library and Worcester College, Oxford.   TIMOTHY CLAYTON

Sources Vertue, *Note books*, 3.38–9, 6.200–01 · A. Bolton and H. D. Hendry, eds., 'Engravings of St. Paul's Cathedral and part II of the building accounts for the years 1685–95', *Wren Society*, 14 (1937), ix–xiv · George Clarke print collection, prints.worc.ox.ac.uk/about. html, Worcester College, Oxford · *A catalogue of maps, prints, copy-books &c. from off copper plates, printed for John Bowles and Son* [1753], 39 · *A catalogue of maps, prints, copy-books, &c. from off copper-plates, which are printed for, and sold by Henry Overton* (1754), 23 · T. Clayton, *The English print, 1688–1802* (1997) · E. Harris and N. Savage, *British architectural books and writers, 1556–1785* (1990) · T. P. Connor, 'The making of *Vitruvius Britannicus*', *Architectural History*, 20 (1977), 14–30

Hulse, Edward (1638–1711), physician, was born in Stanny, Cheshire, in 1638. He matriculated at Emmanuel College, Cambridge, in 1656, graduated BA in 1657, and MA in 1660, and was ejected from the college for nonconformity soon after the Restoration. His name appears in the Leiden register of students of medicine, under the date of 4 July 1668. He graduated MD there about 1669, became physician to the court of the prince of Orange, and was incorporated MD at Oxford on 20 December 1670, on the nomination of the prince. He joined the Royal College of Physicians in 1675, became a fellow in 1677, censor in 1682, and subsequently Harveian orator in 1704, and treasurer from 1704 to 1709. On 28 January 1672 at St Helen's, Bishopsgate, London, he married Dorothy, daughter of Thomas Westrow, of Twittenham, Kent, sheriff of London, and MP for Hythe during the Long Parliament; Sir Edward *Hulse (1682–1759) was their son. Hulse, of Baldwin's Park, Kent, died on 3 December 1711, and is described in the annals of the college as 'a person of great skill in the practice of physick'. CHARLES CREIGHTON, *rev.* MICHAEL BEVAN

Sources Venn, *Alum. Cant.* · Burke, *Peerage* · Munk, *Roll* · IGI
Likenesses oils, *c.*1690, Breamore House, Hampshire

Hulse, Sir Edward, first baronet (1682–1759), physician, was the eldest son of Edward *Hulse (1638–1711), physician, and his wife, Dorothy, daughter of Thomas Westrow. He graduated MB at Emmanuel College, Cambridge, in 1704, and MD in 1717. He married on 15 January 1713 Elizabeth, daughter of Sir Richard Levett, who had been lord mayor in 1700; they had four sons and a daughter. He joined the Royal College of Physicians, London, in 1717, became censor for the first time in 1720, and consiliarius in 1750, 1751, and 1753.

Hulse was one of the leading physicians in London, along with John Freind, Richard Mead, Hans Sloane, and others. He was one of Freind's sureties before the latter was committed to the Tower in 1723 on a charge of high treason. He was described as one of the 'whig doctors' by a later commentator, and is said to have differed so seriously with Freind over the case of Lord Townshend that he withdrew, declaring that Townshend must die if Freind had his way (Townshend recovered, having said he would live or die by the hands of Freind). Hulse was first physician to George II, and was made a baronet on 7 February 1739. In 1745 he was attacked with others in several pamphlets, on their treatment of Robert Walpole, earl of Orford, who had died of kidney stones while in his care.

Hulse retired from practice some years before his death, and lived at his house on Dartford heath, Kent. In 1738 he purchased the estate of Breamore, Hampshire, which was held by his successors in the title. In his old age he became convinced that he would die in penury, a fear which his attendants overcame by putting guineas regularly into the pocket where he used to deposit his fees. Hulse died on 10 April 1759 in Golden Square, London, and was buried along with his wife in the churchyard of Wilmington, Kent, where a monument was erected to his memory. His son Edward, who succeeded to the title, was father of Sir Samuel Hulse. Another son, Richard, inherited his house and manor at Dartford. In 1815 his granddaughter Charlotte married the philanthropist Sir Thomas Barnard (1750–1818).

CHARLES CREIGHTON, *rev.* PATRICK WALLIS

Sources Venn, *Alum. Cant.* · Munk, *Roll* · E. Hasted, *The history and topographical survey of the county of Kent*, 2nd edn, 12 vols. (1797–1801) · Nichols, *Lit. anecdotes* · Burke, *Peerage* (1857) · *GM*, 1st ser., 29 (1759), 194
Likenesses F. Cotes, pastel drawing, 1757, Breamore House, Hampshire · J. Watson, mezzotint, 1757 (after F. Cotes), BM, Wellcome L.

Hulse, John (1708–1790), benefactor, was born at Middlewich, Cheshire, on 15 March 1708, the eldest of the nineteen children of Thomas Hulse of Elworth Hall, Sandbach, Cheshire, and Anne Webb of Middlewich. After attending Congleton and Stockport grammar schools he entered St John's College, Cambridge, in September 1724. Soon afterwards his grandfather, to whom he owed his education, died, and his refusal to comply with his father's wish to sell a part of the entailed estates led to a lifelong alienation. College exhibitions enabled him to continue at Cambridge, and he graduated BA in 1728. He was ordained in 1732 and served first at Yoxall, Staffordshire, and afterwards at Goostry, Cheshire. In 1733 he married Mary Hall of Hermitage, near Holmes Chapel, Cheshire; their only child, a son, Edward, died aged twenty-two. On the death of his father in 1753 Hulse inherited Elworth, and lived there in seclusion on account of his delicate health. Hulse was of diminutive stature and an irritable temperament. He was well versed in medicine, and played the violin, flute, and organ. These accomplishments, coupled with his retired lifestyle, caused him to be regarded by the peasantry as a magician. He died at home on 13 or 14 December 1790 and was buried in the parish church at Middlewich.

In his will Hulse left estates in Cheshire to the University of Cambridge for the advancement and reward of religious learning. The original bequest provided for the maintenance of two divinity scholars at St John's College, the foundation of a dissertation prize, the creation and support of the office of Christian advocate, and finally for the establishment of the post of Hulsean lecturer or Christian preacher. According to the will the advocate was 'to prepare some proper and judicious answers to all … new and popular cavils and objections against Christian Revealed Religion', while the Hulsean lectures were 'to show evidence for Revealed Religion and to demonstrate [in] a most convincing and persuasive manner the Truth and Excellence of Christianity' (Sykes, 347). In their promotion of conservative Anglicanism and criticism of scepticism the Hulsean lectures followed a similar line to the Bampton lectures, established in Oxford in 1780, to which they were probably a response. By a revision of the statute in August 1860 the office of Hulsean professor of divinity was substituted for that of Christian advocate, and the office of Hulsean lecturer was considerably modified. In 1934 a further change saw the merging of the Hulsean and Norrisian professorship to form the Norris–Hulme professorship.

GORDON GOODWIN, *rev.* PHILIP CARTER

Sources Venn, *Alum. Cant.* · *GM*, 1st ser., 60 (1790), 1152 · J. Gascoigne, *Cambridge in the age of the Enlightenment* (1989) · N. Sykes, *Church and state in England in the XVIII century* (1934)

Wealth at death founded professorship and two scholarships at Cambridge

Hulse, Sir Samuel (1747/8–1837), army officer and court official, was the second son of Sir Edward Hulse, second baronet (*d.* 1800), and his wife, Hannah, the daughter of Samuel Vanderplank, a merchant, and the grandson of the physician Sir Edward *Hulse. He entered the army in the 1st foot guards as ensign on 17 December 1761. As captain and lieutenant-colonel he was present with his battalion during the Gordon riots in 1780. In 1793, as brevet-colonel and regimental first major, he commanded the 1st battalion of his regiment with the duke of York at the siege of Valenciennes, in the brilliant affair under Major-General Gerard Lake at Lincelles, and during the operations before Dunkirk, until October, when he returned home on promotion. After returning to Flanders as major-general in May 1794, he commanded a brigade in some minor affairs near Tournai and in the retreat to Bremen. Early in 1795 he was appointed to the home staff, and commanded at Brighton for three years.

In 1798 Hulse became lieutenant-general and was dispatched to Ireland with reinforcements, including a brigade of guards. He returned to his command at Brighton in November of that year, served under the duke of York in the expedition to The Helder in 1799, and afterwards succeeded Lord Grey in command of the south-eastern district. He became a full general in 1803, and was appointed lieutenant-governor of Chelsea Hospital in 1806 and governor in 1820. One of the first to be appointed by George III to the suite of the young prince of Wales (afterwards George IV), he was for many years the prince's treasurer and receiver-general. At the prince's coronation as George IV, Hulse, one of the two eldest generals, was created field marshal. He became treasurer of George IV's household, and was vice-chamberlain from 1827 until the king's death three years later. Hulse was a GCH and a privy councillor and colonel successively of the 56th, 19th, and 62nd foot. He died at his residence in Chelsea Hospital on 1 January 1837, aged eighty-nine, and was buried in the family vault at Erith, Kent. He was survived by his widow, Charlotte, who died on 5 February 1842.

H. M. CHICHESTER, *rev.* PHILIP CARTER

Sources Burke, *Peerage* · *GM*, 2nd ser., 7 (1837), 320 · *Army List* · F. W. Hamilton, *The origin and history of the first or grenadier guards*, 3 vols. (1874)

Likenesses T. Hudson, double portrait, oils (as a child; with his brother), Breamore House, Hampshire · R. J. Lane, lithograph (after S. Lane), BM, NPG · S. Lane, portrait, Breamore House, Hampshire

Hulton, Sir Edward, baronet (1869–1925), newspaper proprietor, was born on 3 March 1869 at 4 Fir Street, Hulme, Manchester, the second son of Edward Hulton (*d.* 1904), newspaper proprietor, and his wife, Mary Mosley.

Hulton, a Roman Catholic, was educated at St Bede's College, Manchester, but left school at sixteen to learn how to manage newspapers, serving an informal apprenticeship in his father's Manchester-based business. Hulton senior was an astute entrepreneur who built up a stable of popular titles, including the *Sporting Chronicle* (1871), the *Athletic News* (1875), and the *Sunday Chronicle* (1885). By the mid-1890s he was ready to relinquish the day-to-day control of his business to Edward, who initiated a period of rapid expansion, adding the *Manchester Evening Chronicle* (1897) and the *Daily Dispatch* (1900) to the Hulton list. The *Evening Chronicle* was especially successful and quickly acquired the largest circulation of any evening paper outside London.

When Hulton senior died in 1904 Edward's two younger sisters indicated that they were unhappy to see the business pass into his hands; they shared, perhaps, their mother's anxieties regarding his interest in racing and coursing. However, he retained the confidence and support of his two elder sisters, and it soon became clear that their judgement was sound. Hulton, who registered his racing colours under the name of Lytham in order not to alarm his mother, devoted much time and expense to his sporting passions but could never have been accused of neglecting the business. His office regime, characterized by an early start to the day and a late finish, with a minimum of delegation, has been described as 'puritanical'. By 1923, when he retired, the Hulton empire had grown to incorporate eight titles generating average pre-tax profits of around £377,000 (Griffiths, *Plant here the Standard*, 210).

It could never be said of the Hultons, father or son, that they grew rich by overestimating public taste. Their approach to the newspaper business perfectly illustrated the idea that journalism was simply 'a branch of commerce' (Jones, 173). Hulton newspapers sought primarily to entertain their readers. They offered an unpretentious diet of human interest news stories, serials, competitions, and other bright features. Though he was a Conservative, Hulton did not seek political influence through his newspapers; he was more interested in sport than politics and correctly judged that most of his readers shared the same innocent priorities. He also recognized the possibilities of picture journalism, establishing the *Daily Sketch* in 1909 in direct competition with Harmsworth's *Daily Mirror* (established in 1903). The *Sketch*, with its front and back pages given over to photographs, was started in Manchester but quickly moved to London, allowing Hulton to establish a base in Fleet Street. Hulton bought the London *Evening*

Standard for £50,000 in 1915, hoping to repeat his earlier success with the *Evening Chronicle* in Manchester. The *Standard* experienced a 'Lancashire invasion' (Colley, 198) as Hulton imported journalistic talent from the north. His management style remained highly personal; it was said that he defused industrial disputes by dispensing racing tips to disgruntled printers (Griffiths, *Plant here the Standard*, 197). He was sufficiently confident of his London base by 1915 to launch a new illustrated paper, the *Sunday Herald*. This was not, however, the success that Hulton anticipated, principally because Rothermere rushed out the rival *Sunday Pictorial* two weeks before the *Herald* made its début, thus gaining the former a flying start which it never lost. Hulton bitterly resented Rothermere's intervention, believing that his rival had made unfair use of confidential information lodged with trade associations (Camrose, 61). This episode helps to explain Hulton's reluctance to sell his newspaper interests to Rothermere when ill health forced him to retire in 1923.

By then Hulton's private company owned eight newspapers. The morning and evening titles had a combined circulation of about 2 million; the circulation of his Sunday and weekly titles was estimated at about 4.5 million. When negotiations with the Berry brothers broke down, Beaverbrook, knowing that Hulton would not sell direct to Rothermere, intervened. Beaverbrook's down payment of £300,000 secured the Hulton papers in a deal worth between £5 million and £6 million. He then sold the titles on to Rothermere, retaining a controlling interest in the *Evening Standard* as commission (Chisholm and Davie, 216).

Hulton was married twice: first to a Miss Turnbull, the daughter of a Manchester solicitor. After that marriage was dissolved (about 1915) he married Millicent Warris, who survived him. There were two children, a son and a daughter, of his second marriage. His son, Sir Edward George Warris *Hulton (1906–1988) was also a magazine publisher, and his publications included *Hulton's Weekly* and *Picture Post*. The elder Sir Edward accepted a baronetcy from Lloyd George in 1921, having been promised it would have a special remainder allowing his son (who had been born out of wedlock) to inherit. However, this did not materialize, and the baronetcy became extinct. His son was awarded a knighthood in 1957.

Hulton retained his interest in sport almost to the end of his life. He owned two winners of the Waterloo cup, the premier prize in hare coursing, and his horses won the Gimcrack Stakes at York three years in succession in 1911, 1912, and 1913. The Epsom Derby eluded him but he did win the wartime substitute race at Newmarket with Finfinella in 1916. His most successful filly was Straitlace, winner of the Oaks in 1924. Hulton was as competitive in sport as he was in business. With his weatherbeaten complexion he could have passed for a north country landowner; he looked every inch the country sportsman.

After purchasing the *Evening Standard* Hulton moved from Manchester to Surrey, taking up residence in Leatherhead, first at Tyrrell's Wood in 1918 and then, a year later, at Downside. He died there on 23 May 1925, after a protracted period of illness and depression. After a funeral at Farm Street, Kensington, he was buried at Putney Vale cemetery. His declining years were stressful; according to his son 'he could not bring himself to think about death in a rational way' (Hulton, 147).

DILWYN PORTER

Sources D. Griffiths, *Plant here The Standard* (1996) · Viscount Camrose [W. E. Berry], *British newspapers and their controllers* (1947) · D. Griffiths, ed., *The encyclopedia of the British press, 1422–1992* (1992) · *The Times* (25 May 1925) · *Dorking Advertiser* (30 May 1925) · *Newspaper World* (30 May 1925) · E. Hulton, *When I was a child* (1952) · A. Chisholm and M. Davie, *Beaverbrook: a life* (1992) · C. Shaw and R. P. T. Davenport-Hines, 'Hulton, Sir Edward', *DBB* · *CGPLA Eng. & Wales* (1925) · K. Jones, *Fleet Street and Downing Street* (1920) · W. Colley, *News hunter* (1936) · *DNB*
Archives FILM BFI NFTVA, amateur film footage
Wealth at death £2,222,471 5s. 4d.: probate, 30 June 1925, *CGPLA Eng. & Wales*

Hulton, Sir Edward George Warris (1906–1988), magazine publisher and writer, was born on 29 November 1906 in London, the only son and elder child (the daughter died when she was twenty-two, in 1932) of Sir Edward *Hulton, baronet (1869–1925), of Downside, Surrey, a Manchester newspaper publisher, whose business expanded to include the London *Evening Standard* and the *Daily Sketch*. His mother, Millicent Warris, a beautiful actress, daughter of John Warris, was Edward Hulton's second wife, but the couple were unable to marry until ten years after their son's birth, and so the baronetcy conferred on Edward Hulton in 1921 became extinct on his death in 1925. Hulton was a lonely, sensitive child. His parents descended at the weekend, when his mother would dote on him, while his father, ambitious for the boy's success, was awkward and irascible. On medical advice his father gave up the newspaper business in 1923, selling it to Lord Beaverbrook. From Harrow School, Hulton won a history scholarship to Brasenose College, Oxford, which he entered in 1925 and where he edited the undergraduate magazine *Cherwell* and spoke frequently in Oxford Union debates. He left in December 1926 without a degree.

Hulton was called to the bar at the Inner Temple in 1936. He had stood unsuccessfully as a Conservative unionist in the general elections of 1929 (the Leek division of Staffordshire) and 1931 (Harwich). Not until he was thirty did he realize control over his father's fortune and set about becoming a publisher in his own right. He founded the Hulton Press in 1937, with the prosaic purchase of *Farmers' Weekly*. The business grew to include a variety of magazines, such as *World Review* and *Leader Magazine*. His children's magazines, notably *Eagle* and *Girl*, were highly successful in their day and set new standards of content and design. But the weekly publication which made Hulton widely known was *Picture Post*, launched on 1 October 1938. Its genius was the Hungarian refugee Stefan Lorant, who had founded (and now sold to Hulton) the popular monthly pocket magazine *Lilliput*. Under the steadying influence of Hulton's manager, Maxwell Raison, and Lorant's successor, Thomas *Hopkinson, *Picture Post* developed a style of photo-journalism in which striking pictures and design were supported by good writing and a progressive editorial line. For more than a decade this formula was popular and profitable, with sales of nearly 1.5 million in the 1940s. Hulton used the magazine to boost the war effort, pioneering (and initially funding) the Home Guard training school at Osterley Park, Middlesex, in 1940, and briefly even organizing the private supply of weapons from the USA. In August 1945 he gave 'a resounding welcome' to the government formed by C. R. Attlee. 'I am not personally a socialist ... Yet I rejoice that latter-day conservatism has been overthrown.' This attitude was foreshadowed by *Picture Post*'s publication of a post-war 'Plan for Britain' in 1941 and by Hulton's involvement in lobbying activities such as the progressive 1941 Committee, of which he was one of the founders and which met regularly in his house, and in support of the report by Sir William Beveridge. His book *The New Age* (1943) summed up his support for a mixed economy and welfare state.

Hulton blamed shifts in reading habits more than the growth of television for *Picture Post*'s decline in the 1950s. His renewed support for the Conservative Party provoked a break with Hopkinson, who resigned in 1950 when Hulton refused to publish a story about the ill-treatment of North Korean prisoners of war. A vacillating market strategy, frequent changes of editor, and mounting losses led Hulton to close the magazine in 1957. Two years later the Hulton Press was taken over by Odhams.

Increasingly Hulton spent time on European affairs. He was editor-in-chief of *European Review* and held office in the European Atlantic Group (president 1969–70), the European League for Economic Cooperation, and the British council of the European Movement. In 1957 he was knighted and in 1969 he received the NATO peace medal. The Hulton Picture Library, later to become the Hulton Getty Collection, which contained photographs taken for *Picture Post*, was founded in 1947.

Hulton had a lively, enquiring mind, as ready to experiment with a model farm at Salperton, his estate village in Gloucestershire, as with the possibilities of a new Sunday newspaper in the 1950s. He belonged to half a dozen London clubs and was fond of social life. He could be brusque and changeable in his opinions. Hopkinson found him donnish and kind-hearted but difficult to work with.

Hulton was stout, shortish, and florid. His manner was vague and authoritative, as if he were accustomed to both giving orders and having them disobeyed. His dress was always formal, as were his manners. He married first, in 1927, Kira Pavlovna, daughter of General Pavel Goudime-Levkovich, of the imperial Russian army. There were no children. The marriage was dissolved in 1932 and in 1941 he again married a Russian, Princess Nika Yuryevich, whose father, Prince Sergey Yuryevich, was a sculptor and had been a chamberlain at the court of the tsar. Of this marriage there were two sons and a daughter. The marriage was dissolved in 1966, but the couple lived together for the last nine years of Hulton's life. Hulton died on 8 October 1988 in his sleep at his home, 11 Carlton Gardens, St James's, London, after a long illness.

COLIN SEYMOUR-URE, *rev.*

Sources E. Hulton, *The new age* (1943) · E. Hulton, *When I was a child* (1952) · T. Hopkinson, ed., *Picture Post* (1970) · *The Times* (10 Oct 1988) · *CGPLA Eng. & Wales* (1988)
Archives HLRO, corresp. with Lord Beaverbrook · King's Lond., Liddell Hart C., corresp. with Sir B. H. Liddell Hart
Likenesses photographs, 1928–54, Hult. Arch.
Wealth at death £1,141,214: probate, 15 Dec 1988, *CGPLA Eng. & Wales*

Hulton, William Adam (1802–1887), lawyer and antiquary, was born in Preston, Lancashire, on 18 October 1802 into one of Lancashire's oldest 'county' families, a son of Lieutenant-Colonel Henry Hulton (*b.* 1765) and his wife, Louisa Caroline, *née* Campbell. Educated at Warrington and then Manchester grammar school, he entered the Inner Temple in 1822, and was called to the bar in 1827. He went on the northern circuit, becoming a commissioner of bankrupts for Bolton. From 1831 to 1849 he was treasurer of the county of Lancaster in succession to his father. He was also assessor to the Lancaster sheriff's court, and on the reform of the county court system in 1847 was one of many judges of local courts who became judges of county courts. In 1832 he married Dorothy Anne, daughter of Edward Gorst of Preston and sister of Sir John Eldon Gorst. The couple lived at Hurst Grange, Penwortham, near Preston, and had eight children.

Hulton wrote *A Treatise on the Law of Convictions* (1835), and edited the travel journal of his late brother Jessop. He joined the council of the Chetham Society in 1848, and edited two of their early publications. He retired in 1886 and died at Hurst Grange, after a long illness, on 3 March 1887. He was buried on 5 March in Penwortham church; the lich-gate there is a memorial to him.

C. W. SUTTON, *rev.* PATRICK POLDEN

Sources *Law Times* (19 March 1887), 367 · *Law Journal* (12 March 1887), 156 · *The Times* (3 July 1887) · *Solicitors' Journal*, 31 (1886–7), 335 · Boase, *Mod. Eng. biog.* · J. Foster, *Men-at-the-bar: a biographical hand-list of the members of the various inns of court*, 2nd edn (1885) · J. F. Smith, ed., *The admission register of the Manchester School, with some notes of the more distinguished scholars*, 3/1, Chetham Society, 93 (1874), 109 · Burke, *Gen. GB* · J. Whishaw, *Synopsis of the members of the English bar* (1835) · *Law Journal* (7 Aug 1886), 188 · *CGPLA Eng. & Wales* (1888) · Allibone, *Dict.* · J. Foster, ed., *Pedigrees of the county families of England*, 1: *Lancashire* (1873) · private information (1891)
Wealth at death £48,399 9s.: resworn probate, April 1888, *CGPLA Eng. & Wales* (1887)

Humberston, Francis Mackenzie. *See* Mackenzie, Francis Humberston, Baron Seaforth and Mackenzie of Kintail (1754–1815).

Humberston, Thomas Frederick Mackenzie (1753–1783), army officer, a lineal descendant of the old Scottish earls of Seaforth, whose estates were forfeited in 1715, was born on 28 September 1753, the eldest son of Major William Mackenzie (*d.* 12 March 1770) and his wife, Mary (*d.* 19 February 1813, at Hartley, Hertfordshire), the daughter of Matthew Humberston of Lincolnshire. In June 1771 he was gazetted cornet, under the name Mackenzie, in the 1st King's dragoon guards, in which he became lieutenant in 1775 and captain in 1777. He appears to have assumed his mother's maiden name of Humberston on coming of age. He helped his chief and kinsman Kenneth Mackenzie, who held the recovered Seaforth estates and had been created Lord Ardlive, Viscount Fortross, and earl of Seaforth, in the peerage of Ireland, to raise a corps of highlanders (the 78th foot) to serve during the American War of Independence. Recruiting in the highlands was difficult—as Humberston wrote in a series of letters to Lord Grenville in 1778–9—but he hoped thereby to advance his army career. The new regiment was officered chiefly from the clan Mackenzie, the men being from the western highlands and isles. Humberston was transferred to the regiment as captain in January 1778, and became major in it the year after. He was present with five companies at the repulse of an attempted French landing in St Ouen's Bay, Jersey, on 1 May 1779. In the same year Lord Seaforth, being greatly embarrassed, made over the Seaforth estates to Humberston for £100,000.

On 5 August 1780 Humberston was appointed lieutenant-colonel commandant of the new 100th foot and on 13 March 1781 he embarked with it as part of an expedition under General Medows and Commodore Johnstone, destined for the Cape of Good Hope. While watering in Porto Praya Bay, Cape Verde Islands, the expedition was attacked by a French naval squadron, which was beaten off after a sharp fight. Humberston, who was on shore, swam under fire back to his ship. On reaching the Cape of Good Hope, they found that the Dutch garrison had been reinforced, and the commodore returned home, leaving the troops to proceed to India under convoy. General Medows and the main body of the troops sailed for Madras while Humberston, commanding parts of two regiments, reached Bombay on 22 January 1782 and six days later also sailed for Madras. The East India Company was engaged in two wars against Indian princes, the Marathas in north-west India and Haidar Ali of Mysore in the Carnatic, in the south-east. Royal troops and naval units were assisting the Madras army against Haidar and against French and Dutch settlements on the eastern Coromandel coast and on the western Malabar coast. Humberston played a small, somewhat inglorious, independent role on the Malabar coast during 1782. The British command structure was also complex and confused, resulting in Humberston's being given contradictory orders and unfulfilled promises of supplies and reinforcements. There was a general agreement that, with the Anglo-Maratha wars winding down, but with the Madras forces stymied in the Carnatic in the south-east, an assault on Haidar Ali's vulnerable conquered lands on the west coast, to be launched by the Bombay council, was highly desirable. But there were profound differences over the kind of assault. General Sir Eyre Coote in the Carnatic wanted only a distraction to draw some of Haidar's forces to the west, which required only a low-level operation on Malabar, probably confined to the coast. The Madras civilian council, however, wanted a major campaign to penetrate inland eastwards from Malabar to link up with a force coming west from the Carnatic to attack Mysore.

Humberston, with forces only suitable for Coote's strategy, strove to realize the grander Madras plan. On 13 February he called in at Calicut, recently captured by an older East India Company army officer, Major Abington, and a body of sepoys, for resupply. But because of strong French naval forces blocking his way round to Madras on the east coast of India, Humberston decided to stay to see what he could do on the western Malabar coast. Abington (later backed by Bombay) disputed Humberston's right to take over command since he had not been ordered to Calicut, and also advised against a penetrative strategy inland given the slim forces at Humberston's disposal compared with the tens of thousands that the French ally Haidar Ali could throw at him, combined with the uncertain support of local rebel forces and the nearness of the monsoon. After resigning his local command, Abington complained to the Bombay council (who were also angry at Humberston's impetuous initiative, because it compromised their plans for an assault on Mangalore, 120 miles north of Calicut, and Haidar's major coastal possession) that Humberston had accused him of 'disgraceful inactivity', and that the colonel was 'possessed full of the ideas of European war, where carrying fire and sword thro' a Country is often the only object of a Campaign', not appreciating the necessity, in India, for 'conciliating the minds of the people to us and strengthening ourselves with their assistance' (Major Abington to Bombay council, 28 May 1782, BL OIOC, range D, 67.417–31).

An initial foray by Humberston in April 1782, with between 1000 and 2000 men plus local rebels, for small loss twice defeated a Mysore force of 7000, inflicting casualties and taking prisoner 2000 men before having to retire to Calicut on the outbreak of the monsoon. Then in September, with the monsoon still raging, the impatient Humberston, after a bout of dysentery, launched an expeditionary force from Paniani, on the coast 50 miles south, up the Paniani River. He aimed to take Palghatcherry Fort, 60 miles inland, guarding the pass into the interior, where, encouraged by the ardent young Madras civil servant in Tanjore John Sulivan, he hoped to link up with a force striking inland from the Carnatic and attack Coimbatore. Humberston, with very sketchy intelligence of the terrain and on the state of Palghatcherry, pressed on another 30 miles when he had to leave his heavy guns behind at Ramgerry owing to inadequate draught oxen. He found the fort stronger than expected and when a well-directed enemy sortie destroyed his provisions on 21 October, he had to withdraw, deluged by the monsoon and spurred on by Bombay orders to return to the coast and by Tipu Sultan, Haidar's son, on his heels with 20,000 cavalry and a French column of infantry and artillery. On 20 November he got his small force back to Paniani without loss; at one point his troops had to ford the torrential river up to their chins. Humberston found himself on his return superseded by Colonel MacLeod, of the 73rd foot, sent round from Madras. Thus ended Humberston's one taste of independent command, creditable for its spirit perhaps but reckless given the caution urged by a junior but more experienced company officer, his lack of reliable intelligence, and the likely hostility of the weather.

As second-in-command, Humberston supported Mac-Leod in repulsing a major attack by Tipu against the only partly fortified Paniani on 29 November, before the sultan withdrew to Seringapatam to take control of Mysore on Haidar's death. In the interim, on Lord Seaforth's death at sea, Humberston learned he had become lieutenant-colonel commandant of his old regiment, the 78th foot, then serving in the Carnatic. Humberston, however, remained on the Malabar coast, where in January 1783 he accompanied MacLeod to join the force of General Mathews, the company commander-in-chief of the Bombay army, in his initially successful attack on the Bednur country and Mangalore to the north. MacLeod and Humberston quarrelled with Mathews over his strategy and distribution of prize money and withdrew to Bombay to complain to the council. In consequence, and because Mathews was disobeying their orders, the council in April 1783 ordered Mathews's suspension and replacement by MacLeod and Humberston. On their way south their ships were attacked by Maratha pirates. Humberston was wounded by a 4 lb ball and later died, aged twenty-eight, at the Maratha port of Gheria on 30 April 1783.

Contemporary accounts describe Humberston as a young man of many accomplishments, and of brilliant promise in his profession. He was unmarried but left an illegitimate son, Thomas B. Mackenzie Humberston, who fell, a captain in the 78th Ross-shire Buffs, at Ahmednagar in 1803. He was succeeded in his estates by his brother Francis Mackenzie Humberston [see Mackenzie, Francis Humberston (1754–1815)], afterwards Lord Seaforth and Mackenzie.   H. M. CHICHESTER, rev. G. J. BRYANT

Sources Fortescue, *Brit. army* · M. Wilks, *Historical sketches of the south of India, in an attempt to trace the history of Mysoor*, 3 vols. (1810–17) · Consultations of the Madras and Bombay select committees, 1782, BL · Anderson, *Scot. nat.* · R. Cannon, ed., *Historical record of the seventy-second regiment, or the duke of Albany's own highlanders* (1848) · A. N. Gilbert, 'Military recruitment and career advancement in the eighteenth century: two case studies', *Journal of the Society for Army Historical Research*, 57 (1979), 34–44 · C. A. Bayly, *Indian society and the making of the British empire* (1988), vol. 2/1 of *The new Cambridge history of India*, ed. G. Johnson
Archives BL OIOC, corresp. and journal, home misc. series | BL, letters to Charles Francis Grenville, etc., Add. MS 42071

Humbert, Albert Jenkins (1821–1877), architect, was born in Lambeth, Surrey, on 4 July 1821, the second among the three children of Lewis Humbert (1789–1875), clerk to the inspector of military stores, East India House, London, and his wife, Louisa (1794/5–1861×71). His parents were both born in London. The loss of Humbert's RIBA nomination papers makes it difficult to document his early architectural training. Between 1846 and 1848 he was an architectural student in Italy with Charles Frederick Reeks, who had studied under James Pennethorne in the Office of Woods and Forests, and Lewis Cubitt. Reeks and Humbert became partners on their return to Britain. Their first major commission was to devise a ground plan and design houses for the crown lands development of Hastings, Sussex, between 1849 and c.1852. They set up an office at 15

Pelham Crescent, Hastings. The development comprises Carlisle Parade, Robertson Terrace, Robertson Street, Trinity Street, and Harold Street.

According to Humbert's obituary in *The Builder* (5 January 1877), Reeks and Humbert 'rebuilt' St Giles, Bodiam, Sussex, in 1853. The chancel had been restored by R. C. Carpenter (1812–1855) before 1845. The later work included rebuilding the fourteenth-century north and south aisles and adding a north porch and vestry.

In 1849 the advowson of St Giles's Church had been purchased by Lewis Cubitt's brother the builder Thomas Cubitt, and in 1851 Thomas Cubitt's son-in-law Charles Parker was installed as rector. The Cubitt connection proved crucial in Humbert's future career, as it was Thomas Cubitt who introduced Humbert to the prince consort in a letter of 9 February 1854. Although still in partnership with Reeks, Humbert's first independent commission was to rebuild John Nash's chancel of St Mildred's, Whippingham, Isle of Wight (1854–5), which Queen Victoria and the royal family attended when residing at Osborne. The chancel was enlarged by the addition of south and north aisles for the use of the royal family and royal household respectively. Later in 1855 the prince appointed Humbert to rebuild Osborne Cottage, Whippingham, in brick (1856–8).

In 1856 Reeks and Humbert entered the public offices competition for a new War Office in Whitehall. Although their design was unsuccessful, it was nevertheless considered worthy of a premium by the three architects appointed by a committee of the House of Commons in 1858 to investigate the competition. In 1859 structural instability prompted the prince consort to demolish the rest of St Mildred's, Whippingham, and to rebuild it. Humbert was again chosen. The prince suggested the basic external form of the new church, but Humbert produced over 200 sketches and working drawings. A contemporary thought that the broad crossing tower with its timber lantern, and the attenuated steeples both on the tower and the west gable, had 'more the appearance of a Continental than an English church' (Field, 5). The main work was undertaken between 1860 and 1861, although the font—apparently inspired by Princess Louise but detailed by Humbert—was not installed until 1864. During this time Humbert also designed a new school at Whippingham, which was constructed in 1861–3.

In 1859 the prince consort invited Humbert to work up initial sketches by Professor Ludwig Gruner from Dresden (Queen Victoria's 'adviser in art') for a mausoleum for the duchess of Kent. The mausoleum is sited on a small artificial mound in the grounds of the duchess's home, Frogmore House, near Windsor. It comprises sixteen granite Ionic columns around a domed cella inspired by the mausoleum at Castle Howard, by Nicholas Hawksmoor, which was admired by the queen. Within the *mount sanctitée* is a vault containing the sarcophagus. That Humbert, rather than Gruner, was primarily responsible for the details in Louis XVI style emerges from drawings in the Royal Library, Windsor, which reveal Humbert experimenting with variant designs for the exterior.

The death of the prince consort on 14 December 1861 deprived Humbert of his most powerful patron, while at the same time presenting him with the opportunity to build his masterpiece: the royal mausoleum at Frogmore (1862–71). Queen Victoria swiftly consulted Gruner and Humbert, and on 13 January 1862 settled on Gruner's design: a central dome on a Latin cross plan with a Romanesque exterior and a High Renaissance interior decorated with Raphaelesque frescoes. Once again Humbert was the executant architect. He refined Gruner's proportions, and undertook all the working drawings. Work began in January, and Humbert produced the finished design by 4 April 1862. Some features, such as the triple lancet windows, are inspired by the mausoleum to Duke Ernest I of Saxe-Coburg and Gotha, which Prince Albert and his brother had commissioned from Gustav Eberhard. The tomb, by Baron Carlo Marochetti, was completed in 1867, but work on the interior decoration continued until 1871. Humbert also designed the nearby lich-gate and royal mausoleum lodge in 1864.

In 1864 Queen Victoria also commissioned Humbert to design a monument to the prince consort for the royal pew at St Mildred's, Whippingham. He produced a classically conceived design with Gothic detailing using various marbles, supporting a niche which houses a bas-relief of a medallion of the prince consort flanked by two angels. William Theed was responsible for the carving. A less elaborate version of Humbert's design was repeated in 1879 for the nearby memorial to Princess Alice.

The prince of Wales (later Edward VII) purchased Sandringham House, Norfolk, in 1862. Humbert was appointed to rebuild the property. He created a brick and stone Jacobean-style country house with details adapted from Blickling Hall, Norfolk. Work started on the service wing in 1866. The main house was completed in 1870, including a bowling alley inspired by one at Trentham, Staffordshire, by Charles Barry. Further additions in the same style were made by Colonel R. W. Edis in 1883 and 1891.

Professionally, Humbert was a diligent and compliant architect. He was not wedded to a particular style, but could transform his clients' ideas into carefully detailed drawings. From c.1854 to 1860 he shared drawing offices in Whitehall, London, with C. F. Reeks. He never married, but lived with his parents, first at 28 Park Road, Stoke Newington, London, then at 27 Fitzroy Square, London, from 1860. On 10 March 1856 Humbert was elected an associate of the RIBA, and he became a fellow on 10 January 1859. His mother died between 1861 and 1871. After the death of his father in 1875 Humbert contracted cirrhosis of the liver (presumably a result of alcoholism) and moved in with his only brother, the Revd Lewis Macnaughton Humbert (1819–1896), author of *Memorials of the Hospital of St Cross … and Alms House of Noble Poverty* (Winchester, 1868), at the rectory, Chiddingfold, Godalming, Surrey. Around October 1877 Humbert contracted dropsy and moved to Castle Mona Hotel, Douglas, Isle of Man, in an attempt to recuperate, but he died there on 24 December 1877. He was buried in grave 899 at Braddan cemetery in

Douglas. Humbert's will was made on 29 July 1876 at Hatchett's Hotel, Piccadilly, and was proved on 7 January 1878.   MICHAEL TURNER

Sources *The Architect* (5 Jan 1878) · *The Builder* (5 Jan 1878) · *Transactions of the Royal Institute of British Architects*, 3rd ser., 15 (1908), 386–539 · *Dir. Brit. archs.*, 1.975; 2.447 · A. J. Humbert, 200 drawings of St Mildred's, Whippingham, 1859–64, English Heritage, Osborne House · C. F. Reeks, crown lands, Hastings street plan, 1849, PRO, MPEE117 · Reeks and Humbert, crown lands, Hastings, 1849–51, PRO, MPE1/958–9, 962–4, 966–7, MR1/1712 · A. J. Humbert, 17 drawings of Sandringham House, Whippingham church, and royal mausoleum, Frogmore, 1860–71, RIBA BAL, drawings collection · A. J. Humbert, drawings of duchess of Kent's mausoleum, 1860–64, Windsor Castle, royal library, 740513–740538 · A. J. Humbert, drawings of royal library, 1862–71, Windsor Castle, royal library, 740539–740594 · A. J. Humbert, drawings of Sandringham House, 1866–7, Windsor Castle, royal library, 930814–930817 · Osborne and Whippingham correspondence, RA, PP/Osborne 36, 47–8, 112–293, *passim* · Royal mausoleum, Frogmore, RA, PP/VIC/2/3494 · W. Ames, *Prince Albert and Victorian taste* (1967) · H. Hobhouse, *Thomas Cubitt master builder*, 2nd edn (1995) · *The royal mausoleum at Frogmore*, 3rd edn (1991) · 'St Giles Church, Bodiam, E Sussex', *The Ecclesiologist*, 4 (1845), 140; 17 (1856), 156–7 · W. Knolly, diary, 1867, RA, Vic/Add. C/7 · W. Field, 'Church of St Mildred Whippingham', *The Church Builder*, 5 (1863), 1–9 · H. M. Colvin, *Royal buildings* (1968) · E. Darby and N. Smith, *The cult of the prince consort* (1983) · *VCH Sussex*, 9.264–5 · *CGPLA Eng. & Wales* (1878) · IGI · Braddon cemetery, Isle of Man, gravestone 899 · Post Office Directories · membership lists, RIBA · d. cert. · will, probate department of the principal registry of the family division

Archives Windsor Castle, royal mausoleum, Frogmore papers, RA PP/VIC/2/3494 · Windsor Castle, Osborne privy purse papers, RA PP/Osborne

Wealth at death £16,000—freehold property in Pomeroy Street, Kent Road, Surrey; 6 Carlisle Parade, Hastings, crown lease: probate, 1878, *CGPLA Eng. & Wales*

Humble, George (*d.* 1640), map- and printseller, dominated the map trade in the first forty years of the seventeenth century and died a very rich man. According to R. A. Skelton he was the son of the London stationer and bookseller Thomas Humble, who published various titles between 1566 and 1581 and was buried in St Michael Cornhill in 1588. George Humble's entry into the print business came when his uncle John Sudbury (*d.* 1620), the earliest known native London print publisher, took him into partnership in 1603. Their address was at the White Horse in Pope's Head Alley, opposite the Royal Exchange.

The first great project of the partnership was the financing of John Speed's *Theatre of the Empire of Great Britaine* over the years 1608–12, for which the plates were engraved in Amsterdam by Jodocus Hondius. Sudbury and Humble were granted a privilege for twenty-one years to protect their investment in 1608. The two men published a series of superb engravings of the royal family by Renold Elstracke in the early 1610s, and in 1617 they managed to secure the services of the brilliant newcomer Simon de Passe, who had arrived in London the previous year to work for their rival, Compton Holland.

In 1615–16 Sudbury was master of the Leathersellers' Company, but there is no sign of his name on new publications after 1618. His will of December 1620 makes no mention of the printselling business or of Humble: evidently he had already transferred his entire interest in it. Humble continued at the same address, but concentrated increasingly on the map business, in which he had a virtual monopoly. In 1626 he sold some of his plates of portraits, together with writing books and drawing books, to William Peake. This may have been to raise funds for his second great project, Speed's *Prospect of the Most Famous Parts of the World*, also engraved in Amsterdam and published in 1627.

Humble had interests in other activities, for in 1639 he and a partner petitioned the House of Lords about a brewery that they wished to set up. In 1628–9 he was master of the Leathersellers' Company and in 1633 deputy of Langborn ward. He died on 7 August 1640, and in his twenty-one-page will—drawn up two years earlier—established scholarships at Oxford and Cambridge for two members of the guild and left £500 for Leathersellers' charities. He also bequeathed the company money to buy four silver tankards, which still survive. He lived in a house in Lombard Street. The business at the White Horse passed to his son William (1612–1687), who continued the map trade through the Commonwealth period but sold it to William Garrett in 1659. In 1660 he was knighted in recognition of £20,000 that he had furnished to Charles II in exile. His will, which is extremely long and complicated, shows that he had property in London, Essex, York, Lincoln, and Surrey.

ANTONY GRIFFITHS

Sources R. A. Skelton, *County atlases of the British Isles, 1579–1830: a bibliography* (1970), 233–5, 242 · A. M. Hind, *Engraving in England in the sixteenth and seventeenth centuries*, 2 (1955), 67–95 · *CSP dom.* · will, PRO, PROB 11/184 [George Humble], fol. 367 · will, PRO, PROB 11/386 [William Humble], fol. 60
Likenesses portrait, Leathersellers' Hall, London
Wealth at death very rich: PRO, PROB 11/184, fol. 367; PRO, PROB 11/386, fol. 60 [William Humble]

Humby [*née* Ayre; *other married name* Hammon], **Anne** (1800–1863?), actress, was born in London; her father was a law stationer, her mother is unknown. She studied music under Domenico Corri. Fitzgerald, who succeeded Tate Wilkinson on the York circuit, engaged her, and she first appeared about 1817 in Hull, as a singer, playing Rosina. During this first season she married William Henry Humby, a member of the Hull company, in York. In 1818 she went to Bath where she was, on 4 November, Rosetta in *Love in a Village*, and subsequently played a variety of roles, some with her husband. In 1820 she left Bath, and in 1821 she was with her husband in Dublin, where a child was born to them. She soon returned to the stage in Dublin, at the New Theatre Royal, where she was described as 'our actress of all work', but gained many good notices. She remained there until 1825. She was engaged at the Haymarket on 18 April 1825, where she appeared for several seasons before moving to Drury Lane in 1830. She had made her reputation in pert chambermaid parts as an experienced and popular soubrette, verses being addressed to her which are reproduced in Mrs Wilson's *Our Actresses*. However, when she attempted Lydia Languish at the Haymarket she failed; Mrs Wilson remembered leaving the theatre saying 'God forgive Mrs Humby

for we never will.' Recorded stage performances thereafter are sporadic.

William Humby became a dentist in Wellington Street, London, in 1831. In 1837 Anne was engaged by Macready for £6 10s. a week. She was to have appeared as Dame Quickly but the overbearing attitude of the actor Foster in Macready's company so overwhelmed her that she renounced the part. On 6 February 1844 she was Lady Clutterbuck in Boucicault's *Used up*. In 1845 she was the original Chicken in Douglas Jerrold's *Time Works Wonders*, Polly Briggs in his *Rent Day*, and Sophy Howes in his *Housekeeper*. Her husband died in Guernsey in 1847 and she appears to have lived at 198 Piccadilly from 1848 to 1851, repeating her role of Lady Clutterbuck at Windsor Castle on 4 January 1849. She last appeared as a Damsel in Barbadoes in *Drop the Curtain* on 29 November 1849. On 3 April 1854 she married, at the Episcopal chapel, St Peter's, Hammersmith, Joseph Hammon of Bridge Road, and from 1854 to 1860 or 1861 she lived at 3 Castlenau Cottages, Barnes. It is probable that she was the Ann Hammon whose death occurred at Downton, Wiltshire, on 29 September 1863, and whose estate was administered by her son John Humby, draper and bootmaker, of Downton. She is described as being a lively and amusing actress, with a pretty face and figure.

JOSEPH KNIGHT, *rev.* J. GILLILAND

Sources Mrs C. Baron-Wilson, *Our actresses*, 2 vols. (1844) · Boase, *Mod. Eng. biog.* · W. Archer, *William Charles Macready* (1890), vol. 1 of *Eminent actors*, ed. W. Archer (1890–91) · Genest, *Eng. stage* · Hall, *Dramatic ports.* · Smith's original letters, Garr. Club · *CGPLA Eng. & Wales* (1863) · *Kelly's directory of Wiltshire* (1855)
Likenesses portrait, Garr. Club, Smith's original letters · seven portraits, Harvard TC
Wealth at death under £450: administration, 22 Dec 1863, *CGPLA Eng. & Wales*

Hume [Home] **family** (*per.* 1424–1516), Scottish nobility, achieved their domination of the south-east of Scotland before the end of the fifteenth century as the result of a determined pursuit of power, at both local and national levels, over three generations.

Rise to prominence, 1424–1461 The architect of the Humes' rise was undoubtedly **Sir Alexander Hume of that ilk** (*d.* 1461), who succeeded his father in 1424 and began a policy of steady expansion in the south-east, starting from a base in the territory of the Merse, north of Berwick. By his marriage to Marion Lauder, granddaughter of Sir Robert Lauder of the Bass, some time before 11 April 1426, Hume eventually acquired lands in Berwickshire and Linlithgowshire. He stepped into the gap created by the forfeiture of Patrick Dunbar, earl of March, in 1435, to support the crown's power-broker in the area, William Douglas, earl of Angus (*d.* 1437), and acquire thereby the lands of Lintlaws, Cruiksfield, and Preston for life; and his piety found expression locally in his transformation of the chapel of St Mary of Dunglass into a collegiate church, a process completed by 1450.

In the major struggle between James II and the Black Douglases (1451–5), Sir Alexander Hume was in a difficult position, for though he had received grants from William, eighth earl of Douglas (d. 1452)—parts of the lordship of Stewarton in Ayrshire—he had also enjoyed continuing patronage from the king. Initially Hume hedged his bets, being named on the safe-conduct to go to Rome with the earl of Douglas for the papal jubilee in 1450; and he may have collected his bull of foundation for Dunglass collegiate church in person from Pope Nicholas V (r. 1447–55). However, 1451 found both Douglas and James II bidding for Hume support; wisely Sir Alexander opted for the royal side, and by 1453 he was in receipt of royal funds for the defence of Hume Castle. No king's friend—he is never to be found as a royal charter witness—Hume was nevertheless a loyal border magnate, and a natural choice to be a Scottish commissioner at the 1458 border talks at Reddenburn, which produced a truce with England and sought to close the door firmly on the forfeited Douglases. When Sir Alexander died, shortly after 3 February 1461, he left a sizeable family (five sons and two daughters) and a secure inheritance.

Consolidation: the Coldingham dispute Sir Alexander was succeeded by his eldest son, **Alexander Hume**, first Lord Hume (d. c.1491), who consolidated the family gains made by his father. Loyalty to James II during the Douglas crisis of the 1450s brought extensive rewards—royal charters of the lands of Dunglass, Hume, Sisterpath, and Kello in 1450, all united into the free barony of Hume at the end of 1451. To these lands were added Chirnside—granted on 4 February 1452, less than three weeks before James II killed the eighth earl of Douglas at Stirling—and Birgham, with a confirmation of the Hume barony in February 1453. In the next reign, Sir Alexander was confirmed in the bailiary of Coldingham, which was made a hereditary office, by the adult James III in November 1472; and Hume's second son, John, was assiduously seeking royal recognition as prior of Coldingham with his father's strong support. A regular attender at parliament since James III's assumption of personal power in 1469, Sir Alexander was created a lord of parliament, as Lord Hume, on 2 August 1473.

However, this elevation may have been little more than an attempt by the king to avoid antagonizing the Humes over a royal plan, first evolved in April 1472, to suppress the priory of Coldingham, a daughter house of Durham (in Berwickshire, where its position had become increasingly uncertain since the beginning of the Anglo-Scottish wars), and reallocate its revenues to the Chapel Royal of St Mary of the Rock, St Andrews. A revised version of this plan in 1473, envisaging a collegiate church—but *not* retaining the priory—at Coldingham, may have been intended as a further royal olive branch. However, any scheme which rejected John Hume's claim to be prior of Coldingham was doomed from the start, for the first lord, bailie of Coldingham for more than a generation, lord of parliament, and (from 1476) a march warden, found royal interference in the growing Hume empire in the southeast unwelcome, and resisted it strenuously with the committed support of his sons. The political struggle over the future of Coldingham was conducted by these younger men. Alexander Hume, the first lord, cannot be shown to

have taken an active part in politics after 1479, though he lived long enough to see Dunglass erected into a burgh of barony in June 1489, a year after James IV's accession.

Hume was the father of seven sons from two marriages. With his first wife, Mariota, heir of Landells in Berwickshire, he had four sons: Alexander, who died before his father, but already married and with two sons, Alexander (second Lord Hume) and John; John, prior of Coldingham; George of Aytoun; and Patrick of Fastcastle. The second marriage, to Margaret, daughter of Alexander, master of Montgomery in Ayrshire, produced three sons, Thomas of Langshaw, Nicholas, and David.

Conflict with James III, 1480–1488 It fell to **Alexander Hume**, second Lord Hume (d. 1506), grandson of the first lord, to steer the family safely through the turbulent 1480s to the calmer political waters of the reign of James IV. Before he succeeded to the lordship in 1492, Alexander and his kin had successfully resisted and seen off one Stewart king and received extensive rewards from his successor.

In the early 1480s the Humes were faced with a stark choice of loyalties: on the one hand James III, who had not abandoned his Coldingham plans, on the other the king's brother Alexander Stewart, duke of Albany (d. 1485), in 1482 claiming King James's throne or, at the least, control of royal government. Albany's initial successes in the 1482 crisis—entering Scotland accompanied by a huge English army—meant that he was a man who could not be ignored by border magnates such as the Humes. However, Albany was also earl of March, and as such his success would represent a threat to the Humes, who had initially come to prominence following the forfeiture of March in 1435. In the event, Alexander Hume performed a dramatic political volte-face at the end of January 1483, first joining Albany and his supporters at Dunbar Castle to plot the seizure or overthrow of James III, then moving swiftly to Edinburgh to reveal the conspiracy to the king. Hume had chosen the right side; by April 1483 Albany was a fugitive, by July he was a forfeited exile, and in a series of grants of territory within the earldom of March to Alexander and his Hume kinsmen, King James expressed his gratitude for recent Hume support. By January 1484, indeed, Alexander Hume was being described as a royal familiar.

However, the Coldingham dispute had not been resolved. It acquired a new and dangerous lease of life in 1484–5, when Alexander's uncle John Hume misused royal letters to obtain a new set of bulls from the pope, confirming his status as prior of Coldingham. In October 1487 James III effectively declared war, not only on the Humes, but on any magnates who were prepared to join them in resisting royal plans for Coldingham. Thus the king himself precipitated the revolt of 1488 which cost him his life at Sauchieburn (11 June). Throughout this crisis the Humes remained rebel hard-liners—given James III's attitude, they had no other choice—and, together with their allies and kinsmen, the Hepburns, they were the major beneficiaries of the uprising and the advent of a new king, the fifteen-year-old James IV. Thus in the parliament of October 1488 Alexander Hume was confirmed as chamberlain for life; over the next two years, he acquired the wardenship of the east march and the custody of Stirling Castle and of James IV's brother, John, earl of Mar; and the Coldingham dispute was at last resolved in favour of John Hume as prior.

Gains and losses, 1488–1516 A spate of royal grants and confirmations to Alexander Hume between 1488 and 1491—the bailiary of Ettrick Forest, the keepership of Newark, the stewardship of Dunbar, an Edinburgh town house, lands in Ayrshire, Stirlingshire, Fife, and the Merse—further increased Hume strength. When Alexander was finally served heir to his grandfather, as second Lord Hume, in 1492, he responded to royal rewards with a career of unswerving loyalty to James IV—in the front line during the Anglo-Scottish wars of 1496–7, taking a leading part in the Scottish naval expedition to Denmark in the summer of 1502, and serving as a commissioner to exchange the ratifications of the 'treaty of perpetual peace', in December of the same year. Alexander, second Lord Hume, died on 9 September 1506. He was twice married: first to Isobel Douglas, a marriage soon dissolved (May 1476) owing to its illegality in canon law; and second to Nichola Ker, daughter and heir of George Ker of Samuelston, with whom the second lord had seven sons—Alexander, who succeeded him as third Lord Hume, George *Hume (the future fourth lord), John, Patrick, William, Andrew, and David—and three daughters, Elizabeth, Mariota, and Nichola.

Alexander Hume, third Lord Hume (*d.* 1516), rapidly succeeded to his father's extensive lands and to the office of chamberlain. The third lord anticipated James IV's invasion of Northumberland in August–September 1513 by taking a large force of borderers into England on a plunder raid early in August; but while withdrawing on 13 August, he was ambushed at Milfield near Wooler by Sir Henry Bulmer, and suffered heavy losses in what came to be known as the 'ill raid'. A month later Hume fought alongside James IV at Flodden, and together with his ally Alexander Gordon, earl of Huntly (*d.* 1524), was one of the few Scottish magnates of note to survive the battle. Later—and extremely dubious—tales suggested that James IV had also survived, and that he had been murdered by the Humes. More believable is Pitscottie's story that Huntly and Hume, having fought and won in their own sector of the battlefield, refused to lend any further assistance to the Scottish army and withdrew from the field. The third lord had, after all, been in the field for a month longer than anyone else, and suffered heavily on the 'ill raid'.

In the tortuous political power struggle which followed Flodden, with the queen mother and her new husband, Archibald Douglas, sixth earl of Angus (*d.* 1557), opposing the return from France of John Stewart, duke of Albany (*d.* 1536), as governor for the infant James V, Alexander, third Lord Hume, at first sided with Albany, but then (possibly because Albany was restored to his father's earldom of March and thereby became a potential local menace to Hume dominance) changed sides, and plotted with others to obtain possession of the king. Failing in this, and once

pardoned, he again took to arms, but, along with his brother William, was tried and convicted for treason, forfeited, and beheaded in Edinburgh on 8 October 1516. He was married, between September 1513 and February 1514, to Agnes Stewart, widow of Adam Hepburn, second earl of Bothwell; they had one daughter, Janet.

Overall, Hume dominance in the south-east of Scotland, and influence in royal politics in general, had been gained—with the notable exception of the Coldingham episode—through service to the crown. Two successive dukes of Albany, acting as earls of March, presented a local threat and proved fatal to one Hume lord in 1516; but the title and many of the estates were restored to Alexander's brother George, who succeeded as fourth Lord Hume in August 1522. NORMAN MACDOUGALL

Sources J. M. Thomson and others, eds., *Registrum magni sigilli regum Scotorum / The register of the great seal of Scotland*, 11 vols. (1882–1914), vol. 2, index · *Manuscripts of the duke of Atholl … and of the earl of Home*, HMC, 26 (1891) · G. Burnett and others, eds., *The exchequer rolls of Scotland*, 23 vols. (1878–1908), vols. 7–13 · T. Dickson and J. B. Paul, eds., *Compota thesaurariorum regum Scotorum / Accounts of the lord high treasurer of Scotland*, 1–4 (1877–1902) · *CDS*, vol. 4 · *Scots peerage*, vol. 4 · W. K. Emond, 'The minority of James V, 1513–1528', PhD diss., U. St Andr., 1988 · *The historie and cronicles of Scotland … by Robert Lindesay of Pitscottie*, ed. A. J. G. Mackay, 1, STS, 42 (1899), 271–2 · C. McGladdery, *James II* (1990) · N. Macdougall, *James III: a political study* (1982) · N. Macdougall, *James IV* (1989) · J. Lesley, *The history of Scotland*, ed. T. Thomson, Bannatyne Club, 38 (1830) · R. Pitcairn, ed., *Ancient criminal trials in Scotland*, 1, Bannatyne Club, 42 (1833)
Archives NA Scot., parliamentary records, R.M.S., E.R., T.A. | PRO, Scots. documents, E39

Hume, Abraham (1614/15–1707), clergyman and ejected minister, was born at Dunbar, Haddingtonshire, and educated at St Andrews University, where he graduated MA. Appointed chaplain to Mary, dowager countess of Home (1596–1645), he accompanied her on a visit to London. On his return to Scotland, he made the acquaintance of John Maitland, the future duke of Lauderdale, who had married Anne, the countess's daughter, in 1632; he travelled abroad with him for two years, visiting Paris and Geneva. In 1643 Lauderdale was selected by the general assembly of Scotland as one of the five Scottish commissioners to visit London for conference with the assembly of divines which had just convened at Westminster. Hume accompanied him to London and was used as a courier in the autumn of 1644 by the commissioner George Gillespie. While in London, Hume was invited to take up the living of Benton, near Newcastle, and on 20 April 1647 he was ordained by the ministers of the fourth London classis, John Ley, Henry Roborough, Nathaniel Hardy, John Hall, Thomas Froysell, and William Wickens. At an unknown date Hume married a woman named Lucy; the only thing known about her is that she died in 1681 and was buried in Bunhill Fields.

From 1651 Hume was vicar of Whittingham, Northumberland. According to Edmund Calamy, he was 'zealous for the King and royal family' and thus earned the enmity of Sir Arthur Hesilrige, a very powerful figure, especially in the north-east, who is said to have forced him for a time from his living, perhaps in 1654. Hesilrige had opposed the dissolution of the Rump but, as a commissioner for triers and ejectors in the four northern counties, he is unlikely to have countenanced Hume's refusal to recognize the authority of Oliver Cromwell as lord protector. Hesilrige's hostility appears to have softened, but if Hume was a royalist he must have been discreet about it. His success in having men of his own presbyterian persuasion installed in neighbouring parishes depended on the acquiescence of the state authorities.

In 1662 Hume refused to conform with the terms of the Act of Uniformity and was ejected from Whittingham. He returned to the household of Lauderdale, who urged him to make his peace with the English church. Hume's determined refusal eventually led to a breach. He travelled in France in 1669 and made the acquaintance of the eminent Calvinist minister Jean Claude, then pastor of the reformed church at Charenton, Paris. In London, Hume found shelter in the house of Thomas Pamplion, a merchant tailor and alderman (January 1670) of the City of London, but Pamplion died the following year. In 1672 Hume was a preacher to a presbyterian congregation in the parish of St Botolph without Bishopsgate, and on 12 April was granted a general licence to preach in any licensed place. It seems that his congregation disintegrated or was forced to disband, possibly in the years of reaction during 1681–5. Hume, it seems, found it advisable to leave London and is known to have preached at Theobalds, Hertfordshire, until 1687. Though there is no record of his ministry at the time of the survey of nonconformist congregations in the years 1690–92, it is reported that in the last years of his life he ministered to a congregation in Drury Lane and, most remarkably, continued past his ninetieth birthday, until 29 January 1707 when he died aged ninety-two, according to the memorial at his burial place in Bunhill Fields.   STEPHEN WRIGHT

Sources *Calamy rev.* · E. Calamy, ed., *An abridgement of Mr. Baxter's history of his life and times, with an account of the ministers, &c., who were ejected after the Restauration of King Charles II*, 2nd edn, 2 vols. (1713) · C. E. Surman, ed., *The register-booke of the fourth classis in the province of London, 1646–59*, 2 vols. in 1, Harleian Society, 82–3 (1953) · *The letters and journals of Robert Baillie*, ed. D. Laing, 3 vols. (1841–2) · G. L. Turner, ed., *Original records of early nonconformity under persecution and indulgence*, 3 vols. (1911–14) · A. B. Beaven, ed., *The aldermen of the City of London, temp. Henry III–*[1912], 2 vols. (1908–13) · W. Wilson, *The history and antiquities of the dissenting churches and meeting houses in London, Westminster and Southwark*, 4 vols. (1808–14)

Hume, Sir Abraham, second baronet (1749–1838), collector of art and precious stones, was born at Hill Street, Berkeley Square, London, on 20 February 1749, the son of Sir Abraham Hume, first baronet (d. 1772), and his wife, Hannah, sixth and youngest daughter of Sir Thomas Frederick (1681–1731), governor of Fort St David, in the East Indies, who married on 9 October 1746. There was also a daughter, Hannah, who married James Hare (bap. 1747, d. 1804), friend of Charles James Fox. The family fortune was made by Hume's uncle Alexander (d. 1766), who was a director of the East India Company and in 1739 acquired the estate of Wormleybury, in Hertfordshire, as well as another at Fernside, in Berwickshire. The house at Wormleybury was rebuilt (1767–9) for Abraham Hume by Robert Mylne, with interiors (1777–9) by Robert Adam and stucco

work based on designs by Angelica Kauffmann. Having been educated at Eton College and, from 1766, at Trinity College, Cambridge, Hume for a time apparently served in the navy, but after inheriting the baronetcy in 1772 he was elected member of parliament for Petersfield (1774–80) and for Hastings (1807–18). On 25 April 1771 he married Amelia (1751–1809), daughter of John *Egerton, bishop of Durham, and sister of the seventh and eighth earls of Bridgewater. She was born on 25 November 1751, and died at Hill Street, London, on 8 August 1809; she was buried at the church of St Laurence, Wormley. Their elder daughter, Amelia (1772–1837) [see Long, Amelia], married Charles Long (1760–1838), later Lord Farnborough; she was a gifted watercolourist. The younger daughter, Sophia (1787/8–1814), married John Cust, first Earl Brownlow. Hume travelled in Italy in 1786–7.

Hume's main interests lay outside politics, in the collection of minerals, and in the arts. Not much is known about his collection of minerals and precious stones, although a catalogue of the diamonds was published by the comte de Bournon in 1815. However, it was for his contribution to natural history and mineralogy that Hume was elected a fellow of the Royal Society on 14 December 1775 and, at his death, was senior fellow; he was also a founder of the Geological Society, serving as vice-president from 1809 to 1813. As regards the arts he was a member of the Society of Dilettanti (1789) and of the Society of Antiquaries.

At the same time Hume, who is often described as an amateur painter, established a reputation as a collector of old master paintings, evidently making his first purchases during the 1770s. He continued to acquire pictures regularly until the early years of the nineteenth century, when other financial demands began to be made on him. An informative catalogue published in 1824 lists 149 paintings, to which twenty-two were added for the revised edition of 1829. Hume's own manuscript catalogue of the collection is in the National Art Library, Victoria and Albert Museum. The most significant holdings were the Renaissance Venetian paintings, which included *Portrait of a Condottiere*, by Giovanni Bellini (National Gallery of Art, Washington), and *The Death of Actaeon*, by Titian (National Gallery, London), as well as works by Cima da Conegliano and Vincenzo Catena. Hume himself published a book on Titian in 1829 that held an honourable place in the earlier Titian scholarship for many years. The quantity and concentration of the Venetian pictures, out of a total of ninety Italian paintings, was notable but Hume did not ignore the Florentine or Roman schools. Neither was he inattentive to the northern schools, although these paintings were less numerous. The outstanding works of the Dutch school were *Aristotle Contemplating the Bust of Homer*, by Rembrandt (Metropolitan Museum of Art, New York) and *The Maas at Dordrecht*, by Aelbert Cuyp (National Gallery of Art, Washington); of the Flemish school, in addition to some oil-sketches by Rubens there was *Portrait of a Woman and Child*, by Van Dyck (National Gallery, London). By contrast there were only small groups by French and British artists. Among the French works was *Les plaisirs du bal* (known as 'Le bal champêtre'), by Watteau, which was exchanged with Noël Desenfans and is now at Dulwich Picture Gallery, London. The British paintings included portraits of Hume and his wife by Sir Joshua Reynolds, dating from 1783 (Belton House, Lincolnshire).

The Italian paintings had for the most part been acquired from leading dealers and agents such as Giovanni Maria Sasso, in Venice, and Giovanni Antonio Armano, in Bologna, but some of the Flemish and Dutch pictures came from a certain Colonel Goldsworthy, who inherited them in 1777 from the widow of Francis Gashry (d. 1762), member of parliament for Looe, Cornwall, and a former colleague at the Admiralty of Sir Charles Wages (1666–1743). Hume's concern for the condition of a painting reveals an unusual degree of aesthetic discrimination for the time; the collection was assessed by Gustav Waagen in his *Works of Art and Artists in England* (1838). Hume's standing as a connoisseur is apparent from his close friendship with Reynolds, his role as a founding director of the British Institution in 1805, and his links with his son-in-law Charles Long, who advised George IV on matters of art and who was a benefactor of the National Gallery. Hume's collection passed, by his second daughter, to his grandson John, Viscount Alford (1812–1851), who also inherited Ashridge House, in Hertfordshire, on the death of the eighth earl of Bridgewater.

The more important paintings were thenceforward housed at Ashridge but thirty lesser works went to Belton House. Although there were isolated sales (the Rembrandt left in 1893 and the Van Dyck in 1914) the core of the collection remained intact until the death, in 1921, of Hume's great-grandson, the third Earl Brownlow, when Ashridge was abandoned and the pictures amalgamated at Belton until eventually dispersed at auction, first at Christies in 1923 (4–7 May) and in 1929 (3 May), and finally at the Belton House sale organized by Christies in 1984 (30 April–2 May). Hume's appearance in the painting *Interior of a Picture Gallery with Portraits* (known as 'Patrons and lovers of art, or, The imaginary picture gallery'), by the Dutch artist P. C. Wonder (priv. coll.), exhibited at the British Institution in 1831 and for which four studies are in the National Portrait Gallery, including one (inv. 793) showing Hume with Charles Long and the fourth earl of Aberdeen, is significant.

Hume died at Wormleybury on 24 March 1838 and was buried at the church of St Laurence, Wormley, where there is a monument with a portrait bust to his memory. Joseph Farington records a contemporary opinion that Hume was 'much beloved by those connected with Him' but 'so restless in disposition as to be always desiring to change from one place to another; never being fixed to any spot or object' (Farington, *Diary*, 5 July 1813).

CHRISTOPHER LLOYD

Sources DNB · *Descriptive catalogue of a collection of pictures* (1824) · J. Ingamells, ed., *A dictionary of British and Irish travellers in Italy, 1701–1800* (1997) · F. Russell, *The dictionary of art*, 14 (1996), 876–7 · *Belton House … property of the Lord Brownlow … which will be sold at auction* (1984), 161–5 [sale catalogue, Christies, 30 April–2 May 1984] · TLS (24 May 1923), 360; (10 Jan 1924), 37 · J. Byam Shaw, *The Italian drawings of the Frits Lugt collection*, 2: *Polidoro album* (Paris, 1983), 7 n. 2

Archives V&A NAL, corresp. and papers | BL, letters to G. Cumberland, Add. MSS 36504–36515, *passim* · National Gallery, London, corresp. with Sasso · V&A NAL, MS catalogue of picture collection and typescripts of corresp. with Sasso and Armano, reserve coll. V. 19 and 19A

Likenesses T. Patch, pen caricature, 1769, Uffizi Gallery, Florence · J. Reynolds, oils, 1783, Belton House, Lincolnshire; replica, Tate collection · C. H. Hodges, mezzotint, pubd 1791 (after J. Reynolds), BM, NPG · T. G. Lupton, mezzotint, pubd 1814 (after J. Reynolds), BM, NPG · P. C. Wonder, portrait, 1831, priv. coll. · S. W. Reynolds, mezzotint, pubd 1837 (after J. Reynolds), BM, NPG · J. Jenkins, stipple (in old age; after H. Edridge), BM, NPG; repro. in W. Jerdan, *National portrait gallery of illustrious and eminent personages* (1830) · P. C. Wonder, group portrait, oil study (*Patrons and lovers of art, 1826*), NPG · memorial with portrait, St Laurence's Church, Wormley, Hertfordshire · mezzotint (after J. Reynolds), NPG

Hume, Abraham (1814–1884), Church of England clergyman and antiquary, was born on 9 February 1814 at Hillsborough, co. Down, Ireland, the son of Thomas F. Hume. Both his parents were of Scottish descent. He was educated at the Royal Belfast Academical Institution, the University of Glasgow, and (from 1835) Trinity College, Dublin. During and after his time at Trinity College he taught mathematics and English at Belfast Academy; from January 1841 he taught English at Liverpool Mechanics' Institute and from 1843 at the Liverpool Institute and Collegiate Institution. He graduated BA from Trinity in 1843 and received an honorary LLD from Glasgow in 1843. Hume was ordained deacon in 1843 and priest in 1844; after serving as curate for four years without a stipend at St Augustine's, Liverpool, he was appointed in 1847 as vicar of the new parish of Vauxhall, also in Liverpool. Here he organized the building of the new church of All Souls (1854–6).

Hume was an enthusiastic antiquary. In 1848, with Joseph Mayer and H. C. Pidgeon, he established the Historic Society of Lancashire and Cheshire, of which he was the main support for many years; he served as president from 1869 to 1875. He was also a fellow of the Royal Society, the Society of Antiquaries, the Royal Society of Northern Antiquaries at Copenhagen, and other similar associations. His antiquarian publications included *Remarks on Certain Implements of the Stone Period* (1851), *Ancient Meols, or, Some Account of the Antiquities near Dove Point* (1863), and several works on Irish and English dialects.

Deeply concerned by the results of the 1851 census of religious worship and the failure of the Church of England to address the problems of urbanization, Hume played a very active role in the religious life of Liverpool. He has been described as 'the Anglican pioneer of religious sociology' (Field, 196): he initiated statistical surveys of several Liverpool parishes, which he published as *Condition of Liverpool, Religious and Social* (1858). This work was followed by a pamphlet in 1860, which reflected on the census, included a map showing the distribution of 'religious' and 'irreligious' areas, and suggested improvements for the 1861 census (which never took place). In addition, in 1857–8 he had sent summaries of his previous year's work in his own parish to *The Times*, thus illustrating the hard working life of a city minister. A keen supporter of church home missions and extension, in 1858 he gave evidence before a select committee of the House of Lords on services in the cities. In the following year he appeared before the committee examining church rates: as an officer of the Church Defence Institution he was a firm opponent of their abolition (and thus a focus for nonconformist and Catholic hostility). In 1867 he was sent on a surveying tour by the South American Missionary Society; he travelled down the west coast of South America, visiting Peru and Chile. On the visit of the church congress to Liverpool in 1869 he acted as secretary, editing its report and reading a paper of his own on the work of the Church of England in Liverpool. He was also secretary to the British Association at Liverpool in 1870; vice-chairman of the Liverpool school board from 1870 to 1876 (and published several works on educational issues, such as the payment of school fees and adult learning classes); and secretary of the Liverpool bishopric committee from 1873 to 1880. An enthusiastic advocate of the formation of the Liverpool diocese, which took place in 1880, he designed the new episcopal seal and published a *Detailed Account of how Liverpool Became a Diocese* (1881). He was an honorary canon of Chester Cathedral from 1874.

Hume died unmarried in Shaw Street, Liverpool, on 21 November 1884, and was buried at Anfield cemetery on 25 November. His concern for the advance of education had allowed him to bridge class divisions in Liverpool: he once suggested that an Irish peasant could understand Shakespeare better than an educated gentleman. But his pugnacious and sometimes abrasive defence of the Anglican establishment had exacerbated religious sectarianism in the city: when he was out in South America in 1867 beleaguered nonconformists in Liverpool hoped that he might be made a bishop there and thus afflict them no more.

C. W. SUTTON, rev. ERIC GLASGOW

Sources J. C. Morley, *A brief memoir of the Rev. Abraham Hume* (1887) • E. Glasgow, *Liverpool people: a miscellany* (1992), 109–13 • *Liverpool Mercury* (22 Nov 1884) • *Men of the time* (1884), 606–7 • Crockford (1876) • Burtchaell & Sadleir, *Alum. Dubl.*, 2nd edn • *The Porcupine*, 9 (1868), 438 • C. D. Field, 'The 1851 religious census of Great Britain: a bibliographical guide for local and regional historians', *Local Historian*, 27/4 (1997), 194–217 • *CGPLA Eng. & Wales* (1885) • private information (2004) [R. Marsh]
Archives Lpool RO, papers and printed works | Elgin Museum, Elgin, letters to George Gordon • LPL, corresp. with A. C. Tait • PRO NIre., corresp. and papers • U. Edin. L., letters to James Halliwell-Phillipps
Likenesses medallion, 1861, City of Liverpool Library • J. de Conte, engraved medallion, 1863 (after Grispi), City of Liverpool Library • stipple, NPG
Wealth at death £1990 19s. 6d.: probate, 13 April 1885, *CGPLA Eng. & Wales*

Hume, Sir Alexander, of that ilk (d. 1461). *See under* Hume family (*per.* 1424–1516).

Hume, Alexander, first Lord Hume (d. c.1491). *See under* Hume family (*per.* 1424–1516).

Hume, Alexander, second Lord Hume (d. 1506). *See under* Hume family (*per.* 1424–1516).

Hume, Alexander, third Lord Hume (d. 1516). *See under* Hume family (*per.* 1424–1516).

Hume, Alexander (c.1557–1609), writer, was the second son of Patrick Hume, fifth baron of Polwarth (d. 1599), Berwickshire, and Agnes, daughter of Alexander Hume of Manderston. He attended St Mary's College, University of St Andrews, graduating BA in 1574. On the apparent biographical evidence of his poem 'Ane Epistle to Maister Gilbert Moncrief' (1599), Hume lived for four years in France, where he probably studied law. His entrance into the ministry was preceded and seemingly fostered by attendance at both the courts of justice and the royal court. Hume's 'Epistle' records the corruption, duplicity, and immorality which he encountered in both spheres. Hume's elder brother, Patrick *Hume of Polwarth, was himself a poet associated with the literary circle around James VI and I's Scottish court.

In 1598 Hume was appointed minister of Logie (an incumbency which he retained until his death). He had by then published several prose treatises, including the *Christian Precepts Serving to the Practise of Sanctification*, spiritual exercises which closed the *Hymnes: Christian Precepts, ane Treatise of Conscience* (1594), and *A Treatise of the Felicitie of the Life to Come* (1594). A manuscript copy survives of a work entitled 'Ane afold admonitioun to the ministerie of Scotland by a deing brother', which also records Hume's political intervention in an ecclesiastical dispute, indicating the position of a moderate reformer.

Hume's devotional ethos and spiritual morality inform all his writing. His *Hymnes, or, Sacred Songs*, published in 1599 by Robert Leprevik, is his unique but substantial contribution to the development of protestant poetics in Scotland. The collection was dedicated to Elizabeth Melville, Lady Colville of Culross, a Calvinist preacher who published *Ane Godlie Dreme* in 1604. Hume's poetry is underpinned by moral antagonism to secular poetry, a conviction expressed in the collection's 'Epistle to the Scottish Youth', and mirrored in the 'Epistle to Maister Gilbert Moncrief' as a polemic against secular court and government. The collection stands as Hume's spiritual, intellectual, and literary attempt to portray the 'high and holie mysteries' (*Poems*, 7). The confession that these 'songs' were begun in his youth and 'prosecuted in my wraslings with the world' (ibid., 8) gives the collection a spiritual trajectory. One poem, 'The Triumph of the Lord, after the Manner of Men', is a fiercely ideological, triumphalistic justification and celebration of the defeat of the Spanish Armada in 1588. Much of Hume's poetry is devoted to the contemplation of divine creation and the miracle of nature ('Of Gods Benefites Bestowed upon Man'). Hume's best-known poem, 'Of the Day Estivall', is a Christian pastoral which delineates the progress of nature and agricultural labour from dawn through to dusk. The poem is symbolically and theologically unified by the revolution of the sun which, in the lyric's underlying opposition between artifice and purity, aesthetically and theologically, is shown to be animated by the 'high and haly on' (ibid., 29), and is therefore not a secular mythological, hence idolatrous, emblem. Hume's poem is renowned for the remarkable fidelity and naturalism of its pastoral description but his depiction of a divinely harmonious nature is also indebted to the tradition of heraldic imagery, suggesting that his work is aesthetically complex in practice.

Celebration of the theocentric universe is not the only subject of the *Hymnes*. A number of lyrics are inward spiritual meditations which record Hume's own afflictions and his anticipation of death which, in 'To his Spiritual Saull for Consolation', is 'rewarded' by a vision of the last judgement and the salvation of the elect. The tension between the absolute conviction of faith and the awareness of physical frailty is often sustained in these lyrics. The persona of 'the godly patient' in one lyric confesses to God 'the medicinar' (*Poems*, 45); this, combined with the poem addressed to Gilbert Moncrieff, physician to James VI, may suggest that Hume himself suffered illness. Hume married Marion Duncanson. He died on 4 December 1609, and was survived by a son and two daughters.

S. M. DUNNIGAN

Sources *The poems of Alexander Hume*, ed. A. Lawson, STS, 48 (1902) · D. Irving, *The lives of the Scotish poets*, 2 vols. (1804) · R. D. S. Jack, 'Poetry under King James VI', *The history of Scottish literature*, ed. C. Craig, 1: *Origins to 1660*, ed. R. D. S. Jack (1987), 125–40 · D. Reid, 'Prose after Knox', *The history of Scottish literature*, ed. C. Craig, 1: *Origins to 1660*, ed. R. D. S. Jack (1988), 183–98 · H. M. Shire, *Song, dance and poetry at the court of Scotland under King James VI*, ed. K. Elliott (1969) · A. A. MacDonald, 'Religious poetry in middle Scots', *The history of Scottish literature*, ed. C. Craig, 1: *Origins to 1660*, ed. R. D. S. Jack (1988), 91–104
Wealth at death approx. £700—inventory of goods: will, *Poems*, ed. Lawson

Hume, Alexander (*d.* 1682), covenanter leader, was a 'portioner' of Hume, Berwickshire. The precise identity of his parents is unknown, but he had at least one brother—George—who was imprisoned in 1690 for publishing antigovernment literature. There is no record of Alexander's early life or education. He married Isobel Hume, and the couple had five children.

A staunch adherent of the covenant, Hume was indicted in 1682 on charges of 'levying war against the king in the counties of Berwick, Roxburgh, and Selkirk' (Anderson, 501). He was captured in November of that year and imprisoned, 'sorely wounded', in the castle of Edinburgh. On 20 December he was accused of having 'commanded a party' at Bothwell Bridge, an offence punishable by death. Despite the earnest plea of his counsel, Sir Patrick Hume of Lumsden, that Hume was not a 'ringleader' of that insurrection (and therefore entitled to leniency under the indemnity of 1679), he was found guilty and condemned to hang. Hume's case might have attracted relatively little attention, were it not for the apparent injustice of the sentence. Lauder of Fountainhall recorded that he 'came not [the] lenth' of a leading player at Bothwell Bridge (*Historical Notices*, 1.86) and—despite the fact that Hume 'own[ed] the presbyterian interest' (*Reg. PCS*, 15.82)—even 'some bishops' interceded before the court on his behalf (*Historical Notices*, 1.86). According to the minister and historian Robert Wodrow, a reprieve was forthcoming but was kept

back by the chancellor, James Drummond, earl of Perth. Whatever the truth of the latter assertion, Hume was hanged on 29 December 1682 at Edinburgh's market cross, where he died 'more composedly and piously then others of them doe'. Fountainhall deplored the execution, noting that (by their martyrdom) such men 'persuade more at their death then they did in life' (ibid.).

The precise value of Hume's estate at the time of his death is unknown, but (since Fountainhall described him as a 'small gentleman in the Merse') it was unlikely to have been extensive. In any case, his property was forfeited on conviction, leaving his wife and five 'small' children 'redacted to extreme necessity [with] no other hopes of livelyhood and subsistence'. In 1686 Isobel Hume petitioned the privy council 'for the small joynter (extending to two hundred and twentie pound Scotts) provided to her by contract of marriage with her deceast husband' (*Reg. PCS*, 13.96). The property of Kennetside was restored to the family after the revolution of 1688.

VAUGHAN T. WELLS

Sources *Reg. PCS*, 3rd ser., vols. 13, 15 · *Historical notices of Scotish affairs, selected from the manuscripts of Sir John Lauder of Fountainhall*, ed. D. Laing, 1, Bannatyne Club, 87 (1848) · R. Wodrow, *The history of the sufferings of the Church of Scotland from the Restoration to the revolution*, ed. R. Burns, 2 (1884) · W. Anderson, *The Scottish nation*, 2 (1884) · M. D. Young, ed., *The parliaments of Scotland: burgh and shire commissioners*, 1 (1992) · DNB

Hume, Alexander (1809–1851), poet, was born at Kelso on 1 February 1809, the son of Walter Hume, a retail trader, and his wife, Janet Edington. He received his early education at Kelso, and was permanently impressed by the beautiful scenery of his native district. While he was still a boy, however, his family moved to London, which was clearly not to Hume's liking, for in 1822 or 1823 he ran away to join a party of strolling players for a few months. While undertaking a variety of characters he sang, especially a song called 'I am such a beautiful boy'. Through the kindness of a relative he obtained a post in 1827 with the London agents of Berwick & Co., brewers of Edinburgh, with whom he remained until 1840.

At some time between 1830 and 1833 Hume joined the Literary and Scientific Institution in Aldersgate Street, became a good debater, and wrote his 'Daft Wattie' for the club's magazine. From this time he found recreation in writing Scottish lyrics, which he collected and published as *Scottish Songs* (1835). In 1837 he married a Miss Scott, and in 1840, owing to ill health, travelled in America. Following his return he became London agent for Messrs Lane, well-known Cork brewers. Meanwhile his fresh songs were becoming increasingly popular, and in 1845 *Songs and Poems, Chiefly Scottish* appeared. 'Sandy Allan', one of his best lyrics, was included in the anthology *Whistle-Binkie* (1832–47).

In 1847 Hume revisited America for the benefit of his health. He died at Northampton Lunatic Asylum on 24 May 1851, survived by his wife and six children.

T. W. BAYNE, *rev.* JAMES HOW

Sources C. Rogers, *The modern Scottish minstrel* (1857) · Boase, *Mod. Eng. biog.* · Irving, *Scots.* · bap. reg. Scot. · d. cert.

Hume, Alexander (1811–1859), poet and composer, was born in Edinburgh on 7 February 1811, the son of William Hume, a wax chandler, and his wife, Elizabeth Robertson. After receiving an elementary education he worked as a cabinet-maker, a trade in which he continued until his death. Early recognized as a singer, he became tenor in St Paul's Episcopal Church, Edinburgh, and chorus master in the Theatre Royal. He devoted much of his leisure to reading. While still young he was associated with the Glasites, and it is likely that the arrangement of their musical manual was his earliest work as a musician. In 1829 he married Ann Lees (d. 1848), with whom he had seven children.

Though self-taught in musical theory Hume was very successful in setting tunes both to standard Scottish lyrics and to songs of his own. He was widely known in his time for popular songs including 'My ain dear Nell' and 'The Scottish Emigrant's Farewell'. He also composed an appropriate melody to Burns's 'Afton Water' and wrote several glees, including 'We fairies come' and 'Tell me where my love reposes'. In 1854 his madrigal 'Round a circle' won a prize.

About 1855 Hume settled in Glasgow, where he worked at his trade and increased his poetical and musical reputation. He frequently published lyrics in the Edinburgh *Scottish Press*, and in 1856 he edited *The Lyric Gems of Scotland*, to which he made over fifty contributions of his own, providing in several cases both words and music, while in others he merely supplied the music or arranged existing compositions. It is not certain that the valuable annotations in the work are Hume's but he probably had a share in them.

Improvident habits ensured that Hume, despite his successes, ended his career in poverty. He died, while working at his bench, on 4 February 1859 at his home, in Great Clyde Street, Glasgow. He was buried in the city's necropolis.   T. W. BAYNE, rev. JAMES HOW

Sources D. Baptie, ed., *Musical Scotland, past and present: being a dictionary of Scottish musicians from about 1400 till the present time* (1894) · D. Baptie, *A handbook of musical biography*, 2nd edn (1887) · J. D. Champlain, *Cyclopedia of music and musicians*, 3 vols. (1888–90) · Boase, *Mod. Eng. biog.* · Irving, *Scots.* · D. Baptie, *Sketches of the English glee composers: historical, biographical and critical (from about 1735–1866)* [1896] · Brown & Stratton, *Brit. mus.* · private information (1891, 2004) [William Hume, son] · bap. reg. Scot. · m. reg. Scot. · d. cert.

Hume, Allan Octavian (1829–1912), administrator in India, founder of the Indian National Congress, and ornithologist, was born on 4 June 1829 at St Mary Cray, Kent, seventh child of Joseph *Hume MP (1777–1855) and his wife, Maria Burnley (b. 1786). He grew up in the radical family environment of 6 Bryanston Square, London, and was educated at University College, London, where his diligence, 'truthfulness, and strict adherence to honourable principles' were commended. Nominated to the Indian Civil Service, he spent two years at the East India College, Haileybury, graduating in the first class and ranking fifth for Bengal. His most admired contemporary thinkers were his boyhood friend John Stuart Mill and Herbert Spencer. Belief in progress, expressed through

Allan Octavian Hume (1829–1912), by unknown photographer

political and social reform, and the intellectual efficacy of science defined Hume's life. He had scant regard for institutional Christianity, but believed in the immortality of the soul and in the idea of a supreme ultimate. On 8 March 1853 Hume married Mary Anne Grindall (1823/4–1890), five years his senior. Their only child, Mary Jane, was born in January 1854. Hume regretted not having a male heir and their daughter had no children.

Hume visited Paris in 1848 and arrived at Calcutta in March 1849. After further studies he was posted to the North-Western Provinces in January 1850. He remained immersed in the Indian rural hinterland until February 1856, when he became magistrate of Etawah. He handled routine administration efficiently but valued his position as an instrument for reform. His main initiatives were the establishment of a district-wide system of secular, voluntarily funded, village vernacular (Hindi and Urdu) education, a press and newspaper in the same languages, the institution of municipal government and extensive redevelopment of the district capital, improved health care facilities, and large-scale improvements to roads and public buildings.

Hume's progressive initiatives were disrupted by the uprising of 1857 and for six months he took refuge in Agra Fort. All but one of Etawah's principal Indian officials remained loyal, and by January 1858 Hume had re-established a tenuous position there. He recruited an irregular force of up to 650 Indian troops and fought with them in many engagements. For his courage and leadership he was made a CB. Hume blamed the uprising on British political ineptitude, believed that the Etawah populace wanted no part of it, and deliberately pursued a policy of 'mercy and forbearance' which some Europeans mistook for a 'want of firmness' or being swayed by 'loyal natives'. Uncontaminated by racism, he admired the executive capabilities of his Indian deputies. To him the rising demonstrated the necessity for greater openness and Indian involvement in government. He worked zealously on reconstruction and reform initiatives from early 1859 until March 1861, when a breakdown from overwork necessitated two years' medical leave in Britain. Before departing he condemned new flogging measures by the provincial government as a reversion to 'barbarous ... torture'. Only after apologizing for the tone of his criticism was he permitted to return to Etawah.

Because of his enterprising district administration, Hume was promoted in 1867 to commissioner of inland customs, and negotiated a major treaty regulating salt sales from Rajputana's Sambhar Lake. This attracted the attention of the viceroy, Lord Mayo, and Hume was selected to head the Indian government's new department of agriculture, revenue, and commerce. Mayo and Hume conceived the department as a vehicle for agricultural reform, but London insisted upon revenue as the top priority. Hume pushed for the development of an integrated system of model farms in every district of India but most provincial governments were unsupportive. Always outspoken, he particularly irritated his superiors by linking land revenue policy with acute poverty in parts of India, condemning indentured emigration practices, and advocating conservation measures. Finally, in 1879 the government utilized ostensible retrenchment measures to abolish Hume's department and demote him to revenue administration in the North-Western Provinces. Hume responded by publishing *Agricultural Reform in India* (1879), an indictment of government neglect of agricultural modernization.

Hume acknowledged that he was considered 'an unsafe, impulsive, insubordinate officer', but scarcely expected a humiliating demotion. Only his desire to finance his costly three-volume publication *The Game Birds of India, Burmah and Ceylon* (1879–81) kept him from resigning immediately. He took early retirement on 1 January 1882, after completing its publication. From 1850 Indian ornithology had been his systematic hobby, and he had assembled a collection of over 80,000 bird skins, eggs and nests, all preserved for scientific study. This unsurpassed collection he donated in 1885 to the British Museum (Natural History), later the Natural History Museum, where it remains. He led pioneering ornithological expeditions to western India, and to the Andaman Islands, the Laccadives, and Manipur, and founded and edited *Stray Feathers*, a scientific journal of Indian ornithology.

During his career crisis of 1879 Hume turned to theosophy, introduced to India that year by its founders, Helena P. Blavatsky and Henry S. Olcott. The Theosophical Society combined interest in the philosophic roots of world religions with scientific exploration of human consciousness and envisaged a new universal brotherhood. Blavatsky claimed transcendental communications with saintly religious leaders who resided in the remote Himalayas. Hume became sufficiently fascinated to school himself for discipleship by forgoing alcohol, becoming a vegetarian, and shooting no more birds, even for science. Theosophy led him into the study of ancient Hinduism and Buddhism. He soon grew distrustful of Blavatsky's honesty and sceptical of her occult phenomena, but then came under the influence of a Vedantist leader, Swami Paramahansa. He had severed association with Blavatsky and Olcott by 1883, but continued to believe, along with independent Indian leaders, in transcendental communication. He remained a vegetarian, and from 1885 was a vice-president of the British Vegetarian Society.

As his involvement in theosophy waned Hume found a new mission in life—fostering the development of Indian national political organization. He was appalled by European opposition to Lord Ripon's Ilbert Bill, by which the viceroy sought to give Indian judges some jurisdiction over white people. Hume sided with Indian leaders and issued an appeal to graduates of Calcutta University to organize for national reform. This initiative led to the creation of the Indian National Congress in 1885. He informed the new viceroy, Lord Dufferin, in advance of the plans for the new organization but contemporary reports that Hume intended it to focus on social reform rather than politics are unconvincing. Hume always attached primacy to politics. He became the general secretary of Congress for its formative first decade. Passionately believing in representative government and constitutional agitation, he was not, as some historians of the 'nationalist school' have claimed, a restraining force on Congress leaders. Rather, he wanted them to exert themselves more vigorously to push the reluctant raj towards substantial political and economic reform. In 1886–7 he initiated a mass publicity campaign designed to broaden the base of Congress by bringing in townsmen, peasant proprietors, and Muslims. This created a backlash among British rulers, and Congress backtracked. Disappointed, Hume was also upset when many Congress members opposed the government's 1891 initiative to raise the age of marriage for Indian girls. He then attempted to make Indian poverty a focus of Congress concern. Disquieted that few leaders took that issue seriously, in early 1892 Hume privately circulated a communication warning that they would be swept aside by violent agrarian revolution unless they mobilized to achieve significant reform. Hume's circular became public, outraged the British establishment, and frightened the Congress élite, who publicly repudiated it. He did not recant, and leaders like B. G. Tilak in India and W. H. Hyndman in Britain supported him. Disappointed that so few Indian leaders were prepared to work full-time in the cause of national emancipation, in 1894 Hume retired permanently to Britain, where he remained involved with the British Congress committee until his death. During his final years he devoted most of his energy and money to establishing a botanical institute for educating working-class youth in south London. He died at his home, The Chalet, 4 Kingswood Road, Upper Norwood, London, on 31 July 1912. His ashes were interred at Brookwood cemetery, Woking, Surrey. EDWARD C. MOULTON

Sources E. C. Moulton, 'Allan O. Hume and the Indian National Congress: a reassessment', *South Asia*, 8 (June–Dec 1985) · J. R. McLane, *Indian nationalism and the early congress* (1977) · S. R. Mehrotra, *Towards India's freedom and partition* (1979) · Mahatma letters, BL, Add. MS 45289B · North-Western Provinces judicial criminal proceedings, 14/9/1861, BL OIOC · A. O. Hume, *Narrative of [mutiny] occurrences in Etawah* (1859) · *The Times* (1 Aug 1912) · *CGPLA Eng. & Wales* (1912) · Desmond, *Botanists*, 328 · certificate of baptism, East India Company, petitions, 2 (1846), fol. 213
Archives BL, corresp. with K. Hoomi, etc., Add. MSS 45284–45289 · BL, Mahatma MSS · BL, corresp. with Lord Ripon · BL OIOC, Dufferin MSS · BL OIOC, Lansdowne MSS · BL OIOC, Lytton MSS · CUL, corresp. with Lord Mayo · National Archives of India, New Delhi, letters to Badruddin Tyabji · NHM, notebooks and papers relating to expeditions in India; MSS and collection of ornithological specimens
Likenesses photograph, 1880–1889?, repro. in W. Wedderburn, *Allan Octavian Hume, C.B., 'father of the Indian National Congress', 1829 to 1912* (1913) · photograph, Hult. Arch. [see illus.]
Wealth at death £18,878 4s. 4d.: probate, 31 Aug 1912, *CGPLA Eng. & Wales*

Hume, Anna (*fl.* 1644), poet, was the daughter of David *Hume of Godscroft (1558–1629x31), himself a prolific writer. Linked with the Humes of Wedderburn, Sir David restyled his Berwickshire property 'Godscroft' from the less eminent 'Gowkscroft' in accordance with his humanist aspirations. One major poetic work by Anna Hume survives, *The Triumphs of Love: Chastitie, Death* (1644), a translation from Petrarch, printed only once. Evidence suggests that she was associated with the literary, social, and political circles around the writer William Drummond of Hawthornden. A letter from Drummond to Hume acknowledges her 'delicate verses' which commend Drummond's own poetry, revealing 'the Highnes of your Spirit, which ever transcendeth mean Measures' (NL Scot., MS 2061).

Hume appears to have been involved in the editorial preparation of her father's somewhat controversial work of historiography, *The History of the Houses of Douglas and Angus*. In 1643 she wrote to Archibald Douglas, earl of Angus, to discuss possible dedicatees for the history, and added:

> It is not the least happinesse I enjoy by my returne to my Countrey, that I have found this Piece amongst my Fathers scattered Papers; it is here in his own method, without addition or change, I cannot say, without defect. (A. Hume to Lord Archibald Douglas, 11 Dec 1643)

None the less, Hume seems to have felt the literary and psychological responsibility onerous. The history was first published in 1644. A letter from Drummond to the marquess of Douglas survives which warns Douglas that he will be 'petitioned for the Gentlewoman (who hath ventured, shee sayes, her whole fortunes) by the Lordes of the State, to suffer the Booke to come abroade, or then to give her satisfaction for her coppyes' (Laing, 97). The marquess may have intended to publish the manuscript history of his family in his possession (written by his father), to counter the influence of Hume's history, and Drummond

writes that this '[would] undoe the poore Woman' (ibid., 98).

A brief letter from Anna Hume to Lord Lauderdale, possibly written about 1665, found among the correspondence of the earl and duke of Lauderdale, asserts with a mixture of humility and ardency that she be allowed to 'present' her 'petition', and implores him 'to own me and to say something in the busines … It was a wrong don me as I was a Scot'. Whether this is related to the publication controversy or another entirely different dispute is uncertain.

Hume dedicates her translation of the first three books of Petrarch's *Trionfi* to Princess Elizabeth of Bohemia (1618–1680), the eldest daughter of Queen Elizabeth of Bohemia (1596–1662) and Frederick V, elector palatine. Hume's preface suggests the possibility of a literary and cultural milieu for her work, and establishes the terms for the defence of women that her translation attempts. The first dedicatory verse exalts Elizabeth as 'True glory of [her] sex', alluding to the princess's intellectual gifts as exemplified by her correspondence with Descartes. The claim that Elizabeth was 'Pleas'd to approve' further writing by Hume suggests that the latter may herself have visited the court of the exiled princess at The Hague. Hume asserts that her translation will 'unveil' or rediscover the figure of Laura for Elizabeth so that the female poet and the female patron appear as just and sensitive interpreters of Petrarch's female beloved. Hume's wholly Anglicized vocabulary is formally contained by an iambic pentameter couplet. The poem shuns elaboration; detail and embellishment are highly refined.

The commentaries which Hume appends to each chapter constitute the intellectual and theoretical underpinnings of her work. Hume's 'glosses' range from the simple identification of mythological figures to semantic interpretation. The 'Italian commentary' to which she refers may be identified as a combination of Bernardino Daniello da Lucca's 1549 edition of the *Trionfi* and that of Alessandro Vellutello (1545). Her commentaries display a piquant humorist at work, a proto-feminist revisionism, and a critical intelligence which takes issue with some exegetical points of the Italian editions. Hume is one of the most important of early Scottish women writers, and her work demonstrates the evolving nature of translation in seventeenth-century Scotland. S. M. DUNNIGAN

Sources A. Hume, *The triumphs of love: chastitie, death translated out of Petrach* (1644) · A. Hume, letter to A. Douglas, 1643, NL Scot.; repr. in D. Hume, *A generall history of Scotland* (1657) · A. Hume, letter to Lord Lauderdale, BL, 23123, fol. 280 · NL Scot., MS 2061; repr. in *The works of William Drummond of Hawthornden* (1711), 139, letter no. 30 · D. Laing, 'Extracts from the Hawthornden manuscripts', *Transactions of the Bibliographical Society of Scotland* (1904), 73–98 · S. M. Dunnigan, 'Scottish women writers, c.1560–c.1650', *A history of Scottish women's writing*, ed. D. Gifford and D. McMillan (1997), 15–43 · G. Greer and others, eds., *Kissing the rod: an anthology of seventeenth-century women's verse* (1988) · D. G. Rees, 'Petrarch's *Trionfo della morte* in English', *Italian Studies*, 7 (1952), 82–96 · R. D. S. Jack, *The Italian influence on Scottish literature* (1972) · D. Irving, *The lives of the Scotish poets*, 2 vols. (1804) · D. Irving, *The history of Scottish poetry*, ed. J. A. Carlyle (1861) · collections on the life of David Hume of Godscroft, U. Glas. L., MSS Gen 1207/38, 1198/359

Hume, Basil. *See* Hume, George Haliburton (1923–1999).

Hume, David, of Godscroft (1558–1629x31), political theorist and poet, was the second son (and second child of eight) of David Hume (1523/4–1574), laird of Wedderburn, and his wife, Mary (*d.* 1564), daughter of Andrew Johnston of Elphinstone. His elder brother, George (*d.* 1616), emerged as a significant political figure, serving as the comptroller of Scotland in the 1590s.

Hume studied with Andrew Simson at Dunbar grammar school some time after 1564, entering St Mary's College at the University of St Andrews about 1569 where he probably took his degree in 1573. From early 1578 to autumn 1579 Hume continued his studies in France, then at the Geneva Academy, when the illness of his elder brother forced his return and prevented him from going on to Italy.

Much of the childhood and early years of both Hume and his siblings was troubled by stormy relations with their stepmother, Margaret Kerr (*fl.* 1754), and also with their aunt, Jean Hepburn (*fl.* 1574–1580), who clung to the title Lady Wedderburn even after their father's succession to his brother's title and her remarriage. The financial insecurity that resulted, he tells us, prevented both him and his brother from marrying the women of their choice. Eventually in 1594 Hume married Barbara Johnston (*d.* 1629) of Elphinstone, daughter of James Johnston of Elphinstone and widow of his close friend James Haldane of Gleneagles, and raised five children.

His mother's determined Calvinism ensured that all the children were raised in the reformed faith, to which all of them would be passionately devoted throughout their lives. Both brothers participated in the Calvinist *coup d'état* of August 1582, subsequently known as the Ruthven raid, that overthrew the crypto-Catholic lords who then controlled the young James VI. A counter-coup in the following June led to the conservative rule of the earl of Arran, and David Hume along with much of the Ruthven leadership fled to England. Subsequently they were joined by Andrew Melville and many of the leading Presbyterian clergy. Hume's brother participated in an abortive rising against the Arran regime in April 1584, and the exiles were only able to return to Scotland as part of yet another coup in November 1585.

Political awakening Hume's intellectual promise was recognized early on, first at grammar school and then at university where George Buchanan, then principal, reputedly praised his Latin poetry. Throughout his life Hume's contemporaries, both friends and opponents, viewed him as a major intellect. Some time between 1581 and 1583 he developed a connection with the staunchly Presbyterian lord Archibald Douglas, eighth earl of Angus, subsequently becoming his companion and secretary. Through Angus he became associated with the Sidney circle during his exile, and it seems he came to be regarded as the potential heir to Buchanan. Undoubtedly it is true that Hume needs to be seen as part of the rich Latin culture and Calvinist humanism signally defined by Buchanan and Melville. While in exile Hume began assembling documents that were initially intended to form an apologia for the exiles and, apparently, for the Presbyterian cause. This collecting of documents continued throughout much of his life and eventually issued in his well-known, posthumously published history of the house of Douglas. One of the more notable features of this vernacular writing is an inserted dialogue with Angus. Written shortly after their return to Scotland, the dialogue touches lightly on the justification of political resistance, but the main thrust of the conversation is the ideal of citizenship and the obligation of civic responsibility. Hume imagined Scotland, effectively, as an aristocratic republic where selfless nobles discussed, determined, and actively pursued the public good. The dialogue provides one of the earliest instances of the neologism 'patriot' and insists on the classical citizen who is at once ruler and ruled. Although Hume's republicanism became increasingly and severely attenuated during the course of the seventeenth century, his commitment to aristocratic governance may even have surpassed that of Buchanan. Where Buchanan regarded the house of Douglas in the fifteenth century as exemplars of baronial gangsterism rightly destroyed by the crown, Hume saw instead a patriot dynasty comparable to the Fabii and the Scipiones of classical antiquity. Much later, when Hume spoke of 'the great Buchanan … great, it's fair to say … in croaking anger', he probably meant Buchanan's historical views rather than the aged scholar's personal irritability (Hume, *Lusus poetici*, 11).

Although Hume's writings were well known in manuscript and well regarded, he published nothing before 1599, and his career as a writer began only in 1603 at James VI's accession to the English crown. Like both Andrew Melville and the king, Hume was a passionate advocate of the British union. But quite unlike the king and virtually all writing about the union at this time, Hume envisioned a fusion of the two realms into a new and highly civic polity whose citizens acquired an altogether new British identity. A self-proclaimed 'Scoto-Britannus', Hume promoted this objective in Latin poetry, historical writings, and outstandingly in his two-part *De unione insulae Britannicae*. Written in part as a response to the anti-unionist sentiment that surfaced in the English House of Commons during the spring of 1604 and assuming its final form in anticipation of the Anglo-Scots Union Commission that met from October to December of that year, the first section delineated the necessity of union. Hume believed that the creation of Britain would lead to an enormous cultural flowering, that it would at last bring civilization to all areas of the realm, and that it would at once derive from and promote civic-mindedness. The work is notable not least for its discussion of learning and the possibility of human improvement, eliding neatly from the Renaissance promotion of humane letters to an almost Enlightenment declaration of human equality:

> I do not disparage the individual of any people whatsoever. I would wish that others would refrain from extolling themselves too much and from denigrating those who are different from them. Mindful of justice and humanity,

rather let all, one with another, strive for moderation.
(Hume, *De unione*, 8)

Hume's determined patriotism in no way qualified his unionist commitments, but rather the reverse. Scotland would realize its great potential through the union, and thus, for Hume, Scottish identity generated British consciousness. Further, Hume argued, as the king's migration to London was incontestable and irresistible, it could only be in Scotland's best interest to create a genuinely British state that assured parity for both realms.

Poet and historian The second part of Hume's union treatise dealt with the specific constitutional measures that would guarantee a union of equals: notably a British parliament based at York that would be superior to all regional assemblies, a British council consisting of equal Scottish and English membership, and, most sensitive, a gradual union of the two churches ideally on the Scottish model. Inevitably the second part of the *De unione* was hugely controversial and could not be printed anywhere in Britain. In the end it was stopped in the press even in France, and existed only in manuscript until the appearance of a modern bilingual edition in 2002.

Hume also promoted the union through poetry. Prominent among these poems is his highly complex *Daphn-Amaryllis* (Hume even provided a guide to its reading suggestive of Edmund Spenser's prefatory remarks to the *Faerie Queene*). In it he adopted a Virgilian tone and spoke of a British crusade against the Roman 'flamen'. This apocalyptic dimension is atypical of his work, and his distrust of prophecy contrasts with the attitudes of such close associates as Andrew Melville. At a more basic level the British crusade points to a fundamental cleavage within Hume's thought. Hume might promote Britain for both patriotic and religious reasons, but the more one spoke of a unified kingdom, the more readily one adopted the voice of Augustan empire rather than of Ciceronian republic, of traditional hierarchical monarchy rather than of egalitarian civic commonwealth. The first part of the *De unione* is suffused with this contradiction, alternately celebrating authoritarian monarchy and then urging civic action. This movement from citizen to subject also found itself reinforced from a still deeper cultural transition associated with the fading of the Renaissance, the quest for stability, and the Counter-Reformation, all leading to a new authoritarianism that increasingly characterized attitudes throughout the British Isles and in Europe generally after 1590.

This changing world manifested itself most dramatically with the king's new religious policies. In 1605 James commenced an attack on Scotland's Presbyterian church and by 1610 had successfully reimposed diocesan episcopacy—a feat vastly more difficult to imagine had he remained simply king of the Scots. Hume played a leading role in resisting this policy of conformity with England. Although he never abandoned his commitment to the British project, Hume perceived the new order as English 'tyranny'. Throughout these years and beyond Hume participated in a widely disseminated correspondence with the new Scottish bishops—effectively a pamphlet war—in which he attacked government policy on patriotic, historical, religious, and philosophical grounds. The Presbyterian cause suffered acutely from the want of a press, and, as a result, only a small portion of Hume's correspondence survives today. But it is abundantly clear that Hume offered a remarkably reflective discussion of the epistemological basis of political authority and even of the nature of language itself. It is also clear that Hume emerged as the terror of the Jacobean clerical establishment.

In 1608 Hume undertook a lengthy critique of William Camden's *Britannia* (first edition 1586) in which he sought to defend Buchanan's *Rerum Scoticarum historia* (1582) and traditional claims for Scotland's vast antiquity (and thus autonomy) against what he perceived as the Englishman's 'mockery'. This defence of Scotland's fabulous history was necessarily less compelling than his exchanges with the bishops. In it Hume made the extraordinary claim that the English language only reached Scotland with Edward I's invasion in the late thirteenth century. His hostility to the *Britannia* was widely shared among Scottish intellectuals of the period. It is an indication of the problems with early modern Scotland's cultural life that virtually none of the responses to Camden secured contemporaneous publication, Hume's *Camdenea* existing only in manuscript even today. There is no small irony in the circumstance that Hume found himself in trouble with the Scottish privy council that year for helping to obtain the publication of John Murray's sermon against episcopacy (*A Godly and Fruitfull Sermon Preached at Lieth* [*sic*]), when so much of his own work would never see print at all. Hume's activism declined as the second decade wore on. Many believed he had won the argument, but few could doubt who was winning the war.

One of Scotland's leading Latin poets, Hume inevitably contributed poetry celebrating James's 1617 visit. In it he continued to promote both the British union and Scottish dignity. His last major work, *Apologia basilica, seu, Machiavelli ingenium, examinatum in libro quem inscriptsit 'Principem'* (Paris, 1626), offers a critique of the Italian thinker and provides an indication of how drastically the political landscape had shifted since the later sixteenth century. Dedicated to Charles I, the tract firmly endorses mixed, limited monarchy and plain-dealing, while rejecting absolutism, irreligion, and, implicitly, republicanism. In 1623 he served as a JP for Berwickshire and devoted much energy during his last decade trying to protect (not altogether successfully) his family's patronage. At the end of his life he was much exercised to publish, at last, his great history of the house of Douglas, apparently because it promoted the civic values he saw as in decline.

Hume's wife died in late June 1629 and was buried at Duns. Hume died some time after 8 August 1629 and before 4 April 1631. He was almost certainly buried at Duns as well. His son and heir, James *Hume (*fl.* 1633–1640), physician, Hebraist, poet, and mathematician, settled in Paris, became famously embroiled in an extended academic dispute with Jean-Baptiste Morin (1583–1656), and, among other things, lamented his father's misman-agement of the estate. His daughter Anna *Hume (*fl.* 1644), a translator of Petrarch's sonnets, worked hard to publish the Douglas history despite its unfashionable pol-itics. A brief truncated version appeared about 1633. Anna succeeded in publishing an apparently full, if Anglicized edition at a more politically congenial moment in 1644, but even then over the objections of the eleventh earl of Douglas. In 1639 James and Anna produced a *Poemata omnia* in Paris, which also included the first part of the *De unione* as well as some of James's own poems and his brief Latin descriptions of several battles of the Thirty Years' War.

During his lifetime contemporaries regarded Hume as a major poet and major political thinker, indeed as being of a stature fully worthy of the medieval scholastic Duns Scotus who was identified with that region. Despite the efforts of his children, Hume's reputation constricted pre-cipitously at his death—a phenomenon also noticed by contemporaries. Only in the last decades of the twentieth century did this original and influential individual begin to be re-evaluated.

PAUL J. MCGINNIS and ARTHUR H. WILLIAMSON

Sources D. Hume, *History of the house of Douglas* (1643–57) · D. Hume, *De unione insulae Britannicae*, Paris edn 1639, tract 1 (1605) · D. Hume, 'De unione insulae Britannicae', tract 2 · D. Hume, *De familia Humia* (1839) · J. Hume, ed., *Poemata omnia* (1639) · D. Hume, *Lusus poetici* (1605) · *Report on the manuscripts of Colonel David Milne Home, of Wedderburn Castle*, HMC, 57 (1902) · D. Calderwood, *The history of the Kirk of Scotland*, ed. T. Thomson and D. Laing, 8 vols., Wodrow Society, 7 (1842–9), vols. 4, 6–7 · *George Buchanan: the political poetry: a translation and commentary*, ed. P. J. McGinnis and A. H. Williamson (2000) · D. Hume, 'Camdenea' · A. H. Williamson, *Scottish national consciousness in the age of James VI* (1979) · A. H. Williamson, 'Patterns of British identity: "Britain" and its rivals in the 16th and 17th centuries', *The new British history: founding a modern state, 1603–1715*, ed. G. Burgess (1999), 138–73 · *The British union: a critical edition and translation of David Hume of Godscroft's 'De unione insulae Britannicae'*, ed. and trans. P. McGinnis and A. Williamson (2002)
Archives NL Scot., 'Origine and descent of the most noble and illustrious familie and name of Douglas', 1644 · Gowkscroft, Berwickshire, papers | BL, Royal MS 12A.53 · NA Scot., GD 267/2/4x · NL Scot., Advocates MSS 31.6.9; 31.6.12; 31.6.13; 34.6.21 · U. Edin., Dc.5.50/1–2; La.III.249; Dc.7.46

Hume, Sir David, of Crossrig. *See* Home, Sir David, of Crossrig, Lord Crossrig (1643–1707).

Hume, David (1711–1776), philosopher and historian, was born in Edinburgh, probably in the family's home in the Lawnmarket, on 26 April 1711. He was the second son and third child of Joseph Home of Ninewells (1681–1713), land-owner and advocate, and Katherine Falconer (1683–1745). (The decision to change the spelling of the surname from Home to Hume was David's alone, and was probably taken when he was in his twenties.) Hume later described him-self as 'of a good family, both by father and mother' ('My own life', in *Essays*, xxxii). The male line were kinsmen of the earls of Home; they had been proprietors of the estate of Ninewells, in Berwickshire, since the fifteenth century. David's grandfather, John Home, had served the house of

David Hume (1711–1776), by Allan Ramsay, 1766

Home and his government in the traditional manner of a borders' laird—which is to say in that order. A Presbyter-ian, but no bigot, he had acquiesced in the rule of James VII, and held several offices under William III. He married three times and had six children, to which his third wife, Mary, widow of Sir David Falconer of Newton, added seven of her own. It was one of her daughters by Sir David, Katherine, who married Joseph, eldest son of John Home by his first wife: David Hume's father, in other words, mar-ried his stepsister. Sir David Falconer had been president of the college of justice as Lord Halkerton, and Joseph Home had likewise been prepared for a career in law, being sent first to college in Edinburgh and then to Utrecht.

Hume's parents were married on 4 January 1708. David's elder brother John was born in 1709 and his sister Kather-ine in 1710; their father died when all three were infants. They grew up at Ninewells, near the village of Chirnside, in the Merse, less than 10 miles from Berwick; the winter months were spent in the house in Edinburgh. These were David Hume's homes (when he was not out of the country) for over half his life, until his elder brother married in 1751; but as the younger brother, David would always have to make his own way in life.

Hume's need to make a living was to result in several attempted careers and a variety of short-term employ-ments; his life was not without incident. But not until the last twelve years of his life did the incidents amount to more than temporary interruptions to his chosen course of study and writing. From an early age Hume's ambitions were pre-eminently intellectual: no less than a revolution in philosophy, and the establishment of a science of man, an enterprise which he gradually extended from metaphysics and moral philosophy to politics, political economy, and history. Accompanying this speculative ambition was a practical determination to become an independent man of letters. The novel element here was independence. Recognizing the opportunities afforded by the expansion of commercial publishing, Hume sought to free himself of the dependence on the patronage of the great which the Renaissance humanist model of the man of letters had presupposed. Once he had achieved independence, he self-consciously made an example of his success to his fellow writers. That he did so as a philosopher without religious belief added an edge to the example which made it harder to carry off. But Hume was usually careful not to flaunt his unbelief in a way which would alienate the open-minded; and he was aided in the effort by his famously but also genuinely equable, sociable, and cheerful character.

Accounts of Hume's life are naturally shaped by his own version of it, 'My own life', which he wrote in April 1776 when close to death. It is often supplemented by the 'Letter to a physician' of 1734, in which Hume reviewed the state of his mind and body in the crucial formative years between 1729 and 1734. 'My own life' was not a philosopher's autobiography in the genre which Descartes had established and Vico had followed; nor was it comparable with any but the shortest of Gibbon's essays in a historian's autobiography. Containing 'little more than the History of my Writings', it made no attempt to explain how he had come to think and write what he did. This may have freed later biographers from the obvious pitfalls of the philosopher's autobiography, in which a complex process of intellectual evolution is rewritten to present the final outcome as predestined. But it is also free of any clues to that intellectual development. On its chosen ground it is not inaccurate, but it does foreshorten important episodes. In so far as it highlights abiding preoccupations, these are the failure of the *Treatise of Human Nature* and its consequences for the presentation of Hume's philosophy, and his gradual acquisition of financial independence. For evidence of Hume's intellectual development the biographer can of course turn to his writings themselves, and to his wonderful letters; but these too have limitations. Convinced of his originality, Hume always restricted his expressions of disagreement with predecessors; and the bulk of his surviving correspondence dates from the last fifteen years of his life, when his works were already written. (It is possible that a new edition of the letters, in preparation, may contain fresh information.) As it is, the most recent biography is *The Life of David Hume* by E. C. Mossner, which was first published in 1954. A personal rather than an intellectual biography, its indulgent tone now makes it look dated. It has been corrected by new scholarship at several important points, but has yet to be replaced.

Early studies It is not known how Hume was educated before he went to Edinburgh University; after the example of his father, he and his brother may well have had a private tutor. But he attended college young, even by

the standards of the time. David's signature appears in the matriculation register under the Greek class of Professor William Scott on 27 February 1723, with the number two alongside his name. This is taken to indicate that David was in his second year at the college, and had entered it, probably at the same time as his older brother, in the 1721–2 session, when as young as ten. The brothers would have lived in the family house in Edinburgh, probably with their mother, during the academic session. Latin was taught in the first year (and it is unlikely that Hume would have been excused the class at that age), Greek in the second. He would then have studied philosophy in the third-year class of Colin Drummond, professor of logic and metaphysics. A recently analysed set of dictates from Drummond's class indicates that his philosophy teaching (delivered in Latin) consisted of a scholasticism that was by then old-fashioned, and was associated with a strenuously orthodox Calvinism (Stewart, 'Hume's intellectual development'). Whether Hume took the optional class in moral philosophy given by William Law, whose orthodoxy was also well attested, is not known. But he did attend the fourth-year natural philosophy class of Professor Robert Steuart in 1724–5. Steuart taught Newtonian optics, mechanics, and astronomy, sometimes direct from Newton but more often using works by his early Scottish commentators John Keill and David Gregory. Perhaps even more important in Steuart's teaching was Boyle, particularly for the experimental part of the course. Works by Boyle headed the catalogue of the Physiological Library which Steuart created for his students, and of which David Hume became a member. Boyle's preoccupations would in turn have provided an entrée to other books in the library, notably Lucretius and the modern interpreters of Epicureanism, headed by Gassendi. While natural history and mathematics predominated, the library also contained works of theology and of modern philosophy, including the *Recherche de la verité* by Malebranche and Locke's *Essay Concerning Human Understanding*. Hume was no more than fourteen when he finished this class, and ten years later described college education as extending little further than the languages; but his access at this stage to works which were later among the few fundamental reference points of his own philosophy is at least suggestive.

Once Hume had finished college in 1725—he did not graduate—the course of his studies becomes much harder to reconstruct. By 1727 his family had arranged for him to receive instruction in the law, no doubt intending him to follow his father and become an advocate. But a letter to his friend Michael Ramsay indicates that Cicero and Virgil, not law textbooks, were his preferred reading, and that he was already trying to write on philosophical topics (letter to Michael Ramsay, 4 July 1727, *Letters*, 1.9–11). A year before, he had acquired a copy of Shaftesbury's *Characteristicks*, a sophisticated statement of a modernized, polite Stoicism. Not until 1729, however, did Hume's reading and thinking begin to come together. Then, as he later described it to an unidentified physician, 'when I was about 18 Years of Age, there seem'd to be open'd up to me a new Scene of Thought, which transported me beyond Measure, & made me, with an Ardor natural to young men, throw up every other Pleasure or Business to apply entirely to it' ('Letter to a physician', March 1734, *Letters*, 1.13).

Unfortunately, the ardour burnt itself out in September, when Hume suffered a sudden loss of energy and confidence. The crisis lasted almost five years. Despite the care with which Hume recalled his changing mental and physical condition in the letter of 1734, it is not clear what exactly was wrong. Various minor physical complaints were identified and apparently cured. Hume took to riding, covering 8 to 10 Scottish miles a day, and in 1731 he developed a vigorous appetite, which transformed his appearance from tall and lean to sturdy and robust. The real problem, however, was his inability to bring his philosophical studies into an order fit for publication. Stoic reflections on the vanity of the world, he discovered, were no help in his predicament; but he evidently found 'diversion and improvement' in reading Bayle, whom he recommended to Michael Ramsay (letter of March 1732, *Letters*, 1.12). It was perhaps not a coincidence that by the time he was twenty, as he later recalled, he had also filled a manuscript book with the progress of his thoughts, or doubts, on the subject of religion (letter to Gilbert Elliot, 10 March 1751, ibid., 1.154).

It is still not known to whom the letter of 1734 was addressed, or if it was ever sent (suggested recipients have included George Cheyne and John Arbuthnot). But by the time it was written Hume had decided to resolve the crisis by trying an active life as a merchant. His move to Bristol in March 1734 may have been precipitated by the accusation by a local Chirnside woman that Hume was the father of her child (although she accused him only after he had left); Hume himself never mentioned the incident. In Bristol he was employed as a clerk to Michael Miller, a sugar merchant, who was probably therefore also involved in the slave trade. The experiment did not last long: Hume's efforts to correct the grammar and spelling of his employer's letters were not appreciated. But Hume had no regrets, as he now went over to France, stopping first in Paris. Bristol had been no more than a convenient temporary staging post.

A Treatise of Human Nature Whatever the difficulties he had encountered since entering upon his 'new Scene of Thought', Hume was by this time well launched on his first great work, *A Treatise of Human Nature*. About the chronology of its genesis, at least, Hume was clear. Planned before he was twenty-one, it was composed before he was twenty-five, during his three years in France (letter to Gilbert Elliot, March or April 1751, *Letters*, 1.158; 'My own life', in *Essays*, xxxiv). After his introduction to Paris, where his guide was the Chevalier Ramsay—Jacobite, metaphysical philosopher, and freemason—Hume moved on in September 1734 to Rheims, where he could hope to live more cheaply. Ramsay gave him several introductions, notably to the Abbé Pluche, and perhaps also to the Pyrrhonist philosopher Lévesque de Pouilly, whose brother was an acquaintance of Ramsay. After a year

Hume moved again, this time to La Flèche, on the Loire: its advantages were that it was still cheaper, and that its Jesuit college had an excellent library even if, as the college of Descartes, it was a stronghold of Cartesianism. Hume stayed at La Flèche for two years, until the work was sufficiently ready to be taken to a publisher. He left in August 1737, and was in London by mid-September.

It was to be a year before Hume signed articles of agreement with a publisher, John Noon, on 26 September 1738, and a further four months before *A Treatise of Human Nature*, books 1 and 2, appeared, anonymously, at the end of January 1739. In the meantime Hume enjoyed 'the pleasures of the town', made new acquaintances, and found several passages in the work which he was able to improve. Among those acquaintances was Pierre Desmaizeaux, the Huguenot journalist and biographer of Bayle, whose circle met at the Rainbow Coffee House, Lancaster Court, where Hume himself lodged. Negotiations with Noon took time because Hume already had views about the terms on which he should publish, and was determined not to surrender the rights to more than the first edition; in return, however, he had to agree that no second edition could be published until the first had been entirely sold.

If Hume was able to give a clear account of the progress of the treatise's composition, he left disappointingly few traces of what is equally important to the biographer of a philosopher: the course and content of his reading while he was writing. At Rheims and at La Flèche he would have had ample opportunity to read French philosophers, including, it has been surmised, works in the clandestine irreligious tradition (Wootton, 210–12). On his way back Hume advised his friend Michael Ramsay that he might prepare himself to understand the metaphysical parts of his philosophy by reading Malebranche, Berkeley, Bayle, and Descartes; but that the rest of it was so little dependent on 'all former systems of Philosophy' that he would have to rely on his own good sense (to Michael Ramsay, 26–31 Aug 1737, in Mossner, *Life of David Hume*, 627). In the introduction to the *Treatise*, and again in the *Abstract* of the *Treatise*, Hume singled out 'some late philosophers in England, who have begun to put the science of man on a new footing': Locke, Shaftesbury, Mandeville, Hutcheson, and Butler. The *Abstract* also mentioned Malebranche and the *Art de penser* of Arnauld. But few of these, or any others, were the subject of more than an occasional reference in the body of the work.

A Treatise of Human Nature was the product of an extraordinary intellectual ambition. The scale of that ambition was explicit in the introduction to book 1. There Hume outlined his conviction that a science of man, the knowledge of human nature, should be the basis for all the others: for mathematics, natural philosophy, and natural religion, as well as for logic, morals, criticism, and politics. Further, he would argue that 'as the science of man is the only solid foundation for the other sciences, so the only solid foundation we can give to this science itself must be laid on experience and observation' (*Treatise*, 4). The consequences of this simple proposition were to be even more radical when applied to moral subjects than they had been when applied to natural ones, a century earlier. The multiplication of philosophical systems, which had brought metaphysical reasoning into disrepute, would be at an end. For a philosophy based on experience cannot discover 'the ultimate original qualities of human nature' (ibid., 5), any more, it was implied, than it can reason about entities, such as God, his qualities, and his operations, of which experience gives us no firm knowledge.

Hume's starting point was to distinguish the perceptions of the mind into impressions and ideas. Impressions are perceptions which strike the mind with the most force and violence, and include all our sensations, passions, and emotions. Ideas are the faint images of these impressions in thinking and reasoning. (A note added that this was perhaps only to restore the word 'idea' to 'its original sense, from which Mr Locke had perverted it, in making it stand for all our perceptions' (Treatise, 7). From this distinction derived the structure of the Treatise. The subject of book 1 was the understanding, treated as the nature and relations of our ideas. Book 2 analysed the passions as impressions. Finally book 3 would treat our moral ideas as derived from feelings, or impressions.

Hume's argument in book 1 was that knowledge consists in relations or connections between ideas, and that only some relations—those of resemblance and quantity—can yield demonstrative knowledge. Others, above all those of contiguity and causation, can yield no more than degrees of probability. At the core of the book, therefore, was a discussion of probability. Our perception of cause and effect is no more than the product of repeated experience, of the constant conjunction of one object with another in the mind. The more constant and regular the conjunction, the more the experience of it will generate a belief in causation; but only when the conjunction is entirely free from doubt and uncertainty may it amount to a proof. On this account, our ideas of cause and effect have nothing to do with any power or efficacy supposed to be in objects themselves: we cannot attribute causality to the nature of matter. Equally we can have no idea of the nature of the mind independent of our perceptions. We can have no impression of the 'substance' of our minds, and therefore the question of the materiality or immateriality of the soul is 'absolutely unintelligible'. Similarly with the idea of the self: 'personal identity' is not natural but artificial, a fiction. In his conclusion to book 1 Hume acknowledged the dangers of excessive scepticism in questions of the understanding, famously responding that nature itself supplied him with the antidote: 'I dine, I play a game of back-gammon, I converse, and am merry with my friends … I find myself absolutely and necessarily determin'd to live, and talk, and act like other people in the common affairs of life'. Yet, he went on, 'in all the incidents of life we ought still to preserve our scepticism'. For philosophy is preferable to superstition of any kind or denomination, and 'generally speaking, the errors in religion are dangerous; those in philosophy only ridiculous' (Treatise, 175–7).

Book 2 treated the passions as 'secondary and reflective impressions', which arise from the original impressions made by bodily pains and pleasures. Hume thus did not attempt to study the passions' natural or physical causes, which would have required him to engage with anatomy and physiology. He first discussed the indirect passions, focusing particularly on pride and humility, love and hatred. These passions are aroused by a complex but intelligible process of association of ideas and impressions. The process, however, is not simply internal to the mind of the individual; our pride, for example, depends to a great extent on our reputation in the opinion of others. This Hume explained through a communication of sentiments between the individual and others, which communication he termed 'sympathy'. (In Hume's usage, therefore, sympathy is not a specific feeling; it is not pity or compassion.) Sympathy likewise explains our esteem for the rich and the powerful, as well as the passions of pity and malice.

When Hume turned to the direct passions—desire and aversion, hope and fear—he immediately faced the problem of the will, and the 'long disputed question concerning liberty and necessity' (Treatise, 257). The question was whether actions of the mind are to be regarded as freely willed or as necessitated, that is determined. Hobbes had notoriously maintained the latter; but it was generally assumed that only if a person's actions were freely willed could he be morally responsible for them. Hume's answer exemplified his conviction that a philosophy based on experience and observation would clarify topics hitherto regarded as abstruse. The will, he argued, is simply an impression, and is influenced only by the passions. Given that the will is determined by the passions, it is incoherent to insist on the liberty of the will. But this does not abrogate moral responsibility. The reverse is true: we cannot ascribe responsibility unless we suppose that the will is caused. ''Tis only upon the principles of necessity, that a person acquires any merit or demerit from his actions, however the common opinion may incline to the contrary' (ibid., 264). It was in this context that Hume made his famous remark that 'reason is, and ought only to be the slave of the passions, and can never pretend to any other office than to serve and obey them' (ibid., 266). The doctrine of free will was not to be rescued by asserting that reason contests the direction of the will with the passions.

In December 1737, while he was preparing books 1 and 2 for the press, Hume had admitted to his friend Henry Home (the future Lord Kames) that he was 'castrating' the work, 'that is, cutting off its noble Parts, that is, endeavouring it shall give as little Offence as possible' (to Henry Home, 2 Dec 1737, New Letters, 3). In particular, he had cut out 'some Reasonings concerning Miracles' (ibid., 2). The immediate motive had been his desire to present the draft to Joseph Butler, though in the event he was unable to do so. But the fear of giving offence was part of a more general anxiety about the reception of the work; he was uneasily aware that two octavo volumes of philosophy, one of 475 pages and the other of 320, would with difficulty attract readers. Wishing to spare himself mortification, he went down to Ninewells shortly after publication, prepared to content himself with the opinion of a few competent judges. Impatience soon got the better of him, and by April he was writing to Desmaizeaux, to whom he had given a copy, to prompt a response. Desmaizeaux did make favourable reference to the *Treatise* in a list of new books in the *Bibliothèque Raisonnée*, a periodical published in Amsterdam by the Irish bookseller William Smith. (The notice, however, breached Hume's anonymity, naming him as the author.) Other, less favourable, notices appeared in periodicals published in Leipzig and The Hague. But full reviews were much slower to appear, and when one did, in *The History of the Works of the Learned* in November and December 1739, it combined incomprehension with mockery. In an attempt to explain as well as to draw attention to the work, Hume prepared an *Abstract* (his authorship of which is now generally accepted) which was published in London in March 1740. In it Hume concentrated on the argument concerning cause and effect, presenting it as a specimen of the whole. The initiative had one outcome. William Smith, who was sent a copy of the *Treatise* and the *Abstract*, published a lengthy review in the *Bibliothèque Raisonnée* for April–June 1740, two-thirds of which was taken straight from the *Abstract*, while the remainder commented critically on the young author's dogmatic Pyrrhonism.

While awaiting the reaction to the first two books, Hume was also finalizing book 3, 'Of morals'. At some point in 1739 a draft of this was sent to Francis Hutcheson, professor of moral philosophy at Glasgow. Although Hutcheson's comments have not survived, Hume's letters in response have. In so far as it can be reconstructed, the exchange is of some significance. For on the relationship between Hume and Hutcheson turned the twentieth-century interpretation of Hume's moral and metaphysical philosophy. In the classic interpretation of Norman Kemp Smith, 'Hume, under the influence of Hutcheson, entered into his philosophy through the gateway of morals' (Kemp Smith, *Philosophy*, 12). In which case Hume's letters to Hutcheson in December 1739 and March 1740 may be read as an ingenuous attempt to persuade the senior philosopher that the arguments of the *Treatise* were a legitimate development of his own. But it is also possible that Hume was aware of important differences between them, and that his deference belied a determination to advance arguments of his own.

Book 3 was published in a third octavo volume of some 310 pages in November 1740, by Thomas Longman. Hume began with the apparently straightforward argument that moral distinctions are derived not from reason but from a moral sense: that is, from the feeling of satisfaction or dissatisfaction we have when contemplating another's behaviour. He was equivocal about the sense in which virtues and vices are 'natural'; it depended on the use of the word 'nature'. There was an important sense, however, in which justice was an 'artificial' virtue. A love of mankind in general is not a natural, universal human motive. Hence the origin of justice, and with it of allegiance to government, must be traced to other principles, and to the operation of custom or habit. In his discussion of property, justice, and government, Hume covered ground familiar to the theorists of natural law and rights; but his argument was quite different from theirs. It was not natural laws, whether divinely ordained or apprehended by reason, or the exchange of rights by contracts, which explained how humans came to form societies regulated by justice; it was self-interest, combined with convention, or agreement reached over time, which established the artifice of justice. In the final part of the book Hume returned to the virtues and vices which could be called 'natural', the qualities of mind which evoke love and pride, or hate and humility. But natural virtues are no less the product of sympathy than artificial ones: we form our ideas of virtue through others' as well as our own judgement of the utility of actions. Moral ideas might be derived from feeling, not reason; but they are not the product of an instinctive benevolence. Virtue is always considered as the means to an end. Hume concluded this book with the observation, previously made in self-defence to Hutcheson, who had accused him of lacking 'Warmth in the Cause of Virtue', that he wrote as an anatomist rather than as a painter. The anatomist dissected human nature, and should not rival the painter in presenting his figures in graceful and engaging attitudes. But the painter could not excel without the anatomist; the latter's speculations were 'subservient to'—that is, the indispensable basis of—practical morality (*Treatise*, 395; to Hutcheson, 17 Sept 1739, *Letters*, 1.32).

Book 3 of the *Treatise* received only one review, again in the *Bibliothèque Raisonnée*, early in 1741. The reviewer identified Hume's reasoning on justice with that of Hobbes, and was insistent on its difference from Hutcheson's; it has been suggested that the reviewer may have been Hutcheson himself, or someone under his influence (Moore and Stewart, 24–6). Whether Hume would have been surprised to discover this is a matter of interpretation; but of the depth and persistence of his disappointment with the reception of the *Treatise* there is no doubt. His last word on it was the most emphatic: it had fallen '*dead-born from the press*, without reaching such distinction, as even to excite a murmur among the zealots' ('My own life', in *Essays*, xxxiv). Yet Hume's disappointment is puzzling, and the second part of that judgement is at least over-simplified. He had not hidden the demands which such a work would place on readers, and he had admitted to friends that his chief reward must be the approbation of the few who would be able to judge it. Moreover Hume cannot have supposed that his 'castration' of the *Treatise* before its publication would be sufficient to allay the doubts of those whose philosophy was founded on religion. Even before book 3 appeared, books 1 and 2 had undercut the arguments required to derive morals from a divine ordering of the world: if experience alone was the basis of knowledge, human beings were on their own.

And in case Hutcheson had missed the point, Hume told him bluntly that his reliance on final causes was 'pretty uncertain & unphilosophical' (to Hutcheson, 17 Sept 1739, *Letters*, 1.33). Hutcheson was no zealot, but he did murmur when he read the *Treatise*. He was not alone.

Whatever his reasons for disappointment, Hume's conviction of the failure of the *Treatise of Human Nature* was decisive for his subsequent approach to publication. Never again did he offer the public a work of abstract philosophy at such length. But he was far from abandoning philosophy; and he clearly continued to believe that any serious treatment of metaphysics or morals should take account of the arguments which he first presented in the *Treatise*.

Essays Following Hume's return to Ninewells in 1739, his concern for the fate of the *Treatise* by no means impeded the pursuit of new projects. Within a year of publication of the final volume of the *Treatise*, he brought out a volume of *Essays, Moral and Political*, published by Alexander Kincaid of Edinburgh in 1741; a second volume followed in 1742. The first volume contained a number of essays on polite behaviour (most of which Hume eventually dropped from later editions); one of these presented the study of history as particularly suitable for women. But the majority were on political topics: on the liberty of the press, on politics as a science, on the independence of parliament, and on parties in general and in Britain in particular. Two explicitly reflected on British government in comparison with French monarchy, asking 'whether the British Government inclines more to Absolute Monarchy, or to a Republic', and whether the difference was simply that between 'liberty and despotism'; in neither case was the answer one-sided. This volume also contained the essay 'Of superstition and enthusiasm', a prelude to the later 'Natural history of religion'. The second volume included a further selection on polite topics, along with four essays of varying weight on philosophical types: the epicurean, the stoic, the platonist, and the sceptic, the last being discussed most fully. There was also a substantial essay on the rise and progress of the arts and sciences, and a short but timely 'character of Sir Robert Walpole'— except that Hume had written it while Walpole was still in power, only for him to fall before it appeared. Embarrassed by seeming to join in the triumph at the great man's expense, Hume subsequently reduced the essay to a footnote to that on politics as a science, and eventually omitted it altogether. The *Essays* attracted more attention than the *Treatise*; but it was some time before Hume could realize his hope that they would prove 'like Dung with Marle, & bring forward the rest of my Philosophy' (to Henry Home, 13 June 1742, *New Letters*, 10).

Nevertheless, the *Essays* staked out a framework for understanding contemporary British politics which was considerably more sophisticated than that which had hitherto dominated public debate, by Viscount Bolingbroke. Against Bolingbroke's marriage of whig constitutional shibboleths and classical republican virtue, Hume emphasized the importance of regular political institutions, of 'civil' liberty, and of the stabilizing force of interest. It was parties of principle, an entirely modern phenomenon, which were dangerous, especially when principle was reinforced with religious enthusiasm (though priests themselves, Hume noted, always acted out of interest). The *Essays* might thus be read as a defence of the government whigs, except that Hume cast doubt on the exceptionalism which was fundamental to any whig view of English liberties: a 'civilised European monarchy' such as that of France, he insisted, was not a despotism.

Since writing was not bringing a significant income, Hume needed to look for a paid position. Tutorships were one obvious possibility, and Hume had canvassed an apparent opportunity in 1739, without success. But in 1744 a much better, less dependent prospect appeared on his horizon: the professorship of moral philosophy at Edinburgh. Hume's 'Affair at Edinburgh' (to Henry Home, 13 June 1745, *New Letters*, 14) proved to be a tangled business, with which scholarship has come to grips only recently. The prospect arose as it became increasingly clear that the incumbent professor, John Pringle, was unwilling to return from the leave which he had first been granted in 1742 in order to serve as a physician with the army in the Netherlands. The appointment was in the hands of the city council, and Hume's candidacy was backed by the lord provost, John Coutts, who in turn was presumed to have the support of the duke of Argyll, the most powerful individual in Scottish politics. In fact Hume's position was never as strong as this might make it appear (and he seems to have supposed). Argyll was out of office and not likely to put his influence on the line for Hume. Coutts's first choice was Francis Hutcheson, not Hume; and though Hutcheson twice declined the post, he was adamantly opposed to the candidacy of Hume. So were William Leechman, professor of divinity at Glasgow, and William Wishart, principal of Edinburgh University, who had hopes of obtaining the post himself. Hume's prospects waned further as Pringle delayed his resignation until March 1745, by which time Coutts's term of office had ended and effective leadership of the council had passed to Gavin Hamilton, who favoured the candidacy of his nephew and one of Pringle's substitutes, William Cleghorn. But the definitive obstacle to Hume was none of these: it was the clergy of Edinburgh, who were called upon to give their *avisamentum* on 28 May. By a majority of twelve to three the ministers vetoed Hume 'on account of his principles'. Cleghorn was duly appointed.

Hume had been surprised to learn that Hutcheson and Leechman were supporting the accusations against him, and had asked his friend William Mure of Caldwell to enquire very discreetly what could be the meaning of the conduct of 'that celebrated & benevolent Moralist' (to Mure of Caldwell, 4 Aug 1744, *Letters*, 1.58). Only at a late stage, however, did he respond: sent a copy of Wishart's objections to the *Treatise* by Coutts, he replied seriatim to the principal's charges, and Henry Home had both printed together as *A Letter from a Gentleman to his Friend in Edinburgh*, published on 21 May 1745. Hume pounced on

Wishart's misunderstandings of his arguments; but he could hardly deny his opponents' underlying point, that the author of the *Treatise* would deprive morals of a religious foundation, when it was one of the duties of the professor to teach the truth of the Christian religion. Nor ought he to have been surprised by the opposition from Glasgow, when he had once admitted to Hutcheson that a man's philosophical speculations were relevant to his character if he was concerned in the instruction of youth, and had more recently commented on a sermon by Leechman in a tone only just short of open mockery (to Hutcheson, 17 Sept 1739; to Mure of Caldwell, 30 June 1743, ibid., 1.34, 50–52).

By the time the Edinburgh 'affair' reached its conclusion, Hume was already in England, having accepted the post of tutor to the marquess of Annandale in February 1745. The marquess was twenty-five, and highly unstable. At first Hume was optimistic: his salary was £300, the marquess was friendly, and he had time to read, if not to write. But matters deteriorated in the autumn, and became increasingly fraught over the winter, spent at Weldehall (or Weld Hall), near St Albans. The marquess was much too ill to be taught. Hume became the enemy of the manager of Annandale's affairs, Captain Philip Vincent; his appeals for help to Sir James Johnstone of Westerhall, brother-in-law to Annandale's mother, went unheeded. Hume held on, even provisionally agreeing to a cut in his salary to £200, until the marquess himself threw him out in April 1746. The job did have the unanticipated advantage of keeping Hume out of Scotland during the Jacobite rising of 1745. This did not prevent him from later writing, with every appearance of authority, a defence of the conduct of the lord provost of Edinburgh during the rebellion: *A True Account of the Behaviour and Conduct of Archibald Stewart Esq.* was published anonymously in 1748.

After Hume's ejection by Annandale, he spent a few weeks in London, and was on the point of returning north when on 18 May 1746 he was unexpectedly invited by General James St Clair to accompany him as his secretary on a military expedition to Canada. Hume welcomed the opportunity. The expedition embarked at Portsmouth in June, was held back by adverse winds, and then cancelled. St Clair thoughtfully made Hume judge advocate, so that he could claim half pay. But at the end of August St Clair was ordered instead to attack the Brittany coast. Siege was laid to Lorient at the end of September, only to be abandoned when the French were on the point of surrender. The episode was later ridiculed in print by Voltaire, and at some point Hume prepared a manuscript in vindication of the 'Descent on the Coast of Brittany' (NL Scot., MS 23159, no. 12); whether he put anything in print is not known. The expedition sailed to Cork, and Hume was back in London early in 1747. He waited there until the summer, seeking his half pay and considering his options. He told Henry Home that he feared he would remain 'a poor philosopher' for ever. He was too late for a career in the army or the law, and 'the Church is my Aversion'. Worst of all, he might fall into 'Dependance, which I have sought all my

Life to avoid' (to Henry Home, June 1747, *New Letters*, 25–6). In July he was back at Ninewells.

In January 1748 St Clair offered Hume another attractive opportunity, to serve as his secretary on an embassy to Vienna and Turin. The purpose of the embassy was to persuade those two courts to fulfil their commitments in the war against France. It set off in February, and went at a leisurely pace through the Netherlands and Germany, reaching Vienna in April. Along the way Hume wrote a journal in the form of a letter to his brother: a sharp and curious observer, he reinforced his conviction that the countries of continental Europe were much more prosperous and civilized than insular English prejudice maintained. Germany, he concluded, was 'a very fine Country, full of industrious honest People, & were it united it woud be the greatest Power that ever was in the World' (to John Home of Ninewells, 3 March – 7 April 1748, *Letters*, 1.114–28). At the end of May the embassy moved on to Turin, by way of Styria, the Tyrol, Trent, and Mantua. Soon after its arrival, news of the peace of Aix-la-Chapelle rendered it redundant; but St Clair awaited a further posting, and Hume hoped they would make the tour of Italy and France. In the meantime Hume became something of a spectacle in his uniform. Now positively fat, he enhanced the comedy by falling for a countess. But, as always, he was also reading. In particular, he read Montesquieu's newly published *Esprit des lois*. When he returned to London he sent Montesquieu a long letter of comments. Some offered Montesquieu additional evidence for his arguments, Hume instancing the abolition of Scotland's hereditary jurisdictions after the late rebellion as confirmation of parliament's hostility to intermediary powers. But Hume also spotted, and criticized, Montesquieu's indulgent view of English commercial policy (to Montesquieu, 10 April 1749, ibid., 1.133–8). A correspondence began, in which Montesquieu was elaborately polite, but clearly recognized the force of Hume's intelligence.

While without paid employment during 1747, Hume had been working on several projects, two of which were published in the following year. One was a 'third edition' of the *Essays, Moral and Political*, including three new essays on national characters, the idea of an original contract, and passive obedience. The essay on national characters disputed the importance which some (notably Montesquieu) attached to physical rather than moral causes in their formation. It also contained two footnotes which were to give much offence: one, on the character of clergymen, to his contemporaries, the other (added in 1753–4) suggesting that 'negroes' were naturally inferior to whites, to later scholars. It was apparently a replacement for an essay on the protestant succession, which Hume had sent to Charles Erskine, Lord Tinwald, asking him to decide whether it should be published. The new essays were also published separately, as *Three Essays*. The publishers were Kincaid and (for the first time) Andrew Millar in London, and (also for the first time) the volumes bore Hume's name.

But the most substantial publication of 1748 was *Philosophical Essays Concerning Human Understanding*, re-titled in

1756 *An Enquiry Concerning Human Understanding*. Though now generally known as the *First Enquiry*, its original title was accurate in suggesting a volume of connected essays. In it Hume abridged and re-cast many of the arguments of book 1 of the *Treatise*. Advising Gilbert Elliot not to read the earlier work, Hume remarked that by shortening and simplifying the questions, he had really rendered them 'much more complete' (to Elliot, March or April 1751, *Letters*, 1.158). But Hume also added matter not in the *Treatise*, including essays on 'the different species of philosophy', on miracles, and on providence and a future state; the second of these was clearly a reworking of the 'reasonings on miracles' which he had thought it prudent to cut out of the *Treatise*. With these contents, the *Philosophical Essays* may be read as Hume's defiant, even contemptuous, response to those who had denied him the Edinburgh chair. The opening section on different species of philosophy was an extended explanation of his earlier distinction between the painter and the anatomist. Ostensibly Hume balanced the merits of those philosophers who make us '*feel* the difference between vice and virtue', and those who treat human nature as a subject of speculation. He conceded that 'ADDISON, perhaps, will be read with pleasure, when LOCKE shall be entirely forgotten'. But his own position was clear: only serious enquiry into the nature of human understanding could subvert that 'abstruse philosophy and metaphysical jargon' which was the handmaid of popular superstition. Philosophy was not obvious and easy, though he hoped that it might be written with clearness (*Enquiry Concerning Human Understanding*, section 1, pp. 1, 4, 12). So much for 'warmth in the cause of virtue'.

Any pretence of reticence in discussing philosophy's relation to religion was abandoned. Those who invoked a divine being to supply a primary cause or a guarantee of our perceptions were swept aside. 'To have recourse to the veracity of the Supreme Being, in order to prove the veracity of our senses', Hume wrote in allusion to Descartes, 'is surely making a very unexpected circuit' (*Enquiry Concerning Human Understanding*, section 12.13). As a matter of probability, the testimony in favour of miracles would never outweigh their unlikelihood; and in any case that testimony was characteristically unreliable. The idea of providence, or 'the religious hypothesis', contributed nothing to our understanding of the course of events, and was of no practical relevance to human life; to deny providence and a future state undermined the foundations of society not at all. Pointedly, Hume put the arguments of this section into the mouth of an imaginary 'Epicurus'. In the final section Hume reviewed the benefits of a moderate or 'mitigated' scepticism—only to end with a proposal anything but moderate. Take in hand any volume of divinity or school metaphysics, he advised, and ask '*Does it contain any abstract reasoning concerning quantity or number? No. Does it contain any experimental reasoning concerning matter of fact and existence? No. Commit it then to the flames: For it can contain nothing but sophistry and illusion*' (ibid., section 12.34). It was, perhaps, a test which the volumes of a Leechman or a Wishart would have struggled to survive.

Yet if Hume expected the *Philosophical Essays* to attract attention, he was again disappointed. He returned from Italy, he recalled, 'to find all England in a ferment, on account of Dr Middleton's Free Enquiry', while his own, more radical, performance was 'entirely overlooked and neglected' ('My own life', in *Essays*, xxxv).

Hume returned to Ninewells in 1749, and resumed writing. By 1751 three further important works had been drafted. The first to appear, in November 1751, was *An Enquiry Concerning the Principles of Morals*. The recasting of book 3 of the *Treatise*, it was clearly conceived on the same lines as the *Philosophical Essays*, as a set of connected essays. No work, it seems, gave Hume himself more pleasure: 'in my own opinion (who ought not to judge on that subject), [it] is of all my writings, historical, philosophical, or literary, incomparably the best' ('My own life', in *Essays*, xxxvi). Instead of abridging the *Treatise*, he redesigned his treatment of morals to concentrate on the virtues of benevolence and justice, and on the argument that the standard of moral judgement is to be found in the principles of utility and agreeableness. The question whether morals are derived from reason or from sentiment now received only cursory treatment; and the discussion of property, justice, and allegiance in the terms of the natural lawyers was abandoned. It has been suggested that Hume's ambition was to rewrite Cicero's *Offices* in a form consistent with his general principles of enquiry founded on experience and observation; and that, in so doing, he was once again at odds with Hutcheson, who had denied that the *Offices* formed a complete system of morals (Moore, 'Utility and humanity'). Whatever his purpose, Hume did not find it necessary to insist anew on the separation of morals from religion: this *Enquiry* was markedly less provocative on that score than its counterpart on the understanding.

As Hume made final revisions to the book in 1751, he may have had an eye on a new academic opportunity, a chair at the University of Glasgow. It became clear in March 1751 that Hutcheson's successor as professor of moral philosophy, Thomas Craigie, was too ill to continue; and in October Adam Smith took up the chair in logic. In November Smith wrote privately that he 'should prefer David Hume to any man for a colleague'; but he doubted of sufficient support for his candidacy (Adam Smith to William Cullen, November 1751, *Correspondence of Adam Smith*, 5–6). Smith's caution was justified: nothing came of the project (except that Smith himself was transferred to the moral philosophy chair).

The second of the works prepared between 1749 and 1751 was the *Political Discourses*, published in 1752. Though subsequently absorbed into the *Essays, Moral and Political*, the *Political Discourses* were another new departure, containing Hume's engagement with political economy. Essays on commerce, luxury, money, interest, and the balance of trade explored the operations of the commercial economy, while a further group on the balance of power, taxes, and public credit examined key features of the political economy of the contemporary British state. The volume opened with a defence of 'abstruse thinkers', a by now familiar signal that Hume expected serious engagement with his arguments; and several of the essays assumed an understanding of the purposes of models in economic thinking. It seems likely that his conception of economic development through commerce and manufactures was framed in opposition to the emphasis laid on agriculture by French economic writers such as Melon. The import of foreign luxuries, Hume argued, played a vital role in stimulating invention among domestic manufacturers. Commenting directly on the luxury debate, Hume maintained that the benefits of innocent luxury far outweighed the dangers of 'vicious' luxury. He questioned the benefits of credit creation in stimulating a poor country's economy; better, he argued, for a poor country to take advantage of the cheapness of its goods on the international market. The primacy accorded to trade was not, however, an endorsement of contemporary British commercial and monetary policies, which Hume regarded as selfish and counter-productive. He was equally sceptical of the advantages and long-term stability of Britain's much-vaunted system of public credit. In addition to these economic essays, the volume included a lengthy contribution to the debate on whether the ancient world had been more populous than the modern, the essay on the protestant succession which had been withheld in 1748, and an apparently whimsical but carefully crafted model of a perfect republic. The *Political Discourses* was the first and, as Hume remembered, the only one of his works to enjoy immediate success, with a second edition later in the year. It was also the first to be translated, two separate French translations appearing in Amsterdam in 1754. It soon attracted the attention of economic writers across Europe, including Josiah Tucker, Vincent de Gournay, Antonio Genovesi, Isaac de Pinto, and Anne-Robert Jacques Turgot.

A third work whose origins lie in this period was the *Dialogues Concerning Natural Religion*. In twelve connected dialogues Hume subjected the widely held belief that the design of the world demonstrates the existence of a divine creator to sustained critical examination. Neither as an argument from experience on behalf of an intelligent agent or artificer, nor as an argument a priori for a first cause whose perfection is beyond human comprehension, could the argument from design be sustained. The dialogues' protagonists were Cleanthes, representing a modern, experimental theist, Demea, a rationalist, and Philo, a sceptic. In March 1751 Hume sent what he called a 'Sample' of the dialogues to Gilbert Elliot, with a request that he strengthen the arguments of Cleanthes, whom Elliot would recognize as 'the Hero of the Dialogue' (to Elliot, 10 March 1751, *Letters*, 1.153–7). In the same letter, however, Hume dropped a strong hint that he identified himself with Philo. Some contemporaries, headed by Dugald Stewart, as well as a number of late nineteenth- and early twentieth-century commentators, were willing to accept Cleanthes' arguments as Hume's. But others were clearly unconvinced; and since the mid-twentieth century scholarship has tended to follow Kemp Smith in supposing that, while at different times Hume used both

Cleanthes and Demea to develop specific points, he intended his readers to be persuaded by Philo's unfailing criticisms of every variety of the argument from design (Kemp Smith, introduction to *Hume's Dialogues*, 58–9). It is likely, therefore, that Hume was being less than ingenuous with Elliot, and that he really wished to test the acceptability of such thoroughly irreligious argument with a friendly member of the Scottish establishment. On this score, at least, Elliot gave Hume a clear answer: the work should not be published. Despite Hume's occasional pleas, this remained the firm view of all those who were shown the book, and the dialogues were not published in his lifetime.

The years of essay writing, between the 'failure' of the *Treatise* and the publication of the *Political Discourses*, had seen Hume cover an extraordinary amount of intellectual ground. But it had still not brought him commercial success. When this finally arrived, it was through the initiative of his publisher, Andrew Millar. In 1753 Millar put together a cheap, four-volume duodecimo edition of *Essays and Treatises on Several Subjects*, in which the *Philosophical Essays* and the *Enquiry Concerning Morals* were placed between the *Essays, Moral and Political* and the *Political Discourses*. Though Hume did not immediately appreciate it, the effect of the edition was to enable his political essays to act as he had once hoped, 'like Dung with Marle', and draw attention to his philosophy in a format which for the first time was both accessible and calculated to encourage sales.

Man of letters In 1751 Hume had removed 'from the country to the town, the true scene for a man of letters'. The move from Ninewells to Edinburgh had been precipitated by his older brother's marriage that year, and was doubtless facilitated by the financial means which Hume had acquired as a result of his office in the embassy to Vienna and Turin. This had made him 'master of near a thousand pounds', sufficient in Hume's eyes for independence ('My own life', in *Essays*, xxxv–vi). After a brief period in lodgings, he took a house in Riddle's Land, in the Lawnmarket, where he was joined by his sister Katherine; in 1753 they moved again to a house in Jack's Land, in the Canongate. The removal was of much more than personal significance: once in Edinburgh, Hume quickly placed himself at the centre of Scottish intellectual life.

Within a year, on 28 January 1752, Hume had been elected keeper of the Library of the Faculty of Advocates and clerk to the faculty. Created in the 1680s by the efforts of Sir George Mackenzie, who had encouraged the acquisition of works of history, criticism, and rhetoric as well as law, the Advocates' Library was the largest in Scotland. Though the keeper's stipend was only £40 per annum, it was, as Hume described it to John Clephane, 'a genteel office', which he regarded as ample compensation for his disappointment at Glasgow. The triumph was all the greater since the opposition, headed by the lord president of the court of session, Lord Arniston, and his son, also Robert Dundas, the dean of the faculty and future lord advocate, had once again raised the cry of 'Deism, atheism, and scepticism' against Hume; but this time they had been overborne by Hume's friends, strongly supported by 'the public' (to John Clephane, 4 Feb 1752, *Letters*, 1.164–7). Hume's tenure of the office proved equally controversial. In 1754 he became embroiled in a row with the curators over the purchase of three works of modern French literature, by La Fontaine, Crébillon, and Bussy-Rabutin. Hume at first acquiesced in their removal, then retracted his agreement. In November he wrote to the lord advocate to demand the books' reinstatement, accusing the curators of 'Insolence of Office' (to Robert Dundas, 20 Nov 1754, ibid., 1.210–12). The row was eventually settled to Hume's satisfaction: he did not resign, but made over his stipend to the blind poet Thomas Blacklock, a gesture which declared Hume's independence. Two of his opponents among the curators were James Burnet, subsequently Lord Monboddo, and Sir David Dalrymple, later Lord Hailes, both scholars of a different cast from Hume; the issue may have been less the decency of the French works than the character of the library. But it would be unwise to infer from Hume's determination to vindicate himself that he was a good librarian: there is no evidence to suggest it (Hillyard, 103–9). What he himself valued was the intellectual opportunity it afforded him: he had become 'master of 30,000 volumes' (to Clephane, 4 Feb 1752, *Letters*, 1.167), many of them relevant to his next great project, the *History of Great Britain*.

Residence in Edinburgh enabled Hume to be active in its literary societies. In December 1751 he became joint secretary of the Philosophical Society. Three years later he was a founding member of the Select Society, formed in 1754 on the initiative of his friend Allan Ramsay, the painter. Hume was made treasurer of the society, and a member of the standing committee responsible for regulations and procedure. It appears, however, that he never actually spoke in the debates. Writing to Ramsay in Rome a year later, he took pride in the popularity of their society, reflected in the demand for membership, and in the formation of a subsidiary society for encouraging arts, sciences, and manufactures; but he probably shared Ramsay's doubts that the society's original purpose of 'understanding' would suffer by such enlargement (to Allan Ramsay, April or May 1755, *Letters*, 1.219–21; Ramsay to Hume, from Rome, 13 March 1756, NL Scot., MS 23156, no. 103).

Much more important to Hume personally—and to his model of a man of letters—were his friendships. Many were already firm; others developed with his coming to Edinburgh. Two older friends who had helped him in his youth were Henry Home, Lord Kames (from 1752), and Patrick Murray, Lord Elibank. Hume's sensitivity to being patronized by his elders, and his critical judgement of their writings, now resulted in occasional coolness between them; but Hume strove to maintain cordial relations. His best and longest friendships, however, were with those of his own generation. Although his earliest known friend, Michael Ramsay, did not live in Scotland, and was now only an occasional correspondent, connections with others almost as early had been much more continuous. This was especially true of James Oswald of Dunnikier, in

Fife, whom Hume had known before he left for France, and of William Mure of Caldwell, near Glasgow, where Hume was a frequent visitor from shortly after his return. Both were landowners and MPs. So too was Gilbert Elliot of Minto, in Selkirk, though Hume's relations with him were perhaps cordial rather than warm. Other close friends were in the professions: John Clephane, a fellow recruit to St Clair's expedition in 1747, was a physician, and Allan Ramsay became the leading British portrait painter of the age (besides maintaining an interest in the philosophy of taste). Ramsay painted Hume twice. The first and better portrait was done in 1754, and depicts Hume in a russet coat with a scholar's cap, his head slightly turned. The second, painted for Hume in 1766 to accompany a portrait of Rousseau, was taken from the front, with Hume wearing a scarlet uniform. It may capture something of the seemingly vacant stare with which Hume fixed those with whom he was conversing, and which so disconcerted Rousseau.

A new set of friendships were those with the 'moderate' clergy of Edinburgh and East Lothian: William Robertson, Adam Ferguson, Hugh Blair, Alexander Carlyle, John Jardine, and, closest of all, Hume's kinsman John Home. A friendship with ministers of the kirk had to overcome some obstacles. The notorious irreligion of Hume's philosophy was perhaps less of one than the anti-clericalism manifest in a footnote to the recently published essay 'Of national characters', and, still more sharply, in the spoof *Bellmen's Petition* of 1751, in which Hume had ridiculed an initiative to raise the stipends of ministers and schoolmasters. Though the *Petition* was issued under a pseudonym, 'Zerobabel MacGilchrist', Hume had proudly intimated his authorship to both Clephane and Elliot (to Clephane and Elliot, both on 18 Feb 1751, *Letters*, 1.149, 153). The insult may indeed have been even greater than first appears. It has been suggested that by combining reference to the biblical Zerubbabel, one of Christ's ancestors, with a surname which translates as 'son of Christ's gillie', or 'servant', the pseudonym mischievously associated the ministers' cause with the esoteric mysteries of freemasonry (Emerson). But the moderates were of a forgiving nature. They were determined to secure the place of polite culture in Scotland, and to contain David Hume within it. When Hume, along with Lord Kames, was the object of a hostile clerical campaign in 1755–6, Robertson and his friends rallied their lay supporters in the general assembly to avert any formal censure. (There are some signs that Hume himself may have regretted the lost opportunity of excommunication.) For his part Hume repaid the moderate clergy by inviting them to suppers at his house, congenial occasions which rarely tested their faith, and by several more tangible expressions of literary solidarity.

Prominent among these was his wholehearted support for John Home's ambitions as a dramatist. Hume readily associated himself with the public performance of Home's *Douglas* in December 1756, acting as a ticket seller and drawing further clerical ire on his own head. In 1762 he acquiesced in the moderates' campaign in support of a

Scottish militia to the extent of becoming a member of the Poker Club. (But he was not otherwise involved: the militia pamphlet known as *Sister Peg* (1761) was by Ferguson, not Hume.) He also lent cautious support to the early stages of Blair's campaign to secure recognition for James Macpherson's 'discovery' of Ossian, the supposedly ancient Gaelic epic poet. Though Hume had backtracked by 1763, realizing that the evidence did not match his own standards of reliable testimony, his initial support was indicative of his uncertain critical standards in relation to literature. Besides John Home's plays, he championed the poetry of Thomas Blacklock and William Wilkie, while ignoring that of Robert Fergusson. Hume was never so uncritical in his support for the moderates' more intellectual endeavours. His generous efforts to introduce Robertson to his London publishers, and the satisfaction he took in the success of Robertson's *History of Scotland*, did not prevent him from continuing to question several of Robertson's interpretations. With this as with every other work by a fellow countryman, Hume was also at pains to alert the author to the presence of Scotticisms in his writing. He was even more severe with Adam Ferguson. When shown a draft 'Treatise on refinement' in 1759, Hume thought that with some amendments it would make 'an admirable book'. But when shown the manuscript of the *Essay on the History of Civil Society* in 1766, he thought better of his earlier judgement, and told an embarrassed Blair that it was not fit to be published, 'neither on account of the Style nor the Reasoning; the Form nor the Matter'. He was none the less gracious when it succeeded, immediately congratulating Ferguson and informing Blair. Although he confided to the latter that he could not change his opinion, he urged Blair to keep this from Ferguson (to Adam Smith, 12 April 1759, to Hugh Blair, 11 Feb 1766, to Ferguson, 10 March 1767, to Blair, 1 April 1767, *Letters*, 1.304, 2.11–12, 125–6, 133).

The one Scottish contemporary whom Hume regarded as both intellectually congenial and his own equal was Adam Smith. Despite the difference of age—Smith was twelve years younger—and the infrequency of Smith's visits to Edinburgh, Hume's letters reveal a friendship of exceptional warmth and respect. Towards Smith, almost alone, Hume could be open and direct in the expression of intellectual disagreement.

Hume certainly did not seek intellectual uniformity among his fellow Scots. Nothing contributed more to the progress of learning, he told Andrew Millar, than disputes and novelties (3 Sept 1757, *Letters*, 1.265). But he did have a clear view of how men of letters should conduct their controversies. His correspondence with Robert Wallace in 1751 and 1753 over their different views on the population of the ancient world provided him with an early model. The two exchanged essays in manuscript, and Hume alerted Wallace to the manner in which he would express disagreement; on publication, they sent each other copies. Grateful for such 'civilities', Hume complimented Wallace on setting 'a new Example of Politeness' (to Robert Wallace, early 1753, *New Letters*, 32). But others required instruction in the etiquette of controversy. One such was

John Stewart, professor of natural philosophy at Edinburgh, who submitted a contribution to the volume of essays Hume was editing for the Philosophical Society, in which he criticized arguments of both Kames and Hume. Hume told him firmly that all railery was to be avoided in philosophical argument, 'both because it is unphilosophical, and because it cannot but be offensive' (February 1754, *Letters*, 1.185–6). Hume was particularly sensitive to the manner in which his own philosophy was criticized, and whenever he could he took the initiative to set the tone of its discussion. A letter to the author of *A Delineation of the Nature and Obligation of Morality* (1753), whom he did not know to be James Balfour of Pilrig, invited him to revive the happy times when the Epicureans, Academics, and Stoics lived together in unreserved friendship (15 March 1753, ibid., 1.172–4). Balfour ignored the invitation, and later returned to the attack. Hume was more successful over George Campbell's *Dissertation on Miracles* (1762). Sent the manuscript in advance by Hugh Blair, he commented on several of its arguments, and urged the author not to denominate him an infidel. On publication he was able to thank Campbell directly for 'the civil and obliging manner' of his disagreement, while reaffirming his resolution, fixed at the beginning of his life, 'always to leave the public to judge between my adversaries and me, without making any reply' (to Hugh Blair, 1761, to George Campbell, 7 June 1762, ibid., 1.348–51, 360–61). A similar pattern was followed a year later with Reid's *Inquiry into the Human Mind* (1764). Blair sent Hume a portion of the manuscript, and Hume commented on it directly to Reid, though in this case with more caution, since he had not seen the whole. His reward was Reid's avowal that he would always be Hume's 'Disciple in Metaphysics' (to Reid, 25 Feb 1763, ibid., 1.375–6; Mossner, *Life of Hume*, 299).

The anti-model of controversy was that practised by William Warburton and his 'gang' of critics in London. Warburton slighted the *Philosophical Essays* and attempted to block publication of the *Four Dissertations*, following this with a public attack on the essay on the natural history of religion, in a letter addressed to himself. Recognizing the subterfuge, Hume was contemptuous of Warburton's failure to 'come into the Field, and dispute concerning the principal Topics of my Philosophy' (to Andrew Millar, 3 Sept 1757, *Letters*, 1.265). To the end of his life he denounced 'the illiberal petulance, arrogance, and scurrility, which distinguish the Warburtonian school' ('My own life', in *Essays*, xxxvii). It was perhaps one of the reasons for Hume's ready encouragement of Edward Gibbon that he too was attacked by the Warburtonians.

There was much more to Hume's concern with the conduct of controversy than good manners: at stake, in his view, was the status of letters and philosophy in the modern world of commercial publishing. It was not simply that men of letters should respect each other if they expected to command the respect of their readers, vital though this was. It was also that philosophy must be taken seriously, not cheapened by railery or undermined by charges of heresy or atheism (which on Hume's principles were mere empty words). In particular, Hume sought recognition of the seriousness of his own arguments. Still smarting from neglect and misrepresentation of the *Treatise*, Hume insisted on the importance of good argument in all matters intellectual. This was why he appreciated Reid and was vexed by Ferguson (who wrote of virtue as if Hume's writings on morals did not exist). And this was why he despised above all those, like Warburton, who had no idea what a good argument might be. As Hume was to discover, however, he could never exert in London the literary authority which he had come to possess in Edinburgh. There Hume's philosophy, and his example of a man of letters, made him the moving force of what is now known as the Scottish Enlightenment. But in London, where the Enlightenment never took hold, he was just another author competing for the attention of publishers and the public, and as vulnerable as anyone else to the slings and arrows of partisan prejudice.

The History of England Hume did not allow the more intensive social life of Edinburgh to break his established habit of hard work. In ten years, from 1751 to 1761, he completed and published two further works. The lesser of these was the *Four Dissertations* of 1757. Hume first suggested the volume to Andrew Millar in 1755, proposing essays on the natural history of religion, the passions, tragedy, and geometry and natural philosophy. The second of these derived from book 2 of the *Treatise*, and completed its abridgement; the fourth may have been a reworking of book 1, part 2. But it was dropped on the advice of Lord Stanhope, a mathematician; and Hume had proposed to replace it with two essays on suicide and on the immortality of the soul. Though 'Five dissertations' were printed in proof, Warburton's interference and Hume's 'abundant prudence' led to their withdrawal, and Hume substituted another, on the standard of taste, to make up the final four dissertations. The most substantial of these was the 'Natural history of religion'. When it was first drafted is uncertain; it may have been contemporary with the still-unpublished *Dialogues*. It offered an experimental history of religious belief and practice, with a comparative analysis of the respective characteristics of polytheism and monotheism. Hume found that polytheism had not only preceded monotheism, but was much less dangerous, being less liable to join a philosophical enthusiasm to a religious superstition. This error he attributed specifically to the Stoics; but all theists were implicated. The only remedy, he concluded, was to set one species of superstition against another, 'while we ourselves … happily make our escape into the calm, though obscure, regions of philosophy' ('The natural history of religion', 351, 363).

The second project of the 1750s was altogether more ambitious. In 1754 Hume published *The History of Great Britain*, volume 1, covering the reigns of James I and Charles I. When Hume first conceived of writing such a history is not known; but he began serious work on it shortly after arriving in Edinburgh. 'I enter upon it', he told Adam Smith in September 1752, 'with great Ardour & Pleasure' (to Adam Smith, 24 Sept 1752, *Letters*, 1.168). Two years later he presented a copy of volume 1 to William Mure,

with a summary of his objectives as a historian. 'The first Quality of an Historian is to be true & impartial; the next to be interesting. If you do not say, that I have done both Parties Justice; & if Mrs Mure be not sorry for poor King Charles, I shall burn all my Papers, & return to Philosophy' (to William Mure, October 1754, ibid., 1.209–10). The impartiality to which he aspired was between whig and tory interpretations of the great conflict between crown and parliament, the former epitomized in the earlier *History of England* (1726–31) by the Huguenot Rapin-Thoyras. Hume had already sketched his own interpretation in several of his essays; now he worked it out in historical detail. Just as important, however, was the eliciting of readers' engagement with the narrative. Hume sought to arouse sympathy with the passions and moral sentiments of past actors, while maintaining the distance which separated them from the present. The fate of Charles I should move readers, but also remind them that those struggles were in the past. Underpinning both Hume's ambitions, moreover, was a sophisticated conceptual framework, in which the rise of commerce and the unleashing of protestant religious enthusiasm were presented as having combined to foster a novel love of liberty in the 1620s and 1630s: while the early Stuarts were not mistaken in their understanding of the constitution they had inherited, the demands of their parliamentary opponents for a new balance between crown and parliament were an explicable product of changing circumstances.

The success of Hume's new work was immediately endangered by his choice of publisher. Despite the increasing success of his relationship with Andrew Millar, Hume accepted an offer of £400 for the first edition of the first volume of the *History* from the Edinburgh publisher Gavin Hamilton. Hamilton would have paid £1200 for three volumes; but Hume would not commit himself beyond one. Very soon it became clear that Hamilton had over-reached himself: the London booksellers, led by Millar, were able to choke off sales, not only in the capital, but among their colleagues in the provinces. The 'conspiracy of the booksellers' may have limited the initial sales; but the *History*'s impact was none the less immediate. 'I was assailed by one cry of reproach, disapprobation, and even detestation; English, Scotch, and Irish, Whig and Tory, churchman and sectary, freethinker and religionist, patriot and courtier, united in their rage against the man, who had presumed to shed a generous tear for the fate of Charles I and the Earl of Strafford' ('My own life', in *Essays*, xxxvii). Hume's letters at the time suggest surprise as well as disappointment, not least at attacks on the work's irreligion; he protested that he had said nothing against revelation. He may have been reassured on this point by receiving messages of encouragement from the primates of England and Ireland. In his frustration he contemplated changing his name and retiring for good to a provincial town in France.

Hume resolved to continue, and two years later published volume 2, covering the period from the death of Charles I to the revolution of 1688. This proved the least controversial of all the volumes, being less offensive to whig susceptibilities. Despite the entreaties of his publishers, Hume now turned back, and devoted himself to the Tudors. 'It is properly at that Period modern History commences', he told Millar (20 May 1757, *Letters*, 1.249). Hume covered these in two volumes, which were published early in 1759 as *The History of England, under the House of Tudor*. In political terms Hume was unequivocal in regarding this as a period of strong monarchy, closer to arbitrary than to mixed government; the hypothesis of a marked slowing-down, if not interruption, in the development of English liberty was confirmed. No less significant, however, was Hume's treatment of the Reformation, which he prefaced with a defence of ecclesiastical establishments supported by the civil magistrate. An Erastian church was the great achievement of the Reformation, in its Lutheran and especially its Anglican forms.

His sails set, Hume completed the *History* with two more volumes, extending the narrative from Julius Caesar to Henry VII; these appeared late in 1761, though bearing the date 1762. While Hume continued in these volumes to emphasize the discontinuities in English constitutional history, he also showed that he could 'whig it with the best' when it came to celebrating King Alfred's laws or Magna Carta (Pocock, 245). As a whole, *The History of England, from the Invasion of Julius Caesar to the Revolution in 1688*, as the complete enterprise was known from 1762, was a remarkable testimony to the coherence of English history across its entire period, despite the evident changes which had occurred in its form of government. But the change of title was an acknowledgement that the same story could not be written of Great Britain, or indeed of Scotland; Hume was close to conceding that his own country did not have a viable history.

To proceed with the *History* after the disappointment of volume 1, Hume had to capitulate to the London publishers. This he very quickly did, encouraging Millar to buy up Hamilton's edition, and agreeing terms for the second volume. In 1757 Hume negotiated the sale of all author's rights to both volumes for 800 guineas; and two years later he accepted £700 for the Tudor volumes, and, in advance, £1400 for the medieval ones. By their means, he recalled, he had become 'not only independent, but opulent' ('My own life', in *Essays*, xxxviii). Millar too hoped to profit, and almost immediately began to produce new editions. The first, the octavo of 1763, was over-produced, and sales were sluggish, to Hume's intense frustration. But a new and lavish quarto in 1770 made amends, and further octavo editions followed in 1773 and 1778. Each of these allowed Hume the opportunity he craved, of making revisions.

Hume was always a stickler for accuracy, both in his own choice of expression and in the printing of his works. He corrected proofs assiduously, and constantly urged the same care from his printers. The better to supervise their publication, he followed both the Tudor and the medieval volumes to London, spending over twelve months there from September 1758 until October 1759, and a further six from June to December 1761. He lodged at the boarding-house kept for Scottish gentlemen by Anne and Peggy Elliot, in Lisle Street, Leicester Fields. Congenial company was at hand, including Oswald, Elliot, St Clair, and Allan Ramsay; Clephane, sadly, had died in 1757. He met, and liked, Edmund Burke, Benjamin Franklin, and Elizabeth Montagu; he disliked and avoided Samuel Johnson and Mrs Mallet. While attending to his own *History* he assisted William Robertson in the publication of his, correcting the proofs and alerting Robertson to new evidence. He was quick to report on its success, and even more pleased by the immediate success of Adam Smith's *Theory of Moral Sentiments*, published in April 1759. He also took the opportunity to use the newly opened British Museum reading-room. During the first visit Hume wondered whether to stay in London permanently; but his second visit settled the question. The anti-Scottish clamour which would soon be exploited by John Wilkes was offensive; and an invitation to join the young earl of Shelburne's coterie was enough to make him take the first available chaise north.

The increasingly xenophobic atmosphere in England in the early 1760s seems to have provoked Hume into adopting a more tory posture. He was particularly concerned to correct mistakes and oversights in the Stuart volumes, which he attributed to 'the plaguy Prejudices of Whiggism, with which I was too much infected when I began' (to Gilbert Elliot, 12 March 1763, *New Letters*, 69). But Hume's repeated declarations of a tory tendency in his revisions may be misleading. Impartiality remained his objective; and in vindicating the coherence, if not the seamless continuity, of English history, he had arguably remained true to his characterization of himself in 1748, in a letter to Henry Home, as 'a Whig, but a very sceptical one' (9 Feb 1748, *Letters*, 1.111). He was certainly a serious historian. He read extensively, purchasing and borrowing books from fellow scholars when the Advocates' Library did not possess them; and he valued exactness in citation. Chided by Horace Walpole for not providing his authorities for the Stuarts, he supplied them for subsequent volumes, and added them to the Stuarts in 1762. If he did not resolve the problems of combining political narrative with social and literary history, he recognized and tackled them by inserting extended appendices at pivotal points in the story. In many respects the *History of England* adhered to the norms of what in the eighteenth century was thought of as a 'civil history', concentrating on one nation's constitutional development, and on relations between the civil power and the church. But Hume had gone further, triumphantly demonstrating that it was possible to write such history in a manner which combined good historical argument with good writing, and thereby appealed to an extensive readership.

Paris and Rousseau Having returned to Edinburgh in December 1761, as he thought for good, the now opulent Hume was able for the first time to purchase a house. The third storey of James's Court, on the Lawnmarket, it commanded a view across the Forth to Adam Smith's Kirkcaldy. There he settled with his sister and long-time housekeeper, Peggy Irvine, to live in some comfort from the income of the stocks in which he invested. He teased

Millar with hints that he might continue his history into the period after the revolution. He also toyed with the idea of an ecclesiastical history. Though he authorized Millar to contradict a report that he was writing it, he also admitted to Mallet that it was 'an Idea I was fond of' (to Andrew Millar, 15 March 1762, to David Mallet, 8 Nov 1762, *Letters*, 1.352, 369). There is no evidence that he made any progress with either, although in the next few years the French *philosophes* were frequently to urge him to take up the ecclesiastical history.

Hume's retirement, however, was premature. Within two years he had embarked on the most dramatic episodes of his life, the visit to Paris between October 1763 and December 1765, and its sequel, the return to England with Rousseau. The three years until the end of 1766 were the one period in which Hume lost his customary (and self-conscious) equanimity; in the early twenty-first century he might even be thought to have experienced a 'midlife crisis'. By the early 1760s Hume was well known in France both by reputation and by his works. He had corresponded with Montesquieu and more recently with Helvétius, but to most purpose with the Abbé Le Blanc, Trudaine de Montigny, and the Abbé Prevost, respectively the translators of the *Political Discourses*, the 'Natural history of religion', and the volumes on the Stuarts. But the summons he received in a letter in 1761 was much more personal. It came from the comtesse de Boufflers, mistress to the prince de Conti and a leading *salonnière* in her own right. Flattering Hume with praise of the style and 'divine impartiality' of his history of the Stuarts, she urged him to fulfil his reported resolution to come to France. Clearly struck, Hume replied courteously, but made no move. Further letters followed in 1762, and in 1763 the comtesse visited England, her intention of meeting Hume in person being conveyed to him by both Lord Elibank and Sir John Pringle. Still Hume avoided her. What overcame his hesitation was an invitation from the earl of Hertford in August 1763 to accompany him as his personal secretary on his embassy to Paris. The invitation was quite unexpected—they had not previously met—and Hume was satisfied that his accepting it would involve no appearance of dependence; perhaps as important, it also meant that he would not be directly beholden to any French host or hostess.

On arrival in Paris, Hume found himself fêted on every side. He was received with the ambassador at court, and introduced to Mme de Pompadour; the children of the dauphin claimed to have read his works. Initially Hume was overwhelmed: his French was rusty, and flattery made him look sheepish. He wrote to Adam Ferguson of his wish for 'the plain roughness of the Poker' (9 Nov 1763, *Letters*, 1.410). But gradually he grew accustomed to the fuss, and began rather to enjoy it. He had an apartment in the embassy, which from March 1764 occupied the Hôtel de Brancas, near the Louvre. He was welcomed at all the major salons, including those of Mme Geoffin, the marquise du Deffand, and Julie de L'Espinasse, but most of all at that of the comtesse de Boufflers.

Once in France, Hume's relations with the comtesse quickly became intense, although there seems to be no evidence that they were ever physical. On paper, at least, his infatuation was at its height during the summer of 1764, when Hume was staying at Compiègne, and Mme de Boufflers was a short distance away at L'Isle Adam. They wrote frequently, and Hume confessed that 'among other obligations ... you have saved me from a total indifference towards every thing in human life' (29 July 1764, *Letters*, 1.457). But the comtesse, far more experienced in such matters, seems to have played fast and loose; and Hume became increasingly confused. In September he returned to Paris to meet Gilbert Elliot, and Elliot clearly recognized that something was amiss. From a safe distance, on his way home, he wrote to warn Hume that he was on the brink of a precipice. Hume's fierce reaction, that he was 'a Citizen of the World', and would live in France if he chose, protested too much (22 Sept 1764, ibid., 1.469–70). Any further prospect of intimacy with de Boufflers was ended, however, by the death of her husband in October. She now hoped to marry the prince de Conti, and Hume was reduced to the role of trusted counsellor to both of them.

Hume's entanglement did not prevent him from also enjoying the company of the *philosophes*. He met Helvétius and dined at the house of the baron d'Holbach, where he was famously taken aback by the dogmatic atheism of the Holbachs' coterie. He had much more respect for Turgot, with whom he later corresponded on political economy. Diderot was a shrewd admirer, likening Hume to 'un gros Bernardin bien nourri' ('a fat, well-fed Bernardine'). But he was probably closest to D'Alembert, subsequently his most assiduous correspondent. By 1765 Hume was also increasingly busy with embassy duties; and in June, after much lobbying, he was officially confirmed as embassy secretary, with an annual salary of £1200, and a further £300 for equipage. From July Hertford was away on leave, and from then until November Hume was chargé d'affaires. As such he was responsible for negotiations and correspondence relating to several outstanding, low-level diplomatic issues arising out of the peace of Paris. During his absence Hertford was appointed lord lieutenant of Ireland, and once again asked Hume to accompany him. But this prospect had far less appeal. 'It is like Stepping out of Light into Darkness to exchange Paris for Dublin', he told his brother (to John Home, 4 Aug 1765, *Letters*, 1.514). In any case, Hume would soon have a new and heavier responsibility.

At Mme de Boufflers's instigation, Hume had offered to find Rousseau a refuge in England in 1762. Hearing that he was once again in difficulties, Hume renewed the invitation in October 1765, and this time Rousseau accepted. Hume therefore waited in Paris, where Rousseau arrived in mid-December. Already some had doubts about the wisdom of the enterprise, and Holbach explicitly warned Hume that he did not understand Rousseau. But Hume went ahead: the two men left Paris on 4 January 1766, and reached London on 13 January. Once in London, Rousseau was treated as something of a curiosity. He sat for Allan Ramsay, who painted his second portrait of Hume at the same time. Hume took him to the theatre, the better that the king and queen might observe him. Not surprisingly, Rousseau demanded to move out of London, and lodgings were found for him in Chiswick, where he was joined by Thérèse Le Vasseur. (Whether Rousseau discovered that Boswell had seduced her while escorting her from Paris is not known, but Hume had foreseen the danger.) By March a more permanent home had been found for him in Wootton, Staffordshire, thanks to the good offices of Richard Davenport, a gentleman with literary connections. The night before he left, Rousseau stayed with Hume in London, and an episode took place which had decisive consequences for their relationship. Rousseau suspected a conspiracy in all the offers of help he was receiving, and accused Hume of connivance in them. Hume denied it, Rousseau suddenly sat down on his knee, and the scene ended with the two in tears. Rousseau had some reason for his suspicions, for Hume, so sensitive to any suggestion of dependence on his own part, had been active in procuring a government pension for the refugee. Hume believed that the crisis had been resolved by Rousseau's apology; but he was increasingly aware of Rousseau's inscrutable depths, and particularly baffled by his strong attachment to religion.

Once at Wootton, Rousseau's suspicions hardened. He ignored, then declined, the offer of the pension. More than once Hume wrote placatory letters, in which partial apologies were offset by efforts to justify himself. Eventually, on 23 June, Rousseau wrote accusing Hume of having brought him to England to dishonour him; and he followed this on 10 July with a much longer account of the many stages and aspects of his mistreatment. Written in the form of a French judicial memoir, the letter was clearly designed for publication. Hume recognized this immediately. His reply was much shorter. He made it clear that he was preparing his defences, and had been in contact with Mme de Boufflers in Paris. His line would be straightforward. 'The Story, as I tell it, is consistent and rational. There is not common Sense in your Account' (to Jean-Jacques Rousseau, 22 July 1766, *Letters*, 2.66–8). Hume then collected the correspondence, had copies made, and sent one set over to Paris; the originals he sought to deposit in the British Museum (an offer which was eventually declined). The affair was discussed in several salons; and after some hesitation a meeting of *philosophes* chaired by D'Alembert decided to publish. In October 1766 there appeared in Paris the *Exposé succinct de la contestation qui s'est élévée entre M. Hume et M. Rousseau, avec les pièces justificatives*; an English version was published in November as *A Concise and Genuine Account of the Dispute between Mr. Hume and Mr. Rousseau*. Since Rousseau's letters were included, the public was effectively invited to judge between them. Hume's appeal was to the evidence, Rousseau's to his own sincerity: the public, that is, the contributors to the ensuing debate, sided overwhelmingly with Rousseau. The same judgement was delivered in London as in Paris: Rousseau was a martyr persecuted by godless atheists, and deserved every sympathy from Christians.

Hume had swithered over publication, and almost certainly regretted it; he omitted all mention of the affair from 'My own life'. He had misread Rousseau, and misread the public. It is quite possible that Parisian flattery of 'le bon David' had turned his head: he believed that he could befriend Rousseau where other *philosophes* had failed, and he may have felt that he owed something to Mme de Boufflers. Rousseau sensed such motives—and rebelled, deviously and hurtfully. By September 1766 Hume had returned to Edinburgh, with the intention of burying himself anew in philosophical retreat.

Last years Once again Hume's retreat did not last long. In February 1767 he was nominated to the office of under-secretary at the northern department by General Conway, the new secretary of state and the earl of Hertford's brother. Hume accepted out of a sense of obligation to the family, and consoled himself with the thought that the ministry, like every other at this time, would soon be out of office. In the event he was in post until January 1768. The office carried no salary, but various fees were divided between the officials, and Hume appears to have earned some £500 in the year. The pace of government was leisurely, and Hume's main activity was the drafting of letters for the minister. One which gave him particular pleasure was the annual 'letter from the throne' to the general assembly of the Church in Scotland in May 1767, which Hume will have regarded as a congenial exercise in practical Erastianism. He also did various good turns, and was able to fulfil a long-standing intention to obtain a pension for Isaac de Pinto. He again lodged with the Misses Elliot, now in Brewer Street, Golden Square. The Conways and the Hertfords, his own circle of London–Scottish friends, and visiting Scottish 'moderate' clergy all kept him entertained, so much so that he stayed on in London for a year and a half after leaving office, until August 1769. A further motive to remain was the opportunity to make revisions for a new edition of the *History*. He also received a pension of £200 from the king, with the clear expectation that he would now continue the work beyond 1688. But there is no evidence of a serious intention to do so, and once he had returned to Scotland, Hume renounced the idea for good.

Back in Edinburgh in James's Court, Hume took renewed pride in his cooking, and decided on a move to the growing New Town. The house he had built for himself and his sister was in St Andrew's Square, at its south-west corner. The adjoining street was not yet named, and one of Hume's female admirers, Nancy Ord, had the wit to name it St David's Street (which it remains, albeit as St David not St David's). Hume was particularly fond of Miss Ord, who was half his age, and there was gossip that he might propose to her. But although he did not discourage the rumours, no marriage occurred. He had several other good female friends in his own generation, including Mrs Mure and Mrs Cockburn, and his housekeeper continued to manage his domestic affairs. Hume was by now a 'weel-kent' figure in Edinburgh, recognized by the general public. On one occasion he was crossing the boggy ground between the Old Town and the New Town and got stuck: calling upon a passing woman for help, he was roundly told that it would depend on his becoming a Christian, and reciting the Lord's prayer and the belief to prove it. As might be expected, Hume had no difficulty in supplying the proofs. He would have delivered them in the distinctively Scots accent he never lost, for all his determination to eliminate Scotticisms from his writing.

Hume had one last attack on his philosophy to endure, James Beattie's *Essay on Truth: in Opposition to Sophistry and Scepticism* (1770). It was exactly the sort of criticism Hume had sought to discountenance, mixing declamation with raillery; and what was worse, its author's 'triumph' over Hume was hailed in London by Burke and Johnson, and portrayed on canvas by Reynolds. Hume memorably dismissed Beattie as 'that bigotted silly Fellow' (to William Strahan, 26 Oct 1775, *Letters*, 2.301); but the episode had a serious, and perhaps unfortunate, consequence. Hume was provoked into composing the 'Advertisement' which he asked William Strahan in 1775 to prefix to the second volume of all future editions of the *Essays and Treatises* (beginning with that of 1777). In it he effectively renounced the *Treatise of Human Nature* as a 'juvenile work', and stated that henceforth only the works in the *Essays and Treatises* were to be regarded as containing his philosophical principles. The practice of his critics in directing their batteries at the *Treatise* had been, he declared, 'contrary to all rules of candour and fair-dealing, and a strong instance of those polemical artifices, which a bigotted zeal thinks itself authorised to employ' (*Enquiry Concerning Human Understanding*, [83]). Political affairs were another source of irritation to Hume in his last years. The faithful Strahan was the recipient of a succession of letters from Edinburgh complaining about the insolence of the London mob, and the way in which the English were abusing their hard-won liberty. Hume was greatly exercised by the growth of the public debt, and more than once prognosticated a general bankruptcy. He was also alert to the growing signs that the American colonies were about to throw off British rule. But while he feared for the consequences should the government attempt to conquer them, he was, like Adam Smith, sanguine about the economic outcome of a separation (for example, to William Strahan, 11 March, 25 June 1771, 26 Oct, 13 Nov 1775, *Letters*, 2.236–7, 244–5, 300–01, 304–5).

Hume's health began to decline in 1772. He lost weight, and suffered from fevers, haemorrhages, and diarrhoea. By 1775 the decline was evident to his friends, and Hume accepted that the end was approaching. Accordingly on 4 January 1776 he redrew his will. His estate was to pass to his brother, or failing him to his brother's son, David *Hume, the future advocate, who was meanwhile to have £1000 to assist his education. His sister Katherine was to receive a legacy of £1200 and the life rent of the house in James's Court, and there were legacies of £200 for Adam Ferguson, D'Alembert, and Adam Smith, who was also entrusted with the publication of the 'Dialogues concerning natural religion'. There were several smaller legacies, and provision of three years' wages for his housekeeper Margaret Irvine. To this he added a codicil on 15 April with provisions for the rebuilding of the bridge at Chirnside and the construction of drains at Ninewells, both subject

to specific conditions. Three days later he composed 'My own life', suggesting in the final sentence that its readers should regard it as his 'funeral oration'.

These measures may have been a response to the death in March of William Mure, 'the oldest and best friend I had in the World' (to John Home, 12 April 1776, *Letters*, 2.314). Yet there was still news to cheer Hume, not least the publication of the first volume of Gibbon's *Decline and Fall*, shortly followed by Adam Smith's *Wealth of Nations*. His letters of congratulation to the two authors have no equal in spontaneous generosity and critical solidarity (to Edward Gibbon, 18 March 1776, to Adam Smith, 1 April 1776, ibid., 2.309–11, 311–12). Moreover his doctors would not be seen to give up hope. Although attended by Joseph Black, William Cullen, and Francis Home in Edinburgh, he was also the recipient of advice from Sir John Pringle (the former professor of moral philosophy whose reluctance to resign had not helped Hume to obtain the chair in 1745), who now practised in London. At Pringle's insistence, Hume agreed to make the journey south for a consultation. He left Edinburgh on 21 April, and two days later acquired the company of John Home. When not reading, Hume entertained Home with political anecdotes, and teased him about his inordinate opinion of the military virtues. In London, Pringle could identify nothing serious, and sent Hume on to take the waters at Bath. There he encountered John Hunter, who identified a tumour in the liver. Satisfied with this, Hume was keen to return home, and was back in Edinburgh by 3 July. His Edinburgh doctors immediately disputed the seriousness of Hunter's diagnosis, but Hume himself was under no illusions. He prepared to die a philosopher's death.

There are two accounts of this, Hume's final achievement, written from almost opposite standpoints, but to the same effect. Soon after Hume's return, on Sunday 7 July, James Boswell, on his way to church, presented himself instead at St David's Street. He was anxious to know if Hume persisted in disbelieving in a future state even in face of death. He asked Hume whether it was not possible there might be a future state. 'He answered it was possible a piece of coal put upon the fire would not burn; and he added that it was a most unreasonable fancy that he should exist for ever.' Boswell tried again, enquiring whether Hume was never uneasy at the thought of annihilation. 'He said not the least; no more than the thought that he had not been, as Lucretius observes.' In the circumstances, Hume's reference to the Epicurean philosopher was almost certainly not casual. After several further attempts Boswell grudgingly conceded defeat; Hume, he concluded, was 'indecently and impolitely positive in incredulity' (Boswell).

With Adam Smith, Hume had no such need to be on his guard. Smith observed that he encouraged his friends to converse with him as with a dying man. As an example, Hume imagined how he might address Charon, boatman of the Styx, after the manner of Lucian's *Dialogues of the Dead*. He would ask him for more time to see how the public would receive his latest revisions, or even to let him see the downfall of some of the prevailing systems of super-stition. But Charon, he knew, would have none of it. 'You loitering rogue, that will not happen these many hundred years. Do you fancy I will grant you a lease for so long a term? Get into the boat this instant, you lazy loitering rogue' ('Letter from Adam Smith, to William Strahan esq., Kirkcaldy, 9 Nov 1776', in *Essays*, xliv–xlvi).

In fact, Hume still had one matter to settle, which he may well have regarded as his very last conversation with his friends and adversaries: the 'Dialogues concerning natural religion'. At some point in 1776 he made further revisions to the manuscript of part 12; and on 7 August he wrote another codicil to his will, in which he retracted his previous charge to Smith to publish the dialogues, and instead requested Strahan to do so, with discretion to add the two suppressed essays on 'Suicide' and the 'Immortal-ity of the soul'. If Strahan did not comply within two years, the property in the dialogues was to pass to Hume's nephew, David, whose duty it would be to publish them. Striking a lighter but still worldly note, he also left John Home a dozen of claret and six dozen of port, on condition that he drink a bottle of port in two sittings, and attest to this as 'John Hume' ('Codicil to my will', NL Scot., MS 23159, no. 24). The more important clause, at least, was duly fulfilled by his nephew: the *Dialogues Concerning Nat-ural Religion* were published in 1779.

David Hume died at his house in St David's Street on 25 August 1776. At his wish, he was buried, on 29 August, in Calton churchyard. He left it to posterity to add any epi-taph, and Adam Smith, overcoming his usual caution, pro-vided it: 'Upon the whole, I have always considered him, both in his lifetime and since his death, as approaching as nearly to the idea of a perfectly wise and virtuous man, as perhaps the nature of human frailty will permit' ('Letter to William Strahan', in *Essays*, xlix).

Reputation The self-deprecatory tone of 'My own life', especially on the subject of the *Treatise*, suggests that Hume had little expectation that his ideas would be better understood after his death. In the short term, it seemed that he had been unduly pessimistic. In 1783 Immanuel Kant published his *Prolegomena to any Future Metaphysics*, in whose preface he famously acknowledged that Hume had awoken him from his 'dogmatic slumber' regarding meta-physics. (Since the *Treatise* would not be translated into German until 1791–2, while the *Enquiry Concerning Human Understanding* had been available in the language since 1755, Kant was almost certainly referring to the latter.) Kant drew radically un-Humean conclusions from his 'awakening', proceeding to reconstruct the concept of reason; before he did so, however, he offered a resounding endorsement of Hume's frequent complaint that his crit-ics—Kant named Reid, Oswald, Beattie, and Priestley—had misunderstood his problem, 'constantly taking for granted just what he doubted, and, conversely, proving with vehemence and, more often than not, great inso-lence exactly what it had never entered his mind to doubt', namely the indispensability of the concept of cause (Kant, 7–12). At the same time Hume's political and

economic essays were being cited with respect in the newly independent United States of America. In particu-lar, it is argued, the conviction of James Madison, one of the authors of *The Federalist*, that the constitution of the union should recognize the existence of factions, and especially factions from interest, was directly indebted to his reading of Hume's political essays.

Nevertheless, the intellectual tide was running against Hume. By 1800 the 'common-sense' philosophy of his crit-ics was established as orthodoxy in both the colleges of America and the universities of Scotland. Unaware of Kant's withering judgement on its begetters, Dugald Stewart took the lead in presenting common-sense philo-sophy as proof against the scepticism and outright irreli-gion which Hume was taken to exemplify, and which might be thought to have been among the intellectual ori-gins of the French Revolution. Equally averse to serious engagement with Hume were the philosophers who con-tinued to uphold the 'experimental' method; these pre-ferred to derive their principles from Locke and from David Hartley's associational psychology. Hume's reputa-tion was further circumscribed by the emergence of a revised 'whig' political and historical philosophy. Devel-oped by Dugald Stewart, Sir James Mackintosh, and T. B. Macaulay, the new whiggism cast Hume firmly in the adversarial role of a 'tory'. The label was pinned with the greatest conviction to Hume's *History*, to which Macau-lay's *History of England* was an explicit rejoinder. It was the notoriety of the *History* which led to Hume's being thought of as a historian rather than a philosopher; and by 1850 its disrepute was synonymous with Hume's own. Writing to his elder son in 1847, Sir James Stephen could dismiss Hume as 'a mere thinking machine', 'a frozen calx' (to James Fitzjames Stephen, 9 Aug 1847, Stephen, 119–20). Stephen's hostility was intensified by distaste for Hume's irreligion, although this continued to attract sym-pathetic readers on the continent, notably Auguste Comte.

Nearly fifty years later, in 1891, the younger son, Leslie Stephen, was more generous, concluding that Hume 'may be regarded as the acutest thinker in Great Britain in the eighteenth century, and the most qualified interpreter of its intellectual tendencies' (*DNB*). Two circumstances prompted this change of attitude. One was the impetus given by Darwinian natural philosophy to agnosticism, stimulating a new appreciation of Hume's this-worldliness. A second was the revival of interest in Hume as a philosopher. By this time Kant's estimate of his importance was known, and under its influence T. H. Green and T. H. Grose had edited the *Philosophical Works* (1874–5), including the *Treatise*. While endorsing the Kant-ian criticism of Hume's limitations, Green's preface explained that Hume still provided the fullest statement of the doctrine of empiricism. Another German critic of empiricism to draw stimulus from Hume was Edmund Husserl. Along with his pupils Adolf Reinach and C. V. Sal-mon, Husserl treated the discussion of ideas and impress-ions in the *Treatise* as an opening to a phenomenological metaphysics. It has been suggested that it was the combined influence of Kant and Husserl which led the Edinburgh professor of philosophy, Norman Kemp Smith, to produce an interpretation of Hume's philosophy as a variant of common sense (Davie, 189–94). On this account, the misunderstanding of Hume by his contemporaries Reid and Beattie was, after all, no more than a failure to recognize that he was one of them. In opposition to the Kantians, there emerged a new and more aggressive version of empiricism, logical positivism, whose Anglo-Saxon adherents no longer hesitated to claim Hume as a predecessor; they were, however, less interested in the study of Hume for his own sake.

By the mid-twentieth century a more sympathetic interest in Hume was once again being shown by political philosophers. Historically minded conservatives, notably Michael Oakeshott, took up Hume's anti-contractarian emphasis on custom and the forging of conventions over time, while liberal individualists, led by F. A. von Hayek, found in Hume's political and economic essays an exemplary formulation of the principle of the spontaneous order of the market. Increasingly, however, philosophical and historical scholarship concentrated on understanding Hume in terms as close as possible to his own. Philosophers focused their attention on the *Treatise*, as the work richest in philosophical puzzles, devoting monographs to its individual books, and articles to its several subordinate parts. A specialist journal, *Hume Studies*, the product of the international Hume Society, exemplifies but by no means exhausts such scholarship. The *Enquiry Concerning Human Understanding* drew fresh attention for its treatment of miracles; this and Hume's other works on religion continued to absorb continental European scholars from anticlerical traditions. A much wider readership was secured by paperback student editions of the *Treatise* and *Enquiries*, available in all major European languages as well as English. The development of philosophy as an academic discipline, the subject of degree courses in its own right, owed much to the use of these texts to induct undergraduates into philosophical problems; in turn, academic prominence has reinforced Hume's reputation as the foremost British philosopher. By contrast, the *History of England* may long since have ceased to be regarded by scholars as an authority; but they have begun to appreciate its originality in the development of historical writing. More generally, intellectual historians have explored the importance of Hume's contribution, as thinker and as man of letters, to the eighteenth-century movement of Enlightenment, in its Scottish and wider European dimensions. Yet even as scholarship finally does justice to Hume's greatness, the attraction of his work continues to transcend academic interest. For scholars no less than laity, the pleasures of reading Hume run deeper, in appreciating the quickness of his intelligence, the humanity of his scepticism, and the lucidity and unforced ease of his writing: such pleasures are not likely soon to be exhausted.

JOHN ROBERTSON

Sources D. Hume, 'My own life', 1776, NL Scot., Hume MSS, MS 23159 [vol. 9] · D. Hume, *Essays moral, political, and literary* (1741–1777), ed. E. F. Miller (1985) [incl. 'My own life'] · *The letters of David Hume*, ed. J. Y. T. Greig, 2 vols. (1932) · *New letters of David Hume*, ed. R. Klibansky and E. C. Mossner (1954) · E. C. Mossner, ed., 'New Hume letters to Lord Elibank, 1748–1776', *Texas Studies in Literature and Language*, 4 (1962), 431–60 · C. Montesquieu and A. Ramsay, letters to D. Hume, NL Scot., Hume MS 23156, nos. 46–8, 103 [vol. 6] · J. Y. T. Greig and H. Benyon, eds., *Calendar of Hume MSS in the possession of the Royal Society of Edinburgh* (1932); repr. (1990) · D. Hume, *A treatise of human nature*, ed. D. F. Norton and M. J. Norton (2000) · D. Hume, *A letter from a gentleman to his friend in Edinburgh* (1745), ed. E. C. Mossner and J. V. Price (1967) · D. Hume, *A true account of the behaviour and conduct of Archibald Stewart Esq., late provost of Edinburgh, in a letter to a friend* (1748) · 'Notes on the expedition to L'Orient', [n.d.], NL Scot., Hume MS 23159, no. 12 [vol. 9] · D. Hume, *An enquiry concerning human understanding*, ed. T. L. Beauchamp (1999) · D. Hume, *An enquiry concerning the principles of morals*, ed. T. L. Beauchamp (1998) · M. A. Stewart, ed., 'Hume's "Bellmen's Petition": the original text', *Hume Studies*, 23/1 (1997), 3–7 · D. Hume, 'The natural history of religion (1757)', *Essays, moral, political and literary*, ed. T. H. Green and T. H. Grose, 2 (1898) · D. Hume, *The history of England from the invasion of Julius Caesar to the revolution in 1688*, new edn, 8 vols. (1778); repr. in 6 vols. (1983–5) · testament of D. Hume, Commissariot Edinburgh: testaments, vol. 125, pt 2 (3 Jan 1781–23 Dec 1782), will of 4 Jan 1776, codicil on 15 April 1776, 'Codicil to my will, 7 August 1776', NL Scot., Hume MS 23159, no. 24 [vol. 9] · *Hume's Dialogues concerning natural religion* (1779); N. Kemp Smith, ed., 2nd edn (1947) · M. A. Stewart, 'The dating of Hume's manuscripts', *The Scottish Enlightenment: essays in reinterpretation*, ed. P. Wood (2000), 267–314 · E. C. Mossner, *The life of David Hume*, 2nd edn (1980) · M. A. Stewart, 'Hume's intellectual development', *Impressions of Hume*, ed. M. Frasca-Spada and P. Kail (2003) · M. Barfoot, 'Hume and the culture of science in the early eighteenth century', *Studies in the philosophy of the Scottish Enlightenment*, ed. M. A. Stewart (1990), 151–90 · D. Wootton, 'Hume's "Of miracles": probability and irreligion', *Studies in the philosophy of the Scottish Enlightenment*, ed. M. A. Stewart (1990), 191–229 · N. Kemp Smith, *The philosophy of David Hume: a critical study of its origins and central doctrines* (1941); repr. (1960) · J. Moore, 'Hume and Hutcheson', *Hume and Hume's connexions*, ed. M. A. Stewart and J. P. Wright (1994), 23–57 · J. Moore and M. A. Stewart, 'William Smith (1698–1741) and the dissenters' book trade', *Bulletin of the Presbyterian Historical Society of Ireland*, 22 (1993), 20–27 · M. A. Stewart, *The kirk and the infidel* (1995) [inaugural lecture delivered at the University of Lancaster, 9 Nov 1994] · R. L. Emerson, 'The "affair" at Edinburgh and the "project" at Glasgow: the politics of Hume's attempts to become a professor', *Hume and Hume's connexions*, ed. M. A. Stewart and J. P. Wright (1994), 1–22 · J. Moore, 'Utility and humanity: the quest for the *honestum* in Cicero, Hutcheson and Hume', *Utilitas*, 14 (2002) · *The correspondence of Adam Smith*, ed. E. C. Mossner and I. S. Ross, 2nd edn (1987), vol. 6 of *The Glasgow edition of the works and correspondence of Adam Smith* · I. Hont, 'The "rich country–poor country" debate in Scottish classical political economy', *Wealth and virtue: the shaping of political economy in the Scottish Enlightenment*, ed. I. Hont and M. Ignatieff (1983), 271–315 · R. B. Sher, 'The book in the Scottish Enlightenment', *The culture of the book in the Scottish Enlightenment*, ed. P. Wood (2000), 40–60 · B. Hillyard, 'The keepership of David Hume', *For the encouragement of learning: Scotland's National Library, 1689–1989*, ed. P. Cadell and A. Matheson (1989), 103–9 · A. Smart, *Allan Ramsay: painter, essayist and man of the Enlightenment* (1992) · R. L. Emerson, 'Hume and the Bellman, Zerobabel MacGilchrist', *Hume Studies*, 23/1 (1997), 9–28 · J. G. A. Pocock, *Barbarism and religion: II, Narratives of civil society* (1999) · D. Goodman, 'The Hume-Rousseau affair: from private *Querelle* to public *procès*', *Eighteenth-Century Studies*, 25 (1991–2), 171–201 · J. Home, 'Journal of the journey with David Hume to Bath, 1776', in *The works of John Home*, 3 vols. (1822), vol. 1, appx · J. Boswell, 'An account of my last interview with David Hume Esq.', *Hume's Dialogues concerning natural religion*, ed. N. Kemp Smith (1947), appx A, 76–9 · A. Smith, 'Letter from Adam Smith to William Strahan Esq., Kirkaldy, 9 Nov 1776', in D. Hume, *Essays moral, political, and literary*, ed. E. F. Miller (1985), xliii–xlix • I. Kant, *Prolegomena to any future metaphysics* (1783), ed. and trans. G. Hatfield (1997) • D. Adair, '"That politics may be reduced to a science": David Hume, James Madison, and the tenth federalist', *Huntington Library Quarterly*, 20 (1956–7), 343–60 • C. E. Stephen, *The first Sir James Stephen* (1906) • *DNB* • G. E. Davie, 'Husserl and Reinach on Hume's *Treatise*', *A passion for ideas: essays on the Scottish Enlightenment*, ed. G. E. Davie and M. Macdonald, 2 (1994), 163–96 • R. Hall, *Fifty years of Hume scholarship: a bibliographic guide* (1978) [suppl. by the same author's bibliographies of Hume scholarship in *Hume Studies* (1978–88), and succeeded by W. E. Morris, 'The Hume literature', *Hume Studies* (annually from 1994)] • old parish register, Midlothian, 685 1/15

Archives BL, diary, Add. MS 36638 • King's AC Cam., corresp. • McGill University, Montreal, McLennon Library, corresp. • NL Scot., corresp. • NL Scot., corresp. and papers • Trinity Cam., corresp. | NA Scot., letters to Lord Kames • NL Scot., copy letters to Jean Jacques Rousseau and to Comtesse de Boufflers • NRA, priv. coll., corresp. with William Strachan • U. Edin. L., letters to R. Wallace

Likenesses C. N. Cochin, pencil and estampe drawing, 1754, Harvard U., Fogg Art Museum • A. Ramsay, oils, 1754, priv. coll. • L. Carrogis, pencil, chalk, and watercolour drawing, 1763?–1765, Scot. NPG • A. Ramsay, oils, 1766, Scot. NPG [*see illus.*] • Lady Abercromby, watercolour drawing (posthumous), U. Edin. • J. Tassie, glass paste medallion, NPG • J. Tassie, two paste medallions, Scot. NPG • tin-plate, Scot. NPG

Hume, David (*bap.* 1757, *d.* 1838), jurist and judge, was baptized on 27 February 1757 at Chirnside, Berwickshire, the third son (of the four sons and four daughters) of John Hume (1709–1786) of Ninewells, Berwickshire, and his wife, Agnes (1725–1785), daughter of Robert Carre of Cavers, Roxburghshire, and Helen Riddell. He was the nephew of the philosopher David *Hume. A pupil at Edinburgh high school from 1765 to 1767, he proceeded to the University of Edinburgh, possibly in 1768, and studying there certainly from 1770 to 1774. In 1774 he studied Roman law with Professor Dick but decided to move to the University of Glasgow to study law with John Millar, then the most celebrated law teacher in the British Isles. He matriculated as a law student in Glasgow in 1775 and studied there until 1777, lodging with Professor Millar. For 1777–8 he registered as a student of Scots law in Edinburgh, studying under Professor William Wallace. On 13 July 1779 he was admitted as an advocate.

Hume's good connections and evident talent brought him early recognition, and on 18 March 1783 he was appointed sheriff-depute of his home county of Berwickshire. To this part-time post he added that of professor of Scots law in the University of Edinburgh, in December 1786. On 24 February 1785 he married Jane (1766?–1816), the only daughter of Thomas Alder of Brentinck, Northumberland. The couple had three sons, John (*d.* 1791), Joseph (1796?–1819), and David (*d.* 1798), and three daughters, Elizabeth (*d.* 1848), Catherine (who in 1819 married Adolphus McDowall Ross MD), and Agnes.

Along with his chair and shrieval appointment Hume maintained a practice as an advocate. In 1793 he exchanged the sheriffdom of Berwickshire for that of Linlithgowshire, which he resigned in 1811 on his appointment as a principal clerk of session (to the chagrin of his friend Walter Scott who also wanted the post, but who joined him as a clerk the next year). Hume long coveted the post of baron of the exchequer, a court noted for its lack of business. He eventually achieved this on 3 January 1822, gaining the label by which he is usually distinguished from his philosopher uncle, Baron David Hume. His resignation from his chair led to quite unprecedented deputations, with addresses from the senate of the university and the Society of Writers to the Signet, and special resolutions of the Faculty of Advocates and the Society of Solicitors to the Supreme Court. The university conferred upon him the degree of LLD; the writers to the signet had his portrait painted by Sir Henry Raeburn; and some former pupils who were judges and advocates had his bust sculpted by Chantrey.

These unparalleled celebrations of Hume's period as professor mark his outstanding success as a teacher of law. There were critics, notably Thomas Carlyle, who described 'his lectures on law [as], (still excepting Erskine's Institute) ... the dullest piece of study I ever saw or heard of' (*Early Letters*, 1.300); but this was the minority view of a man not attracted to the real discipline of law. Others who criticized Hume generally were whig opponents of his high toryism, such as the members of the Speculative Society (of which he had been a member), with whom he had a major dispute. Hume's tory politics led him into leading the opposition to Henry Erskine as dean of the Faculty of Advocates in the charged years of the 1790s. In general, however, his lectures were highly praised and students flocked to them. Sir Walter Scott's judgement that Hume had been 'an architect ... to the law of Scotland' (*Scott on Himself*, 42) is more typical and, to the modern reader, a more just reflection of their status. Hume forbade publication of his lectures, but copies circulated and they were cited in court, many of his pupils reaching the bench. In the 1790s Hume gave a separate course of lectures on criminal law; it provided the foundation for his *Commentaries on the Law of Scotland, Respecting the Description and Punishment of Crimes* (1797) and *Commentaries on the Law of Scotland, Respecting Trial for Crimes* (1800), later published together as his *Commentaries on the Law of Scotland, Respecting Crimes* (1819). Just as the lectures recast Scottish private law ready for the nineteenth century, so the works on criminal law became a foundational statement.

Hume contributed papers to *The Mirror* and *The Lounger*, periodicals edited by Henry Mackenzie, author of *The Man of Feeling* and associated with the cults of sentimentalism and Addisonian politeness in Scotland. He also participated in the reforms of procedure in the court of session and in the steps to commemorate his old friend Sir Walter Scott. Hume had a close and affectionate family life, which was saddened by the early deaths of his wife in 1816 and of his talented advocate son, Joseph, in 1819. On the death of his brother Joseph in 1832 he succeeded to the family estates of Ninewells, Castle Fairney, and others, which ultimately devolved on his daughter Elizabeth. He retired from the exchequer bench on 20 February 1834 and died at his home at 34 Moray Place, Edinburgh, on 27 July 1838. He was buried on 2 August 1838 at Calton cemetery, Edinburgh.   JOHN W. CAIRNS

Sources G. C. H. Paton, 'Biography of Baron Hume', *Baron David Hume's lectures*, Edinburgh Stair Society, 6 (1958) · bap. reg. Scot., OPR index, ext 3063031 · records, U. Edin. · minutes of the Faculty of Advocates, Advocates' Library, Edinburgh · *Early letters of Thomas Carlyle*, ed. C. E. Norton, 2 vols. (1886) · *Scott on himself*, ed. D. Hewitt (1981) · mar. reg. Scot., OPR index
Archives Edinburgh City Archives, law lecture notes, some possibly in his own hand · NL Scot., lectures on Scots law and papers · U. Edin. L., lecture notes
Likenesses H. Raeburn, oils, *c*.1822, Signet Library, Edinburgh · F. Chantrey, marble bust, 1832, Faculty of Advocates, Parliament Hall, Edinburgh
Wealth at death see NA Scot., SC 70/1/57, fol. 330

Hume, Ferguson Wright [Fergus] (1859–1932), author, was born at Powick, Worcestershire, on 8 July 1859, the second son of James Collin Hume (1823–1896), steward at the Worcestershire Pauper Lunatic Asylum, and his wife, Mary Ferguson (d. 1867). Both parents were natives of Glasgow. In 1863 the family emigrated to New Zealand; James Hume founded the first private mental hospital in that country and was also a founder of Dunedin College.

Fergus Hume was educated at the boys' high school in Dunedin before taking a law degree at Otago University. He then served his articles in the office of the attorney-general of New Zealand and was called to the New Zealand bar in 1885. In that year he moved to Melbourne, South Australia, where he took a job as a solicitor's clerk, but his aim was to become the author of plays for the stage. He thought the best way to attract the attention of theatre managers would be to write a successful book, so he:

> took advice of a leading Melbourne bookseller. I enquired what style of book he sold most of. He replied that the detective stories of [Emile] Gaboriau had a large sale … I determined to write a book of the same class, containing a mystery, a murder and a description of low life in Melbourne. (Knight)

The resulting novel, *The Mystery of a Hansom Cab*, was rejected by George Robinson, the leading Melbourne publisher, so in 1886 Hume had it privately printed in Australia and claimed that he sold 5000 copies in three weeks. The novel was dedicated to the novelist James Payn, then editor of the *Cornhill Magazine*, 'in grateful acknowledgement of his kind encouragement to the author'. Hume then sold, for £50, the rights of the novel to a group of London-based entrepreneurs, headed by Frederick Trischler, who promptly established their Hansom Cab Publishing Company in Ludgate Hill. The first London printing (1887) of 25,000 copies was sold out in three days, and subsequent printings were purchased by an eager public across the world. Many editions followed, but Hume did not benefit financially. He was now, however, established as the author of an international best-seller: by the time of his death its sales had reached 500,000. With its 'complex and highly surprising ending' (Knight), it was the first international detective novel, the Australian edition pre-dating Conan Doyle's *Study in Scarlet* (1887) by a year. Critics have questioned just why Hume's 'shoddy pot boiler … received vastly more contemporary attention than

Doyle's *Study in Scarlet*' and became, in the assessment of Willard Huntington Wright, 'the greatest commercial success in the annals of detective fiction' (Haycroft, 63). Such was the success of Hume's novel that a full-length parody, *The Mystery of a Wheelbarrow, or, Gaboriam Gaborooed*, by 'W. Humer Ferguson', was published in 1888. Hume had prudently retained for himself the dramatic rights of *The Mystery of the Hansom Cab* and as a result benefited from the stage versions by the Australian playwright George Darrell, which had long and successful runs in Australia and London.

In 1888 Hume sailed for England and, having settled in London, became a full-time writer. He still considered himself a New Zealand, and not an Australian, author. His best-seller, with its realistic exposé of Melbourne high and low society, was sometimes less well received in the Antipodes, where some criticized how their societies were portrayed by 'one who is representing us in the Old Country' (Robinson and others, 249). Afterwards he wrote 140 novels, half of them mystery and detective stories, but none came close to matching the success of *The Mystery of a Hansom Cab*, which was reprinted and published in new editions through the twentieth century. He tried writing romances, starting with his second novel, *Madame Midas* (1889), which again described Melbourne society and was one of his few books with Australian settings. This was reprinted in 1914 and 1985, but his romances were not particularly successful and, as he later complained, publishers would not hear of him writing anything but detective stories. His ambition to write for the stage continued, and he was the author of eight plays, including one for Sir Henry Irvine, who died before the play could be presented.

Although he travelled in Switzerland, France, and Italy, Hume lived and worked for the rest of his life in the London area. The last of his novels appeared in 1926, yet he is invariably remembered as a one-book author. Following a serious operation for a glandular problem he seemed, to some, to lose his power of writing. After retiring to the Rayleigh area of Essex, he concentrated on lecturing to young people's clubs and debating societies. A deeply religious man, he died of cardiac failure at his home, Rosemary, Grove Road, Thundersley, Essex, on 11 July 1932.

ROBIN WOOLVEN

Sources *The Times* (14 July 1932) · *WW* (1931) · *WWW*, 1929–40 · W. H. Wilde, J. Hooton, and B. Andrews, *The Oxford companion to Australian literature*, 2nd edn (1994) [entries for Hume and *The mystery of a hansom cab*] · 'Detective fiction', 'Hume', *The Oxford companion to New Zealand literature*, ed. R. Robinson and others (1998) · S. Knight, introduction, in F. Hume, *The mystery of a hansom cab* (1985) · H. Haycroft, *The life and times of the detective story* (1941) · b. cert. · d. cert. · J. Thomson, 'Hume, James', *DNZB*, vol. 2
Wealth at death £201 6s.: probate, 31 Aug 1932, *CGPLA Eng. & Wales*

Hume [Home], **George, fourth Lord Hume** (d. 1549), nobleman, was the brother of Alexander *Hume, third Lord Hume (d. 1516), and son of Alexander *Hume, second Lord Hume (d. 1506) [see under Hume family], and his second wife, Nichola Ker of Samuelston. George was restored to his family titles and estates in August 1522, which was not ratified by parliament until 1526. About 1518 he married Mariota Haliburton of Dirleton, coheir of Patrick Haliburton, Lord Haliburton, which brought a third of the lucrative Dirleton estates in Haddingtonshire into Hume ownership. They had three sons: Alexander *Home, fifth Lord Home, Andrew, commendator of Jedburgh Abbey, and Matthew Hume of Cloichtow. Their daughter Margaret married Alexander Erskine of Gogar and was mother of Thomas Erskine, first earl of Kellie. Hume also had an illegitimate son, George.

The power vacuum left by the downfall of the third Lord Hume, executed for treason in 1516, caused unrest in the Scottish east march. Anthoine de Labastie, acting warden of the march, was murdered by the Humes in 1517. An accomplice to this deadly act (Labastie had been exulting in the third lord's downfall), George was denounced a traitor, yet after being offered amnesty in March 1518 he surrendered himself in order to save his life and protect his wife's heritage. He had no other lands at this time, as his brother's forfeiture was still in force. Hume Castle in Berwickshire, for example, was in the custody of Sir James Hamilton of Finnart. He did not regain his family's estates at Hume and Dunglass, Haddingtonshire, until 1522 and had to claim back other lands at Greenlaw, Leitholm, and Birgham in 1524.

In July 1520 Hume came to Edinburgh with others in order to reclaim the honour of his family. One account states that they proceeded to the Tolbooth and removed the heads of the third lord and his brother William. Later they held a proper funeral for them at the Blackfriars with 'greit offeringis and banquets', before returning home (Lesley, 115–16). Another account states that it was the eighteenth earl of Angus who ordered the heads to be removed and delivered to George. Either way this action symbolized the Humes' recovery, underlined when on 12 August 1522 George Hume was restored to his brother's peerage title. During that summer he was praised by Henry VIII for opposing the regent, the fourth duke of Albany, in the name of the young James V. When Albany left Scotland in 1524 the Humes soon fell out with Angus, who succeeded him, resenting the new regent's predominance in the borders. In May 1526 Hume's failure to support Angus led to his being charged with treason, and though a temporary reconciliation followed, with Hume signing a bond of manrent with Angus on 20 June, he later backed the king against the regent. This brought instability to the borders, but strengthened Hume's position during the period 1526–8. He was thanked for preserving the king from Scott of Buccleuch's kidnap attempt in 1526, during which Andrew Ker of Cessford was slain, and he gained from the downfall of Angus in 1528, replacing the earl as warden of the east march.

Hume held that office during the periods 1528–32, 1535–8, 1542–3, and 1546–7, and his deputies were normally his kinsmen. He was displaced only when a higher ranking lieutenant or warden-general was appointed by the crown—magnates such as the earls of Angus, Lennox, or Moray. In 1529, moreover, he was appointed royal lieutenant within the bounds of the Merse, Lauderdale, Teviotdale, Haddingtonshire, and Lammermuir to preserve peace and resist rebels. He was occasionally called to the court to account for border affairs and like other wardens he was warded by the king in 1530 as part of James's programme of strengthening his own authority on the marches. None the less, he was later said to have done good service during the brief Anglo-Scottish war of 1532–3.

The strategic position of Hume Castle in the east marches made it an obvious target for invading English armies. The Scots army lay at Hume Castle, with all the gentlemen of the Merse, just before the battle of Solway Moss in 1542. The following year Hume was described by Sir William Parr as 'a man of a precise, obstinate and froward nature ... very unmeet for his office [wardenship]' (LP Henry VIII, 18/1, no. 592), a hostile view reflecting the fact that he was now a supporter of the pro-French party in Scotland, led by Cardinal Beaton. This guaranteed him French money to defend Hume Castle, but it also led to the deliberate targeting of his property by English raiders. Hume retaliated by attacking settlements in the English east march. However, in May 1544 he could not stop the retreating English army, led by the earl of Hertford, from passing through the strategic pass of Pease near Dunglass.

The Humes were staunch supporters of the Franco-Scottish alliance throughout the 1540s, fighting against the English at Ancrum Moor in 1545, but they paid a heavy price for their loyalty as Lord Hume had 'no goods left undestroyed' by the end of 1545 (LP Henry VIII, 20/2, no. 1009). The compensation that he received from both the Scottish privy council and France could never equal all that he and his kinsmen lost at this time. His family's situation appeared gravest by the autumn of 1547, when French help was expected but did not come. Hume broke his collar bone during a skirmish at Fawside, two days before the battle of Pinkie. The subsequent defeat of the Scots, on 10 September 1547, and the capture of the master of Hume probably led to Lady Hume giving some assurance to Protector Somerset (formerly Hertford) without her husband's knowledge. In a letter to Somerset she wrote with appropriate discretion: 'I dare not let my lord my husband see your last writing about the rendering of Home and the pledges' (CSP Scot., 1547–63, 36). This may be why Hume Castle capitulated with suspicious ease in 1547, even though Hume had been promised £1845 to pay for horsemen, gunners, and victuals there. When French forces finally arrived in 1548 they reconquered southern Scotland, including Hume Castle. When Lord Home died in 1549 he had the satisfaction of knowing that Hume was safe and that his son and heir was back in Scotland.

MAUREEN M. MEIKLE

Sources NA Scot., CH6/6/1, fol. 55 · NA Scot., GD6/24, 38, 47, 60 · NRA Scotland, Home of the Hirsel, 859 · Manuscripts of the duke of Atholl ... and of the earl of Home, HMC, 26 (1891) · APS · CSP Scot., 1547–63 · J. M. Thomson and others, eds., Registrum magni sigilli regum Scotorum / The register of the great seal of Scotland, 11 vols. (1882–1914), vols. 3, 4 · *Reg. PCS*, 1st ser., vol. 1 · M. Livingstone, D. Hay Fleming, and others, eds., *Registrum secreti sigilli regum Scotorum / The register of the privy seal of Scotland*, 1–4 (1908–52) · *LP Henry VIII* · J. B. Paul, ed., *Compota thesaurariorum regum Scotorum / Accounts of the lord high treasurer of Scotland*, 5–9 (1903–11) · R. K. Hannay, ed., *Acts of the lords of council in public affairs, 1501–1554* (1932) · G. Burnett and others, eds., *The exchequer rolls of Scotland*, 23 vols. (1878–1908), vols. 14–18 · J. Lesley, *The history of Scotland*, ed. T. Thomson, Bannatyne Club, 38 (1830) · T. Thomson, ed., *A diurnal of remarkable occurrents that have passed within the country of Scotland*, Bannatyne Club, 43 (1833) · *The historie and cronicles of Scotland … by Robert Lindesay of Pitscottie*, ed. A. J. G. Mackay, 3 vols., STS, 42–3, 60 (1899–1911) · *Scots peerage*, 4.458–60 · *The state papers and letters of Sir Ralph Sadler*, ed. A. Clifford, 3 vols. (1809) · J. Bain, ed., *The Hamilton papers: letters and papers illustrating the political relations of England and Scotland in the XVIth century*, 2 vols., Scottish RO, 12 (1890–92) · *The Scottish correspondence of Mary of Lorraine*, ed. A. I. Cameron, Scottish History Society, 3rd ser., 10 (1927) · J. G. Dalyell, ed., *Fragments of Scottish history* (1798) · J. Cameron, *James V: the personal rule, 1528–1542*, ed. N. Macdougall (1998) · J. Wormald, *Lords and men in Scotland: bonds of manrent, 1442–1603* (1985) · I. Rae, *The administration of the Scottish frontier, 1513–1603* (1966) · M. M. Meikle, 'Lairds and gentlemen: a study of the landed families of the Eastern Anglo-Scottish Borders, c.1540–1603', PhD diss., U. Edin., 1989

Hume, George Haliburton [*name in religion* Basil Hume] **(1923–1999)**, cardinal and Roman Catholic archbishop of Westminster, was born on 2 March 1923 at 4 Ellison Place, Newcastle upon Tyne, the elder son and third of the five children of a distinguished cardiologist from the borders, Sir William Errington Hume (1879–1960), professor of medicine at Durham University and consulting physician at the Royal Victoria Infirmary, Newcastle upon Tyne, and his French wife, Marie Elisabeth, known as Mimi (*b. c.*1896), eldest daughter of Colonel J. R. Tisseyre, army officer and sometime military attaché in Madrid. He was named after his paternal grandfather, George Haliburton Hume, also a distinguished doctor, and the historian of the Newcastle Infirmary, though—like his siblings, Madeleine, Frances, Christine, and John—he was given a first name which could be rendered equally well in French or English.

Family and education Hume's parents met during the First World War in Wimereux, near Boulogne, where William Hume was consulting physician to the First Army (where he was noted for his work on poison gas) and Marie Elisabeth Tisseyre had been evacuated from Lille. Despite initial opposition from her parents—she was seventeen years younger than her husband—they were married in France in 1918, before setting up home in Newcastle. Theirs was a happy, lively, occasionally volatile household; French was the domestic language and the children were expected to be bilingual. The domestic religion was Roman Catholicism, though their father was an Anglican, and the children were also expected to be ecumenical. At the time of their parents' marriage such 'mixed marriages' were strongly discouraged by the Catholic authorities and were disliked almost as much by the Church of England, not least because of the requirement—to which the non-Catholic party was obliged to consent—to bring up the children in the Catholic faith. Having an Anglican father appeared to endow Hume with an instinctive

George Haliburton Hume (1923–1999), by Jeff Stultiens, 1986–7

respect for that faith, though he seems never to have contemplated joining it.

Hume was brought up in Newcastle in a comfortable environment; at one point his parents employed half a dozen domestic servants, as well as a governess for the children. He developed an early interest in sport, especially football, and his lifelong support for Newcastle United originated in his being taken to matches at St James's Park by his father (who also instilled in him a lifelong love of fishing). He was educated at Newcastle preparatory school (1931–3) and at Gilling Castle (1933–4), the preparatory school for Ampleforth College (the public school run by Benedictine monks), which he entered in 1934. At Ampleforth he excelled at sport—he was captain of the rugby first fifteen, and according to a contemporary, 'captain of more or less everything' (*The Tablet*)—was active in the drama and debating societies, and also thrived as a scholar, especially in languages and history, though with characteristic modesty he later put himself as being about average among the brighter boys. He was also noted for a sense of mischief, which went with an ability not to take himself too seriously. But he had heart: what he saw of the great depression as a boy, especially in the Shieldfield and Byker districts of Newcastle (where he was taken by a Dominican priest who had befriended him), gave him a lasting sense of indignation at social injustice and solidarity with its victims. Even at an early age he translated such feelings into a desire to serve his fellow men by means of a religious vocation.

Monk Hume left Ampleforth College in 1941, but returned after the summer to enter the monastery there as a Benedictine novice, taking the name Basil. The choice of Benedictine monasticism must have seemed almost too obvious for him, though his father was disappointed, having hoped that (like his younger brother, John) Hume would follow him into medicine. It was wartime, therefore, when he first sought admission to the Benedictine order, half expecting, even hoping, that the role of Catholic priest in such a violent world could include some form of martyrdom. (His mother was convinced that the Germans would successfully invade England.) Ordinands and clerics were exempt from the wartime obligations of military service, though he later declared that had he joined up, his preference would have been for the Royal Navy. He had no particular pacifist leanings. He made his simple profession as a monk in September 1942, after one year's novitiate, and took solemn vows in 1945. Meanwhile he studied history at St Benet's Hall, Oxford, from 1944 to 1947 (graduating with a second-class degree in the latter year), and then theology (in Latin) at the Catholic University of Fribourg, Switzerland, from 1947 to 1951, when he obtained his licentiate in theology. He was ordained priest on 23 July 1950 at Ampleforth, by Bishop Brunner of Middlesbrough.

As a young monk Hume was assistant priest in Ampleforth village and taught history and modern languages (he was fluent in German as well as French) at Ampleforth College. He became head of the modern languages department in 1952, and in 1955 he became housemaster of St Bede's and professor of dogmatic theology (responsible for teaching the novices and young monks). In 1957 he was elected the Ampleforth monks' delegate to the general chapter of the English Benedictine congregation, which in turn elected him *magister scholarum* of the congregation. He was re-elected to the post in 1961. He also coached Ampleforth College's rugby first fifteen. A characteristic anecdote dates from about this time. He decided to gatecrash an open day for parents at the school, and dressed up as a captain in the army, complete with false moustache. He was chatting to the guest-master when the moustache fell into the teacup he was holding. Hume never quite let go of his adolescence, then or later.

Being a housemaster brought Hume the happiest years of his life—he said later that he was starting to worry at that time that his life was 'too good to last'. Despite the uproar from the music, the truth of one of Thomas Aquinas's 'proofs for the existence of God' came to him while he was allowing boys from his house to watch television (*Six-Five Special*, an early pop-music programme) in his study. The portrait that emerges from his time at Ampleforth is of a man who was relaxed and unstuffy in his relationships, even when he held a position of authority. It was then that he learned a trick which he applied throughout his life, even as a cardinal archbishop: that to have a button missing or undone, or something else slightly askew about his formal clerical attire, was a good

way of signalling to someone who might otherwise be intimidated by him that he was a human being just like them. But it was not an affectation: in early life or later, he was not what might be termed a buttoned-up person. On rising to his feet to make a speech to a distinguished audience of lawyers many years later, he began: 'I feel like an alley-cat who has strayed into Crufts' (*Cardinal Basil Hume*, 14). He had a particular affection for the 'honest rogue' type of character, people who did not pretend to be better than they seemed to be. What was completely lacking from his make-up—a powerful advantage in dealing with those who had it—was personal ambition.

Hume admitted that the one thing he missed from his life was marriage. But he saw priestly celibacy as God's gift to the church, enabling the clergy to be 'there for others' at all times of the day and night. It was, nevertheless, a permanent psychological cross to bear, giving him the sense of openness and vulnerability that made him so attractive. People often said there was a particular chemistry between him and young women, and he could have been a gifted flirt. He was no prude. He knew the language of the locker-room, even if he rarely used it.

Abbot On 17 April 1963 Hume was elected abbot of Ampleforth Abbey, in succession to Abbot Herbert Byrne. As such he became head of a community of more than 150 monks, whose pastoral work included not only the education of boys in Ampleforth College but also the running of some twenty parishes, mostly in the inner cities of northern England. It was a difficult time to take over as abbot: the reforms and updating of the Catholic church brought in by the Second Vatican Council (1962–5) were beginning to make themselves felt, and many religious houses were rent by division. 'One man's renewal is another man's betrayal', he was told by one of his older monks (*The Independent*, 18 June 1999). It needed all his skill to navigate a way through the opposing currents of opinion, doing what he knew had to be done without alienating those opposed to the changes. Such was his success that he was frequently called upon by the abbot primate of the Benedictines, from 1967 his friend the American Rembert Weakland, to visit other monasteries and advise on the resolution of disputes.

'I decided that what unites people has to be very deep. It is the life of prayer. Get that right and much else falls into place', Hume later said of his time as abbot (*The Times*, 18 June 1999). He took his responsibilities as spiritual leader of his community very seriously, and his weekly talks (conferences) to his brethren frequently took some point from the rule of St Benedict as the starting point for a wide-ranging exploration of spiritual values in the modern age. A selection of these talks was later published as *Searching for God* (1977). He kept in close touch with the abbey's various parish missions and became not only a superior but a friend to the mostly older priests working in the parishes. He suffered a rare setback in his attempts to persuade priests to live together in one monastic family where there were reasonably adjoining parishes, though his policy was later taken forward by his successors as abbot. He also played a key role in the development of the priory community at St Louis, Missouri, which had been started in 1955 in order to provide a Catholic day school in the city; he took the decision to allow the priory to have its own novitiate and training, a key stage in transforming the priory into a fully fledged abbey under the leadership of Abbot Luke Rigby, in 1989. Closer to home, Hume continued to take a keen interest in the growth and development of Ampleforth College, and was responsible for the inspired appointment as headmaster of Father Patrick Barry, who led the school successfully through a period of change and consolidation.

Hume played an important role in the wider Benedictine community as chairman of the ecumenical commission and of the commission 'de re monastica', both set up by the confederation of Benedictines in the wake of the Second Vatican Council. His concern for ecumenism was symbolized by his decision to allow a dozen Greek, Serbian, and Russian Orthodox boys to attend Ampleforth College and to live in their own house under the care of a Serbian Orthodox priest. He was also an active member of the ecumenical Council of Churches in Rydale. Through this and other initiatives he gradually became better known in the region, coming to the attention of the archbishop of York, Donald Coggan, with whom he soon developed a close personal friendship.

Coggan was at Canterbury by the time the archbishopric of Westminster became vacant on the death of Cardinal John Carmel Heenan, on 7 November 1975. He put word about that he knew an abbot who would make an excellent candidate. By then Hume had also come to the attention of several prominent Catholic lay people, such as William Rees-Mogg, editor of *The Times*, Norman St John Stevas MP, and the duke of Norfolk, all of whom perceived the need for a change of style after Heenan. They and others lobbied the apostolic delegate in London, Archbishop Bruno Heim, whose job it was to make up the *terna* (the list of three names from which Rome makes episcopal appointments). Their suggestions fell on fertile ground, since Heim was himself already convinced of the need for a change in style, and was (like the pope, Paul VI) deeply interested in the Benedictine tradition. Hume's name duly headed the list. He had been flattered to be asked his opinion of other potential candidates, but when asked to fill the post himself he was 'rather shattered, rather distressed'. He eventually accepted only 'out of a monk's obedience' (*The Times*, 18 June 1999); 'the gap between what is thought and expected of me, and what I know myself to be, is considerable and frightening', he declared (*Cardinal Basil Hume*, 15). His appointment was announced on 17 February 1976, he was ordained archbishop by Heim on 25 March, and on 24 May he was created a cardinal by the pope, with the titular church of San Silvestro in Capite.

Cardinal archbishop At the time of his surprise appointment in 1976, Hume was (apart from his unusual facility with languages) the archetypal public school, Oxford-educated English gentleman—charming, decent, self-deprecating, with a rounded culture, a passion for sport, a sense of fun, and a modicum of eccentricity. In politics he was more a one-nation tory than anything else, though by no means a party man. This English-gentleman side of Hume was a key asset in dealing with Vatican prelates, for he was able to present himself to them as one who understood the complex national character and culture of the English far better than they. 'That is not the way we do things in England' became a trade mark of his, to ward off policies and approaches which were unlikely to endear themselves to the Catholic church at home. At Westminster he was cautious towards the ultra-conservative Catholic organization Opus Dei, and conscious that it had tried to cultivate his support. When reports came to his attention that the organization was recruiting young people without letting their parents know, he issued firm advice discouraging such cult-like practices. He remarked that Opus Dei was too Spanish, not particularly suited to an English culture of understatement and of moderation in all things. He never seemed to take Vatican officials as seriously as they took themselves, though he had a profound reverence for the pope.

Hume sought by such tactics to manage the sensitive relationship between the fears of the papacy and Roman curia that the reforms of the Second Vatican Council were running out of control, and the eagerness of many English priests and lay people to complete the council's vision as fully and as effectively as possible. The fact that the two forces were held together, and that the Catholic community remained united while managing, overall, to be both liberal in style and orthodox in faith, testified to his patient, wise, and good-humoured leadership. The contrast with so many other local churches was striking. It had a price, however. The mild liberalism reached in his early years at Westminster never became a springboard for anything more ambitious, and towards the end there were even signs that some aspects of the life of his archdiocese suffered from neglect. For all the public alarm about paedophilia among a small number of Catholic priests, for instance, he never appointed a child-protection officer for Westminster as he was supposed to do.

That Hume was not an outsider to the British establishment was demonstrated by the fact that Sir John Hunt, secretary to the British cabinet and head of the home civil service, was married to Hume's sister Madeleine. Thus a ready-made network of contacts and influence was in place for him, both through family connections and through the Ampleforth old boys who had known and grown fond of him in his days as housemaster and abbot. For one of such a background, he was remarkably successful at transcending class divisions, and there was never a Hume clique or kitchen cabinet drawn from such upper-crust circles. One of his closest friends and advisers was Mgr George Leonard, a rough-hewn northerner from Shrewsbury diocese, who kept Hume's thinking in touch with the feelings and opinions of ordinary parish clergy. These were not always the easiest of men to deal with. They had reservations about having a monk, unused to running parishes, as archbishop of Westminster. But they warmed to his enthusiasm for the Catholic school system in the archdiocese, though his major regrouping of the school system at sixth-form level led to some untidy and untimely confrontations with certain school governors and the government. They admired his devotion to the poorest of the poor on his own doorstep, especially to the down-and-outs who clustered round (and even inside) Westminster Cathedral. He held regular meetings with the clergy which were filled with good humour; and he supplied them all with an ex-directory telephone number straight to his own desk. But the Catholic priesthood had been losing some of its brighter and more adventurous representatives under Heenan, and Hume never found the secret of reversing that trend, though he slowed it.

Similarly the advance of the Catholic laity into the middle class, largely a success story for the Catholic education system, seemed to go hand in hand with a decline in baptisms, marriages, and habitual mass-going, and hence a steady drop in church numbers. Europe-wide forces were at work, well beyond Hume's control. But he understood the need for a new accommodation between the officers of the church and an articulate and sometimes critical laity. He encouraged adult educational and catechetical initiatives, and gave his full support to the national pastoral congress in Liverpool in 1980, despite rumblings from some conservatives. Far from blocking discussion of the papal encyclical banning contraception, *Humanae vitae* (1968), at the congress, he listened to the debates with open-minded attention. When the congress resolved to ask Rome for some 'development' in that teaching, Hume took the message to the synod on the family in Rome later that year. In a private meeting with the pope he laid the report of the congress before him, open at the two pages on contraception, and asked him to read at least that part of it. The pope took it from him, but put it aside. In the synod hall Hume made a memorable contribution, saying that in a dream he had seen that the church was like a pilgrim, searching for the way. There were signposts to help it.

> The right signs point the way, but signposts become weather-beaten and new paint is needed … My dream became a nightmare, for I saw the wrong paint being put upon the signposts, and the last state was worse than the first (*The Tablet*)

Derek Worlock, archbishop of Liverpool, for his part attempted to raise the question of the pastoral treatment of divorced people who remarried. Hume, like Worlock, felt that ways should be found to lift the canonical ban on such people receiving holy communion, a ban neither took steps to enforce.

Hume did not feel afterwards that the concerns the Catholic community of England and Wales had collectively aired at Liverpool had been given a fair hearing or an adequate response. A more defensive approach in his leadership of the church in England and Wales dated from this time. It was his aim to protect it from disruptive intervention by Rome, particularly in the appointment of bishops. In this he was very successful. But there was a cost: many of the proposals for reform advanced with such enthusiasm by the national pastoral congress were shelved. A sense of disappointment and disillusion lingered for long afterwards.

Nevertheless the papal visit of 1982, at the height of the Falklands conflict, was a triumph for Hume's style and an endorsement of it. He saw that the pope was properly briefed and the people properly prepared; and the pope subsequently talked of this visit as a model never quite matched elsewhere. But the situation in the south Atlantic almost meant that it never happened, because the pope and his Vatican advisers feared giving offence to Argentina. The proposed solution—to add an extra papal visit to Argentina soon afterwards—at first left Hume unhappy, and there were angry words between him and Archbishop Worlock (who favoured and had helped to engineer the arrangement). Hume was convinced that the invasion of the Falklands was an outrage, and did not want to agree to anything that seemed to imply moral equivalence between the two parties to the conflict. A supreme diplomatic effort by the Vatican overcame his objections and calmed his temper. The subsequent success of the visit was one of the many fruits of his productive—though sometimes difficult—relationship with Worlock, upon whom he came to rely and whom he admired but with whom he was never completely at ease. These two led the bishops' conference of England and Wales, Hume supplying the inspiration and directing the broad thrust, Worlock running the machine.

In an age no longer automatically respectful towards senior clergy, Hume was always listened to and only rarely wrong. He quickly learned that submissions to government ministers had to be well researched, and this even discouraged him from raising certain matters that bothered him. He stood up for the family, seeking to strengthen divorce law in favour of marriage stability; he deplored the excesses of the press; and he took the national stage on such occasions as the Gulf War in 1991 and the death of Princess Diana in 1997, with whom he had been photographed on more than one occasion. He fought long and hard to overturn two of the major miscarriages of justice of the twentieth century: the imprisonment of the Guildford four and the Maguire seven following the Guildford IRA bombing in 1974. His successful campaign, for which he recruited two law lords, lords Scarman and Devlin, and two former home secretaries, Roy Jenkins and Merlyn Rees, led not only to freedom for those wrongly convicted (except one, who died in prison) but directly to the appointment of the royal commission on criminal justice, which in turn, led to a major overhaul of the criminal justice system in England and Wales, through the establishment of the Criminal Cases Review Commission.

Hume once said that he was not a prophet. Yet he was an early campaigner for the relief of third world debt; he saw the arms trade as a major international evil; and he repeatedly urged the diminution, pending complete elimination, of nuclear weapons. He was an enthusiastic supporter of the Catholic Fund for Overseas Development throughout his term of office, but more especially after he visited Ethiopia at the height of the famine in 1984. 'You cannot look into the eyes of a starving child and remain the same', he then said (*Cardinal Basil Hume*, 19). Closer to home, he launched various initiatives to help the homeless, young people at risk, people with AIDS, and refugees, including founding the Passage Day Centre for the homeless in Westminster, and the Cardinal Hume Centre for young people at risk. He wrote frequently to ministers and officials to urge action on these and other issues. Yet he stood apart from the politicians of the day, even if tempted, without succumbing, by efforts to lure him into the House of Lords.

Hume was also a heavyweight internationally, one of the most senior and respected cardinals of the international church. Three times he visited Patriarch Alexis of Moscow, twice with Cardinal Danneels of Belgium, once on his own, and their conversations undoubtedly eased tensions between the Orthodox and Catholic churches in Russia. During his time as president of the conferences of the Council of European Bishops (1978–87) he was able to play a role as a representative of European Catholicism with a different style from the Vatican. In that capacity he organized and presided over two European symposia on evangelization.

Hume shared completely Pope John Paul II's stress on human rights, never failing to include the unborn among those needing to be safeguarded. It was in this area that he had his one serious misgiving about the statement *The Common Good and the Catholic Church's Social Teaching*, an influential intervention in British political life before the general election of 1997 which marked a coming of age of the Catholic church in England and Wales. It was published in 1996 with a foreword by Hume and launched by a televised press conference which he handled with his usual stylishness. But on reflection, he said afterwards, he wished it had been tougher over abortion.

In another connection, when asked if he 'regretted' the British government's reliance on condoms in its strategy to resist the spread of AIDS, Hume replied that he 'regretted it was thought necessary' (*The Tablet*). He could be wily and noncommittal when the occasion demanded it. Such questions he often described, with a slightly archaic manner, as 'googlies'. Nevertheless he came close to a reconciliation of his office with the Catholic homosexual community. His 'Observations on the Catholic church's teaching concerning homosexual people' (1993) was a classic example of a pastor going as far as possible to interpret Catholic doctrine creatively without denying it. In whatever context it arises, and always respecting the appropriate manner of its expression, love between two persons, whether of the same sex or of different sexes is to be 'treasured and respected', he wrote. 'When two persons love, they experience in a limited manner in this world what will be their unending delight when one with God in the next'. But he was equally clear that physical expression of homosexual love was ruled out by the teaching of the church, which no one could change because it was 'God given'.

Hume supported the admission of the Catholic church to the new ecumenical instruments which superseded the British Council of Churches in the late 1980s, but only after he was satisfied that his own church would receive equality of treatment and due respect for its principles. In 1987 he stated that the time had come for the Catholic church in England and Wales to move from co-operation to commitment in its relations with other churches. After that point there was a sense that he had become common property, a source of great strength for all the churches in Britain. His commitment was real, though he insisted it was not a commitment to compromise. He preached in several Anglican cathedrals, churches, and chapels, and attended the enthronements in Canterbury Cathedral of Archbishop Robert Runcie in 1980 and Archbishop George Carey in 1991. (He had also attended the enthronement of Archbishop Coggan in 1974, while abbot of Ampleforth.)

A crisis which could have done serious damage to all Hume's work broke after the decision to ordain women in the Church of England in 1992. He sought and gained special dispensation from Rome to allow the ordination of married convert clergy. He gave a series of talks, open to any Anglican clergyman interested enough to attend. He did not entirely overcome the reluctance of some of his diocesan clergy to share his eagerness to admit former Anglican clergy to the Catholic priesthood. When he urged them on, saying in an interview published in *The Tablet* in March 1993 that this could be the 'conversion of England' they had all been praying for, he was perceived as striking an uncharacteristic note of Catholic triumphalism, and he had to withdraw his remark quickly. He was usually extremely tactful towards the Church of England, though careful to manoeuvre so as not to have to play second fiddle to the resident of Lambeth Palace.

That the transfer of Anglican clergy was managed without greatly harming the Catholic church's good relations with the Church of England was largely due to the trust and respect in which he was held inside that 'sister Church'. At awkward moments the archbishop of Canterbury could confide in him. He continued with George Carey the sort of public partnership he had developed first with Donald Coggan and then with Robert Runcie, though Hume did not always feel obliged to fall in with all Carey's wishes. Attempts to make mischief between them were given short shrift, as when he rebuffed the Conservative MP Ann Widdecombe, who had left the Church of England and joined the Church of Rome, for saying that he privately regarded Carey with 'contempt'.

Hume was a member of the Pontifical Council for the Promotion of Christian Unity, and the work of the Anglican Roman Catholic International Commission in overcoming differences both pleased and surprised him. The ordination of women by the Church of England seemed to him an insuperable obstacle, however (though he once said that he had no personal objection to it, and that his opposition was based entirely on canonical law and papal authority). He was keen to be seen as an ally of the Jewish community (and was indeed a personal friend of successive chief rabbis), and spoke sincerely and profoundly about the experience of visiting the concentration camp at Auschwitz, Poland, in 1986.

English Catholics traditionally had little time for English royalty, except when they showed signs of 'coming over'—as indeed the duchess of Kent did, influenced by Hume himself: he received the duchess into communion with the Catholic church at a service in his chapel at Archbishop's House in 1994. But he saw improving relations with Buckingham Palace as an important part of his programme for reacquainting the English with the more positive side of Catholicism. Very few of his co-religionists would have seen it that way, but he thought that one of the highest points of his time at Westminster was the visit of the queen to a service of vespers in November 1995, to celebrate the hundredth anniversary of the foundation of Westminster Cathedral. The award of the Order of Merit, which he received from the queen at Buckingham Palace in June 1999 (despite being by then extremely ill) was an extraordinary tribute, seen against the background of English history.

If one skill defined Hume's ministry, it was his management of extremes and the overcoming of splits and divisions. That undoubtedly reflected his background as a Benedictine abbot, for he regarded the rule of St Benedict as the rule of his life. Though they were less abrasive than in some other Western countries, Britain had its relatively small band of ultra-conservative Catholic dissenters ready to attack their bishops publicly or denounce them secretly to Rome. A crucial test of Hume's leadership came in 1996, therefore, when he accepted an invitation to address a meeting called by conservative Catholic campaigners in London, the other main speaker being the American television evangelist, traditionalist crowd-puller, and thorn in many an episcopal hide, Mother Angelica. His carefully prepared remarks on that occasion amounted to a set of sure signposts for the safe and successful navigation of the minefield that modern Catholicism had become; and therefore they summed up his approach in general. First, there was no going back on the Second Vatican Council: he quoted Pope John Paul II forcefully to that effect. Hence, contrary to the ultra-conservative case, loyalty to the pope was incompatible with rejection of the council's reforms. Second, there was no loyalty to the pope that was not also expressed in loyalty to the bishops. They too were 'vicars of Christ'. Third, Catholics had a right to explore the mysteries of faith and they had no obligation to agree with each other about everything, though it was vital to 'remain in communion with the successor of St Peter' and there would come a point where obedience was required. Fourth, it was important never to damage another's good name, never to be rude or insulting, or seek to exclude people from the church. He enjoined tolerance and charity. Those who made mistakes needed help and guidance, not public condemnation.

Above all, as Hume said time and again in speech after speech, what mattered was the cultivation of a personal relationship with the Lord. One of the chief ways to achieve this was through taking part fittingly in the celebration of mass—though he felt appropriate dignity and reverence were sometimes missing from the liturgy after the Second Vatican Council. His concern for excellence in the work of God translated itself into the world renown that the cathedral choir achieved while he was at Westminster, after he had rescued it from closure at the outset. But he also talked constantly and convincingly of the need for private prayer. It was clear to everyone that he spoke from profound personal knowledge.

By exercising these simple principles with such transparent sincerity, even at times verging on a kind of unselfconscious gaucheness, Hume gradually conditioned the spiritual life of the Catholic community of England and Wales towards the goals set forth in the Second Vatican Council. He was a man of instinct and intuition rather than of strategy and policy. It was his intention, he said at the time of his installation as the archbishop of Westminster, to animate rather than to dominate.

Hume gave many interviews and appeared in many radio and television programmes, most notably the Channel Four film *Return of the Saints* (1984), which he wrote and presented. His books—mainly collections of sermons and addresses, though *Basil in Blunderland* (1997) was a fantasy—included *In Praise of Benedict* (1981), *To be a Pilgrim* (1984), *Towards a Civilisation of Love* (1988), *Light in the Lord* (1991), *Remaking Europe* (1994), and *The Mystery of the Cross* (1998). He received numerous public honours, including honorary doctorates from a dozen universities in Britain and the United States. He was made an honorary bencher of the Inner Temple in 1976, and an honorary freeman of the City of London and Newcastle upon Tyne, both in 1980. (On the latter occasion he was thrilled to meet and to obtain the autograph of the Newcastle United footballer Jackie Milburn, who was created a freeman of the city at the same time.)

Archbishops are required to submit their resignations to the pope at seventy-five, but Hume had been warned that his was unlikely to be accepted (and indeed it was not). In April 1999 he was diagnosed with inoperable cancer. 'It is not in its early stages', he said in his last letter to the clergy of Westminster. 'Above all, no fuss' (*The Tablet*). He endured his last days with characteristic serenity and cheerfulness. He died on 17 June 1999 at the Hospital of St John and St Elizabeth, Westminster, and was buried in St Gregory's Chapel, Westminster Cathedral, on 25 June. Requiem masses were held at Westminster, Newcastle, Middlesbrough, Ampleforth, Oxford, and numerous other places.

Assessment The belief that it was possible to be totally English and totally Catholic had been dimmed during what some saw as the 'ghetto years' in the first half of the twentieth century. This was a time when, under indifferent leadership (with the possible exception of that of Cardinal Arthur Hinsley), English and Welsh Catholicism had been allowed to become obsessively inward looking. The remarkable boldness of Pope Paul VI's appointment of the abbot of a Benedictine monastery in north Yorkshire, whose name was associated with one of the best independent boarding-schools in the land, had the power to transform both this image and the reality it represented. It revealed Vatican shrewdness at its best.

Hume's cultural and religious origins were deeply Benedictine. Of all forms of Catholicism, it is one of the most gentle and least fanatical. The Benedictine spirit ran differently from the mood of the Counter-Reformation, which still cast its dwindling shadow over the Catholic church in the 1940s and 1950s. The uncompromising Counter-Reformation style was what the English were used to in their Roman Catholic neighbours: a social and spiritual snobbery that meant no truck with protestantism and very little with the Church of England. This stiff manner was greatly relaxed by the reforms of the Second Vatican Council but it still needed a Hume to carry the message home.

Hume never forgot, nor let anyone else forget, that he was first of all a Benedictine monk, a member of an ancient religious order whose communities once dotted the English landscape and which built, among many other glories of the Gothic style, Westminster Abbey. There is nobody more English than an English Benedictine: the rule of St Benedict seems to overflow with English common sense. Although the founders of the Church of England were reluctant to admit their debt to previous generations of English churchmen, who were of course Catholics, the pervasive influence of medieval English monasticism on English spirituality was more and more recognized in the twentieth century. One Anglican commentator, Esther de Waal, has written: 'It is hardly too much to claim that the Benedictine spirit is at the root of the Anglican way of prayer.' It is hardly surprising, therefore, that the English at some deep level recognized Hume as one of their own—or that he became, in Hugo Young's words, 'part of the furniture of English life' (Castle, 148).

It was among his greatest achievements that in an increasingly secular age and in a predominantly Anglican culture, Hume cut through cultural and religious prejudice to show the more human face of the Roman Catholic faith. This made it seem less alien and anachronistic to the English, more credible and attractive than it had been for a very long time. His achievement was not so much to have changed it as to have presented it differently. By such means he was able to operate sufficiently close to the high moral ground of public life to inject into national affairs a convincing set of principles. CLIFFORD LONGLEY

Sources T. Castle, *Basil Hume: a portrait* (1986) · S. J. Costello, *Basil Hume: builder of community* (1988) · C. Butler, *Basil Hume: by his friends* (1999) · *Cardinal Basil Hume OSB OM: in memoriam, 1923–1999* (2000) · K. Nichols, *Pilgrimage of grace: Cardinal Basil Hume, 1923–1999* (2000) · *The Times* (18 June 1999) · *Daily Telegraph* (18 June 1999) · *The Guardian* (18 June 1999) · *The Independent* (18 June 1999) · *The Scotsman* (18 June 1999) · *The Tablet* (26 June 1999) · 'Cardinal Basil Hume OSB OM', *Ampleforth Journal* (2000), 1–13 · WWW · b. cert. · d. cert. · personal knowledge (2004) · private information (2004)

Archives Westm. DA, papers

Likenesses D. Clarke, oils, 1970–74, Ampleforth Abbey · M. Boxer, ink drawing, c.1970–1979, NPG · photographs, 1976–87, Hult. Arch. · A. Newman, bromide print, 1978?, NPG · M. Noakes, oils, 1985, Archbishop's House, Westminster · J. Stultiens, oils, 1986–7, NPG [*see illus.*] · photographs (various dates), repro. in *The Times* · photographs (various dates), repro. in *Daily Telegraph* · photographs (various dates), repro. in *The Guardian* · photographs (various dates), repro. in *The Independent* · photographs (various dates), repro. in *The Scotsman* · photographs (various dates), repro. in *The Tablet* · photographs (various dates), repro. in Castle, *Basil Hume*

Wealth at death £13,000: *The Times* (12 Dec 2002)

Hume, Sir George Hopwood (1866–1946), politician, was born on 24 May 1866 in Poltava, south Russia, the son of George Hume, a Scottish-born mechanical engineer who had lived in Russia for many years and who was British vice-consul at Kiev and Kharkov, and his British wife. He was educated in Russia; at the Collège Galliard, Lausanne; and at Finsbury Technical College. As a boy he learned the trade of an engineer working at a bench and lathe in the workshops of Siemens Brothers, and he later became a member of the Institution of Electrical Engineers. In 1900 he was called to the bar at the Middle Temple. In the following year he married Jeanne Alice (d. 1922), the daughter of Professor A. Ladrierre, of Lausanne.

Hume entered politics in 1900, when as a Conservative he became one of the original members of the newly created Greenwich Borough Council. He later emerged as a prominent figure on the London County Council, of which he was a member (1920–22), an alderman (1922–46), and chairman (1926–7). From 1918 to 1925 he was leader of the conservative Municipal Reform Party, which was in a majority on the council. In 1917 the party had formed an effective wartime coalition with the opposition Progressive Party, which had a broadly Liberal base. Hume enjoyed 'an easy working relationship' with J. Scott Lidgett, leader of the Progressive Party, and the two men were largely responsible for continuing in peacetime the consensus born of special circumstances during the war (Young and Garside, 128). Both were advocates of a Greater London authority with powers to develop a co-ordinated response to the pressing problems of traffic, housing, and transport in the capital.

On 4 March 1919 Hume moved, and Lidgett seconded, a council resolution favouring an extension of central power. This, however, met determined resistance from the outlying county councils, notably Middlesex, which opposed the growth of centralization and favoured instead the creation of *ad hoc* committees to deal with individual problems such as housing. At the county council elections in March 1919 the Municipal Reform Party adopted a manifesto committed to reconstruction, which was fully supported by the Progressive Party, and in consequence there was an effective truce at the polls. This consensus was encouraged by the Ministry of Health, which envisaged a greater role for the central government of London in the drive for post-war housing. But the understanding epitomized by Hume and Lidgett found 'barely the palest reflection among the party supporters' (Young and Garside, 135), and an incipient rebellion among the Municipal Reform rank-and-file in March 1922 led to the end of coalition politics in the capital.

At the general election held in November 1922 Hume was elected Conservative MP for Greenwich, with a large majority over the Labour candidate, Edward Timothy Palmer. The two men faced one another at the next five general elections, Palmer narrowly winning on the two occasions (1923 and 1929) when the presence of a Liberal candidate weakened Hume's support. Hume was victorious in 1924, in spite of 'organised rowdyism' at his early meetings that was serious enough to compel the Labour election agent to intervene and call for fair play. Hume also had to contend with the accusations at this poll that he was a foreigner and that he had been idle when first elected to parliament—claims that he could easily refute, though his cosmopolitan upbringing, neat goatee beard, and small, round glasses gave him more the air of a Russian intellectual than a Greenwich Conservative. In 1931, helped by the atmosphere of national crisis and the spoiling presence of a Communist candidate, Hume secured his greatest majority over Labour. He retained the seat in 1935, and retired in 1945, though by 1938 he had already announced his decision not to contest the next election. Moderate and pragmatic, he rejected the collectivist approach of socialist plans to combat unemployment but supported the extension of contributory insurance to provide for benefits and old-age pensions. And he urged conciliation in the case of the Poplar councillors imprisoned for their determination to maintain welfare benefits during a period of severe unemployment.

Hume chaired the executive committee of the London Municipal Society from 1934 to 1938 and the metropolitan division of the National Union of Conservative and Unionist Associations in 1937. He was also a member of the grand council of the Primrose League. He was a member of the Thames Conservancy Board from 1916, the London electricity committee from 1913 to 1926, and the highways committee from 1913 to 1919. He also served on the Ministry of Transport London and home counties traffic advisory committee from 1924 to 1925, and the London and home counties joint electricity authority from 1925 to 1926. In 1924 he was created a knight bachelor, in recognition of his public service. He was chairman of the Mildmay mission hospital, the Trinitarian Bible Society, and the Rachel Macmillan Training College.

After the death of his first wife Hume married, on 1 August 1932, Dorothy Hunt Blundell (b. 1896/7), daughter of Ernest Richard Blundell, an insurance broker. He died on 13 September 1946 at his home, 83 Lee Road, Blackheath, London, survived by his wife. MARK POTTLE

Sources WWBMP · The Times (28 Oct 1924) · The Times (31 Oct 1924) · The Times (9 July 1928) · The Times (14 Sept 1946) · K. Young and P. L. Garside, Metropolitan London: politics and urban change, 1837–1981 (1986) · J. S. Lidgett, My guided life (1936) · J. S. Lidgett, Reminiscences (1928) · F. W. S. Craig, British parliamentary election results, 1918–1949, rev. edn (1977) · N. Branson, Poplarism, 1919–1925: George Lansbury and the councillors' revolt (1979) · m. cert. [D. H. Blundell] · d. cert. · Burke, Peerage (1939) · CGPLA Eng. & Wales (1947)

Likenesses J. Lavery, oils, presented in July 1928, repro. in The Times (9 Dec 1928), 13g · photograph, repro. in Times (28 Oct 1924), 16

Wealth at death £15,232 9s. 10d.: probate, 1947, CGPLA Eng. & Wales

Hume, Hamilton (1797–1873), explorer in Australia, was born at Toongabbie near Parramatta, New South Wales, on 19 June 1797, the son of Andrew Hamilton Hume (1762–1849), superintendent of convicts, and Elizabeth More, née

Kennedy (1760–1847), a clergyman's daughter from Kent who had emigrated in 1795 with her brother, a free settler, and had married in New South Wales on 29 September 1796. Hamilton Hume, the eldest of their five children, was educated at home by his mother. He made his first significant excursion at the age of seventeen from their home at Appin, about 40 miles south-west of Sydney. Such excursions put his services in demand for exploring parties. In March 1818 he accompanied the surveyor James Meehan (1774–1826) to the south-west, when the upper portions of the Shoalhaven River, Lake Bathurst, and the Goulburn plains were discovered. In 1819, with John Oxley and Meehan, he explored Jervis Bay, and returned overland to Sydney with Meehan by way of Bong Bong. Two years later he discovered the Yass plains. In 1822, with Alexander Berry and Thomas Davison, he climbed on to Captain Cook's Pigeon House Mountain from the Clyde River. For his early exploratory work, Hume was granted 400 acres at Appin.

In 1824 Hume undertook the first overland journey from the central coast of New South Wales to the south coast of the continent at Port Phillip on Bass Strait. He was accompanied by **William Hilton Hovell** (1786–1875), a former sailor, born at Great Yarmouth, Norfolk, on 26 April 1786. A seaman from the age of ten, he had been master of trading vessels since he was twenty-two. His first wife was Esther, the daughter of Thomas Arndell, a surgeon on the first fleet, and his wife, Esther Foscari; they had two children, a daughter and a son. Hovell and his family arrived at Sydney in 1813. He was granted 700 acres at Narellan, not far from Appin, though he did not settle there until December 1816, when he forsook the sea to become a merchant. His investigation of the Burragorang valley in 1823 led Governor Brisbane to persuade him to join Hume on the Port Phillip expedition.

The two men left Appin on 2 October 1824, accompanied by six convict assigned servants. They passed Yass plains and crossed the Murrumbidgee River on 19 October. Although they endeavoured to travel in a direct south-west line to Western Port, rugged mountain country forced them south, then at Tumbarumba they had no option but to turn west before weaving across the Murray and Mitta Mitta rivers. Near Tumbarumba, on 8 November, they became the first colonists to see the Australian Alps, clearly snow-clad, some 40 miles to the south. They then crossed the rivers Ovens, King, and Goulburn (3 December), naming the Murray and Goulburn rivers the Hume and Hovell respectively. Turned around by Mount Disappointment, they proceeded by a line further west and reached Corio Bay on the western side of Port Phillip Bay on 16 December, thinking it was Western Port. Hovell corrected this impression in February 1827 during his valuable exploratory probes around Western Port, when he accompanied the expedition which established a short-lived period settlement there. The faster return journey ended at Hume's station north of Lake George on 18 January 1825. Their diagonal trail through six degrees of longitude and four degrees of latitude had lifted the veil from what was to become one of the most vitally important portions of Australia. They each received a grant of 1200 acres, which they sold to defray expedition expenses. Hovell received a further 1280 acres for his later work at Western Port. He had kept a very good record of the route taken in 1824–5, which formed the essential data for William Bland's 1831 book of that journey.

On 8 November 1825 Hume married Elizabeth Dight, the second daughter of John and Hannah Dight of Richmond, New South Wales. They had no children. Hume ably assisted Charles Sturt in the expedition from 7 December 1828 to 21 April 1829 which solved the mystery of the Macquarie marshes and discovered the great Darling River on 1 February 1829. For this and other exploratory work concerning routes over the Blue Mountains he received a further 3200 acres in grants, which he took near Yass. From 1839 he lived as a grazier there at Cooma Cottage, and eventually he held 18,000 acres in this vicinity. Resourceful, courageous, and a great bushman, Hume was jealous of sharing any of his laurels, and when Hovell was feted in Melbourne in 1853 he produced a lengthy pamphlet, *A brief statement of facts in connection with an overland expedition from Lake George to Port Phillip in 1824* (1855), which was excessively unfair to Hovell. Hume became increasingly obsessed with what he believed to be a playing down of his importance, and a second edition followed in 1873. Hovell's published replies (1855 and 1874) had no effect on the tirade, which, with the publication of a third edition of Hume's pamphlet in 1874 and a fourth in 1897, sent influences well into the twentieth century. Hume was made a fellow of the Royal Geographical Society in 1860, and was honoured by his countrymen. He died at Cooma Cottage on 19 April 1873 and was buried in Yass cemetery.

Following the death of his first wife, Hovell married Sophia Wilkinson (*d.* 1876) in 1848; they had no children. After his death, on 9 November 1875 at Sydney, she bequeathed £6000 to the University of Sydney to fund the W. H. Hovell lectureship in geology and physical geography. Hovell was buried at Goulburn.

ALAN E. J. ANDREWS

Sources S. H. Hume, *Beyond the borders: an anecdotal history of the Hume and related pioneering families; from 1790* (1991) · A. E. J. Andrews, ed., *Hume and Hovell, 1824* (1981) · W. Bland, *Journey of discovery to Port Phillip, New South Wales: by Messrs W. H. Hovell, and Hamilton Hume: in 1824 and 1825* (1831) · F. O'Grady, 'Hamilton Hume', *Royal Australian Historical Society Journal and Proceedings*, 49 (1963–4), 337–59 · R. H. Cambage, 'Exploration between the Wingecarribee, Shoalhaven, Macquarie, and Murrumbidgee rivers', *Royal Australian Historical Society Journal and Proceedings*, 7 (1921), 217–88 · C. Sturt, *Two expeditions into the interior of southern Australia, during the years 1828, 1829, 1830 and 1831*, 2 vols. (1833) · A. H. Hume, *A brief statement of … an overland expedition from Lake George to Port Phillip in 1824*, ed. W. Ross, 1st–4th edns (1855–97), 2nd edn 1873; 3rd edn 1874; 4th edn 1897 · W. H. Hovell, *Reply to 'A brief statement of facts, in connection with an overland expedition from Lake George to Port Phillip in 1824' … by 'Hamilton Hume'* (1855) · W. H. Hovell, *Answer to the preface to the second edition of Mr Hamilton Hume's A brief statement of facts, in connection with an overland expedition from Lake George to Port Philip in 1824* [1874] · [F. Watson], ed., *Historical records of Australia*, 1st ser., 7–20 (1916–24) · [F. Watson], ed., *Historical records of Australia*, 3rd ser., 5 (1922) · *AusDB*, vol. 1 [William Hilton Hovell] · A. W. Jose and H. J. Carter, eds., *The Australian encyclopaedia*, new edn, 2 vols. (Sydney, 1927), 628–9 [William Hilton Hovell] · [A. H. Chisholm], ed., *The Australian encyclopaedia*, [new edn], 5 (Sydney, 1963) [William Hilton Hovell]

Archives Mitchell L., NSW · PRO NIre., corresp. and papers relating to exploration of Southern Australia

Likenesses W. P. McIntosh, statue (as a young man), Lands Department, Bridge Street, Sydney, Australia · sketch (aged about seventy-six), repro. in Hume, *Brief statement*, 2nd edn

Wealth at death generally wealthy: Hume, *Beyond the borders*; O'Grady, 'Hamilton Hume'

Hume, Hugh. *See* Campbell, Hugh Hume, third earl of Marchmont (1708–1794).

Hume, James (*fl.* 1633–1640), mathematician, was the son of David *Hume (1558–1629×31) of Gowkscroft, Berwickshire. David Hume spent time in France and his son was living in France at the time when his books were published. He was possibly related to the Thomas Hume then in the service of Louis XIII. James Hume's books were varied in content; his first, published in 1633 and dedicated to Robert Ker, first earl of Ancrum, was a poorly crafted Latin romance, with an appendix on contemporary affairs, a theme to which he returned in several short works issued the following year.

In 1636 Hume published at Paris an explanation of the algebra of François Viète, and a treatise on right-angle and spherical triangles, appending to the latter the titles of nine other mathematical works which he had written in Latin. One of these dealt with fortifications. In 1640, in a book explaining how to make all sorts of clocks and quadrants, Hume admitted to an unpolished style, French not being his native tongue. Nothing is known of his later years.

R. E. ANDERSON, *rev.* ANITA MCCONNELL

Sources F. Michel, *Les écossais en France, les français en Écosse*, 2 vols. (1862), vol. 2, pp. 292–4 · A. De Morgan, *Arithmetical books from the invention of printing to the present time* (1847), 10

Hume, James Deacon (1774–1842), civil servant and free-trader, was born on 28 April 1774 at Newington, Surrey, the son of James Hume, a customs official, and his wife, Elizabeth Capps. He had four sisters. Hume was educated at Westminster School and became a customs clerk in 1791. He rose steadily to reach the grade of comptroller in 1821, with a salary of £1000 p.a. In 1822 he conceived the idea of consolidating customs law. He was given three years' leave to realize this project. Some 1500 acts dating back to Edward I were reduced to ten bills, which received the royal assent in 1825. Though others shared in this work, it bore Hume's stamp throughout. Sir James Stephen considered it 'a masterpiece of legislative skill … he succeeded in the invention of a legal style, so clear … that every one seized his meaning' (Badham, iii). William Huskisson, then president of the Board of Trade, praised his achievement.

Although they worked in different departments, Hume is credited with considerable influence on Huskisson's commercial policy. According to Charles Greville, they 'made the business a science'. In 1828, after Huskisson had left the board, Hume became its joint secretary. Greville continued: 'it is he who advises, directs, legislates. I believe he is one of the ablest practical men who has ever served, more like an American statesman than an English official' (*Greville Memoirs*, 2.84). In 1824 Hume had helped to prepare a bill regulating the duties on silk. Seven years later he toured England, collecting information on silk manufacture, and in 1832 gave evidence on silk duties before a Commons committee. Evidence followed on timber in 1835, fresh fruit in 1839, import duties generally in 1840, and the export of machinery in 1841. Although it was the radical politician Joseph Hume (no relation) who proposed the select committee on import duties in 1840, his namesake seems to have been behind it, supported by John MacGregor, his successor at the Board of Trade. 'They thought it would be for the public interest if those who were, or who had been, in office at the Board of Trade could be transferred ... from their private offices in Whitehall, into a committee room of the House of Commons, for then ... their evidence ... would be ... printed, and circulated through the country' (Badham, 241). Hume retired in 1840 with a pension of £1500 p.a.

In 1815 Hume published a protectionist tract on the corn laws, but he later became a strong advocate of free trade. Richard Cobden recalled a discussion at the Political Economy Club, to which Hume was elected in 1834. Most speakers were opposed to Hume's views. He retorted:

> Gentlemen land-owners, you have your landed estates, they are secured to you by law, you may fence them round and exclude all intruders, why are you not content with the possession of your property, why do you attempt to invade the property of the labourer by interfering with his right to exchange the produce of his own toil for the produce of other lands? (Badham, 159)

In 1809, during the Napoleonic wars, Hume began farming at Pinner. However, he lost money and gave it up in 1822. Three years later parliament voted him £6000 in recognition of his work on consolidating customs law. This sum he lost through unfortunate investments.

Hume was of medium height, with strongly marked features, high forehead, and expressive eyes. A bold rider, he was fond of field sports. He was one of the founders of the Atlas Insurance Company in 1808 and its deputy chairman at the time of his death. The Customs Benevolent Fund was inaugurated under his chairmanship in 1816 and he became its president. On 4 June 1798 he married Frances Elizabeth Ashwell, *née* Whitehouse (d. 1854), a widow with two daughters. From her marriage with Hume she had twelve more daughters. They lived for many years in Russell Square, London, and later at Putney. On retirement Hume moved to Reigate, where he died at Great Doods House of apoplexy on 12 January 1842. He was buried in Reigate churchyard. HENRY PARRIS

Sources C. Badham, *Life of James Deacon Hume, secretary of the board of trade* (1859) · L. Brown, *The board of trade and the free-trade movement, 1830–42* (1958) · *The Greville memoirs, 1814–1860*, ed. L. Strachey and R. Fulford, 8 vols. (1938) · H. Parris, *Constitutional bureaucracy* (1969) · J. C. Sainty, ed., *Officials of the board of trade, 1660–1870* (1974) · *DNB*
Archives LUL, corresp. and papers

Hume, John Robert (1781/2–1857), physician, born in Renfrewshire, Scotland, studied medicine at Glasgow University in 1795, 1798, and 1799, and at Edinburgh University in 1796–7. He entered the medical service of the army, and served in the Peninsular War as surgeon to Wellesley. The University of St Andrews conferred on him the degree of MD on 12 January 1816, and on 22 December 1819 he was admitted a licentiate of the Royal College of Physicians. He settled in London, and became physician to Wellesley, now duke of Wellington, who proved to be a somewhat difficult patient. After once rejecting Hume's advice the duke exclaimed to Mrs Arbuthnot that 'All Doctors are more or less Quacks, and there is nothing more comical than that Dr Hume should have made you believe that I am an Idiot! rather than the truth, that he as well as others of the Medical Profession is a bit of a Charlatan! ... I know what is good for me as well [as] Dr Hume or any Doctor of the Profession' (Thompson, 42).

Hume was created DCL at Oxford on 13 June 1834, the duke being then chancellor of the university. He was admitted a fellow of the Royal College of Physicians on 9 July 1836, and on 1 September 1836 he was appointed one of the metropolitan commissioners in lunacy. He subsequently became inspector-general of hospitals, and was made CB on 16 August 1850. Hume died at his house in Curzon Street, Mayfair, London, on 1 March 1857, aged seventy-five. GORDON GOODWIN, rev. JAMES MILLS

Sources Munk, *Roll* · Foster, *Alum. Oxon.* · *GM*, 3rd ser., 2 (1857), 317 · *GM*, 3rd ser., 3 (1857), 500 · N. Thompson, *Wellington after Waterloo* (1986)

Hume, Joseph (1767–1844), translator and writer, was probably born in London. Nothing is known of his early life but he eventually became a clerk at the victualling office of Somerset House.

From his residence at Montpelier House, Notting Hill, Hume met with literary men such as Charles Lamb, William Hazlitt, and William Godwin. In winter 1807–8 'a singularly strange and melodramatic incident happened' in which Hume and Lamb perpetrated a 'Suicide Joke' on Hazlitt, generating tongue-in-cheek letters in which Hazlitt's death was described and lamented (W. C. Hazlitt, 61). They claimed his forthcoming marriage, what they called his 'unfortunate passion', had driven him to 'put an end to his existence by cutting his throat in a shocking manner' (*Letters of Charles Lamb*, 271). Hazlitt replied in a 'humble petition', setting out the proof of his continued existence. After receiving this 'scrawl of 8 pages ... which ridiculously assumes him to be alive', Hume warned Lamb not to:

> go near his lodgings, lest you might meet with any body there [who would] urge you to be boisterous and pugilistic ... In the meantime, I will not rest till I have discovered who is the author of the manuscript before me (I guess him to be a Quaker). (W. C. Hazlitt, 66)

Responding to Hazlitt's resolution to abandon the services of prostitutes, Hume wrote:

> He was a man of spirit in his better days. He therefore would have been ashamed on his own account and much more so as

an example for the well being of society, to cast out of human contact the habit of wenching.　(Grayling, 121)

Hazlitt does not seem to have been too perturbed by the epistolatory antics of his friends.

Hume published what the *Dictionary of National Biography* considered a 'bad' blank-verse translation of Dante's *Inferno* in 1812 and, two years before his death, *A Search into the Old Testament* (1841), designed to 'establish the truth of those momentous passages, which involve supernatural events' (*A Search*, 1). He had six daughters, one of whom, Julia, became the mother of the poet (Julia) Augusta Webster (pseudonym Cecil Home).

Joseph Hume died in London on 7 August 1844.

JANE POTTER

Sources DNB · *The letters of Charles Lamb*, ed. E. Rhys, 1 (1909) · *The letters of William Hazlitt*, ed. H. M. Sikes, W. H. Bonner, and G. Lahey (1978) · A. C. Grayling, *The quarrel of the age: the life and times of William Hazlitt* (2001) · W. D. Howe, *Charles Lamb and his friends* (1944) · C. A. Prance, *Companion to Charles Lamb* (1983) · W. C. Hazlitt, *Lamb and Hazlitt* (1900) · will, PRO, PROB 11/2005, sig. 705
Wealth at death under £4000: will, PRO, PROB 11/2005, sig. 705

Hume, Joseph (1777–1855), radical and politician, was born at Montrose, Scotland, on 22 January 1777, the younger son of James Hume, a shipmaster of Forfarshire, and Mary Allan. His father died not long after Hume's birth, and his widowed mother supported her children by selling crockery.

Early life Hume attended a parochial school in Montrose, where he obtained a sound education, including natural science, accounting, and navigation. Apprenticed to a surgeon (1790), he went on to study medicine at Aberdeen and then at Edinburgh. His patron David Scott, MP for Forfar and a director of the East India Company, helped him finance his studies through service as a surgeon-mate aboard the *Hawke* (1795) and the *Hope* (1798). He was awarded the MRCS Ed. (1796), the certificate of the London Company of Surgeons (1797), and the degree of MD of Marischal College, Aberdeen (1799).

In August 1799, nominated by the chairman J. Bosanquet, Hume enlisted in the Bengal service of the East India Company. He distinguished himself as purser during an emergency on the outward voyage, and then as medical man with the marine battalion *en route* for Fort St George. Soon fluent in Hindustani and Persian, he was intelligence officer as well as surgeon with the 7th sepoy regiment. He was complimented by Lord Lake on the eve of the Second Anglo-Maratha War (1802), when he used his scientific knowledge for the safe storage of gunpowder. Appointed deputy paymaster at Bundelkhand, Hume also worked for the prize agency and the commissariat. He amassed a fortune of about £40,000, probably legally, and formed an attachment to the Indian subcontinent and its people.

On his return to Scotland, Hume developed a family connection with a clothing company which produced army uniforms and other supplies. In 1809 he went on a fact-finding tour of the manufacturing districts of the midlands and the north of England. He then left for Spain, Portugal, Egypt, Turkey, and Gibraltar, where he participated in the booming economy for a year, and returned in

Joseph Hume (1777–1855), by John Whitehead Walton, 1854

1812, determined to secure a directorship of the East India Company and a seat in parliament.

It was while canvassing East India stockholders in London that Hume met his future wife, Maria Burnley (*b.* 1786), whose father, a merchant, had four votes. They married on 17 August 1815 and had three sons and four daughters, the youngest of whom was the campaigner for medical reform and author Mary Catherine Hume-*Rothery. Mrs Hume became respected as a political hostess and secretary. Hume defended the East India Company's record in the Commons, although his opposition to protectionism and abuses in the court of proprietors prevented his ever obtaining a directorship.

Parliament: radical leader In 1812 Hume purchased the parliamentary seat of Weymouth in the tory interest from the trustees of the late Sir John Lowther Johnstone. After his maiden speech, on 5 March 1812, he was rebuked by Sir Francis Burdett for his representation of a rotten borough. Yet he showed radical leanings by his advocacy of equal rights for men and masters in relation to the Combination Acts, and suggested the extension of popular education to Ireland through the monitorial system. He played a significant part in events surrounding the assassination of the prime minister, Spencer Perceval, by John Bellingham in the lobby of the Commons on 11 May, initialling documents found on the murderer to indicate their authenticity, and giving evidence to official bodies (*The Times*; *Morning Chronicle*, 12–19 May 1812).

In the subsequent general election Hume lost his seat when his patron refused to back him, which resulted in legal action. But he still had important political contacts on the radical side. Francis Place re-introduced him to James Mill, with whom he had been at school in Montrose. With Samuel Whitbread, they reformed the finances of the almost bankrupt West London Lancasterian Association, which promoted free elementary education. After returning to the Commons as MP for the Aberdeen burghs (which included Montrose) in 1818, his links with Burdett and John Cam Hobhouse became stronger, and he was part of the collective radical leadership for the next thirty years. In the Commons party discipline was lacking in the modern sense, but between thirty and almost one hundred MPs voted at various times for radical policies such as economic retrenchment, Catholic emancipation, parliamentary reform, and free trade. Hume developed a network of those open to radical influence through correspondence with individuals and political associations in the country, organizing press handouts, choice of candidates, and tactics at elections. A red-headed Scot, the Apothecary, as he was known, was mocked for frequent slips in speech and etiquette and for being dominated by Francis Place. Hume remained a dull yet dogged orator throughout his political career, and was seemingly impervious to criticism. The suspicion that he had made financial gain from the sale of loan stock intended to finance the struggle for Greek independence during the visit of the Greek deputies in 1824 harmed his reputation, though he assured Edward Ellice that he was only concerned for investors. Place initially disliked and distrusted him, but came to see him as a capable leader compared with Tierney and Burdett.

Hume boldly attacked the government for employing excessive force and a network of spies at the time of Peterloo, the Cato Street conspiracy, and the disturbances surrounding the proceedings against Queen Caroline (1819–21). With the out-of-doors assistance of Francis Place he was able to influence the composition of parliamentary select committees and the substance of the evidence presented to them, furthering the repeal of the Combination Acts, the regulations concerning the emigration of workmen, and the export of machinery (1824–5). He opposed subsequent attempts to revive them. Hume's lengthy comments and questions about waste and sinecures in the army, navy, and other branches of government were to become regular events in debates on the estimates and the reduction of the national debt in years to come. Yet he modified his demands for retrenchment in all branches of administration as time went on, asserting that it should be aimed at the privileges of the ruling class and not designed to take away employment from artisans and unskilled workers. This tallied with his belief that the latter groups deserved fuller representation in parliament.

Hume was able to bring a long and varied experience in the Commons to bear on the question of parliamentary reform, having represented or contested a variety of seats in England, Scotland, and Ireland. He argued that unless the franchise and constituencies were more equal and representative of the country's economic base in the towns, violence might result. From 5 November 1830 he supported Earl Grey and the whigs, working with the metropolitan and other political unions to demand free association and the unfettered expression of radical ideas in the press. He associated himself with the petitioning movement and opposed a property qualification for his own Middlesex electors since all were liable to pay taxes and serve in the militia. Hume voted steadily for the Reform Bill in the Commons during 1831 and 1832. After its first rejection by the Lords in October 1831, he presided over a reform meeting at the Thatched tavern in Westminster. Afterwards he made an ostensibly accidental appearance at the Pall Mall demonstration which ensued, where he used his influence in favour of peaceful conduct. Having enrolled as a member the previous month he presented the National Political Union's petition in favour of reform in December 1831 to increase pressure on the whigs to stand firm and to keep moderate and extreme radicals together.

After the passage of the Reform Act of 1832 and Burdett's retirement, Hume continued to campaign for a wider franchise, a secret ballot, and triennial parliaments (1833). He discovered from his difficulties in Middlesex, where he maintained an uneasy alliance with the whigs, that the newly enfranchised middle class mistrusted radicals. He was narrowly defeated by Colonel Wood in July 1837, and another failure in a populous constituency—at Leeds in 1841—confirmed the point. To intensify a press campaign for reform, Hume gave his patronage to a new newspaper, *The Constitutional* (1836), and supported repeal of stamp duties on newspapers. In the Commons he doubted that unenfranchised working men were 'any better than slaves' (*Hansard 3*, 1839 XLVI, 1077). With Francis Place he attempted to concert parliamentary moves with Chartists and other reform groups in Birmingham and London. As the whig government faltered in May 1839, Hume supported Attwood's motion for a committee on the Charter petition (12 July), which gained the support of about fifty MPs. He repeated his stand in 1840, asserting that the Commons should take heed of agitation and protesting against the mistreatment of Chartists who had been arrested. In June–July 1848 he again defended the Chartist position against Lord John Russell's attack, and unsuccessfully put forward a 'Little Charter' of votes for all householders, secret ballot, triennial parliaments, and equal constituencies. A similar attempt in February 1850 failed by 242 votes to ninety-six. On 20 February 1851 Hume led fifty-three radical MPs who signed a memorial to Russell in favour of a more representative parliament to defend free trade.

Hume also demonstrated consistency on issues of religious toleration. His defence of freethinkers such as Richard and Jane Carlile (1821), Richard Taylor (1827–8 and 1831), Thomas Patterson (1844), and his support for Jewish rights, especially between 1848 and 1851, were notable. Though his advocacy of Catholic emancipation was muted (1828–9), it cost him his Scottish constituency. Hume took a significant part in the Lichfield House compact (18 February 1835), which concerted whig, radical, and Irish nationalist action against Peel and the tories, though he became disillusioned with the whigs as the decade wore on. On the loss of his Middlesex seat, he accepted the offer of an Irish constituency (1837–41) from Daniel O'Connell amid accusations of jobbery. His links with the Catholic Association imbued him with a hatred of coercion in Ireland, which reinforced his reputation as a firebrand in the Commons. He had already begun to speak on land reform, the vexed question of tithes, and the position of the established church in Ireland (April 1832). However, he claimed that he opposed only defects in government that weakened the Union, which he wished to maintain. These included discrimination against Catholics in employment, which he raised on 3 July 1830. Though Hume subsequently made way for O'Connell's son in Kilkenny (1841), he remained committed to justice for Ireland, and opposed Orange sectarianism. From April 1842 until his death he represented his native Montrose.

The philosophic radicals and other connections Hume's association with the philosophic radicalism of Ricardo, Mill, and Bentham led him to support reform of local government, financial assistance for popular education, and alleviation of the harsher aspects of the penal code. He pleaded with Russell for leniency to be shown to the Tolpuddle martyrs, and voted consistently for reform of police and prisons, the abolition of the death penalty (9 March 1847), and the reduction of flogging in the armed services (March 1848). As a physician, he corresponded with Brougham and Chadwick about public health, but opposed Ashley's factory reform as a palliative. His advocacy of self-help and the Poor Law Amendment Act of 1834 seemed harsh and incongruous, especially to the Chartists who campaigned against the background of suffering occasioned by the abolition of outdoor relief. (Hume hoped that the effects of this would be mitigated by cheaper food resulting from the repeal of the corn laws and of other indirect taxes on the poor.) He supported a limited income tax and an inheritance tax on real estate which would have entailed some redistribution of wealth (1842). He campaigned against the corn laws from 1832, and wished to link the Chartists with the Anti-Corn Law League. Though this failed in the London Association, he remained on good terms with Richard Cobden. Hume also co-operated with Huskisson and Spring-Rice on free trade measures. He obtained representation on the select parliamentary committees on banking, associating currency reform with corn-law repeal. Hume welcomed Peel's conversion to repeal at the time of the Irish famine, and paid a glowing tribute to his public spirit when he fell from power in 1846.

The desire for retrenchment and free trade led Hume to support a pacific policy in Europe and the British empire. Upon the abolition of slavery in 1833 he was criticized for demanding compensation for slave owners (his brother-in-law had property in Trinidad) but he was consistent in advocating a measure of self-government for the West Indies and Canada (1840). He objected to the expense of the renewal of the East India Company charter (1833) and showed his concern for native rights in the cases of Satara

(1843), Sind (1847), and Borneo (1851). He took the unpopular line of opposing the Crimean War on the grounds of expense and justice (4 May 1852).

In his later career, Hume recognized the need for a Liberal coalition. He tried to further contact with Gladstone and the Peelites, partly through the committee of the Pentonville working men's testimonial to Sir Robert Peel, and by the publication of Gladstone's speech on the Ecclesiastical Titles Bill (1850). In August 1854 a portrait of him by John Lucas was presented by Lord John Russell to Hume's wife, in his absence through ill health. He alluded to his long labours to change the state of the laws and legislature 'when the popular cause was prostrate and men of liberal views proscribed' (PRO 30/22 11F, fols. 177–9).

Hume was in feeble health from 1853 and died of heart failure on 20 February 1855 at his country residence, Burnley Hall in Norfolk. His wife survived him. He was buried at Kensal Green cemetery in London. He was twice rector of Marischal College, Aberdeen (1824–5), also vice-president of the Society of Arts, FRS, and a member of the Royal Geographical Society. Twelve or more of his speeches to the Commons and East India institutions were published. As a parliamentarian, he was distinguished by muddled speech patterns, particularly in his fiercest orations, but his questioning of ministers and their policies, and his assiduous service on committees strengthened his position in the radical leadership and assured the ultimate success of many of the causes for which he also campaigned in the country. Hume was honoured by the county of Middlesex and the City of London, and was sworn of the privy council shortly before his death. As Palmerston remarked, 'His party feelings were totally independent of any question of political ascendancy' (*Hansard 3*, 1855 CXXXVI, 1879–82).

V. E. CHANCELLOR

Sources V. E. Chancellor, *The political life of Joseph Hume, 1777–1855* (1986) • R. K. Huch and P. R. Ziegler, *Joseph Hume: the people's MP* (1985) • M. Taylor, *The decline of British radicalism, 1847–1860* (1995) • N. McCord, *The Anti-Corn Law League, 1838–46*, 2nd edn (1968) • E. A. Smith, *Lord Grey, 1764–1845* (1990) • N. C. Edsall, *Richard Cobden: independent radical* (1986) • A. D. Macintyre, *The Liberator: Daniel O'Connell and the Irish party, 1830–1847* (1965) • W. Harris, *History of the radical party in parliament* (1885) • I. J. Prothero, *Artisans and politics in early nineteenth-century London: John Gast and his times* (1979) • R. B. McDowell, *Public opinion and government policy in Ireland* (1952) • W. N. Molesworth, *History of the Reform Bill* (1865) • W. N. Molesworth, *History of England since 1830* (1871–3) • D. R. Fisher, 'Hume, Joseph', *HoP, Commons, 1790–1820* • D. Brack and M. Baines, eds., *Dictionary of liberal biography* (1998) • J. Prest, *Lord John Russell* (1972) • A. J. P. Taylor, *The trouble-makers* (1969) • E. P. Thompson, *The making of the English working class* (1963) • D. Close, 'Formation of a two party alignment in the House of Commons, 1832 and 1841', *EngHR*, 84 (1969), 257–77 • D. J. Rowe, 'Class and political radicalism in London, 1831–2', *HJ*, 13 (1970), 31–47 • G. Bartle, 'Bowring and the Greek loans of 1824, 1825', *Balkan Studies* (1962) • M. Brock, *The Great Reform Act* (1973) • J. Morley, *The life of William Ewart Gladstone*, [new edn], 2 vols. (1908) • D. Gray, *Spencer Perceval: the evangelical prime minister, 1762–1812* (1963) • R. Blake, *Disraeli* (1966) • *Hansard 3* • *Hansard 1* • *Hansard 2* • *Morning Chronicle* (Feb 1855) • *The Times* (26 Feb 1855) • *Annual Register* (1855) • bap. reg. Scot. • d. cert.
Archives Duke U., Perkins L., letters • Montrose Museum, Montrose, Angus district council cultural services collection, papers • NL Scot., letters; letters on political subjects • RGS, letters to Royal

Geographical Society • U. Aberdeen, Marischal College, letters • UCL, letters • Yale U., Beinecke L., letters | BL, corresp. with Lord Aberdeen, Add. MS 43200 • BL, corresp. with Charles Babbage, Add. MSS 37188–37195 • BL, corresp. with Richard Cobden, Add. MSS 43667–43668 • BL, letters to W. E. Gladstone, Add. MSS 44363–44584, *passim* • BL, letters to John Charles Herries, Add. MSS 57366–57469 • BL, letters to J. C. Hobhouse, Add. MSS 36457–36472, *passim* • BL, corresp. with Sir Robert Peel, Add. MSS 40344–40600 • BL, letters to Francis Place, Add. MSS 35145–35151, 37949–37950 • Bodl. Oxf., letters to Benjamin Disraeli • Bodl. Oxf., letters to R. Page • Co-operative Union Library, Owen and Holyoake • NL Scot., letters to J. L. Graham • priv. coll., corresp. with Sir John Sinclair and Sir George Sinclair • PRO, corresp. with Lord John Russell, PRO 30/22 • St Deiniol's Library, Hawarden, corresp. with Sir John Gladstone • U. Durham L., letters to Earl Grey • U. Lpool L., corresp. with J. A. Roebuck • UCL, letters to Lord Brougham • UCL, corresp. with Edwin Chadwick • W. Yorks. AS, Leeds, Canning MSS • William Patrick Library, Kirkintilloch, Glasgow, letters to Peter Mackenzie

Likenesses J. Bonomi, bust, *c*.1822, New York Historical Society • A. H. Ritchie, marble bust, *c*.1830, Palace of Westminster, London • F. Bromley, group portrait, etching, pubd 1835 (*The reform banquet*; after B. R. Haydon), NPG • J. Doyle, group portrait, lithograph, pubd 1836 (*A pitiful looking group*; after his earlier portrait), NG Ire. • J. Doyle, caricature, lithograph, 1837, BM • W. Holl, stipple, pubd 1840 (after G. P. A. Healy), BM, NPG • J. Doyle, caricature, pencil drawing, 1849, BM • C. B. Leighton, chalk drawing, 1849–50, NPG • C. B. Leighton, oils, 1849–50, NPG • J. Doyle, chalk drawing, 1851, BM • J. Lucas, oils, 1854, UCL • J. W. Walton, oils, 1854, NPG [*see illus.*] • C. Lucy, oils, 1868, V&A • J. G. Gilbert, oils, Scot. NPG • Gilroy the younger?, caricature, repro. in W. M. Praed, *Political and occasional poems*, ed. G. Young (1888), frontispiece? • G. Hayter, group portrait, oils (*The House of Commons, 1833*), NPG • J. Lucas?, portrait, NL Scot.; repro. in Huch and Ziegler, *Joseph Hume* • statue (after J. W. Walton), Montrose

Wealth at death see probate and will, PRO IR26/7032/323

Hume, Martin Andrew Sharp (1843–1910), historian, was born in London on 8 December 1843, the second son of William Lacy Sharp, an official of the East India Company, and his wife, Louisa Charlotte Hume. He was educated at a private school in Forest Gate, Essex (where by his own account he learned little), was fluent in Spanish from an early age, and developed 'an overmastering passion for books' (M. Hume, Introduction, in G. J. Cayley, *The Bridle Roads of Spain*, 3rd edn, 1908, 5). His maternal ancestor Andrew Hume had been one of the foreign entrepreneurs recruited by the government of Charles III of Spain, being appointed in 1788 as director of a royal button factory at Madrid. The family settled in Spain and took an active part in public life. Sharp's first visit to these hospitable relatives in 1860 was decisive for his future career. Forty years later he recalled having:

> listened open-eyed for hours to the tales of aged relatives and friends who had borne an active part in the great struggle early in the century. Some of them had been friends of Godoy, some of them companions in arms of Wellington and Hill; and from the mouth of one I learned the tragic story of the 2nd of May, at which he had been present. The same aged gentleman and his brother, near relatives of mine, were amongst the victims of the despotism of Ferdinand (VII), and expiated in prison and in exile their adhesion to the cause of the Constitution.   (Hume, xiii–xiv)

On his long annual visits to his kinsmen from 1860 Sharp

was able to observe the continuing drama of Spanish politics at close quarters: he was an eyewitness of the revolution of 1868 and was acquainted with many of its leaders.

The last of the Madrid Humes died in 1876, bequeathing her estate to Sharp, who in compliance with her wishes assumed the name Hume in August 1877. He was now financially independent. For some years after 1868 he served as an officer in the Essex artillery volunteers (3rd battalion of the Essex regiment). In 1877–8 he was attached as an observer to the Turkish forces on the River Lom in northern Bulgaria during the Russo-Turkish War. Subsequently he travelled in west Africa and in Central and South America.

Between 1878 and 1894 Hume was actively involved in Liberal Party politics, standing unsuccessfully as a candidate at Maidstone, Central Hackney, and Stockport. In May 1894 he petitioned Lord Rosebery for some reward for his sixteen years' 'unceasing and unrequited' services (NL Scot., MS 10162, fol. 221). After some practice in business and journalism he fell into literary life 'by accident' (Cunninghame Graham, *True Stories*, vi). His first historical work, the translation of a Spanish chronicle of the reign of Henry VIII (1889), attracted little notice, but he persevered, and his two subsequent books, *The Courtships of Queen Elizabeth* (1896) and *The Year after the Armada* (1896) were sufficiently well received to induce him to adopt historical writing as a profession. Both display his characteristic romanticism, underpinned by patient and thorough archival research. His family background gave him an insight into the Spanish character rare among English historians and though he was a lifelong protestant he dealt with religious matters dispassionately. Having discovered his vocation late in life, he now worked incessantly, publishing seventeen books between 1889 and 1910.

In 1892 Hume succeeded Pascual de Gayangos as editor of the calendar of state papers relating to Spain. Between 1892 and 1896 he published the first three volumes of the Elizabethan series, covering the years 1558–86, and these were followed in 1904 by the eighth and final volume of the series covering the reign of Henry VIII. His official duties did not, however, absorb all his energies. Although his reputation was based on his well-researched work on late sixteenth- and early seventeenth-century history, his readable and vivid survey, *Modern Spain, 1788–1898* (1899; 2nd edn, 1906), shows his narrative gifts to even greater advantage. The tragedies and disappointments he had to relate did not dim his conviction that Spain was 'the most naturally democratic country in Europe' (Hume, 563). A work of wider scope, *The Spanish People: their Origin, Growth and Influence* (1901) was praised by Miguel de Unamuno as 'an excellent psychological study' (M. de Unamuno, *Ensayos*, 4, 1917, 65–86). In 1904 and 1906 Hume contributed chapters on the reigns of Philip II, Philip III, and Philip IV to volumes 3 and 4 of the Cambridge Modern History. In his published lectures, *Spanish Influence on English Literature*, (1905), he strayed on to territory which lay beyond his competence, but *The Court of Philip IV: Spain in Decadence* (1907) has continued to earn praise as a richly documented, if melodramatic, portrait of its age.

Although Hume lectured on Spanish history at Pembroke College, Cambridge, and was an examiner for the universities of Birmingham and London, he failed to obtain chairs in history and Spanish for which he applied at the universities of Glasgow and Liverpool respectively. In his final years, while continuing to work on the state papers, he devoted increasing time to literary productions of a more popular nature. His book of travels *Through Portugal* (1907) is written with affection, and in 1908 he contributed a revealingly personal introduction to a new edition of *The Bridle Roads of Spain*, by G. J. Cayley, a work which had opened his eyes in boyhood to the 'glamour' of that country. He died, unmarried and intestate, on 1 July 1910, at 337 Romford Road, Forest Gate, Essex.

Hume was a dedicated and scrupulous student of Spanish history and did good service in rescuing the subject from neglect. Although he remained on the fringe of the academic world, his work did not go unrecognized. He was made an honorary MA of Cambridge University in 1908, and was a corresponding member of the Royal Spanish Academy, the Royal Spanish Academy of History, and the Royal Galician Academy. He was also awarded the grand cross of the order of Isabel the Catholic. Although he does not appear, according to the army lists, to have risen above the rank of lieutenant in the Essex militia, he was generally known to the public as Major Hume. His last book, *True Stories of the Past*, published posthumously in 1910, carried a short memoir by R. B. Cunninghame Graham who described his friend as:

> erect and soldierly, grave and composed, his thick moustache and olive skin, with something formal in his air, giving him the look of Spanish officers that I have seen long ago in the days of youth, left in command of wretched little forts in which they dragged their weary lives out, passed over by authority and time, and yet contented with their lot. (Cunninghame Graham, *True Stories*, viii)

G. MARTIN MURPHY

Sources DNB · R. B. Cunninghame Graham, preface, in M. A. S. Hume, *True stories of the past* (1910) · M. A. S. Hume, *Modern Spain* (1899), xiii–xiv · R. B. Cunninghame Graham, 'Don Martin', *Saturday Review*, 110 (1910), 43 · *The Times* (4 July 1910) · J. D. Cantwell, *The Public Record Office, 1838–1958* (1991), 318–19, 355 · NL Scot., MS 10162, fol. 221 · *CGPLA Eng. & Wales* (1910)
Archives NL Scot., letters to R. B. Cunninghame Graham
Likenesses drawing, repro. in Graham, *True stories*, frontispiece
Wealth at death £1479 13s. 10d.: administration, 26 July 1910, *CGPLA Eng. & Wales*

Hume, Sir (Hubert) Nutcombe (1893–1967), financier, was born at Southgate, Middlesex, on 4 September 1893, the elder son of Frederick Nutcombe Hume, then a medical superintendent of the North London Fever Hospital, and his wife, Catherine Mary Walton. He was sent to Westminster School and went on to the Royal Military College, Sandhurst, but resigned his commission after two months for want of money. With his mother he clubbed together £100 to finance a journey to Canada, where his jobs ranged from cook to taxi driver, but he identified no long-term opportunity for a penniless immigrant. On the outbreak of war he returned home and was commissioned in the Hampshire regiment; he saw service on the western front and was decorated with the Military Cross.

On demobilization, and using an introduction from a wartime contact, Hume joined the small City issuing house of George Clare & Co., but he soon left to join the well-known stockbrokers Arthur Wheeler & Co. Sir Arthur Wheeler, a controversial City figure, and others, established in 1924 the small issuing house of Gresham Trust Ltd and installed Hume as managing director. A year later, again with Wheeler and respected City and industry figures, Hume established Charterhouse Investment Trust Ltd, of which he was managing director. Hume took charge of transactions while his fellow directors used their contacts to bring in business from medium-sized businesses of good standing. With his entrepreneurial flair, boundless energy, and total commitment, he was Charterhouse's driving force.

Charterhouse, apart from making investments, offered corporate finance advice which specialized in arranging and underwriting issues as a means of raising capital either for organic expansion or for facilitating a merger or acquisition. One early issue, for Selfridges, financed the completion of the eponymous Oxford Street store, while a more complex transaction in 1928 supported the rationalization of part of Britain's malting industry through the establishment of Associated British Maltsters Ltd. Hume's most complex transaction was undoubtedly the 1946 formation of the property company MEPC Ltd.

The 1931 Macmillan committee's report identified the so-called 'Macmillan gap' in the availability of City funding for small businesses; and in 1934 Hume, whose clients included many medium-sized businesses, established Charterhouse Industrial Development Company Ltd (CID) to seek profitable opportunities for financing this sector. This grew to be a core activity of Charterhouse, through CID's taking minority equity stakes in family-owned and family-managed businesses and overseeing them via a boardroom appointment.

In doing this Charterhouse was a pioneer in the City, and from it the firm derived unique strengths which were only seriously rivalled in 1945 when the Industrial and Commercial Finance Corporation was created. In the postwar world, where it was generally more difficult to dispose of small company equity, Charterhouse took much larger investments—sometimes controlling stakes—in the small businesses it financed, which thereby became subsidiary companies. Hume was a rare champion of small businesses but also one whose judgement enabled him to make profitable investments in what others shunned as high risk.

In late 1945 or early 1946 Hume became chairman of Charterhouse and its destiny was for the first time wholly in his hands; he developed it into a major City financial institution. In 1948 and 1952 subsidiaries were established in Australia and Canada to implant Charterhouse's UK model there. The small-business development subsidiary grew apace, and issuing activities were broadened into general merchant banking through the acquisition of the prestigious if somewhat run-down firm of S. Japhet & Co.

This provided Charterhouse with membership of the prestigious Accepting Houses Committee and the status of a full-blooded merchant bank.

However, by the 1960s the Charterhouse Group, as Hume's business was now known, comprised a somewhat haphazard collection of financial and industrial companies which had wide-ranging activities, required a wide spread of management expertise, and exhibited possibly conflicting objectives. One result was the collapse in 1960 of Charterhouse Credit Ltd, due to poor management controls. Hume came to regard this major loss of money and reputation as his only significant business set-back. He retired from Charterhouse in 1964 and was appointed its president.

Hume sat on many boards and was chairman of several others, especially of client companies, which reflected his view that senior financiers should be closely involved in the affairs of industry. The clients included Associated British Maltsters Ltd, Associated Book Publishers Ltd, and MEPC Ltd; he was chairman of the first two. He sat on the council of the Federation of British Industry, of which he was a vice-president, and of its successor, the Confederation of British Industry, where he was involved with the affairs of small businesses.

On the outbreak of the Second World War, Hume, who was still a reserve officer, joined the department of post and telegraph censorship. From 1940 until the end of war he was director of the department of finance (commercial) in the Ministry of Supply, for which he was rewarded with a CBE in 1946. In 1956 he was knighted in recognition of his work for industry.

Hume was a director and later chairman of the Colonial Development Corporation, which was charged with channelling funds for industrial development in the colonies; he was also chairman of the National Film Finance Corporation. Both of these were government-sponsored bodies. In later life he devoted much time to the Salvation Army and headed its London advisory board.

A dynamic personality, Hume's 'enthusiasm was infectious and over the years he became a respected as well as a rumbustious City figure' (DBB, 389). Hume married in 1916 Vera Lilian, daughter of George Hope, a surgeon; his second wife, who he married in 1927, was Jessie Anne Joev (d. 1975), a divorcee, daughter of Donald Campbell. He had no children of his own but had a stepdaughter from his second marriage. Sir Nutcombe Hume died on 22 December 1967 following a heart attack at his London home, Flat 27, 7 Princes Gate. He left estate of only £38,500, an inadequate reflection of the wealth he must have accumulated. He was survived by his second wife.

JOHN ORBELL

Sources L. Dennett, *The Charterhouse Group, 1925–1979: a history* (1979) · L. Dennett, 'Hume, Sir Hubert Nutcombe', *DBB* · *WWW* · *Financial Times* (23 Dec 1967), 11 · *The Times* (23 Dec 1967), 8h · *CGPLA Eng. & Wales* (1968)
Archives Charterhouse Group Archive
Likenesses R. Spear, oils, repro. in Dennett, *Charterhouse Group*
Wealth at death £38,504: probate, 25 March 1968, *CGPLA Eng. & Wales*

Hume, Sir Patrick, of Polwarth (c.1550–1609), courtier and poet, was the eldest son and heir of Patrick Hume (d. 1599) of Polwarth and Redbraes, near Duns, 50 miles south-east of Edinburgh, and Agnes Hume of Manderston. He was one of seven sons and four daughters, all of whom apparently survived childhood. The Hume family in its various branches were, in the sixteenth century, landowners on the east coast of Scotland from North Berwick outside Edinburgh, where a succession of daughters, including Patrick's sister Margaret, were prioresses of the abbey, down to Berwick. Patrick, whose father and uncle were adherents of the regent Moray, seems to have taken a fairly humble position at court, where by 1580 he is recorded as 'familiar servitoir' to the king (*The Promine*, 1580, title-page). In 1585 he received the first of a number of grants of land from the king, and was again referred to as one of his majesty's household servants. He was one of the king's carvers in 1587, and later a gentleman of the bedchamber and cupbearer to the queen. In 1591 he was appointed master of the household at Holyrood Palace, and also warden of the marches. In 1592 he was also appointed keeper of Tantallon Castle, between North Berwick and Dunbar, a post which he held until 1595. He was knighted, probably in 1605. In the celebrated trial for treason, at Linlithgow in January 1606, of the fourteen ministers involved in the Aberdeen assembly of 1605, a trial which generated huge public interest because of the constitutional issues involved, Sir Patrick reluctantly took the lowly, though crucial, position of a juror (protesting that he was 'an ignorant man' and 'of good age') and duly voted for conviction (Calderwood, 391, 477). He seems not to have sought any political or military prominence, and it was in recognition of long service that he was finally made a member of the privy council of Scotland, a year before his death.

Sir Patrick had brought his poetic abilities to the notice of James VI in 1580 with a poem which the king allowed to be printed, called *The Promine* (1580). This poem, in 230 lines of aureate verse and wholesale flattery, was occasioned by the king's 'promenading' on a day in the country near Stirling, 12 June 1579, and contained the promise that he would write more serious poetry or prose if he could find the time. If he did, it has not survived, and he is now known principally as co-author of *The Flyting of Montgomerie and Polwarth* (c.1583), a ritualized, verse-slanging match of about 700 lines between himself and Alexander Montgomerie, when both were members of the king's 'Castalian band' along with Sir Patrick's brother, Alexander Hume (1557?–1609). Flytings required considerable skill in verse manipulation, and a huge vocabulary of obscene and vulgar words, together with the wit to make them sting. Alexander Hume and Montgomerie were much better poets than Sir Patrick, but his versifying abilities, noticeable in *The Promine*, were enough to let him make a very good showing against Montgomerie in *The Flyting*. Montgomerie accused him of cribbing from older authors:

> Thy scrows obscure are borrowed fra some Buik,
> Fra Lindsay thou tuik, thou art Chaucer's Cuik.

Polwarth replied sharply—and, one might think, with some justification:

Also I may be Chaucer's Man,
And yet thy Master not the lesse.

Hume was confirmed in the family estates, including the castle of Redbraes (by the name of which he was often referred to), on 24 October 1599, after his father's death. He married, before 1594, Julian Ker of Ferniehirst (d. 1637); they had nine children, six sons and three daughters. He died in 1609, and was succeeded by his eldest son, Sir Patrick Hume (d. 1648). His will was recorded on 17 December 1611. *The Promine* was reprinted in *The Poems of Alexander Hume*, edited by A. Lawson (Scottish Text Society, 1902), 204–10; his contribution to *The Flyting* is printed with Montgomerie's works. Some of his correspondence survives in the Hume of Marchmont papers in the National Archives of Scotland (GD 158), which also holds his will.

MICHAEL R. G. SPILLER

Sources *Scots peerage* · J. M. Thomson and others, eds., *Registrum magni sigilli regum Scotorum / The register of the great seal of Scotland*, 11 vols. (1882–1914) · *Reg. PCS*, 1st ser., vol. 8 · *CSP Scot. ser.* · NA Scot., Hume of Marchmont papers · D. Calderwood, *The history of the Kirk of Scotland*, ed. T. Thomson and D. Laing, 8 vols., Wodrow Society, 7 (1842–9) · *The Asloan manuscript*, ed. W. A. Craigie, 2 vols., STS, new ser., 14, 16 (1923–5) · S. Mapstone, 'Invective as poetic: the cultural contexts of Polwarth and Montgomerie's flyting', *Scottish Literary Journal*, 26/2 (1999), 18–40

Archives NA Scot., Hume of Marchmont papers

Patrick Hume, first earl of Marchmont (1641–1724), by Sir Godfrey Kneller, 1698

Hume, Patrick, first earl of Marchmont (1641–1724), politician, was born at Redbraes, Berwickshire, on 13 January 1641, the eldest son of Sir Patrick Hume of Polwarth, first baronet (d. 1648), and Christian (d. 1688), youngest daughter of Sir Alexander Hamilton of Innerwick and Ballencrief. Sir Patrick *Hume of Polwarth (c.1550–1609) was his grandfather. Following his father's death in April 1648 he succeeded as second baronet, being brought up by his mother, who before 1656 married Robert Kerr, from 1670 Lord Jedburgh. Polwarth went to Paris to study law; Sir David Hume of Crossrig was one of his fellow students. This may have been before or after his marriage on 29 January 1660 to Grizel (d. 1703), daughter of Sir Thomas Ker of Cavers and his wife, Grizel Halket. Their eldest son, Patrick (d. 1709), was born in November 1664; many of their seventeen children died young.

Early political career On 9 October 1663 parliament appointed Polwarth a justice of the peace for Berwickshire, although the start of his political life is usually dated to 1665. An MP for Berwickshire in the conventions of estates of 1665 (2–4 August) and 1667 (9–23 January), on 23 January 1667 he was appointed a commissioner of supply for the county. The privy council employed him in its action against the Pentland rising in November 1666, commissioned him captain of the horse in the Berwickshire militia on 6 May 1668, and appointed him an excise commissioner in Berwickshire on 26 November. He again represented Berwickshire in Charles II's second parliament in 1669–74. On 23 December 1669 he secured the parliamentary ratification of the barony of Polwarth. That April he was named a commissioner in the trial of one

Henry Wilson, a prisoner in Duns Tolbooth, for witchcraft, while on 20 July 1671 and 7 March 1673 he was appointed a highway commissioner for Berwickshire. He also commanded a troop of horse in the Berwickshire militia in 1672, 1673, 1674, and 1675. With the outbreak of warfare against the United Provinces of the Netherlands in 1672, he was appointed on 4 April an overseer for raising ten men from Berwickshire as part of the total levy of 500 seamen from Scotland.

An opponent of the policies of John Maitland, first duke of Lauderdale, in the administration of Scotland, Polwarth spoke out against him in the 1673 parliamentary session, and in 1674 he was among several Scottish politicians who accompanied William Douglas, third duke of Hamilton, to London to complain about Lauderdale to Charles II. Polwarth fell foul of the authorities in September 1675 when he objected to the privy council garrisoning the houses of several gentlemen, especially in Berwickshire, and refused to support the policy financially. In a letter from Whitehall of 30 September the king referred to Polwarth's 'insolent cariage' (*Reg. PCS*, 4.472), and with Charles's approval, Polwarth was declared to be 'a factious person, having done what may usher in confusion' and 'therefore incapable of all public trust' (*Scots peerage*, 6.13). He was imprisoned first in Edinburgh Castle and then successively in the castles of Dumbarton and Stirling. He was released on 29 February 1676 but re-incarcerated shortly afterwards. On 4 September 1678 Charles II ordered his removal from Edinburgh Tolbooth to Dumbarton Castle; by July 1679 he had been transferred to Stirling Castle, but on 24 July the privy council received royal instructions for his release, largely obtained through the influence of his English relations, especially his cousin, the countess of Northumberland.

Fearful that presbyterian activities and commitment might deny him peaceful possession of his land, Polwarth became involved in the Carolina project with other Scotsmen of like mind. The original plan to purchase New York in conjunction with an English presbyterian for £15,000 sterling was abandoned in favour of a settlement in Carolina. Polwarth went to England to lobby Charles II who gave his approval, but the exposure of the Rye House plot in 1683 brought a swift end to the scheme, as several of its leading promoters, including Polwarth, were supposedly involved in the conspiracy. To the end of his life Polwarth protested that he was guiltless of plotting to kill Charles II and the duke of York, arguing that his 'strict friendship' (Crawford, 241) with Lord Russell, James Scott, duke of Monmouth, and Anthony Ashley Cooper, first earl of Shaftesbury, was only 'to consider what might best be done to secure the kingdom of Scotland against the Papal supremacy and the exercise of arbitrary power, in the event of the succession of a Roman Catholic to the throne' (Warrender, 31). After returning to Scotland, Polwarth only narrowly escaped capture by hiding in the vault beneath Polwarth church, where he was supplied with food by his wife and his eighteen-year-old daughter, Grizel. He then hid under his own house before travelling to London disguised as a surgeon. Thereafter he escaped to France and went via Ostend and Bruges to Brussels, where he hoped to meet Monmouth; failing in this he proceeded to Rotterdam for a time and then to Utrecht. There he enjoyed the protection of the prince of Orange and he sent for his wife and children to join him. Meanwhile, on 13 November 1684 the Scottish privy council set in motion process for treason against him, confirmed when it received royal endorsement for his parliamentary prosecution on 7 January 1685.

In Utrecht when he heard the 'surprising newes' of Charles II's death, Polwarth believed 'base and treacherous means' had effected it as part of a conspiracy for the re-establishment of popery (*A Selection from the Papers of the Earls of Marchmont*, 3.3). He discussed the situation with 'some worthy, liberal spirited gentlemen of our nation' at Utrecht and thereafter met at Rotterdam other members of the exile community, including Monmouth and Archibald Campbell, ninth earl of Argyll. It was resolved to 'endeavour the rescue, defence, and relief, of our religion, rights and liberties, and the many distressed sufferers on their behalf against the Duke of York' (ibid., 5). Polwarth was closely involved in the abortive rebellion of 1685 which ensued, writing an account entitled 'Narrative of the earl of Argyle's expedition', published in *A Selection from the Papers of the Earls of Marchmont*, although he strongly opposed Argyll's strategy of landing in the western highlands, advocating instead a landing in the western lowlands. In the aftermath of the rebellion, Polwarth narrowly escaped with his life. He hid in Ayrshire before escaping from the west coast of Scotland to Ireland, from

where he sailed to Bordeaux and travelled via Geneva back home to his family in the summer of 1686. On 22 May 1685 the Scottish parliament passed a decree of forfeiture against him and legislation of 16 June annexed his lands to the crown. On 3 September 1686 the privy council received instructions from King James giving Polwarth's estate to Kenneth Mackenzie, earl of Seaforth, for a payment of £2000 sterling.

Revolution and the convention Polwarth remained in the Netherlands until the revolution of 1688, living under the alias of Dr Wallace and claiming to be a surgeon. In a letter from Utrecht dated 15 June 1688 and sent to Sir William Denholm of Westshiel, he warned the presbyterian ministers of Scotland against a proposal advocated by Sir James Stewart, 'one who had much power with them', for 'a toleration, which would have included the papists, and thereby acceptable to the King, but as dangerous to the protestant interest' (*A Selection from the Papers of the Earls of Marchmont*, 3.73). In November 1688 Polwarth was among the invasion forces accompanying William of Orange to London. Present at the meeting of the Scottish nobility and gentry with William in the council chamber at Whitehall on 8–9 January 1689, on the second day he spoke out against a motion by James Douglas, earl of Arran, that William should ask King James to return and call a free parliament to secure the protestant religion and heal divisions. Polwarth asked those assembled if anyone would second Arran's motion, but 'none appearing to do it', he argued that the proposal was 'evidently opposite and inimicous to His Highness the Prince of Orange's Undertaking, his Declaration, and the Good Intentions of preserving the Protestant Religion, and of Restoring their Laws and Liberties exprest in it' (Melville Balfour-Melville, 2, appx, 294). His action proved effective in safeguarding William's position: Arran's motion was rejected and he was publicly rebuked by his own father, the duke of Hamilton, the president of the meeting.

In the following two years Polwarth played an important role in Scotland. Despite being a loyal supporter of William, his earlier experiences had led him to resist any encroachment of the royal prerogative on parliamentary rights and powers. He was associated with a political grouping known as 'the Club', whose main aims were the enhancement of Scottish parliamentary powers and the securing of a presbyterian church, and he argued strongly in favour of parliamentary control over the nomination of judges. Although still technically under a sentence of forfeiture, he was an MP for Berwickshire in the 1689 convention of estates. On 16 March he subscribed the act declaring the meeting of the estates to be free and lawful and on 19 March he was appointed captain of the militia troop in Berwickshire. On 23 March he subscribed the convention's letter to William thanking him 'in delyvering us and in perserveing to us the Protestant religion' (*APS*, 9.20). By 19 April Polwarth had offered to levy at his own cost an armed troop of fifty horsemen, requesting that his son Patrick be given the command of these additional men; this was approved by the estates. On 27 April he was named a commissioner of supply for Berwickshire.

Polwarth was included on many of the most important committees of the 1689 convention, especially that of 27 March for settling the government, the so-called 'grand committee'. Polwarth sat on its subcommittee 'to draw the Reasons of the Vacancy' (Melville Balfour-Melville, 2.24), which drew up the Scottish 'Claim of right' and the 'Articles of grievance', the two leading constitutional documents of the Scottish revolutionary settlement. On 16 April Polwarth was appointed to the committee which was to draw up a letter from the estates to William offering him the Scottish crown, and on 23 April to the committee to treat for a union between England and Scotland. Also a member of the committee of estates, on 22 May he was deputed to seize and dispose for the use of the armed forces a quantity of gunpowder which he had discovered. Two days later he was named representative for the shire commissioners in the convention's three-man delegation to brief the king before the forthcoming session of parliament.

Supporter of King William In the first parliament in Scotland of William and Mary, which opened on 5 June 1689, Polwarth once more represented Berwickshire. That day he was appointed to the committee deputed to prepare legislation turning the meeting of the estates into a full parliament. He sat again for Berwickshire in its second and third sessions, from 15 April to 22 July and on 3–10 September 1690. A member of the important committee for settling church government of 9 May 1690, he was appointed a commissioner of supply for Berwickshire on 7 June. On 4 July his forfeiture was rescinded as part of a wider piece of legislation rescinding forfeitures and fines since 1665, while on 8 July an individual act for the same purpose was read. Formal confirmation of this and of the restoration of his lands and estates came on 22 July. He continued to be included on commissions—for the visitation of schools, colleges, and universities (4 July), for the plantation of kirks and valuation of teinds (19 July), and for the preparation of acts in relation to shires and burghs (4 September).

During this period Polwarth was also a member of William's Scottish privy council, where he had a proactive role in military affairs, including the listing of prisoners taken in the first Jacobite rising, auditing military accounts, and reviewing the numbers and condition of the forces of the west-country men. In September 1689 Polwarth and Lord Ruthven reported to the privy council on the condition of the army. They later received a fee of £25 sterling for having mustered and inspected the armed forces in Stirling, Perth, and Dundee. Polwarth was sheriff of Berwick by 11 July 1690, when he was once more put in charge of the Berwickshire militia.

As a reward for his loyal services to King William, Polwarth was promoted into the peerage as Lord Polwarth by a patent dated 26 December 1690. As a special mark of favour, William granted him as an addition to his arms an orange proper, ensigned with an imperial crown. In 1692 he was appointed sheriff of Berwick, and in 1693 he was made an extraordinary lord of session. Lord Polwarth attended the parliamentary sessions of 1693 and 1695 as a member of the noble estate and was a member of the committees for security of the kingdom on both occasions. On 2 May 1696 he gained the highest political office in the kingdom, that of chancellor of Scotland. In his speech to parliament on 8 September, Polwarth extolled the virtues of William as a king who 'has been a Blessing from Heaven to us' (APS, 10, appx, 2). Commenting on the course of the Nine Years' War since 1689, he stated that 'Tis true this War, is the greatest that ever was in Europe' (ibid.). He also gained notoriety that year when his casting vote in the privy council secured the execution of the young student Thomas Aikenhead for his speaking of blasphemous opinions. Macaulay described Polwarth's role in this affair as 'the worst action of his bad life' (Macaulay, 2.621).

However, continued royal favour led to Polwarth's creation on 23 April 1697 as earl of Marchmont, Viscount Blasonberrie, and Lord Polwarth of Polwarth, Redbraes, and Greenlaw. A commissioner of the Treasury and Admiralty that year, he was high commissioner in the 1698 parliamentary session. His parliamentary speeches over the next few years covered foreign affairs as well as domestic Scottish matters, including (19 July 1698) the peace of Ryswick ('an honourable Peace'; APS, 10, appx, 17) and the outbreak of the Great Northern War. Marchmont strenuously defended William's opposition to the Darien project on the grounds that 'it would infallibly disturb the general Peace of Christendome, and bring inevitably upon this Kingdom a heavy War, wherein we could expect no assistance'. It was clear that 'the power of the Spanish Monarchy, and of those concerned in the Support of it, would be united against us, and we in all appearance left to our own strength, without expectation of any Assistants' (ibid., appx, 45).

Career under Anne In 1702 Marchmont was appointed lord high commissioner to the general assembly of the Church of Scotland but its proceedings were interrupted by the death of King William, and although Marchmont was immediately reappointed by Queen Anne, the assembly was dissolved before the warrant arrived. He was chancellor in the first parliamentary session under Queen Anne—also the last of the parliament inaugurated in 1689—and aroused major controversy when he presented an act imposing an oath abjuring the prince of Wales, the Old Pretender (James Stuart). George Lockhart considered it to be 'in the most horrid, scurrilous terms imaginable' ('Scotland's Ruine', 15): Marchmont had suggested that the Pretender had no right or title whatsoever to the Scottish crown, thus implying that the prince was not the son of the forfeited James VII. According to Lockhart, Marchmont acted 'from an headstrong overgrown seal, against the advice of friends' (ibid.) and against the instructions of the high commissioner, James Douglas, second duke of Queensberry. On 11 July 1702 Marchmont sent a memorial to the queen defending and justifying his behaviour, but he was replaced as chancellor by James Ogilvie, first earl of Seafield. Nevertheless, he succeeded in getting an act passed in the 1703 parliamentary session for the security of the presbyterian form of church government.

In the parliamentary sessions of 1704–7 Marchmont proved a strong and consistent supporter of a treaty of union with England; he was a leading figure within the *squadrone volante*, the political group whose votes secured the treaty in the Scottish parliament. According to Lockhart, Marchmont received a payment of £1104 15*s.* 7*d.* sterling out of the £20,000 sterling sent north for distribution by the Scottish treasurer, David Boyle, first earl of Glasgow, but modern calculations indicate that Marchmont had recorded arrears of salary of £2250 sterling and the accusation that Marchmont was bribed was strongly refuted by Sir George Rose. Queen Anne wrote to Marchmont thanking him for his role in the 'great affaire of the Union' (Warrender, 58).

Later years Thereafter, Marchmont's political career declined. Unsuccessful in his attempts to be elected as a representative peer in 1707 and 1708, in 1710 he was deprived of the office of sheriff of Berwickshire and was replaced by the earl of Home. With the accession of George I in 1714, however, Marchmont was restored to that office and he was also made a lord of the court of police, although he took no further prominent role in politics. He died of a fever at his home, Marchmont House, Berwick, on 1 August 1724, aged eighty-three. Some years previously he had moved from Redbraes Castle to Berwick. He was buried with his wife, who had died on 11 October 1703, in the Canongate churchyard in Edinburgh. About 1710 John Macky wrote of Marchmont that:

> he hath been a fine Gentleman, of clear Parts, but always a Lover of set long Speeches, and could hardly give Advice to a private Friend without them; zealous for the Presbyterian Government in the Church, and its Divine Right, which was the great Motive that encouraged him against the Crown ... Business and Years have now almost wore him out; he hath been handsom and lovely; and was so since King William came to the throne.   (*Memoirs of the Secret Services*, 216–17)

Marchmont's eldest son, Patrick, had died on 25 November 1709; he was succeeded as second earl by his third but eldest surviving son, Alexander Hume *Campbell (1675–1740).   JOHN R. YOUNG

Sources M. Warrender, *Marchmont and the Humes of Polwarth by one of their descendents* (1894) · *Scots peerage* · GEC, *Peerage* · *A selection from the papers of the earls of Marchmont, in the possession of the right hon^ble Sir George Henry Rose, illustrative of events from 1685 to 1750*, 3 vols. (1831), vol. 3 · APS, 1661–1707 · *Reg. PCS*, 3rd ser. · E. W. M. Balfour-Melville, ed., *An account of the proceedings of the estates in Scotland, 1689–1690*, 2 vols., Scottish History Society, 3rd ser., 46–7 (1954–5) · *Memoirs of the secret services of John Macky*, ed. A. R. (1733) · R. Wodrow, *The history of the sufferings of the Church of Scotland from the Restoration to the revolution*, ed. R. Burns, 4 vols. (1828–30) · T. B. Macaulay, *The history of England from the accession of James II*, new edn, 2 vols. (1889) · D. Hume of Crossrig, *Domestic details* (1843) · G. Crawford, *The lives and characters of the officers of the crown and the state in Scotland* (1726) · 'Scotland's ruine': *Lockhart of Carnwath's memoirs of the Union*, ed. D. Szechi (1995) · R. S. Rait, *The parliaments of Scotland* (1924) · P. W. J. Riley, *King William and the Scottish politicians* (1979) · P. W. J. Riley, *The union of England and Scotland* (1978) · M. D. Young, ed., *The parliaments of Scotland: burgh and shire commissioners*, 2 vols. (1992–3)

Archives NA Scot., corresp. and papers · NL Scot., corresp. and deeds · NRA, priv. coll., corresp. | Buckminster Park, Grantham, corresp., mainly with duchess of Lauderdale · NRA, priv. coll., letters to Lady Grizell

Likenesses G. Kneller, oils, 1698, priv. coll. [*see illus.*] · W. Aikman, oils, *c.*1720, Scot. NPG · J. Smith, mezzotint (after G. Kneller), BM · R. White, line engraving (after G. Kneller), BM, NPG

Hume, Patrick (*fl.* 1695), literary scholar and poet, was possibly connected to the Polwarth branch of the family (Chambers, *Scots.*) which would suggest Scottish whig affiliations. Rose affirms that Hume kept a school in London. In 1695 *A Poem Dedicated to the Immortal Memory of Her Late Majesty the Most Incomparable Q. Mary* 'by Mr. Hume' was published by Jacob Tonson; if this is his, it indicates a protestant standpoint, with a strong commitment to the majesty of the sovereign.

In the same year there appeared Hume's *Annotations on Milton's Paradise Lost. Wherein the texts of sacred writ, relating to the poem, are quoted; the parallel places and imitations of the most excellent Homer and Virgil, cited and compared; all the obscure parts render'd in phrases more familiar; the old and obsolete words, with their originals, explain'd and made easie to the English reader.* This was also published by Jacob Tonson alongside the sixth edition of *Paradise Lost* in *The Poetical Works of Mr John Milton.* It is unlikely that Hume edited the text of the poem, since he points out errors in it and works from different versions. The separately paginated *Annotations* runs to 321 pages and is longer than the poem on which it forms a line-by-line commentary. There is no preface or dedication; the title-page gives the author merely as 'P. H. *philopoïētēs*'. The commentary virtually eschews any biographical comment on the poet or his historical situation and concentrates solely on textual exegesis. It is the work of an extremely well-educated scholar who can put a solid knowledge of Hebrew, Greek, Latin, French, Italian, Dutch, and Anglo-Saxon to the task of analysing scripture sources, classical allusions, and etymological implications. Alongside this erudition, Hume offers accessible and enthusiastic paraphrases and expansions of Milton's sense, sometimes in verse. There is a strong religious and moralistic cast to the commentary, which however sometimes breaks into facetiousness or imaginative flight. On a very few occasions Hume takes the opportunity to express anti-regicide and patriarchalist views.

Hume's model was essentially the biblical commentary of the seventeenth century; his work itself formed the basis for later commentaries on secular literary works. The *Annotations* were very heavily mined by later commentators such as Bishop Newton, who grudgingly acknowledged some merit in Hume's work; they were comprehensively plagiarized by Joseph Callander in his edition of the first book of *Paradise Lost* (Glasgow, 1750). Thomas Warton praised their value more generously, and current estimation of their interest remains high. Nothing is known of Hume after 1695, and nothing of a biographical nature was collected in the eighteenth century: the author was referred to as Peter and Philip as well as Patrick.   PAUL BAINES

Sources M. Walsh, *Shakespeare, Milton, and eighteenth-century literary editing: the beginnings of interpretative scholarship* (1997), 57–63,

92–5 • M. Walsh, 'Literary annotation and biblical commentary: the case of Patrick Hume's *Annotations* on *Paradise lost*', *Milton Quarterly*, 22/4 (Dec 1988), 109–14 • H. Erskine-Hill, 'On historical commentary: the example of Milton and Dryden', *Presenting poetry: composition, publication, reception*, ed. H. Erskine-Hill and R. McCabe (1995), 52–74 • A. Oras, *Milton's editors and commentators from Patrick Hume to Henry John Todd, 1695–1801* (1931), 22–49 • T., 'Patrick Hume's and Mr Callender of Craigforth's notes on Milton', *Blackwood*, 4 (1819), 658–62 • Chambers, *Scots.* (1855) • H. J. Rose, *A new general biographical dictionary*, ed. H. J. Rose and T. Wright, 12 vols. (1853) • J. Milton, *Paradise lost: a new edition, with notes of various authors*, ed. T. Newton, 2 vols. (1749) • J. Milton, *Poems upon several occasions*, ed. T. Warton (1791) • J. Richardson, *Explanatory notes and remarks on Milton's 'Paradise lost'* (1734) • J. T. Shawcross, ed., *Milton: the critical heritage* (1970)

Hume, Rosemary Ethel (1907–1984), founder of a cookery school and cookery writer, was born on 2 April 1907 at Underriver House, Underriver, near Sevenoaks, Kent, the daughter of Colonel Charles Vernon Hume and his wife, Ursula Wilhelmina Marshall. She was the youngest of three children. Her parents, who had only recently returned from Japan, were staying with her mother's cousins, the Peploes. Her father had been a military attaché at the British legation in Tokyo during the Russo-Japanese War. Her mother was the fourth daughter of Reginald and Mary Jane Dykes of Castlerigg in Keswick, Cumberland.

Born into a class that employed servants to cook and at a time when a woman's interest in kitchen matters was confined to menu planning, Hume was unusual. Family lore says that the child, who would nowadays be classed as dyslexic, first showed an interest in the kitchen at about the age of eight. Often a visitor with her family at large country houses, she became adept at finding her way behind the green baize door that still separated the kitchen from the living area, and wheedling the cooks into teaching her their skills and recipes, many of which found their way into her later books. Such recipes as Belvoir ginger cake, learned from the cook of family friends called Wilson, of Belvoir Castle in Northern Ireland, subsequently appeared in the *Constance Spry Cookery Book* (1956), of which she was co-author.

As she clearly had a vocation, Hume was sent in the late 1920s to Paris to study at the Cordon Bleu School with Henri-Paul Pelleprat, where she gained her diploma. Pelleprat was *professeur* at the cookery school from 1902 to 1932 (with an interruption for military service during the war). The Cordon Bleu was so called to distinguish it from the 'whites' worn by the professional—male—chef, who received a full-time training and had to be physically strong. The aim was not to teach women to cook for a living; paradoxically, girls whose families could afford the school's fees normally employed cooks.

Hume learned the repertory of French dishes derived from Escoffier, and when she returned to England her family's friends often engaged her to pass on her expertise and recipes to their cooks. One of her elder sisters, Gillian Nunn, said that she was astonished to see such 'a shy, unassuming girl gain such rapport with these old pros' (private information).

In 1931 one of these family friends loaned Hume £2000 to set up a school of her own. With Dione Lucas, a fellow student at the Paris Cordon Bleu, she rented two ground-floor rooms in Jubilee Place, Chelsea. The larger room was the kitchen, the smaller the office, and in a corridor to the street 'they set up a few tables and chairs for passers-by to partake of the more edible results of their students' efforts' (private information). Her sister said that their first students consisted largely of 'Cadogan Square' ladies and their daughters; but in only two years the loan was repaid in full.

When in 1935 a tea shop at 11 Sloane Square became vacant the partners moved the busy school there and also opened a restaurant. Pelleprat gave them permission to call it Au Petit Cordon Bleu. This was also the title Lucas and Hume used for a popular book of recipes, published in 1936. There was a revised edition in 1953. In 1939 the school had to be suspended, but the restaurant remained open during the war. In 1942 Lucas went to the USA and set up on her own.

Following the war the school was relaunched in 1945, in partnership with the influential flower arranger Constance *Spry (1886–1960), as the Cordon Bleu Cookery School, a boarding-school at Winkfield Place in Berkshire. Hume had her own flat there, where her mother joined her and, in her declining years, was cared for by Hume and other staff. Au Petit Cordon Bleu, in the meantime, moved to Marylebone Lane, where Hume was joined by a new partner, Muriel Downes; they ran it as a training 'kitchen restaurant' for the students, though it was also open to the public, and Hume commuted between Winkfield and her west London flat in Abingdon Villas. In 1953 they were asked to help with the catering arrangements for the coronation, and Spry is supposed to have invented the famous dish of coronation chicken—cold chunks of chicken in a lightly curried mayonnaise sauce blended with tinned apricot purée. This was served to the guests at the luncheon after the coronation, and Hume was subsequently awarded the MBE. Christopher Driver called her 'an exact and professional cook' (Driver, 10).

During the 1970s food of this sort became unfashionable, as did many of Hume's recipes from the Cordon Bleu and the 1956 *Constance Spry Cookery Book* (co-authored by Hume but given its misleading title by the publishers to the great discomfiture of Mrs Spry, who always acknowledged Hume's share in the work). Even domestic cooks now found uncongenial the recipes' reliance on tinned goods when fresh were now available, and on the flour jar for thickening, instead of reducing natural cooking liquids.

In the 1960s the successful Cordon Bleu School also moved to Marylebone Lane. The style of the recipes taught subsequently changed, as did the students, who were more often interested in a career in catering than in catching and cooking for a man. Having spent most of a lifetime in her kitchens, Hume now bought a house in the Kyles of Bute, Argyll, near family and friends with whom she had been happy in her youth; she lived there with Dr Jan Ayscough Nunn, her brother-in-law, becoming a passionate gardener, and commuting to London until she retired in the 1970s. A series of strokes marred her last years, and she died at her home, Salthouse, Colintraive, Argyll, on 23 February 1984. PAUL LEVY

Sources private information (2004) [G. Barton] · C. Driver, *The British at table* (1983) · A. Barr and P. Levy, *The official foodie handbook* (1984) · b. cert. · *CGPLA Eng. & Wales* (1984)
Wealth at death £268,763: probate, 13 April 1984, *CGPLA Eng. & Wales*

Hume [*née* Wigington], **Sophia** (1702/3–1774), Quaker minister and writer, was born in Charles Town, South Carolina, one of the two children of Henry Wigington (*d.* 1722), deputy secretary of South Carolina, and his wife, Susanna, *née* Bayley (*d.* 1733). Sophia's maternal grandmother was Mary *Fisher, one of the first two Quakers to come to Massachusetts in 1656. On her arrival Fisher and her companion, Ann Austin, had suffered the indignity of having their books burnt and their bodies searched for 'witch-marks' before being banished from Massachusetts. Four years later, on a religious journey, Fisher met the young Sultan Mohammed IV, who was encamped near Adrianople. Unlike the Boston Calvinists he was moved by the visit and impressed by their spirit. One of the important early Quaker 'publishers of truth', Fisher's example and the events of her life had a lasting effect upon her granddaughter. Another influence on Sophia's early life was her father. Though her mother was a Friend, Henry and Susanna Wigington had been married according to the Anglican rite, and Sophia was educated to appreciate 'the pleasures and delusive amusements of this world'.

In 1721 Sophia married Robert Hume (*d.* 1737), a prominent Charles Town lawyer, landowner, and public official. A year later, when Sophia's father died, the couple inherited all his black slaves and 'all moneys due in the province'; as a result they became very wealthy. Sophia's husband died on 1 October 1737 and four years later, aged thirty-eight, Sophia turned her back on Anglicanism and her life as a rich landowner and joined the Society of Friends. Since there were very few Quakers in Charles Town she moved to London.

Like her grandmother Mary Fisher, Sophia Hume was soon drawn to make a religious visit to her natal land, which she did in 1748, despite the fact that her family, friends, and two children—Alexander and Susanna—greatly disapproved of the step that she had taken. While in South Carolina she became convinced of the impossibility for her of accepting a 'pleasure-loving life made possible by slavery'. The result was what became her best-known work, *An Exhortation to the Inhabitants of the Province of South Carolina*, published in Philadelphia in 1748 by Benjamin Franklin and reprinted several times. According to the Quaker historian Rufus Jones the work:

> is a simple little book, with some chaff, but with some real wheat in it, and it gives a clear idea of the type of preaching which was heard in all the meetings of the South as the itinerant messenger came upon them. (Jones, 300–01)

It is said that the anti-slavery pioneer John Woolman (1720–1772) was on the committee of Philadelphia Friends to whom the *Exhortation* was submitted. Like Woolman, Sophia believed that there was 'one truth on which all I

have to say to you greatly depends, namely that *all mankind* have within them a measure and manifestation of the Light, Spirit or Grace of God'.

In Philadelphia, aside from Woolman, Sophia Hume came to know other noteworthy Friends; John Smith speaks of her often in his diary and she made Israel Pemberton's home her residence. She is also credited with an anonymous pamphlet on the practice of inoculation of smallpox, and if this is so it suggests that in her youth she 'languished under a great degree of infection from small-pox'. Ironically on her return to England, by 1772, she again encountered John Woolman, on his fateful journey that ended in York with his death from the disease. Doubt-less the two had much to discuss concerning the slave trade, with Sophia having valuable experience of the situation in South Carolina, where large numbers of slaves were an important aspect of the plantation economy. In a letter of 7 July 1772 she said that she had 'great unity with Woolman' and that it was to her that he entrusted the final portions (the 'sea journey') of his remarkable *Journal*, with permission to revise and reorder his text.

When Sophia Hume was in London in 1772 William Forster (1747–1824), a leading Quaker, described her as 'plain in dress as John Woolman for a man since her convincement'. For Rufus Jones she was 'a person of some refinement and culture, and a woman of very unusual religious experience' (Jones, 300). In addition to the *Exhortation* she published several more religious essays, including *A Caution to such as Observe Days and Times* (c.1763) and *Extracts from Divers Antient Testimonies* (1766). She died suddenly, of apoplexy, on 26 January 1774 at White Hart Court, Grace-church Street, London; she was buried at the Quaker burial-ground at Bunhill Fields. Her son, Alexander, was present but her daughter and son-in-law were in France at the time. William Forster said that the memorial meeting was 'the largest concourse of people I ever saw (at Grace-church Street Meeting) except at Yearly Meeting' (testimony, RS Friends, Lond.). DAVID SOX

Sources 'Dictionary of Quaker biography', RS Friends, Lond. [card index] · *The journal and essays of John Woolman*, ed. A. Mott Gummere (1922) · A. C. Myers, ed., *Hannah Logan's courtship* (1904) · MS testimony of Gracechurch Street monthly meeting, 1774, RS Friends, Lond. · H. J. Cadbury, *John Woolman in England: a documentary supplement* (1971) · D. Sox, *John Woolman: quintessential Quaker* (1999) · R. Larson, *Daughters of light: Quaker women preaching and prophesying in the colonies and abroad, 1700–1775* (1999) · R. M. Jones, *The Quakers in the American colonies* (1911) · parish record, Charleston, South Carolina, St Philip, 1721 [marriage]
Archives RS Friends, Lond. | Swarthmore College, Swarthmore, Pennsylvania, Friends Historical Library, Philadelphia yearly meeting records

Hume, Thomas (1769/70–1850), physician, born in Dublin, was the son of Gustavus Hume, surgeon to the city's Mercers' Hospital. He was educated at Trinity College, Dublin, where he was admitted as a pensioner on 13 October 1787, aged eighteen, and graduated BA in 1792, MB in 1796, and MD on 19 July 1803. On 6 July 1804 he was incorporated DM at Oxford as a member of University College. He was admitted a candidate of the Royal College of Physicians on 25 June 1807, a fellow on 25 June 1808, was censor in 1814,

1821, 1831, and 1832, and was declared an elect on 18 January 1832. In 1808 he sailed for Portugal as physician to the army under Wellesley, but he returned to London during the following year and became physician to the Westminster Hospital. After resigning this office in 1811, he went back to the Peninsula. Shortly afterwards he received from the commander-in-chief the appointment of physician to the London district, which he held until the establishment was broken up by the peace of 1815. He died at Hanwell, Middlesex, on 21 October 1850, aged eighty, and 'was buried in the family vault of his wife, the last descendant of the mathematician, Dr John Wallis (1616–1703)' (*GM*, 2nd ser., 34, 1850, 676).

GORDON GOODWIN, rev. MICHAEL BEVAN

Sources Munk, *Roll* · Foster, *Alum. Oxon.* · Burtchaell & Sadleir, *Alum. Dubl.*, 2nd edn · P. J. Wallis and R. V. Wallis, *Eighteenth century medics*, 2nd edn (1988) · d. cert.

Hume, Tobias (*b.* in or before **1569**, *d.* **1645**), composer and army officer, is of unknown parentage. As a professional soldier he appears to have served in the Swedish and Russian armies, and as a viol player he published two important volumes of music, principally for the lyra viol.

Hume regarded himself primarily as a soldier: 'My Life hath beene a Souldier, and my idlenes addicted to Musicke' (Hume, *The First Part*, sig. B2r). His known musical compositions are contained in his *The First Part of Ayres* (1605) and *Captaine Humes Poeticall Musicke* (1607). In his addresses to the reader his claim for the viol as a worthy rival to the lute was an accurate forecast of change in English musical taste. Taking umbrage, the great composer and lute player John Dowland quoted Hume's words, going so far as to allege that in them the lute had 'been abased' (Traficante, 1968, 21).

Hume's works comprise a variety of instrumental dances, pieces with descriptive, fanciful, and humorous titles, programmatic pieces, and songs. In *The First Part of Ayres* perhaps it was the rough drollery of a soldier that lay behind a title sequence such as 'My Mistresse hath a Prettie Thing', 'She Loues it Well', 'Hit it in the Middle' or the *Lesson for Two to Play upon one Viole*, for the performance of which one player must sit in the lap of the other. This same publication contains what may be the earliest examples of the string instrument playing techniques *pizzicato* and *col legno*. Freed of the rude jocularities of the earlier book and dedicated to Queen Anne, consort of James I, *Captaine Humes Poeticall Musicke* earned for the composer 'according to her highnes comandment and pleasure [by warrant, 6 June 1607]: 100 s[hillings]' (Ashbee, 198). The dedication copy in the British Library bears the handwritten inscription on the verso of the title-page 'I doe in all humylitie beseech your Ma:tie that you woulde bee pleased to heare this Musick by mee; havinge excellent Instruments to performe itt'. Hume's music displays much skill and invention, both in the exploitation of the potential of the viol and in the effectiveness and the variety of sonorities in the ensemble works.

In 1629 Hume entered the Charterhouse almshouse, whose minimum age of entry appears to have been sixty; he remained there until his death. In 1643, presumably at the age of at least seventy-four, Hume published a tragic petition to the 'Lords assembled in the high Court of Parliament'. Identifying himself as 'one of the poore Brethren of that famous Foundation of the Charter House' he made Quixotic requests for military commissions, promising within three months to 'ruine the [Irish] Rebels' and bring 'to his Majestie and the Parliament 20. Millions of Money' (Hume, *True Petition*, title-page). At the same time he described himself as living in great misery, saying 'I have pawned all my best cloathes, and have now no good garment to weare' (ibid., sig. A3). He went on to describe his lack of the barest essentials for food:

> I have not one penny to helpe me at this time to buy me bread, so that I am like to be starved for want of meat and drinke, and did walke into the fields very lately to gather Snailes in the nettles, and brought a bagge of them home to eat, and doe now feed on them for want of other meate. (ibid., sig. A3r)

Hume died at the Charterhouse less than two years later, on 16 April 1645. FRANK TRAFICANTE

Sources T. Hume, *The first part of ayres* (1605) · T. Hume, *Captaine Humes poeticall musicke* (1607) · T. Hume, *The true petition of Colonel Hume, as it was presented to the lords assembled in the high court of parliament* (1642) · W. Sullivan, 'Tobias Hume's *First part of ayres*, 1605', PhD diss., University of Hawaii, 1967; serialized in *Journal of the Viola da Gamba Society of America*, 5 (1968), 5–15; 6 (1969), 13–33; 7 (1970), 92–111; 8 (1971), 64–93; 9 (1972), 16–37 · C. Harris, 'Tobias Hume—a short biography', *Chelys*, 3 (1971), 16–18 · C. Harris, 'A study and partial transcription of *The first part of ayres* by Tobias Hume', diss., U. Lond., 1971 · K. Neumann, 'Captain Hume's *Invention for two to play upon one viole*', *Journal of the American Musicological Society*, 22 (spring 1969), 101–06 · K. Neumann, 'On Captain Hume's "wrong" notes', *Journal of the Viola da Gamba Society of America*, 4 (1967), 21–6 · A. Ashbee, ed., *Records of English court music*, 4 (1991), 197, 198 · F. Traficante, 'Music for the lyra viol: the printed sources', *Lute Society Journal*, 8 (1966), 7–24; repr. in *Journal of the Viola da Gamba Society of America*, 5 (1968), 16–33

Humfrey, John (*bap.* **1621**, *d.* **1719**), clergyman and ejected minister, was baptized on 23 January 1621 at St Albans, Hertfordshire, the son of William Humfrey and his wife, Ann. He went up to Pembroke College, Oxford, in Lent term 1639 and graduated BA in November 1641. The outbreak of the first civil war caused him to leave Oxford briefly but he returned in 1642 when it became the king's capital-in-exile. When Oxford fell to parliament in June 1646 Humfrey again left, in a brief hiatus serving as a chaplain in Devon before returning in July 1647 to proceed MA. Although he was of a godly persuasion, he quickly established himself as a man of no party and refused to take the solemn league and covenant or to join in fellowship with a presbyterian classis. He was, however, ordained in the presbyterian fashion by a classis in 1649; he later claimed that this was because he had no access to a bishop.

Humfrey was admitted to the vicarage of Frome Selwood in Somerset on 27 June 1654. He quickly gained notoriety for reversing the practice of refusing admission to the sacrament of the Lord's supper to those who would not, or could not, come before the elders of the parish to be tested on the fundamentals of faith. Humfrey commented that many parishes in the provinces had not received the Lord's supper for a decade. The predominant view among the godly ministry at the time was that the Lord's supper was a sacrament that was efficacious only to the faithful and could not convert. It followed, therefore, that it should be denied to those who did not possess a basic knowledge of faith. Humfrey disagreed with this view, believing the Lord's supper to be capable of converting the ungodly. After consulting with Richard Baxter he engaged in a long and bitter controversy with the exponents of refusing admission, principally the London presbyterian minister Dr Roger Drake and the godly layman John Timson. Humfrey complained in private correspondence with Baxter that the strictness of the presbyterians' view of the Lord's supper encouraged formalism and dishonesty in the congregation; 'the bottom of all Sir you see is but to save a lye' (Keeble and Nuttall, 1.290). He eventually saw Baxter's own opinions on the rights of the sacraments as unnecessarily strict, and can be seen as an Erastian proponent of mixed communion.

Humfrey opposed both the Commonwealth and the Cromwellian protectorate and made no secret that he sought the return of Charles II. In 1659 after the army coup that removed Richard Cromwell he preached a prophetic sermon on the words: 'I will overturn, overturn, overturn, until the He come whose right it is, and I will give it him.' This language proved too much for Major-General Okey, who issued a warrant for Humfrey's arrest. With the restoration of Charles II in 1660, William Piers, the restored bishop of Bath and Wells, invited Humfrey to assist in the ordination of new priests. This was meant to be a symbol of the reunion of the Church of England. However, Piers took the opportunity to urge Humfrey to renounce his presbyterian ordination and to be episcopally reordained. This caused Humfrey to have a crisis of conscience. After two days of consideration he acceded to the bishop's request with some modifications to the liturgy. His conscience was still affected, however, and so he wrote a paper demonstrating the validity of reordination. Although this received the compliments of a number of bishops, Humfrey could not reconcile himself to his actions and renounced his ordination before Piers's registrar. He burnt his deacon's orders but kept his certificates of priest's orders until after the ejection of 1662. In reply to his own paper on reordination, he wrote a tract echoing the civil war argument of Smectymnuus, stating that the office of presbyter and bishop were synonymous and thus that presbyterian ordination was valid.

Humfrey was ejected from the parish of Frome Selwood in August 1662, to be replaced by Joseph Glanvill. He moved to London and gathered nonconformist congregations at various places there including Duke's Place, Rosemary Lane, and Petticoat Lane. Although in 1669 he considered taking the Oxford oath, to which he devoted his tract *A Case of Conscience* (1669), he does not seem to have done so. He remained a man of no party in nonconformity and sought continually to achieve the union of English protestantism and toleration for those who could not join with the Church of England. He took advantage of the

king's indulgence of 1672 and was licensed as a presbyterian at his house in Kingsbury. His support for the comprehension of nonconformists, announced in the tract *Comprehension Promoted* (1672), earned him a spell of imprisonment in the Gatehouse in 1673 during the Cavalier-Anglican backlash against the indulgence.

Despite being licensed as a presbyterian Humfrey was no exponent of the values of the Westminster assembly's strict doctrinal standards. He was a defender of toleration, even espousing the view that the hated Antinomian Tobias Crisp should have the right to publish his views. In 1700 he wrote a couple of public letters to the American Quakers William Penn and George Keith. Humfrey's letter to Keith, although written in a friendly style, was a criticism of the Quakers' doctrine that the heathen (in particular Native Americans) could have an implicit knowledge of Christ through the inner light. For Humfrey faith could only come through the explicit knowledge of the gospel and the preaching of the ministry. His letter to Penn was a criticism of the belief that the inner light gave a Quaker an infallible guidance in matters of faith; Humfrey also criticized the rejection of the sacraments of baptism and the Lord's supper. He counselled Penn to meditate on the doctrine of predestination as a corrective to Quaker doctrinal errors.

Humfrey was, however, no hardliner in his views on predestination. A debate with Richard Baxter in 1674 shows that he was almost as liberal as Baxter on the doctrine of justification and like Baxter shared a belief in a middle way between Calvinism and Arminianism. This earned him the commendation of the latitudinarian bishops Patrick of Ely, Stillingfleet of Worcester, and Strafford of Chester. In 1681 he returned Stillingfleet's commendation by criticizing him in two long pamphlets co-written with Stephen Lobb. In August 1682 he was fined £100 by the Middlesex sessions for illegal preaching.

Like his moderate nonconformist friend Baxter, Humfrey was a tireless exponent of a new and more comprehensive settlement of the Church of England. He published seemingly endless tracts on the comprehension of moderate nonconformists into the Church of England. His views bore fruit after the revolution of 1688 when discussion for comprehension and toleration resumed during the Convention Parliament. He wrote *Union Pursued* and probably *The Healing Attempt* to try to encourage the parliament to produce a new act of uniformity settling a more ecumenical Church of England. These attempts were all in vain but characteristically Humfrey wrote letters and tracts to almost every session of William's parliaments campaigning for comprehension. In 1709 his work on moderating the sacramental test was burnt by the public hangman, although an apology at the bar of the House of Commons allowed him to escape punishment.

In the years after the 1688 revolution Humfrey lived in Dyot Street, off Great Russell Street. He attended the meeting-house in that street, having a controversy with Joseph Reade over the rights to his seat in the meeting between 1689 and 1691. In 1711 the diarist Ralph Thoresby was sent to Humfrey by the archbishop of York to receive advice on whether or not to conform to the Church of England. Humfrey was still living when Calamy's *Account* (1713) was published; the elderly nonconformist minister Samuel Stancliffe annotated his copy of the *Account* by praising Humfrey as 'a man of such parts, learning, piety, charity, industry and integrity' (*Nonconformist's Memorial*, 190). Humfrey died in 1719, having continued in the ministry until his death. Of all the ministers ejected in 1662 only Nathan Denton survived him.   E. C. VERNON

Sources Calamy rev., 284–5 · *Calendar of the correspondence of Richard Baxter*, ed. N. H. Keeble and G. F. Nuttall, 2 vols. (1991) · *The nonconformist's memorial ... originally written by ... Edmund Calamy*, ed. S. Palmer, 2nd edn, 2 vols. (1777) · E. Calamy, ed., *An abridgement of Mr. Baxter's history of his life and times, with an account of the ministers, &c., who were ejected after the Restauration of King Charles II*, 2nd edn, 2 vols. (1713) · *DNB* · Venn, *Alum. Cant.* · W. Lamont, *Godly rule: politics and religion, 1603–60* (1969)
Archives DWL, corresp. with R. Baxter

Humfrey, Pelham (1647/8–1674), composer, was probably born in London and was a nephew of the parliamentarian Colonel John Humphrey. By late 1660 Humfrey had been admitted to the Chapel Royal as a chorister, where he trained under his future father-in-law, Henry *Cooke (*d.* 1672). It would appear that Humfrey's considerable musical talents were recognized at an early stage, since when the boy's voice broke in 1664 Cooke was assigned an extraordinarily large annual payment of £40 for his maintenance. According to the composer, organist, and music anthologist Thomas Tudway, sometime organist at King's College, Cambridge, Humfrey had already begun composing at this stage. This fact was not in itself unusual: Tudway himself, a contemporary of Humfrey under Cooke, started to compose in his mid-teens, as did John Blow. What was unusual was Humfrey's early fluency of musical technique. On St Cecilia's day 1663 Samuel Pepys heard a setting of Psalm 51 'made for five voices by one of Captain Cooke's boys', which may have been Humfrey's verse anthem 'Have mercy upon me, O God', scored for five solo voices and four-part chorus with an instrumental group comprising strings and organ. James Clifford's *The Divine Services and Anthems* (2nd edition, January 1664) includes texts for five anthems by Humfrey; regrettably, the music for only one of these has survived ('Haste thee, O God', for alto, two tenor and bass soloists, four-part choir, and instruments). Also from this early period are the so-called 'Club Anthem', jointly composed by the fellow Chapel Royal choristers Humfrey, Blow, and William Turner, and a manuscript of Cooke's anthem 'The Lord hear thee in the time of trouble' which contains an instrumental introduction in Humfrey's handwriting (suggesting, therefore, that it is his own, not Cooke's work).

During the years 1664–7 Humfrey was abroad in France and Italy (supported financially by quite substantial sums provided from government coffers). Specific details of his travels are not known, though these were evidently years of study. It has sometimes been claimed that he became a pupil of the French court composer Jean-Baptiste Lully. It is apparent, however, that during these years on the continent Humfrey absorbed all the most important stylistic features of contemporary French and Italian music, facets that were to become of prime importance in his own work and which were to set it somewhat apart from that of his English contemporaries. While still abroad, Humfrey was appointed a lutenist in Charles II's private musick (10 March 1666), and he was officially sworn in as a member of the Chapel Royal on 26 October later that year. Biographical facts relating to the immediate period following his return to England are scarce. Of his appointments, it is known only that he became first an assistant (January 1670) and later a warden (1672) of the Musicians' Company. On 10 March 1672 he became, jointly with Thomas Purcell, composer for the violins; Charles II had established this band of string players, reminiscent of the 'vingt-quatre violons du roy' that he had encountered during his years of exile in France, as an expansion of a smaller string band formed during the civil war. Humfrey's final appointment came on 14 July 1672, when he succeeded Cooke as master of the children of the Chapel Royal and composer in the private musick. Among his responsibilities were teaching the choristers the violin, lute, and theorbo, as well as training them for the daily services. The young Henry Purcell is very likely to have been one of his pupils, and it is clear that Humfrey's knowledge and application of French and Italian styles of composition were to have no small impact on the impressionable chorister. Humfrey married Cooke's daughter Katherine in 1672; a daughter was baptized on 21 November 1673 but died within weeks. Humfrey's own health was fast declining, and on 23 April 1674 he made his will, in which he left his

> deare wife my sole executrix and M[ist]r[es]s of all I have in the world after those few debts I owe (if they are paid. I only desire that 3 Legacye's may bee given: that is to say: to my Cousin Betty Jelfe; to Mr: Blow [John Blow, the composer, also one of the witnesses to Humfrey's will], and to Besse Gill; each of them twenty shillings to buy them Rings.

Within three months he was dead, aged only twenty-six: he died at Windsor on 14 July 1674 and was buried on 17 July in the south cloister of Westminster Abbey.

Of Humfrey's character we have but few glimpses. On the occasion of his marriage, his friend Robert Veel penned 'An Hymeneal to my Dear Friend Mr. P. H.', which describes the dedicatee as 'A Jolly Youth'. The opinion of the diarist Samuel Pepys was less flattering. Following an occasion at which the two men dined together on 15 November 1667, Pepys gave vent to his disgust as follows:

> [Humfrey is] an absolute Monsieur ... full of form and vanity, and [he] disparages everything and everybody's skill but his own ... to hear how he laughs at the King's music here ... that they cannot keep time nor tune ... that Grebus [the Catalan Louis Grabu], the King's Master of Musique ... understands nothing and cannot play on any instrument and so cannot compose, and that he will give him a lift out of his place ... would make a man piss.

Humfrey's most important compositions are his church works, especially the verse anthems, which typically incorporate introductions and interludes for strings, displaying to some extent the influence of the French *grands motets* of Dumont and the court ballets of Lully conceived for the express purpose of reflecting the splendour of the 'Sun King', Louis XIV. His vocal writing, by contrast, is more Italian in idiom, suggesting an acquaintance with the work of Carissimi. His extant output includes in addition five devotional songs (one of which sets a portion of Donne's 'A Hymne to God the Father'); several court odes; two masques, written for the adaptation of Shakespeare's *The Tempest* by Davenant, Dryden, and Shadwell in 1674; and some two dozen secular songs. There is no purely instrumental music. Humfrey was clearly a precocious talent, who, given a longer life, might have developed into a composer of the stature of Purcell. As it is, history will judge his work as an influential, but peripheral, forerunner to his younger contemporary's far greater achievement.   JOHN IRVING

Sources P. Dennison, *Pelham Humfrey* (1986) · P. Dennison, 'The will of Pelham Humfrey', *Royal Musical Association Research Chronicle*, 7 (1969), 28–30 · Pepys, *Diary* · P. Holman, *Henry Purcell* (1995) · A. Ashbee and D. Lasocki, eds., *A biographical dictionary of English court musicians, 1485–1714*, 2 vols. (1998)

Humfrey, William (*c*.1515–1579), mining promoter and assayer, about whom nothing is known before 1560, was a central figure in the Elizabethan government's attempt to revitalize the country's mining and metallurgical industries. In 1560 Humfrey is known to have been a member of the Goldsmiths' Company and a resident of St Vedast's parish in the city of London. His involvement in national affairs owed much to the patronage of Sir William Cecil, with whom he corresponded regularly. Despite evidence to the contrary, Cecil continued to regard Humfrey as an expert on metallurgical matters and provided both financial backing and political support for his projects. In 1561 Humfrey was appointed assay master at the royal mint, where, in 1565, he was implicated in a robbery.

At the mint Humfrey came into contact with the German technologists who had been recruited to assist the recoinage. Both Humfrey and Cecil were convinced of the superiority of German metallurgical techniques, which they believed could be imported to develop new industries in England. In accordance with this policy, two joint-stock companies were incorporated under royal charter in 1568. The Mines Royal Company, which mined copper at Keswick, was financed by Augsburg bankers and operated by German technologists. The Company of Mineral and Battery Works, however, owed its origins to Humfrey's initiative in recruiting the Saxon, Christopher Schütz, to develop brass manufacture and battery in England. The company took over the patents that Humfrey and Schütz had obtained in 1565 covering the manufacture of brass, brass and iron wire, battery (the hammering of metal into plates and utensils), and the introduction of new mining and smelting technology.

Attempts to use German technology to stimulate English industries in this fashion failed. Although deposits of calamine (zinc ore) were discovered in Somerset, Schütz was unable to manufacture brass from English copper and zinc ores. Battery manufacture was similarly abandoned

and the iron-wire mills erected at Tintern struggled to survive. In 1569 Humfrey, smarting from the company's criticism of his extravagant lifestyle at Tintern, leased back part of his original patents and turned his attention to the expanding lead industry.

About 1570 Humfrey and Schütz built a water-powered lead-smelting furnace at Beauchief, near Sheffield, and also introduced a German sieve for processing ore on the Derbyshire mines. Humfrey hoped to persuade the local smelters to adopt his new furnace under licence, but most preferred to retain their traditional wind-powered smelting boles. In response to Humfrey's initiative George Talbot, sixth earl of Shrewsbury, invited smelters from Somerset to erect a Mendip-ore hearth furnace in his park at Chatsworth. Humfrey complained to Burghley that this new furnace, which used foot-powered bellows, infringed his patent. Between 1581 and 1584 the court of exchequer set up four commissions to investigate this complaint and subsequent allegations.

Humfrey's furnace did make lead successfully, but only after he replaced his German workmen with a Mendip smelter. The water-powered smelting mill, as it came to be called, rapidly ousted both traditional boles and footblasts. Despite assistance from Burghley, Humfrey could stop neither the widespread adoption of the smelting mill by the local gentry nor the unlicensed use of his sieve by the miners. The new furnace consumed only half as much fuel as the bole and was far more convenient to operate. It enabled the industry to expand dramatically after 1570 when lead became a major export commodity. Humfrey did not live to see this development or the eventual failure of his patent action. When he died he had already lost interest in Derbyshire and had embarked upon a silver-mining project in Cardiganshire. Humfrey died intestate in July 1579 leaving a wife, Alice, and two daughters. Elizabeth, the elder daughter, married Robert Ledger, a merchant tailor, at St Vedast's on 30 July 1570; Alice, the younger, married Alexander Fownde, an embroiderer.   DAVID KIERNAN

Sources M. B. Donald, *Elizabethan monopolies: the history of the Company of Mineral and Battery Works from 1565 to 1604* (1961) · D. Kiernan, *The Derbyshire lead industry in the sixteenth century* (1989) · W. Rees, *Industry before the industrial revolution*, 2 vols. (1968) · H. Hamilton, *The English brass and copper industries to 1800* (1926) · J. W. Gough, *The rise of the entrepreneur* (1969) · R. Burt, 'The international diffusion of technology during the early modern period: the case of the British non-ferrous mining industry', *Economic History Review*, 2nd ser., 44 (1991), 249–71

Archives PRO, state papers | BL, Lansdowne MSS

Humphery, George Edward Woods (1892–1963), airline executive, was born at 16 St Donatt's Road, Greenwich, on 13 November 1892, the son of George Richard Humphery, tank maker's storekeeper, and his wife, Anne Frances Elizabeth Woods. He was apprenticed to the shipbuilders Yarrow and qualified as a marine engineer. With the outbreak of the First World War he joined the Royal Flying Corps, ending the conflict as a major in the Royal Air Force. He was made an OBE in 1918.

After the war Woods Humphrey became manager of the Handley-Page transport company, which began commercial air services between London and Paris in August 1919. Under pressure from subsidized French airlines Handley-Page was forced to suspend operations in 1921 and Woods Humphrey moved to Daimler Airways. Despite the introduction of British subsidies, Daimler fared little better, and in 1924, following the recommendation of the Hambling committee, the airline was merged with three other British carriers to form Imperial Airways Ltd. Woods Humphrey was appointed general manager of the new company.

Although it received a state subsidy, Imperial Airways was a privately owned airline, and was eventually expected to be self-supporting. In order to gain investors the company needed to be profitable, and Woods Humphrey believed that the best chance of achieving this lay in the operation of long-range empire routes rather than the European services, where competition from foreign airlines, and surface transport, was more intense. Under his management Imperial Airways developed services from the late 1920s onwards to India, Australia, and South Africa, with Cairo as the main junction. Because of the limited range of transport aircraft at this time, these services were operated in short stages between isolated air strips, and were frequently hampered by lack of foreign landing rights. Woods Humphrey, who joined the airline's board in 1929, devoted much of his time, and skill as a negotiator, to the task of gaining better routes for the company.

By the mid-1930s Imperial Airways had the longest network in the world, although its chief cargo was not passengers, but mail. This emphasis culminated in the empire air mail scheme which was introduced from 1937. To facilitate the scheme the Short 'C' Class Empire flying boats were brought into service at the same time. These memorable aircraft offered new standards of comfort, but in general the attachment to flying boats, and loyalty to the British aircraft industry, ensured that Imperial Airways' fleet was technically outclassed by the latest American and German landplanes. In 1938 the report of the civil aviation inquiry chaired by John Cadman was critical of both Imperial Airways and Woods Humphrey, who was accused of taking an excessively commercial view of his responsibilities. As a result of the inquiry, Sir John Reith was persuaded to become chairman of the company and he brought with him a more public-service style of management. Woods Humphrey's place in the airline he had done so much to create became untenable and he resigned in the summer of 1938.

During his fourteen years at Imperial Airways, Woods Humphrey presided over the expansion of its network from 1500 to nearly 25,000 miles. He also made the airline profitable, although it continued to receive a government subsidy—another source of criticism at the time of the Cadman committee. In retrospect Woods Humphrey was a victim of the confusion over policy that characterized British civil aviation, and the unresolved question of whether the nation's flag-carrier was to be run as a commercial enterprise or give priority to the maintenance of national prestige.

An energetic businessman, Woods Humphrey maintained a lifelong interest in aviation; he was also a keen yachtsman, and belonged to the Royal Thames and New York yacht clubs. He was married twice; of his first wife, nothing is known. On 14 December 1929, as a widower, he married Dorothy Josephine, daughter of Colonel Philip Joseph Paterson. The couple had two daughters and one son.

After leaving Imperial Airways, Woods Humphrey moved to the United States. With the outbreak of the Second World War he helped establish the vital Atlantic aircraft ferry service from Canada, but was later forced out of this position. He became a director of Flight Refuelling, a company originally founded by Alan Cobham; and also served on the board of the De Haviland Aircraft Company Ltd. After the war Woods Humphrey remained in the United States, and joined Hubert Scott-Payne in a motorboat enterprise.

Woods Humphrey died of cancer on 25 January 1963 at St Bartholomew's Hospital, Smithfield, London. He was survived by his wife.   PETER J. LYTH

Sources *The Times* (26 Jan 1963) · *The Times* (30 Jan 1963) · 'Report of the committee on the development of civil aviation', *Parl. papers* (1937–8), 8.675, Cmd 5685 · R. Higham, *Britain's imperial air routes, 1918 to 1939* (1960) · *The Hambling Report: report on government financial assistance to civil air transport companies*, Cmd 1811 (1923) · A. J. Quin-Harkin, 'Imperial Airways, 1924–40', *Journal of Transport History*, 1 (1953–4), 197–215 · R. Higham, 'Woods-Humphery, George Edward', *DBB* · b. cert. · m. cert. · d. cert.

Humphrey. *See also* Humfrey, Humphery, Humphry.

Humphrey [Humfrey or Humphrey of Lancaster], **duke of Gloucester** [*called* Good Duke Humphrey] (**1390–1447**), prince, soldier, and literary patron, was the youngest son of Henry, earl of Derby, later *Henry IV, and his first wife, Mary de Bohun (d. 1394). He was protector of England during Henry VI's minority and the first English patron of Italian humanism.

Early years Humphrey was born in the autumn of 1390 while his father was on crusade in Prussia and was raised, along with his elder brothers, in noble households; there is no evidence that he attended Oxford University. His father's seizure of the throne in 1399 determined his early career: he was knighted on 11 October and made a knight of the Garter in 1400. But whereas over the next twelve years his three elder brothers were given important military commands, he had no public employment and remained with his father. Not until Henry V's accession did he receive title or endowment, being appointed chamberlain of England (7 May 1413), duke of Gloucester and earl of Pembroke for life (16 May 1414), with the castle and lordship of Pembroke in tail (20 July 1413).

Military career Gloucester served with a large contingent on the expedition to Harfleur in 1415, and later fought at Agincourt where he was wounded; his life was saved by Henry V in person. On his return he took a steadily more prominent role in affairs of state, being appointed constable of Dover and warden of the Cinque Ports, and chief justice of the forest south of Trent; he also received grants of the Barton in Bristol, the Isle of Wight, and the lordship of Llansteffan. In April 1416 he met and welcomed the emperor Sigismund on his visit to England and at the conference of Henry V, Sigismund, and John the Fearless, duke of Burgundy, at Calais in September and October he became hostage for Duke John's safety. He participated in the conquest of Normandy in 1417 and 1418, and at the age of twenty-seven received his first independent command when, following the surrender of Falaise in February 1418, he was appointed lieutenant and captain-general in the marches of Normandy for the reduction of the Cotentin. He took the surrender of St Lô, Carentan, and Valognes prior to a five-month siege of Cherbourg of which he provided a long description, emphasizing his own resourcefulness and resilience, for the *Vita Henrici quinti* by Tito Livio dei Frulovisi, which he later commissioned. He rejoined Henry V for the siege of Rouen, positioning himself at the Porte St Hilaire. He remained in France during most of 1419: he captured Ivry in May, was present at the Meulan negotiations, and joined the advance towards Paris on the south bank of the Seine, where in November he captured the bridge at Poissy. By the end of the year he had returned to England to replace Bedford as keeper of the realm. As such he held the parliament in December 1420 which ratified the treaty of Troyes while expressing its desire for the king's return. During Henry's presence in England from February to June 1421 Gloucester acted as overseer at the queen's coronation; he returned with the king to France as second in command. He later complained that, since his retinue of 400 men was slightly under strength on sailing, he was not paid wages until it had been mustered in full at the siege of Dreux in July and August. It is not clear whether he accompanied Henry V in the Loire campaign, but in October he was sent to assist Suffolk to repel a dauphinist attack in the Cotentin and recover Avranches. He is not recorded as present at the siege of Meaux and by 22 March 1422 he had returned to England to enable Bedford to accompany Queen Catherine to France in May.

Although Gloucester had held important commands and offices, the limits of his initiative had been closely circumscribed. Only in 1418 was he given an independent command, and his military reputation never attained that of either Clarence or Exeter. Nor, despite almost three years in France, had he been granted any fief there. At home his responsibilities as *custos* (keeper of the realm) were restricted by a flow of orders from the king and the presence of experienced councillors. How Henry V envisaged Gloucester's future role is unclear, although he certainly considered marrying him to *Jacqueline of Hainault who had sought asylum in England after her flight from her husband, John (IV), duke of Brabant, early in 1421.

As protector Henry V's death in August 1422 gave Gloucester the opportunity to shape his own destiny in at least two spheres. In a codicil to his will Henry had bestowed on

him the *tutelam et defensionem nostri filii carissimi principales* ('principal tutelage and protection of our dearest son'; Strong and Strong, 99). Initially the council may have accepted this, but when Gloucester interpreted *tutela* as conferring under Roman law the governance of the kingdom accountable solely to the child monarch, he faced determined opposition from both Bedford and the council, and had to accept merely a pre-eminence in council with the title of protector and defender. Despite being accorded a salary of 8000 marks, Gloucester understandably resented being denied the regency which he believed his brother had intended for him. Gloucester did not withdraw from the council; on the contrary, he is recorded at more sessions in the first two years of the reign than anyone except the officers of state. Yet as the council defined its working procedures—requiring majority decisions, corporate responsibility, and the declaration of vested interests—and as the older and abler Bishop Beaufort built up a following among the regular councillors, Gloucester saw his influence diminish and his natural leadership increasingly usurped.

Gloucester also began to cast his sights wider. By the end of January 1423 he had married Jacqueline, preparing to help her recover Holland and Zeeland from her uncle John of Bavaria, and Hainault from her estranged husband, John of Brabant. Both these could count on support from Philip the Good, duke of Burgundy, who aimed to incorporate these territories into a wider Low Countries state and resisted the intrusion of English interests. Gloucester's plans thus jeopardized the Anglo-Burgundian alliance on which the treaty of Troyes and the English rule in Paris rested, and alarmed both Bedford and Beaufort. None the less Duke Humphrey and Jacqueline landed with a small army at Calais on 18 October 1424; by mid-December much of Hainault was in their hands and they set up their government at Mons. Philip now prepared to support John of Brabant, and by March 1425 he had advanced far into Hainault and challenged Gloucester to single combat. On the grounds of preparing for this duel Gloucester withdrew to England, leaving Jacqueline in Mons. Unable to resist the Burgundian advance she surrendered to Philip and a decision on her marital status was referred to the pope. In September she escaped and briefly revived her cause in Holland, to which an English expedition under Lord Fitzwalter was sent in January 1426. This was repulsed and, without further assistance from Gloucester, Jacqueline was forced to concede defeat.

On his return to England in March 1425 Gloucester played on popular anti-Flemish feeling in London and won support from mercantile interests concerned to protect the market for English cloth in Holland and Zeeland. The council agreed to lend him 20,000 marks over four years to renew his venture though parliament refused taxation. Throughout the summer there was a mounting confrontation with Bishop Beaufort, as chancellor, who had always cultivated friendship with Burgundy. Gloucester construed this as a challenge to his authority as protector, and on 30 October 1425 his attempt to remove the infant Henry VI from Eltham was barred by Beaufort's soldiers on London Bridge. A stand-off was agreed but Beaufort appealed to Bedford to return and take control. Bedford's arrival in January 1426 suspended Gloucester's authority as protector and Gloucester, having declined to accept Bedford's mediation at a council at Northampton, was ordered to attend parliament at Leicester on 18 February. The settlement imposed by Bedford and the lords involved Beaufort's resignation as chancellor and his formal readmission to Gloucester's goodwill, though Gloucester retracted none of his complaints. Although he had successfully removed Beaufort from the council, he was still subordinate to Bedford while the latter remained in England. Moreover the regulations of 1422–4, which underpinned the council's corporate authority, were now re-enacted and the council's members, hearing that Gloucester had declared 'lat my brother governe as hym lust whiles he is in this land, for after his going overe into France I wol governe as me semeth good', required first Bedford and then Gloucester to acknowledge that the execution of royal authority 'stondeth in his lordes assembled in parliament … and in especiale in the lordes of his conseil and resteth not in oon singular persone but in all my said lordes togider' (*Proceedings … of the Privy Council*, 3.231–42). Even so, Gloucester sought to reopen the question of his power as protector in the parliament of 1427–8, refusing to attend until this had been defined. The council, unwilling to be intimidated, recalled him to the settlement of 1422–3 and declined to extend his authority. Concurrently a last appeal from Jacqueline, now widowed by the death of John of Brabant, led the council to offer Gloucester 5000 marks for her assistance, but Bedford swiftly countered this by negotiations with Philip of Burgundy, and on 9 January 1428 a papal verdict affirmed the validity of Jacqueline's earlier marriage to John of Brabant. To pursue his claims Gloucester would have had to remarry her; instead he used his freedom to marry his mistress, Eleanor Cobham [see Eleanor, duchess of Gloucester].

Gloucester's projects in these years had been largely peripheral to the council's preoccupation with financing the war in France. But he was at one with the council in resisting the papal pressure on Archbishop Chichele for the repeal of the Statute of Provisors, and was equally lukewarm about the commission to his rival, Cardinal Beaufort, to raise men and money for a crusade against the Hussites. He did not welcome Beaufort's return to England late in 1428 for this purpose, and in April 1429 raised the question of whether, as cardinal, Beaufort could legally retain the see of Winchester and whether he could be prosecuted under the Statute of Praemunire for obtaining privileges from the Holy See without licence. Although the council deferred any judgment on this, the vulnerability of Beaufort's position had been exposed.

Campaign against Beaufort For the moment the gravity of the military situation in France concentrated the council's efforts on sending a relief expedition and planning a larger force to accompany the king to his coronation in Paris. In the organization of this Beaufort played a prominent and essential role, which increased his influence

with the young king during the two years he remained in France. Henry VI's coronation at Westminster in November 1429 had formally terminated Gloucester's status as protector and he was appointed the king's lieutenant and keeper of England when Henry VI departed in April 1430. However his authority was exercised subject to the assent of the council, the members of which he could not remove. These constraints limited his functions as lieutenant to the suppression of disorders. As protector he had brought to an end the depredations of a notorious gang in Hampshire led by William Wawe in May 1427, and had followed this with sessions held at Norwich in June 1427 and at Chester in September. When, as lieutenant in April 1431, Gloucester was faced with the widespread if poorly organized conspiracy of artisan Lollards intent on an ambitious programme of social and political revolution, commencing with an attack on the abbey of Abingdon, he reacted swiftly. The conspirators, headed by William Perkins under the pseudonym of Jack Sharpe, were hunted down and executed, and widespread commissions of investigation were issued. Gloucester received much credit for his actions. He had also secured some valuable grants. Following the death of Exeter in 1427 he acquired the manor of Greenwich and finally secured custody of the earl of March's lands. Nevertheless the king's absence abroad had marginalized rather than extended his influence and he seized on Henry VI's return to stage a coup against Beaufort and his followers designed to maintain his position. In November 1431 he revived the charges against the cardinal raised in 1429 and persuaded the council to issue writs of *praemunire* following the king's return on 9 February 1432. Already on 6 February Gloucester had impounded the cardinal's treasure, which was being shipped secretly to the continent, and on 25 February Beaufort's supporters were removed from the principal offices of state and household. Beaufort thus faced political and financial ruin. But in his determination to remove his rival Gloucester had overplayed his hand. If the cardinal had been planning to develop his career abroad, he was now forced to return and defend his position, along with his supporters on the council.

Gloucester planned to charge Beaufort with treason, though on what grounds is not clear. He represented himself as the upholder of conciliar authority and defender of the law and the state, and he initiated proceedings in the exchequer against Beaufort's illegal attempt to export his treasure. In the event, after prolonged deliberations, the charges of treason and *praemunire* were dropped and Beaufort's treasure was restored under bond. These decisions reflected the unwillingness of the Lords and Commons to exacerbate divisions and their dependence on Beaufort's loans to finance the war. Although Gloucester had failed to ruin his rival and drive him into exile, the cardinal and his followers for the moment lost their position at the political centre. For the following year, until the middle of 1433, Gloucester and his supporters controlled policy and patronage. In the end their inability to finance the reinforcements needed in France provoked Bedford's return to England with Beaufort in his train.

As in 1426–7, so in 1433–4, Bedford displaced Gloucester as head of the council, and was accorded authority as viceregent to appoint and dismiss councillors and officers of state. He brought back Lord Cromwell, removed by Gloucester in 1432, as treasurer, to revitalize royal finance in preparation for a new offensive in France. Gloucester now turned his resentment against Bedford. At a meeting of the great council in April and May 1434 before Bedford's departure for France he submitted a memorandum highly critical of Bedford's conduct of the war which Bedford took to impugn his honour. Bedford's response deepened the quarrel which the king took into his own hand and suppressed. Gloucester had offered to lead a large army to France, claiming that a bold offensive and decisive victory would eliminate the need for continual taxation for the piecemeal defence of Normandy. In an effort to widen his support Gloucester seems to have publicized this proposal, which had a specious attraction for an impoverished country; for the knights and esquires on the council declared that they had challenged Gloucester to say how the cost of this army, some £50,000, could be met, but had had no answer (*Proceedings … of the Privy Council*, 4.210–16). A later statement by the duke indicates that he had in mind the confiscation of Beaufort's wealth, half of which the crown held on loan and under bond, while the verdict on his smuggling in 1432 remained in suspense. Gloucester's plan to confiscate Beaufort's treasure to finance his own military venture stood little chance of acceptance, and its only result was to alienate Bedford and strengthen his support for Beaufort in the remaining year of his life. With his rival reinstated in the council Gloucester seems to have withdrawn, and it is possible that instead he sought to influence the young king. For on 12 November 1434 the whole council apart from Gloucester took the extraordinary step of riding to Cirencester and solemnly admonishing Henry VI to listen to no 'motions and sturinges' such as had recently been made to him by other parties in matters touching his noble person or estate and the rule and governance of the council (*Proceedings … of the Privy Council*, 4.287–9).

In 1435 the last heroic effort of Bedford to give credibility to Lancastrian rule in France collapsed. At the Congress of Arras (August–September 1435) Burgundy repudiated the treaty of Troyes, in September Bedford died, and there were risings in the Pays de Caux. Gloucester was now heir apparent to Henry VI and his claims to leadership in war and council could not be gainsaid. His long-standing distrust of Burgundy had been vindicated and his advocacy of offensive warfare was winning acceptance. For the moment however his attention was focused on Calais and Flanders rather than Normandy. In November 1435 Gloucester had succeeded Bedford as captain of Calais and in July 1436 Henry VI conferred on him the title of count of Flanders. By March 1436 Duke Philip was known to be preparing to besiege Calais and a general summons to arms was issued to mount what was advertised as a royal expedition under Gloucester's command for its relief. By the end of July a force of some 7500 men had assembled at Dover. But on 28 July a foray by the garrison of Calais

under Edmund Beaufort had seized a bastille held by the men of Ghent, throwing the besieging army into confusion and forcing a Burgundian withdrawal. Gloucester arrived on 2 August to find the siege lifted. He conducted a *chevauchée* into Flanders for three weeks which, though destructive, had little military value and never encountered Duke Philip's army. On his return to England his 'triumph' over the Flemings was celebrated in popular verses, perhaps commissioned from Lydgate, and by the production of a poem in Latin hexameters by his secretary Tito Livio, which portrayed Gloucester as the worthy successor to Henry V.

The ending of Henry VI's minority in 1436–7 did nothing to strengthen Gloucester's position. Although he occasionally attended council and received some small grants of land, he exercised little influence over policy. Cardinal Beaufort's pursuit of a negotiated peace with Charles VII was more congenial to Henry VI than Gloucester's advocacy of war. But by 1439 Gloucester had become the avowed opponent of the negotiations being conducted at Gravelines by Beaufort and the duchess of Burgundy, and of the proposal to release the duke of Orléans to act as mediator with Charles VII in the peace process. The final terms for a perpetual truce transmitted by Beaufort to the English council in August 1439 were opposed by Gloucester and proved unacceptable to the council. Their rejection marked the failure of the cardinal's diplomacy and vindicated Gloucester's opposition. It provided the opportunity for his most comprehensive indictment of his rival's career and policy. Gloucester's charges were probably presented in the parliament at Reading early in 1440 (Stevenson, 2.440–51). Their avowed purpose was to remove Beaufort and Kemp from the council and perhaps allow an impeachment of Beaufort to be framed. But no action was taken on them and there is no evidence that the cardinal was asked or permitted to make a response. Gloucester's attack was stifled; nor did it prevent the release of Orléans. Though treated as a tiresome irrelevance, his criticism was sufficiently damaging to assist the displacement of Beaufort's influence by that of Wiliam de la Pole, earl of Suffolk, as the king attained his majority. Gloucester's accusations stretched back to the time of Henry V and encompassed all his old quarrels and charges, being intended to reveal Beaufort as having undermined rather than upheld the royal estate, and to have been moved not by patriotism but by pride, nepotism, and greed. He accused Beaufort of embezzlement and fraud, of usury and profiteering, of ambition and presumption, of estranging himself and others from the king and diminishing the rights of the crown. He had watched the cardinal carefully and forgotten nothing, but there were no fresh grounds on which a criminal charge or judgment could be made and the cardinal, if not his reputation, emerged unscathed.

These personal accusations were part of a wider challenge to the cardinal's policy. First Gloucester placed on record his objections to the release of the duke of Orléans in June 1440 as a means of furthering peace negotiations with Charles VII by either persuasion or pressure.

Gloucester argued that the reverse was likelier: once released Orléans would join with Charles to expel the English. He recalled that Henry V had forbidden the release of Orléans, now proposed without compensation or exchange. In the event Orléans proved to have little influence over Charles VII and his release had little consequence. Second Gloucester, still holding to an aggressive policy in Normandy, proposed himself for the post of lieutenant-general in France in succession to Warwick. In January 1440 Cardinal Beaufort's nephew, John Beaufort, earl of Somerset, was given a short-term appointment pending Gloucester's arrival. In fact Gloucester withdrew, but it was York, not Somerset, who was appointed in June, frustrating the Beauforts' expectations.

Retirement and death The last of Gloucester's attacks on his rival, though it helped to push Beaufort into retirement, had brought no advantage to himself. The beneficiary was the earl of Suffolk whose influence at court and over the king enabled him to direct policy for the rest of the decade. Yet Gloucester remained heir presumptive to a pliable and unmarried king and the possibility of his succession could never be neglected. It was present in the mind of his ambitious and masterful wife, Eleanor Cobham, whom he had married around 1428. From April 1440, if not before, she had consulted astrologers on the likelihood of the king's demise and these had predicted his severe illness in the summer or autumn of 1441. Her arrest in 1441 and trial for treasonable necromancy resulted in a public penance, her compulsory divorce, and perpetual imprisonment. Although Gloucester was not himself implicated, he was now discredited and distrusted by the king, and his position as heir apparent was fatally prejudiced. His vulnerability had been publicly demonstrated and from 1442 the lands and offices he held from the crown began to be granted in reversion after his death to courtiers with their eyes on his wealth.

Gloucester had been effectively forced into retirement and, though he appeared occasionally in council, took no part in the debates on Somerset's expedition of 1443 or in the discussion of Suffolk's mission to France in 1444 to negotiate a peace and royal marriage. He lent support to the commendation of Suffolk by the Commons in the parliament of June 1445, but his opposition to the peace negotiations in August 1445 was known well enough for Suffolk to assure the French ambassadors that he counted for nothing and to humiliate him publicly in the king's presence. It was only as the prospect of a final peace evaporated and the fateful undertaking to surrender Le Mans became known towards the end of 1446 that his time-honoured opposition to the French seemed once again to be vindicated. The possibility that he might become the figurehead for the embittered war veterans and for the increasing number of Suffolk's enemies proved his eventual undoing. A parliament summoned to meet at Bury St Edmunds in February 1447, in Suffolk's heartland, provided the occasion to silence him. Arriving on 18 February with a strong contingent of Welsh retainers, he was commanded to proceed to lodgings in St Saviour's Hospital. There, after dinner, he was arrested. If it was proposed to charge him with treason, his death on 23 February made this unnecessary. Probably this followed a stroke, for he was said to have lain unconscious for three days; but the circumstances of his death provided the basis for accusations of murder which by 1450 were openly voiced by Cade's rebels and in popular verse. In 1455 a petition formally declaring him to have been a loyal subject was presented by the Commons in the parliament which followed the duke of York's victory at St Albans. The epithet of the 'Good Duke' became attached to his name in recognition of his fidelity to the memory of Henry V and as a victim of Suffolk's regime. His body was taken to St Albans, to which he had been a frequent visitor and a special benefactor and where his tomb had already been constructed near the shrine of the saint; he was buried there on 4 March. Many of his retinue were arrested and convicted of treasonable conspiracy, including his illegitimate son Arthur. Though condemned they were spared execution at the last moment. His wife died in imprisonment at Beaumaris in 1452. Gloucester was stated to have died intestate and his goods were dispersed, but there is evidence that his will was being administered by 1449, though its terms remain unknown. His titles were extinguished and his lands reverted to the crown. The only authentic likeness of Gloucester is in an Arras manuscript.

Gloucester assessed Gloucester was a complex personality whom neither his own nor subsequent generations have found easy to assess. Judged by the dominant military and political standards of his age his failure was the more humiliating because he himself subscribed to them. He wanted others to acknowledge the military genius and boldness that he claimed for himself in his accounts of the Cotentin campaign and the ravaging of Flanders. Yet he lacked not only the incisive mind and steely determination of his hero, Henry V, but the bravado of Clarence and the cautious competence of Bedford. Their different qualities drew men to their service, but Gloucester never commanded a personal following among the professional captains who sustained Lancastrian Normandy. Both his advocacy of a major expedition to Normandy and his offer to lead it commanded little enthusiasm. His arguments might convince but his personality did not. Likewise his chivalric pretensions, though accepted by Waurin, proved hollow. Farce attended his duel with Philip of Burgundy, ignominy his abandonment of Jacqueline, and futility his relief of Calais. The verdict of Pius II, that he was more given to pleasure and letters than to arms, and valued his life more than his honour, was not unwarranted.

Nor did Gloucester win greater recognition as a political leader. Though entitled to pre-eminence in council, his leadership was confined to periods when his rivals were outside England. Within the council he attracted support only from those like Berkeley, Huntingdon, Norfolk, Scrope, and perhaps York, who were excluded from the Beaufort connection. Against Beaufort his enmity was too openly displayed and pursued with insufficient patience and guile. By his personal attacks he convicted himself as factious. As in military strategy, he argued for alternative policies articulately and with plausibility. In claiming the regency in 1422 and 1428, in prosecuting Beaufort between 1429 and 1432, in arguing against the peace terms and the release of Orléans from 1438 to 1440 and in denouncing Beaufort's record in 1440 he often had the better—and the better argued—case. Moreover there are indications that he was able and prepared to appeal to an audience beyond the council: to the Commons in parliament in 1422–3, to Londoners in 1425, to the soldiers and taxpayers in 1434, to the wider political nation over the release of Orléans. It was his ability to create a favourable public image—as the upholder of law and order, the hammer of heretics, the heir of Henry V, the enemy of Burgundy, the protector of St Albans, the patron of Oxford—that provided his most potent weapon. Even his wife's disgrace did not destroy that; in 1447 Suffolk had good reason to fear him as the excluded counsellor, critic, and heir. This ability to win—if also at times to alienate—public support distinguishes Gloucester from other peers, and may have contributed to their distrust of him, though the means by which he sustained his image are not wholly discernible.

Literary patronage Lydgate's pen served Duke Humphrey at a number of levels: in occasional verses to celebrate his marriage in 1423 and perhaps his victory over the Flemings in 1436; in the sustained didactic moralizing of *The Fall of Princes*, and perhaps in promoting the far livelier polemic of *The Libel of English Policy*. His chivalric reputation brought him the dedication of Nicholas Upton's *De studio militari*, and his defence of the church that of Capgrave's *Commentary on Genesis*. It is clear that Duke Humphrey's patronage served to promote his military and political image, but, as Lydgate attests, he was genuinely attracted to the company of clerks and men of letters, eager to read, discuss, and encourage their writings. The miniature court which he and Eleanor held at their Greenwich manor, La Plesaunce, numbered poets, astrologers, physicians, musicians, and men of learning. Nor were these merely accoutrements of his princely state. Gloucester was an intrusive, demanding, and opinionated patron, his personal involvement surpassing his princely munificence. All this—the military and political pretensions, the public image, the personal input—is relevant in assessing his most distinctive achievement, the fostering of Italian humanism in England.

Duke Humphrey's interest in Italian humanism derived largely from his friendship with the papal collectors in England, Simone da Teramo and Piero da Monte, and from his friendship with Zanone di Castiglione, bishop of Bayeux. This was expressed in broadly three ways: the employment of humanists as secretaries, the commissioning and patronage of literary works, and the collection of a library of classical texts. Following Thomas Beckington (d. 1465), who revolutionized the style of English diplomatic writing, Gloucester's first Italian secretary was Tito Livio dei Frulovisi who was in his service as 'poet and orator' from 1436 to 1438 and was followed by Antonio Beccaria from 1439 to 1446. Gloucester commissioned Livio to write a *Vita Henrici quinti* which 'inaugurated an

approach to historical writing hitherto unknown in this country' (Weiss, 'Humphrey … and Tito Livio Frulovisi'), and followed this by a much less successful poem in Latin hexameters, the *Humfroidos*, which celebrated the duke's expedition to Calais and Flanders and presented him as his brother's successor in defending England against its French and Burgundian enemies. For both works Duke Humphrey supplied much information. Over the more distant humanists to whom he extended his patronage he had less influence. Attracted by Leonardo Bruni's translation, *Ethics*, from Aristotle, Gloucester in 1433–4 invited him to England and asked him to undertake further translation. Bruni declined the journey but had completed and dispatched *Politics* three years later. It was through Castiglione that Pier Candido Decembrio came to Gloucester's notice, dedicating to the duke his translation, the *Republic*, in 1438, and eventually following this in 1443 with a sumptuous copy in an Italian hand furnished with a dedication of lavish praise for his learning. Decembrio became Duke Humphrey's principal agent for collecting classical texts; he responded to the duke's requests and pointed out the gaps in his library. Nevertheless both Bruni and Decembrio were disappointed in the meagreness of the rewards they received; the duke displayed even less liberality to his Italian than to his native authors, but he remained in their eyes an important patron. There is no doubt that Humphrey delighted in the acquisition of classical texts: his library contained the newly discovered *Epistolae familiares* of Cicero, all the works of Livy, books of Caesar, Suetonius, and Pliny, and translations of Plato, Aristotle, and Plutarch. It also contained numerous writings of the humanists themselves: of Bruni, Boccaccio, Decembrio, Petrarch, Poggio, and Salutati along with works on medicine and astrology. Gloucester's intellectual bent was essentially lay: towards political philosophy, war, history, and the sciences, rather than theological and devotional works. His importance lies in being the first to patronize the Italian humanists and consciously to collect a library of classical texts. His reputation was underpinned by his gift of the major part of his library to the University of Oxford in two instalments, the first of 129 books in 1439, the second of 134 books in 1444. The university was promised that the residue was to come to it on his death, but, like his other effects, his books were seized by the crown and given to the king's new foundation in Cambridge. Nevertheless the collection was not merely—as the university said—the largest benefaction of its kind but provided the basis for the development of classical studies in the following century. The oldest part of the Bodleian Library is still called Duke Humfrey's Library (preserving the older spelling of his name).

The authenticity of Gloucester's 'humanism' has often been questioned. He certainly knew no Greek and could not write the Latin of the humanists. It is not even known how easily he read it, for he preferred his Latin classics in French translations and all his annotations of his own books are in French. There is little to indicate how far he even understood the aims and outlook of the humanists. Their praise of his learning and discernment, like his own declarations of enthusiasm for their work, were designed to foster the humanists' self-proclaimed 'belief that their art and it alone could confer honour and immortality' on their patrons (Weiss, *Humanism*, 40). Gloucester's ardent desire for both, unsatisfied in war and politics, found a measure of fulfilment here. Yet whatever the limitations of his learning and his concern to enhance his reputation, the catholicity of his reading indicates a measure of intellectual curiosity beyond that of his contemporaries.

G. L. HARRISS

Sources K. H. Vickers, *Humphrey duke of Gloucester: a biography* (1907) · GEC, *Peerage* · G. L. Harriss, *Cardinal Beaufort: a study of Lancastrian ascendancy and decline* (1989) · R. Weiss, *Humanism in England during the fifteenth century*, 2nd edn (1957) · N. H. Nicolas, ed., *Proceedings and ordinances of the privy council of England*, 7 vols., RC, 26 (1834–7) · *RotP*, vols. 4–5 · Chancery rolls: for reigns of Henry V and VI · R. A. Griffiths, *The reign of King Henry VI: the exercise of royal authority, 1422–1461* (1981) · J. Stevenson, ed., *Letters and papers illustrative of the wars of the English in France during the reign of Henry VI, king of England*, 2 vols. in 3 pts, Rolls Series, 22 (1861–4) · *Titi Livii Foro-Juliensis vita Henrici quinti*, ed. T. Hearne (1716) · R. Weiss, 'Humphrey duke of Gloucester and Tito Livio Frulovisi', *Fritz Saxl, 1890–1948: a volume of memorial essays from his friends in England*, ed. D. J. Gordon (1957), 218–27 · P. Strong and F. Strong, 'The last will and codicils of Henry V', *EngHR*, 96 (1981), 79–102 · R. Vaughan, *Philip the Good: the apogee of Burgundy* (1970) · M. R. Thielemans, *Bourgogne et Angleterre: relations politiques et économiques entre les Pays-Bas bourguignons et l'Angleterre, 1435–1467* (Brussels, 1966) · J. A. Doig, 'A new source for the siege of Calais in 1436', *EngHR*, 110 (1995), 404–16 · M. Aston, 'Lollardy and sedition, 1381–1431', *Past and Present*, 17 (1960), 1–44 · *Hist. U. Oxf. 2: Late med. Oxf.* · [A. C. de la Mare and R. W. Hunt], eds., *Duke Humfrey and English humanism in the fifteenth century* (1970) [exhibition catalogue, Bodl. Oxf.] · *Duke Humfrey's Library and the divinity school, 1488–1988* (1988) [exhibition catalogue, Bodl. Oxf., June–Aug 1988] · H. Anstey, ed., *Epistolae academicae Oxon.*, 2 vols., OHS, 35–6 (1898) · G. A. Holmes, 'The Libel of English policy', *EngHR*, 76 (1961), 193–216 · D. Pearsall, *John Lydgate* (1970) · *Memorials of the reign of Henry VI: official correspondence of Thomas Bekynton, secretary to King Henry VI and bishop of Bath and Wells*, ed. G. Williams, 2 vols., Rolls Series, 56 (1872) · J. A. Giles, ed., *Incerti scriptoris chronicon Angliae de regnis trium regum Lancastrensium* (1848) · F. W. D. Brie, ed., *The Brut*, EETS, 2 (1908), 513 · R. A. Griffiths, 'Richard of York and the royal household in Wales', *Welsh History Review / Cylchgrawn Hanes Cymru*, 8 (1976), 14–25; repr. in R. A. Griffiths, *King and country: England and Wales in the fifteenth century* (1991), 265–76 · J. S. Davies, ed., *An English chronicle of the reigns of Richard II, Henry IV, Henry V, and Henry VI*, CS, 64 (1856), 116–18

Archives Bodl. Oxf.

Likenesses J. Le Boucq, crayon drawing, 1500–99 (after drawing), Bibliothèque Municipale d'Arras, France · double portrait, miniature (with his wife), BL, register of St Albans Abbey, Cotton MS Nero D. vii, fol. 154

Humphrey, Sir Andrew Henry (1921–1977), air force officer, was born in Edinburgh on 10 January 1921, the second of the three sons (there were no daughters) of John Humphrey CBE (1879–1956), of Karachi, an exchange broker, and his wife, Agnes Florence, the daughter of Colonel John Beatson-Bell, judge-advocate-general in India. He was educated at Belhaven preparatory school, Dunbar, and Bradfield College. In 1939 he entered the RAF College, Cranwell, from which he graduated in April 1940.

Posted to 266 (Spitfire) squadron, Humphrey flew on active operations in the battle of Britain; after a transfer to night-fighter work he was awarded the DFC in 1941. There followed operational experience on Hurricane fighter bombers with 175 squadron, following which he was transferred to the Middle East as a rocket attack instructor. In 1943 he was awarded the AFC, to which were added bars in 1945 and 1955.

Humphrey served in India, then undertook staff work at home at the headquarters of 106 group and survey work in Africa with 82 squadron. He was appointed OBE in 1951. During a tour as instructor at the RAF Flying College, Manby, he established in 1953 a new record for the Cape Town to London flight flying the twin jet Canberra bomber Aries IV. In 1954 he flew the same aircraft on the first RAF jet flight to the north pole.

Following a course at the RAF Staff College, Bracknell, Humphrey was posted to the Air Ministry, and in 1957 he became deputy director of operational requirements with particular responsibility for the introduction of the Lightning supersonic single-seater fighter. His flair for technical detail and his wide flying experience enabled him to make a major impact on operational efficiency and flight safety standards. For this work he was appointed CB (1959); it was an exceptional recognition for a group captain.

Humphrey commanded the large RAF station at Akrotiri, Cyprus, from 1959 to 1961 and in 1962 attended the Imperial Defence College; that same year he was promoted air commodore. He was then posted to the Ministry of Defence, and served from 1962 to 1965 in senior air planning appointments.

Humphrey's potential as a high flier was by this time well recognized by his seniors; promotion to air vice-marshal in 1965 and selection for appointment as air officer commanding, Middle East, with his headquarters at Aden, reflected their confidence. This tour was not easy: as the last air officer commanding, Humphrey was intimately concerned with the highly complex withdrawal plan for all British forces; he did well. He returned to the Ministry of Defence as air member for personnel in 1968 and was advanced to KCB in June that year, the acting rank of air marshal being confirmed in January 1969. There followed a tour as commander-in-chief strike command, during which he was promoted air chief marshal and created GCB (1974). He was air aide-de-camp to the queen in 1974–6.

The early belief in Humphrey's destiny reached ultimate fulfilment when he became chief of the air staff in April 1974 and then, after promotion to marshal of the Royal Air Force in August 1976, chief of the defence staff in October that year.

Humphrey loved flying and had a personal pride in his flying skill and a deep knowledge of the art. From the earliest days his colleagues and peers came to recognize the emerging human attributes which he had in abundance. An ability to listen, modesty, consideration for others, sensitivity, warmth, love of sport, infectious humour—all these facets developed in him with the years and none was diminished as his responsibilities increased. He had a capacity for dispassionate and unbiased analysis and he thought that the inter-service approach was vital. He was greatly concerned at the ever increasing build-up of Soviet forces, and he spoke and wrote fearlessly and frequently about this.

In March 1952 Humphrey married Agnes Stevenson Wright, a former flight officer in the WRAF and the younger daughter of James Wright, an architect, of Stirling. Agnes Humphrey endeared herself to all by her constant and painstaking care for the needs of service personnel and their families. There were no children. Humphrey died on 24 January 1977 at Princess Mary's RAF Hospital, Halton.   JOHN GRANDY, rev.

Sources Ministry of Defence, air historical branch · *The Times* (25 Jan 1977) · *The Times* (1 Feb 1977) · personal knowledge (1986) **Archives** FILM IWM FVA, documentary footage **Likenesses** J. Hughes-Hallett, oils, strike command headquarters, High Wycombe, officers' mess · M. McGregor, oils, College Hall, Cranwell **Wealth at death** £29,538: probate, 4 April 1977, *CGPLA Eng. & Wales*

Humphrey, Hannah (*c.*1745–1818). *See under* Humphrey, William (*b.* 1742?, *d.* in or before 1814).

Humphrey, Herbert Alfred (1868–1951), mechanical and chemical engineer, was born at Hope Cottage, Lismore Road, Gospel Oak, London, on 2 December 1868, the son of John Charles Humphrey, accountant to the Metropolitan Board of Works, and his wife, Louisa Frost. He was the third son and fifth child of a family of seven. He was educated at Cowper Street middle class school before entering Finsbury Technical College in 1883 under John Perry and W. E. Ayrton. Between 1885 and 1887 he attended the City and Guilds Central Institution in South Kensington, where he was one of the five original students. There he had the advantage of coming into close personal contact with those great teachers W. C. Unwin, W. E. Ayrton, H. E. Armstrong, and O. Henrici. He came top in the exams and John Perry described him 'as almost the best pupil I have ever had' (Humphrey MSS, A1a). To W. E. Ayrton, Humphrey wrote in 1897: 'I desire to prove that the College training, followed by close observation and the reading of current technical literature, will enable any student to cope with almost any work' (ibid., N4). He graduated ACGI (Associate of the City and Guilds of London Institution) in civil and mechanical engineering in 1887. From 1888 he worked for Heenan and Froude of Manchester and Birmingham, becoming manager of the Birmingham works, before joining Brunner Mond & Co. Ltd in 1890. Heenan wrote to Humphrey in 1891: 'I have always felt you would make a name for yourself in the engineering world' (ibid., A8). The founder of the firm, Ludwig Mond, immediately realized that he had found an engineer whose ability and freshness of outlook could be of the greatest use to the chemical industry in developing its many new processes. Humphrey's subsequent career proved this to be the case. For example he installed the first gas engine exceeding 400 hp in Britain. For the next eleven years Humphrey worked at Winnington in connection with Mond Gas Producers.

In 1901 Humphrey became a consulting engineer based in London. His experience with Mond Power Gas and with large gas engines had gained him a worldwide reputation which contributed to his success. It was during this period that he invented the Humphrey gas pump, which overcame many problems of earlier types. Four were installed at the Chingford Reservoir by the Metropolitan Water Board and at the official opening of the installation in 1913 Humphrey was able to explain them to George V. Humphrey pumps were patented in 1906 and the rights were sold to the United States for £100,000.

On the outbreak of war in 1914 Humphrey became technical adviser to the department of explosives supply which was part of the Ministry of Munitions. There he worked with Lord Moulton in ensuring the supply of ammonium nitrate for the making of explosives. Later, with the munitions inventions department he investigated the various known processes for the fixation of nitrogen. The department of explosives supply then intended to build a factory at Billingham where the German Haber process should be used. However, the war ended before construction work began and investigations on the continent were instigated. Humphrey was a member of a British chemical commission sent to look at the synthetic ammonia works at Oppau in May 1919. The commission met with great resistance, culminating in the theft of their report which had to be speedily rewritten.

Later in 1919 the Billingham site was acquired by Brunner Mond & Co. Ltd, who formed a company—Synthetic Ammonia and Nitrates Ltd—to develop the Oppau process. It followed naturally that Humphrey should be offered the posts of consulting engineer and director of the new firm. It was here that his great experience of engineers and their training was of value to the company. He was able to develop his ideas and train other engineers. He therefore played a great part in enabling British chemical engineering to surpass that of Germany and America.

Humphrey's reputation as a great consulting engineer, an innovative and tireless worker in the solving of problems, besides being an inspirational colleague, led to another position, that of consulting engineer to the whole company of Imperial Chemical Industries (ICI) on its formation in 1926. This position he held until his retirement in 1931. One of the most important projects with which he dealt during his latter years with ICI was the construction of the 40,000 kW electric power station at Billingham. It was probably his greatest achievement. It was well in advance of central station design at the time and began to supply power within twelve months of the construction work beginning.

Humphrey was a member of the institutions of civil, mechanical, and electrical engineers and a fellow and vice-president of the Institute of Fuel. He was elected the first fellow of the City and Guilds Institute in 1892 and was also one of the first six fellows of Imperial College in 1932. He read many papers on large gas engines and gas producer plants including an 'epoch making paper' (Humphrey MSS, B10) on the Humphrey gas pump before learned societies which gained for him the Willans, Telford, Watt, and

Constantine gold medals, the Paris premium of the Institution of Electrical Engineers, and the Melchett medal of the Institute of Fuel.

After the end of the Second World War Humphrey visited South Africa and decided to settle at Hermanus, Cape Province. There he, his wife, Mary Elizabeth Horniblow, and their three sons and two daughters became absorbed in the local community. Humphrey was able to indulge in his hobby of wood turning with power machines. He destroyed most of his papers in 1945, and died in South Africa on 9 March 1951. Their eldest son, John Herbert *Humphrey FRS (1915–1987), became deputy director of the National Institute for Medical Research in 1961.   R. E. SLADE, *rev.* ANNE BARRETT

Sources F. H. Bramwell, *The Central* [City and Guilds College] (June 1951), 18–20 • 'Herbert A. Humphrey', *Magazine of the Finsbury Technical College Old Students' Association* [Imperial College Archives] (1913), 173–4 • ICL, H. A. Humphrey MSS • F. H. Bramwell, 'Herbert Alfred Humphrey', *Institution of Mechanical Engineers: Proceedings*, 164 (1951), 463–4 • V. E. Parke, *Billingham: the first ten years* (1957) • personal knowledge (1971) • b. cert.
Archives ICL, corresp., drawings, and papers
Likenesses W. Hester, caricature, mechanical reproduction, NPG; repro. in *VF* (9 April 1913) • photograph, repro. in *The Central* [City and Guilds College], 6 (1909) • photograph, repro. in *The Central* [City and Guilds College] (June 1951)

Humphrey, John Herbert (1915–1987), immunologist and medical scientist, was born on 16 December 1915 in West Byfleet, Surrey, the eldest in the family of three sons and two daughters of Herbert Alfred *Humphrey (1868–1951), inventor and co-founder of Imperial Chemical Industries (ICI) at Billingham, co. Durham, and his wife, Mary Elizabeth Horniblow. He was educated at the International School, Lausanne, Switzerland, before attending Bramcote preparatory school in Yorkshire. Then followed a very formative period at Winchester College. From school he won a scholarship to Trinity College, Cambridge, where he read natural sciences in preparation for medicine. He graduated first class in both part one and part two of the natural sciences tripos (1936 and 1937). It was during this time that he became conscious of the evils and social injustices of his time, and such matters occupied him alongside his scientific career for the rest of his life.

In 1937 Humphrey enrolled at University College Hospital medical school, London (UCHMS), and qualified in medicine (MB, BChir), in 1940 after the start of the Second World War. In 1939 he married Janet Rumney, daughter of Professor Archibald Vivian *Hill CH FRS, Nobel laureate in physiology, and his wife, Margaret Neville, *née* Keynes. They had two sons and three daughters. Humphrey's first clinical appointment at the Royal Postgraduate Medical School (RPMS), Hammersmith, was soon interrupted when an attack of bronchitis was diagnosed as tuberculosis. After convalescence he spent a year (1941–2) as Jenner research fellow at the Lister Institute of Preventive Medicine, Stanmore, Middlesex, carrying out microbiological studies. As he was no longer eligible for service in the armed forces, he accepted in 1942 the post of assistant pathologist at the Central Middlesex Hospital (the chief pathologist having being imprisoned by the Japanese). Under these difficult conditions he still managed to publish ten papers on his hospital work.

After the war Humphrey was able to carry out his passionate wish to do full-time research related to clinical problems. In 1946 he obtained an external Medical Research Council appointment in microbiology at UCHMS to work on bacterial enzymes. He became an MD in 1947. In 1949 he joined the National Institute for Medical Research (NIMR) at Hampstead (later at Mill Hill) as a member of the scientific staff in the division of biological standards, which provided great opportunities for interdisciplinary research. By this time there was an urgent need to standardize biological substances such as antibiotics, and he developed novel techniques for the quantitative analysis of their biological activities. He also found time to initiate collaborations with other institute members on basic immunological problems, which remained a major focus of his life's work.

In 1957 Humphrey was invited to become head of a newly founded immunology department at NIMR, where he served as deputy director from 1961 until 1976, at which time he accepted the chair of immunology at the RPMS, Hammersmith. His official retirement from the chair was in 1981; however, he continued his advisory and immunological activities as emeritus professor at RPMS until his death in 1987. Over many years he became increasingly deaf due to bilateral acoustic neuroma, diagnosed only late with advances in technology. Regardless of a serious cardiac condition, he continued undeterred with all his work, travelling widely, writing, lecturing, encouraging students and colleagues, and providing liberal advice.

Humphrey was a tireless worker; he was interested in all aspects of basic and clinical immunology; his encyclopaedic memory enabled his research to touch on diverse problems, with particular focus on cell-mediated immunity as well as immunopathology. At the time almost nothing was known about the complex cellular interactions responsible for the different immune reactivities. He is best known for his studies with radio-labelled antibodies, the cascade of events in allergic or anaphylactic reactions, the role of complement components in lysing cells, events underlying local antibody/antigen reactions *in vivo* (for example the release of histamine and other substances by different cell types), and the fate of administered foreign molecules or pathogens in relation to the generation of immunity. He published more than 200 papers and several book chapters covering these studies. In 1963 he published a textbook (*Immunology for Students of Medicine*) with R. G. White; it made a great impact, presenting in a dynamic and exciting way the 'new' type of immunology in relation to clinical medicine. He was an important member of many national and international committees connected with the Royal Society, Medical Research Council, World Health Organization, and International Council of Scientific Unions. Most importantly, he exerted a profound influence on his many young associates attracted from all over the world and on the direction of immunological thinking. His enthusiasm for immunology was infectious and he was generous with novel ideas. He always made time for any colleagues or students who sought him out.

In addition to his busy scientific career and influence, Humphrey found time to pursue his passionate concern for many socio-political issues. He was a founder member of the Medical Association for the Prevention of War (1951) and the Medical Campaign against Nuclear Weapons (chairman in 1981 and president from 1985), president of the Society for the Protection of Science and Learning (from 1978), and a supporter of Pugwash (a group of international scientists dedicated to preventing nuclear war). He wrote a number of articles concerning the physicians' peace movement and co-authored, with J. Ziman and P. Sieghart, *The World of Science and the Rule of Law* (1986).

Elected a fellow of the Royal Society in 1963, Humphrey became an honorary member of the American Association of Immunologists in the same year. He was appointed CBE in 1970. He was a fellow of Winchester College (1965–78), the Institute of Biology (1968), and the Royal College of Physicians (1970), and was a foreign honorary member of the American Academy of Arts and Sciences (1981). He had honorary memberships of scientific societies in the Netherlands, Hungary, South Africa, Germany, and Czechoslovakia. He was elected a foreign associate member of the American National Academy of Sciences (1986) and an honorary fellow of Trinity College, Cambridge (1986), and he was awarded an honorary doctorate by Brunel University (1979). Humphrey was tall and thin, with uncombed and wispy light brown hair, lively eyes, and an alert and active stance. His friendly look conveyed genuine interest and concern for the other person. He died on 25 December 1987 at Ducklake House, his country home in Ashwell, near Baldock, Hertfordshire.

B. A. ASKONAS, *rev.*

Sources B. A. Askonas, *Memoirs FRS*, 36 (1990), 273–300 · personal knowledge (1996) · *CGPLA Eng. & Wales* (1988)
Archives Trinity Cam., corresp. with R. L. M. Synge
Wealth at death £330,171: probate, 11 May 1988, *CGPLA Eng. & Wales*

Humphrey, Laurence (1525x7–1589), college head, was born at Newport Pagnell, Buckinghamshire, and educated at Cambridge; he was very probably the Humphrey who matriculated in November 1544 as a pensioner of Christ's College. Soon afterwards, however, he went to Oxford, possibly at the instigation of John Harley, the master of Magdalen School and a fellow native of Newport Pagnell. Humphrey was elected a demy of Magdalen College in 1547, a probationary fellow the following year, and in 1549 he proceeded BA and became a perpetual fellow of the college. In July 1552 he commenced MA; he was also elected lecturer in natural philosophy that year and lecturer in moral philosophy in 1553.

By Edward VI's reign Humphrey was a committed protestant. Over two decades later, he vividly recalled a sermon which Martin Bucer gave in Christ Church in July 1550. That year Humphrey and nine other fellows—including such zealous gospellers as Thomas Bickley, John Mullins, Michael Renniger, and Arthur Saule—sent a letter to the privy council denouncing the hostility of Owen Oglethorpe, the president of Magdalen, to religious reform. They succeeded in having Oglethorpe replaced as president by Walter Haddon, who was much more sympathetic to their views. But the death of Edward VI, and the restoration of Stephen Gardiner as bishop of Winchester, and as such *ex officio* visitor of Magdalen, placed the college in the hands of an unremitting opponent of protestantism. Gardiner duly visited on 26 October 1553; Haddon and over a dozen fellows were ousted. Surprisingly, Humphrey survived this purge, probably because in September he had requested and received permission to retain his fellowship while he travelled overseas.

Exile The exact date of Humphrey's departure from Magdalen is unknown; he was still in residence on 31 October 1553. He arrived in Zürich on 5 April 1554 among a party of English exiles led by Robert Horne, remaining there until autumn 1555 when he journeyed to Basel and enrolled at the university. While in Zürich he and twelve other exiles lodged with the printer Christopher Froschover; in later years he praised Froschover's hospitality and the kindness of the magistrates, ministers, and scholars of Zürich. Humphrey was still receiving a stipend from Magdalen, and on 24 December 1554 the college extended his leave of absence. On 15 June 1555 he received a further extension of his leave, but only upon condition that he would stay away from places infected with heresy and not associate with heretics. Clearly the authorities were beginning to have their suspicions, as well they might, about Humphrey's activities. There were no further extensions, and his name had fallen out of the list of college fellows by July 1556.

Throughout his exile, to supplement and then replace his stipends, Humphrey worked as a corrector and translator for the printers Johann Froben and Johannes Oporinus. (It was probably during this period that he translated three dialogues attributed to Origen, printed in 1571 as part of an *Origensis opera* published by Oporinus.) He became closely associated with John Bale and John Foxe, who were also employees of Oporinus; Humphrey contributed Latin poems to Bale's *Catalogus* (1557–9) and Foxe's *Rerum in ecclesia gestarum … commentarii* (1559). He also began publishing his own works. Two of these, *Epistola de Graecis litteris et Homeri lectione et imitatione* (1558) and *De ratione interpretendi* (1559), from the presses of Oporinus and Froben respectively, are outgrowths of Humphrey's work as a translator. (The latter contains an interesting plea for the use of vernacular languages in divine worship.)

Early writings Another of Humphrey's works, *De religionis conservatione et reformatione vera*, also published by Oporinus in 1559, is more significant. Calling for the purging of popish abuses from the English church, it also attempts to recast the recent works of John Knox, Christopher Goodman, and John Ponet. While maintaining that he is simply presenting these authors' true views, obscured by their occasionally harsh words, he nevertheless contradicts them all by allowing only passive resistance against an evil ruler. And in a politic nod to England's new queen, as well as responding directly to Knox, he argues that although female rule is unusual it is not necessarily monstrous or unnatural: God uses the weak to confound the strong, and has accomplished reformation in England through a female monarch and boy king. The roots of future conflict, however, are revealed in Humphrey's denunciation of the Pharisees who 'put the whole of their religion in vestments, stoles and dramatic pomp' (Humphrey, *De religionis*, 42). Also significant, with hindsight, is Humphrey's dedication of the book to Francis Russell, second earl of Bedford.

In March 1560 Humphrey made another foray into political theory with *Optimates sive de nobilitate*, likewise published by Oporinus. Dedicated to Elizabeth and the 'Christian gentlemen' of the Inner Temple, it is divided into three parts: the first on the value of an aristocracy, the second on the origins of the English nobility, and the third and largest section on the education of the nobility. (Interestingly, especially in view of the dedication, Humphrey insists that the nobility includes both true aristocrats and 'new men', the latter including lawyers.) The greatest significance of the *Optimates* lies in its influence on Sir Thomas Smith's *De republica Anglorum*, but aspects of Humphrey's later career are again foreshadowed in the dedication's exhortation to Elizabeth to complete the godly reformation started by her brother.

Meanwhile, still in exile, Humphrey journeyed to Geneva and was admitted to the English congregation in April 1558. There he married Joan Inkforby (*c*.1537–1611), a member of a family of protestant exiles from Ipswich. The Humphreys would have twelve children, starting with their son John, born *c*.1562. According to Anthony Wood, Humphrey's marriage was unhappy and he was not on good terms with his sons. There is no evidence to support this assertion and little to contradict it, yet Humphrey would later be accused of nepotism, and he certainly surrounded himself at Magdalen with members of his family. Three sons and two brothers-in-law became fellows of the college; the latter also became college bursars. It is impossible to say how much these arrangements owed to familial affection and how much to Humphrey's need for a loyal coterie, but he clearly felt that he could rely on his sons and his wife's family.

By summer 1559 Humphrey had returned to Basel, where in August he penned a preface to Foxe's martyrology, the *Rerum in ecclesiastica gestarum … commentarii*. Possibly he returned to England with Foxe in the autumn of 1559; he was certainly in Oxford, where he would spend the rest of his life, by the summer of 1560.

The vestiarian controversy On his return to England, Humphrey was reaccepted at Magdalen. His star proceeded to rise with celerity in the Oxford firmament, partly because of a dearth of senior academics in the university after three decades of religious change and purges of colleges, and partly because of an even greater shortage of committed protestants. Yet Humphrey also established an impressive reputation for learning and godliness through his

written works, while his considerable talent for networking made him several powerful friends. In May 1560 Archbishop Matthew Parker tried to secure the Lady Margaret chair in divinity for him even though he lacked the required doctorate. When it became clear that Pietro Martire Vermigli (known as Peter Martyr) would not return from Zürich to resume his regius professorship of theology, Humphrey was chosen as his successor.

In 1561, after an energetic campaign spearheaded by the earl of Bedford and abetted by Sir William Cecil, Robert Horne, Edmund Grindal, and Parker, Humphrey was elected president of Magdalen College. In July 1562 he proceeded DTh; it is a sign of the conditions in Oxford at the beginning of Elizabeth's reign that in 1564 he was the senior doctor in the university. Despite this success his financial position remained somewhat precarious; he applied unsuccessfully to Cecil for a prebend at Christ Church, complaining of the heavy expenses the presidency entailed. More altruistically, he appealed in the same letter for increased funding for theology students.

Humphrey's material prospects were to be blighted for a long time by his increasing opposition to the wearing of the surplice and other features of clerical attire which many advanced protestants regarded as superstitious remnants of Catholicism. Humphrey's name appeared on a list, compiled in the early 1560s and submitted to Lord Robert Dudley, of twenty-eight preachers—including Miles Coverdale and John Foxe, among others—'which have utterly forsaken Antichrist and all his Romish rags' in contrast to 'the lord bishops and others that for worldly respects receive and allow them' (*Pepys MSS*, 2–3). In August 1563 Humphrey wrote to the Swiss reformer Heinrich Bullinger, enquiring whether the cap and surplice could be considered indifferent and whether, if commanded by lawful authority, the godly should wear them.

'Lawful authority', however, was already moving to secure Humphrey's compliance. Aware that Humphrey and Thomas Sampson were leading the opposition to vestments, Parker summoned them to Lambeth in December 1564 for an informal conference with other bishops and divines. Those present were asked to sign a document affirming that the vestments were indifferent and could be legitimately imposed by public authority. Some only signed with qualifications, Humphrey and Sampson with the Pauline proviso that if all things were lawful, all things were not expedient.

On 25 January 1565, however, Queen Elizabeth wrote to Parker commanding that order and uniformity in the rites and ceremonies of the church be maintained, and refusing to exempt the universities. Parker immediately sent a commission to Magdalen to investigate the use of vestments there. On 26 February the vice-president and twenty-five fellows sent a letter of complaint to the archbishop, protesting that the bishop of Winchester had sole jurisdiction over the college and refusing the vestments.

On 3 March 1565 Parker summoned Humphrey and Sampson back to Lambeth, but, after further examination, on 8 March they refused to yield, although Parker displayed letters from Martin Bucer and Peter Martyr supporting his position. Parker detained Humphrey and Sampson in London, which may have been a mistake, as the two proceeded to fan opposition to vestments in the capital. On 20 March they asked Parker for liberty to follow their consciences regarding vestments, in a letter also signed by James Calfhill and seventeen prominent London ministers. During Lent, Humphrey and Sampson both preached at Paul's Cross, almost certainly denouncing vestments, since their sermons alarmed Parker, who on 29 April gave them the choice of conformity or deprivation. They refused to conform, and Sampson was ejected from his deanery at Christ Church. Parker also tried to dislodge Humphrey from Magdalen, and during the next year the president scrambled for support from Dudley, now earl of Leicester, and, through his friend Foxe, from the duke of Norfolk. However, by autumn 1566 it must have been apparent that his position was secure. Horne of Winchester, who alone had the authority to deprive Humphrey, made no attempt to do so, despite the opportunity provided by his visitation of Magdalen in September. The previous month, Elizabeth had made a royal progress to Oxford where, according to Wood, she told Humphrey that his doctoral gown became him, and wondered at his resistance to wearing it. This quip, however, if it was even made, marked the extent of the queen's displeasure. Humphrey in his turn presented the queen with a New Testament and prayed publicly that God would open her heart to further reform of the church.

Moving towards conformity Yet Humphrey did not emerge completely unscathed. His role as a leader of the anti-vestiarians stalled further preferment. In December 1565 he was presented to a small living in the diocese of Salisbury but Bishop John Jewel refused to admit him and wrote to Cecil explaining that he respected Humphrey's learning 'but without good assurance of his conformity I mind not in any way to receive him' (*Works*, 4.1265). In a letter to Jewel, dated 20 December 1565, Humphrey promised good behaviour if granted the living, but Jewel still refused to admit him. With a growing family, and his academic posts his sole source of income, the financial pressure on Humphrey during the 1560s must have been persistent.

Humphrey did succeed in consolidating his position at Oxford. As early as 1567 Leicester, as chancellor of the university, recommended Humphrey for the office of vice-chancellor; Humphrey held this post from 1571 to 1576. In 1566 he wrote to Leicester complaining of the decay of 'true' religion in Corpus Christi College; and in the summer of 1568 joined with Horne in purging that college of Catholic fellows and securing the election of William Cole as president. In the same year Humphrey sharply criticized a sermon by Bishop Richard Cheyney of Gloucester on free will, and wrote to his old patron Bedford, urging him to bring the matter before the privy council.

In addition to smiting Catholics and crypto-Catholics, Humphrey was also working to advance the careers of the godly at Oxford. In particular he seems to have introduced John Field, the future presbyterian leader, to Foxe and

helped to facilitate the early steps of Field's remarkable career. Yet despite Humphrey's unimpeachable reformed credentials and his mentoring of the godly, there were signs of tension between Humphrey and a younger generation of reformers. Grindal wrote to Bullinger on 11 June 1568 claiming that while further controversy had arisen over the vestments in London, Humphrey and Sampson refused to support the opposition and were denounced by the new nonconformists as 'semi-papists' (Robinson, *Zurich Letters, 1558–1579*, 201–5).

On 13 March 1571 Humphrey was installed as dean of Gloucester as part of what appears to have been an effort to surround Cheyney, whose theology and administrative ability were both suspect, with reliably reformed senior officials. Guy Eaton, another former Marian exile, was made archdeacon soon afterwards. Humphrey's first significant piece of ecclesiastical preferment did not diminish his reforming zeal: shortly afterwards he was involved with Foxe and Thomas Norton in an attempt to have parliament authorize a reformed Book of Common Prayer.

The failure of this effort (due in part to the disastrous intervention of William Strickland, an uncompromising puritan) may have persuaded Humphrey that further ecclesiastical reform could not be achieved. When Field was imprisoned as a result of the *Admonition to Parliament*, Humphrey visited his former protégé in prison, but in carefully chosen words expressed disapproval of Field's actions. In July 1573 Grindal told Rudolph Gualter that Humphrey and Sampson were completely opposed to the proposals put forth in the *Admonition*.

Episcopal biographer It is a sign of Humphrey's partial rehabilitation in the eyes of the authorities that he was chosen by Parker and Bishop Edwin Sandys of London to write a biography of Jewel. Published in 1573, the book proclaims its author's adherence to religious reform. Unsurprisingly, he discusses in detail Jewel's education at Oxford, and the work's chief historical value is its vivid picture of the university in Edward VI's reign. Humphrey mentions Jewel's recantation but he portrays him as a confessor, giving a detailed and informed account of his flight and exile. And naturally enough (this was why Parker and Sandys had commissioned it) he devotes a great deal of space to Jewel's controversial writings, even buttressing Jewel's arguments with his own.

But the significance of Humphrey's biography lies as much in what is omitted as in what is discussed. Almost nothing is said about Jewel as a diocesan. From Humphrey's pages it would be concluded that Jewel's only episcopal activity was to have used the resources of his diocese to support preachers and scholars. Nothing is said about his intolerance of nonconformity. But there is considerable emphasis on Jewel as preacher; Humphrey's lengthy account of Jewel's death, telling how he insisted on conducting a preaching tour despite severe ill health and medical warnings that such exertions would be fatal was intended to illustrate the bishop's devotion to his preaching ministry. Jewel's death also gave Humphrey an opportunity to emphasize his stoicism; Humphrey's life of

Jewel, that of a man whose life was suffused with the Aristotelian virtue of reasoned moderation, constitutes one of the first, and most important, revivals of Plutarchan biography in Renaissance England.

Controversies at Magdalen Moderation was not a virtue which the fellows of Magdalen found in their president, as events in 1575 would demonstrate. In June that year Humphrey expelled six junior fellows (three of whom were quickly reinstated) who refused to participate in the election of a dean of arts. Ostensibly this dispute turned on the interpretation of a college statute which the six dissenting fellows invoked in an attempt to bar five others (including Roger Inkforby, Humphrey's brother-in-law) from their rights in the college on the eve of the election. In reality they were at loggerheads with Humphrey over his perceived lack of religious zeal and were seizing an opportunity to oust some of his supporters. Because of these underlying tensions two parties swiftly formed. Humphrey was supported by Horne, as college visitor, and twelve of the thirteen senior fellows. The dissidents, however, enjoyed widespread support among the junior fellows, including the future puritan luminaries John Barebon and Edward Gellibrand. More importantly, they had the support of Laurence Tomson, Sir Francis Walsingham's secretary and a former fellow of the college. On 1 July 1575 Tomson wrote to Humphrey, professing friendship and admiration but criticizing his severity in expelling the fellows as an act unworthy of a minister of the gospel. Walsingham told Horne on 11 June that he had written to Humphrey protesting against the expulsions, but that Humphrey would not heed him. In Walsingham's opinion, if Humphrey 'had been so good a governor as he is thought to be a man' this situation would not have arisen (PRO, SP 12/105/16). Walsingham urged Horne to intervene on behalf of the expelled fellows. On the same day, however, Horne wrote to Humphrey criticizing him for having been too lenient and upholding the expulsions. Horne appears to have had second thoughts after receiving Walsingham's letter, for on 16 July he assured Walsingham of his intention to act as a peacemaker and claimed that he was loath to see the dissenting fellows expelled. Horne sent a copy of this letter to Magdalen, with an exhortation to end the quarrel.

The dispute was apparently resolved, but tensions along religious lines persisted at Magdalen, along with a deep suspicion of the radical fellows and their allies. In 1578, at a meeting of college officers, Tomson was accused of planning to alienate the lands and possessions of the church and of all the colleges. But the radicals in Magdalen remained militant, and in August that year, led by John Barebon, the vice-president for 1578, they tried to block the confirmation of John Everie as a fellow. They found that they had overreached themselves. Everie was the son of the queen's serjeant-at-arms and Elizabeth had personally recommended his election as probationary fellow in 1577. Horne descended on the college and Barebon and four supporters were expelled from their fellowships. This time there was no outside intervention on their behalf. In the college elections which followed Humphrey

triumphed. Roger Inkforby was elected vice-president, William Inkforby bursar, and other supporters of Humphrey became the deans of divinity and arts.

In 1581, frustrated by Humphrey's dominance, and completely disillusioned with his regime, the radical fellows engineered the expulsion of Samuel Foxe, son of John Foxe, from his fellowship. Once again the religious divisions are clear: in a letter to an unnamed bishop John Foxe denounced the 'thrice-pure puritans' who had expelled his son, claiming that Samuel had been singled out as part of a campaign to oust the president. Once again Humphrey's opponents had chosen their victim unwisely: John Foxe was not without influence and Samuel was restored at Elizabeth's command.

Complaints and compromises Thomas Cooper became bishop of Winchester in 1584 and conducted a thorough visitation of Magdalen in the autumn of 1585. Depositions were submitted by fellows who disapproved of Humphrey's administration. It is difficult to evaluate their accuracy; claims that Humphrey had allowed Magdalen to become a refuge for Catholic scholars were, at best, gross exaggerations. Complaints about the decline of academic standards at the college were probably more soundly based, although not all the faults alleged were equally serious. Humphrey was also accused of maladministration, of enriching himself at the college's expense, and of allowing his family and supporters to do likewise. There were also allegations that Humphrey appointed negligent or unlearned men to college office.

Humphrey does seem to have become somewhat wealthier—he purchased two Oxfordshire manors in 1575. But whether this affluence was based on peculation or resulted from his recent ecclesiastical preferment is unclear. Much of Humphrey's alleged corruption (if it had any factual basis) probably resulted from his trying to establish a loyal following in the face of persistent attempts to dislodge him. The complaints of rigged elections and partisan appointments may well owe as much to sour grapes as to Humphrey's machinations.

Cooper did not in the event respond directly to these accusations. Instead he issued a series of injunctions imposing conformity on Magdalen but also ending absenteeism and prescribing the regular delivery of lectures. Measures were also enacted to curb financial mismanagement and the mishandling of college records, and to try to ensure fair elections and appointments. The result was peace which lasted until Humphrey's death and the tumultuous election of his successor, Nicholas Bond, under whom Magdalen ceased to be what it had always been under Humphrey: a nursery of godly zeal and an incubator of intense religious division.

Elder statesman Yet while Humphrey's support within Magdalen was evaporating, his career in the Church of England was prospering. In 1574 it was rumoured that he would soon be made a bishop, while Cecil hinted that only his opposition to vestments was blocking his preferment. When Francis Hastings, son of the second earl of Huntingdon and a former pupil of Humphrey's, wrote urging him to accept a bishopric if it was offered, Humphrey replied that it was not sinful to desire the office of a bishop. On 6 February 1576 Humphrey offered Cecil his qualified acceptance of the wearing of vestments by university personnel, provided that they were understood to be worn in obedience to civil policy and not as ecclesiastical garments. This tactical retreat may have been motivated at least as much by concerns over the increasing divisions within the Elizabethan church as by hopes of ecclesiastical preferment. In that same year John Foxe took a very similar position on vestments.

Although a bishopric eluded Humphrey he was entrusted with increasing administrative responsibilities. When a commission for ecclesiastical causes was established for the dioceses of Bristol and Gloucester in 1574 Humphrey was appointed to it. In 1576 he and Arthur Saule conducted a sweeping and rigorous visitation of Gloucester diocese, uncovering much conservative religious nonconformity which had flourished under Cheyney. In October 1580 Humphrey became dean of Winchester. This was no sinecure, and he attended regularly at chapter meetings.

Humphrey was also a major linchpin in the relations between the English church and Oxford University and the protestants on the continent. He provided financial support and patronage for Swiss studying at Oxford, including the sons of Rudolph Gualter and Wolfgang Musculus. In 1578 he was one of four deputies nominated by Elizabeth to attend the Lutheran synod at Schmalkalden (there is no evidence that he went).

Part of Humphrey's international reputation, and much of his utility to the Elizabethan regime, rested on his skill as an anti-Catholic polemicist. In 1582 he published *Jesuitismi pars prima*, which began as a response to Edmund Campion's *Decem rationes*, but developed into a denunciation of Pius V's bull *Regnans in excelsis* (1570) and a rebuttal of Catholic writers who had argued for papal jurisdiction over secular monarchs. Two years later Humphrey published *Jesuitismi pars secunda*, his most highly regarded controversial work. Ostensibly a rebuttal of John Drury's *Concertatio*, itself a riposte to William Whitaker's attacks on Campion, Humphrey's book, over 600 pages long, constitutes an exhaustive criticism of Catholic doctrines and practices. In 1588 he published *A View of the Romish Hydra and Monster*, a collection of seven sermons (hence the title, the hydra being a mythical beast with seven heads) denouncing Catholics as traitors to the queen. The wheel had come full circle: Humphrey the exile had advocated passive resistance to evil rulers, but Humphrey the anti-Catholic polemicist demanded unconditional obedience to the crown.

The struggle against the hydra was the second of Hercules's labours; it was the last of Humphrey's. He died at Oxford, aged sixty-three, on 1 February 1589 and was buried in Magdalen College chapel, where his effigy, high in the chancel wall, still gazes impassively down on the lavish ecclesiastical ceremonies he struggled so hard to purge from the English church.

Humphrey and the Elizabethan church Humphrey was highly esteemed as a scholar—even Anthony Wood, sympathetic neither to Humphrey nor to his legacy, paid tribute to his erudition—and he was an able controversialist. But his historical significance rests on three achievements. The first is his leadership of the anti-vestiarian movement, the first of many protests against the perceived lack of thorough reformation in the English church and an important precedent for future puritan agitation. The second was that Magdalen, under his leadership, became the nursery for several generations of clergy and laity of advanced protestant convictions. While Humphrey should not be given sole credit for this, it remains true that Magdalen was the only Oxford college during Elizabeth's reign of which this could be said; his presidency saw the college by the Cherwell become, metaphorically, the city on the hill. If his godly protégés ultimately turned on him, he was neither the first nor the last reformer to be attacked by the radicals he had mentored. And finally, Humphrey's life of Jewel is an important milestone in the development of English biography. It was a model for later biographies of godly people, notably Simeon Foxe's memoir of his father and the lives edited and written by Samuel Clarke.   THOMAS S. FREEMAN

Sources C. M. Dent, *Protestant reformers in Elizabethan Oxford* (1983) · J. K. Kemp, 'Laurence Humphrey, Elizabethan puritan: his life and political theories', PhD diss., West Virginia University, 1978 · J. R. Bloxam, *A register of the presidents, fellows … of Saint Mary Magdalen College*, 8 vols. (1853–85), vol. 4, pp. 104–32 · W. D. Macray, *A register of the members of St Mary Magdalen College, Oxford*, 8 vols. (1894–1915), vols. 1–2 · Magd. Oxf., MS 730(a) · CCC Cam., MS 114 (B) · Magd. Oxf., Ledger F · BL, Harley MS 416; Lansdowne MS 8; Add. MS 32091 · Inner Temple Library, London, Petyt MS 538, vol. 47 · L. Humphrey, *Joannis Juelli Angli, episcopi Sarisburiensis vita et mors* (1573) · *Correspondence of Matthew Parker*, ed. J. Bruce and T. T. Perowne, Parker Society, 42 (1853) · *Report on the Pepys manuscripts*, HMC, 70 (1911) · H. Robinson, ed. and trans., *The Zurich letters, comprising the correspondence of several English bishops and others with some of the Helvetian reformers, during the early part of the reign of Queen Elizabeth*, 2 vols., Parker Society, 7–8 (1842–5) · C. Litzenberger, *The English Reformation and the laity: Gloucestershire, 1540–1580* (1997) · T. S. Freeman, '"The Reformation of the Church in this Parliament": Thomas Norton, John Foxe and the parliament of 1571', *Parliamentary History*, 16 (1997), 131–47 · J. Strype, *The life and acts of Matthew Parker*, 3 vols. (1822) · C. H. Garrett, *The Marian exiles: a study in the origins of Elizabethan puritanism* (1938) · P. Collinson, *The Elizabethan puritan movement* (1967) · state papers domestic, Elizabeth I, PRO, SP 12/19/55; SP 12/21/28; SP 12/105/16, 19 · CUL, MS Mm I. 43 · LPL, MS 2010 · F. Peck, ed., *Desiderata curiosa*, new edn, 2 vols. in 1 (1779) · *The works of John Jewel*, ed. J. Ayre, 4 vols., Parker Society, 24 (1845–50) · L. Humphrey, *De religionis conservatione et reformatione vera* (1559) · A. Wood, *The history and antiquities of the University of Oxford*, ed. J. Gutch, 2 vols. in 3 pts (1792–6) · *CSP dom.*, 1547–80 · *CPR, 1572–5* · J. Strype, *Annals of the Reformation and establishment of religion … during Queen Elizabeth's happy reign*, new edn, 4 vols. (1824) · Cooper, *Ath. Cantab.*, 2.80 · L. Humphrey, *Epistola de Graecis litteris* (1558) · administration, PRO, PROB 6/4, fol. 88v

Likenesses effigy on funeral monument, 1589, Magd. Oxf. · portrait, 1616–18, Bodl. Oxf., Upper Reading Room · Passe, line engraving, BM, NPG; repro. in H. Holland, *Heröologia Anglica*, 2 vols. (1620) · line engraving, NPG · oils, Christ Church Oxf.; version, Magd. Oxf.

Wealth at death see administration, PRO, PROB 6/4, fol. 88v

Humphrey, William (b. 1742?, d. in or before 1814), engraver and printseller, was probably the child, born on 7 October 1742, baptized on 17 October at the chapel of St George, Mayfair, the son of William Humphries and his wife, Sarah. In 1764 his family ran a shop selling seashells. In that year William Humphrey won a premium from the Society for the Encouragement of Arts, Manufactures, and Commerce for an etching by an artist aged under twenty-four. In the two following years he won prizes for mezzo-tints—the first for a portrait of Rembrandt which was published. A connection with the history painter Robert Edge Pine is suggested by several early mezzotints of Pine's paintings and an etched portrait of his daughter, Charlotte. From 1772 Humphrey published prints from the Shell Warehouse in St Martin's Lane before moving in 1774 to Gerrard Street, where he opened a printshop. His early speciality was droll mezzotints with subjects such as *The Butcher's Wife Dressing for the Pantheon* (1772), and he was soon publishing not only his own engravings but also those of other young artists such as Philip Dawe. During the mid-1770s he was closely associated with John Raphael Smith, and towards the end of the decade he published James Gillray's earliest graphic satires. He had moved to the Strand by 1780 but gave up publishing soon after.

By then Humphrey was dealing in portrait prints. He had already engraved portraits of interesting and rare subjects, such as John Sturt (1780) and George Vertue with his wife (c.1775). According to James Caulfield, Humphrey became an expert in old English portraits, importing a great many from the Netherlands. He

> carried on this trade for many years with great success, and imported more curious English Portraits than any other individual, and was of the greatest service to the collections of the late Earl of Orford, Sir William Musgrave, Messrs Bull, Storer, Cracherode, Bindley, Tighe, Sykes, &c &c &c. (Caulfield, 6)

These were omnivorous portrait collectors, active before James Granger's *Biographical History of England* (1769) popularized the pursuit. Humphrey helped to establish the engraver Charles Howard Hodges in the Netherlands, but received, according to Caulfield, scant gratitude for his help. No ill feeling towards Hodges is evident in a letter written from Amsterdam in 1802 describing the sort of prints that were saleable there and attempting to entice Gillray to join him, with the promise that life there is 'nothing but Singing, Drinking, Music, Balls, Plays—and getting the young Women with Child' (BL, Add. MS 27337, fol. 88). It was probably the decline in the art trade due to the war, rather than addiction to the above pursuits, that reduced Humphrey's financial circumstances in old age. With his wife, Selinda, he had four sons, William, Thomas, Charles, and George, and a daughter, Selinda, all of whom survived him. He died before 1814.

Hannah Humphrey (c.1745–1818), printseller, was the sister of William Humphrey. She is first recorded as having exhibited a basket of flowers in raised paperwork with the Incorporated Society of Artists of Great Britain in 1771. Earlier exhibits of shell work by a Miss Humphreys (1762–

7) were probably the work of Hannah's elder sister Elizabeth, who married about 1768 and subsequently exhibited (1770–72) as Elizabeth Forster.

The date at which Hannah Humphrey began to publish prints is obscured by her practice when she bought old plates of replacing the name of the original publisher with her own without changing the original date of publication. Thus prints apparently issued by her during the 1770s may in fact not have been her property until some years later. Her first publication might have been *A New Academy for Accomplishments*, issued in May 1778 from St Martin's Lane, and about 1779 she seems to have established a printshop at 18 Old Bond Street. She owned high quality portrait and history plates as well as caricatures, and the shop presumably stocked a mixed range of fashionable prints. Increasingly, however, she specialized in caricature, and in 1791 the best graphic satirist, James *Gillray (1756–1815), began to work for her exclusively. From then on she was the leading caricature printseller. Her own caricatured portrait appears in Gillray's *Two-Penny Whist* (1796), in which she appears in a bonnet, bespectacled, tight-lipped, and poker-faced, but the exaggerated impression of spinsterly decrepitude may be a joke. She and Gillray moved in 1797 to the famous shop at 27 St James's Street depicted in *Very Slippy Weather* (1808).

Hannah's later letters to the caricaturist begin affectionately 'Dear Gilly'. One, written from Brighton, demonstrates her familiarity with high-ranking customers: 'His Highness of Clarence did me the honour of asking me how I did as we were walking on the Steine tho he had two Noblemen with Him'. She ended her letter with one of several remarks that suggest she considered Gillray absent-minded: 'PS I hope you take care of the Cat' (BL, Add. MS 27337, fol. 103). The two lived together in circumstances of domestic intimacy for many years, but so discreetly that the prurient gossips of the next generation could find little to say against them. When Gillray made his will in 1807 he left all his possessions 'to my dearest friend Hannah Humphrey'. She died in February or March 1818, leaving her business to her nephew George, substantial allowances to her numerous relatives, especially her sisters-in-law, nieces, and great-nieces, and a very generous living to her servant Betty Marshall.   TIMOTHY CLAYTON

Sources corresp., BL, Add. MS 27337 · will, PRO, PROB 11/1569, fol. 313 [James Gillray] · will, PRO, PROB 11/1602, fols. 154–6 [Hannah Humphrey] · D. Hill, *Mr Gillray the caricaturist* (1965) · F. G. Stephens and M. D. George, eds., *Catalogue of prints and drawings in the British Museum, division 1: political and personal satires*, 1–4 (1870–83) · F. G. Stephens and M. D. George, eds., *Catalogue of political and personal satires preserved … in the British Museum*, 5–11 (1935–54) · J. C. Smith, *British mezzotinto portraits*, 2 (1879), 708–16 · *Engraved Brit. ports.* · J. Caulfield, *Calcographiana: the printsellers chronicle and collectors guide to the knowledge and value of engraved British portraits* (1814) · T. Clayton, *The English print, 1688–1802* (1997) · *A register of the premiums and bounties given by the society instituted at London for the encouragement of arts, manufactures, and commerce from the original institution in the year 1754, to the year 1776 inclusive*, Royal Society for the Encouragement of Arts, Manufactures, and Commerce (1778) · E. G. D'Oench, *Copper into gold: prints by John Raphael Smith, 1751–1812* (1999) · register, Mayfair, St George's Chapel, City Westm. AC, 17 Oct 1742 [baptism]

Archives BL, letters, Add. MS 27337
Likenesses J. Gillray, etching, 1796 (Hannah Humphrey) · C. H. Hodges, mezzotint, pubd 1806 (after C. Imhoff), BM, NPG · drawing (Hannah Humphrey), New College, Oxford
Wealth at death affluent— Hannah Humphrey: will, PRO, PROB 11/1602, fols. 154–6

Humphreys. *See also* Humphries, Humphrys.

Humphreys, (Travers) Christmas (1901–1983), judge, was born in Ealing, Middlesex, on 11 February 1901, the younger son (there were no daughters) of Sir (Richard Somers) Travers Christmas *Humphreys (1867–1956), a barrister, and his wife, Zoë Marguerite (d. 1953), the daughter of Henri Philippe Neumans, an Antwerp artist. The elder son was killed in France in 1917. His father was to become senior Treasury counsel at the central criminal court, a High Court judge, and a member of the privy council. Humphreys was educated at Malvern College and at Trinity Hall, Cambridge, where he obtained a second class in part one of the law tripos (1922) and also a second (division two) in part two (1923).

Humphreys chose the bar as his profession, probably more out of a sense of filial duty than inclination. When he made his decision he knew that his father wanted his son to carry the practice of the law into a third generation. His paternal grandfather, Charles Humphreys, had been the solicitor for Oscar Wilde. He was called to the bar by the Inner Temple in 1924. In 1927 he married Aileen Maude (d. 1975), the daughter of Charles Irvine, a Yorkshire doctor of medicine; they had no children.

Like his father and paternal grandfather Humphreys chose the criminal courts for his practice. He made rapid progress. He was probably helped at first by his father's influence and connections but he had much natural ability. He had a fine presence, being tall and slim, and a pleasant, distinctive voice. In 1934 he was appointed junior Treasury counsel at the central criminal court; in 1942, recorder of Deal (until 1956); in 1947, deputy chairman of east Kent quarter sessions (until 1971); in 1950, senior Treasury counsel at the central criminal court (until 1959); and in 1956, recorder of Guildford.

In 1946 Humphreys was appointed junior counsel, together with A. Comyns Carr KC as his leader, to the war crimes tribunals trying Japanese war criminals. He did much work sifting and evaluating the evidence and drafting the charges but took little part in presenting the cases. His presence in the Far East enabled him to travel widely there and to increase his knowledge of eastern religions which was already extensive.

In 1955 Humphreys joined his father as a bencher of the Inner Temple. All seemed set for him to have a similarly distinguished career in the law but that was not to be. Unlike his father who lived for the law and amid lawyers, he had many interests outside. As the years went by these interests seemed, in the opinion of the director of public prosecutions, to interfere with the performance of his duties as senior Treasury counsel. The resulting loss of confidence, one with the other, led him to decide in 1959 to apply for silk, which by custom necessitated his giving up his appointment. He was given it. By this time he was

fifty-eight, somewhat old for starting practice as a QC. In 1962 he was appointed a judge at the central criminal court and he sat there until he retired in 1976. As a judge he was competent and kindly, too kindly for many who considered that his sentences were over-lenient. His last years on the bench cannot have been satisfying for him. Those in charge of administration at the central criminal court seldom gave him the more interesting cases to try. For about four years before her death in 1975 his wife had been suffering from a terminal illness which had the distressing symptom of loss of memory.

Some lawyers might say that Humphreys did not make the most of his considerable legal talents. He did not consider legal fame worth seeking. From his student days onwards his interests had ranged far beyond the law. As a youth he had become interested in Buddhism. In 1924 he became the founding president of the Buddhist Lodge, now the Buddhist Society. In 1928 he wrote a book, *What is Buddhism?* From that time onwards he led his life according to his Buddhist beliefs. He studied eastern philosophy and learned to appreciate Asian culture, particularly Chinese art. Between 1928 and 1962 he wrote twenty books, including four books of poetry, and numerous pamphlets and articles. He pursued his interests outside the law with enthusiasm and sometimes with more vigour than sound judgement. He was, for example, convinced that the earl of Oxford had written the plays usually attributed to Shakespeare.

In his dealings with people Toby Humphreys, as he was known, was always friendly, courteous, and considerate; but he was not gregarious and in his later years he did not seem to enjoy the company of the lawyers with whom he had worked. He died at his London home, 58 Marlborough Place, St John's Wood, on 13 April 1983. He left his house, which for many years had been a meeting-place for Buddhists, to the Zen Society. FREDERICK LAWTON, *rev.*

Sources C. Humphreys, *Both sides of the circle* (1978) · private information (1990) · personal knowledge (1990)
Archives FILM BFI NFTVA, *Pursuit of happiness*, 29 Sept 1960
Likenesses Ockinden, photograph, 1950, Hult. Arch.
Wealth at death £304,150: probate, 27 May 1983, *CGPLA Eng. & Wales*

Humphreys, David (1690–1740), Church of England clergyman, son of Thomas Humphreys, a London leatherseller, was born on 20 January 1690, and was educated at the Merchant Taylors' School, London, after 1701, and at Christ's Hospital, London, from 1704 until 1707. On 12 September 1707 he was elected to a school exhibition, and on 5 March 1708 he was admitted a sub-sizar of Trinity College, Cambridge. He was elected a scholar in 1709 and graduated BA in 1711, proceeding MA in 1715, BD in 1725, and DD by royal mandate in 1728.

In the quarrels and litigations involving Richard Bentley he was one of the master of Trinity's friends, and on 8 July 1715 he was elected fellow 'provisionally', the arrangement being that he was to take the place of Edmund Miller, Bentley's great opponent, if Miller's fellowship should be decided later by the king to be vacant. The king took no action, but a further arrangement was made on 5

December 1719, by which Miller received £400, in addition to certain other profits, and resigned the fellowship. Humphreys became a major fellow on 2 January 1720.

In 1716 Humphreys was appointed secretary of the Society for the Propagation of the Gospel, and he held this appointment until his death. He does not seem to have been disposed to answer letters while holding this post, but he probably managed the society's affairs efficiently since by the year after his death its income had risen by 50 per cent. In 1725 he sent out a circular letter urging missionaries to instruct in the Christian religion, and baptize, any black slaves working in their houses. He wrote the first book about the society, *An historical account of the incorporated Society for the Propagation of the Gospel in Foreign Parts* (1730). He wrote also *The Apologeticks of Athenagoras with Antiquity Explained* (1714) and *Antiquity Explained and Represented in Sculpture*, a translation from Montfaucon (1721).

Humphreys was ordained deacon on 25 April 1722 and priest on 29 April. He became vicar of Ware in Hertfordshire on 6 January 1730, and of nearby Thundridge on 30 June 1732. He died in 1740.

W. A. J. ARCHBOLD, *rev.* LEONARD W. COWIE

Sources E. P. Hart, ed., *Merchant Taylors' School register, 1851–1920* (1923) · G. A. T. Allan, *Christ's Hospital exhibitioners to the universities of Oxford and Cambridge, 1566–1923* (1924) · Venn, *Alum. Cant.* · E. McClure, ed., *A chapter in English church history: being the minutes of the Society for Promoting Christian Knowledge for … 1698–1704* (1888) · H. P. Thompson, *Into all lands* (1951) · R. J. White, *Dr Bentley: a study in academic scarlet* (1965) · *The correspondence of Richard Bentley*, ed. C. Wordsworth, 2 vols. (1842) · *The diary of E. Rod (1709–1720), fellow of Trinity College*, ed. H. R. Luard, Cambridge Antiquarian Society Publications (1851) · private information (1891) · J. E. Cussans, *History of Hertfordshire*, 3 vols. (1870–81)
Archives Bodl. RH, United Society for the Propagation of the Gospel archives · CUL, Society for the Promotion of Christian Knowledge archives

Humphreys, David (*bap.* 1843, *d.* 1930), Roman Catholic priest and campaigner for social rights, a native of Boher Murroe, co. Limerick, was baptized at Murroe parish church on 18 June 1843, the son of William Humphreys, tenant farmer, and his wife, Bridget Enright. He entered St Patrick's College, Thurles, in September 1863 to become a priest for the diocese of Cashel and Emly. In August 1865 he continued his studies at Maynooth and was ordained at Thurles on 19 September 1869. For the next nine years he was professor of logic at St Patrick's College, Thurles. The application of logic at the expense of common sense was a feature of his life. He subsequently served as curate in Galbally (1878–80), Clonoulty (1880–83), Newport (1883–5), and Tipperary (1885–95), and as parish priest in Killenaule (1895–1930).

In April 1882 Humphreys' father and family were evicted from their farm on the estate of Lord Cloncurry and were forced to live in a Land League hut. Possession of their farm was not regained for over a decade. Humphreys had the previous year written a pamphlet exposing the defects of the 1881 Land Act and the eviction reinforced his hatred of landlordism. In the summer of 1889 the Tipperary tenants of Arthur Hugh Smith-Barry MP withheld their rents as a protest against their landlord's leadership of a landlord syndicate formed to defeat the Plan of Campaign, specifically on the estate of Charles Ponsonby in co. Cork. Humphreys was not central to the decision to abandon the Smith-Barry property and build a 'New Tipperary' on an adjacent site, but he became the driving force behind this action when divisions appeared in the ranks of the tenants. Photographs of Humphreys being closely followed by policemen became a symbol of the nationalist determination to combat landlordism. Along with John Dillon, William O'Brien, and nine others he was arrested and tried for criminal conspiracy in Tipperary in September 1890. He was one of four defendants acquitted—a political decision. Following the split in the Irish Parliamentary Party financial support for New Tipperary began to dry up and Humphreys, a bitter anti-Parnellite, was also increasingly alienated from Dillon and O'Brien. By the time he left Tipperary in 1895 most of the Smith-Barry tenants had returned to their former property. He had not been moved from Tipperary sooner because of the support he received from his archbishop, William Croke.

Humphreys' defining characteristics, intelligence and a refusal to compromise, were seen to their best advantage in his lone campaign to have Catholics benefit from the Erasmus Smith educational endowment, one of the largest in the country. This had been established in 1657, with schools in Tipperary, Galway, and Drogheda, for the benefit of Smith's tenants and had become an exclusively protestant endowment. By agitation among the Smith tenants, public meetings, various publications which showed how deeply he had studied the history of the endowment (the most important of which was *Law in Ireland* (1913), a detailed submission to the educational endowment commission in 1892), and a failed attempt to push the case through the legal system in 1907–10, Humphreys began a process that was eventually resolved—by dividing the endowment between Catholic and protestant interests—after his death. To the end of his life Humphreys continued to do things in his own way. He opposed the Irish-language revival movement and Sinn Féin and was eccentric in his behaviour towards his parishioners. He died at home in the parish house at Killenaule on 22 June 1930 and was buried in the grounds of the church there.

DENIS G. MARNANE

Sources D. G. Marnane, 'Fr David Humphreys and New Tipperary', *Tipperary: history and society*, ed. W. Nolan (1985), 367–78 · D. G. Marnane, 'New Tipperary', *Land and violence: a history of west Tipperary from 1660* (1985), 104–13 · D. G. Marnane, 'A modern town', *Land and violence: a history of west Tipperary from 1660* (1985), 135–44 · M. Bourke, 'Erasmus Smith and Tipperary grammar school', *Tipperary Historical Journal*, 2 (1989), 82–99 · J. O'Shea, *Priest, politics and society in post-famine Ireland* (1983) · private information (2004) · Cashel and Emly diocesan parish records, Tipperary Heritage Centre
Likenesses photograph, repro. in W. Nolan, ed., *Tipperary: history and society* (1985), pl. xxxi
Wealth at death £898 14s. 11d.: probate, 12 Aug 1930, *CGPLA Éire*

Humphreys [*née* Gollan], **Eliza Margaret Jane** [*pseud.* Rita; *known as* Mrs W. Desmond Humphreys] (**1850–1938**), novelist, was born on 14 June 1850 at Gollanfield,

Inverness-shire, the daughter of John Gilbert Gollan, who had been in business in India, and his wife, the daughter of the manager of the Bank of Bengal. John Gollan had returned to Scotland on inheriting the family estate, and his daughter often referred to him as 'the Laird'. As a child, Eliza Gollan accompanied her parents and brother to Sydney, Australia, where her father pursued a business venture, but this proved disappointing, and the family returned to England, settling in London, when she was fourteen. Her Australian experience is reflected in the semi-autobiographical novel *Sheba*, published under the pseudonym Rita in 1889. She had no formal education to speak of, but showed very early a flair for writing stories.

On 23 July 1872 Eliza Gollan married Karl Otto Edmund Booth, a professional musician. His father was German, his mother English, but Eliza's description of her father-in-law as a baron seems unfounded, as was her use of the name von Booth. The marriage lasted long enough to produce three sons, but ended unhappily, later providing material for *Sâba Macdonald* (1906), and also for her Victorian trilogy: *Grandmother* (1927), *The Wand'ring Darling* (1928), and *Jean and Jeanette* (1929). Her second marriage, to an Anglo-Irish professional singer, William Ernest Humphreys (who used the stage name Desmond Humphreys), was a success. A daughter, Dorothy, was born in 1891. After a short stay at Youghal, in Humphreys' native county, Cork, the family lived for several years at Bournemouth, then moved to Bath.

As a writer, Rita greatly admired Ouida, and came to be seen as a rival to Marie Corelli, having much in common with both writers. She was extremely prolific, with nearly 120 titles to her name, and worked in various genres, producing novels, short stories, plays, and essays. Her first published work, which appeared when the author was still in her twenties, was *Vivienne* (1877), and others followed rapidly and frequently, with titles such as *My Lady Coquette* (1881), *My Lord Conceit* (1884), and *Good Mrs. Hypocrite* (1897). Her characters were frequently aristocratic, and the books often had fashionable foreign settings (partly owing to the influence of her European honeymoon). She first began to receive widespread recognition as a popular writer with her *Dame Durden* (1883). *Peg the Rake* (1894) sold 160,000 copies, a large number for those days, and was her first novel with an Irish setting or Irish characters, thereafter a consistent feature of her work.

The year 1894 also saw the appearance of *A Husband of No Importance*, the first of the books in which Rita expressed a critical attitude to current patterns in social life. With a nod to Oscar Wilde's *A Woman of No Importance*, which had opened in 1893, it forms an attack upon the then-prevalent 'new woman' novel. Although Eliza Humphreys herself, by this time, was a successful professional woman (and a founder member of the Writers' Club for Women), she disapproved of women 'aping men', and especially disliked what would later be called polemical feminism. In *Souls* (1903), she scathed pretentious and vicious society women in search of new sensations, following this up with a series of articles ('The sin and scandal of the "smart" set'), in the periodical *The Gentlewoman*, and with

another fictional indictment, *Queer Lady Judas* (1905). In 1907 she produced *Personal Opinions Publicly Expressed*, in which one essay was entitled 'The increase of vulgarity amongst women'. Rita saw the United States as a source of bad examples, a theme to which she returned after a visit to that country, in *America through English Eyes* (1910).

Eliza Humphreys had long been critical of 'Church' Christianity, and considered Mrs Humphry Ward's *Robert Elsmere* (1888) 'one of the bravest and best books of the past century'. She met Madame Blavatsky and became interested in theosophy, and problems of religious belief and conduct dominate Rita's *Calvary: a Tragedy of Sects* (1909), a novel which she maintained meant more to her than any other book that she had written. It was made into a film, as also were *Grim Justice* and *The Iron Stair*, and income from that source helped her through the difficult years of the First World War. In the post-war world, however, with its changed tastes in literature, she found herself in ever greater financial trouble, especially as her husband became an invalid. She was forced to apply to the Royal Literary Fund, and also sought a civil-list pension. These were refused her ('it being obvious that the standard of this lady's work did not qualify her'), but in 1930 she was given an award from the Royal Bounty Fund (her novels had been greatly liked by Queen Mary, who ordered a complete set of them for her private bookcase).

In her *Who's Who* entry (found under Rita), Eliza Humphreys said that she was a great lover of the theatre, and she wrote several plays, none of which, however, enjoyed much success. That was true also of her post-war novels, although they continued to receive respectful notices in the *Times Literary Supplement*. Her last work of fiction was *The Marriage Comedy* (1934), and her final book her autobiography, *Recollections of a Literary Life* (1936). In his preface to this, her friend Sir Philip Gibbs wrote: 'Somehow I think of "Rita"'s readers as lying on deck-chairs in pre-war summers, as tourists in Venice and other pleasant places where well-to-do English people used to take their holidays.'

Rita's writing was always fluent and lively, but occasionally marred by repetitiveness and inconsistencies, and her educational shortcomings sometimes showed. Characters rather than plot were her forte, but, in her prime, she was none the less an extremely popular novelist. Eliza Humphreys died of heart failure at 239 West Brow, Combe Down, Bath, on 1 January 1938; her husband died in the following year. BRIAN PEARCE

Sources Rita [E. M. J. Humphreys], *Recollections of a literary life* (1936) · S. Kemp, C. Mitchell, and D. Trotter, *Edwardian fiction: an Oxford companion* (1997) · Blain, Clements & Grundy, *Feminist comp.* · A. C. Ward, *Longman companion to twentieth-century literature* (1970) · J. Sutherland, *The Longman companion to Victorian fiction* (1988) · *WWW* · *Bath Weekly Chronicle and Herald* (8 Jan 1938) · *The Times* (4 Jan 1938) · *TLS* · BL, Royal Literary Fund archives · Kingham Hill School, Oxfordshire, Dorothy Smith MSS · m. cert. [Eliza Gollan and Karl Otto Edmund Booth] · d. cert.

Humphreys, Humphrey (1648–1712), bishop of Hereford, was born at Hendre Isa, Penrhyndeudraeth, Merioneth, on 24 November 1648, the eldest son of Richard Humphreys and his wife, Margaret, daughter of Robert Wynne of Cesail Gyfarch, Penmorfa, Caernarvonshire. His father was a royalist army officer. He was educated at the free school at Oswestry, Shropshire, where his uncle Humphrey Wynne was the vicar, and after his death at Bangor Free School, Caernarvonshire. He matriculated from Jesus College, Oxford, on 16 February 1666, graduating BA on 19 October 1669. On 12 November 1670 he was ordained deacon and priest by Bishop Morgan in Bangor Cathedral, and on the same day was collated and instituted rector of Llanfrothen, Merioneth. He became rector of Trawsfynydd, Merioneth, in 1672 and proceeded MA on 12 January 1673, and later that year became a fellow at Jesus College. In November 1673 he became chaplain to the new bishop of Bangor, Humphrey Lloyd. In 1677 he became rector of Cricieth, Caernarvonshire, and proceeded BD on 22 May 1679. In 1680 he became rector of Llaniestyn, Caernarvonshire, and dean of Bangor on 16 December 1680. In April 1681 at Bodewryd church, on the Isle of Anglesey, he married Elizabeth, daughter of Robert Morgan, the former bishop of Bangor. She had died by December 1700 when Humphreys wrote that on receiving the news of the death of Dr Wynne it was 'the most afflicting I ever received except that of my wife and child' (BL, Add. MS 41843, fol. 9). The child was his daughter Anne, who died aged sixteen; his other daughter, Margaret, survived him. On 5 July 1682 he was created DD at Oxford. In 1685 he held the rectory of Hope, Flintshire. During his nine-year tenure as dean he rebuilt the deanery and obtained an act of parliament in 1685 for a permanent endowment for the cathedral fabric and choir (1 Jac. II, c. 8).

On 30 June 1689 Humphreys succeeded Lloyd as bishop of Bangor, an appointment which prompted the bishop of St Asaph and Welsh MPs to thank William III for his appointment. He was named a commissioner in September 1689 for talks preparing matters to be laid before convocation concerning the revision of the prayer book and canons. His 1690 visitation was conducted in Welsh, in keeping with his championship of the language and his studies into Welsh history. He supported bards such as Owen Gruffydd and Edward Morris, and prose writers in Welsh, notably Ellis Wynne of Lasynys, Samuel Williams, and Edward Samuel. Edward Lhuyd called him 'incomparably the best skill'd in our Antiquities of any person in Wales' (*DWB*, 396). Humphreys's chronology of the British princes was accepted by the historian James Tyrell. Though he was consulted by the heralds over Welsh pedigrees and claimed that tracing pedigrees was his main diversion in his spare time, Humphreys's main scholarly interest in Welsh history was, as he told one correspondent, 'chiefly with relation to religion and ecclesiastical matters' (E. G. Wright, 81). He collected accounts of the seventh-century north Welsh saints Beuno and Twrog. Humphreys supported the idea of an ancient British church predating St Augustine, and so not corrupted by Rome, which provided a legitimate basis for the sixteenth-century Reformation and so gave Anglicanism its historical foundation.

Politically Humphreys was a loyal bishop, attending parliament with reasonable frequency while bishop of Bangor. He took the oaths of allegiance and supremacy in December 1695 and signed the association in February 1696. He also took the oaths in February 1699 and April 1701, being present on 17 June 1701 to vote for the acquittal of the whig Lord Somers, impeached for his part in King William's foreign policy. Humphreys was thus in London and able to be present at the first meeting of the Society for the Propagation of the Gospel at Lambeth on 27 June 1701. He became a leading figure in the Society for Promoting Christian Knowledge in north Wales. Indeed, an important dimension of Humphreys's support for Welsh language prose writers was his encouragement of translations of English devotional works to further the cause of religious instruction in his homeland.

Humphreys was translated to the see of Hereford on 2 December 1701. During the 1702–3 session of parliament he was a frequent visitor to another scholarly bishop, William Nicolson, where they discussed a whole range of scholarly and ecclesiastical issues. According to Nicolson, Humphreys was an early proponent of a bill 'to prevent the academies of dissenters', initially as a clause to the Occasional Conformity Bill in November 1702. Humphreys did not attend parliament in the following session, but his proxy was cast against the Occasional Conformity Bill in November 1703. Humphreys again appeared in London to take the oaths at the opening of the 1705–6 session; however, he was very irregular in his attendance thereafter. In October 1707 he was pleading his indisposition to the archbishop of Canterbury in order to be excused attendance at the new parliament of Great Britain, even though this meant that he could not assign a proxy. Instead he concentrated on a new Welsh edition of the Book of Common Prayer. He conducted his last visitation in 1710. In a letter to the earl of Sunderland in April 1710 he professed unwillingness to prosecute one of his clergy over a sermon for fear it would prove a 'triumph to his party to begin a prosecution and not be able to prove the charge' (BL, Add. MS 61610, fol. 30).

Although Robert Harley thought Humphreys likely to oppose the new tory ministry in 1710, he did not attend parliament. Ill health and age appear to have confined him to his diocese. According to the testimony of his chancellor, Edward Wynne, he led 'a very busy and active life with quick passions until upwards of fifty' but 'no man took the hint more effectually of taking leave of this world … when he presaged at a distance a decay of his faculties growing upon him' (E. G. Wright, 85). He died on 20 November 1712 at his episcopal palace at Whitbourne, Herefordshire and was buried in Hereford Cathedral. Administration of his estate was granted on 6 December 1712 to his daughter, Margaret, the widow of John Lloyd, son of William Lloyd, the nonjuring bishop of Norwich. Humphreys's additions to Wood's *Athenae* and *Fasti Oxoniensis* were printed by Thomas Hearne in 1730 and incorporated into Bliss's edition of 1813–20 and his catalogue of the deans of Bangor and St Asaph was printed by Hearne in 1732.   STUART HANDLEY

Sources Foster, *Alum. Oxon.* · *DWB* · E. G. Wright, 'Humphrey Humphreys, bishop of Bangor and Hereford', *Journal of the Historical Society of the Church in Wales*, vols. 1–2 (1947–50), vol. 2, pp. 72–86 · *The London diaries of William Nicolson, bishop of Carlisle, 1702–1718*, ed. C. Jones and G. Holmes (1985), 19, 130–98, 258, 317–84 · G. M. Griffiths, 'Eight letters from Edmund Gibson to Bishop Humphreys, 1707–9', *National Library of Wales Journal*, 10 (1957–8), 369–74 · W. M. Marshall, 'Episcopal activity in the Hereford and Oxford dioceses, 1660–1760', *Midland History*, 8 (1983), 113, 116 · G. Wright, 'Humphrey Humphreys, bishop of Bangor and Hereford, 1648–1712', *Transactions of the Anglesey Antiquarian Society and Field Club* (1949), 61–76 · letter of Humphrey Humphreys to Dorothy Wynne, Dec 1700, BL, Add. MS 41843, fol. 9 · letter of Humphrey Humphreys to Lord Sunderland, April 1710, BL, Add. MS 61610, fol. 30 · *The manuscripts of the House of Lords*, new ser., 12 vols. (1900–77), vol. 2, pp. 120; vol. 3, p. 312

Archives NL Wales, corresp. and papers | Glos. RO, letters to Bishop William Lloyd · NL Wales, additions to Welsh biographies in Wood's *Athenae Oxoniensis* · U. Wales, corresp. with Thomas Mostyn · U. Wales, letters to Edward Wynn

Humphreys, James (1768–1830), law reformer, was born in Montgomery, the sixth of the eight children of Charles Gardiner Humphreys, solicitor. Educated at Shrewsbury School, he was articled first to William Pugh of Caerhowell then to Richard Yeomans of Worcester. On his father's death he followed an elder brother Samuel to Lincoln's Inn, where he was admitted on 23 November 1789 and called to the bar on 25 June 1800. The pupil of Charles Butler, he built a chambers practice advising the Montgomeryshire gentlefolk on their property, contributed the conveyancing titles to the six-volume supplement to Charles Viner's *A General Abridgement of Law and Equity* (1799–1806), and lectured on property law at the new University of London in 1828. Described by the *Law Magazine* as 'a bottomless Whig' (*Law Magazine*, 5, 1831, 258), a friend of Fox, Clifford, Horne Tooke, Romilly, and Bentham, he won Henry Brougham's public praise, and hoped in vain to be appointed to the real property commission (1828). In the event, the commissioners were grateful for, but not persuaded by, his evidence before them. In 1822 he married Charlotte Goodrich of Saling Grove, Essex. Seven years later he sustained serious injuries in falling from his horse, and died on 29 November 1830 at 1 Upper Woburn Place, London.

In his lifetime Humphreys was praised by few and reviled by many. In death he was virtually forgotten, until reappraised by later students of nineteenth-century law reform. 1826 saw the publication by John Murray of Humphreys' *Observations on the actual state of the English laws of real property, with the outlines of a code* (a second edition of 1827 prudently replaced the word 'code' with 'systematic reform'). The book first describes critically the law of real property, starting from the realization that by 1825 more wealth was invested in 'the funds' than in land, and was subject to a far simpler legal regime. The second part ('code') includes his substantive reforms within a completely articulated structure. It assumes (what the real property commissioners found hard to accept) that when rules are well settled they can be enacted by parliament instead of being left to judicial precedent. It then drafts a whole set of principles in simple English, and builds them into a coherent system.

The author was not some young firebrand but an experienced chancery lawyer, and his book was ecstatically if incoherently welcomed by Jeremy Bentham in the *Westminster Review* (vol. 6, October 1826), and praised in the other quarterlies. But in its own journals and in pamphlets the legal profession attacked vehemently the substance of Humphreys' reforms, the very notion of a code, and the author's habit of saying things simply. The lawyers' tone was spontaneous, venomous, and almost unanimous: the work was 'rotten', 'a calamity', it would 'sap the essential *manliness* of the common law' (Rudden, 103–4). One of them was even moved to verse:

> These modes of speech are Humphreys', every line;
> For God's sake, reader, take them not for mine!
> (*Law Magazine*, 1, 1828, 3)

Edward Sugden (Lord St Leonards LC) published three versions of his attack, and later ensured that the author was never made bencher of his inn.

Meanwhile, in Albany, Humphreys' ideas inspired the major revision of New York property law of 1828, and from there spread to a dozen other states of the Union.

In retrospect, Humphreys' work presents a paradox. On the one hand, the book crystallized contemporary political and professional opposition, and may thus have delayed reform in his own country. On the other hand the 150 years after his death saw the English legislator accept, piecemeal and without acknowledgement, almost all of Humphreys' substantive proposals. Three of his notions are still beyond us: the idea that uncontentious basic rules might be enacted by parliament; that they can then be stated simply; and that they can be organized in a coherent and self-supporting system.   BERNARD RUDDEN

Sources [E. Humphreys], 'Memoir', *Cambrian Quarterly Magazine and Celtic Repository*, 3 (1831), 288–300 · *GM*, 1st ser., 100/2 (1830), 571 · *GM*, 1st ser., 101/1 (1831), 181–2 · C. Butler, *Reminiscences*, 2 (1827), 284 · B. Rudden, 'A code too soon: the 1826 property code of James Humphreys', *Essays in memory of Professor F. H. Lawson*, ed. P. Wallington and R. M. Merkin (1986), 101–16 · R. B. Lettow, 'Codification and consolidation of English law in the age of Peel and Brougham', MLitt diss., U. Oxf., 1992 · M. Lobban, *The common law and English jurisprudence, 1760–1850* (1991)

Archives UCL, D. M. S. Watson Library, corresp. | BL, Bentham corresp.

Humphreys, Leslie Alexander Francis Longmore (1904–1976), organizer of resistance and Foreign Office official, was born in Budapest on 4 July 1904, the younger child and only son of Richard John Edward Humphreys and his wife, Elizabeth Agnes Lyons. His father, a musician who went first to Austria–Hungary in 1894, taught English in Budapest and subsequently became commercial secretary at The Hague, Budapest, and Bucharest. From Cardinal Vaughan School, Humphreys went to Stonyhurst College. Too young to fight in the war of 1914–18, he became an ardent patriot in his teens and never lost this fierce emotion, nor the deep faith acquired as a 'Jesuit child'. After a year at the Faculté des Lettres in Dijon he went up to Magdalene College, Cambridge. He gained a third class in modern languages in 1925 and a lower second in part two of the history tripos in 1926. Virtually trilingual, he could add to French and German a fair fluency in Romanian.

For six years between periods of business work in London, Humphreys was at the British legation in Bucharest as assistant to his father and attaché to the controller for the League of Nations of an international loan to Romania, a Frenchman. Early in 1939 he joined section D of the British secret service, predecessor of the Special Operations Executive (SOE). Before the outbreak of war he made two operational trips to the Netherlands and one to Poland. He was sent to Paris in September with the rank of major, as liaison with the French fifth bureau, planning sabotage lines from Paris and later a sabotage network inside falling France. He was evacuated on 20 June 1940 by warship from the Gironde amid tumult. On the formation of SOE in July he became head of its F section, charged with organizing subversion in France. Humphreys was preoccupied with one principle—communications are the essential basis of all clandestine work—but he was miscast as executant of Churchill's directive to Hugh Dalton 'to set Europe ablaze'. In December he was moved over to work on clandestine communications (DF section), a task better suited to his temperament and abilities. He visited Lisbon twice during winter 1940–41 to investigate reported lines for passing letters, parcels, and people into France: he decided to construct links of his own. He gradually designed a blueprint of a system that would serve SOE through western Europe for secret travel and secret supply. His first agent, a Maltese schoolteacher, was put ashore near Perpignan in April 1941 and established working contacts with smugglers operating across the Pyrenees. In May he sent the Chilean actress wife of a French Jew, Victor Gerson (Vic), on reconnaissance to Vichy. Gerson followed, and in the course of six separate clandestine visits built SOE's biggest and best escape line. Many of those he recruited were also Jews, more at risk than Gentiles, but determinedly anti-Nazi and used to keeping themselves to themselves. Other helpers included a Swiss social democrat and a Norwegian Quaker ship-broker in Marseilles. Jacques Mitterand, brother of the future president of France, became his chief lieutenant in Paris.

Humphreys, a strong administrator who harped on secrecy, kept his people inconspicuous and this was the main reason for his DF section's run of successes. The effectiveness of his security precautions was demonstrated when the Abwehr in 1943 penetrated the 'Vic' line: none of the eleven arrested sub-agents provided the Germans with exploitable information and the line continued to function unchecked.

DF's methods were sometimes unorthodox. In launching the extremely effective 'Var' escape line which carried seventy people (including François Mitterand) across the beaches of the north Breton coast in the winter and spring of 1943–4, the section's seaborne projects officer dexterously bypassed the proper SOE channels and made his arrangements direct with the naval section of the Secret Intelligence Service (SIS/MI6). At a time when relations

between the two organizations were less than cordial, this tendency to 'play the SIS card within SOE' did not go down well with some of Humphreys's SOE superiors, though there was obviously much less clash of professional interest between DF and SIS than in the case of the other SOE country sections. The results achieved were remarkable: several hundred passengers were carried without loss, and the carrier's casualty rate of 2 per cent was by far the lowest of SOE's French sections. Humphreys attained the rank of lieutenant-colonel and was appointed OBE in 1945.

After the war Humphreys returned to the business world, but in 1950 he accepted an opportunity to serve again under the Foreign Office. His postings took him to Frankfurt, Pusan (South Korea), Vienna, and, finally, London. In 1964 he retired and joined the staff of the Stonyhurst preparatory school. He was, as always, punctilious about his duties. Each day began with mass, and he walked the corridors telling his beads. But his piety did nothing to obscure his habitually jocular, virile approach. Behind the penetrating gaze and powerful jaw he remained pessimistic and thorough, 'with no illusions about man's inevitable progress towards the realms of light or any nonsense about natural innocence' (private information). The boys loved him.

Even after his second retirement in 1973 to Bexhill, Humphreys continued to teach, until the heart attack that caused his death there on 19 December 1976. He was unmarried and his sister kept house for him at both Stonyhurst and Bexhill.   BROOKS RICHARDS, rev.

Sources M. R. D. Foot, *SOE in France: an account of the work of the British Special Operations Executive in France, 1940–1944* (1966) • C. K. Macadam, *Stonyhurst Magazine*, 40/463 (1977) • *The Times* (29 Jan 1977) • R. Huguen, *Par les nuits les plus longues*, 4th edn (1978) • personal knowledge (1986) • private information (1986) • *CGPLA Eng. & Wales* (1977)
Wealth at death £9214: probate, 11 Feb 1977, *CGPLA Eng. & Wales*

Humphreys, (Henry) Noel (1807–1879), graphic artist and author, was born on 4 January 1807 in Birmingham, the son of James Humphreys and Dorothy Ann Knowles. He was educated at King Edward VI's Grammar School, Birmingham, and received artistic training in Brussels.

Following his marriage at Marylebone on 12 July 1833 to Marianne Bland, the couple embarked upon a continental tour which Humphreys then drew upon for the *Architectural Magazine* (1837–9) and *Rome and its Surrounding Scenery* (1840), in which he disclosed his admiration for the Italian Renaissance and baroque—the study of Italy provided inspiration throughout his life. He also wrote about architectural materials and expressed radical sympathy for functionalism and engineering. A contemporary emphasis appeared in *Ten Centuries of Art* (1851) with support for the Pre-Raphaelites, and he discussed the Great Exhibition, where he exhibited.

Apart from an interlude in Pinner, Humphreys spent his career in London. Initially, upon his return from Italy, he lived in Bayswater as a neighbour of a relative, the landscape architect and prolific author J. C. Loudon. Together they mixed with leading literary, artistic, and scientific figures, including the Pre-Raphaelites: his son was the model for Millais's *Christ in the House of his Parents* (1849–50). His family assisted by finding references for his writing, or by completing or transferring designs to the wood block or lithographic surface. They even coloured lithographs.

Humphreys wrote for garden periodicals, beginning with Loudon's *Gardener's Magazine* in 1838 and ending with William Robinson's *The Garden* (1871–9), whose editor dedicated volume 18 (1881) to him. Humphreys' articles for Moore and Ayres's *Gardener's Magazine* (1850–51) were sufficiently interesting to be reprinted in *La Belgique horticole*. Throughout, although open to new ideas, he revealed the influences of Italy and of Loudon. Experiences in Italy and Loudon's encouragement also stimulated an interest in natural history. He discussed natural history illustration in Loudon's *Gardener's Magazine* (1838), and illustrated Jane Loudon's Ladies' Flower Garden series (1839–48) and *British Wild Flowers* (1844), as well as J. O. Westwood's *British Butterflies and their Transformations* (1841) and *British Moths and their Transformations* (1845). These addressed identification and habitat without sacrificing artistry. Humphreys' *The Genera of British Moths* and *The Genera and Species of British Butterflies* (1859) displayed aesthetic qualities. *Ocean Gardens* (1856), *River Gardens* (1857), and *The Butterfly Vivarium* (1858) were cheaper and illustrated with coloured wood-engravings. Humphreys also illustrated other popular natural history books, often in colour.

Humphreys' antiquarianism was broader than his Italian interests implied. He illustrated illuminated manuscripts from many countries, including *Illuminated Illustrations of Froissart* (2 vols., 1844–5), *Illuminated Books of the Middle Ages* (1844–9), *The Art of Illumination and Missal Painting* (1848) and *The Origin and Progress of the Art of Writing* (1852). Other works featured reproductions of printing. *A History of the Art of Printing* (1867), Holbein's *Dance of Death* (1868), and *Masterpieces of the Early Printers and Engravers* (1868–9) used photolithography, but *Rembrandt's Etchings* (1871) was illustrated with photographs. Humphreys also illustrated William Blades's *The Biography and Typography of William Caxton* (1877). These show he understood the contribution words make to page design. In addition he published books on coinage intended as cheap, illustrated guides, such as *The Coin Collector's Manual* (2 vols., 1853), or those that promised a faithful representation through colour printing or embossed metal: *The Coins of England* (1846), *Ancient Coins* (1849), and *The Coinage of the British Empire* (1853).

Humphreys ventured into fiction with *Diamonds and Dust* (1856), *Goethe in Strasbourg* (1860), and *Stories by an Archaeologist and his Friends* (1856), and contributed diversely and extensively to journals, including the *Illuminators' Magazine* and the *Intellectual Observer*. All Humphreys' interests coalesced in gift books, his best-known work. Lithography enabled him to combine illustrations, ornament, and calligraphy into an expressive unity. Some mixed reproductions with page decoration, such as *The Illuminated Calendar and Home Diary* (1845 and 1846) and *A*

Record of the Black Prince (1848). Others contained more original work, notably *Parables of Our Lord* (1846), *Maxims and Precepts of the Saviour* (1848) and *Sentiments and Similes of Shakespeare* (1851). While many owed much to medieval and Renaissance art, a series published by Paul Jerrard from 1851 is rococo in style.

Humphreys ornamented many books illustrated with wood-engravings, mostly editions of poetry aimed at the gift-book market. Examples include Eden Warwick's *The Poets' Pleasaunce* (1847), Martin Tupper's *Proverbial Philosophy* (1853), *The Poetical Works of George Herbert* (1855), *Rhymes and Roundelayes in Praise of a Country Life* (1856), and Thomson's *The Seasons* (1858). Among those using colour are *Christmas with the Poets* (1850), *Rouman Anthology* (1856), and *The Poems of Oliver Goldsmith* (1858). His involvement may have extended to the typography, as with James Anderson's *Ladies of the Reformation* (1854).

Humphreys died at 7 Westbourne Square, London, on 10 June 1879. He is deservedly remembered for his extensive and significant contribution to the commercially produced book. His interest in architectural colour carried over into colour printing and the design of book covers, for which he exploited many techniques and materials. He is less well-known for his other activities, despite their involvement with the culture of his day.

HOWARD LEATHLEAN

Sources R. McLean, *Victorian book design and colour printing*, rev. edn (1972) · H. Leathlean, 'Henry Noel Humphreys and the getting-up of books in the mid-nineteenth century', *Book Collector*, 38 (1989), 192–209 · H. Leathlean, 'The archaeology of the art director', *Journal of Design History*, 6 (1993), 229–45 · H. Leathlean, 'Paul Jerrard, publisher of "special presents"', *Book Collector*, 40 (1991), 169–96 · J. O. Westwood, *The Academy* (21 June 1879), 550 · *The Athenaeum* (21 June 1879), 800 · *The Builder*, 37 (1879), 698 · *The Garden* (14 June 1879) · *Gardeners' Chronicle*, new ser., 11 (1879), 766 · *N&Q*, 5th ser., 11 (1879), 500 · *The Times* (16 June 1879) · H. Leathlean, 'Blood on his hands: the "inimitable pains" of a Pre-Raphaelite episode', *Journal of Pre-Raphaelite and Aesthetic Studies*, 1/2 (1988), 41–53 · H. Leathlean, 'Henry Noel Humphreys and early photolithography', *Book Historian*, 6 (1991), 88–91, 105 · H. Leathlean, 'Loudon's Architectural Magazine and the houses of parliament competition', *Victorian Periodicals Review*, 26 (1993), 145–53 · H. Leathlean, 'Henry Noel Humphreys and some Pre-Raphaelite imagery', *Journal of Pre-Raphaelite Studies*, 7/2 (1987), 41–54 · [W. Robinson ?], 'Henry Noel Humphreys', *The Garden*, 18 (1881), i–xii · private information (2004) · U. Reading, Longman papers

Archives St Bride Institute, London, St Bride Printing Library · U. Reading, Longman archive · V&A, department of prints and drawings · Yale U. CBA

Likenesses R. and E. Taylor, engraving (after portrait by S. T.?), repro. in Robinson?, 'Henry Noel Humphreys', ii

Wealth at death under £800: administration, 17 Feb 1880, *CGPLA Eng. & Wales*

Humphreys, Samuel (*c*.1697–1737), translator and librettist, is of unknown parentage. His poetic output was chiefly limited to the years 1728–32, in which appeared *Canons* (1728), for which the duke of Chandos gave him £20, and two other occasional pieces. His 1733 edition of Matthew Prior's *Poems* contained a life of Prior that was reprinted in Bell's edition of 1777.

Beginning in 1730 Humphreys was George Frideric Handel's chief literary factotum at the King's Theatre; he provided the additional text for Handel's expanded revival of the oratorio *Esther* (1732) and original word books for *Deborah* (1733) and *Athalia* (1733). He also wrote the libretto for John Christopher Smith the younger's oratorio *Ulysses* (1733).

'[S]ome Disappointments' Humphreys met with 'forc'd him to appear as a Translator' (*London Magazine*) as which he had considerable employment. He provided the English translations for the printed librettos of Handel's operas *Poro* (1731), the revised *Rinaldo* (1731), *Ezio* (1732), *Sosarme* (1732), and *Orlando* (1733), as well as *Venceslao* (1731) and Leo's *Catone in Utica* (1732), produced by Handel. In the second half of the decade he published three large folio volumes of biblical commentary, *The Sacred Books of the Old and New Testaments* (1735–9).

Humphreys' most popular work was his *Peruvian Tales* (1734), translated from the French of Thomas-Simon Gueullette; Humphreys's preface provides a defence of such fictions. Humphreys's two volumes were continued with a third by Samuel Kelly. The *Tales* ran through eight editions that century. He also translated the *Spectacle de la nature* by Antoine Noël, abbé de la Pluche (1733) and works by Boccaccio, Crébillon, and La Fontaine.

Humphreys died of consumption at Canonbury House, Islington, where he had rooms, on 11 January 1737, and was buried in Islington churchyard. An auction catalogue of his library was published by the bookseller John Wilcox, probably in 1738.   THOMAS N. McGEARY

Sources *The history and antiquities of Canonbury-house, at Islington* (1788), no. 49 [2/4] of *Bibliotheca topographica Britannica*, ed. J. Nichols (1780–1800), 32–3 · *London Magazine*, 6 (1737), 53 · W. Dean, *Handel's dramatic oratorios and masques* (1959) · R. Smith, *Handel's oratorios and eighteenth-century thought* (1995) · R. Smith, 'Handel's English librettists', *The Cambridge companion to Handel*, ed. D. Burrows (1997), 92–108 · W. Dean, 'Samuel Humphreys', *New Grove* · *DNB* · *ESTC* · *BL cat.*

Humphreys, Sir (Richard Somers) Travers Christmas

(1867–1956), judge, was born on 4 August 1867 in Bloomsbury, London, the fourth son and sixth child of Charles Octavius Humphreys, a solicitor specializing in criminal cases, and his wife, Harriet Ann Grain, sister of the entertainer R. Corney Grain. His father's half-sister was the first wife of the earl of Halsbury. Humphreys was educated at Shrewsbury School and Trinity Hall, Cambridge, where he stroked a trial university eight and graduated with a pass BA in 1889. He was called to the bar by the Inner Temple in 1889 and, joining Archibald Bodkin in the chambers of E. T. E. Besley, soon concentrated on practice in the criminal courts. On 28 May 1896 he married Zoë Marguerite (d. 1953), daughter of Henri Philippe Neumans, the artist, of Antwerp; they had two sons, the elder of whom was killed in France in 1917.

Humphreys was appointed counsel for the crown at the Middlesex and north London sessions in 1905, junior counsel for the crown at the central criminal court in 1908, and a senior counsel in 1916. As a prosecutor it was said of him that 'He's so damned fair that he leaves nothing for the defence to say'. He was recorder of Chichester from 1921 to 1926, when he became recorder of Cambridge. He was elected a bencher of his inn in 1922 and knighted in 1925. There were at this time few judges who specialized in criminal law and in 1928 Humphreys was appointed by Lord Chancellor Cave to the King's Bench Division to redress the balance. In 1946 he was sworn of the privy council and when he retired in 1951 he was the senior and oldest King's Bench judge.

The story of Humphreys's life is the story of the criminal law of his time. He first came into prominence in 1895 when, led by Sir Edward Clarke and Charles Mathews, he appeared as junior counsel in the cases linked with the downfall of Oscar Wilde. In 1910 he was junior counsel in the prosecution of H. H. Crippen for the murder of his wife. He afterwards wrote that he never regarded Crippen as a great criminal; he considered that he was rightly convicted, but in another country would have been given the benefit of 'extenuating circumstances'. In 1912 he was junior counsel in the prosecution of F. H. Seddon for poisoning Eliza Barrow with arsenic. He always regarded the quality of Seddon's guilt as a conclusive justification for retaining capital punishment for murder. In 1915 he appeared with Bodkin for the prosecution at the trial of G. J. Smith, the perpetrator of the 'brides in the bath' murders. In 1916 he was one of the brilliant team who prosecuted Sir Roger Casement for treason. At the central criminal court in 1922 the calm skill of his cross-examination secured the conviction of Horatio Bottomley for fraudulent conversion. In the same year he was junior to the solicitor-general in the prosecution of Frederick Bywaters and Edith Thompson for the murder of her husband. In 1925 he led for the crown in the prosecution of W. C. Hobbs, the blackmailer of Sir Hari Singh.

As a judge Humphreys tried many criminal cases which attracted much public attention. In 1932 he presided at the trial of Mrs Barney, a society woman charged with the murder of her lover but acquitted at the central criminal court. In the following year he tried Leopold Harris and fifteen other persons on charges arising out of systematic arson to defraud insurance companies. The case lasted thirty-three days and his summing-up to the jury took thirteen hours. In 1935 he tried Mrs Rattenbury and her young lover, George Stoner, for the murder of her husband. The man was convicted, but did not hang; the woman was acquitted but committed suicide. At the Lewes assizes in 1949 Humphreys presided at the trial of J. G. Haigh, the acid bath murderer. The defence of insanity, as presented, made the case particularly difficult, but, although eighty-two years old, the judge handled it with conspicuous efficiency and impeccable fairness.

For six years or so following the end of the Second World War Humphreys frequently sat in the court of criminal appeal with Lord Goddard, lord chief justice, as his right-hand man, constituting a formidable court which did much to maintain law and order in the troubled post-war years. By the end of his life Humphreys had become in the public mind the embodiment of English criminal justice.

He was vigorous, spare of figure, and dry in manner, and on the bench quietly efficient, without either vanity or display. Although without deep learning, he was an acknowledged master of the criminal law. He was also a master of the art of summing up and approached every case with a cool good sense and knowledge of the world, unimpressed by drama, romance, or 'glamour'. He was sociable and good company, but his keen sense of humour was always kept rigorously under control. This was characteristic of the habits of discipline inherited from the late Victorian middle class from which he sprang. His views on crime and its consequences were strict and traditional without sadism. He simply believed that punishment, including capital and corporal punishment, helped to diminish crime and that too much emphasis on the comfort of prisoners encouraged it. He also had a firm faith in the jury system and said that 'a jury, rightly directed, is always right'.

In 1946 Humphreys published a book of reminiscences under the title *Criminal Days*, which included a vivid account of his early background and of the courts during his first years at the bar. In 1953 he published *A Book of Trials*. He was a popular member of the Garrick Club and also an enthusiastic yachtsman. He died in London on 20 February 1956. His wife, who was appointed a JP of Middlesex in 1922, predeceased him. His surviving son, (Travers) Christmas *Humphreys, was himself in his turn senior counsel for the crown at the central criminal court for many years and appeared before his father in several of his famous cases; he became an additional judge of the central criminal court.

F. H. COWPER, *rev.* ALEC SAMUELS

Sources *The Times* (21 Feb 1956) • *Law Times* (2 March 1956) • B. Roberts, *Sir Travers Humphreys: his career and cases* (1936) • S. Jackson, *The life and cases of Mr Justice Humphreys* (1952) • D. G. Browne, *Sir Travers Humphreys* (1960) • Burke, *Peerage* (1939) • *CGPLA Eng. & Wales* (1956)
Likenesses W. Stoneman, three photographs, 1931–46, NPG • H. Knight, portrait, Saddlers Company, London
Wealth at death £17,372 5s. 9d.: probate, 4 April 1956, *CGPLA Eng. & Wales*

Humphries, John (*b.* in or after **1706**), composer, published *Six Solos for a Violin and Base with a Thorough Base for the Harpsichord* in 1726, stating in its preface that it was the first work of a young man 'not now above 19'. Authorities are divided as to whether he was also the composer who published various concertos and sonatas for violin, notable for their early use of wind instruments, under the name J. S. Humphries, who was active in the same period. If he was not J. S. Humphries, he probably died *c.*1730. If he was J. S. Humphries, then he probably died *c.*1740. Alfred Moffat published an arrangement of one of John Humphries's violin pieces in his Old English Violin Music series with Novello, and made an early attempt to distinguish between John and J. S. Humphries. The work described as John Humphries's op. 2, twelve concertos for strings, was republished by Garland in 1989.

L. M. MIDDLETON, *rev.* K. D. REYNOLDS

Sources F. Kidson, 'Humphries, John', Grove, *Dict. mus.* (1927) • F. Kidson, 'Humphries, J. S.', Grove, *Dict. mus.* (1927) • O. Edwards,

'Humphries, John', *New Grove* • J. Humphries, preface, *Six solos for a violin and base* (1726)

Humphries, Richard (*c.*1760–1827), prize-fighter, often called the Gentleman Boxer, was probably the son of an army officer who, during his son's boyhood, became destitute on discharge. Humphries appeared as a young boxing instructor at rooms in Panton Street, Haymarket, London, and gained rapid popularity, particularly among upperclass sportsmen, impressing with his fine physique, his elegant boxing style, and—not common among the fistic professors—his polished manners. At first he skirted the edges of the prize-ring, acting as second to the champion, Tom Johnson, before competing himself at the Newmarket spring meeting in May 1786 before the prince of Wales, the duke of York, and a group of French aristocrats. It was an occasion which greatly enhanced the status of a sport which for more than twenty years had been unreliable and ill supported, with just the audience to appreciate the quickness, grace, and skill of Humphries as he wore down his game opponent, Sam Martin, the Bath Butcher.

After this victory Humphries was acknowledged as a leading contestant for the championship along with Daniel Mendoza, who disposed of the unfortunate Martin more quickly than Humphries had done. The two men emerged as ideal foils for each other: Humphries was the clean-limbed Englishman, poised and self-possessed, while Mendoza was the handsome, dashing Jew, dark and darting, highly skilled as a boxer, and volatile by nature. The two were to dominate the boxing scene into the early 1790s with three memorable encounters. Even before the men's first contest, at Odiham in Hampshire on 19 January 1788, the press was carrying almost daily reports of their preparations. At length Humphries was the winner here but, in a contest that was full of incident, the victory was far from decisive. Humphries's second, for example, the rough former champion Johnson, berated his opponent throughout and once even saved his man from falling. Mendoza's defeat, on the other hand, was largely due to a sprained ankle from slipping down. The inevitable rematch took place about fifteen months later in Henry Thornton's Stilton Park in Huntingdonshire. Again the result appeared to have no finality about it, though this time Mendoza was declared the winner, and so the series continued to the final decisive encounter in the large enclosure of an inn near Doncaster on 29 September 1790. Humphries had by then been enjoying a racy lifestyle and had also been quite ill. His fitness and appearance had noticeably suffered and, before a large crowd who had each paid half a guinea entrance fee, Mendoza emerged as the clear winner.

This was one of the few occasions when Humphries's cool judgement deserted him during a fight, though he scarcely justified his title of gentleman when acting as a second, when he went well beyond what the rules allowed in supporting his boxer. During this early part of his boxing life, mixing with the leading young swells of the day and sharing their arrogance, his behaviour could be unreliable and even rude—particularly towards Mendoza—

Richard Humphries (c.1760–1827), by John Hoppner

but prudence was the hallmark of his later years. Aided by his consistent backer, a Mr Bradyl, he invested his gains from the sport wisely and established what proved to be a flourishing coal business at the Adelphi, near the Savoy Steps on the banks of the Thames. He died in 1827, missed by many friends and in what were described as affluent circumstances.   DENNIS BRAILSFORD

Sources Pancratia, or, A history of pugilism, 2nd edn (1815) · H. D. Miles, Pugilistica: the history of British boxing, 3 vols. (1906) · F. Henning, Fights for the championship, 2 vols. (1902) · Sporting Magazine, new ser. (1793) · Daily Universal Advertiser (Dec 1797) · D. Brailsford, Bareknuckles: a social history of prize fighting (1988)
Likenesses J. Young, engraving, 1788 (after J. Hoppner), repro. in T. Sawyer, Noble art (1989), 32 · J. Young, mezzotint, pubd 1788 (after W. Whitby), BM, NPG · J. Hoppner, oils, Metropolitan Museum of Art, New York [see illus.] · double portrait, drawing (with Mendoza), repro. in Brailsford, Bareknuckles, 69 · drawing, repro. in Henning, Fights for the championship, 1.110
Wealth at death in affluent circumstances: Henning, Fights

Humphry, Sir George Murray (1820–1896), surgeon, born at Sudbury in Suffolk on 18 July 1820, was the third son of William Wood Humphry, barrister and distributor of stamps for Suffolk, and Betsy Ann Gilson. He was educated at the grammar schools of Sudbury and Dedham, and in 1836 he was apprenticed to J. G. Crosse, surgeon to the Norfolk and Norwich Hospital. In 1839 he entered as a student at St Bartholomew's Hospital in London. He passed the first MB examination at London University in 1840, obtaining the gold medal in anatomy and physiology, but he never applied for the final examination. He was admitted a member of the Royal College of Surgeons of England on 19 November 1841, and on 12 May 1842 he became a licentiate of the Society of Apothecaries.

On 31 October 1842 Humphry was appointed surgeon at Addenbrooke's Hospital, Cambridge. He was the youngest hospital surgeon in England, and at once began to give clinical lectures and systematic teaching in surgery. In 1847 he acted as deputy to the professor of anatomy, and he gave the lectures and demonstrations on human anatomy from 1847 to 1866. He entered himself a fellow-commoner at Downing College in 1847, graduating MB in 1852 and MD in 1859. From 1866 to 1883 Humphry was professor of human anatomy in the university. He resigned in order to take the newly founded but unpaid professorship of surgery. In 1869 he became the representative of the University of Cambridge on the General Medical Council. In 1880 he delivered the Rede lecture before the University of Cambridge, taking 'Man, past, present, and future' as his subject. He served on the council of the senate of the university, he was an honorary fellow of Downing College, and from 1884 he was a professorial fellow of King's College, Cambridge.

At the Royal College of Surgeons of England Humphry filled all the offices which his health would permit (he suffered attacks of pulmonary tuberculosis, phlebitis, typhoid fever, and pleurisy). Elected FRCS on 26 August 1844, when he was still a year below the statutory age, he served as a member of the council from 1864 to 1884, was Arris and Gale lecturer on anatomy and physiology from 1871 to 1873, a member of the court of examiners from 1877 to 1887, and Hunterian orator in 1879. He declined to be nominated for the offices of vice-president and president.

In September 1849 Humphry married Mary, daughter of Daniel Robert McNab, surgeon, of Epping; they had a daughter and a son. Humphry was elected FRS in 1859, after having written A Treatise on the Human Skeleton, Including the Joints (1858), which had illustrations by his wife. Shortly after, he wrote On the Coagulation of the Blood in the Venous System during Life (1859), a subject of which he had had painful experience during his own illnesses, and The Human Foot and the Human Hand (1861). He became president of the Cambridge and Huntingdon branch of the British Medical Association and in 1867 he presided over the physiological section of the British Association for the Advancement of Science. In 1870 he gave six lectures on the architecture of the human body as a part of the Fullerian course at the Royal Institution of London. At various times he had presidential roles in the Cambridge Medical Society (which he helped to form), the Sanitary Society of Great Britain (1882–3), the Anatomical Society (1887), and the Pathological Society of London (1891–3). He also wrote Observations in Myology (1872), a guidebook to Cambridge (1880), and Old Age (1889). He was knighted in 1891. Humphry died at his residence, Grove Lodge, Cambridge, on 24 September 1896, survived by his wife. He was buried at the Mill Road cemetery, Cambridge.

Humphry began as a general practitioner without a practice, poor and without connections, but became one of the most influential people in the University of Cambridge; he brought its insignificant medical school into world renown, and left an estate valued at £80,000. He was, primarily, a scientist and a collector, particularly of items for the museum of anatomy and surgical pathology. He was one of the first to attempt to bring human anatomy into line with the science of morphology. He was a good surgeon, though major operations always caused him great anxiety; he was the first in England to remove successfully a tumour from the male bladder, and one of the first to advocate the advantages of the suprapubic method. From the 1870s he became a major figure in the vivisection debate. Humphry lived austerely but was hospitable and generous. He was resourceful, and generally succeeded in getting his own way, but always believed that his aims were directed to the greater good of his profession.   D'A. POWER, *rev.* CHRISTIAN KERSLAKE

Sources H. Rolleston, 'Sir George Murray Humphry', *Annals of Medical History*, 9 (1927), 1–11 · *Medico-Chirurgical Transactions*, 80 (1897) · *St Bartholomew's Hospital Reports*, 32 (1896) · personal knowledge (1901) · private information (1901) · *CGPLA Eng. & Wales* (1897) · *DNB*
Likenesses W. W. Ouless, oils, 1886, FM Cam. · C. E. Brock, oils, 1891?, U. Cam., department of pathology · H. Wiles, marble bust, *c.*1891, Addenbrooke's Hospital, Cambridge · H. R. Hope-Pinker, plaster model, 1893 (for a bust, c.1904), RCS Eng. · H. R. Hope-Pinker, bronze bust, *c.*1904, U. Cam., department of pathology · K. M. Humphry, oils, town hall, Sudbury, Suffolk · engraving (after W. W. Ouless) · photograph, Downing College, Cambridge
Wealth at death £80,199 0s. 4d.: resworn probate, Feb 1897, *CGPLA Eng. & Wales* (1896)

Humphry, Ozias (1742–1810), miniature and portrait painter, was born on 8 September 1742 at Honiton, Devon, where he was baptized on 21 September, the eldest surviving child of George Humphry (*d.* 1759), peruke-maker and mercer, and his wife, Elizabeth (*d.* 1790), daughter of Nicholas Hooper of Braunton, Devon. His early aptitude for drawing became evident while he was still attending the grammar school in Honiton; his parents were persuaded to send him to London in 1757 for formal tuition at William Shipley's drawing academy and to study at the duke of Richmond's sculpture gallery in Privy Gardens. The intention was that these studies would enable Humphry to produce patterns for his mother's lace-manufacturing business, but when he returned to Honiton, following the death of his father, he made clear his desire to train as a painter. To this end Humphry and his mother negotiated a three-year apprenticeship with the miniaturist Samuel Collins in Bath, from whom Humphry learnt the art of miniature painting. His earliest miniatures, painted in watercolour on ivory, date from about 1760. In 1762, with a year of the apprenticeship still to run, Collins absconded to Dublin to escape his creditors. As a result the contract with Humphry was formally dissolved and he set up in independent practice in Bath. He took lodgings with the composer Thomas Linley the elder and his family, and through them he met the painters Thomas Gainsborough, whose working practices he recorded, and William Hoare. Although Humphry met with success in Bath, encouraged by Sir Joshua Reynolds, whom he had met on a visit to London in 1763, he decided to settle in London. Reynolds had permitted Humphry to copy some of his paintings and probably also sat to Humphry for the miniature which is

Ozias Humphry (1742–1810), self-portrait, *c.*1770

now at Corsham Court, Wiltshire. Humphry was disappointed by Reynolds's failure to assist him after his arrival in London in August 1764 but despite this set-back he soon established a large clientele, and from 1768 to 1773 he practised from a well-appointed studio at 21 King Street, Covent Garden, exhibiting at the Society of Artists (of which he became a member in 1773) from 1765 to 1771. He worked quickly, usually at this early stage in watercolour on ivory, and occasionally signing his work in monogram, OH. Royal commissions to paint Queen Charlotte (1766) and Charlotte, princess royal (1769) followed the purchase by George III of Humphry's much acclaimed miniature of John Mealing (Royal Collection) from the exhibition of the Society of Artists in 1766. The king's brothers, Henry Frederick, duke of Cumberland, and William Henry, first duke of Gloucester, also became patrons, but it was John Frederick, third duke of Dorset, who was to prove Humphry's most enduring mentor, despite the artist's often belligerent attitude towards his clients. However, this initial pattern of success and prosperity failed to develop throughout Humphry's career, which was interrupted twice by long visits abroad.

A four-year visit to Italy (1773–7), embarked on with his friend George Romney, was prompted by the rejection in 1771 of Humphry's suit to marry Charlotte Paine, the elder sister of his friend the architect James Paine the younger, but more importantly by the serious damage to his eyesight sustained during a riding accident in 1772. This persuaded Humphry that he should work in oils on a large scale rather than in miniature, and he determined to study the old masters in Italy in the hope that this experience would enable him to establish a successful practice as a portrait painter in oils on his return. In fact, unlike Romney, this was not to prove the case; much of Humphry's time in Italy was actually spent working as a miniaturist, furnished with introductions to sitters such as the queen of Naples and Cardinal Albani from the duke of Gloucester, and painting the countess of Albany, wife of Charles Edward Stuart, the Young Pretender, in miniature in 1776. Humphry studied the Borghese collection in Rome in 1773 and copied paintings in the Uffizi in Florence in 1775 in the company of Maria Hadfield, later Mrs Cosway; he also travelled extensively in Italy and formed a broad circle of friends, which included the painters Thomas Jenkins and Henry Tresham, the sculptor Thomas Banks, and the antiquary Charles Townley, before he returned to London in August 1777.

During the period 1777 to 1785 Humphry attempted to concentrate on oil painting, but without the success that he had enjoyed as a miniaturist before his trip to Italy. He failed to translate the qualities that lent such distinction to his miniatures—elegant and inventive compositions, rich colouring, and a grandeur in the presentation of his sitters reminiscent of Reynolds—to the medium of oil. Although 'he was never better at oil portraits than a third-rate echo of Romney's style' (E. Waterhouse, *Painting in Britain, 1530 to 1790*, rev. 4th edn, 1988, 336), Humphry declined to follow the advice of friends, such as the composer William Jackson of Exeter, who recognized that 'you have hurt yourself by changing your branch of painting' (Humphry MS RA HU 2/120). He was, however, elected an associate of the Royal Academy in 1779, the year in which he first exhibited at the academy, and was subsequently elected Royal Academician in 1791. Sensing the downturn in his fortunes, and in pursuit of a more lucrative market for his talents, Humphry followed the suggestion of his friend the engraver Sir Robert Strange that he should work in India, and on 25 January 1785 he sailed for Calcutta, where he arrived in August.

Humphry's letters to Mary Boydell, to whom he had formed an attachment which she broke off while he was in India, record the progress of his career while working as a miniaturist there, and his early anxiety that his rival, the miniaturist John Smart, who also travelled to India in 1785, might compete for Humphry's clients in Calcutta. This fear proved unfounded as Smart remained in Madras, and in 1786 Humphry obtained a commission through the governor-general, Sir John Macpherson, to paint the nabob of Oudh and his courtiers at Lucknow. The fee of 47,000 rupees that was owed to him for this work was never paid, and this outstanding debt, the source of later litigation, was to embitter not only Humphry's stay in India but the remainder of his life. Finding the climate debilitating, and that, as he reported in mid-1786, his employment in India did not match up to his expectations, he returned to London in 1787.

Humphry's career showed every sign of reviving on his return; his old patron the duke of Dorset gave him a large commission to copy ancestral portraits at Knole, Kent, in miniature and applied to Lord Salisbury, recommending Humphry's appointment to the post of miniature painter to the king in 1789. But once again a deterioration in Humphry's sight, in 1791, forced him into a change of direction, and he began to concentrate on drawing in crayon. His success in this medium was marked by his appointment as portrait painter in crayons to the king (1792) through the good offices of the duke of Dorset and Benjamin West, president of the Royal Academy. However, Humphry's correspondence in the mid-1790s is peppered with a series of complaints by clients that his portraits were not reasonable likenesses of his sitters, and his failing talents appeared to have signalled the onset of his almost complete loss of vision in 1797. From then onwards Humphry was forced to make a stream of ever more strident demands to past patrons and to people of influence to supply him with 'some little appointment in the nature of a Sinecure (almost)' to support him in his old age (Humphry MS RA HU 5/115). He failed in his bid for the post of commissioner of the lottery, and in his request for the duke of Dorset to intercede on his behalf with the king to appoint him keeper of the gems, medals, and miniatures in his majesty's collection. His persistent petitioning of those in positions of influence to assist him in his claim against the nabob of Oudh also proved fruitless. His only success was his sale, to Lord Egremont in 1805, of a painting attributed to Raphael, in return for a pension of £100 p.a.

Humphry died, aged sixty-seven, on 9 March 1810 at 39 Thornhaugh Street, Bedford Square, London, after a short illness; he was buried in St James's burial-ground, Hampstead Road. He died unmarried, but left a son, William *Upcott, from his liaison with Delly Wickers (d. 1786). Upcott became a noted collector and antiquary and collated and bound the papers and letters that Humphry had kept meticulously throughout his life (Royal Academy). It is therefore not only as 'one of the best English miniaturists' (Long, 230) that Humphry is now remembered but also as a highly significant chronicler of the artistic environment in which he moved: 'his papers are one of the most significant sources for any study of artistic circles in the second half of the eighteenth century' (*Report on the Papers of Ozias Humphry*, 3). A group of paintings and drawings by Humphry of the Linley family is in the Victoria Art Gallery, Bath; his sketchbooks of India, containing impressions so vivid as to earn him the sobriquet 'a genre and landscape painter manqué' (Archer, 187), are now in the British Museum, together with his copy book, memoranda, and cashbooks (BL, Add. MSS 15958–15969). Examples of his miniatures can be seen at the Victoria and Albert Museum and at the National Portrait Gallery, London.

V. REMINGTON

Sources 'Letters and papers of Ozias Humphry', 8 vols., RA · *Report on the papers of Ozias Humphry … in the Royal Academy of Arts*, HMC (1972) · G. C. Williamson, *Ozias Humphry* (1918) · J. Brewer, *The pleasures of the imagination: English culture in the eighteenth century* (1997), 295–317 · J. Ingamells, ed., *A dictionary of British and Irish travellers in Italy, 1701–1800* (1997), 534–6 · M. Archer, *India and British portraiture, 1770–1825* (1979), 186–204 · W. Foster, 'British artists in India, 1760–1820', *Walpole Society*, 19 (1930–31), 1–88, esp. 51–5 ·

E. Cotton, 'An artist and his fees: the story of the suit brought by Ozias Humphry RA against the governor-general', *Bengal Past and Present*, 34 (1927), 1–19 • B. S. Long, *British miniaturists* (1929), 229–31 • D. Foskett, *Miniatures: dictionary and guide* (1987), 390–400, 572–3 • G. Reynolds, *English portrait miniatures* (1952); rev. edn (1988), 134–8 • *GM*, 1st ser., 80 (1810), 378–80 • *Works by and paintings in the collection of Ozias Humphry* (1810), 1–56 [sale catalogue, Christies, 29 June 1810] • parish register, Honiton, 1734–89 [baptisms and marriages] • Graves, *RA exhibitors*

Archives BL, accounts and notebook, Add. MSS 22947–22952 • BL, catalogue of his art collection, Add. MS 49682 • BL, sketchbooks, Add. MSS 15958–15969 • Bodl. Oxf., corresp. • CKS, papers • RA, corresp. and papers • Yale U., Beinecke L., Indian diary | BL, papers relating to court of Oudh, Add. MS 13532 • FM Cam., letter to Prince Hoare describing visit to Venice and sending greetings to Fuseli

Likenesses O. Humphry, self-portrait, watercolour drawing, *c*.1765–1770, RA • O. Humphry, self-portrait, chalk drawing, *c*.1770, BM [*see illus.*] • V. Green, mezzotint, pubd 1772 (after G. Romney), BM, NPG • G. Romney, oils, 1772, Knole, Kent • H. Spicer, miniature, enamel?, 1772 (after Romney); Sothebys, 12 Oct 1964 • C. Watson, stipple, 1784 (after Romney) • G. Stuart, oils, *c*.1785, Wadsworth Athenaeum, Hertfordshire • H. Edridge, pencil and wash drawing, 1802, BM • W. Daniel, stipple, 1809 (after George Dance) • G. Dance, drawing, RA • D. P. Pariset, stipple (after P. Falconet, 1768), BM, NPG • H. Singleton, group portrait, oils (*Royal Academicians*, 1793), RA

Humphry, William Gilson (1815–1886), Church of England clergyman and biblical scholar, born at Sudbury, Suffolk, on 30 January 1815, was the son of William Wood Humphry, barrister, and his wife, Betsy Ann, *née* Gilson; he was the brother of George Murray *Humphry, professor of surgery in the University of Cambridge. Humphry was educated at Carmalt's school, Putney, and afterwards at Shrewsbury, under Dr Samuel Butler, where he became captain of the school. In 1833 he entered Trinity College, Cambridge, and in 1835 he won the Pitt scholarship. Two years later he graduated as senior classic, second chancellor's medallist, and twenty-seventh wrangler, and in 1839 he was elected a fellow of his college.

Humphry was intended for the legal profession, but this proved distasteful to him after a short period of practice, and in 1842 he took holy orders. He stayed at Trinity, acting as steward and assistant tutor there, and he was proctor of the university in 1845–6. From 1847 to 1855 he was examining chaplain to Bishop C. J. Blomfield of London. In 1852 Humphry became rector of Northolt, Middlesex. From 1855 until his death in 1886 he was vicar of St Martin-in-the-Fields, London. He was appointed Hulsean lecturer for 1849 and 1850 and his lectures were published in 1850 as *The Early Progress of the Gospel* and *The Doctrine of a Future State*; he was Boyle lecturer for 1857 and 1858, publishing *The Character of St Paul*, in 1859. He was a member of the royal commission on clerical subscription in 1865, and of the ritual commission in 1869, and was one of those appointed by convocation in 1870 to revise the Authorized Version of the New Testament. As one of the treasurers of the Society for Promoting Christian Knowledge he steered the society through at least one period of difficulty and danger, and his business capacity and judgement during the thirty years he held the office were of great service to the society. He was a diligent parish priest, and gave special attention to the educational institutions of his parish. In 1852 he married Caroline Maria, only daughter of George *D'Oyly DD, rector of Lambeth; she survived him. Humphry died on 10 January 1886 at the vicarage, Trafalgar Square, London, and was buried in Brompton cemetery.

Humphry published widely on biblical subjects, including *A Commentary on the Acts of the Apostles* (1847) known in its time as 'Humphry on the Acts'; *The Godly Life* was published posthumously (1887) with a brief memoir.

A. M. HUMPHRY, *rev.* H. C. G. MATTHEW

Sources Venn, *Alum. Cant.* • W. G. Humphry, *The godly life* (1887) [with memoir] • Boase, *Mod. Eng. biog.* • Crockford (1886) • *Clergy List* (1885) • *CGPLA Eng. & Wales* (1886)

Archives LPL, annotated copy of Book of Common Prayer | LPL, letters to Tait • LUL, corresp. with Lord Overstone

Wealth at death £45,722 18s. 2d.: probate, 25 Feb 1886, *CGPLA Eng. & Wales*

Humphrys, Sir Francis Henry (1879–1971), colonial administrator and diplomatist, was born in Beatrice Street, Oswestry, Shropshire, on 24 April 1879, the eldest son of the Revd Walter Humphrys, assistant master at Oswestry grammar school, and his wife, Helen Agnes, daughter of the Revd Alfred Francis Boucher. He was educated at Shrewsbury School (1893–8), where he was captain of cricket and head of the school, and at Christ Church, Oxford, where he graduated with a third class in classical honour moderations in 1900. In the same year he joined the 2nd Worcestershire regiment as a second lieutenant and served in the Second South African War.

In 1902 Humphrys began his career in the Indian political service, much of which was spent among the tribes of the North-West Frontier Province. At Peshawar on 2 April 1907 he married Gertrude Mary (*b*. 1882), daughter of Sir Harold Arthur Deane, the first chief commissioner of the North-West Frontier Province. During the First World War he was political agent with the Waziristan frontier force, and also held a temporary commission in the RAF as a pilot (1918), an experience which instilled in him a lifelong enthusiasm for flying, culminating in his being made an honorary air commodore. After the war Humphrys became political agent of the Khyber (1919), and deputy foreign secretary of the government of India (1921), a post which he held until 1922, when he was appointed British minister to Afghanistan.

Three years before Humphrys's arrival in Kabul, King Amanullah had launched the Third Anglo-Afghan War, which ended in Afghanistan's gaining the right to control its own foreign relations. Amanullah's pursuit of his two most cherished objectives—the modernization of his country in the shortest possible time and independence from Britain—soon brought him into headlong conflict with Humphrys, whose previous eighteen years in India, mostly among the tribes across the frontier from Afghanistan, had not prepared him to deal with a ruler of such independence of mind. In addition Humphrys seems to have had some difficulty in adjusting to the fact that Afghanistan was no longer a dependency of British India.

Matters came to a head in summer 1928 after Amanullah's return from an eight-month visit to Europe. He immediately announced a wide-ranging programme of social and political reforms, which appears to have aroused the wrath of the tribes. In late autumn Kabul was besieged by rebel forces, and Amanullah was eventually forced to abdicate. Early in 1929 Humphrys supervised the safe aerial evacuation of several hundred Europeans from the city (a pioneering feat of aviation in sub-zero temperatures over high mountain ranges); both he and his wife were commended for their 'courage and fortitude' in the House of Commons on 4 February, and Gertie, as she was known, was made a DBE. The extent of British involvement in the revolt remains a matter of conjecture, but Humphrys and his colleagues warmly supported the candidature of Nadir Khan, Amanullah's successor, and vigorously opposed Amanullah's attempt to stage a comeback from his retreat in Kandahar. At the time his conduct was given the mark of government approval: having already been appointed KBE in 1924 and GCVO in 1928, he was now promoted to KCMG.

In autumn 1929 Humphrys was appointed high commissioner to the British-mandated state of Iraq. He stayed for six years, becoming the first British ambassador to the newly independent state in 1932. The decision to support Iraq's candidature for the League of Nations had been taken just before Humphrys's arrival, but some misgivings were expressed about the lack of guarantees for the Assyrian and Kurdish minorities after the transition to independence. For his part Humphrys maintained with some justice that any binding provision would not be compatible with the country's independent status. Unfortunately subsequent events, particularly the tragic fate of the Assyrians in the summer of 1933, showed the minorities' fears to have been well founded.

In 1932 Humphrys was further promoted to GCMG, and in 1935 he left public service for a career in the City. He presided over the creation of the British Sugar Corporation, served as its chairman between 1935 and 1949, and was also chairman of a number of other companies, including the Iraq Petroleum Company (1941–50). He took a keen interest in sport throughout his life; he is said to have bowled out W. G. Grace three times while at Oxford. Photographs show a distinguished proconsular figure with a commanding presence. He died after a brief illness on 28 August 1971 at Edgecombe Nursing Home, Hamstead Marshall, near Newbury, Berkshire. He was survived by his wife, a son, and two daughters.

PETER SLUGLETT, rev.

Sources The Times (1 Sept 1971) · Sugar News (Oct 1971) · The Salopian (Jan 1972) · V. Gregorian, The emergence of modern Afghanistan: politics of reform and modernisation, 1880–1946 (1969) · L. B. Poullada, Reform and rebellion in Afghanistan, 1919–1929 (1973) · P. Sluglett, Britain in Iraq, 1914–1932 (1976) · private information (2004) [K. Prior] · WWW · CGPLA Eng. & Wales (1972) · b. cert. · d. cert.
Archives BL OIOC, Halifax collection · BL OIOC, Reading collection
Likenesses group photograph, 1929, BL OIOC, photo s34/7d · photograph (in late middle age), repro. in The Times, 14

Wealth at death £32,295: probate, 5 Jan 1972, CGPLA Eng. & Wales

Humphrys, William (1794–1865), engraver, was born in Dublin, but early in life moved to America and settled in Philadelphia. He was a pupil of the Scots engraver George Murray, who, about 1810, established the firm of Murray, Draper & Co., which undertook banknote engraving. Humphrys's earliest published work appears to be several plates issued in S. F. Bradford's *Encyclopaedia* (1805–18). These were followed by line engraved vignettes for lottery advertisements after Joshua Shaw (1823), when his address was given as the south-west corner of Chesnut and Third streets, Philadelphia. A trade card described him as 'Engraver of history, landscape &c.'. In the same year a portrait of Gregory Bedell was engraved with J. Nesmith in stipple and line.

By October 1824 Humphrys had moved to London, where he engraved *Mother and Child*, after William Brockedon, for the *Literary Souvenir* (1825), in which annual he produced four plates until 1828. In 1826 the Society of Arts presented him with the gold Isis medal for his recipe of etching steel plates, the first menstruum to omit nitric acid. *The Bijou* of 1828 carried three of his engravings, and for S. Rogers's *Italy* (1830) he engraved *The Nun*, after Thomas Stothard, for which he was paid £40. He engraved a plate apiece for *Friendship's Offering* (1831), *Keepsake français* (1831), and *Wreath of Friendship* (c.1832), and for the print publishers, including Ackermann, Colnaghi, and Graves, he engraved *Sancho and the Duchess*, after C. R. Leslie, *Master Lambton*, after Thomas Lawrence, *Spanish Peasant Boy*, after Murillo, *George Washington*, after C. G. Stuart, and, in 1839, *Dowager Duchess of Beaufort*, after Francis Grant. *Magdalen*, after Correggio, was published by Ackermann in 1839.

By this time line engraving was on the wane, and, in common with many other engravers, Humphrys turned to mezzotint on steel, the first of such plates being *Master Lock*, after Lawrence, engraved for the eighth volume of *The Works of Thomas Lawrence* (1839). *The Meet of Melton Hunt*, after Grant, followed in 1840. Humphrys returned to America in 1843 and there contributed illustrations to editions of W. C. Bryant, H. W. Longfellow, and other poets. In 1844 *The Gift* annual carried an engraving of an incident in the early days of Washington after H. Inman. Humphrys was again in London in 1845, and engraved *Egeria*, after Correggio, for the Royal Irish Art Union (1846). Known in London as the American engraver, Humphrys was visited by the eminent engraver Alfred Jones in 1846. *The Coquette*, after Joshua Reynolds (1849), was done for Finden's *Royal Gallery of British Art* (1838–49).

Humphrys devoted the remainder of his artistic career to stamp engraving. He is credited with engraving a portrait of George Washington, possibly for the 1847 American issue, but he went on to work for Perkins, Bacon & Co., for whom he engraved the triangular Cape of Good Hope dies in 1853 and Queen Victoria's head for South Australia in January 1855; he retouched the penny black (February 1855), New Zealand (July 1855), and Queensland (November 1860). He is also credited between 1855 and

1862 with engravings for Van Diemen's Land (later Tasmania), St Helena, Ceylon, Grenada, and others. He then became an accountant in the music firm of Novello. Late in 1864 he suffered a stroke, after which he accepted an invitation to convalesce in Arthur Novello's villa at Genoa, where he died on 21 January 1865, aged seventy-one.

B. HUNNISETT

Sources D. M. Stauffer, *American engravers upon copper and steel*, 2 vols. (1907), vol. 1, pp. 134, 136; vol. 2, p. 246 · M. S. Fielding, *Supplement to American engravers upon copper and steel* (1917), 149 · Redgrave, *Artists* · W. S. Baker, *American engravers and their works* (1875) · Bryan, *Painters* (1903–5) · *Art Union*, 1 (1839), 157, 173 · *Art Union*, 5 (1843), 314 · W. G. Strickland, *A dictionary of Irish artists*, 1 (1913), 535 · R. Lister, *Prints and printmaking: a dictionary and handbook of the art in nineteenth-century Britain* (1984), 235 · *CGPLA Eng. & Wales* (1865)

Wealth at death under £800: probate, 28 Feb 1865, *CGPLA Eng. & Wales*

Humston [Humpston], **Robert** (d. 1606), Church of Ireland bishop of Down and Connor, began his ecclesiastical career in the diocese of Norwich and was possibly a member of the Hunston family of Boston and Walsoken, Norfolk. He is said to have graduated MA at Oxford. He was presented as rector of St Clement's, Norwich, by Sir Robert Woods in 1587, but if he was ever confirmed in this living his spell there was a short one, another presentation to it being made later the same year. His *A Sermon Preached at Reyfham in the Countie of Norfolk the 22 of September 1588* was published in London in 1589. In 1597 he was rector of Barrow, Cheshire. His Calvinist leanings likely encouraged his departure soon afterwards for Ireland, where the established church tended much more in that direction, and for the remainder of his life Humston was connected with the subjugation of Ulster and the associated attempts at establishing the reformed Church of Ireland there.

In 1601 Humston was preacher to the garrison of Carrickfergus. When the bishopric of Down and Connor fell vacant he travelled to London to seek his own nomination. He brought with him letters of recommendation from Adam Loftus, the archbishop of Dublin, the bishop of Chester, Lord Deputy Mountjoy, and Sir Arthur Chichester. The latter spoke of his learning, honesty, and 'the zeal he hath of establishing religion in the minds and understanding of those blind and ignorant people' (*CSP Ire., 1600–01*, 300). He preached at court on 7 June 1601. The following day John Whitgift, archbishop of Canterbury (a fellow student and associate of Loftus at Cambridge), recommended his appointment to Sir Robert Cecil. Nominated bishop of Down and Connor on 17 July 1601, Humston was not consecrated until 5 April 1602. The lack of extant papers makes it very difficult to assess his episcopate. It came at a time when the privately organized plantation of eastern Ulster was bringing large numbers of Scots and English settlers to the region, and when the state was seeking to assert its civil power in the area. To what extent Humston was involved in such developments is difficult to know; at the minimum, diocesan revenues would have needed re-establishing after the violence and destruction of previous years.

He made a Fee-Farm Lease of the Island of Magee, part of his Bishoprik, unto Sir Henry Piers, and Sir Francis Annesty, at 6l 13s 4d rent, which about 20 Years after was returned by a Regal Visitation, to be worth 200l per Annum. (*Whole Works of Sir James Ware*, 207)

but his reasons for so doing may have had more to do with the need speedily to gain income for the church than any impropriety (he received two pardons for such alienations in late 1606). Humston died at Kilroot, near Carrickfergus, co. Antrim, in 1606. His progeny, like his origins, are very difficult to trace: a son Robert is known to have presented a bowl to Trinity College, Dublin, in 1610.

MIHAIL DAFYDD EVANS

Sources J. B. Leslie and H. B. Swanzy, *Biographical succession lists of the clergy of diocese of Down* (1936) · *The whole works of Sir James Ware concerning Ireland*, ed. and trans. W. Harris, 1 (1739) · F. Blomefield and C. Parkin, *An essay towards a topographical history of the county of Norfolk*, [2nd edn], 11 vols. (1805–10), vol. 4 · *Calendar of the manuscripts of the most hon. the marquis of Salisbury*, 24 vols., HMC, 9 (1883–1976) · *CSP Ire., 1600–01; 1603–8* · P. E. McCullough, *Sermons at court: politics and religion in Elizabethan and Jacobean preaching* (1998) [incl. CD-ROM] · J. W. Blench, *Preaching in England in the late fifteenth and sixteenth centuries* (1964) · Wood, *Ath. Oxon.*

Hungerford. For this title name *see* individual entries under Hungerford; *see also* Rawdon, Elizabeth, *suo jure* Baroness Botreaux, *suo jure* Baroness Hungerford, *suo jure* Baroness Moleyns, *suo jure* Baroness Hastings, and countess of Moira (1731–1808).

Hungerford [*other married name* Cotell], **Agnes**, **Lady Hungerford** (d. 1523), murderer, is of unknown parentage. Little or nothing is known of her social background and contemporary genealogists of the Hungerford family remained conspicuously silent about her in an apparent attempt to extinguish her infamy from posterity. Her trial records suggest she may have been a gentlewoman because she maintained servants from Heytesbury, Wiltshire.

Agnes's first husband was John Cotell (d. 1518). They do not appear to have had any children. They both stayed in the household of Sir Edward Hungerford (d. 1522), landowner, soldier, and administrator, son of Sir Walter Hungerford of Heytesbury, Wiltshire, and his wife, Jane, during the summer of 1518. In 1523 Agnes was convicted of inciting and abetting the murder of her first husband, a crime for which she was hanged. A surviving account of her trial records that Cotell was strangled with a neckerchief by William Mathewe and William Ignes, yeomen of Heytesbury, at Farleigh Castle, Somerset, home of Sir Edward Hungerford, on 26 July 1518, 'by the procurement and abetting of Agnes Hungerford'. His body was then burnt in the castle's kitchen furnace. It is conceivable that she killed her first husband in order to marry the second, and that the latter was involved in some way in the murder. She appears to have married Hungerford soon after Cotell's death, since by 28 December she was living at Farleigh and was seemingly able to harbour her servants Mathewe and Ignes within the castle walls. They had no children, but she was stepmother to Hungerford's son and heir from his first marriage, Walter *Hungerford, later first Baron Hungerford of Heytesbury. In her husband's will, made on 14 December 1521 and proved in London on 29 January 1522 by Robert Collet, clerk, Hungerford bequeathed to her 'the residue of all' his 'goodes, detts, catalls, juells, plate, harnesse, and all other moveables whatsoever they be'; he also made her his sole executor (Hardy, 234).

Not until after Hungerford's death on 24 January 1522 were proceedings taken against Lady Hungerford and her accomplices for Cotell's murder. Presumably while he was alive Hungerford had been able to protect her from direct charges being brought. Lady Hungerford, Mathewe, and Ignes were indicted on 25 August 1522 and brought to trial on 27 November. She and Mathewe were both convicted in January 1523 and hanged at Tyburn on 20 February. Ignes claimed benefit of clergy but was later hanged once his plea was disallowed on charges of bigamy. During the trial an inventory was made, apparently from Lady Hungerford's own dictation, of her goods forfeited to the crown. In July 1523 all manors and estates seized and escheated, except for Heytesbury, were restored to Walter Hungerford. Lady Hungerford was buried at Grey Friars in London.   JAMES DAYBELL

Sources BL, Add. MS 6364, fol. 39r · will, PRO, PROB 11/20, sig. 21 [Sir Edward Hungerford] · E. E. Estcourt, 'The tragedy of Lady Hungerford', *GM*, 3rd ser., 4 (1858), 122 · W. J. Hardy, 'Lady Agnes Hungerford', *Antiquary*, 2 (Dec 1880), 233–6 · R. C. Hoare, *Hungerfordiana, or, Memoirs of the family of Hungerford* (1823) · J. E. Jackson, 'The tragedy of Alice Lady Hungerford', *GM*, 2nd ser., 36 (1851), 625–6 · J. G. Nichols, ed., *The chronicle of the grey friars of London*, CS, 53 (1852) · J. G. Nichols and J. E. Jackson, eds., 'Inventory of the goods of Dame Agnes Hungerford, attainted of murder 14 Hen. VIII', *Archaeologia*, 38/2, 353–72 · *DNB*
Wealth at death see inventory of goods forfeited to crown, 1522–3, Nichols and Jackson, eds., 'Inventory of the goods'

Hungerford, Sir Anthony (*bap.* 1567, *d.* 1627), religious convert and author, was baptized on 29 October 1567 at Great Bedwyn, Wiltshire, the second son of Anthony Hungerford (*d.* 1589) of Down Ampney, Gloucestershire, and his wife, Bridget, daughter of John Shelley of Mitchelgrove, Sussex, and granddaughter of Sir William Shelley, justice of the common pleas. Hungerford matriculated at St John's College, Oxford, on 12 April 1583, but left university without taking a degree. Wood suggests that this setback was forced upon him by his father's impoverishment, though Hungerford's own memoirs record that the family had recovered its fortunes by this time (Wood, 2.410). The explanation may have been at least partly religious: his father, though a puritan, had married into a Catholic family, and by 1584 Hungerford, encouraged by his mother, a convicted recusant, had been admitted to the Roman church. None the less, he was created MA on 9 July 1584.

Four years later, however, in 1588, Hungerford abandoned his new faith, arguing in justification that his youth had allowed him to be seduced by the Catholic emphasis on pleasing ceremonies and acts of charity and devotion, but that he could not reconcile himself to the conduct of certain church leaders, particularly the immorality of Pope Alexander VI, nor accept papal claims to infallibility. He subsequently wrote of his conversion in two restrained autobiographies, *The advise of a sonne, now professing the religion established in the present Church of England, to his deare mother, yet a Roman Catholic*, published in 1616, and *The memorial of a father to his deare children, containing an acknowledgement of God his great mercy in bringing him to the profession of the true religion established in the Church of England*, completed in April 1627 but published posthumously in 1639.

Hungerford's experiment with Catholicism had no adverse effect on his temporal advancement. He represented Marlborough in the 1593 parliament, and sat for Great Bedwyn, close to his family's principal estates, in 1597, 1601, and 1604. He made two profitable marriages, through which he secured his financial independence. By 1595 he had married Lucy, daughter of Sir Walter Hungerford of Farleigh, from the senior branch of the family, and widow of Sir John St John. The couple had one son, Edward *Hungerford (1596–1648) and two daughters before Lucy died on 4 June 1598. On 3 May 1605 Hungerford married Sarah, daughter of Giles Crouch, haberdasher, of Cornhill, London, and widow of William Wiseman of Uffington, Berkshire. They had two daughters and four sons, including Anthony *Hungerford (1607/8–1657).

Knighted on 11 December 1606, Sir Anthony was appointed deputy lieutenant of Wiltshire in 1610, a post which he relinquished in 1624 in favour of his heir; he also became a magistrate in three counties. He continued to live in Great Bedwyn until at least 1617, when he moved to his recently bought property at Black Bourton, Oxfordshire, where he died on 27 June 1627, little more than a month after his wife's death on 12 May. He was buried at the church there, where his sons erected a tablet to his memory.

HENRY LANCASTER

Sources A. Hungerford, *The advise of a sonne professing the religion established in the present Church of England … whereunto is added The memorial of a father to his deare children* (1639) · A. Hungerford, *The advice of a sonne* (1616) · J. Jackson, *Hungerford family collections*, 4 vols. · Wood, *Ath. Oxon.*, new edn, 2.410 · L. M. Roberts, 'Sir Anthony Hungerford's "memorial"', *EngHR*, 16 (1901), 292–307 · A. Davidson, 'Roman Catholicism in Oxfordshire', PhD diss., Bristol University, 1970 · Wilts. & Swindon RO, A1/150/2, fol. 224 · PRO, PROB 11/152, fol. 156v. · BL, Add. MS 33412, fols. 68–86; 23690, fols. 87v–88 · Foster, *Alum. Oxon.* · HoP, *Commons, 1558–1603*, 2.353 · W. A. Shaw, *The knights of England*, 2 vols. (1906)
Archives BL, autobiographical treatise, Add. MS 42504 · Devizes Museum Library, Hungerford family collections
Wealth at death £7073: Jackson, *Hungerford family*, vol. 3, pp. 8–9

Hungerford, Anthony (1607/8–1657), politician, was the eldest surviving son of Sir Anthony *Hungerford (*bap.* 1567, *d.* 1627) of Black Bourton, Oxfordshire, and his second wife, Sarah, daughter of Giles Crouch, and widow of William Wiseman of Uffington, Berkshire. His father was a religious convert and author who represented parliament and his half-brother was Sir Edward *Hungerford, MP for Chippenham in 1640 and commander of the parliamentarian forces in Wiltshire in the civil war. Anthony matriculated from Broadgates Hall, Oxford, on 9 May 1623 aged fifteen, but took no degree; on 25 May 1625 he was admitted as a student of the Middle Temple. On 9 April 1629 he married Rachel (d. 1680), daughter of Rice Jones of Asthall, Oxfordshire, with whom he had twelve children. Of their three sons, the eldest was Sir Edward *Hungerford (1632–1711); a second, Anthony (1634–1703), took service with the king's forces in 1655; a daughter, Rachel, married Henry Cary, fourth Viscount Falkland, at Black Bourton on 14 April 1653.

Hungerford was returned to both the Short and Long parliaments of 1640 as a member for Malmesbury in Wiltshire. As a royalist he sat in the king's parliament at Oxford in its first session, December 1643 to March 1644, but soon afterwards surrendered to the parliamentarian forces which controlled his estates at Burford and was imprisoned during the remainder of 1644 in the Tower of London; his later claim to have been carried to Oxford under duress by the king's horse may have owed something to the need to avoid a crippling fine for delinquency. In testimony before the committee for compounding, Hungerford listed estates worth some £333 a year, but local committees found lands in Wiltshire, Oxfordshire, Berkshire, and Gloucestershire to the annual value of £450–500. However, the imposition on 29 January 1646 of a £2532 fine, set at a tenth (confirmed by the Commons on 5 June), implied an income of over twice that much, and may have reflected the fact that he was heir apparent of the estate, which included Farleigh Castle in Somerset, of his half-brother Edward, who died childless in 1648. On 10 October 1648, following 'divers examinations manifesting the good affection of the said Mr Hungerford to the Parliament', the Lords resolved to reduce his fine to £1500 (JHL, 10, 1647–8, 535).

Hungerford found the committee for the advance of money even more accommodating. Following his failure to pay his assessment of £150 for a twentieth, orders were given on 22 June 1649 for the seizure of his estate, but this was stayed and a reduced assessment of £100 imposed. In 1652 he seems to have petitioned Cromwell about his troubles, for the lord general sent a sympathetic (though noncommittal) reply in December of that year. In 1653 on the death of Cecily, widow of Francis, earl of Rutland, his substantial estates were augmented by properties in the area of Malmesbury. The depradations of the Commonwealth did not prevent his leaving the huge sum of £3000 to each of six daughters. He died at Farleigh, Somerset, in 1657, no earlier than 20 August, when he signed his will, and was buried on 16 September at Black Bourton.

A second **Anthony Hungerford** (1614/15?–1657), parliamentarian army officer, may have been the son of Thomas Hungerford, gentleman of Garsdon, Wiltshire. As a young child he was acquainted with Sir John Danvers (d. 1655) of Dauntsey, an estate close to properties owned by a junior branch of the Hungerford family at Garsdon. For this reason he could be the Anthony Hungerford who on 9 November 1632 matriculated from Queen's College, Oxford, at the age of seventeen, the son of Thomas of Garsdon. The army officer is known to have married a wife named Chrisagon and it was quite possibly the same man

who baptized a daughter of that name at Pershore, Worcestershire, on 13 February 1641. The Shropshire connections of Sir John Danvers, through his marriage to Margaret, the widow of Sir Richard Herbert of Chirbury, might help explain Hungerford's appointment as a commissioned officer in the parliamentarian forces of that county.

On 7 November 1644 Hungerford and Robert Fenwick wrote to Lord Denbigh complaining of the poor state of their forces, billeted on the Shropshire villages of Moreton Corbet and Stoke upon Tern. On 23 September 1646 Hungerford wrote again, asking to be commissioned as governor at Stoke, and requesting Denbigh to use his influence to have him appointed major to the Shropshire forces; it is clear that shortly afterwards he received a colonelcy. On 1 March 1647 the committee of both kingdoms wrote ordering the committee at Shrewsbury to co-operate with him in organizing, chiefly from Shropshire forces then awaiting disbandment, a regiment for service in Ireland. Colonel Hungerford and Colonel Long were given detailed instructions as to their possible dealings with Ormond, and landed in Ireland on 30 April 1647. Hungerford was colonel of a foot regiment at Drogheda in May/June 1648, and certainly saw action in Ireland. He survived a shot to the head, though the bullet was still lodged there in 1653, and he appears also to have been permanently lamed. On 9 May 1649 he was granted 'leave to go to the Bath, for recovery of his health, and to be excused from his regiment until the end of July, and have £100 in part of his arrears' (CSP dom., 1649–50, 131). By this time, however, Hungerford's regiment had shrunk to less than half its original strength, and while its colonel was still in England trying to replenish the numbers, it was disbanded on the orders of Cromwell.

Hungerford, meanwhile, employed himself in discovering the efforts of delinquents to evade composition fees by concealing the real value of their estates under the cloak of loans to third parties. This line of work seems to have originated less in zeal than in the desperate financial straits brought on by the non-payment of his arrears for military service. Most of the rest of his life was consumed in legal struggles with the state authorities, both to obtain these arrears, and to secure the entitlements due to original discoverers of the assets of wealthy delinquents. Although the council of state granted him £100 in 1652 to enable him to return to Ireland, he did not do so and in the following year he was in prison in London for debt. Sir John Danvers wrote that same year recalling his long acquaintance with Hungerford, a man 'of most honest and religious conversation, very free from the common vices of swearing, drunkenness, etc, and most valiant and faithful in the service of the parliament' (BL, Add. MS 33412, fol. 81b). In March 1654 Hungerford petitioned Cromwell, drawing his attention to the state's debt to him of £2000 in arrears of pay and costs, his incapacity from wounds sustained in battle, and his inability to support his wife and two children. On 17 April 1655 it was ordered that he be paid a pension of 20s. a week. Hungerford died on 9 June 1657; his pension owed from 30 September 1656 was paid to his widow, Chrisagon. On 24 August 1658 her petition, presumably asking for continued assistance, was passed to the committee at Ely House, but the outcome is not known.   STEPHEN WRIGHT

Sources Keeler, *Long Parliament* · F. Milward-Oliver, *Memoirs of the Hungerford, Milward and Oliver families* (1930) · G. D. Squibb, ed., *Wiltshire visitation pedigrees, 1623*, Harleian Society, 105–6 (1954) · W. H. Turner, ed., *The visitations of the county of Oxford … 1566 … 1574 … and in 1634*, Harleian Society, 5 (1871) · Foster, *Alum. Oxon.* · *Sixth report*, HMC, 5 (1877–8) · M. A. E. Green, ed., *Calendar of the proceedings of the committee for compounding … 1643–1660*, 1, PRO (1889) · M. A. E. Green, ed., *Calendar of the proceedings of the committee for advance of money, 1642–1656*, 1, PRO (1888) · *VCH Wiltshire*, vols. 14–15 · will, PRO, PROB 11/273, sig. 57 [A. Hungerford, *d.* 20 Aug x 16 Sept 1657] · 'The Hungerford family', BL, Add. MS 33412 · BL, Add. MS 42504 · R. C. Hoare, *Hungerfordiana, or, Memoirs of the family of Hungerford* (1823) · *CSP dom.*, 1646–7; 1649–50; 1655–6 · C. T. Martin, ed., *Minutes of parliament of the Middle Temple*, 4 vols. (1904–5), vol. 2 · C. H. Firth and G. Davies, *The regimental history of Cromwell's army*, 2 vols. (1940) · *Fourth report*, HMC, 3 (1874) [earl of Denbigh [pt 1]] · Thurloe, *State papers*, vol. 6
Wealth at death approx. £43,000, incl. £3000 to each daughter: will, PRO, PROB 11/273, sig. 57; Keeler, *Long Parliament*

Hungerford, Anthony (1614/15?–1657). *See under* Hungerford, Anthony (1607/8–1657).

Hungerford, Sir Edward (1596–1648), parliamentarian army officer, was born at Stock, near Great Bedwyn, the eldest of the three children of Sir Anthony *Hungerford MP (*bap.* 1567, *d.* 1627), of Black Bourton, and his first wife and cousin, Lucy (*d.* 1598), daughter of Sir Walter Hungerford of Farleigh (*d.* 1585) and his wife, Eleanor (*d.* 1591), and former wife of Sir John St John of Lydiard, Wiltshire. Having been educated at Queen's College, Oxford (graduated 1611) and the Middle Temple (entered 1613), he became MP for Wootton Bassett in 1614 at the age of eighteen. Thereafter he sat in every parliament (except that of 1626) until his death, representing Chippenham (1621, Short Parliament 1640, Long Parliament 1640); Wiltshire (1624); Bath (1625); and Cricklade (1628). He also served in Wiltshire as justice, deputy lieutenant (from 1624), and sheriff (1632); and was knighted at the coronation of Charles I (1626). In 1620 he married Margaret Halliday (1603–1672), daughter of William Halliday, merchant and lord mayor of London. They had no children. Sir Edward and his wife, who lived at both Corsham House and Farleigh Castle, possessed considerable wealth, inheriting estates in Wiltshire, Somerset, Berkshire, and Gloucestershire.

In the early months of the Long Parliament Hungerford was appointed to a number of committees, including those for ship money and safety. A keen puritan, he took a militant stance on the need to reform abuses in the church, proposed the motion against the new church canons (16 December 1640) and became actively involved in the trial of Archbishop Laud (1644).

In 1642 Hungerford was sent by parliament to execute the militia ordnance in Wiltshire (11 July); he personally pledged money, weapons, and six horses for parliament's use, and led 300 Wiltshire troops at the rendezvous at Chewton Mendip, aimed at expelling the marquess of Hertford from Somerset (5 August). He implemented parliament's propositions in Wiltshire (October), was

Sir Edward Hungerford (1596–1648), by unknown sculptor

excepted by the king from pardon (2 November), and, with other gentry from north Somerset and west Wiltshire, helped to pressurize Bristol council into abandoning its neutralist stance through strongly worded letters and the movement of trained bands near the city (November). In January 1643 he was involved in a bitter personal feud with Sir Edward Baynton, recently appointed parliament's commander-in-chief in Wiltshire—a feud (born in part of Hungerford's jealous nature) which resulted in each being arrested in turn by the other for treason. Parliament eventually adjudicated in favour of Hungerford, who was appointed commander of a new county force to replace Baynton (31 January) and member of county committees for collecting the weekly assessment (24 February) and sequestrating royalist estates (1 April).

Hungerford proved to be an incompetent military commander. He briefly occupied Salisbury (13 February 1643), before abandoning it to the royalists along with both Malmesbury (3 February) and Devizes (23 February). He headed for the safety of Bath, claiming lack of resources as his excuse. After Waller's recapture of Malmesbury for parliament on 23 March Hungerford was made responsible for its defence—only to witness its hasty abandonment by the garrison during his own absence in Bath. He subsequently provided an unconvincing vindication of his part in this episode (written on 28 April and published in London on 6 May). He again retired to Bath, from where he launched spasmodic raids into Wiltshire, gaining the surrender of Wardour Castle after a short siege (8 May) and plundering royalist estates at Woodhouse (28 May) and Longleat (30 May). Although he fought under Waller in the battles of Lansdown (5 July) and Roundway down (13 July), Hungerford's role as a military commander had virtually ceased. Farleigh Castle was occupied by royalists as their grip tightened on the west. In July 1644 he was appointed to parliament's county committees in both Somerset and Wiltshire, aligning himself with the moderates.

On 15 September 1645 he was present with a detachment of the New Model Army to accept the surrender of his castle at Farleigh from his own half-brother, Colonel John Hungerford, who was a royalist (as was his other half-brother, Sir Anthony). Sir Edward died at Farleigh Castle on 23 October 1648. He and his wife were buried within the castle in a splendid tomb with white marble effigies inside St Anne's chapel.   JOHN WROUGHTON

Sources Greaves & Zaller, BDBR, vol. 2 · Keeler, Long Parliament · C. H. Firth, Outline of the civil war in Wiltshire, 1642–1646 (1894) · The memoirs of Edmund Ludlow, ed. C. H. Firth, 2 vols. (1894) · DNB · J. Wroughton, A community at war: the civil war in Bath and north Somerset, 1642–1650, rev. edn (1992) · C. H. Firth and R. S. Rait, eds., Acts and ordinances of the interregnum, 1642–1660, 1 (1911) · R. C. Hoare, Hungerfordiana, or, Memoirs of the family of Hungerford (1823) · The journal of Sir Simonds D'Ewes from the beginning of the Long Parliament to the opening of the trial of the earl of Strafford, ed. W. Notestein (1923) · Sir Edward Hungerford's vindication for the surrendering of Malmesbury (1643) · JHC, 2 (1640–42) · JHL, 5 (1642–3) · PRO, PROB 11/205, fols. 283–7 · common council book, 1642–9, Bristol RO · J. E. Jackson, The Hungerford collection (1885)

Archives Devizes Museum, Wiltshire Archaeological and Natural History Society, Hungerford collection

Likenesses attrib. J. van Ravensteyn?, oils; Christies, New York, 1982 · white marble effigy, St Anne's chapel, Farleigh Castle, Somerset [see illus.]

Hungerford, Sir Edward (1632–1711), politician, merchant, and spendthrift, son and heir of Anthony *Hungerford the royalist (1607/8–1657), and his wife, Rachel Jones (d. 1680), was born on 20 October 1632 at Black Bourton, Oxfordshire. He matriculated at Queen's College, Oxford, in 1649 and was fined £2532 by the commissioners for compounding as reversionary heir to the principal family estates. He sat in Richard Cromwell's parliament for Chippenham, where he had inherited land, and was a commissioner for assessment and the militia in Wiltshire in 1659 and Somerset in 1660. In February 1660 he was one of the Oxfordshire representatives who delivered a petition for a free parliament.

Hungerford was made a knight of the Bath at Charles II's coronation on 23 April 1661, helped by his financial contribution to the king before the Restoration of which Hyde said 'not three men of the nation … made the like present' (Firth, 4.559). He represented Chippenham again in 1660, 1661, 1678, 1679, and 1681 as the leading local patron. Never speaking, he sat on over seventy committees in the Cavalier Parliament and was accounted 'worthy' by Shaftesbury in 1677. In 1670 he joined Hudson's Bay Company through his brother-in-law James Hayes, secretary to Prince Rupert, and was on its committee in 1674–5. In January 1680 he presented an opposition petition for the summoning of parliament, and was one of the members who planned to summon the duke of York before the grand jury of Middlesex as a recusant. This led to his removal from the Wiltshire deputy lieutenancy in May 1681 and from other local offices. In September 1683 his home, Farleigh Castle, was searched for arms after the Rye House plot. Resigning control of Chippenham, in 1685 he sat for New Shoreham near his new estate at Broadwater. He did so again in 1689, and sat for nearby Steyning in 1695, 1698, 1701, and 1702.

Despite correspondence with and support for Sir Robert Harley, Hungerford was politically inactive; immunity from prosecution was probably a principal inducement to stand. A patron of archery, he was lieutenant-colonel of the regiment of archers in 1661, and colonel in 1682; in

1676 he presided at a tournament in Finsbury Fields. Sir Edward was best known for his reckless extravagance, allegedly paying 500 guineas for a wig. By way of restoring his waning fortunes, he obtained an act of parliament in 1677 to hold thrice-weekly markets on the site of the dilapidated Hungerford House, by Charing Cross. In 1682 a market house was erected there, apparently from Sir Christopher Wren's designs; Wren and Sir Stephen Fox purchased the market in 1685. Charing Cross railway station was built on the site in 1862. Hungerford removed to Spring Gardens, within the 'verge of court' and so safe from process by creditors, selling the manor and castle of Farleigh in 1686 to Henry Bayntun of Spye Park for £56,000. Sheldon Manor, Chippenham, and Corsham were sold, and Rowdon, which Hungerford was said to have gambled at the last throw in a bowling match, was mortgaged to Sir Richard Kent. Twenty-eight manors may have been sold, though he retained an estate at Hungerford Engleford, Berkshire, together with funds donated for prayers at St Lawrence's Church, Reading. Broadwater, purchased from his creditor Sir George Pretyman in 1672, was sold in 1709. After the sales Hungerford is stated to have become a poor knight of Windsor, trustees controlling what land remained. He died in 1711, and was buried in the church of St Martin-in-the-Fields.

Hungerford married three times. His first wife, Jane, daughter of Sir John *Hele of Clifton Maybank, Dorset, whom he married before 1658, died on 18 March 1664 and was buried at Farleigh; they had an only son, Edward, who married Lady Alathea Compton at the age of nineteen in 1680 and died in September 1689, and two daughters, Frances and Rachel. He married his second wife, Jane Culme (1637–1674), on 3 February 1666, and his third, Jane Gerard, née Digby (d. 1703), in July 1679; both these subsequent marriages were childless. Hungerford's daughter Rachel married Clotworthy Skeffington, second Viscount Massereene, in March 1684 and on her death on 2 February 1732 she left to her eldest son portraits of her father, her great-uncle (another Sir Edward Hungerford), and other relations.

The last male of the family, Hungerford was a man in whom an unhappy combination of overgenerosity and incompetence with money was offset by political and sporting interests. His reputation has been harshly treated, but he can justifiably be seen as more than just a spendthrift wastrel. Until the 1680s he was active in parliament, and his successive associations with Lord Wharton in the 1660s, Shaftesbury in the 1670s, and Harley about 1690, certainly indicate a sustained line of political beliefs in what can be called a 'country whig' tradition, critical of the court. His activity in the Cavalier Parliament points to a concern with the 'Catholic threat', and anyone who joined in the proposed presentation of the duke of York as a papist recusant in 1680 was certainly putting principle above safety.   TIMOTHY VENNING

Sources JHC, 8 (1660–67), 478 · JHC, 9 (1667–87), 26, 49, 143, 192, 416 · JHC, 10 (1688–93), 83, 165 · CSP dom., 1678; 1683 · M. A. E. Green, ed., Calendar of the proceedings of the committee for advance of money, 1642–1656, 2, PRO (1888); repr. (1967), 867 · W. A. Shaw, ed., Calendar of treasury books, 3, PRO (1908), 911 · Calendar of the manuscripts of the marquess of Ormonde, new ser., 8 vols., HMC, 36 (1902–20), vol. 5, p. 340 · The manuscripts of his grace the duke of Portland, 10 vols., HMC, 29 (1891–1931), vol. 8, pp. 27–8 · GM, 1st ser., 102/1 (1832), 113 · GM, 1st ser., 102/2 (1832), 114–15 · G. H. Gater and F. R. Hiorns, The parish of St Martin-in-the-Fields, 3: Trafalgar Square and neighbourhood, Survey of London, 20 (1940), 22, 43–7, 60 · N. Luttrell, A brief historical relation of state affairs from September 1678 to April 1714, 1 (1857), 32, 89, 395 · F. H. Goldney, Records of Chippenham, 14 (1889), 228–9 · VCH Sussex, 6/1.70 · VCH Berkshire, 3.380; 4.191 · C. H. Firth and R. S. Rait, eds., Acts and ordinances of the interregnum, 1642–1660, 3 vols. (1911), vol. 2, pp. 1335, 1381, 1442 · Calendar of the Clarendon state papers preserved in the Bodleian Library, ed. O. Ogle and others, 5 vols. (1869–1970), vol. 4, p. 559 · N&Q, 4th ser., 6 (1870), 454 · HoP, Commons · J. L. Vivian, ed., The visitations of the county of Devon, comprising the herald's visitations of 1531, 1564, and 1620 (privately printed, Exeter, [1895]), 263 · J. Collinson, The history and antiquities of the county of Somerset, 3 (1791)

Likenesses bust, in or before 1682, repro. in GM, 1st ser., 102/1 (1832), 113; formerly at his town house at Hungerford Market, 1682; demolished, 1833 · portrait; bequeathed to son of Rachel, Viscountess Masserene, in Feb 1732

Wealth at death estate at Hungerford Engleford, Berkshire, passed to distant relative; further twenty-eight manors; subject was in severe difficulties with creditors: VCH Berkshire, vol. 4

Hungerford, John (1657/8–1729), politician, was the son of Richard Hungerford of Wiltshire, and Ann, the daughter of Ellis Price, of Gatcombe, Isle of Wight. Nothing is known of his early education, but on 7 August 1677 he was admitted a student at Lincoln's Inn, and he graduated MA from the University of Cambridge in 1683 by royal mandate. In 1687 (the marriage licence was dated 5 August 1687) he married Mary (d. 1740), the daughter of Abraham Spooner, a vintner of London; there were no children from the marriage. He was called to the bar on 28 November 1687. By 1691 he had become cursitor of Yorkshire and Westmorland.

Hungerford entered parliament on 28 April 1692 as member for Scarborough. He was suspicious of the constitutional innovations that followed the revolution of 1688–9. In his first recorded speech, in December 1692, he rejected the Bill for the Preservation of their Majesties' Persons and Government as a divisive partisan measure. On 2 February 1693 he spoke in favour of the Triennial Bill, although he argued that most of the bill was merely declaratory as triennial parliaments were already part of the ancient constitution. On 1 February 1694, during the debate on the king's answer to the representation of the Commons on the use of the royal veto, he complained that William III had more recourse to the advice of the cabinet or the privy council than to the advice of parliament. His other interests included trade—he later became standing counsel to the East India Company—where he managed a bill on iron exportation through the Commons in February and March 1694, and social issues, where he chaired the committee on the London Orphans Bill in March 1694. Once the bill was through the Commons, on 23 March 1694 he received from its promoters a gift of 20 guineas 'for his pains and services' on their behalf, and was consequently expelled from the house on 26 March 1695, although he denied receiving the sum as a bribe. He was later found guilty of an offence at Lincoln's Inn, on 23

April 1700, when he was expelled from the society for breaking a padlock from the door of his chambers. He was readmitted ten days later, after apologizing. He stood for election again at Scarborough in 1701, when he was unsuccessful, but was returned for Scarborough in the 1702 election. In Anne's reign Hungerford displayed tory opinions but generally supported the court. On 30 December 1702 he spoke for making Prince George of Denmark, the queen's husband, admiral and generalissimo in perpetuity, as an attempt to defuse demands from more extreme tories to make the prince king. He supported the Occasional Conformity Bill in November 1704, but voted against its addition to a supply bill (the tack) in December. Despite his opposition to the tack Daniel Defoe satirized him as an extremist, 'mad Crakerovsky', in his satire The Diet of Poland in 1705. He lost the 1705 election, perhaps because of the tack, but in November 1707 was re-elected, and he continued to represent Scarborough until his death. Meanwhile his status at Lincoln's Inn was enhanced; despite being ordered on 31 May 1706 to remove the dogs he kept in a space under a shared staircase, he was called to the bench on 2 May 1707 and served in several offices over the next few years, including treasurer in 1713 and dean of the chapel in 1715.

In December 1708 and December 1709 Hungerford introduced bills to prevent excessive gaming, the second attempt resulting in an act of parliament. On 13 December 1709 he opposed a whig motion to have Henry Sacheverell's printed sermons declared seditious libels, and he later voted against Sacheverell's impeachment. In June 1710 he was counsel for George Purchase's appeal against conviction for high treason for having taken part in the pro-Sacheverell riots. On 11 April 1711 he introduced a further bill against gaming, to amend the act of 1709 which had proved ineffective. Hungerford, described as a tory patriot advocating British withdrawal from the War of the Spanish Succession, supported the establishment of the Harley ministry, but rapidly became disenchanted with it. In June 1711 he was placated with an appointment as commissioner of the alienation office. However, he remained semi-detached from the administration and sometimes voted with the whigs. He supported the expulsion of Richard Steele from the Commons in March 1714, and was one of the main supporters of the Schism Bill later that year. Following the accession of George I tories were gradually removed from office, and Hungerford lost his place at the alienation office in June 1715.

Following the Hanoverian accession Hungerford opposed the ministry and defended the actions of the Oxford–Bolingbroke government. Much of what he had supported was eroded in the reign of George I, and he became one of the leading tory speakers in the Commons. He was an opponent of the Septennial Bill in 1716, and of the repeal of the Occasional Conformity and Schism Acts in 1719. He introduced a bill for the preservation of game in 1719, having proposed a similar measure in 1711. He was chairman of the Commons committee set up to investigate joint-stock companies in February 1721, leading to the Bubble Act, which sought to defend the South Sea Company. In 1722 he chaired the committee inquiring into the Harburg lottery. His opposition to the repressive measures introduced by ministers after the exposure of the Atterbury plot in 1722 may indicate Jacobite sympathies. Hungerford also defended three men—Francis Francia (1717), John Matthews (1719), and Christopher Sayer (1722)—charged with treasonable relations with James Stuart, the Old Pretender. Francia was acquitted, but Matthews and Sayer were convicted. In 1724 Hungerford was one of nine tory MPs who sat on a parliamentary committee on the employment of farm labourers. He died on 8 June 1729. In his will, dated 24 May 1729, and confirmed on 13 June by his widow, Mary, he left bequests to King's College, Cambridge, to Lincoln's Inn (to be administered by his friend William Melmoth), to his many relatives, and to his executor the Revd Thomas Mangey.

MATTHEW KILBURN

Sources D. W. Hayton, 'Hungerford, John', HoP, Commons, 1690–1715 • N. Luttrell, A brief historical relation of state affairs from September 1678 to April 1714, 6 (1857) • State trials, 15.898–994, 1323–1403; 16.93–322 • R. Sedgwick, 'Hungerford, John', HoP, Commons, 1715–54 • Venn, Alum. Cant. • L. Colley, In defiance of oligarchy: the tory party, 1714–60 (1982) • W. P. Baildon, ed., The records of the Honorable Society of Lincoln's Inn: the black books, 3 (1899), 292, 324, 327 • W. P. Baildon, ed., The records of the Honorable Society of Lincoln's Inn: admissions, 2 vols. (1896) • DNB

Wealth at death manor of Hungerford: BL, Add. MS 33412, fols. 145–7 • left property in trust for wife, then to be sold, two thirds of proceeds to King's College, Cambridge, and one third to Dr Mangley, canon of Durham: Sedgwick, 'Hungerford, John'

Hungerford [née Hamilton], **Margaret Wolfe** [pseud. the Duchess] (1854?–1897), novelist, eldest daughter of Canon Fitzjohn Stannus Hamilton, vicar-choral of Ross Cathedral, co. Cork, Ireland, was born at Milteen, Ross Carbery, co. Cork. She was educated at Portarlington College, Ireland, where she won composition prizes and wrote stories to entertain friends. In 1872 she married Edward Argles (d. 1878), a Dublin solicitor, with whom she had three daughters; and in 1882 she married Thomas Henry Hungerford (b. 1858), with whom she had two sons and one daughter.

Hungerford's first novel, Phyllis (1877), was written before she was nineteen, and became an immediate bestseller. She launched her career on this success, writing first as the 'Author of Phyllis', and later as the 'Duchess', the eponymous heroine of her 1888 novel, which ran to seven editions in ten years. She produced more than forty novels and collections of short stories, often writing on commission, and it was said of her that she sold her books as fast as she could write them. Her works were popular in India, Australia, and America, and all of her novels were reprinted in the Tauchnitz series. Her most successful novel, Molly Bawn (1878), describes the love life of a vivacious Irish girl. In general her fiction wittily portrays courtship and marriage in fashionable society. Although extremely popular and widely read, her novels were treated with scorn by 'serious' critics, causing her to remark that 'reviews are my one great dread and anxiety'

(Black, Notable Women Authors, 116). She died of typhoid fever at her home, St Brenda's, Bandon, co. Cork, on 24 January 1897. Her husband survived her.

ELIZABETH LEE, rev. KATHERINE MULLIN

Sources Boase, Mod. Eng. biog. • A. T. C. Pratt, ed., People of the period: being a collection of the biographies of upwards of six thousand living celebrities, 2 vols. (1897) • P. Schlueter and J. Schlueter, eds., An encyclopedia of British women writers (1988) • H. C. Black, Notable women authors of the day (1893) • The Times (25 Jan 1897) • H. C. Black, 'In memoriam: the late Mrs Hungerford', The Englishwoman, 5 (1897), 102–5 • J. Todd, ed., Dictionary of British women writers (1989) • Blain, Clements & Grundy, Feminist comp. • Allibone, Dict.

Likenesses photograph, repro. in Black, Notable women authors, 106 • wood-engraving (after photograph by Guy & Co.), NPG; repro. in ILN (30 Jan 1897)

Wealth at death £2557 18s. 1d.—in England: administration, 1897, CGPLA Ire.

Hungerford, Robert, second Baron Hungerford (c.1400–1459), landowner, was the eldest son and heir of Walter *Hungerford, first Baron Hungerford (d. 1449), and his first wife, Katherine Peverel. Another son, Sir Walter (d. 1432), was destined for the church in 1415 and was therefore presumably younger. As his parents' marriage agreement dates from 1396 and he was of age by 1423, he was presumably born about 1400. By Michaelmas 1421 he married Margaret (d. 1478), daughter, coheir, and eventually sole heir of William, Lord Botreaux (d. 1462). His career seems particularly undistinguished when compared to those of his ancestors, brothers, and son.

Like his father Hungerford was licensed to go on pilgrimage to the Holy Land in 1423. He served in the French wars and was in the retinue of the duke of Bedford in 1435. In domestic politics he was overshadowed by his father, by his younger brother Sir Edmund Hungerford of Down Ampney, Gloucestershire, and by his heir, Lord Moleyns. Robert Hungerford was summoned to parliament as Lord Hungerford from 1450, but was fined in 1454 for non-attendance. He was appointed to commissions of oyer and terminer both in 1450, to try west-country men implicated in Cade's rebellion, and 1452. His activities and importance, however, seem confined to Somerset and Wiltshire, where the principal Hungerford estates lay. He features regularly on Wiltshire commissions in the 1440s and 1450s. He was a JP for Wiltshire until his father's death and for Somerset thereafter. Robert Hungerford scarcely features in the Hungerford cartularies and few actions are recorded in the public records. Rather more is known of him as feoffee and as a witness for third parties. With the Hungerford estate he inherited the service of a coherent group of family administrators, of whom Gregory Westby and John Mervyn were the most prominent, but the rising lawyer Thomas Tropnell, of Great Chalfield, Wiltshire, and Thomas and Robert South were also significant. All were local men. In contrast to his father's, his long will makes only one modest bequest to a London foundation, Bedlam (Bethlem) Hospital; all other pious benefactions are to monasteries, churches, and hospitals in Somerset and Wiltshire.

A modest jointure settled on Hungerford and his wife at their marriage was amplified in 1437, but he did not attract significant royal grants and was therefore presumably dependent on his father until 1443, when his late mother's Peverel inheritance was settled on him, and on his father's death in 1449 he could not succeed to much of the Hungerford estate until the death in 1455 of his stepmother Eleanor, countess of Arundel, whom his father married in or after 1438. Robert Hungerford thus held the whole inheritance for only four years at most. He never enjoyed the Botreaux inheritance, since his stepfather, who remarried, survived until 1462. He does not seem to have committed himself politically during the 1450s and died before a choice of sides became inescapable. His last years were dominated by the negotiations about the ransom of his eldest son, Robert *Hungerford, Lord Moleyns, eventually set at £6000, for which he raised the first instalment of £3000 by mortgaging his whole estate, his wife, Margaret, having surrendered her dower and jointure. As Hungerford's son and grandson Thomas also suffered forfeiture during the Wars of the Roses, Margaret devoted the last two decades of her life largely to saving the family estate. Hungerford died on 18 May 1459.

Moleyns's ransom explains why Hungerford's will, although long and elaborate, was decidedly modest, making no additional provision for his children and leaving only £158 in pious bequests, much less than his father. He had joined his father in founding St Mary's chantry at Chippenham parish church, Wiltshire, in 1442, but he asked to be buried before the altar of the newly canonized St Osmund in Salisbury Cathedral. This was the justification for his widow's construction of the splendid Hungerford chapel of Jesus and St Mary to the north of the lady chapel and the establishment of a chantry of two priests there. Now demolished, the chapel is recorded in eighteenth-century prints and the statutes survive. Margaret also invoked her husband's authority for the permanent endowment and establishment of Walter, Lord Hungerford's hospital at Heytesbury, Wiltshire. Robert Hungerford's alabaster tomb surmounted by his effigy, formerly set in the wall between the lady and Hungerford chapels, is now in the cathedral nave. Margaret's monument in the body of the chapel has disappeared.

MICHAEL HICKS

Sources J. L. Kirby, *The Hungerford cartulary*, Wilts RS, 49 (1994) · M. A. Hicks, *Richard III and his rivals: magnates and their motives in the Wars of the Roses* (1991) · F. W. Weaver, ed., *Somerset medieval wills*, 1, Somerset RS, 16 (1901) · J. L. Kirby, 'The Hungerford family in the late middle ages', MA diss., U. Lond., 1939 · M. A. Hicks, 'Four studies in conventional piety', *Southern History*, 13 (1991), 1–21 · C. Rawcliffe, 'The politics of marriage in later medieval England', *Huntington Library Quarterly*, 51 (1988), 161–75 · PRO, special collections, ministers' accounts · *Chancery records*
Archives Hunt. L., Hastings MSS · Som. ARS, Hobhouse cartulary · Wilts. & Swindon RO, Radnor MSS
Likenesses alabaster tomb effigy, *c*.1460, Salisbury Cathedral [*see illus.*]
Wealth at death approx. £900 p.a.: PRO, special collections, ministers' accounts

Hungerford, Robert, third Baron Hungerford and Baron Moleyns (*c*.1423–1464), nobleman and administrator, was the eldest son of Robert *Hungerford, second Baron Hungerford (*c*.1400–1459), and Margaret Botreaux (*d*. 1478). He was born in the early 1420s—he was of age by 1445—and was married by 1439 to Eleanor (1428–*c*.1476), heir of Sir William Moleyns (*d*. 1428) of Stoke Poges, Buckinghamshire. In due course he could expect to unite by inheritance the three baronies and estates of Hungerford, Botreaux, and Moleyns in southern England, together worth at least £2000 a year, and would have been the principal magnate in central southern England. Actually his premature death and political miscalculations ensured not only that he never realized these expectations but that none of his descendants did either.

Eleanor Moleyns was a distant descendant of the notorious John Moleyns, the last parliamentary Lord Moleyns, who died in 1362. That Robert Hungerford was summoned to parliament from January 1445 as Lord Moleyns was therefore a signal mark of royal favour; it probably implies an earlier intimacy with Henry VI. In 1446 he was granted £100 a year until he received land of similar value and a further £12 a year in reward for services rendered to the king's foundation of Eton College. His influence at court and easy access to the king also emerge from correspondence among the Paston letters relating to his pursuit of his wife's vestigial title to Gresham, Norfolk, against John Paston (*d*. 1466). Although ultimately unsuccessful, Moleyns twice seized Gresham without punishment, once (according to Paston) with a great display of force, and

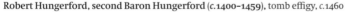

Robert Hungerford, second Baron Hungerford (*c*.1400–1459), tomb effigy, *c*.1460

secured a royal writ to the sheriff to empanel a jury to acquit him. This is one of the more notorious examples of corruption of justice by the powerful associated with the king's favourites. Although Eleanor's estate was mainly in Oxfordshire and Berkshire, Moleyns was residing at this time at Salisbury, where on 3 June 1449 he was murderously attacked at the George Inn, and he features most commonly on commissions in Wiltshire. Until 1449, while his grandfather was still living, Moleyns was both higher in rank and substantially wealthier than his own father. Whereas his father was JP only in Wiltshire, Moleyns was JP from 1447 in the five counties of Buckinghamshire, Dorset, Oxfordshire, Somerset, and Wiltshire, and from 1449 in Berkshire also.

Moleyns was associated with the court in the crises that occurred from 1450. In 1450 itself he was appointed commissioner of array against the rebels and to several oyer and terminer commissions. One of the royal council opposed to the duke of York's rebellion at Dartford in 1452, he was again appointed to several oyer and terminer commissions. This phase in his career ended with his departure on the earl of Shrewsbury's expedition to relieve Aquitaine.

Moleyns may already have served in France, for in 1448 he styled himself lord of Faugernon near Lisieux; however no grant has been found. He shared in Shrewsbury's disastrous defeat at Châtillon on 17 July 1453, when he was wounded and captured, probably by Jean de Bueil, admiral of France, who sold him to Charles VII. He lived as a prisoner in considerable comfort until shortly before 31 March 1459, when a ransom of £6000 had been agreed and the first instalment borrowed from the Medici banker Simone Nori was paid. On the strength of the celebrated but tendentious writing of Margaret, Lady Hungerford, annexed to her will, this ransom has been regarded as overwhelming and the cause of the family's dire financial difficulties. Although large, however, it amounted to only four years' income from the family estates. At least £1000 was raised in cash and the rest was to be financed from a licence to ship wool in 1460, from the sale of his son Thomas's marriage, and from income. The balance was initially paid by borrowing from the Medici factor Simone Nori and English lenders. The first instalment was raised on the security of the Hungerford estates, which were conveyed in mortgage to feoffees by his father, who asked Moleyns not to resent the denial of his hereditary expectations. In 1460 Moleyns himself surrendered his moveables and mortgaged his wife's estates as security for the second instalment of £3000. Although his father died in 1459, so that he was now Lord Hungerford as well as Moleyns, he was thus dependent on his mother.

At once Robert became involved in politics. He and Lord Scales were left by Henry VI as garrison of the Tower of London, where they were besieged by the Yorkists in July 1460. Following the Lancastrian victory at Northampton, he was pardoned on 11 July and the Tower was surrendered on condition that the two lords could depart free, but Scales was murdered. Moleyns was expensive—he had already accumulated £400 in debts—and his politics were

risky, and it was allegedly for these reasons that his mother paid for him to go abroad (licence 25 August 1460). He visited Florence, but unfortunately he returned in time to share in the Lancastrian defeat at Towton, where his brother Sir Arnold Hungerford was killed. Persisting in resistance, he fled with Henry VI and Queen Margaret to Scotland, visited France in the summer on Henry's behalf, and was arrested. Writing to Queen Margaret at the time from Dieppe, he begged her not to lose heart. He was one of the Alnwick garrison evacuated in January and among those who returned there in May 1463. He shared in Somerset's defeat at Hexham in 1464, when he was captured, and was executed at Newcastle upon Tyne on 18 May 1464. His body was reputedly conveyed to Salisbury Cathedral, where it was supposedly buried in an unmarked grave in the chantry chapel of his grandfather Walter, first Baron Hungerford (d. 1449). As a die-hard Lancastrian he had been attainted in 1461, multiplying the problems of his mother and eldest son in England in preserving the Hungerford inheritance, and in 1462 his wife and children had been placed in the custody of Lord Wenlock. By 1469 Eleanor was married to Sir Oliver Maningham. She was defaulting on payments to Nori by 1464 and ultimately repudiated any obligation for Moleyns's debts. She died about 1476. Robert and Eleanor had four children: Sir Thomas [see below], Sir Walter *Hungerford (d. 1516), Leonard, and Frideswide, who became a nun at Syon.

Sir Thomas Hungerford (1439?–1469), Robert Hungerford's eldest son, was styled as of Rowdon near Chippenham. Presumably born in 1439, he was MP for Wiltshire and sheriff of Gloucestershire in 1459, and a knight by January 1465. He married the much younger Anne Percy, daughter of the third earl of Northumberland, before 16 October 1460, when lands were settled in jointure; the marriage portion was 3500 marks, of which only 700 marks were apparently paid. He also inherited properties from his uncle Sir Arnold Hungerford in 1461. He co-operated in the efforts of his grandmother Margaret, Lady Hungerford (d. 1478), to pay off the family's debts and safeguard its patrimony, which was resettled in 1463 with a view to his own eventual succession.

Thomas Hungerford served with Warwick against the northern Lancastrians and was pardoned in 1463 as 'of Salisbury, esquire', but he was arrested with Henry Courtenay for plotting the death of Edward IV with Margaret of Anjou on 21 May 1468 and was tried and executed at Salisbury on 18 January 1469. This second forfeiture compounded his grandmother's problems in saving the Hungerford inheritance. In 1485 the sentences against both Thomas and his father were revoked. He had at least two children, but his only surviving offspring, Mary, six months old at his death, married William, Lord Hastings's son Edward, later first earl of Huntingdon. Hungerford's widow, Anne, married first Sir Lawrence Reynsford (d. 1490) and second Sir Hugh Vaughan. She died in 1522.

MICHAEL HICKS

Sources J. L. Kirby, *The Hungerford cartularies*, Wilts RS (1994), no. 49 · M. A. Hicks, *Richard III and his rivals: magnates and their motives in* the Wars of the Roses (1991) • F. W. Weaver, ed., *Somerset medieval wills*, 1, Somerset RS, 16 (1901) • J. L. Kirby, 'The Hungerford family in the late middle ages', MA diss., U. Lond., 1939 • Emden, *Oxf.* • N. Davis, ed., *Paston letters and papers of the fifteenth century*, 2 vols. (1971–6) • *Chancery records*

Archives Hunt. L., Hastings MSS • PRO • Som. ARS, Somerset Archaeological Society, Hobhouse cartulary • Wilts. & Swindon RO, Radnor MSS

Hungerford, Sir Thomas (*b.* in or before **1328**, *d.* **1397**), landowner and speaker of the House of Commons, was the son of Walter Hungerford and his wife, Elizabeth, daughter of Sir Adam Fitzjohn of Cherhill, Wiltshire. Though best known as speaker of the Bad Parliament of January 1377 (and indeed the first speaker of the Commons recorded in the rolls of parliament) Hungerford is also remarkable for founding the fortunes of a great family by exploiting his expertise as an estate administrator for the nobility.

From his father, Walter, and his more prominent uncle, Sir Robert Hungerford (whose heir he was), Thomas inherited a family tradition of local estate management, of election to parliament for their native Wiltshire, and of links with the house of Lancaster. The family estates bequeathed to him, however, were small: and though he added to them by his marriages to Eleanor Strug of Heytesbury, Wiltshire (before 1352), and (before 1376) to Joan Hussey of Holbrook, Somerset, he acquired most of his eventually considerable lands by purchase.

This Hungerford achieved largely by capitalizing on his position as land agent, during the 1350s and 1360s, for the bishops of Salisbury and Winchester, for William Montagu, second earl of Salisbury, and for Bartholomew, Lord Burghersh. From Burghersh, for example, he purchased important estates at Farleigh Montfort (Somerset) and Heytesbury (Wiltshire), though Burghersh's widow later alleged that he had obtained Heytesbury by sharp practice ('procurement, covyne et malyce') and kept it by exerting his local influence and abusing his office as a Wiltshire JP. Certainly his growing importance was reflected in official appointments: sheriff of Wiltshire (1355–60) and royal escheator there (1355–7), he represented either Wiltshire or Somerset in no less than sixteen parliaments between 1357 and 1393.

After August 1372, moreover, Hungerford's influence spread far beyond his home area. Presumably following previous (but now unrecorded) service to John of Gaunt, duke of Lancaster, he then became the first chief steward of all Gaunt's extensive lands in Wales and in England south of the Thames. In February 1375 his stewardship was extended to all duchy lands south of the Trent (except Derbyshire and Staffordshire), whereupon Gaunt knighted him and made him a member of his council. It was doubtless as Gaunt's representative that he was elected speaker of the Commons in the parliament of January 1377. Thomas Walsingham (a chronicler then hostile to Gaunt) called him 'a knight on the friendliest terms with the duke, since he was his steward', and alleged that Hungerford 'wished nothing to be pronounced, other than what he knew would please his lord's eyes' (Walsingham, 112). This accusation cannot entirely be justified. For

though this 'Bad Parliament' (so called in contradistinction to the 'Good Parliament' which preceded it) generally ratified Gaunt's policies, it also displayed signs of independence.

Hungerford continued as Gaunt's chief steward until 1393, travelling extensively throughout his wide jurisdiction and frequently acting as royal commissioner, escheator, and justice in the duchy lands: his office was a lucrative one, bringing him £66 13s. 4d. a year plus expenses and perquisites. His personal power base, however, remained his nine or more manors in western Wiltshire, Somerset, and Gloucestershire, officially valued at his death at £128 a year but probably worth twice as much. His principal home was Farleigh Montfort, Somerset (subsequently renamed Farleigh Hungerford) whose manor house he converted between 1369 and 1383 into a castle in the currently fashionable quadrangular style. There he was buried after his death on 3 December 1397, beneath a fine effigial monument which still survives in the castle chapel. Survived by his second wife, Joan (*d.* 1412)—whose will provides evidence of the Hungerfords' sheep-farming interests—he was eventually succeeded by his only surviving son Walter *Hungerford, later Baron Hungerford.

CHARLES KIGHTLY

Sources J. S. Roskell, 'Sir Thomas Hungerford', *Parliaments and politics in late medieval England*, 2 (1981), 15–43 • HoP, *Commons, 1386–1421*, 3.443–6 • J. L. Kirby, 'The Hungerford family in the late middle ages', MA diss., U. Lond., 1939 • *Chancery records* • PRO • R. Somerville, *History of the duchy of Lancaster, 1265–1603* (1953) • *John of Gaunt's register*, ed. S. Armitage-Smith, 2 vols., CS, 3rd ser., 20–21 (1911) • *John of Gaunt's register, 1379–1383*, ed. E. C. Lodge and R. Somerville, 2 vols., CS, 3rd ser., 56–7 (1937) • R. C. Hoare, *The history of modern Wiltshire*, 1/2: *Hundred of Heytesbury* (1822) • [T. Walsingham], *Chronicon Angliae, ab anno Domini 1328 usque ad annum 1388*, ed. E. M. Thompson, Rolls Series, 64 (1874) • Reg. Thomas Arundel, LPL, 2, fol. 152 • R. Wilcox, 'Excavations at Farleigh Hungerford Castle', *Proceedings of the Somersetshire Archaeological and Natural History Society*, 124 (1979–80), 87–109

Likenesses stained-glass window, 1360–99, parish church of St Leonard, Farleigh Hungerford, Somerset • tomb effigy, *c.*1397, chapel of Farleigh Hungerford Castle, Somerset, St Anne's chapel

Wealth at death estates valued at £128 p.a.: *CIPM*, Richard II, 17, nos. 15–23

Hungerford, Sir Thomas (1439?–1469). *See under* Hungerford, Robert, third Baron Hungerford and Baron Moleyns (*c.*1423–1464).

Hungerford, Walter, first Baron Hungerford (1378–1449), nobleman, soldier, and administrator, was the fourth but only surviving son of Sir Thomas *Hungerford (*d.* 1397) of Farleigh Montfort, Somerset, being the elder son of his second marriage, to Joan (*d.* 1412), daughter of Sir Edmund Hussey of Holbrook, Somerset. Soldier, diplomat, and administrator, treasurer of England, and trusted servant of the Lancastrian kings, Hungerford was born into the Lancastrian service, since his father was chief steward of the duchy of Lancaster lands in southern England. He also inherited his father's talent for accumulating estates, adding steadily throughout his life to his ancestral property in Somerset and Wiltshire. Through his first marriage, by 1399, to Katherine Peverell, a kinswoman of the Courtenay earls of Devon, Hungerford acquired lands in Somerset, Devon, and Cornwall: judicious marriage settlements arranged for his children and grandchildren brought him revenues from estates all over southern England, and he purchased at least forty manors, mainly in Wiltshire and Somerset. His second marriage (by May 1439) to Eleanor, countess of Arundel, the widow of John, earl of Arundel (d. 1421) more than doubled his landed income, which by 1448 totalled over £1800 a year. Given his other revenues from French lands, royal grants, and substantial emoluments as a government minister, Hungerford clearly died a wealthy man.

Hungerford's wealth and influential contacts were largely the rewards of a long and adventurous career, characterized as much by dutiful devotion to the house of Lancaster as to his own family interests. Born a younger son, he may initially have been educated for the church. Certainly he was literate in Latin, French, and English, owned books of theology, and was a man of great conventional piety, a prolific founder of chantries, and probably (in 1402) a pilgrim to Rome and Jerusalem. But the first decisive action of his career was political, when at the age of twenty-one he supported Henry IV's seizure of the throne in 1399: immediate rewards included knighthood (among the first 'knights of the Bath') on the eve of Henry's coronation. Soon afterwards, in January 1400, he was kidnapped by rebels against the new monarch, but contrived their arrest at Cirencester. Thereafter Hungerford served as JP, MP, and sheriff in his native Wiltshire, though more significantly was employed on military and diplomatic missions. Thus in early 1406 he was rewarded for defeating a French knight at Calais, and later that year escorted the king's daughter Philippa to her wedding in Denmark. Towards the end of Henry IV's reign Hungerford seemingly supported the king's son Prince Henry in disputes at court: for when the prince succeeded as Henry V in March 1413, his career at once shifted into a higher gear.

Immediately appointed to his father's old office of chief steward of the duchy of Lancaster in the south, Hungerford was elected speaker of the parliament of April 1414, and thereafter served with two important embassies, to the German emperor, Sigismund, at Koblenz, and to the Council of Constance. Soon after his return he recruited a retinue for the campaign which culminated at the battle of Agincourt (25 October 1415), on the eve of which he (and not the earl of Westmorland, as Shakespeare alleged) provoked the king's pious rebuke by wishing for 10,000 more archers. During the battle he took several important prisoners, and on 15 August 1416 was again in action against the French, as an admiral at the naval victory off Harfleur.

By now high in Henry V's favour Hungerford was appointed a royal councillor and steward of the king's household in early 1417. He spent the next five years campaigning almost continuously with the king in France, serving at the sieges of Caen and Falaise (1417); at Cherbourg (1418), Rouen (1418–19), and Melun (1420); and at the long siege of Meaux (1421–2), where it was his cannon that finally breached the walls. His labours earned him both honours and rewards, including knighthood of the Garter (1421) and the Norman barony of Hommet (1418): a century later, moreover, Leland was told that Sir Walter's lavish extensions to the family seat at Farleigh Hungerford Castle were financed by the spoils of France. Hungerford's regard for Henry V was subsequently reflected in the 'pseudo-Elmham' life of that king, which he commissioned and for which he probably supplied information. The greatest honour of all, confirmed as Hungerford stood beside Henry V's deathbed on 31 August 1422, was his appointment as joint guardian of the king's infant son, Henry VI. As such (and as a working executor of Henry V's will), he automatically became a member of the council of regency that ruled England during Henry VI's minority. This full-time responsibility brought further promotions. Appointed chamberlain of the duchy of Lancaster in 1425, he was summoned to parliament as Baron Hungerford from January 1426, and two months later became treasurer of England.

Hungerford's championship of the council's authority as against that of the protector (Humphrey, duke of Gloucester) lost him the treasurership in 1432. But 'the wyse lorde baron of Hungerford' (Warner, 57) remained an important member of the government which vainly strove to stem the loss of Henry V's French conquests, and not until after 1440 did he begin to retire from politics and diplomacy. True to his motto 'Devoir' ('Duty')—the title he gave to his personal herald—he remained a royal councillor until his death at Farleigh Hungerford on 9 August 1449. He was succeeded by his eldest son, Robert *Hungerford, and his lengthy will attests both his riches and his piety. Though he had already founded five chantries (including one over his tomb in Salisbury Cathedral), he made legacies to dozens of religious houses (notably of Henry V's favourite Carthusians and Dominicans) and to the poor of eighteen Wiltshire and two London parishes, in each of which bells were tolled and masses said for him. He also passed on the personal drinking-cup of John of Gaunt, duke of Lancaster, a symbol of the continuing—and, as it ultimately proved, disastrous—attachment of the Hungerford family to the house of Lancaster.

CHARLES KIGHTLY

Sources J. S. Roskell, 'Sir Walter Hungerford', *Parliament and politics in late medieval England*, 2 (1981), 95–135 · J. S. Roskell and C. Kightly, 'Hungerford, Sir Walter', HoP, *Commons* · J. L. Kirby, 'The Hungerford family in the late middle ages', MA diss., U. Lond., 1939 · GEC, *Peerage* · *Chancery records* · PRO · R. Somerville, *History of the duchy of Lancaster, 1265–1603* (1953) · will of Walter, Lord Hungerford, LPL, reg. John Stafford, fol. 114 · *RotP*, vols. 4–5 · N. H. Nicolas, ed., *Proceedings and ordinances of the privy council of England*, 7 vols., RC, 26 (1834–7), vol. 4 · F. Taylor and J. S. Roskell, eds. and trans., *Gesta Henrici quinti / The deeds of Henry the Fifth*, OMT (1975) · J. H. Wylie and W. T. Waugh, eds., *The reign of Henry the Fifth*, 3 vols. (1914–29) · A. Gransden, *Historical writing in England*, 2 (1982), 213–17 · G. Warner, ed., *The libelle of Englyshe polycye* (1926) · *The itinerary of John Leland in or about the years 1535–1543*, ed. L. Toulmin Smith, 11 pts in 5 vols. (1906–10), vol. 1, p. 138 · PRO, MS C 136/100 no. 31

Wealth at death £1800—English estates: Kirby, 'The Hungerford family'

Hungerford, Sir Walter (b. in or after 1441, d. 1516), landowner, was the second son of Robert *Hungerford, third

Baron Hungerford and Moleyns (c.1423–1464), and Eleanor Moleyns (1428–c.1476). As he was of age on 2 May 1462 Walter was presumably born in 1441 or earlier. His father was an irreconcilable Lancastrian, who was attainted in 1461 and was executed in 1464, but his womenfolk and children remained in England. Walter's grandmother Margaret, Lady Hungerford, probably supported him. Unlike her, Walter Hungerford was apparently not suspected of Lancastrian leanings, but was able to enter the service either of the crown or of someone influential at court. In 1464 he leased the royal lordship of Corsham, Wiltshire, for five years at a rent of 100 marks, and next year was granted the custody and marriage of a royal ward. Margaret struggled to save the family estate from forfeiture and had apparently succeeded when Walter's elder brother Thomas *Hungerford [see under Hungerford, Robert, third Baron Hungerford and Baron Moleyns] was executed in 1469, which enabled Richard, duke of Gloucester, and William, Lord Hastings, to intervene. Walter Hungerford, however, avoided committing himself to the readeption of Henry VI in 1470–71 and thereafter worked himself back to respectability and even favour. By then he had found a patron in William Fitzalan, earl of Arundel (d. 1487), for whom he and Sir John Scott acted as lieutenants at Dover in 1472–3. In 1475 he served in France with two men-at-arms and twenty archers.

When Hungerford's grandmother died (about 1476) she transmitted Heytesbury, Wiltshire, and other properties to him rather than to Thomas's daughter Mary, whom the king's chamberlain, Lord Hastings, had married to his own son Edward. Hungerford was MP for Wiltshire in 1478, sheriff in 1478–9, and served on Wiltshire commissions from 1480. A squire of the body at Edward IV's death, he bore the king's corpse at his funeral, and in the autumn of 1483 joined Buckingham's rebellion against Richard III as its leader in Wiltshire. He was pardoned and bound by recognizances in 1484, but was apparently briefly confined in the Tower of London. He deserted Richard in 1485, fighting for Henry VII at Bosworth, where he was knighted, and secured the reversal of the attainders of his father and brother. On 24 February 1486 he was licensed to enter Farleigh, Heytesbury, and extensive Hungerford lands in Berkshire, Wiltshire, Somerset, and Cornwall. There ensued lengthy litigation in chancery, between Hungerford as heir male and Mary as heir-general, in which Hungerford made the most of his possession of the family cartularies and of his understanding of Margaret's complex conveyances. In the event Mary, Lady Hastings, secured most of the family's Botreaux, Hungerford, and Moleyns lands, together with all three baronial titles, which were transmitted to later Hastings earls of Huntingdon, but Hungerford was able to keep a substantial estate, including Heytesbury. This gave him the resources of a leading country gentleman rather than those appropriate to the nobility.

Hungerford confirmed the titles of those who had bought family lands from his grandmother, and accepted liability for the remaining debts of his father, which he was still paying in 1487, when he made his will. He was restored to Wiltshire commissions from 1485, sitting until his death, and was sheriff once more in 1510–11. He was also appointed steward and keeper of the park of Corsham in 1485, steward of the Warwick and Salisbury lands in 1493 jointly with Lord Willoughby de Broke, the steward of the royal household, and was granted another wardship in 1505. Henry VII sent him on embassy to the Vatican in 1487, and appointed him a royal councillor from 1504. In 1492 Hungerford again served in France, this time with a retinue of sixty-two men. He was at court on such important occasions as the creation of the future Henry VIII as duke of York (1494), the reception of Katherine of Aragon (1501), and Henry VII's funeral. From 1504 he was bound to the king by recognizances totalling £2500 for various unspecified purposes—in 1509 he was quick to have these cancelled. In 1513 he was active in mustering troops for Henry VIII's expedition to France, but it was actually his son who served. Hungerford had married (by 1487) Jane, widow of Thomas Bulstrode, who predeceased him, and when he died, in 1516, he was succeeded by his son Sir Edward Hungerford. Hungerford was buried in St Michael's chapel in the collegiate church at Heytesbury, Wiltshire. His daughter Isabel had married Lord Fitzwarine's heir.

MICHAEL HICKS

Sources J. C. Wedgwood and A. D. Holt, *History of parliament*, 1: *Biographies of the members of the Commons house, 1439–1509* (1936) • J. L. Kirby, *The Hungerford cartularies*, Wilts RS, 49 (1994) • Chancery records • M. A. Hicks, *Richard III and his rivals: magnates and their motives in the Wars of the Roses* (1991)
Archives Hunt. L., Hastings MSS • Sheffield Central Library, MS 901 • Wilts. & Swindon RO, earl of Radnor MSS

Hungerford, Walter, Baron Hungerford of Heytesbury (1503–1540), alleged traitor, was the only child of Sir Edward Hungerford (d. 1522) of Farleigh Hungerford, Somerset, and his first wife, Jane, daughter of John, Lord Zouche, of Harringworth. He married first Susan, daughter of Sir John Danvers of Dauntsey, Wiltshire; second, in 1527, Alice, daughter of William, Lord Sandys, of the Vine; and third, in October 1532, Elizabeth (d. 1554), daughter of John, Lord Hussey of Sleaford.

Hungerford was nineteen when his father died. He appears as squire of the body to Henry VIII in 1522. He became a magistrate for Wiltshire in 1532 and sheriff of Wiltshire the following year, and was appointed to the county bench for Somerset by 1538. His career was much advanced by Lord Hussey, who in August 1532 recommended his future son-in-law to Thomas Cromwell; by the end of 1533 Walter had entered the minister's service. In June 1536 he was summoned to parliament as Baron Hungerford of Heytesbury. He attended the baptism of Prince Edward in October 1537, the burial of Queen Jane in November 1537, and the reception of Anne of Cleves in January 1540. Throughout this period he enjoyed notable gains in the land market of the day, and by the close of the 1530s his estate in Berkshire, Somerset, and Wiltshire had reached a value of over £1000.

Hungerford's fortunes changed dramatically in summer 1540 when, perhaps as a consequence of the fall of Cromwell or perhaps as part of a series of events that helped lead to the minister's fall, the council investigated rumours that had surrounded him for some time. His wife, Elizabeth, had claimed in an appeal for protection addressed to Cromwell in 1536 that she had been incarcerated in Farleigh Castle by her husband for a period of three to four years and that during that time he had often tried to poison her. He was now accused of being concerned in witchcraft and of having dealings with witches, while other allegations were made that suggested his support for known heretics and his involvement in sexual malfeasance. On 22 March 1540 he was attainted for treason. He was accused first of having employed a Wiltshire clergyman, named William Bird, in his house as chaplain despite knowing him to have spoken against the royal supremacy; second of having instructed another chaplain, named Hugh Wood, and one Dr Maudlin to practise conjuring and magic to determine the king's life and his chances of victory over the rebels of the Pilgrimage of Grace; and third of being guilty of buggery. Contemporary writers, including the French ambassador to the court of King Henry VIII, Charles de Marillac, appear to have considered the crime of buggery the principal charge against him. He was beheaded at Tower Hill on 28 July 1540, his execution staged on the same day as that of his patron, Cromwell. The chronicler Raphael Holinshed noted that 'at the houre of his death [he] seemed unquiet, as manie judged him rather in a frensie than otherwise' (Holinshed, 818). The great chronicle of London recorded that his body, like that of Cromwell, was buried in the grounds of the Tower and that the severed heads of both men were displayed on London Bridge. His widow subsequently married Sir Robert Throgmorton. She died on 23 January 1554 and was buried at Weston Underwood, Buckinghamshire.

Sir Walter Hungerford (d. 1595x7), first son of Walter, Baron Hungerford, and his third wife, Elizabeth Hussey, was popularly named 'the knight of Farley' in recognition of his sporting prowess. The younger Walter, who like his father had been in the service of Thomas Cromwell, was restored in blood in 1542 and recovered the greater part of the Hungerford estate in 1554 at his marriage to Anne Basset, a maid of honour to Mary I. He was knighted in 1554 and sat in parliament for Wiltshire (1554) and for Bodmin, Cornwall (1558). He served as sheriff for Wiltshire in 1557 and as a magistrate for the county from 1564. In 1558 he married again; his second wife was Anne Dormer, the daughter of Jane Dormer, a close friend of Queen Mary. The marriage ended in divorce in 1568 and Hungerford was imprisoned in the Fleet for three years for failure to support his wife in separation. Late in life, wrongly believing that his former wife had died, he was espoused for a third time, to a tenant's daughter named Margery Bright. He died between November 1595, when he made his will, and January 1597, when it was proved. He left two sons and one daughter; one other son was born posthumously.

D. J. ASHTON

Sources PRO, SP 1 · LP Henry VIII · CPR, 1547–58 · Hungerford family collections, Wiltshire Archaeological and Natural History Society Library, Devizes · HoP, Commons, 1509–58, 2.413–14 · DNB · Life and letters of Thomas Cromwell, ed. R. B. Merriman, 2 vols. (1968) · J. E. Jackson, A guide to Farleigh Hungerford, co. Somerset, 3rd edn (1879) · J. E. Jackson, 'Farleigh-Hungerford Castle, Somerset', Somerset Archaeological and Natural History Society, 3 (1852) · R. Warnicke, The marrying of Anne of Cleves: royal protocol in Tudor England (2000) · R. C. Hoare, The history of modern Wiltshire, 6 vols. (1822–44) · R. Holinshed and others, eds., The third volume of chronicles, beginning at Duke William the Norman, ed. J. Hooker (1587) · BL, Cotton MS Titus B 1 388 · J. Kaulek, ed., Correspondance politique de MM. de Castillon et de Marillac, ambassadeurs de France en Angleterre (1537–1542) (Paris, 1885) · A. H. Thomas and I. D. Thornley, eds., The great chronicle of London (1938) · M. L. Robertson, 'Thomas Cromwell's servants: the ministerial household in early Tudor government and society', PhD diss., U. Cal., 1975 · GEC, Peerage · The Antiquary IV, 20 (Aug 1881)

Wealth at death over £1000 in lands in Berkshire, Somerset, and Wiltshire; Sir Walter Hungerford: HoP, Commons, 1509–58

Hungerford, Sir Walter (d. 1595x7). See under Hungerford, Walter, Baron Hungerford of Heytesbury (1503–1540).

Huniades, Johannes [formerly János Bánfi-Hunyadi] (1576–1646), chemist and alchemist, was born at Nagybánya (Baia Mare) in Transylvania, the son of Benedict Bánfi-Hunyadi Mogyoró, from 1590 Calvinist bishop of the Trans-Tisza diocese. He served an apprenticeship as a goldsmith to a Nagybánya coiner and worked as a journeyman at Kassa (Košiche) before deciding to leave in May 1606, when he asked his brother-in-law to look after his Nagybánya vineyard and pressing-house. He settled in London during 1608 and rented a workshop for his goldsmith's trade. In April 1613 he wrote again to his brother-in-law, requesting him to take care of his books, instruments, and gold and silverware until he returned to Nagybánya a year later. He was still in England, however, when on 15 July 1617 he presented the Bodleian Library at Oxford with a handsomely bound Bible published at Hanau, near Frankfurt am Main, in 1608 and completed at Kassel under the patronage of Prince Maurice of Hesse. A Latin poem written in it by Huniades is dedicated to Oxford University and to Prince Maurice, while a Hungarian inscription indicates his imminent departure for Hungary.

Huniades knew the mathematician Thomas Allen of Gloucester Hall, Oxford, and later obtained a copy of Allen's exposition of a work on astronomy by Ptolemy; the John Rylands University Library at Manchester also has a beautifully bound manuscript of Heinrich Khunrath's Amphitheatrum sapientiae aeternae (1609) which belonged to Huniades. Dedicated to John Dee and incorporating his occult 'Monas' symbol, it was printed at Hanau in 1609 and anticipated the Rosicrucian manifestos of 1614–15 published at Kassel, one of Europe's greatest centres of alchemy, which Huniades may well have visited on his way to England in 1608. Both these works, and two pages of alchemical quotes which he inscribed in a family album during 1620, suggest Huniades's strong interest in hermetic philosophy, as does his long relationship with Arthur, John Dee's son, the writer of Rosicrucian alchemical treatises, and physician to Queen Anne, James I's wife, at the time of Huniades's 1617 gift to the Bodleian Library. The 'friend' to whom Arthur Dee paid £100 in travel expenses to collect some 'prime matter' (probably antimony) from Hungary in 1617 was clearly Johannes Huniades (Sloane MS 1876). In 1619 Huniades married Dorothy, a daughter of Sir Francis Colton of Kent. They had a daughter, Elizabeth, born in 1620, and a son, John, born in the same year or in 1621, followed by two more children. Dorothy probably predeceased her husband.

A legal document of 1625 describes Huniades as a Whitechapel goldsmith but by 1635 he was registered as 'John Hunniades borne at Hunger an Alcamist' (SP 16/294). Jon Jonston, a distinguished Polish physician, writing in 1632 about the transmutation of metals in his book, translated in 1657 as *A History of the Constancy of Nature*, described his friend Huniades as 'the chief of all the Chymists in England'. From Jonston's correspondence with Samuel Hartlib in 1633–5 it is evident that he and Huniades shared a marked interest in Paracelsian iatrochemical medicines. During 1633 Prince György Rákóczi invited Huniades to become a professor at a Hungarian academy planned in Kolozsvár (Cluj), Transylvania, but by then Huniades was giving regular courses of chemistry in London attended, for instance, about 1634, by John Webster. Hartlib's 'Ephemerides' for May 1634 mentions a manuscript copy of Huniades's 'Systemata chymi', and an undated note (fol. 47/9/22A) envisages a London 'Publick or City University Laboratory', directed by Huniades, possibly connected with Hartlib's further note that Huniades, backed by Sir Kenelm Digby and others, was constructing a laboratory at Gresham College, Bishopsgate Street, in July 1640. It was in this large laboratory belonging to the medical professorship that Digby, assisted by Huniades, conducted some pioneering experiments on the chemical composition of plants between 1640 and 1641. A notebook of Jonathan Goddard, Gresham professor of physic in 1655, contains several references to Huniades's chemical operations by one of his former students, as well as considerable Latin and old German text, probably in Huniades's hand. One recipe involving a sealed alcohol thermometer (dating from 1641) suggests the earliest recorded use, by Huniades, of temperature measurement in distillation.

In April or May 1642 Huniades, who befriended Hungarian scholars in England, mentioned in a letter to Pál Medgyesi, Prince Rákóczi's chaplain, that he intended leaving Gresham College, where he taught chemistry, to move back into his house in St Mary's parish, Whitechapel, but he retained his post until at least the end of 1644. William Lilly, who had known Huniades since 1633, dedicating his *Anglicus, Peace or No Peace* (1645) to him on the eve of his departure for Hungary, praised his skill and learning as an alchemist which had won him fame in England and abroad. J. P. Gowy's untraced portrait of Huniades was engraved by Hollar in 1644 and a silver medallion struck. The inscriptions and symbols in William Marshall's 1646 engraving of another lost portrait cast much light on Huniades as an alchemist. A tax assessment places him still in London during February 1646. Huniades travelled with his family to Amsterdam that summer (intending to stay there for ten weeks before being joined by Arthur Dee

for the journey back to Hungary) but died suddenly of the plague on 28 August 1646. The administration of his property was granted in London by decree to his son on 11 September 1647. The high esteem in which Huniades was held by his contemporaries may be gauged from the Dutch scientist Henry Appelius's correspondence with Hartlib in 1643, and in 1647 when enquiries were made about replacing Huniades with Johann Rudolph Glauber, the celebrated German chemist working in the Netherlands.

John Huniades (1620/21–1696), according to his acquaintance Aubrey, studied mathematics under William Oughtred, came from 'the familie of the King of Hungrie', and was chemist to the fifth earl of Pembroke, who gave him a pension of £100. Aubrey's 'Faber fortunae' has notes of his chemistry operations in the 1680s applied to industrial processes, activities which brought him into contact with fellows of the Royal Society such as Robert Hooke, Joseph Moxon, and Peter Perkins. Chancery proceedings documents reveal a commercial interest in Portugal (early 1660s) and substantial money made from securing property loans (1660–95). In 1697 Adam Frank, a Hungarian Unitarian minister in London, informed a correspondent that Huniades's sister Elizabeth (1620–1710) had inherited £50,000 from her brother which she spent mostly on founding a hospital for the poor and on a monument to him. Elizabeth Stevenson, as she was when granted the administration of her brother's property on 31 December 1696, married Samuel Benson of Shoreditch soon afterwards. The inscription on the magnificent crypt monumental tomb she raised to her brother gives his age as seventy-five at his death on 15 November 1696; both it and her own striking memorial by Francis Bird in St Leonard's Church, Shoreditch, assert royal Hungarian descent and display the arms of the Benson family impaling the Hunyadi regal device of the black raven, but no evidence has been found to support this claim.

JOHN H. APPLEBY

Sources F. S. Taylor and C. H. Josten, 'Johannes Bánfi Hunyades, 1571–1650', *Ambix*, 5 (1953–6), 44–52 · M. Rady, 'A Transylvanian alchemist in seventeenth-century London', *Slavonic and East European Review*, 72 (1994), 140–51 · J. H. Appleby, 'Arthur Dee and Johannes Bánfi Hunyades', *Ambix*, 24 (1977), 96–109 · G. Gömöri, 'New information on János Bánfihunyadi's life', *Ambix*, 24 (1977), 170–73 · University of Sheffield, Hartlib MSS, fols. 28/1/69a, 29/2/7b, 30/4/51b, 44/1/1a–1b, 2a–2b, 6a–6b, 9b, 10a–10b, 16a–16b, 19a–19b, 20b, 45/1/37b, 45a–45b, 47/9/22a · Jonathan Goddard's notebook, BL, Sloane MS 1139 · J. von Magyary-Kossa, *Ungarische medizinische Erinnerungen* (1935), 247–52 · G. T. Forrest, *The parish of St Leonard, Shoreditch*, ed. J. Bird, Survey of London, 8 (1922), 108, 112 · PRO, PROB 6/22, quire 55, 110 · A. Powell, *John Aubrey and his friends* (1948) · *The diary of Robert Hooke ... 1672–1680*, ed. H. W. Robinson and W. Adams (1935), 438 · PRO, C 24/505, pt 2 (1625) · *The obituary of Richard Smyth ... being a catalogue of all such persons as he knew in their life*, ed. H. Ellis, CS, 44 (1849) · parish register, St Leonard's, Shoreditch, 21 Nov 1696 [burial; John Huniades] · monumental inscription, St Leonard's, Shoreditch [John Huniades]

Archives BL, Jonathan Goddard's notebook, Sloane MS 1139 · Bodl. Oxf., John Aubrey's 'Faber fortunae', Aubrey MS 26 · University of Sheffield, Hartlib MSS

Likenesses W. Hollar, engraving, 1644 (after portrait, now missing), BM; repro. in W. Nicholson, 'The Strand' (1799) · W. Marshall, engraving, 1646 (after portrait; now lost), BM; repro. in Taylor and Josten, 'Johannes Bánfi Hunyades', pl. 2 · silver medallion (after untraced portrait, 1638?), repro. in L. Huszár and G. Varannai, *Medicina in nummis: Hungarian coins and medals related to medicine* (1977), pl. 24

Wealth at death not worth £200: *Calendar of the proceedings of the Committee for Advance of Money, 1642–1656*, pt 2, 679 (1656) · left son and daughter considerable amount of money

Huniades, John (1620/21–1696). *See under* Huniades, Johannes (1576–1646).

Hunne, Richard (*d.* 1514), alleged murder victim, was a merchant tailor of the parish of St Margaret New Fish Street, London, and the son-in-law of Thomas Vincent, a leading member of the city's Lollard community. A wealthy man—Sir Thomas More later wrote that he was worth 1000 marks—Hunne also showed notable Lollard tendencies of his own, a consideration that did much to make him the victim of a widely reported but still problematic scandal of considerable potential significance. On 19 March 1511, following the death of his infant son Stephen, Hunne refused the claim of the rector of St Mary Matfelon, Whitechapel, where Stephen died, to the baby's bearing-sheet as a mortuary. More than a year later, on 26 April 1512, the rector cited Hunne to the archbishop of Canterbury's court of audience, which found against the merchant on 13 May at Lambeth. Then on 27 December Hunne attempted to attend evensong in St Mary Matfelon, but the rector's chaplain refused to begin the service until Hunne left, on the grounds that he had been excommunicated. Hunne's response was to sue the rector for slander in the court of king's bench, thereby implicitly questioning the church's jurisdiction over defamation by drawing attention to its secular consequences, and followed this up with an action of *praemunire* against all those who had been involved in the mortuary case, including the bishop's summoner, Charles Joseph. Archbishop William Warham (*d.* 1532) may have sought to respond by proposing heresy proceedings in June 1514.

On 14 October, following the discovery of a Wyclifite Bible in his house, Hunne was arrested for heresy and put in the 'Lollards' tower' in St Paul's Cathedral. At about the same time the bishop's chancellor, Dr William Horsey, dismissed Joseph, but then seems to have reinstated him. On 2 December Hunne appeared before Bishop Richard Fitzjames (*d.* 1522), apparently ready to admit to extreme speech on such issues as denying tithes, and also to possessing heretical books. On the morning of 4 December his body was discovered, hanging by his silk girdle from a hook in the ceiling of his cell. Fitzjames and Horsey claimed that Hunne had committed suicide, and conducted a swift posthumous trial which found that he had denied transubstantiation and the veneration of saints; his abiding interest in the vernacular scriptures was incontestable circumstantial evidence, and consequently his body was burnt on 20 December. The evidence for the aftermath of his death is full of uncertainties—the extant report dates only from 1539 in an edited version. But on 6 December, against a background of considerable lay hostility towards the London clergy, a coroner's jury allegedly asserted that there had been signs of a struggle, that Hunne had been tortured and then throttled, and that the hanging had been faked *post mortem*. Dr Horsey was committed to prison, and Joseph, arrested while carting his household goods towards Stratford, unsuccessfully pleaded an alibi, and then accused Horsey (against whom he may still have borne a grudge) and his own fellow gaoler, William Stradling, as co-murderers. So noisy was the scandal that Henry VIII ordered an inquiry by his council.

All the official lines of interest petered out, leaving a famous mystery. Attempts to secure the restitution of Hunne's property—forfeited on his posthumous conviction—to his widow and children came to nothing. Dr Horsey remained the bishop's chancellor for another sixteen years. Yet in the late 1530s the verdict of the coroner's court was still thought sufficiently interesting to be published commercially. The martyrologist John Foxe (*d.* 1587) made substantial use of the case to argue for sharp tensions between clergy and laity on the eve of the Reformation. Other historians have done likewise ever since, while yet others have challenged its true nature and typicality. Attempts to show that Hunne had no leanings towards heresy have been unconvincing; none the less the likelihood that he died at the hands of his gaolers (perhaps unintentionally, while seeking further confessions), rather than his own, remains strong. Uncertainties over the order and chronology, not to mention the facts, of the events surrounding his death ensure that it will continue to be sharply disputed. JOHN FINES

Sources E. J. Davis, 'The authorities for the case of Richard Hunne (1514–15)', *EngHR*, 30 (1915), 477–88 · S. Brigden, *London and the Reformation* (1989), 98–103, 172–3 · S. F. C. Milsom, 'Richard Hunne's *praemunire*', *EngHR*, 76 (1961), 80–82 · R. Wunderli, 'Pre-Reformation London summoners and the murder of Richard Hunne', *Journal of Ecclesiastical History*, 33 (1982), 209–24 · R. Hun, *The enquirie and verdite of the quest panneld of the death of R. Hune wich was founde hanged in Lolars tower* (Antwerp, [1537]), 13970 · J. Fines, 'The post-mortem condemnation for heresy of Richard Hunne', *EngHR*, 78 (1963), 528–31 · S. J. Smart, 'John Foxe and "The story of Richard Hun, martyr"', *Journal of Ecclesiastical History*, 37 (1986), 1–14 · C. Haigh, *English reformations: religion, politics, and society under the Tudors* (1993) · J. A. F. Thomson, *The later Lollards, 1414–1520* (1965)

Wealth at death rich; 1000 marks; all possessions forfeited following posthumous trial and conviction

Hünnemann [Hannemann], **Christopher William** (1755–1793), miniature painter, was born in May 1755, the son of a court physician at Hanover. He entered the Royal Academy Schools on 6 December 1773, when his age was given as '18 last May' and where his name was recorded in the register as 'Christr Wilhelm Hanneman', and in the council minutes as 'Hannemann' (Hutchison, 140). He gained the silver medal of the academy in 1776. He was recommended to George III as a copyist and his copies of royal portraits by Gainsborough are at Audley End, Essex, and Hartlebury Castle, Worcestershire. He had an extensive practice as a portrait painter and was a frequent exhibitor at the Royal Academy from 1777 to the year of his death, painting in oil and crayons but principally in miniature. His half-length portrait of Sir John Soane, which portrays the architect holding a pair of calipers, was painted in Rome in 1779 (Sir John Soane's Museum, London). He died in London on 21 November 1793.

L. H. CUST, rev. ANNETTE PEACH

Sources Waterhouse, *18c painters* · S. C. Hutchison, 'The Royal Academy Schools, 1768–1830', *Walpole Society*, 38 (1960–62), 123–91, esp. 140 · R. Walker, *National Portrait Gallery: Regency portraits*, 2 vols. (1985) · A. T. Bolton, ed., *The portrait of Sir John Soane* (1927) · O. Millar, *The later Georgian pictures in the collection of her majesty the queen*, 1 (1969), 35, n. 774

Hunnis, William (d. 1597), musician and conspirator, is of unknown parentage. In his *Certayne Psalmes Chosen out of the Psalter of David*, published in 1550, he states he was servant to William Herbert, earl of Pembroke. By 1552 he was a gentleman of the Chapel Royal, being granted a £10 forfeit that year. He attended the funeral of Edward VI and coronation of Queen Mary in 1553, but in 1555–6 became involved in a plot devised by Sir Henry Dudley to assassinate the king and queen and put Elizabeth on the throne.

In order to provide funds for the conspiracy associates of Nicholas Brigham, a friend of Hunnis and keeper of the Treasure House at Westminster, plotted to rob the treasury. A mint was set up near Dieppe, but Hunnis later testified that he refused the request of a fellow conspirator, John Dethicke, to go there, 'as having skill in alchemy, to make experiments on a foreign coin called ealdergylders to convert them into gold' (PRO, SP 11/7, no. 46). On 18 March 1556 some of the conspirators, including Hunnis, were arrested and imprisoned in the Tower. Another gentleman of the chapel, John Benbowe, was also involved. Hunnis confessed his participation and was indicted on 29 April. His subsequent fate is not recorded, but he escaped execution and probably remained in prison until the accession of Queen Elizabeth. His poem *In Terrors Trapp'd* may date from this time. Brigham died in 1558 and Hunnis married Margaret (possibly *née* Wariner), his widow, at Thaxted, Essex, on 25 April 1559. She in turn died that autumn; her will (of which he was executor) was proved on 12 October.

Hunnis is not listed among the servants attending Mary's funeral or Elizabeth's coronation, but in 1562, as once again a gentleman of the Chapel Royal, he received the office of keeper of the new orchard, the lodge, 'Tholde Gret Garden', and 'the Newe Garden' at Greenwich, at a fee of 12d. per day from Michaelmas 1561. A petition of Westminster almsmen, undated but perhaps of February 1563, complained that Hunnis, through his marriage to Margaret Brigham, had claimed ownership of their house and sought to take the premises 'wherein the priest and three women did commonly lie, with the chapel and garden' (CSP dom., 1601–3, 538), but no more is known of the affair. In the meantime in 1560 Hunnis had married Agnes Blagge or Blancke, a grocer's widow, and was given the freedom of the Grocers' Company on 11 November that

year. From 1563 he had a house and shop on the southern end of London Bridge. He paid dues to the Grocers' Company until the late 1580s; his wife died at Ilford in 1588.

Hunnis succeeded Richard Edwardes as master of the children of the chapel on 15 November 1566; the patent is dated 22 April 1567. On 14 February 1569 he received a grant of arms. He was granted the reversion of collector of the city's rights 'for wheelage and passage' on London Bridge on 30 May 1570, and was later paid £40 in lieu. Hunnis contributed 'a device of the Delivery of the Lady of the Lake' for the entertainment of the queen at Kenilworth on 18 July 1575, published in George Gascoigne's *Princely Pleasures of Kenilworth* (1576–7). He was required to present plays by the children of the chapel, and performances at court directed by him are recorded between 1568 and 1575 and again from 1581 to 1584; the interim years were in the hands of Richard Farrant. Unfortunately only titles of some of the plays are known and Hunnis's authorship of any of them remains unconfirmed. His boys were less in demand at court than the children of St Paul's, but both companies combined for public performances at Blackfriars in 1584; after this Hunnis is not known to have directed plays.

Leases of rents on 14 May 1576 and 10 April 1585 were no doubt intended to alleviate Hunnis's heavy costs of maintaining the chapel boys, voiced in his petition to the privy council in November 1583. His signature appears in the old cheque book of the Chapel Royal on 23 October and 25 December 1592 among witnesses to admissions of gentlemen and vestry officials. He died on 6 June 1597, and was succeeded as master of the children by Nathaniel Giles. If the mock will written on the flyleaf of a copy of Sir Thomas More's works in Trinity College, Oxford, is to be believed, his poverty continued:

To God my soule I doe bequeathe, because it is his owne,
My body to be layd in grave, where to my frends best known.
Executors I wyll none make, thereby great stryffe may
   growe,
Because the goodes that I shall leave wyll not pay all I owe.

Hunnis was a friend of Thomas Newton, the Latin poet, and among the latter's 'Encomia' (verse 177) are lines addressed 'Ad Guliel. Hunnissum amicum integerrimum'. In commendatory verses prefixed to Hunnis's *Hyve Full of Hunnye* (1578) Newton also compliments him on his interludes, as well as on his sonnets, songs, and 'roundletts'.

Hunnis shows a minor talent as the author of several devotional volumes and perhaps some music. Scholars agree that his best work is in *The Paradyse of Daynty Devises* (1576). *Certayne Psalmes* and the *Hyve* are unsuccessful additions to the tradition of English versifying from the scriptures. On the other hand *Seven Sobs of a Sorrowfull Soule for Sinne* (1581?) must have been popular, in view of both the many later editions and the endorsement of imitation by later writers. In addition to the verses it contains twelve single-line tunes which may be by Hunnis. Another of his compositions is a setting, in verse idiom and now incomplete, of his own poem 'Alack, when I look back'. Several of his poems were set by other English composers, such as

Byrd, Morley, Weelkes, and William Mundy, and it has been suggested that *Seven Sobs* may also have influenced John Dowland in setting out his *Lachrimae, or, Seaven Teares Figured in Seaven Passionate Pavans* (1604).

ANDREW ASHBEE

Sources C. C. Stopes, *William Hunnis and the revels of the Chapel Royal* (1910), vol. 29 of *Materialen zur Kunde des älteren englischen Dramas* · C. Leech, T. W. Craik, L. Potter, and others, eds., *The Revels history of drama in English*, 8 vols. (1975–83), vol. 2 · D. M. Loades, *Two Tudor conspiracies* (1965) · A. Ashbee, ed., *Records of English court music*, 9 vols. (1986–96), vols. 6–8 · P. Le Huray, *Music and the Reformation in England, 1549–1660* (1967) · M. Frost, *English and Scottish psalm and hymn tunes, c.1543–1677* (1953) [incl. transcriptions of the music in *Seven sobs*] · P. Brett, ed., *Consort songs*, 2nd edn, Musica Britannica, 22 (1974) · A. Ashbee and J. Harley, eds., *The cheque books of the Chapel Royal*, 2 vols. (2000) · P. Holman, *John Dowland's 'Lachrimae'* (1999) · BL, Harl. MS 1359, fol. 54

Hunsdon. For this title name *see* Carey, Henry, first Baron Hunsdon (1526–1596); Carey, George, second Baron Hunsdon (1546/7–1603) [*see under* Carey, Henry, first Baron Hunsdon (1526–1596)]; Carey, John, third Baron Hunsdon (d. 1617) [*see under* Carey, Henry, first Baron Hunsdon (1526–1596)]; Carey, Elizabeth, Lady Hunsdon (1552–1618); Gibbs, Herbert Cokayne, first Baron Hunsdon of Hunsdon (1854–1935).

Hunt, Dame **Agnes Gwendoline** (1866–1948), worker with physically disabled people, was born in London on 31 December 1866, the sixth child of Rowland Hunt (1828–1878), of Boreatton Park, Baschurch, Shropshire, and his wife, Florence Marianne, daughter of Richard B. Humfrey, of Kibworth Hall, Leicestershire, and Stoke Albany House, Northamptonshire. The Hunts were one of the principal families of north Shropshire.

Agnes Hunt spent her early childhood in the large country house completed by her father in 1857. Although her mother disliked children intensely, the stern regime of Victorian parents was partially mitigated by the companionship of ten brothers and sisters, and many horses, dogs, and other pets. At the age of ten she developed osteomyelitis, which left her severely disabled for the rest of her life. Afterwards Agnes looked back with gratitude to the spartan attitude of her family, and especially of her mother, towards her handicap. She was never allowed to consider herself an invalid, and had to share in every way possible in the normal life of her brothers and sisters, so learning early the self-reliance and independence which she was later to instil into so many others. Her mother was a woman of indomitable spirit and considerable eccentricity. After the death of her husband she left for Australia with seven of her children, including Agnes, with the intention of buying an island and rearing Angora goats. Fortunately for Agnes, who bore the brunt of most of her mother's enterprises, the goats did not materialize, and the family gradually drifted back to England, the elder sisters all to be married—one to Frederic Kenyon, an old friend and neighbour. Agnes, after a year spent with a brother in Tasmania, returned in 1887 to fulfil a long-cherished ambition to become a nurse. Hospital after hospital refused to take her on account of her lameness. The one year's course of a 'lady-pupil' at the Royal Alexander Hospital, Rhyl, took her three years to accomplish owing to repeated breakdowns in health, but at last she succeeded in obtaining her certificate, in 1890. She went on to qualify as a queen's nurse and also in midwifery, and spent several years as a district nurse during which she had experience of epidemics of smallpox and typhoid.

After a visit with Agnes to the United States, her mother announced that she intended henceforth to live with her daughter and suggested that she should open a convalescent home for children in Baschurch. This Agnes did in 1900 with her friend Emily Selina Goodford. From the first the Baschurch Home exerted a magnetic attraction for people with disabilities, whom the building in no way suited by reason of its stairs. To overcome this difficulty, three-sided wooden sheds were erected in the garden, and thus Agnes Hunt founded the world's first open-air hospital for disabled people, the Shropshire Orthopaedic Hospital, in 1907. Four years later Robert Jones, who had recently operated on Agnes, became consulting surgeon to the home. Together they revolutionized the treatment and mental welfare of physically disabled people and the attitude of the general public towards them. On his visits to Baschurch, Jones brought with him distinguished surgeons from all over the world, and soon the remarkable results which were being achieved caused the establishment of similar hospitals in other countries. During the First World War soldiers were also housed in open sheds and tents and in 1918 Agnes Hunt was awarded the Royal Red Cross in recognition of her services. She was appointed DBE in 1926.

In 1921, with the help of a Red Cross grant, the hospital was moved to Oswestry, where it became known as the Robert Jones and Agnes Hunt Orthopaedic Hospital. Gradually during the last years of the war Agnes had started a network of aftercare clinics in the small market towns of Shropshire and the surrounding counties. These clinics were originally intended to obviate the difficulty for disabled people of travelling long distances by train for outpatient supervision; soon the centres also provided preventive treatment. In them, too, Agnes Hunt recognized an opportunity for bringing the concerns of the disabled to the public notice, and around each clinic she formed a committee of local people working for the social welfare of the disabled as distinct from their treatment. Before very long most other orthopaedic hospitals adopted similar systems.

Agnes Hunt realized early that treating disability was not enough. Sufferers should also, she believed, be given independence and made to feel the equal of their more fortunate fellows. This could only be achieved by training them to become self-supporting in competition with the able-bodied. To this end, in 1927 she founded the Derwen Cripples' Training College, near Oswestry, where male and female students were taught a variety of trades best suited to their disability. Before she died Agnes Hunt was able to see many of her trainees successfully employed in the open market.

A woman of outstanding personality and great vision, Agnes Hunt devoted her life to the cause of disabled people with an absolute singleness of purpose, great determination, and a dauntless courage in meeting not only her own physical handicaps and incessant pain, but also the difficulties and set-backs which beset the path of every pioneer. Her autobiography, *This is my life* (1938), reveals her rollicking humour and tremendous sense of fun and joy of life, with which she had the power to imbue almost everyone with whom she came in contact. She was also keenly interested in all social problems, and in politics, world affairs, and natural history. Owing to frequent illness she had little formal education, but she had read widely and had a great love of English verse—much of which she would quote at great length. She had a serene and childlike religious faith—the outcome of some years of doubt and struggle—and an unfaltering conviction that the God whom she served in service to others would never fail her. She died, unmarried, at Baschurch on 24 July 1948.　　　　A. E. Sankey, *rev.* Roger Hutchins

Sources A. Hunt, *This is my life* (1938) · Y. Brown, *Boreatton Park from Dame Agnes Hunt to PGL Adventure Holidays* (1989) · *WWW* · Burke, *Gen. GB* · private information (1959) · personal knowledge (1959) · *CGPLA Eng. & Wales* (1949)

Archives Shrewsbury Local Studies Library, Shrewsbury, family archives

Wealth at death £7144 8s. 11d.: probate, Aug 1949, *CGPLA Eng. & Wales*

Hunt, Alfred William (1830–1896), landscape painter, was born in Bold Street, Liverpool, on 15 November 1830, the youngest of seven children and the only son of Andrew *Hunt (1790–1861), and his wife, Sarah Sanderson (b. 1790). His father was a drawing-master and landscape painter. As a boy Alfred joined his father on painting trips in north-west England and to the west coast of Ireland. He first exhibited at the Manchester Royal Institution, showing views of the lakes at Killarney in 1847. He was educated at Liverpool collegiate school, and he won an exhibition and subsequently a scholarship to read classics at Corpus Christi College, Oxford, going up in 1848 and being awarded his degree in 1852. In 1851 he won the Newdigate prize for his poem 'Nineveh'. In 1853 Hunt was elected as a fellow of Corpus Christi, with an exemption from taking holy orders.

During the 1850s Hunt combined an academic career with that of a landscape painter. At first he was influenced by David Cox, whom his father, a native of Warwickshire himself, knew, and who was invited to comment on Alfred's early drawings. In the mid-1850s, however, Hunt adopted Pre-Raphaelite principles, beginning to favour minute observation and the use of intense colour. Hunt became an associate of the Liverpool Academy in 1854 and a full member in 1856. In 1858 he joined the Hogarth Club as a non-resident member, along with other painters of the Liverpool school. He first exhibited at the Royal Academy in 1854, showing *Wastdale Head from Styhead Pass* (ex Sadler collection, Christies, 8 February 1924). In 1856 his second academy exhibit, *The Stream from Lyn Idwal, Carnarvonshire*, was praised by John Ruskin as 'the best landscape I have seen in the exhibition for many a day—uniting most subtle finish and watchfulness of Nature, with real and rare power of composition' (E. T. Cook and A. Wedderburn, *The Works of Ruskin*, 1903–12, 14.50–51). Hunt's 1857 watercolour *Rock Study: Capel Curig—the Oak Bough* (priv. coll.) reflects the instruction of Ruskin's manual *The Elements of Drawing* published that same year. By the late 1850s Ruskin and Alfred Hunt had commenced a friendship which was to last for twenty years. Hunt was further encouraged to embark on a career as a painter by the Oxford printseller James Wyatt, who sponsored Hunt's tours to north Wales and who exhibited and sold the resulting paintings in his shop in the High. In 1859–60 Hunt—who was concerned about his short-sightedness—consulted the oculist Hofrath de Leeuwe, who practised at Gräfrath near Düsseldorf. He travelled through Germany and Switzerland with his future wife. A series of views of—among other places—Heidelberg, Schloss Eltz, Berncastel, and Lucerne derive from this trip.

Hunt gave up his academic career in 1861, in the first place so as to be able to marry (college fellows were required to remain celibate), but also so as to be able to devote himself to landscape painting. Hunt's wife, Margaret *Hunt (1831–1912), was the daughter of the Revd James *Raine (1791–1858), historian and antiquary of Durham; they were married on 16 November 1861 at St Oswald's Church in Durham, and for the following four years lived in Old Elvet in the same city. Alfred Hunt explored the neighbouring countryside, painting landscape views in oil, such as *Brignal Banks* (Walker Art Gallery, Liverpool), and watercolours, including *Finchale Priory* (priv. coll.). This last work was shown at the Society of Painters in Water Colours in 1862, following Hunt's election as an associate member. In 1865 the Hunts moved to London, living on Campden Hill at 10 Tor Villas (later changed to 10 Tor Gardens), a house owned by J. C. Hook and previously occupied by William Holman Hunt. Margaret Hunt wrote novels, some under the pen-name of Averil Beaumont.

Hunt's works of the early and mid-1860s are finely detailed and richly coloured, mostly of specific topography in northern England. On one occasion, in 1866, he treated a literary subject: his *Childe Roland to the Dark Tower Came* (priv. coll.) shows the mounted figure in a vast and gloomy landscape setting. Robert Browning saw the drawing at the Society of Painters in Water Colours, and wrote to Hunt that he was proud to see his poetry associated with so magnificent a picture. Increasingly, Hunt sought to convey the effects of atmosphere, reducing the range of colour in his compositions and devising techniques to suggest the haziness of light in the brightly lit landscape or the half-light of morning or evening. Among his most dramatic subjects, *Tynemouth Pier: Lighting the Lamps at Sundown* (Yale Center for British Art, New Haven) shows waves crashing on the partially constructed jetty at the mouth of the River Tyne. On occasions he painted views at night, and he had a particular skill in painting rainbows and the effects of passing storms, with beams of light gleaming through cloud and mist.

In 1858 Hunt's painting *Cwm Trifaen: the Track of an Ancient Glacier* (Tate collection) was rejected by the Royal Academy, and from 1863 to 1869 no work by him was shown there. With J. W. Inchbold, he came to be seen as one of the victims of the Royal Academy's indifference towards landscape painters. He was, however, a stalwart of the Society of Painters in Water Colours, acting as deputy president of that institution, and his watercolours were much admired in the summer exhibitions there. Hunt was represented by seventeen works in the display of watercolours that Coutts Lindsay staged as a winter exhibition at the Grosvenor Gallery in 1878–9. An article, 'Modern English landscape-painting', in which Hunt laid out his artistic principles, was published in the *Nineteenth Century* in June 1880.

Hunt spent each summer and autumn away from London, often visiting the north of England and showing a particular preference for the Yorkshire and Northumberland coasts. On other occasions he went to the Scottish highlands, and he also sometimes worked on the upper reaches of the Thames. In the winter of 1869–70 he visited the countries of the Mediterranean, travelling on a friend's yacht. From this trip came a watercolour view of Naples and Vesuvius, entitled *A Land of Smouldering Fire* (priv. coll.). In 1873 Hunt visited Ruskin at Brantwood on Coniston Water, a sojourn that led to Hunt's ethereal watercolour *The Stillness of the Lake at Dawn* (priv. coll.). In 1877 he travelled by yacht up the coast of Norway. On these painting trips, Hunt worked directly from nature on sketches and preparing the outlines and overall treatment of more elaborate paintings which would be completed in his London studio during the winter months.

Hunt depended on a small group of collectors who appreciated the authenticity of his vision of landscape. Most of his patrons were themselves from the north of England, and included men such as John Wheeldon Barnes, Isaac Lowthian Bell, the Revd William Kingsley, and Robert Stirling Newall. His works were consistently praised by sympathetic critics, notably Frederic George Stephens of *The Athenaeum*. A retrospective exhibition was held at the Fine Art Society, New Bond Street, in 1884 (with an accompanying catalogue the introduction of which was written by Edmund Gosse and in which Hunt is presented as the sole Victorian inheritor of the landscape tradition of J. M. W. Turner). In the same year Hunt stood as an associate of the Royal Academy, but was not elected. This was said to have been because the academicians resented the frequent comments of the press on the occasion of the Fine Art Society exhibition, that Hunt had been unfairly neglected by the Royal Academy. In 1895 Hunt was disappointed not to be elected president of the Royal Society of Painters in Water Colours. Edward Burne-Jones, who had known Hunt since Oxford days in the mid-1850s, gave an impression of Hunt to his studio assistant T. M. Rooke when they heard the news of his death in May 1896: 'He always looked to me an anxious kind of man—a regular worry-mutton—took life very heavily I fancy' (M. Lago, ed., *Burne-Jones Talking*, 1982, 100). He died of a brain haemorrhage on 3 May 1896 at 10 Tor Gardens in London and was buried in Brookwood cemetery on 7 May. In 1897 a memorial exhibition of his work was held at the Burlington Fine Arts Club, many of the exhibiting works transferring to the Walker Art Gallery, Liverpool, later in the year. He was survived by his wife and their three daughters (Isabel) Violet *Hunt, Venetia, and Silvia.

CHRISTOPHER NEWALL

Sources E. Gosse, *Notes by Mr Edmund Gosse on the pictures and drawings of Mr Alfred W. Hunt exhibited at the Fine Art Society's* (1884) · F. Wedmore, 'Alfred Hunt', *Magazine of Art*, 14 (1890–91), 104–8 · *The Times* (5 May 1896) · 'Mr Alfred William Hunt', *The Athenaeum* (9 May 1896), 625–6 · *ILN* (16 May 1896), 632 · *Exhibition of drawings in water colour by Alfred William Hunt* (1897) [exhibition catalogue, Burlington Fine Arts Club, London; incl. introduction by C. Monkhouse] · H. C. Marillier, *The Liverpool school of painters: an account of the Liverpool Academy from 1810 to 1867, with memoirs of the principal artists* (1904), 156–68 · V. Hunt, 'Alfred William Hunt, RWS', *Old Water-Colour Society's Club*, 2 (1924–5), 29–47 · D. Goldring, *South Lodge: reminiscences of Violet Hunt, Ford Madox Ford and the English Review Circle* (1943) · A. Staley, *The Pre-Raphaelite landscape* (1973), 144–7 · R. Secor, *John Ruskin and Alfred Hunt: new letters and the record of a friendship* (1982) · S. Wilcox and C. Newall, *Victorian landscape watercolors* (1992) [exhibition catalogue, New Haven, CT, Cleveland, OH, and Birmingham, 9 Sept 1992 – 12 April 1993] · d. cert. · Cornell University, Ithaca, New York, Hunt MSS
Archives Cornell University, Ithaca, New York, family papers · Princeton University, New Jersey, photograph albums | Cornell University, Ithaca, New York, corresp. with Margaret Reine Hunt
Likenesses D. S. Maccoll, pencil drawing, 1890, Athenaeum, London · H. T. Wells, pencil drawing, 1896, BM · photographs, Princeton University, New Jersey, AWH's photograph albums
Wealth at death £25,957 13s. 6d.: probate, 2 July 1896, *CGPLA Eng. & Wales*

Hunt, Andrew (1790–1861), landscape painter, was born at Erdington, near Birmingham. Of his parents, nothing is known. He trained under the engraver Samuel Lines and he maintained a friendship with the landscape painter David Cox the elder throughout his life. He married on 31 October 1813 at Edgbaston, Birmingham, Sarah Sanderson (*b*. 1790), and in 1817 moved to Liverpool, where he practised as a landscape painter and a drawing instructor. He exhibited at the Liverpool Academy, becoming an associate in 1843 and a member in 1850. Between 1852 and 1856 he exhibited genre scenes in London, including three pictures at the Society of British Artists and two at the Royal Academy. Titles include: *Children Playing at Jink-Stones* and *The Butterfly*. He usually painted in oils and he frequently painted views of Cheshire and north Wales, and sometimes Ireland. He died on 22 July 1861 in Liverpool, leaving a son and four daughters, several of whom became artists, most notably the watercolourist Alfred William *Hunt (his seventh child) and also Maria, who was known for her still-life paintings. His painting *The North Shore or Estuary of the River Mersey* is in the Walker Art Gallery, Liverpool.

L. H. CUST, *rev.* CHLOE JOHNSON

Sources Redgrave, *Artists* · Graves, *Artists* · Wood, *Vic. painters*, 3rd edn · H. C. Marillier, *The Liverpool school of painters: an account of the Liverpool Academy from 1810 to 1867, with memoirs of the principal artists* (1904) · private information (1891) · IGI · *CGPLA Eng. & Wales* (1861)

Wealth at death £51,000: probate, 9 Aug 1861, *CGPLA Eng. & Wales*

Hunt, Arabella (1662–1705), singer and musician, was born on 27 February 1662 and baptized on 14 March in the parish of St Martin-in-the-Fields, London, the only surviving child of Richard Hunt, gentleman and landowner, and his wife, Elizabeth, whose maiden name was probably Bell. Two siblings, Elizabeth and Eusebius, did not live to adulthood. Arabella's lifelong association with music at the English court began in adolescence: she was probably the 'mistress Hunt' who sang in the court masque *Calisto* in 1675. Her father died in 1678 or 1679, leaving his house in the Haymarket, London, to his wife and his house and lands at Upton, Buckinghamshire, to his sole remaining child, Arabella.

In 1680 Arabella was courted by a person claiming to be a young man named James Howard. The couple went through a form of marriage at the London parish church of St Marylebone, on 12 September 1680, with Arabella's mother and two female neighbours as witnesses. The bride and groom lived together for about six months 'at bed and board' in Elizabeth Hunt's house in the Haymarket, London. At this point the couple separated, and Arabella Hunt launched a suit for annulment in the London consistory court on the grounds that 'James Howard' was in fact a cross-dressing widow named Amy Poulter, *née* Gomeldon (*d*. 1682/3), that Amy had already been married to Arthur Poulter at the time of her marriage to Arabella, and that Madame Poulter 'went under the suspicion of one of a double gender (being usually called a hermaphrodite)' (Crawford and Mendelson, 371). But examination by a jury of five midwives revealed that Amy Poulter was a 'perfect woman in all her parts', and the marriage was annulled on 15 December 1682 on the grounds that two women could not contract a valid marriage with each other. Both parties were declared free to remarry, so long as they married men.

Despite her great beauty and musical talent, Arabella never remarried. Instead, she pursued a successful career as singer, lutenist, and teacher at the English court. She instructed Princess Anne in singing, and became a special favourite of Queen Mary, who granted her a pension of £100 a year. According to a famous anecdote, the queen became tired of listening to some of Purcell's compositions sung by Hunt (accompanied on the harpsichord by Purcell), and asked Hunt to sing the popular ballad 'Cold and Raw' instead. The composer, 'not a little nettled at the queen's preference of a vulgar ballad to his music', inserted the tune to 'Cold and Raw' into his 1692 birthday song for the queen as a kind of mock homage to the royal taste (Hawkins, 2.564).

Hunt was also a great favourite with the general public, as is indicated by several poetic tributes to her beautiful voice (which was described as 'like the pipe of a bullfinch') (Hawkins, 2.761) and consummate musicianship. John Blow's *Amphion Anglicus* (1700) contains an ode, 'On the Excellency of Mrs Hunt's Voice, and Manner of Singing', in which it is asserted that

Arabella Hunt (1662–1705), by Sir Godfrey Kneller, 1692

> she reigns alone
> is Queen of Musick by the People's choice.
> (pp. 14–15)

William Congreve also celebrated Hunt's musical gifts in an ode, 'On Mrs Arabella Hunt Singing'.

Arabella Hunt died on 26 December 1705 at her home in the Haymarket, London. By her will, dated 15 June 1705, she left all her possessions to her mother, Elizabeth, whom she made her executor. SARA H. MENDELSON

Sources DNB · P. Crawford and S. Mendelson, 'Sexual identities in early modern England: the marriage of two women in 1680', *Gender and History*, 7/3 (1995), 362–77 · Bodl. Oxf., MS Rawl. B. 378, fols. 260–266 · depositions, LMA, DLC/240, fols. 137v–139 · J. Hawkins, *A general history of the science and practice of music*, new edn, 3 vols. (1853); repr. in 2 vols. (1963), vol. 2, pp. 564, 761–2 · will, PRO, PROB 11/359, sig. 58 [will of Richard Hunt, father] · will, PRO, PROB 11/486, sig. 40 · O. Baldwin and T. Wilson, 'Purcell's sopranos', *MT*, 123 (1982), 602–9 · J. Blow, 'On the excellency of Mrs Hunt's voice, and manner of singing', *Amphion Anglicus* (1700), 14–15 · W. Congreve, 'On Mrs Arabella Hunt singing', *Poems upon several occasions* (1752), 26–9 · W. A. Shaw, ed., *Calendar of treasury books*, 10–19, PRO (1935–47) · A. Ashbee and D. Lasocki, eds., *A biographical dictionary of English court musicians, 1485–1714*, 1 (1998), 612–14

Likenesses G. Kneller, portrait, 1692, Gov. Art Coll. [*see illus.*] · John Smith, mezzotint, 1706 (after Kneller), NPG, BM · G. Kneller, portrait, BM; repro. in Crawford and Mendelson, 'Sexual identities', 362

Hunt, Arthur Surridge (1871–1934), papyrologist, was born at Romford, Essex, on 1 March 1871, the eldest son and third of eight children of Alfred Henry Hunt, solicitor, later of Romford Hall, and his wife, Emily Pertwee. His father belonged to an old Essex family and his mother was descended from a French Huguenot family originally named Pertuis. He was educated at Cranbrook School

(1882–8) and Eastbourne College (1888–9), whence in January 1890 he went as a classical scholar to Queen's College, Oxford. In 1891 he obtained a first class in classical moderations, but in 1893 only a second class in *literae humaniores*. Despite this he determined to continue at Queen's, even after his father's sudden death in November 1893, when he decided to help his family by preparing for ordination, supported by the Aubrey Moore studentship for theological study. In 1894, however, he was elected to the Craven travelling fellowship. He chose as his field of study the palaeography of early Latin manuscripts in Spanish libraries, but after his return from Spain, on the invitation of his friend and predecessor in the Craven fellowship, Bernard Pyne *Grenfell (1869–1926), he abandoned Latin palaeography for Greek papyrology. In January 1896 he joined Grenfell and D. G. Hogarth, who were excavating for papyri in the Faiyûm. Thus was formed a partnership memorable in the history of classical scholarship, which made the names of the Dioscuri of Oxford, as they were called, familiar throughout the learned world. They are generally regarded as the fathers of papyrology, although strictly speaking they did not so much found it as establish its methodology and conventions.

From 1896 to 1900 Hunt was a senior demy of Magdalen College, Oxford, and from 1901 to 1906 a research fellow of Lincoln, of which he was elected an honorary fellow in 1918; in 1906 he became a research fellow of Queen's. In 1908, on Grenfell's election as professor of papyrology, Hunt was appointed lecturer in that subject. During Grenfell's absence from 1908 to 1913 he worked alone; then, when Grenfell's appointment lapsed, Hunt was elected professor in his place. During the First World War he volunteered, although over military age, and served from 1915 as an officer in the territorial battalion of the Oxfordshire and Buckinghamshire light infantry; he was attached to the war trade intelligence department (1917–18), the War Office (1918–19), and the intelligence corps in France (1918). In January 1918 he married Lucy Ellen (1880–1959), fourth daughter of Surgeon Major-General Sir Alexander Frederick Bradshaw and Ellen Ewart.

During the war years Grenfell recovered sufficiently to take over the papyrology work in Hunt's absence, and in 1919 they resumed working together; but from 1920 Hunt again had to work alone. He spent the remaining fourteen years of his life editing for the Egypt Exploration Society the immense number of papyri he and Grenfell had brought back from Egypt; in total he edited, alone or in collaboration, at least twenty-two volumes—including the first seventeen of *The Oxyrhynchus Papyri*—for the society's Graeco-Roman Memoirs. His most important works apart from these were the *Catalogue of the Greek Papyri in the John Rylands Library, Manchester* (vol. 1, 1911; vol. 2, with J. de M. Johnson and Victor Martin, 1915); *Tragicorum Graecorum fragmenta papyracea* (1912); and *Select Papyri*, for the Loeb Classical Library (with C. C. Edgar, 2 vols., 1932–4).

Hunt had suffered from heart trouble since childhood, and he never really recovered from the sudden death in May 1932 of his only child, Gerald, from complications after a supposedly minor operation. He himself died on 18 June 1934 at his home, 6 Chadlington Road, Oxford; his funeral was held on 21 June in Queen's College chapel.

Hunt brought several valuable skills to his partnership with Grenfell: experience in Latin palaeography, a flair for piecing together literary fragments, and 'a coolly critical intelligence' (*PBA*, 328). As an editor he was patient and devoted to accuracy, and his skill as a decipherer was revealed both in his war work decoding enemy communications and in his solution to a Greek cryptogram (in *PBA*, 15, 1929). He received one of the first Oxford DLitt degrees in 1900, and later honorary doctorates from the universities of Glasgow, Dublin, Königsberg, Graz, and Athens, and was Drexel medallist of the University of Pennsylvania in 1914. He was elected a fellow of the British Academy in 1913, and was also a member of the Bavarian, Danish, and Roman academies of sciences. Shy, reserved, and cautious, Hunt was quietly humorous and deeply affectionate towards his friends, and was once pronounced 'the only *human* brainy man I've ever met' (*PBA*, 335). He was a loyal Anglican; he loved poetry, which he also wrote, and music; and his main outdoor activities were gardening and shooting. H. I. BELL, *rev.* R. S. SIMPSON

Sources H. I. Bell, *PBA*, 20 (1934), 323–36 · personal knowledge (1949) · private information (1949) · *The Times* (20 June 1934), 9 · W. R. Dawson and E. P. Uphill, *Who was who in Egyptology*, 3rd edn, rev. M. L. Bierbrier (1995) · *WWW* · J. G. Milne, *Journal of Egyptian Archaeology*, 20 (1934), 204–5
Archives Bodl. Oxf., notes on Spanish libraries · U. Oxf., Sackler Library, corresp. and papers | BL, corresp. with Idris Bell, Add. MS 59512 · Egypt Exploration Society, London, corresp. with the Egypt Exploration Society
Likenesses W. Stoneman, photograph, 1917, NPG · Lafayette Ltd, photograph, repro. in Milne, *Journal of Egyptian Archaeology*, pl. 27
Wealth at death £54,780 5s. 3d.: probate, 24 Aug 1934, CGPLA Eng. & Wales

Hunt, Sir David Wathen Stather (1913–1998), diplomatist, was born on 25 September 1913 at Rose Acre, Shincliffe, co. Durham, the son of the Revd Bernard Patteson Wathen Stather Hunt, curate of St Nicholas's, Durham, and his wife, Elizabeth Graham, *née* Milner. Stather was added to his and his father's names after his birth. His education began at home: with typical precocity he was able by the age of three to read and write. His formal education was at St Laurence College, Ramsgate, and at Wadham College, Oxford, where he took firsts in both moderations (1934) and Greats (1936).

Hunt was destined for the home civil service. But, with war on the horizon, he decided it would be more amusing to spend the interim in an Oxford senior commonroom than in the corridors of power. He took up a suggestion of Maurice Bowra and in 1937 (having obtained a diploma in classical archaeology) tried successfully for Magdalen College, where he remained a don until 1947. His deep love of Greece dated to those years before the war when his archaeological pursuits twice took him on visits there. It was appropriate therefore that he should have been transferred from the Welch regiment in 1940 to serve as an intelligence officer in Greece. He remained in intelligence for the rest of the Second World War—in the Middle East, north Africa, and Italy, for much of the time on the staff of

Sir David Wathen Stather Hunt (1913–1998), by Elliott & Fry

Field Marshal Alexander. His war service was chronicled in his most considerable book, *A Don at War* (1966). The book was remarkable for its scrupulous military history, Hunt's deep loyalty to Viscount Alexander, and his occasional flashes of impish humour over, for example, his war injury, sustained when the ball from a lavatory cistern fell on his head. He finished the war with the rank of colonel, three mentions in dispatches, OBE, and the American bronze star. He spent a further year in the army helping Lord Alexander (now governor-general of Canada) to complete his official war dispatches.

The year 1947 marked a turning point in Hunt's career. His second volume of autobiography, *On the Spot*, published in 1975, reveals his conclusion that he could not return to Oxford and his taste for the service of the crown. The option of staying in the army was rejected in favour of the Dominions Office (shortly to be renamed the Commonwealth Relations Office) and Hunt joined as a principal. In 1948 he was posted to South Africa as first secretary. On 29 May the same year he married Pamela Muriel Medawar (*b.* 1920/21), daughter of Nami Medawar. They had two sons.

In 1950 Hunt became foreign affairs private secretary to the prime minister, first Clement Attlee and, after the 1951 general election, Winston Churchill. His autobiography shows his affection and admiration for Attlee and his more distant though admiring relationship with Churchill. He became an assistant secretary in the Commonwealth Relations Office in 1952. Following a posting to Pakistan as deputy high commissioner in 1954, he

returned to the Commonwealth Relations Office as head of the Central African department in 1956, and in 1959 was promoted assistant under-secretary of state, with responsibility for Africa. In that capacity he accompanied Harold Macmillan on his 'wind of change' tour of southern Africa in 1960. He was one of several officials who worked on the draft of Macmillan's speech, originally written by John Johnston, deputy high commissioner in South Africa. Between 1960 and 1962 Hunt served in Nigeria as deputy high commissioner under Viscount Head.

Hunt then embarked on three major Commonwealth missions in a period of tumultuous transition. In 1962, as the first high commissioner in Kampala, he was involved in the suppression of a mutiny by the Ugandan army. He was knighted KCMG in 1963, having been made CMG in 1959. In 1965, as high commissioner in Cyprus, his knowledge of the Greek language and history enabled him to establish so firm a rapport with Archbishop Makarios as to achieve an element of stability in Anglo-Cypriot relations despite a situation of near civil war. After virtual civil war in Cyprus, he encountered on his return to Nigeria as high commissioner in 1967 the real thing. In the face of fierce parliamentary and press criticism he put his job on the line to convince Harold Wilson that Britain must not support rebellion against the established government of General Gowan. Meanwhile, Hunt's first marriage was dissolved in 1967, and he was granted custody of his two sons. In Nigeria he married in 1968 his second wife, Iro Myrianthousis. Together they established a tradition of superb hospitality. This was to serve them well during Hunt's last and only foreign posting, as ambassador to Brazil in 1969. Together with his mastery of Portuguese and his relish for travel in that vast country, it ensured that their mission there was remembered as a notably successful one. Hunt retired from the diplomatic service in 1973.

Hunt's life in retirement might have been more tranquil but it was certainly full. As well as chairman of the board of governors of the Commonwealth Institute (1974–84) he was Montague Burton visiting professor of international relations at Edinburgh (1980), a director of Observer Newspapers (from 1982), and a consultant. His wife's Greek connections rekindled his interests in Greek culture and he was president of the Classical Association (1981–2) and of the Society for the Promotion of Hellenic Studies (1986–90). His last book, published in 1989, was a biography, edited with Iro Hunt, of Caterina Cornaro, the last queen of Cyprus.

Hunt acquired national celebrity as BBC Television's Mastermind in 1977 (answering questions on the Roman revolution as well as general knowledge questions) and then as Mastermind of Masterminds in 1982 (with Alexander the Great as his special subject). Success as Mastermind, he said, could be put down to reading and keeping your nerve. Certainly he read voraciously and his career showed no lack of nerve. But there was more to Hunt than that. He had a marvellously alert mind, a lively interest in everything, a prodigious memory, and instant recall. This ensured an impressive mastery of languages and a capacity to complete the *Times* crossword in about nine minutes, to identify a few bars of music and fine claret with accuracy, and ensure no misquotation passed him by. He loved life and lived it to the full.

Hunt died at the Princess Royal Hospital, Haywards Heath, Sussex, on 30 July 1998, having lived in Lindfield, Sussex, throughout his retirement. He was survived by his wife, Iro, and the two sons from his first marriage. A memorial service was held at St Margaret's Church, Westminster, on 12 November 1998.   ROGER WESTBROOK

Sources D. Hunt, *A don at war* (1966) · D. Hunt, *On the spot: an ambassador remembers* (1975) · *The Times* (31 July 1998) · *Daily Telegraph* (31 July 1998) · *The Independent* (11 Aug 1998) · *WWW* · *FO List* · personal knowledge (2004) · private information (2004) · b. cert. · m. cert. [Pamela Muriel Medawar] · d. cert.
Archives Foreign and Commonwealth Office, official documents | Bodl. Oxf., corresp. with Attlee · IWM, corresp. with official historian relating to Italian campaign
Likenesses photograph, 1977, repro. in *The Independent* · photograph, 1978, repro. in *Daily Telegraph* · Elliott & Fry, photograph, NPG [*see illus.*] · photograph, repro. in *The Times*
Wealth at death £10,097—gross; £7647—net: probate, 23 Dec 1998, *CGPLA Eng. & Wales*

Hunt, Frederick Knight (1814–1854), journalist, was born at Horton, Buckinghamshire, on 3 April 1814, the eldest of six children of John Hunt, an artist, and his wife, Mary Ann. He was baptized at St Pancras, London, on 15 May 1814. His family appear to have been in difficult financial circumstances. At the time of his father's death in 1831 Hunt was a night boy in the printing office of the *Morning Herald*. To support his family, which he continued to do more or less until his death, he took in addition a day job as clerk to a barrister. His employer, fortunately for him, had little practice, and Hunt, who for years together never enjoyed a continuous night's rest more than once a week, filled up his time with study instead of sleep. On 14 July 1835 he married Maria, the daughter of Samuel Meres, a farmer of Rockingham, Northamptonshire. Having secured a literary engagement with a 'short-lived morning newspaper', he found time to study medicine at the North London School of Medicine and on 13 November 1840 he became MRCS.

In 1839 Hunt established the *Medical Times*, which was incorporated in January 1852 with the *Medical Gazette* (and successfully continued as the *Medical Times and Gazette* until 1885). Threats of libel actions by medical figures after he took up the cause of the mesmerist John Elliotson forced him to sell up in 1841 and take a position as surgeon to a poor-law union in Norfolk. He returned to London after a year, and, while continuing to practise medicine, resumed his connection with the press and was briefly employed in the offices of the Anti-Corn Law League. He was successively sub-editor of the *Illustrated London News*, which he helped to launch in May 1842, and editor of the *Pictorial Times*. He edited the *London Journal* in 1844. On the establishment of the *Daily News* in 1846, he was selected by Dickens as one of the assistant editors, probably on the recommendation of Henry Vizetelly. During this period he continued to see patients, at his house in Greenwich. In

1851 he was made chief editor of the *Daily News*, and under him the paper first became prosperous. He launched the journalistic career of Harriet Martineau. He was a contributor to *Household Words* during its first two years and in a letter to R. H. Horne in 1851 Dickens remarked that he had done the publication 'very good service indeed' (Lohrli, 319).

Hunt died of typhus fever at his home in Forest Hill, London, on 18 November 1854, leaving a widow and four children, and was buried at Nunhead cemetery. He was known as an amiable, sanguine, impulsive man, disposed to busy himself with too many projects, and to diffuse his energies over too wide a field, but possessed of sound literary judgement, as well as of extraordinary energy. He was the author of a book on the Rhine, published in 1845, and of other ephemeral publications, but his literary reputation rested on *The fourth estate: contributions towards a history of newspapers and of the liberty of the press* (1850), the first attempt at a fairly thorough history of the British newspaper. It remains useful as a source, although 'discursive and generally unreliable' (Koss, 70).

RICHARD GARNETT, *rev.* C. A. CREFFIELD

Sources *The Athenaeum* (25 Nov 1854), 1432 · *Daily News* (20 Nov 1854) · Boase, *Mod. Eng. biog.* · Ward, *Men of the reign* · A. Lohrli, ed., *Household Words: a weekly journal conducted by Charles Dickens* (1973) · S. E. Koss, *The rise and fall of the political press in Britain*, 1 (1981) · J. Hunt, 'Untamed editor: F. Knight Hunt MRCS (1814–54)', *Journal of Medical Biography*, 5/4 (1997), 210–20 · *IGI*
Archives Wellcome L., certificates and other papers | U. Birm. L., corresp. with Harriet Martineau
Wealth at death modest but sufficient provision made for wife and family: *Athenaeum*

Hunt, George Ward (1825–1877), politician, eldest son of the Revd George Hunt of Winkfield, Berkshire, and Wadenhoe, Northamptonshire, and Emma, youngest daughter of Samuel Gardiner of Coombe Lodge, Oxfordshire, was born at Buckhurst, Berkshire, on 30 July 1825. He was educated at Eton College from 1841 to 1844 and on 31 May 1844 matriculated from Christ Church, Oxford, where he was a student from 1846 to 1857. He graduated BA in 1848 and MA in 1851 and was created DCL on 21 June 1870. He was called to the bar at the Inner Temple on 21 November 1851, and went on the Oxford circuit; on 23 May 1873 he was made a bencher of his inn. He married Alice (*d.* 1894), third daughter of Robert *Eden, bishop of Moray and Ross, on 5 December 1857; they had five sons and five daughters.

Preferring politics to legal studies, Hunt unsuccessfully contested Northampton in 1852 and 1857 as a Conservative, and at last gained a seat on 16 December 1857, as one of the members for the northern division of Northamptonshire, which he represented until his death. His house was at Wadenhoe, Northampton. Hunt's striking achievement as a back-bencher was on 25 March 1866, when he carried a motion defeating the government over regulations controlling foot-and-mouth disease in cattle. He was elected chairman of quarter sessions for Northamptonshire in April 1866 and chairman of the Northamptonshire chamber of agriculture on 18 January 1873.

Hunt was financial secretary to the Treasury in Lord Derby's administration from July 1866 to February 1868, and his correspondence with Disraeli, then chancellor of the exchequer, shows him to have been quite an active economist. When Disraeli became prime minister in February 1868, Hunt, to general surprise, was appointed chancellor of the exchequer; he was sworn of the privy council on 29 December 1868. He was, Lord Stanley noted, 'sensible and laborious' (Vincent, 331) and his sole financial statement, on 23 April, was a low-key affair that levied additional indirect taxation to meet rising expenditure and pay for the military expedition to Abyssinia. He kept the house waiting and it was said that his speech had to be fetched because he had forgotten to bring it. On the return of the Conservatives to power in 1874 he was appointed first lord of the Admiralty (21 February). He was more comfortable conducting the Agricultural Holdings Bill of 1875 through the Commons than he was in dealing with naval matters. His speech on 20 April 1875, which effectively charged his Liberal predecessor with creating a mere paper navy, produced a 'navy scare' and he had to explain that 'it may be that my own niggardly ideas misled the House' (*Hansard 3*, 218, 1875, 1474–5). Even so, Hunt was intent on naval expansion and conducted with some success a campaign for increased naval estimates from 1874 to 1877. He also had to account for a series of naval catastrophes, including the loss of HMS *Vanguard* in a collision in 1875 and the sinking of HMS *Thunderer* after an explosion in 1876. Disraeli unsuccessfully tried to persuade Lord Carnarvon to relieve Hunt at the Admiralty.

Hunt was a vast man who suffered from gout (Disraeli described him as 'reduced … to 25 stone'; *Letters*, 2.24). With the strains of office his health deteriorated further, but even so he was part of what Disraeli called the 'War Party pure and simple' in the cabinet in 1877 (Monypenny, 6.194) and in the Commons on 4 April that year made a strong justification of the case for defending Turkey against Russia. He thus, in Disraeli's view, 'redeemed some peccadilloes' (Monypenny, 6.147). Hunt went to Homburg on 23 June 1877 for treatment and died there from the effects of gout on 29 July 1877; he was buried next morning in the English cemetery.　　H. C. G. Matthew

Sources *The Times* (30–31 July 1877) · *Law Times* (4 Aug 1877) · *ILN* (4 Aug 1877), 119 · W. F. Monypenny and G. E. Buckle, *The life of Benjamin Disraeli*, 6 vols. (1910–20) · H. C. G. Matthew, 'Disraeli, Gladstone, and the politics of mid-Victorian budgets', *HJ*, 22 (1979), 615–43 · R. W. Seton-Watson, *Disraeli, Gladstone and the eastern question: a study in diplomacy and party politics* (1935) · *Disraeli, Derby and the conservative party: journals and memoirs of Edward Henry, Lord Stanley, 1849–1869*, ed. J. R. Vincent (1978) · *Letters of Disraeli to Lady Bradford and Lady Chesterfield*, ed. marquis of Zetland, 2 vols. (1929) · P. W. Clayden, *England under Lord Beaconsfield* (1880) · J. F. Beeler, *British naval policy in the Gladstone–Disraeli era, 1866–1880* (1997) · W. L. Burn, *The age of equipoise* (1964) · *DNB*

Archives Northants. RO, corresp. and papers | Bodl. Oxf., corresp. with Benjamin Disraeli · Lpool RO, corresp. with fifteenth earl of Derby · NMM, corresp. with Sir A. Milne · Suffolk RO, Ipswich, letters to Lord Cranbrook

Likenesses Faustin, chromolithograph, June 1874, NPG · Ape [C. Pellegrini], caricature, watercolour study, V&A · London Stereoscopic Co., carte-de-visite, NPG · G. J. Stodart, stipple and line engraving (after photograph by Maull & Fox), NPG · J. Tenniel, pencil caricature, NPG; repro. in *Punch* (9 June 1877) · lithograph, NPG; repro. in *Civil Service Review* (Feb 1877) · photograph, NPG · portrait, repro. in *ILN* (21 March 1868), 280 · portrait, repro. in *ILN* (18 April 1874), 365 · portrait, repro. in *ILN* (11 Aug 1874), 140 · portrait, repro. in *Graphic* (4 Aug 1877), 113

Wealth at death under £16,000: probate, 6 Oct 1877, *CGPLA Eng. & Wales*

Hunt, George William (*c.*1830–1904), music-hall songwriter, may have been born about 1830, but nothing is known of his parentage or early life. He certainly spent some time in South Africa, and after his return to England in 1860 began writing songs for the music-hall, then in its absolute infancy. He claimed to have written more than 7000 songs by the 1890s, and to have been the first music-hall writer to provide performers with both words and lyrics. Both of these claims are exaggerated, but he clearly had a considerable output, especially in the period from about 1865 to 1885, and, in a popular cultural trade where a division of labour was common, he certainly showed great skill in both departments.

Hunt's first successful song was for Tom MacClagan and expressed sentiments sympathetic to the American anti-slavery movement. Although he was to return to political themes from the late 1870s with great effect, his initial reputation was gained mainly through the comic love songs and 'swell' songs composed for the *lions comiques*, those singers who both celebrated and parodied the lifestyle of leisured young men and their less affluent imitators. Hunt wrote for all the leading male singers of the period to the 1880s and was particularly closely associated with the careers of George Leybourne, The Great Vance, Arthur Lloyd, and G. H. Macdermott. His best-known songs were, at the one extreme, the comic 'The German Band' (1865) for Lloyd, concerning the loss of a loved one to a street musician, and, at the other, 'Macdermott's War Song' (1877), or 'The Jingo Song', as it was usually known. Probably first performed in early May 1877, 'The Jingo Song' dealt with the threat posed to British interests by Russia's declaration of war against Turkey on 24 April 1877. With its strident chorus ('We don't want to fight, but by jingo if we do, We've got the ships, we've got the men, we've got the money too') it became the anthem of those who supported British naval intervention to halt the Russian advance. It was probably the *Daily News* in March 1878 which, aware of the power of the song, dubbed the more bellicose elements in this foreign policy debate 'jingoes', and the use of the term 'jingo' continued well into the twentieth century.

Hunt also wrote a number of music-hall sketches and a small amount of ballet and theatre music. He managed the Cambridge Music Hall from the mid-1870s until 1882 and served as secretary to the Music Hall Provident Fund in the 1890s, retiring from this post in 1901. He died of 'softening of the brain' in Essex County Asylum, Brentwood, on 3 March 1904. Hunt, as one of the earliest, most prolific, and most successful music-hall songwriters, was a key figure in the production of a new genre of popular song, marked by the use of dance rhythms, notably the polka and waltz, a simple tonal and harmonic language, and a vitally important chorus, and which dealt, in varying degrees of seriousness, with the social and emotional aspects of modern urban life. Although he is always remembered in music-hall literature as 'Jingo' Hunt, his contribution to the development of popular songwriting requires that his reputation should extend beyond the role he played in adding to the English language.

DAVE RUSSELL

Sources *The Era* (16 June 1878) · *The Era* (17 March 1894) · *The Era* (5 March 1904) · songs, BL, music collections · *DNB*
Likenesses photograph, repro. in *The Era* (5 March 1901)

Hunt, Henry [*called* Orator Hunt] (**1773–1835**), radical, was born on 6 November 1773 at Widdington Farm, Upavon, Wiltshire, the first of six children of Thomas Hunt (*d.* 1797) and his wife, Elizabeth, *née* Powell (*d.* 1789), of Week, near Devizes. An athletic handsome figure of Wiltshire farming stock, Orator Hunt—the sobriquet seems to have been coined by Robert Southey in 1816—became the most famous and flamboyant figure in early nineteenth-century radical politics, renowned for his stentorian voice, white hat, and disputatious character.

Education, marriage, and separation Hunt's rural upbringing gave no indication of such a notorious public career. Educated at a number of indifferent boarding- and grammar schools in preparation for Oxford and the church, the headstrong young Hunt insisted on following his father into full-time farming. As an innovative gentleman farmer, Hunt enjoyed considerable prosperity in the wartime agricultural boom, when he applied his talents to substantial holdings in the west country. On his father's death, Hunt came into ownership or occupancy of 3000 acres in Wiltshire, including the old family estate at Enford, and property in Bath and Somerset, including the manor and estate of Glastonbury. A hasty and unfortunate *mésalliance*, his marriage (on 12 January 1796) to Ann Halcomb, daughter of the landlord of The Bear inn, Devizes, came under strain on their move to Chisenbury Priory, an elegant mansion where Hunt flaunted his prosperity in 'uninterrupted gaiety and dissipation'. During this 'giddy round of mirth and folly' he fell in love with Mrs Vince, the unhappily married wife of a friend. Unable to conceal their emotions, the couple eloped. Hunt duly arranged a formal separation from his wife in September 1802, with provision for their two sons, Thomas and Henry junior; their first-born child, a girl, died before being baptized, and there was a second daughter, Ann. Thenceforth, extravagance was curtailed. Hunt spent the rest of his life in devoted fidelity to Mrs Vince. Having flouted social convention, however, Hunt found himself ostracized by the Wiltshire establishment, a contributory factor in his conversion to radicalism. His relationship with Mrs Vince and his prowess as a farmer were later the subject of heated dispute with William Cobbett, issues that cut deeper than any political differences in their tempestuous collaboration in the radical cause.

Imprisonment and radicalism A staunch loyalist by upbringing, Hunt first offended the local worthies by excessive zeal in the volunteer movement. This misplaced

Henry Hunt [Orator Hunt] (**1773–1835**), by Adam Buck, *c.*1810

ardour led to six weeks' imprisonment in the king's bench, London, at the end of 1800 for his refusal to apologize to his commanding officer in the Marlborough yeomanry, whom he had challenged to a duel. In prison Hunt encountered new political ideas: Henry Clifford, the distinguished liberal lawyer and doyen of Horne Tooke's Wimbledon circle, took a special interest in his political enlightenment. On return to Wiltshire, however, Hunt placed himself at the head of local defence preparations, an assumption of command that outraged the county notables. After the lord lieutenant refused his services during the invasion scare of 1803, the aggrieved Hunt cast loyalism aside to become a fervent supporter of Sir Francis Burdett and an avid reader of Cobbett. In 1805, in the midst of scandal surrounding the financial misconduct of Lord Melville, the treasurer of the navy, he made his first speech at a Wiltshire county meeting, 'general condemnation of all peculations and peculators' (*Memoirs*, 12.161).

Proud of his independence as a substantial freeholder, Hunt stood forward on the county platform in both Wiltshire and Somerset to protest not only at the war-inflated corruption and incompetence of the 'Pitt system' but also at the factionalism and apostasy of the whigs as evinced by the 'ministry of all the talents'. His radicalism developed apace as the financial difficulties of the Jacob's Well brewery, in which his father-in-law had persuaded him to invest, forced him to spend considerable time in Bristol. In this large freeman borough he endeavoured to emulate the success achieved by the Westminster committee in securing Burdett's election. Having established the Bristol Patriotic and Constitutional Association in 1807, 'Bristol'

Hunt acquired national notoriety in 1812 when he twice contested the seat in demagogic style, taking to the streets as the people's candidate. The champion of the crowd, Hunt finished bottom of the polls; however, in upsetting plans to secure Sir Samuel Romilly's return, he gained a reputation as the scourge of whigs and moderate reformers.

The reputation was confirmed when Hunt transferred his interests to London. After winding up the brewery, Hunt had returned to Wiltshire, where his presence was unwelcome. Wealthy neighbours brought a series of legal actions against him, one of which led in 1810 to his second brief spell of imprisonment (and further political education in discussion with Cobbett and Burdett) in the king's bench, London. Eschewing Wiltshire thereafter, he took a large estate at Rowfant, near East Grinstead, which he farmed with considerable profit until 1813. His next investment, the three-year lease of Cold Henly Farm, Whitchurch, Hampshire, marked a sharp deterioration in fortune: the impact of post-war deflation was compounded by further legal costs in actions brought by Winchester parsons and attorneys who boasted that they had 'driven Cobbett out of the county, and they would try hard to make me follow him' (*Memoirs*, 3.548). Having abandoned Cold Henly and full-time farming, Hunt took up residence at Middleton Cottage, near Andover, intending to spend his time enjoying the sports of the field. 'Bristol' Hunt, however, was increasingly drawn towards London and politics.

At Burdett's suggestion, Hunt entered the Common Hall (as a liveryman of the Loriners' Company) to advocate 'general not partial liberty'. Such independent radicalism brought him into conflict with Robert Waithman, the patriotic linen draper who had transformed the city from a bastion of Pittite loyalism into a stronghold of peace, retrenchment, and reform, but remained subservient to the whigs. Encouraged by Cobbett, Hunt also stood forward to expose the machinations of the Westminster committee, which, having passed into the hands of affluent moderate reformers, sought an accommodation with the progressive whigs by promoting Henry Brougham as Burdett's running mate. Dismayed by Burdett's compliance, Hunt used every public opportunity (which later included Bristol-style intervention in Westminster elections in 1818 and 1819) to condemn the caucus of:

> *petty shopkeepers*, and little *tradesmen*, who under the denomination of *tax-paying housekeepers*, enlisted themselves under the banner of Sir Francis Burdett, in order to set themselves up as a sort of privileged class, above the *operative* manufacturer, the mechanic and the labourer. (*Memoirs*, 2.75)

Development of 'the platform' As post-war distress intensified in 1816, the 'revolutionary party', heirs of the underground 'putsch' tradition, looked to a well-attended public meeting as the best springboard for insurrection, and hence invited all the reform celebrities of the day (Hunt included) to address a meeting of 'Distressed Manufacturers, Mariners, Artisans, and others' at Spa Fields on 15 November 1816. Hunt alone accepted after he had satisfied himself that he was not being drawn into a revolutionary plan to abolish private property in land. In a private interview with Dr Watson, the impecunious apothecary and leading ultra-radical strategist, Hunt insisted there must be no reference to Spencean principles and no incitement to riot. The meeting would be strictly constitutional, a legitimate extension of political activity which would enable the distressed masses to enrol in a campaign of petitions and memorials to 'save the wreck of the constitution' by the instauration of universal (manhood) suffrage, annual parliaments, and the ballot. In an impressive exercise in crowd control, Hunt upstaged the absent moderates and confounded the insurrectionists. When diehards of the revolutionary party tried to implement their original insurrectionary plan at a second meeting on 2 December 1816, their disastrous failure underlined the utility of Hunt's constitutional ways and means.

The format established at the Spa Fields meetings of 1816–17, the disciplined display of numbers, dominated popular agitation until the collapse of Chartism. Open and inclusive, this mass platform deliberately exploited ambiguities in the law and the constitution, facilitating an escalating mobilization of popular support to coerce the otherwise inexorable government, 'peaceably if we may, forcibly if we must'. As mass meetings spread to the industrial districts, radicalism acquired an independent and uncompromising tone. At the Hampden Club convention of 1817 (at which Hunt introduced himself as the delegate of '14,000 petitioners of Bristol, 8000 of Bath and 100,000 at least at Spa Fields'; *Bristol Gazette*, 30 Jan 1817), delegates from the north rejected the direct taxation proposals favoured by Burdett, Cobbett, and the veteran Major Cartwright in favour of Hunt's programme of universal manhood suffrage.

When the radical challenge was crushed by the 'dungeon parliament' of 1817, Hunt returned to the legitimate county meeting platform to register his protest at repression. A forthright critic of the government spy system, his evidence helped to secure the acquittal of Watson and other 'conspirators'. Once the Seditious Meetings Prevention Act had run its course, the Watsonites arranged a mass meeting in Palace Yard, Westminster, in September 1818, where Hunt introduced a stridently worded remonstrance, which reminded the regent of the sovereignty of the people and asserted the worker's right 'to reap the ample and substantial fruits of his virtuous and USEFUL TOIL' (*Sherwin's Political Register*, 12 Sept 1818). The great radical campaign of 1819 began in January, when Hunt took the remonstrance to Manchester to enlist the northern workers.

The Peterloo massacre When denied access to the regent to present the remonstrance, Hunt sanctioned a major escalation of platform activity in the summer of 1819, a cumulative display of irresistible 'pressure from without'. At Hunt's insistence, disciplined good order was the essential feature of the meetings. When the city authorities intervened at Smithfield on 21 July to arrest one of the supporting speakers on the platform, Hunt managed to restrain the crowd, whose numbers were duly enlisted in

'Political Union in the cause of Universal Civil and Religious Liberty' (*Black Dwarf*, 28 July 1819). An escalating exercise in extra-parliamentary agitation, the 'national union' was to be consolidated at regional demonstrations. That planned for St Peter's Field, Manchester, in August, under Hunt's chairmanship, was to be the largest yet, to be followed by a huge London assembly on Kennington Common on his triumphal return. A tense mood of confrontation developed in which each side hoped the other would be the first to overstep the mark, transgress the constitution, and lose public sanction. Well versed in the law, Hunt insisted that radicals abandon arming and drilling on the Lancashire moors: they were to come to the rearranged Manchester meeting on 16 August '*armed* with *no other weapon* but that of a self-approving conscience; determined not to suffer yourselves to be irritated or excited, by any means whatsoever, to commit any breach of the public peace' (*Manchester Observer*, 14 Aug 1819). Having heard a rumour that the magistrates had issued a warrant against him, he offered himself up to the authorities on the Saturday before the meeting in order to leave them no pretext for breaking up the proceedings. On the fateful day, at least eleven people were killed and many hundreds injured when the magistrates sent in the local yeomanry to arrest Hunt and then ordered in the 15th hussars to disperse the peaceable crowd.

The Peterloo massacre inflamed radical spirits, aroused middle-class public opinion, and unnerved the government. The radicals, however, failed to advance beyond this vantage ground. Hunt was soon embroiled in internecine controversy with the Watsonites, as he refused to sanction plans for a full-scale confrontation through simultaneous mass meetings. Hunt, indeed, decided to forgo the platform altogether, resting the radical case on the unsullied moral victory of Peterloo itself. In the courts, however, the authorities were exonerated without question, Hunt's unremitting efforts to bring the 'Manchester murderers' to justice notwithstanding. At his own trial in York in March 1820, Hunt was fined and sentenced to two and a half years' imprisonment.

Later activities, death, and reputation Immured in 'Ilchester Bastille', Orator Hunt turned pamphleteer, journalist, and autobiographer, producing *Memoirs of Henry Hunt, Esq., Written by himself in his Majesty's Jail at Ilchester* (3 vols., 1820–22) and addresses *To the Radical Reformers, Male and Female of England, Ireland and Scotland* (2 vols., 1820–22). These writings, the primary source for his reputation for vanity, were certainly characterized by an interminable concentration on self. At a time of revision in radical ranks, Hunt sought to legitimize his leadership as the best guarantee of the integrity of popular radicalism, otherwise under threat from ideological extremism or moderate opportunism. Furthermore, he needed publicity for his 'gaol politics'. What started as a campaign to secure his political status soon widened into a major exposure of the evils of the prison system which led to the conviction of the governor and the demolition of the gaol.

Hunt left prison hoping to recapture popular support and to recoup the personal fortune he had lost through

agitation and persecution. He enjoyed considerable business success with an extraordinary range of products, including his tax-free Breakfast Powder and his 'matchless' shoe-blacking, bottles of which were embossed with the slogan 'Equal Laws, Equal Rights, Annual Parliaments, Universal Suffrage and the Ballot'. In the absence of a popular radical platform, he campaigned no less energetically within the confines of the unreformed system, insisting on greater accountability at county, city, and vestry level: he condemned the jobbery of the Somerset county establishment, the 'guzzlings and gormandising' of the corporation of London, and the misappropriation of funds in his local parish, Christchurch, Lambeth. In December 1830 he gained election as MP for Preston, a potwalloper constituency that he had contested in 1820 until called away to trial. As champion of the poor Preston electors, Hunt opposed the whig Reform Bill, a stance condemned by other radicals. Expressly addressed to 'the Working Classes and no other', Hunt's opposition to the bill gave voice to an unsophisticated but uncompromising democratic radicalism, upholding the rights of those excluded by the bill with its uniform propertied franchise. Battling against liberal propaganda, reformist sentiment, and popular prejudice, Hunt's democratic opposition to the bill cost him his health, his business, and, at the first elections under the reformed system in December 1832, his parliamentary seat. During his brief parliamentary career Hunt, the 'poor man's protector', spoke over a thousand times, and his activities included the presentation of a pioneer petition for female suffrage.

After the spring of 1834 Hunt was rarely in good health. He suffered a severe stroke on a business trip to Hampshire and died soon afterwards at Alresford on 13 February 1835. A week later he was buried in Colonel Vince's vault at Parham Park, Sussex, after Mrs Vince's own family, the Bishops, had refused to allow the body to be admitted to their vault. Consigned to an early grave, his heart broken by the folly and ingratitude of the people, Hunt was soon elevated to martyrdom. Accorded pride of place in the Chartist pantheon, 'ever-to-be-loved' Hunt was honoured as the great prophet who had tried to warn the non-represented people of the deleterious consequences of middle-class 'liberal' reform. JOHN BELCHEM

Sources J. Belchem, '*Orator*' *Hunt: Henry Hunt and English working-class radicalism* (1985) · W. Proctor, 'Orator Hunt, MP for Preston, 1830–32', *Transactions of the Historic Society of Lancashire and Cheshire*, 114 (1962), 129–54 · J. W. Osborne, 'Henry Hunt, 1815–30: the politically formative years of a radical MP', *Red River Valley Historical Journal of World History*, 5 (1981), 177–94 · *Memoirs of Henry Hunt, esq., written by himself in his majesty's jail at Ilchester*, 3 vols. (1820–22) · *GM*, 2nd ser., 3 (1835), 547

Archives Lancs. RO, corresp., DDX/113 · Man. CL, Manchester Archives and Local Studies, diary · NRA, priv. coll., corresp. and papers · priv. coll., corresp. and papers · University of Chicago Library, corresp. and papers

Likenesses A. Buck, watercolour drawing, c.1810, NPG [*see illus.*] · J. Kennerley, stipple, pubd 1819 (after T. Clater), BM · stipple, pubd 1819, BM · H. Robinson, group portrait, stipple, pubd 1820 (*Political reformers*), BM · A. Buck, watercolour drawings, NPG · bronze plaque, Manchester Reform Club · portraits, BL

Hunt, Sir Henry Arthur (1810–1889), surveyor, was born in Westminster, London, in September 1810, a son of James Hunt, master builder, of the parish of St James's, Westminster. The elder Hunt, with his partner, Bennett, established one of the major building firms of the 1820s, so that his son benefited from an early familiarity with undertakings on the largest scale, such as warehouses at the St Katharine Dock. He was articled to Messrs Thurston, and in 1827 entered the office of John Wallen, the top quantity surveyor of the decade, who took him into partnership before he was eighteen. Hunt married Eliza Susannah (1810/11–1891) probably in the early 1830s; they had three sons and four daughters.

Hunt set up his own practice in 1830, rapidly establishing himself as a leader of his profession. Described in 1835 as 'a surveyor employed very much by architects and builders in making estimates', Hunt himself stated that 'All the large builders in London have taken my quantities' and that Messrs Grissell and Peto had 'uniformly employed me in preference to any other professional man'. He told a select committee that he was involved in numerous projects including two London clubs, the Atlas Fire office, Bermondsey grammar school, hospitals, Westminster prison, the New Hungerford market, and various railways ('Select committee on … the houses of parliament', 21.43–76). He checked Charles Barry's rough estimate for his design for the houses of parliament in 1836 with a thoroughness unusual at that period. Barry's appointment once confirmed, Hunt took out the quantities for a detailed estimate made from a complete set of working drawings and revised it for parliamentary approval. Barry subsequently employed him to measure the work at Westminster in 1851 in order to formulate up-to-date accounts of the expenditure. In 1856, however, Sir Benjamin Hall, first commissioner of works, who was locked in controversy with Barry, secured Hunt's services as part-time surveyor to the office of works. His familiarity with the Westminster buildings enabled him to scrutinize Barry's accounts minutely.

Hunt was engaged at £1000 p.a. to devote one day a week to the government's service, but for years devoted about half his working time to public business. His duties were not defined, but he seems to have been largely responsible for the reorganization of the office of works under Hall. He proved an assiduous and economically minded public servant, advising the minister on a wide range of matters including the comparative merits of schemes for the erection of new public buildings and selection of the most suitable sites.

In 1855 Hunt unsuccessfully but far-sightedly recommended the government to buy the whole district between the river and St James's Park southwards from Downing Street to Great George Street for long-term development as public offices. He drew up the much-criticized specifications for the ill-fated government offices competition of 1856–7 for a smaller site. After George Gilbert Scott obtained the Foreign Office commission with a Gothic design, Hunt claimed to have persuaded ministers to retain Scott when Palmerston insisted on Italianate buildings. Although he had himself designed buildings, Hunt was not qualified to advise on architectural aesthetics. Nevertheless, he frequently gave Hall the benefit of his extensive experience of such matters and was always consulted upon plans for new public buildings.

When W. E. Gladstone appointed Captain Douglas Galton RE, as director of public works (1870–74), Hunt found his unique position undermined. Relations between the two men rapidly deteriorated once the resolute A. S. Ayrton was removed as the first commissioner of works. Hunt's opinions on professional questions were regarded as 'probably the best in England' (NA Scot., Blair Adam MS 4/569), and he resented Galton's control of the technical branch of the office. They were, however, united in criticism of G. E. Street's plans for new law courts in the Strand. Hunt was never afraid of challenging the architectural heavyweights: disapproving of Waterhouse's handling of the erection of the Natural History Museum (for which he had himself in 1862 drawn plans to the brief of Richard Owen), Hunt recommended legal action against him in 1882 for dereliction of duty.

Hunt's official duties also embraced such usual work of a surveyor as valuing properties for purchase. Realizing that there was a potential conflict of interest between his public position and his private practice, he made it a rule in the latter neither to take on government work nor private commissions involving opposition to government proposals. In 1869, however, the Treasury cut his salary to £750, in compensation sanctioning his employment in land-purchase negotiations at the normal fees. This brought him little more than £250 p.a. until 1875, when prospective acquisitions in the Whitehall district promised to yield about £20,000. A departmental committee condemned this uniting of advisory and executive functions as wrong in principle, so that Hunt was thereafter restricted to the role of 'consulting surveyor', his salary being doubled in compensation. Appointed CB in 1871, he was knighted in 1876 and retired ten years later.

In his private practice, operating from offices in Parliament Street, Westminster, Hunt was closely involved in railway development from its earliest stages; on the north Staffordshire line he even designed stations, including the Jacobean-style Stoke-on-Trent Station and hotel; he also constructed Allsopp's gigantic brewery at Burton upon Trent. He was extensively engaged on the London, Brighton, and South Coast, Eastern Counties, District, and Metropolitan railways. An associate of the Institution of Civil Engineers from 1851, Hunt was a founder fellow of the Surveyors' Institution (1868), and vice-president in 1868–70.

Hunt had taken Charles Stephenson into partnership about 1850 and they were later joined by Harry Jones. In 1856 Hunt and Stephenson designed a terrace of fifty-four dwellings, with ground-floor shops, for the duchy of Cornwall in Vauxhall Row, Lambeth. Hunt also, as receiver-general, managed the valuable estates of the dean and chapter of Westminster, and those of the Sons of the

Clergy Corporation. He was much involved in the development of South Kensington: he was surveyor for the builder William Jackson in the 1850s (buying four of his houses as a speculation), and from 1854 to 1887 surveyor to the commissioners for the 1851 exhibition, revising the layout of their main rectangle to improve the financial return, and advising on developers' proposals. Richard Norman Shaw's work on the estate won his admiration.

Hunt's wide range of practical knowledge, coupled with a mastery of detail and a remarkable capability for sustained concentration, made him much in demand as an arbitrator in professional disputes, particularly in the north of England. As his obituary put it: 'He would listen with admirable gravity and patience to the most illogical arguments and the most contradictory statements without betraying his opinion of them either by look or gesture. Never was manner more inscrutable' (*Transactions of the Surveyors' Institution*, 488). On matters of business he habitually spoke with 'extreme brevity and dryness' (ibid.), though in private life he was said to be an entertaining talker.

In middle life, Hunt lived at 54 Eccleston Square with his wife and two unmarried children, supported (in 1871) by an establishment of two male and four female servants. He retired to 16 The Lees, Folkestone, Kent, where, after three or four years of increasing physical debility, he died on 13 January 1889.

M. H. PORT

Sources 'Select committee on … the houses of parliament', *Parl. papers* (1836), 21.43–76, 214, 370, 371, no. 245 • 'Select committee on expenditure for miscellaneous services', *Parl. papers* (1860), 9.473–742, nos. 483, 483-I • *Transactions of the Surveyors' Institution*, 21 (1888–9), 487–9 • M. H. Port, *Imperial London: civil government building in London, 1850–1915* (1995) • census returns for Eccleston Square, Westminster, 1871 • *The museums area of South Kensington and Westminster*, Survey of London, 38 (1975) • Report of Departmental Committee, 1 March 1876, PRO, WORK 22/3/7 • confidential memo by First Commissioner of Works, 4 Nov 1869, PRO, WORK 22/2/18 • Blair Adam MS, 16 Nov 1873, NA Scot., 4/569 • *CGPLA Eng. & Wales* (1889) • *London Directory*

Archives PRO, Office of Works reports and memoranda, WORK

Likenesses F. Grant, oils

Wealth at death £101,053 2s. 8d.: sworn probate, July 1889, *CGPLA Eng. & Wales*

Hunt, Henry George Bonavia (1847–1917), founder of Trinity College of Music, London, was born on 30 June 1847 in Valletta, Malta, the eldest surviving son of William Hunt, former private secretary to the bishop of Jerusalem, and his second wife, Marietta Bonavia, the daughter of a Maltese doctor of Italian extraction. He was educated at King's College School, London, and studied law at the Temple in the early 1870s. On 15 August 1870 he married Louisa Madeline, the daughter of Eugene Carless, a chemical manufacturer, of Stratford. They had two sons and two daughters. On becoming choirmaster at South Hackney parish church in 1872, Hunt gathered the support of leading organists and choirmasters in London and set up an independent institution to provide better training for church musicians known as the Church Choral Society and College of Church Music.

Meanwhile Hunt was studying music in his spare time. He matriculated at Christ Church, Oxford, in 1872 and graduated BMus in 1876. He extended the aims of the College of Church Music, and in 1875 incorporated it for the purpose 'by special licence under Act of Parliament' as Trinity College, London. He was warden from 1872 to 1892. To equip future students to sit for degrees in music made newly available at London University after 1879, he now arranged an 'arts' class at the college to prepare candidates for matriculation, while broadening the music curriculum to conform with the university's new syllabuses. Then in 1879 he sought affiliation with the University of Durham; but objections by the Royal Academy and Royal College of Music prevented his developing stronger links with either university.

Hunt was ordained at Winchester in 1878. Following curacies at Esher in Surrey, St Philip's in Regent Street (1882–3), and St James's, Piccadilly (1884–7), he became minister of St Paul's, Kilburn, in 1887 and vicar in 1897. In all these appointments he was popular both as preacher and pastor, and became well known as a choirmaster. At St James's, Piccadilly, William Ewart Gladstone was often in the congregation, and suggested a royal chaplaincy, but by then Hunt had taken up the Kilburn appointment. He kept up his musical activities, and in 1887 graduated DMus (Trinity College, Dublin).

Energetic and many-sided, Hunt edited or sub-edited several popular magazines and journals, including *The Quiver* (1865–1905) and *Cassell's Magazine* (1874–96), besides founding and, until 1876, editing a children's paper, *Little Folks*. He also composed a little, and his works include a motet, *The Blessed Dead*, and a Magnificat and Nunc dimittis in B♭. Between 1900 and 1906 he was lecturer in music history at London University, and his *Concise History of Music* (1878) was much used; it reached a nineteenth edition in 1915. In addition, he was chairman of Willesden school board from 1899 to 1902, and was the founder and first warden of Kilburn grammar school (1897–1904). On his induction as vicar of the parish church of St John the Evangelist, Burgess Hill, Sussex, in 1905, Hunt resigned his remaining London appointments. He died of heart failure under anaesthetic during a routine operation on 27 September 1917 in Hove.

BERNARR RAINBOW, rev. ANNE PIMLOTT BAKER

Sources M. Bonavia-Hunt, *Henry George Bonavia-Hunt, organist and choirmaster* (1919) • H. Rutland, *Trinity College of Music: the first hundred years* (1972) • *Musical Opinion* (Nov 1917) • P. A. Scholes, *The mirror of music, 1844–1944*, 2 (1947), 696–8 • H. Cox, *Who's who in Kent, Surrey, Sussex* (1911–12) • *Mid-Sussex Times* (2 Oct 1917) • *Mid-Sussex Times* (9 Oct 1917) • m. cert. • *CGPLA Eng. & Wales* (1917)

Likenesses photograph, repro. in Rutland, *Trinity College of Music*

Wealth at death £6432 5s. 7d.: probate, 20 Dec 1917, *CGPLA Eng. & Wales*

Hunt, James [*called* Prophet Hunt] (*bap.* 1591?, *d.* 1649×66), lay preacher and prophet, was probably baptized at St Nicholas's Church, Sevenoaks, on 12 September 1591, the eldest child of John Hunt, a farmer, and Ann Christian. It seems likely that this James Hunt married Parnell Whitehead at the same church on 12 August 1621. On 12 June 1632 Richard Cotton, a servant of James Hunt, was buried in the same parish. Hunt's own writings and reports of his subsequent activities suggest that he was a husbandman, farmer, or yeoman.

Hunt claimed to have been preaching and prophesying since about 1636, but he first came to prominence on 7 May 1640 when the court of high commission, being informed that Hunt was 'a fanatiq, frantiq person … a husbandman, & alltogether illiterate … [who] tooke upon him to … preach and expound the Scriptures, & was lately taken absurdly preaching on a stone in Paulls Church-yard', ordered that he should be committed to Bridewell and held there until further notice (PRO, SP 16/434, 171). How long Hunt was held is unclear, but it is apparent that he had been at liberty for some time when he published his first sermon, *The Sermon and Prophecie* (1641), which he had tried to deliver 'in most Churches in and about London, but since delivered in the Old-Baily. Octob. 9. 1641' (A1r). Shortly after preaching at Westminster Hall where 'his Auditors then seeing the weake madnesse of his giddy-braine, derided and abus'd him there extreamely', and another occasion when he attempted to deliver a sermon at the Old Exchange where he was 'almost pull'd in peices', Hunt once again came to public attention on 19 December 1641 after the sermon at St Pulchers Church. It was noted of this occasion that 'Hunt a Prophet, who have been very troublesome in this City heretofore, and once before committed to the Counter [prison] for a Sermon, which he preached at Christs-Church before, have beene dehorted divers times'. However, 'his sick-brain'd obstinacy' only increased, 'for (as it appeareth) he raised a combustion at this Parish, and standing upcryed with a full voice', exhorting his hearer to listen to his text, taken from Revelation 7: 3. He then 'began to bawle so loud, concerning fire and water with such peremptory confidence, that there did arise a great tumultuous murmur among the Parishioners, and without much prolixity of words he was pulled downe by the Constables and others'. Hunt was then hauled before Richard Gurney, the mayor, who 'perceiving his arrogant protervitie, propounded many interrogations unto him, asking him whether he had the Spirit or no, or how he dare presume to preach having no warrant for the Ministeriall function'. Hunt affirmed 'he had sufficient warrant from God, for he knew that he was his Messenger, and as for the Spirit he was confident that he had that, which he sayd they apparently might conceive by the fruites thereof'. At length the mayor, 'perspicuosly perceiving his erroneous & Schismaticall obstinacie', committed Hunt—who was variously described as 'a mad rusticke fellow', whose 'head and his eares were white, as white wooll … and his eyes were as a flame of fire'—to the Counter (*The Discovery*, A3v–4r; *An Order*, A1r; *New Preachers*, A4v).

Between 1641 and 1648 Hunt published twelve sermons in which he claimed that God and Jesus Christ had raised him to be 'a powerfull instrument … to open the peoples eyes' and 'unfold the mysteries of God, to the praise and glory of his grace, and to the confounding of false doctrine which proceedeth from the devill' (*Sermon Gathered*, 8). To this end Hunt drew a clear distinction between the 'new

law' of the New Testament, or 'booke of life', and the 'Ministration of death' of the Old Testament, which he endeavoured to show were deliberately confused by the universities and clergy to confound the laity (*Sermon and Prophecie*, 1641, 2–3). Hunt claimed that by revealing the 'spiritual Word of God in the doctrine of the new Testament', and explaining it in plain English verse and prose, he could lead all men to know God and thus enjoy 'everlasting joy and glory' (*Sermon and Prophesie*, 1642, 1).

In 1642 Hunt claimed that he had already been confined in gaol eight times and was once again threatened with incarceration, but this time for activity in his home town of Sevenoaks. On 23 July 1642 Hunt was duly indicted by the southern circuit assize court at Maidstone for interrupting William Turner, curate of Sevenoaks, during a service at Sevenoaks church on 20 March 1642 and on other occasions. Notwithstanding these setbacks Hunt continued to publish his sermons intermittently until 1645 when in his sermon *Glorious Light* (George Thomason dated his copy 27 February 1645), he intimated that 'Mr. Kentish' (p. 8)—probably Thomas Kentish who was installed as the rector of Sevenoaks by parliament in 1645—had obtained a mittimus from the county committee to send him to gaol. Hunt then disappeared from view until 5 August 1647 when he once again found himself before the assize court at Maidstone for interrupting Richard Kentish, minister at Sevenoaks (brother of Thomas), during prayers on 11 July 1647. On this occasion Hunt put himself at the mercy of the winter assize of 1648, and was fined. The southern circuit assize continued to issue writs for Hunt's arrest up until 10 July 1649, after which his fate is unknown. Parnell Hunt died a widow in 1666 leaving the bulk of her estate, which included a farm in the liberty of Riverhead, Sevenoaks, leased from Dame Margaret Boswell, to an executor.   IAN L. O'NEILL

Sources *The discovery of a swarme of separatists, or, A leathersellers sermon* (1641) · *The sermon and prophecie of Mr. James Hunt of the county of Kent* (1641) · *The sermon and prophesie of James Hunt: concerning the marriage of the lambe* (1642) · *A sermon gathered and set forth by that divine spirit which God hath given to me James Hunt* (1648) · [J. Hunt], *Glorious light* (1645) · *New preachers, new, Greene the feltmaker, Spencer the horserubber, Quartermine the brewers' clarke, with some few others, that are mighty sticklers in this new kinde of talking trade which many ignorant coxcombs call preaching* (1641) · *An order from the high court of parliament, which was read on Sunday last, in every church, being the 19 day of December, 1641* (1641) · parish records, Sevenoaks, CKS, P330/1/1 · will, CKS, PRS/W/8/108 [Parnell Hunt] · J. S. Cockburn, ed., *Calendar of assize records: Kent indictments, Charles I* (1995) · J. S. Cockburn, ed., *Calendar of assize records: Kent indictments, 1649–1659* (1989) · PRO, SP 16/434, 171

Hunt, James (1833–1869), speech therapist and anthropologist, was born at Godlingston Manor, Swanage, Dorset, the son of Thomas *Hunt (1802–1851), a tenant farmer and speech therapist, and his wife, Mary (1805/6–1855). Nothing is known of his education except that he was trained by his father in the art of curing stammering through breathing exercises, muscle control, and building a patient's confidence, the subject of his *Treatise on Stammering* (1854; 7th edn, 1870) which contained a memoir of his father. In 1856 he purchased a doctorate from the

University of Giessen in Germany, following which he set up practice as a speech therapist at 224 Regent Street, London, and, during the summer months, at Swanage. Among those whom he helped was Charles Kingsley, who spent three weeks with him in January 1857; his *Manual of the Philosophy of Voice and Speech* (1859) was dedicated to Kingsley. Hunt's understanding of speech defects was impressive and the source of his income. In 1858 he settled at Ore House, Ore, near Hastings, where he was a founder and first president of the Hastings Philosophical Society. During the summer season he and his brother-in-law, the Revd Henry F. Rivers (who had married Hunt's sister, Elizabeth), ran a residential clinic at Ore for patients afflicted with speech defects. Charles Dodgson and George Macdonald were notable visitors in 1859.

Hunt's principal interest was in racial differences, and in 1854 he joined the London Ethnological Society; from 1859 to 1862 he was its honorary secretary. Many members disliked his attacks on religious and humanitarian agencies represented by missionaries and the anti-slavery movement. Consequently, in 1863, Hunt founded the Anthropological Society, of which he was the first president; the two societies remained bitter rivals until their unification as the Anthropological Institute in 1871. To further his views that human races had independent points of origin (polygenesis) and that comparative anatomy and physical measurements were needed to create a map of human differences, Hunt published, edited, and took personal responsibility for the *Anthropological Review*. He also encouraged the society to undertake the translation of several foreign books on anthropological subjects. Hunt himself translated and edited Carl Vogt's *Lectures on Man* (1864). Hunt's paper, 'The negro's place in nature', read at the British Association meeting at Newcastle in 1863, was met by hisses and catcalls for defending the subjection and slavery of African-Americans, and supporting belief in the plurality of human species. Hunt, opposed by members of the Ethnological Society, made strenuous endeavours to have anthropology recognized as a distinct section or subsection of the British Association, ethnology being then grouped with geography, and anthropology being largely ignored. In 1866, with T. H. Huxley's independent support, anthropology became a division of section D (biology); it was made a separate section in 1883.

Hunt resigned the presidency of the Anthropological Society in 1867, when the membership numbered over 500, remaining in office as its chief executive officer. He was re-elected president in 1868 but had to meet an acrimonious personal attack on his financial conduct of the society and of the *Anthropological Review*, which he had subsidized at a heavy loss to himself. The controversy in *The Athenaeum* told on his health. In August 1869 he attended the meeting of the British Association at Exeter; on 29 August he died, of inflammation of the brain, at Ore House. He left a widow, Henrietta Maria, and five children. His nephew, William Halse Rivers (1864–1922), inherited his books and was inspired to become an anthropologist. Without being profound Hunt was a serious student, who helped to place anthropology on a sound basis, but his youthful combativeness, fiery temper, racial determinism, and sceptical views on religion roused much personal hostility.

W. H. BROCK

Sources *Anthropological Review*, 8 (1870), lxxix–lxxxiii · E. Dally, *Mémoires de la Société d'Anthropologie de Paris*, 2nd ser., 1 (1873), xxvi–xxxvi · *DSB*, 6.563–4 · D. Rockey, *Speech disorder in nineteenth-century Britain* (1980) · J. W. Burrow, 'Evolution and anthropology in the 1860's', *Victorian Studies*, 7 (1963–4), 137–54 · 'Exchange by William Craft and James Hunt at the annual meeting of the British Association for the Advancement of Science, Newcastle-upon-Tyne, England, 27 August, 1863', *The black abolitionist papers*, ed. C. P. Ripley, 1: *The British Isles, 1830–1865* (1985), 537–43 · *CGPLA Eng. & Wales* (1869) · *DNB* · Boase, *Mod. Eng. biog.*

Archives ICL, corresp. with Thomas Huxley · University of Bristol Library, letters to John Beddoe

Wealth at death under £7000: probate, 19 Nov 1869, *CGPLA Eng. & Wales*

Hunt, James Simon Wallis (1947–1993), racing driver and commentator, was born in Sutton, Surrey, on 29 August 1947, the eldest son and second of six children of Wallis Glynn Gunthorpe Hunt, stockbroker, and his wife, Susan Noel Wentworth, *née* Davis. He was educated in Cheam and at Wellington College, where he excelled at a variety of sports, and represented the college at cross-country running and squash. He was also an accomplished tennis player, and progressed eventually to junior Wimbledon. He was intended by his parents for a career in medicine but opted instead for motor racing, a passion which developed after a friend took him to a meeting at Silverstone as an eighteenth-birthday treat.

Hunt's career in motor sport began modestly in club racing, where he drove a stripped-down Mini before progressing to formula Ford with an Alexis, which he acquired on hire purchase, and then to formula 3. Money was tight in his period as an amateur driver so Hunt took a variety of jobs, including as a hospital porter and as an ice-cream salesman, to fund his tuition in motor racing at Brands Hatch. However, his success in formula 3 was such that for 1970 he acquired sponsorship to race a Lotus 59. Yet it was not until some two years later that Hunt moved up to formula 2, partly, perhaps, because of a number of accidents, most notably at Zandvoort, which led to his acquiring a reputation as Hunt-the-Shunt. Thereafter, progress into the highest level of motor sport was rapid, thanks principally to the patronage of Lord Hesketh, beneficiary of a grocery fortune, motor-racing enthusiast, and a man of similar temperament to Hunt. With Hesketh's support, Hunt soon consolidated his reputation as a skilful and highly competitive driver and, more importantly, began to accumulate points. He was given his first non-championship formula 1 race by Hesketh at Brands Hatch early in 1973, when he finished a highly creditable third in a secondhand Surtees TS9B. During his career in formula 1 motor sport, Hunt took part in 92 grand prix races, had 10 wins, took pole position 14 times, and accumulated a total of 179 points.

Hunt's first victory in grand prix racing was achieved driving a Hesketh Ford at Zandvoort in 1975. However, Hesketh was unable to continue to meet the increasing financial outlay associated with formula 1 racing and so

James Simon Wallis Hunt (1947–1993), by Frank Barratt, 1975

withdrew from the sport at the end of the 1975 season. As a driver of growing reputation—he finished fourth in the 1975 championship—Hunt was quickly taken up by McLaren, with sponsorship provided by Marlboro. The 1976 season began relatively well for Hunt. He achieved the fastest practice lap for the first race, the Brazilian grand prix, and in the actual event appeared to have secured at least second place to Niki Lauda until thwarted by a jammed throttle. After five races, however, Hunt had secured only 8 points to Lauda's 55. The next grand prix, which was in France, saw a change of fortune as Lauda's Ferrari failed to complete the circuit and Hunt drove to victory. This was quickly followed by his reinstatement as winner of the Spanish grand prix as an earlier technical infringement involving the car was overturned. Lauda's near-fatal accident in the German grand prix, which kept him off the circuit for the next two championship races, allowed Hunt the opportunity to retrieve his championship hopes, which he did with style by coming fourth in Austria and winning in the Netherlands. Lauda returned for the Italian grand prix at Monza, where Hunt came off the track. Hunt then won in Canada and the United States. The dash for the championship became so intense that by the final race of the season only three points separated Lauda from Hunt in second place. The race was held in Japan in very poor weather conditions, which led Lauda to withdraw from the race, but, despite two punctured tyres, Hunt managed to secure third place and enough points to become world champion. He was the sixth Briton to

achieve this honour. This was the pinnacle of his racing career. Despite two further years with McLaren, Hunt was unable to repeat his earlier success and, following a short period with the Wolf team, he retired from active participation in motor sport in 1979. During his formula 1 career he was frequently in the public eye, as much for his high living as for his fast driving. He was associated with a series of beautiful women, one of whom, Susan Janet (Suzy) Miller (b. 1947/8), model, and daughter of Frederick Henry Miller, barrister, he married, on 19 October 1974. They were divorced in 1976. She then married the actor Richard Burton. There were no children of her marriage to Hunt.

The reasons for Hunt's retirement from formula 1 racing remain unclear, though it has been speculated that his flamboyant lifestyle was incompatible with the demands of the sport. He also appears to have concluded that the technical aspects of motor vehicle design were degrading the importance of the driver's skills. From 1980 he found a new role as a commentator on motor sport, and developed a rapport with Murray Walker on the BBC grand prix programme, which proved highly popular with the viewing public. This also gave him a platform from which to articulate his often individual and entertaining perceptions of formula 1 racing, as did his magazine articles and newspaper columns. On 17 December 1983 he married, second, Saria Marian (Sarah) Lomax (b. 1957/8), interior decorator, the daughter of Ian Raymond Lomax, insurance broker. There were two sons of the marriage, which ended in divorce in 1990.

Hunt was a brave and naturally gifted racing driver who was motivated by an overwhelming determination to succeed. Although less interested in the technical aspects of motor sport, his exploits and his encouragement of younger drivers, such as Damon Hill, helped to popularize and develop formula 1 racing in Britain. He was said to be a kind man with a social conscience, who returned the money he earned from sales of commentaries to the South African Broadcasting Commission to black-run development projects. Handsome, charismatic, and gregarious, he was remembered as an *enfant terrible* of the motor racing world in his formula 1 days, but he 'matured into a great champion for the sport and a thoroughly likeable fellow' (*The Independent*, 16 June 1993). Motor racing and journalism enabled him to accumulate considerable personal wealth, although much of it was dissipated in failed business ventures, such as the James Hunt Racing Centre at Milton Keynes, which collapsed with debts of £2 million. He died of a heart attack at his home, 4 Bathgate Road, Wimbledon, London, on 15 June 1993. A memorial service was held at St James's, Piccadilly, on 29 September 1993.

DAVID THOMS

Sources J. Hunt, E. S. Young, and D. W. Hodges, *James Hunt: against all odds* (1977) · K. Botsford, *The champions of formula 1* (1988) · P. Silverton, 'James the First', *The Guardian* (28 Aug 1993) · G. Donaldson, *James Hunt: the biography* (1994) · C. Hilton, *James Hunt: portrait of a champion* (1993) · *The Times* (16 June 1993) · *The Times* (19 June 1993) · *The Times* (30 Sept 1993) · *The Independent* (16 June 1993) · *The Independent* (19 June 1993) · *The Guardian* (16 June 1993) · m. certs. · d. cert.

Archives FILM 'The real James Hunt', Channel 4, 14 Aug 2001

Likenesses photographs, 1974–80, Hult. Arch. • F. Barratt, photograph, 1975, Hult. Arch. [*see illus.*] • A. Newman, photograph, 1979, NPG • photograph, repro. in *The Times* (16 June 1993) • photograph, repro. in *The Independent* (16 June 1993) • photograph, repro. in *The Guardian* (16 June 1993) • photograph, repro. in *The Guardian* (28 Aug 1993)

Wealth at death £1,232,942: probate, 8 Nov 1993, *CGPLA Eng. & Wales*

Hunt, Jeremiah (1678–1744), Independent minister, was born in London on 11 June 1678, the only son of Thomas Hunt (*d.* 1680), a member of the Mercers' Company. Following their father's death Hunt and his two sisters were brought up by their mother. After a preliminary classical education, Hunt entered, in 1693, the academy of Thomas Rowe, which was then located in Little Britain, London. From there he proceeded to Edinburgh University; he then completed his education at the University of Leiden, where he matriculated on 19 March 1702. At Leiden he was taught by such distinguished scholars as Frederic Spanheim and Preizonius; he attended the English church and was much influenced by John Milling, the minister there. He was also taught Hebrew by a former rabbi from Lithuania. Hunt began to preach while in the Netherlands and supplied the small English Presbyterian congregation in Amsterdam.

Hunt returned to England, probably in 1704, and in the same year he was chosen to preach at the Independent chapel at Tunstead, near Norwich, as assistant to John Green. According to the church historian Thomas Harmer he was ordained there but there is no record of this in the church archives. In 1707 he accepted the invitation to succeed Richard Wavel at the Independent chapel at Pinners' Hall, London, where he served as minister for the remaining thirty-seven years of his life. How far he deviated from orthodox Calvinism is not clear. He certainly believed in the importance of personal judgement in matters of doctrine and was one of the few Independents to vote with the non-subscribers at Salters' Hall in 1719. This, together with his association with some of the leading antitrinitarians of the time, led to suspicions and accusations of Arianism, if not Socinianism. Hunt, however, admitted to no such charges and looked upon himself as merely a liberal and moderate dissenter. He was awarded the degree of DD from Edinburgh University in 1729, and from 1730 to 1744 he served as a trustee of Dr Williams's Charity. He was one of a group of eminent nonconformist ministers who in 1734–5 delivered at Salters' Hall a course of lectures against the Catholic faith; his chosen subject was what he considered to be the corrupting influence on religion of the Catholic doctrine of penance and pilgrimages.

Hunt appeared to be a master of extemporaneous preaching but, though he preached without notes, his sermons were the result of much study and preparation and, like those of many rational preachers, proved too scholarly, dry, and critical to appeal to the less well educated members of the congregation. As a consequence he had 'few hearers' and these consisted of the 'enlightened and judicious Christians' (Wilson, 2.267). Nevertheless he was well respected by his fellow ministers; he was a close friend of Nathaniel Lardner, who described Hunt as a man of 'extensive erudition' who possessed an 'uncommon strength of judgement and memory' and was 'as useful a minister as any in his time' (Toulmin, *Sketch*, 3–5). Lord Barrington, a member of his congregation, was another whose friendship Hunt could rely on and whose home he visited on numerous occasions. Although a man of considerable learning who excelled in the knowledge of the scriptures Hunt published little; excepting several single sermons his only publication was his *Essay towards Explaining the History and Revelations of Scriptures in their Several Periods* (1734). Four volumes of his sermons were published posthumously in 1748 but, according to Walter Wilson, they were 'little known and less read' (Wilson, 2.270).

Hunt married Catherine Solly, a distant relative of Nathaniel Lardner; they had at least three children, Benjamin, Martha, and Mary. In latter years he was afflicted by severe pain caused by a gallstone. For about a year before his death there was a marked decay in his health. A fall on the way to visit a friend hastened his death, which occurred on 5 September 1744. His funeral sermon, preached by Nathaniel Lardner at Pinners' Hall, was subsequently published. He was survived by his wife.

M. J. MERCER

Sources *DNB* • J. Toulmin, 'A sketch of the life and character of the Rev. Dr Jeremiah Hunt', *Protestant Dissenter's Magazine*, 2 (1795), 1–7 • W. Wilson, *The history and antiquities of the dissenting churches and meeting houses in London, Westminster and Southwark*, 4 vols. (1808–14), vol. 2, pp. 262–7 • C. Surman, index, DWL • W. D. Jeremy, *The Presbyterian Fund and Dr Daniel Williams's Trust* (1885), 29, 131–2 • J. Browne, *A history of Congregationalism and memorials of the churches in Norfolk and Suffolk* (1877), 304–5 • J. Toulmin, 'Memoir of D. Neal', in D. Neal, *Neal's history of the puritans*, rev. E. Parsons, 1 (1811) • J. Aikin and others, *General biography, or, Lives, critical and historical of the most eminent persons*, 10 vols. (1799–1815) • A. Chalmers, ed., *The general biographical dictionary*, new edn, 32 vols. (1812–17) • C. G. Bolam and others, *The English presbyterians: from Elizabethan puritanism to modern Unitarianism* (1968), 163–4, 167, 180 ff., 196, 210 • 'Memoirs of himself, by Mr John Fox … with biographical sketches of some of his contemporaries; and some unpublished letters [pt 8]', *Monthly Repository*, 16 (1821), 569–75, esp. 574 • T. Harmer, 'Historical and biographical accounts of the dissenting churches in the counties of Norfolk and Suffolk', 1774, Norfolk RO • E. Peacock, *Index to English speaking students who have graduated at Leyden University* (1883), 52 • will, PRO, PROB 11/735, fols. 309r–310r

Hunt, Sir John (1548/9–*c.*1615), gentleman, was born at Morcott, Rutland, the second son of John Hunt of Lyndon, Rutland, one of the old Norman family of Le Hunt, and Amy, daughter of Sir Thomas Cave of Stanford, Northamptonshire. At Eton, as a king's scholar, he was one of the contributors of verses to Queen Elizabeth in 1563. On 27 August 1565 he was admitted, aged sixteen, to King's College, Cambridge, but did not take his degree, being admitted as a student to the Middle Temple on 25 November 1567. John was the brother of Thomas, also an Eton scholar admitted to King's College in 1569, aged seventeen. He may have been the man of the same name who sat for Sudbury in the parliament which assembled on 2 April 1571; if so, it was probably through the influence of a relative of his mother, Sir Ambrose Cave, chancellor of the duchy of Lancaster until 1568, a post which carried considerable powers of parliamentary patronage.

Very little is known about Hunt's life. His manor of Lyndon in the parish of the same name had been conveyed to his father in 1553 by a Frances Peyton and her sons. The Hunts were undoubtedly one of the leading families in a very small county. Of the total of £375 raised for the queen's government by the Rutland gentry in 1589, the most eminent magnate, Sir John Harrington, gave £100, but the £25 paid by John Hunt indicates some considerable wealth. Later, he seems to have settled at Newton, Leicestershire. He was not the John Hunt, son of Henry Hunt and Jane, daughter of Hugh Vere, who was accused on 22 July 1611 by Elizabeth, dowager countess of Oxford, of corrupting her young son Henry de Vere, the eighteenth earl. John Hunt of Leicestershire was knighted by James I on 10 November 1611. He is believed to have died about 1615. It is possible that the Sir John Hunt granted the office of serjeant-at-arms for life by a warrant dated 22 December 1615 is to be identified with the subject of this article, for in 1618 a second man, named simply John Hunt, was granted that post in reversion after Edward Grimston. Perhaps this was the son of Sir John, recently deceased.   STEPHEN WRIGHT

Sources Cooper, *Ath. Cantab.*, 3.59 • *VCH Rutland*, vols. 1–2 • HoP, *Commons, 1558–1603* • *CSP dom.*, *1611–18*, 62, 339, 535 • J. Nichols, *The progresses, processions, and magnificent festivities of King James I, his royal consort, family and court*, 2 (1828), 432 • J. Nichols, *The history and antiquities of the county of Leicester*, 3 (1800–04) • C. R. Markham, *The fighting Veres* (1888)

Hunt, John (1775–1848), printer and publisher, probably born in Philadelphia, was the son of Isaac Hunt (1742–1809), a lawyer and political pamphleteer, and his wife, Mary, daughter of Stephen Shewell, a Philadelphia merchant who had been born in Barbados. James Henry Leigh *Hunt (Leigh Hunt) was his brother. Shortly after John's birth, his father's political views caused him to leave America to establish himself as a clergyman in London (he was ordained in 1777). After an interval, his wife followed him across the Atlantic with the children.

Early life John Hunt was apprenticed as a printer to Henry Reynell at 21 Piccadilly, London. In 1804 his mother complained that his health had been damaged by his way of life as a printer: hints of suffering and ill health occur throughout his career. During the Napoleonic scare, he purchased exemption from military service because, according to his mother, he was very busy in the office of John Bell, another important printer and publisher of this period. Hunt once told the painter Benjamin Robert Haydon that no editor could aspire to the status of a gentleman; yet in spite of such apparently realistic recognition of social limitations and some unmistakably radical affiliations, he seems to have fitted comfortably into the Reynell establishment. He married a Miss Hammond, whose first names, if she was the wife who survived him, were Sarah Hoole, and whose sister married Reynell's son. Hunt printed and published a number of books with the Reynells, including the five-volume *Classic Tales* (1806–7),

with introductory essays by his brother Leigh, and several books which Leigh Hunt had authored.

Hunt's career as a printer and publisher was various and influential, although confined to a relatively brief period. In 1805 he established *The News*, to which he appointed Leigh Hunt as theatrical critic; Leigh noted that starting a newspaper had been in his brother's plans for some years. When Henry Brougham approached Hunt to ask him to superintend the establishment of a new whig paper, *The Guardian*, he replied with a stipulation that it should advocate 'Parliamentary Reform, Catholic Emancipation, Religious *Liberty* (not Toleration), the Melioration of the Penal Laws—and in short, what was understood by the cause of the People' (BL, Add. MS 38523, fol. 41). *The Statesman*, for which he solicited the services of his brother, was originally printed by John Hunt but edited by Daniel Lovell. John Hunt was publisher of the quarterly *The Reflector*, which ran from about 1 January 1811 to 23 March 1812 at the price of 6s., was edited by Leigh Hunt, and devoted its attention to philosophy, politics, and 'the Liberal Arts'. Far more expensive than *The Examiner* (which cost 8½ d. at the time), *The Reflector* was intended partly to provide John with 'increased profits through fuller utilization of his printing plant'; it was also intended to stimulate 'The English considered as a Thinking People' (Sullivan, 374). Like a number of Hunt's projects, it did not survive long and the reason for its ultimate failure was at least partly financial.

The Examiner *The Examiner*, a weekly paper (published on Sunday and again on Monday at a price of 7d.), was established at the beginning of 1808. Its politics were not formally defined but were easily identifiable as supportive of reform. The paper flourished: by November its circulation had reached 2200, while by 1812 Jeremy Bentham noted that it had reached between 7000 and 8000, adding that it was the weekly most in vogue 'especially among the high political men' (A. Bain, *James Mill*, 1883, 123). Its readership included women as well as men, and the princess of Wales and Princess Charlotte left behind evidence of a royal interest. Between 1808 and the early 1820s the paper published a regular commentary on politics (British and European), sustained the traditions of impartial theatrical criticism started by *The News* (which now included opera), and introduced occasional 'literary' articles and reviews (contributors included Byron, Shelley, Keats, Hazlitt, Haydon, Lamb, and Thomas Barnes, later editor of *The Times*). The most prevalent and characteristic voice, however, was that of Leigh Hunt, the editor. *The Examiner* profited from a mutually enriching fraternal partnership, as acknowledged by William Blake in his private verses: 'The Examiner whose very name is Hunt' (the reference may encompass a third brother, the art critic Robert).

An associated venture was the *Yellow Dwarf*, an eight-page Saturday paper published at 4d. which ran from 3 January to 23 May 1818 and which included contributions from Keats, J. H. Reynolds, and Hazlitt; many of the pieces collected in Hazlitt's *Political Essays* were first printed here. Its politics were 'reformist and democratic' (Sullivan, 435), and it was obviously inspired by the presence and impact of other journals, including Thomas Wooler's *Black Dwarf* and perhaps also the *White Dwarf*, a tory response, which both started in 1817.

Prosecution and imprisonment The radical and refreshing tone of *The Examiner* resulted in a regular sequence of court appearances. In 1808 the Hunt brothers were prosecuted for an article on the sale of commissions in the army ('Military depravity') which implicated the duke of York, son of George III. This action was dropped, as was that occasioned by an article of October 1809 ('Change of ministry') which suggested the possible benefits of a regency. In September 1810 the reprint of an attack in the *Stamford News* on military flogging ('One thousand lashes!!') led to a trial in which the brothers were successfully defended by Henry Brougham (John Drakard, who had published the original article, was found guilty and imprisoned). But when the Hunts were charged with 'seditious libel' for an article which criticized the prince regent both on personal grounds and for breaking his promises to the Irish ('The prince on St Patrick's day', 22 March 1812), Brougham's defence was to no avail. They were sentenced on 3 February 1813 to two years' imprisonment, fined £500 each, and required to guarantee their future conduct by providing securities. John served his time in Coldbath Fields, which increased the difficulty of producing *The Examiner* as a collaborative effort and removed him from the centre of publicity. He was subjected to rigid discipline, suffered from sciatica, and had his visitors encumbered with heavy restrictions. Leigh was solicitous about the conditions of John's imprisonment and arranged, where possible, for these to be improved or alleviated. But his own success in turning his prison rooms into a kind of literary and political salon deflected attention from John, whose less glamorous imprisonment has been less celebrated. This may have foreshadowed Leigh Hunt's apparent later quarrel with John's widow over her belief that he had always treated his brother unfairly.

John Hunt did not relax in his efforts to tell the truth, and was prosecuted for an attack on the corruption of the House of Commons; members of parliament included, he had asserted, a far greater proportion of 'Public Criminals than Public Guardians' (*The Examiner*, 21 Feb 1821). He was tried on 21 February 1821, found guilty, and imprisoned once again in Coldbath Fields. The offending article had been one of the very few occasions in which he went into print (he used the name 'Ch. Fitzpaine'—probably an allusion to Tom Paine). Leigh Hunt's defence of his brother in *The Examiner* was followed by a transcript of the court proceedings including John's lengthy rehearsal of his history of opposition and a critique of the cost and hypocrisy of the legal system: 'there should at all times be found, in England, men who will make a firm stand for the public liberty, regardless of private considerations, and in despite of personal dangers' (*The Examiner*, 25 Feb 1821). In a subsequent letter from prison Hunt reflected on the implications of the case; it was, he asserted, intended to 'put down the demand for Reform' though, he predicted, 'it will fail' (*The Examiner*, 3 June 1821). He was visited in gaol by Hazlitt and P. G. Patmore; the latter's detailed physical

description suggests a certain moral austerity which also features in other accounts:

> I have never seen in any one else so perfect an outward symbol or visible setting forth of the English character, in its most peculiar and distinguishing features, but also in its best and brightest aspect, as in Mr. John Hunt. A figure tall, robust, and perfectly well-formed; a carriage commanding and even dignified, without the slightest apparent effort or consciousness of being so; a head and a set of features on a large scale, but not in a perfectly regular mould; handsome, open, and full of intelligence, but somewhat hard and severe; an expression of bland benevolence, singularly blended with a marble coldness of demeanour almost repulsive, because almost seeming to be so intended:—such were the impressions produced on me by the first *abord* of John Hunt, as I saw him within his prison walls. (Patmore, 150)

Patmore described too the grim realities of imprisonment in Coldbath Fields; Hunt himself remained unshakeably ascetic. He hung one of Hazlitt's paintings over the mantelpiece (a sign both of his friendship with the essayist and of his susceptibility to art), but a present from a friend met with the gruff response that he had given wine to a man who drank only water. Following his release he continued to dedicate himself to strenuous opposition and complaint. On 26 May 1823 he drew up a petition to the Commons on the selection of juries, taking his own prosecutions as cases in point of the abuse of power.

Other publishers and other publications; fraternal union and strife Unpublished correspondence suggests that the example of Hunt (and to some extent that of his brother) acted as an inspiration and an example to other radical publishers. A grateful letter from Richard Carlile dated 31 May 1819 gives some indication of the moral strength and leadership which *The Examiner* had achieved at this time (although as early as June 1817 John had worried that 'those Articles on Religious topics … have assisted to lower our sale'; *Correspondence*, 1.163–4). About William Hone, who printed Hazlitt's *Political Essays* in 1819 with their flattering dedication to Hunt's virtues, his feelings were ambivalent. He suspected that Hone was 'what is understood by the phrase, "a coarse man"', but acknowledged a greater priority: 'I felt so strongly when I heard he had been arrested, that I called immediately on his wife to inquire about him' (BL, Add. MS 38523, fol. 41). In turn, Hone—and Francis Place—were active in Hunt's defence during his trial in 1821.

Hunt's commitment to reform can be traced through his other publications, which included a detailed transcript of the proceedings against himself and his brother—*The prince of Wales* v. *The Examiner* (1812); *An Essay on Slavery* (1824); *On the Alien Bill* (1824); Jeremy Bentham's *The Book of Fallacies* (1824); *The Church of England Catechism Examined* (1824); *The Rationale of Reward* (translated from the French; 1825); *An Historical Fragment Relative to Her Late Majesty, Queen Caroline* (1824); and *The State of the Jews in the Beginning of the Nineteenth Century* (1825). John Hunt's list also included much of Byron's *Don Juan*, which he took over when the poet finally broke with John Murray; a number of Byron's daring later works; Hazlitt's *Liber amoris*; and Shelley's *Posthumous Poems*. This list is partly indicative of personal loyalties but also demonstrates Hunt's affinity for radical writing and his unwillingness to be shackled by conventional restraints.

John Hunt seems to have retired from a leading role in *The Examiner* in March 1819, preferring to move into the country 'in order that his sons might be better furnished with means for entering into life' (Reiman, 6.791) and to cede managerial responsibility for the weekly to his son Henry Leigh Hunt. Subsequent publishing ventures saw him become the object of several further prosecutions, however, including one for an attack on William Parry, author of *Last Days of Byron*; this led to a trial in June 1827, judgment against Hunt, and the payment of £50 in damages. Hunt seems to have accepted his role as one which necessarily generated conflict with authority; in that way, at least, he seems to have owed something to the influence of his pamphleteering father and to the traditions of revolutionary Philadelphia.

John Hunt was an influential figure who played a significant part in the development of a responsible political press in England and in the larger struggle for freedom of intelligence and strong political principle. Yet he was, and remains, elusive. No portrait of him has been found, he seems to have written very little on his own account, and his correspondence is sporadic and scattered. Quite frequently, he is confused with his younger brother Leigh. The brotherly bond was always important; even in 1825 when Leigh was in dispute with John and felt a strong personal grievance, he acknowledged that 'I cannot bear to vex a brother, a brother-reformer, and the son of my mother' (Brewer, 142). Yet this conjunction, though undoubtedly significant, does not allow sufficiently for John Hunt's individuality. It was he who printed and published *The Examiner* and it was often he, rather than Leigh, who suffered the consequences. Leigh's *Autobiography* is notably silent about his setting out for Italy in 1822 with John still imprisoned in Coldbath Fields.

The respective roles of the brothers were further defined and clarified by the brief history of *The Liberal*, edited by Leigh and printed and published by John. Subtitled 'Verse and Prose from the South', it appeared, priced at 5s., between October 1822 and July 1823. The journal was the main reason for Leigh Hunt's departure for Italy and caused some anxiety in tory circles, but its life was effectively abbreviated by the drowning of Percy Shelley on 8 July. Yet the four numbers produced were unusually rich, including contributions by Byron, Percy and Mary Shelley, Hazlitt, and Leigh Hunt himself. Some of these items carried considerable risk for the publisher, none more than Byron's *The Vision of Judgment*. An intended prefatory note, identifying Southey, not George III, as the main object of satirical attack, was not included in the published version, and another libel action followed; John Hunt was found guilty and fined £100.

It was also during Leigh Hunt's absence in Italy for the purpose of editing *The Liberal* that financial disagreements between the brothers came to a head after John wrote Leigh out of the contract for ownership of *The Examiner*.

The affair was tangled: much of the financial responsibility for the paper seems to have fallen to John, and there was a certain insouciance to Leigh's approach to such matters; yet Leigh's work as editor had contributed significantly to the success of *The Examiner*. Another point of contention was Leigh's forgiving attitude to their father; in John's view a 'bad friend, a bad member of society, a bad father, and a bad husband', with, furthermore, a 'hatred of labour, and a strong feeling for enjoyment' (Gates, 87). This, and other contemporary accounts, are suggestive of a rebarbative but refreshing toughness about John's character—in contrast to the more obviously malleable, and pleasantly sociable, attributes of the 'demi-exotic' Leigh. Mary Shelley, for example, first met him on 11 September 1823 and observed that he was 'very like' his son Henry, who, she noted, was '*not* handsome', and 'stiff in his manners though polite to me'. She told his brother that '*obstinacy* is written on his brow, & reserve in all his solemn address' yet 'he spoke with great affection of you' (*Letters of Mary Wollstonecraft Shelley*, 1.381). John Murray's account of a visit, transmitted back to John by Leigh, conveys still more vividly his personal style:

> He says now, that you looked him in the face as if on purpose to disconcert him; but I told Lord B. that you had a way of looking steadily at people, and that you unfortunately lit upon a man in this instance (as his Lordship knows well) who seems the least able to bear it, and never looks in the face at anybody. (Gates, 155)

Hazlitt and Byron likened him to the seventeenth-century parliamentarians William Prynne and John Pym; Horace Smith detected in him Roman virtues, and Jeremy Bentham praised his indefatigability—and willingness to suffer imprisonment—in the cause of liberty.

Later years Hunt's retirement to Upper Chaddon near Taunton seems to have initiated a long period of relative obscurity. He and his family must have lived modestly; the eighth share of the copyright of *The Examiner* allocated to him by Dr Robert Fellowes on his purchase of the paper in 1828 cannot have amounted to much. Hazlitt reported a visit to Hunt at Upper Chaddon in 1825 when they dined with Francis Place, and there is sporadic later correspondence with Leigh, but little more was heard of John Hunt until his death at 13A Grove Place, Brompton, Middlesex, on 7 September 1848. In addition to health problems brought on by his second imprisonment, he had noted on 5 January 1831: 'Worldly troubles have since multiplied upon me, which, added to increase of years, have worked their usual effect' (Brewer, 161). He suffered from headaches, and his vision was so seriously impaired that 'at times I could see only the upper half of the letters in a book' (ibid.). After his death his son Marriott wrote that his mother had done 'her duty nobly during the last fearful days of my Father's existence', which suggests that he may have been latterly insane, or suffered from a similarly distressing illness (Marriott added that his mother, of whom little else is known, 'bears her loss with much fortitude, and is in pretty good health'; Gates, 475). To Marriott she renounced the administration of her husband's small personal estate, which was valued at £40 (PRO, PROB 6/225, fol. 363r).

Another son, Henry Leigh Hunt, once picked out by Bentham as peculiarly promising, played a significant part in editing *The Examiner*, the short-lived *Literary Examiner* (based on an idea of his father's), and *The Liberal* (which involved significant correspondence from his uncle in Italy). He was closely involved in the family dispute over the finances of *The Examiner* and Leigh Hunt's rights in the matter (which entailed the receipt of further correspondence). Under the publishing imprint of Hunt and Clarke (which he shared with Charles Cowden Clarke, friend and correspondent both of Keats and of his uncle Leigh) he published a number of titles, including the first two volumes of Hazlitt's *The Life of Napoleon Buonaparte*, before both proprietors were declared bankrupt in April 1829.

TIMOTHY WEBB

Sources *The correspondence of Leigh Hunt*, ed. T. L. Hunt, 2 vols. (1862) • *The Examiner* (1808–23) • L. A. Brewer, *My Leigh Hunt library: the holograph letters* (Iowa City, 1938) • K. N. Cameron, D. H. Reiman, and D. D. Fischer, eds., *Shelley and his circle, 1773–1822*, 10 vols. (1961–2002) • E. M. Gates, ed., *Leigh Hunt: a life in letters* (1999) • L. Hunt, *The autobiography of Leigh Hunt; with reminiscences of friends and contemporaries* (1850) • P. G. Patmore, *My friends and acquaintances* (1854) • P. P. Howe, *The life of Hazlitt* (1924) • L. A. Marchand, 'John Hunt as Byron's publisher', *Keats–Shelley Journal*, 8 (1959), 119–32 • W. H. Marshall, *Byron, Shelley, Hunt, and The Liberal* (c.1960) • K. E. Kendall, *Leigh Hunt's 'Reflector'* (1971) • *The letters of Mary Wollstonecraft Shelley*, ed. B. T. Bennett, 1 (1980) • A. Sullivan, ed., *British literary magazines*, [2]: *The Romantic age, 1789–1836* (1984) • PRO, PROB 6/225, fol. 363r • d. cert.
Archives BL, corresp., Add. MSS
Wealth at death £40 personal estate: PRO, PROB 6/225, fol. 363r

Hunt, John (1806–1842), organist and composer, was born in Marnhull, Dorset, on 30 December 1806. At the age of seven he entered the choir of Salisbury Cathedral, where Arthur Thomas Corfe was organist. He was later educated at Salisbury grammar school, and remained there until 1827. During the last five years of this period he was articled to Corfe, from whom he received valuable instruction in music. When he left the grammar school, his fine voice gained him an appointment as lay vicar in the Lichfield Cathedral choir. Hunt resigned from Lichfield on 10 November 1835, when he was elected to succeed Samuel Sebastian Wesley (1810–1876) as organist at Hereford Cathedral. He remained at Hereford until his death, on 17 November 1842, attributed to 'the results of an accident at an audit dinner' (Brown & Stratton, *Brit. mus.*). A collection of his songs, with a memoir, was published in 1843.

R. F. SHARP, *rev.* DAVID J. GOLBY

Sources Brown & Stratton, *Brit. mus.*

Hunt, John (1812–1848), missionary in Fiji, the third child of a farm bailiff, who had previously been a soldier and a sailor, was born at Hykeham Moor, near Lincoln, on 13 June 1812. After a few years in a parish school, Hunt was put to farm labour at the age of ten, and worked for some years as a ploughman at Balderton, near Newark, and Swinderby. He became a Methodist when about sixteen. At Swinderby he educated himself in his spare time, and preached there and afterwards at Potter Hanworth, near

Lincoln. From 1835 to 1838 he attended the Wesleyan Theological Institution, Hoxton, marrying Hannah Summers on 6 March 1838. He was ordained on 27 March 1838 and sailed for Fiji as a missionary.

Hunt travelled extensively in Fiji, but is primarily associated with the mission at Somosomo on Varna Levu, which was unsuccessful and eventually abandoned in 1845, and the flourishing Viwa station, where he lived from 1842 until his death. This was the most productive phase of his career. He and his colleagues enjoyed the patronage of Viwa's rulers, whose most prominent chief, Verani, converted to Christianity in 1845. Viwa was close to the European-Fijian settlement of Levuka, where Hunt conducted marriages and founded a school, and to the headquarters of the Bauan chief Cakobau, the future king of Fiji. Hunt and his colleagues devoted much time to Cakobau, convincing him to restrict practices such as cannibalism and widow strangling, and attempting to obtain permission for a mission station at Bau, near Viwa. This heavy workload had already threatened Hunt's health when he agreed to accompany the captain of HMS *Calypso* on a tour of Fiji in 1848. Hunt made a long overland journey, acting as interpreter, and collapsed from exhaustion afterwards. Dysentery weakened him further and he died at Viwa on 4 October 1848. His wife and two daughters survived him.

Hunt completed various literary projects at Viwa, writing a *Memoir of the Rev. W. Cross, Wesleyan Missionary to the Friendly and Feejee Islands* (1846), completing a colleague's translation of the New Testament into Fijian for printing at Viwa in 1847, beginning work on the Old Testament to complete a Fijian Bible (1864–8), translating prayer book services, and writing a series of theological treatises published posthumously as *Entire sanctification: its nature, the way of its attainment, and motives for its pursuit, in letters to a friend*, edited by James Calvert (1853). He was interested in Fijian art forms, particularly poetry, and published one of his collections of traditional songs in an article, 'Feejeean poetry', in the mission *Vewa Quarterly Letter* (1845).

W. A. J. ARCHBOLD, *rev.* JANE SAMSON

Sources A. Birtwhistle, *In his armour: the life of John Hunt of Fiji* (1954) • J. Nettleton, *John Hunt: pioneer, missionary and saint* (1906) • G. S. Rowe, *The life of John Hunt, missionary to the cannibals* (1860) • N. Gunson, *Messengers of grace: evangelical missionaries in the south seas, 1797–1860* (1978) • J. Calvert, *Copy of a letter ... on the occasion of the death of the Rev. John Hunt* (1855) • SOAS, Wesleyan Methodist Missionary Society archives, Hunt MSS • D. M. Lewis, ed., *The Blackwell dictionary of evangelical biography, 1730–1860*, 2 vols. (1995)
Archives JRL, Methodist Archives and Research Centre, memoranda book and diary • Mitchell L., NSW • NL NZ, Turnbull L., journal and sermons | SOAS, Wesleyan Methodist Missionary Society archives
Likenesses three photographs, SOAS, Wesleyan Methodist Missionary Society archives

Hunt, (Henry Cecil) John, Baron Hunt (1910–1998), mountaineer, was born on 22 June 1910 at Miss Tippet's Nursing Home in Simla, India, the elder son of Captain Cecil Edwin Hunt MC (1880–1914), of the Indian army, and his wife, Ethel Helen, *née* Crookshank (1884–1976). His father was killed in action at Givenchy-la-Bassée, France, in the early months of the First World War.

(**Henry Cecil) John Hunt, Baron Hunt (1910–1998)**, by unknown photographer, 1953 [centre, with Edmund Hillary (left) and Tenzing Norgay (right)]

John Hunt was educated at Marlborough College and passed first of his year into the Royal Military College, Sandhurst, in 1928. He also passed out first as a senior under-officer with the king's gold medal and the Anson memorial sword, setting a personal standard of performance that he maintained throughout his life. In 1930 he was commissioned into the King's Royal Rifle Corps and next year sailed for India. But he soon became bored with cantonment routine and the social round, where hopeful mothers showed off their nubile daughters, and he preferred playing rugby with the other ranks to polo with his fellow officers. He developed his natural gift for languages, adding Urdu and some Bengali to his fluent French and German. When Bengal was in the grip of a wave of revolutionary fervour for which he had some sympathy, Hunt volunteered for secondment to the Indian police. His intelligence work—occasionally squatting unobtrusively in the bazaar in Chittagong, wearing a lunghi and skullcap—led to the award of the Indian police medal. On 3 September 1936 he married Joy Mowbray-Green (*b.* 1913), a former Wimbledon tennis champion; they had four daughters.

After returning to Britain in 1940 Hunt donned a green beret and was appointed chief instructor at the Commando Mountain and Snow Warfare School in Braemar. He was a strong advocate of the value of mountain terrain in preparing troops for war, and wrote a paper on its relevance to the education of youth in general. In 1943 he rejoined his regiment in the Italian campaign, commanding the 11th battalion, King's Royal Rifle Corps, on the Gargliano River in April 1944, and was awarded the DSO in bitter fighting along the Sangro. In the following October his

regiment was sent to Greece following its liberation from the Germans. Keeping the peace between the various dissident groups supported either by the communists or the government-in-exile provided, he said, 'the most tense and difficult period in all my experience, before or since' (Hunt, *Life*, 76). It earned him the CBE.

In 1946 Hunt returned to attend the staff college, after which he became general staff officer I (operations) at the general headquarters Middle East land force, followed by various European staff appointments. It was while serving on the planning staff of the Supreme Headquarters Allied Expeditionary Force (SHAEF) under Montgomery at allied headquarters in Fontainebleau that he was invited to lead the 1953 British Mount Everest expedition. It was a turning point in his life. Hunt had been an enthusiastic mountaineer and skier from his youth, when he had been taken from the age of ten by his mother for summer and winter alpine holidays. At fourteen he was guided up Piz Palu, and his first six climbing seasons were all in the Alps. When he was twenty-three he started climbing guideless at home, and discovered the particular joys of leading on steep rock, which he was then able to test with friends on the Aiguilles above Chamonix, which became a kind of second home. While serving in India he naturally gravitated to the Himalayas. His attempt in 1935, with James Waller's party, on peak 36—now known as Saltoro Kangri—when they reached 24,500 feet, was among the more audacious Himalayan exploits of the 1930s. He was elected to both the Alpine Club and the Royal Geographical Society, but was turned down for Ruttledge's 1936 expedition to Everest after an RAF medical board detected a murmur in his cardiograph: he was advised to be careful going upstairs. In 1937, together with Reggie Cooke, John and Joy Hunt reconnoitred the eastern slopes of Kangchenjunga, climbing the south-western summit of Nepal Peak, and making the third ascent of the Zemu Gap between Kangchenjunga and Simvo, where they came across strange tracks that Sherpa Pasang firmly declared were those of a Yeti.

So Hunt arrived at Everest in 1953 with impressive credentials, despite having been outside the mainstream of Himalayan and alpine climbing after the war. He was appointed leader of the expedition at short notice, after the Himalayan joint committee of the Alpine Club and the Royal Geographical Society decided that he should replace the experienced Eric Shipton. Shipton had presided over the unsuccessful expedition to Cho Oyu in 1952, organized after the Swiss had pre-empted the British by securing permission for Everest in both the spring and autumn of that year. The French had permission for 1954 and the Swiss again for 1955, so 1953 was Britain's last chance to be first to the summit and redeem the failures of the 1920s and 1930s. Hunt was thought to be the leader more likely to ensure success. 'I was able to supply an element of military pragmatism', he said modestly (*The Guardian*, 9 Nov 1998). But it was also greatly to his credit that he was able to win over the core of the Cho Oyu climbers who had understandably remained loyal to Shipton and, with the strength of his personality and determination, mould a group of strong individualists into a happy team. He was not the brusque and conventional military man some people expected. He was a very sensitive and intensely human person. With his engaging blue eyes and confident handshake, warmth, and sincerity, he would immediately put one at ease. He had a real talent for making people from all walks of life seem important to him.

An abiding memory of Hunt on the expedition was at advance base in the western cwm while awaiting reports of progress on the icy Lhotse face. The south col had not yet been attained, and for a critical period in mid-May the impetus of the assault seemed to be running down. He would sit on a packing case, elbows resting on knees, smears of sunblock cream giving him an unnaturally pale face, only partly shaded by a floppy hat, eyes peering through binoculars up at that dazzling backcloth of whiteness. He drove himself hard; at forty-two he was the oldest of the climbers, who wondered at the extent of his reserves. The world had to wait until 2 June for the news of success. 'Everest—the Crowning Glory' was the headline greeting the crowds outside Buckingham Palace. Four days earlier, on 29 May, Edmund Hillary and Sherpa Tenzing had for the first time reached the summit—now surveyed at 29,035 feet. But it was to the leader that the greatest credit was due. Even though he had personally climbed to 27,350 feet in support of the two assaults, it was his battle-hardened powers of leadership and skilful planning that assured success. Both Hunt and Hillary were knighted and Tenzing was awarded the George Medal. Further honours were showered on Hunt for this achievement: the order first-class Gurkha right hand; the Indian Everest medal; the Hubbard medal (US); the founder's medal of the Royal Geographical Society; the Lawrence memorial medal of the Royal Central Asian Society; and honorary degrees from Durham, Aberdeen, and London universities.

Everyone has his critics, and Hunt was no exception. He has been portrayed as a 'terrific thruster' (Daily Telegraph, 9 Nov 1998) but this suggests an aggressive nature or abrasiveness: on the contrary, he could seem almost innocent and diffident at times, but even so always prepared to volunteer to take the lead or speak at any function. He was judged by some to have little appreciation of science and scientists. This impression may have arisen owing to his singleness of purpose when planning the expedition. The objective in 1953 was solely to climb the mountain, undistracted by research projects, however worthy, which did not contribute directly to that aim. His new foreword to the reprint in 1993 of his The Ascent of Everest (1953) included a generous tribute to the contribution of 'our scientific consultants', notably the work of the field physiologist Griffith Pugh. Pugh's seminal report from the Cho Oyu expedition had helped to influence the design of much of the expedition's equipment, clothing, and diet, and to demonstrate the benefits of slow acclimatization and the optimum rates to breathe supplementary oxygen. Hunt himself was a keen naturalist, collecting butterflies

in his early India days and compiling bird lists whenever on trek.

After Everest, Hunt was appointed brigadier and assistant commandant at the Staff College, Camberley. At this time he was increasingly in demand to lecture or respond to invitations to work with young people, and in 1956 he retired from the army to become the first director of the newly created duke of Edinburgh's award scheme, to which he gave ten years. Although a demanding job, it gave him more time to pursue climbing: alpine holidays, leading expeditions to the Caucasus and Pamirs in 1958 and 1962, and trekking parties across Nepal on both the twentieth and twenty-fifth Everest anniversaries. He particularly enjoyed sharing experiences with groups working towards the award, taking them to the Stauning Alps, east Greenland, the Pindus Mountains of Greece, and the Polish Tatras. He delighted in introducing young people to the mountains and must have inspired and influenced thousands to take up and enjoy challenging outdoor pursuits, an interest he sustained into his eighties by editing In Search of Adventure (1990).

Hunt was elected president of both the Alpine Club (1956–8, including its centenary year) and the Royal Geographical Society (1977–80), a distinction shared only by Sir Douglas Freshfield and Lord Chorley. He wrote numerous articles and contributed to several books on mountaineering, including the best-selling The Ascent of Everest, composed in an astonishing thirty days. In 1966 he was created a life peer as Baron Hunt of Llanfair Waterdine; he sat initially as a cross-bencher but joined the Social Democratic Party shortly after its formation. He took his title from the little village near Offa's Dyke among the gentler hills of Radnorshire, where he loved to walk from his country cottage. His record of public service was exceptional: he advised the Harold Wilson government on relief after the Nigerian civil war, served as first chairman of the Parole Board and of the advisory committee on police in Northern Ireland, was a member of the royal commission on the press and president of the Council for National Parks, and served on the Council for Volunteers Overseas and the National Association of Probation Officers. In 1979 he was appointed a knight of the Garter. Above all, he loved his fellow men—and women—calling his autobiography Life is Meeting (1978). The last chapter is devoted to some of his favourite alpine excursions and more than anything expressed his love for climbing.

After heart surgery in 1995 Hunt at last began to show his age, but still attended occasional meetings at the Alpine Club and the Royal Geographical Society. It gave him enormous pleasure to preside with his wife, Joy, over the extended 'Everest family' at its private forty-fifth anniversary reunion in May 1998 near Snowdon. He died later that year on 7 November at his home, Highway Cottage, Aston, Henley-on-Thames. In that very week many of his friends received from him two volumes of his Parliamentary Speeches by an Amateur Politician, transposed and edited from Hansard between the years 1967 and 1994. His body was cremated at Slough crematorium on 13 November

1998 and his ashes were scattered on the hills above Llanfair Waterdine. A service of thanksgiving for his life was held in the Garter knights' chapel of St George's, Windsor Castle, on 26 January 1999. His personal Garter banner, depicting a Himalayan bear, was later rehung in the church at Llanfair Waterdine.　　　GEORGE BAND

Sources WW · J. Hunt, *Life is meeting* (1978) · *Alpine Journal* (1999) · G. Band, *GJ*, 165 (1999), 120–22 · *The Times* (9 Nov 1998) · *The Independent* (10 Nov 1998) · *Daily Telegraph* (9 Nov 1998) · *The Guardian* (9 Nov 1998) · *Daily Express* (9 Nov 1998) · J. Hunt, *The ascent of Everest* (1953) · E. H. Hunt, *A rainbow of memories* (1973) [privately printed autobiography] · I. Cranfield, ed., *Inspiring achievement: the life and work of John Hunt* (2002) · private information (2004) [Lady Hunt; Sue Leyden, daughter] · personal knowledge (2004)

Archives Alpine Club, London, presidential papers etc. · King's Lond., Liddell Hart C., copy notes of life and military career, incl. details of mountaineering expeditions · King's Royal Hussars Museum, Winchester, military medals · priv. coll., Royal Geographical Society founder's medal and Indian Everest medal · RGS, diary and an Everest file · RGS, presidential papers | FILM 'The conquest of Everest' (1953) | SOUND BBC Library, 'Everest 1953', BBC Home Service (24 July 1953), no. 19212 · Empire and Commonwealth Museum, Bristol, Oral History Archive, 'John Hunt' (31 March 1995)

Likenesses photograph, 1953, NPG [*see illus.*] · L. Fildes, oils, *c*.1954, Staff College, Camberley · Cortina Studios, photographs, *c*.1956, Alpine Club, London · J. Schwartz, photograph, *c*.1977, Joint Services Command and Staff College, Watchfield, near Swindon · J. Mendoza, oils, *c*.1983, RGS

Wealth at death £555,300—net: probate, 17 June 1999, *CGPLA Eng. & Wales*

Hunt, John Henderson, Baron Hunt of Fawley (1905–1987), general practitioner and medical politician, was born on 3 July 1905 in Secunderabad, India, the eldest in the family of three sons and two daughters of Edmund Henderson Hunt, surgeon to the Hyderabad state railways, and his wife, Laura Mary Buckingham, the daughter of a tea planter. Mother and children returned to England before the First World War and John was educated at Charterhouse, Surrey, at Balliol College, Oxford (where he obtained a second class in physiology in 1927), and at St Bartholomew's Hospital, London. He qualified BM, BCh and MRCS, LRCP in 1931.

After qualification Hunt seemed destined for a career in neurology and worked at the National Hospital for the Relief and Cure of Diseases of the Nervous System and then at St Bartholomew's, as chief assistant to the neurological clinic. During this period he obtained his MRCP (London, 1934) and a DM (Oxford, 1935). He then decided to be a general practitioner. In 1937 he joined Dr George Cregan in practice at 83 Sloane Street as a partner, but he never went into financial partnership during his career. In 1941 he married Elisabeth Ernestine, daughter of Norman Evill, architect. They had three sons and two daughters, two of whom became medical doctors. Their eldest son died of leukaemia at the age of five; this deeply distressed Hunt, who could never bear to discuss it afterwards. His wife's help was essential in providing the stability on which his achievements were based. In spite of his rate of working, he always had time for his children and took great interest in their achievements, particularly those of a sporting nature.

During the Second World War Hunt served in the Royal Air Force as a neurologist, with the rank of wing commander. He returned to general practice independently in 1945, at 54 Sloane Square. Always in private practice, he never really understood the National Health Service. His patients were in the main well off and had high expectations of health care, which he endeavoured to meet. He had his own laboratory and X-ray facilities and ran a practice where success was measured more by medical than financial standards. He had, as he confided to his brother, the ambition to be the best GP in England, even though his type of practice was vastly different from most. He had a high referral rate of patients for specialist opinions, but this was not because of personal lack of knowledge; his patients expected a second opinion. He consequently had close relationships with specialists. Although he preferred the organic aspects of medicine to the psychosocial, he always considered the personality and character of the patient when deciding the best course of management. Despite being a quick worker he seldom gave the impression he was hurrying or did not have time to listen. He would sit at breakfast with two telephones to hand, one for incoming calls and one for outgoing, and he rarely drove to visits, having a succession of lady drivers while he sat in the back of the car dictating his notes. The notes were typed in the car while he was in a house seeing his next patient.

In 1951 and 1952 Hunt played a crucial role in the establishment of a college of general practitioners. The three royal colleges, which were implacably opposed to a separate college, set up their own committee, with Hunt as a member, to promote a joint faculty. However, he knew that a full and independent college was required and gained support for it through meetings and letters to influential journals and people. Opposition was expressed by the press and in official circles but, with Hunt as the honorary secretary of a steering committee, articles of association were signed on 19 November 1952. Within six months 2000 practitioners joined, a foundation council was formed, and the college was launched. For the next thirteen years Hunt was honorary secretary of council and never missed a meeting. He was a 'workaholic', with obsessional determination and attention to detail, who demanded as much from those who worked with him as he gave. He had an authoritarian demeanour, but his enthusiasm and energy were such that people responded with their best, though several of them became exhausted by the attempt to keep pace.

Hunt received an avalanche of honours. He became an FRCP (1964) and an FRCS (1966) and was recognized by colleges in Canada, the USA, and Australia. He gave numerous important lectures and was the president of many of the prestigious medical societies in London. He was appointed CBE in 1970, was made a life peer in 1973 (which enabled him to steer the Medical Act of 1978 through the House of Lords), and received the gold medal of the British Medical Association in 1980.

Hunt was a big man who, in spite of a hip problem, walked prodigiously, on one occasion from Land's End to

John o' Groats. He played furious tennis and croquet at his country house near Henley-on-Thames. His eyes were always a problem to him. He was short-sighted in youth and lost the sight of one eye in 1967. Ten years later he began to lose the sight of the other and this greatly taxed his patience and that of his family. Later he developed Parkinson's disease. John Hunt died on 28 December 1987 at his home, Seven Steep, in Fawley, Buckinghamshire, near Henley-on-Thames, Oxfordshire.

V. W. M. DRURY, rev.

Sources *The writings of John Hunt*, ed. J. Horder (1992) · J. Fry, J. Hunt, and R. J. F. Pinsent, eds., *A history of the Royal College of General Practitioners* (1993) · private information (1996) · **Wealth at death** £90,890: probate, 9 March 1988, *CGPLA Eng. & Wales*

Hunt, John Higgs (1780–1859), journal editor and translator, was born in Gainsborough, Lincolnshire, the son of Joseph and Martha Hunt. He was educated at Charterhouse School and Trinity College, Cambridge, where he won the Browne medal for a Latin ode (1797), graduated BA in 1801, was elected a fellow in 1803, and obtained the MA in 1804. Hunt was proprietor and editor of the *Critical Review* from 1805 to 1807, when that journal, which finally ceased publication in 1817, began its decline. He attempted to abolish a recent whig stance, reverting to the periodical's original conservatism; but his editorship is chiefly remembered for the favourable notice which it accorded Byron's *Hours of Idleness* (7 September 1807). Hunt would have been well aware of Byron's undergraduate presence at Trinity, which exactly coincided with his editorial career. The whole of 'On Leaving Newstead Abbey' was reproduced in the review, and 'Childish Recollections' was singled out as especially noteworthy. Byron exaggerated, writing to Elizabeth Pigot that he had 'been praised to the Skies in the Critical' (*Byron's Letters and Journals*, ed. Marchand, 1.136), but his happiness has been public knowledge since Moore included that letter in his *Life*, adding the footnote:'This Review in pronouncing upon the young author's future career, showed itself somewhat more "prophet like" than the great oracle of the North [the *Edinburgh Review*]' (*Letters and Journals of Lord Byron*, ed. Moore, 1.58). The article was actually written by John Herman Merivale, though his friend Byron never knew this (A. W. Merivale, 293).

In 1807 Hunt resigned his fellowship to marry the eldest daughter of Samuel Manerty, British resident at Basrah, and was ordained deacon and priest at Chester on 31 December 1815. He and his wife had a daughter, Caroline, and a son, Joseph, who followed his father into the church.

In 1818 J. Mawman, publisher of the *Critical Review*, brought out Hunt's two-volume translation of *Gerusalemme liberata*, the result of only three years' labour. This was favourably reviewed, notably in the *Gentleman's Magazine* for June 1819: 'he has enriched his native language with a work, which has long been greatly wanted, and than which there are few existing which will more delight the poetic reader' (*GM*). Yet he never published anything further, being content with his duties as vicar of Weedon

Beck, Northamptonshire, an incumbency which he held from 20 March 1823 until his sudden death at the parsonage there on 17 November 1859. He was buried in St Peter's churchyard, Weedon Beck.

RALPH LLOYD-JONES

Sources *Charterhouse Register* (1769–1872) · [J. H. Merivale], *Critical Review*, 3rd ser., 12 (1807), 47–53 · *Byron's letters and journals*, ed. L. A. Marchand, 1 (1973), 136 · *Letters and journals of Lord Byron, with notices of his life*, ed. T. Moore, 1 (1830), 58 · A. W. Merivale, *Family memorials* (privately printed, Exeter, 1884) · *GM*, 1st ser., 89/1 (1819), 541–2 · J. O. Hayden, *The Romantic reviewers, 1802–1824* (1969) · D. Roper, 'Politics of the *Critical Review*, 1756–1816', *Durham University Journal*, 53 (1960–61), 117–22 · A. Sullivan, ed., *British literary magazines*, [1]: *The Augustan age and the age of Johnson, 1698–1788* (1983) · *Northampton Herald* (3 Dec 1859) · J. Foster, ed., *Index ecclesiasticus, or, Alphabetical lists of all ecclesiastical dignitaries in England and Wales since the Reformation* (1890) · **Wealth at death** under £3000: probate, 7 Dec 1859, *CGPLA Eng. & Wales*

Hunt, (James Henry) Leigh (1784–1859), poet, journalist, and literary critic, was born on 19 October 1784 at Southgate, Middlesex, the ninth and last child of Isaac Hunt (1742–1809), lawyer and Church of England clergyman, and his wife, Mary (c.1752–1805), daughter of Stephen Shewell, Quaker merchant of Philadelphia.

Hunt's father, who was descended from Church of England ministers on Barbados, studied at the academy in Philadelphia before becoming a successful lawyer in the city. He married Mary on 18 June 1767, and the family lived in a large house on the Delaware river front. Isaac was a talented satirical cartoonist and poet, and an outspoken British loyalist in the American independence controversies. He narrowly avoided being tarred and feathered for his opinions, and escaped from Philadelphia in 1776 travelling via Barbados to London, where his family subsequently joined him. Isaac now took orders in the Church of England (17 January 1777), and his preaching at Bentinck Chapel, Paddington, proved popular. He published loyalist pamphlets, and was for a time tutor to James Henry Leigh (nephew of James Brydges, third duke of Chandos) after whom Leigh Hunt was named. Isaac Hunt was sociable, enjoying drink and tobacco, and he was frequently in debt. The Hunt family received £100 a year from the Loyalist Pension Fund, and Benjamin West the painter and his wife Elizabeth (Mary Hunt's aunt) gave them financial support. Both Isaac and Mary became Unitarians, universalists, and republicans and supported the 'new opinions' and 'new tendency' of the French Revolution (Hunt, *Autobiography*, 1850, 1.34, 80, 136). It is to this background that Leigh Hunt's political radicalism, religious unorthodoxy, and pacifism may be traced.

Early years and education In his *Autobiography* Hunt recalls an unsettled childhood of 'quiet and disturbance … placid readings and frightful knocks at the door, and sickness, and calamity, and hopes, which hardly ever forsook us' (Hunt, *Autobiography*, 1850, 1.19). Pursued by debt collectors, the family was locked up in the king's bench prison, and it was to here that Hunt traced his earliest memories. Given these circumstances it is not surprising that in childhood Hunt was nervous, anxious, afflicted with a

(James Henry) Leigh Hunt (1784–1859), by Samuel Laurence, c.1837

stammer, and generally sickly. As a boy he was taken to Calais to restore his health but 'used hardly to recover from one illness before [he] was seized with another' (ibid., 1.51–2). Hunt's mother described him as 'a steady sensible good boy' (Brewer, 5), but in his *Autobiography* he recalls his 'fearful' imaginings of what a 'porpoise' might be, his terror at ghost stories, and how he was 'unspeakably shocked' by the picture of a mythical beast called the 'Mantichora' (Hunt, *Autobiography*, 1850, 1.54–5, 60). The 'first book' he read was *Paradise Lost* (Hunt, *Correspondence*, 1.1).

Hunt was admitted to Christ's Hospital, London, on 24 November 1791, shortly after Coleridge and Lamb had left. An 'ultra-sympathizing and timid boy', he was bullied at school but soon regarded with esteem for his 'daring in behalf of a friend or a good cause' (Hunt, *Autobiography*, 1850, 1.89, 91). He was taught by Matthew Field, warming to his 'handsome incompetence' (ibid., 1.115), and James Boyer, whom he recalled as 'formidably succinct, hard, and mechanical': 'I should have pitied him, if he had taught us to do anything but fear' (ibid., 1.116). Among his schoolfriends were Thomas Mitchell, who became a classical scholar, Thomas Barnes, later editor of *The Times*, and John Rogers Pitman, preacher and author. Hunt recalled seeing George Dyer 'passing through the school-room … to consult books in the library', and Charles Lamb's 'fine intelligent face' (ibid., 1.98, 128). Making little progress with formal studies ('My grammar seemed always to open at the same place'; ibid., 1.111), Hunt, like John Keats, read eagerly in reference books like Andrew Tooke's *Pantheon*, John Lemprière's *Classical Dictionary*, and Joseph Spence's

Polymetis. He enjoyed collecting Cooke's sixpenny editions of the English poets, and among the poems he wrote at school were 'Winter' and 'The Fairy King' imitating his favourites Thomson and Spenser. Visits to Benjamin West's studio and gallery in Newman Street 'made a great impression' on him, particularly West's paintings *Death on the Pale Horse*, *The Deluge*, and *Ophelia before the King and Queen*. West's engravings and prints encouraged Hunt's lifelong interest in Italian literature and fine arts, and his American sympathies and 'enthusiasm for the Republican chief' Napoleon helped form Hunt's independent stance as a journalist and politician (ibid., 1.147–52; *The Indicator*, 7 June 1820). Hunt's first love, when 'no more than thirteen, if so old' was his cousin Fanny Dayrell (Hunt, *Autobiography*, 1850, 1.168).

Appearance and health As a young man Leigh was tall, lithe, and robust, although described as looking 'slenderer than he really was', and at least one commentator noted an enigmatic presence which he described as an 'elusiveness of face' (Cosmo Monkhouse, *Life of Leigh Hunt*, 1893, 118). His hair was black, shining, and 'inclined to wave', his forehead 'straight and white', and his eyes were 'black and sparkling'. His 'general complexion' revealed the family's Caribbean background and was described by his eldest son as noticeably 'dark', 'a West Indian look' (Hunt, *Autobiography*, 1860, vi; *ILN*, 10 Sept 1859, 249). Hunt was physically vigorous yet his letters and *Autobiography* speak again and again of symptoms such as erysipelas, palpitations, 'throat stiflings', biliousness, giddiness, and a painful sense of pressure in the head which was increased, Hunt said, by 'nervous apprehensions' (for example Hunt, *Correspondence*, 1.17, 25–6, 29; *Autobiography*, 1850, 1.294–6). Hunt's philosophy of easy-going sociability irritated friends like Keats, and provided Dickens with material for one of his best caricatures. But Hunt's cheerfulness, seemingly superficial and unworldly, was a private and courageous effort to control the nervous affliction which in some of its symptoms resembles acute anxiety or panic attacks.

First publications On leaving school in 1799 Hunt 'did nothing but visit [his] schoolfellows, haunt the bookstalls, and write verses' (Hunt, *Autobiography*, 1850, 1.185). His first publication was a verse translation of Horace in *The Juvenile Library* (1800), and the following year his collection *Juvenilia* was published containing poems written between the ages of twelve and sixteen. He was already skilled in forms such as the sonnet, blank verse, and rhyming couplets, and the volume as a whole is ambitious. The concluding poem, 'The Palace of Pleasure; an allegorical poem, in two cantos', is a kind of juvenile *tour de force* in 130 Spenserian stanzas. 'Christ's Hospital', Hunt's blank verse retrospect on the 'honour'd roofs' of his school, bids to be considered alongside Gray's 'Ode on a Distant Prospect of Eton College' and Coleridge's 'Frost at Midnight'. Three odes on friendship announce a theme which Hunt subsequently developed as poet and politician in terms of 'social feeling' and 'sociality'. Among the 800 subscribers gathered by his father were prominent politicians, lawyers, and clergymen, as well as booksellers and publishers, painters and engravers. The book was a success: a second edition was called for within the year, a fourth in 1804, and for a time Hunt 'was introduced to literati, and shown about among parties' (ibid., 1.194). He came to regret this precocity, dismissing *Juvenilia* as 'a heap of imitations' (ibid., 1.186). From this first book can be dated Hunt's uneasy relation to the political and literary establishments, and his (ultimately unsuccessful) determination to resist the kind of patronage on which his father had depended. As editor of *The Examiner* Hunt made much of his independence from party and business interests although, later in life, this principled stance was worn down by necessity.

In 1802 Hunt made a walking tour with John Robertson along the south coast from Ramsgate to Brighton. On his return to London Robertson introduced him to Anne Kent and her daughters Marianne (1787–1857) and Elizabeth (1790–1861). The family looked after Hunt during an attack of 'St Anthony's fire' (the skin inflammation erysipelas), and it is from this time that Hunt's long and fraught courtship of Marianne may be dated. Hunt visited friends at Oxford University (April 1803), meeting in the garden of Trinity College Henry Kett, who said he hoped Hunt would be inspired by 'the muse of [Thomas] Warton'. On the same visit Hunt narrowly escaped from a boating accident on the Thames at Iffley.

Hunt's poems appeared widely in journals such as the *Morning Chronicle*, the *Monthly Mirror*, the *European* and *Monthly* magazines, and the *Poetical Register*. In 1804 he contributed to an evening paper, *The Traveller*, as 'Mr. Town, jnr., Critic and Censor-General' (Hunt, *Autobiography*, 1.255–6). For a short time in 1803 he worked as clerk to his brother Stephen, a lawyer, and from 1805 to 1808 as a clerk in the War Office. From 1805 Leigh wrote theatrical reviews for *The News* and contributed to a short-lived journal *The Statesman*, both papers edited by his brother John (1775–1848). From the first Hunt was a campaigning journalist, announcing his 'impartiality' in seeking to correct 'the universal decline ... of the English drama', which he attributed to 'wretchedly' unoriginal plays and 'histrionic' actors (L. Hunt, *Critical Essays on the Performers of the London Theatres*, 1808, x, xiii, appendix, 15). Instead of 'vehemence of action and voice', Hunt recommended the passionately 'natural carelessness' of Mrs Siddons's performances (ibid., 16, 18). Hunt's reviews were gathered as *Critical Essays on the Performers of the London Theatres* (dated 1807, published early 1808). This book has not received the attention it deserves as a formative statement of Romantic ideas of drama and theatre: Hunt's advice that actors should not be 'confined to surfaces and externals' but should seek to evoke inward 'mental character' (ibid., xi, 2) anticipated the better-known Shakespearian criticism of Samuel Taylor Coleridge, William Hazlitt, and Charles Lamb.

Editor of *The Examiner* and prosecution, 1808–1812 On Sunday 3 January 1808 the first issue of *The Examiner* appeared, edited by Leigh and published by his brother John *Hunt.

The 'Prospectus' announced that *The Examiner* would treat politics with the 'impartiality' that had characterized Leigh's theatre criticism in *The News* (*The Examiner*, 3 Jan 1808, 7). No advertisements would be admitted, lest they should compromise the paper's independence. Like *The News*, *The Examiner* supported parliamentary reform and campaigned for an end to corruption in public life. The paper's reformist opinions and sympathy for Irish independence and Catholic emancipation aroused hostility, so much so that between 1808 and 1812 the government made three (unsuccessful) attempts to prosecute and silence *The Examiner*. Published weekly on a Sunday, by the end of 1808 *The Examiner* had achieved a circulation of 2200 copies, and on 26 December Leigh resigned from his post at the War Office. For the next thirteen years *The Examiner* would be at the centre of his life as a journalist and poet.

On 3 July 1809 Hunt married Marianne Kent, and they went to live (until 1811) at Gowland Cottage in the village of Beckenham. Their first child, Thornton Leigh *Hunt, was born on 10 September 1810 (he died in 1873), and their second, John Horatio, in 1812 (he died in 1846). Besides editing and contributing to *The Examiner* Hunt published in 1809 his pamphlet 'Attempt to show the folly and danger of Methodism', arguing for religious liberty and attacking the 'intolerance' of the Methodists. The following year he edited *The Reflector*, a quarterly magazine published by John Hunt, to which Thomas Barnes, George Dyer, and Charles Lamb contributed. The second issue contained Leigh's poem 'Politics and poetics' on his mutually 'distracting' careers as journalist and poet. His satire on contemporary writers, 'The feast of the poets', appeared in the fourth and final issue (1811). In April 1810 Hunt published a short personal memoir in the *Monthly Mirror*, his first attempt towards the full-scale *Autobiography* of 1850.

An *Examiner* article condemning military flogging, 'One thousand lashes!!' (*The Examiner*, 2 September 1810, 557–8), was prosecuted in February 1811 when Henry Brougham successfully defended the Hunts. After the acquittal Shelley introduced himself to Hunt, sending from Oxford a note of 'sincerest congratulations' on a 'triumph so highly to be prized by men of liberality' (*Letters of Percy Bysshe Shelley*, 1.54). On 19 March 1812 the *Morning Post* hailed the prince regent as the 'Protector of the Arts', the 'Maecenas of the Age', the 'Glory of the People', an 'Adonis of Loveliness', attended by Pleasure, Honour, Virtue, and Truth'. Not everyone was so impressed. At an Irish charity dinner held in the Freemasons' Tavern, London, Richard Brinsley Sheridan's attempt to recommend the prince regent as 'all that Ireland could wish' was greeted with 'hisses' and a 'loud and general clamour' (*The Examiner*, 22 March 1812, 178–9). Hunt now wrote his article 'The prince on St Patrick's day' which contained his devastating portrait of the prince regent as

a violator of his word, a libertine over head and ears in debt and disgrace, a despiser of domestic ties, the companion of gamblers and demireps, a man who has just closed half a century without one single claim on the gratitude of his country or the respect of posterity! (ibid., 179)

A prosecution for libel followed and on 9 December 1812 John and Leigh Hunt were tried before Lord Ellenborough (who ten years earlier had subscribed to the third edition of Leigh's *Juvenilia*). The charge was that the Hunts

> with intention to traduce and vilify his Royal Highness the Prince of Wales, Regent of the United Kingdom, and to bring his Royal Highness into hatred, contempt, and disgrace, on the 22nd of March, in the 52nd year of the King, published a libel against the Prince Regent. (ibid., 13 Dec 1812, 787)

This time Brougham's defence failed. The brothers were found guilty of 'a foul, atrocious, and malignant libel' (ibid., 20 Dec 1812, 808), and on 3 February 1813 Leigh was imprisoned at Horsemonger Lane gaol and John Hunt in the prison at Coldbath Fields; each was fined £500 and required to provide £250 in addition 'for [their] good behaviour' (ibid., 7 Feb 1813, 83). In court the prosecution had dwelt on the Hunts' libellous words, but the trial was also intended to suppress *The Examiner*'s assault on the prince's imperial role as the 'clencher of Irish chains' (ibid., 22 March 1812, 179).

In prison and afterwards, 1813–1815 Horsemonger Lane gaol was just a short distance from the king's bench prison, and Hunt passed his thirtieth birthday in surroundings which surely brought back painful memories of his childhood. The 'perpetual sound' of 'clanking' chains excited nervous attacks and he was moved to rooms in the infirmary (Hunt, *Autobiography*, 1850, 2.146–7; *Correspondence*, 1.73–80). Here he was joined by Marianne and little Thornton, and from time to time by Marianne's sister Elizabeth (of whom Hunt was particularly fond). They transformed the rooms into a 'bower' with a piano and bookcases, rose-patterned wallpaper, clouds and blue sky on the ceiling, and a garden outside. In this accommodation their daughter Mary Florimel (1813–1849) was born. Old school friends visited, as did Jeremy Bentham, Lord Byron, Charles Cowden Clarke (who brought vegetables and eggs), Maria Edgeworth, Benjamin Haydon (who brought his gigantic painting *The Judgment of Solomon*), William Hazlitt, Charles and Mary Lamb, and Thomas Moore. The Hunt brothers continued production of their paper from prison, and Leigh was writing poetry including his sonnets on the Hampstead landscape and his narrative poem *The Story of Rimini* for which Byron supplied books. In January 1814 Hunt published a revised text of *The Feast of the Poets* with extensive notes in which he expressed admiration for 'Mr. Wordsworth's genius' (p. 89) and explored with some care the disparity between Wordsworth's theories and practice as a poet. Notable too is Hunt's recognition that Wordsworth was now 'marked as government property' (p. 99). Hunt's masque *The Descent of Liberty*, on the defeat of Napoleon, was written in prison and published in 1815.

Release from prison came on 3 February 1815 when Hunt went to live at Maida Vale on the Edgware Road, near his brother John. Keats, who had not yet met Hunt, celebrated the occasion in a sonnet 'Written on the day that Mr. Leigh Hunt left prison', but Hunt himself was ill and

later claimed that imprisonment had given a 'shock … to [his] constitution' from which he never recovered (Hunt, *Autobiography*, 1850, 2.159–60). Over the next few years *The Examiner* maintained its liberal opposition while becoming increasingly literary in character. Thomas Barnes and Charles Lamb contributed respectively to the 'Theatrical examiner' and 'Table Talk'. William Hazlitt had joined in 1814 with articles entitled 'On posthumous fame,— whether Shakespeare was influenced by a love of it?' (22 May), 'On Hogarth's Marriage a-la-Mode' (5, 19 June), 'On Mr. Kean's Iago' (24 July, 7 August), and a scathing review of Wordsworth's *The Excursion* (21, 28 August; 2 October). From 1 January 1815 Hunt collaborated with Hazlitt in a series of 'Round table' articles 'on a variety of subjects' relating to 'Manners', 'Morals', and 'Taste' (*The Examiner*, 8 Jan 1815, 26–7). Hunt contributed twelve articles, with titles such as 'On common-place people', 'On Chaucer', 'On the poetical character', 'On death and burial', 'On the night-mare', 'On good nature', 'A day by the fire', 'On washerwomen', 'On the literary character', and 'On poetical versatility'. Hunt adopted a voice which was 'casual and unrestrained' (*The Examiner*, 8 Jan 1815), creating the 'familiar essay' which was to be his principal literary production and source of income in later life. Hunt's and Hazlitt's essays were reprinted in two volumes as *The Round Table* (1817).

Hunt and the 'young poets' On 1 December 1816 *The Examiner* carried Hunt's 'Young poets' article, in which he introduced readers to Shelley, John Hamilton Reynolds, and— 'youngest of them all'—John Keats. Keats had first met Hunt in October 1816, describing the encounter as 'an Era in [his] existence' (*The Letters of John Keats*, ed. Hyder Rollins, 2 vols., 1958, 1.113); he became a frequent visitor to the cottage at the Vale of Health, Hampstead, where Hunt had been living since spring that year. The conclusion of Keats's poem 'Sleep and Poetry' describes Hunt's studio, decorated (like Benjamin West's) with portraits of

> the bards who sung
> In other ages

and busts of King Alfred and the Polish patriot Thaddeus Kosciusko. *The Examiner* for 1 June and 6 and 13 July 1817 printed Hunt's long review of Keats's first collection, *Poems*. Hunt welcomed Keats's 'natural tendency' and 'sensitiveness of temperament', noted reservations about 'super-abundance of detail' and aspects of versification, and drew praising attention to Keats's 'natural touches on the human side of things' (*The Examiner*, 6 July 1817, 428–9) and the 'warm and social feelings' of his poems (*The Examiner*, 13 July 1817, 443). Keats had dedicated this first volume to Hunt and, although their friendship cooled, in 1820 when Keats was ill with tuberculosis Hunt cared for him in his home at Mortimer Terrace.

Hunt's sympathetic presence is well illustrated by his support for Shelley after Harriet Westbrook's suicide on 10 December 1816. From this time their friendship developed swiftly. On 16 December Shelley wrote to Mary Godwin that 'Leigh Hunt has been with me all day & his delicate & tender attentions to me, his kind speeches of you, have sustained me against the weight of the horror of this event' (*Letters of Percy Bysshe Shelley*, 1.520). In the aftermath of the tragedy Percy and Mary Shelley often stayed with Hunt at the Vale of Health, and Shelley wrote to Byron of Hunt's kindly attention describing him as 'a most friendly, and excellent man' (ibid., 1.530). Twice in December 1816 Shelley advanced considerable sums of money to Hunt. On 19 January 1817 Hunt published Shelley's 'Hymn to Intellectual Beauty' in *The Examiner*. Later that year when the Shelleys had moved to Albion House, Marlow, Hunt arranged with his friend Vincent Novello for a piano to be sent down from London. The Hunts stayed with the Shelleys at Marlow from April to July 1817, enjoying an idyllic summer of walks, picnicking, and boating on the Thames.

Literary life and Italy, 1816–1825 In January 1816 Hunt's narrative poem *The Story of Rimini* was published, dedicated to Lord Byron. The poem is based on Dante's encounter in the *Inferno* with the adulterous and quasi-incestuous lovers Paolo and Francesca. In Hunt's version of their story the emphasis is shifted from sin to a sympathetic ('liberal') understanding of their behaviour, affirming—as Hunt explained later—'natural impulses' against the 'authorized selfishness' of religion and law (L. Hunt, *Foliage*, 1818, 17). *Rimini* is Hunt's greatest poem, using the 'freer versification' of run-on couplets and 'a free and idiomatic language' ('with tip-toe looks the people gaze'; 'the fond air'; 'the pouting rose') to create a brisk and colourful narrative (*Rimini*, xv). The poem was well received, except in the tory press where Hunt's 'free' versification and language were linked to his liberal politics and the poem's supposedly 'loose' morals. In *Blackwood's Magazine* (October 1817) John Lockhart's first 'cockney school' essay associated *Rimini*'s 'extreme moral depravity' with Hunt's 'sour Jacobinism' as editor of *The Examiner*.

In *The Examiner* between 1813 and 1817 Hunt explored how poetry might further the paper's liberal campaign, so resolving the problem he had articulated in 'Politics and poetics'. Hunt's sonnet on Kosciusko's 'patient valour' in the cause of freedom (*The Examiner*, 19 Nov 1815) was straightforward panegyric, admitting him to a pantheon of liberal heroes which, for Hunt, included King Alfred, Chaucer, Shakespeare, and Milton. Elsewhere, Hunt's more subtle lyrical interpretations of *The Examiner*'s politics may be traced, for example in the preface to his collection of poems *Foliage* (1818) where he argues that the 'properties of poetry' might encourage 'health and sociality', thus countering the 'melancholy and partial systems' of unrepresentative government (pp. 13, 15–16). *Foliage* was followed by a three-volume *Poetical Works* (1819) and four issues of the *Literary Pocket-Book, or, Companion for the Lover of Nature and Art* (1819–22). 'The calendar of nature' in the 1819 volume was reprinted as a separate volume *The Months* (1821), a publishing strategy that Hunt would often use in later life. Some of his finest essays appeared in his weekly journal *The Indicator*, published in seventy-six issues between 13 October 1819 and 21 March 1821 when illness forced him to give up the journal. Keats's 'La belle dame sans merci' first appeared here (*The Indicator*, 10 May

1820) and Hunt and Keats collaborated on one essay, 'A now, descriptive of a hot day' (*The Indicator*, 28 June 1820). *Amyntas, a Tale of the Woods; from the Italian of Torquato Tasso* appeared in 1820, and was dedicated to Keats.

Following his release from prison Hunt's family had grown. Percy (1816–1827) was followed on 4 December 1817 by Percy Bysshe (d. 1899), on 28 September 1819 by Henry Sylvan, and on 9 June 1823 by Vincent (d. Oct 1852). On 26 August 1821 Shelley wrote to Hunt from Pisa reporting Byron's proposal 'that you should come and go shares with him and me, in a periodical work [*The Liberal*] to be conducted here' (*Letters of Percy Bysshe Shelley*, 2.344). The circulation of *The Examiner* was 'lamentably falling off' (Hunt, *Correspondence*, 1.163), and Hunt had been in poor health. Having resigned his editorship of *The Examiner*, he set sail on 15 November 1821 with Marianne (who was showing symptoms of tuberculosis) and their six children. A severe storm drove their ship into Dartmouth, from where they went on to Plymouth. They passed the winter living 'very quietly at Stone-house, opposite Mount Edgecumbe', where some 'friends of the *Examiner*' in the locality presented Hunt with a silver cup (Hunt, *Autobiography*, 1850, 2.268). On 13 May 1822 the Hunts resumed their voyage, arriving at Genoa on 15 June and Leghorn on 1 July.

They were rapturously welcomed by Shelley: Thornton, who was a favourite of Shelley's, recalled 'his crying out that he was "so *inexpressibly* delighted!—you cannot think how *inexpressibly* happy it makes me!"' (Thornton Hunt, 'Shelley. By one who knew him', *Atlantic Monthly*, 11, 1863, 189–90). Together they went on to Pisa, where the Hunts occupied rooms on the ground floor of Byron's palace. Just one week later Shelley was drowned on 8 July, a loss that for Hunt was 'as hard a blow from fortune as could well be given' and which set the later course of his life and writing (Gates, 164). Hunt attended Shelley's cremation on the beach at Viareggio on 16 August, and in the years following he sought to assuage his grief by 'dematerializing' his friend and creating the '*religion* ... towards Mr. Shelley's memory' which would emerge in *Christianism* and *The Religion of the Heart*.

In September 1822 the Hunts, Byron, and Mary Shelley left Pisa for Albaro, near Genoa, where the Hunts lived with Mary Shelley. Four issues of *The Liberal* were published (1822–3), containing numerous contributions by Hunt including his four 'Letters from abroad', Byron's *The Vision of Judgment*, and Hazlitt's *My First Acquaintance with Poets*. But friendship in this circle was becoming strained, and financial difficulties led to their parting. Byron described Hunt's circumstances at this time succinctly:

> I have done all I can for Leigh Hunt—since he came here—but it is almost useless—his wife is ill—his six children not very tractable and in the affairs of this world he himself is a child. The death of Shelley left them totally aground—and I could not see them in such a state without using the common feelings of humanity—& what means were in my power to set them afloat again. (*Byron's Letters and Journals*, ed. Marchand, 10.13)

In July 1823 Byron left for Greece, Mary Shelley set off for England, and in September the Hunts moved to Florence where they remained 'living in a primitive manner'

(Hunt, *Correspondence*, 2.225) until their return to England two years later. Money was short, and Hunt quarrelled with his brother John about ownership of *The Examiner* and payment for his articles. Charles Armitage Brown, who was then living in Florence, patiently helped to sort out their differences. Hunt's poetry from this period includes *Ultra-Crepidarius; a Satire on William Gifford* (1823), *Bacchus in Tuscany* (1825), contributions to the *Literary Examiner* (1823), and 'The wishing cap' papers in *The Examiner* (1824–5). His many contributions to the *New Monthly Magazine* began at this time.

Return to England, 1825–1830 The Hunts left Italy in September 1825, travelling in stages by *vettura*. They were at Paris on 8 October, and arrived in England on a steamboat from Calais on 12 October. A daughter, Julia, was born in 1826 but did not survive; two years later their last child, Jacintha (1828–1914), was born. The Hunts settled at Highgate where Hunt published his journal *The Companion* from 9 January to 23 July 1828, and contributed two essays—'Pocket-books and keepsakes' and 'Dreams on the borders of the land of poetry'—to a literary annual *The Keepsake*. In that year Hunt's controversial *Lord Byron and some of his Contemporaries* was published in which, 'agitated by grief and anger' (Hunt, *Autobiography*, 1850, 3.3) at Byron's having abandoned him in Italy, Hunt presented an embittered portrait of his former friend and patron. Hunt's *Autobiography* had its origins in this work, which also contained essays on Shelley and Keats, and Hunt's own memoirs. Hunt tried to make money with two short-lived periodicals, the *Chat of the Week* (5 June–28 August 1830) and *The Tatler* (4 October 1830–13 February 1832), 'a literary and theatrical paper' which Hunt wrote entirely himself: 'the work, slight as it looked, nearly killed me', he recalled (ibid., 3.215).

The man of letters, 1830–1850 From 1828 to 1832 Hunt lived first at Epsom, then at Old Brompton, St John's Wood, and finally New Road, Marylebone. At Epsom he began his novel *Sir Ralph Esher*, which was published in 1832 and reached a third edition in 1836. In 1832 he printed for private circulation seventy-five copies of a pamphlet entitled *Christianism*, 'a set of aspirations, or thoughts and feelings, connected with the best hopes of man' (p. iii) which grew out of Hunt's coming to terms with Shelley's death. It was reprinted as *The Religion of the Heart* in 1853. A copy of *Christianism* was sent to Thomas Carlyle, leading to a life-long friendship. In 1832 the *Poetical Works of Leigh Hunt* appeared, with a long 'gossiping' preface in which Hunt reflects on imagination, versification, rhyme, and his own poems in the volume. Hunt also published Shelley's *Masque of Anarchy* in 1832, thirteen years after the Peterloo massacre which prompted the poem. Shelley originally submitted the poem to *The Examiner* but, as Hunt now explained, publication of 'this flaming robe of verse' in 1819 would have incited 'the suffering part of the people' to violence rather than to 'a calm, lawful, and inflexible preparation for resistance in the shape of a protesting multitude,—the few against the many,—the laborious and suffering against the spoilt children of monopoly,—

Mankind against Tory-kind' (Shelley, *Masque of Anarchy*, 1832, vi, x).

Hunt settled in 1833 at 4 Upper Cheyne Row, Chelsea, next door to Carlyle, and remained there until 1840 when he moved to 33 Edwardes Square, Kensington, where he stayed for eleven years until 1851. In this period Hunt's journalistic productions and his financial struggles continued. He contributed articles to many journals including *Court Magazine* (1832–3), *Tait's Edinburgh Magazine* (January–September 1833), the *True Sun* (1833–4), and the *Monthly Chronicle* (1838–40). His health was so bad that he had 'to be carried every morning to the *True Sun* office in a hackney-coach' (Hunt, *Autobiography*, 1850, 3.222). Selections from Hunt's *Indicator* and *Companion* reappeared in two volumes (1834). His next venture was *Leigh Hunt's London Journal* (2 April 1834–31 December 1835), 'a miscellany of essays, criticism, and passages from books' (ibid., 3.231). Rumours of war sparked Hunt's remarkable protest ballad *Captain Sword and Captain Pen* (1835). The poem circles between scenes of 'military gaiety' (ibid., 3.237) and the horrors of the battlefield:

> Now see what crawleth, well as it may,
> Out of the ditch, and looketh that way

and it concludes with 'the bullet-sense' of warmongers succeeded by the peaceful 'line of Captain Pen'—that is, the company of sages, patriots, and poets:

> Twas only for many-souled Captain Pen
> To make a world of swordless men.

He edited the *Monthly Repository* (1837–8), and among his contributions was his poem *Blue-Stocking Revels, or, The Feast of the Violets*, described by Hunt as 'a kind of female *Feast of the Poets*, which nobody took any notice of' (ibid., 3.241). Selections from Hunt's journalism were gathered in *The Seer, or, Common-Places Refreshed* (1840).

On 7 February 1840 Hunt's play *A Legend of Florence* was performed at Covent Garden Theatre, and attended by Queen Victoria two or three times in its successful first season. It was revived in 1850 at Sadler's Wells, and in 1852 in a command performance at Windsor Castle. Hunt wrote the introductory biographical and critical material for Moxon's editions of *The Dramatic Works of Wycherley, Congreve, Vanbrugh, and Farquhar* and *The Dramatic Works of Richard Brinsley Sheridan* (both 1840). *The Palfrey; a Love Story of Old Times* appeared in 1842, and the following year Hunt republished essays from his *London Journal* (1834–5) in *One hundred romances of real life, comprising remarkable historical and domestic facts illustrative of human nature*. Another edition of his *Poetical Works* was published in 1844.

One of the most influential publications of Hunt's later life was his book *Imagination and Fancy* (1844). Hunt's introductory essay 'An answer to the question what is poetry?' draws on Romantic theory (especially Coleridge's) in presenting poetry as 'the operation of feeling' modified by imagination and the 'playful creativeness' of fancy. Hunt's comments are illustrated by extensive quotations from English, Italian, and classical poetry. High points in the book are his brilliant account of the 'mysterious returns of importunate feeling' in *Christabel*, and his close criticism of Keats's poem *Eve of St Agnes* which is reproduced in full in the book.

Later life to 1859 Hunt's health was always precarious, and in the last two decades of his life illness was accompanied by 'other domestic anxieties': he had a 'morbid dread of fire', a 'fiend of fear' associated with Marianne's illness and, particularly, her alcoholism (Hunt, *Correspondence*, 2.164; Gates, 35). In a letter of 1851 Hunt mentions that Marianne is 'sometimes confined to her bed for months … and has not quitted the house for years except in a carriage' (Brewer Collection, MS LH 94 SW). Hunt's income was fitful, alternating between 'handsome earnings' from his publications and periods when he received 'no income at all' (Hunt, *Correspondence*, 2.168). On two occasions a royal grant of £200 had been secured for him, and from 1844 he received an annuity of £120 from the Shelley family. Carlyle wrote a petition drawing attention to Hunt's services 'as Poet, Essayist, Public Teacher', and pointing out his 'domestic burdens', 'weak health', and want of 'economical resources' (BL, Add. MS 38110). On 22 June 1847 the prime minister, Lord John Russell, wrote to Hunt that a pension of £200 a year would be granted him. In summer 1847 Charles Dickens and a company of amateur players performed Ben Jonson's *Every Man in his Humour* for Hunt's benefit; the performances in London, Manchester, and Liverpool raised some £900.

Hunt's publications in the 1840s included *Stories from the Italian Poets, with Lives of the Writers* (1845) and *Wit and Humour, Selected from the English Poets; with an Illustrative Essay and Critical Comments* (1846). *Men, Women, and Books: a Selection of Sketches, Essays and Critical Memoirs* (1847) was a two-volume miscellany drawn from Hunt's 'uncollected prose writings' (preface). *A Jar of Honey from Mount Hybla* (1847) reprinted Hunt's articles from *Ainsworth's Magazine* (1844) on the mythology, history, and biography of Sicily, and ancient legends and examples of pastoral poetry. *The Town: its Memorable Characters and Events* (1848) was a 'topographical and historical' account of London, with 'memories of remarkable characters and events associated with its streets between St. Paul's and St. James's' ('Advertisement' to *The Town*). Most of this work had appeared thirteen years before in Hunt's *London Journal*. His anthologizing continued in 1849 with *A Book for a Corner, or, Selections in Prose and Verse* and *Readings for railways, or, Anecdotes and other short stories, reflections, maxims, characteristics, passages of wit, humour, and poetry, etc.* This last is significant for showing Hunt's versatility in adapting to the new market of readers encouraged by railway travel.

In June 1850 Smith, Elder & Co. published *The Autobiography of Leigh Hunt, with Reminiscences of Friends and Contemporaries* in three volumes. Hunt begins by observing that 'a more involuntary production it would be difficult to conceive' (Hunt, *Autobiography*, 1850, 1.1) although the book drew on and carefully revised material from *Lord Byron and some of his Contemporaries* and other memoirs and journalism dating back as far as 1810. Thomas Carlyle thought it 'by far the best of the autobiographic kind [he remembered] to have read', an 'altogether *human* and worthy Book' (*Collected Letters*, 25.97). Of particular interest are

Hunt's accounts of his parents, of his schooldays at Christ's Hospital, and of theatregoing in the early nineteenth century. His imprisonment and literary friendships with Shelley, Keats, Lamb, and others take up most of the second volume, and form the heart of the book. The third volume covers his time in Italy, while the twenty-five years of hardship and literary endeavour following his return to England are dealt with in just three short concluding chapters. The *Autobiography* repays close reading: Carlyle was right to point to the 'graceful honesty' of the book (ibid.), which unobtrusively notices many harrowing and painful episodes without disrupting the genial tone of the whole. A revised edition with an introduction by his eldest son, Thornton, was published in 1860; notable in it are Hunt's revisions to his portrait of his father, emphasizing his 'honest' loyalism and mentioning only 'defects' of character rather than 'faults'.

In 1851 Hunt (now living at 2 Phillimore Terrace, off Kensington High Street) published *Table-Talk, to which are Added Imaginary Conversations of Pope and Swift*, a gathering of short pieces first published in the newspaper *The Atlas* and other periodicals. *Leigh Hunt's Journal: a Miscellany for the Cultivation of the Memorable, the Progressive, and the Beautiful* ran from 7 December 1850 until the 'luckless Journal' ceased on 22 March 1851 (Gates, 508). In October 1852 Hunt's youngest son, Vincent, died after 'wasting before [his] eyes for two years'; Hunt said that the death 'haunted [him] like a monomania for eight months' (Hunt, *Correspondence*, 2.153, 214). He now published *The Religion of the Heart: a Manual of Faith and Duty* (1853), an elaboration of his *Christianism* pamphlet which followed the death of Shelley. *The Religion of the Heart* harks back to the universalist beliefs of his parents, and responds to Vincent's death by spiritualizing Hunt's philosophy of cheerfulness. In the same year Dickens's *Bleak House* caricatured Hunt as the 'perfect child', Harold Skimpole. Dickens denied in *All the Year Round* (24 December 1859) that Hunt's unworldly character had suggested any of Skimpole's disagreeable attributes. But he had already admitted in a letter of 21 September 1853 that Skimpole was 'the most exact portrait that ever was painted in words! … It is an absolute reproduction of a real man' (*The Letters of Charles Dickens*, ed. M. House, G. Storey, and others, 12 vols., 1965–2002, 7.154). *The Old Court Suburb, or, Memorials of Kensington—Royal, Critical, and Anecdotical* appeared in 1855, and in the same year Hunt's selection from Beaumont and Fletcher. As in *Imagination and Fancy* Hunt quotes generously, sometimes reproducing whole scenes from the plays. *Stories in Verse* (1855) reprinted Hunt's narrative poems.

Vincent's death encouraged Hunt's move in 1853 to 7 Cornwall Road, Hammersmith, his last home. The Cowden Clarkes recalled his living here with 'his books and papers about him, engravings and plaster-casts around his room' (C. Cowden Clarke and M. Cowden Clarke, 263). On 2 December 1856 Hunt wrote to his old friend Charles Ollier, 'Mrs Hunt and myself have both suffered more than commonly, she with cough as well as rheumatism, and I with cough and bronchoroea' (Hunt, *Correspondence*, 2.206). Marianne, who had been in ill health for most of her life (and was described in 1851 as 'sodden with drink'; Tatchell, 45) died on 26 January 1857 aged sixty-nine and was buried in Kensal Green cemetery. Hunt's tribute to Marianne appears in his *Autobiography* (1860, 448). American editions of Hunt's *Works* (1856) and *Poetic Works* (1857) appeared, and in 1858 he contributed to *Fraser's Magazine* two poems in the manner of Chaucer and Spenser, 'The Tapiser's Tale' and 'The Shewe of Fair Seeming'. A series of articles entitled 'The occasional' appeared in *The Spectator* in 1859, the last of which appeared on 20 August one week before his death.

Early in August 1859 Hunt went for a change of air to his old friend Charles Reynell at Putney, taking 'his work and the books he more immediately wanted' (Hunt, *Autobiography*, 1860, 452). He died at Reynell's home in the High Street on 28 August 1859, aged seventy-four. The cause of his death 'was simply exhaustion'. Thornton Hunt wrote: 'he broke off his work to lie down … he said that his only "uneasiness" was failing breath' (ibid.). Leigh Hunt was buried, as he had requested, in Kensal Green cemetery. On 19 October 1869 a monument was unveiled by Lord Houghton, with a bust of Hunt by Joseph Durham and an epitaph from his own poem 'Abou-ben-Adhem': 'Write me as one who loves his fellow-men'.

Reputation Hunt outlived Keats, Shelley, and Byron, and the later decades of his life may seem lacklustre by comparison with years when he was lionized as 'Libertas', the martyr to liberty. His long life connected the Romantic period with the nineteenth-century Victorian era, and he had a wide and decisive influence in both periods. His editorship of *The Examiner* was a high point in the history of English journalism, and his campaigning on a variety of liberal and human issues marks him out as one of the great reformers. His theatrical and literary criticism, his championing of poets such as Keats, Shelley, Tennyson, and D. G. Rossetti, and his enthusiasm for Italian arts all had a formative effect on British culture in the nineteenth and twentieth centuries. Apart from a few anthology pieces like 'Abou-ben-Adhem', Hunt's own poetry has not been widely read. Poets, however, have taken much from Hunt: the Pre-Raphaelites learned from his interest in Italian arts, and in the twentieth century the socialized 'suburban' scene of his 'Hampstead sonnets' was adapted by Philip Larkin and John Betjeman. Rather than the sublimities of Romantic nature in the Lake District or the Alps it is Hunt's domesticated, urbanized landscape that corresponds to the reality of modern England. Hazlitt said in *The Spirit of the Age* (1825) that Hunt 'improves upon acquaintance'; everyone can gain from knowing him better.

NICHOLAS ROE

Sources *The autobiography of Leigh Hunt, with reminiscences of friends and contemporaries*, 3 vols. (1850) · *The correspondence of Leigh Hunt*, ed. T. L. Hunt, 2 vols. (1862) · *Leigh Hunt: a life in letters, together with some correspondence of William Hazlitt*, ed. E. M. Gates (1998) · A. L. Brewer, *My Leigh Hunt library: the holograph letters* (Iowa City, 1938) · L. Landré, *Leigh Hunt (1784–1859): contribution à l'histoire de romantisme anglais*, 2 vols. (Paris, 1936) · *The letters of Percy Bysshe Shelley*, ed. F. L. Jones, 2 vols. (1964) · *The poetical works of Leigh Hunt*, ed. H. S. Milford [1923] [incl. bibliography of the poetry of Leigh Hunt] · *The Examiner* (1808–1822), facs. edn, 15 vols. (1996–8) · E. Blunden, *Leigh Hunt: a biography* (1930) · E. Blunden, *Leigh Hunt's 'Examiner' examined, 1808–1825* (1928) · *The autobiography of Leigh Hunt*, new edn (1860) · J. Cox, *Poetry and politics in the cockney school: Shelley, Hunt, and their circle* (1998) · N. Roe, *John Keats and the culture of dissent* (1997) · Brewer Collection, University of Iowa Library, Iowa City · BL, Add. MSS · *The collected letters of Thomas and Jane Welsh Carlyle*, ed. C. R. Sanders, K. J. Fielding, and others, [30 vols.] (1970–) · M. Tatchell, *Leigh Hunt and his family in Hammersmith* (1969) · R. Russell, *The wider family of Leigh Hunt* (1989) · C. Cowden Clarke and M. Cowden Clarke, *Recollections of writers* (1878) · W. Hazlitt, *The spirit of the age* (1825) · presentation papers for entry to Christ's Hospital, 1791, Christ's Hospital School

Archives BL, commonplace book, RP1713 · BL, corresp., literary and biographical papers, Add. MSS. 33515, 38105–38111, 38523–38524, 46202 · Duke U., Perkins L., papers · Hist. Soc. Penn., papers · Hunt. L., letters and literary MSS · Keats House, Hampstead, London, literary MSS and letters · Man. CL, papers · NYPL, corresp. · NYPL, Pforzheimer collection, papers · University of Iowa Libraries, corresp. and literary papers · University of Virginia, Charlottesville, papers · V&A, literary corresp. · V&A NAL, literary corresp. and MS of 'A legend of Florence' | BL, corresp. with Lady Holland, Add. MSS 51853–51855 · BL, letters to his wife, Marianne, Ashley MSS 3393, 3398 · BL, letters to his son, Thornton Leigh Hunt, Add. MS 47671 · BL, corresp. with Macvey Napier, Add. MSS 34621–34626 · BL, letters to Thomas Powell, RP 2008, 2090 [copies] · BL, letters to Royal Literary Fund, loan 96 · BL, corresp. with Mary Shelley, Add. MSS 38523–38524 · Chatsworth House, Derbyshire, letters to the sixth duke of Devonshire · FM Cam., letters to James Bailey · Herts. ALS, letters to Lord Lytton · Manchester Co-operative Union, Holyoake House, letters to G. J. Holyoake · NL Scot., letter to Archibald Constable · NYPL, Berg collection · U. Leeds, Brotherton L., letters to Charles Cowden Clarke · UCL, letters to Lord Brougham and Henry Brougham · University of Iowa, Iowa City, Brewer collection

Likenesses T. C. Wageman, pencil drawing, 1815, NPG · H. H. Meyer, line engraving, pubd 1828 (after J. Hayter), BM, NPG · S. Laurence, oils, *c*.1837, NPG [*see illus.*] · J. Durham, bust, 1869, Chelsea town hall, London · D. Maclise, lithograph, pubd 1873, NPG · S. Freeman, stipple (after J. Jackson), BM, NPG · M. Gillies, miniature, NPG · B. R. Haydon, oils, NPG · D. Maclise, pencil drawing, V&A · H. Meyer, stipple (after J. Hayter), BM, NPG; repro. in *Byron and his contemporaries* (1828) · oils, Christ's Hospitals, Horsham, Sussex · watercolour drawing, NPG

Wealth at death under £200: administration, 29 Oct 1859, *CGPLA Eng. & Wales*

Hunt [*née* Raine], **Margaret** (1831–1912), novelist, was born on 14 October 1831 in Durham, the second daughter of the four children of James *Raine (1791–1858), antiquary and topographer, and Margaret Peacock, eldest daughter of the Revd Thomas Peacock (1756–1851), curate and headmaster of a school in Denton. James Raine was second master at Durham School from 1812 to 1827. He was ordained in 1818, held the living of St Mary's in Durham, and became librarian to the dean and chapter of Durham Cathedral.

Churchmen and educationists predominated in the family. Margaret Raine's uncle George Peacock (1791–1858) was a reformer, both as a fellow of Trinity College, Cambridge, teaching mathematics, then as dean of Ely Cathedral. Her only brother, James (1830–1896), became rector of All Saints' Pavement Church, York, and chancellor and canon-residentiary.

Three years after Margaret's birth, the family moved to the medieval manor Crook Hall, which was visited by John

Ruskin, Walter Scott, and William and Dorothy Wordsworth. Margaret was tutored at home. At twenty she took
drawing lessons in Durham from William Bell Scott, master of the Government School of Design in Newcastle,
from whom she heard about the Pre-Raphaelites.

Margaret Raine had many eligible suitors, but broke off
her engagement to Canon Greenwell after she met Alfred
William *Hunt (1830–1896) in 1856 or 1857. She and Hunt
were married on 16 November 1861, in St Oswald's
Church, near Durham Cathedral. Hunt, the son of landscape artist Andrew Hunt, was already an established
painter and a member of the Liverpool Academy from
1856. Alfred Hunt had gone to Corpus Christi College,
Oxford, intending to enter the church. He did not take
holy orders, but the college nevertheless made him a fellow. He taught classics, but painting was his vocation. He
was influenced by Ruskin's *Modern Painters*, Turner, and
the Pre-Raphaelites, though he was never a member of the
Brotherhood. When he married, he gave up his fellowship
and the couple settled in Durham.

The Hunts' eldest daughter, (Isabel) Violet *Hunt (1862–
1942), fictionalized their love match in her novel *Their
Hearts* (1921). He was modest and self-effacing, but depressive. She was confident and outgoing, with a north country wit as blunt as it was sharp. They moved to a narrow
Georgian house at 29 Old Elvet and had two more daughters: Venetia ('Venice') Margaret (b. 1864), whose godfather
was Ruskin, and Silvia (1865–1920). They took regular
painting and sketching tours in the summers. Favourite
haunts were Wales, Northumberland, north Yorkshire,
and the Lake District.

In 1865 the Hunts moved to London, renting 1 Tor Villas
in Kensington from their friend William Holman Hunt.
Ruskin became a close friend, as did Robert Browning, the
Alma Tademas, the Ford Madox Browns, the Burne-
Joneses, the Millais, and Lord Leighton. Margaret persuaded Browning, Millais, and Burne-Jones to sign a
women's rights petition. Ford Madox Ford said Margaret
had 'a brilliant social popularity—if that can be called
popularity which consisted in having most of the great
men of her day constantly in her drawing room and
equally constantly afraid of her biting and nimble
tongue', and that they all thought her 'the wittiest woman
in London' (preface to *The Governess*, Margaret Hunt's
novel completed by Violet Hunt, 1912).

Alfred Hunt aspired to become a member of the Royal
Academy, but was never elected. Landscape painting was
out of fashion, and the hanging committee found his
work too Pre-Raphaelite. After their persistent rejection
of his oils, he turned mainly to watercolour, and became a
member of the Old Watercolour Society from 1864.

In 1869 the Hunts accepted an invitation from Sidney
Courtauld to go on a Mediterranean cruise. Margaret went
to find the two sisters she had read about when reviewing
Edward Lear in Corsica, Reine and Catherine Dausoigne, and
brought them to London hoping to find them advantageous matches. Unfortunately the only proposals they
received were to sit as models for Pre-Raphaelite painters
and the photographer Julia Margaret Cameron.

Margaret took up writing to supplement her family's
income. She wrote for *The Spectator* and *Gentleman's Annual*
and worked with Andrew Lang on versions of *Grimms'
Fairy Tales*. Her fiction 'is generally exuberantly comic and
satirical' (Sutherland, 314). The first of her twelve novels,
Magdalen Wynyard, or, The Provocations of a Pre-Raphaelite
(1872), caused a scandal for its thinly veiled portrayal of
Durham Cathedral close. *Thornicroft's Model* followed in
1873, broadly based on Dante Gabriel Rossetti and Elizabeth Siddall. (Both were published under the pseudonym
Averil Beaumont.) *The Leaden Casket* (1880) satirizes London
artistic and literary worlds. From 1887 to 1897 she contributed regularly to *Longman's Magazine*.

Three episodes suggest Margaret's attraction to literary
celebrities overrode her maternal sense. In 1873 she had
sent Venice to console Ruskin for being rejected by Rose La
Touche. In 1875, when Ruskin had seen Rose for the last
time, Margaret then encouraged Violet's idea that *she*
should offer herself as a substitute child-bride in three
years' time. From 1879 Oscar Wilde became a friend and
correspondent. When he became taken with Violet, Margaret appears to have thought him a good match.

In 1888 Alfred became deputy president of the Royal
Watercolour Society. In 1893 he was invited to be art juror
at the Great Chicago Exhibition. He and Margaret sailed to
the USA for two months, visiting New York and Niagara
Falls. But despite such recognition, Alfred was devastated
by the Royal Academy's exclusion. With his eyesight failing, he struggled to make a living. He died of apoplexy on
3 May 1896. The strain told on Margaret, who became
increasingly cantankerous and her writing suffered. *Mrs
Juliet* (1892) was her last completed novel.

Margaret moved with Violet to South Lodge, Campden
Hill Road, in 1896. The attempt by Venice to try to get her
committed in 1901 was perhaps premature. But Margaret's eccentricity advanced inexorably.

> Once, on being handed a cup of tea, the old lady sniffed it
> suspiciously and then in a deep and tragic voice said: 'What
> is this, poison? Well, never mind, I'll drink it if you like',
> downing it all in a single hearty gulp.   (Fraser, 128)

Eventually Violet had to have her committed to the court
of lunacy and herself made her receiver. After that, Margaret took to her own rooms. She died at South Lodge on 1
November 1912, aged eighty-one. Her funeral and burial
were on 4 November at Brookwood cemetery, where she
was buried alongside Alfred.

Margaret Hunt's style of light Victorian fiction went
quickly out of fashion. In the twenty-first century she is
remembered chiefly in biographical research on Violet
Hunt or Ford Madox Ford.   MAX SAUNDERS

Sources B. Belford, *Violet* (1990) · J. Hardwick, *An immodest violet*
(1990) · *DNB* · J. Sutherland, *The Longman companion to Victorian fiction* (1988) · *WWW*, 1897–1916 · G. L. Fraser, *In the days of my youth*
(1970) · A. Mizener, *The saddest story* (1971)
Archives Cornell University, Ithaca, New York, Carl A. Kroch Library, papers
Wealth at death £23,589 0s. 4d.: probate, 22 Feb 1913, *CGPLA Eng.
& Wales*

Hunt, Martita (1900–1969), actress, was born in Buenos
Aires, Argentina, on 30 January 1900, to Alfred Hunt and

his wife, Marta, *née* Burnett. She came to England to attend Queenwood boarding-school, Eastbourne, and she then trained for a theatrical career under Dame Geneviève Ward and Lady Benson. After acting at Liverpool repertory theatre and with a touring company, she made her London début for the Stage Society in Ernst Toller's *The Machine Wreckers* at the Kingsway in May 1923. She spent the next six years working in the West End, giving performances as the Principessa della Cercola in W. Somerset Maugham's *Our Betters* (Globe, 1924) and as Mrs Linden in Ibsen's *A Doll's House* (Playhouse, 1925), interspersed with engagements at club theatres such as the Q and the Arts and, in 1926, a short season of Chekhov plays at the small Barnes Theatre, directed by Victor Komisarjevsky, who cast her as Charlotta Ivanovna, the eccentric governess in *The Cherry Orchard* and as Olga in *Three Sisters*.

In September 1929 Hunt joined the Old Vic company under Harcourt Williams, and in the following eight months played a challenging succession of Shakespearian roles (the Nurse in *Romeo and Juliet*, Portia in *The Merchant of Venice*, the Queen in *Richard II*, Helena in *A Midsummer Night's Dream*, Portia in *Julius Caesar*, and, opposite John Gielgud, Rosalind in *As You Like It*, Lady Macbeth in *Macbeth*, and Queen Gertrude in *Hamlet*), together with the parts of Béline in Molière's *The Imaginary Invalid*, Queen Elizabeth in Shaw's *The Dark Lady of the Sonnets*, and Lavinia in his *Androcles and the Lion*. With an arresting appearance and a dominant stage presence, she proved most effective as strong, tragic characters, her Gertrude in *Hamlet* being accounted by some critics the finest they had seen.

Returning to the West End, Hunt featured in an extraordinary range of productions in the 1930s and during the war years, notably as Edith Gunter in Dodie Smith's *Autumn Crocus* (Lyric, 1931), the countess of Rousillon in *All's Well that Ends Well* (Arts, 1932), Lady Strawholme in Ivor Novello's *Fresh Fields* (Criterion, 1933), Liz Frobisher in John Van Druten's *The Distaff Side* (Apollo, 1933), Barbara Dawe in Clemence Dane's *Moonlight is Silver* (Queen's, 1934), Theodora in Elmer Rice's *Not for Children* (Fortune, 1935), Masha in Chekhov's *The Seagull* (New, 1936), Emilia in *Othello* (when she rejoined the Old Vic briefly in 1938), the Mother in Garcia Lorca's *Marriage of Blood* (Savoy, 1939), Miss Havisham in a dramatization of Dickens's *Great Expectations* at the Rudolf Steiner Hall (1939), Léonie in Cocteau's *Les parents terribles* (Gate, 1940), Mrs Cheveley in Wilde's *An Ideal Husband* (Westminster, 1943), and Cornelia in Webster's *The White Devil* (Duchess, 1947). During the same period Hunt made innumerable films, the majority unworthy of her talents, though some, like *Good Morning, Boys* (1937), *Trouble Brewing* (1939), *The Man in Grey* (1943), and *The Wicked Lady* (1945), achieved considerable popularity and enabled her to sparkle in supporting or cameo roles, and in David Lean's *Great Expectations* (1946) she took the opportunity to develop her stage characterization of Miss Havisham into an unforgettable study in alienation. For all this resourcefulness, stardom continued to elude her until, in 1948, an American management hired her to play Countess Aurelia, the eponymous heroine of Giraudoux's *The Madwoman of Chaillot*, for its

English-speaking première, a compelling performance which won her a Tony award on her Broadway début, but sadly left London audiences relatively unmoved three years later. Ironically, this very success served only to type-cast her as the *grande dame* or patrician grotesque in a string of subsequent films, including *Anna Karenina* (1948), *Lady Windermere's Fan* (1949), *Folly to be Wise* (1952), *The March Hare* (1956), *Anastasia* (1956), *The Admirable Crichton* (1957), *The Prince and the Showgirl* (1957)—contributing a witty reprise of her stage performance as the Grand Duchess in its source, Rattigan's *The Sleeping Prince* (Phoenix, 1953)—*The Brides of Dracula* (1960), *Becket* (1964), and *The Unsinkable Molly Brown* (1964). After 1950 her stage appearances became more infrequent and she made her last as Angélique Boniface in *Hotel Paradiso*, an adaptation from Feydeau, alongside Alec Guinness at the Winter Garden in May 1956. She died of bronchial asthma at her home, 7 Primrose Hill Studios, Fitzroy Road, Hampstead, London, on 13 June 1969.　　　　　　　　　　DONALD ROY

Sources *Who was who in the theatre, 1912–1976*, 2 (1978), 1241–2 · W. Rigdon, *The biographical encyclopedia* (1966), 556 · D. Quinlan, *The illustrated directory of film character actors* (1985), 152 · S. D'Amico, ed., *Enciclopedia dello spettacolo*, 11 vols. (Rome, 1954–68) · P. Hartnoll, ed., *The concise Oxford companion to the theatre* (1972), 259 · *The Times* (14 June 1969), 1, 10 · J. Willis, ed., *Theatre world*, 26 (1970), 268–9 · F. Gaye, ed., *Who's who in the theatre*, 14th edn (1967), 769–70 · E. M. Truitt, *Who was who on screen*, 3rd edn (1983), 360 · *The Guardian* (14 June 1969), 5 · R. May, *A companion to the theatre* (1973), 110 · J.-L. Passek, ed., *Dictionnaire du cinéma* (1991), 334

Likenesses Sasha, photograph, 1931, Hult. Arch. · group portrait, photograph, 1937, Hult. Arch. · photograph, 1939 (as Miss Havisham in *Great expectations*), repro. in *Theatre World* (Jan 1940), 19 · photograph, 1948 (as Countess Aurelia in *The mad woman of Chaillot*), repro. in *Theatre Arts* (March 1949), 14 · photograph, *c*.1953, Hult. Arch. · photograph, repro. in Willis, ed., *Theatre world*, 269

Wealth at death £5390: administration, 18 Dec 1969, *CGPLA Eng. & Wales*

Hunt, Nicholas (1596–1648), mathematician, was born in the parish of St Mary Steps, Exeter, Devon. He entered Exeter College, Oxford, on 12 April 1612, and graduated BA on 19 April 1616. Hunt was described on the title page of his first, devotional, work as 'preacher of Christ's Word', but his next, *Newe Recreations, or, The Mindes Release and Solacing* (1631), was dedicated to Charles I and contained arithmetical conundrums and problems. His *Handmaid to Arithmetick Refin'd* (1633) dealt principally with weights and measures, coinage, and other commercial matters. His last publication, in 1634, was again devotional.

By 1639 Hunt was living at Camberwell, in Surrey, where he was one of the proctors of the court of arches. He died there in 1648, leaving a widow, Margery, a son, William, and several daughters.

R. E. ANDERSON, *rev.* ANITA McCONNELL

Sources A. De Morgan, *Arithmetical books from the invention of printing to the present time* (1847), 39–40 · Wood, *Ath. Oxon.* · W. H. Blanch, *Ye parish of Camberwell* (1875), 103 · will, PROB 11/207/ sig. 14

Hunt, Norman Crowther, Baron Crowther-Hunt (1920–1987), constitutional scholar and television and radio broadcaster, was born on 13 March 1920 at Bradford, Yorkshire, the elder son (there were no daughters) of Ernest

Angus Hunt, master butcher, of Eccleshill, Bradford, and his wife, Florence, *née* Crowther. He was educated at Belle Vue high school, Bradford, and at Sidney Sussex College, Cambridge, where he was an exhibitioner (1939–40) and, after war service in the Royal Artillery and the War Office, a scholar (1945–7). He married Joyce, daughter of the Revd Joseph Stackhouse, of Walsall Wood, Staffordshire, in 1944; they had three daughters. Hunt took a first in both parts of the history tripos (1946 and 1947), was a research fellow of Sidney Sussex (1949–51), and then spent a year as Commonwealth Fund fellow at Princeton, studying American politics. In 1952 he was elected to a tutorial fellowship in politics at Exeter College, Oxford, where he spent the rest of his academic career.

Hunt was the very antithesis of the cloistered don, however. A square, stocky, round-faced man of enormous energy and indefatigable good humour, he took delight in challenging closed establishments, devising schemes and drafting papers for reform of matters great and small, and proving his stamina in new fields. He had won a Cambridge football blue as goalkeeper (1940), and continued to be an agile opponent in most ball games and in politics at every level. His years as domestic bursar of Exeter (1954–70) were christened the Norman Conquest by those who felt their impact. He was not a man for the long-considered haul of quiet research. He published part of his historical Cambridge PhD thesis (1951) as *Two Early Political Associations* (1961), edited *Whitehall and Beyond* (1964), and (with Graham Tayar) *Personality and Power* (1971), and wrote (with Peter Kellner) *The Civil Servants* (1980). But his academic gifts lay in teaching, not scholarship.

Hunt was an invigorating, forceful tutor for generations of Oxford undergraduates, and, thanks to the BBC, a challenging political guide and familiar voice to a much wider audience. From 1961 he appeared regularly on both television and radio, and his *People and Politics* was a weekly feature of the World Service for many years. His long service to the BBC culminated in his appointment as chairman of its General Advisory Council in 1986. It had also initiated a lasting friendship with Harold Wilson, a fellow Yorkshireman, whom Hunt interviewed (and greatly impressed) shortly after Wilson's election as leader of the Labour Party in 1963. While Wilson was prime minister (1964–70, 1974–6) Hunt was able to promote the two constitutional issues about which he felt most deeply, and which he helped to place firmly on the political agenda: reform of the civil service and devolution.

Hunt's was the chief radical voice in the committee on the civil service (1966–8) chaired by Lord Fulton. He led its management consultancy group and drafted much of the final report which condemned the 'generalist' (and Oxbridge) bias of civil service recruitment and sought to open senior posts to specialists. In 1969 he was appointed to the royal commission on the constitution, chaired first by Lord Crowther and then by C. J. D. Shaw (later Lord Kilbrandon). Hunt was once again on the radical wing, though this time in a minority. He was principal author of a long memorandum of dissent to the final report (1973), in which he argued that devolution to the English regions must go hand in hand with the devolution to elected assemblies in Scotland and Wales which Kilbrandon recommended.

In 1973 Hunt was made a life peer (he took the title Baron Crowther-Hunt of Eccleshill), and on Wilson's return to power in 1974 he was appointed constitutional adviser to the government (March–October), with a brief to develop its devolution proposals. He dealt with the same issue as minister in the privy council office in 1976. In the interim, from 1974 to 1976, he was minister of state at the Department of Education and Science; but he was less successful at handling the public controversies aroused by his proposals for manpower planning in higher education than he had been as a backroom advocate and elaborator of policy. He was disillusioned also by the extent to which narrowly party-political considerations determined the government's attitude to devolution, and although civil service reform had proceeded further, he chafed at what he saw as continuing Whitehall obstruction. He returned to full-time teaching at Exeter College in 1976, not disappointed (he was the last man ever to have regrets), but with some relief.

Hunt's election as rector of the college in 1982 began the final, and personally most satisfying, part of his career. He enjoyed the distinction, as he enjoyed his honorary fellowship of Sidney Sussex (1982) and his honorary degrees from Bradford University (1974) and Williams College, Massachusetts, USA (1985). But he was as determined as ever to use his position to reshape institutions and open their doors to fresh talent. He helped to reform the university's admissions procedures, and initiated an ambitious and successful college appeal. He made the rector's lodgings a welcoming centre of college activity, where undergraduates met public figures, where he could share his interests in music, and where his closeness to his family, and dependence upon them, were visible. Still full of plans for the college, and with seven months to go before retiring from office, he died suddenly of a heart attack in the John Radcliffe Hospital, Oxford, on 16 February 1987 and was buried at Wolvercote cemetery in Oxford.

PAUL SLACK, *rev.*

Sources *The Times* (18 Feb 1987) · *WWW* · *Exeter College Association Register* (1987) · personal knowledge (1996) · private information (1996) [family]
Archives Bodl. Oxf., papers
Likenesses T. Rames, oils, 1986, Exeter College, Oxford
Wealth at death £233,653: probate, 8 June 1987, *CGPLA Eng. & Wales*

Hunt, Richard William (1908–1979), palaeographer, was born at Spondon, Derbyshire, on 11 April 1908, the second of three sons and one daughter born to Sydney Hunt, the local doctor, and his wife, Mabel Mary Whitely. From school at Haileybury College he went to read classics at Balliol College, Oxford, in 1927. Tutored by R. A. B. Mynors, he took a second class in honour moderations and a first class in Greats. Mynors encouraged Hunt's enthusiasm for the study of manuscripts, the transmission of texts, and medieval libraries, and Hunt, armed with a senior scholarship at Christ Church, went to Munich to work under the direction of Paul Lehmann. After a year he returned to Oxford and began research for a doctorate on Alexander Nequam (1157–1217) under F. M. Powicke. The thesis, which was not completed until 1936 and remained unpublished until after his death, was described by Beryl Smalley as 'a monument to the scholarship of the 1930s' (Smalley, viii) and became in the post-war years one of the most frequently consulted of any from an arts faculty deposited in the Bodleian.

In 1934 Hunt moved to Liverpool University as lecturer in palaeography and together with Mynors, N. R. Ker, C. R. Cheney, and J. R. Liddell undertook pioneering work on the availability of manuscripts, and thus knowledge, through libraries in the medieval period—work which appeared under Ker's editorship as *Medieval Libraries of Great Britain: a List of Surviving Books* in 1941. At the same time, together with Raymond Klibansky he initiated and edited *Medieval and Renaissance Studies* (*MARS*) which appeared spasmodically from 1941 to 1968.

Hunt remained at Liverpool throughout the Second World War and on 11 December 1939 he married Edith Irene Joyce Twamley, a 28-year-old Liverpool social worker. The marriage, which took place at Spondon, was, however, short-lived. Joyce Hunt, together with an unborn baby, died on 7 December 1940. On 14 February 1942 Hunt remarried. His wife was Katharine (Kit) Eva (*b.* 1913/14), a chartered masseuse, daughter of Harry Rowland of Parkgate, Cheshire, and three sons were born to them. It was a happy and hospitable marriage.

In September 1945 Hunt returned to Oxford as keeper of Western manuscripts at the Bodleian Library—a post he held together with a senior research fellowship at Balliol until retirement in September 1975. The attraction of the position for him was its function of 'helping and advising readers' (Southern, *PBA*, 67.390) and during his thirty-year tenure he made his wide and detailed knowledge of medieval manuscripts and scholars available personally to researchers in Duke Humfrey's Library while striving to make the Bodleian's manuscripts from all periods more easily accessible through catalogues. His own introductory volume to the *Summary Catalogue of Western Manuscripts in the Bodleian Library* is a masterly elucidation of the growth of the library's collections. He recruited a group of learned curatorial staff and together they expanded the Bodleian's manuscript holdings in all periods. The department also became one of the leading centres for the training of archivists to staff the growing number of county record offices in the 1950s and 1960s.

Though no great administrator, Hunt twice acted as Bodley's librarian during vacancies in that post, and if his published output diminished over the years his influence, measured by acknowledgements to him in the work of others, was immense. From 1948 to 1975 he was university lecturer in palaeography and the transmission of classical Latin texts, and he was Sandars reader in bibliography at Cambridge in 1959–60, lecturing on manuscripts of the Latin classics in England in the middle ages. A modest and kindly man, though one capable of a surprising fierceness

at a lack of intellectual precision, he was a devout Christian who inspired great loyalty in his staff. Except when on holiday on the Isle of Wight he was unhappy when away from the Bodleian; there his untidy desk, his expressive eyebrows, his succession of corduroy jackets, and his battered bicycle were famous. A charming description of his somewhat eccentric lecturing style appears in Peter Levi's *The Flutes of Autumn* (pp. 85–6).

Elected a fellow of the British Academy in 1961, Hunt also chaired the manuscripts sub-committee of the Standing Conference of National and University Libraries from 1957 until 1975, and under its auspices set in train N. R. Ker's *Medieval Manuscripts in British Libraries* and A. G. Watson's *Dated and Datable Manuscripts in the British Library*, and *Dated and Datable Manuscripts in Oxford Libraries*.

His wife died in December 1977 and Hunt on 13 November 1979 in Oxford. An excellent photograph of Hunt by J. W. Thomas forms the frontispiece to the *Festschrift* (1976) in his honour, and a somewhat more severe pencil drawing of him made by Joy Finzi in 1978 hangs in the Bodleian Library.   DAVID VAISEY

Sources R. W. Southern, 'Richard William Hunt, 1908–1979', *PBA*, 67 (1981), 371–97 · R. W. Southern, foreword, *Medieval learning and literature: essays presented to Richard William Hunt*, ed. J. J. G. Alexander and M. T. Gibson (1976) · B. Smalley, preface, in R. W. Hunt, *The schools and the cloister: the life and writings of Alexander Nequam*, rev. M. Gibson (1984) · R. W. Hunt, *The history of grammar in the middle ages: collected papers*, ed. G. L. Bursill-Hall (1980) [see also *Bodleian Library Record*, 11 (1982–5), 9–19] · *WWW, 1971–80* · E. Lemon, ed., *The Balliol College register, 1916–1967*, 4th edn (privately printed, Oxford, 1969) · J. Jones and S. Viney, eds., *The Balliol College register, 1930–1980*, 5th edn (privately printed, Oxford, 1983?) · P. Levi, *The flutes of autumn* (1983) · A. C. de la Mare and B. C. Barker-Benfield, eds., *Manuscripts at Oxford: an exhibition in memory of Richard William Hunt (1908–1979)* (1980) [exhibition catalogue, Bodl. Oxf.] · Bodl. Oxf., MSS R. W. Hunt · R. W. Hunt, personal file, archives, Bodl. Oxf. · m. certs. · d. cert. [E. I. J. Hunt] · d. cert. · personal knowledge (2004) **Archives** Bodl. Oxf., papers | Bodl. Oxf., N. R. Ker papers · Bodl. Oxf., corresp. with Graham Pollard **Likenesses** Oxford Mail, photograph, 1975 (with wife, Kit), repro. in De la Mare and Barker-Benfield, eds., *Manuscripts at Oxford* · J. W. Thomas, photograph, 1976, repro. in Southern, 'Richard William Hunt' · J. Finzi, pencil drawing, 1978, Bodl. Oxf. **Wealth at death** £121,827: probate, 9 July 1980, *CGPLA Eng. & Wales*

Hunt, Robert (1568/9–1608), Church of England clergyman and first minister at James Town, Virginia, was probably the Robert Hunt of Hampshire admitted to Magdalen College, Oxford, in 1589. He matriculated on 14 February 1589, aged twenty, and proceeded BA on 23 November 1592 and MA on 4 July 1595. He was married in Canterbury on 18 January 1597 to Elizabeth Edwards of St Margaret's parish. Collated to the vicarage of Reculver, Kent, on 18 January 1595, he resigned in 1602. Instituted to the vicarage of Heathfield in the diocese of Chichester on 5 October 1602, Hunt held that post until his death.

It remains unclear how Hunt or his early seventeenth-century colleagues were selected to serve ecclesiastical assignments in Virginia, as no prelate had been made responsible for supervising the overseas church. As Reculver was an archiepiscopal living and as several of Hunt's family continued to live in the community perhaps Archbishop Richard Bancroft had a hand in the appointment. According to Captain Edward-Maria Wingfield, the first president of the council of Virginia, it was at his own suggestion that Hunt was chosen for the assignment:

> For my firste worke (Wch was to make a right choice of a spirituall pastor) I appeale to the remembrance of my Lord of Canterbury his grace, who gave me very gracious audience in my request. And the world knoweth whome I took wth me; truly, in my opinion, a man not any waie to be touched wth the rebellious humors of a popish spirit, nor blemished wth the least suspicion of a factius Scismatick whereof I had spiall care.   (Wingfield, 102)

Captain John Smith, however, offers another view, saying that the position was offered to Richard Hakluyt, prebendary of Westminster, 'who by his authority sent master Robert Hunt, an honest, religious, and couragious Divine' (Arber, 2.958). On 21 November 1606 a patent was issued to Richard Hakluyt 'and to Robert Hunt clerk M. A. vicar of the parish church of Heathfield co. Suss. dioc. Chichester', granting them 'full and free license' to go to Virginia and, without giving up their parishes in England, to hold 'one or more benefices, church dignities, or cures in the said parts of Virginia. or America' (Parks, 256). It is quite likely that Hakluyt was consulted regarding the appointment.

The colonists sailed from Blackwall in the *Susan Constant* on 19 December 1606, and in the course of the passage Hunt became seriously ill. The ship arrived in Virginia on 27 April 1607, and a settlement was established and called James Town. Hunt conducted daily common prayer morning and evening, with sermons on Sundays, and every three months administered the holy communion. He probably celebrated the first known service of holy communion in what is today the United States of America on 21 June 1607. On that occasion an old sail provided shelter, but by Hunt's efforts a rude church was erected, which was burnt down, however, in the fire of January 1608, together with the greater part of the dwellings of the new colony. Hunt lost his library and all that he had except the clothes on his back. A new church was built in the spring of 1608, but Hunt did not long survive. The exact date of his death is uncertain, but it probably occurred between January and April 1608; he was buried in James Town.

On 20 November 1606, one month before the expedition sailed for Virginia, Hunt signed a will making bequests to his wife and to a son, Thomas, and a daughter, Elizabeth (Barbour, 60–62). The fact that in this will Hunt laid down that his wife was to be disinherited if she were to 'commit the act of incontinency', or even be suspected of it, and specifically should she consort with one John Taylor of Heathfield, suggests an unhappy state of affairs in the home, which may have been a factor in his deciding to go to America. Probate was granted in London on 14 July 1608.

JAMES B. BELL

Sources C. W. F. Smith, 'Chaplain Robert Hunt and his parish in Kent', *Historical Magazine of the Protestant Episcopal Church*, 26 (1957) · G. MacLaren Brydon, *Virginia's mother church and the political conditions under which it grew* (1947), vol. 1 · E.-M. Wingfield, 'A discourse of Virginia', *Archaeologia Americana: Transactions and Collections of the American Antiquarian Society*, 4 (1860) · *Virginia Magazine of History and Biography*, 25 (1917) · E. Arber, ed., *Travels and works of Capt. John Smith* (1910) · G. B. Parks, *Richard Hakluyt and the English voyages* (New York, 1928) · P. L. Barbour, ed., *The Jamestown voyages under the first charter, 1606–1609*, 2 vols., Hakluyt Society, 2nd ser., 136–7 (1969)

Wealth at death £50–£100: will, Barbour, *Jamestown voyages*

Hunt, Robert (1807–1887), chemist and photographer, was born at Plymouth Dock (Devonport) on 6 September 1807, the posthumous only child of Robert Hunt (*bap.* 1781, *d.* 1807), carpenter on the *Moucheron*, and his wife, Honour Thomas (1781–1842). Left to support herself and her infant son on a small naval pension, Hunt's mother remained at Devonport until 1816, then moved to Penzance where she had relatives. At school at Plymouth and then at one run by a Wesleyan minister at Penzance, Hunt early showed a love of poetry and literature, an enquiring mind, determination, and ambition.

When he was twelve Hunt was placed with a surgeon at Paddington but harsh treatment led to his leaving after eighteen months. After some months of unemployment and a brief spell as a wharfinger's clerk he obtained a position which enabled him to continue to learn dispensing. The firm closed suddenly but, through the influence of the Quaker philanthropists Elizabeth Fry (1780–1845) and William Allen (1770–1843), Hunt became manager of a West End dispensary. A fall into the icy Thames in January 1827 (when attempting to find a vantage point to see the funeral procession of the duke of York) caused a lengthy illness, but his grandfather's death provided him the means to keep himself while he convalesced, and in 1829 he spent ten months in Cornwall, visiting each relic of Old Cornwall and gathering up tales of its ancient people. He also obtained subscriptions, many from the Cornish gentry, to enable him to publish *The Mounts Bay*, a descriptive poem in three books, but it failed to find favour with the public.

After another short stay in London, Hunt returned to Penzance where, in 1831, his mother had married Stephen Weaver and his uncle had married Ann Davy. (She was a niece of Edmund Davy who for some years was assistant to his cousin Sir Humphry Davy at the Royal Institution, and this connection with the Davy family provided Hunt with information used later in writing the *Dictionary of National Biography* articles on Sir Humphry Davy and others.) In Penzance, Hunt set up in business with his uncle James Thomas as a chemist and druggist, entered actively into the life of the town and played a prominent role in the Penzance Literary and Scientific Society. On 16 March 1834 he married Harriet Swanson (1808–1896) and their first child, Robert, was born on Christmas day. Family disputes caused the business to fail, and Hunt returned to work in London, where he tried his hand at writing plays, but without success. He rejoined his wife at Devonport, where she was living with her father, after the birth of their second son, Charles (*b.* 1837). He opened a druggist's shop, advertised his services as an analyst, and began some research, publishing the first of many papers in the *Philosophical Magazine* in January 1838. Later he contributed articles to the *Art Journal*, *The Athenaeum*, *British Association Reports*, *Chemist*, *Pharmaceutical Times*, and the *Photographic*

1884); a fourth daughter, Elizabeth (1846–1921), was born in London, completing the family.

In 1845 Hunt was appointed keeper of the mining record office, part of the geological survey under Henry De la Beche, his duties being to keep the documents in order and to conduct correspondence with survey officers. He began the compilation of statistics on mineral production—the first being published in volume one of the *Memoirs of the Geological Survey of Great Britain and of the Museum of Economic Geology* in 1846 as a notice of the copper and tin raised in Cornwall. In 1848 he published *The Poetry of Science*. Conceived as an attempt to popularize science it was well received by the public. *Panthea, the Spirit of Nature* (1849) was a poetical romance of little merit. He produced an elementary physics textbook in 1851 and also handbooks for the Great Exhibition.

When, in 1851, the School of Mines was opened Hunt, while remaining keeper of the survey's museum and record office, was appointed professor of mechanical science. From 1854, following recognition of the importance of the office, he devoted his whole time to it. In that year he was also elected a fellow of the Royal Society. From 1855 Hunt's mineral statistics were a separate publication and in that year he was elected a fellow of the Royal Statistical Society. Hunt's role in the preparation of the statistics was recognized by a testimonial from the mining industry in 1860. The volumes of statistics and collection of mine plans stand as a lasting memorial of his labours.

Some years earlier, Hunt had become interested in the education of working miners. In 1841 he gave lectures on chemistry in a short-lived evening school supported by the president of the Royal Cornwall Polytechnic Society and his sister. In 1853 he had been associated with an attempt to establish a school of mines at Truro and after it closed proposed the formation of a miners' association of Cornwall and Devonshire to provide local classes for working miners. It was established in 1859 and had considerable success, Hunt retaining a keen interest in it until his death. It indirectly inspired the establishment of Camborne School of Mines (later part of Exeter University and home of the Robert Hunt memorial collection of geological specimens). From 1860 Hunt edited *Ures Dictionary of Arts, Manufactures and Mines*, considerably increasing its size. In 1865 he published *Popular Romances of the West of England*, an immediate success which passed through numerous editions; based on the stories he had collected in 1829 with additional material supplied to him by William Bottrell and others, it remains an invaluable record of the folklore of early nineteenth-century Cornwall. Indeed, Hunt noted that some stories he had collected in 1829 were already forgotten locally.

Hunt retired in 1883 and in the following year brought together the fruits of his long connection with the mining industry in *British Mining*. A monumental work of 944 pages, it gives an authoritative picture of the industry. Hunt died on 17 October 1887 at 26 St Leonards Terrace, Chelsea, London.   ALAN PEARSON

Robert Hunt (1807–1887), by Ernest Edwards, pubd 1864

Journal. Following the announcement of the discovery of photographic processes, Hunt concentrated on research in this field and opened a correspondence with Sir John Herschel, who encouraged him and submitted a paper by Hunt which was published in the *Philosophical Transactions* of the Royal Society in 1840. In the following year Hunt published *A Popular Treatise on the Art of Photography*, a comprehensive record of all the important contributions to photography from 1839 and incorporating much of his own research. It was an immediate success and in 1851 was revised and enlarged to form volume sixteen of the *Encyclopaedia Metropolitana*. Another of Hunt's works, *Researches on Light* (1844), surveyed in detail the early history of light and photochemistry.

Hunt was a founder member of the Calotype Club (1847) and of the Photographic Society of Great Britain (1853); he was elected a vice-president of the latter in 1854 and in 1873 he and Fox Talbot became its first honorary members. Late in 1840 he became secretary of the Royal Cornwall Polytechnic Society at Falmouth, a position which gave time for research and brought him into contact with leading scientific figures (as did his active participation in British Association meetings from 1841, when he was secretary of a section and presented the results of some of his research). Hunt's work received official recognition in 1844 when his son Robert was granted a place at Christ's Hospital by patronage of the prince of Wales.

During the 1840s Hunt's family continued to grow: three daughters were born at Falmouth, Charlotte Fisher (1841–1932), Harriet (1842–1926), and Emma Jane (1844–

Sources A. Pearson, *Robert Hunt* (1976) · R. Hunt, *A popular treatise on the art of photography* (1841); facs. edn with introduction and notes by J. Y. Tong (1973) · Boase & Courtney, *Bibl. Corn.* · G. C. Boase, *Collectanea Cornubiensia: a collection of biographical and topographical notes relating to the county of Cornwall* (1890) · parish register (baptism), 2 Aug 1809 and 24 Jan 1781, Stoke Damerel, Devon [also father] · parish register (baptism), 13 July 1781, St Levan, Cornwall [mother] · d. cert. · R. Hunt, correspondence with J. F. W. Herschel, RS, HS10.80; HS10.124

Archives NHM, papers, on various men of eminence · Sci. Mus. · Sci. Mus., Lacock Abbey collection | Elgin Museum, Elgin, letters to George Gordon · ICL, letters to Sir Andrew Ramsay · International Museum of Photography, New York, Herschel corresp. · RS, corresp. with Sir J. F. W. Herschel

Likenesses E. Edwards, photograph, NPG; repro. in L. Reeve, ed., *Portraits of eminence*, 2 (1864) [*see illus.*] · photograph, repro. in T. G. Chambers, *Register of the associates and old students of the Royal College of Chemistry, the Royal School of Mines and the Royal College of Chemistry, etc.* (1896)

Wealth at death £1605 8s. 8d.: probate, 29 Nov 1887, *CGPLA Eng. & Wales*

Hunt, Roger (d. **1455/6**), lawyer and speaker of the House of Commons, was of obscure origins. His first interests were probably in Huntingdonshire, where he acquired the manor of Molesworth and became member of parliament in 1407 and 1413 (the first two of fifteen occasions between then and 1433). His interests in Bedfordshire, which he represented on three occasions (November 1414, March 1416, and 1420) when not sitting for Huntingdonshire, perhaps came later. By 1436 his landed income was some £68—insufficient for him to regard the post of sheriff of Cambridgeshire and Huntingdonshire (1433–5) as anything but a burden he sought to resign. About 1402 he leased a London house, perhaps while training at Lincoln's Inn, and he became royal attorney for the common pleas, from 17 August 1408 to 18 February 1410, under the patronage of his Huntingdonshire neighbour Sir John Tiptoft (d. 1443), the treasurer (for whom he acted extensively), before the rise of Prince Henry displaced them both.

Between 1413 and 1433 Hunt was elected to every parliament except one (December 1421), and was appointed speaker in 1420 and again in 1433. In 1420, uniquely in the period, a poll was required to prefer his candidacy over that of John Russell. From about 1415 he was 'of counseill' to John (V) Mowbray, earl marshal and later duke of Norfolk (d. 1432), whose claim to precedence over Richard Beauchamp, earl of Warwick (d. 1439), he helped to uphold in the parliament of 1425. In political life he was closer to Henry Beaufort, bishop of Winchester (d. 1447), than to Humphrey, duke of Gloucester (d. 1447), but more than either he favoured John, duke of Bedford (d. 1435), to whom in 1426 Hunt led a deputation of the Commons urging his mediation, and whose beneficial influence he extolled as speaker in 1433. Following his parliamentary career Hunt was second baron of the exchequer (3 November 1439), and died about 1455. With his wife Margery, whose surname was probably Bullock and whom he had married before 1419, he had a son, Roger, who succeeded to his father's estates in July 1456. JULIAN LOCK

Sources C. Rawcliffe, 'Roger Hunt', HoP, *Commons, 1386–1421* · J. S. Roskell, *The Commons and their speakers in English parliaments, 1376–1523* (1965) · J. S. Roskell, *The Commons in the parliament of 1422*

[1954] · *CPR, 1405–52* · G. L. Harriss, *Cardinal Beaufort: a study of Lancastrian ascendancy and decline* (1988) · R. E. Archer, 'Parliamentary restoration: John Mowbray and the dukedom of Norfolk in 1425', *Rulers and ruled in late medieval England: essays presented to Gerald Harriss*, ed. R. E. Archer and S. Walker (1995), 99–116

Wealth at death landed income at least £68 in 1436: Rawcliffe, 'Hunt, Roger'

Hunt, Thomas (1611–1683), schoolmaster, was born in Worcester, the son of Henry Hunt. He entered Wadham College, Oxford, subscribing to the Thirty-Nine Articles, on 29 January 1630; there is no record of his matriculation. He graduated BA from Wadham on 4 December 1632, proceeding MA from Pembroke College on 8 July 1636.

After teaching in a private school in Salisbury, Hunt moved to London, where by 1661 he was master of the church school at St Dunstan-in-the-East. His *Libellus orthographicus, or, The Diligent School-Boy's Directory* (1661; reprinted 1968), a work on spelling and punctuation, was written in the form of a dialogue. Hunt's own prefatory remarks and the dedicatory verses of his former pupils portray a gentle and dedicated teacher who had been much distressed by the turmoil of the English civil wars and interregnum.

By 1671 Hunt was master of the free school of St Saviour's, Southwark. Anthony Wood remarked that he 'did much good among the youth there, as elsewhere he hath done' (Wood, *Ath. Oxon.*, 4.81). Also in 1671 his *Abecedarium scholasticum, or, The Grammar-Scholar's Abecedary* appeared, with a second edition in 1681. He died in Southwark on 23 January 1683 and was buried in St Saviour's Church.

FRANCES HENDERSON

Sources J. Chambers, *Biographical illustrations of Worcestershire* (1820), 587 · Foster, *Alum. Oxon.* · matriculation register, 1645–8, Oxf. UA, SP 2 · subscription register, Oxf. UA, SP 39 · register of congregation, 1630–34, Oxf. UA, NEP/supra/RegO · register of congregation, 1634–47, Oxf. UA, NEP/supra/RegQ · Wood, *Ath. Oxon.*, new edn, 4.81 · R. C. Alston, *A bibliography of the English language from the invention of printing to the year 1800*, 4: *Spelling books* (1967); repr. with corrections (1974), 12 · E. Arber, ed., *The term catalogues, 1668–1709*, 3 vols. (privately printed, London, 1903–6), vol. 1, pp. 58, 445 · Wing, STC

Hunt, Thomas (1626/7–1688), lawyer and whig polemicist, was born in Austin Friars, London, the son of Richard Hunt, citizen and mercer of London, and his wife, Mary Gascoyne, daughter of William Gascoyne of Cleveland, Yorkshire. He was admitted a pensioner at Queens' College, Cambridge, on 2 November 1645, graduating BA in 1650 and proceeding MA in 1653. On 8 July 1650 he translated to Peterhouse, where he became Ramsey fellow. Hunt was admitted to Gray's Inn in November 1650 and he was called to the bar in 1658. He was appointed clerk to the Oxford assize circuit in 1659. He was ejected from that office upon the Restoration and from 1660 to 1683 he practised law in Banbury and was a steward to the duke of Buckingham and to the duke of Norfolk.

In 1679, in his *The Honours of the Lords Spiritual Asserted*, Hunt entered the debate in the press over the jurisdiction of the bishops in parliament, asserting their right to judge capital cases, a position challenged by the enemies of the earl of Danby, who wished to remove the episcopal block vote in Danby's impeachment for treason. The following year he served as a member of the counsel for the Catholic Lord Stafford, who was impeached for treason by the House of Commons, and he followed his first defence of the bishops with another entitled *The Rights of the Bishops to Judge in Capital Cases in Parliament Cleared*. Yet for all his support of the bishops, Hunt was clearly active in whig circles in the early 1680s. In March 1681 he was a witness at the Fitzharris impeachment trial, where he described a meeting at a whig tavern with Sir William Waller. He was also a frequent visitor of the notorious Titus Oates and a friend of the whig antiquarian William Petyt. In 1680 he published a powerful pamphlet in support of the Exclusion Bill, designed to bar the Catholic James, duke of York, from the throne, entitled *Great and Weighty Considerations Relating to the Duke of York*.

Hunt not only threw his legal acumen behind the whig bid for exclusion, he also proved himself a hardened enemy of the lower clergy when, in 1682, he attached his most famous contribution to whig ideology, *Postscript for Rectifying some Mistakes in some of the Inferior Clergy, Mischievous to our Government and Religion*, to another defence of the bishops, *An Argument for the Bishops' Right in Judging in Capital Causes in Parliament*. Hunt's *Postscript* attacked parish divines for using the pulpit to propagate royalist tenets, particularly the divine right of kings and passive obedience. The *Postscript* made Hunt a hero among whigs and earned him the epithet Postscript Hunt. Royalists such as the tory divine Edward Pelling were astonished to learn that Postscript Hunt and the Thomas Hunt of Gray's Inn, who had so strongly supported the bishops' rights, were one and the same. 'But of all men living,' wrote Pelling in his *The Apostate Protestant* (1682),

> I wonder at Mr. Hunt, a person whose name I cannot mention without due respect because of his *Argument for the Bishops Rights etc* where he hath shewed a great deal of good learning in the laws, and hath exprest his just zeal for the Church. (p. 21)

The 'anti-monarchical and seditious' (p. 40) nature of the *Postscript*, as Pelling described it, alarmed other royalists as well. Roger L'Estrange vehemently attacked Hunt in his weekly *Observator* and charged that Hunt had only converted from a champion of the Anglican clergy to an exclusionist as the result of thwarted ambition, claiming that Charles II had nominated Hunt for the position of lord chief baron of the exchequer in Ireland in 1681 but that the duke of York had prevented his candidacy. The *Postscript*, L'Estrange asserted, was Hunt's revenge. Considering, however, that Hunt had published his first pro-exclusion tract in 1680 and was already infamous in the whig community by 1681, the story seems unlikely.

In 1683 Hunt earned further notoriety when he published an impassioned diatribe in support of London's city charter (the surrender of which was demanded by the crown), *A Defence of the Charter and Municipal Rights of the City of London*. A long digression is devoted to an attack upon Dryden's play *The Duke of Guise*. Dryden replied in an elaborate vindication in which he concluded that Hunt was 'crack'd and if he should return to England … his only

prison might be bedlam' (p. 39). Indeed, Hunt had left England, absconding to Holland in January 1683. In April a warrant was issued for Hunt's arrest for seditious libel for his *Defence of the Charter* and his house was searched. A second warrant was issued in August for the *Postscript* and his house was searched again. In Holland Hunt took the alias Mr Briggs, and he associated with whig and dissenter refugees. He reportedly returned to England incognito in 1686 to discover if James II's general pardon for participants in Monmouth's failed rebellion was applicable to rebels hiding in Holland. Hunt later visited Germany with Slingsby Bethel. He died in Utrecht in 1688, aged sixty-one, only a few weeks short of the prince of Orange's invasion.

Hunt was a sophisticated polemicist whose two pro-exclusion tracts, *Great and Weighty Considerations* and *Postscript*, sought to undermine the basic pillars of royalist ideology in the 1680s: the divine appointment of kings, an unalterable hereditary succession, and the obligation of subjects to passively obey their sovereigns. He also challenged the ideas of Sir Robert Filmer, whose book *Patriarcha* was published for the first time in 1680. Whereas Filmer had used scripture to support his justification of absolute monarchy, Hunt built his contractual theory of government on the simple notion that 'men make governments' (Hunt, *Great and Weighty Considerations*, 8). 'God', wrote Hunt, 'hath made government necessary in the general order of things, but the specification thereof is from men.' Hunt further asserted that 'the succession to the crown is the people's right'. 'It belongs to the people to make a new king, under what limitations they please, or to make none; for the polity is not destroyed if there is no king created' (Hunt, *Postscript*, 38, 43). Hunt also promoted the people's right of resistance to unlawful magistrates. In his final published work, *An Apology for the English Government* (1686), Hunt warned other whig polemicists against adopting historical arguments to support their cause. Hunt, like John Locke, believed that human reason alone was enough to discern the nature of government.

MELINDA ZOOK

Sources Wood, *Ath. Oxon.*, new edn, 2.72–3 · T. Hunt, *The honours of the lords spiritual asserted* (1679) · T. Hunt, *Great and weighty considerations relating to the duke of York* (1680) · T. Hunt, *An argument for the bishops' right in judging in capital cases in parliament … to which is added a postscript* (1682) · T. Hunt, *A defence of the charter* (1683) · T. Hunt, *An apology for the English government* (1686) · E. Pelling, *The apostate protestant* (1682) · J. Dryden, *A vindication* (1683) · T. Hunt, *The rights of the bishops to judge in capital cases in parliament cleared* (1680) · CSP dom., 1680–81, 627; 1683, 240–42; 1683, 17; 1683–4, 217 · BL, Add. MS 41817, fol. 165 · BL, Add. MS 41818, fol. 17 · BL, Add. MS 41804, fol. 158 · BL, Add. MS 41819, fol. 272 · BL, Add. MS 41820, fol. 87 · BL, Add. MS 23619 · N. Luttrell, *A brief historical relation of state affairs from September 1678 to April 1714*, 1 (1857), 247 · J. Foster, *The register of admissions to Gray's Inn, 1521–1889, together with the register of marriages in Gray's Inn chapel, 1695–1754* (privately printed, London, 1889), 255 · *State trials*, 8.364–5 · Venn, *Alum. Cant.* · T. A. Walker, ed., *Admissions to Peterhouse or St Peter's College in the University of Cambridge* (1912), 96 · DNB
Archives BL, 'The character of popery', a handwritten folio, Add. MS 23619

Hunt, Thomas (1696–1774), orientalist, was born on 18 September 1696 at Horsington in the county of Somerset, the son of Thomas Hunt. His mother's name is unknown. He was educated at the free school in Bruton, and then privately by the rector of Yeovilton. He matriculated at Christ Church, Oxford, on 24 May 1715, where he took the degree of BA on 6 February 1718. On 13 March 1718, at the invitation of Richard Newton, he became a tutor at Hart Hall, from where he proceeded MA on 26 October 1721. He was ordained deacon by the bishop of Oxford on 10 April 1720, and priest by George Hooper, bishop of Bath and Wells, on 18 February 1721. He was inducted as rector of Chelwood, Somerset, on 19 February 1721, and on 12 January 1726 was appointed prebend of White Lackington, which post he held until his death. In 1728 he became chaplain to Thomas Parker, earl of Macclesfield, and tutor to his grandsons. He was installed as rector of Bix Gibwin and Bix Brand, Oxfordshire, on 24 October 1729 and as rector of Shirburn on 30 December 1731. He graduated BD at Hertford College on 15 March 1743 and DD on 8 May 1744. In 1738 he was elected Laudian professor of Arabic at the University of Oxford and in 1740 was appointed to the lord almoner's professorship in Arabic. On 30 July 1747 he became regius professor of Hebrew and a canon of the sixth stall in Christ Church Cathedral. He gave his inaugural lecture on 23 February 1748. On moving to Christ Church he resigned the lord almoner's professorship and his rectorship at Shirburn. He held both the Laudian and the regius professorships until his death. He was elected a fellow of the Royal Society in 1740 and a fellow of the Society of Antiquaries in 1757. If Hearne's report is correct Hunt married Sarah Adkins, his laundress, after she had given birth to his child in the summer of 1727. His marriage on 8 October 1743 to Hannah Hatrell of Newcastle under Lyme, Staffordshire, is securely documented. His will mentions no children from either marriage. Hunt, who for many years suffered from gravel, died at Oxford on 31 October 1774, aged seventy-eight. He was buried in Christ Church Cathedral, where he has a simple memorial stone.

Hunt's chief publications were *De antiquitate, elegantia, utilitate, linguae Arabicae, oratio* (1739) (a defence of the teaching and study of Arabic), the text of his inaugural lecture as Laudian professor, delivered on 7 August 1738; *De usu dialectorum orientalium, ac praecipue Arabicae, in Hebraico codice interpretando, oratio* ('On the use of Arabic, in particular, in elucidating the Hebrew text of the Bible') (1748); and *A Dissertation on Proverbs Vii. 22,23* (1743). In addition he published *A Fragment of Hippolytus*, printed in Parker's *Bibliotheca biblica*, vol. 4 (1728), and a Latin translation of al-Razi's treatise on smallpox and measles, included in Richard Mead's work on the same topic *De variolis et morbillis liber* (1747). In 1746 Hunt issued *Proposals for Printing by Subscription, 'Abdollatiphi historiae Aegypti compendium'*, the description of Egypt by ʿAbd al-Latif al-Baghdadi, which was to contain a full edition of the Arabic text, together with a Latin translation. The work remained unpublished at the time of Hunt's death and subscribers were compensated with the posthumous *Observations on Several Passages in the Book of Proverbs* (1775), which was edited from Hunt's

papers by Benjamin Kennicott, a friend and former student. A Latin grammar which Hunt compiled for the use of Lord Macclesfield's grandsons was printed, in a limited edition, in London about 1730. Hunt published, in an edition of 100 copies, George Hooper's *De benedictione patriarchae Jacobii Genes. xlix. conjecturae* ('Conjectures on Genesis 49') (1728), adding his own footnotes in accordance with Hooper's wishes. He subsequently published Hooper's complete *Works* (1757; reprinted 1855). Hunt assisted in the publication of works by John Gagnier (1713) and Leonard Twells (1740), and collaborated with George Costard in producing a second edition of Thomas Hyde's *Veterum Persarum et Parthorum et Medorum religionis historia* (1760), on the religion of the ancient Persians. His collaboration with Gregory Sharpe on an edition of Hyde's *Dissertations* (1767) led to a rift in their friendship. Among notable visitors to his rooms at Christ Church was the French scholar Anquetil Duperron, who went to Oxford in January 1762. In his *Zend-Avesta* (1771) Duperron wrongly accused Hunt of claiming a knowledge of the language of the Avesta, a charge that was answered by William Jones.

Hunt, an amiable and learned man, was held in high regard during his lifetime. Generous with criticism and advice, he was instrumental in persuading the university press to print Kennicott's variorum edition of the Hebrew Bible, *Vetus Testamentum Hebraicum* (1776–80), and John Channing's *Albucasis de chirurgia* (1778), comprising an edition of the Arabic text, with Latin translation, of the section on surgery in Abu'l-Qasim al-Zahrawi's general work on medicine. His conspicuous failure to produce a major work of scholarship has been ascribed to a lack of self-confidence. He was an Anglican divine and biblical scholar very much in the mould of his seventeenth-century predecessors at Oxford. As an orientalist his importance lies not so much in the value of his own modest output as in his encouragement of fellow scholars, notably Benjamin Kennicott, John Channing, and, later, William Jones. Hunt's oriental manuscripts are preserved in the Bodleian Library, as are a number of his letters to Richard Rawlinson and Gregory Sharpe. Letters to Philip Doddridge and William Jones have been published (1790 and 1804). His private papers are lost. Hunt's library of printed books was sold at Oxford on 30 October 1775 by Daniel Prince. COLIN WAKEFIELD

Sources Bodl. Oxf., MS Rawl. J, fol. 3, 326–8 · Bodl. Oxf., MS Rawl. letters 96, fols. 38, 144, 288, 291 · Bodl. Oxf., MS Eng. lett. d. 145, fols. 16–17 · Foster, *Alum. Oxon.* · *Hist. U. Oxf.* 5: *18th-cent. Oxf.* · H. Carter, *A history of the Oxford University Press*, 1: *To the year 1780* (1975) · *Remarks and collections of Thomas Hearne*, ed. C. E. Doble and others, 9, OHS, 65 (1914), 376 · F. Madan, *A summary catalogue of Western manuscripts in the Bodleian Library at Oxford*, 3 (1895), 603; 5 (1905), 385, 909–11 · *GM*, 1st ser., 71 (1801), 101–3 · A. H. A. Duperron, *Zend-Avesta, ouvrage de Zoroastre*, 1 (1771) · [W. Jones], *Lettre à monsieur A*** du P*** (1771) · A. N. L. Munby and L. Coral, eds., *British book sale catalogues, 1676–1800: a union list* (1977) · PRO, PROB. 11/1002 · W. E. Daniel, *The parish register of Horsington* (1907) · parish register, Newcastle under Lyme, pt 2, 1939

Archives Bodl. Oxf., Oriental MSS

Hunt, Thomas Frederick (*bap.* 1790, *d.* 1831), architect, was baptized on 10 October 1790 at St Mary's Church,

Marylebone, Middlesex, the son of Thomas Hunt and his wife, Mary. Details of his early life and professional training are unclear but in 1813 he was appointed one of the 'labourers in trust' attached to the board of works at St James's Palace. He remained in the royal service for the rest of his life, attaining, in 1829, the position of clerk of works at Kensington Palace. In addition to his official duties he entered and won, in 1815, a competition to design the mausoleum 'over the remains of Burns, the Scottish poet' in St Michael's churchyard in Dumfries (Graves, *RA exhibitors*, 4.198). The design for this handsome domed edifice was exhibited at the Royal Academy in 1816 and three working drawings survive in Dumfries Museum. When funds proved insufficient, a subscription was raised by Hunt's 'intimate friend' the journalist William Jerdan, and the architect himself 'would not accept of any reward for all his work … to render the work complete' (Jerdan, 2.121, 261). The Burns mausoleum, now roofless, once contained a monument to the poet by Peter Turnerelli. It was fully finished in September 1819 and remains Hunt's most important work. He was also responsible for the design of the old Episcopal (now Wesleyan) church in Buccleuch Street, Dumfries, with an impressive villa-like Ionic portico (1817; now derelict). His design for a 'house at Chiswick' was exhibited at the Royal Academy in 1824 and the following year he submitted a design for 'cottages, etc., in Hertfordshire'—neither of which, if built, can now be identified (Graves, *RA exhibitors*, 4.198). According to Jerdan, one of Hunt's best works was the recasting of Bifrons, near Patrixbourne in Kent, for the dowager Marchioness Conyngham, work which took place c.1825 (dem. 1948, although estate buildings survive).

In 1825 Hunt published a pattern book of fanciful estate buildings in the 'Olde English' style entitled *Half-a-dozen hints on picturesque domestic architecture in a series of designs for gate lodges, gamekeeper's cottages, and other rural residences* (2nd edn, 1826; 3rd edn, 1833; repr. 1841), illustrated with lithographs by the author. In the introductory 'Address' to the book Hunt refers to one of his lodge designs having been built at Bromley Hill in Kent, the seat of Lord Farnborough (formerly Sir Charles Long), 'under the immediate superintendance of Lady Long'. His second publication, another illustrated work promoting the picturesque Tudor style entitled *Designs for parsonage-houses, alms houses, etc. etc. with examples of gables and other curious remains of old English architecture* (1827), is dedicated to Lord Farnborough. Hunt exhibited three works in the Royal Academy in 1828; a house 'in the old English domestic style' to be erected at Sydney, New South Wales, Australia, 'for one of the principal government officers'; a design for Danehurst, near Danehill, Surrey, for someone called Davies; and 'Redrice, Hants, the seat of the Rt. Hon. William Noel Hill', afterwards third Baron Berwick (rebuilt 1844; Graves, *RA exhibitors*, 4.198). His design for Danehurst was illustrated in the expanded third edition of *Hints*. Hunt's third foray into print, a volume called *Architettura campestre, displayed in lodges, gardener's houses etc. in the modern or Italian style*, came out in the same year and was dedicated to his superior in the office of works Lieutenant-

Colonel Stephenson, the surveyor-general. In this work he eschewed his familiar picturesque idiom in favour of 'economic' designs, 'without carving or other embellishment' (*Architettura campestre*, 12), inspired by farm buildings in the Italian campagna. However, Hunt's most ambitious publication is undoubtedly *Exemplars of Tudor architecture adapted to modern habitations, with illustrative details, selected from ancient edifices; and observations on the furniture of the Tudor period* (1830; 2nd edn, 1841) which combines the function of an architectural pattern book with a learned commentary on Tudor architecture, furnishings, and customs, much of it being drawn from contemporary manuscript sources, which establishes Hunt as much as an antiquary as an architectural polemicist.

Hunt's private life remains shadowy but for anecdotes in Jerdan's *Autobiography* which describe him as extravagant and perpetually pursued by creditors, who walked abroad only on Sundays for fear of arrest and on one occasion was forced to take sanctuary in the gatehouse of St James's Palace so as to escape their attentions. Given his importunity, Hunt must have welcomed a chance encounter on the continent with J. M. W. Turner, who, despite his reputation for parsimony, took 'a fancy to so excellent a boon companion, invited him to travel together and treated him in a princely style, without costing him a shilling through the whole of their tour' (Jerdan, 2.261).

Thomas Hunt died at Kensington Palace, where he was living, on 4 January 1831 but no will can be traced. His obituary in the *Gentleman's Magazine* describes him as an 'ingenious architect' (*GM*, 1st ser., 101/1, 1831, 376) and gives his age as forty.   TIM KNOX

Sources review of *Designs for parsonage-houses*, *GM*, 1st ser., 97/1 (1827), 605–6 · review of *Exemplars*, *GM*, 1st ser., 100/1 (1830), 33–6 · *GM*, 1st ser., 101/1 (1831), 376 · Graves, *RA exhibitors*, 4 (1906), 198 · [W. Papworth], ed., *The dictionary of architecture*, 11 vols. (1853–92) · Colvin, *Archs.*, 520–1 · W. Jerdan, *The autobiography of William Jerdan: with his literary, political, and social reminiscences and correspondence during the last fifty years*, 4 vols. (1852–3), vol. 2, pp. 110–23, 261; vol. 4, pp. 52–5 · P. Gray, *Dumfriesshire illustrated* (1894), 70 · W. MacDowall, *Memorials of St Michael's churchyard, Dumfries* (1876), 103 · cutting from *Literary Chronicle* [1828?] in copy of T. F. Hunt, *Archittura campestre* (1828), RIBA BAL · *Dumfries and Galloway*, Pevsner (1996), 241 · *IGI*

Archives Dumfries Museum, working drawings for Burns mausoleum

Hunt, Thomas Perkins Lowman (1802–1851), speech therapist, was born at Whitchurch, Dorset, and is said to have been educated at Winchester College. He was admitted as a pensioner, aged twenty, at Trinity College, Cambridge, on 7 June 1822, with the intention of becoming a minister of the Church of England. However, the affliction of a fellow collegian who suffered from stammering is said to have captured his attention, and he left Cambridge without taking a degree in order to devote himself to the study and cure of defective speech.

Hunt found that the lips, the tongue, the jaws, and the breath were in different cases the causes of the problems. Believing in his ability to cure stammering, he sought wider experience in a provincial tour, and finally in 1827 settled in Regent Street, London. He relied on simple common-sense directions. Each case was studied separately. Sometimes slow and sometimes rapid articulation was recommended to his patients; some were taught to place their tongues in particular positions, and others practised improved means of breathing. Hunt held that not one case in fifty was the consequence of deformity, and objected to surgical operations. He was patronized from 1828 by Sir John Forbes MD FRS, who sent him pupils for twenty-four years. When George Pearson, the chief witness in the case respecting the attempt on the life of Queen Victoria made by John Francis on 30 May 1842, was brought into court he was incapable of giving his evidence, but after a fortnight's instruction from Hunt he spoke easily, a fact certified by the sitting magistrate. *The Lancet* of 16 May 1846 made a severe attack on Hunt as an unlicensed practitioner. Hunt ably replied in the *Literary Gazette* of 30 May.

Hunt's leisure was spent in Dorset, where he cultivated land and undertook agricultural improvements and experiments. In 1849 his numerous pupils, in commemoration of his twenty-two years' service, subscribed for his bust in marble, which was modelled by Joseph Durham and exhibited in the Royal Academy. He died at Godingston, near Swanage, Dorset, on 18 August 1851, leaving his practice to his son James *Hunt. He was survived by his wife, Mary, who died on 25 January 1855, aged forty-nine.

G. C. BOASE, rev. ROGER HUTCHINS

Sources Venn, *Alum. Cant.* · J. Hunt, *A treatise on the cure of stammering, etc., with a memoir of the late T. Hunt* (1854) · *ILN* (23 Aug 1851), 238 · C. Kingsley, *Fraser's Magazine*, 60 (1859), 1–14
Likenesses J. Durham, marble bust · portrait, repro. in *ILN*

Hunt, Thornton Leigh (1810–1873), journalist, was born on 10 September 1810, the first of the seven children of (James Henry) Leigh *Hunt (1784–1859), Romantic poet and essayist, and his wife, Marianne (d. 1857), the daughter of Thomas and Ann Kent. The family lived in Hampstead.

In February 1813 Leigh Hunt was imprisoned in Surrey gaol on the charge of seditious libel against the prince regent. His wife and two sons, Thornton and John, resided with him until Thornton became so ill that Marianne Hunt departed with her children for a seaside vacation in Brighton. In his autobiography Leigh Hunt recalls that Thornton was his constant companion during his imprisonment. The occasion inspired Charles Lamb's poem 'To T. L. H.—a Child'.

In 1822 the financially unstable elder Hunt took his wife and seven children to Italy at the invitation of Percy Bysshe Shelley. Hunt was to edit *The Liberal*, an organ for publications by Shelley and Byron, but Shelley's death later that year left the Hunts without adequate financial support. Not until 1825 was their return to England made possible by an advance from a London publisher.

Thornton Hunt aspired to become a painter, but suffered allergic reactions to the pigments he was using. Though he continued to produce pencil sketches and designed eight woodcuts to illustrate his father's poem 'Captain Sword and Captain Pen', he turned to writing as a vocation. His most significant contribution to *belles-lettres* was his editorship of his father's autobiography (1859),

poetry (1860), and correspondence (1862). He preserved strong financial and emotional ties to his father, with whom he continued to reside after his marriage in 1834 to Katharine Gliddon.

In addition to editing his father's works, Thornton Hunt was known to his contemporaries for his journalism. From September 1836 until 1 July 1837 he served as subeditor of *The Constitutional*, a vehicle for the promotion of radical ideas, such as extension of the suffrage and vote by ballot. In 1838 he went north to edit first the *Cheshire Reformer* and then the *Glasgow Argus*.

In 1840 Hunt returned to London. For the next twenty years he was associated with newspapers such as *The Spectator*, a weekly edited by progressive radical Stephen Rintoul; *The Globe*; *The Atlas*; the *Morning Chronicle*; and *The Leader*, a weekly which he founded with George Henry Lewes in 1850. Other periodicals to which he contributed include the *Monthly Repository*, *The Atlantic*, the *Illustrated Family Journal*, and *Cornhill Magazine*. His writings explore a variety of topics, such as Shelley, Leigh Hunt, the transportation system, coats of arms, and the Irish convict system. Hunt also published a fourteenth-century romance, *The Foster-Brother* (1845), probably inspired by his childhood years in Italy. He was a founding member of the Association for the Promotion of the Repeal of the Taxes on Knowledge, and in 1855 began an association with one of the major beneficiaries of this repeal, the *Daily Telegraph*. Though he became its editor, his chief involvement with the *Telegraph* was as a leader writer. His influence is displayed in the newspaper's strong support of Gladstone during the 1860s, which owed much to the contacts which developed between Hunt and Gladstone from 1860. They corresponded on a range of issues, including the paper duty repeal (1861), the ecclesiastical commissioners (1862), and annuities legislation (1865). They were in frequent, often daily, contact during the Reform Bill crisis, and during the Irish church resolutions and church rate debates (1868). Throughout his career Hunt advocated political freedom and social improvement and allied himself with groups such as the Chartists and the People's International League, organizations which fostered democratic social reform.

In the 1840s and 1850s Hunt participated in a communal living experiment known as the Phalanstery. Already the father of several children with his wife, he became the lover of Agnes Jervis Lewes (1822–1902), the wife of Hunt's collaborator on *The Leader*. In 1850 Hunt's first child with Agnes was born, but was registered as Edmund Alfred Lewes. In 1851 and 1853 Hunt had children with both Agnes and Kate. Altogether he fathered fourteen children, ten with Kate and four with Agnes.

Hunt died on 25 June 1873 at 41 Victoria Road, Kilburn, London, and was buried at Kensal Green in a grave beside his father's. His unpublished and unfinished works include a volume on the progress of society, an edition of William Maginn's writings, and a novel.

CARROLL VIERA

Sources M. Tatchell, 'Thornton Hunt', *Keats–Shelley Journal*, 20 (1969), 13–20 · E. Blunden, 'Leigh Hunt's eldest son', *Essays by Divers*

Hands, being the Transactions of the Royal Society of Literature of the United Kingdom, new ser., 19 (1942), 53–75 · A. Blainey, 'The wit in the dungeon: Leigh Hunt in Surrey gaol', *Books at Iowa*, 34 (April 1981), 9–14 · *The Athenaeum* (28 June 1873), 825 · E. Blunden, *Leigh Hunt and his circle* (1930) · E. Blunden, *Leigh Hunt: a biography* (1930) · G. J. Holyoake, *Sixty years of an agitator's life*, 2 vols. (1892) · W. J. Linton, *Memories* (1895) · H. R. Fox Bourne, *English newspapers: chapters in the history of journalism*, 2 vols. (1887) · A. Andrews, *The history of British journalism*, 2 vols. (1859); repr. (1968) · W. B. Thomas, *The story of The Spectator, 1828–1928* (1928) · G. S. Haight, *George Eliot: a biography* (1968) · D. Griffiths, ed., *The encyclopedia of the British press, 1422–1992* (1992) · H. C. G. Matthew, *Gladstone*, 2 vols. (1986–95); repr. in 1 vol. as *Gladstone, 1809–1898* (1997) · Gladstone, *Diaries* · *CGPLA Eng. & Wales* (1873) · Boase, *Mod. Eng. biog.* · d. cert.

Archives BL, corresp., Add. MS 47671 · Bodl. Oxf., corresp. · McGill University, Montreal, McLennan Library, papers relating to political economy | BL, letters to W. E. Gladstone, Add. MSS 44397–44425 · BL, letters to Sir A. H. Layard, Add. MSS 38991–38996, 39115–39116 · Co-operative Union, Holyoake House, Manchester, Co-operative Union archive, letters to George Holyoake · Keats House, Hampstead · University of Iowa, Iowa City, Brewer-Leigh Hunt collection · Yale U., George Henry Lewes collection

Likenesses W. M. Thackeray, group portrait, pencil, *c.*1844, NPG; repro. in Haight, *George Eliot* · S. Laurence, chalk drawing, AM Oxf.; repro. in Haight, *George Eliot*, 162a · portrait (with Kate Hunt), priv. coll.; repro. in Tatchell, 'Thornton Hunt', 16

Wealth at death under £1000: administration, 20 Sept 1873, *CGPLA Eng. & Wales*

Hunt, (Isabel) Violet (1862–1942), author and literary hostess, was born on 28 September 1862 at 29 Old Elvet, Durham, the eldest of the three daughters of Alfred William *Hunt (1830–1896), landscape watercolourist, and Margaret Raine *Hunt (1831–1912), novelist and translator. She was tutored at home and in 1877 graduated from Notting Hill and Ealing high school, one of London's first public day schools for girls, going on to study at the Kensington Art School (1877–9).

Violet Hunt had literary aspirations, a sharp tongue, and the magnetism to attract influential people. An early admirer was the young Oscar Wilde, who called her 'the sweetest Violet in England' (*Letters of Oscar Wilde*, 64). In her memoirs she asserted that she was 'as nearly as possible escaped the honour of being Mrs. Wilde' (Hunt, 168). In fact she really preferred older married men, including her first lover, George Henry Boughton, a Royal Academy artist, and Oswald John Frederick *Crawfurd (1834–1909), a diplomatist and publisher, from whom she contracted syphilis during their relationship (1890–1900). She seduced Somerset Maugham, and was in turn seduced by H. G. Wells; later she was known as the self-proclaimed wife of Ford Madox *Ford (1873–1939), then known as Hueffer. Her ten-year affair with the writer, eleven years her junior, was one of the saddest stories in literary history: it resulted in scandal, lawsuits, and tabloid headlines.

Violet Hunt wrote short stories, seventeen novels, a memoir of her Edwardian years, and a biography of Elizabeth *Siddal, wife of Dante Gabriel Rossetti. Novels such as *The Maiden's Progress* (1894) and *A Hard Woman* (1895) are typical examples of the 'new woman' genre, exploring various routes of resistance to the constraints placed on women by late nineteenth-century society. *The Human Interest* (1899), its heroine 'a great Ibsenite', frankly explores sexual problems, as does much of her fiction, including her later novel *White Rose of Weary Leaf* (1908), felt by many to be her best work, and the short-story collection *Tales of the Uneasy* (1911). Her autobiographical novels, *Their Lives* (1916), where Wilde appears as Philip Wynyard, and *Their Hearts* (1921) are of interest for their depictions of notable figures.

Violet Hunt's literary reputation stems, however, more from her Kensington salons at South Lodge, Campden Hill, where she entertained Rebecca West, Ezra Pound, Joseph Conrad, Wyndham Lewis, D. H. Lawrence, and Henry James; she founded the Women Writers' Suffrage League, and in 1921 she co-founded PEN with Mrs C. A. 'Sappho' Dawson, electing John Galsworthy as president. In 1908 she helped Ford to start the *English Review*, the literary magazine that discovered D. H. Lawrence, with the publication of 'The Odour of Chrysanthemums'. Lawrence said wryly of Hunt: 'I rather like her—she's such a real assassin' (*Collected Letters*, 98). Violet Hunt appears as the manipulative Florence in Ford's *The Good Soldier* and the termagant Sylvia in *Parade's End*. In *The Moon and Sixpence* Maugham used her as the original for Rose Waterford, a Pre-Raphaelite beauty who looked on life as an opportunity for writing novels. Her features inform the paintings of Edward Burne-Jones and Walter Sickert, for both of whom she modelled.

Violet Hunt died of pneumonia at South Lodge during the blitz at the age of seventy-nine on 16 January 1942, and was buried in the Brookwood cemetery. *The Times*'s obituary noted that, artistically, 'certain types—especially of disagreeable worldly women—she drew with extreme skill', and accurately concluded that, personally, 'kindness of heart and feeling for the troubles of others lay behind her often acid speeches' (*The Times*, 19 Jan 1942).

BARBARA BELFORD

Sources B. Belford, *Violet: the story of the irrepressible Violet Hunt and her circle of lovers and friends — Ford Madox Ford, H. G. Wells, Somerset Maugham, and Henry James* (1990) · Violet Hunt diaries, Cornell University, Ithaca, New York, Olin Library · V. Hunt, *The flurried years* (1926) · *The letters of Oscar Wilde*, ed. R. Hart-Davis (1962) · *The collected letters of D. H. Lawrence*, ed. H. T. Moore, 2 vols. (1962) · B. J. Robinson, 'Hunt, Violet', *The 1890s: an encyclopedia of British literature, art, and culture*, ed. G. A. Cevasco (1993) · J. Sutherland, *The Longman companion to Victorian fiction* (1988) · b. cert. · d. cert.

Archives Cornell University, Ithaca, New York, Olin Library, corresp., MSS, diaries, etc. · Pennsylvania State University, Patee Library | Georgetown University, Washington, DC, Lauinger Library, letters to Graham Greene · HLRO, letters to Catherine Hueffer · Princeton University, Edward Naumburg Jun. collection of Ford Madox Ford · U. Glas. L., letters to D. S. MacColl · U. Reading L., letters to Bodley Head Ltd

Wealth at death £8664 13s. 9d.: probate, 30 April 1942, *CGPLA Eng. & Wales*

Hunt, Violet Edith Gwynllyn Brooke- (1870/71–1910), writer, social worker, and political activist, was born at Bowden Hall in Gloucester, the eldest daughter of Charles George Brooke-Hunt, a lieutenant in the Royal Navy. Brooke-Hunt was educated privately and then attended Cheltenham College until the age of seventeen, when she became actively involved in the education of working-class boys and young men. This work began with the formation of a reading-room for the servants and labourers living on the family estate, and the opening of a club for the artisans of Gloucester. After moving to London in the early 1890s, her work was continued among the soldiers of the Knightsbridge barracks. Her pamphlet *Clubs for Boys and Young Men* (1897), read as a paper to the National Union of Women Workers in October 1896, argued strongly for the importance of clubs in raising 'the bodies and minds and spirits of their members' (Brooke-Hunt, *Clubs*, 6). It envisaged clubs equipping members with practical skills, offering non-compulsory religious instruction, and encouraging participation in athletics and games. The latter was understood to be essential if boys and young men were to be attracted away from the 'degrading' influences of the public house and the music-hall. A devout Anglican, Brooke-Hunt also published a number of homilies during the 1890s, including *Goals and Tries* (1897) and *Egerton's Brother* (1899). These fictional works, written in simple, sometimes rather patronizing, language, were published under the auspices of the Society For Promoting Christian Knowledge. They were aimed at young male readers, who were exhorted to self-improvement under the inspiration and example of Christ.

With the encouragement of Florence Nightingale, Brooke-Hunt set sail for South Africa at the beginning of the Second South African War (1899–1902) to help care for British soldiers. Beginning in Naauwport, she played an important role in improving the facilities, and in particular the food, of the station hospital and the convalescent camp. She then travelled to Bloemfontein and to Pretoria to set up soldiers' institutes, the latter specifically at the request of Lord Roberts. The institutes proved popular with soldiers, providing cheap meals and entertainments, reading-rooms, and a place to worship on Sundays. Brooke-Hunt was later awarded a war medal and the order of Lady of Grace of St John of Jerusalem for her services in South Africa.

Brooke-Hunt returned to Britain in time to organize the Colonial Troops Club at the coronation of Edward VII in August 1902. She then immersed herself in the organization of various extra-parliamentary associations, including the Union Jack Club, the Navy League, and the Tariff Reform League. Her role as secretary of the Women's Unionist and Tariff Reform Association established her as one of the more prominent Edwardian female political activists. Displaying formidable energy and organizational zeal, Brooke-Hunt helped to form over forty women's branches of the Tariff Reform League. She also showed herself to be a gifted public speaker, and regularly took to the platform to publicize her views on the fiscal question and the navy. Despite this self-assertiveness, Brooke-Hunt does not appear to have been connected with the suffragette movement, although neither is there any evidence to suggest that she was an anti-suffragist. In fact, the issue of the vote for women was not central to her political concerns. Her contribution to female emancipation proved more subtle, taking the form of broadening

and politicizing the public role of women, and of acclimatizing some men to women's political activism.

Brooke-Hunt died unmarried on 9 June 1910 at the Gabled House, the home of her brother-in-law at The Holt, in Alverstoke, Hampshire. Her early death, at the age of thirty-nine (from infective enteritis and exhaustion), came as a shock to many political friends, particularly those associated with the tariff reform movement, whom she had greatly impressed with her drive and determination. In an obituary in the *Morning Post*, Mary Maxse, erstwhile chairman of the Women's Tariff Reform League, described her as one of the most vivid personalities of her day, who was 'able to a remarkable degree to inspire with her own enthusiasm those with whom she worked'.

ANDREW S. THOMPSON

Sources *Monthly Notes on Tariff Reform* (July 1910) • V. Brooke-Hunt, *A woman's memories of the war* (1901) • *WWW* • V. Brooke-Hunt, *Clubs for boys and young men* (1897) • Baroness Burdett-Coutts [A. G. Burdett-Coutts], ed., *Woman's mission: a series of congress papers on the philanthropic work of women* (1893) • *Morning Post* (11 June 1910) • d. cert.

Likenesses photograph, 19 Dec 1900, repro. in Brooke-Hunt, *A woman's memories of the war*

Wealth at death £10,475 16s. 9d.: probate, 2 July 1910, *CGPLA Eng. & Wales*

Hunt [Venantius], **Walter** (*d.* 1478), Carmelite friar and theologian, was born in the west of England and joined the Carmelites at Oxford. He commenced his studies in London, for on 24 September 1418 he was ordained deacon in St Paul's Cathedral. But he completed his theology course at Oxford and incepted as DTh there on 11 November 1434, when a benediction was written for the occasion by another Carmelite, John Haynton. In 1438 Walter Hunt was one of four doctors who represented the English province at the Council of Ferrara–Florence. Owing to political difficulties, the other delegations from England did not attend, and the Carmelites were the only English representatives there. Hunt played a prominent part in the negotiations between the Latin and Greek Orthodox churches, and his efforts won him the praise of Pope Eugenius IV. Afterwards he composed an account of the council, which was probably that consulted by Thomas Rudborne for his *Historia major* (*c*.1450). In 1446 Hunt represented the Oxford Carmelite distinction at a meeting held to discuss the reform of the English province. By 1450 he was chaplain to John Kemp, archbishop of York (*d.* 1454), and received a papal dispensation to hold a benefice. He held various livings, while in 1465 he was appointed to the canonry and prebend of Moreton and Whaddon by the Carmelite bishop of Hereford, John Stanbury. Later, on Stanbury's death in 1474, Hunt was an executor of his will. In 1475 he witnessed the new statutes for University College, Oxford. He died on 28 November 1478 in the Carmelite house at Oxford, where he was buried and Bale preserves his epitaph. The name Venantius sometimes attributed to him is a Latinate rendering of his surname.

Hunt was a prolific writer and Bale, who saw his works in the Carmelite library at Oxford, records twenty-five titles. Sadly only two short *quaestiones* survive; probably written for his students, these rely heavily on the

Doctrinale of Thomas Netter (*d.* 1430). Hunt's other works were concerned with issues raised at the Council of Ferrara–Florence, papal supremacy and the authority of the church, and with the theological preoccupations of his day, predestination, the rights of religious orders, the kingship, and poverty of Christ; there is also a tract against preaching by women, a Latin dictionary, and a commentary on the *Sentences* of Peter Lombard. Hunt seems to have been a gifted writer and teacher rather than an original thinker, a preacher in demand by the king and nobility, and one whose efforts at the Council of Ferrara–Florence earned him a lasting reputation for diplomacy.

RICHARD COPSEY

Sources J. Bale, Bodl. Oxf., MS Bodley 73 (SC 27635), fols. 11*v*, 108*v*, 109, 196*v*, 200*v*, 201–201*v*, 209*v* · J. Bale, Bodl. Oxf., MS Selden supra 41, fol. 181*v* · J. Bale, BL, Harley MSS, MS 1819, fol. 200*v* · J. Bale, BL, Harley MSS, MS 3838, fols. 104*v*–105*v*, 209–209*v* · A. Bostius, 'Speculum historiale', *Speculum Carmelitanum*, ed. Daniel a Virgine Maria, 1 (Antwerp, 1680), 896 · Emden, *Oxf.*, 2.986–7 · J. Greatrex, 'Thomas Rudborne, monk of Winchester, and the Council of Florence', *Schism, heresy and religious protest*, ed. D. Baker, SCH, 9 (1972), 171–6 · M. M. Harvey, 'Harley Manuscript 3049 and two *questiones* of Walter Hunt, O.Carm.', *Transactions of the Architectural and Archaeological Society of Durham and Northumberland*, new ser., 6 (1982), 45–7 · J. Bale, *Illustrium Maioris Britannie scriptorum … summarium* (1548), 207–8 · Bale, *Cat.*, 1.615–16 · *Commentarii de scriptoribus Britannicis, auctore Joanne Lelando*, ed. A. Hall, 2 (1709), 468
Archives BL, Harley MS 3049, fols. 237*v*–240

Hunt, William (*fl.* 1696), author, published *Demonstration of astrology, or, A brief discourse, proving the influence of the sun, moon, and stars, over this terraqueous globe* (1696), in which he describes himself as 'a Lover of the Mathematicks and Natural Philosophy' (Hunt, title-page). As the preface was written in Alconbury, Essex, he may have lived there at the time. The work was dedicated to Charles, Viscount Mandevill and earl of Manchester, with thanks for his support. Otherwise, biographical details of Hunt are conjectural. Since it seems probable that he had a university education, he may have been the William Hunt, born the son of William Hunt at Sutton, Cambridgeshire, who attended a private school there and matriculated from Magdalene College, Cambridge, on 7 August 1674, aged nineteen, and who probably graduated LLB from Trinity Hall in 1679. This man's father may be identified as the Oxford-educated clergyman William Hunt who was ejected from his living at Sutton in 1662, but who remained there as a schoolmaster and was licensed as a presbyterian minister in 1672; his two sons, William and John, entered the ministry. A William Hunt of Little Beddow, Essex, 'minister of the gospell', drew up his will on 2 March 1698, mentioning his two brothers, Edward and John, also 'minister of the gospell', two daughters from his first marriage to 'E. T.', and a son, John. The executor was his (second) wife, Abigail, and the overseers included Francis Barrington, esquire. The will was proved on 19 April the same year.

Hunt's treatise was part of a general movement at the time among the better-educated astrologers to rescue the subject from its parlous state, which he described as 'now so sullied over with Innovations and Superstitions, that it's hard to find the Truth from the Falsehood' (Hunt, v–vi).

As a result, there were left 'but few students or lovers of this art' (ibid., A3). Other tracts from this period with the same aim (if not always the same means) include John Goad's *Astro-Meteorologica* (1686), John Partridge's *Opus reformatum* (1693) and *Defectio geniturarum* (1697), and Robert Godson's *Astrologia reformata* (1697). Hunt claimed that 'I through my diligent Study and Observation have gained more select Arcana's than ever were known to the late (tho Learned) Dr. Goad' (ibid., iv) and, like Goad, he sought to rectify the disrepute into which partisan and sectarian astrologers had brought their subject by concentrating upon 'chiefly this most useful and innocent Part, the Knowledg of the Weather' (ibid., A2).

Hunt's particular contribution was his claim to ground astrology 'on the Fundamental Rules of the Copernican System and Philosophy. … Whereby the Art is rendered almost Mathematically Demonstrable' (Hunt, title). It was not original, however; Joshua Childrey's *Indago astrologica* (1652) and Vincent Wing's *Harmonicon coeleste* (1651) had both attempted to give astrology a new footing in the heliocentric cosmos. The 'almost' of his title gives away the enormous gap between Hunt's ambition—which is what it might have taken actually to re-establish astrology as a reputable subject—and his accomplishment. So too does his appendix, 'treating of this Summer's Effects. … Wherein we have great cause to fear, that the Sword, Pestilence, and Famine, will annoy our European Territories this ensuing Summer': just the kind of prognostication that had brought astrology into lasting disfavour among the intellectual, religious, and political élites of the day.

PATRICK CURRY

Sources W. Hunt, *Demonstration of astrology* (1696) · will of W. Hunt, *d.* 1698, PRO, PROB 11/445, fols. 83*v*–84*r* · *Calamy rev.*, 285 · Venn, *Alum. Cant.* · Foster, *Alum. Oxon.* · P. Curry, *Prophecy and power: astrology in early modern England* (1989) · B. S. Capp, *Astrology and the popular press: English almanacs, 1500–1800* (1979)

Hunt, William (1842–1931), historian and biographer, was born on 3 March 1842 at Hotwells, Clifton, Bristol, the elder son of the Revd William Hunt (*d.* 1889), then curate of Holy Trinity, Hotwells, and subsequently vicar of Holy Trinity, Weston-super-Mare, Somerset, and his wife, Maria Simpson. He was educated at Harrow School in Dr Vaughan's house. He matriculated at Trinity College, Oxford, in March 1861, obtained a second in classical moderations in 1862, and graduated with a first class in law and modern history in 1864. He married first, in 1865, Emma (*d.* 1893), daughter of the Revd Arthur Ramsay. He was made deacon in 1865 and was ordained priest in 1866 while serving for two years as his father's curate. Between 1867 and 1882 he held his only parochial cure, the vicarage of Congresbury, Somerset, where he was responsible for restoring the parish church and building a school. While at Congresbury he served as honorary general secretary of the Somersetshire Archaeological and Natural History Society (1872–9) and as public examiner in the school of modern history at Oxford (1877–9 and 1881–2).

In 1882 Hunt moved to London, where he lived at 24 Phillimore Gardens, Kensington, until his death. For the next twenty-five years he wrote or edited historical textbooks on both medieval and modern subjects, and was a regular contributor to the *Saturday Review*, in which he attempted to acquire a controlling interest. For a short time in 1885 he gave sub-editorial assistance to the *Dictionary of National Biography* and was subsequently a substantial contributor. He was awarded the degree of DLitt by Oxford University in 1903, served as president of the Royal Historical Society (1905–9), and was an honorary fellow of his college from 1921.

Hunt's work was remarkably wide-ranging, and he had a 'well-nigh national reputation' as a historian and biographer (*Proceedings*, 145). He was one of only seven contributors to the *Dictionary of National Biography* whose work appeared in all the original sixty-three volumes, his contributions calculated as amounting to approximately 830 pages divided between 595 articles mostly on medieval subjects (including Edward I and Edward III) but also on English divines of the sixteenth and seventeenth centuries (including Thomas Ken). Hunt also contributed articles to the 1901–11 supplement on Professor E. A. Freeman and Dean W. R. W. Stephens, with both of whom he had acted as editor of historical series.

Between 1883 and 1905 Hunt published a number of monographs and textbooks which remain useful, including *The Somerset Diocese: Bath and Wells* (1885) in the Diocesan Histories series, a history of *Bristol* (1887) in the Historic Towns series, edited jointly with E. A. Freeman, the first volume of the widely acceptable *History of the English Church* (1899–1910), which he edited with W. R. W. Stephens, and the tenth volume, on the reign of George III, in the notable twelve-volume *Political History of England* (1905–10), a series which he edited with R. L. Poole. His least successful work by modern academic standards, and the only text published, was his edition of *Two Chartularies of the Priory of St. Peter at Bath* (1893) for the Somerset Record Society.

Hunt's commanding figure with flowing beard was well known at the Savile Club, where his circle of friends, mostly scientists and men of letters, included Sir Edmund Gosse. His views, both political and ecclesiastical, were conservative; his main recreation even in old age was foreign travel. Hunt's second marriage, in 1895, was to Katharine, daughter of Thomas Rae of Melbourne. There were no children of either union. He died at home on 14 June 1931 and was buried in Kensington Hanwell cemetery, Ealing. His second wife survived him.

ROBERT W. DUNNING

Sources *The Times* (16 June 1931) · *The Times* (19 June 1931) · *Proceedings of the Somersetshire Archaeological and Natural History Society*, 77 (1931), 145–6 · DNB · CGPLA Eng. & Wales (1931)

Archives BL, corresp. with Macmillans, Add. MS 55080 · Bodl. Oxf., letters to P. S. Allen · U. Leeds, Brotherton L., letters to E. Gosse; corresp. with Edith Thompson · UCL, letters to David Hannay

Likenesses Elliott & Fry, photograph, repro. in *Proceedings of the Somersetshire Archaeological and Natural History Society*, facing p. 145 · photograph, UCL, Royal Historical Society

Wealth at death £125,070 1s. 1d.: probate, 31 July 1931, CGPLA Eng. & Wales

Hunt, William Henry (1790–1864), watercolour painter, was born in March 1790 and baptized on 28 March 1790 at 8 Old Belton Street (now Endell Street), London, son of John Hunt, tin-plate worker and japanner, and his wife, Judith. Sickly and lame from childhood, he was regarded as too weak to follow his father's profession. J. L. Roget records a remark made by one of Hunt's uncles that his 'nevvy, little Billy Hunt … was always a poor cripple, and as he was fit for nothing, they made an artist of him' (Roget, 1.390). At the age of sixteen he was apprenticed to the landscape painter John Varley for seven years for £200, and for a time he lived with Varley at 18 Broad Street, Golden Square, London. Here he made close friends with William Mulready and John Linnell, and he worked with Linnell on a transparency for an illumination celebrating a victory over the French in 1807; later Hunt did scene painting for the Theatre Royal, Drury Lane. Also in 1807 he exhibited at the Royal Academy three oils of views near Hounslow, Reading, and Leatherhead, and in 1808 he entered the Royal Academy Schools, though it seems likely that he did not attend life classes. (He later regretted his lack of proficiency in depicting the human form.)

At the same time Hunt was also drawing at the 'Monro academy', at 8 Adelphi Terrace, London—the house of Dr Thomas Monro, an enthusiastic patron of watercolourists: here he copied drawings by Gainsborough and Canaletto. At Monro's country house, Merry Hill, near Bushey in Hertfordshire, he was paid 7s. 6d. a day for his pictures; work—landscape drawings—from this period includes *Merry Hill, Bushey* (British Museum, London) and *Bushey Church* (Bradford Art Galleries and Museums). Monro's patronage led to further similar commissions: Hunt was also employed by the earl of Essex to paint views of his estate and interiors of his house at nearby Cassiobury. (When in 1839 John Britton published *A History and Description of Cassiobury Park*, it included illustrations by Hunt, as well as Turner, Henry Edridge, and Pugin.) In 1822 Hunt met the sixth duke of Devonshire, and for him made interior studies of the duke's four houses (now in the Devonshire collection at Chatsworth, Derbyshire).

Apart from the period spent with Varley, Hunt lived in the family home in London until 1822; he then moved to 36 Brownlow Street, Drury Lane, and in 1825 to 6 Marchmont Street, Brunswick Square. Between 1807 and 1825 he showed fourteen works, both oils and watercolours, at the Royal Academy, and from 1814 he also exhibited at the Society of Painters in Oil and Water Colours. In 1824 he was elected an associate of the Society of Painters in Water Colours (known as the Old Watercolour Society); he became a full member in 1826. His early technique was described by F. G. Stephens as 'thin in handling, sober and delicate in colour, warm and grey according as the subject or even the motive of the theme required' (Stephens, 531). From this time onward he dedicated himself more or less exclusively to painting in watercolours.

In line with contemporary fashion Hunt's work moved away from topographical scenes to ones of human interest, including rural or domestic characters, as well as still lifes and figure studies. Examples include *The Vegetable*

William Henry
Hunt (1790–1864),
self-portrait

Seller (1825?, Courtauld Inst.), *Still Life with Earthenware Pitcher, Coffee Pot and Basket* (Ashmolean Museum, Oxford), and *James Holland, Painter* (1828, Victoria and Albert Museum, London). For some years he spent the winter months at Hastings in Sussex, where he did many drawings of boats, the seashore, and fishermen. Three brothers he met in Hastings, who became known as 'Hunt's boys', posed as models for many of his drawings, such as *The Turnip Lantern* (1838, Leicestershire Museums and Art Galleries).

On 13 September 1830 Hunt married his eighteen-year-old cousin Sarah Holloway, whose father was a miller and farmer at Bramley in Hampshire. A daughter, Emma Effie, was born in 1832. From 1851 Hunt also had an address at Parkgate, Bramley, and after Sarah's death her sister kept house for him. According to Stephens's account, Hunt was

> probably about five foot. He was broad as well as round shouldered and his head was large beyond proportion to the rest of his figure of which the torso was that of a larger man. His large and long frock coats and loose trousers although favourable to him on other accounts, did not add to his outward graces.   (Witt, 48)

Self-conscious about his looks, it is noticeable that his self-portraits (National Portrait Gallery and British Museum, London) are much more flattering than his appearance in photographs (National Portrait Gallery and Bankside Gallery, London) would suggest. In a memoir Ann Mary Wood also recollected him as 'grotesque' and:

> a Quilp like dwarf but … [he] possessed the tenderest heart and the most sympathetic and delicate nerves. Like Paul Dombey he was addicted to low company, and street conjurors, acrobats and nigger minstrels were always welcome at the tea table of his humble lodging, and a certain 'Bones' in the latter troop was his especial friend.
> ('Reminiscences')

He was, she recalled, an 'unaggressive but immoveable agnostic' (ibid.).

In 1845 Hunt moved to 62 Stanhope Street, Hampstead Road, London, where his studio was described by Walter Sickert (in 1910) as 'a little box lit from above that cannot

have measured more than seven foot square' (Witt, 56). He worked tirelessly from early morning until dusk, though a drawing might take him more than a fortnight to complete. As this diligence suggests, his late drawings are much tighter than his earlier works: he became renowned for his finish, particularly for the bloom on his fruit, an effect he achieved by stippling pure watercolour onto an opaque surface of Chinese white mixed with gum. His still lifes were now his most lucrative drawings and his many portrayals of fruit, flowers, nests, and birds' eggs earned him the nickname Bird's Nest Hunt. Examples of such work include *Peach and Grapes* (Brantwood Trust, Coniston) and *Bird's Nest and Blossom* (Manchester City Galleries). The former belonged to John Ruskin, a great admirer of Hunt's acute powers of observation. Hunt himself was unassuming about his work. Samuel Palmer told a story about a lady who asked Hunt about his technique only to receive the down-to-earth reply that the only thing to do 'is to Fudge it out … we must all fudge it out, there is no other way than Fudging it out!' (Hunt to Joseph Jenkins, 1 March 1864, Royal Society of Painters in Water Colours MS J55/22). But his drawings remain remarkable for their exquisite sense of poise and colour.

By the end of his life Hunt had exhibited 791 works with the Old Watercolour Society. Roget recorded his remark in 1858 that pictures which he had sold for 25 guineas ten years earlier now brought him 35. (He disliked cheques, preferring to be paid in cash.) However, within a few years of his death, his drawings were fetching hundreds of pounds; one was sold for 750 guineas at an auction in 1875. This financial success was crowned by artistic honours. He had eleven works in the Paris Universal Exhibition of 1855, where he was awarded a certificate of merit. The celebrated French poet and art critic Charles Baudelaire described him as 'a stubborn realist', and another French critic, Edmond About, noted that his pictures sold for more than those of Ingres and Delacroix. In the following year Hunt was made an honorary member of the Koninklijke Academie van Beeldende Kunsten in Amsterdam. In 1857 he had thirty pictures in the Manchester Art Treasures Exhibition, where only Turner and David Roberts had more work exhibited.

William Henry Hunt died of a stroke on 10 February 1864 at 62 Stanhope Street, Hampstead Road, London, and was buried in Highgate cemetery, Middlesex, on 15 February. According to an account by W. J. Wainwright, he died in his daughter's arms in anguished regret that his will had been unjust to her (Royal Society of Painters in Water Colours MS B120). (She herself died in squalor in New York in 1873.) Hunt's obituarists were generous: the art critic of *The Athenaeum* (20 February 1864) said that he had 'the art of Titian in colour and of the Dutchmen in finish', whereas *The Reader* (27 February 1864) declared him one of the greatest artists of the century. Remaining works and the contents of Hunt's studio were sold by Christie, Manson and Woods on 16 and 17 May 1864.

Hunt's influence on his contemporaries can scarcely be overestimated: in his landscape, genre, and still-life drawings he reflected supremely well the taste of the age. The heightened realism of his nature studies and his technical creativity anticipated the work of the Pre-Raphaelites, as well as artists such as John Frederick Lewis, Myles Birket Foster, and Frederick Walker. Ruskin himself took lessons from Hunt, regarding him as the greatest ever painter of still life. The influence of his method of stippling can be traced in the works of pointillist painters such as Seurat, Signac, and Pissarro. Hunt's reputation was at its highwater mark at the time of his death, however, and his work is now not quite so highly regarded as that of other watercolourists whose drawings appear less varied in their range and content. Significant public collections of his many works are in the British Museum and the Victoria and Albert Museum in London, and the Yale Center for British Art in New Haven, Connecticut.

SIMON FENWICK

Sources J. L. Roget, *A history of the 'Old Water-Colour' Society*, 2 vols. (1891) · J. Witt, *William Henry Hunt (1790–1864): life and work* (1982) · Bankside Gallery, London, Royal Society of Painters in Water Colours MSS · 'Reminiscences of Mrs A. Wood', c.1905, priv. coll. · F. G. Stephens, 'William Henry Hunt, water-colour painter', *Fraser's Magazine*, 72 (1865), 525–36; repr. in *Old Water-Colour Society's Club*, 12 (1933), 17–50 · *DNB*

Archives Bankside Gallery, London, Royal Society of Painters in Water Colours MSS · BL, letters to J. H. Maw, Add. MS 45883 · Yale U., Beinecke L., letters to T. William

Likenesses W. H. Hunt, self-portrait, oils, c.1825, V&A · W. H. Hunt, self-portraits, watercolour drawings, c.1840, BM, NPG · W. H. Hunt, self-portrait, oils, c.1850, NPG · photograph, c.1860, NPG · photograph, c.1860, Bankside Gallery, London · A. Munro, marble bust, 1861, Bankside Gallery, London · Cundall & Downes, carte-de-visite, NPG · J. G. P. Fischer, pencil drawing, BM · W. H. Hunt, self-portrait, watercolour, NPG [*see illus.*] · W. H. Hunt, self-portrait, watercolour drawing, Lady Lever Art Gallery, Port Sunlight · W. Jeffrey, photograph, carte-de-visite, NPG · A. Munro, bust, Royal Society of Painters in Water Colours, London

Wealth at death under £20,000: resworn probate, July 1864, *CGPLA Eng. & Wales* · under £18,000: double probate, 5 April 1864, *CGPLA Eng. & Wales*

Hunt, William Holman (1827–1910), painter, was born on 2 April 1827 at Love Lane, Wood Street, Cheapside, in the City of London, the third of the seven children of William Hunt (1800–1856) and his wife, Sarah (*bap.* 1798, *d.* 1884), daughter of William and Ann Hobman of Rotherhithe. He was baptized at St Giles Cripplegate on 10 June, the church register giving his father's profession as warehouseman. William Hunt's employer was the haberdashery manufacturer James Chadwick & Brother, of 3 Little Love Lane.

Early years and first paintings From a very early age Holman Hunt was continually drawing. But in 1839 his father, who disapproved of his ambition to become a professional painter, decided that he should leave boarding-school and earn his living in a city warehouse. The twelve-year-old Hunt arranged instead to be taken on as a copying clerk to a Spitalfields estate agent and auctioneer, James Labram, who encouraged his artistic talent and introduced him to oil painting. At this period Hunt studied drawing at a mechanics' institute in the evenings and spent his salary on weekly lessons with a City portrait painter, Henry Rogers.

Hunt left his first job at the end of 1840, and from 1841 to

William Holman Hunt (1827–1910), self-portrait, 1867–75

1843 found employment as a clerk in the muslin and calico printing works of Richard Cobden, at 40 Cateaton Street, Aldermanbury. He then undertook his first attempts at landscape painting, but his striving for truth to nature was frowned upon by Henry Rogers, who set him to copy (c.1842–1843; priv. coll.) his copy of Van Dyck's *Virgin and Child with St Catherine* (original then in the collection of the marquess of Westminster, now in the Metropolitan Museum, New York). Most of Hunt's earliest known oils are portraits, including one of old Hannah, a local orange seller (c.1843). This striking likeness was drawn to the attention of William Hunt, and during the ensuing confrontation the young clerk was at last able to overrule his father's objections to his choice of career.

In 1844 Hunt was issued with a ticket authorizing him to paint in the National Gallery. One of the first copies he made there was of David Wilkie's *The Blind Fiddler* (1806; Tate collection), which, he learned, was painted without a monochrome lay-in of the whole design, 'finishing each bit thoroughly in the day' (*Pre-Raphaelitism*, 1st edn, 1.53). This piecemeal technique, employed by Renaissance fresco painters, stimulated Hunt's interest in quattrocento painting and led to the Pre-Raphaelites' adoption of a similar method.

In the summer of 1844, while studying in the British Museum, Hunt met John Everett Millais, who was to become his closest friend and colleague. Millais encouraged the slightly older artist to reapply to the Royal Academy Schools; at the third attempt Hunt was enrolled as a probationer, on 11 July, becoming a full student on 18 December. The following year he made his exhibition début at the Royal Manchester Institution with *Pity the Sorrows of a Poor Old Man*. The subject suggests that from the start he was attracted to themes dealing with the oppressed.

Youth and foundation of the Pre-Raphaelite Brotherhood At the Royal Academy Schools, Hunt met Frederic George Stephens, who, as a critic, was to become his great supporter, and whose portrait Hunt painted in 1846–7 (Tate collection). In 1847 Hunt completed *Dr Rochecliffe Performing Divine Service in the Cottage of Joceline Joliffe, at Woodstock* (priv. coll.), a subject from Sir Walter Scott. It was well received at that year's Royal Academy exhibition and immediately found a buyer.

In the summer of 1847 Hunt was lent a copy of the critic John Ruskin's *Modern Painters* and later recalled that 'of all its readers none could have felt more strongly that it was written expressly for him' (*Pre-Raphaelitism*, 1st edn, 1.73). Reading the Old Testament in search of characters or incidents that prefigure the life of Christ or any persons or events in the Christian dispensation was standard practice in evangelical circles. But Ruskin's way of applying this method (known as typology) in his analysis of Tintoretto's *Annunciation* (Scuola di San Rocco, Venice) had a profound effect on Hunt's artistic development. It showed him that it was possible to combine realism and symbolism into a coherent whole without distorting the realism by resorting to outdated allegorical modes. It was probably the cause of Hunt's setting aside *Christ and the Two Marys* (1847–c.1897; Art Gallery of South Australia, Adelaide), his largest painting to date and his first religious subject, on realizing that its traditional iconography would lack emotional impact.

Ruskin also converted Hunt to a moralistic approach to his painting, which is immediately apparent in *The Flight of Madeline and Porphyro during the Drunkenness Attending the Revelry* (Guildhall Art Gallery, London), begun in February 1848. Hunt's attempt at portraying a dramatic situation in a convincingly realized setting, and the rich deep colours of the costumes, prefigure the works of high Pre-Raphaelitism. The cramped picture space was a compositional format that also came to be associated with the works of the Pre-Raphaelite Brotherhood.

At the Royal Academy exhibition of 1848 *The Flight of Madeline and Porphyro* was much admired by the painter and poet Dante Gabriel Rossetti. Hunt and Rossetti became close friends and in August began sharing a studio in Cleveland Street, Fitzroy Square. By the end of the year Hunt and Rossetti, together with Millais, William Michael Rossetti, F. G. Stephens, James Collinson, and Thomas Woolner, formed the Pre-Raphaelite Brotherhood. The aims of the movement were elucidated in 1895 by W. M. Rossetti as follows:

1, To have genuine ideas to express; 2, to study Nature attentively, so as to know how to express them; 3, to sympathize with what is direct and serious and heartfelt in previous art, to the exclusion of what is conventional and self-parading and learned by rote; and 4, and most

indispensable of all, to produce thoroughly good pictures and statues.   (*Family Letters*, 1.135)

Achievements of the period of high Pre-Raphaelitism In the summer of 1848 Hunt began his only oil painting bearing the initials of the brotherhood, PRB: *Rienzi vowing to obtain justice for the death of his young brother, slain in a skirmish between the Colonna and Orsini factions* (priv. coll.). The source was Edward Bulwer Lytton's novel *Rienzi, the Last of the Roman Tribunes* (1835). Hunt would have been attracted by Rienzi's youth and humble origins, as well as by his struggle for the political freedom of his country. Indeed the picture was conceived as a reflection of the populist-inspired uprisings that were convulsing Europe in 1848; Hunt had been caught up in them that April, when he and Millais witnessed the Chartist gathering on Kennington Common. Fittingly, three members of the brotherhood—Millais and D. G. and W. M. Rossetti—posed for a work planned as revolutionary in terms of a rejection of artistic convention. The landscape was painted out of doors, in full sunlight, and the style was suited to the trecento subject matter. At the Royal Academy in 1849 *Rienzi* attracted the attention of the academician Augustus Egg, who managed to sell it that August, on Hunt's behalf, to the industrialist John Gibbons.

The 100 guineas that Hunt received for the painting enabled him to buy the canvas for *A converted British family sheltering a Christian missionary from the persecution of the Druids* (AM Oxf.), and he now went down to Homerton, Middlesex, to work on the landscape out of doors. In the autumn he visited Paris and Belgium with D. G. Rossetti. On his return to London he took rooms in Brompton, and on 5 January 1850 moved to 5 Prospect Place, Cheyne Walk, Chelsea, where he painted the figures in his druids picture. The two missionaries were conceived as types of the persecuted Saviour, and, on its exhibition at the Royal Academy of 1850, Hunt's use of typological symbolism was rightly linked with that of Millais in *Christ in the House of his Parents* (Tate collection). The critical response was generally savage, exacerbated by the uneasy religious climate of a time when conversions to Rome were widespread.

The prevailing hostility was probably responsible for the cancellation of a commission in late May from the academician Thomas Creswick. For this Hunt had designed two highly-finished pen-and-ink drawings that focused on the psychological trauma engendered by the conflict between passion and duty. The first was *The Lady of Shalott* (National Gallery of Victoria, Melbourne), whose theme was to be of lifelong significance for Hunt. He regarded Tennyson's eponymous heroine as a paradigm of the role of the artist, necessarily cloistered from the world yet dedicated to interpreting it. The second design, a compositional study for *Claudio and Isabella* (FM Cam.), from Shakespeare's *Measure for Measure*, was developed into a painting (1850–53; Tate collection), Augustus Egg having taken over the original commission from Creswick.

In September 1850 Hunt received 150 guineas for *A Converted British Family*, which became the cornerstone of the Pre-Raphaelite collection of Thomas Combe, printer to the University of Oxford and a prominent high-churchman. Combe played an important role in Hunt's life, as a father figure and adviser as well as staunch patron. Hunt now had the means to begin another Shakespearian subject: *Valentine Rescuing Sylvia from Proteus* (Birmingham Museum and Art Gallery), the landscape of which was executed between September and November in the grounds of Knole Park, near Sevenoaks. The sparkling colouring of the work is heightened by Hunt's use, in parts, of a wet white ground, adapting a technique employed by Renaissance fresco painters. On its exhibition at the Royal Academy in 1851, Rossetti's mentor Ford Madox Brown advised his friend Lowes Dickinson to adopt this method:

> at once, as I can assure you you will be forced to do so ultimately, for Hunt and Millais, whose works already kill everything in the exhibition for brilliancy, will in a few years force every one who will not drop behind them to use their methods. (*Pre-Raphaelitism*, 1st edn, 1.256n.)

Valentine Rescuing Sylvia was warmly praised by Ruskin in his letters to *The Times* of 13 and 30 May 1851 in defence of the Pre-Raphaelite exhibits, which had once again been strongly attacked. His intervention finally turned the critical tide in the artists' favour.

From then onwards most of Hunt's major paintings were based on a complex intellectual framework that he worked out in advance. In May 1851 he wrote to the poet Coventry Patmore, who had been responsible for enlisting Ruskin's support, asking to borrow a copy of the works of the seventeenth-century theologian Richard Hooker. He added: 'As however I am obliged to read for my next year's subjects much just now, I hope you will be able to spare it some time' (Bodl. Oxf., MS Eng. lett. d. 40, fol. 31). Hooker provided the theme of *The Hireling Shepherd* (1851–2; Manchester City Galleries), with its underlying attack on sectarianism for deflecting the clergy from the task of tending their flock. The picture marks out a new direction, in which the symbolism is so arcane as to be virtually impenetrable without a literary gloss. The painting can, however, be enjoyed on many levels. Its sunlit landscape, with its closely observed blue shadows, was painted at Ewell, Surrey, between June and December 1851 and was Hunt's most ambitious attempt at naturalism to date.

The Light of the World (1851–3; Keble College, Oxford), arguably the most famous religious image of the nineteenth century, was also begun at Ewell in 1851, and Hunt was concerned to render the night effects with total fidelity. The figure of Christ was, however, deliberately 'mystic in aspect and not suggesting any single person' (*Pre-Raphaelite Friendship*, 246). The painting of the Saviour knocking on a door overgrown with brambles, a symbol of the human heart, was executed as the result of a conversion experience. From now onwards, Hunt's deeply felt Christianity fuelled his obsessive desire to go to the Holy Land to put his Pre-Raphaelite principles into practice *in situ*. *The Light of the World* was purchased by Thomas Combe in August 1853 and was exhibited at the Royal Academy in

the following year. On 5 May 1854 *The Times* published a letter from Ruskin that explained the symbolism at length and championed the picture as 'one of the very noblest works of sacred art ever produced in this or any other age' (*Works*, 12.330).

In the summer of 1852 Hunt stayed with Thomas and Martha Combe in Oxford and executed *New College Cloisters, 1852* (Jesus College, Oxford), a highly accomplished portrait of the curate John David Jenkins. He then travelled to Fairlight, near Hastings, where he painted his greatest landscape, *Our English Coasts, 1852*, later known as *Strayed Sheep* (Tate collection). At the 1853 Royal Academy exhibition these works, together with *Claudio and Isabella*, attracted the attention of the Mancunian engineer Thomas Fairbairn, who immediately gave Hunt 'an unlimited commission for some work to be undertaken at my convenience' (Bronkhurst, 'Fruits of a connoisseur's friendship', 588). With this in mind Hunt began *The Awakening Conscience* (1853–4; Tate collection), which he planned as a pendant to *The Light of the World*, in order 'to show how the still small voice speaks to a human soul in the turmoil of life' (*Pre-Raphaelitism*, 1st edn, 1.347). It depicts a man with his mistress in a room in a St John's Wood villa. The model for the woman was Annie Miller, whom Hunt had discovered in a Chelsea slum and with whom he was deeply in love.

Artist–explorer in the Near East, 1854–1856 Avid for adventure, in January 1854 Hunt embarked for the East, and the following month joined the artist Thomas Seddon in Cairo. He was initially enchanted by the beauty of the city, which he depicted in the watercolour *Cairo: Sunset on the Gebel Mokattum* (1854–7; Whitworth Art Gallery, Manchester). However, his protestant beliefs and conviction of Anglo-Saxon superiority ill equipped him for his first encounter with the Arab way of life. He had difficulty in persuading the local inhabitants to sit for *A Street Scene in Cairo: the Lantern-Maker's Courtship* (1854–61; Birmingham Museum and Art Gallery). Despite this, by late April the picture was well advanced. The carefully delineated bazaar setting added exoticism to what was basically a conventional courtship theme. *The Afterglow in Egypt* (1854–63; Southampton Art Gallery), begun on Hunt's second visit to Giza, of April–May 1854, marks, however, a new direction: it was painted from a model posed in the open air, developing his earlier preference for painting the landscape settings of his subjects directly from nature.

For Hunt his first sight of Jerusalem—on 3 June 1854—was an intensely moving religious experience. He rented a house inside the city gates with views over the mosques of the Haram al-Sharif (the site of the temple) towards the Mount of Olives, and wrote to his sculptor friend John Lucas Tupper on 24 July:

> The course of events seem so much more comprehensible—the journeys of the Saviour, in the last days of his ministration, from Bethany to Jerusalem to the Temple around the Mount of Olives … seem so real as to appear like an event of the day. (*Pre-Raphaelite Friendship*, 45)

His many drawings of sites redolent with biblical associations were a means of capturing the essence of the landscape of the Holy Land, which had a profound effect on his own beliefs. He was greatly influenced by Ruskin's call, in *Pre-Raphaelitism* (1851), for artists to record faithfully 'every scene of the slightest historical interest' (*Works*, 12.349). He wrote to W. M. Rossetti on 12 August 1855 that a painter's duty was 'to give you a truer notion of the thing' and stated that in landscape this 'must be done … most religiously, in fact with something like the spirit of the Apostles' (Bronkhurst, 'An interesting series', 123).

By this date Hunt's major painting *The Finding of the Saviour in the Temple* (1854–60; Birmingham Museum and Art Gallery) had been in hand for over a year. Most contemporary spectators would have realized the importance of the view of the Mount of Olives in the right background, since it was from there that the Saviour, just before the crucifixion, prophesied the destruction of the temple (Matthew 24). The work is suffused with similar examples of typological symbolism. Hunt's attempt to visualize the scene as accurately as possible, both in terms of the architecture of the second temple and of the costumes and features of the protagonists, broke new ground.

In view of the difficulties that Hunt experienced in finding Semitic models prepared to sit for a painting containing seven rabbis as well as the Holy Family, the subject of *The Scapegoat* (1854–5; Lady Lever Art Gallery, Port Sunlight), his second major oil begun on this visit to Syria, was a welcome contrast. The setting—Usdum, on the southern shores of the Dead Sea—was an essential part of the conception, since it was thought to be the site of Sodom. As Hunt noted in his journal of 19 November 1854, 'No one can stand and say it is not accursed of God' (Landow, 15). At the time the area was exceptionally dangerous—because of the threat from aggressive Bedouins—and Hunt's trip had to be curtailed before he could finish the landscape part of his picture. The typological link between the scapegoat (a subject from Leviticus) and the persecuted Saviour was crucial to the artist, and in order to convey his meaning he employed biblical quotations on the frame (which he himself designed), as well as providing a long explanatory note in the 1856 Royal Academy catalogue. The painting is a haunting and timeless image of desolation, which W. M. Rossetti, for one, regarded as one of Hunt's 'finest performances … an act of singular genius' (Rossetti, 'Reminiscences', 389).

London and Italy, 1856–1869 In October 1855 Hunt left Jerusalem and travelled north through Galilee to the Lebanon. After visiting Constantinople and the battle site of Balaklava, in the Crimea, he arrived back in London on 29 January 1856, 'looking older and altered with a leonine beard' (*Letters of Christina Rossetti*, 1.106). In March he took rooms at 49 Claverton Terrace, Lupus Street, Pimlico, with Michael Halliday and Robert Braithwaite Martineau, who were to become his disciples. This was a steamer ride away from Annie Miller in Chelsea. Hunt had been paying for her education and had proposed to her by letter the previous autumn. On his return he was distressed to find that in his absence she had been flirting with D. G. Rossetti and

fellow artist George Price Boyce. He confided in Madox Brown, who noted in his diary of 6 July: 'They all seem mad about Annie Millar & poor Hunt has had a fever about it' (*Diary of Ford Madox Brown*, 181).

In the summer of 1856 *The Scapegoat* was sold for 450 guineas, Hunt's highest price to date. But despite the impact that the picture had made at that year's Royal Academy exhibition, in the elections for associate membership on 3 November, Hunt received only one vote. His opposition to the Royal Academy on the grounds of its hostility to artistic innovation was well known, and he had only put his name forward at the instigation of Thomas Combe. He was, however, deeply hurt by the rejection and now determined to make his reputation without standing again, even though he realized that exclusion carried financial risks. He did not have the means to concentrate on *The Finding of the Saviour in the Temple*, and in the late 1850s had to work on small-scale paintings that would command a ready sale. These include *The School Girl's Hymn* (1858; AM Oxf.), and replicas of *The Light of the World* (1853–7; Manchester City Galleries) and *The Eve of St Agnes* (c.1856–1857; Walker Art Gallery, Liverpool), which were exhibited in the United States in 1857–8, in a show of contemporary British art organized by W. M. Rossetti.

In the summer of 1857 Hunt moved to 1 Tor Villa, Campden Hill, Kensington. At the same period Edward Moxon's edition of Tennyson's *Poems* was published with illustrations by the three major Pre-Raphaelites (D. G. Rossetti, Millais, and Hunt) and five academicians (Creswick, John Callcott Horsley, Daniel Maclise, William Mulready, and Clarkson Stanfield). Hunt's seven designs include the celebrated headpiece to *The Lady of Shalott*, a powerful image of frustrated sexuality. Illustrations were an important source of income for Hunt during these years, and between 1858 and 1866 he executed thirteen more designs for engravings. Two of these, *Lost* (for Dinah Mulock's *Studies from Life*, 1862) and *A Morning Song* (for Isaac Watts's *Divine and Moral Songs for Children*, 1866), explore the effects on young women of contemporary sexual morality.

The subject of the fallen woman was an understandable obsession, considering Hunt's tortuous relationship with Annie Miller, which finally broke up acrimoniously in the autumn of 1859. She was one of the models for *Il dolce far niente* (c.1859–1866; ex Christies, 19 Feb 2003), a sensuous, life-size figure painting which was almost certainly inspired by Frederic Leighton's *A Roman Lady* (*La Nanna*) (exh. RA, 1859; Philadelphia Museum of Art). Hunt was engaged in an artistic dialogue with Leighton at this time, and his sensitivity to aesthetic trends in avant-garde British art of the late 1850s and early 1860s has seldom been recognized, largely because of his later efforts to divorce himself from the second generation Pre-Raphaelites, under D. G. Rossetti's leadership. Like Rossetti and William Morris, Hunt had a flair for furniture design; the Egyptian chair (Birmingham Museum and Art Gallery) which features prominently in *Il dolce far niente* was designed by him in 1857. Moreover, his attention to the frames for his pictures is a preoccupation shared by

Rossetti and Whistler. Hunt's important frame designs are intensely individual and innovative, incorporating symbolism appropriate to the subject without losing sight of the decorative ensemble.

The Finding of the Saviour in the Temple (1854–60; Birmingham Museum and Art Gallery) has an elaborate gilt frame full of symbolic details. It was designed by Hunt in 1859 as an integral part of his picture, which in April of the following year was sold to the dealer Ernest Gambart for £5500. This was a record sum at the time for any contemporary painting. The price included copyright, and Gambart was shrewdly aware of the profits to be made from sales of the engraving (which was published in a massive edition in 1867). The exhibition of *The Finding* at his German Gallery in 1860 jammed New Bond Street with carriages. Woolner wrote to Emily Tennyson:

> You must have heard of the prodigious success of Hunt's picture in a popular sense, nothing like it in modern times … it is so unusual that a fashionable public goes mad about anything more dignified than a Crystal Palace, crinoline, or a Railway King. (Woolner, 193)

On 11 February 1860 Hunt told his friend William Bell Scott: 'I always try to paint every thing as unlike the thing I last painted as possible' (Troxell collection, MS, Princeton University Library). The watercolours executed on a walking tour of the west country that autumn—for example, *Asparagus Island* (priv. coll.)—provided a respite from his eastern work. So did two oils of 1862–3, *The King of Hearts* (priv. coll.) and a portrait of the retired judge and whig politician Stephen Lushington (NPG). In 1864 Hunt organized an exhibition at the New Gallery, 16 Hanover Street, of two of his recently completed paintings. *The Afterglow in Egypt* must have contrasted oddly with *The Sea King's Peaceful Triumph* (*London Bridge on the Night of the Marriage of the Prince and Princess of Wales*) (1863–4; AM Oxf.), a crowd scene influenced by W. P. Frith. The one new work in his small retrospective show at the New Gallery the following year was *The Children's Holiday* (1864–5; Torbay borough council, Torquay), a large group portrait of Mrs Thomas Fairbairn and five of her children.

In June 1865 Hunt proposed to and was accepted by Fanny (1833–1866), daughter of a prosperous chemist, George Waugh (d. 1873), and his wife, Mary Walker (1805–1886), and sister-in-law of Thomas Woolner. They had known each other for six years, were utterly devoted, and ideally suited. The marriage took place on 28 December 1865, and the following August they left England *en route* for the East. A cholera outbreak in Marseilles prevented them from reaching their goal, and in October they settled in Florence. At the end of the month Fanny gave birth to a son, Cyril Benoni; she never recovered her strength and on 20 December died of miliary fever. The heartbroken widower plunged 'deep into work hoping to keep the hard fixed sorrow at bay' (Allingham and Williams, 292). He channelled all his anguish into *Isabella, or, The Pot of Basil* (1866–8; Laing Art Gallery, Newcastle upon Tyne), a magnificent life-size portrayal of a young woman mourning her murdered lover.

On his return to London in October 1867 Hunt began a portrait of his late wife from a carte-de-visite photograph (1867–8; Toledo Museum of Art, Ohio), as a pendant to his *Portrait of the Artist* (1867–75; Uffizi, Florence). The self-portrait depicts Hunt in his favourite role of artist–explorer, dressed in a turquoise-striped cross-over gown of oriental cloth (*qumbaz*), secured by a cashmere scarf. If the costume suggests that he wished to base his reputation on his Near Eastern works, the setting, reminiscent of a Renaissance palazzo, places the artist in a European context, while his luxuriant auburn beard, piercing blue eyes, and pale complexion proclaim his Anglo-Saxon origins.

In June 1868 Hunt returned to Florence to supervise the elaborate marble tomb that he had designed for his wife in the shape of an ark on the waters (English cemetery, piazzale Donatello). He now took the opportunity to explore further the effects of light on landscape, in such watercolours as *Festa at Fiesole* (priv. coll.) and *Sunset at Chimalditi*. These were shown in 1870 at the Old Watercolour Society—without putting his name forward, Hunt had been elected an associate member in February of the previous year.

Religious works inspired by further visits to Jerusalem, 1869–1872, 1875–1878, and 1892 On 21 July 1869 Hunt left Florence, and on 31 August he arrived in Jerusalem. He had already devoted several months to thinking about the major religious paintings that he intended undertaking in the Holy Land, and he now began the preparatory oil for *The Shadow of Death* (1869–73; Leeds City Art Gallery). The depiction of the Saviour and Virgin in the interior of a carpenter's workshop was influenced by Ruskin, who in the third volume of *Modern Painters* (1856) had called for a sacred art 'representing events historically recorded, with solemn effort at a sincere and unartificial conception' (*Works*, 5.85). Hunt's reading of Ernest Renan's *Vie de Jésus* (1863) in 1869 encouraged him to depict the Saviour as a working man, an image that he was well aware would appeal to a wide audience. Indeed, the engraving published in 1878 was Agnews' most widely circulated nineteenth-century print. But by imbuing his picture with typological symbolism Hunt wanted to convey to his audience the spiritual as well as archaeological aspects of his subject.

The definitive painting of *The Shadow of Death* (1870–73; Manchester City Galleries) was begun in Jerusalem in April 1870. The figures of Christ and the Virgin were painted out of doors, the models posing on the roof of Hunt's house in the Muslim quarter. Two movable huts were constructed in an attempt to regulate the light, since the artist was determined to capture faithfully the impression of the setting afternoon sun. This was a heroic but virtually impossible task on such a large canvas and involved Hunt in continual reworking of both versions. They were completed after his return to London in July 1872, and in March 1873 were sold to Agnews for 10,000 guineas. The large canvas, which was on view at their Bond Street gallery from December 1873 to August 1874, was described that May in an American periodical as 'probably the most talked-about painting in the world' ('Holman Hunt and his "Shadow of death"', 657).

The other religious subject conceived in Florence in 1868–9 was *The Triumph of the Innocents*, based on chapter 2 of the gospel of St Matthew. Hunt transformed the traditional iconography of angels attending the Holy Family on their flight into Egypt, substituting a spiritualist vision of the infants condemned to death by Herod at the time of Christ's birth. He researched extensively to secure what he regarded as the correct setting for this subject, and between February and March 1870 encamped at Gaza, painting at night the background of the first version (1870–1903; Harvard U., Fogg Art Museum). On this trip he also carefully studied the local costumes and customs that he was to incorporate into the picture.

The composition was developed on Hunt's return to Jerusalem at the end of 1875, and in the following March he began a much larger version (1876–87; Walker Art Gallery, Liverpool). The series of preparatory drawings for *The Triumph of the Innocents* reflects his study of the old masters, which influenced his new determination to paint a digest of his ideas rather than a transcript from nature. The second version was begun on defective canvas, necessitating continual repainting both in Jerusalem and London, to which he had returned in April 1878. A third version, begun in 1883 (Tate collection), was shown at the Fine Art Society in 1885. It was accompanied by a descriptive pamphlet written by the artist, which attempted to explain the symbolism of the picture, with its consoling message of the existence of the afterlife.

An even longer pamphlet was on sale at the New Gallery in 1899, when Hunt's last major original composition, *The Miracle of the Sacred Fire in the Church of the Holy Sepulchre, Jerusalem* (Harvard U., Fogg Art Museum), was first shown. On his arrival in Jerusalem in 1892, for a fourth and final visit, he 'felt it would be a pity if I … should not take the opportunity of perpetuating for future generations the astounding scene which many writers have so vividly described' (*Pre-Raphaelitism*, 1st edn, 2.380–81). This was the fraudulent ceremony that for centuries had taken place on (the Greek) Easter Saturday in the presence of hordes of credulous and often hysterical pilgrims, when the light that usually burns over the sepulchre of Christ was apparently spontaneously rekindled. The crowded composition of Hunt's picture—incorporating over 200 figures—reflects the chaotic nature of the ceremony. He worked on it sporadically from 1893 to 1899, and it can be viewed as the culmination of his mission as artist-ethnographer. His attention to the details of the church architecture and of the costumes of the different races is as acute as ever, even if his personal involvement with the subject prevented him from realizing that the significance of the ceremony could not be successfully conveyed by purely pictorial means.

Later career and writings, 1872–1910 In 1874 Ruskin, deeply impressed by *The Shadow of Death*, wrote to J. A. Froude:

Among the men I know, or have known, he is the *One* (literal) Christian, of intellectual power. I have known many Christians—many men of capacity: only Hunt who is both, and who is sincerely endeavouring to represent to our eyes the things which the eyes were blessed which saw. (*Works*, 37.83)

Hunt, however, soon alienated the Anglican establishment. His late wife's youngest sister (Marion) Edith (1846–1931) had been in love with him since 1868, and in June 1873 they became engaged, even though union with a deceased wife's sister was (until 1907) proscribed under English law. Their courageous decision to proceed isolated them from both their families. The marriage took place in Neuchâtel on 8 November 1875, and in the following month they sailed from Venice to Alexandria *en route* for Jerusalem. Edith proved a strong and supportive partner, and Hunt was an uxorious husband. Their first child, Gladys Millais Mulock Holman Hunt, was born in Jerusalem on 20 September 1876; their second, a boy, Hilary Lushington, in London on 6 May 1879. Edith and both children posed for Hunt's subject pictures as well as for portraits. Edith, for example, was the first model for *The Bride of Bethlehem* (1879–84; priv. coll.), an attempt at an image that would appeal to devotees of the aesthetic movement; it was exhibited at the Grosvenor Gallery in 1885. Two years later Hunt showed there the large *Master Hilary: the Tracer* (c.1885–1887; priv. coll.), the last and most successful of a trio of paintings of his children. Hilary posed in the drawing room of the house in which the Hunts had lived since November 1881—Draycott Lodge, Fulham—looking out at his father, who was painting him from the garden.

Hilary also posed for the chorister holding a lily in *May Morning on Magdalen Tower*, the first version of which (1888–92; Birmingham Museum and Art Gallery) was begun in Oxford in May 1888. As with nearly all Hunt's late major subjects there was a long gestation period—his interest in the May day ceremony and his desire to paint it had begun in 1851. According to his letter of 19 November 1906 to Barrow Cadbury, the first owner of the large version (1888–91; Lady Lever Art Gallery, Port Sunlight), 'The subject itself is, in my mind, one of peculiar interest because it testifies to a latent but strong racial poetic feeling in the English nature' (Bennett, 59). Hunt's nationalism in the 1880s was very pronounced, fuelled by the growing influence of contemporary French art, which he deplored, on the British art scene. But at the same time his respect for, and interest in, religions other than Christianity increased. The pamphlet accompanying the picture's exhibition in 1891 (at the Gainsborough Gallery in Bond Street) makes clear that he considered *May Morning* a religious work, celebrating 'a reverent act of worship [that accepts] the sun as a perfect symbol of creative power' (*Pre-Raphaelitism*, 2nd edn, 2.418). The composition includes an elderly, bearded Parsi (an adherent of sun worship) next to a group of Oxford academics singing the 'Hymnus eucharisticus'.

The denial of sectarianism and the emphasis on the positive value of religious worship expressed in this work look forward to the nearly life-size replica of *The Light of the World* (c.1900–1904; St Paul's Cathedral, London). This, Hunt's last oil painting, was begun as a protest against the treatment of the original by Keble College. He was incensed that visitors had been asked to pay to see it, and in a letter of 28 February 1894 to a relative of Thomas Combe he described the authorities there as 'bigotted Goths' (Maas, 97). He signalled his own liberalism by adding to the replica a crescent aperture in the lantern held by the Saviour, suggesting that the light of the world was available to all, Muslim as well as Christian. The painting was bought in 1904 by the shipowner and sociologist Charles Booth, who paid for it to tour Canada, Australasia, and South Africa. It was seen by millions of people, many of whom had never previously entered an art gallery.

Hunt's advancing glaucoma necessitated employing Edward Robert Hughes as a studio assistant on this picture and on the large oil of *The Lady of Shalott* (c.1888?–1905; Wadsworth Atheneum, Hartford, Connecticut), which *The Times* of 22 May 1905 rightly judged 'a fine thing, the crown of a fine life's work'. In letters of November 1897 to the Birmingham MP J. T. Middlemore, Hunt described it as 'a picture with deep significance', but stressed that he had 'no intention of explaining the details' (MSS, Birmingham Museum and Art Gallery). This suggests that he wanted the image to be judged on aesthetic grounds. It synthesizes elements of classical, Eastern, and Christian cultures, each of which had a precise meaning for the artist, but which he declined to elucidate in his 1905 pamphlet on the painting. For once Hunt had moved away from didacticism towards an open-ended approach which allies this picture with *fin de siècle* European symbolism.

In 1903 the Hunts moved to 18 Melbury Road, Kensington, where the artist worked on his memoirs. This major project had been in his mind since the mid-1880s, when he published a series of articles entitled 'The Pre-Raphaelite Brotherhood: a fight for art' in the *Contemporary Review*, to coincide with his first comprehensive one-man exhibition held at the Fine Art Society in 1886. His agenda, in *Pre-Raphaelitism and the Pre-Raphaelite Brotherhood*, was first to promote the Hunt–Millais wing of the brotherhood at the expense of Rossetti and Madox Brown; and second to attack foreign influence on contemporary British art, since he felt that the role of the artist was to give 'a tangible and worthy image of the national body and mind' (*Pre-Raphaelitism*, 1st edn, 1.xiii). The two volumes were published in December 1905. Their self-aggrandizing tone caused deep offence, and particularly incensed F. G. Stephens (who had been alienated from Hunt since 1880). But commercially the book was a success: 1500 copies out of a print run of 2000 were sold within a month, and by April 1906 Hunt was preparing a second edition. This appeared posthumously in 1913.

On 28 June 1905 Hunt received an honorary DCL from Oxford University, and on 24 July he was awarded the Order of Merit. In October–November 1906 a retrospective exhibition of his works was shown at the Leicester Galleries in London. It attracted 30,000 visitors and was followed by successful one-man shows on a larger scale at Manchester (1906–7), Liverpool, and Glasgow (1907).

From 1901 the Hunts had spent their summers at Sonning-on-Thames, Berkshire, in a house designed by Edith and Gladys Holman Hunt for the artist's retirement.

On 22 August 1910 Hunt caught what appeared to be a slight chill in the garden there. He became critically ill, and on 6 September was brought back to his home, 18 Melbury Road, Kensington, where he died at 12.30 p.m. the following day. The cause of death was given as emphysema, chronic bronchitis, and respiratory and cardiac failure. Unusually for this period Hunt had left instructions that he should be cremated. The funeral took place on 10 September at Golders Green crematorium; following a campaign by his friends his ashes were buried in the crypt of St Paul's Cathedral two days later, next to the grave of Turner. William Michael Rossetti, sole survivor of the Pre-Raphaelite Brotherhood, was one of the pall-bearers. A report in *The Times* of 13 September 1910 makes Hunt's place in popular consciousness quite clear:

> The thousands who assembled in St. Paul's Cathedral yesterday, and the crowds in the churchyard outside, were the representatives of many millions who had never seen Holman Hunt in the flesh but to whom he was far more than a name; for his pictures had carried him, a revered and familiar friend, into homes without number all over the world.

Character, aims, and reputation The popular appeal of his pictures was crucially important to Hunt, whose youthful study of Shakespeare had led him 'to rate lightly that kind of art devised only for the initiated' (*Pre-Raphaelitism*, 1st edn, 1.148). He never forgot his own relatively humble origins, and was a convinced egalitarian, committed to widening working-class access to the arts. The way in which he overcame opposition to his choice of career shows remarkable determination and foreshadows his habit in maturity of setting himself almost insuperable artistic challenges. His memoirs give a misleading impression of an intensely serious young man, but contemporary accounts stress his sense of humour as well as his gregarious nature and his wide circle of friends. An acquaintance described him in her journal of 28 September 1860 as:

> a very genial, young-looking creature, with a large, square, yellow beard, clear blue laughing eyes, a nose with a merry little upward turn in it, dimples in the cheek, and the whole expression sunny and full of simple boyish happiness. His voice is most musical, and there is nothing in his look or bearing, spite of the strongly-marked forehead, to suggest the High Priest of Pre-Raphaelitism. (*Journals of Caroline Fox*, 231–2)

Hunt did, however, regard himself in this light and had declared, in the diary of his visit to the Dead Sea in November 1854: 'I regard my occupation as somewhat akin to that of the priests' (Bronkhurst, 'An interesting series', 115). He took on himself a priestlike role because he believed that factual information conveyed visually was valuable in itself, nature being a repository of transcendent truth. Like the priests, what he sought was no less than 'the power of undying appeal to the hearts of living men' (*Pre-Raphaelitism*, 1st edn, 1.48). One of the most immediate means of achieving this in the Victorian age was by painting pictures that told a story. Indeed, Hunt claimed that 'The Literature and Art of an age are ever inspired by a kindred spirit, the latter faithfully following the former' (ibid., 1.325–6), a view that in his later years isolated him from progressive trends in English painting. He was committed to incorporating meaning in his major works, but not at the expense of conveying a convincing representation of nature, whether in terms of landscape or an intensely realized human situation. In a pamphlet issued in 1865, *An Apology for the Symbolism Introduced into the Picture called The Light of the World*, he stated that 'The first ambition of the painter … should be to give a delightsome aspect to all his representations' (p. 2). Whether he consistently achieved this aim is questionable but what is beyond doubt is his power to create some unforgettable images.

In the same pamphlet Hunt declared that 'It is for each artist to decide for himself which principle he will adopt, not to make laws for others' (*An Apology*, 2). His intellectually questing nature was never content to take anything on trust, whether in terms of art or religion. Although he regarded himself as an Anglican this did not 'forbid a feeling of fellowship with any other communities that call upon the God of Abraham as their God' ('Religion and art', 41). His dislike of narrow sectarianism—which underlies the composition of *The Hireling Shepherd* and *Our English Coasts, 1852*—deepened into disgust on his first visit to Jerusalem, where he found squabbling Christian sects vying with each other to convert the poverty-stricken Jews. Bribery was endemic and Hunt was so incensed by the activities of Samuel Gobat, Anglican bishop of Jerusalem, in this respect that in 1858 he published a pamphlet unmasking him (*Jerusalem: Bishop Gobat in re Hanna Hadoub*). This almost certainly ruined Hunt's chances of ever receiving a major church commission. In a letter of 1890 he criticized Anglican church decoration for 'using Art—not for instruction—only in a sort of heraldic form. This is—in my eyes—a very grave defect, for it makes unbelievers treat our divine faith as only a fossilised myth' (Brumbaugh, 89). The implication is that his own instructive religious art had such a powerful impact because it stemmed from an intensely personal form of protestantism, which enabled him to reinvigorate sacred themes.

The influence of *The Light of the World* as a protestant icon cannot be overestimated. For many years it was illustrated in the Book of Common Prayer, and reproductions of the image continue to sell in their thousands. It has inspired artists ranging from G. F. Watts to Henry Moore, and together with *The Awakening Conscience* and *The Scapegoat* it is regularly caricatured in the British press (for example, in a cartoon by Peter Brookes in *The Times* of 29 January 1983). This suggests that these images are considered part of the national consciousness, and it is certainly true that in the late twentieth century Hunt's reputation recovered from the backlash that it suffered in the early and mid-twentieth century, when his didacticism and meticulous technique were generally regarded as unacceptable. In 1969 Mary Bennett's pioneering exhibition of Hunt's works, at the Walker Art Gallery, Liverpool, included 63 oil paintings (out of a relatively small output of less than 170 known works), and displayed his versatility, which ranged from the accomplished, hard-edged drawings of the late 1840s to portraits and watercolours, etchings and illustrations.

But, despite the sums that his major works fetch at auction, by the start of the twenty-first century Hunt had not regained the sort of popularity that the British public accords to paintings of alluring women by more decorative Victorian artists. Yet works such as *The Afterglow in Egypt*, *The Scapegoat*, *Isabella, or, The Pot of Basil*, and *The Shadow of Death*, as well as those of the high Pre-Raphaelite period, are deeply memorable on all levels. Together with *The Lady of Shalott* they have an enduring place in the history of British art.

Hunt's significance as one of the three original founders of the Pre-Raphaelite Brotherhood, and the only one to have remained true to its original principles, was acknowledged on 19 July 1879, when *Vanity Fair* published a caricature of him entitled *The Pre-Raphaelite of the World*. The way in which many of his major paintings focus on highly dramatic situations, fusing truth to nature with a serious moral message, struck such a chord with the Victorians that his influence during his lifetime can be compared to that of Thomas Carlyle, Ruskin, and Charles Dickens.

JUDITH BRONKHURST

Sources J. Bronkhurst, *William Holman Hunt: a catalogue raisonné* (2004) • W. H. Hunt, *Pre-Raphaelitism and the Pre-Raphaelite Brotherhood*, 2 vols. (1905) • W. Holman-Hunt, *Pre-Raphaelitism and the Pre-Raphaelite Brotherhood*, 2nd edn, ed. M. E. Holman-Hunt, 2 vols. (1913), 2.384, 401–5, 411–33 [incl. appxs with ed. repr. of Hunt's pamphlets on his pictures] • G. P. Landow, *William Holman Hunt and typological symbolism* (1979), 2–7, 15 [incl. bibliography] • D. Holman-Hunt, *My grandfather, his wives and loves* (1969), 154, 169, 238, 243, 252 [first pubd account of Hunt's relationship with Annie Miller] • J. Maas, *Holman Hunt and The light of the world* (1984) • *A Pre-Raphaelite friendship: the correspondence of William Holman Hunt and John Lucas Tupper*, ed. J. H. Coombs and others (1986), 45, 246 • [M. Bennett], *William Holman Hunt: an exhibition arranged by the Walker Art Gallery* (1969) • J. Bronkhurst, '"An interesting series of adventures to look back upon": William Holman Hunt's visit to the Dead Sea in November 1854', *Pre-Raphaelite papers*, ed. L. Parris (1984), 123 • W. H. Hunt, letter to C. Patmore, [9–12 May 1851], Bodl. Oxf., MS Eng. lett. d. 40, fol. 31 • A. Woolner, *Thomas Woolner, R.A., sculptor and poet: his life in letters* (1917), 193 • *The diary of Ford Madox Brown*, ed. V. Surtees (1981), 181 • *The works of John Ruskin*, ed. E. T. Cook and A. Wedderburn, library edn, 39 vols. (1903–12), vol. 4, pp. 263–5; vol. 5, p. 85; vol. 12, p. 330, 349; vol. 37, p. 83 • *The journals of Caroline Fox, 1835–71: a selection*, ed. W. Monk (1972), 231–2 • W. H. Hunt, 'Religion and art', *Contemporary Review*, 71 (1897), 41 • W. H. Hunt, letters to J. T. Middlemore, 10 and 22 Nov 1897, MSS, Birmingham Museum and Art Gallery • [W. H. Hunt], *An apology for the symbolism introduced into the picture called The light of the world* [1865] [copy in Kenneth Spencer Research Library, University of Kansas] • *The Times* (8–10 Sept 1910) • *The Times* (12–13 Sept 1910) • W. H. Hunt, letter to W. B. Scott, 11 Feb 1860, MS, Princeton University Library, Troxell collection • T. B. Brumbaugh, 'Two William Holman Hunt letters to John Clifford, chiefly concerning Henry Wentworth Monk', *Pre-Raphaelite Review*, 3 (1979), 89 • *The letters of Christina Rossetti*, ed. A. H. Harrison, 1 (1997), 106 • W. M. Rossetti, *Dante Gabriel Rossetti: his family letters, with a memoir*, 2 vols. (1895), 1.135 • H. Allingham and E. B. Williams, eds., *Letters to William Allingham* (1911), 292 • 'Holman Hunt and his "Shadow of death"', *Appleton's Journal*, 11 (23 May 1874), 656–8 • 'Mr. Holman Hunt's *Lady of Shalott*', *The Times* (22 May 1905) • W. M. Rossetti, 'Reminiscences of Holman Hunt', *Contemporary Review*, 98 (1910), 389 • J. Bronkhurst, 'Fruits of a connoisseur's friendship: Sir Thomas Fairbairn and William Holman Hunt', *Burlington Magazine*, 125 (1983), 586–97, esp. 588 • parish register, St Giles Cripplegate, 10 June 1827, GL · parish register, St Paul's Deptford, 18 Feb 1798 [baptism: Sarah Hobman, mother] **Archives** Getty Center for the History of Art and the Humanities, Los Angeles, Archives of the History of Art, papers, MSS · Hunt. L., MSS collection and Hunt/Tupper collection · Hunt. L., corresp. · Hunt. L., letters · JRL, MSS · Tate collection, papers · University of British Columbia, papers · University of Kansas, Kenneth Spencer Research Library, albums, MS 60:1/3 | BL, letter to Sir Alfred Fripp, Add. MS 46445 · BL, corresp. with Macmillans, Add. MS 55231 · BL, letters to Ford Madox Brown, Add. MS 38794 · BL, letters to F. G. Stephens and Sir Charles Dilke, Add. MS 43910 · Bodl. Oxf., letters to H. W. Acland · Bodl. Oxf., corresp. with Thomas Combe and Martha Combe, MS Eng. lett. c. 296 · Bodl. Oxf., letters to Coventry Patmore · Bodl. Oxf., letters to F. G. Stephens, MS Don. e 66–68 · CUL, letters to H. V. Tebbs · JRL, letters to Mr and Mrs G. L. Craik · JRL, letters to Thomas Seddon · Morgan L., Millais papers, MSS · Princeton University, New Jersey, Troxell collection, MSS · Theatre Museum, London, letters to the lord chamberlain's licensee · U. Birm., letters to M. H. Spielmann · U. Newcastle, Robinson L., letters to Sir Walter and Lady Trevelyan · University of British Columbia, Angeli-Dennis papers · University of British Columbia, letters to James Leathart · University of Kansas, Lawrence, Kenneth Spencer Research Library, Shields corresp. collection · V&A NAL, letters to C. R. Ashbee · V&A NAL, letters to Ford Madox Brown

Likenesses W. H. Hunt, self-portrait, oils, c.1841–1842, AM Oxf. · W. H. Hunt, self-portrait, oils, 1845, Birmingham Museums and Art Gallery · J. E. Millais, graphite, 1853, NPG · D. G. Rossetti, graphite drawing, 1853, Birmingham Museums and Art Gallery · W. H. Hunt, self-portrait, pen and ink, 1854, Arizona State University · J. E. Millais, graphite and watercolour drawing, 1854, AM Oxf. · C. L. Dodgson, photograph, 1860, Princeton University, New Jersey, Morris L. Parrish collection of Victorian novelists · D. W. Wynfield, photograph, c.1862–1864, NPG · W. H. Hunt, group portrait, oils, 1863 (*London Bridge on the night of the marriage of the prince and princess of Wales*), AM Oxf. · J. M. Cameron, two photographs, 1864, NPG · J. Ballantyne, oils, 1865, NPG · Elliott & Fry, carte-de-visite, 1865, priv. coll. · W. H. Hunt, self-portrait, oils, 1867–75, Uffizi Gallery, Florence [*see illus.*] · W. B. Richmond, oils, c.1879, NPG · Kingsbury & Notcutt, photograph, 1890, NPG · Walery, photograph, 1891, priv. coll. · F. Hollyer, double portrait, photograph, 1894 (with Ruskin), priv. coll. · W. B. Richmond, oils, 1900, NPG · R. Peacock, oils, exh. Liverpool Autumn Exhibition 1902, Walker Art Gallery, Liverpool · G. Reid, oil sketch, c.1903–1904, repro. in A. S. Walker, 'The portraits of Sir George Reid, R.S.A.', *Studio*, 55 (1912) · G. Reid, oils, exh. New Gallery 1904; Sothebys, 16 Dec 1987 · E. J. M. Hallé, drawing, 1907, Royal Collection · H. Speed, oils, 1909, Birmingham Museums and Art Gallery · E. R. Hughes, miniature watercolour on vellum, c.1911 ('aged 53'), Scot. NPG; repro. in *Secret passion to noble fashion* (1999), 227 [exhibition catalogue, Holburne Museum, Bath]; on loan to Scot. NPG from Albion collection of portrait miniatures · Barraud, photograph, NPG; repro. in *Men and Women of the Day*, 3 (1890) · H. J. Brooks, group portrait, oils (*Private view of the Old Masters Exhibition, Royal Academy, 1888*), NPG · Elliott & Fry, photograph, NPG · Elliott & Fry, W. Jeffrey, and London Stereoscopic Co., photographs and cartes-de-visite, NPG · Spy [L. Ward], chromolithograph caricature, NPG; repro. in *VF* (19 July 1879)

Wealth at death £16,169 1s. 4d.: probate, 25 Oct 1910, *CGPLA Eng. & Wales*

Hunter, Alexander (1729?–1809), physician, was born in Edinburgh, the son of a druggist. After a grammar-school education he trained as a physician at Edinburgh, pursuing additional anatomical training in Rouen and Paris, before graduating MD in Edinburgh in 1753, with a thesis entitled 'De cantharidibus'. After practising as a physician for a few months in Gainsborough, Lincolnshire, and for several years in Beverley, Yorkshire, he moved in 1763 to York, where he practised successfully in the city and among the county gentry until his death. He was a physician at the York Dispensary from its inception in 1788. Later, in 1793, he founded a private house in Acomb, for the care of 'persons of condition only' who were mentally ill. But it was his actions as a founder in 1777 of the York Lunatic Asylum, and thereafter as first physician, that aroused controversy.

Although the York asylum was a public institution, a policy of increasing secrecy in its medical and financial management was adopted, while it began to admit affluent patients, as well as those in impoverished or moderate circumstances for whom the asylum had supposedly been created. This attracted a growing amount of criticism, and Hunter led the defence in a polemical war of words that included his anonymously published pamphlets of 1788 and 1792, *A Letter from a Subscriber to the York Lunatic Asylum* and *The History of the Rise and Progress of the York Lunatic Asylum*. The controversy began locally in 1788, built up to a local inquiry in 1813–14, and was subsumed into a national investigation conducted by the select committee on madhouses in 1813–15. Although Hunter died before the reforming impulse had come to a climax, his posthumous reputation both as a man of financial probity, and as a solicitous specialist, suffered. Significantly, both in his introduction to *Sylva* (1786) and in his *Culina famulatrix medicinae* (1804; fourth edn, 1806) Hunter justified the right of the professional man to use his time in liberal rather than medical pursuits.

Hunter's life corresponded to an early Georgian image of the physician as a genteel member of a learned profession whose interests were not bounded by occupation; an ideal that was becoming outdated with increasing medical specialism. His first book, *A Treatise on the Buxton Waters* (1761) was timely in investigating a popular practice of taking the waters, and so went through seven editions. Less well-known medical publications were on phthisis (1795) and the Harrogate waters (1806). However, most of his writing was on non-medical matters. His *Georgical Essays* of 1770–72 were a product of his activities as a founder member of the York Agricultural Society. A continuing interest in notable contemporary innovations in farming led in the 1790s to an honorary membership of the newly founded board of agriculture, and also to three further agricultural publications: *A New Method of Raising Wheat* (1796); *Outlines of Agriculture* (1795); and *An Illustration of the Analogy between Vegetable and Animal Parturition* (1800?). He is best known, however, for his illustrated editions with notes of John Evelyn's *Sylva* (1776) and *Terra* (1778). He was elected a fellow of the Royal Society of London in 1775, and of that of Edinburgh in 1792.

In 1765 Hunter married Elizabeth Dealtry (d. 1794), of Gainsborough, with whom he had two sons, John and George; and in 1799 he married Ann Bell (d. 1814). Hunter died on 7 May 1809 and was buried in the York parish church of St Michael le Belfry. ANNE DIGBY

Sources O. Allen, *History of the York dispensary* (1845) · A. Digby, 'Changes in the asylum: the case of York', *Economic History Review*, 2nd ser., 36 (1983), 218–39 · A. Digby, *Madness, medicine and morality*

(1985) • A. Digby, *From York Lunatic Asylum to Bootham Park Hospital*, Borthwick Papers, 69 (1986) • [A. Hunter], *A letter from a subscriber to the York lunatic asylum* (1788) • A. Hunter, 'Memoir', *Culina famulatrix medicinae, or, Receipts in modern cookery, with a medical commentary*, 4th edn (1806) • *York Courant* (1772–1815) • will, proved, 22 Sept 1809, Borth. Inst. • [A. Hunter], *The history of the rise and progress of the York lunatic asylum* (1792) • *DNB* • F. Bennet and M. Melrose, *Index of fellows of the Royal Society of Edinburgh: elected November 1783 – July 1883*, ed. H. Frew, rev. edn (1984) • *The record of the Royal Society of London*, 4th edn (1940) • memorial tablet, St Michael le Belfry, York
Archives Wellcome L., Smythe MSS
Likenesses J. R. Smith, mezzotint, pubd 1805, Wellcome L. • portrait, Bootham Park Hospital, York
Wealth at death under £3500—incl. house in Petergate, York, and two estates in Lincolnshire est. at c.£2100; private madhouse at Acomb (income from which not given); small monetary bequests amounting to £345 specified and possibly another £150; a few bequests, notably of books: will, Borth. Inst., proved 22 Sept 1809

Hunter, Andrew (1744–1809), Church of Scotland minister and university teacher, was born on 15 February 1744 in Edinburgh, the fourth son (but the eldest to survive infancy) of Andrew Hunter (1695–1770), writer to the signet and eighth in the Abbotshill branch of the Hunters of Hunterston, and his wife, Grizel, daughter of Colonel William Maxwell of Cardoness. He attended James Mundell's school in West Bow, Edinburgh, from 1750 and intermittent classes in Edinburgh University between 1758 and 1766 but he did not graduate. His studies were guided by Robert Walker of St Giles's, Edinburgh, a noted evangelical. He then spent a year studying theology in Utrecht but without having matriculated. Ample means and filial piety may explain why, although licensed by Edinburgh presbytery on 25 March 1767, he remained at home until after his father's death.

Hunter was active among Edinburgh's literary and debating clubs—a practice he later recommended to his students—from at least 1760, when he was a founder member of the Newtonian Society. He attended the Belles Lettres Society and in 1783 was a founder member of the Royal Society of Edinburgh in the short-lived literary class. He may also have belonged to the earlier Philosophical Society, which paved the way for the Royal Society. He moved easily in the circles of Edinburgh's literati in its 'age of improvement'; James Boswell certainly found his company congenial enough.

On 20 September 1770 Hunter was ordained to the second charge (New Church) of Dumfries. In 1772 he sold the family property at Abbotshill and bought Barjarg, south of Thornhill, in Dumfriesshire. He improved the estate by reforestation, by bringing upland into cultivation, and by lime quarrying. The last proved highly profitable. He later made innovative use of machinery, some of which was salvaged for preservation in the late twentieth century; a water-wheel features in Edinburgh's Museum of Scotland.

On 18 February 1779 Hunter was awarded the DD by Edinburgh University and on 14 April he married Mainie Schaw (1756–1806), eldest daughter of William Napier, seventh Baron Napier of Merchistoun (1730–1775), army officer, and Mary Anne Cathcart (1727–1774). Later in the same year he was translated to New Greyfriars, Edinburgh, and appointed joint professor of divinity in the university. His senior colleague, Robert Hamilton, died in 1787. Hunter's patrons on the town council ensured his election to the chair in the face of opposition from moderates but his conservative Calvinism (he lectured from Benedict Pictet's *Theologia Christiana*) and stolid style made him an unappealing lecturer. Eleven manuscript volumes of his exegetical and theological lectures survive in the university library. His personal dealings with students, including financial support, displayed his cordiality and fairness to better effect but moderate critics of his theology, like Alexander Carlyle, took less kindly to Hunter than Edinburgh's clubbable circles. He published only a handful of sermons.

On 2 April 1786, after much altercation, Hunter was translated to the Tron Church as colleague and, from 1788, successor to John Drysdale. In 1792 he was elected moderator of the general assembly. He backed many evangelical causes—Lady Glenorchy's Chapel, the British and Foreign Bible Society, Edinburgh Missionary Society—and was a strong advocate of Sunday observance. His support of Charles Simeon's visits in 1796 and 1798 could not prevent the assembly of 1799 debarring Church of England clergymen and ministers of other denominations from kirk pulpits. In church controversies, notably the John Leslie case of 1805, Hunter's candour and refined liberality earned wide respect. In temper an evangelical moderate, he had the good fortune to live a generation before the Disruption. His son, John, of similar cast, was to remain in the establishment.

Hunter died in his grand house in New Street, one of the sights of the city, on 21 (or possibly 22) April 1809 and was buried in Canongate churchyard on 25 April. His son William Francis succeeded to the estate and added the name Arundell on marriage. The family retains the home and estate to the present day, apart from Barjarg Tower, whose library Thomas Carlyle relished while resident nearby in bleak Craigenputtoch.

D. F. WRIGHT

Sources D. F. Wright, 'Andrew Hunter of Barjarg (1744–1809): evangelical divine in an age of improvement', *Records of the Scottish Church History Society*, 26 (1996), 135–68 • A. A. Hunter, *The pedigree of Hunter of Abbotshill and Barjarg* (1905) • D. Butler, *The Tron Kirk of Edinburgh* (1906) • J. Kay, *A series of original portraits and caricature etchings … with biographical sketches and illustrative anecdotes*, ed. [H. Paton and others], 2 vols. in 4 (1837–8) • A. Bower, *The history of the University of Edinburgh*, 3 (1830) • Newtonian Society, minute book, 1760–64, U. Edin. L., MS Gen. 1423 • *DNB* • *Scots Magazine and Edinburgh Literary Miscellany*, 71 (1809), 320
Archives Ewart Library, Dumfries, collection • NA Scot., family MSS, GD 78 • U. Edin. L., lecture notes, Dc.3.22–32
Likenesses J. Kay, caricature, etching, 1785, BM, NPG • J. Kay, caricature, etching, 1789, NPG • J. Tassie, plaster medallion, 1791 (after H. Raeburn), Scot. NPG • plaster medallion, 1791 (after J. Tassie), Scot. NPG • Dawe & Hodgetts, mezzotint, pubd 1810 (after H. Raeburn), BM, Scot. NPG • J. Kay, caricature, 1837, repro. in Kay, *Series of original portraits* • Dawe & Hodgetts, engraving, Scot. NPG • J. Kay, caricature, etching, BM • H. Raeburn, oils, repro. in Hunter, *Pedigree of Hunter*
Wealth at death see wills, NA Scot., family MSS, GD 78/229 and 232

Hunter [*née* Home], **Anne** (1742–1821), poet, was born in Greenlaw, Berwickshire, the eldest daughter of Robert Boyne Home, surgeon, and his wife, Mary, *née* Hutchinson. Her brothers included Sir Everard *Home (1756–1832) and Robert *Home (1752–1834), painter. Little is known of her early life, but on 22 July 1771, after a long engagement, she married John *Hunter (1728–1793), surgeon. Before her marriage she had gained some note as a lyrical poet, her 'Flower of the Forest' appearing in *The Lark*, an Edinburgh periodical, in 1765. Her social literary parties were among the most enjoyable of her time, though not always to the taste of her taciturn and work-driven husband. She counted Elizabeth Carter, Mary Delany, Elizabeth Montagu, and Hester Thrale among her closest friends. In the 1790s she became acquainted with Haydn during his visits to England, and he set a number of her songs to music, including 'My mother bids me bind my hair', originally written to an air of Pleydell's. She also anonymously provided the lyrics for his *Six Original Canzonettas* (1794), which he dedicated to her, and for some of his *Second Set of Canzonettas* (1795).

On her husband's death in 1793, Anne Hunter was left ill provided for, and for some time she was indebted for a maintenance partly to the queen's bounty and to the generosity of Dr Maxwell Garthshore (1732–1812), and partly to the sale of her husband's furniture, library, and curiosities. In 1799 parliament voted £15,000 for the Hunterian museum, which placed Anne Hunter in fair circumstances. She collected her *Poems* in 1802 (2nd edn, 1803), dedicating them to her son Captain John Banks. In 1804 she published *The Sports of the Genii*, in memory of Susan MacDonald, who had died in 1803 at the age of twenty-one, and whose drawings had inspired the poems, originally written in 1797. Her poetry was praised for its natural feeling and simplicity of expression, although some reviewers were harsher in their judgements, the reviewer in the *Edinburgh Review* of January 1803, for instance, stating that 'Poetry ... appears to have been studied as an accomplishment than pursued from any natural propensity' (Todd, 170).

Anne Hunter had four children, and the familial themes and dedications found throughout her *Poems* would seem to contradict the assertion by Roodhouse Gloyne, her husband's biographer, that her children played little part in her life. She did, however, later become estranged from her surviving son, John, although her daughter, who married Sir James Campbell, was one of her main supports in her old age. Anne Hunter lived in retirement in London until her death on 7 January 1821.

G. T. BETTANY, *rev.* M. CLARE LOUGHLIN-CHOW

Sources J. Todd, ed., *A dictionary of British and American women writers, 1660–1800* (1984) • R. Lonsdale, ed., *Eighteenth-century women poets: an Oxford anthology* (1989) • *IGI* • D. Baptie, *A handbook of musical biography*, 2nd edn (1887) • O. Ebel, *Women composers: a biographical handbook of woman's work in music*, 3rd edn (1913) • *GM*, 1st ser., 91/1 (1821), 89–90 • C. Rogers, *The modern Scottish minstrel, or, The songs of Scotland of the past half-century*, 1 (1855), 39–40 • S. R. Gloyne, *John Hunter* (1950)

Archives RCS Eng., papers, esp. letters

Hunter, Sir Archibald (1856–1936), army officer, was born in Kilburn, London, on 6 September 1856, the eldest son of Archibald Hunter (*d.* 1868) of Cannon Street, London, a cloth merchant, calico printer, and friend of Cobden, and his wife and first cousin, Mary Jane (*c.*1834–1905), daughter of Major Duncan Grahame, late of the 6th foot. Both his parents were from Scottish lowland families. Known to his family (and later to the army) as Archie, he was educated at Glasgow Academy (1869–73) and Sandhurst (1874–5), and on 27 August 1875 was commissioned lieutenant in the 4th foot (the King's Own), joining the 1st battalion at Gibraltar. He quickly made his mark as a keen and efficient officer. From 1879 to 1881 he served with the battalion in Barbados, and from April 1880 to November 1882 served as adjutant. The battalion lost a tenth of its fighting strength in a yellow fever epidemic and was recalled to England. Hunter was promoted captain on 30 August 1882.

In February 1884 Hunter joined the new British-officered Egyptian army, and served with it until 1899, initially with the 9th Sudanese. He served on the Gordon relief expedition (1884–5)—when the Egyptian army was largely on the line of communication—working on transport, administration, and intelligence, and was for the first time in action. Then and subsequently he gained a reputation for bravery and efficiency. He was made brevet major on 15 June 1885. Hunter was severely wounded during a skirmish with Mahdists at Koshe in December 1885 (so missing the battle of Giniss) and was awarded the DSO. He commanded a brigade, and was again wounded at the battle of Toski on 3 August 1889, when the emir Wad al-Nejumi was defeated. On 17 August he was made brevet lieutenant-colonel, in recognition of his services. He was promoted substantive major on 15 June 1892, and obtained the further brevet of colonel on 6 January 1894.

From August 1892 to July 1894 Hunter served as governor of Suakin and the Red Sea littoral, and from July 1894 to November 1896 he commanded the Sudan frontier field force. On leave in Cairo he enjoyed prostitutes and, he wrote to his brother, 'always got the clap' (Hunter, 38); at Suakin he had an Abyssinian mistress.

In the 1896–8 operations which culminated in the recapture of Khartoum, Hunter was Kitchener's right-hand man. At Firket, on 7 June 1896, he successfully commanded the infantry. He was promoted major-general on 18 November 1896, when aged only forty, the youngest major-general since Wellington. In 1897 he led the flying column which defeated the Mahdists at Abu Hamed on 7 August and went on to occupy Berber on 5 September. At the battles of the Atbara (8 April 1898)—when he rode into battle at the head of his troops—and of Omdurman (2 September) he commanded the Egyptian division with great ability. He was mentioned in dispatches, received the thanks of parliament, and was appointed KCB in 1898 (GCB, 1911). The Sudan War, and British press reporting of it, established Hunter's reputation. G. W. Steevens, the *Daily Mail's* brilliant correspondent, praised him as 'the true knight-errant ... short and thick-set ... he is all energy', and 'renowned as a brave man even among

British officers … one of the finest leaders of troops in the army' (Steevens, 55–6). Back in Britain he was lionized and awarded military and civic honours.

On 23 May 1899 Hunter was appointed to command the Quetta division in India. However, in September, with war apparently imminent in South Africa, he was designated chief of staff to Sir Redvers Buller in case of war there, and left for South Africa with a contingent of British troops. He reached Durban on 5 October, before Buller had left England. Pending his own arrival, Buller ordered Hunter to join Sir George White's staff. Hunter became White's chief of staff and accompanied him to Ladysmith. Hunter wanted to join Buller, but White refused. He also refused, despite the urging of Hunter and French, to send his cavalry south. During the siege of Ladysmith (November 1899 to February 1900), with White despondent and largely inactive, Hunter as second in command had a crucial role: according to Sir Henry Rawlinson he was 'such a splendid leader' (Maurice, 49). He wanted more active measures. Early on 8 December he led a very risky, but lucky and successful, night raid to silence Boer artillery on Gun Hill: a brave but arguably unwise action for a senior officer in so responsible a position. He also had a key role in the defeat of the Boer assault on 6 January 1900.

Shortly after the relief of Ladysmith (28 February 1900) Hunter was promoted lieutenant-general and given command of the 10th division. His column's advance over the Vaal at Windsorten and defeat of the Boers at Rooidam on 5 May contributed significantly to the relief of Mafeking and Roberts's advance on Pretoria. In June Hunter succeeded Major-General Sir Ian Hamilton as commander of the columns in the north-eastern Orange Free State. Although he failed to capture de Wet he achieved the second great Boer surrender, that of General Martinius Prinsloo and more than 4000 men in Brandwater Basin on 30 July: the greatest haul of prisoners in the war, achieved with very low British casualties. He later commanded counter-guerrilla operations—including house and farm burning for resource denial and reprisals—in the central Orange Free State. Following trouble with an old wound and an attack of malaria, in January 1901 he was invalided home. Among the best British commanders in the war, he had enhanced his reputation.

From 6 May 1901 to September 1903 Hunter was general officer commanding the Scottish district. He was awarded honorary LLDs by Glasgow and Cambridge universities. In February 1903 he gave evidence to the (Elgin) royal commission on the war in South Africa, urging greater professionalism and the use of motor transport. Sometimes tactlessly outspoken, he criticized the naval gunners at Ladysmith, remarking that schoolgirls could have shot as well; following indignant naval protest he had to apologize.

Hunter commanded in India from 30 October 1903 the western army, then from 1 June 1907 until 29 October 1908 the southern army. He supported Kitchener against the military department and Curzon, assisted Kitchener in his Indian army reorganization, and enjoyed big-game hunting. On 8 December 1905 he was promoted general.

On 30 September 1910 Hunter was appointed governor and commander-in-chief of Gibraltar. On 1 November, with Kitchener as his best man, he married in London, a lowland Scot, Mary (known as Mazie), daughter of Hickson Fergusson of the Knowe, Ayrshire, formerly a Glasgow merchant, and wealthy widow of George Arbuthnot Burns, second Baron Inverclyde (1861–1905), formerly chairman of the Cunard Steamship Company. They had no children, and she died on 30 November 1924. Obsessive about cleanliness, and concerned for the efficiency of the fortress and the welfare of its garrison, in early 1913 Hunter offended Gibraltarians by regulations which resulted in shopkeepers losing trade and by publicly criticizing, 'in plain, soldierly terms' (The Times, 16), Gibraltarians as dishonest and insanitary: 'this town is like the Augean stables' (Hunter, 211). Following Gibraltarian protests, on Colonial Office advice the Liberal government recalled Hunter and made him resign in June 1913. Also in 1913 he became colonel of his old regiment, the King's Own.

After the outbreak of war, in August 1914 Hunter was appointed commander of the Aldershot training centre, and in January 1917 general officer commanding-in-chief, Aldershot command, and trained men for the 'New Armies'. He wanted, and repeatedly requested, a command in France. His Aldershot posting ended in September 1917. From 1917 to 1919 he was aide-de-camp general to the king, who wanted to make him a field marshal. He retired from the army in October 1920, though continued colonel of the King's Own until 1926. GCVO (1912) and an Egyptian pasha, he had French and Egyptian orders.

In the December 1918 'coupon' election Hunter was elected coalition Conservative MP for Lancaster. A conscientious MP, though not speaking in the house, he voted with the majority at the Carlton Club meeting (19 October 1922) for Conservative withdrawal from the coalition. He did not stand in the 1922 election. After his wife's death, in his last years he lived in London and sought consolation in drink and Mrs Sinclair Westcott, a middle-aged Irish widow. He died at his home, 52 Draycott Place, Chelsea, London, on 28 June 1936 and was cremated on 1 July. Hunter was a brave and professional soldier, popular in the army, and a successful fighting general against both Mahdists and Boers. Yet away from war he sometimes lacked judgement and was unwisely outspoken. Given the opportunity, he might well have been an effective commander in the First World War.   ROGER T. STEARN

Sources A. Hunter, Kitchener's sword-arm: the life and campaigns of General Sir Archibald Hunter (1996) · Army List · Indian Army List · The Times (29 June 1936) · G. W. Steevens, With Kitchener to Khartum (1898) · T. Pakenham, The Boer War (1979) · L. I. Cowper and J. M. Cowper, eds., The King's Own: the story of a royal regiment, 3 vols. (1939–57) · P. Warner, Dervish: the rise and fall of an African empire (1973) · M. Barthorp, War on the Nile: Britain, Egypt and the Sudan, 1882–1898 (1984) · G. Sharp, The siege of Ladysmith (1976) · W. S. Churchill, The river war, 2nd edn (1902) · J. F. Maurice and M. H. Grant, eds., History of the war in South Africa, 1899–1902, 4 vols. (1906–10) · WWBMP · K. Griffith, Thank God we kept the flag flying: the siege and relief of Ladysmith, 1899–1900 (1974) · F. Maurice, The life of General Lord Rawlinson of Trent (1928)

Archives Bodl. Oxf., corresp. · priv. coll. | IWM, corresp. with Sir Henry Wilson · U. Durham L., corresp. with Sir Reginald Wingate
Likenesses W. Stoneman, photograph, 1921, NPG · Bassano, photograph, Convent, Gibraltar · Spy [L. Ward], caricature, watercolour study, NPG; repro. in *VF* (27 April 1899) · Spy [L. Ward], group portrait, caricature, chromolithograph (*A general group*), NPG; repro. in *VF* (29 Nov 1900) · photograph, repro. in *The Times*, 16 · photographs, repro. in Hunter, *Kitchener's sword-arm* · photographs, repro. in *Navy and Army Illustrated* (1898–1901) · photographs, repro. in *ILN* (1898–1901) · portrait, repro. in Churchill, *River war*
Wealth at death £9469 17s. 7d.: confirmation, 15 Sept 1936, *CCI*

Hunter, Christopher (*bap.* 1675, *d.* 1757), antiquary and physician, baptized on 8 July 1675, was the only son of Thomas Hunter (*bap.* 1637, *d.* 1685) of Medomsley, Durham, and his second wife, Margaret Readshaw (*c.*1653–1676). He was educated at the free grammar school of Kepier in Houghton-le-Spring, co. Durham. In 1693 he was admitted a pensioner of St John's College, Cambridge, and became a favourite pupil of Thomas Baker, whose sister Margaret was the wife of John Hunter, Christopher's elder brother. From this connection he derived a taste for antiquarian pursuits. He took the degree of bachelor of medicine in 1698, and soon afterwards settled in practice at Stockton-on-Tees. He had a licence, dated 7 October 1701, from Dr John Brookbank, spiritual chancellor of Durham, to practise physic throughout the diocese of Durham. On 1 August 1702 he married, at Durham Abbey, Elizabeth Elrington, one of the two daughters and coheirs of John Elrington of Espersheales in the parish of Bywell, Northumberland.

A few years later Hunter and his wife moved from Stockton to Durham, a place much more congenial to his social and antiquarian tastes. 'His life was a pattern of simple and inflexible integrity; and his remarkable moderation in respect of his professional fees, and his extreme disinterestedness in all matters of worldly oeconomy, kept and left him [relatively] poor' (Surtees, 2.288). He abandoned alcohol, but frequently drank twenty-four cups of coffee a day. He became a regular frequenter of the fine library of the dean and chapter, but he was refused access for a while for spilling a bottle of ink over the 1225 (Henry III) confirmation of Magna Carta. He was among the first archaeological field workers. He discovered coins and inscriptions, excavated altars, and traced roads and stations at Lanchester and Ebchester. To the success of his researches on Roman ground, the altars preserved in the cathedral library at Durham bear solid testimony; while his local knowledge was extremely valuable to John Horsley in compiling his *Britannia Romana* and to Alexander Gordon in his *Itinerarium septentrionale* (Gordon, 13). Hunter visited a number of the forts on Hadrian's Wall, including Chesters and Birdoswald. Horsley knew him personally and reviewed his work on the inscriptions found on the wall, and those which he found at Ebchester and Lanchester in co. Durham. His drawings of eleven of these inscriptions were included in Gibson's second edition of Camden's *Britannia* (1722) with comments. Horsley referred to him as a 'judicious antiquary' (Horsley, 291) and thought highly of his work on Roman inscriptions. Hunter also rendered considerable assistance to David Wilkins in his *Concilia*, and he contributed materials for Henry Bourne's *History of Newcastle upon Tyne*. On 15 December 1725 he was elected FSA.

In April 1743 Hunter circulated proposals for printing by subscription in two quarto volumes a parochial history of the diocese of Durham, collected from the archives of the church of Durham, the chancery rolls there, and the records in the consistory court. With a view probably to the completion of this work he was entrusted by Thomas Bowes of Streatlam with the valuable Bowes manuscripts. His intended history, however, never saw the light. His publications were confined to an anonymous reissue, with considerable additions, of John Davies's *Rites and Monuments of the Church of Durham* (1733), five papers in the *Philosophical Transactions*, and *An illustration of Mr. Daniel Neal's 'History of the Puritans', in the article of Peter Smart, A. M. … from original papers, with remarks* (1736), also published anonymously. He was also a botanist with a particular interest in fossil plants. He contributed a list of wild plants of co. Durham to Gibson's second edition of Camden's *Britannia* (1722).

In the spring of 1757 Hunter retired from Durham to his wife's estate at Unthank in the parish of Shotley, Northumberland, where he died on 13 July 1757, aged eighty-two, and was buried in Shotley church. His wife survived him, together with their elder son, Thomas. John, their younger son, and Anne, their only daughter, had died long before him.

Hunter's manuscript topographical collections in twenty-one closely written volumes in folio were after his death offered for sale by his executors. Two volumes of transcripts from the chartularies of the church of Durham, written in an extremely neat hand, and a bundle of loose papers, were purchased by the dean and chapter of Durham for 12 guineas; but Thomas Randal, one of the executors, perceiving that the dean and chapter were likely to become the purchasers of the whole, for some reason stopped the sale of the remaining volumes. Another volume was in the possession of the family in 1820, but many appear to be irretrievably lost. Surtees pays a high tribute to the value of Hunter's labours. The greater portion of Hunter's library was sold to John Richardson, bookseller, of Durham, for £360. His cabinets of Roman antiquities and coins were acquired by the dean and chapter of Durham.

GORDON GOODWIN, rev. F. HORSMAN

Sources R. Surtees, *The history and antiquities of the county palatine of Durham*, 1 (1816), 7–8; 2 (1820), 287–9 · Nichols, *Lit. anecdotes*, 8.282–5; 9.690–91 · J. Rogan, 'Christopher Hunter: antiquary', *Archaeologia Aeliana*, 4th ser., 32 (1954), 116–25 · R. C. Norris, 'The library of the dean and chapter of Durham', 1988 [stencil] · *The family memoirs of the Rev. William Stukeley*, ed. W. C. Lukis, 2, SurtS, 76 (1883), 272 · J. Horsley, *Britannia Romana* (1732) · A. Gordon, *Itinerarium septentrionale* (1726) · D. Wilkins, ed., *Concilia Magnae Britanniae et Hiberniae*, 4 vols. (1737) · H. Bourne, *The history of Newcastle upon Tyne* (1736) · [R. Gough?], *A list of the members of the Society of Antiquaries of London, from their revival in 1717, to 19 June 1796* (1798)

Archives Bodl. Oxf. · Durham Cath. CL, papers and collections · Northumbd RO, Newcastle upon Tyne, transcripts of records, capitularia · RS | Bodl. Oxf., letters to Browne Willis; copy of Wharton's *Anglia sacra*

Hunter, Sir Claudius Stephen, first baronet (1775–1851), lawyer and lord mayor of London, born at Beech Hill, near Reading, on 24 February 1775, was the youngest son of Henry Hunter (1739–1789) of Beech Hill, Berkshire, a barrister, and his wife, Mary, third daughter of William Sloane, the great-nephew of Sir Hans Sloane, bt. His sister Mary (d. 1847) was second wife of William Manning, MP for Lymington, and he was thus the uncle of Cardinal Manning. Hunter was educated at Newcome's school at Hackney, and afterwards by a protestant clergyman in Switzerland. He entered as a student of the Inner Temple, but was subsequently articled for five years to Beardsworth, Burley, and Moore, solicitors, of Lincoln's Inn. He commenced business in 1797 as a solicitor in Lincoln's Inn, in partnership with George Richards. On 15 July that year he married Penelope Maria, only daughter of James Free; she brought him considerable wealth and his practice grew very large.

Hunter was solicitor to the commercial commissioners under the income duty acts, the London Dock Company, the Royal Institution, the Society for the Promotion of Religion and Virtue and Suppression of Vice, the Linnean Society, and the Royal Exchange Assurance Company. In September 1804 he was chosen alderman of the ward of Bassishaw, and then relinquished the general management of his business to his partner. Two years afterwards he was appointed lieutenant-colonel of the Royal East regiment of London militia (becoming colonel on 10 January 1810); he was a devoted militiaman. In June 1808 he was elected sheriff of London. He retired from business as a solicitor on 11 January 1811, and was called to the bar. On 9 November 1811 he became lord mayor of the City of London and revived various ceremonies for his pageant, which was exceptionally magnificent. He was created a baronet on 11 December 1812 and made an honorary DCL of the University of Oxford on 23 June 1819. In 1835 he removed from the ward of Bassishaw to that of Bridge Without, and at the time of his death was the 'father of the City'. From 1835 he was president of the London Life Association.

Hunter's first wife died in 1840; on 25 October 1841 he married Janet, second daughter of James Fenton of Hampstead; she died at Cambridge Terrace, Hyde Park, on 21 January 1859. He and his first wife had two sons and a daughter. He died at Mortimer Hill, Reading, on 20 April 1851. His elder son John (1798–1842) left a son, Claudius Stephen Paul, who succeeded his grandfather in the baronetcy.   G. C. BOASE, *rev.* H. C. G. MATTHEW

Sources *The Times* (11 Nov 1811) · *GM*, 2nd ser., 36 (1851), 88 · Boase, *Mod. Eng. biog.* · *ILN* (26 April 1851), 329
Likenesses W. Beechey, oils, Merchant Taylor's Hall, London · T. Blood, stipple (after S. Drummond), BM, NPG; repro. in *European Magazine* (Sept 1812)

Hunter, Colin (1841–1904), painter, was born on 16 July 1841 in Glasgow, the youngest of the seven children of John Hunter, a cabinet maker, and his wife, Anne MacArthur. His father's ill health prompted a move to the seaside town of Helensburgh about 1844, where John Hunter opened a library and bookshop and also became the postmaster. On leaving school Colin Hunter began a four-year apprenticeship in a shipping office in Glasgow, but he spent his leisure time sketching from nature and, at the age of twenty, abandoned business to become a landscape painter. He often painted out of doors with his friend John Milne Donald and throughout the late 1860s he also sketched with his friend William McTaggart at Tarbert. Hunter spent a few months studying in Paris. He worked in the studio of Léon Bonnat, but this artist's work had little effect on his own.

Most of Hunter's early work depicts the coastal landscape around Helensburgh, but soon he ventured further afield and painted scenes all around the Scottish coastline—on Iona, Skye, and the Shetland Islands—and even journeyed as far as Cornwall and Connemara. He did occasionally paint studies of poor crofters struggling against the elements—a subject favoured by his friend Joseph Farquharson at this date—but more often he chose to depict poor people struggling to make a living on the coastal fringes—fishing for lobster, salmon, and herring, gathering mussels, or baiting lines. Much of this work recalls the Hague school of artists, particularly Jozef Israëls, whose paintings Hunter would have seen in the homes of Aberdeen artists and collectors, including George Reid and Alexander Macdonald, whom he visited, with Farquharson, in October 1879.

Hunter worked mainly in oils, applying his paint generously, using thick impasto rather than thin glazes. Like his Dutch and Scottish contemporaries, he emphasized tone rather than colour in his paintings, and he preferred to set his pictures in the half-light of dusk—the intrinsic sadness of this time of day emphasizing the potential pathos of seafaring life. Hunter did, however, occasionally paint in watercolour and from 1879 was a member of the Royal Scottish Watercolour Society. He also etched, with great economy of line, similar fishing scenes to those he selected for his paintings.

Until 1870 Hunter lived principally at Helensburgh, although from 1868 to 1872 he had a studio in Edinburgh. He first exhibited at the Royal Academy in 1868 and again in 1870, thereafter exhibiting every year without fail until his last showing, in 1903. In 1872 he went to London, although he continued to spend some time in Edinburgh, where he attended William McTaggart's life study classes at the Royal Scottish Academy. London, however, was increasingly his home; after occupying studios in Langham Place and Carlton Hill he moved, in 1877, to 14 Melbury Road, Kensington, where he built a house. He named it Lugar, no doubt after the village and picturesque small river of that name in Ayrshire. On 20 November 1873, in Glasgow, Hunter married Isabella Rattray (b. 1851/2), daughter of John H. Young, who was a surgeon–dentist. They had two daughters and two sons, the elder of whom, John Young Hunter (1874–1955), became a professional artist. Also in 1873 Hunter's *Trawlers Waiting for Darkness* was hung at the Royal Academy and was greatly admired, so much so that it was engraved by T.-N. Chauval. This marked a turning point in Hunter's career and from then on his paintings achieved public recognition and were bought both by private collectors and for public collections. The city art galleries in Manchester, Preston, Liverpool, and Glasgow all acquired his work, as did the Chantrey Bequest, buying the dramatic *Their Only Harvest* of 1878 (Tate collection). Hunter also achieved recognition abroad, his paintings being acquired for the public art galleries in Sydney, Adelaide, and Cape Town.

In 1884 Hunter was elected an associate of the Royal Academy and that autumn visited the United States of America and Canada, marking his visit there with paintings such as *The Rapids of Niagara above the Falls* (exh. RA, 1885). As well as landscapes Hunter painted some portraits and, in 1892, one historical painting, *The Burial of the Macdonalds of Glencoe on St Munda Island, Loch Leven, 1692* (exh. RA, 1892). Some time before his death Hunter's right hand became paralysed. This was followed by an extended period of ill health. Hunter died at his London home on 24 September 1904, and was buried at Helensburgh; his wife survived him. JENNIFER MELVILLE

Sources DNB · P. J. M. McEwan, *Dictionary of Scottish art and architecture* (1994) · J. L. Caw, *Scottish painting past and present, 1620–1908* (1908) · D. Irwin and F. Irwin, *Scottish painters at home and abroad, 1700–1900* (1975) · J. Halsby, *Scottish watercolour, 1740–1940* (1986) · L. Errington, *William McTaggart, 1835–1910* (1989) [exhibition catalogue, Royal Scot. Acad., 11 Aug – 29 Oct 1989] · W. Armstrong, 'Colin Hunter', *Art Journal*, new ser., 5 (1885), 117–20 · CGPLA Eng. & Wales (1904) · *The exhibition of the Royal Academy* [exhibition catalogues] · b. cert. · m. cert.

Archives Aberdeen Art Gallery, archives of George Reid

Likenesses J. Pettie, oils, c.1878 · C. Hunter, self-portrait, oils, 1882, Aberdeen Art Gallery · R. W. Robinson, photograph, NPG; repro. in R. W. Robinson, *Members and associates of the Royal Academy of Arts, 1891* (1892)

Wealth at death £11,400 12s. 6d.: probate, 17 Oct 1904, CGPLA Eng. & Wales

Hunter, Donald (1898–1978), physician and expert in occupational medicine, was born on 11 February 1898 at Forest Gate, London, the second of the five sons (there were no daughters) of George Hunter, Post Office executive engineer, of East Ham, and his wife, Maria-Louisa Edwards. After school at Forest Gate he became a student at the London Hospital in 1915, but spent a year at sea serving as a probationary surgeon lieutenant before qualifying MB BS (Lond.) in 1920. He gained his MD (Lond.) in 1922 and MRCP (Lond.) in 1923.

Hunter married, in 1925, Dr Mathilde (Thilo) Eglantine Freda, daughter of the Revd Gustave Adolphe Bugnion, a Swiss pastor in Lausanne. Of their two sons and two daughters, one daughter, Elizabeth, became a consultant in psychiatry at St George's Hospital, and one son, Peter, a consultant in endocrinology at Shrewsbury Royal Infirmary. Hunter went to Harvard as a research fellow in 1926, working with J. Aub on lead poisoning. In 1927 he was elected assistant physician to the London Hospital, which he served until retirement in 1963. He became FRCP in 1929.

In 1943 Hunter was appointed director of the Medical Research Council's department for research in industrial medicine, which he established at the London and ran until it was closed on his retirement, after which he taught for a period at the Middlesex Hospital, then became research fellow in the occupational health department at Guy's Hospital, until finally returning to an office at the London where he worked until shortly before his death.

Hunter is rightly considered the father of occupational medicine in Britain. He was the first editor, in 1944, of the *British Journal of Industrial Medicine*, later to become one of the world's leading journals on the subject, which he advanced also through many important lectures, including the Goulstonian (1930), Croonian (1942), and Ernestine Henry (1949), and the Harveian oration (1957) of the Royal College of Physicians. He was Sims Commonwealth travelling professor in 1955 and in the same year published his major work, *The Diseases of Occupations*, the comprehensive classic textbook on the subject, which reached its seventh edition not long before his death.

Hunter himself made a great contribution to the knowledge of occupational medicine through his own research into industrial toxicology, particularly the clinical investigation of poisoning by lead, mercury, and organic mercury compounds. Even greater was the impact of his lucid and fascinating record of the immense amount of information he gleaned throughout the world on the way people work, on the diseases to which they thus become vulnerable, and on how these can be prevented. Greater still was the influence of the man himself on the attitudes of those with whom he came into personal contact as a teacher and examiner. Despite his commitment to research, Hunter never ceased to be a practising doctor, and had the supreme gift of being able to kindle in others his own joy in medicine and to fire them with his unceasing curiosity. He built up a remarkable teaching collection at the London Hospital. His hospital rounds were conducted at a great pace, without losing the attention or enthusiasm of his students. He was also well known as an examiner and a medical traveller, being an enthusiastic member of the Medical Pilgrims' Travelling Club.

Hunter was appointed CBE in 1957 and was awarded an honorary DSc by the University of Durham in 1960. He was commemorated by the Donald Hunter memorial lecture of the faculty of occupational medicine.

Hunter died in Norwood and District Hospital, south London, on 12 December 1978. JOHN ELLIS, rev.

Sources BMJ (6 Jan 1979), 60; (13 Jan 1979), 134 · *The Times* (19 Nov 1979) · *Daily Telegraph* (15 Dec 1978) · personal knowledge (1986) · CGPLA Eng. & Wales (1979)

Archives Wellcome L., papers, corresp.

Wealth at death £62,262: probate, 5 April 1979, CGPLA Eng. & Wales

Hunter, Sir Ellis (1892–1961), industrialist, was born on 18 February 1892 at Great Ayton, Yorkshire, the younger son of William Hunter, the headmaster of the village school, and his wife, Alice Davison. He attended the village school and Middlesbrough high school and in 1914 qualified as an accountant at a local firm. During the First World War he joined the steel department of the Ministry of Munitions, where he worked on profit limitation and steelwork extensions. From this experience came his poor opinion of the government's ability to supervise manufacturing activity. On 8 August 1918 he married Winifred Grace, daughter of John William Steed, of Essex; they had two daughters. Hunter became a local partner in W. B. Peat & Co. after the war and in 1927 he gained his fellowship of the Institute of Chartered Accountants. On the creation of the enlarged firm of Peat, Marwick, Mitchell & Co. in 1928 he became a general partner.

In the early 1930s Hunter's expertise was brought to bear on the vast, loosely structured, and ailing combine Dorman, Long & Co. in the aftermath of its acquisition of Bolckow, Vaughan & Co. It dominated the iron and steel industry on Teesside and Hunter undertook to safeguard the interests of capital lenders. His secretaryship of the Dorman Long Debenture Holders Association in 1935 was followed, with remarkable alacrity, by his appointment as deputy chairman and managing director in 1938. His early work at Dorman Long focused on rectifying the deficiencies of financial control, establishing reliable data flow on productive activity, and creating specific spheres of managerial responsibility. Plans for the re-equipment of plants were, however, forestalled by the outbreak of war.

During the Second World War, Hunter's advisory work at the British Iron and Steel Federation (BISF) in London brought him into close contact with the Ministry of Supply and the complexity of government–industry relations. In 1945 he became president of the BISF on the sudden death of the incumbent. He held the presidency for the unusually long period of seven years and gradually assumed a significance in negotiations which belied the presumption that his post was subordinate to the independent chairman, Sir Andrew Duncan. As soon as the war ended the steel industry came under close political scrutiny. The BISF presented a seven-year development plan to the Labour government in 1945, which was eventually published as a white paper in May 1946. Hunter played a leading part in the formulation of this comprehensive scheme for industrial reorganization, which recognized that the rampant individualism characteristic of the steel industry needed to be tempered with some acceptance of public supervision, short of state ownership. Hunter was sensitively alert, in an era of planning and quotas, to the need for mutuality, and he accepted the importance of national needs. Yet the problem remained of obtaining larger scale production and specialization among firms which manufactured a wide mix of products in a variety of plants and locations, and the planning framework for the rationalization of an inorganic steel industry remained unclear.

In 1946 the government moved to the view that the steel industry could not be controlled unless it was state owned. Hunter, with Duncan, became embroiled in a series of fierce exchanges with Labour ministers, who sought to storm Steel House, or the 'citadel of power', as Stafford Cripps described the London office of the BISF (Chester, 168). Clement Attlee, the prime minister, had hoped that a

hybrid solution would emerge, but the provisional agreement was defeated in cabinet in July 1947 and on 11 August Hunter and Duncan were informed that public ownership of the steel industry would proceed. Hunter tenaciously opposed the consequent Iron and Steel Act of 1949. In his condemnation of state control this dour, reserved industrialist became a forthright, cogent critic of government policy, who eloquently highlighted the benefits of decentralized managerial accountability and the 'enlightened cooperative approach' of the existing Iron and Steel Board (*The Times*, 11 Nov 1948). Far from dissociating the issue from politics, Hunter drew attention to the intention of the Conservative opposition to denationalize the industry, criticized the 'expropriation' of shareholders by poor compensation levels, and highlighted the diminished political authority of the short-lived Labour government of 1950–51. In addition, he challenged the government's refusal to allow the 'hiving off' of Dorman Long's assets in structural engineering.

Hunter's forceful resistance to nationalization placed more emphasis on property rights and managerial autonomy than on the imperatives of modernization. After vesting day—15 February 1951—the BISF quietly obstructed, with much constitutional propriety, the emergence of the state holding company—British Iron and Steel Corporation—and, in early informal contact with advisers to the Bank of England, won reassurance that City institutions would co-operate in denationalization, despite the threat of renationalization. Hunter saw Winston Churchill, then prime minister, on 12 May 1952, who confirmed the government's reversal of this aspect of labour industrial policy. He undertook a substantial amount of preparatory work for the Iron and Steel Act of 1953. The BISF commentary on the new proposals noted the need to 'harness jointly individual effort and public responsibility' (BISF, 1). Hunter regarded this contribution, at the end of his presidency, as his most important achievement.

Hunter remained managing director and chairman (from 1948) of the Dorman Long group until six months before his death, and his only other business interest was a directorship of Royal Exchange Assurance after 1951. After the war Dorman Long improved existing plant with beneficial results but was slow to start the construction of modern blast furnaces and to concentrate production in large units. Its much vaunted priority in 1945–6 for the first wide flange beam mill in Britain finally became operative in 1958–9. Progress was made on new wharves and a central unloading plant for imported ore on the south bank of the River Tees. However, the integration of operations around the Cleveland works was slow despite the compact geographical homogeneity of the company. This cautious evolutionary programme fell short of urgent modernization, but Dorman Long remained at the forefront of heavy constructional steelmaking. Hunter financed expansion from retained profits with determination in the face of some criticism from shareholders.

Hunter had a resolutely meritocratic approach to making senior appointments in a web of companies which, not long before, was dominated by founding families. In

1944 he initiated a system of special directorships, which gave chief officers close contact with board members. He was knighted in 1948 and appointed GBE in 1961. He exemplified the rise of the accountant–manager in manufacturing industry and the irrelevance of university education to this process in mid-twentieth-century Britain. In common with many businessmen, his acceptance of wartime roles led to a recognition of the state's supervisory powers in the economy but not to any relish for thoroughgoing corporatism. His calm, thoughtful, unostentatious outlook stemmed from ascetic and individualistic principles and he cared little for the values of emergent affluent society. Hunter derived great pleasure from country life around his home, Howden Gate, Northallerton, where he died of cancer on 21 September 1961.

KEITH GRIEVES

Sources C. Wilson, *A man and his times: a memoir of Sir Ellis Hunter* (1962) · *DNB* · British Iron and Steel Federation (BISF), *The policy for steel* (1953) · *The Times* (22 Sept 1961) · 'Iron and steel industry reports by the British Iron and Steel Federation and the Joint Iron Council to the ministry of supply', *Parl. papers* (1945–6), 13.429, Cmd 6811 · 'Iron and steel industry', *Parl. papers* (1951–2), 25.419, Cmd 8619 · N. Chester, *The nationalisation of British industry, 1945–51* (1975) · H. Dalton, *High tide and after: memoirs, 1945–1960* (1962) · J. Fforde, *The Bank of England and public policy, 1941–1958* (1992) · C. Barnett, *The audit of war: the illusion and reality of Britain as a great nation* (1986) · D. McEachern, *A class against itself: power and the nationalisation of the British steel industry* (1980) · D. Burn, *The steel industry, 1939–1959: a study in competition and planning* (1961) · *The Times* (11 Nov 1948) · *The Times* (4 Dec 1948) · *The Times* (17 Dec 1948) · *The Times* (24 May 1949) · *The Times* (16 Dec 1949) · *The Times* (15 Sept 1950) · b. cert. · m. cert. · d. cert.

Archives British Steel Northern Regional Centre, Skippers Lane Industrial Estate, Middlesbrough, Dorman, Long & Co. Ltd, statutory records · Cleveland Archives, Exchange House, Middlesbrough, Dorman, Long & Co. Ltd, minutes, reports, and accounts · HLRO, corresp. with Viscount Davidson · PRO, denationalization of iron and steel industry, 1951–5, corresp. with British Iron and Steel Federation, Supp 16/16 · PRO, Iron and Steel Act, 1949–50, AVIA 12/9 · PRO, iron and steel denationalization, 1952, AVIA 12/13

Likenesses A. W. D. Hunter, portrait, 1960, British Steel Records Centre, Irthlingborough, Northamptonshire, east midlands region · W. Bird, photograph, 1961, NPG

Wealth at death £106,884 10s. 11d.: probate, 13 April 1962, CGPLA Eng. & Wales

Hunter, Sir George Burton (1845–1937), shipbuilder, was born in Cousin Street, Sunderland, co. Durham, on 19 December 1845, the third son of Thomas Hunter (1805–1887), shipowner, and Elizabeth, the daughter of William Rowntree, master mariner. It is recorded that 'from infancy he gave evidence of an energetic if somewhat serious and taciturn disposition' (Rutherford, 27). When he was eight years old his father took the whole family on a voyage round the world on the ship he owned, the 454 ton *William and Jane*, which also carried emigrants.

Hunter's education was thus confined to the period between his return and the time when, at the age of thirteen, he became a pupil under Thomas Meek, engineer to the River Wear commissioners. He supplemented his knowledge with a study of *Cassell's Popular Educator* and in later life also learned French and shorthand. After two

years he commenced an apprenticeship in the Sunderland shipyard belonging to his cousin, William Pile. He quickly made his mark, and he took charge of the drawing office and became acting manager before he moved to Clydeside in 1869 to spend two years at the Govan yard of R. Napier & Sons as an assistant to the manager, Sir William Pearce. He then returned to his old employer in Sunderland, as manager, until the business failed on Pile's death in 1873.

This was particularly unfortunate timing, as on 15 April 1873 Hunter married Annie Hudson (*d.* 1927), the daughter of Charles Hudson of Whitby and niece of the 'railway king', George Hudson; they had four daughters and two sons. A partnership that Hunter formed in 1874 with S. P. Austin, another Sunderland shipbuilder, eventually restored his fortunes, however. It was in the course of this partnership that Hunter devised a system of cellular double-bottom construction, for water ballast, first used on the screw-steamer *Fenton* in 1876. At the end of 1879 the partnership was dissolved and Hunter moved to Tyneside, where he became managing partner in a new enterprise, C. S. Swan and Hunter, with a shipyard at Wallsend.

Wallsend was at that time a pit village and the shipyard occupied no more than a a 7 acre site but, under Hunter's guidance and in boom conditions, the business expanded steadily. The yard concentrated initially on the production of iron cargo steamers, of which nearly forty had been built by 1883. In that year more land was acquired and the East Yard laid out. Soon afterwards ships were being built in steel and fitted with triple-expansion engines. Oil tankers and refrigerated cargo ships quickly followed. In 1893 the firm became the leading Tyneside yard, in terms of tonnage constructed, for the first time.

In 1895 the business was incorporated as a private limited liability company, C. S. Swan and Hunter Ltd, with Hunter as chairman. Two years later it took over the neighbouring yard of Schlesinger, Davis & Co., which was thereafter used for the construction of floating docks. Two roofed-in building berths were constructed in the East Yard, followed by a further two capable of building vessels up to 750 feet. The company built its first passenger liner for Cunard, the *Ultonia*, in 1898 and several more were built before the *Mauretania* was laid down. The scale of that contract led to amalgamation with another Tyneside shipbuilder and engineer, Wigham Richardson & Co. Ltd, to form Swan, Hunter, and Wigham Richardson Ltd in 1903. By now the enterprise occupied 78 acres, with 1400 yards of river frontage. About this time the new company also took control of the Tyne Pontoons and Dry Docks Company Ltd and the Wallsend Slipway and Engineering Company Ltd. In 1912 the Clyde shipbuilders Barclay, Curle & Co. Ltd were acquired and a new yard opened at Southwick, Sunderland. After the First World War the company extended its interests in, or took control of, a number of other concerns throughout the British Isles, including the Glasgow Iron and Steel Company Ltd and the North British Diesel Engine Works Ltd.

Hunter was involved in the wider affairs of the shipbuilding industry. He was one of the founders, in 1884, of the North East Coast Institution of Engineers and Ship-builders. He served from 1900 to 1924 on the council of the Institution of Naval Architects and he was their representative on the technical committee of Lloyd's Register of Shipping and the Merchant Shipping Advisory Committee. He was also a member of the Institution of Civil Engineers.

The development of Wallsend was so bound up with the fortunes of the shipyard that Hunter's role has been likened to that of Lord Leverhulme towards Port Sunlight. Certainly it was the object of much of his philanthropy, and he set up and subsidized the Wallsend Café to provide the means of non-alcoholic refreshment and self-improvement to those who wished to take advantage of it. Much involved in local government, after Wallsend was created a borough in 1901 Hunter became its second mayor and he was made a freeman of the borough in 1911. He also served as a JP. In 1906 Durham University awarded him an honorary DSc, in recognition of his support of Armstrong College, and in 1918 he was knighted for his wartime services.

Invariably dressed in a blue reefer suit, often wearing a yachting cap, Hunter presented a tall, robust figure with a full beard and deep-set grey eyes. He was the archetypal self-made man, with a passion for his work which still left room for numerous other enthusiasms. A lifelong Anglican of evangelical tendency, he was also a rigid teetotaller and non-smoker. It is little wonder that his obituary commented that 'those who accompanied him on the trial trips of ships he built will remember the air of grave detachment with which he would survey his guests enjoying themselves in the smoking room after dinner' (*The Times*). He served as president of the National Temperance Federation and favoured prohibition. Similarly, he championed the cause of spelling reform as chairman of the Simplified Spelling Society. He was naturally drawn to the public platform and was a frequent correspondent to newspapers. Never short of an opinion and never shy in volunteering one, it is perhaps surprising that he did not pursue a political career. But his only attempt, when he stood as a Liberal candidate for Sunderland in 1900, ended in a narrow defeat.

In 1928, following his wife's death, he gave up the chairmanship of Swan Hunter. However, he remained a director and enjoyed life with scarcely diminished energy, crossing the Atlantic for the last time at the age of eighty-six. He died at his home, The Willows, Clayton Road, Jesmond, Newcastle upon Tyne, on 21 January 1937 at the age of ninety-one and was survived by three daughters and two sons. He was buried on 25 January in St Andrew's cemetery, Newcastle upon Tyne, alongside his wife and a daughter who had predeceased him.

LIONEL ALEXANDER RITCHIE

Sources W. Rutherford, *The man who built the 'Mauretania'* (1934) · *Newcastle Journal* (22–6 Jan 1937) · *The Times* (22 Jan 1937) · *The Engineer* (29 Jan 1937), 137 · *Engineering* (29 Jan 1937), 116 · *Shipbuilding and Shipping Record* (28 Jan 1937) · *Transactions of the Institution of Naval Architects*, 79 (1937), 338–9 · *Launching ways: published on the occasion of their jubilee*, Swan, Hunter, and Wigham Richardson Ltd (1953) · W. Richardson, *History of the parish of Wallsend and Willington* (1923) ·
WWW · Swan, Hunter, and Wigham Richardson Ltd, *Swan, Hunter & Wigham Richardson, Limited* (1906) · D. H. Pollock, *Modern shipbuilding and the men engaged in it* (1884), 15 · L. A. Ritchie, ed., *The shipbuilding industry: a guide to historical records* (1992) · D. Dougan, *The history of north-east shipbuilding* (1968) · J. F. Clarke, 'Hunter, Sir George Burton', *DBB* · *CGPLA Eng. & Wales* (1937)
Archives Tyne and Wear Archives Service, Newcastle upon Tyne, Swan, Hunter records
Likenesses W. Stoneman, photograph, 1920, NPG · photographs, repro. in Rutherford, *The man who built the 'Mauretania'*
Wealth at death £152,363 11s. 11d.: probate, 12 March 1937, *CGPLA Eng. & Wales*

Hunter, George Orby (1773?–1843), army officer and translator, was possibly the illegitimate son of Captain Charles Orby Hunter (d. 1791), of Croyland Abbey, Lincolnshire, his mother possibly being his father's French mistress. The Orby baronetcy, created in 1658, expired in 1724; other forms of this ancient name were Orreby and Arpe. His legitimate younger brother, Thomas Orby Hunter (1774–1847), married Fanny, third daughter of John Modyford Heywood of Maristowe House, Devon: her eldest sister was the celebrated Sophia Musters to whom the young Byron wrote four 'Caroline' poems, first published in *Fugitive Pieces* (*Byron's Letters and Journals*, 116). Hoping to fight Tipu, sultan of Mysore, George Orby Hunter joined the 100th regiment of foot in 1784, but peace was signed with Mysore in March, and the regiment disbanded. He transferred to the 7th fusiliers. His entire military career was spent in the British Isles; between 1786 and 1790 he was stationed in Aberdeen, where Catherine Byron and her baby son arrived in 1789. Hunter resigned his commission in 1790 before his regiment went to Gibraltar.

Thereafter Hunter's life, spent on the continent, remains obscure, but Byronic connections doubtless encouraged his translations of some minor and several major poems (including the first 186 stanzas of *Don Juan*), published two years after his death in France. Though Byron disliked translation of his works, Hunter's verse attempt is certainly better than Amédée Pichot's prose version (1819–25), and it played an important role in furthering European understanding of Byron. At his death on 26 April 1843 at 6 Grande Rue, Dieppe, the Dieppe registrar promoted Hunter to 'colonel of English infantry', but in truth he never rose above lieutenant. He was buried at All Saints' Church in Dieppe.   RALPH LLOYD-JONES

Sources *Army List* · *Registre des actes de décès de la ville de Dieppe* · W. Wheater, ed., *Historical record of the seventh or royal regiment of fusiliers* (1875) · *The Farington diary*, ed. J. Greig, 5 (1925) · J. Burke and J. B. Burke, *A genealogical and heraldic history of the extinct and dormant baronetcies of England, Ireland and Scotland*, 2nd edn (1841); repr. (1844) · *Byron's letters and journals*, ed. L. A. Marchand, 1 (1973), 116 · S. Pakenham, *60 miles from England: the English at Dieppe, 1814–1914* (1967) · R. Escarpit, 'Misunderstanding in France', *Byron Journal*, 3 (1975) · O. Manning and W. Bray, *The history and antiquities of the county of Surrey*, 3 (1814)

Hunter, Henry (1741–1802), Church of Scotland minister and translator, was born at Culross, Perthshire, on 25 August 1741, the fifth of seven children of David and Agnes Hunter. He was recognized to be an intelligent child and, though his was a humble family, he was sent, aged thirteen, to Edinburgh University. In 1758, at seventeen, he became tutor to Claude Irvine Boswell, later Lord Balmuto (from which position he was recalled by the illness and death of his father), and then to the family of the earl of Dundonald at Culross Abbey. On 2 May 1764 he was licensed to preach, and was ordained on 9 January 1766 as minister of South Leith. In May that year he married Margaret (d. 1803), daughter of the Revd Thomas Charters of Inverkeithing, with whom he raised a large family. In 1769 curiosity drove Hunter to London, where he preached to several of the Scottish communities, and in 1771, about the time the University of Edinburgh created him DD, he accepted an invitation to minister to the congregation at London Wall, with whom he thereafter remained. A tall, slender man, Hunter was known for his ability to fit in with all classes of society, and to enliven any conversation with knowledge, wit, and humour.

In 1784, while composing the first of his seven volumes of *Sacred Biography*, Hunter encountered the French edition of J. G. Lavater's *Essai sur la physiognomonie*, which he much admired. Having decided to translate it, he negotiated with Thomas Holloway to engrave the plates, and with John Murray to publish it. While the first parts were in press, he decided to visit Lavater at Zürich; expecting a warm welcome, he was rather taken aback by Lavater's hostility to a project that, he believed, would rob him of sales of the original edition. Hunter none the less proceeded, and the complete work, in five volumes with over 800 engravings, was issued between 1789 and 1798. Meanwhile he embarked on a German text: Euler's *Letters to a German Princess on Different Subjects in Physics and Philosophy*, a simple exposition of these topics, to which Hunter added notes and a glossary of foreign and scientific terms; its two volumes appeared in 1795. Other translations, of varying quality, of both sacred and scientific works poured from his pen. His last production, in 1790, was of J. H. Castéra's *Life of Catherine II of Russia*.

During these years Hunter did not neglect his flock; indeed his eloquence always drew a full house. He undertook various philanthropic duties, officiating as chaplain to the Scots Corporation in London, and, in 1790, serving as secretary to the Society for Promoting Christian Knowledge in respect of the highlands and islands of Scotland. The Hunters' personal life was marked by tragedy. Their first-born died in infancy. In 1791 their eldest son, Samuel, who had been nine years with the East India Company, returned to England on leave; he was to travel back overland, and Hunter accompanied him as far as Venice. Problems beset Samuel later in the journey and he died shortly afterwards. Three other children died in succession: Henry, a barrister, in 1797; Christine, in 1798; and Thomas, a merchant, in Jamaica in 1800. Hunter himself began to suffer attacks of faintness in June 1802. He gave up preaching in September and in early October went to Bath in hope of a cure; when this was not forthcoming he moved on to Bristol, where he died on 27 October 1802. He was buried at Bunhill Fields, London, on 6 November. He was survived by his wife, who died on 25 July 1803, and by two sons and a daughter.

GORDON GOODWIN, rev. ANITA McCONNELL

Sources 'Biographical sketch and critical account of his writings', H. Hunter, *Sermons and other miscellaneous pieces*, 2 vols. (1804), 1.i–lxxx · *Monthly Magazine*, 14 (1802), 456 · Chambers, *Scots.* (1856), 3.144–7 · Anderson, *Scot. nat.*, 516–17 · *GM*, 1st ser., 72 (1802), 1072–4
Likenesses plaster medallion, 1795 (after J. Tassie), Scot. NPG · Holloway, line engraving (after Stevenson), NPG · W. Platt, stipple (after A. Buck), NPG; repro. in *Gospel Magazine* (1799) · T. Trotter, line engraving, BM, NPG · engraving, repro. in Hunter, *Sermons*

Hunter, John (1728–1793), surgeon and anatomist, was born during the night of 13 February 1728, the youngest of ten children of John Hunter (1662/3–1741) and his wife, Agnes Paul (c.1685–1751), in the family holding at Long Calderwood in East Kilbride, a small village near Glasgow. The Hunters were descended from an old Ayrshire family, and through the mother were related to members of the Glasgow middle class, her father being the city treasurer. Of John's siblings only three survived into adulthood. Despite the hopes of his parents, as a boy John disliked—and largely ignored—the classical book education common to children of his class. He preferred the outdoors—sports and the treasures of nature that he could find in his tramps through the countryside. A brief trial as an apprentice cabinet-maker to his brother-in-law in Glasgow failed.

Medical education and early career Unable to find a vocation in Scotland and still undecided on his future John Hunter moved to London in 1748 to assist his brother William *Hunter (1718–1783), already making a career as a teacher of anatomy and an accoucheur. Capitalizing on the need for more surgeons, William, a couple of years before his brother's arrival, had taken over a small anatomical school to serve the needs of a growing number of medical students and the curiosity of an occasional visitor. Rowlandson's well-known and widely circulated cartoon, purportedly of William's anatomy class, with its partially dissected cadavers, observers, and surgical apprentices, catches something of the interest of the participants as some watched and others engaged in the varied dissections in process. It was something of a show, to which William's excellence as a lecturer added content that attracted the occasional onlooker from London's intellectual community.

Beyond the ten-year difference in their ages the brothers were very different in their personalities. William possessed an agreeable public persona which served him well as an anatomical lecturer and man-midwife. He enjoyed the social life of Hanoverian London, initially in the bustle around a changing Covent Garden and then, two years after John joined him, in more substantial quarters on Jermyn Street. Although a Scotsman in a city where anti-Scottish sentiment was strong, his good humour and *joie de vivre* allowed him entry into both its social and intellectual society. John, on the other hand, with little formal education and a heavy Scottish accent, found his social equals in the coffee houses behind the Great Piazza and the theatres nearby. It was there too that he met those who could procure the bodies always needed for his brother's anatomy demonstrations. The primary locus of

John Hunter (1728–1793), by Sir Joshua Reynolds, 1786, reworked 1789

his activity, however, was the dissecting room. There he learned the value of precise observation and description and to that his commitment soon became total.

Recognizing John's precocious skill in dissection, his brother adopted him as his assistant and prosector. The position suited John's needs and his temperament. Over the next decade, as William's reputation as a surgical lecturer increased and his anatomy school flourished, John pursued with his usual intensity, although in relative obscurity, a series of novel investigations both alone and in co-operation with his brother; these reflected his particular talents and the promise of future success.

Meanwhile, almost certainly pressed by his brother as well as the promise of the greater rewards due to the practitioner, John took steps to qualify as a surgeon. During the summers of 1749 and 1750, when the heat of London made anatomy impossible, he was a pupil first of the Chelsea Army Hospital's William Cheselden—then at the end of his career as the finest surgical operator in London—and a year later of Percivall Pott, the highly regarded surgeon at St Bartholomew's. From the one he learned the importance of well-trained technique to avoid as much pain to the patient as possible; from the other he learned that in the healing process nature was the surgeon's friend and helper; and from both he learned the Hippocratic injunction to do no unnecessary harm or injury to the patient.

While valuable in setting the tone for Hunter's future as a surgeon, such an episodic and pragmatic course of surgical training did little to qualify him professionally. To that end, in 1754, he entered St George's Hospital as a surgical pupil. Again the situation was apparently unsatisfactory, for in summer 1755 he was induced by his brother to become a student in St Mary Hall, Oxford, where he might obtain the credentials for practice as a physician. The classicist and non-scientific bookishness of the university, where he was expected to learn Greek and Latin along with the traditional medical texts and philosophy, fitted neither his temperament nor, he thought, was it relevant to his goal. He later commented: 'They wanted to make an old woman of me, or that I should stuff Latin and Greek', but, pressing his thumbnail on the table, 'these schemes I cracked like so many vermin as they came before me' (Gloyne, 23). Hunter left after only a few months, returning to St George's in 1756.

The wounds of war By 1760 Hunter had been in London for a dozen years. He was thirty-two, and hardly better off professionally than when he had arrived. He was no longer the untrained young Scot who had come down to London on horseback to seek his future and his fortune. But the first was still unsure and the second non-existent. To live in London required more than an assistant's income, and to be a man of social substance more than an assistant's position. His brother offered him a partnership in the school, but recognizing his own deficiencies as a lecturer he refused. His goal had been to become a practising surgeon and yet, despite his talent and despite his experiences in the laboratory and the hospital, he could still not qualify as a member of the Company of Surgeons or practise in the city as a fully fledged professional. By now Hunter's workload had affected his health and he was advised to take a complete rest, go abroad, and occupy his mind 'with less exacting pursuits' (Dobson, *Clift*, 45). Hunter did no work for several months. However, with England at war and in need of surgeons, he joined the army as a staff surgeon in October 1760, and was part of the expedition which sailed for Belle Île in 1761.

The Seven Years' War, during which England was engaged primarily with France for imperial dominance, was already winding down. England's victory was virtually assured, although the war continued for another three years, and surgeons to treat the wounded were still in demand. Hunter served with the army in Portugal in 1762. For Hunter such service promised, among other things, the formal qualification for surgical practice he required, and its pay of the (hardly munificent) 10s. a day allowed him greater financial independence.

In the dissecting room, demonstrating the structural details of the human body, he had dealt with only the dead. In the army, whether in the field, aboard ship, or in the base hospital, as a surgeon, Hunter dealt always with the trauma of battle: the open wounds, the shattered limbs, the bullet holes. In the schools, anatomy was all. The medical venues of war were, however, laboratories of the living where experiment was immediate and unplanned, but where too ignorance was often profound, and success infrequent and inexplicable. Traditional methods of treatment were of limited use. With his leg amputated, the blood vessels tied, and the stump painfully cauterized with the red-hot iron, the patient more often died than survived; the gunshot wound cut to extract the ball did more harm than good. It was from such experiences that he initiated his most important research on the inflammation of the blood and gunshot wounds. Following the advice of Pott, Hunter found that left to itself nature did better than the surgeon. What was nature's secret? For the anatomist each organ, each part, could be teased out with a delicate hand and faithfully described. What and how their purposes were served, however, was still largely unknown. Despite his anatomical knowledge and his skills as a practising surgeon with scalpel or saw Hunter was forced to confront his own ignorance.

Hunter was not a learned man. His literary background was meagre, his linguistic skills inferior to the manual. Moreover, he was not the autobiographical type nor given to introspection. There is virtually nothing of a personal comment on his wartime experience, especially of the failures to heal and the pervasive pain and death—only, as his subsequent publications indicate, a stronger commitment to discover the processes of life through which the normal become the abnormal. So he came to physiology, the search for an understanding of the processes of life. It was not enough to know the role played by each part of the whole, but how that role was effected. Although a copy of Bacon's work was in his library when he died it is unlikely that Hunter had read it, and yet it was the Baconian concept of an inductive natural history that he re-created as his method. The war years, particularly those spent in Portugal, where he began seriously to collect specimens in the field, gave him the opportunities to apply it in earnest.

Thus, the war years were the capstone of an educational process that not only prepared him as the leading surgeon he soon became but also served as an introduction to the human and comparative physiology that became the primary interest for the rest of his life. As he remarked later and continually emphasized to his students, 'To perform an operation, is to mutilate a patient we cannot cure; it should therefore be considered an acknowledgement of the imperfection of our art' (Works, 2.93). It was to perfect the art that he turned to natural history and comparative anatomy.

A London surgeon With the war about to end, in spring 1763, Hunter returned to London. He found rooms in Golden Square only a few streets from his brother's now successful Jermyn Street establishment. The war experience had made him a surgeon. It had also provided a career path within the army structure which, beginning with limited duty on half pay, would over the next thirty years lead him to increasingly responsible and respectable offices of authority: as surgeon-extraordinary to the king in 1776, surgeon-general of the army, and inspector of its hospitals in 1790, positions earned as much by political skills and patronage as by qualification.

More immediate was the difficult task of developing a successful career in a London where surgical practice was dominated, if not controlled, by surgeons of well-established reputations at the major hospitals. Without patients of his own and with a new found collecting habit to support, Hunter joined the dental practice of James Spence, a respectable operator in an occupation in which quackery was common. Although he respected Spence, the alliance was a comedown because in the hierarchy of medical practice dental surgery occupied the lowest level. To earn a few more guineas, Hunter gave some lectures on anatomy and took on temporary students to pay for additions to his growing collection. Through royal favour he had first refusal of the animals dying in the king's menagerie, but in order to study the living specimens he acquired a small country cottage and property in Earls Court beyond the western edge of the city, which over the following years he expanded into a small country estate where he kept a variety of exotic specimens. With the live animals at Earls Court and from his varied and expanding collection of dried and wet specimens, he was creating the laboratory of comparative anatomy and physiology that for the rest of his life, in one venue or another, was the focus of his professional activity.

Primarily from his work during these years Hunter produced his first major scientific work, A Treatise on the Natural History of the Human Teeth. Like all his more comprehensive works, necessarily supported by a long series of continued observations, the publication of the Treatise was not hurried; the first part, a slim volume, appeared in 1771, from the sale of which he reportedly received £1000, and the second in 1778, when both were issued as a single volume. Hunter was never secretive of his research, whose aim was to provide the information documented by experiment and disciplined observation for the improvement of surgical practice. Although his treatises were the culmination of a long series of observations, their content had been disseminated through his annually updated lectures and personal discussions. It is the reputation he won as a virtually unpublished researcher through such informal means that earned him election as a fellow of the Royal Society on 5 February 1767 (earlier than his brother William). He received the Copley medal in 1787. From 1776 to 1782 Hunter gave the Croonian lectures which were based on his research on muscular motion. In 1768 he became a member of the Company of Surgeons and a member of the surgical staff of St George's Hospital.

The Treatise laid out the form of all but the most limited of his future publications: an ordered record of his sometimes long-continued observations or experiments as preliminary to functional generalizations. Their detail bewildered critics, who derided what seemed a senseless piling of one apparently irrelevant descriptive detail on another. Hunter rejoined that

Too much attention cannot be paid to facts; yet too many facts crowd the memory without advantage, ... [unless] they lead us to establish principles ... [from which] we learn the causes of diseases. Without this knowledge a man cannot be a surgeon. (Kobler, 169)

This method—the translation of the anatomical to the

physiological, the operational interdependence of both and, perhaps, the hesitant extraction of the general from the precisely defined particulars—runs throughout his subsequent treatises: *Treatise on Venereal Disease* (1786) and the most important, *Treatise on the Blood, Inflammation, and Gunshot Wounds* (1794). Hunter shared the scepticism of his fellow Scotsman David Hume about the generally assumed precedence of ideas over experience, together with his emphasis on the need to separate matters of meaning from essential matters of fact from which the former are always inferred. Hunter's world was that of matters of fact; he was very cautious in moving to the level of generalization occupied by matters of meaning.

In 1785 Hunter carried out experiments on the mode of growth of deer's antlers which resulted in his discovery of collateral circulation by anastomosing branches of the arteries. This discovery led him in December to tie the femoral artery of a patient suffering from popliteal aneurysm, trusting to the development of the collateral circulation. The patient recovered in six weeks.

The Spence years provided Hunter also with a sense of systemic focus. From the initial descriptive emphasis on the teeth, for example, he moved to the mouth, the throat, and eventually the stomach, viewing them all as interacting parts of a major physiological system of food ingestion and digestion, characteristic in one form or another of all animal life. Subsequently, in his contributions both to the Royal Society and in his surgical lectures, his research data led him to define similarly related structures as the cerebrally centred nervous system, the circulatory system whose fluids both fed the organism and cleansed it of wastes, the musculoskeletal system which moved it, and the process which propagated the species. His was a holistic view of the organism, each part playing its own role in a constantly interacting systemic whole that was the living organism. It was also a teleological view, but with no external assigner of some predetermined purpose. He allowed himself, however, a rare speculation that the whole was energized by some life-force, inherent perhaps in the blood that moves through the whole organism, but without design or designer. In Hunter's view the concepts of function and form were inseparable. Pathology reflected the failure of a part to perform its function just as death reflected the failure of the whole system itself through the loss of blood's vitality. The art of surgery was to correct the failures, and, as a natural philosopher, it was his own role to discover through science the matters of fact of the normal process in order to correct where possible its aberration.

As his comparative anatomy collection increased Hunter used this systemic approach as a means of ordering it. By the end of his life, using the human system, which he considered the most advanced, as a reference point, he sought to construct the progressive order within the animal kingdom in each of the several systems illustrated by his own preparations. The concept of a functional improvement in each major system, describable in nature, was to be the primary novelty in the arrangement of his museum collection. Lacking for most of his life any

real concept of geological time Hunter's system, unlike that of J. B. Lamarck, was non-transformational, but rather a classificatory device much fuller and more natural than those which followed in one way or another the popular but arbitrary Linnaean model. In the next century, Richard Owen, curator of the Hunterian collection for twenty-five years and the most celebrated advocate of his method, after reviewing all Hunter's works, saw him as

> the first of the moderns who treated the organs of the animal body under their most general relations, and who pointed out the anatomical conditions which were characteristic of great groups or classes of animals; as one, in short, throughout whose works we meet with general propositions in comparative anatomy, the like of which exist in none of his contemporaries or predecessors, save in those of Aristotle. (Owen, xl)

Resettled as a surgical practitioner By 1770 the increase in both Hunter's practice and the continuing expansion of his collection forced a change in residence and practice. Fortunately William decided to move his school to grander quarters on Great Windmill Street. Hunter took over the few remaining years of the Jermyn Street lease. The new space provided ample room for his growing collection, which, by the time of the lease's end ten years later, had taken over much of the building; and the expanding practice allowed him to settle his domestic life.

After a courtship of several years, on 22 July 1771 Hunter married Anne Home (1742–1821) [*see* Hunter, Anne], the daughter of Robert Boyne Home, an army surgeon, whom Hunter had met during the war. The two men had kept up a friendship in London and it was in such a context of family friendship that Hunter had met his future wife. Anne's personality and interests usefully complemented those of her husband. A poet, she became active in the socially amorphous group of actors, writers, artists, and musicians who frequented the salons and clubs in the city. The Hunters had four children, but only two survived infancy: John Banks Hunter (d. 1838), who found a career in the army, and Agnes Margaretta (d. 1838), who married first Captain James Campbell and later Lieutenant-Colonel Benjamin Charlewood.

In new quarters, Hunter's work space arranged, his domestic life settled, and a surgeon at St George's, he set up shop as surgeon, researcher, and teacher, all in the same establishment. For the first time he could take on paying house pupils. His first and most famous student was Edward Jenner in 1770, up to London from Gloucestershire to become a surgeon. The close friendship and tuitional relationship between the two lasted until Hunter's death. For Jenner, as with many other students, the association with Hunter was the major influence in his professional life. Hunter's nephew Matthew *Baillie and his brother-in-law Everard *Home were early students; one of the last to attend his lectures was the polymath and prodigy Thomas Young. There were also such distinguished surgeons of the next generation as Astley Cooper, Anthony Carlisle, John Abernethy, William Blizard, Henry

Cline, and William Lawrence, all of whom, as oligarchs of the Royal College of Surgeons, became protectors of the Hunterian legacy. To them all he had preached as he had demonstrated the indissoluble relationship between form and function, and always the dictum that observation and experiment must precede generalization. As he wrote in the often quoted response to Jenner's request for comment on an idea of his, 'I *think* your solution is just. But why think? Why not try the experiment? Repeat the experiments … they will give you the solution' (*Works*, 1.56). His lectures, delivered in the early years at various venues, on the theory and practice of surgery, beginning in 1772, were works in progress, not infrequently changing viewpoints and correcting data from year to year. Unlike the shorter lecture series of his medical colleagues, Hunter's more serious lectures were ambitious, consisting of eighty-six one-hour evening lectures three times a week from October to April. To these lectures he devoted a great deal of time and energy since they were designed to teach students not only the elements of their art but also the methods and results of the science from which it must proceed. He was not, however, a successful lecturer. Too uncomfortable as a public speaker and too much interested in detail, however animated he might be in informal conversation, his delivery, read nervously from his detailed notes and text, made him a dull lecturer. Few auditors began the course and fewer stayed on to the end. His métier as a teacher was to establish a working relationship with the student, to teach him through experience rather than by written word.

In 1780 an incident occurred which led to Hunter's becoming estranged from his brother. In January that year John read a paper before the Royal Society on the structure of the placenta. On 3 February William wrote to the secretary of the Royal Society claiming that the discovery was well known to be his. John Hunter replied that he had made the discoveries in 1754, discussed them with William, and repeated the experiment. John also asserted that William had 'accurately delineated and minutely described the parts in that very accurate and elaborate work which he published on the Gravid uterus, without mentioning the mode of discovery' (Dobson, *Clift*, 350). Neither Hunter's paper nor the correspondence was published by the Royal Society.

The Hunterian establishment in Leicester Square Hunter prospered both as surgeon and as man of science in Jermyn Street—so much so that by the time the lease expired in 1783 he required more space. He found a large house, 28 Leicester Fields or Square, as it became, a short distance away. The property, on the east side of the square, consisted of the main house fronting the square, a large lot behind it, and a small house on Castle Street. Over the next three years he renovated the entire property at a cost of £3000. The major change was to unite the two existing houses through constructing a building which could display his expanding natural history collection arranged in specially built cases on the upper level, and house a lecture theatre and reception room on the lower, all lit by a skylight. The smaller Castle Street house

was divided into several rooms or laboratories in which Hunter and his assistants prepared and studied specimens. However, as his interests in the relation between anatomical form and physiological function increased he spent more time at Earls Court, its original small cottage expanded into a country villa, with its menagerie and laboratory, where he could get away from the distracting hurly-burly of the busy city and from his wife's social life. There he could observe directly the living animal as an extension of his work with the dead.

Two years after the move Hunter was fully established—his family in the large house on the square, with his consulting room on the ground floor, his lecture hall and natural history collection in the new space in the rear. He had become a public scientific man and his wife an active member of society. By the time of his death, eight years later, some fifty people had become a part of his expanded enterprise, for all of whom he was financially responsible—a responsibility that kept Hunter working harder and harder in order to stay out of ruinous debt. Although the income from his practice and his pupils reached as high as £6000 a year in the last years of his life, his zeal to add to his collection left little to support family or staff, and his estate was encumbered by debt at his death.

It was in the Leicester Square establishment that Hunter's career both as surgeon and naturalist reached its climax. In 1786 he published his timely *Treatise on Venereal Disease*, based on cases and treatments that he had been compiling for several years, and he was still working on his more important *Treatise on the Blood, Inflammation, and Gunshot Wounds*, containing his most significant contributions to surgical theory and practice, materials for which he had been storing away in his notes since the war years. Virtually completed, prepared for publication, and with a brief laudatory biographical preface by Home, it was published posthumously in 1794. Already in 1786 Hunter had brought together the nine memoirs he had contributed to the Royal Society into a single volume, *Observations on Certain Parts of the Animal Oeconomy*. Its title reflected his concern with the overall functioning of various interdependent parts of the whole organic system; a year before his death, certainly aware of how ill he was, he published a second edition, adding two more pieces. By the time of his death he had extended his interests to the study and explication of fossils, a varied collection of which he had assembled. In his last paper intended for the Royal Society, he identified them as representing animal species unknown in the present world, evidence suggesting an antiquity of the earth of 'thousands of centuries'. In an intellectual climate increasingly critical of theological heterodoxy, it was too radical even for his friends. Advised that such an idea would be abhorrent to the orthodox, it was not published until its rediscovery more than half a century later.

Hunter's working life Hunter was addicted to work. His working day was divided into discrete parts. It might begin at five and certainly by six when his assistant arrived. These early hours until he breakfasted at nine were usually devoted to the dissections, of which more than 500 were documented. After breakfast he would see patients until midday; and then to his rounds, visiting patients at home or in hospital. Dinner was at four, after which he took his usual hour's sleep 'a sacred hour, in which he was only to be disturbed in matters of utmost emergency. Thus refreshed, the philosopher returned to his study, and passed the hours from eight o'clock to midnight in the business of writing or dictation' (Owen, 1.293). He usually worked up the scribbled notes from his dissections into some more philosophical treatment designed as a memoir or lecture through dictation to one or another of his assistants, of which William Clift was the last and the most tenacious in keeping the memory of the great man alive. Hunter kept his notes and manuscript drafts in cabinets in his study, Clift recalled,

> that he might have ready access to them in the evenings; and scarcely a single evening occurred, except Sundays, during my attendance on Mr. Hunter for the last twenty months of his life, in which something was not added to the contents of those volumes of papers. I wrote constantly for him during that period from seven o'clock until eleven p.m., and sometimes an hour or two later; as did also Mr. Haynes for a great part of that period.   (Owen, 2.497)

Most of his initial notes were scribbled on the 'blank pages and envelopes of letters', then copied into the manuscripts. The scraps were then used to light candles from the fire in the fireplace and the rough drafts of memoirs, once clean copied, were 'taken into his private dissecting room as waste paper to dissect upon'.

Hunter's personality and manner As the best of Hunter's nineteenth-century biographers described him from recollections of his students and others who knew him, Hunter

> was deficient in those refined gentlemanly feelings, and those conciliatory manners … especially requisite in the medical profession. Conscious of great mental superiority, he was too apt to show this in a rude and overbearing manner, towards men who in their station were his equals, and exhibited somewhat too large a share of his self definition. Though he had a few admirers and friends, his apparent arrogance created many enemies and prevented him from ever becoming a general favourite of the profession.   (*Works*, 1.26–7)

Home, after Hunter's death, was more generous, but even he had to acknowledge Hunter's faults: 'His disposition was candid and free from reserve even to a fault', he wrote. 'He hated deceit, and as he was above every kind of artifice, he detested it in others, and too often avowed his sentiments' (Home, 64). He could be a difficult person to deal with. His success as surgeon, comparative anatomist, and natural historian excited hostility and provoked a malicious biography by a fellow surgeon, Jesse *Foot, to many of whose observations and charges verging on malpractice and fraud his conservative colleagues could agree. However, certain of his own rectitude Hunter gave as much as he got. His comments regarding his enemies were caustic and acerbic. Although he would correct factual errors of his own when subsequent dissections or comment by others demanded, he remained certain that his method and principles were correct, and had little or

no respect for those who disagreed with him. A tory in politics, he 'wished all the rascals who were dissatisfied with their country would be good enough to leave' (*DNB*). He would rather have seen his museum on fire than show it to a democrat.

The fine portrait of Hunter which his Leicester Square neighbour and friend Sir Joshua Reynolds painted in 1786 (and reworked in 1789) became his public image, thanks to the hundred or more impressions of William Sharp's even more expressive print. It is itself a biographical document. Here Hunter is seated at his writing table, pen in hand, specimens of his collection and significant publications on the shelves and table beside him, all showing examples of his idea of systemic progression. Reynolds caught the facial expression as Clift and his earlier long-time assistant, William Bell, may often have seen him: virtually motionless, his mind fully focused on the particular dissection on which he was engaged or the idea, the principle, to which it led.

Beyond the dissecting room Once returned from the war the pressures of time and the discovery of his true vocation narrowed his social activities to those most directly associated with his professional interests and practice. Still fond of the theatre Hunter could attend only occasionally the mainly comedic and melodramatic performances that he enjoyed. Hunter was also a collector of paintings and rare books, although the motive for collecting appears to have been acquisitiveness rather than connoisseurship. The collection was auctioned after Hunter's death. As his reputation grew Hunter met many important figures in London's intellectual world, but his interests were too narrowly focused to foster any close relationship. He was neither a great conversationalist nor a frequenter of the fashionable salons, not even those hosted by his wife.

In the smaller, more intimate informal groups, coming together in the popular coffee-house clubs to discuss the novelties of the new sciences, however, he was much more comfortable. There Hunter could discuss his own work and argue his own ideas with associates with similar interests. One of these was a small exclusive group that met first at Jack's Coffee House, moving later to Slaughter's Coffee House. Richard Lovell Edgeworth, a wealthy Anglo-Irish landowner and intellectual, described a meeting he attended in the 1770s:

> John Hunter was our chairman. Sir Joseph Banks, Solander, Sir C. Blagden, Dr. George Fordyce, Milne, Maskelyne, Captain Cook, Sir G. Shuckburgh, Lord Mulgrave, Smeaton, and Ramsden, were among our numbers. Many other gentlemen of talents belonged to this club … [among them and through their discussions] a certain *esprit de corps*, uncontaminated with jealousy, in some degree, combines the talents of numbers to forward the views of a single member … We tried every means in our power, except for personal insult, to try the temper and understanding of each candidate for admission. Every prejudice, which his profession or situation in life might have led him to cherish, was attacked, exposed to argument and ridicule. The argument was always ingenious, and the ridicule sometimes coarse.   (R. L. Edgeworth, *Memoirs*, 1820, 1.188–9)

It was a period when such small specialized groups flourished, if only for a season or two. And Hunter played an important role in their meetings. There was the Lyceum Medicum Londinenses for the Advancement of Medical Knowledge, of which he was a founder in 1785 and whose meetings he hosted in Leicester Square. Another was the more formal and somewhat more successful Society for the Improvement of Medical and Chirurgical Knowledge, of which he was also a founding member in 1783. The society met once a month to hear research papers from its members, some of which would be published in its short-lived *Transactions*. And most prestigious of all, there was the Royal Society, where the honour was great, but the proceedings dull.

Within such select groups, more heterodox in their medical views, his active participation suggests that Hunter felt much more comfortable than among the large number of surgeons operating within the orthodox traditions of medical practice. While they might respect him as a politically and professionally successful practitioner, they could neither understand nor appreciate his approach, nor his collecting mania, which was for them a matter of amusement, the rumoured sums paid for a single specimen a subject of malicious gossip.

Hunter's death From the early 1770s, shortly after his marriage, Hunter suffered from the heart disease that eventually killed him. As an experienced surgeon, who had autopsied many of his patients with the symptoms he was himself increasingly experiencing, he would have known how serious his condition was.

With episodes of angina occurring with greater intensity and frequency, Hunter wrote out his final will during summer 1793. The family property in Scotland that he half inherited from his brother he willed to his son; his personal assets, which in the event were few, he willed to his wife and children; and to his nephew Matthew Baillie and his brother-in-law, Everard Home, he willed the Earls Court property. More concerned about the fate of his natural history collection and its documentation he willed the whole of it to Baillie and Home as trustees with instructions that it be sold to the government for the public or, failing that, to any foreign government, with the hope that it would be taken as a whole with no threat of dispersal. Unwanted by the family, and with no value in themselves, the manuscripts and papers were unmentioned, though recognized as an essential part of the material collection.

On 16 October 1793 Hunter went into his dissecting room before dawn as usual, and continued a dissection until breakfast at nine; he left at noon, 'as well as I ever saw him in my life' (Dobson, *Clift*, 11), wrote Clift a few days later, for what was to be an important meeting with his colleagues at St George's. The meeting promised to be contentious. Since becoming house surgeon of St George's twenty-five years earlier he had often diverged from his colleagues over the increasing restrictions on the admission of students and the teaching offered them when they arrived. Hunter stressed the need for better clinical training for the students and considered that his colleagues

were not doing enough to attract students to the hospital, even though 'the surgeons were very ready to receive their share of the profits, but would do nothing to earn it' (Dobson, *Clift*, 324). It had been a continuing battle—and a losing one. He had become a member of the hospital staff, not 'to augment my income', Hunter wrote,

> but to acquire opportunities of acquiring knowledge that I might be more useful to mankind, not only by improving [the quality of] my private practice, but if I should be enabled to make discoveries even in the art itself. I had a view also to the instruction of those who were studying under me … whose improvement is one principal benefit accruing to the public from such instruction … My motive was in the first place to serve the hospital, and in the second to diffuse the knowledge of the art that all might be partakers of it; thus indeed is the highest office in which the surgeon can be employed.   (Wells, 137)

In this last meeting with his colleagues he was frustrated by the refusal to accept two young students from Scotland, who, like Hunter almost fifty years before, had travelled to London to become surgeons.

In the past Hunter's angina attacks had usually been triggered by the mental excitement of intense argument. On this occasion, soon after the beginning of what would have been a repetition of the continuing disagreement, in the middle of a personal verbal attack by an opponent, Hunter felt ill and went off to a neighbouring room where he soon collapsed and died. Home's autopsy confirmed the arteriosclerosis that Hunter himself, from his symptoms and his experience, must have already known. No great public notice was taken of his death, and after a simple funeral six days later his body, in its leaden coffin, was placed in the vault of St Martin-in-the-Fields church, to be found there sixty years later by Frank Buckland and, in a different intellectual climate, removed for interment in Abbot Islip's chapel, on the north side of the nave of Westminster Abbey. In 1877 a memorial window to Hunter was placed in the north transept of Kensington parish church by public subscription.

The Hunterian Museum At his death Hunter's career was already moving in two directions: the successful surgeon who commanded high fees for his services; and the compulsive collector whose bottled preparations, dried specimens, and Earls Court menagerie, though ridiculed by many of his colleagues, attracted foreign naturalists on their visits to London. Through it he had become a friend of and consultant to both Sir Joseph Banks and Captain James Cook on their return with their treasures in 1771 from their long exploratory trip in the south Pacific. Hunter subsequently served future expeditions as an adviser on what to collect, how to collect, preserve, and analyse the more remarkable natural history specimens acquired. Earlier in his career, in 1775, he had written to Jenner of a 'great scheme' to found a programme 'to teach natural history, in which will be included anatomy, both human and comparative' of which his collection would be the physical text (24 May 1775, quoted in *Works*, 1.55). That idea went nowhere, superseded by more immediate practical needs.

In his instructions to his executors Hunter hoped that his collection might still serve the purpose for which he had assembled it. With its own political and economic problems the government had little interest in purchasing a collection of exotica that most experts thought of little use or consequence. In 1796 Sir Joseph Banks did not consider Hunter's museum to be 'an object of importance to the general study of natural history' (*DNB*). It was left to a few friends, especially the politically active Lord Auckland, finally to persuade the government, in 1799, to acquire the collection for £15,000 and to place it in the trust of the Company of Surgeons (soon to become the Royal College of Surgeons) for its preservation; this was only after the Royal College of Physicians had refused the collection. A dozen years later the government provided a similar amount for the construction of a building for its arrangement and exhibit. The collection was given on condition that a proper catalogue be made, a conservator appointed, and that twenty-four lectures on comparative anatomy should be delivered annually at the college.

Except for a few dedicated students of Hunter's there was little interest in the collection as it was left at his death. It remained for Clift to care for the collection with an almost single-minded dedication to the reputation of the man he revered above all others for the rest of his long life. Clift remained virtually alone with the collection and Hunter's papers until, with the expiry of the lease in 1807, he supervised its move to a college owned building in Lincoln's Inn Fields and then, in 1813, into the new expanded galleries, built by the surgeons as a monument to the man whose efforts, interests, and talents they felt had made them gentlemen. For most of that time, shifted from place to place, the natural history and comparative anatomy portion of the collection remained uncatalogued, most of the 13,682 specimens unexamined since Hunter's death and many having lost their identifying labels. Of the original collection, about two-thirds were destroyed in a bombing raid on 11 May 1941. Hunter's more substantive notes, the drafts of papers never published, and his correspondence, all important documentation for his unfinished work, were maintained with an equal dedication. Alone with the collection and without guidance as to its future, Clift began to copy them out in his legible hand as a continuing reminder of his master's greatness. When in 1800 the collection was transferred to the care of the College of Surgeons, Home, no longer executor, had a cartload of Hunter's manuscripts carried to his house, where, after plagiarizing them to make his own reputation, he burnt them in 1823. Only Clift's copies, safely in his own possession until his death, remained as evidence of Hunter's range of interests and constructive scientific imagination.

Through these two decades after his death Hunter's image was recast from that of a professionally unpopular medical radical into that of the profession's totemic ancestor. His teaching and empirical approach were now available to a wider public through the museum's arrangement, promised in the anticipated catalogue, and

perpetuated by his students, now prominent in the profession. At the installation of the collection in its specially designed galleries of the college, his brother-in-law, Home, and his nephew, Baillie, established the Hunterian orations to be delivered on his birthday, first annually and later bi-annually, each to burnish some small part of the image symbolically paraded before the community as demonstration of how far the surgeons had grown in social respectability. The achievement of full professional status, almost a century after the separation of surgeons from the artisan barbers, was confirmed with the long-awaited completion of the collection's catalogues in time for the opening of the new expanded Hunterian Museum and the establishment of a Hunterian professorship of comparative anatomy and physiology in 1837, to be held for the next twenty years by Richard Owen. In the first series of his annual lectures in 1837, he ranked Hunter with Aristotle as a major contributor to natural philosophy. In support he brought together, in a new edition of the *Animal Oeconomy*, all Hunter's published memoirs as the fourth volume of J. F. Palmer's *The Works of John Hunter*. Together with Owen's publication in 1861 of all Hunter's unpublished work saved by Clift from Home's piracy and destruction, they constitute—with the Hunterian collection—the whole of Hunter's extant contributions to comparative physiology in the service of surgical practice. Paradoxically, even as his greatness was being celebrated his vision was being clouded. The art of surgical practice, and the science that Hunter had hoped would aid it, were breaking apart. For a younger generation of surgeons, a half century after Hunter's death, the collection itself was an anachronism to be enshrined in a museum. Hunter's aim of improving surgical practice through integrating it with natural science was deemed impracticable, even undesirable. Owen's continuation of Hunter's comparative anatomy was subject to the criticism of the college's membership. Responding to Owen's concern over the charge of irrelevance of a seemingly esoteric anatomical study, Sir Anthony Carlisle, one of the last surviving Hunterian students, and a major force in the college and its museum, wrote that he should not mind the criticism:

> It is an excellent specimen of the Hunterian-Cuvierian Natural History, but, as I at first foresaw, your *pearls* are thrown before swine. If the medical hog-trough should be cleared out in our time, there is a gleam of hope for science among a *small* few, but you must not be disappointed by the general neglect of your researches. (Owen correspondence, NHM, 6.298)

Despite Carlisle's gloomy words the museum remains, at the start of the twenty-first century, a fitting memorial to John Hunter, a major figure in the development of experimental medicine.   JACOB W. GRUBER

Sources *The works of John Hunter*, ed. J. F. Palmer and others, 4 vols. (1835–7) • J. Kobler, *The reluctant surgeon* (1960) • *DNB* • S. R. Gloyne, *John Hunter* (1950) • G. Quist, *John Hunter: 1728–1793* (1981) • R. Owen, *Essays and observation on natural history* (1861) • J. Adams, *Memoirs of the life and doctrines of the late John Hunter, esq.* (1817) • E. Home, 'Introduction', in J. Hunter, *Treatise on the blood, inflammation, and gunshot wounds* (1794) • J. Dobson, *William Clift* (1954) • J. Dobson, 'John Hunter's museum', in Z. Cope, *The Royal College of Surgeons: a history*

(1959), 274–306 · F. H. Butler, 'John Hunter', *Encyclopaedia Britannica*, 11th edn (1910–11) · J. Finlayson, 'Account of a MS volume by William Clift', *BMJ* (29 March 1890) · L. A. Wells, 'Why not try the experiment? The scientific education of Edward Jenner', *Proceedings of the American Philosophical Society*, 118 (1974) · L. S. Jacyna, 'Images of John Hunter in the nineteenth century', *History of Science*, 21 (1983), 85–108 · E. Allen, R. S. Murley, and J. L. Turk, *The case books of John Hunter FRS* (1873) · sexton's register book, London, St Martin-in-the-Fields

Archives BL, anatomical notes, Add. MS 34407 · Bodl. Oxf., lecture notes [copies] · King's Lond., lecture notes · National Library of Medicine, Maryland, lecture notes · NHM, corresp. and papers · RCS Eng., corresp. and papers · Royal College of Physicians of Edinburgh, lecture notes · RS, papers · St George's Hospital, papers · Wellcome L., lecture notes · Wellcome L., notes on principles of surgery and venereal diseases | RCS Eng., letters to Edward Jenner

Likenesses bronze and plaster casts of life mask, c.1785, NPG · J. Reynolds, oils, 1786 (reworked 1789), RCS Eng. [*see illus.*] · attrib. G. Dance, pencil drawing, 1793, RCS Eng. · J. Flaxman, marble bust, c.1800–1805, RCS Eng. · F. Chantrey, marble bust, 1820, RCS Eng. · H. Weekes, statue, 1864 (after J. Reynolds), RCS Eng. · R. Home, oils, RCS Eng. · J. Jackson (after oils by J. Reynolds), NPG · oils, RCS Eng.

Wealth at death liabilities of approx. £19,000; property sold for approx. £14,000, collection purchased in 1799 for £15,000

Hunter, John (1737–1821), naval officer and colonial governor, was born on 29 August 1737 in Leith, Scotland, the son of William Hunter, ship's master, and Helen Drummond, the daughter of a prominent Edinburgh family. As a child Hunter accompanied his father on a voyage which ended in shipwreck on the coast of Norway. While living with his uncle Robert Hunter he attended school in King's Lynn, and afterwards he was at a school in Edinburgh. He studied briefly at the University of Aberdeen before joining the Royal Navy.

In 1754 Hunter entered the *Grampus* as captain's servant. From 1757 to 1759 he was in the *Neptune*, and saw action at Rochefort and in Canada. He was then midshipman in the *Royal George*. In 1767 he was master's mate in the *Launceston*. On obtaining his Trinity House certificate in 1769 he was appointed master of the *Carysfort*, in which he sailed to the West Indies. For the next two years he charted some of the islands and sections of the American coast. From 1772 to 1775 Hunter was master of the *Intrepid*, which sailed to India. In 1775, at John Jervis's request, he was appointed to the *Kent*. He then followed Jervis to the *Foudroyant*, where he met Evan Nepean. In 1776 Richard Howe appointed Hunter master of his flagship, the *Eagle*, so that he had senior responsibilities in the North American squadron for some years.

In 1779, after he had failed in his request to be made a lieutenant, Hunter joined the *Berwick*, after which Sir Charles Hardy gave him a temporary commission as lieutenant in the *Union*. In 1780 he sailed as a volunteer in the *Berwick* to the West Indies, where Sir George Brydges Rodney commissioned him in 1782. Howe then appointed him third lieutenant of the *Victory*, where he rose to first lieutenant. On 12 November 1782 he was promoted master and commander, receiving the command of the *Marquis de Seignelay*.

In 1786 Hunter was promoted post captain and given the unusual appointment of second captain (under Arthur Phillip) of the *Sirius*, the frigate intended to escort the first fleet of convict transports to Botany Bay. Hunter evidently had the reputation of a good manager of ships, for Phillip wrote that 'there are not many Officers in the Line of Service so equal to the Task' (1 Nov 1786, State Library of New South Wales, Dixson MS, Q 162, p. 1). Phillip drew on Hunter's experience to see that the first fleet was just about as well-equipped as it could have been for the long voyage out and the tasks of colonization; Hunter also helped to keep the death-rate on the voyage strikingly low.

Aiming to arrive several weeks earlier than Hunter, so as to prepare storehouses and gardens, Phillip pressed on ahead from the Cape of Good Hope with four ships, leaving Hunter to escort the six remaining transports. But Hunter, sailing in a higher latitude than Phillip, and thus finding stronger winds, reached Botany Bay only three days after Phillip. To him too, therefore, goes some of the credit for the success 'of a voyage which, before it was undertaken, the mind hardly dared venture to contemplate, and on which it was impossible to reflect without some apprehensions as to its termination' (D. Collins, *An Account of the English Colony in New South Wales*, 1798, 1).

In 1788 Hunter filled in his time by assisting Phillip, and in exploring Sydney harbour and its nearby coast, drawing charts and fauna and flora as he did so. In October Phillip sent him in the *Sirius* to the Cape of Good Hope to obtain additional food supplies. Sailing east below Cape Horn, then across the southern Indian Ocean, Hunter made a rapid circumnavigation. None the less the voyage was difficult. By the time the *Sirius* reached Cape Town (2 January 1789), the crew was afflicted with scurvy; and as it returned to Sydney the ship leaked badly in the rough weather, and was nearly lost off the coast of Van Diemen's Land.

In March 1790 the colony had still not been resupplied from Britain, so Phillip sent Hunter with some 220 marines and convicts to Norfolk Island, hoping they would the more readily be able to support themselves there. The *Sirius* was wrecked on the reef at Sydney Bay on 19 March. Through the heroic actions of some of the crew many of the supplies were saved, but the ship's crew was also now added to the number on the island. The next twelve months were exceptionally difficult, as the people struggled to feed themselves, and as Lieutenant Philip King (the commander of the convicts), Major Robert Ross (commander of the marines), and Hunter contended for authority. At one point the settlers suffered under four different disciplines—civil, military, naval, and an odd hybrid that Ross insisted on.

In March 1791 Phillip chartered the Dutch transport *Waaksamheyd* to return Hunter and the crew of the *Sirius* to England which, after vicissitudes, they reached in April 1792. In 1793 Hunter went with Howe into the *Queen Charlotte* as a volunteer, where he remained until early 1795. He thus participated in Howe's triumph over the French squadron on 1 June 1794. In February 1795 Hunter sailed again for New South Wales, having been appointed governor in succession to Arthur Phillip. He arrived in September, and remained at Sydney until recalled in September 1800 owing to his failure to follow instructions or reduce the cost of the colony to the British Treasury. He arrived back in England in May 1801. The less than admirable circumstances of his recall did not prevent a new ministry from seeking his advice about the colony, nor the Admiralty from appointing him captain of the *Venerable* (74 guns) in 1804. Hunter lost this ship also, when it ran aground in heavy fog at Paignton in November. Another court martial exonerated him of blame. Hunter rose by seniority to rear-admiral on 2 October 1807, and vice-admiral on 31 July 1810, but he did not serve actively again.

John Hunter voyaged widely, but so did many others in the age. He had the beginnings of a classical education; and wrote a competent if rather dull journal of his time in New South Wales. His charts and drawings constitute a significant part of the region's visual record at the moment of European colonization. However, it is to his time as governor of the convict colony that we must look for any substantial historical import; and here the view is clouded.

Hunter's character exhibited a strange mixture of compassion and cruelty, determination and vacillation. At Cape Town in 1789 he excused Jacob Nagle's desertion; yet back in Sydney he refused to extend compassion to a female convict, who was accordingly hanged for theft. On Norfolk Island he stood up to the impossible Major Ross, yet when governor of the whole colony he acquiesced in injustice, legal and otherwise. In this Hunter resembled David Collins, first deputy judge advocate of the colony, then lieutenant-governor of the Van Diemen's Land settlement. Perhaps governing convicts in difficult conditions at a great distance from the metropolis unduly strained the character of mediocre men, who lost the ability to cope with bad behaviour, insubordination, adversity, and loneliness.

Hunter did assume the direction of the convict colony at a difficult time. The French revolutionary war meant that Sydney was scarcely in the forefront of government attention; and in 1796 much work still remained to secure the colony's food supply. On the other hand the war reduced the influx of new convicts, and he should have been able to govern more effectively than he did.

Some of Hunter's troubles arose from the nature and activities of the soldiers and officers serving in the colony. Of the character of the troops, he made bitter plaint to the Colonial Office: 'Soldiers from the Savoy, and other characters who have been considered as disgraceful to every other regiment in his Majesty's service, have been thought fit and proper recruits for the New South Wales Corps' (10 Aug 1796, *Historical Records of New South Wales*, 3.65). And the officers of this force, who should have imposed discipline, were effectively a law unto themselves, acquiring land by dubious as well as legal means, and 'speculat[ing] and traffic[king] in grain, live stock, and

spirits' (ibid., Lord Portland to Hunter, 18 Sept 1798, 3.490).

By the time Hunter arrived the young colony's notorious rum trade was well established, spirits assuming the role of currency. Although he was firmly instructed to contain this trade and recall the officers to their duty, Hunter could not do so. Indeed, in the face of the most explicit instructions to the contrary, he actually encouraged the officers in their activities in that he allowed each up to thirteen convict servants, victualled by the government store, whereas they should have been supported by the settlers themselves. As Lord Portland tartly pointed out, with a convict costing the government at least £20 per annum to maintain in the colony, the cost of an officer's allocation was £260 or more per year—'which is to be multiplied according to the number of persons to whom that quota of convicts is allowed' (31 Aug 1797, *Historical Records*, 3.295). Hunter's excuse was that as it was the officers who had wrought significant improvements in the colony's husbandry and agriculture, the common good justified the continuation of the practice. There was some truth to this view; but Hunter's pursuit of it did constitute a distinct dereliction of duty.

There were others. With the myriad costs of war, the home government was keen to cut the cost of the colony. Portland repeatedly complained about what he saw as unwarranted, heavy expenditure. This he ascribed partly to the government store buying produce at inflated prices from the officers, partly to Hunter's not maintaining a 'strict adherence' to his instructions (31 Aug 1797, *Historical Records*, 3.294). Government officials at home could not have fully appreciated the difficulties Hunter faced. Still, their sense of general profligacy was not unfounded. Hunter compounded this by failing properly to document his expenditure—as Portland again told him, 'You must be sensible that great inconveniences have arisen from the bills which have been drawn from New South Wales on the … Treasury having been unaccompanied with the proper accounts and vouchers in support of them' (ibid., 3 Dec 1798, 3.512). It does not appear that Hunter profited personally from his lax practices. Sydney Smith's assessment is the better one: 'the Governor, who appears to be an extremely well-disposed man, is not quite so conversant in the best writings on political oeconomy as we could wish' (Smith, 'Account of the English colony of New South Wales', *Edinburgh Review*, 2, 1803). In the face of Hunter's lack of control and failure to follow instructions, Portland recalled him.

John Hunter was a good subordinate officer, but a poor leader. He gains his historical significance mainly from being in the company of greater men. He was much less able than Arthur Phillip as governor of the early convict colony. Hunter died, unmarried, at his last residence at Judd Street, New Road, Hackney, Middlesex, on 13 March 1821, and was buried at Hackney old cemetery.

ALAN FROST

Sources F. M. Bladen, ed., *Historical records of New South Wales*, 3 (1895) · J. Hunter, *An historical journal of the transactions at Port Jackson and Norfolk Island … in 1787 … 1792* (1793) · PRO, ADM and CO ·

J. Bach, introduction, in J. Hunter, *An historical journal of events at Sydney and at sea, 1787–1792* (1968), xi–xxvi · J. J. Auchmuty, 'Hunter, John', *AusDB*, vol. 1 · *The Hunter sketchbook: birds and flowers of New South Wales drawn on the spot in 1788, 89 and 90*, ed. J. Calaby and others (Canberra, 1988)

Archives NL Aus., sketchbook · State Library of New South Wales, Sydney, Dixson Wing, journal | NMM, letters to Lord Nelson · NRA, corresp. with Sir Joseph Banks

Likenesses D. Orme, stipple, pubd 1792 (after R. Dighton), BM, NPG; repro. in J. Hunter, *An historical journal of transactions at Port Jackson and Norfolk Island* (1793) · Ridley, stipple, pubd 1801 (after unknown artist), NPG · W. M. Bennett, oils, 1815, Public Library of New South Wales, Sydney · engraving, repro. in Hunter, *Historical journal*, frontispiece

Hunter, John (1745–1837), classical scholar and university teacher, was born in the autumn of 1745 at Closeburn, Dumfriesshire, where his father is said to have been a farmer. Although left an orphan in boyhood, he received a good elementary education before entering Edinburgh University, where he was a distinguished student, although he supported himself largely by private teaching. His scholarship attracted the attention of Lord Monboddo who employed him as his private secretary for several years after he left college.

In 1775 Hunter was elected professor of humanity at St Andrews University, holding the post until 1835. In 1788 he contributed an article called 'The nature, import, and effect of certain conjunctions' to *Edinburgh Philological Transactions*. In 1796 he published at St Andrews a complete edition of Sallust, followed a year later with an edition of Horace, which he reissued in 1813 in two volumes. In 1809 he published Caesar's *De bello Gallico et civili commentarii* in two volumes; a year on he sent out in similar form his edition of Virgil, first edited in 1797. In 1820 he edited Thomas Ruddiman's *Latin Rudiments*, adding a scholarly and logical disquisition, 'Moods and tenses of the Greek and Latin verb'. Hunter's edition of Livy—*Historiarum libri quinque priores*—appeared two years later and enjoyed a scholarly reputation for much of the nineteenth century. The article 'Grammar' in the seventh edition of the *Encyclopaedia Britannica*, though not written by Hunter, was in large measure constructed from his teaching.

In addition to his duties at the university, Hunter helped in municipal work at St Andrews, and to him was largely due the introduction of the Pipeland water supply. He was also an accomplished horticulturist, and a potato called after him the 'Hunter kidney' was long a favourite in Scotland.

In 1835 Hunter left his post and was appointed principal of the united colleges of St Salvator's and St Leonard's. He was twice married, first to Elizabeth Miln. They had seventeen children, one of whom, James, became professor of logic at St Andrews; a daughter, Elizabeth, was the first wife of Thomas *Gillespie (1778–1844) who succeeded his father-in-law to the chair of humanity. John Hunter's second marriage was to Margaret, daughter of George Hadow, professor of divinity at St Andrews. He died of cholera on 18 January 1837.

T. W. BAYNE, *rev.* PHILIP CARTER

Sources Anderson, *Scot. nat.* · Irving, *Scots.* · IGI

Likenesses J. Brown, chalk sketch, Scot. NPG · J. Brown, pencil drawing, Scot. NPG · J. Watson-Gordon, oils, U. St Andr.

Hunter, John (1754–1809), physician, was born in early 1754 at Knap, parish of Longforgan, Perthshire, and baptized on 27 or 28 February 1754 at Longforgan, the younger of two sons of John Hunter (*c*.1712–*c*.1767) of Knap, landowner, and his wife, Euphemia, daughter of Alexander Jack of Glamis. From 1770 Hunter studied at Edinburgh and he graduated MD in 1775, with the thesis *De hominum varietatibus et harum causis*. He was admitted a licentiate of the Royal College of Physicians in London on 22 March 1777, after which he was appointed physician to the army, through the influence of Sir George Baker and William Heberden. From 1781 to 1783 he was superintendent of the military hospitals in Jamaica. After returning to England he settled in practice as a physician in London, from 1783 at 9 Charles Street, St James's, and from 1804 at 14 Hill Street, Berkeley Square, Mayfair. In the same year as Hunter's return to Britain, the Society for Medical and Chirurgical Knowledge was founded, and in the first volume of its *Transactions* Hunter is credited as the sole author of a paper which for the first time recommended the rational experiments to determine the path of transmission of rabies, or 'canine madness', which were later carried out in Germany. On 30 July 1784 Hunter married Elizabeth LeGrand (*c*.1756–1802), daughter of Robert LeGrand, at Ash, Kent.

In 1787 Hunter contributed three papers to the *Medical Transactions* published by the Royal College of Physicians. One concerned the common occurrence of typhus fever in the crowded and unventilated houses of the London poor, another was on morbid anatomy, and a third addressed the cause of the 'Dry-belly-ach' of the tropics. In the last of these the discovery made by Baker two years earlier, that lead in the cider was the cause of 'Devonshire colic', was extended by Hunter to include rum which had been distilled through a leaden worm; this, he observed, had been the cause of 'Dry-belly-ach' in the troops in Spanish Town and Kingston, Jamaica, during his time of service there.

Hunter's principal work, *Observations on the Diseases of the Army in Jamaica*, appeared in 1788. This provided an amplified account of the 'Dry-belly-ach' and it included a copy of Benjamin Franklin's letter of 1786 on the subject of lead poisoning. Hunter's *Observations* also dealt with yellow fever and other diseases of the troops, as well as briefly with some of the illnesses which afflicted the indigenous population. The work was translated into German in Leipzig in 1792. Hunter also contributed to volume 78 of the *Philosophical Transactions* (1788) the paper, 'Some observations on the heat of wells and springs in the island of Jamaica, and on the temperature of the earth below the surface in different climates'. This subject had originally been suggested to him in 1780, on the eve of his departure for Jamaica, by the chemist and natural philosopher Henry Cavendish.

Admitted a fellow of the Royal College of Physicians *speciali gratia* in 1793, Hunter was made censor in the same year. As Goulstonian lecturer in 1796 he lectured on 'softening of the brain', which he is said to have been the first to treat as a distinct pathological condition. The lecture was not published. He delivered the Croonian lectures from 1799 to 1801. Hunter was elected a fellow of the Royal Society on 12 January 1786. Among the twenty-five signatories on his election form were George Baker, William Heberden, and John Hunter (1728–1793) the anatomist. Hunter died in London at 14 Hill Street on 29 January 1809, and was buried at St James's, Piccadilly, on 6 February. As physician-extraordinary to the prince of Wales he bequeathed £50 to the Brighton Chapel Royal. Ninety years after Hunter's death, his original thesis at Edinburgh, which had been praised by contemporaries, was published, in English, as an appendix to J. F. Blumenbach's treatise *De generis humani varietate nativa*. The latter had originally been published in 1775 and was regarded as a landmark in the development of modern anthropology; its republication was one of a series of translations of anthropological treatises commissioned by James Hunt's Anthropological Society in London in the 1860s.   CHARLES CREIGHTON, rev. LISE WILKINSON

Sources C. A. H. Franklyn, *A genealogical history of the families of Montgomerie of Garboldisham, Hunter of Knap and Montgomerie of Fittleworth* (1967), 31–76 · L. Wilkinson, 'The other John Hunter, MD, FRS (1754–1809)', *Notes and Records of the Royal Society*, 36 (1981–2), 227–41 · Munk, *Roll* · *GM*, 1st ser., 72 (1802), 185 · *GM*, 1st ser., 79 (1809), 188

Archives U. Edin. L., lecture notes
Likenesses J. Mitan, stipple, 1805 (after G. Slovs), Wellcome L.

Hunter, Sir (Ernest) John (1912–1983), shipbuilder, was born on 3 November 1912 at 19 Haldane Terrace, Newcastle upon Tyne, the second son of George Ernest Hunter (1875–1954), engineer and director of Swan, Hunter, and Wigham Richardson, and his wife, Elsie Emma May, *née* Edwards (1881–1957). Hunter was the grandson of Sir George Burton *Hunter (1845–1937), founder of Swan, Hunter, and Wigham Richardson in Wallsend on Tyneside, one of the largest shipbuilders in the north-east, which launched the famous Cunard liner *Mauretania* in 1906. Educated at Oundle School, Hunter did one year's apprenticeship in the company from 1930 to 1931, before spending a year at St John's College, Cambridge, followed by three years at Durham University from 1932 to 1935, graduating BSc.

Returning to Swan, Hunter, and Wigham Richardson in 1935, Hunter worked for two years as a draughtsman. On 20 November 1937 he married Joanne Winifred (*b.* 1915/16), daughter of Cornelius Garbutt Wilkinson, a shipbroker; they had one son. Following their divorce, on 19 March 1949 he married Sybil, daughter of Charles William Gordon, a London stockbroker, and divorced wife of Camille Enright Malfroy; they also had one son. Hunter moved to Scotland to work as assistant manager of the Clyde shipbuilders Barclay, Curle & Co. Ltd, a subsidiary of Swan, Hunter, and Wigham Richardson, and remained there until 1939. During the Second World War he was based at the company's dry docks on Tyneside, becoming assistant manager of the dry docks in 1941, and general

Sir (Ernest) John Hunter (1912–1983), by Walter Bird, 1964

manager in 1943, responsible for the wartime repairs. In 'Shipgrafting—some wartime repairs', published in the *Transactions of the North East Coast Institution of Engineers and Shipbuilders* (1947), he described some of the innovations in the dry docks during the war, including the grafting of new forward halves on to surviving end halves, as with MV *Pontfield*, whose after half survived an enemy attack in September 1941, and with a new front half built and grafted on at the yard was ready for active service again in June 1942.

Hunter became a director of the company in 1945. There was plenty of demand for new ships after the war, and the order-books were full in the 1940s and 1950s with new ships and conversions from wartime to peacetime use. With twelve berths, Swan, Hunter, and Wigham Richardson dominated shipbuilding on the Tyne. Twelve ships were launched in 1947, including an aircraft-carrier, an oil tanker, and passenger and cargo ships. After a brief lull between 1948 and 1949, the upward trend continued during most of the 1950s, and the company won the contract for a passenger liner for the Norwegian America Line. Launched in 1956, the MV *Bergensfjord* became the flagship of the line. Hunter was responsible for the planning and construction of a large new dry dock, opened in 1957.

When Hunter became chairman and managing director in 1957, output was at its peak, but there was a downward trend in annual tonnage after 1957, and the tonnage launched between 1957 and 1965 was only one third of the company's maximum capacity. With the help of a government loan, Swan, Hunter, and Wigham Richardson won the contract for two cargo vessels for Ghana, launched in 1964, but it was getting harder to find customers, and a design for a nuclear-powered ship never became a commercial possibility. The company developed its ship-repairing activities abroad, including the conversion of the Malta dry docks and the naval dockyards in Singapore, and built ship-repairing yards in South Africa and Trinidad. Following the publication of the Geddes report (1966) on the future of the shipbuilding industry, Swan, Hunter, and Wigham Richardson merged with Smith's Docks Company, with yards on the Tees and the Tyne, to form the Swan Hunter Group, and in 1967 three other shipbuilders, Vickers Armstrong, Hawthorn-Leslie, and John Readhead, agreed to amalgamate their Tyneside yards with Swan Hunter, under Hunter's chairmanship, also taking over the Furness repair yards on the Tees. Swan Hunter Shipbuilders, as it was called from 1969, became the largest shipbuilding group in Britain, with a workforce of more than 20,000 in 1968, and after four bad years it began to make a profit in 1971. In 1972 Hunter stepped down as managing director, but remained as executive chairman. The revival in the fortunes of the group was short-lived, and an attempt to get orders from the navy in 1973 failed when the government decided not to build warships on the Tyne. A crisis in world shipbuilding followed the increase in the price of oil in 1974 and the collapse of the market for oil tankers, and when the government nationalized the shipbuilding industry in 1977 Swan Hunter Shipbuilders became a member company of British Shipbuilders. Hunter formed an industrial holding group, Swan Hunter Shiprepairers Tyne, with interests in shipbuilding in Britain and abroad, which he chaired until his retirement in 1979.

Hunter played an important part in public life. He was chairman of the Tyne Shipbuilders' Association from 1956 to 1957, the North East Coast Ship Repairers' Association from 1957 to 1958, and the Dry Dock Owners and Repairers' Central Council from 1961 to 1962. As chairman of the British Employers' Federation from 1962 to 1964 he took part in talks with the Federation of British Industry which led to the formation of the Confederation of British Industry in 1965. He was a member of the National Economic Development Council from 1962 to 1964, and served for three years on the board of British Railways. He was also the first chairman of the Central Training Council, from 1964 to 1968, and a member of the North East Coast Institution of Engineers and Shipbuilders, serving on the council, and as president from 1958 to 1960, and he was president of the Shipbuilders and Repairers National Association from 1968. His business interests included directorships of the Wallsend Slipway and Engineering Company and the Glasgow Iron and Diesel Company, and he was chairman of M. W. Swinburne & Sons, brassfounders, and the Hopemount Shipping Company.

Hunter was appointed CBE in 1960 and was knighted in 1964. He received the degree of DSc from the University of Newcastle in 1968 and was given the freedom of the borough of Wallsend in 1972. He died on 19 December 1983 at his home, Beech Close Farm, Newton, Stocksfield, Northumberland, and was buried at St Andrew's Church, Corbridge, on 23 December. Swan Hunter returned to private ownership in 1986. ANNE PIMLOTT BAKER

Sources J. F. Clarke, *Building ships on the north east coast, 2: c.1914–1980* (1997) · J. F. Clarke, 'Hunter, Sir Ernest John', *DBB* · *The Times* (21 Dec 1983) · J. F. Clarke, *A century of service to engineering and shipbuilding: a centenary history of the North East Coast Institution of Engineers and Shipbuilders, 1884–1984* (1984) · *WWW* · L. A. Ritchie, ed., *The shipbuilding industry: a guide to historical records* (1992) · b. cert. · m. cert. · d. cert.
Likenesses W. Bird, photograph, 1964, NPG [*see illus.*] · photograph, repro. in Clarke, 'Hunter, Sir Ernest John', 3, 394 · photograph, repro. in D. Dougan, *The history of north east shipbuilding* (1967), facing p. 193
Wealth at death £158,725: probate, 21 June 1984, *CGPLA Eng. & Wales*

Hunter, John Alexander (1882–1963), hunter, was born on 3 June 1882 at Shearington, on the coast of the Solway Firth near Dumfries, one of the five children of David Hunter, a farmer, and his wife, Elizabeth. He was educated at local schools, after which he joined his father working the family farm, but his heart was not in agriculture. By his teens he was a keen hunter and a good shot, especially of geese and duck, and spent more time shooting and poaching than ploughing. At the age of twenty-six he was discovered to be having an affair with a married woman, and his parents persuaded him to emigrate to avoid a scandal. Having a distant relative dairy farming in British East Africa, he sailed for Mombasa, and arrived in 1908 with little more than his clothes and a Purdey shotgun. After working on the farm for a short time, he obtained employment on the railway. With the co-operation of locomotive drivers he shot big game from the trains and then sold the ivory and hides.

In the First World War, Hunter fought with distinction in German East Africa (now Tanzania) and then, upon demobilization, co-founded a transportation company delivering goods by wagon to outlying regions and began working for Safariland, one of the earliest safari operators. He married on 3 June 1918 Hilda Banbury (d. 1985), whose parents founded east Africa's first music shop in Nairobi in 1912; they had six children. In 1920, in collaboration with the famous gunmaker Morrison Shaw, he established the well-known Nairobi gunsmiths Shaw and Hunter. Two years later he set himself up as a professional hunter and joined the colonial government's game department.

Hunter's primary responsibility was to shoot marauding game, especially crop-destroying elephant or rhino and stock-killing lions. An expert shot with extraordinarily acute eyesight, he rarely failed to kill with a single bullet. He aided the cattle-herding Maasai, shooting 360 lion in one year and becoming a tribal legend. For a small fee tribal chiefs offered him ownership of the world-famous Ngorongoro crater by way of gratitude but Hunter could not afford the minimal payment. As a professional hunter he accompanied the famous explorers Martin and Osa Johnson to the Congo.

Widely known and liked in the hunting fraternity,

Hunter was a member of the Professional Hunters' Association and a close friend of many prominent colonials. He was an intimate confidant of Denys Finch-Hatton, with whom he opened up Masai, and was the last person to see Finch-Hatton alive before his aircraft crashed at Voi in 1931. His acute sense of humour made him very popular and he was a great practical joker. On one occasion he came upon a fellow hunter's lion bait, a dead zebra. Creeping up, he placed a tobacco pipe in the zebra's mouth and withdrew to nearby cover to observe the consequences. The hunter arrived, approaching the bait with extreme caution—then he saw the pipe. Hunter burst into uncontrollable laughter, his victim lost his temper and opened fire on him: Hunter fled, tears of mirth streaming down his face.

In addition to hunting, Hunter owned a small coffee farm near Kiambu and Clairmont, a guest house (which was also the family home) in Nairobi, much frequented by hunters. He also founded Hunter's Lodge, a celebrated wayside inn on the Nairobi–Mombasa Road near Makindu. In later life he wrote four books about his hunting exploits, most famously his autobiographical *Hunter* (1952) and *Hunter's Tracks* (1957). He decried the destruction of wildlife and habitat by increased farming and population pressures, and was a dedicated naturalist and conservationist, frequently collecting specimens for the Natural History Museum in London. He died at Hunter's Lodge on 27 June 1963 and is buried at Langata cemetery, near Nairobi. MARTIN BOOTH

Sources private information (2004) • J. A. Hunter, *Hunter* (1952) • J. A. Hunter, *Hunter's tracks* (1957) • *The Times* (29 June 1963), 10 **Likenesses** H. Hunter, photograph, repro. in Hunter, *Hunter's tracks*, frontispiece • photographs, priv. coll.

Hunter, John Kelso (1802–1873), portrait painter and author, was born on 15 December 1802 at Dankeith, Ayrshire, the seat of Colonel William Kelso. His father, who died about 1810, had moved there from Chirnside, Berwickshire, in 1799 to work as a gardener. Hunter worked as a herd-boy on the estate, and was then apprenticed to a shoemaker. After his apprenticeship he moved to Kilmarnock and set himself up as a shoemaker, and also taught himself portrait painting. He later moved to Glasgow, where he worked both as an artist and as a shoemaker.

In 1847 Hunter exhibited at the Royal Academy a portrait of himself as a cobbler. He exhibited five portraits at the Royal Scottish Academy between 1849 and 1872, and seven at the Glasgow (later Royal Glasgow) Institute of the Fine Arts. Following the success of his autobiography, *The retrospect of an artist's life: memorials of west country men and manners of the past half century* (1868), he published *Life Studies of Character—Recollections of Burns and other Scottish Literary Heroes* (1870): as a young man he had known many who had known Burns, and in this book he describes the society in which Burns lived; it also includes information on minor poets such as the Scottish songwriter Robert Tannahill. Hunter died on 3 February 1873 at Pollokshields, Glasgow. G. C. BOASE, *rev.* ANNE PIMLOTT BAKER

Sources P. J. M. McEwan, *Dictionary of Scottish art and architecture* (1994) • *The Times* (6 Feb 1873), 7 • *ILN* (8 Feb 1873), 126 • C. B. de

Laperriere, ed., *The Royal Scottish Academy exhibitors, 1826–1990*, 4 vols. (1991) • Graves, *RA exhibitors*

Hunter, Joseph (1783–1861), antiquary and record scholar, was born at Sheffield on 6 February 1783, the son of Michael Hunter, a cutler, and his wife, Elizabeth (*née* Girdler). His mother died in 1787, and he, the only surviving child, was left in the guardianship of the Revd Joseph Evans, a local dissenting Presbyterian minister, although his father remarried and is known still to have been alive in 1802. He received a basic classical education at a school at Attercliffe and served a full apprenticeship as a cutler. He had access to a subscription library, and by the age of fifteen he was developing an interest in the history and antiquities of the area. By about 1800 he was corresponding with local antiquaries and collecting historical and genealogical materials.

After deciding against a career as a cutler, Hunter went in 1805 to New College, York, a Presbyterian college under strong Unitarian influence, to study for the ministry. On completing his studies in 1809 he became minister of a Presbyterian congregation at Trim Street in Bath, where he remained for twenty-three years. In 1814 he visited Paris, and on 26 December of the following year he married Mary (d. 1840), daughter of Francis Hayward, a doctor of Bath. Their first child, Evan, was born in 1816, and they had six children in all, of whom three sons and a daughter survived him. While in Bath, Hunter published some sermons and, in 1826, a religious manual based on the works of earlier writers. He became a leading member of the Bath Literary and Scientific Institution, and also became a member of the 'Stourhead circle' of Sir Richard Colt Hoare, who held annual meetings of gentlemen scholars from Somerset and Wiltshire at his house at Stourhead in the latter county. Despite living in Somerset, Hunter continued work on south Yorkshire, visiting the area when he could and sometimes borrowing Yorkshire manuscripts from their owners. During his holidays he also visited the British Museum in London and the Bodleian Library in Oxford, where the collections of Roger Dodsworth, the seventeenth-century Yorkshire antiquary, were housed. This work culminated in the publication in 1819 of his history of the Sheffield area, *Hallamshire: the History and Topography of the Parish of Sheffield*, and in 1828 and 1831 of his two-volume work on the deanery of Doncaster, *South Yorkshire*, which served to establish his reputation. In 1830 he also published an edition of the diary of an earlier West Riding antiquary, Ralph Thoresby. His genealogical researches into the ancestry of the Cavendishes, the family of the dukes of Devonshire, of Chatsworth and Hardwick in neighbouring Derbyshire, helped him to prove, in an important paper published in 1814, that Cavendish's *Life of Wolsey* was written by George Cavendish, not his brother William.

Until the 1830s Hunter had made no firsthand use of the records of government departments and courts held at various repositories in London because he found access to them difficult to obtain. In 1833, however, he was appointed as a subcommissioner of the public records, under the sixth and last of the record commissions (1831–7), and moved to London. He was in favour of the full publication of the texts of government records as a means of making the information they contained more accessible to scholars such as himself, and he was responsible for various editions of records, in many of which he found himself revising unsatisfactory work originally undertaken by others. He also catalogued various collections of manuscripts for the commissioners, although he regarded such work as of lesser importance. Among the record publications with which he was concerned were the *valor ecclesiasticus*; the oldest pipe roll, that for the thirty-first year of Henry I, which he securely dated for the first time, and the earliest pipe rolls of the reign of Henry II; and many of the earliest feet of fines for the reigns of Richard I and John. None of these editions has yet been replaced. The commission attracted criticism for extravagance, leading to the appointment of a parliamentary select committee of inquiry in 1836. He gave evidence to it in defence of the commission, which in any case lapsed after the death of William IV in 1837. During that year his work moved away from the editing of records for publication to the sorting and cataloguing of the records of the exchequer, which had recently been abolished. At the Augmentation Office, he began work on the 'ancient miscellanea' of the king's/ queen's remembrancer's department, which remained his principal activity for the remainder of his life. In 1840, after a period of great uncertainty about his future, he was confirmed as one of the first generation of assistant keepers of the new Public Record Office, established by an act of parliament in 1838. In 1843 his office moved to the branch record office at Carlton Ride, where he remained for over fifteen years before moving to the new Public Record Office building in Chancery Lane at the end of 1858. He spent little time there, frequently being absent because he was afflicted with gallstones.

While living in London, Hunter continued his antiquarian pursuits as a prominent fellow and a vice-president of the Society of Antiquaries, and read many papers to the society. He studied English literature of the sixteenth and seventeenth centuries, particularly Shakespeare and Milton, and made important genealogical discoveries about the former. He also made significant discoveries among the public records concerning the early settlements in New England, which attracted considerable attention in America. He identified documents which, he suggested, proved that the original Robin Hood was a porter working in the household of Edward II in 1324, and he thus initiated attempts to identify the outlaw through references in early official records. He also found the time to publish in 1834 a historical defence of his old college in York, whose endowment was at the time under threat in a charity case in the court of chancery. His numerous publications, official and private, were listed in the *Dictionary of National Biography*.

A passage Hunter wrote in a letter written to the deputy keeper of public records in March 1860 might serve as his obituary: 'I am one of those who have ever from my childhood delighted in minute historical research, and who have devoted my hours of relaxation from the absolute duties of life to this search of historic truth' (PRO, 1/24, 14 March 1860). Hunter died on 9 May 1861 at his home in 30 Torrington Square, Bloomsbury. Despite his nonconformity, he was buried in the grounds of the parish church at Ecclesfield, near Sheffield. A brief memorial of him was printed privately in 1861 by his son Sylvester. The sale of his library in December 1861 realized £1105. Founded in 1912, the Sheffield local history society honoured his memory by naming itself the Hunter Archaeological Society.

DAVID CROOK

Sources D. Crook, 'The Reverend Joseph Hunter and the public records', *Transactions of the Hunter Archaeological Society*, 12 (1982), 1–15 · J. Hunter, *Hunter's pedigrees: a continuation of Familiae minorum gentium*, ed. J. W. Walker, Harleian Society, 88 (1936), 76, 142 · R. Doncaster, 'The Hunter Archaeological Society: the society crest and the Joseph Hunter portraits', *Transactions of the Hunter Archaeological Society*, 14 (1987), 32–42 · J. D. Cantwell, *The Public Record Office, 1838–1958* (1991) · D. Evans, 'Joseph Hunter, assistant keeper of the records, 1838–1861', *Transactions of the Hunter Archaeological Society*, 8 (1960–63), 263–71 · G. R. Potter, 'Joseph Hunter centenary, 6 May 1861', *Transactions of the Hunter Archaeological Society*, 8 (1960–63), 288–96 · S. Schoenbaum, *Shakespeare's lives*, new edn (1991), 266–9 · C. Roberts to the treasury, 9 May 1861, PRO, PRO 1/25

Archives BL, genealogical, literary, and antiquarian corresp., collections, and papers, Add. MSS 24436–24630, 24864–24885, 25459–25481, 25676–25677 · BL, corresp., diaries, and papers, Add. MSS 31021, 33600–33601, 35161–35163, 36305, 36527, 39818–39820 · Leeds Leisure Services, notebook and collections for the history of the wapentakes of Stafford and Tickhill · PRO, PRO 1 · Sheff. Arch., antiquarian MSS, notes, extracts, and pedigrees relating to Yorkshire · Sheff. Arch., corresp., notebook relating to Agincourt · Sheff. Arch., heraldic notes, corresp., papers, and pedigrees · University of Sheffield, anecdotes relating to his contemporaries · W. Yorks. AS, Leeds, Yorkshire Archaeological Society · Yale U., Beinecke L., anecdotes relating to his contemporaries · York Minster Library, papers | BL, letters to Philip Bliss, Add. MSS 34567–34579, *passim* · BL, letters to H. A. Napier, Add. MS 47780 · BL, letters to E. D. Protheroe, Add. MS 31021 · Bodl. Oxf., corresp. with Sir Thomas Phillipps and related papers · NL Wales, letters to J. M. Traherne · Sheff. Arch., Baronagium Anglicanum and notes on Lupset · Sheff. Arch., Leader MSS · UCL, letters to Society for the Diffusion of Useful Knowledge

Likenesses [H. W.?] Pickersgill, portrait, 1852, Graves Art Gallery, Sheffield · H. Smith, oils, 1852, S. Antiquaries, Lond. · H. Meyes, stipple (after S. C. Smith), NPG

Wealth at death £9000: probate, 3 June 1861, *CGPLA Eng. & Wales*

Hunter, (George) Leslie (1877–1931). *See under* Scottish colourists (*act.* 1900–1935).

Hunter, Leslie Stannard (1890–1983), bishop of Sheffield, was born in Glasgow on 2 May 1890, the younger son and younger child of John William Hunter, Congregational minister at Trinity Congregational Church in Glasgow, and his wife, Marian Martin, formerly of Hull. J. W. Hunter was a liberal preacher, concerned for women's rights, and of considerable civic influence. Educated at Kelvinside Academy, and from 1909 at New College, Oxford, Leslie Hunter obtained a second-class honours degree in theology in 1912. He spent time in France with the YMCA in 1916, and also became a friend of Baron von Hügel, growing to admire his liberal Catholicism and mysticism. His elder brother was killed in the First World War.

Charles Gore confirmed Hunter into the Anglican

church in 1913. His first post as study secretary of the Student Christian Movement (SCM; 1913–20) was a decisive influence. After ordination in 1916 he also served part-time curacies in Brockley and St Martin-in-the-Fields (hero-worshipping H. R. L. Sheppard, the vicar) and as a hospital chaplain. He published the first of many books, *The Artist and Religion* (1915), arising from work with students in colleges of art.

In 1919 Hunter married Grace Marion (d. 1975), a Cambridge graduate and SCM staff member, the daughter of Mary and Samuel McAulay, a farmer of Aylesby, Lincolnshire. Her hospitality complemented Hunter's taciturnity, which could alarm visitors. She became a much respected JP on the Sheffield bench. They had no children.

A Newcastle upon Tyne canonry (1922–6) preceded four creative years as vicar of Barking (1926–30). During the depression Hunter returned to the north as archdeacon of Northumberland (1931–9), where he became the effective force in the diocese. *A Parson's Job* (1931) argued for a strongly led team ministry approach in growingly secularized communities. In Newcastle he founded the Tyneside council of social service, recruiting the sociologist Henry Mess, and committed himself to bringing the needs of the north-east—unemployment relief and more generous and imaginative policies in health, housing, and education—to the attention of the government. He defended the 1936 Jarrow march as a necessary expression of frustration at indifference by government and City. He preached a Sandringham sermon and wrote letters to *The Times* querying establishment attitudes. He forged links with the German church resistance, joined those working to create the World Council of Churches, and led the 'Men, Money, and the Ministry' movement within the Church of England for the sake of a more militant church with new methods of paying and deploying the clergy. Reforms he suggested were later adopted.

As bishop of Sheffield (1939–62) Hunter transformed the diocese into the most forward-looking and strategy-conscious within the established church. He was haunted by the gulf between workers and the church. He created a team which included Oliver Tomkins, Alan Ecclestone, and others who respected his convictions and shared his aims. Trade union leaders were invited to his home, though at first they were prepared to come only at night. He brought in Edward R. Wickham to build a new type of industrial mission, enabling the church to meet workers on their own ground in factories and mines. Unfortunately, timorous ecclesiastical authority later modified this industrial mission, making it pietistic rather than pioneering.

Sociologically, Hunter understood the alienation of working-class people and worked tirelessly to alter the restricted attitudes of churchgoers. He helped to found William Temple College, Whirlow Grange conference centre, and Hollowford youth centre. In the House of Lords he pleaded the cause of German prisoners of war, the need for clean air, and justice in industrial relations. He was deeply disappointed when introverted central church leadership at Lambeth concentrated on canon law.

Distrusting narrow ecclesiastical attitudes, he looked forward to a ministry which would include ordained women; in this, as in the range of his concerns, this unassuming man became the heir of Archbishop William Temple. He ordained more than 200 men and also attracted a number of outstanding women and men to the service of the diocese. He was the founder and first inspirer of the board of social responsibility at Church House, Westminster. He was one of the originators of Christian Aid, the most effectual ecumenical movement for famine relief.

Short of stature, with piercing eyes, often difficult to hear, Hunter was no orator, but, as a listener with an imaginative and critical approach, he valued and resolutely used episcopal office to relate Christian faith and activity to twentieth-century life. Of his fourteen books, the most perceptive is *A Mission of the People of God* (1961). His italic handwriting, often inviting the reader to accept some difficult task, was known as the 'snare of the hunter'. Critics detected Machiavellian skill, but the young appreciated being taken seriously. Honorary degrees (DCL Durham 1940; DD Lambeth 1949; LLD Sheffield 1953; DD Trinity College, Toronto, 1954) indicated the respect in which he was held by universities and policy makers. The European Bursary Fund set up in his memory witnessed to his lifelong interest in Scandinavian and continental Christianity, and his admiration of the Taizé community. Hunter died at York on 15 July 1983.

ALAN WEBSTER, rev.

Sources G. Hewitt, ed., *Strategist for the spirit* (1985) · *The Times* (19 July 1983) · private information (1983) · personal knowledge (1983) · *CGPLA Eng. & Wales* (1983)
Archives Sheff. Arch., papers
Likenesses painting, Sheffield Cathedral; repro. in G. Hewitt, ed., *Strategist for the spirit* (1985)
Wealth at death £52,377: probate, 13 Oct 1983, *CGPLA Eng. & Wales*

Hunter [*née* Anderson], **Margaret Annie** (1922–1986), communist activist and politician, was born on 11 November 1922 in Reid Street, Bridgeton, Glasgow, the only surviving daughter (another died in infancy) and youngest of five children of James Anderson, a theatrical performer from Montrose, and his wife, Margaret Josephine Rippey, from Strabane, Northern Ireland. Margaret's father was injured in the First World War and was often unemployed. A foundation member of the Communist Party of Great Britain, involved in tenants' struggles, he was an obvious influence on the young Margaret, who was involved with the Young Pioneers in the Gorbals before joining the Young Communist League aged fourteen. The family moved from Bridgeton to Calder Street in Polmadie, Glasgow, where Margaret grew up. She attended Queen's Park high school and then went to work as a typist for British Oxygen.

Margaret Anderson was elected secretary of the Knightswood, Glasgow, branch of the Communist Party in 1940. During the Second World War she was called up and worked for the engineering firm of Barr and Stroud in Anniesland, Glasgow, where she became a member of the Transport and General Workers' Union and convener for the women in the factory. She spoke regularly at lunchtime factory-gate meetings and it was at one of these that she met her future husband James McCartney Hunter (*b.* 1921), an engineer who was a member of the Communist Party in Dalmuir, Clydebank. They married in Glasgow in 1946 and lived at Albert Road in Shawlands, Glasgow.

After the war Margaret Hunter became a full-time secretary for the Communist Party and worked in the Glasgow office. Elected to the Glasgow committee of the party and serving as its secretary, she stood unsuccessfully in Dalmarnock ward in the local council elections of 1947 and 1949. During the same period she was also involved in a campaign for squatters and helped to house them by forcibly opening empty properties. In the 1950s Margaret became a Scottish organizer for the party, dealing with press and publicity, and sat on the Scottish secretariat (1956–63). She was responsible for industrial and branch activity, and continued to shine as a public speaker at factory-gate and public meetings. In 1959 she organized the Communist Party's bicentenary celebrations of Robert Burns's birth with a concert held in St Andrew's Hall in Glasgow, attended by over 3000 people. Her work involved campaigning and recruiting for the party in the evenings and at weekends, and she also acted as an election agent at council elections. In the early 1960s Margaret Hunter was sent by the national committee of the party to sort out a dispute in the Lancashire district, and in consequence she herself served as district secretary there for six months.

In 1963, in recognition of her great political and organizational ability, Margaret Hunter was elected to the post of national women's officer of the party, the first person to be so. She and her husband were deeply reluctant to leave Scotland, where they had been wholly devoted to the party, and had endured living in poverty and illness. They were won over, however, by the arguments of Scottish party leaders and more particularly by Margaret's admiration for the party's general secretary, John Gollan, a fellow Scot.

Margaret Hunter stood for parliament in the Gorbals constituency in Glasgow in the 1964 and 1966 general elections. Though unsuccessful, she managed through her candidacy to highlight the desperate housing plight of the area. In London she joined the Fawcett Society which fought for equality between men and women, and she campaigned among MPs and trade unions on women's issues. A member of the national executive of the Communist Party from 1964 to 1968, she also organized educational weekend schools for women throughout Britain, at which prominent speakers lectured on history, politics, and literature. She co-ordinated the activities of the party's women's advisory committee and worked generally to raise the profile of women in the party and the labour movement. She regularly contributed articles to the party's publications, usually on women's issues.

Margaret Hunter was 5 feet 8 inches tall, of striking sharp features, with short black hair and blue eyes. Her work involved travel abroad on behalf of the party, and

while on an official delegation to the GDR in 1967 she became very ill. She suffered increasingly from hypertension and nephritis, and her career was soon tragically cut short. After receiving treatment in Czechoslovakia and in the Soviet Union at the behest of the party, in 1968 she suffered a stroke. She returned to work but was forced to retire five years later after suffering a massive stroke when she was only fifty. She later succumbed to Alzheimer's disease and spent her last three years in Tooting Bec Hospital in London, dying there of pneumonia on 21 February 1986. She was cremated at Golders Green crematorium on 3 March 1986. She was survived by her husband.

NEIL RAFEEK

Sources private information (2004) · *Comment* (15 Oct 1966), 666–7 · *Comment* (18 March 1967), 166 · *Comment* (23 March 1968), 181–2 · *Comment* (6 July 1968), 419–20 · *World News* (16 April 1960), 191 · d. cert.
Likenesses photographs, 1966, William Gallacher Memorial Library, Glasgow

Hunter, Sir Martin (1757–1846), army officer and colonial administrator, was born on 7 September 1757 in Medomsley, co. Durham, the second son and heir of Cuthbert Hunter and his wife, Anne, the daughter of the Revd John Nixon of Haltwhistle, Northumberland. He was educated in Newcastle upon Tyne and later at a school in Bishop's Waltham, Hampshire. On 30 August 1771 he was commissioned as an ensign in the 52nd foot. In April 1775 he was with his regiment at Lexington at the outbreak of the American War of Independence. He was heavily involved in subsequent encounters, notably at Bunker Hill in June 1775, when he was appointed lieutenant, at the evacuation of Boston in March 1776, the storming of Fort Washington in August 1776, and the battle of Brandywine in September 1776. On 21 November 1777 he was promoted captain, and later the following year he returned to England.

In 1783 Hunter accompanied his regiment to India, where he served as brigade major during the Third Anglo-Mysore War. In February 1792 he took part in, and was wounded at, the attack on Tipu Sahib's camp near the walls of Seringapatam. On 17 July 1794 Hunter was appointed lieutenant-colonel in the newly raised 91st foot (disbanded in 1796), and in 1796 he was transferred to the 60th Royal Americans. He served with his battalion of that corps in the West Indies, and commanded a brigade under Sir Ralph Abercromby at the capture of Trinidad and the failed siege of Puerto Rico. On 13 September 1797 he married Jean (*d.* 1845), the heir of James Dickson of St Anton's Hill, Berwickshire; the couple had seven sons and four daughters.

Having exchanged into the 48th foot, Hunter commanded that regiment in Minorca, at Leghorn, and at the siege of Malta in 1800. Three years later he was appointed a brigadier-general in North America and commanded the troops in Nova Scotia. Also in 1803 he was appointed colonel of the New Brunswick fencibles, and in 1810 he was made colonel of the old 104th foot, formed out of the New

Brunswick fencibles at that time and disbanded at Montreal in May 1817. The regiment's success, epitomized by a celebrated march to Quebec and distinguished service in Upper Canada (1813–14), owed much to Hunter's practical leadership.

Hunter's administrative career began in early 1808, when he was appointed to the council of New Brunswick. From then until 1812 he acted as lieutenant-governor in all but name, the position being officially held by Thomas Carleton until 1817. Hunter's administration was characterized by its harmonious relations with the assembly at a time of little contentious legislation and growing economic prosperity. In 1825 Hunter was appointed general. Later he was awarded a GCH (1832), a GCMG (1837), and the governorship of Stirling Castle. He died at his home, St Anton's Hill, on 9 December 1846.

H. M. CHICHESTER, rev. PHILIP CARTER

Sources D. M. Young, 'Hunter, Sir Martin', *DCB*, vol. 7 · *The journal of Martin Hunter, G.C.M.G., C.H., and some letters of his wife Lady Hunter*, ed. A. Hunter and E. Bell (1894) · *Army List* (1771–1837) · W. A. Squires, *The 104th regiment of foot, 1803–1817* (1962)

Hunter, Philip Vassar (1883–1956), electrical engineer, was born in the Norfolk village of Emneth Hungate on 3 August 1883, the eldest son of Josiah Hunter, a farmer, and his wife, Sarah, daughter of Philip Vassar, a neighbouring farmer. He was educated at Wisbech grammar school, and determined at an early age, despite his father's misgivings, to follow his boyhood idol, Sebastian de Ferranti, in the new and exciting career of an electrical engineer. From school, he enrolled in 1900 at Faraday House, a private engineering college at Charing Cross, London, where in 1903 he gained his diploma with first-class honours. After a brief period of practical training under Robert Hammond, a well-known consulting engineer and founder of Faraday House, he joined in 1904 the staff of C. H. Merz and William McLellan in Newcastle upon Tyne. Here he made rapid progress and in 1909 became head of the electrical department, specializing in high-voltage systems and inventing new types of system protection, such as the Merz–Hunter and split-conductor methods. He developed an interest in electric traction and was sent to work on railways in Argentina and Australia.

In 1915 Hunter was seconded to the Admiralty, as the engineering director in a team of three formed within the anti-submarine division under the eventual leadership of William W. Fisher. Their work culminated in the evolution of the ASDIC system of submarine detection, and for his part in this development, Hunter was in 1920 appointed CBE.

In 1919 Hunter joined Callender's Cable and Construction Company, where, as chief engineer and joint manager, and later as a director, he devoted his energies to the development of high-voltage power cables. The scope of his work during this period ranged from a preoccupation, in 1920, with improving the design of 33,000 volt cables, to the invention of the buoyant cable used for sweeping magnetic mines, and to sponsoring in 1943 the world's first three-core cable for 132,000 volts. In 1934 he initiated the company's research laboratories at Wood Lane, Shepherd's Bush, and maintained the keenest interest in their work until his death. In 1946, on the merging of the company with British Insulated Cables Ltd, he became engineer-in-chief of British Insulated Callender's Cables, and from 1947 to 1952 was joint deputy chairman of the new company. He was also chairman of nine, and director of many other, electrical companies. He retained a life-long interest in Faraday House, serving as a special lecturer during the post-war years, and was active in its old students' association. He collaborated with J. Temple Hazell on a comprehensive history entitled *The Development of Power Cables* (1956). Much of the subject matter was derived from their collection, garnered over a period of some twenty years, illustrating the development of cable making from 1882 onwards; this was eventually presented to the Science Museum, London.

As a sportsman Hunter was, in his younger days, a keen skater and curler; and in 1935, after some years as secretary and treasurer, he became president of the British Ice Hockey Association. He was well known as an enthusiastic golfer, and was chairman of Addington Golf Club, of which he was for some years captain.

Hunter married twice: first, in 1904, Helen Maud, daughter of Charles Golder; and second, in 1947 (after the death of his first wife), Ruby Phyllis Petty, *née* Hudson, of Herne Bay, Kent. He had three daughters—two with his first wife and one from his second marriage.

Hunter had a high reputation, both in his own country and internationally, not least for his ability to select the vital and essential facts from a complex situation, and having done so, to put forward a solution with clarity and decisiveness. This gift of his was almost legendary, and many a harassed committee was grateful for it. He possessed in the highest degree the quality of leadership, selecting his lieutenants with care and judgement, trusting them with a large measure of individual responsibility, and helping them not only with wise advice but with unfailing support. Although he was a man of compelling personality, he would never use it to beat down opposition. Indeed, one of his greatest pleasures was to stimulate discussion; and his junior engineers gratefully recognized that their opinions would always be received with courtesy and understanding, so long as they were to the point and honestly held. Quick to detect promise in his younger staff, he took every opportunity of fostering their ability and helping them to greater responsibility in their profession.

Imperturbability was one of Hunter's notable characteristics. He steadfastly refused to be diverted from the work in hand, whether by present danger or by apprehension about the future, and those who remembered him in the dark days of 1940 recalled with gratitude the steadying influence he exerted on all who worked with him then. This attitude of mind informed all that he did. He was a man of astonishingly equable temper, courteous, tolerant, and disdainful of provocation and malice. Few ever saw him angry.

Hunter was president (1933–4) of the Institution of Electrical Engineers, and in 1951 achieved the ultimate distinction of honorary membership. He was chairman of many professional committees and a fellow of the American Institute of Electrical Engineers. He died at his home, Springhurst, 180 Shirley Church Road, Addington, Surrey, on 22 October 1956. His wife, Ruby, survived him.

J. T. HAZELL, rev. ANITA McCONNELL

Sources private information (1971) · personal knowledge (1971) · F. W. Lipscomb, *Wise men of the wires: the story of Faraday House* (1973) · m. certs. · d. cert.
Likenesses photograph, c.1933–1934, Inst. EE
Wealth at death £42,502 12s. 9d.: probate, 28 Feb 1957, *CGPLA Eng. & Wales*

Hunter, Rachel (c.1754–1813), novelist, was born in London, but little, not even her maiden name, is known of her early life. She married an English merchant resident in Lisbon, but her husband died after they had been married for ten years and Rachel Hunter returned to England. She took up residence in Norwich in either 1794 or 1795, and devoted herself thenceforth to literary pursuits. She wrote both Gothic novels as well as more didactic pieces characterized by a 'strictly moral tendency'. Jane Austen knew and joked about Hunter's books, which included *Letitia, or, The Castle without a Spectre* (1801), *History of the Grubthorpe Family* (1802), *Letters from Mrs Palmerstone to her Daughter, Inculcating Morality by Entertaining Narratives* (1803), *The Unexpected Legacy* (1804), and *Lady Maclairn, the Victim of Villany* (1806). The prefaces to her novels are interesting, with the narrator acting as a kind of characterized critic. *Letitia*, for instance, features a preface on Gothic and moral fiction, and *The Unexpected Legacy* is prefaced by an attack by an ostensible male friend of the author. Sometimes confused with Maria Hunter, actor and novelist, Rachel Hunter died at Norwich in 1813.

THOMAS SECCOMBE, rev. REBECCA MILLS

Sources Blain, Clements & Grundy, *Feminist comp.* · Watt, *Bibl. Brit.*, vol. 1 · D. Le Faye, 'Jane Austen and Mrs Hunter's novel', *N&Q*, 230 (1985), 335–6 · Allibone, *Dict.*

Hunter, Robert (1666–1734), army officer and colonial governor, was born in October 1666 in Edinburgh, the son of James Hunter (d. 1671) and Margaret Spalding of Dreghorn. James Hunter was the third of four sons born to Robert Hunter, twentieth laird of Hunterston. As a younger son, James Hunter did not inherit the family's extensive estates in Ayrshire, and was trained as an attorney. At his death in April 1671 James left a modest estate of only £30 Scots.

Landless and in need of income, Robert Hunter found a career in the military. He possessed the firmness of character, clear judgement, intelligence, and ruthlessness that would make him a top-flight officer. Hunter had the necessary physical and mental attributes that would enable him to rise in the military. He was also a poet and playwright, a classical scholar, a linguist, an amateur scientist who was a member of the Royal Society, a mathematician, and a connoisseur of the arts.

Robert Hunter's first known military service occurred

during the revolution of 1688, when he formed part of the guard that escorted Princess Anne from London as she fled from her father, James II. An ardent whig, Hunter was in favour of the accession to the throne of William of Orange and Mary, James's daughter. Hunter's military service to William and Mary began on 19 April 1689, when he was commissioned an aide major in the regiment of dragoons of Henry Erskine, Baron Cardross. He later served in General John Hill's regiment of foot at Fort William. In 1694 he was commissioned as a captain and then promoted to major of the brigade of the Royal Scots Dragoons, commanded by Colonel Sir Thomas Livingston. In 1698 Hunter was commissioned a major in Colonel Charles Ross's Irish dragoons and a captain of a troop in that same regiment. Hunter's most noted service occurred as a member of the Irish dragoons during the War of the Spanish Succession (1702–13) when he served as aide-de-camp to the commander-in-chief, John Churchill, duke of Marlborough. This close relationship with Marlborough brought Hunter into contact with the most influential men in Great Britain. Under Marlborough, Hunter rose to the rank of lieutenant-colonel and saw active duty at the battles of Blenheim and Ramillies in 1704 and 1706, respectively. Hunter was also instrumental in securing the surrender of the city of Antwerp in 1706.

This last event caused a break between Marlborough and Hunter. Hunter later claimed that he, leading six squadrons of horse, arrived at Antwerp well before any other forces. At Antwerp, Hunter personally met the Spanish governor and arranged the surrender of the city. Marlborough was pleased to accept the surrender but wanted credit for the capitulation to go to William Cadogan. When Marlborough ignored Hunter's role while rewarding Cadogan, Hunter realized he had no future in the military, and in 1706 he retired from active service.

Marlborough, who handled colonial appointments during the early years of Queen Anne's reign, had appointed George Hamilton, earl of Orkney, as governor-general of Virginia. Orkney offered Hunter, a close friend, the post of lieutenant-governor. Hunter accepted, and prior to his departure he married in London Lady Elizabeth Hay, née Orby, the widow of another of Hunter's close friends, John, Lord Hay. Lady Hay was the sole heir of her father, Thomas Orby, who had extensive landholdings in England and Jamaica. The couple had five children. Lady Hay died in August 1716 at Perth Amboy, New Jersey.

While in London waiting to sail for Virginia, Hunter furthered his friendships with such literary figures as Jonathan Swift, Richard Steele, and Joseph Addison. Hunter wrote several pieces that were later published in *The Tatler*, and began a correspondence with Swift that lasted several years.

Hunter sailed for Virginia in 1707 but was captured *en route* by French pirates. Having been taken prisoner to Paris, he was exchanged in 1709. While he was prisoner the Jamaica governorship had fallen vacant. Hunter, anxious to oversee the Orby property on that island, applied for the post. When Marlborough awarded the Jamaica post to another person, Hunter, with the duke's approval, received the highly profitable joint governorship of New York and New Jersey. Prior to sailing, Hunter presented a plan to the ministry to employ some of the thousands of displaced Palatine refugees who found their way to England after being forced from their homeland by marauding French armies. His suggestion, eagerly accepted by the whig ministry, was to transport approximately three thousand Palatines to New York to establish a naval stores programme there. The ministry, headed by treasurer Sidney Godolphin, agreed to provide financial support for the mission.

Hunter, with 2814 Palatine refugees, sailed for New York in the spring of 1710. He arrived on 13 June 1710. On the next day the whig ministry fell at Westminster and the tories took power. The tory dominance left Hunter without financial support for the Palatine project. Unaware at first of the end of the whig ministry, Hunter extended his own credit to purchase land for the project along the Hudson River in New York, and to arrange for the provisioning of the Palatines. In vain did he submit bills for his expenses to the home government. Before he finally decided to end the project in 1712, Hunter incurred a personal debt on the crown's behalf of over £21,000. Despite his continual pleas to the tory ministry, the money was never repaid.

New York politicians were well aware that Hunter had little or no influence with the tory ministry. Despite resistance, Hunter, with the aid of allies, was able to take control of the colony. These allies, usually appointed to the council, were the nucleus of a provincial 'court' party; the opposition, or 'country' party, was centred in the assembly. That body was intent on increasing its power at the expense of the royal prerogative that Hunter represented. An early disagreement between assembly and governor developed over the disbursement of the colony's money. Hunter insisted that, according to the terms of his commission, the crown's representative alone should be responsible for the payment of the colony's debts. The assemblymen, who had watched Lord Cornbury, one of Hunter's predecessors in New York, misappropriate public money, were equally determined that their treasurer take responsibility for debt repayment. The assembly also disputed the council's right to amend its money bills, demanded the right to appoint and control the province's London agent, and insisted that the governor could not erect courts without its consent. Hunter disagreed with the assembly on all these issues, recognizing that to give way would compromise the royal prerogative he represented.

Until independence colonists insisted that their local houses of assembly were similar to the House of Commons. Hunter and other royal officials recognized no such comparison. While Hunter in Britain favoured the rise of parliamentary authority, he did not support the rise of the assembly in the colony. To limit that power he refused to concede to the assembly's demands. The assembly, responsible for raising all money for government expenses, including the governor-general's income, retaliated by refusing to pay Hunter's salary or to raise money for other necessary government expenses. To contain the assembly's power Hunter suggested to the ministry that the British parliament take direct control of the colonies.

The assembly's refusal to raise money for necessary government expenses, including the military, put the colony at risk, since Britain was still engaged in war with the French. Hunter ensured the allegiance of the Five Nations of the Iroquois and recruited them for a major, but futile, land and sea expedition against Canada in 1711. The result of the assembly's intransigence was that Hunter frequently paid for necessary expenses out of his own pocket.

Without backing from the tory government, Hunter worked out his own local solution for his problems with the assembly. He was also assisted in 1714 by the accession of George I and the re-establishment of a whig ministry. In 1715 the governor used compromise and humour to defeat his enemies. He conceded the assembly's demand to retain control of the disbursement of funds, but in return got from the assembly long-term, or five-year, support of government. He also wrote a satirical play, *Androboros*, the first play to be printed in America. In the play Hunter made laughing-stocks of his tory enemies, who included the former governor Lord Cornbury, now earl of Clarendon, and Francis Nicholson, erstwhile governor of Maryland and Virginia. An amused public read the play and Hunter won widespread support among New York's voters. This support was apparent at the polls in 1716. Hunter called new assembly elections and achieved a pro-administration 'court' majority in that body. From 1716 to the time he left the colony, the New York assembly was a fairly obedient tool in Hunter's hands. The opposition was rendered largely ineffectual and key enemies were forced to travel personally to London to voice complaints to the ministry in the hope of having Hunter recalled.

In New Jersey, unlike New York, Hunter met opposition principally from the council. His solution was to discharge the councillors and appoint new men who were loyal to him. The displaced councillors immediately ran for and achieved seats in the assembly, and then tried to halt legislative proceedings by not attending sessions. Hunter solved that problem by hounding dissident leaders out of the province. He then called new assembly elections to achieve a 'court' majority in that body, as he had in New York. Opposition leaders in New Jersey were again forced to lodge complaints personally against Hunter in England.

Hunter, probably the most effective royal governor to serve in New York and New Jersey, returned to England in 1719 to answer the criticisms of his provincial opponents, and for personal reasons. In 1720 he exchanged posts with William Burnet, comptroller of customs. In his new post Hunter worked closely with Robert Walpole, first lord of the Treasury from 1722 to 1742. In 1727 Hunter's connections with Walpole, who controlled colonial patronage, brought him the long-desired post of governor of Jamaica.

Hunter experienced difficulty in governing Jamaica both because of his own advanced age and because Jamaica's absentee landowners provided him with few allies. He was also hampered because the nature of colonial administration had changed since he held office in New York and New Jersey. Walpole, unlike Marlborough, favoured expanding the empire through trade, not by military conquests. There was little interference from the home government in colonial affairs as long as trade prospered. Hence Hunter had even less support from the home government than he had received when in New York and New Jersey.

As in New York, Hunter faced defiance from the politically sophisticated Jamaica assembly, which tried to gain control of the appointment of militia officers and of military operations. Like the New York assembly, the Jamaica body insisted it alone had the right to frame money bills. Despite this opposition, Hunter was able in 1728 to wrest from the assembly a permanent revenue bill, making him the only eighteenth-century British royal governor to achieve such a victory. He was less successful in reducing the threat that the maroons presented to the colony. The maroons, largely composed of escaped slaves, lived in Jamaica's mountains and made frequent raids on plantations. The raids became so severe that Hunter was forced to ask for the help of British regulars. The regiments arrived in Port Royal in February 1731. The men, immediately prey to rum and the island's many diseases, were weakened and their ranks depleted even before they faced what proved to be an elusive enemy. When the British finally engaged their opponents they were forced to retreat in great disorder, as the maroons employed tactics of guerrilla warfare.

Hunter, despite age, increasing ill health, and the grief caused by the death of his eldest son in 1732, proved an active governor of Jamaica. He held an assembly session in February 1734 in which he encouraged the representatives to petition the king for additional military assistance in their continuing battle against the maroons. One of the last measures he signed was a bill to cut additional roads and build more barracks in the eastern half of Jamaica. Though ill, he held a council meeting on 19 March 1734 to plan yet another offensive against the maroons. He died less than two weeks later, on 31 March 1734, at St Jago de la Vega, and was buried there in the churchyard of the Anglican church. Having risen from an obscure and impoverished childhood to positions of power and influence, Hunter was at his death a wealthy, propertied, and respected man.

Robert Hunter was a man of principle who knew when it was necessary to make concessions. His ability to compromise was his most valuable asset. Like all royal governors, however, Hunter was placed in an impossible position. Given more theoretical power in the colonies than the monarch enjoyed at home, he lacked the means to enforce that authority. His suggestions to establish a strong central government in the colonies were ignored.

Hunter astutely observed that the opposition he and other royal governors faced in the colonies was not so much directed at them as at British government. He feared that colonies which were permitted to continue challenging crown authority would ultimately provoke rebellion. The failure of parliament to act until 1763 ensured that Robert Hunter's prediction was fulfilled. MARY LOU LUSTIG

Sources *DNB* · BL, Blenheim papers · privy council register, PRO, 2/82, 2/83, 5/4 · PRO, admiralty papers, ADM 1/231 · PRO, colonial office papers, CO 5/1050, CO 5/1085, CO 137/17, CO 137/18, CO 138/17, CO 140/23 · NA Scot., Stair muniments · New York State Library, Albany, New York, colonial documents, LX, LXI · New York Historical Society, New York, Jay papers · New York Historical Society, New York, Rutherfurd collection · New York Historical Society, New York, Hunter MSS · letter-book, Hist. Soc. Penn., Logan papers · Hist. Soc. Penn., Simon Gratz MSS · E. B. O'Callaghan and B. Fernow, eds. and trans., *Documents relative to the colonial history of the state of New York*, 15 vols. (1853–87) · E. B. O'Callaghan, ed., *The documentary history of the state of New York*, 4 vols. (1849–51) · W. A. Whitehead and others, eds., *Documents relating to the colonial, revolutionary and post-revolutionary history of the state of New Jersey*, 1–10 (1880–86) · *Journals of the Assembly of Jamaica*, ed. Assembly of Jamaica, 14 vols. (1811–29), vol. 4 · M. L. Lustig, *Robert Hunter (1666–1734), New York's Augustan statesman* (1983) · L. H. Leder, 'Robert Hunter, *Androborus*, a biographical farce in three acts', *Bulletin of the New York Public Library*, 68 (1964), 153–90 · J. Paterson, *History of the county of Ayr: with a genealogical account of the families of Ayrshire*, 2 vols. (1847–52)

Archives National Library of Jamaica, dispatches and instructions · NRA, priv. coll., report on and account of claim for maintenance of Palatines in New York province | LPL, corresp. with SPG

Likenesses attrib. G. Kneller, oils, *c*.1720, New York Historical Society

Wealth at death property in Lincolnshire, London, New York, New Jersey, and Jamaica

Hunter, Robert (*d.* after **1803**), portrait painter, was described as from Ulster and taught by Justin Pope Stevens (Pasquin, 13). The establishment portrait painter in Dublin for the second half of the eighteenth century, he was much admired by his contemporaries and slightly later critics, including William Carey, who saw him as 'a walking chronicle of everything relative to the Irish artists and arts' (Carey, 226), and W. B. Sarsfield Taylor, who said he took 'excellent likenesses' and that his practice was extensive (Taylor, 284). He was sufficiently well known to be commissioned to paint a whole-length of Sir Charles Burton, lord mayor of Dublin, in 1753 (now known from a mezzotint by James McArdell). The group of six portraits of the King family (priv. coll.), long attributed to Hunter, were painted about 1748 and are lively and strong in colour. His three-quarter-length (his favourite size) of the illustrious philanthropist and writer Samuel Madden (Trinity College, Dublin) is a portrait worthy of the sitter and was engraved with some alterations by Richard Purcell in 1756. Hunter was much influenced by English painters such as Thomas Hudson, Reynolds, and Arthur Devis, whose work he knew through engravings and frequently used as a source for his own compositions. It is uncertain whether he ever visited England. He exhibited between 1765 and 1777 at the Society of Artists in Ireland many portraits, a few subject pictures (all now lost), and many small whole-lengths, often of sitters in fancy dress such as Thomas Conolly of Castletown (1771) in Van Dyck costume. In some cases the small whole-lengths may have been made as copies for the sitter's family, as there are several which are duplicates of larger portraits, for example that of Henry de Burgh, first marquess of Clanricarde (1783); the larger version is at Harewood House, Yorkshire, and the smaller was sold at Sothebys (9 March 1988), when it was incorrectly identified as the marquess of Buckingham (c.1783) whose whole-length portrait by Hunter (the deanery, St Patrick's Cathedral, Dublin) also has a small version (National Gallery of Ireland, Dublin).

From his early, somewhat baroque, manner Hunter moved to a simpler style in which his sitters are often set in a well-observed and painted landscape, as, for example, in the whole-length, probably of Peter La Touche, where the figure is resting while out shooting with his dog (1775, National Gallery of Ireland, Dublin). His masterpiece is his three-quarter-length portrait of Lord Newbottle, later fifth marquess of Lothian, painted in uniform (1762, priv. coll.). His half-lengths include several versions of Lord Harcourt, lord lieutenant from 1772 to 1777, engraved by Edward Fisher in 1775 (versions Ulster Museum, Belfast; National Gallery of Ireland, Dublin; and elsewhere), and Henry Haughton, Hunter's last known dated work (1790, ex Christies, 1 March 1985, lot 113). A few double portraits can be attributed to him. Although it is not known how much he charged for a portrait, he was paid £7 7s. 10d. in 1788 for repairing a portrait of Charles II for Dublin corporation.

Although Ireland was visited by the portraitists Robert Home (1779–89) and Gilbert Stuart (1789–93) who had great success with commissions, it was probably age and not competition (as has been suggested) which reduced Hunter's output in the late 1780s. No work by him is known after 1790. According to Strickland, Hunter held an exhibition of his work in 1792, though no evidence for this has been traced. If such an exhibition did take place it would have been the first one-man show to have been held in Dublin. Hunter exhibited pictures for the last time at the Society of Artists in 1800, and continued to leave his name in the Dublin directory until 1803, soon after which date he must have died. He had lived in Dublin all his working life.

Hunter married about 1750 and his only child, Mary Anne Hunter [**Mary Anne Trotter** (*b.* 1752, *d.* before 1792)], painter, exhibited at the Society of Artists in Ireland between 1765, when she was thirteen, and 1777. She married the portrait painter John Trotter (*d.* 1792) in 1774, after which time she exhibited under the name Mary Anne Trotter. She predeceased her husband, whose second wife, Elizabeth, survived him. Mary Anne was probably the mother of **Eliza H. Trotter** (*fl.* 1800–1815), portrait painter, who was the daughter of John Trotter. Eliza Trotter exhibited in Dublin between 1800 and 1809, trained at the Royal Academy Schools in London from 1809 to 1812, and exhibited between 1811 and 1815 at the Royal Academy and British Institution from addresses in

Westminster and Hammersmith. Her portrait of Lady Caroline Lamb (exh. 1811) is in the National Portrait Gallery, London.   L. H. CUST, *rev.* ANNE CROOKSHANK

Sources A. Crookshank, 'Robert Hunter', *GPA Irish Arts Review Yearbook*, 6 (1989–90), 169–85 · W. G. Strickland, *A dictionary of Irish artists*, 2 vols. (1913) · A. Pasquin [J. Williams], *An authentic history of the professors of painting, sculpture, and architecture who have practiced in Ireland … to which are added, Memoirs of the royal academicians* [1796]; facs. edn as *An authentic history of painting in Ireland* with introduction by R. W. Lightbown (1970), 13 · W. Carey, *Some memoirs of the patronage and progress of the fine arts in England and Ireland* (1826), 226 · W. B. S. Taylor, *The origin, progress and present condition of the fine arts in England and Ireland*, 2 vols. (1841), 2.284 · G. Breeze, *Society of Artists in Ireland: index of exhibits, 1765–80* (1985) · B. Stewart and M. Cutten, *The dictionary of portrait painters in Britain up to 1920* (1997) · Graves, *RA exhibitors*

Hunter, Robert (1823–1897), Free Church of Scotland missionary, geologist, and lexicographer, was born at Newburgh, Fife, on 3 September 1823, son of John Hunter, a clerk of the Inland Revenue and a native of Wigtownshire, and his wife, Agnes Strickland of Ulverston, Lancashire. He was educated at Marischal College, Aberdeen, probably from 1837 and was awarded his MA in 1841. He then went to Bermuda for two years, where he showed himself to be a promising naturalist. He returned to Edinburgh to study divinity at New College in 1843, and in October 1846 was ordained a minister and sent to join Stephen Hislop at the Free Church's recently established mission station at Nagpur in central India, where he arrived in March 1847.

Hunter, who was said to have been 'of a gentle, poetical, sensitive temperament, great refinement of mind, and extraordinary accuracy and readiness in the use of his extensive acquirements, spiritual in his conversation', was seen as 'altogether a sort of Melancthon to Mr Hislop. They seem admirably suited to each other from their diversity of character, and oneness of purpose' (Mackenzie, 3.298). Their fellowship was strengthened by a shared interest in geology and they began to collect fossils which they sent to the Geological Society of London. The two men published a joint memoir of their research in the society's *Quarterly Journal*. In May 1855 Hunter was forced to leave India because of ill health, but he did not resign from the mission until September 1857. Although he made no reference to the fact in his writing, his decision was probably influenced by the death, in July, of his brother Thomas, a Church of Scotland missionary to the Punjab who was killed at Sialkot, along with his wife and child, during the Indian mutiny. After returning home Hunter helped Alexander Duff to form missionary associations in the Free Church. He drew on his missionary experiences to write *The History of India* (1863), intended for school use, and *History of the Missions of the Free Church of Scotland in India and Africa* (1873).

From 1864 to 1866 Hunter served as resident tutor in the theological college of the Presbyterian Church of England in London. He also established a Presbyterian congregation at Victoria docks, London, and conducted Sunday services in a schoolroom at the hamlet of Sewardstone, Essex, for over twenty years. His later years were mainly

Robert Hunter (1823–1897), by G. Haworth

taken up with preparing a seven-volume *Encyclopaedic Dictionary* (1879–88), which took seventeen years to finish. He also published *The Sunday School Teacher's Bible Manual* (1894), later reissued as *Cassell's Concise Bible Dictionary* (1901). He was a frequent contributor to religious periodicals, in particular the *British and Foreign Evangelical Review*.

Hunter became a fellow of the Geological Society in 1868 and was granted an honorary degree (LLD) from Aberdeen University in 1883. He was also a member of the British Archaeological Association. Hunter seems never to have married, and was of a retiring, scholarly disposition. He died at his home, Forest Retreat, Staple's Road, in Loughton, Essex, on 25 February 1897.

T. B. JOHNSTONE, rev. LIONEL ALEXANDER RITCHIE

Sources The Times (1 March 1897) · R. Hunter, *History of the missions of the Free Church of Scotland in India and Africa* (1873) · C. Mackenzie, *Life in the mission, the camp, and the zenana, or, Six years in India*, 3 vols. (1853) · W. Ewing, ed., *Annals of the Free Church of Scotland, 1843–1900*, 1 (1914), 188 · *Fasti Scot.* · *Kelly's directory of Essex* (1890) · CGPLA Eng. & Wales (1897)
Likenesses G. Haworth, photograph, GS Lond. [see illus.]
Wealth at death £296 12s. 5d.: resworn probate, Aug 1897, CGPLA Eng. & Wales

Hunter, Sir Robert (1844–1913), lawyer and authority on commons and public rights of way, was born at 3 Addington Square, Camberwell, on 27 October 1844, the elder of two children of Robert Lachlan Hunter, master mariner and shipowner, and his wife, Anne, daughter of Joseph Lachlan. He was educated at a private school and tutored by the author and barrister Leonard Seeley. Hunter

matriculated in 1861, entering University College, London, where he gained first-class honours in logic and moral philosophy. After taking the MA degree in 1865 he studied law and was admitted solicitor in 1867. Public opinion at that time was stirred by the enclosure of many metropolitan London commons, and Henry Peek offered prizes for essays on the subject. Hunter, among many rising lawyers, competed; his essay gained a prize and was selected for publication. This led to Hunter's becoming in 1869 a partner in the firm of Fawcett, Horne, and Hunter, solicitors to the Commons Preservation Society which had been founded in 1865. He was entrusted with the conduct of the suits that led to the protection of Hampstead Heath, Berkhamsted, Plumstead, and Wimbledon commons, and other threatened open spaces and established the principles of public interest on which the law related to commons is now based. The most notable case effected the recovery from enclosure of 3000 acres of Epping Forest on the suit of the corporation of the City of London. Hunter acted with the City solicitor in the conduct of the protracted legal proceedings (1871–4). He was subsequently instrumental in the preservation and protection from enclosure of Ashdown Forest, the New Forest, and Burnham Beeches. Whenever common land or ancient woodland was threatened the aggrieved parties therefore naturally turned to Hunter for help, for while they received plenty of 'sympathy and indignation' from members of parliament and philanthropists, Hunter provided them with the necessary 'sinews of war'. His wise counsel was always given willingly and free of charge.

In 1869 Hunter married Emily Browning, who died in childbirth on 2 January 1872. On 19 May 1877 he married Ellen Cann (1851–1932), the daughter of a land surveyor, Samuel Thomas Cann. There were three daughters of this second marriage. Four years later in 1881 Hunter purchased Meadfields Hanger, a substantial property in Haslemere, Surrey, where he lived for the remainder of his life. An active Liberal in politics, Hunter was a committed broad-church Anglican, supporting the work of his parish church insofar as his other commitments allowed. However, in spite of his success in preventing the spoliation of the countryside, he failed in his effort to impede the enlargement and 'modernization' of his own church building.

On 1 February 1882 Henry Fawcett, then postmaster-general, appointed Hunter solicitor to the General Post Office. He held the position until shortly before his death, and was concerned in the drafting and passage of over fifty acts of parliament dealing with the department. These measures included the Conveyance of Mails Act (1893), which ensured that all differences between the railway companies and the state as to remuneration for the carriage of mails should be referred for settlement to the Railway and Canal Commission. By his initiative and able handling of this measure Hunter saved the country in excess of £10 million. His most striking achievement, however, was his successful negotiation, in conjunction with Sir Henry Babington Smith, of the terms for the purchase of the National Telephone Company's system under the powers conferred on the Post Office by the Telegraph Arbitration Act (1909). The compensation claimed by the company was £21 million, but the amount awarded to them was reduced to £12½ million, after the contract, drafted by Hunter, had stood the test of bitterly fought arbitration proceedings lasting for seventy-two days. The value to the Post Office of Hunter's acumen and persuasive personality was well recognized, Fawcett once declaring that nothing in his official career had given him greater pleasure than the securing of a man of Hunter's character and ability for the country's service.

From 1875 onwards, Hunter was Octavia Hill's adviser on the protection of open spaces in London. She introduced him to countryside campaigners in the Lake District, where in 1883 he gave support to protests against the construction of slate railways through Wordsworth's Vale of Newlands and elsewhere, spearheaded by H. D. Rawnsley. A year later, in a paper read on his behalf to the National Association of Social Science in Birmingham, he outlined what were eventually to become, in the National Trust, the guiding principles of an institution expressly established for the purchase of open spaces to ensure their permanent protection from development.

On 16 November 1893 Hunter, Rawnsley, and Hill met in the offices of the Commons Preservation Society to discuss the formation of a 'National Trust for Places of Historic Interest or Natural Beauty', an organization which was on 16 July 1894 at Grosvenor House formally inaugurated under the chairmanship of the duke of Westminster. Hunter, knighted that year for his services to the conservation of open spaces, acted as chairman of the executive committee, in which capacity he drafted the 1907 National Trust Act. As adviser to the Hindhead Preservation Committee, he was closely associated with the acquisition of 750 acres of Hindhead Common, including the Devil's Punchbowl, presented to the National Trust in 1906.

Although slightly built and frail in appearance, Hunter was an energetic fell walker and president of the first Federation of Rambling Clubs, precursor of the Ramblers' Association. Rawnsley describes him as having a fierce fighting spirit, a cheery optimism, and 'an almost child's power of simple enjoyment'. His comprehensive guide to laws governing access to the countryside (*Open Spaces, Footpaths and Rights of Way*, 1896) shows his clarity of thought and expression. He was made CB in 1909 and promoted KCB in 1911.

Even after his official retirement, Hunter continued his work for the Post Office until his death from toxaemia at the age of sixty-nine at Meadfields Hanger on 6 November 1913. As befitted a man who had all his life been truly modest and self-effacing, Sir Robert Hunter was buried in an unmarked grave four days later in the parish churchyard of St Bartholomew at Haslemere. Fourteen acres of water and woodland at Waggoner's Wells, near Haslemere, were purchased by public subscription and given to the National Trust in honour of his memory.

L. W. CHUBB, *rev.* GRAHAM MURPHY

Sources G. Murphy, *Founders of the National Trust* (1987) • H. D. Rawnsley, 'A national benefactor—Sir Robert Hunter', *Cornhill Magazine*, [3rd] ser., 36 (1914), 230–39 • *The Times* (7 Nov 1913) • private information (2004) • b. cert. • d. cert.
Archives Surrey HC, corresp. and papers
Likenesses Caswall Smith, photograph, c.1865, Guildford Muniment Room • photograph, c.1865, Guildford Muniment Room • Mesenbach, photograph, c.1896, National Trust photographic library, London • photograph, c.1900, National Trust • photograph, 1907, Guildford Muniment Room • E. H. Mills, photograph, c.1912, priv. coll.
Wealth at death £13,216 12s. 8d.: probate, 30 Jan 1914, *CGPLA Eng. & Wales*

Hunter, Samuel (1769–1839), newspaper editor, was the son of John Hunter (1716–1781), parish minister of Stoneykirk, Wigtownshire. He was educated at the parochial school in Stoneykirk, and then at Glasgow University, graduating MA in 1795 and later qualifying as a surgeon. He joined the North Lowland fencibles as a surgeon, and fought with them in suppressing the Irish rising in 1798. The regiment was disbanded in 1800 and Hunter retired with the rank of captain. He was briefly and unsuccessfully involved in a calendering business, rolling and pressing machinery. His 18 stones and his geniality made him a popular figure in Glasgow. It was said that he had to take two seats in the London coach to accommodate his bulk.

On 10 January 1803 Hunter was announced as part proprietor and editor of the *Glasgow Herald and Advertiser*, which he edited for thirty-four years. Hunter was a strong tory. He resumed his military involvement in the face of radical unrest, becoming major in a corps of gentlemen sharpshooters, and then colonel-commandant of the 4th regiment of Highland local militia. After election to Glasgow town council, Hunter rose to be a magistrate, and was very successful and popular on the bench. In 1820 fresh military activity again brought him forward as commander of a corps of gentlemen sharpshooters.

Hunter was a successful editor, on the whole circumspectly conveying a tory point of view to a liberal city (though his opposition to parliamentary reform led to his effigy being burned at Glasgow Cross). John Strang believed that 'as a guide and controller of public opinion in the west of Scotland he was regarded as little less than an oracle' (Phillips, 43). After retiring as editor in 1836, Hunter settled at Rothesay; he died on 9 June 1839 when visiting his nephew, Archibald Blair Campbell, parish minister of Kilwinning, Ayrshire. He was buried in Kilwinning churchyard.

H. C. G. MATTHEW

Sources *Glasgow Herald* (14 June 1839) • Irving, *Scots.* • A. Phillips, *Glasgow's Herald, 1783–1983* (1982) • *DNB*
Likenesses D. Macnee, oils, U. Glas.

Hunter, Thomas (1666–1725), Jesuit and religious controversialist, was born in Northumberland on 6 June 1666 and studied at the English College at St Omer. He entered the Society of Jesus in 1684, was appointed professor of logic and philosophy at Liège, and was professed of the four vows on 2 February 1702. He became chaplain to the Sherburne family at Stonyhurst, Lancashire, in 1704. After the marriage in 1709 of Sir Nicholas Sherburne's daughter and heir, Mary Winifred Frances, to Thomas, eighth duke of Norfolk, Hunter generally resided with the duchess as her chaplain. He died on 21 February 1725.

Described as 'a man of powerful mind, remarkable industry and extensive information' (Gillow, *Lit. biog. hist.*, 3.484), Hunter was the author of a number of published and unpublished works. They included *A Modest Defence of the Clergy and Religious against R. C.'s History of Doway* (1714). This was a reply to the anonymous work of Charles Dodd, a Catholic priest and historian, entitled *The History of the English College at Doway, from its First Foundation in 1568 to the Present Time* (1713). Dodd then replied to Hunter in *The Secret Policy of the English Society of Jesus* (1715). According to Charles Butler, Dodd's pamphlet was written at a time 'when the secular clergy were suffering under charges of Jansenism, which they supposed were installed by the Jesuits' (ibid., 3.485). Another work by Hunter, *An English Carmelite: the Life of Catharine Burton, Mother Mary Xaveria of the Angels, of the English Teresian Convent at Antwerp*, remained unpublished until 1876, when it was issued in London. THOMPSON COOPER, *rev.* ROBERT BROWN

Sources Gillow, *Lit. biog. hist.* · G. Holt, *The English Jesuits, 1650–1829: a biographical dictionary*, Catholic RS, 70 (1984) · G. Oliver, *Collections towards illustrating the biography of the Scotch, English and Irish members of the Society of Jesus* (1835) · C. Butler, *Historical memoirs of the English, Irish, and Scottish Catholics since the Reformation*, 3rd edn, 4 vols. (1822) · H. Foley, ed., *Records of the English province of the Society of Jesus*, 7 vols. in 8 (1875–83)

Hunter, Thomas (1711/12–1777), Church of England clergyman and schoolmaster, was born in Kendal, Westmorland, where he was baptized on 30 or 31 March 1712, the eldest son of William and Margaret Hunter. Having been educated at Kendal grammar school he matriculated from Queen's College, Oxford, on 2 July 1734, aged twenty-two. In 1737 he was appointed headmaster of Blackburn grammar school. One of his pupils was the classical scholar Edward Harwood, who had a very high regard for his 'most worthy preceptor' and regarded Blackburn as 'the best School … of any gentleman in the country' (Nichols, *Lit. anecdotes*, 9.579). On 28 February 1738 Hunter married Mary, the widow of Hugh Baldwin.

Hunter left Blackburn grammar school in 1750, when he was appointed vicar of Garstang, Lancashire, and in 1755 he was preferred to the vicarage of Weaverham, Cheshire. In the 1750s he published several sermons, a pamphlet on image worship in the Roman Catholic church, and a comparative study of Tacitus and Livy. Although he went blind later in life it was then that he published his most significant works, namely *A Sketch of the Philosophical Character of the Late Viscount Bolingbroke* (1770) and *Reflections Critical and Moral on the Letters of the Late Earl of Chesterfield* (1776; 2nd edn, 1777). While acknowledging the literary merits of both Bolingbroke and Chesterfield, Hunter was unabashed in attacking the political and moral propositions contained in their most celebrated works. In the former work he set out to expose Bolingbroke as 'an avowed and undissembled enemy both to church and state, to his country and to mankind' (preface, viii) and in the latter to portray Chesterfield's example and precepts as irreligious

and pernicious. He also published two volumes of *Moral Discourses on Providence and other Important Subjects* (1774).

Hunter died at Weaverham on 1 September 1777. Of his children William Hunter was a fellow of Brasenose College, Oxford, and vicar of St Paul's, Liverpool, and Thomas Hunter succeeded his father as vicar of Weaverham.

C. W. SUTTON, *rev.* RICHARD S. TOMPSON

Sources J. Garstang, *A history of Blackburn grammar school, founded AD 1514* (1897), 63–4 · G. F. Eastwood, *Queen Elizabeth's: a new history of the ancient grammar school of Blackburn* [n.d., 1967?] · W. A. Abram, *A history of Blackburn, town and parish* (1877), 339, 347, 478 · Foster, *Alum. Oxon.* · G. Ormerod, *The history of the county palatine and city of Chester*, 3 vols. (1819), 2.58 · *GM*, 1st ser., 47 (1777), 459 · G. A. Stocks, ed., *The records of Blackburn grammar school*, Chetham Society (1909), 66–8 · Nichols, *Lit. anecdotes*, 9.577–9 · H. Fishwick, *The history of the parish of Garstang in the county of Lancaster*, 2, Chetham Society, 105 (1879), 93 · J. P. Earwaker, ed., *Local gleanings relating to Lancashire and Cheshire*, rev. edn, 1 (1876), ii · IGI

Hunter, William (1718–1783), physician, anatomist, and man-midwife, was born on 23 May 1718 at Long Calderwood, East Kilbride, Lanarkshire, the seventh of ten children of John Hunter (*d.* 1741), farmer, and Agnes (*d.* 1751), a woman of wide education, daughter of Mr Paul, a treasurer of Glasgow. He was the elder brother of John *Hunter (1728–1793). Intended by his father for the church, he attended the local Latin school before matriculating at Glasgow University in 1731. There he received an excellent education from the outstanding body of professors that included Francis Hutcheson.

Medical education and establishment of career Deciding against the church, Hunter left the university in 1736 without graduating. William Cullen, in medical practice in Hamilton, offered Hunter an apprenticeship. So well did they work together that they decided to go into partnership when Hunter completed his medical education. In 1739 Hunter attended the anatomy lectures of Alexander Monro primus in Edinburgh and in 1740 went to London to learn midwifery from William Smellie. He also attended the anatomy lectures of Frank Nicholls and the Newtonian John Desaguliers's natural philosophy course. An introduction to James Douglas led to his being offered employment as Douglas's anatomy assistant and tutor to his son William George. Cullen, seeing the advantage to Hunter, released him from the proposed partnership. Hunter joined the Douglas household in 1741. Many of Hunter's interests stemmed from work he did with Douglas, who also arranged for him to become a surgical pupil of David Wilkie at St George's Hospital. Douglas died in April 1742 but had already arranged that William George and Hunter should go to Paris to study anatomy and surgery. Hunter continued to live with the Douglas family, and on 3 June 1743 gave a paper to the Royal Society (*PTRS*, 42, 1743, 514–21) on articular cartilages on which he had worked for Douglas. In September 1743 Hunter and Douglas left for Paris, where Hunter attended the lectures of Antoine Ferrein on anatomy and of H. F. Le Dram on surgery. Hunter was back in London by early summer 1744 and continued to live with the Douglas family. He may have been engaged to Douglas's daughter Martha Jane, but she had died while he was in Paris, and Hunter never

William Hunter (1718–1783), by Allan Ramsay, *c.*1764

married. Hunter began building a surgical and midwifery practice, and investigating female reproductive anatomy using animals. At the time Monro primus held that in the human gravid uterus no maternal blood reached the placenta. Experiments on the lymphatic system convinced Hunter that it was an absorbent system. He believed this to be a discovery but, finding Francis Glisson in 1654 had concluded the same, he surrendered priority to him. It fell to William Cruikshank, who later assisted Hunter and who also worked on the lymphatics, to give an account of the work of Hunter and his assistants on the system in his *Anatomy of the Absorbing Vessels of the Human Body* (1786).

In October 1746 Hunter took advantage of the split between the barbers and the surgeons and advertised his first anatomy course in which 'Gentlemen may have the opportunity of learning the Art of Dissecting during the whole winter season in the same manner as in Paris' (Lawrence, 184). The 'Paris manner' meant that students could practise on human corpses. Lecturing regularly for the rest of his life, Hunter initially gave two courses a year; from 1767 one course lasted from October until March. He was described as 'the most perfect demonstrator as well as lecturer the world has ever known' (Adams, 120), attracting pupils from the continent and North America. Pupils' notes of his lectures are the only record of some of his discoveries.

A member of the Company of Surgeons by 1747 and temporary man-midwife at the Middlesex Hospital in 1748, Hunter was by now firmly settled in what he termed his 'darling London' (Brock, 38), and expressed his ambitions in a letter that year to William Cullen in which he told him that 'I want to tell you many things about colleges, hospitals, professorships, chariots, wives, etc. I am busy forming a plan for being an author. In short my head is full of a thousand things' (Porter, 15). In the summer of 1748 Hunter visited Leiden and saw W. Noortwyk's preparation of a human gravid uterus showing maternal blood in the placenta. After calling on Albinus, whose injections had impressed him, he visited Paris, but he was back in London for his autumn course and to welcome his brother John into the Douglas household. In 1749 Hunter became man-midwife to the new British Lying-in Hospital, an appointment he held until 1759, after which he was consultant physician. During the summer of 1749 the Hunter brothers moved to a house in Covent Garden that provided accommodation and lecturing facilities. Hunter took with him all Douglas's papers.

Work on the gravid uterus and priority disputes Hunter had his first opportunity to dissect a full-term human gravid uterus in 1750 and was able to determine the relationship between the maternal and foetal blood systems in the placenta. This work confirmed that maternal blood reached the placenta but did not pass to the foetus. The dissections, beautifully illustrated by Jan van Rymsdyk, his main anatomical artist, were engraved (two by Robert Strange), and exhibited in 1752 to solicit subscriptions for their publication. They form the first ten plates in Hunter's *Anatomia uteri humani gravidi tabulis illustrata* (1774), which covered all stages of pregnancy. A draft of his *Anatomical Description of the Human Gravid Uterus* was found after his death. An edition, unsatisfactorily edited by Matthew Baillie, was published in 1794. Hunter's understanding of female anatomy certainly contributed to his successful midwifery practice. However, a pupil's notes of Hunter's lectures later suggested to John Hunter that his brother did not understand placental anatomy. In a paper to the Royal Society in 1780 he claimed that it was he, in a dissection with Colin Mackenzie in 1754, who elucidated it, rather than his brother. His description in no way differs from that shown in plates of the 1750 dissection at which he may have assisted. Hunter had indeed acknowledged his brother's help in dissections of gravid uteri.

Family matters took Hunter to Scotland for the summer of 1750. During the visit Edinburgh made him a guild brother of the city, and Glasgow University awarded him the degree of MD. It was also to be the last time he saw William Cullen, but their friendship and correspondence continued. Hunter's elder brother James died about this time and William inherited Long Calderwood. When Hunter's mother died in 1751 Cullen arranged the funeral and took Dorothea, Hunter's sister, into his family until she could move to London. In London, Hunter canvassed for Cullen's appointment to the professorship of chemistry at Edinburgh and later for the professorship of the practice of medicine. Cullen's sons Harry and Archie attended Hunter's lectures and received favoured treatment. Hunter offered, if Cullen died, to take care of Archie's education. Hunter also promoted Cullen's election to a fellowship of the Royal Society in 1777.

In 1752 John Hunter, working on behalf of William, injected the semeniferous tubules in a human testis connecting with the epididymus, a procedure which he acknowledged Henry Watson had shown him in a dissection. Alexander Monro secundus, who came to hear about Hunter's unpublished work, claimed priority for a similar preparation in a publication of 1755, though priority rested with Albrecht von Haller (1745). Monro's 1755 Edinburgh thesis also claimed the discovery that lymphatics were absorbents. Joseph Black, who saw the draft thesis, told Monro that he must remove the claim as Hunter had been teaching that view since 1746. Monro clung to priority. He further claimed the discovery of the ducts from the lachrymal gland to the human eye that Hunter had demonstrated in 1747. These were not the only priority disputes in which Hunter was involved. Following a suggestion by Haller, he set John to discover how congenital hernias were formed. After seeing John's preparations, in 1757 Percivall Pott published a claim to the discovery of their formation. Tobias Smollett, a great friend of Hunter, reviewed the publications of Monro and Pott in the *Critical Review* (1757), pointing out Hunter's priority in both these fields. This led to very public disputes, documented in Hunter's *Medical Commentaries* (1762) and its supplement (1764).

Medical observations and a high-class practice In 1754 Hunter became a member of the Society of London Physicians, which in 1757 started publishing *Medical Observations and Inquiries*, in which he was to publish some of his important cases and, on behalf of former pupils, forty-four accounts of interesting cases they had sent him. Hunter published two important papers in *Medical Observations and Inquiries*, 6: in 'Three cases of malformation of the heart' he speculated on the importance of the survival of the fittest to procreate, while 'The uncertainty of signs of murder in bastard children' became a classic of forensic medicine. He saved two mothers of dead bastards from execution, gave an expert opinion in three cases of possible murder, and confirmed the births of bastards in three divorce cases. Hunter's surgical practice became so successful that it was not until 1756 that he left the Company of Surgeons and became a licentiate of the Royal College of Physicians, possibly because of his growing midwifery practice among the aristocracy. Hunter certainly seems to have developed personal qualities which brought him patients such as the Pitts, Hertfords, Lady Ossory, the Fitzroys, the earl of Sandwich, Lord North, the Coutts, and the Hollands. He was also someone who was aware of the benefits which could arise from cultivating persons of influence: 'I have', he wrote, 'the pleasure of thinking that every soul of my acquaintance wishes me well and would be ready to serve me' (Porter, 33). Hunter moved to a house in Jermyn Street in 1756 but kept on the Covent Garden house as a home for John and for delivering lectures. Accused in 1757 in the *Monthly Review* of ignorance in holding that Paulus Aegineta, not Galen, first described a true aneurysm, he was defended by Smollett in the *Critical Review*. Hunter detected an error in the Greek text of Paulus that caused the confusion. He was right but

Paulus was quoting Antylus, hardly known in the eighteenth century, who first described the true aneurysm.

When his brother John, who assisted him with lecturing and experimental work, enlisted as an army surgeon, Hunter took on William Hewson, a former pupil, as an assistant, and when Hewson went to Edinburgh in 1760 to attend lectures, Hunter decided to end his own lecturing and vacated the Covent Garden premises. His pupils were so devastated that he felt compelled to continue in new premises when Hewson returned.

Hunter now formed a connection with the royal family. In 1761 Queen Charlotte became pregnant and the king was advised to employ Hunter to look after her. The safe birth of a son in August 1762 was followed on 18 September by Hunter's appointment, on the recommendation of Sir Caesar Hawkins, as physician-extraordinary to the queen. He attended all her pregnancies until his death and was on friendly terms with both the king and queen. Hunter had previously been a whig, and his involvement in court circles led him to adopt more ministerialist sentiments, to the scorn of his whig friend Horace Walpole, who accused him of peddling 'political anatomy from the dais' (Porter, 30). Hunter, credited by Dr Johnson as having 'good intelligence' at court (ibid., 12), was also able to mix with the likes of Henry Fielding, Joshua Reynolds, Hester Thrale, Charles Burney, and David Hume.

In 1763 John Hunter left the army but did not rejoin William. William helped John—who had only his half pay as regular income—financially, and they sometimes worked together. Through his practice, lectures, financial prudence—John claimed, 'he was in the strictest sense a miser' (Porter, 12)—and possibly a win in the state lottery, Hunter was by now a rich man: his balance at Drummond's Bank in 1762 stood at £28,148 13s. 3d. Wishing to immortalize his name, he applied to the government for land on which to build and equip, at his own expense, a public school of anatomy. The government was not interested; even the king would not help. Disappointed, Hunter withdrew the offer. He toyed briefly with the idea of establishing an anatomy school in Glasgow.

Hunter had left the Company of Surgeons in order to become a fellow of the Royal College of Physicians. On discovering that as an accoucheur he could not become a fellow he joined the Society of Collegiate Physicians, which had the objective of opening up the fellowship. First steward, then treasurer, and finally president, Hunter played an important part in the society's activities and helped finance legal action against the Royal College of Physicians. By 1771 a few concessions had been won but the college would not accept man-midwives as fellows (Clark, 566). On 3 April 1767 Hunter was elected a fellow of the Royal Society. He gave the society three papers on comparative anatomy, proving that the large bones from the Ohio River banks were not those of an elephant but were from an unknown animal, probably extinct (*PTRS*, 58, 1768, 34–45), and that bones from the Rock of Gibraltar were not human but quadruped bones (*PTRS*, 60, 1770, 414–16). Interested in the formation of species, he suggested that the Indian nilgai might be a cross between deer and black cattle (*PTRS*, 61, 1770, 170–81). Hunter believed that venereal disease was in Europe before the return of Columbus from America but withdrew his paper on this subject from publication when told that the dating of some of his evidence was uncertain. Through the society he also brought to public notice the work of former pupils and of friends such as Charles Burney, James Bruce, and Professor Crell, chemist from Helmstadt.

Great Windmill Street James Mylne, friend and architect, designed for Hunter a residence in Great Windmill Street with anatomy theatre and preparation rooms and one large room as a museum in which to house the fast-growing collections in which he invested his wealth. His collection of anatomy preparations was vast. His collection of coins was second only to that of the king of France. Hunter purchased minerals and curiosities brought back from Cook's voyages. In 1781 he acquired John Fothergill's collection of shells and corals, and in 1782 part of Henry Yates's insect collection. His picture collection was small but choice. His library came to contain over 10,000 books, including 534 incunabula and 656 manuscripts. He received many gifts for the museum, and his library and museum were open to all who wished to use them. Duplicates were given to universities, institutions, and friends.

Hunter began lecturing in the new anatomy theatre in 1767, and lived on the site from 1768. His *Two Introductory Lectures* were published posthumously in 1784. He was elected a fellow of the Society of Antiquaries in 1768 and in December that year, when the king founded the Royal Academy of Art, Hunter was appointed professor of anatomy. 'I am', he said, 'pretty much acquainted with all the best artists and live in friendship with them' (Porter, 31). The importance of the visual should not be underestimated in Hunter's work. He stressed the necessity of achieving a natural appearance in anatomical preparations and in the plates which illustrated his own work. He wrote that:

> In explaining the structure of the parts, if a teacher would be of real service, he must take care, not barely to describe but to shew or demonstrate every part. What the student acquires in this way is solid knowledge, arising from the information of his own senses. (Jordanova, 386)

Anatomical pictures ought to reveal 'true nature, that is, the peculiar habit and composition of parts, as well as the outward form situation and connection of them' (ibid., 395). It must also be said that Hunter had numerous portraits painted of himself.

After relations between them soured Hunter replaced Hewson in 1772 with William Cruikshank. In 1776 Hunter lent his brother the use of his anatomy theatre to lecture on physiology and surgery. A dispute developed, possibly over John's lectures, which had little foundation in fact or experiment. Hunter, a deist, held 'speculation' an indignity against the 'Great Author of All Things. ... It is not showing what we are but what we should have been' (W. Hunter, *Two Introductory Lectures*, 1784, 95). John moved his lectures to the Haymarket in 1778. The Société Royale de Médecine, Paris, elected Hunter an associate member despite his opposition to the French practice of cutting the pubic symphysis in difficult births. Hunter had demonstrated that it provided little extra space in the pelvic cavity and discouraged its use in Britain.

Hunter's sister Dorothea had married the Revd James Baillie. Hunter promoted his appointment as professor of divinity at Glasgow, and when Baillie died in 1778 Hunter took over the education of his son Matthew *Baillie (1761–1823), training him to take over the anatomy lectures. Hunter died on 30 March 1783 at Great Windmill Street, his death possibly hastened by giving a surgery lecture despite being ill. For years he had suffered from kidney stones and gout, and he may have died from renal failure. He was buried on 5 April in a vault in St James's Church, Piccadilly, where there is a monument to his memory. His English will left to Glasgow University his museum and library, after remaining in London for thirty years to allow Baillie and Cruikshank to use the anatomy preparations to continue the lectures. They now form the Hunterian Museum, Glasgow. His Scottish will, covering property and mortgages held in Scotland, left £8000 to Glasgow University for building a museum, and provided an annuity for Dorothea and legacies for her two daughters. Matthew Baillie was residuary legatee.

Hunter was short and slim with pleasing manners, and he won the affection of his pupils, who went into mourning at his death. His contempt for those who offended him brought enemies. Some thought he was glib and lacked frankness and generosity (Porter, 12).

> Though he lived surrounded by a magnificent library and a fine collection of pictures, well, if soberly dressed ... maintaining a carriage, his general style of living was very modest. When he dined with a club of Scottish physicians that he met at the British Coffee House, his meal consisted of a couple of eggs and a glass of claret. Dining at home he never had more than one dish, and even when he had guests he never regaled them with more than two. (Brock, 42)

Hunter's reputation has suffered through his failure to publish much of his work and through ignorant latter-day historians accepting at face value the accusations of the Monros and John, branding him a thief of other men's work.

HELEN BROCK

Sources U. Glas., Hunter MSS · RCS Eng., Hunter–Baillie papers · S. Foart-Simmons and J. Hunter, *William Hunter, 1718–1783: a memoir*, ed. C. H. Brock (1983) · J. Thomson, *An account of the life, lectures and writings of William Cullen* (1832), 548 · Hunter's bank account, 1756–83, Drummond's bank, now Royal Bank of Scotland, Charing Cross, London · Hunter's bank account, 1764–6, Bank of England · G. C. Peachey, *A memoir of William and John Hunter* (1924) · J. Adams, *Memoirs of the life and doctrines of the late John Hunter, esq.* (1817), 120 · R. Porter, 'William Hunter: a surgeon and a gentleman', *William Hunter and the eighteenth-century medical world*, ed. W. Bynum and R. Porter (1985), 7–34 · L. Jordanova, 'Gender, generation and science: William Hunter's obstetrical atlas', *William Hunter and the eighteenth-century medical world*, ed. W. Bynum and R. Porter (1985), 385–412 · C. H. Brock, 'The happiness of riches', *William Hunter and the eighteenth-century medical world*, ed. W. Bynum and R. Porter (1985), 35–54 · J. H. Teacher, *Catalogue of the anatomical and pathological preparations of Dr William Hunter in the Hunterian Museum*, 2 vols. (1900) · S. F. Simmons, *An account of the life and writings of the late William Hunter* (1783) · G. Clark and A. M. Cooke, *A history of the Royal College of Physicians of London*, 2 (1966) · S. C. Lawrence, *Charitable knowledge: hospital pupils and practitioners in eighteenth-century London* (1996)

Archives Bodl. Oxf., papers relating to aneurysms · Glasgow Royal Infirmary Museum · RCS Eng., letter-book, lecture notes · Royal College of Physicians of Edinburgh, lecture notes · RS, papers · St George's Hospital, London, medical school, lecture notes · U. Glas. L., corresp. and papers · Uppsala University, Waller Library · Wellcome L., lecture notes | Berger Bibliothek, Bern, MSS His. Helv. · Bibliothèque Nationale, Paris, corresp. with l'Abbé Barthélemey · FM Cam., Spencer–Percival MSS

Likenesses oils, *c.*1756–1759, Hunterian Museum and Art Gallery, Glasgow; version, RCP Lond. · M. Chamberlain, oils, 1763–9, RA · A. Ramsay, oils, *c.*1764, Hunterian Museum and Art Gallery, Glasgow [*see illus.*] · E. Burch, bronze medal, 1774, NPG · J. Zoffany, oils, *c.*1775, RCP Lond. · attrib. J. Barry, oils, *c.*1784, RCP Lond. · J. Bogle, miniature, 1785, priv. coll. · J. Reynolds, oils, *c.*1788–1789 (posthumous), U. Glas. · J. Barry, group portrait, oils (*The Society for the Encouragement of Arts*), RS · H. Bone, miniature, Hunterian Society, London · E. Burch, copper medal, Scot. NPG · attrib. R. Cross, miniature, RCP Lond. · C. Grignion, pencil drawing, U. Glas. · N. Hone, miniature; copy, RCP Lond. · G. M. Moser, miniature, U. Glas. · R. E. Pine, oils, RCS Eng. · T. Rowlandson, caricature, etching, RCS Eng. · J. Zoffany, group portrait, oils (*Royal Academicians, 1772*), Royal Collection · silhouette, wash drawing, RCP Lond.

Wealth at death £1464 11*s.* 5*d.*—final balance: 1783, bank account, Drummond's bank, now Royal Bank of Scotland, Charing Cross, London · £25,000—mortgages and possessions in Scotland: RCS Eng., Hunter–Baillie papers, vol. 6, F. 37

Hunter, William (1755–1812), orientalist, was born at Montrose, Forfarshire. Nothing is known of his parents. He was educated at Marischal College, Aberdeen, where he took the degree of MA in 1777. After serving as apprentice to a surgeon for four years, he became doctor on board an East Indiaman. On his arrival in India in 1781 he was transferred to the service of the East India Company, and gazetted assistant surgeon in Bengal on 6 April 1783. For some time he was surgeon to the British residency at Agra, and accompanied the resident in a march with Mahadji Sindhia from Agra to Ujjain and back, during a struggle for leadership of the Maratha confederacy. Of this expedition, which lasted from February 1792 to April 1793, Hunter gave a detailed account in the sixth volume of the *Asiatic Researches*. He was gazetted surgeon to the marines on 21 October 1794, and held the post until 1806. In 1808, being then surgeon at the general hospital of Bengal, he received the degree of MD from his old college. On the conquest of Java from the Dutch in 1811, he received the special appointment of superintendent-surgeon in the island and its territories.

Hunter had begun his career with mechanical contrivances, and an improvement of the screw invented by him was noticed in the *Philosophical Transactions* in 1780. He wrote a variety of scientific articles, many of them contributions to the *Asiatic Researches*. His *Concise Account of the Kingdom of Pegu* (1785), a volume of other works, contained 'An enquiry into the cause of the variety observable in fleeces of sheep in different climates'. His astronomical writings included the results of his own observations and an article entitled 'An account of the labours of Jayasimha' on the Hindu astronomer, with a detailed description of his observatory in Delhi, published in *Asiatic Researches*. Hunter's *Essay on Diseases Incident to Indian Seamen, or Lascars, on Long Voyages* (1804), printed at the expense of the government in Calcutta, was the first British attempt to write about the health of Indians. He contributed to the *Memoirs* of the Medical Society a 'History of an aneurism of the aorta' and to the *Transactions of the Linnean Society* a paper entitled 'On *Nauclea gambir*, the plant producing the drug called gutta gambier'. He was a foreign member of the Medical Society of London and an honorary member of the Academical Society of Sciences of Paris.

But Hunter's main intellectual interests were orientalist. In 1782 the ship in which he was serving as medical officer went, while on the way from Bengal to the Carnatic, far off course in a storm. It had to put into the River Syriam in Pegu (later part of Burma) and stay there for a month. In the interval Hunter gathered materials for his *Concise Account*, to which he added a description of the caves at Elephanta, Ambola, and Kanheri in western India. This book attained considerable popularity and was translated into French in 1793. In 'Some artificial caverns near Bombay', an essay he contributed to *Archaeologia* (7, 1785, 291), Hunter admired the ability of Indian sculptors to render anatomical detail and emotional expression, providing a basis for aesthetic analysis thus far lacking in the British reception of the subcontinent's plastic art.

During two periods (May 1798 to March 1802, and April 1804 to April 1811) Hunter acted as secretary to the Asiatic Society of Bengal. In 1801, soon after the foundation of Fort William College, he was appointed regular examiner in Persian and Hindustani, and in July 1807 succeeded as public examiner. In November 1805 he became secretary of the college, a post which he retained until his resignation in 1811. In 1805 he compared with the original Greek and thoroughly revised the Hindustani New Testament by Mirza Mohummed Fitrut. He also superintended the publication of the *Mejmua shemsi*, a summary of the Copernican system of astronomy translated into Persian by Maulavi Abul Khwa. The earliest attempt to compile a dictionary of the Afghan language was made by Amir Muhammad of Peshawar in accordance with Hunter's advice. His own two-volume Hindustani and English dictionary was published at Calcutta in 1808. For some years Hunter was engaged in compiling a *Collection of Proverbs and Proverbial Phrases in Persian and Hindustani, with Translations*, but left the work incomplete at his death. It was finished and published by his friend Captain Roebuck and by Horace Hayman Wilson in 1824. Hunter died in Java in December 1812. E. J. Rapson, rev. Michael Fry

Sources Dodwell [E. Dodwell] and Miles [J. S. Miles], eds., *Alphabetical list of the Honourable East India Company's Bengal civil servants, from the year 1780 to the year 1838* (1839) · *Asiatic Researches*, 1–16 (1788–1828) · P. Mitter, *Much maligned monsters: history of European reactions to Indian art* (1977) · *European Magazine and London Review*, 64 (1813), 180

Hunter, William Alexander (1844–1898), jurist, born in Aberdeen on 8 May 1844, was the eldest son of James Hunter, granite merchant, and his wife, Margaret Boddie, of Aberdeen. After attending Aberdeen grammar school he entered the University of Aberdeen at the age of sixteen, with a high place in the bursary competition. In

1862–3 he was first prizeman in logic, moral philosophy, Christian evidences, botany, and chemistry, and in 1864 he graduated MA with the highest honours in mental philosophy and in natural science. Besides several prizes he gained the Ferguson scholarship in mental philosophy, and the Murray scholarship, awarded by the university after a competitive examination in all the subjects of the arts curriculum. With this successful record he was encouraged to read for the bar, and he entered the Middle Temple in London in 1865. After taking numerous exhibitions awarded by the Council of Legal Education, and passing his examinations with first-class honours, he was called to the English bar in 1867, and joined the south-eastern circuit.

For some years Hunter's work was almost entirely educational. In 1868 he gained the *proxime accessit* to the Shaw fellowship in philosophy, which, like the Ferguson, was open to graduates of all Scottish universities. Shortly afterwards he took the Blackwell prize for the best essay on the philosophy of Leibniz, and on 7 August 1869 he was appointed professor of Roman law at University College, London. His class was never large, but he devoted much time to the preparation of his lectures and elaborated a logical arrangement of the subject, which afterwards appeared in his textbooks. In 1878 he resigned the chair of Roman law, and on 2 November was appointed professor of jurisprudence in the same college. Hunter's lectures on his subject during the four years he held the chair contained much valuable criticism of Austin and other writers, but the matter was not published except in a few magazine articles. Under the influence of John Stuart Mill, Hunter also took an active part in the agitation for the political enfranchisement of women, and helped to obtain for them opportunities of higher education. In 1875, following the example of Professor John Eliot Cairnes, he admitted women to his class in Roman law, and he extended to them the same privilege when he afterwards became professor of jurisprudence. In 1882 he resigned his chair of jurisprudence at University College, and in the same year he received the degree of LLD from the University of Aberdeen.

While professor at University College, Hunter acted from time to time as examiner in Roman law and jurisprudence at the University of London, and he wrote on social and political subjects in *The Examiner* and other newspapers. He was for five years editor of the *Weekly Dispatch*. In 1875 he wrote a pamphlet entitled *The Law of Master and Servant*, and he gave much attention to the interpretation of the law as it affected labour disputes.

After retiring from his chair in 1882 Hunter gave whatever time was not occupied in professional pursuits to political controversy. In conjunction with his friend James Barclay, MP for Forfarshire, he took part in the attempts then being made by English and Scottish tenant farmers to obtain compensation for improvements. He also took up in the same interest the question of railway rates, and succeeded in obtaining important improvements in restrictions on charges and in the classification of goods and rates. He collected some materials for a work on private bill legislation, but this was never completed.

In 1885 Hunter was elected the advanced radical MP for the north division of Aberdeen by a majority of 3900 over the Conservative candidate. His friendship with Charles Bradlaugh and his close acquaintance with Indians who had been his law students had familiarized him with Indian questions, and on 21 January 1886 he began his career in the House of Commons by moving an amendment to the address expressing regret that the revenues of India had been applied to defray the expenses of the military operations in Ava without the consent of parliament. This was withdrawn at Gladstone's suggestion.

At the 1886 general election Hunter declared himself in favour of home rule, and was returned for North Aberdeen unopposed. In 1888 he was appointed by the Council of Legal Education as reader in Roman law, international law, and jurisprudence. Next year the government, when legislating on local government in Scotland, appropriated probate duty to the payment of the fees of children taking the three lowest standards in elementary schools. In 1890 Hunter saw the chance of completely freeing elementary education from the payment of fees, and urged that the increase in the duties, which the government then imposed on spirits, should pay the fees in elementary schools on the standards above the three lowest. This he succeeded in carrying, and thus secured wholly free elementary education for Scotland. For this service he received the freedom of his native city in 1890. On 27 January 1891 Hunter moved that the resolution refusing permission to Bradlaugh to take the oath or make affirmation should be expunged from the records of the House of Commons, and this was carried without a division. Hunter had always been interested in old-age pensions, which he was the first to press upon the attention of parliament, and he gave valuable assistance to those attempting to bring forward a feasible scheme. But his health was rapidly failing, and he seldom intervened in debate during his remaining years in parliament. He was re-elected as member for North Aberdeen by a majority of 3548 in 1895 but retired from parliament in the following year owing to the state of his health. On the recommendation of A. J. Balfour he was awarded a civil-list pension of £200. He died on 21 July 1898 at Cults in Aberdeenshire.

Hunter's most important work was *A systematic and historical exposition of Roman law in the order of a code embodying the institutes of Gaius and of Justinian* (1876). The chief characteristic of this work was its order of arrangement, which was based on that recommended by Bentham for a civil code. Under the heading 'contracts' some important criticisms of Maine's theory of the origin of *stipulatio* are given, and under 'ownership' a new theory respecting bona fide *possessio* is put forward entirely opposed to that of Savigny.   ELIZA ORME, rev. C. A. CREFFIELD

Sources personal knowledge (1901) · *The Times* (22 July 1898), 10 · *The Times* (25 July 1898), 8 · *Law Journal* (23 July 1898), 388 · *CCI* (1898)

Wealth at death £1351 16s. 4d.: confirmation, 28 Dec 1898, *CCI*

Hunter, Sir William Guyer (1827–1902), army medical officer, born at Calcutta, India, was the eldest son of Thomas Hunter of Catterick, Yorkshire. Educated in London at King's College School, he began his training at Charing Cross Hospital in 1844, became MRCS in 1849, FRCS (Edinburgh) in 1858, MD at Aberdeen and MRCP (London) in 1867, and FRCP in 1875.

After enlisting as an assistant surgeon in the Bombay medical service in May 1850, Hunter served through the Second Anglo-Burmese War of 1852–3 which led to the annexation of Pegu. For this campaign, during which he nearly died of cholera, he received a medal and clasp. In 1854 he received a commendation from the Bombay medical board for successfully establishing dispensaries in Raligaum, Alighur, and Shikarpur, and in 1857 the thanks of the government for his zeal and skill during a fever epidemic in Shikarpur, and for repressing a revolt of 800 prisoners in the gaol there. During the Indian mutiny he acted as civil surgeon in Upper Sind, and he obtained brevet rank of surgeon in 1864. He again received the thanks of the government for his actions and was awarded a medal.

Hunter's health had been shattered by the experiences of the year and he came home on furlough, but he was soon recalled to Bombay to take up the appointments of physician to the Jamsetji Jijibhoy Hospital and professor of medicine in the Grant Medical College, of which he became principal in 1876. The institution prospered under his administration and expanded from 16 students to 200. He was made surgeon-major in 1870 and deputy surgeon-general in 1876, and he was promoted to the rank of surgeon-general in 1877, when he received the thanks of the government for organizing the medical and hospital equipment for troops in active service when they were sent to Malta from India. His scheme was ultimately adopted throughout India.

In 1880 Hunter was appointed by Sir Richard Temple as vice-chancellor of the University of Bombay, a distinction usually reserved for members of the legislative council and judges of the high court in India. On his retirement from the service in 1880 he was appointed honorary surgeon to Queen Victoria; the inhabitants of Bombay presented him with a public address, gave his portrait to the Grant Medical College, and founded a scholarship. On his return to England, Hunter was elected a consulting physician to the Charing Cross Hospital, London.

In 1883, following the outbreak of a cholera epidemic in Egypt, Hunter, at the request of the Indian medical board, was sent on a special mission to investigate it. He wrote an able report showing the urgent need for efficient sanitation in Egypt and emphasizing the superior value of sanitary measures to quarantine regulations. The report was criticized, but its main conclusions seem justified. In 1885 Hunter put forward his views at the sanitary conference at Rome, which he attended as the official representative of Great Britain. He was made KCMG in 1884 and honorary LLD of Aberdeen in 1894.

In his last years Hunter was prominent in English public life. From 1886 to 1887 he was a member of the London school board for the Westminster division, and from 1885 to 1892 he was Conservative MP for Central Hackney in east London. While in parliament he was chairman of the water inquiry committee of the City of London, and a member of the departmental committee to 'enquire into the best mode of dealing with habitual drunkards'. He also did much work in connection with the vaccination commission, the Shop Hours Bill, and the Midwives' Registration Bill, and he continued to take an active interest in sanitary questions. During 1884–5 he was especially interested in the formation of the Volunteer Medical Staff Corps, drawn largely from Charing Cross Hospital students to begin with (later the Royal Army Medical Corps, territorial), of which he was the first honorary commandant.

Hunter married first, in 1856, a daughter of Christopher Packe, vicar of Ruislip, Middlesex; and second, in 1871, Mary Louisa, second daughter of Joseph Stainburn. Hunter died at his residence, Marnhull, Anerley Hill, Upper Norwood, Surrey, on 14 March 1902, and was buried at Paddington cemetery. He was survived by his second wife. D'A. POWER, rev. PATRICK WALLIS

Sources Munk, *Roll* · *BMJ* (22 March 1902), 748–9 · *The Lancet* (22 March 1902), 856 · R. J. Minney, *The two pillars of Charing Cross* (1967) · D. G. Crawford, *A history of the Indian medical service, 1600–1913*, 2 vols. (1914) · *Medico-Chirurgical Transactions*, 86 (1903), cvii–cix · Burke, *Peerage* · CGPLA Eng. & Wales (1902)

Archives BL OIOC, letters to Sir George Birdwood, MS Eur. F 216 · UCL, manuscript room, letters to E. Chadwick

Wealth at death £692 9s. 10d.: probate, 1 May 1902, CGPLA Eng. & Wales

Hunter, Sir William Wilson (1840–1900), administrator in India and historian, was born on 15 July 1840, the son of Andrew Galloway Hunter, a Glasgow manufacturer from Denholm, Roxburghshire, and his wife, Isabella Wilson, a younger sister of James Wilson (1805–1860). He was educated at Glasgow, first at the academy and later at the university. After graduating in 1860, he spent some months as a student in Paris and Bonn, acquiring a useful knowledge of Sanskrit. In the open competition for the Indian Civil Service in 1861, he passed at the head of the list.

Hunter arrived in India in November 1862, and was posted to Birbhum district in the lower provinces of Bengal as assistant magistrate. On 4 December 1863 he married Jessie, daughter of Thomas *Murray. They were to have two surviving sons. He began to show an interest in historical research, studying old records and collecting local traditions. His first literary venture, *The Annals of Rural Bengal* (1868), was a considerable historical work and was intended as the precursor of a series. It was well received, due to Hunter's ability to make the details of administration both intelligible and attractive. Less successful was another publication of the same year, *A Comparative Dictionary of the non-Aryan Languages of India and High Asia*, which was a glossary based mainly on the collections of Brian Houghton Hodgson, with a political commentary on the relationship between the Indian government and the indigenous people. Hunter later withdrew some of the linguistic inductions, and acknowledged the

Sir William Wilson Hunter (1840–1900), by Barraud, pubd 1893

influential exercises in imperial information gathering undertaken in the nineteenth century, and supervised the work of the local editors in gathering statistical and other data. Moreover, he undertook the volumes on Bengal and Assam himself: the former were published as *The Statistical Account of Bengal* (excluding Calcutta) in twenty volumes between 1875 and 1877; *The Statistical Account of Assam* (1879) comprised a further two volumes. The other local gazetteers brought the total number of volumes to 128. At the same time, the work of condensing this mass of information into the *Imperial Gazetteer* went ahead. The first edition appeared in nine volumes in 1881, and a second edition of fourteen volumes, incorporating the latest statistics and the results of the 1881 census, was published in 1885–7. By the time of the final edition in 1931 the *Gazetteer* had expanded to twenty-six volumes. Of course, Hunter was not personally responsible for the entirety of this monumental achievement, but his was the mind which conceived the whole plan, and his the energy which caused it to appear so promptly; he also had the gift of motivating his assistants. His own special contribution was the introductory article, which was re-issued separately in an expanded form as *The Indian Empire: its Peoples, History and Products* (1895). In this work he gave a summary of his opinions about many controversial questions in the ethnic and religious history of early India. Of continuing interest is his account of the growth of Christianity in southern India. A version of this work produced for schools in England and India and published under the title *A Brief History of the Indian Peoples* (1880) sold widely in many editions and was translated into several Indian languages.

In 1881 Hunter was appointed an additional member of the executive council, which seat he retained for six years. In 1882 he was appointed president of the commission on education, which was intended to regulate the divergent systems which had grown up in the several provinces. The viceroy, Lord Ripon, believed that it was the duty of the state to provide education for all the people of India, and that while those able to do so should provide for their own education, the state should devote its attention and resources to the spread of primary education among the masses. By contrast, official policy had been clearly élitist: over 80 per cent of public funding for education had been spent on less than a sixth of the total number of students. Any change of policy was likely to generate considerable opposition and be interpreted as a triumph for the Christian missionaries' priorities. The report of the commission, drafted by Hunter and accepted almost in its entirety by the government, affirmed that, without checking higher education, the provision, extension, and improvement of elementary education for the masses should be the priority of the state. As funds were limited, once a district had an efficient high school, the state should do no more than bestow grants-in-aid. With free scope and cordial encouragement, private enterprise might produce satisfactory results: private agencies—but not missionary bodies—should therefore be encouraged to take over higher education. The recommendations also provided

inadequacy of his research. Hunter recognized the atmosphere of tension created by the Wahabis in northern India in the early 1870s, and in his book *The Indian Mussalmans* (1871) he announced that the Muslims in India formed a source of chronic danger to British power, as they were 'seditious masses in the heart of an Empire'. He added that they had good reasons for their profound sense of grievance. Lord Mayo's government, which was more optimistic in its assessment, considered proscribing the book, but soon abandoned the idea. Meanwhile, in 1869 Mayo had selected Hunter to organize a statistical survey of India, a task which was to occupy the next twelve years of his life. His first duty was to travel over the whole of India, in order to see things for himself and talk with local officials. These tours, which he often repeated, gave him an unrivalled knowledge of every corner of the subcontinent. He encountered some opposition and personal criticism, directed chiefly against the introduction of a uniform system of spelling place names. His enthusiasm and diplomacy finally triumphed, and his compromise, based on the transliteration of vernacular names without any diacritical marks but with a concession to the old spelling of place names of historical significance, gradually won a general acceptance which survived until the British withdrawal from India in 1947.

In September 1871 the post of director-general of statistics to the government of India was created for Hunter, who thereafter spent considerable periods in Britain for the furtherance of his work. He drew up the scheme for the *Imperial Gazetteer of India*, one of the largest and most for the withdrawal of a child from religious instruction if a denominational school was the only one of its class available in the locality, for the preparation of a moral textbook, based on the fundamental principles of natural religion, to be used in all colleges, and for lectures to be given on the duties of citizenship.

These principles generally pleased Indian opinion, and indeed, in 1949, the first university commission of free India made very similar recommendations. However, the Hunter commission's 'conscience clause' was resisted by missionaries. They were formally prepared to concede it when the institution was the only one of its kind in the locality, but the author of the clause, Dr William Miller, a leading missionary in south India, informed the viceroy that he did not wish the government to act on his recommendation. In England too there was considerable resistance to the 'baneful idea' that the highest form of education was compatible with the entire absence of religious culture. As a result, matters were left as they were, despite the fact that the viceroy considered the decision judicious, but mistaken.

In 1884 Hunter gave evidence in London before a House of Commons committee on Indian railways; in the same year he was made a CSI. In 1886 he was a member of the commission on finance, and also in that year served as vice-chancellor of the University of Calcutta. He finally retired from the Indian Civil Service in 1887, at the early age of forty-seven, and was promoted KCSI. He devoted the remainder of his life to working up the materials he had accumulated for an authoritative history of India. He moved from Edinburgh, where he had previously spent his time in Britain, to Oxford, where he eventually built himself a house on the slopes of Wytham Woods. He became a regular contributor to *The Times*, writing weekly articles on Indian affairs. He also arranged for the publication of the Rulers of India series by the Clarendon Press, initiating the series himself with a memoir of the administration of Lord Dalhousie (1890); this was followed by a biography of Lord Mayo, a précis of his full-length study of 1875. In *Bombay, 1885 to 1890* (1892) he examined in detail the administration of Bombay presidency under the governorship of Lord Reay. He had hoped to write a life of Sir Bartle Frere, but instead wrote a biography of the veteran orientalist Brian Houghton Hodgson (1800–1894). His other publications included, in a lighter vein, *The Old Missionary* (1895) and *The Thackerays in India* (1897), and a bibliography of books about India which he contributed to James Samuelson's *India Past and Present* (1890).

Despite all this literary activity, Hunter still hoped to execute the projected history of India he had planned during his early years of service at Birbhum. *Bengal Ms. Records*, three volumes of records which he had calendared at that time, were published in 1894 with a dissertation on the permanent settlement of the revenue. He also compiled a catalogue of 380 historical manuscripts in the India Office Library. But he reluctantly came to realize that he could not cover the entire field of Indian history, and confined himself to tracing the period of British rule. Even this limited design, as sketched out by Hunter,

would have taken five volumes; only two were completed.

In the winter of 1898–9 Hunter undertook the long rail journey across Europe to Baku on the Caspian Sea, where one of his sons was ill. On his return he fell victim to influenza and died at his home, Oaken Holt, at Cumnor, near Oxford, on 7 February 1900. He was buried in the churchyard at Cumnor, Berkshire. He was survived by his wife, who edited a volume of his essays published under the title *The India of the Queen* (1903).

J. S. COTTON, rev. S. GOPAL

Sources F. H. Skrine, *Life of Sir William Wilson Hunter* (1901) · S. Gopal, *The viceroyalty of Lord Ripon, 1880–1884* (1953) · S. Gopal, *British policy in India, 1858–1905* (1965) · *DNB*
Likenesses Barraud, photograph, pubd 1893, NPG [*see illus.*] · W. H. Thornycroft, bronze bust, 1900, Indian Institute, Oxford
Wealth at death £34,298 0s. 8d.: probate, 24 April 1900, *CGPLA Eng. & Wales*

Hunting, Sir Percy Llewellyn (1885–1973), shipping and aviation entrepreneur, was born on 6 March 1885, at Deep Dene House, Newcastle upon Tyne, the eldest son of Charles Samuel Hunting (1853–1921), a successful shipowner of Newcastle upon Tyne, and his wife, Agnes Mona Arthur. The family's enterprise had been set up in the days of sail, but by the time Percy Hunting began to be involved in the business, its fleet was exclusively steam-powered, and the firm had begun to take a particular interest in the shipping of oil, a line of business which he and his younger brother Gerald Lindsay Hunting were to make its hallmark after the First World War.

Percy Hunting received a fairly conventional middle-class education in his early years, being sent first of all to Loretto School and, in 1903, to Paris to perfect his French. But thereafter he was apprenticed to the North Eastern Marine Engineering Company at Wallsend-on-Tyne, and went on to study marine engineering at Armstrong College, later the University of Newcastle upon Tyne. Having completed his engineering training, Hunting married in 1910 Dorothy Edith (d. 1958), daughter of Daniel Moule Birkett JP, of Bexhill; the couple had two sons. In 1912 he was sent, in the company of his brother Gerald Lindsay Hunting, to the USA, Canada, and Mexico. One aim of the trip seems to have been to identify possible new business opportunities, with particular reference to oil.

The outbreak of war in 1914 saw Hunting, as a member of the Territorial Army, commissioned into the 4th battalion, Northumberland Fusiliers. He appears to have remained on the home establishment of his unit for two years, perhaps because officers were needed in Britain to train the new volunteer armies raised in response to Lord Kitchener's famous appeal. Seeking more active involvement in the war, Hunting in 1916 joined the Royal Flying Corps (RFC), in which his brother also served. He was posted to 30 squadron RFC and served with it and with 3rd wing general headquarters in Mesopotamia, primarily as a wireless officer. His military career was evidently not undistinguished, as he was twice mentioned in dispatches.

When Percy and Lindsay Hunting returned from war in

1918, they found the family business in poor shape. Like many shipping lines, the company had suffered severely from enemy action, and only two of its ships were still afloat. The brothers, taking over the enterprise after the death in 1921 of their father, embarked on a rebuilding programme in which oil tankers figured prominently. The firm itself was restructured from a family partnership to a private limited company in 1926, with Percy Hunting as chairman, a position he occupied for the next thirty-five years. The firm also acquired new interests in shipbroking.

The firm fared badly as the slump of 1929–32 hit the world shipping trades, and by the latter year every unit of the fleet was laid up. As a result, Hunting began to seek more promising business opportunities and shifted the focus of his activities from Tyneside to London. In the process, he moved his family home from Glebe House, Edmondbyers, in Northumberland, to Old Whyly in the Sussex village of East Hoathly. He remained active in the shipping business, serving as vice-chairman, then chairman, of the British chamber of shipping's tanker committee from 1933 to 1940, and as deputy chairman of the International Tanker Owners Association from 1934 to 1950. But he also invested successfully in oil production, through the British Oil Development Company and Brazos Young Oil Company of Texas. On the distribution side, Huntings also took over a company based in Preston which operated a chain of filling-stations in Lancashire and Yorkshire.

The most important step in the diversification of the Hunting enterprise, however, took place in 1938, when a minority shareholding was taken in a small aircraft servicing company based at Croydon airport called Rollasons. By that time the likelihood of war was becoming increasingly apparent. This, coupled with a recognition of the impact its outbreak would have on the aviation industry, inspired the conversion of the minority stake into a majority holding in 1939. The war indeed generated the expected expansion both at Croydon and at a new factory in Llanberis in north Wales, especially in the manufacture of airframe components for a variety of military aircraft. Hunting accordingly assumed complete control of the firm in 1941, changing its name to Field Air Services. Then in 1944 Hunting made a move into the manufacture of complete aircraft through the acquisition of Percival Aircraft Ltd of Luton.

Simultaneously with the purchase of a stake in Rollasons in 1938, Hunting also acquired a shareholding in the Aircraft Operating Company and its subsidiary Aerofilms, which took the group into aerial survey and mapping. As with Rollasons, the initial minor shareholding became complete control in 1942. The company's efforts were initially devoted to war work under government control, but after 1945, as Hunting Aerosurveys, it developed a leading reputation in air survey work involving mapping, geophysical, soil, forestry, and mineral surveys not only in Britain but in Canada, Africa, Australasia, and Antarctica.

As the war progressed, Hunting's new ventures seem to have started to eclipse his interest in shipping. The group certainly remained active in that field, but Percy Hunting himself appeared to be running down his prominent role in shipping circles after leaving the chairmanship of the tramp tanker committee in 1943. The war also brought him personal grief, with the loss of his younger son in the sinking of HMS *Repulse* off the Malayan coast in 1941.

When hostilities ended Hunting took a very active role in his group's aviation interests, which he lost no time in expanding further. The year 1945 saw the creation of an airline, Hunting Air Travel. The immediate post-war climate was not especially favourable to private enterprise in civil aviation, and Hunting Air Travel met considerable opposition from the Ministry of Civil Aviation and the nationalized airlines—British European Airways (BEA) and British Overseas Airways Company (BOAC)—in obtaining access to worthwhile routes and purchasing the latest aircraft. Nevertheless, the new airline had its successes. It developed worthwhile business in Africa, where Field Air Services was also prominent, in a joint venture—Hunting Clan Air Holdings—with the Clan Line shipping company. It also became the first British independent airline to operate the highly successful Vickers Viscount airliner.

The Hunting group was also very prominent in the years after the war in aircraft design and manufacturing. Hunting Percival produced a series of primary training aircraft for the Royal Air Force, culminating in the Jet Provost, which served in the basic training role through the 1970s and 1980s. The twin-engined Prince feeder liner was also very successful, being adapted for a variety of other roles such as air survey (not least with Hunting Aerosurveys Ltd), training, and communications work with the RAF, the Royal Navy, and, like the Jet Provost, various foreign and Commonwealth air forces. On the eve of its absorption into the British Aircraft Corporation in 1960, Hunting Aircraft was engaged in a design study which was eventually to emerge as the BAC 1–11 jet airliner.

Hunting seems never to have been content to take a merely commercial interest in all the businesses in which he became involved, but to have thrown himself into their technical aspects as well. He was a fellow of the Institute of Chartered Secretaries, a companion of the Royal Aeronautical Society, and held memberships of the Institute of Petroleum Technology, of the Photogrammetric Society of Great Britain, and of the American Society of Naval Architects and Marine Engineers, as well as being an associate member of the Independent Petroleum Association of America. He also took an interest in arboriculture, and planted around his house in Sussex specimens of trees from all parts of the world to which his business activities had taken him. He was also active in a variety of companies outside the Hunting group itself, in fields as diverse as rope making, marine insurance, and house building.

Hunting's wife, Dorothy, died in 1958, and he retired from the chairmanship of the Hunting group of companies in 1960, to be succeeded in that capacity in 1962 by his son, Charles. In the year of his retirement he was knighted, and married Evelyn Marion Birkett, his first wife's sister. He suffered a heart attack at Old Whyly on 2 January 1973, and was declared dead at the Royal Sussex County Hospital, Brighton. ALEX J. ROBERTSON

Sources D. J. Rowe, 'Hunting, Sir Percy Llewellyn', *DBB* · *The Times* (3 Jan 1973) · P. L. Hunting, *The group and I: an account of the Hunting Group with which is interwoven my own life and thoughts* (1968) · *WWW*, 1981–90 · b. cert. · d. cert.
Likenesses F. Eastman, oils (after photograph), Hunting Group of Companies, London
Wealth at death £468,032: probate, 12 April 1973, *CGPLA Eng. & Wales*

Huntingdon. For this title name *see* Senlis, Simon (I) de, earl of Northampton and earl of Huntingdon (*d.* 1111x13); Senlis, Simon (II) de, earl of Northampton and earl of Huntingdon (*d.* 1153); David, earl of Huntingdon and lord of Garioch (1152–1219); Clinton, William, earl of Huntingdon (*d.* 1354); Leybourne, Juliana, countess of Huntingdon (1303/4–1367); Angle, Guichard (IV) d', twelfth earl of Huntingdon (*c*.1308x15–1380); Holland, John, first earl of Huntingdon and duke of Exeter (*c*.1352–1400); Hastings, George, first earl of Huntingdon (1486/7–1544); Hastings, Francis, second earl of Huntingdon (1513/14–1560); Hastings, Henry, third earl of Huntingdon (1536?–1595); Hastings, Katherine, countess of Huntingdon (*c*.1538–1620); Hastings, Henry, fifth earl of Huntingdon (1586–1643); Stanley, Elizabeth, countess of Huntingdon (*bap.* 1587, *d.* 1633); Hastings, Lucy, countess of Huntingdon (1613–1679); Hastings, Theophilus, seventh earl of Huntingdon (1650–1701); Hastings, Selina, countess of Huntingdon (1707–1791); Hastings, Hans Francis, twelfth earl of Huntingdon (1779–1828); Hastings, Francis John Clarence Westenra Plantagenet, sixteenth earl of Huntingdon (1901–1990); Lane, Margaret Winifred [Margaret Winifred Hastings, countess of Huntingdon] (1907–1994).

Huntingdon, Gregory of. See Gregory (*fl. c*.1300).

Huntingdon, Jack. See Hastings, Francis John Clarence Westenra Plantagenet, sixteenth earl of Huntingdon (1901–1990).

Huntingfield, William of (*d.* in or before **1225**), landowner, was the son of Roger of Huntingfield (*d. c*.1203). They held knights' fees of several baronies in the king's hand, notably seven fees of the honour of Eye, including the manor of Huntingfield, Suffolk, which supplies William's toponym; other fees were held of the honour of Lancaster, the honour of Henry of Essex, and the honour of Freiston.

William entered King John's service in September 1203 as temporary custodian of Dover Castle during Hubert de Burgh's absence; he surrendered his son and daughter to the king as hostages. He was an itinerant justice on the eastern circuit of the eyre of 1208–9 and sheriff of Norfolk and Suffolk, 1209–10. During the interdict he had custody of the abbey of St Benet of Hulme, Norfolk, and of the property of his brother Roger, a cleric. He sent knights on John's expedition to Ireland in 1210, and he accompanied the king in 1214 on his expedition to Poitou, where he was a leading witness to royal charters. Following his return from France he witnessed the king's grant of liberties to the English church in November 1214.

The next spring William turned against the king, and joined the rebel barons at Stamford in Easter week 1215. He had ties with the rebel leader Robert Fitzwalter (*d.* 1235), a fellow East Anglian landholder, and with another rebel, Oliver de Vaux, who was lord of his Lincolnshire lands as second husband of Petronilla de Craon. Like some other rebels William had offered speculative fines to the king for favours, though King John pardoned him of 100 marks of his father's debt in 1203. In 1205 he offered four palfreys and a falcon for royal confirmation of the manor of Stokes, Norfolk, and in 1206 he made an offering for custody of the land and heir of Osbert fitz Hervey, another East Anglian knight and royal justice. William paid £80 on behalf of Isolda Biset in 1211, obtaining in return custody of her son William and of one of her manors. Also in 1211 he offered the king six 'beautiful Norwegian hawks' for having his widowed daughter's dower lands and the right to her remarriage.

Following the baronial defiance King John ordered that William's lands be seized on 12 May 1215. In June 1215 William was named one of the committee of twenty-five charged with enforcing Magna Carta. In February 1216 the king handed over custody of William's castle at Frampton to Nicola de la Haie, hereditary sheriff of Lincolnshire: after the civil war she was accused of having seized chattels of his to a value in excess of £270. William joined William de Mandeville and Robert Fitzwalter in extending rebel control over East Anglia in 1216 after the landing of Louis of France. Shortly before John's death, however, the king took vengeance, ravaging William's property in the region. William was taken prisoner by royalist forces at Lincoln in May 1217, and in September two of his knights came before the royal agents seeking his ransom. In November 1218 he was present at the great council that issued regulations restricting use of the great seal during Henry III's minority.

William died before October 1225, leaving as heir a son, Roger of Huntingfield (*d.* 1257), and a daughter, Alice, who had been married to a Lincolnshire knight, Richard de Solariis (*d. c*.1211). RALPH V. TURNER

Sources Pipe rolls · Chancery records (RC) · H. C. M. Lyte and others, eds., *Liber feodorum: the book of fees*, 3 vols. (1920–31) · H. Hall, ed., *The Red Book of the Exchequer*, 3 vols., Rolls Series, 99 (1896) · *Rogeri de Wendover liber qui dicitur flores historiarum*, ed. H. G. Hewlett, 3 vols., Rolls Series, [84] (1886–9) · *The historical works of Gervase of Canterbury*, ed. W. Stubbs, 2 vols., Rolls Series, 73 (1879–80) · *CIPM*, vol. 1 · T. D. Hardy, ed., *Rotuli litterarum clausarum*, RC, 2 (1834), 83b

Huntingford, George Isaac (1748–1832), college head and bishop of Hereford, was born at Winchester on 9 September 1748, the son of James Huntingford (1723/4–1772), a dancing-master, and his wife, Sarah. According to family tradition, later recorded by his nephew Thomas Huntingford, the Huntingfords had been prosperous farmers ruined by attempting to match the high-living lifestyle of their patrons the Wyndhams. The nickname by which Huntingford was known to Winchester boys, Tiptoe, may derive from his father's profession. He was educated at the grammar school at Odiham, Hampshire, and then at St Bartholomew's Grammar School, Newbury, Berkshire. Both schools sometimes acted as preparatory schools for Winchester College, where Huntingford was admitted as a scholar in 1762. On 19 July 1768 he matriculated at New College, Oxford, from where he graduated BA in 1773, MA in 1776, and BD and DD in 1793.

Huntingford was elected fellow of New College in 1770, but while reading for his BA returned to Winchester as tutor in commoners, a post in which he was paid directly by the headmaster, Joseph Warton. At about this time he was ordained and became curate of Compton, near Winchester, for which parish he must have held affection, for he was eventually buried there. In 1776 he was formally appointed sub-praeceptor at Winchester, and began to teach scholars as well as commoners. This dual position was resented by the scholars, who saw it as a breach of their privileges, and for a while Huntingford withdrew to London, from where he negotiated his return with Warton. He also began to publish, but although his *A Short Introduction to the Writing of Greek* (1778) became Winchester's preferred textbook for sixty years, his compositional style was not highly regarded. His edition of the *Monostrophics* was reviewed so harshly in the *Monthly Review* (June and August 1783) by the younger Charles Burney, that when a second edition appeared in 1784 it was accompanied by *An Apology for the Monostrophics*. Despite Burney's disparagement of Huntingford as a Greek scholar, the two maintained a friendly correspondence.

In 1785, on the expiry of his Oxford fellowship, Huntingford was elected a fellow of Winchester and seems to have resided in his rooms in Chamber Court, which was unusual for the period. Without any formal requirement to teach at Winchester, he planned to spend three years as a private tutor in Salisbury, but in 1787 the death of his brother Thomas, master of Warminster School, Wiltshire, left him with responsibility for Thomas's pregnant widow, Mary, *née* Seagram (d. 1814), and her six children. He applied to the patron at Warminster, Thomas Thynne, third Viscount Weymouth, and was appointed master there. He ran the school with diligence—'sound education and morals will be my objects; the graces I must leave for less old-fashioned masters' (Huntingford to Henry Addington, 21 March 1787, Winchester College archives). He was devoted to his brother's children: he sent four of his five nieces to school and married them into prominent families associated with Winchester College, and energetically supported his nephews' careers in the Church of England.

One of Huntingford's early pupils at Winchester was Henry Addington, speaker of the House of Commons from June 1789. Huntingford wrote over 600 letters to Addington over the course of his career. The letters are warm and, to some readers, even romantic, but the relationship between Huntingford and Addington has been assessed as one of 'formidable chastity, conducted on a level of idealism which may have sometimes been enervating to the participants but left not the slightest ground for the efforts of gossips and scandalmongers' (Ziegler, 21). It was perhaps through Addington's influence that Huntingford was elected warden of Winchester College by the fellows of New College, Oxford, on 5 December 1789, although he later credited another former pupil, Gilbert Heathcote, fellow of New College from 1785, with having brought him the post.

Huntingford moved into the warden's lodgings at Winchester with his sister-in-law and her young family, and set out to be an active warden, attempting to restore discipline among the boys and ensure adherence to the statutes of William of Wykeham. He gained a reputation for lack of imagination and severity that has become part of Winchester College legend. In 1793, faced with a rising in college, when it was said a cap of liberty on the model of the French revolutionaries was carried, he reasserted order with the help of a deputation of gentlemen from the town and the threat of intervention by the Buckinghamshire militia. Thirty-five members of college were expelled. Following the rebellion William Stanley Goddard, the second master, who was sympathetic to Huntingford's aims but seems not to have been regarded by the boys with hostility, was promoted to headmaster to replace Warton.

Addington's patronage brought Huntingford opportunities to preach official sermons. He preached before the House of Commons on the occasion of the general fast on Good Friday 1793, when he was forthright about the expected fate of the French revolutionary government: 'National iniquity shall lead on to national ruin' (G. Huntingford, *A Sermon Preached before the Honourable House of Commons, on Friday April 19th 1793*, 1793, 20). In 1797 he gave the annual sermon to the charity school children of London and Westminster at St Paul's Cathedral, on the subject of 'Education, as necessary and beneficial to man'. He advocated self-discipline, conformity to the divinely ordained social order, and repression of the 'wayward fancies of an age capricious and volatile as that of childhood and youth' (Stowell, 28).

Huntingford has been described as perhaps 'politically not a wholesome influence' on Addington, who 'continued throughout his life to believe in his tutor's wisdom and good judgement' (Bell, 355). Addington's appointment as prime minister in 1801 sat well with Huntingford, a lifelong defender of the Church of England and opponent of Roman Catholic emancipation. George III had at first wanted Huntingford to become bishop of St David's in 1800, but had then preferred Lord George Murray to the see. In 1802 Addington proposed that Huntingford become bishop of Bath and Wells; George III instead suggested the see of Gloucester, declaring him 'a valuable acquisition to the bench' who should not 'withdraw his attention to that excellent seminary at Winchester' (*Later Correspondence of George III*, 4.2617). Huntingford acted as an apologist for the ministry, and soon after he became a bishop published anonymously *Brief Memoirs of the Rt Hon Henry Addington's Administration through the First Fifteen Months since its Commencement* in 1802.

As a lever of tory sentiment during Addington's ministry and in the years after 1804, Huntingford was able to exert much pressure against an alteration of the ecclesiastical status quo for Catholics and dissenters. A charge, delivered to the clergy of the diocese of Gloucester, on the petition of the English Roman Catholics, published in 1807, ran to three editions, and sparked a response from John Lingard. In 1809 he made representations on behalf of Viscount Sidmouth (as Addington had become) over the latter's commitment to Catholic emancipation, and in 1813 published *A Protestant Letter Addressed to Lord Somers* in response to that peer's agitation for the admission of Catholics to parliament. At the same time he was wary of protestant dissent: *A Call for Union with the Established Church Addressed to English Protestants*, published in 1800, reached a second edition in 1808, and with Shute Barrington, bishop of Durham, he represented to Sidmouth the need for tighter control of Methodist operations in 1811.

As a bishop, Huntingford was non-resident outside the summer months, and preferred to perform his ordinations in Winchester College chapel rather than in his diocese. He appeared negligent to later critics, who compared him to subsequent nineteenth-century prelates and to contemporaries such as Beilby Porteus, but his letters show a concern for detail and knowledge of law and precedent which dispel this impression. In 1815 he was translated from Gloucester to the larger diocese of Hereford, where he renovated the bishop's palace. He continued to spend most of his time at Winchester, but was represented in the diocese by his nephew Thomas Huntingford, whom he appointed prebendary of Ewithington.

Huntingford remained committed to Winchester, where he supported first Goddard and then, from 1809, Henry Dison Gabell in their efforts to enforce adherence to the college statutes in the face of well-established traditions that undermined authority. He wrote to Gilbert Heathcote in 1816 that, although aware of the imperfections of the college, 'I have in no department found means adequate to my ideas of melioration: so I have long acquiesced in that which was practicable, and have ceased to attempt more' (Stowell, 37). In that spirit he opposed Henry Brougham's parliamentary enquiries into education, beginning in 1816, as being based on unachievable and false premises; they also raised expectations of reform among the boys at Winchester. In 1818 there was a further rising at Winchester College. Huntingford calmed it by promising that he would redress the rebels' grievances if they dispersed, but the boys found that they were escorted back to college by troops armed with bayonets supplied at Huntingford's request by Sidmouth. This they considered dishonourable, contributing to Huntingford's reputation among Wykehamists as 'a lickspittle to the great and a bully to the young, a pedant, a liar and a cheat' (Firth, 92).

Huntingford's supposed retort to one of the rebellious boys of 1818—'Do you know, Sir, that you are assaulting a Peer of the Realm?' (Cook, 90)—is suggestive of both his respect for the established order and his inability to appreciate the positions of those who did not share his regard.

He did not appreciate the additional workload placed upon bishops by the Clergy Residence Act of 1817, which made bishops directly responsible for the appointment of curates to non-resident clergy: in 1827 he wrote to Thomas Burgess, bishop of Salisbury, that 'My chief and sore complaint now is that I am compelled to waste in signatures that precious time which divines who lived before the Act 57 George III was passed had the happiness, the luxury, of devoting to biblical and other professional reading' (Huntingford to Burgess, Bodl. Oxf., MS Eng. lett. c.136, fols. 103–4). That year he was laid low by a severe illness from which he never fully recovered. His frailty probably prevented him from joining Sidmouth in voting against the Reform Bill in 1831. He died, unmarried, at Winchester College, in the same room in which he had first been admitted as a scholar, on 29 April 1832, and was buried in the parish church at his old curacy at Compton. His maxim, recalled by Thomas Adolphus Trollope in 1877, was said to have been 'No innovation' (T. A. Trollope, *What I Remember*, 2 vols., 1887, 1.131). Although many Wykehamists would remember him as an uncompromising reactionary, Huntingford's conduct reveals a more complex man, convinced of the need to restore the eroded principles of the constitution in Winchester College as in church and state, and devoted to confounding those who thought the established order itself was at fault. ANDREW ROBINSON

Sources A. Bell, 'Warden Huntingford and the old conservatism', *Winchester College: sixth-centenary essays*, ed. R. Custance (1982), 351–74 · *DNB* · *GM*, 1st ser., 102/1 (1832), 559–61 · *Annual Biography and Obituary*, 17 (1833), 42–6 · J. D'E. Firth, *Winchester College* (1949) · P. Ziegler, *Addington* (1965) · A. Robinson, 'The episcopate in the age of Pitt', MLitt diss., U. Cam., 1991 · H. M. Stowell, *George Isaac Huntingford, warden of Winchester College* (1970) · *Hansard 1* (1817), 26.88–92, 683–5, 1277 · T. F. Kirby, *Annals of Winchester College, from its foundation in the year 1382 to the present time* (1892) · A. K. Cook, *About Winchester College* (1917) · *The later correspondence of George III*, ed. A. Aspinall, 5 vols. (1962–70)

Archives Winchester College, corresp., notebooks, and papers | Bodl. Oxf., corresp. with Thomas Burgess · Devon RO, corresp. with Lord Sidmouth

Likenesses T. Lawrence, oils, 1807, Winchester College, Hampshire · J. Wood, engraving, 1807 (after T. Lawrence)

Wealth at death income of bishop of Gloucester and Windsor must have been approx. £2000 p.a.

Huntingford, Henry (1787–1867), classical scholar and Church of England clergyman, was born at Warminster, Wiltshire, on 19 September 1787, son of the Revd Thomas Huntingford, master of Warminster School, and a nephew of George Isaac Huntingford, bishop of Hereford. He became a scholar of Winchester College in 1802, and matriculated at New College, Oxford, on 16 April 1807, subsequently becoming a fellow both of New College and (5 April 1814) of Winchester. He took the degree of BCL on 1 June 1814, and relinquished his fellowship at New College later in that month. In 1822 he was appointed rector of Hampton Bishop, Herefordshire, and in 1838 a residentiary canon of Hereford Cathedral. He was also rural dean and prebendary of Colwall. He died at Goodrest, Great Malvern, on 2 November 1867, and was buried at Hampton

Bishop. He left a widow, Eugenia Jane Huntingford. Huntingford published various works, including an edition of Pindar (1814) and of Damm's *Lexicon Pindaricum* (1814), and edited his uncle's *Thoughts on the Trinity* (1832).

GORDON GOODWIN, *rev.* RICHARD SMAIL

Sources Foster, *Alum. Oxon.* • Boase, *Mod. Eng. biog.* • *GM*, 4th ser., 4 (1867), 830 • T. F. Kirby, *Winchester scholars: a list of the wardens, fellows, and scholars of … Winchester College* (1888) • *CGPLA Eng. & Wales* (1867)
Archives Bodl. Oxf., travel diaries • Winchester College, diary
Wealth at death under £8000: resworn probate, Dec 1870, *CGPLA Eng. & Wales* (1867)

Huntington, George (1825–1905), Church of England clergyman, was born at Elloughton, near Hull, on 25 August 1825, the youngest of the four sons and three daughters of Charles William Huntington of Elloughton and his wife, Harriet, daughter of William Mantle, curate-in-charge of Siderston, Norfolk. After education at home he studied from 1846 to 1848 at St Bees Theological College (closed in 1896). Ordained deacon in 1848 and priest in 1849 by the bishop of Manchester, he served as curate at St Stephen's, Salford, before moving in 1850 to Wigan, where his work in the mining community came to the notice of the earl of Crawford and Balcarres, who made him his domestic chaplain. On 26 April 1849 he married Charlotte Elizabeth, daughter of John Henry Garton of Hull.

After acting as clerk in orders of Manchester Cathedral from 1855 to 1863, and receiving the Lambeth degree of MA in 1855, Huntington became rector of St Stephen's, Salford, in 1863. He was active in Manchester during the cotton famine, and this experience was reflected in his book *The Church's Work in our Large Towns* (1863). On 6 January 1867 he was appointed by the crown to the rectory of Tenby, Pembrokeshire, where he remained until his death.

Huntington was a devout high-churchman who initially provoked evangelical opposition in Tenby. A mission conducted there in 1877 by ritualist clergy under his auspices led to a controversy involving the bishop of St David's (see *Three Letters on the Subject of the Late Tenby Mission*, 1877). The hostility gradually disappeared, however, and Huntington was able to restore his church with the support of his parishioners. He was an impressive preacher, at once practical and somewhat mystical. He was also a governor of the county school, chairman of the managers of the parish schools, and an energetic freemason. Huntington published two works of edifying fiction, *Autobiography of John Brown, Cordwainer* (1867), which went into five editions, and *Autobiography of an Alms-Bag* (1885), followed by *Random Recollections* (1895).

Huntington died at 8 Edward Street, Bath, on 8 April 1905. His wife survived him, together with their five daughters and two sons.

E. S. HOOPER, *rev.* G. MARTIN MURPHY

Sources *The Times* (14 April 1905) • *Church Times* (14 April 1905) • *Tenby and County News* (12 April 1905) • *CGPLA Eng. & Wales* (1905)
Wealth at death £2137 16s.: probate, 24 May 1905, *CGPLA Eng. & Wales*

Huntington, Jabez (1719–1786), merchant and revolutionary politician in America, was born on 7 August 1719 at Norwich, Connecticut, the eldest son of Joshua Huntington, merchant, and his wife, Hannah Perkins. The large Huntington family was prominent in eastern Connecticut, and especially important in the settling and growth of Norwich, the hub of the region. Jabez entered Yale College in 1737, aged eighteen, older than most of his peers, and graduated BA in 1741, when he was last among the twenty members of his class ranked according to the prominence of their families; he returned to Norwich to pursue a career as a merchant. These were years of great religious excitement in New England, as the revival called the Great Awakening spurred many to look into the state of their souls. Jabez may have shared in this enthusiasm; in later years, at least, he became identified with the New Lights, as proponents of the Awakening were called. He may have been influenced by his future wife, Elizabeth (1721–1745), the daughter of Samuel Backus and Elizabeth Tracy; her younger brother was Isaac *Backus, the great New England Baptist minister who waged a lifelong fight against the aridity of the standard of preaching. Married on 20 January 1742, Jabez and Elizabeth had two sons before she died on 1 July 1745. A little over a year later, on 10 July 1746, Jabez married Hannah (1726–1807), daughter of Ebenezer Williams, the first minister of Pomfret, Connecticut, and his wife, Penelope Chester. The couple had three sons and three daughters.

Huntington's rise as a merchant paralleled the development of Norwich's trading connections. Situated 14 miles inland from Long Island Sound, at the head of navigation for ocean-going ships on the Thames River, Norwich thrived as the entrepôt for eastern Connecticut and western Rhode Island, exporting livestock, produce, and lumber to other British colonies in North America and the West Indies. Huntington participated in this trade with Norwich's other great mercantile families—Backus, Leffingwell, and Tracy—and became particularly noted as a merchant in the West Indies trade, from which he amassed a sizeable fortune, and as a landowner. At his death in 1786 he had an estate worth 11,919 pounds Connecticut currency, substantial wealth in an era of post-war deflation.

Huntington's particular significance lies in his political career, which illustrates how a man who rose to prominence in the old colonial political culture of deference and family connections made the transition to an age of revolution. In eighteenth-century Connecticut prominent local men were expected to participate in serving the public, because they were presumed to have both the talent and the time to do so. Huntington's neighbours chose him to be lieutenant of the first militia company in Norwich, an appointment the assembly confirmed in October 1745. In May 1750 the town sent him as one of its two deputies to the assembly, where his new colleagues named him a justice of the peace, an appointment based entirely on his local standing not his legal acumen. Although he was a justice continuously until 1763, for the next six years he served only intermittently in the assembly, in October

1753 and again in October 1754, a low average. In the meantime, in early 1754 he was elected captain of the local troop of horse, a more expensive and therefore more prestigious form of militia service than the foot companies. Apparently militia service was not to his liking; he resigned and was replaced by February 1757.

With his election to the colony's assembly in October 1756 Huntington began what would become nearly a quarter century of continuous service in ever more important public offices. He was chosen a Norwich deputy at each biannual election from October 1756 to October 1763, fifteen consecutive elections by one of the most prosperous towns in the colony, a telling indication of political clout on the local level. In May 1757 his assembly colleagues named him their clerk, a post he held for three years until they elected him their speaker, a post he held for four more years until his election by colony-wide ballot in May 1764 as the twelfth, and last, member of the governor's council.

Other men from prominent families received high public office more rapidly, of course, but few rose as quickly from a near standing start so relatively late in life (Huntington was thirty-seven in 1756). His success was due in part to his own abilities and Norwich's growing prosperity, but his affiliation with the New Lights, evangelical men of the Great Awakening, was also an important factor. He became and remained a firm opponent of Britain's attempts in the mid-1760s to tighten imperial trade regulation and controls over the internal activities of the colonies. In 1765–6 he rallied support for the Sons of Liberty, men primarily from eastern Connecticut who opposed increased imperial control, by extra-legal means if necessary; his exact role is not clear. Nor is it clear why the assembly chose in May 1765 to appoint him as lieutenant-colonel of the 3rd militia regiment, the senior militia officer in Norwich, a position he would fill until October 1774; it may have been an attempt by the Sons of Liberty to grasp the levers of official authority. Huntington certainly did profit politically from the upwelling of opposition to those more conservative leaders such as Governor Thomas Fitch, who thought there was no alternative to accepting increased British control. At the climactic election in May 1766, when Fitch and four assistants were denied re-election, Huntington jumped from twelfth to sixth place on the governor's council. His place in the revamped ruling élite of Connecticut was enhanced on 1 May 1766 when his eldest son, Jedidiah (1743–1818), married Faith Trumbull (1743–1775), the eldest daughter of the about-to-be-elected lieutenant-governor, Jonathan Trumbull.

Huntington's most important public service began shortly after the fighting between British troops and American colonists in April 1775 at Lexington and Concord led to the creation of a New England patriot army around Boston. Joseph Trumbull, the commissary of the Connecticut forces (the son of now-Governor Trumbull and the brother of Huntington's daughter-in-law), was responsible for supplying provisions and equipment to the Connecticut soldiers, including the regiment commanded by his brother-in-law, Jedidiah. He let contracts around the colony; in Norwich they went to Huntington and Christopher Leffingwell. From May 1775 to the following March, when the American army marched from Boston through Connecticut on its way to New York, Huntington used his mercantile connections to help the army survive. In May 1775, too, the assembly appointed him a member of Governor Trumbull's council of safety, a group of senior leaders in eastern Connecticut who lived close enough to Trumbull's home in Lebanon to serve as his advisers between sessions of the assembly. Huntington was involved in every aspect of Connecticut's war effort from the council's first meeting on 7 June 1775 to the last day he attended, 16 February 1780, a period of over four and a half years. In December 1776 the assembly gave him the added responsibility of being second major-general of the militia; political skill and administrative competence must have been the reasons, as Huntington had no actual military experience. In May 1777 it promoted him to first major-general after his predecessor, David Wooster, was killed resisting the British raid on the state's supply depot at Danbury. Huntington never represented Connecticut in any interstate conventions or congresses; rather, he was among those who, like Governor Trumbull himself, stayed close to home and made the myriad of decisions that helped Connecticut contribute so much to the American patriot war effort.

Some time in February 1779 Huntington was afflicted with some sort of 'nervous disorder' which gradually disabled him in body and mind and rendered him progressively less able to conduct public business (Hoadley, *Public Records of the State of Connecticut*, 3.5) In May 1779 he resigned as probate judge of the Norwich district, a position he had held since 1773. In June he laid down his commission as major-general. In May 1780 he resigned as an assistant, to which post he had just been re-elected for the seventeenth consecutive time. Long removed from active participation in Connecticut's political life, he died at Norwich on 5 October 1786. His wife died over two decades later, on 25 March 1807.   HAROLD E. SELESKY

Sources E. Gray and A. C. Bates, eds., *Huntington papers: correspondence of the brothers Joshua and Jedediah Huntington during the period of the American Revolution*, Connecticut Historical Society Collections, 20 (1923) · J. H. Trumbull and C. J. Hoadly, eds., *The public records of the colony of Connecticut*, 15 vols. (1850–90), vols. 9–15 · C. J. Hoadly and others, eds., *The public records of the state of Connecticut*, 11 vols. (1894–1967), vols. 1–3 · F. B. Dexter, 'Jabez Huntington', *Biographical sketches of the graduates of Yale College*, 1 (1885) · O. Zeichner, *Connecticut's years of controversy, 1750–1776* (1949) · R. L. Bushman, *From puritan to Yankee: character and the social order in Connecticut, 1690–1765* (1967) · F. M. Caulkins, *History of Norwich* (1866) · F. Monaghan, 'Huntington, Jabez', *DAB* · L. R. Gerlach, *Connecticut congressman: Samuel Huntington, 1731–1796* (1976) · B. P. Stark, *Connecticut signer: William Williams* (1975) · C. M. Destler, *Connecticut: the provisions state* (1973)

Archives L. Cong., Peter Force transcripts; Jonathan Trumbull papers

Wealth at death £11,919—presumably Connecticut money: Dexter, 'Jabez Huntington', 676

Huntington, John (*fl.* 1538–1561), poet and Church of England clergyman, was known as Huntington the Preacher. There is no evidence to support Wood's claim that he was educated at Oxford. He is first documented on his ordination to the priesthood by Bishop John Stokesley at London in 1538. Around 1540 he composed a polemical poem against protestantism under the title *The Genealogy of Heretics*, which survives only in a later refutation penned by John Bale, *A Mysterye of Inyquyte Contayned within the Heretycall Genealogye of Ponce Pantolabus*. This effort includes the immortal verse,

> O braynlesse nodye
> Christ sayd my bodye
> Is verely meate
> For manne to eate.
> (Bale, *Mysterye*)

Huntington's early religious sympathies were thus clearly Catholic, as he was one of those who informed against the Scottish protestant former friar Alexander Seton, in 1541. However, Bale remarked in 1545 that Huntington had since 'converted to repentance', and a later reference to him as 'meus in Christo filius' suggests Bale himself won him over (Bale, *Cat.*, 1.742). That same year Anne Askew, soon to be burned as a heretic, named him as one of those to whom she was prepared to make her confession. In 1547 he was preaching reformed doctrine at Boulogne, where his intercession saved a gunner, William Hastlen, from a charge of heresy.

Huntington proved troublesome under regimes of each religious hue. In December 1549 he was reported for 'lewd and slanderous' remarks made about the mayor and aldermen of London during his sermons. In December 1553 he was summoned before Mary Tudor's privy council for writing a poem against Dr Stokes and the sacrament of the altar, but he recanted and thus survived to flee to Germany. After his return from exile he preached before large audiences at Paul's Cross in August and September 1559, and may have won the favour of Queen Elizabeth. She promoted him to a prebend at Exeter Cathedral in May 1560 (*sede vacante*), and also conferred upon him the rectory of Streate (Bath and Wells diocese) in March 1561.

RICHARD REX

Sources J. Foxe, *Actes and monuments* (1563) · J. Bale, *A mysterye of inyquyte* (1545) · Bale, *Cat.* · S. House, 'An unknown Tudor propaganda poem, *c.*1540', *N&Q*, 237 (1992), 282–5 · *CPR, 1558–63* · S. Brigden, *London and the Reformation* (1989) · *The diary of Henry Machyn, citizen and merchant-taylor of London, from AD 1550 to AD 1563*, ed. J. G. Nichols, CS, 42 (1848) · *DNB*

Huntington, Robert (*c.*1616–1684), army officer, came from an obscure background in East Anglia, probably from Battisford, Suffolk. A freeman of Great Yarmouth in 1640, he was a merchant before joining the parliamentarian army in 1643; his younger brother and apprentice Richard (*d.* 1690) became bailiff of Yarmouth in 1666 and MP for the borough in 1679. Robert Huntington served in Cornelius Vermuyden's regiment in the eastern association army, and was appointed captain of horse in the New Model on 11 March 1645 in Vermuyden's regiment, later commanded by Oliver Cromwell. With the rank of major he served at Naseby, Bristol, and Basing House. Clarendon described him as 'one of the best officers they had, upon whom [Cromwell] relied in any enterprise of importance more than upon any man' (*Clarendon State Papers*, 4.260). In April 1647 parliament voted not to disband the regiment but to transfer command to Huntington.

Huntington was Fairfax's choice to divert Charles I's escort from Cambridge after the king had been seized by Cornet Joyce. He acted as the senior officers' usual intermediary with Charles that summer and autumn, his role being that of a messenger rather than participant, though the king clearly trusted him more than his superiors. When it became evident that Charles was playing for time, Huntington reproached Cromwell in 'very sharp terms' for his sudden coldness to Charles and according to Clarendon warned that Cromwell 'would destroy him [Charles] if he were not prevented' (*Clarendon State Papers*, 4.261). He chose a moment of maximum inconvenience, during the second civil war, to resign his commission in June 1648, and in August delivered a paper to the Lords, published as *Sundry Reasons Inducing Major Robert Huntington to Lay Down his Commission*. This attack detailed the officers' alleged double-dealing with Charles, and condemned Cromwell for hypocrisy, breaking promises, greed for power, and ordering Joyce to seize the king. He maintained that Cromwell had no loyalty to any constitution and believed that 'every honest man' could resolve the kingdom's crisis. The army's intentions, and particularly Ireton's, were 'very repugnant and destructive to the honour and safety of Parliament' (Thurloe, *State papers*, 1.94–8).

Possibly co-ordinated with presbyterian plans, Huntington's broadside led to official riposte that he had arranged Charles's seizure, and on 7 May 1650 parliament seized his papers, preventing him from claiming land as a military veteran. Cromwell's council lifted the order on his petition on 24 July 1654. He settled at Stanton Harcourt, Oxfordshire, and resumed mercantile activity with participation in a Greenland venture. By 1657 royalist plotters seeking presbyterian assistance had opened discussions with him, but the royalist agent Guy Carleton claimed that 'when we expected present action upon Major Huntington's promise. … they were flatly denied assistance. … alleging that he would meddle no more in the business' (*Clarendon State Papers*, 3.372). In July 1659 he was recalled as militia commissioner for Berkshire and Oxfordshire, searching Lord Falkland's house for illegal weaponry, and in December aided Sir Henry Ingoldsby in seizing Windsor Castle for Monck. He was named as major in his old regiment in January 1660. Offering service to Charles II in February 1660, his claim on royal gratitude led to the grant of an estate in Windsor Great Park in 1661.

In 1666 Huntington was among the new commissioners for the ale and beer excise around London, in 1667 he became farmer of the duty on French wines, and in 1668 he joined the excise commissioners. In 1671 he became a chief commissioner for excise, and he was receiver-general of customs from 1677 to 1679. It is possible, but not certain, that he was knighted about this time. On 4 March 1669 he married, as a widower, Dorothy (*née* Styles), widow of Sir Robert Dicer, bt, master of the Drapers' Company 1656–7, at Hackney, where he chiefly resided thereafter. He died in 1684. TIMOTHY VENNING

Sources R. Huntington, ed., *Sundry reasons inducing Major Robert Huntingdon to lay down his commission* (1648); repr. F. Maseres, ed., *Select tracts relating to the civil wars in England*, 2 (1815) · *CSP dom.*, 1650; 1654; 1659–62; 1666–7; 1670–72 · W. A. Shaw, ed., *Calendar of treasury books*, 1–8, PRO (1904–23) · Clarendon, *Hist. rebellion* · J. L. Chester and J. Foster, eds., *London marriage licences, 1521–1869* (1887) · Thurloe, *State papers* · *Calendar of the Clarendon state papers preserved in the Bodleian Library*, 3: 1655–1657, ed. W. D. Macray (1876) · *JHL*, 10 (1647–8) · *JHC*, 5 (1646–8) · *A calendar of the freemen of Great Yarmouth, 1429–1800*, Norfolk and Norwich Archaeological Society (1910) · H. Swinden, *The history and antiquities of the ancient burgh of Great Yarmouth*, ed. J. Ives (1772) · *The letter-book of John, Viscount Mordaunt, 1658–1660*, ed. M. Coate, CS, 3rd ser., 69 (1945) · GEC, *Baronetage* · J. Foster, *The register of admissions to Gray's Inn, 1521–1889, together with the register of marriages in Gray's Inn chapel, 1695–1754* (privately printed, London, 1889) · W. H. Rylands, ed., *The visitation of the county of Suffolk, begun … 1664, and finished … 1668*, Harleian Society, 61 (1910) · J. Foster, ed., *Visitation of Middlesex* (1887) · M. E. Grimwade, *Index of the probate records … Suffolk*, 2 vols. (1979–80) · E. Cruickshanks and B. D. Henning, 'Huntington, Richard', HoP, *Commons, 1660–90*, 2.620–21 · D. Lysons, *The environs of London*, 3 (1795) · R. Simpson, *Some account of the monuments in Hackney church* (1881) · M. Fitch, ed., *Index of wills proved in the prerogative court of Canterbury*, 12: 1694–1700, British RS, 80 (1960)

Wealth at death house and *c*.125 acres at Paddock Walk, Windsor Great Park, valued at £100 at grant, 1661; house, Stanton Harcourt, Oxfordshire; residence, Hackney, Middlesex, probably wife's property from first husband: *CSP dom.*, 1661–2, 70; Shaw, ed., *Calendar of treasury books*, 1606; Foster, *Register of admissions*; Simpson, *Some account of the monuments*, 88; Lysons, *Environs of London*, vol. 2 p. 497; Chester and Foster, eds., *London*, 371

Huntington, Robert (*bap.* 1637, *d.* 1701), orientalist and bishop of Raphoe, was born at Deerhurst, near Tewkesbury, and was baptized on 27 February 1637, the second of the four sons of Robert Huntington (1592–1664), curate of Deerhurst and subsequently, from 1648 until his death, vicar of the neighbouring parish of Leigh. After attending Bristol grammar school—a student of exceptional diligence, he 'passed through the school unwhipped, which no one had done before' (Bodl. Oxf., MS Smith 50, p. 217)—Huntington went to Merton College, Oxford, where he matriculated on 20 July 1654. He proceeded BA on 9 March 1658 and was elected to a fellowship the same year. In 1660 he signed the decree condemning all the proceedings of convocation under the Commonwealth, and received his MA degree on 21 January 1663.

At Oxford, Huntington was liked for what his friend and biographer Thomas Smith described as 'his easy carriage, sweet disposition, and progress in learning' (Smith, 11). In 1663 he devoted himself to the study of theology and eastern languages under the supervision of Edward Pococke, the professor of Hebrew and Arabic. As a fellow of Merton he occupied various functions, including that of Greek lecturer in 1662, dean in 1663, 1664, and 1666, bursar in 1665, and librarian in 1667. Like his three brothers, John, Benjamin, and Dennis, who were also at Oxford, Huntington was ordained. Having applied for the vacant post of chaplain to the Levant Company in Aleppo, Syria, he was

elected on 1 August 1670. He left Oxford on 12 August, set sail on 21 September, and, after stopping on the Turkish mainland and in Rhodes and Cyprus, disembarked in Iskenderun to arrive in Aleppo in January 1671. He took up residence in the company's factory just south of the great mosque, in the Khan al-Gumruk. The convivial atmosphere there was described by the naval chaplain Henry Teonge who visited the town in 1675.

Huntington intended to gather as much information about the Levant as possible—topographical details, botanical and zoological specimens, coins and antiquities, and above all manuscripts. In one of his first letters from Aleppo, to John Locke, he said he was awaiting Robert Boyle's 'Commands and Instructions for the right improvement of my time in these Parts' (*Correspondence of John Locke*, 353), and he was to answer the questions of his many English friends with modesty and exactitude. He remained in touch with Smith, Pococke, Thomas Marshall, Edward Bernard, John Fell, and Narcissus Marsh, and exchanged numerous letters with John Covel, his brother chaplain in Constantinople.

In the course of the eleven years in which he served the Levant Company, Huntington obtained a sound command of Arabic and Turkish and established a formidable network of advisers and informants across the Middle East—Jesuits in Mardin, Franciscans in Damascus, Capuchins in Rosetta, Maronite monks in the Lebanon, and Coptic monks in Egypt; all assisted him in his quest for manuscripts and knowledge. Thanks to the Discalced Carmelite missionaries in Basrah he acquired books and information about the Mandaeans of Iraq. With the help of the Maronite chronicler and patriarch of Antioch, Estefan al-Duwayhi, he collected a number of codices, including some important texts by Ephraem. He corresponded with the Greek Orthodox primate of Cyprus, Hilarion Cigala. In 1674, on his way to Jerusalem, he visited the Samaritan community in Sichem (Nablus) and initiated a correspondence with them which was pursued by Thomas Marshall.

As a result of his travels throughout the Levant, Huntington assembled well over 600 manuscripts, mainly Arabic and Hebrew, but also Coptic, Syriac, Samaritan, Persian, and Turkish. He had donated fourteen (seven Arabic, six Hebrew, and one Syriac) to Merton College in 1673, and made further donations to the Bodleian Library in 1678, 1680, and 1683. The majority of his manuscripts, however, were purchased by Oxford University in 1692 for almost £1100. It was the largest and most spectacular collection acquired by the university to date and was of inestimable value to future scholars. The twenty-nine Coptic codices included an illustrated twelfth-century Bohairic version of the gospels, MS Huntington 17, which is among the finest of its kind. Also to Huntington the Bodleian owes its earliest Arabic manuscript on paper, apparently dated 983 (Huntington MS 228), an unusual illustrated treatise on weaponry especially commissioned by Saladin for his own library (Huntington MS 264), and a celebrated Hebrew manuscript containing the signature of Maimonides (Huntington MS 80).

One of Huntington's principal concerns when he was in the Levant was the propagation of Anglicanism among the eastern Christians, his interest in whom is attested by his choice of manuscripts. This was an ideal which he shared with Boyle. Among the Christians he distributed Pococke's Arabic translations of the Anglican catechism and Grotius's *De veritate religionis Christianae* as well as William Seaman's Turkish translation of John Ball's *Short Catechisme* sponsored by Boyle. He himself urged Pococke to translate the Anglican liturgy into Arabic and offered £20 towards the costs. After the translation had been completed (in 1675 and at the expense of Oxford University) Huntington gave copies to his Christian acquaintances such as the Greek Orthodox archbishop of Mount Sinai, Johannes Lascaris, whom he met on his first visit to Cairo in 1680 and who was astounded to discover that there was such a thing as the Church of England.

Having resigned his chaplaincy on 14 July 1681 Huntington made his way back to England by way of Italy and France. In Paris he made friends with the orientalists Louis Dufour de Longuerue and Louis Picques, the learned book collector Melchisédec Thévenot, and above all the Huguenot scholar Pierre Allix with whom he remained in correspondence for the rest of his life. Arriving back in Oxford on 22 July 1682 he again took up residence at Merton and presented the Ashmolean with a number of Egyptian antiquities. On 15 June 1683 he proceeded BD and DD. Appointed sub-warden of his college, he was regarded as a strong competitor for the chair of Hebrew which, however, went to Humphrey Prideaux. On 24 July he was sent by the university to read a letter of congratulation to Charles II on his escape from the Rye House plot.

On the recommendation of John Fell, bishop of Oxford, Huntington was appointed provost of Trinity College, Dublin. He accepted reluctantly and set sail on 13 August 1683 to be sworn in on 24 September. Soon after his arrival he and his predecessor Narcissus Marsh assisted the mathematician and astronomer William Molyneux in founding the Dublin Philosophical Society. Its inaugural meeting was held in Huntington's lodgings on 15 October. Besides the encouragement he gave the new society he took part in yet another venture sponsored by Boyle, a result of the same missionary zeal he had displayed in the Levant: he superintended, together with Marsh, a translation into Irish of the Old Testament. Although he embarked on the plan with high hopes, he was disappointed by the results, informing Boyle in November 1686 that he still had half the copies he had been sent to distribute and that he could 'find but few, to whom they can be given with any probable hopes that they shall be well employd' (*Correspondence of Robert Boyle*, 6.198). But for all his protestant fervour and his hatred of Roman Catholicism—'a religion distructive to reason and piety, and certainly strikes at the root of boath'—Huntington, who had many Catholic friends, was opposed to protestant segregation of the Irish Catholics, arguing that 'the more a Protestant knows of the intrigues and policies and devices and managery of their Church, the more he will love his own' (Bodl. Oxf., MS Eng. misc. c.23, pp. 393–4).

Huntington was an active and scrupulous provost of Trinity. He presented the library with thirteen manuscripts from his collection (one Coptic, one Syriac, and eleven Arabic). He obtained funds to complete the new chapel and various other college buildings, and was responsible for having a plot of ground which had served as the college kitchen garden turned into a physic garden. Faced with a rapidly growing number of students which did little to improve the standard of the university, he circulated a letter in 1684 urging local Irish schoolmasters to provide their scholars with better instruction in the classical languages as well as in 'their good behaviour and deportment too' (Barnard, 72). But Ireland never suited him. He complained to Boyle of 'the moisture and fogginess of the air, which I more dread, than any thing els in the Country' (*Correspondence of Robert Boyle*, 6.2). He described himself as 'sentenced to live (if a man may be said to live) in banishment from his beloved Country', and he informed his French friends that 'I am not dead, tho perhaps buryed alive in Ireland' (Bodl. Oxf., MS Eng. misc. c.23, pp. 342, 400).

After a period of increasing difficulty at the university, which suffered from the hostility of James II and growing Catholic discontent in the country at large, Huntington was deputed to announce his election to the new chancellor of Trinity, James Butler, second duke of Ormond, chosen to succeed his grandfather. He set sail for England on 26 September 1688 and returned to Ireland only after the battle of the Boyne in the summer of 1690. On 22 September 1691, however, his friend Sir Edward Turnour, son of the former solicitor-general, offered him the living of Great Hallingbury in Essex, which had just fallen vacant through the death of his kinsman Grandison Turnour, whom Huntington had known at Merton. Huntington accepted the offer on 3 October, assuring his patron that 'there is not a soul in the whole Parish for whose Welfare I shall not be solicitous' (W. Sussex RO, Shillinglee MS 602). With the regretful but understanding consent of Sir Charles Porter, the lord chancellor of Ireland, Huntington made his way back to England. In April 1692 he refused the bishopric of Kilmore on discovering that the incumbent, William Sheridan (whose father, Dennis, had worked on the Irish translation of the Old Testament), was ejected for refusing to take the oath of allegiance, and on 19 August he was instituted rector of Great Hallingbury. He resigned the provostship of Trinity in September, leaving the college a silver salver engraved with his arms.

On 6 June 1692 Huntington married Mary, the daughter of an old family friend, John Powell, and the sister of Sir John Powell, a judge of the king's bench. He was clearly devoted to the woman to whom he referred in his letters as 'my Governess', and they had a daughter, Anna Maria. Huntington's name as a fellow had disappeared from the Merton registers in 1685, and in October 1693 he hoped, but failed, to obtain the college wardenship.

From Great Hallingbury Huntington continued his learned correspondence, the literary activity in which he excelled. His sole publication, a short letter 'concerning the Porphyry Pillars in Egypt' which appeared in the *Philosophical Transactions* of the Royal Society (no. 161, 20 July 1684, pp. 264–9), hardly fulfilled the high expectations of his friends. 'It is from you that we expect an account of the state of the poor Christians in Syria', Thomas Smith had written to him in 1673. 'All our hopes are fixed upon you, who are most able to performe this and a great deal more' (Bodl. Oxf., MS Smith 60, p. 34). But Huntington was too diffident ever to do justice to his immense learning. Its breadth emerges from his letters, some of which, including the description of Egypt addressed to Pierre Allix in March 1696, were published posthumously by Smith in 1704.

In June 1701 the queen appointed Huntington bishop of Raphoe. He returned to Ireland to take up his post in the same conscientious spirit with which he had accepted his other offices. 'I shall be glad if I can do more good here than I did at Hallingbury' he wrote, with customary modesty, to Sir Edward Turnour on 15 July shortly after his arrival (W. Sussex RO, Shillinglee MS 622). Five days later, on 20 July, he was consecrated in Dublin by the archbishop, Narcissus Marsh, but soon afterwards he fell ill. He died in Dublin on 2 September 1701, and was buried in Trinity College chapel. He was survived by his wife. His library of over 1700 books was sold at auction on 27 January 1702. ALASTAIR HAMILTON

Sources G. J. Toomer, *Eastern wisedome and learning: the study of Arabic in seventeenth-century England* (1996) · T. Smith, 'The life and travels of the right rev. and learned Dr Robert Huntington', *GM*, 1st ser., 95/1 (1825), 11–15, 115–19, 218–21 · R. Huntington, *Epistolae*, ed. T. Smith (1704) · L. Twells and S. Burdy, *The lives of Dr Edward Pocock … Dr Zachary Pearce … Dr Thomas Newton … and of the Rev Philip Skelton*, 2 vols. (1816) · C. Wakefield, 'Arabic manuscripts in the Bodleian Library: the seventeenth-century collections', *The 'Arabick' interest of the natural philosophers in seventeenth-century England*, ed. G. A. Russell (1994), 128–46 · M. Feingold, 'Oriental studies', *Hist. U. Oxf. 4: 17th-cent. Oxf.*, 449–503 · H. L. Murphy, *A history of Trinity College, Dublin from its foundation to 1702* (1951) · *The correspondence of Robert Boyle (1636–91)*, ed. M. Hunter, A. Clericuzio, and L. M. Principe (2001), vols. 4 and 6 · *The life and times of Anthony Wood*, ed. A. Clark, 3, OHS, 26 (1894) · T. C. Barnard, 'Provost Huntington's injunction to schoolmasters in 1684', *Hermathena*, 119 (1975), 71–3 · *The correspondence of John Locke*, ed. E. S. de Beer, 1 (1976) · *DNB* · will, PRO, PROB 11/462, sig. 139 · *Catalogus vetus*, Merton Oxf., 4.16 · college register, 1567–1713, Merton Oxf., 1.3 · C. H. Holland, ed., *Trinity College Dublin and the idea of a university* (1991) · R. B. McDowell and D. A. Webb, *Trinity College, Dublin, 1592–1952: an academic history* (1982) · *Catalogue of the library of the reverend and learned Huntington, late lord bishop of Raphoe* (1702) · T. K. Abbot, *Catalogue of the manuscripts in the library of Trinity College, Dublin* (1900) · H. O. Coxe, ed., *Catalogus codicum MSS qui in collegiis aulisque Oxoniensibus hodie adservantur*, 1 (1852)
Archives Bodl. Oxf., collections and papers · Bodl. Oxf., letters, MS Rawl. B497 · Bodl. Oxf., letters from and concerning him, MS Smith 50 · Bodl. Oxf., letters from and concerning him, MS Eng. misc. c.23, fols. 327–416 | Bodl. Oxf., letter to William Sancroft, MS Tanner 34, fol. 179 · Kongelige Bibliotek, Copenhagen, letters to Edward Bernard, MS NKS 1675 2° · NL Scot., letters to Robert Boyle [copies] · W. Sussex RO, corresp. with Sir Edward Turnour, Shillinglee MSS 600–628
Wealth at death total bequests over £1067 10s.; total estate (incl. library) far more: will, PRO, PROB 11/462, sig. 139

Huntington, Samuel (1731–1796), lawyer and revolutionary politician in America, was born on 5 July 1731 in the 'Scotland society' of Windham, Connecticut, the second son and fourth child of nine born to Nathaniel Huntington (1691–1767), farmer and tailor, and Mehetable Thurston (1700–1781). His father put three sons through Yale College, but not Samuel. None the less, Samuel received instruction from the Old Light minister Ebenezer Devotion, who prepared his brothers for college and whose daughter, Martha (d. 1794), he subsequently married, on 17 April 1761. At twenty-two he began a legal apprenticeship and in 1754 he started pleading before the Windham county superior court. However, Huntington's legal practice languished until after he moved to neighbouring Norwich in 1758.

As one of Connecticut's emerging port towns during the eighteenth century, Norwich offered more opportunities for a young lawyer than rural Windham. Norwich also contained an extended network of Huntington kin, and soon after settling there Samuel Huntington began serving as town counsel. This led to appearances before the general assembly and in 1765 to election to the lower house. Both made him known beyond New London county and by 1770 he was as likely to represent clients living in other parts of Connecticut—and even in other colonies—as local ones.

In 1773 the general assembly appointed Huntington to a vacancy on the colony's superior court. Its judges rode circuit, visiting each of Connecticut's six counties twice a year. His growing visibility on the bench together with the developing revolutionary crisis led to his election as assistant or member of the upper house of the legislature in 1775, just after the outbreak of the American War of Independence. Although Huntington had not hitherto been prominent in the revolutionary movement, he found himself in the thick of the colony's military mobilization after the legislature appointed him to the council of safety charged with directing Connecticut's war effort. As 1775 drew to a close he was also named to the colony's congressional delegation.

Huntington arrived in Philadelphia in January 1776 and, after recovering from smallpox, quickly adjusted to congress's hectic routines. During the spring he supported all measures leading to independence and became one of the original signers of the Declaration of Independence. He returned to Connecticut in November 1776 and spent the next year coping with problems that the war was creating at home. He went back to congress briefly between February and July 1778 and again in late May 1779. On 28 September his colleagues selected him to be their president.

Huntington's election stemmed from the nationalist profile that he had established with his fellow delegates. He supported the free navigation of the Mississippi and the appointment of an ambassador to the Spanish court, opposed recognizing Vermont's independence from New York, and distanced himself from the controversy over whether Silas Deane, also from Connecticut, had abused his powers in France. Huntington's presidency coincided with the darkest period of the revolution when congress lost effective direction of the war effort owing to bankruptcy. His colleagues valued Huntington's dignity at a time when the assistance of foreign powers, particularly France and Spain, had become critical, and they extended his original year-long term, though not without opposition. He finally retired from congress on 9 July 1781 after more than two years of uninterrupted service.

Aside from another stint with congress between July and November 1783, Samuel Huntington spent the rest of his career in Connecticut. Of all the state's leaders associated with continental institutions, he was least affected by the populist backlash of 1783–4. Endorsed by both nationalists and localists, he was elected lieutenant-governor and chief justice of the state in 1784 and succeeded to the governorship in 1786. Although he never attended college, the college of New Jersey awarded him an LLD in 1780; Yale and Dartmouth followed in 1787. He supported Connecticut's ratification of the constitution in 1788 and was annually re-elected as the state's chief executive until his death on 5 January 1796. He was buried on 8 January in the burial-ground of the First Congregational Church, Norwich.   RICHARD BUEL JUN.

Sources L. R. Gerlach, *Connecticut congressman: Samuel Huntington, 1731–1796* (1976) · L. Cong., manuscript division, Continental Congress MSS · P. H. Smith and others, eds., *Letters of delegates to congress, 1774–1789*, 26 vols. (1976–2000), vols. 14–17 · G. M. Cuthbertson, 'Huntington, Samuel', *ANB* · *The Huntington family in America: a genealogical memoir of the known descendants of Simon Huntington from 1633 to 1915* (1915) · A. G. Van Dusen, 'Samuel E. Huntington: a leader of revolutionary Connecticut', *Bulletin of the Connecticut Historical Society*, 19 (1954), 38–62 · J. Strong, *A sermon delivered at the funeral of His Excellency Samuel Huntington, governor of the state of Connecticut* (1796)
Archives Connecticut Historical Society, Hartford · Hunt. L. | Connecticut State Library, Hartford, Connecticut Archives, revolutionary war, 1st ser. · L. Cong., Continental Congress MSS
Likenesses C. W. Peale, portrait, 1783, National Parks Service, Independence National Park, Philadelphia · G. F. Wright, portrait (after C. W. Peale), Museum of Connecticut History, Hartford, Connecticut, Governor's Portrait Collection · portrait, repro. in P. E. Du Simitière, *Thirteen portraits of American legislators* (1783)
Wealth at death £8988 [$32,509]: Connecticut probate estate papers, Connecticut State Library, Hartford, 1796

Huntington, William (1745–1813), preacher and religious writer, was born on 2 February 1745 in a cottage at the Four Wents, on the road between Goudhurst and Cranbrook, Kent, the natural son of Barnabas Russel, farmer, and baptized on 14 November 1750 at Cranbrook church in the name of his putative father, William Hunt (an agricultural labourer employed by Russel). After acquiring a rudimentary education at the Cranbrook grammar school, he worked successively as a gentleman's servant, gunmaker's apprentice, sawyer's pitman, coachman, hearse driver, tramp, gardener, coalheaver, and popular preacher. At Frittenden, Kent, he had an affair with Susan Fever, a tailor's daughter, which produced a child. Prevented from marrying her, he decamped and changed his name to Huntington (1769): with that peculiar attitude to language evident in his religious writings, he added 'ing' by analogy with words for vices (such as lying and swearing), and 'ton' to indicate he was a vessel of the Lord.

William Huntington (1745–1813), by Domenico Pellegrini, 1803

In the same year Huntington married a servant named Mary Short (1742/3–1806), with whom he settled at Mortlake, working intermittently as a gardener. Here he suffered acutely from poverty and conviction of sin. He moved to Sunbury and in winter 1773 experienced a vision of brilliant light while pruning a pear tree: after praying fervently, Christ appeared to him 'in a most glorious manner, with his body all stained with blood', and he felt assured he was 'brought under the covenant love of God's elect'. In *The Kingdom of Heaven Taken by Prayer* (1784) he gives a detailed account of this conversion experience and its confirmation of his belief in predestination. His readings of the Bible, dissatisfaction with the Thirty-Nine Articles, and conversations with local Calvinists led him to give up attending the established church. His encounters with Methodists in Kingston were unsatisfactory and he moved to Ewell. Gradually his ability to expound the Bible prompted invitations to preach, though these small gatherings also attracted fierce opposition. On moving to Thames Ditton he worked as a coalheaver until his religious practices led to his dismissal; afterwards he combined preaching with casual work and cobbling.

Huntington was so poor that for two years he and his growing family lived on gleaned barley; but his distress was irregularly relieved by windfall appearances of food and money which he attributed to the interposition of Providence. In *God the Guardian of the Poor and the Bank of Faith* (2 pts, 1785–1802) he describes how his early career as a preacher developed thanks to Providence supplying him with a horse, riding breeches, and other necessaries (these attributions were later denounced by Robert Southey in a very hostile article in the *Quarterly Review*, 48, April 1821, but approved in an edition of 1913 which celebrated the book as 'a household treasure'). Huntington's circuit took in Thames Ditton, Richmond, Cobham, Worplesdon, Petworth, Horsham, and Margaret Street Chapel, London; with scanty clothing and meagre rations he often walked more than 100 miles a week. To his most loyal adherents Huntington confided his affair in Frittenden, and added to his name the letters SS (Sinner Saved). The persecutions he endured from those who resented his preaching, and their untimely or violent ends, he later described in *The Naked Bow, or, A Visible Display of the Judgments of God on the Enemies of Truth* (1794).

In 1782, after what he took to be a heavenly call telling him to 'Prophesy upon the thick boughs', Huntington moved to London, where he soon accumulated enough credit to build a chapel in Titchfield Street, consecrated in 1783. Here at Providence Chapel he officiated for more than a quarter of a century, while living in Church Street, Paddington. Huntington's ministry flourished: his preaching attracted the rich and fashionable. Princess Amelia was a regular; others, like Lord Liverpool, came out of curiosity. Even George III read some of his works (which a footman left on a chair). Huntington himself expressed greater attachment to poorer souls: in 1794 he claimed a following in London of 3000; in 1808 he was preaching to over 1200 people at a time. In his later years he had a comfortable annual income of £2000 from his pew rents and publications, and from 1799 he lived in a handsome villa in Cricklewood. On 13 July 1810 Providence Chapel burnt to the ground. It was uninsured, but Huntington easily raised more than £10,000 with which he built a larger chapel in Gray's Inn Lane, between Wilson Street and Calthorpe Street. New Providence Chapel, as it was called, opened on 20 June 1811.

With his wife, Mary, Huntington had thirteen children, of whom seven were living at his death. In 1802 he became close to Elizabeth (widow of Sir James Sanderson, lord mayor of London in 1792). This liaison, which had upset Mary (who died on 9 December 1806), was not popular among his congregation; it lost him the support of his closest follower, the Revd William Brook of Brighton. However, Huntington married Lady Sanderson on 15 August 1808, though she continued to use her own name until her death on 9 November 1817. She was buried at a cottage Huntington gave her near Cranbrook.

In a characteristically paradoxical letter of 20 December 1812 Huntington described himself as 'a child of wrath, but yet a child of God'. His belligerent Christianity manifested itself in controversies with many antagonists, including Jeremiah Learnoult Garrett, Rowland Hill, Timothy Priestley, and Maria de Fleury. His own aggression provoked some of the persecution he endured, but after Garnett Terry threatened him with a libel action in 1806 he was more cautious. His extensive correspondence with men and women convinced by his experimental religion was printed in *Epistles of Faith* (2 pts, 1785–97), *Living Testimonies* (2 pts, 1794–1806), *Correspondence between Noctua Aurita and Philomela* (1799), and other works. Avoiding

theological authorities in favour of his own Calvinist exegesis, he developed an original style full of allegory, metaphor, paradox, and biblical texts: in later life he was known as the Walking Bible, according to his grandson and biographer Ebenezer Hooper.

An admirer of John Bunyan and George Whitefield, Huntington attacked Arminians and antinomians for what he saw as their inadequate stress on the intercessionary powers of Christ. His preaching style was described as fluent, solemn, and surprisingly placid; his only eccentricity in the pulpit was running a white handkerchief through his fingers. Described even by his enemies as an original, he styled himself 'the Doctor', sported a clerical hat over his black wig, and was a heavy snuff-taker. Upright in posture, solid in figure, with a florid complexion and blue eyes, he was more a charismatic than an imposing figure. Unusually for a dissenter, he was an ardent tory.

Huntington opened chapels at Lewes (1802), Brighton (1805), Newark (1806), Leicester, Grantham, and Sleaford (1806), Chichester (1809), and Bristol (1810). His influence outside London was sufficient to attract an attack by George Crabbe in *The Borough* (1810). In 1811 he published a collected edition of his works complete to the year 1806, in twenty volumes. He continued to publish during his life, and six more volumes appeared after his death (*Gleanings of the Vintage*, 2 vols., 1814; *Posthumous Letters*, 3 vols. in 1815 and 1 in 1822). He died at Tunbridge Wells on 1 July 1813 and was interred on 8 July in the burial-ground of Jireh Chapel, Lewes, next to his friend and fellow preacher the Revd Jenkin Jenkins. His epitaph, composed by himself, was as follows:

> Here lies the coalheaver, who departed this life July 1st, 1813, in the 69th year of his age, beloved of his God, but abhorred of men. The omniscient Judge at the grand assize shall ratify and confirm this to the confusion of many thousands, for England and its metropolis shall know that there hath been a prophet among them.

His prophecies, concerned with Napoleon and the papacy, were not fulfilled; his reputation, still controversial in the wake of Hooper's biography in the 1870s, was based rather on his pastoral and polemical writings, and on his representations of Providence as closely concerned in the transformation of his life from coalheaver to popular preacher. CLARE BRANT

Sources DNB · E. Hooper, *The celebrated coalheaver* (1871) · E. Hooper, *Facts, letters and documents (chiefly unpublished) concerning William Huntington* (1872) · W. Huntington, *The substance of the last or farewell sermon of the late Reverend William Huntington, SS* (1813) · *The Sinner Saved: a memoir of the Rev. William Huntington* [1813] · two letters to Mr Beasley, 5 July 1813, BL, Add. MS 46886 · *A catalogue of the genteel household furniture … and various other effects … of the Rev William Huntington* [sale catalogue, 22 Sept 1813] · *The poetical works of … George Crabbe, with … his life*, ed. [G. Crabbe], 1, 3 (1834) · GM, 1st ser., 83/2 (1813), 190–94, 702–3 · G. M. Ella, *William Huntington, pastor of Providence* (1994)

Archives BL, letters to congregation, Add. MS 46886 · CKS, corresp. and papers

Likenesses J. Borgnis, stipple, pubd 1791, BM, NPG · D. Pellegrini, oils, 1803, NPG [*see illus.*] · T. Overton, stipple, pubd 1814, BM, NPG ·

T. Rowlandson, caricature, etching, pubd 1825, NPG · J. S. Reynolds, portrait, Providence Chapel, Chichester · bust, V&A · caricature, repro. in *The Satirist* (1 June 1808)
Wealth at death effects sold for £1800: Hooper, *Celebrated coalheaver*; *Catalogue of the genteel household furniture*, MS annotations

Huntley, Francis (*c.*1783–1831), actor, was born in Barnsley, Yorkshire. He lost his father while young, and claimed to have been educated at Douglas's academy in South Audley Street, London, and articled to a surgeon. After some practice in the capital as an amateur actor he began his professional career at Brecon about 1806, under R. Phillips. He made a bad start, and appeared with no more success at the Lyceum under Laurent. He remained for some time with Beverley at the Richmond Theatre, studying and rising in his profession. He then performed at Stamford and Nottingham and played Othello to the Iago of Edmund Kean (then using the name Carey) at the Birmingham Theatre, under Watson. Under Ryley at Bolton he was seen by R. W. Elliston, who engaged him for Manchester, and brought him subsequently to the Olympic and to the Surrey, where in the summer of 1809 he appeared as Lockit in *The Beggar's Opera* to Elliston's Macheath. On 25 November 1811, as King James in *The Knight of Snowdoun*—an operatic adaptation by Morton of *The Lady of the Lake*—he made his début at Covent Garden. The part of Romaldi in Thomas Holcroft's *The Tale of Mystery* followed on the 27th, and, on 11 December, Wilford in Colman's *The Iron Chest*. On 31 January 1812 he was the original Don Alonzo in Reynolds's *Virgin of the Sun*. At Easter Huntley returned to the Surrey, and went from there to Dublin, where during two seasons he played leading business at the Smock Alley Theatre. After this he was seen at the Olympic, again, with Thomas Dibdin, at the Surrey, at the Coburg, the Royalty, the West London—where he opened as Oedipus to the Jocasta of Julia Glover—Astley's, and then again at the Coburg and the Surrey.

In his later years Huntley was known as the 'Roscius of the Coburg', at which house he was principally seen. He was a well-built man, about 5 feet 10 inches in height, dark, with an expressive face, great command of feature, and a clear and powerful voice, the undertones of which had much sweetness. Before ruining himself by drunkenness and other irregularities of life, and by playing to vulgar audiences, he had great powers of expressing rage, fear, despair, and other strong passions. When at the Surrey his terms are said to have been a guinea a night and as much brandy as he could drink (Honeyman, the lessee, was also a publican). He married about 1808, but separated from his wife, with whom he had a child. Another Frank Huntley, who was subsequently on the stage, may have been his son. Huntley's death, which took place 'lately, aged 48', according to the *Gentleman's Magazine* of April 1831 (1.376), was hastened by intemperance. Oxberry (*Dramatic Biography*) doubtfully says that he was born in 1785, that he died in 1823, and that he was buried in Walworth.

JOSEPH KNIGHT, *rev.* KATHARINE COCKIN

Sources *Oxberry's Dramatic Biography*, new ser., 1/13 (1827), 217–28 · Genest, *Eng. stage* · Hall, *Dramatic ports.* · *GM*, 1st ser., 101/1 (1831), 376–7

Likenesses twelve prints, Harvard TC

Huntley, Sir Henry Vere (1795–1864), naval officer and colonial governor, was the third son of Richard Huntley (1776–1831) of Boxwell Court, Boxwall, near Wotton under Edge, Gloucestershire, and his wife, Anne, daughter of the Ven. James Webster, archdeacon of Gloucester. He entered the navy in March 1809, when he served on the North America and West Indies station. In 1815 he was in the *Northumberland* when she carried Napoleon to St Helena. In 1818 he was made lieutenant, and served in the Mediterranean successively in the brigs *Redpole* and *Parthian*. In the latter he was wrecked on the Egyptian coast on 15 May 1828. Huntley was afterwards at Portsmouth in the *Ganges* with Captain John Hayes, whom he followed to the *Dryad* (42 guns), on the west coast of Africa, where, for the greater part of the time, he commanded one of her tenders, the schooner *Fair Rosamond*. Although he later wrote in his *Seven Years' Service on the Slave Coast* that maintaining the anti-slave-trade squadron was 'an idle absurdity' (Lloyd, *The Navy and the Slave Trade*, 73), he cruised successfully against slavers.

On 20 September 1832 Huntley married Anne (d. 1855), eldest daughter of Lieutenant-General John Skinner. They had two sons and a daughter. In 1833 he was appointed to command of the 3-gun brigantine *Lynx*, also on the west coast of Africa, and in her captured several slavers. In 1837 he was employed, with Commander Craigie of the *Scout*, in negotiating a treaty with the king of Bonny (on the coast of what later became Nigeria), and was sent home with the treaty for ratification. On 28 June 1838 he was promoted commander, and in 1839 was appointed lieutenant-governor of the settlements on the River Gambia, during which appointment he had to repel tribal incursions. In August 1841 he was appointed lieutenant-governor of Prince Edward Island, and before leaving was knighted, on 9 October 1841. He was afterwards arbitrator of the mixed courts at Luanda, and later became consul at Santos in Brazil. In 1859 he married the daughter of the Revd Henry Drury, rector of Fingest, Buckinghamshire; they had no children.

While in command at Prince Edward Island, Huntley apparently took to writing as an amusement; and on his return to England published in rapid succession: *Peregrine Scramble, or, Thirty Years' Adventures of a Bluejacket* (2 vols., 1849), in an obvious and feeble imitation of Marryat; *Observations upon the Free Trade Policy of England in Connection with the Sugar Act of 1846* (1849), a protest against the controversial policy which favoured slave-grown sugar; *Seven Years' Service on the Slave Coast of Western Africa* (2 vols., 1850), a personal narrative; and *California, its Gold and its Inhabitants* (2 vols., 1856). Many of Huntley's official reports on African questions were published in the parliamentary papers.

He died at Santos, Brazil, on 7 May 1864. The eldest son from his first marriage, Lieutenant Spencer Robert Huntley RN, died in command of the *Cherub* on the North America and West Indies station in 1869.

J. K. LAUGHTON, *rev.* ANDREW LAMBERT

Sources O'Byrne, *Naval biog. dict.* · *GM*, 3rd ser., 17 (1864), 112 · H. Temperley, *British antislavery, 1833–1870* (1972) · K. O. Dike, *Trade* *and politics in the Niger delta, 1830–1885* (1956) • Boase, *Mod. Eng. biog.* • C. Lloyd, *The nation and the navy* (1949) • C. Lloyd, *The navy and the slave trade* (1949), 73

Archives Glos. RO, corresp. and family papers

Wealth at death under £800: resworn probate, Oct 1873, *CGPLA Eng. & Wales* (1864)

Huntly. For this title name *see* Seton, Alexander, first earl of Huntly (*d.* 1470); Gordon, George, second earl of Huntly (1440/41–1501); Gordon, Alexander, third earl of Huntly (*d.* 1524); Gordon, George, fourth earl of Huntly (1513–1562); Gordon, George, fifth earl of Huntly (*d.* 1576); Gordon, George, first marquess of Huntly (1561/2–1636); Gordon, George, second marquess of Huntly (*c.*1590–1649); Gordon, George, ninth marquess of Huntly (1761–1853); Gordon, (Mary) Pamela, marchioness of Huntly (1918–1998) [*see under* Berry, (James) Gomer, first Viscount Kemsley (1883–1968)].

Hunton, Louis [Lewis] (*bap.* **1814**, *d.* **1838**), geologist and chemist, was born at Hummersea House, Loftus, North Riding of Yorkshire, and baptized on 6 August 1814. He was the son of William Hunton (1789–1863), manager of the local alum works and ship-owner, and Jane, *née* March (1791–1878). Little is known of his earliest years but he was probably educated at the school provided for children at the alum works by Lord Dundas. In 1832 Hunton entered King's College, London. He is said to have spent two years at King's, during the period when Charles Lyell and John Phillips were teaching geology there. However, he is recorded only as an occasional student of German language and literature. In 1835 Hunton went, for one year, to University College, London, where he attended courses on comparative anatomy, fossil zoology (both taught by Robert Grant), and natural philosophy.

On 25 May 1836 Hunton's only geological paper was communicated to the Geological Society of London by J. F. Royle (1799–1858) of King's College. Published the following year, it recorded the results Hunton had obtained from detailed study of the Upper Lias and Marlstone strata exposed at Rockcliff, to the east of his father's Loftus works on the Yorkshire coast. Nearly one hundred years later, this paper was described as 'a truly remarkable document' showing 'remarkable qualities' (Arkell). Hunton was the first to urge that accurate information about the distributions of fossils in rocks could only come from the study of samples taken from material still *in situ* within the beds in question; loose materials accumulated at the foot of cliffs should never be used. When *in situ* materials were used, they demonstrated how certain species, especially ammonites, showed much more limited vertical distributions through rocks than had previously been realized. Such discoveries greatly helped the more accurate discrimination of both strata and time in the geology of the next decade. Hunton's geological paper brought him election as a fellow of the Geological Society in November 1836; he was proposed by Robert Grant. The same year he discovered a fine 5 metre long ichthyosaur, which was presented to the Whitby Museum in 1867.

Hunton's only other published scientific work appeared in the *London and Edinburgh Philosophical Magazine* in 1837.

The paper, on his other interest, chemistry, discussed combinations of sugar (of interest to any alum maker) with alkalis and metallic oxides. By this time, however, Hunton was ill with consumption and had had to abandon further scientific research. He travelled to Nîmes in the south of France hoping his health would recover. It did not and on 18 February 1838 he died at rue des Lombards 12, Nîmes, aged twenty-three. He was posthumously remembered by an ammonite named after him by Martin Simpson in 1843.   H. S. TORRENS

Sources H. S. Torrens and T. A. Getty, 'Louis Hunton, 1814–1838: English pioneer in ammonite biostratigraphy', *Earth Sciences History*, 3 (1984), 58–68 • A. Long and R. Long, *A shipping venture: Turnbull Scott and Company, 1872–1972* (1974) • G. Smales, *Whitby authors and their publications* (1867), 226–7 • 'Whitby Museum', *Whitby Repository*, new ser., 1 (1867), 279–80 • W. J. Arkell, *The Jurassic system in Great Britain* (1933), 8–15 • M. Simpson, *A monograph of the ammonites of the Yorkshire Lias* (1843), 41 • H. B. Browne, *The story of Whitby Museum* (1949) • R. Osborne, *The floating egg* (1998)

Hunton, Philip (*bap.* **1602**, *d.* **1682/3**), polemicist, was baptized at Andover, Hampshire, on 12 September 1602, the son of Philip Hunton, yeoman. He was admitted as a batteler or servitor at Wadham College, Oxford, in 1622; he matriculated on 31 January 1623, graduated BA in 1626, and proceeded MA in 1629. He was ordained priest at Salisbury on 21 September 1628, after which he acted as schoolmaster at Avebury in Wiltshire and as curate at Clyffe Pypard. He was nominated to the prebend of Tytherington in 1631. Having been licensed to preach at Devizes on 27 December 1638 Hunton was presented to the living at Westbury on 12 July 1641. Although he was to remain there for many years, his time at Westbury was not without problems, as is evident from the statement he issued in 1647 of his terms for resuming his ministry, including the assertion of his right to refuse the sacrament as he saw fit.

Hunton's reputation rests primarily upon two pamphlets published during the early phase of the civil wars. *A Treatise of Monarchy* was published in May 1643 in response to the debate between such parliamentarians as Henry Parker, William Bridge, Jeremiah Burroughes, and Charles Herle on the one hand and royalist divines like Henry Ferne on the other. In reply to Ferne's *Reply unto Several Treatises* (November 1643) Hunton published *A Vindication of the 'Treatise of Monarchy'* in March 1644. In essence Hunton's treatises centred upon his analysis of the nature of a mixed constitution, and he arguably possessed the keenest sense of any of his contemporaries that England was a mixed monarchy, the central dilemma of the civil war. In playing down 'election' and 'representation' as legitimating principles Hunton's theory can be called the presbyterian parliamentarian theory, and ultimately paved the way for the later ideas of John Locke.

Hunton's *Treatise* was divided into two parts: an analysis of abstract forms of government, and an analysis of the English monarchy. He based his theory upon the notion that while authority was divinely sanctioned, particular forms of government were not, and he argued that consent determined the mode and personnel of government but that human choices were approved by God, from whence came authority. Hunton thus accepted the logical possibility of a simple monarchy, a simple aristocracy, or a simple democracy. However, even in an absolute monarchy he granted a right of resistance, whether by an individual or an entire community, on grounds of self-defence. In limited monarchies, Hunton argued that the ruler's powers were restricted by fundamental laws rather than by the monarch's own free will. He thus accepted the possibility of resistance, although he specified situations in which such resistance ought to be passive, and stressed that active resistance ought never extend to the person of the monarch, since those constituted with sovereign power were sacred and thus out of the reach of positive resistance or violence. While Ferne argued that limitations on a monarch's power required a sanction to enforce them, Hunton's novelty lay in recognizing that resistance was not an act of public jurisdiction. In a limited monarchy 'there can be no stated internal judge of the monarch's actions if there grow a fundamental variance betwixt him and the community', since the existence of such a judge would import supremacy and destroy monarchy (Hunton, 17).

Hunton proceeded by asserting that 'experience' had taught people to devise a mixed system, such as he considered England to possess. He denied the importance of the Norman 'conquest' by demonstrating both William's legitimate claim and the people's consent, and by accepting the Tacitean understanding of the origins of English liberties. In a mixed monarchy the sovereign power lay in all three estates, each of which shared the supreme power and moderated and restrained the others. This was encapsulated in the fact that English laws required parliamentary consent, with each estate possessing a negative voice. Although Hunton did not invent the idea of the supremacy of 'king in parliament', he nevertheless saw its implications and grasped the supremacy of legislation more clearly than other parliamentarians.

While regarding this mixed monarchy as the best possible system, Hunton nevertheless understood its key weakness. He recognized that 'there can be no constituted, legal, authoritative judge of the fundamental controversies arising betwixt the three estates ... for the established being of such authority would *ipso facto* overthrow the frame, and turn it into absoluteness' (Hunton, 28–9). Although the English benefited from the stabilizing force of custom and the common law, Hunton nevertheless recognized that in the absence of an authoritative judge, such 'fundamental controversies' represented 'the fatal disease of these governments for which no salve can be prescribed' (ibid.). In this situation there were only two possible outcomes—civil war or a return to the state of nature—and Hunton explicitly justified resistance by arguing that if one estate sought dominance and exorbitant power, 'the power of restraint and providing for the public safety should be in the rest'. He did not argue that resistance represented an authoritative civil act or that it could be justified on the grounds of possessing supreme authority, but rather that it was undertaken in order 'to

preserve the state from ruin' and in order to preserve the mixed constitution. Hunton was somewhat inconsistent, however, in establishing who was permitted to initiate resistance, and retreated from his initial position that such power lay in individuals in order to stress that resistance to threats to the constitution could be instigated only by the king or parliament. In mixed constitutions as in monarchies, however, Hunton stressed that the person of the monarch was 'above the reach of violence in its utmost exorbitances'. He argued that 'when a people have sworn allegiance and invested a person or line with supremacy, they have made it sacred, and no abuse can divest him of that power, irrevocably communicated ... he is *de jure* exempt from any penal hand' (ibid., 28). Hunton thus opposed the use of force against an English monarch such as Charles I, but asserted that parliament could resist the king's advisers and assistants in order to protect the mixed constitution.

Having allowed for the possibility of resistance by one or more estates against the unbearable proceedings of another, Hunton was forced to address, at the climax of his analysis, how the people could arbitrate a conflict initiated by either king or parliament, and adjudicate their competing claims regarding the accused estate in the civil war. Royalists such as Ferne sought to convince the public that ultimate power lay with the king, while parliamentarian theorists such as Parker contested that final judgements lay with parliament. Hunton rejected both positions, since both tended towards the idea of a legally constituted judge and would create an absolute government and destroy the mixed monarchy. Hunton's conclusion was that an appeal needed to be made to 'every man's conscience' (Hunton, 28–9) and to the community at large; that individuals should follow their consciences, make moral and rational decisions regarding their own and the community's rights and safety, and support whichever side they judged to stand for the public good. The outcome of civil war should thus depend upon the verdict of the community. Hunton himself supported the parliamentarian cause, but this was less a reflection of the legality of parliament's actions than his personal opinion that the judgement of two houses was greater than that of a private man. The ambiguity of his position, however, stemmed from his justification of the legal force of parliamentarian measures such as the militia ordinance of 1642. Since such measures required obedience, Hunton came close to implying that parliament was supreme within the constitution, something which he avoided only by arguing that parliament's current powers were extraordinary and temporary. In doing so, he adopted precisely the line of argument pursued by parliament itself.

Richard Baxter later claimed that Hunton's *Treatise of Monarchy*, Henry Parker's *Observations*, and Nathaniel Bacon's *Historical Discourse* were the most important parliamentarian tracts of the civil war, but after the appearance of the *Vindication* Hunton produced no further known work, even though he was one of the targets for the royalist Sir Robert Filmer in *The Anarchy of a Limited or Mixed Monarchy* (1648). Nevertheless Hunton did not withdraw from public life, and under the protectorate acted as one of the clerical assistants to the commissioners for the ejection of scandalous clergy in Wiltshire (1654). More importantly, he was made founding provost of the abortive scheme for Durham College in 1657, and preacher at Durham in March 1658, and he was granted the lucrative living of Sedgefield. Hunton's colleague Ezerel or Israel Tonge, later a close associate of Titus Oates, called him 'an indisputable scholar' (Webster, 237), and wrote of Hunton's interest in medical and veterinary studies as well as divinity. That Hunton retained his ties with Westbury, however, is evident from his having promoted a petition against interference in the local clothworking industry in 1658.

Hunton was ejected from Westbury in 1662, and thereafter gathered a congregation of dissenters at his house in Westbury, although he was reported to have disputed with local Quakers. His preaching led to him being cited before the bishop of Salisbury in 1669, but no action was taken against him then or during the remainder of his life. Indeed, having signed a petition from several Wiltshire ministers in 1672 for acknowledgement as nonconformists, Hunton was licensed to preach at his house in Westbury in October 1672. Hunton did not resurface as a controversialist during these years even though his work took on new importance in the late 1670s and early 1680s, not least through the republication of Filmer's attack in 1679. Neither did he live to see his book burnt in public for its damnable doctrines, according to the judgment of the University of Oxford in July 1683, as part of the tory reaction to the Popish Plot and exclusion crises.

Hunton died between 29 June 1682, when he wrote his will, and 28 June 1683, when it was proved. He left property in his native Andover, as well as in Warbledon and Hailsham, Sussex. His bequests in Westbury included a plot of land for his nonconformist colleagues, which was later sold to raise money for a chapel. His personal estate was valued for the purposes of probate at £545, including a library worth £50. Hunton left a widow, Anne (d. 1689), whom he had married at an unknown date, and she herself left money to three nonconformist ministers on her death. Hunton's works remained influential after his death, and his *Treatise* was republished twice in 1689. Anthony Wood recorded that it 'hath been and is still in great vogue among many persons of commonwealth and levelling principles' (Wood, *Ath. Oxon.*, 4.50).

J. T. PEACEY

Sources P. Hunton, *A treatise of monarchy*, ed. I. Gardner (2000) · H. Ferne, *A reply unto several treatises* (1643) · R. Filmer, *The anarchy of a limited or mixed monarchy* (1648) · *Calamy rev.* · VCH *Wiltshire*, vol. 3 · J. H. Franklin, *John Locke and the theory of sovereignty* (1978) · D. Wootton, ed., *Divine right and democracy* (1986) · C. H. McIlwain, *Constitutionalism and the changing world* (1969) · Wood, *Ath. Oxon.*, new edn, 4.49–51 · G. L. Turner, ed., *Original records of early nonconformity under persecution and indulgence*, 3 vols. (1911–14) · C. Webster, *The great instauration: science, medicine and reform, 1626–1660* (1975) · will, PRO, PROB 4/12438

Wealth at death £545: will, PRO, PROB 4/12438

Huntsman, Benjamin (1704–1776), steel manufacturer, was born at Epworth, Lincolnshire, on 4 June 1704, the third son of a Quaker farmer, William Huntsman. At the age of fourteen he was apprenticed to an Epworth clockmaker for a premium of £4. At the end of his apprenticeship he set up as a clockmaker in Doncaster, where he was recorded as taking on his own apprentice in 1725. He married Elizabeth Haigh (d. 1760) of Doncaster at a Church of England ceremony in 1729 at Retford. Their children, Elizabeth and William, were born in 1730 and 1733 respectively. Benjamin Huntsman appears in the records of Doncaster corporation, when he was appointed to look after the town clock in 1727 and the new town clock in 1735. In 1739 he rented a house in Doncaster High Street and two years later he purchased the freehold.

Huntsman is remembered as the inventor of crucible steel, or 'cast steel' as it was known at the time, since no steel had ever before been cast into ingots. A traditional story is that he was dissatisfied with the quality of the steel that he needed for the springs and pendulums of his clocks and that he therefore started experiments to make a more reliable metal. The steel at this time was 'cementation' steel, sometimes known as 'German steel' as it was imported via the Rhine, but which had been made in south Yorkshire in modest quantities since at least 1642. The quality of such steel was not uniform, since it was produced by forging a number of bars bound together. Huntsman took this steel and melted it down in clay crucibles in the manner of the brass-founders. This was the first time that molten steel had been manufactured, allowing the constituent parts to mix properly. The temperature at which the steel became molten was much higher than that required for melting brass. Local glass makers had already proved that clay crucibles were capable of withstanding such heat.

It is not known when Huntsman began his experiments, but in 1742 he moved west from Doncaster to a cottage at Handsworth on the outskirts of Sheffield. He continued his trade of clockmaker, but by 1751 he had moved to Worksop Road, Attercliffe Green, in the eastern part of the parish of Sheffield, and set up as a steel maker. The first reference to his steel-making activities occurs in the records of the Cutlers' Company of Hallamshire for 1750. He made another short move about 1770 to premises known later as Huntsman's Row, which he and his descendants occupied until 1899.

Despite later legends about the secrecy of his experiments Huntsman did not patent his process. He and his son developed a thriving business, but he did not achieve—and possibly did not seek—the great commercial success of some contemporary entrepreneurs. His invention attracted interest abroad and a number of foreign visitors came to see him. They included the Swedish engineer Ludwig *Robsahm (1761) and probably the Frenchman Gabriel *Jars (1765) [*see under* Industrial spies], both of whom made written reports. Huntsman's steel was not at first used by local cutlers, who found it difficult to work. The earliest ledgers of the firm date from ten years after Huntsman's death, but they confirm earlier evidence that crucible steel was used only for special applications and that sales were made to French and Swiss customers. By that time, much of the firm's profits came from the manufacture of metal buttons. The Huntsman method remained the only way of producing steel ingots until Bessemer's invention in 1856 enabled steel to be made in bulk. Crucible output continued to grow up to 1873, when over 100,000 tons per annum were being made in the Sheffield area, in well over 3000 crucible holes. During the First World War crucible production soared to new heights, but then declined and eventually disappeared.

Huntsman died at Attercliffe on 20 June 1776 and was buried in Attercliffe chapel yard (now known as Hill Top cemetery), the Church of England chapel of ease which served the eastern part of the parish of Sheffield. His wife, who had died on 3 November 1760, was buried in the same grave. Their son, William Huntsman (1733–1809), carried on and expanded the family business. Benjamin Huntsman was recognized in the nineteenth century for his outstanding contribution to the steel industry. Praised by Samuel Smiles, he was the man most responsible for Sheffield's pre-eminence in the manufacture of steel.

DAVID HEY

Sources K. C. Barraclough, *Benjamin Hunstman, 1704–1776* (1976) · K. C. Barraclough, *Steelmaking before Bessemer*, 2 (1984)

Huquier, Jacques-Gabriel [James-Gabriel; *known as* Huquier *fils*] (**1730–1805**), engraver and portrait painter, was born in Paris, the son of Marie-Anne Desvignes (*d.* 1775) and Gabriel Huquier (1695–1772). His father was a well-known painter, etcher, print publisher, printseller, and collector who played a crucial role in the publication of design drawings and artists' *œuvres*, including those of Juste-Aurèle Meissonnier and Gilles-Marie Oppenord. The numerous series of ornament prints issued by Huquier the elder include plates with rococo borders to be mounted on screens. Huquier *fils* was trained by François Boucher in drawing and by his father, in whose atelier he worked until 1756. From that year his prints were published by Denis-Charles Buldet (*fl.* 1745–1781). Pierre-Jean Mariette attributed to Huquier *fils* the *Lettre sur l'exposition des tableaux au Louvre avec des notes historiques* (1753), but this seems unlikely. In 1758 Huquier married Anne-Louise Chéreau (1740–1775), daughter of the engraver and print publisher Jacques Chéreau (1688–1776); he received from his father 10,000 livres, of which 3000 were in cash and the remainder in engraved copperplates, prints, and valuable drawings. Huquier assisted his father-in-law in managing his stock of plates from 1758 to 1761, at 'rue St. Jacques au dessus de celle des Mathurins' with the sign 'au Grand Saint-Rémy', and he settled afterwards at the 'grand rue du faubourg St. Martin', specializing in fan leaves and optical views. These prints are known by an announcement in the *Avant Coureur* (6 December 1762), but none of the fan leaves has been located. In 1762 a reissue of Vignola's *Règles des cinq ordres d'architecture*, drawn and etched by Babel, first issued by Jacques Chéreau in 1747, bears as his address 'A Paris chez Huquier fils, rue St. Jacques au grand St. Rémy'. In 1764 he settled at the 'porte Saint-Martin à côté de la Barrière'. Huquier supplied notably the Spanish and Portuguese markets, but he encountered serious difficulties in managing his stock. On 17 May 1763 his creditors gave him three years to settle his debts. His stock then comprised 1141 plates, estimated at 17,000 livres, including numerous devotional subjects, fan leaves, decorations for fire- and wall-screens, and prints after Boucher, Watteau, and Natoire. In 1766 Huquier fils & Compagnie established a wallpaper manufactory at Suresnes near Paris and he sold his papers partly through the shop of his father at the rue des Mathurins. On 21 March 1768 several paintings, drawings, and prints were auctioned in Paris, probably from his private collection, and on 30 May the remainder of his stock was sold at auction, including thirty-one copperplates. He made several trips to England and in 1772 he moved permanently to London, leaving his wife and children behind, never to return to France again. He exhibited from 1771 at the Royal Academy as a painter of pastel portraits. He drew a portrait of the Chevalier d'Eon, which was engraved in mezzotint by T. Burke. In 1782 he etched a portrait of Richard Tyson, master of the ceremonies at Bath, for Anstey's *New Bath Guide*. The vast majority of his prints predate his move to England in 1772. He moved in 1783 to Cambridge and died in Shrewsbury on 7 June 1805. His engraved *œuvre* is only partly identified and notably the more ephemeral (fan leaves, frontispieces) and popular subjects (optical prints) have escaped the attention of collectors and cataloguers.

PETER FUHRING

Sources *Avant-Coureur* (1760), 14–15 · *Avant-Coureur* (6 Dec 1762), 788 · J. M. Papillon, *Traité historique et pratique de la gravure en bois*, 1 (1766); repr. (1985), 536 · 'Inventaire après décès de Gabriel Huquier, 8–29 Juillet 1772', MS, Archives Nationales, Paris, minutier central, étude XCVIII · M. Huber and C. C. H. Rost, *Manuel des curieux et des amateurs de l'art*, 8 (Zürich, 1804), 77–8 · G. G. Gandellini, *Notizie degli intagliatori*, ed. L. De Angelis, rev. edn (1812), 173–4 · F. E. Joubert, 'Huquier, G.', *Manuel de l'amateur d'estampes*, 2 (Paris, 1821), 145–6 · C. Le Blanc, *Manuel de l'amateur d'estampes*, 2 (Paris, 1855–6), 403–5 · H. Herluison, *Actes d'état civil d'artistes français, peintres, graveurs, architectes, etc. extraits des registres de l'Hôtel-de-Ville de Paris, détruits dans l'incendie du 24 mai 1871* (1873), 186–7 · Redgrave, *Artists* · R. Portalis and H. Béraldi, *Les graveurs du dix-huitième siècle*, 2 (Paris, 1888), 449–50 · J. Guiffrey, 'Scellés et inventaires d'artistes', *Nouvelles Archives de l'Art Français*, 2nd ser., 6/3 (vol. 12 of collection) (1885), 67–8 [reprint 1973] · Graves, *RA exhibitors* · Bénézit, *Dict.* · Thieme & Becker, *Allgemeines Lexikon* · Y. Bruand, 'Un grand collectionneur, marchand et graveur du XVIIIe siècle: Gabriel Huquier (1695–1772)', *Gazette des Beaux-Arts*, 6th ser., 37 (1950), 99–104 · Y. Bruand and M. Hébert, *Graveurs du XVIIIe siècle* (1970), vol. 11 of *Inventaire du fonds français*, 538–45, nos. 1–46 · P. Jean-Richard, *L'œuvre gravé de François Boucher dans la collection Edmond de Rothschild au Musée du Louvre* (1978), 285–93, nos. 1162–92 · 'Huquier, J.-G.', M. Préaud, P. Casselle, M. Grivel, and C. Le Bitouze, *Dictionnaire des éditeurs d'estampes à Paris sous l'ancien régime* (1987), 165–6 · N. McWilliam, ed., *A bibliography of salon criticism in Paris from the ancien régime to the restoration, 1699–1827* (1991), 0077

Likenesses J. B. Perronneau, pastel drawing, 1747, Louvre, Paris · J. Greenwood, pencil drawing, BM

Hurcomb, Cyril William, Baron Hurcomb (**1883–1975**), civil servant, was born in Oxford on 18 February 1883, the eldest of three children of William Hurcomb, bookseller, and his wife, Sarah Ann Castle. He was educated at Oxford high school and, as a scholar, at St John's College, Oxford, where he obtained a first in classical moderations in 1903 and a second in *literae humaniores* in 1905. He entered the civil service in the Post Office in 1906, and was briefly outposted before being assigned to the secretary's office; after five years he became private secretary to the postmaster-general, and was thus marked out for promotion. He was strongly influenced in this period by Sir Matthew Nathan and Herbert Samuel. In 1911 he married Dorothy Ethel (*d.* 1947), daughter of Alfred Brooke, solicitor. They had two daughters.

After the outbreak of the First World War Hurcomb was transferred to the Admiralty and then, in 1916, to the newly formed Ministry of Shipping. There he became deputy director and, later, director of commercial services, working closely with a group of men who were to play important parts in shaping his future career, such as his Oxford contemporary J. A. Salter. His work was operational rather than conventionally administrative, and he showed an aptitude for managerial duties which characterized all his later posts. It was here also that he acquired an ease and skill for working with and winning the confidence of colleagues drawn from business, the professions, and other walks of life. The international aspects of the work appealed to him, and he developed a remarkable capacity for forming relations of close trust with a wide variety of foreigners, especially Europeans. The challenges presented to him by wartime shipping problems determined the rest of his career.

Hurcomb's work at Shipping had brought him to the notice of Sir Eric Geddes who in 1919 persuaded him to join the new Ministry of Transport which Geddes headed. His main task there was to negotiate the regrouping of the railway companies in 1921. He was appointed permanent secretary of the Ministry of Transport in 1927, at the early age of forty-four. He had then to face an immediate challenge from the Treasury, which proposed to abolish his ministry as a measure of economy. Making full use of the impact at that time of the motor vehicle on society, Hurcomb fought a skilful and patient holding action. In 1929 the tables were turned with the arrival, as minister in the new Labour government, of the able and energetic Herbert Morrison, with whom he quickly established a close personal friendship. Jointly they piloted the pioneering legislation to establish the London Passenger Transport Board, which amalgamated a large number of separate concerns. Simultaneously they pushed through parliament the Road Traffic Act of 1930, which introduced tests for drivers, compulsory third-party insurance, licensing of road passenger services, a highway code, and a speed limit for built-up areas. Further legislation in the 1930s led to trouble with the Home Office which objected to the growing burden placed upon the police by some of these measures. The result was an increased number of negotiations which he found wearying.

In 1937 therefore Hurcomb was glad to take the opportunity of transferring to the Electricity Commission where, as chairman from 1938, he was at one remove from politics. Although he retained this post for ten years, from 1939 his time was to be pre-empted for most of them by war and post-war responsibilities as director-general of the Ministry of Shipping (later War Transport), where he was able to apply the principles which he had learnt in the First World War. In this he was greatly helped by the renewed collaboration of Salter, now in parliament, who as a junior minister in the department provided strong intellectual support. The necessity of deploying the British-controlled and United States merchant fleets as if they were one made it imperative to establish close relations of trust with the shipping authorities in Washington, and this task was excellently performed from April 1941 by Salter, whose intimate understanding of Hurcomb's thoughts and style enabled him to act as head of the British merchant shipping mission in full harmony with London. One of Hurcomb's main concerns was to block outside interference, and this he achieved with entire success, even in face of determined attempts at encroachment by F. A. Lindemann (later Viscount Cherwell).

The post-war Attlee administration embarked on a major programme of nationalization under Herbert Morrison, who turned naturally to Hurcomb to bring into operation the British Transport Commission, which he served as chairman from 1947 to 1953. Partly owing to a reversal of policy by the succeeding Conservative government this was probably the least successful of his official assignments, and certainly the least enduring. Although his robust health continued he was less ready to tackle trouble than in his earlier years. Having become keenly interested in the growing movement for conservation of nature he was not unwilling to relinquish his thankless task at the commission under the post-war Churchill government, and at the age of seventy to move elsewhere.

Hurcomb had already taken a first step in April 1947 by becoming chairman of the committee of bird sanctuaries in the royal parks, and he took great pains to produce an authoritative annual report, and to ensure that the bailiff and each of his officers was fully advised of anything relevant to bird protection. In 1953 he joined the official Nature Conservancy, serving as chairman of its committee for England and in 1961–2 as chairman of its council. From 1954 to 1960 he was vice-president of the International Union for the Conservation of Nature and Natural Resources, and his disarming intervention with a vintage House of Lords speech at a moment of crisis helped to avert a threatened split in the union at its meeting in Poland in 1960. He was president of the Society for the Promotion of Nature Reserves in 1950–61, of the Field Studies Council from 1957, and of the Royal Society for the Protection of Birds in 1961–6. He was also active in several other naturalist and conservation bodies. Apart from his lifelong devotion to fishing, and his renewal in later life of an early interest in bird-watching, he was deeply read in the classics and in English literature and was fond of serious conversation. His tolerance and sense of humour were shown by his choice as supporters for his coat of arms of 'a heron proper gorged' on either side, upholding a branch of willow on which sat a kingfisher with wings elevated, with the motto 'Quoad potero perferam' ('For as long as I can bear').

Hurcomb's pallid complexion and worn appearance belied his toughness and stamina, just as his austere mien disguised his receptiveness as a listener and his great consideration for others. These, combined with his clarity of mind and tenacity of purpose, made him an outstanding negotiator. His manner was never ingratiating, but his arguments were fair and persuasive, winning respect if not always affection. Without being an expert on any subject he learned enough of a number to be taken seriously by experts, and to complement their expertise with his own wisdom.

Hurcomb was appointed CBE in 1918, CB in 1922, KBE in 1929, KCB in 1938, GCB in 1946, and he was created Baron Hurcomb in 1950. He also had many foreign decorations. In 1938 St John's College, Oxford, made him an honorary fellow. The barony became extinct upon Hurcomb's death at Horsham, Sussex, on 7 August 1975.

MAX NICHOLSON, rev.

Sources C. W. Hurcomb, MS autobiographical notes, priv. coll. · *The Times* (8 Aug 1975) · *The Times* (21 Aug 1975) · R. Harrod, *The prof: a personal memoir of Lord Cherwell* (1959) · personal knowledge (1986) · private information (1986, 2004) · *CGPLA Eng. & Wales* (1975)
Likenesses W. Stoneman, three photographs, 1930–47, NPG
Wealth at death £45,521: probate, 25 Sept 1975, *CGPLA Eng. & Wales*

Hurd, Dorothy Iona. *See* Campbell, Dorothy Iona (1883–1945).

Hurd, Richard (1720–1808), bishop of Worcester, was born on 13 January 1720 at Congreve, in the parish of Penkridge, Staffordshire, the second of the three children of John Hurd (1685–1755), a yeoman farmer, and his wife, Hannah (c.1685–1773). He was educated at a 'good Grammar school at Brewood' ('Dates of some occurrences') by Mr Hillman and then by William Budworth. On 3 October 1733 he was admitted to Emmanuel College, Cambridge, but he did not go up to the university until 1735, when he matriculated; he was admitted BA in February 1739 and MA in July 1742. In June 1742 he had been ordained deacon by Bishop Joseph Butler on the title of the curacy of Reymerston, Norfolk, obtained for him through the influence of his early patron, the collector Cox Macro. But in December he returned to Emmanuel, having been elected to a fellowship, and he remained there for the next fourteen years, during which time he was moderately active in college and in university politics. While there he also forged a number of friendships that were to endure for, and colour, the rest of his life. Two of these, with William Mason and Thomas Gray, suggest the interest in literary and critical matters that particularly occupied Hurd at this time and in which he was to establish his intellectual reputation.

In 1749 Hurd published an edition of Horace's *Ars poetica* modelled on William Warburton's editing of Pope's *Dunciad*. His acknowledgement of Warburton's influence initiated a correspondence and close friendship—revealed

Richard Hurd (1720–1808), by Thomas Gainsborough, exh. RA 1781

most clearly in Hurd's defence of Warburton, *On the Delicacy of Friendship* (1755)—which lasted until the latter's death in 1779. The *Ars poetica* was followed in 1751 by an edition of Horace's *Epistola ad Augustum*; these two texts eventually went through five editions. Hurd's major literary works, however, all appeared between 1759 and 1764. First came a series of imaginary conversations, the popular *Moral and Political Dialogues* (1759), followed in 1764 by another set, *The Uses of Foreign Travel*. Between these he produced his most influential critical work, *Letters on Chivalry and Romance* (1762), which was an immediate success. This was significant not least for its appreciation of 'Gothic Romance' (R. Hurd, *Works*, 4.329) and consequently its role in stimulating a revival of interest in medieval and Renaissance English literature. But the main drive of the *Letters* was its affirmation of the power of the imagination, and the justification of the realms into which it can lead us.

Literary interests, however, did not inhibit the development of Hurd's clerical career. He had been ordained priest in 1744, and in 1750, thanks to Warburton's recommendation, he was appointed to a Whitehall preachership, an institution designed to encourage promising young clergy from the universities. He also revealed a taste for religious controversy. His first work, published in 1746, had been a reply to William Weston's *Enquiry into the Rejection of the Christian Miracles*. Then, in 1757, in collaboration with Warburton, he produced *Remarks on Mr David Hume's Essay on the Natural History of Religion*: this was written primarily by Warburton but with additions by Hurd. In the previous year he had been nominated to the college living of Thurcaston, in Leicestershire. This took Hurd away from the scholarly atmosphere of Cambridge to a rural 'retirement' (*Early Letters*, 328), the solitude of which allowed him to devote himself to his studies. Four years later, in 1760, Warburton appointed him his chaplain, and then, in 1765, he was appointed preacher at Lincoln's Inn. The acquisition of this London pulpit does not appear to have spurred his ambition. In 1769 he wrote to Thomas Balguy in mild admonition of what appear to have been the grumblings of thwarted ambition: 'are there no objects of desire ... but deaneries or bishoprics?' (Kilvert, 106). None the less the appointment to the preachership marks a decisive point in Hurd's life: he all but abandoned his critical writing and committed himself to a career in the church.

As preacher at Lincoln's Inn, Hurd soon attracted favourable attention. He had chambers where he could entertain such literary friends as Thomas Warton. Preferment soon followed: in 1767 he was made archdeacon of Gloucester and rector of Dursley, in that diocese. In the following year the degree of DD was conferred on him by Cambridge University and he was appointed the first of the Warburtonian lecturers, whose brief was 'for the illustration of the argument in favour of Christianity derived from prophecy' (Kilvert, 101). His twelve sermons were preached in the chapel of Lincoln's Inn, drew large audiences, and in 1772 were published as *An Introduction to the Study of the Prophecies Concerning the Christian Church, and in Particular Concerning the Church of Rome*. A fifth edition appeared in 1788. This work provoked a private—and friendly—debate with Edward Gibbon over the authenticity of the book of Daniel; Hurd's letter to Gibbon on this subject (29 August 1772) was published in the latter's *Miscellaneous Works* in 1796. In fact in common with many clergymen Hurd disapproved of Gibbon's *History of the Decline and Fall of the Roman Empire*, describing the third volume in particular as 'polluted everywhere by the most immoral as well as irreligious insinuations' (to Balguy, 7 July 1788; Kilvert, 166).

In 1774, through the influence of Lord Mansfield and with the warm approval of George III, Hurd was nominated in succession to the prime minister's half-brother Brownlow North to the bishopric of Coventry and Lichfield; he was consecrated on 12 February 1775. He described Lichfield as 'on all accounts an eligible see, the value about eighteen hundred pounds a year' (Kilvert, 123). In the House of Lords he was a loyal supporter of Lord North's administration, dismissing opposition as factious and malignant. He was strongly critical of the American rebels and when preaching the fast sermon before the Lords on 13 December 1776 described the colonial revolt as a divine punishment for British sin. His courtier-like qualities led to his appointment in June 1776 as preceptor to George, prince of Wales, and to Prince Frederick, while his theological orthodoxy appealed to the king, with whom he developed a warm personal friendship. Although he had expressed some private sympathy with the Feathers tavern petitioners in 1772 he privately expressed vehement distaste for the Dissenters Relief Bill of 1779, which substituted a simple declaration of belief in the scriptures for subscription to the Thirty-Nine Articles. While accepting that 'Nobody ... ought to be punished for religious opinions' he complained that the dissenters operated on the 'horrid principle' of the independence of the civil power and the separation of church and state (ibid., 134–5).

It was apparent that Hurd was destined for higher ecclesiastical preferment, and in 1781 the elevation of Brownlow North to Winchester led to Hurd's succeeding him a second time. He was George III's personal choice as bishop of Worcester, a situation in which he remained for the rest of his life. He discharged his episcopal functions dutifully, holding visitations in person in 1782, 1785, 1790, 1796, and 1800 and carrying out regular confirmations and ordinations. He recognized the economic necessity that lay behind the extensive pluralism in his diocese. At the bishop's residence, Hartlebury Castle, near Stourport, he greatly extended the library, added to it Warburton's books (which he had purchased on the latter's death in 1779), and in 1805 enhanced it further with a gift of books from George III. He did not abandon his literary interests, and maintained a lively correspondence with Thomas Warton and William Mason. He had edited Abraham Cowley's works in 1772, and a six-volume edition of the works of Joseph Addison, based on manuscripts compiled by Hurd, was published in 1811.

In May 1783 George III entreated Hurd to succeed Frederick Cornwallis as archbishop of Canterbury. He declined the offer as 'not suited to his temper and talents' and excessively onerous; he considered the episode as an 'escape' (Kilvert, 146). Dr Johnson is reported to have observed 'I am glad he did not go to Lambeth; for, after all, I fear he is a Whig in his heart' (Boswell, *Life*, 4.190). He voted against the Fox–North coalition's India Bill in both closely contested Lords divisions, on 15 and 17 December 1783, thus helping to precipitate the coalition's dismissal by the king. The cordiality of his relations with George III is evident in the king's published correspondence, and was marked by a royal visit to Hartlebury on 2 August 1788, followed by the royal family's stay at the palace in Worcester from 5 to 9 August. Hurd loyally attended the Lords to support William Pitt's ministry over the Regency Bill in the winter of 1788–9. He was predictably hostile to the French Revolution and deplored the attitude taken by the Foxite opposition. At the time of the renewal of war with France in 1803 the king proposed, in the event of invasion, to retire with his family to Hartlebury Castle.

Although several of Hurd's sermons were printed and his charges survive in manuscript he did not produce a great deal of original theological work. In 1788 he published an edition of Warburton's works, in seven volumes, with a flattering biographical account of their author. His correspondence with Warburton, *Letters from an Eminent Prelate to One of his Friends*, appeared in 1808. He showed himself a true disciple of the author of *The Alliance between Church and State* when he affirmed to George III in 1801 'Toleration should be allowed to those who dissent from an Establishment & ... such Establishments should be guarded by a Test Law' (*Later Correspondence of George III,*

3.501). He was no friend to Catholic emancipation. In later life he was badly afflicted by gout and he frequently complained of weakness and infirmity. In his visitations of 1803 and 1806 he needed the assistance of the archdeacon and chancellor of the diocese, while in 1803 he admitted that he did not enforce the regulations governing non-residence. He died at Hartlebury Castle, apparently of a bronchial disorder (Kilvert, 190) that had been aggravated by 'frequent attacks of gout and dizziness', on 28 May 1808, and was buried in Hartlebury churchyard on 10 June. He had never married. In a codicil to his will he bequeathed £2000 to Emmanuel College. An edition of his works, in eight volumes, was published in 1811.

Hurd was 'below the middle height, of slight make, but well proportioned' (Kilvert, 194). According to his obituary in the *Gentleman's Magazine* he possessed 'a kind of veneration which in times like the present, could neither be acquired nor preserved but by the exercise of great virtue' (*GM*, 563). Fanny Burney described his manner as 'dignified, placid, grave and mild, but cold, and rather distancing' (*Diary and Letters*, 2.260). In private conversation he was urbane, good-humoured, and fond of witty gossip. Though increasingly unsympathetic to dissent in either its rationalistic or enthusiastic forms he was not a high-churchman. His commonplace book contains a carefully worded critique of Archbishop Laud. He regarded the Church of England as the classic *via media* between Catholic authoritarianism and dissenting libertarianism. By the meritorious nature of his promotion, as well as by his learning and conscientiousness, he represented an important element within the eighteenth-century Anglican tradition.   G. M. DITCHFIELD and SARAH BREWER

Sources *The early letters of Bishop Richard Hurd, 1739–1762*, ed. S. Brewer (1995) · F. Kilvert, *Memoirs of the life and writings of the Right Rev. Richard Hurd* (1860) · Venn, *Alum. Cant.*, 1/2 · *GM*, 1st ser., 78 (1808) · *Fasti Angl., 1541–1857*, [Ely] · *Fasti Angl., 1541–1857*, [Bristol] · *The correspondence of King George the Third from 1760 to December 1783*, ed. J. Fortescue, 6 vols. (1927–8) · *The later correspondence of George III*, ed. A. Aspinall, 5 vols. (1962–70) · M. Ransome, ed., *The state of the bishopric of Worcester, 1782–1808* (1968) · *The correspondence of Thomas Warton*, ed. D. Fairer (1995) · E. H. Pearce and L. Whibley, eds., *The correspondence of Richard Hurd and William Mason, and letters of Richard Hurd to Thomas Gray* (1932) · Nichols, *Lit. anecdotes* · Nichols, *Illustrations* · Boswell, *Life* · N. Sykes, *Church and state in England in the XVIII century* (1934) · [R. Hurd], 'Dates of some occurrences in my own life', MS, Hartlebury Castle, Worcestershire · D. Eddy, *A bibliography of Richard Hurd* (1999) · A. W. Evans, *Warburton and the Warburtonians: a study in some eighteenth-century controversies* (1932) · *Diary and letters of Madame D'Arblay*, ed. C. Barrett, 4 vols. (1893)
Archives Emmanuel College, Cambridge, records and MSS · Hartlebury Castle, Worcestershire, corresp. and MSS · Worcs. RO, corresp. and MSS | BL, corresp. with C. Macro, Add. MSS 32556–32557 · BL, letters to W. Warburton and his wife, MS Egerton 1958 · BL, letters to T. Warton, Add. MS 42560–42561 · BL, letters to C. Yorke, Add. MSS 35635–35639 · NL Scot., letters to Lord Hailes · NL Wales, letters to J. Potter · Royal Arch., letters to George III · Staffs. RO, letters to E. Littleton · Yale U., Beinecke L., letters to T. Balguy
Likenesses W. Hoare, 1764, Hartlebury Castle, Worcestershire · engraving, *c.*1776 · I. Gosset, wax medallion, 1778, Hartlebury Castle, Worcestershire · T. Gainsborough, oils, exh. RA 1781, Royal Collection [*see illus.*] · J. Barry, group portrait, oils, *c.*1783 (*The distribution of premiums in the Society of Arts*), RSA · engraving, pubd 1783 (after painting formerly at the Queen's Palace, 1783) · T. Gainsborough, oils, *c.*1788, Emmanuel College, Cambridge · engraving, pubd 1801 (as Bishop of Worcester) · J. Neagle, engraving, pubd 1808 (as Bishop of Worcester; after wax model by I. Gosset, 1788) · J. Hall, engraving, pubd 1811 (after T. Gainsborough)
Wealth at death under £35,000: IR 27/136, fol. 267v; will, PRO, PROB 11/1481, fols. 449v–450v

Hurd, Thomas Hannaford (*bap.* 1747, *d.* 1823), naval officer and hydrographer, was born in Plymouth and baptized on 30 January 1747 at the town's St Andrew's Church, the son of Edward and Jane Hurd. He joined the navy on 1 September 1768 as an able seaman in the *Cornwall* (Captain Molyneux Shuldham). Between 1771 and 1774, while serving on the Newfoundland and North American stations, he took part in hydrographic surveys under Samuel Holland in the armed vessel *Canceaux* (Lieutenant Henry Mowat). Hurd passed for lieutenant on 1 March 1775 and on 30 January 1777 he was appointed first lieutenant of the *Unicorn* by Lord Howe, in whose flagship the *Eagle* he was serving at the time. The *Unicorn*, a copper-bottomed ship under the command of Captain John Ford, cruised with remarkable success against the enemy's privateers and merchant ships, and on her return to England was one of the small squadron engaged under Sir James Wallace in the capture of the *Danaé* and the destruction of two other French frigates in Cancale Bay on the north coast of France on 13 May 1779.

In the battle of the Saints off Dominica, on 12 April 1782, Hurd was second lieutenant of the *Hercules* (Captain Savage) in command of the main-deck guns. After the battle he was appointed first lieutenant of one of the prizes, the *Ardent* (64 guns; Captain Lucas) for the voyage to England during which the ill-fated convoy suffered dreadfully in the hurricane of 17 September 1782. In 1785, on the recommendation of Lord Howe, Hurd was appointed surveyor-general of Cape Breton, but he was dismissed the following year by J. F. W. Des Barres, the province's lieutenant-governor.

In 1789 Hurd was sent by the Admiralty to carry out a detailed hydrographic survey of Bermuda, which took nine years to complete. His survey resulted in the founding of the navy's Bermuda base. He may have married his wife, Elizabeth, during this period. On his return to England in 1798 Hurd spent the next three years in the hydrographic office laying down and compiling his survey of the islands. He was promoted commander on 18 August 1795 and captain on 29 April 1802. Between 1804 and 1806 Hurd carried out a detailed survey of the approaches to Brest during William Cornwallis's blockade of the port, the results of which were published in two charts and sailing directions. Simultaneously he carried out a detailed survey of Falmouth harbour and its approaches, which was also published.

In November 1807 Hurd was appointed to a committee to advise Alexander Dalrymple, hydrographer to the Admiralty, on the selection of charts for issue to the navy. In May 1808 Hurd was appointed to the post of hydrographer in succession to Dalrymple. During his appointment there was a significant increase in the number of charts engraved and issued to the navy. He was also able to organize a regular system of surveys under his control by specialist naval officers in command of ships specially allocated for their use. In 1821 he persuaded the Admiralty to place Admiralty charts on sale to the public so that they could be used by ships of the mercantile marine.

At the time of his death, probably in London, on 29 April 1823 Hurd was also superintendent of chronometers and a commissioner for the discovery of longitude. He was survived by his wife.   ANDREW C. F. DAVID

Sources DNB · 1817 survey of officer's service, PRO, ADM MS 9/2, 202 · G. S. Ritchie, *The Admiralty chart: British naval hydrography in the nineteenth century*, new edn (1995) · L. S. Dawson, *Memoirs of hydrography*, 2 vols. (1885) · S. Fisher, 'Captain Thomas Hurd's survey of the Bay of Brest during the blockade in the Napoleonic wars', *Mariner's Mirror*, 79 (1993), 293–304 · G. N. D. Evans, *Uncommon obdurate: the several public careers of J. F. W. Des Barres* (1969) · GM, 1st ser., 93/1 (1823), 475 · muster list of the *Cornwall*, ADM 36/8517 · baptism register, St Andrew's Church, Plymouth · will, PRO, PROB 11/1670
Archives Hydrographic Office, Taunton, MSS surveys, and survey notebook | NMM, chart of Hurd's achievement off Brest · PRO, ADM MS 9/2, 202
Likenesses portrait, repro. in A. Day, *The Admiralty Hydrographic Service 1795–1919* (1967)
Wealth at death plantations in West Indies and North America: will, PRO, PROB 11/1670

Hurdis, James (*bap.* 1763, *d.* 1801), Church of England clergyman and poet, was baptized on 27 April 1763 at Bishopstone near Seaford in Sussex, the only son of James Hurdis (1710–1769), collector of customs at Newhaven, and his second wife, Jane, *née* Artlett (*bap.* 1732, *d.* 1815). His father's estate at Little Halland was small, and on his death his first wife's brother the Lewes barrister Henry Humphrey settled an annuity of £40 on James. His uncle Dr Thomas Hurdis was a canon of Chichester and James lived with him between 1770 and 1780 when attending the city's prebendal school. A frail and studious child, James gave most of his spare time to writing poetry; only music, according to his sister, could induce him to leave his books.

In June 1780 Hurdis went up to St Mary Hall, Oxford, where he was a contemporary of Daniel Lysons, with whom he remained friendly. Two years later Hurdis was elected a demy of Magdalen College, of which his tutor Dr John Rathbone was chaplain. While at Oxford he remained part of the Chichester household of Dr Hurdis, who contributed to his education, and his migration to Magdalen was eased by a payment of £60 from Steere's exhibition, a Lewes charity. At the beginning of every vacation Hurdis would return to Bishopstone to visit his mother and continue the education of his sisters.

In March 1784 Hurdis left Oxford for Stanmer House near Brighton, to prepare George Pelham, who had renounced a commission in the guards for a career in the church, for entry to Cambridge. On 30 November 1785 Hurdis was ordained deacon, and in 1786 became curate at Burwash, a Pelham living enjoyed by John Courtail, the archdeacon of Lewes and canon of Chichester (Hurdis's grandfather and uncle had also both owed preferment to the Pelhams). A year later he brought three of his five sisters to live with him in a house to the north of the village.

This, probably the happiest time of his life, was recorded in *The Village Curate*, a poem in blank verse published anonymously in 1788 and very favourably noticed in the *Monthly Review*. As well as a blissful evocation of the wealden landscape, this conveys the simple pleasures of Hurdis's 'little Paradise'. These included reading and music (he played several instruments and had built an organ while at school). The poem also records and celebrates the duties that come with ordination, denouncing the indolence of 'pampered Priests'. In the same year Hurdis published an edition of Michael Drayton's *English Heroic Epistles*, with elementary notes probably based on his didactic experience with his sisters.

In his own work Hurdis consciously imitated the style of William Cowper, and saluted *The Task* in the opening lines of the *Curate*, of which a second edition appeared in 1790, pirated in Dublin the same year. Their publisher, Joseph Johnson, sent Cowper the manuscript of *Sir Thomas More*, a tragedy in which Hurdis had dramatized his sisters as More's daughters. Johnson's stratagem initiated a correspondence, and when *More* appeared in 1792 it was dedicated to Cowper. Hurdis in turn made extensive comments on Cowper's translation of Homer. His letters to his mentor were frank, self-revealing, and indiscreet. Hurdis attacked his rector's parsimony and selfishness, and satirized the corruption of his bishop. At the same time, he published a pamphlet deploring his limited Hebrew scholarship, an article censuring the fashion for immodest necklines, and an audacious but misguided attempt to challenge Malone's scholarship in a pamphlet entitled *Cursory Remarks* on the chronological order of Shakespeare's plays.

In February 1792, while visiting his publisher, Hurdis dined with Tom Paine, whose *Rights of Man* the apprehensive Johnson had delayed in the press. Paine's declaration that he could judge any poem by reading two lines did not endear him to Hurdis, who that night sent Cowper a vituperative narrative of his encounter, likening the radical's complexion to the coat of a Seville orange, with eyes of 'a strange ideotish obliquity' (*Letters*, 16). Hurdis preached against Paine at Bishopstone in a sermon on equality, published in 1794.

Hurdis's wealden idyll was terminated by the death of Catherine, his favourite sister, on 7 August 1792. The previous year he had been appointed to the living of his native village and, convinced that he could never again enter the house at Burwash, resigned his curacy and returned to his mother and sisters at Bishopstone. His long letter to Cowper describing Catherine's last days produced a pressing invitation to William Hayley's house at Eartham near Chichester, where Cowper, George Romney, and Charlotte Smith were guests. Hurdis's broken heart dominated his stay, and he left on a feigned excuse. At the end of September he wrote to the president of Magdalen, expressing his intention to return to Oxford and requesting help in recruiting pupils. Unable to find a suitable home, Hurdis spent a miserable winter in Sussex, composing the blank verse *Tears of Affection* (published 1794) in Catherine's memory.

On 31 January 1793 Hurdis became senior dean of arts at Magdalen and soon began to canvass support for the professorship of poetry, to which he was elected on 31 October. Cowper, who had aided his campaign, declared that none 'has more sincerely rejoiced in your success than I' (*Letters*, 34). The chair was worth £76, bringing Hurdis's annual income to over £300 from which, threatening his solvency, he supported his sisters at Temple Cowley, near Oxford, and his mother and a sister at Bishopstone. The suit of Dr Thomas Sheppard, the holder of the richest college living, to Hurdis's sister would have solved these problems; but at sixty-seven Sheppard was more than twice her age, and Hurdis 'decidedly opposed' the union as 'preposterous' (Whitaker, 46). Perhaps it was his failure to cultivate college friendships that caused Magdalen, which had supported his candidacy, to deny him further college offices, a unique occurrence in the 1790s. He nevertheless sprang to its defence, and to that of the university, when in 1796 Lord Sheffield's edition of Gibbon's posthumous memoirs attacked the Oxford of the 1750s. Sheffield's wife was Lucy Pelham, and Hurdis wished his *Vindication*, which was ready for the press by August 1796, to appear anonymously. No publisher was forthcoming, and in November Hurdis installed a printing press at Bishopstone and in three weeks had run off 500 copies. The splenetic work, full of personal abuse, was welcomed by the *Gentleman's Magazine* but pilloried, along with Hurdis's ode in honour of the duke of Portland, by the young W. S. Landor.

The appearance of the *Vindication* paradoxically coincided with a dispute with the governing body, which required Hurdis to apologize for a letter to the vice-president which had been seen as offensive. The episode still rankled a year later, when Hurdis pronounced 'the measures adopted to humiliate me' (Whitaker, 40) inconsistent with justice and humanity. Hurdis graduated doctor of divinity on 26 January 1797 but was to spend little time in college. He retreated to Little Halland, where he printed a fourth edition of the *Curate*, fascicules of his Oxford poetry lectures, and the text of his act sermon, stressing the importance of a knowledge of Hebrew for biblical study. But no advancement came his way, and as he wrote from Sussex at the end of the year, 'I must resign myself to chance and be content to *starve on*. It is the lot of every poet, and the peculiar endowment of my chair' (ibid., 47).

On 5 May 1798 Hurdis made a rare appearance at a college meeting to discuss participation in the Oxford Volunteers, evidence of his increasing preoccupation with the danger of treason and sedition; to the end of his life he sought 'to stay the contagion by engaging in continual combat with the most subtle advocates of anarchy and irreligion' (BL, Add. MS 33108, fols. 235–7). He began to write anonymously in the *Anti-Jacobin Review*, where his comments on Richard Polwhele's works appeared in 1799.

On 19 July 1799 Hurdis, who had admitted to Cowper that he loved 'to cast my eyes on the female part of the creation' (*Letters*, 9), married Harriet Taylor (1777–1855), the illegitimate daughter (she had passed as his ward) of Hughes Minet of Austin Friars and Fulham Lodge. They were accompanied on their honeymoon, to co. Durham and Scotland, by the poet's sister Elizabeth. Although the settlement, which provided an income of £525 a year and £80 for Harriet's own use, gave Hurdis financial security for the first time in his life, his wife seems rapidly to have become a source of irritation and pain to him and his family. It is clear that Harriet and her father sought to terminate Hurdis's dependence on his sisters, who in October 1801 were moved out of the house at Cowley into apartments in the grounds. By July 1801, conscious of a heart condition, Hurdis had drafted a will by which he attempted to make his family independent of his wife, and to commit the upbringing of his baby son to Elizabeth; although he repeatedly showed it to his sisters and referred them to Blackstone for its validity, he carried it with him, 'when only going to the next door to tea' (PRO, PROB 24/111), to keep it from his wife.

The Favourite Village, Hurdis's tender eulogy of his birthplace and the downland, was published from his own press in April 1800 with an elaborately double-edged dedication to Archdeacon Courtail; it is regarded as his best work, and extends to 210 pages. But with familiar irony, his letter sending a copy to Thomas Pelham also announced his decision to leave Bishopstone, where a long-running dispute with one of the churchwardens had culminated in a violent argument. He returned to Cowley where his eldest son, James Henry *Hurdis, was born on 5 June. Bishop Douglas of Salisbury had encouraged Hurdis's Hebrew studies and promised support for his attempt on the Oxford professorship, which came vacant in September 1801. But Pelham, to whom Hurdis had written of his anti-Jacobin warfare, received a damning reply from the prime minister, Henry Addington, who found himself unable 'to gratify the wishes of [Hurdis] as I am no stranger to his literary and personal character' (BL, Add. MS 33108, fol. 173).

The intensity of Hurdis's feelings, and his inability to control them, resulted in repeated strife with all but his mother and sisters, by whom alone he seems not to have felt threatened. Indeed, his behaviour in his final years seems to have verged on the deranged. But that same sensitivity produced an acute observer of his native county in both its aspects, weald and down, a tender feeling for nature, and a love of animals and his subordinate fellow man. In Sussex, Hurdis would free wheatears from shepherds' traps, substituting a penny for the disappointed captor; at Oxford, he declared that his lectures would 'not be obscured by quotation from any dead language' (*Hist. U. Oxf.* 5: *18th-cent. Oxf.*, 800) and so delivered them in English. Even at the university, the scholar had given place to the man of sensibility. Hurdis had grown up in a society of patronage and deference, and his poetry was a lyrical expression of that orderly world; by nature a conservative, he grew increasingly reactionary as men like Gibbon and Paine sought to shake its foundations. He described himself as having been a 'silent, shamefaced, hesitating boy' (*Letters*, 13), was never comfortable in company, and hated public debate.

Preferment came too late for Hurdis. On 17 November 1801 his former tutor Dr John Rathbone presented him to the living of Buckland in Berkshire. He was inducted a month later, and died suddenly at the vicarage on 23 December. His body was returned to Bishopstone and buried on 3 January 1802 in the parish church there under an epitaph by Hayley, in the vault which he had enlarged to accommodate his whole family on Catherine's death a decade before. Harriet Hurdis retreated to her father's house at Fulham, where in 1802 she gave birth to a posthumous daughter and established the validity of her husband's will by litigation in the prerogative court. In 1808, with the assistance of William Hayley, Hurdis's sisters published a selection of his work, prudently omitting the juvenilia, to which he had been particularly partial; dedicated to the queen, the three volumes bore the names of over twelve hundred subscribers.

CHRISTOPHER WHITTICK

Sources A. P. Whitaker, *James Hurdis: his life and writings* (1960) · *Letters of the Revd. James Hurdis, D.D., vicar of Bishopstone, Sussex, to William Cowper, 1791–1794*, ed. J. F. Tattersall [1927, reprinted from the *Sussex County Magazine*, 1926–7] · W. H. Challen, 'James Hurdis (1763–1801)', *Sussex Notes and Queries*, 15 (1963), 229–32 · PRO, PROB 11/1402; PROB 18/109 no 28, 18/110 no 21; PROB 24/111; PROB 31/941 no 275, 31/964 no 559 [case papers in *Hurdis v. Hurdis* in the prerogative court of Canterbury, 1802–1803] · E. Sussex RO, PAR 247/1/1/2, 1/5/1; QDS 1/3 · W. Sussex RO, Add. MS 2758 [copy of Hayley's epitaph and commentary by Hayley], Par 70/1/1/2 · M. A. Lower, 'James Hurdis, D. D. and Catherine Hurdis', *The Worthies of Sussex* (1865), 161–71 · Magd. Oxf., MS 480 · BL, Add. MS 33106, fols. 340, 365, 370; 33108, fols. 172–5, 107, 235–7; 33090, fol. 348 · N. Plumley and J. Lees, *The organs and organists of Chichester Cathedral* (1988) · A. C. Piper, 'Private presses in Sussex', *The Library*, 3rd ser., 5 (1914), 70–79 · J. Betjeman, *First and last loves* (1952) · *Hist. U. Oxf.* 5: *18th-cent. Oxf.* · T. W. Horsfield, *The history, antiquities and topography of the county of Sussex* (1835), 1.272
Likenesses J. Sharples, chalk drawing, 1784 · Teed, miniature, 1792, repro. in Whitaker, *James Hurdis*, frontispiece · J. Romney, engraving, pubd 1809 (after miniature by F. Nash) · J. H. Hurdis, engraving, 1842 (after J. Sharples), repro. in Whitaker, *James Hurdis*, following p. 16 · J. Goodyear, group portrait, engraving (after W. Harvey), repro. in *The life and works of William Cowper*, 7, ed. R. Southey (1836), frontispiece · T. Spink, portrait (after miniature by Teed, 1792), repro. in *Letters*, ed. Tattersall, frontispiece
Wealth at death annual income at death approaching £1000

Hurdis, James Henry (1800–1857), engraver, was born on 5 June 1800 at Temple Cowley near Oxford, the eldest child of the Revd James *Hurdis DD (bap. 1763, d. 1801), professor of poetry at Oxford University, and his wife, Harriet Taylor (1777–1855), the illegitimate daughter of Hughes Minet of Fulham and a Miss or Mrs Taylor, gentlewoman. Dr Hurdis died on 23 December 1801 and, noting in his will that James had been 'entirely nourished and brought up by the hand of his aunt Elizabeth, and is attached to her as a mother', charged him not to forget the kindness of his aunt 'and never to imagine that he has sufficiently repaid her for her maternal attentions' (PRO, PROB 11/1402). Dr Hurdis's widow gave birth to their posthumous daughter, Harriet, at her father's house in Fulham in August 1802, and subsequently married Storer Ready (1777–1857),

briefly an army surgeon, at St Bartholomew-the-Great, London, on 14 March 1805. Ready practised at Southampton, and under his aegis James and his brother John Lewis Hurdis (1801–1889), later controller of customs in Bermuda and a naturalist, attended King Edward VI School, Southampton, until 1816 when, following Ready's bankruptcy, the family took up residence at the Château Bagatelle near Abbeville, France. Despite opposition from some members of his family, Hurdis was apprenticed to the engraver Charles Heath, in whose company he made the acquaintance of George Cruikshank, much of whose humour he shared. He completed Cruikshank's engravings of the humorous title-page of editions of the *Universal Songster* in both 1826 and 1827, but thereafter seems to have restricted his artistic sense of humour to his private sketchbooks. He did not publish again for a number of years thereafter.

On 30 November 1826, from the home of his paternal aunts Elizabeth and Sarah in Southover near Lewes, Hurdis married Sarah's niece Eliza (1788–1841), daughter of William Hutton of Gate Burton in Lincolnshire. Hurdis acquired with his wife a small income from land, and they settled at Greenfield Cottage in Newick near Lewes where, after a long and painful illness, Eliza died of dropsy on 12 June 1841. On 8 November 1843 at Margate, Hurdis married Charlotte (1804–1870), the fifth daughter of Henry Jackson of Lewes, barrister; their daughter Harriet Charlotte (1847–1929) was born at Newick. Before their marriage her mother had committed Charlotte to an asylum, and her uncertain mental health involved Hurdis closely in the care and upbringing of their daughter. The marriage considerably augmented his income, and the year after their daughter's birth the family moved to Ketches House in the village, where Hurdis became the tenant of the antiquary William Henry Blaauw.

In 1833 Hurdis published engraved views of Beechlands in Newick, and in 1838 he produced and dedicated to the inhabitants a view of the banquet at Southover to celebrate the coronation. He engraved a number of portraits, including portraits of his father James Hurdis (1842) and his neighbours Thomas Partington (1841) and Sir George Shiffner (1844). With the encouragement of his friend Mark Anthony Lower, the antiquary, he engraved a picture of the looting of the *Nympha Americana*, wrecked at Birling Gap in 1747, depicting his grandfather James Hurdis (1710–1767), customs officer at Newhaven, as the central figure, attempting to restrain the pillagers. But by far his best-known work did not appear until 1853, an engraving of Frederick Colvin's imaginary scene of the burning of ten protestants at Lewes in 1557. The print was influential in Lower's creation of the cult of the Sussex Martyrs, and became a virtual icon in the dissenting homes of the county. Hurdis's sketchbooks reveal that his published output formed only a small proportion of his work, which seems to have been undertaken out of antiquarian interest or to oblige his friends. In Lower's words, 'he was not compelled to engage professionally in the drudgery of the burin' (Lower, *Worthies*, 170), and his resources enabled him to preside over an artistic milieu at

Newick which provided a creative refuge for his old friend George Cruikshank, and a fruitful source of instruction to such young local artists as E. W. J. Hopley.

In 1846 Hurdis and his wife became individual founder members, with Lower and Blaauw, of the Sussex Archaeological Society, whose *Collections* were frequently illustrated by his work. The following year he engraved a view by the stonemason John Latter Parsons of the chapel he had designed at Southover to house the remains of Countess Gundrada, the discovery of which by railway navvies had provoked the society's foundation. Late in the 1840s Hurdis began to experiment with photography, and became an accomplished portraitist in that medium.

In December 1852, in order to save money, James and Charlotte Hurdis left 'dull, unsocial Newick' (MS letter, E. Sussex RO, ADA box 953) and moved to a smaller house at Southampton, where James indulged his interests in yachting, shooting, and photography, and continued to provide engravings for Lower. Hurdis died of a fever on 30 November 1857 and was buried in the old cemetery, The Common, Southampton, on 7 December. Despite the paucity of his published work, Hurdis was regarded by his contemporaries as an amateur of the highest class, an artist of great originality and talent, and one of the greatest etchers of his time.   CHRISTOPHER WHITTICK

Sources MSS family papers, priv. coll. · A. P. Whitaker, *James Hurdis: his life and writings* (1960) · M. A. Lower, *The worthies of Sussex* (1865) · C. R. Russell, *A history of King Edward VI School [Southampton]* (1980), 298–300 · E. Sussex RO, PAR 247 (Bishopstone), 410 (Lewes, All Saints), 413 (Southover), and 428 (Newick); SHR 3048-3051; LT Newick; TD 42 · Canterbury Cathedral, archives, U3/140/1/19 · W. H. Godfrey, 'James Hurdis', *Sussex Notes and Queries*, 15 (1958–62), 229–33 · MSS, PRO, B 4/35; PROB 11/1402; HO 107/1643, fol. 189v · A. W. Hutton, *The Huttons of Gate Burton* (privately printed, 1898) · E. Sussex RO, PDA L52 · *Sussex Archaeological Collections*, 10 (1858), 89 · M. A. Lower, *Memorials of the town, parish, and cinque-port of Seaford* (1855) · *Sussex Agricultural Express* (15 May 1869) [obit. of E. W. J. Hopley] · E. Sussex RO, ADA box 953
Archives E. Sussex RO, original copper plate and first pull, with annotations, of subject's engraved portrait of George Shiffner, SHR 3048–3051
Likenesses self-portrait, photograph, priv. coll.
Wealth at death under £7000: probate, 13 Feb 1858, *CGPLA Eng. & Wales*

Hurlbatt, Ethel (1866–1934), college head, was born in Bickley, Bromley, Kent, on 1 July 1866, one of seven children of Charles Hurlbatt, mining engineer, and his wife, Sophia Margaret Smith. She was educated at Minshall House, Beckenham, and at a private school in Bromley. She studied modern history at Somerville College, Oxford, between 1888 and 1892, gaining a second in 1891. She stayed on in Oxford for another year as a student, during which time she also started work calendaring medieval charters and rolls for the Bodleian Library. Her BA and MA were conferred upon her by Trinity College, Dublin, in 1905, and she received an honorary MA from Oxford University in 1925.

In 1892 Ethel Hurlbatt became principal of Aberdare Hall, the residence for women students at Cardiff University College. During the next six years, as well as running Aberdare Hall, she was a member of the committee of the Training School of Cookery and Domestic Arts, Cardiff; she was a governor of Howell's School, Llandaff, and honorary secretary of the South Wales Association for Promoting the Education of Women in Wales.

Ethel Hurlbatt became principal of Bedford College, London, in 1898. She also taught economics at the college. During her period as principal, the college became one of the recognized schools of London University, and she became a member of the college council and all college committees. Her time at Bedford left her with many happy memories, but it took its toll on her health. Though in appearance robust, she suffered all her life from what her obituarist Susan Vaughan referred to as 'certain constitutional weaknesses, especially in the nervous system'. She was forced to take extended leave before resigning in 1906.

In 1907 Ethel Hurlbatt began work as warden of Royal Victoria College, the women's college in McGill University in Montreal, having travelled to Canada with the founder of the college, Lord Strathcona. She remained in this post until her retirement in 1929. As warden of the college she promoted the study of the French language, and the French government showed their gratitude for her services to education in Montreal during the First World War by appointing her *officier de l'instruction publique* in 1918. The Serbian government also acknowledged her war work by awarding her the cross of mercy. Illness continued to affect her work, and she was admitted to hospital in 1928. When she retired she was presented with $2000 which had been raised by the Alumnae Society of Royal Victoria College to fund the travels designed to restore her to good health. Her service to the college was further recognized in 1930 when she received an honorary LLD from McGill University. After her death the Alumnae Society paid tribute to her by establishing the Ethel Hurlbatt scholarship.

Ethel Hurlbatt's commitment to the higher education of women and to the place of women's colleges within universities was unwavering. She believed that women's colleges should make every effort to conserve their early records, and hence their history. She acknowledged that she had 'done something near' (Hurlbatt) to pioneering work in women's education; but Susan Vaughan noted that she did not generally hold radical political views, and was not a rebel, giving her allegiance to long-established institutions . During her retirement Ethel Hurlbatt travelled widely, and pursued her interest in sketching. She spent her last days in Tours in France, where she enrolled as a pupil at the Institute de Touraine. She was a tall, imposing figure whose presence commanded attention and respect among her students at Royal Victoria College. She suffered a series of heart attacks, complicated by influenza, in the year before she died. Ethel Hurlbatt died peacefully in her sleep at Tours on 22 March 1934. Her sister, **Kate Hurlbatt** (1865–1957), college head, was born on 24 March 1865. She attended Somerville College, Oxford, from 1884 to 1887 as a clothworkers' scholar, gaining a pass in the university examination for women in 1886. She undertook teacher training at Somerville for two terms, and went on to become a governess for several families, and assistant mistress at St John's College for Girls in St Leonards and at Wimbledon high school. She was lady superintendent of Queen Margaret Hall at Glasgow University from 1895 to 1897. In 1898 she succeeded her sister as principal of Aberdare Hall, a position she held until her retirement in 1934. Her contribution to the higher education of women in Wales was recognized when she was awarded an honorary MA from the University of Wales in 1933. Like her sister she remained unmarried. Kate Hurlbatt died at the General Hospital in Monmouth on 17 January 1957.

SOPHIE BADHAM

Sources S. Vaughan, 'Ethel Hurlbatt, LLD, warden of Royal Victoria College, 1907–1929', *The McGill News* (1934) · M. J. Tuke, *A history of Bedford College for Women, 1849–1937* (1939) · C. Dyhouse, *No distinction of sex? Women in British universities, 1870–1939* (1995) · b. cert. [Ethel Hurlbatt] · 'Hurlbatt, Kate', *Somerville College register* · E. Hurlbatt, speech given at McGill University, personal file, 1930, Royal Holloway College, Egham, Surrey, AR150/D113
Archives Royal Holloway College, Egham, Surrey, personal file, AR150/D113
Likenesses Forster Morley, portrait, 1906, Royal Holloway College, Egham, Surrey · photograph, repro. in Vaughan, 'Ethel Hurlbatt, LLD' · three photographs, Royal Holloway College, Egham, Surrey, personal file, AR150/D113
Wealth at death £1503 12s. 4d.—Kate Hurlbatt: probate, 6 March 1957, *CGPLA Eng. & Wales*

Hurlbatt, Kate (1865–1957). *See under* Hurlbatt, Ethel (1866–1934).

Hurleston, Richard (*bap.* 1746?, *d.* in or after 1780), painter, was possibly the Richard Hurleston who was baptized on 9 March 1746, at St Martin-in-the-Fields, Westminster, London, the son of William Hurleston, and his wife, Mary. His father lived in Carey Street, Lincoln's Inn Fields, London. Hurleston obtained in 1764 a premium from the Society of Arts, and on 3 November 1769 he entered the Royal Academy Schools. He principally painted portraits, and exhibited a few at the Royal Academy. In 1773 he accompanied his intimate friend Joseph Wright ARA, of Derby, and John Downman to Italy, arriving in Rome in February 1774. He made copies in the Uffizi Gallery, Florence, in 1775 and 1776, and was again in Rome in November 1776. He returned to England about 1780. In that year he exhibited *Maria*, a picture from Lawrence Sterne's *Sentimental Journey*, which was engraved in mezzotint by W. Pether, and painted a portrait of Edward Easton, mayor of Salisbury, which was engraved in mezzotint by J. Dean. Shortly afterwards he was killed by lightning while riding over Salisbury Plain during a storm. He was great-uncle to the painter Frederick Yeates Hurlstone.

L. H. CUST, rev. J. DESMARAIS

Sources Redgrave, *Artists* · W. Bemrose, *The life of Joseph Wright of Derby* (1885) · J. C. Smith, *British mezzotinto portraits*, 4 (1882–4) · *The exhibition of the Royal Academy* (1771–80) [exhibition catalogues] · Bryan, *Painters* (1886–9) · Graves, *RA exhibitors* · J. Ingamells, ed., *A dictionary of British and Irish travellers in Italy, 1701–1800* (1997) · *Checklist of British artists in the Witt Library*, Courtauld Institute, Witt Library (1991) · S. C. Hutchison, 'The Royal Academy Schools, 1768–1830', *Walpole Society*, 38 (1960–62), 123–91, esp. 134 · *IGI*

Hurlestone, Randall (1525/6–1587?), religious writer, was one of seven children of Richard Hurlston of Picton, Cheshire, and Elizabeth, daughter of James Shawcrosse of Manchester. The records of Hurlestone's education, and indeed of his entire career, are obscured by some uncertainty, in no small degree because of the many variant spellings of his name. Both Venn and Sterry claim that he is the Ralph Hurleton who attended Eton College between approximately 1539 and 1543, and who was admitted to King's College, Cambridge, on 12 August 1543, aged seventeen, and left without a degree, despite having been made a fellow, in 1546–7.

About 1550 Hurlestone published *Newes from Rome concerning the blasphemous sacrifice of the papisticall masse with dyvers other treatises very godlye and profitable*, a pamphlet containing four dialogues which he claimed to have translated. The first dialogue, writes Hurlestone:

> teacheth playnly that the papisticall Masse is no sacrifice, but rather a blasphemie of Christes passion invented by man. The next techeth how God must be worshypped aryght. The third how sayntes ought to be worshypped. The last what is Christian lybertie.

The introductory matter also attacks popish practices. In a preface to Thomas Howard, Hurlestone berates the 'beggerly ceremonies fetched out of the bottome of hell'. He writes that he has published the pamphlet, so that 'your hole posteritie may knowe what religion your lordshyp followed: forsakynge throughly the Romisshe ydoll, with al his toyes and invencions contrary to gods holy worde'. In a subsequent letter to the reader, Hurlestone calls for Christian teaching to be grounded in the reading of the scripture; he also attacks Catholic teaching, ceremony, and icons, in particular the assumption that the Catholic mass is 'a ful sacrifice *ex opere operato*'.

In 1551 Hurlestone appears to have been in the employment of Lord Dacre: his name is appended to an order for certain items of clothing for Lord Dacre (BL, Add. MS 5751A, fol. 55). One Ranulph or Randulph Hurleston, who is said to come from Picton and who may very well be the same as the Randall Hurlestone above, was admitted to the Inner Temple in November 1553. He was called to the bench in 1569, and made reader in 1572 and treasurer in 1582. He appears frequently in the Inner Temple records until 1587, when he appears to have died. He had no children, but his nephew, John Hurlestone, also applied for admission to the Inner Temple.

CHRISTOPHER BURLINSON

Sources F. A. Inderwick and R. A. Roberts, eds., *A calendar of the Inner Temple records*, 1 (1896) · G. J. Armytage and J. P. Rylands, eds., *Pedigrees made at the visitation of Cheshire, 1613* (1909) · *The visitation of Cheshire in the year 1580, made by Robert Glover, Somerset herald*, ed. J. P. Rylands, Harleian Society, 18 (1882) · Venn, *Alum. Cant.* · W. Sterry, ed., *The Eton College register, 1441–1698* (1943) · *STC, 1475–1640* · *CSP dom., 1547–80*

Hurley, James Francis [Frank] (1885–1962), photographer and film producer, was born on 15 October 1885 in Glebe, Sydney, Australia, the third in the family of three sons and two daughters of Edward Harrison Hurley, a typesetter at the *Sydney Morning Herald* and a trade union official, and his wife, Margaret Agnes Bouffier, from a family of wine growers from Alsace Lorraine. At thirteen he ran away

James Francis Hurley (1885–1962), self-portrait, 1929–31

from home and found work as a fitter's handyman in R. W. Sandford's ironworks in Lithgow, where he spent two years before being transferred to work on a ship in the Sydney docks. He remained in Sydney, taking evening classes in engineering, and became a partner in a picture-postcard business in 1905.

When Douglas Mawson advertised for an official photographer to accompany the Australasian Antarctic Expedition in 1911 Hurley applied, and was accepted. On the *Aurora*, the expedition reached Cape Denison, in Commonwealth Bay, and set up a base from which to make sledging journeys during the Antarctic summer. Despite ferocious winds Hurley managed to take a series of dramatic photographs, including 'In the Blizzard'—a shot of two men trying to cut ice from a glacier—and a panorama colour photograph of the foreshore of Commonwealth Bay, featuring penguins and sea elephants. He was one of the party of three that made an eight-week sledging expedition to the interior in November 1912 to make magnetic observations at the south magnetic pole. In the face of continuous blizzards and sub-zero temperatures, and suffering from snow-blindness and frostbite, he always remained cheerful: 'he was an ideal mate for such a trip. His fertile brain and imagination made a comedy of the most desperate situation' (Laseron, 199). An imaginative cook, his *tour de force* was the 'plum pudding' that he concocted for Christmas dinner on the way back from the south pole, when rations were running low, by grating three biscuits with a saw, adding sugar and seven raisins flavoured with methylated spirits, mixing them with

snow, and boiling them in an old sock over the primus stove. On his return to Australia in 1913 he put together his ciné film of the expedition, *Home of the Blizzard*.

It was the success of this film that led Sir Ernest Shackleton to invite Hurley in 1914 to join his Antarctic expedition, during which he hoped to cross the south polar continent on foot. Hurley made a photographic record of life on board the *Endurance*, the beauty of the Antarctic scenery, and the hardships suffered by the party after the destruction of the ship in the ice; these included a five-month drift on ice floes until they were able to launch the lifeboats and reach Elephant Island, where they waited while Shackleton took one of the boats to South Georgia to get help. The photographs show scenes of dogs being exercised on the ice, the crew playing soccer on the ice floe, seals being skinned to extract the blubber to fuel the stove that Hurley had created out of materials salvaged from the wreck, and the *Endurance* covered with rime on a moonlit night; he thought the ship was at its most beautiful 'when the bright moonlight etched her inky silhouette, or transformed her into a vessel from fairyland' (Hurley, 158–9). He also filmed the *Endurance* as it was forced out of the ice and crushed by moving slabs of ice, and the masts crashing down before the ship eventually sank. Although Shackleton had made Hurley leave his glass negatives on board when they abandoned ship, he went back in before the ship broke up, and 'bared from head to waist probed in the mushy ice' to retrieve them, only to be forced to select what could be stored in one tin; he was able to save only 150 out of more than 500, and smashed the remaining negatives lest he should change his mind. After his return he made a special expedition to South Georgia to take pictures for his book and to finish shooting the film of the voyage, *In the Grip of the Polar Ice*. He also printed his still photographs, often using 'combination printing' to enhance their effect; these were montages made by superimposing several negatives to combine into one picture. He published his account of the expedition, *Argonauts of the South*, in 1925 and rewrote it as a children's book, *Shackleton's Argonauts* (1948).

In 1917 Hurley was appointed official war photographer to the Australian Imperial Force and given the honorary rank of captain, a title that he continued to use for the rest of his life. He covered the third battle of Ypres, and his colour slides are among the very few colour photographs of the First World War. Still making composite pictures, he superimposed clouds, exploding shells, and fighter aircraft onto the original images to increase the drama of the battle scenes, as in his most famous photograph of the war in France, 'Over the Top'. In December 1917 he was sent to Cairo to cover the participation of General Chauvel's light horse in Allenby's drive on Jerusalem, and turned the film that he shot into *With the Australians in Palestine*. In Cairo, in April 1918, he married Antoinette Thierault, an opera singer, daughter of a French army officer and his Spanish wife, of Alexandria, whom he had met ten days earlier; they had three daughters and one son.

Having returned to Sydney, Hurley was asked by the

Anglican missions to make a film about their work in New Guinea. The success of *Pearls and Savages* (later retitled *The Lost Tribe*), completed in 1921, led to tours of the United States in 1923 and England in 1924, during which he gave live commentaries during showings of the silent film; he also published *Pearls and Savages* as a book, in 1924. The Stoll Film Company financed his two feature films, *The Jungle Woman* and *Hound of the Deep*, which was filmed in New Guinea and released in 1926 to great acclaim.

After a year working as pictorial editor of *The Sun* in Sydney, in 1929 Hurley joined the British Australian and New Zealand Antarctic Research Expedition (BANZARE), led by Sir Douglas Mawson, which was aiming to continue the exploration of the Antarctic region to the south of Australia and claim more territory for the British crown. Hurley was on both voyages of the *Discovery*, in 1929–30 and 1930–31. On the second cruise he was able to make a filming trip in a whaling cruiser while the *Discovery* was taking on coal, and also shot a film sequence of Mawson on a reconnaissance flight in bad weather. He made two films of these expeditions: *Southward Ho! with Mawson* (1930) and his first film with a soundtrack, *Siege of the South* (1931), 'in story, sound and song', billed as 'An Epic of Man's Glorious Struggle with Nature in the Frozen South'.

After the success of these films Cinesound, in Sydney, appointed Hurley chief cameraman, and for the next eight years he wrote, filmed, and produced documentaries, as well as several feature films, including *Lovers and Luggers* (1937), which included underwater photography. His first documentary for Cinesound was *Jewel of the Pacific* (1931), about the inhabitants of Lord Howe Island; others included *Symphony in Steel* (1932), about the building of the Sydney harbour bridge (reviewers said he must have clung to every girder to get some of his shots); *Pageant of Power* and *Brown Coal to Briquettes*, both produced in 1935 for the state electricity commission of Victoria; *Oasis* and *Here is Paradise*, tourist films for the South Australian government, made in 1936; and *A Nation is Built* (1938), commissioned by the Australian government as part of the 150th anniversary celebrations.

In 1941, following the outbreak of the Second World War, Hurley was put in charge of the Australian Broadcasting Commission's photographic unit in the Middle East; he spent three years with the Australian forces there, making two-reel films to be shown on newsreels. *Advance into Libya* (1941) was the first film of the fighting in the western desert to be shown in Australia, and *The Siege of Tobruk* (1941) was shown all over the world. He was awarded the OBE in 1941. In 1943 the British Ministry of Information appointed him director of British army features and propaganda films; he travelled over 250,000 miles in the Middle East during the next three years, filming contributions for British newsreels and making documentary films, including *The Holy Land*, a history of Palestine under the British mandate.

Hurley returned to Australia in 1946, after six years in the Middle East, and embarked on a project to photograph its different regions; he produced a series of lavishly illustrated photographic books between 1949 and 1956, of which *Australia* (1955) ran to four editions. As he grew older he lost his joviality and became less sociable. Restless and tireless, he lived for photography and spent more time away from home than he did with his wife and family. He died on 16 January 1962 at his home, Stonehenge, Edgecliffe Boulevarde, Collaroy Plateau, Sydney. His wife survived him. ANNE PIMLOTT BAKER

Sources F. Legg and T. Hurley, *Once more on my adventure* (1966) · L. Bickel, *In search of Frank Hurley* (1980) · E. Shackleton, *South: the story of Shackleton's last expedition, 1914–17*, ed. P. King (1991) · F. Hurley, *Argonauts of the south* (1925) · H. Fletcher, *Antarctic days with Mawson: a personal account of the British, Australian and New Zealand Antarctic Research Expedition of 1929–31* (1984) · D. Mawson, *Home of the blizzard: being the story of the Australasian Antarctic expedition, 1911–1914*, 2 vols. [1915] · *Mawson's Antarctic diaries*, ed. F. Jacka and E. Jacka (1988) · R. Huntford, *Shackleton* (1985) · P. Ayres, *Mawson* (1999) · C. Alexander, *The Endurance* (1998) · C. F. Laseron, *South with Mawson: reminiscences of the Australasian Antarctic Expedition, 1911–1914* (1947) · WW

Archives Scott Polar RI, Cambridge, photograph collection | RGS, negative plates

Likenesses photograph, 1911–13, repro. in Mawson, *Home of the blizzard*, 62–3 · photograph, 1914–16, Scott Polar RI; repro. in Shackleton, *South*, 123 · photograph, 1914–16, repro. in Hurley, *Argonauts of the south*, facing p. 8 · self-portrait, photograph, 1929–31; Christies, 21 Sept 2000, lot 121 [*see illus.*] · photograph (during first Banzare voyage), repro. in Jacka and Jacka, eds., *Mawson's Antarctic diaries*, 348

Hurley, William (*d.* 1354), master carpenter, is first recorded *c.*1315 in the exchequer plea rolls, among a list of London craftsmen acting as 'sureties' on behalf of imprisoned masons employed at the king's manor of Eltham, Kent. Although no works can be associated with Hurley before 1322/3, his status and income must already have been substantial for him to act as a financial guarantor in 1315. In 1322/3 Hurley's name appears in the royal accounts for works at the Tower of London and at Westminster Palace, where between 1323 and 1325 he was employed upon St Stephen's Chapel. Thereafter it is possible to trace Hurley's career as a designer and overseer of major carpentry structures undertaken for royal, noble, urban, and ecclesiastical patrons; his achievements made him a typical member of a high-status artisan class which was closely associated with court culture and aristocratic households and allow him a place in the first rank of English craftsmen of the fourteenth century.

As master carpenter at Westminster, Hurley's tasks at the palace chapel included the erection of scaffolding and work tables, designing the roof, the complex timber vault, and later (in 1351) the choir stalls. As was customary, the structural carpentry was prefabricated, all timbers marked, and the whole stored until the time of assembly. However, political circumstances in Edward II's reign and the resulting hiatus of works at St Stephen's Chapel delayed the erection of Hurley's ornate vault and roof until 1345–8, some twenty years after their original fabrication. In the meantime, Hurley undertook carpentry works for Edward II's favourite, Hugh Despenser the younger, at Caerphilly Castle, where he may well have designed the great hall roof, *c.*1325/6.

In 1336 Hurley was appointed for life to be Edward III's

chief carpenter at the Tower and the overseer of all works of carpentry in the king's castles south of the Trent; in that capacity he was responsible for maintenance and transport of the siege engines, as well as domestic works such as Edward III's new chapel and chamber in the privy palace at Westminster, begun in 1342. Before the king's grandiose projects at Windsor, Hurley was engaged by the city of London to work on the Guildhall Chapel and received in 1331–3 the large payment of £8 14s. 2d. for his services. At this time, John Pulteney, mayor of London, lent money to the Guildhall for repairs and also built himself a grand residence at Penshurst, Kent. Because of Hurley's employment at the Guildhall when Pulteney was mayor (1330–37), it has been suggested that Hurley may have designed the great roof of the hall; however, this must remain only a tempting speculation.

Hurley's work at Ely is documented with certainty from 1334 until 1354, but considerable disagreement remains as to what role, if any, he played in devising the ingenious support system for the octagonal lantern, with its span of just over 70 feet. The general dates of construction can be firmly established between 1322, when the Norman crossing tower collapsed, and 1340/41, when the lantern windows were glazed. How early Hurley was employed at Ely cannot be resolved because of lacunae in the accounts for the critical years 1326 to 1334. It is known, however, that the stone octagon, which provides grooves for seating the framing, was finished in 1328 and archaeological evidence demonstrates that the masonry and carpentry must have been designed together. The sacrist rolls for 1322/3 name several carpenters and masons, including an anonymous *quidam* ('someone') who came from London to ordain the new work and who was paid a total of 3s. 4d., that is, half a master's normal salary of 6s. 8d. to 7s. a week (which was Hurley's salary as chief carpenter at Windsor). Efforts have been made to identify Hurley with this unnamed Londoner, in a desire to credit him with the octagon and its brilliant engineering, but the documents cannot support this interpretation. But the sources do permit the assigning to Hurley of the tierceron (lower) vault of the crossing which conceals the structural framing of the lantern and which was painted in 1334/5; also the upper star-patterned vault of the lantern and the roof of the entire 'campanile'.

At Windsor Castle, where Edward III provided a model for the international chivalry of Europe, Hurley was engaged in various projects until his death in 1354. His largest work there was certainly the tournament pavilion, or 'domus' of the Round Table, erected between 1344 and 1345. The purchase of 40,000 tiles and vast quantities of laths, pegs, and nails demonstrate that this immense 'house' was to be roofed, at least partially, in order to provide Edward's court with a sheltered space to observe the jousting. The sources, however, do not indicate the plan, or, indeed, whether the structure was ever actually completed. Apart from this romantic project, Hurley, assisted by his warden, William Herland, was responsible for carpentry works in general and particularly for the choir stalls of St George's Chapel (*c.*1350–52). Hurley had a

chamber in Windsor Castle and also a 'house' where it was said that he 'turns the chapiters [capitals] for the stalls' (*History of the King's Works*, 1.873, n. 4). As well as his salary, robe, and privileges as a member of the king's household, Hurley received £1 annually from the Ely fabric accounts until his death in 1354.   LYNN T. COURTENAY

Sources [H. Wharton], ed., *Anglia sacra*, 2 vols. (1691) · R. Brown, H. M. Colvin, and A. J. Taylor, eds., *The history of the king's works*, 1–2 (1963) · F. R. Chapman, ed., *Sacrist rolls of Ely*, 2 vols. (1907) · N. Coldstream, 'Ely Cathedral: the fourteenth-century work', *Medieval art and architecture at Ely Cathedral*, ed. N. Coldstream and P. Draper, British Archaeological Association Conference Transactions [1976], 2 (1979), 28–46 · F. Devon, ed. and trans., *Issues of the exchequer: being payments made out of his majesty's revenue, from King Henry III to King Henry VI inclusive*, RC (1837) · J. Harvey and A. Oswald, *English mediaeval architects: a biographical dictionary down to 1550*, 2nd edn (1984) · J. H. Harvey, 'The king's chief carpenters', *Journal of the British Archaeological Association*, 3rd ser., 11 (1948), 13–34 · J. H. Harvey, 'The mediaeval carpenter and his work as an architect', *RIBA Journal*, 45 (1937–8), 733–43 · W. H. St J. Hope, *Windsor Castle, an architectural history*, 2 vols. (1913) · W. R. Lethaby, *Westminster Abbey and the king's craftsmen* (1906) · *English historical documents*, 4, ed. A. R. Myers (1969) · PRO, king's remembrancer accounts various, E101/485, rolls 14–15 [roof of St Stephen's, upper chapel] · Chancery records · L. F. Salzman, *Building in England down to 1540* (1952) · J. T. Smith, *Antiquities of Westminster ...: containing two hundred and forty-six engravings of topographical objects* (1807) · *VCH Cambridgeshire and the Isle of Ely*, vol. 4 · G. Webb, *Architecture in Britain: the middle ages* (1962)

Archives PRO, king's remembrancer, accounts various, E101/485, rolls 14–15

Hurlstone, Frederick Yeates (1800–1869), portrait and history painter, was born in London, the eldest son of Thomas Y. Hurlstone, one of the proprietors of the *Morning Chronicle*, and his second wife, Elizabeth Willet. He began life in the office of that journal, but while still very young became a pupil of William Beechey, and afterwards studied under Thomas Lawrence and Benjamin Robert Haydon. His first original work was an altarpiece, painted in 1816, for which he received £20. In 1820 he was admitted to the Royal Academy Schools; there, in 1822, he gained the silver medal for the best copy made in the school of painting, and in 1823 the gold medal for his historical painting *The Contention between the Archangel Michael and Satan for the Body of Moses*.

Hurlstone first exhibited in 1821, sending to the Royal Academy *Le malade imaginaire* and to the British Institution a *View near Windsor*. These were followed at the academy in consecutive years by several portraits and biblical pieces. One of his best early works was *A Venetian Page with a Parrot*, exhibited at the British Institution in 1824, later purchased by the duke of Westminster. In 1824 he also contributed *The Bandit Chief* to the first exhibition of the Society of British Artists. Hurlstone continued to send portraits to the Royal Academy until 1830, but in 1831 he was elected a member of the Society of British Artists, after which he seldom exhibited elsewhere. He was elected president in 1836, and again in 1840, retaining the office until his death. He contributed to the society's exhibitions upwards of 300 portraits and other works,

Frederick Yeates Hurlstone (1800–1869), self-portrait

among them *The Enchantress Armida*, exhibited in 1831, *Eros*, 1836, and the *Prisoner of Chillon*, purchased by the earl of Tankerville in 1837. In 1844 and 1845 he again sent portraits to the Royal Academy. His subsequent works at the Society of British Artists consisted mainly of literary, historical, and anecdotal paintings.

Hurlstone's later works, which were much inferior to those of his earlier years, consisted mainly of Spanish and Italian rustic and fancy subjects, the outcome of several visits to Italy, Spain, and Morocco, made between 1835 and 1854. At the Paris Exhibition of 1855 he was awarded a gold medal for his works *The Last Sign of the Moor* (*Boabdil el Chico, Mourning Over the Fall of Granada, Reproached by his Mother*), *La Mora*, and *Constance and Prince Arthur*. As a portrait painter he was successful, one of his best heads being that of Richard, seventh earl of Cavan, exhibited at the Society of British Artists in 1833, and at the National Portrait Exhibition of 1868.

In 1836 Hurlstone married Jane Coral, who exhibited watercolours and portraits at the Royal Academy and the Society of British Artists between 1846 and 1850, but from 1850 to 1856 she contributed to the latter only fancy subjects in oils. She died on 2 October 1858, leaving two sons: Frederick Bradley Hurlstone, also an artist, and Martin de Galway Hurlstone, a surgeon, father of the composer William Yeates Hurlstone.

Always opposed to the constitution and management of the Royal Academy, Hurlstone gave evidence before the select committee of the House of Commons in 1836, complaining about the unjust preference shown to the Royal Academy, and resenting especially the privileges attached to being an Academician, and the allocation to a private

institution of a public building. He died at Stoke Newington, London, on 10 June 1869, and was buried in Norwood cemetery.   R. E. GRAVES, rev. PATRICIA MORALES

Sources *Art Journal*, 31 (1869), 271 · W. Sandby, *The history of the Royal Academy of Arts*, 2 (1862) · Redgrave, *Artists* · J. E. Hodgson and F. A. Eaton, *The Royal Academy and its members, 1768–1830* (1905) · *The works of John Ruskin*, ed. E. T. Cook and A. Wedderburn, library edn, 39 vols. (1903–12), vol. 5, p. xvi · Graves, *Artists*, new edn · H. Hubbard, *An outline history of the Royal Society of British Artists* (1937) · exhibition catalogues (1824–70) [Society of British Artists] · *CGPLA Eng. & Wales* (1869)

Likenesses F. Y. Hurlstone, self-portrait, Royal Society of British Artists [*see illus.*]

Wealth at death under £7000: probate, 8 July 1869, *CGPLA Eng. & Wales*

Hurlstone, William Martin Yeates (1876–1906), composer and pianist, was born on 7 January 1876 at 12 Richmond Gardens, Fulham, London, the only son of Martin de Galway Hurlstone (1839–1899) and his wife, Maria Bessy Styche. He was the grandson of Frederick Yeates *Hurlstone (1800–1869), first president of the Society (later Royal Society) of British Artists. His father was a surgeon, but lost his sight and his fortune; William suffered throughout his short life from poverty and bronchial asthma. The family moved to Wilton, near Salisbury, where he made his mark in a local choir; in 1884 the vicar brought Hubert Parry and Sir George Grove to hear the young prodigy. When William was nine his father published his op. 1, *Five Easy Waltzes* for piano.

Though self-taught in composition, Hurlstone won a scholarship to the Royal College of Music (RCM; 1894–8), where Parry was now director; he studied with Charles Stanford and, for piano, with Algernon Ashton and Edward Dannreuther. His fellow student Thomas Dunhill recalled that his 'dark visage, and somewhat awkward presence, modest and unassertive though they were, seemed to dominate the mental picture' (Hurlstone, 37). While he was there, his *Five Dances for Orchestra* (1895), his piano concerto (9 December 1895), his piano and wind quintet (1897), and his violin sonata (1897) were performed. He played the concerto himself, and performed it again at St James's Hall on 6 March 1896 (Gustav Holst playing the trombone, Ralph Vaughan Williams the triangle), but his asthma made concert appearances exhausting for him. The concerto was a remarkably assured work for a nineteen-year-old, in sound and style beneficially reminiscent of Brahms, whose B♭ major concerto had received its first performance only fourteen years before. Hurlstone showed a ruminative cast of mind, and worked with genuine impetus in ample, strong forms.

After leaving the RCM Hurlstone became a jobbing musician, teaching and conducting in Croydon, Anerly, and Norwood, the district where the family had settled. Modest, gifted, poor, he was helped by generous local well-to-do amateurs, who invited him to play at their homes and financially supported him and his now widowed mother. Towards the end of the First World War Elgar told the poet Robert Nichols to 'look out for some Variations' by Hurlstone (Hurlstone, 49). The *Variations on an Original*

Theme (1896) should indeed be considered alongside Parry's (1897) and Elgar's (1899), even if Hurlstone's invention was less striking than that of the older composers. Richter gave the more forceful and concise *Hungarian Variations* in Manchester, after the first performance, under Stanford, at the RCM in 1899.

Hurlstone was unusual among British composers of his period in his predilection for instrumental music; his only big choral work was *Alfred the Great*, composed in 1901. His abstract music, which includes a piano trio and cello and bassoon sonatas, is mature and shapely. When the Patron's Fund was established to give performances of young British composers, Hurlstone won places in the first two concerts. Stanford conducted the *Fantasie-Variations on a Swedish Air* on 20 May 1904 at St James's Hall; the critic of *The Times* considered that Hurlstone's variations and Holst's orchestral suite in E♭ 'towered' over the rest of the programme. The second Patron's Fund concert, later that year, included the piano quartet in E minor. The fanciful *Magic Mirror* suite, first performed at the RCM in 1901, was given in 1904 by the Strolling Players, an orchestra led by W. W. Cobbett. In 1905 Cobbett established a competition for a 'phantasy' quartet, and Hurlstone's quartet in A won the first prize.

In 1903 Hurlstone became accompanist to the Bach Choir, and in 1905 he was appointed to the staff of the RCM. In order to be nearer his work he moved to 23 Park Mansions, Prince of Wales Road, Battersea Park, London. There he died from bronchial asthma on 30 May 1906, unmarried and survived by his mother; he was buried on 1 June at the Croydon new cemetery. So he joined the group of English composers who died young, their promise unfulfilled.   DIANA McVEAGH

Sources K. Hurlstone, ed., *William Hurlstone, musician: memories and records by his friends* (c.1947) · H. G. Newell, *William Yeates Hurlstone: musician and man* (1936) · Royal College of Music, London, Hurlstone archive
Archives Royal College of Music, London, MSS
Likenesses E. Norton Collins, photograph, 1900, Royal College of Music, London · E. Morley, photograph (aged fifteen), Royal College of Music, London
Wealth at death £299 10s. 8d.: administration, 14 June 1906, *CGPLA Eng. & Wales*

Hurrion, John (1676–1731), Independent minister and religious writer, was born at Rendham, Suffolk, on 15 or 16 November 1676, the son of John Hurrion and his wife, a daughter of Edmund Whincop, ejected curate of Leiston, Suffolk. In his youth he decided on becoming a minister and received part of his training for the ministry from the Revd Mr Robinson (or Robertson) of Walpole, Norfolk. In 1696 he settled as minister to the Independent congregation at Denton, Norfolk, and at about the same time married Jane Baker, daughter of Samuel Baker of Wattisfield Hall, Suffolk. Hurrion found the church in Denton in a 'low and declining condition' (Ridgley, 36), but through hard work and accomplished preaching and pulpit talents brought it into a flourishing state. He was also a scholar of some repute and was held in high regard by his fellow clergymen, but his increasingly reclusive nature did little to endear him to his parishioners.

In 1724 Hurrion became assistant to John Nesbitt at Hare Court, Aldersgate, London, and on Nesbitt's death in 1727 succeeded him. He was chosen one of the Merchants' lecturers at Pinners' Hall in 1726, and eight of the sermons he preached during his first year there were published in 1727 under the title *The Knowledge of Christ and him Crucified*. In 1730 he was commissioned to deliver a course of four sermons at Lime Street entitled 'The scripture doctrine of particular redemption', but ill health prevented him completing his assignment. However, the sermons were published posthumously in 1773. Among Hurrion's other publications were several single sermons occasioned mainly by the death of friends and colleagues, such as that preached for his predecessor, John Nesbitt, in 1728. His most successful work was *The Scripture Doctrine of the Proper Divinity*, a collection of sixteen sermons delivered at Pinners' Hall in 1729, 1730, and 1731 and published posthumously in 1734.

Hurrion's ministry at Hare Court was not successful or happy. His health was broken before his move from Norfolk and grew steadily worse in London, where his 'infirm constitution rendered him very unfit for the constant discharge of his ministerial work' (Ridgley, 38). He suffered in particular from dropsy, which ultimately brought about his death in London on 31 December 1731. His funeral sermon was preached by Thomas Ridgley at Hare Court on 9 January 1732. He left two sons, John and Samuel, both of whom became dissenting ministers.

W. A. J. ARCHBOLD, rev. M. J. MERCER

Sources T. Ridgley, *A sermon occasioned by the death of Revd. John Hurrion* (1732) · A. Taylor, *A discourse occasioned by the death of Mr John Hurrion* (1733) · A. Taylor, 'The life of John Hurrion', in *The whole works of the Rev. John Hurrion*, 1 (1823) · W. Wilson, *The history and antiquities of the dissenting churches and meeting houses in London, Westminster and Southwark*, 4 vols. (1808–14), vol. 3, pp. 288–96 · Allibone, *Dict.*, 1.926 · IGI · J. Browne, *A history of Congregationalism and memorials of the churches in Norfolk and Suffolk* (1877), 437–40
Archives BL, funeral sermon for S. May, Add. MS 19205, fol. 24

Hurry, Leslie George (1909–1978), painter and theatre designer, was born on 10 February 1909 at 53 High Street, St John's Wood, London, the third and last child of Alfred George Hurry (c.1880–1951/2), funeral director, and his wife, Edith Louise Perry, *née* Butcher (c.1880–1954). Sickly and perhaps unwanted, he was largely brought up by his elder sister. He remained devoted to her. At Haberdashers' Aske School (1920–25) he knew he had to paint, and with his sister's help resisted pleas to join the family's undertaking business. He went to St John's Wood Art School (1925–7), then won a five-year scholarship to the Royal Academy Schools, but left after his third year (1927–31). A small allowance let him continue painting, including landscape murals for public houses. Between 1934 and 1936 he painted further watercolour landscapes in Britain and Ireland, which were exhibited in London and praised by Herbert Read (*The Listener*, 31 March 1937). Commissions for more landscapes followed, but Hurry became depressed, feeling that his art lacked 'a rhythmic organisation of colour from the tensions between himself' and his subjects (Lindsay, 9). He fled to Thaxted, Essex, and

Leslie George Hurry (1909–1978), self-portrait, 1944

sought ways to depict the workings of his mind within his increasingly abstract pictures. Many he destroyed. There followed moves to Brittany and then Paris, but illness forced him home. When war was declared in 1939, Hurry's poor health meant that he was not recruited; however, a flood of surreal paintings appeared. Waste, destruction, and the plight of humanity troubled him deeply, and even the portrait of *Grace Sholto Douglas* (1940; exh. Royal Festival Hall, 1990; Tate collection) shows the dying patroness, clad in crimson and with hands so like Hurry's own, looking away from strange ritual figures.

In 1941 Hurry had two London exhibitions; here dancer–choreographer Robert Helpmann realized that Hurry's paintings matched his preparations for a dance-mime *Hamlet* for Sadler's Wells. The action was within the prince's dying brain, with characters and events overlapping. The nervous Hurry knew nothing of theatre, but agreed to submit designs, provided that Helpmann destroyed them if they displeased him. When *Hamlet* opened at the New Theatre in 1942, Hurry found himself 'greatly congratulated on his décor and costumes' (*Punch*, 3 June 1942). The phantasmagoric set, in blood-red and crimson, evoked a 'decadent palace' (Beaumont, 8), dominated by a Janus-faced figure, Revenge; all characters wore asymmetrical Gothic-style costumes in contrasting colours. *Hamlet* proved Hurry's intuitive grasp of stage design. In 1943 he designed Sadler's Wells' new *Swan Lake*, and was hailed for his 'quite outstanding imagination' (*The Spectator*, 18 Sept 1943). Three further Sadler's Wells–Covent Garden *Swan Lakes* followed: 1952, 1965, and 1971. From the adventurous

surrealism of 1943 to the autumnal romanticism of 1971, Hurry's *Swan Lakes* have influenced greatly fifty years' worth of ballet-goers.

Over a period of thirty-five years Hurry designed for major companies more than sixty productions, though he always stressed he was not a designer but a painter. Until 1950 he did just one show a year and his paintings flourished; partly influenced by designs, they placed a growing emphasis on mankind. *Bombers* and *War* (both 1944; exh. The Minories, Colchester, 1987; IWM) show war's destructiveness; *Atom Bomb* (1946; exh. Barbican, 1987; priv. coll.) his horror; and *Liberation* (1945; V&A) owes much to his *Hamlet* schemes (see also Shakespeare's play, 1944, Old Vic at New Theatre). Two emotive oil *Self-Portraits* (1944; both exh. The Minories, Colchester, 1987; NPG and Tate collection) stress further Hamlet-like qualities. In October 1950 he joined a delegation of artists to visit Moscow, and later addressed the Society for Cultural Relations Between Peoples of the British Commonwealth and the USSR. Hurry was not a communist but was deeply egalitarian; this incident prevented him from entering the USA in 1955. It arose because the director Tyrone Guthrie staged Marlowe's *Tamburlaine the Great* (at the Old Vic in 1951), where 'the golden glory of Hurry's décor will haunt the memory of all' (*Theatre World*, November 1951). This production was remounted in 1955–6 for Toronto and New York; Hurry visited Canada but the United States banned him. By now he was designing full-time, including Wagner's *Ring Cycle* (Covent Garden, 1954) which let him buy his Suffolk cottage, fourteen Old Vic and five Sadler's Wells productions, plus new works like the set for Graham Greene's *The Living Room* (Wyndham's Theatre, 1953) and costumes for Lionel Bart's *Maggie May* (Adelphi, 1964).

In 1960 Hurry became a Royal Shakespeare Company associate designer; he contributed, among others, his 'sandpit *Troilus and Cressida*' (1960–62) (*The Times*, 24 Nov 1978). Urged to become more sculptural, he achieved this, particularly after 1964, by designing six productions for the thrust stage of Canada's Stratford Festival, Ontario. Included were Sheridan's witty *School for Scandal* (1970–71) and a magnificent *Pericles* (1973–4). His final Canadian commission was *Caesar and Cleopatra* (Shaw festival, Niagara on the Lake, Ontario, 1975). British design had ended earlier with Humphrey Searle's opera, *Hamlet* (Covent Garden, 1969). Its rich, vivid, but fractured sets and costumes matched the paintings which again preoccupied Hurry. Still he tried to reflect, in their detailed sensibility, both the visible and psychological worlds he perpetually experienced. Landscape again reasserts itself, but the pictures now have a breathing openness, whether expressing regret in the surreal *Egypt/Israel War, October 6–22* (1973; exh. The Minories, Colchester, 1987; priv. coll.) or delight in the more representational Suffolk scenes (1968–78). When he died, his cottage was crammed with unseen works.

Tall, gaunt, and always breathless, Hurry's moods were volatile. In the theatre he could be very funny, very ironic, but always praised those who interpreted his designs. When painting, he still lacked confidence. Unmarried, he really trusted only a few women friends and his sister. He died on 20 November 1978 at the London Chest Hospital and was cremated a week later at Golders Green. His sister's son took his ashes home to Suffolk. In life, Hurry had paintings and designs exhibited throughout Britain and in Ontario, Canada; posthumously, major retrospectives have occurred. His paintings can be found in many British galleries, and his designs are well represented in London's Theatre Museum, Stratford upon Avon's Shakespeare Birthplace Trust, and the Metropolitan Library's art department in Toronto.   RAYMOND INGRAM

Sources J. Lindsay, 'Introduction', in L. Hurry, *Paintings and drawings* (1950) · C. W. Beaumont, 'Introduction', in L. Hurry, *Settings and costumes for Sadler's Wells ballets Hamlet* (1942), *Le lac des cygnes and the Old Vic Hamlet* (1944) (1947) · R. Ingram, *The stage designs of Leslie Hurry* (1990) · J. H. Armstrong, 'Leslie Hurry: his family', *Leslie Hurry* (1987) [exhibition catalogue, The Minories, Colchester, 24 Oct – 29 Nov 1987] · D. Mellor, 'Leslie Hurry: towards the nuclear future', *A paradise lost* (1987) [exhibition catalogue, Barbican Art Gallery, London] · R. Ingram, *Leslie Hurry: an exhibition of theatrical designs and illustrations* (1990) [exhibition catalogue, Royal Festival Hall, London, 1 May – 10 June 1990] · D. W. Ladell, 'Biography', *Leslie Hurry: a painter for the stage* (Stratford, Ontario, [1982]) [exhibition catalogue, The Gallery, Stratford, Ontario, 7 June – 6 Sept 1982] · J. Pettigrew and J. Portman, *Stratford: the first thirty years* (Toronto, 1985) · E. Coranthiel, 'Creative artists in the theatre: Leslie Hurry', *Theatre World* (May 1953), 17–19 · H. Read, 'The present state of watercolour', *The Listener* (31 March 1937) · E. Johns, 'The scourge and terror of the world', *Theatre World* (Nov 1951), 11–18, 34 · *CGPLA Eng. & Wales* (1979) · private information (2004) [nephew]

Archives priv. coll., collection of diaries and MSS | Stratford Festival Archives, Ontario | FILM priv. coll., recording of the Service of Thanksgiving for Hurry, 24 May 1979, St Paul's Church, Covent Garden, 16mm film · Stratford Festival Archives, Ontario, single stationary camera of *The School for Scandal*, 1970 (good); *Pericles*, 1973 (poor) · Thames Video (VHS/TV8012) of Hurry's Royal Ballet *Swan Lake* (1971/modified 1979)

Likenesses L. G. Hurry, self-portrait, oils, *c*.1943, NPG · L. G. Hurry, self-portrait, oils, 1944, Tate collection [*see illus.*] · M. Ambler, photograph, *c*.1950, repro. in *Shakespeare Memorial Theatre souvenir programme 1950* · R. Eastham, photograph, *c*.1977, repro. in *Leslie Hurry* (National Theatre, 1979), cover [exhibition catalogue]

Wealth at death £55,950: probate, 20 April 1979, *CGPLA Eng. & Wales* · £64,186: private information (2004)

Hurst [*formerly* Hertz], **Sir Arthur Frederick** (1879–1944), physician, was born at 3 Oak Mount, Manningham, Bradford, on 23 July 1879, the third son of William Martin Hertz, wool merchant, and his wife, Fanny Mary, daughter of Julius Baruch Halle, merchant, of Clapham Park, London. His Jewish grandparents on both sides came from Germany in the mid-nineteenth century. Sir Gerald Hurst was his elder brother. His father's cousin Heinrich Rudolph Hertz was the discoverer of electromagnetic waves. Hertz was educated at Bradford and Manchester grammar schools, and at Magdalen College, Oxford, where he was awarded a demyship and placed in the first class in the final honour school of physiology in 1901. From Oxford he went to Guy's Hospital with a university science scholarship and graduated BM (Oxon.) in 1904, winning gold medals in medicine and surgery; he became DM in 1907. Awarded the Radcliffe travelling scholarship in 1905 he studied at Munich, Paris, and in the United

States, and in 1909 he was given the Radcliffe prize. His name was changed by deed poll to Hurst in 1916, and he also took British nationality. He was appointed assistant physician to Guy's Hospital in 1906 in charge of the neurological department, and he remained on the staff as physician from 1918 until his retirement as senior physician in 1939, when he became consulting physician to the hospital and joined the board of governors. On 2 October 1912 he married Cushla Harriette Strotter (*b*. 1893/4), daughter of the late Frederick Riddiford, a farmer of Hawera, New Zealand. They had one son and two daughters.

His contemporaries at Guy's saw Hurst as continuing the traditions of such famous physicians of the previous century as Richard Bright, Thomas Addison, and Thomas Hodgkin. Hurst was one of the London physicians responsible for starting the disinterested study of clinical phenomena by the methods of exact physiology, while at the same time he ran a large private consulting practice. His first major piece of work was on the sensibility of the alimentary tract, delivered as the Goulstonian lectures in 1911; he showed that the common stimulus for the production of abdominal pain was muscular tension.

During the First World War Hurst was consulting physician at Salonika, then, from 1916 to 1918 was in charge of the neurological section at Netley. Between 1918 and 1919 he worked at the Seale Hayne Military Hospital for war neuroses, where he achieved remarkable results in the treatment of shell-shock by suggestion.

After the war Hurst continued his studies on the alimentary tract using the new method of radiological examination. Much of his clinical work was directed to the treatment of peptic ulcer and constipation. He introduced the concept of achalasia, or absence of relaxation, to explain troublesome dilation of the oesophagus, and devised special methods for its treatment. He maintained that pernicious anaemia and subacute combined degeneration of the spinal cord were primarily diseases of the alimentary tract and felt himself vindicated by the introduction by Minot and Murphy in the United States of liver treatment for that condition.

Hurst soon became dissatisfied with the conditions of a single-handed consulting practice and he concentrated his work at New Lodge Clinic, Windsor Forest, where he built up a team of colleagues for the investigation of disease by contemporary methods. Another of his great interests was the *Guy's Hospital Reports*. Under his editorship from 1921 to 1939 they increased greatly in size and scope. Deafness spared him from committee work and examining. Hurst had a disconcerting habit of switching off his hearing aid if he considered a presentation at a medical meeting to be unimportant. He was an enthusiastic member of the Association of Physicians of Great Britain and Ireland, of which he was made an honorary member, and he was founder of the Medical Pilgrims Club, with which he made many visits abroad. He was elected FRCP (London) in 1910, and was Goulstonian (1911) and Croonian (1920) lecturer, Harveian orator (1937), and Moxon medallist (1939) of the college. He was president of the medical section of the Royal Society of Medicine (1927–9), and of the International Society of Gastro-Enterology, and an honorary member of many foreign medical societies. In 1935 he was awarded the Osler memorial medal, and in 1937 he was knighted in the coronation honours.

Hurst's retirement from Guy's in 1939 coincided with the beginning of the Second World War. New Lodge Clinic was disbanded and Hurst went to live at Oxford, where he taught in the newly established clinical school. There he drew large crowds to his ward rounds at the Radcliffe Infirmary. Always a ready source of ideas Hurst was prepared to talk on any subject within his speciality and at short notice, without notes. He was the physician primarily responsible for establishing gastroenterology as a speciality in Britain. Throughout his life Hurst was subject to intractable asthma. He was slight of build and bowed from his disorder. While at the home of T. L. Hardy, first professor of gastroenterology and secretary to the newly founded Gastroenterological Club, 35 Calthorpe Road, Edgbaston, Birmingham, he died suddenly, on 17 August 1944. He was cremated in Oxford, where his ashes were scattered. He was survived by his wife.

Undoubtedly Hurst will be most remembered for his foundation of the Gastroenterological Club. Starting with forty members in 1937, it grew into the British Society of Gastroenterology, which by the end of the century had 2500 members and had become the leading such society in Europe. The society's most prestigious lecture is named the Arthur Hurst lecture.

L. J. WITTS, *rev.* CHRISTOPHER C. BOOTH

Sources W. N. Mann, 'Arthur Hurst: a personal note', *Guy's Hospital Gazette*, [3rd ser.], 94 (1979), 281–6 · F. A. Jones, 'Gastroenterology in Britain before 1937 and the founding of the Gastro-Enterological Club', *Gut*, golden jubilee issue (1987), 3–6 · private information (2004) [W. N. Mann, Christopher Hurst] · *A twentieth century physician: being the reminiscences of Sir Arthur Hurst* (1949) · T. Hunt, ed., *Selected writings of Sir Arthur Hurst* (1969) [biographical] · J. A. Ryle, 'Sir Arthur Hurst', *Guy's Hospital Reports*, 4th ser., 24 (1945), 1–11 · personal knowledge (1959) · private information (2004) · *WWW* · T. Hunt, 'Sir Arthur Hurst', *Gut*, 20 (1979), 463–6 · b. cert. · m. cert. · d. cert. · *CGPLA Eng. & Wales* (1945)

Likenesses Vandyk, photograph, Guy's Hospital medical school, London · photograph, repro. in Ryle, 'Sir Arthur Hurst', facing p. 1

Wealth at death £35,444 3s. 8d.: probate, 11 April 1945, *CGPLA Eng. & Wales*

Hurst, Sir Cecil James Barrington (1870–1963), international lawyer, was born at Horsham Park, Sussex, on 28 October 1870, the third and youngest son of Robert Henry Hurst (1817–1905), barrister, recorder of Hastings and Rye from 1862 to 1905, and member of parliament for Horsham between 1865 and 1876, and his wife, Matilda Jane, daughter of James Scott, of The Nunnery, Rusper, Sussex. From Westminster School he went on to Trinity College, Cambridge, where he obtained a second in part one and a first in part two (1891–2) of the law tripos.

Called to the bar by the Middle Temple in 1893, Hurst's masters in chambers were the future Lord Justice Scrutton and Mr Justice Bray. After a year as junior counsel to the Post Office on the south-eastern circuit in 1901, he was appointed, in 1902, as assistant legal adviser to the Foreign Office. In this capacity he became active in international

Sir Cecil James Barrington Hurst (1870–1963), by Walter Stoneman, 1935

affairs, first, in 1907, as legal secretary to the British plenipotentiaries at the second Hague peace conference, then, in 1908, as a British delegate at the London naval conference. In 1910 he was appointed a member of the commission to report on the *Alsop* claim which had been referred to his majesty's arbitrament by the United States and Chilean governments. After 1912 he was much involved as British agent in the work of the British–American claims arbitration tribunal. He took silk in 1913.

Hurst was promoted legal adviser to the Foreign Office in 1918. He had served in 1917–18 on the Phillimore committee which prepared an early draft for the covenant of the League of Nations. But the work which had the most direct reflection in the covenant as eventually adopted was his co-operation with David Hunter Miller, the American delegate, the outcome of which was presented, early in 1919, to the League of Nations commission of the peace conference in the form of the so-called 'Hurst-Miller' draft. Among Hurst's own proposals was one for a Permanent Court of International Justice. As a member of the Paris peace conference he played an important part also in the drafting of the peace treaties. Writing to the Foreign Office in May 1919 James Headlam-Morley remarked 'Hurst really carried the thing through entirely on his own shoulders, and it is owing to him more than to anyone else that there is a treaty of any kind to present to the Germans' (Headlam-Morley, 99).

In 1919–20 Hurst visited Egypt as a member of the mission headed by Lord Milner. When a commission of jurists was set up under the Washington conference on naval disarmament of 1921–2 to examine and report on the laws of war, Hurst was nominated a British member. He attended the assembly of the League of Nations as a substitute delegate in 1922, 1924, and 1925, and as a delegate in 1926, and always played a leading creative role. He was prominent in the negotiation of the treaty of Locarno of 1925.

A man of immense energy and dedication, endowed with a strong sense of moral principle and a devotion to public service, Hurst enjoyed the constant respect of his colleagues. Kindness, courtesy, and absolute integrity characterized his work, in which he set himself an exacting standard of scholarly perfection. He became assistant legal adviser at the Foreign Office at a time when legal institutions were powerful in policy making, and it was largely he who invested the post of legal adviser with the prestige and eminence it subsequently carried. For Hurst regarded his function as that of a jurist involved in international affairs; not merely a writer of opinions, but a representative of his government and a creator of policy at international conferences. One of his successors, Sir Gerald Fitzmaurice, observed that by the time Hurst left the Foreign Office he had established an influence comparable to that of the permanent under-secretary. Foreign lawyers particularly were impressed by Hurst's lack of insularity and his receptiveness to foreign ideas. Indeed, his friendship with Henri Fromageot, his French counterpart, did much, in the words of Lord McNair, 'to ensure the co-operation, or minimize the divergence, of the British and French governments in implementing the Treaty of Versailles' (McNair, 401).

Anxious to foster the development of an integrated and authoritative literature of international law, Hurst was convinced that there existed a vital need for the participation in the development of the subject by Foreign Office lawyers who were so closely involved with its practical application. He actively encouraged his colleagues to shed light on the purely legal aspects of their work, without ever jeopardizing the essential secrecy of political transactions. Within the limitations which the nature of his work imposed, Hurst himself published a number of important articles on a wide range of international legal questions. These have been republished as his *Collected Papers* (1950). It was largely because of his happy blend of scholarship with practical experience that Hurst was able to exert such a marked influence on the growth both of policy and of legal thought.

In 1919 Hurst provided the initiative in founding the *British Year Book of International Law*, the first English periodical specifically devoted to this field of study. He himself served until 1928 as its chief editor. He also took an active part in the establishment of the Grotius Society, of which he became president in 1940.

In his last four years at the Foreign Office, Hurst appeared as counsel in several cases heard before the Permanent Court of International Justice. In 1929 he was elected a judge of the court, of which he was president from 1934 to 1936. Appropriately, it was the first Viscount Finlay, who had been his former leader at the bar, whom

Hurst succeeded in 1929 as the second British judge elected to the court. There his gifts of diplomacy and scholarship were to be combined to even greater effect than hitherto. Hurst's aim as a judge was to strengthen the prestige and authority of the court's pronouncements, striving always to achieve unity and minimize disagreement by means of exhaustive deliberation. It was the example he set by his far-sighted judicial philosophy which earned him the presidency after so short a time. He played a decisive part in formulating the many majority judgments with which he associated himself. While recognizing that the right to dissent was essential to the viability of any international tribunal, he was convinced that the ultimate effect of the indiscriminate production of dissenting opinions would be to undermine the standing of the court's decisions. Yet, being conscientious in his adherence to principle, Hurst himself occasionally found it necessary to have recourse to this liberty. His preference for the textual method of treaty interpretation, which involved him in meticulous analysis of several important international conventions, bears out Lord McNair's view of him as a traditionalist. Hurst remained a judge until the dissolution of the court in 1946, upon its replacement by the International Court of Justice. In the meantime, during the Second World War he spent three years as chairman of a Home Office panel for appeals against orders of detention under regulation 18B; then became the first president of the war crimes commission, in 1943–5.

Throughout his career Hurst enjoyed the full support of his wife, Sibyl Gabriel Lumley Smith, daughter of Sir Lumley Smith, a judge of the City of London court, whom he married on 21 December 1901. She died in 1947, leaving two sons and a daughter. Hurst was appointed CB (1907), KCB (1920), KCMG (1924), and GCMG (1926); he was elected a bencher in 1922 and was treasurer of the Middle Temple in 1940. He was president of the Institute of International Law and an honorary LLD of Cambridge and Edinburgh. Hurst lived to be ninety-two, and died at his home, South Grove, Brighton Road, Horsham, Sussex, on 27 March 1963 from pneumonia.　　　　ELIHU LAUTERPACHT, rev.

Sources W. E. Beckett, 'Sir Cecil Hurst's services to international law', *British Year Book of International Law*, 26 (1949), 1–5 · Lord McNair [A. D. McNair], 'Sir Cecil James Barrington Hurst', *British Year Book of International Law*, 38 (1962), 400–06 · G. Fitzmaurice, *Annuaire de l'Institut de Droit International*, 13 (1963), 462–77 [obituary] · 'Sir Cecil Hurst: two tributes', *International and Comparative Law Quarterly*, 13 (1964), 1–5 · D. Hunter Miller, *The drafting of the covenant*, 1 (1928) · J. Headlam-Morley, *A memoir of the Paris peace conference, 1919*, ed. A. Headlam-Morley, R. Bryant, and A. Ciencicila (1972) · CGPLA Eng. & Wales (1963) · *Old Westminsters*, vol. 1 · d. cert.
Archives BL, corresp. with Lord Cecil, Add. MS 51090 · NA Scot., letters to Philip Kerr
Likenesses W. Stoneman, photograph, 1935, NPG [see illus.] · W. Dring, portrait, 1948, repro. in Beckett, 'Sir Cecil Hurst's services'
Wealth at death £14,365 1s. 11d.: probate, 28 May 1963, CGPLA Eng. & Wales

Hurst, Henry (1629–1690), clergyman and ejected minister, was born at Mickleton, Gloucestershire, on 31 March 1629, the eldest son of Henry Hurst (d. 1685), vicar of that parish, and his wife, Elenor Wells. He entered Merchant

Taylors' School in October 1644, then about 1646 went to Magdalen Hall, Oxford, where he submitted to the authority of the parliamentary visitors on 4 May 1648 and matriculated on 29 January 1649. Having graduated BA on 11 June, he was examined on 6 August 1649 as candidate for a fellowship at Merton College, in which he enjoyed the support of Henry Wilkinson (d. 1690), soon to be principal of Magdalen Hall. The visitors recorded that he was elected on 12 November, but Hurst and others encountered determined obstruction by college administrators, and in April 1651 he was still trying to extract the allowances due.

Hurst proceeded MA on 18 November 1652, starting soon afterwards to preach, from a presbyterian standpoint, and on 22 October 1656 was admitted rector of Aston Subedge, Gloucestershire. Before the end of 1658, however, he had been admitted as rector of St Matthew's, Friday Street, London, following an election in which the parishioners, by a majority, preferred him to Ezekiel Hopkins. He was formally collated on 11 March 1661 but was ejected under the Act of Uniformity before 28 August 1662, having been unable to comply with its requirements despite 'much prayer and fasting' (Palmer, 1.164). Samuel Pepys reported on 24 August 'a great many young people knotting together and crying out "Porridge" [nickname for the prayer book] often and seditiously in the church, and took the Common Prayer Book, they say, away; and, some say, did tear it'. The churchwardens recorded payment of 'a Reader for Readinge the Common prayer on Bartholomew daye 6s' and their enforced purchase of a surplice for £2 18s. 6d. (Calamy rev., 286).

By a licence of 8 January 1662 Hurst married Anne Bate, of the parish of St Edmund the King, Lombard Street, London. He is reported to have preached in his native Gloucestershire and at Ashford, Kent, where his wife had relations, and to have given a weekly lecture at Highgate, Middlesex. It seems that by the end of the 1660s Hurst was at Mickleton, for Anne was buried there on 17 January 1669. By April 1674 Hurst had become chaplain to the countess of Manchester at Waltham Abbey, Essex, signing from his study there a dedication to John Maynard's Law of God Ratified by Gospel of Christ (1674) from which it is clear that Hurst also knew several of Maynard's parishioners at Mayfield, Sussex. He contributed one of a collection of sermons preached in Southwark, published the following year, and provided the commentary upon Ezekiel as part of the continuation of the annotations on the Bible begun by Matthew Poole.

In 1676 Hurst was a signatory of The Judgement of Nonconformists of the Interest of Reason in the Matter of Religion. In a sermon on flattery, first printed in 1677, he concluded epigrammatically, 'holy principles may set you above vain praises, and humble self denial may content you without them' (Annesley, 3.198). In another, undated, sermon, amid observations on the supposed character of the ancient Athenians and on the ethics of news-gathering, Hurst noted sadly the 'great partiality and falsehood in ecclesiastical historians' of his day, wishing there were 'a

college of judicious, impartial, diligent and able historians, employed and encouraged to search out the truth of all misreported parties, and tell the world the best, as well as their worst' (ibid., 3.543). By June 1677 he had become chaplain to the earl of Anglesey, who refers several times to him between that date and August 1684. His second marriage may have taken place during this period: since his second wife was called Dorothy, he may well have been the Henry Hurst who married Dorathy Kidley on 12 February 1679 at All Hallows, London Wall.

In 1687 Hurst was one of the presbyterian ministers who wrote thanking James II for his declaration of indulgence, an initiative very controversial among dissenters. In 1689 he was certified as preacher in Lincoln's Inn Fields, London, but the next year he suffered an apoplectic fit during a sermon and died the following day, 14 April 1690. He was buried three days later at St Paul's, Covent Garden, where the sermon was preached by Richard Adams (d. 1698). His death also inspired Daniel Burgess's Christian Commemoration and Imitation of Saints Departed (1691), in which it is reported that there was not enough room in the church for the mourners seeking to attend his funeral. By his will, dated 9 November 1689, Hurst left small parcels of land in and around Mickleton to his son, Henry, and daughter, Elizabeth; the will was proved by his widow, Dorothy, on 19 April 1690.

STEPHEN WRIGHT

Sources Calamy rev., 286 · M. Burrows, ed., The register of the visitors of the University of Oxford, from AD 1647 to AD 1658, CS, new ser., 29 (1881) · C. J. Robinson, ed., A register of the scholars admitted into Merchant Taylors' School, from AD 1562 to 1874, 2 vols. (1882–3) · Foster, Alum. Oxon. · G. C. Brodrick, Memorials of Merton College, OHS, 4 (1885) · Calendar of the correspondence of Richard Baxter, ed. N. H. Keeble and G. F. Nuttall, 2 vols. (1991) · Wood, Ath. Oxon., new edn, 2.120, 171 · Wood, Ath. Oxon.: Fasti, new edn · The nonconformist's memorial … originally written by … Edmund Calamy, ed. S. Palmer, [3rd edn], 3 vols. (1802–3) · S. Annesley, ed., The morning-exercise at Cripple-gate, 4th edn (1677) · will, PRO, PROB 11/399, sig. 59 · D. Burgess, Christian commemoration and imitation of saints departed (1691) · IGI [parish register of All Hallows, London Wall]

Wealth at death small landholdings: will, PRO, PROB 11/399, sig. 59

Hurst [née Berney; other married name Baines], **Margery** (1913–1989), recruitment agency founder, was born on 23 May 1913, probably in Portsmouth, the second of the four daughters (there were no sons) of Samuel Berney, cinema owner and builder, of Portsmouth, and his wife Deborah, née Rose. Her grandparents on both sides were Russian Jewish immigrants. She was educated at Brondesbury and Kilburn high school, London, and the Royal Academy of Dramatic Art (RADA). While at RADA she acted two nights a week with the repertory company at Collins's music-hall, which her father had just bought, but decided that she was too self-conscious to become an actress, and got a job as a typist. From there she moved on to work for her father, running the clerical side of his building business, and then became his office manager.

At the outbreak of the Second World War Margery Berney became a secretary in an ambulance unit, and in 1940 she married Major William Baines, an army officer.

Margery Hurst (1913–1989), by Baron Studios, 1961

In 1943 she was commissioned into the Auxiliary Territorial Service (ATS). She later claimed that running a business was not very different from being in charge of a platoon. In 1944 she was invalided out of the army after having a nervous breakdown, worn out by the constant battle against army red tape.

In 1946, three weeks after the birth of Margery Baines's twin daughters (one of whom was stillborn), her husband deserted her for another woman, and, driven by the need to support herself and her surviving baby, she borrowed £50 and an old typewriter from her father, rented a small room in Mayfair, London, at 62 Brook Street, opposite Claridge's Hotel, and started a typing agency. But overwork and the stress involved in leaving her baby with a nanny in Portsmouth while she spent the week in London led to another breakdown, and the typing agency collapsed. She started again, and founded the Brook Street Bureau of Mayfair, this time supplying other businesses with temporary secretaries. From the beginning she would take on only secretaries with several years' experience who had passed her skills test in shorthand and typing. In the meantime, having been divorced from her first husband, she married, on 26 September 1948, Eric Kenneth Isaac Hurst (b. 1913/14), barrister and later her business partner, the son of Wilfred Hurst, cotton merchant; there was one daughter from this marriage, which also ended in divorce.

In the early 1950s the Brook Street Bureau began to open branches in the London suburbs and then in other parts of the country. By 1961 there were thirty-three branches, providing about one-third of Britain's agency-supplied staff,

both temporary and permanent. In the early 1960s Margery Hurst opened branches in New York and Australia. In 1965 the company, now the largest office employment agency in the world, was floated on the London stock exchange. Because she was persuaded that it would be impossible to have a woman as chairman of a public company, she reluctantly agreed to remain as managing director, with her husband as chairman. The flotation was a success, and share prices doubled in fifteen months. There were financial problems in the early 1970s, but profits rose again with the highly successful 'Brook Street got big by bothering' advertising campaign on London underground trains, which lasted for a decade. The Brook Street Bureau suffered during the recession of the early 1980s and was forced to close 100 branches in Britain, as well as most of the branches in Australia and the United States. In 1985 it was sold for more than £19 million to the Blue Arrow recruitment group. The Hursts, who owned 61 per cent of the shares, made £10 million out of the sale. Brook Street kept its identity, and Margery Hurst stayed on as non-executive chairman and consultant until 1988.

A member of the London county council children's committee for several years from 1956, Margery Hurst was involved in charities concerned with child welfare, and in 1973 she bought and founded a house in Gravesend, Kent, to train autistic school-leavers for jobs. She was on the executive committee of the Mental Health Research Fund from 1967 to 1972. She also campaigned against discrimination in recruitment against former psychiatric patients, and in the 1970s the Brook Street Bureau started a special project for the placement of those who had been mentally ill. She was appointed OBE in 1976 and was one of the first women to become a member of Lloyd's, in 1970. She was elected the first female member of the Worshipful Company of Marketors in 1981, became a freeman of the City of London in the same year, and was also the first woman to be elected to the New York chamber of commerce.

Margery Hurst was very small (5 feet tall) but had a dominating, if not domineering, personality. She was assertive and competitive, and even as a child she wanted to be in charge, not just part of a team. She was hot-tempered and liable to have violent arguments with members of her staff. Restless and energetic, she found it hard to relax and had a series of mental breakdowns. She died on 11 February 1989 at her London home in Eaton Square; her funeral took place three days later.

ANNE PIMLOTT BAKER, *rev.*

Sources *The Independent* (16 Feb 1989) · *The Times* (14 Feb 1989) · M. Hurst, *No glass slipper* (1967) · M. Hurst and S. Brompton, *Walking up Brook Street* (1988) · m. cert. [M. Baines and E. K. I. Hurst] · *CGPLA Eng. & Wales* (1989)
Likenesses Baron Studios, photograph, 1961, NPG [*see illus.*] · photographs, repro. in Hurst and Brompton, *Walking up Brook Street*, following p. 88
Wealth at death £3,826,389: probate, 21 Dec 1989, *CGPLA Eng. & Wales*

Hurst, William (*bap.* 1787, *d.* 1844), architect, was baptized on 2 May 1787 in Doncaster, the son of William Hurst, keeper of The Salutation inn, and his wife, Mary. He was articled to William Lindley (c.1739–1818), who had been a long-serving assistant of John Carr of York before establishing his own practice in Doncaster. In 1811 Hurst exhibited two drawings at the Royal Academy. From c.1810 Lindley was in partnership with John Woodhead (d. c.1838) and, on the former's death in 1818, the practice became Woodhead and Hurst. On 27 April 1820 Hurst married Sophia Elizabeth Pearson (bap. 1796, d. 1822), who died when their only child, Mary Sophia, was born. Two years later, on 16 November 1824, he married Charlotte Jane Innes (d. 1856). Hurst took a great interest in civic affairs, served on numerous committees, was mayor of Doncaster for the year 1828–9, and became a magistrate for the borough. He acquired several houses and pieces of land in the town and, after his father's death (probably in 1828), became owner of The Salutation inn.

The Woodhead and Hurst practice was based at South Parade, Doncaster, and around the 1820s designed various improvements for the town, such as a library (1819–21), substantial additions to the racecourse buildings (1823–4), a gasworks (1826–7), betting rooms in High Street (1826), and a new gaol (1829). The latter is known to have been by Hurst (then mayor), as was the imposing Christ Church (1827–9), which shows Hurst's early assurance in the handling of Gothic (and is the only survivor of the buildings listed above). The practice was not confined to the Doncaster area and carried out work elsewhere in Yorkshire and in Derbyshire. The partners could turn their hands to a variety of styles. About 1820 they remodelled Firbeck Hall, West Riding, Yorkshire, with Jacobethan detailing, for Henry Gally Knight and built the church in Firbeck, using a mixture of late Norman and Early English. For Colonel James Wilson, also about 1820, they built the castellated mansion of Sneaton Castle 1½ miles west of Whitby, North Riding, Yorkshire, complete with a curtain wall separating the grounds from the road. Sneaton church, also for Wilson, is a mixture of Perpendicular and Early English. Churches formed an important element in the work of the practice, with examples in Sheffield (St George's, 1821–5), Pateley Bridge (1825–7), and Stannington (1828) in the West Riding, and New Brampton (1830–31) and Ridgeway (1838–40) in Derbyshire. In 1824 Woodhead and Hurst planned the new town of Goole, Yorkshire, for the Aire and Calder Navigation Company, whose first docks there opened in 1826. The first houses were occupied in 1826, the year the docks and canal were officially opened, and building continued until the early 1840s.

In 1836 Hurst was elected a fellow of the Institute of British Architects. The following year he proposed an ambitious scheme to redevelop the area of Doncaster market with new buildings and roads but this remained unexecuted. On the death of Woodhead about 1838, Hurst took on a new partner, William Lambie Moffatt (1808–1882), a Scot and a pupil of William Burn. The practice continued to undertake a mixture of secular and ecclesiastical commissions, most of them away from Doncaster. Hurst and Moffatt designed the Greek revival New Independent Chapel in East Parade, Leeds (1839–41), Gothic churches at Grosmont (North Riding, 1840), Woodsetts

and Ardsley (both West Riding, 1841), and a Romanesque church at Rock Ferry (Cheshire, 1841–2). In 1842–4 they were responsible for the Clipstone archway in the drive at Welbeck Abbey for the duke of Portland. There were also various public buildings in Leeds and Wakefield, but these were mainly the work of Moffatt. Their grandest work, for the new town of Goole, is the church of St John (1843–8), which Pevsner found 'remarkably large and stately' (Pevsner, 223). Although its Perpendicular detail was passing out of fashion, the generous scale and the fine proportions of the tall crossing tower and spire might have impressed the choosy critics of the day. But long before the church was complete, Hurst died of 'disorder of the heart' at his home at 6 Regent Terrace, South Parade, Doncaster, on 8 December 1844, aged fifty-seven. He was buried five days later in Doncaster.

GEOFFREY K. BRANDWOOD

Sources P. Coote, 'Doncaster's architects, no. 1: William Hurst', *Doncaster Civic Trust Newsletter*, 29 (Nov 1979) • Colvin, *Archs.* • [W. Papworth], ed., *The dictionary of architecture*, 11 vols. (1853–92) • registers of baptisms, marriages and burials, Doncaster Archives, St George, Doncaster, P1/1 • *Doncaster, Nottingham and Lincoln Gazette* (13 Dec 1844) • *Doncaster Chronicle and Farmers' Journal* (13 Dec 1844) • d. cert. • *Yorkshire: the West Riding*, Pevsner (1959) • IGI • Doncaster Archives
Archives Doncaster Central Library, account book • RIBA BAL, papers

Hurter, Ferdinand (1844–1898), industrial chemist, was born on 15 March 1844 in Schaffhausen, Switzerland, the only son of the two children of Tobias Hurter, bookbinder, and his wife, Anna Oechslein. He went to the *Gymnasium* at Schaffhausen, and then, after apprenticeship with a dyer in Winterthur, he moved to Zürich to work with a silk firm. He attended the Zürich Polytechnic under G. Staedler, and then studied at Heidelberg University under R. W. Bunsen. He graduated PhD (*summa cum laude*) at the age of twenty-one.

Hurter refused a professorship in Switzerland and went instead to Manchester, armed only with a few letters of introduction. In 1867 he joined Deacon and Gaskill, alkali manufacturers at Widnes. He became chief chemist, and with Henry Deacon developed the process by which the by-product, hydrochloric acid, was converted to marketable chlorine and bleaching powder—an important contribution to the survival of the Leblanc soda process.

On 3 August 1871 Hurter married Hannah, daughter of R. Garnett of Farnworth; they had six children. Hurter was a pioneer in applying the disciplines of physical chemistry and thermodynamics to industrial processes. By 1880 he was recognized as an international authority on alkali manufacture. Competition from the more cost-effective ammonia-soda process forced the many Leblanc soda manufacturers to combine, and in 1891 the United Alkali Company was formed, with Hurter in charge of its research centre at Widnes. Soon afterwards he was asked to assess a new process, the production of caustic soda and chlorine by the electrolysis of brine. At a time when his health was failing, Hurter's judgement was affected by emotional loyalty to the Leblanc process, to which he had made such valuable contributions in the past, and following his advice, the company made a disastrous decision to decline the investment opportunity.

Hurter collaborated with Vero Driffield, an engineer, in research into photography; they published many papers and were awarded the progress medal of the Royal Photographic Society in 1895.

Hurter, who remained a Swiss citizen, was a sociable man, loved music, and played the clarinet and piano. He campaigned for free education, and for the introduction into Britain of the metric system. He was active in founding the Society of Chemical Industry, and read an important paper at the first meeting of the Liverpool section in 1881; he was its chairman in 1889–91. He died at his home, Holly Lodge, Cressington Park, Liverpool, on 12 March 1898 and was buried at Farnworth churchyard. The Hurter Laboratory of the United Alkali Company of Widnes was named in his memory, and the Society of Chemical Industry endowed the triennial Hurter memorial lecture.

N. J. TRAVIS, rev.

Sources D. W. F. Hardie, *A history of the chemical industry in Widnes* (1950) · 'Life and work of Ferdinand Hurter', *Journal of the Society of Chemical Industry*, 17 (1898), 406–11 · *Journal of the Society of Chemical Industry* (July 1931) [jubilee number] · D. W. Broad, *Centennial history of the Liverpool section, Society of Chemical Industry* (1981)
Likenesses photograph, repro. in Hardie, *History* (1950), facing p. 136
Wealth at death £6272 13s. 4d.: probate, 7 April 1898, *CGPLA Eng. & Wales*

Hurwitz, Hyman (1770–1844), biblical scholar, was born at Posen in Poland and raised in the Jewish community there. He came to England about 1800 and opened a private academy for Jews at Highgate, Middlesex, where he became a close friend of the poet Coleridge. Hurwitz's early works included *A Grammar of the Hebrew Language* (2nd edn, 1835), a Hebrew dirge for Princess Charlotte's funeral (chanted in the Great Synagogue, Aldgate, and afterwards translated into English verse by Coleridge), and another elegy, on George III, which was translated into English by W. Smith as 'The Knell'. Further contributions to Hebrew scholarship included *Vindiciae Hebraicae, being a Defence of the Hebrew Scriptures as a Vehicle of Revealed Religion* (1820) and *Hebrew Tales from the Writings of the Hebrew Sages* (1826). In 1828 he was elected professor of Hebrew language and literature at University College, London, where he wrote his most enduring work, *Elements of the Hebrew Language* (1829; 4th edn, 1848). Hurwitz died on 18 July 1844.

[ANON.], rev. SINÉAD AGNEW

Sources *Voice of Jacob*, 3/79 (2 Aug 1844), 196–7 · [J. Watkins and F. Shoberl], *A biographical dictionary of the living authors of Great Britain and Ireland* (1816) · Allibone, *Dict.* · Watt, *Bibl. Brit.*, 1.529a

Husband, Sir (Henry) Charles (1908–1983), civil engineer, was born on 30 October 1908 at 98 Mona Road, Sheffield, the youngest of the three children (all sons) of Joseph Husband (1871–1961) and his wife, Ellen Walton, née Harby. His father was the founder, in 1892, of the civil engineering department of the Sheffield Technical School. This eventually merged with the University of Sheffield of which he

was the first professor of civil engineering from 1921 to 1936. Charles was educated at King Edward VII School, Sheffield, and read engineering at Sheffield University, graduating BEng in 1929.

After gaining early experience with the Barnsley Water Board, Husband served from 1931 to 1933 as an assistant to the civil engineer and architect Sir (Evan) Owen Williams. On 19 March 1932 he married Eileen Margaret Nowill (b. 1906/7), daughter of Henry Nowill, architect, of Sheffield; they had two sons and two daughters. In 1933 he was appointed engineer and surveyor to the First National Housing Trust Ltd, with responsibility for the planning and construction of large housing schemes in England and Scotland. In 1936 he founded the firm of Husband and Clark, consulting engineers, in Sheffield. Other offices were subsequently opened in London and in Colombo in Ceylon. As a partner in this firm with his father and Antony Clark he was involved in a variety of public works varying from major road and railway bridges to drainage and water supply schemes. During the Second World War he was a principal technical officer in the central register of the Ministry of Labour and National Service (1939–40); from 1943 to 1945 he was assistant director on the directorate of aircraft-production factories of the Ministry of Works.

After the war, with Clark having retired from the partnership, Husband, who had become senior partner in 1937, sought to develop the firm, now Husband & Co., into one of the foremost engineering consultancies in the country. Under his leadership it quickly became involved in a wide range of construction projects. In 1946 he designed the first high-altitude testing plant for the continuous running of complete jet engines. From 1947 the firm received extensive commissions from the National Coal Board. It was also responsible for the construction of new buildings for various industrial organizations, and for the research establishments of the British Iron and Steel Research Association and the Production Engineering Research Association.

In 1949 Husband met Bernard Lovell at Jodrell Bank, Manchester University's research station north of Holmes Chapel in Cheshire. Lovell had been unable to interest a number of major engineering firms in the project to construct a large, steerable altazimuth radio telescope. They had felt that it was an impossible task, for the dish had to be not only mobile, which had not been achieved before with one of such size, but also rigid and free of any vibration which would blur the signals being received. Husband did not deem it impossible and in the autumn of 1957 the aperture telescope of 250 foot diameter came into operation. He subsequently presented a paper to the Institution of Civil Engineers (ICE) which dealt in depth with the engineering problems (*PICE*, 9, 1958–9, 65–86) and for which he was awarded the ICE's Benjamin Baker gold medal. The success of the telescope was a tribute to his engineering skill, determination, and courage, for, being designed before the age of digital computers, enormous difficulties had to be surmounted. Wind-tunnel experiments in particular had a considerable influence on the design, but structural, mechanical, and electrical techniques all had to be closely correlated. At the time of his death twenty-six years later it had worked with great success and, apart from standard maintenance, without interruption. He went on to design other large radio telescopes, at home and abroad, including the steerable aerials for the General Post Office's satellite/earth station at Goonhilly downs in Cornwall.

When Robert Stephenson's Britannia rail bridge across the Menai Strait to Anglesey in north Wales was severely damaged by fire in May 1970, Husband won the competition for its reconstruction. He described the design of the new bridge, and the associated problems, in half of another paper presented to the ICE (*PICE*, 58, 1975–6, 25–49); in the other half (49–66) his son Richard described its construction. When it opened ten years later the new bridge, with an added road deck above the rail deck, was not universally liked. Husband was accused of altering the design but he claimed to have been faithful to Stephenson's original plan. For his work he was awarded the James Watt medal of the ICE in 1976. At this time, in addition to many engineering projects in Britain, he was also involved with a variety of overseas activities, particularly in Sri Lanka where he was responsible for a number of public works. In 1964 he was appointed a CBE and in 1975 was knighted.

In 1964 Husband was made an honorary DSc at the University of Manchester and, in 1967, an honorary DEng at the University of Sheffield. At the latter he was a member of court of the university and was chairman of its advisory committee on engineering and metallurgy. In 1965 he was the first recipient of the Royal Society's queen's gold medal for distinguished contributions to the applied sciences. In 1966 he received the Wilhelm Exner medal for science and technology from the University of Vienna and the gold medal of the Institution of Structural Engineers in 1974. Husband was a founder fellow of the Fellowship of Engineering and a fellow of the ICE, the Institution of Mechanical Engineers, the Institution of Structural Engineers (of which he was president in 1964–5 and whose gold medal he received in 1974), and the American Society of Civil Engineers. In 1967 he was chairman of the Association of Consulting Engineers. He was a member of the Council of Engineering Institutions in 1965–6 and a board member from 1979.

Husband's outside interests were walking and, in particular, sailing. He undertook a number of sea voyages under difficult conditions. He died in Heatherleigh Nursing Home, Nether Padley, Derbyshire, on 7 October 1983. His elder son, Richard William Husband, succeeded him as head of the firm.   ROBERT SHARP

Sources *The Times* (8 Oct 1983), 10g · *The Times* (15 Oct 1983), 10g · personal knowledge (1990) [*DNB*] · private information (1990, 2004) · *WWW* · b. cert. · m. cert. · d. cert. · *CGPLA Eng. & Wales* (1984)
Wealth at death £568,339: probate, 17 Feb 1984, *CGPLA Eng. & Wales*

Husband, William (1822–1887), civil and mechanical engineer, was born at Mylor Bridge, Cornwall, on 13 October 1822, the eldest son of James Husband (d. 1859), shipbuilder and surveyor for Lloyd's Register at Falmouth. He was educated first by Edgcombe Rimell, curate of Mabe, and afterwards at Bellevue Academy, Penryn.

Husband showed an early and strong interest in engineering, and declining to be either a sailor or a shipbuilder, as his father desired, was in 1839 apprenticed for four years to Harvey & Co., engineers and ironfounders, of Hayle, Cornwall. His steadiness and ability soon won for him the esteem of his employers, and in 1843 he was sent to the Netherlands to superintend the erection of a large steam pumping-engine which they had constructed for the draining of Haarlem Lake. As the machinery could not be landed for some time because of ice, he went to the village school at Sassenheim to learn Dutch. In six months he wrote and spoke it with fluency. On the death in 1845 of the mechanical engineer in charge of the steam machinery on the drainage works he succeeded to that post, and successfully supervised the complex erection of the drainage engine. The lake when drained added 47,000 acres of rich alluvial soil to the country, and proved of great benefit to the economy of the region. William II of the Netherlands expressed his satisfaction, and on 13 March 1848 Husband was elected a member of the Koninklijk Instituut van Ingenieurs. While in the Netherlands, in conjunction with his friends Colonel Wiebeking and Professor Munnich, he also invented an inexpensive system for drying and warehousing grain, and preserving it in good condition for years.

In 1849 ill health forced Husband to return to England. The following year, on 20 June, he married Ann, fifth daughter of Edward Nanney; they had four children. In May 1851 he developed a plan for a floating powder magazine in the Mersey, on the recommendation of the Liverpool town council. He was also invited to go to Clifton to assist in some works in the Bristol docks, when he planned a bridge for the Cumberland basin. In September 1852 he undertook the management of the London business of Harvey & Co., and in June 1854 returned to Hayle to take charge of the engineering department. In 1863 he became managing partner. He resumed the management of the business in London in October 1885, and remained there until his death.

During his lifetime Husband was one of the leading authorities on hydraulic and mining machinery. In June 1859 he submitted to the Admiralty a plan for a floating battery, and patented a number of significant inventions, many intended to improve the safety of pumping machinery. He also effected many improvements in the pneumatic ore stamps used in tin, copper, iron, and other ore mines. During the last two years of his life he was employed in carrying out contracts for the pumping machinery at the Severn Tunnel, and at the time of his death was planning further improvements in Cornish mine pumping engines. On 1 May 1866 he was elected a member of the Institution of Civil Engineers, and during

1881 and 1882 served as president of the Mining Association and Institute of Cornwall. He was an active supporter of improved technical education as a member of the Royal Cornwall Polytechnic Society, and he established science classes in Hayle in connection with the Royal College of Science at South Kensington. In 1855 he planned and superintended the erection of a breakwater at Porthleven in Mounts Bay, Cornwall, thereby making it a safe harbour. He helped to secure a water supply for Hayle and a system of drainage. He originated and became first captain of the 8th Cornwall artillery volunteers in April 1860, a post which he held until 1865. He took a great interest in astronomy and spectrum analysis, and made many observations with a 10¼ inch telescope.

He died at his lodgings, 26 Sion Hill, Clifton, Bristol, on 10 April 1887 of an attack of gallstones and was buried at St Erth, Cornwall, on 16 April. In 1890 a sum of £800 was raised to establish a Husband scholarship for the technical education of miners.

G. C. BOASE, rev. RALPH HARRINGTON

Sources The Times (3 May 1887) • PICE, 89 (1886–7), 470–73 • The Engineer (6 May 1887) • Iron (6 May 1887) • Boase, Mod. Eng. biog. • private information (1891) • DNB
Wealth at death £22,204 12s. od.: probate, 11 May 1887, CGPLA Eng. & Wales

Husbands, John (1706–1732), critic, was born at Marsh Baldon, Oxfordshire, on 29 January 1706 and baptized there on 12 February 1706, the son of the Revd Thomas Husbands (1677–1728), vicar of Canon Pyon, Herefordshire, and his wife, Elizabeth. Thomas was formerly chaplain of New College, Oxford, and preached in the university two days before John was baptized.

John Husbands was educated at a Mr Rodd's school in Hereford, matriculated from Pembroke College, Oxford, on 28 July 1721, graduated BA in 1725 and MA in 1728, and was elected fellow on 7 June 1728; he took deacon's orders in 1728 and priest's a year later. He contributed Latin verses to an Oxford University collection marking the death of George I and accession of George II (1727). In 1731 he published in Oxford, by subscription, A Miscellany of Poems 'by several hands' in which all but about fifteen of the sixty-one poems were by himself. Strangely, Richard Savage subscribed for twenty copies. The only poem in the volume now remembered is a college exercise by Samuel Johnson: a Latin version of Pope's 'Messiah' and Johnson's first appearance in print. Boswell was told it was printed for Johnson's father, who was acquainted with some of the fellows of Pembroke, and Johnson, who had gone down in December 1729, 'was very angry when he heard of it' (Boswell, Life, 1.61, 59).

Husbands's preface, 120 pages long, reveals advanced critical opinions, for it is an enthusiastic dissertation on 'natural' primitive poetry, especially the Hebrew scriptures. He intended to carry this line of criticism further because at the time of his death 'he was preparing for the press a Comparison of the Eastern and Western Poetry' (GM, 1st ser., 2.1083). He died, unmarried, on 21 November 1732 in Compton Bassett, Wiltshire, at the seat of William Northey. His father had died at Canon Pyon on 26 April 1728, leaving his widow with very limited means; she was still alive in 1734.

JAMES SAMBROOK

Sources Remarks and collections of Thomas Hearne, ed. C. E. Doble and others, 11 vols., OHS, 2, 7, 13, 34, 42–3, 48, 50, 65, 67, 72 (1885–1921), vol.1, p. 182; vol. 4, p. 326; vol. 5, p. 268; vol. 11, p. 136 (quoting Northampton Mercury, 4 Dec 1732) • Foster, Alum. Oxon. • GM, 1st ser., 2 (1732), 1083 • J. Husbands, A miscellany of poems (1731), 170 • A. L. Reade, Johnsonian gleanings, 5 (privately printed, London, 1928), 194–5 • W. P. Courtney and D. Nichol Smith, A bibliography of Samuel Johnson (1915), 1 • Boswell, Life, 1.61, 527 • MS biography of Thomas Husbands, Hereford Cathedral Library, HCA 7003/4/3 • E. H. Fellowes and E. R. Poyser, The baptism, marriage, and burial registers of St George's chapel, Windsor (1957) • HoP, Commons, 1715–54 • R. S. Crane, 'An early 18th century enthusiast for primitive poetry: John Husbands', Modern Language Notes, 37 (1922), 27–36

Husenbeth, Frederick Charles (1796–1872), Roman Catholic writer, was born at Bristol on 30 May 1796, the son of Frederick Charles Husenbeth (d. 1848), a German emigré, and his wife, Elizabeth James (d. 1876), a convert to Roman Catholicism of Cornish origin. The elder Husenbeth, a native of the grand duchy of Hesse, was a teacher of classics and languages at Mannheim before settling at Bristol, where he established a wine business. He was an excellent musician, and is said to have been a friend of Samuel Taylor Coleridge. In 1803 the younger Husenbeth was sent to the Catholic school at Sedgley Park, near Wolverhampton, for which he retained a lifelong affection. In 1810 he was placed in his father's business, but three years later, on declaring his wish to become a priest, he was allowed to resume his studies, first at Sedgley Park, and then, from 1814, at St Mary's College, Oscott, where he was ordained priest in 1820. Soon afterwards he was sent to Costessey Hall, Norfolk, as chaplain to Sir George Jerningham, who in 1824 succeeded to the barony of Stafford. He arrived at Costessey on 7 July 1820 and remained there for fifty-two years, residing not at the hall, like previous chaplains, but in his own quarters in the village. In 1827 he was appointed grand vicar to Thomas Walsh, vicar apostolic of the Midland district, and in 1841 opened the new chapel of St Wulstan at Costessey. In 1850 Pope Pius IX conferred on him the degree of DD. After the re-establishment of the Catholic hierarchy in England in 1850 he was appointed on 24 June 1852 provost of the new diocesan chapter of Northampton. He was also a member of the Old Brotherhood of the English secular clergy and became its president shortly before his death.

In his funeral sermon Canon John Dalton described Husenbeth as 'a priest of the old school', perhaps more suited to a college life than to that of a priest on the mission. Exact and methodical, Husenbeth was an indefatigable antiquary and one of the most valued contributors to Notes and Queries, for which he wrote 1305 articles. Fifty-four works written, translated, or edited by him are listed in Gillow's Bibliographical Dictionary of the English Catholics. His works of controversy included several replies to George Stanley Faber and a Defence of the Creed and Discipline of the Catholic Church, countering the attacks of Joseph Blanco White. His talents were more fitted, however, for work of an antiquarian or historical nature. His Emblems of

Saints by which they are Distinguished in Works of Art (1850) became a widely used work of reference and was republished after his death by the Norfolk Archaeological Society in an extended third edition by the Revd A. Jessopp. Husenbeth's life of Joseph Milner, published in 1862, though written in a spirit of hero-worship, remains valuable for its first-hand biographical detail, as does his life of Henry Weedall (1860), which covers the early history of Old Oscott College but pointedly omits all mention of the new Oscott created by Nicholas Wiseman. Like many of the older English clergy, Husenbeth regarded Wiseman with some suspicion. His nostalgic *History of Sedgley Park School* (1856) vividly evokes what he saw as the homely piety characteristic of the Catholic middle class on the eve of emancipation. He also produced a much-reprinted missal for the use of the laity (1837) and a revision (1853) of the edition of the Douai Bible published by George and Thomas Haydock. Though the son of a wine merchant he became an advocate of total abstinence and a warm supporter of the apostle of the movement, Father Theobald Mathew.

A man of outspoken prejudices, which included a dislike of new-fangled devotional practices and a distrust of the growing influence of the religious orders, Husenbeth embodied the virtues as well as the limitations of the old secular clergy, to whose interests he was devoted. He died at Costessey on 31 October 1872 and was buried there on 6 November.   G. Martin Murphy

Sources Gillow, *Lit. biog. hist.* · J. Dalton, *Funeral sermon* (1872) · *N&Q*, 4th ser., 10 (1872), 441–2 · *The Tablet* (16 Nov 1872), 628–9 · *DNB* · *CGPLA Eng. & Wales* (1872)
Archives Norfolk RO, notes on Norfolk churches; original poetry and translations | Ushaw College, Durham, corresp. with Nicholas Wiseman
Likenesses photograph, repro. in *The Oscotian* [magazine of St Mary's College, Oscott], 5th ser., 4 (1934), 1
Wealth at death under £1500: probate, 20 Dec 1872, *CGPLA Eng. & Wales*

Husk, William Henry (1814–1887), writer on music, was born on 4 November 1814 in London, the son of a solicitor's clerk. He was employed as clerk to Manning and Dalston, a firm of solicitors, from 1833 until the year before his death. In 1834 he joined the Sacred Harmonic Society of which he was librarian from 1852 until the dissolution of the society in 1882. He spent ten years compiling a *Catalogue of the Library of the Sacred Harmonic Society* (1862), with a revised and expanded edition published in 1872, and wrote prefaces to the wordbooks of the oratorios performed at the Sacred Harmonic Society's concerts. He also wrote an *Account of the Musical Celebrations on St Cecilia's Day in the Sixteenth, Seventeenth, and Eighteenth Centuries*, with *A Collection of Odes on St Cecilia's Day* (1857), and edited *Songs of the Nativity* (1864). He supplied many entries for the first edition of Grove's *Dictionary of Music and Musicians* (1879).

Husk died on 12 August 1887 at 20 Westmoreland Place, Pimlico, London, and was buried in Brompton cemetery on 19 August.

L. M. Middleton, *rev.* Anne Pimlott Baker

Sources *New Grove* · Boase, *Mod. Eng. biog.* · *MT*, 28 (1887), 539 · *Musical World* (27 Aug 1887), 680 · D. Baptie, *A handbook of musical biography* (1883) · *CGPLA Eng. & Wales* (1888)
Wealth at death £282 14s. 2d.: probate, 12 Jan 1888, *CGPLA Eng. & Wales*

Huske, Ellis (1700–1755). *See under* Huske, John (1692?–1761).

Huske, John (1692?–1761), army officer, is unheard of before he first entered the army on 7 April 1708 as an ensign in Colonel Toby Caulfeild's regiment of foot. He next appears as a cornet in Colonel William Cadogan's regiment of horse (later the 5th dragoon guards), his commission dated 18 March 1709. However, according to Charles Dalton, on 24 March 1709 he transferred to the Grenadier Guards with whom he served at the battle of Malplaquet later that year.

On 22 July 1715 Huske was appointed captain and lieutenant-colonel of one of the four new companies then added to the Coldstream Guards. At that time and afterwards he was aide-de-camp to the regiment's commanding officer, William Cadogan. Cadogan's role as a leading supporter of the Hanoverian succession saw Huske heavily involved as a confidential agent in the suppression of Jacobitism both in England and on the continent after the rising of 1715. In August he was sent to Paris on secret government business and in October he was ordered to Minehead to arrest Sir William Wyndham, the leader of English Jacobitism in the west country. Wyndham escaped after giving Huske his parole, but later gave himself up. Huske was with Cadogan in Scotland with forces brought over from the Netherlands and when the latter returned there in April 1716 as envoy and minister-plenipotentiary, Huske was sent on a series of anti-Jacobite missions. Thus in April 1717 he travelled to Paris to inform the ambassador, John Dalrymple, second earl of Stair, of James Stuart's movements. In 1718 he received Treasury payments for expenses incurred on government service in the Low Countries. In April 1719 following rumours of a Spanish descent upon the English coast, in concert with Charles Whitworth, the British plenipotentiary at the Hague, he organized the payment for and transport of three Dutch and two Swiss battalions taken into British service.

In March 1720 Huske accompanied Cadogan's diplomatic mission to Berlin and Vienna to arrange terms for the accession of Spain to the Quadruple Alliance. He was appointed lieutenant-governor of Hurst Castle on 8 July 1721. He was made second major (in the Coldstream Guards) on 30 October 1734 and first major on 5 July 1739. On 25 December 1740 he became colonel of the 32nd regiment of foot (later the Cornwall light infantry). He commanded a brigade of infantry at Dettingen in 1743 where according to an account by an officer with the 23rd foot (later the Royal Welch Fusiliers), he 'behaved quite gloriously and quite cool, was shot through the foot at the time that our colonel fell, yet continued his post' (*GM*, 1st ser., 13, 1743, 386). In recognition of his conduct, on 28 July 1743 he was appointed colonel of the 23rd foot and promoted major-general.

At the Jacobite rising in 1745 Huske was appointed to serve under General George Wade at Newcastle. As a senior staff officer he was kept busy by the sequence of futile marches and counter-marches in pursuit of the Jacobite army—recorded for posterity in correspondence between his aide-de-camp, Captain Richard Webb, and his regimental agent, William Adam, in London. His solicitude for the junior officers and soldiers who served under him was well known and earned him the nickname Daddy Huske.

According to Speck he was considered for the appointment of general of the army to be sent to Scotland, but was discounted because of his lesser rank; instead he went as second in command to Lieutenant-General Henry Hawley.

Following the siege of government forces at Stirling Castle, on 13 January 1746, Huske was sent with the vanguard of the government army to Linlithgow. Hawley arrived with reinforcements near Falkirk on the evening of 16 January. However, he failed to anticipate an attack by the Jacobite army. On the afternoon of 17 January the government force, caught off guard by news that the approaching highlanders were attempting to take command of Falkirk muir above the town, was hurriedly formed up and marched out to battle. However, the matter was poorly conducted and the situation was made worse by the onset of a severe storm. An initial charge by Hawley's cavalry was repulsed and their falling back caused disorder among the foot regiments of Hawley's left flank. These regiments together with the whole of the second line then turned and ran as several Highland regiments charged down upon them. A total rout was only averted by Huske, together with Brigadier James Cholmondeley, who rallied the right flank and stalled the highlanders' advance with a steady flanking fire. Huske maintained a rearguard on the field which allowed the royal army to retreat unpursued to Linlithgow.

Huske only narrowly avoided death himself:

> for a rebel officer, putting on a red coat, mixt himself with ours … and being come the General, drew a pistol to shoot him but Brigadier Cholmondeley was as near the General, struck up his pistol in the air, where it went off, and the daring officer was secured. (*Egmont Diary*, 3.313)

Huske further distinguished himself at the battle of Culloden. Following the charge of the highlanders against the royal army's left wing, Huske brought up the second line to seal off their advance by a flanking movement, which effectively won the battle.

According to one report, after the battle both Huske and Hawley gave orders for the slaying of the enemy wounded, who, whatever the truth of this, were left without aid and under guard on Drummossie Moor for several days. Following the battle he commanded the garrison at Fort Augustus where he proposed the idea of a £5 bounty for the head of every rebel brought into camp. This measure was not adopted but, as John Prebble wrote, Huske:

> who was a good soldier and an otherwise kindly man, was merely acting in character, a general officer outraged and bewildered by men in rebellion against the simple decencies of God, King, Country and Flag. His savage proposal was also symptomatic of the army's general mood and behaviour. (Prebble, 203)

Huske was made a lieutenant-general on 11 May 1747, and served in Flanders during 1747–8. He was absent from his regiment, the 23rd foot, when it took part in the unsuccessful defence of Minorca in 1756. He became a full general on 12 December 1756.

In 1753 Huske purchased Ealing House, in the parish of the same name in Middlesex, together with an estate valued at £4000 in 1761. Huske died, unmarried, at Ealing House on 18 January 1761. He left an estate valued at £41,842, full particulars of which were published in the *Gentleman's Magazine* of January 1761. He was particularly generous to his many servants and friends. Ealing House was devised to his regimental agent, William Adam, an executor of his will. He left a sum of £3200 to be divided among his family, the children of his late brothers Ellis and Richard Huske.

Ellis Huske (1700–1755), judge, younger brother of Major-General John Huske, was born in England; by 1720 he had emigrated to Massachusetts where, on 25 October at Salem, he married Mary (*b.* 1702), daughter of Ichabod Plaisted, judge of probate in New Hampshire. Ellis Huske became postmaster at Boston in 1734. He preceded Benjamin Franklin as deputy postmaster-general of the colonies. He was a member of the New Hampshire provincial council from 1733 to 1755, justice of the superior court (1739–49), and chief justice (1749–54). He was the publisher of the *Boston Weekly Postboy*, and reputed author of *The Present State of North America*, published in London in 1755. He died in America in 1755.

From his marriage to Mary Plaisted, Huske had a son, **John Huske** (1724–1773), politician, born at Portsmouth, New Hampshire, on 3 July 1724. He came to England in 1748 after a period as a Boston merchant. He became a political ally of Charles Townshend and gained a reputation as a 'tough, unscrupulous adventurer' (Namier, 659). He was appointed deputy treasurer of the chamber, to Townshend as treasurer, in December 1756. He was a ruthless election manager but his interventions tended to alienate electorates. General John Huske pointedly excluded his nephew John from the provisions of his will. Huske was eventually elected member for Maldon on 26 April 1763, often speaking on American issues, but voting with government on most issues. He was burned in effigy by his fellow colonists in Boston for supporting the Stamp Act, but Namier argued that the evidence demonstrated Huske was actually a consistent opponent. He died in Paris in October 1773, having left England in 1769 under threat of arrest for reputedly embezzling £30,000–£40,000 during his time as secretary to Charles Townshend when the latter was treasurer to the chamber. He was probably unmarried, but left one son, apprenticed to a man called Hooper in North Carolina.

JONATHAN SPAIN

Sources C. Dalton, ed., *English army lists and commission registers, 1661–1714*, 6 (1904) • C. Dalton, *George the First's army, 1714–1727*, 2 vols. (1910–12) • A. D. L. Cary, S. McCance, and others, eds., *Regimental records of the Royal Welch Fusiliers (late the 23rd foot)*, 7 vols. (1921–), vol. 1 • S. Reid, *1745: a military history of the last Jacobite rising* (1996) • K. Tomasson and F. Buist, *Battles of the '45* (1962) • D. Mackinnon,

Origin and services of the Coldstream guards, 2 vols. (1833) • J. Black, *Culloden and the '45* (1990) • W. A. Speck, *The Butcher: the duke of Cumberland and the suppression of the 45* (1981) • J. Prebble, *Culloden* (1961) • C. Sinclair-Stevenson, *Inglorious rebellion: the Jacobite risings of 1708, 1715 and 1719* (1971) • C. Petrie, *The Jacobite movement*, 3rd edn (1958) • J. Redington, ed., *Calendar of Treasury papers*, 6 vols., PRO (1868–89), vol. 5, p. 133; vol. 6, p. 1 • W. A. Shaw, ed., *Calendar of treasury books*, 31/2, PRO (1960), 280; 32/2 (1957), 272 • *GM*, 1st ser., 13 (1743), 386 • *GM*, 1st ser., 31 (1761), 44 • L. B. Namier, 'Huske, John', HoP, *Commons, 1754–90* • *Report on manuscripts in various collections*, 8 vols., HMC, 55 (1901–14), vol. 8, pp. 141, 163 • *Manuscripts of the earl of Egmont: diary of Viscount Percival, afterwards first earl of Egmont*, 3 vols., HMC, 63 (1920–23), vol. 3, p. 313 [Falkirk] • *Report on the Laing manuscripts*, 2, HMC, 72 (1925), 352–7, 367 • *Report on the manuscripts of Lord Polwarth*, 5 vols., HMC, 67 (1911–61), vol. 2, pp. 119, 506 • *VCH Middlesex*, 7.130–31

Archives BL, dialogue on his killing of the wounded at Culloden in verse, 1746, Add. MS 33954, fol. 82 • BL, opinion in favour of a march into Germany, Add. MS 22537, fol. 240 • BL, corresp. with duchess of Marlborough, Add. MS 61351, fols. 225–235b • BL, letters to duke of Newcastle • BL, letters to J. Yorke, Add. MS 35431 • U. Nott., letters to Henry Pelham

Wealth at death £41,842: *GM*, 31

Huske, John (1724–1773). *See under* Huske, John (1692?–1761).

Huskisson, Thomas (1784–1844), naval officer, son of William Huskisson (*d.* 1790) of Oxley, near Wolverhampton, and half-brother of William *Huskisson, the politician, was born on 31 July 1784. He attended Wolverhampton grammar school, and entered the navy in July 1800 (under the patronage of Admiral Mark Milbanke) on the sloop *Beaver*. A few months later, he was moved to the *Romney*, and went to the East Indies under the command of Captain Sir Home Popham. On the *Romney*'s being paid off he was appointed to the *Defence* with Captain George Hope, and was present at Trafalgar, when he was stationed on the poop in charge of the signals. Huskisson was afterwards moved into the *Foudroyant*, flagship of Sir John Borlase Warren, in which he was present at the capture of the *Marengo* and *Belle Poule* on 13 March 1806. In August he received a commission as acting lieutenant of the *Foudroyant*, which was confirmed by the Admiralty on 15 November. In 1807 he was signal lieutenant to Lord Gambier on the *Prince of Wales* in the expedition to Copenhagen, and in 1808 went to the West Indies in the *Melpomene*, from which he was promoted to the command of the *Pelorus* (18 guns) on 18 January 1809. In her he assisted in the capture of a French ship under the battery at Pointe-à-Pitre, and in the capture of Guadeloupe.

In 1810 Huskisson was appointed acting captain of the *Blonde* which he brought home, and on 14 March 1811 he was posted to the *Garland* (28 guns). In June 1812, still in the West Indies, he was moved into the *Barbadoes* (24 guns), which, as the French privateer *Brave*, had won a wide reputation for exceptional speed in 1804. As war was just then declared against the United States, Huskisson hoped that this remarkable speed might win him distinction and profit, and he was cruelly disappointed when, sent with a small convoy to Halifax, the ship was lost in a fog on Sable Island (Nova Scotia) on 28 September 1812, a misfortune which deprived him of active service for the rest of the war.

Huskisson married, in 1813, Elizabeth, daughter of Francis Wedge of Aqualate Park, Staffordshire. They had four sons and two daughters. In the summer of 1815 he commanded the *Euryalus* (42 guns), on the coast of France, and from 1818 to 1821 was in her in the West Indies, where for two periods of six months he was senior officer of the station, with a broad pennant. In 1821–2 he commanded the *Semiramis* (42 guns) at Cork, as flag captain to Lord Colville, and in March 1827 was appointed paymaster of the navy by his brother William, then treasurer of the navy. In October 1830, when the office of paymaster was abolished, Huskisson was promised the first vacant commissionership of the navy; but the Navy Board itself was abolished at about the same time, and he was appointed one of the captains of the Royal Naval Hospital, Greenwich, a less valuable office. The death of his brother and the change of ministry were fatal to his prospects, and he remained at the Greenwich hospital, combining his duties between 1831 and 1840 with that of superintendent of the hospital schools. He died at Greenwich on 21 December 1844. His manuscript memoirs up to 1808 were published in 1985.

J. K. LAUGHTON, *rev.* ANDREW LAMBERT

Sources T. Huskisson, *Eyewitness to Trafalgar* (1985) • O'Byrne, *Naval biog. dict.* • J. Marshall, *Royal naval biography*, suppl. 2 (1828), 338 • J. Marshall, *Royal naval biography*, 4/2 (1835), 452 • private information (1891)

Archives Worcs. RO, draft for his biography

Huskisson, William (1770–1830), politician, was born on 11 March 1770 at Birtsmorton Court, Worcestershire, the eldest of four sons of William Huskisson (1743–1790), gentleman, and his first wife, Elizabeth (*c.*1743–1774), who was daughter of John Rotton of Oxley, Staffordshire, and his wife, Jane. As a young boy Huskisson was sent away to school, in turn to Brewood, in Staffordshire; Albrighton, in Shropshire; and Appleby, in Leicestershire. Following his father's second marriage he was sent in 1783, with his brother Richard, to be educated by their mother's uncle, Richard Gem, who had settled as a doctor in Paris in 1762. Under his guidance Huskisson received an unorthodox education which would later mark him out from his political colleagues. For Gem's friends included the freethinking Baron d'Holbach and other *philosophes*, as well as Franklin and Jefferson. In the light of subsequent ultra-tory charges that he had been a Jacobin, Huskisson prudently claimed that his ideas had been formed in England. But it is difficult to believe that he was untouched by the intellectual currents of late Enlightenment France. He witnessed the fall of the Bastille, was an early critic of Burke's 'strange romantic doctrines' (Melville, 9), and was befriended by the radical poet William Hayley. He made his first public mark as a member of the liberal Société de 1789, contributing in August 1790 a strong criticism of the new French paper currency. The leading light in this club was Condorcet, at whose home Talleyrand claimed Huskisson learned his system of public economy, while it was

William Huskisson (1770–1830), by Richard Rothwell, 1830

less credibly rumoured that Madame Condorcet taught him the arts of love. Huskisson's political outlook, albeit subsequently modulated by other influences, retained much in common with that of the French school of political economy of Turgot, Say, and the Idéologues. More importantly for his immediate political career, in late 1790 Huskisson became private secretary to the British ambassador, Earl Gower, sharing intimately in the *événements* of the early revolution before returning to London in September 1792, after Britain severed diplomatic relations with France.

The making of a Pittite, 1793–1814 Under the patronage of Gower, Huskisson was introduced to Pitt and Dundas. His grasp of French as well as his administrative promise led to his appointment as superintendent of the aliens office in January 1793, overseeing arrangements for the influx of French émigrés and helping to set up Britain's modern secret service. In July 1794 Huskisson moved with Dundas and Nepean to the War Office, where he became chief clerk. He had impressed his seniors so much that when Nepean subsequently moved to the Admiralty he was able to lay claim to his post as under-secretary in March 1795, a remarkable promotion for a 24-year-old recommended by talent rather than by pedigree. In 1796, through Gower's friend the earl of Carlisle, Huskisson was elected to parliament for Morpeth. It was also at Gower's Wimbledon home that Huskisson first met Canning, forming a strong personal attachment that became the lodestar of his later political trajectory. But his first loyalty lay to Pitt and Dundas, while his administrative responsibilities brought

him to the heart of the war effort against France, including close involvement in military planning and strategy as well as counter-revolutionary activity.

Huskisson's official success was not yet complemented by financial security. In 1793 he had sold his father's Oxley estates for £13,500, and received a further £2500 on the death of his brother Richard in 1794. Imprudently as it turned out, he lent these sums to his Paris-based friend the banker Walter Boyd, incurring charges of stockjobbing and eventually losing some £14,000. This was largely made good by the £10,000 he inherited on the death of Gem in 1800. Having also secured a government pension and the agency to the Cape of Good Hope, Huskisson had sufficient prospects to marry, on 6 April 1799, Eliza Emily (1777–1856), the daughter of Admiral Mark Milbanke and his wife, Mary Webber. Their marriage was childless, but provided the sometimes neurotic and paranoic Huskisson with welcome domestic tranquillity. Huskisson also inherited from Gem substantial landed property, including the mortgage on Eartham, in Sussex, then occupied by his friend Hayley. Eartham provided Huskisson with landed status and an indispensable venue for political entertaining. Tall and ungainly in appearance, and often cold and dry in his public manner, he was a ready and occasionally playful host, a good shot, and enjoyed country house visits. Even so, social routine was always subordinate to Huskisson's overriding ethic of hard work and public duty, designed to secure stability and prosperity for Britain at a time of revolutionary political and economic change.

As one of Pitt's confidential group, Huskisson resigned in January 1801, receiving a pension of £1200 p.a. and the lucrative Ceylon agency (in place of that of the Cape). But his career now reached a hiatus, for while he toyed with taking office under Addington, he found himself without a seat in parliament, Morpeth having passed to Carlisle's son. Not wishing to owe his seat to the new ministry, he unsuccessfully contested Dover, with the encouragement of Pitt, losing £3000 in the process, and receiving much adverse publicity as Cobbett's *Political Register* exposed his dealings with Boyd. Huskisson, a fervent admirer of Pitt's 'superior virtue and superior sense' (Fay, 71), was rewarded on Pitt's return to office in May 1804 by appointment as joint secretary to the Treasury. By this time he had found a seat in parliament, this time for Liskeard, which was placed at his disposal by Lord Eliot. While not a prominent orator in the Commons, he played a leading part in securing the important Warehousing Act of 1804. He saw Pitt's approaching death in January 1806 as 'the end of all things' (Melville, 59), and when Grenville succeeded Pitt in February 1806 Huskisson once more found himself in opposition.

'[S]et loose by the death of Pitt' (Thorne, 272), Huskisson attached himself politically to Canning, one of a number of potential leaders of 'Mr Pitt's friends'. Besides their early friendship and their temperamental complementarity, they had recently worked together when Canning was treasurer of the navy in 1804–6. But Huskisson also set out to make an independent mark in the Commons, proposing in July 1806 his scheme for the rationalization of government accounting. When the Portland ministry succeeded that of Grenville, he returned in April 1807 to his position at the Treasury, and was elected for the Treasury borough of Harwich. Acknowledged as the leading Pittite financial expert, he played an important part in 'cleaning up' relations between the government and the Bank of England, and in supervising Ireland's finances. Yet, once again Huskisson's stay in office proved short-lived. For having attached himself to Canning, he proved disinterested and loyal when Canning's bid both to oust Castlereagh from the ministry and to take the lead himself resulted in the infamous duel between the two rivals, and to Canning's and Huskisson's resignations in September 1809.

Huskisson was confined to the political wilderness for the next five years, but the pattern of his future career was now set. First, his prospects for office remained tied fast to those of Canning. They acted in concert in parliament, while Huskisson declined office in 1809, in 1811, and, above all, in 1812 in what many saw as a factious refusal to join Lord Liverpool's re-creation of the Pittite coalition. This was a crucial turning point—with Huskisson's career now 'thrown out of the course' (Huskisson to Canning, 25 April 1821, BL, Add. MS 38742, fol. 206) and men he considered his juniors promoted ahead of him. In addition, having forfeited Treasury support Huskisson needed a constituency, which he eventually found at Chichester, conveniently near Eartham. Second, Huskisson consolidated his reputation as the 'first financier of the age' (Speeches, 54). In particular, he emerged as a leading bullionist, attacking the evils of depreciation of the currency following the wartime resort to paper money in 1797 and advocating the speedy resumption of cash payments. Huskisson believed that only convertibility would remedy the evils of inflation, which he regarded as not only ruinous to creditors but possibly revolutionary in its consequences. He played a major part in the proceedings of the famous bullion committee in 1810, and published his important pamphlet, The Question Concerning the Depreciation of our Currency Stated and Examined, in October 1810, which soon went through seven editions. In 1811 he also joined Canning and others in defending the report in the Quarterly Review. He now became the leading critic of Vansittart's management of the economy, displaying the financial grasp that marked him out by 1814 as Pitt's administrative heir among the tories, while in parliament he had secured an important niche for himself as Canning's leading lieutenant. Yet Huskisson was not a politician to thrive in opposition, for he was a man of business par excellence. It was to be Lord Liverpool who now set him to constructive work.

'The best practical man of business in England', 1814–1823 In 1814 Canning, on accepting office under Liverpool, had stipulated that Huskisson should also be offered a post. Eventually he was appointed first commissioner of the woods and forests in August. This office entailed important responsibilities which Huskisson undertook with typical conscientious devotion to detail and duty—perambulating the king's forests and assisting in the rebuilding of later Georgian London. His career in that post might therefore appear, as some have seen it, as relatively 'thankless' (Thorne, 277). But in reality he rapidly became a pivotal figure, one of the group of advisers upon whom Liverpool depended for the formulation and execution of detailed policy, 'the little committee by which all the parliamentary business has been settled' (Correspondence of Charles Arbuthnot, 19 n.2). For Liverpool, policy making was essentially a task for those outside the cabinet, and Huskisson felt he was treated 'not as belonging to a political party, but simply as chairman of an executive board'. This irked him, as he saw himself as a career politician, and a colleague in no way less valuable than socially superior but ineffectual cabinet ministers. Yet however frustrated he became, Huskisson remained indefatigable, and his imprint was fundamental to the economic and financial policies of Liverpool's government.

Huskisson's mark was first felt with regard to the corn law of 1815, when he supported a graduated scale of duties on corn as the best means to ensure stability of supply. In 1814 he had composed crucial parts of the Commons' committee report on corn, and by February 1815 he and Liverpool had 'forged a "cordial" and lifelong alliance on economic policy' (Hilton, Corn, 12). In deference to Huskisson's views, Vansittart abandoned his own proposal for a small fixed duty on corn in favour of Huskisson's sliding scale, but eventually this was also replaced by duties of 80s. on foreign corn and 67s. on imperial corn. Huskisson also secured the free warehousing of corn, vital as a spur to investment in the corn trade and as a guarantee of supplies in case of scarcity, a fear reinforced by Huskisson's experience of conditions in pre-revolutionary France.

If the corn law was for Huskisson a necessary part of the transition from war to peace, far more vital was the return to sound money. From 1816, with Canning's support, he crusaded for a swift return to cash payments, and when Peel's committee was set up in 1819 he seized the initiative, ensuring that the committee viewed the question simply as a matter of timing, not of principle. In drawing up its report he pressed for immediate resumption, but was happy with the compromise outcome of mid-1823, a date advanced by the Bank of England to 1821. Huskisson also aimed to put government finances back on what he considered a proper footing; this included an effective sinking fund (a touchstone of loyalty to Pitt) and stringent government retrenchment, including that of royal expenditure. Huskisson won an important victory when the cabinet in May 1819 endorsed his scheme for devoting a £5 million surplus to debt redemption. Through such policies Huskisson had won the 'undergame' for Liverpool's ear, defeating the Vansittart–Herries–Rothschild faction—but ensuring a residue of long-running resentment in these circles. Yet Huskisson had clear long-term goals in view—to stabilize existing social relations, to cut the government free from the monied power and the Bank of England, and to make London the chief financial centre of the world. He consolidated his victory in 1822, when he carried an amendment that parliament should not alter the standard of value, ensuring that the gold standard would last (until 1914) as a symbol of fiscal and political rectitude.

In 1821 Huskisson also returned to the question of the corn laws, taking the 'labouring oar' (Melville, 138) in the select committee of that year and producing, with Ricardo, a report which foreshadowed eventual free trade in corn. This marked a substantial change in Huskisson's views on the corn laws, for he favoured abandoning the inefficient margins of cultivation, accepting Ricardo's law of diminishing returns, while looking to Europe to feed industrial Britain's growing population if suitably encouraged by the lowering of Britain's protective duties. Huskisson accepted that Britain's economic future was geared to manufacturing exports and the vicissitudes of the international economy. This perspective would vitally underpin his subsequent work at the Board of Trade, while it also ended the prospects of increased agricultural protection, further alienating Huskisson from the strong tory rural interest.

By 1822 Huskisson, a tireless and efficient administrator, admirably deployed by the skilful leadership of Lord Liverpool, had imparted a new decisiveness to tory economic policy. But however devoted an executive politician, Huskisson was also driven by ambition which looked to the highest offices of state, hitherto forfeited by his loyalty to Canning. It was therefore with Canning's prospective return to high office in 1821–2 that Huskisson looked for his own elevation to the cabinet, and the end of 'nearly eight years of lingering expectation' (Melville, 134). In the extensive political intrigues of 1821–2 Huskisson had set his heart on the Board of Control, but this was denied him. Canning urged him to accept the Board of Trade, an office eminently congenial to Huskisson, although one he believed should be accompanied by cabinet rank. But he was kept out of the cabinet, largely because Liverpool, irritated by his desire for promotion, kept him back in order to accommodate Charles Wynn, a member of the Grenvillite squad, which had lately adhered to the ministry. This episode induced much angry self-pity and heightened Huskisson's strong sense of social inferiority, but he was eventually assuaged by the promise of the next cabinet vacancy or admission after one year. In February 1823 Huskisson therefore became president of the Board of Trade, with the treasurership of the navy, before eventually joining the cabinet in November of the same year.

The Board of Trade, 1823–1827 Huskisson's work at the Board of Trade, long hailed as central both to 'liberal toryism' and to Britain's gradual adoption of free trade, was based firmly on the economic and financial policies he had put in place between 1814 and 1823. Those policies had been shaped largely by principles drawn from Smith and Ricardo, although Huskisson, like many of his contemporaries, occasionally attended the sermons of the evangelical Thomas Chalmers. But Huskisson was no doctrinaire, and his work at the board, as even his critic Herries noted, 'steered a steady course' between practicality and abstraction (Hilton, *Corn*, 182). He built purposefully on the work of colleagues such as Wallace and Robinson, but now put the board at the centre of the governmental machine. Significantly, too, in 1823 Huskisson succeeded Canning as MP for Liverpool. He had previously deputized for him on Liverpool parliamentary business, forming valuable links with merchants such as John Gladstone, and he was well equipped to consolidate mercantile support for Lord Liverpool's government as well as to advance his constituents' local concerns. But Huskisson entered office with the needs of a rapidly industrializing state uppermost in mind. Those needs dictated the removal of impediments to the growth of domestic industries and the export economy. In the first place, this led to an overhaul of the tariff. This began with the equalization of British and Irish duties in 1823, and was followed by a policy of substituting moderately protective duties for prohibitory ones. Thus silk and gloves were now admitted at duties of 30 per cent, arousing considerable opposition against Huskisson. Duties on raw materials were also lowered, and many export duties and bounties were abolished, although with significant exceptions, such as those on machinery and the whale and herring fisheries. With the assistance of Deacon Hume at the customs department, Huskisson codified the tariff under eight heads and repealed over 1000 separate customs acts. Through such measures he sought to create a self-regulating economic order, removing, so far as prudent, the hand of the state from the workings of the economy. In this spirit, in 1824 he moved to abolish the Spitalfields Acts regulating wages in the silk industry and to repeal the combination laws, which had largely prohibited trade union activity. The latter were in 1825 speedily, if partially, reinstated, restoring some of the prerogatives of capital but also achieving a *modus vivendi* with labour that lasted until 1871.

Second, Huskisson undertook the first major overhaul of the Navigation Acts, in place since the seventeenth century and unmodified, despite what he interpreted as the American revolt against them in the 1770s. In 1822 the new Latin American states had been allowed to ship directly to Britain, and the United States had been allowed to trade directly with the West Indies. But Huskisson now contemplated a far greater departure from the mercantilist past by offering equality of duties on goods and shipping to any country that agreed to grant the same to British shipping. The Reciprocity of Duties Act of 1823 led therefore to a series of treaties, especially with Prussia, France, and the northern European states. However, importantly Huskisson reserved the right to retaliate against those countries which retained discriminatory duties against British shipping, and put this into effect against both the Netherlands and the United States. He met much resistance from the shipping interest (which later attributed depression to his changes), but also much support from many mercantile groups, who saw in reciprocity and retaliation a means towards 'real free trade'. Huskisson also sought avidly to open new markets to British goods, especially in Latin America. His commercial policy formed an integral part of Canningite diplomacy, involving him in important reforms of the consular service and extensive negotiations with the United States concerning the slave trade, the St Lawrence navigation, and the North American border.

Third, Huskisson's policies had important implications for the British empire. On the one hand, he had consciously dismantled the bastions of 'our ancient colonial system', but on the other he sought to reshape a new empire of trade and colonization. As its agent he had seen Ceylon as a prototypical 'small spearhead of the imperial economy' (Fay, 99), and at the Board of Trade he had undertaken a close scrutiny of colonial legislation. Above all, in his commercial policy Huskisson had retained the principle of imperial preference, with regard to Canadian timber, and in 1825 he had extended this to Canadian corn. Much more sensitive was the issue of preference for the West Indies, for this was intimately linked with the slavery question. While not keen to promote immediate abolition, Huskisson accepted that the West Indies would need to make a painful withdrawal from slavery, encouraged by the gradual reduction of preference. His brief spell as colonial secretary made clearer his vision of empire, with support for the gradual ending of slavery and the extension of colonization. He also reinstituted the Passenger Acts, whose repeal he had undertaken while at the Board of Trade. A strong case can therefore be made for the view that Huskisson was *par excellence* an 'imperial statesman' with a vision of Britain as the dynamic centre of an expanding colonial horizon, with empire offering tangible economic and political resources to the British state.

Huskisson's vigorous reforms left him increasingly open to attack, partly because he did occasionally stumble (as he complained, he had so much to do compared with other ministers, it was not surprising if he sometimes came unstuck, as on the Combination Acts in 1824 or the budget in 1826). Above all, they provided an obvious target in the wake of the commercial crisis of late 1825. His tory critics now rounded on the 'French Jacobin in the English cabinet', venting, as Creevey put it, 'the rage of the old Tory high flyers against the liberal jaw of Canning and Huskisson' (*Creevey Papers*, 2.99). Huskisson had, in fact, predicted the financial panic, but now resolutely defended cash payments against attempts to suspend them, while encouraging the bank to discount liberally to surmount the crisis. But this panic also brought renewed long-term fears for the convertibility of the pound. Ironically this now led Huskisson to support a bimetallic standard in order to broaden the monetary foundations of the currency. His scheme was to be revived by late nineteenth-century supporters of bimetallism, but in the late 1820s, as the bank came under the control of directors who leaned towards stricter monetary management, this proved unnecessary.

Corn therefore remained the outstanding issue for the liberal tories to resolve. In August 1825 Huskisson had edged the cabinet towards allowing more bonded corn onto the market in advance of an attack on the corn laws themselves, but the panic of 1825 and the coming election forestalled further action, other than once more allowing in bonded corn. After these temporary measures Huskisson's memorandum of October 1826 paved the way for a major reconstruction of the laws, with the goal of equalizing home and foreign prices. He proposed a new sliding scale, but in the light of his unpopularity among the landed tories Canning took the lead in the House of Commons, introducing the new bill on 1 March 1827 and securing an unopposed third reading on 12 April. However, proceedings were interrupted by the elevation of Canning to the premiership following Lord Liverpool's illness and resignation. Huskisson now found himself in a difficult position—for this was his long-awaited opportunity to press for one of the great offices of state. But with much unfinished business at the Board of Trade, not least corn, he somewhat ungraciously relinquished his immediate claims to promotion, 'I prefer and am determined for the present, to remain at the post which I occupy, because it is that against which an attack is threatened' (Melville, 122). However, the attack came unexpectedly in the form of an amendment to the Corn Bill by Wellington in the House of Lords. Wellington claimed he was acting with Huskisson's approval, but this purported 'misunderstanding' of Huskisson's intentions was probably a deliberate death blow against the bill. Ironically, therefore, the battle over corn had to be fought again, this time within Wellington's cabinet, with the Corn Bill of 1828 embodying a modified version of Huskisson's proposed scale. That scale had aimed to safeguard food supplies by regular imports, with regularity an important guarantee of exchange stability, a line of reasoning still of vital importance for Peel in the 1840s. After the corn law fiasco of 1827 Huskisson, nervous and exhausted, left for a recuperative tour of the continent, only to be stopped in the Austrian Tyrol by news of Canning's approaching death. As leader presumptive of the Canningites, he immediately turned back to England.

Political disintegration and death, 1827–1830 Having learned of Canning's death, and of Goderich's (and so not his own) succession, Huskisson rested in Paris with his friend the ambassador Lord Granville, pondering his political future. On his return to London on 26 August, he accepted office as colonial secretary and leader of the House of Commons, thus becoming the mainstay of the government. But the ministry was soon destroyed by a combination of Goderich's inept leadership and the bitter rivalry between Huskisson and Herries. Huskisson enjoyed the brief illusion that he might become prime minister before George IV offered this to the safer aristocratic hands of Wellington in January 1828. To accusations of desertion by the whigs and of personal betrayal by Lady Canning, Huskisson, with his Canningite friends, accepted office under Wellington in January 1828. But the high-tory animus against Huskisson had not receded, and in May 1828 Wellington took the opportunity, inadvertently provided by Huskisson himself, to oust him from the government. This occurred over the East Retford Bill, when Huskisson, having voted against the government, offered as a matter of form, not substance, to resign. Wellington, however, took him at his word, and gratefully rid himself of an uncomfortable colleague. Out of office for the first time since 1814, Huskisson led, in dithering fashion, his small group of followers. He supported in its eventual success the old Canningite cause of Catholic emancipation in 1829, while it has been suggested, although the evidence is far from conclusive, that he employed his new leisure to compose the anonymously published *Essays on Political Economy* (1830). Yet he did not relinquish the quest for office, especially as the political value of his supporters rose, and he now spoke more frequently and more wide-rangingly in the Commons. When the death of George IV opened up the prospect of office to the whigs, there was even some plausibility in the idea of a Huskisson-led fusion between the 'liberal' tories and the 'liberal' whigs. More realistically, he was presented with the separate blandishments of the whigs and Wellingtonians. Both parties travelled to the opening of the Liverpool to Manchester railway in September 1830 in hope of securing his support. Huskisson, dogged throughout his life by accidents and ill health, steeled himself for his visit to Liverpool, dutifully anxious to please his constituents, who had re-elected him in his absence in August. Nor was he without curiosity about a project he had done much to promote. On 15 September, in an atmosphere of technological excitement compounded by political intrigue, Huskisson, having alighted from the train during a stop at Parkside, fell into the path of the oncoming *Rocket* engine while attempting to re-enter the duke of Wellington's carriage. He died later that evening at the home of the Revd Thomas Blackburne, facing death stoically but with characteristic attention to detail, correcting the signature to the hasty codicil to his will. He was the first fatality of the railway age. His widow reluctantly acceded to civic request, and Huskisson was buried at St James's Church, Liverpool, on 24 September. A monument stands by the track near the scene of the accident.

Huskisson has remained more famed for the manner of his death than for the achievements of his life. Always suspect in high-tory eyes, he was a figure of obloquy for memoirists such as Mrs Arbuthnot and for the supposed victims of his actions, such as the glovemakers of Worcester, whose laments were echoed in Mrs Henry Wood's popular Victorian novels. The rapid publication of his *Speeches* (1831) by his secretary Edward Leeves, with the assistance of his widow, did much to establish his reputation as a systematic politician, devoted to the establishment of free trade. His policies won the admiration of free-traders such as the 'Corn Law Rhymer' Ebenezer Elliot and Richard Cobden. In Liverpool, Huskisson's memory was cherished, both in the Gladstone household—he was an early paragon for the young William—and in the public sphere, with a splendid mausoleum and statue by Gibson. Huskisson's substantial contribution to the making of the modern British state was later overshadowed by those of Peel and Gladstone, but both had been strongly influenced by him, especially through the luminous clarity of his memoranda. This relative neglect was partly remedied by Alexander Brady's *William Huskisson and Liberal Reform* (1928), but George Veitch's intended biography did not progress beyond article form. In 1931 Lewis Melville edited *The Huskisson Papers*. Charles Ryle Fay's *Huskisson and his Age* (1951) offered an affectionate portrait and much discursive information, although a companion volume on Huskisson and Canning was not completed. Huskisson's importance and the pragmatic, rather than doctrinaire, origins of his policies have been more fully appreciated by recent historians, above all by Boyd Hilton in *Corn, Cash, Commerce* (1977). But alone of major nineteenth-century statesmen, Huskisson has yet to attract a modern biographer.

A. C. HOWE

Sources *The speeches of the Rt. Hon. William Huskisson with a biographical memoir*, 3 vols. (1831) · BL, Huskisson MSS · *The Huskisson papers*, ed. L. Melville [L. S. Benjamin] (1931) · C. R. Fay, *Huskisson and his age* (1951) · G. S. Veitch, 'Huskisson and Liverpool' (1929); repr. from *Transactions of the Historic Society of Lancashire and Cheshire*, 80 (1928), 1–50 · B. Hilton, *Corn, cash, commerce: the economic policies of the tory governments, 1815–1830* (1977) · A. Brady, *William Huskisson and liberal reform*, (1928), 2nd edn (1967) · W. Yorks. AS, Leeds, Canning papers · PRO, Granville MSS · PRO, Board of Trade papers · S. M. Hardy, 'William Huskisson (1770–1830), imperial statesman and economist', PhD diss., U. Lond., 1943 · R. G. Thorne, 'Huskisson, William', HoP, *Commons, 1790–1820* · A. L. Lingelbach, 'William Huskisson as president of the board of trade', *American Historical Review*, 43 (1937–8), 759–74 · [William Huskisson (?)], *Essays on political economy* (1976) [introduction by G. S. L. Tucker] · B. Gordon, *Economic doctrine and tory liberalism, 1824–1830* (1979) · B. Hilton, 'The political arts of Lord Liverpool', *TRHS*, 5th ser., 38 (1988), 147–70 · *Despatches, correspondence, and memoranda of Field Marshal Arthur, duke of Wellington*, ed. A. R. Wellesley, second duke of Wellington, 8 vols. (1867–80) · *The correspondence of Charles Arbuthnot*, ed. A. Aspinall, CS, 3rd ser., 65 (1941) · *The Creevey papers*, ed. H. Maxwell, 2nd edn, 2 vols. (1904) · *The journal of Mrs Arbuthnot, 1820–1832*, ed. F. Bamford and the duke of Wellington [G. Wellesley], 2 vols. (1950) · BL, Add. MS 38742, fol. 206 · *GM*, 5th ser., 23 (1879), 264–5, 366–70, 650

Archives BL, corresp. and papers, Add. MSS 38734–38770, 39948–39949 · Lpool RO, corresp.; letters received through Liverpool parliamentary office · Yale U., Beinecke L., papers relating to American–Canadian boundary | Birm. CA, letters to Boulton family · BL, letters to Sir James Gordon, Add. MS 49480 · BL, corresp. with second duke of Liverpool, Add. MSS 38191, 38267–38320, 38425, *passim* · BL, letter to Lord Liverpool, loan 72 · BL, corresp. with Robert Peel, Add. MSS 40333–40397 · Derbys. RO, letters to Sir Robert Wilmot-Horton; corresp. with Sir R. J. Wilmot-Horton · Leeds Central Library, Canning MSS · NA Scot., corresp. with Lord Dalhousie · NRA, priv. coll., corresp. with earl of Haddington · NRA, priv. coll., corresp. with Spencer Perceval · PRO, Chatham MSS · PRO, letters to William Dacres Adams · PRO, letters to Lord Granville, 30/29 · PRO NIre., corresp. with John Foster · St Deiniol's Library, Hawarden, corresp. with Sir John Gladstone · Staffs. RO, Hatherton MSS · U. Birm. L., letters to David Scott, etc. · U. Durham L., letters to first Earl Grey · U. Mich., Clements L., letters to Lord Melville

Likenesses T. Lawrence, oils, c.1828, priv. coll.; repro. in *Speeches*, frontispiece · R. Rothwell, oils, 1830, NPG [*see illus.*] · S. Joseph, marble bust, 1831, Petworth House, Sussex · W. J. Ward, mezzotint, pubd 1831 (after J. Graham), BM, NPG · J. Carew, monument,

1832, Chichester Cathedral • J. Gibson, marble statue, c.1836, Pimlico Square, London; repro. in Fay, *Huskisson and his age*, frontispiece • J. Gibson, statue, 1847, Custom House, Liverpool • J. Doyle, pencil caricature, BM • J. Gibson, marble statue, St James's cemetery, Liverpool; repro. in Veitch, *Huskisson and Liverpool*, 5 • W. Spence, relief bust on marble plaque, Athenaeum Library, Liverpool; repro. in Veitch, *Huskisson and Liverpool*, 12

Wealth at death   under £60,000: Fay, *Huskisson and his age*, 14

Hussein ibn Ali (1853–1931), emir of Mecca and founder of the Hashemite kingdom of the Hejaz, was born in Constantinople in 1853, the first son of Ali ibn Muhammad (*d.* 1861) and Salha. His parents were descendants of the prophet Muhammad, as denoted by their titles sherif and sherifa respectively, and members of the Aouni branch of the house of Hashim, the head of which ruled Mecca as emir (or grand sherif). Their income came from religious endowments in the form of property. Private tutors taught Hussein calligraphy, the Koran, science, and poetry. He was also educated in the political rivalry with the Zaidi branch of the ruling family, which competed to secure the succession to the emirate. These dynastic intrigues were played out in the relationship with their sovereign overlord the sultan of Turkey. Between 1856 and 1858, and again from 1861, members of Hussein's Aouni branch, the junior of the two, became emir, prompting the family to live in Mecca.

In 1880 the Zaidi branch became ascendant, excluding Hussein from a prominent political role, and he spent the next decade shuttling between Constantinople and Mecca. He had married his first cousin Abdiyya bint Abdullah (*d.* 1886) in Mecca in 1879 and they had three sons—Ali (*b.* 1879), Abdullah (*b.* 1882), and Feisal (*b.* 1886)—before his wife's death soon after the birth of Feisal. Hussein's grandmother subsequently helped to raise the children. By the start of the 1890s relations between the two branches of the family had deteriorated to the point that disturbances in the Hejaz became a distinct possibility. To calm the situation, in 1891 Sultan Abdul Hamid II ordered Hussein to reside in Constantinople and provided him with a luxurious villa overlooking the Bosphorus. In 1894 Hussein married a Circassian, Adleh Hanum, and a fourth son, Zeid, was born two years later. His ambitions remained unfulfilled, however, and the sultan's spies regarded him as wilful and recalcitrant.

Hussein's political fortunes were transformed in 1908 by the Young Turk revolution, coupled with the deposition of the emir of Mecca. The appointment of a successor was in the gift of the sultan—the conservatively inclined Hussein was preferred to the more liberal candidate favoured by the Young Turks. On 1 November 1908 Hussein, aged fifty-five, became emir of Mecca. As such, he was one of the Muslim world's leading spiritual leaders, a matter of some interest to Britain because of the large Muslim population in India. His immediate concern was to consolidate power. This entailed subduing unruly tribes in and adjacent to the Hejaz, while also resisting the centralizing tendencies of Constantinople. The increasing likelihood of European war and the prospect of Turkey's siding with the central powers complicated these local struggles. In February 1914 Hussein's son Abdullah,

during a visit to Khedive Abbas Hilmi II in Cairo, sounded out Lord Kitchener on Britain's attitude to greater Arab autonomy in Arabia. Kitchener renewed these contacts in September prior to London's declaration of war on Turkey in November. Hussein was receptive to British feelers but also wary of provoking Turkish military intervention in Mecca. His family therefore maintained contacts with both sides.

Between July 1915 and March 1916 Hussein exchanged ten letters with Sir (Arthur) Henry McMahon, Kitchener's replacement as consul-general in Egypt. This correspondence negotiated the terms for the Hashemite-led Arab revolt against the Turkish empire. Encouraged by British financial backing and the possibility of territorial gains (the latter imprecisely delineated), Hussein raised the banner of revolt in June 1916. It was a classic example of an over-mighty subject seeking to throw off the overlord and assume complete control of his home region. The Arab rebels were led in the field by Hussein's sons. For Britain, the 'sherifian policy' began as backing for a limited guerrilla war in the Hejaz and ended up as a king-making project across the Arab world. Its architects were T. E. Lawrence (remembered by the Bedouin as the man who brought the gold) and his superior David George Hogarth at the Cairo-based Arab Bureau, a British intelligence organization established in early 1916.

From the start the British found Hussein to be the most troublesome element in the scheme. On 29 October he proclaimed himself 'king of the Arab lands' in the grand mosque at Mecca, but Britain, anxious about the reaction of other Arab leaders, would only recognize him as 'king of the Hejaz' (on 6 November 1916). In Arabic Hejaz means 'barrier', a reference to the harsh desert. Though disparaging the lesser title as 'a meaningless phantom', Hussein was already unable to control the tribes within his truncated kingdom. While his frontiers extended northwards to what became southern Transjordan, it was the Nejd border in the east that proved particularly difficult. Here the local tribes preferred a rival leader, ʿAbd al-ʿAziz (Ibn Saʿud), and his brand of strict Wahabi Islam, to a man they regarded as an upstart Sunni governor appointed by Constantinople and now in league with the infidel British. Hussein demanded a higher subsidy from Britain in order to alleviate these difficulties. From January 1917 £200,000 per month was paid, compared to the half million given in four instalments after June 1916.

After the seizure of ʿAqabah in July 1917, the Arab campaign shifted northwards to Palestine. Faced with reduced funds during 1918, Hussein ceased to pay wavering tribes within his borders, while also raising taxes on the loyal population. The upshot was that tribal unrest spread throughout the Hejaz. A major rout of his forces occurred at Khurma in August, made worse when Feisal, who was leading the campaign in Palestine, failed to send help. This apparent family disloyalty damaged Hashemite prestige. Nevertheless, because of his military achievements Feisal remained Hussein's trump card with the British and he therefore represented his father at the Paris peace conference in 1919. Feisal's brief was simple: to make Britain adhere to its pledges regarding Arab independence. Meanwhile, Hashemite fighters led by Abdullah drove out the Turks from Medina in April 1919, allowing an attempt to recapture Khurma the following month. The 3000-strong force—supposedly the best in the Hejaz—was massacred in a surprise night attack by forces loyal to Ibn Saʿud. The blow to Hussein was enormous and his downfall seemed imminent. To forestall this, Britain dispatched H. St John Philby to negotiate a territorial division between the protagonists. Embittered by the lack of support from Britain, Hussein refused to accept arbitration and instead detained Philby. In London, Lord Curzon fumed that Britain had been made to look ridiculous because of the stubbornness of a sensitive old man.

In early 1920 the Arab Bureau was disbanded, leaving King Hussein isolated from British official circles. His regular monthly subsidies were replaced from February by occasional lump sums. He strongly disapproved of Britain's Middle Eastern policies (Feisal had been unsuccessful in Paris) and was especially furious at the Anglo-French carve-up of Syria and Palestine, despite being briefed by British officials on the Sykes–Picot 'spheres of influence' agreement in May 1917, a year after its conclusion. After setbacks in Syria in 1920, his sons fared well when the British grafted a new political framework onto the region in March 1921: Feisal became king of Iraq, while Abdullah settled for being emir of Transjordan. These developments failed to assuage Hussein's sense of betrayal and he continued to style himself 'king of the Arab lands'. Feisal's and Abdullah's countries went unrecognized by their father. In an effort to raise revenues for his ailing administration, Hussein levied extra customs duties on pilgrims *en route* for Mecca, even though he was unable to guarantee safe passage. A stream of tribal incidents turned Muslim opinion increasingly against him. Mindful of its Muslim subjects in India, Britain halted aid to his administration in 1924. He was subsequently left isolated in his struggle with Ibn Saʿud.

A short and stocky, well-dressed townsman, Hussein was physically, psychologically, and politically ill matched against the tall and powerful desert sheikh thirty years his junior. Whereas Ibn Saʿud proudly bore the scars of hand-to-hand fights, Hussein looked down on tribal people. In March 1924 a half-hearted attempt by Hussein (pushed by Abdullah) to claim the caliphate exacerbated hostility towards him in the Islamic world. Seizing the moment, Ibn Saʿud attacked Taʿif in August, easily defeating the defending force. Britain's neutrality permitted Hussein no relief and the previously loyal notables of Mecca switched their support to his eldest son. On 3 October, after eight years of unrelenting conflict, Hussein abdicated in favour of Ali, who reigned until the kingdom of the Hejaz was completely overrun by Ibn Saʿud on 19 December 1925, so ending 1100 years of Hashemite rule in Mecca. Except for the final days, Hussein lived out his remaining years in Cyprus, a British crown colony. After suffering a stroke he was allowed to visit Abdullah in Transjordan. He died in Amman on 4 July 1931 and was buried, amid a large crowd of mourners, in Jerusalem at the Dome of the Rock.

The ambiguous 'Hussein–McMahon correspondence' became a key element in Arab discontent over the Zionist project in Palestine during the inter-war period. So great was the controversy that the British government, eager to shore up support in the region on the eve of the Second World War, published the letters in a white paper of 1939 (*Parl. papers*, (1938–9), 27, Cmd 5957). Despite this move, the allegation of bad faith continued to taint Britain's standing in the Middle East long after the end of empire. Yet Hussein, like the British officials, deliberately used vague and obscure language in pursuit of his ambitions. He was also well aware of Britain's supposedly conflicting promises while the Arab revolt was being waged. The ambiguity was mutual and self-serving. But whereas Britain refined its policies as the Turkish empire collapsed, Hussein doggedly clung to misplaced dreams of a unified Arabia with himself as king. Irrespective of the realities of European penetration in the region, Hussein's ambition failed to take account of local political forces. Tellingly, his downfall came at the hands not of the French or the British, but of Ibn Saʿud.   MICHAEL T. THORNHILL

Sources D. Fromkin, *A peace to end all peace: creating the modern Middle East, 1914–1922* (2000) · R. Baker, *King Husain and the kingdom of Hejaz* (1979) · E. Kedourie, *In the Anglo-Arab labyrinth: the McMahon–Husayn correspondence and its interpretations, 1914–1939* (2000) · A. Susser and A. Shmuelevitz, eds., *The Hashemites in the modern Arab world* (1995) · D. G. Hogarth, *Hejaz before World War I: a handbook* (1917) · R. Bullard, *The camels must go* (1961) · H. Montgomery-Massingberd, *Burke's royal families of the world*, 2: *Africa and the Middle East* (1980) · T. E. Lawrence, *Seven pillars of wisdom* (1962) · R. Storr, *Orientations* (1939) · B. Westrate, *The Arab Bureau* (1992) · J. Morris, *The Hashemite kings* (1959)
Archives IWM, T. E. Lawrence papers · Jesus College, Oxford, T. E. Lawrence papers · Pembroke Cam., corresp. and diaries of R. Storr · St Ant. Oxf., D. G. Hogarth papers
Likenesses photograph, repro. in Baker, *King Husain* · photographs, repro. in Fromkin, *Peace to end all peace* · portraits, IWM

Hussey family (*per. c.*1150–1349), gentry, held land mainly in Berkshire, Hampshire, Sussex, and Wiltshire in the twelfth and thirteenth centuries. The surname, now usually written Hussey, is variously attested in early records as Hoese, Hose, Huse, and Husee. It has been suggested that the family was originally from Normandy and that it took its name from a fief called Le Hosu (now Le Houssel), near Rouen. Another theory, however, holds that the family name is the same as the Old French (and English) *hose*, 'boot, stocking', a term which, in the middle ages, also referred to a kind of wineskin (presumably resembling a boot). Supporting this line of argument is the expression 'serjeanty of the hose', referring to lands held in return for carrying wine, a service a Hussey ancestor may have performed for the king's household. The two etymologies are not mutually exclusive as the name of the fief in Normandy may have been erroneously taken to be the word for 'boot'.

At all events the family is first represented in England by **Henry** [i] **Hussey** (*fl.* 1156–1166), who between 1156 and 1166 was given two knights' fees in Harting, Sussex, by William d'Aubigny, first earl of Arundel (*d.* 1176). In 1165

Henry founded nearby Durford Abbey, which flourished for 400 years in part due to his munificence and to that of his descendants. Henry's younger son, **Geoffrey Hussey** (*fl.* 1166–1167), held the manor of Stapleford, Wiltshire, in 1166–7, and also inherited the manors of Ablington, Figheldean, and Knighton, all in Wiltshire, from his father in the later twelfth century. That the family was already well connected is evidenced by the fact that Geoffrey married Gundred, daughter of William (II) de *Warenne, second earl of Surrey (*d.* 1138). Henry [i]'s great-grandson **Henry [ii] Hussey** (*d.* 1235) married Cecily, daughter of Emma de Stanton, who brought him the manor of Eling in Hampshire. Henry forfeited his lands in Berkshire, Hampshire, Nottinghamshire, and Wiltshire for rebelling against King John, but they were restored after the king died in 1216. Henry's and Cecily's son, **Sir Matthew Hussey** (*d.* 1252), married, as his second wife, Agnes de Sanford, younger daughter and coheir of Hugh de Sanford (*d.* 1233/4). Agnes inherited half of the manor of Great Missenden, Buckinghamshire, later known as Overbury (the other moiety was subsequently referred to as Netherbury). Matthew's coat of arms figures among the shields believed to have been painted by Matthew Paris himself to illustrate his manuscript histories and which constitute the earliest English roll of arms (*c.*1244).

Sir Matthew's son and heir, **Sir Henry [iii] Hussey** (1240–1290), served under two kings. He was a loyal supporter of Henry III during the barons' war in 1264–5. At the instance of the Lord Edward, he was licensed to crenellate his manor at Harting in 1266. In 1269 he increased his holdings in Hampshire when he acquired the manor of Freefolk from Nicholas de Sifrewast. He was also granted a weekly market and an annual fair there to last three days on the eve, day, and morrow of the feast of St Simon and St Jude in 1271. He acquitted himself well with Edward I during the Welsh wars which began in 1276, but, being infirm in 1282, made fine instead of serving in person. He was constable of Portchester Castle, Hampshire, situated on a small point of land running into Portsmouth harbour, in 1289. He was ordered to repair the houses of the castle there on this occasion. His first wife, Joan (*d.* 1278), daughter and coheir of Alard le Fleming, inherited Pulborough in Sussex. He later married Agnes, who held the manor of Standen Hussey, Wiltshire, in dower and who survived him.

Sir Henry's and Joan's son and heir, **Henry [iv] Hussey**, first Lord Hussey (1265–1332), had a long and distinguished military career, also serving under two kings. He was several times knight of the shire in Sussex, beginning perhaps as early as 1290, served in Gascony in 1294, and campaigned with Edward I in Scotland in the later 1290s and early 1300s. He entertained King Edward at Harting in September 1302. Summoned to parliament by writs from 1295 to 1325, he is thereby held to have become Lord Hussey. In 1308 he attended, with his wife, Isabel, the coronation of Edward II and processed with her in the train of the king and queen. Late in life he was sheriff of Sussex (1320–21), and was summoned to a great council at Westminster in 1324, and to serve in Gascony in 1324 and 1325.

His son and heir, **Henry [v] Hussey**, second Lord Hussey (1302–1349), and other descendants down to at least about 1466, inherited the barony.

Modern sources generally list the family arms as barry ermine and gules and that is the form attested in St George's roll and Charles's roll, both compiled in the thirteenth century. However, many rolls, the earliest of which is that of Matthew Paris, paint or blazon the coat ermine, three bars gules and even reverse the tinctures. Moreover, in the Public Record Office, a seal of Henry Hussey, lord of Harting, Sussex, dated 1337, has a shield of arms ermine, three bars. Evidently, the distinction between barry, which in modern heraldry consists of an even number of pieces, and a field with, for instance, three or four bars (seven or nine pieces), did not always matter at the time. Nicholas Hussey of Rowde, Wiltshire (*d.* 1300), an individual with the same surname but whose relationship to this family has not been established, bore argent, three boots (or stockings) gules, a classic example of canting arms.

GERARD J. BRAULT

Sources GEC, *Peerage*, new edn, 7.1–11 · C. Moor, ed., *Knights of Edward I*, 2, Harleian Society, 81 (1929), 257–61 · W. Dugdale, *The baronage of England*, 2 vols. (1675–6); repr. (1977), 1.622–4 · W. H. Blaauw, 'Dureford Abbey, its fortunes and misfortunes with some particulars of the Premonstratensian order in England', *Sussex Archaeological Collections*, 8 (1856), 41–96 · VCH *Sussex*, vols. 2, 4 · G. J. Brault, ed., *Rolls of arms of Edward I (1272–1307)*, 2 vols. (1998) · T. D. Tremlett, H. Stanford London, and A. Wagner, eds., *Rolls of arms, Henry III*, Harleian Society, 113–14 (1967), pp. 47–8, no. 56; p. 57, no. 113 · R. H. Ellis, ed., *Catalogue of seals in the Public Record Office: personal seals*, 1 (1978), 35 (P420) · VCH *Berkshire*, vol. 4 · H. Kurath and S. M. Kuhn, eds., *Middle English dictionary*, [13 vols.] (1952–2001), pt G–H, 958–9 · J. H. Round, *The king's serjeants and officers of state* (1911); repr. (1970), 177–83 · VCH *Wiltshire*, vols. 3, 15 · VCH *Buckinghamshire*, vol. 2 · VCH *Hampshire and the Isle of Wight*, vol. 3

Hussey, Christopher Edward Clive (1899–1970), architectural historian, was born at 113 Park Street, Grosvenor Square, Mayfair, London, on 1 October 1899, the only son and elder of the two children of Major William Clive Hussey of the Royal Engineers and his wife, Mary Ann, eldest daughter of the Very Revd George Herbert, dean of Hereford. His father was the second son of Edward Hussey of Scotney Castle, Kent. His parents encouraged his interest in buildings, writing, drawing, and the theatre, all of which had developed before he went to Eton College; and it was through his activity as a journalist there that he sent his first, non-architectural, contribution to *Country Life* in 1917. In 1918 Hussey served as second lieutenant in the Royal Field Artillery. At the instigation of H. Avray Tipping, who was the principal architectural writer on *Country Life* and a family friend, and who wanted him to join the editorial staff, he then went up to Oxford, where he spent the years 1919–21 at Christ Church. He read modern history (in which he gained second-class honours in 1921) and devoted time to dramatics and journalism; and while an undergraduate he wrote his first country-house articles for *Country Life*. In 1920 he became a member of the editorial staff. During the next fifty years he contributed nearly 1400 signed articles, as well as being editor from 1933 to 1940, and only his exceptional powers of concentration and industry enabled him to write on planning, landscape, historic towns, preservation issues, and the modern movement as well as country houses—with a regular flow of notes on topical subjects for the leader page, and occasional letters signed Curious Crow, Tunbridge Wells. The list of his articles rightly dominated the bibliographical tribute to him in *Architectural History* (1970). Not only did he sustain the standard already set out by Avray Tipping and Lawrence Weaver, whose notice Hussey later wrote for the *Dictionary of National Biography*, but he made the weekly country-house article into a tradition which was strengthened as architectural history became established as a subject and as documentary research became accepted as an integral part of it. It is particularly remarkable that he was able to sustain the theme throughout the Second World War.

In the late 1920s Hussey became increasingly concerned at the threats to country houses and landscape as well as at destruction in London. In addition to writing numerous signed articles published over the following forty years—in effect pleas or obituaries for places—he contributed many leaders that are unsigned and so can be attributed only to him. At that time few people shared his concerns and views on the need for tax relief for country houses or saw country houses as part of an unrecognized national heritage, but those leaders are prophetic of thinking that attracted political attention in the 1970s only after he had died. He did, however, find one contemporary listener in Philip Kerr, eleventh marquess of Lothian, who had recently inherited Blickling Hall, Norfolk, about which Hussey wrote in 1930. There is strong evidence of Hussey's thinking and writing in Lord Lothian's speech at the National Trust's annual meeting in 1934 which led to the formulation of the National Trust's country houses scheme.

Hussey's regular articles were the basis of a number of his books: *Eton College* (1922), *Petworth House* (1926), and *English Country Houses: Early Georgian* (1955), *Mid Georgian* (1956), and *Late Georgian* (1958). That trilogy was the distillation of over thirty years' work, and the last volume helped prepare the way for the reassessment of the Victorian country house. His most important book was *The Picturesque* (1927). It was also the most revealing in showing how much he owed to his paternal and maternal background and the links which they forged with eighteenth-century attitudes to literature and landscape. From the early 1920s his grandfather's house and garden at Scotney, to which he was the heir, played an increasingly important role in his life; it inspired and influenced much of his writing, particularly on landscape. This culminated in his *English Gardens and Landscapes, 1700–1750* (1967), the counterpart of his trilogy on Georgian country houses. Scotney also lay behind his concern for the practical issues of property management and preservation.

Although moved by the past, Hussey was never a remote aesthete: he believed in the continuity of tradition and its practical application. That is apparent in his lifelong admiration for and enjoyment of the architecture of Edwin Lutyens, whose *Life* he wrote in 1950 in connection

with the three memorial volumes on his architecture by A. S. G. Butler and which remains a classic of architectural biography; his articles on Lutyens span a period of forty-nine years. Similarly, he wrote about Robert Lorimer in 1931, and later contributed the notices of both Lutyens and Lorimer to the *Dictionary of National Biography*. By 1931 Hussey had also become interested in modern architecture, and in 1933 he chaired an exhibition of industrial art at Dorland Hall, London. He took an active part in public work, particularly for the National Trust and the Historic Buildings Council for England, where his sound judgement was highly valued. His presidency of the Society of Architectural Historians from 1964 to 1966 recognized not only his special contribution to the establishment of a subject which did not exist in England when he began work, but also his influence on growing public awareness of the need for preservation. Hussey was an honorary ARIBA (1935) and an associate of the Institute of Landscape Architects. He was also FSA (1947) and was appointed CBE in 1956.

In fact, Hussey was a remarkably rounded figure, who enjoyed all he did and did all he enjoyed, whether it was writing and research, painting in watercolour, which was a strong family tradition, gardening and planting trees, shooting, writing verse and lyrics, or choosing cattle for his prize Sussex herd at Scotney. On 23 April 1936 he married Elizabeth Maud (b. 1906/7), daughter of Major P. Kerr-Smiley. They had no children. Hussey inherited his uncle's property in 1952, and thereafter he and his wife devoted much effort to maintaining and improving the untouched early Victorian house and its picturesque setting, which he left to the National Trust. He died at Scotney Castle on 20 March 1970.   JOHN CORNFORTH

Sources *The Times* (21 March 1970) • *The Times* (25 March 1970) • *The Times* (23 April 1970) • *Newsletter of the Society of Architectural Historians* (May 1970) • *Victorian Society Annual* (1969–70) • J. M. Crook, ed., 'Christopher Hussey: a bibliographical tribute', *Architectural History*, 13 (1970), 5–29 • J. Cornforth, 'The Husseys and the picturesque', *Country Life*, 165 (1979), 1522–5 • b. cert. • m. cert. • personal knowledge (2004) • private information (1981) • D. Watkin, *The rise of architectural history* (1980) • J. Cornforth, 'Continuity and progress: Christopher Hussey and modern architecture', *Country Life*, 170 (1981), 1366–8 • J. Cornforth, 'Qualities of generalship: Christopher Hussey and modern architecture', *Country Life*, 170 (1981), 1468 • J. Cornforth, 'Country-house enthusiasms: Christopher and Betty Hussey's visiting albums (1936–1970)', *Country Life*, 175 (1984), 197–200 • J. Cornforth, 'Whig vitality: Christopher and Betty Hussey's visiting albums (1936–1970)', *Country Life*, 175 (1984), 274–7 • J. Cornforth, 'Lutyens and *Country Life*: 81 not out', in P. Gough and R. Huggett, *Lutyens: the work of the English architect Sir Edwin Lutyens* (1981), 25–31

Archives U. Birm. L., corresp. with Lord and Lady Avon

Likenesses T. McKenzie, bronze bust, Scotney Castle Gardens, Kent • J. Ward, portrait, Scotney Castle Gardens, Kent

Wealth at death £446,477: probate, 15 May 1970, *CGPLA Eng. & Wales*

Hussey, Eric Robert James (1885–1958), educationist, was born at White Cliff, Mill Street, Blandford, in Dorset, on 26 April 1885, the eldest son of the Revd James Hussey (1846–1920) and his wife, Martha Ellen Hewett. He won scholarships to Repton School (1899–1904) and then to Hertford College, Oxford, from where he graduated BA in *literae* *humaniores* with third-class honours in 1908 (MA 1923). At both Repton and Oxford he was an outstanding athlete, specializing in the 110 yards hurdles, and competed for the United Kingdom in the Olympic games held in London in the summer of 1908. In the same year he joined the Sudan educational service as a tutor at Gordon College, Khartoum. After four years he was seconded to the administration for a period as a district officer and later as district commissioner at Sennar. By then he had acquired a spoken knowledge of Arabic. During the First World War he was retained at his post. Thereafter he became senior inspector in the education department in Khartoum. In November 1920 he went on a special mission to Somaliland to advise on education, and made similar visits to Uganda and Kenya in 1924. On 19 July 1922 Hussey married Christine Elizabeth Justice Morley (1892–1977). They had a son, Marmaduke, and a daughter. Marmaduke Hussey subsequently became a prominent figure in the newspaper industry and later chairman of the BBC (1986–96); in 1996 he was created a life peer as Lord Hussey of North Bradley.

In 1925 Hussey became Uganda's first director of education. He successfully established a department of education and drafted the first education ordinance in a colony in which rival Anglican and Roman Catholic churches exercised a monopoly over schooling. He subsequently won the support of both churches and also formed a lasting friendship with J. H. Oldham, the highly influential secretary of the International Missionary Council. Hussey was a firm advocate of the 'adaptation' theory of African education as espoused in the 1925 memorandum *Education Policy in British Tropical Africa* and sought to avoid at all costs a policy of reckless Westernization accomplished through the medium of education. He also worked hard to consolidate the recently established Makerere College.

In 1929 Hussey was transferred to west Africa as the first overall director of education in Nigeria. The task awaiting him was no less challenging. A new education ordinance and a new grants-in-aid scheme had to be drafted and major changes made to the structure of schooling while simultaneously reassuring long established and powerfully entrenched missions that their educational interests would be respected. Unfortunately, much of his work, including the establishment of Yaba College, which he hoped would ultimately achieve the status of a university college, and his equally enthusiastic efforts to expand the education of girls, was adversely affected by the prolonged economic recession of the early 1930s which resulted in severe financial and staff retrenchments. In 1932 Hussey was a member of the commission which inspected the Prince of Wales College at Achimota in the Gold Coast Colony. A year later he was made a CMG for his services to colonial education. His term of office in Nigeria ended in February 1936 and with it his career in the colonial education service.

Thereafter Hussey found employment first as assistant secretary (March 1936) and subsequently as secretary (December 1936) of the National Society, which was responsible for the administration of numerous Anglican schools throughout England and Wales. He served with distinction as the Anglican church's 'Minister for Education' until June 1942 when he was asked by the British government to go to Ethiopia for two years to act as the emperor's educational adviser. The 1943 annual report of the National Society claimed that he achieved 'an administrative triumph' in reshaping the affairs of the society to meet new demands under the 1934 charter, and that he steered it safely through the difficult period of transition with unostentatious ability and faithfulness. Between 1940 and April 1942 he also served with distinction on the Colonial Office's advisory committee on education in the colonies.

In 1944 Hussey returned to London to a position with the British Council as director of the Middle East section which he retained until his retirement in 1949. Between 1945 and 1947 he also served a second term on the Colonial Office's advisory committee on education. In 1940 he began a long association with the London School of Oriental and African Studies (SOAS) as the Nigerian representative on the governing board, a position he retained until his death. His last overseas mission was to Eritrea in 1953 to advise on education in the territory's first year of independence. In the immediate post-war years Hussey was active in the Royal African Society as both a council member and vice-president, and represented the society at the Solway Conference on Education in Africa held in Brussels in 1950. In July 1948 he became a fellow of the Woodard Corporation and in 1951 chairman of the governing board of Hurstpierpoint School. Between 1950 and 1956 he also served on the Africa committee of the Conference of British Missionary Societies.

In 1935 Hussey delivered one of the three Joseph Paine lectures at the London Institute of Education ('Some aspects of education in Nigeria'), and in 1939 the sixth of the Heath Clark lectures at SOAS, entitled 'The role of education in assisting the people of west Africa to adjust themselves to the changing conditions due to European contacts'. He was also a frequent contributor to *African Affairs* and *African World*, especially in the post-war years, and recorded several radio talks for the BBC in 1954 on Ethiopian affairs. In 1959 Christine Hussey arranged for publication and private circulation of his memoirs of service in Africa.

As a young man Hussey acquired a reputation for outstanding athletic prowess and his quiet demeanour and genial disposition won him friends wherever he went. They were qualities that endured throughout his life. Sir Christopher Cox visited him in Ethiopia in early 1944 when he was in his sixtieth year and commented that he quite thrived on a 16 mile walk over the mountains (Hussey, 129); Michael E. Okorodudu, a Nigerian chief, claimed that Hussey was the first director of education who wore shorts and an open-neck shirt and sat to eat Nigerian meals with Nigerian boys and girls in Nigerian schools (Hussey, 155). Finally, it was James A. Gray, the editor of *African World*, who referred to him as 'an educationist of distinction' but who was quick to add that it was the man himself who made the fullest impact, the big, unruffled man with the quick smile, eager approach, and quiet chuckle who was courteous and friendly to everyone. He was, Gray suggested, a living example of the truth of how much a man can accomplish if he does not care who gets the credit (*African World*, 10 July 1958). Hussey died of heart disease at his home, Painswold, Broad Street, Cuckfield, Sussex, on 19 May 1958, aged seventy-three years. He was cremated, and his ashes scattered in the churchyard of Cuckfield parish church.   CLIVE WHITEHEAD

Sources private information (2004) [family] · E. R. J. Hussey, *Tropical Africa, 1908–44: memoirs of a period* (1959) · records of the advisory committee on education in the colonies, 1940–42, 1945–7, PRO, Sir Christopher Cox MSS, CO1045 · *Annual reports of the Ugandan department of education* (1925–9) · *Annual reports of the Nigerian department of education* (1930–36) · Church of England Records Centre, 15 Galleywell Road, Bermondsey, London, Archives of the National Society · Woodard Corporation Archives, 1 Sanctuary, Westminster, London · SOAS, Archives of the Joint International Missionary Council and Conference of British Missionary Societies · *British Council annual reports* (1945–9) · *Annual reports of the School of Oriental and African Studies* (1940–41) · *Annual reports of the School of Oriental and African Studies* (1957–8) · *WW* (1997) · *African World* (10 July 1958) · b. cert. · m. cert. · d. cert. · M. Messiter, ed., *Repton School register, 1557–1910* (1910)
Archives Church of England Records Centre, 15 Galleywell Road, Bermondsey, London, Archives of the National Society · SOAS, Archives of the Joint International Missionary Council and Conference of British Missionary Societies · Woodard Corporation Archives, 1 Sanctuary, Westminster, London
Likenesses photograph (probably in his late fifties), repro. in Hussey, *Tropical Africa*, frontispiece
Wealth at death £16,860 5s. 5d.: probate, 16 Jan 1959, CGPLA Eng. & Wales

Hussey, Geoffrey (*fl.* 1166–1167). *See under* Hussey family (*per. c.*1150–1349).

Hussey, Giles (1710–1788), history and portrait painter, was born on 10 February 1710 at Marnhull, Dorset, the tenth of thirteen children of John Hussey (*d.* 1736) and his wife, Mary, daughter of Thomas Burdett. The family was Roman Catholic and between the ages of seven and twelve Hussey was educated at the English Benedictine College at Douai (1717–19) and at the Jesuit college of St Omer (1719–22), both in France. He then studied briefly under Jonathan Richardson before working successively with two Italian painters in London, Francesco Riari and Vincenzo Damini. In 1728 he assisted Damini with the paintings in Lincoln Cathedral, and in the following year travelled with him to Italy. Damini evidently abandoned Hussey as soon as the funds advanced by his father had been spent. Hussey enrolled at the Accademia di Belle Arti in Bologna and there won prizes for drawing in 1731 and 1732. His drawing of *Apollo Guarding the Flocks of Admetus* inscribed 'Egidio Hussey Inglese 1731 Pa. Clse.' has since remained in their collection. Other drawings Hussey made in Bologna are in the British Museum and in the Royal Collection. Towards the end of 1732 he moved to Rome as a pupil of the painter, sculptor, and engraver Ercole Lelli, and developed his drawing skills by studying anatomy and copying antique sculpture and Renaissance and later painting. He

Giles Hussey (1710–1788), self-portrait, *c*.1745

also became an accomplished portrait draughtsman, producing the first of the profile heads for which he is best remembered. These indicate that he moved in Jacobite circles for among his sitters were James Stuart and Charles Edward Stuart, the Old and Young Pretenders (versions listed in Kerslake, 42). After several years of copying in monochrome from prescribed models he had just begun to use colour when, in 1736, his father died leaving him without financial support.

Hussey returned to England, and from then on what had promised to be a successful artistic career came to a standstill. In March 1738 George Vertue referred disparagingly to Hussey's idling in the country and talking of 'mighty things' (Vertue, 82–3); in October 1745 he recorded that:

> much discourse we had upon the Subject of the art of drawing, and concerning the ancient artists ... he found & discovered many gross errors in those famous ... Statues ... he coud demonstrate ... (by Triangles or Triangular or trigonometry) to every one—the faults imperfections or defects in the proportion or in the perspective part of humane bodies ... but meets with no encouragement ... he has done one painting or so, for Sr Hu Smithson who Friendly—knew him at Rome.   (ibid., 138)

Hussey outlined his theories of proportion in a series of letters, and an album in the British Museum contains many drawings annotated with complicated calculations. The drawings are almost all based on copies of antique sculpture, obsessively repeated with variations of proportion, hairstyle, and other details. The theories earned the disapprobation not only of Vertue, but also of William Hogarth, who introduced a jibe at Hussey in the first of the plates accompanying his *Analysis of Beauty* (1753). The paintings for Smithson, later duke of Northumberland, were *Bacchus*, *Ariadne*, and a self-portrait (Syon House, Middlesex). Hussey earned a living as a portraitist, charging 10 guineas for a half-length in oil and 5 guineas for a drawing in black or red chalk. Portraits in oil include *Sir John Swinburne* (Swinburne Collection, Newcastle) and *William Meredith* (Raby Castle, Durham). The number of surviving versions of his drawing of Charles Edward Stuart gives credence to the statement that he was reduced to earning 'the scantiest meals by no other means but making copies from a likeness he had taken of the Pretender when at Rome' (Britton, 1.291). He also provided designs for engraved gems by Edward Burch and Robert Bateman Wray (drawings in the British Museum, London).

In the mid-1760s Hussey befriended the young James Barry, whose own depressive character led him to identify with the older artist's lack of recognition and to blame Hussey's 'opponents' for 'a tendency to mental derangement', as he stated in a letter to the Dilettanti Society in 1793 (Barry, 2.562). Barry introduced Hussey's portrait behind the figure of Phidias in his allegorical *Elysium* (1777–84; Society of Arts, London).

Hussey spent a good deal of his time at the family seat of Nash Court at Marnhull in Dorset, where he settled in 1773 after inheriting the property from his brother. He was on close terms with prominent local Roman Catholics: Henry, Baron Arundell of Wardour, and the Weld family of Lulworth, for whom he drew a number of portraits.

The numismatist Matthew Duane owned a collection of Hussey's drawings (sold Greenwoods, 24–25 May 1785, and Christies, 1 May 1787), a group of which were bought by Benjamin West (Yale U. CBA). Hussey's spare and delicate style appealed to the neo-classical taste of the period and prices were high, two drawings of the Old and Young Pretenders fetching as much as 30 guineas.

In 1787 Hussey transferred his property to his nephew John Rowe, who took the name of Hussey. He moved to Beaston, near Broadhempston, Devon, and in June 1788 died there of a stroke while working in his garden. He was buried in Broadhempston. Rowe was the beneficiary of Hussey's will, dated 12 September 1787. The change in taste that had led to a late appreciation of Hussey's drawings during his lifetime also accounts for a posthumous interest in his theories: his letters were published in Hutchins (4.154–9, 424), the *Monthly Magazine*, 4 (October and December 1799), and Webb (p. 5).

SHEILA O'CONNELL

Sources Vertue, *Note books*, 3.122 · J. Barry, *Works* (1809), 1.171, 176, 201; 2.244, 390–92, 562 · E. Croft-Murray, 'Catalogue of British drawings in the British Museum', vol. 2, BM, department of prints and drawings · Gillow, *Lit. biog. hist.*, 3.507–10 · J. Hutchins, *History and antiquities of Dorset*, 4 (1792), 154–9 · J. Britton, *Beauties of Wiltshire* (1801), 1.187, 287–8, 291, 296, 301 · W. G. Maton, *Natural history, picturesque scenery, and antiquities of the western counties of England* (1797), 35, 39 · F. Webb, *Panharmonicon* (1815), 4, 10, 13 · S. O'Connell, 'An explanation of Hogarth's *Analysis of beauty*, pl. 1, fig. 66', *Burlington Magazine*, 126 (1984), 32–4 · J. Kerslake, *National Portrait Gallery: early Georgian portraits*, 2 vols. (1977), 42 · J. Ingamells, ed., *A dictionary of British and Irish travellers in Italy, 1701–1800* (1997), 539–40 · DNB

Archives BM, department of prints and drawings, drawings, letters | BL, letters to Lord Arundell concerning local Roman Catholic community, Add. MS 48212
Likenesses G. Hussey, self-portrait, oils, c.1745, Syon House, Brentford, Middlesex [*see illus.*] · J. Barry, oils, 1777–84, RSA · engraving, c.1815 (after G. Hussey), repro. in Webb, *Panharmonicon*, frontispiece · stipple (after G. Hussey), BM, NPG; repro. in Hutchins, *History and antiquities*, 185
Wealth at death see will, PRO, PROB 11/1178

Hussey, Henry (*fl.* 1156–1166). *See under* Hussey family (*per.* c.1150–1349).

Hussey, Henry (*d.* 1235). *See under* Hussey family (*per.* c.1150–1349).

Hussey, Sir Henry (1240–1290). *See under* Hussey family (*per.* c.1150–1349).

Hussey, Henry, first Lord Hussey (1265–1332). *See under* Hussey family (*per.* c.1150–1349).

Hussey, Henry, second Lord Hussey (1302–1349). *See under* Hussey family (*per.* c.1150–1349).

Hussey, John, Baron Hussey (1465/6–1537), nobleman and alleged rebel, was the elder son of Sir William *Hussey (*d.* 1495), justice, of Sleaford in Lincolnshire, and his wife, Elizabeth, daughter of Thomas Berkeley of Wymondham, Leicestershire. His year of birth is estimated from his age of sixty-three years in 1529. He had a younger brother, Sir William Hussey (*b.* in or before 1473, *d.* 1531?), a courtier and MP. While it would not be unreasonable to infer that he attended the inns of court, nothing specific is known on this point, nor of his early life generally except that he was appointed surveyor of the Lincolnshire lands of George, duke of Clarence, on 12 June 1481. He entered the service of Henry VII and fought for him at the battle of Stoke on 16 June 1487. He married, by 4 August 1492, Margaret (*d.* 1503x5), daughter and heir of Simon Blount of Mangotsfield, Gloucestershire, and his wife, Eleanor. The couple had at least two sons, including Sir William Hussey (*b.* in or before 1493, *d.* 1556). There is some ambiguity over when Margaret Hussey died because a pardon roll dated 18 May 1509 names her as still living. However, Hussey remarried in 1505. In 1492 Hussey was present at peace negotiations with France and attended other ceremonial occasions, including the reception of Philip the Fair of Burgundy in 1496. He was an esquire for the body by 1494, was knighted after the battle of Blackheath on 17 June 1497, and was a knight of the body by December 1503. He was promoted banneret in 1511.

Early career, 1497–1509 Hussey's major claim to prominence in Henry's reign was as an administrator. By 1497 he had secured enough visibility at court to be named among the 'caitiffs and villains of simple birth' around the king who were denounced by Perkin Warbeck. His first formal administrative post came with his appointment as master of the wards in December 1503. This appointment, held at pleasure, made Hussey 'chief immediate officer for overseeing, managing and selling the wardships of all lands which be in the king's hands' (Richardson, 169). By 1511 he was receiving a salary for the post of £100 per annum.

Hussey held the mastership until he was succeeded by Sir Thomas Lovell in 1513, despite rumours that he was to be deprived in 1510. He was also made comptroller of the household in the last months of the old king's reign.

That Hussey was a member of Henry's court and conciliar élite is reflected in the marriage of his eldest son, William, to Lovell's niece, Ursula, the daughter and coheir of Sir Robert Lovell. The settlement for this marriage—which was made in 1503—cost Hussey 1000 marks. Similarly, the feoffees appointed when Hussey settled his estate later the same year were court figures, among them Richard Fox, bishop of Winchester, William Warham, Sir Giles Daubeney, and the Lovell brothers again. He was at this time able to raise large sums of money. Apart from his son's marriage, he spent 2000 marks to secure the settlement for his own second marriage (by 18 February 1505) and £1100 in 1506 on lands of his new brother-in-law Richard *Grey, third earl of Kent (b. in or before 1478, d. 1524). His second wife was Lady Anne (d. 1546), daughter of George *Grey, second earl of Kent (d. 1503), and his second wife, Katherine. The couple had at least one son, Thomas Hussey (b. in or before 1530, d. 1572×6), a lawyer and MP, and four daughters. In 1515 John Hussey was forced to assign lands to trustees for the settlement of debts due to the crown totalling £3019.

Courtier and diplomat, 1509–1534 Hussey was among the old king's servants who successfully transferred to the new monarch, although it is not certain how long he remained comptroller. He went to France in 1513 as captain of a force of 328 men in arms; on 9 October 1514 he was present at the marriage of Mary Tudor to Louis XII of France. He was one of the commissioners employed in 1520 to settle disputes with the Hanse and he attended Henry VIII at the Field of Cloth of Gold. In 1522 he was present when the king met Charles V at Canterbury. On 1 June 1521 Hussey was appointed chief butler of England, an office he retained until his death. He was a councillor from before the death of Henry VII and was active hearing Star Chamber cases under Cardinal Thomas Wolsey. In 1518 it was claimed before the council that he had protected the murderers of the husband of one Alice Hardman. The council asked him not to sit on this case, but while not convicting him, asked that he should pay Hardman £6 13s. 4d. out of 'pity and compassion' (BL, Lansdowne MS 639, fol. 47v). It was as a councillor sitting as an MP in the House of Commons that he proposed the granting of a further year's subsidy charged on lands only in the deadlocked parliament of 1523.

Lincolnshire was Hussey's county. He was sheriff from 1493 to 1494 and appears on the commissions of the peace for Kesteven from 1495, Holland from 1497, and Lindsey from 1501. By 1513 he was custos rotulorum. Complaints about his conduct as a JP were made to the council in 1519. In 1523 (and possibly also in 1515) he was returned as a knight of the shire for Lincolnshire; he was elected again in 1529, but was elevated to the House of Lords as Baron Hussey on 1 December 1529, reflecting his local prominence, wealth, and abilities. While no systematic work has yet been done on his estates, he seems to have ignored no

opportunity to extend his landholdings in Lincolnshire and Rutland. His father's estate at Dagenhams and Cockerells in Havering, Essex, was exchanged by Hussey for a manor in Lincolnshire in 1512. The estates in Gloucestershire, Somerset, and Wiltshire which descended to Hussey's son from his mother, Margaret Blount, were sold by Hussey, probably to fund the acquisition of additional lands nearer home. He was among those who preyed on the estates of the weak-willed third earl of Kent, but as his brother-in-law, it is not clear how far Hussey's involvement was driven by self-interest. He also bought lands from Thomas West, eighth Baron de la Warr, in 1504. At his death he held lands only in Lincolnshire, Rutland, and a sole manor in Nottinghamshire worth, on the evidence of his own accounts, about £400 per annum. These accounts show that he also held a large number of monastic leases. His total annual income, before costs, at the end of his life, was about £1100.

While we know that Hussey was seriously alienated from Henry VIII by 1534, there is no real evidence that this was so in 1529 or the years immediately following. His elevation to the Lords surely suggests that he retained Henry's confidence, as does his appointment as chamberlain to the household of Princess Mary, which had taken place by autumn 1530. In this role he was the king's man: it was he who drew to Henry's attention Mary's continued determination to be called princess and her claim to be the king's heir; this led to the winding up of the household and Hussey's loss of office late in 1533. Hussey was in attendance when the submission of the clergy was presented to Henry on 11 May 1532; he was present at the coronation of Anne Boleyn and the christening of Princess Elizabeth on 10 September 1533, when he held the canopy over the infant (although it has been suggested that those who found the Boleyn marriage unpalatable were assigned prominent roles).

Alienation, 1534–1536 At some time during 1534 Hussey resolved not to die a heretic. By September his dislike of the direction of policy was so set that he was willing to discuss his alienation with the imperial ambassador, Eustace Chapuys. Hussey told Chapuys that he hoped Charles could be persuaded to intervene in England; he expressed disappointment that the emperor had not already done so, holding that the English Commons would welcome him throwing his weight against Henry on behalf of Mary. When pressed further, Hussey referred Chapuys to another peer, also a survivor of Henry VII's court, Thomas Darcy, Baron Darcy, who was also anxious for Charles to invade. Darcy believed that Henry could be overthrown if Charles would land in the Thames estuary and the north. Darcy and Hussey were clearly in cahoots, and Darcy at least thought that they might be able to call on the support of other older noblemen among their circle. Nothing came from these private conversations, but Hussey's wife was indiscreet in her support for Mary, persisting in calling her Princess Mary, and she suffered a short period of imprisonment during the summer of 1536 as punishment. (By the beginning of October she was living with Hussey at Sleaford.) It was perhaps a reflection of Hussey's distaste for the direction of politics, especially the religious changes of the Reformation Parliament, that caused him to plead illness and ask to be excused attendance from the final session, which dissolved the monasteries. He did, though, attend the parliament which met after the fall of Anne Boleyn, perhaps in the hope that royal policies would be reversed.

The general character of Hussey's religious preferences is clear: he was devout, but by the standards of the 1530s old-fashioned. There is no evidence to show that he shared Darcy's predilection for the mendicant orders, but it may be significant that he asked to be buried among the Gilbertines at Sempringham, Lincolnshire. In 1534 John Fewterer dedicated his *The Mirror or Glass of Christes Passion* to Hussey. Hence it is possible that, like Darcy, Hussey's hostility to the king's policy and to the direction religious reform was taking was well known before the rebellion in Lincolnshire broke out at Louth on 2 October 1536, and that this knowledge coloured contemporaries' interpretation of his actions. Hussey wrote his own detailed account of his response to the rebellion and this forms the basis of any assessment of his behaviour.

The Lincolnshire rising, 1536–1537 Hussey was at his house at Sleaford when reports reached him from Edward Fiennes de Clinton, ninth Baron Clinton, of the disturbance at Louth on 2 October and from George Heneage, dean of Lincoln, the following morning. Later that same day he also had a letter from a JP, Thomas Moigne, written in ignorance of the capture of a large number of gentry at Caistor after Moigne had left them, but trying to arrange a meeting to resist the commons. Hussey attempted to call his own meetings of the local gentry to assess the situation; he also ordered a mobilization against the commons and the breaking down of bridges and opening of sluices to stop the passage of people into East Anglia. However, most of the people Hussey tried to reach either had fled or were under house arrest at Louth. The Louth commons sent him a letter written in the name of the gentry on 4 October telling him to throw in his lot with them or threatening to come to Sleaford and take Hussey as their enemy. Hussey also established contact with the secondary rising at Horncastle and met a delegation from the town during 4 October.

While Hussey has been seen to vacillate in these days, his language shows that he had no truck with the commons. In his letter to Heneage, which fell into the hands of the commons at Louth, he referred to them as rebels: he told the Horncastle commons that they should 'walk home knaves, for the king is used not to condition with no such rebellious' (PRO, SP 1/109, fol. 71r). He offered to ride to the king and plead for their pardon if they would submit, a suggestion which they refused. It was also reported that at this meeting Hussey refused to betray Henry by joining the rebels, but he also admitted that he was impotent to resist them because his tenants would not serve against them. On the other hand, there is other evidence to show that Hussey was right to believe that his tenants and the townspeople of Sleaford would not join him if he threw in his weight with the rebels, as shown by a report

written on 6 October by Christopher Ayscough (who carried letters to Hussey) that 'he dare not stir and none of his tenants will rise for him' (*LP Henry VIII*, 11, no. 567). Ayscough believed that Hussey would be captured in the following days. In fact he fled, disguised as a priest, during 7 October to George Talbot, fourth earl of Shrewsbury, who was mustering troops at Nottingham. After his flight, a party of commons went to Sleaford to take him. They swore his wife to go after him to bring him back, but he ignored her persuasions. By flight Hussey secured what had become his prime objective: he kept himself out of the hands of the commons. He may have decided that flight was the only option a day or two previously, for his household servants had been progressively sent away on 5 and 6 October.

Hussey justified remaining at Sleaford with the comment 'as for my tarrying so long, it was for staying of the country, for as long as I remained at home, there was no rising in Kesteven nor Holland' (PRO, SP 1/109, fol. 73r). While we may see that his situation was hopeless, his behaviour might have seemed less ambiguous to contemporaries if he had fled earlier to Shrewsbury. Hussey was sent to London on 18 October, confident that he could vindicate himself, but Shrewsbury, Thomas Manners, first earl of Rutland, and George Hastings, first earl of Huntingdon, expressed doubts about his earlier behaviour when they said that he had been the king's true subject since his arrival among them. Hussey was certainly examined by the council. In early November he was used by them to establish contact with Darcy; the letter which Hussey wrote at their direction said that he had been accused of conspiracy with Darcy but had been defended from these accusations by the favourable testimony of Thomas Howard, third duke of Norfolk.

It is finally not certain whether Hussey failed to convince, or whether he was tried for the larger offence—unknown to the statute book—of inactivity in the face of overwhelming difficulties. He was indicted on 12 May 1537 of conspiracy against the king and raising a rebellion against him at Lincoln. Both Darcy and he were tried by their peers on 15 May and, despite pleading not guilty, were convicted. Hussey was taken back to Lincoln and executed there on 29 June 1537. His estates were seized for the crown and he was posthumously attainted, as were others involved in the Pilgrimage of Grace, in the parliament of 1539. Hussey's eldest son, Sir William Hussey, was restored in blood by statute of 3 Edward VI and his other sons and daughters by a further statute of 5 Elizabeth I. None of Hussey's estates were recovered by the family.

Hussey made a will on 22 October 1535 in which, after entailing lands on his eldest son, with the remainder to his younger sons and brothers, he left his daughters Mary and Bridget 500 marks apiece. He also requested that he be interred in Sempringham church, that is, in the church of the Gilbertine priory there, some 8 miles south of Sleaford, where his father had been buried.   R. W. HOYLE

Sources GEC, *Peerage* · HoP, *Commons, 1509–58*, 2.423–4, 426–8 · R. W. Hoyle, *The Pilgrimage of Grace and the politics of the 1530s* (2001) ·

M. James, 'Obedience and dissent in Henrician England: the Lincolnshire rebellion, 1536', *Society, politics and culture: studies in early modern England* (1986), 188–269 • *LP Henry VIII*, vols. 1–12/2 • *CCIR, 1485–1509* • W. C. Richardson, *Tudor chamber administration, 1485–1547* (1952) • G. W. Bernard, 'The fortunes of the Greys, earls of Kent, in the early sixteenth century', *HJ*, 25 (1982), 671–85

Archives PRO, composition with the crown, E 211/130, 152 [duplicate copies] • PRO, deposition, JP1/109, fols. 70r–74r • PRO, estate and household accounts, E 36/95 • PRO, family settlements, E 315/237, pp. 85–107 [copies] • PRO, private deeds, E 326 • PRO, rental, E 315/393

Hussey, Sir Matthew (d. 1252). *See under* Hussey family (*per. c.*1150–1349).

Hussey, Philip (1713–1783), portrait painter, was born in Cloyne, co. Cork, the son of a clothier; his parents separated and he lived with his mother and her relatives. His mother was clever and musical, playing the violin. Hussey was sent to sea as a boy and was three times shipwrecked. His first drawings were of ship figureheads. Gradually he taught himself to paint; he became a protégé of Lord Chancellor Bowes, who encouraged him to become a portrait painter. As the source of information on Hussey's early life, Strickland further noted that Hussey 'twice visited England, and improved himself by the study of the works of old masters … On his second visit he was introduced to the Prince of Wales and made many friends' (Strickland, 1.450).

Hussey's earliest dated portrait is a whole length of Master Edward O'Brien (1746; priv. coll.). A competent work with a column and drapery, this portrait is clearly not by a beginner. He also painted small whole lengths such as Judge Blennerhasset (priv. coll.), which also has baroque trappings. Unfortunately he frequently signed on the back of his canvases and many signatures have been destroyed by relining. Hussey owned a self-portrait by his friend James Latham, which Pasquin said 'was exceedingly valued by the possessor' (Pasquin, 10–11). Their work can be close in manner: in the case of a pair of portraits, *Lord Carlow* appears to be the work of Latham while *Lady Carlow* was painted by Hussey. Hussey's love of flower painting, jewellery, and lace led to him being more successful with female portraits than those of men. The sensitivity that this implies also enabled him to convey old age, as in the portrait of the eighty-year-old Sarah, Lady Meredyth (1764; Christies 9 October 1981, lot 82). Pasquin's remark that he was a botanist suggests the possibility that he produced flower paintings, but as yet no such signed work by Hussey has been identified. His numerous half-length male portraits are extraordinarily alike and rather dull. His later work was characterized by a shiny, enamel-like finish. A conversation piece attributed to Hussey (National Gallery of Ireland, Dublin), which came from Rathbeale Hall, co. Dublin, shows a more varied talent.

Hussey died, apparently unmarried, in 1783 in Earl Street, Dublin. In his will he left £25 to his servant, Ann Hynds. Pasquin recorded that he was a musician and that 'his house, on every Sunday morning, was the rendezvous of the literati and painters of Dublin' (Pasquin, 10–11).

There is some evidence that he cleaned, framed, and copied pictures for families like the Edgeworths of Edgeworthstown, co. Longford, and was even involved in auctioneering, making £35 9s. 2d. by assisting in the O'Hara sale at Portglenone, co. Antrim, in 1763.

L. H. CUST, rev. ANNE CROOKSHANK

Sources A. Pasquin [J. Williams], *An authentic history of the professors of painting, sculpture, and architecture who have practiced in Ireland … to which are added, Memoirs of the royal academicians* [1796]; facs. edn as *An authentic history of painting in Ireland* with introduction by R. W. Lightbown (1970), 10–11, 29 • W. G. Strickland, *A dictionary of Irish artists*, 2 vols. (1913) • A. Crookshank and the Knight of Glin [D. Fitzgerald], *The painters of Ireland, c.1660–1920* (1978), 44–6

Archives NL Ire., MSS 1521–1522, 1524 • PRO NIre., account book of O'Hara of Portglenone, co. Antrim, D10/22/4a

Hussey, Richard (*bap.* 1715, *d.* 1770), lawyer and politician, baptized at St Mary's, Truro, Cornwall, on 17 November 1715, was the elder son of John Hussey and his wife, Elizabeth Gregor, who married in Truro on 3 September 1713. His father, an attorney, was town clerk of Truro from 1722 to 1727 and its mayor in both 1728 and 1733. Hussey matriculated from Balliol College, Oxford, on 30 October 1730. At the Middle Temple he was admitted as a student in 1731, called to the bar in 1742, and elected a bencher in 1760. He held a number of appointments as counsel: to the duchy of Cornwall (1752), the Admiralty (1757), and the East India Company. After George III's accession he received a silk gown and was appointed attorney-general to the queen. He was suggested as a possible solicitor-general in 1761 and attorney-general in 1765. He was also auditor of the Royal Naval Hospital, Greenwich, and in 1768 of the duchy of Cornwall.

Hussey, who never married, became mayor of Truro in 1748 and built up an interest in the local tin mines, including those at St Agnes. He was also concerned in the practical assessment of proposals for steam engines to work the mines. In the 1760s he constructed Killiganoon in the parish of St Feock, a few miles to the south of Truro, as his country seat. He was soon recognized to have 'a good personal interest in many parts of Cornwall', and his ambition to sit at Westminster led Henry Pelham to describe him as 'Parliament mad' (BL, Add. MS 35423, fol. 162). At the general election in 1754 he contested the Cornish borough of Mitchell, but was seated on petition on 24 March 1755 only after a long and bitter parliamentary struggle. In 1761 he was returned by Lord Falmouth for St Mawes, and in 1768 was given a government seat at East Looe, which he retained until his death.

Hussey's reputation among politicians was universally high: Horace Walpole, the duke of Newcastle, and Lord John Cavendish all praised his honesty and abilities. In 1766 Chatham, whom he generally supported, eulogized that his 'ability and weight are great indeed; and my esteem and honour for his character [are] the highest imaginable' (*Correspondence of William Pitt*, 3.110); while in 1768 Lord North considered that 'He is a most amiable, estimable man, and gives a credit to every question he supports' (Lord North to duke of Grafton, 26 April 1768, Suffolk RO, Bury St Edmunds, Grafton MS 472). Initially regarded as a government supporter, Hussey opposed Grenville's administration over the cider excise, Wilkes, and general warrants. On 24 November 1763 he spoke impressively in the debate on Wilkes's privilege: 'He was copious and learned, and reasoned well. No one on his side [of] the question made so able a figure' (Hants. RO, Malmesbury MSS). On 29 January 1765, in the debate on the motion to declare general warrants illegal, he warned against leaving the question of legality doubtful for the future. On 25 April 1768, at a meeting called by Grafton to discuss the expulsion of Wilkes from parliament, Hussey made an impact by declaring that he 'was strongly against a second expulsion for the same offence, *in being the author of a political libel*' (*Autobiography … of Grafton*, 198), but he later followed the government line.

On American policy Hussey declared on 3 February 1766 that there was no precedent for taxing a country that had its own assembly, and on 24 February he reiterated his view that the Stamp Act had been 'unjust in its original'. None the less, he maintained that British authority and the right of taxation should be asserted. On 26 January 1769 he argued that the Townshend duties were 'inexpedient and impolitic', but not unjust. Resolute action would force the Americans to 'acknowledge their error, and own the supreme power of the mother country' (*Cavendish's Debates*, 1.197–8).

When his friend Camden was dismissed as lord chancellor in January 1770, Hussey resigned the attorney-generalship to the queen. He died at Truro on 11 September 1770 and was buried at its parish church of St Mary on 14 September.
PATRICK WOODLAND

Sources J. Brooke, 'Hussey, Richard', HoP, *Commons* • H. Walpole, *Memoirs of the reign of King George the Third*, ed. G. F. R. Barker, 4 vols. (1894) • 'The parliamentary papers of Nicholas Ferrar, 1624', ed. D. R. Ransome, *Camden miscellany, XXXIII*, CS, 5th ser., 7 (1996) • 'Parliamentary memorials of James Harris', Hants. RO, Malmesbury papers [transcript, History of Parliament Trust, London] • Suffolk RO, Bury St Edmunds, Grafton papers • *Sir Henry Cavendish's Debates of the House of Commons during the thirteenth parliament of Great Britain*, ed. J. Wright, 2 vols. (1841–3) • *Correspondence of William Pitt, earl of Chatham*, ed. W. S. Taylor and J. H. Pringle, 4 vols. (1838–40) • *Autobiography and political correspondence of Augustus Henry, third duke of Grafton*, ed. W. R. Anson (1898) • J. Polsue, *A complete parochial history of the county of Cornwall*, 4 vols. (1867–72) • J. Palmer, *Truro in the eighteenth century* (1990) • parish register, Truro, St Mary's, Cornwall RO [baptism, 1715; death, 1770] • correspondence re steam engines, 1766–7, Cornwall RO, Accession AD 55/21 and 22 • tin bounds map of St Agnes, Royal Institution of Cornwall, Truro, Courtney Library, HJ/8/5 • Foster, *Alum. Oxon.* • *GM*, 1st ser., 40 (1770), 441 • Boase & Courtney, *Bibl. Corn.*, 1.260–61 • H. Walpole, *Memoirs of the reign of King George the Second*, ed. Lord Holland [H. R. Fox], 2 vols. (1846) • *The letters of Horace Walpole, earl of Orford*, ed. P. Cunningham, 9 vols. (1857–9) • *DNB* • IGI

Archives Cornwall RO, St Mary's, Truro, parish registers • Cornwall RO, Accession AD 55/21 and 22 | Royal Institution of Cornwall, Truro, Courtney Library, tin bounds map of in St Agnes, HJ/8/5

Hussey, Robert (1801–1856), ecclesiastical historian, born on 7 October 1801, was fourth son of William Hussey, a member of an old Kentish family, and his wife, Charlotte, *née* Twopenny; the father was for forty-nine years rector of Sandhurst, near Hawkhurst in Kent. (His eldest sister,

Charlotte, who married Alexander Sutherland FSA, gave to the Bodleian Library in 1837 a magnificent collection of historical prints and drawings, in sixty-one folio volumes, illustrating the works of Clarendon and Burnet.) Hussey was for a time at Rochester grammar school; but in 1814 he was sent to Westminster School, in 1816 became a king's scholar, and in 1821 went to Christ Church, Oxford. There he resided for the remainder of his life. He obtained a double first-class in 1824, and proceeded MA in 1827 and BD in 1837. After a few years spent in private tuition he was appointed one of the college tutors, and held that office until he became censor in 1835. He was appointed select preacher before the university in 1831 and again in 1846. He was proctor in 1836, in which year he was an unsuccessful candidate for the headmastership of Harrow School. In 1838 he was appointed one of the classical examiners at Oxford, and from 1841 to 1843 was one of the preachers at Whitehall. Hussey supported the extension of the professoriate, and in 1842 was appointed to the newly founded regius professorship of ecclesiastical history. It was a timid appointment. Hussey was, Tuckwell recalled, 'a monument of erudition' in the Christ Church common room (Tuckwell, 150), but he was not an ecclesiastical historian to rival the Germans. He was a source of information to students rather than a writer of histories.

For the students attending his lectures Hussey edited the histories of Socrates (1844), Evagrius (1844), Bede (1846), and Sozomen (3 vols. finished after his death, 1860). The preface to his *Sermons, Mostly Academical* (1849) was a contribution to Syriac studies and the controversy surrounding the fragments discovered by William Cureton. He also published on Roman and Greek weights and measures (1836) and on Roman remains in the Dorchester area (1841). In 1851, at the time of the 'papal aggression', he published a manual on *The Rise of the Papal Power Traced in Three Lectures* (reissued, with additions, in 1863).

Hussey was a protestant high-churchman of an old-fashioned and cautious kind. He took part when proctor in the censure of R. D. Hampden in 1836. He gave some support to the Tractarians in 1845 (in his *Reasons*, published that year). He opposed Benjamin Jowett's plan for a final honour school of theology, although he moderated his view shortly before his death.

In 1845 Hussey became (in addition to his existing duties) perpetual curate of Binsey, by Oxford, and he was later rural dean to Bishop Samuel Wilberforce. He was elected a member of the new hebdomadal council of 1854.

Hussey was married to Elizabeth, sister of his friend and Christ Church contemporary the Revd Jacob Ley. 'Grimly saturnine' (Tuckwell, 150) in later years, Hussey died rather suddenly of heart disease on 2 December 1856. He left to his college his substantial library on patristics and ecclesiastical history, for use of his professorial successors. His wife and one daughter survived him.
H. C. G. MATTHEW

Sources J. Ley, 'Memoir', in R. Hussey, *Rise of the papal power*, 2nd edn (1863) • J. W. Burgon, *Lives of twelve good men*, [new edn], 2 vols.

(1888–9) · Foster, *Alum. Oxon.* · W. R. Ward, *Victorian Oxford* (1965) · W. Tuckwell, *Reminiscences of Oxford*, 2nd edn (1907) · *DNB*

Hussey, Thomas (1746–1803), Roman Catholic bishop of Waterford and Lismore, was born in Ballybogan, Harristown, co. Meath, Ireland. Having completed his studies at the English College in Seville he was ordained to the priesthood on 25 March 1769 and immediately appointed one of the ordinary chaplains to the Spanish ambassador in London; fifteen years later he was made principal chaplain. This appointment placed him within a circle that included Lord Chatham, the duke of Portland, Charles James Fox, and Dr Johnson. It was at this time, too, that he established a lasting friendship with Edmund Burke, to whom Hussey was reputed to have administered the sacraments in his last illness (*Irish Magazine*, February 1808). But while Hussey rose to the top echelon of British society (in March 1792 he was admitted a fellow of the Royal Society) he was despised by some. William Drennan, the Belfast Presbyterian United Irishman, dismissed the 'native broadness and vulgarity' of Hussey's brogue; 'strange that someone of the most ancient strain of Ireland and in foreign courts all his life should smack so strongly of the bogtrotter' (Chart, 228).

During the American war a secret embassy was sent to Spain under Richard Cumberland in an effort to break the Franco-Spanish Alliance. At the special request of George III, Hussey joined this delegation and, despite its failure, he made an impression in the Spanish court. Cumberland, who acknowledged Hussey's ability and incorruptibility, believed the cleric had acted disingenuously towards himself, claiming that he would have willingly headed a revolution with the object of disestablishing the protestant religion in Ireland.

Hussey immersed himself in the affairs of the Catholics of England and Ireland. In 1790 he declined a request to represent the English Catholic Committee in Rome in an attempt to defuse the crisis produced by their 'Protestation'. In the same year the Catholic Committee of Ireland appealed to Hussey to secure the services of Edmund Burke's son Richard in the removal of their disabilities. Hussey's role in the establishment of the Catholic seminary at Maynooth ranked among his proudest achievements. His association with the project began in December 1793, when Edmund Burke recommended his services to the Irish bishops as 'the best clergyman I know' (*The Correspondence of Edmund Burke*, ed. T. W. Copeland and others, 10 vols., 1958–78, 7.499). His contribution was duly recognized in his appointment as first president of the college in 1795; Hussey's delight was reflected in his reference to Maynooth as his 'favourite spot, this *punctum saliens* of the salvation of Ireland from Jacobinism and anarchy' (ibid., 9.141).

In August 1796 Hussey received a vicarial authority over the crown forces in Ireland from Pius VI; two months later Pitt confirmed this appointment in the confidence that he would stamp out disaffection in the army. Hussey championed the cause of Catholic soldiers and militia, who bitterly complained to him that they had been flogged for failing to attend protestant services. These exertions roused the wrath of the executive in Dublin, and Hussey's increasing isolation led to a protracted correspondence with Burke in which he dismissed this Dublin Castle 'junto', which he claimed was 'Jacobinising Ireland' (*The Correspondence of Edmund Burke*, ed. T. W. Copeland and others, 10 vols., 1958–78, 9.141).

Nominated to the diocese of Waterford and Lismore in December 1796 Hussey devoted the emoluments of his office to ecclesiastical purposes; a keen pastor, his views on Catholic education expressed in a pastoral address (published in April 1797) inspired Edmund Rice to establish the Irish Christian Brothers. Of more immediate consequence was the pastoral's condemnation of the penal laws, the Church of Ireland, and the rejection of the right of Ireland's temporal rulers to exercise jurisdiction in spiritual matters. Such blunt remarks aroused immediate criticism, prompting the publication of at least five pamphlets.

Hussey was oblivious to loyalist criticism, which he dismissed as 'vomiting ... malice', but his position in Ireland became increasingly difficult. His 'unpastoral letter' (Keogh, 414) was the source of acute embarrassment for the Catholic hierarchy, and there were calls for his resignation as president of Maynooth and bishop of Waterford. Both were resisted but Hussey quit Ireland shortly after the publication of the pastoral and did not return until late 1802. Hussey's absence from Ireland explains his delay in condemning the rising of 1798. Yet during the period of his absence he busied himself with a host of ambitious projects, including the restoration of the Irish College in Paris. There were rumours, too, that he had assisted Cardinal Golsalvi in the negotiations of the concordat with Napoleon, a task for which it was incorrectly rumoured that he had received a red hat.

Hussey returned to Ireland in 1802 and died suddenly at Dunmore East, co. Waterford, on 11 July. Even in death he managed to rouse strong feelings, and his funeral became the scene of violent protest. As his remains were being brought to Waterford for burial on 12 July, drunken soldiers returning from an Orange meeting, who attempted to toss his coffin into the Suir, disrupted the proceedings. A party of the local militia, who recovered Hussey's remains and escorted them to their final resting place, in Waterford Cathedral, spared him this indignity.

J. T. Gilbert, *rev.* Dáire Keogh

Sources Waterford Diocesan Archive, Waterford, Ireland, Hearn MSS · Burke papers, Sheff. Arch., Wentworth Woodhouse muniments · C. Butler, *Historical memoirs of the English, Irish, and Scottish Catholics since the Reformation*, 3rd edn, 4 (1822), 39–45 · *The Drennan letters*, ed. D. A. Chart (1931), 228 · R. Cumberland, *Memoirs of Richard Cumberland written by himself*, 2 vols. (1806–7) · S. Flagg Bemis, *The Hussey–Cumberland mission and American independence* (1931) · J. Healy, *Centenary history of Maynooth* (1895) · D. Keogh, 'Thomas Hussey, bishop of Waterford and Lismore, 1797–1803', *Waterford: history and society*, ed. W. Nolan (1992), 403–26 · *Propaganda scritture referite nei congressi Irlanda*, Vatican Archives, vol. 18, fol. 125 · J. J. Silke, 'The Irish College Seville', *Archivium Hibernicum*, 24 (1961), 103–47 · *DNB*

Archives Sheff. Arch., Burke papers · Sheff. Arch., corresp. with Earl Fitzwilliam · Waterford Diocesan Archive, Hearn MSS

Likenesses W. Hincks, stipple, pubd 1783 (after T. Collopy), BM, NPG · S. W. Reynolds, mezzotint, pubd 1796 (after C. F. de Breda), BM, NG Ire. · oils, St Patrick's College, Maynooth
Wealth at death approx. £2000: W. Carrigan, ed., 'Catholic episcopal wills, province of Cashel', *Archivium Hibernicum*, 3 (1914), 201–2

Hussey, (John) Walter Atherton (1909–1985), dean of Chichester and patron of the arts, was born at St Matthew's Parade, Northampton, on 15 May 1909, son of Canon John Bowden Hussey (1864–1950), vicar of St Matthew's, Northampton, and his wife, Lilian Mary Atherton (d. 1946). The second of two sons, he attended the Knoll, a preparatory school at Woburn Sands, and Marlborough College, before reading philosophy, politics, and economics at Keble College, Oxford (1927–1930). For a short period he served as a schoolmaster at Charleston, Sussex, then went to study theology at Cuddesdon (1931–2). He was ordained to a curacy at St Mary Abbots, Kensington (1932), and was in charge of the daughter church of St Paul (1935–6). In 1937 he succeeded his father as vicar of St Matthew's parish church, Northampton, remaining there until nominated dean of Chichester in 1955.

Hussey's role as an ecclesiastical patron of the arts began in earnest when, in 1943, he commissioned Benjamin Britten to write the cantata *Rejoice in the Lamb* to mark the fiftieth anniversary of St Matthew's Church. The words of the cantata, from an eighteenth-century poem by Christopher Smart, came to epitomize Hussey's own attitude to the relationship between religion and the arts, and between sanctity and aesthetics:

> Hallelujah from the heart of God,
> and from the hand of the artist inimitable,
> and from the echo of the heavenly harp
> in sweetness magnifical and mighty.

At a time when church decoration was languishing in mass-produced Victorianism, and when art itself was often considered unjustifiable luxury work, Hussey sought to re-establish the church's connection with modern artists, musicians, and writers of high calibre. Henry Moore's sculpture *Madonna and Child* (1943), with its neo-romantic emphasis on the nurturing body, and Graham Sutherland's painting *The Crucifixion* (1947), which consciously alluded to the atrocities of the Nazi death camps, were installed in opposite transepts of the parish church. These images echoed Hussey's own sacramental, catholic theology, and attested to his astuteness as a patron. At the time of their unveiling, both works were heavily criticized in the press: the *Madonna* for being 'grotesque' and 'an insult to every woman', and the *Crucifixion* for its modernist style and uncompromising portrayal of suffering and degradation (Hussey, *Patron of Art*, 45, 67–73). However, Hussey had the support of his congregation, and of Kenneth Clark, director of the National Gallery. Moreover, the unity of these art works with their liturgical and architectural context has been attested by more recent critics. They certainly document the catholic preoccupation with synthesis and balance: between the Christian doctrines of incarnation and redemption, between neo-romanticism and artistic modernism, between peaceful detachment and impassioned protest, and between the consciousness of beatitude and the conviction of the sin which perpetrates the most horrifying atrocities.

These commissions, combined with a broadcast from the church by the BBC Symphony Orchestra in 1943, two performances by the soprano Kirsten Flagstad in 1947 and 1948, a litany and anthem written by the poet W. H. Auden for the patronal festival in 1946, and the publication in pamphlet form of Norman Nicholson's poem 'The Outer Planet' in 1949, served to place St Matthew's Church at the centre of a small renaissance of religious art. It was not a coincidence that this occurred amid 1940s austerity; Hussey's sacramental aesthetic, like that of Bishop Bell of Chichester, was nourished by a conviction that the vision of the artist, in conjunction with that of the church, was a weapon in the spiritual arsenal of 'Christian civilization', essential for combating the cultural influence of totalitarianism.

Hussey's reputation for inspired art patronage, combined with highly aesthetic catholic liturgical celebration, was firmly established by the 1950s, and his appointment as dean of Chichester in 1955 transformed the cathedral into a thriving centre of ecclesiastical and artistic co-operation. By his retirement in 1977 Hussey's vision of a renewed tradition of religious art was amply attested by the decoration of the church itself, which contained significant works of modern art alongside medieval sculptures and architectural features, painstakingly restored. Ceri Richards designed a set of copes in 1960, Graham Sutherland contributed a painting, *Noli me tangere* (1961), John Piper designed an imposing tapestry for the altar reredos (1966), and 1978 saw the unveiling of a window illustrating Psalm 150, designed by Marc Chagall. As Alan Doig has commented, the artistic objects commissioned by Hussey for the cathedral possess a 'calm completeness' which enhances the sense of continuity between the medieval and the modern (Doig, 18). At Hussey's instigation, a Victorian wooden choir screen was replaced by the restored fifteenth-century stone screen, two twelfth-century Romanesque carvings of New Testament scenes were newly displayed, and, among other musical commissions, Leonard Bernstein wrote settings for the *Chichester Psalms* in 1965, and William Albright a *Chichester Mass* in 1975.

In the year of his retirement, Hussey wrote movingly of the relationship between the church and the arts:

> [The artist] can purge our imagination. He may, by forcing us to share his vision, lead us to the spiritual reality that lies behind the sounds and sights that we perceive with our senses. If all this be so, the true artist is one of the most valuable and honourable members of society and his work one of the highest activities of man … Art of high standard can and should be offered to God and in the offering symbolise all that should be offered by mankind. (Hussey, 'The arts and the church', 1)

That uncomplicated theological perception was the driving force behind Hussey's determination to invite modern artists to rejoin the life of the church, and the enthusiasm with which he approached that task is evident in his one book, *Patron of Art* (1985). Following a stroke, Hussey died on 25 July 1985 at St Stephen's Hospital, Chelsea, London. After his death his enormous private collection (which had become very valuable) was inherited by Pallant House in Chichester, and by the Northampton City Museum and Art Gallery. His estate was valued for probate at £1,370,620.   GILES C. WATSON

Sources W. Hussey, *Patron of art: the revival of a great tradition among modern artists* (1985) · A. Doig, 'Architecture and performance: Dean Walter Hussey and the arts', *Theology*, 99 (1996), 16–21 · G. Turner, '"Aesthete, impresario and indomitable persuader": Walter Hussey at St Matthew's, Northampton, and Chichester Cathedral', *The church and the arts* (1995) · M. Day, *Modern art in English churches*, ed. D. Wood (1984) · W. Hussey, 'The church and the artist: an association too much neglected', *The Churchman* (June 1946), 9–10 · W. Abrahams and P. Stansky, *London's burning: life, death and art in the Second World War* (1994) · W. Hussey, 'The arts and the church', *Chichester News* (June 1977), 1 · G. Watson, 'Catholicism in Anglican culture and theology: responses to crisis in England, 1937–1949', PhD diss., Australian National University, 1998 · b. cert. · d. cert. · W. Sussex RO, W. Hussey papers · *Oxford University Calendar* (1927–30)
Archives W. Sussex RO, corresp. and papers | Tate collection, corresp. with Lord Clark
Likenesses G. Sutherland, portrait, Pallant House, Chichester · photograph (with Henry Moore's *The falling warrior*), W. Sussex RO, W. Hussey papers, Hussey MS 375
Wealth at death £1,370,620: probate, 21 Nov 1985, *CGPLA Eng. & Wales*

Hussey [Huse], **Sir William** (*d.* 1495), justice, was the son of John Huse, of Old Sleaford, Lincolnshire, and Elizabeth Nesfield (or Neffield) of Yorkshire. He married Elizabeth, daughter of Thomas Berkeley of Wymondham, Leicestershire; they had two daughters and three sons, one of whom, John *Hussey, became Lord Hussey of Sleaford and was executed in 1537 after the Pilgrimage of Grace. Hussey attended parliament for Bramber (1460) and Grantham (1467 and 1478) and was regularly summoned between 1472 and 1491. As well as receiving numerous royal commissions (for instance, to arrest rebels in Sussex in 1461), he was a justice of the peace for Lincolnshire, for Kesteven from 1460, and for Rutland in 1470 and again from 1473 onwards, and was appointed to the bench of a dozen counties in 1483. His views on the office of justice of the peace are preserved in William Lambarde's *Eirenarcha* of 1581. A member of Gray's Inn, and possibly a reader there in 1455 and 1464, Hussey was attorney-general from 1471 to 1478, surrendering his office in 1478 to become a serjeant and later, perhaps in the same year, king's serjeant. He was made chief justice of the king's bench in 1481, the year in which he was knighted, and he was reappointed in 1483 and 1485. A feoffee for Sir John Audley, Sir Robert Tailboys, and Sir Reginald Bray, he was retained by the third duke of Buckingham, by William, Lord Hastings (1468–9), and by Richard of Gloucester, and was deputy chief steward for the southern part of the duchy of Lancaster from 1474 to 1480. He was a member of the great council during Edward IV's absence in France in 1475 and was granted the manor of Burton Pedwardine, Lincolnshire, by the king on his return; Richard III later granted him estates in Leicestershire and Lincolnshire.

Hussey was an influential and independent-minded judge. In 1482 he indicated that if the chancellor committed a suitor for breach of an injunction not to sue at common law, the king's bench would release him. He recalled in 1485 his sympathy with Edward IV's attempts to control retaining and, in the same year, maintained that the king of England was superior, concerning temporalities in his realm, to the pope (though in 1489 he declined to comment on 'the authority of the bishop of Rome'). He protested in 1486 against Henry VII's consultation of judges before they decided crown cases. The proceedings which followed, in the case of Humphrey Stafford, hastened the demise of sanctuary.

In 1484 Hussey was licensed to found a perpetual chantry at Old Sleaford, but he instructed that he was to be buried in the London Charterhouse or, if he died at home, in Sempringham or Peterborough. He died on 8 September 1495, bequeathing £10 yearly to found a lectureship at Cambridge.   NORMAN DOE

Sources A. W. B. Simpson, ed., *Biographical dictionary of the common law* (1984) · J. C. Wedgwood and A. D. Holt, *History of parliament*, 1: *Biographies of the members of the Commons house, 1439–1509* (1936) · *The reports of Sir John Spelman*, ed. J. H. Baker, 2 vols., SeldS, 93–4 (1977–8) · C. Rawcliffe, *The Staffords, earls of Stafford and dukes of Buckingham, 1394–1521*, Cambridge Studies in Medieval Life and Thought, 3rd ser., 11 (1978) · E. W. Ives, *The common lawyers of pre-Reformation England* (1983) · Holdsworth, *Eng. law* · *Les reports des cases en ley* (1680), Michaelmas 22, Edward IV, fol. 37, plea 21; Easter 22, Edward IV, fol. 6, plea 18 [year books] · *Les reports des cases* (1679), Michaelmas 1, Henry VII, fol. 3, plea 3; Trinity 4, Henry VII, fol. 15, plea 12; Hilary 9, Henry VII, fol. 20, plea 15 [year books] · *CIPM, Henry VII*, 1 · Chancery records
Likenesses miniature (on 1487 plea roll), repro. in Simpson, ed., *Biographical dictionary*, 256

Hussey, Sir William (*b.* in or after **1640**, *d.* **1691**), merchant and diplomat, was the second surviving son of Thomas Hussey (*b. c.*1613, *d.* in or before 1641) of Honnington, Lincolnshire, and his wife, Rhoda (*c.*1617–1686), daughter of Thomas Chapman of London. He came from a well-established Lincolnshire family, but the premature death of his father and the upheavals of the civil wars probably hastened his entry into the world of commerce. Perhaps aided by his mother's metropolitan connections, he was apprenticed to Levant trader Thomas Murthwaite in May 1655, and in 1662 was listed as a member of the factory at Aleppo. By July 1675 he had returned to London, from where he wrote to his elder brother, Thomas, revealing a keen interest in public affairs. In March 1677 he became a freeman of the Levant Company, and only two years later was elected to the board of assistants, on which he served until 1687. He clearly had made a name for himself, for in May 1680 the king intervened to prevent the company from nominating him as ambassador to the Ottoman Porte, insisting that any person who had lived in the Levant at a sub-ambassadorial rank could not stand. Hussey was cited as 'the most likely person to carry it with the young men who are the major part of the company', but the royal pronouncement quashed his ambitions on this occasion (*Finch MSS*, 2.75–6). Some compensation came in the form of his marriage in August 1682 to Mary (*c.*1660–1731), daughter of Sir John Buckworth, a leading figure within the Turkey trade. There is no evidence to suggest that there were any children of the marriage.

Although Hussey's hopes of public advancement were frustrated, his stature within the City continued to grow, and he served as one of the assistants of the Royal Africa Company from 1683 to 1685 and from 1688 to 1690. However, he did not appear eager for office in the London corporation, and was not prominent amid the bitter factionalism which gripped the capital during the 1680s. In contrast, his standing within the Turkey trade was recognized by his election to the deputy governorship of the Levant Company in 1688, and in that capacity he demonstrated support for the Williamite regime after the revolution of that year. The ensuing war with France clearly troubled him, and in February 1690 he lamented the 'very great difficulties' under which the country now laboured (*Downshire MSS*, 1.336). Personal uncertainty also greeted news of his subsequent appointment as ambassador to the Porte, although domestic concerns were blamed for his initial hesitation to take the post. Bowing to the royal will, in April he was formally named as ambassador, and knighted at Whitehall in accordance with his new dignity. His elevation probably owed little to personal fitness for the role, and can be read more directly as a sign of the king's impatience for the return to England of the current incumbent, Sir William Trumbull. Hussey's main task was to broker a peace between the Turks and the Austrian Habsburgs, which would allow the latter to contribute more fully to the allied offensive against the French. However, even before he left London, Hussey betrayed serious misgivings about the likelihood of success, pointing out that the timing of his embassy left him little chance of arresting the Balkan war at the height of the campaigning season. His protestations were waved aside, and in early October he embarked on his fateful journey east.

Having spent part of the winter in Vienna to sound out the Austrian position, Hussey eventually began to parley with Turkish officials on reaching Adrianople in May 1691. The following month he was granted an audience with the grand vizier, who appeared amenable towards a treaty. However, while both sides talked of peace, military operations continued, and Habsburg successes in the summer campaigns rendered the emperor less willing to settle with the Turks. Hussey's subsequent dispatches from Constantinople remained optimistic, but he found it difficult to prevail in such trying circumstances, and railed against the interference of the French, who were prepared to use any means to keep the Austrians pegged down in the east. Nobody could doubt his attachment to diplomatic duty, and while on another futile trip to Adrianople to secure peace terms he succumbed to a fever, dying on 14 September 1691. In England, rumour circulated that he had been poisoned by the French, even though it appears that his whole entourage had fallen ill in the heat of the Turkish summer. Administration of his estate was granted to his brother-in-law the following November, but it was not until 16 May 1695 that Hussey's body was finally laid to rest in the family vault at Honnington.

Shortly before his death Hussey had bitterly complained of crippling personal expenditure during the embassy, and within days of his demise his widow, Mary, argued that at least £6500 was owed to him on account of his diplomatic endeavours. She continued to pursue this suit after her eventual return to England in the winter of 1694–5, and, having married another Levant merchant, John Evans, reputedly Hussey's former business partner, made a claim for over £10,000 expenses for the 1690–91 embassy. There is no evidence that she had been repaid these charges by the time of her own death on 10 June 1731.   PERRY GAUCI

Sources R. E. G. Cole, *History of the manor and township of Doddington* (1897), 70–122 · SOAS, Paget MSS · *Report on the manuscripts of the marquis of Downshire*, 6 vols. in 7, HMC, 75 (1924–95), vol. 1 · *Report on the manuscripts of Allan George Finch*, 5 vols., HMC, 71 (1913–2003), vols. 1–3 · PRO, SP 105/154, fol. 11v · PRO, PROB 6 · Bodl. Oxf., MS Top. Linc. c. 3, fols. 32–3 · D. B. Horn, ed., *British diplomatic representatives, 1689–1789*, CS, 3rd ser., 46 (1932), 150 · *The manuscripts of the Marquess Townshend*, HMC, 19 (1887), 130 · *CSP dom., 1689–91* · S. P. Anderson, *An English consul in Turkey: Paul Rycaut at Smyrna, 1667–1678* (1989), 254 · K. G. Davies, *The Royal African Company* (1957), 303 · GL, MSS 15860/5 · A. R. Maddison, ed., *Lincolnshire pedigrees*, 2, Harleian Society, 51 (1903), 529–30 · G. J. Armytage, ed., *Allegations for marriage licences issued by the vicar-general of the archbishop of Canterbury, July 1679 to June 1687*, Harleian Society, 30 (1890), 104 · N. Luttrell, *A brief historical relation of state affairs from September 1678 to April 1714*, 6 vols. (1857)
Archives SOAS, corresp. with Lord Paget
Wealth at death reportedly 'a good estate': HMC, *Downshire*, vol. 1, p. 385 · widow later claimed that he was owed £10,863 by government for diplomatic expenses

Hustler, John (1715–1790), wool stapler and canal promoter, was born on 5 October 1715 at the family farm, Apple Tree Farm, Low Fold, Bolton, near Bradford, Yorkshire, the eldest son of William Hustler of Steeton (*d.* 11 May 1759), wool stapler and merchant, and his wife, Jane (1685–1745), *née* Jowett, whose family were farmers in Bradford. His parents were members of the Society of Friends (Quakers), and John received an education at the Friends' school in Goodmanend, Bradford. On completing his apprenticeship as a sorter and stapler of wool, he joined his father and uncle, John, in their wool merchanting business at the family farm. For almost a century the Hustlers were the leading wool staplers of the town, profiting from their resale of raw wool purchased from farms and wool fairs all over England.

At the age of forty-eight John Hustler married Christiana Hird (1732–1811), a minister in the Quaker faith and the daughter of Leeds landowner William Hird. They had six children, two sons, William (*b.* 1766) and John (*b.* 1768), and four daughters, Sarah (*b.* 1765), Anne (*b.* 1772), Patience (*b.* 1775), and Christiana. Shortly after his marriage Hustler bought an estate of 90 acres at Eccleshill and built Undercliffe House, living there for the rest of his life, and playing host to itinerant Quaker ministers.

By 1780 Bradford's outdated market facilities were forcing local tradesmen and farmers to take their business elsewhere. Hustler and others therefore built a new market hall, shops, and a shambles in a newly laid-out street (now Market Street). Before 1773 Bradford's clothmakers sold their rolls of finished cloth from the upper rooms of local public houses, but in that year Hustler initiated the funding for a proper retail outlet for finished worsted pieces. The 100 stalls of the first Bradford piece hall were in such demand that Hustler and his committee were soon forced to extend the premises.

Perhaps the single most important project launched by Hustler for the benefit of the Bradford region in the eighteenth century was that linking the town to the national network of canals. Bradford was badly located for transport to either coast. Although not the original author of the scheme, Hustler was the prime mover in the formation of the Leeds to Liverpool Canal Company. He was an original subscriber and publicist for the idea of a trans-Pennine canal, and following the death of another Bradford colliery owner he took responsibility for its promotion nationwide, writing a prospectus, *A Summary View of the Proposed Canal from Leeds to Liverpool* (1770) in favour of the parliamentary legislation establishing the company. Hustler was chairman and treasurer of the Yorkshire committee which invited subscriptions, placed newspaper advertisements, and enlisted the financial support of Quakers across the nation. Despite a late secession by the Lancashire committee Hustler went ahead, and by May 1770 his parliamentary lobbying paid off when his canal bill became law (10 Geo. III c. 114). Four years later he locked Bradford into the canal system with the opening of the small Bradford Canal, and until his death he worked assiduously to raise sufficient funds to complete the Leeds to Liverpool Canal, travelling to the continent to raise the necessary capital.

Hustler's colliery interests in Bradford and Wigan had motivated his commitment to the canal scheme, but his primary business as a wool merchant made him a spokesman for that industry for most of his life. As early as 1752 he gave evidence before a parliamentary committee dealing with the false practices of wool growers, and in 1764 he was largely instrumental in pressing parliament for legislation against the closed-shop activities of domestic textile workers, particularly wool combers. In 1777 two acts of parliament (17 Geo. III c. 11 and c. 56) established the formation of the worsted committee to act as a policing agency on behalf of worsted manufacturers. At its first meeting at The Talbot inn, Halifax, on 9 June 1777 Hustler was elected chairman, an office he held for many years. In 1782 and 1787 Hustler wrote several pamphlets against the exportation of English long wool resulting in successful legislation in 1788.

Hustler took little part in politics, although as a protestant dissenter he was firmly against the Jacobite rising of 1745, heading the Bradford subscription towards the defence of the Hanoverian succession. Also in 1767 he wrote an important pamphlet on the issue of the corn bounty entitled *The Occasion of the Dearness of Provisions*, considering reasons for and against the imposition of such a bounty. Apart from his active work as a Quaker minister Hustler helped to found Ackworth School, and, having

amassed great wealth from his successful wool business, promoted numerous commercial schemes which benefited the industrial and economic transformation of the West Riding of Yorkshire, and of Bradford in particular. He died on 6 November 1790 at Undercliffe House, leaving two sons and a widow who survived him by twenty-one years. He was interred at the Quaker burial-ground in Bradford.　　　　　　　　　　　　　　　　GARY FIRTH

Sources J. James, *Continuation and additions to the history of Bradford, and its parish* (1866), 90–92 · W. Hustwick, 'An eighteenth-century woolstapler', *Bradford Textile Society Journal* (1956–7), 117–25 · J. Maffey, 'On some decayed families of Bradford', *Bradford Antiquary*, 1 (1881–8), 26–32 · A. Robinson, 'The Hustlers, a great Quaker family', *Bradford and Halifax Chamber of Commerce Journal*, 2/2 (1975) · A. Raistrick, *Quakers in science and industry* (1950); repr. (1968), 78–80 · *GM*, 1st ser., 60 (1790), 1055 · J. Smith, ed., *A descriptive catalogue of Friends' books*, 1 (1867), 1024–5 · *DNB* · G. Field, 'Incidents in the history of Bradford Quakerism over 250 years', lecture transcript, Bradford Central Library, B 289.6 FIE
Archives University of Bradford, J. B. Priestley Library, worsted committee MSS · York Minster, Hailstone MSS

Hutcheson, Archibald (*c*.1660–1740), lawyer and economist, was the son of Archibald Hutcheson of Stranocum, co. Antrim. He was admitted to the Middle Temple in 1680, was called to the bar in 1683, and for the next five years practised as a barrister in England and Ireland. At the beginning of 1688 he was chosen attorney-general of the Leeward Islands by the governor, Sir Nathaniel Johnson, and he became noted for implementing a policy of complete leniency towards the islands' Catholic populace. A protestant, and possibly of Ulster–Scots presbyterian stock, he had a deep antipathy to religious persecution, which seems to have been a strong recommendation to the lords of trade in London. He retained his position after the revolution, although not without becoming caught up in the accusations of disloyalty to William III directed at Johnson's successor, Colonel Christopher Codrington, being himself accused of aspersing the king's name and of bias towards Catholics and Jacobites. Hutcheson was cleared of these denunciations, however, and continued his official legal duties on the islands until 1704 when he returned to England, settling permanently at St James's, Westminster, and re-establishing his legal practice. Having first married Mary Smith on 29 June 1697 at St Martin-in-the-Fields, he had following her death married Rebecca Bankes (*d*. in or before 1715), a widow, on 19 August 1701 at Topsham, Devon. His interest in economic and mathematical questions led to his election as FRS in 1708.

About 1710 Hutcheson became a legal adviser to the duke of Ormond, thus joining the extensive retinue of advisers, lawyers, and agents whom the duke employed to administer his vast, mainly Irish estate. Hutcheson's own Irish background and the close proximity to Ormond's London residence in St James's Square doubtless assisted what remained primarily a professional rather than political association. Hutcheson spent the early months of 1713 touring Germany in the company of the young duke of Montagu. During these travels, which included visits to several princely courts, he acted as a kind of self-appointed ambassador in support of the protestant Hanoverian succession to the British crown. At Frankfurt he was welcomed by the exiled duke of Marlborough, Montagu's father-in-law, who regarded him as a potentially useful tool in parliament. He also made a favourable impression with courtiers and politicians at Hanover. Upon his return to England, the duke of Ormond, as newly appointed warden of the Cinque Ports, was able to procure Hutcheson's return for Hastings in the autumn general election.

Although Hutcheson had been regarded as a tory, presumably on the grounds of his pronounced attachment to the church, he had little liking for the administration of the earl of Oxford, and once in parliament co-operated closely with the whigs in opposition. Indeed, his intimacy with senior whig politicians, combined with the strong whiggish line which he took in the Commons during the 1714 session, set him apart from most other 'whimsical' or moderate tories, and political observers regarded him more as a whig. Hutcheson's sterling parliamentary services in helping to rally tories against the ministry were rewarded after the accession of George I with his appointment (in December 1714) as a lord commissioner of the Board of Trade with a salary of £1000. His accord with the new whig administration rapidly disintegrated, however, when proceedings were commenced in June 1715 to impeach the duke of Ormond, who, having aligned himself with the Stuart dynasty, was now in exile. Hutcheson gave a fulsome defence of his patron, and in January 1716 resigned from the Board of Trade.

Hutcheson's marriage in August 1715 (by a licence dated 18 August) to Mary, Lady Gayre (d. 1727), the widow of the wealthy West Indian merchant Sir John Gayre, gave him access to a fortune said to be worth £40,000 and obviated any further need he might have for a government salary. For the remainder of his career in parliament he cast himself as an independent critic of government. Hutcheson's continuing association with Ormond and his family inevitably prompted accusations that he was a crypto-Jacobite, but as he had become one of the duke's principal creditors and an authority on his tangled finances, it was no longer an association he could renounce without considerable personal loss. In July 1718 Hutcheson added fuel to public concern about the size of the national debt with the publication of his essay *The Present State of the Public Debts and Funds*, the main thrust of which was his argument that the debt had escalated sharply under the management of George I's whig ministers. Responding for the government, John Crookshanks, an excise official, claimed to detect flaws in Hutcheson's accounting methodology and demonstrated that the recent accumulations of debt had in fact been incurred during Queen Anne's reign. In advancing his case, Crookshanks played upon Hutcheson's supposed Jacobitism by exposing passages in Hutcheson's text which seemed redolent of a sympathy for the Stuarts. However, by the time Hutcheson published his *Answer* in December 1719, the chief concern was not with

responsibility for the debt but with the agency selected for its reduction: the South Sea Company.

Hutcheson strongly opposed the company's proposals for taking over the national debt, and in a further pamphlet published as stock prices soared he warned that since stock values bore little or no relationship to their 'intrinsic' worth, financial disaster was inevitable. In the aftermath of the 'bubble' he proposed his own radical 'engraftment' scheme, and with several other prominent opposition MPs and peers led demands for the company's directors to be stripped of their estates and effects. He subsequently participated in the Commons' secret committee which investigated the scandal. His idiosyncratic efforts during 1721–2 to persuade Lord Sunderland to inaugurate a popular ministry, embracing 'country principles' and capable of governing a nation traumatized by the South Sea crisis, produced nothing but his own disillusion. His candidacy in tandem with a tory in a particularly violent contest for the populous constituency of Westminster during the election in the spring of 1722 only revived taunts of Jacobitism; and the following year, amid exposure of the Atterbury plot, he was forced to publish a strong denial of any involvement with the Jacobite conspirators.

Hutcheson remained MP for Hastings, continuing to participate actively in proceedings until he stood down in 1727. In 1726 he was made a bencher at the Middle Temple, and on 30 October 1727, eight months after the death of his third wife, from whom he had previously separated by decree of chancery, he married another widow, Elizabeth Stewart, thereby acquiring property interests on the islands of Montserrat and St Kitts. Despite the jibes of certain detractors, his connection with Jacobitism was more apparent than real, for it was on the basis of his deep involvement in the complex financial affairs of Ormond and his brother, the earl of Arran, which continued into the early 1730s, that other prominent Jacobites whom he encountered presumed upon his personal support for their cause. He remained publicly active until almost the end of his life. He was one of the lords proprietors of Carolina and a member of the court of St George's Hospital, and in 1739 became treasurer of the Middle Temple. He died, probably aged eighty, on 12 August 1740; his fourth wife, Elizabeth, survived him. A. A. HANHAM

Sources 'Hutcheson, Archibald', HoP, *Commons, 1690–1715* [draft] · [A. Hutcheson], *A collection of advertisements, letters and papers ... relating to the late election at Westminster and Hastings* (1722) · HoP, *Commons, 1715–54*, 2.163–4 · J. D. Alsop, 'The politics of whig economics: the national debt on the eve of the South Sea Bubble', *Durham University Journal*, new ser., 46 (1985), 211–18 · 'A declaration signed by Archibald Hutcheson', 1723, BL, BS 91/8/3

Archives BL, problems relating to right-angled triangles, Add. MS 4436, fols. 149–150b · BL, speeches, St MS 372; Add. MS 18682 | Berks. RO, corresp. and accounts with M. S. Pleydell, D/EPb/E68–71 · BL, corresp. with W. Matthew relating to claims upon property in Montserrat and St Kitts, Add. MS 18683 · BL, corresp. with Lord Sunderland, Add. MS 61496, fols. 48–9, 62–5; Add. MS 61547, fols. 206–7 · NL Ire., letters documenting his involvement in the duke of Ormond's estate and financial affairs, Ormond MSS 2474, pp. 349–69, 383–4, 513; MS 2476, pp. 91, 37–8, 107, 315–27, 375–6, 399–400, 407–8, 415–16; MS 2518, pp. 1–14

Hutcheson, Francis (1694–1746), moral philosopher, was born in Ulster, in the township of Drumalig, near Saintfield, co. Down, on 8 August 1694. His father was John Hutcheson (d. 1729), minister of the Presbyterian church in Downpatrick (1690–97) and Armagh (1697–1729). His mother was the daughter of Lieutenant-Colonel James Trail of Killyleagh; she bore John Hutcheson three sons: Hans (the eldest), Francis, and Robert. She was the first of three wives of the Revd John Hutcheson; by his second wife, the daughter of Robert Wilson of Tully, co. Longford, he had three children: two sons, Alexander and John, and a daughter, Rhoda; he was married a third time to Rachel Graham, daughter of Arthur Graham of Ballyharridan. (wills of Hutcheson family; *Fasti of the Irish Presbyterian Church*, 68; Stuart, 487).

Early years and education Francis Hutcheson spent some years of his youth in the company of his grandfather, Alexander Hutcheson (d. 1711), Presbyterian minister of Saintfield. In 1702 Francis was sent with his elder brother, Hans, to live with their grandfather and attend a preparatory school in Saintfield; they remained with Alexander Hutcheson until 1707. Francis went on to attend a dissenting academy in Killyleagh, co. Down conducted by the Revd James McAlpine. It was there, no doubt, in the household of his aunt Margaret Trail and his uncle the Revd James *Bruce that he began to form a lifelong friendship with his cousin, William *Bruce (*Belfast Monthly Magazine*, 11, 1813; MSS minutes of the presbytery of Down, 5 Aug 1707, cited in Witherow, 345n.).

An education at an academy in England, Ireland, or Wales prepared Presbyterians and other nonconformists for study at a Scottish university. The curriculum was designed to substitute for the syllabus of the university that students would ultimately attend. For most Irish Presbyterian students, the university of choice was that of Glasgow. When Francis Hutcheson was admitted to the University of Glasgow in 1710/11, he had already satisfied the course requirements for the first three years of university study: in logic, metaphysics, and moral philosophy. He entered in the fourth and final year, in the natural philosophy class of John Loudon. Accordingly, his studies at the academy in Killyleagh would have given him some mastery of the texts assigned students at the University of Glasgow in the first decade of the eighteenth century: in logic, the *Ars cogitandi* or Port Royal logic, amended by the writings of John Locke and Jean Leclerc; in metaphysics, the *Determinationes ontologicae et pneumatologicae* of Gerard de Vries, qualified by the writings of Locke and Malebranche; in moral philosophy, Samuel Pufendorf's *De officio hominis et civis*, supplemented by the Reformed scholastic treatises of Adrien Heereboord and Francis Burgersdyck and modified by the political writings of John Locke.

Following completion of the prescribed course of study at Glasgow, Hutcheson spent a year studying the classics. He would later recall that it was in Glasgow, that

> I had my first taste of the immortal sublimities of Homer and Virgil, of the charms, the felicity and dexterity … of Xenophon, Horace, Aristophanes and Terence; likewise the

Francis Hutcheson (1694–1746), by Allan Ramsay, c.1745

> abundant grace and breadth of Cicero in every branch of philosophy. (*De naturali hominum socialitate*, inaugural lecture, Glasgow, 1730, 2)

His love of classical literature and philosophy would have an abiding influence on his thought and his career. In 1712/13 he began six years of training to become a minister in the Presbyterian church. His teacher was the controversial professor of divinity John Simson, twice tried for heresy before the general assembly of the Church of Scotland: in 1714–17 for teaching the doctrines of Arminius (and Grotius) that the fall of man did not leave mankind bereft of reason, will power, and natural affection, in the absence of saving grace; in 1726–9 for teaching Arianism, the doctrine that Christ was not consubstantial with nor of the same substance as God. Simson was suspended from his teaching duties in 1729.

The Dublin years and philosophical treatises, 1720–1730 Hutcheson returned to Ulster in 1718. He was licensed as a probationer by the presbytery of Armagh in 1719 but he never accepted a ministerial charge. Ulster Presbyterians were at that time engaged in a controversy concerning the obligation of ministers to subscribe to the articles of the Westminster confession of faith. Some ministers, led by the Revd John Abernethy and the Revd Samuel Haliday, declared it to be the right of ministers and of all Christians to exercise private judgement in matters of faith. Hutcheson found himself in the company of the non-subscribers; both Abernethy and Haliday became his friends; their names appear frequently in his correspondence. The non-subscription movement in Ulster was supported by ministers of the Presbyterian churches in Dublin: Joseph Boyse, Richard Choppin, and Nathaniel Weld. They invited

Hutcheson to come to Dublin and conduct an academy for Presbyterian and other nonconformist students. Hutcheson accepted the invitation. His abilities as a teacher and thinker soon came to the attention of prominent figures of Dublin society: among them were John Carteret, lord lieutenant of Ireland, and his chaplain, Edward Synge. Both men attempted to persuade Hutcheson to accept a living in the Church of Ireland, an invitation that caused concern to his father, the Revd John Hutcheson. Francis Hutcheson assured his father that he had no such intention; but that his father should not be distressed if his son or another should accept such a ministry: for the 'true end' of any church was after all the promotion of 'real Piety and Virtue' (F. Hutcheson to J. Hutcheson, 4 Aug 1726, PRO NIre., D971/34/G/1/1). There is no reason to suppose that his father, a strict Presbyterian, was reassured by this letter. Francis Hutcheson had close relations with other notable members of the established church: with Hugh Boulter, archbishop of Armagh and primate of all Ireland, and Richard West, the lord chancellor (Leechman, ix). Of all his Dublin acquaintants, the most significant influence upon his writing and his career was no doubt Robert, Viscount Molesworth. Through the 1720s Molesworth, a friend and correspondent of the third earl of Shaftesbury, entered into an exchange of letters with Scottish professors and Irish students in Scottish universities: he recommended that they read moral and political authors in the classical republican tradition (Machiavelli, Harrington, Milton, and Sidney), that they work for the reform of the Scottish universities, so that students might be inspired to pursue truth, beauty, and virtue for their own sake.

It was in this social, educational, and ecclesiological milieu that Hutcheson wrote his first philosophical work, *An Inquiry into the Original of our Ideas of Beauty and Virtue* (1725). In the first of the two treatises contained in the *Inquiry* he argued that there is an internal sense, analogous to the five external senses, which brings to mind ideas of beauty, order, harmony, and design, whenever one perceives objects, artefacts, scenes, and compositions which exhibit uniformity amid variety. In the second treatise he argued for the presence in human nature of a moral sense which determines one to recognize virtue whenever one observes a character or an action prompted by benevolence or kind affection. He found no merit in arguments which reduce virtue to self-interest, however useful or serviceable to others such interested conduct might appear. 'If there be any Benevolence at all, it must be *disinterested*; for the most useful Action imaginable, loses all appearance of *Benevolence*, as soon as we discern that it only flowed from Self-Love, or Interest' (p. 129). His argument that the moral sense forms a natural or instinctive part of human nature was directed pointedly against the contention of Bernard Mandeville that virtue and vice are artificial distinctions, the inventions of politicians, who employ these terms for no other reason than to curb the appetites and ambitions of unruly subjects.

Hutcheson's *Inquiry* provoked an extended, mutually respectful exchange with the Revd Gilbert Burnet (1690–

1726) in the *London Journal* (April–December, 1725). Burnet (using the pseudonym Philaretus) argued that Hutcheson's determination to ground moral distinctions upon sensibility and feeling left moral life without an adequate foundation. He proposed that antecedently to any sensation or feeling of virtue there must be a reason or a rational apprehension of goodness and rectitude. Hutcheson (writing as Philanthropus) countered that in order for the terms reason, reasonable, and rational to be meaningful they must refer to the happiness of persons or moral agents; an individual who prefers his own happiness to the general or public happiness might be considered reasonable but he could not be considered moral; one who prefers the greater or public happiness to his own happiness is properly considered not only reasonable but also moral or virtuous. The latter judgement cannot be based upon reason: it must derive from a still more basic feeling that benevolent or public-spirited action is singularly or particularly virtuous.

In 1728 Hutcheson's *Essay on the Nature and Conduct of the Passions and Affections, with Illustrations on the Moral Sense* was published in Dublin and London. In the *Essay* Hutcheson answered the arguments of John Clarke of Hull, who had contended that benevolence is traceable to self-love; one feels uneasiness when one perceives that others are in misery or in distress; benevolence or kind affection for others is prompted by a desire to satisfy or relieve this uneasiness in oneself; accordingly, benevolence or kind affection is derived not from an original or distinct or irreducible instinct, it is traceable, like all affections and passions, to self-love. Hutcheson thought Clarke's 'Scheme' of deducing disinterested affection from self-love 'more ingenious than any which the Author of the *Inquiry* ever yet saw in print' (*Essay*, Preface, xii). His answer, adumbrated in section I of the *Essay*, was that there are different classes of desires; that the desire to assist the afflicted or distressed or to act for the benefit of the public is entirely different from the desire to seek happiness or satisfaction or pleasure for oneself. He connected the desire to act in a spirit of kindness or benevolence to a public sense; this was a new sense, introduced together with a sense of honour for the first time in the *Essay*. In the preface to *Illustrations on the Moral Sense* Hutcheson returned to his differences with Gilbert Burnet, endeavouring, he said, 'to leave no Objections of his unanswer'd' (p. xxxi). He also continued his argument against moral rationalists to register his disagreement with Samuel Clarke's theory that virtue and vice may be discovered in relations of ideas, and with William Wollaston's theory that virtue and vice are signified by the truth or falsehood of actions and assertions. Hutcheson maintained that both theories overlooked or abstracted from the qualities of character that are truly relevant for moral judgement; that, if these theories were correct, one could not exclude from 'the Class of Virtues, all the practical Mathematicks, and the Operations of Chymistry' (*Illustrations*, 248).

The *Inquiry* had been published in Dublin by William and John Smith. When the senior partner left the firm, in

1725, to become a partner with the Amsterdam booksellers Rudolf and Jacob Wetstein, his place was taken in the Dublin firm by William Bruce, Hutcheson's cousin; Smith and Bruce were the publishers of the *Essay*. John Smith, now the senior partner, had been expelled from the University of Glasgow in 1722, for celebrating a reported election victory of Viscount Molesworth and for scuffling, on that occasion, with one of the professors, Gershom Carmichael. John Smith and William Bruce were part of a literary circle which included James Arbuckle, the editor of the *Dublin Weekly Journal*, in which essays of Hutcheson's, critical of Thomas Hobbes on laughter and of Bernard Mandeville, were published in 1725 and 1726. The intensive literary activities of this circle, the continued agitation for reform of the University of Glasgow by former students of Hutcheson's academy, and the influence exerted by his students and by friends in the highest levels of government in London resulted in a commission of visitation of the University of Glasgow in 1727. The commission abolished the regenting system in philosophy and created professorships of logic and metaphysics, moral philosophy, and natural philosophy. Following the death of the first occupant of the chair of moral philosophy, Gershom Carmichael (1672–1729), the faculty of the University of Glasgow determined by majority vote, on 19 December 1729, 'that Mr. Francis Hutchinson of Dublin should be Elected to Succeed to the said Vacancy' (U. Glas., Archives and Business Records Centre, MS 26635, fol. 147).

Professor at Glasgow and theological controversy, 1730–1738
The choice of Hutcheson was controversial: he was thought by many to be suspect in his theological principles: 'how the principles he goes on agree with the truths generally received in this Church, and what influence his teaching them here may have, time will discover' (Wodrow, 4.99). His candidacy had been contested by the son of the previous occupant of the chair, by the principal, and by half of the masters. It was due to the influence of the earl of Ilay that the friends of Hutcheson, led by Alexander Dunlop, the professor of Greek, were able to secure his election. Hutcheson arrived in Glasgow in October 1730. He introduced himself to the faculty, students, and friends of the University of Glasgow in an inaugural lecture, delivered in Latin, 'On the natural sociability of mankind'. Although Robert Wodrow considered the lecture to be on 'a very safe general subject' (ibid., 4.187), Hutcheson was not reluctant to take up controversial themes. It had been one of the dogmas of reformed theology that the natural condition of mankind was a fallen or sinful condition; the only remedy for this condition was salvation, made available to some, not to all, by the atonement made for our sins by Christ. Hutcheson ascribed to the reformed theologians a different view. He acknowledged that

> though in popular language they sometimes call our fallen and corrupt state natural, ... they do not deny thereby that the original fabric of our nature was, by the divine art and plan, designed for every virtue, for all honest and illustrious things. (*De naturali hominum socialitate*)

He also used the occasion of his inaugural lecture to answer new arguments advanced by Archibald Campbell and Bernard Mandeville, moralists convinced of the primacy of self-love or self-esteem. He concluded with an appeal to youth

> to follow nature and God as your leader, applying your minds to honest studies, gathering a store of multifarious, useful things which you may bring forth in all honest, temperate, modest and brave service to our country and to the human race. (ibid.)

In his lectures at the University of Glasgow, Hutcheson was not obliged to teach logic, metaphysics, and natural philosophy, as had been the case at Dublin, in his academy. The particular subject of his lectures in Glasgow was moral philosophy, his speciality. He continued to offer private classes and examine theses in Latin. It was the opinion of a former student that 'he wrote and spoke, at least we thought so, better in Latin than English' (J. Wodrow to the earl of Buchan, 28 May 1808, Glasgow, Mitchell Library, Baillie MS 32225). But some time during the 1730s, Hutcheson introduced to the University of Glasgow and to Scottish university education generally the practice of lecturing in English (S. Kenrick to J. Wodrow, 28 Sept 1786, DWL, MS 24.157). When Hutcheson's students defended him from the charge that he taught doctrines contrary to religion and morality, in 1738, they cited his 'very expression' in English (*A Vindication of Mr. Hutcheson*, 13). Hutcheson had been accused of teaching that 'we have a notion of moral goodness prior in the order of knowledge to any notion of the will or law of God' (ibid., 7). His students agreed that this was indeed his teaching, but they found nothing objectionable in the charge. It is true, they argued, that we have a notion of goodness as benevolence, independent of God's will; we judge God to be good because we recognize a benevolent scheme in the order of the creation; if we had no notion of goodness apart from God's will, we would have no more to say in praise of God than that his will is consistent with itself (ibid., 7–8). Hutcheson himself dismissed the accusation as 'some whimsical Buffoonery about my Heresy' (F. Hutcheson to T. Drennan, 5 March 1739, Glasgow University Library, MS Gen. 1018).

A System of Moral Philosophy Earlier in the same year, Hutcheson had sent to Ireland and to William Bruce a manuscript of a work which would remain unpublished during his lifetime. It was entitled *A System of Moral Philosophy, in Three Books* (1755). It is the most voluminous of Hutcheson's writings (738 pages); it is also the most ambitious in scope. It contains his most comprehensive account of human nature, the supreme good and greatest happiness, divine providence, natural rights, and civil government. His design in the *System* appears to have been to delineate a theodicy, in which God or providence is shown to have made provision for the happiness of the human race. It is curious that after taking the time and trouble to compose so large a work Hutcheson should have decided not to publish it. He told Drennan (letter of 15 June 1741) that he was dissatisfied with the argument. He also indicated that while making revisions of the manuscript he was refreshing his memory of particular subjects for incorporation in his lectures. If the purpose of the exercise was simply to put his thoughts on ethics, natural jurisprudence, and civil government into English for classroom use, then publication would have no point. There may also be significance in the circumstance that he was determined that the manuscript be circulated in Ireland, notwithstanding the very sensible advice given him by William Bruce that 'all the advantage that can possibly arise from the perusal of them on this side of the water is not worth the hazard of their being lost' (W. Bruce to F. Hutcheson, 12 Jan 1738, NL Scot., MS 9252). Once his manuscript had been read in Ireland by Edward Synge and others, Hutcheson may have concluded that his ideas on this subject had been communicated to the readers whom he had primarily in mind when he composed it. He may also have been disturbed by arguments put to him by his younger contemporary David Hume, and decided to pursue his differences with Hume in a different idiom.

Pedagogical writings In 1742 two works written in Latin by Hutcheson were published by Robert Foulis of Glasgow. They were *Philosophiae moralis institutio compendiaria, ethices & jurisprudentiae naturalis elementa continens*, book 3, and *Metaphysicae synopsis: ontologiam, et pneumatologiam, complectens*. A third text of Hutcheson's, *Logicae compendium*, was published posthumously, in 1756, by the same firm; a student transcription of a variant of this text, entitled 'Logica', was available in the late 1740s. In each of these texts, Hutcheson made it clear that they were intended for the use of students only. This specification of their use presents a problem. It has been observed that Hutcheson did not teach logic or metaphysics at Glasgow. He had begun lecturing in moral philosophy, in English, some time in the 1730s. It may be wondered when these writings were composed and what use Hutcheson would have had for them? Each of these works may be recognized to be adaptations of texts that had been assigned to students at the University of Glasgow earlier in the century and were still in use at that institution. His *Logicae compendium* or 'Logica' was a modification of the logic course dictated to his students by John Loudon in 1711 and 1729. The *Metaphysicae synopsis* was an adaptation of the *Determinationes ontologicae et pneumatologicae* of the Dutch metaphysician Gerard de Vries, the text assigned again by John Loudon, during the several decades of his teaching career at Glasgow (1699–1750). The *Philosophia moralis* was much indebted for its structure and its argument to Gershom Carmichael's edition of Samuel Pufendorf's *De officio hominis et civis* (1718; 2nd edn, 1724), as Hutcheson acknowledged, freely and generously, in the dedication (*Philosophia moralis*, ii). These were texts that a tutor or instructor might have dictated to substitute for lectures on these subjects at the University of Glasgow through the early decades of the eighteenth century. One may surmise that Hutcheson's texts had been composed by him for the use of his students in his academy in Dublin, when he taught all the parts of philosophy, in Latin, and prepared many of his students to enter the University of Glasgow (as he had done) in the final or natural philosophy year.

If Hutcheson's Latin texts date from the 1720s, why did he arrange or accede to their publication in the 1740s? At least three considerations may have prompted him to agree to their publication. One, he was eager to give Robert Foulis, his former student, support in his new publishing initiative; Hutcheson wrote to Drennan that 'if you knew Foulis you would think he well deserved all encouragement' (F. Hutcheson to T. Drennan, 31 May 1742, Glasgow University Library, MS Gen. 1018). Second, the health of his colleague John Loudon had become frail in the 1740s. His classes had come to appear, to some of his students at least, to be uninspired. Loudon also taught his classes in logic and metaphysics, entirely in Latin (S. Kenrick to J. Wodrow, 27 April 1808, Glasgow, Mitchell Library, Baillie MS 32225). It may be supposed that there would have been curiosity in the student body to learn what a popular teacher, like Hutcheson, thought on these subjects. Third, Hutcheson may also have been prompted to return to his earlier writings on metaphysics and morals by reading David Hume's very different treatment of those subjects. Hutcheson confessed to Henry Home that 'these metaphysical subjects have not been much in my thoughts of late; tho' a great many of these sentiments and reasonings had employed me about 10 or 12 years ago'; that is, when he taught metaphysics, in Dublin, at his academy (F. Hutcheson to H. Home, April 1739?, Edinburgh, Register House, Abercairny collection, GD 24/no. 55). He sent Hume a copy of his *Philosophia moralis*, a gift which Hume perceived to be a further contribution to their exchange of views on moral subjects that had occurred when Hume was preparing Book III of *A Treatise of Human Nature* for publication (D. Hume to F. Hutcheson, 10 Jan 1743; *Letters*, 1.45–8). At least some of the revisions which Hutcheson made to his metaphysics, and particularly to his morals, suggest that opinions put to him by Hume were very much in his mind as he prepared second editions of these texts for publication, in 1744 and 1745.

Hutcheson and Hume The relationship between Francis Hutcheson and David Hume has been interpreted differently in different centuries. In the eighteenth century, their contemporaries and successors—James Balfour, Adam Smith, Thomas Reid, Adam Ferguson—perceived them to have been propounding very different systems of morals. In the twentieth century, following the scholarship of Norman Kemp Smith, historians of philosophy were more inclined to recognize common themes in their approaches to moral subjects. They were perceived to have been naturalists (Norman Kemp Smith), empiricists (David Daiches Raphael), emotivists (William Frankena), and moral realists (David Fate Norton). But however mutually supportive their systems may appear in light of more recent controversies in moral philosophy, their writings were very different in inspiration. Hutcheson adamantly opposed Hume's candidacy for the professorship of pneumatics and ethical philosophy at the University of Edinburgh: 'as to Mr. Hutcheson', Hume remarked, 'all my Friends think, that he has been rendering me bad Offices to the utmost of his Power' (D. Hume to W. Mure of Caldwell, 4 Aug 1744; *Letters*, 1.55–9). Hutcheson had considerable influence in Edinburgh in the 1740s; the principal of the university, William Wishart, had been associated with Hutcheson and the Molesworth circle in the 1720s; Hutcheson found himself not only invited to apply for the chair, he was even appointed to it, although he did not apply. He declined the appointment, but submitted at the request of the University of Edinburgh a list of potential appointees. David Hume's name did not appear on the list. Hutcheson's principal complaint against Hume as a moral philosopher, as he expressed it in a letter to Hume (known to us only from Hume's reply), was that Hume's moral philosophy lacked 'a certain Warmth in the Cause of Virtue' (D. Hume to F. Hutcheson, 17 Sept 1739; *Letters*, 1.32–5). Hume responded that this was not an accident: his philosophy was not designed to recommend virtue but to explain the operations of the understanding, the passions, and morals. In the event Hume was not appointed to the chair of moral philosophy at the University of Edinburgh; the appointment went to William Cleghorn, one of several candidates recommended by Hutcheson.

Marriage, death, and estate Hutcheson married in 1725. His wife was Mary Wilson, eldest daughter of Francis Wilson, of Tully, co. Longford. She was the niece of the Revd John Hutcheson's second wife; as such, she was Hutcheson's first cousin (step-cousin) or cousin-german. His own marriage may have inspired his later defence of marriages between cousins-german, in which 'multitudes of families are beautifully interwoven with each other in affection and interest, and friendly ties are much further diffused' (*System of Moral Philosophy*, 2.171–2). By his marriage, Hutcheson acquired extensive property in Ireland. The townlands of Drumnacross, Garrinch, and Knockeagh, in co. Longford, were part of the dowry brought to her marriage by Mary Wilson. Francis Hutcheson and his wife had seven children; only one survived (F. Hutcheson to the Revd T. Steward, 12 Feb 1740, Magee College, MS 46). This was Francis *Hutcheson, fellow of Trinity College, Dublin. His fellowship of Trinity College, Dublin, indicates that Francis Hutcheson the younger became a member of the Church of Ireland.

Francis Hutcheson died on 8 August 1746, of a fever, during a visit to Dublin. He was buried the following day in the churchyard of St Mary's Church, Dublin. In his will he left his wife an annuity of £20 on the lands of Ballyhackmer, in co. Down, and 'all the Rents, Issues and Profits' of the lands in co. Longford during her life; together with the remainder of his personal estate after payment of his debts. He appointed his brother Robert trustee of the lands in co. Longford. He left his son Francis the lands of Ballyhackmer, subject to the annuity assigned to his wife. He also left his son his half of the lands of Drumalig, inherited from his father and grandfather; with the provision that if his son should agree, when he is of legal age, to be a life tenant only, and settle his half of Drumalig upon Hans Hutcheson, testator's brother, then his brother Robert should 'make over and convey' the lands of co. Longford to his son Francis. 'But if my son Francis refuse to concur in such Deeds as to settle the Lands of Drumalig aforesaid that then my brother Robert shall retain the said Lands … to himself and his heirs and Assignees forever.'

He left William Bruce £100 'to be disposed among his Friends at his discretion'. He also left sums of money to his other brothers, his sister Rhoda, his aunts and relations. The will was witnessed by his colleague James Moor and by the booksellers Robert and Andrew Foulis (PRO NIre., D/971/34/D/I).

Hutcheson was succeeded as professor of moral philosophy at the University of Glasgow by Thomas Craigie (1746–52), Adam Smith (1752–64), and Thomas Reid (1764–80). His textbooks on logic, metaphysics, and moral philosophy were reprinted in successive editions through the eighteenth century. These texts, together with *A System of Moral Philosophy*, published by subscription in 1755, and his *Inquiries*, *Essay*, and *Illustrations*, were widely used in Scottish and American universities in the eighteenth century. The interpretation and relevance of his moral philosophy remains a subject of active scholarly interest and controversy. JAMES MOORE

Sources *Collected works of Francis Hutcheson*, ed. B. Fabian, facs. edn, 7 vols. (1969–71) · *Collected works and correspondence of Francis Hutcheson*, ed. K. Haakonssen, 7 vols. (2003) [ongoing] · W. R. Scott, *Francis Hutcheson: his life, teaching and position in the history of philosophy* (1900) · W. Leechman, 'Account of the life, writings and character of the author', in F. Hutcheson, *A system of moral philosophy* (1755), i–xlviii · J. M. Barkley, 'Francis Hutcheson (1694–1746), professor of moral philosophy, University of Glasgow', *Bulletin of the Presbyterian Historical Society of Ireland*, 14 (1985), 1–14 · PRO NIre., D/971/34/D/I ['probat of will of Francis Hutcheson, 30th of June 1746'] · PRO NIre., T/403 [legal abstracts of the wills of Alexander, John, and Francis Hutcheson] · J. McConnell and others, eds., *Fasti of the Irish Presbyterian church, 1613–1840*, rev. S. G. McConnell, 2 vols. in 12 pts (1935–51) · J. Stuart, *Historical memoirs of the city of Armagh, for a period of 1373 years* (1819) · 'Progress of non-subscription to creeds', *Christian Moderator*, 2 (1827–8), 348–54 · R. Wodrow, *Analecta, or, Materials for a history of remarkable providences, mostly relating to Scotch ministers and Christians*, ed. [M. Leishman], 4 vols., Maitland Club, 60 (1842–3) · C. Innes, ed., *Munimenta alme Universitatis Glasguensis / Records of the University of Glasgow from its foundation till 1727*, 3, Maitland Club, 72 (1854), 196, 253 · H. M. B. Reid, *The divinity professors in the University of Glasgow, 1640–1903* (1923), chap. 6 · *Shaftesbury's ghost conjur'd* (1788) · *A vindication of Mr. Hutcheson from the calumnious aspersions of a late pamphlet, by several of his scholars* (1738) · T. Witherow, *Historical and literary memorials of presbyterianism in Ireland, 1623–1731* (1879) · T. Mautner, ed., *Francis Hutcheson: two texts on human nature* (1993), introduction, 3–87, and appxs, 148–68 · M. A. Stewart, 'John Smith and the Molesworth circle', *Eighteenth-Century Ireland*, 2 (1987), 89–102 · J. Moore, 'The two systems of Francis Hutcheson: on the origins of the Scottish Enlightenment', *Studies in the philosophy of the Scottish Enlightenment*, ed. M. A. Stewart (1990), 37–59 · D. Smyth, ed., *Francis Hutcheson: a special symposium … supplement to Fortnight*, 308 (1992) · Norman K. Smith, 'Hutcheson's teaching and its influence on Hume', *The philosophy of David Hume* (1941), chap. 2 · D. D. Raphael, *The moral sense* (1947), chap. 2 · W. Frankena, 'Hutcheson's moral sense theory', *Journal of the History of Ideas*, 16 (1955), 356–75 · D. F. Norton, 'Hutcheson's moral realism', *David Hume: common-sense moralist, sceptical metaphysician* (1982), chap. 2 · J. Moore, 'Hume and Hutcheson', *Hume and Hume's connexions*, ed. M. A. Stewart and J. P. Wright (1994), 23–57 · K. Haakonssen, *Natural law and moral philosophy: from Grotius to the Scottish Enlightenment* (1996), chap. 2 · I. McBride, 'The school of virtue: Francis Hutcheson, Irish Presbyterians and the Scottish Enlightenment', *Political thought in Ireland since the seventeenth century*, ed. D. G. Boyce, R. Eccleshall, and V. Geoghegan (1993), 73–99 · J. Moore, 'Hutcheson's theodicy: the argument and the contexts of *A system of moral philosophy*', *The Scottish enlightenment: essays in reinterpretation*, ed. P. Wood (2002), 239–66 ·

M. Brown, *Francis Hutcheson in Dublin, 1719–1730* (2002) · registry book of St Mary's, Dublin, Representative Church Body Library, Dublin · lease of land, PRO NIre., D 971/34/B/28 · memorial inscription, PRO NIre., D 2673/1/14–16 · U. Glas., Archives and Business Records Centre, 43228; 43170; 26635; 26647–9 · F. Hutcheson, letters to Thomas Drennan, U. Glas. L., MS Gen. 1018 · W. Bruce, letters to F. Hutcheson, NL Scot., MS 9252 · F. Hutcheson, letter to Rev John Hutcheson, 4 Aug 1726, PRO NIre., D 971/34/G/1/1 · F. Hutcheson, letter to the Revd Thomas Steward, 12 Feb 1740, Magee College, Londonderry, MS 46 · F. Hutcheson, letter to Henry Home, General Register Office for Scotland, Edinburgh, Abercairny Collection, GD 24/no. 55 [April 1739?; printed in I. Ross, 'Hutcheson on Hume's *Treatise*: an unnoticed letter', *Journal of the History of Philosophy*, 4 (1966), 69–72] · *The letters of David Hume*, ed. J. Y. T. Greig, 1 (1932), 32–5, 45–8, 55–9 [letters to Francis Hutcheson and William Mure] · J. Wodrow, letter to the earl of Buchan, 28 May 1808, Mitchell L., Glas., Baillie MS 32225 · S. Kenrick, letter to James Wodrow, 28 Sept 1786, DWL, MS 24.157 · S. Kenrick, letter to James Wodrow, 27 April 1808, Mitchell L., Glas., Baillie MS 32225
Archives U. Glas. L., letters to Thomas Drennan
Likenesses J. Latham, portrait, oils, *c*.1740, NG Ire. · A. Ramsay, oils, *c*.1745, Hunterian Museum and Art Gallery, Glasgow [*see illus.*] · A. Selvi, bronze medallion, 1746 (after I. Gosset), Scot. NPG · J. Tassie, plaster medallion, 1746 (after I. Gosset), Scot. NPG · A. Selvi, stipple, 1780 (after F. Bartolozzi), BM, NPG; repro. in F. Blackburne, ed., *Memoirs of Thomas Hollis*, 2 vols. (1780) · F. Bartolozzi, stipple, BM, NPG; repro. in F. Blackburne, ed., *Memoirs of Thomas Hollis*, 2 vols. (1780) · J. Foulis, oils (after Barkley), U. Glas., Senate Room · I. Gosset, copper medal, BM
Wealth at death extensive property in land in co. Down and co. Longford

Hutcheson, Francis [*pseud.* Francis Ireland] (**1721–1780**), composer, was born in Dublin on 13 August 1721, the only son of Francis *Hutcheson (1694–1746), philosopher, and his wife, formerly Miss Wilson. He graduated MA from Glasgow University in 1744, and MD in 1750; in the latter year he published a medical work at Glasgow. In 1755 he published his father's *System of Moral Philosophy*, which had been left in manuscript on the elder Hutcheson's death. In July 1760 he was appointed lecturer in chemistry at Trinity College, Dublin, and in 1775 consulting physician to the Rotunda Hospital. He was twice president of the Royal College of Physicians of Ireland.

Hutcheson wrote many partsongs, three of which won prizes at the Noblemen's and Gentlemen's Catch Club: 'As Colin one evening' (1771), 'Jolly Bacchus' (1772), and 'Where weeping yews' (1773). Nineteen of his songs appeared in Thomas Warren's *Collection of Catches and Glees* (vols. 2–4, 1764–6), and in *Vocal Harmony*. His four-part madrigal 'Return, return, my lovely maid' has been picked out as a particularly fine example of his art. His songs were published under the name Francis Ireland, presumably to distance his compositions from his professional life. He was probably the Dr Hutcheson who was a founder member and violinist in Lord Mornington's Musical Academy (founded 1757). He died in Dublin in 1780.

L. M. MIDDLETON, *rev.* K. D. REYNOLDS

Sources 'Ireland, Francis', Grove, *Dict. mus.* (1927) · B. Boydell, 'Ireland, Francis', *New Grove* · Burtchaell & Sadleir, *Alum. Dubl.*

Hutcheson, George (**1550x60–1639**), philanthropist, was the son of Thomas Hutcheson (*c*.1520–*c*.1595) of Lambhill and his wife, Helen Herbertsone. He became a public writer and notary in Glasgow. He was judge-depute in the commissary courts of Glasgow and Hamilton, and branched out into banking and moneylending, which in turn led to extensive landed estates in addition to the inheritance in Lambhill from his father. He had a house on the north side of Trongate from which he carried on his business, plus a house on the south side of Trongate. At a session of the kirk in Glasgow on 28 August 1588, Hutcheson pronounced himself willing to marry Elizabeth Craig (*d.* 1632), probably the sister or daughter of John Craig, writer and public notary of Glasgow, after she had given birth to a girl (this was presumably not the natural daughter mentioned in his will). He was ordered to marry her within a month. In 1611 Hutcheson built a house at Partick, probably on the site of the old bishop's palace.

Hutcheson died in Glasgow on 26 December 1639 and was buried in Glasgow Cathedral. In a deed of 16 December 1639 he had mortified and disposed a tenement of land on the west side of the old west port of Glasgow for building a 'hospital for entertainment of the poor, aged, decrepit men', together with 20,000 merks to provide for the institution's running costs. Further funds were contributed by his younger brother, Thomas *Hutcheson, and in 1641 the foundation stone was laid of what became Hutcheson's Hospital. STUART HANDLEY

Sources W. Hill, *History of the hospital and school in Glasgow founded by George and Thomas Hutcheson of Lambhill, 1639–41* (1881) · A. MacGeorge, *Old Glasgow: the place and the people* (1888)
Likenesses portrait (after Scougal), Hutcheson's Hospital, Glasgow

Hutcheson, George (*c*.1615–1674), Church of Scotland minister, was born in Ireland, the son of a humble weaver. He was sent to the Latin school in Irvine, where he boarded with the parish minister, the eminent David Dickson. He was educated at the University of Edinburgh, where he graduated MA on 20 July 1638. In 1642 he was admitted minister of Colmonell, Ayrshire. At an unknown date, but possibly about this time, he married his first wife, Catherine Kininmont.

In August 1647 Hutcheson was appointed a member of the general assembly's powerful standing committee, the commission for the public affairs of the kirk. He was translated to Edinburgh's Tolbooth parish on 4 April 1649 and, in February 1650, was chosen to be one of the kirk's commissioners to the treaty of Breda. After his return to Scotland in June he was appointed by the general assembly to be one of the chaplains of Charles II. During the heated controversy between radical and moderate covenanters following the king's return he became a leading radical, supporting the western remonstrance and denouncing the public resolutions that led to the repeal of the acts of classes. When the kirk was bitterly divided between resolutioners and protesters at the 1651 general assembly, he joined with the latter party in declining the assembly's authority. For reasons unknown he transferred his allegiance to the resolutioner party some time before the 1652 general assembly and, for the remainder of the decade, was an outspoken critic of the protesters.

Soon after this 'conversion', Hutcheson published his first contribution to a series of popular biblical commentaries, *A Brief Exposition of the Twelve Minor Prophets* (London, 1653–5). His second instalment appeared two years later under the title *An Exposition of the Gospel According to St. John* (London, 1657). He also collaborated with James Wood in writing two polemical pamphlets against the protesters: *A True Representation* (London, 1657) and *A Review and Examination of … Protesters No Subverters* (Edinburgh, 1659).

Following the Restoration, Hutcheson attended the marquess of Argyll during his last days and accompanied him to the scaffold on 27 May 1661. Soon thereafter he was offered a bishopric, but declined. He later refused to conform to episcopacy, and was deprived by parliament on 7 August 1662. After supporting the government's plan to settle deposed presbyterian ministers in vacant parishes, he accepted the resultant indulgence and, on 27 July 1669, was admitted to the parish of Irvine, Ayrshire. Also in 1669 he published his third and last popular commentary, *An Exposition of the Book of Job* (London, 1669). His first wife having died, Hutcheson married, on 19 January 1672, Rachael, daughter of Robert Baillie of Jerviswood, and widow of Andrew Gray (1633–1656). Hutcheson died at Irvine on 1 March 1674 after an illness of only two hours; his wife survived him.

K. D. HOLFELDER

Sources *Fasti Scot.*, new edn, 1.118; 3.99 · R. Wodrow, *Analecta, or, Materials for a history of remarkable providences, mostly relating to Scotch ministers and Christians*, ed. [M. Leishman], 4 vols., Maitland Club, 60 (1842–3), vol. 1, pp. 45–6, 168; vol. 2, pp. 119; vol. 3, pp. 12–16 · R. Wodrow, *The history of the sufferings of the Church of Scotland from the Restoration to the revolution*, ed. R. Burns, 1 (1828), 155; 2 (1829), 133, 178–216, 222, 278n. · *The letters and journals of Robert Baillie*, ed. D. Laing, 3 (1842) · W. Stephen, ed., *Register of the consultations of the ministers of Edinburgh*, 2 vols., Scottish History Society, 3rd ser., 1, 16 (1921–30) · A. F. Mitchell and J. Christie, eds., *The records of the commissions of the general assemblies of the Church of Scotland*, 3 vols., Scottish History Society, 11, 25, 58 (1892–1909) · *Diary of Sir Archibald Johnston of Wariston*, 2, ed. D. H. Fleming, Scottish History Society, 2nd ser., 18 (1919)

Archives NL Scot., Wodrow collection, letters and papers

Hutcheson, Thomas (1589/90–1641), philanthropist, was the son of Thomas Hutcheson (*c*.1520–*c*.1595) and his wife, Helen Herbertstone, and the younger brother of George *Hutcheson, and with him the joint founder of Hutcheson's Hospital in Glasgow. His brother, who was much older, looked after Thomas's education. Thomas entered Glasgow University in 1607 and graduated in 1610. He followed his brother and became a public writer, becoming about 1627 register of sasines of the regality of Glasgow. Hutcheson acted as an agent for the University of Glasgow, like his brother, and in August 1640 he was named a commissioner for visiting the university. On 24 April 1640 he was made a burgess of Glasgow for his work in setting up the hospital (and in September got his cousin made a burgess as well). On 27 June 1640 Hutcheson ratified the deeds of his brother relating to the foundation of the hospital, and on 9 March 1641 mortified certain bonds for 20,000 merks to add to the hospital by erecting 'a commodious and distinct house of itself for educating and harbouring twelve male children, indigent orphans, or others of the like condition and quality, sons of burgesses'. On 3 March 1641 he laid the foundation stone of the hospital. He added 1000 merks by a mortification dated 3 July 1641 and a further 10,500 merks on 14 July. Hutcheson died on 1 September 1641, in his fifty-second year, and was buried next to his brother in Glasgow Cathedral. He left a widow, Marion, daughter of James Stewart of Blackhall, who lived until November 1670.

STUART HANDLEY

Sources W. Hill, *History of the hospital and school in Glasgow founded by George and Thomas Hutcheson of Lambhill, 1639–1641* (1881) · J. R. Anderson, ed., *The burgesses and guild brethren of Glasgow, 1573–1750*, Scottish RS, 56 (1925), 102

Likenesses G. Jamesone, oils, Glasgow Art Gallery

PICTURE CREDITS

Hope, Sir Alexander (1769–1837)—in the collection of the Hopetoun House Preservation Trust; photograph courtesy the Scottish National Portrait Gallery

Hope, Charles, first earl of Hopetoun (1681–1742)—in the collection of the Hopetoun House Preservation Trust; photograph courtesy the Scottish National Portrait Gallery

Hope, Sir James, of Hopetoun, appointed Lord Hopetoun under the protectorate (1614–1661)—in the collection of the Hopetoun House Preservation Trust; photograph courtesy the Scottish National Portrait Gallery

Hope, Sir John, Lord Craighall (1603x5–1654)—private collection; photograph courtesy the Scottish National Portrait Gallery

Hope, John Adrian Louis, seventh earl of Hopetoun and first marquess of Linlithgow (1860–1908)—published by permission of the Hopetoun House Preservation Trust

Hope, Sir Thomas, of Craighall, first baronet (1573–1646)—Scottish National Portrait Gallery

Hope, Victor Alexander John, second marquess of Linlithgow (1887–1952)—Estate of the Artist; HSBC Group Archives. Photograph: Photographic Survey, Courtauld Institute of Art, London

Hopkins, Esek (1718–1802)—Ashmolean Museum, Oxford

Hopkins, Sir Frederick Gowland (1861–1947)—© The Royal Society

Hopkins, Gerard Manley (1844–1889)—© National Portrait Gallery, London

Hopkins, Matthew (d. 1647)—© National Portrait Gallery, London

Hopkins, Sir Richard Valentine Nind (1880–1955)—© National Portrait Gallery, London

Hopkinson, Eirene Adeline [Antonia White] (1899–1980)—© National Portrait Gallery, London

Hopkinson, John (1849–1898)—© National Portrait Gallery, London

Hoppner, John (1758–1810)—© Royal Academy of Arts, London, 2002. Photographer: J. Hammond

Hopps, John Page (1834–1911)—by permission of Dr Williams's Library

Hopton, Ralph, Baron Hopton (bap. 1596, d. 1652)—photograph by courtesy Sotheby's Picture Library, London

Horder, Thomas Jeeves, first Baron Horder (1871–1955)—St Bartholomew's Hospital Archives and Museum. Photograph: Photographic Survey, Courtauld Institute of Art, London

Hordern, Sir Michael Murray (1911–1995)—© Alistair Morrison; collection National Portrait Gallery, London

Horlick, Sir James, first baronet (1844–1921)—© National Portrait Gallery, London

Hornby, Albert Sydney (1898–1978)—© reserved; photograph National Portrait Gallery, London

Hornby, Frank (1863–1936)—© reserved

Hornby, Sir Geoffrey Thomas Phipps (1825–1895)—© National Portrait Gallery, London

Hornby, James John (1826–1909)—© National Portrait Gallery, London

Horne, George (1730–1792)—© National Portrait Gallery, London

Horne, Henry Sinclair, Baron Horne (1861–1929)—Scottish National Portrait Gallery

Horne, (Charles) Kenneth (1907–1969)—© Lewis Morley, courtesy of The Akehurst Bureau; collection National Portrait Gallery, London

Horne, Robert (1513x15–1579)—© Copyright The British Museum

Horne, Robert Stevenson, Viscount Horne of Slamannan (1871–1940)—© National Portrait Gallery, London

Horneck, Anthony (1641–1697)—© National Portrait Gallery, London

Horner, Arthur Lewis (1894–1968)—© National Portrait Gallery, London

Horner, Frances Jane, Lady Horner (1854/5–1940)—Christie's Images Ltd. (2004)

Horner, Francis (1778–1817)—© National Portrait Gallery, London

Horner, Leonard (1785–1864)—Heriot-Watt University Archive

Horniman, Annie Elizabeth Fredericka (1860–1937)—© National Portrait Gallery, London

Horovitz, Frances Margaret (1938–1983)—photograph courtesy Mike Golding

Horrocks, Sir Brian Gwynne (1895–1985)—© National Portrait Gallery, London

Horsbrugh, Florence Gertrude, Baroness Horsbrugh (1889–1969)—© National Portrait Gallery, London

Horsell, William (1807–1863)—The Vegetarian Society

Horsey family (per. c.1500–c.1640)—Collection Sherborne Abbey; © reserved in the photograph

Horsley, John Callcott (1817–1903)—© National Portrait Gallery, London

Horsley, Samuel (1733–1806)—© National Portrait Gallery, London

Horsley, Sir Victor Alexander Haden (1857–1916)—Wellcome Library, London

Horsman, Edward (1807–1876)—© National Portrait Gallery, London

Hort, Fenton John Anthony (1828–1892)—by permission of the Master, Fellows, and Scholars of Emmanuel College in the University of Cambridge

Horton, Sir Max Kennedy (1883–1951)—© National Portrait Gallery, London

Horton, Robert Forman (1855–1934)—© National Portrait Gallery, London

Horton, Sir Robert John Wilmot-, third baronet (1784–1841)—© Copyright The British Museum

Horwood, Sir William Thomas Francis (1868–1943)—© National Portrait Gallery, London

Hoste, Sir William, first baronet (1780–1828)—© National Portrait Gallery, London

Hotham, Beaumont, second Baron Hotham (1737–1814)—Ashmolean Museum, Oxford

Hotham, Sir Richard (1722–1799)—Town Hall, Bognor Regis; photograph © National Portrait Gallery, London

Houblon, Sir John (1632–1712)—© National Portrait Gallery, London

Hough, John (1651–1743)—reproduced by kind permission of His Grace the Archbishop of Canterbury and the Church Commissioners. Photograph: Photographic Survey, Courtauld Institute of Art, London

Houldsworth, Sir Hubert Stanley, first baronet (1889–1956)—© National Portrait Gallery, London

Houldsworth, Margaret Marshall (1839–1909)—from St George's School for Girls, Edinburgh, Archive

Housman, Alfred Edward (1859–1936)—© National Portrait Gallery, London

Housman, Laurence (1865–1959)—© National Portrait Gallery, London

Houston, Dame Fanny Lucy (1857–1936)—© National Portrait Gallery, London

Houston, Renée (1902–1980)—© Kenneth Hughes / National Portrait Gallery, London

How, William Walsham (1823–1897)—© National Portrait Gallery, London

Howard [Dacre], Anne, countess of Arundel (1557–1630)—© Copyright The British Museum

Howard, Bernard Marmaduke Fitzalan-, sixteenth duke of Norfolk (1908–1975)—© National Portrait Gallery, London

Howard, Charles, second Baron Howard of Effingham and first earl of Nottingham (1536–1624)—© National Maritime Museum, London, Greenwich Hospital Collection

Howard, Charles, third earl of Carlisle (1669–1738)—private collection; © reserved in the photograph

Howard, Sir Ebenezer (1850–1928)—First Garden City Heritage Museum, Letchworth

Howard, Esme William, first Baron Howard of Penrith (1863–1939)—© National Portrait Gallery, London

Howard, Frances, countess of Somerset (1590–1632)—© National Portrait Gallery, London

Howard, Francis, fifth Baron Howard of Effingham (bap. 1643, d. 1695)—The Virginia Historical Society, Richmond, Virginia

Howard, Frederick, fifth earl of Carlisle (1748–1825)—© National Portrait Gallery, London

Howard, George William Frederick, seventh earl of Carlisle (1802–1864)—© National Portrait Gallery, London

Howard, Henrietta, countess of Suffolk (c.1688–1767)—© National Portrait Gallery, London

Howard, Henry, earl of Surrey (1516/17–1547)—© National Portrait Gallery, London

Howard, Henry, earl of Northampton (1540–1614)—© Warburg Institute

Howard, Henry, seventh duke of Norfolk (1655–1701)—Ashmolean Museum, Oxford

Howard, Henry, twelfth earl of Suffolk and fifth earl of Berkshire (1739–1779)—unknown collection; photograph Sotheby's Picture Library, London / National Portrait Gallery, London

Howard, Henry Granville Fitzalan-, fourteenth duke of Norfolk (1815–1860)—reproduced by kind permission of His Grace the Duke of Norfolk. Photograph: Photographic Survey, Courtauld Institute of Art, London

Howard, Hugh (1675–1738)—© Copyright The British Museum

Howard, John (1726?–1790)—© Copyright The British Museum

Howard, Kenneth Alexander, first earl of Effingham (1767–1845)—© National Portrait Gallery, London

Howard, Leslie (1893–1943)—© Estate of Frederick William Daniels; collection National Portrait Gallery, London

Howard, Luke (1772–1864)—in the possession of the Royal Meteorological Society

Howard, Philip [St Philip Howard], thirteenth earl of Arundel (1557–1595)—reproduced by kind permission of His Grace the Duke of Norfolk. Photograph: Photographic Survey, Courtauld Institute of Art, London

Howard, Philip (1629–1694)—© National Portrait Gallery, London

Howard, Sir Robert (1626–1698)—© National Portrait Gallery, London

Howard, Rosalind Frances, countess of Carlisle (1845–1921)—© National Portrait Gallery, London

Howard, Thomas, third duke of Norfolk (1473–1554)—The Royal Collection © 2004 HM Queen Elizabeth II

Howard, Thomas, fourth duke of Norfolk (1538–1572)—private collection

Howard, Thomas, first earl of Suffolk (1561–1626)—Rangers House / © English Heritage Photo Library

Howard, Thomas, fourteenth earl of Arundel, fourth earl of Surrey, and first earl of Norfolk (1585–1646)—© National Portrait Gallery, London

Howard, Trevor (1913–1988)—© Cornel Lucas; collection National Portrait Gallery, London

Howard, William, first Baron Howard of Effingham (c.1510–1573)—unknown collection / Christie's; photograph National Portrait Gallery, London

Howe, (Mary Sophia) Charlotte, Viscountess Howe (1703–1782)—

private collection. Photograph: Photographic Survey, Courtauld Institute of Art, London

Howe, John (1630–1705)—© National Portrait Gallery, London

Howe, Joseph (1804–1873)—© National Portrait Gallery, London

Howe, Richard, Earl Howe (1726–1799)—© National Maritime Museum, London

Howell, Denis Herbert, Baron Howell (1923–1998)—© Godfrey Argent Studios; collection National Portrait Gallery, London

Howell, George (1833–1910)—© National Portrait Gallery, London

Howell, James (1594?–1666)—© National Portrait Gallery, London

Howells, Herbert Norman (1892–1983)—© National Portrait Gallery, London

Howerd, Frankie (1917–1992)—© Vincent Gillet Photography; collection National Portrait Gallery, London

Howitt, William (1792–1879)—Nottingham City Museums and Galleries

Howley, William (1766–1848)—by permission of the Warden and Scholars of Winchester College

Howson, John (1556/7–1632)—Christ Church, Oxford

Hoy, Thomas (b. 1659, d. in or after 1721)—by permission of the Royal College of Physicians, London

Hubback, Eva Marian (1886–1949)—© Robin Adler; photograph National Portrait Gallery, London

Hubbard, Louisa Maria (1836–1906)—© National Portrait Gallery, London

Huddart, Joseph (1741–1816)—unknown collection / Christie's; photograph National Portrait Gallery, London

Huddesford, George (bap. 1749, d. 1809)—© Tate, London, 2004

Huddleston, John (1608–1698)—private collection; © reserved in the photograph

Huddleston, (Ernest Urban) Trevor (1913–1998)—© National Portrait Gallery, London

Hudson, Charles (1828–1865)—private collection

Hudson, George (d. 1672/3)—Faculty of Music, University of Oxford

Hudson, George [the Railway King] (1800–1871)—York City Art Gallery

Hudson, Jeffery (1619–1682)—The Royal Collection © 2004 HM Queen Elizabeth II

Hudson, (Arthur) Kenneth (1916–1999)—Theo Richmond

Hudson, Sir Robert Arundell (1864–1927)—© National Portrait Gallery, London

Hudson, Thomas (bap. 1701, d. 1779)—Derby Museum and Art Gallery

Hudson, William Henry (1841–1922)—© National Portrait Gallery, London

Hügel, Friedrich Maria Aloys François Charles von, Baron von Hügel in the nobility of the Holy Roman empire (1852–1925)—© National Portrait Gallery, London

Hugessen, Edward Hugessen Knatchbull-, first Baron Brabourne (1829–1893)—© National Portrait Gallery, London

Hugessen, Sir Hughe Montgomery Knatchbull- (1886–1971)—© National Portrait Gallery, London

Huggins, Godfrey Martin, first Viscount Malvern (1883–1971)—© National Portrait Gallery, London

Huggins, Sir William (1824–1910)—© National Portrait Gallery, London

Hughes, David Edward (1831–1900)—Heritage Images Partnership

Hughes, Sir Edward (c.1720–1794)—© National Maritime Museum, London, Greenwich Hospital Collection

Hughes, Edward James (1930–1998)—© Henri Cartier-Bresson / Magnum Photos; collection National Portrait Gallery, London

Hughes, Hugh Price (1847–1902)—© National Portrait Gallery, London

Hughes, John (c.1816–1889)—© National Portrait Gallery, London

Hughes, Thomas (1822–1896)—© National Portrait Gallery, London

Hughes, William Morris (1862–1952)—Historic Memorials Collection, Canberra. Courtesy of the Parliament House Art Collection, Joint House Department Canberra ACT

Huish, Mark (1808–1867)—© National Portrait Gallery, London

Hull, John (1764–1843)—Wellcome Library, London

Hullah, John Pyke (1812–1884)—© National Portrait Gallery, London

Hullmandel, Charles Joseph (1789–1850)—Ashmolean Museum, Oxford

Hulme, Thomas Ernest (1883–1917)—Getty Images – Hulton Archive

Hume, Allan Octavian (1829–1912)—Getty Images – Hulton Archive

Hume, David (1711–1776)—© Scottish National Portrait Gallery

Hume, George Haliburton (1923–1999)—© National Portrait Gallery, London

Hume, Joseph (1777–1855)—© National Portrait Gallery, London

Hume, Patrick, first earl of Marchmont (1641–1724)—reproduced by kind permission of the Trustees of the Paxton Trust

Humphries, Richard (c.1760–1827)—The Metropolitan Museum of Art, The Alfred N. Punnett Endowment Fund, 1953. (53.113) Photograph © 1998 The Metropolitan Museum of Art

Humphry, Ozias (1742–1810)—© Copyright The British Museum

Hungerford, Sir Edward (1596–1648)—courtesy of John Wroughton

Hungerford, Robert, second Baron Hungerford (c.1400–1459)—© English Heritage. NMR

Hunt, Arabella (1662–1705)—© Crown copyright in photograph: UK Government Art Collection

Hunt, Sir David Wathen Stather (1913–1998)—© National Portrait Gallery, London

Hunt, Henry [Orator Hunt] (1773–1835)—© National Portrait Gallery, London

Hunt, James Simon Wallis (1947–1993)—Getty Images – Frank Barratt

Hunt, (Henry Cecil) John, Baron Hunt (1910–1998)—© reserved; photograph National Portrait Gallery, London

Hunt, (James Henry) Leigh (1784–1859)—© National Portrait Gallery, London

Hunt, Robert (1807–1887)—© National Portrait Gallery, London

Hunt, William Henry (1790–1864)—© National Portrait Gallery, London

Hunt, William Holman (1827–1910)—Bridgeman Art Library / Alinari

Hunter, John (1728–1793)—reproduced by kind permission of the President and Council of the Royal College of Surgeons of London

Hunter, Sir (Ernest) John (1912–1983)—© National Portrait Gallery, London

Hunter, Robert (1823–1897)—by permission of the Geological Society of London

Hunter, William (1718–1783)—© Hunterian Art Gallery, University of Glasgow

Hunter, Sir William Wilson (1840–1900)—© National Portrait Gallery, London

Huntington, William (1745–1813)—© National Portrait Gallery, London

Hurd, Richard (1720–1808)—The Royal Collection © 2004 HM Queen Elizabeth II

Hurley, James Francis (1885–1962)—Christie's Images Ltd. (2004)

Hurlstone, Frederick Yeates (1800–1869)—Federation of British Artists; photograph National Portrait Gallery, London

Hurry, Leslie George (1909–1978)—by courtesy of the Tate Gallery, London / © reserved

Hurst, Sir Cecil James Barrington (1870–1963)—© National Portrait Gallery, London

Hurst, Margery (1913–1989)—© National Portrait Gallery, London

Huskisson, William (1770–1830)—unknown collection / Christie's; photograph National Portrait Gallery, London

Hussey, Giles (1710–1788)—Collection of the Duke of Northumberland. Photograph: Photographic Survey, Courtauld Institute of Art, London

Hutcheson, Francis (1694–1746)—© Hunterian Art Gallery, University of Glasgow